The Minor Prophets
A Commentary

E. B. Pusey

Volume 1
HOSEA TO JONAH

Heritage Edition

Fourteen Volumes 0834-4

1. Genesis (Murphy)	0835-2	8. Minor Prophets (Pusey)	0842-5
2. Exodus to Esther (Cook)	0836-0	9. The Gospels	0843-3
3. Job	0837-9	10. Acts and Romans	0844-1
4. Psalms	0838-7	11. I Corinthians to Galatians	0846-8
5. Proverbs to Ezekiel (Cook)	0839-5	12. Ephesians to Philemon	0847-6
6. Isaiah	0840-9	13. Hebrews to Jude	0848-4
7. Daniel	0841-7	14. Revelation	0849-2

When ordering by ISBN (International Standard Book Number), numbers listed above should be preceded by 0-8010-.

Reprinted from the 1847 edition published
by Blackie & Son, London

Reprinted 2005 by Baker Books
a division of Baker Book House Company
P.O. Box 6287, Grand Rapids, MI 49516-6287

Printed in the United States of America

CONTENTS.

INTRODUCTORY STATEMENT

ON THE

PRINCIPLES AND OBJECT

OF

THE COMMENTARY.

THE object of the following pages is to evolve some portion of the meaning of the Word of God. In regard to the literal meaning of the sacred text, I have given that which, after a matured study spread over more than thirty years, I believe to be the true, or, in some cases, the more probable only. In so doing, I have purposely avoided all show of learning or embarrassing discussion, which belong to the dictionary or grammar rather than to a commentary on Holy Scripture. Where it seemed to mé necessary, on some unestablished point, to set down in some measure, the grounds of the rendering of any word or phrase, I have indicated it very briefly in the lower margin[a]. I hoped, in this way, to make it intelligible to those acquainted with the sacred language, without interrupting the development of the meaning of the text, which presupposes a knowledge of the verbal meaning. Still less have I thought the discussion of different renderings of ancient Versions suited to a commentary of this sort. As soon as one is satisfied that any given rendering of an ancient version does not correctly represent the Hebrew original, the question how the translators came so to render it, by what misreading or mishearing, or guess, or paraphrase, belongs to a history of that Version, not to the explanation of the sacred original. Still more distracting is a discussion of the various expositions of modern commentators, or an enumeration of names, often of no weight, who adhere to one or the other rendering, or perhaps originated some crotchet of their own. These things, which so often fill modern commentaries, have a show of learning, but embarrass rather than aid a reader of Holy Scripture. I have myself examined carefully every commentator, likely or unlikely to contribute any thing to the understanding of the sacred text; and, if I have been able to gain little from modern German commentaries, (except such as Tholuck, Hengstenberg, Keil, Delitzsch, and Hävernick) it is not that I have not sifted them to the best of the

[a] As time went on, and the use and abuse of Hebrew increased, I increased the remarks on the Hebrew in the lower margin, as I hoped might be useful to those who had some knowledge of Hebrew, without distracting those who had not. 1877.

ability which God gave me. Even Luther said of his adherents, that they were like Solomon's fleet; some brought back gold and silver; but the younger, peacocks and apes. On the other hand, it has been pleasurable to give (at times somewhat condensed) the expositions of Pococke, extracted from the folio, in which, for the most part, they lie entombed amid the heaps of other explanations which his learning brought together. Else it has been my desire to use what learning of this sort I have, in these many years, acquired, to save a student from useless balancing of renderings, which I believe that no one, not under a prejudice, would adopt.

If, in the main, I have adhered to the English Version, it has been from the conviction that our translators were in the right. They had most of the helps for understanding Hebrew, which we have, the same traditional knowledge from the ancient Versions, Jewish commentators or lexicographers or grammarians, (with the exception of the Jewish-Arabic school only,) as well as the study of the Hebrew Scriptures themselves; and they used those aids with more mature and even judgment than has mostly been employed in the subsequent period. Hebrew criticism has now escaped[b], for the most part, from the arbitrariness, which detected a various reading in any variation of a single old Version, or in the error of some small fraction of MSS., which disfigured the commentaries of Lowth, Newcome, and Blayney. But the comparison of the cognate dialects opened for the time an unlimited licence of innovation. Every principle of interpretation, every rule of language, was violated. The Bible was misinterpreted with a wild recklessness, to which no other book was ever subjected. A subordinate meaning of some half-understood Arabic word was always at hand to remove whatever any one misliked. Now, the manifoldness of this reign of misrule has subsided. But interpretations as arbitrary as any which have perished still hold their sway, or from time to time emerge, and any revisal of the authorized Version of the O. T., until the precarious use of the dialects should be far more settled, would give us chaff for wheat, introducing an indefinite amount of error into the Word of God. In some places, in the following pages, I have put down what I thought an improvement of the Eng. Version; in others, I have marked, by the word, *or*, a rendering which I thought equally or more probable than that which our Translators adopted. Where I have said nothing, it has not been that I have been unaware of any other translation (for I have proved all), but that I thought the received Version most in accordance with the Hebrew, or at least the most probable. For the most part, I have pointed out simple things, which any one would see, who could read the Hebrew text, but which cannot mostly be preserved in a translation without a cumbrousness which would destroy its beauty and impressiveness.

The literal meaning of the words lies, of course, as the basis of any further developement of the whole meaning of each passage of Holy Scripture. Yet any thoughtful reader must have been struck by observing, how independent that meaning is of single words. The general

[b] Ewald re-opened a system of boundless licence which has been copied by his followers; only, instead of drawing from some mistake or paraphrase of an ancient version, such draw from their own imagination. It comes to this, "Had I been the prophet, I would have written so and so." As the pious and original Claudius pictures the commentators on the Gospels in his day,

"There crossed my mind a random thought:
Had I been Christ, so had *I* taught."

It is very piteous, that a mind, with such rare grammatical gifts, which, at 19, laid the foundation of scientific study of Hebrew grammar, should, by over-confidence in self, have become so misled and misleading. 1877.

meaning remains the same, even amid much variation of single words. This is apparent in the passages which the Apostles quote from the LXX, where it is not an exact translation of the Hebrew. The variation arising from any single word does not mostly extend beyond itself.

This is said, that I may not seem to have neglected the letter of Holy Scripture, because I have not set down what is now commonly found in books, which profess to give an explanation of that letter. My wish has been to give the results rather than the process by which they were arrived at; to exhibit the building, not the scaffolding. My ideal has been to explain or develop each word and sentence of Holy Scripture, and, when it should be required, the connection of verses, to leave nothing unexplained, as far as I could explain it; and if any verse should give occasion to enter upon any subject, historical, moral, doctrinal, or devotional, to explain this, as far as the place required or suggested. Then, if any thoughtful writers with whom I am acquainted, and to whom most English readers have little or no access, have expanded the meaning of any text in a way which I thought would be useful to an English reader, I have translated them, placing them mostly at the end of the comment on each verse, so that the mind might rest upon them, and yet not be sensible of a break or a jar, in passing on to other thoughts in the following verse.

The nature of the subjects thus to be expanded must, of course, vary with the different books of Holy Scripture. The prophets are partly teachers of righteousness and rebukers of unrighteousness; partly they declared things then to come, a nearer and a more distant future, God's judgments on unrighteousness, whether of His own sinful people or of the nations who unrighteously executed God's righteous judgments upon them, and the everlasting righteousness which He willed to bring in through the Coming of Christ. Of these, the nearer future, by its fulfillment of their words, accredited to those who then would hear, the more distant; to us, (with the exception of those more lasting visitations, as on Nineveh and Babylon and God's former people, whose destructions or dispersion have lived on to the present day) the then more distant future, the prophecies as to Christ, which are before us in the Gospels, or of the Church among all nations, whose fulfillment is around us, accredit the earlier. The fulfillments of these prophecies, as they come before us in the several prophets, it lies within the design of the present work, God giving us strength, to vindicate against the unbelief, rife in the present day. Where this can be done without disturbing the interpretation of the Scripture itself, the answers may often be tacitly supplied for those who need them, in the course of that interpretation. Where a fuller discussion may be necessary, it will probably be placed in the Introduction to the several books.

To this employment, which I have had for many years at heart, but from which the various distresses of our times, and the duties which they have involved, have continually withheld me, I hope to consecrate the residue of the years and of the strength which God may give me. "Vitæ summa brevis spem vetat inchoare longam." The wonderful volume of the twelve prophets, "brief in words, mighty in meaning," and, if God continue my life, the Evangelical Prophet, are what I have specially reserved for myself. The New Testament except the Apocalypse, and most of the rest of the Old Testament, have been undertaken by friends whose names will be published, when the arrangement shall finally be completed[c]. The Commentary on the Minor

[c] It is useless to say, *how* these hopes, as to myself, or others have failed. God removed some, by

Prophets is in the course of being printed; the Commentary on S. Matthew is nearly ready for the press. Other portions are begun. But the object of all, who have been engaged in this work, is one and the same, to develop, as God shall enable us, the meaning of Holy Scripture out of Holy Scripture itself; to search in that deep mine and—not bring meanings into it, but—(Christ being our helper, for "the well is deep,") to bring such portions, as they may, of its meaning out of it; to exhibit to our people, truth side by side with the fountain, from which it is drawn; to enable them to see something more of its riches, than a passer-by or a careless reader sees upon its surface.

To this end, it is our purpose to use those more thoughtful writers of all times, who have professedly, or, as far as we know, incidentally developed the meaning of portions or texts of the sacred volume, men who understood Holy Scripture through that same Spirit by Whom it was written, to whom prayer, meditation, and a sanctified life laid open its meaning. For He, Who first gave to man the words of eternal life, still hides their meaning from those who are wise and prudent in their own eyes, and giveth wisdom to the simple. "Lord, to whom shall we go? Thou hast the words of eternal life." "The reading of the Scripture is the opening of Heaven." "In the words of God, we learn the Heart of God."

death, as my friend C. Marriott, that beautiful mind and ripe scholar, James Riddell of Balliol, and when he, at last, had accomplished his 16 years' labor of love for the memory of the Apostolic Bishop Wilson, the revered John Keble. Some thought the plan on too large a scale for them. I myself have only to thank God for enabling me to do the little I could do, praying Him to accept anything which He gave, and to forgive anything amiss for Jesus' sake. 1877.

"O Eternal Truth, and True Love, and loving Light, our God and our All, enlighten our darkness by the brightness of Thy light; irradiate our minds by the splendor of holiness, that in Thy Light we may see light, that we, in turn, may enlighten others, and kindle them with the love of Thee. Open Thou our eyes, that we may see wondrous things out of Thy law, Who makest eloquent the minds and tongues of the slow of speech. To Thee, to Thy glory, to the good of Thy Church and people, may we labor, write, live. Thou hast said, Lord, to Thine Apostles and Prophets, their followers and interpreters, 'Ye are the salt of the earth; ye are the light of the world.' Thou hast said it, and, by saying it, hast done it. Grant to us, then, Lord, that we too, like them, may be preachers of heaven, sowers for eternity, that they who read, may, by the knowledge of Thy Scriptures, through the graveness and the weight of Thy promises and threats, despise the ensnaring entanglements of earth, and be kindled with the love of heavenly goods, and the effectual earnest longing for a blessed eternity. This be our one desire, this our prayer, to this may all our reading and writing and all our toil tend, that Thy Holy Name may be hallowed, Thy Holy Will be done, as in heaven, so in earth, Thy Holy kingdom of grace, glory, and endless bliss, where Thou wilt be all things in all, may come to us. Amen."

CHRIST CHURCH,
EASTER, 1860.

gleamed over the fall of Israel and Judah, shone in their captivity, and set at last, with the prediction of him, who should precede the rising of the Sun of Righteousness.

In the reign of Jeroboam II., Hosea, Amos, Jonah, prophesied in the kingdom of Israel. Joel was probably called at the same time to prophesy in Judah, and Obadiah to deliver his prophecy as to Edom; Isaiah, a few years later: Micah, we know, began his office in the following reign of Jotham, and then prophesied, together with Isaiah, to and in the reign of Hezekiah.

The order, then, of "the twelve" was probably, for the most part, an order of time. We know that the greater prophets are placed in that order, as also the three last of the twelve, Haggai, Zechariah, and Malachi. Of the five first, Hosea, Amos and Jonah were nearly contemporary; Joel was prior to Amos[f]; and of the four remaining, Micah and Nahum were later than Jonah, whom they succeed in order; Nahum refers to Jonah; Zephaniah quotes Habakkuk. It may be from an old Jewish tradition, that S. Jerome says[g], "know that those prophets, whose time is not prefixed in the title, prophesied under the same kings, as those other prophets, who are placed before them, and who have titles."

Hosea, the first of the twelve, must have prophesied during a period, as long as the ordinary life of man. For he prophesied (the title tells us) while Uzziah king of Judah and Jeroboam II., king of Israel, were both reigning, as also during the reigns of Jotham, Ahaz, and Hezekiah. But Uzziah survived Jeroboam, 26 years. Jotham and Ahaz reigned, each, 16 years. Thus we have already 58 years complete, without counting the years of Jeroboam, during which Hosea prophesied at the beginning of his office, or those of Hezekiah which elapsed before its close. But since the prophecy of Hosea is directed almost exclusively to Israel, it is not probable that the name of Jeroboam would alone have been selected for mention, unless Hosea had prophesied for some time during his reign. The house of Jehu, which sunk after the death of Jeroboam, was yet[h] standing, and in its full strength, when Hosea first prophesied. Its might apparently is contrasted with the comparative weakness of Judah[i]. On the other hand, the office of Hosea probably closed before the end of the 4th year of Hezekiah[k]. For in that year, B. C. 721, the judgment denounced by Hosea upon Samaria was fulfilled, and all his prophecy looks on to this event as yet to come: the 13th chapter closes with the prophecy of the utter destruction of Samaria; and of the horrible cruelties which would befall her helpless ones. The last chapter alone winds up the long series of denunciations by a prediction of the future conversion of Israel. This chapter, however, is too closely connected with the preceding, to admit of its being a consolation after the captivity had begun. If then we suppose that Hosea prophesied during 2 years only of the reign of Hezekiah, and 10 of those in which the reigns of Jeroboam II. and Uzziah coincided, his ministry will have lasted 70 years. A long and heavy service for a soul full of love like his, mitigated only by his hope of the Coming of Christ, the final conversion of his people, and the victory over the grave! But the length is nothing incredible, since, about this time, Jehoiada "[l]did good in Israel both towards God and towards His House;" until he "was 130 years." The shortest duration of Hosea's office must have been some 65 years. But if God called him quite young to his office, he need but have lived about 95 years, whereas Anna the Prophetess served God in the temple with fasting and prayer night and day, after a widowhood probably of 84 years[m]; and S. John the Evangelist lived probably until 104 years; and S. Polycarp became a martyr, when he was about 104 years old, having served Christ for 86 years[n], and having, when 95, sailed from Asia to Italy. Almost in our own days, we have heard of 100 centenarians, deputed by a religious order who ate no animal food, to bear witness that their rule of life was not unhealthy. Not then the length of Hosea's life, but his endurance, was superhuman. So long did God will that His prophets should toil; so little fruit were they content to leave behind them. For these few chapters alone remain of a labour beyond the ordinary life of man. But they were content to have God for their exceeding great reward.

The time, during which Hosea prophesied, was the darkest period in the history of the kingdom of Israel. Jeroboam II. was almost the last king who ruled in it by the appointment of God. The promise of God to Jehu[o] in reward of his partial obedience, that his "[p]children of the fourth generation should sit on the throne of Israel," expired with Jeroboam's son, who reigned but for 6 months[q] after an anarchy of 11 years. The rest of Hosea's life was passed amid the decline of the kingdom of Israel. Politically all was anarchy or misrule; kings made their way to the throne through the murder of their pre-

[f] See Introd. to Joel. [g] Præf. in duod. Proph.
[h] Ch. i. 4, 5. [i] Ch. i. 7.
[k] 2 Kgs xviii. 9. [l] 2 Chron. xxiv. 15.
[m] So S. Ambrose and others understand the words "a widow of about fourscore and four years;" (S. Luke ii. 37.) and it seems the most natural. If, according to Jewish law and practice, she was married at 12, her widowhood, after "7 years" began when she was 19, and when she was permitted to see our Lord, she was 103.
[n] Ep. Eccl. Smyrn. in Eus. H. E. iv. 15.
[o] 2 Kgs x. 30. [p] 2 K. xv. 8. [q] See Ib. 10, 14, 25, 30.

decessors, and made way for their successors through their own[p]. Shallum slew Zechariah; Menahem slew Shallum; Pekah slew the son of Menahem; Hoshea slew Pekah. The whole kingdom of Israel was a military despotism, and, as in the Roman empire, those in command came to the throne. Baasha, Zimri, Omri, Jehu, Menahem, Pekah, held military office before they became kings[r].

Each usurper seems to have strengthened himself by a foreign alliance. At least, we find Baasha in league with Benhadad, king of Syria[s]; Ahab marrying Jezebel, daughter of a king of Tyre and Zidon[t]; Menahem giving Pul king of Assyria tribute, that he might "confirm the kingdom in his hand[u];" Pekah confederate with Rezin[v]. These alliances brought with them the corruptions of the Phœnician and Syrian idolatry, wherein murder and lust became acts of religion. Jehu also probably sent tribute to the king of Assyria, to secure to himself the throne which God had given him. The fact appears in the cuneiform inscriptions[w]; it falls in with the character of Jehu and his half-belief, using all means, human or divine, to establish his own end. In one and the same spirit, he destroyed the Baal-worshippers, as adherents of Ahab, retained the calf-worship, courted the ascetic Jonadab son of Rechab, spoke of the death of Jehoram as the fulfilment of prophecy, and sought help from the king of Assyria.

These irreligions had the more deadly sway, because they were countenanced by the corrupt worship, which Jeroboam I. had set up as the state religion, over against the worship at Jerusalem. To allow the people to go up to Jerusalem, as the centre of the worship of God, would have risked their owning the line of David as the kings of God's appointment. To prevent this, Jeroboam set up a great system of rival worship. Himself a refugee in Egypt[x], he had there seen nature (i. e. what are God's workings in nature) worshiped under the form of the calf[y]. He adopted it, in the words in which Aaron had been overborne to sanction it, as the worship of the One True God under a visible form: "These be thy gods, O Israel, which brought thee up out of the land of Egypt[z]." With great human subtlety, he laid hold of Israel's love for idol-worship, and their reverence for their ancestors, and words which even Aaron had used, and sought to replace, by this symbol of God's working. His actual presence over the mercy-seat. Around this he gathered as much of the Mosaic ritual as he could. The Priests and Levites remaining faithful to God[a], he made others priests, not of the line of Aaron[b]. Then, while he gratified the love of idolatry, he decked it out with all the rest of the worship which God had appointed for Himself. He retained the feasts which God had appointed, the three great festivals[c], their solemn assemblies[d], the new moons and sabbaths[e]; and these last feasts were observed even by those, to whose covetousness the rest on the festival was a hindrance[f]. Every kind of sacrifice was retained, the daily sacrifice[g], the burnt-offering[h], the meal-offering[i], the drink-offering[j], thank-offerings[k], peace-offerings[h], free-will offerings[k], sin-offerings[l]. They had hymns and instrumental music[m]. They paid the tithes of the third year[n]; probably they gave the first fruits[o]; they had priests[p] and prophets[q] and temples[r]; the temple at Bethel was the king's chapel, the temple of the state[s]. The worship was maintained by the civil authority[t]. But all this

[r] Nadab was with the army besieging Gibbethon, when Baasha slew him (1 Kgs xv. 27.); Zimri was "captain of half the chariots of Elah son of Baasha" (Ib. xvi. 9.); "all Israel made Omri, the captain of the host, king over Israel in the camp" (Ib. 16.). Jehu seems to have been chief among the captains (2 Kgs ix. 5.). Menahem "went up from Tirzah" (the residence of the kings of Israel until Omri built Samaria) Ib. xvi. 14. Pekah was a captain of Remaliah (Ib. 25.).

[s] 1 Kgs xv. 19. [t] 1 Kgs xvi. 31. [u] 2 Kgs xv. 19.

[v] Is. vii. 1, 9, 16. 2 Chron. xxviii. 5, 6.

[w] Sir H. Rawlinson and Dr. Hincks separately decyphered the name "Jahua (יהוא) son of Khumri," as one of those whose tribute is recorded on the Black obelisk [probably of Shalmanubar,] now in the British Museum. In the same inscription Beth-Khumri i. e. house or city of Omri (ק for ע) occurs for Samaria. Jehu may be so named from his capital, or from supposed or claimed descent from Omri. See Layard Nin. and Bab. p. 613. Rawlins. Herod. i. 465. Dr. Hincks Dublin Univ. Mag. 1853. p. 426. Scripture ascribes to Jehu personal might (גבורה), but in his days Israel lost to Hazael all the country beyond Jordan. The attack of Hazael may have been the cause or the effect of his seeking help of Assyria.

[x] 1 Kgs xi. 40. xii. 2.

[y] Two living bulls, Apis and Mnevis, were worshiped as symbols of Osiris and the sun at Memphis and Heliopolis. Diod. Sic. i. 21. Strabo xvii.

[z] Ex. xxxii. 4. 1 Kgs xii. 28. [a] 2 Chron. xi. 13–15.

[b] 1 Kgs xii. 31. "He made priests out of the lowest of the people," (lit. "the end of the people") should be rendered "from the whole of the people" [indiscriminately] "which were not of the sons of Levi."

[c] Hosea ii. 11. ix. 5. Amos v. 21. Jeroboam transferred, apparently, the feast of tabernacles from the 15th of the seventh month (Lev. xxiii. 34.) to the 15th of the eighth month (1 Kgs xii. 32, 33.)

[d] Amos v. 21. [e] Hosea ii. 11. [f] Amos viii. 5.

[g] Ib. iv. 4. [h] Ib. v. 22. [i] Hosea ix. 4. Amos v. 22.

[j] Hosea ix. 4. [k] Hosea v. 6, vi. 6, perhaps iv. 8.

[l] Amos iv. 5, and of this class generally, Hosea viii. 13.

[m] Amos v. 23. viii. 3. [n] Amos iv. 4.

[o] These were brought to Elisha (2 Kgs iv. 42.) from Baal-Shalisha in the mountainous country of Ephraim, where "the land of Shalisha" was, (1 Sam. ix. 4.) by one probably who could not own the calf-priests. The prophets acted as priests in the kingdom of Israel. 1 Kgs xviii. 36. 2 Kgs iv. 23.) Hence the mention of "altars of the Lord" in Israel also, 1 Kgs xviii. 30. xix. 20.

[p] 1 Kgs xii. 32. Hosea iv. 6, 9. v. 1. vi. 9. x. 5.

[q] Hosea iv. 5. ix. 7, 8.

[r] 1 Kgs xii. 31, 32. Hosea viii. 14.

[s] Amos vii. 13. [t] Hosea v. 11. xiii. 2.

outward shew was rotten at the core. God had forbidden man so to worship Him, nor was it He Who was worshiped at Bethel and Dan, though Jeroboam probably meant it. People, when they alter God's truth, alter more than they think for. Such is the lot of all heresy. Jeroboam probably meant that God should be worshiped under a symbol, and he brought in a worship, which was not, in truth, a worship of God at all. The calf was the symbol, not of the personal God, but of ever-renewed life, His continued vivifying of all which lives, and renewing of what decays. And so what was worshiped was not God, but much what men now call "nature." The calf was a symbol of "nature;" much as men say, "nature does this or that;" "nature makes man so and so;" "nature useth simplicity of means;" "nature provides," &c.; as if "nature were a sort of semi-deity," or creation were its own Creator. As men now profess to own God, and do own Him in the abstract, but talk of "nature," till they forget Him, or because they forget Him, so Jeroboam, who was a shrewd, practical, irreligious man, slipped into a worship of nature, while he thought, doubtless, he was doing honor to the Creator, and professing a belief in Him.

But they were those same workings in creation, which were worshiped by the neighboring heathen, in Baal and Ashtaroth; only there the name of the Creator was altogether dropped. Yet it was but a step from one to the other. The calf was the immediate and often the sole object of worship. They "sacrificed to the calves[u];" "kissed the calves[v]," in token of worship; swore by them as living gods[w]. They had literally "[x]changed their Glory [i. e. God] into the similitude of a bull which eateth hay." Calf-worship paved the way for those coarser and more cruel worships of nature, under the names of Baal and Ashtaroth, with all their abominations of consecrated child-sacrifices, and degrading or horrible sensuality. The worship of the calves led to sin. The heathen festival was one of unbridled licentiousness. The account of the calf-festival in the wilderness agrees too well with the heathen descriptions. The very least which can be inferred from the words "Aaron had made them naked to their shame before their enemies[y]," is an extreme relaxedness, on the borders of further sin.

And now in Hosea's time, these idolatries had yielded their full bitter fruits. The course of iniquity had been run. The stream had become darker and darker in its downward flow. Creature worship (as S. Paul points out[z]), was the parent of every sort of abomination; and religion having become creature-worship, what God gave as the check to sin became its incentive. Every commandment of God was broken, and that, habitually. All was falsehood[a], adultery[b], bloodshedding[c]; deceit to God[d] produced faithlessness to man; excess[e] and luxury[f] were supplied by secret[g] or open robbery[h], oppression[i], false dealing[j], perversion of justice[k], grinding of the poor[l]. Blood was shed like water, until one stream met another[m], and overspread the land with one defiling deluge. Adultery was consecrated as an act of religion[n]. Those who were first in rank were first in excess. People and king vied in debauchery[o], and the sottish king joined and encouraged the freethinkers and blasphemers of his court[p]. The idolatrous priests loved and shared in the sins of the people[q]; nay, they seem to have set themselves to intercept those on either side of Jordan, who would go to worship at Jerusalem, laying wait to murder them[r]. Corruption had spread throughout the whole land[s]; even the places once sacred through God's revelations or other mercies to their forefathers, Bethel[t], Gilgal[u], Gilead[v], Mizpah[w], Shechem[x], were especial scenes of corruption or of sin. Every holy memory was effaced by present corruption. Could things be worse? There was one aggravation more. Remonstrance was useless[y]; the knowledge of God was wilfully rejected[z]; the people hated rebuke[a]; the more they were called, the more they refused[b]; they forbade their prophets to prophesy[c]; and their false prophets hated God greatly[d]. All attempts to heal all this disease only shewed its incurableness[e].

Such was the condition of the people among whom Hosea had to prophesy for some 70 years. They themselves were not sensible of their decay[f], moral or political. They set themselves, in despite of the Prophet's warning, to prop up their strength by aid of the two heathen nations, Egypt or Assyria. In Assyria they chiefly trusted[g], and Assyria, he had to denounce to them, should carry them captive[h]; stragglers at least,

[u] 1 Kgs xii. 32. [v] Hosea xiii. 2. [w] Amos viii. 4.
[x] Ps. cvi. 20. [y] Ex. xxxii. 25. [z] Rom. i.
[a] Hosea iv. 1. vii. 1, 3.
[b] Ib. iv. 11. v. 3. 4. vii. 4. ix. 10. Amos ii. 7.
[c] Hosea v. 2. vi. 8. [d] Ib. iv. 2. x. 13. xi. 12.
[e] Ib. iv. 11. vii. 5. Amos iv. 1.
[f] Hosea iii. 15. vi. 4–6.
[g] Ib. iv. 2. vii. 1.
[h] Ib. vii. 1. [i] Ib. xii. 7. Amos iii. 9, 10. iv. 1. v. 11.
[j] Hosea xii. 7. Amos viii. 5.
[k] Hosea x. 4. Amos. ii. 6, 7. v. 7, 12. vi. 3, 12.
[l] Amos ii. 7. viii. 6. [m] Hosea iv. 2.

[n] See on iv. 14. [o] Hosea vii. 5. [p] Ib. vii. 5.
[q] Ib. iv. 8, 9. [r] Ib. v. 1. vi. 9. [s] Ib. v. 1.
[t] Hosea iv. 15. x. 5, 8. 15. xii. 4. Amos iii. 14. v. 5. vii. 10. 13.
[u] Hosea iv. 15. ix. 15. xii. 11. [v] Hosea vi. 8. xii. 11.
[w] v. 1. [x] See on vi. 9. [y] Ib. iv. 4. [z] Ib. 6.
[a] Amos v. 10. [b] Hosea xi. 2, add 7.
[c] Amos ii. 12. [d] Hosea ix. 7, 9.
[e] Ib. vii. 1. [f] Ib. vii. 9.
[g] Ib. v. 13. viii. 9, 10. xiv. 3. and with Egypt, vii. 11. xii. 1.
[h] Hosea x. 6. xi. 9. (denying it of Egypt.)

from them fled to Egypt[i], and in Egypt they should be a derision[j], and should find their grave[k]. This captivity he had to foretell as imminent[l], certain[m], irreversible[n]. Once only, in the commencement of his prophecy, does he give any hope, that the temporal punishment might be averted through repentance. This too he follows up by renewing the declaration of God expressed in the name of his daughter, "I will not have mercy[o]," He gives them in God's Name, a distant promise of a spiritual restoration in Christ, and forewarns them that it is distant[p]. But, that they might not look for any temporal restoration, he tells them, on the one hand, in peremptory terms, of their dispersion; on the other, he tells them of their spiritual restoration without any intervening shadows of temporal deliverance. God tells them absolutely, "[q] I will cause the kingdom of the house of Israel to cease;" "I will no more have mercy upon the house of Israel;" "they shall be wanderers among the nations;" "they shall not dwell in the Lord's land;" "Israel is swallowed up; she shall be among the nations like a vessel in which is no pleasure." On the other hand, the promises are markedly spiritual[r]; "Ye are the sons of the living God;" "I will betroth her to Me for ever;" "they shall fear the Lord and His goodness;" "He will raise us up, and we shall live in His sight;" "till He come and rain righteousness upon you." "I will ransom them from the power of the grave, I will redeem them from death." Again, God contrasts[s] with this His sentence on Israel, His future dealings with Judah, and His mercies to her, of which Israel should not partake, while of Judah's spiritual mercies, He says, that Israel should partake by being united with Judah[t].

The ground of this difference was, that Israel's separate existence was bound up with that sin of Jeroboam, which clave to them throughout their history, and which none of their least bad kings ventured to give up. God tried them for two centuries and a half; and not one king was found, who would risk his throne for God. In merciful severity then, the separate kingdom of Israel was to be destroyed, and the separate existence of the ten tribes was to be lost.

This message of woe gives a peculiar character to the prophecies of Hosea. He, like St. Paul, was of the people, whose temporary excision he had to declare. He calls the wretched king of Israel "our king[u];" and God calls the rebellious people "*thy* people[v]." Of that people, he was specially the prophet. Judah he mentions incidentally, when he does mention them, not in his warnings only, but in his prophecies of good also. His main commission lay among the ten tribes. Like Elijah and Elisha whom he succeeded, he was raised up out of them, for them. His love could not be tied down to them; and so he could not but warn Judah against sharing Israel's sin. But it is, for the most part, incidentally and parenthetically[w]. He does not speak of them equally, except as to that which was the common sin of both, the seeking to Assyria for help, and unfulfilled promise of amendment[x]. And so, on the other hand, mercies, which belong to all as God's everlasting betrothal of His Church[y], and our redemption from death[z] and the grave, he foretells with special reference to Ephraim, and in one place only expressly includes Judah[a].

The prophecies of Hosea (as he himself collected them) form one whole, so that they cannot be distinctly separated, In one way, as the second chapter is the expansion and application of the first, so the remainder of the book after the third is an expansion and application of the third, The first and third chapters illustrate, summarily, Ephraim's ingratitude and desertion of God and His dealings with her, by likening them to the wife which Hosea was commanded to take, and to her children. The second chapter expands and applies the picture of Israel's unfaithfulness, touched upon in the first, but it dwells more on the side of mercy; the remaining chapters enlarge the picture of the third, although, until the last, they dwell chiefly on the side of judgment. Yet while the remainder of the book is an expansion of the third chapter, the three first chapters, (as every reader has felt) are united together, not by their narrative form only, but by the prominence given to the history of Hosea which furnishes the theme of the book, the shameful unfaithfulness of Israel, and the exceeding tenderness of the love of God, Who, "in wrath, remembers mercy."

The narrative leads us deep into the Prophet's personal sorrows. There is no ground to justify our taking as a parable, what Holy Scripture relates as a fact. There is no instance in which it can be shewn, that Holy Scripture relates that a thing was done, and *that*, with the names of persons, and yet that God did not intend it to be taken as

[i] Hosea ix. 3. [j] Hosea vii. 16.
[k] Hosea ix. 6. [l] i. 4. v. 7.
[m] v. 9. ix. 7. [n] i. 6. v. 6.
[o] i. 2–4. [p] iii. 4. 5..
[q] i. 4, 6. ix. 17. ix. 3. viii. 8. and of distant captivity iv. 19 and 16.
[r] i. 10. ii. 19. sqq. iii. 5. vi. 1–3. x. 12. xiii. 14.
[s] i. 7. vi. 11. [t] i. 11. iii. 5. [u] vii. 5.

[v] iv. 4. The words, "I have seen a horrible thing in the house of Israel" (vi. 10.), are words of God, not the prophet's own observation.
[w] iv. 15. v. 5, 10. vi. 11. "Judah also;" viii. 14. xi. 12. "Judah *yet* ruleth;" xii. 2. "with Judah also."
[x] v. 13. 14. vi. 4. [y] ii. 19, 20.
[z] xiii. 14.
[a] i. 11. Judah is included virtually in iii. 5.

literally true[b]. There would then be no test left of what was real, what imaginary; and the histories of Holy Scripture would be left to be a prey to individual caprice, to be explained away as parables, when men misliked them. Hosea, then, at God's command, united to himself in marriage, one who, amid the widespread corruption of those times, had fallen manifoldly into fleshly sin. With her he was commanded to live holily, as his wife, as Isaac lived with Rebecca whom he loved. Such an one he took, in obedience to God's command, one Gomer. At some time after she bore the prophet's children, she fell into adultery, and forsook him. Perhaps she fell into the condition of a slave[c]. God anew commanded him to shew mercy to her, to redeem her from her fallen condition, and, without restoring to her the rights of marriage[d], to guard and protect her from her sins. Thus, by the love of God and the patient forbearance which He instructed the prophet to shew, a soul was rescued from sin unto death, and was won to God; to the children of Israel there was set forth continually before their eyes a picture and a prophecy of the punishment upon sin, and of the close union with Himself which He vouchsafes to sinners who repent and return to Him.

"Not only in visions which were seen," says S. Irenæus[e], "and in words which were preached, but in acts also was He [the Word] seen by the Prophets, so as to prefigure and foreshew things future, through them. For which cause also, the Prophet Hosea took 'a wife of whoredoms,' prophesying by his act, that the earth, i. e. the men who are on the earth, shall commit whoredoms, departing from the Lord; and that of such men God will be pleased to take to Himself a Church, to be sanctified by the communication of His Son, as she too was sanctified by the communion of the Prophet. Wherefore Paul also saith, that [f]the unbelieving woman is sanctified in her believing husband." "What," asks S. Augustine[g] of the scoffers of his day, "is there opposed to the clemency of truth, what contrary to the Christian faith, that one unchaste, leaving her fornication, should be converted to a chaste marriage? And what so incongruous and alien from the faith of the Prophet, as it would have been, not to believe that all the sins of the unchaste were forgiven, when she was converted and amended? So then, when the Prophet made the unchaste one his wife, a kind provision was made for the woman to amend her life, and the mystery [of the union of Christ Himself with the Church of Jews and Gentiles] was expressed." "[h]Since the Lord, through the same Scripture, lays clearly open what is figured by this command and deed, and since the Apostolic Epistles attest that this prophecy was fulfilled in the preaching of the New Testament, who would venture to say that it was not commanded and done for that end, for which He who commanded it, explains in the holy Scripture that He commanded, and that the Prophet did it?"

The names which Hosea, by God's command gave to the children who were born, expressed the temporal punishment, which was to come upon the nation. The prophet himself, in his relation to his restored yet separated wife, was, so long as she lived, one continued, living prophecy of the tenderness of God to sinners. Fretful, wayward, jealous, ungovernable, as are mostly the tempers of those who are recovered from such sins as her's, the Prophet, in his anxious, watchful charge, was a striking picture of the forebearing loving-kindness of God to us amid our provocations and infirmities. Nay, the love which the Prophet bare her, grew the more out of his compassion and tenderness for her whom God had commanded him to take as his own. Certain it is, that Holy Scripture first speaks of her as the object of his love, when God commanded him a second time to take charge of her who had betrayed and abandoned him. God bids him shew active love to her, whom, amid her unfaithfulness, he loved already. *Go yet, love a woman, beloved of her husband, yet an adulteress.* Wonderful picture of God's love for us, for whom He gave His Only-begotten Son, loving us, while alien from Him, and with nothing in us to love!

Such was the tenderness of the Prophet, whom God employed to deliver such a message of woe; and such the people must have known to be *his* personal tenderness, who had to speak so sternly to them.

The three first prophecies, contained severally in the three first chapters, form each, a brief circle of mercy and judgment. They do not enter into any detail of Israel's sin, but sum up all in the one, which is both centre and circumference of all sin, the all-comprehending sin, departure from God, choosing the creature rather than the Creator. On this, the first prophecy foretells the entire irrevocable destruction of the kingdom; God's temporary rejection of His people, but their acceptance, together with Judah, in One Head, Christ. The second follows the same outline, rebuke, chastisement, the cessation

[b] "The prophet obeys and marries one impure, whose name and her father's name he tells, that what he says might seem not to be a mere fiction, but a true history of facts." Theod. Mops.
[c] See on iii. 2. [d] See on iii. 3.

[e] iv. 20. 12. p. 374 O. T. [f] 1 Cor. vii. 14.
[g] c. Faust. xxii. 80. Not only S. Ambrose (Apol. David. ii. 10. p. 726.) Theodoret, S. Cyril Alex., but even Theodore of Mopsuestia understood the history as fact. [h] S. Aug. ib. 89.

of visible worship, banishment, and then the betrothal for ever. The third speaks of offence against deeper love, and more prolonged punishment. It too ends in the promise of entire restoration; yet only in the latter days, after *many days* of separation, both from idolatry and from the true worship of God, such as is Israel's condition now. The rest is one continuous prophecy, in which the Prophet has probably gathered into one the substance of what he had delivered in the course of his ministry. Here and there, yet very seldom in it[i], the Prophet refers to the image of the earlier chapters. For the most part he exhibits his people to themselves, in their varied ingratitude, folly, and sin. The prophecy has many pauses, which with one exception coincide with our chapters[j]. It rises and falls, and then bursts out in fresh tones of upbraiding[k], and closes mostly in notes of sorrow and of woe[l], for the destruction which is coming. Yet at none of these pauses is there any complete break, such as would constitute what preceded, a separate prophecy; and on the other hand, the structure of the last portion of the book corresponds most with that of the first three chapters, if it is regarded as one whole. For as there, after rebuke and threatened chastisement, each prophecy ended with the promise of future mercy, so here, after finally foreannouncing the miseries at the destruction of Samaria, the Prophet closes his prophecy and his whole book with a description of Israel's future repentance and acceptance, and of his flourishing with manifold grace.

The brief summary, in which the Prophet calls attention to all which he had said, and foretells, who would and who would not understand it, the more marks the prophecy as one whole.

Yet, although these prophecies, as wrought into one by the Prophet, bear a strong impress of unity, there yet seem to be traces, here and there, of the different conditions of the kingdom of Israel, amid which different parts were first uttered. The order, in which they stand, seems, upon the whole, to be an order of time. In the first chapters, the house of Jeroboam is still standing in strength, and Israel appears to have trusted in its own power, as the prophet Amos[m] also, at the same time, describes them. The fourth chapter is addressed to the "house of Israel[n]" only, without any allusion to the king, and accords with that time of convulsive anarchy, which followed the death of Jeroboam II. The omission of the king is the more remarkable, inasmuch as the "house of the king" *is* included in the corresponding address in ch. v.[o] The "rulers[p]" of Israel are also spoken of in the plural; and the bloodshed[q] described seems to be more than individual insulated murders. In this case, the king upbraided in ch. v. would, naturally, be the next king, Zechariah, in whom God's promise to the house of Jehu expired. In the seventh chapter a weak and sottish king is spoken of, whom his princes misled to debauchery, disgusting drunkenness and impiety. But Menahem was a general of fierce determination, energy and barbarity. Debauchery and brutal ferocity are natural associates; but this sottishness here described was rather the fruit of weak compliance with the debauchery of others. "The princes made him sick[r]," it is said. This is not likely to have been the character of successful usurpers, as Menahem, or Pekah, or Hoshea. It is far more likely to have been that of Zechariah, who was placed on the throne for 6 months, "did evil in the sight of the Lord," and then was "slain publicly before the people[s]," no one resisting. Him, as being the last of the line of Jehu, and sanctioned by God, Hosea may the rather have called "our king[t]," owning in him, evil as he was, God's appointment. The words, "they have devoured their judges, all their kings have fallen[u]," had anew their fulfillment in the murder of Zechariah and Shallum (B.C. 772) as soon as the promise to the house of Jehu had expired. The blame of Judah for "[v] multiplying fenced cities," instead of trusting in God, probably relates to the temper in which they were built in the days of Jotham[w], between B.C. 758, and 741. Although Jotham was a religious king, the corruption of the people at this time is especially recorded; "the people did corruptly." Later yet, we have mention of the dreadful battle, when Shalman, or Shalmanezer, took and massacred women and children at Betharbel[x] in the valley of Jezreel, about B.C. 729. Hosea, thus, lived to see the fulfillment of his earlier prophecy, "[y] I will break the bow of Israel in the valley of Jezreel." It has been thought that the question "where is thy king?" relates to the captivity of Hoshea, three years before the destruction of Samaria. This sort of question, however, relates not to the actual place where the king was, but to his ability or inability to help.

It belongs to the mournful solemnity of

[i] iv. 5. v. 3. 7. ix. 1.
[j] c. v. and vi. alone seems to be one.
[k] See the beginnings of cc. v. vii. viii. ix. x. xi. xii. xiii.
[l] See iv. ult. vii. 16. viii. 14. ix. 17. x. 15. xii. 14. xiii. 16. Chapters vi. and xi. close with the contrast with Judah, ch. vi., declaring that for Judah only was there a harvest reserved on its return from captivity; ch. xi. that it alone maintained the true religion.
[m] ii. 14, 16. vi. 13.
[n] Hosea iv. 1.
[o] v. 1.
[p] iv. 18.
[q] iv. 2.
[r] vii. 5.
[s] 2 Kgs xv. 10.
[t] Hosea vii. 5.
[u] vii. 7.
[v] viii. 14.
[w] 2 Chron. xxvii. 2–4.
[x] Hosea x. 14.
[y] Ib. i. 4. see on x. 14.

Hosea's prophecy, that he scarcely speaks to the people in his own person. The ten chapters, which form the centre of the prophecy, are almost wholly one long dirge of woe, in which the prophet rehearses the guilt and the punishment of his people. If the people are addressed, it is, with very few exceptions, God Himself, not the Prophet, Who speaks to them; and God speaks to them as their Judge[*]. Once only does the Prophet use the form, so common in the other Prophets, "[a]saith the Lord." As in the three first chapters, the Prophet, in his relation to his wife, represented that of God to His people, so, in these ten chapters, after the first words of the fourth and fifth chapters, "Hear the word of the Lord, for the Lord hath a controversy with the inhabitants of the land," "Hear ye this, O priests[b]," whenever the prophet uses the first person, he uses it not of himself, but of God. "I" "My[c]" are not Hosea, and the things of Hosea, but God and what belongs to God. God addresses the Prophet himself in the second person[d]. In four verses only of these chapters does the Prophet himself apparently address his own people Israel, in two[e] expostulating with them; in two[f], calling them to repentance. In two other verses he addresses Judah[g], or foretells to him judgment mingled with mercy[h]. The last chapter alone is one of almost unmingled brightness; the Prophet calls to repentance[i], and God in His own Person[j] accepts it, and promises large supply of grace. But this too closes the prophecy with the warning, that righteous as are the ways of God, the transgressors should stumble in them.

It is this same solemn pathos, which has chiefly occasioned the obscurity, complained of in Hosea. The expression of S. Jerome has often been repeated; "[k]Hosea is concise, and speaketh, as it were, in detached sayings." The words of upbraiding, of judgment, of woe, burst out, as it were, one by one, slowly, heavily, condensed, abrupt, from the Prophet's heavy and shrinking soul, as God commanded and constrained him, and put His words, like fire, in the Prophet's mouth. An image of Him Who said, "[l]O Jerusalem, Jerusalem, thou that killest the Prophets and stonest them which are sent unto thee, how often would I have gathered thy children together, even as a hen gathers her chickens under her wings, and ye would not," he delivers his message, as though each sentence burst with a groan from his soul, and he had anew to take breath, before he uttered each renewed woe. Each verse forms a whole for itself, like one heavy toll in a funeral knell. The Prophet has not been careful about order and symmetry, so that each sentence went home to the soul. And yet the unity of the prophecy is so evident in the main, that we cannot doubt that it is not broken, even when the connection is not apparent on the surface. The great difficulty consequently in Hosea is to ascertain that connection in places where it evidently exists, yet where the Prophet has not explained it. The easiest and simplest sentences[m] are sometimes, in this respect, the most difficult. It is in remarkable contrast with this abruptness in the more mournful parts, that when Hosea has a message of mercy to deliver, his style becomes easy and flowing. Then no sign of present sin or impending misery disturbs his brightness. He lives wholly in the future bliss which he was allowed to foretell. Yet, meanwhile, no prophet had a darker future to declare. The prophets of Judah could mingle with their present denunciations a prospect of an early restoration. The ten tribes, as a whole, had no future. The temporal part of their punishment was irreversible. Hosea lived almost to see its fulfillment. Yet not the less confidently does he foretell the spiritual mercies in store for his people. He promises them as absolutely as if he saw them. It is not matter of hope, but of certainty. And this certainty Hosea announces, in words expressive of the closest union with God; an union shadowed by the closest union which we know, that, whereby a man and his wife are *no more twain, but one flesh*. Here, as filled and overfilled with joy, instead of abrupt sentences, he gladly lingers on his subject, adding in every word something to the fulness of the blessing contained in the preceding[n]. He is, indeed, (if one may venture so to speak) eminently a prophet of the tenderness of the love of God. In foretelling God's judgments, he ventures to picture Him to us, as overcome (so to speak) by mercy, so that He would not execute His full sentence[o]. God's mercies he predicts in the inmost relation of love, that those whom He had rejected, He would own, as "sons of the living God;" that He would betroth them to Himself in righteousness, in judg-

[*] Ib. iv. 5, 6, 13, 14. v. 3, 13. vi. 4, 5. viii. 5. ix. 10. xiii. 4, 5, 9, 11. In xi. 8, 9, God speaks to them, in mitigation of His sentence; x. 9, is uncertain, but in x. 10, God speaks.

[a] Hosea xi. 11.

[b] Hosea iv. 1. v. 1.

[c] In fifty-seven verses, iv. 5–9, 12–14. 17. v. 2, 3, 9, 10, 12, 14, 15. vi. 4–7, 10, 11. vii. 1, 2, 12–15. viii. 1, 2, 4, 5, 10, 12, 14. ix. 10, 12, 15, 16. x. 10, 11. xi. 1, 3. 4. 7–9, 12. xii. 9, 10. xiii. 4, 9, 11. There are apparently only ten verses, in which the Prophet speaks of *the Lord* in the third person, iv. 10. v. 4, 6, 7. ix. 3, 4. x. 12. xii. 2, 13. xiii. 15. He says, "My God" ix. 8, 17.

[d] iv. 4, 17. viii. 1.

[e] ix. 1, 5.

[f] Hosea x. 12; (but followed by a declaration of the fruitlessness of his call 13, 15.) xii. 6.

[g] Hosea iv. 13.

[h] See on vi. 11.

[i] Hosea xiv. 1, 3.

[j] Ib. xiv. 4, 8.

[k] Osee commaticus est, et quasi per sententias loquitur. Præf. in xii. Proph.

[l] S. Matt. xxiii. 37.

[m] e. g. xii. 9, 12, 13.

[n] ii. 14–20. xiv. 1–7.

[o] xi. 8, 9.

ment, loving-kindness, mercies, faithfulness, and that, for ever; that He would raise us up on the third day, and that we should live in His sight, ransoming us, Himself, and redeeming us, as our Kinsman, from death and the grave[p].

In this prophecy of the betrothal of the Church to God, he both applies and supplies the teaching of the forty-fifth Psalm and of the Song of Solomon. Moses had been taught to declare to his people that God had, in a special way, made them His people, and was Himself their God. The violation of this relation, by taking other Gods, Moses had also spoken of under the image of married faithlessness. But faithlessness implies the existence of the relation, to which they were bound to be faithful. The whole human family, however, had once belonged to God, and had fallen away from Him. And so Moses speaks of the heathen idolatry also under this name, and warned Israel against sharing their sin. "[q] Lest thou make a covenant with the inhabitants of the land, and they go a whoring after their gods,—and their daughters go a whoring after their gods, and make thy sons go a whoring after their gods." The relation itself of betrothal Moses does not mention; yet it must have been suggested to the mind of Israel by his describing this special sin of choosing other gods, under the title of married faithlessness[r] and of desertion of God[s], and by his attributing to God the title of "Jealous[t]." It was reserved to Hosea, to exhibit at once to Israel under this image, God's tender love for them and their ingratitude, to dwell on their relation to God Whom they forsook[u], and explicitly to foretell to them that new betrothal in Christ which should abide for ever.

The Image, however, presupposes an acquaintance with the language of the Pentateuch; and it has been noticed that Hosea incidentally asserts that the written Pentateuch was still used in the kingdom of Israel. For God does not say, "I have *given* to him," but "I have *written*," or "I write[v] to him the great" or "manifold[w]" things of the law. The "ten thousand things" which God says that He had written, cannot be the decalogue only, nor would the word "written" be used of an unwritten tradition. God says moreover, "I write," in order to express that the law, although written once for all, still came from the ever-present authority of Him Who wrote it.

The language of Hosea is, for the most part, too concise and broken, to admit of his employing actual sentences of the Pentateuch. This he does sometimes[x], as has been pointed out[y]. On the other hand, his concise allusions would scarcely be understood by those who were not familiar with the history and laws of the Pentateuch[z]. Since then plainly a prophet spoke so as to be understood by the people, this is an evidence of the continual use of the Pentateuch in Israel, after the great schism from Judah. The schools of the Prophets, doubtless, maintained the teaching of the law, as they did the public worship. The people went to Elisha on new-moons and sabbaths, and so to other prophets also[a]. Even after the great massacre of the prophets by Jezebel[b], we have incidental notices of schools of the prophets at Bethel[c], Jericho[d], Gilgal[e], Mount Ephraim[f], Samaria[g], from which other schools were formed[h]. The selection of Gilgal, Bethel, and Samaria, shews that the spots were chosen, in order to confront idolatry and corruption in their chief abodes. The contradiction of men's lives to the law, thus extant and taught among them, could scarcely have been greater than that of Christians now to the Bible which they have in their houses and their hands and their ears, but not in their hearts.

p See on i. 10. ii. 19. sqq. vi. 2. xiii. 14.
q Ex. xxxiv. 15, 16.
r Lev. xvii. 7. xx. 5, 6. Num. xiv. 33.
s Deut. xxxi. 16.
t Ex. xx. 5. xxxiv. 14. Deut. iv. 24. v. 9. vi. 15. Num. xxv. 2.
u The language "went a whoring *from* God" &c. occurs in Ps. lxxiii. 27. Hos. i. 2. iv. 12. ix. 1. not in the Pentateuch. In Ezek. xxiii. 5, "when she was Mine."
v viii. 12.
w lit. "ten thousand" according to the textual reading.

x See iii. 1. iv. 8, 10. v. 6, 10, 11, 14. vi. 2, 3. x. 14. xi. 7, 8. xii. 4, 6. xiii. 6, 9. xiv. 2.
y Hengstenberg Authentie des Pentateuches, i. 48. sqq. although, naturally, all his instances will not seem to all to have the force of proof.
z See i. 10, 11. iii. 2. iv. 4, 8. viii. 6, 11, 13. ix. 3, 10. x. 4, 11. xi. 8, xii. 4–6, 10, 11, 12. xiv. 3, 4.
a 2 Kgs iv. 23. b 1 Kgs xviii. 13. c 2 Kgs ii. 3 d Ib. 5. e Ib. iv. 38. f Ib. v. 22.
g Elisha dwelt in Mount Carmel, 2 Kgs ii. 25. iv. 25. but also at Samaria, 2 Kgs ii. 25. (probably v. 9.) vi. 32. He had a school of "sons of the prophets" with him, vi. 1. ix. 1. h Ib. vi. 1.

HOSEA.

Before CHRIST cir. 785.

CHAPTER I.

1 *Hosea, to shew God's judgment for spiritual whoredom, taketh Gomer,* 4 *and hath by her Jezreel,* 6 *Lo-ruhamah,* 8 *and Lo-ammi.* 10 *The restoration of Judah and Israel.*

THE word of the LORD
that came unto Hosea,
the son of Beeri, in the
days of Uzziah, Jotham,
Ahaz, *and* Hezekiah, kings
of Judah, and in the days
of Jeroboam the son of
Joash, king of Israel.
2 The beginning of the
word of the LORD by
Hosea. And the LORD
said to Hosea, [a] Go, take

[a] So ch. 3. 1.

CHAP. 1., ver. 1. *The word of the Lord, that came unto Hosea.* Hosea, at the very beginning of his prophecy, declares that all this, which he delivered, came, not from his own mind but from God. As S. Paul says, *Paul an Apostle, not of men neither by man, but by Jesus Christ, and God the Father.* He refers all to God, and claims all obedience to Him. That word *came* to him; it existed then before, in the mind of God. It was first God's, then it became the Prophet's, receiving it from God. So it is said, *the word of God came to John*[1].

Hosea, i. e. *Salvation,* or, *the Lord saveth.* The Prophet bare the name of our Lord Jesus, Whom he foretold and of Whom he was a type. *Son of Beeri,* i. e. *my well or welling-forth.* God ordained that the name of his father too should signify truth. From God, as from the Fountain of life, Hosea drew the living waters, which he poured out to the people. *With joy shall ye draw water out of the wells of salvation*[2].

In the days of Uzziah, &c. Hosea, although a Prophet of Israel, marks his prophecy by the names of the kings of Judah, because the kingdom of Judah was the kingdom of the theocracy, the line of David to which the promises of God were made. As Elisha, to whose office he succeeded, turned away from Jehoram[3], saying, *get thee to the prophets of thy father, and to the prophets of thy mother,* and owned Jehoshaphat king of Judah only, so, in the title of his prophecy, Hosea at once expresses that the kingdom of Judah alone was legitimate. He adds the name of Jeroboam, partly as the last king of Israel whom, by virtue of His promise to Jehu, God helped; partly to shew that God never left Israel unwarned. Jeroboam I. was warned first by the prophet[4], who by his own untimely death, as well as in his prophecy, was a witness to the strictness of God's judgments, and then by Ahijah[5]; Baasha by Jehu, son of Hanani[6]; Ahab, by Elijah and Micaiah son of Imla; Ahaziah by Elijah[7]; Jehoram by Elisha who exercised his office until the days of Joash[8]. So, in the days of Jeroboam II, God raised up Hosea, Amos and Jonah. "The kings and people of Israel then were without excuse, since God never ceased to send His prophets among them; in no reign did the voice of the prophets fail, warning of the coming wrath of God, until it came." While Jeroboam was recovering to Israel a larger rule than it had ever had since it separated from Judah, annexing to it Damascus[9] which had been lost to Judah even in the days of Solomon, and from which Israel had of late so greatly suffered, Hosea was sent to forewarn it of its destruction. God alone could utter "such a voice of thunder out of the midst of such a cloudless sky." Jeroboam doubtless thought that his house would, through its own strength, survive the period which God had pledged to it. "But temporal prosperity is no proof either of stability or of the favor of God. Where the law of God is observed, there, even amid the pressure of outward calamity, is the assurance of ultimate prosperity. Where God is disobeyed, *there* is the pledge of coming destruction. The seasons when men feel most secure against future chastisement, are often the preludes of the most signal revolutions."

2. *The beginning of the word of the Lord by Hosea* or *in Hosea.* God first revealed Himself and His mysteries to the prophet's soul, by His secret inspiration, and then declared, through him, to others, what He had deposited in him. God enlightened him, and then others through the light in him.

And the Lord said unto Hosea. For this thing was to be done by Hosea alone, because God had commanded it, not by others of their own mind. To Isaiah God first revealed Himself, as sitting in the temple, adored by the Seraphim: to Ezekiel God first appeared, as enthroned above the Cherubim in the Holy of Holies; to Jeremiah God announced that, ere yet he was born, He had sanctified him for this office: to Hosea He enjoined, as the beginning of his prophetic office, an act contrary to man's natu-

[1] S. Luke iii. 2. [2] Isa. xii. 3. [3] 2 Kgs iii. 13, 14. [4] 1 Kgs xiii. [5] Ib. xiv. [6] Ib. xvi. [7] 2 Kgs i. [8] Ib. xiii. 14. [9] Ib. xiv. 28.

Before CHRIST cir. 785.

unto thee a wife of whoredoms and children of whoredoms: for [b]the land hath committed great whoredom, *departing* from the LORD.

[b] Deut. 31. 16. Ps. 73. 27. Jer. 2. 13. Ezek. 23. 3, &c.

3 So he went and took Gomer the daughter of

ral feelings, yet one, by which he became an image of the Redeemer, uniting to Himself what was unholy, in order to make it holy.

Go take unto thee. Since Hosea prophesied some eighty years, he must now have been in early youth, holy, pure, as became a prophet of God. Being called thus early, he had doubtless been formed by God as a chosen instrument of His will, and had, like Samuel, from his first childhood, been trained in true piety and holiness. Yet he was to unite unto him, so long as she lived, one greatly defiled, in order to win her thereby to purity and holiness; herein, a little likeness of our Blessed Lord, Who, in the Virgin's womb, to save us, espoused our flesh, in us sinful, in Him All-holy, without motion to sin; and, further, espoused the Church, formed of us who, *whether Jews or Gentiles, were all under sin*, aliens from God and gone away from Him, *serving divers lusts and passions*, [1] *to make it a glorious Church, without spot or wrinkle.*

A wife of whoredoms, i. e. take as a wife, one who up to that time had again and again been guilty of that sin. So *men of bloods*[2] are "men given up to bloodshedding;" and our Lord was *a Man of Sorrows*[3], not occasional only, but manifold and continual, throughout His whole life. She must, then, amid the manifold corruption of Israel, have been repeatedly guilty of that sin, perhaps as an idolatress, thinking of it to be in honour of their foul gods[4]. She was not like those degraded ones, who cease to bear children; still she must have manifoldly sinned. So much the greater was the obedience of the Prophet. Nor could any other woman so shadow forth the manifold defilements of the human race, whose nature our Incarnate Lord vouchsafed to unite in His own Person to the perfect holiness of the Divine Nature.

And children of whoredoms; for they shared the disgrace of their mother, although born in lawful marriage. The sins of parents descend also, in a mysterious way, on their children. Sin is contagious, and, unless the entail is cut off by grace, hereditary. The mother thus far portrays man's revolts, before his union with God; the children, our forsaking of God, after we have been made His children. The forefathers of Israel, God tells them, *served* other *gods, on the other side of the flood*[5], (i. e. in Ur of the Chaldees, whence God called Abraham) *and in Egypt.* It was out of such defilement, that God took her[6], and He says, *Thou becamest Mine*[7]. Whom He maketh His, He maketh pure; and of her, not such as she was in herself by nature, but as such as He made her, He says[8], *I remember thee, the kindness of thy youth, the love of thine espousals, when thou wentest after Me, in the wilderness.* But she soon fell away; and thenceforth there were among them (as there are now among Christians,) the children of God, *the children of the promise*, and the *children of whoredoms*, or *of the devil.*

For the land, &c. This is the reason why God commands Hosea to do this thing, in order to shadow out their foulness and God's mercy. What no man would dare to do[9], except at God's bidding, God in a manner doth, restoring to union with Himself those who had gone away from Him. *The land*, i. e., Israel, and indirectly, Judah also, and, more widely yet, the whole earth.

Departing from lit. *from after the Lord.* Our whole life should be, [10]*forgetting the things which are behind, to follow after* Him, Whom here we can never fully attain unto, God in His Infinite Perfection, yet so as, with our whole heart, *fully to follow after Him.* To depart from the Creator and to serve the creature, is adultery; as the Psalmist says, [11] *Thou hast destroyed all them, that go a whoring from Thee.* He who seeks any thing out of God, turns from following Him, and takes to him something else as his god, is unfaithful, and spiritually an adulterer and idolater. For he is an adulterer, who becomes another's than God's.

3. *So he went.* He did not demur, nor excuse himself, as did even Moses[12], or Jeremiah[13], or S. Peter[14], and were rebuked for it, although mercifully by the All-Merciful. Hosea, accustomed from childhood to obey God and every indication of the Will of God, did at once, what he was bidden, however repulsive to natural feeling, and became, thereby, the more an image of the obedience of Christ Jesus, and a pattern to us, at once to believe and obey God's commands, however little to our minds.

Gomer, the daughter of Diblaim. Gomer is completion; *Diblaim*, a double lump of figs; which are a figure of sweetness. These names may mean, that "the sweetness of sins is the parent of destruction;" or that Israel,

[1] Eph. v. 27 [2] Ps. v. 6. [3] Isa. liii. 3. [4] See on iv. 13, 24. [5] Josh. xxiv. 14. [6] Ezek. xxiii. 3, 8.

[7] Ezek. xvi. 8. [8] Jer. ii. 2. [9] Ib. iii. 1. [10] Phil. iii. 13. [11] Ps. lxxiii. 27. [12] Ex. iv. 18. [13] Jer. i. 6. [14] Acts x. 4.

Before CHRIST cir. 785.

Diblaim; which conceived,
and bare him a son.
4 And the LORD said
unto him, Call his name
Jezreel; for yet a little
while, [c]and I will † avenge
the blood of Jezreel upon
the house of Jehu, [d]and

Before CHRIST cir. 785.

c 2 Kings 10. 11.
† Heb. *visit*.
d 2 Kings 15. 10, 12.

---

or mankind had completely forsaken God, and were children of corrupting pleasure.

Holy Scripture relates that all this was done, and tells us the births and names of the children, as real history. As such then, must we receive it. We must not imagine things to be unworthy of God, because they do not commend themselves to us. God does not dispense with the moral law, because the moral law has its source in the Mind of God Himself. To dispense with it would be to contradict Himself. But God, Who is the absolute Lord of all things which He made, may, at His Sovereign Will, dispose of the lives or things which He created. Thus, as Sovereign Judge, He commanded the lives of the Canaanites to be taken away by Israel, as, in His ordinary Providence, He has ordained that the magistrate should not bear the sword in vain, but has made him His *minister, a revenger to execute wrath upon him that doeth evil*[1]. So, again, He, Whose are all things, willed to repay to the Israelites their hard and unjust servitude, by commanding them to *spoil the Egyptians*[2]. He, Who created marriage, commanded to Hosea, *whom* he should marry. The Prophet was not defiled, by taking as his lawful wife, at God's bidding, one defiled, however hard a thing this was. "He who remains good, is not defiled by coming in contact with one evil; but the evil, following his example, is turned into good." But through his simple obedience, he foreshadowed Him, God the Word, Who was called [3]*the Friend of publicans and sinners;* Who warned the Pharisees, that[4] *the publicans and harlots should enter unto the kingdom of God before them;* and who now vouchsafes to espouse, dwell in, and unite Himself with, and so to hallow, our sinful souls. The acts which God enjoined to the Prophets, and which to us seem strange, must have had an impressiveness to the people, in proportion to their strangeness. The life of the Prophet became a sermon to the people. Sight impresses more than words. The Prophet, being in his own person a mirror of obedience, did moreover, by his way of life, reflect to the people some likeness of the future and of things unseen. The expectation of the people was wound up, when they saw their Prophets do things at God's command, which they themselves could not have done. When Ezekiel was bidden to shew no sign of mourning, on the sudden death of [5]*the desire of his eyes*, his wife; or when he dug through the wall of his house, and carried forth his household stuff in the twilight, with his face covered[6]; the people asked, [7]*Wilt thou not tell us what these things are to us, that thou doest so?* No words could so express a grief beyond all power of grieving, as Ezekiel's mute grief for one who was known to be "*the desire of his eyes*," yet for whom he was forbidden to shew the natural expressions of grief, or to use the received tokens of mourning. God Himself declares the ground of such acts to have been, that, rebellious as the house of Israel was[8], *with eyes which saw not, and ears which heard not*, they might yet consider such acts as these.

4. *Call his name Jezreel;* i.e. in its first sense here, "God will scatter." The life of the prophet, and his union with one so unworthy of him, were a continued prophecy of God's mercy. The names of the children were a life-long admonition of His intervening judgments. Since Israel refused to hear God's words, He made the prophet's sons, through the mere fact of their presence among them, their going out and coming in, and the names which He gave them, to be preachers to the people. He depicted in them and in their names what was to be, in order that, whenever they saw or heard of them, His warnings might be forced upon them, and those who would take warning, might be saved. If, with their mother's disgrace, these sons inherited and copied their mother's sins, then their names became even more expressive, that, being such as they were, they would be scattered by God, would not be owned by God as His people, or be pitied by Him.

I will avenge the blood of Jezreel upon the house of Jehu. Yet Jehu shed this blood, the blood of the house of Ahab, of Joram and Jezebel and the seventy sons of Ahab, at God's command and in fulfillment of His Will. How was it then sin? Because, if we do what is the Will of God for any end of our own, for any thing except God, we do, in fact, our own will, not God's. It was not lawful for Jehu to depose and slay the king his master, except at the command of God, Who, as the Supreme King, sets up and puts down earthly rulers as He wills. For any other end, and done otherwise than at God's express command, such an act is sin. Jehu was rewarded for the measure in which he fulfilled God's

1 Rom. xiii. 4. 2 Ex. iii. 22. 3 S. Matt. xi. 19. 4 Ib. xxi. 31. 5 Ezek. xxiv. 16–18.

6 Ib. xii. 3–7. 7 Ib. xxiv. 19. add xii. 10. 8 Ib. xii. 2.

Before CHRIST cir. 785.

will cause to cease the
kingdom of the house of
Israel.

e 2 Kings 15. 29.

5 [e]And it shall come to
pass at that day, that I
will break the bow of
Israel in the valley of
Jezreel.

Before CHRIST cir. 785.

commands, as Ahab who had *sold himself to work wickedness*, had yet a temporal reward for humbling himself publicly, when rebuked by God for his sin, and so honoring God, amid an apostate people. But Jehu, by cleaving, against the Will of God, to Jeroboam's sin, which served his own political ends, shewed that, in the slaughter of his master, he acted not, as he pretended, out of *zeal*[1] for the Will of God, but served his own will and his own ambition only. By his disobedience to the one command of God, he shewed that he would have equally disobeyed the other, had it been contrary to his own will of interest. He had no principle of obedience. And so the blood, which was shed according to the righteous judgment of God, became sin to *him* who shed it in order to fulfill, not the Will of God, but his own. Thus God said to Baasha[2] *I exalted thee out of the dust, and made thee prince over My people Israel*, which he became by slaying his master, the son of Jeroboam, and all the house of Jeroboam. Yet, because he followed the sins of Jeroboam[3], *the word of the Lord came against Baasha, for all the evil that he did in the sight of the Lord, in being like the house of Jeroboam, and because he killed him.* The two courses of action were inconsistent; to destroy the son and the house of Jeroboam, and to do those things, for which God condemned him to be destroyed. Further yet. Not only was *such* execution of God's judgments itself an offence against Almighty God, but it was sin, whereby he condemned himself, and made his other sins to be sins against the light. In executing the judgment of God against another, he pronounced His judgment against himself, in that he *that judged*, in God's stead, *did the same things*[4]. So awful a thing is it, to be the instrument of God in punishing or reproving others, if we do not, by His grace, keep our own hearts and hands pure from sin.

And will cause to cease the kingdom of the house of Israel. Not the kingdom of the house of Jehu, but all Israel. God had promised that the family of Jehu should sit on the throne to the fourth generation. Jeroboam II., the third of these, was now reigning over Israel, in the fulness of his might. He *restored the coast of Israel from the entering of Hamath*[5], i. e. from the Northern extremity, near Mount Hermon, where Palestine joins on to Syria, and, which Solomon only in all his glory had won for Israel[6], *unto the sea of the plain*, the Dead sea, regaining all which Hazael had conquered[7], and even subduing Moab also[8], *according to the word of the Lord by Jonah the son of Amittai.* He had recovered to Israel, Damascus, which had been lost to Judah, ever since the close of the reign of Solomon[9]. He was a warlike prince, like that first Jeroboam, who had formed the strength and the sin of the ten tribes. Yet both his house and his kingdom fell with him. The whole history of that kingdom afterwards is little more than that of the murder of one family by another, such as is spoken of in the later chapters of Hosea; and Israel, i. e. the ten tribes, were finally carried captive, fifty years after the death of Zechariah, Jeroboam's son. Of so little account is any seeming prosperity or strength.

5. *I will break the bow of Israel in the valley of Jezreel.* The valley of Jezreel is a beautiful and a broad valley or plain, stretching, from W. to E., from Mount Carmel and the sea to the Jordan, which it reaches through two arms, between the Mountains of Gilboa, little Hermon, and Tabor; and from S. to N. from the Mountains of Ephraim to those of Galilee. Nazareth lay on its Northern side. It is called "[10]the great plain," "[11]the great plain of Esdraelon." There God had signally executed His judgments against the enemies of His people, or on His people, when they became His enemies. There He gave the great victories over the invading hosts of Sisera[12], and of Midian, with the children of the East[13]. There also He ended the life and kingdom of Saul[14], visiting upon him, when his measure of iniquity was full, his years of contumacy, and his persecution of David, whom God had chosen. Jezreel became a royal residence of the house of Ahab[15]. There, in the scenes of Ahab's wickedness and of Jehu's hypocritical zeal; there, where he drave furiously, to avenge, as he alleged, on the house of Ahab, the innocent blood which Ahab had shed in Jezreel, Hosea foretells that the kingdom of Israel should be broken In the same plain, at the battle with Shalmaneser, near Betharbel[16], Hosea lived to see his prophecy fulfilled. The strength of the kingdom was

[1] 2 Kings x. 16. [2] 1 Kings xvi. 2. [3] Ib. xvi. 7.
[4] Rom. ii. 1. [5] 2 Kings xiv. 25. [6] 2 Chr. viii. 3, 4.
[7] 2 Kings x. 32, 33. [8] See on Am. vi. 14.
[9] 1 Kings xi. 24. [10] 1 Macc. xii. 49.
[11] Judith i. 8. [12] Jud. iv. 4 sqq.
[13] Jud. vi. 33.
[14] 1 Sam. xxix. 1. xxxi. 1, 7, 10.
[16] 1 Kings xviii. 46. xxi. 1, 2, 3. 2 Kings ix. 10, 25, 30. x. 1, 11.
[16] See on x. 14.

Before CHRIST cir. 785.

6 ¶ And she conceived
again, and bare a daughter.
And *God* said unto him,
Call her name || Lo-ruha-
mah: [f]for † I will no more
have mercy upon the house
of Israel; || but I will ut-
terly take them away.

|| That is, *Not having obtained mercy.*
[f] 2 Kings 17. 6, 23.
† Heb. *I will not add any more to.*
|| Or, *that I should altogether pardon them.*

7 [g]But I will have mer-
cy upon the house of Ju-
dah, and will save them
by the LORD their God,
and [h]will not save them
by bow, nor by sword, nor
by battle, by horses nor by
horsemen.

Before CHRIST cir. 785.
[g] 2 Kings 19. 35.
[h] Zech. 4. 6. & 9. 10.

---

there finally broken; the sufferings there endured were one last warning before the capture of Samaria[1].

The name of Jezreel blends the sins with the punishment. It resembles, in form and in sound, the name of Israel, and contains a reversal of the promise contained in the name of Israel, in which they trusted. *Yisrael* (as their name was originally pronounced[2]) signifies, *he is a prince with God; Yidsreel, God shall scatter.* They who, while they followed the faith, for which their forefather Jacob received from God the name of Israel, had been truly Israel, i. e. "princes with God," should now be *Yidsreel*, "scattered by God."

6. *Call her name Lo-ruhamah.* The name is rendered in St. Paul[3], *not beloved*, in St. Peter[4], *hath not obtained mercy. Love* and *mercy* are both contained in the full meaning of the intensive form of the Hebrew word, which expresses the deep tender yearnings of the inmost soul over one loved; as in the words, "[5]*As a father pitieth* [*yearneth over*] *his own children, so the Lord pitieth* [*yearneth over*] *them that fear Him.* It is *tender love* in Him Who pitieth; *mercy*, as shewn to him who needeth mercy. The punishment, foretold under the name of the daughter, *Unpitied*, is a great enlargement of that conveyed under the name of the first son, *God shall scatter.* Judah too was carried captive, and scattered; but after the 70 years, she was restored. The 10 tribes, it is now foretold, when scattered, should, as a whole, be cut off from the tender mercy of God, scattered by Him, and as a whole, never be restored. Those only were restored, who, when Judah returned from captivity, clave to her, or subsequently, one by one, were united to her.

But I will utterly take them away. Lit., *for,* [6]*taking away, I will take away from them*, or *with regard to them*, viz., everything. He specifies nothing; He excepts nothing; only, with that awful emphasis, He dwells on the taking away, as that which He had determined to do to the utmost. This is the thought, which He wills to dwell on the mind. As a little while after, God says, that He would be nothing to them, so here, where He in fact repeats this one thought, *take away, take away, from them*, the guilty conscience of Israel would at once, supply, "all." When God threatens, the sinful or awakened soul sees instinctively what draws down the lightning of God's wrath, and where it will fall.

7. *I will have mercy on the house of Judah.* For to them the promises were made in David, and of them, according to the flesh, Christ was to come. Israel, moreover, as being founded in rebellion and apostacy, had gone on from bad to worse. All their kings clave to the sin of Jeroboam; not one did right in the sight of God; not one repented or hearkened to God. Whereas Judah, having the true Worship of God, and the reading of the law, and the typical sacrifices, through which it looked on to the great Sacrifice for sin, was on the whole, a witness to the truth of God[7].

And will save them by the Lord their God, not by bow, &c. Shortly after this, God did, in the reign of Hezekiah, save them by Himself from Sennacherib, when the Angel of the Lord smote in one night 185,000 in the camp of the Assyrians. "Neither in that night, nor when they were freed from the captivity at Babylon, did they bend bow or draw sword against their enemies or their captors. While they slept, the Angel of the Lord smote the camp of the Assyrians. At the prayers of David and the prophets and holy men, yea, and of the angels[8] too, the Lord stirred up the spirit of Cyrus king of Persia, to set them free *to go up to Jerusalem, and build the temple of the Lord God of Israel*[9].

---

[1] See on x. 15.

[2] The two names would either be pronounced, *Yisrael, Yidsreel*; or both, *Israel, Idsreel.*

[3] Romans ix. 25.

[4] 1 S. Peter ii. 10.

[5] Ps. ciii. 13.

[6] This mode of speech is often used in Holy Scripture. First, a negative is used; then, the opposite is said in this emphatic way affirmatively, *Thou shalt not spare him, for killing thou shalt kill him,* Deut. xiii. 8, 9. [9, 10. Heb.] *Thou shalt not escape out of his hand; for, taking, thou shalt be taken.* Jer. xxxiv. 3. *We will not hearken unto thee; for, doing, we will do whatsoever,* &c. Ib. xliv. 17. Add Jer. xlix. 12. Ex. xix. 13. Deut. xx. 17. This uniform usage, doubtless, determined our Translators to prefer the rendering of the text to that in the margin, "That I should altogether pardon them," which would require the two כִּי's to be taken in different senses.

[7] See on xi. 12.

[8] Zech. i. 12.

[9] Ezr. i. 3.

Before CHRIST cir. 785.

8 ¶ Now when she had
weaned Lo-ruhamah, she
conceived, and bare a
son.

9 Then said *God*, Call
his name ‖ Lo-ammi: for
ye *are* not my people, and
I will not be your *God*.

‖ That is, *Not my people.*

But much more, this is the special promise of the Gospel, that God would deliver, not outwardly, but inwardly; not by human wars, but in peace; not by man, but by Himself. *By the Lord their God*, by Himself Who is speaking, or, The Father by the Son, (in like way as it is said, [1] *The Lord rained upon Sodom fire from the Lord.*) They were saved in Christ, the Lord and God of all, not by carnal weapons of warfare, but by the might of Him Who saved them, and shook thrones and dominions, and Who by His own Cross triumpheth over the hosts of the adversaries, and overthroweth the powers of evil, and giveth to those who love Him, to *tread on serpents and scorpions and all the power of the enemy.* They were saved, not for any merits of their own, nor for anything in themselves. But when human means, and man's works, such as he could do of his own free-will, and the power of his understanding, and the natural impulses of his affections, had proved unavailing, then He redeemed them by His Blood, and bestowed on them gifts and graces above nature, and filled them with His Spirit, and gave them *to will and to do of His good pleasure.* But this promise also was, and is, to the true Judah, i. e. to those who, as the name means, *confess* and *praise* God, and who, receiving Christ, Who, as Man, was of the tribe of Judah, became His children, being re-born by His Spirit."

8. *Now when she had weaned, &c.* Eastern women very commonly nursed their children two, or even three[2] years. The weaning then of the child portrays a certain interval of time between these two degrees of chastisement; but after this reprieve, the last and final judgment pictured here was to set in irreversibly.

9. *Call his name Lo-ammi*, i. e. *not My people.* The name of this third child expresses the last final degree of chastisement. As *the scattering by God* did not involve the being wholly *unpitied;* so neither did the being wholly *unpitied* for the time involve the being wholly rejected, so as to be *no* more *His people.* There were corresponding degrees in the actual history of the kingdom of Israel. God withdrew his protection by degrees. Under Jeroboam, in whose reign was this beginning of Hosea's prophecy, the people was yet outwardly strong. This strength has been thought to be expressed by the sex of the eldest child, that he was a son. On this, followed extreme weakness, full of mutual massacre and horrible cruelty, first, in a long anarchy, then under Zechariah, Shallum, Menahem, Pekahiah, Pekah, Hosea, within, and through the invasions of Pul, Tiglathpileser, Shalmaneser, kings of Assyria, from without. The sex of the daughter, *Lo Ruhamah, Unpitied*, corresponds with this increasing weakness, and breaking of the spirit. 3. When she was *weaned*, i. e. when the people were deprived of all consolation and all the spiritual food whereby they had hitherto been supported, prophecy, teaching, promises, sacrifices, grace, favour, consolation, it became wholly *Lo-ammi, not My people.* As a distinct part of God's people, it was cast off for ever; and yet it became outwardly strong, as the Jews became powerful, and often were the persecutors of the Christians. The same is seen in individuals. God often first chastens them lightly, then more heavily, and brings them down in their iniquities; but if they still harden themselves, He withdraws both His chastisements and His grace, so that the sinner even prospers in this world, but, remaining finally impenitent, is cast off for ever.

I will not be your God; lit. *I will not be to you*, or, *for you; for you*, by Providence; *to you*, by love. The words say the more through their silence. They do not say what God will not be to those who had been His people. They do not say that He will not be their Defender, Nourisher, Saviour, Deliverer, Father, Hope, Refuge; and so they say that He will be none of these, which are all included in the English, *I will not be your God.* For, as God, He is these, and all things, to us. *I will not be to you.* God, by His love, vouchsafes to give all and to take all. He gives Himself wholly to His own, in order to make them wholly His. He makes an exchange with them. As God the Son, by His Incarnation, took the Manhood into God, so, by His Spirit dwelling in them, He makes men gods, *partakers of the Divine Nature*[3]. They, by His adoption, belong to Him; He, by His promise and gift, belongs to them. He makes them His; He becomes their's. This mutual exchange is so often expressed in Holy Scripture, to shew how God loveth to give Himself to us, and to make us His; and that where the one is, there is the other; nor can the one be without the other. This was the original covenant with Israel: *I will be your God, and you shall be My people*[4];

[1] Gen. xix. 24. [2] 2 Macc. vii. 27.

[3] 2 S. Pet. i. 4. [4] Lev. xxvi. 12. add Ex. vi. 7.

Before CHRIST cir. 785.

10 ¶ Yet [l]the number of the children of Israel shall be as the sand of the sea, which cannot be measured or numbered; [k]and it shall come to pass, *that* || in the place where it was said unto them, [l]Ye *are* not my people, *there* it shall be said unto them, *Ye are* [m]the sons of the living God.

[l] Gen. 32. 12. Rom. 9. 27, 28.

[k] Rom. 9. 25, 26. 1 Pet. 2. 10.

Before CHRIST cir. 785.

|| Or, *instead of that*.

[l] ch. 2. 23.

[m] John 1. 12. 1 John 3. 1.

---

and as such, it is often repeated in Jeremiah[1] and Ezekiel[2]. Afterwards, this is expressed still more affectionately. *I will be a Father unto you, and ye shall be My sons and daughters*[3]. And in Christ the Son, God saith, *I will be his Father, and he shall be My son*[4]. God, Who saith not this to any out of Christ, nor even to the holy Angels, (as it is written[5], *Unto which of the Angels said He at any time, I will be to him a Father, and he shall be to Me a son?*) saith it to us in Christ. And so, in turn, the Church and each single soul which is His, saith, or rather He saith it in them[6], *My beloved is mine, and I am His*, and more boldly yet, *I am my Beloved's, and my Beloved is mine*[7]. Whence also at the Holy Communion we say, "then we dwell in Christ and Christ in us; we are one with Christ, and Christ with us;" and we pray that "we may evermore dwell in Him, and He in us."

10. *Yet* [lit. *and*] *the number of the children of Israel, &c.* Light springeth out of darkness; joy out of sorrow; mercy out of chastisement; life out of death. And so Holy Scripture commonly, upon the threat of punishment, promises blessings to the penitent. "Very nigh to the severest displeasure is the dispersion of sorrows and the promised close of darkness." What God takes away, He replaces with usury; things of time by things eternal; outward goods and gifts and privileges by inward; an earthly kingdom by Heaven. Both St. Peter[8] and St. Paul[9] tell us that this prophecy is already, in Christ, fulfilled in those of Israel, who were the true Israel, or of the Gentiles, to whom the promise was made[10], *In thy Seed shall all the nations be blessed*, and who, whether Jews or Gentiles, believed in Him. The Gentiles were adopted into the Church, which, at the Day of Pentecost, was formed of the Jews, and in which Jews and Gentiles became one in Christ[11]. Yet of the Jews alone, not only did *many tens of thousands in Jerusalem believe*[12], but S. Peter and S. James both write *to the dispersed of the ten tribes*[13]; and the Apostles themselves were Jews. Although, then, those Jews who believed in Christ were few in comparison of those who rejected Him, yet they were, in themselves, many, and, through those who, in Christ Jesus, were *begotten* by them *through the Gospel*[14], they were numberless. Yet this prophecy, although accomplished in part, will, according to S. Paul[15], be yet more completely fulfilled in the end.

In the place where it was said [or *where it shall be said*, i. e. at the first] *unto them, ye are not My people*, there *it shall*, in after-time, *be said unto them*, ye are *the sons of the living God.* Both the times here spoken of by the Prophet were yet future; for Israel, although they had apostatised from God, had not yet been disowned by God, Who was still sending to them prophets, to reclaim them. They ceased to be owned as God's people, when, being dispersed abroad, they had no share in the sacrifices, no Temple-worship, no prophets, no typical reconciliation for sin. God took no more notice of them than the heathen. The Prophet then speaks of two futures; one, when it shall be said to them, *ye are not My people;* and a yet further future, in which it should be said, *ye are the sons of the living God.* The place of both was to be the same. The place of their rejection, the dispersion, was to be the place of their restoration. And so S. Peter says that this Scripture was fulfilled in them, while still *scattered abroad through Pontus, Galatia, Cappadocia, Asia, and Bithynia.* The place, then, where they shall be called *the sons of the living God*, is, wheresoever they should believe in Christ. Although separated in body, they were united by faith. And so it shall be unto the end. "Nothing now constraineth to go up to Jerusalem, and still to seek for the temple of stones; for neither will they worship God, as aforetime, by sacrifices of sheep or oxen; but their worship will be faith in Christ and in His commandments, and the sanctification in the Spirit, and the regeneration through Holy Baptism, making the glory of sonship their's, who are worthy thereof and are called thereto by the Lord[16]."

It shall be said, ye are the sons of the living God. It was the special sin of Israel, the source of all his other sins, that he had left the *living God*, to serve dead idols. In the times of the Gospel, not only should he own God

---

[1] Jer. xi. 4, 5. xxiv. 7. xxx. 22. xxxi. 1, 33. xxxii. 38.
[2] Ezek. xi. 20. xiv. 11. xxxvi. 28. xxxvii. 23, 27.
[3] 2 Cor. vi. 18.
[4] 2 Sam. vii. 14.
[5] Heb. i. 5.
[6] Cant. ii. 16.
[7] Ib. vi. 3.
[8] 1 S. Pet. ii. 10.
[9] Rom. ix. 25, 6.
[10] Gen. xxii. 18.
[11] Gal. iii. 28.
[12] Acts xxi. 20.
[13] S. James i. 1, 1 S. Pet. i. 1.
[14] 1 Cor. iv. 15.
[15] Rom. xi. 25, 6.
[16] S. Cyr.

Before CHRIST cir. 785.

a Is. 11. 12, 13. Jer. 3. 18. Ezek. 34. 23. & 37. 16–24.

11 [a]Then shall the
children of Judah and the
children of Israel be gathered together, and appoint
themselves one head, and
they shall come up out of
the land: for great *shall be*
the day of Jezreel.

as his God, but he should have the greatest of all gifts, that the *living God*, the fountain of all life, of the life of nature, of grace, of glory, should be his Father, and as being his Father, should communicate to him that life, which He has and Is. For He Who Is Life, imparts life. God doth not only pour into the souls of His elect, grace and faith, hope and love, or all the manifold gifts of His Spirit, but He, *the living God*, maketh them to be His living sons, by His Spirit dwelling in them, by Whom He adopteth them as His sons, through Whom He giveth them grace. For by His Spirit He adopteth them as sons. [1] *We have received the spirit of adoption of sons, whereby we cry, Abba, Father. And if sons, then heirs; heirs of God and joint-heirs of Christ.* God not only giveth us grace, but adopteth us as sons. He not only accounteth us, but He maketh us sons; He maketh us sons, not outwardly, but inwardly; not by inward grace only, but by His Spirit: not only by the birth from the Spirit, but *in* the Only-Begotten Son; sons of God, because members of Christ, the Son of God; sons of God, by adoption, as Christ is by Nature; but actual sons of God, as Christ is actually and eternally *the* Son of God. God is our Father, not by nature, but by grace; yet He is really our Father, since we are born of Him, *sons of the living God*, born of the Spirit. He giveth us of His Substance, His Nature, although not by nature; not united with us, (as it is, personally, with His Son,) but dwelling in us, and making us *partakers of the Divine Nature. Sons of the living God* must be living by Him and to Him, by His life, yea, through Himself living in them, as our Saviour saith[2], *If any man love Me, he will keep My words, and My Father will love him, and We will come unto him, and make Our abode with him.*

11. *Then shall the children of Judah and the children of Israel be gathered together.* A little image of this union was seen after the captivity in Babylon, when some of the children of Israel, i. e. of the ten tribes, were united to Judah on his return, and the great schism of the two kingdoms came to an end. More fully, both literal Judah and Israel were gathered into one in the one Church of Christ, and all the spiritual Judah and Israel; i. e. as many of the Gentiles as, by following the faith, became the sons of faithful Abraham, and heirs of the promise to him.

And shall make themselves one Head. The act of God is named first, *they shall be gathered;* for without God we can do nothing. Then follows the act of their own consent, *they shall make themselves one Head;* for without us God doth nothing in us. God gathereth, by the call of His grace; they make to themselves one Head, by obeying His call, and submitting themselves to Christ, the one Head of the mystical body, the Church, who are His members. In like way, Ezekiel foretells of Christ, of the seed of David, under the name of David[3]; *I will set up one Shepherd over them, and He shall feed them, even My servant David; and I the Lord will be their God, and My servant David a Prince among them;* and again[4]; *I will make them one nation in the land, upon the mountains of Israel; and one king shall be king to them all; and they shall be no more two nations, neither shall they be divided into two kingdoms any more at all.* But this was not wholly fulfilled, until Christ came; for after the captivity they were under Zorobabel as chief, and Joshua as High-Priest.

And shall come up out of the land. To *come up* or *go up* is a title of dignity; whence, in our time, people are said to go up to the metropolis, or the University; and in Holy Scripture, to "come up," or "go up," out of Egypt[5], or Assyria[6], or Babylon[7], to the land of promise, or from the rest of the land to the place which God chose[8] to place His name there, Shiloh[9], or, afterwards, Jerusalem[10]; and it is foretold that *the mountain of the Lord's house shall be exalted above the hills; and many nations shall come and say, Come, and let us go up to the mountain of the Lord*[11]. The land from which they should go up is, primarily and in image, Babylon, whence God restored the two tribes; but, in truth and fully, it is the whole aggregate of lands, the earth, the great *city of confusion*, which Babel designates. Out of which they shall go up, "not with their feet but with their affections," to the *city set upon a hill*[12], *the heavenly Jerusalem*[13] and Heaven itself, where we are *made to sit together with Christ*[14], and where *our conversation is*[15], that *where* He *is*, there may we *His servants be*[16]. They ascend in mind above the earth and the

[1] Rom. viii. 15.
[2] S. John xiv. 23.
[3] Ezek. xxxiv. 23, 24.
[4] Ib. xxxvii. 22.
[5] Gen. xiii. 1. xlv. 25. &c.
[6] 2 Kgs xvii. 3. xviii. 9, 13. Isa. xxxvi. 1, 10.
[7] 2 Kgs xxiv. 1. Ezr. ii. 1. vii. 6. Neh. vii. 6. xii. 1.
[8] Ex. xxxiv. 24.
[9] 1 Sam. i. 22.
[10] 2 Sam. xix. 34. 1 Kgs xii. 27, 28. Ps. cxxii. 4, &c.
[11] Isa. ii. 2, 3. Mic. iv. 1, 2.
[12] S. Matt. v. 14.
[13] Heb. xii. 22.
[14] Eph. ii. 6.
[15] Phil. iii. 20.
[16] S. John xii. 26.

Before CHRIST cir. 785.

CHAPTER II.

1 *The idolatry of the people.* 6 *God's judgments against them.* 14 *His promises of reconciliation with them.*

‖ That is, *My people.*
‖ That is, *Having obtained mercy.*

SAY ye unto your brethren, ‖ Ammi; and to your sisters, ‖ Ruhamah.

2 Plead with your mother, plead; for ᵃshe *is* not my wife, neither *am* I her husband: let her therefore put away her ᵇwhoredoms out of her sight, and her adulteries from between her breasts;

Before CHRIST cir. 785.

ᵃ Isai. 50. 1.
ᵇ Ezek. 16. 25.

---

things of earth, and the lowness of carnal desires, that so they may, in the end, come up out of the earth, *to meet the Lord in the air, and for ever be with the Lord*[1].

For great is the day of Jezreel. God had denounced woe on Israel, under the names of the three children of the prophet, Jezreel, Lo-Ammi, Lo-Ruhamah; and now, under those three names, He promises the reversal of that sentence, in Christ. He begins with the name, under which He had begun to pronounce the woe, the first son, *Jezreel. Jezreel* means *God shall sow*, either for increase, or to scatter. When God threatened, *Jezreel* necessarily meant, *God shall scatter;* here, when God reverses His threatening, it means, *God shall sow.* But the issue of the seed is either single, as in human birth, or manifold, as in the seed-corn. Hence it is used either of Him Who was eminently, *the Seed of Abraham, the Seed of the woman*, or of the manifold harvest, which He, the seed-corn[2], should bring forth, when sown in the earth, by His vicarious Death. It means, then, Christ or His Church. Christ, the Only-Begotten Son of God before all worlds, was, in time, also "conceived by the Holy Ghost, of the Virgin Mary," the Son of God Alone, in a way in which no other man was born of God. Great then should be the day, when "God should sow," or give the increase in mercy, as before He scattered them, in His displeasure. The great Day wherein *God should sow*, was, first, *the day which the Lord hath made*[3], the Incarnation, in which God the Son became Man, *the seed of the woman;* then, it was the Passion, in which, like a seed-corn, He was sown in the earth; then, the Resurrection, when He rose, *the Firstborn among many brethren;* then, all the days in which He *bare much fruit.* It is the one day of salvation, in which, generation after generation, *a* new *seed* hath been or *shall be born* unto Him, and *shall serve Him*[4]. Even unto the end, every time of any special growth of the Church, every conversion of Heathen tribe or people, is *a day of Jezreel*, a day in which "the Lord soweth." Great, wonderful, glorious, thrice-blessed is the day of Christ; for in it He hath done great things for us, gathering together under Himself, the Head, those scattered abroad, *without hope and without God in the world;* making "*not* My people" into "My people" and those *not beloved* into His *beloved*, the objects of His tender, yearning compassion, full of His grace and mercy. For so it follows,

II. 1. *Say ye unto your brethren, Ammi*, i. e. *My people, and to your sisters, Ruhamah*, i. e. *beloved or tenderly pitied.* The words form a climax of the love of God. First, the people scattered[5], unpitied[6], and disowned by God[7], is re-born of God; then it is declared to be in continued relation to God, *My people;* then to be the object of his yearning love. The words, *My people*, may be alike filled up, "ye are My people," and "be ye My people." They are words of hope in prophecy, "ye shall be again My people;" they become words of joy in each stage of fulfillment. They are words of mutual joy and gratulation, when obeyed; they are words of encouragement, until obeyed. God is reconciled to us, and willeth that we be reconciled to Him. Among those who already are God's people, they are the voice of the joy of mutual love in the oneness of the Spirit of adoption; *we are His people;* to those without (whether the ten tribes, or the Jews or heretics,) they are the voice of those who know in Whom they have believed, *Be ye also His people.* "Despair of the salvation of none, but, with brotherly love, call them to repentance and salvation."

This verse closes what went before, as God's reversal of His own sentence, and anticipates what is to come[8]. God commands the prophets and all those who love Him, to appeal to those who forget Him, holding out to them the mercy in store for them also, if they will return to Him. He bids them not to despise those yet alien from Him, "but to treat as brethren and sisters, those whom God willeth to introduce into His house, and to call to the riches of His inheritance."

2. *Plead with your mother, plead.* The prophets close the threats of coming judgments with the dawn of after-hopes; and from hopes

[1] 1 Thess. iv. 17.
[2] S. John xii. 24.
[3] Ps. cxviii. 24.
[4] Ps. xxii. 30, 31.
[5] Jezreel.
[6] Lo-Ruhamah.
[7] Lo-Ammi.
[8] v. 14 sqq.

Before CHRIST cir. 785.

[c] Jer. 13. 22, 26. Ezek. 16. 37, 39.
[d] Ezek. 16. 4.

3 Lest [c] I strip her naked, and set her as in the
day that she was [d] born, and
make her [e] as a wilderness,
and set her like a dry land,
and slay her with [f] thirst.

Before CHRIST cir. 785.

[e] Ezek. 19. 13.
[f] Amos 8. 11, 13.

they go back to God's judgments against sin, pouring in wine and oil into the wounds of sinners. The *mother* is the Church or nation; the *sons*, are its members, one by one. These, when turned to God, must plead with their mother, that she turn also. When involved in her judgments, they must plead with her, and not accuse God. God *had not forgotten to be gracious;* but she "kept not His love, and refused His friendship, and despised the purity of spiritual communion with Him, and would not travail with the fruit of His Will." "[1] The sons differ from the mother, as the inventor of evil from those who imitate it. For as, in good, the soul which, from the Spirit of God, conceiveth the word of truth, is the mother, and whoso profiteth by hearing the word of doctrine from her mouth, is the child, so, in evil, whatsoever soul inventeth evil is the mother, and whoso is deceived by her is the son. So in Israel, the adulterous mother was the Synagogue, and the individuals deceived by her were the sons."

"Ye who believe in Christ, and are both of Jews and Gentiles, say ye to the broken branches and to the former people which is cast off, *My people,* for it is your brother; and *Beloved,* for it is *your sister.* For when [2] the fulness of the Gentiles shall have come in, then shall all Israel be saved. In like way we are bidden not to despair of heretics, but to incite them to repentance, and with brotherly love to long for their salvation [3]."

For she is not My wife. God speaketh of the spiritual union between Himself and His people whom He had chosen, under the terms of the closest human oneness, of husband and wife. She was no longer united to Him by faith and love, nor would He any longer own her. Plead therefore with her earnestly as orphans, who, for her sins, have lost the protection of their Father.

Let her therefore put away her whoredoms. So great is the tender mercy of God. He says, let her but put away her defilements, and she shall again be restored, as if she had never fallen; let her but put away all objects of attachment, which withdrew her from God, and God will again be All to her.

Adulteries, whoredoms. God made the soul for Himself; He betrothed her to Himself through the gift of the Holy Spirit; He united her to Himself. All love, then, out of God, is to take another, instead of God. *Whom have I in heaven but Thee? and there is none upon earth that I desire besides Thee. Adultery* is to become another's than His, the Only Lord and Husband of the soul. *Whoredom* is to have many other objects of sinful love. Love is one, for One. The soul which has forsaken the One, is drawn hither and thither, has manifold objects of desire, which displace one another, because none satisfies. Hence the prophet speaks of "fornications, adulter*ies*;" because the soul, which will not rest in God, seeks to distract herself from her unrest and unsatisfiedness, by heaping to herself manifold lawless pleasures, out of, and contrary to the Will of, God.

From before her, lit. *from her face.* The face is the seat of modesty, shame, or shamelessness. Hence in Jeremiah God says to Judah, [4] *Thou hadst a harlot's forehead; thou refusedst to be ashamed;* and [5] *they were not at all ashamed, neither will they blush.* The eyes, also, are the [6] *windows, through* which *death,* i. e. lawless desire, *enters into* the soul, and takes it captive.

From her breasts. These are exposed, adorned, degraded in disorderly love, which they are employed to allure. Beneath too lies the heart, the seat of the affections. It may mean then, that she should no more gaze with pleasure on the objects of her sin, nor allow her heart to dwell on things which she loved sinfully. Whence it is said of the love of Christ, which should keep the soul free from all unruly passions which might offend him, [7] *My Well-beloved shall lie all night betwixt my breasts,* [8] *as a seal upon* the *heart* beneath.

3. *Lest I strip her naked.* "There is an outward visible nakedness, and an inward, which is invisible. The invisible nakedness is, when the soul within is bared of the glory and the grace of God." The visible nakedness is the privation of God's temporal and visible gifts, the goods of this world, or outward distinction. God's inward gifts the sinful soul or nation despises, while those outward gifts she prizes. And therefore, when the soul parts with the inward ornaments of God's grace, He strips her of the outward, His gifts of nature, of His Providence and of His Protection, if so be, through her outward misery and shame and poverty, she may come to feel that deeper misery and emptiness and disgrace within, which she had had no heart to feel. So, when our first parents lost the robe of innocence, *they knew that they were naked* [9].

[1] Rup.
[2] Rom. xi. 25, 26.
[3] S. Jer.
[4] Jer. iii. 3.
[5] Ib. vi. 15.
[6] Ib. ix. 21.
[7] Cant. i. 13.
[8] Ib. viii. 6.
[9] Gen. iii. 7.

Before CHRIST cir. 785.

4 And I will not have mercy upon her children; for they *be* the [g]children of whoredoms.

Before CHRIST cir. 785.

[g] John 8. 41.

And set her, (lit. "I will *fix* her," so that she shall have no power to free herself, but must remain as a gazing stock,) *as in the day that she was born*, i. e. helpless, defiled, uncleansed, uncared for, unformed, cast out and loathsome. Such she was in Egypt, which is in Holy Scripture spoken of, as her birthplace[1]; for there she first became a people; thence the God of her fathers called her to be His people. There she was naked of the grace and of the love of God, and of the wisdom of the law; indwelt by an evil spirit, as being an idolatress; without God; and under hard bondage, in works of mire and clay, to Pharaoh, the type of Satan, and her little ones a prey. For when a soul casts off the defence of heavenly grace, it is an easy prey to Satan.

And make her as a wilderness, and set her as a dry land, and slay her with thirst. The outward desolation, which God inflicts, is a picture of the inward. Drought and famine are among the four sore judgments, with which God threatened the land, and our Lord forewarned them, [2] *Your house is left unto you desolate;* and Isaiah says, [3] *Whereas thou hast been forsaken and hated, so that no man went through thee.* But the Prophet does not say, *make her a wilderness*, but *make her as a wilderness.* The soul of the sinner is solitary and desolate, for it has not the presence of God; unfruitful, bearing briars and thorns only, for it is unbedewed by God's grace, unwatered by the Fountain of living waters; athirst, *not with thirst for water, but of hearing the word of the Lord*, yet also, burning with desire, which the foul streams of this world's pleasure never slake. In contrast with such thirst, Jesus says of the Holy Spirit which He would give to them that believe in Him, *Whosoever drinketh of the water, that I shall give him, shall never thirst; but the water, that I shall give him, shall be in him a well of water, springing up into everlasting life*[4].

"[5] But was not that certain, which God had said, *I will no more have mercy on the house of Israel?* How then does God recall it, saying, '*Let her put away her fornications, &c.* lest I do to her this or that which I have spoken?' This is not unlike to that, when sentence had been passed on Nebuchadnezzar, Daniel saying, *This is the decree of the Most High, which is come upon my Lord the king; they shall drive thee from men, and thy dwelling;* the same Daniel says, *Wherefore, O king, let my counsel be acceptable unto thee, and redeem thy sins by righteousness, and thine iniquities by shewing mercy on the poor, if it may be a lengthening of thy tranquillity*[6]. What should we learn hereby, but that it hangs upon our own will, whether God suspend the judgment or no? For we ought not to impute our own evil to God, or impiously think that fate rules us. In other words, this or that evil comes, not because God foreknew or foreordained it; but, because this evil was to be, or would be done, therefore God both foreknew it, and prefixed His sentence upon it. Why then does God predetermine an irrevocable sentence? Because He foresaw incorrigible malice. Why, again, after pronouncing sentence, doth God counsel amendment? That we may know by experience, that they are incorrigible. Therefore, He waits for them, although they will not return, and with much patience invites them to repentance." Individuals also repented, although the nation was incorrigible.

4. *I will not have mercy upon her children.* God visits the sins of the parents upon the children, until the entailed curse be cut off by repentance. God enforces His own word *lo-ruhamah*, *Unpitied*, by repeating it here, *lo-arahem*, "I will not pity." Reproaches, which fall upon the mother, are ever felt with especial keenness. Whence Saul called Jonathan, [7] *Thou son of the perverse rebellious woman.* Therefore, the more to arouse them, he says, *for they are the children of whoredoms*, evil children of an evil parent, as S. John Baptist calls the hypocritical Jews, *ye generation of vipers*[8]. "This they were, from their very birth and swaddling-clothes, never touching any work of piety, nor cultivating any grace." As of Christ, and of those who, in Him, are nourished up in deeds of righteousness, it is said, *I was cast upon Thee from the womb; Thou art my God from my mother's belly;* so, contrariwise, of the ungodly it is said, *The wicked are estranged from the womb; they go astray as soon as they be born, speaking lies.* And as they who *live honestly, as in the day and in the light*, are called *children of the day and of the light*, so they who live a defiled life are called *the children of whoredoms.* "[5] To call them *children of whoredoms* is all one with saying, that they too are incorrigible or unchangeable. For of such, Wisdom, after saying, *executing Thy judgments upon them by little and little*, added forthwith, [9] *not being ignorant that they were a naughty generation, and that their malice was bred in them, and that their cogitation would never be changed, for it was a*

[1] Ezek. xvi. 4.
[2] S. Matt. xxiii. 38.
[3] Is. lx. 15.
[4] S. John iv. 14. vii. 38, 39.
[5] Rup.
[6] Dan. iv. 24, 25, 27.
[7] 1 Sam. xx. 30.
[8] S. Matt. iii. 7.
[9] Wisd. xii. 10, 11.

Before CHRIST cir. 785.

5 [h]For their mother
hath played the harlot:
she that conceived them
hath done shamefully: for
she said, I will go after my
lovers, [i]that give *me* my
bread and my water, my
wool and my flax, mine oil
and my † drink.

6 ¶ Therefore, behold,
[k]I will hedge up thy way
with thorns, and † make a
wall, that she shall not find
her paths.

[h] Isai. 1. 21. Jer. 3. 1, 6, 8, 9. Ezek. 16. 15, 16. &c.

[i] ver. 8. 12. Jer. 44. 17.

† Heb. *drinks.*

[k] Job 3. 23. & 19. 8. Lam. 3. 7, 9.

† Heb. *wall a wall.*

cursed seed from the beginning. All this is here expressed briefly by this word, *that they are the children of whoredoms,* meaning that their *malice* too was inbred, and that they, as much as the Ammorite and Hittite, were *a cursed seed.* Nor yet, in so speaking, did he blame the nature which God created, but he vehemently reproves the abuse of nature, that malice, which cleaves to nature but was no part of it, was by custom changed into nature."

5. *She that conceived them hath done shamefully,* lit. *hath made shameful.* The silence as to *what* she *made shameful* is more emphatic than any words. She *made shameful* every thing which she could *make shameful,* her acts, her children, and herself.

I will go [lit. *let me go, I would go*] *after my lovers.* The Hebrew word *Meahabim* denotes intense passionate love; the plural form implies that they were sinful loves. Every word aggravates the shamelessness. Amid God's chastisements, she encourages herself, *Come, let me go,* as people harden and embolden, and, as it were, lash themselves into further sin, lest they should shrink back, or stop short in it. *Let me go after.* She waits not, as it were, to be enticed, allured, seduced. She herself, uninvited, unbidden, unsought, contrary to the wont and natural feeling of woman, follows after those by whom she is not drawn, and refuses to follow God Who would draw her[1]. The *lovers* are, whatever a man loves and courts, out of God. They were the idols and false gods, whom the Jews, like the heathen, took to themselves, besides God. But in truth they were devils. Devils she sought; the will of devils she followed; their pleasure she fulfilled, abandoning herself to sin, shamefully filled with all wickedness, and travailing with all manner of impurity. These she professed that she loved, and that they, not God, loved her. For whoever receives the gifts of God, except from God and in God's way, receives them from devils. Whoso seeks what God forbids, seeks it from Satan, and holds that Satan, not God, loves him; since God refuses it, Satan encourages him to possess himself of it. Satan, then, is his *lover.*

That gave me my bread and my water. The sense of human weakness abides, even when Divine love is gone. The whole history of man's superstitions is an evidence of this, whether they have been the mere instincts of nature, or whether they have attached themselves to religion or irreligion, Jewish or Pagan or Mohammedan, or have been practised by half-Christians. "She is conscious that she hath not these things by her own power, but is beholden to some other for them; but not remembering Him (as was commanded) Who had *given her power to get wealth,* and *richly all things to enjoy,* she professes them to be the gifts of her lovers." *Bread and water, wool and flax,* express the necessaries of life, *food and clothing; mine oil and my drink* [Heb. *drinks*], its luxuries. Oil includes also ointments, and so served both for health, food and medicine, for anointing the body, and for perfume. In perfumes and choice drinks, the rich people of Israel were guilty of great profusion; whence it is said, *He that loveth wine and oil shall not be rich*[2]. For such things alone, the things of the body, did Israel care. Ascribing them to her false gods, she loved those gods, and held that they loved her. In like way, the Jewish women shamelessly told Jeremiah[3], *we will certainly do whatsoever thing goes out of our own mouth, to burn incense unto the queen of heaven, and to pour out drink-offerings unto her, as we have done, we and our fathers, our kings and our princes, in the cities of Judah and in the streets of Jerusalem. For then had we plenty of victuals, and were well, and saw no evil. But since we left off to burn incense to the queen of heaven, and to pour out drink-offerings unto her, we have wanted all things, and have been consumed by the sword and by the famine.*

6. *Therefore,* i. e. because she said, *I will go after my lovers, behold I will hedge up thy ways;* lit. *behold, I hedging.* It expresses an immediate future, or something which, as being fixed in the mind of God, is as certain as if it were actually taking place. So swift and certain should be her judgments.

Thy way. God had before spoken *of* Israel; now He turns to her, pronouncing judgment upon her; then again He turneth away from her, as not deigning to regard her. "If the sinner's way were plain, and the soul

[1] See Ezek. xvi. 31–4.

[2] Pr. xxi. 17.

[3] Jer. xliv. 17, 18.

Before CHRIST cir. 785.

7 And she shall follow after her lovers, but she shall not overtake them; and she shall seek them, but shall not find *them*: then shall she say, [l]I will go and return to my [m] first husband; for then *was it* better with me than now.

[l] ch. 5. 15. Luke 15. 18. [m] Ezek. 16. 8.

had still temporal prosperity, after it had turned away from its Creator, scarcely or never could it be recalled, nor would it *hear the* voice *behind it*, warning it. But when adversity befalls it, and tribulation or temporal difficulties overtake it in its course, then it remembers the Lord its God." So it was with Israel in Egypt. When *they sat by the flesh pots, and did eat bread to the full*, amid *the fish, which they did eat freely, the cucumbers and the melons*, they forgat the God of their fathers, and served the idols of Egypt. Then He raised up *a new king*, who *made their lives bitter with hard bondage, in mortar and in brick and in all the service of the field*; then *they groaned by reason of the bondage, and they cried, and their cry came up unto God by reason of their bondage, and God heard their groaning*[1]. So in the book of Judges the ever-recurring history is, they forsook God; He delivered them into the hands of their enemies; they cried unto Him; He sent them a deliverer. A way may be found through a *hedge* of *thorns*, although with pain and suffering; through a stone *wall* even a strong man cannot burst a way. *Thorns* then may be the pains to the flesh, with which God visits sinful pleasures, so that the soul, if it would break through to them, is held back and torn; the *wall* may mean, that all such sinful joys shall be cut off altogether, as by bereavement, poverty, sickness, failure of plans, &c. In sorrows, we cannot find our idols, which, although so near, vanish from us; but we may find our God, though we are so far from Him, and He so often seems so far from us. "God hedgeth with thorns the ways of the elect, when they find prickles in the things of time, which they desire. They attain not the pleasures of this world which they crave." They cannot *find their paths*, when, in the special love of God, they are hindered from obtaining what they seek amiss. "I escaped not Thy scourges," says St. Augustine, as to his heathen state[2], "for what mortal can? For Thou wert ever with me, mercifully rigorous, and besprinkling with most bitter alloy all my unlawful pleasures, that I might seek pleasure without alloy. But where to find such, I could not discover, save in Thee, O Lord, Who teachest by sorrow, and woundest us, to heal, and killest us, lest we die from Thee."

7. *And she shall follow after*. The words rendered *follow after* and *seek*[3], are intensive, and express "eager, vehement pursuit," and "diligent search." They express, together, a pursuit, whose minuteness is not hindered by its vehemence, nor its extent and wideness by its exactness. She shall seek far and wide, minutely and carefully, everywhere and in all things, and shall fail in all. For eighteen hundred years the Jews have chased after a phantom, a Christ, triumphing, after the manner of the kings of the earth, and it has ever escaped them. The sinful soul will too often struggle on, in pursuit of what God is withdrawing, and will not give over, until, through God's persevering mercy, the fruitless pursuit exhausts her, and she finds it hopeless. Oh the wilfulness of man, and the unwearied patience of God!

Then shall she say, I will go and return. She encourages herself tremblingly to return to God. The words express a mixture of purpose and wish. Before, she said, "Come, *let me go after my lovers;*" now, she says, "Come *let me go and let me return,*" as the prodigal in the Gospel, *I will arise and go to my Father*.

To my first husband. "God is the *first Husband* of the soul, which, while yet pure, He, through the love of the Holy Ghost, united with Himself. Him the soul longeth for, when it findeth manifold bitternesses, as thorns, in those delights of time and sense which it coveted. For when the soul begins to be gnawed by the sorrows of the world which she loveth, then she understandeth more fully, how it was better with her, with her former husband. Those whom a perverse will led astray, distress mostly converts." "Mostly, when we cannot obtain in this world what we wish, when we have been wearied with the impossibility of our search of earthly desires, then the thought of God returns to the soul; then, what was before distasteful, becomes pleasant to us; He Whose commands had been bitter to the soul, suddenly in memory grows sweet to her, and the sinful soul determines to be a faithful wife." And God still vouchsafes to be, on her return, the Husband even of the adulterous soul, however far she had strayed from Him.

For then it was better with me than now. It is the voice of the prodigal son in the Gospel, which the Father hears, *How many hired servants of my Father have bread enough and to spare, and I perish with hunger!* "I will

[1] Ex. xvi. 3. Nu. xi. 5. Ex. i. 8, 14. ii. 23, 4.

[2] Conf. ii. 4.

[3] רדף, בקש.

Before CHRIST cir. 785.

ⁿ Isa. 1. 3.
° Ezek. 16. 17, 18, 19.
† Heb. *new wine.*
‖ Or, wherewith *they made Baal,* ch. 8. 4.

8 For she did not ⁿ know
that ° I gave her corn, and
† wine, and oil, and multiplied her silver and gold,
‖ *which* they prepared for
Baal.
9 Therefore will I re-
turn, and ᵖ take away my
corn in the time thereof,
and my wine in the sea-
son thereof, and will ‖ recover my wool and my flax
given to cover her nakedness.

Before CHRIST cir. 785.

ᵖ ver. 3.
‖ Or, *take away.*

serve," Israel would say, "the living and true God, not the pride of men, or of evil spirits; for even in this life it is much sweeter to bear the yoke of the Lord, than to be the servant of men." In regard to the ten tribes, the "then" must mean the time before the apostacy under Jeroboam. God, in these words, softens the severity of His upbraiding and of His sentences of coming woe, by the sweetness of promised mercy. Israel was so impatient of God's threats, that their kings and princes slew those whom He sent unto them. God wins her attention to His accusations by this brief tempering of sweetness.

8. *For she did not know.* The prophet having, in summary[1], related her fall, her chastisement, and her recovery, begins anew, enlarging both on the impending inflictions, and the future mercy. She *did not know,* because she would not; she *would not retain God in her knowledge*[2]. *Knowledge,* in Holy Scripture, is not of the understanding, but of the heart and the will.

That I gave her corn, &c. The *I* is emphatic[3]. *She did not know, that it was I Who gave her.* God gave them the *corn, and wine, and oil,* first, because He gave them the land itself. They held it of Him as their Lord. As He says[4], *The land is Mine, and ye* are *strangers and sojourners with Me.* He gave them also in the course of His ordinary Providence, wherein He also gave them *the gold and silver,* which they gained by trading. *Silver* He had so multiplied to her in the days of Solomon, that it was *in Jerusalem as stones, nothing accounted of*[5], and *gold,* through the favor which He gave him[6], was in abundance above measure.

Which they prepared for Baal. Rather, as in the E. Margin, *which they made into Baal*[7]. "Of that gold and silver, which God had so multiplied, Israel, revolting from the house of David and Solomon, made, first the calves of gold, and then Baal." Of God's own gifts they made their gods. They took God's gifts as from their gods, and made them into gods to them. *Baal,* Lord, the same as Bel, was an object of idolatry among the Phœnicians and Tyrians. Its worship was brought into Israel by Jezebel, daughter of a king of Sidon. Jehu destroyed it for a time, because its adherents were adherents of the house of Ahab. The worship was partly cruel, like that of Moloch, partly abominable. It had this aggravation beyond that of the calves, that Jezebel aimed at the extirpation of the worship of God, setting up a rival temple, with its 450 prophets and 400 of the kindred idolatry of Ashtaroth, and slaying all the prophets of God.

It seems to us strange folly. They attributed to gods, who represented the functions of nature, the power to give what God alone gives. How is it different, when men now say, "nature does this, or that," or speak of "the operations of nature," or the laws of "nature," and ignore God Who appoints those laws, and *worketh hitherto*[8] "those operations?" They attributed to planets (as have astrologers at all times) influence over the affairs of men, and worshiped a god, Baal-Gad, or Jupiter, who presided over them. Wherein do those otherwise, who displace God's Providence by fortune or fate or destiny, and say "fortune willed," "fortune denied him," "it was his fate, his destiny," and, even when God most signally interposes, shrink from naming Him, as if to speak of God's Providence were something superstitious? What is this, but to ascribe to Baal, under a new name, the works and gifts of God? And more widely yet. Since "men have as many strange gods as they have sins," what do they, who seek pleasure or gain or greatness or praise in forbidden ways or from forbidden sources, than make their pleasure or gain or ambition their god, and offer their time and understanding and ingenuity and intellect, yea, their whole lives and their whole selves, their souls and bodies, all the gifts of God, in sacrifice to the idol which they have made? Nay, since whosoever believes of God otherwise than He has revealed Himself, does, in fact, believe in another god, not in the One True God, what else does all heresy, but form to itself an idol out of God's choicest gift of nature, man's own mind, and worship, not indeed the works of man's own hands, but the creature of his own understanding?

9. *Therefore I will return.* God is, as it

[1] ver. 5–7. [2] Rom. i. 28. [3] אנכי. [4] Lev. xxv. 23. [5] 1 Kgs x. 27, 21.
[6] Ib. ix. 14. x. 10, 14. [7] See viii. 4. Ezek. xvi. 17–19. [8] S. John v. 17.

Before CHRIST cir. 785.

10 And now [q] will I discover her † lewdness in the sight of her lovers, and none shall deliver her out of mine hand.

[q] Ezek. 16. 37. & 23. 29.
† Heb. *folly*, or *villany*.

11 [r] I will also cause all her mirth to cease, her [s] feast days, her new moons, and her sabbaths, and all her solemn feasts.

Before CHRIST cir. 785.

[r] Amos 8. 10.
[s] 1 Kgs 12. 32. Amos 8. 5.

---

were, absent from men, when He lets them go on in their abuse of His gifts. *His judgments are far above out of their sight.* He *returns* to them, and His Presence is felt in chastisements, as it might have been in mercies. He is not out of sight or out of mind, then. Others render it, *I will turn*, i. e. *I will do other than before; I will turn* from love to displeasure, from pouring out benefits to the infliction of chastisements, from giving abundance of all things to punishing them with the want of all things.

I will take away My corn in the time thereof. God shews us that His gifts come from Him, either by giving them when we almost despair of them, or taking them away, when they are all but our's. It can seem no chance, when He so doeth. The chastisement is severer also, when the good things, long looked-for, are, at the last, taken out of our very hands, and that, when there is no remedy. If in harvest-time there be dearth, what afterwards! "God taketh away all, that they who knew not the Giver through abundance, might know Him through want."

And will recover My wool. God *recovers*, and, as it were, *delivers* the works of His Hands from serving the ungodly. While He leaves His creatures in the possession of the wicked, they are holden, as it were, in captivity, being kept back from their proper uses, and made the handmaidens and instruments and tempters to sin. God made His creatures on earth to serve man, that man, on occasion of them, might glorify Him. It is against the order of nature, to use God's gifts to any other end, short of God's glory; much more, to turn God's gifts against Himself, and make them serve to pride or luxury or sensual sin. It is a bondage, as it were, to them. Whence of them also St. Paul saith [1], *The creature was made subject to vanity, not willingly;* and, *all creation groaneth and travaileth in pain together until now.* Penitents have felt this. They have felt that they deserve no more that the sun should shine on them, or the earth sustain them, or the air support them, or wine refresh them, or food nourish them, since all these are the creatures and servants of the God Whom themselves have offended, and they themselves deserve no more to be served by God's servants, since they have rebelled against their common Master, or to use even rightly what they have abused against the will of their Creator.

My flax, given *to cover her nakedness*, i. e. which God had given to that end. Shame was it, that, covered with the raiment which God had given her to hide her shame, she did deeds of shame. The white linen garments of her Priests also were symbols of that purity, which the Great High Priest should have and give. Now, withdrawing those gifts, He gave them up to the greatest visible shame, such as insolent conquerors, in leading a people into captivity, often inflicted upon them. Thereby, in act, was figured that loss of the robe of righteousness, heavenly grace, wherewith God beautifies the soul, whereof when it is stripped, it is indeed foul.

10. *Her lewdness.* The word originally means *folly*, and so *foulness.* For sin is the only real folly, as holiness is the only true wisdom. But the folly of sin is veiled amid outward prosperity, and men think themselves, and are thought, wise and honorable and in good repute, and are centres of attraction and leaders of society, so long as they prosper; as it is said, [2] *so long as thou doest well unto thyself, men will speak of thee.* But as soon as God withdraws those outward gifts, the mask drops off, and men, being no longer dazzled, despise the sinner, while they go on to hug the sin. God says, *I will discover*, as just before He had said, that His gifts had been given to *cover her.* He would then lay her bare outwardly and inwardly; her folly, foulness, wickedness, and her outward shame; and that, *in the sight of her lovers*, i. e. of those whom she had chosen instead of God, her idols, the heavenly bodies, the false gods, and real devils. Satan must jeer at the wretched folly of the souls whom he deceives.

And none shall deliver her out of My hand. Neither rebel spirits nor rebel men. The evil spirits would prolong the prosperity of the wicked, that so they might sin the more deeply, and might not repent, (which they see men to do amid God's chastisements,) and so might incur the deeper damnation.

11. *I will also cause her mirth to cease, her feast days, &c.* Israel had forsaken the temple of God; despised His priests; received from Jeroboam others whom God had not chosen; altered, at least, one of the festivals; celebrated all, where God had forbidden; and

[1] Rom. viii. 20, 22.

[2] Ps. xlix. 18.

Before CHRIST cir. 785.

12 And I will † destroy her vines and her fig trees, [t] whereof she hath said, These *are* my rewards that my lovers have given me: and [u] I will make them a forest, and the beasts of the field shall eat them.

† Heb. *make desolate.*
[t] ver. 5.
[u] Ps. 80. 12, 13. Isai. 5. 5.

13 And I will visit upon her the days of Baalim, wherein she burned incense to them, and she [x] decked herself with her earrings and her jewels, and she went after her lovers, and forgat me, saith the LORD.

Before CHRIST cir. 785.

[x] Ezek. 23. 40, 42.

worshiped the Creator under the form of a brute creature[1]. Yet they kept the great *feast-days*, whereby they commemorated His mercies to their forefathers; the *new moons*, whereby the first of every month was given to God; *the sabbaths*, whereby they owned God as the Creator of all things; and *all the* other *solemn feasts*, whereby they thanked God for acts of His special Providence, or for His annual gifts of nature, and condemned themselves for trusting in false gods for those same gifts, and for associating His creatures with Himself. But man, even while he disobeys God, does not like to part with Him altogether, but would serve Him enough to soothe his own conscience, or as far as he can without parting with his sin which he loves better. Jeroboam retained all of God's worship, which he could combine with his own political ends; and even in Ahab's time Israel *halted between two opinions*, and Judah *sware both by the Lord and by Malcham*[2], the true God and the false. All this their worship was vain, because contrary to the Will of God. Yet since God says, *I will take away all her mirth*, they had, what they supposed to be, religious *mirth* in their *feasts*, fulfilling as they thought, the commandment of God, *Thou shalt rejoice in thy feasts*[3]. She could have no real joy, since true joy is *in the Lord*[4]. So, in order that she might not deceive herself any more, God says that He will take away that feigned formal service of Himself, which they blended with the real service of idols, and will remove the hollow outward joy, that, through repentance, they might come to the true joy in Him.

12. *And I will destroy her vines and her fig trees.* Before, God had threatened to take away the fruits in their seasons; now He says, that He will take away all hope for the future; not the fruit only, but the trees which bare it. "The vine is a symbol of joy, the fig of sweetness[5]." It was the plague, which God in former times laid upon those, out of the midst of whom He took them to be His people. [6]*He smote their vines also and their fig trees, and brake the trees of their coasts.* Now that they had become like the heathen, He dealt with them as with the heathen.

Of which she said, these are my rewards; lit. *my hire.* It is the special word, used of the payment to the adulteress, or degraded woman, and so continues the likeness, by which he had set forth the foulness of her desertion of God.

And I will make them a forest. The vines and fig-trees which had aforetime been their wealth, and full of beauty, should, when neglected, run wild, and become the harbour of the wild beasts which should prey upon them. So to the wicked God causes, *that the things which should have been for their wealth should be an occasion of falling*[7]. They contain in themselves the sources of their own decay.

13. *I will visit upon her the days of Baalim,* or *Baals.* When men leave the one true God, they make to themselves many idols. They act, as if they could make up a god piece-meal out of the many attributes of the One God, and create their Creator. His power of production becomes one God; His power of destroying, another; His Providence, a third; and so on, down to the very least acts. So they had many Baals or Lords; a *Baal-berith*[8], *Lord of covenants*, who was to guard the sanctity of oaths; *Baal-zebub*[9], *Lord of flies*, who was to keep off the plague of flies, and *Baal-Peor*[10], who presided over sin. All these their various idolatries, and all the time of their idolatries, God threatens to visit upon them at once. "The days of punishment shall equal the days of the wanderings, in which she burnt incense to Baal." God spares long. But when persevering impenitence draws down His anger, He punishes not for the last sin only, but for all. Even to the penitent, God mostly makes the chastisement bear some proportion to the length and greatness of the sin.

Wherein she burnt incense unto them. Incense was that part of sacrifice, which especially denoted thanksgiving and prayer ascending to God.

And she decked herself with her ear-rings and

[1] See Introduction, p. 11.
[2] Zeph. i. 5.
[3] Deut. xvi. 14.
[4] Phil. iv. 4.
[5] See Jud. ix. 11, 13.
[6] Ps. cv. 33. See Jer. v. 17.
[7] Ps. lxix. 22.
[8] Jud. viii. 33.
[9] 2 Kgs. i. 2.
[10] Num. xxv. 3.

Before CHRIST cir. 785.

y Ezek. 20. 25.

14 ¶ Therefore, behold, I will allure her, and [y]bring her into the wilderness, and speak ‖ † comfortably unto her.

Before CHRIST cir. 785.

‖ Or, *friendly.*
† Heb. *to her heart.*

her jewels. Christ says to the bride[1], *Thy cheeks are comely with rows of jewels, thy neck with chains of gold.* But what He gave her, she threw away upon another, and *cast* her *pearls before swine.* She *decked herself,* i. e. made God's ornaments her own, used them not as He gave them, but artificially as an adulteress. And what else is it, to use wit or beauty or any gift of God, for any end out of God? "[2]The ornament of souls which choose to serve idols, is to fulfill those things which seem good to the unclean spirits.—Very beautiful to devils must be the sin-loving soul, which chooses to think and to do whatsoever is sweet to, and loved by them." Sins of the flesh being a part of the worship of Baal, this garish trickery and pains to attract had an immediate offensiveness, besides its belonging to idols. He still pictures her as seeking, not sought by her lovers. *She went after her lovers, and forgat Me.* The original has great emphasis. *She went after her lovers, and Me she forgat, saith the Lord.* She went after vanities, and God, her All, she forgat. Such is the character of all engrossing passion, such is the course of sin, to which the soul gives way, in avarice, ambition, worldliness, sensual sin, godless science. The soul, at last, does not rebel against God; it *forgets* Him. It is taken up with other things, with itself, with the objects of its thoughts, the objects of its affections, and it has no time for God, because it has no love for Him. So God complains of Judah by Jeremiah, *their fathers have forgotten My name for Baal*[3].

14. *Therefore.* The inference is not what we should have expected. Sin and forgetfulness of God are not the natural causes of, and inducements to mercy. But God deals not with us, as we act one to another. Extreme misery and degradation revolt man; man's miseries invite God's mercies. God *therefore* has mercy, not because we deserve it, but because we need it. He *therefore* draws us, because we are so deeply sunken. He prepareth the soul by those harder means, and then the depths of her misery cry to the depths of His compassion, and because chastisement alone would stupify her, not melt her, He changes His wrath into mercy, and speaks to the heart which, for her salvation, He has broken.

I will allure her. The original word is used of one readily enticed, as a simple one, whether to good or ill. God uses, as it were, Satan's weapons against himself. As Satan had enticed the soul to sin, so would God, by holy enticements and persuasiveness, allure her to Himself. God too hath sweetnesses for the penitent soul, far above all the sweetnesses of present earthly joys; much more, above the bitter sweetnesses of sin.

I Myself (such is the emphasis) *will allure her.* God would shew her something of His Beauty, and make her taste of His Love, and give her some such glimpse of the joy of His good-pleasure, as should thrill her and make her, all her life long, follow after what had, as through the clouds, opened upon her.

And will bring her into the wilderness. God, when He brought Israel out of Egypt, led her apart from the pressure of her hard bondage, the sinful self-indulgences of Egypt and the abominations of their idolatries, into the wilderness, and there, away from the evil examples of the nation from which He drew her and of those whom she was to dispossess, He gave her His law, and taught her His worship, and brought her into covenant with Himself[4]. So in the beginning of the Gospel, Christ allured souls by His goodness in His miracles, and the tenderness of His words, and the sweetness of His preaching and His promises, and the attractiveness of His sufferings, and the mighty manifestations of His Spirit. So is it with each penitent soul. God, by privation or suffering, turns her from her idols, from the turmoil of the world and its distractions, and speaks, Alone to her alone.

And speak to her heart; lit. *on* her heart, making an impression *on* it, soothing it, in words which will dwell in it, and rest there. Thus within, not without, [5]*He putteth His laws in the mind, and writeth them in the heart,* not *with ink,* but *with the Spirit of the living God.* God speaks to the heart, so as to reach it, soften it, comfort it, tranquilize it, and, at the last, assure it. He shall speak to her, not as in Sinai, amid *blackness and darkness and tempest, and the sound of a trumpet, and the voice of words, which voice they that heard intreated that the word should not be spoken to them any more*[6], but *to the heart.* But it is in solitude that He so speaks to the soul and is heard by her, warning, reproving, piercing, penetrating through every fold, until He reaches the very inmost heart and dwells there. And then he infuseth hope of pardon,

[1] Cant. i. 10. [2] S. Cyr.
[3] Jer. xxiii. 27. add Jud. iii. 7. 1 Sam. xii. 9, 10. Jer. ii. 32. iii. 20. xiii. 25. xviii. 15. Ezek. xxii. 12. xxiii. 35. Isa. xvii. 10. Ps. ix. 17. l. 22. lxxviii. 11. cvi. 13, 21. [4] See Ezek. xx. 34–36.
[5] Heb. viii. 10. 2 Cor. iii. 3. [6] Heb. xii. 18, 19.

Before CHRIST cir. 785.

z Josh. 7. 26. Isai. 65. 10.

15 And I will give her
vineyards from thence, and
[z]the valley of Achor for a
door of hope: and she shall
sing there, as in [a]the days
of her youth, and [b]as in
the day when she came up
out of the land of Egypt.

Before CHRIST cir. 785.

a Jer. 2. 2. Ezek. 16. 8, 22, 60.
b Ex. 15. 1.

kindleth love, enlighteneth faith, giveth feelings of child-like trust, lifteth the soul tremblingly to cleave to Him Whose voice she has heard within her. Then His infinite Beauty touches the heart; His Holiness, Truth, Mercy, penetrate the soul; in silence and stillness the soul learns to know itself and God, to repent of its sins, to conquer self, to meditate on God. *Come out' from among them and be ye separate, saith the Lord, and touch not the unclean thing, and I will receive you*[1].

"[2] Search we the Scriptures, and we shall find, that seldom or never hath God spoken in a multitude; but so often as He would have anything known to man, He shewed Himself, not to nations or people, but to individuals, or to very few, and those severed from the common concourse of men, or in the silence of the night, in fields or solitudes, in mountains or vallies. Thus He spake with Noah, Abraham, Isaac, Jacob, Moses, Samuel, David, and all the Prophets. Why is it, God always speaketh in secret, except that He would call us apart? Why speaketh He with a few, except to collect and gather us into one? In this solitude doth God speak to the soul, from the beginning of its conversion to the loneliness of death. Here the soul, which, overspread with darkness, knew neither God nor itself, learns with a pure heart to know God. Here, placed aloft, she sees all earthly things flee away beneath her, yea, herself also passing away in the sweeping tide of all passing things." Here she learns, and so unlearns her sins, sees and hates herself, sees and loves God. Only "[3] the solitude of the body availeth not, unless there be the solitude of the heart." And if God so speak to the penitent, much more to souls, who consecrate themselves wholly, cleave wholly to Him, meditate on Him. By His presence "[4] the soul is renewed, and cleaving, as it were, to Him, feels the sweetness of an inward taste, spiritual understanding, enlightening of faith, increase of hope, feeling of compassion, zeal for righteousness, delight in virtue. She hath in orison familiar converse with God, feeling that she is heard, and mostly answered: speaking face to face with God, and hearing what God speaketh in her, constraining God in prayer and sometimes prevailing."

15. *And I will give her her vineyards from thence.* God's mercies are not only in word, but in deed. He not only speaks to her heart, but He restores to her what He had taken from her. He promises, not only to reverse His sentence, but that He would make the sorrow itself the source of the joy. He says, I will give her back her vineyards *thence*, i. e. from the wilderness itself; as elsewhere, He says, *The wilderness shall be a fruitful field*[5]. Desolation shall be the means of her restored inheritance and joy in God. Through fire and drought are the new flagons dried and prepared, into which the new wine of the Gospel is poured.

And the valley of Achor [lit. *troubling*] for a *door of hope.* As, at the first taking possession of the promised land, Israel learnt through the transgression and punishment of Achan, to stand in awe of God, and thenceforth all went well with them, when they had wholly freed themselves from the accursed thing, so to them shall "sorrow be turned into joy, and hope dawn there, where there had been despair." "Therefore only had they to endure chastisements, that through them they might attain blessings." It was through the punishment of those who *troubled* the true *Israel*, "the destruction of Jerusalem, that to the Apostles and the rest who believed, the hope of victory over the whole world was opened." "*Hope.*" The word more fully means, a "patient, enduring longing." To each returning soul, *the valley of trouble*, or the lowliness of repentance, becometh *a door of* patient longing, not in itself, but because *God giveth* it to be so; a longing which *reacheth on, awaiteth on*, entering within the veil, and bound fast to the Throne of God. But then only, when none of the *accursed thing*[6] cleaveth to it, when it has no reserves with God, and retains nothing for itself, which God hath condemned.

And she shall sing there, as in the days of her youth. The song is a responsive song, choir answering choir, each stirring up the other to praise, and praise echoing praise, as Israel did after the deliverance at the Red Sea. "[7] *Then sang Moses and the children of Israel this song unto the Lord. I will sing unto the Lord, for He hath triumphed gloriously. And Miriam the prophetess, the sister of Aaron, took a timbrel, and all the women went out after her. And Miriam answered them, Sing ye to the Lord, for He hath triumphed gloriously.* So *the Seraphim sing one to another, Holy, holy, holy*[8]; so

1 2 Cor. vi. 17.
2 Hugo de S. Vict. de Arc. Noe. iv. 4. in Lap.
3 S. Greg. Mor. xxx. 12. Lap.
4 Ric. Vict. in Cant. iii. 4. Lap.
5 Isa. xxxii. 15.
6 Josh. vii. 11-15.
7 Ex. xv. 1, 20, 1.
8 Is. vi. 3.

Before CHRIST cir. 785.

‖ That is, *My husband.*

16 And it shall be at that day, saith the LORD, *that* thou shalt call me ‖ Ishi; and shalt call me no more ‖ Baali.

17 For [e] I will take

Before CHRIST cir. 785.

‖ That is, *My lord.*

[e] Ex. 23. 13. Josh. 23. 7. Ps. 16. 4. Zech. 13. 2.

S. Paul exhorts Christians *to admonish one another in psalms and hymns and spiritual songs, singing with grace in their hearts to the Lord*[1]; so the Jewish psalmody passed into the Christian Church, and the blessed in heaven, having on the Cross passed the troublesome sea of this world, *sing the new song of Moses and of the Lamb*[2].

She shall sing there. Where? There, where He *allureth* her, where He *leadeth* her, where He *speaketh to her heart,* where He inworketh in her that hope. There, shall she sing, there, give praise and thanks.

As in the days of her youth. Her *youth* is explained, in what follows, to be *the days when she came up out of the land of Egypt,* when she was first born to the knowledge of her God, when the past idolatries had been forgiven and cut off, and she had all the freshness of new life, and had not yet wasted it by rebellion and sin. Then God first called *Israel, My firstborn son. My son, My firstborn*[3]. *She came up* into the land which God chose, out of Egypt, since we *go up* to God and to things above; as, on the other hand, the Prophet says, *Woe to those who go* down *to Egypt*[4], for the aids of this world; and the man who was wounded, the picture of the human race, was *going* down *from Jerusalem to Jericho*[5].

16. *And it shall be—thou shall call Me Ishi* [*my Husband,*] *and shalt call Me no more Baali* [*my Baal, Lord.*] *Baal,* originally Lord, was a title sometimes given to the husband. "The lord of the woman," "her lord," "the heart of her lord," stand for "the husband," "her husband[6]." God says, "so wholly do I hate the name of idols, that on account of the likeness of the word Baal, *my Lord,* I will not be so called even in a right meaning, lest, while she utter the one, she should think on the other, and calling Me her Husband, think on the idol." Yet, withal, God says that He will put into her mouth the tenderer name of love, *Ishi,* lit. *my Man.* In Christ, the returning soul, which would give herself wholly to God, however far she had wandered, should not call God so much her Lord, as her Husband. "[7] Every soul, although laden with sins, meshed in vices, snared by enticements, a captive in exile, imprisoned in the body, sticking fast in the mud, fixed in the mire, affixed to its earthly members, nailed down by cares, distracted by turmoils, narrowed by fears, prostrated by grief, wandering in errors, tossed by anxieties, restless through suspicions, in fine, a captive *in the land of the enemy, defiled with the dead, accounted with them who go down in the grave*[8],—although she be thus condemned, in state thus desperate, yet she may perceive *that* in herself, whence she may not only respire to hope of pardon and of mercy, but whence she may dare to aspire to the nuptials of the Word, tremble not to enter into alliance with God, be not abashed to take on her the sweet yoke of love with the Lord of Angels. For what may she not safely dare with Him, with Whose image she seeth herself stamped, and glorious with His likeness? To this end God Himself, the Author of our being, willed that the ensign of our Divine nobleness of birth should ever be maintained in the soul, that she may ever have *that* in herself from the Word, whereby she may ever be admonished, either to stand with the Word, or to return to Him, if she have been moved. Moved, not as though removing in space, or walking on foot, but moved (as a spiritual substance is moved) with its affections, yea, its defections, it goes away from itself, as it were, to a worse state, making itself unlike itself and degenerate from itself, through pravity of life and morals; which unlikeness, however, is the fault, not the destruction, of nature. Contrariwise, the return of the soul is its conversion to the Word, to be re-formed by Him, conformed to Him. Wherein? In love. For He saith, *be ye followers of me, as dear children, and walk in love, as Christ also hath loved us.* Such conformity marries the soul to the Word, when she, having a likeness to Him by nature, also maketh herself like to Him in will, loving as she is loved. Wherefore, if she loveth perfectly, she is married. What sweeter than this conformity? What more desirable than this love? For by it, not content with human guidance, thou approachest, by thyself, O soul, confidentially to the Word; to the Word thou constantly cleavest; of the Word thou familiarly enquirest, and consultest as to all things, as capacious in understanding as emboldened in longing. This is contract of marriage, truly spiritual and holy. Contract! I have said too little. It is embrace. For embrace it is, when to will the same and nill the same, maketh of twain, one spirit."

17. *For I will take away the names of Baalim out of her mouth.* It is, then, of grace. He

[1] Col. iii. 16. [2] Rev. xv. 3.
[3] Ex iv. 22. [4] Isa. xxxi. 1.
[5] Luke x. 30. See above on i. 11.
[6] Ex. xxi. 22. 2 Sam. xi. 26. Prov. xxxi. 11, &c.
[7] S. Bern. in Cant. Serm. 83. Lap.
[8] Baruch iii. 10, 11.

Before CHRIST cir. 785.

away the names of Baalim
out of her mouth, and
they shall no more be
remembered by their
name.

d Job. 23. Is. 11. 6–9. Ezek. 34. 25.

18 And in that day will
I make a [d]covenant for
them with the beasts of the
field, and with the fowls of
heaven, and *with* the creeping things of the ground:
and [e]I will break the bow
and the sword and the
battle out of the earth, and

e Ps. 46. 9. Isai. 2. 4. Ezek. 39. 9, 10. Zech. 9. 10.

does not only promise the ceasing of idolatry, but that it shall be the fruit of His converting grace, the gift of Him from Whom *is both to will and to do. I will take away*, as God saith elsewhere[1], *I will cut off the names of the idols out of the land, and they shall be no more remembered;* and, [2]*the idols He shall utterly abolish.* In like way God foretells of Judah that the fruit of her captivity should be, that her idols should cease, that He would cleanse them from their idols, and renew them by His grace. [3]*In all your dwelling places the cities shall be laid waste, and the high places shall be desolate; that your altars may be laid waste and made desolate, and your idols may be broken and cease, and your images may be cut down, and your works may be abolished.* And, [4]*Then I will sprinkle clean water upon you, and ye shall be clean: from all your filthiness, and from all your idols will I cleanse you. A new heart also will I give you, and a new spirit will I put within you. Neither shall they defile themselves any more with their idols, nor with their detestable things, nor with any of their transgressions.*

And they shall be no more remembered, or, *made mention of.* The names of Baal and the idols, through which Israel sinned, are remembered now, only in the history of their sin.

18. *And in that day.* "[5]Truly and properly is the time of the Incarnation of the Only-Begotten called *the Day,* wherein darkness was dispelled in the world, and the mist dispersed, and bright rays shed into the minds of believers, and the Sun of Righteousness shone upon us, pouring in the light of the true knowledge of God, to those who could open wide the eye of the mind."

And I will make a covenant for them with the beasts of the field, &c. God promises to do away the whole of the former curse. Before, He had said that their vineyards should be laid waste by *the beasts of the field;* now, He would make an entire and lasting peace with them. He, Whose creatures they are, would renew for them in Christ the peace of Paradise, which was broken through Adam's rebellion against God, and would command none to hurt them. The blessings of God do not correspond only, they go beyond the punishment. The protection is complete. Every kind of evil animal, beast, bird and reptile, is named. So S. Peter *saw all manner of fourfooted beasts of the earth, and wild beasts, and creeping things, and fowls of the air.* All were to be slain to their former selves, and pass into the Church. Together the words express, that God would withhold the power of all enemies, visible or invisible; worldly or spiritual. Each also may denote some separate form or character of the enemy. Thus *wild beasts* picture savageness or bloodthirstiness, the ceasing whereof [6]Isaiah prophesies under the same symbols of beasts of prey, as the leopard, lion, wolf, and bear, or of venomous reptiles, as the asp or the basilisk. The *fowls of heaven* denote stealthy enemies, which, unperceived and unawares, take the word of God out of the heart; *creeping things*, such as entice to degrading, debasing sins, love of money or pleasure or appetite, *whose god is their belly, who mind earthly things*[7]. All shall be subdued to Christ or by Him; as He says, *I give you power over serpents and scorpions, and all the power of the enemy:* and *Thou shalt go upon the lion and the adder; the young lion and the adder shalt thou trample under feet*[8].

I will break the bow and the sword and the battle out of the earth. God foretells much more the greatness of what He would do for man, than the little which man receives. The Gospel brings peace within, and, since [9]*wars and fightings come from* evil passions and *lusts*, it brings peace, as far it prevails, without also; *peace*, as the *borders of* the Church[10]; peace in the world, as far as it is won to Christ by the Church; peace to the soul of the believer, so far as he loves God and obeys the Gospel.

And will make them to lie down safely, i. e. in confidence. God gives not outward peace only, but fearlessness. Fearless, the Christian lies down during life, at peace with God, his neighbour, and his own conscience; fearless, because *perfect love casteth out fear*[11]; and fearless in death also, because resting in Jesus, in everlasting, unfailing, unfading peace.

[1] Zech. xiii. 2. [2] Is. ii. 18.
[3] Ezek. vi. 6. [4] Ib. xxxvi. 25, 26. xxxvii. 23.
[5] S. Cyr. [6] c. x.
[7] Phil. iii. 19. [8] S. Luke x. 19. Ps. xci. 13.
[9] S. James iv. 1. [10] Ps. cxlvii. 14.
[11] 1 S. John iv. 18.

Before CHRIST cir. 785.

will make them to [f] lie down safely.

[f] Lev. 26. 5. Jer. 23. 6.

19 And I will betroth thee unto me for ever; yea, I will betroth thee unto me in righteousness, and in judgment, and in loving-kindness, and in mercies.

19. *And I will betroth her unto Me for ever.* God does not say here, "I will forgive her;" "I will restore her;" "I will receive her back again;" "I will again shew her love and tenderness." Much as these would have been, He says here much more. He so blots out, forgets, abolishes all memory of the past, that He speaks only of the future, of the new betrothal, as if it were the first espousal of a virgin. Hereafter God would make her wholly His, and become wholly her's, by an union nearer and closer than the closest bond of parent and child, that, whereby *they are no more twain, but one flesh;* and through this oneness, formed by His own indwelling in her, giving her Himself, and taking her into Himself, and so bestowing on her a title to all which is His. And this, *for ever.* The betrothal and union of grace in this life passeth over into the union of glory, of which it is said [1], *Blessed are they who are called to the marriage supper of the Lamb.* He, by His Spirit, shall be with His Church *unto the end of the world,* and so bind her unto Himself that *the gates of hell shall not prevail against her.* The whole Church shall never fail. This *betrothal* implies and involves a new covenant, as God says [2], *Behold the days come, that I will make a new covenant with the house of Israel and the house of Judah, not according to My covenant which I made with their fathers, which My covenant they brake,* and which vanisheth away. To those who had broken His covenant and been unfaithful to Him, it was great tenderness, that He reproached them not with the past; as neither doth He penitents now. But beyond this, in that He speaks of *espousing* her who was already espoused to Him, God shews that He means something new, and beyond that former espousal. What God here promised, He fulfilled, not as God the Father, but in Christ. What God promised of Himself, He only could perform. God said to the Church, *I will betroth thee unto Me.* He Who became the *Bridegroom* [3] of the Church was Christ Jesus; she became *the wife of the Lamb* [4]; to Him the Church was *espoused, as a chaste Virgin* [5]. He then Who fulfilled what God promised that He would Himself fulfill, was Almighty God.

I will betroth thee unto Me in righteousness, or rather, (which is more tender yet and more merciful,) *by, with,* righteousness, &c. These are the marriage-dowry, the bridal gifts, *with* [6] which He purchaseth and espouseth the bride unto Himself. Righteousness then and Judgment, loving-kindness and mercies, and faithfulness or truth, are attributes of God, wherewith, as by gifts of espousal, He maketh her His own. *Righteousness* is *that* in God, whereby He is Himself righteous and just; *Judgment,* that whereby He puts in act what is right against those who do wrong, and so judges Satan; as when the hour of His Passion was at hand, He said, *when the Comforter is come, He will reprove the world of sin, and of righteousness, and of judgment; of judgment, because the prince of this world is judged* [7]. *Loving-kindness* is that tender affection, wherewith He cherisheth His children, the works of His hands; *Mercies,* His tender yearnings over us [8], wherewith He hath compassion on our weakness; *Faithfulness,* that whereby He *keepeth covenant for ever* [9], and *loveth His own unto the end* [10]. And these qualities, as they are His, whereby He saved us, so doth He impart them to the Church in her measure, and to faithful souls. These are her dowry, her jewels, her treasure, her inheritance. He giveth to her and to each soul, as it can receive it, and in a secondary way, His Righteousness, Judgment, Loving-kindness, Mercies, Faithfulness. His *Righteousness,* contrary to her former unholiness, He poureth into her, and giveth her, with it, grace and love and all the fruits of the Spirit. By His *Judgment,* He giveth her a right judgment in all things, as contrary to her former blindness. *Know ye not,* says the Apostle [11], *that we shall judge angels? how much more, things that pertain to this life? Loving-kindness* is tender love, wherewith we *love one another, as Christ loved us* [12]. *Mercies* are that same love to those who need mercy, whereby we are *merciful,* as our *Father is merciful* [13]. *Faithfulness* is that constancy, whereby the elect shall *persevere unto the end,* as He saith, *Be thou faithful unto death, and I will give thee a crown of life* [14].

The threefold repetition of the word *betroth* is also, doubtless mysterious, alluding chiefly to the Mystery of the All-Holy Trinity, so often and so manifoldly, in Holy Scripture, foreshadowed by this sacred number. To them is the Church betrothed, by the pronouncing of Whose Names each of her members is, in Holy Baptism, *espoused as a chaste*

[1] Rev. xix. 9. [2] Jer. xxxi. 31, 32. [3] S. John iii. 29. [4] Rev. xxi. 9. [5] 2 Cor. xi. 2. [6] As in 2 Sam. iii. 14.

[7] S. John xvi. 8, 11. [8] See ab. on i. 6. [9] Ps. cxi. 9. [10] S. John xiii. 1. [11] 1 Cor. vi. 3. [12] S. John xv. 12. [13] S. Luke vi. 36. [14] Rev. ii. 10.

Before CHRIST cir. 785.

20 I will even betroth
thee unto me in faithful-
ness: and [g] thou shalt
know the LORD.
21 And it shall come to
pass in that day, [h] I will
hear, saith the LORD, I
will hear the heavens, and
they shall hear the earth;
22 And the earth shall

[g] Jer. 31, 33, 34. John 17. 3.

[h] Zech. 8. 12.

virgin unto Christ. At three times especially did our Lord espouse the Church unto Himself. "[1] First in His Incarnation, when He willed to unite His own Deity with our humanity," and "in the Virgin's womb, the nature of the woman, our nature, human nature, was joined to the nature of God," and that *for ever.* "He will be for ever the Word and Flesh, i. e. God and Man." Secondly, in His Passion, when He washed her with His Blood, and bought her for His own by His Death. Thirdly, in the Day of Pentecost, when He poured out the Holy Spirit upon her, whereby He dwelleth in her and she in Him. And He Who thus espoused the Church is God; she whom He espoused, an adulteress, and He united her to Himself, making her a pure virgin without spot or blemish. "[2] Human marriage makes those who were virgins to cease to be so; the Divine espousal makes her who was defiled, a pure virgin." *I have espoused you,* says S. Paul to those whom he had won back from all manner of heathen sins[3], *to one Husband, that I may present you a chaste virgin unto Christ.* O the boundless clemency of God! "[4] How can it be possible, that so mighty a King should become a Bridegroom, that the Church should be advanced into a Bride? That alone hath power for this, which is All-powerful; *love, strong as death*[5]. How should it not easily lift her up, which hath already made Him stoop? If He hath not acted as a Spouse, if He hath not loved as a Spouse, been jealous as a Spouse, then hesitate thou to think thyself espoused."

20. *And thou shalt know the Lord.* This knowledge of God follows on God's act of betrothal and of love. *We love God, because God first loved us.* And the true knowledge of God includes the love of God. "To love man, we must know him: to know God, we must love Him." To *acknowledge* God, is not yet to *know* Him. They who love not God, will not even acknowledge Him as He Is, "Supreme Wisdom and Goodness and Power, the Creator and Preserver; the Author of all which is good, the Governor of the world, Redeemer of man, the most bounteous Rewarder of those who serve Him, the most just Retributor of those who persevere in rebellion against Him." They who will not love God, cannot even *know* aright *of* God. But to *know God*, is something beyond this. It is to know by experience that God is good; and this God makes known to the soul which He loves, while it meditates on Him, reads of Him, speaks of Him, adores Him, obeys Him. "This knowledge cometh from the revelation of God the Father, and in it is true bliss. Whence, when Peter confessed Him to be the Son of Man and Son of God, He said, *Blessed art thou; for flesh and blood hath not revealed it unto thee, but My Father which is in heaven.*" Yea, this knowledge is life eternal, as He said, [6] *This is life eternal, that they might know Thee the only true God, and Jesus Christ Whom Thou hast sent.*

21, 22. *I will hear the heavens, &c.* As all nature is closed, and would refuse her office to those who rebel against her God, so, when He hath withdrawn His curse and is reconciled to man, all shall combine together for man's good, and, by a kind of harmony, all parts thereof join their ministries for the service of those who are at unity with Him. And, as an image of love, all, from lowest to highest, are bound together, each depending on the ministry of that beyond it, and the highest on God. At each link, the chain might have been broken; but God Who knit their services together, and had before withheld the rain, and made the earth barren, and laid waste the trees, now made each to supply the other, and led the thoughts of men through the course of causes and effects up to Himself, Who ever causes all which comes to pass.

The immediate want of His people, was the corn, wine and oil; these needed the fruitfulness of the earth; the earth, by its parched surface and gaping clefts, seemed to crave the rain from heaven; the rain could not fall without the Will of God. So all are pictured as in a state of expectancy, until God gave the word, and His Will ran through the whole course of secondary causes, and accomplished what man prayed Him for. Such is the picture. But, although God's gifts of nature were gladdening tokens of His restored favor, and now too, under the Gospel, we rightly thank Him for the removal of any of His natural chastisements, and look upon it as an earnest of His favor toward us, the Prophet who had just spoken of the highest things, the union of man with God in Christ, does not here speak only of the

[1] Rup. [2] S. Jer. [3] 2 Cor. xi. 2. see Jer. iii. 1, 2.

[4] S. Bern. de dedic. Eccl. S. 5. Lap. [5] Cant. viii. 6. [6] S. John xvii. 3.

Before CHRIST cir. 785.

hear the corn, and the wine,
and the oil; [i] and they
shall hear Jezreel.
23 And [k] I will sow her
unto me in the earth; [l] and
will have mercy upon her
that had not obtained
mercy; and I [m] will say to
them which were not my
people, Thou *art* my people; and they shall say,
Thou art my God.

[i] ch. 1. 4.
[k] Jer. 31. 27. Zech. 10. 9.
[l] ch. 1. 6.
[m] ch. 1. 10. Zech. 13. 9. Rom. 9. 26. 1 Pet. 2. 10.

Before CHRIST cir. 785.

---

lowest. What God gives, by virtue of an espousal *for ever*, are not gifts in time only. His gifts of nature are, in themselves, pictures of His gifts of grace, and as such the Prophets employ them. So then God promiseth, and this in order, a manifold abundance of all spiritual gifts. Of these, *corn and wine*, as they are the visible parts, so are they often, in the Old Testament, the symbols of His highest gift, the Holy Eucharist; and *oil*, of God's Holy Spirit, through Whom they are sanctified.

God here calls *Israel* by the name of *Jezreel*, repealing, once more in the close of this prophecy, His sentence, conveyed through the names of the three children of the Prophet. The name *Jezreel* combines in one, the memory of the former punishment and the future mercy. God did not altogether do away the temporal part of His sentence. He had said, "I will scatter;" and, although some were brought back with Judah, Israel remained scattered in all lands, in Egypt and Greece and Italy, Asia Minor, and the far East and West. But God turned His chastisement into mercy to those who believed in Him. Now He changes the meaning of the word into, *God shall sow.* Israel, in its dispersion, when converted to God, became everywhere the preacher of Him Whom they had persecuted; and in Him,—the true Seed Whom God sowed in the earth and It *brought forth much fruit*,—converted Israel also bore, *some a hundred-fold; some sixty; some thirty.*

23. *And I will sow her unto Me in the earth. She* whom God sows, is the Church, of whom God speaks as *her*, because she is the Mother of the faithful. After the example of her Lord, and by virtue of His Death, every suffering is to increase her. "The blood of Christians was their harvest-seed [1]." "The Church was not diminished by persecutions, but increased, and the field of the Lord was even clothed with the richer harvest, in that the seeds, which fell singly, arose multiplied [2]."

In the earth. "[3] He does not say *in their own land*, i. e. Judæa, but *the earth.* The whole earth was to be the seed-plot of the Church, where God would sow her to Himself, plant, establish, cause her to increase, and multiply her mightily." As he said [4], *Ask of Me, and I will give Thee the heathen for Thine inheritance, and the utmost parts of the earth for Thy possession.* Of this sowing, Jews were the instruments. Of them according to the flesh, Christ came; of them were the Apostles and Evangelists and all writers of Holy Scripture; of them was the Church first formed, into which the Gentiles were received, being, with them, knit into one in Christ.

I will have mercy upon her that had not obtained mercy. This which was true of Israel in its dispersion, was much more true of the Gentiles. These too, the descendants of righteous Noah, God had cast off for the time, that they should be no more His people, when He chose Israel out of them, to make known to them His Being, and His Will, and His laws, and, (although in shadow and in mystery,) Christ Who was to come. So God's mercies again overflow His threatenings. He had threatened to Israel, that he should be *unpitied*, and no more His people; in reversing His sentence, He embraces in the arms of His mercy all who were not His people, and says of them all, that they should be *My people* and *beloved*. At one and the same time, was Israel to be thus multiplied, and *pity* was to be shewn to those *not pitied*, and those who were *not God's people*, were to become *His people.* At one and the same time were those promises fulfilled in Christ; the one through the other; Israel was not multiplied by itself, but through the bringing-in of the Gentiles. Nor was Israel alone, or chiefly, brought into a new relation with God. The same words promised the same mercy to both, Jew and Gentile, that all should be *one in Christ*, all one Jezreel, one Spouse to Himself, one Israel of God, one Beloved; and that all, with one voice of jubilee, should cry unto Him, "my Lord and my God."

And they shall say, Thou art my God, or rather, *shall say, my God.* There seems to be more affectionateness in the brief answer, which sums up the whole relation of the creature to the Creator in that one word, *Elohai, my God.* The prophet declares, as before, that, when God thus anew called them His people, they by His grace would obey His call, and surrender themselves wholly to

[1] Tertull. Apol. end. p. 105. Oxf. Tr.
[2] S. Leo. See others quoted Ib. p. 105, 6. note a.
[3] Poc. Not כארצם but כארץ.
[4] Ps. ii. 8.

Before CHRIST cir. 785.

CHAPTER III.

1 *By the expiation of an adulteress,* 4 *is shewed the desolation of Israel before their restoration.*

THEN said the LORD
unto me, [a] Go yet,
love a woman beloved of
her [b] friend, yet an adulteress, according to the love
of the LORD toward the
children of Israel, who look
to other gods, and love
flagons † of wine.
2 So I bought her to me
for fifteen *pieces of* silver,
and *for* an homer of barley,
and an † half homer of barley:

a ch. 1. 2.

b Jer. 3. 20.

† Heb. of *grapes.*

† Heb. *lethech.*

Him. For to say, *my God,* is to own an exclusive relation to God alone. It is to say, my Beginning and my End, my Hope and my Salvation, my Whole and only Good, in Whom Alone I will hope, Whom Alone I will fear, love, worship, trust in, obey and serve, with all my heart, mind, soul and strength; my God and my All.

III. 1. *Go yet, love a woman, beloved of* her *friend, yet an adulteress.* This *woman* is the same Gomer, whom the Prophet had before been bidden to *take,* and whom, (it appears from this verse) had forsaken him, and was living in adultery with another man. The *friend*[1] is the husband himself, the Prophet. The word *friend* expresses, that the husband of Gomer treated her, not harshly, but mildly and tenderly so that her faithlessness was the more aggravated sin. *Friend* or *neighbour* too is the word chosen by our Lord to express His own love, the love of the good Samaritan, who, not being akin, became *neighbour to Him who fell among thieves,* and had mercy upon him. Gomer is called *a woman, ishah,* not, thy wife, *ishteca*[2], in order to describe the state of separation, in which she was living. Yet God bids the Prophet to *love her,* i. e. shew active love to her, not, as before, to *take* her; for she was already and still his wife, although unfaithful. He is now bidden to buy her back, with the price and allowance of food, as of a worthless slave, and so to keep her apart, on coarse food, abstaining from her former sins, but without the privileges of marriage, yet with the hope of being, in the end, restored to be altogether his wife. This prophecy is a sequel to the former, and so relates to Israel, after the coming of Christ, in which the former prophecy ends.

According to the love of the Lord toward the children of Israel. The Prophet is directed to frame his life, so as to depict at once the ingratitude of Israel or the sinful soul, and the abiding, persevering, love of God. The woman, whom God commands him to *love,* he had loved before her fall; he was now to love her after her fall, and amid her fall, in order to rescue her from abiding in it. His love was to outlive her's, that he might win her at last to him. Such, God says, is *the love of the Lord* for *Israel.* He loved her, before she fell; for the woman was *beloved of her friend, and* yet *an adulteress.* He loved her after she fell, and while persevering in her adultery. For God explains His command to the Prophet still to love her, by the words, *according to the love of the Lord toward the children of Israel, while they look to other gods,* lit., *and they are looking.* The words express a contemporary circumstance. God was loving them and looking upon them; and they, all the while, were looking to other gods.

Love flagons of wine; lit. *of grapes,* or perhaps, more probably, *cakes of grapes,* i. e. dried raisins. Cakes were used in idolatry[3]. The *wine* would betoken the excess common in idolatry, and the bereavement of understanding: the *cakes* denote the sweetness and lusciousness, yet still the dryness, of any gratification out of God, which is preferred to Him. Israel despised and rejected the true Vine, Jesus Christ, the source of all the works of grace and righteousness, and *loved the dried cakes,* the observances of the law, which, apart from Him, were dry and worthless.

2. *So I bought her to me for fifteen* pieces of *silver.* The fifteen shekels were half the price of a common slave[4], and so may denote her worthlessness. The homer and half-homer of barley, or forty-five bushels, are nearly the allowance of food for a slave among the Romans, four bushels a month. Barley was the offering of one accused of adultery, and, being the food of animals, betokens that she was *like horse and mule which have no understanding.* The Jews gave dowries for their wives; but she was the Prophet's wife already. It was then perhaps an allowance, whereby he bought her back from her evil freedom, not to live as his wife, but to be honestly

[1] רע as in Jer. iii. 20. Cant. v. 16.
[2] אשה not אשתך.

[3] Jer. vii. 18. xliv. 19.
[4] Ex. xxi. 32.

Before CHRIST cir. 785.

c Deut. 21. 13.

3 And I said unto her,
Thou shalt [c] abide for me
many days; thou shalt not
play the harlot, and thou
shalt not be for *another*
man: so *will* I also *be* for
thee.
4 For the children of

Before CHRIST cir. 785.

maintained, until it should be fit, completely to restore her.

3. *Thou shalt abide for me many days;* lit. *thou shalt sit,* solitary and as a widow [1], quiet and sequestered; not going after others, as heretofore, but waiting for him [2]; and *that,* for an undefined, but long season, until he should come and take her to himself.

And thou shalt not be for another *man;* lit. *and thou shalt not be to a man*, i. e. not even to thine own man or husband. She was to remain without following sin, yet without restoration to conjugal rights. Her husband would be her guardian; but as yet, no more. *So* will *I also* be *for thee or toward thee.* He does not say "*to* thee," so as to belong to her, but "towards thee;" i. e. he would have regard, respect to her; he would watch over her, be kindly disposed towards her; he, his affections, interests, thoughts, would be directed *towards* her. The word *towards* expresses regard, yet distance also. Just so would God, in those times, withhold all special tokens of His favor, covenant, Providence; yet would he secretly uphold and maintain them as a people, and withhold them from falling wholly from Him into the gulf of irreligion and infidelity.

4. *For the children of Israel shall abide many days.* The condition described is one in which there should be no civil polity, none of the special Temple-service, nor yet the idolatry, which they had hitherto combined with it or substituted for it. *King* and *prince* include both higher and lower governors. Judah had *kings* before the Captivity, and a sort of *prince* in her governors after it. Judah remained still a polity, although without the glory of her kings, until she rejected Christ. Israel ceased to have any civil government at all. *Sacrifice* was the centre of worship before Christ. It was that part of their service, which, above all, fore-shadowed His love, His Atonement and Sacrifice, and the reconciliation of God by His Blood, Whose merits it pleaded. *Images,* were, *contrariwise,* the centre of idolatry, the visible form of the beings, whom they worshipped instead of God. The *Ephod* was the holy garment which the High-priest wore, with the names of the twelve tribes and the Urim and Thummim, over his heart, and by which he enquired of God. The *Teraphim* were idolatrous means of divination. So then, *for many days,* a long, long period, *the children of Israel* should *abide,* in a manner waiting for God, as the wife waited for her husband, kept apart under His care, yet not acknowledged by Him; not following after idolatries, yet cut off from the sacrificial worship which He had appointed for forgiveness of sins, through faith in the Sacrifice yet to be offered, cut off also from the appointed means of consulting Him and knowing His Will. Into this state the ten tribes were brought upon their Captivity, and (those only excepted who joined the two tribes or have been converted to the Gospel,) they have ever since remained in it. Into that same condition the two tribes were brought, after that, by *killing the Son,* they had *filled up the measure of their father's* sins; and the second temple, which His Presence had hallowed, was destroyed by the Romans. In that condition they have ever since remained; free from idolatry, and in a state of waiting for God, yet looking in vain for a Messias, since they had not and would not receive Him Who came unto them; praying to God; yet without sacrifice for sin; not owned by God, yet kept distinct and apart by His Providence, for a future yet to be revealed. "No one of their own nation has been able to gather them together or to become their king." Julian the Apostate attempted in vain to rebuild their temple, God interposing by miracles to hinder the effort which challenged His Omnipotence. David's temporal kingdom has perished and his line is lost, because *Shiloh,* the Peace-maker, is come. The typical Priesthood ceased, in presence of the true *Priest after the order of Melchisedek.* The line of Aaron is forgotten, unknown, and cannot be recovered. So hopelessly are their genealogies confused, that they themselves conceive it to be one of the offices of their Messiah to disentangle them.. Sacrifice, the centre of their religion, has ceased and become unlawful. Still their characteristic has been to *wait.* Their prayer as to the Christ has been, "may He soon be revealed." Eighteen centuries have flowed by. *Their eyes have failed with looking* for God's promise, whence it is not to be found. Nothing has changed this character, in the mass of the people. Oppressed, released, favoured; despised, or aggrandised; in East or West; hating Christians, loving to blaspheme Christ, forced (as they would remain Jews,) to explain away the prophecies which speak of Him, deprived of the sacrifices which, to their forefathers, spoke of Him and His Atonement;—still, as a mass, they blindly wait for Him, the true

1 Deut. xxi. 13.

2 Such is the force of ישׁב ל Ex. xxiv. 14. Jer iii. 2.

Before CHRIST cir. 785.

Israel shall abide many
days [d] without a king, and
without a prince, and
without a sacrifice, and
without † an image, and
without an [e] ephod, and
without [f] teraphim:

5 Afterward shall the
children of Israel return,
and [g] seek the LORD their
God, and [h] David their
king; and shall fear the
LORD and his goodness in
the [i] latter days.

[d] ch. 10. 3.
† Heb. *a standing*, or, *statue*, or, *pillar*, Isai. 19. 19.
[e] Exod. 28. 6.
[f] Judg. 17. 5.
[g] Jer. 50. 4, 5. ch. 5. 6.
[h] Jer. 30. 9. Ezek. 34. 23, 24. & 37. 22, 24.
[i] Isai. 2. 2. Jer. 30. 24. Ezek. 38. 8, 16. Dan. 2. 28. Mic. 4. 1.

knowledge of Whom, His Offices, His Priesthood, and His Kingdom, they have laid aside. And God has been *towards them.* He has preserved them from mingling with idolaters or Mohammedans. Oppression has not extinguished them, favor has not bribed them. He has kept them from abandoning their mangled worship, or the Scriptures which they understand not, and whose true meaning they believe not; they have fed on the raisin-husks of a barren ritual and unspiritual legalism since the Holy Spirit they have grieved away. Yet they exist still, a monument to *us*, of God's abiding wrath on sin, as Lot's wife was to them, encrusted, stiff, lifeless, only that we know that *the dead shall hear the voice of the Son of God, and they that hear shall live.*

True it is, that idolatry was not the immediate cause of the final punishment of the two, as it was of the ten, tribes. But the words of the prophecy go beyond the first and immediate occasion of it. The sin, which God condemned by Hosea, was alienation from Himself. He loved them, and they *turned to other gods.* The outward idolatry was but a fruit and a symbol of the inward. The temptation to idolatry was not simply, nor chiefly, to have a visible symbol to worship, but the hope to obtain from the beings so symbolised, or from their worship, what God refused or forbade. It was a rejection of God, choosing His rival. "The adulteress soul is whoever, forsaking the Creator, loveth the creature." The rejection of our Lord was moreover the crowning act of apostacy, which set the seal on all former rejection of God. And when the sinful soul or nation is punished at last, God punishes not only the last act, which draws down the stroke, but all the former accumulated sins, which culminated in it. So then they who "despised the Bridegroom, Who came from heaven to seek the love of His own in faith, and, forsaking Him, gave themselves over to the Scribes and Pharisees who *slew Him, that the inheritance,* i. e. God's people, *might be* theirs," having the same principle of sin as the ten tribes, were included in their sentence.

5. *Afterward shall the children of Israel return.* Elsewhere it is said more fully, *return to the Lord.* It expresses more than *turning* or even conversion to God. It is not conversion only, but *re*version too, a turning *back from* the unbelief and sins, for which they had left God, and a return to Him Whom they had forsaken.

And shall seek the Lord. This word, *seek,* expresses in Hebrew, from its intensive form, a diligent search; as used with regard to God, it signifies a religious search. It is not such seeking as our Lord speaks of [1], *Ye seek me, not because ye saw the miracles, but becaus ye did eat of the loaves and were filled,* or [2], *many shall seek to enter in and shall not be able,* but that earnest seeking, to which He has promised, *Seek and ye shall find.* Before, she had diligently sought her false gods. Now, in the end she shall as diligently seek God and His grace, as she had heretofore sought her idols and her sins.

And David their King. David himself, after the flesh, this could not be. For he had long since been gathered to his fathers; nor was he to return to this earth. *David* then must be *the Son of David,* the same, of Whom God says [3], *I will set up One Shepherd over them, and He shall feed them, even My servant David, and He shall be their Shepherd, and I the Lord will be their God, and My servant David a Prince among them.* The same was to be *a witness, leader, commander to the people* [4]; He Who was to be *raised up to David* [5], *a righteous Branch,* and Who was to *be called the Lord our Righteousness*; *David's Lord* [6] as well as *David's Son.* Whence the older Jews, of every school, Talmudic, mystical, Biblical, grammatical, explained this prophecy, of Christ. Thus their received paraphrase is: "[7] Afterward the children of Israel shall repent, or turn by repentance, and shall seek

[1] S. John vi. 26. [2] S. Luke xiii. 24.
[3] Ezek. xxxiv. 23, 24. [4] Isa. lv. 4.
[5] Jer. xxiii. 5, 6. [6] Ps. cx. 1.
[7] Jon. Targ. "This is the King Messiah; whether he be from among the living, his name is David, or whether he be from the dead, his name is David." Jerus. Berachoth in Martini Pug. Fid. f. 277. and Schöttg. Horæ Hebr. T. ii. ad loc. So also the mystical books, Zohar, Midrash Shemuel (ap. Schöettg. ii. p. 22.), and Tanchuma, which has, "God said to the Israelites; In this world ye fear for your sins; but in the world to come [i. e. the time of Christ] when the evil nature shall no longer be, ye shall be amazed at that good which is reserved for you, as it is written, 'Afterwards the children of Israel shall return, &c.'" It is also one of the passages, which, they say, a voice from heaven, *Bath col,* revealed to them, as relating to the Messiah, Schöttg. Ib. p. 141. See also Ibn Ezra and Kimchi in Pococke, p. 139.

Before CHRIST cir. 780.

CHAPTER IV.

1 *God's judgments against the sins of the people,* 6 *and of the priests,* 12 *and against their idolatry.* 15 *Judah is exhorted to take warning by Israel's calamity.*

HEAR the word of the LORD, ye children of Israel: for the LORD hath a [a] controversy with the inhabitants of the land, because *there is* no truth, nor mercy, nor

Before CHRIST cir. 780.

[a] Isai. 1. 18. & 3. 13, 14. Jer. 25. 31. ch. 12. 2. Mic. 6. 2.

the service of the Lord their God, and shall obey Messiah the Son of David, their King."

And shall fear the Lord; lit. *shall fear toward the Lord and toward His goodness.* It is not then a servile fear, not even, as elsewhere, a fear, which makes them shrink back *from* His awful Majesty. It is a fear, the most opposed to this; a fear, whereby "they shall flee to Him for help, from all that is to be feared;" a reverent holy awe, which should even impel them *to* Him; a fear of losing Him, which should make them hasten to Him. "[1] They shall fear, and wonder exceedingly, astonied at the greatness of God's dealing, or of their own joy." Yet they should *hasten tremblingly,* as bearing in memory their past unfaithfulness and ill deserts, and fearing to approach, but for the greater fear of turning away. Nor do they hasten with this reverent awe and awful joy to God only, but *to His Goodness* also. His Goodness draws them, and to it they betake themselves, away from all cause of fear, their sins, themselves, the Evil one. Yet even His Goodness is a source of awe. *His Goodness!* How much it contains. All whereby God is good in Himself, all whereby He is good to us. That whereby He is essentially good, or rather Goodness; that whereby He is good to us, as His creatures, as yet more as His sinful, ungrateful, redeemed creatures, re-born to bear the Image of His Son. So then His Goodness overflows into beneficence, and condescension, and graciousness and mercy and forgiving love, and joy in imparting Himself, and complacence in the creatures which He has formed, and re-formed, redeemed and sanctified for His glory. Well may His creatures *tremble towards* it, with admiring wonder that all this can be made their's!

This was to take place *in the latter days.* These words, which are adopted in the New Testament, where Apostles say, [2] *in the last days, in these last days,* mean this, the last dispensation of God, in contrast with all which went before, the times of the Gospel[3]. The prophecy has all along been fulfilled during this period to those, whether of the ten or of the two tribes, who have been converted to Christ, since God ended their temple-worship. It *is* fulfilled in every soul from among them, who now *is converted and lives.* There will be a more full fulfillment, of which S. Paul speaks, when the eyes of all Israel shall be opened to the deceivableness of the last Anti-Christ; and Enoch and Elias, the two witnesses[4], shall have come to prepare our Lord's second Coming, and shall have been slain, and, by God's converting grace, *all Israel shall be saved*[5].

IV. 1. *Hear the word of the Lord, ye children of Israel.* The Prophet begins here, in a series of pictures as it were, to exhibit the people of Israel to themselves, that they might know that God did not do without cause all this which He denounced against them. Here, at the outset, He summons, the whole people, their prophets and priests, before the judgment-seat of God, where God would condescend, Himself to implead them, and hear, if they had ought in their defence. The title *children of Israel* is, in itself, an appeal to their gratitude and their conscience, as the title "Christian" among us is an appeal to us, by Him Whose Name we bear. Our Lord says, [6] *If ye were Abraham's children, ye would do the works of Abraham;* and S. Paul[7], *let every one that nameth the name of Christ, depart from iniquity.*

For the Lord hath a controversy. God wills, in all His dealings with us His creatures, to prove even to our own consciences, the righteousness of His judgments, so as to leave us without excuse. Now, through His servants, He shews men their unrighteousness and His justice; hereafter our Lord, the righteous Judge, will shew it through the book of men's own consciences.

With the inhabitants of the land. God had given *the land* to the children of Israel, on account of the wickedness of those whom He drave out before them. He gave it to them [8] *that they might observe His statutes and keep His laws.* He had promised that His [9] *Eyes* should *always* be *upon it from the beginning of the year unto the end of the year.* This land,

[1] Rup. [2] Acts ii. 17. Heb. i. 2.
[3] "It is a rule given by Kimchi on Isa. ii. 2. 'Whenever it is said *in the latter days,* it is meant the days of the Messiah.' The same rule is also on that place given by Abarbanel, and backed by the authority of Moses Ben Nachman, who, on Gen. xlix. 1, gives it as a general rule of all their Doctors." Poc.
[4] Rev. xi. 3. [5] Rom. xi. 26. [6] S. John viii. 39.
[7] 2 Tim. ii. 19. [8] Ps. cv. ult. [9] Deut. xi. 12.

Before CHRIST cir. 780.

[b] knowledge of God in the
land.

[b] Jer. 4. 22. & 5. 4.

2 By swearing, and
lying, and killing, and
stealing, and committing
adultery, they break out,
and †blood toucheth
blood.

† Heb. *bloods.*

Before CHRIST cir. 780.

the scene of those former judgments, given to them on those conditions, [1] the land which God had given to them as their God, they had filled with iniquity.

Because there is no truth, nor mercy. Truth and mercy are often spoken of, as to Almighty God. *Truth* takes in all which is right, and to which God has bound Himself; *mercy,* all beyond, which God does out of His boundless love. When God says of Israel, *there is no truth nor mercy,* He says that there is absolutely none of those two great qualities, under which He comprises all His own Goodness. *There is no truth,* none whatever, "no regard for known truth; no conscience, no sincerity, no uprightness; no truth of words; no truth of promises; no truth in witnessing; no making good in deeds what they said in words."

Nor mercy. The word has a wide meaning; it includes all love of one to another, a love issuing in acts. It includes loving-kindness, piety to parents, natural affection, forgiveness, tenderness, beneficence, mercy, goodness. The Prophet, in declaring the absence of this grace, declares the absence of all included under it. Whatever could be comprised under love, whatever feelings are influenced by love, of that there was nothing.

Nor knowledge of God. The union of right knowledge and wrong practice is hideous in itself; and it must be especially offensive to Almighty God, that His creatures should know Whom they offend, how they offend Him, and yet, amid and against their knowledge, choose that which displeases Him. And, on that ground, perhaps, He has so created us, that when our acts are wrong, our knowledge becomes darkened [2]. The *knowledge of God* is not merely to know some things of God, as that He is the Creator and Preserver of the world and of ourselves. To know things of God is not to know God Himself. We cannot know God in any respect, unless we are so far made like unto Him. *Hereby do we know that we know Him, if we keep His commandments. He that saith, I know Him, and keepeth not His commandments, is a liar and the truth is not in him. Every one that loveth is born of God, and knoweth God. He that loveth not, knoweth not God; for God is love* [3]. Knowledge of God being the gift of the Holy Ghost, he who hath not grace, cannot have that knowledge. A certain degree of speculative knowledge of God, a bad man may have, as Balaam had by inspiration, and the Heathen who, *when they knew God, glorified Him not as God.* But even this knowledge is not retained without love. Those who *held the truth in unrighteousness* ended (S. Paul says [4]) by corrupting it. *They did not like to retain God in their knowledge, and so God gave them over to a reprobate,* or undistinguishing *mind,* that they could not. Certainly, the speculative and practical knowledge are bound up together, through the oneness of the relation of the soul to God, whether in its thoughts of Him, or its acts towards Him. Wrong practice corrupts belief, as misbelief corrupts practice. The Prophet then probably denies that there was any true knowledge of God, of any sort, whether of life or faith or understanding or love. Ignorance of God, then, is a great evil, a source of all other evils.

2. *By swearing, and lying; &c,* lit. *swearing* or *cursing* [5], *and lying, and killing, and stealing, and committing adultery!* The words in Hebrew are nouns of action. The Hebrew form is very vivid and solemn. It is far more forcible than if he had said, "They swear, lie, kill, and steal." It expresses that these sins were continual, that nothing else (so to speak) was going on; that it was all one scene of such sins, one course of them, and of nothing besides; as we say more familiarly, "It was all, swearing, lying, killing, stealing, committing adultery." It is as if the Prophet, seeing with a sight above nature, a vision from God, saw, as in a picture, what was going on, all around, within and without, and summed up in this brief picture, all which he saw. This it was and nothing but this, which met his eyes, wherever he looked, whatever he heard, *swearing, lying, killing, stealing, committing adultery.* The Prophet had before said, that the ten tribes were utterly wanting in all truth, all love, all knowledge of God. But where there are none of these, *there,* in all activity, will be the contrary vices. When the land or the soul is empty of the good, it will be full of the evil. *They break out,* i.e. burst through all bounds, set to restrain them, as a river bursts its banks and overspreads all things or sweeps all before it. *And blood toucheth blood,* lit. *bloods touch bloods* [6]. The

[1] See Deut. iv. 1, 40. vi. 21-25. &c.
[2] Rom. i. 21.
[3] 1 S. John ii. 3, 4. iv. 7, 8.
[4] Rom. i. 21, 18, 28.
[5] The word rendered swearing, *aloh,* is derived from the Name of God, *Eloah,* and signifies, using His name; invoking him, probably in a *curse,* which the noun *alah* signifies.
[6] "Bloods" is ever, in Holy Scripture, used of blood-shed. On the history, see Introd. p. 5, and below p. 148.

Before CHRIST cir. 780.

3 Therefore [c] shall the
land mourn, and [d] every
one that dwelleth therein
shall languish, with the
beasts of the field, and with
the fowls of heaven; yea,
the fishes of the sea also
shall be taken away.
4 Yet let no man strive,
nor reprove another: for
thy people *are* as [e] they that
strive with the priest.

[c] Jer. 4. 28. & 12. 4. Amos 5. 16. & 8. 8.
[d] Zeph. 1. 3.
[e] Deut. 17. 12.

---

blood was poured so continuously and in such torrents, that it flowed on, until stream met stream and formed one wide inundation of blood.

3. *Therefore shall the land mourn.* Dumb inanimate nature seems to rejoice and to be in unison with our sense of joy, when bedewed and fresh through rain and radiant with light; and, again, to mourn, when smitten with drought or blight or disease, or devoured by the creatures which God employs to lay it waste for man's sins. Dumb nature is, as it were, in sympathy with man, cursed in Adam, smitten amid man's offences, its outward show responding to man's inward heart, wasted, parched, desolate, when man himself was marred and wasted by his sins.

With the beasts of the field, lit. "*in* the beasts," &c. God included *the fowl and the cattle and every beast of the field* in His covenant with man. So here, in this sentence of woe, He includes them in the inhabitants of the land, and orders that, since man would not serve God, the creatures made to serve him, should be withdrawn from him. "General iniquity is punished by general desolation."

Yea, the fishes of the sea also. Inland seas or lakes are called by this same name, as the Sea of Tiberias and the Dead Sea. Yet here the Prophet probably alludes to the history of man's creation, when God gave him dominion [1] *over the fish of the sea, and over the fowl of the heaven, and over every living thing* (*chaiah*), in just the inverse order, in which he here declares that they shall be taken away. There God gives dominion over all, from lowest to highest; here God denounces that He will take away all, down to those which are least affected by any changes. Yet from time to time God has, in chastisement, directed that the shoals of fishes should not come to their usual haunts. This is well known in the history of sea-coasts; and conscience has acknowledged the hand of God and seen the ground of His visitation. Of the fulfillment S. Jerome writes: "Whoso believeth not that this befell the people of Israel, let him survey Illyricum, let him survey the Thraces, Macedonia, the Pannonias, and the whole land which stretches from the Propontis and Bosphorus to the Julian Alps, and he will experience that, together with man, all the creatures also fail, which afore were nourished by the Creator for the service of man."

4. *Yet let no man strive, nor reprove another,* lit. "*Only man let him not strive, and let not man reprove.*" God had taken the controversy with His people into His own hands; *the Lord,* He said [2], *hath a controversy* (*rib*) *with the inhabitants of the land.* Here He forbids man to intermeddle; *man let him not strive.* (He again uses the same word [3].) The people were obstinate and would not hear; warning and reproof, being neglected, only aggravated their guilt: so God bids man to cease to speak in His Name. He Himself alone will implead them, Whose pleading none could evade or contradict. Subordinately, God, teaches us, amid His judgments, not to strive or throw the blame on each other, but each to look to his own sins, not to the sins of others.

For thy people are as they that strive with the priest. God had made it a part of the office of the priest, to *keep knowledge* [4]. He had bidden, that all hard causes should be taken *to* [5] *the priest who stood to minister there before the Lord their God;* and whoso refused the priest's sentence was to be put to death. The priest was then to judge in God's Name. As speaking in His Name, in His stead, with His authority, taught by Himself, they were called by that Name, in Which they spoke, Elohim [6], God, not in regard to themselves but as representing Him. To *strive* then *with the priest* was the highest contumacy; and such was their whole life and conduct. It was the character of the whole kingdom of *Israel.* For they had thrown off the authority of the family of Aaron, which God had appointed. Their political existence was based upon the rejection of that authority. The national character influences the individual. When the whole polity is formed on disobedience and revolt, individuals will not tolerate interference. As they had rejected the priest, so would and did they reject the prophets. He says not, they *were* priest-strivers, (for they had no lawful priests, against whom to strive,) but they were *like priest-strivers,* persons whose habit it was to strive with those who spoke in God's Name. He says in fact, let not *man* strive with those who strive with God. The uselessness of

[1] Gen. i. 28. [2] iv. 1 ריב [3] ירב [4] Mal. ii. 7. [5] Deut. xvii. 8–12. [6] Ex. xxi. 6. xxii. 8, 9.

Before CHRIST cir. 780.

5 Therefore shalt thou
fall [f] in the day, and the
prophet also shall fall with
thee in the night, and I
will † destroy thy mother.
6 ¶ [g] My people are † destroyed for lack of knowledge: because thou hast rejected knowledge, I will also reject thee, that thou shalt be no priest to me: seeing thou hast forgotten the law of thy God, I will also forget thy children.

f See Jer. 6. 4, 5. & 15. 8.
† Heb. *cut off*.
g Isai. 5. 13.
† Heb. *cut off*.

such reproof is often repeated. [1] *He that reproveth a scorner getteth to himself shame, and he that rebuketh a wicked man getteth himself a blot. Reprove not a scorner, lest he hate thee.* [2] *Speak not in the ears of a fool, for he will despise the wisdom of thy words.* S. Stephen gives it as a characteristic of the Jews[3], *Ye stiff-necked and uncircumcised in heart and ears, ye do always resist the Holy Ghost; as your fathers did, so do ye.*

5. *Therefore shalt thou fall.* The two parts of the verse fill up each other. "By day and by night shall they fall, people and prophets together." Their calamities should come upon them successively, day and night. They should stumble by day, when there is least fear of stumbling[4]; and night should not by its darkness protect them. Evil should come *at noon-day*[5] upon them, seeing it, but unable to repel it; as Isaiah speaks of it as an aggravation of trouble[6], *thy land strangers devour it in thy presence;* and the false prophets, who saw their visions in the night, should themselves be overwhelmed in the darkness, blinded by moral, perishing in actual, darkness.

And I will destroy thy mother. Individuals are spoken of as the children; the whole nation, as the mother. He denounces then the destruction of all, collectively and individually. They were to be cut off, root and branch. They were to lose their collective existence as a nation; and, lest private persons should flatter themselves with hope of escape, it is said to them, as if one by one, "thou shalt fall."

6. *My people are destroyed for lack of knowledge.* "My people *are*," not, "*is*." This accurately represents the Hebrew[7]. The word "people" speaks of them as a whole; *are*, relates to the individuals of whom that whole is composed. Together, the words express the utter destruction of the whole, one and all. They are destroyed *for lack of knowledge*, lit. "of *the* knowledge," i. e. the only knowledge, which in the creature is real knowledge, that knowledge, of the want of which he had before complained, the knowledge of the Creator. So Isaiah mourns in the same words[8], *therefore my people are gone into captivity, because they have no knowledge.* They are destroyed for lack of it; for the true knowledge of God is the life of the soul, true life, eternal life, as our Saviour saith, *This is life eternal, that they should know Thee, the only true God, and Jesus Christ Whom Thou has sent.* The source of this lack of knowledge, so fatal to the people, was the wilful rejection of that knowledge by the priest;

Because thou hast rejected knowledge, I will also reject thee, that thou shalt be no priest to Me. God marks the relation between the sin and the punishment, by retorting on them, as it were, their own acts; and that with great emphasis, *I will utterly reject thee*[9]. Those, thus addressed, must have been true priests, scattered up and down in Israel, who, in an irregular way, offered sacrifices for them, and connived at their sins. For God's sentence on them is, *thou shalt be no priest to ME.* But the priests whom Jeroboam consecrated out of other tribes than Levi, were priests not to God, but to the calves. Those then, originally true priests to God, had probably a precarious livelihood, when the true worship of God was deformed by the mixture of the calf-worship, and the people *halted between two opinions;* and so were tempted by poverty also, to withhold from the people unpalatable truth. They shared, then, in the rejection of God's truth which they dissembled, and made themselves partakers in its suppression. And now, they *despised, were disgusted with*[10] the knowledge of God, as all do in fact despise and dislike it, who prefer ought besides to it. So God repaid their contempt to them, and took away the office, which, by their sinful connivances, they had hoped to retain.

Seeing thou hast forgotten the law of thy God. This seems to have been the sin of the people. For the same persons could not, at least in the same stage of sin, despise and forget. They who despise or *reject*, must have before their mind that which they *reject*. To *reject* is wilful, conscious, deliberate sin, with a high hand; to *forget*, an act of negligence.

[1] Prov. ix. 7, 8. [2] Ib. xxiii. 9. [3] Acts vii. 51.
[4] S. John xi. 9, 10. [5] Jer. xv. 8. [6] Is. i. 7.
[7] The singular noun, as being a collective, is joined with the plural verb.

[8] מבלי דעת vi. 13. The absence of the article makes no difference
[9] Such is probably the force of the unusual form אמאסאך. [10] Such is the first meaning of the word.

Before CHRIST cir. 780.

[h] ch. 13. 6.
[i] 1 Sam. 2. 30. Mal. 2. 9. Phil. 3. 19.

7 [h] As they were increased,
so they sinned against me:
[i] *therefore* will I change
their glory into shame.

8 They eat up the sin of
my people, and they † set
their heart on their ini-
quity.

Before CHRIST cir. 780.

† Heb. *lift up their soul to their iniquity.*

The rejection of God's law was the act of the understanding and will; forgetfulness of it comes from the neglect to look into it; and this, from the distaste of the natural mind for spiritual things, from being absorbed in things of this world, from inattention to the duties prescribed by it, or shrinking from seeing *that* condemned, which is agreeable to the flesh. The priests knew God's law and *despised* it; the people *forgat* it. In an advanced stage of sin, however, man may come to forget what he once despised; and this is the condition of the hardened sinner.

I will also forget thy children, lit. *I will forget thy children, I too.* God would mark the more, that His act followed on their's; they, first; then, He saith, *I too.* He would requite them, and do what it belonged not to His Goodness to do first. Parents who are careless as to themselves, as to their own lives, even as to their own shame, still long that their children should not be as themselves. God tries to touch their hearts, where they are least steeled against Him. He says not, *I will forget thee*, but I will forget those nearest thy heart, *thy children.* God is said to *forget*, when He acts, as if His creatures were no longer in His mind, no more the objects of His Providence and love.

7. *As they were increased, so they sinned against Me.* The *increase* may be, either in actual number or in wealth, power or dignity. The text includes both. In both kinds of increase, the bad abuse God's gifts against Himself, and take occasion of them to offend Him. The more they were increased in number, the more there were to sin, the more they were who sinned. God promised to make Abraham's seed, *as the stars of heaven.* They were to shine in the world through the light of the law, and the glory which God gave them while obeying Him. [1] *Thy fathers went down into Egypt with threescore and ten persons; and now the Lord thy God hath made thee like the stars of heaven for multitude. Therefore thou shalt love the Lord thy God, and keep His charge, and His statutes, and his judgments and His commandments alway.* God multiplied them, that there might be the more to adore Him. But instead of multiplying subjects, He multiplied apostates. "As many men as Israel had, so many altars did it build to dæmons, in the sacrifices to whom it sinned against Me." "The more sons God gave to Israel, the more enemies He made to Himself; for Israel brought them up in hatred to God, and in the love and worship of idols." "As too among the devout, one provokes another, by word and deed, to good works, so, in the congregation of evil doers, one incites another to sins." Again, worldlings make all God's gifts minister to pride, and so to all the sins, which are the daughters of pride. [2] *Jeshurun*, God says, *waxed fat and kicked; then he forsook God which made him, and lightly esteemed the Rock of his salvation.* In this way too, the increase of wealth which God gives to those who forget Him, increases the occasions of ingratitude and sins.

I will turn their glory into shame. Such is the course of sin and chastisement. God bestows on man, gifts, which may be to him matter of praise and glory, if only ordered aright to their highest and only true end, the glory of God; man perverts them to vainglory and thereby to sin; God turns the gifts, so abused, to shame. He not only gives them shame *instead* of their glory; He makes the glory itself the means and occasion of their shame. Beauty becomes the occasion of degradation; pride is proverbially near a fall; "vaulting ambition overleaps itself, and falls on th'other side;" riches and abundance of population tempt nations to wars, which become their destruction, or they invite other and stronger nations to prey upon them. *Thou hast indeed smitten Edom*, was the message of Jehoash to Amaziah [3], *and thine heart hath lifted thee up; glory of this, and tarry at home; for why shouldest thou meddle to thy hurt, that thou shouldest fall, even thou and Judah with thee? But Amaziah would not hear.* He lost his own wealth, wasted the treasures in God's house; and the walls of Jerusalem were broken down.

8. *They eat up the sin of My people.* The priests made a gain of the sins of the people, lived upon them and by them, conniving at or upholding the idolatries of the people, partaking in their idol-sacrifices and idolatrous rites, which, as involving the desertion of God, were *the sin of* the *people*, and the root of all their other sins. This the priests did knowingly. True or false, apostate or irregularly appointed, they knew that there was no truth in the golden calves; but they withheld the truth, they held it down in unrighteousness, and preached Jeroboam's falsehood, *these be thy gods, O Israel.* The reputation, station, maintenance of the false priests depended upon it. Not being of the line of

[1] Deut. x. 22. xi. 1.

[2] Ib. xxxii. 15.

[3] 2 Kings xiv. 10, 11.

Before CHRIST cir. 780.

9 And there shall be,
[k] like people, like priest:
and I will † punish them
for their ways, and † re-
ward them their doings.
10 For [l] they shall eat,
and not have enough: they
shall commit whoredom,
and shall not increase:
because they have left
off to take heed to the
LORD.

Before CHRIST cir. 780.

k Isai. 24. 2. Jer. 5. 31.
† Heb. *visit upon*
† Heb. *cause to return.*
l Lev. 26. 26. Mic. 6. 14. Hag. 1. 6.

Aaron, they could be no priests except to the calves, and so they upheld the sin whereby they lived, and, that they might themselves be accounted priests of God, taught them to worship the calves, as representatives of God.

The word, *sin*, may include indirectly the sin-offerings of the people, as if they loved the sin or encouraged it, in order that they might partake of the outward expiations for it.

And they set their heart on their iniquity, as the source of temporal profit to themselves. "Benefited by the people, they reproved them not in their sinful doings, but charged themselves with their souls, saying, on us be the judgment, as those who said to Pilate, *His blood be upon us*." That which was, above all, *their iniquity*, the source of all the rest, was their departure from God and from His ordained worship. On this they *set their hearts;* in this they kept them secure by their lies; they feared any misgivings, which might rend the people from them, and restore them to the true worship of God. But what else is it, to extenuate or flatter sin now, to dissemble it, not to see it, not openly to denounce it, lest we lose our popularity, or alienate those who commit it? What else is it to speak smooth words to the great and wealthy, not to warn them, even in general terms, of the danger of making Mammon their god; of the peril of riches, of parade, of luxury, of immoral dressing, and, amid boundless extravagance, neglect of the poor; encouraging the rich, not only in the neglect of Lazarus, but in pampering the dogs, while they neglect him? What is the praise of some petty dole to the poor, but connivance at the withholding from God His due in them? "We see now," says an old writer, "[1] how many prelates live on the oblations and revenues of the laity, and yet, whereas they are bound, by words, by prayers, by exemplary life, to turn them away from sin, and to lead them to amendment, they, in various ways, scandalize, corrupt, infect them, by ungodly conversation, flattery, connivance, co-operation, and neglect of due pastoral care. Whence Jeremiah says[2], *My people hath been lost sheep: their shepherds have caused them to go astray.* O how horrible and exceeding great will be their damnation, who shall be tormented for each of those under their care, who perish through their negligence."

9. *And there shall be like people, like priest.* Priest and people were alike in sin. Yea they are wont, if bad, to foment each other's sin. The bad priest copies the sins which he should reprove, and excuses himself by the frailty of our common nature. The people, acutely enough, detect the worldliness or self-indulgence of the priest, and shelter themselves under his example. Their defence stands good before men; but what before God? Alike in sin, priest and people should be alike in punishment. "Neither secular greatness should exempt the laity, nor the dignity of his order, the priest." Both shall be swept away in one common heap, in one disgrace, into one damnation. *They shall bind them in bundles to burn them.*

And I will punish them for their ways, and reward them their doings; lit. *I will visit upon him his ways, and his doings I will make to return to him.* People and priests are spoken of as one man. None should escape. The judgment comes down *upon* them, overwhelming them. Man's deeds are called his *ways*, because the soul holds on the tenor of its life along them, and those ways lead him on to his last end, heaven or hell. The word rendered *doings*[3] signifies *great doings*, when used of God; *bold doings*, on the part of man. Those bold presumptuous doings against the law and Will of God, God will bring back to the sinner's bosom.

10. *For they shall eat, and not have enough.* This is almost a proverbial saying of Holy Scripture, and, as such, has manifold applications. In the way of nature, it comes true in those, who, under God's afflictive Hand in famine or siege, *eat* what they have, but *have not enough*, and perish with hunger. It comes true in those, who, through bodily disease, are not nourished by their food. Yet not less true is it of those who, through their own insatiate desires, are never satisfied, but crave the more greedily, the more they have. Their sin of covetousness becomes their torment.

They shall commit whoredom and not increase; lit. *they have committed whoredom.* The time spoken of is perhaps changed, because God would not speak of their future sin, as certain. There is naturally too a long interval between this sin and its possible fruit,

[1] Dionys. Carth.

[2] l. 6.

[3] מעלליו.

Before CHRIST cir. 780.

11 Whoredom and wine
and new wine [m] take away
the heart.
12 ¶ My people ask
counsel at their [n] stocks,
and their staff declareth
unto them: for [o] the spirit
of whoredoms hath caused

[m] Isai. 28. 7. See Eccles. 7. 7.

[n] Jer. 2. 27. Hab. 2. 19.

[o] Isai. 44. 20. ch. 5. 4.

which may be marked by this change of time. The sin was past, the effect was to be seen hereafter. They used all means, lawful and unlawful, to increase their offspring, but they failed, even because they used forbidden means. God's curse rested upon those means. Single marriage, according to God's law, *they twain shall be one flesh*, yields in a nation larger increase than polygamy. Illicit intercourse God turns to decay. His curse is upon it.

Because they have left off to take heed to the Lord, lit. *to watch, observe, the Lord.* The eye of the soul should be upon God, watching and waiting to know all indications of His Will, all guidings of His Eye. So the Psalmist says[1], *As the eyes of servants look unto the hand of their masters, and as the eyes of a maiden unto the hands of her mistress, even so our eyes wait upon the Lord our God, until He have mercy upon us.* The Angels of God, great and glorious as they are, *do alway behold the Face of* the *Father*[2], at once filled with His love, and wrapt in contemplation, and reading therein His Will, to do it. The lawless and hopeless ways of Israel sprang from their neglecting to watch and observe God. For as soon as man ceases to watch God, he falls, of himself, into sin. The eye which is not fixed on God, is soon astray amid the vanities and pomps and lusts of the world. So it follows;

11. *Whoredom and wine and new wine take away* (lit. *takes away*) *the heart.* Wine and fleshly sin are pictured as blended in one, to deprive man of his affections and reason and understanding, and to leave him brutish and irrational. In all the relations of life toward God and man, reason and will are guided by the affections. And so, in God's language, the "heart" stands for the "understanding" as well as the "affections," because it directs the understanding, and the understanding, bereft of true affections, and under the rule of passion, becomes senseless. Besides the perversion of the understanding, each of these sins blunts and dulls the fineness of the intellect; much more, both combined. The stupid sottishness of the confirmed voluptuary is a whole, of which each act of sensual sin worked its part. The Heathen saw this clearly, although, without the grace of God, they did not act on what they saw to be true and right. This, the sottishness of Israel, destroying their understanding, was the ground of their next folly, that they ascribed to *their stock* the office of God. "Corruption of manners and superstition" (it has often been observed) "go hand in hand."

12. *My people ask counsel at* [lit. *on*] *their stocks.* They ask habitually[3]; and that, in dependence *on their stocks.* The word *wood* is used of the idol made of it, to bring before them the senselessness of their doings, in that they asked counsel of the senseless wood. Thus Jeremiah[4] reproaches them for *saying to a stock, my father;* and Habakkuk[5], *Woe unto him that saith to the wood, awake.*

And their staff declareth unto them. Many sorts of this superstition existed among the Arabs and Chaldees. They were different ways of drawing lots, without any dependence upon the true God to direct it. This was a part of their senselessness, of which the Prophet had just said, that their sins took away their hearts. The tenderness of the word, *My people*, aggravates both the stupidity and the ingratitude of Israel. They whom the Living God owned as His own people, they who might have asked of Him, asked of a stock or a staff.

For the spirit of whoredoms. It has been thought of old, that the evil spirits assault mankind in a sort of order and method, different spirits bending all their energies to tempt him to different sins[6]. And this has been founded on the words of Holy Scripture, "a lying spirit," "an unclean spirit," "a spirit of jealousy," and our Lord said of the evil spirit whom the disciples could not cast out[7]; *This kind goeth not out but by prayer and fasting.* Hence it has been thought that "[6]some spirits take delight in uncleanness and defilement of sins; others urge on to blasphemies; others, to anger and fury; others take delight in gloom; others are soothed with vainglory and pride; and that each instills into man's heart that vice in which he takes pleasure himself; yet that all do not urge their own perversenesses at once, but in turn, as opportunity of time or place, or man's own susceptibility, invites them." Or the word, *spirit of whoredoms*, may mean the vehemence with which men were whirled along by their evil passions, whether by their passionate love of idolatry, or by the fleshly sin which was so often bound up with their idolatry.

They have gone a whoring from under their

[1] Ps. cxxiii. 2. [2] S. Matt. xviii. 10.
[3] The Hebrew tense expresses action which is repeatedly resumed.
[4] ii. 27. [5] ii. 19.
[6] Cassian Collat. vii. 17.
[7] S. Matt. xvii. 21.

Before CHRIST cir. 780.

them to err, and they have
gone a whoring from under
their God.

p Isai. 1. 29. & 57. 5, 7. Ezek. 6. 13. & 20. 28.

13 p They sacrifice upon
the tops of the mountains,
and burn incense upon the
hills, under oaks and poplars and elms, because the
shadow thereof *is* good:
q therefore your daughters
shall commit whoredom,
and your spouses shall commit adultery.

q Amos 7. 17. Rom. 1. 28.

14 || I will not punish
your daughters when they
commit whoredom, nor
your spouses when they
commit adultery: for them-

|| Or, *Shall I not, &c.*

God. The words *from under* continue the image of the adulteress wife, by which God had pictured the faithlessness of His people. The wife was spoken of as *under her husband*[1], i. e. under his authority; she withdrew herself *from under* him, when she withdrew herself from his authority, and gave herself to another. So Israel, being wedded to God, estranged herself from Him, withdrew herself from His obedience, cast off all reverence to Him, and prostituted herself to her idols.

13. *They sacrifice upon the tops of the mountains.* The tops of hills or mountains seemed nearer heaven, the air was purer, the place more removed from the world. To worship the Unseen God upon them, was then the suggestion of natural feeling and of simple devotion. God Himself directed the typical sacrifice of Isaac to take place on a mountain; on that same mountain He commanded that the temple should be built; on a mountain, God gave the law; on a mountain was our Saviour transfigured; on a mountain was He crucified; from a mountain He ascended into heaven. Mountains and hills have accordingly often been chosen for Christian churches and monasteries. But the same natural feeling, misdirected, made them the places of heathen idolatry and heathen sins. The Heathen probably also chose for their star and planet-worship, mountains or large plains, as being the places whence the heavenly bodies might be seen most widely. Being thus connected with idolatry and sin, God strictly forbade the worship on the high places, and (as is the case with so many of God's commandments) man practised it as diligently as if He had commanded it. God had said[2], *Ye shall utterly destroy all the places, wherein the nations, which ye shall possess, served their gods upon the high mountains, and upon the hills and under every green tree.* But[3] *they set them up images and groves* [rather *images of Ashtaroth*] *in every high hill and under every green tree, and there they burnt incense in all the high places, as did the heathen whom the Lord carried away before them.* The words express, that this which God forbade they did diligently; *they sacrificed much and diligently; they burned incense much and diligently*[4]; and that, not here and there, but generally, *on the tops of the mountains*, and, as it were, in the open face of heaven. So also Ezekiel complains[5], *They saw every high hill and all the thick trees, and they offered there their sacrifices, and there they presented the provocation of their offering; there also they made their sweet savor, and poured out there their drink-offerings.*

Under oaks, [*white*] *poplars and elms* [probably *the terebinth or turpentine tree*] *because the shadow thereof is good.* The darkness of the shadow suited alike the cruel and the profligate deeds which were done in honor of their false gods. In the open face of day, and in secret they carried on their sin.

Therefore their daughters shall commit whoredoms, and their spouses [or more probably, *daughters-in-law*] *shall commit adultery,* or (in the present) *commit adultery.* The fathers and husbands gave themselves to the abominable rites of Baal-peor and Ashtaroth, and so the daughters and daughters-in-law followed their example. This was by the permission of God, Who, since they *glorified not God* as they ought, *gave them up,* abandoned them, *to vile affections.* So, through their own disgrace and bitter griefs, in the persons of those whose honor they most cherished, they should learn how ill they themselves had done, in departing from Him Who is the Father and Husband of every soul. The sins of the fathers descend very often to the children, both in the way of nature, that the children inherit strong temptations to their parents' sin, and by way of example, that they greedily imitate, often exaggerate, them. Wouldest thou not have children, which thou wouldest wish unborn, reform thyself. The saying may include too sufferings at the hands of the enemy. "What thou dost willingly, that shall your daughters and your daughters-in-law suffer against thine and their will."

14. *I will not punish your daughters.* God threatens, as the severest woe, that He will not punish their sins with the correction of a Father in this present life, but will leave

[1] Num. v. 19, 29. Ezek. xxiii. 5.
[2] Deut. xii. 2.
[3] 2 Kings xvii. 10, 11.
[4] *yezabbechu*, not *izbechu; yekatteru*, not *yaktiru*.
[5] xx. 28.

Before CHRIST cir. 780.

selves are separated with whores, and they sacrifice with harlots: therefore the people *that* [r] doth not understand shall || fall.

[r] ver. 1, 6.

|| Or, *be punished.*

15 ¶ Though thou, Israel, play the harlot, *yet* let not Judah offend; [s] and come not ye unto Gilgal, neither go ye up to [t] Beth-aven, [u] nor swear, The LORD liveth.

Before CHRIST cir. 780.

[s] ch. 9. 15. & 12. 11. Amos 4. 4. & 5. 5.

[t] 1 Kings 12. 29. ch. 10. 5.

[u] Amos 8. 14. Zeph. 1. 5.

the sinners, unheeded, to follow all iniquity. It is the last punishment of persevering sinners, that God leaves them to prosper in their sins and in those things which help them to sin. Hence we are taught to pray[1], *O Lord, correct me, but in judgment, not in Thine anger.* For since God chastiseth those whom He loveth, it follows[2], *if we be without chastisement, whereof all are partakers, then are we bastards, and not sons.* To be chastened severely for lesser sins, is a token of great love of God toward us; to sin on without punishment is a token of God's extremest displeasure, and a sign of reprobation. [3] "Great is the offence, if, when thou hast sinned, thou art undeserving of the wrath of God."

For themselves are separated with whores. God turns from them as unworthy to be spoken to any more, and speaks of them, They *separate themselves*, from Whom? and with whom? They separate themselves *from* God, and *with* the degraded ones and *with* devils. Yet so do all those who choose wilful sin.

And they sacrifice [*continually*, as before] *with* [*the*] *harlots.* The unhappy women here spoken of were such as were[4] *consecrated* (as their name imports) to their vile gods and goddesses, and to prostitution. This dreadful consecration, yea desecration, whereby they were taught to seek honor in their disgrace, was spread in different forms over Phœnicia, Syria, Phrygia, Assyria, Babylonia. Ashtaroth, (the Greek Astarte) was its chief object. This horrible worship prevailed in Midian, when Israel was entering the promised land, and it suggested the devilish device of Balaam[5] to entangle Israel in sin whereby they might forfeit the favor of God. The like is said to subsist to this day in heathen India. The sin was both the cause and effect of the superstition. Man's corrupt heart gave rise to the worship: and the worship in turn fostered the corruption. He first sanctioned the sin by aid of a degrading worship of nature, and then committed it under plea of that worship. He made his sin a law to him. Women, who never relapsed into the sin, sinned in obedience to the dreadful law[6]. Blinded as they were, individual heathen had the excuse of their hereditary blindness; the Jews had imperfect grace. The sins of Christians are self-sought, against light and grace.

Therefore the people that doth not understand shall fall. The word comprises both, *that doth not understand*, and, *that will not understand.* They might have understood, if they *would.* God had revealed Himself to them, and had given to them His law, and was still sending to them His prophets, so that they could not but have known and understood God's Will, had they willed. Ignorance, which we might avoid or cure, if we would, is itself a sin. It cannot excuse sin. They shall, he says, *fall*, or *be cast headlong.* Those who blind their eyes, so as not to see or understand God's Will, bring themselves to sudden ruin, which they hide from themselves, until they fall headlong in it.

15. *Let not Judah offend.* The sentence of Israel had been pronounced; she had been declared incorrigible. The Prophet turns from her now to Judah. Israel had abandoned God's worship, rejected or corrupted His priests, given herself to the worship of the calves; no marvel what further excess of riot she run into! But Judah, who had the law and the temple and the service of God, let not her, (he would say,) involve herself in Israel's sin. If Israel, in wilful blindness, had plunged herself in ruin, let not Judah involve herself in her sin and her ruin. He turns (as elsewhere) incidentally to Judah.

Come ye not unto Gilgal. Gilgal lay between Jericho and the Jordan. There, ten furlongs from the Jordan, first in all the promised land, the people encamped; there Joshua placed the monument of the miraculous passage of the Jordan; there he renewed the circumcision of the people which had been intermitted in the wilderness, and the feast of the passover; thither the people returned, after all the victories by which God gave them possession of the land of promise[7]. There Samuel habitually sacrificed, and there, *before the Lord*, i. e. in His special covenanted Presence, he publicly made Saul king[8]. It was part of the policy of Jeroboam to take hold of all these associations, as a sort of setoff against Jerusalem and the Temple, from which he had separated his people. In op-

[1] Jer. x. 24. [2] Heb. xii. 8.
[3] S. Jer. [4] הקדשות
[5] Num. xxv. xxxi. 8, 16.
[6] Herod. i. 199. It may have been in some such way, that Gomer, whom the prophet was bidden to marry, had fallen.
[7] Josh. iv. 19, 20. v. 9, 10. ix. 6. x. 6–9. 43. xiv. 6.
[8] 1 Sam. x. 8. xi. 14, 15. xiii. 4–9. xv. 21, 33.

Before CHRIST cir. 780.

16 For Israel [x] slideth
back as a backsliding heifer: now the LORD will feed
them as a lamb in a large
place.

x Jer. 3. 6. & 7. 24. & 8. 5. Zech. 7. 11.

17 Ephraim *is* joined to
idols: [y] let him alone.
18 Their drink † is
sour: they have commit-
ted whoredom continually:

Before CHRIST cir. 780.

y Matt. 15. 14.
† Heb. *is gone.*

---

position to this idolatry, Elisha for a time, established there one of the schools of the Prophets [1].

Neither go ye up to Bethaven. Bethaven, lit. *house of vanity*, was a city East of *Bethel* [2], *the house of God.* But since Jeroboam had set up the worship of the calves at Bethel, Bethel had ceased to be *the house of God*, and had become *a house* or *temple of vanity;* and so the Prophet gave it no more its own name which was associated with the history of the faith of the Patriarchs, but called it what it had become. In Bethel God had twice appeared to Jacob, when he left the land of promise [3] to go to Laban, and when he returned [4]. Thither also the ark of God was for a time in the days of the judges removed from Shiloh [5], near to which on the south [6] Bethel lay. It too Jeroboam profaned by setting up the calf there. To these places then, as being now places of the idolatry of Israel, Judah is forbidden to go, and then to *swear, the Lord liveth.* For to swear by the Lord in a place of idolatry would be to associate the living God with idols [7], which God expressly forbade.

16. *For Israel slideth back, as a backsliding heifer.* The calves which Israel worshiped were pictures of itself. They represented natural, untamed, strength, which, when put to service, started back and shrank from the yoke. "Untractable, petulant, unruly, wanton, it withdrew from the yoke, when it could; if it could not, it drew aside or backward, instead of forward." So is it rare, exceeding rare, for man to walk straight on in God's ways; he jerks, writhes, twists, darts aside hither and thither, hating nothing so much as one straight, even, narrow tenor of his ways.

Now the Lord will feed them as a lamb in a large place. The punishment of Israel was close at hand, *now.* It would not have the straitness of God's commandments; it should have the wideness of a desert. God would withdraw His protecting Providence from them: He would rule them, although unfelt in His mercy. At *large*, they wished to be; at large they should be; but it should be the largeness of *a wilderness where is no way.* There, like a lamb, they should go astray, wandering up and down, unprotected, a prey to wild beasts. Woe is it to that man, whom, when he withdraws from Christ's easy yoke, God permits to take unhindered the broad road which leadeth to destruction. To Israel, this *wide place* was the wide realms of the Medes, where they were withdrawn from God's worship and deprived of His protection.

17. *Ephraim is joined to idols*, i. e. banded, bound up with them, *associated*, as the word means, with them so as to cleave to them, willing neither to part with, nor to be parted from, them. The *idols* are called by a name, denoting *toils;* with toil they were fashioned, and, when fashioned, they were a toil and grief.

Let him alone, lit. *give him rest*, i. e. from all further expostulations, which he will not hear. It is an abandonment of Israel for the time, as in the prophet Ezekiel [8], *As for you, O house of Israel, thus saith the Lord God, go ye, serve ye every one his idols.* Sinners often long not to be tormented by conscience or by God's warnings. To be left so, is to be abandoned by God, as one whose case is desperate. God will not, while there is hope, leave a man to sleep in sin; for so the numbness of the soul increases, until, like those who fall asleep amid extreme cold of the body, it never awakes.

18. *Their drink is sour*, lit. *turned*, as we say of milk. So Isaiah says [9], *Thy silver is become dross; thy wine is mingled*, i. e. adulterated, *with water;* and our lord speaks of *salt which had lost its savor.* The wine or the salt, when once turned or become insipid, is spoiled, irrecoverably, as we speak of "dead wine." They had lost all their life, and taste of goodness.

Her rulers with shame do love, give ye. Avarice and luxury are continually banded together according to the saying, "covetous of another's, prodigal of his own." Yet it were perhaps more correct to render, *her rulers do love, do love, shame* [10]. They love that which brings shame, which is bound up with shame, and ends in it; and so the Prophet says that they *love* the *shame* itself. They act, as if they were in love with the shame, which, all their lives long, they are unceasingly and, as it were, by system, drawing upon themselves. They chase diligently after all the occasions of sins and sinful pleasures which end in shame; they omit nothing

---

[1] 2 Kgs. iv. 38. [2] Josh. vii. 2. [3] Gen. xxviii. 10, 19. [4] Ib. xxxv. 1 and 9. [5] Jud. xx. 26, 7. [6] Jud. xxi. 19. [7] Zeph. i. 5. [8] xx. 39. [9] i. 22.

[10] אהבוהבו is probably one of the earliest forms of the intensive verb, repeating a part of a verb itself, with its inflection.

Before CHRIST cir. 780.

a Mic. 3. 11. & 7. 3.
† Heb. *shields*, Ps. 47. 9.
a Jer. 4. 11, 12. & 51. 1.
b Isai. 1. 29. Jer. 2. 26.

[a] her † rulers *with* shame do
love, Give ye.
19 [a] The wind hath
bound her up in her wings,
and [b] they shall be ashamed
because of their sacrifices.

CHAPTER V.

1 *God's judgments against the priests, the people, and the princes of Israel, for their manifold sins,* 15 *until they repent.*

Before CHRIST cir. 780.

HEAR ye this, O priests; and hearken, ye house of Israel; and give ye ear, O house of the king; for judgment *is* toward you, because [a] ye have been a snare on Mizpah, and a net spread upon Tabor.

a ch. 6. 9.

which brings it, do nothing which can avoid it. What else or what more could they do, if they *loved* the *shame* for its own sake?

19. *The wind hath bound her up in her wings.* When God brought Israel out of Egypt, He *bare them on eagle's wings, and brought them unto Himself*[1]. Now they had abandoned God, and God abandoned them as chaff to the wind. The certainty of Israel's doom is denoted by its being spoken of in the past. It was certain in the Divine judgment. Sudden, resistless, irreversible are God's judgments, when they come. As if "imprisoned in the viewless winds, and" borne "with resistless violence," as it were on the wings of the whirlwind, Israel should be hurried by the mighty wrath of God into captivity in a distant land, bound up so that none should escape, but, when arrived there, dispersed hither and thither, as the chaff before the wind.

And they shall be ashamed because of their sacrifices. They had sacrificed to the calves, to Baal, or to the sun, moon, stars, hoping aid from them rather than from God. When then they should see, in deed, that from those their sacrifices no good came to them, but evil only, they should be healthfully ashamed. So, in fact, in her captivity, did Israel learn to be ashamed of her idols; and so does God, by healthful disappointment, make us ashamed of seeking out of Him, the good things, which He alone hath, and hath in store for them who love Him.

V. 1. *Hear ye this, O ye priests.* God, with the solemn threefold summons, arraigns anew all classes in Israel before Him, not now to repentance but to judgment. Neither the religious privileges of the priests, nor the multitude of the people, nor the civil dignity of the king, should exempt any from God's judgment. The priests are, probably, the true but corrupted priests of God, who had fallen away to the idolatries with which they were surrounded, and, by their apostacy, had strengthened them. The king, here first mentioned by Hosea, was probably the unhappy Zechariah, a weak, pliant, self-indulgent, drunken scoffer[2], who, after eleven years of anarchy, succeeded his father, only to be murdered.

For judgment is toward you, lit. *the judgment.* The kings and the priests had hitherto been the judges; now they were summoned before Him, Who is *the* Judge of judges, and the King of kings. To teach the law was part of the priest's office; to enforce it, belonged to the king. The guilt of both was enhanced, in that they, being so entrusted with it, had corrupted it. They had the greatest sin, as being the seducers of the people, and therefore have the severest sentence. The Prophet, dropping for the time the mention of the people, pronounces the judgment on the seducers.

Because ye have been a snare on Mizpah. Mizpah, the scene of the solemn covenant of Jacob with Laban, and of his signal protection by God, lay in the mountainous part of Gilead on the East of Jordan. Tabor was the well-known Mountain of the Transfiguration, which rises out of the midst of the plain of Jezreel or Esdraelon, one thousand feet high, in the form of a sugar-loaf. Of Mount Tabor it is related by S. Jerome, that birds were still snared upon it. But something more seems intended than the mere likeness of birds, taken in the snare of a fowler. This was to be seen everywhere; and so, had this been all, there hath no ground to mention these two historical spots. The Prophets has selected places on both sides of Jordan, which were probably centres of corruption, or special scenes of wickedness. Mizpah, being a sacred place in the history of the Patriarch Jacob[3], was probably, like Gilgal and other sacred places, desecrated by idolatry. Tabor was the scene of God's deliverance of Israel by Barak[4]. There, by encouraging idolatries, they became hunters, not pastors, of souls[5]. There is an old Jewish tradition[6], that lyers-in-wait were set in these two places, to intercept and murder

[1] Ex. xix. 4. Deut. xxxii. 11. [2] See Introd. p. 15. [3] Gen. xxxi. 23–49. [4] Jud. iv. [5] Ezek. xiii. 18, 20.

[6] Rashi, Ibn Ezra, Kimchi "out of ancienter Rabbins." Poc.

Before CHRIST cir. 780.

2 And the revolters are
[b] profound to make slaugh-
ter, || though I *have been*
† a rebuker of them all.
3 [c] I know Ephraim, and
Israel is not hid from me:
for now, O Ephraim, [d] thou
committest whoredom, *and*
Israel is defiled.
4 † || They will not frame
their doings to turn unto
their God: for [e] the spirit

[b] Isai. 29. 15.
|| Or, *and, &c.*
† Heb. *a correction.*
[c] Amos 3, 2.

Before CHRIST cir. 780.

[d] Ezek. 23. 5. &c. ch. 4. 17.
† Heb. *They will not give.*
|| Or, *Their doings will not suffer them.*
[e] ch. 4. 12.

---

those Israelites, who would go up to worship at Jerusalem. And this tradition gains countenance from the mention of slaughter in the next verse.

2. *And the revolters are profound to make slaughter;* lit. "*They made the slaughter deep,*" as Isaiah says, "*they deeply corrupted themselves* [1];" and our old writers say "He smote deep." They willed also doubtless to "make it deep," hide it so deep, that God should never know it, as the Psalmist says of the ungodly, "that *the inward self and heart of the workers of iniquity is deep*," whereon it follows, that God should *suddenly wound them,* as here the prophet subjoins that God rebuked them. Actual and profuse murder has been already [2] mentioned as one of the common sins of Israel, and it is afterward [3] also charged upon the priests.

Though I have been a rebuker, lit. *a rebuke,* as the Psalmist says [4], *I am prayer,* i. e "I am all prayer." The Psalmist's whole being was turned into prayer. So here, all the attributes of God, His mercies, love, justice, were concentrated into one, and that one, *rebuke.* Rebuke was the one form, in which they were all seen. It is an aggravation of crime to do it in the place of judgment or in the presence of the judge. Israel was immersed in his sin and heeded not, although God rebuked him continually by His voice in the law, forbidding all idolatry, and was now all the while, both in word and deed, rebuking him.

3. *I know Ephraim.* There is much emphasis on the *I.* It is like our, "*I* have known," or "I, I, have known." God had known him all along, if we may so speak. However deep they may have laid their plans of blood, however they would or do hide them from man, and think that no Eye seeth them, and say, *Who seeth me? and who knoweth me? I, to* Whose *Eyes all things are naked and opened* [5], have all along known them, and nothing of them has been hid from Me. *For,* He adds, even now, *now* when, under a fair outward shew, they are veiling the depth of their sin, *now,* when they think that their way is hid in darkness, I know their doings, that they are defiling themselves. Sin never wanted specious excuse. Now too unbelievers are mostly fond of precisely those characters in Holy Scripture, whom God condemns. Jeroboam doubtless was accounted a patriot, vindicating his country from oppressive taxation, which Rehoboam insolently threatened. Jerusalem, as lying in the Southernmost tribe, was represented, as ill-selected for the place of the assemblage of the tribes. Bethel, on the contrary, was hallowed by visions; it had been the abode, for a time, of the ark. It lay in the tribe of Ephraim, which they might think to have been unjustly deprived of its privilege. Dan was a provision for the Northern tribes. Such was the exterior. God says in answer, *I know Ephraim.* [6] *Known unto God are all his works from the beginning of the world.* Although (in some way unknown to us) not interfering with our free-will, known unto God are our thoughts and words and deeds, before they are framed, while they are framed, while they are being spoken and done; known to Him is all which we do, and all which, under any circumstances, we should do. This he knows with a knowledge, before the things were. "[7] All His creatures, corporeal or spiritual, He doth not therefore know, because they are; but they therefore are, because He knoweth them. For He was not ignorant, what He was about to create; nor did He know them, after He had created them, in any other way than before. For no accession to His knowledge came from them; but, they existing when and as was meet, that knowledge remained as it was." How strange then to think of hiding from God a secret sin, when He knew, before He created thee, that He created thee liable to this very temptation, and to be assisted amidst it with just that grace which thou art resisting! God had known Israel, but it was not with the knowledge of love, of which He says, *The Lord knoweth the way of the righteous* [8], and [9], *if any man love God, the same is known of Him,* but with the knowledge of condemnation, whereby He, the Searcher of hearts, knows the sin which He judges.

4. *They will not frame their doings, &c.* They were possessed by an evil spirit, impelling and driving them to sin; *the spirit of whoredoms is in the midst of them,* i. e. in their very inward self, their centre, so to speak; in their souls, where reside the will, the reason, the judgment; and so long as they did not, by the strength of God, dislodge him, they

[1] xxxi. 6. [2] iv. 2. [3] vi. 9. [4] Ps. cix. 4. [5] Heb. iv. 13. [6] Acts xv. 18. [7] S. Aug. [8] Ps. i. 6. [9] 1 Cor. viii. 3.

Before CHRIST cir. 780.

of whoredoms *is* in the midst of them, and they have not known the LORD.

f ch. 7. 10.

5 And f the pride of Israel doth testify to his face: therefore shall Israel and Ephraim fall in their iniquity; Judah also shall fall with them.

Before CHRIST cir. 780.

would and could not frame their acts, so as to repent and turn to God. For a mightier impulse mastered them and drove them into sin, as the evil spirit drove the swine into the deep.

The rendering of the margin, although less agreeable to the Hebrew, also gives a striking sense. *Their doings will not suffer them to turn unto their God.* Not so much that their habits of sin had got an absolute mastery over them, so as to render repentance impossible; but rather, that it was impossible that they should turn inwardly, while they did not turn outwardly. Their evil doings, so long as they persevered in doing them, took away all heart, whereby to turn to God with a solid conversion.

And yet He was *their God;* this made their sin the more grievous. He, Whom they would not turn to, still owned them, was still ready to receive them as *their God.* For the Prophet continues, *and they have not known the Lord.* Him, *their God,* they knew not. For the spirit which possessed them hindered them from thought, from memory, from conception of spiritual things. They did not turn to God, 1) because the evil spirit held them, and so long as they allowed his hold, they were filled with carnal thoughts which kept them back from God. 2) They did not know God; so that, not knowing how good and how great a good He is in Himself, and how good to us, they had not even the desire to turn to Him, for love of Himself, yea even for love of themselves. They saw not, that they lost a loving God.

5. *And the pride of Israel.* Pride was from the first the leading sin of Ephraim. Together with Manasseh, (with whom they made, in some respects, one whole, as *the children of Joseph*[1],) they were nearly equal in number to Judah. When numbered in the wilderness, Judah had 74,600 fighting men, Ephraim and Manasseh together 72,700. They speak of themselves as *a great people, forasmuch as the Lord has blessed me hitherto*[2]. God having chosen, out of them, the leader under whom He brought Israel into the land of promise, they resented, in the following time of the Judges, any deliverance of the land, in which they were not called to take a part. They chode with Gideon[3], and suffered very severely for insolence[4] to Jephthah and the Gileadites. When Gideon, who had refused to be king, was dead, Abimelech, his son by a concubine out of Ephraim, induced the Ephraimites to make Him king over Israel, as being *their bone and their flesh*[5]. Lying in the midst of the tribes to the North of Judah, they appear, in antagonism to Judah, to have gathered round them the other tribes, and to have taken, with them, the name of Israel, in contrast with Judah[6]. Shiloh, where the ark was, until taken by the Philistines, belonged to them. Samuel, the last judge, was raised up out of them[7]. Their political dignity was not aggrieved, when God gave Saul, out of *little Benjamin,* as king over His people. They could afford to own a king out of the least tribe. Their present political eminence was endangered, when God chose David out of their great rival, the tribe of Judah; their hope for the future was cut off by His promise to the posterity of David. They accordingly upheld, for seven years[8], the house of Saul, knowing that they were acting against the Will of God[9]. Their religious importance was aggrieved by the removal of the ark to Zion, instead of its being restored to Shiloh[10]. Absalom won them by flattery[11]; and the rebellion against David was a struggle of Israel[12] against Judah. When Absalom was dead, they had scarcely aided in bringing David back, when they fell away again, because their advice had not been first had in bringing him back[13]. Rehoboam was already king over Judah[14], when he came to Shechem to be made king over Israel[15]. Then the ten tribes sent for Jeroboam of Ephraim[16], to make him their spokesman, and, in the end, their king. The rival worship of Bethel provided, not only for the indolence, but for the pride of his tribe. He made a state-worship at Bethel, over-against the worship ordained by God at Jerusalem. Just before the time of Hosea, the political strength of Ephraim was so much superior to that of Judah, that Jehoash, in his pride, compared himself to the cedar of Lebanon, Amaziah king of Judah to the thistle[17]. Isaiah speaks of "jealousy[18]" or "envy," as the characteristic sin of Israel, which perpetuated that

1 Josh. xvi 4. xvii. 14. 2 Josh. xvii. 14.
3 Jud. viii. 1 sqq. 4 Ib. xii. 1 sqq.
5 Ib. viii. 31. ix. 1–3, 22.
6 2 Sam. ii. 9, 10. iii. 17. 7 1 Sam. i. 1.
8 2 Sam. v. 5. 9 Ib. iii. 9. 10 Ps. lxxviii. 60, 67–69.
11 2 Sam. xv. 2, 5, 10, 12, 13.
12 xvi. 15. xvii. 15. xviii. 6.
13 Ib. xix. 41–3. xx. 1, 2. 14 1 Kgs xi. 43.
15 1 Kgs xii. 1. 16 1 Kgs xi. 26.
17 2 Kgs xiv. 9. 18 xi. 13.

Before CHRIST cir. 780.

6 [g]They shall go with their flocks and with their herds to seek the LORD; but they shall not find *him;* he hath withdrawn himself from them.

[g] Prov. 1. 28. Isai. 1. 15. Jer. 11. 11. Ezek. 8. 18. Mic. 3. 4. John 7. 34.

Before CHRIST cir. 780.

division, which, he foretold, should be healed in Christ. Yet although such was the power and pride of Israel, God foretold that he should first go into captivity, and so it was.

This pride, as it was the origin of the schism of the ten tribes, so it was the means of its continuance. In whatever degree any one of the kings of Israel was better than the rest, still *he departed not from the sins of Jeroboam, who made Israel to sin.* The giving up of any other sin only shewed, how deeply rooted this sin was, which even then they would not give up. As is the way of unregenerate man, they would not give themselves up without reserve to God, to do *all* His will. They could not give up *this* sin of Jeroboam, without endangering their separate existence as *Israel,* and owning the superiority of Judah. From this complete self-surrender to God, their pride shrank and held them back.

The pride, which Israel thus shewed in refusing to turn to God, and in preferring their sin to *their God,* itself, he says, witnessed against them, and condemned them. In the presence of God, there needeth no other witness against the sinner than his own conscience. It *shall witness to his face,* "openly, publicly, themselves and all others seeing, acknowledging, and approving the just judgment of God and the recompense of their sin." Pride and carnal sin are here remarkably united.

"[1]The Prophet having said, *the spirit of fornication is in the midst of them,* assigns as its ground, *the pride of Israel will testify to his face,* i. e. the sin which, through pride of mind, lurked in secret, bore open witness through sin of the flesh. Wherefore the cleanness of chastity is to be preserved by guarding humility. For if the spirit is piously humbled before God, the flesh is not raised unlawfully above the spirit. For the spirit holds the dominion over the flesh, committed to it, if it acknowledges the claims of lawful servitude to the Lord. For if, through pride, it despises its Author, it justly incurs a contest with its subject, the flesh."

Therefore shall Israel and Ephraim fall in [or *by*] *their iniquity.* Ephraim, the chief of the ten tribes, is distinguished from the whole, of which it was a part, because it was the rival of Judah, the royal tribe, out of which Jeroboam had sprung, who had formed the kingdom of Israel by the schism from Judah. All Israel, even its royal tribe, where was Samaria, its capital and strength, should fall, their iniquity being the stumbling-block, on which they should fall.

Judah also shall fall with them. "Judah also, being partaker with them in their idolatry and their wickedness, shall partake with them in the like punishment. Sin shall have the like effect in both." Literally, he saith, *Judah hath fallen,* denoting, as do other prophets, the certainty of the future event, by speaking of it, as having taken place already; as it had, in the Mind of God.

6. *They shall go with their flocks.* "They had let slip the day of grace, wherein God had called them to repentance, and promised to be found of them and to accept them. When then the decree was gone forth and judgment determined against them, all their outward shew of worship and late repentance shall not prevail to gain admittance for them to Him. He will not be found of them, hear them, nor accept them. They stopped their ears obstinately against Him calling on them, and proffering mercy in the day of mercy: He will now stop His ear against them, crying for it in the Day of judgment." Repenting thus late, (as is the case with most who repent, or think that they repent, at the close of life) they did not repent out of the love of God, but out of slavish fear, on account of the calamity which was coming upon them. But the main truth, contained in this and other passages of Holy Scripture which speak of a time when it is too late to turn to God, is this: that "[2]it shall be too late to knock when the door shall be shut, and too late to cry for mercy when it is the time of justice." God waits long for sinners; He threatens long before He strikes; He strikes and pierces in lesser degrees, and with increasing severity, before the final blow comes. In this life, He places man in a new state of trial, even after His first judgments have fallen on the sinner. But the general rule of His dealings is this; that, when the time of each judgment is actually come, then, as to *that* judgment, it is too late to pray. It is *not* too late for other mercy, or for final forgiveness, so long as man's state of probation lasts; but it is too late as to this one. And thus, each judgment in time is a picture of the Eternal Judgment, when the day of mercy is past for ever, to those who have finally, in this life, hardened themselves against it. But temporal mercies correspond with temporal judgments; eternal mercy with

[1] S. Greg.

[2] Commination Service.

Before CHRIST cir. 780.

7 They have [h] dealt treacherously against the LORD: for they have begotten strange children:
now shall [i] a month devour them with their portions.

8 [k] Blow ye the cornet in Gibeah, *and* the trumpet

[h] Isai. 48. 8. Jer. 3. 20. & 5. 11. ch. 6. 7. Mal. 2. 11.

[i] Zech. 11. 8.

[k] ch. 8. 1. Joel 2. 1.

eternal judgment. In time, it may be too late to turn away temporal judgments; it is not too late, while God continues grace, to flee from eternal; and the desire not to lose God, is a proof to the soul that it is not forsaken by God, by Whom alone the longing for Himself is kept alive or re-awakened in His creature.

They shall not find Him. This befell the Jews in the time of Josiah. Josiah himself[1] *turned to the Lord with all his heart and with all his soul and with all his might, according to all the law of Moses.* He put away idolatry thoroughly; and the people so far followed his example. He held such a Passover, as had not been held since the time of the judges. *Notwithstanding the Lord turned not from the fierceness of His great wrath, wherewith His anger was kindled against Judah because of all the provocations that Manasseh had provoked Him withal. And the Lord said, I will remove Judah out of My sight, as I have removed Israel, and will cast off this city Jerusalem, which I have chosen, and the house of which I said, My name shall be there.*

The Prophet describes the people, as complying with God's commands; *they shall go,* i. e. to the place which God had chosen and commanded, *with their flocks and their herds,* i. e. with the most costly sacrifices, *the flocks* supplying the sheep and goats prescribed by the law; the *herds* supplying the bullocks, calves and heifers offered. They seem to have come, so far, sincerely. Yet perhaps it is not without further meaning, that the Prophet speaks of those outward sacrifices only, not of the heart; and the reformation under Josiah may therefore have failed, because the people were too ingrained with sin under Manasseh, and returned outwardly only under Josiah, as they fell back again after his death. And so God speaketh here, as He does by David[2], *I will take no bullock out of thine house, nor he-goat out of thy fold. Thinkest thou, that I will eat bulls' flesh, or drink the blood of goats?* and by Isaiah[3], *To what purpose is the multitude of your sacrifices unto Me? I am full of the burnt offerings of rams, and the fat of fed beasts.*

He hath withdrawn Himself from them. Perhaps he would say, that God, as it were, *freed Himself* from them, as He saith in Isaiah[4], *I am weary to bear them,* the union of sacrifices and of sin.

7. *They have dealt treacherously;* lit. *have cloaked,* and so, acted deceitfully. The word is used of treachery of friend towards his friend, of the husband to his wife, or the wife to her husband[5]. *Surely as a wife treacherously departeth from her husband, so have ye dealt treacherously with Me, O house of Israel, saith the Lord.* God, even in His upbraiding, speaks very tenderly to them, as having been in the closest, dearest relation to Himself.

For they have begotten strange children. God had made it a ground of the future blessing of Abraham[6], *I know him, that he will command his children and his household after him, and they shall keep the way of the Lord, to do justice and judgment.* But these, contrariwise, themselves being idolaters and estranged from God, had children, who fell away like themselves, strangers to God, and looked upon as strangers by Him. The children too of the forbidden marriages with the heathen were, by their birth, *strange* or foreign children, even before they became so in act; and they became so the more in act, because they were so by birth. The next generation then growing up more estranged from God than themselves, what hope of amendment was there?

Now shall a month devour. The word *now* denotes the nearness and suddenness of God's judgments; the term *month,* their rapidity. A *month* is not only a brief time, but is almost visibly passing away; the moon, which measures it, is never at one stay, waxing till it is full, then waning till it disappears. Night by night bears witness to the month's decay. The iniquity was full; the harvest was ripe; *now,* suddenly, rapidly, completely, the end should come. One month should *devour them with their portions.* God willed to be the Portion of His people; He had said[7], *the Lord's portion is His people; Jacob is the lot of His inheritance.* To Himself He had given the title[8], *the portion of Jacob.* Israel had chosen to himself *other portions* out of God; for these, he had forsaken his God; therefore he should be consumed with them. "All that they had, all that they possessed, enjoyed, trusted in, all, at once, shall that short space, suddenly and certainly to come, devour, deprive and bereave them of; none of them shall remain with them or profit them in the Day of wrath."

8. *Blow ye the cornet in Gibeah.* The evil

1 2 Kgs xxiii. 25–27.
2 Ps. l. 9, 13.
3 i. 11.
4 i. 14.
5 Jer. iii. 20.
6 Gen. xviii. 19.
7 Deut. xxxii. 9.
8 Jer. x. 16.

Before CHRIST cir. 780.

in Rama: [l] cry aloud *at*
[m] Bethaven, [n] after thee, O
Benjamin.
9 Ephraim shall be des-
olate in the day of rebuke:
among the tribes of Israel
have I made known that
which shall surely be.
10 The princes of Judah
were like them that [o] remove the bound: *therefore*
I will pour out my wrath
upon them like water.
11 Ephraim *is* [p] op-
pressed *and* broken in
judgment, because he willingly walked after [q] the
commandment.

l Isai. 10. 30.
m Josh. 7. 2. ch. 4. 15.
n Judg. 5. 14.
o Deut. 19. 14. & 27. 17.
p Deut. 28. 33.
q 1 Kgs. 12. 28. Mic. 2. 16.

day and destruction, denounced, is now vividly pictured, as actually come. All is in confusion, hurry, alarm, because the enemy was in the midst of them. The *cornet*, an instrument made of horn, was to be blown as the alarm, when the enemy was at hand. The *trumpet* was especially used for the worship of God. *Gibeah* and *Ramah* were cities of Benjamin, on the borders of Ephraim, where the enemy, who had possessed himself of Israel, would burst in upon Judah. From *Beth-aven* or Bethel, the seat of Ephraim's idolatry, on the border of Benjamin, was to break forth the outcry of destruction, *after thee, O Benjamin;* the enemy is upon thee, just behind thee, pursuing thee. God had promised His people, if they would serve Him [1], *I will make all thine enemies turn their backs unto thee*, and had threatened the contrary, if they should *walk contrary to Him.* Now that threat was to be fulfilled to the uttermost. The ten tribes are spoken of, as already in possession of the enemy, and he was *upon Benjamin* fleeing before them.

9. *Ephraim shall be desolate.* It shall not be lightly rebuked, nor even more grievously chastened; it shall not simply be wasted by famine, pestilence, and the sword; it *shall be* not simply desolate, but *a desolation*, one waste, *in the day of rebuke*, when God brings home to it its sin and punishment. Ephraim was not taken away for a time; it was never restored.

I have made known that which shall surely be. "[2] Doubt not that this which I say shall come upon thee, for it is a sure saying which I have made known;" lit. one *well-grounded*, as it was, in the mind, the justice, the holiness, the truth of God. All God's threatenings or promises are grounded in past experience. So it may also be, as though God said, "Whatever I have hitherto promised or threatened to Israel, has come to pass. In all I have proved Myself true. Let no one then flatter himself, as though this were uncertain; for in this, as in the rest, I shall be found to be God, faithful and true."

10. *The princes of Judah were like them that remove the bound.* All avaricious encroachment on the paternal inheritance of others, was strictly forbidden by God in the law, under the penalty of His curse. [3] *Cursed is he that removeth his neighbor's landmark. The princes of Judah*, i.e. those who were the king's counsellors and chief in the civil polity, had committed sin, *like* to this. Since the prophet had just pronounced the desolation of Israel, perhaps that sin was, that instead of taking warning from the threatened destruction, and turning to God, they thought only how the removal of Ephraim would benefit them, by the enlargement of their borders. They might hope also to increase their private estates out of the desolate lands of Ephraim, their brother. The unregenerate heart, instead of being awed by God's judgment on others, looks out to see, what advantages it may gain from them. Times of calamity are also times of greediness. Israel had been a continual sore to Judah. The princes of Judah rejoiced in the prospect of their removal, instead of mourning their sin and fearing for themselves. More widely yet, the words may mean, that the *princes of Judah* "burst all bounds, set to them by the law of God, to which nothing was to be added, from which nothing was to be diminished," transferring to idols or devils, to sun, moon and stars, or to the beings supposed to preside over them, the love, honor, and worship, due to God Alone.

I will pour out My wrath like water. So long as those bounds were not broken through, the Justice of God, although manifoldly provoked, was yet stayed. When Judah should break them, they would, as it were, make a way for the chastisement of God, which should burst in like a flood upon them, overspreading the whole land, yet bringing, not renewed life, but death. Like a flood, it overwhelmed the land; but it was a flood, not of water, but of the wrath of God. They had burst the bounds which divided them from Israel, and had let in upon themselves its chastisements.

11. *Ephraim is oppressed and broken in judg-*

[1] Ex. xxiii. 27.
[2] Rup.
[3] Deut. xxvii. 17.

Before CHRIST cir. 780.

12 Therefore *will* I *be*
unto Ephraim as a moth,
and to the house of Judah
[r] as || rottenness.

13 When Ephraim saw
his sickness, and Judah *saw*
his [s] wound, then went
Ephraim [t] to the Assyrian,
[u] and sent || to king Jareb:
yet could he not heal
you, nor cure you of your
wound.

[r] Prov. 12. 4.
|| Or, *a worm.*

[s] Jer. 30. 12.
[t] 2 Kings 15. 19. ch. 7. 11. & 12. 1.
[u] ch. 10. 6.
|| Or, *to the king of Jareb;* or, *to the king that should plead.*

ment, lit. *crushed in judgment.* Holy Scripture, elsewhere also, combines these same two words, rendered *oppressed* and *crushed*[1], in speaking of man's oppression by man. Ephraim preferred man's commands and laws to God's; they obeyed man and set God at nought; therefore they should suffer at man's hands, who, while he equally neglected God's will, enforced his own. The *commandment,* which *Ephraim willingly went after,* was doubtless that of Jeroboam[2]; *It is too much for you to go up to Jerusalem; behold thy gods, O Israel, which brought you out of the land of Egypt; and Jeroboam ordained a feast unto the children of Israel.* Through this *commandment,* Jeroboam earned the dreadful title, *who made Israel to sin.* And Israel *went willingly after it,* for it is said; *This thing became a sin; and the people went to worship before the one, even unto Dan:* i. e. while they readily accepted Jeroboam's plea. *It is too much for you to go up to Jerusalem,* they *went willingly* to the Northernmost point of Palestine, *even to Dan.* For this sin, God judged them justly, even through the unjust judgment of man. God mostly punishes, through their own choice, those who choose against His. The Jews said, *we have no king but Cæsar,* and Cæsar destroyed them.

12. *Therefore I will be unto Ephraim a moth,* lit. *and I as a moth.* This form of speaking expresses what God was doing, while Ephraim was *willingly following* sin. *And I* was all the while *as a moth.* The moth in a garment, and the decay in wood, corrode and prey upon the substance, in which they lie hid, slowly, imperceptibly, but, at the last, effectually. Such were God's first judgments on Israel and Judah; such are they now commonly upon sinners. He tried, and now too tries at first, gentle measures and mild chastisements, uneasy indeed and troublesome and painful, yet slow in their working; each stage of loss and decay, a little beyond that which preceded it; but leaving long respite and time for repentance, before they finally wear out and destroy the impenitent. The two images, which He uses, may describe different kinds of decay, both slow, yet the one slower than the other, as Judah was, in fact, destroyed more slowly than Ephraim. For the *rottenness,* or caries in wood, preys more slowly upon wood, which is hard, than the moth on the wool. So God visits the soul with different distresses, bodily or spiritual. He impairs, little by little, health of body, or fineness of understanding; or He withdraws grace or spiritual strength; or allows lukewarmness and distaste for the things of God to creep over the soul. These are the gnawing of the moth, overlooked by the sinner, if he persevere in carelessness as to his conscience, yet in the end, bringing entire decay of health, of understanding, of heart, of mind, unless God interfere by the mightier mercy of some heavy chastisement, to awaken him. "[3]A moth does mischief, and makes no sound. So the minds of the wicked, in that they neglect to take account of their losses, lose their soundness, as it were, without knowing it. For they lose innocency from the heart, truth from the lips, continency from the flesh, and, as time holds on, life from their age." To Israel and Judah the moth and rottenness denoted the slow decay, by which they were gradually weakened, until they were carried away captive.

13. *When Ephraim saw his sickness,* lit. *And Ephraim saw,* i. e. perceived it. God proceeds to tell them, how they acted when they felt those lighter afflictions, the decline and wasting of their power. The *sickness* may further mean the gradual inward decay; the *wound,* blows received from without.

And sent to king Jareb, or, as in the E. M. *a king who should plead,* or, *an avenging king.* The *hostile king* is, probably, the same Assyrian Monarch, whom both Israel and Judah courted, who was the destruction of Israel and who weakened Judah. Ahaz king of Judah did send to Tiglath-Pileser king of Assyria to come and save him[4], when *the Lord brought Judah low; and Tiglath-Pileser king of Assyria came unto him and distressed him, but strengthened him not.* He who held his throne from God sent to a heathen king[5], *I am thy servant and thy son; come up and save me out of the hand of the king of Syria, and out of the hand of the king of Israel, which rise up against me.* He emptied his own treasures,

[1] Deut. xxviii. 33. 1 Sam. xii. 3, 4. Is. lviii. 6 Am. iv. 1. עשק and its derivatives are scarcely used of anything else.

[2] 1 Kgs xii. 28, 32, 33.
[3] S. Greg. on Job iv. 19.
[4] 2 Chr. xxviii. 19, 20.
[5] 2 Kings xvi. 7, 8.

Before CHRIST cir. 780.

14 For [x] I *will be* unto Ephraim as a lion, and as a young lion to the house of Judah: [y] I, *even* I, will tear and go away; I will take away, and none shall rescue *him*.

[x] Lam. 3. 10. ch. 13. 7, 8.
[y] Ps. 50. 22.

15 ¶ I will go *and* return to my place, † till [z] they acknowledge their offence, and seek my face: [a] in their affliction they will seek me early.

† Heb. *till they be guilty.*
[z] Lev. 26. 40, 41. Jer. 29, 12, 13. Ezek. 6. 9. & 20. 43. & 36. 31.
[a] Ps. 78. 34.

and pillaged the house of God, in order to buy the help of the Assyrian, and he taught him an evil lesson against himself, of his wealth and his weakness. God had said that, if they were faithful[1], *five shall chase an hundred, and an hundred put ten thousand to flight.* He had pronounced him *cursed, who trusted in man, and made flesh his arm, and whose heart departed from the Lord*[2]. But Judah sought man's help, not only apart from God, but against God. God was bringing them down, and they, by man's aid, would lift themselves up. *The king* became an *avenger*, for "[3] whoso, when God is angry, striveth to gain man as his helper, findeth him God's avenger, who leadeth into captivity God's deserters, as though he were sworn to avenge God."

14. *For I* will be *unto Ephraim as a lion.* He who would thus strengthen himself by outward help against God's chastisements, challenges, as it were, the Almighty to a trial of strength. So then God, unwilling to abandon him to himself, changes His dealings, and "[4] He Who had heretofore, in His judgments, seemed but as a tender moth or a weak worm," now shews forth His resistless power, imaged by His creatures in whom the quality of power is most seen. It may again be, that the fiercer animal (lit. *the roaring*) is associated with the name of Ephraim; that of the younger lion, fierce and eager for prey, yet not full-grown, with that of Judah.

I, I will tear. It is a fearful thing, to fall into the Hands of the Living God[5]. *The Assyrian was* but *the rod of God's anger, and the staff*, He says, *in thine hand is His indignation*[6]. Whatever is done, is done or overruled by God, Who gives to the evil his power to do, in an evil way, what He Himself overrules to the end of His wisdom or justice. God, Himself would tear them asunder, by giving the Assyrians power to carry them away. And since it was God Who did it, there was no hope of escape. He Who was faithful to his word would do it. There is great emphasis on the *I, I.* God and not man; He, the author of all good, would Himself be the Cause of their evil. What hope then is there, when He, Who is Mercy, becomes the Avenger?

15. *I will go* and *return to My place.* As the wild beast, when he has taken his prey, returns to his covert, so God, when He had fulfilled His Will, would, for the time, withdraw all tokens of his Presence. God, Who is wholly everywhere, is said to dwell *there*, relatively to us, where He manifests Himself, as of old, in the Tabernacle, the Temple, Zion, Jerusalem. He is said to *go and return*, when He withdraws all tokens of His Presence, His help, care, and Providence. This is worse than any affliction on God's part, "[4] a state like theirs who, in the lowest part of hell, are *delivered into chains of darkness*, shut out from His Presence, and so from all hope of comfort; and this must needs be their condition, so long as He shall be absent from them; and so perpetually, except there be a way for obtaining again His favorable Presence."

Till they acknowledge their offence. "[4] He Who *hath no pleasure in the death of the wicked, but that the wicked turn from his way and live*, withdraws Himself from them, not to cast them off altogether, but that they might know and acknowledge their folly and wickedness, and, seeing there is no comfort out of Him, prefer His Presence to those vain things." which they had preferred to Him. To say, that God would hide His Face from them, *till they should acknowledge their offence*, holds out in itself a gleam of hope, that hereafter they would turn to Him, and would find Him.

And seek My Face. The first step in repentance is confession of sin; the second, turning to God. For to own sin without turning to God is the despair of Judas.

In their affliction they shall seek Me early. God does not only leave them hopes, that He would shew forth his Presence, when they sought him, but He promises that they shall seek Him, i. e. He would give them His grace whereby alone they could seek Him, and that grace should be effectual. Of itself affliction drives to despair and more obdurate rebellion and final impenitence. Through the grace of God, "evil brings forth good; fear, love; chastisement, repentance." *They shall seek Me early*, originally, *in the morning*, i. e. with all diligence and earnestness, as a

[1] Lev. xxvi. 8. [2] Jer. xvii. 5. [3] Rup. [4] Poc. [5] Heb. x. 31. [6] Is. x. 5.

Before CHRIST cir. 780.

CHAPTER VI.

1 *An exhortation to repentance.* 4 *A complaint of their untowardness and iniquity.*

[a] Deut. 32. 39. 1 Sam. 2. 6. Job 5. 18. ch. 5. 14.
[b] Jer. 30. 17.

COME, and let us return unto the LORD: for [a]he hath torn, and [b]he will heal us; he hath smitten, and he will bind us up.

2 [c]After two days will he revive us: in the third day he will raise us up, and we shall live in his sight.

[c] 1 Cor. 15. 4.

---

man riseth early to do what he is very much set upon. So these shall "shake off the sleep of sin and the torpor of listlessness, when the light of repentance shall shine upon them."

This was fulfilled in the two tribes, toward the end of the seventy years, when many doubtless, together with Daniel[1], *set* their *face unto the Lord God to seek by prayer and supplication with fasting and sackcloth and ashes;* and again in, those [2]*who waited for redemption in Jerusalem,* when our Lord came; and it will be fulfillment in all at the end of the world. "The first flash of thought on the power and goodness of the true Deliverer, is like the morning streaks of a new day. At the sight of that light, Israel shall arise early to seek his God; he shall rise quickly like the Prodigal, out of his wanderings and his indigence."

VI. 1. *Come and let us return unto the Lord.* These words depend closely on the foregoing. They are words put into their mouth by God Himself, with which or with the like, they should exhort one another to return to God. Before, when God smote them, they had gone to Assyria; now they should turn to Him, owning, not only that He Who *tore* has the power and the will to *heal* them, but that He tore, *in order to* heal them; He smote them, *in order to* bind them up. This closeness of connection is expressed in the last words; lit. *smite He and He will bind us up.* "He smiteth the putrefaction of the misdeed; He healeth the pain of the wound. Physicians do this; they cut; they smite; they heal; they arm themselves in order to strike; they carry steel, and come to cure."

They are not content to return singly or to be saved alone. Each encourageth another to repentance, as before to evil. The dry bones, scattered on the face of the earth, reunite. There is a general movement among those *who sat in darkness and the shadow of death,* to return together to Him, Who is the Source of life.

2. *After two days will He revive us* or *quicken us, give us life, in the third day He will raise us up.* The Resurrection of Christ, and our resurrection in Him and in His Resurrection, could not be more plainly foretold. The Prophet expressly mentions *two days,* after which life should be given, and a *third day, on* which the resurrection should take place. What else can this be than the two days in which the Body of Christ lay in the tomb, and the third day, on which He rose again, as [3]*the Resurrection and the life,* [4]*the first fruits of them that slept,* the source and earnest and pledge of our resurrection and of life eternal? The Apostle, in speaking of our resurrection in Christ, uses these self-same words of the Prophet; [5]*God, Who is rich in mercy, for His great love wherewith He loved us—hath quickened us together with Christ, and hath raised us up and made us to sit together in heavenly places in Christ Jesus.* The Apostle, like the Prophet, speaks of that which took place in Christ our Head, as having already taken place in us, His members. "If we unhesitatingly believe in our heart," says a father[6], "what we profess with our mouth, *we* were crucified in Christ, *we* died, *we* were buried, *we* also were raised again on that very third day. Whence the Apostle saith[7], *If ye rose again with Christ, seek those things which are above, where Christ sitteth at the right hand of God.*" As Christ died for us, so He also rose for us. "Our old man was nailed to the wood, in the flesh of our Head, and the new man was formed in that same Head, rising glorious from the tomb." What Christ, our Head, did, He did, not for Himself, but for His redeemed, that the benefits of His Life, Death, Resurrection, Ascension, might redound to all. He did it for them; they partook of what He did. In no other way, could our participation of Christ be foretold. It was not the Prophet's object here, nor was it so direct a comfort to Israel, to speak of Christ's Resurrection in itself. He took a nearer way to their hearts. He told them, "all we who turn to the Lord, putting our whole trust in Him, and committing ourselves wholly to Him, to be healed of our wounds and to have our griefs bound up, shall receive life from Him, shall be raised up by Him." They could not understand *then,* how He would do this. The *after two days* and, *in the third day,* remained a mystery, to be explained by the event. But the promise itself was not the less distinct, nor the less full of hope, nor did it less fulfill all cravings for

[1] Dan. ix. 2, 3.
[2] S. Luke ii. 25, 38.
[3] S. John xi. 25.
[4] 1 Cor. xv. 20.
[5] Eph. ii. 4–6.
[6] S. Leo.
[7] Col. iii. 1.

Before CHRIST cir. 780.

3 [d]Then shall we know,
if we follow on to know the
LORD: his going forth is
prepared [e]as the morning;
and [f]he shall come unto us
[g]as the rain, as the latter
and former rain unto the
earth.

d Is. 54. 13.
e 2 Sam. 23. 4.
f Ps. 72. 6.
g Job 29. 23.

life eternal and the sight of God, because they did not understand, *how shall these things be.* Faith is unconcerned about the "*how.*" Faith believes what God says, because He says it, and leaves Him to fulfill it, "how" He wills and knows. The words of the promise which faith had to believe, were plain. The life of which the Prophet spoke, could only be life from death, whether of the body or the soul or both. For God is said to *give life*, only in contrast with such death. Whence the Jews too have ever looked and do look, that this should be fulfilled in the Christ, though they know not that it has been fulfilled in Him. They too explain it; "[1]He will quicken us in the days of consolation which shall come; in the day of the quickening of the dead; He will raise us up, and we shall live before Him."

In shadow, the prophecy was never fulfilled to Israel at all. The ten tribes were never restored; they never, as a whole, received any favor from God, after He gave them up to captivity. And unto the two tribes, (of whom, apart from the ten, no mention is made here) what a mere shadow was the restoration from Babylon, that it should be spoken of as the gift of life or of resurrection, whereby we should live before Him! The strictest explanation is the truest. The *two days* and *the third day* have nothing in history to correspond with them, except that in which they were fulfilled, when Christ, "rising on the third day from the grave, raised with Him the whole human race[2]."

And we shall live in His sight, lit. *before His Face.* In the face, we see the will, and mind, the love, the pleasure or displeasure of a human being whom we love. In the holy or loving face of man, there may be read fresh depths of devotion or of love. The face is turned away in sorrowful displeasure; it is turned full upon the face it loves. Hence it is so very expressive an image of the relation of the soul to God, and the Psalmists so often pray, *Lord lift up the light of Thy countenance upon us; make Thy Face to shine upon Thy servant; God bless us, and cause His Face to shine upon us; cast me not away from Thy Presence* or *Face; look Thou upon me and be merciful unto me; look upon the Face of thine anointed; how long wilt Thou hide Thy Face from me? hide not Thy Face from Thy servant*[3]; or they profess, *Thy Face, Lord, will I seek*[4]; or they declare that the bliss of eternity is in *the Face of God*[5].

God had just said, that He would withdraw His Presence, until they should *seek His Face;* now He says, they should *live before His Face.* To Abraham He had said[6], *Walk before Me*, lit. *before My Face, and be thou perfect.* Bliss from the Creator, and duty from the creature, answer to one another. We *live in His sight*, in the way of duty, when we refer ourselves and our whole being, our courses of action, our thoughts, our love, to Him, remembering that we are ever in His Presence, and ever seeking to please Him. *We live in His sight*, in the bliss of His Presence, when we enjoy the sense of His favor, and know that His Eye rests on us in love, that He cares for us, guides us, guards us; and have some sweetness in contemplating Him. Much more fully shall we live in His sight, when, in Him, we shall be partakers of His Eternal Life and Bliss, and shall behold Him *face to face*, and *see Him as He is*, and the sight of Him shall be our bliss, *and in His light we shall see light*[7].

3. *Then shall we know*, if *we follow on to know the Lord;* rather, *Then shall we know, shall follow on to know the Lord*, i. e. we shall not only know Him, but we shall grow continually in that knowledge. Then, in Israel, God says, *there was no knowledge* of Him; His *people* was *destroyed for lack of* it[8]. In Christ He promises, that they should have that inward knowledge of Him, ever growing, because the grace, through which it is given, ever grows, and *the depth of the riches of His wisdom and knowledge is unsearchable, passing knowledge.* We *follow on*, confessing that it is He who maketh us to follow Him, and draweth us to Him. We know, in order to follow; we follow, in order to know. Light prepares the way for love. Love opens the mind for new love. The gifts of God are interwoven. They multiply and reproduce each other, until we come to the perfect state of eternity. For here *we know in part* only; then *shall we know, even as we are known. We shall follow on.* Whither shall we *follow on?* To the fountains of the water of life, as another Prophet saith; *For He that hath*

[1] Targ.
[2] S. Jer. so Tertull. adv. Jud. c. 13. Orig. Hom. 5. in Exod. S. Cypr. Test. ii. 25. S. Cyr. Jer. Cat. xiv. 14. S. Greg. Nyss. de cogn. Dei. S. Aug. de Civ. D. xviii. 28. Ruf. de exp. Symb. S. Cyr. Al. in S. Joh. L. ii. S. Greg. in Ezek. Hom. 20.
[3] Ps. iv. 6; xxxi. 16 (from Num. vi. 25.); lxvii. 1. lxxx. 7. cxix. 135; li. 11; cxix. 132; lxxxiv. 9; xiii. 1. lxix, 17. &c.
[4] Ps. xxvii. 8. See xxiv. 6. cv. 4.
[5] Ps. xi. 7. xvi. 11. xvii. 15.
[6] Gen. xvii. 1.
[7] Ps. xxxvi. 9.
[8] ch. iv. 1, 6.

Before CHRIST cir. 780.

[h] ch. 11. 8.

4 ¶ [h] O Ephraim, what shall I do unto thee? O Judah, what shall I do unto thee? for your ‖ goodness *is* [i] as a morning cloud, and as the early dew it goeth away.

‖ Or, *mercy*, or *kindness*.
[i] ch. 13. 3.

mercy upon them shall lead them, even by the springs of water shall He guide them [1]. And in the Revelations we read, that *the Lamb Who is in the midst of the throne shall feed them, and shall lead them unto living fountains of waters* [2]. The bliss of eternity is fixed; the nearness of each to the throne of God, the *mansion* in which he shall dwell, admits of no change; but, through eternity, it may be, that we shall *follow on to know* more of God, as more shall be revealed to us of that which is infinite, the Infinity of His Wisdom and His Love.

His going forth, i. e. the going forth of God, *is prepared*, firm, fixed, certain, established, (so the word means) *as the morning*. Before, God had said, He would withdraw Himself from them; now, contrariwise, He says, that He would *go forth*. He had said, *in their affliction they shall seek Me early* or *in the morning;* now, *He shall go forth as the morning*. "[3] They shall seek for Him, as they that long for the morning; and He will come to them as the morning," full of joy and comfort, of light and warmth and glorious radiance, which shall diffuse over the whole compass of the world, so that *nothing shall be hid from its light* and *heat*. He Who should so go forth, is the same as He Who was to *revive them* and *raise them up*, i. e. Christ. Of Him it is said most strictly, that He *went forth*, when from the Bosom of the Father He came among us; as of Him holy Zacharias saith, (in the like language,) *The Dayspring from on high hath visited us, to give light to them that sit in darkness and in the shadow of death, to guide our feet into the way of peace.* Christ goeth forth continually from the Father, by an eternal, continual, generation. In time, He *came forth* from the Father in His Incarnation; He *came forth* to us from the Virgin's womb; He *came forth*, from the grave in His Resurrection. His *coming forth, as the morning*, images the secrecy of His Birth, the light and glow of love which He diffuseth throughout the whole new creation of His redeemed. "[4] As the dawn is seen by all and cannot be hid, and appeareth, that it may be seen, yea, that it may illuminate, so His going forth, whereby He proceeded from His own invisible to our visible condition, became known to all," tempered to our eyes, dissipating our darkness, awakening our nature as from a grave, unveiling to man the works of God, making His ways plain before his face, that he should no longer *walk in darkness, but have the light of life.*

He shall come unto us as the rain, as the latter and *former rain unto the earth.* So of Christ it is foretold [5], *He shall come down like rain upon the mown grass, as showers that water the earth.* Palestine was especially dependent upon rain, on account of the cultivation of the sides of the hills in terraces, which were parched and dry, when the rains were withheld. The *former*, or autumnal *rain*, fell in October, at the seed-time; the *latter* or spring *rain*, in March and April, and filled the ears before harvest. Both together stand as the beginning and the end. If either were withheld, the harvest failed. Wonderful likeness of Him Who is the Beginning and the End of our spiritual life; from Whom we receive it, by Whom it is preserved unto the end; through Whom the soul, enriched by Him, hath abundance of all spiritual blessings, graces, and consolations, and yieldeth all manner of fruit, each after its kind, to the praise of Him Who hath given it life and fruitfulness.

4. *O Ephraim, what shall I do unto thee?* It is common with the prophets, first to set forth the fullness of the riches of God's mercies in Christ, and then to turn to their own generation, and upbraid them for the sins which withheld the mercies of God from *them*, and were hurrying them to their destruction. In like way Isaiah [6], having prophesied that the Gospel should go forth from Zion, turns to upbraid the avarice, idolatry, and pride, through which the judgment of God should come upon them.

The promises of God were to those who should turn with true repentance, and seek Him early and earnestly. Whatever of good there was, either in Ephraim or Judah, was but a mere empty shew, which held out hope, only to disappoint it. God, Who *willeth not that any should perish, but that all should come to repentance*, appeals to His whole people, *What shall I do unto thee?* He had shewn them adundance of mercies; He had reproved them by His prophets; He had chastened them; and all in vain. As he says in Isaiah [7], *What could have been done more to My vineyard, that I have not done in it?* Here He asks them Himself, what He could do to convert and to save them, which He had not done. He would take them on their own terms, and whatever they would prescribe to His Almightiness and Wisdom, as means for their conversion, *that* He would use, so that they would but turn to Him. "What means

[1] Is. xlix. 10. [2] Rev. vii. 17. [3] Poc. [4] Rup.

[5] Ps. lxxii. 6. [6] ch. ii. [7] ch. v.

Before CHRIST cir. 780.

5 Therefore have I hewed *them* [k] by the prophets; I have slain them by [l] the words of my mouth: || and thy judgments *are as* the light *that* goeth forth.

Before CHRIST cir. 780.

6 For I desired [m] mercy, and [n] not sacrifice; and

k Jer. 1. 10 & 5. 14.
l Jer. 23. 29. Heb. 4. 12.
|| Or, *that thy judgments might be, &c.*

m 1 Sam. 15. 22. Eccles. 5. 1. Mic. 6. 8. Matt. 9. 23. & 12. 7. n Ps. 50. 8, 9. Prov. 21. 3. Is. 1. 11.

shall I use to save thee, who wilt not be saved?" It has been a bold saying, to describe the *love of Christ which passeth knowledge*, "Christ so loveth souls, that He would rather be crucified again, than allow any one (as far as in Him lies) to be damned."

For your goodness is *as a morning cloud. Mercy* or *loving-kindness*, (which the E. M. suggests as the first meaning of the word) stands for all virtue and goodness toward God or man. For love to God or man is one indivisible virtue, issuing from one principle of grace. Whence it is said[1], *love is the fulfilling of the law. He that loveth another hath fulfilled the law.* And[2], *Beloved, let us love one another; for love is of God, and every one that loveth is born of God, and knoweth God.* Of this their goodness, he says the character was, that it never lasted. The *morning cloud* is full of brilliancy with the rays of the rising sun, yet quickly disappears through the heat of that sun, which gave it its rich hues. The *morning dew* glitters in that same sun, yet vanishes almost as soon as it appears. Generated by the cold of the night, it appears with the dawn; yet appears, only to disappear. So it was with the whole Jewish people; so it ever is with the most hopeless class of sinners; ever beginning anew, ever relapsing; ever making a shew of leaves, good feelings, good aspirations, but yielding no fruit. "There was nothing of sound, sincere, real, lasting goodness in them;" no reality, but all shew; quickly assumed, quickly disused.

5. *Therefore have I hewed* them *by the prophets*. Since they despised God's gentler warnings and measures, He used severer. *He hewed* them, He says, as men hew stones out of the quarry, and with hard blows and sharp instruments overcome the hardness of the stone which they have to work. Their piety and goodness were light and unsubstantial as a summer cloud; their stony hearts were harder than the material stone. The stone takes the shape which man would give it; God hews man in vain; he will not receive the image of God, for which and in which he was framed.

God, elsewhere also, likens the force and vehemence of His word to [3] *a hammer which breaketh the rocks in pieces;* [4] *a sword which pierceth even to the dividing asunder of soul and spirit.* He "[5] continually hammered, beat upon, disquieted them, and so vexed them (as they thought) even unto death, not allowing them to rest in their sins, not suffering them to enjoy themselves in them, but forcing them (as it were) to part with things which they loved as their lives, and would as soon part with their souls as with them."

And thy judgments are as *the light* that *goeth forth*. The *judgments* here are the acts of justice executed upon a man; the "judgment upon him," as we say. God had done all which could be done, to lay aside the severity of His own judgments. All had failed. Then His judgments, when they came, would be manifestly just; their justice clear as *the light which goeth forth* out of the darkness of night, or out of the thick clouds. God's past loving-kindness, His pains, (so to speak,) His solicitations, the drawings of His grace, the tender mercies of His austere chastisements, will, in the Day of judgment, stand out clear as the light, and leave the sinner confounded, without excuse. In this life, also, God's final *judgments are as a light which goeth forth*, enlightening, not the sinner who perishes, but others, heretofore in the darkness of ignorance, on whom they burst with a sudden blaze of light, and who reverence them, owning that *the judgments of the Lord are true and righteous altogether*[6].

And so, since they would not be reformed, what should have been for their wealth, was for their destruction. *I slew them by the words of My mouth.* God spake yet more terribly to them. He slew them in word, that He might not slay them in deed; He threatened them with death; since they repented not, it came. The stone, which will not take the form which should have been imparted to it, is destroyed by the strokes which should have moulded it. By a like image Jeremiah compared the Jews to ore which is consumed in the fire which should refine it, since there was no good in it. [7] They are *brass and iron; they* are *all corrupted; the bellows are burned, the lead is consumed of the fire; the founder melteth in vain; for the wicked are not plucked away. Reprobate silver shall* men *call them, because the Lord hath rejected them.*

6. *For I desired mercy and not sacrifice.* God had said before, that they should *seek* Him *with their flocks and herds, and not find*

1 Rom. xiii. 10, 8. 2 1 S. John iv. 7. 3 Jer. xxiii. 29. 4 Heb. iv. 12. 5 from Poc.

6 Ps. xix. 9.
7 Jer. vi. 28–30.

Before CHRIST cir. 780. the °knowledge of God more than burnt offerings. Before CHRIST cir. 780.

° Jer. 22. 16. John 17. 3.

Him. So here He anticipates their excuses with the same answer wherewith He met those of Saul, when he would compensate for disobedience by burnt offerings. The answer is, that all which they did to win His favor, or turn aside His wrath, was of no avail, while they wilfully withheld what He required of them. Their mercy and goodness were but a brief, passing, shew; in vain He had tried to awaken them by His Prophets; therefore judgment was coming upon them; for, to turn it aside, they had offered Him what He desired not, sacrifices without love, and had not offered Him, what He did desire, love of man out of love for God. God had Himself, after the fall, enjoined sacrifice, to foreshew and plead to Himself the meritorious Sacrifice of Christ. *He* had not contrasted *mercy* and *sacrifice,* Who enjoined them both. When then they were contrasted, it was through man's severing what God united. If we were to say, "Charity is better than Church-going," we should be understood to mean that it is better than such Church-going as is severed from charity. For, if they were united, they would not be contrasted. The soul is of more value than the body. But it is not contrasted, unless they come in competition with one another, and their interests (although they cannot in trust *be,*) *seem* to be separated. In itself, *Sacrifice* represented all the direct duties to God, all the duties of the first table. For Sacrifice owned Him as the One God, to Whom, as His creatures, we owe and offer all; as His guilty creatures, it owned that we owed to Him our lives also. *Mercy* represented all duties of the second table. In saying then, *I will have mercy and not sacrifice,* he says, in effect, the same as S. John[1], *If a man say, I love God, and hateth his brother, he is a liar; for he that loveth not his brother, whom he hath seen, how can he love God Whom he hath not seen?* As the love, which a man pretended to have for God, was not real love, if a man loved not his brother, so *sacrifice* was not an offering, to God at all, while man withheld from God that offering, which God most required of him, the oblation of man's own self. They were, rather, offerings to satisfy and bribe a man's own conscience. Yet the Jews were profuse in making these sacrifices, which cost them little, hoping thereby to secure to themselves impunity in the wrongful gains, oppressions, and unmercifulnesses which they would not part with. It is with this contrast, that God so often rejects the sacrifices of the Jews, [2] *To what purpose is the multitude of your oblations unto Me? Bring no more vain oblations unto Me; new moons and sabbaths, the calling of assemblies, I cannot away with; iniquity and the solemn meeting.* [3] *I spake not to your fathers, nor commanded them, in the day that I brought them out of the land of Egypt, concerning burnt-offerings or sacrifices; but this thing commanded I them, saying, Obey My voice, and I will be your God, and ye shall be My people.* And the Psalmist; [4] *I will not reprove thee for thy sacrifices or thy burnt-offerings, to have been continually before Me. Offer unto God thanksgiving, &c. But unto the wicked God saith, What hast thou to do, to declare My statutes, &c.*

But, further, the prophet adds, *and the knowledge of God more than burnt-offerings.* The two parts of the verse fill out one another, and the latter explains the former. *The knowledge of God* is, as before, no inactive head-knowledge, but that knowledge, of which S. John speaks, [5]*Hereby we do know that we know Him, if we keep His commandments.* It is a knowledge, such as they alone can have, who love God and do His Will. God says then, that He prefers the inward, loving, knowledge of Himself, and loving-kindness toward man, above the outward means of acceptableness with Himself, which He had appointed. He does not lower those His own appointments; but only when, emptied of the spirit of devotion, they were lifeless bodies, unensouled by His grace.

Yet the words of God go beyond the immediate occasion and bearing, in which they were first spoken. And so these words, [6]*I will have mercy and not sacrifice,* are a sort of sacred proverb, contrasting *mercy,* which overflows the bounds of strict justice, with *sacrifice,* which represents that stern justice. Thus, when the Pharisees murmured at our Lord for eating with Publicans and sinners, He bade them, *Go and learn what that meaneth. I will have mercy and not sacrifice.* He bade them learn that deeper meaning of the words, that God valued mercy for the souls for which Christ died, above that outward propriety, that He, the All-Holy, should not feast familiarly with those who profaned God's law and themselves. Again, when they found fault with the hungry disciples for breaking the sabbath by rubbing the ears of corn, He, in the same way, tells them, that they did not know the real meaning of that saying. [7] *If ye had known what this meaneth, I will have mercy and not sacrifice, ye would not have condemned the guiltless.* For as, before, they were envious as to mercy to the souls of sinners,

[1] 1 S. John iv. 20.
[2] Is. i. 11–3.
[3] Jer. vii. 22, 3.
[4] Ps. l. 8. 14. 16.
[5] Eph. ii. 3.
[6] S. Matt. ix. 13.
[7] Ib. xii. 7.

Before CHRIST cir. 780.

7 But they ‖ like men
[p] have transgressed the
covenant: there [q] have they
dealt treacherously against
me.
8 [r] Gilead *is* a city of

‖ Or, *like Adam.* Job 31. 33.
p ch. 8. 1. q ch. 5. 7.
r ch. 12. 11.

so now they were reckless as to others' bodily needs. Without that love then, which shews itself in acts of mercy to the souls and bodies of men, all sacrifice is useless.

Mercy is also more comprehensive than *sacrifice*. For sacrifice was referred to God only, as its end; *mercy*, or love of man for the love of God, obeys God Who commands it; imitates God, "Whose property it is always to have mercy;" seeks God Who rewards it; promotes the glory of God, through the thanksgiving to God, from those whom it benefits. "Mercy leads man up to God, for mercy brought down God to man; mercy humbled God, exalts man." Mercy takes Christ as its pattern, Who, from His Holy Incarnation to His Precious Death on the Cross, *bare our griefs, and carried our sorrows*[1]. Yet neither does mercy itself avail without true knowledge of God. For as mercy or love is the soul of all our acts, so true knowledge of God and faith in God are the source and soul of love. "Vain were it to boast that we have the other members, if faith, the head, were cut off[2]."

7. *But they like men*, or (better as in the E. M.) *like Adam, have transgressed the covenant.* As Adam our first parent, in Paradise, not out of any pressure, but wantonly, through self-will and pride, broke the covenant of God, eating the forbidden fruit, and then defended himself in his sin against God, casting the blame upon the woman: so these, in the good land which God had given them, *that they should* therein *keep His covenant and observe His laws*[3], wantonly and petulantly broke that covenant; and then obstinately defended their sin. Wherefore, as Adam was cast out of Paradise, so shall these be cast out of the land of promise.

There have they dealt treacherously against Me. There! He does not say, *where*. But Israel and every sinner in Israel knew full well, where. *There*, to Israel, was not only Bethel or Dan, or Gilgal, or Mizpah, or Gilead, or any or all of the places, which God had hallowed by His mercies, and they had defiled. It was every high hill, each idol-chapel, each field-altar, which they had multiplied to their idols. To the sinners of Israel, it was every spot of the Lord's land which they had defiled by their sin. God points out to the conscience of sinners the place and time, the very spot where they offended Him. Wheresoever and whensoever they broke God's commands, *there they dealt treacherously against* God Himself. There is much emphasis upon the *against Me*. The sinner, while breaking the laws of God, contrives to forget God. God recalls him to himself, and says, *there*, where and when thou didst those and those things, thou didst deal falsely with, and against, *Me*. The sinner's conscience and memory fills up the word *there*. It sees the whole landscape of its sins around; each black dark spot stands out before it, and it cries with David, *there*, in this and this and this, *against Thee, Thee only, have I sinned, and done this evil in Thy sight*[4].

8. *Gilead is a city of them that work iniquity.* If we regard "Gilead," (as it elsewhere is,) as the country beyond Jordan, where the two tribes and a half dwelt, this will mean that the whole land was banded in one, as one city of evil-doers. It had an unity, but of evil. As the whole world has been pictured as divided between "the city of God" and the city of the devil, consisting respectively of the children of God and the children of the devil; so the whole of Gilead may be represented as one city, whose inhabitants had one occupation in common, to work evil. Some think that there was a city so called, although not mentioned elsewhere in Holy Scripture, near that Mount Gilead, dear to the memory of Israel, because God there protected their forefather Jacob. Some think that it was Ramoth in Gilead[5], which God appointed as "a city of refuge," and which, consequently, became a city of Levites and priests[6]. Here, where God had preserved the life of their forefather, and, in him, had preserved them; here, where He had commanded the innocent shedder of blood to be saved; here, where He had appointed those to dwell, whom He had hallowed to Himself, all was turned to the exact contrary. It, which God had hallowed, was become *a city of workers of iniquity*, i. e. of men, whose habits and wont was to work iniquity. It, where God had appointed life to be preserved, was *polluted* or *tracked with blood*. Everywhere it was marked and stained with the bloody footsteps of those, who (as David said) *put* innocent *blood in their shoes which were on their feet*[7], staining their shoes with blood which they shed, so that, wherever they went, they left marks and signs of it." *Tracked with blood* it was, through the sins of its inhabitants; *tracked with blood* it was again, when it first was taken

[1] Is. liii. 4. [2] S. Jer. [3] Ps. cv. 44. [4] Ib. li. 4.
[5] Deut. iv. 43. Jos. xx. 8. S. Jerome instances Ramoth and the deeds there, but does not identify Gilead with it, since he supposes the prophet to speak of "the Province itself."
[6] Jos. xxi. 38. [7] 1 Kgs ii. 5.

Before CHRIST cir. 780.

them that work iniquity,
and is || polluted with
blood.

|| Or, *cunning for blood.*

9 And as troops of rob-
bers wait for a man, *so* [s] the
company of priests murder
in the way † by consent:

[s] Jer. 11. 9. Ezek. 22. 25. ch. 5. 1, 2.

† Heb. *with* one *shoulder*, or, *to Shechem.*

for they commit || lewdness.
10 I have seen [t] an horrible thing in the house of
Israel: there *is* [u] the whoredom of Ephraim; Israel is
defiled.
11 Also, O Judah, [x] he

Before CHRIST cir. 780.

|| Or, *enormity.*

[t] Jer. 5. 30.

[u] ch. 4. 12, 13, 17.

[x] Jer. 51. 33. Joel 3. 13. Rev. 14. 15.

---

captive[1], and "*it*, which had swum with the innocent blood of others, swam with the guilty blood of its own people." It is a special sin, and especially avenged of God, when what God had hallowed, is made the scene of sin.

9. *And as troops of robbers wait for a man, so the company of priests murder in the way by consent;* or (more probably) *in the way to Shechem*[2]. Shechem too was a "city of refuge[3]," and so also a city of Levites and priests[4]. It was an important city. For there Joshua assembled all Israel for his last address to them, and made a covenant with them[5]. There, Rehoboam came to be accepted by Israel as their king[6], and was rejected by them. There Jeroboam after the schism, for a time, made his residence[7]. The priests were banded together; their counsel was one; they formed one company; but they were bound together as a band of robbers, not to save men's lives but to destroy them. Whereas the way to the cities of refuge was, by God's law, to be *prepared*[8], clear, open, without let or hindrance to the guiltless fugitive, to save his life, the priests, the guardians of God's law, obstructed the way, to rob and destroy. They, whom God appointed to teach the truth that men might live, were banded together against His law.

Shechem, besides that it was a city of refuge, was also hallowed by the memory of histories of the patriarchs who walked with God. There, was Jacob's well[9]; there Joseph's bones were buried[10]; and the memory of the patriarch Jacob was cherished there, even to the time of our Lord[9]. Lying in a narrow valley between Mount Ebal and Gerizim, it was a witness, as it were, of the blessing and curse pronounced from them, and had, in the times of Joshua, an ancient sanctuary of God[11]. It was a halting-place for the pilgrims of the northern tribes, in their way to the feasts at Jerusalem; so that these murders by the priests coincide with the tradition of the Jews, that they who would go up to Jerusalem were murdered in the way.

For they commit lewdness, lit. *For they have done deliberate sin*[12]. The word literally means *a thing thought of*, especially an evil, and so, deliberate, contrived, bethought-of, wickedness. They did deliberate wickedness, gave themselves to do it, and did nothing else.

10. *I have seen a horrible thing*, lit. *what would make one shudder.* God had seen it; therefore man could not deny it. In the sight of God, and amid the sense of His Presence, all excuses fail.

In the house of Israel. "[13] For what more horrible, more amazing than that this happened, not in any ordinary nation but *in the house of Israel*, in the people of God, in the portion of the Lord, as Moses said, *the Lord's portion is His people, Jacob is the lot of His inheritance?* In another nation, idolatry was error. In Israel, which had the knowledge of the one true God and had received the law, it was horror." *There is the whoredom of Ephraim*, widespread, over the whole land, wherever the house of Ephraim was, through the whole kingdom of the ten tribes, *there* was its spiritual adultery and defilement.

11. *Also, O Judah, He hath set a harvest for thee, when I returned* (rather, *when I return*) *the captivity of My people.*

The *harvest* may be either for good or for bad. If the harvest is spoken of, as bestowed upon the people, then, as being of chief moment for preserving the life of the body, it is a symbol of all manner of good, temporal or spiritual, bestowed by God. If the people is spoken of, as themselves being the harvest which is ripe and ready to be cut down, then it is a symbol of their being ripe in sin, ready for punishment, to be cut off by God's judgments. In this sense, it is said of Babylon[14], *Yet a little while, and the time of her harvest shall come;* and of the heathen, [15] *put ye in the sickle, for their harvest is ripe, for their wickedness is great;* and of the whole earth, [16] *the harvest of the earth is ripe.* Here God must be

---

[1] 2 Kgs xv. 29.

[2] This translation accounts for the grammatical form שְׁכֶמָה "*towards* Shechem;" (as in Gen. xxvii. 14. &c.). The consent of many in doing a thing is indeed expressed by saying "they did it with *one* shoulder," (Zeph. iii. 9.) Yet the word *one* (which is not used here,) is essential to the figure, which is, that many did the act, as if they were one.

[3] Joh. xx. 7.
[4] Ib. xxi. 21.
[5] Ib. xxiv. 1. 25.
[6] 1 Kgs xii. 1.
[7] Ib. 25.
[8] Deut. xix. 3.
[9] S. Joh. iv. 5, 6.
[10] Josh. xxiv. 32.
[11] Ib. 26.
[12] It is used of sins of the flesh in Lev. xix. 29. xx. 14. Job xxxi. 11. and especially in Ezek.
[13] Rup.
[14] Jer. li. 33.
[15] Joel iii. 13.
[16] Rev. xiv. 15.

Before CHRIST cir. 780.

hath set an harvest for thee, [y] when I returned the captivity of my people.

[y] Ps. 126. 1.

speaking of a *harvest*, which he willed hereafter to give *to* Judah. For the time of the harvest was to be, when He should *return the captivity of His people*, restoring them out of their captivity, a time of His favor and of manifold blessings. *A harvest* then *God appointed for Judah*. But when? Not at that time, not for a long, long period, not for any time during the life of man, but at the end of the captivity of 70 years. God promises relief, but after suffering. Yet He casts a ray of light, even while threatening the intermediate darkness. He foreshews to them a future harvest, even while their coming lot was captivity and privation. *Now* Judah, His people, was entangled in the sins of Ephraim, and, like them, was to be punished. Suffering and chastisement were the condition of healing and restoration. But whereas the destruction of the kingdom of Israel was final, and they were no more to be restored as a whole, God Who loveth mercy, conveys the threat of impending punishment under the promise of future mercy. He had rich mercies in store for Judah, yet not until after the captivity, when He should again own them as *My people*. Meantime, there was withdrawal of the favor of God, distress, and want.

The distinction between Judah and Israel lay in the promise of God to David. [1] *The Lord hath sworn in truth to David, He will not turn from it; of the fruit of thy body will I set upon thy throne.* It lay in the counsels of God, but it was executed through those who knew not of those counsels. The ten tribes were carried away by the Assyrians into Media; Judah, by Nebuchadnezzar, into Babylon. The Babylonian empire, which, under Nebuchadnezzar, was the terror of Asia, was but a continuation of the Assyrian, being founded by a revolted Assyrian general[2]. The seat of empire was removed, the policy was unchanged. In man's sight there was no hope that Babylon would give back her captives, any more than Assyria, or than the grave would give back her dead. To restore the Jews, was to reverse the human policy, which had removed them; it was to re-create an enemy; strong in his natural position, lying between themselves and Egypt, who could strengthen, if he willed, their great rival. The mixed multitude of Babylonians and others, whom the king of Assyria had settled in Samaria, in their letter to a successor of Cyrus, appealed to these fears, and induced the impostor Smerdis to interrupt the restoration of Jerusalem. They say; [3] *We have sent and certified the king, that search may be made in the book of the records of thy fathers. So shalt thou find in the book of the records, and know that this city is a rebellious city, and hurtful unto kings and provinces, and that they have moved sedition within the same of old time; for which cause was this city destroyed.* The king did find in his records, that Judah had been of old powerful, and had refused the yoke of Babylon. [4] *I commanded, and search hath been made, and it is found that this city of old time hath made insurrection against kings, and that rebellion and sedition hath been made therein. There have been mighty kings over Jerusalem, which have ruled over all countries beyond the river, and toll, tribute, and custom, hath been given to them.* Conquerors do not think of restoring their slaves, nor of reversing their policy, even when there is no constraining motive to persevere in it. What is done, remains. This policy of transplanting nations, when once begun, was adopted, as a regular part of Assyrian, Babylonian, and Persian policy [5]. Yet no case is known, in which the people once removed were permitted to return, save the Jews. But God first foretold, that Cyrus should restore His people and build His temple; then, through men's wills He ordered the overthrow of empires. Cyrus overcame the league against him, and destroyed first the Lydian, then the Babylonian, empire. God then brought to his knowledge the prophecy concerning him, given by Isaiah 178 years before, and disposed his heart to do, what Isaiah had foretold that he should do. *Cyrus made his proclamation throughout all his kingdom.* The terms were ample. [6] *Who is there among you of all His people? His God be with him, and let him go up to Jerusalem, which is in Judah, and build the house of the Lord God of Israel (He is the God) which is in Jerusalem.* The proclamation must have reached *the cities of the Medes*, where the ten tribes were. But they only, *whose spirit God had raised*, returned to their land. Israel remained, of his own free will, behind; and fulfilled unwittingly the prophecy that they should be *wanderers among the nations*, while in Judah *the Lord brought again the captivity of His people*, and gave them *the harvest* which He had *appointed* for them. A Psalmist of that day speaks of the strangeness of the deliverance to them. [7] *When the Lord turned again the*

[1] Ps. cxxxii. 11.
[2] Nabopolassar. See Abyden. in Eus. Chron. Arm. i. p. 54.
[3] Ezra iv. 14, 15.
[4] Ib. 19, 20.
[5] See instances in Rawlinson Herod. T. ii. p. 564.
[6] Ezra i. 3.
[7] Ps. cxxvi. 1, 5.

Before CHRIST cir. 780.

CHAPTER VII.

1 *A reproof of manifold sins.* 11 *God's wrath against them for their hypocrisy.*

WHEN I would have healed Israel, then the iniquity of Ephraim was discovered, and the †wickedness of Samaria: for [a]they commit falsehood; and the thief cometh in, *and* the troop of robbers †spoileth without.

Before CHRIST cir. 780.

† Heb. *evils.*
[a] ch. 5. 1. & 6. 10.
† Heb. *strippeth.*

captivity of Zion, we were like them that dream. And primarily of that *bringing* back *the captivity of His people*, he uses Hosea's image of the *harvest. They which sow in tears shall reap in joy.* To the eye of the politician, it was an overthrow of empires and convulsion of the world, the herald of further convulsions, by which the new-established empire was in its turn overthrown. In the real, the religious, history of mankind, of far greater moment were those fifty thousand souls, to whom, with Zorobabel of the line of David, Cyrus gave leave to return. In them he fulfilled prophecy, and prepared for that further fulfillment, after his own empire had been long dissolved, and when, from the line of Zorobabel, was that Birth which was promised in Bethlehem of Judah.

VII. 1. *When I would have healed Israel.* God begins anew by appealing to Israel, that all which He had done to heal them, had but served to make their sin more evident, and *that*, from highest to lowest, as to all manners and ways of sin. When the flash of God's light on the sinner's conscience enlightens it not, it only discloses its darkness. The name *Israel* includes the whole people; the names, Ephraim and Samaria, probably are meant to designate the chief among them, Ephraim having been their royal tribe, and being the chief tribe among them; Samaria being their royal city. The sins, which Hosea denounces in this chapter, are chiefly the sins of the great, which, from them, had spread among the people. Whatever healing methods God had used, whether through the teaching of the prophets or through His own fatherly chastisements, they "[1]would not hearken nor be amended, but ran on still more obstinately in their evil courses. The disease prevailed against the remedy, and was irritated by it, so that the remedy served only to *lay open* the extent of its malignity, and to shew that there was worse in it, than did at first appear." So. S. Paul says of all human nature. [2]*When the commandment came, sin revived.* Apart from grace, the knowledge of good only enhances evil. "[3]So, when God, made Man, present and visible, willed to *heal Israel*, then that iniquity of the Jews and wickedness of the Scribes and Pharisees was discovered, whereof this iniquity of Ephraim and wickedness of Samaria was a type. For an evil spirit goaded them to mock, persecute, blaspheme the Teacher of repentance Who, together with the word of preaching, did works, such as none other man did. For Christ pleased them not, a Teacher of repentance, persuading to poverty, a Pattern of humility, a Guide to meekness, a Monitor to mourn for sins, a Proclaimer of righteousness, a Requirer of mercy, a Praiser of purity of heart, a Rewarder of peace, a Consoler of those who suffered persecution for righteousness' sake. Why did they reject, hate, persecute, Him Who taught thus? Because they loved all contrary thereto, and wished for a Messiah, who should exalt them in this world, and disturb the peace of nations, until he should by war subdue to their empire all the rest of the world, build for them on earth a Jerusalem of gold and gems, and fulfill their covetousness in all things of this sort. This their mind He once briefly expressed; [4]*How can ye believe which receive honor one of another, and seek not the honor which cometh from God only?* They persecuted Him then Who willed to heal them, as madmen strike the physician offering them medicine, nor did they cease, until they required Him their King to be crucified. Thus was *the iniquity of Ephraim and wickedness of Samaria discovered*, yet filled up by them; and so they filled up the measure of their fathers, and discovered and testified, that they were of the same mind with their fathers.—In all these things they *committed falsehood*, lying against their King Whom they denied, and accused as seditious."

For they [i. e. all of them] *commit falsehood.* Falsehood was the whole habit and tissue of their lives. "[5]They dealt falsely in all their doings both with God and man, being hypocritical and false in all their words and doings, given to fraud and deceit, from the highest to the lowest." Night and day; in silence and in open violence; *within*, where all seemed guarded and secure, and *without*, in open defiance of law and public justice; these deeds of wrong went on in an unceasing round. In the night, *the thief cometh in*, breaking into men's houses and pillaging secretly; *a troop of robbers spoileth without*, spreading their ravages far and wide, and desolating without resistance. It was all one state of anarchy, violence, and disorganization.

[1] Poc. [2] Rom. vii. 9. [3] Rup.

[4] S. John v. 24. [5] Poc.

Before CHRIST cir. 780.

† Heb. *say not to.*
[b] Jer. 17. 1.
[c] Ps. 9. 16. Prov. 5. 22.

2 And they † consider
not in their hearts *that* I
[b] remember all their wickedness: now [c] their own
doings have beset them
about; they are [d] before my
face.
3 They make the king

Before CHRIST cir. 780.

[d] Ps. 90. 8.

2. *And they consider not in their hearts*, lit. (as in the E. M.) *they say not to their hearts*. The conscience is God's voice to the heart from within; man's knowledge of the law of God, and his memory of it, is man's voice, reminding his heart and rebellious affections to abide in their obedience to God. God speaks through the heart, when by His secret inspirations He recalls it to its duty. Man speaks to his own heart, when he checks its sinful or passionate impulses by the rule of God's law, *Thou shalt not*. "At first, men feel the deformity of certain sorts of wickedness. When accustomed to them, men think that God is indifferent to what no longer shocks themselves." *They say not to their heart* any more, that *God remembers them.*

I remember all their wickedness. This was the root of *all their wickedness*, want of thought. They would not stop to say to themselves, that God not only saw, but *remembered their wickedness*, and not only this, but that He remembered it *all*. Many will acknowledge that God *sees* them. He sees all things, and so them also. This is a part of His natural attribute of omniscience. It costs them nothing to own it. But what God *remembers, that* He will repay. This belongs to God's attributes, as the moral Governor of the world; and this, man would gladly forget. But in vain. God does *remember*, and remembers in order to punish. *Now*, at the very moment when man would not recall this to his own heart, *their own doings have beset them about; they are before my face.* Unless or until man repent, God sees man continually, encompassed by all his past evil deeds; they surround him, accompany him, whithersoever he goeth; they attend him, like a band of followers; they lie down with him, they await him at his awakening; they live with him, but they do not die with him; they encircle him, that he should in no wise escape them, until he come attended by them, as witnesses against him, at the judgment-seat of God. [1] *His own iniquities shall take the wicked himself, and he shall be holden with the cords of his sins.* God *remembers all their wickedness*. Then He will requite *all;* not the last sins only, but all. So when Moses interceded for his people after the sin of the calf, God says to him, [2] *go lead the people unto the place, of which I have spoken unto thee; behold My Angel shall go before thee; nevertheless, in the day when I visit, I will visit their sin upon them;* and of the sins of Israel and their enemies; [3] *Is not this laid up in store with Me,* and *sealed up among My treasures? to Me* belongeth *vengeance and recompense; their foot shall slide in* due *time.* The sins, forgotten by man, are remembered by God, and are requited all together in the end. A slight image of the Day of Judgment, *the Day of wrath and revelation of the righteous judgment of God, against* which the hard and impenitent heart *treasures up unto* itself *wrath!*

They are before My face. All things, past, present, and to come, are present before God. He sees all things which have been, or which are, or which shall be, or which could be, although He shall never will that they should be, in one eternal, unvarying, present. To what end then for man to cherish an idle hope, that God will not *remember*, what He is ever seeing? In vain wouldest thou think, that the manifold ways of man are too small, too intricate, too countless, to be remembered by God. God says, *They are before My Face.*

3. *They make the king glad with their wickedness.* Wicked sovereigns and a wicked people are a curse to each other, each encouraging the other in sin. Their king, being wicked, had pleasure in their wickedness; and they, seeing him to be pleased by it, set themselves the more, to do what was evil, and to amuse him with accounts of their sins. Sin is in itself so shameful, that even the great cannot, by themselves, sustain themselves in it, without others to flatter them. A good and serious man is a reproach to them. And so, the sinful great corrupt others, both as aiding them in their debaucheries, and in order not to be reproached by their virtues, and because the sinner has a corrupt pleasure and excitement in hearing of tales of sin, as the good joy to hear of good. Whence S. Paul says, [4] *who, knowing the judgment of God that they which commit such things are worthy of death, not only do the same, but have pleasure in them that do them.*

But whereas, they all, kings, princes, and people, thus agreed and conspired in sin, and the sin of the great is the most destructive, the prophet here upbraids the people most for this common sin, apparently because they were free from the greater temptations of the great, and so their sin was the more wilful. "An unhappy complaisance was the ruling character of Israel. It preferred its kings to God. Conscience was versatile, ac-

[1] Prov. v. 22. [2] Ex. xxxii. 34. [3] Deut. xxxii. 34. 5. [4] Rom. i. 32.

Before CHRIST cir. 780.

glad with their wickedness,
and the princes [e] with their
lies.
4 [f] They *are* all adulterers, as an oven heated by
the baker, || *who* ceaseth
|| from raising after he hath
kneaded the dough, until
it be leavened.
5 In the day of our king
the princes have made *him*
sick || with bottles of wine;
he stretched out his hand
with scorners.
6 For they have || made
ready their heart like an
oven, whiles they lie in
wait: their baker sleepeth

[e] Rom. 1. 32.

[f] Jer. 9. 2.

|| Or, *the raiser will cease.*

|| Or, *from waking.*

|| Or, *with heat through wine.*

|| Or, *applied.*

commodating. Whatever was authorized by those in power, was approved." Ahab added the worship of Baal to that of the calves; Jehu confined himself to the sin of Jeroboam. The people acquiesced in the legalized sin. Much as if now, marriages, which by God's law are incest, or remarriages of the divorced, which our Lord pronounces adultery, were to be held allowable, because man's law ceases to annex any penalty to them.

4. *They* are *all adulterers.* The Prophet continues to picture the corruption of all kinds and degrees of men. *All of them,* king, princes, people; all were given to adultery, both spiritual, in departing from God, and actual, (for both sorts of sins went together,) in defiling themselves and others. *All of them* were, (so the word [1] means,) habitual *adulterers.* One only pause there was in their sin, the preparation to complete it. He likens their hearts, inflamed with lawless lusts, to the heat of *an oven* which *the baker* had already *heated.* The unusual construction "burning *from* the baker [2]" instead of "heated *by* the baker" may have been chosen, in order to express, how the fire continued to burn of itself, as it were, (although at first kindled by the baker,) and was ever ready to burn whatever was brought to it, and even now was all red-hot, burning on continually; and Satan, who had stirred it, gave it just this respite, *from the time when he had kneaded the dough* [3], until the leaven, which he had put into it, had fully worked, and the whole was ready for the operation of the fire.

The world is full of such men now, ever on fire, and pausing only from sin, until the flatteries, whereby they seduce the unstable, have worked and penetrated the whole mind, and victim after victim is gradually leavened and prepared for sin.

5. *In the day of our king, the princes have made* him *sick with bottles of wine* [or, *with heat from wine.*] Their holydays, like those of so many Englishmen now, were days of excess. *The day of* their *king* was probably some civil festival; his birthday, or his coronation-day. The Prophet owns the king, in that he calls him *our king;* he does not blame them for keeping the day, but for the way in which they kept it. Their festival they turned into an irreligious and anti-religious carousal; making themselves like *the brutes which perish,* and tempting their king first to forget his royal dignity, and then to blaspheme the majesty of God.

He stretched out his hand with scorners, as it is said [4], *Wine is a mocker* (or *scoffer*). Drunkenness, by taking off all power of self-restraint, brings out the evil which is in the man. The *scorner* or *scoffer* is one who *neither fears God nor regards man* [5], but makes a jest of all things, true and good, human or divine. Such were these corrupt princes of the king of Israel; with these *he stretched out the hand,* in token of his good fellowship with them, and that he was one with them. He withdrew his hand or his society from good and sober men, and *stretched* it *out,* not to punish these, but to join with them, as men in drink reach out their hands to any whom they meet, in token of their sottish would-be friendliness. With these the king drank, jested, played the buffoon, praised his idols, scoffed at God. The flattery of the bad is a man's worst foe.

6. *For they have made ready their heart like an oven.* He gives the reason of their bursting out into open mischief; it was ever stored up within. They *made ready,* (lit. *brought near*) *their heart.* Their heart was ever brought nigh to sin, even while the occasion was removed at a distance from it. "The *oven* is their heart; the fuel, their corrupt affections, and inclinations, and evil concupiscence, with which it is filled; *their baker,* their own evil will and imagination, which stirs up whatever is evil in them." The Prophet then pictures how, while they seem for a while to rest from sin, it is but *whilst they lie in wait;* still, all the while, they made and kept their hearts ready, full of fire for sin and passion; any breathing-time from actual sin was no real rest; the heart was still all on fire; *in the*

[1] מנאפים

[2] בערה מאפה.

[3] The E. V. *who ceaseth from raising,* and the E. M. *the raiser will cease,* mean the same thing.

[4] Prov. xx. 1. The word is the same, לץ or לוצץ.

[5] S. Luke xviii. 4.

Before CHRIST cir. 780.

all the night; in the morning it burneth as a flaming
fire.

Fulfilled 772.

7 They are all hot as an
oven, and have devoured
their judges; [g] all their kings
[h] are fallen: [i] *there is* none
among them that calleth
unto me.
8 Ephraim, he [k] hath

Before CHRIST cir. 780.

g ch. 8. 4.
h 2 Kgs 15, 10, 14, 25, 30.
i Is. 64. 7.
k Ps. 106. 35.

morning, right early, as soon as the occasion came, it burst forth.

The same truth is seen where the tempter is without. Such, whether Satan or his agents, having lodged the evil thought or desire in the soul, often feign themselves asleep, as it were, "letting the fire and the fuel which they had inserted, work together," that so the fire pent-in might kindle more thoroughly and fatally, and, the heart being filled and penetrated with it, might burst out of itself, as soon as the occasion should come.

7. *They are all hot as an oven, and have devoured their judges.* Plans of sin, sooner or later, through God's overruling Providence, bound back upon their authors. The wisdom of God's justice and of His government shews itself the more, in that, without any apparent agency of His own, the sin is guided by Him, through all the intricate mazes of human passion, malice, and cunning, back to the sinner's bosom. Jeroboam, and the kings who followed him, had corrupted the people, in order to establish their own kingdom. They had heated and inflamed the people, and had done their work completely, for the Prophet says, *They are all hot as an oven;* none had escaped the contagion; and they, thus heated, burst forth and, like the furnace of Nebchadnezzar, devoured not only what was cast into it, but those who kindled it. The heathen observed, that the "artificers of death perished by their own art."

Probably the Prophet is describing a scene of revelry, debauchery, and scoffing, which preceded the murder of the unhappy Zechariah; and so fills up the brief history of the Book of Kings. He describes a profligate court and a debauched king; and him doubtless, Zechariah [1]; those around him, delighting him with their wickedness; all of them habitual adulterers; but one secret agent stirring them up, firing them with sin, and resting only, until the evil leaven had worked through and through. Then follows the revel, and the ground why they intoxicated the king, viz. their lying-in-wait. "*For*," he adds, "they prepared their hearts like a furnace, *when they lie in wait.*" The mention of dates, of facts, and of the connection of these together; "the day of our king;" his behavior: their lying in wait; the secret working of one individual; the bursting out of the fire in the morning; the falling of their kings; looks, as if he were relating an actual history. We know that Zechariah, of whom he is speaking, was slain through conspiracy publicly in the open face of day, "before all the people," no one heeding, no one resisting. Hosea seems to supply the moral aspect of the history, how Zechariah fell into this general contempt; how, in him, all which was good in the house of Jehu expired.

All their kings are fallen. The kingdom of Israel, having been set up in sin, was, throughout its whole course, unstable and unsettled. Jeroboam's house ended in his son; that of Baasha, who killed Jeroboam's son, Nadab, ended in his own son, Elah; Omri's ended in his son's son, God having delayed the punishment on Ahab's sins for one generation, on account of his partial repentance; then followed Jehu's, to whose house God, for his obedience in some things, continued the kingdom to *the fourth generation.* With these two exceptions, in the houses of Omri and Jehu, the kings of Israel either left no sons, or left them to be slain. Nadab, Elah, Zimri, Tibni, Jehoram, Zechariah, Shallum, Pekahiah, Pekah, were put to death by those who succeeded them. Of all the kings of Israel, Jeroboam, Baasha, Omri, Menahem, alone, in addition to Jehu and the three next of his house, died natural deaths. So was it written by God's hand on the house of Israel, *all their kings have fallen.* The captivity was the tenth change after they had deserted the house of David. Yet such was the stupidity and obstinacy both of kings and people, that, amid all these chastisements, none, either people or king, turned to God and prayed Him to deliver them. Not even distress, amid which almost all betake themselves to God, awakened any sense of religion in them. *There is none among them, that calleth unto Me.*

8. *Ephraim, he hath mixed himself among the people;* i.e. with the heathen; he *mixed* or *mingled* himself among or with them, so as to corrupt himself [2], as it is said [3], *they were mingled among the heathen and learned their works.* God had forbidden all intermarriage with the heathen [4], lest His people should corrupt

[1] See Introd. p. 5.

[2] The word בלל is used not of mingling only, but of a mingling which involved confusion, (as in the origin of the name *Babel*, Gen xi. 7,) or contamination, (as in תבל.)

[3] Ps. cvi. 35

[4] Ex. xxxiv. 12-16.

Before CHRIST cir. 780.

mixed himself among the
people; Ephraim is a cake
not turned.

l ch. 8. 7.

9 [l]Strangers have de-
voured his strength, and
he knoweth *it* not: yea,

† Heb. *sprinkled.*

gray hairs are † here and
there upon him, yet he
knoweth not.

m ch. 5. 5.

10 And the [m] pride of
Israel testifieth to his face:

n Is. 9. 13.

and [n] they do not return to
the Lord their God, nor
seek him for all this.

themselves: they thought themselves wiser than He, intermarried, and were corrupted. Such are the ways of those who put themselves amid occasions of sin.

Ephraim is (lit. *is become*) *a cake* (lit. *on the coals*) *not turned.* The Prophet continues the image.[1] *Ephraim* had been *mingled,* steeped, kneaded up into one, as it were, *with the heathen,* their ways, their idolatries, their vices. God would amend them, and they, withholding themselves from His discipline, and not yielding themselves wholly to it, were but spoiled. The sort of cake, to which Ephraim is here likened, *uggah*[2], lit. *circular,* was a thin pancake, to which a scorching heat was applied on one side; sometimes by means of hot charcoal heaped upon it; sometimes, (it is thought,) the fire was within the earthen jar, around which the thin dough was fitted. If it remained long *unturned,* it was burnt on the one side; while it continued unbaked, doughy, reeking, on the other; the fire spoiling, not penetrating it through. Such were the people; such are too many so-called Christians; they united in themselves hypocrisy and ungodliness, outward performance and inward lukewarmness; the one overdone, but without any wholesome effect on the other. The one was scorched and black; the other, steamed, damp, and lukewarm; the whole worthless, spoiled irremediably, fit only to be cast away. The fire of God's judgment, with which the people should have been amended, made but an outward impression upon them, and reached not within, nor to any thorough change, so that they were the more hopelessly spoiled through the means which God used for their amendment.

9. *Strangers have devoured his strength, and he knoweth* it *not.* Like Samson, when, for sensual pleasure, he had betrayed the source of his strength and God had departed from him, Israel knew not how or wherein his alliances with the heathen had impaired his strength. He thought his losses at the hand of the enemy, passing wounds, which time would heal; he thought not of them, as tokens of God's separation from him, that his time of trial was coming to its close, his strength decaying, his end at hand. Israel was not only incorrigible, but *past feeling*[3], as the Apostle says of the heathen. The marks of wasting and decay were visible to sight and touch; yet he himself perceived not what all saw except himself. Israel had sought to strangers for help, and it *had turned to his decay.* Pul and Tiglath-pileser had *devoured his strength,* despoiling him of his wealth and treasure, the flower of his men, and the produce of his land, draining him of his riches, and hardly oppressing him through the tribute imposed upon him. But "like men quite stupified, they, though thus continually gnawed upon, yet suffered themselves willingly to be devoured, and seemed insensible of it." Yet not only so, but the present evils were the forerunners of worse. Grey hairs, themselves the effects of declining age and tokens of decay, are the forerunners of death. "[4] Thy grey hairs are thy passing-bell," says the proverb.

The Prophet repeats, after each clause, *he knoweth not.* He knoweth nothing; he knoweth not the tokens of decay in himself, but hides them from himself; he knoweth not God, Who is the Author of them; he knoweth not the cause of them, his sins; he knoweth not the end and object of them, his conversion; he knoweth not, what, since he knoweth not any of these things, will be the issue of them, his destruction. Men hide from themselves the tokens of decay, whether of body or soul. And so death, whether of body or soul or both, comes upon them unawares. "[5] Looking on the surface, he imagines that all things are right with him, not feeling the secret worm which gnaws within. The outward garb remains; the rules of fasting are observed; the stated times of prayer are kept; but the heart is far from Me, saith the Lord. Consider diligently what thou lovest, what thou fearest, whereat thou rejoicest or art saddened, and thou will find, under the habit of religion, a worldly mind; under the rags of conversion, a heart of perversion."

10. *And the pride of Israel testifieth to his face.* His pride convicted him. All the afflictions of

[1] The word, *hath mingled,* includes also doubtless the meaning of *kneaded up with,* בלול ב, as in Lev. ii. 4, 5. &c.

[2] עֻגָה.

[3] Eph. iv. 19.

[4] lit. "Thy grey hairs are the proclaimer of thy death," an Arabic proverb.

[5] S. Bern. Serm. 2. in cap. jej. § 2, 3.

Before CHRIST cir. 780.

11. ¶ [o] Ephraim also is
like a silly dove without
heart: [p] they call to Egypt,
they go to Assyria.

[o] ch. 11. 11.
[p] See 2 Kings 15. 19. & 17. 4. ch. 5. 13. & 9. 3. & 12. 1.

12 When they shall go,
[q] I will spread my net upon
them; I will bring them
down as the fowls of the

Before CHRIST cir. 780.

[q] Ezek. 12. 13.

God humbled him not; yea, they but brought out his pride, which "[1] kept him from acknowledging and repenting of the sins which had brought those evils upon him, and from *turning to God and seeking to Him* for remedy." Men complain of their "fortune" or "fate" or "stars," and go on the more obstinately, to build up what God destroys, to prop up by human means or human aid what, by God's Providence, is failing; they venture more desperately, in order to recover past losses, until the crash at last becomes hopeless and final.

Nor seek Him for all this. God had exhausted all the treasures of His severity, as, before, of His love. He Himself marvels at His incorrigible and contumacious servant, as He says in Isaiah [2], *Why should ye be stricken any more? Ye will revolt more and more.* How is this? It follows, because they have *no heart.*

11. *Ephraim is* [*become*] *like a silly dove.* "There is nothing more simple than a dove," says the Eastern proverb. Simplicity is good or bad, not in itself, but according to some other qualities of the soul, good or evil, with which it is united, to which it opens the mind, and which lead it to good or mislead it to evil. The word [3] describes one, easily persuaded, open, and so, one who takes God's word simply, obeys His Will, without refinement or subtlety or explaining it away; in which way it is said [4], *The Lord preserveth the simple;* or, on the other hand, one who lets himself easily be led to evil, as the heathen said of youth, that they were "like wax to be bent to evil." In this way, it is said [5], *How long, ye simple ones, will ye love simplicity?* Our Lord uses this likeness of the dove, for good [6], *be wise as serpents, simple,* or *harmless as doves.* Hosea speaks of simplicity without wisdom; for he adds, *a silly dove without understanding,* (lit. *without a heart,*) whereby they should love God's Will, and so should understand it. Ephraim *became,* he says, like a silly dove. Neglecting God's calls, unmoved by calamity or sufferings, and not *seeking* to God *for all this* which He has done to recall them, they grew in folly. Man is ever *growing in wisdom* or in folly, in grace or in gracelessness. This new stage of folly lay in their flying to Assyria, to help them, in fact, against God; as it follows,

They call to Egypt. Instead of *calling to* God Who could and would help, they *called to Egypt* who could not, and *went to Assyria* who would not. So God complains by Isaiah [7], *To Me, thou hast not called, O Jacob.* This was their folly; they called not to God, Who had delivered them out of Egypt, but, alternately, to their two powerful neighbors, of whom Egypt was a delusive promiser, not failing only, but piercing, those who leant on it; Assyria was a powerful oppressor. Yet what else is almost the whole history of Christian states? The "balance of power," which has been the pride of the later policy of Europe, which has been idolized as a god, to which statesmen have looked, as a deliverance out of all their troubles; as if it were a sort of Divine Providence, regulating the affairs of men, and dispensing with the interference of God; what is it but the self-same wisdom, which balanced Egypt against Assyria?

12. *When they go,* (lit. *according as* they go, in all circumstances of time or place or manner, when whithersoever or howsoever they shall go,) *I will spread My net upon them,* so as to surround and envelop them on all sides and hold them down. The *dove* soaring aloft, with speed like the storm-wind [8], is a picture of freedom, independence, impetuous, unhindered, following on its own course; weak and timid, it trusts in the skillfulness with which it guides its flight, to escape pursuit; the *net,* with its thin slight meshes, betokens how weak instruments become all-sufficient in the hands of the Almighty; the same dove, brought down from its almost viewless height, fluttering weakly, helplessly and hopelessly, under those same meshes, is a picture of that same self-dependent spirit humiliated, overwhelmed by inevitable evils, against which it impotently struggles, from which it seems to see its escape, but by which it is held as fast, as if it lay motionless in iron.

As their congregation hath heard. Manifoldly had the message of reward on obedience, and of punishment on disobedience, come to Israel. It was spread throughout the law; it fills the book of Deuteronomy; it was concentrated in the blessing and the curse on mount Ebal and Gerizim; it was put into their mouths in the song of Moses; it was inculcated by all the prophets who had already prophesied to them, and now it was being enforced on that generation by Hosea himself. Other kingdoms have fallen; but their fall, apart from Scripture, has not been the subject of prophecy. Their ruin has come

[1] Poc. [2] i. 5. [3] פתה. [4] Ps. cxvi. 6. [5] Prov. i. 22. [6] S. Matt. x. 16. [7] Isai. xliii. 22. [8] Ps. lv. 6–8.

Before CHRIST cir. 780.

heaven; I will chastise
them, [r] as their congregation hath heard.
13 Woe unto them! for
they have fled from me:
† destruction unto them!
because they have trans-
gressed against me: though
[s] I have redeemed them,
yet they have spoken lies
against me.
14 [t] And they have not
cried unto me with their
heart, when they howled
upon their beds: they as-
semble themselves for corn

[r] Lev. 26. 14, &c. Deut. 28. 15, &c. 2 Kings 17. 13, 18.
† Heb. *spoil.*
[s] Mic. 6. 4.
[t] Job 35. 9, 10. Ps. 78. 36. Jer. 3. 10. Zech. 7. 5.

---

mostly unexpected, either by themselves or others.

13. *Woe unto them, for they have fled from Me.* The threatening rises in severity, as did the measure of their sin. Whereas [1] *Salvation belonged to God* alone, and they only [2] *abide under His shadow,* who make Him their *refuge, woe* must needs come on them, who leave Him. [3] *They forsake their own mercy. Woe* they draw upon themselves, who forget God; how much more then they, who wilfully and with a high hand transgress against Him! *Destruction unto them, for they have transgressed against Me.* To be separated from God is the source of all evils; it is the "pain of loss" of God's Presence, in hell; but *destruction* is more than this; it is everlasting death.

And I have redeemed them and they have spoken lies against Me. The *I* and *they* are both emphatic in Hebrew; [4] "*I* redeemed;" "*they* spoke lies." Such is man's requital of His God. Oft as He redeemed, so often did they traduce Him. Such was the history of the passage through the wilderness; such, of the period under the Judges; such had it been recently, when God delivered Israel by the hand of Jereboam II [5]. The word, *I have redeemed,* denotes "habitual oft-renewed deliverance," "that He was their constant Redeemer, from Whom they had found help, did still find it, and might yet look to find it, if they did not, by their ill behavior, stop the course of His favor towards them [6]." God's mercy overflowed their ingratitude. *They* had spoken lies against Him, often as He had delivered them; *He* was still their abiding Redeemer. *I do redeem them.*

They have spoken lies against Me. Men *speak lies* against God, in their hearts, their words, their deeds, whenever they harbor thoughts, speak words, or act, so as to deny that God is what He is, or as to imply that He is not what He has declared Himself to be. Whoever seeks anything out of God or against His Will; whoever seeks from man, or from idols, or from fortune, or from his own powers, what God alone bestows; whoever acts as if God was not a good God, ready to receive the penitent, or a just God Who will avenge the holiness of His laws and *not clear the guilty,* does in fact, *speak lies against God.* People, day by day, *speak lies against* God, against His Wisdom, His Providence, His Justice, His Goodness, His Omniscience, when they are thinking of nothing less. Jeroboam spake lies against God, when he said, *these be thy gods, O Israel, which brought thee out of the land of Egypt,* whereas God had so often enforced upon them [7], *the Lord redeemed you out of the house of bondmen, from the hand of Pharaoh king of Egypt;* [8] *the Lord thy God brought thee out thence with a mighty hand and stretched out arm.* Israel *spake lies against God,* when he said [9], *these are my rewards which my lovers have given me,* or when, *they returned not to Him* but *called on Egypt,* as though God would not help them, Who said that He would, or as though Egypt could help them, of whom God said that it should not. Sometimes, they *spoke* out *lies* boldly, telling God's true prophets that He had not sent them, or forbidding them to speak in His Name; sometimes covertly, as when they turned to God, not sincerely but feignedly; but always perversely. And when God the Son came on earth to *redeem them,* then still more, they spoke lies against Him, all His life long, saying, *He deceiveth the people,* and all their other blasphemies, and "[10] when He forgave them the sin of His death, saying, *Father, forgive them for they know not what they do,* they persevered in *speaking lies* against Him, and bribed the soldiers to speak lies against Him," and themselves do so to this day.

14. *And they have not cried unto Me with their heart, when they howled upon their beds,* or, in the present time, *they cry not unto Me when they howl.* They did *cry,* and, it may be, they *cried* even *unto God.* At least, the prophet does not deny that they cried to God at all; only, he says, that they did *not cry to* Him *with their heart.* Their cries were wrung from them by their temporal distresses, and ended in them, not in God. There was no sincerity in their hearts, no change in their doings.

[1] Ps. iii. 8. [2] Ib. xci. 1, 2.
[3] Jon. ii. 8.
[4] ואנכי אפדם והמה דברו.
[5] 2 Kings xiv. 25–27. [6] Poc.

[7] Ex. xx. 2. Lev. xix. 36. xxiii. 43. Num. xv. 41. Deut. v. 6, 15.
[8] Deut. vii. 8; add. xiii. 5. xv. 15. xxiv. 18.
[9] ch. ii. 12. [10] Rup.

Before CHRIST cir. 780.

and wine, *and* they rebel
against me.

‖ Or, *chastened.*

15 Though I ‖ have
bound *and* strengthened
their arms, yet do they imagine
mischief against me.

[u] ch. 11. 7.

16 [u] They return, *but* not
to the most High: [x] they
are like a deceitful bow:
their princes shall fall by
the sword for the [y] rage of
their tongue: this *shall be*
their derision [z] in the land
of Egypt.

[x] Ps. 78. 57.
[y] Ps. 73. 9.
[z] ch. 9. 3, 6.

Their *cry* was a mere *howling.* The secret complaint of the heart is a loud cry in the ears of God. The impetuous *cry* of impatient and unconverted suffering is a mere brutish *howling.* Their heart was set wholly on their earthly wants; it did not thank God for giving them good things, nor cry to Him truly when He withheld them.

But, it may be, that the Prophet means also to contrast the acts of the ungodly, private and public, amid distress, with those of the godly. The godly man implores God in public and in private. The prayer on the *bed,* expresses the private prayer of the soul to God, when, the world being shut out, it is alone with Him. In place of this, there was the *howling,* as men toss fretfully and angrily on their beds, roar for pain; but, instead of complaining *to* God, complain *of* Him, and are angry, not with themselves, but with God. In place of the public prayer and humiliation, there was a mere tumultuous assembly, in which they clamored *for corn and wine,* and *rebelled against* God. *They assemble themselves;* (lit. *they* [1] *gather themselves tumultuously together*). *They rebel against Me;* (lit. *they turn aside against Me*). They did not only (as it is expressed elsewhere) "turn aside *from* God." *They turn aside against Me* [2], He says, flying, as it were, in the very face of God. This *tumultuous assembly* was either some stormy civil debate, how to obtain the corn and wine which God withheld, or a tumultuous clamoring to their idols and false gods, like that of the priests of Baal, when arrayed against Elijah on Mount Carmel; whereby they removed the further from God's law, and rebelled with a high hand against Him.

"[3] What is to *cry to the Lord,* but to long for the Lord? But if any one multiply prayers, crying and weeping as he may, yet not with any intent to gain God Himself, but to obtain some earthly or passing thing, he cannot truly be said to *cry unto the Lord,* i. e. so to cry that his cry should come to the hearing of the Lord. This is a cry like Esau's, who sought no other fruit from his father's blessing, save to be rich and powerful in this world. When then He saith, *They cried not to Me in their heart, &c.,* He means, they were not devoted to Me, their heart was not right with Me; they sought not Myself, but things of Mine. They howled, desiring only things for the belly, and seeking not to have Me. Thus they belong not to *the generation of those who seek the Lord, who seek the face of the God of Jacob* [4], but to the generation of Esau."

15. *Though I have bound,* rather, (as in the E. M.) *And I have chastened* [5], *I have strengthened their arms, and they imagine mischief against Me.* God had tried all ways with them, but it was all one. He chastened them in love, and in love He strengthened them; He brought the enemy upon them, (as aforetime in the days of the Judges,) and He gave them strength to repel the enemy; as He raised up judges of old, and lately had fulfilled His promise which He had made to Joash through Elisha. But it was all in vain. Whatever God did, Israel was still the same. All only issued in further evil. The Prophet sums up in four words all God's varied methods for their recovery, and then sets over against them the one result, fresh rebellion on the part of His creatures and His people.

They imagine or *devise mischief against Me.* The order in the Hebrew is emphatic, *and against Me they devise evil;* i. e. *against Me,* Who had thus tried all the resources and methods of Divine wisdom to reclaim them, *they devise evil.* These are words of great condescension. For the creature can neither hurt nor profit the Creator. But since God vouchsafed to be their King, He deigned to look upon their rebellions, as so many efforts to injure Him. All God's creatures are made for His glory, and on earth, chiefly man; and among men, chiefly those whom He had chosen as His people. In that, then, they set themselves to diminish that glory, giving to idols [6], they, as far as in them lay, *devised evil against* Him. Man would dethrone God, if he could.

16. *They return,* but *not to the most High.*

[1] גור, when used of assembling, is always used of tumultuous assembling, as in Ps. lvi. 7. lix. 4. cxl. 3. Is. liv. 15.

[2] This is in two words in Hebrew, יסורו בי.

[3] Rup.

[4] Ps. xxiv. 6.

[5] The two words *asar,* אסר, *bound,* and *issar,* יסר, *chastened,* differ but by a letter in the Hebrew. Yet one is never put for the other. The Heb. Comm., whom the E. V. followed, did but guess from the context.

[6] See Is. xlii. 8.

Before CHRIST cir. 760.

CHAPTER VIII.

1, 12 *Destruction is threatened for their impiety,* 5 *and idolatry.*

SET [a] the trumpet to † thy mouth. *He shall come*
[b] as an eagle against the house of the LORD, because
[c] they have transgressed my covenant, and trespassed against my law.

[a] ch. 5. 8.
† Heb. *the roof of thy mouth.*
[b] Deut. 28. 49. Jer. 4. 13. Hab. 1. 8.
[c] ch. 6. 7.

God exhorts by Jeremiah [1], *If thou wilt return, O Israel, saith the Lord, return unto Me.* They changed, whenever they did change, with a feigned, hypocritical conversion, but not to God, nor acknowledging His Majesty. Man, until truly converted, *turns* to and fro, unstably, hither and thither, changing from one evil to another, from the sins of youth to the sins of age, from the sins of prosperity to the sin of adversity; but he remains himself unchanged. *He turns, not to the most High.* The Prophet says this in three, as it were, broken words, *They turn,* [2] *not most High.* The hearer readily filled up the broken sentence, which fell, drop by drop, from the Prophet's choked heart.

They are like a deceitful bow, which, "howsoever the archer directs it, will not carry the arrow right home to the mark," but to other objects clean contrary to his will. "[3] God had, as it were, bent Israel, as His own bow, against the tyranny of the devil and the deceit of idolatry. For Israel alone in the whole world cast aside the worship of idols, and was attached to the true and natural Lord of all things. But they turned themselves to the contrary. For, being bound to this, they fought against God for the glory of idols. They became then as a warped bow, shooting their arrows contrariwise." In like way doth every sinner act, using against God, in the service of Satan, God's gifts of nature or of outward means, talents, or wealth, or strength, or beauty, or power of speech. God gave all for His own glory; and man turns all aside to do honor and service to Satan.

Their princes shall fall by the sword for the rage of their tongue. The word, rendered [4] *rage,* is everywhere else used of the wrath of God; here, of the *wrath* and *foaming* of man against God. Jeremiah relates how, the nearer their destruction came upon Judah, the more madly the politicians and false prophets cantradicted what God revealed. Their tongue was *a sharp sword.* They sharpened their tongue like a sword; and the sword pierced their own bosom. The phrensy of their speech not only drew down God's anger, but was the instrument of their destruction. They misled the people; taught them to trust in Egypt, not in God; persuaded them to believe themselves, and to disbelieve God; to believe, that the enemy should depart from them and not carry them away captive. They worked up the people to their will, and so they secured their own destruction. The princes of Judah were especially judged and put to death by Nebuchadnezzar [5]. The like probably took place in Israel. In any case, those chief in power are chief objects of destruction. Still more did these words come true before the final destruction of Jerusalem by the Romans. They were maddened by their own curse, *the rage of their tongue* against their Redeemer, *His blood be on us and on our children.* Phrensy became their characteristic. It was the amazement of the Romans, and their own destruction.

This shall be their derision in the land of Egypt. This, i. e. all this, their boasting of Egypt, their failure, their destruction, shall become their *derision.* In Egypt had they trusted; to Egypt had they gone for succor; in Egypt should they be derided. Such is the way of man. The world derides those who trusted in it, sued it, courted it, served it, preferred it to their God. Such are the wages, which it gives. So Isaiah prophesied of Judah [6], *the strength of Pharaoh shall be your shame, and the trust in the shadow of Egypt your confusion. They were all ashamed of a people that could not profit them, nor be an help nor profit, but a shame and also a reproach.*

VIII. 1. *The trumpet to thy mouth!* So God bids the prophet Isaiah [7], *Cry aloud, spare not, lift up thy voice like a trumpet.* The prophets, as watchmen, were set by God to give notice of His coming judgments [8]. As the sound of a war-trumpet would startle a sleeping people, so would God have the Prophet's warning burst upon their sleep of sin. The ministers of the Church are called to be "watchmen [9]" "They too are forbidden to keep a cowardly silence, when *the house of the Lord* is imperilled by the breach of the covenant or violation of the law. If fear of the wicked or false respect for the great silences the voice of those whose office it is to *cry aloud,* how shall such cowardice be excused?"

He shall come *as an eagle against the house of the Lord.* The words "he shall come" are inserted for clearness. The Prophet beholds the enemy speeding with the swiftness of an eagle, as it darts down upon its prey. *The*

[1] ch. iv. 1. [2] ישובו לא על. [3] S. Cyr. [4] זעם. [5] Jer. lii. 10. [6] xxx. 3, 5.

[7] ch. lviii. 1. [8] Ezek. xxxiii. 3, Am. iii. 6. [9] Service for Ordering Priests.

Before CHRIST cir. 760.

2 [d] Israel shall cry unto
me, My God, [e] we know
thee.
3 Israel hath cast off *the*
thing that is good: the
enemy shall pursue him.
4 [f] They have set up
kings, but not by me: they

[d] Ps. 78. 34. ch. 5. 15.
[e] Tit. 1. 16.
[f] 2 Kings 15. 13, 17, 25. Shallum, Menahem, Pekahiah.

house of the Lord is, most strictly, the Temple, as being *the place which God had chosen to place His name there.* Next, it is used, of the kingdom of Judah and Jerusalem, among whom the Temple was; whence God says[1], *I have forsaken My house, I have left Mine heritage; I have given the dearly-beloved of My soul into the hands of her enemies*, and[2], *What hath My beloved to do in Mine house, seeing she hath wrought lewdness with many?* Yet the title of *God's house* is older than the Temple; for God Himself uses it of His whole people, saying of Moses[3], *My servant Moses is not so, who is faithful in all Mine house.* And even the ten tribes, separated as they were from the Temple-worship, and apostates from the true faith of God, were not, as yet, counted by Him as wholly excluded from *the house of God.* For God, below, threatens that removal, as something still to come; *for the wickedness of their doings I will drive them out of My house*[4]. The eagle, then coming down *against* or *upon* the house of the Lord, is primarily Shalmaneser, who came down and carried off the ten tribes. Yet since Hosea, in these prophecies, includes Judah, also, *the house of the Lord* is most probably to be taken in its fullest sense, as including the whole people of God, among whom He dwelt, and the Temple where His Name was placed. The *eagle* includes then Nebuchadnezzar also, whom other prophets so call[5]; and (since, all through, the principle of sin is the same and the punishment the same) it includes the Roman eagle, the ensign of their armies.

Because they have transgressed My covenant. "God, Whose justice is always unquestionable, useth to make clear to men its reasonableness." Israel had broken the covenant which God had made with their fathers, that He would be to them a God, and they to Him a people. The *covenant* they had broken chiefly by idolatry and apostacy; the *law*, by sins against their neighbor. In both ways they had rejected God; therefore God rejected them.

2. *Israel shall cry unto Me, My God, we know Thee.* Or, according to the order in the Hebrew, *To Me shall they cry, we know Thee, Israel*, i. e. *we, Israel*, Thy people, *know Thee.* It is the same plea which our Lord says that He shall reject in the Day of Judgment[6]. *Many shall say unto Me, in that Day, Lord, Lord, have we not prophesied in Thy Name, and in Thy Name cast out devils, and in Thy Name done many wonderful works.* In like way, when our Lord came in the flesh, they said of God the Father, *He is our God.* But our Lord appealed to their own consciences[7]; *It is My Father Who honoreth Me, of Whom ye say, He is our God, but ye have not known Him.* So Isaiah, when speaking of his own times, prophesied of those of our Lord also[8]; *This people draweth nigh unto Me, with their mouth and honoreth Me with their lips; but their heart is far from Me.* "God says, that they shall urge this as a proof, that they know God, and as an argument to move God to have respect unto them, viz. that they are the seed of Jacob, who was called Israel, because he prevailed with God, and they were called by his name." As though they said, "*we*, Thy *Israel, know thee.*" It was all hypocrisy, the cry of mere fear, not of love; whence God, using their own name of Israel which they had pleaded, answers the plea, declaring what *Israel* had become.

3. *Israel has cast off the* thing that is *good*, or (since the word means "to cast off with abhorrence") *Israel hath cast off and abhorred Good*, both "Him who is Good" and "that which is good." The word *tob* includes both. They rejected good in rejecting God, "[9] Who is simply, supremely, wholly, universally good, and good to all, the Author and Fountain of all good, so that there is nothing simply good but God; nothing worthy of that title, except in respect of its relation to Him Who is *good and doing good*[10]. So then whatsoever any man hath or enjoys of good, is from his relation to Him, his nearness to Him, his congruity with Him. [11] *The drawing near to God is good to me.* All that any man hath of good, is from his being near to God, and his being, as far as human condition is capable of, like unto Him. So that they who are far from Him, and put Him far from them, necessarily *cast off* all that is *good.*"

The enemy shall pursue him. "Forsaking God, and forsaken by Him, they must needs be laid open to all evils." *The enemy*, i. e. the Assyrian, *shall pursue him.* This is according to the curse, denounced against them in the law, if they should forsake the Lord, and break His covenant, and *not hearken to His voice to observe to do His commandments*[12].

4. *They have set up kings, but not by ME.*

[1] Jer. xii. 7. [2] Ib. xi. 15.
[3] Num. xii. 7. [4] ch. ix. 15.
[5] Ezek. xvii. 3, 12. Jer. xlviii. 40. Hab. i. 8.
[6] S. Matt. vii. 22. [7] S. John viii. 54.
[8] S. Matt. xv. 8. Is. xxix. 13. [9] Poc. [10] Ps. cxix. 68.
[11] Ps. lxxiii. 28. [12] Deut. xxviii. 15–25.

Before CHRIST cir. 760.

have made princes, and I knew *it* not: [g] of their silver and their gold have they made them idols, that they may be cut off.

[g] ch. 2. 8. & 13. 2.

Before CHRIST cir. 760.

God Himself foretold to Jeroboam by Ahijah the prophet, that He would *rend the kingdom out of the hands of Solomon, and give ten tribes* to him, *and* would *take* him, *and* he *should reign according to all that* his *soul desired and* should *be king over Israel*[1]; and, after the ten tribes had made Jeroboam king, God said by Shemaiah the prophet to Rehoboam and the two tribes[2], *Ye shall not go up, nor fight against your brethren the children of Israel; return every man to his house; for this thing is from Me.*

Yet although here, as everywhere, man's self-will was overruled by God's Will, and fulfilled it, it was not the less self-will, both in the ten tribes and in Jeroboam. It was so in the ten tribes. For they cast off Rehoboam, simply of their own mind, because he would not lessen the taxes, as they prescribed. If he would have consented to their demands, they would have remained his subjects[3]. *They set up kings, but not by* or *through* God, Whom they never consulted, nor asked His Will about the rules of the kingdom, or about its relation to the kingdom of Judah, or the house of David. They referred these matters no more to God, than if there had been no God, or than if He interfered not in the affairs of man. It was self-will in Jeroboam himself, for he received the kingdom (which Ahijah told him, he *desired*) not from God, not inquiring of him, how he should undertake it, nor anointed by Him, nor in any way acknowledging Him, but from the people. And as soon as he had received it, he set up rebellion against God, in order to establish his kingdom, which he founded in sin, whereby he made Israel to sin.

In like way, the Apostle says[4], *against Thy holy Child Jesus, Whom Thou hast anointed, both Herod and Pontius Pilate, with the Gentiles and the people of Israel, were gathered together, for to do whatsoever Thy hand and Thy counsel determined before to be done.* Yet not the less did they sin in this Deicide; and the Blood of Jesus has ever since, as they imprecated on themselves, been on the Jews and on their children, as many as did not repent.

As was the beginning of the kingdom of Israel, such was its course. *They made kings, but not from God.* Such were all their kings, except Jehu and his house. During 253 years, for which the kingdom of Israel lasted, eighteen kings reigned over it, out of ten different families, and no family came to a close, save by a violent death. The like self-will and independence closed the existence of the Jewish people. The Roman Emperor being afar off, the Scribes and Pharisees hoped, under him, without any great control, to maintain their own authority over the people. They themselves, by their *God forbid!* [5] owned that our Lord truly saw their thoughts and purpose, *This is the heir; come let us kill Him, that the inheritance may be ours.* They willed to reign without Christ, feared the Heathen Emperor less than the holiness of Jesus, and in the words, *We have no king but Cæsar,* they deposed God, and shut themselves out from His kingdom.

And I knew it not. "As far as in them lay, they did it without His knowledge.[6]" They did not take Him into their counsels, nor desire His cognizance of it, or His approbation of it. If they could, they would have had Him ignorant of it, knowing it to be against His Will. And so in His turn, God knew it not, owned it not, as He shall say to the ungodly, *I know you not*[7].

Of their silver and their gold have they made them idols. God had multiplied them, (as He said before[8]) and they ungratefully abused to the dishonor of the Giver, what He gave them to be used to His glory.

That they may be cut off, lit. *that he may be cut off.* The whole people is spoken of as one man, "one and all," as we say. It is a fearful description of obstinate sin, that their very object in it seemed to be their own destruction. They acted with one will as one man, who had, in all he did, this one end,—to perish. "[9] As if on set purpose they would provoke destruction, and obstinately run themselves into it, although forewarned thereof." Holy Scripture speaks of that, as men's end, at which all their acts aim. [10] *They see not, nor know, that they may be ashamed;* i. e. they blind themselves, as though their whole object were, what they will bring upon themselves, their own shame. [11] *They prophesy a lie in My Name, that I might drive you out, and that ye might perish, ye, and the prophets that prophesy unto you.* This was the ultimate end of those false prophecies. The false prophets of Judah filled them with false hopes; the real and true end of those prophecies, that in which they ended, was the ruin of those who uttered, and of those who listened to them. We ourselves say almost proverbially, "he goes the way to ruin himself;" not that such is the man's own object, but that he obstinately chooses a course of conduct, which,

[1] 1 Kings xi. 31, 37. [2] xii. 22–4. [3] Ib. 4
[4] Acts iv. 27, 8. [5] S. Luke xx. 16.

[6] S. John viii. 54. [7] S. Matt. xxv. 12.
[8] ch. ii. 8. [9] Poc. [10] Is. xliv. 9. [11] Jer. xxvii. 15.

Before CHRIST cir. 760.

5 ¶ Thy calf, O Samaria, hath cast *thee* off; mine anger is kindled against them: [h] how long *will it be* ere they attain to innocency?

[h] Jer. 13. 27.

6 For from Israel *was* it also: the workman made

others see, must end in utter ruin. So a man chooses destruction or hell, if he chooses those things which, according to God's known law and word, end in it. Man hides from his own eyes the distant future, and fixes them on the nearer objects which he has at heart. God lifts the veil, and discovers to him the further end, at which he is driving, which he is, in fact, compassing, and which is in truth *the* end; for his own fleeting objects perish in the using; this and this alone abides.

5. *Thy calf, O Samaria, hath cast thee off.* Israel had cast off God, his good. In turn, the Prophet says, the *calf,* which he had chosen to be his god instead of the Lord his God, *has cast* him *off.* He repeats the word, by which he had described Israel's sin, [1] *Israel hath cast off and abhorred good,* in order to shew the connection of his sin and its punishment. "*Thy* calf," whom thou madest for thyself, whom thou worshipest, whom thou lovest, of whom thou saidst[2], *Behold thy gods, O Israel, which brought thee up out of the land of Egypt; thy* calf, in whom thou didst trust instead of thy God, it has requited thee the dishonor thou didst put on thy God; it hath *cast thee off* as a thing *abhorred.* So it is with all men's idols, which they make to themselves, instead of God. First or last, they all fail a man, and leave him poor indeed. Beauty fades; wealth fails; honor is transferred to another; nothing abides, save God. Whence our own great poet of nature makes a fallen favorite say, "had I but serv'd my God with half the zeal I served my king, He would not in mine age have left me naked to mine enemies."

Mine anger is kindled against them. Our passions are but some distorted likeness of what exists in God without passion; our anger, of His displeasure against sin. And so God speaks to us after the manner of men, and pictures His Divine displeasure under the likeness of our human passions of anger and fury, in order to bring home to us, what we wish to hide from ourselves, the severe and awful side of His Being, His Infinite Holiness, and the truth, that He will indeed avenge. He tells us, that He will surely punish; as men, who are extremely incensed, execute their displeasure if they can.

How long will it be ere they attain to innocency? lit. *how long will they not be able innocency?* So again it is said, *him that hath an high look and a proud heart, I cannot*[3]; we supply, *suffer. New moons and Sabbaths I cannot*[4]; our version adds, *away with,* i. e. endure. So here probably. As they had with abhorrence cast off God their good, so God says, *they cannot endure innocency;* but He speaks as wondering and aggrieved at their hardness of heart and their obdurate holding out against the goodness, which He desired for them. *How long will they not be able to endure innocency?* "What madness this, that when I give them place for repentence, they will not endure to return to health of soul!"

6. *For.* This verse may assign the reasons of God's displeasure, *mine anger is kindled;* or of Israel's impenitency, *How long will it be?* This indeed is only going a little further back; for Israel's incorrigibleness was the ground of God's displeasure. And they were incorrigible; because they had themselves devised it; *for from Israel was it also.* Those are especially incorrigible, who do not fall into error through ignorance, but who through malice devise it out of their own heart. Such persons act and speak, not as seduced by others, but seducing themselves, and condemned by their own judgment. Such were Israel and Jeroboam his king, who were not induced or seduced by others to deem the golden calf to be God, but devised it, of malicious intent, knowing that it was not God. Hence Israel could be cured of the worship of Baal, for this was brought from without by Jezebel; and *Jehu destroyed Baal out of Israel.* But of the sin of the calf they could not be healed. In this sin all the kings of Israel were impenitent.

From Israel was it also. Their boast, that they were of Israel, aggravated their sin. They said to God, *we, Israel, know thee.* So then their offence, too, their brutishness also, was from those who boasted themselves of bearing the name of their forefather, Israel, who were the chosen people of God, so distinguished by His favor. The name of Israel, suggesting their near relation to God, and the great things which He had done for them, and their solemn covenant with Him to be His people as He was their God, should, in itself, have made them ashamed of such brutishness. So S. Paul appealeth to us by our name of Christians[5], *Let every one who nameth the Name of Christ depart from iniquity.*

The workman made it, therefore it is not God. The workman was rather a god to his idol, than it to him; for *he* made it; *it* was a thing made. To say that it was made, was to deny that it was God. Hence the prophets so often

[1] ver. 3. זנח. [2] 1 Kings xii. 28–31. [3] Ps. ci. 5.

[4] Is. i. 13. [5] 2 Tim. ii. 19.

Before CHRIST cir. 760.

it; therefore it *is* not God:
but the calf of Samaria
shall be broken in pieces.
7 For [i]they have sown
the wind, and they shall
reap the whirlwind: it hath
no ‖ stalk: the bud shall
yield no meal: if so be it
yield, [k]the strangers shall
swallow it up.
8 [l]Israel is swallowed
up: now shall they be

[i] Prov. 22. 8. ch. 10, 12, 13.

‖ Or, *standing corn.*

[k] ch. 7. 9.

[l] 2 Kgs. 17. 6.

Before CHRIST cir. 760.

---

urge this special proof of the vanity of idols. No creature can be God. Nor can there be anything, between God and a creature. "[1]Every substance which is not God is a creature; and that which is not a creature, is God." God Himself could not make a creature who should be God. The Arian heresy, which imagined that God the Son could be a creature and yet an object of our worship, or that there could be a secondary god, was folly[2] as well as blasphemy. They did not conceive what God is. They had low, debased notions of the Godhead. They knew not that the Creator must be removed as infinitely above His most exalted creature, as above the lowest.

Nor do the prophets need any subtleties (such as the heathen alleged) that their idol might be indwelt by some influence. Since God dwelt not in it, any such influence could only come from a creature, and that, an evil one.

The calf of Samaria shall be broken in pieces. The calves were set up at Bethel and at Dan, but they were the sort of tutelar deity of the ten tribes; therefore they are called *the calf of Samaria.* They represented one and the same thing; whence they are called as one, *the calf,* not "calves." A thing of nought it was in its origin, for it had its form and shape from man; a thing of nought it should be in its end, for it should be *broken in pieces,* or become *chips, fragments,* for fire[3].

7. *For they have sown the wind, and they shall reap the whirlwind. They shall reap,* not merely as *they have sown,* but with an awful increase. They sowed folly and vanity, and shall reap, not merely emptiness and disappointment, but sudden, irresistible destruction[4]. *They sowed the wind,* and, as one seed bringeth forth many, so the wind, "penn'd up," as it were, in this destructive tillage, should "burst forth again, reinforced in strength, in mightier store and with greater violence." Thus they *reaped the whirlwind,* yea, (as the word means) *a mighty whirlwind*[5]. But the whirlwind which they reap doth not belong to *them;* rather they belong to it, blown away by it, like chaff, the sport and mockery of its restless violence.

It hath no stalk. If their design should for the time seem to prosper, all should be but empty shew, disappointing the more, the more it should seem to promise. He speaks of three stages of progress. First, the seed should not send forth the corn with the ear; *it hath no stalk* or *standing corn;* even if it advanced thus far, still the ear should yield no meat; or should it perchance yield this, the enemy should devour it. Since the yielding fruit denotes doing works, the fruit of God's grace, the absence of the *standing corn* represents the absence of good works altogether; the absence of the *meal,* that nothing is brought to ripeness; the *devouring* by *the enemy,* that what would otherwise be good, is, through faulty intentions or want of purity of purpose, given to Satan and the world, not to God. "[6]When hypocrites make a shew of good works, they gratify therewith the longings of the evil spirits. For they who do not seek to please God therewith, minister not to the Lord of the field, but to *strangers.* The hypocrite, then, like a fruitful but neglected "ear," cannot retain his fruit, because the "ear" of good works lieth on the ground. And yet he is fed by this very folly, because for his good works he is honored by all, eminent above the rest; men's minds are subject to him; he is raised to high places; nurtured by favors. But *then* will he understand that he has done foolishly, when, for the delight of praise, he shall receive the sentence of the rebuke of God."

8. *Israel is swallowed up.* Not only shall all which they have, be swallowed up by the enemy, but themselves also; and this, not at any distant time, but *now. Now,* at a time all but present, *they shall be among the Gentiles, as a vessel wherein is no pleasure,* or, quite strictly, *Now they have become, among the Gentiles.* He speaks of what should certainly be, as though it already were. *A vessel wherein is no pleasure,* is what S. Paul calls[7] *a vessel to dishonor,* as opposed to *vessels to honor* or honorable uses. It is then some vessel put to vile uses,

[1] S. Aug. de Trin. i. 6.

[2] See S. Athanas. against Arians, p. 3. n. f. 10. u. 191. d. 301. c. 411. b. 423. m. Oxf. Tr.

[3] Some derive the word שְׁבָבִים from an Arabic root, *kindled,* others from a Talmudic word, *fragment.* The word is the same as the Arabic *Shebab,* "that whereby fire is kindled," fuel for fire. The Talm. word may be no original word, but formed from the Heb. in the sense which those writers conceived it to have in this place.

[4] Hosea expressed this in four words; רוח יזרעו וסופתה יקצרו.

[5] The form סופתה is intensive of סופה.

[6] S. Greg. Mor. viii. 71.

[7] 2 Tim. ii. 20.

Before CHRIST cir. 760.

among the Gentiles [m] as a
vessel wherein *is* no pleasure.
9 For [n] they are gone
up to Assyria, [o] a wild
ass alone by himself:
Ephraim [p] hath hired
† lovers.

Before CHRIST cir. 760.

m Jer. 22. 28. & 48. 38.
n 2 Kgs. 15. 19.
o Jer. 2. 24. cir. 771.
p Isai. 30. 6. Ezek. 16. 33, 34.
† Heb. *loves.*

such as people turn away from with disgust. Such has been the history of the ten tribes ever since: *swallowed up*, not destroyed; *among* the nations, yet not of them; despised and mingled among them, yet not united with them; having an existence, yet among that large whole, *the nations*, in whom their national existence has been at once preserved and lost; everywhere had in dishonor; the Heathen and the Mohammedan have alike despised, outraged, insulted them; avenging upon them, unconsciously, the dishonor which they did to God. The Jews were treated by the Romans of old as offensive to the smell, and are so by the Mohammedans of North Africa still. "Never," says a writer of the fifth century [1], "has Israel been put to any honorable office, so as, after losing the marks of freedom and power, at least to have the rank of honorable servitude; but, like a vessel made for dishonorable offices, so they have been filled with revolting contumelies." "The most despised of those in servitude" was the title given by the Roman historian to the Jews, while yet in their own land. Wealth, otherwise so coveted, for the most part has not exempted them from dishonor, but exposed them to outrage. Individuals have risen to eminence in philosophy, medicine, finance; but the race has not gained through the credit of its members; rather, these have, for the most part, risen to reputation for intellect, amid the wreck of their own faith. When Hosea wrote this, two centuries had passed, since the fame of Solomon's wisdom (which still is venerated in the East) spread far and wide; Israel was hated and envied by its neighbors, not despised; no token of contempt yet attached to them; yet Hosea foretold that it should shortly be; and, for two thousand years, it has, in the main, been the characteristic of their nation.

9. *For they are gone up to Assyria.* The ground of this their captivity is that wherein they placed their hope of safety. They shall be presently swallowed up; *for* they went to Asshur. The Holy Land being then honored by the special presence of God, all nations are said to *go up* to it. Now, since Israel forgetting God, their strength and their glory, went to the Assyrian for help, he is said to *go up* thither, whither he went as a suppliant.

A wild ass alone by himself. "As *the ox* which *knoweth its owner, and the ass its Master's crib*, represents each believer, of Jew or Gentile; Israel, who would not know Him, is called the *wild ass*." The *pere*, or *wild ass* of the East, is "[2] heady, unruly, undisciplinable [3], obstinate, running with swiftness far outstripping the swiftest horse [4], whither his lust, hunger, thirst, draw him without rule or direction, hardly to be turned aside from his intended course." Although often found in bands, one often breaks away by himself, exposing itself for a prey to lions, whence it is said, *the wild ass is the lion's prey in the wilderness* [5]. Wild as the Arab was, a "wild ass's colt by himself [6]," is to him a proverb for one "[7] singular, obstinate, pertinacious in his purpose." Such is man by nature [8]; such, it was foretold to Abraham, Ishmael would be [9]; such Israel again became; "stubborn, heady, selfwilled, refusing to be ruled by God's law and His counsel, in which he might find safety, and, of his own mind, running to the Assyrian," there to perish.

Ephraim hath hired lovers or *loves.* The plural, in itself, shews that they were sinful loves, since God had said, *a man shall cleave unto his wife and they twain shall be one flesh.* These sinful *loves* or *lovers* she was not tempted by, but she herself invited them [10]. It is a special and unwonted sin, when woman, forsaking the modesty which God gives her as a defence, becomes the temptress. "Like such a bad woman, luring others to love her, they, forsaking God, to Whom, as by covenant of marriage, they ought to have cleaved, and on Him alone to have depended, sought to make friends of the Assyrian, to help them in their rebellions against Him, and so put themselves to that charge (as sinners usually do) in the service of sin, which in God's service they need not to have been at."

And yet that which God pictures under colors so offensive, what was it in human eyes? The *hire* was presents of gold to powerful nations, whose aid, humanly speaking, Israel needed. But wherever it abandoned its trust in God, it adopted their idols. "Whoever has recourse to human means, without consulting God, or consulting whether He will, or will not bless them, is guilty of unfaithfulness which often leads to many

[1] Orosius App. Ruf. p. 439. Lap. [2] Poc.
[3] Pallas, Reisen iii. p. 511.
[4] See Ker Porter, Travels, i. p. 459. Its Hebrew names פרא and perhaps ערוד are from swiftness.
[5] Ecclus. xiii. 19.
[6] The root in Arabic is the same as that here, ברר, Poc. [7] See in Poc. [8] Job xi. 12.
[9] Gen. xvi. 12. [10] See Ezek. xvi. 33, 4.

Before CHRIST cir. 760.

10 Yea, though they
have hired among the na-
tions, now [p] will I gather
them, and they shall || sor-
row || a little for the burden
of [r] the king of princes.

[q] Ezek. 16. 37.
[p] ch. 10. 10.
|| Or, *begin.*
|| Or, *in a little while*, as Hag. 2. 6.
[r] Isai. 10. 8. Ezek. 26. 7. Dan. 2. 37.

11 Because Ephraim
hath made [s] many altars to
sin, altars shall be unto
him to sin.
12 I have written to him
[t] the great things of my

Before CHRIST cir. 760.

[s] ch. 12. 11.
[t] Deut. 4. 6, 8. Ps. 119. 18. & 147. 19, 20.

others. He becomes accustomed to the tone of mind of those whose protection he seeks, comes insensibly to approve even their errors, loses purity of heart and conscience, sacrifices his light and talents to the service of the powers, under whose shadow he wishes to live under repose."

10. *Yea, though they have hired*, or better, *because* or *when they hire among the heathen, now will I gather them;* i.e. I will gather the nations together. The sin of Israel should bring its own punishment. He sent presents to the king of Assyria, in order to strengthen himself against the will of God; "he thought himself secured by his league made with them; but he should find himself much deceived in his policy;" he had *hired among them* only; *now*, ere long, very speedily, God Himself would *gather them*, i.e. those very nations, not in part, but altogether; not for the help of Israel, but for its destruction. As though a man would let out some water from a deep lake ponded up, the water, as it oozed out, loosened more and more the barriers which withheld it, until, at length, all gave way, and the water of the lake was poured out in one wide wild waste, desolating all, over which it swept. It may be, that Assyria would not have known of, or noticed Israel, had not Israel first invited him.

And they shall sorrow a little for the burden of the king of princes. So great shall be the burden of the captivity hereafter, that they shall then sorrow but little for any burdens put upon them now, and which they now feel so heavy. *The king of princes* is the king of Assyria, who said [1], *Are not my princes altogether kings?* The burden of which they complained will then be the thousand talents of silver which Menahem gave to Pul, king of Assyria, to support him in his usurpation, and in order to pay which, he *exacted the money of Israel, even of all the mighty men of wealth, of each man fifty shekels of silver* [2].

If we adopt the E. M., *begin*, we must render, *and they shall begin to be minished through the burden of the king of the princes*, i. e. they shall be gradually reduced and brought low through the exactions of the Assyrians, until in the end they shall be carried away. This describes the gradual decay of Israel, first through the exactions of Pul, then through the captivity of Gilead by Tiglathpileser.

11. *Because Ephraim hath made many altars to sin, altars shall indeed be unto him to sin*, i.e. they shall be proved to him to be so, by the punishment which they shall draw upon him. The prophet had first shewn them their folly in forsaking God for the help of man; now he shews them the folly of attempting to "secure themselves by their great shew and pretences of religion and devotion in a false way." God had appointed *one* altar at Jerusalem. There He willed the sacrifices to be offered, which He would accept. To multiply altars, much more to set up altars against the one altar, was to multiply sin. Hosea charges Israel elsewhere with this multiplying of altars, as a grievous sin. *According to the multitude of his fruit, he hath increased altars. Their altars are as heaps in the furrows of the field* [3]. They pretended doubtless, that they did it for a religious end, that they might thereon offer sacrifices for the expiation of their sins and appeasing of God. They endeavored to unite their own selfwill and the outward service of God. Therein they might deceive themselves; but they could not deceive God. He calls their act by its true name. To make altars at their own pleasure and to offer sacrifices upon them, under any pretence whatever, was to sin. So then, as many altars as they reared, so often did they repeat their sin; and this sin should be their only fruit. They should be, but only for sin. So God says of the two calves, *This thing became a sin* [4], and of the indiscriminate consecration of Priests (not of the family of Aaron), *This thing became sin unto the house of Jeroboam, even to cut it off and to destroy it from the face of the earth* [5].

12. *I have written to him the great things of My law*, lit. *I write.* Their sin then had no excuse of ignorance. God had written their duties for them in the ten commandments with His own Hand; He had written them of old and *manifoldly* [6], often repeated and in divers manners. He wrote those manifold things *to them* [or *for them*] by Moses, not for that time only, but that they might be con-

[1] Is. x. 8. [2] 2 Kgs xv. 19, 20. [3] x. 1. xii. 11.
[4] 1 Kgs xii. 30. [5] Ib. xiii. 33, 34.
[6] The E. V. translates the Kri, or marginal correction. The meaning is much the same, but the reading of the text, although often more difficult, is almost always right. Here, רבו, "ten thousand things," as we say, "a thousand times," manifoldly, i. e. again and again.

Before CHRIST cir. 760.

law, *but* they were counted
as a strange thing.
13 [u] || They sacrifice flesh
for the sacrifices of mine
offerings, and eat *it*; [x] *but*
the LORD accepteth them
not; [y] now will he remember
their iniquity, and visit
their sins: [z] they shall return
to Egypt.

u Jer. 7. 21. Zech. 7. 6.
|| Or, *In the sacrifices of mine offerings, they, &c.*
x Jer. 14. 10, 12. c. 5. 6. & 9. 4. Amos 5. 22.
y ch. 9. 9. Amos 8, 7.
z Deut. 28. 68. ch. 9, 3, 6. & 11. 5.

tinually before their eyes, as if He were still writing. He had written to them since, in their histories, in the Psalms. His words were still sounding in their ears through the teaching of the prophets. God did not only give His law or revelation once for all, and so leave it. By His providence and by His ministers He continually renewed the knowledge of it, so that those who ignored it, should have no excuse. This ever-renewed agency of God He expresses by the word, *I write*, what in substance was long ago written. What God then wrote, were *the great things of His law* (as the converted Jews, on the day of Pentecost speak of *the great* or *wonderful things of God*[1]) or *the manifold things of His law*, as the Apostle speaks of *the manifold wisdom of God*[2], and says, that [3] *God at sundry times and in divers manners spake in time past unto the fathers by the prophets.*

They were counted as a strange thing by them. These *great*, or *manifold things of God's law*, which ought to have been continually before their eyes, in their mind and in their mouth[4], they, although God had written them for them, *counted as a strange thing*, a thing quite foreign and alien to them, with which they had no concern. Perhaps this was their excuse to themselves, that it was *foreign* to *them.* As Christians say now, that one is not to take God's law so precisely; that the Gospel is not so strict as the law; that men, before the grace of the Gospel, had to be stricter than *with* it; that *the liberty of the Gospel* is freedom, not from sin, but from duty; that such and such things belonged to the early Christians, while they were surrounded by heathen, or to the first times of the Gospel, or to the days when it was persecuted; that riches were dangerous, when people could scarcely have them, not now, when every one has them; that "vice lost half its evil, by losing all its grossness[5];" that the world was perilous, when it was the Christian's open foe, not now, when it would be friends with us, and have us friends with it; that, *love not the world* was a precept for times when the world hated us, not now, when it is all around us, and steals our hearts. So Jeroboam and Israel too doubtless said, that those prohibitions of idolatry were necessary, when the heathen were still in the land, or while their forefathers were just fresh out of Egypt; that it was, after all, God, Who, was worshiped under the calves; that state-policy required it; that Jeroboam was appointed by God, and must needs carry out that appointment, as he best could. With these or the like excuses, he must doubtless have excused himself, as though God's law were good, but *foreign* to *them.* God counts such excuses, not as a plea, but as a sin.

13. *They sacrifice flesh* for *the sacrifices of Mine offerings, and eat* it; but *the Lord accepteth them not.* As they rejected God's law, so God rejected their *sacrifices*, which were not offered according to His law. They, doubtless, thought much of their sacrifices; and this the prophet perhaps expresses by an intensive form[6]; *the sacrifices of My gifts, gifts*, as though they thought, that they were ever giving. God accounted such sacrifices, not being hallowed by the end for which He instituted them, as mere *flesh.* They *offered flesh* and *ate* it. Such was the beginning, and such the only end. *He* would *not accept them.* Nay, contrariwise, *now*, now while they were offering the sacrifices, God would shew in deed that He *remembered* the sins, for which they were intended to atone. God seems to man to forget his sins, when He forbears to punish them; to *remember* them, when He punishes.

They shall return to Egypt. God had commanded them to return no more to Egypt[7] of their own mind. But He had threatened that, on their disobedience, *the Lord would bring them back to Egypt by the way, whereof He spake unto them, Thou shalt see it no more again*[8]. Hosea also foretells to them, that they (i. e. many of them) should go to Egypt and perish there[9]. Thence also, as from Assyria, they were to be restored[10]. Most probably then, Hosea means to threaten an actual return to Egypt, as we are told, that some of the two tribes did go there for refuge, against the express command of God[11]. The main part of the ten tribes were taken to Assyria, yet as they were, even under Hosea, conspiring with Egypt[12], such as could, (it is likely) took refuge there. Else, as future

1 τὰ μεγαλεῖα τοῦ θεοῦ Acts ii. 11.
2 Eph. iii. 10.
3 Heb. i. 1.
4 Deut. vi. 7–9.
5 Burke on the French Revolution.
6 הבהבי is an intensive form from יהב *gave.* See above on iv. 18. The word occurs here only, and was probably made by Hosea.
7 Deut. xvii. 16.
8 Ib xxviii. 68.
9 ch. ix. 3, 6.
10 ch. xii. 11.
11 Jer. xlii. xliii.
12 2 Kgs xvii. 4.

Before CHRIST cir. 760.

a Deut. 32. 18.
b Isai. 29. 23. Eph. 2. 10.
c 1 Kgs. 12. 31.
d Jer. 17. 27. Amos 2. 5.

14 [a] For Israel hath forgotten [b] his Maker, and [c] buildeth temples; and Judah hath multiplied fenced cities; but [d] I will send a fire upon his cities, and it shall devour the palaces thereof.

CHAPTER IX.

The distress and captivity of Israel for their sins and idolatry.

Before CHRIST cir. 760.

REJOICE not, O Israel, for joy, as *other* people; for thou [a] hast gone a whoring from thy God, thou hast loved a [b] reward ‖ upon every cornfloor.

a ch. 4. 12. & 5. 4, 7.
b Jer. 44. 17. ch. 2. 12.
‖ Or, *in, &c.*

deliverance, temporal or spiritual, is foretold under the image of the deliverance out of Egypt, so, contrariwise, the threat, *they shall return to Egypt*, may be, in figure, a cancelling of the covenant, whereby God had promised, that *His* people should not return: a threat of renewed bondage, *like* the Egyptian; an abandonment of them to the state, from which God once had freed them and had made them His people.

14. *For Israel hath forgotten his Maker.* God was his Maker, not only as the Creator of all things, but as the Author of his existence as a people, as He saith[1], *hath He not made thee, and established thee?*

And buildeth temples; as for the two calves, at Bethel and at Dan. Since God had commanded to build one temple only, that at Jerusalem, to *build temples* was in itself sin. The sin charged on Ephraim is idolatry; that of Judah is self-confidence[2]; whence Isaiah blames them, that they were busy in repairing the breaches of the city, and cutting off the supplies of water from the enemy; *but ye have not looked unto the Maker thereof, neither had respect unto Him, that fashioned it long ago*[3]. Jeremiah also says[4], *that they shall impoverish* [or, *crush*] *the fenced cities, wherein thou trustedst, with the sword.*

But I will send a fire upon his cities. In the letter, the words relate to Judah; but in substance, the whole relates to both. Both had forgotten God; both had offended Him. In the doom of others, each sinner may read his own. Of the cities of Judah, Isaiah says, *your country is desolate, your cities are burned with fire*[5] and *in the fourteenth year of Hezekiah,* (some twelve years probably after the death of Hosea) *Sennacherib came up against all the cities of Judah and took them*[6]; and of Jerusalem it is related, that Nebuchadnezzar[7] *burnt the house of the Lord, and the king's house, and all the houses of Jerusalem, and every great man's house he burnt with fire.* Man set them on fire; God brought it to pass; and, in order to teach us that He doeth all things, giving all good, overruling all evil, saith that He was the doer of it.

1 Deut. xxxii. 6. 2 See Introd. p. 5. 3 ch. xxii. 11. 4 ch. v. 17. 5 ch. i. 7. 6 2 Kgs xviii. 13. 7 Ib. xxv. 8, 9.

IX. 1. *Rejoice not, O Israel, for joy, as* other *people.* lit. *rejoice not to exultation,* so as to bound and leap for joy[8]. The prophet seems to come across the people in the midst of their festivity and mirth, and arrests them by abruptly stopping it, telling them, that they had no cause for joy. Hosea witnessed days of Israel's prosperity under Jeroboam II; the land had peace under Menahem after the departure of Pul; Pekah was even strong, so as, in his alliance with Rezin, to be an object of terror to Judah[9], until Tiglath-Pileser came against him. At some of these times, Israel seems to have given himself to exuberant mirth, whether at harvest-time, or on any other ground, enjoying the present, secure for the future. On this rejoicing Hosea breaks in with his stern, *rejoice not.* "[10] *In His Presence is fulness of joy,* true, solid, lasting joy." How then could Israel joy, *who had gone a whoring from his God?* Other nations might joy; for they had no imminent judgment to fear. Their sins had been sins of ignorance; none had sinned like Israel. They had not even [11] *changed their gods, which were no gods. If* other *people* did not thank God for His gifts, and thanked their idols, they had not been taught otherwise. Israel had been taught, and so his sin was sin against light. Whence God says by Amos[12], *You only have I known of all the families of the earth; therefore I will punish you for all your iniquities.* "[13] It was ever the sin of Israel to wish to joy as other nations. So they said to Samuel, *make us a king to judge us, like all the nations.* And when Samuel *told the people the word of God, they have rejected Me that I should not reign over them,* they still said, *Nay, but we will have a king over us, that we may be like all the nations*[14]. This was the joy of the nations, to have another king than God, and with this joy Israel wished to exult, when it asked for Saul as king; when it followed Jeroboam; when it *denied* Christ *before the presence of Pilate, saying, we have no king but Cæsar.* But the people who received the law, and professed the worship of God, might not exult as other people who had not

8 as in Job iii. 22. 9 Is. vii. 10 Ps. xvi. 11. 11 Jer. ii. 11. 12 iii. 2. 13 Rup. 14 1 Sam. viii. 5, 10, 7, 19, 20.

Before CHRIST cir. 760.

2 [c] The floor and the
‖ winepress shall not feed
them, and the new wine
shall fail in her.
3 They shall not dwell
in [d] the LORD's land; [e] but
Ephraim shall return to
Egypt, and [f] they shall
eat unclean *things* [g] in
Assyria.

[c] ch. 2. 9, 12.
‖ Or, *winefat.*
[d] Lev. 25. 23. Jer. 2. 7. & 16. 18.
[e] ch. 8. 13, & 11. 5. Not in Egypt itself, but into another bondage as bad as that.
[f] Ezek. 4. 13. Dan. 1. 8.
[g] 2 Kgs. 17. 6. ch. 11. 11.

the knowledge of God, that, like them, it should, after forsaking God, be allowed to enjoy temporal prosperity, like theirs. He says, *rejoice not like the nations*, viz. for it is not allowed thee. Why? *for thou hast gone a whoring from thy God.* The punishment of the adulteress, who departs by unfaithfulness from her husband, is other than that of the harlot, who had never plighted her faith, nor had ever been bound by the bond of marriage. Thou obtainedst God for thy Husband, and didst forsake Him for another, yea, for many others, in the desert, in Samaria, even in Jerusalem, for the golden calves, for Baal, and the other monstrous gods, and lastly, when, denying Christ, thou didst prefer Barabbas. *Rejoice not* then, with the *joy* of the *nations;* for the curses of the law, written against thee, allow thee not. [1] *Cursed shalt thou be in the city, cursed in the field; cursed thy basket and thy store; cursed shall be the fruit of thy body, and the fruit of thy land; the increase of thy kine and the flocks of thy sheep; cursed thou in thy coming in, and cursed thou in thy going out.* Other nations enjoyed the fruit of their own labors; thou *tookest the labors* of others as a hire, *to observe His laws* [2]."

Thou hast loved a reward [lit. *the hire* [3] of a harlot] *on every corn-floor.* Israel had no heart, except for temporal prosperity. This he loved, wheresoever he found it; and so, *on every corn-floor*, whereon the fruits of the earth were gathered for the threshing, he received it from his idols, as the *hire*, for which he praised them "for the good things which he had received from a better Giver." "[4] Perverse love! Thou oughtest to *love* God to use His rewards. *Thou lovedst the reward*, despisedst God. So then thou *wentest a whoring from thy God*, because thou didst turn away the love, wherewith thou oughtest to love God, to love the hire: and this not sparingly, nor any how, but *on every barn-floor*, with avarice so boundless and so deep, that all the barn-floors could not satisfy thee." The first-fruits, and the free-will-offering, they retained, turned them away from the service of God, and offered them to their idols.

2. *The floor and winepress shall not feed them.* God turneth away wholly from the adulterous people, and telleth others, how justly they shall be dealt with for this. "Because she loved My reward, and despised Myself, the reward itself shall be taken away from her." When the blessings of God have been abused to sin, He, in mercy and judgment, takes them away. He cut them off, in order to shew that He alone, Who now withheld them, had before given them. When they thought themselves most secure, when the corn was stored on the floor, and the grapes were in the press, then God would deprive them of them.

And the new wine shall fail in her, or *shall fail her*, lit. *shall lie to her.* It may be, he would say, that as Israel had lied to his God, and had *spoken lies against Him* [5], so, in requital, the fruits of the earth should disappoint her, and holding out hopes which never came to pass, should, as it were, lie to her, and in the bitterness of her disappointment, represent to her her own failure to her God. The prophet teaches through the workings of nature, and gives, as it were, a tongue to them [6].

3. *They shall not dwell in the Lord's land. The earth is the Lord's and the fulness thereof.* Yet He had chosen the land of Canaan, there to place His people; there, above others, to work His miracles; there to reveal Himself; there to send His Son to take our flesh. He had put Israel in possession of it, to hold it under Him on condition of obedience. Contrariwise, God had denounced to them again and again; [7] *if thine heart turn away, so that thou wilt not hear, but shalt be drawn away, ye shall not prolong your days upon the land, whither thou passest over Jordan to possess it.* The fifth commandment, [8] *the first commandment with promise*, still implies the same condition, *that thy days may be long in the land which the Lord thy God giveth thee.* God makes the express reserve that the land is His. *The land shall not be sold for ever; for the land is Mine; for ye are strangers and sojourners with Me* [9]. It was then an aggravation of their sin, that they had sinned in God's land. It was to sin in His special

[1] Deut. xxviii. 16–19.
[2] Ps. cv. 45.
[3] ii. 12. viii. 9. Ezek. xxi. 31, 34. Mic. i. 7.
[4] Rup
[5] vii. 13.
[6] The fact that Greek or Latin poets use the same language without any moral reference, is no reason why there should be none such in a prophet's. *They* spoke the language of earthly disappointment; *he* declares the judgment of God.
[7] Deut. xxx. 17, 18.
[8] Eph. v. 2.
[9] Lev. xxv. 23.

Before CHRIST cir. 760.

4 [h] They shall not offer
wine *offerings* to the LORD,
[i] neither shall they be pleasing unto him: [k] their sacrifices *shall be* unto them as
the bread of mourners; all
that eat thereof shall be
polluted: for their bread

[h] ch. 3. 4.
[i] Jer. 6. 20. ch. 8. 13.
[k] Deut. 26. 14.

Presence. To offer its first-fruits to idols, was to disown God as its Lord, and to own His adversary. In removing them, then, from His land, God removed them from occasions of sin.

But Ephraim shall return to Egypt. He had broken the covenant, whereon God had promised, that they should not return there [1]. They had recourse to Egypt against the Will of God. Against their own will, they should be sent back there, in banishment and distress, as of old, and in separation from their God.

And they shall eat unclean things in Assyria. So in Ezekiel, [2] *The children of Israel shall eat their defiled bread among the Gentiles, whither I will drive them. Not to eat things common or unclean* was one of the marks which God had given them, whereby he distinguished them as His people. While God owned them as His people, He would protect them against such necessity. The histories of Daniel, of Eleazar and the Maccabees [3], shew how sorely pious Jews felt the compulsion to eat things unclean. Yet this doubtless Israel had done in his own land, if not in other ways, at least in eating things offered to idols. Now then, through necessity or constraint, they were to be forced, for their sustenance, to eat things unclean, such as were, to them, all things killed with the blood in them, i. e. as almost all things are killed now. They who had wilfully transgressed God's law, should now be forced to live in the habitual breach of that law, in a matter which placed them on a level with the heathen. People, who have no scruple about breaking God's moral law, feel keenly the removal of any distinction, which places them above others. They had been as heathen; they should be in the condition of heathen.

4. *They shall not offer wine-offerings to the Lord.* The *wine* or *drink-offering* was annexed to all their burnt-offerings, and so to all their public sacrifices. The burnt-offering (and with it the meal and the wine-offering,) was *the* daily morning and evening sacrifice [4], and the sacrifice of the Sabbath [5]. It was offered, together with the sin-offering, on the first of the month, the Passover, the feast of the first-fruits, of trumpets, of tabernacles, and the Day of Atonement, besides the special sacrifices of that day [6]. It entered also into private life [7]. The drink-offering accompanied also the peace-offering [8]. As the burnt-offering, on which the offerer laid his hand [9], and which was wholly consumed by the sacred fire which at first fell from heaven, expressed the entire self-devotion of the offerer, that he owed himself wholly to his God; and as the peace-offering was the expression of thankfulness, which was at peace with God; so the outpouring of the wine betokened the joy, which accompanies that entire self-oblation, that thankfulness in self-oblation of a soul accepted by God. In denying, then, that Israel should *offer wine-offerings*, the prophet says, that all the joy of their service of God, nay all their public service should cease. As he had before said, that they should be *for many days without sacrifice* [10], so now, he says, in fact, that they should live without the prescribed means of pleading to God the Atonement to come. Whence he adds,

Neither shall they be pleasing to the Lord; for they should no longer have the means prescribed for reconciliation with God [11]. Such is the state of Israel now. God appointed one way of reconciliation with Himself, the Sacrifice of Christ. Sacrifice pictured this, and pleaded it to Him, from the fall until Christ Himself *appeared, once in the end of the world, to put away sin by the sacrifice of Himself* [12]. Soon after, when time had been given to the Jews to learn to acknowledge Him, all bloody sacrifices ceased. Since then the Jews have lived without that means of reconciliation, which God appointed. It availed, not in itself, but as being appointed by God to foreshadow and plead that one sacrifice. So He Who, by our poverty and void, awakens in us the longing for Himself, would through the anomalous condition, to which He has, by the orderings of His Divine Providence, brought His former people, call forth in them that sense of need, which would bring them to Christ. In their half-obedience, they remain under the ceremonial law which He gave them, although He called them, and still calls them, to exchange the shadow for the substance in Christ. But in that they cannot fulfill the requirements of the law, even in its outward form, the law, which

1 See ab. on viii. 13. 2 iv. 13.
3 Dan. i. 8. 2 Macc. vi. vii.
4 Ex. xxix. 38–41. Nu. xxviii. 3–8. 5 Ib. 9.
6 Ib. 11, 15, 16, 19, 22, 26, 7, 30. xxix. 11, 1. 2, 5, 7, 8, 12–38. 7 Lev. i. Nu. xv. 3, 10.
8 Nu. xv. 8, 10. 9 Lev. i. 4. 10 iii. 4.

11 The word יערבו *shall be pleasing* is most naturally understood of the persons of whom it had just been said, *they shall not offer*, not of the *wine:* for this is the object, not the subject; and is in the singular, not the plural.
12 Heb. ix. 26.

Before CHRIST cir. 760.

[l]for their soul shall not
come into the house of the
LORD.
5 What will ye do in
[m]the solemn day, and in
the day of the feast of the
LORD?
6 For, lo, they are gone
because of † destruction:
[n]Egypt shall gather them
up, Memphis shall bury
them: ‖ † the pleasant
places for their silver, [o]net-
tles shall possess them: †
thorns *shall be* in their
tabernacles.

[l] Lev. 17. 11.
[m] ch. 2. 11.
† Heb. *spoil.*
[n] ch. 7. 16. ver. 3.
‖ Or, *their silver shall be desired, the nettle, &c.*
† Heb. *the desire.*
[o] Is. 5, 6. & 32. 13. & 34. 13. ch. 10. 8.

they acknowledge, bears witness to them, that they are not living according to the mind of God.

Their sacrifices shall be *unto them as the bread of mourners.* He had said that they should not sacrifice to God, when no longer in the Lord's land. He adds that, if they should attempt it, their sacrifices, so far from being a means of acceptance, should be defiled, and a source of defilement to them. *All* which was *in* the same *tent* or house with a dead body, was *unclean for seven days*[1]. The bread, which they ate then, was defiled. If *one unclean by a dead body touched bread or pottage or any meat, it* was *unclean*[2]. In offering the tithes, a man was commanded to declare, *I have not eaten of it in my mourning*[3]. So would God impress on the soul the awfulness of death, and man's sinfulness, of which death is the punishment. He does not say, that they would offer sacrifices, but that their sacrifices, if offered as God did not command, would defile, not atone. It is in human nature, to neglect to serve God, when He wills it, and then to attempt to serve Him when He forbids it. Thus Israel, affrighted by the report of the spies[4], would not go up to the promised land, when God commanded it. When God had sentenced them, not to go up, but to die in the wilderness, *then* they attempted it. Sacrifice, according to God's law, could only be offered in the promised land. In their captivity, then, it would be a fresh sin.

For their bread for their soul, or *is for their soul*, i. e. *for themselves;* it is for whatever use they can make of it for this life's needs, to support life. Nothing of it would be admitted *into the house of the Lord*, as offered to Him or accepted by Him.

5. *What will ye do in the solemn day?* Man is content to remain far from God, so that God do not shew him, that He has withdrawn Himself from him. Man would fain have the power of drawing near to God in time of calamity, or when he himself likes. He would fain have God at his command, as it were, not be at the command of God. God cuts off this hope altogether. He singles out the great festivals, which commemorated His great doings for His people, as though they had no more share in those mercies. The more solemn the day, the more total man's exclusion, the more manifest God's withdrawal. To one shut out from His service, the days of deepest religious joy became the days of deepest sorrow. Mirth is turned into heaviness. To be deprived of the ordinary daily sacrifice was a source of continual sorrow; how much more, *in the days of* their *gladness*[5], in which they were bidden to rejoice before the Lord, and "in which they seemed to have a nearer and more familiar access to God." True, that having separated themselves from the Temple, they had no right to celebrate these feasts, which were to be held in the place *which God had chosen to place His name there.* Man, however, clings to the shadow of God's service, when he has parted with the substance. And so God foretold them before[6], that He would *make all their mirth to cease.*

6. *For lo, they are gone because of destruction.* They had fled, for fear of destruction, to destruction. For fear of the destruction from Assyria, they were fled away and gone to Egypt, hoping, doubtless, to find there some temporary refuge, until the Assyrian invasion should have swept by. But, as befalls those who flee from God, they fell into more certain destruction.

Egypt shall gather them up, Memphis shall bury them. They had fled singly, in making their escape from the Assyrian. Egypt shall receive them, and shall gather them together, but only to one common burial, so that none should escape. So Jeremiah says[7], *They shall not be gathered nor buried; and* Ezekiel[8], *Thou shalt not be brought together, nor gathered. Memphis* is the Greek name for the Egyptian *Mamphta*, whence the Hebrew *Moph*[9]; or *Manuph*, whence the Hebrew *Noph*[10]. It was at this time the capital of Egypt, whose idols God threatens[11]. Its name, "the dwelling of Phta," the Greek Vulcan, marked it, as a

[1] Nu. xix. 14.
[2] Hagg. ii. 12, 13.
[3] Deut. xxvi. 15.
[4] Nu. xiv.
[5] Num. x. 10.
[6] ch. ii. 11.
[7] viii. 2.
[8] xxix. 5.
[9] here.
[10] Is. xix. 13. Jer. ii. 16. xliv. 1. xlvi. 14. Ezek. xxx. 13 sqq.
[11] Ezek. l. c.

Before CHRIST cir. 760.

7 The days of visitation are come, the days of recompence are come; Israel shall know *it:* the prophet *is* a fool, [p] the † spiritual man *is* mad, for the multitude of thine iniquity, and the great hatred.

p Ezek. 13. 3, &c. Mic. 2. 11. Zeph. 3. 4.
† Heb. *man of the spirit.*

---

seat of idolatry; and in it was the celebrated court of Apis [1], the original of Jeroboam's calf. There in the home of the idol for whom they forsook their God, they should be gathered to burial. It was reputed to be the burial-place of Osiris, and hence was a favorite burial-place of the Egyptians. It once embraced a circuit of almost 19 miles [2], with magnificent buildings; it declined after the building of Alexandria; its very ruins gradually perished, after Cairo rose in its neighborhood.

The pleasant places *for their silver, nettles shall possess them.* The E. M. gives the same sense in different words; *their silver shall be desired;* (as Obadiah saith [3], *his hidden* treasures *were searched out) nettles shall inherit them.* In either way, it is a picture of utter desolation. The long rank grass or the nettle, waving amid man's habitations, looks all the sadder, as betokening that man once was there, and is gone. The desolate house looks like the grave of the departed. According to either rendering, the silver which they once had treasured, was gone. As they had *inherited* and *driven* out (the word is one) the nations, whose land God had given them, so now nettles and thorns should *inherit them.* These should be the only tenants of their treasure-houses and their dwellings.

7. *The days of visitation are come.* The false prophets had continually hood-winked the people, promising them that those days would never come. *They had put far away the evil day* [4]. Now it was not at hand only. In God's purpose, those *days* were *come,* irresistible, inevitable, inextricable; days in which God would visit, what in His long-suffering, He seemed to overlook, and would *recompense* each *according to his works.*

Israel shall know it. Israel would not know by believing it; now it should *know,* by feeling it.

The prophet is *a fool, the spiritual man* is *mad.* The true Prophet gives to the false the title which they claimed for themselves, *the prophet* and *the man of the spirit.* Only the event shewed what spirit was in them, not the spirit of God but a lying spirit. The men of the world called the true prophets, *mad,* lit. maddened, *driven mad* [5], as Festus thought of S. Paul [6]; *Thou art beside thyself; much learning doth make thee mad.* Jehu's captains called by the same name the young prophet whom Elisha sent to anoint him. *Wherefore came this mad fellow unto thee* [7]? Shemaiah, the false prophet, who deposed God's priest, set false priests to *be officers in the house of the Lord,* to have an oversight as to *every man who is mad and maketh himself a prophet,* calling Jeremiah both a false prophet and a *madman* [8]. The event was the test. Of our Lord Himself, the Jews blasphemed, *He hath a devil and is mad* [9]. And long afterward, "madness," "phrensy" were among the names which the heathen gave to the faith in Christ [10]. As S. Paul says, that *Christ crucified* was *to the Greeks* and to *them that perish, foolishness,* and that *the things of the Spirit of God, are foolishness to the natural man, neither can he know* them, *because they are spiritually discerned* [11]. The man of the world and the Christian judge of the same things by clean contrary rules, use them for quite contrary ends. The slave of pleasure counts him mad, who foregoes it; the wealthy trader counts him mad, who gives away profusely. In these days, profusion for the love of Christ has been counted a ground for depriving a man of the care of his property. One or the other *is* mad. And worldlings must count the Christian mad; else they must own themselves to be so most fearfully. In the Day of Judgment, Wisdom says [12], *They, repenting and groaning for anguish of spirit, shall say within themselves, This was he whom we had sometimes in derision and a proverb of reproach. We fools counted his life madness, and his end to be without honor. How is he numbered among the children of God, and his lot is among the saints!*

For the multitude of thine iniquity and the great hatred. The words stand at the close of the verse, as the reason of all which had gone before. Their *manifold iniquity* and their *great hatred* of God were the ground why *the days of visitation* and *recompense* should *come.* They were the ground also, why God allowed such prophets to delude them. The words, *the great hatred,* stand quite undefined, so that they may signify alike the hatred of Ephraim against God and good men and His true prophets, or God's hatred of them. Yet it,

1 Herod. ii. 153.
2 Diod. Sic. i. 51.
3 ver. 6.
4 Am. vi. 3.
5 The form מְשֻׁגָּע in passive. It is used of one driven to distraction through distress, (Deut. xxviii. 34,) and of loss of reason, 1 Sam. xxi. 16.
6 Acts xxvi. 24.
7 2 Kings ix. 11.
8 Jer. xxix. 25, 6. The word is the same.
9 S. John x. 20.
10 See Tertul. Apol. 1. p. 4. and on de Test. An. p. 136. not. s. t. Oxf. Tr.
11 1 Cor. i. 18, 23. ii. 14.
12 Wisd. v. 3–6.

Before CHRIST cir. 760.

8 The [q] watchman of Ephraim *was* with my God: but the prophet *is* a snare of a fowler in all his ways *and* hatred || in the house of his God.

[q] Jer. 6. 17. & 31. 6. Ezek. 3. 17. & 33. 7.

|| Or, *against*.

most likely, means, *their* great hatred, since of them the Prophet uses it again in the next verse. The sinner first neglects God; then, as the will of God is brought before him, he wilfully disobeys Him; then, when, he finds God's Will irreconcilably at variance with his own, or when God chastens him, he hates Him, and (the Prophet speaks out plainly) *hates* Him *greatly*.

8. *The watchman of Ephraim* was *with my God.* These words may well contrast the office of the true prophet with the false. For Israel had had many true prophets, and such was Hosea himself now. The true prophet was at all times *with God.* He was *with God,* as holpen by God, *watching* or looking out and on into the future by the help of God. He was *with God,* as walking with God in a constant sense of His Presence, and in continual communion with Him. He was *with God,* as associated by God with Himself, in teaching, warning, correcting, exhorting His people, as the Apostle says[1], *we then as workers together* with *Him.*

It might also be rendered in nearly the same sense, *Ephraim was a watchman with my God,* and this is more according to the Hebrew words[2]. As though the whole people of Israel had an office from God, "[3] and God addressed it as a whole, 'I made thee, as it were, a watchman and prophet of God to the neighboring nations, that through My Providence concerning thee, and thy living according to the law, they too might receive the knowledge of Me. But thou hast acted altogether contrary to this, for thou hast become a snare to them.'"

Yet perhaps, if so construed, it would rather mean, "Ephraim is a watchman, beside my God," as it is said, [4] *There is none upon earth, that I desire with Thee,* i. e. beside Thee. In God the Psalmist had all, and desired to have nothing *with,* i. e. beside God. Ephraim was not content with God's revelations, but would himself be *a seer, an espier* of future events, the Prophet says with indignation, *together with my God.* God, in fact, sufficed Ephraim not. Ahab hated God's prophet, because *he did not speak good concerning him but evil*[5]. And so the kings of Israel had court-prophets of their own, an establishment, as it would seem, of four hundred and fifty prophets of Baal, and four hundred prophets of Ashtaroth[6], which was filled up again by new impostors[7], when after the miracle of Mount Carmel, Elijah, according to the law[8], put to death the prophets of Baal. These false prophets, as well as those of Judah in her evil days, flattered the kings who supported them, misled them, encouraged them in disbelieving the threatenings of God, and so led to their destruction. By these means, the bad priests maintained their hold over the people. They were the Anti-Christs of the Old Testament, disputing the authority of God, in Whose Name they prophesied. Ephraim encouraged their sins, as God says of Judah by Jeremiah, *My people love to have it so*[9]. It willed to be deceived, and was so.

"On searching diligently ancient histories," says S. Jerome, "I could not find that any divided the Church, or seduced people from the house of the Lord, except those who have been set by God as priests and prophets, i. e. watchmen. These then are turned into a snare, setting a stumbling-block everywhere, so that whosoever entereth on their ways, falls, and cannot stand in Christ, and is led away by various errors and crooked paths to a precipice." "No one," says another great father[10], "doth wider injury than one who acteth perversely, while he hath a name or an order of holiness." "God endureth no greater prejudice from any than from priests, when He seeth those whom He has set for the correction of others, give from themselves examples of perverseness, when *we* sin, who ought to restrain sin.—What shall become of the flock, when the pastors become wolves?"

The false *prophet* is *the snare of a fowler in* (lit. *upon*) *all his ways;* i. e. whatever Ephraim would do, wherever the people, as a whole or any of them, would go, there the false prophet beset them, endeavoring to make each and everything a means of holding them back from their God. This they did, *being hatred in the house of his God.* As one says[11]. *I am* (all) *prayer,* because he was so given up to prayer that he seemed turned into prayer; his whole soul was concentrated in prayer; so of these it is said, *they* were *hatred.* They hated so intensely, that their whole soul was turned into hatred; they were as we say, hatred personified; hatred was embodied in them, and they ensouled with hate. They were also the source of hatred against God

[1] 2 Cor. vi. 1.
[2] צֹפֶה not being in construction with Ephraim.
[3] Theod.
[4] Ps. lxxiii. 25.
[5] 1 Kgs. xxii. 8, 18.
[6] Ib. xviii. 19.
[7] 2 Kgs. iii. 13. x. 19.
[8] Deut. xiii. 5. xvii. 5.
[9] v. 31.
[10] S. Greg. Past. i. 2; in Evang. Hom. xvii. 14.
[11] Ps. cix. 4.

Before CHRIST cir. 760.

9 [r]They have deeply
corrupted *themselves*, as in
the days of [s]Gibeah: [t]*there-*
fore he will remember their
iniquity, he will visit their
sins.

10 I found Israel like
grapes in the wilderness; I
saw your fathers as [u]the
first-ripe in the fig tree [x]at
her first time: *but* they
went to [y]Baal-peor, and
[z]separated themselves [a]un-
to *that* shame; [b]and *their*
abominations were accord-
ing as they loved.

r Isai. 31. 6. ch. 10. 9.
s Judg. 19. 22.
t ch. 8. 13.

u Isai. 28. 4. Mic. 7. 1.
x See chap. 2. 15.
y Num. 25. 3. Ps. 106. 28.
z ch. 4. 14.
a Jer. 11. 13. See Judg. 6. 32.
b Ps. 81. 12. Ezek. 20. 8. Amos 4. 5.

---

and man. And this each false prophet was *in the house of his God!* for God was still his God, although not owned by him as God. God is the sinner's God to avenge, if he will not allow Him to be his God, to convert and pardon.

9. *They have deeply corrupted* themselves; lit. *they have gone deep, they are corrupted.* They have deeply immersed themselves in wickedness; have gone to the greatest depth they could, in it; they are sunk in it, so that they could hardly be extricated from it; and this, of their own deliberate intent; they contrived it deeply, hiding themselves, as they hoped, from God.

As in the days of Gibeah, when Benjamin espoused the cause of *the children of Belial* who had wrought such horrible brutishness in Gibeah towards the concubine of the Levite. This they maintained with such obstinacy, that, through God's judgment, the whole tribe perished, except six hundred men. Deeply they must have already corrupted themselves, who supported such guilt. Such corruption and such obstinacy was their's still.

Therefore *he will remember their iniquity.* God seemed for a time, as if He overlooked the guilt of Benjamin in the days of Gibeah; for at first He allowed them to be even victorious over Israel, yet in the end, they were punished, almost to extermination, and Gibeah was destroyed. So now, although He bore long with Ephraim, He would, in the end shew that He remembered all by visiting all.

10. *I found Israel like grapes in the wilderness.* God is not said to find anything, as though *He* had lost it, or knew not where it was, or came suddenly upon it, not expecting it. *They* were lost, as relates to Him, when they were found by Him. As our Lord says of the returned prodigal, *This my son was lost and is found*[1]. He *found* them and made them pleasant in His own sight, "as grapes which a man finds unexpectedly, in *a great terrible wilderness of fiery serpents and drought*[2]," where commonly nothing pleasant or refreshing grows; or *as the first ripe in the fig-tree at her fresh time,* whose sweetness passed into a proverb, both from its own freshness and from the long abstinence[3]. God gave to Israel both richness and pleasantness in His own sight; but Israel, from the first, corrupted God's good gifts in them. This generation only did as their fathers. So S. Stephen, setting forth to the Jews how their fathers had rebelled against Moses, and persecuted the prophets, sums up; *as your fathers did, so do ye*[4]. Each generation was filling up the measure of their fathers, until it was full; as the whole world is doing now[5].

But *they went to Baal-Peor. They,* the word is emphatic; these same persons to whom God shewed such love, to whom He gave such gifts, *went.* They left God Who called them, and *went* to the idol, which could not call them. Baal-Peor, as his name probably implies, was "the filthiest and foulest of the heathen gods." It appears from the history of the daughters of Midian, that his worship consisted in deeds of shame[6].

And separated themselves unto that *shame,* i. e. to Baal-Peor, whose name of *Baal, Lord,* he turns into *Bosheth, shame*[7]. Holy Scripture gives disgraceful names to the idols, (as *abominations, nothings, dungy things, vanities, uncleanness*[8],) in order to make men ashamed of them. *To this shame they separated themselves* from God, in order to unite themselves with it. The Nazarite *separated himself from* certain earthly enjoyments, and consecrated himself, for a time or altogether, to *God*[9]; these *separated themselves from* God, and united, devoted, consecrated themselves *to shame.* "They made themselves, as it were, Nazarites to shame." Shame was the object of their worship and their God, *and their abominations were according as they loved,* i. e. they had as many *abominations* or abominable idols, *as* they had *loves.* They multiplied

---

1 S. Luke xv. 32.
2 Deut. viii. 15.
3 See Is. xxviii. 4.
4 Acts vii. 51.
5 Rev. xiv. 15.
6 Num. xxv.
7 as in 2 Sam. xi. 21.
8 הבלים, גלולים אלילים, שקוצים all common names of idols; (also, און,) נדה 2 Chr. xxix. 5.
9 הנזר ל Num. vi. 2, 5, 6. מן Ib. 3. See on Am. ii. 11.

Before CHRIST cir. 760.

11 *As for* Ephraim, their
glory shall fly away like a
bird, from the birth, and
from the womb, and from
the conception.
12 [c] Though they bring

Before CHRIST cir. 760.

[c] Job 27. 14.

abominations, *after their heart's desire;* their abominations were manifold, because their passions were so; and their love being corrupted, they loved nothing but abominations. Yet it seems simpler and truer to render it, *and they became abominations, like their loves;* as the Psalmist says, [1] *They that make them are like unto them.* "[2] The object which the will desires and loves, transfuses its own goodness or badness into it." Man first makes his god like his own corrupt self, or to some corruption in himself, and then, worshiping this ideal of his own, he becomes the more corrupt through copying that corruption. He makes his god *in his* own *image and likeness*, the essence and concentration of his own bad passions, and then conforms himself to the likeness, not of God, but of what was most evil in himself. Thus the Heathen made gods of lust, cruelty, thirst for war; and the worship of corrupt gods reacted on themselves. They forgot that they were *the work of their own hands*, the conception of their own minds, and professed to "do gladly [3]" "what so great gods" had done.

And more widely, says a father [4], "what a man's love is, that he is. Lovest thou earth? thou art earth. Lovest thou God? What shall I say? thou shalt be god." "[5] Naught else maketh good or evil actions, save good or evil affections." Love has a transforming power over the soul, which the intellect has not. "He who serveth an abomination is himself an abomination [6]," is a thoughtful Jewish saying. "The intellect brings home to the soul the knowledge on which it worketh, impresses it on itself, incorporates it with itself. Love is an impulse whereby he who loves is borne forth towards that which he loves, is united with it, and is transformed into it." Thus in explaining the words, *Let Him kiss me with the kisses of* His *Mouth* [7], the fathers say, "[8] Then the Word of God kisseth us, when He enlighteneth our heart with the Spirit of Divine knowledge, and the soul cleaveth to Him and His Spirit is transfused into him."

11. As for *Ephraim, their glory shall fly away, like a bird.* Ephraim had parted with God, his true Glory. In turn, God would quickly take from him all created glory, all which he counted glory, or in which he gloried. When man parts with the substance, his true honor, God takes away the shadow, lest he should content himself therewith, and not see his shame, and, boasting himself to be something, abide in his nothingness and poverty and shame to which he had reduced himself. *Fruitfulness*, and consequent strength, had been God's especial promise to Ephraim. His name, Ephraim, contained in itself the promise of his future fruitfulness [9]. With this Jacob had blessed him. He was to be greater than Manasseh, his elder brother, *and his seed shall become a multitude of nations* [10]. Moses had assigned to him *tens of thousands* [11], while to Manasseh he had promised *thousands* only. On this blessing Ephraim had presumed, and had made it to feed his pride; so now God, in his justice and mercy, would withdraw it from him. It should *make* itself *wings, and fly away* [12], with the swiftness of a bird, and *like a bird*, not to return again to the place, whence it has been scared.

From the birth. Their children were to perish at every stage in which they received life. This sentence pursued them back to the very beginning of life. First, when their parents should have joy in *their birth*, they were to come into the world only to go out of it; then, their mother's womb was to be itself their grave; then, stricken with barrenness, the womb itself was to refuse to conceive them.

"[13] The glory of Ephraim passes away, from the birth, the womb, the conception, when the mind which before was, for glory, half-deified, receives, through the just judgment of God, ill report for good report, misery for glory, hatred for favor, contempt for reverence, loss for gain, famine for abundance. Act is the *birth*; intention the *womb*; thought the *conception*. *The glory of Ephraim* then *flies away from the birth, the womb, the conception*, when, in those who before did outwardly live nobly, and gloried in themselves for the outward propriety of their life, the acts are disgraced, the intention corrupted, the thoughts defiled."

12. *Though they bring up children.* God had threatened to deprive them of children, in every stage before or at their birth. Now, beyond this, he tells them, as to those who should escape this sentence, he would bereave them of them, or make them childless.

That there shall *not* be a *man* left; lit. *from man.* The brief word may be filled up, as the E. V. has done, (by an idiom not infrequent) 1) "*from* there *being a man;*" or

[1] Ps. cxv. 8. [2] Lap. from Aq. [3] Ter. Eun.
[4] S. Aug. in Ep. S. Joh. Tr. ii.
[5] S. Aug. Ep. 155. ad Macedon. § 13. amores, mores; amours, mœurs.
[6] Kimchi, MS. in Poc. [7] Cant. i. 2.
[8] S. Ambr. de Isaac. c. 3. Lap. [9] Gen. xli. 52.
[10] Ib. xlviii. 19. [11] Deut. xxxiii. 17.
[12] Prov. xxiii. 5. [13] Julian. Tolet. in Nah. Lap.

Before CHRIST cir. 760.

up their children, yet [d] will I bereave them, *that there shall* not *be* a man *left:* yea, [e] woe also to them when I [f] depart from them!

[d] Deut. 28.41, 62.
[e] Deut. 31. 17. 2 Kgs. 17. 18. ch. 5. 6.
[f] See 1 Sam. 28. 15, 16.

13 Ephraim, [g] as I saw Tyrus, *is* planted in a pleasant place: [h] but Ephraim shall bring forth his children to the murderer.

[g] See Ezek. 26, & 27, & 28.
[h] ver. 16. ch. 13. 16.

2) *from* among *men;* as Samuel said to Agag [1], *as thy sword has made women childless, so shall thy mother be childless among women;* or 3) *from* becoming *men,* i. e. from reaching man's estate. The Prophet, in any case, does not mean absolute excision, for he says, *they shall be wanderers among the nations,* and had foretold, that they should abide, as they now are, and be converted in the end. But since their pride was in their numbers, he says, that these should be reduced in every stage from conception to ripened manhood. So God had forewarned Israel in the law [2], *If thou wilt not observe to do all the words of this law,—ye shall be left few in number, whereas ye were as the stars of heaven for multitude.* A sentence, felt the more by Ephraim, as being the head of the most powerful division of the people, and himself the largest portion of it.

Yea, [lit. *for*] *woe also unto them, when I depart from them.* This is, at once, the ground and the completion of their misery, its beginning and its end. God's departure was the source of all evil to them; as He foretold them [3], *I will forsake them, and I will hide My face from them, and they shall be devoured, and many evils and troubles shall befall them, so that they shall say in that day, Are not these evils come upon us, because our God is not among us?* But His departure was itself above all. For the Prophet says *also; for woe also unto them.* This was the last step in the scale of misery. Beyond the loss of the children, whom they hoped or longed for, beyond the loss of their present might, and all their hope to come, there is a further undefined, unlimited, evil, *woe to them also,* when God should *withdraw,* not His care and Providence only, but Himself also from them; *when I depart from them.* They had *departed* and turned away, from or *against* God [4]. It had been their characteristic [5]. Now God Himself would requite them, as they had requited Him. He would depart from them. This is the last state of privation, which forms the "punishment of loss" in Hell. When the soul has lost God, what has it?

13. *Ephraim, as I saw Tyrus, is planted in a pleasant place;* or (better) *as I saw* (her) *towards Tyre,* or *as I saw as to Tyre.* Ephraim stretched out, in her dependent tribes, *towards* or *to* Tyre itself. Like to Tyrus she was, "in her riches, her glory, her pleasantness, her strength, her pride," and in the end, her fall. The picture is that of a fair tree, not chance-sown, but *planted* carefully by hand in a pleasant place [6]. Beauty and strength were blended in her. On the tribe of Joseph especially, Moses had pronounced the blessing [7]; *Blessed of the Lord be his land, for the precious things of heaven, for the dew, and for the deep which coucheth beneath, and for the precious fruits brought forth by the sun, and for the precious things put forth by the moons* (*i. e.* month by month) *and for the chief things of the ancient mountains, and for the precious things of the lasting hills and for the precious things of the earth and the fulness thereof, and for the good pleasure of Him who dwelt in the bush.* Beautiful are the mountains of Ephraim, and the rich valleys or plains which break them. And chief in beauty and in strength was the valley, whose central hill its capital, Samaria, crowned; *the crown of pride* to the *drunkards of Ephraim, whose glorious beauty is a fading flower which is on the head of the fat valleys of them that are overcome with wine* [8]. The blessing of Moses pointed perhaps to the time when Shiloh was the tabernacle of Him, Who once dwelt and revealed Himself in the Bush. Now that it had exchanged its God for the calves, the blessings which it still retained, stood but in the more awful contrast with its future.

But Ephraim shall bring forth his children to the murderer; lit. *and Ephraim is to bring forth &c.* i. e. proud though her wealth, and high her state, pleasantly situated and firmly rooted, one thing lay before her, one destiny, she *was to bring forth children* only *for the murderer.* Childlessness in God's Providence is the appropriate and frequent punishment of sins of the flesh. Pride too brought Peninnah, the adversary of Hannah, low, even as to that which was the ground of her pride, her children. [9] *The barren hath born seven, and she that hath many children is waxed feeble.* So as to the soul, "pride deprives of grace."

[1] 1 Sam. xv. 33. מנשים; as here מאדם. add Prov. xxx. 14. [2] Deut. xxviii. 58, 62. [3] Ib. xxxi. 17.

[4] See on vii. 13.

[5] Hos. iv. 16. The word in each place, is virtually the same, סור, written here שור, and סיר.

[6] שתל is always used of *planting* with choice of situation. See Ezek. xvii. 8, 22, 23. xix. 10 and in a bad soil, of set purpose, Ib. 13. See Jer. xvii. 8. Ps. i. 3. and in a figure, *They who are planted in the house of the Lord,* Ps. xcii. 14.

[7] Deut. xxxiii. 13–16. [8] Is. xxviii. 1.

[9] 1 Sam. ii. 5.

Before CHRIST cir. 760.

14 Give them, O LORD:
what wilt thou give? give
them[l] a †miscarrying
womb and dry breasts.
15 All their wickedness
[k]*is* in Gilgal: for there I
hated them: [l]for the wickedness of their doings I will
drive them out of mine
house, I will love them no
more: [m]all their princes
are revolters.
16 Ephraim is smitten,
their root is dried up, they

[l] Luke 23. 29.
† Heb. *that casteth the fruit.*
[k] ch. 4. 15. & 12. 11.
[l] ch. 1. 6.
[m] Is. 1. 23.

14. *Give them a miscarrying womb.* The Prophet prays for Israel, and debates with himself what he can ask for, amid this their determined wickedness, and God's judgments. Since *Ephraim* was *to bring forth children to the murderer*, then it was mercy to ask for them, that they might have no children. Since such are the evils which await their children, grant them, O Lord, as a blessing, the sorrows of barrenness. What God had before pronounced as a punishment, should, as compared to other evils, be a mercy, and an object of prayer. So our Lord pronounces as to the destruction of Jerusalem[1]. *Behold the days are coming, in which they shall say, Blessed are the barren, and the wombs that never bare, and the paps that never gave suck.* "O unhappy fruitfulness and fruitful unhappiness, compared with which, barrenness, which among them was accounted a curse, became blessedness."

15. *All their wickedness is in Gilgal. Gilgal*, having been the scene of so many of God's mercies, had been, on that very ground, chosen as a popular scene for idol-worship[2]. And doubtless, Ephraim still deceived himself, and thought that his idolatrous worship, in a place once so hallowed, would still be acceptable with God. "There, where God of old was propitious, He would be so still, and whatever they did, should, even for the place's sake, be accepted; the hallowed place would necessarily sanctify it." In answer to such thoughts, God says, *all their wickedness*, the very chief and sum, the head from which the rest flowed, their desertion of God Himself, whatever they hoped or imagined, *all their wickedness is* there.

For there I hated them. "*There*, in the very place where heretofore I shewed such great tokens of love to, and by My gracious presence with, them, *even there I have hated them* and now hate them." "He saith not, there was I angry, or displeased with them, but in a word betokening the greatest indignation, *I hated them.* Great must needs be that wickedness which provoked the Father of mercies to so great displeasure as to say, that He *hated them;* and severe must needs be those judgments which are as effects of hatred and utter aversation of them, in Him."

For the wickedness of their doings. The sin of Israel was no common sin, not a sin of ignorance, but against the full light. Each word betokens evil. The word *doings* expresses *great bold doings.* It was *the wickedness of their wicked works*, a deeper depth of wickedness in their wickedness, an essence of wickedness, for which, God saith, *I will drive them out of My house*, i. e. as before, out of His whole land[3].

I will love them no more. So He saith, in the beginning[4]; *I will have no more mercy upon the house of Israel, but I will utterly take them away.* "[5]This was a national judgment, and so involved the whole of them, as to their outward condition, which they enjoyed as members of that nation, and making up one body politic. It did not respect the spiritual condition of single persons, and their relation, in this respect, to God." As individuals, they were, "not cut off from God's favor and tokens of His love, nor from the power of becoming members of Christ, whenever any of them should come to Him. It only struck them for ever out of that *house of the Lord* from which they were then driven," or from hopes that that kingdom should be restored, which God said, He would cause to cease.

All their princes are revolters. Their case then was utterly hopeless. No one of their kings *departed from the sin of Jeroboam who made Israel to sin.* The political power which should protect goodness, became the fountain of corruption. "[6]None is there, to rebuke them that offend, to recall those that err; no one who, by his own goodness, and virtue, pacifying God, can turn away His wrath, as there was in the time of Moses." "[7]Askest thou, why God cast them out of His house, why they were not received in the Church or the house of God? He saith to them, because they *are all revolters, departers*, i.e. because, before they were cast out visibly in the body, they departed in mind, were far away in heart, and therefore were cast out in the body also, and lost, what alone they loved, the temporal advantages of the house of God."

16. *Ephraim is smitten.* The Prophet, under the image of a tree, repeats the same sentence of God upon Israel. The word *smitten* is used of the smiting of the tree from above, especially by the visitation of God, as by *blasting* and *mildew*[8]. Yet such smiting, although it

[1] S. Luke xxiii. 29. [2] ab. iv. 15. [3] See ab. viii. 1. [4] i. 6. [5] Poc. [6] S. Cyr. [7] Rup. [8] Am. iv. 9.

Before CHRIST cir. 760.

shall bear no fruit: yea, [n] though they bring forth, yet will I slay *even* † the beloved *fruit* of their womb.

n ver. 13.
† Heb. *the desires*.
Ezek. 24. 21.

17 My God will cast them away, because they did not hearken unto him: and they shall be [o] wanderers among the nations.

Before CHRIST cir. 760.

o Deut. 28. 64, 65.

falls heavily for the time, leaves hope for the future. He adds then, *their root is* also *withered*, so that *they should bear no fruit;* or if, perchance, while the root was still drying up and not quite dead, any fruit be yet found, *yet will I slay*, God says, *the beloved*, fruit *of their womb*, the desired fruit of their bodies, that which their souls longed for. "[1] So long as they have children, and multiply the fruit of the womb, they think that they bear fruit, they deem not that *their root is dried*, or that they have been severed by the axe of excision, and *rooted out of the land of the living;* but, in the anguish at the *slaying* of those they most loved, they shall say, better had it been to have had no children."

17. *My God hath cast them away. My God* (he saith) as if God were *his* God only who clave to him, not their's who had, by their disobedience, departed from Him. *My God.* "He had then authority from Him," Whom he owned and Who owned *him*, and Who bade him so speak, as though God were *his* God, and no longer their's. God *casts them away*, lit. *despises them*, and so rejects them as an object of aversion to Him, *because they did not hearken to him.* "God never forsakes unless He be first forsaken." When they would not hearken, neither doing what God commanded, nor abstaining from what He forbade, God at last rejected them, as worthless, wanting altogether to that end for which He created them.

And they shall be wanderers among the nations. This was the sentence of Cain[2]; a *fugitive and a vagabond shalt thou be in the earth.* So God had forewarned them[3]. *The Lord shall scatter thee among all people, from the one end of the earth even unto the other end of the earth—and among these nations shalt thou find no ease, neither shall the sole of thy foot have rest.*

The words of the Prophet imply an abiding condition. He does not say, *they shall wander*, but, *they shall be wanderers*[4]. Such was to be their lot; such has been their lot ever since; and such was not the ordinary lot of those large populations whom Eastern conquerors transported from their own land. Those conquerors took away with them into their own land, portions of the people whom they conquered, for two ends. When a people often rebelled, they were placed where they could rebel no more, among tribes more powerful than they, and obedient to the rule of the conqueror. Or they were carried off, as slaves to work in bricks, like Israel in Egypt[5]. Their workmen, smiths, artificers, were especially taken to labor on those gigantic works, the palaces and temples of Nineveh or Babylon. But, for both these purposes, the transported population had a settled abode allotted to it, whether in the capital or the provinces. Sometimes new cities or villages were built for the settlers[6]. Israel at first was so located. Perhaps on account of the frequent rebellions of their kings, the ten tribes were placed amid a wild, warlike, population, *in the cities of the Medes*[7]. When the interior of Asia was less known, people thought that they were still to be found there. The Jews fabled, that the ten tribes lay behind some mighty and fabulous river, Sambatyon[8], or were fenced in by mountains[9]. Christians thought that they might be found in some yet unexplored part of Asia. Undeceived as to this, they still asked whether the Afghans, or the Yezides, or the natives of North America were the ten tribes, or whether they were the Nestorians of Kurdistan. So natural did it seem, that they, like other nations so transported, should remain as a body, near or at the places, where they had been located by their conquerors. The Prophet says otherwise. He says their abiding condition shall be, *they shall be wanderers among the nations*, wanderers among them, but no part of them. Before the final dispersion of the Jews at the destruction of Jerusalem,

[1] Rup. [2] Gen. iv. 12. The word נוד or נדד occurs in both. [3] Deut. xxviii. 64, 5.
[4] Not ידדו, but יהיו נודדים בגוים.
[5] This appears both from the sculptures of Nineveh in which multitudes of workmen, of countenance and form distinct from the Assyrians, are represented as working in chains, and from the inscriptions of the kings. "I [Sennacherib] carried off into captivity a great number of workmen. All the young active men of Chaldæa and Aramea, Manna, &c. who had refused to submit to my government, I carried them all away, to make bricks for me." (Bellino Cylinder in Fox Talbot's Assyr. Texts. p. 9.) "I carried them off as slaves, and compelled them to make bricks for me." (Cyl. of Esarhad. Ib. p. 17.) "By the labor of foreign slaves, my captives, who lifted up their hands in the name of the great gods, my lords, I built thirty temples in Assyria and in—" (Ib. p. 16.)
[6] "A city I built. City of Esarhaddon I called it. Men who were—, natives of the land of [Caramania?] and of the sea of the rising sun, in that city I caused to dwell. I appointed my secretaries to be magistrates over them." (Cyl. of Esarh. Ib. p. 11. et al.)
[7] 2 Kings xvii. 6. [8] Jon. in Ex. xxxiv. 14.
[9] Peritsol Orchot Olam. c. 4. 9. quoted by Basnage, Hist. d. Juifs. vi. 3. 3.

Before CHRIST cir. 740.

CHAPTER X.

Israel is reproved and threatened for their impiety and idolatry.

ISRAEL *is* [a] || an empty vine, he bringeth forth fruit unto himself: according to the multitude of his fruit [b] he hath increased the altars; according to the goodness of his land [c] they have made goodly † images.

[a] Nah. 2. 2.
|| Or, *a vine emptying the fruit which it giveth.*

Before CHRIST cir. 740.

[b] ch. 8. 11. & 12. 11.
[c] ch. 8. 4.
† Heb. *statues, or, standing images.*

"the Jewish race," Josephus says [1], "was in great numbers through the whole world, interspersed with the nations." Those assembled at the day of Pentecost had come from all parts of Asia Minor but also from Parthia, Media, Persia, Mesopotamia, Arabia, Egypt, maritime Lybia, Crete, and Italy [2]. Wherever the Apostles went, in Asia or Greece, they found Jews, in numbers sufficient to raise persecution against them. S. James writes to those whom, with a word corresponding to that of Hosea, he calls, "the dispersion." *James—to the twelve in the dispersion* [3]. The Jews, scoffing, asked, whether our Lord would go to *the dispersion among the Greeks* [4]. They speak of it, as a body, over against themselves, to whom they supposed that He meant to go, to teach them, when He said, *Ye shall seek Me and shall not find Me.* The Jews of Egypt were probably the descendants of those who went thither, after the murder of Gedaliah. The Jews of the North, as well as those of China, India, Russia, were probably descendants of the ten tribes. From one end of Asia to the other and onward through the Crimea, Greece and Italy, the Jews by their presence, bare witness to the fulfillment of the prophecy. Not like the wandering Indian tribe, who spread over Europe, living apart in their native wildness, but settled, among the inhabitants of each city, they were still distinct, although with no polity of their own; a distinct, settled, yet foreign and subordinate race. "[5] Still remains unreversed this irrevocable sentence, as to their temporal state and face of an earthly kingdom, that they remain still *wanderers* or dispersed among other nations, and have never been restored, nor are in likelihood of ever being restored to their own land, so as to call it their own. If ever any of them hath returned thither, it hath been but as strangers, and all, as to any propriety that they should challenge in it, to hear the ruins and waste heaps of their ancient cities to echo in their ears the Prophet's words, [6] *Arise ye and depart, for this is not your rest;* your ancestors polluted it, and ye shall never return as a people thither, to inhabit it, as in your former condition."

"Meanwhile Ephraim here is an example, not only to particular persons, that as they will avoid personal judgments, so they take care faithfully to serve God and hearken unto Him; but to nations and kingdoms also, that as they will prevent national judgments, so they take care that God be truly served, and the true religion maintained in purity and sincerity among them. Ephraim, or Israel, held their land by as good and firm tenure as any people in the world can theirs, having it settled on them by immediate gift from Him Who is the Lord of the whole earth, Who promised it to their forefathers, Abraham and his seed for ever [7], called therefore the land which the Lord sware unto them [8]; and which He had promised them [9], the land of Promise [10]. Who could have greater right to a place, better and firmer right, than they had to the Lord's land, by *His* promise which never fails, and *His* oath Who will not repent, confirmed to them? Certainly, if they had observed conditions and kept covenant with Him, all the people in the world could never have driven them out, or dispossessed them of it. But, seeing they revolted and brake His covenant, and did not hearken to Him, He would not suffer them longer to dwell in it, but drave and cast them out of it, so that they could never recover it again, but continue to this day *wandering among the nations,* having no settled place of their own, nowhere where they can be called a people, or are for such owned. If God so dealt with Israel on their disobedience and departing from His service, to whom He had so particularly engaged himself to make good to them the firm possession of that land; how shall any presume on any right or title to any other, or think to preserve it to themselves by any force or strength of their own, if they revolt from Him, and cast off thankful obedience to Him? The Apostle cautioneth and teacheth us so to argue, *if God spared not the natural branches, take heed lest He also spare not thee,* and therefore warneth, *be not high-minded,* and presumptuous, *but fear* [11]."

X. 1. *Israel is an empty vine,* or, in the same sense, *a luxuriant vine;* lit. *one which poureth out,* poureth itself out into leaves, abundant in switches, (as most old versions explain it,) luxuriant in leaves, emptying itself in them,

[1] de B. J. vii. 33.
[2] Acts ii. 9–11.
[3] ἐν τῇ διασπορᾷ. S. James i. 1.
[4] διασποράν. S. John vii. 35.
[5] Poc.
[6] Mic. ii. 10.
[7] Gen. xiii. 14. 15. Deut. xxxiv. 4.
[8] Num. xiv.
[9] Deut. ix. 28.
[10] Heb. xi. 9.
[11] Rom. xi. 20, 21.

Before CHRIST cir. 740.

2 ‖ Their heart is [d] divided; now shall they be found faulty: he shall † break down their altars, he shall spoil their images.

‖ Or, *He hath divided their heart.* [d] 1 Kgs. 18. 21. Matt. 6. 24.

Before CHRIST cir. 740.

† Heb. *behead.*

---

and empty of fruit; like the fig-tree, which our Lord cursed. For the more a fruit tree putteth out its strength in leaves and branches, the less and the worst fruit it beareth. "[1] The juices which it ought to transmute into wine, it disperseth in the ambitious idle shew of leaves and branches." The sap in the vine is an emblem of His Holy Spirit, through Whom alone we can bear fruit. *His grace which was in me,* says St. Paul, *was not in vain.* It is in vain to us, when we waste the stirrings of God's Spirit in feelings, aspirations, longings, transports, "which bloom their hour and fade[2]." Like the leaves, these feelings aid in maturing fruit; when there are leaves only, the tree is barren and *nigh unto cursing, whose end is to be burned*[3].

It bringeth forth fruit for itself, lit. *setteth fruit to,* or *on itself.* Luxuriant in leaves, its fruit becomes worthless, and is from itself to itself. It is uncultured; (for Israel refused culture,) pouring itself out, as it willed, in what it willed. It had a rich shew of leaves, a shew also of fruit, but not for the Lord of the vineyard, since they came to no size or ripeness. Yet to the superficial glance, it was rich, prosperous, healthy, abundant in all things, as was the outward state of Israel under Jehoash and Jeroboam II.

According to the multitude of his fruit, or more strictly, *as his fruit was multiplied, he multiplied altars; as his land was made good, they made goodly their images.* The more of outward prosperity God bestowed upon them, the more they abused His gifts, referring them to their idols; the more God lavished His mercies on them, the more profuse they were in adoring their idols. The superabundance of God's goodness became the occasion of the superabundance of their wickedness. They rivalled and competed with, and outdid the goodness of God, so that He could bestow upon them no good, which they did not turn to evil. Men think this strange. Strange it is, as is all perversion of God's goodness; yet so it is now. Men's sins are either the abuse of what God gives, or rebellion, because He withholds. In the sins of prosperity, wealth, health, strength, powers of mind, wit, men sin in a way in which they could not sin, unless God continually supplied them with those gifts which they turn to sin. The more God gives, the more opportunity and ability they have to sin, and the more they sin. They are *evil,* not only in despite of God's goodness, but *because* He is *good.*

2. *Their heart is divided* between God and their idols, in that they would not wholly part with either, as Elijah upbraided them[4], *How long halt ye between the two opinions?* When the heathen, by whom the king of Assyria replaced them, had been taught by one of the priests whom the king sent back, in order to avert God's judgments, they still propagated this division. Like Jeroboam, [5] *they became fearers of the Lord,* His worshipers, *and made to themselves out of their whole number* (i. e. indiscriminately) *priests of the high places. They were fearers of the Lord, and they were servers of their gods, according to the manner of the nations whom they carried away from thence.—These nations were fearers of the Lord, and they were servers of their idols, both their children and their children's children. As did their fathers, so do they unto this day.* This divided allegiance was their hereditary worship. These heathen, as taught by one of the priests of Israel, added the service of God to that of their idols, as Israel had added the service of the idols to that of God. But God rejecteth such half service; whence he adds, *now,* in a brief time, all but come, *they shall be found faulty,* lit. *they shall be guilty,* shall be convicted of guilt and shall bear it. They thought to *serve at once God and Mammon;* but, in truth, they served their idols only, whom they would not part with for God. God Himself then would turn away all their worship, bad, and, as they thought, good. *He,* from Whom their heart was divided, He Himself, by His mighty power which no man can gain-say, *shall break down their altars,* lit. shall *behead* them. As they out of His gifts multiplied their altars and slew their sacrifices upon them against His will, so now should the altars themselves be demolished; and *the images* which they had decked with the gold which He had given, should, on account of that very gold, tempt the spoiler, through whom God would spoil them.

He shall break down. He Himself[6]. The word is emphatic. "[7] God willeth not that, when the merited vengeance of God is inflicted through man, it should be ascribed to man. Yea, if any one ascribeth to himself what, by permission of God, he hath power to do against the people of God, he draweth down on him the displeasure of God, and, at

[1] S. Jer. [2] Lyra Apost. N. 67. [3] Heb. vi. 8.
[4] 1 Kings xviii. 21.
[5] 2 Kgs. xvii. 32, 33, 41. The form היו יראים את יי expresses that they were habitual worshipers of God.
[6] הוא. [7] Rup.

Before CHRIST cir. 740.

3 [e] For now they shall
say, We have no king, be-
cause we feared not the
LORD; what then should a
king do to us?
4 They have spoken
words, swearing falsely in
making a covenant: thus
judgment springeth up [f] as
hemlock in the furrows of
the field.
5 The inhabitants of Sa-
maria shall fear because of
[g] the calves of [h] Beth-aven:
for the people thereof shall
mourn over it, and ‖ the
priests thereof *that* rejoiced
on it, [i] for the glory thereof,

e ch. 3. 4. & 11. 5. Mic. 4. 9. ver. 7.
f See Deut. 29. 18. Amos 5. 7. & 6. 12. Acts 8. 23. Heb. 12. 15.
g 1 Kgs. 12. 28. 29. ch. 8. 5, 6.
h ch. 4. 15.
‖ Or, *Chemarim*, 2 Kgs. 23. 5. Zeph. 1. 4.
i 1 Sam. 4. 21. 22. ch. 9. 11.

times, on that very ground, can hurt the less[1]." The prophet then says very earnestly, *He Himself shall break*, meaning us to understand, not the lofty hand of the enemy, but that the Lord Himself did all these things.

3. *For now they shall say, we have no king.* These are the words of despair, not of repentance; of men terrified by the consciousness of guilt, but not coming forth out of its darkness; describing their condition, not confessing the iniquity which brought it on them. In sin, all Israel had asked for a king, when the Lord was their king; in sin, Ephraim had made Jeroboam king; in sin, their subsequent kings were made, without the counsel and advice of God; and now as the close of all, they reflect how fruitless it all was. They had a king, and yet, as it were, they had no king, since, God being angry with them, he had no strength to deliver them. And now, without love, the memory of their evil deeds crushes them beyond hope of remedy. They groan for their losses, their sufferings, their fears, but do not repent. Such is the remorse of the damned. All which they had is lost; and what availed it now, since, when they had it, they feared not God?

4. *They have spoken words.* The words which they spoke were eminently *words;* they were mere *words*, which had no substance; *swearing falsely in making a covenant*, lit. *swearing falsely, making a covenant, and judgment springeth up as hemlock in the furrows of the field.* "[2] There is no truth in words, no sanctity in oaths, no faithfulness in keeping covenants, no justice in giving judgments." Such is the result of all their oaths and covenants, that *judgment springeth up*, yea, flourisheth; but, what judgment? Judgment, bitter and poisonous as hemlock, flourishes, as hemlock would flourish on ground broken up and prepared for it. They break up the ground, make the *furrows*. They will not have any chance self-sown seed; they prepare the soil for harvest, full, abundant, regular, cleared of all besides. And what harvest? Not any wholesome plant, but poison. They cultivate injustice and wickedness, as if these were to be the fruits to be rendered to God from His own land. So Amos says[3], *Ye have turned judgment into gall* or *wormwood*, and Habakkuk, *Judgment went forth perverted*[4].

5. *The inhabitants of Samaria shall fear because of* [i. e. *for*] *the calves of Beth-aven.* He calls them in this place *cow-calves*[5], perhaps to denote their weakness and helplessness. So far from their idol being able to help *them*, *they* shall be anxious and troubled for their idols, lest these should be taken captive from them. The *Bethel* (*House of God*) of the Patriarch Jacob, was now turned into *Beth-aven, the house of vanity.* This, from its old sacred memories, was a more celebrated place of the calf-worship than Dan. Hosea then gives to the calf of Bethel its precedence, and ranks both idols under its one name, as *calves of the house of vanity.*

For the people thereof shall mourn over it. They had set up the idols, instead of God; so God calls them no longer His people, but *the people of the calf* whom they had chosen for their god; as Moab was called [6] *the people of Chemosh*, its idol. They had joyed in it, not in God; now they, *its people* and its priests, should *mourn over* it, when unable to help itself, much less, them. Both their joy and their sorrow shewed that they were without excuse, that they had *gone willingly after the king's commandment*, serving it of their own free-will out of love, not out of fear of the king, and, neither out of love or fear, serving God purely.

For the glory thereof, because it is departed from it. The true glory of Israel was God; the Glory of God is in Himself. *The glory of the calves*, for whom Ephraim had exchanged their God, was something quite outward to them, the gold of which they were made, and the rich offerings made to them. Both together became an occasion of their being carried captive. They mourned, not because they had offended God by their sin, but for the loss of that dumb idol, whose

[1] See Deut. xxxii. 26, 7. Is. x. 5 sqq. [2] Osorius.

[3] vi. 12. v. 7. [4] i. 4. [5] עגלות. [6] Num. xxi. 29.

Before CHRIST cir. 740.

because it is departed from
it.

6 It shall be also car-
ried unto Assyria *for* a
present to [k]king Jareb:
Ephraim shall receive
shame, and Israel shall
be ashamed [l]of his own
counsel.

7 [m]*As for* Samaria, her
king is cut off as the foam
upon † the water.

k ch. 5. 13.

l ch. 11. 6.

m ver. 3, 15.

† Heb. *the face of the water.*

worship had been their sin, and which had brought these heavy woes upon them. Impenitent even under chastisement! The Prophet does not mention any grief for "the despoiling of their country, the burning of their cities, the slaughter of their people, their shame[1]." One only thing he names as moving them. Even then their one chief anxiety was, not that God was departed from them, but that their calf in which they had set their *glory*, whereupon they so franticly relied, on which they had lavished their substance, their national distinction and disgrace, was gone. Without the grace of God men mourn, not their sins, but their idols.

6. *It shall be also carried;* [i. e. *Itself*[2] *also shall be carried.*] Not Israel only shall be carried into captivity, but its god also. The victory over a nation was accounted of old a victory over its gods, as indeed it shewed their impotence. Hence the excuse made by the captains of Benhadad, that the *gods of Israel* were *gods of the hills, and not gods of the valleys*[3], and God's vindication of His own Almightiness, which was thus denied. Hence also the boast of Sennacherib by Rabshakeh, [4] *have any of the gods of the nations delivered at all his land out of the hand of the king of Assyria? Where are the gods of Hamath and of Arpad? where are the gods of Sepharvaim, Hena, and Ivah? have they delivered Samaria out of mine hand? Who are they among all the gods of the countries,* [5]*that have delivered their country out of mine hand, that the Lord should deliver Jerusalem out of mine hand?* When God then, for the sin of His people, gave them into the hand of their enemies, He vindicated His own glory, first by avenging any insult offered to His worship, as in the capture of the ark by the Philistines, or Belshazzar's insolent and drunken abuse of the vessels of the temple; or by vindicating His servants, as in the case of Daniel and the three children, or by chastening pride, as in Nebuchadnezzar, and explaining and pointing His chastisement through His servant Daniel, or by prophecy, as of Cyrus by Isaiah and Daniel. To His own people, His chastisements were the vindication of His glory which they had dishonored, and the close of the long strife between the true prophets and the false. The captivity of the calf ended its worship, and was its final disgrace. The destruction of the temple and the captivity of its vessels and of God's people ended, not the worship, but the idolatries of Judah, and extended among their captors, and their captors' captors, the Medes and Persians, the knowledge of the One true God.

Unto Assyria, for a present to king Jareb or *to a hostile* or *strifeful*[6] *king.* Perhaps the name *Jareb* designates the Assyrian by that which was a characteristic of their empire, love of *strife.* The history of their kings, as given by themselves in the newly-found inscriptions, is one warfare. To that same king, to whom they sent for aid in their weakness, from whom they hoped for help, and whom God named as what He knew and willed him to be to them, *hostile, strifeful,* and *an avenger,* should the object of their idolatry be carried in triumph[7]. They had trusted in the calf and in the Assyrians. The Assyrian, to whom they looked as the protector of their liberties, was to carry away their other trust, their god[1].

Ephraim shall receive shame. This shall be all his gain; this his purchase; this he had obtained for himself by his pride and wilfulness and idolatry and ambition and wars: this is the end of all, as it is of all pursuits apart from God; this he *shall receive* from the Giver of all good, *shame. And Israel shall be ashamed of his own counsel.* Ephraim's special *counsel* was that which Jeroboam *took* with the most worldly-wise of his people, a counsel which admirably served their immediate end, the establishment of a kingdom, separate from that of Judah. It was acutely devised; it seemed to answer its end for 230 years, so that Israel, until the latter part of the reign of Pekah, was strong, Judah, in comparison, weak. But it was *the sin wherewith he made Israel to sin,* and for which God scattered him among the heathen. His wisdom became his destruction and his shame. The policy which was to establish his family and his kingdom, destroyed his own family in the next generation, and ultimately, his people, not by its failure, but by its success.

7. *Her king is cut off like foam* (or, more

[1] from Osor. [2] The *itself,* אתו, is emphatic.
[3] 1 Kgs. xx. 23, 28.
[4] 2 Kgs. xviii. 33-35. add. xix. 10-13.
[5] Num. xxi. 29. [6] See ab. v. 13.

[7] יובל is used of solemn stately processions, as of a royal bride, Ps. xlv. 15, 16; or a burial, Job x. 19. xxi. 30, 32. and so of the lengthened train of presents, Ps. lxviii. 30.

Before CHRIST cir. 740.

n ch. 4. 15.
o Deut. 9. 21. 1 Kgs. 12. 30.
p ch. 9. 6.

8 [n] The high places also of Aven, [o] the sin of Israel, shall be destroyed: [p] the thorn and the thistle shall come up on their altars; [q] and they shall say to the mountains, Cover us; and to the hills, Fall on us.

Before CHRIST cir. 740.

q Is. 2. 19. Luke 33. 30. Rev. 6. 16. & 9. 6.

probably, [1] *a straw*) *on the* [lit. *face of the*] *water*. A bubble, or one of those little shreds which float in countless numbers on the surface of the water, give the same image of lightness, emptiness, worthlessness, a thing too light to sink, but driven impetuously, and unresistingly, hither and thither, at the impulse of the torrent which hurries it along. Such was the king, whom Israel had set in the highest place, in whom it had trusted, instead of God. So easily was Hoshea, their last king, swept away by the flood, which broke in on Ephraim, from Assyria. Piety is the only solidity; apart from piety all is emptiness.

8. *The high places of Aven*, i.e. of vanity or iniquity. He had before called *Bethel*, *house of God*, by the name of *Bethaven*, *house of vanity;* now he calls it *Aven*, *vanity* or *iniquity*, as being the concentration of those qualities. Bethel was situated on a *hill*, the *mount of Bethel*, and, from different sides, people were said to *go up* [2] to it. *The high place* often means the shrine, or *the house of the high places*. Jeroboam had built such at Bethel [3]; many such already existed in his time, so that, *whoever would, he consecrated* as their *priests* [4]. The high-place or shrine, is accordingly said to be *built* [5], *broken down and burnt* [6]. At times, they were tents, and so said to be *woven* [7], *made* of *garments* of *divers colors* [8]. The calf then, probably, became a centre of idolatry; many such *idol-shrines* were formed around it, on its mount, until Bethel became a metropolis of idolatry. This was *the sin of Israel*, as being the source of all its sins.

The thorn and the thistle shall come up upon their altars. This pictures, not only the desolation of the place, as before [9], but the forced cessation of idolatry. Fire destroys, down to the root, all vegetable life which it has once touched. The thorn, once blackened by fire, puts out no fresh shoot. But now, these idol fires having been put out for ever, from amid the crevices of the broken altars, *thorn and thistle* [10] should grow freely as in a fallow soil. Where the victims aforetime *went up* [11], or were offered, now the wild briars and thistles alone should *go up*, and wave freely in undisputed possession. Ephraim had *multiplied altars*, as God multiplied their *goods;* now their altars should be but monuments of the defeat of idolatry. They remained, but only as the grave-stones of the idols, once worshiped there.

They shall say to the mountains, cover us. Samaria and Bethel, the seats of the idolatry and of the kingdom of Israel, themselves both on heights, had both, near them, mountains higher than themselves. Such was to Bethel, the mountain on the East, where Abraham built an altar to the Lord [12]; Samaria was encircled by them. Both were probably scenes of their idolatries; from both, the miseries of the dwellers of Bethel and Samaria could be seen. Samaria especially was in the centre of a sort of amphitheatre; itself, the spectacle. No help should those high places now bring to them in their need. The high hills round Samaria, when the tide of war had filled the valley around it, hemmed them in, the more hopelessly. There was no way, either to break through or to escape. The narrow passes, which might have been held, as flood gates against the enemy, would then be held against them. One only service could it seem, that their mountains could then render, to destroy them. So should they be freed from evils worse than the death of the body, and escape the gaze of men upon their misery. "They shall wish rather to die, than to see what will bring death." "They shall say to the mountains on which they worshiped idols, fall on us, and anticipate the cruelty of the Assyrians and the extreme misery of captivity." Nature abhors annihilation; man shrinks from the violent marring of his outward form; he clings, however debased, to the form which God gave him. What misery, then, when men long for, what their inmost being shrinks from!

The words of the Prophet become a sort of proverbial saying for misery, which longs for death rather than life. The destruction of Samaria was the type of the destruction of Jerusalem by the Romans, and of every other final excision, when the measure of iniquity was filled, and there was neither

[1] From the use of קצפה "shredding," Joel i. 7. and the Arab.
[2] Josh. xvi. 1. 1 Sam. xiii. 2. ab. iv. 13. Gen. xxxv. 1. Judg. i. 22. 1 Sam. x. 3. 2 Kgs. ii. 23.
[3] 1 Kgs. xii. 31. [4] Ib. xiii. 32, 33. [5] Ib. xi. 7.
[6] 2 Kgs. xxiii. 15. [7] Ib.7.
[8] Ezek. xvi. 16. [9] ch. ix. 6.
[10] These same two plants are named together in the cursing of the ground for Adam's sin (Gen. iii. 18.) and there alone does the word, translated *thistle*, occur. Hosea, probably, was using the words of Genesis, in that, as a sort of proverb, he joins these two, out of sixteen names of the class of plant which occur in the Old Testament.
[11] עלה (whence עֹלָה *whole burnt offering*, lit. that which *goeth up*) is also a sacrificial term.
[12] Gen. xii. 8.

Before CHRIST cir. 740.

9 [r] O Israel, thou hast
sinned from the days of
Gibeah: there they stood:
[s] the battle in Gibeah
against the children of iniquity did not overtake
them.

[r] ch. 9. 9.
[s] See Judg. 20.

10 [t] *It is* in my desire
that I should chastise them;
and [u] the people shall be
gathered against them,
‖ when they shall bind
themselves in their two furrows.

[t] Deut. 28. 63.
[u] Jer. 16. 16. Ezek. 23. 46, 47. ch. 8. 10.
‖ Or, *when I shall bind them for their two transgressions, or, in their two habitations.*

hope nor remedy. This was the characteristic of the destruction of Samaria. They had been God's people; they were to be so no more. This was the characteristic of the destruction of Jerusalem, not by the Babylonians, after which it was restored, but by the Romans, when they had rejected Christ, and prayed, *His Blood be on us and on our children.* So will it be in the end of the world. Hence our Lord uses the words [1], to forewarn of the miseries of the destruction of Jerusalem, when the Jews hid themselves in caves for fear of the Romans [2]; and S. John uses them to picture man's despair at the end of the world [3]. "I dread" says S. Bernard [4], "the gnawing worm, and the living death. I dread to fall into the hands of a living death, and a dying life. This is *the second death*, which never out-killeth, yet which ever killeth. How would they long to die once, that they may not die for ever! *They who say to the mountains, fall on us, and to the hills, cover us,* what do they will, but, by the aid of death, either to escape or to end death? *They shall seek death, but shall not find it, and shall desire to die, and death shall flee from them,* saith S. John [5]."

9. *O Israel, thou hast sinned from the days of Gibeah.* There must have been great sin, on both sides, of Israel as well as Benjamin, when Israel punished the atrocity of Gibeah, since God caused Israel so to be smitten before Benjamin. Such sin had continued ever since, so that, although God, in His long-suffering, had hitherto spared them, "it was not of late only that they had deserved those judgments, although now at last only, God inflicted them." *There* in Gibeah, *they stood.* Although smitten twice at Gibeah, and heavily chastened, *there* they were avengers of the sacredness of God's law, and, in the end, *they stood; chastened but not killed.* But *now,* none of the ten tribes took the side of God. Neither zeal for God, nor the greatness of the guilt, nor fear of judgment, nor the peril of utter ruin, induced any to set themselves against sin so great. The sin devised by one, diffused among the many, was burnt and branded into them, so that they never parted with it [6]. *The battle in Gibeah against the children of iniquity did not overtake them,* i. e. it did not overtake them then, but it shall overtake them now. Or if we render, (as is more probable,) *shall not overtake them,* it will mean, not a battle like that in Gibeah, terrible as that was, *shall* now *overtake them;* but one far worse. For, although the tribe of Benjamin was then reduced to six hundred men, yet the tribe still survived and flourished again; now the kingdom of the ten tribes, and the name of Ephraim, should be utterly blotted out.

10. *It is in My desire that I should chastise them.* God *doth not afflict willingly, nor grieve the children of men* [7]. Grievous then must be the cause of punishment, when God not only chastens men, but, so to speak, longs to chasten them, when He chastens them without any let or hindrance from His mercy. Yet so God had said [8]; *It shall come to pass, that as the Lord rejoiced over you to do you good and to multiply you, so the Lord will rejoice over you to destroy you and to bring you to nought.* God willed to enforce His justice, with no reserve whatever from His mercy. His whole mind, so to speak, is to punish them. God is "without passions." Yet, in order to impress on us the truth, that one day there will, to some, be *judgment without mercy* [9], He speaks as one, whose longing could not be satisfied, until the punishment were executed. So He says [10], *I will ease Me of Mine adversaries;* [11] *Mine anger shall be accomplished and I will cause My fury to rest upon them, and I will be comforted.*

And the people shall be gathered against him. "As all the other tribes were gathered against Benjamin at Gibeah to destroy it, so, although that war did not overtake them, now *against him,* i. e. against Ephraim or the ten tribes, *shall be gathered* divers *peoples* and nations, to destroy them." The number gathered against them shall be as overwhelming, as that of all the tribes of Israel against the one small tribe of Benjamin. "[6] As of old, they ought to have bound themselves to extinguish this apostacy in its birth, as they bound themselves to avenge the horrible wickedness at Gibeah. But since they bound themselves not against sin, but to it, God says

[1] S. Luke xxiii. 30. [2] Jos. de B. J. vi. 9. [3] Rev. vi. 16. [4] De consid. v. 12. [5] Rev. ix. 6.

[6] Osor. [7] Lam. iii. 33. [8] Deut. xxviii. 63. [9] S. James ii. 13. [10] Is. i. 24. [11] Ezek. v. 13.

Before CHRIST cir. 740.

11 And Ephraim *is as*
[x] an heifer *that is* taught,
and loveth to tread out *the*
corn; but I passed over
upon †her fair neck: I will
make Ephraim to ride;
Judah shall plow, *and*
Jacob shall break his clods.

[x] Jer. 50. 11. Mic. 4. 13.

† Heb. *the beauty of her neck.*

that He would gather Heathen nations against them, to punish their obstinate rebellion against Himself. They who will neither be drawn by piety, nor corrected by moderate chastisements, must needs be visited by sharper punishments, that some, who will not strive to the uttermost against the mercy of God, may be saved."

When they shall bind themselves in their two furrows. They *bind themselves* and Satan *binds them* to their sin. In harmony and unity in nothing else, they will bind themselves, and plough like two oxen together, adding furrow to furrow, joining on line to line of sin. They who had thrown off the light and easy yoke of God, who were ever like a restive, untamed, heifer, starting aside from the yoke, would *bind* and band themselves steadily in their own ways of sin, cultivating sin, and in that sin should destruction overtake them. Men who are unsteady and uneven in every thing besides, will be steadfast in pursuing sin; they who will submit to no constraint, human or Divine, will, in their slavery to their passions, submit to anything. No slavery is so heavy as that which is self-imposed.

This translation has followed an old Jewish tradition, expressed by the vowels of the text,[1] and old Jewish authorities. With other vowels, it may be rendered, lit. *in their binding to their two transgressions*, which gives the same sense, "because they bound themselves to their two transgressions," or, passively, *when they are bound, on account of their two transgressions.* The *two transgressions*, may designate the two calves, *the sin of Israel*, or the twofold guilt of fornication, spiritual, and in the body; the breach of both tables of God's law; or as Jeremiah says[2], *My people hath committed two evils; they have forsaken Me, the Fountain of living waters, and hewed them out cisterns, broken cisterns, which can hold no water.* "[3]This could not be said of any other nation, which knew not God. For if any such worshiped false gods, they committed only one transgression; but this nation, in which God was known, by declining to idolatry, is truly blamed as guilty of *two transgressions;* they left the true God, and for, or against, Him they worshiped other gods. For he hath twofold guilt, who, knowing good, rather chooseth evil; but *he* single, who, knowing no good, taketh evil for good. That nation then, both when, after seeing many wonderful works of God, it made and worshiped one calf in the wilderness; and when, forsaking the house of David and the temple of the Lord, it made itself two calves; yea, and so often as it worshiped those gods of the heathen; and yet more, when it asked that Barabbas should be released but that Christ should be crucified, committed two transgressions, rejecting the good, electing the evil; [4]*setting sweet for bitter, and bitter for sweet; setting darkness as light, and light as darkness.*"

11. *Ephraim is an heifer that is taught and that loveth to tread out the corn.* The object of the metaphor in these three verses seems to be, to picture, under operations of husbandry, what God willed and trained His people to do, how they took as much pains in evil, as He willed them to do for good. One thing only they did *which* He willed, but not because He willed it,—what pleased themselves. Corn was threshed in the East chiefly by means of oxen, who were either driven round and round, so as to trample it out with their feet, or drew a cylinder armed with iron, or harrow-shaped planks, set with sharp stones which at the same time cut up the straw for provender. The treading out the corn was an easy and luxurious service, since God had forbidden to *muzzle the ox*[5], while doing it. It pictures then the sweet gentle ways by which God wins us to His service. Israel would serve thus far; for she liked the service, *she was accustomed* to it, and *she loved it*, but she would do no more. *She waxed fat and kicked*[6].

"[7]The heifer when accustomed to the labor of treading out the corn, mostly, even unconstrained, returns to the same labor. So the mind of the ungodly, devoted to the slaveries of this world, and accustomed to the fatigues of temporal things, even if it may have leisure for itself, hastens to subject itself to earthly toils, and, inured to its miserable conversation, seeks the renewal of toil, and will not, though it may, cease from the yoke of this world's slavery. This yoke our Lord would remove from the necks of His disciples, saying[8], *Take heed, lest at any*

[1] in that they have pointed עוֹנותם not עֲונותם *iniquities.* Another rendering *before their two eyes*, is altogether wrong. 1. It would, at least, be, עֵינֵיהֶם. not עינותם which means *their fountains.* 2. There is probably no such reading as עינותם, the merely indicating a reading ענותם without י. Hiller. Arc. Cethib. p. 233.

[2] ii. 13. [3] Rup. [4] Is. v. 20.

[5] Deut. xxv. 4. [6] Ib. xxxii. 15.

[7] S. Greg. Mor. xx. 16. Rib. [8] S. Luke xxi. 34.

Before CHRIST cir. 740.

[y] Prov. 11. 18.

12 [y] Sow to yourselves in righteousness, reap in mercy; [z] break up your fallow ground: for *it*

Before CHRIST cir. 740.

[z] Jer. 4. 3.

time your hearts be overcharged with cares of this life, and that Day come upon you unawares. And again, *Come unto Me, all ye who labor and are heavy laden, and I will refresh you. Take My yoke upon you.*" "[1] Some, in order to appear somewhat in this world, overload themselves with earthly toils, and although, amid their labors, they feel their strength fail, yet, overcome by love of earthly things, they delight in their fatigue. To these it is said by the Prophet, *Ephraim is a heifer taught and loving to tread out the corn.* They ask that they may be oppressed; in rest, they deem that they have lighted unto a great peril."

And I passed over her fair neck, handling her gently and tenderly, as men put the yoke gently on a young untamed animal, and inure it softly to take the yoke upon it. Yet "[2] to *pass over,* especially when it is said of God, always signifies inflictions and troubles." To pass over sins, is to remit them; to pass over the sinner, is to punish him. *I will make Ephraim to ride* or *I will make* it, i. e. the yoke, to *ride* on *Ephraim's* neck, as the same word is used for "[3] place the hand on the bow;" or, perhaps better, *I will set a rider on Ephraim,* who should tame and subdue him. Since he would not submit himself freely to the easy yoke of God, God would set a ruler upon him, who should be his master. Thus, the Psalmist complains, [4] *Thou hast made men to ride on our head,* directing us at their pleasure.

"[5] The *beauty of the neck* designates those who sin and take pleasure in their sins. That passing over or ascending, said both in the past and the future, *I passed, I will make to ride,* signifies that what He purposes is most certain. It expresses that same vengeance as, [6] *Ye are a stiffnecked people; I will come up into the midst of thee in a moment, and consume thee.* The *beauty* of the *neck* here is the same as the ornament there, when the Lord says, *therefore now put off thy ornaments from thee, that I may know what to do unto thee.* As long as the sinner goes adorned, i. e. is proud in his sins, as long as he stiffens his fair neck, self-complacent, taking pleasure in the ills which he has done, God, in a measure, knows not what to do to him; mercy knows not how, apart from the severity of judgment, to approach him; and so after the sentence of the judge, *thou art a stiffnecked people, &c.* He gives the counsel *put off thine ornaments &c.* i. e. humble thyself in penitence, that I may have mercy upon thee."

Judah shall plow, Jacob shall break his clods. In the Will of God, Judah and Israel were to unite in His service, Judah first, Jacob, after him, breaking the clods, which would hinder the seed from shooting up. Judah being mentioned in the same incidental way, as elsewhere by Hosea, it may be, that he would speak of what should follow on Ephraim's chastisement. "[7] When they shall see this, the two tribes shall no longer employ themselves in treading out the corn, but shall plow. To *tread out the corn* is to" act "in hope of present gain; to *plow,* is to labor in that, which has no instant fruit, but promiseth it hereafter, i. e. the fulfillment of God's commands." *Jacob* will then be the remnant of the ten tribes, who, at Hezekiah's invitation, out of Ephraim, Manasseh, Issachar, Asher, and Zebulun, joined in celebrating the passover at Jerusalem, and subsequently in destroying idolatry[8]. Hosea had already foretold that Judah and Israel shall be *gathered together,* under *one Head*[9]. Here, again, he unites them in one, preparing His way first in themselves, then, in others. Judah is placed first; for to him was the promise in his forefather, the Patriarch, and then in David. Ephraim was to be partaker of his blessings, by being united to him. The image of the heifer has been dropped. He had spoken of them as husbandmen; as such he addresses them.

12. *Sow to yourselves in righteousness, reap in mercy;* lit. *in the proportion of mercy,* not in proportion *to* what you have sown, nor what justice would give, but beyond all deserts, *in the proportion of mercy;* i. e. "according to the capacity and fullness of the mercy of God; what becometh the mercy of God, which is boundless," which overlooketh man's failings, and giveth an infinite reward for poor imperfect labor. As our Lord says[10], *Give, and it shall be given unto you; good measure, pressed down, and shaken together and running over, shall men give into your bosom.* "[11] If the earth giveth thee larger fruits than it has received, how much more shall the requiting of mercy repay thee manifold more than thou gavest!" Sowing and reaping always stand over against each other, as labor and reward. [12] *He that soweth sparingly shall reap also sparingly; and he which soweth bountifully shall reap also bountifully.* And, [13] *whatsoever*

[1] S. Greg. in Ezek. Hom. x. Ib.
[2] S. Jer. See Job ix. 11. xiii. 13. Ps. lxxxviii. 17. Heb. Is. xxviii. 18.
[3] הרכב 2 Kings xiii. 16. twice. [4] Ps. lxvi. 12.

[5] Rup. [6] Ex. xxxiii. 5. [7] Rib.
[8] 2 Chron. xxx. xxxi. [9] i. 11. [10] S. Luke vi. 38.
[11] S. Ambr. de Naboth, § 7. Rib.
[12] 2 Cor. ix. 6. [13] Gal. vi. 7, 8, 9.

Before CHRIST cir. 740.

is time to seek the LORD, till he come, and rain righteousness upon you.

a man soweth, that shall he also reap. For he that soweth to the flesh, shall of the flesh reap corruption; but he that soweth to the Spirit shall of the Spirit reap life everlasting. In due season we shall reap, if we faint not.* We are bidden *to sow to ourselves*, for, [1] *our goodness reacheth not to God;* our's is the gain, if we love God, the Fountain of all good. This reward, *according to mercy*, is in both worlds. It is in this world also. For "grace well used draws more grace." God giveth *grace upon grace*[2]; so that each good deed, the fruit of grace, is the seed-corn of larger grace. "If thou humble thyself, it stimulates thee to humble thyself more. If thou prayest, thou longest to pray more. If thou givest alms, thou wishest to give more." It is in the world to come. For, says a holy man[3], "our works do not pass away as it seems, but each thing done in time, is sown as the seed of eternity. The simple will be amazed, when from this slight seed he shall see the copious harvest arise, good or evil, according as the seed was." "Thou seekest two sheaves, rest and glory. They shall reap glory and rest, who have sown toil and self-abasement[4]."

Break up your fallow ground. This is not the order of husbandry. The ground was already plowed, harrowed, sown. Now he bids her anew, *Break up your fallow ground.* The Church breaks up her own fallow ground, when she stirs up anew the decaying piety of her own members; she breaks up fallow ground, when, by preaching the Gospel of Christ, she brings new people into His fold. And for us too, one sowing sufficeth not. It must be no surface-sowing. And "the soil of our hearts must ever be anew cleansed; for no one in this mortal life is so perfect, in piety, that noxious desires will not spring up again in the heart, as tares in the well-tilled field."

For it is time to seek the Lord, until He come and rain righteousness upon you, or better, *until He shall come and teach you righteousness.* To *rain righteousness* is the same image as Solomon uses of Christ; [5] *He shall come down like rain upon the mown grass, as showers that water the earth,* and Isaiah, [6] *drop down ye heavens from above and let the skies pour down righteousness.* It expresses in picture-language how He, Who is *our Righteousness,* came down from heaven, to give life to us, who were dried and parched up and withered, when the whole face of our mortal nature was as dead.

Yet there is nothing to indicate that the Prophet is here using imagery. The Hebrew word is used very rarely in the meaning, to *rain;* in that of teaching, continually, and that, in exactly the same idiom as here[7]. One office of our Lord was to teach. Nicodemus owned Him, *as a teacher sent from* God[8]. The Samaritans looked to the Messiah, as one who should *teach all things*[9]. The prophets foretold that He should *teach us His ways*[10], that He should be *a witness unto the people*[11].

The Prophet bids them *seek diligently*[12], and perseveringly, "not leaving off or desisting," if they should not at once find, but continuing the search, quite *up to*[13] the time when they should find. His words imply the need of perseverance and patience, which should stop short of nothing but God's own time for finding. The Prophet, as is the way of the prophets, goes on to Christ, who was ever in the prophets' hearts and hopes. The words could only be understood improperly of God the Father. God does not *come,* Who is everywhere. He ever was among His people, nor did He will to be among them otherwise than heretofore. No coming of God, *as* God, was looked for, to *teach righteousness.* Rather, the time was coming, when He would be less visibly among them than before. Among the ten tribes, as a distinct people, He would shortly be no more, either by prophecy, or in worship, or by any perceptible token of His Providence. From Judah also He was about, although at a later period, to withdraw the kingdom of David, and the Urim and Thummim, and the Shechinah, or visible Presence. Soon after the Captivity, prophecy itself was to cease. But "the coming of Christ the Patriarchs and holy men all along desired to see: Abraham saw it and was glad[14]. Jacob longed for it[15]. The law and the Prophets directed to it, so that there were always in Israel such as waited for it, as appears by the example of old Simeon and Joseph of Arimathæa, and those many prophets and righteous men whom our Saviour speaks of[16]. *He that should come* seems to have been a known title for Him; since John Baptist sent two of his disciples, to say unto Him, *Art thou He that shall come, or do we look for another*[17]?"

The Prophet saith then, "Now is the time to seek the Lord, and prepare for the coming

[1] Ps. xvi. 2. [2] S. John i. 16.
[3] S. Bern. de Conv. c. 8. Lap.
[4] Id. Serm. de S. Bened. § 11. Ib.
[5] Ps. lxxii. 6. [6] xlv. 8.
[7] with accusat. of that which is taught and dat. of the person, Deut. xxxiii. 10.

[8] S. John iii. 2. [9] Ib. iv. 25. [10] Is. ii. 3.
[11] Ib. lv. 4. [12] דרש.
[13] This is the force of עד.
[14] S. John viii. 56. [15] Gen. xlix. 18.
[16] S. Luke ii. 25. S. Mark xv. 43. S. Matt. xiii. 17.
[17] S. Matt. xi. 3.

Before CHRIST cir. 740.

13 [a] Ye have plowed wickedness, ye have reaped iniquity; ye have eaten the fruit of lies: because thou

Before CHRIST cir. 740.

[a] Job 4. 8. Prov. 22. 8. ch. 8. 7. Gal. 6. 7, 8.

of Christ; for He, when He cometh, will teach you, yea, will give you true righteousness, whereby ye shall be righteous before God, and heirs of His kingdom." "[1] So God speaketh through Isaiah, *keep ye judgment and do justice, for My salvation is near to come, and my righteousness to be revealed.* In both places, men are warned, *to prepare the way* to receive Christ, which was the office assigned to the law. As S. Paul saith, *Whereunto was the law? It was added because of transgressions.* It was given to restrain the passions of men by fear of punishment, lest they should so defile themselves by sin, as to despise the mercy and office of Christ. It was given to prepare our souls by love of righteousness and mercy to receive Christ, that he might enrich them with the Divine wealth of righteousness." "[2] If Israel of old were so to order their ways in expectation of Him, and that they might be prepared for His coming; and if their neglecting to do this made them liable to such heavy judgments, how much severer judgments shall they be worthy of, who, after His Coming and raining upon them the plentiful showers of heavenly doctrine, and abundant measure of His grace and gifts of His Holy Spirit, do, for want of breaking up the fallow ground of their hearts, suffer His holy word to be lost on them. The fearful doom of such unfruitful Christians is set down by S. Paul[3]."

The present is ever the time to seek the Lord. [4] *Behold now is the accepted time; behold now is the Day of Salvation.* As Hosea says, *it is time to seek the Lord till He come,* so S. Paul saith, [5] *unto them that look for Him, shall he appear the second time, without sin, unto salvation.*

13. *Ye have plowed wickedness.* They not only did not that which God commanded, but they did the exact contrary. They cultivated wickedness. They broke up their fallow ground, yet to sow, not wheat, but tares. They did not leave it even to grow of itself, although even thus, on the natural soil of the human heart, it yields a plenteous harvest; but they bestowed their labor on it, plowed it, sowed, and as they sowed, so they reaped, an abundant increase of it. "They brought their ill doings to a harvest, and laid up as in provision the fruits thereof." Iniquity and the results of iniquity, were the gain of all their labor. Of all their toil, they shall have no fruits, except the iniquity itself. "[6] By the plowing, sowing, eating the fruits, he marks the obstinacy of incorrigible sinners, who begin ill, go on to worse, and in the worst come to an end. Then too, when the corrupted soul labors with the purpose of a deed of sin, and resolves in its inmost thoughts, how it may bring the ungodly will into effect in deed, it is like one plowing or sowing. But when, having completed the work of iniquity, it exults that it has done ill, it is like one reaping. When further it has broken out so far as, in pride of heart to defend its sins against the law of God prohibiting them, and goes on unconcerned in impenitence, he is like one who, after harvest, eats the fruits stored up."

Ye have eaten the fruit of lies. They had been full of *lies*[7]; they had *lied* against God by hypocrisy[8] and idolatry; they had *spoken lies against Him*[9]*;* by denying that He gave them what He bestowed upon them, and ascribing it to their idols[10]. All iniquity is a lie. Such then should be *the fruit* which they tasted, on which they fed. It should not profit, nor satisfy them. It should not merely be empty, as in the case of those who are said to *feed on ashes*[11], but hurtful. As Isaiah saith[12], *they conceive mischief and bring forth iniquity. They hatch cockatrice' eggs, and weave the spider's web; he that eateth of their eggs dieth, and that which is crushed, breaketh out into a viper.* "Gain deceives, lust deceives, gluttony deceives; they yield no true delight; they satisfy not, they disgust; and they end in misery of body and soul." "Bodily delights," says a father[13], "when absent, kindle a vehement longing; when had and eaten, they satiate and disgust the eater. Spiritual delights are distasteful, when unknown; when possessed, they are longed for; and the more those who hunger after them feed upon them, the more they are hungered for. Bodily delights please, untasted; when tasted, they displease; spiritual, when untasted, are held cheap; when experienced, they please. In bodily delights, appetite generates satiety; satiety, disgust. In spiritual, appetite produceth satiety; satiety appetite. For spiritual delights increase longing in the soul, while they satisfy. For the more their sweetness is perceived, so much the more is *that* known which is loved more eagerly. Unpossessed, they cannot be loved, because their sweetness is unknown."

Because thou didst trust in thy way. Thy way, i. e. not God's. They forsook God's

[1] Osor. [2] Poc. [3] Heb. vi. 4–8. [4] 2 Cor. vi. 2. [5] Heb. ix. 28. [6] Rup. [7] ch. iv. 1, 2. vii. 3. [8] v. 7. vi. 7. vii. 16. x. 4.

[9] vii. 13. [10] ii. 5, 12. [11] Is. xliv. 20. [12] Ib. lix. 4, 5. [13] S. Greg. in Evang. Hom. 36. init. L.

Before CHRIST cir. 740.

didst trust in thy way, in
the multitude of thy mighty
men.
14 [b]Therefore shall a
tumult arise among thy
people, and all thy fortresses
shall be spoiled, as Shalman
spoiled [c]Betharbel in the

[b] ch. 13. 16.

[c] 2 Kgs. 18. 34. & 19. 13.

way, followed "ways of wickedness and misbelief." While displeasing God, they trusted in the worship of the calves and in the help of Egypt and Assyria, *making flesh their arm, and departing from the living God.* So long as a man mistrusts his ways of sin, there is hope of his conversion amid any depths of sin. When he *trusts in his ways*, all entrance is closed against the grace of God. He is as one dead; he not only justifies himself, but is self-justified. There is nothing in him, neither love nor fear, which can be awakened

14. *Therefore shall a tumult arise among thy people*, lit. *peoples.* Such was the immediate fruit of departing from God and trusting in men and idols. They trusted in their own might, and the multitude of their people. That might should, through intestine division and anarchy, become their destruction. As in the dislocated state of the Roman empire under the first emperors, so in Israel, the successive usurpers arose out of their armies, [1]*the multitude of their mighty ones*, in whom they trusted. The *confused noise*[2] of *war* should first *arise in* the midst of their own *peoples.* They are spoken of not as one, but as many; *peoples*[3], not, as God willed them to be, one people, for they had no principle of oneness or stability, who had no legitimate succession, either of kings or of priests; who had *made kings, but not through* God. Each successor had the same right as his predecessor, the right of might, and furnished an example and precedent and sanction to the murderer of himself or of his son.

All thy fortresses shall be spoiled, lit. *the whole of thy fortresses shall be wasted.* He speaks of the whole as one. Their fenced cities, which cut off all approach[4], should be one waste[5]. They had forsaken God, their *fortress and deliverer*, and so He gave up their fortresses to the enemy, so that all and each of them were laid waste. The confusion, begun among themselves, prepared for destruction by the enemy. Of this he gives one awful type.

As Shalman spoiled (or *wasted*) *Beth-Arbel in the day of battle. Shalman* is, no doubt, *Shalmaneser king of Assyria,* who came up against Hoshea, early in his reign, *and he became a servant to him and brought him a present*[6]. *Shalman* being the characteristic part of the name[7], the Prophet probably omitted the rest, on the ground of the rhythm. *Beth-Arbel* is a city, which the Greeks, retaining, in like way, only the latter and characteristic half of the name, called Arbela[8]. Of the several cities called Arbela, that celebrated in Grecian history, was part of the Assyrian empire. Two others, one "[9] in the mountain-district of Pella" and so on the East side of Jordan, the other between Sepphoris and Tiberias[10], (and so in Naphthali) must, together with the countries in which they lay, have fallen into the hands of the Assyrians in the reign of *Tiglath-pileser*, who *took—Gilead and Galilee, all the land of Naphtali*[11], in the reign of Pekah. The whole country, East of Jordan, being now in the hands of Shalmaneser, his natural approach to Samaria was over the Jordan, through the valley or plain of Jezreel. Here was the chief wealth of Israel, and the fittest field for the Assyrian horse. Over the Jordan then, whence Israel itself came when obedient to God, whence came the earlier instruments of God's chastisements, came doubtless the host of Shalmaneser, along the "great plain" of Esdraelon. "In that plain" also

[1] See Introd. p. 2.

[2] as in Am. ii. 2.

[3] בעמין plural. The corruption in some MSS. בעמך (sing.) and the rendering of the old Versions (as of our own) in the singular, (with the same general sense,) illustrate the peculiarity of the idiom for which they substituted an easier, and nearly equivalent, phrase.

[4] The Etymology of מבצר, as of *Bozrah.*

[5] expressed by the union of כל with the genitive plur. and the sing. verb, which is very rare. Is. lxiv. 7. Nah. iii. 7. Prov. xvi. 2. have been cited as the only instances.

[6] 2 Kings xvii. 3.

[7] *Eser* occurs in *Esar*haddon, Tiglath pil*eser* and, probably, is the same as *ezzar* and *ezer* in Nebuchadnezzar, and Sharezer. It probably signifies "help." A much stronger omission occurs probably in the name of the parricide Sharezer, 2 Kings xix. 37. whose whole name was Nergal Sharezer. Merodach Baladan is probably the Mardocempal of Ptol. Rawl. Herod. i. p. 502. *Chedorlaomer* (Gen. xiv. 1. 9.) is very probably the same as the *kudurmapula* of the Babylonian bricks, *mapula* being omitted, and *laomer*, i. e. *el-omer* "the ravager" being equivalent to the meaning of *abda Mactu* of the bricks, "waster of the West." See Rawl. Herod. i. 436.

[8] as Beth Aven, (although on other grounds,) was called Aven (ver. 8.) Beth Baal Meon is called more commonly Baal Meon, but also Beth Meon and now *Maein* or *Myun; Gilgal* is probably called *Beth Haggilgal*, Neh. xii. 29; *Diblathaim* (afterward *Diblatai*) is *Beth Diblathaim*, Jer. xlviii. 22; the people of *Bethcar* are called by Josephus (Ant. vi. 2. 2.) *Corræi*; *Ophrah* is probably Bethle *aphrah*, Mic. i. 10; *Beth Millo*, 2 Kings xii. 21. *Millo*; *Beth Nimra*, now *Nemrin*; *Beth Eden*, now *Eden*; *Beth Azmaveth*, *Azmaveth*; *Beth-eked-harohim*, 2 Kings x. 12. *Beth-eked*, 14 in Eus. *Baithakath*; *Beeshterah*, (for *Beth Ashtarah*) *Ashtaroth.* See all these in Ges. Lex. v. בית pp. 193–6.

[9] Eus. Onom. s. v.

[10] Jos. B. J. i. 16. 2. Vit. 37. 66.

[11] 2 Kings xv. 29.

Before CHRIST cir. 740.

day of battle: [d] the mother was dashed in pieces upon *her* children.

15 So shall Bethel do unto you because of † your great wickedness: in a morning [e] shall the king of Israel utterly be cut off.

[d] ch. 13. 16.
† Heb. *the evil of your evil.*
[e] ver. 7.

CHAPTER XI.

Before CHRIST cir. 740.

1 *The ingratitude of Israel unto God for his benefits.* 5 *His judgment.* 8 *God's mercy toward them.*

WHEN [a] Israel *was* a child, then I loved him, and [b] called my [c] son out of Egypt.

[a] ch. 2. 15.
[b] Matt. 2. 15.
[c] Ex. 4. 22, 23.

lay an *Arbela*, "nine miles from Legion[1]." Legion itself was at the Western extremity of the plain, as Scythopolis or Bethshean lay at the East[2]. It was about fifteen miles West of Nazareth[3], and ten miles from Jezreel[4]. Beth-Arbel must accordingly have lain somewhere in the middle of the valley of Jezreel. Near this Arbela, then, Israel must have sustained a decisive defeat from Shalmaneser. For the Prophet does not say only, that he *spoiled Beth-Arbel*, but that he did this *in a day of battle.* Here Hosea, probably in the last years of his life, saw the fulfillment of his own earlier prophecy; and God *brake the bow of Israel in the valley of Jezreel*[5].

The mother was dashed to pieces on the children. It was an aggravation of this barbarity, that, first the infants were dashed against the stones before their mother's eyes, then the mothers themselves were dashed upon them. Syrians[6], Assyrians[7], Medes[8], Babylonians[9], used this barbarity. India has borne witness to us of late, how heathen nature remains the same.

It may be that, in the name *Beth*arbel, the Prophet alludes to the name *Bethel*[10]. As *Betharbel*, i. e. *the house*, or it may be the idolatrous *temple of Arbel*, rescued it not, but was rather the cause of its destruction, so shall Bethel. The holy places of Israel, the memorials of the free love of God to their forefathers, were pledges to *them*, the children of those forefathers, that, so long as they continued in the faith of their fathers, God the Unchangeable, would continue those same mercies to them. When they *turned* Bethel, *the house of God*, into Bethaven, *house of vanity*, then it became, like Betharbel, lit. *house of ambush of God*, the scene and occasion of their desolation.

15. *So shall Bethel do unto you.* God was the Judge, Who condemned them so to suffer from the enemy. The Assyrian was the instrument of the wrath of God. But, in order to point out the moral government of God, the Prophet says, neither that God did it, nor that the Assyrian did it, but Bethel, once *the house of God*, now the place where they dishonored God, *because of your great wickedness*, lit. *the wickedness of your wickedness.* In their wickedness itself, there was an essence of wickedness, malice within malice.

In a morning shall the king of Israel be cut off. Hoshea was cut off finally, leaving neither root nor branch. His kingdom perished; he left no memorial. Like the morning, he seemed to dawn on the troubles of his people: he sinned against God: and *in a morning*, the kingdom, in *the multitude of* whose *mighty men* he trusted, *was cut off* for ever.

XI. 1. *When Israel* was *a child, then I loved him.* God loved Israel, as He Himself formed it, ere it corrupted itself. He loved it for the sake of the fathers, Abraham, Isaac, and Jacob, as he saith[11], *Jacob have I loved, but Esau have I hated.* Then, when it was weak, helpless, oppressed by the Egyptians, afflicted, destitute, God loved him, cared for him, delivered him from oppression, and called him out of Egypt. "[10] When did He love Israel? When, by His guidance, Israel regained freedom, his enemies were destroyed, he was fed with *food from heaven*, he heard the voice of God, and received the law from Him. He was unformed in Egypt; then he was informed by the rules of the law, so as to be matured there. He was a child in that vast waste. For he was nourished, not by solid food, but by milk, i. e. by the rudiments of piety and righteousness, that he might gradually attain the strength of a man. So that law was a schoolmaster, to retain Israel as a child, by the discipline of a child, until the time should come when all, who despised not the heavenly gifts, should receive the Spirit of adoption. The Prophet then, in order to shew the exceeding guilt of Israel," says, " *When Israel was a child*, (in the wilderness, for then he was born when he bound himself to conform to the Divine law, and was not yet matured) *I loved him*, i. e. I gave him the law, priesthood, judgments, precepts, instructions; I loaded him with most ample

[1] Eus. l. c.
[2] Eus. (v. Ἰεσραὴλ) assigns these, as the two extremities. [3] Reland, p. 873. [4] Itin. Hieros. p. 586.

[5] ch. i. 5. [6] 2 Kgs. viii. 12. [7] here and xiii. ult.
[8] Is. xiii. 16. [9] Ps. cxxxvii. 8, 9.
[10] Osor. [11] Mal. i. 2.

Before CHRIST cir. 740.

d 2 Kgs 17. 16. ch. 2. 13. & 13. 2.

2 *As* they called them, so they went from them: [d]they sacrificed unto Baalim, and burned incense to graven images.

Before CHRIST cir. 740.

benefits; I preferred him to all nations, expending on him, as on My chief heritage and peculiar possession, much watchful care and pains."

I called My son out of Egypt, as He said to Pharaoh [1], *Israel is My son, even My firstborn; let My son go, that he may serve Me.* God chose him out of all nations, to be His peculiar people. Yet also God chose him, not for himself, but because He willed that Christ, His only Son, should *after the flesh* be born of him, and for, and in, the Son, God called His people, *My son.* "[2] The people of Israel was called a son, as regards the elect, yet only for the sake of Him, the Only-Begotten Son, Begotten, not adopted, Who, *after the flesh*, was to be born of that people, that, through His Passion, He might bring many sons to glory, disdaining not to have them as brethren and co-heirs. For, had He not come, Who was to come, the Well Beloved Son of God, Israel too could never, any more than the other nations, have been called the son of so great a Father, as the Apostle, himself of that people, saith [3], *For we were, by nature, children of wrath, even as others.*"

Since, however, these words relate to literal Israel, the people whom God brought out by Moses, how were they fulfilled in the infant Jesus, when He was brought back out of Egypt, as S. Matthew teaches us, they were [4]?

Because Israel himself was a type of Christ, and for the sake of Him Who was to be born of the seed of Israel, did God call Israel, *My son;* for His sake only did He deliver him. The two deliverances, of the whole Jewish people, and of Christ the Head, occupied the same position in God's dispensations. He rescued Israel, whom He called His son, in its childish and infantine condition, at the very commencement of its being, as a people. His true Son by Nature, Christ our Lord, He brought up in His Infancy, when He began to shew forth His mercies to us in Him. Both had, by His appointment, taken refuge in Egypt; both were, by His miraculous call, to Moses in the bush, to Joseph in the dream, recalled from it. S. Matthew apparently quotes these words, not to prove anything, but in order to point out the relation of God's former dealings with the latter, the beginning and the close, what relates to the body, and what relates to the Head. He tells us that the former deliverance had its completion in Christ, that in His deliverance was the full solid completion of that of Israel; and that then indeed it might, in its completest fullness, be said, *Out of Egypt have I called My Son.*

When Israel was brought out of Egypt, the figure took place; when Christ was called, the reality was fulfilled. The act itself, on the part of God, was prophetic. When He delivered Israel, and called him His firstborn, He willed, in the course of time, to bring up from Egypt His Only-Begotten Son. The words are prophetic, because the event which they speak of, was prophetic. "They speak of Israel as one collective body, and, as it were, one person, called by God *My son*, viz. by adoption, still in the years of innocency, and beloved by God, called of God out of Egypt by Moses, as Jesus, His true Son, was by the Angel." The following verses are not prophetic, because in them the Prophet no longer speaks of Israel as one, but as composed of the many sinful individuals in it. Israel was a prophetic people, in regard to this dispensation of God towards him; not in regard to his rebellions and sins.

2. *As they called them, so they went from them.* The Prophet changes his tone, no longer speaking of that one first call of God to Israel as a whole, whereby He brought out Israel as one man, His one son; which one call he obeyed. Here he speaks of God's manifold calls to the people, throughout their whole history, which they as often disobeyed, and not disobeyed only, but went contrariwise. *They called them.* Whether God employed Moses, or the judges, or priests, or kings, or prophets, to call them, it was all one. Whenever or by whomsoever they were called, they turned away in the opposite direction, to serve their idols. They proportioned and fitted, as it were, their disobedience to God's long-suffering. "[5]Then chiefly they threw off obedience, despised their admonitions, and worked themselves up the more franticly to a zeal for the sin which they had begun." *They*, God's messengers, *called; so*, in like manner, *they went away from them. They sacrificed unto Baalim*, i. e. their many Baals, in which they cherished idolatry, cruelty, and fleshly sin. So "[6]when Christ came and called them manifoldly, as in the great day of the feast, *If any man thirst, let him come unto Me and drink*, the more diligently He called them, the more diligently they went away from Him, and returned to their idols,

[1] Ex. iv. 22, 3. [2] Rup. [3] Eph. ii. 3. [4] ii. 15. [5] Osor. [6] Rib.

Before CHRIST cir. 740.

3 [e]I taught Ephraim also to go, taking them by their arms; but they knew not that [f]I healed them.

4 I drew them with cords of a man, with bands of love: and [g]I was to them as they that † take off the yoke on their jaws, and [h]I laid meat unto them.

e Deut. 1. 31. & 32. 10, 11, 12. Is. 46. 3.
f Ex. 15. 26.
g Lev. 26. 13.
† Heb. *lift up*.
h Ps. 78. 25. ch. 2. 8.

to the love and possession of riches and houses and pleasures, for whose sake they despised the truth."

3. *I taught Ephraim also to go*, lit. *and I set Ephraim on his feet;* i. e. while they were rebelling, I was helping and supporting them, as a nurse doth her child, teaching it to go with little steps, step by step, "accustoming it to go by little and little without weariness;" and not only so, but *taking them by their arms;* or it may be equally translated, *He took them in His arms*, i. e. God not only gently *taught* them *to walk*, but when they were wearied, *He took them up in His arms*, as a nurse doth a child when tired with its little attempts to walk. Such was the love and tender care of God, guiding and upholding Israel in His ways which He taught him, guarding him from weariness, or, if wearied, taking him in the arms of His mercy and refreshing him. So Moses says[1], *In the wilderness thou hast seen, how that the Lord thy God bare thee, as a man doth bear his son, in all the way that ye went, until ye came unto this place;* and he expostulates with God, [2] *Have I conceived all this people? have I begotten them, that Thou shouldest say unto me, Carry them in thy bosom, as a nursing father beareth his sucking child, unto the land which Thou swarest unto their fathers?* "[3] Briefly yet magnificently doth this place hint at the wondrous patience of God, whereof Paul too speaks, [4]*for forty years suffered He their manners in the wilderness.* For as a nursing father beareth patiently with a child, who hath not yet come to years of discretion, and, although at times he be moved to strike it in return, yet mostly he sootheth its childish follies with blandishments, and, ungrateful though it be, carries it in his arms, so the Lord God, Whose are these words, patiently bore with the unformed people, ignorant of the spiritual mysteries of the kingdom of heaven, and although He slew the bodies of many of them in the wilderness, yet the rest He soothed with many and great miracles, *leading them about*, and *instructing them*, (as Moses says) *keeping them as the apple of His eye*[5]."

But they knew not that I healed them. They laid it not to heart, and therefore what they knew with their understanding was worse than ignorance. "[6]I Who was a Father, became a nurse, and Myself carried My little one in My arms, that he should not be hurt in the wilderness, or scared by heat or darkness. By day I was a cloud; by night, a column of fire, that I might by My light illumine, and heal those whom I had protected. And when they had sinned and had made the calf, I gave them place for repentance, and they knew not that I healed them, so as, for forty years, to close the wound of idolatry, and restore them to their former health."

"[7] The Son of God carried us in His arms to the Father, when He went forth carrying His Cross, and on the wood of the Cross stretched out His arms for our redemption. Those too doth Christ carry daily in His arms, whom He continually entreateth, comforteth, preserveth, so gently, that with much alacrity and without any grievous hindrance they perform every work of God, and with heart enlarged run, rather than walk, the way of God's commandments. Yet do these need great caution, that they be clothed with great circumspection and humility, and despise not others. Else Christ would say of them, *They knew not that I healed them.*"

4. *I drew them with the cords of a man.* "[8]Wanton heifers such as was Israel, are drawn with ropes; but although Ephraim struggled against Me, I would not draw him as a beast, but I drew him as *a man*, (not a servant, but a son) *with cords* of love." "Love is the magnet of love." "[9]The first and chief commandment of the law, is not of fear, but of love, because He willeth those whom He commandeth, to be sons rather than servants." "[10] Our Lord saith, *No man cometh unto Me, except the Father Who hath sent Me, draw him.* He did not say, lead *him*, but *draw him.* This violence is done to the heart, not to the body. Why marvel? Believe and thou comest; love and thou art drawn. Think it not a rough and uneasy violence: it is sweet, alluring; the sweetness draws thee. Is not a hungry sheep drawn, when the grass is shewn it? It is not, I ween, driven on in body, but is bound tight by longing. So do thou too come to Christ. Do not conceive of long journeyings. When thou believest, then thou comest. For to Him Who is everywhere, men come by loving, not by traveling." So the Bride saith, [11]*draw me and I will run after Thee.* "How sweet," says S. Augustine, when converted [12], "did it at once

[1] Deut. i. 31. [2] Num. xi. 12. [3] Rup. [4] Acts xiii. 18. [5] Deut. xxxii. 10. [6] S. Jer. [7] Dion. [8] Lap.
[9] Rib. [10] S. Aug. Serm. 81. on N. T. § 2. Oxf. Tr. [11] Cant. i. 4. [12] Conf. ix. 1.

Before CHRIST cir. 740.

5 ¶ [l]He shall not return into the land of Egypt, but the Assyrian shall be his king, [k]because they refused to return.

[l] See ch. 8. 13. & 9. 3.
[k] 2 Kgs. 17. 13, 14.

6 And the sword shall abide on his cities, and shall consume his branches, and devour *them*, [l]because of their own counsels.

Before CHRIST cir. 740.

cir. 728. They became tributaries to Salmanasser.
[l] ch. 10. 6.

become to me, to want the sweetnesses of those toys; and what I feared to be parted from, was now a joy to part with. For Thou didst cast them forth from me, Thou true and highest Sweetness. Thou castedst them forth, and for them enteredst in Thyself, sweeter than all pleasure, though not to flesh and blood; brighter than all light, but more hidden than all depths; higher than all honor, but not to the high in their own conceits."

"[1] Christ *drew* us also *with the cords of a man*, when for us He became Man, our flesh, our Brother, in order that by teaching, suffering, dying for us, He might in a wondrous way bind and draw us to Himself and to God; that He might redeem the earthly Adam, might transform and make him heavenly;" "[2] giving us ineffable tokens of His love. For He giveth Himself to us for our Food; He giveth us sacraments; by Baptism and repentance He conformeth us anew to original righteousness. Hence He saith [3], *I, if I be lifted up from the earth, shall draw all men unto me;* and Paul [4], *I live by the faith of the Son of God, Who loved me and gave Himself for me*. This most loving drawing, our dullness and weakness needeth, who ever, without grace, grovel amidst vile and earthly things."

"All the methods and parts of God's government are twined together, as so many twisted cords of love from Him, so ordered, that they ought to draw man with all his heart to love Him again." "[5] Man, the image of the Mind of God, is impelled to zeal for the service of God, not by fear, but by love. No band is mightier, nor constrains more firmly all the feelings of the mind. For it holdeth not the body enchained, while the mind revolteth and longeth to break away, but it so bindeth to itself the mind and will, that it should will, long for, compass, nought beside, save how, even amid threats of death, to obey the commands of God. Bands they are, but bands so gentle and so passing sweet, that we must account them perfect freedom and the highest dignity."

And I was to them as they that take off (lit. *that lift up*) *the yoke on their jaws, and I laid meat unto them*. Thus explained, the words carry on the description of God's goodness, that He allowed not the yoke of slavery to weigh heavy upon them, as He saith [6], *I am the Lord your God, Which brought you out of the land of Egypt, that ye should not be their bondmen, and I have broken the bands of your yoke, and made you go upright;* and God appealeth to them [7], *Wherein have I wearied thee? testify against Me.*

But the words seem more naturally to mean, *I was to them*, in their sight, I was regarded by them, *as they that lift up the yoke on their jaws*, i. e. *that raise the yoke*, (not being already upon them) to place it *over their jaws*. "For plainly the yoke never rests on the jaws, but only passed over them, either when put on the neck, or taken off." This, God seemed to them to be doing, ever placing some new yoke or constraint upon them. *And I*, God adds, all the while *was placing meat before them;* i. e. while God was taking all manner of care of them, and providing for them *all things richly to enjoy*, He was regarded by them as one who, instead of *laying food before them*, was *lifting the yoke over their jaws*. God did them all good, and they thought it all hardship.

5. *He shall not return to Egypt*. Some had probably returned already to Egypt; the rest were looking to Egypt for help, and rebelling against the Assyrian, (whose servant their king Hoshea had become), and making alliance with So king of Egypt. The Prophet tells them, as a whole, that they shall not return to Egypt to which they looked, but should have the Assyrian for their king, whom they would not. *They refused to return* to God, Who lovingly called them; therefore, what they desired, they should not have; and what they feared, that they should have. They would not have God for their king; therefore *the Assyrian* should *be their king*, and a worse captivity than that of Egypt should befall them. For, from *that* they were delivered; from this, now hanging over them, never should they be restored.

6. *And the sword shall abide on his cities*, lit. *shall light, shall whirl* down upon. It shall come with violence upon them as a thing whirled with force, and then it shall alight and abide, to their destruction; as Jeremiah says [8], *a whirlwind of the Lord is gone forth in fury, a grievous whirlwind; it shall fall grievously* [lit. *whirl down*] *on the head of the wicked*. As God said to David, after the murder of Uriah [9], *Now therefore the sword shall never de-*

[1] Rup. Lap. [2] Dion. [3] S. John xii. 32.
[4] Gal. ii. 20. [5] Osor.
[6] Lev. xxvi. 13. [7] Mic. vi. 3.
[8] Jer. xxiii. 19. [9] 2 Sam. xii. 10.

Before CHRIST cir. 740.

7 And my people are bent to [m]backsliding from me: [n]though they called them to the most High, †none at all would exalt him.

[m] Jer. 3. 6, &c. & 8. 5. ch. 4. 16.
[n] ch. 7. 16.
† Heb. *together they exalted not.*

8 [o]How shall I give thee up, Ephraim? *how* shall I deliver thee, Israel? How shall I make thee as [p]Admah? *how* shall I set thee as Zeboim? [q]mine heart is

Before CHRIST cir. 740.

[o] Jer. 9. 7. ch. 6. 4.
[p] Gen. 14. 8. & 19. 24, 25. Deut. 29. 23. Amos 4. 11.
[q] Deut. 32. 36. Is. 63. 15. Jer. 31. 20.

part from thy house, so as to Israel, whose kings were inaugurated by bloodshed. By God's appointment, "blood will have blood." Their own sword first came down and rested upon them; then the sword of the Assyrian. So after they *had killed the Holy One and the Just,* the sword of the Zealots came down and rested upon them, before the destruction by the Romans.

And shall consume his branches, i. e. his mighty men. It is all one, whether the mighty men are so called, by metaphor, from the *branches* of a tree, or from the *bars* of a city, made out of those branches. Their mighty men, so far from escaping for their might, should be the first to perish.

And devour them, *because of their own counsels.* Their counsels, wise after this world's wisdom, were without God, against the counsels of God. Their destruction then should come from their own wisdom, as it is said[1], *Let them fall by their own counsels,* and Job saith[2], *He taketh the wise in their own craftiness, and the counsel of the cunning is carried headlong,* i. e. it is the clean contrary of what they intend or plan; they purpose, as they think, warily; an unseen power whirls their scheme on and precipitates it. *And his own counsel shall cast him down*[3]; and above; [4] *Israel shall be ashamed through his own counsels.* Hoshea's conspiracy with So, which was to have been his support against Assyria, brought Assyria against him, and his people into captivity.

7. *And My people are bent to backsliding from Me,* lit. *are hung to it!* as we say, "a man's whole being *hangs* on a thing." A thing *hung to* or *on* another, sways to and fro within certain limits, but its relation to that on which it is hung, remains immovable. Its power of motion is restrained within those limits. So Israel, so the sinner, however he veer to and fro in the details and circumstances of his sin, is fixed and immovable in his adherence to his sin itself. Whatever else Israel did, on one thing his whole being, as a nation, depended, on *backsliding* or aversion[5] from God. The political existence of Israel, as a separate kingdom, depended on his worship of the calves, *the sin wherewith* Jeroboam *made Israel to sin.* This was the ground of their[6] *refusing to return,* that, through habitual sin, they were no longer in their own power: they were fixed in evil.

Though they called them to the most High, lit. *called him.* As one man, the prophets called Israel; as one man, Israel refused to return; *none at all would exalt* Him, lit. *together he exalteth* Him *not.*

8. *How shall I give thee up, Ephraim?* "[7]God is infinitely just and infinitely merciful. The two attributes are so united in Him, yea, so one in Him Who is always One, and in Whose counsels *there is no variableness, nor shadow of turning,* that the one doth not ever thwart the proceeding of the other. Yet, in order to shew that our ills are from our own ill-deserts, not from any pleasure of His in inflicting ill, and that what mercy He sheweth, is from His own goodness, not from any in us, God is represented in this empassioned expression as in doubt, and (so to say) divided betwixt justice and mercy, the one pleading against the other. At the last, God so determines, that both should have their share in the issue, and that Israel should be both justly punished and mercifully spared and relieved."

God pronounces on the evil deserts of Israel, even while He mitigates His sentence. The depth of the sinner's guilt reflects the more vividly the depth of God's mercy. In saying, *how shall I make thee as Admah? how shall I set thee as Zeboim?* He says, in fact, that they were, for their sins, worthy to be utterly destroyed, with no trace, no memorial, save that eternal desolation like the five *cities of the plain,* of which were Sodom and Gomorrah, which God[8] *hath set forth for an example, suffering the vengeance of eternal fire.* Such was their desert. But God says, with inexpressible tenderness, *Mine heart is turned within Me* lit. *upon Me* or *against Me,* so as to be a burden to Him; as we say of the heart, that it is "heavy." God deigneth to speak as if His love was heavy, or a weight upon Him, while He thought of the punishment which their sins deserved.

My heart is turned. "[9]As soon as I had spoken evil against thee, mercy prevailed, tenderness touched Me; the tenderness of the Father overcame the austerity of the Judge."

[1] Ps. v. 10. [2] v. 13. [3] Ib. xviii. 7. [4] ch. x. 6.
[5] The Rabbins observe that משובה is used in an evil sense of *aversion* from God, תשובה of conversion to Him. [6] ver. 5. [7] Poc. [8] S. Jude 7. [9] Rup.

Before CHRIST cir. 740.

turned within me, my re-
pentings are kindled to-
gether.
9 I will not execute the
fierceness of mine anger, I
will not return to destroy
Ephraim: [r] for I *am* God,
and not man; the Holy One
in the midst of thee: and
I will not enter into the city.

Before CHRIST cir. 740.

[r] Num. 23. 19. Is. 55. 8, 9. Mal. 3. 6.

My repentings are kindled together, or *My strong compassions*[1] *are kindled*, i.e. with the heat and glow of love; as the disciples say[2], *Did not our hearts burn within us?* and as it is said of Joseph *his bowels did yearn*[3] (lit. *were hot*) *towards his brother;* and of the true mother before Solomon, *her bowels yearned*[4] (E. M. *were hot*) *upon her son.*

Admah and *Zeboim* were cities in the same plain with Sodom and Gomorrah, and each had their petty king[5]. In the history of the destruction of Sodom and Gomorrah, they are not named, but are included in the general title *those cities and all the plain*[6]. The more then would Hosea's hearers think of that place in Moses where he does mention them, and where he threatens them with the like end; [7] *when the stranger shall see*, that *the whole land thereof* is *brimstone and salt and burning, that it is not sown, nor beareth, nor any grass groweth therein, like the overthrow of Sodom and Gomorrah, Admah and Zeboim, which the Lord overthrew in His anger and His wrath.* Such was the end, at which all their sins aimed; such the end, which God had held out to them; but His *strong compassions were kindled.*

9. *I will not execute the fierceness of Mine anger.* It is the voice of *mercy, rejoicing over judgment.* Mercy prevails in God over the rigor of His justice, that though He will not suffer them to go utterly unpunished, yet He will abate of it, and not utterly consume them.

I will not return to destroy Ephraim. God saith that He will not, as it were, glean Ephraim, going over it again, as man doth, in order to leave nothing over. As it is in Jeremiah[8], *They shall thoroughly glean the remnant of Israel, as a vine. Turn back thine hand, as a grapegatherer into the baskets;* and, *If grapegatherers come to thee, would they not leave some gleaning-grapes? but I have made Esau bare*[9].

For I am *God and not man*, "[10] not swayed by human passions, but so tempering His wrath, as, in the midst of it, to remember mercy; so punishing the iniquity of the sinful children, as at once to make good His gracious promises which He made to their forefathers." "[11] Man punishes, to destroy; God smites, to amend."

The Holy One in the midst of thee. The holiness of God is at once a ground why He punishes iniquity, and yet does not punish to the full extent of the sin. Truth and faithfulness are part of the holiness of God. He, the Holy One Who was *in the midst* of them, by virtue of His covenant with their fathers, would keep the covenant which He had made, and for their father's sakes would not wholly cut them off. Yet the holiness of God hath another aspect too, in virtue of which the unholy cannot profit by the promises of the All-Holy. "I will not," paraphrases S. Cyril, "use unmingled wrath. I will not *give* over Ephraim, wicked as he has become, to entire destruction. Why? Do they not deserve it? Yes, He saith, but *I am God and not man*, i. e. Good, and not suffering the motions of anger to overcome Me. For that is a human passion. Why then dost Thou yet punish, seeing Thou art God, not overcome with anger, but rather following Thine essential gentleness? I punish, He saith, because I am not only Good, as God, but Holy also, hating iniquity, rejecting the polluted, turning away from God-haters, converting the sinner, purifying the impure, that he may again be joined to Me. We, then, if we prize the being with God, must, with all our might, fly from sin, and remember what He said, *Be ye holy, for I am holy.*"

And I will not enter the city. God, Who is everywhere, speaks of Himself, as present to *us*, when He shews that presence in acts of judgment or of mercy. He visited His people in Egypt, to deliver them; He visited Sodom and Gomorrah as a Judge, making known to us that He took cognizance of their extreme wickedness. God says, that He would *not enter the city*, as He did *the cities of the plain*, when He overthrew them, because He willed to save them. As a Judge, He acts as though He looked away from their sin, lest, seeing their city to be full of wickedness, He should be compelled to punish it. "[12] I will not smite indiscriminately, as man doth, who when wroth, bursts into an offending city, and destroys all. In this sense, the Apostle says[13], *Hath God cast away His people? God forbid! For I also am an Israelite, of the seed of Abraham, of the tribe of Benjamin. God hath not cast away His people, whom He foreknew.*

1 The word נחומי is an intensive.
2 S. Luke xxiv. 32.
3 Gen. xliii. 30.
4 1 Kings iii. 26. The word is the same in all three places נכמרו.

5 Gen. xiv. 2.
6 Ib. xix. 25.
7 Deut. xxix. 22, 3.
8 vi. 9.
9 Ib. xlix. 9, 10.
10 Poc.
11 S. Jer.
12 Rup.
13 Rom. xi. 1, 2, 4, 5.

Before CHRIST cir. 740.

10 They shall walk after the LORD: [s] he shall roar like a lion: when he shall roar, then the children shall tremble [t] from the west.

[s] Is. 31. 4. Joel 3. 16. Amos 1. 2.
[t] Zech. 8. 7.

11 They shall tremble as a bird out of Egypt, [u] and as a dove out of the land of Assyria: [x] and I will place them in their houses, saith the LORD.

Before CHRIST cir. 740.

[u] Is. 60. 8. ch. 7. 11.
[x] Ezek. 28. 25, 26. & 37. 21, 25.

What saith the answer of God to Elias! I have reserved to Myself seven thousand men, who have not bowed the knee to Baal. Even so then, at this present time also, there is a remnant according to the election of grace. God then was wroth, not with His people, but with unbelief. For He was not angered in such wise, as not to receive the remnant of His people, if they were converted. No Jew is therefore repelled, because the Jewish nation denied Christ; but whoso, whether Jew or Gentile, denieth Christ, he himself, in his own person, repels himself."

10. *They shall walk after the Lord.* Not only would God not destroy them all, but a remnant of them should *walk after the Lord*, i. e. they shall believe in Christ. The Jews of old understood this of Christ. One of them saith [1], "this pointeth to the time of their redemption." And another [2], "Although I will withdraw from the midst of them My Divine Presence for their iniquity, and remove them out of their own land, yet shall there be a long time in which they shall seek after the Lord and find Him." This is what Hosea has said before [3], that they should *abide many days without a king and without a prince, and without a sacrifice;—afterward shall the children of Israel return and seek the Lord their God, and David their king.* "[4] Whereas now they *fled from God*, and *walked after other gods after the imagination of their evil hearts, after their own devices* [5], then He promises, they shall *walk after* God *the Lord*, following the will, the mind, the commandments, the example of Almighty God. As God says of David, He *kept My commandments, and walked after Me with all his heart* [6]; and Micah foretells that *many nations shall say, we will walk in His paths* [7]." They shall *follow after* Him, Whose Infinite perfections none can reach; yet they shall *follow after*, never standing still, but reaching on to that which is unattainable; by His grace, attaining the more by imitating what is inimitable, and stopping short of no perfection, until, in His Presence, they be perfected in Him.

He shall roar like a lion. Christ is called *the Lion of the tribe of Judah* [8]. His *roaring* is His loud call to repentance, by Himself and by His Apostles. The voice of God to sinners, although full of love, must be full of awe too. He calls them, not only to flee to His mercy, but to *flee from the wrath to come.* He shall call to them with a voice of Majesty and command.

When He shall roar, the children shall tremble from the West, i. e. they shall come in haste and fear to God. "[9] *His word is powerful, sharper than any two-edged sword, piercing even to the dividing asunder of soul and spirit, and of the joints and marrow.* Whence those whose hearts were pricked at the preaching of St. Peter, said to him with trembling [10], *Men and brethren what shall we do?* So did the preaching of judgment to come terrify the world, that from all places some did come out of the captivity of the world and did fly to Christ [11]." He says, *from the West;* for *from the West* have most come in to the Gospel. Yet the Jews were then about to be carried to the East, not to the West; and of the West the prophets had no human knowledge. But the ten tribes, although carried to the East into Assyria, did not all remain there, since before the final dispersion, we find Jews in Italy, Greece, Asia Minor; whither those who had been restored to their own land, would not have anew exiled themselves. In these, whenever they were converted, this prophecy was fulfilled.

11. *They shall tremble as a bird out of Egypt.* The West denoted Europe; Egypt and Assyria stand, each for all the lands beyond them, and so for Africa and Asia; all together comprise the three quarters of the world, whence converts have chiefly come to Christ. These are likened to birds, chiefly for the swiftness with which they shall then haste to the call of God, who now turned away the more, the more they were called. The dove, especially, was a bird of Palestine, proverbial for the swiftness of its flight, easily affrighted, and flying the more rapidly, the more it was frightened, and returning to its cot from any distance whither it might be carried; whence Isaiah also says of the converts [12], *Who are these that fly as a cloud, and as the doves to their windows?* "The Hebrews," says S. Jerome, "refer this to the coming of the Christ, Who, they hope, will come; we shew that it hath taken place already. For both from Egypt and Assyria, i. e.

[1] Tanchum, in Poc. [2] Kimchi.
[3] Hos. iii. 4, 5. [4] Poc.
[5] Hos. vii. 13. Jer. vii. 9. iii. 17. xviii. 12.
[6] 1 Kings xiv. 8. [7] iv. 2. [8] Rev. v. 5.
[9] Heb. iv. 12. [10] Acts ii. 37.
[11] Poc. [12] Is. lx. 8.

Before CHRIST cir. 740.

12 [y] Ephraim compasseth me about with lies, and the house of Israel with deceit: but Judah yet ruleth with God, and is faithful || with the saints.

y ch. 12. 1.

|| Or, *with the most holy.*

CHAPTER XII.

1 *A reproof of Ephraim, Judah, and Jacob.* 3 *By former favors*

from East and West, from North and South, have they come, and daily do they come, who sit down with Abraham, Isaac and Jacob."

And I will place them in their houses. Their houses may be their own particular Churches, in the one Church or *House of God*[1]. In this house, God says, that He will make them to dwell, not again to be removed from it, nor shaken in it, but in a secure dwelling-place here until they be fitted to be removed to everlasting habitations. "[2] *In their houses,* i. e. in the mansions prepared for them. For from the beginning of the world, when He created our first parents, and blessed them and said, *Increase and multiply and replenish the earth,* He prepared for them everlasting *houses* or mansions. Whereof He said, just before His Death, *In My father's house are many mansions,* and in the last Day, He will say, *Come ye blessed of My Father, inherit the kingdom prepared for you from the foundation of the world.*

12. *Ephraim compasseth Me about with lies.* Having spoken of future repentance, conversion, restoration, he turns back to those around him, and declares why they can have no share in that restoration. Nothing about them was true. If ever they approached God, it was *with lies.* "[3] God, being infinite, cannot really be *compassed about.*" The Prophet so speaks, to describe the "great multitude of those who thus lied to God, and the multitude and manifoldness of their lies. Wherever God looked, in all parts of their kingdom, in all their doings, all which He could see was lying to Himself." All was, as it were, one throng of lies, heaped on one another, jostling with one another. Such is the world now. "Their sin was especially a lie, because they sinned, not through ignorance, but through malice." Their chief lie was the setting up of the worship of the calves, with a worldly end, yet with pretence of religion towards God; denying Him, the One true God, in that they joined idols with Him, yet professing to serve Him. And so all their worship of God, their repentance, their prayers, their sacrifices were all one lie. For one lie underlay all, penetrated all, corrupted all. All half-belief is unbelief; all half-repentance is unrepentance, all half-worship is unworship; and, in that each and all give themselves out for that Divine whole, whereof they are but the counterfeit, each and all are *lies,* wherewith men, on all sides, encompass God. From these wrong thoughts of God all their other deceits flowed, while yet, "they deceived, not Him but themselves, in that they thought that they could deceive Him, Who cannot be deceived." When Christ came, the house of Israel surrounded Him with lies, the scribes and lawyers, the Pharisees and Sadducees and Herodians, vying with one another, *how they might entangle Him in His talk*[4].

But Judah yet ruleth with God. Ephraim had cast off the rule of God, the kings and priests whom He had appointed, so that his whole kingdom and polity was without God and against Him. In contrast with this, Judah, amid all His sins, was outwardly faithful. He adhered to the line of kings, from whom was to spring the Christ, David's Son but David's Lord. He worshiped with the priests whom God had appointed to offer the typical sacrifices, until *He* should come, *the High Priest forever, after the order of Melchisedek,* Who should end those sacrifices by the Sacrifice of Himself. Thus far Judah *ruled with God*; he was on the side of God, maintained the worship of God, was upheld by God. So Abijah said to Jeroboam[5], *The Lord is our God, and we have not forsaken Him, and the priests which minister unto the Lord are the sons of Aaron, and the Levites wait upon their business. For we keep the charge of the Lord our God, but ye have forsaken Him, and behold God is with us for our Captain, &c.*

And is faithful with the saints; or [better perhaps, with the E. M.] *with the All-Holy.* The same plural is used of God elsewhere[6]; and its use, like that of the ordinary name of God, is founded on the mystery of the Trinity. It does not teach it, but neither can it be accounted for in any other way. This faithfulness of Judah was outward only, (as the upbraiding of the Prophet to Judah testifies,) yet did it much favor inward holiness. *The body without the soul is dead;* yet the life, even when seeming to be dying out, might be brought back, when the body was there; not, when it too was dissolved. Hence Judah had many good kings, Israel none. Yet, in that he says, *yet ruleth with God,* he shews that a time was coming when Judah too would be, not *with God* but against Him, and also would be cast off.

XII. 1. *Ephraim feedeth on wind, and fol-*

[1] 1 Tim. iii. 15. [2] Rup. [3] Poc.
[4] S. Matt. xxii. 15. [5] 2 Chron. xiii. 10–12.

[6] קדושים Josh. xxiv. 19. and in Prov. xxx. 3. where our translators too render it *the holy.*

Before CHRIST cir. 725.

he exhorteth to repentance. 7 Ephraim's sins provoke God.

[a] ch. 8. 7.

EPHRAIM [a] feedeth on wind, and followeth after the east wind: he daily increaseth lies and desolation; [b] and they do make a covenant with the Assyrians, and [c] oil is carried into Egypt.

[b] 2 Kgs. 17. 4. ch. 5. 13. & 7. 11.

2 [d] The LORD hath also a controversy with Judah, and will † punish Jacob according to his ways; according to his doings will he recompense him.

Before CHRIST cir. 725.

[c] Is. 30. 6. & 57. 9.
[d] ch. 4. 1. Mic. 6. 2.
† Heb. *visit upon.*

loweth after the east wind. The East wind in Palestine, coming from Arabia and the far East, over large tracts of sandy waste, is parching, scorching, destructive to vegetation, oppressive to man, violent and destructive on the sea[1], and, by land also, having the force of the whirlwind. [2] *The East wind carrieth him away and he departeth, and as a whirlwind hurleth him out of his place.* In leaving God and following idols, Ephraim *fed on* what is unsatisfying, and chased after what is destructive. If a hungry man were to *feed on wind,* it would be light food. If a man could overtake the East wind, it were his destruction. Israel "[3] *fed on wind,* when he sought by gifts to win one who could aid him no more than the wind; *he chased the East wind,* when, in place of the gain which he sought, he received from the patron whom he had adopted, no slight loss." Israel sought for the scorching wind, when it could betake itself under the shadow of God. "[4] The scorching wind is the burning of calamities, and the consuming fire of affliction."

He increaseth lies and desolation. Unrepented sins and their punishment are, in God's government, linked together; so that to multiply sin is, in fact, to multiply desolation. Sin and punishment are bound together, as cause and effect. Man overlooks what he does not see. Yet not the less does he [5] *treasure up wrath against the Day of wrath and revelation of the righteous Judgment of God.* "[3] *Lying* will signify false speaking, false dealing, false belief, false opinions, false worship, false pretences for color thereof, false hopes, or relying on things that will deceive. In all these kinds, was Ephraim at that time guilty, adding one sort of lying to another."

They do make a covenant with the Assyrians and oil is carried into Egypt. Oil was a chief product of Palestine, whence it is called [6] *a land of oil olive;* and *oil* with balm was among its chief exports to Tyre[7]. It may also include precious ointments, of which it was the basis. As an export of great value, it stands for all other presents, which Hoshea sent to So, King of Egypt. Ephraim, threatened by God, looked first to the Assyrian, then to Egypt, to strengthen itself. Having dealt falsely with God, he dealt falsely with man. First, he *made covenant with* Shalmaneser, king of *Assyria;* then, finding the tribute, the price of his help, burdensome to him, he broke that covenant, by sending to Egypt. Seeking to make friends out of God, Ephraim made the more powerful, the Assyrian, the more his enemy, by seeking the friendship of Egypt; and God executed His judgments through those, by whose help they had hoped to escape them.

2. *The Lord hath also a controversy with Judah, and will punish Jacob.* The guilt of Judah was not open apostasy, nor had he filled up the measure of his sins. Of him, then, God saith only, that He *had a controversy with* him, as our Lord says to *the Angel of the Church of Pergamos*[8], *I have a few things against thee. Repent, or else I will come unto thee quickly, and fight against thee with the sword of My mouth.* Of Ephraim, whose sin was complete, He says, that the Lord *is to punish.* God had set His mind, as we say, on punishing him; He had (so to speak) set Himself to do it[9]. Jacob, like Israel, is here the name for the chief part of Israel, i. e. the ten tribes. Our Lord uses the same gradation in speaking of different degrees of evil-speaking[10]; *Whosoever of you is angry without a cause, shall be in danger of the judgment; and whosoever shall say to his brother, Raca, shall be in danger of the council; but whosoever shall say, Thou fool, shall be in danger of hell-fire.* "[11] The justice of God falls more severely on those who degenerate from a holy parent, than on those who have no incitement to good from the piety of their home." To amplify this, "[12] The Prophet explains what good things Jacob received, to shew both the mercy of God to Jacob, and the hardness of Ephraim towards God. While Jacob was yet in his mother's womb, he took his brother by the heel, not by any strength of his own, but by the mercy of God, Who knows and loves those whom he hath predestinated."

[1] Ps. xlviii. 7. [2] Job xxvii. 21. See Jer. xviii. 17.
[3] Poc. [4] S. Cyr.
[5] Rom. ii. 5. [6] Deut. viii. 8.

[7] Ezek. xxvii. 17. See ab. ii. 8.
[8] Rev. ii. 12, 16. [9] The force of ל.
[10] S. Matt. v. 22. [11] Osor. [12] S. Jer.

Before CHRIST cir. 725.

3 ¶ He took his brother
[e] by the heel in the womb,
and by his strength he
† [f] had power with God:

[e] Gen. 25. 26.
† Heb. *was a prince*, or, *behaved himself princely.*
[f] Gen. 32, 24, &c.

4 Yea, he had power
over the angel, and pre-
vailed: he wept, and made
supplication unto him: he

Before CHRIST cir. 725.

3. *He took his brother by the heel in the womb.* Whether or no the act of Jacob was beyond the strength, ordinarily given to infants in the womb, the meaning of the act was beyond man's wisdom to declare. Whence the Jews paraphrased, "[1] Was it not predicted of your father Jacob, before he was born, that he should become greater than his brother?" Yet this was not fulfilled until more than 500 years afterwards, nor completely until the time of David. These gifts were promised to Jacob out of the free mercy of God, antecedent to all deserts. But Jacob, thus chosen without desert, shewed forth the power of faith; *By his strength he had power with God.* "[2] The strength by which he did this, was God's strength, as well as that by which God contended with him; yet it is well called *his*, as being by God given to him. Yet *he had power with God*, God so ordering it, that the strength which was in Jacob, should put itself forth with greater force, than that in the assumed body, whereby He so dealt with Jacob. God, as it were, bore the office of two persons, shewing in Jacob more strength than He put forth in the Angel." "By virtue of that faith in Jacob, it is related that God *could* not prevail against him. He could not because He would not overthrow his faith and constancy. By the touch in the hollow of his thigh, He but added strength to his faith, shewing him Who it was Who wrestled with him, and that He willed to bless him." For thereon Jacob said those words which have become a proverb of earnest supplication[3], *I will not let thee go, except thou bless me*, and, *I have seen God, face to face, and my life is preserved.* "[4] He was strengthened by the blessing of Him Whom he overcame."

4. *He wept and made supplication unto Him.* Jacob's weeping is not mentioned by Moses. Hosea then knew more than Moses related. He could not have gathered it out of Moses; for Moses relates the words of earnest supplication; yet the tone is that of one, by force of earnest energy, wresting, as it were, the blessing from God, not of one weeping. Yet Hosea adds this, in harmony with Moses. For "vehement desires and earnest petitions frequently issue in tears." "[5] To implore means to ask with tears." "Jacob, learning, that God Himself thus deigned to deal with him, might well out of amazement and wonder, out of awful respect to Him, and in earnest desire of a blessing, pour out his supplication with tears." Herein he became an image of Him, *Who, in the days of His flesh, offered up prayers and supplications, with strong crying and tears unto Him that was able to save Him from death, and was heard in that He feared*[6].

"[7] This which he saith, *he prevailed*, subjoining, *he wept and made supplication*, describes the strength of penitents; for in truth they are strong by weeping earnestly and praying perseveringly for the forgiveness of sins, according to that, *From the days of John the kingdom of heaven suffereth violence, and the violent take it by force.* Whosoever so imitates the Patriarch Jacob, who wrestled with the Angel, and, as a conqueror, extorted a blessing from him, he, of whatever nation he be, is truly Jacob, and deserveth to be called Israel." "[8] Yea, herein is the unconquerable might of the righteous, this his wondrous wrestling, herein his glorious victories, in glowing longings, assiduous prayers, joyous weeping. Girt with the might of holy orison, they strive with God, they wrestle with His judgment, and will not be overcome, until they obtain from His goodness all they desire, and extort it, as it were, by force, from His hands."

He found him in *Bethel.* This may mean either that "God found Jacob," or that "Jacob found God;" which are indeed one and the same thing, since we find God, when He has first found us. God *found*, i. e. made Himself known to Jacob twice in this place; first, when he was going toward Haran, when he saw the vision of the ladder and the angels of God ascending and descending, *and the Lord stood above it and said, I* am *the Lord God of Abraham and the God of Isaac;* and Jacob first called the place *Bethel;* secondly, on his return, when God spake with him, giving him the name of Israel. Both revelations of God to Jacob are probably included in the words, *He found him in Bethel*, since, on both occasions, God did *find him*, and come to him, and he *found* God. In Bethel, where God *found* Jacob, Israel deserted Him, setting up the worship of the calves; yea, he deserted God the more there, because of God's mercy to his forefather, desecrating to false worship the place which had been consecrated by the revelation of the true God; and

[1] Jon. [2] Poc. [3] Gen. xxxii. 26, 30. [4] S. Jer.
[5] Implorare est fletu rogare. Imploro is formed from ploro, which relation is retained in the French Implorer, pleurer, pleurs. So we have *cry* (i. e. weep) and *cry on him*, [R. Glouc.] *cry unto.*
[6] Heb. v. 7. [7] Rup. [8] Osor.

Before CHRIST cir. 725.

found him *in*[g] Beth-el, and there he spake with us;

g Gen. 28. 12, 19. & 35. 9, 10, 15.

5 Even the LORD God of hosts; the LORD *is* his [h] memorial.

h Ex. 3. 15.

choosing it the rather, because it had been so consecrated.

And there He spake with us. For what He said to Jacob, He said not to Jacob only, nor for Jacob's sake alone, but, in him, He spake to all his posterity, both the children of his body and the children of his faith. Thus it is said[1], *There did we rejoice in Him*, i. e. we, their posterity, rejoiced in God there, where He so delivered our forefathers, and, [2] *Levi also, who receiveth tithes, paid tithes in Abraham, for he was yet in the loins of his father, when Melchizedek met him.* And S. Paul saith, that what was said to Abraham, *therefore it was imputed to him for righteousness, was not written for his sake alone, but for us also, to whom it shall be imputed, if we believe on Him that raised up Jesus our Lord from the dead*[3]. There He spake with us, how, in our needs, we should seek and find Him. In loneliness, apart from distractions, in faith, rising in proportion to our fears, in persevering prayer, in earnestness, which "clings so fast to God, that if God would cast us into Hell, He should, (as one said) Himself go with us, so should Hell not be Hell to us," God is sought and found.

5. *Even the Lord God of Hosts, the Lord* is *His memorial.* The word, here as elsewhere, translated and written LORD, is the special and, so to say, the proper Name of God, that which He gave to Himself, and which declares His Being. God Himself authoritatively explained its meaning. When Moses inquired of Him, what he should say to Israel, when they should ask him, *what is the Name* of *the God of their fathers*, Who, he was to tell them, had sent him to them[4], *God said*, I AM THAT I AM; *thus shalt thou say*, I AM (EHYeH) *hath sent me unto you*; *and God said again unto Moses, Thus shalt thou say unto the children of Israel; The* LORD [lit HE IS, YeHeVeH[5],] *the God of your fathers, the God of Abraham, the God of Isaac, and the God of Jacob, hath sent me unto you; This is My Name for ever, and this is My memorial unto all generations.* I AM, expresses Self-existence; He Who Alone IS. I AM THAT I AM, expresses His Unchangeableness, the necessary attribute of the Self-existent, Who, since HE IS, ever IS all which He IS. "To Be," says S. Augustine[6], "is a name of unchangeableness. For all things which are changed, cease to be what they were, and begin to be what they were not. True Being, pure Being, genuine Being, no one hath, save He Who changeth not. He hath Being to Whom it is said, *Thou shalt change them and they shall be changed, but Thou art the Same.* What is, I AM THAT I AM, but, I am Eternal? What is, I AM THAT I AM, save, I cannot be changed? No creature, no heaven, no earth, no angel, *nor Power, nor Throne, nor Dominion, nor Principality.* This then being the name of eternity, it is somewhat more, than He vouchsafed to him a name of mercy, *I am the God of Abraham, the God of Isaac, the God of Jacob. That*, He is in Himself, *this*, to us. If he willed only to be That which he is in Himself, what should we be? Since Moses understood, when it was said to him, I AM THAT I AM, HE Who IS hath sent me unto you, he believed that this was much to men, he saw that this was far removed from men. For whoso hath understood, as he ought, That which IS, and which truly IS, and, in whatever degree, hath even transiently, as by a lightning flash, been irradiated by the light of the One True Essence, sees himself far below, in the utmost farness of removal and unlikeness." This, the Self-existent, the Unchangeable, was the meaning of God's ancient Name, by which He was known to the Patriarchs, although they had not in act seen His unchangeableness; for theirs was a life of faith, hoping for what they saw not. The word, HE IS, when used of Him by His creatures, expresses the same which He says of Himself, I AM. This He willed to be *His memorial forever.* This the way in which He willed that we should believe in Him and think of Him as HE Who IS, the Self-existing, the Self-Same.

The way of pronouncing that Name is lost[7]. The belief has continued, wherever

1 Ps. lxvi. 6. 2 Heb. vii. 9, 10.
3 Rom. iv, 23, 4. 4 Ex. iii. 13–15.

5 יהוה "HE IS," from an old verb הוה "*is*," which exists in Chaldee and Syriac, and which in Hebrew became היה, as חוה "lives" (whence the name of Eve חַוָּה) became חיה. The old form remained in poetic language in the Imperative (Gen. xxvii. 19. Job xxxvii. 6. Is. xvi. 4.) and in the Participle, Eccl. ii. 22. Neh. vi. 6. The root הוה must have been almost out of use in the time of Moses, since the word is explained in Exodus by the use of the verb היה, not by הוה. The vowels, by which the consonants are to be pronounced, must remain uncertain. It might be pronounced *Yihveh* (like יִהְיֶה) or *Yeheveh* (after the analogy of יֶהֱמֶה) or less probably, *Yehveh* like יֶהְגֶּה. Another pronunciation, *Yahaveh* or *Yahveh*, might seem to be favored by Theodoret's statement, that the Samaritans pronounced it IABE (Quæst. 15. in Exod.); but on the other hand the Samaritans, like the Galileans, had probably a broader pronunciation than the Jews.

6 Serm. 7. § 7.

7 The popular pronunciation *Jehovah*, is altogether a mistake. When a word in the text is not read by the Jews, (and this ceased to be read before the vowels were written) the vowels belong, not to the word itself, but to another, which is to be substituted for it. Those placed under this word, יהוה, vary.

Before CHRIST cir. 725.

6 [l] Therefore turn thou
to thy God: keep mercy
and judgment, and [k] wait
on thy God continually.

[l] ch. 14. 1. Mic. 6. 8.

Before CHRIST cir. 725.

[k] Ps. 37. 7.

---

the LORD is named. For by the Lord we mean the Unchangeable God. That belief is contradicted, whenever people use the name Jehovah, to speak of God, as though the belief in Him under the Old Testament differed from that of the New. Perhaps God allowed it to be lost, that people might not make so familiar with it, as they do with the word Jehovah, or use it irreverently and anti-Christianly, as some now employ other ways of pronouncing it. The Jews, even before the time of our Lord, ceased ordinarily to pronounce it. In the translations of the Old Testament, and in the Apocrypha, the words, "the Lord," were substituted for it. Jewish tradition states, that in later times the Name was pronounced in the Temple only, by the priests, on pronouncing the blessing commanded by God in the law [1]. On the great Day of atonement, it was said that the High Priest pronounced it ten times [2], and that when the people heard it, they fell on their faces, saying, "Blessed be the glorious name of His kingdom for ever and ever [3]." They say, however, that in the time of Simeon the Just [i. e. Jaddua [4].] who died about B. C. 322, the High Priests themselves disused it, for fear of its being pronounced by some irreverent person [5].

Our Lord Himself sanctioned the disuse of it, (as did the inspired Apostles yet more frequently,) since, in quoting places of the Old Testament in which it occurs, He uses instead of it the Name, *the Lord* [6]. It stands, throughout the Old Testament, as the Name which speaks of God in relation to His people, that He ever IS; and, since He ever IS, then He IS unchangeably to us, all which He ever was, *The Same, yesterday and to-day and for ever* [7].

He then Who appeared to Jacob, and Who, in Jacob, spake to all the posterity of Jacob, was God; whether it was (as almost all the early fathers thought [8],) God the Son, Who thus appeared in human form to the Patriarchs, Moses, Joshua, and in the time of the Judges, under the name of *the Angel of the Lord*, or whether it was the Father. God Almighty thus accustomed man to see the form of Man, and to know and believe that it was God. He it was, the Prophet explains, *the Lord*, i. e. the Self-existent, the Unchangeable, *Who was, and is and is to come* [9], Who Alone Is, and from Whom are all things, "[10] the Fullness of Being, both of His own, and of all His creatures, the boundless Ocean of all which is, of wisdom, of glory, of love, of all good."

The Lord of Hosts, i. e. of all things visible and invisible, of the angels and heavenly spirits, and of all things animate and inanimate, which, in the history of the Creation, are called *the host of heaven and earth* [11], the one host of God. This was the way in which He willed to be had in mind, thought of, remembered. On the one hand then, as relates to Ephraim's sin, not by the calves, nor by any other created thing, did He will to be represented to men's minds or thoughts. On the other hand, as relates to God's mercies, since He, who revealed Himself to Jacob, was the unchangeable God, Israel had no cause to fear, if he returned to the faith of Jacob, whom God there accepted. Whence it follows;

6. *Therefore turn thou to thy God* [lit. *And thou, thou shalt turn* so as to lean *on thy God* [12].] *And thou* unlike, he would say, as thou art to thy great forefather, now at least, *turn to thy God;* hope in Him, as Jacob hoped; and thou too shalt be accepted. God was the Same. They then had only to turn to Him in truth, and they too would find Him, such as Jacob their father had found Him, and then *trust in him continually. Mercy and judgment* include all our duty to our neighbor, love and justice. The Prophet selects the duties of the second table, as Micah also places them first [13], *What doth the Lord require of thee, but to do justly and love mercy, and walk humbly with thy God?* and our Lord chooses those same commandments, in answer to the rich young man, who asked him, *What shall I do*, in order to *enter into life* [14]? For men

They direct mostly, that the word *Adonai*, LORD, is to be read for it. But if this has just occurred, other vowels are placed, directing that it should be read *Elohim*, God. The placing of the vowels under the word are an indication, not that they *are* to be used with the word, but that they are *not* to be used with it. The vowels of a textual reading, when there is also a marginal reading, are always to be supplied by conjecture. It is better to own ignorance, how this name of God is pronounced, than to use the name Jehovah, which is certainly wrong, or any other which can only be conjectural. The subject is fully discussed in the disputations, edited by Reland, Decas Exercit. de nom. Jeh., esp. those of Drusius, Amama and Buxtorf.

[1] Num. vi. 24–26. see Massecheth Sota in Amama, l. c. p. 173.

[2] Massecheth Yoma, f. 39. p. 2. ib. p. 177.

[3] Lib. prec. 356. 2 Drus. Ib. p. 51.

[4] Drus. Tetr. c. 10. ib. 59.

[5] Maim. Yad Chazaka, c. 14. §10. Ib 174. Drus. p. 59.

[6] S. Matt. iv. 7. from Deut. vi. 16, and S. Matt. xxii. 44. from Ps. cx. 1.

[7] Heb. xiii. 8.

[8] See Bp. Bull, Def. Fid. Nic. i. 1. 3–8. 12. ii. 4, 5. Tertullian de Præscr. §13. p. 447. note. Oxf. Tr. [p. 463. ed. 2.] S. Athan. de Conc. Arim. p. 120 note q. Orat. l. c. Arian. pp. 235. 418. note h. Oxf. Tr.

[9] Rev. i. 4, 8.

[10] Lap.

[11] Gen. ii. 1.

[12] באלהיך תשוב.

[13] vi. 8.

[14] S. Matt. xix. 17.

Before CHRIST cir. 725.

‖ Or, *Canaan:* See Ezek. 16. 3.
[l] Prov. 11. 1. Amos 8. 5.
‖ Or, *deceive.*

7 ¶ *He is* ‖ a merchant,
[l] the balances of deceit *are*
in his hand: he loveth to
‖ oppress.
8 And Ephraim said,
[m] Yet I am become rich, I
have found me out sub-
stance: ‖ *in* all my labors
they shall find none iniquity
in me † that *were* sin.

Before CHRIST cir. 725.

[m] Zech. 11. 5. Rev. 3. 17.
‖ Or, *all my labors suffice me not: he shall have punishment of iniquity in whom is sin.*
† Heb. *which.*

---

cannot deceive themselves so easily about their duties to their neighbor, as about their duty to God. It was in love to his neighbor that the rich young man failed.

Thou shalt turn, i.e. it is commonly said, thou oughtest to turn; as our's has it, *turn.* But it may also include the promise that, at one time, *Israel shall turn to the Lord,* as S. Paul says, *so shall all Israel be saved.*

And wait on thy God continually. If they did so, they should not wait in vain. "[1] This word, *continually,* hath no small weight in it, shewing with what circumstances or properties their waiting or hope on God ought to be attended; that it ought to be on Him alone, on Him always, without doubting, fainting, failing, intermission or ceasing, in all occasions and conditions which may befall them, without exception of time, even in their adversity." "Turn to *thy* God," he saith, "wait on *thy* God," as the great ground of repentance and of trust. *God had avouched them for His peculiar people*[2], and they had *avouched Him for* their only *God.* He then was still their God, ready to receive them, if they would return to Him.

7. He is *a merchant,* or, indignantly, *a merchant in whose hands* are *the balances of deceit!* How could they love *mercy and justice,* whose trade was *deceit,* who weighed out deceit with their goods? False in their dealings, in their weights and measures, and, by taking advantage of the necessities of others, oppressive also. Deceit is the sin of weakness, oppression is the abuse of power. Wealth does not give the power to use naked violence, but wealthy covetousness manifoldly grinds the poor. When for instance, wages are paid in necessaries priced exorbitantly, or when artizans are required to buy at a loss at their masters' shops, what is it but the union of deceit and oppression? The trading world is full of oppression, scarcely veiled by deceit. *He loveth to oppress.* Deceit and oppression have, each, a devilish attractiveness to those practiced in them; deceit, as exercising cleverness, cunning, skill in overreaching, outwitting; oppression, as indulging self-will, caprice, love of power, insolence, and the like vices. The word *merchant,* as the Prophet spoke it, was *Canaan*[3]*;* merchants being so called, because the Canaanites or Phœnicians were the then great merchant-people, as astrologers were called Chaldeans. The Phœnicians were, in Homer's time, infamous for their griping in traffic. They are called "gnawers[4]" and "money-lovers[5]." To call Israel, *Canaan,* was to deny to him any title to the name of Israel, "reversing the blessing of Jacob, so that, as it had been said of Jacob, *Thy name shall be called no more Jacob, but Israel,* he would in fact say, 'Thy name shall be called no more Israel, but *Canaan*'*;* as being, through their deeds, heirs, not to the blessings of Israel but to the curse of Canaan." So Ezekiel saith[6], *Thy father was an Amorite, and thy mother a Hittite.*

8. *And Ephraim said, Yet am I become rich,* lit. *I am simply rich.* As if he said, "the only result of all this, with which the Prophets charge me, is that *I am become rich:* and since God thus prospers me, it is a sure proof that he is not displeased with me, that *no iniquity* can be *found in me;*" the ordinary practical argument of men, as long as God withholds His punishments, that their ways cannot be so displeasing to Him. With the men of this world, with its politicians, in trade, it is the one decisive argument: "I was in the right, for I succeeded." "It was a good speculation, for he gained thousands." "It was good policy; for, see its fruits." An answer, at which the heathen laughed, "the people hisses me, but I, I, safe at home, applaud myself, when the coin jingles in my chest[7]." The heathen ridiculed it; Christians enact it. But in truth, the fact that God does not punish, is often the evidence of His extremest displeasure.

They shall find none iniquity in me, that were *sin.* The merchants of Ephraim continue their protest; "In all the toil of my hands, all my buying and selling, my bargains, contracts, they can bring no iniquity home to me," and then, in a tone of simple innocence, they add, *that* were *sin,* as though they *could* not do, what to do were sin. None suspect themselves less, than those intent on gain. The evil customs of other traders, the habits of trade, the seeming necessity for some frauds, the conventional nature of others, the minuteness of others, with their frequent repetition, blind the soul, until it sees no sin, while, with every smallest sale, "they sell their own souls into the bargain[8]."

[1] Poc. [2] Deut. xxvi. 17, 18. [3] כנען.
[4] Philostratus in Grot.
[5] Od. xiv. 283. xv. 413. [6] xvi. 3.
[7] Hor. Sat. i. 1. 66. [8] South's Sermons.

Before CHRIST cir. 725.

9 And [n] I *that am* the LORD thy God from the land of Egypt [o] will yet make thee to dwell in tabernacles, as in the days of the solemn feast.

Before CHRIST cir. 725.

[n] ch. 13. 4.
[o] Lev. 23. 42, 43. Neh. 8. 17. Zech. 14. 16.

9. *And I, the Lord thy God from the land of Egypt.* God, in few words, comprises whole centuries of blessings, all, from the going out of Egypt to that very day, all the miracles in Egypt, in the wilderness, under Joshua, the Judges; one stream of benefits it had been, which God had poured out upon them from first to last. The penitent sees in one glance, how God had been *his* God, from his birth till that hour, and how he had all along offended God.

Will yet make thee to dwell in tabernacles. The feast of tabernacles was the yearly remembrance of God's miraculous guidance and support of Israel through the wilderness. It was the link, which bound on their deliverance from Egypt to the close of their pilgrim-life and their entrance into their rest. The passage of the Red Sea, like Baptism, was the beginning of God's promises. By it Israel was saved from Egypt and from bondage, and was born to be a people of God. Yet, being the beginning, it was plainly not the completion; nor could they themselves complete it. Enemies, more powerful than they, had to be dispossessed; *the great and terrible wilderness, the fiery serpents and scorpions, and the land of exceeding drought, where was no water* [1], had to be surmounted; no food was there, no water, for so vast a multitude. It was a time of the visible Presence of God. He promised [2]; *I send an Angel before thee to keep thee in the way and to bring thee into the place which I have prepared.* He *brought* them *forth water out of the rock of flint, and fed them with Manna which,* He says, *thy fathers knew not* [3]. *Thy raiment,* He appeals to them, *waxed not old, nor did thy foot swell these forty years* [4]; *thy shoe is not waxen old upon thy foot; ye have not eaten bread, neither have ye drunk wine or strong drink, that ye may know that I am the Lord your God* [5]. It was a long trial-time, in which they were taught entire dependence upon God; a time of sifting, in which God proved His faithfulness to those who persevered. Standing there between the beginning and the end of the accomplishment of God's promise to Abraham and to them, it was a type of His whole guidance of His people at all times. It was a pledge that God would lead His own, if often *by a way which they knew not* [6], yet to rest, with Him. The yearly commemoration of it was not only a thanksgiving for God's past mercies; it was a confession also of their present relation to God, that *here we have no continuing city* [7]; that they still needed the guidance and support of God; and that their trust was not in themselves, nor in man, but in Him. This they themselves saw. "[8] When they said, 'Leave a fixed habitation, and dwell in a chance abode,' they meant, that the command to dwell in tabernacles was given, to teach us, that no man must rely on the height or strength of his house, or on its good arrangements though it abound in all good; nor may he rely on the help of any man, not though he were lord and king of the whole earth, but must trust in Him by Whose word the worlds were made. For with Him alone is power and faithfulness, so that, whereinsoever any man may place his trust, he shall receive no consolation from it, since in God alone is refuge and trust, as it is said, *Whoso putteth his trust in the Lord, mercy embraceth him on every side,* and *I will say unto the Lord, my Refuge and my Fortress, my God, in Him will I trust.*"

The feast of Tabernacles was also a yearly thanksgiving for the mercies with which God had *crowned the year.* The joy must have been even the greater, since it followed, by five days only, after the mournful day of Atonement, its rigid fast from evening to evening, and its confession of sin. Joy is greater when ushered in by sorrow; sorrow for sin is the condition of joy in God. The Feast of Tabernacles was, as far it could be, a sort of Easter after Lent. At the time when Israel rejoiced in the good gifts of the year, God bade them express, in act, their fleeting condition in this life. It must have been a striking confession of the slight tenure of all earthly things, when their kings and great men, their rich men and those who lived at ease, had all, at the command of God, to leave their ceiled houses, and dwell for seven days in rude booths, constructed for the season, pervious in some measure to the sun and wind, with no fixed foundation, to be removed when the festival was passed. "Because," says a Jewish writer [9], "at the time of the gathering of the increase from the field, man wishes to go from the field to his house to make a fixed abode there, the law was anxious, lest on account of this fixed abode, his heart should be lifted up at hav-

[1] Deut. viii. 15.
[2] Ex. xxiii. 20.
[3] Deut. viii. 15, 16.
[4] Ib. 4.
[5] Ib. xxix. 5, 6.
[6] Is. xlii. 16.
[7] Heb. xiii. 14. comp. xi. 9, 10.
[8] Menorat Hammaor, f. 39, col. 2 in Dachs Succa, pp. 527, 8.
[9] R. Sal. Ephr. Keli Yakar in Lev. l. c. in Dachs, p. 546.

Before CHRIST cir. 725.

p 2 Kgs. 17. 13.

10 p I have also spoken
by the prophets, and I have
multiplied visions, and used
similitudes, † by the ministry of the prophets.
11 q *Is there* iniquity *in*

† Heb. *by the hand.*

q ch. 5. 1. & 6. 8.

ing found a sort of palace, and he should *wax fat and kick.* Therefore it is written, *all that are Israelites born shall dwell in booths.* Whoso begins to think himself a citizen in this world, and not a foreigner, him God biddeth, leaving his ordinary dwelling, to remove into a temporary lodging, in order that, leaving these thoughts, he may learn to acknowledge that he is only a stranger in this world and not a citizen, in that he dwells as in a stranger's hut, and so should not attribute too much to the shadow of his beams, but *dwell under the shadow of the Almighty.*"

Every year, the law was publicly read in the feast. Ephraim was living clean contrary to all this. He boasted in his wealth, justified himself on the ground of it, ascribed it and his deliverance from Egypt to his idols. He would not keep the feast, as alone God willed it to be kept. While he existed in his separate kingdom, it could not be. Their political existence had to be broken, that they might be restored.

God then conveys the notice of the impending punishment in words which promised the future mercy. He did not, *then, make* them *to dwell in tabernacles.* For all their service of Him was out of their own mind, contrary to His Will, displeasing to Him. This, then, "I will *yet* make thee dwell in tabernacles," implies a distant mercy, beyond and distinct from their present condition. Looking on beyond the time of the Captivity, He says that they shall yet have a time of joy, *as in the days of the solemn feast.* God would give them a new deliverance, but out of a new captivity.

The feast of Tabernacles typifies this our pilgrim-state, the life of simple faith in God, for which God provides; poor in this world's goods, but rich in God. The Church militant dwells, as it were, in tabernacles; hereafter, we hope to be *received into everlasting habitations,* in the Church triumphant.

10. *I have also spoken by the prophets,* lit. *upon the prophets,* the revelation coming down from heaven upon them. Somewhat like this, is what Ezekiel says, *the hand of the Lord was strong upon me*[1]. God declares, in what way He had been their God *from the land of Egypt.* Their ignorance of Him was without excuse; for He had ever taught them, although they ever sought the false prophets, and persecuted the true. He taught them continually and in divers ways, if so be any impression might be made upon them. He taught them, either in plain words, or in the *visions* which He *multiplied* to the prophets; or in the *similitudes* or parables, which He taught through their ministry. In the *vision,* God is understood to have represented the things to come, as a picture, to the prophet's mind, "[2]whether the picture were presented to his bodily eyes, or impressed on his imagination, and that, either in a dream, or without a dream." The *similitude,* which God says that He repeatedly, continually, used[3], seems to have been the parable, as when God compared His people to a vine, Himself to the Lord of the vineyard, or when He directed His prophets to do acts which should shadow forth some truth, as in the marriage of Hosea himself. God had said to Aaron, that He would thus make Himself known by the prophets. [4] *If there be a prophet among you, I, the Lord, will make Myself known unto him in a vision, and will speak unto him in a dream. My servant Moses is not so, who is faithful in all My house. With him will I speak mouth to mouth, even apparently, and not in dark speeches. The dark speech* in Moses answers to the *similitude* of Hosea; the *vision* and *dream* in Moses are comprehended in *visions,* as used by Hosea. The prophet Joel also says[5], *your old men shall dream dreams, your young men shall see visions.* So little ground then have they, who speak of the visions of Daniel and Zechariah, as if they belonged to a later age. "[6]I have instructed," God saith, "men of God, to form thee to piety, enlightening their minds with manifold knowledge of the things of God. And because the light of Divine wisdom could not otherwise shine on men placed here below in the prison-house of the body, I had them taught through figures and corporeal images, that, through them, they might rise to the incorporeal, and receive some knowledge of Divine and heavenly things. And thou, how didst thou requite me? How didst thou shew thy teachableness? It follows;"

11. Is there *iniquity* in *Gilead?* The Prophet asks the question, in order to answer it the more peremptorily. He raises the doubt, in order to crush it the more impressively. Is there *iniquity* in *Gilead?* Alas, there was nothing else. *Surely they are vanity,* or, strictly, *they have become merely vanity.* As he said before, *they become abominations like their love.* "For such as men make their idols, or conceive their God to

[1] iii. 14, etc. [2] Poc.
[3] Such is the force of the Heb. אַדַּמֶּה.
[4] Num. xii. 6–8.
[5] ii. 28. [6] Osor.

Before CHRIST cir. 725.

Gilead? surely they are
vanity: they sacrifice bullocks in [r]Gilgal: yea, [s]their
altars *are* as heaps in the
furrows of the fields.
12 And Jacob [t]fled into
the country of Syria, and
Israel [u]served for a wife,
and for a wife he kept
sheep.

r ch. 4. 15. & 9. 15. Amos 4. 4. & 5. 5.
s ch. 8. 11. & 10. 1.
t Gen. 28. 5. Deut. 26. 5.
u Gen. 29. 20, 28.

13 [x]And by a prophet
the LORD brought Israel
out of Egypt, and by a
prophet was he preserved.
14 [y]Ephraim provoked
him to anger † most bitterly: therefore shall he
leave his † blood upon him,
[z]and his [a]reproach shall
his Lord return unto him.

Before CHRIST cir. 725.

x Ex. 12. 50, 51. & 13. 3. Ps. 77. 20. Is. 63. 11. Mic. 6. 4.
y 2 Kgs. 17. 11–18.
† Heb. *with bitternesses.*
† Heb. *bloods.* See Ezek. 18. 13. & 24. 7, 8.
z Dan. 11. 18.
a Deut. 28. 37.

be, such they become themselves. As then he who worships God with a pure heart, is made like unto God, so they who worship stocks and stones, or who make passions and lusts their idols, lose the mind of men and become *like the beasts which perish.*" *In Gilgal they have sacrificed oxen. Gilead* represents all the country on its side, the East of Jordan; *Gilgal*, all on its side, the West of Jordan. In both, God had signally shewn forth His mercies; in both, they dishonored God, sacrificing to idols, and offering His creatures, as a gift to devils.

Yea, their altars are *as heaps in the furrows of the field.* Their altars are like the heaps of stones, from which men clear the ploughed land, in order to fit it for cultivation, as numerous, as profuse, as worthless, as desolate. *Their* altars they were, not God's. They did, (as sinners do,) in the service of devils, what, had they done it to God, would have been accepted, rewarded, service. Full often they sacrificed oxen[1]; they threw great state into their religion; they omitted nothing which should shed around it an empty shew of worship. They multiplied their altars, their sins, their ruins; many altars over against His one altar; "[2]rude heaps of stones, in His sight; and such they should become, no one stone being left in order upon another." In contrast with their sins and ingratitude, the Prophet exhibits two pictures, the one, of the virtues of the Patriarch whose name they bore, from whom was the beginning of their race; the other, of God's love to them, in that beginning of their national existence, when God brought those who had been a body of slaves in Egypt, to be His own people.

12. *And Jacob fled into the country of Syria.* Jacob chose poverty and servitude rather than marry an idolatress of Canaan. He knew not whence, except from God's bounty and Providence, he should have *bread to eat, or raiment to put on*[3]*; with his staff alone he passed over Jordan*[4]. His voluntary poverty, bearing even unjust losses[5], and *repaying the things which he never took*, reproved their dishonest traffic; his trustfulness in God, their mistrust; his devotedness to God, their alienation from Him, and their devotion to idols. And as the conduct was opposite, so was the result. Ill-gotten riches end in poverty; stable wealth is gained, not by the cupidity of man, but by the good pleasure of God. Jacob, having *become two bands*, trusting in God and enriched by God, returned from Syria to the land promised to him by God; Israel, distrusting God and enriching himself, was to return out of the land which the Lord his God had given him, to Assyria, amid the loss of all things.

13. *By a Prophet was he preserved* or *kept.* Jacob *kept sheep* out of love of God, sooner than unite himself with one, alien from God; his posterity *was kept* like a sheep by God, as the Psalmist said[6], *He led His people like sheep by the hand of Moses and Aaron.* They were *kept* from all evil and want and danger, by the direct power of God; *kept* from all the might of Pharaoh in Egypt and the Red Sea, "[2]not through any power of their own, but by the ministry of a single prophet; *kept, in that great and terrible wilderness*[7], wherein were *fiery serpents and scorpions and drought, where* was *no water*, but what God brought out of the rock of flint; no bread, but what he sent them from heaven." All this, God did for them *by a* single *Prophet; they* had many Prophets, early and late, calling upon them in the name of God, but they would not hearken unto them."

14. *Ephraim provoked* the Lord *most bitterly*, lit. *with bitternesses*, i. e. with most heinous sins, such as are most grievously displeasing to God, and were a most bitter requital of all His goodness. Wherefore *He shall leave* [or, *cast*] *his blood* [lit. *bloods*] *upon him.* The plural *bloods*[8] expresses the manifoldness of

[1] The force of זִבֵּחוּ. [2] Poc. [3] Gen. xxviii. 20.
[4] Ib. xxxii. 10. [5] Ib. xxxi. 39.
[6] Ps. lxxvii. 20. [7] Deut. viii. 15.
[8] דמים. When David said to the Amalekite, *Thy bloods be upon thy head*, 2 Sam. i. 16. it was the blood-guiltiness in slaying Saul, which he had imputed to himself. When the spies said, *his blood* [sing.] *be upon his head*, (Josh. ii. 19.) they meant, let himself and no other be guilty of the loss of his life.

Before CHRIST cir. 725.

CHAPTER XIII.

1 *Ephraim's glory, by reason of idolatry, vanisheth.* 5 *God's anger for their unkindness.* 9 *A promise of God's mercy.* 15 *A judgment for rebellion.*

WHEN Ephraim spake
trembling, he exalted
himself in Israel; but
[a] when he offended in Baal,
he died.

Before CHRIST cir. 725.

[a] Kgs. 17. 16, 18. ch. 11. 2.

the bloodshed. It is not used in Holy Scripture of mere guilt. Ephraim had shed blood profusely, so that it ran like water in the land[1]. He had sinned with a high hand against God, in destroying man made in the image of God. Amid that bloodshed, had been the blood not of the innocent only, but of those whom God sent to rebuke them for their idolatry, their rapine, their bloodshed. *Jezebel cut off the prophets of the Lord*[2], as far as in her lay, with a complete excision. Ephraim thought his sins past; they were out of his sight; he thought that they were out of God's also; but they were laid up with God; and God, the Prophet says, would *cast* them down *upon him*, so that they would crush him.

And his reproach shall his Lord return unto him. For the blood which he had shed, should his own blood be shed; for the reproaches which he had in divers ways cast against God or brought upon Him, he should inherit reproach. Those who rebel against God, bring reproach on Him by their sins, reproach Him by their excuses for their sins, reproach Him in those whom He sends to recall them from their sins, reproach Him for chastening them for their sins. All who sin against the knowledge of God, bring reproach upon Him by acting sinfully against that knowledge. So Nathan says to David[3], *Thou hast given much occasion to the enemies of God to blaspheme.* The reproachful words of the enemies of God are but the echo of the opprobrious deeds of His unfaithful servants. The reproach is therefore, in an especial manner, *their reproach* who caused it. All Israel's idolatries had this aggravation. Their worship of the calves or of Baal or of any other gods of the nations, was a triumph of the false gods over God. Then, all sin must find some plea for itself, by impugning the wisdom or goodness of God who forbad it. Jeroboam, and Ephraim by adhering to Jeroboam's sin, reproached God, as though the going up to Jerusalem was a hard service. *It is too much for you to go up to Jerusalem; Behold thy gods, O Israel, which brought thee up out of the land of Egypt.* "[4] It was an open injury and reproach to God, to attribute to dead lifeless things those great and wonderful things done by Him for them." All the reproach, which they, in these ways, brought, or cast upon God, he says, *his Lord shall return* or *restore* to them. Their's it was; He would give it back to them, as He says[5], *Them that honor Me, I will honor; and they that despise Me, shall be lightly esteemed.* Truly shame and reproach have been for centuries the portion of God's unfaithful people. To those who are lost, He gives back their reproach, in that they *rise to reproaches*[6] *and everlasting abhorrence*[7]. It is an aggravation of this misery, that He Who shall *give back to him* his reproach, had been *his God.* Since *his God* was against him, who could be for him? "For whither should we go for refuge, save to Him? If we find wrath with Him, with whom should we find ruth?" Ephraim did not, the sinner will not, allow God to be *his God* in worship and service and love: but whether he willed or no, God would remain his Lord. He was, and might still have been their Lord for good; they would not have Him so, and so they should find Him still their Lord, as an Avenger, returning their own evil to them.

XIII. 1. *When Ephraim spake trembling,* i. e. probably "there was *trembling.*" "[8] Ephraim was once very awful, so as, while he spake, the rest of the tribes were ready to tremble." The prophet contrasts two conditions of Ephraim, of prosperity, and destruction. His prosperity he owed to the undeserved mercy of God, Who blessed him for Joseph's sake; his destruction, to his own sin. There is no period recorded, *when Ephraim spake tremblingly,* i. e. in humility. Pride was his characteristic, almost as soon as he had a separate existence as a tribe[9]. Under Joshua, it could not be called out, for Ephraim gained honor, when Joshua, one of themselves, became the captain of the Lord's people. Under the Judges, their pride appeared. Yet God tried them, by giving them their hearts' desire. They longed to be exalted, and He satisfied them, if so be they would thus serve Him. They had the chief power, and were a *terror* to Judah. *He exalted himself,* (or perhaps *he was exalted,*) *in Israel; but when he offended in Baal he died;* lit. *and he offended in Baal and died.* He abused the goodness of God; his sin followed as a consequence of God's goodness to him. God raised him, and he offended. The alliance with a king of Tyre

[1] See ab. iv. 2. v. 2.
[2] 1 Kings xviii. 4.
[3] 2 Sam. xii. 14.
[4] S. Cyr.
[5] 1 Sam. ii. 30.
[6] Dan. xii. 2.
[7] The word is the same as in Is. lxvi. 24.
[8] Bp. Hall.
[9] See on v. 5.

Before CHRIST cir. 725.

† Heb. *they add to sin.*
b ch. 2. 8. & 8. 4.

2 And now † they sin
more and more, and [b] have
made them molten images
of their silver, *and* idols
according to their own understanding, all of it the
work of the craftsmen:
they say of them, Let ‖ the
men that sacrifice [c] kiss the
calves.

‖ Or, *the sacrificers of men.*
c 1 Kgs. 19. 18.

and Sidon, which brought in the worship of Baal, was a part of the worldly policy of the kings of Israel [1]. *As if it had been a light thing for him to walk in the sins of Jeroboam the son of Nebat, he took to wife the daughter of Ethbaal, king of the Zidonians, and went and served Baal and worshiped him.* The twenty-two years of Ahab's reign established the worship. The prophets of Baal became 450; the prophets of the kindred idolatry of Ashtoreth, or Astarte, became 400; Baal had his one central temple, large and magnificent [2], a rival of that of God. The prophet Elijah thought the apostacy almost universal; God revealed to him that He had *reserved* to Himself *seven thousand in Israel.* Yet these were *all the knees which had not bowed to Baal, and every mouth which had not kissed him* [3].

And died. Death is the penalty of sin. Ephraim *died* spiritually. For sin takes away the life of grace, and separates from God, the true life of the soul, the source of all life. He "died more truly, than he who is dead and at rest." Of this death, our Lord says [4], *Let the dead bury their dead;* and S. Paul [5], *She who liveth in pleasure is dead while she liveth.* He *died* also as a nation and kingdom, being sentenced by God to cease to be.

2. *And now they sin more and more.* Sin draws on sin. This seems to be a third stage in sin. First, under Jeroboam, was the worship of the calves. Then, under Ahab, the worship of Baal. Thirdly, the multiplying of other idols [6], penetrating and pervading the private life, even of their less wealthy people. The calves were of gold; now they *made them molten images of their silver,* perhaps plated with silver. In Egypt, the mother of idolatry, it was common to gild idols, made of wood, stone, and bronze. The idolatry, then, had become more habitual, daily, universal. These idols were made of *their silver;* they themselves had had them *molten* out of it. Avaricious as they were [7], they lavished *their silver,* to make them their gods. *According to their own understanding,* they had had them formed. They employed ingenuity and invention to multiply their idols. They despised the wisdom and commands of God Who forbad it. The rules for making and coloring the idols were as minute as those, which God gave for His own worship. Idolatry had its own vast system, making the visible world its god and picturing its operations, over against the worship of God its Creator. But it was all, *their own understanding.* The conception of the idol lay in its maker's mind. It was his own creation. He devised, what his idol should represent; how it should represent what his mind imagined; he debated with himself, rejected, chose, changed his choice, modified what he had fixed upon; all *according to his own understanding.* Their own understanding devised it; the labor of the craftsmen completed it.

All of it the work of the craftsmen. What man could do for it, he did. But man could not breathe into his idols the breath of life; there was then no spirit, nor life, nor any effluence from any higher nature, nor any deity residing in them. From first to last it was *all* man's *work;* and man's own wisdom was its condemnation. The thing made must be inferior to its maker. God made man, inferior to Himself, but lord of the earth, and all things therein; man made his idol of the things of earth, which God gave him. It too then was inferior to *its* maker, man. He then worshiped in it, the conception of his own mind, the work of his own hands.

They say of them. Strictly, *Of them,* (i. e. of these things, such things, as these,) *they, say, Let the men that sacrifice kiss the calves.* The prophet gives the substance or the words of Jeroboam's edict, when he said, *It is too much for you to go up to Jerusalem, behold thy gods, O Israel.* "Whoever would sacrifice, let him do homage to the calves." He would have calf-worship to be the only worship of God. Error, if it is strong enough, ever persecutes the truth, unless it can corrupt it. Idol-worship was striving to extirpate the worship of God, which condemned it. Under Ahab and Jezebel, it seemed to have succeeded. Elijah complains to God in His own immediate presence; *the children of Israel have forsaken Thy covenant, thrown down Thine altars, and slain Thy Prophets with the sword; and I, even I, only am left, and they seek my life, to take it away* [8]. Kissing was an act of homage in the East, done upon the hand or the foot, the knees or shoulder. It was a

[1] 1 Kings xvi. 31. see Introd. p. 2.
[2] 2 Kings x. 21, 22, 25.
[3] 1 Kings xix. 18.
[4] S. Matt. viii. 22.
[5] 1 Tim. v. 6.
[6] See 2 Kings xvii. 9, 10.
[7] Above xii. 7, 8.
[8] 1 Kings xix. 10, 14.

Before CHRIST cir. 725.

d ch. 6. 4.

e Dan. 2. 35.

3 Therefore they shall be [d]as the morning cloud, and as the early dew that passeth away, [e]as the chaff *that* is driven with the whirlwind out of the floor, and as the smoke out of the chimney.

f Is. 43. 11. ch. 12. 9.

4 Yet [f]I *am* the LORD thy God from the land of

token of Divine honor, whether to an idol[1] or to God[2]. It was performed, either by actually kissing the image, or when the object could not be approached, (as the moon) kissing the hand[3], and so sending, as it were, the kiss to it. In the Psalm, it stands as a symbol of worship, to be shewn towards *the* Incarnate *Son*, when God should make Him *King upon* His *holy hill of Sion.*

3. *Therefore they shall be as the morning cloud.* There is often a fair show of prosperity, out of God; but it is short-lived. "The third generation," says the heathen proverb, "never enjoys the ill-gotten gain." The highest prosperity of an ungodly state is often the next to its fall. Israel never so flourished, as under Jeroboam II. Bright and glistening with light is *the early dew;* in an hour it is gone, as if it had never been. Glowing and gilded by the sun is *the morning cloud;* while you admire its beauty, its hues have vanished. *The chaff* lay in one heap *on the floor* with the wheat. Its owner casts the mingled chaff and wheat against the strong wind; in a moment, it *is driven by the wind out of the floor.* While every grain falls to the ground, the chaff, light, dry, worthless, unsubstantial, is hurried along, unresisting, the sport of the viewless wind, and itself is soon seen no more. The *smoke*, one, seemingly solid, full, lofty, column, ascendeth, swelleth, welleth, vanisheth[4]. In form, it is as solid, when about to be dispersed and seen no more, as when it first issued *out of the chimney.* "[5]It is raised aloft, and by that very uplifting swells into a vast globe; but the larger that globe is, the emptier; for from that unsolid, unbased, inflated greatness it vanisheth in air, so that its very greatness injures it. For the more it is uplifted, extended, diffused on all sides into a larger compass, so much the poorer it becometh, and faileth, and disappeareth." Such was the prosperity of Ephraim, a mere show, to vanish for ever. In the image of *the chaff*, the Prophet substitutes the *whirlwind* for the wind by which the Easterns used to winnow, in order to picture the violence with which they should be whirled away from their own land.

While these four emblems, in common, picture what is fleeting, two, the *early dew* and the *morning cloud*, are emblems of what is in itself good, but passing[6]; the two others, the chaff and the smoke, are emblems of what is worthless. The dew and the cloud were temporary mercies on the part of God which should cease from them, "good in themselves, but to their evil, soon to pass away." If the dew have not, in its brief space, refreshed the vegetation, no trace of it is left. It gives way to the burning sun. If grace have not done its work in the soul, its day is gone. Such dew were the many prophets vouchsafed to Israel; such was Hosea himself, most brilliant, but soon to pass away. The chaff was the people itself, to be carried out of the Lord's land; the smoke, "its pride and its errors, whose disappearance was to leave the air pure for the household of God." "[7]So it is written[8]; *As the smoke is driven away*, so *shalt thou drive* them *away*; as *wax melteth before the fire, so shall the ungodly perish before the presence of God;* and in Proverbs[9]; *As the whirlwind passeth*, so is *the wicked no* more; *but the righteous* is *an everlasting foundation.* Who although they live and flourish, as to the life of the body; yet spiritually they die, yea, and are brought to nothing; for by sin man became a nothing. Virtue makes man upright and stable; vice, empty and unstable. Whence Isaiah says[10], *the wicked are like the troubled sea, which cannot rest;* and Job[11]; *If iniquity be in thy hand, put it far away; then shalt thou be steadfast.*"

4. *Yet*, [lit. *and*] *I* am *the Lord thy God from the land of Egypt.* God was still the same God Who had sheltered them with His providence, ever since He had delivered them from Egypt. He had the same power and will to help them. Therefore *their* duty was the same, and their destruction arose, not from any change in Him, but from themselves. "God is the God of the ungodly, by creation and general Providence."

And thou shalt [i. e. oughtest to] *know no God but Me, for* [lit. *and*] there is *not a Saviour but ME.* "To be God and Lord and Saviour are incommunicable properties of God. Wherefore God often claimed these titles to Himself, from the time He revealed Himself to Israel. In the song of Moses, which they were commanded to rehearse, He says[12], *See now that I, I am He, and there is no*

[1] 1 Kings xix. 18 and here.
[2] Ps. ii. 12.
[3] Job xxxi. 26, 27.
[4] S. Aug.
[5] Id. in Ps. xxxvi. S. ii. § 12.
[6] Rup.
[7] Dion.
[8] Ps. lxviii. 2.
[9] Prov. x. 25.
[10] Is. lvii 20..
[11] xi. 14, 15.
[12] Deut. xxxii. 39.

Before CHRIST cir. 725.

Egypt, and thou shalt know
no god but me: for [g] there
is no saviour beside me.
5 ¶ [h] I did know thee in
the wilderness, [i] in the land
of † great drought.

g Is. 43. 11. & 45. 21.
h Deut. 2. 7. & 32. 10.
i Deut. 8. 15. & 32. 10.
† Heb. *droughts.*

6 [k] According to their
pasture, so were they filled;
they were filled, and their
heart was exalted; there-
fore [l] have they forgotten
me.

Before CHRIST cir. 725.

k Deut. 8. 12. 14. & 32. 15.
l ch. 8. 14.

God with Me: I kill, and I make alive; I wound, and I heal; neither is there any that can deliver out of My hand. Isaiah repeats this same [1], *Is there a God besides Me? yea there is no God; I know not any;* and [2] *There is no God else besides Me, a just God and a Saviour; there is none else. Look unto Me and be ye saved; for I am God and there is none else;* and [3], *I am the Lord, that is My Name; and My glory will I not give to another; neither My praise to graven images.* "[4] That God and Saviour is Christ; God, because He created; Saviour, because, being made Man, He saved. Whence He willed to be called Jesus, i. e. Saviour. Truly *beside* Him, *there is no Saviour; neither is there salvation in any other; for there is none other name under heaven, given among men, whereby we must be saved* [5]." "It is not enough to recognize in God this quality of a Saviour. It must not be shared with *any other*. Whoso associates with God any power whatever to decide on man's salvation makes an idol, and introduces a new God."

5. *I did know thee in the wilderness.* "God so knew them, as to deserve to be known by them. By *knowing* them, He shewed how He ought to be acknowledged by them." *As we love God, because He first loved us,* so we come to know and own God, having first been owned and known of Him. God shewed His knowledge of them, by knowing and providing for their wants; He knew them *in the wilderness, in the land of great drought,* where the land yielded neither food nor water. He supplied them with the *bread from heaven* and with *water from the flinty rock.* He knew and owned them all by His Providence; He knew in approbation and love, and fed in body and soul those who, having been known by Him, knew and owned Him. "[4] No slight thing is it, that He, Who knoweth all things and men, should, by grace, know us with that knowledge according to which He says to that one true Israelite, Moses [6], *thou hast found grace in My sight, and I know thee by name.* This we read to have been said to that one; but what He says to one, He says to all, whom now, before or since that time, He has chosen, being foreknown and predestinate; for He wrote the names of all in the book of life. All these elect are *known in the wilderness,* in the land of loneliness, in the wilderness of this world, where no one ever saw God, in the solitude of the heart and the secret of hidden knowledge, where God alone, beholding the soul tried by temptations, exercises and proves it, and accounting it, when *running lawfully,* worthy of His knowledge, professes that He *knew it.* To those so known, or named, He Himself saith in the Gospel, *rejoice, because your names are written in heaven* [7]."

6. *According to their pasture, so were they filled.* "[4] He implies that their way of being *filled* was neither good nor praiseworthy, in that he says, *they were filled according to their pastures.* What or of what kind were these *their pastures?* What they longed for, what they murmured for, and spoke evil of God. For instance, when they said, *who will give us flesh to eat? We remember the flesh which we did eat in Egypt freely. Our soul is dried up, because our eyes see nothing but this manna* [8]. Since they desired such things in such wise, and, desiring, were filled with them to loathing, well are they called '*their* pastures.' For they sought God, not for Himself, but for them. They who follow God for Himself, things of this sort are not called *their* pastures, but the word of God is their pasture, according to that [9], *Man shall not live by bread alone, but by every word, which proceedeth out of the mouth of God.* These words, *according to their pastures,* convey strong blame. It is as if he said, 'in their eating and drinking, they received their whole reward for leaving the land of Egypt and receiving for a time the law of God.' It is sin, to follow God for such *pastures.* Blaming such in the Gospel, Jesus saith [10], *Verily, verily, I say unto you, ye seek Me, not because ye saw the miracles, but because ye did eat of the loaves and were filled. Labor not for the meat which perisheth, but for that which endureth unto everlasting life.* In like way, let all think themselves blamed, who attend the altar of Christ, not for the love of the sacraments which they celebrate, but only to *live of the altar.* This fullness is like that of which the Psalmist says [11], *The Lord gave them their desire and sent leanness withal into their bones.* For such fullness of the belly generates elation of spirit; such satiety produces forgetfulness of God." It is

1 xliv. 8. 2 xlv. 21, 2. 3 xlii. 8. 4 Rup. 5 Acts iv. 12. 6 Ex. xxxiii. 17. 7 S. Luke x. 20.

8 Num. xi. 4–6. 9 Deut. viii. 3. 10 S. John vi. 26, 27. 11 Ps. cvi. 15.

Before CHRIST cir. 725.

7 Therefore [m] I will be unto them as a lion: as [n] a leopard by the way will I observe *them*:

[m] Lam. 3. 10. ch. 5 14.
[n] Jer. 5. 6.

8 I will meet them [o] as a bear *that is* bereaved *of her whelps*, and will rend the caul of their heart, and

Before CHRIST cir. 725.

[o] 2 Sam. 17. 8. Prov. 17. 12.

more difficult to bear prosperity than adversity. They who, in the waste howling wilderness, had been retained in a certain degree of duty, forgat God altogether in the good land which He had given them. Whence it follows;

They were filled, and their heart was exalted; therefore have they forgotten Me. For they owned not that they had all from Him, therefore they were puffed up with pride, and forgot Him in and by reason of His gifts. This was the aggravation of their sin, with which Hosea often reproaches them[1]. They abused God's gifts, (as Christians do now) against Himself, and did the more evil, the more good God was to them. God had forewarned them of this peril[2], *When thou shalt have eaten and be full, beware lest thou forget the Lord which brought thee forth out of the land of Egypt, from the house of bondage.* He pictured it to them with the song of Moses[3]; *Jeshurun waxed fat and kicked; thou art waxen fat; thou art grown thick; thou art covered with fatness; then he forsook God which made him;—thou hast forgotten God that formed thee.* They acted (as in one way or other do most Christians now,) as though God had commanded what He foretold of their evil deeds, or what He warned them against. [4] *As their fathers did, so did they.* [5] *They walked in the statutes of the heathen, whom the Lord cast out from before the children of Israel, and of the kings of Israel which they made. They wrought wicked things to provoke the Lord to anger. And the Lord testified against Israel and against Judah by all the prophets and by all the seers, saying, turn ye from your evil ways. And they hearkened not, and hardened their necks, like to the neck of their fathers, that did not believe in the Lord their God.* "[6] The words are true also of those rich and ungrateful, whom God hath filled with spiritual or temporal goods. But they, *being in honor, and having no understanding,* abuse the gifts of God, and, becoming unworthy of the benefits which they have received, have their hearts uplifted and swollen with pride, despising others, *glorying as though they had not received,* and not obeying the commands of God. Of such the Lord saith in Isaiah, *I have nourished and brought up children and they have rebelled against Me.*"

7. *I will be unto them as a lion.* They had waxen fat, were full; yet it was, to become themselves a prey. Their wealth which they were proud of, which they abused, allured their enemies. To cut off all hopes of God's mercy, He says that He will be to them, as those creatures of His, which never spare. The fierceness of the lion, and the swiftness of the leopard, together portray a speedy inexorable chastisement. But what a contrast! He Who bare Israel in the wilderness like a Father, Who bare them on eagle's wings, Who drew them with the cords of a man, with bands of love, He, the God of mercy and of love, their Father, Protector, Defender, Avenger, He it is Who will be their Destroyer.

8. *As a bear bereaved* of her whelps. The Syrian bear is fiercer than the brown bears to which we are accustomed. It attacks flocks[7], and even oxen[8]. The fierceness of the she-bear, *bereaved of her whelps,* became a proverb[9]. "[10] They who have written on the nature of wild beasts, say that none is more savage than the she-bear, when she has lost her whelps or lacks food." It blends wonderfully most touching love and fierceness. It tenderly protects its wounded whelps, reckless of its life, so that it may bring them off, and it turns fiercely on their destroyer. Its love for them becomes fury against their injurer. Much more shall God avenge those who destroy His sons and daughters, leading and enticing them into sin and destruction of body and soul.

Rend the caul of [what encloses] *their heart,* i. e. the pericardium. They had closed their hearts against God. Their punishment is pictured by the rending open of the closed heart, by the lion which is said to go instinctively straight to the heart, tears it out, and sucks the blood[11]. Fearful will it be in the Day of Judgment, when the sinner's heart is laid open, with all the foul, cruel, malicious, defiled, thoughts which it harbored and concealed, against the Will of God. *It is a fearful thing to fall into the hands of the living God*[12].

And there will I devour them. There, where they sinned, shall they be punished. *The wild beast shall tear them.* What God does, He does mostly through instruments, and what His instruments do, they do fulfilling His Will through their own blind will or appetite. Hitherto, He had spoken, as being

[1] ii. 5. iv. 7. x. 1.
[2] Deut. vi. 11, 12, add viii. 11, &c.
[3] Ib. xxxii. 15, 18.
[4] Acts vii, 51.
[5] 2 Kings xvii. 8, 11, 13, 14.
[6] Rib.
[7] 1 Sam. xvii. 34.
[8] Plin. viii. 54.
[9] 2 Sam. xvii. 8, Prov. xvii. 12. and here.
[10] S Jer.
[11] See in Boch. iii. 2. pp. 740, 1.
[12] Heb. x. 31.

Before CHRIST cir. 725.

there will I devour them
like a lion: † the wild beast
shall tear them.
9 ¶ O Israel, [p] thou hast
destroyed thyself; [q] but in
me † *is* thine help.

† Heb. *the beast of the field.*
[p] Prov. 6. 32. ch. 14. 1. Mal. 1. 9.
[q] ver. 4.
† Heb. *in thy help.*

10 ‖ I will be thy king:
[r] where *is any other* that
may save thee in all thy
cities? and thy judges of
whom [s] thou saidst, Give
me a king and princes?

[s] 1 Sam. 8. 5, 19.

Before CHRIST cir. 725.

‖ Rather, *Where is thy king?* King Hoshea being then in prison. 2 Kgs. 17. 4.
[r] Deut. 32. 38. ch. 10. 3. ver. 4.

Himself their Punisher, although laying aside, as it were, all His tenderness; now, lest the thought, that still it was He, the God of love Who punished, should give them hope, He says, *the wild beast shall devour them.* He gives them up, as it were, out of His own hands to the destroyer.

9. *O Israel, thou hast destroyed thyself, but in Me* is *thy help.* This is one of the concise sayings of Hosea, which is capable of many shades of meaning. The five words, one by one, are lit. *Israel, thy destruction, for* or *that, in* or *against Me, in* or *against thy help.* Something must be supplied any way; the simplest seems; *O Israel, thy destruction* is, *that* thou hast been, hast rebelled *against Me, against thy help* [1]. Yet, in whatever way the words are filled up, the general sense is the same, that God alone is our help, we are the sources of our own destruction; and *that,* in separating ourselves from God, or rebelling against Him Who is our help until we depart from Him, Who Alone could be, and Who if we return, will be, our help. The sum of the meaning is, all our destruction is from ourselves; all our salvation is from God. "[2] Perdition, reprobation, obduration, damnation, are not, properly and in themselves, from God, dooming to perdition, reprobating, obdurating, damning, but from man sinning, and obduring or hardening himself in sin to the end of life. Contrariwise, predestination, calling, grace, are not from the foreseen merits of the predestinate, but from God, predestinating, calling, and, by His grace, forecoming the predestinate. Wherefore although the cause or ground, why they are predestinated, does not lie in the predestinate, yet in the not-predestinated does lie the ground or cause why they are not predestinated."

"This saying then, *O Israel, thou hast destroyed thyself, but in Me* is *thy help,* may be thus unfolded;

Thy captivity, Israel, is from thee; thy redemption from Me.

Thy perishing is from thee; thy salvation from Me.

Thy death from thee; thy life from Me.

Thy evil from thee; thy good from Me.

Thy reprobation from thee; thy predestination from Me, Who ever stand at the door of thy heart and in mercy knock.

Thy dereliction from thee; thy calling from Me.

Thy misery from thee; thy bliss from Me.

Thy damnation from thee, thy salvation and beatifying from Me."

For "[3] many good things doeth God in man, which man doeth not, but none doeth man, which God endueth not man to do." "[4] The first cause of the defect of grace is from us; but the first cause of the gift of grace is from God." "[5] Rightly is God called, not the Father of judgments or of vengence, but the *Father of mercies,* because from Himself is the cause and origin of His mercy, from us the cause of His judging or avenging."

"Blessed the soul which comprehendeth this, not with the understanding only, but with the heart. Nothing can destroy us before God, but sin, the only real evil; and sin is wholly from us, God can have no part in it. But every aid to withdraw us from sin, or to hinder us from falling into it, comes from God alone, the sole Source of our salvation. The soul then must ever bless God, in its ills and its good; in its ills, by confessing that itself is the only cause of its suffering; in its good, owning that, when altogether unworthy of it, God prevented it by His grace, and preserves it each instant by His Almighty goodness."

"[6] No power, then, of the enemy could harm thee, unless, by thy sins, thou calledst forth the anger of God against thee to thy destruction. Ascribe it to thyself, not to the enemy. So let each sinful city or sinful soul say, which by its guilt draws on it the vengeance of God."

This truth, that in Him alone is help, He confirms by what follows:

10. *I will be* [lit. *I would be*] *thy King; Where* is any other that &c. Better, [7] *Where now is thy king, that he may save thee in all thy cities; and thy judges, of whom thou saidst, give me a king and princes.*

As Israel was under Samuel, such it remained. *Then* it mistrusted God, and looked

[1] Rashi. [2] Lap. from Theologians on 1 p. q. 23.
[3] S. Aug. c. 2 Epp. Pet. ii. 21. Ib.
[4] Aq. 1. 2. q. 112. a. 3. ad. 2 Ib.
[5] S. Bern. Serm. 8 in Nat. Dom. Ib. [6] Lap.

[7] אפוא, which our Version renders *where?* never occurs alone as an interrogative, but always as subjoined to איה, with which אהי is identical and identified by great Jewish authorities, as Abulvalid.

Before CHRIST cir. 725.

11 [t]I gave thee a king
in mine anger, and took
him away in my wrath.

[t] 1 Sam. 8. 7. & 10. 19. & 15. 22, 23. & 16. 1. ch. 10. 3.

12 [u]The iniquity of
Ephraim *is* bound up; his
sin *is* hid.

Before CHRIST cir. 725.

[u] Deut. 32. 34. Job 14. 17.

---

to man for help, saying[1], *Nay, but we will have a king over us, that we also may be like other nations, and that our king may judge us, and go out before us, and fight our battles.* In choosing man they rejected God. The like they did, when they chose Jeroboam. In order to rid themselves of the temporary pressure of Rehoboam's taxes, they demanded anew *king and princes.* First they rejected God as their king; then they rejected the king whom God appointed, and Him in His appointment. *In all thy cities.* It was then to be one universal need of help. They had chosen a king *to fight their battles,* and had rejected God. Now was the test, whether their choice had been good or evil. One cry for help went up from *all their cities.* God would have heard it; could man?

"[2]This question is like that other[3], *Where are their gods, their rock in whom they trusted, which did eat the fat of their sacrifices,* and *drink the wine of their drink offerings?* As there, when no answer could be made, He adds, *See now that I, I am He, and that there is no god with Me,* so here He subjoins;"

11. *I gave thee a king in Mine anger.* "[4]God, when He is asked for ought amiss, sheweth displeasure, when He giveth, hath mercy, when He giveth not." "The devil was heard," [in asking to enter into the swine] "the Apostle was not heard," [when he prayed that the messenger of Satan might depart from him.] "[5]God heard him whom He purposed to condemn; and He heard not him whom He willed to heal." "[6]God, when propitious, denieth what we love, when we love amiss; when wroth, He giveth to the lover, what he loveth amiss. The Apostle saith plainly, *God gave them over to their own hearts' desire.* He gave them then what they loved, but, in giving, condemned them." God did appoint Jeroboam, although not in the way in which Israel took him. Jeroboam and Israel took, as from themselves, what God appointed; and, so taking it, marred God's gift. Taking it to themselves from themselves, they maintained it for themselves by human policy and sin. As was the beginning, such was the whole course of their kings. The beginning was rebellion; murder, intestine commotion, anarchy, was the oft-repeated issue. God was against them and their kings; but he let them have their way. In His displeasure with them He allowed them their choice; in displeasure with their evil kings He took them away. Some He smote in their own persons, some in their posterity. So often as He gave them, so often He removed them[7], until, in Hoshea, He took them away for ever. This too explains, how what God *gave in anger,* could be *taken away* also *in anger.* The civil authority was not a thing wrong in itself, the ceasing whereof must be a mercy. Israel was in a worse condition through its separate monarchy; but, apart from the calf-worship, it was not sin. The changing of one king for another did not mend it. Individual kings were taken away in anger against themselves; their removal brought fresh misery and bloodshed. Nations and Churches and individuals may put themselves in an evil position, and God may have allowed it in His anger, and yet, it may be their wisdom and humility to remain in it, until God change it, lest He should *take* it away, not in forgiveness, but in *anger.* "[8]David they neither asked for, nor did the Lord give him in His anger; but the Lord first chose him in mercy, gave him in grace, in His supreme good-pleasure He strengthened and preserved him." "[9]Let no one who suffereth from a wicked ruler, accuse *him* from whom he suffereth; for it was from his own ill deserts, that he became subject to such a ruler. Let him accuse then his own deeds, rather than the injustice of the ruler; for it is written, *I gave thee a king in Mine anger.* Why then disdain to have as rulers, those whose rule we receive from the anger of God?" "[10]When a reprobate people is allowed to have a reprobate pastor, that pastor is given, neither for his own sake, nor for that of the people; inasmuch as he so governeth, and they so obey, that neither the teacher nor the taught are found meet to attain to eternal bliss. Of whom the Lord saith by Hosea, *I gave thee a king in Mine anger.* For in the anger of God is a king given, when the bad have a worse appointed as their ruler. Such a pastor is then given, when he undertakes the rule of such a people, both being condemned alike to everlasting punishment."

12. *The iniquity of Ephraim* is *bound up* (as in a bag or purse, and so, *treasured up*), as Job saith, using the same word, [11] *My trans-*

---

[1] 1 Sam. viii. 19.
[2] Rup.
[3] Deut. xxxii. 37-9.
[4] Sent. 252. ap. S. Aug. Apo. T. x. p. 239 Lap.
[5] Id. in Ps. lxxxv. § 9.
[6] Id. in Ps. xxvi. § 7.
[7] The words אתן, אקח, express this oft-renewed dealing of God.
[8] Rup.
[9] S. Greg. in Job L. xxv. c. 20. Rib.
[10] Id. in 1 Reg. ix. T. iii. pp. 215, 16. Ib.
[11] Job xiv. 17. בצרור as here צרור.

Before CHRIST cir. 725.

13 [x]The sorrows of a
travailing woman shall
come upon him: he *is* [y]an unwise son; for he should not [z]
stay† long in *the place of* the
breaking forth of children.

[x] Is. 13. 8. Jer. 30. 6.
[y] Prov. 22. 3.
[z] 2 Kgs 19. 3.
† Heb. *a time.*

gression is sealed up in a bag, and Thou sewest up mine iniquity. His sin is *hid,* i. e. as people lay up hidden treasure, to be brought out in its season. What Job feared for himself, was to be the portion of Ephraim. All his sins should be counted, laid by, heaped up. No one of them should escape His Eye Who sees all things as they pass, and with Whom, when past, they are present still. One by one, sins enter into the treasure-house of wrath; silently they are stored up, until the measure is full; to be brought out and unfolded in the Great Day. Ephraim thought, as do all sinners, that because God does not punish at once, He never will. They think, either that God will bear with them always, because He bears with them so long; or that He does not see, does not regard it, is not so precise about His laws being broken. [1] *Because sentence against an evil work is not executed speedily, therefore the heart of the sons of men is fully set in them to do evil.* But God had forewarned them [2]; *Is not this laid up in store with Me, and sealed up among My treasures? To Me belongeth vengeance and recompense; their foot shall slide in due time:* and [3], *These things hast thou done, and I kept silence; and thou thoughtest wickedly that I was altogether* such an one *as thyself; I will reprove thee, and set them in order before thine eyes.* Unrepented sin is an evergrowing store of the wrath of God, hid out of sight in the depths of the Divine judgments, but of which nothing will be lost, nothing missing. Man treasures it up, lays it up in store for himself, as the Apostle saith [4]; *Despisest thou the riches of His goodness and forbearance and long-suffering, not knowing that the goodness of God leadeth thee to repentance; but after thy hardness and impenitent heart treasurest up unto thyself wrath against the Day of wrath and revelation of the righteous judgment of God, Who will render to every man according to his deeds?* "[5] *Sin* is *hidden,* when it is laid open by no voice of confession; yea, when it is covered with a shield of proud self-defence. Then iniquity is bound up, so that it cannot be loosed or forgiven. Contrariwise a holy man saith [6], *I acknowledged my sin unto Thee, and my iniquity have I not hid. I said, I will confess my transgressions unto the Lord; and Thou forgavest the iniquity of my sin.* But these hide their sin in the sight of men, and since they cannot hide it in the sight of God, they defend it with impenitent hearts, but *the pangs of a travailing woman,* he saith, *shall come upon him.* For as a woman can conceal her conception for a time, but, at last, the travail-pangs betraying her, she discloses what was concealed, so these can dissemble and conceal for a time their sin, but in their time all the hidden things of their hearts shall, with anguish, be revealed, according to that [7], *There is nothing covered, that shall not be revealed, and hid, that shall not be known.*"

13. *The sorrows of a travailing woman are come upon him.* The travail-pangs are violent, sudden, irresistible. A moment before they come, all is seemingly perfect health; they come, increase in vehemence, and, if they accomplish not that for which they are sent, end in death, both to the mother and the child. Such are God's chastisements. If they end not in the repentance of the sinner, they continue on in his destruction. But never is man more secure, than just before the last and final throe comes upon him. "The false security of Israel, when Samaria was on the point of falling into the hands of its enemies, was a picture of that of the Synagogue, when greater evils were coming upon it. Never did the Jews less think that the axe was laid to the root of the trees." This blind presumption is ever found in a people whom God casts off. At the end of the world, amid the awful signs, the fore-runners of the Day of Judgment, people will be able to reassure themselves, and say [8], *Peace and safety; then sudden destruction cometh upon them as travail upon a woman with child, and they shall not escape.*

The prophet first compares Israel to the mother, in regard to the sufferings which are a picture of the sudden overwhelming visitations of God; then to the child, on whose staying or not staying in the womb, the welfare of both depends.

He is an unwise son, for he should not stay long. Senseless would be the child, which, if it had the power, lingered, hesitated, whether to come forth or no. While it lingers, at one time all but coming forth, then returning, the mother's strength is wasted, and both perish. Wonderful picture of the vacillating sinner, acted upon by the grace of God, but resisting it; at one time all but ready to pour out before his God the hidden burthen which oppresses him, at the next, withholding it; impelled by his sufferings, yet presenting a passive resistance; almost constrained at times by some mightier pang, yet still withheld; until, at the last, the impulses become

[1] Eccl. viii. 11.
[2] Deut. xxxii. 34, 5.
[3] Ps. l. 21.
[4] Rom. ii. 4–6.
[5] Rup.
[6] Ps. xxxii. 5.
[7] S. Matt. x. 26.
[8] 1 Thess. v. 3.

Before CHRIST cir. 725.

14 [a] I will ransom them
from † the power of the
grave; I will redeem them
from death: [b] O death, I
will be thy plagues; O
grave, I will be thy de-
struction: [c] repentance
shall be hid from mine eyes.

[a] Is. 25. 8. Ezek. 37. 12.
† Heb. *the hand.*
[b] 1 Cor. 15. 54, 55.
[c] Jer. 15. 6. Rom. 11. 29.

weaker, the pangs less felt, and he perishes with his unrepented sin.

"[1] He had said, that the unwise cannot bring forth, that the wise can. He had mentioned *children*, i. e. such as are not still-born; who come forth perfect into the world. These, God saith, shall by His help be redeemed from everlasting destruction, and, at the same time, having predicted the destruction of that nation, He gives the deepest comfort to those who will to retain firm faith in Him, not allowing them to be utterly cast down."

14. *I will ransom them from the power of the grave;* lit. *from the hand*, i. e. the grasp *of the grave*, or *of hell.* God, by His prophets, mingles promises of mercy in the midst of His threats of punishment. His mercy overflows the bounds of the occasion upon which He makes it known. He had sentenced Ephraim to temporal destruction. This was unchangeable. He points to that which turns all temporal loss into gain, their eternal redemption. The words are the fullest which could have been chosen. The word rendered *ransom*, signifies, rescued them by the payment of a price, the word rendered *redeem*, relates to one, who, as the nearest of kin, had the right to acquire anything as his own, by paying that price. Both words, in their exactest sense, describe what Jesus did, buying us *with a price*, a full and dear price, *not of corruptible things, as of silver and gold, but with His precious blood* [2]; and that, becoming our near kinsman, by His Incarnation, *for which cause He is not ashamed to call us brethren* [3], and *little children* [4]. This was never done by God at any other time, than when, out of love for our lost world, [5] *He gave His Only Begotten Son, that whosoever believeth in Him should not perish but have everlasting life;* and He *came to give His life a ransom for many* [6]. Then only was man really delivered from the *grasp* of the *grave;* so that *the first death* should only be a freedom from corruption, an earnest, and, to fallen man, a necessary condition of immortality; and *the second death* should *have no power over* them [7]. Thenceforward "[8] death, the parent of sorrow, ministers to joy; death, our dishonor, is employed to our glory; the *gate of hell* is the portal to the kingdom of heaven; the *pit of destruction* is the entrance to salvation; and that to man, a sinner." At no other time, "[9] were men freed from death and the grave, so as to make any distinction between them and others subject to mortality." The words refuse to be tied down to a temporal deliverance. A little longer continuance in Canaan is not a redemption from the power of the grave; nor was Ephraim so delivered. Words of God "[10] cannot mean so little, while they express so much." Then and then alone were they, in their literal meaning, fulfilled when God the Son *took* our flesh [11], *that, through death, He might destroy him that had the power of death, that is the devil; and deliver them who, through fear of death, were all their lifetime subject to bondage.*

The Jews have a tradition wrapped up in their way, that this was to be accomplished in Christ. "[12] I went with the angel Kippod, and Messiah son of David went with me, until I came to the gates of hell. When the prisoners of hell saw the light of the Messiah, they wished to receive him, saying, this is he who will bring us out of this darkness, as it is written, *I will redeem them from the hand of hell.*"

"[13] Not without reason is the vouchsafed mercy thus once and again outspoken to us, *I will ranson them from the power of the grave; I will redeem them from death.* It is said in regard to that twofold death whereby we all died in Adam, of the body and of the soul." *O death, I will be thy plagues; O grave, I will be thy destruction.* So full is God's word, that the sense remains the same, amid much difference of rendering. Christ was the death of death, when He became subject to it; the destruction of the grave when He lay in the tomb. Yet to render it in the form of a question is most agreeable to the language [14]. *O death, where are thy plagues? O grave, where is thy destruction?* It is a burst of triumph at the promised redemption, then fulfilled to us in earnest and in hope, when *Christ*, being *risen from the dead, became the First-fruits of them that slept* [15], and we rose in Him. But the Apostle teaches us, that then it shall be altogether fulfilled, when, at the last Day, *this corruptible*

[1] Osor. [2] 1 Pet. i. 18, 19. [3] Heb. ii. 11.
[4] S. John xiii. 33. [5] S. John iii. 16.
[6] S. Matt. xx. 28. add 1 Tim. ii. 6.
[7] Rev. xx. 6. [8] S. Bern. Serm. 26 in Cant. Lap.
[9] Poc. [10] Davison on Prophecy.
[11] Heb. ii. 14, 15.
[12] Bereshith Rabba, in Martin. Pug. Fid. f. 605, 6.

[13] Rup.
[14] אהי is most naturally taken in the sense in which Hosea had just used it, as equivalent to איה. As a verb, it would mean, *I would be*, which would not agree with the absolute declaration just before, *I will ransom, I will redeem.*
[15] 1 Cor. xv 20.

Before CHRIST cir. 725.

[d] See Gen. 41. 52. & 48. 19.
[e] Jer. 4. 11. Ezek. 17. 10. & 19. 12. ch. 4. 19.

15 ¶ Though [d] he be
fruitful among *his* brethren, [e] an east wind shall
come, the wind of the
LORD shall come up from
the wilderness, and his
spring shall become dry
and his fountain shall be
dried up: he shall spoil
the treasure of all † pleasant
vessels.
16 ‖ Samaria shall be-

Before CHRIST cir. 725.

† Heb. *vessels of desire.*
Nah. 2. 9.
‖ Fulfilled, cir. 721. 2 Kgs 17. 6.

shall have put on incorruption, and this mortal shall have put on immortality[1]. *Then* shall *death and hell deliver up the dead which* shall be *in them, and themselves* be *cast into the lake of fire*[2]. "Then shall there be no sting of death; sorrow and sighing shall flee away; fear and anxiety shall depart; tears shall be no more, and in place thereof shall be boundless pleasure, everlasting joy, praise of the glory of God in most sweet harmony." But now too, through death, the good man "ceases to die, and begins to live;" he "[3] dies wholly to the world, that he may live perfectly with God; the soul returns to the Author of its being, and is hidden in the hidden Presence of God."

Death and hell had no power to resist, and God says that He will not alter His sentence; *Repentance shall be hid from Mine eyes;* as the Apostle says[4], *the gifts and calling of God are without repentance.*

15. *Though* [lit. *when*] *he* [*shall*] *be fruitful among his brethren.* Fruitfulness was God's promise to Ephraim, and was expressed in his name. It was fulfilled, abused, and, in the height of its fulfillment, was taken away. Ephraim is pictured as a fair and fruitful tree. An *East wind*, so desolating in the East, and that, no chance wind, but *the wind of the Lord*, a wind, sent by God and endued by God with the power to destroy, *shall come up from the wilderness*, parching, scorching, fiery, from the burning sands of "Arabia the desert," from which it came, *and shall dry up the fountain* of his being. Deep were the roots of this fair and flourishing tree, great its vigor, ample and perpetual the fountain of its waters, over which it grew and by which it was sustained. He calls it "*his* spring, *his* fountain," as though this source of its life were made over to it, and made its own. It *was planted by the water side;* but it was not of God's planting. *The East wind from the Lord* should dry up the deepest well-spring of its waters, and the tree should wither. Such are ungodly greatness and prosperity. While they are fairest in show, their life-fountains are drying up.

He shall spoil the treasure of all pleasant vessels. He, emphatically[5], the enemy whom the Prophet had ever in his mind, as the instrument of God's chastisement on His people, and who was represented by the East wind; the Assyrian, who came from the East, to whom, as to the East wind, the whole country between lay open, for the whirlwinds of his armies to sweep over in one straight course from the seat of his dominion.

16. *Samaria shall become desolate*, or *shall bear her iniquity.* Her iniquity should now find her out, and rest upon her. Of this, "desolation" was, in God's judgments, the consequence. Samaria, "the nursery of idolatry and rebellion against God," the chief in pride should be chief in punishment. *For she hath rebelled against her God.* It aggravated her sin, that He *against* Whom *she rebelled*, was *her* own *God.* He Who had chosen her to be His, and made Himself her God; Who had shewed Himself *her God* in the abundance of His loving-kindness, from the deliverance out of Egypt to that day. This her desolation, it is again said, should be complete. Hope remains, if the men of a generation are cut off; yet not only should these fall by the sword; those already born were to be dashed in pieces; those as yet unborn were to be sought out for destruction, even in their mother's womb. Such atrocities were common then. Elisha foretold to Hazael that he would perpetrate both cruelties[6], Shalmaneser dashed the young children in pieces[7], as did the conqueror of No-Ammon[8], and the Babylonians[9] afterward. The children of Ammon ripped up the women with child in Gilead[10], and the usurper Menahem in Tiphsah and its coasts[11]. Isaiah prophesies that Babylon should undergo, in its turn, the same as to its children[12], and the Psalmist pronounces God's blessing on its destroyer who should so requite him[9].

Such was to be the end of the pride, the ambition, the able policy, the wars, the oppressions, the luxury, the self-enjoyment, and, in all, the rebellion of Samaria against *her God.* She has stood the more in opposition to God, the nearer she might have been to Him, and *bare her iniquity.* As a city of God's people, it was never restored. The spot, in its heathen colonists, with which Assyrian policy repeopled it[13], was still the abode of a mingled religion. Corruption clung, by inheritance,

[1] 1 Cor. xv. 54. [2] Rev. xx. 13, 14.
[3] de dign. Div. Am. fin. ap. S. Bern. ii. 274.
[4] Rom. xi. 29. [5] הוּא [6] 2 Kings viii. 12.

[7] Above x. 14. [8] Nah. iii. 10. [9] Ps. cxxxvii. 9.
[10] Am. i. 13. [11] 2 Kings xv. 16.
[12] xiii. 16. [13] 2 Kings xvii. 24.

Before CHRIST cir. 725.

come desolate; [f]for she hath rebelled against her God: [g]they shall fall by the sword: their infants shall be dashed in pieces, and their women with child shall be ripped up.

f 2 Kgs 18. 12.
g 2 Kgs 8. 12, & 15. 16. Is. 13. 16. ch. 10. 14, 15. Amos 1. 13. Nah. 3. 10.

CHAPTER XIV.

1. *An exhortation to repentance.*
4. *A promise of God's blessing.*

Before CHRIST cir. 725.

O ISRAEL, [a]return unto the LORD thy God; [b]for thou hast fallen by thine iniquity.

a ch. 12. 6. Joel 2. 13.
b ch. 13. 9.

to its site. This too was destroyed by John Hyrcanus. "He effaced the marks that it had ever been a city[1]." It was rebuilt by the Romans, after Pompey had taken Jerusalem[2]. Herod reinclosed a circuit of two miles and a half of the ancient site; fortified it strongly, as a check on the Jews; repeopled it, partly with some who had served in his wars, partly with the people around; gave them lands, revived their idolatry by replacing their poor temple by one remarkable for size and beauty, in an area of a furlong and a half; and called the place Sebaste in honor of his heathen patron, Augustus[3]. A coin of Nero, struck there, bears the figure (it is thought) of its old idol, Ashtaroth[4]. S. Jerome says, that S. John the Baptist was buried there[5]. The heathen, who were encouraged in such desecrations by Julian the Apostate[6], opened the tomb, burned the bones, and scattered the dust[7]. The city became a Christian see, and its Bishops were present at the four first General Councils [8]. It is now but a poor village, connected with the strongly-fortified town of Herod by its heathen name Sebastieh, a long avenue of broken pillars, and the tomb of the great Forerunner[9]. Of the ancient capital of Ephraim, not even a ruin speaks.

The Prophet closes this portion of his prophecy, as other prophets so often do, with the opposite end of the righteous and the wicked. He had spoken of the victory over death, the irrevocable purpose of God for good to his own; then he speaks of utter final destruction. Then when the mercy of God shall be shewn to the uttermost, and the victory over sin and death shall be accomplished, then shall all the pomp of the world, its riches, joys, luxuries, elegance, glory, dignity, perish, and not a wreck be left behind of all which once dazzled the eyes of men, for which they forsook their God, and sold themselves to evil and the evil one.

XIV. 1. *O Israel, return* [*now, quite*] *unto the Lord your God.* The heavy and scarcely interrupted tide of denunciation is now past. Billow upon billow have rolled over Ephraim; and the last wave discharged itself in the overwhelming, indiscriminating destruction of the seat of its strength. As a nation, it was to cease to be. Its separate existence was a curse, not a blessing; the offspring of rivalry, matured by apostacy; the parent, in its turn, of jealousy, hatred, and mutual vexation.

But while the kingdom was past and gone, the children still remained heirs of the promises made to their fathers. As then, before, Hosea declared that Israel, after having long remained solitary, should in the end *seek the Lord and David their king*[10], so now, after these manifold denunciations of their temporal destruction, God not only invites them to repentance, but foretells that they should be wholly converted.

Every word is full of mercy. God calls them by the name of acceptance, which He had given to their forefather, Jacob; *O Israel.* He deigns to beseech them to return; *return now*; and that not "towards" but *quite up to* [11]Himself, the Unchangeable God, Whose mercies and promises were as immutable as His Being. To Himself, the Unchangeable, God invites them to return; and that, as being still their God. They had cast off their God; God had *not cast off His people Whom He foreknew*[12].

"[13]He entreats them not only to turn back and look toward the Lord with a partial and imperfect repentance, but not to leave off till they were come quite home to Him by a total and sincere repentance and amendment." He bids them *return quite to* Himself, the Unchangeable God, and their God. "Great is repentance," is a Jewish saying[14], "which maketh men to reach quite up to the Throne of glory."

For thou hast fallen by thine iniquity. "This is the first ray of Divine light on the sinner. God begins by discovering to him the abyss into which he has fallen," and the way by which he fell. Their own iniquity it was, on which they had stumbled and so had fallen, powerless to rise, except through *His* call, Whose *voice is with power*[15], and "Who giveth what He commandeth." "[16]Ascribe

1 Jos. Ant. 13. 10. 3.
2 Ib. 14. 4. 4. and 5. 3.
3 Ib. 15. 8. 5.
4 Vaillant, Num. Imp. p. 370 in Reland, Pal. p. 981.
5 On Hos. i. 5. Obad. init. Mic. i. 6. Onom. v. Semeron.
6 Misopog. p. 95.
7 Theod. H. E. iii. 7.
8 See in Reland, p. 983.
9 Stanley, Palestine, p. 245.
10 iii. 5.
11 Not אל but עד.
12 Rom. xi. 2.
13 Poc.
14 Yoma, c. 8. in Poc.
15 Ps. xxix. 4.
16 Osor.

Before CHRIST cir. 725.

2 Take with you words,
and turn to the LORD: say
unto him, Take away all
iniquity, and ‖ receive *us*
graciously: so will we render
der the [c] calves of our lips.

Before CHRIST cir. 725.

‖ Or, *give good.*
c Heb. 13. 15.

not thy calamity," He would say, "to thine own weakness, to civil dissension, to the disuse of military discipline, to want of wisdom in thy rulers, to the ambition and cruelty of the enemy, to reverse of fortune. These things had not gone against thee, hadst not thou gone to war with the law of thy God. Thou inflictest the deadly wound on thyself; thou destroyedst thyself. Not as fools vaunt, by fate, or fortune of war, but *by thine iniquity hast thou fallen.* Thy remedy then is in thine own hand. *Return to thy God.*"

"[1] In these words, *by thine iniquity,* he briefly conveys, that each is to ascribe to himself the iniquity of all sin, of whatsoever he has been guilty, not defending himself, as Adam did, in whom we all, Jews and Gentiles, have sinned and fallen, as the Apostle says[2], *For we were by nature the children of wrath, even as others.* By adding actual, to that original, sin, Israel and every other nation falleth. He would say then, O Israel, be thou first converted, for thou hast need of conversion; *for thou hast fallen;* and confess this very thing, that *thou hast fallen by thine iniquity;* for such confession is the beginning of conversion."

But wherewith should he return?

2. *Take with you words.* He bids them not bring costly offerings, that they might regain His favor; not whole burnt offerings of bullocks, goats or rams; with which, and with which alone, they had before gone to seek Him[3]; not the silver and gold which they had lavished on their idols; but what seems the cheapest of all, which any may have, without cost to their substance; *words;* worthless, as mere words; precious when from the heart; words of confession and prayer, blending humility, repentance, confession, entreaty and praise of God. God seems to assign to them a form, with which they should approach Him. But with these words, they were also to turn inwardly *and turn unto the Lord,* with your whole heart, and not your lips alone. "After ye shall be converted, confess before Him."

Take away all iniquity [lit. and pleadingly, *Thou wilt take away all iniquity.*] They had *fallen by their iniquities;* before they can rise again, the stumbling-blocks must be taken out of their way. They then, unable themselves to do it, must turn to God, with Whom alone is power and mercy to do it, and say to Him, *Take away all iniquity,* acknowledging that they had manifold iniquities, and praying Him to forgive all, *take away all. All iniquity!* "not only then the past, but what we fear for the future. Cleanse us from the past, keep us from the future. Give us righteousness, and preserve it to the end."

And receive us *graciously,* [lit. *and receive good*[4]]. When God has forgiven and taken away iniquity, He has removed all hindrance to the influx of His grace. There is no vacuum in His spiritual, any more than in His natural, creation. When God's good Spirit is chased away, the evil spirits enter the house, which is *empty, swept, and garnished*[5] for them. When God has forgiven and taken away man's evil, He pours into him grace and all good. When then Israel and, in him, the penitent soul, is taught to say, *receive good,* it can mean only, the good which Thou Thyself hast given; as David says, *of Thine own we have given Thee*[6]. As God is said to "crown in us His own gifts;" ("His own gifts," but "in us[7];") so these pray to God to receive from them His own good, which they had from Him. For even the good, which God giveth to be in us, *He* accepteth in condescension and forgiving mercy, *Who crowneth thee in mercy and loving-kindness*[8]. "They pray God to accept their service, forgiving their imperfection, and mercifully considering their frailty. For since *our righteousnesses are filthy rags,* we ought ever humbly to entreat God, not to despise our dutifulness, for the imperfections, wanderings, and negligences mingled therewith. For exceedingly imperfect is it, especially if we consider the majesty of the Divine Nature, which should be served, were it possible, with infinite reverence." They plead to God, then, to accept what, although from Him they have it, yet through their imperfection, were, but for His goodness, unworthy of His acceptance. Still, since the glory of God is the end of all creation, by asking Him to accept it, they plead to Him, that this is the end for which He made and remade them, and placed the good in them, that it might redound to His glory. As, on the other hand, the Psalmist says[9], *What profit is there in my blood, if I go down into the pit,* as though

[1] Rup. [2] Eph. ii. 3. [3] See ab. v. 6.

[4] The rendering, *And receive us graciously,* overlooks the contrast of the two clauses. Israel is bidden to pray God, to *take away,* and to *receive.* On the two verbs, there follow two nouns, which stand naturally as the object of each; עון וקח טוב תשא. No one would have doubted that קח טוב means, *receive good,* as just before, קחו דברים means, *take words,* but for the seeming difficulty, "what good had they?"

[5] S. Matt. xii. 44.

[6] 1 Chr. xxix. 14. [7] S. Aug.

[8] Ps. ciii. 4. [9] xxx. 9.

Before CHRIST cir. 725.

3 [d] Asshur shall not save us; [e] we will not ride upon horses; [f] neither will we say any more to the work of our hands, *Ye are* our gods: [g] for in thee the fatherless findeth mercy.

Before CHRIST cir. 725.

[d] Jer. 31. 18, &c. ch. 5. 13. & 12. 1.
[e] Deut. 17. 16. Ps. 33. 17. Is. 30. 2, 16. & 31. 1.
[f] ch. 2. 17. ver. 8.
[g] Ps. 10. 14. & 68. 5.

his own perishing were a loss to God, his Creator, since thus there were one creature the less to praise Him. "[1] *Take from us all iniquity*, leave in us no weakness, none of our former decay, lest the evil root should send forth a new growth of evil; *and receive good;* for unless Thou take away our evil, we can have no good to offer Thee, according to that[2], *depart from evil, and do good.*"

So will we render the calves of our lips, lit. *and we would fain repay, calves, our lips;* i. e. when God shall have *forgiven us all our iniquity*, and *received* at our hands what, through His gift, we have to offer, the *good* which through His good Spirit we can do, then would we *offer* a perpetual thank-offering, *our lips*. This should be the substitute for the thank-offerings of the law. As the Psalmist says[3], *I will praise the Name of God with a song, and magnify Him with thanksgiving. This also shall please the Lord, better than a bullock that hath horns and hoofs.* They are to bind themselves to perpetual thanksgiving. As the morning and evening sacrifice were continual, so was their new offering to be continual. But more. The material sacrifice, *the bullock*, was offered, consumed, and passed away. Their *lips* were offered, and remained; a perpetual thank-offering, even a *living sacrifice*, living on like the mercies for which they thanked; giving forth their "endless song" for never-ending mercies.

This too looks on to the Gospel, in which, here on earth, our unending thanksgiving is beginning, in which also it was the purpose of God to restore those of Ephraim who would return to Him. "[4] Here we see law extinguished, the Gospel established. For we see other rites, other gifts. So then the priesthood is also changed. For three sorts of sacrifices were of old ordained by the law, with great state. Some signified the expiation of sin; some expressed the ardor of piety; some, thanksgiving. To those ancient signs and images, the truth of the Gospel, without figure, corresponds. Prayer to God, *to take away all iniquity*, contains a confession of sin, and expresses our faith, that we place our whole hope of recovering our lost purity and of obtaining salvation in the mercy of Christ. *Receive good.* What other good can we offer, than detestation of our past sin, with burning desire of holiness? This is the burnt offering. Lastly, *we will repay the calves of our lips*, is the promise of that solemn vow, most acceptable to God, whereby we bind ourselves to keep in continual remembrance all the benefits of God, and to render ceaseless praise to the Lord Who has bestowed on us such priceless gifts. For *the calves of* the *lips* are orisons well-pleasing unto God. Of which David says[5], *Then shalt Thou be pleased with the sacrifices of righteousness, with burnt offerings and whole burnt offerings; then shall they offer bullocks upon Thine altar.*"

3. *Asshur shall not save us.* After prayer for pardon and for acceptance of themselves, and thanksgiving for acceptance, comes the promise not to fall back into their former sins. Trust in man, in their own strength, in their idols, had been their besetting sins. Now, one by one, they disavow them.

First, they disclaim trust in man, and making[6] *flesh their arm*. Their disclaimer of the help of the Assyrian, to whom they had so often betaken themselves against the will of God, contains, at once, that best earnest of true repentance, the renewal of the confession of past sins, and the promise to rely no more on any princes of this world, of whom he was then chief. The horse, in like way, is the symbol of any warlike strength of their own. As the Psalmist says[7], *Some put their trust in chariots and some in horses, but we will remember the name of the Lord our God;* and[8], *a horse is a vain thing for safety, neither shall he deliver any by his great strength;* and Solomon[9], *The horse is prepared for the day of battle, but salvation is of the Lord.* War was almost the only end for which the horse was used among the Jews. If otherwise, it was a matter of great and royal pomp. It was part of a standing army. Their kings were especially forbidden to *multiply horses*[10] *to* themselves. Solomon, indeed, in his prosperity, broke this, as well as other commands of God. The pious king Hezekiah, although possessed at one time of large treasure, so kept that command as to furnish matter of mockery to Rabshakeh, the blaspheming envoy of Assyria, that he had neither horses nor horsemen[11]. The horses being procured from Egypt[12], the commerce gave fresh occasion for idolatry.

Neither will we say any more to the work of our hands, ye are *our gods*. This is the third disavowal. Since it was folly and sin to trust

[1] S. Jer. [2] Ps. xxxvii. 27. [3] lxix. 30, 1. [4] Osor. [5] Ps. li. ult. [6] Jer. xvii. 5. [7] Ps. xx. 7. [8] Ps. xxxiii. 17. [9] Prov. xxi. 31. [10] Deut. xvii. 16. [11] 2 Kings xviii. 23. [12] 1 Kings x. 28.

Before CHRIST cir. 725.

4 ¶ I will heal [h] their
backsliding, I will love
them [i] freely: for mine

[h] Jer. 5. 6. & 14. 7. ch. 11. 7. [i] Eph. 1. 6.

anger is turned away from
him.
5 I will be as [k] the dew

Before CHRIST cir. 725.

[k] Job 29. 19. Prov. 19. 12.

---

in the creatures which God had made, apart from God, how much more, to trust in things which they themselves had made, instead of God, and offensive to God!

For in Thee [or, *O Thou, in Whom*] *the fatherless findeth mercy.* He is indeed fatherless who hath not God for his Father. They confess then, that they were and deserved to be thus *fatherless* and helpless, a prey to every oppressor; but they appeal to God by the title which He had taken, *the Father of the fatherless*[1], that He would have mercy on them, who had no help but in Him. "[2] We promise this, they say, hoping in the help of Thy mercy, since it belongeth to Thee and is for Thy Glory to have mercy on the people which believeth in Thee, and to stretch forth Thine Hand, that they may be able to leave their wonted ills and amend their former ways."

4. *I will heal their backsliding.* God, in answer, promises to *heal* that wound of their souls, whence every other evil came, their fickleness and unsteadfastness. Hitherto, this had been the characteristic of Israel. [3] *Within a while they forgat His works, and would not abide His counsels.* [4] *They forgat what He had done. Their heart was not whole with Him; neither continued they steadfast in His covenant. They turned back and tempted God. They kept not His testimonies, but turned back and fell away like their forefathers, starting aside like a broken bow.* Steadfastness to the end is the special gift of the Gospel. *Lo, I am with you alway, even unto the end of the world. The gates of hell shall not prevail against it*[5]. And to individuals, *Jesus, having loved His own, loved them unto the end*[6]. In healing that disease of unsteadfastness, God healed all besides. This He did to all, wheresover or howsoever dispersed, who received the Gospel; this He doth still; and this He will do completely in the end, when *all Israel shall be saved.*

I will love them freely; i.e. as the word means, *impelled*[7] thereto by Himself alone, and so, (as used of God) moved by His own Essential Bountifulness, the exceeding greatness of His Goodness, largely, bountifully. God *loves* us *freely* in loving us against our deserts, because He *is love;* He *loves* us *freely* in that He freely became Man, and, having become Man freely shed His Blood for the remission of our sins, freely forgave our sins; He *loves* us *freely*, in *giving us grace, according to the good pleasure of His will*[8], to become pleasing to Him, and causing all good in us; He *loves* us *freely*, in rewarding infinitely the good which we have from *Him.* "[9] More manifestly here speaketh the Person of the Saviour Himself, promising His own Coming to the salvation of penitents, with sweetly sounding promise, with sweetness full of grace."

For Mine anger is turned away from him. As He says[10], *In My wrath I smote thee; but in My favor have I had mercy on thee.* He doth not withhold only, or suspend His anger, but He taketh it away wholly. So the Psalmist saith[11], *Thou hast forgiven the iniquity of Thy people; Thou hast covered all their sin; Thou hast taken away all Thy wrath; Thou hast turned from the fierceness of Thine anger.*

5. *I will be as the dew unto Israel.* Before, He had said[12], *his spring shall become dry and his fountain shall be dried up.* Now again He enlarges the blessing; their supply shall be unfailing, for it shall be from God; yea, God Himself shall be that blessing; *I will be the dew; descending on the mown grass*[13], to quicken and refresh it; descending, Himself, into the dried and parched and sere hearts of men, as He saith, *We will come unto him and make Our abode in him*[14]. The grace of God, like the dew, is not given once for all, but is, day by day, waited for, and, day by day, renewed. Yet doth it not pass away, like the fitful goodness[15] of God's former people, but turns into the growth and spiritual substance of those on whom it descends.

He shall grow as the lily. No one image can exhibit the manifold grace of God in those who are His own, or the fruits of that grace. So the Prophet adds one image to another, each supplying a distinct likeness of a distinct grace or excellence. The *lily* is the emblem of the beauty and purity of the soul in grace; the *cedar* of Lebanon, of its strength and deep-rootedness, its immovableness and uprightness; the evergreen *olive tree* which "remaineth in its beauty both winter and summer," of the unvarying presence of Divine Grace, continually, supplying an ever-sustained freshness, and issuing in fruit; and the fragrance of the aromatic plants with which the lower parts of Mount Lebanon are decked, of its loveliness and sweetness; as a native explains this[16], "he takes a sec-

[1] Ps. lxviii. 5.
[2] Rup.
[3] Ps. cvi. 13.
[4] Ps. lxxviii. 12, 37, 42, 57, 58.
[5] S. Matt. xxviii. 20. xvi. 18.
[6] S. John xiii. 1.
[7] נדבה.
[8] Eph. i. 5.
[9] Rup.
[10] Is. lx. 10.
[11] lxxxv. 2, 3.
[12] xiii. 15.
[13] Ps. lxxii. 6.
[14] S. John xiv. 23.
[15] Above vi. 4.
[16] R. Tanchum, in Poc.

Before CHRIST cir. 725.

unto Israel: he shall ‖ grow
as the lily, and † cast forth
his roots as Lebanon.

‖ Or, *blossom.*
† Heb. *strike.*
† Heb. *shall go.*

6 His branches † shall
spread, and [l]his beauty
shall be as the olive tree,

l Ps. 52. 8. & 128. 3.

and [m]his smell as Leba-
non.

7 [n]They that dwell un-
der his shadow shall re-
turn; they shall revive *as*
the corn, and ‖ grow as the

m Gen. 27. 27. Cant. 4. 11.
n Ps. 91. 1.
‖ Or, *blossom.*

ond comparison from Mount Lebanon for the abundance of aromatic things and odoriferous flowers." Such are the myrtles and lavender and the odoriferous reed; from which "[1] as you enter the valley" [between Lebanon and Anti-lebanon] "straightway the scent meets you." All these natural things are established and well-known symbols of things spiritual. The lily, so called in Hebrew from its dazzling whiteness, is, in the Canticles[2], the emblem of souls in which Christ takes delight. The lily multiplies exceedingly[3]; yet hath it a weak root and soon fadeth. The Prophet, then, uniteth with these, plants of unfading green, and deep root. The seed which *had no root,* our Lord says, *withered away*[4], as contrariwise, St. Paul speaks of these, who are *rooted and grounded in love*[5], and of being *rooted and built up in Christ*[6]. The wide-spreading branches are an emblem of the gradual growth and enlargement of the Church, as our Lord says[7], *It becometh a tree, so that the birds of the air come and lodge in the branches thereof.* The symmetry of the tree and its outstretched arms express, at once, grace and protection. Of the *olive* the Psalmist says[8], *I am like a green olive tree in the house of God;* and Jeremiah says[9], *The Lord called thy name a green olive tree, fair and of goodly fruit;* and of "fragrance" the spouse says in the Canticles[10], *because of the savor of Thy good ointments, Thy name is as ointment poured forth;* and the Apostle says[11], *thanks be to God, which maketh manifest the savor of His knowledge by us in every place.* Deeds of charity also are *an odor of good smell*[12]*;* the prayers of the saints also are *sweet odors*[13]. All these are the fruits of the Spirit of God Who says, *I will be as the dew unto Israel.* Such reunion of qualities, being beyond nature, suggests the more, that that, wherein they are all combined, the future Israel, the Church, shall flourish with graces beyond nature, in their manifoldness, completeness, unfadingness.

7. *They that dwell under his shadow,* i. e. the shadow of the restored Israel, who had just been described under the image of a magnificent tree uniting in itself all perfections. "[14] They that are under the shadow of the Church are together under the shadow of Christ the Head thereof, and also of God the Father." The Jews, of old, explained it[15], "they shall dwell under the shadow of their Messias." These, he says, *shall return,* i. e. they shall turn to be quite other than they had been, even back to Him, to Whom they belonged, Whose creatures they were, God. *They shall revive* as *the corn.* The words may be differently rendered, in the same general meaning. The simple words, *They shall revive* [lit. *give life* to, or *preserve in life,*] *corn,* have been filled up differently. Some of old, (whence ours has been taken) understood it, *they shall revive* themselves, [16]and so, *shall live,* and that either *as corn,* (as it is said, *shall grow as the vine*); or *by corn*[17] which is also very natural, since "bread is the staff of life," and our spiritual Bread is the support of our spiritual life. Or lastly, (of which the grammar is easier, yet the idiom less natural) it has been rendered *they shall give life to corn,* make corn to live, by cultivating it. In all ways the sense is perfect. If we render, *shall revive* as *corn,* it means, being, as it were, dead, they shall not only live again with renewed life, but shall even increase. Corn first dies in its outward form, and so is multiplied; the fruit-bearing branches of the vine are pruned and cut, and so they bear richer fruit. So through suffering, chastisement, or the heavy hand of God or man, the Church, being purified, yields more abundant fruits of grace. Or if rendered, *shall make corn to grow,* since the Prophet, all around, is under figures of God's workings in nature, speaking of His workings of grace, then it is the same image, as when our Lord speaks of those *who receive the seed in an honest and true heart and bring forth fruit, some an hundredfold, some sixty, some thirty*[18]. Or if we were to render, *shall produce life through wheat,* what were this, but that seed-corn, which, for us and for our salvation, was sown in the earth, and died, and *brought forth much fruit;* the Bread of life, of which our Lord says[19], *I am the Bread of life, Whoso eateth of this bread shall live for ever, and the bread which I will give is My Flesh, which I will give for the life of the world?*

The scent thereof shall be *as the wine of Lebanon.* The grapes of Lebanon have been of the size of plums; its wine has been spoken

1 Theophr. Hist. Plant. x. 7. 2 Cant. ii. 1. 2.
3 Plin. in Poc. 4 S. Matt. xiii. 6.
5 Eph. iii. 17. 6 Col. ii. 7. 7 S. Matt. xiii. 32.
8 Ps. lii. 8. 9 xi. 16. 10 i. 3.
11 2 Cor. ii. 14. 12 Phil. iv. 18. 13 Rev. v. 8.
14 Poc. 15 Jon. 16 Kimchi.
17 As the old versions, LXX. Vulg. Syr.
18 S. Matt. xiii. 23. 19 S. John vi. 48, 51.

Before CHRIST cir. 725.

vine: the ‖ scent thereof
shall be as the wine of Lebanon.
8 Ephraim *shall say*,
° What have I to do any
more with idols? ᵖ I have
heard *him*, and observed
him: I *am* like a green fir
tree. ᑫ From me is thy
fruit found.

‖ Or, *memorial*.
° ver. 3.
ᵖ Jer. 31. 18.
ᑫ Jam. 1. 17.

of as the best in the East or even in the world[1]. Formerly Israel was as a luxuriant, but empty, vine, bringing forth no fruit to God[2]. God [3]*looked that it should bring forth grapes, and it brought forth wild grapes.* Now its glory and luxuriance should not hinder its bearing fruit, and *that*, the noblest of its kind. Rich and fragrant is the odor of graces, the inspiration of the Spirit of God, and not fleeting, but abiding.

8. *Ephraim* shall say, *what have I to do any more with idols?* So Isaiah fortells[4], *The idols He shall utterly abolish.* Aforetime Ephraim said obstinately, in the midst of God's chastisements[5]; *I will go after my lovers, who give me my bread and my water, my wool and my flax, mine oil and my drink.* Now she shall renounce them wholly and for ever. This is entire conversion, to part wholly with everything which would dispute the allegiance with God, to cease to look to any created thing or being, for what is the gift of the Creator alone. So the Apostle says[6], *what concord hath Christ with Belial?* This verse exhibits in few, vivid, words, converted Ephraim speaking with God, and God answering; Ephraim renouncing his sins, and God accepting him; Ephraim glorying in God's goodness, and God reminding him that he holds all from Himself.

I have heard and observed him. God answers the profession and accepts it. *I*, (emphatic) *I Myself have heard* and *have answered*, as He says[7], *Before they call I will answer.* Whereas God, before, had hid His face from them, or had *observed*[8] them, only as the object of His displeasure, and as ripe for destruction, now He reverses this, and *observes* them, in order to forecome the wishes of their hearts before they are expressed, to watch over them and survey and provide for all their needs. To this, Ephraim exulting in God's goodness, answers, *I* am *like a green fir tree*, i. e. evergreen, ever-fresh. The *berosh*, (as S. Jerome, living in Palestine, thought) one of the large genus of the *pine* or *fir*, or (as others translated) the *cypress*[9], was a tall stately tree[10]; in whose branches the stork could make its nest[11]; its wood precious enough to be employed in the temple[12]; fine enough to be used in all sorts of musical instruments[13]; strong and pliant enough to be used for spears[14]. It was part of the glory of Lebanon[15]. A Greek historian says that Lebanon "[16]was full of cedars and pines and cypresses, of wonderful beauty and size." A modern traveller says, of "the cypress groves of Lebanon;" "[17]Each tree is in itself a study for the landscape painter—some, on account of their enormous stems and branches. —Would you see trees in all their splendor and beauty, then enter these wild groves, that have never been touched by the pruning knife of art." This tree, in its majestic beauty, tenacity of life, and undying verdure, winter and summer, through the perpetual supply of sap, pictures the continual life of the soul through the unbroken supply of the grace of God. Created beauty must, at best, be but a faint image of the beauty of the soul in grace; for this is from the indwelling of God the Holy Ghost.

From Me is thy fruit found. Neither the pine nor the cypress bear any fruit, useful for food. It is probable then that here too the Prophet fills out one image by another and says that restored Israel, the Church of God, or the soul in grace, should not only have beauty and majesty, but what is not, in the way of nature, found united therewith, fruitfulness also. *From Me is thy fruit found;* as our Lord says[18], *I am the vine, ye are the branches.* Human nature, by itself, can as little bear fruit well-pleasing to God, as the pine or cypress can bear fruit for human use. As it were a miracle in nature, were these trees to bring forth such fruit, so, for man to bring forth fruits of grace, is a miracle of grace. The presence of works of grace attests the immediate working of God the Holy Ghost, as much as any miracle in nature.

[1] See in Œdmann, ii. 193. Germ. and Maronites in Lap.
[2] x. 1. [3] Is. v. 2. [4] ii. 18. [5] ch. ii. 5.
[6] 2 Cor. vi. 15. [7] Is. lxv. 24. [8] xiii. 7.
[9] S. Jerome uniformly renders abies. The LXX. and Syr. vary, rendering both cypress and pine. The Syriac *berutho* (doubtless the same tree and used sometimes for it in the Peshito) is said by Bar Bahlul to be the Arabic *Abuhul;* and this Ibn Baithar describes as "a large tree with leaves like the tamarisk." He identifies it also with the βράθυ of Dioscorides, who mentions a second sort, "with leaves like the cypress, more prickly than the other." Pliny (xxv. 11) says that some called this "the Cretan cypress." The bratum is commonly called the "Juniperus Sabina," which, however, is not known to be a tall tree, although some of the Juniper tribe are.
[10] Is. lv. 13. [11] Ps. civ. 17.
[12] 1 Kings v. 22, 24. [8. 10. Eng.] vi. 15, 34.
[13] 2 Sam. vi. 5. [14] Nah. ii. 3.
[15] Is. xxxvii. 24. lx. 13. [16] Diod. Sic. xix. 58.
[17] Van de Velde Syr. and Pal. ii. 475.
[18] S. John xv. 5.

Before CHRIST cir. 725.

9 [r] Who *is* wise, and he shall understand these *things?* prudent, and he shall know them? for [s] the

[r] Ps. 107. 43. Jer. 9. 12. Dan. 12. 10. John 8. 47. & 18. 37.

[s] Prov. 10. 29. Luke 2. 34. 2 Cor. 2. 16. 1 Pet. 2. 7, 8.

9. *Who is wise and he shall understand these* things? The Prophet says this, not of the words in which he had spoken, but of the substance. He does not mean that his style was obscure, or that he had delivered the message of God in a way difficult to be understood. This would have been to fail of his object. Nor does he mean that human acuteness is the key to the things of God. He means that those only of a certain character, those *wise*, through God, unto God, will understand the things of God. So the Psalmist, having related some of God's varied chastenings, mercies and judgments, sums up [1], *Whoso is wise and will observe these things, even they shall understand the loving kindness of the Lord.* So Asaph says that God's dealings with the good and bad in this life were *too hard* for him to *understand, until* he *went into the sanctuary of God;* then *understood* he *their end* [2]. In like way Daniel, at the close of his prophecy, sums up the account of a sifting-time [3], *Many shall be purified and made white and tried, and the wicked shall do wickedly; and none of the wicked shall understand, but the wise shall understand.* As these say that the wise alone understand the actual dealings of God with man, so Hosea says, that the wise alone would understand what he had set forth of the mercy and severity of God, of His love for man, His desire to pardon, His unwillingness that any should perish, His longing for our repentance, His store of mercies in Christ, His gifts of grace and His free eternal love, and yet His rejection of all half-service and His final rejection of the impenitent. *Who is wise?* "[4] The word *who* is always taken, not for what is impossible, but for what is difficult." So Isaiah saith [5], *Who hath believed our report, and to whom is the Arm of the Lord revealed?* Few are wise with *the wisdom which is from above;* few understand, because few wish to understand, or seek wisdom from Him *Who giveth to all men liberally, and upbraideth not* [6]. The question implies also, that God longs that men should *understand* to their salvation. He inquires for them, calls to them that they would meditate on His mercies and judgments. As S. Paul says [7], *Behold the goodness and severity of God; on them which fell, severity; but toward thee, goodness, if thou continue in His goodness. O the depth of the riches both of the wisdom and knowledge of God! how unsearchable are His judgments, and His ways past finding out. Unsearchable* to intellect and theory; intelligible to faith and for acting on.

And he shall understand, (i. e. *that he may understand* [8]) *these* things. The worldly-wise of that generation, too, doubtless, thought themselves too wise to need to understand them; as the wise after this world counted the Cross of Christ foolishness.

Prudent. Properly "gifted with understanding," the form of the word expressing, that he was *endowed with* this *understanding* [9], as a gift from God. *And He shall know them.* While the wise of this world disbelieve, jeer, scoff at them, in the name of human reason, he who has not the natural quickness of man only, but who is endued with the true wisdom, shall *know* them. So our Lord says [10], *If any man will do His will, he shall know of the doctrine whether it is of God.* The word, *wise,* may specially mean him who contemplates these truths and understands them in themselves, yet plainly so as to act upon them; and the word *endued with prudence,* may specially describe such as are gifted with readiness to apply that knowledge to practice, in judgment, discrimination, act [11]. By uniting both, the Prophet joins contemplative and practical wisdom, and intensifies the expression of God's desire that we should be endowed with them.

For the ways of the Lord are *right.* If in the word, *ways,* the figure is still preserved [12], the Prophet speaks of the *ways,* as "direct and straight;" without a figure, as "just and upright."

The ways of the Lord are, what we, by a like figure, call "the *course* of His Providence;" of which Scripture says [13], *His ways are judgment;* [14] *God, His ways are perfect;* [15] *the Lord is righteous in all His ways, and holy in all His works;* [16] *Thy way is in the sea, and Thy paths in the great waters, and Thy footsteps are not known;* [17] *lo, these are parts of His ways, but how little a portion is heard of Him, and the thunder of His power who can understand?* [18] *Who hath enjoined Him His way, and who can say, Thou hast wrought iniquity?* These *ways of God* include His ordering for us, in His eternal wisdom, that course of life, which leads most directly to Himself. They include, then, all God's commandments, pre-

[1] Ps. cvii. 43. [2] Ib. lxxiii. 16, 17. [3] Dan. xii. 10.
[4] S. Jer. on Eccl. iii. 21. [5] liii. 1.
[6] S. James i. 5. [7] Rom. xi. 22, 33.
[8] The force of the abbreviated form, ויבן.
[9] נבון, the passive of the יבן which had just preceded. [10] S. John vii. 17.

[11] As in their degree, the heathen too distinguish σοφία and φρόνησις.
[12] ישר is both used of physical and moral straightness.
[13] Deut. xxxii. 4. Dan. iv. 37. [14] Ps. xviii. 30.
[15] Ib. cxlv. 17. [16] Ib. lxxvii. 19.
[17] Job xxvi. 14. [18] Ib. xxxvi. 23.

Before CHRIST cir. 725.

ways of the LORD *are* right, and the just shall walk in them: but the transgressors shall fall therein.

Before CHRIST cir. 725.

cepts, counsels, His whole moral law, as well as His separate purpose for each of us. In the one way, they are God's ways toward us; in the other they are God's ways for us.

The just shall walk in them. God reveals His ways to us, not that we may know them only, but that we may do them. "The end of moral science is not knowledge, but practice," said the Heathen philosopher[1]. But the life of grace is a life of progress. The word, *way*, implies not continuance only, but advance. He does not say, "they shall *stand* in God's ways," but *they shall walk in them.* They shall go on in them "upright, safe, and secure, in *great peace* and with *nothing whereat to stumble*[2]. In God's ways there is no stumbling block, and they who walk in them, are free from those of which other ways are full. Whereas, out of God's ways, all paths are tangled, uneven, slippery, devious, full of snares and pitfalls, God maketh His *way straight*, a royal highway, smooth, even, direct unto Himself.

But [*and*] *the transgressors shall fall therein,* lit. *shall stumble thereon*[3]. *Transgressors*, i. e. those who rebel against the law of God, *stumble* in divers manners, not *in*, but *at*[4] the ways of God. They stumble at God Himself, at His All-Holy Being, Three and One; they stumble at His attributes; they stumble at His Providence, they stumble at His acts; they stumble at His interference with them; they stumble at His requirements. They rebel against His commandments, as requiring what they like not; at His prohibitions, as refusing what they like. They stumble at His Wisdom, in ordering His own creation; at His Holiness, in punishing sin; but most of all, they stumble at His Goodness and condescension. They have a greater quarrel with His condescension than with all His other attributes. They have stumbled, and still stumble at God the Son, becoming Man, and taking our flesh in the Virgin's womb; they stumble at the humility of the Crucifixion; they stumble at His placing His Manhood at the Right Hand of God; they stumble at the simplicity, power and condescension, which He uses in the Sacraments; they stumble at His giving us His Flesh to eat; they stumble at His forgiving sins freely, and again and again; they stumble at His making us members of Himself, without waiting for our own wills; they stumble at His condescension in using our own acts, to the attainment of our degree of everlasting glory. Every attribute, or gift, or revelation of God, which is full of comfort to the believer, becomes in turn an occasion of stumbling to the rebellious. *The things which should have been for his wealth, become to him an occasion of falling*[5]. "They cannot attemper their own wishes and ways to the Divine law, because, obeying what they themselves affect, *the law of their members*, they stumble at that other law, which leadeth unto life[6]." With this the Prophet sums up all the teaching of the seventy years of his ministry. This is the end of all which he had said of the severity and mercy of God, of the Coming of Christ, and of our resurrection in Him. This is to us the end of all; this is thy choice, Christian soul, to walk in God's ways, or to stumble at them. As in the days when Christ came in the Flesh, so it is now; so it will be to the end. So holy Simeon prophesied, "[7] *This Child is set for the fall and rising again of many in Israel;* and our Lord said of Himself, [8]*For judgment I am come into this world, that they which see not might see, and that they which see might be made blind.* And S. Peter[9]; *Unto you which believe* He is *precious; but unto them which be disobedient, the stone which the builders disallowed, the same is made the head of the corner, and a stone of stumbling and rock of offence,* to them *which stumble at the word, being disobedient. Christ crucified* was *unto the Jews a stumbling block, and unto the Greeks foolishness, but unto them which are called, both Jews and Greeks, Christ the Power of God, and the Wisdom of God*[10]. *The commandment, which* was ordained *to life*, Paul, when yet unregenerate, *found* to be *unto death*[11]. "[12] Pray we then the Eternal Wisdom, that we may be truly wise and understanding, and receive not in vain those many good things which Christ has brought to the race of man. Let us cleave to Him by that *faith, which worketh by love;* let us seek the Good, seek the Just, *seek the Lord while He may be found, and call upon Him while He is near.* Whatever God doeth toward ourselves or others, let us account right; *for the ways of the Lord are right,* and *that* cannot be unjust, which pleaseth the Just. Whatever He teacheth, whatever He commandeth, let us believe without discussion, and embrace most firmly for *that* cannot be false, which the Truth hath taught. Let us walk in His ways;" for Christ Himself is *the Way* unto Himself, *the Life*. "[13] Look up to heaven; look down to Hell; live for Eternity." "[14] Weigh a thousand, yea thousands of years against eternity what dost thou, weighing a finite, how vast soever, against Infinity?"

[1] Aristot. Eth. i. 3. [2] Poc. [3] Ps. cxix. 165.
[4] As in Nah. iii. 3. Prov. iv. 19. [5] Ps. lxix. 22.
[6] from Sanct. [7] S. Luke ii. 34.
[8] S. John ix. 39. [9] 1 Ep. ii. 7, 8. [10] 1 Cor. i. 23, 24.
[11] Rom. vii. 10. [12] Rib. [13] Lap.
[14] S. Aug. in Ps. xxxvi. L.

INTRODUCTION

TO

THE PROPHET

JOEL.

THE Prophet Joel relates nothing of himself. He gives no hints as to himself, except the one fact which was necessary to authenticate his prophecy, that the word of the Lord came to him, and that the book to which that statement is prefixed is that "word of the Lord." *The word of the Lord, which came to Joel, son of Pethuel.* Like Hosea, he distinguished himself from others of the same name, by the mention of the name of his unknown father. But his whole book bears evidence, that he was a prophet of Jerusalem. He was living in the centre of the public worship of God: he speaks to the priests as though present, *Come ye, lie all night in sackcloth*[a]; he was, where the *solemn assembly*[b], which he bids them *proclaim*, would be held; *the house of the Lord*[c], from which *meat-offering and drink-offering* were *cut off*, was before his eyes. Whether for alarm[d], or for prayer[e], he bids, *blow ye the trumpet in Zion. The city*[f], which he sees the enemy approaching to beleaguer and enter, is Jerusalem. He addresses the *children of Zion*[g]; he reproaches Tyre, Zidon, and Philistia, with selling to the Greeks *the children of Zion and Jerusalem*[h]. God promises by him to *bring back the captivity of Judah and Jerusalem*[i]. Of Israel, in its separated existence, he takes no more notice, than if it were not. They may be included in the three places in which he uses the name; *Ye shall know that I am in the midst of Israel; I will plead for My people and My heritage, Israel; the Lord will be the strength of Israel*[k]; but, (as the context shews) only as included, together with Judah, in the one people of God. The promises to Judah, Jerusalem, Zion, with which he closes his book, being simply prophetic, must, so far, remain the same, whomsoever he addressed. He foretells that those blessings were to issue from Zion, and that the Church was to be founded there. Yet the absence of any direct promise of the extension of those blessings to the ten tribes, (such as occur in Hosea and Amos) implies that he had no office in regard to them.

Although a prophet of Jerusalem, and calling, in the name of God, to a solemn and strict fast and supplication, he was no priest. He mentions the priests as a class to which he did not belong[l], *the priests, the Lord's ministers; ye priests; ye ministers of the altar; ye ministers of my God; let the priests, the ministers of the Lord, weep between the porch and the altar*, the place where they officiated. He calls upon them to proclaim the fast, which he enjoined in the Name of God. *Sanctify ye a fast, call a solemn assembly*[m], he says to those, whom he had just called to mourn, *ye priests, ye ministers of the altar.* As entrusted with a revelation from God, he had an authority superior to that of the priests. While using this, he interfered not with their own special office.

Joel must have completed his prophecy in its present form, before Amos collected his prophecies into one whole. For Amos takes as the key-note of his prophecy, words with which Joel almost closes his; *The Lord shall roar from Zion, and utter His voice from Jerusalem*[n]. Nor only so, but Amos inserts at the end of his own prophecy some of Joel's closing words of promise. Amos thus identi-

[a] i. 13, 14. [b] ii. 15–17. [c] i. 9. [d] ii. 1. [e] ii. 15. [f] ii. 9. [g] ii. 23. [h] iii. 4, 6.

[i] iii. 1. [k] ii. 27, iii. 2, 16. [l] i. 9, 13, ii. 17. [m] i. 14. [n] Joel iii. 16.

fied his own prophecy with that of Joel. In the threatening with which he opens it, he retains each word of Joel, in the self-same order, although the words admit equally of several different collocations, each of which would have had an emphasis of its own[o]. The symbolic blessing, which Amos takes from Joel at the close of his prophecy *the mountains shall drop with new wine*[p], is found in these two prophets alone; and the language is the bolder and more peculiar, because the word *drop*[q] is used of dropping from above, not of flowing down. It seems as if the picture were, that the mountains of Judæa, *the* mountains, instead of mist or vapor, should *distill* that which is the symbol of joy, *wine which maketh glad the heart of man*[r]. The ground why Amos, in this marked way, joined on his own book of prophecy to the book of Joel, must remain uncertain, since he did not explain it. It may have been, that, being called in an unusual way to the Prophetic office, he would in this way identify himself with the rest of those whom God called to it. A prophet, out of Judah but for Israel, Amos identified himself with the one prophet of Judah, whose prophecy was committed to writing. Certainly those first words of Amos, *The Lord shall roar from Zion, and utter His voice from Jerusalem*, pointed out to the ten tribes, that Zion and Jerusalem were the place *which God had chosen to place His Name there*, the visible centre of His government, whence proceeded His judgments and His revelation. Others have supposed that bad men thought that the evil which Joel had foretold would not come, and that the good may have looked anxiously for the fulfillment of God's promises; and that on that ground, Amos renewed, by way of allusion, both God's threats and promises, thereby impressing on men's minds, what Habakkuk says in plain terms[s], *The vision is for the* [t] *appointed time, and it hasteth to the end*[u]*: though it tarry, wait for it; for it will come, it will not tarry*, or *be behindhand*[v].

However this may have been, such marked renewal of threatenings and promises of Joel by Amos, attests two things; 1) that Joel's prophecy must, at the time when Amos wrote, have become part of Holy Scripture, and its authority must have been acknowledged; 2) that its authority must have been acknowledged by, and it must have been in circulation among, those to whom Amos prophesied; otherwise he would not have prefixed to his book those words of Joel. For the whole force of the words, as employed by Amos, depends upon their being recognized by his hearers, as a renewal of the prophecy of Joel. Certainly bad men jeered at Amos, as though his threatenings would not be fulfilled[w].

Since, then, Amos prophesied during the time, when Azariah and Jeroboam II. reigned together, the book of Joel must have been at that time written, and known in Israel also. Beyond this, the brief, although full, prophecy of Joel affords no clue as to its own date. Yet probably it was not far removed from that of Amos. For Amos, as well as Joel, speaks of the sin of Tyre and Zidon and of the Philistines in selling the children of Judah into captivity[x]. And since Amos speaks of this, as the crowning sin of both, it is perhaps likely that some signal instance of it had taken place, to which both prophets refer. To this, the fact that both prophets speak of the scourge of locusts and drought[y], (if this were so) would not add any further evidence. For Joel was prophesying to Judah; Amos, to Israel. The prophecy of Joel may indeed subordinately, although very subordinately at the most, *include* real locusts; and such locusts, if he meant to include them, could have been no local plague, and so could hardly have passed over Israel. But Amos does not speak of the ravages of the locusts, by which, in addition to drought, mildew, pestilence, God had, when he prophesied, recently chastened Israel, as distinguished above others which God had sent upon this land. There is nothing therefore to identify the locusts spoken of by Amos with those which Joel speaks of as an image of the terrible, successive, judgments of God. Rather Amos enumerates, one after the other, God's ordinary plagues in those countries, and says that all had failed in the object for which God sent them, the turning of His people to Himself.

Nor, again, does anything in Joel's own prophecy suggest any particular date, beyond what is already assigned through the relation which the book of Amos bears to his book. On the contrary, in correspondence, perhaps, with the wide extent of his prophecy, Joel says next to nothing of what was temporary or local. He mentions, incidentally, in one place the *drunkards*[z] of his people; yet in this case too, he speaks of the sin as especially affected and touched by the chastisement, not

[o] ויהוה מציון ישאג ומירושלם יתן קולו. Amos, since he opens his prophecy with these words, omits the ו (and that alone,) with which Joel joins them on with what preceded.

[p] Joel iv. 18. יטפו ההרים עסיס Am. ix. 13. והטיפו ההרים עסיס.

[q] חטיף נטף, are used of "the heavens," Jud. v. 4, Ps. lxviii. 9; of "the fingers trickling," Cant. v. 5, 13; "the lips dropping honey," Cant. iv. 11, Prov. v. 3; then of speech.

[r] Ps. civ. 15.

[s] Hab. ii. 3.

[t] לַמּוֹעֵד.

[u] lit. *breatheth*, as we say "panteth," יָפֵחַ.

[v] יְאַחֵר.

[w] v. 18, vi. 3, ix. 10.

[x] Jo. iii. 4–6. Am. i. 6, 9.

[y] "drought," Joel i. 17, 20, Am. iv. 7, 8; "locusts," Am. iv. 9.

[z] i. 5.

of the chastisement, as brought upon the sinner or upon the sinful people by that sin. Beyond this one case, the Prophet names neither sins nor sinners among his own people. He foretells chastisement, and exhorts to repentance as the means of averting it, but does not specify any sins. His prophecy is one declaration of the displeasure of God against all sin, and of His judgments consequent thereon, one promise of pardon upon earnest repentance; and so, perhaps, what is individual has, for the most part been purposely suppressed.

The notices in the book of Joel, which have been employed to fix more precisely the date of the Prophet, relate 1) to the proclamation of the solemn assembly, which, it is supposed, would be enjoined thus authoritatively in a time when that injunction would be obeyed; 2) to the mention of certain nations, and the supposed omission of certain other nations, as enemies of Judah. Both arguments have been overstated and misstated.

1) The call to public humiliation implies, so far, times in which the king would not interfere to prevent it. But ordinarily, in Judah, even bad and irreligious kings did not interfere with extraordinary fasts in times of public distress. Jehoiakim did not; the king, who hesitated not to cut in shreds the roll of Jeremiah's prophecies when three or four columns or chapters[a] had been read before him, and burnt it on the hearth by which he was sitting. The fast-day, upon which that roll had been read in the ears of all the people, was an extraordinary *fast before the Lord, proclaimed to all the people in Jerusalem, and to all the people that came from the cities of Judah unto Jerusalem*[b]. This fasting day was not their annual fast, the day of Atonement. For the day of Atonement was in the seventh month; this, Jeremiah tells us, *was in the ninth month*[c]. When such a king as Jehoiakim tolerated the appointment of an extraordinary fast, not for Jerusalem only, but for *all the people who came from the cities of Judah*, we may well think that no king of ordinary impiety would, in a time of such distress as Joel foretells, have interfered to hinder it. There were, at most, after Athaliah's death, two periods only of decided antagonism to God. The first was at the close of the reign of Joash, after the death of Johoiada, when Joash with the princes gave himself to the idolatry of Ashtaroth and put to death Zechariah, the son of Jehoiada, upon whom *the Spirit of God came*, and he foretold their destruction; *Because ye have forsaken the Lord, He had also forsaken you*[d]. The period after the murder of Zechariah was very short. *As the year came round*, the Syrians came against them; and *when they departed, his own servants slew him*[e]. The only space, left uncertain, is the length of time, during which the idolatry lasted, before the murder of Zechariah. The second period, that in which Amaziah fell away to the idolatry of the Edomites, silenced the prophet of God, and was abandoned by him to his destruction[f], was also brief, lasting probably some sixteen years.

2) The argument from the Prophet's mention of some enemies of God's people[g] and the supposed omission of other later enemies, rests partly on a wrong conception of prophecy, partly on wrong interpretation of the Prophet. On the assumption that the Prophets did not speak of nations, as instruments of God's chastisements on His people, until they had risen above the political horizon of Judah, it has been inferred that Joel lived before the time when Assyria became an object of dread, because, mentioning other enemies of God's people, he does not mention Assyria. The assumption, which originated in unbelief, is untrue in fact. Balaam prophesied the captivity through Assyria[h], when Israel was entering on the promised land; he foretold also the destruction of Assyria or the great empire of the East through a power who should come from Europe[i]. The prophet Ahijah foretold to Jeroboam I. that the Lord would *root up Israel out of the good land which He gave to their fathers, and* would *scatter them beyond the river*[k]. Neither in temporal nor spiritual prophecy can we discern the rules, by which, *at sundry times and in divers manners, God* revealed Himself *through the Prophets*, so that we should be able to reduce to one strict method *the manifold wisdom* of God, and infer the age of a prophet from the tenor of the prophecy which God put into his mouth.

It is plain, moreover, from the text of Joel himself, that God had revealed to him, that other more formidable enemies than had yet invaded Judah would hereafter come against it, and that those enemies whom he speaks of, he mentions only, as specimens of hatred against God's people and of its punishment. There can really be no question, that by *the Northern*[l] army, he means the Assyrian. God foretells also by him the capture of Jerusalem, and the punishment of those who *scattered Israel, My heritage, among the heathen, and divided My land*[m]. Such words can only be understood of an entire removal of Judah, whereby others could come and take possession of his land. In connection with these great powers occurs the mention of Tyre Sidon and Philistia, petty yet vexatious enemies, contrasted with the more powerful.

[a] Jer. xxxvi. 23. [b] Ib. 9. [c] Ib.
[d] 2 Chron. xxiv. 17–21. [e] Ib. 23, 25.
[f] Ib. xxv. 14–16, 23.

[g] Tyre, Zidon, Philistia, iii. 4; Egypt and Edom, iii. 19. [h] Nu. xxiv. 22. [i] Ib. 24. [k] 1 Kgs xiv. 15.
[l] ii. 20. [m] iii. 2.

The very formula with which that mention is introduced, shews that they are named only incidentally and as instances of a class. *And also*[n], *what are ye to Me, O Tyre, and Zidon, and all the coasts of Philistia?* The mighty nations were to come as lions, to lay waste; these, like jackals, made their own petty merchants gain. The mighty divided the land; these were plunderers and men-stealers. In both together, he declares that nothing, either great or small, should escape the righteous judgments of God. Neither shall might save the mighty, nor shall the petty malice of the lesser enemies of God be too small to be requited. But not only is there no proof that Joel means to enumerate all the nations who had hitherto infested Judah, but there is proof that he did not.

One only has been found to place Joel so early as the reign of Jehoshaphat. But in his reign, after the death of Ahab, (B. C. 897,) *Moab and Ammon and with them* others, *a great multitude*[o], invaded Judah. Since then it is tacitly admitted, that the absence of the mention of Moab and Ammon does not imply that Joel prophesied before their invasion (B. C. 897,) neither is the non-mention of the invasion of the Syrians any argument that he lived before the end of the reign of Jehoash (B. C. 840). Further, not the mere invasion of Judah, but the motives of the invasion or cruelty evinced in it, drew down the judgments of God. The invasion of Hazael was directed not against Judah, but *against Gath*[p]. But *a small company of men*[p] went up against Jerusalem; *and the Lord delivered a very great company into their hand, because they had forsaken the Lord God of their fathers. They executed*, we are told, *judgment against Joash.* Nor does it appear, that they, like the Assyrians, exceeded the commission for which God employed them. [r] *They destroyed all the princes of the people from among the people*, the princes who had seduced Joash to idolatry and were the authors of the murder of Zechariah. [s] *They conspired against him, and stoned him (Zechariah) with stones at the commandment of the king.* Amos mentions, as the last ground of God's sentence against Damascus, not this incursion, but the cruelty of Hazael to Gilead[t]. The religious aspect of the single invasion of Judah by this band of Syrians was very different from the perpetual hostility of the Philistines, or the malicious cupidity of the Phœnicians.

Still less intelligible is the assertion, that Joel would not have foretold any punishment of Edom, had he lived after the time when Amaziah smote 20,000 of them *in the valley of salt, and took Selah*[u], or Petra B. C. 838. For Amos confessedly prophesied in the reign of Azariah, the son of Amaziah. Azariah recovered Elath also from Edom[v]; yet Amos, in his time, foretells the utter destruction of Bozra and Teman[w]. The victory of Amaziah did not humble Edom. They remained the same embittered foe. In the time of Ahaz, they again invaded Judah and *smote* it and *carried away a captivity*[x]. Prophecy does not regard these little variations of conquest or defeat. They do not exhaust its meaning. It pronounces God's judgment against the abiding character of the nation; and while that continues unchanged, the sentence remains. Its fulfillment seems often to linger, but in the end, it does not fail nor remain behind God's appointed time. Egypt and Edom moreover, in Joel, stand also as symbols of nations or people like themselves. They stand for the people themselves, but they represent also others of the same character, as long as the struggle between "the city of God" and "the city of the devil[y]" shall last, i. e. to the end of time.

There being then no internal indication of the date of Joel, we cannot do better than acquiesce in the tradition, by which his book is placed next to that of Hosea, and regard Joel as the prophet of Judah, during the earlier part of Hosea's office toward Israel, and rather earlier than Isaiah. At least, Isaiah, although he too was called to the prophetic office in the days of Uzziah, appears to have embodied in his prophecy, words of Joel, as well of Micah, bearing witness to the unity of prophecy, and, amid the richness and fullness of his own prophetic store, purposely borrowing from those, of whose ministry God did not will that such large fruit should remain. The remarkable words[z], *Near is the Day of the Lord, like destruction from the Almighty shall it come*, Isaiah inserted, word for word[a], from Joel[b], including the remarkable alliteration, ceshod mishshaddai, "like *a mighty* destruction from the *Almighty*."

The prophecy of Joel is altogether one. It extends from his own day to the end of time. He gives the key to it in a saying, which he casts into the form of a proverb, that judgment shall follow after judgment[c]. Then he describes that first desolation, as if present, and calls to repentance[d]; yet withal he says expressly, that the day of the Lord is not come, but is at hand[e]. This he repeats at the beginning of the second chapter[f], in

[n] וגם iv. 4 Heb.; iii. 4 Eng.
[o] 2 Chron. xx. 1, 2. [p] 2 Kgs xii. 17.
[q] 2 Chron. xxiv. 24. [r] Ib. 23; add 17, 18.
[s] Ib. 21. [t] i. 3. [u] 2 Kgs xiv. 7. 2 Chron. xxv. 11.
[v] 2 Kgs xiv. 22. 2 Chron. xxvi. 2. [w] i. 12.
[x] 2 Chron. xxviii. 17.
[y] See S. Aug. de Civ. Dei. i. 1. [z] Isaiah xiii. 6.
[a] קרוב יום יהוה כשד משדי יבוא Isaiah has omitted the "and" only. Other correspondences, as the use of ברכה Is. lxv. 8. Jo. ii. 14, and that between Is. xiii. 10 and Jo. ii. 31, which is an agreement in substance not of words, have no force of proof. [b] Joel i. 15. [c] i. 4.
[d] i. 5 sqq. [e] i. 15. [f] ii. 1.

which he describes the coming judgment more fully, speaks of it, as coming[g], and, when, he has pictured it as just ready to break upon them, and God, as giving the command to the great camp assembled to fulfill His word[h], he calls them, in God's name, yet more earnestly to repentance[i], and promises, upon that repentance, plenary forgiveness and the restoration of everything which God had withdrawn from them[k]. These promises culminate in the first Coming of Christ, the outpouring of the Spirit upon all flesh, and the enlarged gift of prophecy at the same time among the sons and daughters of Judah[l]. Upon these mercies to His own people, follow the judgments upon His and their enemies, reaching on to the second Coming of our Lord.

An attempt has been made to sever the prophecy into two discourses, of which the first is to end at c. ii. 17, the second is to comprise the remainder of the book[m]. That scheme severs what is closely united, God's call to prayer and His promise that He will answer it. According to this severance of the prophecy, the first portion is to contain the exhortation on the part of God, without any promise; the second is to contain an historical relation that God answered, without saying what He answered. The notion was grounded on unbelief, that God absolutely foretold, that He would, beyond the way of nature, bring, what He would, upon repentance, as certainly remove. It is rested on a mere error in grammar[n]. The grammatical form was probably chosen, in order to express how instantaneously God would hearken to real repentance, *that the Lord is jealous for His land.* The words of prayer should not yet have escaped their lips, when God answered. As He says, [o] *And it shall be, before they shall call, I will answer; while they are yet speaking, I will hear.* Man has to make up his mind on a petition; with God, hearing and answering are one.

The judgments upon God's people, described in the two first chapters of Joel, cannot be limited to a season of drought and a visitation of locusts, whether one or more. i) The prophet includes all which he foretells, in one statement, which, both from its form and its preternatural character, has the appearance of a proverbial saying[p]. It does stand, as a summary. For he draws the attention of all to *this*[q]; *Hear* this, *ye old men, and give ear, all ye inhabitants of the land. Hath* this *been in your days? &c.* He appeals to the aged, whether they had heard the like, and bids all transmit it to their posterity[r]. The summary is given in a very measured form, in three divisions, each consisting of four words, and the four words standing, in each, in the same order[s]. The first and third words of the four are the same in each; and the fourth of the first and second four become the second of the second and third four, respectively. Next to Hebrew, its force can best be seen in Latin;

Residuum	erucæ	comedit	locusta;
Residuumque	locustæ	comedit	bruchus;
Residuumque	bruchi	comedit	exesor.

The structure of the words resembles God's words to Elijah[t], whose measured rhythm and precise order of words may again be best, because most concisely, exhibited in Latin. Each division contains five words in the same order; and here, the first, second, and fourth words of each five remain the same, and the Proper name which is the fifth in the first five becomes the third in the second five[u].

Profugum	gladii	Hazaelis	occidet	Jehu;
Profugumque	gladii	Jehu	occidet	Elisha.

In this case, we see that the form is proverbial, because the slaying by Elisha is different in kind from the slaying by Jehu and Hazael, and is the same of which God speaks by Hosea[v], *I hewed them by the Prophets; I slew them by the words of my mouth.* But so also is it with regard to the locust. Except by miracle, what the Prophet here describes, would not happen. He foretells, not only that a scourge should come, unknown in degree and number, before or afterward, in Palestine, but that four sorts of locusts should come successively, the latter destroying what the former left. Now this is not God's ordinary way in bringing this scourge. In His ordinary Providence different sorts of locusts do not succeed one another. Nor would it be any increase of the infliction, anything to record or forewarn of. At times, by a very rare chastisement, God has brought successive flights of the same insect from the same common birthplace; and generally, where the female locusts deposit their eggs and die,

[g] ii. 2–10. [h] ii. 11. [i] ii. 12–17. [k] ii. 18-27. [l] ii. 28, 29. [m] Ewald, p. 65.

[n] Forms, like וַיְקַנֵּא, וַיַּעַן are only used of the past, when a past has been already expressed or implied, as, in English, we may use a present in vivid description, in which the mind, as it were, accompanies and sees the action, although past. The past having once been expressed, we might say "and he goes" &c. without ambiguity. But the form being relative, it must be understood of the same time, as that which has preceded. Here the time, which has preceded, is future. So also then is the word. The same form is used of the future, Hos. viii. 10, Am. ix. 5, Is. ix. 5, 10, 13. Hæv. Einl. ii. 232.

[o] Isa. lxv. 24. [p] i. 4. [q] i. 2. [r] i. 3.

[s] יתר הגזם אכל הארבה
ויתר הארבה אכל הילק
ויתר הילק אכל החסיל

[t] 1 Kgs. xix. 17.

[u] הנמלט מחרב חזאל ימית יהוא
והנמלט מחרב יהוא ימית אלישע

[v] vi. 5.

unless a moist winter or man's forethought destroy the eggs, the brood which issues from them in the next spring, being as voracious as the full grown locusts, but crawling through the land, does, in that immediate neighborhood, destroy the produce of the second year, more fatally than the parent had that of the preceding. This however is, at most, the ravage of two stages of the same insect, not four successive scourges, the three last destroying what the former had spared. What the Prophet predicted, if taken literally, was altogether out of the order of nature, and yet its literal fulfillment has not the character of a miracle; for it adds nothing to the intensity of what is predicted. The form of his prediction is proverbial; and this coincides with the other indications that the Prophet did not intend to speak of mere locusts.

1) In order to bring down this summary of the Prophet to the level of an ordinary event in God's ordinary Providence, a theory has been invented, that he is not here speaking of different sorts of locusts, but of the same locust in different stages of its growth, from the time when it leaves the egg, until it attains its full development and its wings. According to the inventor of this theory [w], the first, the *gazam* (the *palmer-worm* of our version) was to be the migratory locust, which visits Palestine (it was said) chiefly in Autumn; the second, *arbeh*, (the ordinary name of the locust) was to stand for the young locust, as it first creeps out of the shell; the *yelek* (translated *cankerworm*) was to be the locust, in what was supposed to be the third stage of development; the *chasil* (translated *caterpillar*) was to be the full-grown locust. According to this form of the theory, the *gazam* was to be the same as the *chasil*, the first as the last; and two of the most special names of the locust, *gazam* and *chasil*, were, without any distinction, to be ascribed to the full-grown locust, of one and the same species. For, according to the theory, the *gazam* was to be the full-grown locust which arrived by flight and deposited its eggs; the *arbeh*, *yelek*, *chasil*, were to be three chief stages of development of the locusts which left those eggs. So that the *chasil*, although not the same individual, was to be exactly the same insect as the *gazam*, and at the same stage of existence, the full-grown locust, the gryllus migratorius with wings. But while these two, more special, names were appropriated to the self-same species of locust, in the same, its full-grown stage (which in itself is unlikely, when they are thus distinguished from each other) one of the two names which remained to describe (as was supposed) the earlier, (so to speak) infantine or childish [x] stages of its development, *arbeh*, is the most general name of locust. This was much as if, when we wished to speak of a "colt" as such, we were to call it "horse," or were to use the word "cow" to designate a "calf." For, according to this theory, Joel, wishing to mark that he was speaking of the pupa, just emerged from the egg, called it "arbeh," the most common name of the locust tribe.

This theory then was tacitly modified [y]. In the second form of the theory, which is more likely to be introduced among us, *gazam* was to be the locust in its first stage; *arbeh* was to be the second, instead of the first; *yelek* was to be the last but one; *chasil* was, as before, to be the full-grown locust. This theory escaped one difficulty, that of making the *gazam* and *chasil* full-grown locusts of the same species. It added another. The three moultings which it assumes to be represented by the *arbeh*, *yelek*, and *gazam*, correspond neither with the actual moults of the locust, nor with those which strike the eye. Some observers have noticed four moultings of the locust, after it had left the egg [z]. Some write, as if there were yet more [a]. But of marked changes which the eye of the observer can discern, there are two only, that by which it passes from the larva state into the pupa, and that by which it passes from the pupa to the full-grown locust. The *three* names, arbitrarily adapted to the natural history of the locust, correspond neither with the *four* actual, nor with the *two* noticeable changes.

But even these terms larva and pupa, if taken in their popular sense, would give a wrong idea of the moults of the locust. The changes with which we are familiar under these names, take place in the locust, before it leaves the egg [b]. "[c] The pupæ are equally capable of eating and moving with the larvæ, which they resemble except in having rudiments of wings or of wings and elytra:" having in fact "complete wings, only folded up longitudinally and transversely, and inclosed in membranous cases." "The pupæ of the orthoptera" [to which the locust belongs] "resemble the perfect insect, both as to shape and the organs for taking their food,

[w] Credner on Joel i. 4. p. 102. followed by Scholz only.

[x] The expression of Van der Hœven, Handbook of Zoology i. 273, to convey the idea of growth, rather than of change.

[y] Gesenius (Thesaur. p. 1257. v. ארבה) tacitly corrects Credner. Maurer, Ewald, Umbreit, follow Gesenius; yet Ewald thinks that the *gazam*, *yelek*, *chasil*, *need* not belong to the proper locust tribe *arbeh*, (which is in fact an abandonment of the theory).

[z] Thomson, The Land and the book, ii. p. 104. Rœsel Insecten Belustigungen T. ii. Heuschrecken § 7. 8. pp. 69, 70. Van der Hœven. i. 4.

[a] "Après plusieurs mues." Nouveau Dict. d'hist. natur. 1817. viii. 446. The Encyclopédie Méthodique v. Criquet (Ib. p. 706) says that the number was not ascertained.

[b] Owen Invertebrata Lect. 18. pp. 424, 435, 6.

[c] See Spence and Kirby, Introd. to Entomol. iii. 240, 1. Van der Hœven, i. p. 273.

except in not having their wings and elytra fully developed."

These changes regard only its outward form, not its habits. Its voracity begins almost as soon as it has left the egg. The first change takes place "a few days[d]" after they are first in motion. "They fast, *for a short time*[d]," before each change. But the creature continues, throughout, the same living, devouring, thing[e]. From the first, "creeping and jumping in the same general direction, they begin their destructive march[d]." The change, when it is made, takes place "in seven or eight minutes" by the creature disengaging itself from its former outward skin[f]. All the changes are often completed in six weeks. In the Ukraine, six weeks after it has left the egg, it has wings and flies away[g]. In the warmer climate of Palestine, the change would be yet more rapid. "They attain their natural size," Niebuhr says of those in Mosul[h], "with astonishing rapidity." "Tis three weeks," says Le Bruyn[i], "before they can use their wings."

But 2) the Prophet is not writing on "natural history," nor noticing distinctions observable only on minute inspection. He is foretelling God's judgments. But, as all relate, who have described the ravages of locusts, there are not three, four or five, but two stages only, in which its ravages are at all distinct, the unwinged and the winged state.

3) Probably, only in a country which was the birthplace of locusts, and where consequently they would, in all the stages of their existence, be, year by year, before the eyes of the people, would those stages be marked by different names. Arabia was one such birthplace, and the Arabs, living a wild life of nature, have invented, probably beyond any other nation, words with very special physical meanings. The Arabs, who have above fifty names for different locusts, or locusts under different circumstances, as they distinguished the sexes of the locust by different names, so they did three of its ages. "[j] When it came forth out of its egg, it was called *doba;* when its wings appeared and grew, it was called *ghaugha;* and this, when they jostled one another; and when their colors appeared, the males becoming yellow, the females black, then they were called *jerad.*" This is no scientific description; for the wings of the locust are not visible, until after the last moult. But in the language of other countries, where this plague was not domestic, these different stages of the existence of the locust are not marked by a special name. The Syrians added an epithet "the flying," "the creeping," but designated by the "creeping" the *chasil* as well as the *yelek*[k], which last the Chaldees render by (*parecha*) "the flying." In Joel where they had to designate the four kinds of locusts together, they were obliged, like our own version, in one case to substitute the name of another destructive insect; in another, they use the name of a different kind of locust, the *tsartsuro*, or *tsartsero*, the Syrian and Arabic way of pronouncing the Hebrew *tselatsal*[l]. In Greek the Βροῦχος and Ἀττέλαβος have been thought to be two stages of the unwinged, and so, unperfected, locusts. But S. Cyril[m] and Theodoret[m] speak of the Βροῦχος as having wings; Aristotle[n] and Plutarch[o] speak of the eggs of the Ἀττέλαβος.

4) The Prophet is speaking of successive ravagers, each devouring what the former left. If the theory of these writers was correct, the order in which he names them, would be the order of their development. But in the order of their development, they never destroy what they left in their former stages. From the time when they begin to move, they march right onward "creeping and jumping, all in the same general direction[p]." This march never stops. They creep on, eating as they creep, in the same tract of country, not in the same spot. You could not say of creatures (were we afflicted with such,) who crawled for six weeks, devouring, over two counties of England, that in their later stage they devoured what in their former they left. We should speak of the plague "spreading" over two counties. We could not use the Prophet's description, for it would not be true. This mere march, however destructive in its course, does not correspond

[d] Thomson, l. c. "*No sooner were any of them hatched*, than they immediately collected themselves together, each of them forming a compact body of several hundred yards in square, which, marching afterwards directly forward, climbed over trees, walls and houses, eat up every plant in their way, *and let nothing escape them.*" Shaw, Travels p. 257.

[e] "This is a character of the whole of the hemoptera and orthoptera. The development is attended with no loss of activity or diminution of voracity." Owen, p. 423. "The whole life of the orthopterous insect from the exclusion [from the egg] to flight, may be called an active nymphhood." Ib. 436.

[f] Shaw, Ib. He is speaking of the last and chief change to the winged state.

[g] About mid-April "they hatch and leap all about, being six weeks before they can fly," de Beauplan, Ukraine, in Churchill's Voyages i. 600.

[h] Descr. de l' Arab. p. 149.

[i] Travels, p. 179.

[j] Demiri, quoted by Bochart. iv. 1.

[k] In Joel i. 2, ii. 25, the Syriac renders the *arbeh*, *kamtso porecho* (the flying locust), and the *yelek*, *kamtso dsochelo*, (the creeping locust). In 1 Kgs viii. 37 and 2 Chron. vi. 28, it renders *chasil* by *dsochelo*, *creeping*. In Ps. lxxviii. 46, it renders *chasil* by *kamtso*, *locust*, and *arbeh*, by *dsochelo*, *creeper*. In Ps. cv. 34, it renders *arbeh*, by *kamtso* only [as also in 2 Chron. vi.] and *yelek* again by *dsochelo*.

[l] צלצל Deut. xxviii. 42.

[m] on Nah. iii. 16, quoted by Bochart, iii. 262.

[n] Hist. Anim. v. 29. Ib.

[o] de Isid. ib.

[p] Thomson, l. c.

with the Prophet's words. The Prophet then must mean something else. When the locust becomes winged it flies away, to ravage other countries. So far from destroying what, in its former condition, it left, its ravages in that country are at an end. Had it been ever so true, that these four names, *gazam, arbeh, yelek, chasil*, designated four stages of being of the one locust, of which stages *gazam* was the first, *chasil* the last, then to suit this theory, it should have been said, that *gazam*, the young locust, devoured what the *chasil*, by the hypothesis the full-grown locust, left, not the reverse, as it stands in the Prophet. For the young, when hatched, do destroy in the same place which their parents visited, when they deposited their eggs; but the grown locust does not devastate the country which he wasted before he had wings. So then, in truth, had the Prophet meant this, he would have spoken of two creatures, not of four; and of those two he would have spoken in a different order from that of this hypothesis.

5) Palestine not being an ordinary breeding place of the locusts, the locust arrives there by flight. Accordingly, on this ground also, the first mentioned would be the winged, not the crawling, locust. 6) The use of these names of the locust, elsewhere in Holy Scripture, contradicts the theory, that they designate different stages of growth, of the same creature. a) The *arbeh* is itself one of the four kinds of locust, allowed to be eaten, having subordinate species. [q] *The locust* (arbeh) *after his kind, and the bald locust* (sol'am *the devourer*) *after his kind, and the beetle* (chargol, lit. *the springer*) *after his kind, and the grasshopper* (chagab, perhaps, *the overshadower*) *after his kind.* It is to the last degree unlikely, that the name *arbeh*, which is the generic name of the most common sort of the *winged* locust, should be given to one imperfect, unwinged, stage of one species of locust.

b) The creeping, unwinged, insect, which has just come forth from the ground, would more probably be called by yet another name for "locust," *gob, gobai*, "the creeper," than by that of *gazam*. But though such is probably the etymology of *gob*, probably it too is winged [r].

c) Some of these creatures here mentioned by Joel are named together in Holy Scripture as distinct and winged. The *arbeh* and *chasil*, are mentioned together [s]; as are also the *arbeh* and the *yelek* [t]. The *arbeh*, the *yelek*, and the *chasil*, are all together mentioned in regard to the plague of Egypt [u], and all consequently, as winged, since they were brought by the wind. The prophet Nahum also speaks of the *yelek*, a *spoiling and fleeing away* [v]. According to the theory, the *yelek*, as well as the *arbeh*, ought to be unwinged.

Nor, again, can it be said, that the names are merely poetic names of the locust. It is true that *arbeh*, the common name of the locust, is taken from its number; the rest, *gazam, yelek, chasil*, are descriptive of the voracity of that tribe. But both the *arbeh* and the *chasil* occur together in the historical and so in prose books. We know of ninety sorts of locusts [w], and they are distinguished from one another by some epithet. It would plainly be gratuitous to assume that the Hebrew names, although epithets, describe only the genus in its largest sense, and are not names of species. If moreover these names were used of the same identical race, not of different species in it, the saying would the more have the character of a proverb. We could not say, for instance, "what the horse left, the steed devoured," except in some proverbial meaning.

This furnishes a certain probability that the Prophet means something more under the locust, than the creature itself, although this in itself too is a great scourge of God.

ii. In the course of the description itself, the Prophet gives hints, that he means, under the locust, a judgment far greater, an enemy far mightier, than the locust. These hints have been put together most fully, and supported in detail by Hengstenberg [x], so that here they are but re-arranged.

1) Joel calls the scourge, whom he describes, *the Northern* or Northman. But whereas the Assyrian invaders of Palestine did pour into it from the North, the locust, almost always, by a sort of law of their being, make their inroads there from their birth-place in the south [y].

2) The Prophet directs the priests to pray, *O Lord give not Thine heritage to reproach, that the heathen should rule over them* [z]. But there is plainly no connection between the desolation caused by locusts, and the people being given over to a heathen conqueror.

3) The Prophet speaks of, or alludes to, the agent, as one responsible. It is not likely that, of an irrational scourge of God, the Prophet would have assigned as a ground of its destruction, *he hath magnified to do* [a]; words used of human pride which exceeds the measure appointed to it by God. On the other hand, when God says, *a nation is come up upon My land* [b] *then will the Lord be jealous for His land* [c], the words belong rather to a heathen invader of God's land, who

[q] Lev. xi. 22. [r] Nah. iii. 17.
[s] 1 Kings viii. 37, 2 Chr. vi. 28, Ps. lxxviii. 46.
[t] Nah. iii. 16, 17, Ps. cv. 34. [u] Ps. l. c. [v] iii. 16.
[w] Encyclopédie Méthodique Hist. Nat. Insectes, T. vi. v. Criquet pp. 209–33. [x] Christol. iii. 352–58. ed. 2.
[y] See on ii. 20, p. 123. [z] ii 17.
[a] See on ii. 20, p. 124. [b] i. 6.
[c] ii. 18.

disputed with His people the possession of the land which He had given them, than to an insect, which was simply carried, without volition of its own, by the wind. With this, falls in the use of the title *people, goi*[d], used often of heathen, not (as is *'am*[e]) of irrational creatures.

4) After the summary which mentions simply different kinds of locusts, the prophet speaks of *fire, flame, drought*[f], which shew that he means something beyond that plague.

5) The imagery, even where it has some correspondence with what is known of locusts, goes beyond any mere plague of locusts. a) People are terrified at their approach; but Joel says not *people*, but *peoples*[g], nations. It was a scourge then, like those great conquering Empires, whom God made *the hammer of the whole earth*[h]. b) The locusts darken the air as they come; but the darkening of the sun and moon, the withdrawing of the shining of the stars[i] (which together are incompatible) are far beyond this, and are symbols elsewhere of the trembling of all things before the revelation of the wrath of God.[k] c) Locusts enter towns and are troublesome to their inhabitants[l]; but the fields are the scenes of their desolation, in towns they are destroyed[m]. These in Joel are represented as taking *the city*, Jerusalem[l], symbols of countless hosts, but as mere locusts, harmless.

6) The effects of the scourge are such as do not result from mere locusts. a) The quantity used for *the meat-offering and drink-offering*[n] was so small, that even a famine could not occasion their disuse. They were continued even in the last dreadful siege of Jerusalem. Not materials for sacrifice, but sacrificers were wanting[o]. b) God says, *I will restore the years which the locust hath eaten*[p]. But the locust, being a passing scourge, did not destroy the fruits of several *years*, only of that one year. c) The *beasts of the field* are bidden to rejoice, *because the tree beareth her fruit*[q]. This must be metaphor, for the trees are not food for cattle. d) The scourge is spoken of as greater than any which they or their fathers knew of, and as one to be ever remembered[r]; but Israel had many worse scourges than any plague of locusts, however severe. God had taught them by David, It is better to fall into the hands of God, than into the hands of men.

7) The destruction of this scourge of God is described in a way, taken doubtless in its details from the destruction of locusts, yet, as a whole, physically impossible in a literal sense[s].

8) The Day of the Lord, of which he speaks, is identical with the scourge which he describes, but is far beyond any plague of locusts. It includes the captivity of Judah[t], the division of their land[u], its possession by strangers, since it is promised that these are *no more to pass through her*[v]. It is a day of utter destruction, such as the Almighty alone can inflict. *It shall come like a mighty destruction from the Almighty*[w].

Attempts have been made to meet some of these arguments; but these attempts for the most part only illustrate the strength of the arguments, which they try to remove.

I. 1) *Northern* has been taken in its natural sense, and it has been asserted, contrary to the fact, that locusts did come from the North into Palestine[x]; or it has been said[y], that the locusts were first driven from their birthplace in Arabia Deserta through Palestine *to* the North, and then brought back again into Palestine *from* the North; or that *Northern* meant that part of the whole body of locusts which occupied the Northern parts of Palestine[z], Judea lying to the extreme south.

But an incidental flight of locusts, which should have entered Palestine from the North, (which they are not recorded to have done) would not have been called "*the* Northern." The object of such a name would be to describe the locale of those spoken of, not a mere accident or anomaly. Still less, if this ever happened, (of which there is no proof) would a swarm of locusts be so called, which had first come from the South. The regularity, with which the winds blow in Palestine, makes such a bringing back of the locusts altogether improbable. The South wind blows chiefly in March; the East wind in Summer, the North wind mostly about the Autumnal equinox. But neither would a body so blown to and fro, be the fearful scourge predicted by the Prophet, nor would it have been called *the Northern*. The *i* of the word *tsephoni*, like our *ern* in North*ern*, designates that which is spoken of, not as coming incidentally from the North, but as having an habitual relation to the North. A flight of locusts driven back, contrary to continual experience, from the North, would not have been designated as *the Northern*, any more than a Lowlander who passes some time in the Highlands would be called a Highlander, or a Highlander, passing into the South, would be called a "Southron." With regard to the third explanation, Joel was especially a prophet of Judah. The supposition that, in predicting the destruction of the locusts, he spoke of the Northern not of the Southern portion of them,

[d] גוי i. 6. [e] עם. [f] i. 19, 20. [g] ii. 6. [h] Jer. l. 23. [i] ii. 10. [k] Is. xiii. 10. [l] See on ii. 9, p. 117. [m] Niebuhr, Descr. de l' Arabie, p. 149. [n] i. 9. [o] Hengst. from Jos. B. J. 6, 2, 1. [p] ii. 25.

[q] ii. 22. [r] i. 2, 3, ii. 2. [s] See on ii. 20. [t] iii. 1. [u] iii. 2. [v] iii. 17. [w] i. 15. [x] Aben Ezra, Kimchi, followed by Lightfoot, Chron. V. T. i. 94. Cast. Scholz. [y] Credner. [z] Bochart (Hieroz. P. ii. L. iv. c. 5.), Lively.

implies that he promised on the part of God, as the reward of the humiliation of Judah, that God would remove this scourge from the separated kingdom of the ten tribes, without any promise as to that part which immediately concerned themselves. Manifestly also, *the Northern* does not, by itself, express the Northern part of a whole.

It is almost incredible that some have understood by *the Northern*, those driven toward the North, and so those actually in the South [a]; and *I will remove far from you the Northern*, "I will remove far from *you* who are in the South, the locusts who have come to you from the South, whom I will drive to the North."

2) Instances have been brought *from other lands*, to which locusts have come from the North. This answer wholly misstates the point at issue. The question is not as to the direction which locusts take, *in other countries*, whither God sends them, but as to the quarter from which they enter Judea. The direction which they take, varies in different countries, but is on one and the same principle. It is said by one observer, that they have power to fly against the wind [b]. Yet this probably is said only of light airs, when they are circling round in preparation for their flight. For the most part, they are carried by the prevailing wind, sometimes, if God so wills, to their own destruction, but, mostly, to other counties as a scourge. "When they can fly, they go," relates Beauplan [c] of those bred in the Ukraine, "wherever the wind carries them. If the North-east wind prevails, when they first take flight, it carries them all into the Black Sea; but if the wind blows from any other quarter, they go into some other country, to do mischief." Lichtenstein writes [d], "They never deviate from the straight line, so long as the same wind blows." Niebuhr says, "[e] I saw in Cairo a yet more terrible cloud of locusts, which came by a South-west wind and so from the desert of Libya." "[f] In the night of Nov. 10, 1762, a great cloud passed over Jidda with a West wind, consequently over the Arabian gulf which is very broad here." Of two flights in India which Forbes witnessed, he relates [g], "Each of these flights were brought by an East wind; they took a Westerly direction, and, without settling in the country, probably perished in the gulf of Cambay." Dr. Thomson who had spent 25 years in the Holy Land, says in illustration of David's words, [h] *I am tossed up and down like the locust*, "[i] This refers to the flying locust. I have had frequent opportunities to notice, how these squadrons are tossed up and down, and whirled round and round by the ever-varying currents of the mountain winds." Morier says, "[k] The South-east wind constantly brought with it innumerable flights of locusts," but also "[l] a fresh wind from the South-west which had brought them, so completely drove them forward that not a vestige of them was to be seen two hours afterward." These were different kinds of locusts, the first "at Bushire," having "legs and body of a light yellow and wings spotted brown [l];" the second at Shiraz (which "the Persians said came from the Germesir,") being "larger and red."

The breeding country for the locust in South-western Asia, is the great desert of Arabia reaching to the Persian gulf. From this, at God's command, *the East wind brought the locust* [m] to Egypt. They are often carried by a West or South-west wind into Persia. "I have often in spring," relates Joseph de S. Angelo [n], "seen the sun darkened by very thick clouds (so to say) of locusts, which cross the sea from the deserts of Arabia far into Persia." In Western Arabia, Burckhard [o] writes, "the locusts are known to come invariably from the East," i. e. from the same deserts. The South wind carries them to the different countries Northward. This is so general, that Hasselquist wrote; "[p] The locusts appear to be directed—in a direct meridian line by keeping nearly from South to North, turning very little either to the East or West. They come from the deserts of Arabia, take their course on through Palestine, Syria, Carmania, Natolia, go sometimes through Bithynia. They never turn from their course, for example, to the West, wherefore Egypt is not visited by them, though so near their usual tract. Neither do they turn to the East, for I never heard that Mesopotamia or the confines of the Euphrates are ravaged by them." And Volney reports, as the common observation of the natives [q]; "The inhabitants, of Syria remarked that the locusts only came after overmild winters, and that they always came from the deserts of Arabia." Whence S. Jerome, himself an inhabitant of Palestine, regarded this mention of the North as an indication that the prophet intended us to understand under the name of locusts, the

[a] Jun. Trem. Justi.
[b] "They fly high and quick, even against the wind, or in circles; but often so low, that one, riding through them, can see nothing before him, and is often hit in the face." Schlatter, Bruchstucke aus einigen Reisen nach d. sudl. Russland, p. 320.
[c] Description of Ukraine in Churchill's voyages, i. 600.
[d] Travels in S. Africa, c. xlvi. p. 251.
[e] Descr. de l' Arabie, p. 148.
[f] Ib. p. 149. Of the other flights, which Niebuhr mentions, he does not specify whether they came with or without wind. Ib.
[g] ii. 273, 4.
[h] Ps. cix. 23.
[i] The Land and the Book, T. ii. 106.
[k] 2d Journey, p. 43.
[l] Ib. 98.
[m] Ex. x. 13.
[n] Gazoph. Pers. v. Locusta, quoted by Ludolf Comm. in Hist. Æth. pp. 175, 6.
[o] Notes, ii. 90.
[p] Travels, pp. 446, 7.
[q] Voyages en Syrie, i. 277, 8.

great Conquerors who did invade Palestine from the North. "[r] According to the letter, the South wind, rather than the North, hath been wont to bring the flocks of locusts, i. e. they come not from the cold but from the heat. But since he was speaking of the Assyrians, under the image of locusts, therefore he inserted the mention of the North, that we may understand, not the actual locust, which hath been wont to come from the South, but under the locust, the Assyrians and Chaldees."

On the same ground, that the locusts came to Palestine from the South, they were brought from Tartary, (the breeding-place of the locust thence called the Tartarian locust) by an East or South-east wind to the Ukraine. "[s] They generally come [to the Ukraine] from toward Tartary, which happens in a dry spring; for Tartary and the countries East of it, as Circassia, Bazza and Mingrelia, are seldom free from them. The vermin being driven by an East or South-east wind come into the Ukraine." To the coasts of Barbary or to Italy for the same reason they come from the South; to Upper Egypt from Arabia; and to Nubia from the North [t], viz. from Upper Egypt. "In the summer of 1778," Chenier says of Mauritania [u], there "were seen, coming from the South, clouds of locusts which darkened the sun. Strabo states, that, "[v] the strong S. W. or W. winds of the vernal equinox drive them together into the country of Acridophagi." To the Cape of Good Hope they come from the North, whence alone they could come [w]; to Senegal they come with the wind from the East [x]. "They infest Italy," Pliny says [y], "chiefly from Africa;" whence of course, they come to Spain also [z]. Shaw writes of those in Barbary [a]; "Their first appearance was toward the latter end of March, the wind having been for some time Southerly." "As the direction of the marches and flight of them both," [i. e. both of the young brood and their parents, their "marches" before they had wings, and their "flight" afterward] "was always to the Northward, it is probable that they perished in the sea."

All this, however, illustrates the one rule of their flight, that they come with the wind from their birthplace to other lands. On the same ground that they come to Italy or Barbary from the South, to the Ukraine or Arabia Felix from the East, to Persia from the South or South-west, to Nubia or to the Cape, or Constantinople sometimes, from the North, they came to Judea from the South. The word "Northern" describes the habitual character of the army here spoken of. Such *was* the character of the Assyrian or Chaldean conquerors, who are described oftentimes, in Holy Scripture, as coming "out of the North," and such was not the character of the locusts, who, if described by the quarter from which they habitually came, must have been called "the Southern."

3) The third mode of removing the evidence of the word "Northern," has been to explain its meaning. But in no living, nor indeed in any well-known language, would any one have recourse to certain or uncertain etymology, in order to displace the received meaning of a word. Our "North" originally meant "narrowed, contracted;" the Latin "Septentrionalis" is so called from the constellation of the Great Bear; yet no one in his right mind, if he understood not how anything was, by an English author, called "Northern," would have recourse to the original meaning of the word and say "Northern" might signify "hemmed in," or that "septentrionalis" or septentrional meant "belonging to the seven plowers," or whatever other etymology might be given to septentrio. No more should they, because they did not or would not understand the use of the word *tsephoni*, have had recourse to etymologies. *Tsaphon* [b] as uniformly signifies the North, as our word "North" itself. *Tsephoni* signifies *Northern*, the *i* having the same office as our ending *ern* in *Northern*. The word *Tsaphan* originally signified *hid;* then, *laid up;* and, it may be, that *the North* was called *tsaphon*, as *the hidden*, "shrouded in darkness." But to infer from that etymology, that *tsephoni* here may signify the *hider* [c], "that which obscures the rays of the sun," is, apart from its grammatical incorrectness, much the same argument as if we were to say that Northern meant, that which "narrows, contracts, hems in," or "is fast bound."

Equally capricious and arbitrary is the coining of a new Hebrew word to substitute for the word *tsephoni;* as one [d], first reading it *tsipponi*, supposes it to mean *captain*, or *main army*, because in Arabic or Aramaic, *tsaphpha* means, "set things in a row," "set an army in array," of which root there is no trace in Hebrew. Stranger yet is it to identify the well-known Hebrew word *Tsaphon* with the Greek *τύφων*, and *tsephoni* with *τυφωνικός*; and because Typhon was, in Egyptian mythology, a principle of evil, to infer that *tsephoni*

[r] in Joel ii. 20. [s] Beauplan, Ib. i. 599.
[t] Burckhardt, Notes, ii. 89, 90.
[u] Sur les Maures, iii. 495. [v] xvi. 4. 12. Kr.
[w] Sparrmann, p. 366. [x] Adansson, Voyage, p. 88.
[y] Hist. Nat. xi. 35. Liv. xlii. 10.
[z] Asso y del Rio, von der Heuschrecken, ed. Tychsen.

[a] Nat. Hist. of Algiers and Tunis. Travels, pp. 256, 8. [b] צפון.

[c] Justi, Maurer, adopted by Gesenius sub. v. Maurer, in his commentary of 1838, suggested two yet more improbable etymologies.

[d] Ewald. "Van Cölln and Meier would also alter the text." Hengst.

meant a *destroyer*[e]. Another[f], who would give to *tsephoni* the meaning of "Barbarian," admits in fact the prophetic character of the title; since the Jews had as yet, in the time of Joel, no external foe on their North border; no one, except Israel, as yet invaded them from the North. Not until the Assyrian swept over them, was *the Northern* any special enemy of Judah. Until the time of Ahaz, Syria was the enemy, not of Judah, but of Israel.

This varied straining to get rid of the plain meaning of the word *the Northern*, illustrates the more the importance of the term as one of the keys of the prophecy.

One and the same wind could not drive the same body of locusts, to perish in three different, and two of them opposite, directions. Yet it is clear that the Prophet speaks of them as one and the same. The locusts are spoken of as one great army, (as God had before called them[g],) with front and rear. The resource has been to say that the van and rear were two different bodies of locusts, destroyed at different times, or to say that it is only Hebrew parallelism. In Hebrew parallelism, each portion of the verse adds something to the other. It does not unite things incompatible. Nor is it here the question of two but of three directions, whither this enemy was to be swept away and perish.

But Joel speaks of them first as one whole. *I will drive him into a land barren and desolate*, the wastes South of Judah, and then of the front and rear, as driven into the two seas, which bound Judah on the East and West. The two Hebrew words, *panaiv vesopho*[h], *his front and his rear*, can no more mean two bodies, having no relation to one another and to the whole, than our English words could, when used of an army.

II. Equally unsuccessful are the attempts to get rid of the proofs, that the invader here described is a moral agent. In regard to the words assigned as the ground of his destruction, *for he hath magnified to do*, 1) it has been denied, contrary to the Hebrew idiom and the context, that they do relate to moral agency, whereas, in regard to creatures, the idiom is used of nothing else, nor in any other sense could this be the ground why God destroyed them. Yet, that this their pride was the cause of their destruction, is marked by the word *for*. 2 (Strange to say) one has been found who thought that the Prophet spoke of the locusts as moral agents. 3) Others have applied the words to God, again contrary to the context. For God speaks in this same verse of Himself in the first person, of the enemy whom He sentences to destruction, in the third. "And *I* will remove far off from you the Northern army, and *I* will drive *him* into a land barren and desolate, *his* face towards the Eastern sea, and *his* rear towards the Western sea, and *his* stink shall come up, and *his* ill savor shall come up, because *he* hath magnified to do." Joel does not use rapid transitions. And rapid transitions, when used, are never without meaning. A sacred writer who has been speaking of God, does often, in holy fervor, turn suddenly to address God; or, having upbraided a sinful people, he turns away from them, and speaks, not *to* them any more but *of* them. But it is unexampled in Holy Scripture, that in words in the mouth of God, God should speak of Himself first in the first person, then in the third.

III. Instead of "*that the heathen should rule over them*," they render, "*That the heathen should* jest at *them*," But besides this place, the phrase occurs fifty times in the Hebrew Bible, and in every case means indisputably "rule over[i]." It is plainly contrary to all rules of language, to take an idiom in the fifty-first case, in a sense wholly different from that which it has in the other fifty. The noun also signifying "proverb," is derived from a root entirely distinct from the verb to *rule*; the verb which Ezekiel perhaps formed (as verbs are formed in Hebrew) from the noun, is never used except in connection, direct or implied, with that noun[k]. The idiom "became a proverb," "make a proverb of," is always expressed, not by the verb, but by the noun with some other verb, as "became, give, set, place[l]." It is even said[m], *I will make him desolate to a proverb*, or *shall take up a parable against him*[n], but in no one of these idioms is the verb used.

IV. The word "jealousy" is used twenty times in the Old Testament, of that attribute in God, whereby He does not endure the love of His creatures to be transferred from Him, or divided with Him. Besides this place, it is used by the Prophets fifteen times, of God's love for His people, as shewn against the Heathen who oppressed them. In all the thirty-five cases it is used of an attribute of Almighty God toward His rational creatures. And it is a violation of the uniform usage of Holy Scripture in a matter which relates to the attributes of Almighty

[e] Hitzig on Joel ii. 20.

[f] Umbreit on Joel, Ib.

[g] ii. 11. [h] פניו וספו. [i] משל ב׳.

[k] The phrase is משל משל in 6 of the places in Ezekiel. In the 7th, Ezek. xvi. 44, a proverb is spoken of. It is used by no other of the sacred writers. In this sense it corresponds with the Arab. *mathala*, Syr. *methal*. Mashal, *rule*, occurs in Phœnician only, and, (as Ges. pointed out) in the Greek βασιλεύς.

[l] היה Deut. xxviii. 37. 1 Kgs. ix. 7. Ps. lxix. 12. נתן 2 Chr. vii. 20. Jer. xxiv. 9. הצין Job xvii. 6. שים Ps. xliv. 15.

[m] השמתי Ezek. xiv. 8, combining the two, "I will make him a desolation and a proverb."

[n] ישא משל Mich. ii. 4. Hab. ii. 6.

God and His relation to the creatures which He has made, to extend it to His irrational creation. It is to force on Holy Scripture an unauthorized statement as to Almighty God.

Of these hints that the prophecy extends beyond any mere locusts, five are given in the space of four verses at the close of that part of the prophecy, and seem to be condensed there, as a key to the whole. Joel began his prophecy by a sort of sacred enigma or proverb, which waited its explanation. At the close of the description of God's judgments on His people, which he so opened, he concentrates traits which should indicate its fullest meaning. He does not exclude suffering by locusts, fire, drought, famine, or any other of God's natural visitations. But he indicates that the scourge, which he was chiefly foretelling, was man. Three of these hints combine to shew that Joel was speaking of Heathen scourges of God's people and Church. The mention *of the Northern* fixes the prophecy to enemies, of whom Joel had no human knowledge, but by whom Judah was carried away captive, and who themselves were soon afterward destroyed, while Judah was restored. Not until after Joel and all his generation were fallen asleep, did a king of Assyria come up against Israel, nor was the North a quarter whence men would then apprehend danger. Pul came up against Menahem, king of Israel, at the close of the reign of Uzziah. The reign of Jotham was victorious. Not until invited by his son Ahaz, did Tiglath-pileser meddle with the affairs of Judah. In yet another reign, that of Hezekiah, was the first invasion of Judah. Sennacherib, first the scourge of God, in his second invasion blasphemed God, and his army perished in one night, smitten by the Angel of God.

It seems then probable, that what Joel describes was presented to him in the form of a vision, the title which he gives to his prophecy. There, as far as we can imagine what was exhibited by God to His prophets, he saw before him the land wasted and desolate; pastures and trees burned up by fire; the channels of the rivers dried up, the barns broken down as useless, and withal, the locusts, such as he describes them in the second chapter, advancing, overspreading the land, desolating all as they advanced, marching in the wonderful order in which the locust presses on, indomitable, unbroken, unhindered; assaulting the city Jerusalem, mounting the walls, possessing themselves of it, entering its houses, as victorious. But withal he knew, by that same inspiration which spread this scene before his eyes, that not mere locusts were intended, and was inspired to intermingle in his description expressions which forewarned his people of invaders yet more formidable.

It may be added, that S. John, in the Revelation, not only uses the symbol of locusts as a type of enemies of God's Church and people, whether actual persecutors or spiritual foes or both, but, in three successive verses of his description, he takes from Joel three traits of the picture. *The shapes of the locusts were like unto horses prepared unto battle; their teeth were as the teeth of lions; the sound of their wings was as the sound of chariots of many horses running to battle* [o]. It seems probable, that as S. John takes up anew the prophecies of the Old Testament, and embodies in his prophecy their language, pointing on to a fulfillment of it in the Christian Church, he does, by adopting the symbol of the locusts, in part in Joel's own words, express that he himself understood the Prophet to speak of enemies, beyond the mere irrational scourge.

The chief characteristic of the Prophet's style is perhaps its simple vividness. Every thing is set before our eyes, as though we ourselves saw it. This is alike the character of the description of the desolation in the first chapter; the advance of the locusts in the second; or that more awful gathering in the valley of Jehoshaphat, described in the third. The Prophet adds detail to detail; each, clear, brief, distinct, a picture in itself, yet adding to the effect of the whole. We can, without an effort, bring the whole of each picture before our eyes. Sometimes he uses the very briefest form of words, two words, in his own language, sufficing for each feature in his picture. One verse consists almost of five such pairs of words [p]. Then, again, the discourse flows on in a soft and gentle cadence, like one of those longer sweeps of an Æolian harp. This blending of energy and softness is perhaps one secret, why the diction also of this Prophet has been at all times so winning and so touching. Deep and full, he pours out the tide of his words, with an unbroken smoothness, carries all along with him, yea, like those rivers of the new world, bears back the bitter, restless billows which oppose him, a pure strong stream amid the endless heavings and tossings of the world.

Poetic as Joel's language is, he does not much use distinct imagery. For his whole picture is one image. They are God's chastenings through inanimate nature, picturing the worse chastenings through man. So much had he, probably, in prophetic vision, the symbol spread before his eyes, that he likens it in one place to that which it represents, the men of war of the invading army. But

[o] Rev ix. 7–9. Joel ii. 4. i. 6. ii. 5.

[p] i. 10. In one of them *For*, is added. Other pairs of words in Hebrew occur i. 11, 12, 14, 17. ii. 9, 15, 16.

this too adds to the formidableness of the picture.

Full of sorrow himself, he summons all with him to repentance, priests and people, old and young, bride and bridegroom. Yet his very call, *let the bridegroom go forth out of his chamber, and the bride out of her closet*, shews how tenderly he felt for those, whom he called from the solaces of mutual affection to fasting and weeping and girding with sackcloth. Yet more tender is the summons to all Israel [q], *Lament like a virgin girded with sackcloth for the husband of her youth.* The tenderness of his soul is evinced by his lingering over the desolation which he foresees. It is like one, counting over, one by one, the losses he endures in the privations of others. Nature to him "seemed to mourn;" he had a feeling of sympathy with the brute cattle which in his ears mourn so grievously; and, if none else would mourn for their own sins, he himself would mourn to Him Who is full of compassion and mercy. He announces to the poor cattle the removal of the woe, *Fear not, fear ye not* [r]. Few passages in Scripture itself are more touching, than when, having represented God as marshalling His creatures for the destruction of His people, and just ready to give the word, having expressed the great terribleness of the Day of the Lord, and asked *who can abide it?* he suddenly turns, *And now too* [s], and calls to repentance.

Amid a wonderful beauty of language, he employs words not found elsewhere in Holy Scripture. In one verse, he has three such words [t]. The degree to which the prophecies of Joel reappear in the later prophets has been exaggerated. The subjects of the prophecy recur; not, for the most part, the form in which they were delivered. The subjects could not but recur. For the truths, when once revealed, became a part of the hopes and fears of the Jewish Church; and the Prophets, as preachers and teachers of their people, could not but repeat them. But it was no mere repetition. Even those truths which, in one of their bearings, or, again, in outline were fully declared, admitted of subordinate enlargement, or of the revelation of other accessory truths, which filled up or determined or limited that first outline. And as far as anything was added or determined by any later prophet, such additions constituted a fresh revelation by him. It is so in the case of the wonderful image, in which, taking occasion of the fact of nature, that there was a fountain under the temple [u], which carried off the blood of the sacrifices, and, carrying it off, was intermingled with that blood, the image of the All-atoning Blood, Joel speaks of *a fountain* flowing forth *from the House of the Lord and watering the valley of Shittim*, whither by nature its waters could not flow. He first describes the holiness to be bestowed upon Mount Zion; then, how from the Temple, the centre of worship and of revelation, the place of the shadow of the Atonement, the stream should gush forth, which, pouring on beyond the bounds of the land of Judah, should carry fertility to a barren and thirsty land. (For in such lands the shittah grows.) To this picture Zechariah [v] adds the permanence of the life-giving stream and its perennial flow, *in summer and in winter shall it be.* Ezekiel, in his full and wonderful expansion of the image [w], adds the ideas of the gradual increase of those waters of life, their exceeding depth, the healing of all which could be healed, the abiding desolation where those waters did not reach; and trees, as in the garden of Eden, yielding food and health. He in a manner anticipates our Lord's prophecy, *ye shall be fishers of men.* S. John takes up the image [x], yet as an emblem of such fullness of bliss and glory, that, amid some things, which can scarcely be understood except of this life, it seems rather to belong to life eternal.

Indeed, as to the great imagery of Joel, it is much more adopted and enforced in the New Testament than in the Old. The image of the locust is taken up in the Revelation; that of the "pouring out of the Spirit" (for this too is an image, how largely God would bestow Himself in the times of the Gospel) is adopted in the Old Testament by Ezekiel [y], yet as to the Jews only; in the New by St. Peter and St. Paul [z]. Of those condensed images, under which Joel speaks of the wickedness of the whole earth ripened for destruction, the harvest and the wine-treading, that of the harvest is employed by Jeremiah [a] as to Babylon, that of the wine-press is enlarged by Isaiah [b]. The harvest is so employed by our Lord [c] as to explain the imagery of Joel; and in that great embodiment of Old Testament prophecy, the Revelation [d], St. John expands the image of the wine-press in the same largeness of meaning as it is used by Joel.

The largeness of all these declarations remains peculiar to Joel. To this unknown Prophet, whom in his writings we cannot but love, but of whose history, condition, rank, parentage, birth-place, nothing is known, nothing beyond his name, save the name of an unknown father, of whom moreover God has allowed nothing to remain save these few chapters,—to him God reserved the prerogative, first to declare the out-pouring

[q] i. 8. [r] ii. 21, 22. [s] ii. 12.
[t] i. 16. [u] See on iii. 18.
[v] xiv. 8. [w] xlvii. 1–12.
[x] Rev. xxii. 1–5. [y] xxxix. 29.
[z] "On the Gentiles also is *poured out* (ἐκκέχυται) the gift of the Holy Ghost," Acts x. 45; "the love of God is poured out (ἐκκέχυται) in our hearts by the Holy Ghost Who hath been given to us," Rom. v. 5.
[a] li. 33. [b] lxiii. 1–6.
[c] S. Matt. xiii. 39. [d] xiv. 18–20.

of the Holy Ghost upon all flesh, the perpetual abiding of the Church, the final struggle of good and evil, the last rebellion against God, and the Day of Judgment. *The Day of the Lord, the great and terrible day,* the belief in which now forms part of the faith of all Jews and Christians, was a title first revealed to this unknown Prophet.

The primæval prophecy on Adam's expulsion from Paradise, had been renewed to Abraham, Jacob, Moses, David, Solomon. In Abraham's seed were all nations of the earth to be blessed[e]; the obedience[f] of the nations was to be rendered to Shiloh the Peacemaker[g]; the nations were to rejoice with the people of God[h]; God's anointed king was from Mount Zion to have the heathen for his inheritance[i]; David's Son and David's Lord was to be a king and priest forever after the order of Melchizedek[k]; the peoples were to be willing in the Day of His power. All nations were to serve him[l]. This had been prophesied before. It was part of the body of belief in the time of Joel. But to Joel it was first foreshewn that the Gentiles too should be filled with the Spirit of God. To him was first declared that great paradox, or mystery, of faith, which, after his time, prophet after prophet insisted upon, that while deliverance should be in Mount Zion, while sons and daughters, young and old, should prophesy in Zion, and the stream of God's grace should issue to the barren world from the Temple of the Lord, those in her who should be delivered should be a remnant only[m].

[e] Gen. xxii. 18.
[f] Such must be the meaning of יקהה in the other place in which it occurs, Prov. xxx. 17, as it is of the corresponding Arabic root. Onkelos so understood it.

Marvelous faith, alike in those who uttered it and those who received it; marvelous, disinterested faith! The true worship of God was, by the revolt of the ten tribes, limited to the two tribes, the territory of the largest of which was but some 50 miles long, and not 30 miles broad; Benjamin added but 12 miles to the length of the whole. It was but 12 miles from Jerusalem on its Southern Border to Bethel on its Northern. They had made no impression beyond their own boundaries. Edom, their "brother", was their bitterest enemy, wise in the wisdom of the world[n], but worshiping false gods[o]. Nay they themselves still borrowed the idolatries of their neighbors[p]. Beset as Judah was by constant wars without, deserted by Israel, the immediate band of worshipers of the one God within its narrow borders thinned by those who fell away from Him, Joel foretold, not as uncertainly, not as anticipation, or hope, or longing, but absolutely and distinctly, that God would *pour out* His *Spirit upon all flesh;* and that the healing stream should issue forth from Jerusalem. Eight centuries rolled on, and it was not accomplished. *He* died, of Whom it was said, *we trusted that it had been He Who should have redeemed Israel*[q]; and it was fulfilled. Had it failed, justly would the Hebrew Prophets have been called fanatics. The words were too distinct to be explained away. It could not fail; for God had said it.

[g] Gen. xlix. 10.
[h] Deut. xxxii. 43.
[i] Ps. ii.
[k] Ps. cx.
[l] Ps. lxxii. 11.
[m] ii. 32.
[n] Obad. 8. Jer. xlix. 7.
[o] Chr. xxv. 14, 20.
[p] Ib.
[q] S. Luke xxiv. 21.

JOEL.

Before CHRIST cir. 800.

CHAPTER I.

1 *Joel, declaring sundry judgments of God, exhorteth to observe them,* 8 *and to mourn.* 14 *He prescribeth a fast for complaint.*

THE word of the LORD
that came to Joel the
son of Pethuel.
2 Hear this, ye old men,
and give ear, all ye inhabitants of the land. [a] Hath
this been in your days, or
even in the days of your
fathers?
3 [b] Tell ye your children
of it, and *let* your children
tell their children, and
their children another generation.
4 [c] † That which the
palmerworm hath left hath

Before CHRIST cir. 800.

[a] ch. 2, 2.

[b] Ps. 78. 4.

[c] Deut. 28. 38. ch. 2. 25.

† Heb. *The residue of the palmerworm.*

CHAP. I. Ver. I. *The word of the Lord that came to Joel.* Joel, like Hosea, mentions the name of his father only, and then is silent about his extraction, his tribe, his family. He leaves even the time when he lived, to be guessed at. He would be known only, as the instrument of God. *The word of the Lord came to* him [1], and he willed simply to be the voice which uttered it. He was "content to live under the eyes of God, and, as to men, to be known only in what concerned their salvation." But *this* he declares absolutely, that the Word of God came to him; in order that we may give faith to his prophecy, being well assured that what he predicted, would come to pass. So the Saviour Himself says, "*My words shall not pass away* [2]. For truth admits of nothing false, and what God saith, will certainly be. For *He confirmeth the word of His servant, and performeth the counsel of His messengers* [3]. The Prophet claimeth belief then, as speaking not out of his own heart, but out of the mouth of the Lord speaking in the Spirit." *Joel* signifies, *The Lord is God.* It owns that God Who had revealed Himself, is alone the God. The Prophet's name itself, embodied the truth, which, after the miraculous answer to Elijah's prayer, all the people confessed, *The Lord He is the God, The Lord He is the God. Pethuel* signifies, "persuaded of God." The addition of his father's name distinguished the Prophet from others of that name, as the son of Samuel, of king Uzziah, and others.

2. *Hear this, ye old men.* By reason of their age they had known and heard much; they had heard from their fathers, and their father's fathers, much which they had not known themselves. Among the people of the East, memories of past times were handed down from generation to generation, for periods, which to us would seem incredible. Israel was commanded, so to transmit the vivid memories of the miracles of God. The Prophet appeals *to the old men, to hear,* and, (lest, anything should seem to have escaped them) to the whole people of the land, to give their whole attention to *this* thing, which he was about to tell them, and then, reviewing all the evils which each had ever heard to have been inflicted by God upon their forefathers, to say whether *this* thing had happened in their days or in the days of their fathers.

3. *Tell ye your children of it.* In the order of God's goodness, generation was to declare to generation the wonders of His love. [4] *He established a testimony in Jacob, and appointed a law in Israel, which He commanded our fathers that they should make them known to their children, that the generation to come might know them, the children which should be born, who should arise and declare them to their children that they might—not forget the works of God.* This tradition of thankful memories God, as the Psalmist says, enforced in the law [5]; *Take heed to thyself, lest thou forget the things which thine eyes have seen, but teach them thy sons and thy sons' sons.* This was the end of the memorial acts of the ritual, that their sons might inquire the meaning of them, the fathers tell them God's wonders [6]. Now contrariwise, they are, generation to generation, to tell *concerning it,* this message of unheard-of woe and judgment. The memory of God's deeds of love should have stirred them to gratitude; now He transmits to them memories of woe, that they might entreat God against them, and break off the sins which entail them.

4. *That which the palmerworm hath left, hath the locust eaten.* The creatures here spoken of are different kinds of locusts, so named from their number or voracity. We, who are free from this scourge of God, know them only by the generic name of locusts. But the law mentions several sorts of locusts, each

[1] See on Hos. i. 1.
xliv. 26.
[2] S. Matt. xxiv. 35
[4] Ps. lxxviii. 5–7.
[5] Deut. iv. 9. add vi. 6, 7. xi. 19.
[6] Ib. vi. 20–24.

Before CHRIST cir. 800.

the locust eaten; and that which the locust hath left hath the cankerworm eaten; and that which the cankerworm hath left hath the caterpillar eaten.

after its kind, which might be eaten[1]. In fact, above eighty different kinds of locusts have been observed[2], some of which are twice as large as that which is the ordinary scourge of God[3]. Slight as they are in themselves, they are mighty in God's Hand; beautiful and gorgeous as they are, floating in the sun's rays[4], they are a scourge, including other plagues, famine, and often, pestilence.

Of the four kinds, here named by the Prophet, that rendered *locust* is so called from its multitude, (whence Jeremiah says[5], *they are more numerous than the locust;*) and is, probably, the creature which desolates whole regions of Asia and Africa. The rest are named from their voracity, the "gnawer," "licker," "consumer," but they are, beyond doubt, distinct kinds of that destroyer. And this is the characteristic of the Prophet's threatening, that he foretells a succession of destroyers, each more fatal than the preceding; and that, not according to the order of nature. For in all the observations which have been made of the locusts, even when successive flights have desolated the same land, they have always been successive clouds of the same creature.

Over and above the fact, then, that locusts are a heavy chastisement from God, these words of Joel form a sort of sacred proverb. They are the epitome of his whole prophecy. It is *this* which he had called the old men to hear, and to say whether they had known anything like *this*; that scourge came after scourge, judgment after judgment, until man yielded or perished. The visitation of locusts was one of the punishments threatened in the law, *Thou shall carry much seed out into the field, and shalt gather but little in; for the locust shall consume it*[6]. It was one of God's ordinary punishments for sin, in that country, like famine, or pestilence, or blight, or mildew, or murrain, or (in this) potato disease. Solomon, accordingly, at the dedication of the Temple mentions the locust among the other plagues, which he then solemnly entreated God to remove, when individuals or the whole people should spread forth their hands in penitence towards that house[7]. But the characteristic of *this* prophecy is the successiveness of the judgments, each in itself, desolating, and the later following quick upon the earlier, and completing their destructiveness. The judgments of God are linked together by an invisible chain, each drawing on the other; yet, at each link of the lengthening chain, allowing space and time for repentance to break it through. So in the plagues of Egypt, God, *executing His judgments upon them by little and little, gave them time for repentance*[8]; yet, when Pharaoh hardened his heart, each followed on the other, until he perished in the Red Sea. In like way God said[9], *him that escapeth the sword of Hazael shall Jehu slay; and him that escapeth from the sword of Jehu* shall *Elisha slay*. So, in the Revelation, the *trumpets* are sounded[10], and *the vials of the wrath of God* are *poured out upon the earth*, one after the other[11]. Actual locusts were very likely one of the scourges intended by the Prophet. They certainly were not the whole; but pictured others fiercer, more desolating, more overwhelming. The proverbial dress gained and fixed men's attention on the truth, which, if it had been presented to the people nakedly, they might have turned from. Yet as, in God's wisdom, what is said generally, is often fulfilled specially, so here there were four great invaders which in succession wasted Judah; the Assyrian, Chaldæan, Macedonian and Roman.

Morally, also, four chief passions desolate successively the human heart. "[12] For what is designated by the *palmerworm*, which creeps with all its body on the ground, except it be lust, which so pollutes the heart which it possesses, that it cannot rise up to the love of heavenly purity? What is expressed by the *locust*, which flies by leaps, except vain glory which exalts itself with empty presumptions? What is typified by the *cankerworm*, almost the whole of whose body is gathered into its belly, except gluttony in eating? What but anger is indicated by mildew, which burns as

[1] Lev. xi. 22. ארבה [the ordinary name] חרגל "hopper," סלעם "devourer," (these two occur in that place of Lev. only) and חגב so called, it is thought, from veiling the sun in its flight.
[2] Dict. de l' Hist. Natur. v. Criquet.
[3] "The Gryllus Tartaricus is almost twice as large as the ordinary locust" [gryllus gregarius.] Clarke, Travels, i. 437. Beauplan speaks of those which, for several years, he observed in the Ukraine, as being "as thick as a man's finger and twice as long." Churchill, i. 600.
[4] "The gryllus Migratorius has red legs, and its inferior wings have a lively red color, which gives a bright fiery appearance to the animals when fluttering in the sun's rays." Clarke, i. 438. Schlatter has much the same description, Bruchstucke aus einigen Reisen nach dem sudlichen Russland, A. D. 1820–28. p. 326. in Ersch, Encycl. v. Heuschreckenzüge, p. 315. Those mentioned by Fr. Alvarez as the great scourge of Æthiopia were different. They had yellow under-wings, which also reflected the sun's rays, c. 32.
[5] xlvi. 23. רבו כארבה. See Jud. vi. 5. vii. 12. Ps. cv. 34. Nah. iii. 15. It is a proverb in Arabic also.
[6] Deut. xxviii. 38.
[7] 1 Kings viii. 37, 8.
[8] Wisd. xii. 10.
[9] 1 Kings xix. 17.
[10] Rev. viii. ix. xi. 15.
[11] Ib. xvi.
[12] S. Greg. Mor. xxxiii. 65. p. 614. Oxf. Tr.

Before CHRIST cir. 800.

5 Awake, ye drunkards, and weep; and howl, all ye drinkers of wine, because of the new wine; [d] for it is cut off from your mouth.

[d] Is. 32. 10.

6 For [e] a nation is come up upon my land, strong, and without number, [f] whose teeth *are* the teeth of a lion, and he hath the cheek teeth of a great lion.

[e] So Prov. 30. 25, 26, 27. ch. 2. 2. 11, 25.
[f] Rev. 9. 8.

it touches? What *the palmerworm* then *hath left the locust hath eaten*, because, when the sin of lust has retired from the mind, vain glory often succeeds. For since it is not now subdued by the love of the flesh, it boasts of itself, as if it were holy through its chastity. And *that which the locust hath left, the cankerworm hath eaten*, because when vain glory, which came, as it were, from holiness, is resisted, either the appetite, or some ambitious desires are indulged in too immoderately. For the mind which knows not God, is led the more fiercely to any object of ambition, in proportion as it is not restrained by any love of human praise. *That which the cankerworm hath left*, the mildew consumes, because when the gluttony of the belly is restrained by abstinence, the impatience of anger holds fiercer sway, which, like mildew, eats up the harvest by burning it, because the flame of impatience withers the fruit of virtue. When then some vices succeed to others, one plague devours the field of the mind, while another leaves it."

5. *Awake, ye drunkards, and weep.* All sin stupefies the sinner. All intoxicate the mind, bribe and pervert the judgment, dull the conscience, blind the soul and make it insensible to its own ills. All the passions, anger, vain glory, ambition, avarice and the rest are a spiritual drunkenness, inebriating the soul, as strong drink doth the body. "[1] They are called drunkards, who, confused with the love of this world, feel not the ills which they suffer. What then is meant by, *Awake, ye drunkards and weep*, but, 'shake off the sleep of your insensibility, and oppose by watchful lamentations the many plagues of sins, which succeed one to the other in the devastation of your hearts?'" God arouse those who will be aroused, by withdrawing from them the pleasures wherein they offended Him. Awake, the Prophet cries, from the sottish slumber of your drunkenness; awake to weep and howl, at least when your feverish enjoyments are dashed from your lips. Weeping for things temporal may awaken to the fear of losing things eternal.

6. *For a nation is come up upon my land.* He calls this scourge of God *a nation*, giving them the title most used in Holy Scripture, of heathen nations. The like term, *people, folk*, is used of the *ants* and the *conies*[2], for the wisdom with which God teaches them to act. Here it is used, in order to include at once, the irrational invader, guided by a Reason above its own, and the heathen conqueror. This enemy, he says, is *come up* (for the land as being God's land, was exalted in dignity, above other lands,) *upon My land*, i. e. *the Lord's land*[3], hitherto owned and protected as God's land, *a land which*, Moses said to them[4], *the Lord thy God careth for; the eyes of the Lord thy God are always upon it, from the beginning of the year even unto the end of the year.* Now it was to be bared of God's protection, and to be trampled upon by a heathen foe.

Strong and without number. The figure is still from the locust, whose numbers are wholly countless by man. Travellers sometimes use likenesses to express their number, as clouds darkening the sun[5] or discharging flakes of snow[6]; some grave writers give it up, as hopeless. "[7] Their multitude is incredible, whereby they cover the earth and fill the air; they take away the brightness of the sun. I say again, the thing is incredible to one who has not seen them." "It would not be a thing to be believed, if one had not seen it." "On another day, it was beyond belief: they occupied a space of eight leagues [about 24 English miles]. I do not mention the multitude of those without wings, because it is incredible." "[8] When we were in the Seignory of Abrigima, in a place called Aquate, there came such a multitude of locusts, as cannot be said. They began to arrive one day about terce [nine] and till night they cease not to arrive; and when they arrived, they bestowed themselves. On the next day at the hour of prime they began to depart, and at midday there was not one, and there remained not a leaf on the trees. At this instant others began to come, and stayed like the others to the next day at the same hour; and these left not a stick with its bark, nor a green herb, and thus did they five days one after another; and the people said that they were the sons, who went to seek their fathers, and they took the road towards the others which had no wings.

[1] S. Greg. Mor. xxxiii. 66.
[2] Prov. xxx. 25, 6.
[3] Hos. ix. 3.
[4] Deut. xi. 12.
[5] See on ii. 10.
[6] Clarke's Travels, l. c. p. 437. Beauplan, Ukraine, in Churchill, i. 599. Lichtenstein, c. 46.
[7] Fr. Alvarez do Preste Joan, das Indias, c. 32.
[8] Ib. c. 33.

Before CHRIST cir. 800.

7 He hath [g] laid my vine waste, and † barked my fig tree: he hath made it clean bare, and cast *it* away; the branches thereof are made white.

[g] Is. 5. 6.
† Heb. laid *my fig tree for a barking.*

Before CHRIST cir. 800.

After they were gone, we knew the breadth which they had occupied, and saw the destruction which they had made, it exceeded three leagues [nine miles] wherein there remained no bark on the trees." Another writes of South Africa[1]; "Of the innumerable multitudes of the incomplete insect or larva of the locusts, which at this time infested this part of Africa, no adequate idea could be conceived without having witnessed them. For the space of ten miles on each side of the Sea-Cow river, and eighty or ninety miles in length, an area of 16, or 1800 square miles, the whole surface might literally be said to be covered with them. The water of the river was scarcely visible on account of the dead carcasses which floated on the surface, drowned in the attempt to come at the weeds which grew in it." "[2] The present year is the third of their continuance, and their increase has far exceeded that of a geometrical progression whose whole ratio is a million." A writer of reputation says of a "column of locusts" in India; "[3] It extended, we were informed, 500 miles, and so compact was it when on the wing, that, like an eclipse, it completely hid the sun; so that no shadow was cast by any object, and some lofty tombs, not more than 200 yards distant, were rendered quite invisible." In one single neighborhood, even in Germany, it was once calculated that near 17,000,000 of their eggs were collected and destroyed [4]. Even Volney writes of those in Syria[5], "the quantity of these insects is a thing incredible to any one who has not seen it himself; the ground is covered with them for several leagues." "The steppes," says Clarke[6], an incredulous traveler, "were entirely covered by their bodies, and their numbers falling resembled flakes of snow, carried obliquely by the wind, and spreading thick mists over the sun. Myriads fell over the carriage, the horses, the drivers. The Tartars told us, that persons had been suffocated by a fall of locusts on the *steppes*. It was now the season, they added, in which they began to diminish." "[7] It was incredible, that their breadth was eight leagues."

Strong. The locust is remarkable for its long flights. "Its strength of limbs is amazing; when pressed down by the hand on the table, it has almost power to move the fingers[8]".

Whose teeth are *the teeth of a lion.* The teeth of the locust are said to be "harder than stone." "[9] They appear to be created for a scourge; since to strength incredible for so small a creature, they add saw-like teeth admirably calculated to *eat up all the herbs in the land.*" Some near the Senegal, are described as "[10] quite brown, of the thickness and length of a finger, and armed with two jaws, toothed like a saw, and very powerful." The Prophet ascribes to them the sharp or prominent eye-teeth of the lion and lioness, combining strength with number. The ideal of this scourge of God is completed by blending numbers, in which creatures so small only could exist together, with the strength of the fiercest. "[11] Weak and short-lived is man, yet when God is angered against a sinful people, what mighty power does He allow to man against it!" "And what more cruel than those who endeavor to slay souls, turning them from the Infinite and Eternal Good, and so dragging them to the everlasting torments of Hell?"

7. *He hath laid my vine waste, and barked my fig tree.* This describes an extremity of desolation. The locusts at first attack all

[1] Barrow, S. Africa, p. 257. [2] Ib. 258.
[3] Major Moor in Kirby on Entomology, Letter vi.
[4] 16,690,905. They were collected near Droschen. Half a peck was found to contain 39,272. Ersch, Heuschreckenzüge, p. 314. Beauplan says (Ib.) "wheresoever they come, in less than 2 hours they crop all they can, which causes great scarcity of provisions; and if the locusts remain there in Autumn when they die, after laying at least 300 eggs apiece, which hatch next spring, if it be dry, then the country is 300 times worse pestered."
[5] Voyage en Syrie, i. 277.
[6] Travels, c. 18. i. 437. "At Vienna they were half an hour's journey in breadth, but, after 3 hours, though they seemed to fly fast, one could not yet see the end of the column." Philosophical Transactions, T. 46. p. 36. "In Cyprus, in going in a chaise 4 or 5 miles, the locusts lay swarming above a foot deep in several parts of the high road, and thousands were destroyed by the wheels of the carriage driving over them." Russell, Nat. Hist. of Aleppo, ii. 229. "I have seen them at night when they sit to rest them, that the roads were 4 inches thick of them one upon another, so that the horses would not trample over them, but as they were put on with much lashing—the wheels of our carts and the feet of our horses bruising those creatures, there came from them such a stink, as not only offended the nose but the brain." Beauplan, 599, 600. "This place stands on a high hill, whence large tracts and many places could be seen all yellow with locusts." Fr. Alvarez, c. 32. "The face of the country is covered with them for many miles." Forbes, ii. 273. "In Senegal, they come almost every three years, and when they have covered the ground, they gnaw almost every thing, and are in such numbers as to shadow the heaven for xii. [Italian] miles. If they came every year, all would be consumed and desert. I have seen them sometimes fly in a troop over the sea; their number was almost infinite." Aluise da cà da Mosto, Navig. c. 13. "The locusts cover the ground, so that it can scarcely be seen." Le Bruyn, Lev. 252.
[7] Alvarez, c. 32. [8] Clarke, i. 438.
[9] Morier, 2d. Journey, p. 99.
[10] Adansson, Voyage au Sénégal, p. 88. [11] Rup.

which is green and succulent; when this has been consumed, then they attack the bark of trees. "[1] When they have devoured all other vegetables, they attack the trees, consuming first the leaves, then the bark." "[2] A day or two after one of these bodies were in motion, others were already hatched to glean after them, gnawing off the young branches and the very bark of such trees as had escaped before with the loss only of their fruit and foliage." "[3] They carried desolation wherever they passed. After having consumed herbage, fruit, leaves of trees, they attacked even their young shoots and their bark. Even the reeds, wherewith the huts were thatched, though quite dry, were not spared." "[4] Every thing in the country was devoured; the bark of figs, pomegranates, and oranges, bitter hard and corrosive, escaped not their voracity." The effects of this wasting last on for many years [5].

He hath made it clean bare. "[6] It is sufficient, if these terrible columns stop half an hour on a spot, for everything growing on it, vines, olive trees, and corn, to be entirely destroyed. After they have passed, nothing remains but the large branches, and the roots which, being under ground, have escaped their voracity." "[7] After eating up the corn, they fell upon the vines, the pulse, the willows and even the hemp, notwithstanding its great bitterness." "[8] They are particularly injurious to the palm trees; these they strip of every leaf and green particle, the trees remaining like skeletons with bare branches." "[9] The bushes were eaten quite bare, though the animals could not have been long on the spot.—They sat by hundreds on a bush gnawing the rind and the woody fibres."

The branches thereof are made white. "[10] The country did not seem to be burnt, but to be much covered with snow, through the whiteness of the trees and the dryness of the herbs. It pleased God that the fresh crops were already gathered in."

The *vine* is the well-known symbol of God's people [11]; the fig too, by reason of its sweetness, is an emblem of His Church and of each soul in her, bringing forth the fruit of grace [12]. When then God says, *he hath laid My vine waste,* He suggests to us, that He is not speaking chiefly of the visible tree, but of that which it represents. The locusts, accordingly, are not chiefly the insects, which bark the actual trees, but every enemy which wastes the heritage of God, which He calls by those names. His vineyard, the Jewish people, was outwardly and repeatedly desolated by the Chaldæans, Antiochus Epiphanes, and afterward by the Romans. The vineyard, which the Jews had, was, (as Jesus foretold,) *let out to other husbandmen* when they had killed Him; and, thenceforth, is the Christian Church, and, subordinately each soul in her. "[13] Heathen and heretical Emperors and heresiarchs wasted often the Church of Christ. Anti-Christ shall waste it. They who have wasted her are countless. For the Psalmist says, *They who hate me without a cause are more than the hairs of my head* [14]."

"[15] The nation which cometh up against the soul, are the princes of this world and of darkness and spiritual wickedness in high places, whose *teeth* are the teeth of a lion, of whom the Apostle Peter saith, *Our adversary the devil, as a roaring lion, walketh about seeking whom he may devour* [16]. If we give way to this nation, so that they should come up in us, forthwith they will make our vineyard where we were wont to make *wine to gladden the heart of man* [17], a desert, and bark or break our fig tree, that we should no more have in us those most sweet gifts of the Holy Spirit. Nor is it enough for that nation to destroy the vineyard and break the fig tree, unless it also destroy whatever there is of life in it, so that, its whole freshness being consumed, the switches remain white and dead, and that be fulfilled in us, *If they do these things in a green tree, what shall be done in the dry?* [18]" "[19] The Church, at least a part of it, is turned into a desert, deprived of spiritual goods, when the faithful are led, by consent to sin, to forsake God. *The fig tree* is *barked,* when the soul which once abounded with sweetest goods and fruits of the Holy Ghost, hath those goods lessened or cut off. Such are they who, having *begun in the Spirit* [20], are perfected by the flesh."

"[21] By spirits lying in wait, the vineyard of God is made a desert, when the soul, replenished with fruits, is wasted with longing for the praise of men. That *people barks* the *fig tree* of God, in that, carrying away the misguided soul to a thirst for applause, in proportion as it draws her on to ostentation, it strips her of the covering of humility. *Making it clean bare, it despoils it,* in that, so long as it lies hidden in its goodness, it is, as it

[1] Jackson's Travels to Morocco ap. Kirby.
[2] Shaw's Travels, p. 257. [3] Adansson, Ib.
[4] Chénier, Recherches Historiques sur les Maures, iii. 496. "They destroyed the leaves and bark of the olive." Dr. Freer, in Russell's Aleppo, p. 230.
[5] "The wine of Algiers, before the locusts in 1723 wasted the vineyards, was, in flavor not inferior to the best Hermitage. Since that time the wine has much degenerated and has not yet (1732) recovered its usual qualities." Shaw, p. 227.
[6] Constitutionnel, May, 1841, of locusts in Spain in that year. K.
[7] Phil. Trans. 1686. T. xvi. p. 148.
[8] Burckhardt, Notes, ii. 90.
[9] Lichtenstein, Trav. in S. Afr. c. 46. p. 251.
[10] Fr. Alvarez, c. 33.
[11] Ps. lxxx. 8, 14. Cant. ii. 13, 15. Hos. x. 1. Is. v. 1-7. xxvii. 2.
[12] Hos. ix. 10. S. Matt. xxi. 19. S. Luke xiii. 6, 7.
[13] Rib. [14] Ps. lxix. 4. [15] S. Jer.
[16] 1 S. Pet. v. 8. [17] Ps. civ. 15.
[18] S. Luke xxiii. 31. [19] Dion.
[20] Gal. iii. 3.
[21] S. Greg. on Job L. viii. § 82.

Before CHRIST cir. 800.

h Is. 22. 12.
i Prov. 2. 17. Jer. 3. 4.
k ver. 13. ch. 2. 14.

8 ¶ h Lament like a vir-
gin girded with sackcloth
for i the husband of her
youth.
9 k The meat offering
and the drink offering is
cut off from the house
of the LORD; the priests,
the LORD's ministers,
mourn.

Before CHRIST cir. 800.

were, clothed with a covering of its own, which protects it. But when the mind longs that which it has done should be seen by others, it is as though *the fig tree despoiled* had lost the bark that covered it. And so, as it follows, *The branches thereof are made white;* in that his works, displayed to the eyes of men, have a bright shew; a name for sanctity is gotten, when good actions are published. But as, upon the bark being removed, the branches of the fig tree wither, so observe that the deeds of the arrogant, paraded before human eyes, wither through the very act of seeking to please. Therefore the mind which is betrayed through boastfulness is rightly called a fig tree barked, in that it is at once fair to the eye, as being seen, and within a little of withering, as being bared of the covering of the bark. Within, then, must our deeds be laid up, if we look to a reward of our deeds from Him Who seeth within."

8. *Lament like a virgin.* The Prophet addresses the congregation of Israel, as one espoused to God[1]; "*Lament thou,* daughter of Zion," or the like. He bids her lament, with the bitterest of sorrows, as one who, in her virgin years, was just knit into one with the husband of her youth, and then at once was, by God's judgment, on the very day of her espousal, ere yet she ceased to be a virgin, parted by death. The mourning which God commands is not one of conventional or becoming mourning, but that of one who has put away all joy from her, and takes the rough garment of penitence, girding the haircloth upon her, enveloping and embracing, and therewith, wearing the whole frame. The haircloth was a coarse, rough, formless, garment, girt close round the waist, afflictive to the flesh, while it expressed the sorrow of the soul. God regarded as a virgin, the people which He had made holy to Himself[2]; He so regards the soul which He has regenerated and sanctified. The people, by their idolatry, lost Him Who was a Husband to them; the soul, by inordinate affections, is parted from its God. "[3]God Almighty was the Husband of the Synagogue, having espoused it to Himself in the Patriarchs and at the giving of the law. So long as she did not, through idolatry and other heavy sins, depart from God, she was a spouse in the integrity of mind, in knowledge, in love and worship of the true God." "[4]The Church is a Virgin; Christ her Husband. By prevailing sins, the order, condition, splendor, worship of the Church, are, through negligence, concupiscence, avarice, irreverence, worsened, deformed, obscured." "The soul is a virgin by its creation in nature; a virgin by privilege of grace; a virgin also by hope of glory. Inordinate desire maketh the soul a harlot; manly penitence restoreth to her chastity; wise innocence, virginity. For the soul recovereth a sort of chastity, when through thirst for righteousness, she undertakes the pain and fear of penitence; still she is not as yet raised to the eminence of innocence.—In the first state she is exposed to concupiscence; in the second, she doth works of repentance; in the third, bewailing her Husband, she is filled with the longing for righteousness; in the fourth, she is gladdened by virgin embraces and the kiss of Wisdom. For Christ is the Husband of her youth, the Betrother of her virginity. But since she parted from Him to evil concupiscence, she is monished to return to Him by sorrow and the works and garb of repentance." "[5]So should every Christian weep who has lost Baptismal grace, or has fallen back after repentance, and, deprived of the pure embrace of the Heavenly Bridegroom, *embraced* instead these earthly things which are as *dunghills*[6], *having been brought up in scarlet,* and *being in honor, had no understanding*[7]. Whence it is written[8], *let tears run down like a river day and night; give thyself no rest.* Such was he who said[9]; *rivers of waters run down mine eyes, because they keep not Thy law.*"

9. *The meat offering and the drink offering is cut off.* The meat offering and drink offering were part of every sacrifice. If the materials for these, the corn and wine, ceased, through locusts or drought or the wastings of war, the sacrifice must become mangled and imperfect. The priests were to mourn for the defects of the sacrifice; they lost also their own subsistence, since the altar was, to them, in place of all other inheritance. The meat and drink offerings were emblems of the materials of the Holy Eucharist, by which Malachi foretold that, when God had rejected the offering of the Jews, there should be a *pure offering*

[1] The Hebrew אלי is feminine. [2] Jer. ii. 2. [3] Rup. [4] Huge de S. Vict. [5] Dion. [6] Lam. iv. 5. [7] Ps. xlix. 12, 20. [8] Lam. ii. 18. [9] Ps. cxix. 136.

Before CHRIST cir. 800.

10 The field is wasted,
[l] the land mourneth; for
the corn is wasted: [m] the
new wine is ‖ dried up, the
oil languisheth.
11 [n] Be ye ashamed, O
ye husbandmen; howl, O
ye vinedressers, for the
wheat and for the barley;
because the harvest of the
field is perished.
12 [o] The vine is dried
up, and the fig tree lan-
guisheth; the pomegranate
tree, the palm tree also,
and the apple tree, *even* all

[l] Jer. 12. 11. & 14. 2.
[m] Is. 24. 7. ver. 12.
‖ Or, *ashamed.*
[n] Jer. 14. 3, 4.
[o] ver. 10.

among the heathen[1]. When then Holy Communions become rare, the meat and drink offering are literally cut off from the house of the Lord, and those who are indeed priests, the ministers of the Lord, should mourn. Joel foretells that, however love should wax cold, there should ever be such. He forsees and foretells at once, the failure, and the grief of the priests. Nor is it an idle regret which he foretells, but a mourning unto their God. "[2] Both meat offering and drink offering hath perished from the house of God, not in actual substance but as to reverence, because, amid the prevailing iniquity there is scarcely found in the Church, who should duly celebrate, or receive the Sacraments."

10. *The field is wasted, the land mourneth.* As, when God pours out His blessings of nature, all nature seems to smile and be glad, and as the Psalmist says, *to shout for joy and sing*[3], so when He withholds them, it seems to mourn, and, by its mourning, to reproach the insensibility of man. Oil is the emblem of the abundant graces and gifts of the Holy Spirit, and of the light and devotion of soul given by Him, and spiritual gladness, and overflowing, all-mantling charity.

11. *Be ye ashamed, O ye husbandmen.* The Prophet dwells on and expands the description of the troubles which he had foretold, setting before their eyes the picture of one universal desolation. For the details of sorrow most touch the heart, and he wished to move them to repentance. He pictures them to themselves; some standing aghast and ashamed of the fruitlessness of their toil, others giving way to bursts of sorrow, and all things around waste and dried. Nothing was exempt. Wheat and barley, wide-spread as they were (and the barley in those countries, "more fertile[4]" than the wheat,) perished utterly. The rich juice of the vine, the luscious sweetness of the fig the succulence of the ever-green pomegranate, the majesty of the palm tree, the fragrance of the Eastern apple, exempted them not. All, fruitbearing or barren, were dried up; for joy itself, and every source of joy was dried up from the sons of men.

All these suggest a spiritual meaning. For we know of a spiritual *harvest*, souls born to God, and a spiritual *vineyard*, the Church of God; and spiritual *husbandmen* and *vinedressers*, those whom God sends. The trees, with their various fruits were emblems of the faithful, adorned with the various gifts and graces of the Spirit. All well-nigh were dried up. Wasted without, in act and deed, the sap of the Spirit ceased within; the true laborers, those who were jealous for the vineyard of the Lord of hosts were ashamed and grieved. "[5] *Husbandmen* and *vinedressers*, are priests and preachers; *husbandmen* as instructors in morals, *vinedressers* for that joy in things eternal, which they infuse into the minds of the hearers. *Husbandmen*, as instructing the soul to deeds of righteousness; *vinedressers*, as exciting the minds of hearers to the love of wisdom. Or, *husbandmen*, in that by their doctrine they uproot earthly deeds and desires; *vinedressers*, as holding forth spiritual gifts." "The vine is the richness of divine knowledge; the fig the sweetness of contemplation and the joyousness in things eternal." The pomegranate, with its manifold grains contained under its one bark, may designate the variety and harmony of graces, disposed in their beautiful order. "The palm, rising above the world." "[6] Well is the life of the righteous likened to *a palm*, in that the palm below is rough to the touch, and in a manner enveloped in dry bark, but above it is adorned with fruit, fair even to the eye; below it is compressed by the enfoldings of its bark; above, it is spread out in amplitude of beautiful greenness. For so is the life of the elect, despised below, beauti.ul above. Down below, it is, as it were, enfolded in many barks, in that it is straitened by innumerable afflictions. But on high it is expanded into a foliage, as it were, of beautiful greenness by the amplitude of the rewarding."

Because joy is withered away. "[5] There are four sorts of joy, a joy in iniquity, a joy in vanity, a joy of charity, a joy of felicity. Of the first we read, *Who rejoice to do evil,* and *delight in the forwardness of the wicked*[7]. Of

[1] i. 11.
[2] Hugo de S. V. A. D. 1120.
[3] Ps. lxv. 13.
[4] S. Jer.
[5] Hugo de S. V.
[6] S. Greg. on Job L. xix. § 49.
[7] Prov. ii. 14.

Before CHRIST cir. 800.

the trees of the field, are
withered: because [p] joy is
withered away from the
sons of men.
13 [q] Gird yourselves,
and lament, ye priests:
howl, ye ministers of the
altar: come, lie all night
in sackcloth, ye ministers
of my God: for [r] the meat
offering and the drink offering is withholden from the
house of your God.
14 ¶ [s] Sanctify ye a fast,
call [t] a ‖ solemn assembly,
gather the elders *and* [u] all
the inhabitants of the land
into the house of the LORD
your God, and cry unto
the LORD.

p Is. 24. 11. Jer. 48. 33. See Ps. 4. 7. Is. 9. 3.
q Jer. 4. 8. ver. 8.
r ver. 9.
s 2 Chr. 20. 3, 4. ch. 2. 15, 16.
t Lev. 23. 36.
‖ Or, *day of restraint.*
u 2 Chr. 20. 13.

the second, *They take the timbrel and harp, and rejoice at the sound of the organ*[1]. Of the third, *Let the saints be joyful in glory*[2]. Of the fourth, *Blessed are they that dwell in Thy house; they will be still praising Thee*[3]. The joy of charity and the joy of felicity *wither from the sons of men*, when the virtues aforesaid failing, there being neither knowledge of the truth nor love of virtue, no reward succeedeth, either in this life or that to come."

Having thus pictured the coming woe, he calls all to repentance and mourning, and those first, who were to call others. God Himself appointed these afflictive means, and here He "gives to the priest a model for penitence and a way of entreating mercy." "[4] He invites the priests first to repentance through whose negligence chiefly the practice of holiness, the strictness of discipline, the form of doctrine, the whole aspect of the Church was sunk in irreverence. Whence the people also perished, hurrying along the various haunts of sin. Whence Jeremiah says, *The kings of the earth and all the inhabitants of the world would not have believed that the adversary and the enemy should have entered into the gates of Jerusalem. For the sins of her Prophets and the iniquities of her priests that have shed the blood of the just in the midst of her, they have wandered as blind men in the streets, they have polluted themselves with blood*[5].

13. *Gird yourselves*, i. e. with haircloth, as is elsewhere expressed[6]. The outward affliction is an expression of the inward grief, and itself excites to further grief. This their garment of affliction and penitence, they were not to put off day and night. Their wonted duty was, to *offer up sacrifice for their own sins and the sins of the people*[7], and to entreat God for them. This their office the Prophet calls them to discharge day and night; to *come* into the court of the Temple, and there, where God shewed Himself in majesty and mercy, *lie all night* prostrate before God, not at ease, but in sackcloth. He calls to them in the Name of his God, *Ye ministers of my God;* of Him, to Whom, whosoever forsook Him, he himself was faithful. "[8] The Prophets called the God of all, their own God, being united to Him by singular love and reverential obedience, so that they could say, *God is the strength of my heart and my portion for ever*[9]." He calls Him, further, *their* God, (*your God*) in order to remind them of His special favor to them, and their duty to Him Who allowed them to call Him *their* God.

14. *Sanctify ye a fast.* He does not say only, "proclaim," or "appoint a fast," but *sanctify it.* Hallow the act of abstinence, seasoning it with devotion and with acts meet for repentance. For fasting is not accepted by God, unless done in charity and obedience to His commands. "[10] *Sanctify* it, i. e. make it an offering to God, and as it were a sacrifice, a holy and blameless fast." "[11] To sanctify a fast is to exhibit abstinence of the flesh, meet toward God, with other good. Let anger cease, strife be lulled. For in vain is the flesh worn, if the mind is not held in from evil passions, inasmuch as the Lord saith by the Prophet[12], *Lo! in the day of your fast you find your pleasures.* The fast which the Lord approveth, is that which lifteth up to Him hands full of almsdeeds, which is passed with brotherly love, which is seasoned by piety. What thou substractest from thyself, bestow on another, that thy needy neighbor's flesh may be recruited by means of that which thou deniest to thine own."

Call a solemn assembly. Fasting without devotion is an image of famine. At other times *the solemn assembly* was for festival-joy. Such was the last day of the feast of the Passover[13] and of Tabernacles[14]. No servile work was to be done thereon. It was *then* to be consecrated to thanksgiving, but now to sorrow and supplication. "[8] The Prophet commands that all should be called and gathered into the Temple, that so the prayer

[1] Job xxi. 12. [2] Ps. cxlix. 5. [3] Ib. lxxxiv. 4. [4] Hugo de S. V. [5] Lam. iv. 13, 14. [6] Is. xxii. 12. Jer. iv. 8. vi. 26. [7] Heb. vii. 27. [8] Dion. [9] Ps. lxxiii. 26.

[10] S. Cyr. [11] S. Greg. in Ev. Hom. 16. [12] Is. lviii. 3. [13] Deut. xvi. 8. [14] Lev. xxiii. 36. Num. xxix. 35. 2 Chr. vii. 9. Neh. viii. 18.

Before CHRIST cir. 800.

x Jer. 30. 7.
y Is. 13. 6, 9. ch. 2. 1.

15 [x] Alas for the day! for [y] the day of the LORD *is* at hand, and as a destruction from the Almighty shall it come.

Before CHRIST cir. 800.

might be the rather heard, the more they were who offered it. Wherefore the Apostle besought his disciples to pray for him, that so what was asked might be obtained the more readily through the intercession of many."

Gather the elders. Age was, by God's appointment [1], had in great reverence among the Hebrews. When first God sent Moses and Aaron to His people in Egypt, He bade them collect the elders of the people [2] to declare to them their own mission from God; through them He conveyed the ordinance of the Passover to the whole congregation [3]; in their presence was the first miracle of bringing water from the rock performed [4]; then He commanded Moses to choose seventy of them, to appear before Him before He gave the law [5]; then to bear Moses' own burden in hearing the causes of the people, bestowing His spirit upon them [6]. The elders of each city were clothed with judicial authority [7]. In the expiation of an uncertain murder, the elders of the city represented the whole city [8]; in the offerings for the congregation, the elders of the congregation represented the whole [9]. So then, here also, they are summoned, chief of all, that "the authority and example of their grey hairs might move the young to repentance." "[10] Their age, near to death and ripened in grace, makes them more apt for the fear and worship of God." All however, *priests, elders,* and the *inhabitants,* or *people of the land* [11], were to form one band, and were, with one heart and voice, to cry unto God; and that *in the house of God.* For so Solomon had prayed, that God would *in Heaven* His *dwelling place, hear whatever prayer and supplication* might there be *made by any man or by all His people Israel* [12]; and God had promised in turn, [13] *I have hallowed this house which thou hast built, to put My name there for ever, and Mine eyes and Mine heart shall be there perpetually.* God has given to united prayer a power over Himself, and "prayer overcometh God [14]." The Prophet calls God *your God,* shewing how ready He was to hear; but he adds, *cry unto the Lord;* for it is not a listless prayer, but a loud earnest *cry,* which reacheth to the throne of God.

15. *Alas for the day! for the Day of the Lord* is *at hand.* The judgment of God, then, which they were to deprecate, was still to come. "[15] All times and all days are God's. Yet they are said to be our days, in which God leaves us to our own freedom, to do as we will," and which we may use to repent and turn to Him. "Whence Christ saith [16], *O Jerusalem—if thou hadst known in this thy day the things which belong unto thy peace.* That time, on the contrary, is said to be God's Day, in which He doth any new, rare, or special thing, such as is the Day of Judgment or vengeance." All judgment in time is an image of the Judgment for eternity. "The Day of the Lord" is, then, each "day of vengeance in which God doth to man according to His will and just judgment, inflicting the punishment which he deserves, as man did to Him in his day, manifoldly dishonoring Him, according to his own perverse will." That Day *is at hand;* suddenly to come. Speed then must be used to prevent it. Prevented it may be by speedy repentance before it comes; but when it does come, there will be no avoiding it; for

As a destruction from the Almighty shall it come. The name *the Almighty* or *God Almighty* is but seldom used in Holy Scripture. God revealed Himself by this Name to Abraham, when renewing to him the promise which was beyond nature, that he should be a father of many nations, when he and Sarah were *old and well stricken in age.* He said, *I am God Almighty; walk before Me and be thou perfect* [17]. God Almighty uses it again of Himself in renewing the blessing to Jacob [18]; and Isaac and Jacob use it in blessing in His Name [19]. It is not used as a mere name of God, but always in reference to His might, as in the book of Job which treats chiefly of His power [20]. In His days of judgment God manifests Himself as the All-mighty and All-just. Hence in the New Testament, it occurs almost exclusively in the Revelations, which reveal His judgments to come [21]. Here the words form a sort of terrible proverb, whence they are adopted from Joel by the prophet Isaiah [22]. The word *destruction, shod,* is formed from the same root as *Almighty,*

1 Lev. xix. 32.
2 Ex. iii. 16. iv. 29. comp. Deut. xxxi. 28.
3 Ex. xii. 3. 21.
4 Ex. xvii. 5. add. xviii. 12.
5 Ib. xxiv. 1. 9.
6 Num. xi. 16 sqq.
7 Deut. xix. 12. xxii. 15. xxv. 7.
8 Ib. xxi. 3–6.
9 Lev. iv. 15. ix. 1.
10 S. Jer.
11 Jer. i. 18.
12 1 Kings viii. 39.
13 Ib. ix. 3.
14 Tert. de orat. § 29. p. 321. O. T.
15 Dion.
16 S. Luke xix. 42.
17 Gen. xvii. 1–6. 16–21. xviii. 10–14. Rom. iv. 17–21.
18 Gen. xxxv. 11.
19 Gen. xxviii. 3. xliii. 14. xlviii. 3. xlix. 25.
20 In the book of Job, it occurs 31 times; else it is used twice by the heathen Ruth, i. 20, 1; twice by Balaam, Num. xxiv. 4, 16; twice by Ezekiel of God revealing Himself in Majesty, i. 24. x. 5; and twice in the Psalms, of God putting forth His might, lxviii. 15. or protecting, xci. 1.
21 Eight times, else only in 2 Cor. vi. 18, referring to the O. T.
22 xiii. 6.

Before CHRIST cir. 800.

16 Is not the meat cut
off before our eyes, *yea*,
[z] joy and gladness from the
house of our God?
17 The † seed is rotten
under their clods, the garners are laid desolate, the
barns are broken down;
for the corn is withered.

z See Deut. 12. 6, 7. & 16, 11, 14, 15.

† Heb. *grains*.

18 How do [a] the beasts
groan! the herds of cattle
are perplexed, because they
have no pasture; yea, the
flocks of sheep are made
desolate.
19 O LORD, [b] to thee
will I cry: for [c] the fire
hath devoured the ‖ pas-

Before CHRIST cir. 800.

a Hos. 4. 3.

b Ps. 50. 15.

c Jer. 9. 10. ch. 2. 3.

‖ Or, *habitations*.

Shaddai[1]. *It shall come as might from the Mighty*. Only, the word *might* is always used of "might" put forth to destroy, a *mighty destruction*. He says then, in fact, that that Day shall come, like might put forth by the Almighty Himself, to destroy His enemies, irresistible, inevitable, unendurable, overwhelming the sinner.

16. *Is not the meat cut off before our eyes?* The Prophet exhibits the immediate judgment, as if it were already fulfilled in act. He sets it in detail before their eyes. "When the fruits of the earth were now ripe, the corn now calling for the reaper, and the grapes fully ripe and desiring to be pressed out, they were taken away, when set before their eyes for them to enjoy." Yea, *joy and gladness from the house of our God*. The joy in the abundance of the harvest was expressed in one universal thanksgiving to God, by fathers of families, sons, daughters, menservants, maidservants, with the priest and Levite. All this was to be cut off together. The courts of God's house were to be desolate and silent, or joy and gladness were to be turned into sorrow and wailing.

"[2] So it befell those who rejected and insulted Christ. *The Bread of life Which came down from Heaven and gave life to the world*[3], *the corn of wheat, which fell into the ground and died, and brought forth much fruit*[4], that spiritual *wine* which knoweth how to *gladden the heart of man*, was already in a manner before their eyes. But when they ceased not to insult Him in unbelief, He, as it were, disappeared from their eyes, and they lost all spiritual sustenance. All share in all good is gone from them. *Joy and gladness* have also gone *from the House* which they had. For they are given up to desolation, and *abide without king or prince or sacrifice*[5]. Again, the Lord said[6], *Man shall not live by bread alone, but by every word which cometh forth out of the Mouth of God*. The word of God then is food. This hath been taken away from the Jews; for they understood not the writings of Moses, but *to this day the veil is upon their heart*[7]. For they hate the oracles of Christ. All spiritual food is perished, not in itself but to *them*. To them, it is as though it were not. But the Lord Himself imparts to those who believe in Him a right to all exuberance of joy in the good things from above. For it is written[8], *The Lord will not suffer the soul of the righteous to famish; but He thrusts away the desire of the wicked*."

17. *The seed is rotten under the clods*. Not only was all to be cut off for the present, but, with it, all hope for the future. The scattered seed, as it lay, each under its clod known to God, was dried up, and so decayed. The garners lay desolate, nay, were allowed to go to ruin, in hopelessness of any future harvest.

18. *How do the beasts groan!* There is something very pitiable in the cry of the brute creation, even because they are innocent, yet bear man's guilt. Their groaning seems to the Prophet to be beyond expression. *How* vehemently *do* they *groan! The herds of cattle are perplexed*, as though, like man, they were endued with reason, to debate where to find their food. *Yea*, not these only, but *the flocks of sheep*, which might find pasture where the herds could not, these too shall *bear the punishment of guilt*. They suffered by the guilt of man; and yet so stupid was man, that he was not so sensible of his own sin for which they suffered, as they of its effect. The beasts cried to God, but even their cries did not awaken His own people. The Prophet cries for them;

19. *O Lord, to Thee will I cry*. This is the only hope left, and contains all hopes. From the Lord was the infliction; in Him is the healing. The Prophet appeals to God by His own Name, the faithful Fulfiller of His promises, Him Who Is, and Who had promised to hear all who call upon Him. Let others call to their idols, if they would, or remain stupid and forgetful, the Prophet would cry unto God, and that earnestly.

For the fire hath devoured the pastures. The gnawing of locusts leaves things, as though

---

1 שׁד, שׁדי, This last is from an old root, שׁדי i. q. שׁדד. 2 S. Cyr. 3 S. John vi. 48, 51.

4 Ib. xii. 24. 5 Hos. iii. 4. 6 S. Matt. iv. 4. 7 2 Cor. iii. 15. 8 Prov. x. 3.

Before CHRIST cir. 800.

tures of the wilderness, and
the flame hath burned all
the trees of the field.
20 The beasts of the
field [d] cry also unto thee:
for [e] the rivers of waters
are dried up, and the fire
hath devoured the pastures
of the wilderness.

[d] Job 38. 41. Ps. 104. 21. & 145. 15.
[e] 1 Kings 17. 7. & 18. 5.

CHAPTER II.

Before CHRIST cir. 800.

1 *He sheweth unto Zion the terribleness of God's judgment.* 12 *He exhorteth to repentance,* 15 *prescribeth a fast,* 18 *promiseth a blessing thereon.* 21 *He comforteth Zion with present,* 28 *and future blessings.*

1 [a] BLOW ye the ‖ trumpet
in Zion, and [b] sound
an alarm in my holy moun-

[a] Jer. 4. 5. ver. 15.
‖ Or, *cornet.*
[b] Num. 10. 5, 9.

scorched by fire[1]; the sun and the East wind scorch up all green things, as though it had been the actual contact of fire. Spontaneous combustion frequently follows. The Chaldees wasted all before them with fire and sword. All these and the like calamities are included under *the fire,* whose desolating is without remedy. What has been scorched by fire never recovers. "[2]The famine," it is said of Mosul, "was generally caused by fire spreading in dry weather over pastures, grass lands, and corn lands, many miles in extent. It burnt night and day often for a week and sometimes embraced the whole horizon."

20. *The beasts of the field cry also unto Thee.* "[3]There is an order in these distresses. First he points out the insensate things wasted; then those afflicted, which have sense only; then those endowed with reason; so that to the order of calamity there may be consorted an order of pity, sparing first the creature, then the things sentient, then things rational. The Creator spares the creature; the Ordainer, things sentient; the Saviour, the rational." Irrational creatures joined with the Prophet in his cry. The beasts of the field cry to God, though they know it not; it is a cry to God, Who compassionates all which suffers. God makes them, in act, a picture of dependence upon His Providence, "seeking to It for a removal of their sufferings, and supply of their wants." So He saith[4], *the young lions roar after their prey, and seek their meat from God,* and[5], *He giveth to the beast his food and to the young ravens that cry,* and[6], *Who provideth for the raven his food? when his young ones cry unto God.* If the people would not take instruction from him, he "bids them learn from the beasts of the field how to behave amid these calamities, that they should cry aloud to God to remove them."

II. 1. The Prophet begins anew in this chapter, first delineating in greater detail the judgments of God; then calling to repentance. The image reaches its height in the capture of Jerusalem by the Babylonians, itself an image only of worse judgments, first on the Jews by the Romans; then on particular Churches; then of the infliction through Anti-Christ; lastly on the whole world. "[3]The Prophet sets before them the greatness of the coming woe, of the approaching captivity, of the destruction imminent, in order to move the people to terror at the judgment of God, to compunction, to love of obedience. This he does from the manifoldness of the destruction, the quality of the enemy, the nature of the victory, the weight of the misery, the ease of the triumph, the eagerness for ill, the fear of the besieged princes, the sluggishness of the besieged people. He exhorts all in common to prostrate themselves at the feet of the Divine judgment, if so be God would look down from His dwelling place, turn the storm into a calm, and at length out of the shipwreck of captivity bring them back to the haven of consolation." "[7]It is no mere prediction. Everything stands before them, as in actual experience, and before their eyes." Things future affect men less; so he makes them, as it were, present to their souls. "[7]He will not let them vacillate about repentance, but bids them, laying aside all listlessness, set themselves courageously to ward off the peril, by running to God, and effacing the charges against them from their old sins by ever-renewed amendment."

Blow ye the trumpet. The trumpet was wont to sound in Zion, only for religious uses; to call together the congregations for holy meetings, to usher in the beginnings of their months and their solemn days with festival

[1] See on ii. 3. [2] Ainsworth, ii. 127. "The whole of the mountain is thickly covered with dry grass which readily takes fire, and the slightest breath of air instantly spreads the conflagration far over the country. The Arabs who inhabit the valley of the Jordan invariably put to death any person who is known to have been even the innocent cause of firing the grass, and they have made it a public law among themselves, that even in the height of intestine warfare, no one shall attempt to set his enemy's harvest on fire. One evening at Tabaria, I saw a large fire on the opposite side of the lake, which spread with great velocity for two days, till its progress was checked by the Wady Feik." Burckhardt, Travels in Syria, pp. 331, 2. See also Thomson, i. 529.

[3] Hugo de S. V. [4] Ps. civ. 21. [5] Ps. cxlvii. 9. [6] Job xxxviii. 41. [7] S. Cyr.

Before CHRIST cir. 800.

tain: let all the inhabitants of the land tremble:
for [c] the day of the LORD
cometh, for *it is* nigh at
hand;
2 [d] A day of darkness

[c] ch. 1. 15. Obad. 15. Zeph. 1. 14, 15.

[d] Amos 5. 18, 20.

gladness. Now in Zion itself, the stronghold of the kingdom, the Holy City, the place which God chose to put His Name there, which He had promised to establish, the trumpet was to be used, only for sounds of alarm and fear. Alarm could not penetrate there, without having pervaded the whole land. With it, the whole human hope of Judah was gone.

Sound an alarm in My holy mountain. He repeats the warning in varied expressions, in order the more to impress men's hearts and to stir them to repentance. Even *the holy mountain* of God was to echo with alarms; the holiness, once bestowed upon it, was to be no security against the judgments of God; yea, in it rather were those judgments to begin. So St. Peter saith [1], *The time* is come, *that judgment must begin at the house of God.* The alarm being blown in Zion, terror was to spread to all the inhabitants of the land, who were, in fear, to repent. The Church of Christ is foretold in prophecy under the names of *Zion* and of the holy *mountain.* It is the *stone cut out without hands, which became a great mountain, and filled the whole earth* [2]. Of it, it is said [3], *Come ye and let us go up to the mountain of the Lord, to the house of the God of Jacob!* And St. Paul says, *ye are come unto mount Zion and unto the city of the living God* [4]. The words then are a rule for all times. The judgments predicted by Joel represent all judgments unto the end; the conduct, prescribed on their approach, is a pattern to the Church at all times. "[5] In this mountain we must wail, considering the failure of the faithful, in which, *iniquity abounding, charity waxeth cold.* For now (A. D. 1450) the state of the Church is so sunken, and you may see so great misery in her from the most evil conversation of many, that one who burns with zeal for God, and truly loveth his brethren, must say with Jeremiah [6], *Let mine eyes run down with tears night and day, and let them not cease, for the virgin daughter of my people is broken with a great breach.*"

Let all the inhabitants of the land tremble. "[5] We should be troubled when we hear the words of God, rebuking, threatening, avenging, as Jeremiah saith [7], *my heart within me is broken, all my bones shake, because of the Lord and because of the words of His holiness.* Good is the trouble which shaketh carnal peace, vain security, and the rest of bodily delight, when men, weighing their sins, are shaken with fear and trembling, and repent."

For the Day of the Lord is at hand. The Day of the Lord is any day in which He avengeth sin, any day of Judgment, in the course of His Providence or at the end; the day of Jerusalem from the Chaldees or Romans, the day of Anti-Christ, the day of general or particular judgment, of which St. James says [8], *The coming of the Lord draweth nigh. Behold the Judge standeth before the door.* "[9] Well is that called *the day of the Lord,* in that, by the Divine appointment, it avengeth the wrongs done to the Lord through the disobedience of His people."

2. *A day of darkness and of gloominess.* "[5] A day full of *miseries;* wherefore he accumulates so many names of terrors. There was inner darkness in the heart, and the darkness of tribulation without. They hid themselves in dark places. There was the cloud between God and them; so that they were not protected nor heard by Him, of which Jeremiah saith [10], *Thou hast covered Thyself with a cloud, that our prayers should not pass through.* There was the whirlwind of tempest within and without, taking away all rest, tranquillity and peace. Whence Jeremiah hath [11], *A whirlwind of the Lord is gone forth in fury, it shall fall grievously upon the head of the wicked. The anger of the Lord shall not return, until He have executed it.*" [12] *The Day of the Lord* too *shall come as a thief in the night. Clouds and darkness are round about Him* [13].

A day of clouds and of thick darkness. The locusts are but the faint shadow of the coming evils, yet as the first harbingers of God's successive judgments, the imagery, even in this picture is probably taken from them. At least there is nothing in which writers, of every character, are so agreed, as in speaking of locusts as clouds darkening the sun. "[14] These creatures do not come in legions, but in whole clouds, 5 or 6 leagues in length and 2 or 3 in breadth. All the air is full and darkened when they fly. Though the sun shine ever so bright, it is no brighter than when most clouded." "[15] In Senegal we have seen a vast multitude of locusts shadowing the air; for they come almost every three years, and darken the sky." "[16] About 8 o'clock there arose above us a thick cloud, which darkened the air, depriving us of the

[1] 1 Pet. iv. 17. [2] Dan. ii. 34, 5. [3] Is. ii. 3.
[4] Heb. xii. 22. [5] Dion. [6] xiv. 17.
[7] xxiii. 9. [8] v. 8, 9. [9] Hugo de S. V.
[10] Lam. iii. 44. [11] xxiii. 19. [12] 1 Thess. v. 2.

[13] Ps. xcvii. 2.
[14] Beauplan, Ukraine, l. c. p. 599.
[15] Aluise, da cà da Mosto Navig. c. 13.
[16] Adansson, Voyage au Sénégal, p. 87, 8,

Before CHRIST cir. 800.

and of gloominess, a day of clouds and of thick darkness, as the morning spread upon the mountains:

Before CHRIST cir. 800.

rays of the sun. Every one was astonished at so sudden a change in the air, which is so seldom clouded at this season; but we soon saw that it was owing to a cloud of locusts. It was about 20 or 30 toises from the ground [120–180 feet] and covered several leagues of the country, when it discharged a shower of locusts, who fed there while they rested, and then resumed their flight. This cloud was brought by a pretty strong wind, it was all the morning passing the neighborhood, and the same wind, it was thought, precipitated it in the sea." "[1] They take off from the place the light of day, and a sort of eclipse is formed." "[2] In the middle of April their numbers were so vastly increased, that in the heat of the day they formed themselves into large bodies, appeared like a succession of clouds and darkened the sun." "[3] On looking up we perceived an immense cloud, here and there semi-transparent, in other parts quite black, that spread itself all over the sky, and at intervals shadowed the sun." The most unimaginative writers have said the same; "[4] When they first appear, a thick dark cloud is seen very high in the air, which, as it passes, obscures the sun. Their swarms were so astonishing in all the steppes over which we passed in this part of our journey [the Crimea,] that the whole face of nature might have been described as concealed by a living veil." "[5] When these clouds of locusts take their flight to surmount some obstacle, or traverse more rapidly a desert soil, one may say, to the letter, that the heaven is darkened by them."

As the morning spread upon the mountains. Some have thought this too to allude to the appearance which the inhabitants of Abyssinia too well knew, as preceding the coming of the locusts[6]. A sombre yellow light is cast on the ground, from the reflection, it was thought, of their yellow wings. But that appearance itself seems to be peculiar to that country, or perhaps to certain flights of locusts. The image naturally describes, the suddenness, universality of the darkness, when men looked for light. As the mountain-tops first catch the gladdening rays of the sun, ere yet it riseth on the plains, and the light spreads from height to height, until the whole earth is arrayed in light, so wide and universal shall the outspreading be, but it shall be of darkness, not of light; the light itself shall be turned into darkness.

A great people and a strong. The imagery throughout these verses is taken from the flight and inroad of locusts. The allegory is so complete, that the Prophet compares them to those things which are, in part, intended under them, warriors, horses and instruments of war; and this, the more, because neither locusts, nor armies are exclusively intended. The object of the allegory is to describe the order and course of the Divine judgments; how they are terrific, irresistible, universal, overwhelming, penetrating everywhere, overspreading all things, excluded by nothing. The locusts are the more striking symbol of this, through their minuteness and their number. They are little miniatures of a well-ordered army, unhindered by what would be physical obstacles to larger creatures, moving in order inimitable even by man, and, from their number, desolating to the uttermost. "What more countless or mightier than the locusts," asks S. Jerome, who had seen their inroads, "which human industry cannot resist?" "It is a thing invincible," says S. Cyril, "their invasion is altogether irresistible, and suffices utterly to destroy all in the fields." Yet each of these creatures is small, so that they would be powerless and contemptible, except in the Hands of Him, Who brings them in numbers which can be wielded only by the Creator. Wonderful image of the judgments of God, Who marshals and combines in one, causes each unavailing in itself, but working together the full completion of His inscrutable Will.

There hath not been ever the like. The courses of sin and of punishment are ever recommencing anew in some part of the world and of the Church. The whole order of each, sin and punishment, will culminate once only, in the Day of Judgment. Then only will these words have their complete fulfillment. The Day of Judgment alone is that Day of terror and of woe, such as never has been before, and shall never be again. For there will be no new day or time of terror. Eternal punishment will only be the continuation of the sentence adjudged *then*. But, in time and in the course of

[1] Nieuhoff, China, p. 377. [2] Shaw, p. 256.
[3] Morier, Second Journey, p. 98.
[4] Clarke, i. c. 18. p. 437.
[5] Volney, i. 277. "While I was at Sale in Morocco, after midday the sun was darkened, we knew not why, until we saw very many kinds of locusts, exceeding great." R. Anania of Fez, in Lud. Comm. p. 176. "The wagons passed directly through them, before which they rose up in a cloud which darkened the air on each side." Barrow, S. Afr. i. 242. "A. D. 1668, there were, in the whole country of Cyprus, such numbers of locusts, that when they flew, they were like a dark cloud, through which the rays of the sun could scarcely penetrate." Le Bruyn, Lev. c. 72. "The swarm had exactly the appearance of a vast snow-cloud hanging on the slope of a mountain from which the snow was falling in very large flakes." Lichtenstein, c. 46. "The air at a distance had the appearance of smoke." Forskäl, p. 8.
[6] See on ver. 6.

Before CHRIST cir. 800.

[e] a great people and a
strong; [f] there hath not
been ever the like, neither
shall be any more after it,
even to the years † of many
generations.

3 [g] A fire devoureth before them; and behind

[e] ch. 1. 6. ver. 5, 11, 25.
[f] Ex. 10. 14.
† Heb. *of generation and generation.*
[g] ch. 1. 19, 20.

God's Providential government, the sins of each soul or people or Church draw down visitations, which are God's final judgments there. Such to the Jewish people, before the Captivity, was the destruction of the Temple, the taking of Jerusalem by Nebuchadnezzar, and that Captivity itself. The Jewish polity was never again restored as before. Such, to the new polity after the Captivity, was the destruction by the Romans. Eighteen hundred years have seen nothing like it. The Vandals and then the Mohammedans swept over the Churches of North Africa, each destructive in its own way. Twelve centuries have witnessed one unbroken desolation of the Church in Africa. In Constantinople, and Asia Minor, Palestine, Persia, Churches of the Redeemer became the mosques of the false prophet. Centuries have flowed by, *yet we see not our signs, neither is there any among us, that knoweth how long*[1]. Wealthy, busy, restless, intellectual, degraded, London, sender forth of missionaries, but, save in China, the largest heathen city in the world; converter of the isles of the sea, but thyself unconverted; fullest of riches and of misery, of civilization and of savage life, of refinements and debasement; heart, whose pulses are felt in every continent, but thyself diseased and feeble, wilt thou, in this thy day, anticipate by thy conversion the Day of the Lord, or will It come upon thee, *as hath never been the like, nor shall be, for the years of many generations?* Shalt thou win thy lost ones to Christ, or be thyself the birthplace or abode of Anti-Christ? *O Lord God, Thou knowest.*

Yet the words have fulfillments short of the end. Even of successive chastisements upon the same people, each may have some aggravation peculiar to itself, so that of each, in turn, it may be said, in *that* respect, that no former visitation had been like it, none afterwards should resemble it. Thus the Chaldæans were chief in fierceness, Antiochus Epiphanes in his madness against God, the Romans in the completeness of the desolation. The fourth beast which Daniel saw *was*[2] *dreadful and terrible and strong exceedingly, and it was diverse from all the beasts that were before it.* The persecutions of the Roman Emperors were in extent and cruelty far beyond any before them. They shall be as nothing, in comparison to the deceivableness and oppression of Anti-Christ. The Prophet, however, does not say that there should be absolutely *none like it*, but only not *for the years of many generations.* The words *unto generation and generation* elsewhere mean *for ever;* here the word "years" may limit them to length of time. God, after some signal visitation, leaves a soul or a people to the silent workings of His grace or of His Providence. The marked interpositions of His Providence, are like His extraordinary miracles, rare; else, like the ordinary miracles of His daily operations, they would cease to be interpositions.

3. *A fire devoureth before them, &c.* Travelers, of different nations and characters, and in different lands, some unacquainted with the Bible words, have agreed to describe under this image the ravages of locusts. "[3] They scorch many things with their touch." "[4] Whatever of herb or leaf they gnaw, is, as it were, scorched by fire." "[5] Wherever they come, the ground seems burned, as it were with fire." "[6] Wherever they pass, they burn and spoil everything, and that irremediably." "[7] I have myself observed that the places where they had browsed were as scorched, as if the fire had passed there." "[8] They covered a square mile so completely, that it appeared, at a little distance, to have been burned and strewn over with brown ashes. Not a shrub, nor a blade of grass was visible." "[9] A few months afterwards, a much larger army alighted and gave the whole country the appearance of having been burned." "Wherever they settled, it looks as if fire had devoured and burnt up everything." "[10] It is better to have to do with the Tartars, than with these little destructive animals; you would think that fire follows their track," are the descriptions of their ravages in Italy, Æthiopia, the Levant, India, S. Africa. The locust, itself the image of God's judgments, is described as an enemy, invading, as they say, "with fire and sword," "breathing fire," wasting all, as he advances, and leaving behind him the blackness of ashes, and burning villages. "[11] Whatsoever he seizeth on, he shall consume as a devouring flame and shall leave nothing whole behind him."

[1] Ps. lxxiv. 9. [2] Dan. vii. 7–19. [3] Plin. xi. 35.
[4] Lud. Hist. Æth. i. 13. [5] Alvarez, c. 32.
[6] Villamont, Voyage, p. 226.
[7] Le Bruyn, Lev. c. 72.
[8] Barrow, S. Afr. i. 242. "According to all accounts, wherever the swarms of locusts arrive, the vegetables are sometimes entirely consumed and destroyed, appearing as if they had been burnt up by fire." Sparrman, i. 367.
[9] Forbes, ii. 274. [10] Volney, i. 177. [11] S. Jer.

Before CHRIST cir. 800.

h Gen. 2. 8. & 13. 10. Is. 51. 3.
i Zech. 7. 14.

them a flame burneth: the land *is* as [h] the garden of Eden before them, [i] and behind them a desolate wilderness; yea, and nothing shall escape them.

Before CHRIST cir. 800.

The land is as the garden of Eden before them. In outward beauty the land was like that Paradise of God, where He placed our first parents; as were Sodom and Gomorrah, before God overthrew them[1]. It was like a garden enclosed and protected from all inroad of evil. They sinned, and like our first parents forfeited its bliss. *A fruitful land* God *maketh barren, for the wickedness of them that dwell therein*[2]. Ezekiel fortells the removal of the punishment, in connection with the Gospel-promise of[3] *a new heart and a new spirit. They shall say, This land that was desolate is become like the garden of Eden.*

And behind them a desolate wilderness. The desolation caused by the locust is even more inconceivable to us, than their numbers. We have seen fields blighted; we have known of crops, of most moment to man's support, devoured; and in one year we heard of terrific famine, as its result. We do not readily set before our eyes a whole tract, embracing in extent several of our counties, in which not the one or other crop was smitten, but every green thing was gone. Yet such was the scourge of locusts, the image of other and worse scourges in the treasure-house of God's displeasure. A Syrian writer relates[4], "A. D. 1004, a large swarm of locusts appeared in the land of Mosul and Bagdad, and it was very grievous in Shiraz. It left no herb nor even leaf on the trees, and even gnawed the pieces of linen which the fullers were bleaching; of each piece the fuller gave a scrap to its owner: and there was a famine, and a cor [about two quarters] of wheat was sold in Bagdad for 120 gold dinars, [about £54]:" and again[5], "when it [the locust of A. D. 784,] had consumed the whole tract of Edessa and Sarug, it passed to the W. and for three years after this heavy chastisement there was a famine in the land." "[6] We traveled five days through lands wholly despoiled; and for the canes of maize, as large as the largest canes used to prop vines, it cannot be said how they were broken and trampled, as if asses had trampled them; and all this from the locusts. The wheat, barley, tafos[7], were as if they had never been sown; the trees without a single leaf; the tender wood all eaten; there was no memory of herb of any sort. If we had not been advised to take mules laden with barley and provisions for ourselves, we should have perished of hunger, we and our mules. This land was all covered with locusts without wings, and they said that they were the seed of those who had all gone, who had destroyed the land." "[8] Everywhere, where their legions march, verdure disappears from the country, like a curtain which is folded up; trees and plants stripped of leaves, and reduced to their branches and stalks, substitute, in the twinkling of an eye, the dreary spectacle of winter for the rich scenes of spring." "Happily this plague is not very often repeated; for there is none which brings so surely famine and the diseases which follow it." "[9] Desolation and famine mark their progress; all the expectations of the husbandman vanish; his fields, which the rising sun beheld covered with luxuriance, are before evening a desert; the produce of his garden and orchard are alike destroyed; for where these destructive swarms alight, not a leaf is left upon the trees, a blade of grass in the pastures, nor an ear of corn in the field." "[10] In 1654 a great multitude of locusts came from the N. W. to the Islands Tayyovvan and Formosa, which consumed all that grew in the fields, so that above eight thousand men perished by famine." "[11] They come sometimes in such prodigious swarms, that they darken the sky as they pass by and devour all in those parts where they settle, so that the inhabitants are often obliged to change their habitations for want of sustenance, as it has happened frequently in China and the Isle of Tajowak." "[12] The lands, ravaged throughout the West, produced no harvest. The year 1780 was still more wretched. A dry winter produced a new race of locusts which ravaged what had escaped the inclemency of the season. The husbandman reaped not what he had sown, and was reduced to have neither nourishment, seed, nor cattle. The people experienced all the horrors of famine. You might see them wandering over the country to devour the roots; and, seeking in the bowels of the earth for means to lengthen their days, perhaps they rather abridged them. A countless number died of misery and bad nourishment. I have seen countrymen on the roads and in the streets dead of starvation, whom others were laying across asses, to

1 Gen. xiii. 10.
2 Ps. cvii. 34.
3 Ezek. xxxvi. 26, 35.
4 Barhebr. Chron. Syr. p. 214.
5 Ib. p. 134.
6 Alvarez, c. 33.
7 One of the best Æthiopian grains.
8 Volney, i. 277.
9 Forbes, c. 22. ii. 273.
10 Nieuhoff, 2d. Emb. to China, p. 29.
11 Nieuhoff, Voyage in Churchill, ii. 359.
12 Chénier, iii. 496–8.

Before CHRIST cir. 800.

[k] Rev. 9. 7.

4 [k] The appearance of
them *is* as the appearance
of horses; and as horse-
men, so shall they run.

5 [l] Like the noise of
chariots on the tops of
mountains shall they leap,
like the noise of a flame

Before CHRIST cir. 800.

[l] Rev. 9. 9.

---

go bury them. Fathers sold their children. A husband, in concert with his wife, went to marry her in some other province as if she were his sister, and went to redeem her, when better off. I have seen women and children run after the camels, seek in their dung for some grain of indigested barley and devour it with avidity."

Yea, and nothing shall escape them; or (which the words also include) *none shall escape him,* lit. *and also there shall be no escaping as to him* or *from him.* The word [1], being used elsewhere of the *persons* who escape, suggests, in itself, that we should not linger by the type of the locusts only, but think of enemies more terrible, who destroy not harvests only, but men, bodies or souls also. Yet the picture of devastation is complete. No creature of God so destroys the whole face of nature, as does the locust. A traveler in the Crimea uses unconsciously the words of the Prophet [2]; "On whatever spot they fall, the whole vegetable produce disappears. Nothing escapes them, from the leaves of the forest to the herbs on the plain. Fields, vineyards, gardens, pastures, everything is laid waste; and sometimes the only appearance left is a disgusting superficies caused by their putrefying bodies, the stench of which is sufficient to breed a pestilence." Another in S. Africa says [3], "When they make their appearance, not a single field of corn remains unconsumed by them. This year the whole of the Sneuwberg will not, I suppose, produce a single bushel." "[4] They had [for a space 80 or 90 miles in length] devoured every green herb and every blade of grass; and had it not been for the reeds on which our cattle entirely subsisted while we skirted the banks of the river, the journey must have been discontinued, at least in the line that had been proposed." "[5] Not a shrub nor blade of grass was visible." The rapidity with which they complete the destruction is also observed [6]. "In two hours, they destroyed all the herbs around Rama."

All this which is a strong, but true, image of the locusts is a shadow of God's other judgments. It is often said of God [7], *A fire goeth before Him and burneth up His enemies on every side.* [8] *The Lord will come with fire; by fire will the Lord plead with all flesh.* This is said of the Judgment-day, as in S. Paul [9], *The Lord Jesus shall be revealed from heaven with His mighty angels, in flaming fire taking vengeance on them that know not God, and that obey not the Gospel of our Lord Jesus Christ.* That awful lurid stream of fire shall burn up *the earth and all the works that are therein* [10]. All this whole circuit of the globe shall be enveloped in one burning deluge of fire; all gold and jewels, gardens, fields, pictures, books, "the cloud-capt towers and gorgeous palaces, shall dissolve, and leave not a rack behind." The good shall be removed beyond its reach; for they shall be *caught up to meet the Lord in the air* [11]. But all which is in the earth and those who are of the earth shall be swept away by it. It shall go before the army of the Lord, the Angels whom [12] *the Son of man shall send forth, to gather out of His kingdom all things that shall offend and them that do iniquity.* It *shall burn after them.* For it shall burn on during the Day of Judgment until it have consumed all for which it is sent. *The land will be a garden of Eden before it.* For they will, our Lord says, be eating, drinking, buying, selling, planting, building, marrying and giving in marriage [13]; the world will be *glorifying itself and living deliciously,* full of riches and delights, when it *shall be utterly burned with fire,* and *in one hour so great riches shall come to nought* [14]. *And after it a desolate wilderness,* for there shall be none left. *And none shall escape.* For our Lord says [15], *they shall gather all things that offend; the angels shall come forth and sever the wicked from among the just, and shall cast them into the furnace of fire.*

4. *The appearance of them* is *as the appearance of horses.* "If you carefully consider the head of the locust," says Theodoret, a Bishop in Syria, "you will find it exceedingly like that of a horse." Whence the Arabs, of old [16] and to this day [17], say; "In the locust, slight as it is, is the nature of ten of the larger animals, the face of a horse, the eyes of an elephant, the neck of a bull, the horns of a deer, the chest of a lion, the belly of a scorpion, the wings of an eagle, the thighs of a camel, the feet of an ostrich, the tail of a serpent."

5. *Like the noise of chariots on the tops of the mountains shall they leap.* The amazing noise

[1] פליטה as "captivity" for "captives."
[2] Clarke, i. 428, 9. [3] Barrow, i. 248, 9. [4] Ib. 257.
[5] Ib. 242. [6] Le Bruyn, c. 46. [7] Ps. xcvii. 3.
[8] Is. lxvi. 15, 16. [9] 2 Thess. i. 7, 8.
[10] 2 Pet. iii. 10. [11] 1 Thess. iv. 17.
[12] S. Matt. xiii. 41. [13] S. Luke xvii. 27, 8, 30.
[14] Rev. xviii. 7, 8, 17. [15] S. Matt. xiii. 41, 49, 50.
[16] Demiri in Bochart, ii. iv. 4.
[17] The Arabs remarked to Niebuhr, the likeness to the horse, the lion, the camel, the serpent, the scorpion; and foremost that of the head to the horse's. Descr. de l' Arabie, p. 153.

Before CHRIST cir. 800.

of fire that devoureth the stubble, [m] as a strong people set in battle array.

[m] ver. 2.

6 Before their face the people shall be much pained: [n] all faces shall gather † blackness.

Before CHRIST cir. 800.

[n] Jer. 8. 21. Lam. 4. 8. Nah. 2. 10.
† Heb. *pot.*

---

of the flight of locusts is likened by those who have heard them, to all sorts of deep sharp rushing sounds. One says[1], "their noise may be heard six miles off." Others, "[2] within a hundred paces I heard the rushing noise occasioned by the flight of so many millions of insects. When I was in the midst of them, it was as loud as the dashing of the waters occasioned by the mill-wheel." "[3] While passing over our heads, their sound was as of a great cataract." "[4] We heard a noise as of the rushing of a great wind at a distance." "[5] In flying they make a rushing rustling noise, as when a strong wind blows through trees." "[6] They cause a noise, like the rushing of a torrent." To add another vivid description[7], "When a swarm is advancing, it seems as though brown clouds were rising from the horizon, which, as they approach, spread more and more. They cast a veil over the sun and a shadow on the earth. Soon you see little dots, and observe a whizzing and life. Nearer yet, the sun is darkened; you hear a roaring and rushing like gushing water. On a sudden you find yourself surrounded with locusts."

Like the noise of a flame of fire that devoureth the stubble. The sharp noise caused by these myriads of insects, while feeding, has also been noticed. "[8] You hear afar the noise which they make in browsing on the herbs and trees, as of an army which is foraging without restraint." "[9] When they alight upon the ground to feed, the plains are all covered, and they make a murmuring noise as they eat, when in two hours they devour all close to the ground." "[10] The noise which they make in devouring, ever announces their approach at some distance." "[11] They say, that not without a noise is their descent on the fields effected, and that there is a certain sharp sound, as they chew the corn, as when the wind strongly fanneth a flame."

Their noise, Joel says, is *like the noise of chariots.* Whence St. John says[12], *the sound of their wings was as the sound of many horses rushing to battle.* Their sound should be like the sound of war-chariots, bounding in their speed; but their inroad should be, where chariots could not go and man's foot could rarely reach, *on the tops of the mountains*[13]. A mountain range is, next to the sea, the strongest natural protection. Mountains have been a limit to the mightiest powers. The Caucasus of old held in the Persian power; on the one side, all was enslaved, on the other, all was fearlessly free[14]. Of late it enabled a few mountaineers to hold at bay the power of Russia. The pass of Thermopylæ, until betrayed, enabled a handful of men to check the invasion of nearly two millions. The mountain-ridges of Spain were, from times before our Lord, the last home and rallying-place of the conquered or the birth-place of deliverance[15]. God had assigned to His people a spot, central hereafter for the conversion of the world, yet where, meantime, they lay enveloped and sheltered *amid the mountains* which *His Right-Hand purchased*[16]. The Syrians owned that *their God* was *the God of the hills*[17]; and the people confessed[18], *as the hills are round about Jerusalem, so the Lord is round about His people. Their* protection was a symbol of His. But His protection withdrawn, nothing should be a hindrance to those whom He should send as a scourge. The Prophet combines purposely things incompatible, the terrible heavy bounding of the scythed chariot, and the light speed with which these countless hosts should in their flight bound over the tops of the mountains, where God had made no path for man. Countless in number, boundless in might, are the instruments of God. The strongest national defences give no security. Where then is safety, save in fleeing from God displeased to God appeased?

6. *Before their face the people shall be much pained.* The locust being such a scourge of God, good reason have men to be terrified at their approach; and those are most terrified who have most felt the affliction. In Abyssinia, some province of which was desolated every year, one relates[19], "When the locusts travel, the people know of it a day before, not

[1] Remigius, ad loc. "as they relate," he adds, "into whose country they have been often wont to come."
[2] Lichtenstein, c. 46.
[3] Forskäl, p. 81.
[4] Morier, 2d Journey, p. 98.
[5] Nieuhoff, 2d. Emb. p. 29.
[6] Forbes, ii. 273.
[7] Schlatter. Pliny says (probably of some smaller sort which reached Italy,) "they fly with such clashing of wings, that they are believed to be other large winged creatures." xi. 35.
[8] Volney, i. 177.
[9] Beauplan, i. 599.
[10] Chénier, iii. 82.
[11] S. Cyr.
[12] Rev. ix. 9.
[13] It should be read, *Like the noise of chariots, on or over the tops of mountains shall they leap.*
[14] Herod. iii. 97.
[15] See Alison's Hist. of Europe, c. 53. beg.
[16] Ps. lxxviii. 54.
[17] 1 Kings xx. 23.
[18] Ps. cxxv. 2.
[19] Fr. Alvarez, c. 32. "In this part and in the whole seignory of Prester John, there is a very great plague of locusts, which destroy every fresh

Before CHRIST cir. 800.

7 They shall run like
mighty men; they shall
climb the wall like men of
war; and they shall march

Before CHRIST cir. 800.

because they see them, but they see the sun yellow and the ground yellow, through the shadow which they cast on it (their wings being yellow) and forthwith the people become as dead, saying, 'we are lost, for the Ambadas (so they call them) are coming.' I will say what I have seen three times; the first was at Barva. During three years that we were in this land, we often heard them say, 'such a realm, such a land, is destroyed by locusts:' and when it was so, we saw this sign, the sun was yellow, and the shadow on the earth the same, and the whole people became as dead." "The Captain of the place called Coiberia came to me with men, Clerks, and Brothers [Monks] to ask me, for the love God, to help them, that they were all lost through the locusts." "[1] There were men, women, children, sitting among these locusts, [the young brood] as stupefied. I said to them 'why do you stay there, dying? Why do you not kill these animals, and avenge you of the evil which their parents have done you? and at least when dead, they will do you no more evil.' They answered, that they had no courage to resist a plague which God gave them for their sins. We found the roads full of men, women, and children, (some of these on foot, some in arms) their bundles of clothes on their heads, removing to some land where they might find provisions. It was pitiful to see them." Burkhardt relates of S. Arabia, "[2] The Bedouins who occupy the peninsula of Sinai are frequently driven to despair by the multitudes of locusts, which constitute a land-plague. They remain there generally for forty or fifty days, and then disappear for the rest of the year." Pliny describes their approach, "[3] they overshadow the sun, the nations looking up with anxiety, lest they should cover their lands. For their strength suffices, and as if it were too little to have passed seas, they traverse immense tracts, and overspread them with a cloud, fatal to the harvest."

All faces shall gather blackness. Others, of high-authority, have rendered, shall *withdraw* [their] *beauty*[4]. But the word signifies to *collect together*, in order that what is so collected should be present, not absent[5]; and so is very different from another saying, *the stars shall withdraw their shining*[6]. He expresses how the faces contract a livid color from anxiety and fear, as Jeremiah says of the Nazarites[7], *Their visage is darker than blackness.* "[8] The faces are clothed with lurid hue of coming death; hence they not only grow pale, but are blackened." A slight fear drives the fresh hue from the cheek: the livid hue comes only with the deepest terror. So Isaiah says[9]; *they look amazed one to the other; faces of flame are their faces.*

green thing most grievously. Their multitude is past belief, they cover the ground and fill the air; they take away the brightness from the sun. I say again, it would not be a thing to be believed, if one had not seen it. They are not general in all the realms every year; for if they were, the land would be desert, according to the destruction which they make; but in one year they are in one part; in another year, in another;—sometimes in 2 or 3 parts of these provinces."

7. *They shall run like mighty men.* They are on God's message, and they linger not, *but rejoice to run their course*[10]. "The height of walls cannot hinder the charge of the mighty; they enter not by the gates but over the walls[11]," as of a city taken by assault. Men can mount a wall few at a time; the locusts scale much more steadily, more compactly, more determinately, and irresistibly. The picture unites the countless multitude, condensed march, and entire security of the locust with the might of warriors.

They shall march every one on his ways. There is something awful and majestic in the well-ordered flight of the winged locusts, or their march while yet unwinged. "This," says S. Jerome, "we have seen lately in this province [Palestine]. For when the hosts of locusts came, and filled the air between heaven and earth, they flew, by the disposal of God ordaining, in such order, as to hold each his place, like the minute pieces of mosaic, fixed in the pavement by the artist's hands, so as not to incline to one another a hair's breadth." "You may see the locust," says Theodoret, "like enemies, both mounting the walls, and marching on the roads, and not allowing itself to be dispersed by any violence, but making the assault by a sort of concert." "It is said," says S. Cyril, "that they go in rank, and fly as in array, and are not severed from each other, but attend one on the other, like sisters, nature infusing into them this mutual love." "[12] They seemed to be impelled by one common instinct, and moved in one body, which had the appearance of being organized by a leader." "[13] There is something frightful in the appearance of these locusts proceeding in divisions, some of which are a league in length and 200 paces in breadth." "[14] They continued their journey, as if a signal had been actually given

[1] Ib. c. 33. [2] Burckhardt, Notes, ii. 91.
[3] N. H. xi. 35.
[4] Abulwalid, Aben Ezra, see Poc.
[5] Jos. Kimchi, Ib.
[6] אספו (ii. 10, iii. 15.) The *their* had also needed to be expressed.
[7] Lam. iv. 8. see Margin. [8] Oros.
[9] xiii. 8. [10] Ps. xix. 5. [11] S. Jer.
[12] Morier, p. 98. [13] Constitutionnel, 1841.
[14] Philos. Trans. xlvi. 9. p. 31.

Before CHRIST cir. 800.

every one on his ways, and they shall not break their ranks:

8 Neither shall one thrust another; they shall walk every one in his path:

them to march." So, of the young brood it is related; "[1] In June, their young broods begin gradually to make their appearance; no sooner were any of them hatched than they immediately collected themselves together, each of them forming a compact body of several hundred yards square, which, marching afterward directly forward, climbed over trees, walls and houses, ate up every plant in their way, *and let nothing escape them.*" "[2] They seemed to march in regular battalions, crawling over everything that lay in their passage, in one straight front." So the judgments of God hold on their course, each going straight to that person for whom God in the awful wisdom of His justice ordains it. No one judgment or chastisement comes by chance. Each is directed and adapted, weighed and measured, by Infinite Wisdom, and reaches just that soul, for which God appointed it, and no other, and strikes upon it with just that force which God ordains it. As we look on, God's judgments are like a heavy sleet of arrows; yet as each arrow, shot truly, found the mark at which it was aimed, so, and much more, does each lesser or greater judgment, sent by God, reach the heart for which He sends it and pierces it just as deeply as He wills.

8. When *they fall upon the sword* [lit. *among the darts*] *they shall not be wounded.* It may be that the Prophet would describe how the locust seems armed as in a suit of armor. As one says, "[3] Their form was wondrous; they had a sort of gorget round their neck like a lancer, and a helm on their head, such as soldiers wear." But, more, he exhibits their indomitableness and impenetrableness, how nothing checks, nothing retards, nothing makes any impression upon them. "[4] They do not suffer themselves to be impeded by any obstacles, but fly boldly on, and are drowned in the sea when they come to it." "[5] When on a march during the day, it is utterly impossible to turn the direction of a troop, which is generally with the wind." "[6] The guard of the Red Town attempted to stop their irruption into Transylvania by firing at them; and indeed when the balls and shot swept through the swarm, they gave way and divided; but having filled up their ranks in a moment, they proceeded on their journey." And in like way of the young swarms; "[7] The inhabitants, to stop their progress, made trenches all over their fields and gardens and filled them with water; or else, placing in a row great quantities of heath, stubble, and such like combustible matter, they set them on fire on the approach of the locusts. But all this was to no purpose, for the trenches were quickly filled up, and the fires put out by infinite swarms, succeeding one another; whilst the front seemed regardless of danger, and the van pressed on so close, that a retreat was impossible." "[8] Like waves, they roll over one another on and on, and let themselves be stopped by nothing. Russians and Germans try many means with more or less success against them, when they come from the waste against the cornlands. Bundles of straw are laid in rows and set on fire before them; they march in thick heaps into the fire, but this is often put out thro' the great mass of the animals and those advancing from behind march away over the corpses of their companions, and continue the march." "[9] Their number was astounding; the whole face of the mountain was black with them. On they came like a living deluge. We dug trenches, and kindled fires, and beat and burned to death heaps upon heaps, but the effort was utterly useless. Wave after wave rolled up the mountain side, and poured over rocks, walls, ditches and hedges, those behind covering up and bridging over the masses already killed. After a long and fatiguing contest, I descended the mountain to examine the *depth* of the column, but I could not see to the end of it." "It was perfectly appalling to watch this animated river, as it flowed *up* the road and ascended the hill." Both in ancient and modern times, armies have been marched against them [10]; but in vain, unless they destroyed them, before they were full-grown.

Since the very smallest of God's judgments are thus irreversible, since creatures so small

[1] Shaw, p. 237.
[2] Morier, p. 100.
[3] Nieuhoff, 2d. Emb. p. 29.
[4] Sparrman, Cape of G. Hope, i. 366.
[5] Barrow, p. 258. [6] Phil. Trans.
[7] Shaw, l. c. p. 257. [8] Schlatter.
[9] Thomson, The Land and the Book, ii. 103.
[10] "The inhabitants of Asia, as well as Europe, sometimes take the field against locusts with all the dreadful apparatus of war. The Bashaw of Tripoli in Syria, some years ago, raised 4000 soldiers against these insects, and ordered those to be hanged who refused to go." Hasselq. p. 447. "In Cyrenaica, there is a law to wage war with them thrice in the year; first crushing the eggs, then the young, then when full grown; whoso neglects this, lies under the penalty of a deserter. At Lemnos too a certain measure is filled, which each is to bring of these creatures killed, to the magistrates. In Syria too, they are compelled, under military command, to kill them." Plin. xi. 35. "The marches cannot be stopped; only quite early, during the dew, when the locust can neither fly nor hop, they must be killed in masses." Ersch, 34.

Before CHRIST cir. 800.

and *when* they fall upon
the || sword, they shall not
be wounded.

9 They shall run to and
fro in the city; they shall
run upon the wall, they
shall climb up upon the
houses; they shall [o] enter
in at the windows [p] like a
thief.

|| Or, *dart.*

[o] Jer. 9. 21.
[p] John 10. 1.

---

cannot be turned aside, since we cannot turn away the face of one of the least of our Master's servants, since they are each as a *man of might* [1] (so he calls them, it is the force of the word rendered *each*) what of the greater? what of the whole?

9. *They shall run to and fro in the city.* "*The* city" is questionless Jerusalem. So to the Romans, "the city" meant Rome; to the Athenians, Athens; among ourselves, "town" or "the city" are idiomatic names for the whole of London or "the city of London." In Wales "town" is, with the country-people, the neighboring town with which alone they are familiar. There is no ambiguity in the living language. In Guernsey, one who should call Port St. Pierre by any other name than "the town," would betray himself to be a stranger. In Hosea, and Amos, prophets for Israel, *the city* is Samaria [2]. In Solomon [3] and the prophets of Judah [4], *the city* is Jerusalem; and that the more, because it was not only the capital, but the centre of the worship of the One True God. Hence it is called *the city of God* [5], *the city of the Lord* [6], then *the city of the Great King* [7], *the holy city* [8]; and God calls it *the city I have chosen out of all the tribes of Israel* [9], *the city of righteousness* [10]. So our Lord spake [11], *go ye into the city*, and perhaps, [12] *tarry ye in the city.* So do His Evangelists [13], and so does Josephus [14].

All around corresponds with this. Joel had described their approach; they had come over "the tops of *the* mountains," those which protected Jerusalem; and now he describes them scaling "*the* wall," "mounting *the* houses," "entering *the* windows," "running to and fro in *the* city." Here the description has reached its height. The city is given over to those who assault it. There remaineth nothing more, save the shaking of the heaven and the earth.

They shall enter in at the windows. So in that first great judgment, in which God employed the locust, He said, [15] *They shall cover the face of the earth, that one cannot be able to see the earth; and they shall fill thy houses, and the houses of all thy servants, and the houses of all the Egyptians.* "[16] For nothing denies a way to the locusts, inasmuch as they penetrate fields, cornlands, trees, cities, houses, yea, the retirement of the bed-chambers." "Not that they who are victors, have the fear which thieves have, but as thieves are wont to enter through windows, and plunder secretly, so shall these, if the doors be closed, to cut short delay, burst with all boldness through the windows." "[17] We have seen this done, not by enemies only, but often by locusts also. For not only flying, but creeping up the walls also, they enter the houses through the openings for light." "[18] A.D. 784, there came the flying locust, and wasted the corn and left its offspring; and this came forth and crawled, and scaled walls and entered houses by windows and doors; and if it entered the house on the S. side, it went out on the N.; together with herbs and trees it devoured also woolen clothing, and men's dresses." Modern travelers relate the same. "[19] They entered the inmost recesses of the houses, were found in every corner, stuck to our clothes and infested our food." "[20] They overwhelm the province of Nedjd sometimes to such a degree, that having destroyed the harvest, they penetrate by thousands into the private dwellings, and devour whatsoever they can find, even the leather of the water-vessels." "[21] In June 1646, at Novogorod it was prodigious to behold them, because they were hatched there that spring, and being as yet scarce able to fly, the ground was all covered, and the air so full of them, that I could not eat in my chamber without a candle, all the houses being full of them, even the stables, barns, chambers, garrets, and cellars. I caused cannon-powder and sulphur to be burnt, to expel them, but all to no purpose. For when the door was opened, an infinite number came in, and the others went fluttering about; and it was a troublesome thing when a man went abroad, to be hit on the face by

---

[1] גבר.
[2] Hos. xi. 9. Am. iii. 6.
[3] Ps. lxxii. 16. Prov. i. 21. viii. 3.
[4] Mic. vi. 9. Lam. i. 1, &c. Ezek. vii. 23. xxxiii. 21.
[5] Ps. xlvi. 4. xlviii. 1, 8. lxxxvii. 3.
[6] Ps. ci. 8. Is. lx. 14.
[7] Ps. xlviii. 2. S. Matt. v. 35.
[8] Is. xlviii. 2. lii. 1. Neh. xi. 1, 18. Dan. ix. 24.
[9] 1 Kings xi. 32.
[10] Is. i. 26.
[11] S. Matt. xxvi. 18. S. Mark xiv. 13. S. Luke xxii. 10.
[12] S. Luke xxiv. 49. Important MSS. omit "Jerusalem."
[13] S. Matt. xxi. 17, 18. xxviii. 11. S. Mark xi. 1, 19. S. Luke xix. 41. Acts vii. 58. S. John xix. 20.
[14] Ant. x. 31, no mention of Jerusalem having immediately preceded. He calls Manasseh's mother πολῖτις, "a citizen," i. e. of Jerusalem.
[15] Ex. x. 5, 6.
[16] S. Jerome, ad loc.
[17] Theod. ad loc.
[18] Barh. Chron. Syr. p. 134.
[19] Morier, p. 100.
[20] Burckhardt, Notes, ii. 90.
[21] Beauplan, p. 599.

Before CHRIST cir. 800.

q Ps. 18. 7.
r Is. 13. 10. Ezek. 32. 7. ver. 31. ch. 3. 15. Matt. 24. 29.

10 [q] The earth shall quake before them; the heavens shall tremble: [r] the sun and the moon shall be dark, and the stars shall withdraw their shining:

11 [s] And the Lord shall

Before CHRIST cir. 800.

s Jer. 25. 30. ch. 3. 16. Amos 1 2.

those creatures, on the nose, eyes, or cheeks, so that there was no opening one's mouth, but some would get in. Yet all this was nothing; for when we were to eat, they gave us no respite; and when we went to cut a piece of meat, we cut a locust with it, and when a man opened his mouth to put in a morsel, he was sure to chew one of them." The Eastern windows, not being glazed but having at most a lattice-work[1], presented no obstacle to this continuous inroad. All was one stream of infesting, harassing foes.

As the windows are to the house, so are the senses and especially the sight to the soul. As the strongest walls and battlements and towers avail not to keep out an enemy, if there be an opening or chink through which he can make his way, so, in vain is the protection of God's Providence or His Grace[2], if the soul leaves the senses unguarded to admit unchallenged sights, sounds, touches, which may take the soul prisoner. "[3] *Death*, says Jeremiah[4], *entereth through the window*. Thy window is thy eye. If thou seest, to lust, death hath entered in; if thou hearest enticing words, death hath entered in: if softness gain possession of thy senses, death has made his way in." The arrow of sin is shot through them. "[5] When the tongue of one introduces the virus of perdition, and the ears of others gladly drink it in, *death enters in*; while with itching ears and mouth men minister eagerly to one another the deadly draught of detraction, *death enters in at the windows*." "[6] Eve had not touched the forbidden tree, except she had first looked on it heedlessly. With what control must we in this dying life restrain our sight, when the mother of the living came to death through the eyes! The mind of the Prophet, which had been often lifted up to see hidden mysteries, seeing heedlessly another's wife, was darkened," and fell. "To keep purity of heart, thou must guard the outward senses." An enemy is easily *kept out* by the barred door or window, who, having entered in unawares, can only by strong effort and grace be *forced out*. "It is easier," said the heathen philosopher[7], "to forbid the beginnings of feelings than to control their might."

Like a thief, i. e. they should come unawares, so as to take men by surprise, that there should be no guarding against them. As this is the close of this wonderful description, it may be that he would, in the end, describe the suddenness and inevitableness of God's judgments when they do come, and of the final judgment. It is remarkable that our Lord, and His Apostles from Him adopt this image of the Prophet, in speaking of the coming of the Day of Judgment and His own. *Behold I come as a thief. This know, that if the goodman of the house had known what hour the thief would come, he would have watched. Be ye therefore ready also; for the Son of man cometh at an hour when ye think not. Yourselves know perfectly that the Day of the Lord so cometh as a thief in the night. Ye are not in darkness, that that Day should overtake you as a thief*[8].

10. *The earth shall quake before them.* "Not," says S. Jerome, "as though locusts or enemies had power to move the heavens or to shake the earth; but because, to those under trouble, for their exceeding terror, the heaven seems to fall and the earth to reel. But indeed, for the multitude of the locusts which cover the heavens, sun and moon shall be turned into darkness, and the stars shall withdraw their shining, while the cloud of locusts interrupts the light, and allows it not to reach the earth." Yet the mention of moon and stars rather suggests that something more is meant than the locusts, who, not flying by night except when they cross the sea, do not obscure either. Rather, as the next verse speaks of God's immediate, sensible, Presence, this verse seems to pass from the image of the locusts to the full reality, and to say that heaven and earth should shake at the judgments of God, before He appeareth. Our Lord gives the same description of the forerunners of the Day of Judgment[9]; *there shall be signs in the sun and in the moon and in the stars; and upon the earth distress of nations with perplexity; the sea and the waves roaring, men's hearts failing them for fear and for looking after those things which are coming on the earth; for the powers of heaven shall be shaken.*

11. *And the Lord shall utter His voice.* The Prophet had described at length the coming

[1] S. Jerome, in Ezek. xli. 16. אֲרֻבָּה and הרכים are both derived from "twisting" and so reticulating.
[2] from Lap. on Jer.
[3] S. Ambr. de fug Sæc. § 3
[4] ix. 21.
[5] S. Bern. in Cant. S. 24.
[6] from S. Greg. on Job L. xxi. § 4.
[7] Senec. Ep. 96. L.
[8] Rev. xvi. 15. (add iii. 3.) S. Matt. xxiv. 43, 44. S. Luke xii. 39. 1 Thess. v. 2. 2 Pet. iii. 10.
[9] S. Luke xxi. 25, 6.

Before CHRIST cir. 800.

[t] ver. 25.
[u] Jer. 50. 34. Rev. 18. 8.

utter his voice before [t] his army: for his camp *is* very great: [u] for *he is* strong that executeth his word: for the [x] day of the LORD *is* great and very terrible; and [y] who can abide it?

Before CHRIST cir. 800.

[x] Jer. 30. 7. Amos 5. 18. Zeph. 1. 15.
[y] Num. 24. 23. Mal. 3. 2.

of God's judgments, as a mighty army. But lest amid the judgments, men should, (as they often do) forget the Judge, he represents God, as commanding this His army, gathering, ordering, marshalling, directing them, giving them the word, when and upon whom they should pour themselves. Their presence was a token of His. They should neither anticipate that command, nor linger. But as an army awaits the command to move, and then, the word being given, rolls on instantly, so God's judgments await the precise moment of His Will, and then fall. *The voice of the Lord* is elsewhere used for the thunder; because in it He seems to speak in majesty and terror to the guilty soul. But here the voice refers, not to us, but to the army, which He is imaged as marshalling; as Isaiah, referring perhaps to this place, says *The Lord of hosts mustereth the host of the battle*[1]. God had spoken, and His people had not obeyed; now He speaks not to them any more, but to their enemies. He calls the Medes and Persians, *My sanctified ones, My mighty ones*[2], when they were to exercise His judgments on Babylon; and our Lord calls the Romans His armies. *He sent forth His armies and destroyed those murderers and burned up their city*[3]. Then follow as threefold ground of terror. *For His camp is very great.* All the instruments wherewith God punishes sin, are pictured as His one camp, each going, as *He* commands, *Who bringeth forth the host* of heaven *by number: He calleth them all by names, by the greatness of His might, for that He is strong in power; not one faileth*[4]. For he is *strong, that executeth His word,* or, *for* it (His camp) is *strong, executing His word.* Weak though His instruments be in themselves, they are mighty when they do His commands, for He empowers them, as S. Paul saith, *I can do all things through Christ instrengthening me*[5]. *For the Day of the Lord* is *great,* great, on account of the great things done in it. As those are called *evil days, an evil time,* in which evil comes; as it is called *an acceptable time;* in which we may be accepted; so the Day of God's judgment is *great and very terrible,* on account of the great and terrible acts of His justice done in it. *Who can abide it?* The answer is implied in the question. "No one, unless God enable him."

This is the close of the threatened woe. The close, so much beyond any passing scourge of any created destroyer, locusts or armies, suggests the more what has been said already, that the Prophet is speaking of the whole aggregate of God's judgments unto the Day of Judgment.

"[6] The Lord saith, that He will send an Angel with the sound of a trumpet, and the Apostle declares that the resurrection of the dead shall take place amid the sound of a trumpet. In the Revelation of John too, we read that the seven Angels received seven trumpets, and as they sounded in order, that was done which Scripture describes. The priests and teachers accordingly are here bidden to lift up their voice like a trumpet in Zion, that is, the Church, that so all the inhabitants of the earth may be troubled or confounded, and this confusion may draw them to Salvation. By *the Day of the Lord,* understand the Day of judgment, or the day when each departeth out of the body. For what will be to all in the Day of judgment, this is fulfilled in each in the day of death. It is a *day of darkness and gloominess, a day of clouds and of thick darkness,* because everything will be full of punishment and torment. The *great and strong people* of the angels will come, to render to each according to his works; and as the rising morn first seizes the mountains, so judgment shall begin with the great and mighty, so that *mighty men shall be mightily tormented*[7]. *There hath not been ever the like, neither shall be any more after it.* For all evils, contained in ancient histories and which have happened to men, by inundation of the sea, or overflow of rivers, or by pestilence, disease, famine, wild beasts, ravages of enemies, cannot be compared to the Day of judgment. *A fire devoureth,* or *consumeth before* this people, to consume in us *hay, wood, stubble.* Whence it is said of God[8], *thy God is a consuming fire.* And *after* him *a flame burneth,* so as to leave nothing unpunished. Whomsoever this people toucheth not, nor findeth in him what is to be burned, shall be likened to the garden of God, and the paradise of pleasure, i. e. of Eden. If it burn any, it will reduce this (as it were) wilderness to dust and ashes, nor can any escape its fury. For they shall run to and fro to torture those over whom they shall receive power, like horsemen flying hither and thither. Their sound shall be terrible, as *chariots* hurrying along level places, and

[1] Is. xiii. 4.
[2] Ib. 3.
[3] S. Matt. xxii. 7.
[4] Is. xl. 26.
[5] Phil. iv. 13.
[6] S. Jer.
[7] Wisd. vi. 6.
[8] Deut. iv. 24.

Before CHRIST cir. 800.

12 ¶ Therefore also now, saith the LORD, [z] turn ye *even* to me with all your heart, and with fasting, and with weeping, and with mourning:

Before CHRIST cir. 800.

[z] Jer. 4. 1. Hos. 12. 6. & 14. 1.

upon the tops of the mountains they *shall leap,* longing to torment all who are lofty and set on high in the Church. And since *before them there is a devouring fire,* they will destroy everything, *as the fire devoureth the stubble.* They shall come to punish, *as a strong people in battle array.* Such will be the fear, of all, such the conscience of sinners, that none shall shine or have any brightness of joy, but his face shall be turned into darkness. They shall not turn aside, in fulfilling the office enjoined them, but each shall carry on the punishments on sinners entrusted to him.—At the presence of that people, *the earth shall quake* and *the heavens tremble.* For *heaven and earth shall pass away, but the word of the Lord shall endure for ever.* The sun and moon also shall not endure to see the punishments of the miserable, and shall remove and, for bright light, shall be shrouded in terrible darkness. *The stars also shall withdraw their shining,* in that the holy also shall not without fear behold the presence of the Lord. Amid all this, *The Lord shall utter His voice* before His army. For as the Babylonians, in punishing Jerusalem, are called the army of God, so the evil angels (of whom it is written [1], *He cast upon them the fierceness of His anger, wrath, and indignation, and trouble, by sending evil angels among them*) are called the army of God and His camp, in that they do the Will of God."

The Day of the Lord, is great and terrible, of which it is written elsewhere [2], *to what end do ye desire the Day of the Lord? it is darkness and not light and very terrible,* and few or none *can abide it,* but will furnish some ground of severity against himself.

12. *Therefore* [*And*] *now also.* All this being so, one way of escape there is, true repentance. As if God said [3], "All this I have therefore spoken, in order to terrify you by My threats. Wherefore *turn unto Me with all your hearts,* and shew the penitence of your minds *by fasting and weeping and mourning,* that, fasting now, ye may *be filled* hereafter; *weeping now,* ye may *laugh* hereafter; *mourning now,* ye may hereafter be *comforted* [4]. And since it is your wont to *rend your garments* in sorrow, I command you to rend, not them but your hearts which are full of sin, which, like bladders, unless they be opened, will burst of themselves. And when ye have done this, return unto the Lord your God, whom your former sins alienated from you; and despair not of pardon for the greatness of your guilt, for mighty mercy will blot out mighty sins."

"[5] The strict Judge cannot be overcome, for He is Omnipotent; cannot be deceived, for He is Wisdom; cannot be corrupted, for He is Justice; cannot be sustained, for He is Eternal; cannot be avoided, for He is everywhere. Yet He can be entreated, because He is Mercy; He can be appeased, because He is Goodness; He can cleanse, because He is the Fountain of grace; He can satisfy, because He is the Bread of life; He can soothe, because He is the Unction from above; He can beautify, because He is Fullness; He can beatify because He is Bliss. Turned from Him, then, and fearing His Justice, turn ye to Him, and flee to His Mercy. Flee from Himself to Himself, from the rigor of Justice to the Bosom of Mercy. The Lord Who is to be feared saith it. He Who is Truth enjoins what is just, profitable, good, *turn ye to Me,* &c."

Turn ye even *to Me,* i. e. so as to return *quite to* [6] God, not halting, not turning half way, not in some things only, but from all the lusts and pleasures to which they had turned from God. "[7] *Turn quite to Me,* He saith, *with all your heart,* with your whole mind, whole soul, whole spirit, whole affections. For I am the Creator and Lord of the heart and mind, and therefore will, that that whole should be given, yea, given back, to Me, and endure not that any part of it be secretly stolen from Me to be given to idols, lusts or appetites." "It often happens with some people," says S. Gregory [8], "that they stoutly gird themselves up to encounter some vices, but neglect to overcome others, and while they never rouse themselves up against these, they are re-establishing against themselves, even those which they had subdued." Others, "in resolve, aim at right courses, but are ever doubling back to their wonted evil ones, and being, as it were, drawn out without themselves, they return back to themselves in a round, desiring good ways, but never forsaking evil ways." In contrast to these half conversions, he bids us turn to God with our whole inmost soul, so that all our affections should be fixed on God, and all within us, by a strong union, cleave to Him; for "in whatever degree our affections are scattered among created things, so far is the conversion of the heart to God impaired."

[1] Ps. lxxviii. 49. [2] from Am. v. 18. [3] S. Jer.
[4] S. Luke vi. 21. S. Matt. v. 4. [5] Hugo de S. V.

[6] The force of עַד. See on Hos. xiv. 2. [7] Lap.
[8] on Job vii. § 35. 34. p. 390. O. T.

Before CHRIST cir. 800.

13 And [a]rend your
heart and not [b]your garments, and turn unto the
LORD your God: for he *is*

Before CHRIST cir. 800.

a Ps. 34. 18. & 51. 17.   b Gen. 37. 34. 2 Sam. 1. 11. Job. 1. 20.

"Look diligently," says S. Bernard[1], "what thou lovest, what thou fearest, wherein thou rejoicest or art saddened, and under the rags of conversion thou wilt find a heart perverted. The whole heart is in these four affections; and of these I think we must understand that saying, *turn to* the Lord *with all thy heart.* Let then thy love be converted to Him, so that thou love nothing whatever save Himself, or at least for Him. Let thy fear also be converted unto Him; for all fear is perverted, whereby thou fearest anything besides Him or not for Him. So too let thy joy and sorrow equally be converted unto Him. This will be, if thou only grieve or joy according to Him." "[2] There is a conversion with the whole heart, and another with a part. The conversion with the whole heart God seeketh, for it suffices to salvation. That which is partial he rejecteth, for it is feigned and far from salvation. In the heart, there are three powers, reason, will, memory; reason, of things future; will, of things present; memory, of things past. For reason seeks things to come; the will loves things present; memory retains things past. Reason illumines; will loves; memory retains. When then the reason seeks that Highest Good and finds, the will receives and loves, the memory anxiously keeps and closely embraces, then the soul turns with the whole heart to God. But when the reason slumbers and neglects to seek heavenly things, or the will is tepid and cares not to love them, or the memory is torpid and is careless to retain them, then the soul acts false, falling first into the vice of ignorance, secondly into the guilt of negligence, thirdly into the sin of malice. In each, the soul acts false; else ignorance would be expelled by the light of reason, and negligence be excluded by zeal of will, and malice be quenched by diligence of memory [of Divine things]. Reason then seeking begetteth knowledge; will embracing produceth love; memory holding fast, edification. The first produceth the light of knowledge, the second, the love of righteousness; the third preserveth the treasure of grace. This is that conversion of heart, which God requireth; this is that, which sufficeth to salvation."

And with fasting. "[3] In their returning to Him, it is required in the first place, that it be with the heart in the inward man, yet so that the outward man is not left unconcerned, but hath his part also, in performance of such things whereby he may express, how the inward man is really affected; and so by the concurrence of both is true conversion made up. *With fasting,* which shall make for the humbling of the heart, which pampering of the flesh is apt to puff up and make insensible of its own condition, and forgetful of God and His service, as Jeshurun who, being *waxed fat, kicked, and forsook the God which made him and lightly esteemed the God of his salvation*[4]. To waiting then on God's service and prayer, it is usually joined in Scripture, as almost a necessary accompaniment, called for by God, and by holy men practised."

And with weeping and with mourning; i. e. by *beating*[5] on the breast, (as the word originally denoted,) *as the publican smote upon his breast*[6], and *all the people that came together to that sight* [of Jesus on the Cross], *beholding the things which were done, smote their breasts*[7]. "[8] These also, in themselves signs of grief, stir up in the heart more grief, and so have their effects on the person himself, for the increase of his repentance, as well as for shewing it." It also stirs up in others like passions, and provokes them also to repentance." "[9] These things, done purely and holily, are not conversion itself, but are excellent signs of conversion." "[10] We ought *to turn in fasting,* whereby vices are repressed, and the mind is raised. We ought to *turn in weeping,* out of longing for our home, out of displeasure at our faults, out of love to the sufferings of Christ, and for the manifold transgressions and errors of the world." "What avails it," says S. Gregory[11], "to confess iniquities, if the affliction of penitence follow not the confession of the lips? For three things are to be considered in every true penitent, conversion of the mind, confession of the mouth, and revenge for the sin. This third sort is as a necessary medicine, that so the imposthume of guilt, pricked by confession, be purified by conversion, and healed by the medicine of affliction. The sign of true conversion is not in the confession of the mouth, but in the affliction of penitence. For then do we see that a sinner is well converted, when by a worthy austerity of affliction he strives to efface what in speech he confesses. Wherefore John Baptist, rebuking the ill-converted Jews who flock to him says, *O generation of vipers—bring forth therefore fruits worthy of repentance.*"

13. *And rend your hearts and not your garments,* i. e. *not your garments* only[12]. The

1 Serm. 2. de Quadr. Lap. 2 Hugo de S. V. 3 Poc. 4 Deut. xxxii. 15. 5 ספד. 6 S. Luke xviii. 13. 7 Ib. xxiii. 48. 8 Poc. 9 Mont. ap. Poc. 10 Dion.

11 in 1 Reg. L. vi. c. 2. § 33. See Tertullian Note K. Oxf. Tr.

12 See on Hos. vi. 6.

Before CHRIST cir. 800.

[e] gracious and merciful, slow to anger, and of great kindness, and repenteth him of the evil.

Before CHRIST cir. 800.

[e] Ex. 34. 6. Ps. 86. 5, 15. Jonah 4. 2.

rending of the clothes was an expression of extraordinary uncontrollable emotion, chiefly of grief, of terror, or of horror. At least, in Holy Scripture it is not mentioned as a part of ordinary mourning, but only upon some sudden overpowering grief, whether public or private [1]. It was not used on occasion of death, unless there were something very grievous about its circumstances. At times it was used as an outward expression, one of deep grief, as when the leper was commanded to keep his clothes rent [2], or when David, to express his abhorrence at the murder of Abner, commanded *all the people with him, rend your clothes;* Ahab used it, with fasting and haircloth, on God's sentence by Elijah and obtained a mitigation of the temporal punishment of his sin; Jeremiah marvels that neither *the king,* Jehoiakim, *nor any of his servants, rent their garments* [3], on reading the roll containing the woes which God had by him pronounced against Judah. The holy garments of the priests were on no occasion to be rent [4]; (probably because the wholeness was a symbol of perfection, whence care was to be taken that the ephod should not accidentally be rent [5]) so that the act of Caiaphas was the greater hypocrisy [6]. He used it probably to impress his own blasphemous accusation on the people, as for a good end, the Apostles Paul and Barnabas rent their [7] clothes, when they heard that, after the cure of the impotent man, the priest of Jupiter with the people would have done sacrifice unto them. Since then apostles used this act, Joel plainly doth not forbid the use of such outward behavior, by which their repentance might be expressed, but only requires that it be done not in outward shew only, but accompanied with the inward affections. "[8] The Jews are bidden then to rend their hearts rather than their garments, and to set the truth of repentance in what is inward, rather than in what is outward." But since the rending of the garments was the outward sign of very vehement grief, it was no commonplace superficial sorrow, which the Prophet enjoined, but one which should pierce and rend the inmost soul, and empty it of its sins and its love for sin. [9] Any very grieving thing is said to cut one's heart, to "cut him to the heart." A truly penitent heart is called *a broken and a contrite heart.* Such a penitent rends and "rips up by a narrow search the recesses of the heart, to discover the abominations thereof," and pours out before God "the diseased and perilous stuff" pent up and festering there, "expels the evil thoughts lodged in it, and opens it in all things to the reception of Divine grace. This rending is no other than the spiritual circumcision to which Moses exhorts. Whence of the Jews, not thus rent in heart, it is written in Jeremiah [10], *All the nations are uncircumcised, and all the house of Israel are uncircumcised in heart.* This *rending* then is the casting out of the sins and passions."

And turn unto the Lord your God. God owns Himself as still *their* God, although they had turned and were gone from Him in sin and were alienated from Him. To Him, the true, Unchangeable God, if they returned, they would find Him still *their God. Return, ye backsliding children, I will heal your backsliding,* God saith by Jeremiah [11]; *Behold,* Israel answers, *we come unto Thee, for Thou* art *the Lord our God.*

For He is *very gracious and very merciful.* Both these words are intensive [12]. All the words, *very gracious, very merciful, slow to anger, and of great kindness,* are the same and in the same order as in that revelation to Moses, when, on the renewal of the two tables of the law, *the Lord descended in the cloud and proclaimed the name of the Lord* [13]. The words are frequently repeated, shewing how deeply that revelation sunk in the pious minds of Israel. They are, in part, pleaded to God by Moses himself [14]; David, at one time, pleaded them all to God [15]; elsewhere he repeats them of God, as in this place [16]. Nehemiah, in praising God for His forgiving mercies, prefixes the title, *God of pardons* [17], and adds, *and Thou forsakedst them not;* as Joel, for the special object here, adds, *and repenteth Him of the evil.* A Psalmist, and Hezekiah in his message to Isaiah, and Nehemiah in the course of that same prayer, repeat the two words of intense mercy, *very gracious and very merciful* [18], which are used of God only, except once by that same Psalmist [19], with the express object of shewing how the good man conformeth himself to God. The word *very gracious* ex-

[1] The instances are; Gen. xxxvii. 29, 34. xliv. 13. Num. xiv. 6. Josh. vii. 6. Jud. xi. 35. 1 Sam. iv. 12, 25. 2 Sam. i. 2, 11. iii. 31. xiii. 19, 31. xv. 32. 1 Kings xxi. 27. 2 Kings v. 7, 8. vi. 30. xi. 14. xviii. 37.. xix. 1. xxii. 11, 19. Ezr. ix. 3, 5. Esth. iv. 1. Job i. 20. ii. 12. Jer. xli. 5.

[2] Lev. xiii. 45. The word is not, as here, קרע, but פרם, used only in Leviticus.

[3] Jer. xxxvi. 24.

[4] Lev. x. 6. xxi. 10.

[5] Ex. xxviii. 32. xxxix. 23.

[6] S. Matt. xxvi. 65. S. Mark xiv. 63.

[7] Acts xiv. 14.

[8] Dion.

[9] Poc. and Dion.

[10] ix. 26.

[11] iii. 22.

[12] רחום חנון.

[13] Ex. xxxiv. 5, 6.

[14] Num. xiv. 18.

[15] Ps. lxxxvi. 15.

[16] Ps. ciii. 8. cxlv. 8.

[17] Neh. ix. 17.

[18] Ps. cxi. 4. 2 Chr. xxx. 9. Neh. ix. 31.

[10] Ps. cxii. 4.

Before CHRIST cir. 800.

14 [d] Who knoweth *if* he
will return and repent,
and leave [e] a blessing
behind him; *even* [f] a meat
offering and a drink offering
unto the LORD your
God?

15 ¶ [g] Blow the trumpet
in Zion, [h] sanctify a fast,
call a solemn assembly:

d Josh. 14. 12. 2 Sam. 12. 22. 2 Kings 19. 4. Amos 5. 15. Jonah 3. 9. Zeph. 2. 3.
e Is. 65. 8.
f Hag. 2. 19. ch. 1. 9. 13.
g Num. 10. 3. ver. 1.
h ch. 1. 14.

presses God's free love, whereby He sheweth Himself good to us; *very merciful* expresses the tender yearning of His love over our miseries [1]; *great kindness*, expresses God's tender love, as love. He first says, that God is *slow to anger* or *long-suffering*, enduring long the wickedness and rebellion of man, and waiting patiently for the conversion and repentance of sinners. Then he adds, that God is *abundant in kindness*, having manifold resources and expedients of His tender love, whereby to win them to repentance. Lastly He is *repentant of the evil*. The evil which He foretells, and at last inflicts, is (so to speak) against His Will, Who *willeth not that any should perish*, and, therefore, on the first tokens of repentance He *repenteth Him of the evil*, and doeth it not.

The words rendered, *of great kindness*, are better rendered elsewhere, *abundant, plenteous in goodness, mercy* [2]. Although the mercy of God is in itself one and simple, yet it is called *abundant* on account of its divers effects. For God knoweth how in a thousand ways to succor His own. Whence the Psalmist prays, *According to the multitude of Thy mercies, turn Thou unto me* [3]. *According to the multitude of Thy tender mercies, do away mine offences* [4].

14. *Who knoweth if He will return.* God has promised forgiveness of sins and of eternal punishment to those who turn to Him with their whole heart. Of this, then, there could be no doubt. But He has not promised either to individuals or to Churches, that He will remit the temporal punishment which He had threatened. He forgave David the sin. Nathan says, *The Lord also hath put away thy sin.* But he said at the same time, *the sword shall never depart from thy house* [5]; and the temporal punishment of his sin pursued him, even on the bed of death. David thought that the temporal punishment of his sin, in the death of the child, might be remitted to him. He used the same form of words as Joel [6], *I said, who can tell* whether *God will be gracious unto me, that the child may live?* But the child died. The king of Nineveh used the like words [7], *Who can tell if God will return and repent and turn away from His fierce anger, that we perish not?* And he was heard. God retained or remitted the temporal punishment, as He saw good for each. This of the Prophet Joel is of a mixed character. The *blessing* which they crave, he explains to be *the meat offering and the drink offering*, which had been *cut off or withholden from the house of their God*. For "[8] if He gave them wherewith to serve Him," after withdrawing it, it was clear that "He would accept of them and be pleased with their service." Yet this does not imply that He would restore all to them. A Jewish writer [9] notes that after the Captivity, "the service of sacrifices alone returned to them," but that "prophecy, [soon after], the ark, the Urim and Thummim, and the other things [the fire from heaven] were wanting there." As a pattern, however, to all times, God teaches them to ask first what belongs to His kingdom and His righteousness, and to leave the rest to Him. So long as the means of serving Him were left, there was hope of all. Where the Sacrament of the Body and Blood of Christ (whereof *the meat offering and the drink offering* were symbols) remains, there are "[10] the pledges of His love," the earnest of all other blessing.

He says, *leave a blessing behind Him*, speaking of God as one estranged, who had been long absent and who returns, giving tokens of His forgiveness and renewed good-pleasure. God often visits the penitent soul and, by some sweetness with which the soul is bathed, leaves a token of His renewed Presence. God is said to repent, not as though He varied in Himself, but because He deals variously with us, as we receive His inspirations and follow His drawings, or no.

15. Before, he had, in these same words [11], called to repentance, because the Day of the Lord was coming, was nigh, *a day of darkness, &c.* Now [12], because God is *gracious and merciful, slow to anger and plenteous in goodness*, he agains exhorts, *Blow ye the trumpet;* only the call is more detailed, that every sex and age should form one band of suppliants to the mercy of God. "[13] Most full abolition of sins is then obtained, when one prayer and one confession issueth from the whole Church. For since the Lord promiseth to the pious agreement of two or three, that He will grant whatever is so asked, what shall be denied to a people of many thousands, fulfilling together one observance, and supplicating in

1 See on Hos. ii. 19.
2 Ex. xxxiv. 6. Ps. lxxxvi. 15. ciii. 8.
3 Ps. xxv. 7, 16.
4 Ps. li. 1.
5 2 Sam. xii. 13, 10.
6 Ib. 22.
7 Jon. iii. 9.
8 Poc.
9 Abarb. in Poc.
10 Communion Service.
11 ii. 1. i. 14.
12 S. Jer.
13 S. Leo Serm. 3 de jej. 7 mens. § 3. Lap.

Before CHRIST cir. 800.

16 Gather the people, [i] sanctify the congregation, [k] assemble the elders, [l] gather the children, and those that suck the breasts: [m] let the bridegroom go forth of his chamber, and the bride out of her closet.

[i] Ex. 19. 10, 22.
[k] ch. 1. 14.
[l] 2 Chr. 20. 13.
[m] 1 Cor. 7. 5.

17 Let the priests, the ministers of the LORD, weep [n] between the porch and the altar, and let them say, [o] Spare thy people, O LORD, and give not thine heritage to reproach, that the heathen should || rule

Before CHRIST cir. 800.

[n] Ezek. 8. 16. Matt. 23. 35.
[o] Ex. 32. 11, 12. Deut. 9. 26–29.
|| Or, *use a byword against them.*

---

harmony through One Spirit?" "We come together," says Tertullian[1] of Christian worship, "in a meeting and congregation as before God, as though we would in one body sue Him by our prayers. This violence is pleasing to God."

16. *Sanctify the congregation.* "[2] Do what in you lies, by monishing, exhorting, threatening, giving the example of a holy life, that the whole people present itself holy before its God," "[3] lest your prayers be hindered, and a little leaven corrupt the whole lump."

Assemble the elders. "[4] The judgment concerned all; all then were to join in seeking mercy from God. None were on any pretence to be exempted; not the oldest, whose strength was decayed, or the youngest, who might seem not yet of strength." The old also are commonly freer from sin and more given to prayer.

Gather the children. "[4] He Who feedeth the young ravens when they cry, will not neglect the cry of poor children. He assigns as a reason, why it were fitting to spare Nineveh, the [5] *six-score thousand persons that could not discern between their right hand and their left.*" The sight of them who were involved in their parents' punishment could not but move the parents to greater earnestness. So when Moab and Ammon[6], *a great multitude, came against Jehoshaphat, he proclaimed a fast throughout all Judah, and Judah gathered themselves together to ask help of the Lord; even out of all the cities of Judah, they came to seek the Lord. And all Judah was standing before the Lord, their little ones also, their wives, and their children.* So it is described in the book of Judith, how "[7] with great vehemency did they humble their souls, both they and their wives and their children—and every man and woman and the little children—fell before the temple, and cast ashes upon their heads and spread out their sackcloth before the Face of the Lord."

Let the bridegroom go forth. He says not even, the married, or the newly married, he who had taken a new wife, but he uses the special terms of the marriage-day, *bridegroom and bride.* The new-married man was, during a year, exempted from going out to war, or from any duties which might *press upon him*[8]. But nothing was to free from this common affliction of sorrow. Even the just newly married, although it were the very day of the bridal, were to leave the marriage-chamber and join in the common austerity of repentance. It was mockery of God to spend in delights time consecrated by Him to sorrow. He says[9], *In that day did the Lord God of hosts call to weeping, and to mourning, and to baldness, and to girding with sackcloth. And behold joy and gladness—surely this iniquity shall not be purged from you till ye die, saith the Lord God of Hosts.* Whence, in times of fasting or prayer, the Apostle suggests the giving up of pure pleasures[10], *that ye may give yourselves to fasting and prayer.*

"[3] He then who, by chastisement in food and by fasting and alms, says that he is doing acts of repentance, in vain doth he promise this in words, unless he *go forth out of his chamber* and fulfill a holy and pure fast by a chaste penitence."

17. *Let the priests, the ministers of the Lord, weep between the porch and the altar.* The porch in this, Solomon's temple, was in fact a tower, in front of the Holy of Holies, of the same breadth with the Temple, viz. 20 cubits, and its depth half its breadth, viz. 10 cubits[11], and its height 120 cubits, the whole *overlaid within with pure gold*[12]. The brazen altar for burnt offerings stood in front of it[13]. The altar was of brass, twenty cubits square; and so, equal in breadth to the Temple itself, and ten cubits high[14]. The space then *between the porch and the altar* was inclosed on those two sides[15]; it became an inner part of the court of the priests. Through it the priests or the high priest passed, whenever they went to sprinkle the blood, typifying the Atonement, before the veil of the tabernacle, or for any other office of the tabernacle. It seems to have been a place of prayer for the priests. It is spoken of as an aggravation of the sins of those 25 idolatrous priests, that here, where they ought to worship God, they turned

---

[1] Apol. c. 39. p. 80. Oxf. Tr. [2] Lap. [3] S. Jer. [4] Poc. [5] Jon. iv. 11. [6] 2 Chr. xx. 1–4, 13. [7] iv. 9–11. [8] Deut. xxiv. 5. [9] Is. xxii. 12–14.

[10] 1 Cor. vii. 5. [11] 1 Kings vi. 3. [12] 2 Chr. iii. 4. [13] Ib. viii. 12. [14] Ib. iv. 1. [15] Ib. vii. 7.

Before CHRIST cir. 800.

[p] Ps. 42. 10. & 79. 10. & 115. 2. Mic. 7. 10.
[q] Zech. 1. 14. & 8. 2.
[r] Deut. 32. 36. Is. 60. 10.

over them: [p] wherefore
should they say among the
people, Where *is* their God?
18 ¶ Then will the
LORD [q] be jealous for his
land, [r] and pity his people.
19 Yea, the LORD will
answer and say unto his
people, Behold, I will send
you [s] corn, and wine, and
oil, and ye shall be satisfied therewith: and I will no
more make you a reproach
among the heathen:

Before CHRIST cir. 800.

[s] See ch. 1. 10. Mal. 3. 10, 11, 12.

---

their backs toward the Temple of the Lord, to worship the sun[1]. Here, in the exercise of his office, Zechariah was standing[2], when the Spirit of God came upon him and he rebuked the people and they stoned him. Here the priests, with their faces toward the Holy of Holies and the Temple which He had filled with His Glory, were to *weep*. Tears are a gift of God. In holier times, so did the priests weep at the Holy Eucharist in thought of the Passion and Precious Death of our Lord Jesus, which we then plead to God, that they bore with them, as part of their dress, linen wherewith to dry their tears[3].

And let them say. A form of prayer is provided for them. From this the words, *spare us, good Lord, spare thy people,* enter into the litanies of the Christian Church.

And give not thine heritage to reproach. The enmity of the heathen against the Jews was an enmity against God. God had avouched them as His people and His property. Their land was an heritage from God. God, in that He had separated them from the heathen, and revealed Himself to them, had made them His especial heritage. Moses[4], then Joshua[5], the Psalmists[6], plead with God, that His own power or will to save His people would be called in question, if he should destroy them, or give them up. God, on the other hand, tells them, that not for any deserts of theirs, but for His own Name's sake, He delivered them, lest the Heathen should be the more confirmed in their errors as to Himself[7]. It is part of true penitence to plead to God to pardon us, not for anything in ourselves, (for we have nothing of our own but our sins) but because we are the work of His hands, created in His image, the price of the Blood of Jesus, called by His Name.

That the heathen should rule over them. This, and not the rendering in the margin, *use a byword against them,* is the uniform meaning of the Hebrew phrase. It is not to be supposed that the Prophet Joel would use it in a sense contrary to the uniform usage of all the writers before him. Nor is there any instance of any other usage of the idiom in any later writer[8]. "The enigma which was closed," says St. Jerome, "is now opened. For who that people is, manifold and strong, described above under the name of the *palmerworm, the locust, the canker-worm* and the *catterpillar,* is now explained more clearly, *lest the heathen rule over them.* For the heritage of the Lord is given to reproach, when they serve their enemies, and the nations say, *Where is their God,* Whom they boasted to be their Sovereign and their Protector?" Such is the reproach ever made against God's people, when He does not visibly protect them, which the Psalmist says was as a sword in his bones[9]; his *tears* were his *meat day and night* while they said it. The Chief priests and scribes and elders fulfilled a prophecy by venturing so to blaspheme our Lord[10], *He trusted in God; let Him deliver Him now, if He will have Him.*

18. *Then will the Lord be jealous for His land.* Upon repentance, all is changed. Before, God seemed set upon their destruction. It was His great army which was ready to destroy them; He was at its head, giving the word. Now He is full of tender love for them, which resents injury done to them, as done to Himself. The word might more strictly perhaps be rendered, *And the Lord is jealous*[11]. He would shew how instantaneous the mercy and love of God for His people is, restrained while they are impenitent, flowing forth upon the first tokens of repentance. The word, *jealous for,* when used of God, jealous for My holy Name[12], jealous for Jerusalem[13], is used, when God resents evil which had been actually inflicted.

19. *I will send you corn, &c.* This is the beginning of the reversal of the threatened judgments. It is clear from this, and still

[1] Ezek. viii. 16.
[2] 2 Chr. xxiv. 20, 1. S. Matt. xxiii. 35.
[3] Amalar. de Eccl. Off. iii. 22.
[4] Ex. xxxii. 12. Num. xiv. 13–16. Deut. ix. 28, 9.
[5] Josh. vii. 9.
[6] Ps. lxxiv. lxxix. cxv.
[7] Ezek. xx. 5. xxxvi. 21–3.
[8] See Introd. to Joel, p. 102.
[9] Ps. xlii. 3, 10; add Ps. lxxix. 10. cxv. 2. Mic. vii. 16.
[10] S. Matt. xxvii. 43, from Ps. xxii. 8.
[11] It is not an absolute past. For the ו *conversive* only denotes a past, by connecting the word with some former past, as we could say in vivid description of the past, "then he goes." But here no past has preceded, except the prophetic past mixed with the future, in the description of the inroad of this scourge.
[12] Ezek. xxxix. 25.
[13] Zech. i. 14. viii. 2.

Before CHRIST cir. 800.

20 But [t] I will remove
far off from you [u] the
northern *army*, and will
drive him into a land barren and desolate, with his
face [x] toward the east sea,

[t] See Ex. 10. 19.
[u] Jer. 1. 14.
[x] Ezek. 47. 18. Zech. 14. 8

more from what follows, that the chastisements actually came, so that the repentance described, was the consequence, not of the exhortations to repentance, but of the chastisement. What was removed was the chastisement which had burst upon them, not when it was ready to burst. What was given, was what before had been taken away. So it ever was with the Jews; so it is mostly with the portions of the Christian Church or with individuals now. Seldom do they take warning of coming woe; when it has begun to burst, or has burst, then they repent and God gives them back upon repentance what He had withdrawn or a portion of it. So the Prophet seems here to exhibit to us a law and a course of God's judgments and mercies upon man's sin. He takes away both temporal and spiritual blessings symbolized here by the corn and wine and oil; upon repentance He restores them. "[1] Over and against the wasting of the land, he sets its richness; against hunger, fullness; against reproach, unperiled glory; against the cruelty and incursion of enemies, their destruction and putrefaction; against barrenness of fruits and aridity of trees, their fresh shoots and richness; against the hunger of the word and thirst for doctrine, he brings in the fountain of life, and the Teacher of righteousness; against sadness, joy; against confusion, solace; against reproaches, glory; against death, life; against ashes, a crown." "O fruitful and manly penitence! O noble maiden, most faithful intercessor for sins! A plank after shipwreck! Refuge of the poor, help of the miserable, hope of exiles, cherisher of the weak, light of the blind, solace of the fatherless, scourge of the petulant, axe of vices, garner of virtues. Thou who alone bindest the Judge, pleadest with the Creator, conquerest the Almighty. While overcome, thou overcomest; while tortured, thou torturest; while wounding, thou healest; while healthfully succumbing, thou triumphest gloriously. Thou alone, while others keep silence, mountest boldly the throne of grace. David thou leadest by the hand and reconcilest; Peter thou restorest; Paul thou enlightenest; the Publican, taken from the receipt of custom, thou boldly insertest in the choir of the Apostles; Mary, from a harlot, thou bearest aloft and joinest to Christ; the robber nailed to the cross, yet fresh from blood, thou introducest into Paradise. What more? At thy disposal is the court of heaven."

And I will no more make you a reproach. All the promises of God are conditional. They presuppose man's faithfulness. God's pardon is complete. He will not, He says, for these offences, or for any like offences, give them over to the heathen. So after the Captivity He no more made them a reproach unto the heathen, until they finally apostatized, and leaving their Redeemer, owned no king but Cæsar. They first gave themselves up; they chose Cæsar rather than Christ, and to be servants of Cæsar, rather than that *He* should not be crucified; and so God left them in *his* hands, whom they had chosen.

20. *And I will remove far off from you the northern* army. God speaks of the human agent under the figure of the locusts, which perish in the sea; yet so as to shew at once, that He did not intend the locust itself, nor to describe the mode in which He should overthrow the human oppressor. He is not speaking of the locust itself, for the Northern is no name for the locust which infested Palestine, since it came from the South; nor would the destruction of the locust be in two opposite seas, since they are uniformly driven by the wind into the sea, upon whose waves they alight and perish, but the wind would not carry them into two opposite seas; nor would the locust perish in a *barren and desolate land*, but would fly further; nor would it be said of the locust that he was destroyed, *Because he had done great things* [2]. But He represents to us, how this enemy should be driven quite out of the bounds of His people, so that he should not vex them more, but perish. The imagery is from the Holy Land. The *East sea* is the Dead Sea, once the fertile *vale of Siddim* [3], "[4] in which sea were formerly Sodom and Gomorrah, Admah and Zeboim, until God overthrew them." This, in the Pentateuch, is called *the salt sea* [5], or *the sea of the plain*, or *desert* [6], explained in Deuteronomy and Joshua to be *the salt sea* [7]; Ezekiel calls it *the East sea* [8], and in Numbers it is said of it [9], *your south border shall be the salt sea eastward. The utmost*, or rather, *the hinder sea* [10] (i. e. that which is behind one who is looking toward the East whose Hebrew name [11] is from "fronting" you) is the Mediterranean, "on whose shores are Gaza and Ascalon, Azotus and Joppa and Cæsarea." The *land barren and desolate*, lying

[1] Hugo de S. Victor.
[2] See Introduction to Joel, p. 153.
[3] Gen. xiv. 3.
[4] S. Jer.
[5] Gen. Ib. Num. xxxiv. 3, 12.

[6] Deut. iii. 17. iv. 49. Josh. iii. 16. xii. 3. xv. 25. xviii. 19, also in 2 Kings xiv. 25.
[7] Deut. iii. Josh. iii. xii.
[8] xlvii. 18.
[9] xxxiv. 3.
[10] Deut. xi. 24. xxxiv. 2.
[11] קדם.

Before CHRIST cir. 800.

y Deut. 11. 24.

and his hinder party
y toward the utmost sea,
and his stink shall come up,
and his ill savor shall
come up, because † he hath
done great things.

Before CHRIST cir. 800.

† Heb. *he hath magnified to do.*

between, is the desert of Arabia, the southern boundary of the Holy Land. The picture then seems to be, that the *Northern* foes filled the whole of Judæa, in numbers like the locust, and that God drove them violently forth, all along the bounds of the Holy Land, into the desert, the Dead Sea, the Mediterranean. S. Jerome relates a mercy of God in his own time which illustrates the image; but he writes so much in the language of Holy Scripture, that perhaps he only means that the locusts were driven into the sea, not into both seas. "In our times too we have seen hosts of locusts cover Judæa, which afterward, by the mercy of the Lord, when the priests and people, *between the porch and the altar*, i. e. between the place of the Cross and the Resurrection prayed the Lord and said, *spare Thy people*, a wind arising, were carried headlong *into the Eastern sea, and the utmost sea.*" Alvarez relates how, priests and people joining in litanies to God, He delivered them from an exceeding plague of locusts, which covered 24 English miles, as He delivered Egypt of old at the prayer of Moses. "[1] When we knew of this plague being so near, most of the Clerks of the place came to me, that I should tell them some remedy against it. I answered them, that I knew of no remedy except to commend themselves to God, and to pray Him to drive the plague out of the land. I went to the Embassador and told him that to me it seemed good that we should make a procession with the people of the land and that it might please our Lord God to hear us; it seemed good to the Embassador; and, in the morning of the next day, we collected the people of the place and all the Clergy; and we took our Altar-stone, and those of the place theirs, and our Cross and theirs, singing our litany, we went forth from the Church, all the Portuguese and the greater part of the people of the place. I said to them that they should not keep silence, but should, as we, cry aloud saying in their tongue Zio marinos, i. e. in our's, Lord Jesus Christ, have mercy on us. And with this cry and litany, we went through an open wheat-country for the space of one third of a league.—It pleased our Lord to hear the sinners, and while we were turning to the place, because their [the locusts'] road was toward the sea whence they had come, there were so many after us, that it seemed no otherwise than that they sought to break our ribs and heads with blows of stones, such were the blows they dealt us. At this time a great thunderstorm arose from toward the sea, which came in their face with rain and hail, which lasted three good hours; the river and brooks filled greatly; and when they had ceased to drive, it was matter of amazement, that the dead locusts on the bank of the great river measured two cubits high; and so for the rivulets, there was a great multitude of dead on their banks. On the next day in the morning there was not in the whole land even one live locust."

And his stink shall come up. The image is still from the locust. It, being such a fearful scourge of God, every individual full of activity and life repeated countlessly in the innumerable host, is, at God's will and in His time, cast by His word into the sea, and when thrown up by the waves on the shore, becomes in a few hours one undistinguishable, putrefying, heaving mass. Such does human malice and ambition and pride become, as soon as God casts aside the sinful instrument of His chastisement. Just now, a world to conquer could not satisfy it; superior to man, independent, it deems, of God. He takes away its breath, it is a putrid carcase. Such was Sennacherib's army; *in the evening* inspiring *terror; before the morning, he is not* [2]. *They were all dead corpses* [3].

The likeness stops here. For the punishment is at an end. The wicked and the persecutors of God's people are cut off, the severance has taken place. On the one side, there is the putrefying mass; on the other, the jubilee of thanksgiving. The gulf is fixed between them. The offensive smell of the corruption ascends; as Isaiah closes his prophecy, *the carcases* of the wicked, the perpetual prey of *the worm* and *the fire, shall be an abhorring* to *all flesh.* The righteous behold it, but it reaches them not, to hurt them. In actual life, the putrid exhalations at times have, among those on the sea-shore, produced a pestilence, a second visitation of God, more destructive than the first. This, however, has been but seldom. Yet what must have been the mass of decay of creatures so slight, which could produce a wide-wasting pestilence! What an image of the numbers of those who perish, and of the fetidness of sin! S. Augustine, in answer to the heathen who imputed all the calamities of the later Roman Empire to the displeasure of the gods, because the world had become Christian, says [4], "They themselves have recorded that the

[1] c. 32. [2] Is. xvii. 14. [3] Ib. xxxvii. 36.
[4] de Civ. Dei. iii. 71. fin. He is referring, doubtless, to Julius Obsequens, a heathen writer, (de prodig. c. xc.) "Immense armies of locusts in Africa, which, cast by the wind into the sea, and thrown up by the waves, through the intolerable

Before CHRIST cir. 800.

21 ¶ Fear not, O land; be glad and rejoice: for the LORD will do great things.

Before CHRIST cir. 800.

multitude of locusts was, even in Africa, a sort of prodigy, while it was a Roman province. They say that, after the locusts had consumed the fruits and leaves of trees, they were cast into the sea, in a vast incalculable cloud, which having died and being cast back on the shores, and the air being infected thereby, such a pestilence arose, that in the realm of Masinissa alone 800,000 men perished, and many more in the lands on the coasts. Then at Utica, out of 30,000 men in the prime of life who were there, they assert that 10 only remained." S. Jerome says of the locusts of Palestine [1]; "when the shores of both seas were filled with heaps of dead locusts which the waters had cast up, their stench and putrefaction was so noxious as to corrupt the air, so that a pestilence was produced among both beasts and men." Modern writers say [2], "The locusts not only produce a famine, but in districts near the sea where they had been drowned, they have occasioned a pestilence from the putrid effluvia of the immense numbers blown upon the coast or thrown up by the tides." "[3] We observed, in May and June, a number of these insects coming from the S. directing their course to the Northern shore; they darken the sky like a thick cloud, but scarcely have they quitted the shore before they who, a moment before, ravaged and ruined the country, cover the surface of the sea with their dead bodies, to the great distress of the Franks near the harbor, on account of the stench from such a number of dead insects, driven by the winds close to the very houses." "[4] All the full-grown insects were driven into the sea by a tempestuous N. W. wind, and were afterward cast upon the beach, where, it is said, they formed a bank of 3 or 4 feet high, extending—a distance of near 50 English miles. It is asserted that when this mass became putrid and the wind was S. E. the stench was sensibly felt in several parts of Sneuwberg. The column passed the houses of two of our party, who asserted that it continued without any interruption for more than a month." "[5] The South and East winds drive the clouds of locusts with violence into the Mediterranean,

smell produced a grievous pestilence to the cattle; and of man it is related that 800,000 perished through this plague." Orosius says, "In Numidia, 800,000 perished; on the sea coast, especially that near Carthage and Utica, it is said that more than 200,000 perished. In Utica itself, 30,000 soldiers, placed as a guard for all Africa, were destroyed. At Utica in one day, at one gate, more than 1500 of their corpses were carried out." (v. 11.)

[1] ad. loc. [2] Forbes, ii. 373. [3] Hasselquist, p. 445.
[4] Barrow, S. Afr. p. 239. [5] Volney, i. 278.
[6] ii. 21. Ps. cxxvi. 2, 3. 1 Sam. xii. 24.

and drown them in such quantities that when their dead are cast on the shore, they infect the air to a great distance." Wonderful image of the instantaneous, ease, completeness, of the destruction of God's enemies; a mass of active life exchanged, in a moment, into a mass of death.

Because he hath done great things; lit. (as in the E. M.) *because he hath magnified to do,* i. e. as used of man, *hath done proudly.* To do greatly [6], or to magnify Himself [7], when used of God, is to display His essential greatness, in goodness to His people, or in vengeance on their enemies. Man's great deeds are mostly deeds of great ambition, great violence, great pride, great iniquity; and so of him, the words *he magnified himself* [8], *he did greatly* [9], mean, he did ambitiously, proudly, and so offended God. In like way *great doings,* when used of God, are His great works of good [10]; of man, his great works of evil [11]. "[12] Man has great deserts, but evil." To *speak great things* [13], is to speak proud things: *greatness of heart* [14] is pride of heart. He is speaking then of man who was God's instrument in chastening His people; since of irrational, irresponsible creatures, a term which involves moral fault, would not have been used, nor would a moral fault have been set down as the ground why God destroyed them. The destruction of Sennacherib or Holofernes have been assigned as the fulfillment of this prophecy. They were part of its fulfillment, and of the great law of God which it declares, that instruments, which He employs, and who exceed or accomplish for their own ends, the office which He assigns them, He casts away and destroys.

21. *Fear not, O land.* Before, they were bidden to tremble [15], now they are bidden, *fear not;* before, *to turn in weeping, fasting and mourning;* now, to *bound for joy and rejoice;* before, *the land mourned;* now, *the land* is bidden to *rejoice.* The enemy had *done great things;* now the cause of joy is that God had *done great things;* the Almightiness of God overwhelming and sweeping over the might put forth to destroy. It is better rendered, *the Lord hath*

[7] Ezek. xxxviii. 23. [8] Is. x. 15. Dan. xi. 36, 37.
[9] Lam. i. 9. Zeph. ii. 8. Dan. viii. 4, 8, 11, 25.
[10] עלילות Ps. ix. 12. lxxvii. 13. lxxviii. 11. ciii. 7. Is. xii. 4; מעללים Ps. lxxvii. 12. lxxviii. 7.
[11] עלילות Ps. cxli. 4. 1 Sam. ii. 3. Ezek. xiv. 22. 23. xx. 43. xxi. 29. Zeph. iii. 11; מעללים Jer. iv. 18. xi. 18. xxi. 14, see Hos. xii. 2.
[12] S. Aug. [13] Ps. xii. 3. Dan. vii. 8, 11, 20.
[14] Is. ix. 9. x. 12. [15] ii. 1.

Before CHRIST cir. 800.

22 Be not afraid, [z] ye
beasts of the field: for [a] the
pastures of the wilderness
do spring, for the tree beareth her fruit, the fig tree
and the vine do yield their
strength.
23 Be glad then, ye
children of Zion, and [b] rejoice in the LORD your

[z] ch. 1. 18, 20.
[a] Zech. 8. 12. See ch. 1. 19.
[b] Is. 41. 16. & 61. 10. Hab. 3. 18. Zech. 10. 7.

done great things. If Joel includes herein God's great doings yet to come, he speaks of them as, in the purpose of God, already in being; or he may, in this verse, presuppose that this new order of God's mercies has begun, in the destruction of the Heathen foe.

22. The reversal of the whole former sentence is continued up to man. The beasts of the field *groaned, were perplexed, cried unto* God; now they are bidden, *be not afraid;* before, *the pastures of the wilderness* were *devoured by fire;* now, they *spring* with fresh tender life; before, *the fig tree* was *withered, the vine languished*; now, they should *yield their strength, put out their full* vigor. For God was reconciled to His people; and all things served them, serving Him.

23. *Be glad then and rejoice in the Lord your God.* All things had been restored for their sakes; they were to rejoice, not chiefly in these things, but in God; nor only in God, but in the Lord their God. *For He hath given you the former rain moderately.* The word rendered *moderately* should be rendered *unto righteousness;* the word often as it occurs never having any sense but that of *righteousness;* whether of God or man. The other word *moreh*, rendered *the former rain*, confessedly has that meaning in the latter part of the verse, although *yoreh* is the distinctive term for *latter rain* [1]. *Moreh* mostly signifies *a teacher* [2], which is connected with the other ordinary meanings of the root, *torah, law, &c.* The older translators then agreed in rendering, *of righteousness*, or, *unto righteousness* [3], in which case the question as to *moreh*, is only, whether it is to be taken literally of *a teacher*, or figuratively of spiritual blessings, as we say, "the dew of His grace." Even a Jew paraphrases, "[4] But ye, O children of Zion, above all other nations, be glad and rejoice in the Lord your God. For in Him ye shall have perfect joy, in the time of your captivity. For He will give you an *instructor to righteousness;* and He is the king Messias, which shall teach them the way in which they shall walk, and the doings which they shall do." The grounds for so rendering the word are; 1) such is almost its uniform meaning. 2) The righteousness spoken of is most naturally understood of righteousness in man; it is a condition which is the result and object of God's gifts, not the Righteousness of God. But "He hath given you the early rain unto righteousness," i. e. that ye may be righteous, is an unwonted expression. 3) There is a great emphasis on the word [5], which is not used in the later part of the verse, where rain, (whether actual, or symbolical of spiritual blessings) is spoken of. 4) The following words, *and He maketh the rain to descend for you*, according to the established Hebrew idiom [6], relates to a separate action, later, in order of time or of thought, than the former. But if the former word *moreh* signified *early rain*, both would mean one and the same thing. We should not say, "He giveth you the former rain to righteousness, and then He maketh the rain, the former rain and the latter rain to descend;" nor doth the Hebrew.

It seems then most probable, that the Prophet prefixes to all the other promises, that first all-containing promise of the Coming of Christ. Such is the wont of the Prophets, to go on from past judgments and deliverances, to Him Who is the centre of all this cycle of God's dispensations, the Son manifest in the Flesh. He had been promised as a Teacher when that intermediate dispensation of Israel began, the Prophet like unto Moses. His Coming old Jacob looked to, *I have longed for Thy salvation, O Lord.* Him, well known and longed for by the righteous of old, Joel speaks of as the subject of rejoicing, as Zechariah did afterward, *Rejoice greatly, daughter of Zion; behold thy King cometh unto thee.* So Joel here, *Exult and joy in the Lord thy God; for He giveth*, or *will give thee, the Teacher unto righteousness*, i. e. the result and object of Whose Coming is righteousness; or, as Daniel says, *to bring in everlasting righteousness;* and Isaiah, *By His knowledge*, i. e. by the knowledge of Him, *shall My righteous Servant justify many*, i. e. make many righteous. How His coming should issue in righteousness, is not here said. It is presupposed. But Joel speaks of His Coming, as a gift, *He shall give you;* as Isaiah says, *unto us a Son is given;* and that, as *the Teacher*, as Isaiah says [7], *I have given Him a witness to the peoples,*

[1] Deut. xi. 14. Jer. v. 24.
[2] 2 Kings xvii. 28. Job xxxvi. 22. Prov. v. 13. Is. ix. 15. xxx. 20. (twice) Hab. ii. 18.
[3] Jon. "has restored to you your instructor (or instructors) in righteousness;" Vulg. "teacher of righteousness;" LXX. "the foods unto righteousness;" followed by Syr. and Arab.
[4] Abarb. in Poc. so also Jon. and, (following him,) Rashi, R. Japhet.
[5] את המורה.
[6] The ו conv.
[7] Is. lv. 4.

Before CHRIST cir. 800.

God, for he hath given you || the former rain † moderately, and he [e] will cause to come down for you [d] the rain, the former rain and the latter rain in the first *month*.

|| Or, *a teacher of righteousness.*
† Heb. *according to righteousness.*
[e] Lev. 26. 4. Deut. 11. 14. & 28. 12.

Before CHRIST cir. 800.

[d] Jam. 5. 7.

---

a Prince and a Commander unto the people; and that, *for righteousness.*

"It is the wont of the holy prophets," says S. Cyril, "on occasion of good things promised to a part or a few, to introduce what is more general or universal. And these are the things of Christ. To this then the discourse again proceeds. For when was ground given to the earth to rejoice? When did the Lord do mighty things, but when the Word, being God, became Man, that, flooding all below with the goods from above, He might be found to those who believe in Him, as a river of peace, a torrent of pleasure, as the former and latter rain, and the giver of all spiritual fruitfulness?"

The early rain and the latter rain. "[1] He multiplies words, expresssive of the richness of the fruits of the earth, that so we may understand how wondrous is the plenteousness of spiritual goods." Being about to speak of the large gift of God the Holy Ghost as an *out-pouring*, he says here that "[2] the largeness of the spiritual gifts thereafter should be as abundant as the riches temporal blessings" hitherto, when God disposed all things to bring about the fruitfulness which He had promised. *The early and latter rain*, coming respectively at the seed-time and the harvest, represent the beginning and the completion; and so, by the analogy of earthly and spiritual sowing, growth and ripeness, they represent [3] preventing and perfecting grace; the inspiration of good purposes and the gift of final perseverance, which brings the just to glory consummated; *the principles of the doctrine of Christ* and *the going on unto perfection* [4].

In the first month. This would belong only to the latter rain, which falls about the first month, Nisan, or our April, *the former rain* falling about 6 months earlier, at their seed time [5]. Or, since this meaning is uncertain [6], it may be, *at the first* [7], i. e. as soon as ever it is needed, or in contrast to the more extensive gifts afterward; or, *as at first* [8], i. e. all shall, upon their penitence, be restored as at first. These lesser variations leave the sense of the whole the same, and all are supported by good authorities. It is still a reversal of the former sentence, that, whereas afore the rivers of water were dried up, now the rains should come, each in its season. *In the first month*, and *at the beginning*, express the same thought, the one with, the other without a figure. For no one then needed to be told that the latter rain, if it fell, should fall *in the first month*, which was its appointed season for falling. If then the words had this meaning, there must have been this emphasis in it, that God would give them good gifts punctually, instantly, at man's first and earliest needs, at the first moment when it would be good for him to have them. *As at the beginning*, would express the same which he goes on to say, that God would bestow the same largeness of gifts as He did, before they forfeited His blessings by forsaking Him. So He says [9], *I will restore thy judges as at the first, and thy counsellors as at the beginning;* and [10], *She shall sing there as in the days of her youth, and as in the day when she come up out of the land of Egypt;* and [11], *then shall the offering of Judah and Jerusalem be pleasant unto the Lord, as in the days of old and as in the former years.* Likeness does not necessarily imply equality [12], as in the words [13], *The Lord thy God will raise up unto thee a Prophet like unto me;* and [14] *that they may be one, even as We are One.* The good things of the Old Testament had a likeness to those of the New, else *the law* would not have been even *the shadow of good things to come* [15]; they had not equality, else they would have been the very things themselves. "[16] Christ is the whole delight of the soul, from Whom and through Whom there cometh to those who love Him, all fullness of good and supply of heavenly gifts, represented in *the early and latter rain*, and *the full floor of wheat*, and *the fats overflowing with wine and oil.* It is true also as to the fullness of the mysteries. For the living water of Holy Baptism is given us as in rain; and as in corn, the Bread of Life, and as in wine the Blood." Before, *the barns were broken down*, since there was nothing to store therein. As other parts of the natural and spiritual husbandry correspond, and our Lord Himself compares His gracious trials of those who bear fruit, with the pruning of the vine [17]; it may be that the *vat* wherein the grape or the olive, through pressure, yield

---

1 Rib. 2 Lap. 3 Dion. Castr. Lap.
4 Heb. vi. 1. 5 See on Hos. vi. 3.
6 In the known cases, where, *in the first*, בראשון, stands for *in the first month*, (Gen. viii. 13. Num. ix. 5. Ezek. xxix. 17. xlv. 18, 21) this is marked in the sentence itself.

7 S. Jer. R. Tanchum, in Poc.
8 Abarb. R. Tanch. LXX. Syr. Vulg.
9 Is. i. 26. Rib. 10 Hos. ii. 15. 11 Mal. iii. 4.
12 Rib. 13 Deut. xviii. 15.
14 S. John xvii. 22. 15 Heb. x. 1.
16 S. Cyr. 17 S. John xv. 2.

Before CHRIST cir. 800.

24 And the floors shall
be full of wheat, and the
fats shall overflow with
wine and oil.

25 And I will restore to
you the years [e] that the
locust hath eaten, the cankerworm, and the cater-

Before CHRIST cir. 800.

[e] ch. 1. 4.

their rich juice, is a symbol of the *tribulations*, through which we *must enter the kingdom of God*[1]. "[2] The holy mind, placed as if in a winefat, is pressed, refined, drawn out pure. It is pressed by calamity; refined from iniquity, purified from vanity. Hence are elicited the groans of pure confession; hence stream the tears of anxious compunction; hence flow the sighs of pleasurable devotion; hence melt the longings of sweetest love; hence are drawn the drops of purest contemplation. Wheat is the perfecting of righteousness; wine, the clearness of spiritual understanding; oil, the sweetness of a most pure conscience."

25. *And I will restore to you the years that the locust hath eaten.* The order in which these destroyers are named not being the same as before, it is plain that the stress is not on the order, but on the successiveness of the inroads, scourge after scourge. It is plain too that they did not come in the same year, or two years, but year after year; for he says, not *year*, but in the plural, *years*. The locusts, although not the whole plague, intended, are not exclu led. "[3] As the power of God was shewn in the plagues of Egypt by small animals, such as the cyniphes, gnats so small as scarce to be seen, so also now," in creatures so small "is shown the power of God and weakness of man. If a creature so small is stronger than man, *why are earth and ashes proud?*" The locusts, small as they are, are in God's hands *a great army*, (and from this place probably, Mohammed[4] taught his followers so to call them) and mighty empires are but "[5] the forces of God and messengers of His Providence for the punishing of" His people "by them," *the rod of His* Anger; and when they have done their commission and are cast away by Him, they are as the vilest worms.

"[3] Since then after repentance God promises such richness, what will Novatus say, who denies repentance or that sinners can be re-formed into their former state, if they but do works meet for repentance? For God in such wise receives penitents, as to call them His people, and to say, that they *shall never be confounded*, and to promise, that He will dwell in the midst of them, and that they shall have no other God, but shall, with their whole mind, trust in Him Who abides in them forever."

[1] Acts xiv. 22. [2] Hugo de S. V. [3] S. Jer.
[4] Mohammed probably had it from the apostate Jew who helped him in composing the Coran.

Through repentance all which had been lost by sin, is restored. In itself deadly sin is an irreparable evil. It deprives the soul of grace, of its hope of glory; it forfeits heaven, it merits hell. God, through Christ, restores the sinner, blots out sin, and does away with its eternal consequences. He replaces the sinner where he was before he fell. So God says by Ezekiel[6]; *If the wicked will turn from all the sins which he hath committed and keep all My statutes, and do that which is lawful and right, he shall surely live, he shall not die; all his transgressions that he hath committed shall not be mentioned unto him;* and[7], *as for the wickedness of the wicked, he shall not fall thereby in the day that he turneth from his wickedness.* God forgives that wickedness, as though it had never been. If it had never been, man would have all the grace, which he had before his fall. So then also, after he has been forgiven, none of his former grace, no store of future glory, will be taken from him. The time which the sinner lost, in which he might have gained increase of grace and glory, is lost for ever. But all which he had gained before, returns. All his lost love returns through penitence; all his past attainments, which were before accepted by God, are accepted still for the same glory. "Former works which were deadened by sins following, revive through repentance[8]." The penitent begins anew God's service, but he is not at the beginning of that service, nor of his preparation for life eternal. If the grace which he had before, and the glory corresponding to that grace, and to his former attainments through that grace, were lost to him, then, although eternally blessed, he would be punished eternally for forgiven sin, which, God has promised, should *not be remembered.* God has also promised to reward all which is *done in the body*[9]. What is evil, is effaced by the Blood of Jesus. What, through His Grace, was good, and done for love of Himself, He rewards, whether it was before any one fell, or after his restoration. Else He would not, as He says He will, reward all. And who would not believe, that, after David's great fall and great repentance, God still rewarded all that great early simple faith and patience, which He gave him? Whence writers of old say, "[10] It is pious to believe that the recovered grace of God which destroys a man's former evils, also reintegrates

[5] Abarb. in Poc. [6] xviii. 21, 22. [7] Ib. xxxiii. 12.
[8] Gloss in Ep. ad Heb. [9] 2 Cor. v. 10.
[10] de ver. et fals. pœnit. c. 14.

Before CHRIST cir. 800.

pillar, and the palmer-
worm, [f] my great army
which I sent among
you.
26 And ye shall [g] eat in
plenty, and be satisfied,
and praise the name of the
LORD your God, that hath
dealt wondrously with you:

[f] ver. 11.

[g] Lev. 26. 5. Ps. 22. 16. See Lev. 26. 26. Mic. 6. 14.

and my people shall never
be ashamed.
27 [h] And ye shall know
that I *am* [i] in the midst of
Israel, and *that* [k] I *am* the
LORD your God, and none
else: and my people shall
never be ashamed.
28 ¶ [l] And it shall come

Before CHRIST cir. 800.

[h] ch. 3. 17.

[i] Lev. 26. 11, 12. Ezek. 37. 26, 27, 28.

[k] Is. 45. 5, 21, 22. Ezek. 39. 22, 23.

[l] Is. 44. 3. Ezek. 39. 29. Acts 2. 17.

---

his good, and that God, when He hath destroyed in a man what is not His, loves the good which He implanted even in the sinner." "[1] God is pleased alike with the virtue of the just, and the meet repentance of sinners, which restored to their former estate David and Peter." "Penitence is an excellent thing which recalleth to perfection every defect." "[2] God letteth His sun arise on sinners, nor doth He less than before, give them, most large gifts of life and salvation." Whence, since the cankerworm, &c. are images of spiritual enemies, this place has been paraphrased; "[3] I will not allow the richness of spiritual things to perish, which ye lost through the passions of the mind." Nay, since none can recover without the grace of God and using that grace, the penitent, who really rises again by the grace of God, rises with larger grace than before, since he has both the former grace, and; in addition, this new grace, whereby he rises.

26. *And ye shall eat in plenty and be satisfied.* It is of the punishment of God, when men eat and are *not* satisfied [4]; it is man's sin, that they are satisfied, and do not to praise God, but the more forget Him [5]. And so God's blessings become a curse to him. God promises to restore His gifts, and to give grace withal, that they should own and thank Him.

Who hath dealt wondrously with you. "First, wonderfully He afflicted and chastened them, and then gave them wonderful abundance of all things, and very great and miraculous consolation after vehement tribulation, so that they might truly say, *This is the change of the Right Hand of the Most High.*"

And My people shall never be ashamed. "[6] So that they persevere in His service. Although he incur temporal confusion, yet this shall not last for ever, but the people of the predestinate, penitent, and patient in adversity, will be saved for ever."

27. *And ye shall know that I* am *in the midst of Israel.* God had foretold their rebellions, His forsaking them, *the troubles* which should *find* them, and that *they* should *say* [7], *Are not these evils come upon us, because our God is not among us?* It had been the mockery of the Heathen in their distress [8], *Where is their God?* "Now, by the fulfillment of His promises and by all God's benefits, they should know that He was among them by special grace as His own peculiar people." Still more was this to be fulfilled to Christians, in whose heart He dwells by love and grace, and of whom He says, *Where two or three are gathered together in My name, there will I be in the midst of them.* In the highest sense, *God was in the midst of them,* in that "[9] God the Son, equal to God the Father as touching His Godhead, did, in the truth of human nature, take our flesh. This to see and know, is glory and bliss ineffable. Therefore He repeats, and by repeating, confirms, what he had said, *And My people shall never be ashamed.* Yea, glorious, magnified, honored, shall be the people, to whom such a Son was promised, and of whom He was born. Glorious to them is that which the Apostle saith, that *He took not on Him the nature of Angels, but He took the seed of Abraham,* and this glory shall be eternal."

28. *And it shall come to pass afterward.* After the punishment of the Jews through the Heathen, and their deliverance; after the Coming of the Teacher of righteousness, was to follow the outpouring of the Spirit of God.

I will pour out My Spirit on all flesh. "[9] This which He says, *on all flesh,* admits of no exception of nations or persons. For before Jesus was glorified, He had poured His Spirit only on the sons of Zion, and out of that nation only were there Prophets and wise men. But after He was glorified by His Resurrection and Ascension, He made no difference of Jews and Gentiles, but willed that remission of sins should be preached to all alike."

All flesh is the name of all mankind. So

[1] Gloss on Lev. vii. init.
[2] S. Aug. Ep. 153, ad Macedon. § 7.
[3] Gloss hic. The above passages are quoted by Medina, de pœnit. q. 8. who uses these arguments.
[4] See Hos. iv. 10.
[5] Hos. xiii. 6.
[6] Dion.
[7] Deut. xxxi. 17.
[8] ii. 17.
[9] Rup.

Before CHRIST cir. 800.

to pass afterward, *that* I [m] will pour out my spirit upon all flesh; [n] and your sons and [o] your daughters shall prophesy, your old men shall dream dreams, your young men shall see visions:

m Zech. 12. 10. John 7. 39.
n Is. 54. 13.
o Acts 21. 9.

in the time of the flood, it is said *all flesh had corrupted his way: the end of all flesh is come before Me.* Moses asks, *who of all flesh hath heard the voice of the Lord God, as we have, and lived?* So in Job; *in Whose Hand is the breath of all flesh of man. If He set His heart upon man, if He gather to Himself his spirit and his breath, all flesh shall perish together.* And David; *Thou that hearest prayer, to Thee shall all flesh come; let all flesh bless His Holy Name for ever and ever*[1]. In like way speak Isaiah, Jeremiah, Ezekiel, Zechariah[2]. The words *all flesh* are in the Pentateuch, and in one place in Daniel, used, in a yet wider sense, of everything which has life[3]; but, in no one case, in any narrower sense. It does not include every individual in the race, but it includes the whole race, and individuals throughout it, in every nation, sex, condition, *Jew or Gentile, Greek or Barbarian*, i. e. educated or uneducated, rich or poor, bond or free, male or female. As *all* were to be *one in Christ Jesus*[4], so on all was to be poured the Holy Spirit, the Bond Who was to bind all in one. He names our nature from that which is the lowest in it, *the flesh*, with the same condescension with which it is said, *The Word was made flesh*[5], whence we speak of the *Incarnation* of our Blessed Lord, i. e. "His taking on Him our Flesh." He humbled Himself to take our flesh; He came, as our Physician, to heal our flesh, the seat of our concupiscence. So also God the Holy Ghost vouchsafes to dwell in our flesh, to sanctify it and to heal it. He, Whom God saith He will pour out on all flesh, is the Spirit of God, and God. He does not say that He will pour out graces, or gifts, ordinary or extraordinary, influences, communications, or the like. He says, *I will pour out My Spirit;* as S. Paul says, *know ye not that ye are the temple of God, and the Spirit of God dwelleth in you*[6]*? Ye are not in the flesh but in the Spirit, if so be that the Spirit of God dwell in you. Now if any man have not the Spirit of Christ, he is none of His*[7]. It is said indeed, *on the Gentiles also was poured out the gift of the Holy Ghost*, but the gift of the Holy Ghost was the Holy Ghost Himself, as it had been just said, *the Holy Ghost fell on all them that heard the word*[8]. It is said, *the love of God is shed abroad in our hearts by the Holy Ghost, which is given us*[9]; but the *Holy Ghost* is first *given*, and He poureth out into the soul *the love of God.* As God the Word, when He took human nature, came into it personally, so that *the fullness of the Godhead dwelt bodily in it*[10]; so, really, although not personally, "doth the Holy Spirit, and so the whole Trinity, enter into our mind by sanctification, and dwelleth in it as in His throne." No created being, no Angel, nor Archangel could dwell in the soul. "[11] God Alone can be poured out into the soul, so as to possess it, enlighten it, teach, kindle, bend, move it as He wills," sanctify, satiate, fill it. And "as God is really present with the blessed, when He sheweth to them His Essence by the beatific vision and light of glory, and communicates it to them, to enjoy and possess; so He, the Same, is also in the holy soul, and thus diffuseth it in His grace, love, and other divine gifts." At the moment of justification, "the Holy Ghost and so the whole Holy Trinity entereth the soul at His temple, sanctifying and as it were dedicating and consecrating it to Himself, and at the same moment of time, although in the order of nature subsequently, He communicates to it His love and grace. Such is the meaning of, *We will come unto him, and make Our abode with him.* This is the highest union of God with the holy soul; and greater than this can none be given to any creature, for by it we become *partakers of the divine Nature*, as S. Peter[12] saith. See here, O Christian, the dignity of the holiness whereunto thou art called and with all zeal follow after, preserve, enlarge it."

This His Spirit, God says, *I will pour*, i.e. give largely, as though He would empty out Him Who is Infinite, so that there should be no measure of His giving, save our capacity of receiving. So He says of converted Israel[13], *I have poured out My Spirit upon the house of Israel*, and[14], *I will pour out upon the house of David and upon the inhabitants of Jerusalem the Spirit of grace and supplication.*

And your sons and your daughters shall prophesy. This cannot limit what he has said, that God would pour out His Spirit upon all flesh. He gives instances of that out-pouring, in those miraculous gifts, which were at the first to be the tokens and evidence of His

1 Gen. vi. 12, 13. Deut. v. 26. Job xii. 10. xxxiv. 14, 15. Ps. lxv. 2. cxlv. 21.
2 Is. xl. 5, 6. xlix. 26. lxvi. 16, 23, 24. Jer. xxv. 31. xxxii. 27. xlv. 5. Ezek. xx. 48. xxi. 4, 5. Zech. ii. 13.
3 Gen. vi. 17, 19. vii. 15, 16, 21. viii. 17. ix. 11, 15, 16, 17. Lev. xvii. 14. Num. xviii. 15. Dan. iv. 12; probably Ps. cxxxvi. 25.
4 Gal. iii. 28.
5 S. Aug. Ep. 140. c. 4. Lap.
6 1 Cor. iii. 16.
7 Rom. viii. 9, 10.
8 Acts x. 44, 45.
9 Rom. v. 5.
10 Col. ii. 9.
11 Lap.
12 2 S. Pet. i. 4.
13 Ezek. xxxix. 29.
14 Zech. xii. 10.

Before CHRIST cir. 800.

29 And also upon [p] the servants and upon the handmaids in those days will I pour out my spirit.

Before CHRIST cir. 800.

p 1 Cor. 12. 13. Gal. 3. 28. Col. 3. 11.

inward Presence. These gifts were at the first bestowed on the Jews only. The highest were reserved altogether for them. Jews only were employed as Apostles and Evangelists; Jews only wrote, by inspiration of God, *the oracles of God*, as the source of the faith of the whole world. "[1] The Apostles were sons of Israel; the Mother of our Lord Jesus Christ, and the other women who abode at the same time and prayed with the Apostles, were daughters. S. Luke mentions, *All these were persevering with one accord in prayer with the women and Mary the Mother of Jesus, and His brethren.* These sons and daughters of the Sons of Zion, having received the Spirit, prophesied, i. e. in divers tongues they spoke of the heavenly mysteries." In the narrower sense of "[2] foretelling the future, the Apostles, the Blessed Virgin [3], Zacharias [4] and Anna [5], Elizabeth [6], the virgin daughters of Philip [7], Agabus [8], S. John in the Apocalypse," Simeon [9], and S. Paul also oftentimes [10] prophesied. At Antioch, there were certain *prophets* [11]; and [12] *the Holy Ghost in every city witnessed, saying, that bonds and afflictions awaited him* in Jerusalem. "But it is superfluous," adds Theodoret [13] after giving some instances, "to set myself to prove the truth of the prophecy. For down to our times also hath this gift been preserved, and there are among the saints, men who have the eye of the mind clear, who foreknow and foretell many of the things which are about to be." So the death of Julian the Apostate, who fell, as it seemed, by a chance wound in war with the Persians was foreseen and foretold [14]; and S. Cyprian foretold the day of his own martyrdom and the close of Decian persecution, which ended through the death of the Emperor in a rash advance over a morass, when victory was gained [15]. The stream of prophecy has been traced down through more than four centuries from the Birth of the Redeemer. One of the Bishops of the Council of Nice was gifted with a prophetic spirit [16].

Your old men shall dream dreams, and your young men shall see visions. "[8] God often attempers Himself and His oracles to the condition of men, and appears to each, as suits his state." It may then be, that to old men, while sleeping by reason of age, He appeared most commonly in dreams; to young men, while watching, in visions. But it is so common in Hebrew, that each part of the verse should be filled up from the other, that perhaps the Prophet only means, that their old and young should have dreams and see visions, and both from God. Nor are these the highest of God's revelations; as He says, that to the prophet He would *make* Himself *known in a vision* and would *speak in a dream*, but to Moses *mouth to mouth; even apparently, and not in dark speeches; and the similitude of the Lord shall he behold* [17].

The Apostles also saw waking visions, as S. Peter at Joppa [18]; (and that so frequently, that when the Angel delivered him, he thought that it was one of his accustomed visions [19],) and S. Paul after his conversion, and calling him to Macedonia; and the Lord appeared unto him in vision at Corinth, revealing to him the conversions which should be worked there, and at Jerusalem foretelling to him the witness he should bear to Him at Rome. In the ship, the Angel of the Lord foretold to him his own safety, and that God had given him all who sailed with him [20]. Ananias [21] and Cornelius [22] also received revelations through visions. But all these were only revelations of single truths or facts. Of a higher sort seems to be that revelation, whereby our Lord revealed to S. Paul Himself and His Gospel which S. Paul was to preach, and *the wisdom of God*, and the glories of the world to come, and the conversion of the Gentiles; and when he was *caught up to the third heaven*, and *abundance of revelations* were vouchsafed to him [23].

29. *And also upon the servants.* God tells beforehand that he would be no respecter of persons. He had said, that He would endow every age and sex. He adds here, and every condition, even that of slaves, both male and female. He does not add here, that they shall prophesy. Under the law, God had provided for slaves, that, even if aliens, they should by circumcision be enrolled in His family and people; that they should have the rest and the devotion of the sabbath; and share the joy of their great festivals, going up with their masters and mistresses to the place which God appointed. They were included in one common ordinance of joy; *Ye shall rejoice before the Lord your God, ye and your sons and your daughters, and* [lit.]

1 Rup. 2 Lap. 3 S. Luke i. 48.
4 Ib. 67 sqq. 5 Ib. ii. 36, 38.
6 Ib. i. 42-45. 7 Acts xxi. 9.
8 Ib. xi. 28. xxi. 10, 11. 9 S. Luke ii. 27-35.
10 Acts xx. 29, 30. 2 Thess. ii. 3-12. 2 Tim. iii. 1, 4. 1 Tim. iv. 1.
11 Acts xiii. 1. 12 Ib. xx. 23. 13 ad loc.
14 Theodoret H. E. iii. 18, 19.
15 See Pref. to S. Cyprian's Epistles and Ep. xi. p. 27. note k. Oxf. Tr.
16 S. Greg. Naz. Orat. 18. in fun. patr. § 12.
17 Num. xii. 6, 8. 18 Acts x. 10 sqq. xi. 5 sqq.
19 Ib. xii. 9.
20 Acts ix. 12. xvi. 6, 7, 9. xviii. 9. xix. 21. xxiii. 11. xxvii. 24. 21 Ib. ix. 10. 22 Ib. x. 3.
23 Gal. i. 12, 16. 1 Cor. ii. 7. Eph. iii. 3. 2 Cor. xii. 1-7.

Before CHRIST cir. 800.

30 And [q] I will shew
wonders in the heavens
and in the earth, blood, and
fire, and pillars of smoke.

Before CHRIST cir. 800.

q Matt. 24. 29. Mark 13. 24. Luke 21. 11, 25.

---

your men slaves and your women slaves, and the Levite which is within your gates[1]. In the times before the Gospel, they doubtless fell under the contempt in which the Pharisees held all the less educated class; *These people who knoweth not the law* (i. e. according to the explanation of their schools) *is cursed.* Whence it was a saying of theirs, "[2] Prophecy doth not reside except on one wise and mighty and rich." As then elsewhere it was given as a mark of the Gospel, *the poor have the Gospel preached unto them,* so here. It was not what the Jews of his day expected; for he says, *And on the servants too.* But he tells beforehand, what was against the pride both of his own times and of the time of its fulfillment, that[3] *God chose the foolish things of the world to confound the wise, and God hath chosen the weak things of the world to confound the things which are mighty; and base things of the world and things which are despised hath God chosen, and things which are not, to bring to naught things that are, that no flesh should glory in His presence.* The prophetic word circles round to that wherewith it began, the all-containing promise of the large out-pouring of the Spirit of God; and that, upon those whom the carnal Jews at all times would least expect to receive it. It began with including the heathen; *I will pour out My Spirit on all flesh;* it instances individual gifts; and then it ends by resting on the slaves; *and on* these *too in those days will I pour out My Spirit.* The order of the words is significant. He begins, *I will pour out My Spirit upon all flesh,* and then, in order to leave the mind resting on these same great words, he inverts the order, and ends, *and upon the servants and upon the handmaidens I will pour out My Spirit.* It leaves the thoughts resting on the great words, *I will pour out My Spirit.*

The Church at Rome, whose *faith was spoken of throughout the whole world*[4], was, as far as it consisted of converted Jews, made up of slaves, who had been set free by their masters. For such were most of the Roman Jews, "[5] who occupied that large section of Rome beyond the Tiber." Most of these, Philo says, "having been made freemen, were Roman citizens. For having been brought as captives to Italy, set free by their purchasers, without being compelled to change any of their country's rites, they had their synagogues and assembled in them, especially on the sabbath."

S. Peter, in declaring that these words began to be fulfilled in the Day of Pentecost, quotes them with two lesser differences. *I will pour out* of *My Spirit,* and *upon* My *servants and* My *handmaidens.* The words declare something in addition, but do not alter the meaning, and so S. Peter quotes them as they lay in the Greek, which probably was the language known by most of the mixed multitude, to whom he spake on the day of Pentecost. The words, *I will pour out My Spirit,* express the largeness and the fullness of the gift of Him, "[6] Who is Very God, Unchangeable and Infinite, Who is given or poured out, not by change of place but by the largeness of His Presence." The words, *I will pour out* of *My Spirit,* express in part, that He Who is Infinite cannot be contained by us who are finite; in part, they indicate, that there should be a distribution of gifts, although *worked by One and the Same Spirit,* as the Prophet also implies in what follows. Again, the words, *the servants and the handmaidens,* mark the outward condition; the words *My servants and My handmaidens,* declare that there should be no difference between *bond and free.* The servants and handmaidens should have that highest title of honor, that they should be the servants of God. For what more can the creature desire? The Psalmist says to God[7], *Lo I am Thy servant and the son of Thine handmaid;* and God gives it as a title of honor to Abraham and Moses and Job and David and Isaiah[8], and Abraham and David call themselves the servants of God[9], and S. Paul, S. Peter, and S. Jude, *servants of Jesus Christ*[10], and S. James, *the servant of God*[11]; and the blessed Virgin, *the handmaid of the Lord*[12]; yea, and our Lord Himself, in His Human Nature is spoken of in prophecy as [13] *the Servant of the Lord.*

30. *And I will shew wonders.* Each revelation of God prepares the way for another, until that last revelation of His love and of His wrath in the Great Day. In delivering His people from Egypt, *the Lord shewed signs and wonders, great and sore, upon Egypt*[14]. Here, in allusion to it, He says, in the same words[15], of the new revelation, *I will shew,* or *give, wonders,* or *wondrous signs,* (as the word

1 Gen. xvii. 23, 27. Ex. xx. 10. Deut. xii. 12, 18. xvi. 11, 14.
2 Moreh Nebochim, ii. 32. in Poc.
3 1 Cor. i. 27–30.
4 Rom. i. 8.
5 Philo leg. ad Caium, p. 1014. ed. Paris.
6 Dion.
7 Ps. cxvi. 16.
8 Gen. xxvi. 24. Num. xii. 7, 8. Josh. i. 2. 2 Kings xxi. 8. Job i. 8. ii. 3. xlii. 7, 8. 2 Sam. vii. 5. &c. Is. xx. 3.
9 Gen. xix. 19. Ps. lxxxvi. 2, 4.
10 Rom. i. 1. Gal. i. 10. 2 S. Pet. i. 1. S. Jude 1.
11 S. Jam. i. 1, also Tit. i. 1.
12 S. Luke i. 38, 48.
13 Is. xlii. 1. xlix. 6. lii. 13. Zech. iii. 8. Ezek. xxxiv. 23, 4. xxxvii. 24, 5.
14 Deut. vi. 22.
15 ויתן יי אותת ומפתים Deut., ונתתי מופתים Joel.

Before CHRIST cir. 800.

31 [r]The sun shall be turned into darkness, and the moon into blood, [s]before the great and the terrible day of the LORD come.

[r] Is. 13. 9, 10. ch. 3. 1, 15. ver. 10. Matt. 24. 29. Mark. 13. 24. Luke 21. 25. Rev. 6. 12.

[s] Mal. 4. 5.

includes both) wonders beyond the course and order of nature, and portending other dispensations of God, of joy to His faithful, terror to His enemies. As when Israel came out of Egypt, [1] *the pillar of the cloud was a cloud and darkness to the camp of the Egyptians*, but *gave light by night* to the *camp of Israel*, so all God's workings are light and darkness at once, according as men are, who see them or to whom they come. These wonders in heaven and earth "began in" the First Coming and "Passion of Christ, grew in the destruction of Jerusalem, but shall be perfectly fulfilled toward the end of the world, before the final Judgment, and the destruction of the Universe." At the birth of Christ, there was *the star* which appeared unto the wise men, and *the multitude of the heavenly host*, whom the shepherds saw. At His Atoning Death, *the sun was darkened*, there was the three hours' darkness over the whole land; and on earth *the veil of the temple was rent in twain from the top to the bottom, and the earth did quake, and the rocks rent, and the graves were opened*[2]: and the Blood and water issued from the Saviour's side. After His Resurrection, there was the vision of Angels, terrible to the soldiers who watched the sepulchre, comforting to the women who sought to honor Jesus. His Resurrection was a sign on earth, His Ascension in earth and heaven. But our Lord speaks of signs both in earth and heaven, as well before the destruction of Jerusalem, as before His second Coming.

With regard to the details, it seems probable that this is an instance of what we may call an inverted parallelism, that having mentioned generally that God would give *signs in* 1) *heaven and* 2) *earth*, the Prophet first instances the *signs in earth*, and then those *in heaven*. A very intellectual Jewish expositor[3] has suggested this, and certainly it is frequent enough to be, in conciser forms, one of the idioms of the sacred language. In such case, *the blood and fire and pillars of smoke*, will be *signs in earth; the turning* of *the sun into darkness and the moon into blood* will be *signs in heaven*. When fortelling the destruction of Jerusalem, the Day of vengeance, which fell with such accumulated horror on the devoted city, and has for these 1800 years dispersed the people of Israel to the four winds, our Lord mentions first the signs on earth, then those in heaven. *Nation shall arise against nation, and kingdom against kingdom, and great earthquakes shall be in divers places, and famines, and pestilences; and fearful sights and great signs shall there be from heaven*[4]. Before the Day of Judgment our Lord also speaks of both[5]; 1) *there shall be signs in the sun and in the moon and in the stars;* 2) *and upon the earth distress of nations with perplexity; the sea and the waves roaring; men's hearts failing them for fear and for looking after those things which are coming on the earth; for the powers of heaven shall be shaken.*

The Jewish historian relates signs both in heaven and in earth, before the destruction of Jerusalem[6]. "A star stood like a sword over Jerusalem;" "a light which, when the people were assembled at the Passover at 9 at night, shone so brightly around the altar and the temple, that it seemed like bright day, and this for half an hour; the Eastern door of the temple, which 20 men scarcely shut at eventide, stayed with iron-bound bars and very deep bolts let down into the threshhold of one solid stone, was seen at 6 o'clock at night to open of its own accord; chariots and armed troops were seen along the whole country, coursing through the clouds, encircling the cities; at the feast of Pentecost, the priests entering the temple by night, as their wont was for worship, first perceived a great movement and sound, and then a multitudinous voice, 'Let us depart hence.'" These signs were authenticated by the multitude or character of those who witnessed them.

31. *Before the great and terrible Day of the Lord come.* "[7]The days of our life are our days wherein we do what we please; *that* will be the *Day of the Lord*, when He, our Judge, shall require the account of all our doings. It will be *great*, because it is the horizon of time and eternity; the last day of time, the beginning of eternity. It will put an end to the world, guilt, deserts, good or evil. It will be *great*, because in it great things will be done. Christ with all His Angels will come down and sit on His Throne; all who have ever lived or shall live, shall be placed before Him to be judged; all thoughts, words, and deeds shall be weighed most exactly; on all a sentence will be passed, absolute, irrevocable throughout eternity; the saints shall be assigned to

[1] Ex. xiv. 19, 20.
[2] S. Luke xxiii. 44, 5. S. Matt. xxvii. 45, 51, 52.
[3] Aben Ezra.
[4] S. Luke xxi. 10, 11.
[5] Ib. 25, 26.
[6] Jos. de bell. Jud. vi. 5. 3; also in Euseb. H. E. iii. 8.
[7] Lap.

Before CHRIST cir. 800.

32 And it shall come to pass, *that* [t] whosoever shall call on the name of the LORD shall be delivered:

[t] Rom. 10. 13.

Before CHRIST cir. 800.

heaven, the ungodly to hell; a great gulf shall be placed between, which shall sever them for ever, so that the ungodly shall never see the godly nor heaven nor God; but shall be shut up in a prison for ever, and shall burn as long as heaven shall be heaven, or God shall be God." "[1] That day shall be great to the faithful, terrible to the unbelieving; great to those who said, *Truly this is the Son of God;* terrible to those who said, *His blood be upon us and upon our children.*" "[2] When then thou art hurried to any sin, think on that terrible and unendurable judgment-seat of Christ, where the Judge sits on His lofty Throne, and all creation shall stand in awe at His glorious Appearing and we shall be brought, one by one, to give account of what we have done in life. Then by him who hath done much evil in life, there will stand terrible angels.—*There* will be the deep gulf, the impassable darkness, the lightless fire, retaining in darkness the power to burn, but reft of its rays. *There* is the empoisoned and ravenous worm insatiably devouring and never satisfied, inflicting by its gnawing pangs unbearable. There that sharpest punishment of all, that shame and everlasting reproach. Fear these things; and, instructed by this fear, hold in thy soul as with a bridle from the lust of evil."

32. *Whosoever shall call upon the name of the Lord. To call upon the name of the Lord,* is to worship Him, as HE IS, depending *upon* Him. *The name of the Lord,* expresses His True Being, That which He IS. Hence so often in Holy Scripture, men are said to *call on the Name of the Lord, to bless the Name of the Lord, to praise the Name of the Lord, to sing praises to His Name, to make mention* of *His Name, to tell of His Name, to know His Name*[3]; but it is very rarely said *I will praise the Name of God*[4]. For the Name rendered *the Lord,* expresses that HE IS, and that He Alone IS, the Self-Same, the Unchangeable; the name rendered *God* is not the special Name of God. Hence as soon as men were multiplied and the corrupt race of Cain increased, men *began,* after the birth of Enos, the son of Seth, *to call upon the Name of the Lord*[5], i.e. in public worship. Abraham's worship, in the presence of the idolatries of Canaan, is spoken of, under the same words, *he called upon the Name of the Lord*[6]. Elijah says to the prophets of Baal, *call ye on the name of your gods, and I will call on the Name of the Lord*[7]. Naaman the Heathen says of Elisha[8], *I thought that he would come out to me, and stand and call on the Name of the Lord his God.* Asaph and Jeremiah pray God[9]; *Pour out Thy wrath upon the heathen that have not known Thee, and upon the kingdoms* [*families* Jer.] *which have not called upon Thy Name;* and Zephaniah fortells the conversion of the Heathen[10], *that they may all call upon the Name of the Lord, to serve Him with one consent.*

To *call* then *upon the Name of the Lord* implies right faith, to call upon Him as He IS; right trust in Him, leaning upon Him; right devotion, calling upon Him as He has appointed; right life, ourselves who call upon Him being, or becoming by His Grace, what He wills. They *call* not *upon the Lord,* but upon some idol of their own imagining, who call upon Him, as other than He has revealed Himself, or remaining themselves other than those whom He has declared that He will hear. For such deny the very primary attribute of God, His truth. *Their* God is not a God of truth. But whosoever shall in true faith and hope and charity have in this life worshiped God, *shall be delivered,* i.e. out of the midst of all the horrors of that Day, and the horrible damnation of the ungodly. The *deliverance* is by way of *escape* (for such is the meaning of the word[11],) *he shall be made to escape, slip through* (as it were) perils as imminent as they shall be terrible. Our Lord uses the like word of the same Day[12], *Watch ye therefore and pray always, that ye may be accounted worthy to escape all these things that shall come to pass, and to stand before the Son of man.* Those who so call upon Him in truth shall be heard in that day, as He says[13], *Ask and it shall be given you; Whatsoever ye shall ask the Father in My Name, He will give it you.*

"[14] That calling on God whereon salvation depends, is not in words only, but in heart and in deed. For what the heart believeth, the mouth confesseth, the hand in deed fulfilleth, The Apostle saith[15], *No man can say that Jesus is the Lord, but by the Holy Ghost;* yet this very *saying* must be weighed not by words, but by the affections. Whence we read of Samuel, *And Samuel among those who call upon His Name,* and of Moses and Aaron[16], *These called upon the Lord, and He heard them.*

For in Mount Zion—shall be deliverance. Re-

[1] Hugo de S. V. [2] S. Basil in Ps. xxxiii. § 8. Lap.

[3] אודה, אזכירה, אכפדה שמך, יודעי שמך, קרא בשם יי. ברך, הלל את שם יי. אזמרה

[4] Ps. lxix. 31. Heb. [5] Gen. iv. 26.

[6] Ib. xii. 8. xiii. 4. xxi. 33. xxvi. 25.

[7] 1 Kings xviii. 24. [8] 2 Kings v. 11.

[9] Ps. lxxix. 6. Jer. x. 25. [10] iii. 9.

[11] ימלט [12] S. Luke xxi. 36.

[13] S. Matt. vii. 7. S. John xvi. 23.

[14] Hugo de S. V. partly from S. Jer.

[15] 1 Cor. xii. 3. [16] Ps xcix. 6.

Before CHRIST cir. 800.

for [u] in mount Zion and in Jerusalem shall be deliverance, as the LORD hath said, and in [x] the remnant whom the LORD shall call.

Before CHRIST cir. 800.

[u] Is. 46. 13. & 59. 20. Obad. 17. Rom. 11. 26.

[x] Is. 11. 11, 16. Jer. 31. 7. Mic. 4. 7. & 5. 3, 7, 8. Rom. 9. 27. & 11. 5, 7.

pentance and remission of sins were to *be preached in the Name* of Jesus, *in all nations, beginning at Jerusalem*[1]. *There* was, under the Old Testament, the centre of the worship of God; *there* was the Church founded; thence it spread over the whole world. The place[2], *whither the tribes went up, the tribes of the Lord, unto the testimony of Israel, to give thanks unto the Name of the Lord,* where God had set His Name, where alone sacrifice could lawfully be offered, stands, as elsewhere, for the whole Church. Of that Church, we are in Baptism all made members, when we are made members of Christ, children of God, and heirs of heaven. Of that Church all remain members, who do not, by viciousness of life, or rejecting the truth of God, cast themselves out of it. They then are members of the *soul* of the Church, who, not being members of the visible Communion and society, know not, that in not becoming members of it, they are rejecting the command of Christ, to Whom by faith and love and in obedience they cleave. And *they*, being members of the *body* or visible communion of the Church, are not members of the *soul* of the Church, who, amid outward profession of the faith, do, in heart or deeds, deny Him Whom in words they confess. The deliverance promised in that Day, is to those who, being in the body of the Church, shall by true faith in Christ and fervent love to Him belong to the soul of the Church also, or who, although not in the body of the Church shall not, through their own fault, have ceased to be in the body, and shall belong to its soul, in that through faith and love they cleave to Christ its Head.

As the Lord hath said, by the Prophet Joel himself. This which he had said, is not man's word, but God's; and what God had said, shall certainly be. They then who have feared and loved God in this their day, shall not need to fear Him in that Day, for He is the Unchangeable God; as our Blessed Saviour says[3]; *Heaven and earth shall pass away, but My words shall not pass away.* God had said of both Jews and Gentiles, united in one[4]; *Rejoice, O ye nations, with His people, for He will avenge the blood of His servants, and will render vengeance to His adversaries, and will be merciful to His land and unto His people.*

And in the remnant. While foretelling His mercies in Christ, God foretells also, that[5] *few they be that find* them. It is evermore *a remnant, a residue, a body which escapes;* and so here, the mercies should be fulfilled, literally, *in the fugitives*, in those who flee from the wrath to come. All prophecy echoes the words of Joel; all history exemplifies them. Isaiah, Micah, Zephaniah, Jeremiah, Ezekiel, Zechariah, all foretell with one voice, that a remnant, and a remnant only, shall be left. In those earlier dispensations of God, in the flood, the destruction of Sodom and Gomorrah; in His dealings with Israel himself at the entrance into the promised land, the return from the Captivity, the first preaching of the Gospel, the destruction of Jerusalem, *a remnant* only was saved. It is said in tones of compassion and mercy, that *a remnant should be saved. The remnant should return, the remnant of Jacob, to the Mighty God*[6]. *The Lord of hosts shall be for a crown of glory to the residue of His people*[7]. *The Lord shall set His Hand to recover the remnant of His people which shall be left*[8]. *I will gather the remnant of My flock out of all countries whither I have driven them*[9]. *Publish ye, praise ye, and say, O Lord, save Thy people, the remnant of Israel*[10]. *Yet I will leave a remnant, that ye may have some that escape the sword among the nations*[11]. *Therein shall be left a remnant which shall be brought forth*[12]. *I will surely gather the remnant of Israel*[13]. *Who is a God like Thee, that pardoneth iniquity, and passeth by the transgression of the remnant of His heritage*[14]? *The remnant of Israel shall not do iniquity*[15]. *The residue of the people shall not be cut off from the city*[16]. It is then a summary of the declarations of the Prophets, when S. Paul says[17], *Even so, at this present time also, there is a remnant according to the election of grace. Israel hath not obtained that which he seeketh for; but the election hath obtained it, and the rest were blinded.* And so the Prophet says here;

Whom the Lord shall call. He had said before, *whosoever shall call upon the Name of the Lord shall be delivered.* Here he says, that they who should *so call on God*, shall themselves have been first *called by God.* So S. Paul[18], *to them that are sanctified in Christ Jesus, called* to be *Saints, with all that in every place call upon the Name of Jesus Christ our Lord.* It is all of grace. God must first call by His

1 S. Luke xxiv. 47. 2 Ps. cxxii. 4.
3 S. Mark xiii. 31. 4 Deut. xxxii. 43.
5 S. Matt. vii. 14.
6 Is. x. 20; add 21, 22. vi. 9–13, &c.
7 Ib. xxviii. 5. 8 Ib. xi, 11, add 16.
9 Jer. xxiii. 3. 10 Ib. xxxi. 7.
11 Ezek. vi. 8. 12 Ib. xiv. 22.
13 Mic. ii. 12; add iv. 7. v. 3, 7, 8. 14 Ib. vii. 18.
15 Zeph. iii. 13. add ii. 9. 16 Zech. xiv. 2.
17 Rom. xi. 5, 7. 18 1 Cor. i. 2.

Before CHRIST cir. 800.

CHAPTER III.

1 *God's judgments against the enemies of his people.* 9 *God will be known in his judgment.* 18 *His blessing upon the Church.*

[a] Jer. 30. 3. Ezek. 38. 14.

FOR, behold, [a] in those
days, and in that time,
when I shall bring again
the captivity of Judah and
Jerusalem,

Before CHRIST cir. 800.

2 [b] I will also gather all
nations and will bring them
down into [c] the valley of
Jehoshaphat, and [d] will
plead with them there for
my people and *for* my her-

[b] Zech. 14. 2, 3, 4.

[c] 2 Chr. 20. 26. ver. 12.

[d] Isai. 66. 16. Ezek. 38. 22.

---

grace; then we obey His call, and call upon Him; and He has said [1], *call upon Me in the day of trouble, and I will deliver thee, and thou shalt glorify Me.* God accounts our salvation His own glory.

III. 1. *For, behold.* The Prophet by the word, *for,* shews that he is about to explain in detail, what he had before spoken of, in sum. By the word, *behold,* he stirs up our minds for something great, which he is to set before our eyes, and which we should not be prepared to expect or believe, unless he solemnly told us, *Behold.* As the detail, then, of what goes before, the prophecy contains all times of future judgment on those who should oppose God, oppress His Church and people, and sin against Him in them and all times of His blessing upon His own people, until the Last Day. And this it gives in imagery, partly describing nearer events of the same sort, as in the punishments of Tyre and Sidon, such as they endured from the kings of Assyria, from Nebuchadnezzar, from Alexander; partly using these, His earlier judgments, as representatives of the like punishments against the like sins unto the end.

In those days and in that time. The whole period of which the Prophet had been speaking, was the time from which God called His people to repentance, to the Day of Judgment. The last division of that time was from the beginning of the Gospel unto that Day. He fixes the occasion of which he speaks by the words, *when I shall bring again the captivity of Judah and Jerusalem.* This form was used, before there was any general dispersion of the nation. For all captivity of single members of the Jewish people had this sore calamity, that it severed them from the public worship of God, and exposed them to idolatry. So David complains, *they have driven me out this day from abiding in the inheritance of the Lord, saying, go serve other gods* [2]. The restoration then of single members, or of smaller bodies of captives, was, at that time, an unspeakable mercy. It was the restoration of those shut out from the worship of God; and so was an image of *the deliverance from the bondage of corruption into the glorious liberty of the sons of God* [3], or of any *return* of those who had gone astray, *to the Shepherd and Bishop of* their *souls* [4]. The grievous captivity of the Jews, now, is to Satan, whose servants they made themselves, when they said, *we have no king but Cæsar; His Blood be upon us and upon our children.* Their blessed deliverance will be *from the power of Satan unto God* [5]. It is certain from S. Paul [6], that there shall be a complete conversion of the Jews, before the end of the world, as indeed has always been believed. This shall probably be shortly before the end of the world, and God would here say, "when I shall have brought to an end *the captivity of Judah and Jerusalem,* i.e. of that people *to whom were the promises* [7], and shall have delivered them from the bondage of sin and from blindness to light and freedom in Christ, then will I gather all nations to judgment."

2. *I will gather all nations and bring them down to the valley of Jehoshaphat.* It may be that the imagery is furnished by that great deliverance which God gave to Jehoshaphat, when *Ammon and Moab and Edom come against* him, *to cast God's people out of* His *possession,* which *He gave* them *to inherit* [8], and Jehoshaphat appealed to God, *O our God, wilt Thou not judge them?* and God said, *the battle is not your's but God's,* and God turned their swords everyone against the other, *and none escaped. And on the fourth day they assembled themselves in the valley of Berachah* (blessing); *for there they blessed the Lord* [9]. So, in the end, He shall destroy Anti-Christ, not by human aid, but *by the breath of His mouth,* and then the end shall come and He shall sit on the throne of His glory to judge all nations. Then shall none escape of those gathered against Judah and Jerusalem, but shall be judged of their own consciences, as those former enemies of His people fell by their own swords.

That valley, however, is nowhere called *the valley of Jehoshaphat.* It continued to be *called the valley of Berachah,* the writer adds, *to this day.* And it is so called still. Caphar Barucha, "the village of blessing," was still known in that neighborhood in the time of S. Jerome [10];

[1] Ps. l. 15. [2] 1 Sam. xxvi. 19. [3] Rom. viii. 21 [4] 1 S. Pet. ii. 25. [5] Acts xxvi. 18. [6] Rom. xi. 26.

[7] Ib. ix. 4. [8] 2 Chr. xx. 11. [9] Ib. 24, 26. [10] Ep. 108. ad Eustoch. § 11.

Before CHRIST cir. 800.

itage Israel, whom they have scattered among the nations, and parted my land.

Before CHRIST cir. 800.

it had been known in that of Josephus[1]. S. W. of Bethlehem and E. of Tekoa are still 3 or 4 acres of ruins[2], bearing the name Bereikut[3], and a valley below them, still bearing silent witness to God's ancient mercies, in its but slightly disguised name, "the valley of Bereikut" (Berachah). The only valley called the *valley of Jehoshaphat*[4], is the valley of Kedron, lying between Jerusalem and the Mount of Olives, encircling the city on the East. There Asa, Hezekiah, and Josiah cast the idols, which they had burned[5]. The valley was the common burying-place for the inhabitants of Jerusalem[6]. *There* was the garden whither Jesus oftentimes resorted with His disciples; *there* was His Agony and Bloody Sweat; there Judas betrayed Him; thence He was dragged by the rude officers of the High Priest. The Temple, the token of God's presence among them, the pledge of His accepting their sacrifices which could only be offered there, overhung it on the one side. There, under the rock on which that temple stood, they dragged Jesus, *as a lamb to the slaughter*[7]. On the other side, it was overhung by the Mount of *Olives*, whence *He beheld the city and wept over it*, because it *knew* not *in* that its *day, the things which belong to its peace;* whence, after His precious Death and Resurrection, Jesus ascended into Heaven. There the Angels foretold His return[8], *This same Jesus which is taken up from you into heaven shall so come in like manner as ye have seen Him go into heaven.* It has been a current opinion, that our Lord should descend to judgment, not only in like manner, and in the like Form of Man, but in the same place, over this valley of Jehoshaphat. Certainly, if so it be, it were appropriate, that He should appear in His Majesty, where, for us, He bore the extremest shame; that He should judge *there*, where for us, He submitted to be judged. "He sheweth," says S. Hilary[9], "that the Angels bringing them together, the assemblage shall be in the place of His Passion; and meetly will His Coming in glory be looked for *there*, where He won for us the glory of eternity by the sufferings of His humility in the Body." But since the Apostle says, *we shall meet the Lord in the air*, then, not *in* the valley of Jehoshaphat, but *over* it, in the clouds, would His throne be. "[10] Uniting, as it were, Mount Calvary and Olivet, the spot would be well suited to that judgment wherein the saints shall partake of the glory of the Ascension of Christ and the fruit of His Blood and Passion, and Christ shall take deserved vengeance of His persecutors and of all who would not be cleansed by His Blood."

God saith, *I will gather all nations*, of the gathering together of the nations against Him under Anti-Christ, because He overrules all things, and while they, in *their* purpose, are gathering themselves against His people and elect, He, in His purpose secret to them, is gathering them to sudden destruction and judgment, *and will bring them down;* for their pride shall be brought down, and themselves laid low. Even Jewish writers have seen a mystery in the word, and said, that it hinteth "the depth of God's judgments," that God "would descend with them into the depth of judgment[11]," "a most exact judgment even of the most hidden things."

His very Presence there would say to the wicked, "[12] In this place did I endure grief for you; here, at Gethsemane, I poured out for you that sweat of water and Blood; here was I betrayed and taken, bound as a robber, dragged over Cedron into the city; hard by this valley, in the house of Caiaphas and then of Pilate, I was for you judged and condemned to death, crowned with thorns, buffeted, mocked and spat upon; here, led through the whole city, bearing the Cross, I was at length crucified for you on Mount Calvary; here, stripped, suspended between heaven and earth, with hands, feet, and My whole frame distended, I offered Myself for you as a Sacrifice to God the Father. Behold the Hands which ye pierced; the Feet which ye perforated; the Sacred prints which ye anew imprinted on My Body. Ye have despised My toils, griefs, sufferings; ye have counted the Blood of My covenant an unholy thing; ye have chosen to follow your own concupiscences rather than Me, My doctrine and law; ye have preferred momentary pleasures, riches, honors, to the eternal salvation which I promised; ye have despised Me, threatening the fires of hell. Now ye see Whom ye have despised; now ye see that My threats and promises were not vain, but true; now ye see that vain and fallacious were your loves, riches, and dignities; now ye see that ye were fools and senseless in the love of them; but too late. *Depart, ye cursed, into everlasting fire, prepared for the devil and his*

[1] Jos. Ant. ix. 1. 3. [2] Robins. Pal. iii. 275.
[3] in Seetzen's map (Ritter, Erdk. xv. 635), Wolcott, Excurs. to Hebron, p. 43
[4] Euseb. Onom. κοιλὰς Ἰωσαφάτ.
[5] 1 Kings xv. 13. 2 Chr. xxx. 14. 2 Kings xxiii. 6, 12.
[6] Williams, H. C. ii. 523. Thomson, The Land, &c. ii. 481. Josephus places the death of Athaliah in that valley. Ant. ix. 7. 3.
[7] Is. liii. 7. [8] Acts i. 11. [9] in S. Matt. c. 25.
[10] Suarez, in 3. p. q. 59. art. 6. disp. 53. sect. 3.
[11] Rashi and Abarbanel in Poc.
[12] abridged from Lap.

Before CHRIST cir. 800.

[e] Obad. 11. Nah. 3. 10.

3 And they have [e] cast
lots for my people; and
have given a boy for an
harlot, and sold a girl for
wine, that they might
drink.

Before CHRIST cir. 800.

---

angels. But ye who believed, hoped, loved, worshiped Me, your Redeemer, who obeyed My whole law; who lived a Christian life worthy of Me; who lived soberly, godly and righteously in this world, looking for the blessed hope and this My glorious Coming, *Come ye blessed of My Father, inherit the kingdom of heaven prepared for you from the foundation of the World.—And these shall go into everlasting fire; but the righteous into life eternal.* Blessed he whoso continually thinketh or foreseeth, provideth for these things."

And will plead with them there. Woe to him, against whom God pleadeth! He saith not, "judgeth" but *pleadeth*, making Himself a party, the Accuser as well as the Judge, "[1] Solemn is it indeed when Almighty God saith, *I will plead. He that hath ears to hear let him hear.* For terrible is it. Wherefore also that *Day of the Lord* is called *great and terrible.* For what more terrible than, at such a time, the pleading of God with man? For He says, *I will plead*, as though He had never yet pleaded with man, great and terrible as have been His judgments since that first destruction of the world by water. Past are those judgments on Sodom and Gomorrah, on Pharaoh and his hosts, on the whole people in the wilderness from twenty years old and upward, the mighty oppressions of the enemies into whose hands He gave them in the land of promise; past were the four Empires; but now, in the time of Anti-Christ, *there shall be tribulation, such as there had not been from the beginning of the world.* But all these are little, compared with that *great and terrible Day;* and so He says, *I will plead*, as though all before had not been, to *plead*."

God maketh Himself in such wise a party, as not to condemn those unconvicted; yet the *pleading* has a separate awfulness of its own. God impleads, so as to allow Himself to be impleaded and answered; but there is no answer. He will set forth what He had done, and how we have requited Him. And we are without excuse. Our memories witness against us; our knowledge acknowledges His justice; our conscience convicts us; our reason condemns us; all unite in pronouncing ourselves ungrateful, and God holy and just. For a sinner to see himself is to condemn himself; and in the Day of Judgment, God will bring before each sinner his whole self.

For My people. "[1] God's people are the one true Israel, *princes with God*, the whole multitude of the elect, foreordained to eternal life." Of these, the former people of Israel, once chosen of God, was a type. As St. Paul says[2], *They are not all Israel which are of Israel;* and again[3], *As many as walk according to this rule* of the Apostle's teaching, *peace be on them and mercy, and upon the Israel of God*, i. e. not among the Galatians only, but in the whole Church throughout the world. Since the whole people and Church of God is one, He lays down one law, which shall be fulfilled to the end; that those who, for their own ends, even although therein the instruments of God, shall in any way injure the people of God, shall be themselves punished by God. God makes Himself one with His people. *He that toucheth you, toucheth the apple of My eye*[4]. So our Lord said, [5] *Saul, Saul, why persecutest thou Me?* and in the Day of Judgment He will say[6], *I was an hungered and ye gave me no meat. Forasmuch as ye did it not unto one of the least of these My brethern, ye did it not to Me.* "[7] By calling them *My heritage*, He shews that He will not on any terms part with them or suffer them to be lost, but will vindicate them to Himself for ever."

Whom they have scattered among the nations. Such was the offence of the Assyrians and Babylonians, the first *army*, which God sent against His people. And for it, Nineveh and Babylon perished. "[8] Yet he does not speak of that ancient people, or of its enemies only, but of all the elect both in that people and in the Church of the Gentiles, and of all persecutors of the elect. For that people were a figure of the Church, and its enemies were a type of those who persecute the Saints." The dispersion of God's former people by the heathen was renewed in those who persecuted Christ's disciples *from city to city*, banished them, and confiscated their goods. Banishment to mines or islands were the slightest punishments of the early Christians[9].

3. *And they have cast lots.* They treated God's people as of no account, and delighted in shewing their contempt toward them. They chose no one above another, as though all alike were worthless. *They cast lots*, it is said elsewhere[10], *upon their honorable men*, as a special indignity, above captivity or slavery. A *girl* they sold for an evening's revelry, and a *boy* they exchanged for a night's debauch.

[1] from Rup. [2] Rom. ix. 6. [3] Gal. vi. 16. [4] Zech. ii. 8. [5] Acts ix. 4. [6] S. Matt. xxv. 34, 35. [7] Poc. [8] Rib.

[9] See Tertull. Apol. c. 12. p. 30. Oxf. Tr. S. Cypr. Ep. x. 1. xi. 1. xx. 3. xxii. xxxi. xxxvii. 2. 3. xxxix. 1. lxxvi. 2. p. 304. n. y. [10] Nah. iii. 10.

Before CHRIST cir. 800.

4 Yea, and what have
ye to do with me, [f] O Tyre,
and Zidon, and all the
coasts of Palestine? [g] will
ye render me a recom-
pense? and if ye recom-
pense me, swiftly *and* speedily will I return your recompense upon your own head;
5 Because ye have taken
my silver and my gold, and
have carried into your temples my goodly † pleasant
things:

f Amos 1. 6, 9.
g Ezek. 25. 15, 16, 17.
† Heb. *desirable*: Dan. 11. 38.

4. *Yea, and what have ye to do with Me?* lit. *and also, what are ye to Me?* The words, *And also*, shew that this is something additional to the deeds of those before spoken of. Those, instanced before, were great oppressors, such as dispersed the former people of God and *divided their land.* In addition to these, God condemns here another class, those who, without having power to destroy, harass and vex His heritage. The words, *what are ye to Me?* are like that other phrase [1], *what is there to thee and me?* i. e. what have we in common? These words, *what are ye to Me?* also declare, that those nations had no part in God. God accounts them as aliens, *what are ye to Me?* Nothing. But the words convey, besides, that they would, unprovoked, have to do with God, harassing His people without cause. They obtruded themselves, as it were, upon God and His judgments; they challenged God; they thrust themselves in, to their destruction, where they had no great temptation to meddle, nothing, but inbred malice, to impel them. This was, especially, the character of the relations of Tyre and Zidon and Philistia with Israel. They were allotted to Israel by Joshua, but were not assailed [2]. On the contrary, *the Zidonians* are counted among those who *oppressed* Israel, and *out of* whose *hand* God *delivered* him, when he *cried* to God [3]. The Philistines were the unwearied assailants of Israel in the days of the Judges, and Saul, and David [4]; during 40 years Israel was given into the hands of the Philistines, until God delivered them by Samuel at Mizpeh. When David was king of all Israel, the Philistines still acted on the offensive, and lost Gath and her towns to David in an offensive war [5]. To Jehoshaphat some of them voluntarily paid tribute [6]; but in the reign of Jehoram his son, they, with some Arabians, marauded in Judah, plundering the king's house and slaying all his sons, save the youngest [7]. This is the last event before the time of Joel. They stand among the most inveterate and unprovoked enemies of God's people, and probably as enemies of God also hating the claim of Judah that their God was the One God.

Will ye render Me a recompense? Men never want pleas for themselves. The Philistines, although the aggressors, had been signally defeated by David. Men forget their own wrong-doings and remember their sufferings. It may be then, that the Philistines thought that they had been aggrieved when their assaults were defeated, and looked upon their own fresh aggressions as a requital. If moreover, as is probable, they heard that the signal victories won over them were ascribed by Israel to God, and themselves also suspected, that these *mighty Gods* [8] were the cause of their defeat, they doubtless turned their hatred against God. Men, when they submit not to God chastening them, hate Him. This belief that they were retaliating against God, (not, of course, knowing Him as God,) fully corresponds with the strong words, "will ye render Me *a recompense* [9]?" Julian's dying blasphemy, "Galilean, thou hast conquered," corresponds with the efforts of his life against the gospel, and implies a secret consciousness that He Whose religion he was straining to overthrow *might* be, What he denied Him to be, God. The phrase [10] *swiftly*, lit. *lightly, and speedily, denotes* the union of easiness with speed. The recompense is returned *upon* their head, coming down upon them from God.

5. *Ye have taken My silver and My gold.* Not the silver and gold of the temple, (as some have thought.) At least, up to the Prophet's time, they had not done this. For the inroad of the Philistines in the reign of Jehoram was, apparently, a mere marauding expedition, in which they slew and plundered, but are not said to have besieged or taken any city, much less Jerusalem. God calls the *silver and gold* which He, through His Providence, had bestowed on Judah, *My* gold and silver; as He said by Hosea [11],

[1] Josh. xxii. 24, &c. S. Matt. viii. 29, &c.
[2] Zidon, Josh. xix. 28. xiii. 6. see Judg. i. 31. iii. 3. Tyre, Josh. xix. 29. the Philistines, Josh. xiii. 2, 3. xv. 45–7. xix. 43. see Jud. iii. 3.
[3] Judg. x. 12.
[4] Ib. xiii. 1. 1 Sam. iv. xiii. xvii. xxiii. 1. xxx. xxxi.
[5] 2 Sam. v. 17–end. viii. 1. 1 Chr. xviii. 1. 2 Sam. xxi. 18. xxiii. 9–16.
[6] 2 Chr. xvii. 11.
[7] 2 Chr. xxi. 16, 17. xxii. 1.
[8] 1 Sam. iv. 7, 8.
[9] גמל, rendered *recompense*, is used, although rarely, of one who "begins good or evil," but, as united with the word שלם *repay, make good*, it can only denote *requited*.
[10] It recurs Is. v. 26.
[11] ii. 8.

Before CHRIST cir. 800.

6 The children also of Judah and the children of

Before CHRIST cir. 800.

She knew not that I multiplied her silver and gold, whereof she made Baal; and by Haggai[1], *The silver is Mine, and the gold is Mine, saith the Lord of Hosts.* For they were His people, and what they had, they held of Him; and the Philistines too so accounted it, and dedicated a part of it to their idols, as they had the ark formerly, accounting the victory over God's people to be the triumph of their idols over God.

6. *The children also,* lit. *And the sons of Judah and the sons of Jerusalem have ye sold to the sons of the Greeks.* This sin of the Tyrians was probably old and inveterate. The Tyrians, as they were the great carriers of the world's traffic, so they were slave-dealers, and, in the earliest times, men-stealers. The Greek ante-historic tradition exhibits them, as trading and selling women, from both Greece[2] and Egypt[3]. As their trade became more fixed, they themselves stole no more, but, like Christian nations, sold those whom others stole or made captive. Ezekiel speaks of their trade in *the souls of men*[4] with *Greece* on the one side, and *Tubal and Mesech* near the Black Sea on the other. The beautiful youth of Greece of both sexes were sold even into Persia[5]. In regard to the Moschi and Tibareni, it remains uncertain, whether they sold those whom they took in war (and, like the tribes of Africa in modern times, warred the more, because they had a market for their prisoners,) or whether, like the modern Circassians, they sold their daughters. Ezekiel however says, *men,* so that he cannot mean, exclusively, women. From the times of the Judges, Israel was exposed in part both to the violence and fraud of Tyre and Sidon. The tribe of Asher seems to have lived in the open country among fortified towns of the Zidonians. For whereas of Benjamin, Manasseh, Ephraim, Zabulon, it is said that the old inhabitants of the land *dwelt among them*[6], of Asher it is said, that they *dwelt among the Canaanites,* the *inhabitants of the land*[7], as though these were the more numerous. And not only so, but since they did *not drive out the inhabitants* of seven cities, *Accho, Zidon, Ahlab, Achzib, Helbah, Aphek, Rehob,* they must have been liable to incursions from them. The Zidonians were among those who *oppressed Israel*[8]. Sisera's army came from their territory, (for Jabin was king of Hazor,) and Deborah speaks of *a damsel or two,* as the expected prey of each man in the whole multitude of his host. An old proverb, mentioned B. C. 427, implies that the Phœnicians sent circumcised slaves into the fields to reap their harvest[9]. But there were no other circumcised there besides Israel.

But the Phœnician slave-trade was also probably, even in the time of the Judges, exercised against Israel. In Joel and Amos, the Philistines and Tyrians appear as combined in the traffic. In Amos, the Philistines are the robbers of men; the Phœnicians are the receivers and the sellers[10]. Heathen nations retain for centuries the same inherited character, the same natural nobleness, or, still more, the same natural vices. The Phœnicians, at the date of the Judges, are known as dishonest traders, and that, in slaves. The Philistines were then also inveterate oppressors. On one occasion *the captivity of the land* coincided with the great victory of the Philistines, when Eli died and the ark of God was taken. For these two dates are given in the same place as the close of the idolatry of Micah's graven image. It endured *unto the captivity of the land*[11] and, *and all the time that the house of God was at Shiloh,* whence the ark was removed, never to return, in that battle when it was taken. But *the captivity of the land* is not merely a subdual, whereby the inhabitants would remain tributary or even enslaved, yet still remain. A captivity implies a removal of the inhabitants; and such a removal could not have been the direct act of the Philistines. For dwelling themselves in the land only, they had no means of removing the inhabitants from it, except by selling them; and the only nation, who could export them in such numbers as would be expressed by the words *a captivity of the land,* were the Zidonians. Probably such acts were expressly prohibited by the *brotherly covenant*[12] or treaty between Solomon and Hiram King of Tyre. For Amos says that Tyre forgot that treaty, when she sold wholesale the captive Israelites whom the Philistines had carried off. Soon after Joel, Obadiah speaks of a captivity at *Sepharad,* or *Sardis*[13], the capital of the Lydian empire. The Tyrian merchants were *the* connecting link between Palestine and the coasts of Asia-minor. The Israelites must have been sold thither as slaves, and that by

1 ii. 8.
2 Herod. i. 1. Eurip. Helen. 190. Movers quotes these and the following authorities Phœnic. Alterthum. c. 4. p. 71.
3 Herod. ii. 54.
4 xxvii. 13.
5 Bochart Phaleg. iii. 3. p. 154.
6 Judg. i. 21, 27, 29, 30.
7 Ib. 31, 2.
8 Judg. v. 30. see iv. 3, 7, 13, 15, 16.
9 "Cuckoo; ye circumcised, to field." The Cuckoo's note was, in Phœnicia, the signal for harvest, (Aristoph. Av. 505–7,) and those sent out, with a term of contempt, to gather it, were "circumcised."
10 Am. i. 6, 9.
11 Judg. xviii. 30, 31.
12 See on Am. i. 9.
13 See on Ob. 20.

Before CHRIST cir. 800.

Jerusalem have ye sold unto † the Grecians, that ye might remove them far from their border.

† Heb. *the sons of the Grecians.*

Before CHRIST cir. 800.

the Phœnicians. In yet later times the Tyrian merchants followed, like vultures, on the rear of armies to make a prey of the living, as the vultures of the dead. They hung on the march of Alexander as far as India[1]. In the wars of the Maccabees, at Nicanor's proclamation, a thousand[2] merchants gathered to the camp of Gorgias[3] *with silver and gold, very much, to buy the children of Israel as slaves*, and with chains[4] wherewith to secure them. They assembled in the rear of the Roman armies, "[5] seeking wealth amid the clash of arms, and slaughter, and fleeing poverty through peril." Reckless of human life, the slave-merchants commonly, in their wholesale purchase of captives, abandoned the children as difficult of transport, whence the Spartan king was praised for providing for them[6].

The temptation to Tyrian covetousness was aggravated by the ease with which they could possess themselves of the Jews, the facility of transport, and, as it seems, their value. It is mentioned as the inducement to slave-piracy among the Cilicians. "The export of the slaves especially invited to misdeeds, being most gainful; for they were easily taken, and the market was not so very far off and was most wealthy[7].

The Jewish slaves appear also to have been valued, until those times after the taking of Jerusalem, when they had become demoralized, and there was a plethora of them, as God had predicted[8]. The post occupied by the *little maid* who *waited on Naaman's wife*[9], was that of a favorite slave, as Greek tradition represented Grecian maidens to have been an object of coveting to the wife of the Persian Monarch[10]. The *damsel or two* for the wives of each man in Jabin's host appear as a valuable part of the spoil. The wholesale price at which Nicanor set the Jews his expected prisoners, and at which he hoped to sell some 180,000[11], shews the extent of the then traffic and their relative value. £2. 14*s.* 9*d.* as the average price of each of ninety slaves *in* Judea, implies a retail-price at the place of sale, above the then ordinary price of man. This wholesale price for what was expected to be a mixed multitude of nearly 200,000, (for "[12] Nicanor undertook to make so much money of the captive Jews as should defray the tribute of 2000 talents which the king was to pay to the Romans,") was nearly 5 times as much as that at which Carthaginian soldiers were sold at the close of the first Punic war[13]. It was two-thirds of the retail price of a good slave at Athens[14], or of that at which, about B. C. 340, the law of Greece prescribed that captives should be redeemed[15]; or of that, (which was nearly the same) at which the Mosaic law commanded compensation to be made for a slave accidentally killed[16]. The facility of transport increased the value. For, although Pontus supplied both the best and the most of the Roman slaves[17], yet in the war with Mithridates, amid a great abundance of all things, slaves were sold at 3*s.* 3*d.*[18] The special favors also shewn to the Jewish captives at Rome and Alexandria shew the estimation in which they were held. At Rome, in the reign of Augustus, "[19] the large section of Rome beyond the Tiber was possessed and inhabited by Jews, most of them Roman citizens, having been brought as captives into Italy and made freedmen by their owners." On whatever ground Ptolemy Philadelphus redeemed 100,000 Jews whom his father had taken and sold[20], the fact can hardly be without foundation, or his enrolling them in his armies, or his employing them in public offices or about his own person.

Joel lived before the historic times of Greece. But there are early traces of slave-trade carried on by Greeks[21]. According to Theopompus, the Chians, first among the Greeks, acquired barbarian slaves in the way of trade[22]. The Ionian migration had filled the islands and part of the coasts of Asia Minor with Greek traders about two centuries before Joel, B. C. 1069[23]. Greeks inhabited both the coasts and islands between Tyre and Sardis, whither we know them to have been carried. Cyprus and Crete, both inhabited by Greeks and both in near intercourse with Phœnicia, were close at hand.

The demand for slaves must have been enormous. For wives were but seldom allowed them; and Athens, Ægina, Corinth alone had in the days of their prosperity

1 Arr. Exped. vi. 22. 8.
2 2 Macc. viii. 34.
3 1 Macc. iii. 41.
4 Jos. Ant. xii. 7. 3. and 1 Macc. see Eng. Marg.
5 S. Jer. on Ezek. xxvii. 16.
6 Xenoph. Agesil. i. 21.
7 Strabo xiv. 5. 2.
8 Deut. xxviii. 68. Glycas says that Adrian sold 4 Jews for a modius [two gallons] of barley. Ann. iii. p. 448. M.
9 2 Kgs v. 2.
10 Herod. iii. 134.
11 Ninety being offered for a talent, this would be the number whose sale would bring in 2000 talents.
12 2 Macc. viii. 10.
13 18 Denarii, i. e. 11*s.* 3*d.* Liv. xxi. 41. Boeckh Econ. of Ath. i. 92.
14 Boeckh i. 94.
15 Aristot. Eth. v. 7. 1.
16 Ex. xxi. 30.
17 Polyb. iv. 38.
18 Plutarch Lucull. § 14.
19 Philo Leg. ad Caium Opp. ii. 568.
20 Jos. Ant. xii. 2. and 4.
21 Movers quotes instances from Samos, Lesbos, Ephesus, Miletus, p. 81.
22 In Athenæus vi. 88. p. 574. Mov.
23 Eus. Chron. ii. 304–18.

Before CHRIST cir. 800.

[h] Isai. 43. 5, 6. & 49. 12. Jer. 23. 8.

7 Behold, [h] I will raise
them out of the place
whither ye have sold them,
and will return your recompense upon your own
head:
8 And I will sell your
sons and your daughters

1,330,000 slaves [1]. At the great slave-mart at Delos, 10,000 were brought, sold, removed in a single day [2].

That ye might remove them far from their border. The Philistines hoped thus to weaken the Jews, by selling their fighting men afar, whence they could no more return. There was doubtless also in this removal an anti-religious malice, in that the Jews clung to their land, as *the Lord's land*, the land given by Him to their fathers; so that they, at once, weakened their rivals, aggravated and enjoyed their distress, and seemed again to triumph over God. Tyre and Sidon took no active share in making the Jews prisoners, yet, partaking in the profit and aiding in the disposal of the captives, they became, according to that true proverb "the receiver is as bad as the thief," equally guilty of the sin, in the sight of God.

7. *Behold I will raise them.* If this promise relates to the same individuals who had been sold, it must have been fulfilled silently; as indeed the return of captives to their own land, unless brought about by some historical event, belongs not to history, but to private life. The Prophet, however, is probably predicting God's dealings with the nations, not with those individuals. The enslaving of these Hebrews in the time of Joram was but one instance out of a whole system of covetous misdeeds. The Philistines carried away captives from them again in the time of Ahaz [3], and yet again subsequently [4]; and still more at the capture of Jerusalem [5].

8. *I will sell your sons.* God Himself would reverse the injustice of men. The sons of Zion should be restored, the sons of the Phœnicians and of the Philistines sold into distant captivity. Tyre was taken by Nebuchadnezzar, and then by Alexander, who sold "more than 13,000" of the inhabitants into slavery [6]; Sidon was taken and destroyed by Artaxerxes Ochus, and it is said, above 40,000 of its inhabitants perished in the flames [7]. The like befell the Philistines [8]. The Sabæans are probably instanced, as being the remotest nation in the opposite direction, a nation, probably, the partner of Tyre's traffic in *men*, as well as in their other merchandise, and who (as is the way of unregenerate nature) would as soon trade *in* Tyrians, as *with* Tyrians. The Sabæans were like the Phœnicians, a wealthy merchant people, and, of old, united with them in the trade of the world, the Sabæans sending forth their fleets across the Indian Ocean, as the Tyrians along the Mediterranean. Three fathers of distinct races bore the name Sheba; one, a descendant of Ham, the other two, descended from Shem. The Hamite Sheba was the son of Raamah, the son of Cush [9], and doubtless dwelt of old in the country on the Persian gulf called by the name Raamah [10]. Traces of the name Sheba occur there, and some even after our era [11]. The Shemite Sabæans, were, some descendants of Sheba, the tenth son of Joktan [12]; the others from Sheba, the son of Abraham and Keturah [13]. The Sabæans, descended from Joktan, dwelt in the S. W. extremity of Arabia, extending from the Red Sea to the Sea [14] of Babel-mandeb. The country is still called "ard-es-Seba [15]," "land of Saba;" and Saba is often mentioned by Arabic writers [16]. To the Greeks and Latins they were known by the name of one division of the race (Himyar) Homeritæ [17]. Their descendants still speak an Arabic, acknowledged by the learned Arabs to be a distinct language from that which, through Mohammed, prevailed and was diffused [18]; a "species [19]" of Arabic which they attribute "to the times of (the Prophet) Hud [perhaps Eber] and those before him." It belonged to them as descendants of Joktan. Sabæans are mentioned, distinct from both

[1] Athens, 400,000. (Ctesicles in Athen. vi. 103,) Corinth, 460,000. (Timæus ib.) Ægina, 470,000. (Aristot. ib.)
[2] Strabo xiv. 5. 2.
[3] 2 Chr. xxviii. 18.
[4] Ezek. xvi. 27, 57.
[5] Ib. xxv. 15.
[6] Diod. Sic. xvii. 46. Arrian says 30,000. ii. 24.
[7] Diod. xvi. 45.
[8] See on Zeph. ii. 4–7.
[9] Gen. x. 7.
[10] Regma, Steph. Byz. sub v. רעמה is pronounced Ῥέγμα by the LXX. "Regma," Vulg.
[11] In the names "The promontory of Ἀσαβώ, or Ἀσαβῶν" in Ptolemy vi. 7, and Marcian Heracl. p. 16. "The black mountains called Ἀσαβῶν," Ptol. Ib. "a very great mountain, called Σαβώ," at the entrance of the Persian gulf. (Arrian. Peripl. p. 20) Batra*saves* or Batra*sabbes* a city in Pliny, (vi. 28. 32.) *Sabis*, a river in Carmania on the opposite side of the Persian gulf. (Mela iii. 8.) Dionysius Perieg. also places the Sabæ next to the Pasargadæ, v. 1069. see Bochart, iv. 7.
[12] Gen. x. 28.
[13] Ib. xxv. 3.
[14] Plin. vi. 28, 32.
[15] Cruttenden in Journ. Geogr. Soc. 1838. viii. 268.
[16] See De Sacy below.
[17] Philostg. ii. 6. iii. 4. (Arr.) Peripl. p. 13. Marcian 13. Plin. vi. 28. 32.
[18] Authorities referred to by Soiuthi, quoted by Fresnel Lettre iv. in Journal Asiatique T. v. p. 512. Fresnal says that the grammatical forms most resemble Æthiopic, although it is richer than Arabic both in consonants and vowels, and has more Hebrew roots than ordinary Arabic. Ib. 533, sqq. De Sacy observed that the difference was one of language, (not of dialect only.) Acad. d. Inscr. T. 48. p. 509. note.
[19] Soiuthi Ib.

Before CHRIST cir. 800.

into the hand of the children of Judah, and they shall sell them to the [l]Sabeans, to a people [k]far off: for the LORD hath spoken *it.*

[l] Ezek. 23. 42.
[k] Jer. 6. 20.

9 ¶ [l]Proclaim ye this among the Gentiles; † Prepare war, wake up the mighty men, let all the men of war draw near; let them come up:

Before CHRIST cir. 800.

[l] See Isaiah 8, 9, 10. Jer. 46. 3, 4. Ezek. 38. 7.
† Heb. *Sanctify.*

of these, as "[1]dwelling in Arabia Felix, next beyond Syria, which they frequently invaded, before it belonged to the Romans." These Sabæans probably are those spoken of as marauders by Job[2]; and may have been descendants of Keturah. Those best known to the Greeks and Romans were, naturally, those in the South Western corner of Arabia. The account of their riches and luxuries is detailed, and, although from different authorities[3], consistent; else, almost fabulous. One metropolis is said to have had 65 temples[4], private individuals had more than kingly magnificence[5]. Arabic historians expanded into fable the extent and prerogatives[6] of their Paradise lands, before the breaking of the artificial dike, made for the irrigation of their country[7]. They traded with India, availing themselves doubtless of the Monsoon, and perhaps brought thence their gold, if not also the best and most costly frankincense[8]. The Sheba of the Prophet appears to have been the wealthy Sheba near the Red Sea. Indeed, in absence of evidence to the contrary, it is natural to understand the name of those best known. Solomon unites it with Seba[9], (the Æthiopian Sabæ.) The known frankincense-districts are on the S. W. corner of Arabia[10]. The tree has diminished, perhaps has degenerated through the neglect consequent on Mohammedan oppression, diminished consumption, change of the line of commerce; but it still survives in those districts[11]; a relic of what is passed away. Ezekiel indeed unites *the merchants of Sheba and Raamah*[12], as trading with Tyre. *The merchants of Sheba and Raamah, they were thy merchants; with the chief of all spices and with all precious stones and gold they occupied in thy fairs.* It may be that he joins them together as kindred tribes; yet it is as probable that he unites the two great channels of merchandise, East and West, Raamah on the Persian Gulf, and Sheba near the Red Sea. Having just mentioned the produce of Northern Arabia as poured into Tyre, he would, in this case, enumerate North, East, and West of Arabia as combined to enrich her. Agatharcides unites the Sabæans of S. W. Arabia with the Gerrhæans, who were certainly on the Persian Gulf[13]. "No people," he says[5], "is apparently richer than the Sabæans and Gerrhæans, who dispense forth everything worth speaking of from Asia and Europe. These made the Syria of Ptolemy full of gold. These supplied the industry of the Phœnicians with profitable imports, not to mention countless other proofs of wealth." Their caravans went to Elymais, Carmania; Charræ was their emporium; they returned to Gabala and Phœnicia[14]. Wealth is the parent of luxury and effeminacy. At the time of our Lord's Coming, the softness and effeminacy of the Sabæans became proverbial. The "soft Sabæans" is their characteristic in the Roman poets[15]. Commerce, navigation, goldmines, being then carried on by means of slaves, and wealth and luxury at that time always demanding domestic slaves, the Sabæans had need of slaves for both. They too had distant colonies[16], whither the Tyrians could be transported, as far from Phœnicia, as the shores of the Ægean are from Palestine. The great law of Divine Justice[17], *as I have done, so God hath requited me,* was again fulfilled. It is a sacred proverb of God's overruling Providence, written in the history of the world and in men's consciences.

9. *Proclaim ye this among the Gentiles.* God having before said that He would *gather all nations,* now, by a solemn irony, bids them prepare, if, by any means, they can fight

[1] Strabo, xvi. 4. 21. [2] Job i. 15. Bochart iv. 9.
[3] Agatharcides (p. 61,) Strabo from Metrodorus and Eratosthenes, (xvi. 4. 19.) Diodorus "from memoirs in the Alexandrian library or eye witnesses." iii. 38. 47. The account of their natural productions is exaggerated, yet with a mixture of truth, e. g. as to a very venomous sort of serpent.
[4] Thomna. Plin. vi. 28. 32. Movers, p. 300.
[5] Geogr. Vet. Scriptt. Min. T. i. p. 64, 5. Oxon.
[6] See Kazvini, the Turkish Jehan-numa from older writers, Masudi, in de Sacy Mem. de l'Acad. d. Inscr. T. 48. p. 506, note 629.
[7] De Sac. Ib.
[8] see Ritter's Diss. Erdk. xii. 356–372. Strabo however (quoted there p. 364) says, that most *cassia* came from India; "the best frankincense is that near Persia.
[9] Ps. lxxii. 10.
[10] Theophr. Hist. Plant. ix. 4. Agartharc. p. 61–4, 5. Eratosthenes in Strabo xvi. 4. 4.
[11] Capt. Haines in Geogr. Soc. ix. 154. Wellsted. Travels in Arabia. Survey in Bombay Geogr. Soc. 1839. p. 55. quoted Ritter, Erdk. xii. 259, 60.
[12] xxvii. 22.
[13] Ptol. vi. 7. Strabo, xvi. 3. 3.
[14] Juba in Plin. H. N. xii. 18. n. 40.
[15] Virg. Geogr. i. 57. also Metrodorus in Strabo xvi. 4. 19. See other authorities in Smith, Dict. of Geogr. Art. Saba, p. 862.
[16] Agatharc. p. 64. [17] Judg, i. 7.

Before CHRIST cir. 800.

[m] See Is. 2. 4. Mic. 4. 3.
‖ Or *scythes*.

10 [m] Beat your plowshares into swords, and your ‖pruninghooks into spears: [n] let the weak say, I *am* strong.

Before CHRIST cir. 800.

[n] Zech. 12. 8.

against Him. So in Isaiah[1]; *Associate yourselves, O ye people, and ye shall be broken in pieces ; and give ear, all ye of far countries ; gird yourselves, and ye shall be broken in pieces; gird yourselves, and ye shall be broken in pieces; take counsel together, and it shall come to nought ; speak the word, and it shall not stand ; for God is with us.*

Prepare, lit. *hallow, war*. To *hallow war* was to make it holy, either in appearance or in truth, as the prophet bade them, *sanctify a fast*, i. e. keep it holily. So God calls the Medes, whom He employed against Babylon[2], *My sanctified ones*, and bids[3], *sanctify the nations against her ;* and the enemies of Judah encourage themselves[4], *sanctify ye war against her ;* and Micah says, that whosover bribed not the false prophets, *they sanctify war against him*[5], i. e. proclaim war against him in the Name of God. The enemies of God, of His people, of His truth, declare war against all, in the Name of God. The Jews would have stoned our Lord for blasphemy, and, at the last, they condemned Him as guilty of it. [6] *He hath spoken blasphemy. What further need have we of witnesses? behold, now ye have heard His blasphemy.* And He foretold to His disciples[7], *Whosoever killeth you, will think he doeth God service.* St. Stephen was persecuted for speaking[8] *blasphemous words against Moses and against God, this holy place and the law.* St. Paul was persecuted for[9] *persuading men to worship God contrary to the law and polluting this holy place.* Anti-Christ shall set himself up as God, [10] *so that he, as God, sitteth in the temple of God, shewing himself that he is God.* Heretics and unbelievers declaim against the Gospel, as though it, and not themselves, were opposed to the holiness and Majesty and love of God. The Gnostics of old spake against the Creator in the Name of God. Arians affected reverence for the glory of God[11], being, on their own mis-belief, idolaters or polytheists[12]. The Apollinarians charged the Church with ascribing to our Lord a sinful soul, as though the soul must needs be such[13], and themselves held the Godhead to have been united to a soulless, and so a brute, nature. Manichæans accused her of making God the author of evil, and themselves, as do Pantheists now, invented a god who sinned[14]. Novatians and Donatists accused the Church of laxity. Pelagians charged her with denying the perfectibility of man's nature, themselves denying the grace whereby it is perfected. Mohammed arrayed the truth of the Unity of God against His Being in Three Persons, and fought against the truth as Idolatry. Some now array "Theism," i.e. truths as to God which they have stolen from Holy Scripture, against the belief in God as He has revealed Himself. Indeed, no imposture ever long held its ground against truth, unless it masked itself under some truth of God which it perverted, and so *hallowed* its *war* against God in the Name of God.

Wake up the mighty men ; arouse them, as if their former state had been a state of sleep; arouse all their dormant powers, all within them, that they may put forth all their strength, if so be they may prevail against God.

Let all the men of war draw near, as if to contend, and close, as it were, with God and His people[15], as, on the other hand, God says[16], *I will come near to you to judgment. Let them come up* into His very Presence. Even while calling them to fulfill this their vain purpose of striving with God, the Prophet keeps in mind, into Whose Presence they are summoned, and so calls them to *come up*, as to a place of dignity.

10. *Beat your ploughshares into swords.* Peace had been already promised, as a blessing of the gospel. *In His days*, foretold Solomon[17], *shall the righteous flourish, and abundance of peace, so long as the moon endureth.* And another[18], *He maketh thy borders peace.* Peace within with God flows forth in peace with man. *Righteousness and peace kissed each other*[19]. Where there is not rest in God, all is unrest. And so, all which was needful for life, the means of subsistence, care of health, were to be forgotten for war.

Let the weak say, I am strong. It is one last gathering of the powers of the world against their Maker; the closing scene of man's rebellion against God. It is their one universal gathering. None, however seemingly unfit, was to be spared from this conflict; no one was to remain behind. The husbandman was to forge for war the instruments of his peaceful toil ; the sick was to forget his weakness and

[1] viii. 9, 10. see also Ezek. xxxviii. 7–end.
[2] Is. xiii. 3. [3] Jer. li. 27. [4] Ib. vi. 4.
[5] Mic. iii. 5. [6] S. Matt. xxvi. 65.
[7] S. John xvi. 2. [8] Acts vi. 11, 13.
[9] Ib. xviii. 13. xxi. 28. xxiv. 6. [10] 2 Thess. ii. 4.
[11] See Arius Thalia in S. Ath. Counc. of Arim. § 15. p. 94. Oxf. Tr. S. Ath. ag. Ar. i. 28. p. 221. and the full note f.
[12] Ib. p. 191. n. d. p. 206. 301. c. 310. h. 411. b. 423. m. n.
[13] See in S. Ath. p. 221. n. f. O. T.
[14] See S. Aug. Conf. Note at the end.
[15] See 1 Sam. xvii. 41. 2 Sam. x. 13.
[16] Mal. iii. 5. see Is. xli. 1. l. 8.
[17] Ps. lxxii. 7.
[18] Ib. cxlvii. 14. [19] Ib. lxxxv. 10.

Before CHRIST cir. 800.

11 [o]Assemble your-
selves, and come, all ye
heathen, and gather your-
selves together round
about: thither || cause [p]thy
mighty ones to come down,
O LORD.
12 Let the heathen be
wakened, [q]and come up to
the valley of Jehoshaphat:
for there will I sit to [r]judge
all the heathen round
about.
13 [s]Put ye in the sickle,
for [t]the harvest is ripe:
come, get you down; for

o ver. 2.
|| Or, *the LORD shall bring down.*
p Ps. 103. 20. Isa. 13. 3.
q ver. 2.
r Ps. 96. 13. & 98. 9. & 110. 6. Is. 2. 4. & 3. 13. Mic. 4. 3.
s Matt. 13. 39. Rev. 14. 15, 18.
t Jer. 51. 33. Hos. 6. 11.

to put on a strength which he had not, and that to the uttermost. But as weakness is, in and through God, strength, so all strength out of God is weakness. Man may say, *I am strong;* but, against God, he remains weak as, it is said, that *weak man*[1] *from the earth may no more oppress.*

11. Once more all the enemies of God are summoned together. *Assemble yourselves*[2], (Others in the same sense render, *Haste ye,*) *and come, all ye heathen, round about,* lit. *from round about,* i.e. from every side, so as to compass and hem in the people of God, and then, when the net had been, as it were, drawn closer and closer round them, and no way of escape is left, the Prophet prays God to send His aid; *thither cause Thy mighty ones to come down, O Lord.* Against *the mighty ones* of the earth, or *the weak* who *say* they are *mighty,* (the same word is used throughout,) there *come down the mighty ones of God.* The *mighty ones of* God, whom He is prayed to *cause to come down,* i.e. from heaven, can be no other than the mighty angels, of whom it is said, they *are mighty in strength*[3] (still the same word,) to whom God gives *charge over*[4] His own, *to keep* them *in all* their *ways,* and one of whom, in this place, slew[5] *one hundred and fourscore and five thousand* of the Assyrians. So our Lord saith[6], *The Son of man shall send forth His Angels, and they shall gather out of His kingdom all things that offend, and them that do iniquity.*

12. *Let the heathen be awakened.* This emphatic repetition of the word, *awaken,* seems intended to hint at the great awakening, to Judgment[7], when they *who sleep in the dust of the earth shall awake, being awakened* from the sleep of death. Another word is used of *awakening*[8]. On the destruction of Anti-Christ it is thought that the general Judgment will follow, and *all who are in the graves shall hear the voice of the Son of Man and shall come forth*[9]: They are bidden to *come up* into the valley of Jehoshaphat, "[10] for to come into the Presence of the most High God, may well be called *a coming up.*" *For there will I sit to judge all the heathen round about,* (again lit. *from round about,*) *from every side,* all nations from all the four quarters of the world. The words are the same as before. There *all nations from every side* were summoned to come, as they thought, to destroy God's people and heritage. Here the real end is assigned, for which they were brought together; for God would sit to judge them. In their own blind will and passion they came to destroy; in God's secret overruling Providence, they were dragged along by their passions,—to be judged and to be destroyed. So our Lord says[11], *When the Son of Man shall come in His Glory, and all the Holy Angels with Him, then shall He sit on the throne of His Glory and before Him shall be gathered all nations.* Our Lord, in that He uses words of Joel, seems to intend to direct our minds to the Prophet's meaning. What follows are nearly His own words;

13. *Put ye in the sickle, for the harvest is ripe.* So Jesus saith, *let both grow together until the harvest, and in the time of the harvest I will say to the reapers, Gather ye together the tares and bind them in bundles to burn them;* and this He explains[12], *The harvest is the end of the world; and the reapers are the Angels.* He then Who saith, *put ye in the sickle, for the harvest is ripe,* is the Son of Man, Who, before He became the Son of Man, was, as He is now, the Son of God, and spake this and the other things by the Prohets; they to whom He speaketh are His reapers, the Angels; and the ripeness of the harvest is the maturity of all things here, good and evil, to be brought to their last end.

In itself, the harvest, as well as the vintage, might describe the end of this world, as to both the good and the bad, in that the wheat is severed from the chaff and the tares, and the treading of the winepress separates the wine which is stored up from the husks which are cast away. Yet nothing is said,

1 Ps. x. 18. אנוש.

2 The word עושו occurs here only. The E. V. follows the chief authorities.

3 Ps. ciii. 20. 4 Ib. xci. 11. 5 2 Kings xix. 35.

6 S. Matt. xiii. 41.

7 This same word is used Job xiv. 12. Even Abarbanel understands this of the Resurrection; see in Poc. on ver. 11.

8 הקיץ, also Job Ib. Ps. xvii. 15. Is. xxvi. 19. Dan. xii. 2.

9 S. John v. 27–9. 10 Poc.

11 S. Matt. xxv. 31, 2. 12 Ib. xiii. 30, 39.

Before CHRIST cir. 800.

the [u]press is full, the fats
overflow; for their wickedness *is* great.
14 Multitudes, multi-
tudes, in [x]the valley of
|| decision: for [y] the day of
the LORD *is* near in the
valley of decision.
15 The [z]sun and the
moon shall be darkened,
and the stars shall with-
draw their shining.

u Is. 63. 3. Lam. 1 15. Rev. 14. 19, 20.
x ver. 2.
|| Or, *concision*, or, *threshing*.
y ch. 2. 1.
z ch. 2. 10, 31.

here of storing up aught, either the wheat or the wine, but only of the ripeness of the harvest, and that *the fats overflow, because their wickedness is great.* The harvest is sometimes, although more rarely, used of destruction[1]; the treading of the winepress is always used as an image of God's anger[2]; the vintage of destruction[3]; the plucking off the grapes, of the rending away of single lives or souls[4]. It seems probable then, that the ripeness of the harvests and the fullness of the vats are alike used of the ripeness for destruction, that "[5]they were ripe in their sins, fit for a harvest, and as full of wickedness as ripe grapes, which fill and overflow the vats, through the abundance of the juice with which they swell." Their ripeness in iniquity calls, as it were, for the sickle of the reaper, the trampling of the presser.

For great is their wickedness. The whole world is flooded and overflowed by it, so that it can no longer contain it, but, as it were, cries to God to end it. The long suffering of God no longer availed, but would rather increase their wickedness and their damnation. So also, in that first Judgment of the whole world by water, when *all flesh had corrupted his way upon the earth, God said, the end of all flesh is before Me*[6]; and when the hundred and twenty years of the preaching of Noah were ended without fruit, *the flood came.* So Sodom was *then* destroyed, when not ten righteous could be found in it; and the seven nations of Canaan were spared above four hundred years, because the *iniquity of the Amorites was not yet full*[7]; and our Lord says[8], *fill ye up the measure of your fathers,—that upon you may come all the righteous blood shed upon the earth.* So "[9]God condemneth each of the damned, when he hath filled up the measure of his iniquity."

14. The prophet continues, as in amazement at the great throng assembling upon one another, *multitudes, multitudes, in the valley of decision,* as though, whichever way he looked, there were yet more of these *tumultuous masses,* so that there was nothing beside them. It was one living, surging, boiling, sea: throngs upon throngs, mere throngs[10]! The word rendered *multitudes* suggests, besides, the thought of the hum and din[11] of these masses thronging onward, blindly, to their own destruction. They all *tumultuously rage together, and imagine a vain thing, against the Lord and against His Christ*[12]; but the place whither they are gathered, (although they know it not,) is *the valley of decision,* i. e. of "sharp, severe judgment." The valley is the same as that before called *the valley of Jehoshaphat;* but whereas that name only signifies *God judgeth,* this further name denotes the strictness of God's judgment. The word signifies "cut," then "decided;" then is used of severe punishment, or destruction decided and decreed[13], by God.

For the Day of the Lord is near in the valley of decision. Their gathering against God shall be a token of His coming to judge them. They come to fulfill their own ends; but His shall be fulfilled on them. They are left to bring about their own doom; and being abandoned by Him, rush on the more blindly because it is at hand. When their last sin is committed, their last defiance of God spoken or acted against Him, it is come. At all times, indeed, *the Lord is at hand*[14]. It may be, that we are told, that the whole future revealed to us *must shortly come to pass*[15], in order to show that all time is a mere nothing, a moment, a dream, when it is gone. Yet here it is said, relatively, not to us, but to the things foretold, that it *is near* to come.

15. *The sun and the moon shall be darkened.* This may be, either that they shall be outshone by the brightness of the glory of Christ, or that they themselves shall undergo a change, whereof the darkness at the Crucifixion was an image. An ancient

1 Is. xvii. 5. Jer. li. 33.
2 Lam. i. 15. Is. lxiii. 3. Rev. xix. 15.
3 Is. xvii. 6. Judg. viii. 2. Mic. vii. 1.
4 Ps. lxxx. 12. 5 Poc. 6 Gen. vi. 12, 13.
7 Gen. xv. 16. 8 S. Matt. xxiii. 32, 35. 9 Dion.
10 As Gen. xiv. 10, *pits, pits,* i. e. *full of pits,* nothing but pits; 2 Kings iii. 16, *ditches, ditches,* i. e. *full of ditches.* By another idiom, it has been taken to mean that the *multitudes* were of two sorts; whence Abarbanel explains it, "a multitude of living, and a multitude of dead," in Poc. Others, the good and the bad.

11 The word המה (whence המון) is identical with our *hum;* then, "noise," and, among others, "the hum of a multitude;" then, a multitude even apart from that noise. It is used of the throng of a large army, Judg. iv. 7, Dan. xi. 11, 12, 13; of whole peoples, Ezek. xxxii. 12, 16, 18, 20, 22, 26.
12 Ps. ii. 1, 2.
13 *destruction determined,* Is. x. 22; *destruction, and that determined,* Is. x. 23, xxviii. 22, Dan. ix. 27; *that which is decreed of desolations,* i. e. *the desolations decreed,* Ib. 26.
14 Phil. iv. 5. 15 Rev. i. 1.

Before CHRIST cir. 800.

16 The LORD also shall
[a] roar out of Zion, and utter
his voice from Jerusalem;
and [b] the heavens and the
earth shall shake: [c] but the
LORD *will be* the † hope of
his people, and the strength
of the children of Israel.
17 So [d] shall ye know
that I *am* the LORD your
God dwelling in Zion, [e] my
holy mountain: then shall

[a] Jer. 25. 30. ch. 2. 11. Amos 1. 2.
[b] Hag. 2. 6.
[c] Is. 51. 5, 6.
† Heb. *place of repair.* or, *harbor.*

Before CHRIST cir. 800.

[d] ch. 2. 27.
[e] Dan. 11. 45. Obad. 16. Zech. 8. 3.

writer says[1]; "As in the dispensation of the Cross the sun failing, there was darkness over all the earth, so when *the sign of the Son of man* appeareth in heaven in the Day of Judgment, the light of the sun and moon and stars shall fail, consumed, as it were by the great might of that sign." And as the failure of the light of the sun at our Lord's Passion betokened the shame of nature at the great sin of man, so, at the Day of Judgment, it sets before us the awfulness of God's judgments, as though "[2] it dared not behold the severity of Him Who judgeth and returneth every man's work upon his own head;" as though "[3] every creature, in the sufferings of others, feared the judgment on itself."

16. *The Lord shall roar out of Zion.* As in the destruction of Sennacherib, when he was now close upon his prey, and *shook his hand against the mount of the daughter of Zion, the hill of Jerusalem, the Lord of hosts lopped the bough with terror, and the high ones of stature* were *hewn down, and the haughty* were *humbled*[4], so at the end. It is foretold of Anti-Christ, that his destruction shall be sudden[5], *Then shall that Wicked one be revealed, whom the Lord shall consume with the spirit of His mouth, and shall destroy with the brightness of His Coming.* And Isaiah saith of our Lord[6], *He shall smite the earth with the rod of His mouth, and with the breath of His lips shall He slay the wicked.* When the multitudes of God's enemies were thronged together, then would He speak with His Voice of terror. The terrible voice of God's warnings is compared to the roaring of a lion[7]. *The lion hath roared, who will not fear? the Lord hath spoken, who can but prophesy?* Much more, when those words of awe are fulfilled. Our Lord then, *The Lion of the tribe of Judah*[8], Who is here entitled by the incommunicable Name of God, I AM, shall utter His awful Voice, as it is said[9]; *The Lord Himself shall descend from heaven with a shout, with the voice of the Archangel and with the Trump of God;* and He Himself says, [10] *The hour is coming, in the which all that are in the graves shall hear His voice and shall come forth, they that have done good unto the Resurrection of life, and they that have done evil unto the resurrection of damnation.*

And shall utter His voice from Jerusalem, i. e. either from His Throne aloft *in the air* above the holy city, or from the heavenly Jerusalem, out of the midst of the tens of thousands of His holy angels[11], and saints[12], who shall *come with Him.* So terrible shall that voice be, that *the heavens and the earth shall shake,* as it is said[13], *the heavens shall pass away with a great noise, and the elements shall melt with fervent heat, the earth also and the works that are therein shall be burned up;* and "[14] heaven shall open for the coming of the saints," and *hell shall be moved at the coming*[15] of the evil. "[16] Nor shall it be a slight shaking of the earth at His Coming, but such that all the dead shall be roused, as it were from their sleep, yea, the very elect shall fear and tremble, but, even in their fear and trembling, shall retain a strong hope. This is what he saith forthwith, *The Lord will be the hope* (or *place of refuge*) of His *people, and the strength* (or *strong hold*) *of the children of Israel,* i. e. of the true Israel, the whole people of the elect of God. All these He will then by that His Majesty at once wonderfully terrify and strengthen, because they ever hoped in God, not in themselves, and ever trusted in the strength of the Lord, never presumed on their own. Whereas contrariwise the false Israelites hope in themselves, while, *going about to establish their own righteousness, they submitted themselves not to the righteousness of God*[17]. The true Israel shall trust much more than ever before; yet none can trust then, who in life, had not trusted in Him Alone.

17. God Himself wondrously joins on His own words to those of the Prophet, and speaks to His own people; *so* (lit. *and*) *ye shall know,* by experience, by sight, face to face, what ye now believe, *that I am the Lord your God, dwelling in Zion, My holy mountain.* So He saith in the second Psalm[18], *Then shall he speak unto them* (the enemies of His Christ) *in His wrath, and vex them in His sore displeasure; And I have set My king on My holy hill of Zion;* and[19], *Behold the tabernacle of*

[1] Orig. Tr. 30. in S. Matt.
[2] S. Jer.
[3] Hugo de S. V.
[4] Is. x. 32, 3.
[5] 2 Thess. ii. 8.
[6] Is. xi. 4.
[7] Am. iii. 8.
[8] Rev. v. 5.
[9] 1 Thess. iv. 16.
[10] S. John v. 28, 29.

[11] S. Matt. xvi. 27. xxv 31. S. Mark viii. 38. 2 Thess. i. 7.
[12] Zech. xiv. 5. Jude 14.
[13] 2 Pet. iii. 10.
[14] Lyr. Lap.
[15] Is. xiv. 9.
[16] Rup.
[17] Rom. x. 3.
[18] Ps. ii. 5, 6.
[19] Rev. xxi. 3.

Before CHRIST cir. 800.

Jerusalem be †holy, and
there shall no [f]strangers
pass through her any more.

† Heb. *holiness.*

[f] Is. 35. 8 & 52. 1. Nah. 1. 15. Zech. 14. 21. Rev. 21. 27.

18 ¶ And it shall come
to pass in that day, *that*
the mountains shall [g]drop

Before CHRIST cir. 800.

[g] Amos 9. 13.

God is with men, and He will dwell with them, and they shall be His people, and God Himself shall be with them, their God, dwelling with them and in them, by an unvarying, blissful, hallowing Presence, never withdrawn, never hidden, never shadowed, but ever shining upon them. *Your God*, your own, as much as if possessed by none besides, filling all with gladness, yet fully possessed by each, as though there were none besides, so that each may say, *Thou art my Portion, O Lord*[1]; my *Lord, and my God*[2], as He saith, *I am thy exceeding great Reward*[3].

And Jerusalem shall be holy, lit. *holiness* as John saith[4], *He carried me away in the Spirit to a great and high mountain, and shewed me that great city, the holy Jerusalem, descending out of heaven from God, having the glory of God.*

And there shall no stranger pass through her any more. Without, says S. John[5], *are dogs and sorcerers, and whoremongers, and murderers, and idolaters, and whosoever loveth and maketh a lie.* None alien from her shall pass through her, so as to have dominion over her, defile or oppress her.

This special promise is often repeated. [6]*It shall be called the way of holiness, the unclean shall not pass over it.* [7]*Henceforth there shall no more come into thee the uncircumcised and the unclean.* [8]*The wicked shall no more pass through thee.*[9] *In that day there shall be no more the Canaanite in the house of the Lord of hosts.* [10]*And there shall in no wise enter into it any thing that defileth.* These promises are, in their degree and in the image and beginning, made good to the Church here, to be fully fulfilled when it shall be[11] *a glorious Church, not having spot or wrinkle or any such thing, but holy and without blemish.* Here they do not pass through her, so as to overcome; *the gates of hell shall not prevail against her.* However near, as hypocrites, they come to her, they feel in themselves that they *are not of her*[12]. There they shall be severed from her for ever. "[13]Heretics came, armed with fantastic reasons and deceitful arguments; but they could not pass through her, repelled by the truth of the word, overcome by reason, cast down by the testimonies of Scripture and by the glow of faith." They fell backward to the ground before her. They[14] *go out from her, because they are not of her.* They who are not of her can mingle with her, touch her sacraments, but their power and virtue they partake not. They are inwardly repelled.

18. *And it shall come to pass in that Day.* After the destruction of Anti-Christ, there will, it seems, still be a period of probation, in which the grace of God will abound and extend more and more widely. The Prophet Zechariah, who continues on the image, of the *living waters going out from Jerusalem*[15], places this gift after God had gathered all nations against Jerusalem, and had visibly and miraculously overthrown them[16]. But in that the blessings which he speaks of, are regenerating, they belong to time; the fullness of the blessing is completed only in eternity; the dawn is on earth, the everlasting brightness is in heaven. But though the prophecy belongs eminently to one time, the imagery describes the fulness of spiritual blessings which God at all times diffuses in and through the Church; and these blessings, he says, shall continue on in her for ever; her enemies shall be cut off for ever. It may be, that Joel would mark a fresh beginning and summary by his words, *It shall be in that Day.* The prophets do often begin, again and again, their descriptions. Union with God, which is their theme, is one. Every gift of God to His elect, except the beatific vision, is begun in time, union with Himself, indwelling, His Spirit flowing forth from Him into His creatures, His love, knowledge of Him, although here through a glass darkly.

The promise cannot relate to exuberance of temporal blessings, even as tokens of God's favor. For he says, *a fountain shall come forth of the house of the Lord, and shall water the valley of Shittim.* But *the valley of Shittim* is on the other side Jordan, beyond the Dead Sea, so that by nature the waters could not flow thither. The valley of Shittim or acacia trees is a dry valley; for in such the Easten Acacia, i. e. the sant or sandal wood grows. "It is," says S. Jerome[17], "a tree which grows in the desert, like a white thorn in color and leaves, not in size. For they are of such size, that very large planks[18], are cut out of them. The wood is very strong, and of incredible lightness and beauty. They do not grow in cultivated places, or in the Roman soil, save only in the desert of

[1] Ps. cxix. 57. Lam. iii. 24.
[2] S. John xx. 28.
[3] Gen. xv. 1.
[4] Rev. xxi. 10, 11.
[5] Ib. xxii. 15.
[6] Is. xxxv. 8.
[7] Ib. lii. 1.
[8] Nah. i. 15.
[9] Zech. end.
[10] Rev. xxi. 27.
[11] Eph. v. 27.
[12] 1 S. John ii. 19.
[13] Hugo Vict.
[14] 1 S. John ii. 19.
[15] Zech. xiv. 8.
[16] Ib. 2–4.
[17] on Is. xli. 19.
[18] 12 els long. Theophr. plant. iv. 3.

Before CHRIST cir. 800.

down new wine, and the hills shall flow with milk, [h] and all the rivers of Judah shall † flow with waters, and [i] a fountain shall come forth of the house of the

h Is. 30. 25.

† Heb. *go.*

i Ps. 46. 4. Ezek. 47. 1. Zech. 14. 8. Rev. 22. 1.

Arabia." It does not decay [1]; and when old becomes like ebony [2]. Of it the Ark of God was made, its staves, the table of Shewbread, the tabernacle and its pillars, the altar for burnt offerings, and of incense [3]. The valley is about six miles from Livias [4], seven and a half beyond the Dead Sea [5]. It was the last station of Israel, before entering the land of promise [6], whence Joshua sent out the spies [7]; where God turned the curse of Balaam into a blessing [8]; and he prophesied of the Star which should arise out of Israel, even Christ [9]; where Israel sinned in Baal Peor, and Phineas turned aside His displeasure [10].

The existence of a large supply of water under the Temple is beyond all question. While the Temple was still standing, mention is made of a "[11] fountain of ever-flowing water under the temple," as well as pools and cisterns for preserving rain-water. One evidently well acquainted with the localities says [12], "The pavement has slopes at befitting places, for the sake of a flush of water which takes place in order to cleanse away the blood from the victims. For on festivals many myriads of animals are sacrificed. But of water there is an unfailing supply, a copious and natural fountain within gushing over, and there being moreover wonderful underground-receptacles in a circuit of five furlongs, in the substructure of the temple, and each of these having numerous pipes, the several streams inter-communicating, and all these closed up below and on the sides.—There are also many mouths toward the base, invisible to all except those to whom the service of the temple belongs. So that the manifold blood of the sacrifices being brought together are cleansed by the gush [of water down] the slope." This same writer relates that, more than half a mile from the city, he was told to stoop down and heard the sound of gushing waters underground. The natural fountain, then, beneath the temple was doubtless augmented by waters brought from a distance, as required for the "divers washings" both of the priests and other things, and to carry off the blood of the victims. Pools near the temple are mentioned by writers of the third and fourth century [13]; and Omar, on the surrender of Jerusalem, A. D. 634, was guided to the site of the ancient temple (whereon he built his Mosk) by the stream of water which issued through a water-channel from it [14]. Whencesoever this water was derived, whether from a perennial spring beneath the temple itself, or whether brought thither from some unfailing source without, it afforded Jerusalem an abundant supply of water. Much as Jerusalem suffered in sieges by famine, and its besiegers by thirst, thirst was never any part of the sufferings of those within [15]. The superfluous water was and still is carried off underground, to what is now "the fountain of the Virgin [16]," and thence again, through the rock, to the pool of Siloam [17]. Thence it carried fertility to the gardens of Siloam, in Joel's time doubtless *the king's gardens* [18], still "[19] a verdant spot, refreshing to the eye in the heat of summer, while all around is parched and dun." The blood of the victims flowed into the same brook Kidron, and was a known source of fertility, before the land was given to desolation. The waters of Kidron, as well as all the waters of Palestine, must have been more abundant formerly. Isaiah speaks of it as *flowing softly* [20]; Josephus [21], of the "abundant fountain;" an official report [22], of the "fountain gushing forth with abundance of water." Still its fertilizing powers formed but one little oasis, where all around was arid. It fertilized those gardens five miles from the city, but the mid-space was waterless [23], thirsty, mournful [24]. Lower down, the rivulet threaded its way to the Dead Sea, through a narrow ravine which became more and more wild, where St. Saba planted his monastery. "A howling wilderness, stern desolation, stupendous perpendicular cliffs, terrific chasms, oppressive solitude" are the terms by which one endeavors to characterize "the heart of this stern desert of Judæa [25]."

1 Jos. Ant. iii. 6. 2 Vell. Pat. ii. 56.
3 Ex. lxxv. 5, 10, 13, 23, 28. xxvi. 15, 26, 32, 37. xxvii. 1, 6. xxx. 1. xxxv. 7, 24. xxxvi. 20, 31, 36. xxxvii. 1, 4, 10, 15, 25, 28. xxxviii. 1, 6. Deut. x. 3.
4 S. Jer. 5 Josh. Ant. v. 1. 1.
6 Num. xxxiii. 49. 7 Jos. ii. 1.
8 Num. xxiii. xxiv. Mic. vi. 5.
9 Num. xxiv. 17.
10 Ib. xxv. 1, 7, 11.
11 fons perennis aquæ. Tac. Hist. v. 12.
12 Aristeas in App. ad Joseph. ed. Hav. p. 112.
13 The Bourdeaux Pilgrim and Philostorg. ap. Phot. vii. 14. Itin. Hieros. p. 152. quoted in Williams' full account of the waters of the Holy City and their connection. Holy City, ii. 466 sqq.
14 Williams, H. C. i. 216. Arabic authorities.
15 Williams, H. C. ii. 453, 4.
16 Ib. 468. Robinson i. 344.
17 Robinson i. 231, 2. 338, 9.
18 2 Kgs xxv. 4. Jer. xxxix. 4. lii. 7. Neh. iii. 15. Williams ii. 477.
19 Williams ii. 456. 20 viii. 6. 21 B. J. v. 4. 1.
22 in Eus. Præp. Ev. ix. 36. Williams ii. 464.
23 Timochares in Eus. ix. 35 Williams ii. 478.
24 Strabo xvi. c. 2. § 36. 40. p. 761, 3. W. ii. 453.
25 Thomson ii. 435. 431.

Before CHRIST cir. 800.

k Num. 25. 1.
l Is. 19. 1, &c.

LORD, and shall water [k] the
valley of Shittim.
19 [l] Egypt shall be a
desolation, and [m] Edom
shall be a desolate wilderness, for the violence *against*

Before CHRIST cir. 800.

m Jer. 49. 17. Ezek. 25. 12, 13. Amos 1. 11. Obad. 10.

Such continues to be its character, in the remaining half of its course, until it is lost in the Dead Sea, and is transmuted into its saltness. Its valley bears the name of desolation, Wady en Nar[1], "valley of fire." No human path lies along it. The Kidron flows along "[2] a deep and almost impenetrable ravine," "in a narrow channel between perpendicular walls of rock, as if worn away by the rushing waters between those desolate chalky hills." That little oasis of verdure was fit emblem of the Jewish people, itself bedewed by the stream which issued from the Temple of God, but, like Gideon's fleece, leaving all around dry. It made no sensible impression out of, or beyond itself. Hereafter, *the stream*[3], the Siloah, whose *streamlets*, i. e. the artificial fertilizing divisions[4], *made glad the city of God*, should make the wildest, driest spots of our mortality *like the garden of the Lord*. Desolation should become bright and gay; the parched earth should shoot up fresh with life; what was by nature barren and unfruitful should bring forth good fruit; places heretofore stained by sin should be purified; nature should be renewed by grace; and that, beyond the borders of the promised land, in that world which they had left, when Joshua brought them in thither. This, which it needs many words to explain, was vivid to those to whom Joel spoke. They had that spot of emerald green before their eyes, over which the stream which they then knew to issue from the Temple trickled in transparent brightness, conducted by those channels formed by man's diligence. The eyes of the citizens of Jerusalem must have rested with pleasure on it amid the parched surface around. Fresher than the gladliest freshness of nature, brighter than its most kindled glow, is the renewing freshness of grace; and this, issuing from mount Zion, was to be the portion not of Judæa only, but of the world.

The vision of Ezekiel[4], which is a comment on the prophecy of Joel, clearly belongs primarily to this life. For in this life only is there need for healing; in this life only is there a desert land to be made fruitful; death to be changed into life; death and life, the healed and unhealed, side by side; life, where the stream of God's grace reacheth, and death and barrenness, where it reacheth not. The fishers who spread their nets amid *the fish, exceeding many*, are an emblem which waited for and received its explanation from the parables of our Lord.

In the Revelation, above all, the peace, glory, holiness, vision of God, can only be fulfilled in the sight of God. Yet here too the increase of the Church, and the healing of the nations[5], belong to time and to a state of probation, not of full fruition.

But then neither can those other symbols relate to earthly things.

The mountains shall drop down new wine, lit. *trodden* out. What is ordinarily obtained by toil, shall be poured forth spontaneously. *And the hills shall flow with milk*, lit. *flow milk*, as though they themselves, of their own accord, gushed forth into the good gifts which they yield. *Wine* ever new, and ever renewing, sweet and gladdening the heart; *milk*, the emblem of the spiritual food of childlike souls, of purest knowledge, holy devotion, angelic purity, heavenly pleasure. And these shall never cease. These gifts are spoken of, as the spontaneous, perpetual flow of the mountains and hills; and as the fountain gushes forth from the hill or mountain-side in one ceaseless flow, day and night, streaming out from the hidden recesses to which the waters are supplied by God from His treasure-house of the rain, so day and night, in sorrow or in joy, in prosperity or adversity, God pours out, in the Church and in the souls of His elect, the riches of His grace. *All the rivers*, lit. *channels*[6], *of Judah shall flow with water*. Every *channel*, however narrow and easily drying up, shall *flow with water*, gushing forth unto everlasting life; the love of God shall stream through every heart; each shall be full according to its capacity, and none the less full, because a larger tide pours through others. How much more, "[7] in those everlasting hills of heaven, *the heavenly Jerusalem*, resting on the eternity and Godhead of the Holy Trinity, shall that long promise be fulfilled of the land flowing with milk and honey, where God, through the beatific vision of Himself, shall pour into the blessed *the torrent of pleasure*, the unutterable sweetness of joy and gladness unspeakable in Himself; and *all the rivers of Judah*, i. e. all the powers, capacities, senses, speech of the saints who *confess* God, shall flow with a perennial stream of joy, thanksgiving, and jubilee, as of all pleasure and bliss."

19. *Egypt shall be a desolation. Egypt* and *Edom* represent each a different class of enemies of the people of God, and both together exhibit the lot of all. Egypt was the powerful oppressor, who kept Israel long time in

[1] Robinson i. 531. [2] Ps. xlvi. 4. [3] פלגיו. [4] Ezek. xlvii. 1–12.

[5] Rev. xxi. 24–26. xxii. 21. [6] אפיקי. [7] from Lap.

Before CHRIST cir. 800.

the children of Judah, because they have shed innocent blood in their land.

Before CHRIST cir. 800.

hard bondage, and tried, by the murder of their male children, to extirpate them. Edom was, by birth, the nearest allied to them, but had, from the time of their approach to the promised land, been hostile to them, and shewed a malicious joy in all their calamities[1]. *Their land*, in which Egypt and Edom shed the *innocent blood of the children of Judah*, may either be Edom, Egypt, or Judæa. If the land was Judæa, the sin is aggravated by its being God' s land, the possession of which they were disputing with God. If it was Egypt and Edom, then it was probably the blood of those who took refuge there, or, as to Edom, of prisoners delivered up to them[2].

This is the first prophecy of the humiliation of Egypt. Hosea had threatened, that Egypt should be the grave of those of Israel who should flee there[3]. He speaks of it as the vain trust, and a real evil to Israel[4]; of its own future he says nothing. Brief as Joel's words are, they express distinctly an abiding condition of Egypt. They are expanded by Ezekiel[5]; particular chastisements are foretold by Isaiah[6], Jeremiah[7], Ezekiel[8], Zechariah[9]. But the three words of Joel[10], *Egypt shall become desolation*, are more comprehensive than any prophecy, except those by Ezekiel. They foretell that abiding condition, not only by the force of the words, but by the contrast with an abiding condition of bliss. The words say, not only "it shall be desolated," as by a passing scourge sweeping over it, but "it shall itself *pass over into* that state;" it shall become what it had not been[11]; and this, in contrast with the abiding condition of God's people. The contrast is like that of the Psalmist[12], *He turneth a fruitful land into barrenness for the wickedness of them that dwell therein. He turneth the wilderness into a standing water, and dry ground into water-springs.* Judah should overflow with blessing, and the streams of God's grace should pass beyond its bounds, and carry fruitfulness to what now was dry and barren. But what should reject His grace should be itself rejected.

Yet when Joel thus threatened Egypt, there were no human symptoms of its decay; the instruments of its successive overthrows were as yet wild hordes, (as the Chaldees, Persians, and Macedonians,) to be consolidated thereafter into powerful empires, or (as Rome) had not the beginnings of being. The "[13] continuous monumental history of Egypt" went back seven centuries before this, to about 1520, B. C. They had had a line of conquerors among their kings, who subdued much of Asia, and disputed with Assyria the country which lay between them[14]. Even after the time of Joel, they had great conquerors, as Tirhaka; Psammetichus won Ashdod back from Assyria[15], Neco was probably successful against it, as well as against Syria and king Josiah; for he took Cadytis on his return[16] from his expedition against Carchemish[17]; Pharaoh Hophra, or Apries, until he fell by his pride[18], renewed for a time the prosperity of Psammetichus[19]; the reign of Amasis, even after Nebuchadnezzar's conquest, was said to be "the most prosperous time which Egypt ever saw[20];" it was still a period of foreign conquest[21], and its cities could be magnified into 20,000. The Persian invasion was drawn upon it by an alliance with Lydia, whither Amasis sent 120,000 men[22]; its, at times, successful struggles against the gigantic armies of its Persian conquerors[23] betoken great inherent strength; yet it sank for ever, a perpetual desolation. "Rent, twenty-three centuries ago, from her natural proprietors," says an unbelieving writer[24], "she has seen Persians, Macedonians, Romans, Greeks, Arabs, Georgians, and at length, the race of Tartars, distinguished by the name of Ottoman Turks, establish themselves in her bosom." "The system of oppression is methodical;" "an universal air of misery is manifest in all which the traveler meets." "[25] Mud-walled cottages are now the only habitations, where the ruins of temples and palaces abound. The desert covers many extensive regions, which once raised Egypt among the chief of the kingdoms." The desolation of Egypt is the stranger, because exceeding misrule alone could have effected it.

Egypt, in its largest dimensions, has been calculated to contain 123,527 square miles or 79,057,339 acres, and to be three fourths of

1 Ob. 10–14. Ez. xxv. 12. xxxv. 15. xxxvi. 5. Lam. iv. 22. Ps. cxxxvii. 7. See on Am. i. 11.
2 See on Amos i. 9.
3 ix. 6.
4 vii. 11, 12, 16. viii. 13. ix. 3. xi. 5.
5 xxix. 9–12. 15.
6 xix. xx.
7 xlvi.
8 xxix.–xxxii.
9 x. 11.
10 מצרים לשממה תהיה.
11 Such is the force of היה ל.
12 Ps. cvii. 33–5.
13 Sir G. Wilkinson Hist. Notice of Eg. in Rawl. Herod. ii. 354.
14 See Ib. pp. 356–377.
15 Herod. ii. 157.
16 Ib. 159.
17 2 Kgs xxiii. 29.
18 Ezek. xxix. 3.
19 Herod. ii. 161 and p. 248. n. 8. Rawl.
20 Her. ii. 177.
21 Ib. 182.
22 Cyrop. vi. 2. 10. vii. 1. 30–45.
23 Sir G. Wilkinson in note in Rawl. Herod. ii. p. 393.
24 Volney Voyage c. 6. also c. 12. 18. quoted by Keith.
25 Keith on Prophecy, Egypt. p. 500–3.

the size of France[1]. The mountains which hem in Upper Egypt, diverge at Cairo, parting, the one range, due East, the other N. W. The mountains on the West sink into the plains; those on the East retain their height as far as Suez. About 10 miles below Cairo, the Nile parted, inclosing within the outside of its seven branches, that triangle of wondrous fertility, the Delta. A network of canals, formed by the stupendous industry of the ancient Egyptians, inclosed this triangle in another yet larger, whose base, along the coast, was 235 miles, in direct distance about 181. East of the Eastern-most branch of the Nile, lay the *land of Goshen,* formerly, at least for cattle, *the good of the land*[2], a part, at least, of the present esh-Sharkiyyeh, second in size of the provinces of Egypt, but which, A. D. 1375, yielded the highest revenue of the state[3]. On the Western side of the Nile, and about a degree South of the apex of the Delta, a stupendous work, the artificial lake of Mœris[4], inclosing within masonry 64¾ square miles of water, received the superfluous waters of the river, and thus at once prevented the injury incidental on any too great rise of the Nile, and supplied water during six months for the irrigation of 1724 square miles, or 1,103,375, acres[5]. The Nile which, when it overflowed, spread like a sea over Egypt[6], encircling its cities like islands, carried with it a fertilizing power, attested by all, but which, unless so attested, would seem fabulous. Beneath a glowing heat, greater than its latitude will account for, the earth, supplied with continual moisture and an ever renewed alluvial deposit which supersedes all need of "dressing" the soil, yields, within the year, three harvests of varied produce[7]. This system of canalising Egypt must have been of very early antiquity. That giant conception of the water system of lake Mœris is supposed to have been the work of Ammenemhes, perhaps about 1673, B. C.[8]. But such a giant plan presupposes the existence of an artificial system of irrigation which it expanded. In the time of Moses, we hear incidentally of *the streams* of Egypt, *the canals*[9] (that is, those used for irrigation), and *the ponds*[10], the receptacles of the water which was left when the Nile retired. Besides these, an artificial mode of irrigation *by the foot*[11] is mentioned, now no longer distinctly known, but used, like the present plans of the water-wheel and the lever[12], to irrigate the lands for the later harvests. This system of irrigation had, in the time of Joel, lasted probably for above 1000 years. The Egyptians ascribed the first turning of the Nile to their first king, Menes[13], of fabulous antiquity. But while it lasted in any degree, Egypt could not become barren except by miracle. Even now it recovers, whenever water is applied. "Wherever there is water, there is fertility." "[14] The productive powers of the soil of Egypt are incalculable. Wherever water is scattered, there springs up a rapid and beautiful vegetation. The seed is sown and watered, and scarcely any other care is requisite for the ordinary fruits of the earth. Even in spots adjacent to the desert and which seem to be taken possession of by the sands, irrigation brings rapidly forth a variety of green herbs and plants." For its first crop, there needed but to cast the seed, and have it trodden in by cattle[15].

Nothing then could desolate Egypt, except man's abiding negligence or oppression. No passing storm or inroad could annihilate a fertility, which poured in upon it in ever-renewing richness. For 1000 years, the Nile had brought to Egypt unabated richness. The Nile overflows still, but in vain amid depopulation, and grinding, uniform, oppression. Not the country is exhausted, but man.

"If" says Mengin[16], "it is true that there is no country richer than Egypt in its territorial productions, still there is perhaps no one whose inhabitants are more miserable. It is owing solely to the fertility of its soil and the sobriety of its cultivators, that it retains the population which it still has." The marked diminution of the population had begun before the Birth of our Lord. "Of old," says Diodorus[17], "it far exceeded in denseness of population all the known countries in the world, and in our days too it seems to be inferior to no other. For in ancient times it had more than 18,000 considerable villages and towns, as you may see registered in the sacred lists. In the time of Ptolemy Lagus more than 30,000 were counted, a number which has continued until now. But the

[1] Descript. de l' Egypte (Col. Jacotin) Etat Moderne. T. ii. P. ii. p. 571. ed. fol.
[2] Gen. xlvii. 6. 11.
[3] Etat de l' Eg. from the Arabic. De Sac. Abdal. p. 595.
[4] This is the interesting discovery of M. Linant de Bellefonds, Mémoire sur le lac de Mœris. 1843.
[5] 967,948 feddans. The feddan, an Arabic acre (i. q. פדן) varied at different times. M. Linant counts it at 4200 mètres 83 centimètres carrés, 1 1/27 Eng. Acre. Col. Jacotin estimates it at 5929 mètres carrés, a little under 1½ Eng. Acre, 1. 42577. (Descr. de l' Eg. Ib. 573). Mr. Lane states it at 1 1/10 Eng. Acre a little before 1836, "more at an earlier period," (i. 158) less than an acre now (ii. 371).
[6] Herod. ii. 97.
[7] Lane Egypt ii. 26.
[8] Lepsius Kœnigsbuch d. alten Ægypt. Synopt. Tafeln p. 5.
[9] יארים, the Egyptian word *ior*, "ditch" or "river."
[10] Ex. vii. 19 viii. 1.
[11] Deut. xi. 40.
[12] Sackiyeh and shadoof. See Lane ii. 24.
[13] Herod. ii. 4. 99.
[14] Bowring Report on Egypt. 1840. p. 12.
[15] Herod. ii. 14. and Sir G. Wilk. Rawl. Herod. ii. 18.
[16] Hist. de l' Eg. ii. 342.
[17] i. 31. He wrote, in part, 20 B. C. i. 44.

whole people are said of old to have been about seven millions, and in our days not less than three[1]." A modern estimate supposes that Egypt, if cultivated to the utmost, would, in plentiful years, support eight millions [2]. It is difficult to calculate a population where different ranks wish to conceal it. It has been guessed however that, two centuries ago, it was four millions; that, at the beginning of this century, it was two millions and a half; and that, in 1845, it was 1,800,000[3]. The great diminution then had begun 1900 years ago. Temporary causes, plague, smallpox, conscription, have, in this last century, again halved the population; but down to that time, it had sunk to no lower level than it had already reached at least 18 centuries before. The land still, for its fruitfulness, continues to supply more than its inhabitants consume; it yields over and above cotton [4], for strangers to employ. Yet its brilliant patches of vegetation are but indications how great the powers implanted in it. In vain "the rising Nile overflows (as it is thought) a larger proportion of the soil [5]" than heretofore; in vain has the rich alluvial deposit encroached upon the gradual slope of the desert; in vain, in Upper Egypt has a third been added since about the time of the Exodus. Egypt is stricken. Canals and even arms of the Nile, were allowed to choke up. Of the seven branches of the Nile, two only, at first artificial, remain [6]. "The others have either entirely disappeared or are dry in summer." The great Eastern arm, the Pelusian, is nearly effaced "[7] buried almost wholly beneath the sands of the desert." "[8] The land at the mouth of the canal which represents it, is a sand waste or a marsh." "[9] There is now no trace of vegetation in the whole Pelusian plain. Only one slight isolated rise has some thickets on it, and some shafts of columns lie on the sand." "[10] In the midst of a plain the most fertile, they want the barest necessaries of life." The sand of the desert, which was checked by the river and by the reeds on its banks, has swept over lands no longer fertilized. "[11] The sea has not been less destructive. It has broken down the dykes, wherewith man's labor held it in, and has carried barrenness over the productive lands, which it converted into lakes and marshes." A glance at the map of Egypt will shew how widely the sea has burst in, where land once was. On the East, the salt lake Menzaleh, (itself from W. N. W. to S. E. about 50 miles long, and above 10 miles from N. to S.) absorbs two more of the ancient arms of the Nile, the Tanitic and the Mendesian [12]. The Tanitic branch is marked by a deeper channel below the shallow waters of the lake [13]. The lake of Burlos "[14] occupies from E. to W. more than half the basis of the Delta." Further Westward are a succession of lakes, Edkou, Madyeh (above $12\frac{1}{2}$ miles) Mareotis ($37\frac{1}{2}$ miles). "[15] The ancient Delta has lost more than half its surface, of which one-fifth is covered with the waters of the lakes Mareotis, Madyeh, Edkou, Bourlos, and Menzaleh, sad effects of the carelessness of the rulers or rather spoilers of this unhappy country." Even when the lake Mareotis was, before the English invasion in 1801, allowed nearly to dry up, it was but an unhealthy lagoon; and the Mareotic district, once famous for its wine and its olives and papyrus [16], had become a desert. So far from being a source of fertility, these lakes from time to time, at the low Nile, inundate the country with salt water, and are "surrounded by low and barren plains [17]."

The ancient populousness and capabilities of the Western province are attested by its ruins. "[18] The ruins which the French found everywhere in the military reconnaissances of this part of Egypt attest the truth of the historical accounts of the ancient population of the Province, now deserted;" "[19] so deserted, that you can scarce tell the numbers of ruined cities frequented only by wandering Arabs."

According to a calculation lower than others, $\frac{1}{3}$ of the land formerly tilled in Egypt has been thrown out of cultivation, i. e. not less than 1,763,895 acres or $2755\frac{7}{10}$ square miles [20]. And this is not of yesterday. Towards the end of the 14th century, the extent of the land taxed was 3,034,179 feddans [21], i. e. $4,377,836\frac{5}{6}$ acres or $6840\frac{1}{3}$ square miles. The list of lands taxed by the Egyptian government in 1824 yields but a sum of 1,956,340 feddans [22], or 2,822,171 acres or 4409 square miles. Yet even this does not represent the land actually cultivated. Some even of the taxed land is left wholly, some partially, uncultivated [23]. In an official

[1] Only one late MS. omits the word τριακοσίων, making the sense, that the number was still no less than seven millions. It has no weight against the greater authority of MSS.

[2] Lane's Egypt i. 27.

[3] Sir G. Wilkinson Modern Egypt i. 257. M. Jomard (Descr. de l' Eg. ii. 2. p. 364.) sets it at 2,422,200.

[4] 100,000 bales of a cwt. each in one year. Lane i. 28.

[5] Wilkinson Anc. Eg. i. 218, 9.

[6] Wilkinson mod. Eg. i. 403.

[7] Malus sur l'état anc. et mod. des Provinces Orient. de la Basse Eg. Descr. Eg. ii. p. 305.

[8] Ritter Erdk. i. 824. 6.

[9] Ib. 827.

[10] Malus Ib. p. 310.

[11] Col. Jacotin in Descr. de l' Eg. M. ii. p. 576.

[12] Andréossy in Descr. Eg. M. i. pp. 261 sqq.

[13] Ib. § 4.

[14] Ritter i. 821.

[15] Le Père Ib. ii. 1. 471.

[16] Athen. i. 60. pp. 76, 7. Dind. Strab. xvii. 1, 14, 15. Ritter i. 871.

[17] Le Père Ib. ii. 2. 482.

[18] Id. ib. ii. p. 10.

[19] Ib. 7.

[20] 474. 24 square leagues. Col. Jacotin ii. 2. p. 577.

[21] from the Arabic list published by De Sacy at the end of his Abdallatif, p. 597–704.

[22] Mengin Hist. de l' Eg. ii. 343.

[23] Sir G. Wilkinson, says, "The land N. and S. of the canal, particularly round Menzaleh, is little productive, and in parts perfectly barren. The increase of nitre in the soil seems to doom to

report[1], 2,000,000 feddans are stated to be cultivated, when the overflow of the Nile is the most favorable, i. e. 4/7 only of the estimated cultivable amount. The French, who surveyed Egypt minutely, with a view to future improvement, calculated that above 1,000,000 feddans (1,012,887) might be proximately restored by the restoration of the system of irrigation, and nearly 1,000,000 more (942,810) by the drainage of its lakes, ponds and marshes, i. e. nearly as much again as is actually cultivated. One of the French surveyors sums up his account of the present state of Egypt[2]; "without canals and their dykes, Egypt, ceasing to be vivified throughout, is only a corpse which the mass of the waters of its river inundates to superfluity, and destroys through fullness. Instead of those ancient cultivated and fertile plains, one only finds, here and there, canals filled up or cut in two, whose numerous ramifications, crossing each other in every direction, exhibit only some scarcely distinguishable traces of a system of irrigation; instead of those villages and populous cities, one sees only masses of bare and arid ruins, remnants of ancient habitations reduced to ashes; lastly, one finds only lagoons, miry and pestilential, or sterile sands which extend themselves, and unceasingly invade a land which the industry of man had gained from the desert and the sea."

Yet this is wholly unnatural. In the Prophet's time, it was contrary to all experience. Egypt is alike prolific in its people and in the productions of the earth. The Egyptian race is still accounted very prolific[3]. So general is this, that the ancients thought that the waters of the Nile must have some power of fecundity[4]. Yet with these powers implanted in nature unimpaired, the population is diminished, the land half-desert. No one doubts that man's abiding misgovernment is the cause of Egypt's desolation. Under their native princes, they were happy and prosperous[5]. Alexander, some of the Ptolemies, the Romans, saw, at least, the value of Egypt. The great conception of its Greek conqueror, Alexandria, has been a source of prosperity to strangers for above 2000 years. Prosperity has hovered around Egypt. Minds, the most different, are at one in thinking that, with a good government, internal prosperity and its famed richness of production might at once be restored. Conquerors of varied nations, Persians, Macedonians, Romans, Greeks, Arabs, Georgians, Tartars, or Turks have tried their hands upon Egypt. Strange that selfishness or powerlessness for good should have rested upon all; strange that no one should have developed its inherent powers! Strange contrast. One long prosperity, and one long adversity. One scarcely broken day, and one troubled night. And that doom foretold in the midday of its prosperity, by these three words, *Egypt shall be a desolation.*

Edom shall be a desolate wilderness. Edom, long unknown, its ancient capital, its rock-dwellings, have been, within these last forty years, anew revealed. The desolation has been so described to us, that we have seen it, as it were, with our own eyes. The land is almost the more hopelessly desolate, because it was once, artificially, highly cultivated. Once it had *the fatness of the earth and the dew of heaven from above*[6]: it had [7]*cornfields* and *vineyards* in abundance, and *wells* of water; its vegetation, its trees, and its vineyards, attracted the dew by which they were supported. "Petra," says Strabo[8], "lies in a spot precipitous and abrupt without, but within possessed of abundant fountains for watering and horticulture." The terrace-cultivation, through which each shower which falls is stored to the uttermost, clothing with fertility the mountain-sides, leaves those steep sides the more bare, when disused. "We saw," says a traveler[9], "many ruined terraces, the evidences and remains of a flourishing agriculture, which, in the prosperous days of Edom and Petra, clothed many of these now sterile mountains with fertility and beauty.—Fields of wheat and some agricultural villages still exist in the eastern portion of Edom; but, with very slight exceptions, the country is blighted with cheerless desolation and hopeless sterility. The hill-sides and mountains, once covered with earth and clothed with vineyards, are now bare rocks. The soil no longer supported by terraces and sheltered by trees, has been swept away by the rains. The various contrivances for irrigation, which even now might restore fertility to many considerable tracts, have all disappeared. Sand from the desert, and the debris of the soft rock of the

destruction even that which is still deserving of cultivation. Some land scarcely repays the labor of tilling, and some has been found so unproductive that, *though rated for taxation and annually paying firdeh*, it has been left uncultivated." Mod. Eg. i. 441, 2. Again, of the province of Behnesa; "The land for the most part lies fallow, for three months before the inundation, partly from the indolence of the people, and partly from the want of hands to cultivate." ii. 30.

[1] "When the Nile rises from 23 to 24 coudées, 2,000,000 feddans are cultivated. But often the Nile does not rise above 19 coudées, and the inundation is not permanent enough to produce the effect desired. Egypt is calculated to have 3,500,000 feddans of cultivable land, if cultivation were pushed to its greatest extent." Bowring Report p. 13.

[2] Le Père Mémoire sur les lacs et les deserts de la basse Egypte in Descr. de l' Eg. Mod. ii. 1. p. 481.

[3] Bowring p. 5. Lane i. 195.

[4] Aristotle and Aristobulus in Strabo xv. 1. § 22. Plin. vii. 3. and others.

[5] Wilkinson Anc. Eg. c. 3. end.

[6] Gen. xxvii. 39.

[7] Nu. xx. 17.

[8] xvi. 4. 21.

[9] Olin T. ii. pp. 15, 55. Keith p. 308.

Before CHRIST cir 800.

20 But Judah shall || dwell [n] for ever, and Jerusalem from generation to generation.

|| Or, *abide*. [n] Amos 9. 15.

Before CHRIST cir. 800.

mountains, cover the valleys which formerly smiled with plenty." Now "[1] the springs have been dried up to such an extent, as to render the renewal of the general fertility of Edom [well nigh] impossible. In places along the course of the stream, reeds and shrubs grow luxuriantly, oleanders and wild figs abound, and give proof that a little cultivation would again cover the rock, and fill the cliffs with the numberless gardens which once adorned them. The traces of former fertility are innumerable; every spot capable of sustaining vegetable life was carefully watered and cultivated. There are numerous grooves in the rocks to carry rainwater to the little clefts in which even now figs are found. Every spot capable of being so protected has been walled up, however small the space gained, or however difficult the means of securing it. The ancient inhabitants seem to have left no accessible place untouched. They have exhibited equal art and industry in eliciting from the grand walls of their marvelous capital whatever the combination of climate, irrigation and botanical skill could foster in the scanty soil afforded them. The hanging gardens must have had a wondrous effect among the noble buildings of the town when it was in all its glory." This desolation began soon after the captivity of Judah and Edom's malicious joy in it. For Malachi appeals to Judah, that whereas God had restored him, He had[2] *laid the mountains and the heritage* of Esau *waste for the jackals of the wilderness*.

Yet Edom was the centre of the intercourse of nations. Occupying, as it did in its narrowest dimensions, the mountains between the S. end of the Dead Sea and the Ælanitic gulf, it lay on the direct line between Egypt and Babylonia. A known route lay from Heroopolis to Petra its capital, and thence to Babylon[3]. Elath and Ezion-geber discharged through its vally, the Arabah, the wealth which they received by sea from India or Africa. Petra was the natural halting-place of the caravans. "The Nabatæans," says Pliny[4], "inclose Petra, in a valley of rather more than two miles in extent, surrounded by inaccessible mountains, through which a stream flows. Here the two roads meet of those who go to Palmyra of Syria, and of those who come from Gaza." Eastward again, he says[5], "they went from Petra to Fora, and thence to Charax" on the banks of the Tigris, near the Persian gulf. Yet further the wealth of Arabia Felix poured by a land-route through Petra. "[6] To Petra and Palestine, Gerræns and Minæans and all the neighboring Arabs brought down from the upper country the frankincense, it is said, and all other fragrant merchandise." Even after the foundation of Alexandria had diverted much of the stream of commerce from Leuce Come, the Ælanitic gulf, and Petra to Myos Hormus[7] on the Egyptian side of the Red Sea, the Romans still connected Elath and Petra with Jerusalem by a great road, of which portions are still extant[8], and guarded the intercourse by military stations[9]. Of these routes, that from Arabia Felix and from Egypt to Babylonia had probably been used for above 1000 years before the time of Joel. Elath and Eziongeber were well-known towns at the time of the Exodus[10]. The intercourse was itself complex and manifold. The land exports of Arabia Felix and the commerce of Elath necessarily passed through Edom, and thence radiated to Egypt, Palestine, Syria. The withdrawal of the commerce of Egypt would not alone have destroyed that of Petra, while Tyre, Jerusalem, Damascus still received merchandise through her. To them she was the natural channel; the pilgrim-route from Damascus to Mecca lies still by Petra. In Joel's time, not the slightest shadow was cast on her future. Then Babylon destroyed her for a time; but she recovered. The Babylonian and Persian Empires perished; Alexander rose and fell; Rome, the master alike of Alexandria and Petra, meant Petra still to survive. No human eye could even then tell that it would be finally desolate; much less could any human knowledge have foreseen it in that of Joel. But God said by him, *Edom shall be a desolate wilderness*, and it is so!

As, however, Egypt and Edom are only instances of the enemies of God's people and Church, so their desolation is only one instance of a great principle of God's Government, that[11] *the triumphing of the wicked* is *short, and the joy of the ungodly for a moment;* that, after their short-lived office of fulfilling God's judgment on His people, the judgment rolls round on themselves, *and they that hate the righteous shall be desolate*[12].

20. *Judah shall dwell for ever.* Not earthly Judah, nor earthly Jerusalem; for these must come to an end, together with the earth itself, of

[1] Lord C. Hamilton Journal in Keith Ib. Idumæa pp. 338, 9. see also Count Portalis, Ib. p. 332.
[2] Mal. i. 3.
[3] Strabo xvi. 4. 2.
[4] vi. 28.
[5] Ib.
[6] Agatharcides p. 57 in Geogr. Min. ed. Oxen, quoted in Vincent's Periplus ii. 262.
[7] Strab. xvi. 4. 24.
[8] Robins. Pal. ii. 161.
[9] Reland p. 230.
[10] Deut. ii. 8.
[11] Job xx. 5.
[12] Ps. xxxiv. 21.

Before CHRIST cir. 800.

21 For I will [o]cleanse
their blood *that* I have not
cleansed: [p] ‖ for the LORD
dwelleth in Zion.

[o] Is. 4. 4.

[p] Ezek. 48. 35. ver. 17. Rev. 21. 3.
‖ Or, *even I the Lord that dwelleth in Zion.*

whose end the Prophets well knew. It is then the one people of God, the true Judah, the people who praise God, the Israel, which is indeed Israel. Egypt and Edom and all the enemies of God should come to an end; but His people shall never come to an end. *The gates of hell shall not prevail against her.* The enemy shall not destroy her; time shall not consume her; she shall never decay. The people of God shall abide before Him and through Him here, and shall dwell with Him for ever.

21. *For I will cleanse her blood that I have not cleansed.* The word rendered *cleansed* [1] is not used of natural cleansing, nor is the image taken from the cleansing of the body. The word signifies only to pronounce innocent, or to free from guilt. Nor is *blood* used of sinfulness generally, but only of the actual guilt of shedding blood. The whole then cannot be an image taken from the cleansing of physical defilement, like the words in the prophet Ezekiel [2], *then washed I thee with water; yea, I thoroughly washed away thy blood from thee.* Nor again can it mean the forgiveness of sins generally, but only the pronouncing innocent the blood which had been shed. This, the only meaning of the words, fall in with the mention of the *innocent blood*, for shedding which, Egypt and Edom had been condemned. The words are the same. There it was said, *because they have shed innocent blood; dam naki;* here, *I will pronounce innocent their blood, nikkethi damam. How*, it is not said. But the sentence on Egypt and Edom explains how God would do it, by punishing those who shed it. For in that He punishes the shedding of it, He declared the *blood* innocent, whose shedding He punished. So in the Revelation it is said [3], *I saw under the altar the souls of them that were slain for the word of God, and for the testimony which they held, and they cried with a loud voice, saying, How long, O Lord, holy and true, dost Thou not judge and avenge our blood on them that dwell on the earth?* "[4] Then, at the last judgment, when the truth in all things shall be made manifest, He shall *declare the blood* of His people, who clave to Him and His truth, which blood their enemies thought they had shed justly and deservedly as the blood of guilty persons, to have indeed been innocent, by absolving them from eternal destruction to which He shall then adjudge their enemies for shedding of it."

For [lit. *and*] *the Lord dwelleth in Zion.* He closes with the promise of God's abiding dwelling. He speaks, not simply of a future, but of an ever-abiding present. He Who IS, the unchangeable God, "[4] the Lord, infinite in power and of eternal Being, Who gives necessary being to all His purposes and promises," dwelleth now in [5] *Mount Zion, the city of the living God, the heavenly Jerusalem,* now by grace and the presence of His Holy Spirit, hereafter in glory. Both of the Church militant on earth and that triumphant in heaven, it is truly to be said, that the Lord dwelleth in them, and that, perpetually. Of the Church on earth will be verified what our Saviour Christ saith [6], *lo I am with you always, even unto the end of the world;* and of its members S. Paul saith, that *they* are *of the household of God, an holy temple in the Lord, in Whom they are builded together for an habitation of God through the Spirit* [7]. Of the Church triumphant, there is no doubt, that *He* doth and will there dwell, and manifest His glorious Presence for ever, *in* Whose *Presence is the fullness of joy, and at His Right Hand* there are *pleasures for evermore* [8]. It is an eternal dwelling of the Eternal, varied as to the way and degree of His Presence by our condition, now imperfect, there perfected in Him; but He Himself dwelleth on for ever. He, the Unchangeable, dwelleth unchangeably; the Eternal, eternally.

"[9] *Glorious things are spoken of thee, thou city of God* [10]. Jerusalem, our mother, we thy children now groan and weep in this valley of tears, hanging between hope and fear, and, amid toil and conflicts, *lifting up our eyes* to thee and greeting thee from far. Truly *glorious things are spoken of thee.* But whatever can be said, since it is said to men and in the words of men, is too little for the *good things* in thee, which *neither eye hath seen, nor ear heard, nor hath entered into the heart of man* [11]. Great to us seem the things which we suffer; but one of thy most illustrious citizens, placed amid those sufferings, who knew something of thee, hesitated not to say [12], *Our light affliction, which is but for a moment, worketh out for us a far more exceeding and eternal weight of glory.* We will then *rejoice in hope*, and *by the waters of Babylon,* even while *we sit and weep,* we will *remember thee, O Zion. If I forget thee, O Jerusalem, may my right hand forget* her cunning. *Let my tongue cleave to the roof of my mouth, I do*

[1] נקיתי. [2] xvi. 9. [3] vi. 10. 11. [4] Poc.
[5] Heb. xii. 22. add Gal. iv. 26. Rev. iii. 12. xiv. 1. xxi. 2. 10.
[6] S. Matt. xxviii. 20. [7] Eph. ii. 19, 21, 2.
[8] Ps. xvi. 12. [9] Rib. [10] Ps. lxxxvii. 3.
[11] 1 Cor. ii. 9. [12] 2 Cor. iv. 17.

not remember thee, if I prefer not Jerusalem above my chief joy[1]. O blessed longed-for day, when we shall enter into the city of the saints, *whose light is the Lamb*, where *the King is seen in His beauty*, where *all tears are wiped off from* the *eyes* of the saints, *and there shall be no more death neither sorrow nor pain; for the former things have passed away*[2]. *How amiable are Thy tabernacles, O Lord of Hosts! My soul longeth, yea fainteth for the courts of the Lord; my heart and my flesh crieth out for the living God*[3]. *When shall I come and appear before God*[4]*?* when shall I see that Father, Whom I ever long for and never see, to Whom out of this exile, I cry out, *Our Father, which art in Heaven?* O true Father,[5], *Father of our Lord Jesus Christ*, [6]*Father of mercies and God of all comfort!* When shall I see *the Word*, Who *was in the beginning with God*, and Who *is God*[7]*?* When may I kiss His sacred Feet, pierced for me, put my mouth to His sacred Side, sit at His Feet, never to depart from them? O Face, more Glorious than the sun! Blessed is he, who beholdeth Thee, who hath never ceased to say[8], *I shall see Him, but not now; I shall behold Him, but not nigh.* When will the day come, when, cleansed from the defilement of my sins, I shall, [9]*with unveiled face, behold the glory of the Lord*, and see the sanctifying Spirit, the Author of all good, through Whose sanctifying we are cleansed, that [10] *we may be like Him, and see Him as He is?* [11] *Blessed are all* they *that dwell in Thy house*, O Lord, *they shall ever praise Thee;* for ever shall they behold Thee and love Thee."

[1] Ps. cxxxvii.
[2] Rev. xxi. 23. Is. xxxiii. 17. Rev. xxi. 4.
[3] Ps. lxxxiv. 1, 2. [4] Ps. xlii. 2. [5] Rom. xv. 6. &c.
[6] 2 Cor. i. 3. [7] S. Joh. i. 1.
[8] Nu. xxiv. 17. [9] 2 Cor. iii. 18.
[10] 1 Joh. iii. 2. [11] Ps. lxxxiv. 4.

INTRODUCTION

TO

THE PROPHET

AMOS.

"[a] He *Who made*, one by one, *the hearts of men*, and *understandeth all their works*, knowing the hardness and contrariousness of the heart of Israel, reasoneth with them not through one Prophet only, but, employing as His ministers many, and those, wondrous men, both monisheth them and foretelleth the things to come, evidencing through the harmony of many the truthfulness of their predictions."

As the contradiction of false teachers gave occasion to S. Paul to speak of himself, so the persecution of the priest of Bethel has brought out such knowledge as we have of the life of Amos, before God called him to be a prophet. *I*, he says[b], *was no prophet, neither was I a prophet's son.* He had not received any of the training in those schools of the prophets which had been founded by Samuel, and through which, amid the general apostacy and corruption, both religious knowledge and religious life were maintained in the remnant of Israel. He was a herdsman, whether (as this word would naturally mean[c]) *a cowherd* or (less obviously) *a shepherd.* He was *among the herdsmen of Tekoah; among* them, and, outwardly, as they, in nothing distinguished from them. The sheep which he tended (for he also kept sheep) may have been his own. There is nothing to prove or to disprove it. But any how he was not like the king of Moab, "a sheep-master[d]," as the Jews, following out their principle, that "[e] prophecy was only bestowed by God on the rich and noble," wish to make him. Like David, he was following the sheep[f], as their shepherd. But his employment as *a gatherer* (or, more probably, *a cultivator) of sycamore fruit*, the rather designates him, as one living by a rural employment for hire. The word, probably, designates the artificial means by which the sycamore fruit was ripened, irritating, scraping, puncturing, wounding it[g]. Amos does not say that these were his food, but that one of his employments was to do a gardener's office in maturing them. A sort of gardener then he was, and a shepherd among other shepherds. The sheep which he fed were also probably a matter of trade. The breed of sheep and goats, *nakad*, from keeping which his peculiar name of shepherd, *noked*, was derived, is still known by the same name in Arabia; a race, small, thin, short-legged, ugly, and stunted. It furnished a proverb, "viler than a nakad;" yet the wool of the sheep was accounted the very best. The goats were found especially in Bahrein. Among the Arabs also, the shepherd of these sheep was known by a name derived from them. They were called "nakad;" their shepherd "nokkad[h]."

The prophet's birthplace, Tekoah, was a town which, in the time of Josephus and of S. Jerome, had dwindled into a "village[i],"

[a] Theod. [b] vii. 14. [c] בקר being used always of the "ox" or "herd," in contrast with the "flocks" of sheep or goats, and the name being derived from "ploughing."

[d] The term נוקד is used of the king of Moab 2 K. iii. 4. [e] See on Joel ii. 29.

[f] vii. 15. *He took me* מאחרי הצאן.

[g] κνίζων. LXX. vellicans, S. Jer. See Theophr. iv. 2. Dioscor. L. i. Plin. xiii. 7. in Bochart ii. 39. p. 384. The Hebrew word בולס (from בלס "a fig" or sycamore in Arab. and Æthiop. signifies only "employed about figs" or sycamores.

[h] See Arabic authorities in Bochart L. ii. c. 34. pp. 442, 3. and Freytag Lexicon. [i] Josephi Vit. § 75.

"a little village[j]," on a high hill, twelve miles from Jerusalem, "which," S. Jerome adds, "we see daily." "It lay," S. Jerome says[k], "six miles southward from holy Bethlehem where the Saviour of the world was born, and beyond it is no village save some rude huts and movable tents. Such is the wide waste of the desert which stretcheth to the Red Sea, and the bounds of the Persians, Ethiopians, and Indians. And no grain whatever being grown upon this dry and sandy soil, it is all full of shepherds, in order, by the multitude of the flocks, to make amends for the barrenness of the land." From Tekoah Joab brought the *wise woman*[l] to intercede for Absalom; Rehoboam built it[m]; i. e. whereas it had been before (what it afterward again became) a village, and so was not mentioned in the book of Joshua, he made it a fortified town toward his South-Eastern border. The neighboring wilderness was called after it[n]. Besides its sycamores, its oil was the best in Judah[o]. War and desolation have extirpated both from this as well as from other parts of Palestine[p]. Its present remains are Christian, "[q]ruins of 4 or 5 acres." It, as well as so many other places near the Dead Sea, is identified by the old name, slightly varied in pronunciation, Theku'a, as also by its distance from Jerusalem[r]. In the sixth century we hear of a chapel in memory of the holy Amos at Tekoa[s], where the separated monks of the lesser laura of S. Saba communicated on the Lord's day. The wide prospect from Tekoa embraced both the dead and the living, God's mercies and His judgments. To the South-East "[t]the view is bounded only by the level mountains of Moab, with frequent bursts of the Dead Sea, seen through openings among the rugged and desolate mountains which intervene." On the North, the Mount of Olives is visible, at that time dear to sight, as overhanging the place, which God had *chosen to place His Name there*. Tekoah, however, although the birthplace, was not the abode of the prophet. He was *among the herdsmen from Tekoah*[u], their employment, as shepherds, leading them away *from Tekoah*. In the wilds of the desert while he was following his sheep, God saw him and revealed Himself to him, as he had to Jacob and to Moses, and said to him, *Go prophesy unto My people Israel*. And as the Apostle left their nets and their father, and Matthew the receipt of custom, and followed Jesus, so Amos left his sheep and his cultivation of sycamores, and appeared suddenly in his shepherd's dress at the royal but idolatrous[v] sanctuary, the temple of the state, to denounce the idolatry sanctioned by the state, to foretell the extinction of the Royal family, and the captivity of the people. This, like Hosea, he had to do in the reign of the mightiest of the sovereigns of Israel, in the midst of her unclouded prosperity. Bethel was but twelve miles Northward from Jerusalem[w], as Tekoah was twelve miles toward the South-East. Six or seven hours would suffice to transport the shepherd from his sheep and the wilderness to that fountain of Israel's corruption, the high places of Bethel, and to confront the inspired peasant with the priests and the prophets of the state-idolatry. There doubtless he said[x], *the sanctuaries of Israel shall be laid waste;* and there, like the former *man of God*, while standing over against *the altar*, he renewed the prophecy against it, and prophesied that in its destruction it should involve its idolatrous worshipers[y]. Yet although he did deliver a part of his prophecy at Bethel, still, like his great predecessors Elijah and Elisha, doubtless he did not confine his ministry there. His summons to the luxurious ladies of Samaria, whose expenses were supported by the oppressions of the poor[z], was questionless delivered in Samaria itself. The call to the heathen to look down into Samaria from the heights which girt in the valley out of which it rose[a], thence to behold its din and its oppressions, to listen to the sound of its revelries and the wailings of its oppressed, and so to judge between God and His people, would also be most effectively given within Samaria. The consciences of the guilty inhabitants to whom he preached, would people the heights around them, their wall of safety, as they deemed, between them and the world, with heathen witnesses of their sins, and heathen avengers. The Prophet could only know by inspiration the coming destruction of the house of Jeroboam and the captivity of Israel. The sins which he rebuked, he probably knew from being among them. As S. Paul's *spirit was stirred in him* at Athens, *when he saw the city wholly given to idolatry*[b], so that of Amos must have been stirred in its depths by that grievous contrast of luxury and penury side by side, which he describes in such vividness of detail. The sins which he rebukes are those of the outward prosperity especially of a capital, the extreme luxury[c], revelries[d], debauchery[e], of the rich, who sup-

j S. Jer. on Jerem. vi. 1.
k Præf. ad. Amos.
l 1 Sam. xiv. 2.
m 2 C. xi. 6.
n 2 C. xx. 20, 1 Macc. ix. 33.
o Menachot viii. 3. in Reland p. 1029.
p See Keith land of Israel c. 3. 4. 5. Stanley Palestine p. 120. Robinson i. 552.
q Robinson i. 486.
r Ritter Erdk. xv. p. 629.
s Vita S. Sabæ in Cotelre. Ecc. Græc. Mon. iii. p. 272.
t Rob. Ib.
u מתקוע.
v vii. 13.
w Euseb. sub. v.
x vii. 9.
y ix. 1.
z iv. 1.
a See on iii. 9.
b Acts xvii. 16.
c iii. 12, 15, iv. 1. v. 11. vi. 4–6.
d ii. 8. iii. 9.
e ii. 7.

ported their own reckless expenditure by oppression of the poor [f], extortion [g], hard bargains with their necessities [h], perversion of justice [i], with bribing [k], false measures [l], a griping, hard-fisted, and probably usurious sale of corn [m]. In grappling with sin, Amos deals more with the details and circumstances of it than Hosea. Hosea touches the centre of the offence; Amos shews the hideousness of it in the details into which it branches out. As he is everywhere graphic, so here he points out the events of daily life in which the sin shewed itself, as the vile price or, it may be, the article of luxury, *the pair of sandals* [n], for which the poor was sold, or *the refuse of wheat* (he invents the word) which they sold, at high prices and with short measure to the poor [o].

According to the title which Amos prefixes to his prophecy, his office fell within the 25 years, during which Uzziah and Jeroboam II. were contemporary, B.C. 809-784. This falls in with the opinion already expressed [p], that the bloodshed mentioned by Hosea in the list of their sins, was rather blood shed politically in their revolutions after the death of Jeroboam II., than individual murder. For Amos, while upbraiding Israel with the sins incidental to political prosperity and wealth, (such as was the time of Jeroboam II.) does not mention bloodshed.

It has been thought that the mention of the earthquake, two years before which Amos began his prophecy, furnishes us with a more definite date. That earthquake must have been a terrible visitation, since it was remembered after the captivity, two centuries and a half afterward. *Ye shall flee,* says Zechariah [q], as of a thing which his hearers well knew by report, *as ye fled before the earthquake in the days of Uzziah king of Judah.* Josephus connects the earthquake with Uzziah's act of pride in offering the incense, for which God smote him with leprosy. He relates it as a fact. "[r] Meanwhile a great earthquake shook the ground, and, the temple parting, a bright ray of the sun shone forth, and fell upon the king's face, so that forthwith the leprosy came over him. And before the city, at the place called Eroge, the Western half of the hill was broken off and rolled half a mile to the mountain Eastward, and there stayed, blocking up the ways and the king's gardens." This account of Josephus, however, is altogether unhistorical. Not to argue from the improbability, that such an event as the rending of the temple itself should not have been mentioned, Josephus has confused Zechariah's description of an event yet future with the *past* earthquake under Uzziah. Nor can the date be reconciled with the history. For when Uzziah was stricken with leprosy [s], *Jotham, his son, was over the king's house, judging the people of the land.* But Jotham was only twenty-five years at his father's death, *when he* himself *began to reign* [t]. And Uzziah survived Jeroboam 26 years. Jotham then, who judged for his father after his leprosy, was not born when Jeroboam died. Uzziah then must have been stricken with leprosy some years after Jeroboam's death; and consequently, after the earthquake also, since Amos, who prophesied *in the* days of Jeroboam, prophesied *two years before the earthquake.*

An ancient Hebrew interpretation [u] of the prophecy of Isaiah [v], *within threescore and five years shall Ephraim be broken that it be no more a people,* assumed that Isaiah was foretelling the commencement of the captivity under Tiglath-Pileser or Sargon, and since the period of Isaiah's own prophecy to that captivity was not 65 years, supposed that Isaiah counted from a prophecy of Amos [w], *Israel shall surely be led captive out of his own land.* This prophecy of Amos they placed in the 25th year of Uzziah. Then his remaining 27 years, Jotham's 16, Ahaz 16, and the six first of Hezekiah would have made up the 65. This calculation was not necessarily connected with the error as to the supposed connection of the earthquake and the leprosy of Uzziah. But it is plain from the words of Isaiah, *in yet* [x] *threescore and five years,* that he is dating from the time when he uttered the prophecy; and so the prophecy relates, not to the imperfect captivity which ended the *kingdom* of Israel, but to that more complete deportation under Esarhaddon [y], when the ten tribes ceased to be *any more a people* (Ahaz 14, Hezekieh 29, Manasseh 22, in all 65). Neither then does this fix the date of Amos.

Nor does the comparison, which Amos bids Israel make between his own borders, and those of Calneh, Hamath and Gath, determine the date of the prophecy. Since Uzziah brake down the walls of Gath [z], and Hamath was recovered by Jeroboam II. to Israel [a], it is probable that the point of comparison lay between the present disasters of these nations, and those with which Amos threatened Israel, and which the rich men of Israel practically did not believe. For it follows [b], *ye that put far away the evil day.* It is probable then that Calne (the very ancient city [c] which subsequently became Ctesiphon,) on the other side of the Euphrates, had lately

[f] ii. 7. 8. iii. 9. iv. 1. v. 11. vi. 3. viii. 4–6. [g] iii. 10.
[h] ii. 8. [i] ii. 7. v. 7, 12. [k] ii. 6. v. 12.
[l] viii. 5. [m] viii. 5. 6. [n] ii. 6. viii. 6. [o] viii. 6.
[p] See Introd. to Hos. p. 15.
[q] xiv. 5. [r] Ant. ix. 10.
[s] 2 C. xxvi. 21. [t] Ib. xxvii. 1.

[u] in Euseb. & S. Jer. ad. loc. found also in Rashi, Aben Ezra, Abarbenel.
[v] vii. 8. [w] vii. 11. 17. [x] בעוד.
[y] Ezr. iv. 2. 2 Chr. xxxiii. 11. 2 Kgs xvii. 24.
[z] 2 Chr. xxvi. 6. [a] 2 Kgs xiv. 28.
[b] Am. vi. 3. [c] Gen. x. 10.

suffered from Assyria, as Gath and Hamath from Judah and Israel. But we know none of these dates. Isaiah speaks of the Assyrian as boasting that *Calno* was *as Carchemish*[d], *Hamath as Arpad, Samaria as Damascus*. But this relates to times long subsequent, when Hamath, Damascus, and Samaria, had fallen into the hands of Assyria. Our present knowledge of Assyrian history gives us no clue to the event, which was well known to those to whom Amos spoke.

Although, however, the precise time of the prophetic office of Amos cannot thus be fixed, it must have fallen within the reign of Jeroboam, to whom Amaziah, the priest of Bethel, accused him[e]. For this whole prophecy implies that Israel was in a state of prosperity, ease, and security, whereas it fell into a state of anarchy immediately upon Jeroboam's death. The mention of *the entering in of Hamath*[f] as belonging to Israel implies that this prophecy was after Jeroboam had recovered it to Israel[g]; and the ease, pride, luxury, which he upbraids, evince that the foreign oppressions[h] had for some time ceased. This agrees with the title of the prophecy, but does not limit it further. Since he prophesied while Uzziah and Jeroboam II. reigned together, his prophetic office must have fallen between B.C. 809 and B.C. 784, in the last 25 years of the reign of Jeroboam II. His office, then, began probably after that of Hosea, and closed long before its close. He is, in a manner then, both later and earlier than Hosea, later than the earliest period of Hosea's prophetic office, and long earlier than the latest.

Within this period, there is nothing to limit the office of Amos to a very short time. The message of Amaziah, the priest of Bethel, implies that Amos' words of woe had shaken Israel through and through. [i]*Amos hath conspired against thee in the midst of the house of Israel; the land is not able to bear all his words.* It may be that God sent him to the midst of some great festival at Bethel, as, at Jeroboam's dedication-feast, He sent the prophet who afterward disobeyed Him, to foretell the desecration of the Altar, which Jeroboam was consecrating, in God's Name, against God. In this case, Amos might, at once, like Elijah, have been confronted with a great concourse of the idol-worshipers. Yet the words of Amaziah seem, in their obvious meaning, to imply that Amos had had a more pervading influence than would be produced by the delivery of God's message in one place. He says of *the land*, i. e. of all the ten tribes generally, it *is not able to bear all his words.* The accusation also of a *conspiracy* probably implies, that some had not been shaken only, but had been converted by the words of Amos, and were known by their adherence to him and his belief.

Amos seems also to speak of the prohibition to God's prophets to prophesy, as something habitual, beyond the one opposition of Amaziah, which he rebuked on the spot. *I raised up of your sons for prophets; but ye commanded the prophets, saying, Prophesy not*[k]. Nor, strictly speaking, was Amos a *son* of Ephraim. The series of images in the 3d chapter seem to be an answer to an objection, why did he prophesy among them? People, he would say, were not, in the things of nature, surprised that the effect followed the cause. God's command was the cause; his prophesying, the effect[l]. Then *they put away from them the evil day*[m], forgetting future evil in present luxury; or they professed that God was with them; "the LORD, the God of hosts, shall be with you, *as ye have spoken*[n];" or trusting in their half-service of God and His imagined Presence among them, they jeered at Amos's prophecies of ill, and professed to desire the Day of the Lord, with which he threatened them; they said that evil should not reach them; *Woe unto you that desire the Day of the Lord! to what end is it to you*[o]*? All the sinners of My people shall die by the sword, which say, the evil shall not overtake nor prevent us*[p]. They shewed also in deed that they hated those who publicly reproved them[q]; and Amos, like Hosea, declares that they are hardened, so that wisdom itself must leave them to themselves[r]. All this implies a continued intercourse between the prophet and the people, so that his office was not discharged in a few sermons, so to say, or inspired declarations of God's purpose, but must have been that of a Pastor among them during a course of years. His present book, like Hosea's, is a summary of his prophecies.

That book, as he himself subsequently gathered into one his prophetic teaching, is one well-ordered whole. He himself, in the title, states that it had been spoken before it was written. For in that he says, these are *the words* which in prophetic vision he *saw, two years before the earthquake,* this portion of his prophecies must have preceded his writings by those two years at least. That terrible earthquake was probably the occasion of his collecting those prophecies. But that earthquake doubtless was no mere note of time. Had he intended a date only, he would probably have named, as other prophets do, the year of the king of Judah. He himself mentions earthquakes[s], as one of the warnings of God's displeasure. This more destructive earthquake was probably the first great token of God's displeasure during the

[d] Is. x. 9. [e] vii. 10. 11. [f] vi. 14. [g] 2 Kgs xiv. 25. [h] Ib. 26. [i] vii. 10.

[k] ii. 11, 12. [l] iii. 3–8. [m] vi. 3. [n] v. 14. [o] v. 18. [p] ix. 10. [q] v. 10. [r] v. 13. [s] iv. 11.

prosperous reign of Jeroboam II., the first herald of those heavier judgments which Amos had predicted, and which brake upon Israel, wave after wave, until the last carried him away captive. For two years, Israel had been forewarned; now *the beginning of sorrows*[t] had set in.

Amos, at the beginning of his book, (as has been already noticed) joins on his book with the book of the prophet Joel. Joel had foretold, as instances of God's judgments on sin, how He would recompense the wrongs, which Tyre, Zidon, Philistia and Edom had done to Judah, and that He would make Egypt desolate. Amos, omitting Egypt, adds Damascus, Ammon and Moab, and Judah itself. It may be, that he selects seven nations in all, as a sort of whole (as that number is so often used), or that he includes all the special enemies of the Theocracy, the nations who hated Israel and Judah, *because* they were the people of God, and God's people itself, as far as it too was alienated from its God. Certainly, the sins denounced are sins against the Theocracy or government of God[v]. It may be, that Amos would exhibit to them the truth, that *God is no respecter of persons;* that He, the Judge of the whole earth, punishes every sinful nation; and that he would, by this declaration of God's judgments, prepare them for the truth, from which sinful man so shrinks;—that God punishes most, where He had most shewn His light and love[w]. The thunder-cloud of God's judgments, having passed over all the nations round about, Syria and Philistia, Tyre, Edom, Ammon, Moab, and even discharged the fire from heaven on Judah and Jerusalem, settles at last on Israel. The summary which closes this circle of judgments on Israel, is fuller in regard to *their* sins, since they were the chief objects of his mission. In that summary he gathers in one the sins with which he elsewhere upbraids them, and sets before them their ingratitude and their endeavors to extinguish the light which God gave them.

Our chapters follow a natural division, in that each, like those of Hosea, ends in woe. The 3d, 4th, and 5th are distinguished by the three-fold summons, *Hear ye this word.* In each, he sets before them some of their sins, and in each pronounces God's sentence upon them. *Therefore thus saith the Lord God; Therefore thus will I do unto thee, O Israel; Therefore the Lord, the God of hosts, the Lord, saith thus*[x]. On this follows a two-fold woe, *Woe unto you that desire*[y]*; Woe to them that are at ease*[z]*;* both which sections alike end in renewed sentences of God's judgment; the first, of the final captivity of Israel *beyond Damascus;* the second, of their nearer afflictions through the first invasion of Tiglath-pileser[a]. In the 7th chapter he begins a series of visions. In the two first, God forgives, at the intercession of the prophet[b]. The 3d vision God interprets, that He would forgive no more[c]. On this followed the prohibition from Amaziah to prophesy, and God's sentence against him. In the 8th chapter, Amos resumes (as though nothing had intervened), the series of visions, upon which Amaziah had broken in. He resumes them exactly where he had been stopped. Amaziah broke in, when he declared that God would not *pass by* the house of Israel *any more,* but would desolate the idol-sanctuaries of Israel and bring a sword against the house of Jeroboam. The vision in which Amos resumes, renews the words[d], *I will not again pass by them any more,* and foretells that the songs of the idol-temple should be turned into howlings. The last chapter he heads with a vision, that not only should the idol-altar and temple be destroyed, but that it should be the destruction of its worshipers[e]. Each of these visions Amos makes a theme which he expands, both ending in woe; the first, with the utter destruction of the idolaters of Israel[f]; the 2d, with that of the sinful *kingdom* of Israel[g]. With this he unites the promise to the *house* of Israel, that, *sifted* as they should be *among the nations, not one grain should fall to the earth*[h]. To this he, like Hosea, adds a closing promise, the first in his whole book, that God would raise the fallen tabernacle of David, convert the heathen, and therewith restore the captivity of Israel, amid promises, which had already, in Joel, symbolized spiritual blessings[i].

Amos, like Hosea, was a prophet for Israel. After the 2d chapter in which he includes Judah in the circle of God's visitations, because he had *despised the law of the Lord*[k], Amos only notices him incidentally. He there foretells that Jerusalem should (as it was) be burned with fire. Judah also must be included in the words, "[l]against the *whole* family which God brought up out of the land of Egypt," and *woe* is pronounced against those who are *at ease in Zion*[m]. Else, *Israel, the house of Israel, the virgin of Israel, the sanctuaries of Israel, Jacob, the house of Jacob,* and (in the same sense) *the high places of Isaac, the house of Isaac; the house of Joseph, the remnant of Joseph, the affliction of Joseph, the mountain,* or *the mountains of Samaria, Samaria* itself, *Bethel*[n], occur interchangeably as the object of his prophecy. Amaziah's

[t] S. Matt. xxiv. 8.
[v] See below in the Commentary.
[w] iii. 2. [x] iii. 11. iv. 12. v. 16. as before, ii. 14.
[y] v. 18. [z] vi. 1. [a] See on vi. 14. [b] vii. 3, 6.
[c] Ib. 8. [d] viii. 2. [e] ix. 1. [f] viii. 14. [g] ix. 8.
[h] Ib. 9. [i] Ib. 13. [k] ii. 4, 5. [l] iii. 1. [m] vi. 1.
[n] iii. 9, 12, 13, 14. iv. 1, 4, 5, 12. v. 1, 4, 6, 15, 25. vi. 1, 6, 8, 14. vii. 2, 5, 8, 9, 16, 17. viii. 2, 14. ix. 7, 8, 9.

taunt, that his words, as being directed against Israel and Bethel, would be acceptable in the kingdom of Judah, implies the same; and Amos himself declares that this was his commission, *go, prophesy unto My people Israel.* In speaking of the idolatry of Beersheba, he uses the word, *pass not over to Beersheba*[o], adding the idolatries of Judah to their own. The word, *pass not over*, could only be used by one prophesying in Israel. It must have been then the more impressive to the faithful in Israel, that he closed his prophecy by the promise, not to them primarily, but to the house of David, and to Israel through its restoration. Amos, like Hosea, foretells the utter destruction of *the kingdom* of Israel, even while pronouncing that God would not utterly destroy *the house* of Jacob[p], but would save the elect in it.

The opposition of Amaziah stands out, as one signal instance of the manifold cry, *Prophesy not,* with which men sought to drown the Voice of God. Jeroboam left the complaint unheeded. His great victories had been foretold to him by the Prophet Jonah; and he would not interfere with the Prophet of God, although he predicted, not as Amaziah distorted his words, that *Jeroboam* should *die by the sword*, but that *the house of Jeroboam*[p] should so perish. But his book is all comprised within the reign of Jeroboam and the kingdom of Israel. He was called by God to be a prophet there; nor is there any, the slightest, trace of his having exercised his office in Judah, or having retired thither in life.

A somewhat late tradition places Amos among the many prophets, whom, our Lord says, His people slew. The tradition bore, "that after he had been often beaten (the writer uses the same word[r] which occurs in Heb. xi. 35) by Amaziah the priest of Bethel, the son of that priest, Osee, broke his temples with a stake. He was carried half-dead to his own land, and, after some days, died of the wound, and was buried with his fathers." But the anonymous Greek writer who relates it, (although it is in itself probable) has not, in other cases, trustworthy information, and S. Jerome and S. Cyril of Alexandria knew nothing of it. S. Jerome[s] relates only that the tomb of Amos was still shewn at Tekoa, his birthplace.

The influence of the shepherd-life of Amos appears most in the sublimest part of his prophecy, his descriptions of the mighty workings of Almighty God[t]. With those awful and sudden changes in nature, whereby what to the idolaters was an object of worship, was suddenly overcast, and *the day made dark with night*, his shepherd-life had made him familiar. The starry heavens had often witnessed the silent intercourse of his soul with God. In the calf, the idolaters of Ephraim worshiped "nature." Amos then delights in exhibiting to them *his* God, Whom they too believed that they worshiped, as the Creator of "nature," wielding and changing it at His Will. All nature too should be obedient to its Maker in the punishment of the ungodly[v], nor should any thing hide from Him[w]. The shepherd-life would also make the Prophet familiar with the perils from wild beasts which we know of as facts in David's youth. The images drawn from them were probably reminiscences of what he had seen or met with[x]. But Amos lived, a shepherd in a barren and for the most part treeless wild, not as a husbandman. His was not a country of corn, nor of cedars and oaks; so that images from stately trees[y], a heavy-laden wain[z], or the sifting of corn[a], were not the direct results of his life amid sights of nature. The diseases of corn, locusts, drought, which, the Prophet says, God had sent among them, were inflictions which would be felt in the corn-countries of Israel, rather than in the wilderness of Tekoah. The insensibility for which he upbraids Israel was, of course, their hardness of heart amid their own sufferings[b]; the judgments, with which he threatens them in God's Name[c], can have no bearing on his shepherd-life in his own land.

Even S. Jerome, while laying down a true principle, inadvertently gives as an instance of the images resulting from that shepherd-life, the opening words of his book, which are in part words of the Prophet Joel. "It is natural," he says, "that all who exercise an art, should speak in terms of their art, and that each should bring likenesses from that wherein he hath spent his life.—Why say this? In order to shew, that Amos the Prophet too, who was a shepherd among shepherds, and that, not in cultivated places, or amid vineyards, or woods, or green meadows, but in the wide waste of the desert, where were witnessed the fierceness of lions and the destruction of cattle, used the language of his art, and called the awful and terrible Voice of the Lord, the roaring of lions, and compared the overthrow of the cities of Israel to the lonely places of shepherds or the drought of mountains."

The truth may be, that the religious life of Amos, amid scenes of nature, accustomed him, as well as David, to express his thoughts in words taken from the great picture-book of nature, which, as being also written by the Hand of God, so wonderfully expresses the things of God. When his Prophet's life

[o] v. 5. [p] ix. 8–10. [q] vii. 9.
[r] τυμπανίσας, Auct. de vit. Proph. ap. S. Epiph. ii. 145. [s] de loc. Hebr. T. iii. 206. ed. Vall.

[t] iv. 13. v. 8. ix. 5, 6. [v] viii. 8. [w] ix. 2, 3, 5.
[x] iii. 4, 5, 12. v. 19. [y] ii. 9. [z] ii. 13.
[a] ix. 9. [b] iv. 7–9. [c] vii. 1–3.

brought him among other scenes of cultivated nature, his soul, so practiced in reading the relations of the physical to the moral world, took the language of his parables alike from what he saw, or from what he remembered. He was what we should call "a child of nature," endued with power and wisdom by his God. Still more mistaken has it been, to attribute to the Prophet any inferiority even of outward style, in consequence of his shepherd-life. Even a heathen has said, "words readily follow thought;" much more, when thoughts and words are poured into the soul together by God the Holy Ghost. On the contrary, scarcely any Prophet is more glowing in his style, or combines more wonderfully the natural and moral world, the Omnipotence and Omniscience of God[d]. Visions, if related, are most effectively related in prose. Their efficacy depends, in part, on their simplicity. Their meaning might be overlaid and hidden by ornament of words. Thus much of the book of Amos, then, is naturally in prose. The poetry, so to speak, of the visions of Amos or of Zechariah is in the thoughts, not in the words. Amos has also chosen the form of prose for his upbraidings of the wealthy sinners of Israel. Yet, in the midst of this, what more poetic than the summons to the heathen enemies of Israel, to people the heights about Samaria, and behold its sins[e]? What more graphic than that picture of utter despair which dared not name the Name of God?[f] What bolder than the summons to Israel to come, if they willed, at once to sin and to atone for their sin[g]? What more striking in power than the sudden turn[h], "You only have I known: *therefore* I will punish you for all your iniquities? or the sudden summons[i], "because I will do *this* unto thee," (the silence, what the *this* is, is more thrilling than words) "prepare to meet thy God, O Israel?" Or what more pathetic than the close of the picture of the luxurious rich, when, having said, how they heaped luxuries one on another, he ends with what they did *not* do[k]; *they are not grieved for the afflictions of Joseph?*

S. Augustine selects Amos, as an instance of unadorned eloquence. Having given instances from S. Paul, he says[l], "These things, when they are taught by professors, are accounted great, bought at a great price, sold amid great boasting. I fear these discussions of mine may savor of the like boasting. But I have to do with men of a spurious learning, who think meanly of our writers, not because they have not, but because they make no shew of the eloquence which these prize too highly.—

"I see that I must say something of the eloquence of the prophets. And this I will do, chiefly out of the book of that prophet, who says that he was a shepherd or a cowherd, and was taken thence by God and sent to prophesy to His people.

"When then this peasant, or peasant-prophet, reproved the ungodly, proud, luxurious, and therefore most careless of brotherly love, he cries aloud, *Woe to them that are at ease in Zion, &c.* Would they who, as being learned and eloquent, despise our prophets as unlearned and ignorant of elocution, had they had aught of this sort to say, or had they to speak against such, would they, as many of them as would fain not be senseless, wish to speak otherwise? For what would any sober ear desire more than is there said? First, the inveighing itself, with what a crash is it hurled as it were, to awaken their stupefied senses!"

Then, having analysed these verses, he says, "How beautiful this is, and how it affects those who, reading, understand, there is no use in saying to one who does not himself feel it. More illustrations of the rules of rhetoric may be found in this one place, which I have selected. But a good hearer will not be so much instructed by a diligent discussion of them, as he will be kindled by their glowing reading. For these things were not composed by human industry, but were poured forth in eloquent wisdom from the Divine mind, wisdom not aiming at eloquence, but eloquence not departing from wisdom." "For if, as some most eloquent and acute men could see and tell, those things which are learned as by an art of rhetoric, would not be observed and noted and reduced to this system, unless they were first found in the genius of orators, what wonder if they be found in those also, whom *He* sends, Who creates genius? Wherefore we may well confess that our canonical writers and teachers are not wise only but eloquent, with that eloquence which beseems their character."

S. Jerome, in applying to Amos words which S. Paul spake of himself[m], *rude in speech but not in knowledge*, doubtless was thinking mostly of the latter words; for he adds, "For the same Spirit Who spake through all the Prophets, spake in him." Bp. Lowth says happily[n], "Jerome calls Amos, *rude in speech but not in knowledge*, implying of him what Paul modestly professed as to himself, on whose authority many have spoken of this Prophet, as though he were altogether rude, ineloquent, unadorned. Far otherwise! Let any fair judge read his writings, thinking not who wrote them, but what he wrote, he will think that our shepherd was *in no wise behind the very chiefest* Prophets; in the loftiness of his thoughts and the mag-

[d] iv. 13. [e] iii. 9. [f] vi. 9, 10. [g] iv. 4. [h] iii. 2. [i] iv. 12. [k] vi. 6. [l] De doctr. Christ. iv. 7. n. 15–21.

[m] 2 Cor. xi. 6.
[n] de S. Poesi Hebr. Præl. xxi.

nificence of his spirit, nearly equal to the highest, and in the splendor of his diction and the elegance of the composition scarcely inferior to any. For the same Divine Spirit moved by His Inspiration Isaiah and Daniel in the court, David and Amos by the sheepfold; ever choosing fitting interpreters of His Will and sometimes perfecting praise out of the mouth of babes. Of some He useth the eloquence; others He maketh eloquent."

It has indeed been noticed that in regularity of structure he has an elegance peculiar to himself. The strophaic form, into which he has cast the heavy prophecies of the two first chapters adds much to their solemnity; the recurring "burden" of the fourth[o], *Yet have ye not returned unto Me, saith the Lord*, gives it a deep pathos of its own. Indeed no other prophet has bound his prophecies into one, with so much care as to their outward form, as this inspired shepherd. Amos (to use human terms) was not so much the poet as the sacred orator. One of those energetic turns which have been already instanced, would suffice to stamp the human orator. Far more, they have shaken through and through souls steeped in sin from the Prophet's time until now. It has been said of human eloquence, "he lightened, thundered, he commingled Greece." The shepherd has shaken not one country, but the world; not by a passing earthquake, but by the awe of God which, with electric force, streamed through his words.

Some variation of dialect, or some influence of his shepherd-life on his pronunciation, has been imagined in Amos. But it relates to five words only. In three, his orthography differs by a single letter from that found elsewhere in Hebrew. In two cases, the variation consists in the use of a different sibilant[p]; the 3d in the use of a weaker guttural[q]. Besides these, he uses a softer sound of the name Isaac[r], which also occurs in Jeremiah and a Psalm; and in another word, he, in common with two Psalms, employs a root with a guttural[s], instead of that common in Hebrew which has a strong sibilant. In four of these cases, Amos uses the softer form; in the 5th, we only know that the two sibilants were pronounced differently once, but cannot guess what the distinction was. The two sibilants are interchanged in several Hebrew words, and on no rule, that we can discover[t]. In another of the sibilants, the change made by Amos is just the reverse of that of the Ephraimites who had only the pronunciation of s for sh; "sibboleth" for "shibboleth." But the Ephraimites could not pronounce the sh at all; the variation in Amos is limited to a single word. The like variations to these instances in Amos are also found in other words in the Bible. On the whole, we may *suspect* the existence of a softer pronunciation in the South of Judæa, where Amos lived; but the only safe inference is, the extreme care with which the words have been handed down to us, just as the Prophet spoke and wrote them.

It has been noticed already that Amos and Hosea together shew, that all the Mosaic festivals and sacrifices, priests, prophets, a temple, were retained in Israel, only distorted to calf-worship[u]. Even the third-year's tithes they had not ventured to get rid of[v]. Amos supplies some yet more minute traits of ritual; that they had the same rules in regard to leaven[w]; that their altar too had horns (as prescribed in the law), on which the blood of the sacrifices was to be sprinkled[x], they had the altar-bowls[y] whence the blood of the victim was sprinkled[z], such as the princes of the congregation offered in the time of Moses[a], and *their* rich men, at times at least, plundered to drink

[o] iv. 6, 8, 9, 10, 11.

[p] a) בושסכם for what would elsewhere be בוססכם v. 10. (the actual form does not occur elsewhere). b) מסרף for משרף vi. 10.

[q] מתאב for מתעב vi. 8. The use of the common word פתאם, from פתע, and אודות probably from איד i. q. עוד, are instances of the like change within the language itself, from its earliest times. Isaiah probably uses אגם (xix. 10) for עגם (Job xxx. 25). (גאל for געל is used by Isaiah (lix. 3, lxiii. 3,) Zephaniah (iii. 1) and Jeremiah (Lam iv. 14) as well as after the captivity by Malachi (i. 7, 12) Ezra (ii. 62) Nehemiah (vii. 64).

[r] ישחק for יצחק, Am. vii. 9, 16. The verb, צחק, from which יצחק is formed, occurs twice only out of the Pentateuch (Jud. xvi. 25, Ez. xxiii. 32). The form which Amos and Jeremiah (xxxiii. 26) use, (as also Ps. cv. 9) is from the verb, as it was subsequently written, שחק.

[s] מעיק from a root עוק i. q. צוק whence עקה Ps. lv. 4. מועקה Ps. lxvi. 11.

[t] כעש occurs four times in Job for כעס, but contrariwise הסיג (Job xxiv. 2) for השיג; שור in Hos. ix. 12 for סור; פרש in Mic. iii. 4, Lam. iv. 4 for פרם; סבך and שבך passim; סדר and שדרה, 3ce in Kings; שוג 2 S. i. 22. and שיג 1 K. xviii. 27, for סוג; שכך Ex. xxxiii. 22; else סכך Ex. xl. 3, xxv. 20 &c. סעפם 1 K. xviii. 21 and שעפים Job iv. 13, xx. 2; סער and שער; ספח and שפח Is. iii. 17, v. 7.

[u] Introd. to Hosea, p. 2. [v] Ib. [w] iv. 5.

[x] iii. 14. See Ex. xxvii. 2. xxix. 12. Lev. iv. 25.

[y] vi. 6.

[z] מזרק is only used of such a bowl; and its meaning "a vessel for *sprinkling*," agrees herewith. Its employment by the rich, when it had once been desecrated to idolatry, is nothing strange; far less, than the use of chalices to adorn the side-boards of rich English, when Church-plate had been plundered in England or Spain.

[a] Nu. vii. 13 sqq.

wine from. They had also true Nazarites, raised up among them, as well as true prophets; and they felt the weight of the influence of these Religious against them, since they tried by fraud or violence to make them break their vow [b]. Amos, while upbraiding their rich men for breaking the law between man and man, presupposes that the law of Moses was, in this respect also, acknowledged among them. For in his words, "they turn aside the way of the meek [c]," "they turn aside the poor in the gate [e]," "they take a ransom [d]" (from the rich for their misdeeds), he retains the peculiar term of the Pentateuch; as also in that, "on clothes laid to pledge [e] they lie down by every altar;" "who make the Ephah small [f]." "Balances of deceit [g]" are the contrary of what are enjoined in the law, "balances of right [h]." In upbraiding them for a special impurity, forbidden in principle by the law [i], he uses the sanction often repeated in the law, "[k] to profane My Holy Name." In the punishments which he mentions, he uses terms in which God threatens those punishments. The two remarkable words, rendered "blasting and mildew [l]," occur only in Deuteronomy, and in Solomon's prayer founded upon it [m], and in Haggai [n] where he is referring to Amos. In the words, "[o] as God overthrew Sodom and Gomorrah," the peculiar term and form of Deuteronomy, as well as the threat, are retained. The threat, "Ye have built houses of hewn stone, and ye shall not dwell therein; ye have planted pleasant vineyards, but ye shall not drink the wine thereof;" but blends and enlarges those in Deuteronomy [p]. The remarkable term describing their unrepentance is taken from the same [q]. So also the image of "gall and wormwood [r]," two bitter plants, into which they turned judgment and righteousness. There are other verbal reminiscences of the Pentateuch, interwoven with the words of Amos, which presuppose that it was in the memory of both the Prophet and his hearers in Israel [s]. Indeed, after that long slavery of four hundred years in Egypt, the traditions of the spots, hallowed by God's intercourse with the Patriarchs, probably even their relations to "Edom [t] their brother," must have been lost. The book of Genesis did not embody popular existing traditions of this sort, but must have revived them. The idolatry of Beersheba [u], as well as that of Gilead, alluded to by Hosea, as also Jeroboam's choice of Bethel itself for the calf-worship [u], imply on the part of the idolaters a knowledge and belief of the history, which they must have learned from the Pentateuch. Doubtless it had been a part of Jeroboam's policy to set up, over-against the exclusive claim for the temple at Jerusalem, rival places of traditionary holiness from the mercies of God to their forefathers, much as Mohammed availed himself of the memory of Abraham, to found his claim for an interest in Jerusalem. But these traditions too must have been received by the people not derived from them. They were not brought with them from Egypt. The people, enslaved, degraded, sensualized, idolatry-loving, had no hearts to cherish the memories of the pure religion of their great forefathers, who worshiped the un-imaged Self-existing God.

As Amos employed the language of the Pentateuch and cited the book of Joel, so it seems more probable, that in the burden of his first prophecies, "[v] I will send a fire upon——and it shall devour the palaces of——" he took the well-known words of Hosea [w], and, by their use, gave an unity to their prophecies, than that Hosea, who uses no language except that of the Pentateuch, should, in the one place where he employs this form, have limited the "burden" of Amos to the one case of Judah. Besides, in Hosea, the words, declaring the destruction of the cities and palaces of Judah, stand in immediate connection with Judah's wrong temper in building them whereas in Amos they are insulated. Beside this, the language of the two prophets does not bear upon each other, except that both have the term "[x] balances of deceit," which was originally formed in contrast with what God had enjoined in the law, "balances of right," and which stands first in the Proverbs of Solomon [y].

Of later prophets, Jeremiah renewed against Damascus the prophecy of Amos in his own words; only, the memory of Hazael having been obliterated perhaps in the destruction under Tiglath-Pileser, Jeremiah

[b] ii. 12. [c] ii. 7. v. 12. הטו. See Ex. xxiii. 6. Deut. xvi. 19. xxiv. 17. xxvii. 19.

[d] v. 12. לקחי כפר; Nu. xxxv. 31. לא תקחו כפר.

[e] ii. 8. על בגדים חבלים. See Ex. xxii. 26, 7.

[f] viii. 5. See Deut. xxv. 14. 15. [g] Am. Ib.

[h] Lev. xix. 36. [i] Deut. xxiii. 1.

[k] להלל את שם קדשי ii. 7. Lev. xx. 3.

[l] שדפון, ירקון. iv. 9. Deut. xxviii. 22.

[m] 1 K. viii. 37. [n] ii. 17.

[o] iv. 11. Deut. xxix. 23. כמהפכת סדם ועמרה.

[p] v. 11. Deut. xxviii. 30, 39. [q] לא שבתם עדי iv. 6, 8, 9, 10. See Deut. iv. 29.

[r] vi. 12, from Deut. xxix. 18. לענה occurs alone, in the same image, Am. v. 7 and ראש in Hos. x. 4. They are used together as an image of the bitter draught of affliction (Jer. ix. 15, xxiii. 15, Lam. iii. 19, and לענה Lam. iii. 15) and of the bitter end of sin, Prov. v. 4. Not elsewhere.

[s] See ii. 2, 10, 11. iii. 2. vi. 1. vii. 16. ix. 8, 12.

[t] i. 11.

[u] v. 8. The above instances are selected from Hengstenberg, Auth. d. Pent. i. 83–104.

[v] i. 4, 7, 10, 12, ii. 2, 5. It is slightly varied in i. 14.

[w] Hos. vii. 14. [x] Hos. xii. 8. [7 Eng.] Am. viii. 5.

[y] Prov. xi. 1. xx. 23.

calls it not after Hazael, but by its own name and that of Benhadad[z]. The words of Amos had once been fulfilled, and its people had been transported to Kir. Probably fugitives had again repeopled it, and Jeremiah intended to point out, that the sentence pronounced through Amos was not yet exhausted. On the like ground probably, when upbraiding Ammon for the like sins and for that for which Amos had denounced woe upon it, its endeavor to displace Israel[a], Jeremiah used the words of Amos, *their king shall go into captivity,—and his princes together*[b]. In like way Haggai upbraids the Jews of his day for their impenitence under God's chastisements, in words varied in no essential from those of Amos[c]. The words of Amos, so repeated to the Jews upon their restoration, sounded, as it were, from the desolate heritage of Israel, *Sin no more, lest a worse thing happen unto thee.*

Other reminiscences of the words of Amos are only a part of the harmony of Scripture[d], the prophets in this way too indicating their unity with one another, that they use the words, the one of the other.

The might of his teaching at the time, the state-priest Amaziah impressed on Jeroboam. Contemptuous toward Amos himself, Amaziah admitted the truth to Jeroboam. *The land is not able to bear all his words.* Doubtless, as the Jews were mad against S. Stephen, *not* being *able to resist the wisdom and Spirit by which he spake*[e], so God accompanied with power His servant's words to His people. They had already seen God's words fulfilled against the houses of Jeroboam I., of Baasha, of Ahab. That same doom was now renewed against *the house of Jeroboam,* and with it the prophecy of the dispersion of the ten tribes[f], which Hosea contemporaneously foretold[g]. The two prophets of Israel confirmed one another, but also left themselves no escape. They staked the whole reputation of their prophecy on this definite issue. We know it to have been fulfilled on the house of Jeroboam; yet the house of Jeroboam was firmer than any before or after it. We know of the unwonted captivity of the ten tribes. Had they not been carried captive, prophecy would have come to shame; and such in proportion is its victory. Each step was an instalment, a pledge, of what followed. The death of Zechariah, Jeroboam's son, was the first step in the fulfillment of the whole; then probably, in the invasion of Pul against Menahem[h], followed the doom of Amaziah. God is not anxious to vindicate His word. He does not, as to Shebna[i], or Amaziah, or the false prophets Ahab, Zedekiah[j] or Shemaiah[k], or Pashur[l] or other false prophets[m]. At times, as in the case of Hananiah[n], Scripture records the individual fulfillment of God's judgments. Mostly, it passes by unnoticed the execution of God's sentence. The sentence of the criminal, unless reprieved, in itself implies the execution[o]. The fact impressed those who witnessed it; the record of the judgment suffices for us.

Then followed, under Tiglath-pileser, the fulfillment of the prophecy as to Damascus[p], and Gilead[q]. Under Sargon was fulfilled the prophecy on the ten tribes[r]. That on Judah[s] yet waited 133 years, and then was fulfilled by Nebuchadnezzar. A few years later, and he executed God's judgments foretold by Amos on their enemies, Moab, Ammon, Edom, Tyre[t]. [u]Kings of Egypt, Assyria, and the Macedonian Alexander fulfilled in succession the prophecy as to Philistia. So various were the human wills, so multitudinous the events, which were to bring about the simple words of the shepherd-prophet. Amos foretells the events; he does say, why the judgments should come; he does not foretell "when," or "through whom:" but the events themselves he foretells absolutely, and they came. Like Joel, he foretells the conversion of the Heathen and anticipates so far the prophecies of Isaiah, that God would work this through the restoration of the house of David, when fallen. Strange comment on human greatness, that the royal line was not to be employed in the salvation of the world, until it was fallen! The Royal Palace had to become the hut of Nazareth, ere the Redeemer of the world could be born, Whose glory and kingdom were not of this world, Who came, to take from us nothing but our nature, that He might sanctify it, our misery, that He might bear it for us. Yet flesh and blood could not foresee it ere it came, as flesh and blood could not believe it, when He came.

[z] Jer. xlix. 27. [a] Am. i. 13. Jer. xlix. 1.
[b] Am. i. 15. Jer. xlix. 3. Jeremiah retains the idiom הלך בַנולה, only adding "his priests," before the words "and his princes." He retains also the characteristic word תרועה Am. i. 14, and for בָאש תצתנה,הִצַּתִּי אש. [c] Am. iv. 9. Hagg. ii. 19.
[d] Such are, the use of the words of Amos ii. 14 in Jer. xlvi. 6; the use of the idiom of Amos, *I take up a lamentation* נשֵׂא עליכם קינה (v. 1.) three times by Ezekiel, xxvii. 2, xxviii. 12, xxxii. 2; the use of the image, *a brand plucked out of the burning,* Am. iv. 11, Zech. iii. 2. [e] Acts vi. 10. [f] v. 27. vii. 8, 9, 17.

[g] Hos. i. 6. ix. 17. [h] 2 Kgs xv. 19.
[i] Is. xxii. 17, 18. [j] Jer. xxix. 20–22. [k] Ib. 32.
[l] Ib. xx. 6. [m] Ib. xiv. 15. [n] Ib. xxviii. 17.
[o] A recent writer "on the interpretation of Scripture" (Essays and Reviews, p. 343.) ventures to give this (Amos vii. 10–17) as one of three instances in proof that "the failure of prophecy is never admitted *in spite of Scripture and of history.*" Certainly, no Christian thinks that God's word can have failed. But unless the execution of God's sentence on one of the many calf-priests of Bethel is necessarily matter of history, it has rather to be shewn why it should be mentioned, than why it was omitted. [p] i. 5. [q] vi. 14.
[r] v. 27. vii. 8, 9, 17. ix. 8. [s] ii. 5. [t] i. 9. ii. 3. [u] i. 6–8.

AMOS.

Before CHRIST cir. 787.

CHAPTER I.

1 *Amos sheweth God's judgment upon Syria,* 6 *upon the Philistines,* 9 *upon Tyrus,* 11 *upon Edom,* 13 *upon Ammon.*

THE words of Amos,
[a] who was among the
herdmen of [b] Tekoa, which
he saw concerning Israel
[c] in the days of Uzziah king
of Judah, and in the days
of [d] Jeroboam the son of
Joash king of Israel, two
years before the [e] earthquake.
2 And he said, The
LORD will [f] roar from Zion,
and utter his voice from

[a] ch. 7. 14.
[b] 2 Sam. 14. 2. 2 Chr. 20. 20.
[c] Hos. i. 1.
[d] ch. 7. 10.
[e] Zech. 14. 5.
[f] Jer. 25. 30. Joel 3. 16.

CHAP. I. ver. 1. *The words of Amos, who was among the herdmen.* "Amos begins by setting forth his own nothingness, and withal the great grace of his Teacher and Instructor, the Holy Spirit, referring all to His glory." He, like David, Peter, Paul, Matthew, was one of *the weak things of the world, whom God chose to confound the mighty.* He was himself a herdsman only *among herdsmen;* but the words which he spake were not his own. They were words which he saw, not with eyes of flesh, but "with that vision wherewith words can be seen, the seer's vision in the mind." They were *words concerning,* or rather *upon Israel,* heavy words coming upon the heavy transgressions of Israel. The Hebrew word *saw*[1] is not of mere sight, but of a vision given by God. Amos only says that they were *his* words, in order immediately to add, that they came to him from God, that he himself was but the human organ through which God spake.

Two years before the earthquake. This earthquake must plainly have been one of the greatest, since it was vividly in men's memories in the time of Zechariah, and Amos speaks of it as "*the* earthquake." The earthquakes of the East, like that of Lisbon, destroy whole cities. In one, a little before the birth of our Lord, "[2] some ten thousand were buried under the ruined houses." This terrific earthquake (for as such Zechariah describes it) was one of the preludes of that displeasure of God, which Amos foretold. A warning of two years, and time for repentance, were given, *before the earthquake* should come, the token and beginning of a further shaking of both kingdoms, unless they should repent. In effect, it was the first flash of the lightning which consumed them.

2. *The Lord will roar.* Amos joins on his prophecy to the end of Joel's, in order at once in its very opening to attest the oneness of their mission, and to prepare men's minds to see, that his own prophecy was an expansion of those words, declaring the nearer and coming judgments of God. Those nearer judgments, however, of which he spake, were but the preludes of the judgments of the Great Day which Joel foretold, and of that last terrible voice of Christ, *the Lion of the tribe of Judah,* of Whom Jacob prophesies; *He couched, He lay down as a lion, and as a young lion; who shall raise Him up*[3]? God is said to *utter His* awful *voice from Zion and Jerusalem,* because there He had set His Name, there He was present in His Church. It was, as it were, His own place, which He had hallowed by tokens of His Presence, although *the heaven and the heaven of heavens cannot contain Him.* In the outset of his prophecy, Amos warned Israel, that there, not among themselves in their separated state, God dwelt. Jeremiah, in using these same words toward Judah, speaks not of Jerusalem, but of heaven; [4] *The Lord shall roar from on high, and utter His voice from His holy habitation.* The prophecy is to the ten tribes or to the heathen: God speaks out of the Church. He uttereth His Voice out of Jerusalem, as He saith, [5] *Out of Zion shall go forth the law, and the word of the Lord from Jerusalem,* "where was the Temple and the worship of God, to shew that God was not in the cities of Israel, i.e. in Dan and Bethel, where were the golden calves, nor in the royal cities of Samaria and Jezreel, but in the true religion which was then in Zion and Jerusalem."

And the habitations of the shepherds shall mourn. Perhaps, with a feeling for the home which he had loved and left, the Prophet's first thought amid the desolation which he predicts, was toward his own shepherd-haunts. The well-known Mount Carmel[6]

[1] חזה, whence חֹזֶה *seer,* חזון, חזיון, vision.
[2] Jos. Ant. xv. 5. 2.
[3] Gen. xlix. 9.
[4] Jer. xxv. 30.
[5] Is. ii. 3.
[6] The mention of the *head of Carmel* marks out that the Mount Carmel is meant (see ix. 3, 1 Kgs xviii. 42) not the town Carmel (now Kurmul) in the south of Judah, lying around the head and sides of a valley of some width and depth. The whole plain around it is high, and it seems probable that a district was called by its name (1 Sam. xxv. 2, 7, 2 Chr. xxvi. 10), but the hill of Main is only 200 feet above the plain. Robinson, i. 433.

Before CHRIST cir. 787.

Jerusalem; and the habitations of the shepherds shall mourn, and the top of [g]Carmel shall wither.

[g] 1 Sam. 25. 2. Is. 33. 9.

3 Thus saith the LORD; For three transgressions of [h]Damascus, || and for four, I will not || turn away

[h] Is. 8. 4. & 17. 1. Jer. 49. 23. Zech. 9. 1.

|| Or, *yea, for four.* || Or, *convert it*, or, *let it be quiet:* and so ver. 6, &c.

was far in the opposite direction in the tribe of Asher. Its name is derived from its richness and fertility, perhaps "a land of vine and olive yards[1]." In S. Jerome's time, it was "[2]thickly studded with olives, shrubs and vineyards." "Its very summit of glad pastures." It is one of the most striking natural features of Palestine. It ends a line of hills, eighteen miles long, by a long bold headland reaching out far into the Mediterranean, and forming the South side of the Bay of Acco or Acre. Rising 1200 feet above the sea[3], it stands out "like some guardian of its native strand;" yet withal, it was rich with every variety of beauty, flower, fruit, and tree. It is almost always called "*the Carmel*," "the rich garden-ground." From its neighborhood to the sea, heavy dews nightly supply it with an ever-renewed freshness, so that in mid-summer it is green and flowery[4]. Travelers describe it, as "[5]quite green, its top covered with firs and oaks, lower down with olives and laurels, and everywhere excellently watered." "There is not a flower," says Van de Velde[6], "that I have seen in Galilee or on the plains along the coasts, that I do not find here again on Carmel. It is still the same fragrant lovely mountain as of old." "[5] Its varied world of flowers attracts such a number of the rarer varicolored insects that a collector might for a whole year be richly employed." "It is a natural garden and repository of herbs." Its pastures were rich, so as to equal those of Bashan[7]. "It gives rise to a number of crystal streams, the largest of which gushes from the spring of Elijah." It had abundant supplies in itself. If it too became a desert, what else would be spared? [8] *If they do these things in a green tree, what shall be done in the dry?* All, high and low, shall be stricken in one common desolation; all the whole land, from *the pastures of the shepherds* in the South to Mount *Carmel* in the North. And this, as soon as God had spoken. *He spake, and it was made.* So now, contrariwise, He uttereth His Voice, and Carmel hath languished. Its glory hath passed away, as in the twinkling of an eye. God hath spoken the word, and it is gone.

What depended on God's gifts, abides; what depended on man, is gone. There remains a wild beauty still; but it is the beauty of natural luxuriance. "All," says one who explored its depths[9], "lies waste; all is a wilderness. The utmost fertility is here lost for man, useless to man. The vineyards of Carmel, where are they now? Behold the long rows of stones on the ground, the remains of the walls; they will tell you that here, where now with difficulty you force your way through the thick entangled copse, lay, in days of old, those incomparable vineyards to which Carmel owes its name."

3. The order of God's threatenings seems to have been addressed to gain the hearing of the people. The punishment is first denounced upon their enemies, and that, for their sins, directly or indirectly, against themselves, and God in them. Then, as to those enemies themselves, the order is not of place or time, but of their relation to God's people. It begins with their most oppressive enemy, Syria; then Philistia, the old and ceaseless, although less powerful, enemy; then Tyre, not an oppressor, as these, yet violating a relation which they had not, the bonds of a former friendship and covenant; malicious also and hardhearted through covetousness. Then follow Edom, Ammon, Moab, who burst the bonds of blood also. Lastly and nearest of all, it falls on Judah, who had the true worship of the true God among them, but despised it. Every infliction on those like ourselves finds an echo in our own consciences. Israel heard and readily believed God's judgments upon others. It was not tempted to set itself against believing them. How then could it refuse to believe of itself, what it believed of others like itself? "Change but the name, the tale is told of thee[10]," was a heathen saying which has almost passed into a proverb. The course of the prophecy convicted *them*, as the things written in Holy Scripture *for our ensamples* convict Christians. *If they* who [11] *sinned without law, perished without law*, how much more should they who *have sinned in the law, be judged by the law*. God's judgments rolled round like a thunder-cloud, passing from land to land, giving warning of their ap-

[1] כרם lit. "a rich and fertile land" (as in Arabic) is used of the olive-*garden* Jud. xv. 7, as well as of the more ordinary vineyard. כרמל is probably a collective from it.

[2] in Jer. iv. 26.

[3] Schubert in Ritter, xvi. 721. Porter says 1750. (Handb. 371).

[4] Thomson, The Land, &c. ii. 231.

[5] O. v. Ritchter.

[6] i. 317, 8.

[7] Jer. l. 19. Nah. i. 4.

[8] S. Luke xxiii. 31.

[9] Van de Velde, i. 318.

[10] Horace.

[11] Rom. ii. 12.

Before CHRIST cir. 787.

the punishment thereof; [1]because they have threshed Gilead with threshing instruments of iron:

[1] 2 Kings 10. 33 & 13. 7.

Before CHRIST cir. 787.

proach, at last to gather and centre on Israel itself, except it repent. In the visitations of others, it was to read its own; and that, the more, the nearer God was to them. *Israel* is placed the last, because on it the destruction was to fall to the uttermost, and rest there.

For three transgressions and for four. These words express, not four transgressions added to the three, but an additional transgression beyond the former, the last sin, whereby the measure of sin, which before was full, overflows, and God's wrath comes. So in other places, where the like form of words occurs, the added number is one beyond, and mostly relates to something greater than all the rest. So, [1]*He shall deliver thee in six troubles; yea, in seven there shall no evil touch thee.* The word, *yea*, denotes, that the seventh is some heavier trouble, beyond all the rest, which would seem likely to break endurance. Again [2], *give a portion to seven, and also to eight. Seven* is used as a symbol of a whole, since *on the seventh day God rested from all which He had made*, and therefore the number seven entered so largely into the whole Jewish ritual. All time was measured by seven. The rule then is; "give without bounds; when that whole is fulfilled, still give." Again in that series of sayings in the book of Proverbs [3], the fourth is, in each, something greater than the three preceding. *There are three* things that *are never satisfied; yea, four* things *say not*, it is *enough* [4]. The other things cannot be satisfied; the fourth, fire, grows fiercer by being fed. Again [5], *There be three* things *which go well; yea, four are comely in going.* The moral majesty of a king is obviously greater than the rest. So [6]*the handmaid which displaceth her mistress* is more intolerable and overbearing than the others. The art and concealment of man in approaching a maiden is of a subtler kind than things in nature which leave no trace of themselves, the eagle in the air, the serpent on the rock, the ship in its pathway through the waves [7]. Again [8], *Sowing discord among brethren*, has an especial hatefulness, as not only being sin, but causing wide-wasting sin, and destroying in others the chief grace, love. Soul-murder is worse than bodily murder, and requires more devilish art.

These things, Job says [9], *worketh God twice and thrice with man, to bring back his soul from the pit.* The last grace of God, whether sealing up the former graces of those who use them, or vouchsafed to those who have wasted them, is the crowning act of His love or forbearance.

In heathen poetry also, as a trace of a mystery which they had forgotten, three is a sacred whole; whence "thrice and fourfold blessed" stands among them for something exceeding even a full and perfect blessing, a super-abundance of blessings.

The fourth trangression of these Heathen nations is alone mentioned. For the Prophet had no mission to *them;* he only declares to Israel the ground of the visitation which was to come upon them. The three transgressions stand for a whole sum of sin, which had not yet brought down extreme punishment; the fourth was the crowning sin, after which God would no longer spare. But although the fourth drew down His judgment, God, at the last, punishes not the last sin only, but all which went before. In that the Prophet says, not, *for the fourth*, but *for three transgressions and for four*, he expresses at once, that God did not punish until the last sin, by which *the iniquity* of the sinful nation became *full* [10], and that, *then*, He punished for all, for the whole mass of sin described by the three, and for the fourth also. God is long-suffering and ready to forgive; but when the sinner finally becomes a *vessel of wrath* [11], He punishes all the earlier sins, which, for the time, He passed by. Sin adds to sin, out of which it grows; it does not overshadow the former sins, it does not obliterate them, but increases the mass of guilt, which God punishes. When the Jews slew the Son, there [12] *came on* them *all the righteous bloodshed upon the earth, from the blood of righteous Abel unto the blood of Zacharias, son of Barachias.* All the blood of all the prophets and servants of God under the Old Testament came upon that generation. So each individual sinner, who dies impenitent, will be punished for all which, in his whole life, he did or became, contrary to the law of God. Deeper sins bring deeper damnation at the last. So St. Paul speaks [13] of those who *treasure up to* themselves *wrath against the Day of wrath and revelation of the righteous judgment of God.* As good men, by the grace of God, do, through each act done by aid of that grace, gain an addition to their everlasting reward, so the wicked, by each added sin, add to their damnation.

Of Damascus. Damascus was one of the

[1] Job v. 19. [2] Eccl. xi. 2. [3] xxx. [4] Ib. 15, 16. [5] Ib. 29–31. [6] Ib. 21–23. [7] Ib. 18, 19. [8] Ib. vi. 16–19. [9] xxxiii. 29.

[10] Gen. xv. 16. [11] Rom. ix. 22. [12] S. Matt. xxiii. 35, 6. S. Luke xi. 50, 1. [13] Rom. ii. 5.

oldest cities in the world, and one of the links of its intercourse. It lay in the midst of its plain, a high table-land [1] of rich cultivation, whose breadth, from Anti-libanus Eastward, was about half a degree. On the W. and N. its plain lay sheltered under the range of Anti-libanus; on the East, it was protected by the great desert which intervened between its oasis-territory and the Euphrates. Immediately, it was bounded by the three lakes which receive the surplus of the waters which enrich it. The Barada [the "cold"] having joined the Fijeh, (the traditional Pharpar [2], a name which well designates its tumultuous course) [3], runs on the N. of, and through the city, and then chiefly into the central of the three lakes, the Bahret-el-kibliyeh, [the "South" lake;] thence, it is supposed, but in part also directly, into the Bahret-esh-Shurkiyeh [the "East" lake [4]]. The 'Awaj [the "crooked"] (perhaps the old Amana, "the never-failing," in contrast with the streams which are exhausted in irrigation) runs near the old South boundary of Damascus [5], separating it probably from the Northern possessions of Israel beyond Jordan, Bashan (in its widest sense), and Jetur or Ituræa. The area has been calculated at 236 square geographical miles [6]. This space rather became the centre of its dominions, than measured their extent. But it supported a population far beyond what that space would maintain in Europe. Taught by the face of creation around them, where the course of every tiny rivulet, as it burst from the rocks, was marked by a rich luxuriance [7], the Damascenes of old availed themselves of the continual supply from the snows of Hermon or the heights of Anti-libanus, with a systematic diligence [8], of which, in our Northern clime, as we have no need, so we have no idea. "Without the Barada," says Porter [9], "the city could not exist, and the plain would be a parched desert; but now aqueducts intersect every quarter, and fountains sparkle in almost every dwelling, while innumerable canals extend their ramifications over the vast plain, clothing it with verdure and beauty. Five of these canals are led off from the river at different elevations, before it enters the plain. They are carried along the precipitous banks of the ravine, being in some places tunnelled in the solid rock. The two on the Northern side water Salahiyeh at the foot of the hills about a mile from the city, and then irrigate the higher portions of the plain to the distance of nearly twenty miles. Of the three on the S. side, one is led to the populous village Daraya, five miles distant; the other two supply the city, its suburbs, and gardens." The like use was made of every fountain in every larger or lesser plain. Of old it was said, "[10] the Chrysorrhoas [the Barada] "is nearly expended in artificial channels." "[11] Damascus is fertile through drinking up the Chrysorrhoas by irrigation." Fourteen names of its canals are still given [12]; and while it has been common to select 7 or 8 chief canals, the whole have been counted up even to 70 [13]. No art or labor was thought too great. The waters of the Fijeh were carried by a great aqueduct tunnelled through the side of the perpendicular cliff [14]. Yet this was as nothing. Its whole plain was intersected with canals, and tunnelled below. "[15] The waters of the river were spread over the surface of the soil in the fields and gardens; underneath, other canals were tunnelled to collect the superfluous water which percolates the soil, or from little fountains and springs below. The stream thus collected is led off to a lower level, where it comes to the surface. "[16] The whole plain is filled with these singular aqueducts, some of them running for 2 or 3 miles underground. Where the water of one is diffusing life and verdure over the surface, another branch is collecting a new supply." "In former days these extended over the whole plain to the lakes, thus irrigating the fields and gardens in every part of it."

Damascus then was, of old, famed for its beauty. Its white buildings, embedded in the deep green of its engirdling orchards, were like diamonds encircled by emeralds. They reach nearly to Anti-libanus [17] West-

[1] "2200 feet above the sea." Porter, Five years in Dam. i. 26.

[2] G. Williams. Ibn. Haukal says, "*the* river of Damascus rises under a Christian church, called al-Fijat. It unites with the river, called Barada." in Abulf. Tab. Syr. p. 15. The Fijeh is "pure, sweet and limpid" (Rob. ii. 476); the Barada is undrinkable, producing goitre. (G. Will. in Smith Geogr. Dict. v. Damascus.)

[3] Unsteady and in part headlong motion is the central meaning of the Arabic "pharphara;" "parting asunder, and so flight," of the Arabic "pharra." On the bursting forth of the Fijeh, see Porter, Five years, i. 260.

[4] Ib. 375–82. Journ. of Sacr. Lit. 1853. July. Oct.

[5] Five years i. 26. 318. 321. 389. ii. 13, 247, 8.

[6] Ib. 27.

[7] "Nothing can be conceived more dreary than the ravines near Damascus, except when streams flow through them, which are always fringed with green." Ld. Lindsay, Holy Land, p. 330. See Porter, Five years, i. 324. 280.

[8] "Every stream that descended from the hills (in the upper valley of the Barada) was made available to the irrigation of long slips of green which marked its course." Ib. p. 332. See Porter, Five years, i. 21, 277, 8, 9, 321. 358. 375. ii. 276. 306, 7, and accounts of canals i. 23, 372. 376. 321. 393. ii. 14. 16. 247. (at Lebweh ii. 322.) and aqueducts i. 329. in Hauran ii. 29. 77.

[9] Ib. 27, 8.

[10] Strabo xvi. 2. 16.

[11] Plin. v. 18. 16.

[12] Wilson, Lands of the Bible, ii. 325. note.

[13] Hajji Chalifa, See Ritter's Diss. Erdk. xvii p. 1303 sqq.

[14] Ib. 257.

[15] Five years, i. 394, 5. See further i. 159, 162. 371. ii. 11. [54. 205. of Hauran] 248, 9. 358.

[16] Porter, Handbook, p. 497.

[17] Five years, i. 27.

ward, "[1] and extend on both sides of the Barada some miles Eastward. They cover an area at last 25 [or 30] miles in circuit, and make the environs an earthly Paradise." Whence the Arabs said[2], "If there is a garden of Eden on earth, it is Damascus; and if in Heaven, Damascus is like it on earth." But this its beauty was also its strength. "The river," says William of Tyre[3], "having abundant water, supplies orchards on both banks, thick-set with fruit-trees, and flows Eastward by the city wall. On the W. and N. the city was far and wide fenced by orchards, like thick dense woods, which stretched four or five miles toward Libanus. These orchards are a most exceeding defence; for from the density of the trees and the narrowness of the ways, it seemed difficult and almost impossible to approach the city on that side." Even to this day it is said[4], "The true defence of Damascus consists in its gardens, which, forming a forest of fruit-trees and a labyrinth of hedges, walls and ditches, for more than 7 leagues in circumference, would present no small impediment to a Mussulman enemy."

The advantage of its site doubtless occasioned its early choice. It lay on the best route from the interior of Asia to the Mediterranean, to Tyre, and even to Egypt. Chedorlaomer and the four kings with him, doubtless, came that way, since the first whom they smote were at Ashteroth Karnaim[5] in Jaulan or Gaulonitis, and thence they swept on Southward, along the west side of Jordan, smiting, as they went, first the *Zuzim*, (probably the same as the Zamzummim[6]) in Ammonitis; then *the Emim in the plain of Kiriathaim* in Moab[7], then *the Horites in Mount Seir unto Elparan* (probably Elath on the Gulf called from it.) They returned that way, since Abraham overtook them at Hobah near Damascus[8]. Damascus was already the chief city, through its relation to which alone Hobah was known. It was on the route by which Abraham himself came at God's command from Haran (Charræ of the Greeks) whether over Tiphsach ("the passage," Thapsacus) or any more Northern passage over the Euphrates. The fact that his chief and confidential servant whom he entrusted to seek a wife for Isaac, and who was, at one time, his heir, was a Damascene[9], implies some intimate connection of Abraham with Damascus. At the time of our era, the name of Abraham was still held in honor in the country of Damascus[10]; a village was named from him "Abraham's dwelling;" and a native historian Nicolas[11] said, that he reigned in Damascus on his way from the country beyond Babylon to Canaan. The name of his servant "Eliezer" "my God is help," implies that at this time too the servant was a worshiper of the One God. The name Damascus probably betokened the strenuous[12], energetic character of its founder. Like the other names connected with Aram in the Old Testament[13], it is, in conformity with the common descent from Aram, Aramaic. It was no part of the territory assigned to Israel, nor was it molested by them. Judging, probably, of David's defensive conquests by its own policy, it joined the other Syrians who attacked David, was subdued, garrisoned, and became tributary[14]. It was at that time probably a subordinate power, whether on the ground of the personal eminence of Hadadezer king of Zobah, or any other. Certainly Hadadezer stands out conspicuously; the Damascenes are mentioned only subordinately. Consistently with this, the first mention of the kingdom of Damascus in Scripture is the dynasty of Rezon son of Eliada's, a fugitive servant of Hadadezer, who formed a marauding band, then settled and reigned in Damascus[15]. Before this, Scripture speaks of the people only of Damascus, not of their kings. Its native historian admits that the Damascenes were, in the time of David, and continued to be, the aggressors, while he veils over their repeated defeats, and represents their kings, as having reigned successively from father to son, for ten generations, a thing unknown probably in any monarchy. "[16] A native, Adad, having gained great power, became king of Damascus and the rest of Syria, except Phœnicia. He, having carried war against David, king of Judæa, and disputed with him in many battles, and that finally at the Euphrates where he was defeated, had the character of a most eminent king for prowess and valor. After his death, his descendants reigned for ten generations, each receiving from his father the name [Hadad] together with the kingdom, like the Ptolemies of Egypt. The third, having gained the greatest power of all, seeking to repair the defeat of his grandfather, warring against the Jews, wasted what is now called Samaritis." They could not brook a defeat, which they had brought upon themselves. Rezon renewed, throughout the later part of Solomon's reign, the aggression of Hadad. On the schism of the

[1] Porter, Five years, i. 29, add pp. 152, 3.
[2] in R. Pethakiah in Journ. As. 1831. viii. 388, and Ibn Batuta in Ritter, xvii. 1346, with much more.
[3] xvii. 3. [4] Ali Bey travels, ii. 282.
[5] Gen. xiv. 5, 6. [6] Deut. ii. 20. [7] Ib. 9, 11.
[8] Gen. xiv. 15. [9] Gen. xv. 2, 3,
[10] Jos. Ant. i. 7, 2. [11] L. iv. ap. Jos. ibid.
[12] Dimashko, Damshako, "swift, ready, strenuous." Arab.
[13] as Aram Naharaim, Aram Beth Rehob, Aram Maachah, Padan Aram, Hamath, Tadmor, Tiphsach, &c. The Arabic form of the name Mabug [Hierapolis], Manbej, is probably the original; so that Hitzig is wrong as to the three which he assumed to be proofs of a non-Semitic origin of the cities on this line of traffic. (quoted by Ritter, xvii. 1337.)
[14] 2 Sam. viii. 5, 6. [15] 1 Kgs xi. 23, 24.
[16] Nicolaus, Damasc. Hist. iv. in Jos. Ant. vii. 2. 2.

ten tribes, the hostility of Damascus was concentrated against Israel who lay next to them. Abijam was in league with the father of Benhadad[1]. Benhadad at once broke his league with Baasha at the request of Asa in his later mistrustful days[2], and turned against Baasha[3]. From Omri also Benhadad I. took cities and extorted *streets*, probably a Damascus-quarter, in Samaria itself[4]. Benhadad II. had *thirty-two* vassal *kings*[5], (dependent kings like those of Canaan, each of his own city and little territory,) and led them against Samaria, intending to plunder it[6], and, on occasion of the plundering, probably to make it his own or to destroy it. By God's help they were twice defeated; the second time, when they directly challenged the power of God[7], so signally that, had not Ahab been flattered by the appeal to his mercy[8], Syria would no more have been in a condition to oppress Israel. Benhadad promised to restore the cities which his father had taken from Israel, and to make an Israel-quarter in Damascus[9]. If this promise was fulfilled, Ramoth-Gilead must have been lost to Syria at an earlier period, since, three years afterward, Ahab perished in an attempt, by aid of Jehoshaphat, against the counsels of God, to recover it[10]. Ramoth-Gilead being thus in the hands of Syria, all North of it, half of Dan and Manasseh beyond Jordan, must also have been conquered by Syria. Except the one great siege of Samaria, which brought it to extremities and which God dissipated by a panic which He infused into the Syrian army[11], Benhadad and Hazael encouraged only marauding expeditions against Israel during the 14 years of Ahaziah and Jehoram. Benhadad was, according to Assyrian inscriptions defeated thrice, Hazael twice, by Shalmanubar king of Assyria[12]. Benhadad appears to have acted on the offensive, in alliance with the kings of the Hittites, the Hamathites and Phœnicians[12]; Hazael was attacked alone, driven to take refuge in Anti-libanus, and probably became tributary[13]. Assyrian chronicles relate only Assyrian victories. The brief notice, that through Naaman[14] *the Lord gave deliverance to Syria*, probably refers to some signal check which Assyria received through him. For there was no other enemy, from whom Syria had to be *delivered*. Subsequently to that retreat from Samaria, he even lost Ramoth[15] to Jehoram after a battle before it[16], in which Jehoram was wounded. It is a probable conjecture[17] that Jehu, by his political submission to Assyria, drew on himself the calamities which Elisha foretold. Hazael probably became the instrument of God in chastening Israel, while he was avenging Jehu's submission to a power whom he dreaded and from whom he had suffered. Israel, having lost the help of Judah, became the easier prey. Hazael not only took from Israel all East of Jordan[18], but made the whole open country unsafe for the Israelites to dwell in. Not until God *gave Israel a saviour*, could they *dwell in their tents as beforetime*[19]. Hazael extended his conquests to Gath[20], intending probably to open a connecting line with Egypt. *With a small company of men* he defeated a large army of Judah[21]. Joash king of Judah bought him off, when advancing against Jerusalem, with everything of gold, consecrated or civil, in the temple or in his own treasures[22]. Jehoash recovered from Benhadad III. the cities this side Jordan[23]; Jeroboam II., all their lost territories and even Damascus and Hamath[24]. Yet after this, it was to recover its power under Rezin, to become formidable to Judah, and, through its aggressions on Judah, to bring destruction on itself. At this time, Damascus was probably, like ourselves, a rich, commercial, as well as warlike, but not as yet a manufacturing[25] nation. Its wealth, as a great emporium of transit-commerce, (as it is now) furnished it with sinews for war. The *white wool*[26], in which it traded with Tyre, implies the possession of a large outlying tract in the desert, where the sheep yield the whitest wool. It had then doubtless, beside the population of its plain, large nomadic hordes dependent upon it.

I will not turn away the punishment *thereof;* lit. *I will not turn it back.* What was this, which God would not turn back? Amos does not express it. Silence is often more emphatic than words. Not naming it, he leaves it the rather to be conceived of by the mind, as something which had been of old coming upon them to overwhelm them, which God had long stayed back, but which, since He would now stay it no longer, would burst in, with the more terrific and overwhelming might, because it had been restrained before. Sin and punishment are by a great law of God bound together. God's mercy holds back the punishment long, allowing only some slight tokens of His displeasure to shew themselves, that the sinful soul or people may not be unwarned. When He no longer withholds it, the law of His moral government holds its course. "Seldom[27]," said heathen experience, "hath punishment with linger-

1 1 Kgs xv. 19. 2 1 Chr. xvi. 2–7. 3 Ib. and 1 Kgs xv. 20. 4 1 Kgs xx. 34. 5 Ib. 1, 24. 6 Ib. 6, 7. 7 Ib. 22–25, 28. 8 Ib. 31, 32. 9 Ib. 34. 10 1 Kgs xxii. 11 2 Kgs vii. 6. 12 See Rawl. Herod. i. 464. 13 Ib. Dr. Hincks, Dubl. Univ. Mag. Oct. 1853, pp. 422, 5, 6.

14 2 Kgs v. 1. 15 Ib. ix. 14, 15. 16 Ib. viii. 29. 17 Rawl. Herod. i. p. 465. 18 2 Kgs x. 32, 33. 19 Ib. xiii. 5. 20 Ib. xii. 17. 21 2 Chr. xxiv. 23, 24. 22 2 Kgs xii. 18. 23 Ib. xiii. 25. 24 Ib. xiv. 28. 25 See on iii. 12. 26 Ezek. xxvii. 18. 27 Horace.

Before CHRIST cir. 787.

4 [k] But I will send a fire into the house of Hazael, which shall devour the palaces of Benhadad.

[k] Jer. 17. 27. & 49. 27. ver. 7. 10. 12. ch. 2. 2. 5.

ing foot parted with the miscreant, advancing before."

Because they have threshed Gilead with threshing instruments of iron. The instrument, St. Jerome relates here, was "a sort of wain, rolling on iron wheels beneath, set with teeth; so that it both threshed out the grain and bruised the straw and cut it in pieces, as food for the cattle, for lack of hay." A similar instrument, called by nearly the same name[1], is still in use in Syria and Egypt. Elisha had foretold to Hazael his cruelty to Israel[2]; *Their strong holds thou wilt set on fire, and their young men wilt thou slay with the sword, and wilt dash their children, and rip up their women with child.* Hazael, like others gradually steeped in sin, thought it impossible, but did it. In the days of Jehu[3], *Hazael smote them in all the coasts of Israel from Jordan Eastward; all the land of Gilead, the Gadites and the Reubenites and the Manassites, from Arorer which is by the river Arnon, even Gilead and Bashan;* in those of Jehoahaz, Jehu's son[4], *he oppressed them, neither did he leave of the people to Jehoahaz but fifty horsemen and ten chariots, and ten thousand footmen; for the king of Syria had destroyed them, and had made them like the dust by threshing.* The death here spoken of, although more ghastly, was probably not more severe than many others; not nearly so severe as some which have been used by Christian Judicatures. It is mentioned in the Proverbs, as a capital punishment[5]; and is alluded to as such by Isaiah[6]. David had had, for some cause unexplained by Holy Scripture, to inflict it on the Ammonites[7]. Probably not the punishment in itself alone, but the attempt so to extirpate the people of God brought down this judgment on Damascus.

Theodoret supposes the horrible aggravation, that it was thus that the women with child were destroyed with their children, "casting the aforesaid women, as into a sort of threshing-floor, they savagely threshed them out like ears of corn with saw-armed wheels."

Gilead is here doubtless to be taken in its widest sense, including all the possessions of Israel, E. of Jordan, as, in the account of Hazael's conquests, *all the land of Gilead*[3] is explained to mean, all which was ever given to the two tribes and a half, and to include Gilead proper, as distinct from Basan. In like way Joshua relates[8], that *the children of Reuben and the children of Gad and the half tribe of Manasseh returned to go into the country of Gilead, to the land of their possessions.* Throughout that whole beautiful tract, including 2½ degrees of latitude, Hazael had carried on his war of extermination into every peaceful village and home, sparing neither the living nor the unborn.

4. *And I will send a fire on the house of Hazael.* The *fire* is probably at once material fire, whereby cities are burned in war, since he adds, *it shall devour the palaces of Benhadad,* and also stands as a symbol of all other severity in war as in the ancient proverb[9], *a fire is gone out from Heshbon, a flame from the city of Sihon; it hath consumed Ar of Moab, the lords of the high places of Arnon;* and again of the displeasure of Almighty God, as when He says[10], *a fire is kindled in Mine anger, and it shall burn unto the lowest hell.* For the fire destroys not the natural buildings only, but *the house of Hazael,* i. e. his whole family. In these prophecies, a sevenfold vengeance by fire is denounced against the seven people, an image of the eternal fire into which all iniquity shall be cast.

The palaces of Benhadad. Hazael, having murdered Benhadad his master and ascended his throne, called his son after his murdered master, probably in order to connect his own house with the ancient dynasty. Benhadad, i. e. *son* or worshiper of the idol *Hadad,* or "the sun," had been the name of two of the kings of the old dynasty. Benhadad III. was at this time reigning. The prophet foretells the entire destruction of the dynasty founded in blood. The prophecy *may* have had a fulfillment in the destruction of the house of Hazael, with whose family Rezin, the king of Syria in the time of Ahaz, stands in no known relation. Defeats, such as those of Benhadad III. by Jeroboam II. who took Damascus itself, are often the close of an usurping dynasty. Having no claim to regard except success, failure vitiates its only title. The name Hazael, "whom God looked upon," implies a sort of owning of the One God, like Tab-el, "God is good," El-iada', "whom God knoweth," even amid the idolatry in the names, Tab-Rimmon, "good is Rimmon;" Hadad-ezer, "Hadad is help;" and Hadad, or Benhadad. Bad men abuse every creature, or ordinance, or appointment of God. It may be then that, as Sennacherib boasted[11], *am I now come up without the Lord against this land*

[1] Nauraj, probably a corruption from the Heb. מורג. The חרוץ and the מורג חרוץ are plainly the same. See the last woodcut in Thomson, The Land, ii. 315, and Wilkinson, ii. 190.

[2] 2 Kgs viii. 12. [3] Ib. x. 32, 3. [4] Ib. xiii. 7. [5] xx. 26. [6] xxviii. 28. [7] 2 Sam. xii. 31. 1 Chr. xx. 3. [8] Josh. xxii. 9. [9] Nu. xxi. 28. [10] Deut. xxxii. 22. [11] Is. xxxvi. 10.

Before CHRIST cir. 787.

5 I will break also the [l] bar of Damascus, and cut off the inhabitant from ‖ the plain of Aven, and

[l] Jer. 51. 30. Lam. 2. 9.

‖ Or, *Bikath-aven.*

Before CHRIST cir. 787.

to destroy it? the Lord said unto me, Go up against this land and destroy it; so Hazael made use of the prophecy of Elisha, to give himself out as the scourge of God, and thought of himself as one "on whom God looked." Knowledge of futurity is an awful gift. As "Omniscience alone can wield Omnipotence," so superhuman knowledge needs superhuman gifts of wisdom and holiness. Hazael seemingly hardened himself in sin by aid of the knowledge which should have been his warning. Probably he came to Elisha, with the intent to murder his master already formed, in case he should not die a natural death; and Elisha read him to himself. But he very probably justified himself to himself in what he had already purposed to do, on the ground that Elisha had foretold to him that he should be king over Syria[1], and, in his massacres of God's people, gave himself out as being, what he was, the instrument of God. "Scourges of God" have known themselves to be what they were, although they themselves were not the less sinful, in sinfully accomplishing the Will of God[2]. We have heard of a Christian Emperor, who has often spoken of his "mission," although his "mission" has already cost the shedding of much Christian blood.

5. *I will also break the bar of Damascus.* In the East, every city was fortified; the gates of the stronger cities were cased in iron, that they might not be set on fire by the enemy; they were fastened within with bars of brass[3] or iron[4]. They were flanked with towers, and built over, so that what was naturally the weakest point and the readiest access to an enemy became the strongest defence. In Hauran the huge doors and gates of a single stone 9 and 10 feet high[5], and 1½ foot thick[6], are still extant, and "[6] the place for the ponderous bars," proportioned to such gates, "may yet be seen." The walls were loosened with the battering-ram, or scaled by mounds: the strong gate was seldom attacked; but, when a breach was made, was thrown open from within. The *breaking* of *the bar* laid open the city to the enemy, to go in and come out at his will. The whole strength of the kingdom of Damascus lay in the capital. It was itself the seat of empire and was the empire itself. God says then, that He Himself would shiver all their means of resistance, whatever could hinder the inroad of the enemy.

And cut off the inhabitant from the plain of Aven; lit. *from the vale of vanity,* the *Bik'ah* being a broad vale between hills[7]. Here it is doubtless the rich and beautiful valley, still called el-bukâa by the Arabs, La Boquea by William of Tyre[8], lying between Lebanon and Anti-libanus, the old Cœle-Syria in its narrowest sense. It is, on high ground, the continuation of that long deep valley which, along the Jordan, the Dead sea, and the Arabah, reaches to the Red Sea. Its extreme length, from its Southern close at Kal'at-esh-shakîf to Hums (Emesa) has been counted at 7 days journey[9]; it narrows toward its Southern extremity, expands at its Northern, yet it cannot any how be said to lose its character of a valley until 10 miles N. of Riblah[10]. Midway, on its highest elevation about 3800 feet above the sea[11], was Baalbek, or Heliopolis, whither the Egyptian worship is said to have been brought of old times from their "city of the sun[12]." Baalbek, as the ruins still attest, was full of the worship of the sun. But the whole of that beautiful range, "[13] a magnificent vista," it has been said, "carpeted with verdure and beauty," "[14] a gem lying deep in its valley of mountains," was a citadel of idolatry. The name Baal-Hermon connects Mount Hermon itself, the snow-capt height which so towers over its S. E. extremity, with the worship of

[1] 2 Kgs viii. 13.
[2] See on Hos. i. 4.
[3] 1 Kgs iv. 13.
[4] Ps. cvii. 16. Is. xlv. 2; comp. Is. xlviii. 14. Jer. li. 30.
[5] Burckhardt's Syria, 90. quoted in Five years, ii. 201.
[6] Five years, ii. 196.
[7] Etymologically, it would mean "cleft." It does mean a valley, as contrasted with hills, Deut. viii. 7. xi. 11. Is. xl. 4. xli. 18. lxiii. 14. Ezek. iii. 22, 3. It is used of the "valley of the Chebar," in contrast with the *hill* of *Tel*-Abib. As united with proper names, it answers to our "vale," a broad valley between hills; as "the vale of Megiddo," "of Jericho," "of Mizpeh," "under Hermon," (Jos. xi. 8, 3.) probably the upper part of the valley of the Jordan above the lake Merom (v. 7), along the course of the river Hasbany; the "vale of Lebanon" being probably the Southern part of the great Bik'ah, where Baal-gad lay under Hermon (Ib. xi. 17), and east of Lebanon (Ib. xiii. 5). So also probably the "vale of Dura." (Dan. iii. 1.) A long valley, though broad, if seen from a height, looks like a cleft. In Arabic, the original force of the root is altogether lost. In nouns, we have, in different forms, the varying meanings assigned, bekâ, "a plateau;" bak'a, "low ground, where water stagnates;" baki'a, "a plain." See Freytag Lex. Burckhardt mentions "a broad valley called El Bekka [Bek'a] N. and N. E. of Ssafout [near Amman] at the foot of the mountain on which it stands." Syria, 362.
[8] xviii. 17.
[9] Berggren, Guide Franc. Arab. p. 458. in Ritter, xvii. 154.
[10] The "end of the central ridge of Anti-lebanon." Porter, Handb. p. 578.
[11] See V. de Velde, Memoir, p. 175.
[12] (Lucian) de Syria Dea § 5. Macr. Sat. i. 23. Robins. iii. 518.
[13] Robins. iii. 493.
[14] Ib. 504.

Before CHRIST cir. 787.

him that holdeth the sceptre from || the house of Eden: and [m] the people of Syria shall go into captivity [n] unto Kir, saith the LORD.

|| Or, *Beth-eden.*
[m] Fulfilled, 2 Kings 16. 9.
[n] ch. 9. 7.

Baal or the sun, and that, from the time of the Judges[1]. The name Baal-gad connects *the valley of Lebanon*, i. e. most probably the S. end of the great valley, with the same worship, anterior to Joshua[2]. The name Baalbek is probably an abbreviation of the old name, Baal-bik'ah[3], "Baal of the valley," in contrast with the neighboring Baal-hermon. "[4]The whole of Hermon was girded with temples." "[5]Some eight or ten of them cluster round it," and, which is more remarkable, one is built "[6]to catch the first beams of the sun rising over Hermon;" and temples on its opposite sides face toward it, as a sort of centre[7]. In S. Jerome's time, the Heathen still reverenced a celebrated temple on its summit[8]. On the crest of its central peak, 3000 feet above the glen below, in winter inaccessible, beholding far asunder the rising and the setting sun on the Eastern desert and in the Western sea, are still seen the foundations of a circular wall or ring of large stones, a rude temple, within which another of Grecian art was subsequently built[9]. "On three other peaks of the Anti-libanus range are ruins of great antiquity[10]." "[11]The Bukâa and its borders are full of the like buildings." "Lebanon, Anti-lebanon and the valleys between are thronged with ancient temples[12]." Some indeed were Grecian, but others Syro-Phœnician. The Grecian temples were probably the revival of Syro-Phœnician. The "[13]massive substructions of Baalbek are conjectured to have been those of an earlier temple." The new name *Heliopolis* only substituted the name of the object of worship (the *sun*) for its title Lord. The Heathen emperors would not have lavished so much and such wondrous cost and gorgeous art on a temple in Cœle-Syria, had not its Pagan celebrity recommended it to their superstition or their policy. On the W. side of Lebanon at Afca, (Apheca) was the temple of Venus at the source of the river Adonis[14], a centre of the most hateful Syrian idolatry, "[15]a school of misdoing for all profligates." At Heliopolis too, men "[16]shamelessly gave their wives and daughters to shame." The outburst of Heathenism there in the reign of Julian the Apostate[17] shows how deeply rooted was its idolatry. Probably then, Amos pronounces the sentence of the people of that whole beautiful vale, as *valley of vanity* or *iniquity*[18], being wholly given to that worst idolatry which degraded Syria. Here, as the seat of idolatry, the chief judgments of God were to fall. Its inhabitants were to be *cut off*, i. e. utterly destroyed; on the rest, captivity is the only sentence pronounced. The Assyrian monarchs not unfrequently put to death those who despised their religion[19], and so may herein have executed blindly the sentence of God.

From the house of Eden, a Proper, but significant, name, "Beth-Eden," i. e. "house of pleasure." The name, like the Eden of Assyria[20], is, in distinction from man's first home, pronounced ĕden, not ēden[21]. Two places near, and one in, the Bik'ah have, from similarity of name, been thought to be this "house of delight." 1. Most beautiful now for situation and climate, is what is probably mispronounced Ehden; a Maronite Village "[22]of 4 or 500 families, on the side of a rich highly-cultivated valley" near Beshirrai on the road from Tripolis to the Cedars. Its climate is described as a ten

[1] Jud. iii. 3. [2] Jos. xi. 17. xii. 7. xiii. 5.

[3] The older Eastern names often re-appear, when the Greek names, which their conquerors gave, passed away with themselves. This is not a revival of the old name, but a continuance of it. During the reign of their conquerors, we hear from *them* the names which they gave. When they are gone, we hear from the Easterns the old Eastern name which lived on among them. The name Baalbek re-appears in the tenth century in Mohammedan writers (Rob. iii. 524.) But in none but Pagan times would a pagan name have been given to it.

[4] Robins. iii. 432.

[5] Porter, Handb. 451.

[6] Porter, 452. Stonehenge is said to be built so that the first rays of the sun on the longest day fell through the entrance on the altar.

[7] Ib. 457. Rob. iii. 417, 8.

[8] Euseb. Onom. v. Ἀερμὼν. "It is said that on its summit there is a celebrated temple, which is the object of reverence to the Heathen towards Paneas and Libanus." S. Jerome. S. Hilary also mentions the reverence to Hermon, (or, as he says, worship of it,) up to his day, in Ps. 133. Reland, 323.

[9] Porter, 454.

[10] Ib. and p. 451. "At Kula't Bustra, 1000 feet above" the road, "is a groupe of ruined temples, simple in form, and rude in style." Add Rob. iii. 414, 5.

[11] Rob. iii. 438. [12] Ib. 417.

[13] Ib. 520. [14] Rob. iii. 606.

[15] Eus. Vit. Const. iii. 55. Ib.

[16] Ib. iii. 58.

[17] Soz. v. 10. Theod. H. E. iii. 7. Rob. iii. 52.

[18] It has been conjectured, that, with the worship of the sun, the Egyptian name for Heliopolis, On, (Light) *may* have been brought from Egypt, and that, as Ezekiel calls the Heliopolis of Egypt, *Aven*, *vanity*, for "On," (xxx. 17) and Hosea calls "Bethel," "Bethaven," (iv. 15, x. 5) so Amos *may* have called this "the valley of vanity" "for the valley of On." But this is mere conjecture. There is no trace of the name "On" in the whole tract. Baalbek must have been an ancient name.

[19] See authorities in Rawl. Herod. i. 495.

[20] 2 Kgs xix. 12. Is. xxxvii. 12. Ezek. xxvii. 23.

[21] עֶדֶן not עֵדֶן.

[22] Irby and Mangles, Travels in Syria, p. 64.

months spring[1]; "the hills are terraced up to their summits;" and every place full of the richest, most beautiful, vegetation; "grain is poured out into the lap of man, and wine into his cup without measure." "The slopes of the valleys, one mass of verdure, are yet more productive than the hills; the springs of Lebanon gushing down, fresh, cool and melodious in every direction[2]." The wealthier families of Tripoli still resort there for summer, "the climate being tempered by the proximity of the snow-mountains, the most luxuriant vegetation favored by the soft airs from the sea[3]." It is still counted "[4]the Paradise of Lebanon." 2. Beit-el-Janne, lit. "house of Paradise," is an Arabic translation of Beth-Eden. It "lies under the root of Libanus, [Hermon] gushing forth clear water, whence," says William of Tyre[5], "it is called 'house of pleasure.'" It lies in a narrow valley, where it widens a little, about ¾ of an hour from the plain of Damascus[6], and about 27 miles[7] from that city on the way from Banias. "[8]Numerous rock-tombs, above and around, bear testimony to the antiquity of the site." It gives its name to the Jennani (Paradise-river), one of two streams which form the second great river near Damascus, the Awadj. 3. The third, the Paradisus of the Greeks, one of the three towns of Laodicene[9], agrees only accidentally with the Scripture name, since their Paradisus signifies not an earthly Paradise, but a hunting-park. For this the site is well suited; but in that country so abounding in water, and of soil so rich that the earth seems ready, on even slight pains of man, to don itself in luxuriant beauty, what probably is the site[10] of the old Paradisus, is hopelessly barren[11]. Beth-eden may have been the residence of one of the subordinate kings under the king of Damascus, who was to be involved in the ruin of his suzerain; or it may have been a summer-residence of the king of Damascus himself, where, in the midst of his trust in his false gods, and in a Paradise, as it were, of delight, God would cut him off altogether. Neither wealth nor any of a man's idols protect against God. As Adam, for sin, was expelled from Paradise, so the rulers of Damascus from the place of their pleasure and their sin.

And the people of Syria shall go into captivity. Syria or Aram perhaps already included, under the rule of Damascus, all the little kingdoms on this side of the Euphrates, into which it had been formerly sub-divided. At least, it is spoken of as a whole, without any of the additions which occur in the earlier history, Aram-beth-rehob, Aram-zobah, Aram-Maachah. Before its captivity Damascus is spoken of as *the head of Syria*[12].

Into Kir. Kir has been identified 1) with the part of Iberia near the river Kur[13] which unites with the Araxes, not far from the Caspian, to the North of Armenia; 2) a city called by the Greeks Kourēna[14] or Kourna on the river Mardus[15] in Southern Media; 3) a city, Karine[16], the modern Kerend[17]. The first is the most likely, as the most known; the Kur is part probably of the present name Kurgistan, our "Georgia." Armenia at least which lay on the South of the River Kur, is frequently mentioned in the cuneiform inscriptions, as a country where the kings of Assyria warred and conquered[18]. The two parricide sons of Sennacherib are as likely to have fled[19] to a distant portion of their father's empire, as beyond it. Their flight thither may have been the ground of Esarhaddon's war against it[20]. It has at all times afforded a shelter to those expelled from others' lands[21]. The domestic, though late, traditions of the Armenians count as their first inhabitants some who had fled out of Mesopotamia to escape the yoke of Bel, king of Babylon[22]. Whatever be the value of particular traditions, its mountain-valleys form a natural refuge to fugitives. On occasion of some such oppression, as that from which Asshur fled before Nimrod[23], Aram may have been the first of those who took shelter in the mountains of Armenia and Georgia, and thence spread themselves, where we afterward find them, in the lowlands of Mesopotamia. The name Aram however is in no way connected with Armenia, which is itself no indigenous name of that country, but was probably formed by the Greeks, from a name which

[1] Ritter, Erdk. xvii. 650. from Roth, Reise in v. Schubert, iii. 306. I. and M. ib. "It seemed as though the spring never left this country." De la Roque.
[2] Lord Lindsay, Holy Land, p. 355 more fully.
[3] Ritter, ib.
[4] Wilson, Lands of the Bible, p. 394.
[5] xxi. 10, in Gesta Dei per Francos, pp. 1002, 3. He calls it Bedegene.
[6] Burckhardt, Syria, pp. 45–7.
[7] See Burckhardt, corrected in Five years, i. 313.
[8] Porter, Handb. p. 449.
[9] Ptol. v. 15. 20.
[10] A monument at its site "near the source of the Orontes" (Strabo xvi. 2. 19.) has hunting-scenes on its four sides. G. Williams, in Smith's Geogr. Dict. v. Orontes.
[11] "A more dreary and barren situation could scarcely be imagined. There is no stream or fountain within miles of it, and the inhabitants were wholly dependent upon wells and cisterns for supply of water." Porter, Handb. p. 577.
[12] Is. vii. 8.
[13] Dion. L. 36. Boch. Phal. iv. 32.
[14] Ptol. vi. 2.
[15] Boch. Phal. iv. 32.
[16] Vitr. on Is. xxii. 6.
[17] Ritt. Erdk. ix. 359. 391.
[18] See in Rawl. Herod. i. 464. 470. 473. 475. 481. 484.
[19] Is. xxxvii. 38.
[20] The subdual of Armenia by Esarhaddon is mentioned in the cuneiform Inscr., Rawl. Herod. i. 481.
[21] See Ritter, x. 584 sqq.
[22] Moses Choren i. 9. Ib.
[23] Gen. x. 11. See Introd. to Nahum.

they heard[1]. The name Aram, "lofty," obviously describes some quality of the son of Shem, as of others who bore the name[2]. Contrariwise, Canaan, (whether or no anticipating his future degraded character as partaking in the sin of Ham) may signify "crouching." But neither has Aram any meaning of "highland," nor Canaan of "lowland," as has of late been imagined[3].

From Kir the forefathers of the Syrians had, of their own will, been brought by the good all-disposing Providence of God; to Kir should the Syrians, against their will, be carried back. Aram of Damascus had been led to a land which, for its fertility and beauty, has been and is still praised as a sort of Paradise. Now, softened as they were by luxury, they were to be transported back to the austere though healthy climate, whence they had come. They had abused the might given to them by God, in the endeavor to uproot Israel; now they were themselves to be utterly uprooted. The captivity which Amos foretells is complete; a captivity by which (as the word means[4]) the land should be *bared* of its inhabitants. Such a captivity he foretells of no other, except the ten tribes. He foretells it absolutely of these two nations alone[5], of the king and princes of Ammon[6], not of Tyre, or the cities of Philistia, or Edom, or Ammon, or Moab. The punishment did not reach Syria in those days, but in those of Rezin who also oppressed Judah. The sin not being cut off, the punishment too was handed down. Tiglath-pileser carried them away, about fifty years after this, and *slew Rezin*[7]. In regard to these two nations, Amos foretells the captivity absolutely. Yet at this time, there was no human likelihood, no ground, except of a Divine knowledge, to predict it of these two nations especially. They went into captivity too long after this for human foresight to predict it; yet long enough before the captivity of Judah for the fulfillment to have impressed Judah if they would. The transportation of whole populations, which subsequently became part of the standing policy of the Persian and of the later Assyrian Empires, was not, as far as we know, any part of Eastern policy at the time of the prophet. Sesostris, the Egyptian conqueror, some centuries before Amos, is related to have brought together "[8] many men," "a crowd," from the nations whom he had subdued, and to have employed them on his buildings and canals. Even this account has received no support from the Egyptian monuments, and the deeds ascribed by the Greeks to Sesostris have been supposed[9] to be a blending of those of two monarchs of the xix. Dynasty, Sethos I. and Raamses II., interwoven with those of Ousartesen III. (Dynasty xii.) and Tothmosis III. (Dyn. xviii). But the carrying away of any number of prisoners from fields of battle is something altogether different from the political removal of a nation. It had in it nothing systematic or designed. It was but the employment of those whom war had thrown into their hands, as slaves. The Egyptian monarchs availed themselves of this resource, to spare the labor of their native subjects in their great works of utility or of vanity. But the prisoners so employed were but a slave population, analogous to those who, in other nations, labored in the mines or in agriculture. They employed in the like way the Israelites, whom they had

[1] Xen. An. iv. 5. Armenia is probably i. q. הר מני har-minni, "mountain of Minni" (i. q. Minyas) a name of one portion of Armenia (Jer. li. 27). Aram has only the *m* in common with Minni.

[2] A son of Kemuel, Gen. xxii. 21; and son of Shemer, 1 Chr. vii. 34.

[3] The theory that Aram means "highland," Canaan "lowland," 1) ignores that, in the Bible, they are the names of men, not of lands. 2) It is contrary to the facts, as they appear in Holy Scripture. The borders of Canaan extended from Zidon Southwards to Gaza, and thence to the S. of the Dead Sea (Gen. x. 19) and, according to their own coins, included Laodicea ad Libanum (Ges. Thes. s. v.). Damascus (2400 feet above the sea), the highest place in Aram, was lower than Jerusalem (2610) or Bethlehem (2704) or Ramah (2800) or Hebron (3029) (See V. de Velde Memoir, p. 176–80), and the common names of Aram, "plain of Aram," "field of Aram," (Padan Aram, Sedeh Aram,) "Aram between the two rivers," (Aram Naharaim) all agree in describing a flat country. Aram Naharaim or Mesopotamia is only about 435 Eng. feet above the sea (408 Fr. feet Ritter, viii. 16) i. e. ⅙ of the height of Jerusalem. Heights are spoken of once in connection with Aram (*from Aram, from the mountains of the East* Nu. xxiii. 7) and Mesopotamia is bounded on the N. by Mt. Masius, but it is itself a plain. 3) The root from which the word Canaan is derived has in no case the sense of physical depression. Its very varied Arabic meanings centre in that of "contracted;" thence "bowed," bowed towards, "i. e. was submissive," "was *bent* upon a thing." In Hebrew it is used of wares "compressed," "packed together;" of bowing down an enemy, or one's self in submission. 4) For the real lowland of Canaan, that near the coast (from Joppa to Gaza) there is specific term, שפלה, "the low," which occurs in the first detailed descriptions of Canaan in Joshua, is the received Hebrew word, thence passed into Greek, ἡ Σεφηλά 1 Macc. xii. 38, of which Eusebius says "and it is yet called Sephela. This is the whole low country, N. and W. around Eleutheropolis." (Onom. See Reland, p. 307, add 372) whence the Carthaginians carried it to Spain, (Seville) with many other names (See Movers, Phœnic. iii. 640, 1.). It is used also of that same part of Palestine by Arabic authors.

The idea then that Canaan is used for lowland, as contrasted with Aram, highland, is contrary to the fact (in that Aram mostly was low, Canaan, high), contrary to the meaning of the word (which is never used in this sense, for which another word is employed), contrary to the simple sense of Scripture, where the names are originally those of the fathers of the races who lived in those countries.

[4] גלה.

[5] See below as to Israel, or its rich men. v. 5, 27. vi. 7. vii. 11, 17.

[6] i. 15.

[7] 2 Kgs xvi. 9.

[8] Herod. ii. 107, 8.

[9] Brugsch, Hist. de l' Eg. c. 8. p. 153.

Before CHRIST cir. 787.

6 ¶ Thus saith the
LORD; For three trans-
gressions of °Gaza, and
for four, I will not turn
away *the punishment* there-
of; because they || carried

°2 Chr. 28. 18. Is. 14. 29. Jer. 47. 4, 5. Ezek. 25. 15. Zeph. 2. 4.

|| Or, *carried them away with an entire captivity*, 2 Chron. 21. 16, 17. Joel 3. 6.

Before CHRIST cir. 787.

received peacefully. Their earlier works were carried on by native labor[1]. After Tothmosis III., in whose reign is the first representation of prisoners employed in forced labor[2], they could, during their greatness, spare their subjects. They imported labor, not by slave trade, but through war. Nubia was incorporated with Egypt[3], and Nubian prisoners were, of course, employed, not in their own country but in the North of Egypt; Asiatic prisoners in Nubia[4]. But they were prisoners made in a campaign, not a population; a foreign element in Egyptian soil, not an interchange of subject-populations. Doubtless, the *mixed multitude*[5], which *went up with* Israel from Egypt, were in part these Asiatic captives, who had been subjected to the same hard bondage. The object and extent of those forced transportations by the later Assyrians, Babylonians, and Persians were altogether different. Here the intention was to remove the people from their original seat, or at most to leave those only who, from their fewness or poverty, would be in no condition to rebel. The cuneiform inscriptions have brought before us, to a great extent, the records of the Assyrian conquests, as given by their kings. But whereas the later inscriptions of Sargon, Sennacherib, Esarhaddon, mention repeatedly the deportation of populations, the earlier annals of Asshurdanipal or Asshurakhbal relate the carrying off of soldiers only as prisoners, and women as captives[6]. They mention also receiving slaves as tributes, the number of oxen and sheep, the goods and possessions and the gods of the people which they carry off[7]. Else the king relates, how he crucified or impaled or put to death[6] men at arms or the people generally, but in no one of his expeditions does he mention any deportation. Often as modern writers *assume*, that the transportation of nations was part of the hereditary policy of the Monarchs of Asia, no instances before this period have been found. It appears to have been a later policy, first adopted by Tiglath-pileser towards Damascus and East and North Palestine, but foretold by the Prophet long before it was adopted. It was the result probably of experience, that they could not keep these nations in dependence upon themselves while they left them in their old abodes. As far as our knowledge reaches, the prophet foretold the removal of these people, at a time when no instance of any such removal had occurred.

6. *Gaza* was the Southernmost city of the Philistines, as it was indeed of Canaan[8] of old, the last inhabited place at the beginning of the desert, on the way from Phœnicia to Egypt[9]. Its situation was wonderfully chosen, so that, often as a Gaza has been destroyed, a new city has, if even after long intervals, risen up again in the same immediate neighborhood[10]. The fragments of the earlier city became materials for the later. It was first Canaanite[8]; then Philistine; then, at least after Alexander, Edomite[11]; after Alexander Janneus, Greek[12]; conquered by Abubekr the first Khalif, it became Arabian; it was desolated in their civil wars, until the Crusaders rebuilt its fort[13]; then again, Mohammedan. In the earliest times, before the destruction of Sodom and Gomorrah, Gaza was the S. angle of the border of the Canaanites, whence it turned to the S. of the Dead Sea. Even then it was known by its name of strength, 'Azzah "the strong," like our "Fort." For a time, it stood as an island-fort, while the gigantic race of the Avvim wandered, wilder probably than the modern Bedaween, *up to* its very gates. For since it is said[14], *the Avvim dwelt in open villages*[15] *as far as Gaza*, plainly they did not dwell in Gaza itself, a fortified town. The description assigns the bound of their habitations, up to the furthest town on the S. E., Gaza. They prowled around it, infested it doubtless, but did not conquer it, and were themselves expelled by the Caphtorim[14]. The fortress of the prince of Gaza is mentioned in the great expedition of Tothmosis III.[16], as the conquest of Ashkelon was counted worthy of mention in the monuments of Raamses II[17]. It was strengthened

[1] See Ib. p. 35, 51, 2, 68, 9. The first mention which we have as yet of numerous captives is in the victory in Mesopotamia by Tothmosis I. (Ib. 90.)

[2] See in Brugsch, p. 106.

[3] Ib. pp. 8, 9.

[4] Ib. p. 154.

[5] Ex. xii. 38.

[6] Fox Talbot, Assyrian texts translated, p. 22, 24, &c.

[7] So also the Egyptian inscriptions, in remarkable conformity with the account given by the priests to Germanicus, "There were read also the tributes imposed on the nations, the weight of silver and gold, the number of arms and horses, and gifts to the temples, ivory and incense, and what quantity of corn and all utensils each nation paid, on a scale not less magnificent than is now prescribed by the violence of the Parthians or the power of the Romans." Tac. Ann. ii. 60.

[8] Gen. x. 19.

[9] Arr. ii. 27.

[10] See further on Zeph. ii. 4.

[11] Alexander repeopled it from its own neighborhood.

[12] Jos. Ant. xvii. 11. 4.

[13] Will. Tyre. xvii. 12.

[14] Deut. ii. 23.

[15] חצרים.

[16] Brugsch, Hist. de l' Eg. p. 96.

[17] Ib. p. 146.

Before CHRIST cir. 787.

away captive the whole captivity, [p] to deliver *them* up to Edom:

[p] ver. 9.

7 [q] But I will send a fire on the wall of Gaza, which shall devour the palaces thereof:

Before CHRIST cir. 787.

[q] Jer. 47. 1.

doubtless by giving refuge to the Anakim, who, after Joshua had expelled them *from Hebron* and neighboring cities, *and the mountains of Judah and Israel, remained in Gaza, in Gath, and in Ashdod*[1]. Its situation, as the first station for land-commerce to and from Egypt, whether toward Tyre and Sidon, or Damascus and the upper Euphrates, or towards Petra, probably aggrandized it early. Even when the tide of commerce has been diverted into other channels, its situation has been a source of great profit. A fertile spot, touching upon a track through a desert, it became a mart for caravans, even those which passed, on the pilgrim-route to Mekka, uniting traffic with their religion Where the five cities are named together as unconquered, Gaza is mentioned first, then Ashdod[2]. Samson, after he had betrayed his strength, was *brought down to Gaza*[3], probably as being their strongest fortress, although the furthest from *the valley of Sorek*[4], where he was ensnared. There too was the vast temple of Dagon, which became the burying-place of so many of his worshipers. In Solomon's reign it was subject to Israel[5]. After the Philistine inroad in the time of Ahaz[6], and their capture of towns of Judah in the south and the low country, Shephelah[7], Hezekiah drove them back as far as Gaza[8], without apparently taking it. Its prince was defeated by Sargon[9], whose victory over Philistia Isaiah foretold[10]. Sennacherib gave to its king, together with those of Ascalon and Ekron[11], "fortified and other towns which" he "had spoiled," avowedly to weaken Judah; "so as to make his (Hezekiah's) country small;" probably also as a reward for hostility to Judah. Greek authors speak of it, as "a very large city of Syria[12]," "a great city[13]." Like other cities of old, it was, for fear of pirates, built at some distance from the sea (Arrian says "2½ miles"), but had a port called, like that of Ascalon[14], Maiuma[15], which itself too in Christian times became a place of importance[16].

Because they carried away the whole captivity; lit. *a complete captivity;* complete, but for evil; a captivity in which none were spared, none left behind; old or young, woman or child; but a whole population (whatever its extent) was swept away. Such an inroad of the Philistines is related in the time of Jehoram[17].

To deliver them up to Edom; lit. *to shut them up to Edom,* in the power of Edom, their bitter enemy, so that they should not be able to escape, nor be restored. The hands, even if not the land, of Edom were already dyed in the blood of Jacob[18] *their brother.* "Any whither but there," probably would cry the crowd of helpless captives. It was like driving the shrinking flock of sheep to the butcher's shambles, reeking with the gore of their companions. Yet therefore were they driven there to the slaughter. Open markets there were for Jewish slaves in abundance. "Sell us, only not to slaughter." "Spare the greyheaded;" "spare my child," would go up in the ears of those, who, though enemies, understood their speech. But no! Such was the compact of Tyre and Philistia and Edom against the people of God. Not one was to be spared; it was to be a *complete captivity;* and that, to Edom. The bond was fulfilled. *Whoso stoppeth his ears at the cry of the poor, he too shall cry and shall not be heard*[19]. Joel mentions the like sin of the Philistines and Phœnicians, and foretold its punishment[20]. That in the reign of Jehoram is the last which Scripture mentions, but was not therefore, of necessity or probably, the last. Holy Scripture probably relates only the more notable of those border-raids. Unrepented sin is commonly renewed. Those strong Philistine fortresses must have given frequent, abundant opportunity for such inroads; as now too it is said in Arabia, "the harvest is to the stronger;" and while small protected patches of soil in Lebanon, Hauran, &c. are cultivated, the open fertile country often lies uncultivated[21], since it would be cultivated only for the marauder. Amos renews the sentence of Joel, forewarning them that, though it seemed to tarry, it would come.

7. *But* lit. *and.* Thus had Gaza done, *and* thus would God do; *I will send a fire upon Gaza.* The sentence on Gaza stands out, probably in that it was first in power and in sin. It was the merchant-city of the five; the caravans parted from it or passed

[1] Josh. xi. 21-23. [2] Josh. xiii. 3. [3] Jud. xvi. 21.
[4] Ib. 4. Its situation was marked in S. Jerome's time, by a "village" named from it "Capharsorech," village of Sorech, "N. of Eleutheropolis near Saraa [Zorah Jud. xiii. 2.] whence Samson was." de loc. Hebr. [5] 1 K. iv. 21. [6] 2 Chr. xxviii. 18.
[7] See ab. p. 160. note 25. [8] 2 Kgs xviii. 8.
[9] Rawl. Her : 473. from Cuneif. Inscr.
[10] xiv. 29.
[11] Cuneif. Inscr. in Layard, Nin. & B. p. 144.
[12] Plut. Alex. 25.
[13] Arr. l. c. Mela (i. 11) calls it "large and well fortified." [14] See Reland, p. 530, note 2.
[15] lit. "Place on the sea" (in Egyptian), Quatremère in Ritt. xvi. 60.
[16] Soz. v. 3. [17] 2 Chr. xxi. 16. [18] Joel iii. 19.
[19] Pr. xxi. 13. [20] iii. 4. 6.
[21] See e. g. Five years in Damasc. ii. 175.

Before CHRIST cir. 787.

8 And I will cut off the inhabitant [r] from Ashdod, and him that holdeth the sceptre from Ashkelon, and

[r] Zeph. 2. 4. Zech. 9. 5, 6.

through it; and so this sale of the Jewish captives was ultimately effected through them. First in sin, first in punishment. Gaza was strong by nature and by art. "The access to it also," Arrian notices [1], "lay through deep sand." We do not hear of its being taken, except in the first times of Israel under the special protection of God [2], or by great conquerors. All Philistia, probably, submitted to David; we hear of no special conquest of its towns [3]. Its siege cost Alexander 2 months [4], with all the aid of the engines with which he had taken Tyre, and the experience which he had there gained. The Egyptian accounts state, that when besieged by Tothmosis III. it capitulated [5]. Thenceforth, it had submitted neither to Egypt nor Assyria. Yet Amos declared absolutely, that Gaza should be destroyed by fire, and it was so. Sennacherib first, then, after Jeremiah had foretold anew the destruction of Gaza, Ashkelon, and the Philistines, Pharaoh Necho *smote Gaza* [6]. Yet who, with human foresight only, would undertake to pronounce the destruction of a city so strong?

8. *And I will cut off the inhabitant from Ashdod.* Ashdod, as well as Ekron, have their names from their strength; Ashdod, "the mighty," like Valentia; Ekron, "the firm-rooted." The title of Ashdod implied that it was powerful to inflict as to resist. It may have meant, "the waster." It too was eminent in its idolatry. The ark, when taken, was first placed in its Dagon-temple [7]; and, perhaps, in consequence, its lord is placed first of the five, in recounting the trespass-offerings which they sent to the Lord [8]. Ashdod (Azotus in the N. T. now a village, Esdud or Shdood [9],) lay 34 or 36 miles from Gaza [10], on the great route from Egypt Northward, on that which now too is most used even to Jerusalem. Ashkelon lay to the left of the road, near the sea, rather more than half-way. Ekron (Akir, now a village of 50 mud-houses [11],) lay a little to the right of the road North-ward from Gaza to Lydda (in the same latitude as Jamnia, Jabneel) on the road from Ramleh to Beit Jibrin (Eleutheropolis). Ekron, the furthest from the sea, lay only 15 miles from it. They were then a succession of fortresses, strong from their situation, which could molest any army, which should come along their coast. Transversely, in regard to Judah, they enclosed a space parallel to most of Judah and Benjamin. Ekron, which by God's gift was the Northern line of Judah [12], is about the same latitude as Ramah in Benjamin; Gaza, the same as Carmel (Kurmul). From Gaza lay a straight road to Jerusalem; but Ashkelon too, Ashdod, and Ekron lay near the heads of valleys, which ran up to the hill-country near Jerusalem [13]. This system of rich valleys, in which, either by artificial irrigation or natural absorption, the streams which ran from the mountains of Judah westward fertilised the corn-fields of Philistia, afforded equally a ready approach to Philistine marauders into the very heart of Judah. The Crusaders had to crown with castles the heights in a distant circle around Ashkelon [14], in order to restrain the incursions of the Mohammedans. On such occasions doubtless, the same man-stealing was often practised on lesser scales, which here, on a larger scale, draws down the sentence of God. Gath, much further inland, probably formed a centre to which these maritime towns converged, and united their system of inroads on Judah.

These five cities of Philistia had each its own petty king (Seren, our "axle"). But all formed one whole; all debated and acted together on any great occasion; as in the plot against Samson [15], the sacrifice to Dagon in triumph over him, where they perished [16]; the inflictions on account of the ark [17]; the great attack on Israel [18], which God defeated at Mizpeh; the battle when Saul fell, and the dismissal of David [19]. The cities divided their idolatry also, in a manner, between

[1] l. c. [2] Jud. i. 1, 2, 18. [3] 2 Sam. viii. 1.

[4] Jos. Ant. xi. 8, 4. Arrian's description of the siege implies a longer time.

[5] "He entered this place by combat, by force, and by convention," Karnac Inscr. in Brugsch, p. 96, after Birch.

[6] Jer. xlvii. 1. [7] 1 Sam. v. 1–7. [8] Ib. vi. 17.

[9] Kinnear, Kairo, &c. p, 214. Ali bey, "Zedoud." Travels, ii. 208. Ritt. xvi. 90.

[10] Reland, p. 608. from Itin. Anton. and Hieros. and Diod. Sic.

[11] Porter, Handb. 275.

[12] Josh. xv. 11.

[13] Ashkelon, at the head of Wadi Simsim which joins on to the Wady el Hasy and drains all the country round Beit Jibrin and Tel-es-Safieh (Rob. ii. 48, 9) which reaches on beyond Ajjar (Ritt. xvi. 68) near Yarmuth. Ashdod, at the head of the valley called from it, meeting the valley of Ashkelon at Beit Jibrin. (Ritt. 91.) Ekron near the Wady-es-Surrar, the trunk of the system of valleys in N. Philistia, reaching on into the mountains of Judah, and ramifying greatly. (Ritt. 102, 3.)

[14] viz. Blanche Garde, Tel-es-Safieh. (Robinson, ii. 31, 32.) South of this, Beit-Jibrin (Eleutheropolis) on the road from Gaza; (Rob. ii. 28, 9. This was fortified by the Turks probably to restrain Bedaween incursions, as late as A. D. 1551. Robins. Ib. 25.) Castellum Arnaldi at Beit Nube on the Ramleh road to Jerusalem, (Ritter, xvi. 92, 3) and Ibelin (Jamnia, or Yebna) on the North. (Rob. Ib. 66. note 5.) [15] Jud. xvi. 5, 8, 18. [16] Ib. 23, 27, 30.

[17] 1 Sam. v. 8, 11. vi. 4, 12, 16, 18. [18] Ib. vii. 7.

[19] Ib. xxxi. 2, 6, 7. 1 Chr. xii. 19.

Before CHRIST cir. 787.

I will [s]turn mine hand against Ekron: and [t]the

[s] Ps. 81. 14. [t] Jer. 47. 4. Ezek. 25. 16.

them, Ashdod being the chief seat of the worship of Dagon[1], Ashkelon, of the corresponding worship of Derceto[2] the fish-goddess, the symbol of the passive principle in re-production. Ekron was the seat of the worship of Baalzebub and his oracle, whence he is called "*the* god of Ekron[3]." Gaza, even after it had become an abode of Greek idolatry and had seven temples of Greek gods, still retained its worship of its god Marna ("our Lord") as the chief[4]. It too was probably "nature[5]," and to its worship they were devoted. All these cities were as one; all formed one state; all were one in their sin; all were to be one in their punishment. So then for greater vividness, one part of the common infliction is related of each, while in fact, according to the wont of Prophetic diction, what is said of each is said of all. King and people were to be cut off from all; all were to be consumed with fire in war; on all God would, as it were, *turn* (lit. *bring back*) *His Hand*, visiting them anew, and bringing again the same punishment upon them. In truth these destructions came upon them, again and again, through Sargon, Hezekiah, Pharaoh, Nebuchadnezzar, Alexander, the Maccabees.

Ashdod. Uzziah about this time *brake down* its *walls and built cities about*[6] it, to protect his people from its inroads. It recovered, and was subsequently besieged and taken by Tartan, the Assyrian General under Sargon[7] (about B.C. 716). Somewhat later, it sustained the longest siege in man's knowlege, for 29 years, from Psammetichus[8] king of Egypt (about B.C. 635). Whence, probably Jeremiah, while he speaks of Ashkelon, Gaza, Ekron, mentions *the remnant of Ashdod*[9] only. Yet, after the captivity, it seems to have been the first Philistine city, so that the Philistines were called Ashdodites[10], and their dialect Ashdodite[11]. They were still hostile to the Jews[10]. The war, in which Judas Maccabæus spoiled Ashdod and other Philistine cities[12], was a defensive war against a war of extermination. "The nations round about[13]," it is said at the beginning of the account of that year's campaign, "thought to destroy the generation of Jacob that was among them, and thereupon they began to slay and destroy the people." Jonathan, the brother of Judas, "set fire to Azotus and the cities round about it[14]," after a battle under its walls, to which his enemies had challenged him. The temple of Dagon in it was a sort of citadel[15].

Ashkelon is mentioned as a place of strength, taken by the great conqueror, Raamses II. Its resolute defence and capture are represented, with its name as a city of Canaanites, on a monument of Karnac[16]. Its name most naturally signifies "hanging." This suits very well with the site of its present ruins, which "hang" on the side of the theatre or arc of hills, whose base is the sea. This, however, probably was not its ancient site. [17] Its name occurs in the wars of the Maccabees, but rather as submitting readily[18]. Perhaps the inhabitants had been changed in the intervening period. Antipater, the Edomite father of Herod, courted, we are told[19], "the Arabs and the Ascalonites and the Gazites." "Toward the Jews their neighbors, the inhabitants of the Holy Land," Philo says[20] to the Roman emperor, "the Ascalonites have an irreconcilable aversion, which will come to no terms." This abiding hatred[21] burst out at the beginning of the war with the Romans, in which Jerusalem perished. The Ascalonites massacred 2500 Jews dwelling among them[22]. The Jews "fired Ascalon and utterly destroyed Gaza[23]."

Ekron was apparently not important enough in itself to have any separate history. We hear of it only as given by Alexander Balas "with the borders thereof in possession[24]" to Jonathan the Maccabee. The valley of Surâr gave the Ekronites a readier entrance into the centre of Judæa, than Ascalon or Ashdod had. In S. Jerome's time, it had sunk to "a very large village."

The residue of the Philistines shall perish. This has been thought to mean *the rest*[25], i. e. Gath, (not mentioned by name any more as having ceased to be of any account[26]) and the towns, dependent on those chief cities[27]. The common (and, with a proper name, universal[28]) meaning of the idiom is, *the rem-*

[1] See p. 162. [2] Herod. i. 105 Diod. ii. 4.
[3] 2 Kgs i. 2, 3, 16.
[4] Vit. S. Porph. Gaz. c. 9 (in Act. Sanct. v. 655.) Rel. p. 793. See also S. Jer. in Is. 17. Ep. ad Læt.
[5] See Movers, Phœn. i. pp. 662, 3.
[6] 2 Chr. xxvi. 6. [7] Is. xx. 1.
[8] Herod. ii. 157. [9] Jer. xxv. 20. [10] Neh. iv. 7.
[11] Ib. xiii. 24. [12] 1 Macc. v. 68. [13] Ib. 1, 2.
[14] Ib. x. 82, 4. [15] Ib. 83.
[16] Brugsch, Hist. de l'Eg. p. 146.
[17] See on Zeph. ii. 4. [18] 1 Macc. x. 86. xi. 60.
[19] Jos. Ant. xiv. 1. 3.
[20] Leg. ad Cai. p. 1021. Rel. p. 587.
[21] Jos. B. S. iii. 2. 2. [22] Ib. ii. 18. 5.
[23] Ib. 1. This occurred first, unless the account be a summary. [24] 1 Macc. x. 89.
[25] as in Jer. xxxix. 3. Neh. vii. 72.
[26] See on Am. vi. 3. [27] So S. Jer. Theod.
[28] as, "the remnant of Judah," Jer. xl. 15. xlii. 15. xliv. 28; "the remnant of Jerusalem," Jer. xxiv. 8; "the remnant of Israel," Is. xlvi. 3. Jer. vi. 9. xxxi. 7. Ez. ix. 8. Mic. ii. 12; "of Jacob," Mic. v. 6, 7, (7, 8 Eng.); "the remnant of the house of Judah," Zeph. ii. 7; "the remnant of Mine inheritance," 2 K. xxi. 14; "of My flock," Jer. xxiii. 3; "the remnant which is left," Is. xxxvii. 4; "go forth a remnant,"

Before CHRIST cir. 787.

remnant of the Philistines
shall perish, saith the Lord
God.
9 ¶ Thus saith the
Lord; For three trans-
gressions of [u] Tyrus, and
for four, I will not turn
away *the punishment* thereof; [x] because they delivered
up the whole captivity to
Edom, and remembered
not † the brotherly cove-
nant;
10 [y] But I will send a

[u] Is. 23. 1. Jer. 47. 4. Ezek. 26, & 27, & 28. Joel 3. 4. 5.

[x] ver. 6.

† Heb. *the covenant of brethren*, 2 Sam. 5. 11. 1 Kings 5. 1. &. 9. 11–14.

[y] ver. 4, 7, &c.

nant, those who remain over after a first destruction. The words then, like those just before, *I will bring again my hand against Ekron*, foretell a renewal of those first judgments. The political strength which should survive one desolation should be destroyed in those which should succeed it. In tacit contrast with the promises of mercy to the remnant of Judah[1], Amos foretells that judgment after judgment should fall upon Philistia, until the Philistines ceased to be any more a people; as they did.

9. The last crowning sin, for which judgment is pronounced on Tyre, is the same as that of Philistia, and probably was enacted in concert with it. In Tyre, there was this aggravation, that it was a violation of a previous treaty and friendship. It was not a covenant only, nor previous friendliness only; but a specific covenant, founded on friendship which they forgat and brake. If they retained the memory of Hiram's intercourse with David and Solomon, it was a sin against light too. After David had expelled the Jebusites from Jerusalem[2], *Hiram King of Tyre sent messengers to David, and cedar trees and carpenters and masons; and they built David a house.* The Philistines contrariwise invaded him[3]. This recognition of him by Hiram was to David a proof[4], *that the Lord had established him king over Israel, and that He had exalted his kingdom for His people, Israel's sake.* Hiram seems, then, to have recognized something super-human in the exaltation of David. *Hiram was ever a lover of David*[5]. This friendship he continued to Solomon, and recognized his God as *the* God. Scripture embodies the letter of Hiram[6]; *Because the Lord hath loved his people, He hath made thee king over them. Blessed be the Lord God of Israel, that made heaven and earth, who hath given to David a wise son—that he might build an house for the Lord.* He must have known then the value which the pious Israelites attached to the going up to that temple. A later treaty, offered by Demetrius Nicator to Jonathan, makes detailed provision that the Jews should have "[7] the feasts and sabbaths and new moons and the solemn days and the three days before the feast and the three days after the feast, as days of immunity and freedom." The three days before the feast were given, that they might go up to the feast. Other treaties guarantee to the Jews religious privileges[8]. A treaty between Solomon and Hiram, which should not secure any religious privileges needed by Jews in Hiram's dominion, is inconceivable. But Jews were living among the Zidonians[9]. The treaty also, made between Hiram and Solomon, was subsequent to the arrangement by which Hiram was to supply cedars to Solomon, and Solomon to furnish the corn of which Hiram stood in need[10]. *The Lord gave Solomon wisdom, as He promised him*[11]; and, as a fruit of that wisdom, *there was peace between Hiram and Solomon; and they two made a covenant*[12]. The terms of that covenant are not there mentioned; but a covenant involves conditions. It was not a mere peace; but a distinct *covenant*, sanctioned by religious rites and by sacrifice[12]. This *brotherly covenant* Tyre *remembered not*, when they delivered up to Edom *a complete captivity*, all the Jews who came into their hands. It seems then, that that covenant had an especial provision against selling them away from their own land. This same provision other people made[13] for love of their country or their homes; the Jews, for love of their religion. This covenant Tyre remembered not, but brake. They knew doubtless why Edom sought to possess the Israelites; but the covetousness of Tyre fed the cruelty of Edom, and God punished the broken appeal to Himself.

10. *I will send a fire upon the wall of Tyre.* Tyre had long ere this become tributary to Assyria. Asshur-dan-ipal (about B.C.

Ib. 32; "of Moab," Is. xv. 9; "of Philistia," Is. xiv. 30; and in Amos himself, "the remnant of Joseph," v. 15; "the remnant of Edom," ix. 12.

[1] See ab. on Joel ii. 32.

[2] Sam. v. 11. [3] Ib. 17. [4] Ib. 12. [5] 1 Kgs v. 1.

[6] 2 Chr. ii. 11. *Hiram answered in writing, which he sent to Solomon.* [7] 1 Macc. x. 34. Jos. Ant. xiii. 2, 3.

[8] 1 Macc. xi. 34. Jos. Ant. xiii. 4, 9. renewed to Simon, 1 Macc. xiii. 35–40.

[9] See on Joel iii. 6.

[10] 1 Kgs v. 7–11. [11] Ib. 12. [12] כרתו ברית.

[13] Strabo xii. 3, 4. "This too is said, that the Milesians who first founded Heraclea constrained the Mariandyni, who possessed it before, to act as serfs, and to be liable even to be sold by them, *but not beyond their borders (for they covenanted as to this)*, in likeway as the so-called Mnoan-union became serfs to the Cretans, and the Penestæ to the Thessalians." quoted by Movers, Phœn. ii. 1. pp. 313, 4. who so interprets Amos.

Before CHRIST cir. 787.

fire on the wall of Tyrus, which shall devour the palaces thereof.

11 ¶ Thus saith the Lord: For three transgressions of [z] Edom, and

[z] Is. 21. 11. & 34. 5. Jer. 49. 8. &c. Ezek. 25. 12, 13, 14. & 35. 2, &c. Joel 3. 19. Obad. 1, &c. Mal. 1. 4.

930,) records his "[1] taking tribute from the kings of all the chief Phœnician cities as Tyre, Sidon, Biblus and Aradus." His son Shalmanubar records his taking tribute from them in his 21st year[2] about 880, B.C.), as did Ivalush III.[3], and after this time Tiglath-pileser II.[4], the same who took Damascus and carried off its people, as also the East and North of Israel. The Phœnicians had aided Benhadad, in his unsuccessful war or rebellion against Shalmanubar[5], but their city had received no hurt. There was nothing, in the time of Amos, to indicate any change of policy in the Assyrian conquerors. They had been content hitherto with tribute from their distant dependencies; they had spared them, even when in arms against them. Yet Amos says absolutely in the name of God, *I will send a fire upon the wall of Tyre*, and the fire did fall, first from Shalamaneser or Sargon his successor, and then from Nebuchadnezzar. The Tyrians (as is men's wont) inserted in their annals their successes, or the successful resistance which they made for a time. They relate that "[6] Elulæus, king of Tyre, reduced the Kittiæans (Cypriotes) who had revolted. The king of Assyria invaded all Phœnicia, and returned, having made peace with all. Sidon and Ace and old Tyre, and many other cities revolted from the Tyrians, and surrendered to the king of Assyria. Tyre then not obeying, the king returned against them, the Phœnicians manning 60 ships for him." These, he says, were dispersed, 500 prisoners taken; the honor of Tyre intensified. "The king of Assyria, removing, set guards at the river and aqueducts, to hinder the Tyrians from drawing water. This they endured for 5 years, drinking from the wells sunk." The Tyrian annalist does not relate the sequel. He does not venture to say that the Assyrian King gave up the siege, but, having made the most of their resistance, breaks off the account. The Assyrian inscriptions say, that Sargon took Tyre[7], and received tribute from Cyprus, where a monument has been found, bearing the name of Sargon[8]. It is not probable that a monarch, who took Samaria and Ashdod, received tribute from Egypt, the "Chief of Saba," and "Queen of the Arabs," overran Hamath, Tubal, Cilicia, Armenia, reduced Media, should have returned baffled, because Tyre stood out a blockade for 5 years. Since Sargon wrested from Tyre its newly-recovered Cyprus, its insular situation would not have protected itself. Nebuchadnezzar took it after a thirteen years' siege[9].

11. *Edom.* God had impressed on Israel its relation of brotherhood to Edom. Moses expressed it to Edom himself[10], and, after the suspicious refusal of Edom to allow Israel to march on the highway through his territory, he speaks as kindly of him[11], as before; *And when we passed by from our brethren, the children of Esau.* It was the unkindness of worldly politics, and was forgiven. The religious love of the Egyptian and the Edomite was, on distinct grounds, made part of the law. [12] *Thou shalt not abhor an Edomite; for he* is *thy brother: thou shalt not abhor an Egyptian; because thou wast a stranger in his land.* The grandchild of an Egyptian or of an Edomite was religiously to become as an Israelite[13]. Not a foot of Edomite territory was Israel to appropriate, however provoked. It was God's gift to Edom, as much as Canaan to Israel. [14] *They shall be afraid of you, and ye shall take exceeding heed to yourselves. Quarrel not with them, for I will give you of their land, no, not so much as the treading of the sole of the foot; for I have given Mount Seir unto Esau for a possession.* From this time until that of Saul, there is no mention of Edom; only that the Maonites and the Amalekites, who oppressed Israel[15], were kindred tribes with Edom. The increasing strength of Israel in the early days of Saul seems to have occasioned a conspiracy against him, such as Asaph afterward complains of[16]; *They have said, come and let us cut them off from* being *a nation, that the name of Israel may be no more in remembrance. For they have consulted together with one consent, they are confederate against Thee; the tabernacles of Edom and the Ishmaelites; of Moab and the Hagarenes; Gebal and Ammon and Amalek; the Philistines with the inhabitants of Tyre; Assur also is joined with them; they have been an arm to the children of Lot.* Such a combination began probably in the time of Saul. [17] *He fought against all his enemies on every side;*

[1] Rawl. Herod. T. i. Ess. vii. § 11. from Cuneiform Inscr.
[2] Rawl. Ib. § 14. p. 463.
[3] Rawl. Ib. § 19. p. 467.
[4] Rawl. § 22. p. 470.
[5] Rawl. § 15. p. 464.
[6] Menander in Jos. Ant. ix. 14. 2.
[7] Rawl, § 24. p. 474.
[8] "The statue of Sargon, now in the Berlin Museum, brought from Idalium, commemorates the Cyprian expedition" Rawl. Ib.
[9] Ezek. xxvi. 7–12, see on Is. xxiii.
[10] Nu. xx. 14. *thus saith thy brother Israel.*
[11] Deut. ii. 8.
[12] Ib. xxiii. 7.
[13] Ib. 8.
[14] Ib. ii. 4, 5.
[15] Jud. vi. 3. x. 12.
[16] Ps. lxxxiii. 4–8.
[17] 1 Sam. xiv. 47.

Before CHRIST cir. 787.

for four, I will not turn away *the punishment* thereof; because he did pursue [a]his brother [b]with the

Before CHRIST cir. 787.

[a] Gen. 27. 41. Deut. 23. 7. Mal. 1. 2. [b] 2 Chr. 28. 17.

against Moab, and against the children of Ammon, and against the king of Edom, and against the Philistines. They were *his enemies*, and that, round about, encircling Israel, as hunters did their prey. *Edom*, on the S. and S. E.; *Moab* and *Ammon* on the East; the Syrians of *Zobah* on the N.; the Philistines on the W. enclosed him as in a net, and he repulsed them one by one. *Whichever way he turned, he worsted*[1] them. It follows[2], *he delivered Israel out of the hands of them that spoiled them.* The aggression was from Edom, and that in combination with old oppressors of Israel, not from Saul[3]. The wars of Saul and of David were defensive wars. Israel was recovering from a state of depression, not oppressing. *The valley of salt*[4], where David defeated the Edomites, was also doubtless within the borders of Judah, since *the city of salt* was[5]; and the valley of salt was probably near the remarkable "mountain of salt," 5⅗ miles long, near the end of the Dead Sea[6], which, as being Canaanite, belonged to Israel. It was also far north of Kadesh, which was *the utmost boundary* of Edom[7]. From that Psalm too of mingled thanksgiving and prayer which David composed after the victory, *in the valley of salt*[8], it appears that, even after that victory, David's army had not yet entered Edom. [9]*Who will bring me into the strong city? who will lead me into Edom?* That same Psalm speaks of grievous suffering before, *in* which God had *cast* them *off* and *scattered* them; *made the earth tremble and cleft it;* so that *it reeled*[10]. Joab too had *returned* from the war in the North against the Syrians of Mesopotamia, to meet the Edomites. Whether in alliance with the Syrians, or taking advantage of the absence of the main army there, the Edomites had inflicted some heavy blow on Israel; a battle in which Abishai slew 18,000 men[11] had been indecisive. The Edomites were repulsed by the rapid countermarch of Joab. The victory, according to the Psalm, was still incomplete[12]. David put *garrisons in Edom*[13], to restrain them from further outbreaks. Joab avenged the wrong of the Edomites, conformably to his character[14]; but the fact that *the captain of the host* had *to go up to bury the slain*[15], shews the extent of the deadly blow, which he so fearfully avenged.

The store set by the king of Egypt on Hadad, the Edomite prince who fled to him[16], shews how gladly Egypt employed Edom as an enemy to Israel. It has been said that he rebelled and failed[17]. Else it remained under a dependent king appointed by Judah, for 1½ century[18]. One attempt against Judah is recorded[19], when those of Mount Seir combined with Moab and Ammon against Jehoshaphat after his defeat at Ramoth-gilead. They had penetrated beyond Engedi[20], on the road which Arab marauders take now[21], toward the wilderness of Tekoa, when God set them against one another, and they fell by each other's hands[22]. But Jehoshaphat's prayer at this time evinces that Israel's had been a defensive warfare. Otherwise, he could not have appealed to God[23], *the children of Ammon and Moab and mount Seir, whom Thou wouldest not let Israel invade when they came out of the land of Egypt, but they turned from them, and destroyed them not, behold, they reward us, to come to cast us out of Thy possession, which Thou hast given us to inherit.* Judah held Edom by aid of garrisons, as a wild beast is held in a cage, that they might not injure them, but had taken no land from them, nor expelled them. Edom sought to cast Israel out of God's land. Revolts cannot be without bloodshed; and so it is perhaps the more probable, that the words of Joel[24], *for the violence against the children of Judah, because they have shed innocent blood in their land*, relate to a massacre of the Jews, when Esau revolted from Jehoram[25]. We have seen, in the Indian Massacres, how every living being of the ruling power may, on such occasions, be sought out for destruction. Edom gained its independence, and Jehoram, who sought to recover his authority, escaped with his life by cutting through the Edomite army by night[26]. Yet in Amaziah's time they were still on the offensive, since the battle wherein he defeated them, was again *in the valley of salt*[27]. Azariah, in whose reign Amos prophesied, regained Elath from them, the port for the Indian trade[28]. Of the origin of that war, we know nothing; only the brief words as to the Edomite invasion against Ahaz[29], *and yet again had the Edomites come, and smitten in Judah, and carried captive a captivity*, attest previous and, it may be,

[1] ירשיע. [2] ver. 48.
[3] as has often been carelessly assumed.
[4] 2 Sam. viii. 13. [5] Josh. xv. 62.
[6] Robinson, ii. 108, 9. [7] Nu. xx. 16.
[8] Ps. lx. title. [9] Ib. 9. [10] Ib. 1–3, 10.
[11] 1 Chr. xviii. 12. [12] Ib. 1, 5, 9–12.
[13] 2 Sam. viii. 14. [14] 1 Kgs xi. 16.
[15] Ib. 15. It should be rendered, not, *after he had slain*, but, *and he slew*, &c.

[16] 1 Kgs xi. 14–20. [17] Jos. Ant. viii. 7. 6.
[18] 1 Kgs xxii. 47. 2 Kgs iii. 9 sqq.
[19] 2 Chr. xx. 10.
[20] Ib. 2, 16, 20.
[21] Rob. i. 508. [22] ver. 22–24.
[23] Ib. 10, 11. [24] iii. 19.
[25] 2 Kgs viii. 20–22. [26] Ib. 21.
[27] Ib. xiv. 7. 2 Chr. xxv. 11, 14.
[28] 2 Chr. xxvi. 2. [29] Ib. xxviii. 17.

Before CHRIST cir. 787.

sword, and †did cast off all pity, [c]and his anger did tear perpetually, and he kept his wrath for ever:

† Heb. *corrupted his compassions.* c Ezek. 35. 5.

Before CHRIST cir. 787.

habitual invasions. For no *one* such invasion had been named. It may probably mean, "they did *yet again*, what they had been in the habit of doing." But in matter of history, the prophets, in declaring the grounds of God's judgments, supply much which it was not the object of the historical books to relate. *They* are histories of God's dealings with His people, His chastisements of them or of His sinful instruments in chastising them. Rarely, except when His supremacy was directly challenged, do they record the ground of the chastisements of heathen nations. Hence, to those who look on the surface only, the wars of the neighboring nations against Israel look but like the alternations of peace and war, victory and defeat, in modern times. The Prophets draw up the veil, and shew us the secret grounds of man's misdeeds and God's judgments.

Because he did pursue his brother. The characteristic sin of Edom, and its punishment are one main subject of the prophecy of Obadiah, inveterate malice contrary to the law of kindred. Eleven hundred years had passed since the birth of their forefathers, Jacob and Esau. But, with God, eleven hundred years had not worn out kindred. He Who willed to knit together all creation, men and angels, in one in Christ[1], and, as a means of union[2], *made of one blood all nations of men for to dwell on all the face of the earth,* used all sorts of ways to impress this idea of brotherhood. *We* forget relationship mostly in the third generation, often sooner; and we think it strange when a nation long retains the memories of those relationships[3]. God, in His law, stamped on His people's minds those wider meanings. To slay a man was to slay a *brother*[4]. Even the outcast Canaan was a *brother*[5] to Shem and Ham. Lot speaks to the men of Sodom amidst their iniquities, *my brethren*[6]; Jacob so salutes those unknown to him[7]. The descendants of Ishmael and Isaac were to be brethren; so were those of Esau and Jacob[8]. The brotherhood of blood was not to wear out, and there was to be a brotherhood of love also[9]. Every Israelite was a brother[10]; each tribe was a brother to every other[11]; the force of the appeal was remembered, even when passion ran high[12]. It enters habitually into the Divine legislation. *Thou shall open thy hand wide unto thy brother*[13]; *if thy brother, a Hebrew, sell himself to thee*[14]; *thou shalt not see thy brother's ox or his sheep go astray and hide thyself from them*[15]; *if thy brother be waxen poor, then shalt thou relieve him,* though *a stranger and a sojourner, that he may live with thee*[16]. In that same law, Edom's relationship as a brother was acknowledged. It was an abiding law that Israel was not to take Edom's land, nor to refuse to admit him into the congregation of the Lord. Edom too remembered the relation, but to hate him. The nations around Israel seem to have been little at war with one another, bound together by common hatred against God's people. Of their wars indeed we should not hear; for they had no religious interest. They would be but the natural results of the passions of unregenerate nature. Feuds there doubtless were and forays, but no attempts at permanent conquest or subdual. Their towns remain in their own possession[17]. Tyre does not invade Philistia; nor Philistia, Tyre or Edom. But all combine against Israel. The words, *did pursue his brother with the sword,* express more than is mentioned in the historical books. To *pursue* is more than to fight. They followed after, in order to destroy a remnant, *and cast off all pity,* lit. and more strongly, *corrupted his compassions, tendernesses.* Edom did violence to his natural feelings, as Ezekiel, using the same word, says of Tyre, *corrupting*[18] *his wisdom,* i. e. perverting it from the end for which God gave it, and so destroying it. Edom "steeled himself," as we say, "against his better feelings," "his better nature," "deadened" them. But so they do not live again. Man is not master of the life and death of his feelings, any more than of his natural existence. He can destroy; he cannot re-create. And he does, so far, *corrupt,* decay, do to death, his own feelings, whenever, in any signal instance, he acts against them. Edom was not simply unfeeling. He destroyed all *his tender yearnings*[19] over suffering, such as God has put into every human heart, until it destroys them. Ordinary anger is satisfied and slaked by its indulgence; malice is fomented and fed and invigorated by it. Edom ever, as occasion came, gratified his anger; *his anger did tear continually;* yet, though raging as some wild ravening animal, without control, *he kept his wrath for ever,* not within bounds, but to let it loose anew. He retained it when he ought

[1] Eph. i. 10. [2] Acts xvii. 26. [3] as the Scotch.
[4] Gen. ix. 5. [5] Ib. 25. [6] Ib. xix. 7.
[7] Ib. xxix. 4. [8] Ib. xvi. 12. xxv. 18.
[9] Ib. xxvii. 29, 37.
[10] Ex. ii. 11. iv. 18; the king and his people, Deut. xvii. 20. 1 Chr. xxviii. 2.
[11] Deut. x. 9. xviii. 2. Jud. xx. 23, 28.
[12] 2 Sam. ii. 26. [13] Deut. xv. 11. [14] Ib. 12.
[15] Ib. xxii. 1–4.
[16] Lev. xxv. 35–39. add Lev. xix. 17. Deut. xxiv. 7, 10, 14. [17] On Moab and Edom see on ii. 1.
[18] Ez. xxviii. 17. [19] שחת רחמיו.

Before CHRIST cir. 787.

d Obad. 9, 10.

12 But [d] I will send a
fire upon Teman, which
shall devour the palaces of
Bozrah.

Before CHRIST cir. 787.

e Jer. 49. 1, 2. Ezek. 25. 2. Zeph. 2. 9.

13 ¶ Thus saith the
LORD; For three trans-
gressions of [e] the children
of Ammon, and for four, I

to have parted with it, and let it loose when he ought to have restrained it.

"What is best, when spoiled, becomes the worst," is proverbial truth. "[1] As no love wellnigh is more faithful than that of brothers, so no hatred, when it hath once begun, is more unjust, no odium fiercer. Equality stirs up and inflames the mind; the shame of giving way and the love of pre-eminence is the more inflamed, in that the memory of infancy and whatever else would seem to gender good will, when once they are turned aside from the right path, produce hatred and contempt." They were proverbial sayings of Heathenism, "fierce are the wars of brethren [2]," and "they who have loved exceedingly, they too hate exceedingly [2]." "[3] The Antiochi, the Seleuci, the Gryphi, the Cyziceni, when they learnt not to be all but brothers, but craved the purple and diadems, overwhelmed themselves and Asia too with many calamities."

12. *But* [*And I*, in My turn and as a consequence of these sins] *will send a fire upon Teman.* "Teman," say Eusebius and S. Jerome [4], "was a country of the princes of Edom, which had its name from Teman son of Eliphaz, son of Esau [5]. But even to this day there is a village, called Teman, about 5 (Eusebius says 15) miles from Petra, where also is a Roman garrison, from which place was Eliphaz, king of the Themanites." It is, however, probably the district which is meant, of which Bozra was then the capital. For Amos when speaking of cities, uses some word to express this, as *the palaces of Benhadad, the wall of Gaza, of Tyrus, of Rabbah;* here he simply uses the name Teman, as he does those of Moab and Judah. Amos does not mention Petra, or Selah; for Amaziah had taken it, and called it Joktheel, "which God subdued," which name it for some time retained [6].

Bozrah (lit. which cuts off approach) is mentioned, as early as Genesis [7], as the seat of one of the elective kings who, in times before Moses, reigned over Edom. It lay then doubtless in Idumea itself, and is quite distinct from the Bozrah of Hauran or Auranitis, from which S. Jerome also distinguishes it [4]. "There is another Bosor also, a city of Esau, in the mountains of Idumea, of which Isaiah speaks." There is yet a small village of the like name (Busaira "the little Bozrah") which "appears," it is said [8], "to have been in ancient times a considerable city, if we may judge from the ruins which surround the village." It has now "some 50 houses, and stands on an elevation, on the summit of which a small castle has been built." The name however, "little Bozrah," indicates the existence of a "great Bozrah," with which its name is contrasted, and is not likely to have been the place itself [9]. Probably the name was a common one, "the strong place" of its neighborhood [10]. The Bozrah of Edom is either that little village, or is wholly blotted out.

13. *Ammon.* Those who receive their existence under circumstances, in any way like those of the first forefathers of Moab and Ammon, are known to be under physical as well as intellectual and moral disadvantages. Apart from the worst horrors, on the one side reason was stupefied, on the other it was active in sin. He who imprinted His laws on nature, has annexed the penalty to the infraction of those laws. It is known also how, even under the Gospel, the main character of a nation remains unchanged. The basis of natural character, upon which grace has to act, remains, under certain limits, the same. Still more in the unchanging East. Slave-dealers know of certain hereditary good or evil qualities in non-Christian nations in whom they traffic. What marvel then that Ammon and Moab retained the stamp of their origin, in a sensual or passionate nature? Their choice of their idols grew out of this original character and aggravated it. They chose them gods like themselves, and worsened themselves by copying these idols of their sinful nature. The chief god of the fierce Ammon was Milchom or Molech, the

[1] F. Petrarch. Dial. ii. 45. Bas. 1554. Lap.
[2] in Arist. Pol. vii. 7. Lap.
[3] Plut. de frat. amore. Ib.
[4] de locis Hebr.
[5] Gen. xxxvi. 11, 15.
[6] 2 Kgs xiv. 7.
[7] xxxvi. 33.
[8] Burckhardt, Syria, 407.
[9] as has been assumed since Robinson, ii. 167.
[10] i. "Bezer in the wilderness" or "plain" in Reuben opposite to Jericho, one of the cities of refuge. (Deut. iv. 43. Josh. xx. 8.) ii. Bosor, a "strong and great city" of Gilead. (1 Macc. v. 26, 36. Ant. xii. 8. 4.) iii. Besara, on the confines of Ptolemais, 2½ miles from Geba (Jos. Vit. § 24.) iv. Bozrah of Moab, (Jer. xlviii. 24.) The Bostra which the Romans rebuilt, 24 miles from Edrei, which became the Metropolis of Arabia, and, in Arabic times of Hauran, (see the description of the remains, Porter, Five years, ii. 140 sqq.) lay too far North to be any of these. It is probably a corruption of בעשתרה, "house of Ashtoreth" in Manasseh (Jos. xxi. 27. see Reland, v. Bostra p. 666.); and Bosorra (distinct from Bosor, 1 Macc. v. 26, 28.) may be another corruption of the name.

Before CHRIST cir. 787.

will not turn away *the punishment* thereof; because they have ||[f] ripped up the women with child of Gilead, [g] that they might enlarge their border:

|| Or, *divided the mountains.*

[f] Hos. 13. 16.

[g] Jer. 49. 1.

principle of destruction, who was appeased with sacrifices of living children, given to the fire to devour. Moab, beside its idol Chemosh, had the degrading worship of Baal Peor [1], re-productiveness the counterpart of destruction. And, so, in fierce or degrading rites, they worshiped the power which belongs to God, to create, or to destroy. Moab was the seducer of Israel at Shittim [1]. Ammon, it has been noticed, shewed at different times a peculiar wanton ferocity [2]. Such was the proposal of Nahash to the men of Jabesh-Gilead, when offering to surrender [3], *that I may thrust out all your right eyes and lay it* for *a reproach unto all Israel.* Such was the insult to David's messengers of peace, and the hiring of the Syrians in an aggressive war against David [4]. Such, again, was this war of extermination against the Gileadites. On Israel's side, the relation to Moab and Ammon had been altogether friendly. God recalled to Israel the memory of their common descent, and forbade them to war against either. He speaks of them by the name of kindness, *the children of Lot,* the companion and friend of Abraham. [5] *I will not give thee of their land* for *a possession, because I have given it unto the children of Lot* for *a possession.* Akin by descent, their history had been alike. Each had driven out a giant tribe; Moab, the Emim; Ammon, the Zamzummim [6]. They had thus possessed themselves of the tract from the Arnon, not quite half way down the Dead Sea on its East side, to the Jabbok, about half way between the Dead Sea and the Sea of Galilee [7]. Both had been expelled by the Amorites, and had been driven, Moab, behind the Arnon, Ammon, behind the *strong border* [8] of the upper part of the Jabbok, what is now the Nahr Amman, "the river of Ammon," Eastward. The whole of what became the inheritance of the 2½ tribes, was in the hands of the Amorites, and threatened very nearly their remaining possessions; since, at *Aroer that* is *before Rabbah* [9], the Amorites were already over against the capital of Ammon; at the Arnon they were but 2½ hours [10] from Ar-Moab, the remaining capital of Moab. Israel then, in destroying the Amorites, had been at once avenging and rescuing Moab and Ammon; and it is so far a token of friendliness at this time, that, after the victory at Edrei, the great *iron bedstead* of Og was placed *in Rabbah of the children of Ammon* [11]. Envy, jealousy, and fear, united them to *hire Balaam to curse* Israel [12], although the king of Moab was the chief actor in this [13], as he was in the seduction of Israel to idoltary [14]. Probably Moab was then, and continued to be, the more influential or the more powerful, since in their first invasion of Israel, the Ammonites came as the allies of Eglon king of Moab. *He gathered unto him the children of Ammon and Amalek* [15]. *And* they *served Eglon.* Yet Ammon's subsequent oppression must have been yet more grievous, since God reminds Israel of His delivering them from the Ammonites [16], not from Moab. There we find Ammon under a king, and in league with the Philistines [17], *crashing and crushing* [18] *for* 18 *years all the children of Israel in Gilead.* The Ammonites carried a wide invasion across the Jordan against Judah, Benjamin and Ephraim [19], until they were subdued by Jephthah. Moab is not named; but the king of Ammon claims as *my land* [20], the whole which Moab and Ammon had lost to the Amorites, and they to Israel, *from Arnon unto Jabbok and unto Jordan* [20]. The range also of Jephthah's victories included probably all that same country from the Arnon to the neighborhood of Rabbah of Ammon [21]. The Ammonites, subdued then, were again on the offensive in the fierce siege of Jabesh-Gilead and against Saul [22]. Yet it seems that they had already taken from Israel what they had lost to the Amorites; for Jabesh-Gilead was beyond the Jabbok [23]; and *Mizpeh of Moab,* whither David went

[1] Nu. xxv. 1–3.
[2] Grote in Smith, Bibl. Dict. v. Ammon.
[3] 1 Sam. xi. 1–3. [4] 2 Sam. x. 1–6.
[5] Deut. ii. 9, 19. [6] Ib. 10, 11, 20. 1.
[7] Nu. xxi. 23–30. Of this, Moab had the part from the Arnon to the N. of the Dead Sea, including *the plains of Moab* (עַרְבוֹת מוֹאָב) i.e. the part of the valley of the Jordan on the E. side, opposite to Jericho, the subsequent possession of Reuben. Gilead, to the S. and E. of the Jabbok, had belonged to Ammon, whence it is said that Moses gave to the 2½ tribes the land *unto the border of the children of Ammon,* (Jos. xiii. 10.) i.e. Westward, and yet *half the land of the children of Ammon,* (Ib. 25.) i.e. what they had lost to the Amorites.
[8] Nu. xxi. 24. [9] Jos. xiii. 25.
[10] Porter, Handb. 302. [11] Deut. iii. 11.
[12] Ib. xxiii. 4. [13] Nu. xxii.–xxiv. [14] Ib. xxv. 1–3.
[15] Jud. iii, 13. [16] Ib. x. 11. [17] Ib. 7.
[18] וַיִּרְעֲצוּ וַיְרֹצְצוּ. Ib. 8. The two alliterate and equivalent words are joined as intensive.
[19] Ib. 9. [20] Ib. xi. 13.
[21] Ib. 33. *He smote them from Aroer to Minnith,* (Minnith was "4 miles from Heshbon on the way to Philadelphia," i.e. Rabbah) *twenty cities and unto Abel-keramim* "7 (Eus. 6.) miles from Rabbah." S. Jer. If Aroer is here the best known, that by the Arnon, the account describes one line from the Arnon to a little beyond Heshbon and then to a place near the Jabbok. [22] See above on ver. 11.
[23] "6 miles from Pella on a hill towards Gerasa" (Jerash). S. Jer. de loc. Hebr. Both places were

Before CHRIST cir. 787.

14 But I will kindle a
fire in the wall of [h] Rabbah, and it shall devour
the palaces thereof, [i] with

[h] Deut. 3. 11. 2 Sam. 12. 26. Jer. 49. 2. Ezek. 25. 5.

[i] ch. 2. 2.

to seek the king of Moab[1], was probably no other than the Ramoth-Mizpeh[2] of Gad, the Mizpeh[3] whence Jephthah went over to fight the Ammonites. With Hanan, king of Ammon, David sought to remain at peace, on account of some kindness, interested as it probably was, which his father Nahash had shewn him, when persecuted by Saul[4]. It was only after repeated attempts to bring an overwhelming force of the Syrians against David, that Rabbah was besieged and taken, and that awful punishment inflicted. The severity of the punishment inflicted on Moab and Ammon, in that two-thirds of the fighting men of Moab were put to death[5], and fighting men of *the cities of Ammon*[6] were destroyed by a ghastly death, so different from David's treatment of the Philistines or the various Syrians, implies some extreme hostility on their part, from which there was no safety except in their destruction. Moab and Ammon were still united against Jehoshaphat[7], and with Nebuchadnezzar against Jehoiakim[8], whom they had before sought to stir up against the king of Babylon[9]. Both profited for a time by the distresses of Israel, *magnifying* themselves *against her border*[10], and taking possession of her cities[11], after the 2½ tribes has been carried away by Tiglath-pileser. Both united in insulting Judah, and (as it appears from Ezekiel[12]) out of jealousy against its religious distinction. When some of the scattered Jews were reunited under Gedaliah, after the destruction of Jerusalem by Nebuchadnezzar, it was a king of Ammon, Baalis, who instigated Johanan to murder him[13]. When Jerusalem was to be rebuilt after the return from the captivity, Ammonites and Moabites[14], *Sanballat the Horonite* (i. e. out of Horonaim, which Moab had taken to itself[15],) *and Tobiah the servant, the Ammonite*, were chief in the opposition to it. They helped on the persecution by Antiochus[16]. Their anti-religious character, which shewed itself in the hatred of Israel and the hire of Balaam, was the ground of the exclusion of both from admission *into the congregation of the Lord forever*[17]. The seduction of Solomon by his Ammonite and Moabite wives illustrates the infectiousness of their idolatry. While he made private chapels *for all his strange wives, to burn incense and sacrifice to their gods*[18], the most stately idolatry was that of Chemosh and Molech, the abomination of Moab and Ammon[19]. For Ashtoreth alone, besides these, did Solomon build high-places in sight of the temple of God, on a lower part of the Mount of Olives[20].

They have ripped up the women with child in Gilead. Since Elisha prophesied that Hazael would be guilty of this same atrocity, and since Gilead was the scene of his chief atrocities[21], probably Syria and Ammon were, as of old, united against Israel in a war of extermination. It was a conspiracy to displace God's people from the land which He had given them, and themselves to replace them. The plan was effective; it was, Amos says, executed. They expelled and *inherited Gad*[22]. Gilead was desolated for the sins for which Hosea rebuked it; "blood had blood." It had been *tracked with blood*[23]; now life was sought out for destruction, even in the mother's womb. But, in the end, Israel, whose extermination Ammon devised and in part effected, survived. Ammon perished and left no memorial.

That they might enlarge their border. It was a horror, then, exercised, not incidentally here and there, or upon a few, or in sudden stress of passion, but upon system and in cold blood. We have seen lately, in the massacres near Lebanon, where male children were murdered on system, how methodically such savageness goes to work. A massacre, here and there, would not have *enlarged their border*. They must have carried on these horrors then, throughout all the lands which they wished to possess, making place for themselves by annihilating Israel, that there might be none to rise up and thrust them from their conquests, and claim their old inheritance. Such was the fruit of habitually indulged covetousness. Yet who beforehand would have thought it possible?

14. *I will kindle a fire in the wall of Rabbah.* Rabbah, lit. *the great*, called by Moses[24] *Rabbah of the children of Ammon*, and by later Greeks, *Rabathammana*[25], was a strong city

beyond the Jabbok. The name Jabesh, "dry," still survives in the valley *Yabes*, (the Arabic pronunciation) which, with its brook, ends in the Jordan 7 or 8 geogr. miles N. of the Jabbok.

[1] 1 Sam. xxii. 3. [2] Josh. xiii. 26. [3] Jud. xi. 29.
[4] 2 Sam. x. 2. [5] Ib, viii. 2. [6] Ib. xii. 31.
[7] 2 Chr. xx. [8] 2 Kgs xxiv. 2. [9] Jer. xxvii. 3.
[10] Zeph. ii. 8.
[11] On Ammon see below. When Isaiah prophesied, Moab was in possession of all the cities of Reuben, Is. xv. xvi.
[12] Ez. xxv. 2–8. [13] Jer. xl. 11–14. xli. 10.
[14] Neh. ii. 10, 19. iv. 1–3.
[15] Is. xv. 5. Jer. xlviii. 3, 5, 34.
[16] 1 Macc. v. 6. [17] Deut. xxiii. 3.
[18] 1 Kgs xi. 8.
[19] Solomon's worship of Ashtoreth as well as of Milcom is mentioned 1 Kgs xi. 5. The high places of Chemosh and Molech are alone mentioned there, ver. 7; that of Ashtoreth is mentioned in the account of its defilement by Josiah.
[20] Kgs xxiii. 13. [21] Ab. 3. [22] Jer. xlix. 1.
[23] See on Hos. vi. 8. p. 42. [24] Deut. iii. 11.
[25] Polyb. v. 71. 4. Steph. Byz.

Before CHRIST cir. 787.

shouting in the day of battle, with a tempest in the day of the whirlwind:

15 And [k] their king shall go into captivity, he and his princes together, saith the LORD.

Before CHRIST cir. 787.

k Jer. 49. 3.

with a yet stronger citadel. Ruins still exist, some of which probably date back to these times. The lower city "[1] lay in a valley bordered on both sides by barren hills of flint," at ½ an hour from its entrance. It lay on a stream, still called by its name Moyet or Nahr Ammân, "waters" or "river of Ammon," which ultimately falls into the Zurka (the Jabbok.) "[2] On the top of the highest of the Northern hills," where at the divergence of two valleys it abuts upon the ruins of the town, "stands the castle of Ammon, a very extensive rectangular building," following the shape of the hill and wholly occupying its crest. "Its walls are thick, and denote a remote antiquity; large blocks of stone are piled up without cement, and still hold together as well as if they had been recently placed; the greater part of the wall is entire. Within the castle are several deep cisterns." There are remains of foundations of a wall of the lower city at its Eastern extremity [3]. This lower city, as lying on a river in a waterless district, was called the *city of waters* [4], which Joab had taken when he sent to David to come and besiege the Upper City. In later times, that Upper City was resolutely defended against Antiochus the Great, and taken, not by force but by thirst [5]. On a conspicuous place on this castle-hill, stood a large temple, some of its broken columns 3½ feet in diameter [6], probably the Grecian successor of the temple of its idol Milchom. Rabbah, the capital of Ammon, cannot have escaped, when Nebuchadnezzar, "[7] in the 5th year of his reign, led an army against Cœle-Syria, and, having possessed himself of it, warred against the Ammonites and Moabites, and having made all these nations subject to him, invaded Egypt, to subdue it." Afterward, it was tossed to and fro in the desolating wars between Syria and Egypt. Ptolemy II. called it from his own surname Philadelphia [8], and so probably had had to restore it. It brought upon itself the attack of Antiochus III. and its own capture, by its old habit of marauding against the Arabs in alliance with him. At the time of our Lord, it, with "Samaria, Galilee and Jericho," is said by a heathen [9] to be "inhabited by a mingled race of Egyptians, Arabians and Phœnicians." It had probably already been given over to *the children of the East*, the Arabs, as Ezekiel had foretold [10]. In early Christian times Milchom was still worshiped there under its Greek name of Hercules [11]. Trajan recovered it to the Roman empire [12], and in the 4th century it, with Bostra [13], was still accounted a "vast town most secured by strong walls," as a frontier fortress "to repel the incursions of neighboring nations." It was counted to belong to Arabia [14]. An Arabic writer says that it perished before the times of Mohammed, and covered a large tract with its ruins [15]. It became a station of pilgrims to Mecca, and then, till now, as Ezekiel foretold [16], *a stable for camels* and *a couching place for flocks*.

I will kindle a fire in the wall. It may be that the prophet means to speak of some conflagration from within, in that he says not, as elsewhere [17], *I will send a fire upon*, but, *I will kindle a fire in.* But *the shouting* is the battle-cry [18] of the victorious enemy, the cheer of exultation, anticipating its capture. That onslaught was to be resistless [19], sweeping, like a whirlwind, all before it. The fortress and walls of Rabbah were to yield before the onset of the enemy, as the tents of their caravans were whirled flat on the ground before the eddying of the whirlwinds from the desert, burying all beneath them.

15. *And their king.* The king was commonly, in those nations, the centre of their energy. When *he and his princes* were *gone into captivity*, there was no one to make head against the conqueror, and renew revolts. Hence, as a first step in the subdual, the reigning head and those who shared his counsels were removed. Ammon then, savage as it was in act, was no ill-organized horde. On the contrary, barren and waste as all that country now is, it must once have been

1 Burckhardt, Syria, 358, 8.
2 Ib. 359, 60. and see plan p. 357.
3 Buckingham, Trav. Ritter, xv. 1150.
4 2 Sam. xii. 27.
5 Polyb. l. c. A prisoner shewed how the access of the garrison to the water might be cut off.
6 Burckhardt, 360.
7 Jos. Ant. x. 9. 7.
8 S. Jer. in Ezek. xxv.
9 Strabo, xvi. 2. 34. Ritt. 1156.
10 xxv. 4.
11 Coins from Trajan to Commodus, see authorities, Ritt. 1157.
12 Amm. xiv. 8. 13.
13 "and Gerasa," Ib.
14 S. Epiph. Synops. L. ii. adv. Hær. p. 397. Anaceph. p. 145. Reland, 612.
15 Abulfeda, (who, at Hamath, must have known it, as lying on the pilgrim-road to Mecca) Tab. Syr. p. 91.
16 Ezek. xxv. 5. See Lord Lindsay. 278–82. Porter, Handb. 304, 5. Lord C. Hamilton's Journal in Keith on Prophecy, 270, 1.
17 i. 4, 7, 10, 12. ii. 2, 5.
18 Job xxxix. 25. Jer. xx. 16. Zeph. i. 16, &c.
19 The etymol. of סופה.

Before CHRIST cir. 787.

CHAPTER II.

1 *God's wrath against Moab,* 4 *upon Judah,* 6 *and upon Israel.* 9 *God complaineth of their unthankfulness.*

THUS saith the LORD: For three transgressions of [a]Moab, and for four, I will not turn away

[a] Is. 15, & 16. Jer. 48. Ezek. 25. 8. Zeph. 2. 8.

highly cultivated by a settled and laborious people. The abundance of its ruins attests the industry and habits of the population. "The whole of the country," says Burckhardt[1], "must have been extremely well cultivated, to have afforded subsistence to the inhabitants of so many towns." "The low hills are, for the most part, crowned with ruins." Of the "[2]thirty ruined or deserted places, which including Ammân," have been even lately "counted East of Assalt" (the village which probably represents Ramoth-Gilead, "about 16 miles West of Philadelphia[3]" i.e. Ammân,) several are in Ammonitis. Little as the country has been explored, ruins of large and important towns have been found S.S.E. and S. of Ammân[4]. Two hours S.E. of Ammân, Buckingham relates[5], "an elevation opened a new view before us, in the same direction. On a little lower level, was a still more extensive track of cultivated plain than that even which we had already passed—Throughout its whole extent were seen ruined towns in every direction, both before, behind, and on each side of us; generally seated on small eminences; all at a short distance from each other; and all, as far as we had yet seen, bearing evident marks of former opulency and consideration. There was not a tree in sight as far as the eye could reach; but my guide, who had been over every part of it, assured me that the whole of the plain was covered with the finest soil, and capable of being made the most productive corn land in the world—For a space of more than thirty miles there did not appear to me a single interruption of hill, rock or wood, to impede immediate tillage. The great plain of Esdraelon, so justly celebrated for its extent and fertility, is inferior in both to this plain of Belkah. Like Esdraelon, it appears to have been once the seat of an active and numerous population; but in the former the monuments of the dead only remain, while here the habitations of the living are equally mingled with the tombs of the departed, all thickly strewn over every part of the soil from which they drew their sustenance." Nor does the crown, of *a talent of gold weight, with precious stones*[6], belong to an uncivilized people. Such hordes too depend on the will and guidance of their single Skeikh or head. This was a hereditary kingdom[7]. The kings of Ammon had their constitutional advisers. These were they who gave the evil and destructive counsel to insult the ambassadors of David. Evil kings have evermore evil counsellors. It is ever the curse of such kings to have their own evil, reflected, anticipated, fomented, enacted by bad advisers around them. [8]*Hand in hand the wicked shall not be unpunished.* They link together, but to drag one another into a common destruction. Together they had counselled against God; *king and princes together*, they should *go into captivity.*

There is also doubtless, in the word Malcham, a subordinate allusion to the god whom they worshiped under the title Molech or Malchom. Certainly Jeremiah *seems* so to have understood it. For, having said of Moab, [9]*Chemosh shall go into captivity, his priests and his princes together*, he says as to Ammon, in the self-same formula and almost in the words of Amos; [10]*Malcham shall go into captivity, his priests and his princes together.* Zephaniah [11] also speaks of the idol under the same name Malcham, "their king." Yet since Ammon had kings before this time, and just before their subdual by Nebuchadnezzar, and king Baalis [12] was a murderer, it is hardly likely that Jeremiah too should not have included him in the sentence of his people, of whose sins he was a mainspring. Probably, then, Amos and Jeremiah foretell, in a comprehensive way, the powerlessness of all their stays, human and idolatrous. All in which they trusted should not only fail them, but should be carried captive from them.

II. 1. *Moab.* The relation of Moab to Israel is only accidentally different from that of Ammon. One spirit actuated both, venting itself in one and the same way, as occasion served, and mostly together[13]. Beside those more formal invasions, the history of Elisha mentions one probably of many in-

[1] Syria, 357. (See also Porter, Hdb. 307.)

[2] Keith, c. 6. end 274. Of the 30 in Dr. Smith's list (Robinson App. iii. 168. ed. i.) several are clearly W. of Ammon, in Gilead, several are not in the maps; some are clearly in Ammonitis.

[3] Eus. Onom. Our copies of S. Jerome have by mistake, East. "6 hours" Porter, 307. See 309. and Ritter, xv. 1136–8.

[4] Buckingham, p. 83–96.

[5] Ib. 85.

[6] 2 Sam. xii. 30.

[7] Ib. x. 1.

[8] Pr. xi. 21.

[9] xlviii. 7.

[10] xlix. 3. מַלְכָּם בַּגּוֹלָה ילך כהניו ושריו יחדיו. Am. הלך מַלְכָּם בַּגּוֹלָה הוא ושריו יחדו. They use the same idiom and words, including the word הלך, not יצא which Jeremiah has xxix. 16. xlviii. 7. S. Jerome here renders Chemosh, and so did the Greek copies which Theodoret used. Aq. Sym. and Syr.

[11] i. 5.

[12] Jer. xl. 14.

[13] See on i. 13.

Before CHRIST cir. 787.

the punishment thereof; because he [b]burned the bones of the king of Edom into lime:

[b] 2 Kgs 3. 27.

roads of *bands of the Moabites.* It seems as though, when *the year entered in*, and with it the harvest, *the bands of the Moabites entered in*[1] too, like *the Midianites and Amalekites and the children of the East*[2] in the time of Gideon, or their successors the Bedaweens, now. This their continual hostility is related in the few words of a parenthesis. There was no occasion to relate at length an uniform hostility, which was as regular as the seasons of the year, and the year's produce, and the temptation to the cupidity of Moab, when Israel was weakened by Hazael.

Because he burned the bones of the king of Edom. The deed here condemned, is unknown. Doubtless it was connected with that same hatred of Edom, which the king of Moab shewed, when besieged by Israel. Men are often more enraged against a friend or ally who has made terms with one whom they hate or fear, than with the enemy himself. Certainly, *when the king of Moab saw that the battle was too sore for him*[3], his fury was directed personally against the king of Edom. He *took with him* 700 chosen men *to cut through to the king of Edom, and they could not.* Escape was not their object. They sought not *to cut through* the Edomite contingent into the desert, but *to the king of Edom.* Then *he took his eldest son,* i. e. probably the eldest son of the king of Edom[4] whom he captured, *and offered him up as a burnt offering on the wall.* Such is the simplest structure of the words; *He strove to cut through to the king of Edom, and they could not, and he took his eldest son, &c, and there was great indignation against Israel.* That *indignation* too on the part of Edom (for there was no other to be indignant *against Israel*) is best accounted for, if this expedition, undertaken because Moab had rebelled against Israel, had occasioned the sacrifice of the son of the king of Edom, who took part in it only as a tributary of Judah. Edom would have had no special occasion to be indignant with Israel, if on occasion of an ordinary siege, the king of Moab had, in a shocking way, performed the national idolatry of child-sacrifice. That hatred the king of Moab carried beyond the grave, hatred which the heathen too held to be unnatural in its implacableness and unsatiableness. The soul being, after death, beyond man's reach, the hatred, vented upon his remains, is a sort of impotent grasping at eternal vengeance. It wreaks on what it knows to be insensible, the hatred with which it would pursue, if it could, the living being who is beyond it. Its impotence evinces its fierceness, since, having no power to wreak any real revenge, it has no object but to shew its hatred. Hatred, which death cannot extinguish, is the beginning of the eternal hate in hell. With this hatred Moab hated the king of Edom, seemingly because he had been, though probably against this will, on the side of the people of God. It was then sin against the love of God, and directed against God Himself. The single instance, which we know, of any feud between Moab and Edom was, when Edom was engaged in a constrained service of God. At least there are no indications of any conquest of each other. The Bozrah of Moab, being in the Mishor, *the plain*[5], is certainly distinct from the Bozrah of Edom, which Jeremiah speaks of at the same time, as belonging to Edom[6]. Each kingdom, Edom and Moab, had its own strong city, Bozrah, at one and the same time. And if "the rock," which Isaiah speaks of as the strong hold of Moab[7], was indeed the Petra of Edom, (and the mere name, in that country of rock-fortresses is not strong, yet is the only, proof,) they won it from Judah who had taken it from Edom, and in whose hands it remained in the time of Amos[8], not from Edom itself. Or, again, the tribute *may* have been only sent through Petra, as the great centre of commerce. Edom's half-service gained it no good, but evil; Moab's malice was its destruction.

The proverb, "speak good only of the dead," shews what reverence human nature dictates, not to condemn those who have been before their Judge, unless He have already openly condemned them. "Death," says S. Athanasius[9] in relating the death of Arius on his perjury, "is the common end of all men, and we ought not to insult the dead, though he be an enemy; for it is uncertain whether the same event may not happen to ourselves before evening."

[1] 2 Kgs xiii. 20. lit. *And the bands of Moab were wont to come in,* (the force of יבאו) as *the year came in* (בא). [2] Jud. vi. 3, 4, 11. [3] 2 Kgs iii. 26, 7.

[4] Josephus understands it of the king of Moab's own son; but then he misses the force of every expression. He supposes that the king of Moab tried to cut his way to escape only, and explains the great indignation against Israel, of the compassion of Israel himself (Ant. ix. 3, 2.) Theodoret supposes that the Moabites took the king of Edom [i. e. the heir apparent] prisoner, and so sacrificed him.

[5] Jer. xlviii. 21, 24. [6] Ib. xlix. 13. [7] Is. xvi. 1.

[8] 2 Kgs xiv. 7. See ab. on i. 12.

[9] ad. Ep. Æg. § 19, in S. Ath. Hist. Tracts, p. 147. Oxf. Tr.

Before CHRIST cir. 787.

c Jer. 48. 41.
d ch. 1. 14.

2 But I will send a fire
upon Moab, and it shall
devour the palaces of [c] Kirioth: and Moab shall die
with tumult, [d] with shouting, *and* with the sound of
the trumpet:
3 And I will cut off [e] the
judge from the midst
thereof, and will slay all

Before CHRIST cir. 787.

e Num. 24. 17.
Jer. 48. 7.

2. *It shall devour the palaces of Kerioth;* lit. *the cities,* i. e. a collection of cities. It may have received a plural form upon some enlargement, as Jerusalem received a dual form, as a double city. The name is, in different forms, very common[1]. In the plain or high downs of Moab itself, there were both Kiriathaim, "double city" and Kerioth[2]; in Naphthali, a Kiriathaim[3], or Kartan[4]; in Judah, the Kerioth [5] whence the wretched Judas has his name Iscariot[6]; in Zebulon, Kartah[7] also, which reappears as the Numidian Cirta. Moab had also a Kiriath-huzoth[8], "city of streets," within the Arnon[9]. This alone was within the proper border of Moab, such as the Amorites had left it. Kerioth and Kiriathaim were in the plain country which Israel had won from the Amorites, and its possession would imply an aggression of Moab. Jeroboam II. had probably at this time brought Moab to a temporary submission[10]; but Israel only required fealty and tribute of Moab; Moab appears even before the captivity of the 2½ tribes,to have invaded the possessions of Israel. Kerioth was probably a new capital, beyond the Arnon, now adorned with *palaces* and enlarged, as "Paris, Prague, Cracow[11]," London, are composed of different towns. In S. Jerome's time, it had probably ceased to be[12].

Shall die with tumult. Jeremiah, when prophesying the destruction of Moab, designates it by this same name *sons of tumult*[13]. *A flame shall devour the corner of Moab and the crown of the sons of tumult.* And probably herein he explains the original prophecy of Balaam[14], *shall smite the corners of Moab, and destroy all the children of tumult*[15]. As they had done, so should it be done to them; tumults they caused, *in tumult* they should perish.

After the subdual of Moab by Nebuchadnezzar, it disappears as a nation, unless indeed Daniel in his Prophecy[16], *Edom and Moab and the chief of the children of Ammon shall escape out of his hand* [Antiochus Epiphanes,] means the nations themselves, and not such as should be like them. Else the inter-marriage with Moabitish women[17] is mentioned only as that with women of other heathen nations which had ceased to be. The old name, Moabitis, is still mentioned; but the Arabs had possessed themselves of it, and bore the old name. Alexander Jannæus "subdued[18]," we are told, "of the Arabians, the Moabites and Gileadites," and then, again, when in difficulty, made it over with its fortified places, to the king of the Arabians[19]. Among the cities which Alexander took from the king of the Arabians[20], are cities throughout Moab, both in that part in which they had succeeded to Israel, and their proper territory S. of the Arnon[21].

3. *And I will cut off the judge.* The title *judge* (shophet) is nowhere used absolutely of a king. Holy Scripture speaks in several places of *all the judges of the earth*[22]. Hosea[23], under *judges,* includes *kings and princes,* as *judging the people.* The word *judge* is always used as one invested with the highest, but not regal authority, as of all the judges from the death of Joshua to Samuel. In like way it (Sufetes) was the title of the chief magistrates of Carthage[24], with much the same authority as the Roman Consuls[25]. The Phœnician histories, although they would not own that Nebuchadnezzar conquered Tyre, still own that, after his thirteen years' siege[26], Baal reigned 10 years, and after him *judges* were set up, one for two months, a second for ten, a third, a high-priest, for three, two more for six, and between these one reigned for a year. After his death, they sent for Merbaal from Babylon, who reigned for four years, and on

1 Besides the following, there is a Kuryetein, about half-way between Damascus and Palmyra (See Five years, i. 252 sqq. ii. 358.) and a Kureiyeh "in a broad valley at the S. W. base of the Jebel Hauran," near the Roman Bostra with "remains of remote antiquity." Ib. ii. 191. 8. add Burckhardt, Syria, 103, 4.

2 Jer. xlviii. 23, 24.
3 1 Chr. vi. 76. (61. Heb.)
4 Josh. xxi. 32.
5 Josh. xv. 25.
6 אִישׁ קְרִיּוֹת.
7 Josh. xxi. 34.
8 Nu. xxii. 39.

9 Balak met Balaam at *a city of Moab in the border of Arnon,* and then returned apparently to Kiriath-Huzoth.

10 See on vi. 14.
11 Lap.

12 Kiriathaim was according to S. Jerome in his time "a Christian village called Coraiatha, 10 miles W. of Medaba, near Baare" [perhaps the valley so called, near Machærus, Jos. B. J. vii. 6. 3. Ritter, xv. 582.] Of Kerioth he only says, "in the country of Moab, as Jeremiah writes." The present Korriath lies under the Jebel Attarus, S. W. of Medeba, by the streamlet el Wal. Ritter, Ib. and map in Robinson.

13 xlviii. 45.
14 Nu. xxiv. 17.
15 שֵׁת i. q. שְׁאוֹן.
16 xi. 41.
17 Ezr. ix. 1.
18 Jos. Ant. xiii. 13. 5.
19 Ib. 14. 2.
20 xiv. 1. 1. comp. xiii. 15, 4.

21 Medaba and Livias N. of the Arnon; Agalla [Eglaim] "8 miles S. of it" (Eus.); Zoar, near the South of the Dead Sea; Oronæ [Horonaim] on Edom's boundary. Is. xv. 5.

22 Job ix. 24. Ps. ii. 10. cxlviii. 11. Pr. viii. 16. Is. xl. 23.
23 xiii. 10.
24 Liv. xxviii. 37. Phœnic. Inscr. in Ges. Lex.
25 Liv. xxx. 7.
26 Jos. c. Ap. i. 21.

Before CHRIST cir. 787.

the princes thereof with
him, saith the LORD.

4 ¶ Thus saith the
LORD; For three trans-
gressions of Judah, and for
four, I will not turn away
the punishment thereof; [f] because they have despised
the law of the LORD, and
have not kept his com-
mandments, and [g] their
lies caused them to err,
[h] after the which their
fathers have walked:

[f] Lev. 26. 14, 15. Neh. 1. 7. Dan. 9. 11.

[g] Is. 28. 15. Jer. 16. 19, 20. Rom. 1. 25.

[h] Ezek. 20. 13, 16, 18, 24, 30.

---

his death, they sent for Hiram his brother who reigned for twenty. The judges then exercised the supreme authority, the king's sons having been carried away captive. Probably, then, when Jeroboam II. recovered the old territory of Israel, Moab lost its kings. It agrees with this, that Amos says, *the princes thereof*, lit. *her princes*, the princes of Moab, not as of Ammon, *his princes*, i.e. the princes of the king.

4. *For three transgressions of Judah, &c.* "[1] Here too there is no difference of Jew and Gentile. The word of God, a just judge, spareth no man's person. Whom sin joins in one, the sentence of the Judge disjoins not in punishment." [2] *As many as have sinned without law, shall also perish without law, and as many as have sinned in the law, shall be judged by the law.* "[3] Those other nations, Damascus and the rest, he upbraids not for having *cast away the law of God*, and *despised His commandments;* for they had not the written law, but that of nature only. So then of them he says, that *they corrupted all their compassions*—and the like. But Judah, who, at that time, had the worship of God and the temple and its rites, and had received the law and commandments and judgments and precepts and testimonies, is rebuked and convicted by the Lord, for that it had *cast aside His law and not kept His commandments;* wherefore it should be punished as it deserved. And since they rejected and despised these, then, in course, *their lies deceived* them, i.e. their idols;" *lies* on their part who made them and worshiped them for the true God, and *lies* and lying to them, as deceiving their hopes. For *an idol is nothing in the world*[4], as neither are all the vanities in the world whereof men make idols, but they deceive by a vain shew, as though they were something. "[3] They would not have been deceived by their idols, unless they had first *rejected the law of the Lord and not done His commandments.*" They had sinned with a high hand, *despising* and so rejecting the law of God; and so He despised and rejected them, leaving them to be deceived by the lies which they themselves had chosen. So it ever is with man. Man must either[5] *love* God's *law* and *hate and abhor lies*, or he will despise God's law and cleave to lies. He first in act *despises* God's law, (and whoso does not keep it, despises it,) and then he must needs be deceived by some idol of his own, which becomes his God. He first chooses wilfully his own *lie*, i.e. whatever he chooses out of God, and then his own *lie* deceives him. So, morally, liars at last believe themselves. So, whatever false maxim any one has adopted against his conscience, whether in belief or practice, to justify what he wills against the Will of God, or to explain away what God reveals and he mislikes, stifling and lying to his conscience, in the end deceives his conscience, and at the last, a man believes that to be true, which, before he had lied to his conscience, he knew to be false. The Prophet uses a bold word in speaking of man's dealings with his God, *despises.* Man carries on the serpent's first fraud, *Hath God indeed said?* Man would not willingly own, that he is directly at variance with the Mind of God. Man, in his powerlessness, at war with Omnipotence, and, in his limited knowledge, with Omniscience! It were too silly, as well as too terrible. So he smoothes it over to himself, *lying* to himself. "God's word must not be taken so precisely;" "God cannot have meant;" "the Author of nature would not have created us so, if He had meant;" and all the other excuses, by which he would evade owning to himself that he is directly rejecting the Mind of God and trampling it under foot. Scripture draws off the veil. Judah had the law of God, and did not keep it; then, he *despised* it. On the one side was God's Will, His Eternal Wisdom, His counsel for man for good; on the other, what debasements! On the one side were God's awful threats, on the other, His exceeding promises. Yet man chose whatever he willed, lying to himself, and acting as though God had never threatened or promised or spoken. This ignoring of God's known Will and law and revelation is to despise them, as effectually as to *curse God to His face*[6]. This rejection of God was hereditary. Their lies were those *after which their fathers walked*, in Egypt and from Egypt onwards, in the wilderness[7], "[3] making the image of the calf of Egypt and worshiping Baalpeor and Ashtoreth and Baalim." Evil

[1] Rup. [2] Rom. ii. 12. [3] S. Jer. [4] 1 Cor. viii. 4. [5] Ps. cxix. 163. [6] Job. ii. 5. [7] See on v. 25, 6.

Before CHRIST cir. 787.

5 [l] But I will send a fire
upon Judah, and it shall
devour the palaces of Je-
rusalem.
6 ¶ Thus saith the
LORD; For three trans-
gressions of Israel, and for
four, I will not turn away
the punishment thereof; because [k] they sold the righteous for silver, and the
poor for a pair of shoes;

[l] Jer. 17. 27. Hos. 8. 14.

[k] Is. 29. 21. ch. 8. 6.

acquires a sort of authority by time. Men become inured to evils, to which they have been used. False maxims, undisputed, are thought indisputable. They are in possession; and "possession" is held a good title. The popular error of one generation becomes the axiom of the next. The descent *of the image of the great goddess Diana from Jupiter*, or of the Coran, becomes a *thing* which *cannot be spoken against*[1]. The *lies after which the fathers walked* deceive the children. The children canonize the errors of their fathers." Human opinion is as dogmatic as revelation. The second generation of error demands as implicit submission as God's truth. The transmission of error against Himself, God says, aggravates its evil, does not excuse it. "[10] Judah is the Church. In her the Prophet reproves whosoever, worshiping his own vices and sins, cometh to have that as a god by which he is overcome; as St. Peter saith[2], *Whereby a man is overcome, of the same is he brought in bondage*. The covetous worshipeth mammon; the glutton, his belly[3]; the impure, Baalpeor; she who, *living in pleasure, is dead while she liveth*[4], the pleasure in which she liveth." Of such idols the world is full. Every fair form, every idle imagination, everything which gratifies self-love, passion, pride, vanity, intellect, sense, each the most refined or the most debased, is such a *lie*, so soon as man loves and regards it more than his God.

5. *I will send a fire upon Judah.* All know now, how Jerusalem, its temple, and its palaces perished by fire, first by Nebuchadnezzar, then by the Romans. Yet some two centuries passed, before that first destruction came. The ungodly Jews flattered themselves that it would never come. So we know that a *fiery stream*[5] will issue and come forth from Him; *a fire* that *consumeth to destruction*[6] all who, whether or no they are in the body of the Church, are not of the heavenly Jerusalem; dead members in the body which belongs to the Living Head. And it will not the less come, because it is not regarded. Rather, the very condition of all God's judgments is, to be disregarded and to come, and then most to come, when they are most disregarded.

6. 7. *For three transgressions of Israel, and for four.* In Israel, on whom the Divine sentence henceforth rests, the Prophet numbers four classes of sins, running into one another, as all sins do, since all grievous sins contain many in one, yet in some degree distinct. 1) Perversion of justice; 2) oppression of the poor; 3) uncleanness; 4) luxury with idolatry.

They sold the righteous for silver. It is clear from the opposite statement, *that we may buy the poor for silver and the needy for a pair of shoes*, that the Prophet is not speaking of judicial iniquity, but of actual buying and selling. The law allowed a Hebrew who was poor to sell himself[7], and a Hebrew to buy him until the year of release; yet this too with the express reserve, that the purchaser was forbidden to *serve himself with him with the service of a slave, but as a hired servant and a sojourner shall he be with thee*[8]. The thief who could not repay what he stole, was to *be sold for his theft*[9]. But the law gave no power to sell an insolvent debtor. It grew up in practice. The sons and daughters of the debtor[10], or *his wife and children*[11], nay even the sons of a deceased debtor[12], were sold. Nehemiah rebuked this sharply. In that case, the hardness was aggravated by the fact that the distress had been fomented by usury. But the aggravation did not constitute the sin. It seems to be this merciless selling by the creditor, which Amos rebukes. The *righteous* is probably one who, without any blame, became insolvent. The *pair of shoes*, i.e. sandals, express the trivial price, or the luxury for which he was sold. They had him sold *for the sake of*[13] *a pair of sandals*, i.e. in order to procure them. Trivial in themselves, as being a mere sole, the sandals of the Hebrew women were, at times, costly and beautiful[14]. Such a sale expressed contempt for man, made in the image of God, that he was sold either for some worthless price, or for some needless adornment.

[1] Acts xix. 35, 6.
[2] 2 Pet. ii. 19.
[3] Phil. iii. 19.
[4] 1 Tim. v. 6.
[5] Dan. vii. 10.
[6] Job xxxi. 12.
[7] In Lev. xxv. 39. Deut. xv. 12. נמכר should be rendered, according to the first sense of the conjugation, *sell himself*, not, *be sold*.
[8] Lev. xxv. 39, 40.
[9] Ex. xxii. 2, 3.
[10] Neh. v. 5.
[11] S. Matt. xviii. 25.
[12] 2 Kgs iv. 1.
[13] בעבור
[14] Cant. vii. 1. Ez. xvi. 10. Judith xvi. 9.

Before CHRIST cir. 787.

7 That pant after the
dust of the earth on the
head of the poor, and [l]turn
aside the way of the meek:
[m]and a man and his father
will go in unto the *same*
‖ maid, [n]to profane my
holy name:

[l] Is. 10. 2. ch. 5. 12.

[m] Ezek. 22. 11.
‖ Or, *young woman.*
[n] Lev. 20. 3. Ezek. 36. 20. Rom. 2. 24.

7. *That pant after the dust of the earth;* lit. *the panters!* with indignation. Not content with having rent from him the little hereditary property which belonged to each Israelite, these creditors grudged him even the *dust*, which, as a mourner, he strewed on his head[1], since it too was *earth.* Covetousness, when it has nothing to feed it, craves for what is absurd or impossible. What was Naboth's vineyard to a king of Israel with his *ivory palace?* What was Mordecai's refusal to bow to one in honor like Haman? What a trivial gain to a millionaire? The sarcasm of the Prophet was the more piercing, because it was so true. Men covet things in proportion, not to their worth, but to their worthlessness. No one covets what he much needs. Covetousness is the sin, mostly not of those who have not, but of those who have. It grows with its gains, is the less satisfied, the more it has to satisfy it, and attests its own unreasonableness, by the uselessness of the things it craves for.

And turn aside the way of the meek. So Solomon said[2], *A wicked* man *taketh a bribe out of the bosom, to pervert the ways of judgment.* God had laid down the equality of man, made in His own image, and had forbidden to favor either poor[3] or rich[4]. Amos calls these by different names, which entitled them to human sympathy; *poor, depressed, lowly; poor,* in their absolute condition; *depressed*[5], as having been brought low; *lowly,* as having the special grace of their state, the wonderful meekness and lowliness of the godly poor. But all these qualities are so many incentives to injury to the ungodly. They hate the godly, as a reproach to them; because [6]*he is clean contrary to their doings, his life is not like other men's; his ways are of another fashion.* Wolves destroy, not wolves, but sheep. Bad men circumvent, not the bad, but the good. Besides the easiness of the gain, there is a devilish fascinating pleasure to the bad, to overreach the simple and meek, because they are such. They love also to *turn aside the way of the meek,* by "[7]turning them from what is truly right and good;" or from the truth; or again to thwart them in all their ways and endeavors, by open injustice or by perverting justice. Every act of wrong prepares the way for the crowning act; and so *the turning aside the way of the meek* foreshadowed and prepared for the unjust judgment of Him Who was *the Meek and Lowly One*[8]; the selling the righteous for a trifling sum prepared for the selling[9] *the Holy One and the Just* for the *thirty pieces of silver.* "[10]Contrariwise, whoso is truly wise, cordially venerates the humble and abject, the poor and simple, and prefers them in his own heart to himself, knowing that God has [11]*chosen the poor, and the weak things of the world, and things despised, and things which are not;* and that Christ hath likened Himself to such, saying in the Psalm, [12]*I am poor and sorrowful.*"

The same damsel. This is not expressly forbidden by the law, except in the case of marriage, the father being forbidden to marry his son's widow, and the son to take his father's widow to wife[13]. Abominations, unless they had become known to Israel in Egypt, were not expressly forbidden, but were included in the one large prohibition, which, as our Lord explains, forbade every offence, bearing upon it. Israel must have so understood the law, since Amos could upbraid them with this, which is not forbidden by the letter of the law, as a wilful insult to the Majesty of God. Reverence was due from the son to the father, example from the father to the son. But now the father was an example of evil to the son; and the son sinned in a way which had no temptation except its irreverence. Men, sated with ordinary sin seek incitement to sin, in its very horrors. Probably this sin was committed in connection with their idolworship[14]. The sin of marrying the father's widow was *fornication not so much as named among the Gentiles*[15]; it was unknown, as seemingly legalizing what was so unnatural. Oppression of the poor, wronging the righteous, perverting the way of the meek, laid the soul open for any abomination.

To profane My Holy Name, i. e. as called upon them, as the people of God. God had said, *ye shall keep My commandments and do them*[16]. *I am the Lord, and ye shall not defile My Holy Name. For I will be sanctified among the children of Israel. I am the Lord Who sanctify you.* The sins of God's people are a reproach upon Himself. They bring Him,

1 Job ii. 12.
2 Pr. xvii. 23. להטות ארחות with the same image as here דרך יטו.
3 Ex. xxiii. 3.
4 Ib. 6.
5 דל
6 Wisd. ii. 12, 15.
7 S. Cyr.
8 S. Matt. xi. 29.
9 Acts iii. 14.
10 Dion.
11 1 Cor. i. 27, 8.
12 Ps. lxix, 29.
13 Lev. xviii. 8, 15.
14 See on Hosea iv. 14.
15 1 Cor v. 1.
16 Levit. xxii. 31, 32. add Ib. xx. 3. xviii. 21. xxi. 6.

Before CHRIST cir. 787.

8 And they lay *themselves* down upon clothes °laid to pledge ᵖby every altar, and they drink the wine of ‖the condemned *in* the house of their god.

° Ex. 22. 26.
ᵖ Ezek. 23. 41. 1 Cor. 8. 10 & 10. 21.

‖ Or, *such as have fined*, or *mulcted.*

so to say, in contact with sin. They defeat the object of His creation and revelation. He created man in His Image, to bear His likeness, to have one will with Himself. In effect, through sin, He has created rebels, deformed, unlike. So long as He bears with them, it seems as if He were indifferent to them. Those to whom He has not revealed Himself, must needs think that He takes no account of what He permits unnoticed. Israel, whom God had separated from the Heathen, did, by *mingling with the Heathen and learning their works*[1], all which in them lay, to *profane* His *Holy Name.* They acted as if they had no other purpose than to defile it[2]. Had such been their object, they could not have done it more effectually, they could not have done otherwise. In deliberate sin men act, at last, in defiance of God, in set purpose to dishonor Him. The Name of God has ever since been blasphemed, on account of the sins of the Jews, as though it were impossible that God should have chosen for His own, a people so *laden with iniquities*[3]. Nathan's words to David[4], *Thou hast given great occasion to the enemies of the Lord to blaspheme*, have been fulfilled till this day. How much more, Christians, who not only are called "the people of God," but bear the name of Christ incorporated in their own. Yet have we not known Mohammedans flee from our Christian capital, in horror at its sins? "He lives like a Christian," is a proverb of the Polish Jews, drawn from the debased state of morals in Socinian Poland. The religion of Christ has no such enemies as Christians. "[5] As the devout by honoring God, shew that He is Holy, Great, Most High, Who is obeyed in holiness, fear and reverence, so the ungodly, by dishonoring God, exhibit God as far as in them lies, as if He were not Holy. For they act so as if evil were well-pleasing to Him, and induce others to dishonor Him. Wherefore the Apostle saith; *the name of God is blasphemed among the Gentiles through you*[6]; and by Ezekiel the Lord saith oftentimes, *Ye have profaned My Holy Name. And I will sanctify My great Name which was profaned among the heathen, which ye have profaned in the midst of them*[7]. The devout then are said to *magnify*, sanctify, *exalt God;* the unrighteous to *profane*[8], *despise*, God."

8. *They lay* themselves *down.* They condensed sin. By a sort of economy in the toil of sinning, they blended many sins in one; idolatry, sensuality, cruelty, and, in all, the express breach of God's commandments. The *clothes* here are doubtless the same as the *raiment* in the law, the large enfolding cloak, which by day was wrapped over the long loose shirt[9], the poor man's only dress besides, and by night was his only bedding[10]. God had expressly commanded[11], *If the man be poor, thou shalt not sleep with his pledge;* in any case *thou shalt deliver him the pledge again, when the sun goeth down, that he may sleep in his own raiment, and bless thee; and it shall be righteousness to thee before the Lord thy God.* Here the *garments laid to pledge* are treated as the entire property of the creditors. They *stretch*[12] their listless length along upon them in their idol-feasts *by every altar.* Ezekiel speaks of a *stately bed*, upon which they *sat, and a table prepared before it*[13]. Isaiah; *Upon a lofty and high mountain hast thou set up thy bed; even thither wentest thou up to offer sacrifice;— thou hast enlarged thy bed; thou hast loved their bed; thou providedst room*[14]. In luxury and state then, and withal in a shameless publicity, they *lay on the garments* of the despoiled *by every altar.* The multiplication of altars[15] was, in itself, sin. By each of these multiplied places of sin, they committed fresh sins of luxury and hard-heartedness, (perhaps, from the character of the worship of nature, yet grosser sins,) *and drink the wine of the condemned*, or (as the E. M. more exactly) *the amerced*, those whom, unjustly, persons in any petty judicial authority had *amerced*, expending in revelry and debauchery in the idol's temple what they had unjustly

1 Ps. cvi. 35.
2 See on Hos. viii. 4.
3 Is. i. 4.
4 2 Sam. xii. 14.
5 Dion.
6 Rom. ii. 24.
7 Ezek. xxxvi. 23.
8 Ib. xiii. 19.

9 כתנת χιτών. בגד, as well as שמלה, is used of the outside cloak, Gen. xxxix. 12, 13, 15. It is the more generic name, like our "clothes," except that it is chiefly used of large raiment and even of the outside covering, in which the ark, the table of shew-bread, &c. were covered in the journeys in the wilderness (E. V. cloth) Nu. iv. 6, 11, 13; and of the bed-coverings of the great. 1 Sam. xix. 13. 1 Kgs. i. 1. It is used also of state robes, 1 Kgs. xxii. 10. 2 Chr. xviii. 9. It is the word commonly used in the plural of "rending the clothes;" שמלה being used Gen. xxxvii. 34. xliv. 13. Josh. vii. 6 and מדין 1 Sam. iv. 12; else בגדים, whether of kings or others. It is the word used of "washing the clothes," except in Ex. xix. 10, 14. where שמלות is used.

10 Ex. xxii. 26. 7.
11 Deut. xxiv. 12, 13.

12 יטו, הטה is not used elsewhere of stretching out the person, but it is used intrans. of "turning aside," Is. xxx. 11. Job xxiii. 11. Ps. cxxv. 5; and מטה (like κλίνη, κλισία from κλίνω) is a place where one reclines at full length, bed, sofa, litter, or bier.

13 xxiii. 41.
14 lvii. 7, 8.
15 Hos. viii. 11. x. 1. xii. 11.

Before CHRIST cir. 787.

q Num. 21. 24. Deut. 2. 31. Josh. 24. 8.
r Num. 13. 28, 32, 33.

9 ¶ Yet destroyed I the
q Amorite before them,
r whose height *was* like the
height of the cedars, and
he *was* strong as the oaks;
yet I s destroyed his fruit
from above, and his roots
from beneath.

s Is. 5. 24. Mal. 4. 1.

extorted from the oppressed. There is no mask too transparent to serve to hide from himself one who does not wish to see himself. Nothing serves so well as religion for that self-deceit, and the less there is of it, or the more one-sided it is, the better it serves. For the narrower it is, the less risk of impinging on the awful reality of God's truth; and half a truth as to God is mostly, a lie which its half-truth makes plausible. So this dreadful assemblage of cruelty, avarice, malice, mockery of justice, unnatural debauchery, hard-heartedness, was doubtless smoothed over to the conscience of the ten tribes by that most hideous ingredient of all, that *the house of their god* was the place of their ill-purchased revelry. Men do not serve their idols for nothing; this costly service at Bethel was not for nought. They did all these things; but they did something for "the Deity" or "Nature" or "Ashtoreth;" and so "the Deity" was to be at peace with them. Amos, with wonderful irony, marks the ghastly mixture of sin and worship, *they drank the wine of the amerced*—where? *in the house of their God*, condemning in five words[1] their luxury, oppression, perversion of justice, cruelty, profaneness, unreal service and real apostacy. What hard-heartedness to the wilfully-forgotten poor is compensated by a little Church-going!

9. *Yet* [*and I*] *I* (Emphatic) *destroyed.* Such were *their* doings; such their worship of *their God.* And what had *God done?* what was it, which they thus requited?

The Amorite. These, as one of the mightiest of the Canaanite tribes, stand in Moses for all. Moses, in rehearsing to them the goodness of God and their backsliding, reminds them, how he had said[2], *Ye have come to the mountain of the Amorites, which the Lord your God giveth you;* and that they, using this same word, said[3], *Because the Lord hateth us, He hath brought us forth out of the land of Egypt, to give us into the hand of the Amorite to destroy us.* The aged Joshua, in rehearsing God's great deeds for Israel, places first by itself the destruction of the Amorite before them, with the use of this same idiom, [4]*I brought you into the land of the Amorites which dwelt on the other side of Jordan—and I destroyed them before you.* The Amorites were descended from the 4th son of Canaan[5]. At the invasion of Chedorlaomer, a portion of them[6] dwelt at Hazezon-Tamar or Engedi, half way on the W. side of the Dead Sea, and at Hebron near it[7]. Their corruption had not yet reached its height, and the return of Israel was delayed to the four hundredth year, *because the iniquity of the Amorite* was *not yet full*[8]. When Israel returned, the Amorites, (together with the Hittites and the Jebusites) held the hill country[9], Jerusalem, Hebron, Gibeon[10], and, on the skirts of the mountains Westward[11], Jarmuth, Lachish, and Eglon[12]. They dwelt on the side of the Jordan Westward[13], besides the two kingdoms which they had formed East of Jordan, reaching to Mount Hermon[14] and Bashan up to the territory of Damascus. Afterward a small remnant remained only in the portion of Dan, and in the outskirts of Judah, from the South of the Dead Sea, Maaleh Akrabbim (Scorpion-pass) and Petra[15]. Those near Idumea were probably absorbed in Edom; and the remnant in Dan, after becoming tributary to Ephraim[15], lost their national existence perhaps among the Philistines, since we have thenceforth only the single notice in the days of Samuel after the defeat of the Philistines, *there was peace between Israel and the Amorites*[16].

Whose height was *like the height of the cedars.* The giant sons of Anak were among the Amorites at *Hebron*[17] (called for a time Kiriath Arba[18] from their giant father) *Debir, Anab, and the mountains of Judah and Israel*[19]. *The valley of Rephaim*[20], S. W. of Jerusalem, connects this giant race with the Amorites, as does the fact that Og, king of the Amorites in Basan, was *of the remnant of the Rephaim*[21]. Basan and Argob were, in Moses' time, still called *the land of Rephaim*[22]. The Rephaim, with the Perizzites, dwelt still in woody mountains near Ephraim; whence,

1 ויין ענושים ישתו בית אלהיהם.
2 Deut. i. 20. 3 Ib. 27.
4 Josh. xxiv. 8. אל ארץ האמרי-ואשמידם מפניכם
Josh. ואנכי השמדתי את האמרי מפניכם Am.
Moses has the same idiom of God's act on behalf of Ammon and Edom. Deut. ii. 21, 22.
5 Gen. x. 16.
6 האמרי הישב "those Amorites who dwelt."
7 Ib. xiv. 7, 13. comp. xiii. 18. 2 Chr. xx. 2.
8 Ib. xv. 16.
9 Nu. xiii. 29. Deut. i. 7. 44. 10 2 Sam. xxi. 2.
11 Jarmuth, 10 miles N. of Eleutheropolis (Beth Jabrin); Eglon, 10 miles West; and Lachish, 7 miles S. Eus. S. Jer.
12 Josh. x. 3, 5. 13 Ib. v. 1. 14 Deut. iii. 8.
15 Jud. i. 35, 6. 16 1 Sam. vii. 14. 17 Nu. xiii. 22.
18 Josh. xiv. 15. xv. 13, 14. 19 Ib. xi. 21.
20 2 Sam. v. 18. 21 Deut. iii. 11. Josh. xii. 4. xiii. 12.
22 Deut. iii. 13.

Before CHRIST cir. 787.

[t] Ex. 12. 51. Mic. 6. 4.
[u] Deut. 2. 7. & 8. 2.

10 Also [t] I brought you
up from the land of Egypt,
and [u] led you forty years
through the wilderness, to
possess the land of the
Amorite.

Before CHRIST cir. 787.

---

on the complaint that the lot of the sons of Joseph was too narrow, Joshua bade his tribe to expel them[1]. The Rephaim are mentioned between the Perizzites and the Amorites[2], in God's first promise of the land to Abraham's seed, and perhaps some intermixture of race gave the giant stature to the Amorites. It is clear from Amos that the report of the spies, *all the people that we saw in it were men of stature*[3], was no exaggeration, nor did Joshua and Caleb deny *this*. The name of the Amorite[4], is probably connected with "commanding," describing some quality of their forefather, which descended to his race.

Whose height was *like the height of cedars.* Giant height is sometimes a cause of weakness. Amos, in a degree like Hosea[5], combines distinct images to make up the idea of stateliness and strength. The cedar is the ideal of Eastern trees for height[6], stretching forth its arms as for protection. "[7] It groweth to an exceeding height, and with increasing time ever riseth higher." The oak has its Hebrew name from strength[8]. The more majestic the tall strength of the Amorite, the more manifest that Israel[9] *gat not the land in possession by their own sword*, who had counted themselves, in sight of the Amorite, *as grasshoppers*[10]. God, Who gave him that strength, took it away, as we say, "root and branch," leaving him no shew above, no hope of recovered life below[11]. Having compared each Amorite to a majestic tree, he compares the excision of the whole nation to the cutting down of that one tree[12], so swift, so entire, so irrecoverable. Yet the destruction of the Amorite, a mercy to Israel in the purpose of God, was a warning to Israel when it became as they. God's terrors are mercies to the repentant; God's mercies are terrors to the impenitent. [13] *Ye shall keep My statutes and My judgments and shall not commit* any *of these abominations*, was the tenure upon which they held the Lord's land, *that the land spue not you out also, when ye defile it, as it spued out the nations that were before you.*

10. *Also I* (lit. *And I, I*, emphatic; thus and thus did ye to Me; and thus and thus, with all the mercy from the first, did *I* to you,) *I brought you up from the land of Egypt.* It is this language in which God, in the law, reminded them of that great benefit, as a motive to obedience[14]; *I brought thee forth out of the land of Egypt, out of the house of bondage;* only there, since God has not as yet *brought them up* into the land which He promised them, but they were yet in the wilderness, He says, *brought them forth;* here, *brought them up*[15], as to a place of dignity, His own land.

And led you forty years through the wilderness. These are the very words of the law[16], and reminded them of so many benefits during the course of those *forty years*, which the law rehearsed; the daily supply of manna, the water from the rock, the deliverance from the serpents and other perils, the manifold forgivenesses. To be *led forty years through*

---

[1] Josh. xvii. 15, 18. [2] Gen. xv. 20, 1. [3] Nu. xiii. 32.

[4] The idea of physical height does not exist in the root *amar* in any Semitic language. In the only word alleged in Hebrew, it has been inferred from the context, rather than from any knowledge as to the word itself, that אמיר (which occurs in Is. xvii. 6, 9. only) signifies *uppermost branch*. The Vulg. however, Chald. and Saadia render it "branch" only, in which case אמיר would be equivalent to the Syriac 'Amiro. The LXX. alone has μετεώρου. Even if אמיר have the meaning "uppermost," this would probably be by way of metaphor from the Arabic *Emir* (from which Aben Ezra derives it) as we speak of "a *commanding* height," and so would not imply that the idea of physical elevation ever existed in the root. 2) If the word had had the meaning of height, it would describe the high stature of the forefather of the tribe and the tribe itself, as Rephaim from Rapha' (tall), Enakim from Anek (long-necked). We use the word "heights," but we should not infer that "high" meant "a dweller on heights," a "mountaineer." 3) This meaning, which writers of late have, one after the other, ascribed to אמרי, would obviously have been expressed by the word הררי, as derived from the common Hebrew word for mountain, הר. (Perhaps this does exist 2 Sam. xxiii. 11. 33.) 4) The word (even if it had the meaning,) would not be characteristic of the Amorites, since the Jebusites and the Hittites and the Rephaim equally dwelt in the mountains: and the Amorites did not dwell in the mountains only. The apparent object of this unlikely inference from imagined etymology is to find a meaning for the names of the Canaanite nations, expressive of some local circumstance. But as to the names of the sons of Canaan as also that of Canaan himself, the attempt obviously fails as to all enumerated in Gen. x. 15–18. The Perizzites, who are perhaps persons "living in the open country," are not there mentioned.

[5] See ab. p. 90.

[6] Is. ii. 13. Ezek. xvii. 22. xxxi. 3. 1 Kgs iv. 33. 2 Kgs xiv. 9.

[7] Comm. in Is. ii. 13. ap. S. Basil. Opp.

[8] אלון from אלל i. q. אול as the Latin, "robur."

[9] Ps. xliv. 3. [10] Nu. xiii. 33.

[11] See Hos. ix. 16. Job xviii. 16. Ezek. xvii. 9.

[12] Dion. [13] Lev. xviii. 26, 38.

[14] Ex. xx. 2. Deut. v. 6. vi. 12.

[15] In the Pentateuch, הוצאתיך מארץ מצרים; here, העליתי אתכם מארץ מצרים.

[16] Deut. xxix. 4. [5 Eng.] only slightly transposing the במדבר. In Deut. ואולך אתכם ארבעים שנה במדבר; here, ואולך אתכם במדבר ארבעים שנה.

Before CHRIST cir. 787.

11 And I raised up of your sons for prophets, and

the wilderness, alone, had been no kindness, but a punishment. It was a blending of both. The abiding in the wilderness was punishment or austere mercy, keeping them back from the land which they had shewn themselves unqualified to enter: God's *leading* them was, His condescending mercy. The words, taken from the law, must have re-awakened in the souls of Israelites the memory of mercies which they did not mention, how that same book relates[1] *He found him in a desert land, and in the waste howling wilderness; He led him about; He instructed him; He kept him as the apple of His eye. The Lord alone did lead him.* [2] *In the wilderness, where thou hast seen how that the Lord thy God bare thee, as a man doth bear his son, in all the way that ye went until ye came to this place;* or that minute tender care, mentioned in the same place[3], *your clothes are not waxen old upon you, and thy shoe is not waxen old upon thy foot.* But unless Israel had known the law well, the words would only have been very distantly suggestive of mercy, that it must have been well with them even in the wilderness, since God *led them*. They had then the law in their memories, in Israel also[4], but distorted it or neglected it.

11. *And I raised up of your sons for Prophets.* Amos turns from outward mercies to inward, from past to present, from miracles of power to miracles of grace. God's past mercies live on in those of to-day; the mercies of to-day are the assurance to us that we have a share in the past; His miracles of grace are a token that the miracles of His power are not our condemnation. God had, from the time of Moses, *raised up* prophets. Eldad and Medad[5] were images of those, whom God would raise up beyond the bounds of His promise. The divine Samuel was an Ephrathite[6]; Ahijah the Shilonite, i. e. of Shiloh in Ephraim, lived on to old age[7] in the kingdom of the ten tribes after their schism, the witness against the apostacy of Jeroboam[8], yet acknowledged by the king whose rise and of the destruction of whose house he prophesied[7]. Jehu, son of Hanani, was the prophet of both kingdoms[9]; Micaiah, son of Imlah, was well known to Ahab, as *prophesying evil concerning him*[10] continually; unknown to Jehoshaphat[11]. That wondrous pair, marvelous for superhuman sanctity and power among the marvelous miracles of God, Elijah and Elisha, were both *sons* of Israel, whom God *raised up; Elijah the Tishbite*[12], born doubtless at Thisbe, a village of Naphthali[13], and one of the sojourners[14] in Gilead; Elisha of Abelmeholah[15], on the West side of the valley of the Jordan[16]. And even now He had raised up to them of their own *sons*, Hosea and Jonah. Their presence was the presence of God among them, Who, out of the ordinary way of His Providence, *raised* them *up* and filled them with His Spirit; and where the Presence of God is, if there is fear, yet there is also hope.

And of your young men for Nazarites. The Nazarite was a fruit of the grace of God in its moral and religious workings, superhuman in holiness and self-denial, as the Prophets were of that same grace, conferring superhuman wisdom and knowledge also. Of both, God says, *I raised up*, teaching that both alike, holiness of life and superhuman wisdom, were His own special gift to each individual, His own creation. God surveyed His people, called, and *raised up*, by His grace, out of the crowd, those souls which responded to His call. The life of the Nazarites was a continual protest against the self-indulgence and worldliness of the people. It was a life above nature. Unless any prophet like Samuel[17], was also a Nazarite, they had no special office except to live that life. Their life taught. Nay, it taught in one way the more, because they had no special gifts of wisdom or knowledge, nothing to distinguish them from ordinary men, except extraordinary grace. They were an evidence, what all might do and be, if they used the grace of God. The power of the grace of God shews itself the more wondrously in those who have nought beside. The essence of the Nazarite life, as expressed by its name[18], was "separation," separation from things of the world, with a view to God. The separation was not, necessarily, for more than a limited time. In such case, it answered to the strictness of the Christian Lent. It was a considerable discipline for a time. In those simpler days, when luxury

[1] Deut. xxxii. 10, 12. [2] Ib. i. 31.
[3] Deut. xxix. 4. [5. Eng.] only slightly transposing the במדבר. In Deut. ואולך אתכם ארבעים שנה במדבר; here, ואולך אתכם במדבר ארבעים שנה.
[4] See Introd. to Amos p. 152. [5] Nu. xi. 26–9.
[6] 1 Sam. i. 1. [7] 1 Kgs xiv. 2, 4.
[8] Ib. 7-14. xv. 29.
[9] Ib. xvi. 1, 7, 12. 2 Chr. xix. 2. xx. 34.
[10] 1 Kgs xxii. 8, 18. [11] Ib. 7. [12] Ib. xvii. 1.
[13] Tob. i. 2. See Reland, 1035. Eus. and S. Jer. mention the village Thisbe.
[14] מתושבי. [15] 1 Kgs xix. 16.
[16] See 1 Kgs iv. 12. Eus. S. Jer. say, "it is now a village, in the valley of the Jordan, 10 miles South of Scythopolis [Bethshean] and is now called Bethmaela [our copies of Jerome have Bethaula]. There is also [a little village S. Jer.]. Abelmea, on the way from Neapolis [Nablus] to Scythopolis."
[17] 1 Sam. i. 11. [18] נזיר.

Before CHRIST cir. 787.

of your young men for [x]Nazarites. *Is it* not even thus, O ye children of Israel? saith the Lord.

Before CHRIST cir. 787.

x Num. 6. 2. Judg. 13. 5.

had not been so busy[1], the absolute prohibition of anything fermented[2], whether from the grape or any other substance[3], or vinegar made of either, or any liquor or refreshing food or drink, made in any way from the grape, fresh or dry, its husks or its kernels, while it cut off every evasion, involved the giving up not only every drink, in any way exciting or stimulating, but very much also, which was refreshing. Water, which in the East has seldom the freshness of ours, was their only drink. This, which to individuals may be an easy rule, would not be so in the main. Those only think an undeviating rule slight, who have never tried one, nor set themselves on system to conquer self-will. Such a rule would not be acted upon, except for God. The long never-shorn hair was probably intended to involve the neglect of personal appearance. Yet this was the body only of the vow; its soul was the dedication to God. The Nazarite not only *separated himself from*[4] those earthly things; he *separated himself to* the Lord[5]: he *consecrated to the Lord the days of his separation*[6]: *all the days of his separation he* was *holy to the Lord*[7]: *the separation of his God* was *upon his head*[8]. The vow was a great and singular thing. *When man or woman shall vow a special vow of a Nazarite*[9]. The ritual of the Nazarite likened him to the priest. Giving him no priestly office, it yet even intensified some of the rules of the priesthood. The priest was to abstain from wine and strong drink, only *when* he *went into the tabernacle of the congregations*, that he might *put difference between holy and unholy, and teach Israel the statutes* of the Lord[10]: the Nazarite, so long as he remained such. The priest might defile himself for certain very near dead[11]; the high priest alone and the Nazarite, *neither for father nor mother*[12]: and that for the kindred reason; the high priest, *because the crown of the anointing oil of his God* was *upon him;* the Nazarite, *because the consecration of his God* was *upon his head!* His consecrated hair was called by the self-same name[13] as the mitre of the priest. It appears to have been woven into *seven locks*[14], itself a number of consecration. If his consecration came to an end, that hair was mingled with the sacrifice[15], and on *his* hands alone, besides the priest's at his consecration, was part of the offering laid[16]. All Israel was, in God's purpose, *a kingdom of priests*[17]; and, among them, the Nazarite was brought yet nearer, not to the priest's office, but to his character. This must have diffused itself indefinitely through the outward and inward life. Further strictness probably lay in the spirit of the vow. The outward appearance of the Nazarites appears to have been changed by their abstemiousness[18]. *Her Nazarites were purer than snow; they were whiter than milk.* Their countenance had that transparent[19] purity, which sometimes results from a pure abstemious life; as S. Athanasius is said to have been "bloodless." S. John Baptist, the counterpart of Elijah, ate only of the food of the wilderness, *locusts and wild honey;* his clothing was the hair cloth[20]. Of S. James the Just it is related with reference to the Nazarite vow; "[21]He was holy from his mother's womb; wine and strong drink he drank not, nor ate any living thing; the razor came not up upon his head; he anointed him not with oil, and he used not a bath." Nazarites there had been in the most disorganized times of Israel. The histories of Samson and Samuel stand over against one another, as Nazarites who, the one forfeited, the other persevered in, his vocation. Elijah's ascetic character is as if he had been one of them, or deepened the lines of their rule. Ahaziah's ungodly messengers described him contemptuously as *a man, lord of hair*, as though he had nothing but his prophet's broad mantle of hair, and *the leathern girdle about his loins*[22]. The Rechabites, although Kenites by origin[23], had been enrolled in the people of God, and had received a rule from their father, uniting with

1 Coffee, though invented for vigils, was adopted as a compensation for Mohammed's prohibition of wine. See the history in de Sacy, Chrest. Arab. T. i. p. 412. ed. 2.

2 Nu. vi. 3, 4.

3 The *strong drink* (שכר) was the more comprehensive, because it was undefined. S. Jerome enumerates, as prohibited under it, "every inebriating drink, whether made of barley, or juice of apples, or when honey is decocted into a sweet barbarian drink, or liquor is expressed from the date, or when water is colored and thickened by boiled fruit." (Ep. ad Nepotian.) Accordingly beer, cider, mead (οἰνόμελι) or "dibs," datewine, and any other fermented liquor, of whatever, (like our British wines,) it might be made, was forbidden.

4 Nu. vi. 3. 5 Ib. 2, 5, 6. 6 Ib. 12. 7 Ib. 8. 8 Ib. 7.

9 Ib. 2. כי יפלא לנדר נדר נזיר. In Lev. xxvii. 2. the E. V. renders the same word and form, יפלא נדר *make a singular vow.*

10 Lev. x. 9–11. 11 Lev. xxi. 1–3.

12 Ib. 11, 12. Nu. vi. 7. 13 נזר Nu. vi. 19.

14 Jud. xvi. 13. 15 Nu. vi. 18. 16 Ib. 19.

17 Ex. xix. 6. 18 Lam. iv. 7.

19 The LXX. render זכה Ex. xxx. 34 by *διαφανής*.

20 S. Luke i. 15. vii. 33. S. Matt. iii. 4.

21 Hegesippus in Eus. H. E. ii. 23.

22 2 Kgs. i. 8. The mention of the girdle shews that the *hair* was the "garment of hair," (Zech. xiii. 4. Heb. xi. 37) not the Nazarite's hair.

23 1 Chr. ii. 55.

Before CHRIST cir. 787.

12 But ye gave the Nazarites wine to drink;

Before CHRIST cir. 787.

the abstinence of the Nazarites, a mode of life which kept them aloof from the corruptions of cities[1]. The rules of their Nomadic life were consecrated to God, for He says[2], *There shall not be cut off from Jonadab, the son of Rechab, a man standing before Me for ever,* i. e. as the servant of God. God uses as to them the term which marks the service of the Levites[3], Priests[4], and Prophets[5]. Jonadab, the author of their rule, was plainly an ascetic, through whose presence Jehu hoped to cast a religious character over his ambitious execution of God's command[6]. But the value which the artful, though impetuous[7], bloodstained, captain attached to the presence of the ascetic shews the weight which they had with the people. Strange sight it must have been, the energetic warrior in his coat of mail, and the ascetic, as energetic, in his hair-cloth. Deeper far the contrast within. But the more marvelous the contrast, the more it attests the influence which the unworldly ascetic had over the world. Like the garb of the prophets, their appearance was a standing rebuke to a life of sense. Like the patriarchs, it professed that they were *strangers and pilgrims upon the earth.* They who sought nothing of the world or of time, were a witness to the belief in their eternal home. The Nazarites must now have been a numerous body, since Amos speaks of them, as a known class, like the prophets, of whose numbers we hear incidentally[8]. Yet the memory of these, who, amid the general corruption, were, each in his own sphere, centres of pure faith and life, is embalmed in these few words only. So little reason is there to think that God's commands were neglected by all, because their observance is not related. Amos appeals publicly to the people that the fact was so, that God had raised up Nazarites as well as prophets among them. He had His *little flock*[9], His *seven thousand*[10], who escaped the eye even of Elijah. The gift of the Nazarites was a special favor to Israel, as a memorial what the grace of God could do for man, what man could do, with the grace of God. His *raising up Nazarites, out of their young men,* men in their first bloom of unmarried[11], virgin[12], life, their picked "very chosen men[13]," such as furnished the prime of their warriors[14], strengthened that teaching. Even now, one devoted to God in his youth is a witness for God, leaven of the world around him. But the Nazarite had also to bear an outward mark for good, to be singular. His appearance bespoke that he had chosen God. His vow was not only a living up to the law; it lay beyond the law, the free-will offering of those whom God called. At an age, when so many do things unlawful, to gratify passion, these abstained even from things lawful. "Canst thou not do what these youths and these maidens can? or can they either in themselves, and not rather in the Lord their God?" was St. Augustine's upbraiding of himself[15], on the eve of his conversion, in thought of those who were living a devoted virgin life.

Is it not even thus? It were enough that God, the Truth, said it. But He condemns not, without giving space for excuse or defense. So he describes the Day of Judgment[16]. *The books were opened,—and the dead were judged out of those things which were written in the books, according to their works*[17]. Now, in the time of grace, the question asks, what, written under the picture of Christ crucified, once converted a sinner; "This have I done for thee: What doest thou for Me?" What did they? What had they done? What would they do?

12. *But ye gave the Nazarites wine to drink;* lit. *and,* (this, on their part, was the consequence of what God did for them) *ye caused the Nazarites to drink wine.* God appointed; Israel strove to undo His appointment. God *raised up Nazarites,* as a testimony to them; they sought to make His servants break their vow, in order to rid themselves of that testimony. Their pains to destroy it, is a strong proof of its power. The world is mad against true religion, because it feels itself condemned by it. Men set themselves against religion and the religious, the Church or the Priesthood, only when and because they feel their power

1 Jer. xxxv. 7, 9. 2 Ib. 19. 3 Deut. x. 8.
4 Jud. xx. 28. 5 I Kgs xvii. 1.
6 2 Kgs x. 15, 16, 23. Jehonadab, beforehand, was present to observe if there were any worshipers of God, in Baal's temple; his influence was not with the Baal-worshipers, but with the vacillating people.
7 Ib. ix. 20.
8 See Introduction to Hosea, p. 6. Obadiah saved the lives of *an hundred prophets.* 1 Kgs xviii. 4.
9 S. Luke xii. 32. 10 1 Kgs xix. 18.
11 Ruth iii. 10. (in ii. 9. where there was no emphasis, נְעָרִים is used) Is. lxii. 5.
12 Hence joined with בתולה "virgin," Deut. xxxii. 25. 2 Chr. xxxvi. 17. Jer. li. 22. and in the plur. Ps. lxxviii. 63. cxlviii. 12. Is. xxiii. 4. Jer. xxxi. 13. Lam. i. 18. ii. 21. Zech. ix. 17. and by Amos himself, viii. 13.
13 בחור is, by its form, intensive, not "chosen" only, but "greatly chosen." It is nowhere used without emphasis.
14 Hence in the idiom "shall slay their young men with the sword," &c. 2 Kgs. viii. 12. Jer. xi. 22. xv. 8. xviii. 21. &c. Ezek. xxx. 17, and in the remaining place in Amos iv. 10.
15 Conf. viii. 27. p. 152. Oxf. Tr.
16 S. Matt. xxv. 24–30. 41–5. xxii. 11.
17 Rev. xx. 12.

Before CHRIST cir. 787.

and commanded the prophets,[y] saying, Prophesy not.

[y] Is. 30. 10. Jer. 11. 21. ch. 7. 12, 13. Mic. 2. 6.

on God's side against them. What men despise, they do not oppose. "They kill us, they do not despise us," were true words of a French priest, as to the "reign of reason" in the first French revolution. Had the men in power not respected the Nazarites, or felt that the people respected them, they would not have attempted to corrupt or to force them to break their vow. The word, *cause* them *to drink*, does not express whether they used constraint or seduction. Israel's consciences supplied it. Yet since they *persecuted the prophets* and put them to death, it seems likely that Amos means that they used violence, either by forcing the wine into their mouths, as the swine-flesh was forced into the mouth of Eleazar[1], and, in the Decian persecution an infant was made to eat of the idol oblation[2], or by threat of death.

And commanded the prophets, saying, Prophesy not. God had commanded the prophets to prophesy. Israel issued and laid upon them his commands against the commands of God. The more God reveals His Will, the directer and more determinate the opposition of those who will not yield. God's perseverance in trying to win them irritates them; they oppose grace, and are angered at not being let alone. This large statement of Amos means much more than the prohibition of Amaziah to himself[3]. Jeroboam I. was prevented only by miracle[4] from seizing the prophet who denounced the altar at Bethel. Ahab, during the famine foretold by Elijah, sought him everywhere to destroy him[5], and Jezebel, after the miracle at Carmel and the death of her prophets, swore by her gods to do so[6]. Ahab's last act was to imprison Micaiah[7], the son of Imlah, for prophesying his death, when adjured by himself to speak truly. Ahaziah, his son, undeterred by the fire from heaven which destroyed two captains, each with his fifty, sent yet a 3d to take Elijah, when he prophesied that the king would not recover from his sickness[8]. Jehoram, his 2d son, swore by God to destroy Elisha[9], laying the evils of the siege to the Prophet, as the Romans did the evils of their decaying empire to the Christian. Micah and Isaiah, a little later, speak of such opposition, in Judah, as habitual[10]; much more in Israel, where the opposition to God's law was more fundamental, and where God's prophet's had been all but exterminated. Even Asa, in his degenerate days, imprisoned Hanani for prophesying that he would *have wars*[11]; Joash slew Zechariah son of Jehoiada[12]; Amaziah silenced the prophet who rebuked him[13], *Art thou made of the king's counsel? forbear. Why shouldest thou be smitten?* Jehoiakim sent even into Egypt to fetch Uriah and slew him[14]. Jeremiah's life was one continuous encounter with false accusations[15], contradictions by false prophets[16], hatred[17], mockery[18], persecution[19], imprisonment[20], attempts to destroy him[21]. The complaint was, as here, *wherefore dost thou prophesy*[22]? What, when our Lord gives it as the characteristic of Jerusalem[23], that she was "the slayer of the prophets, the stoner of those sent unto her?" They would not have slain the prophets, if they could have silenced them. Men are loth to go to extremities with God; they will make an armistice with Him; their awe of holiness makes them inwardly shrink from laying hands on it. Like the wolf in the fable, they must have a plea against it; and that plea against those who have the truth is obstinacy[24]. If the Christians would have abstained from converting the world, they would not have been persecuted. The Chief-priests at first sought simply to silence the Apostles[25]; then they enforced their command with scourges[26]; then persecuted them and the Christians to death[27]. Direct contumacy to God's known voice and silencing His messenger, is a last stage of obduracy and malice, which leaves God no further avenue to the soul or the people. His means of grace are exhausted when the soul or people not only deaden His voice within, but obstruct it without. One who, through vehemence of his passions, refuses to hear, is within the reach of the grace of God, afterward. He who stifles God's word to others has mostly hardened his heart deliberately and maliciously in unlove to man, as well as contempt of God. Hence God speaks, as though this brought the day of grace to a close.

[1] 2 Macc. vi. 18.
[2] S. Cyprian on the lapsed § 16. p. 169. Oxf. Tr.
[3] vii. 13.
[4] 1 Kgs xiii. 4.
[5] Ib. xviii. 10–12.
[6] Ib. xix. 2, 3.
[7] Ib. xxii. 26, 7.
[8] 2 Kgs i. 9–13.
[9] Ib. vi. 31.
[10] Mic. ii. 6. Is. xxx. 10, 11.
[11] 2 Chr. xvi. 7, 10.
[12] Ib. xxiv. 20, 1.
[13] Ib. xxv. 15, 16.
[14] Jer. xxvi. 20–3.
[15] Ib. xx. 10. xxxvii. 13. xxxviii. 4.
[16] Ib. xxiii. 17 sqq. xxvii. 9, 10, 14–16. xxviii. xxix.
[17] Ib. xv. 10.
[18] Ib. xvii. 15. xx. 7, 8. xxiii. 33.
[19] Ib. xvii. 18.
[20] Ib. xx. 2. xxxii. 3. xxxiii. 1. xxxvii. 15–21. xxxviii. 6–13.
[21] Ib. xi. 18–21 xviii. 18, 20–23. xxvi. 8 sqq. xxxvi. 26.
[22] Ib. xxxii. 3.
[23] S. Matt. xxiii. 37. *ἡ ἀποκτείνουσα τοὺς προφήτας καὶ λιθοβολοῦσα.*
[24] See on Tert. de spect. 1. p. 189. n. f. Oxf. Tr.
[25] Acts iv. 18, 21.
[26] Ib. v. 40.
[27] Ib. vii. 57–9. viii. 1–4. ix. 1, 2. xii. 1–3. xxii. 4, 5.

Before CHRIST cir. 787.

13 [z] Behold, || I am
pressed under you, as a
cart is pressed *that is* full
of sheaves.
14 [a] Therefore the flight
shall perish from the swift,
and the strong shall not
strengthen his force, [b] neither shall the mighty de-
liver † himself:
15 Neither shall he
stand that handleth the
bow; and *he that is* swift
of foot shall not deliver
himself: [c] neither shall he
that rideth the horse de-
liver himself.
16 And *he that is* † courageous among the mighty
shall flee away naked
in that day, saith the
LORD.

z Is. 1. 14.
|| Or, *I will press your place, as a cart full of sheaves presseth.*
a Jer. 9. 23. ch. 9. 1, &c.
b Ps. 33. 16.
† Heb. *his soul*, or, *life.*
c Ps. 33. 17.
† Heb. *strong of his heart.*

13. *Behold, I am pressed under you.* God bore His people, as the wain bears the sheaves. *Ye yourselves have seen,* He said to them by Moses[1], how *I bare you on eagle's wings, and brought you unto Myself.* [2] *Thou hast seen how the Lord thy God bare thee, as a man doth bear his son, in all the way that ye went, until ye came into this place.* And by Isaiah[3], *He bare them and carried them all the days of old;* and [4], *which are born* by Me *from the belly, which are carried from the womb.* Now, He speaks of Himself as wearied by them, as by Isaiah[5], *thou hast wearied Me with thine iniquities;* and by Malachi[6], *ye have wearied the Lord: yet ye say, wherewith have we wearied Him?* His long-suffering was, as it were, worn out by them. He was straitened under them, as the wain groans under the sheaves with which it is over-full. The words are literally, *Behold I, I* [emphatic *I*, your God, of Whom it would seem impossible] *straiten myself* [i. e. of My own Will allow Myself to be straitened] *under you*[7], *as the wain full for itself,* i. e. as full as ever it can contain, is *straitened, groans,* as we say. God says, (the word in Hebrew is half active) that He allows Himself to be straitened, as in Isaiah He says, *I am weary to bear,* lit., "I let Myself be wearied." *We* are simply passive under weariness or oppressiveness: God endures us, out of His own free condescension in enduring us. But it follows, that when He shall cease to endure our many and grievous sins, He will cast them and the sinner forth from Him.

14-16. Israel relied, against God, on his own strength. *Have we not,* they said[8], *taken to us horns by our own strength?* Amos tells them then, that every means of strength, resistance, flight, swiftness of foot, of horse, place of refuge, should fail them. Three times he repeats, as a sort of dirge, *he shall not deliver himself.*

Therefore the flight (probably *place of flight*[9],) *shall perish.* They had despised God, as their *place of refuge*[10], so *the place of refuge should perish from the swift,* as though it were not. He should flee amain, but there would be *no place to flee unto.* God alone *renews strength;* therefore *the strong* man should not *strengthen his force* or *might,* should not be able to gather or "collect his strength[11]," as we say. Fear should disable him. *The handler of the bow*[12], and who by habit is a skilled archer, although himself out of the immediate reach of the enemy, and able, unharmed, to annoy him and protect the fugitives, *shall not stand*[13]. Panic should overtake him. The *mighty* man, the *fleet of foot* should *not deliver,* yea, *the horseman* should not *deliver himself;* yea, he who, *among the mighty,* was *strongest of his heart,* firm-souled among those of mightiest prowess, *shall flee away naked,* i. e. bared of all, armor[14] or dress, which might encumber his flight *in that day,* which the Lord made a day of terror, His own day.

Saith the Lord. Probably lit. *the secret utterance*[15] *of the Lord.* Amos, more than Hosea, uses this special authentication of his words[16], which is so common in Isaiah, Jeremiah,

[1] Ex. xix. 4. [2] Deut. i. 31. [3] lxiii. 9.
[4] xlvi. 3. [5] xliii. 24. [6] ii. 17.

[7] The E. M. gives as a choice, the rendering, "I will press your place, as a cart full of sheaves presseth." But 1) תחת never occurs as the first object of a verb. In Job xxxvi. 20. xl. 12. it stands absolutely, as with the intrans. verb, Hab. iii. 7. 2) Nor is the object pressed down omitted, as if "press down under you," could stand for "press *you* down." 3) Nor is the slight track made by a two-wheeled cart (such as is used in the East and in many mountainous countries) likely to be an image of the utter crushing of a people. [8] vi. 13.

[9] So מנוס probably means in the same idiom, Job xi. 20. Ps. cxlii. 5. Jer. xxv. 35.

[10] מנוס is so used as to God, 2 Sam. xxii. 3. Ps. lix. 17. Jer. xvi. 19.

[11] So Prov. xxiv. 5.

[12] As in Jer. xlvi. 9. תפשי מגן.

[13] As in Jer. xlvi. 21. Nah. ii. 8.

[14] As Livy speaks of persons "unarmed and naked," iii. 23; or S. Peter is said to be "naked," before he had girt on his upper garment, (ἐπενδυτης) S. Joh. xxi. 7; and Virgil directs his husbandmen to "plough and sow naked," Georg. i. 229. i. e. unencumbered with the upper dress.

[15] From the Arab.

[16] At the end of the sentence, here and iii. 13, 15. iv. 3, 5, 6, 8, 9, 10, 11. ix. 8. 12; in the middle, iii. 10. vi. 8, 14, viii. 3, 9, 11. ix. 7, 13.

Before CHRIST cir. 787.

CHAPTER III.

1 *The necessity of God's judgment against Israel.* 9 *The publication of it, with the causes thereof.*

HEAR this word that the
LORD hath spoken
against you, O children of
Israel, against the whole
family which I brought up
from the land of Egypt,
saying,
2 [a] You only have I

[a] Deut. 7. 6. & 10, 15. Ps. 147. 19, 20.

Ezekiel, and Zechariah. He claims a knowledge, which those around him had not, and ratifies it by the express appeal to the direct, though secret, revelation of God; what those who were not of God, would deny; what they who were of God, would believe.

III. 1. Amos, like Hosea, rebukes Israel directly, Judah indirectly. He had warned each nation separately. Now, ere he concentrates himself on Israel, he sums up what he had before said to Judah and in the Person of God. "Ye have been alike in My gifts to you, alike in your waste of them and your sins; alike ye shall be in your punishment." What was said to Israel was said also to Judah: what was directed first to the former people, belongs to us, the later. What Jesus said to the Apostles, He said also to the Church, and to single souls, [1] *What I say unto you, I say unto all, Watch.*

1. *Hear ye this word.* With that solemn threefold call, so frequent in the Old Testament, he summons them thrice [2], as in the Name of the Holy Trinity, to hear God's words. "[3] The Prophet, at the outset of the chapter, rouses the hearers to anxious consideration. For the words of the most High God are to be heard, not with a superficial, unawed, wandering mind, but with reverence, fear, and love."

That the Lord hath spoken against (and upon [4]) *you,* (coming down *from heaven* [5], both *upon* and *against* them) *the whole family which I brought up from the land of Egypt.* To Abraham God had said [6], *in thee shall all the families of the earth be blessed.* So now, in withdrawing that blessing from them. He takes it away from them, family by family [7]. He includes them, one and all, and Judah also, since all had been *brought out of Egypt.*

2. *You only have I known of all the families of the earth; therefore I will punish you for all your iniquities.* Such is the one law of God. The nearer any is brought unto God, the worse is his fall, and, his trial over, the more heavily is he punished. Nearness to God is a priceless, but an awful gift. The intensest blessing becomes, by the abuse of free will, the most dreadful woe. For the nearer God places any one to His own light, the more malignant is the choice of darkness instead of light. The more clearly any one knows the relation to God, in which God has placed him, the more terrible is his rejection of God. The more God reveals to any, what He IS, His essential perfections, His holiness and love, the more utter, fearful malignity it is, to have been brought face to face with God, and to have in deed said to Him, "On Thy terms I will have none of Thee." The angels who sinned against fullest light, had no redemption or repentance; but became devils. [8] *He took not on Him the nature of angels.* [9] *The angels which kept not their first estate, but left their own habitations, He hath reserved in everlasting chains under darkness unto the judgment of the great Day.* Of the former people, when their first day of grace was past, Daniel says [10]; *under the whole heaven hath not been done, as hath been done upon Jerusalem. Begin,* God saith in Ezekiel [11], *at My sanctuary. Then they began at the ancient men which* were *before the house.* So our Lord lays down the rule of judgment and punishment hereafter [12]: *the servant which knew his Lord's will, and prepared not* himself, *neither did according to His will, shall be beaten with many* stripes. *But he that knew not, and did commit things worthy of stripes, shall be beaten with few* stripes. *For unto whomsoever much has been given, of him shall much be required, and to whom men have committed much, of him they will ask the more. The time* is come, says S. Peter [13], *that judgment must begin at the house of God.*

You only I have known. Such care had God had of Israel, so had He known them, and made Himself known to them, as if He had, in comparison, disregarded all besides, as He remained unknown by them. Knowledge, among men, is mutual, and so it seemed as if God knew not those, of whom He was not known. Knowledge, with God, is love, and so He seemed not to have known those, to whom, although *He left not Himself without witness* [14], He had shown no such love [15]. Whence our Lord shall say to the wicked [16], *I never knew you;* and contrariwise, He says [17], *I am the good Shepherd and know My sheep, and am known of Mine.* "[18] Myriads of cities and lands are there under the whole heaven, and

[1] S. Mark xiii. 37. [2] iii. 1. iv. 1. v. 1. [3] Dion. [4] עליכם. [5] Heb. xii. 25. [6] Gen. xii. 3. [7] Zech. xii. 12. [8] Heb. ii. 16. [9] S. Jude 6.

[10] ix. 12. [11] ix. 6. [12] S. Luke xii. 47, 8. [13] 1 Ep. iv. 17. [14] Acts xiv. 17. [15] See on Hos. xiii. 5. p. 83. [16] S. Matt. vii. 23. [17] S. John x. 14. see 2 Tim. ii. 19. [18] S. Cyr.

Before CHRIST cir. 787.

known of all the families of the earth: [b] therefore I will † punish you for all your iniquities.

[b] See Dan. 9. 12. Matt. 11. 22. Luke 12. 47. Rom. 2. 9. 1 Pet. 4. 17.

† Heb. *visit upon.*

in them countless multitudes; but you alone have I chosen out of all, made Myself known and visible among you by many miracles, chosen you out of a bitter unbearable bondage, trained you by My law to be well-pleasing to Me, fenced you with protection, brought you into the land promised to your fathers, enlightened you with prophecies." "[1] Not, I deem, as though in the time of Israel and of the Old Testament, there were not, in the whole world, some good men and predestinated; but because God did not then choose any nation or whole people, save the children of Israel. For it was meet that that people, of which God willed to be Incarnate, should be distinguished by some special grace."

Therefore I will punish you. "[2] To depise God and to neglect the Lord's Will procureth destruction to those who have known Him or been known of Him, and been spiritually made His own." "I made you My own people, friends, sons. As a Father, I cherished, protected, exalted, you. Ye would not have Me as a Father, ye shall have Me as a Judge." "[3] As Israel has, in its elect, been glorious above all, so, in the reprobate, has it been made viler than all, both before God and before men." How much more Christians, and, among Christians, priests! It has of old been believed, that the deepest damnation will be that of ungodly priests.

Yet since almost all punishment in this life is remedial, the saying admits another meaning that God would leave no sin unchastened in those whom He had made His own. Both are true meanings, fulfilled at different times. God chastens in proportion to His love, in the Day of grace. He punishes, in proportion to the grace and love despised and trampled upon without repentance in eternity. Here, "[4] the most merciful Physician, cutting away the cancrous flesh, spareth not, that He may spare; He pitieth not, that He may the more pity. For *whom the Lord loveth He chasteneth, and scourgeth every son whom He receiveth.*" Hence the prayer [5] "Burn, cut, here; and spare forever." Contrariwise, "[6] we should esteem any sinner the more miserable, when we see him left in his sin, unscourged. Whence it is said [7], *The turning away of the simple shall slay them, and the prosperity of fools shall destroy them.* For whoso *turneth away* from God and is *prosperous*, is the nearer to perdition, the more he is removed from the severity of discipline."

[1] Dion. [2] S. Cyr. [3] Rup.
[4] S. Jerome in Ezek. vii. Sanct. in Hos. iv. 14.
[5] Ap. S. Aug. Bp. Andrewes, Prayers.

"[8] This is the terrible, this the extreme case, when we are no longer chastened for sins, when we are no more corrected for offending. For when we have exceeded the measure of sinning, God, in displeasure, turneth away from us His displeasure." "[9] When you see a sinner, affluent, powerful, enjoying health, with wife and circle of children, and that saying is fulfilled, [10] *They* are *not in trouble* as other *men, neither are they plagued like* other *men*, in him is the threat of the Prophet fulfilled, *I will not visit.*"

3. Sacred parables or enigmas must have many meanings. They are cast on the mind, to quicken it and rouse it by their very mystery. They are taken from objects which in different lights, represent different things, and so suggest them. This series of brief parables have, all of them, this in common, that each thing spoken of is alternately cause and effect, and where the one is found, *there* must be the other. From the effect you can certainly infer the cause, without which it could not be, and from the cause you may be sure of the effect. Then, further, all the images are of terror and peril to the objects spoken of. The Prophet impresses upon their minds both aspects of these things; "evil will not befall, unless it has been prepared;" "signs of evil will not shew themselves, unless the evil be at hand." The bird will not fall without the snare; if the snare rises and so shews itself, the bird is as good as taken. As surely then (the Prophet would say) as the roaring of the lion, the rising of the snare, the alarm of the trumpet, betokens imminent peril, so surely does the warning Voice of God. *The lion hath roared; who will not fear?* Again, as surely as these are the effects of their causes, so surely is all infliction sent by Him Who Alone has power over all things, and is the cause of all. *Shall there be evil in a city, and the Lord hath not done* it? Again, as these tokens are given before the evil comes, and the God of nature and of grace has made it a law in nature, that what is fearful should give signs of coming evil, so has He made it a law of His own dealings, not to inflict evil, without having fore-announced it. *Surely the Lord God will do nothing, but He revealeth His secret unto His servants the prophets.* As nothing else is by chance, nor happens without cause, much less the acts of God. The lion or young lion when they roar, the bird when it falls to the ground, the snare when it rises, the trumpet's

[6] S. Greg. in Ezek. L. i. Hom. xii. 18.
[7] Pr. i. 32. [8] Orig. Hom. viii. 5. in Ex. xx. S.
[9] S. Jer. in Hos. iv. 14. S. [10] Ps. lxxiii. 5.

Before CHRIST cir. 787.

3 Can two walk together,
except they be agreed?
4 Will a lion roar in the
forest, when he hath no
prey? will a young lion
† cry out of his den, if he
have taken nothing?
5 Can a bird fall in a
snare upon the earth, where
no gin *is* for him? shall
one take up a snare from
the earth, and have taken
nothing at all?
6 Shall a trumpet be
blown in the city, and the
people || not be afraid?

† Heb. *give forth his voice.*

|| Or, *not run together?*

sound, all have their cause and ground: shall not then much more the acts and works of God? Shall evil happen in the city, and have no ground in the Cause of all causes, God in His righteous judgments? As there is fear, whenever there are tokens and causes of fear, so fear ye now and watch, lest the fear overtake you and it be too late. The first words then,

3. *Can* [*Will*] *two walk together, except they be agreed?* are at once a general rule for all which follows, and have different bearings according to those its several aspects. And, before all these, it is an appeal at once to the conscience which feels itself parted from its God; "so neither will God be with thee, unless thou art agreed and of one mind with God. Think not to have God with thee, unless thou art with God;" as He saith[1], *I will not go up in the midst of thee, for thou art a stiff-necked people, lest I consume thee in the way;* and[2], *if ye walk contrary unto Me, then will I also walk contrary unto you, and will punish you yet seven times for your sins.* And on the other hand[3], *They shall walk with Me in white, for they are worthy.* "[4]God cannot be agreed with the sinner who justifies himself. "[5]God Who rebuketh, and Israel who is rebuked, are two. God saith, We are not agreed, in that Israel, when rebuked, heareth not Me, God, rebuking. Herein we are not agreed, that I rebuke, Israel justifieth himself. Lo, for so many years since Jeroboam made the golden calves, have I sent Prophets, and none agreeth, for no one king departed from the sin of Jeroboam. So then I came Myself, God made Man, rebuking and reproving: but[6] *ye are they which justify yourselves before men,* and, being sick, ye say to the Physician, we need Thee not." "[7] So long as thou confessest not thy sins, thou art in a manner litigating with God. For what displeaseth Him, thou praisest. Be at one with God. Let what displeaseth Him, displease thee. Thy past evil life displeaseth Him. If it please thee, thou art disjoined from Him; if it displease thee, by confessing thy sins, thou art joined to Him." So He awakens and prepares the soul for the following words of awe.

In connection with what follows, the words are also the Prophet's defence of his Mission. Israel *said to the Prophets, prophesy not*[8], or, *The Lord our God hath not sent thee*[9], because, while it disobeyed God, the Prophets must *speak concerning* it *not good, but evil.* Amos prepares the way for his answer; ye yourselves admit, that *two will* not *walk together, unless they be agreed.* The seen and the unseen, the words of the Prophets and the dealings of God, would not meet together, unless the Prophets were of one mind with God, unless God had admitted them into His counsels, and *were agreed* with them, so that their words should precede His deeds, His deeds confirm His words by them.

Then, further, each question by itself suggests its own thought. Amos had already, in repeating Joel's words, spoken of God's Voice, under the image of a lion roaring[10]. Hosea had likened Israel to *a silly dove without heart*[11]; on the other hand, he had likened God's loud call to repentance to the roaring of the lion, the conversion of Israel to the return of the dove to its home[12]. As the roaring of the lion causeth terror, for he sendeth forth his terrible roar when he is about to spring on his prey[13], so God threatens by His Prophets, only when He is about to punish. Yet the lion's roar is a warning to escape. God's threatening is a warning to betake them to repentance, and so to escape from all fear, by fleeing from their sins. If the season is neglected, wilt thou rescue the prey from the lion's grasp, or thyself from the wrath of God?

Again, the bird taken in the snare is the image of those drawn down from heaven, where *our conversation is*[14] and the soul may rise free toward its God, "[15]drawn up by the Spirit to high and heavenly things." Such souls being allured by the things of earth, are entangled and taken by Satan; as, on the other hand, *the soul, escaped as a bird out of the snare of the fowler*[16], is a soul, set free by Christ and restored to Heaven.

[1] Ex. xxxiii. 3. [2] Lev. xxvi. 23, 4. [3] Rev. iii. 4. [4] Lap. [5] Rup. [6] S. Luke xvi. 15. [7] S. Aug. in Ps. lxxv. Lap. [8] See ab. on ii. 12. [9] Jer. xliii. 2.

[10] i. 2. Hos. xi. 10 (add v. 14. vi. 1. xiii. 7.) Jer. xxv. 30. [11] vii. 11. [12] xi. 10, 11. [13] Boch. Hieroz. i. iii. 2. [14] Phil. iii. 20. [15] Art. xvii. [16] Ps. cxxiv. 7.

Before CHRIST cir. 787.

[c]shall there be evil in a
city, ‖ and the LORD hath
not done *it?*
7 Surely the Lord GOD

c Is. 45. 7.
‖ Or, *and shall not the LORD do* somewhat.

will do nothing, but [d]he
revealeth his secret unto
his servants the prophets.
8 [e]The lion hath roared,

Before CHRIST cir. 787.

d Gen. 6. 13. & 18. 17. Ps. 25. 14. John 15. 15.
e ch. 1. 2.

In the last likeness, the Prophet comes nearer to the people themselves, and the trumpet is, at once, the well-known token of alarm among men, and of the loud voice of God, wakening them to repentance[1] and still oftener, warning them of the approach of judgment[2], or summoning man before Him[3]. "[4]God's Voice will not always be *a still small voice*, or whispered only among the Angels, or heard as from the ground. It will be heard terribly in the whole world." "[5]Whatever is said in Holy Scripture is a trumpet threatening, and with loud voice sinking into the hearts of believers. If we are righteous, we are called by the trumpet of Christ to bliss. If we are sinners, we know that we are to suffer torment." *Is there evil in the city and the Lord hath not done it?* Evil is of two sorts, evil of sin, and evil of punishment. There is no other; for evil of nature, or evil of fortune, are evils, by God's Providence, punishing the evil of sin. "[6]Evil, which is sin, the Lord hath not done; evil, which is punishment for sin, the Lord bringeth." The Providence of God governing and controlling all things, man doth ill which he wills, so as to suffer ill which he wills not. Only, evil which is by God's Providence the punishment of sin is in this life remedial, and through final impenitence alone becomes purely judicial.

"[7]Refer not, the Prophet would say, the ills which ye suffer and will suffer, to any other causes, as men are wont to do. God, in His displeasure, sends them upon you. And that ye may know this the more certainly, whatever He shall send He will first reveal to the Prophets and by them ye shall be forewarned. See then that ye despise not my words, or the words of the other prophets. Men ascribe their sufferings to fortune, accident, any cause, rather than the displeasure of God. The intemperate will think anything the cause of their illness rather than their intemperance. Men love the things of the world and cannot and will not be persuaded that so many evils are brought on them by the things which they love. So then God explains through the prophets the punishment which He purposes to bring on men."

7. *Surely the Lord God will do* [*For* the Lord GOD *doeth*] *nothing*, but *He revealeth His secret unto His servants the prophets.* So our Lord saith[8], *And now I have told you before it come to pass, that, when it is come to pass, ye may believe.* While it is yet a *secret* counsel within Himself, He admitteth to it His servants the prophets. The same word signifies "secret[9]" and "secret counsel with a friend." So "[10]God revealed to Noah that He would bring the deluge, and to Abraham and Lot, that He would destroy the cities of the plain, and to Joseph the 7 years' famine in Egypt, and to Moses its plagues, and to Moses and Joshua all the chastisements of His people, and to Jonah the destruction of Nineveh, that they who heard of the coming punishment, might either avoid it by repentance, or, if they should despise it, might be more justly punished. And so now the Lord is about to reveal through Amos, His servant and prophet, what He willeth to do to the 10 tribes, that forsaking their idols and turning to Him, they might be freed from the impending peril; which is of the great mercy of God. He foretelleth evil to come, that He may not be compelled to inflict it. For He Who forewarneth, willeth not to punish sinners."

"[11]So He inflicted not on Egypt any plagues by the hand of Moses, but He first forewarned Pharaoh and the Egyptians by him; nor the sufferings by the Ammonites, Midianites and Philistines, related in the book of Judges, but He foremonished Israel by Joshua; [12]nor did He inflict on the Jews that destruction by Titus and the Romans, but He foremonished them by Christ[13] and the Apostles. So neither will He bring that last destruction on the world, without having first sent the Prophets and Angels, who, sounding with the seven trumpets, shall proclaim it throughout the world[14]."

8. *The Lion hath roared: who will not fear? The Lord God hath spoken: who can but prophesy?* i. e. there is cause for you to fear, when the Lord *roareth from Zion;* but if ye fear not, God's prophets dare not but fear. So S. Paul saith[15], *necessity is laid upon me; yea, woe is unto me if I preach not the Gospel! For if I do this thing willingly, I have a reward; but if against my will, a dispensation* of the Gospel *is committed unto me;* and SS. Peter and John[16], *whether it be right in the sight of*

1 Is. lviii. 1. Joel ii. 15.
2 Is. xviii. 3. Jer. iv. 5. vi. 1. Ez. xxxiii. 2–6. Hos. v. 8. viii. 1. Rev. viii.
3 1 Cor. xv. 52. 1 Thess. iv. 16.
4 Rup.
5 S. Jer.
6 S. Aug. c. Adim. 26.
7 Rib.

8 S. John xiv. 29. comp. Ib. xiii. 19.
9 סוד, used here.
10 S. Jer.
11 Lap.
12 Jos. xxiii. 12–16. xxiv. 19, 20.
13 S. Luke xix. 42–44.
14 Rev. viii. 2.
15 1 Cor. ix. 16, 17.
16 Acts iv. 19, 20.

Before CHRIST cir. 787.

who will not fear? the
Lord GOD hath spoken,
[f] who can but prophesy?
9 ¶ Publish in the
palaces at Ashdod, and in
the palaces in the land of
Egypt, and say, Assemble
yourselves upon the moun-

[f] Acts 4. 20. & 5. 20, 29. 1 Cor. 9. 16.

Before CHRIST cir. 787.

God to hearken unto you more than unto God, judge ye! For we cannot but speak the things which we have seen and heard. Moses was not excused, though slow of speech; nor Isaiah, though of polluted lips; nor Jeremiah, because he was a child; but God said [1], *Say not, I am a child; for thou shalt go to all that I shall send thee, and whatsoever I command thee, thou shalt speak.* And Ezekiel was bidden [2], *be not rebellious, like that rebellious house.* And when Jeremiah would keep silence, he saith [3], *His Word was in mine heart as a burning fire, shut up in my bones, and I was weary with forbearing and I could not* stay.

9. *Publish* [*ye*, they are the words of God, commissioning His prophets,] *in* [*on*] *the palaces of Ashdod,* [i. e. *on* the flat roofs of their high buidings, whence all can hear] *and in* [*on*] *the palaces in the land of Egypt.* "[4] Since ye disbelieve, I will manifest to Ashdodites and Egyptians the transgressions of which ye are guilty." Amos had already pronounced God's sentence on *the palaces of Ashdod* and all Philistia, for their sins against Himself in His people [5]. Israel now, or a little later, courted Egypt [6]. To friend then and to foe, to those whom they dreaded and those whom they courted, God would lay open their sins. Contempt and contumely from an enemy aggravate suffering: man does not help whom he despiseth. *They were all ashamed of a people who could not profit them,* saith Isaiah [7] subsequently, of Egypt in regard to Judah. From those palaces, already doomed to destruction for their sins, the summons was to go, to visit Samaria, and see her sins, amid grace which those people had not. As our Lord says [8], *It shall be more tolerable for Sodom and Gomorrah in the Day of Judgment, than for that city.* Shame toward man survives shame toward God. What men are not ashamed to do, they are, apart from any consequences, ashamed to confess that they have done. Nay, to avoid a little passing shame, they rush upon *everlasting shame.* So God employs all inferior motives, shame, fear, hope of things present, if by any means He can win men, not to offend Him.

Assemble yourselves upon the mountains of Samaria, i. e. those surrounding it. Samaria was chosen with much human wisdom for the strong capital of a small people. Imbedded in mountains, and out of any of the usual routes [9], it lay, a mountain-fastness in a rich valley. Armies might surge to and fro in the valley of Jezreel, and be unconscious of its existence. The way from that great valley to Samaria lay, every way, through deep and often narrowing valleys [10], down which the armies of Samaria might readily pour, but which, like Thermopylæ, might be held by a handful of men against a large host. The broad vale near the hill of Dothan [11], along which the blinded Syrian army followed Elisha to Samaria, contracts into "a narrow valley [12]," before it reaches Samaria. The author of the book of Judith, who knew well the country, speaks of "the passages of the hill-country" near Dothaim, "by" which "there was an entrance into Judæa, and it was easy to stop them that would come up, because the passage was strait for two men at the most [13]." "[14] A series of long winding ravines open from the mountains to the plain; these were the passes so often defended by the 'horns of Joseph, the ten thousands of Ephraim, and the thousands of Manasseh' against the invaders from the North." Within these lay "[15] the wide rocky rampart" which fenced in Samaria from the N. "[16] The fine round swelling hill of Samaria, now cultivated to the top, [about 1100 feet above the sea [17], and 300 from its own valley [18],] stands alone in the midst of a great basin of some two hours [or 5 miles] in diameter surrounded by higher mountains on every side." "[19] The view from its summit presents a splendid panorama of the fertile basin and the mountains around, teeming with large villages, and includes not less than 25 degrees of the Mediterranean." Such a place, out of reach, in those days, from the neighboring heights,

[1] Jer. i. 7. [2] ii. 8. [3] xx. 9. [4] Theod.
[5] See on i. 6–8. [6] Hos. vii. 11. xii. 1. [7] xxx. 5.
[8] S. Matt. x. 15.
[9] Even the route from Beisan [Beth-shean] and Zerin [Jezreel] to Ramleh and Egypt lay N. of Samaria, passing through the valley of Yabud to Ferasin and Zeita. (Rob. iii. 122–4.)
[10] Maundrell "passed through narrow valleys for four hours," before he reached Caphar Arab, taking the road to the left of Arab (Arrabeh) and Rama and "over Selee." pp. 77, 8. "The way from Sanur to Jenin ran uniformly through a narrow wadi ("a sort of defile," Wilson, Lands, &c. ii. 84.), opening into the plain of Esdraelon." (V. de Velde i. 367. Rob. ii. 314.)
[11] "A huge hill, covered over with ruins." V. de Velde, i. 364. [12] Ib. 370.
[13] iv. 7. This was probably a proverbial expression.
[14] Porter, Hdb. 350. "Almost all travelers are compelled to draw conclusions from the well-known descent from Sebaste through Sanur to Jenin. But the general nature of the ground cannot be doubted." Stanley, Pal. 246.
[15] V. de V. 373. [16] Rob. ii. 304.
[17] Poole, in V. de Velde, Memoir, 178.
[18] Porter, 344. [19] Rob. ii. 307.

Before CHRIST cir. 787.

tains of Samaria, and be-
hold the great tumults in the
midst thereof, and the || op-
pressed in the midst thereof.

|| Or, *oppressions.*

10 For they [g] know not
to do right, saith the LORD,
who store up violence and
|| robbery in their palaces.

Before CHRIST cir. 787.

g Jer. 4. 22.

|| Or, *spoil.*

was well-nigh impregnable, except by famine. But its inhabitants must have had handed down to them the memory, how those heights had once been peopled, while their valleys were thronged with *all the hosts* [1] of Benhadad, his chariots and his horsemen; and the mountains, in which they had trusted to shut out the enemy, were the prison-walls of their famished people. From those heights, "[2] the Syrians could plainly distinguish the famishing inhabitants of the city. The adjacent circle of hills were so densely occupied, that not a man could push through to bring provisions to the beleaguered city." The city, being built on the summit and terraced sides of the hill, unfenced and unconcealed by walls which, except at its base, were unneeded, lay open, unsheltered in every part from the gaze of the besiegers. The surrounding hills were one large amphitheatre, whence to behold the tragedy of Israel [3], and enemies were invited to be the spectators. They could see its famine-stricken inhabitants totter along those open terraces. Sin had brought this chastisement upon them. God had forgiven them then. When God Who had, by His Prophet, foretold their relief then [4], now by His Prophet called anew those enemies of Samaria to those same heights to behold her sins, what could this mean but that He summoned them to avenge what He summoned them to behold? It was no figure of speech. God avenges, as He comforts, not in word, but in deed. The triumph of those enemies David had especially deprecated [5], *Tell* it *not in Gath, publish* it *not in the streets of Askelon; lest the daughters of the Philistines rejoice, lest the daughters of the uncircumised triumph.* To these Israel was to be a gazing-stock. They were like *the woman set in the midst* [6], amid one encircling sea of accusing insulting faces, with none to pity, none to intercede, none to shew mercy to them who *had shewed no mercy.* Faint image of the shame of that Day, when not men's deeds only, but [7] *the secrets of all hearts shall be revealed,* and [8] *they shall begin to say to the mountains, Fall on us, and to the hills, Cover us;* and of that *shame* there will be no end; for it is *everlasting* [9].

And behold the great tumults, i. e. the alarms, restlessness, disorders and confusion of a people intent on gain; turning all law upside down, the tumultuous noise of the oppressors and oppressed. It is the word which Solomon uses [10], *Better is little with the fear of the Lord, than great treasure and tumult therewith,* the tumults and restlessness of continual gaining. *And the oppressed,* or better (as in the E. M.) *the oppressions* [11], the manifold ever-repeated acts by which men were crushed and trampled on.

In the midst thereof, admitted within her, domiciled, reigning there in her very centre, and never departing out of her, as the Psalmist says [12], *Wickedness is in the midst thereof; deceit and guile depart not from her streets.* Aforetime, God spared His people, that His *Name* [13] *should not be polluted before the heathen, among whom they were, in whose sight I made Myself known unto them in bringing them forth out of the land of Egypt.* Now He summons those same heathen as witnesses that Israel was justly condemned. These sins, being sins against the moral law, the Heathen would condemn. Men condemn in others, what they do themselves. But so they would see that God hated sin, for which He spared not His own people, and could the less triumph over God, when they saw the people whom God had established and protected, given up to the king of Assyria.

10. *For* [*and*] *they know not to do right.* They *have not known* [14], they have lost all sense and knowledge, how *to do right* (lit. what is *straight-forward* [15]) because they had so long ceased to do it. It is part of the miserable blindness of sin, that, while the soul acquires a quick insight into evil, it becomes, at last, not paralyzed only to *do* good, but unable to perceive it. So Jeremiah says [16], *they are wise to do evil, but to do good they have no knowledge.'* Whence of the Christian S. Paul says, *I would have you wise unto that which is good, and simple concerning evil* [17]. People, step by step, lose the power of understanding either good or evil, the love of the world or the love of God. Either becomes "a strange language" to ears accustomed to the *songs of Zion* or the din of the world. When our Lord and God came to His own, they said, [18] *we know that God spake unto Moses: as for this man we know not whence He is.* And this blindness was wrought by covetousness which *blindeth the eyes* even of *the wise* [19], as he adds;

[1] 2 Kings vi. 24. [2] V. de Velde, i. 377. [3] Mont. [4] 2 Kgs vii. 1, 2. [5] 2 Sam. i. 20. [6] S. John viii. 3. [7] Rom. ii. 16. [8] S. Luke xxiii. 30. [9] Dan. xii. 2. [10] Prog. xv. 16. [11] As in Job xxxv. 9. Eccl. iv. 1. The word, like our *oppressions,* is a passive, made active by its use as an abstract. [12] Ps. lv. 11. [13] Ezek. xx. 9. [14] לא ידעו. [15] נכחה. [16] iv. 22. [17] Rom. xvi. 19. [18] S. John ix. 29. [19] Ex. xxiii. 8.

Before CHRIST cir. 787.

11 Therefore thus saith the Lord GOD; [h] An adversary *there shall be* even round about the land; and he shall bring down thy strength from thee, and thy palaces shall be spoiled.

[h] 2 Kings 17. 3, 6. & 18. 9, 10, 11.

Before CHRIST cir. 787.

Who store [lit. with indignation, *the storers* [1]] *with violence and robbery.* They could not understand what was right, while they habitually did what was wrong. They *stored up*, as they deemed, the gains and fruits; the robbery and injustice they saw not, because they turned away from seeing. But what is *stored* up, is not what wastes away, but what abides. Who doubts it? Then, what they treasured, were not the perishing things of earth, but, in truth, the sins themselves, as a [2] *treasure of wrath against the Day of wrath and revelation of the righteous judgment of God.* Strange treasure, to be so diligently accumulated, guarded, multiplied! Yet it is, in fact, all which remains. [3] *So is he that layeth up treasure for himself and is not rich towards God.* He adds, as an aggravation, *in their palaces.* Deformed as in all oppression, yet *to oppress the poor, to increase his riches* [4], has an unnatural hideousness of its own. What was wrung from the poor, laid up *in palaces!* Yet what else is it to cheapen luxuries at the cost of the wages of the poor?

11. *Therefore thus saith the Lord God.* There was no human redress. The oppressor was mighty, but mightier the Avenger of the poor. Man would not help; therefore God would. *An adversary* there shall be, *even round about the land;* lit. *An enemy, and around the land!* The Prophets speaks, as seeing him. The abruptness tells how suddenly that enemy should come, and *hem* [5] in the whole land on all sides. What an unity in their destruction! He sees one *enemy, and* him everywhere, all *around*, encircling, encompassing, as with a net, their whole land, narrowing in, as he advanced, until it closed around and upon them. The corruption was universal, so should be the requital.

And he shall bring down thy strength from (i. e. *away from*) *thee.* The word *bring down* implies a loftiness of pride which was to be brought low, as in Obadiah [6], *thence will I bring thee down;* and in Isaiah [7], *I will bring down their strength to the earth.* But further, their strength was not only, as in former oppressions, to be *brought down*, but *forth from thee. Thy palaces shall be spoiled;* those palaces, in which they had heaped up the spoils of the oppressed. Man's sins are, in God's Providence, the means of their punishment. [8] *Woe to thee that spoilest and* [i.e. whereas] thou wert *not spoiled, and dealest treacherously, and they dealt not treacherously with thee! when thou perfectest spoiling, thou shalt be spoiled; when thou accomplishest dealing treacherously, they shall deal treacherously with thee.* Their spoiling should invite the spoiler, their oppressions should attract the oppressor, and they, with all which they held to be their strength, should go *forth* into captivity.

"[9] *The Lord will be justified in His sayings*, and in His works, when He executeth judgment on *us and shall be cleared*, even by the most unjust judges, *when He is judged* [10]. He cites the Ashdodites and Egyptians as judges, who were witnesses of His benefits to this people, that they might see how justly He punished them. And now the hardened Jews themselves, Turks and all Hagarenes, might be called to behold at once our iniquities, and *the mercies of the Lord, that we are not consumed* [11]. If these were gathered on the mountains of Samaria, and surveyed from aloft our sins, who worship Mammon and Vain-glory and Venus for God, doubtless the Name of God would through us be blasphemed among the heathen. 'Imagine yourselves withdrawn for a while to the summit of some lofty mountain,' says the blessed martyr Cyprian [12], 'view thence the face of things, as they lie beneath you, yourself free from contact of earth, cast your eyes hither and thither, and mark the turmoils of this billowy world. You too, recalled to self-remembrance, will pity the world; and, made more thankful to God, will congratulate yourself with deeper joy that you have escaped it. See thou the ways obstructed by bandits, the seas infested by pirates, war diffused everywhere by the camp's bloodstained fierceness: a world reeking with mutual slaughter; and homicide, a crime in individuals, called virtue when wrought by nations. Not innocence but the scale of its ferocity gains impunity for guilt. Turn thy eyes to the cities, thou wilt see a peopled concourse more melancholy than any solitude.' This and much more which he says of the life of the Gentiles, how it fits in with our's, any can judge. What greater madness than that men, called to heavenly thrones, should cling to trifles of earth? immortal man glued to passing, perishable things! men, redeemed by the Blood of Jesus Christ, for lucre wrong their brethren, redeemed by the same Price,

[1] האצרים, as before (ii. 7) השאפים.
[2] Rom. ii. 5.
[3] S. Luke xii. 21.
[4] Pr. xxii. 16.
[5] צר.
[6] ver. 4.
[7] Is. lxiii. 6.
[8] Ib. xxxiii. 1.
[9] Rib.
[10] Ps. li. 4.
[11] Lam. iii. 22.
[12] ad Don. Treatises, p. 5. Oxf. Tr.

Before CHRIST cir. 787.

12 Thus saith the LORD; as the shepherd † taketh out of the mouth of the lion two legs, or a piece of an ear; so shall the children of Israel be taken out that dwell in Samaria in the corner of a bed, and ‖ in Damascus *in* a couch.

† Heb. *delivereth.*

‖ Or, *on the bed's feet.*

the same Blood! No marvel then, that the Church is afflicted, and encompassed by unseen enemies, and her strength drawn down from her spoiled houses."

"Samaria is also every soul, which willeth to please man by whom it thinketh it may be holpen, rather than God, and, boasting itself to be Israel, yet worshipeth the golden calves, i. e. gold, silver, honors, and pleasures. Let men alien from the light of the Gospel survey *its tumults,* with what ardor of mind riches, pleasures are sought, how ambition is served, how restless and disturbed the soul is in catching at nothings, how forgetful of God the Creator and of heavenly things and of itself, how minded, as if it were to perish with the body! What tumults, when ambition bids one thing, lust another, avarice another, wrath another, and, like strong winds on the sea, strong, unbridled passions strive together! They *know not to do right,* bad ends spoiling acts in themselves good. They *treasure up violence,* whereas they ought to treasure up grace and charity against that Day when God shall judge the secrets of men. And when they ascribe to themselves any benefits of the Divine mercy, and any works pleasing to God, which they may have done or do, what else do they than *store up robbery?* So then the powers of the soul are *spoiled,* when truths as to right action, once known and understood by the soul, fade and are obscure, when the memory retaineth nothing useful, when the will is spoiled of virtues and yields to vicious affections."

12. *As the shepherd taketh* [rather, *rescueth*[1]] *out of the mouth of the lion two legs* [properly, the shank, the lower part of the leg below the knee, which in animals is dry, and bone only and worthless] *or a piece* [the tip] *of an ear, so* [i. e. so few and weak, so bared and spoiled, a mere remnant,] *shall the children of Israel be taken out* [rather, *rescued*[1]] *that* now *dwell* at ease *in Samaria in the corner of a bed, and in Damascus*[2], in *a couch,* or rather *in Damascus, a couch.* Now, that soft, rounded, oblong, hill of Samaria, was one large luxurious couch, in which its rich and great rested securely, propped and cushioned up on both sides, *in,* what is still the place of dignity, *the corner of a bed,* or "Divan," i. e. the inner corner where the two sides meet. Damascus also, which Jeroboam had won for Israel, was a canopied couch to them, in which they stayed themselves. It is an image of listless ease and security, like that of those whom the false prophetesses lulled into careless stupidity as to their souls; *sewing pillows to all armholes,* or *wrists*[3], whereon to lean in a dull inertness. In vain! Of all those who then dwelt at ease and in luxury, the Good Shepherd Himself should rescue from *the lion,* (the enemy, in the first instance the Assyrian,) a small remnant, in the sight of the enemy and of man of little account, but precious in the sight of God. The enemy would leave them perhaps, as not worth removing, just as, when the lion has devoured the fat and the strong, the shepherd may recover from him some slight

[1] The uniform meaning of הציל with מִן, as also of the Niphal.

[2] The LXX. Aq. Symm. Theod. Syr. Ch. S. Jer. retain "Damascus" as a proper name. Of late, it has become a fashion to render it, "and in the damask of a couch." But 1) the fact that Ezekiel (xxvii. 18) speaks of *wine* and *white wool,* (the raw material) as the exports of Damascus to Tyre, seems a decisive proof, that the manufactures, for which Damascus has in modern times been so celebrated, did not exist there then. 2) It does not appear that the manufacture, which in modern European language is called from the city, "damask" or the like, is so called in Arabic. There has been a two-fold error in comparing an Arabic word. *a*) The word which, though foreign, had been naturalized in Arabia before Mohammed, was "Dimakso." This occurs in old poets [Amrulkeis v. 10. Ham. pp. 265, 6, 556.] Scholiasts or Lexica mention corruptions of this; "midakso," "dikamso," "dimkâso," but no trace of these has yet been observed in the actual language. The alleged forms, Dimssâko, Dimssako, Dimasko, (which alone would have corresponded with the Hebrew word) have no existence, except in error. See Freyt. Lex. Arab. ii. 57. The word "dimakso" is probably, from its different forms, a corrupted and foreign word. But the corruption has no near relation to the name of the city, Dimashko. It would have been strange that Arabs, speaking the same, and Hebrews, a kindred dialect, should have corrupted the name, as Europeans have not. Nor does any native Scholiast connect Dimakso with the city Damascus. *b*) The meaning of this word Dimakso, was not "manufactured," but "*raw* silk." Freyt. from Kam. Dj. It is silk "thread," which can be "twisted." Amrulk. "raw white silk or what is like it in whiteness and softness." Abulala in Tebriz. Scholl. ad. Ham. p. 566. The garment made of it was called, in the passive participle, "modamkaso," i. e., made of "dimakso." The punctuation of the Hebrew word is certainly varied here, דְּמֶשֶׁק, for what is elsewhere and in Amos himself (i. 3, 5. v. 27.) דַּמֶּשֶׂק. Yet there are two other variations in pronouncing the name, דרמשק 1 Chr. xviii. 5. דומשק 2 Kgs. xvi. 10. It may have been pointed so by those who, like Aben Ezra, guessed from the context, that ברמשק was i. q. בפאת. On the other hand, very old and very accurate MSS. have here too the usual punctuation. See De Rossi.

[3] Ezek. xiii. 18.

Before CHRIST cir. 787.

13 Hear ye, and testify
in the house of Jacob,
saith the Lord GOD, the
God of hosts,

14 That in the day that
I shall || visit the trans-
gressions of Israel upon
him I will also visit the

Before CHRIST cir. 787.

|| Or, *punish Israel for.*

piece of skin or extremity of the bones. Amos then, as well as Joel[1], preaches that same solemn sentence, so repeated throughout the prophets, *a remnant* only *shall be saved.* So doubtless it was in the captivity of the ten tribes, as in the rest. So it was in Judah, when certain *of the poor of the land* only were *left for vinedressers and for husbandmen*[2]. In the Gospel, *not many wise men after the flesh, not many mighty, not many noble were called*[3], but *God chose the poor of this world, rich in faith*[4]: and the Good Shepherd rescued from the mouth of the lion those whom man despised, yet who *had ears to hear.* After the destruction of Jerusalem by the Romans, a poor remnant only escaped. "[5]The spirit of prophecy foresaw both captivities, the end whereof was to confirm the faith, not in one place only but in all the earth, and so a slight remnant was *rescued from the mouth of the lion,* i. e. from the slaughter of the destroyers, and permitted to live, that through them, as a witness and monument, the justice of God might be known from age to age, and the truth of the Scriptures might be everywhere borne about by them, still witnessing to Christ the Son of God, Who is known by the law and the prophets. Hapless remnants, so *taken out* for the good of others, not their own!" As these remnants of the animal shew what it was which the lion destroyed, yet are of no further profit, so are they now a memorial of what they once were, what grace through their sins they have lost.

"[6]Many souls will perish, because they trust in their own strength, and no more call on God to have mercy on them than if they could rise of themselves and enter the way of salvation without God. They trust in the power of their friends, or the friendship of princes, or the doctrines of philosophers, and repose in them as in a couch of Damascus. But Christ the Good Shepherd will rescue out of the mouth of *the lion,* who *goeth about seeking whom he may devour,* what is last and of least esteem in this world, who have any thing whereby the Good Shepherd can hold them. The *legs* signify the desire to go to hear the Word of God; the extremity of the ear, that obedience was not wholly lost. For if any begin even in part to obey the word of God which he hath heard, God, of His fatherly mercy, will help him and lead him on to perfect obedience. The legs also denote desire[7], whereby, as by certain steps, the soul approacheth to God or departeth from Him. Yet if a soul would be saved, desires suffice not; but if to these obedience to the heavenly commands be added, it shall be rescued from the mouth of the lion."

13. *Hear ye and testify ye in* [rather *unto* or *against*[8]] *the house of Israel;* first *hear* yourselves, then *testify,* i. e. solemnly *protest,* in the Name of God; and *bear witness unto* and *against* them, so that the solemn words may sink into them. It is of little avail to *testify,* unless we first *hear;* nor can man *bear witness* to what he doth not know; nor will words make an *impression,* i. e. leave a trace of themselves, be stamped in or on men's souls, unless the soul which utters them have first hearkened unto them.

Saith the Lord God of hosts. "So [9]thundereth, as it were, the authority of the Holy Spirit, through the mouth of the shepherd. Foretelling and protesting the destruction of the altar of Bethel, he sets his God against the god whom Israel had chosen as theirs and worshiped there, *the Lord God of hosts,* against [10]*the similitude of a calf that eateth hay.* Not I, a shepherd, but so speaketh my God against your god."

14. *In the day that I shall visit the transgression of Israel upon him, I will also visit* [*upon*] *the altars of Bethel.* Israel then hoped that its false worship of "nature" would avail it. God says, contrariwise, that when He should punish, all their false worship, so far from helping them, should itself be the manifest object of His displeasure. Again God attests, at once, His long-suffering and His final retribution. Still had He foreborne to punish, *being slow to anger and of great goodness;* but when that day, fixed by the divine Wisdom, should come, wherein He should vindicate His own holiness, by enduring the sin no longer, then He would *visit their transgressions,* i. e. all of them, old and new, forgotten by man or remembered, *upon them.* Scripture speaks of "visiting offences upon" because, in God's Providence, the sin returns upon a man's own head. It is not only the cause of his being punished, but it becomes part of his punishment. The memory of a man's sins will be part of his eternal suffering.

[1] See on Joel ii. 32. p. 199.
[2] 2 Kgs xxv. 12. Jer. lii. 16.
[3] 1 Cor. i. 26.
[4] S. Jam. ii. 5.
[5] Rup.
[6] Rib.
[7] S. Greg. on Job L. vi. n. 25.

[8] As in Deut. viii. 19, *I testify against you this day that ye shall utterly perish;* Ps. l. 7, *hear, O Israel, and I will testify against thee; I am God, thy God.* Comp. Ps. lxxxi. 8. *I will testify unto thee.*
[9] From Rup.
[10] Ps. cvi. 20.

Before CHRIST cir. 787.

altars of Beth-el: and the
horns of the altar shall be
cut off, and fall to the
ground.

[i] Jer. 36. 22.

15 And I will smite [i] the
winter house with [k] the summer house; and [l] the houses
of ivory shall perish, and
the great houses shall have
an end, saith the LORD.

Before CHRIST cir. 787.

[k] Judg. 3. 20.
[l] 1 Kings 22. 39.

Even in this life, "remorse," as distinct from repentance, is the "gnawing" of a man's own conscience for the folly of his sin. Then also God would visit upon the false worship. It is thought that God visits less speedily even grave sins against Himself, (so that man does not appeal falsely to Him and make Him, in a way, a partner of his offence,) than sins against His own creature, man. It may be that, All-Merciful as He is, He bears the rather with sins, involving corruption of the truth as to Himself, so long as they are done in ignorance, on account of the *ignorant worship*[1] of Himself, or the fragments of truth which they contain, until the evil in them have its full sway in moral guilt[2]. "[3] Wonderful is the patience of God in enduring all those crimes and injuries which appertain directly to Himself; wonderful His waiting for repentance. But the deeds of guilt which violate human society, faith, and justice, hasten judgment and punishment, and, as it were, with a most effectual cry call upon the Divine Mind to punish, as it is written, [4] *The voice of thy brother's blood crieth unto Me from the ground, And now cursed* art *thou*, &c. If then upon that very grave guilt against God Himself there be accumulated these other sins, this so increases the load, that God speedily casts it off. However long then Israel had, with impunity, given itself to that vain, alien worship, this evinced the patience, not the approval, of God. Now, when they are to be punished for the fourth transgression, they will be punished for the first, second and third, and so, most grievously; when brought to punishment for their other sins, they should suffer for their other guilt of impiety and superstition."

And the horns of the altar. This was *the* one great *altar*[5] for burnt offerings, set up by Jeroboam, in imitation of that of God at Jerusalem, whose doom was pronounced in the act of its would-be consecration. He had copied faithfully its outward form. At each corner, where the two sides met in one, rose the *horn*, or pillar, a cubit high[6], there to sacrifice victims[7], there to place the blood of atonement[8]. So far from atoning, they themselves were *the* unatoned *sin* of *Jeroboam* whereby[9] he *drave Israel from following the Lord, and made them sin a great sin.* These were to be *cut off*, hewn down, with violence. A century and a half had passed, since the man of God had pronounced its sentence. They still stood. The day was not yet come; Josiah was still unborn; yet Amos, as peremptorily, renews the sentence. In rejecting these, whereon the atonement was made, God pronounced them out of covenant with Himself. Heresy makes itself as like as it can to the truth, but is thereby the more deceiving, not the less deadly. Amos mentions *the altars of Bethel*, as well as *the altar*. Jeroboam made but *one altar*, keeping as close as he could to the Divine ritual. But false worship and heresy ever hold their course, developing themselves. They never stand still where they began, but *spread, like a cancer*[10]. It is a test of heresy, like leprosy, that *it spreads abroad*[11], preying on what at first seemed sound. The oneness of the Altar had relation to the Unity of God. In Samaria, they worshiped, they *knew not what*[12], not God, but some portion of His manifold operations. The many altars, forbidden as they were, were more in harmony with the religion of Jeroboam, even because they were against God's law. Heresy develops, becoming more consistent, by having less of truth.

15. *And I will smite the winter house with the summer house.* Upon idolatry, there follow luxury and pride. "So wealthy were they," says S. Jerome, "as to possess two sorts of houses, *the winter house* being turned to the South, *the summer house* to the North, so that, according to the variety of the seasons, they might temper to them the heat and cold." Yet of these luxuries, (so much more natural in the East where summer-heat is so intense, and there is so little provision against cold) the only instance expressly recorded, besides this place, is *the winter house*[13] of Jehoiakim. In Greece[14] and Rome[15], the end was attained, as with us, by North and South rooms in the same house. These, which Amos rebukes, were like our town and country houses, separate residences, since they were to be destroyed, one on the other. *Ivory houses* were houses, pannelled, or inlaid,

[1] Acts xvii. 23. 30. xiv. 16. [2] Rom. i. [3] Mont.
[4] Gen. iv. 10, 11. [5] 1 Kgs xii. 32, 3. xiii. 1–5.
[6] The size under the second temple.
[7] Ps. cxviii. 27. [8] Ex. xxix. 12.
[9] 2 Kgs xvii. 21. [10] 2 Tim. ii. 17. [11] Lev. xiii.

[12] S. John. iv. 22.
[13] Jer. xxxvi. 22. Eglon, king of Moab, had only "a cool upper room," עלית המקרה. Jud. iii. 24.
[14] Xen. Mem. iii. 8. 9. [15] Pall. de re rust. i. 8.

Before CHRIST cir. 787.

CHAPTER IV.

1 *He reproveth Israel for oppression,* 4 *for idolatry,* 6 *and for their incorrigibleness.*

[a] Ps. 22. 12. Ezek. 39. 18.

HEAR this word, ye
[a] kine of Bashan, that
are in the mountain of Samaria,
which oppress the
poor, which crush the
needy, which say to their
masters, Bring, and let us
drink.

Before CHRIST cir. 787.

with ivory. Such a palace Ahab built[1]. Even Solomon *in all his glory* had but an ivory throne[2] Else *ivory palaces*[3] are only mentioned, as part of the symbolical glory of the King of glory, the Christ. He adds, *and the great* [or *many*] [4] *houses shall have an end, saith the Lord.* So prosperous were they in outward shew, when Amos foretold their destruction. The desolation should be wide as well as mighty. All besides should pass away, and the Lord Alone abide in that Day. "[5] What then shall we, if we would be right-minded, learn hence? How utterly nothing will all earthly brightness avail, all wealth, glory, or ought besides of luxury, if the love of God be wanting, and righteousness be not prized by us! For *treasures of wickedness profit nothing; but righteousness delivereth from death*[6]."

IV. 1. *Hear ye this, ye kine of Bashan.* The pastures of Bashan were very rich, and it had its name probably from its richness of soil[7]. The Batanea of later times was a province only of the kingdom of Bashan, which, with half of Gilead, was given to the half tribe of Manasseh. For the Bashan of Og included Golan[8], (the capital of the subsequent Gaulonitis, now Jaulân) Beeshterah[9] (or Ashtaroth[10],) very probably Bostra[11], and Edrei[12], in Hauran or Auranitis; the one on its S. border, the other perhaps on its Northern boundary towards Trachonitis[13]. Its Eastern extremity at Salkah[14], (Sulkhad[15]) is the Southern point of Batanea (now Bathaniyyeh); Argob, or Trachonitis[16], (the Lejah) was its N. Eastern fence. Westward it reached to Mount Hermon[17]. It included the subsequent divisions, Gaulonitis, Auranitis, Batanea, and Trachonitis. Of these the mountain range on the N. W. of Jaulân is still "[18] everywhere clothed with oak-forests." The Ard-el-Bathanyeh, "[19] the country of Batanea or Bashan, is not surpassed in that land for the beauty of its scenery, the richness of its pastures, and the extent of its oak-forests." "The Arabs of the desert still pasture their flocks on the luxuriant herbage of the Jaulân[20]." Its pastures are spoken of by Micah[21] and Jeremiah[22]. The animals fed there were among the strongest and fattest[23]. Hence the male animals became a proverb for the mighty on the earth[24], the bulls furnished a type for fierce, unfeeling, enemies[25]. Amos however speaks of *kine;* not, as David, of *bulls.* He upbraids them not for fierceness, but for a more delicate and wanton unfeelingness, the fruit of luxury, fullness of bread, a life of sense, which destroy all tenderness, dull the mind, "banker out the wits," deaden the spiritual sense.

The female name, *kine,* may equally brand the luxury and effeminacy of the rich men, or the cruelty of the rich women, of Samaria. He addresses these *kine* in both sexes, both male and female[26]. The reproachful name was then probably intended to shame both; men, who laid aside their manliness in the delicacy of luxury; or ladies, who put off the tenderness of womanhood by oppression. The character of the oppression was the same in both cases. It was wrought, not directly by those who revelled in its fruits, but through the seduction of one who had authority over them. To the ladies of Samaria, *their lord* was their husband, as the husband is so called; to the nobles of Samaria, he was their king, who supplied their extravagances and debaucheries by grants, extorted from the poor.

Which oppress, lit. *the oppressing!* The word expresses that they habitually oppressed and crushed the poor. They did it not directly; perhaps they did not know that it was done; they sought only, that their own thirst for luxury and self-indulgence should be gratified, and knew not, (as those at ease often know not now,) that their luxuries are continually watered by the tears of the poor, tears shed, almost unknown except by the

[1] 1 Kgs xxii. 39. [2] Ib. x. 18. [3] Ps. xlv. 8.
[4] As the same words בתים רבים are translated, Is. v. 9.
[5] S. Cyr. [6] Pr. x. 2.
[7] In Arab. "a soft smooth soil." On the richness of the Ard-el-Bathanyeh, see Five years, ii. 52, 7, 8, 60, 71, 82, 146, 9; on Jaulân, Port. Hdb. 461, 4.
[8] Deut. iv. 43 [9] Josh. xxi. 27. [10] 1 Chr. vi. 71.
[11] See ab. on i. 12. [12] Deut. i. 4.
[13] Five years, ii. 220–3.
[14] Deut. iii. 10. Jos. xiii. 11,
[15] Five years, ii. 184–8. "Szalkhat" Burckh. Syr. 99.
[16] Five years, ii. 268–72, 240–3.
[17] Deut. iii. 8. Josh. xii. 5. xiii. 11. 1 Chr. v. 23.
[18] Five years, ii. 259.
[19] Ib. 267; add. 57, 8, 67, 133.
[20] Porter, Hdb. 460, 2. On the Jebel Hauran, see Burckh. Syr. 309.
[21] vii. 14. [22] Jer. l. 19.
[23] Deut. xxxii. 14.
[24] Ez. xxxix. 18. [25] Ps. xxii. 12.
[26] "Hear *ye*, *your* Lord, upon *you*, they shall take *you*," are masculine; "*that* oppress, *that* crush, *that* say, *your* posterity, *ye* shall go out, *each* before *her*, and *ye* shall be cast forth," feminine.

Before CHRIST cir. 787.

2 [b] The Lord GOD hath
sworn by his holiness, that
lo, the days shall come
upon you, that he will
take you away [c] with
hooks, and your posterity
with fishhooks.
3 And [d] ye shall go out
at the breaches, every *cow*
at that which is before her;

b Ps. 89. 35.
c Jer. 16. 16. Hab. 1. 15.
d Ezek. 12. 5, 12.

Maker of both. But He counts wilful ignorance no excuse. "He who doth through another, doth it himself," said the heathen proverb. God says, they did *oppress*, were *continually oppressing*[1], *those in low estate*[2], and *crushing the poor* (a word is used expressing the vehemence with which they *crushed*[3] them.) They *crushed* them, only through the continual demand of pleasures of sense, reckless how they were procured; *bring and let us drink*. They invite their husband or lord to joint self-indulgence.

2. *The Lord God hath sworn by His holiness.* They had sinned to profane His *Holy Name*[4]. God swears by that holiness which they had profaned in themselves on whom it was called, and which they had caused to be profaned by others. He pledges His own holiness, that He will avenge their unholiness. "[5] In swearing *by His holiness*, God sware by Himself. For He is the supreme uncreated Justice and Holiness. This justice each, in his degree, should imitate and maintain on earth, and these had sacrilegiously violated and overthrown."

Days shall come [lit. *are among*] *upon you*. God's Day and eternity are ever coming. He reminds them of their continual approach. He says not only that they *will* certainly come, but they *are* ever *coming*. They are holding on their steady course. Each day which passes, they advance a day closer upon the sinner. Men put out of their minds what *will come;* they *put far the evil day*. Therefore God so often in His notices of woe to come[6], brings to mind, that those *days are* ever *coming*[6]; they are not a thing which shall be only; in God's purpose, they already *are;* and with one uniform steady noiseless tread *are coming upon* the sinner. Those *days shall come upon you*, heavily charged with the displeasure of God, crushing you, as ye have crushed the poor. They come doubtless, too, unexpectedly upon them, as our Lords says, *and so that day come upon you unawares.*

He [i. e. *one*] *will take you away*. In the midst of their security, they should on a sudden be taken away violently from the abode of their luxury, as the fish, when hooked[7], is lifted out of the water. The image pictures[8] their utter helplessness, the contempt in which they would be had, the ease with which they would be lifted out of the flood of pleasures in which they had immersed themselves. People can be reckless, at last, about themselves, so that their *posterity* escape, and they themselves survive in their offspring. Amos foretells, then, that these also should be swept away.

3. *Ye shall go out through the breaches.* Samaria, the place of their ease and confidence, being broken through, they should go forth one by one, *each straight before her*, looking neither to the right nor to the left, as a herd of cows go one after the other through a gap in a fence. Help and hope have vanished, and they hurry pell-mell after one another, reckless and desperate, as the animals whose life of sense they had chosen.

And ye shall cast them *into the palace*, or, better, (since nothing has been named which they could cast) *cast yourselves*[9]. The word may describe the headlong motion of the animal, and the desperate gestures of the hopeless. They should cast themselves from palace to palace, from the palace of their luxuries to the palace of their enemies, from a self-chosen life of sensuousness to be concubines in the harem. If the rulers are still included, it was reserved for the rich and noble to become eunuchs in the palace of their Assyrian or Babylonian conquerors, as Isaiah foretold to Hezekiah[10]. It is another instance of that great law of God[11], *wherewithal a man sinneth, by the same shall he be tormented.* They had lived in luxury and wantonness; in luxury and wantonness they should live, but amid the jealousies of an Eastern harem, and at the caprice of their sensual conquerors.

The word however rendered, *to the palace*[12], occurring only here, is obscure. The other

1 The force of the participles הרצצות העשקות.

2 דלים. 3 רצץ. 4 See on ii. 7.

5 From Lap. who applies it to princes and judges.

6 1 Sam. ii. 31. Is. xxxix. 6. Jer. vii. 32. ix. 25. xvii. 14. xix. 6. xxiii. 5, 7. xxx. 3. xxxi. 27–31, 38. xxxiii. 14. xlviii. 12. xlix. 2. li. 47, 52. [Ges.] Am. viii. 11.

7 The fem. צנות. סירות, were probably used to distinguish the artificial hook from the actual thorns, סירים, צנים.

8 See Hab. i. 15. Ezek. xxix. 4, 5.

9 השלכתנה is rendered actively by the rigid Aquila, and so pointed in all collated MSS. but one. It is rendered passively by the LXX; impersonally, by Jon. "they shall carry you captive;" both as paraphrases. The Hiphil is used of a person's own actions, in regard to certain qualities, their acting on themselves.

10 Is. xxxix. 7. 11 Wisd. xi. 16.

12 ההרמונה. Kimchi accounts הרמון to be only a stronger pronunciation of ארמון. It is some objection to this, that Amos five times wrote the word in its ordinary way. Yet there is abundant

Before CHRIST cir. 787.

and ‖ ye shall cast *them*
into the palace, saith the
LORD.
4 ¶ [e] Come to Beth-el
and transgress; at [f] Gilgal
multiply transgression;
and [g] bring your sacrifices
every morning, [h] *and* your
tithes after † three years:
5 [i] And † offer a sacrifice of thanksgiving with
leaven, and proclaim *and*
publish [k] the free offerings:
[l] for † this liketh you, O

‖ Or, *ye shall cast away the things of the palace.*
[e] Ezek. 20. 39.
[f] Hos. 4. 15. & 12. 11. ch. 5. 5.
[g] Num. 28. 3, 4.

Before CHRIST cir. 787.

[h] Deut. 14. 28.
† Heb. *three years of days.*
[i] Lev. 7. 13. & 23. 17.
† Heb. *offer by burning.*
[k] Lev. 22. 18, 21. Deut. 12. 6.
[l] Ps. 81. 12.
† Heb. *so ye love.*

most probable conjecture is, that it is a name of a country, *the mountains of Monah*, i. e. perhaps Armenia. This would describe accurately enough the country to which they were to be carried; *beyond Damascus; the cities of the Medes.* The main sense is the same. They should be cast forth from the scene of their pleasures and oppression, to be themselves oppressed. The whole image is one, which an inspired prophet alone could use. The reproof was not from man, but from God, unveiling their sins to them in their true hideousness. Man thinks nothing of being more degraded than the brutes, so that he can hide from himself, that he is so.

4 *Come to Gilgal and transgress.* Having foretold their captivity, the prophet tries irony. But his irony is in bidding them go on to do, what they were doing earnestly, what they were set upon doing, and would not be withdrawn from. As Micaiah in irony, until adjured in the name of God, joined Ahab's court-priests, bidding him *go to Ramoth-Gilead*[1], where he was to perish; or Elijah said to the priests of Baal[2], *Cry aloud, for he is a god;* or our Lord[3], *Fill ye up then the measure of your fathers;* so Amos bids them do all they did, in their divided service of God, but tells them that to multiply all such service was to multiply transgression. Yet they were diligent in their way. Their offerings were daily, as at Jerusalem; the tithes of the third year[4] for the poor was paid, as God had ordained[5]. They were punctual in these parts of the ritual, and thought much of their punctuality. So well did they count themselves to stand with God, that there is no mention of sin offering or trespass offering. Their sacrifices were *sacrifices of thanksgiving* and *free will offerings*, as if out of exuberance of devotion, such as David said that Zion would *offer*, when God had been *favorable and gracious unto* her[6]. These things they did; they *proclaimed* and *published* them, like the hypocrites whom our Lord reproves, *sounding a trumpet before them*[7], when they did alms; proclaiming these private offerings, as God bade proclaim the solemn assemblies. *For so ye love.* They did it, because they liked it, and it cost them nothing, for which they cared. It was more than most Christians will sacrifice, two fifteenths of their yearly income, if they gave the yearly tithes, which were to be shared with the poor also. But they would not sacrifice what God, above all, required, the fundamental breach of God's law, on which their kingdom rested, *the sin which Jeroboam made Israel to sin.* They did what they liked; they were pleased with it, and they had that pleasure for their only reward, as it is of all which is not done for God.

But amid this boastful service, all was self-will. In little or great, the calf-worship at Bethel, or the use of leaven in the sacrifice, they did as they willed. The Prophet seems to have joined purposely the fundamental change, by which Jeroboam substituted the worship of nature for its God, and a minute alteration of the ritual, to shew that one and the same temper, self-will, reigned in all, dictated all they did. The use of leaven in the things sacrificed was forbidden, out of a symbolic reason, i. e. not in itself, but as representing something else. The Eastern leaven, like that used in France, consisting of what is sour, had the idea of decay and corruption connected with it. Hence it was unfit to be offered to God. For whatever was the object of any sacrifice, whether of atonement or thanksgiving, perfection in its kind was essential to the idea of offering. Hence it was expressly forbidden[8]. *No meat offering, which ye shall bring unto the Lord, shall be made with leaven; for ye shall burn no leaven in an offering of the Lord made by fire.* At other

analogy for the change of ה and א. Most of the old Versions regard the word as a proper Name, simple or compound; "the mountains of Armenia," Ch. Syr. Symm.; "the hill of Romman or Remman," LXX.; Armon i. e. Armenia, S. Jer. as if כונה i. q. מני. "The hill Mona," Theod. in S. Jerome. To that also the article is an objection. Another Greek rendering, "to a lofty mountain," is obviously a conjecture.

[1] 1 Kings xxii. 15.
[2] Ib. xviii. 27.
[3] S. Matt. xxiii. 32.
[4] So E. V. rightly, according to the idiomatic use of ימים, "days," for one circle of days, i. e. a year. Lev. xxv. 29. Jud. xvii. 10. 1 Sam. xxvii. 7. &c. To "bring tithes every three days," would be too strong an irony, as being a contradiction.
[5] Deut. xiv. 28. xxvi. 12.
[6] Ps. li. 18, 19.
[7] S. Matt. vi. 2.
[8] Lev. ii. 11; add. vi. 17.

Before CHRIST cir. 787.

ye children of Israel, saith the Lord GOD.

6 ¶ And I also have given you cleanness of teeth in all your cities, and want of bread in all your

Before CHRIST cir. 787.

---

times it is expressly commanded, that *unleavened bread* should be used. In two cases only, in which the offering was not to be burned, were offerings to be made of leavened bread, 1) the two loaves of first-fruits at Pentecost[1], and 2) an offering with which the thank offering was accompanied, and which was to be the priest's[2]. The special meat offering of the thank offering was to be without leaven[3]. To *offer a sacrifice of thanksgiving with leaven* was a direct infringement of God's appointment. It proceeded from the same frame of mind, as the breach of the greatest. Self-will was their only rule. What they willed, they kept; and what they willed, they brake. Amos bids them then go on, as they did in their wilfulness, breaking God's commands of set purpose, and keeping them by accident.

"[4]This is a most grave mode of speaking, whereby He now saith, 'Come and do so and so, and He Himself Who saith this, hateth those same deeds of their's. He so speaketh, not as willing, but as abandoning; not as inviting, but as expelling; not in exhortation, but in indignation. He subjoins then, (as the case required,) *for so ye loved.* As if He said, 'I therefore say, *come to Bethel* where is your god, your calf, because *so ye loved*, and hitherto ye have come. I therefore say, *transgress*, because ye do transgress, and ye will to transgress. I say, *come to Gilgal*, where were idols[5] long before Jeroboam's calves, because ye come and ye will to come. I say, *multiply transgressions*, because ye do multiply it, and yet will to multiply it. I say, *bring your sacrifices*, because ye offer them and ye will to offer them, to whom ye ought not.—I say, *offer a sacrifice of thanksgiving with leaven*, because ye so do, and ye will do it, leavened as ye are with *the old leaven of malice and wickedness*, against the whole authority of the holy and spiritual law, which forbiddeth to offer in sacrifice anything leavened. This pleaseth your gods, that ye be leavened, and without [6]*the unleavened bread of sincerity and truth.* To them then *sacrifice the sacrifice of thanksgiving with leaven*, because to Me ye, being sinners, cannot offer a seemly sacrifice of praise. And so doing, *proclaim and publish the free offerings*, for so ye do, and so ye will to do, honoring the sacrifices which ye offer to your calves with the same names, whereby the authority of the law nameth those which are offered unto Me; *burnt offerings*, and *peace offerings;* and *proclaim* them[7] *with the sound of trumpet and harp, with timbrel and dancing, with strings and organ, upon the well tuned cymbals and the loud cymbals*, that so ye may be thought to have sung louder and stronger than the tribe of Judah or the house of David in the temple of the Lord, because ye are more.' All these things are said, not with the intention of one willing, but with the indignation of One forsaking, as in many other instances. As that which the same Lord said to His betrayer[8]; *what thou doest, do quickly.* And in the Revelations[9] we read, *He that is unjust, let him be unjust still; and he that is filthy, let him be filthy still.* These things, and the rest of the like sort, are not the words of one commanding, or, of His own Will, conceding, but permitting and forsaking. *For He was not ignorant,* (*Wisdom saith*[10]) *that they were a naughty generation, and their malice was inbred, and that their cogitation never would be changed.*"

Proclaim and publish the free offerings. "[11]Account much of what ye offer to God, and think that ye do great things, as though ye honored God condignly, and were under no obligation to offer such gifts. The whole is said in irony. For some there are, who appreciate magnificently the gifts and services which they offer to God, and think they have attained to great perfection, as though they made an adequate return to the Divine benefits, not weighing the infinite dignity of the Divine Majesty, the incomparable greatness of the Divine benefits, the frailty of their own condition and the imperfection of their service. Against whom is that which the Saviour saith[12], *When ye shall have done all those things which are commanded you, say, We are unprofitable servants, we have done that which was our duty to do.* Hence David saith[13] *all things* come *of Thee, and of Thine own have we given Thee.*"

6. *And I, I too*[14] *have given you.* Such had been their gifts to God, worthless, because destitute of that which alone God requires of His creatures, a loving, simple, single-hearted, loyal obedience. So then God had but one gift which He could bestow, one only out of the rich storehouse of His mercies, since all besides were abused,—chastisement. Yet this too is a great gift of God, a pledge of *His* love, Who willed not that they should perish; an earnest of greater favors, had they used it. It is a great gift of God, that He should care for us, so as to chasten us. The chastisements too were no ordinary chastisements, but

[1] Lev. xxiii. 17. [2] Ib. vii. 13, 14.
[3] Ib. 12. [4] Rup.
[5] Jud. iii. 19 E. M. [6] 1 Cor. v. 8. [7] Ps. cl.

[8] S. John xiii. 27. [9] xxii. 11. [10] xii. 10.
[11] Dion. [12] S. Luke xvii. 10.
[13] 1 Chr. xix. 14. [14] וגם אני emphatic.

Before CHRIST cir. 787.

places: [m] yet have ye not
returned unto me, saith the
LORD.
7 And also I have with-
holden the rain from you,
when *there were* yet three
months to the harvest: and
I caused it to rain upon
one city, and caused it not
to rain upon another city:

[m] Is. 26. 11. Jer. 5. 3. ver. 8, 9. Hag. 2. 17.

those which God forewarned in the law, that He would send, and, if they repented, He would, amid the chastisements, forgive. This famine God had sent everywhere, *in all their cities*, and *in all their places*, great and small. Israel thought that its calves, i. e. nature, gave them these things. *She did not know*, God saith, *that I gave her corn and wine and oil;* but said, *These* are *my rewards that my lovers have given me*[1]. In the powers and operations of "nature," they forgat the God and Author of nature. It was then the direct corrective of this delusion, that God withheld those powers and functions of nature. So might Israel learn, if it would, the vanity of its worship, from its fruitlessness. Some such great famines in the time of Elijah and Elisha[2] Scripture records; but it relates them, only when God visibly interposed to bring, or to remove, or to mitigate them. Amos here speaks of other famines, which God sent, as He foretold in the law, but which produced no genuine fruits of repentance.

And ye returned not unto Me. He says not, that they "*returned not* at all," but that they *returned not wholly, quite back to God*[3]. Nay, the emphatic saying, *ye did not return quite to Me*, so as to reach Me, implies that they did, after a fashion, return. Israel's worship was a half, halting[4], worship. But a half-worship is no worship; a half-repentance is no repentance; repentance for one sin or one set of sins is no repentance, unless the soul repent of all which it can recall wherein it displeased its God. God does not half-forgive; so neither must man half-repent. Yet of its one fundamental sin, the worship of nature for God, Israel would not repent. And so, whatever they did was not that entire repentance, upon which God, in the law, had promised forgiveness; repentance which stopped short of nothing but God.

7. *And I, I too*[5] *have withholden the rain.* S. Jerome, dwelling in Palestine, says, that "this rain, when *three months yet remained until harvest*, was the *latter rain*, of the very greatest necessity for the fields of Palestine and the thirsty ground, lest, when the blade is swelling into the crop, and gendering the wheat, it should dry up through lack of moisture. The time intended is the spring, at the end of April, whence, to the wheat-harvest, there remain three months, May, June, July." "God withheld the rain that they might endure, not only lack of bread, but burning thirst and penury of drink also. For in these places, where we now live, all the water, except small fountains, is of cisterns; and if the wrath of God should withhold the rain, there is greater peril of thirst than of hunger, such as Scripture relates to have endured for three years and six months in the days of the prophet Elijah. And lest they should think that this had befallen their cities and people, by a law of nature, or the influence of the stars, or the variety of the seasons, He says, that He rained upon one city and its fields, and from another withheld the rain."

This was a second visitation of God. First, a general famine, *in all their cities;* secondly, a discriminating visitation. "Nature" possesses no discrimination or power over her supplies. Seeming waste is one of the mysteries of God in nature, [6] *to cause it to rain on the earth* where *no man* is; on *the wilderness wherein* there *is no man*. Ordinarily too, God[7] *maketh His sun to rise on the evil and on the good, and sendeth rain on the just and on the unjust.* But God does not enslave Himself, (as men would have it) to His own laws. Amos appeals to them, that God had dealt with them, not according to His ordinary laws; that not only God had given to one city the rain which He had withheld from another, but that He had made the same difference as to smaller *pieces* of ground, the inherited *portions* of individuals[8]. Some such variations have been observed in Palestine now[9]. But this would have been no indication of God's Providence, had not the consciences of men responded to the Prophet's appeal, and recognized that the rain had been given or withholden according to the penitence or impenitence, the deeper or more mitigated idolatry, the greater or less sinfulness of the people. We have, then, in these few words a law of God's dealing with Israel. God, in His word, reveals to us the meaning of His daily variations in the workings of nature; yet, hardly even in such instances, as men can scarcely elude, do they think of God

[1] Hos. ii. 8, 12.
[2] 1 Kgs xvii. xviii. 2 Kgs viii. 1–6.
[3] עד; see on Joel ii. 12, and Introd. to Am. p. 152.
[4] 1 Kgs xviii. 21.
[5] וגם אנכי.
[6] Job xxxviii. 26.
[7] S. Matt. v. 45.
[8] Such is the common force of חלקה, "the portion of ground, belonging to one." Deut. xxxiii. 21. Ruth ii. 3. iv. 3. 2 Sam. xiv. 30, 1. 2 Kgs ix 21, 25.
[9] Thomson, The Land, ii. 66.

Before CHRIST cir. 787.

one piece was rained upon,
and the piece whereupon
it rained not withered.
8 So two *or* three cities
wandered unto one city, to
drink water: but they
were not satisfied: [n] yet
have ye not returned unto
me saith the LORD.
9 [o] I have smitten you
with blasting and mildew:
|| when your gardens and
your vineyards and your
fig trees and your olive
trees increased, [p] the palm-
erworn devoured *them*:
yet have ye not returned
unto me, saith the LORD.
10 I have sent among
you the pestilence || [q] after
the manner of Egypt:
your young men have I
slain with the sword, † and
have taken away your

n ver. 6, 10, 11.

o Deut. 28. 22. Hag. 2. 17.

|| Or, *the multitude of your gardens, &c. did the palmerworm, &c.*

Before CHRIST cir. 787.

p Joel 1. 4. & 2. 25.

|| Or, *in the way.*

q Ex. 9. 3, 6. & 12. 29. Deut. 28. 27, 60. Ps. 78. 50.

† Heb. *with the captivity of your horses,* 2 Kings 13. 7.

---

the Creator, rather than of "nature," His creation.

8. *Two or three cities wandered into one city.* Those then who were punished, were more than those who were reprieved. The word *wandered* lit. *trembled*, expresses the unsteady reeling gate of those exhausted, in quest of food[1]. They staggered through weakness, and uncertain, amid the general drought, whither to betake themselves. This was done, not in punishment but to heal. God paused, in order to give them opportunity to repent; in deed, His long-suffering only shewed to themselves and to others, that they would not; *and ye returned not unto Me; saith the Lord.*

9. *I have smitten you with blasting;* lit. *an exceeding scorching*, such as the hot East wind produced, and *an exceeding mildew*, a blight, in which the ears turn untimely a pale yellow, and have no grain. Both words are doubly intensive. They stand together in the prophecy of Moses[2], among the other scourges of disobedience; and the mention of these would awaken, in those who would hear, the memory of a long train of other warnings and other judgments.

When your gardens—increased; better, as E. M. *the multitude*[3] *of your gardens.* The garden of the East united the orchard[4], herb[5], and flower garden. It comprised what was necessary for use as well as what was fragrant. It furnished part of their support[6]. Its trees[7], as well as the garden[8] generally, being mostly watered artificially, it was beyond the reach of ordinary drought. The tree, *planted by the channels of waters*[9], was an image of abiding freshness and fertility. Yet neither would these escape God's sentence. On these He sent the locusts, which, in a few hours, leaves all, flower, herb or tree, as dead[10].

10. *I have sent among you the pestilence after the manner of Egypt;* i. e. after the way in which God had dealt with Egypt[11]. God had twice promised, when the memory of the plagues which He sent on Egypt was still fresh[12], *if thou wilt diligently hearken to the voice of the Lord thy God,—I will put none of the diseases upon thee which I have brought upon the Egyptians.* Contrariwise, God had forewarned them in that same prophecy of Moses, that, if they disobeyed Him[13], *He will bring upon thee all the diseases of Egypt which thou was afraid of, and they shall cleave unto thee.* Egypt was, at times, subject to great visitations of the plague[14]; it is said to be its birthplace[15]. Palestine was, by nature, healthy. Hence, and on account of the terribleness of the scourge, God so often speaks of it, as of His own special sending. He had threatened in the law; [16] *I will send a pestilence upon you*[17]; *the Lord thy God will make the pestilence cleave unto you.* Jeremiah says to the false prophet Hananiah[18]; *The prophets that have been before me and before thee of old prophesied both against many countries and against great kingdoms, of war and of evil and of pestilence.* Amos bears witness that those visitations came. Jeremiah[19] and Ezekiel[20] prophesied them anew, together with the sword and with famine. Israel, having sinned like Egypt, was to be punished like Egypt.

[1] Ps. lix. 15. cix. 10; of one blind, Lam. v. 14.
[2] Deut. xxviii. 22.
[3] הרבות (here, and Pr. xxv. 7.) is i. q. הרבא. The word and the construction are probably the same as in Eccl. i. 16.
[4] Job viii. 16. Cant. iv. 13, 14. vi. 11.
[5] Deut. xi. 10. Cant. iv. 14. vi. 2.
[6] Am. ix. 14. Jer. xxix. 5, 28.
[7] Eccl. ii. 6.
[8] Cant. iv. 15. Ecclus. xxiv. 30.
[9] Ps. i. 3. Jer. xvii. 8; add Is. lviii. 11. Jer. xxxi. 12, contrariwise Is. i. 30.
[10] See on Joel i. 7. p. 106.
[11] דרך "way" with the gen. is either act. "the way of a man," i. e. his way of acting, dealing, &c. or pass. "the way in which he is dealt with or it fares with him," as in Isa. x. 24. Gen. xxxi. 35.
[12] Ex. xv. 26. Deut. vii. 15.
[13] Deut. xxviii. 60, add 27.
[14] "A violent plague used formerly to occur about once in 10 or 12 years. It was always less frequent at Cairo than at Alexandria." Sir G. Wilk. Hdb. Eg. p. 7.
[15] Prosp. Alp. rer. Æg. i. 19. Win.
[16] Lev. xxvi. 25.
[17] Deut. xxviii. 21.
[18] xxviii. 8.
[19] xiv. 12. xxix. 17, 18. xxxiv. 17.
[20] v. 12, vi. 11, &c.

Before CHRIST cir. 787.

horses; and I have made
the stink of your camps to
come up unto your nos-
trils: [r] yet have ye not returned unto me, saith the
LORD.
11 I have overthrown
some of you, as God overthrew [s] Sodom and Gomorrah, [t] and ye were as a
firebrand plucked out of
the burning: [u] yet have ye
not returned unto me, saith
the LORD.

r ver. 6.

Before CHRIST cir. 787.

s Gen. 19. 24, 25. Is. 13. 19. Jer. 49. 18.

t Zech. 3. 2. Jude 23.

u ver. 6.

And have taken away your horses; lit. as E. M. *with the captivity of your horses.* After famine, drought, locust, pestilence, followed that worst scourge of all, that through man. The possessions of the plain of Jezreel, so well fitted for cavalry, probably induced Israel to break in this respect the law of Moses. Hazael *left to Jehoahaz but fifty horsemen and ten chariots and ten thousand footmen; for the king of Syria had destroyed them, and had made them like the dust by threshing.* Their armies, instead of being a defence, lay unburied on the ground, a fresh source of pestilence.

11. *I have overthrown* some *of you.* The earthquake is probably reserved to the last, as being the rarest, and so the most special, visitation. Frequent as earthquakes have been on the borders of Palestine, the greater part of Palestine was not on the line, which was especially shaken by them. The line, chiefly visited by earthquakes, was along the coast of the Mediterranean or parallel to it, chiefly from Tyre to Antioch and Aleppo. Here were the great historical earthquakes, which were the scourges of Tyre, Sidon, Beirut, Botrys, Tripolis, Laodicea on the sea; which shattered Litho-prosopon, prostrated Baalbek and Hamath, and so often afflicted Antioch and Aleppo [1], while Damascus was mostly spared [2]. Eastward it may have reached to Safed, Tiberias, and the Hauran. Ar-Moab perished by an earthquake in the childhood of S. Jerome [3]. But, at least, the evidence of earthquakes, except perhaps in the ruins of the Hauran [4], is slighter. Earthquakes there have been (although fewer) at Jerusalem. Yet on the whole, it seems truer to say that the skirts of Palestine were subject to destructive earthquakes, than to affirm this of central Palestine [5]. The earthquake must have been the more terrible, because unwonted. One or more terrible earthquakes, overthrowing cities, must have been sent, before that, on occasion of which Amos collected his prophecies. For his prophecies were uttered *two years before* that *earthquake;* and this earthquake had preceded his prophecy. *I overthrew,* God says, *among you, as God overthrew Sodom and Gomorrah.* He uses the word, especially used by Moses and the prophets of that dread overthrow of Sodom and Gomorrah, when they were turned, as it were, upside down. The earthquake is at all times the more mysterious, because unseen, unannounced, unlooked for, instantaneous, complete. The ground under a man's feet seems no longer secure: his shelter is his destruction; men's houses become their graves. Whole cities

[1] See authorities in Ritter, Erdk. xvi. 731. xvii. 37. 119. 225. 249. 334–6. 365. 437. 599. 600, 7. 836. 925. 1034. 1155–7. 64. 74, 5. 83, 8. 1206. 1504. 1654, 68. 1711, 35, 44. 52, 6. The terrible earthquake of 1837 which reached the interior of Palestine from Tyre to Bethlehem and Hebron, and northward to Beirut, Cyprus and Damascus (auth. in Ritter, xv. 254, 305. xvi. 210, 28. 647. xvii. 334, 5. 365, 406.) was, from its extent, exceptional. 250,000 perished at Antioch in one earthquake which destroyed Beirut, Biblos with all its inhabitants, and Sidon in part. Ritt. xvii. 437, 8. [2] Ritter, xvii. 1315. [3] S. Jer. on Is. xv.

[4] The Hauran, besides being basaltic, has on the East a very remarkable volcanic country, occupying 2 degrees of latitude (32–34) and 1⅓ longitude, "surpassed perhaps in extent, but scarcely in intensity by any like formation in the world." See Wetzstein, [its discoverer] Reisebericht des Hauran, p. 6–20, and woodcuts of extinct volcanoes.

[5] Baronius, Pagi, Fleuri, Tillemont, the Univ. Hist. (Mod.) only mention the following earthquakes as afflicting Palestine. i. an earthquake on Julian's attempt to rebuild the temple, A. D. 363. (from Ruf. H. E. i. 38, 9.) ii. a shock only, A. D. 394. (from S. Jer. c. Vigil.) iii. "strong shocks," A. D. 633. (from Elmacin p. 19.) iv. a severe one "in Palestine and Syria" (locality undefined) A. D. 658, from Theophanes; [A. D. 650. Theoph. i. 531.] v. "in Palestine round the Jordan and throughout Syria," A. D. 746. (Bar. i. Pag. ii.) also from Theoph. "many thousands, yea, countless. perished; Churches and monasteries fell in; and chiefly in the desert of the Holy City." (Theoph. A. 738. i. 651. ed. Class. Paul. Diac. L. xxii. Bibl. Patr. xii. 311.) vi. "no slight one," A. D. 756. (Bar. xv.) from the same. [A. D. 748. i. 662 Class.] vii. a severe earthquake at Ramleh and its vicinity, A. D. 1066. radiating along the coast Southwards, from Renaud. Hist. Patr. Al. 433. Von Raumer (Palest. 91. ed. 4) quotes Vitriaco, who speaks chiefly of the sea-coast, and specifies Tyre (in Gesta Dei p. 1097.); a shock A. D. 1105, another A. 1114, destructive in Cilicia and Antioch (Ib. 419, 424, 610.) frequent shocks at Nablus, A. 1120. (Ib, 824.) The list of earthquakes given by Von Hoff in his Chronik der Erdbeben vom. J. 3460 vor bis 1759 unserer Zeitrechnung in his Gesch. d. Veränd. d. Erdöberfl. (T. iv. 122–430.) (as extracted for me) adds, at most, one only affecting Palestine (in common with Syria), A. D. 1182, but does not name the authority. (That of 1353, 4, is not related to have affected Palestine.) Cedrenus also only adds one A. D. 532, 3, "pervading the whole world and lasting 40 days." He mentions Arabia, Palestine, Mesopotamia, Antioch as suffering by it. (i. 674 ed. Bekk.) Abulfaraj (Hist. Dyn.) adds none. The list in Berryat, Collection Académique T. vi. pp. 488–675, adds one, A. D. 650, "in Syria, Persia, especially in Judæa; but without naming any authority."

Before CHRIST cir. 787.

12 Therefore thus will I
do unto thee, O Israel:
and because I will do
this unto thee, [x] prepare
to meet thy God, O
Israel.
13 For, lo, he that
formeth the mountains,

x See Ezek. 13. 5. & 22. 30. Luke 14. 31, 32.

must have been utterly overthrown, for He compares the overthrow wrought *among* them, to the overthrow of *the cities of the plain*. Other visitations have heralds sent before them. War, pestilence, famine, seldom break in at once. The earthquake at once, buries, it may be, thousands or tens of thousands, each stiffened (if it were so) in that his last deed of evil; each household with its own form of misery; each in its separate vault, dead, dying, crushed, imprisoned; the remnant indeed "surviving," for most whom they loved were gone. So he says;

And ye, who escaped, *were as a firebrand, plucked out of the burning*. Once it had been green, fresh, fragrant, with leaf or flower; now scorched, charred, blackened, all but consumed. In itself, it was fit for nothing, but to be cast back into the fire whence it had been rescued. Man would so deal with it. A re-creation alone could restore it. Slight emblem of a soul, whose freshness sin had withered, then God's severe judgment had half-consumed; in itself, meet only for the everlasting fire, from which yet God withdraws it.

12. *Therefore thus will I do unto thee*. God says more by His silence. He had enumerated successive scourges. Now, with His hand uplifted to strike, He mentions none, but says, *thus*. "[1] So men too, loth to name evils, which they fear and detest, say, *God do so to me, and more also*. God using the language of men," "[2] having said, *thus will I do unto thee*, is silent as to what He will do; that so, Israel hanging in suspense, as having before him each sort of punishment (which are the more terrible, because he imagines them one by one), may indeed repent, that God inflict not what He threatens."

Prepare to meet thy God, in judgment, face to face, final to them. All the judgments which had been sent hitherto were but heralds, forerunners of the judgment to come. He Himself was not in them. In them, He passed no sentence upon Israel. They were medicinal, corrective; they were not His final sentence. Now, having tried all ways of recovering them in vain, God summons them before His tribunal. But although the judgment of the ten tribes, as a whole, was final, to individuals there was place for repentance. God never, in this life, bids people or individuals *prepare to meet Him*, without a purpose of good to those who do prepare to receive His sentence aright. He saith not then, "come and hear your doom," but *prepare to meet thy God*. It has hope in it, to be bidden to *prepare;* yet more, that He Whom they were to prepare to meet, was *their God*. It must have recurred full often to the mind of the ten tribes during their unrestored captivity of above seven centuries before the Coming of our Lord; a period as long as the whole existence of Rome from its foundation to its decay; as long as our history from our king Stephen until now. Full oft must they have thought, "we have not met Him yet," and the thought must have dawned upon them; "It is because He willed to *do thus* with us, that He bid us *prepare to meet* Him. He met us not, when He did it. It was then something further on; it is in the Messiah that we are to meet and to see Him." "[2] *Prepare to meet thy God*, receiving with all eagerness the Lord coming unto thee." So then, is this further sense which lay in the words, "[1] he (as did Hosea at the end) exhorts the ten tribes, after they had been led captive by the Assyrians, not to despond, but to *prepare to meet their God*, i. e. to acknowledge and receive Christ their God, when the Gospel should be preached to them by the Apostles." "[1] God punisheth, not in cruelty, but in love. He warns then those whom He strikes, to understand what He means by these punishments, not thinking themselves abandoned by God, but, even when they seem most cast away and reprobate, rousing themselves, in the hope of God's mercy through Christ, to call upon God, and *prepare to meet their God*. For no one's salvation is so desperate, no one is so stained with every kind of sin, but that God cometh to him by holy inspirations, to bring back the wanderer to Himself. Thou therefore, O Israel, whoever thou art, who didst once serve God, and now servest vilest pleasures, when thou feelest God coming to thee, *prepare to meet* Him. Open the door of thy heart to that most kind and benevolent Guest, and, when thou hearest His Voice, deafen not thyself: flee not, like Adam. For He seeketh thee, not to judge, but to save thee."

13. *For lo, He that formeth the mountains*. Their God whom they worshiped was but nature. Amos tells them, Who *their God* is, Whom they were to prepare to meet. He describes Him as the Creator of that, which to man seems most solid, to go furthest back in times past. Before the everlasting moun-

[1] Rib.

[2] S. Jer.

Before CHRIST cir. 787.

and createth the ‖ wind,
[y] and declareth unto man
what *is* his thought, [z] that
maketh the morning dark-
ness, [a] and treadeth upon
the high places of the
earth, [b] The LORD, The
God of hosts, *is* his name.

‖ Or, *spirit*.
y Ps. 139. 2. Dan. 2. 28.
z ch. 5. 8. & 8. 9.
a Deut. 32. 13. & 33. 29. Mic. 1. 3.
b Is. 47. 4. Jer. 10. 16. ch. 5. 8. & 9. 6.

CHAPTER V.

1 *A lamentation for Israel.* 4 *An exhortation to repentance.* 21 *God rejecteth their hypocritical service.*

Before CHRIST cir. 787.

HEAR ye this word which I [a] take up against you, *even* a lamentation, O house of Israel.

2 The virgin of Israel
is fallen; she shall no
more rise: she is forsaken
upon her land; *there is*
none to raise her up.

a Jer. 7. 29. Ezek. 19. 1. & 27. 2.

tains were, God IS; for He made them. Yet God is not a Creator in the past alone. He is a continual Worker. *And formeth the wind*, that finest subtlest creature, alone invisible in this visible world; the most immaterial of things material, the breath of our life, the image of man's created immaterial spirit, or even of God's uncreated presence, the mildest and the most terrific of the agents around us. But the thought of God, as a Creator or Preserver without, affects man but little. To man, a sinner, far more impressive than all majesty of Creative power, is the thought that God knows his inmost soul. So he adds; *and declareth unto man what is his thought*, i. e. his meditation, before he puts it into words. God knows our thoughts more truly than we ourselves. We disguise them to ourselves, know not our own hearts, wish not to know them. God reveals us to ourselves. As He says[1], *The heart is deceitful above all things;—who can know it? I, the Lord, search the heart; I try the reins, even to give every man according to his ways and according to the fruit of his doings.* Man's own conscience tells him that God's knowledge of his inmost self is no idle knowledge. [2] *If our heart condemn us, God is greater than our heart and knoweth all things.*

That maketh the morning darkness. If the light become *darkness, how great that darkness!* From the knowledge of man's heart, the Prophet goes on to retribution. Morning is the symbol of all which is beautiful, cheering, radiant, joyous to man; darkness effaces all these. Their God, he tells them, can do all this. He can quench in gloom all the magnificent beauty of His own creation and make all which gladdened the eyes of man, "one universal blot." *And treadeth upon the high places of the earth.* He *treadeth* them, to tread them under. He humbleth all which exalteth itself. "God walketh, when He worketh. He is without all, within all, containeth all, worketh all in all. Hence it is said, *He walketh on the wings of the wind*[3]; *He walketh on the heights of the sea*[4]; *He walketh on the circuit of Heaven*[5].

Such was He, Who made Himself *their God*, The Author of all, the Upholder of all, the Subduer of all which exalted itself, Who stood in a special relation to man's thoughts, and Who punished. At His command stand all the hosts of heaven. Would they have Him for them, or against them? Would they be at peace with Him, before they met Him, face to face?

V. 1. In order to impress Israel the more, Amos begins this his third appeal by a *dirge* over its destruction, mourning over those who were full of joy, and thought themselves safe and enviable. As if a living man, in the midst of his pride and luxury and buoyant recklessness of heart, could see his own funeral procession, and hear, as it were, over himself the "earth to earth, ashes to ashes, dust to dust." It would give solemn thoughts, even though he should impatiently put them from him. So must it to Israel, when after the tide of victories of Jeroboam II., Amos said, *Hear this word which I am lifting up*, as a heavy weight, to cast it down *against* or *upon you*, a funeral *dirge*, O house of Israel. Human greatness is so unstable, human strength so fleeting, that the prophet of decay finds a response in man's own conscience, however he may silence or resent it. He would not resent it, unless he felt its force.

"[6] Amos, an Israelite, mourneth over Israel, as Samuel over Saul[7], or as Isaiah says[8], *I will weep bitterly; labor not to comfort me, because of the spoiling of the daughter of my people;* images of Him Who wept over Jerusalem." "So are they bewailed, who know not why they are bewailed, the more miserable, because they know not their own misery."

2. *She hath fallen, she shall rise no more, the virgin of Israel; she hath been dashed down upon her land*, there is *none to raise her up.*

1 Jer. xvii. 9, 10.
2 1 S. John iii. 20.
3 Ps. civ. 3.
4 Job ix. 8.
5 Ib. xxii. 14.
6 from Dion.
7 1 Sam. xv. 35.
8 Is. xxii. 4.

Before CHRIST cir. 787.

3 For thus saith the
Lord GOD; The city that
went out *by* a thousand
shall leave an hundred,
and that which went forth
by an hundred shall leave
ten, to the house of Israel.
4 ¶ For thus saith the
LORD unto the house of
Israel, [b] Seek ye me, [c] and
ye shall live:
5 But seek not [d] Beth-el,

Before CHRIST cir. 787.

b 2 Chr. 15. 2. Jer. 29. 13. ver. 6.
c Is. 55. 3.
d ch. 4. 4.

Such is the dirge, a dirge like that of David over Saul and Jonathan, over what once was lovely and mighty, but which had perished. He speaks of all as past, and that, irremediably. Israel is one of the things which had been, and which would never again be. He calls her tenderly, *the virgin of Israel,* not as having retained her purity or her fealty to God; still less, with human boastfulness, as though she had as yet been unsubdued by man. For she had been faithless to God, and had been many times conquered by man. Nor does it even seem that God so calls her, because He once espoused her to Himself. For Isaiah so calls Babylon. But Scripture seems to speak of cities, as women, because in women tenderness is most seen; they are most tenderly guarded; they, when pure, are most lovely; they, when corrupted, are most debased. Hence "[1] God says on the one hand, [2] *I remember thee, the love of thine espousals;* on the other [3], *Hear, thou harlot, the word of the Lord.* When He claims her faithfulness He calls her, betrothed." Again, "[1] when He willeth to signify that a city or nation has been as tenderly loved and anxiously guarded, whether by Himself or by others, He calleth it *virgin,* or when He would indicate its beauty and lovely array. Isaiah saith [4], *come down and sit in the dust, virgin daughter of Babylon,* i.e. thou who livedest before in all delicacies, like a virgin under the shelter of her home. For it follows, *for thou shalt no more be called tender and delicate.*" More pitiable, for their tenderness and delicacy, is the distress of women. And so he pictures her as already fallen, *dashed* (the word imitates the sound [5]) to the earth *upon her own ground.* An army may be lost, and the nation recover. She was *dashed down upon her own ground.* In the abode of her strength, in the midst of her resources, in her innermost retreat, she should fall. In herself, she fell powerless. And he adds, she has *no one to raise her up;* none to have ruth upon her; image of the judgment on a lost soul, when the terrible sentence is spoken and none can intercede! *She shall not rise again.* As she fell, she did not again rise. The Prophet beholds beyond the eighty-five years which separated the prosperity under Jeroboam II. from her captivity. As a people, he says, she should be restored no more; nor was she.

3. *The city that went out* by a *thousand,* (i.e. probably that sent out a thousand fighting men, as the word *went out* is often used for, *went out* [6] to fight,) *shall have* lit. *shall retain, an hundred.* She was to be decimated. Only, the tenth alone was to be reserved alive; the nine-tenths were to be destroyed. And this, alike in larger places and in the small. The city *that went forth an hundred shall retain ten.* Smaller places escape for their obscurity, the larger from their strength and situation. One common doom was to befall all. Out of all that multitude, one tithe alone was to be preserved, "[1] dedicated to God," that remnant which God always promised to reserve.

4. *Seek ye Me and ye shall live;* lit. *seek Me and live.* Wonderful conciseness of the word of God, which, in two words [7], comprises the whole of the creature's duty and his hopes, his time and his eternity. The Prophet uses the two imperatives, inoncing both, man's duty and his reward. He does not speak of them, as cause and effect, but as one. Where the one is, there is the other. To seek God is to live. For to seek God is to find Him, and God is Life and the source of life. Forgiveness, grace, life, enter the soul at once. But the seeking is diligent seeking [8]. "[9] It is not to seek God anyhow, but as it is right and meet that He should be sought, longed for, prayed for, Who is so great a Good, constantly, fervently, yea, to our power, the more constantly and fervently, as an Infinite Good is more to be longed for, more loved than all created good." The object of the search is God Himself. *Seek Me,* i.e. seek God for Himself, not for anything out of Him, not for His gifts, not for anything to be loved with Him. This is not to seek Him purely. All is found in Him, but by seeking Him first, and then loving Him in all, and all in Him. *And ye shall live,* first by the life of the body, escaping the enemy; then by the life of grace now, and the life of glory hereafter, as in that of the Psalmist [10], *your heart shall live who seek God.*

5. *But* [*And*] *seek not Bethel.* Israel pretended to seek God in Bethel. Amos sets the two seekings, as incompatible. The god, worshiped at Bethel, was not the One God.

[1] from Rib. [2] Jer. ii. 2. [3] Ezek. xvi. 35.
[4] Is. xlvii. 1. [5] נטשה.

[6] See in Ges. Thes. v. יצא. [7] דרשוני וחיו.
[8] דרש. [9] Dion. [10] Ps. lxix. 32.

Before CHRIST cir. 787.

nor enter into Gilgal, and
pass not to [e] Beersheba:
for Gilgal shall surely
go into captivity, and
[f] Beth-el shall come to
nought.

[e] ch. 8. 14.
[f] Hos. 4. 15. & 10. 8.

6 [g] Seek the LORD, and
ye shall live; lest he break
out like fire in the house
of Joseph, and devour *it*,
and *there be* none to quench
it in Beth-el.

Before CHRIST cir. 787.

[g] ver. 4.

To seek God there was to lose Him. "Seek not God," he would say, "and a phantom, which will lead from God."

And pass not to Beersheba. Jeroboam I. pretended that it was too much for Israel to go up to Jerusalem. And yet Israel thought it not too much to go to the extremest point of Judah toward Idumæa[1], perhaps, four times as far South of Jerusalem, as Jerusalem lay from Bethel. For Beersheba is thought to have lain some thirty miles South of Hebron[2], which is twenty-two miles South of Jerusalem[3]; while Bethel is but twelve to the North. So much pains will men take in self-willed service, and yet not see that it takes away the excuse for neglecting the true. At Beersheba, Abraham[4] *called upon the name of the Lord, the everlasting God.* There God revealed Himself to Isaac and Jacob[5]. There, because He had so revealed Himself, Judah made a place of idolatry, which Israel, seeking nought besides from Judah, sought. Beersheba was still a town[6] or large village[7] in the time of S. Jerome. Now all is swept away, except "[8] some foundations of ruins," spread over ¾ of a mile, "with scarcely one stone upon another[9]." The wells alone remain[10], with the ancient names.

Gilgal shall surely go into captivity. The verbal allusions in the Prophets are sometimes artificial; sometimes, they develop the meaning of the word itself, as when Zephaniah says[11], *Ekron* [probably the *firm-rooting*] *shall be uprooted;* sometimes, as here, the words are connected, although not the same. In all cases, the likeness of sound was calculated to fix them in men's memories. It would be so, if one with authority could say, "Paris périra[12]," "Paris shall perish," or "London is undone." Still more would the words, Hag-gilgal galo yigleh, because the name Gilgal still retained its first meaning, *the great rolling*[13], and the word joined with it had a kindred meaning[14]. Originally it probably means, "swept clear away." God first *rolled away the reproach of Egypt*[15] from His people there. Then, when it made itself like the heathen, it should itself be rolled clear away[16]. Gilgal was originally in Benjamin, but Israel had probably annexed it to itself, as it had Bethel and Jericho[17], both of which had been assigned by Joshua to Benjamin[18].

And Bethel shall come to nought. Hosea had called *Bethel, God's house,* by the name of *Bethaven*[19], *Vanity-house.* Amos, in allusion to this probably, drops the first half of the name, and says that it shall not merely be *house of vanity,* but *Aven, vanity* itself. "By sin the soul, which was the house or temple of God, becomes the temple of vanity and of devils."

6. *Seek ye the Lord and ye shall live;* lit. *seek the Lord and live;* being united to Him, the Fountain of life. He reimpresses on them the one simple need of the creature, *seek God,* the one true God as He revealed Himself, not as worldly men, or the politicians of Jeroboam's court, or the calf-priests, fabled of Him. *Seek Him.* For in Him is all; without Him, nothing.

Lest He break out like fire in Bethel. Formerly the Spirit of God came vehemently down[20] upon Sansom[21] and Saul[22] and David[23], to fit them as instruments for God; as did the Evil spirit, when God departed from Saul[24]. So now, unless they repented, God Himself would suddenly shew His powerful Presence among them, but, as He had revealed Himself to be[25], *the Lord thy God* is *a consuming Fire. And devour* it, lit. *and it* [the fire] *shall devour, and* there be *none to quench* it *in* [better, *for*] *Bethel.* Bethel, the centre of their idol-hopes, so far from aiding them then, shall not be able to help itself, nor shall there be any to help it. The fire of God kindles around it, and there is none to quench it for her[26].

"[27] The whole place treateth of mercy and justice. The whole ground of men's punish-

[1] Jos. Ant. 8. 13. 7.
[2] Robinson, i. 206. Eus. and S. Jer. have twenty.
[3] Euseb. S. Jer. v. Arbo.
[4] Gen. xxi. 33.
[5] Ib. xxvi. 23, 4. xlvi. 1.
[6] S. Jer. Qu. ad Gen. xxii. 30.
[7] de loc. Hebr.
[8] Van de Velde, ii. 127.
[9] Robinson, i. 204.
[10] There are now seven wells, 2 large and separate from the other 5. But Moses speaks of one well only, dug by Abraham and reopened by Isaac. Gen. xxi. 30. xxvi. 18, 32, 3.
[11] ii. 4.
[12] instanced by Mercier here.
[13] The article is prefixed to proper names, which are still in a degree appellatives.
[14] גלה and גלל both from a biliteral root, גל.
[15] Josh. v. 9.
[16] See גלגלתיך Jer. li. 25.
[17] 1 Kgs xvi. 34.
[18] Josh. xviii. 21, 22.
[19] iv. 15. x. 5.
[20] The same word is used in all these places.
[21] Jud. xiv. 6, 19. xv. 14.
[22] 1 Sam. x. 6. xi. 6.
[23] Ib. xvi. 13.
[24] Ib. xviii. 10.
[25] Deut. iv. 24.
[26] as in Jer. iv. 4.
[27] Mont.

Before CHRIST cir. 787.

7 Ye who [h] turn judg-
ment to wormwood, and
leave off righteousness in
the earth,
8 *Seek him* that maketh
the [i] seven stars and Orion,
and turneth the shadow of
death into the morning,
[k] and maketh the day dark
with night: that [l] calleth

[h] ch. 6. 12.

[i] Job 9. 9. & 38. 31.
[k] Ps. 104. 20.
[l] Job 38. 34. ch. 9. 6.

ment, calamities, condemnation is ascribed to their own fault and negligence, who neglect the deliverance often promised and offered them by God, and [1] *love darkness rather than light, because their deeds are evil.* Whoever is not saved, the whole blame lies in their own will and negligence and malice. God, Who [2] *willeth not that any should perish, but that all should come to repentance,* Himself unsought, seeks, entreats, ceases not to monish, exhort, set before them their guilt, that they may cease to prepare such evil for themselves. But they neither give Him entrance, nor hear His entreaties, nor admit the warnings of the Divine mercy, which if they neglect, they must needs be made over to His justice. The goodness of God is wanting to no one, save those who are wanting to themselves. Wherefore, having often besought them before, He invites them yet again to salvation, putting forth that His Name, so full of mysteries of mercy; *Seek the Lord and live,*" seek Him Who IS, the Unchangeable. He Who had willed their salvation, still willed it, for He *changes not* [3]. "He adds threatenings, that those whom He calls to life, He might either allure by promises, or scare from death through fear of the impending evil."

7. *Ye who turn.* Those whom he calls to seek God, were men filled with all injustice, who turned the sweetness of justice into the bitterness of wormwood [4]. Moses had used *gall* and *wormwood* as a proverb [5]; *lest there be among you a root that beareth gall and wormwood; the Lord will not spare him, but then the anger of the Lord and His jealousy shall smoke against that man, and all the curses that are written in this book shall lie upon him.* The word of Amos would remind them of the word of Moses.

And leave off righteousness in the earth; better, *and set righteousness to rest on the ground* [6]. They dethroned righteousness, the representative and vice-gerent of God, and made it rest on the ground. The *little horn,* Daniel says [7], should *cast truth to the ground.* These seem to have blended outrage with insult, as when *the Lord our Righteousness* [8] took our flesh, they *put on Him* the *scarlet robe, and* the *crown of thorns* upon His Head, *and bowed the knee before Him, and mocked Him,* and then *crucified Him.* They "deposed" her, "set her down," it may be, with a mock make-believe deference, as men now-a-days, in civil terms, depose God, ignoring Him and His right over them. They set her on the ground and so left her, the image of God. This they did, not in one way only, but in all the ways in which they could. He does not limit it to the *righteousness* shewn in doing justice. It includes all transactions between man and man, in which right enters, all buying and selling, all equity, all giving to another his due. All the bands of society were dissolved, and *righteousness* was placed on the ground, to be trampled on by all in all things.

8. Seek Him *that maketh the seven stars.* Misbelief effaces the thought of God as He Is. It retains the name God, but means something quite different from the One True God. So men spoke of "the Deity," as a sort of First Cause of all things, and did not perceive that they only meant to own that this fair harmony of things created was not (at least as it now exists,) self-existent, and that they had lost sight of the Personal God Who had made known to them His Will, Whom they were to believe in, obey, fear, love. "The Deity" was no object of fear or love. It was but a bold confession that they did not mean to be Atheists, or that they meant intellectually to admire the creation. Such confessions, even when not consciously Atheistic, become at least the parents of Atheism or Panotheism, and slide insensibly into either. For a First Cause, who is conceived of as no more, is an abstraction, not God. God *is* the Cause of all causes. All things *are,* and have their relations to each other, as cause and effect, because He so created them. A "Great First Cause," who is only thought of as a Cause, is a mere fiction of a man's imagining, an attempt to appear to account for the mysteries of being, without owning that, since our being is from God, we are responsible creatures whom He created for Himself, and who are to yield to Him an account of the use of our being which He gave us. In like way, Israel had probably so mixed up the thought of God with Nature, that it had lost sight of God, as distinct from the creation. And so Amos, after appealing to their consciences, sets forth God to them as the Creator, Disposer

[1] S. John iii. 19. [2] 2 S. Pet. iii. 9.
[3] Mal. iii. 6. [4] S. Jer.
[5] Deut. xxix. 18, 20.
[6] הניח is used of casting forth, Nu. xix. 9; casting violently to the ground, Is. xxviii. 2; casting into a furnace, Ez. xxii. 20. Yet ordinarily it has the simple meaning "placed, made to rest."
[7] viii. 12. [8] Jer. xxiii. 6.

Before CHRIST cir. 787.

for the waters of the sea,
and poureth them out upon
the face of the earth:
m ch. 4. 13. [m] The LORD *is* his name:

9 That strengtheneth the
† spoiled against the strong,
so that the spoiled shall
come against the fortress.

† Heb. *spoil.*

of all things, and the Just God, who redresseth man's violence and injustice. The *seven stars*, lit. *the heap*, are the striking cluster of stars, called by Greeks and Latins the Pleiades[1], which consist of seven larger stars, and in all of above forty. Orion[2], a constellation in one line with the Pleiades, was conceived by the Arabs and Syrians also, as a gigantic figure. The Chaldee also renders, the "violent" or "the rebel." The Hebrew title *Cesil, fool*, adds the idea of an irreligious man, which is also the meaning of Nimrod, *rebel*, lit. "let us rebel." Job, in that he speaks of *the bands of Orion*[3], pictures him as "bound," the "belt" being the *band.* This falls in with the later tradition, that Nimrod, who, as the founder of Babel, was the first rebel against God[4], was represented by the easterns in their grouping of the stars, as a giant chained[5], the same constellation which we call Orion.

And turneth the shadow of death into the morning. This is no mere alternation of night and day, no "kindling" of "each day out of night." The *shadow of death* is strictly the darkness of death, or of the grave[6]. It is used of darkness intense as the darkness of the grave[7], of gloom[8], or moral benightening[9] which seems to cast *the shadow of death* over the soul, of distress which is as the forerunner of death[10], or of things, hidden as the grave, which God alone can bring to light[11]. The word is united with darkness, physical, moral, mental, but always as intensifying it, beyond any mere darkness. Amos first sets forth the power of God, then His goodness. Out of every extremity of ill, God can, will, does, deliver. He Who said, *let there be light and there was light,* at once changeth any depth of darkness into light, the death-darkness of sin into the dawn of grace, the hopeless night of ignorance into *the day-star from on high,* the night of the grave into the eternal morn of the Resurrection which knoweth no setting. But then on impenitence the contrary follows;

And maketh the day dark with night; lit. *and darkeneth day into night.* As God withdraws *the shadow of death,* so that there should be no trace of it left, but all is filled with His light, so, again, when His light is abused or neglected, He so withdraws it, as at times, to leave no trace or gleam of it. Conscience becomes benighted, so as to sin undoubtingly: faith is darkened, so that the soul no more even suspects the truth. Hell has no light.

That calleth for the waters of the sea. This can be no other than a memory of the flood, *when the waters prevailed over the earth*[12]. The Prophet speaks of nothing partial. He speaks of *sea* and *earth*, each, as a whole, standing against the other. *God calleth the waters of the sea and poureth them over the face of the earth.* They seem ever threatening the land, but for Him[13] *which hath placed the sand for the bound of the sea, that it cannot pass it.* Now God calls them, and *pours them over the face,* i. e. the whole surface. The flood, He promised, should not again be. But it is the image of that universal destruction, which shall end man's thousands of years of rebellion against God. The words then of Amos, in their simplest sense, speak of a future universal judgment of the inhabitants of the earth, like, in extent, to that former judgment, when God *brought in the flood upon the world of the ungodly*[14].

The words have been thought also to describe that daily marvel of God's Providence, how, from the salt briny sea, which could bring but barrenness, He, by the heat of the Sun, draws up the moisture, and discharges it anew in life-giving showers on the surface of the earth. God's daily care of us, in the workings of His creatures, is a witness[15] of His relation to us as our Father; it is an earnest also of our relation, and so of our accountableness, to Him.

The Lord is *His name.* He, the One Self-existent Unchangeable God, who revealed Himself to their forefathers, and forbade them to worship Him under any form of their own device.

9. *That strengtheneth the spoiled,* (lit. *spoil*

[1] כימה (i. q. Arab. koumah, "heap,") is rendered πλειάδα by Symm. Theod. here; by the LXX. Aq. and S. Jer. in Job xxxviii. 31; by the LXX. also Job ix. 9 (the two names Ἀρκτοῦρον and πλειάδα, being transposed). The Syr. and Ch. retain the Hebrew word, which the Arab. Transl. in Job renders "Thorayya," "little multitude," the Arabic name of the Pleiades.

[2] Aquila and S. Jerome here, S. Jer. in Job ix. 9, the LXX. in Is. xiii. 10 and Job xxxviii. 31, render, "Orion." The Ch. in Job has נפולא; its plural here; in Isaiah, the Heb. word. The Syr. here and in Job has "jaboro" (the Heb. גביר. Mighty, Gen. x. 8). The Arab. in Job, the same.

[3] xxxviii. 31.

[4] Gen. x. 9, 10. xi. 4–9. Josephus (Arch. i. 4. 2.) does but develop Genesis.

[5] Chron. Pasch. p. 36.

[6] Job iii. 5. x. 21, 22. xxxiv. 22 xxxviii. 17. Ps. xxiii. 4. Jer. xiii. 16.

[7] Job xxviii. 3.

[8] Ib. xxiv. 17.

[9] Is. ix. 2. (1 Heb.)

[10] Job xvi. 16. Ps. xliv. 19. cvii. 10, 14. Jer. ii. 6. xiii. 16.

[11] Job xii. 22.

[12] Gen. vii. 24.

[13] Jer. v. 22.

[14] 2 S. Pet. ii. 5.

[15] Acts xiv. 17.

Before CHRIST cir. 787.

n Is. 29. 21.
o 1 Kings 22. 8.

10 n They hate him that rebuketh in the gate, and they o abhor him that speaketh uprightly.

11 Forasmuch therefore as your treading *is* upon

Before CHRIST cir. 787.

E. M.) probably *That maketh devastation to smile on the strong*[1]. The *smile*, in anger, attests both the extremity of anger, and the consciousness of the ease, wherewith the offence can be punished. They were strong in their own strength; strong, as they deemed, in their *fortress;* "[2] strong with an evil strength, like one phrensied against his physician." But their strength would be weakness. *Desolation*, when God willed, would *smile at* all which they accounted *might*, and would *come against the fortress*, which, as they deemed, *cut off*[3] all approach.

10. *They hate him that rebuketh. The gate* is the well-known place of concourse, where just or, in Israel now, unjust judgment was given[4], where all was done which was to be done publicly[5]. Samaria had a large area[6] by its chief gate, where two kings could hold court, and the 400 false prophets and the people, in great numbers, could gather[7], and a market could be held[8]. Josiah brake down an idol-shrine, which was in one of the gates of Jerusalem[9]. The prophets seized the opportunity of finding the people together, and preached to them there. So it was even in the days of Solomon[10]. *Wisdom crieth without; she uttereth her voice in the streets; she crieth in the chief place of concourse, in the openings of the gates, in the city she uttereth her words, How long, ye simple ones, will ye love simplicity? &c.*, and again[11], *She standeth in the top of high places, by the way, in the meeting of the paths. She crieth at the gates, at the entry of the city, at the coming in at the doors; Unto you, O men, I call, &c.* Jeremiah mentions two occasions, upon which God bade him reprove the king and people in the gates of Jerusalem[12]. There doubtless Amos and Hosea *reproved* them, and, for reproving, were *hated.* As Isaiah says[13], *they lay a snare for him that reproveth in the gate.* They sinned publicly, and therefore they were to be rebuked publicly. They sinned *in the gate* by injustice and oppression, and therefore were to be *rebuked before all, that others also might fear*[14].

And they abhor him that speaketh uprightly, lit. *perfectly.* The prophets spoke *perfectly*, "[15] for they spoke the all-perfect word of God, of which David says[16], *The law of the Lord is perfect, converting the soul.*" "Carnal eyes hate the light of truth, which they cast aside for execrable lies, closing to themselves the fountain of the Divine mercy[15]." "[2] This is the sin which hath no remission; this is the sin of the strong and mighty, who sin not out of ignorance or weakness, but with impenitent heart proudly defend their sin, and *hate him that rebuketh and abhor him who* dareth to *speak perfectly*, i. e. not things which please them, but resisting their evil." This, like all other good of God and evil of man, met most in and against Christ. "[2] Who is he who *rebuked in the gate* or who *spake perfectly?* David rebuked them, and spake much perfectly, and so they hated him and said[17], *what portion have we in David, or what inheritance have we in the son of Jesse?* Him also who spake these very words, and the other prophets they hated and abhorred. But as the rest, so this too, is truly and indubitably fulfilled in Christ, rebuking justly and speaking perfectly. He Himself saith in a Psalm[18], *They that sat in the gate spake against Me*, wherefore, when He had said[19], *he that hateth Me hateth My Father also*, and, *now they have both seen and hated both Me and My Father*, He subjoined, *that the word might be fulfilled that is written in their law, they hated Me without a cause.* Above all then, we understand Christ, Whom they hated, *rebuking in the gate*, i. e. openly and in public; as He said[20], *I spake openly to the world, and in secret have I said nothing.* He alone spake perfectly, *Who did no sin, neither was guile found in His mouth*[21]. In wisdom also and doctrine, He alone spake perfectly, perfectly and so wonderfully, that *the officers of the chief priests and Pharisees* who were *sent to take Him, said, Never man spake like this Man*[22]."

"[23] It is a great sin to hate him who rebuketh, especially if he rebuke thee, not out of dislike, but out of love, if he doth it *between thee and him alone*[24], if, *taking with* him a brother, if afterward, in the presence of the Church, so that it may be evident that he does not blame thee out of any love of detraction, but out of zeal for thine amendment."

11. *Forasmuch therefore*, (since they rejected reproof, he pronounces the sentence of God upon them,) *as your treading* is *upon the poor.*

[1] The E. V. has followed a conjecture of Jon. and Kimchi, founded on the context of Job ix. 27, x. 20. Aquila, ὁ μειδιῶν, and S. Jerome, *subridens*, agree with the Arabic use, which suits all the places in Heb. "smiled, was gladdened, was cheered." Others here, "made to dawn," from the Arab.

[2] Rup.

[3] The force of מבצר.

[4] Deut. xxv. 7. Job v. 4. xxxi. 21. 2 Sam. xv. 2. Pr. xxii. 22. Is. xxix. 21.

[5] Ruth iv. 1, 11.

[6] גרן.

[7] 1 Kgs xxii. 10. 2 Chr. xviii. 9.

[8] 2 Kgs vii. 1.

[9] Ib. xxiii. 8.

[10] Pr. i. 20–22.

[11] Ib. viii. 2–4.

[12] xvii. 19. xix. 2.

[13] xxix. 21.

[14] 1 Tim. v. 20.

[15] Lyr.

[16] Ps. xix. 7.

[17] 1 Kgs xii. 16.

[18] lxix. 12.

[19] S. John xv. 23–25.

[20] Ib. xviii. 20.

[21] 1 S. Pet. ii. 22.

[22] S. John vii. 45, 6.

[23] S. Jer.

[24] S. Matt. xviii. 15–17.

Before CHRIST cir. 787.

the poor, and ye take from
him burdens of wheat: [p] ye
have built houses of hewn
stone, but ye shall not
dwell in them; ye have
planted † pleasant vineyards, but ye shall not
drink wine of them.

12 For I know your
manifold transgressions
and your mighty sins:
[q] they afflict the just, they

p Deut. 28. 30, 38, 39. Mic. 6. 15. Zeph. 1. 13. Hag. 1. 6.
† Heb. *vineyards of desire.*
q ch. 2. 6.

This expresses more habitual trampling on the poor, than if he had said, *ye tread upon the poor*. They were ever trampling on those who were already of low and depressed condition. *And ye take from him burdens of wheat, presents of wheat.* The word always signifies presents, voluntary [1], or involuntary [2], what was *carried*, offered to any one. They received *wheat* from the poor, cleansed [3], winnowed, and *sold the refuse* [4], requiring what it was wrong to receive, and selling what at the least it was disgraceful not to give. God had expressly forbidden to [5] *lend food for interest.* It may be that, in order to evade the law, the interest was called *a present.*

Ye have built houses of hewn stone. The houses of Israel were, perhaps most commonly, built of brick [6] dried in the sun only. As least, houses built of hewn stone, like most of our's, are proverbially contrasted with them, as the more solid with the more ordinary building. [7] *The white bricks are fallen down, and we will build with hewn stones.* And Ezekiel is bidden to dig through the wall of his house [8]. Houses of stone there were, as appears from the directions as to the unhealthy accretions, called the leprosy of the house [9]. It may be, however, that their houses of *hewn stone*, had a smoothed surface, like our "ashlar." Anyhow, the sin of luxury is not simply measured by the things themselves, but by their relation to ourselves and our condition also; and wrong is not estimated by the extent of the gain and loss of the two parties only, but by the injury inflicted. These men, who built houses, luxurious for them, had wrung from the poor their living, as those do, who beat down the wages of the poor. Therefore they were not to take possession of what was their own; as Ahab, who by murder possessed himself of Naboth's vineyard, forfeited his throne and his life. God, in the law, consulted for the feeling which desires to enter into the fruit of a man's toil. When they should go to war they were to proclaim, [10] *what man* is there *that hath built a new house, and hath not dedicated it? let him go and return to his house, lest he die in the battle, and another man dedicate it. And what man* is he *that hath planted a vineyard and hath not eaten of it? let him go. and return unto his house, lest he die in the battle and another man eat of it.* Now God reversed all this, and withdrew the tender love, whereby He had provided it. The words, from their proverbial character, express a principle of God's judgments, that wrong dealing, whereby a man would secure himself or enlarge his inheritance, destroys both. Who poorer than our Lord, bared of all upon the Cross, of Whom it had been written, [11] *They persecuted the poor helpless man, that they might slay him who was vexed at the heart*, and of whom the Jews said [12], *Come let us kill Him, that the inheritance may be our's?* They killed Him, they said [13], lest *the Romans take away our place and nation. The vineyard was taken from them;* their *place* destroyed, their *nation* dispersed.

12. *For I know;* lit. *I have known.* They thought that God did not know, because He did not avenge; as the Psalmist says, [14] *Thy judgments are far above out of his sight.* Men who do not act with the thought of God, cease to know Him, and forget that He knows them. *Your manifold transgressions;* lit. *many* are *your transgressions and mighty your sins.* Their deeds, they knew, were mighty, strong, vigorous, decided. God says, that their *sins* were so, not many and great only, but *mighty, strong,* "[15] issuing not out of ignorance and infirmity, but out of proud strength:" "[16] *strong* in the oppression of the poor and in provoking God," and bringing down His wrath. So Asaph says of the prosperous [17]; *Pride encompasseth them, as a chain; they are corrupt, they speak oppression wickedly; they speak from on high.*

They afflict the just, lit. *afflicters of the just,* i. e. such as habitually afflicted him; whose habit and quality it was to afflict him. Our version mostly renders the word *enemies.* Originally, it signifies *afflicting, persecuting* enemies. Yet it is used also of the enemies of

1 of the "mess" sent, Gen. xliii. 34, 2 Sam. xi. 8; of the gifts of one superior in rank, Esth. ii. 18, Jer. xl. 5.

2 of a contribution appointed by Divine law, 2 Chr. xxiv. 6–9, Ez. xx. 40. The masc. משא is used, of tribute, 2 Chr. xvii. 11

3 Such is בר as distinct from חטה, the name of the grain, "wheat."

4 Am. viii. 6.
5 Lev. xxv. 37. Deut. xxiii. 19.
6 לבנים.
7 Is. ix. 10.
8 xii. 5, 7.
9 Lev. xiv. 34–48.
10 Deut. xx. 5, 6.
11 Ps. cix. 15.
12 S. Matt. xxi. 38.
13 S. John xi. 48.
14 Ps. x. 5.
15 Rup.
16 Hug.
17 Ps. lxxiii. 6, 8.

Before CHRIST cir. 787.

‖ Or, *a ransom.*
r Is. 29. 21. ch. 2. 7.
s ch. 6. 10.

take ‖ a bribe, and they
r turn aside the poor in the
gate *from their right.*
13 Therefore s the prudent shall keep silence in
that time: for it *is* an evil
time.
14 Seek good, and not
evil, that ye may live: and
so the LORD, the God of

God, perhaps such as persecute Him in His people, or in His Son when in the flesh. The unjust hate the just, as is said in the book of Wisdom[1]; *The ungodly said, Therefore let us lie in wait for the righteous, because he is not for our turn, and is clean contrary to our doings: he upbraideth us with our offending the law. He professeth to have the knowledge of God, and he calleth himself the child of the Lord. He was made to reprove our thoughts. He is grievous unto us even to behold; for his life is not as other men's, his ways are of another fashion.* So when the Truth and Righteousness came into the world, the Scribes and Pharisees hated Him because He reproved them, *denied*[2] and crucified *the Holy one and the Just, and desired a murderer to be granted unto* them, haters and *enemies of the Just,* and preferring to Him the unjust.

That take a bribe, lit. *a ransom.* It may be that, contrary to the law, which forbade, in these same words[3], *to take any ransom for the life of a murderer,* they took some ransom to set free rich murderers, and so, (as we have seen for many years to be the effect of unjust acquittals,) blood was shed with impunity, and was shed the more, because it was disregarded. The word, however, is used in one place apparently of any bribe, through which a man connives at injustice[4].

13. *Therefore the prudent shall keep silence in that time.* The *time* may be either the time of the obduracy of the wicked, or that of the common punishment. For a time may be called *evil,* whether evil is done, or is suffered in it, as Jacob says[5], *Few and evil have the days of the years of my life been.* Of the first, he would perhaps say, that the oppressed poor would, if wise, be silent, not complaining or accusing; for, injustice having the mastery, complaint would only bring on them fresh sufferings. And again also he may mean that, on account of the incorrigibleness of the people, the wise and the prophets would be silent, because the more the people were rebuked, the more impatient and worse they became. So our Lord was silent before His judges, as had been foretold of Him; for since they would not hear, His speaking would only increase their condemnation[6]. *If I tell you, ye will not believe; and if I also ask you, ye will not answer Me, nor let Me go.* So God said by Solomon[7]: *He that reproveth a scorner getteth himself shame, and he that rebuketh a wicked* man getteth *himself a blot.* And our Lord bids[8], *Give not that which is holy unto dogs, and cast not your pearls before swine.* They hated and rejected those who rebuked them[9]. Since then rebuke profited not, the prophets should hold their peace. It is a fearful judgment, when God withholds His warnings. In times of punishment also the prudent keep silence. Intense affliction is *dumb and openeth not its mouth,* owning the hand of God. It may be too, that Amos, like Hosea[10], expresses the uselessness of all reproof, in regard to the most of those whom he called to repentance, even while he continued earnestly to rebuke them.

14. *Seek good and not evil,* i.e. *and seek not evil*[11]. Amos again takes up his warning, *seek not Bethel; seek the Lord.* Now they not only *did evil,* but they *sought*[12] it diligently; they were diligent in doing it, and so, in bringing it on themselves; they sought it out and the occasions of it. Men "[13]cannot seek good without first putting away evil, as it is written[14], *cease to do evil, learn to do well.*" *Ye cannot serve God and Mammon.* He bids them use the same diligence in seeking good which they now used for evil. Seek it also wholly, not seeking at one while good, at another, evil, but wholly good, and Him Who is Good. "He seeketh good, who believeth in Him Who saith[15], *I am the good Shepherd.*"

That ye may live, in Him Who is *the Life; and so the Lord, the God of hosts, shall be with you,* by His holy Presence, grace and protection, *as ye have spoken.* Israel looked away from the sins whereby he displeased God, and looked to his half-worship of God as entitling him to all which God had promised to full obedience. "[16]They gloried in the nobleness of their birth after the flesh, not in imitating the faith and lives of the patriarchs. So then, because they were descended from Abraham, they thought that God must defend them. Such were those Jews, to whom the Saviour said[17], *If ye were Abraham's seed, ye would do the works of Abraham;* and His forerunner[18], *think not to say within yourselves, we have Abraham for our father.*" They

1 ii. 1, 12–15.
2 Acts iii. 14.
3 Num. xxxv. 22, לא תקחו כפר.
4 1 Sam. xii. 3.
5 Gen. xlvii. 9.
6 S. Luke xxii. 67, 8.
7 Pr. ix. 7.
8 S. Matt. vii. 6.
9 ver. 10.
10 iv. 4, 17.
11 אל implying the verb.
12 דרש.
13 S. Jer.
14 Is. i. 16, 17.
15 S. John x. 11.
16 Dion.
17 S. John viii. 39.
18 S. Matt. iii. 9.

Before CHRIST cir. 787.

hosts, shall be with you,
[t] as ye have spoken.
15 [u] Hate the evil, and
love the good, and estab-
lish judgment in the gate:
[x] it may be that the LORD
God of hosts will be gra-
cious unto the remnant of
Joseph.
16 Therefore the LORD,
the God of hosts, the Lord,
saith thus; Wailing *shall
be* in all streets; and they
shall say in all the high-

t Mic. 3. 11.
u Ps. 34. 14. & 97. 10. Rom. 12. 9.
x Ex. 32 30. 2 Kings 19. 4. Joel 2. 14.

wished that God should abide with them, that they might[1] *abide in the land*, but they cared not to abide with God.

15. *Hate the evil and love the good.* Man will not cease wholly to *seek evil*, unless he *hate* it; nor will he *seek good*, unless he *love* it. "[2] He *hateth evil*, who not only is not overcome by pleasure, but hates its deeds; and he *loveth good*, who, not unwillingly or of necessity or from fear, doth what is good, but because it is good." "[3] Evil of sin must be hated, in and for itself; the sinner must not be hated in himself, but only the evil in him." They hated him, who reproved them; he bids them hate sin. They *set down righteousness on the ground;* he bids them, *establish*, lit. *set up firmly, judgment in the gate.* To undo, as far as any one can, the effects of past sin, is among the first-fruits of repentance.

It may be that the Lord God of Hosts will be gracious. "[3] He speaks so, in regard of the changeableness and uncertainty, not in God, but in man. There is no question but that God is gracious to all who *hate evil and love good*; but He doth not always deliver them from temporal calamity or captivity, because it is not for their salvation. Yet had Israel *hated evil and loved good*, perchance He would have delivered them from captivity, although He frequently said, they should be carried captive. For so He said to the two tribes in Jeremiah[4], *Amend your ways, and your doings, and I will cause you to dwell in this place.*" But since God knew that most of them would not repent, He saith not, *will be gracious unto Israel*, but, *unto the remnant of Joseph*, i. e.[5] *the remnant, according to the election of grace;* such as had been *the seven thousand who bowed not the knee unto Baal;* those who repented, while *the rest were hardened.* He says, *Joseph*, not Ephraim, in order to recall to them the deeds of their father. Jacob's blessing on Joseph descended upon Ephraim, but was forfeited by Jeroboam's *sin wherewith he made Israel to sin.* "[6] Joseph in his deeds and sufferings was a type of Jesus Christ, in Whom the remnant is saved." *A remnant*, however only, *should be saved;* so the Prophet says;

16. *Therefore the Lord, the God of Hosts, the Lord.* For the third time in these three last verses Amos again reminds them, by Whose authority he speaks, His Who had revealed Himself as *I AM*, the Self-existent God, God by nature and of nature, the Creator and Ruler and Lord of all, visible or invisible, against their false gods, or fictitious substitutes for the true God. Here, over and above those titles, *HE IS*, i. e. HE Alone IS, *the God of Hosts*, God *of all things, in heaven and earth*, the heavenly bodies from whose influences the idolaters hoped for good, and the unseen evil beings[7], who seduced them, he adds the title, which men most shrink from, *Lord.* He Who so threatened, was the Same who had absolute power over His creatures, to dispose of them, as He willed. It costs men nothing to own God, as a Creator, the Cause of causes, the Orderer of all things by certain fixed laws. It satisfies certain intellects, so to own Him. What man, a sinner, shrinks from, is that the God is Lord, the absolute disposer and Master of his sinful self.

Wailing in all streets, lit. *broad places*, i.e. market-places[8]. *There*, where judgments were held, where were the markets, where consequently had been all the manifold oppressions through injustice in judgments and in dealings, and the wailings of the oppressed; *wailing* should come on them.

They shall say in all the highways, i. e. *streets, alas! alas!* our, *woe, woe.* It is the word so often used by our Lord; *woe unto you.* This is no imagery. Truth has a more awful, sterner, reality than any imagery. The terribleness of the prophecy lies in its truth. When war pressed without on the walls of Samaria, and within was famine and pestilence, woe, woe, woe, must have echoed in every street; for in every street was death and fear of worse. Yet imagine every sound of joy or din or hum of men, or mirth of children, hushed in the streets, and woe, woe, going up from every street of a metropolis, in one unmitigated, unchanging, ever-repeated monotony of grief. Such were the present fruits of sin. Yet what a mere shadow of the inward grief is its outward utterance!

[1] Ps. xxxvii. 3, [2] S. Jer. [3] Dion. [4] vii. 3. [5] Rom. xi. 4, 5. [6] Rup. [7] Is. xxiv. 21.
[8] The רחב might be a "broad" street (πλατεῖα) as Gen. xix. 2, Jud. xix. 15, 17, 20, but, contrasted with חוצות, it is probably the "broad place" near the gate.

Before CHRIST cir. 787.

ways, Alas! alas! and they
shall call the husbandman
to mourning, and [y] such as
are skillful of lamentation
to wailing.

17 And in all vineyards
shall be wailing: for [z] I
will pass through thee,
saith the LORD.
18 [a] Woe unto you that

[y] Jer. 9 17.

[z] Ex. 12. 12. Nah. 1. 12.
[a] Is. 5. 19. Jer. 17. 15. Ezek. 12. 22, 27. 2 Pet. 3. 4.

And they shall call the husbandman to mourning. To cultivate the fields would then only be to provide food for the enemy. His occupation would be gone. One universal sorrow would give one universal employment. To this, they would call those unskilled, with their deep strong voices; they would, by a public act, *proclaim wailing to* [1] *those skillful in lamentation.* It was, as it were, a dirge over the funeral of their country. As, at funerals, they employed minstrels, both men and women [2], who, by mournful anthems and the touching plaintiveness of the human voice, should stir up deeper depths of sorrow, so here, over the whole of Israel. And as at the funeral of one respected or beloved, they used exclamations of woe [3], *ah my brother!* and *ah sister, ah lord, ah his glory,* so Jeremiah bids them [4], *call and make haste and take up a wailing for us, that our eyes may run down with tears: for a voice of wailing is heard out of Zion. How are we spoiled!* "[5] In joy, men long to impart their joys to others, and exhort them to joy with them. Our Lord sanctions this, in speaking of the Good Shepherd, Who called His friends and neighbors together, *rejoice with Me, for I have found the sheep which I had lost.* Nor is it anything new, that, when we have received any great benefit from God, we call even the inanimate creation to thank and praise God. So did David ofttimes and the three children. So too in sorrow. When anything adverse has befallen us, we invite even senseless things to grieve with us, as though our own tears sufficed not for so great a sorrow." The same feeling makes the rich now clothe those of their household in mourning, which made those of old hire mourners, that all might be in harmony with their grief.

17. *And in all vineyards* shall be *wailing.* All joy should be turned into sorrow. Where aforetime was the vintage-shout in thankfulness for the ingathering, and anticipating gladness to come, there, in the source of their luxury, should be wailing, the forerunner of sorrow to come. It was a vintage, not of wine, but of woe.

For I will pass through thee. In the destruction of the firstborn in Egypt, God did not *pass through* but *passed over* them, and they kept, in memory thereof, the feast of the Passover. Now God would no longer *pass over* them and their sins. He says, *I will pass through thee,* as He then said [6], *I will pass through the land of Egypt this night, and will smite all the firstborn of the land of Egypt—and against all the gods of Egypt I will execute judgment.* As God says by Hosea [7], *I will not enter the city,* i. e. He would not make His Presence felt, or take cognizance, when to take cognizance would be to punish, so here, contrariwise, He says, *I will pass through,* taking exact and severe account, in judgment. S. Jerome further says, "so often as this word is used in Holy Scripture, in the person of God, it denotes punishment, that He would not abide among them, but would pass through and leave them. Surely, it is an image of this, that, when the Jews would have cast our Lord headlong from the brow of the hill whereon their city was built, *He passed through the midst of them* [8], so that they could not see Him nor know Him, *and so went His way.* And this, when He had just told them, that none of the widows of Israel were fed by Elias, or the lepers cleansed by Elisha, save the widow of Sarepta, and Naaman the Syrian. So should their leprosy cleave to them, and the famine of the word of God and of the oil of the Holy Spirit abide among them, while the Gentiles were washed by His laver and fed with the bread of life."

18. *Woe unto you that desire* [*for yourselves* [9]] *the Day of the Lord.* There were *mockers in those days* [10], as there are now, and as there shall be in the last. And as the *scoffers in the last days* [10] shall say, *Where is the promise of His coming?* so these said [11], *let Him make speed and hasten His work, that we may see it, and let the council of the Holy One of Israel draw nigh and come, that we may know it.* Jeremiah complained [12]; *they say unto me, where is the word of the Lord? let it come now!* And God says to Ezekiel [13], *Son of man, what is that proverb that ye have in the land of Israel, saying, the days are prolonged, and every*

[1] This is the Hebrew construction. The E. V. has followed Kimchi in assuming a transposition, which is, however, only as much as to say that the two idioms are equivalent, as they are. To "call the husbandman to mourning," or to "proclaim mourning to the husbandman" mean the same thing, though the Hebrew words can grammatically only mean the last.

[2] 2 Chr. xxxv. 25. The word *skillful* is masculine, יודעי so in S. Matt. ix. 23.

[3] הוי 1 Kgs xiii. 29. Jer. xxii. 18. Amos uses a shorter form, found here only, הו הו. [4] ix. 17–19.

[5] from Sanct. [6] Ex. xii. 12. [7] xi. 9.

[8] S. Luke iv. 30. [9] The force of מתאוים.

[10] 2 S. Pet. iii. 3, 4, S. Jude 18. [11] Is. v. 19.

[12] xvii. 15. [13] xii. 22, 27.

Before CHRIST cir. 787.

desire the day of the LORD! to what end *is* it for you? [b] the day of the LORD *is* darkness, and not light.

[b] Jer. 30. 7. Joel 2. 2. Zeph. 1. 15.

vision faileth? The vision that he seeth is for many days, and he prophesieth of the times far off. "They would shew their courage and strength of mind, by longing for the Day of the Lord, which the prophets foretold, in which God was to shew forth His power on the disobedient." "[1] Let it come, what these prophets threaten till they are hoarse, let it come, let it come. It is ever held out to us, and never comes. We do not believe that it will come at all, or if it do come, it will not be so dreadful after all; it will go as it came." It may be, however, that they who scoffed at Amos, cloked their unbelief under the form of desiring the good days, which God had promised by Joel afterward. "[2] There is not," they would say, "so much of evil in the captivity, as there is of good in what the Lord has promised afterward." Amos meets the hypocrisy or the scoff, by the appeal to their consciences, *to what end is it to you?* They had nothing in common with it or with God. Whatever it had of good, was not for such as them. *The Day of the Lord* is *darkness, and not light.* Like the pillar of the cloud between Israel and the Egyptians, which betokened God's Presence, every day in which He shews forth His Presence, is a day of light and darkness to those of different characters. The prophets foretold both, but not to all. These scoffers either denied the Coming of that day altogether, or denied its terrors. Either way, they disbelieved God, and, disbelieving Him, would have no share in His promises. To *them*, the Day of the Lord would be unmixed darkness, distress, desolation, destruction, without one ray of gladness. The tempers of men, their belief or disbelief, are the same, as to the Great Day of the Lord, the Day of Judgment. It is all one, whether men deny it altogether or deny its terrors. In either case, they deny it, such as God has ordained it. The words of Amos condemn them too. *The Day of the Lord* had already become the name for every day of judgment, leading on to the Last Day. The principle of all God's judgments is one and the same. One and the same are the characters of those who are to be judged. In one and the same way, is each judgment looked forward to, neglected, prepared for, believed, disbelieved. In one and the same way, our Lord has taught us, will the Great Day come, as the judgments of the flood or upon Sodom, and will find men prepared or unprepared, as they were then. Words then, which describe the character of any day of Judgment, do, according to the Mind of God the Holy Ghost, describe all, and the last also. Of this too, and that chiefly, because it is the greatest, are the words spoken, *Woe unto you, who desire*, amiss or rashly or scornfully or in misbelief, *the Day of the Lord, to what end is it for you? The Day of the Lord is darkness and not light.*

"[3] This sounds a strange woe. It had not seemed strange, had he said, 'Woe to you, who fear not the Day of the Lord.' For, 'not to fear,' belongs to bad, ungodly men. But the good may desire it, so that the Apostle says [4], *I desire to depart and to be with Christ.* Yet even *their* desire is not without a sort of fear. For [5] *who can say, I have made my heart clean?* Yet that is the fear, not of slaves, but of sons; *nor hath* it *torment* [6], for it hath [7] *strong consolation through hope.* When then he says, *Woe unto you that desire the Day of the Lord*, he rebuketh *their* boldness, [8] *who trust in themselves, that they are righteous.*" "At one and the same time," says S. Jerome, "the confidence of the proud is shaken off, who, in order to appear righteous before men, are wont to long for the Day of Judgment and to say, 'Would that the Lord would come, would that we might be dissolved and be with Christ,' imitating the Pharisee, who spake in the Gospel [9], *God, I thank Thee, that I am not as other men are.* For the very fact, that they *desire*, and do not fear, *the Day of the Lord*, shews, that they are worthy of punishment, since no man is *without* sin [10], and *the stars are not pure in His sight* [11]. And He [12] *concluded all under sin, that He might have mercy upon all.* Since, then, no one can judge concerning the Judgment of God, and we are to *give account of every idle word* [13], and Job *offered sacrifices* [14] daily for his sons, lest they should have thought something perversely against the Lord, what rashness it is, to long to reign alone [15]!—In troubles and distresses we are wont to say, 'would that we might depart out of the body and be freed from the miseries of this world,' not knowing that, while we are in this flesh, we have place for repentance; but if we depart, we shall hear that of the prophet, [16] *in hell who will give Thee thanks?* That is *the sorrow of this world* [17], which worketh *death*, wherewith the Apostle would not have him sorrow who had sinned with his father's wife; the sorrow whereby the wretched Judas too perished, who, *swallowed up with overmuch sorrow* [18], joined mur-

[1] from Lap. [2] S. Jer. [3] Rup. [4] Phil. i. 23. [5] Prov. xx. 9. [6] 1 S. John iv. 18. [7] Heb. vi. 18, Rom. v. 2. [8] S. Luke xviii. 9.

[9] S. Luke xviii. 11, 12. [10] 2 Chr. vi. 36. [11] Job xxv. 5. [12] Gal. iii. 22, Rom. xi. 32. [13] S. Matt. xii. 36. [14] Job i. 5. [15] 1 Cor. iv. 8. [16] Ps. vi. 5. [17] 2 Cor. vii. 10. [18] Ib. ii. 7.

Before CHRIST cir. 787.

19 [e] As if a man did
flee from a lion, and a
bear met him; or went
into the house, and leaned
his hand on the wall, and
a serpent bit him.

20 *Shall* not the day of
the LORD *be* darkness, and
not light? even very dark,
and no brightness in it?

e Jer. 48. 44.

21 ¶ [d] I hate, I despise
your feast days, and [e] I
will not ‖ smell in your
solemn assemblies.

22 [f] Though ye offer me
burnt offerings and your
meat offerings, I will not
accept *them:* neither will
I regard the ‖ peace offerings of your fat beasts.

Before CHRIST cir. 787.

d Prov. 21. 27. Is. 1. 11–16. Jer. 6. 20. Hos. 8. 13.
e Lev. 26. 31.
‖ Or, *smell your holy days.*
f Is. 66. 3. Mic. 6. 6, 7.
‖ Or, *thank offerings.*

---

der[1] to his Betrayal, a murder the worst of murders, so that where he thought to find a remedy, and that death by hanging was the end of ills, there he found the lion and the bear, and the serpent, under which names I think that different punishments are intended, or else the devil himself, who is rightly called a lion or bear or serpent."

19. *As if a man did flee from a lion.* The Day of the Lord is a day of terror on every side. Before and behind, without and within, abroad under the roof of heaven, or under the shelter of his own, everywhere is terror and death. The Syrian bear is said to have been fiercer and more savage than the lion. For its fierceness and voracity[2], God made it, in Daniel's vision, a symbol of the empire of the Medes. From both lion and bear there might be escape by flight. When the man had *leaned his hand* trustfully *on the wall* of his own house, *and the serpent bit him*, there was no escape. He had fled from death to death, from peril to destruction.

20. Shall *not the Day of the Lord* be *darkness?* He had described that Day as a day of inevitable destruction, such as man's own conscience and guilty fears anticipate, and then appeals to their own consciences, "is it not so, as I have said?" Men's consciences are truer than their intellect. However they may employ the subtlety of their intellect to dull their conscience, they feel, in their heart of hearts, that there is a Judge, that guilt is punished, that they are guilty. The soul is a witness to its own deathlessness, its own accountableness, its own punishableness[3]. Intellect carries the question out of itself into the region of surmising and disputings. Conscience is compelled to receive it back into its own court, and to give the sentence, which it would fain withhold. Like the god of the heathen fable, who changed himself into all sorts of forms, but when he was still held fast, gave at the last, the true answer, conscience shrinks back, twists, writhes, evades, turns away, but, in the end, it will answer truly, when it must. The Prophet then, turns quick round upon the conscience, and says, "tell me, for you know."

21. *I hate, I despise your feasts.* Israel clave to its heart's sin, the worship of the true God, under the idol-form of the calf; else, it would fain be conscientious and scrupulous. It had its *feasts of* solemn *joy*[4], and the *restraint* of its *solemn assemblies*[5], which all were constrained to keep, abstaining from all servile work. They offered *whole burnt offerings*, the token of self-sacrifice, in which the sacrificer retained nothing to himself, but gave the whole freely to God. They offered also *peace offerings*, as tokens of the willing thankfulness of souls at peace with God. What they offered, was the best of its kind, *fatted beasts*. Hymns of praise, full-toned chorus, instrumental music! What was wanting, Israel thought, to secure them the favor of God? Love and obedience. *If ye love Me, keep My commandments.* And so those things, whereby they hoped to propitiate God, were the object of His displeasure. *I hate, I despise, I will not accept* with good pleasure[6]; *I will not regard*, look toward, *I will not hear, will not smell.* The words, *I will not smell*, reminded them of that threat in the law[7], *I will make your cities waste and bring your sanctuaries unto desolation, and I will not smell the savor of your sweet odors.* In so many ways does God declare that He would not accept or endure, what they all the while were building upon, as grounds of their acceptance. And yet so secure were they, that the only sacrifice which they did *not* offer, was the sin or trespass offering. Worshiping "nature," not a holy, Personal, God, they had no sense of unholiness, for which to plead the Atoning Sacrifice to come. Truly each Day of Judgment unveils much self-deceit. How much more the Last!

---

1 S. Matt. xxvii. 3–5.
2 Dan. vii. 5.
3 See Tertullian's short but remarkable treatise "of the witness of the soul," p. 132–42. Oxf. Tr.

4 חג.
5 עצרה lit. restraint.
6 ארצה.
7 Lev. xxvi. 31.

Before CHRIST cir. 787.

23 Take thou away from
me the noise of thy songs;
for I will not hear the melody of thy viols.

[g] Hos. 6. 6. Mic. 6. 8.
† Heb. *roll.*

24 [g] But let judgment
† run down as waters, and
righteousness as a mighty
stream.

25 [h] Have ye offered unto
me sacrifices and offerings
in the wilderness forty
years, O house of Israel?

[h] Deut. 32. 17. Josh. 24. 14. Ezek. 20. 8, 16, 24. Acts 7. 42, 43. See Is. 43. 23.

23. *Take thou away from Me*, lit. *from upon Me*, i. e. from being a burden to Me, a weight *on* Me. So God says by Isaiah[1], *your new moons and your appointed feasts My soul hateth; they are a burden upon Me; I am weary to bear them.* Their *songs* and hymns were but a confused, tumultuous, *noise*[2], since they had not the harmony of love.

For [*And*] *the melody of thy viols I will not hear.* Yet the *nebel*, probably a sort of harp, was almost exclusively consecrated to the service of God, and the Psalms were God's own writing. Doubtless they sounded harmoniously in their own ears; but it reached no further. Their melody, like much Church-music, was for itself, and ended in itself. "[3] Let Christian chanters learn hence, not to set the whole devotion of Psalmody in a good voice, subtlety of modulation and rapid intonation, &c, quavering like birds, to tickle the ears of the curious, take them off to themselves and away from prayer, lest they hear from God, *I will not hear the melody of thy viols.* Let them learn that of the Apostle[4], *I will sing with the Spirit, and I will sing with the understanding also.*" "[5] If the Psalm prays, pray; if it sorrows, sorrow; if it is glad, rejoice; if full of hope, hope; if of fear, fear. For whatever is therein written, is our mirror." "[6] How many are loud in voice, dumb in heart! How many lips are silent, but their love is loud! For the ears of God are to the heart of man. As the ears of the body are to the mouth of man, so the heart of man is to the ears of God. Many are heard with closed lips, and many who cry aloud are not heard." "[7] God says, *I will not hear*, as He says[8], *praise is not seemly in the mouth of a sinner*, and[9], *to the ungodly saith God, what hast thou to do, to declare My statutes?* and[10], *he that turneth away his ear from hearing the law, even his prayer* shall be *abomination.* It is not meant hereby that the wicked ought wholly to abstain from the praise of God and from prayers, but that they should be diligent to amend, and know that through such imperfect services they cannot be saved." The Prophet urges upon them the terribleness of the Day of Judgment, that they might feel and flee its terribleness, before it comes. He impresses on them the fruitlessness of their prayers, that, amending, they might so pray, that God would hear them.

24. *But* [*And*] *let judgment run down* [lit. *roll* E. M.] *like water.* The duties of either table include both; since there is no true love for man without the love of God, nor any real love or duty to God without the love of man. Men will exchange their sins for other sins. They will not break them off unless they be converted to God. But the first outward step in conversion, is to break off sin. He bids them then *let judgment*, which had hitherto ever been perverted in its course, *roll on like* a mighty tide of *waters*, sweeping before it all hindrances, obstructed by no power, turned aside by no bribery, but pouring on in one perpetual flow, reaching all, refreshing all, and *righteousness like a mighty* [or ceaseless] *stream.* The word *ethan* may signify *strong* or *perennial.* Whence the seventh month, just before the early rain, was called *the month Ethanim*[11], i. e. the month of *the perennial streams*, when they alone flowed. In the meaning *perennial*, it would stand tacitly contrasted with *streams which fail* or *lie*[12]. True righteousness is not fitful, like an intermitting stream, vehement at one time, then disappearing, but continuous, unfailing.

25. *Have ye offered* [better, *Did ye offer*] *unto Me sacrifices and offerings?* Israel justified himself to himself by his half-service. This had been his way from the first. [13] *Their heart was not whole with God, neither abode they in His covenant.* He thought to be accepted by God, because he did a certain homage to Him. He acknowledged God in his own way. God sets before him another instance of this half-service and what it issued in;—the service of that generation which He brought out of Egypt, and which left their bones in the wilderness. The idolatry of the ten tribes was the revival of the idolatry of the wilderness. The ten tribes owned as the forefathers of their worship those first idolaters[14]. They identified themselves with sin which they did not commit. By approving it and copying it, they made that sin their own. As the Church of God in all

[1] i. 14. [2] המון. [3] Lap.
[4] 1 Cor. xiv. 15.
S. Aug. in Ps. xxx. Enarr. iv. [p. 263. Oxf. Tr.] L.
S. Aug. in Ps. cxix. [n. 9. T. v. p. 470. O. T.] L.

[7] Dion. [8] Ecclus. xv. 9. [9] Ps. l. 16.
[10] Prov. xxviii. 9. [11] 1 Kgs viii. 2.
[12] אכזב. Jer. xv. 18, כזב. Is. lviii. 11.
[13] Ps. lxxviii. 37. [14] See Introd. to Hos. p. 2.

Before CHRIST cir. 787.

26 But ye have borne || the tabernacle [i] of your

|| Or, *Siccuth your king.* [i] 1 Kings 11.33.

Before CHRIST cir. 787.

times is one and the same, and Hosea says of God's vision to Jacob[1], *there He spake with us,* so that great opposite camp, the city of the devil, has a continuous existence through all time. These idolaters were *filling up the measure of* their forefathers, and in the end of those forefathers, who perished in the wilderness where they sinned, they might behold their own. As God rejected the divided service of their forefathers, so He would their's.

God does not say that they did not offer sacrifice at all, but that they did not offer unto *Him.* The *unto Me* is emphatic. If God is not served wholly and alone, He is not served at all. "[2] He regardeth not the offering, but the will of the offerer." Some sacrifices were offered during the thirty-eight years and a half, after God had rejected that generation, and left them to die in the wilderness. For the rebellion of Korah and his company was a claim to exercise the priesthood, as Aaron was exercising it[3]. When atonement was to be made, the *live coals* were already on the altar[4]. These, however, were not the free-will offerings of the people, but the ordinance of God, performed by the priests. The people, in that they went after their idols, had no share in nor benefit from what was offered in their name. So Moses says[5], *they sacrificed to devils, not to God;* and Ezekiel[6], *Their heart went after their idols.* Those were the gods of their affections, whom they chose. God had taken them for His people, and had become their God, on the condition that they should not associate other gods with Him[7]. Had they loved God Who made them, they would have loved none beside Him. Since they chose other gods, these were the objects of their love. God was, at most, an object of their fear. As He said by Hosea[8], *their bread is for themselves, it shall not enter into the house of the Lord,* so here He asks, and by asking denies it, *Did ye offer unto Me?* Idolatry and heresy feign a god of their own. They do not own God as He has revealed Himself; and since they own not God as He is, the god whom they worship, is not the true God, but some creature of their own imaginings, such as they conceive God to be. Anti-Trinitarianism denies to God His essential Being, Father, Son, and Holy Ghost. Other heresies refuse to own His awful holiness and justice; others, the depth of His love and condescension. Plainly, their god is not the one true God. So these idolaters, while they associated with God gods of cruelty and lust, and looked to them for things which God in His holiness and love refused them, did not own God, as the One Holy Creator, the Sole Disposer of all things.

26. *But ye have borne* [lit. *And ye bare*] *the tabernacle of your Moloch* [lit. *your king,* whence the idol Moloch had its name.]. He assigns the reason, why he had denied that they sacrificed to God in the wilderness. *Did ye offer sacrifices unto Me, and ye bare?* i. e. seeing that ye bare. The two were incompatible. Since they did *carry about the tabernacle of their king,* they did not really worship God. He whom they chose as "their king," was their god. The *tabernacle* or *tent* was probably a little portable shrine, such as Demetrius the silversmith and those of his craft made for the little statues of their goddess Diana[9]. Such are mentioned in Egyptian idolatry. "They carry forth," we are told[10], "the image in a small shrine of gilt wood."

Of your Moloch and Chiun. The two clauses must be read separately, *the tabernacles of Moloch* [strictly, *of your king,*] *and Chiun your images.* The two clauses, *the tabernacle of your king, and Chiun your images*[11], are altogether distinct. They correspond to one another, but they must not be read as one whole, in the sense, *the tabernacle of your king and of Chiun your images.* The rendering of the last clause is uncertain. God has so *utterly abolished the idols*[12], through whom Satan contested with Him the allegiance of His people, that we have no certain knowledge, what they were. There may be some connection between the god whom the Israelites in the wilderness worshiped as *their king,* and him whose worship Solomon, in his decay, brought into Jerusalem, the god whom the Ammonites worshiped as *the king, Hammolech,* or, as he is once called, *Molech*[13], and three times *Milchom*[14] (perhaps an abstract, as some used to speak of "*the Deity*"). He is mostly called *Hammolech,* the Ammonite way of pronouncing what the Hebrews called *Hammelech, the king.* But since the name designates the god only as *the king,* it may have been given to different gods, whom the heathen worshiped as their chief god. In Jewish idolatry, it became equivalent to Baal[15], *lord;* and to avert his displeasure, the Hebrews (as did the Carthaginians, a Phœnician people, down to

[1] xii. 4. See ab. p. 76.
[2] S. Jer.
[3] Num. xvi. 5, 9, 10.
[4] Ib. 46.
[5] Deut. xxxii. 17.
[6] xx. 16.
[7] Ex. xx. 2–5.
[8] ix. 4. see ab. p. 56.
[9] Acts xix. 24.
[10] Herod. ii. 63.
[11] את סכות מלככם ואת כיון צלמיכם
[12] Is. ii. 18.
[13] The idol, called *Molech,* 1 Kgs xi. 7. had been called *Milchom,* Ib. 5.
[14] 1 Kgs xi. 5, 33, 2 Kgs xxiii. 13.
[15] Jer. xix. 5. xxxii. 35.

Before CHRIST cir. 787.

Moloch and Chiun your images, the star of your god, which ye made to yourselves.

Before CHRIST cir. 787.

the time of our Lord [1],) burnt their own children, *their sons and their daughters*, alive to him. Yet, even in these dreadful rites, the Carthaginian worship [2] was more cold-blooded and artificial than that of Phœnicia. But whether *the king*, whom the Israelites worshiped in the wilderness, was the same as the Ammonite Molech or no, those dreadful sacrifices were then no part of his worship; else Amos would not have spoken of the idolatry, as *the carrying about his tabernacle* only. He would have described it by its greatest offensiveness. *The king* was a title also of the Egyptian Deity, Osiris [3], who was identified with the sun, and whose worship Israel may probably have brought with them, as well as that of the calf, his symbol. Again most of the old translators have retained the Hebrew word *Chiyyun* [4], either regarding it as a proper name, or unable to translate it. Some later tradition identifies it with the planet Saturn [5], which under a different name, the Arabs propitiated as a malevolent being [6]. In S. Ephrem's time, the heathen Syrians worshiped "the child-devouring Chivan [7]." Israel however, did not learn the idolatry from the neighboring Arabs, since it is not the Arab name of that planet [8]. In Egyptian, the name of Chunsu, one of the 12 gods who severally were thought to preside over the 12 months, appears in an abridged form Chuns or Chon [9]. He was, in their mythology, held to be "the eldest son of Ammon [10];" his name is said to signify, "[11] power, might;" and he to be that ideal of might, worshiped as the Egyptian Hercules [12]. The name Chun extended into Phœnician [13] and Assyrian [14] proper names. Still Chon is not Chiyyun; and the fact that the name was retained as Chon or Chun in Phœnicia (where the worship was borrowed) as well as in Assyria, is a ground for hesitating to identify with it the word of Chiyyun, which has a certain likeness only to the abridged name. S. Jerome's Hebrew teacher on the other hand knew of no such tradition, and S. Jerome renders it *image* [15]. And certainly it is most natural to render it not as a name, but as a common noun. It may probably mean, *the pedestal* [16], the *basis of your images*. The prophet had spoken of their images, as covered over with their little *shrines, the shrines of your king*. Here he may, not improbably, speak of them, as fastened to a pedestal. Such were the gods, whom they chose for the One true God, gods, *carried about*, covered over, fixed to their place, lest they should fall.

The worship was certainly some form of star-worship, since there follows, *the star of your god*. It took place after the worship of the calf. For S. Stephen, after having spoken of that idolatry says [17], *Then God turned and gave them up to worship the host of heaven, as it is written in the book of the prophets*. Upon their rebellions, God at last gave them up to themselves. S. Stephen calls the god whom they worshiped, *Rephan*, quoting the then existing Greek translation, "having regard," S. Jerome says, "to the meaning rather than the words. This is to be observed in all Holy Scripture, that Apostles and Apostolic men, in citing testimonies from the Old Testament, regard, not the words, but the meaning, nor do they follow the words, step by step, provided they do not depart from the meaning."

Of the special idolatry there is no mention in Moses, in like way as the mention of the worship of the "goat [18]," a second symbol of

[1] "Even to the days of a Proconsul under Tiberius." Tertull. Apol. 9. pp. 20, 1. Oxf. Tr. and note k. Ges. quotes 3 Phœnician inscriptions, attesting the Punic child-sacrifices to Baal, Thes. p. 795.

[2] As described Diod. xx. 14. The Rabbins, however, speak of the sacrifices to Molech in exactly the same way, Carpzoff, Ant. 87. 484.

[3] Plutarch. Is. et Os. c. 10.

[4] The Syr. writes *Chevon;* Jon. *Chiun;* Aq. and Symm. in S. Jer. *Chion*. The *Rephan* of the LXX. may be only a different way of writing Chevan, the Greek translator, here as elsewhere, substituting ר for כ; or it may be an Egyptian equivalent.

[5] In Persian, in the Dabistan, it is said, "The image of Keiwan was of black stone." Lee's Lex. v. אשרה. The Bundehesh, in enumerating the planets, places *Kivan*, the fifth, as does the Codex Nasoræus (ed. Norb. p. 54.) but all these are comparatively modern. The Copt-Arabic list of planets, which explains Rephan by the Arabic *Zochal* i. q. Saturn, may very probably have its name Rephan from the Greek.

[6] Poc spec. Hist. Arab. p. 103. 120. ed. White.

[7] Serm. 8 adv. Hær. Opp. Syr. ii. 458.

[8] The Kamoos explains the Persian *Kaivan* by the Arabic name *Zochal*.

[9] "The Coptic name Paschôns or Pachon is resolved into Pa-chons," "that of Chons or Chonsou; the name of the god who, according to the monuments, presided over this month." Brugsch, Eg. p. 162.

[10] Birch, from slab in the Brit. Mus. (quoted by Bunsen, Æg. Stella, i. 460.)

[11] Birch, Ib.

[12] "They say that Hercules is in Ægyptian called Chon, χῶν." Etym. M. See Sir G. Wilk. in Rawl. Herod. ii. 78. note. "The Egyptians called Hercules Chon." L. Girald [Opp. ii. 327.] from Xenophan. Antioch. Drus. but the authority given is wrong.

[13] San*chon*iathon, *Chuna*sun. Movers, Phœn. i. 291.

[14] Chinzer כן־אצר, Cinneladan כון-אל-ארן in Ptol. Id. ib.

[15] Theodotion also translates it as a noun.

[16] כיון from כון.

[17] Acts vii. 42.

[18] שְׂעִירִים Lev. xvii. 7. rendered in the E. V. "devils;" but שְׂעִיר lit. "the hairy," is the Hebrew name of the goat, as hircus from hirtus, hirsutus. The name for "devils" in the Pentateuch is שֵׁדִים Deut. xxxii. 17. Jeroboam endeavored fruitlessly to revive the worship. *He made him priests for the high places and the Seirim and 'Agalim which he had*

Before CHRIST cir. 787.

27 Therefore will I cause you to go into captivity [k] beyond Damascus, saith the LORD, [l] whose name *is* The God of hosts.

k 2 Kings 17. 6.

Before CHRIST cir. 787.

l ch. 4. 13.

the Pantheistic worship of Egypt[1], is contained only incidentally in the prohibition of that worship. After the final rebellion, upon which God rejected that generation, Holy Scripture takes no account of them. They had failed God; they had forfeited the distinction, for which God had created, preserved, taught them, revealed Himself to them, and had, by great miracles, rescued them from Egypt. Thenceforth that generation was cast aside unnoticed.

Which ye made to yourselves. This was the fundamental fault, that they *made it for themselves.* Instead of the tabernacle, which God, their king, appointed, they *bare about the tabernacle* of *him* whom they took for their king; and for the service which He gave, they *chose new gods*[2] for themselves. Whereas God made them for Himself, they made for themselves gods out of their own mind. All idolatry is self-will, first choosing a god, and then enslaved to it.

27. *Therefore* [*And*] this being so, such having been their way from the beginning until now, *will I cause you to go into captivity beyond Damascus.* Syria was the most powerful enemy by whom God had heretofore chastened them[3]. From Syria He had recently, for the time, delivered them, and had given Damascus into their hands[4]. That day of grace had been wasted, and they were still rebellious. *Now* God would bring against them a mightier enemy. Damascus, the scene of their triumph, should be their pathway to captivity. God would *cause* them *to go into captivity*, not to *Damascus*, whence they might have easily returned, but *beyond* it, as He did, *into the cities of the Medes.* But Israel had, up to the time of Amos and beyond it, no enemy, no war, *beyond Damascus.* Jehu had probably paid tribute to Shalmanubar king of Assyria, to strengthen himself[5]. The Assyrian monarch had warred against Israel's enemies, and seemingly received some check from them[6]. Against Israel he had shewn no hostility. But for the conspiracy of one yet to be born in private life, one of the captains of Israel who, by murder, became its sovereign, it might have continued on in its own land. The Assyrian monarchs needed tribute, not slaves; nor did they employ Israel as slaves. Exile was but a wholesale imprisonment of the nation in a large but safe prison-house. Had they been still, they were more profitable to Assyria, as tributaries in their own land. There was no temptation to remove them, when Amos prophesied. The temptation came with political intrigues which had not then commenced. The then Assyrian monarch, Shamasiva, defeated their enemies the Syrians, united with and aiding the Babylonians[7]; *they* had then had no share in the opposition to Assyria, but lay safe in their mountain-fastness. It has been said, "[8] Although the kingdom of Israel had, through Jeroboam, recovered its old borders, yet careless insolence, luxury, unrighteousness, *must* bring the destruction of the kingdom which the Prophet foretells. The Prophet does but dimly forebode the superior power of Assyria." Solomon had declared the truth[9], *Righteousness exalteth a nation, but sin is a reproach to any people.* But there are many sorts of decay. Decay does not involve the transportation of a people. Nay, decay would not bring it, but the contrary. A mere luxurious people rots on its own soil, and would be left to rot there. It was the little remnant of energy, political caballing, warlike spirit, in Israel, which brought its ruin from man. Idolatry, "insolence, luxury, unrighteousness," bring down the displeasure of God, not of man. Yet Amos foretold, that God would bring the destruction through man. They were, too, no worse than their neighbors, nor so bad; not so bad as the Assyrians themselves, except that, God having revealed Himself to them, they had more light. The sin then, the punishment, the mode of punishment, belong to the Divine revelation. Such sins and worse have existed in Christian nations. They were in part sins directly against God. God reserves to Himself, how and when He will punish. He has annexed no such visible laws of punishment to a nation's sins that man could, of his own wisdom or observation of God's ways, foresee it. They through whom He willed to inflict it, and whom Amos pointed out, were not provoked by *those* sins. There was no connection between Israel's present sins, and Assyria's future vengeance. No Eastern despot cares for the oppressions of his subjects, so that his own tribute is collected.

made. (2 Chr. xi. 15.) *Seirim* is doubtless to be taken in its literal sense, "he goats," as *'Agalim*, with which it is joined, is of "calves."

[1] Pan, or Mendes, worshiped under the goat, was nature in one great aggregate, the oldest of their gods, according to themselves (Herod. ii. 145. add 46), as being, in fact, the principle of life, apart from its Author. In Egyptian idolatry, the goat was accounted a special manifestation of that principle.

[2] Jud. v. 8. [3] 2 Kgs xiii. 7. [4] Ib. xiv. 25, 28.
[5] See Introd. to Hosea, p. 2. [6] See ab. on i. 3.
[7] Rawl. Herod. i. 466, from Cuneif. Inscr.
[8] De Wette, Einl. § 232. [9] Prov. xiv. 34.

Before CHRIST cir. 787.

CHAPTER VI.

1 *The wantonness of Israel,* 7 *shall be plagued with desolation,* 12 *and their incorrigibleness.*

WOE [a] to them *that* ‖ *are*
at ease in Zion, and
trust in the mountain of
Samaria, *which are* named

Before CHRIST cir. 787.

[a] Luke 6. 24.
‖ Or, *are secure.*

See the whole range of Mohammedan rule now. As far too as we know, neither Assyria nor any other power had hitherto punished rebellious nations by transporting them[1]; and certainly Israel had not yet rebelled, or meditated rebellion. He only Who controls the rebellious wills of men, and through their self-will works out His own all-wise Will and man's punishment, could know the future of Israel and Assyria, and how through the pride of Assyria He would bring down the pride of Samaria.

It has been well said by a thoughtful observer of the world's history, "Whosoever attempts to prophesy, not being inspired, is a fool." We English know our own sins, many and grievous; we know of a vast reign of violence, murder, blasphemy, theft, uncleanness, covetousness, dishonest dealing, unrighteousness, and of the breach of every commandment of God: we know well [2] now of an instrument in God's Hands, not far off, like the Assyrian, but within two hours of our coast; armaments have been collected; a harbor is being formed; our own coast openly examined; iron-sheeted vessels prepared; night-signals provided; some of our own alienated population organized; with a view to our invasion. We recognize the likelihood of the invasion, fortify our coast, arm, not as a profession, but for security. Our preparations testify, how wide-spread is our expectation. No one scarcely doubts that it will be. Yet who dare predict the issue? Will God permit that scourge to come? will he prevail? What would be the extent of our sufferings or loss? how would our commerce or our Empire be impaired? Would it be dismembered? Since no man can affirm anything as to this which is close at hand, since none of us would dare to affirm in God's Name, in regard to any one stage of all this future, that this or that would or would not happen, then let men have at least the modesty of the magicians of Egypt, and seeing in God's prophets these absolute predictions of a future, such as their own wisdom, under circumstances far more favorable, could not dare to make, own; [3] *This is the finger of God.* Not we alone. We see all Europe shaken; we see powers of all sorts, heaving to and fro; we see the Turkish power ready to dissolve, stayed up, like a dead man, only by un-Christian jealousies of Christians. Some things we may partially guess at. But with all our means of knowing what passes everywhere, with all our knowledge of the internal impulses of nations, hearing, as we do, almost every pulse which beats in the great European system, knowing the diseases which, here and there, threaten convulsion or dissolution, no one dare stake his human wisdom on any *absolute* prediction, like these of the shepherd of Tekoa as to Damascus[1] and Israel. To say the like in God's Name, unless inspired, we should know to be blasphemy. God Himself set the alternative before men. [4] *Let all the nations be gathered together, and let the people be assembled; who among them that can declare this, and shew former things? Let them bring forth their witnesses, that they may be justified; or let them hear, and say,* It is *truth.*

S. Stephen, in quoting this prophecy, substitutes, Babylon for Damascus, as indeed *the cities of the Medes* were further than Babylon. Perhaps he set the name, in order to remind them, that as God had brought Abraham [5] *out of the land of the Chaldeans,* leaving the idols which his *fathers* had *served* [6], to serve God only, so they, serving idols, were carried back, whence Abraham had come, forfeiting, with the faith of Abraham, the promises made to Abraham; aliens and outcasts.

Saith the Lord, the Lord of hosts, the Lord of the heavenly hosts for whose worship they forsook God; the Lord of the hosts on earth, whose ministry He employs to punish those who rebel against Him. "[7] For He hath many hosts to execute His judgments, the hosts of the Assyrians, the Medes and Persians, the Greeks and Romans." All creatures in heaven and in earth are, as He says of the holy Angels, [8] *ministers of His, that do His pleasure.*

VI. 1. *Woe to them* that are *at ease.* The word [9] always means such as are recklessly at their ease, *the careless ones,* such as those whom Isaiah bids, [10] *rise up, tremble, be troubled; for many days and years shall ye be troubled.* It is that luxury and ease, which sensualize the soul, and make it dull, stupid, hard-hearted. By one earnest, passing word, the Prophet warns his own land, that present sinful ease ends in future woe. [11] *Woe unto them that laugh now: for they shall mourn and weep.* "[7] He foretells the destruction and

[1] See ab. on i. 5. pp. 160, 1.
[2] Written in 1860.
[3] Ex. viii. 19.
[4] Is. xliii. 9.
[5] Acts vii. 4.
[6] Josh. xxiv. 14.
[7] Rup.
[8] Ps. ciii. 21.
[9] שאננים.
[10] Is. xxxii. 9–11.
[11] S. Luke vi. 25.

Before CHRIST cir. 787.

[b] || chief of the nations, to whom the house of Israel came!

2 [c] Pass ye unto [d] Calneh, and see; and from thence go ye to [e] Hamath the great: then go down to [f] Gath of the Philis-

Before CHRIST cir. 787.

[b] Ex. 19. 5.
|| Or, *firstfruits*,
[c] Jer. 2. 10.
[d] Is. 10. 9. Taken cir. 794.
[e] 2 Kings 18. 34.
[f] 2 Chr. 26. 6.

captivity of both Judah and Israel at once; and not only that captivity at Babylon, but that whereby they are dispersed unto this day." Luxury and deepest sins of the flesh were rife in that generation[1], which slew Him Who for our sakes became poor.

And trust in the mountain of Samaria, not in God. Samaria was strong[2], resisted for three years, and was the last city of Israel which was taken. *The king of Assyria came up throughout all the land and went up to Samaria, and besieged it*[3]. Benhadad, in that former siege, when God delivered them[4], attempted no assault, but famine only.

Which are *named the chief of the nations;* lit. *the named of the chief of the nations*, i. e. those who, in Israel, which by the distinguishing favor of God were *chief of the nations*, were themselves, marked, distinguished, *named*. The Prophet, by one word, refers them back to those first princes of the congregation, of whom Moses used that same word[5]. They were *heads of the houses of their fathers*[6], *renowned of the congregation, heads of thousands in Israel*[7]. As, if any one were to call the Peers, "Barons of England," he would carry us back to the days of Magna Charta, although six centuries and a half ago, so this word, occurring at that time[8], here only in any Scripture since Moses, carried back the thoughts of the degenerate aristocracy of Israel to the faith and zeal of their forefathers, *what* they ought to have been, and *what* they were. As Amalek of old was *first of the nations*[9] in its enmity against the people of God[10], having, first of all, shewn that implacable hatred, which Ammon, Moab, Edom, evinced afterward, so was Israel *first of nations*, as chosen by God. It became, in an evil way, *first of nations*, i. e. distinguished above the heathen, by rejecting Him.

To whom the house of Israel came, or *have come*. They were, like those princes of old, raised above others. Israel *came* to them for judgment; and they, regardless of duty, lived only for self-indulgence, effeminacy, and pride. S. Jerome renders in the same sense, "that enter pompously the house of Israel," lit. *enter for themselves*, as if they were lords of it, and it was made for them.

2. *Pass over to Calneh*. He bids them behold, East, North, and West, survey three neighboring kingdoms, and see whether God had not, even in the gifts of this world, dealt better with Israel. Why then so requite Him? *Calneh*, (which Isaiah calls *Calno*[11], Ezekiel, *Canneh*[12],) was one of the four cities, built by Nimrod *in the land of Shinar*[13], *the beginning of his kingdom*. From that time, until this of Amos, no mention of it occurs. It, probably, was more than once conquered by the Assyrians[14], lying, as it did, on the Tigris, some 40 miles perhaps from Babylon. Hence it was said, under its new name Ctesiphon[15], to have been built, i. e. rebuilt, by the Macedonians[16], and again by the Parthians[17], whose "[18] kings made it their winter residence on account of its good air." It was anew destroyed by Severus[19], rebuilt by Sapor II. in the 4th Century[20]. Julian's generals held it impregnable[21], being built on a peninsula, surrounded on three sides by the Tigris[22]. It became the scene of repeated persecutions of Christianity[23]; Nestorianism was favored[24]. A centre of Persian luxury, it fell at once and for ever before Omar[25], and the Persian empire perished with it. It was replaced by the neighboring Bagdad. The history illustrates the tenacity of life in those well-chosen sites, and the character of the place, of whose conquest Sennacherib boasted, with which Amos compared the land of Israel.

Go thence to Hamath the great, originally, a Canaanite kingdom[26]. *The entrance to* it was assigned as the Northern border of Israel[27]. In David's time its king was at war with the king of Zobah[28], and made presents to David on his subdual. In Solomon's time it had fallen under the power of the king of Zobah,

[1] See S. John viii. 9, Rom. ii. 21–24, S. Luke xi. 39, 42, S. Matt. xxiii. 14, 23, 26.
[2] See ab. on iii. 9.
[3] 2 Kgs xvii. 5.
[4] Ib. vii. 6.
[5] Num. i. 17.
[6] Ib. 4.
[7] Ib. 16.
[8] The phrase of Num. i. 17. occurs only in the books of Chronicles (1 Chr. xii. 31, xvi. 41, 2 Chr. xxviii. 15, xxxi. 19) and Ezra (viii. 20) as taken from the Pentateuch. See Hengst. Auth. d. Pent. i. 97.
[9] Nu. xxiv. 20.
[10] Ex. xvii. 8–16. So Onk. S. Jer. Pseud-Jon.
[11] x. 9.
[12] xxvii. 23.
[13] Gen. x. 10.
[14] See ab. Introd. p. 149.
[15] S. Jer. here. S.Ephr. Jon.
[16] Procop. B. Pers. ii. 28.
[17] Plin. vi. 26. n. 30. It certainly existed before, Polyb. v. 46.
[18] Strabo, xvi. 1. 26, who speaks of it as existing already.
[19] Dio Cass. lxxv. Sev. 9.
[20] Mirkhond, Hist. d. Sass. in De Sacy, Men. sur la Perse, p. 316.
[21] Amm. xxiv. 7. 1.
[22] Kinneir, Geogr. Mem. of the Persian Empire, p. 252.
[23] Ass. B. O. i. 185 sqq. iii. 2. lii. sqq. Acta Mart.
[24] Ass. iii. 2. lxxxvii.
[25] Abulf. i. 233–5, Ritt. x. 172.
[26] Gen. x. 18.
[27] Num. xxxiv. 7, 8, Josh. xiii. 5.
[28] 2 Sam. viii. 9, 10.

Before CHRIST cir. 787.

tines: [g] *be they* better than these kingdoms? or their border greater than your border?

[g] Nah. 3. 8.

whence it was called Hamath-zobah. Solomon won it from him, incorporated it with Israel, and built towns in its territory [1]. The "Hamathites" were, under their own king, united with Benhadad, the Hittites, and the Phœnicians in their war with Shalmanubar, and defeated by him [2]. Ezekiel speaks of the *border of Damascus* and *the coast of Hamath* [3], as of places of like importance, and Zechariah [4], of their joint subdual by Alexander. To judge from the present site, it in some respects resembled Samaria. It lay in a narrow oval valley of the Orontes; its citadel on a round hill in the centre. The city rises up the steep sides of the hills which inclose it [5]. Vast water-wheels [6], some of a diameter of 67 [7], 80, 90 [8], feet, raise the water of the Orontes to supply, by aid of aqueducts, the upper city, or to water the neighboring gardens. "[9] The Western part of its territory is the granary of Northern Syria." Even when Antiochus Epiphanes called it after himself Epiphania, its inhabitants called it after its old name [10]. Mention occurs of it in the crusades [11]. In the 13th century it had its own well-known prince [12]; and has still a population of some 30,000 [13].

Gath [*Winepress*] must, from its name, have been situated in a rich country. It lay on the confines of Judea and Philistia; for Rehoboam fortified it as a border-fortress [14]. It had been contrariwise fortified by the Philistines against Judah, since, when David took it *out of the hand of the Philistines*, it had the title [15] *methegammah*, "bridle of the mother city," or metropolis. It had at that time *daughter towns* [16] dependent upon it. It must also have been near Micah's birthplace, *Moresheth Gath*, i.e. Moresheth of Gath, which in S. Jerome's [17] time was "a small village near Eleutheropolis," [Bethgabrin.] Of Gath itself S. Jerome says, "[18] It is one of the five cities of Philistia, near the confines of Judea, and now too a very large village on the way from Eleutheropolis to Gaza." Eusebius says [19], "about the 5th milestone from Eleutheropolis to Diospolis" [Lydda]. Since the Philistines carried the Ark of God from Ashdod to Gath, and thence to Ekron [20], it seems likely that Gath lay nearer to Ashdod than Ekron, although necessarily more inland than either, since it was a border-city to Judah. The Tel-es-Safiyeh corresponds with these conditions, lying at the entrance of the Shephēlah, about 5 miles from Beit-Jibrin on the road to Lydda, [Ludd]. It "[21] rises about 100 feet above the Eastern ridge which it terminates, and perhaps 200 over the plain which terminates its Western base. The ruins and subterranean reservoirs shew that it is a site of high antiquity, great strength, and importance." Gath had at this time probably been taken by Uzziah who *broke down* its *wall* [22]; and since it is not mentioned with the other four Philistine cities, whose sentence is pronounced by Amos [23] himself, Zephaniah [24], and Zechariah [25], it is probable that it never recovered.

Be they *better than these kingdoms?* The prophet seems purposely to say less than he might, in order that his hearers might have to supply the more. Calneh, Hamath, Gath, had not been more guilty against God than Ephraim, yet probably they had all been conquered: Gath by Judah; Hamath by Israel [26] himself; Calneh by Assyria. Both Shalmanubar and Shamasiva conquered in Babylonia [27]; and Shamasiva "[28] declares that he took above 200 towns" in Babylonia. Amos, then, upbraids Israel for their ingratitude, both as to the original gift of their good land, and its continuance. The Heathen had suffered; *they*, the guiltier, had been spared; yet still they acted no otherwise than these Heathen.

"[29] What spacious, what wide border have we, boundless as the life of God and eternity!" "[30] Our hopes and the bounds of our bliss are measured, not like those of the worldly and ungodly, by the limits of a petty time or by this dot of earth, but by the

[1] 2 Chr. viii. 3, 4.
[2] Cuneif. Inscr. in Rawl. Her. i. 463, 4.
[3] Ezek. xlvii. 16, xlviii. 1. [4] ix. 1, 2.
[5] Col. Squire, in Walpole Mem. 323-5.
[6] Seetzen puts them at 250. Nachlass, i. 13-15. in Ritt. xvii. 1042. Burckhardt (Syria 146.) says, "about a dozen" supply the city itself.
[7] Squire, l. c. "at least 70 feet," Burckh. l. c.
[8] Thomson, The Land, ii. 278.
[9] Burckh. 147.
[10] Jos. Ant. i. 6, 2. S. Jer. Qu. in Gen. x. 15.
[11] Ritter. 1033. [12] Abulfeda. [13] Burckhardt, Ib.
[14] 2 Chr. xi. 8.
[15] 2 Sam. viii. 1. comp. 1 Chr. xviii. 1.
[16] בנתיה 1 Chr. Ib. [17] Præf. ad Mic.
[18] In Mic. i. 10.
[19] v. Γέθ (in Joshua) where he explains it to be the place where the Enakim dwelt, i.e. the Philistine Gath. Under "the Kings" v. Γεθθὰ, "whither the Philistines removed the Ark from Ashdod," he says, "there is yet a very large village called Giththa, on the road between Antipatris and Jamnia. And another, Geththaim." This which Eusebius, found probably in some other authority, would make Gath the most Northern of the Philistine towns, and near the sea, which is inconsistent with its being near Moresheth and a frontier-town of Judah.
[20] 1 Sam. v. 8, 10. [21] Porter, Hdb. 253, 4.
[22] 2 Chr. xxvi. 6. [23] i. 7, 8. [24] ii. 4. [25] ix. 5.
[26] See bel. ver. 14.
[27] Cuneif. Inscr. in Rawl. Her. i. 464.
[28] Ib. 466. [29] Rib. [30] Lap.

Before CHRIST cir. 787.

3 Ye that [h] put far away
the [i] evil day, [k] and cause
[l] the || seat of violence to
come near;
4 That lie upon beds of
ivory, and || stretch them-
selves upon their couches,
and eat the lambs out of
the flock, and the calves
out of the midst of the
stall;
5 [m] That || chant to the

[h] Ezek. 12. 27.
[i] ch. 5. 18. & 9. 10.
[k] ch. 5. 12. ver. 12.
[l] Ps. 94. 20.
|| Or, *habitation*.
|| Or, *abound with superfluities*.

Before CHRIST cir. 787.

[m] Is. 5. 12.
|| Or, *quaver*.

boundless space of eternity and of heaven; so that we may say confidently to the ungodly, *Is not our border wider than your border?*"

3. *Ye that put far away.* Probably *with aversion*[1]. They bade that day as it were, be gone. The Hebrew idiom expresses, how they would put it off, if they could; as far as in them lay, they *assigned a distance to it*[2], although they could not remove the day itself. The *evil day* is that same *day of the Lord*, which the scoffers or misbelievers professed to long for[3]. The thought that the Lord has a Day, in which to judge man, frets or frightens the irreligious, and they use different ways to get rid of it. The strong harden themselves against it, distort the belief in it, or disbelieve it. The weak and voluptuous shut their eyes to it, like the bird in the fable, as if what they dread would cease to be there, because they cease to see it.

And cause the seat [lit. *the session, sitting*] *of violence to come near.* They dismissed the thought of the Day of account, in order that they might sin with less fear. They put from them the judgment of God, that they might exercise violence over His creatures. Men do not put away the thought of God, except to invite His Enemy into their souls. But therewith, they *brought near* another *seat of violence*, not their own, but upon them. They brought near what they wished to put away, the day, in which, through the violence of the Assyrians, God would avenge their own.

"[4] Let *them* consider this, who put no bound to their sins. For the more they obey their own will, the more they hasten to destruction; and while they think they draw nigh to pleasures, they draw nigh to everlasting woes."

4. *That lie upon beds* (i.e. *sofas*) *of ivory*, i.e. probably inlaid with ivory. The word might, in itself, express either the bed, in which they slept by night, or the Divan, on which the Easterns lay at their meals; *and stretch themselves*, lit. *are poured* out[5], stretching their listless length, dissolved, unnerved, in luxury and sloth, *upon their couches*, perhaps under an awning[6]: *and eat the lambs*, probably *fatted lambs*[7], *out of the flock*, chosen, selected out of it as the best, and *calves out of the midst of the stall;* i.e. the place where they were tied up (as the word[8] means) to be fatted. They were stall-fed, as we say, and these people had the best chosen for them.

"[9] He shews how they *draw nigh the seat of violence.* They lay on beds or couches of ivory, and expended thereon the money wherewith their poor brethren were to be fed. Go now, I say not into the houses of nobles, but into any house of any rich man, see the gilded and worked couches, curtains woven of silk and gold, and walls covered with gold, while the poor of Christ are naked, shivering, shrivelled with hunger. Yet stranger is it, that while this is everywhere, scarce anywhere is there who *now* blames it. *Now* I say; for there were formerly. 'Ye array,' S. Ambrose says[10], 'walls with gold, men ye bare. The naked cries before your door and you neglect him; and are careful with what marbles you clothe your pavement. The poor seeketh money, and hath it not; man asketh for bread, and thy horse champeth gold. Thou delightest in costly ornaments, while others have not meal. What judgment thou heapest on thyself, thou man of wealth! Miserable, who hast power to keep so many souls from death, and hast not the will! The jewel of thy ring could maintain in life a whole population.' If such things are not to be blamed now, then neither were they formerly."

5. *That chant to the voice of the lyre*, accompanying *the voice of the lyre* with the human voice, giving vocal expression and utterance to what the instrumental music spoke without words. The word, which Amos alone uses in this one place, describes probably [11] a hurried flow of unmeaning, unconsidered

[1] As in נִדָּה from נדד, i. q. נדה. In the other place where it occurs, Is. lxvi. 5, it is united with hatred, "expelled with aversion." In 2 Kgs xxii. 21, Cheth. נדא is used of Jeroboam *driving* the people away from following God.

[2] The force of ל.

[3] ch. v. 18.

[4] Rib.

[5] As in Arab. and Syr. In Heb, it is used of a vine pouring itself out, in luxuriance, Ezek. xvii. 6; of a curtain overlapping, Ezek xxiv. 12, 13; of a headdress hanging over, Ezek. xxiii. 15; of wisdom poured away and gone, Jer. xlix. 7.

[6] ערש like the Arab. 'arsh. See Judith xvi. 23.

[7] As in Deut. xxxii. 14, Ps. xxxvii. 20, 1 Sam. xv. 9, Jer. li. 40.

[8] מרבק.

[9] Rib.

[10] de Nabuthe, c. 13.

[11] The central meaning of the Arabic root is "anticipating another;" then hurry, negligence, excess, inadvertence in act, and, in speech, exaggeration

Before CHRIST cir. 787.

sound of the viol, *and* invent to themselves instruments of musick, [n] like
David;

[n] 1 Chr. 23. 5.

6 That drink ‖ wine in
bowls, and anoint them-
selves with the chief
ointments: [o] but they

Before CHRIST cir. 787.

‖ Or, *in bowls of wine.*

[o] Gen. 37. 25.

---

words, in which the rhythm of words and music was everything, the sense, nothing; much like most glees. The E. M. "quaver" has also some foundation in the root, but does not suit the idiom so well, which expresses that the act was something done *to the voice of the lyre*, accompanying the music, not altering the music itself. In fact, they would go together. An artificial, effeminate music which should relax the soul, frittering the melody, and displacing the power and majesty of divine harmony by tricks of art, and giddy, thoughtless, heartless, soulless versifying would be meet company. Debased music is a mark of a nation's decay, and promotes it. The Hebrew music seems to have been very simple; and singing appears to have been reserved almost exclusively for solemn occasions, the Temple-service, or the greeting of victory [1]. *Singing men and singing women* were part of the state of David and Solomon [2]. Else the music at the feasts of the rich appears rather to be mentioned with blame [3]. Songs they had [4]; but the songs, for which the Hebrew exiles were celebrated, and which their Babylonian masters required them to sing, *the songs of Zion* [5], were the hymns of the temple, *the Lord's song.*

And invent to themselves instruments of music. The same pains, which David employed on music to the honor of God, they employed on their light, enervating unmeaning music, and, if they were in earnest enough, justified their inventions by the example of David. Much as people have justified our degraded, sensualizing, immodest dancing, by the religious dancing of Holy Scripture! The word can mean no other than *devised* [6]. David then did *devise* and *invent* instruments of music for the service of God. He introduced into the Temple-service the use of the stringed instruments, the *kinnor*, (the *lyre*) and the *nebel* (the *harp*) in addition to the cymbals. Whence these, in contrast with the trumpets, are called *the instruments of David* [7]. Probably, in adapting them to the Temple-service, he, in some way, improved the existing instrument; having been, in early youth, remarkable for his skill upon the harp [8]. As *he* elevated the character and powers of the, perhaps rude, instrument which he found, and fitted it to the service of God, so these men refined it doubtless, as they thought, and fitted it for the service of luxury and sensuality. But what harm, they thought, in amending the music of their day, since so did David?

6. *That drink wine in bowls* (lit. as E. M. *drink in bowls*, lit. *sprinkling vessels, of wine*). The word is elsewhere used only of the *bowls*, out of which the blood of the sacrifice was sprinkled. Probably Amos was referring to the first offering of the Princes in the wilderness, with whom he had already tacitly contrasted these Princes [9]. *They* had shewn zeal for God in offering the massive bowls for the service of the tabernacle: the like zeal had these princes for the service of their own *god* [10], *their belly.* It may be too, (since misbelief and sensuality are necessarily irreverent) that they used for their revels vessels which had at one time been employed in sprinkling the blood of their idol-sacrifices. There was no additional desecration in it. The gold and silver vessels of the Temple were consecrated by being offered to God, by His hallowing of the Temple through His Presence, by being used in the typical sacrifices. The gold and silver, creatures of God, were desecrated by being employed in idol-worship, of which indeed sensuality was a part. Their employment in this luxury was only a continuance of their desecration, which it did but illustrate. It is nothing incredible, since among Christians, the fonts of the Church have been turned into horse-troughs by sects who disbelieved in Baptism. The vessels were, probably, large, since those offered for the tabernacle weighed 70 shekels. Private luxury vied with the ficti-

---

in praise, and (conj. iii.) "got the first word," "spoke precipitately, the tongue outrunning the sense." Abu'l Walid applies this last meaning, that "they, poured out words and measured out defilements." He says also that the corresponding Arabic participle is used of those "who extemporise poetry, i. e. sing extempore without thought." See the Arabic in Ges.

[1] 1 Sam. xviii. 7. [2] 2 Sam. xix 35, Eccl. ii. 8.

[3] Is. v. 12, xxiv. 9. [4] Pr. xxv. 20.

[5] Ps. cxxxvii. 3, 4.

[6] It is commonly used with abstract nouns as מחשבות, רעה, און, מזמה, *devices, evil, vanity*, or with ל and the inf.; but always in the meaning of "devising," "inventing." It is used of those gifted by God "to devise devices," i. e. as it is explained, *to work in gold and in silver and in brass and in setting of stones.* Ex. xxxi. 4, 5. It is used also of war-like machines, and their inventor; as our Engineer, Engine comes from ingenium. An embroiderer, who needed continual invention, is called חושב; his work, the work of an inventor (see Ex. xxvi. 1. E. M. &c.) S. Jerome's rendering, "like David, they think that they have instruments of music,' does not suit the Hebrew idioms.

[7] 2 Chr. xxix. 26, comp. 25. and 1 Chr. xv. 16, 19–21, 24.

[8] 1 Sam. xvi. 16, 18, 23.

[9] Hengst. Auth. d. Pent. p. 99. See ab. p. 152.

[10] Phil. iii. 19.

Before CHRIST cir. 787.

are not grieved for the † affliction of Joseph.

† Heb. *breach*.

Before CHRIST cir. 787.

tious sanctuary, which aped the sanctuary of God. Perhaps Amos would express the capacity of these vessels by saying, *that drink in bowls of wine.* Like swine in the trough, they immersed themselves in their drink, "[1] swimming in mutual swill."

All this they did, he expresses, habitually. He speaks of these their acts in a form expressing an ever-renewed present, *the putters off, the liers on couches of ivory, the out-stretched, the eating, the drinking*, men whose lives were spent in nothing else; the voluptuaries, sensualists, "good-fellows" of Israel.

Anoint themselves with the chief ointments. Anointing the body was a sort of necessary[2] in the hot climate of the East, for bodily health. *Not* to anoint the body was the exception, as in mourning[3]. But necessaries become a vehicle for luxury. For health, olive-oil sufficed[4]. For the service of God, a rich ointment was appointed, to which odorous substances, myrrh, cinnamon, the odoriferous reed, and cassia[5] gave a scent emblematic of the fragrance of holiness. In order to separate what was sacred from ordinary uses, God forbade, on pain of death, to imitate this ointment, or *pour it on the flesh of man*[6]. Luxury vied with religion, and took to itself either the same, or ointment more costly. *They anointed themselves with the chief* [kind] *of ointments*[7]; those which held the first, highest rank among them. Nothing better or so good was left for what they thought to be the service of God, as, in times a little past, anything was thought good enough for a Church, nothing too good for a dwelling-house. Gorgeous adornments of man's house were thought splendor and good taste and fit employment of wealth; slight adornment of the house of God was thought superstition.

But [*And*] *they are not grieved* [lit. *grieve not themselves*[8],] admit no grief[9], shut out all grief, *for the affliction* [lit. *breach*] of *Joseph.* The name of the Patriarch, Ephraim's father, recalled his suffering from his brethren. [9] His brethren cast him into a *pit without water*[10], probably an empty leaking well, (much as was that into which Jeremiah[11] was cast,) damp, fetid, and full of loathsome creatures. They [12] *saw the anguish of his soul when he besought* them, *and would not hear.* But what did they? [13] *They sat down to eat bread.* So did these rich men deal with all their brethren, all Ephraim. They suffered not in, or with, any sufferings, present or future, of individuals or the whole. "Cast off thought," "cast off care," is the motto of sensualists and of the worldly; "seize joyous the present hour, and leave the future," said the heathen[14]. This was the effect of their luxury and life of sense. The Prophet recounts, they stretched themselves listlessly, ate choice food, sang glees, drank deep, anointed themselves with the very best ointment, *and grieved* not themselves for any sufferings of their own flesh and blood. It followed, of necessity, from the rest. Luxury shuts out suffering, because any vivid knowledge of or dwelling upon sufferings must needs disturb its ease. Selfish wealth persuades itself that there is no suffering, lest it should be forced to think of it; it *will* think distress either too little, so that it can relieve itself, or so great that it cannot be relieved; or it will philosophise upon distress and misery, as though it were best relieved by its own luxuries. Any how it will not know or hear of its details, it will not admit grief. "[15] Mercilessness is the own daughter of pleasure." [16] *This was the iniquity of thy sister Sodom; pride, fullness of bread, and careless ease had she and her daughters; and the hand of the poor and needy she strengthened not.* "Seest thou," says S. Chrysostom[17], "how he blames a delicate life? For in these words he accuses not covetousness, but prodigality only. And thou eatest to excess, Christ not even for need; thou various cakes, He not so much as dry bread; thou drinkest choice wine, but on Him thou hast not bestowed so much as a cup of cold water in His thirst. Thou art on a soft, embroidered bed; He is perishing with the cold. Be then the banquets clear from covetousness, yet they are accursed, because, while *thou* doest all beyond thy need, to Him thou givest not even His need; and that, living in luxury on what is His!"

And yet what was this luxury, which the Prophet so condemns? What, in us, were simplicity. What scarce any one thought of diminishing, while two millions, close by, were wasting away by famine's horrors;—chairs or sofas inlaid, fat lamb or veal; wine; perfumes; light music. The most delicate ingredient of those perfumes, cinnamon, enters into our food. "Looking at *our* times," says a writer at the close of the 16th century[18], "I marvel at the spareness of the ancients, and think that it would be well with us, if any above the poor were content with what were, of old, delicacies to kings and

1 Thomson, Autumn.
2 2 Chr. xxviii. 15.
3 2 Sam. xiv. 2.
4 Deut. xxviii. 40.
5 Ex. xxx. 23–5.
6 Ib. 32, 3.
7 ראשית שמנים.

8 לא נחלו.
9 from Sanct.
10 Gen. xxxvii. 24.
11 Jer. xxxviii. 6.
12 Gen. xlii. 21.
13 xxxvii. 25.
14 Hor.
15 Lap.
16 Ez. xvi. 49.
17 Hom. 48. in S. Matt.
18 Ribera.

Before CHRIST cir. 787.

7 ¶ Therefore now shall
they go captive with the
first that go captive, and
the banquet of them that
stretched themselves shall
be removed.

p Jer. 51. 14. Heb. 6. 13, 17.

8 p The Lord GOD hath
sworn by himself, saith the
LORD the God of hosts, I
abhor q the excellency of
Jacob, and hate his palaces:
therefore will I deliver up
the city with all † that is
therein.

q Ps. 47. 4. Ezek. 24. 21. ch. 8. 7.

† Heb. *the fulness thereof.*

nobles. Happy were these times, if they could imitate even what the prophets blame in nobles.—In the Gospel, *the King* Who *made a marriage feast for His Son said, I have prepared My dinner, My oxen and fatlings are killed, and all things are ready; come unto the marriage*[1]. When a *fatted calf* was killed for a feast, it was thought the best cheer, as when Abraham entertained Angels, or in that feast of the Father Who, when He had received back His son, said[2], *bring hither the fatted calf and kill it, and let us eat and be merry: for this My son was dead and is alive again.* So then the Prophet accuses the nobles of luxury, because they ate fat oxen and lambs. For the table of Solomon, the wealthiest of monarchs, there were brought *fat oxen, and oxen out of the pastures, sheep, besides hart and roebuck and fallow deer and fatted fowls*[3]. *Now* whatever is produced in sea or earth or sky, men think to be born to satisfy their appetites. Who could recount the manifold forms of food and condiments, which all-inventing gluttony has devised? Books had to be written; no memory sufficed. In this ocean, wealthiest patrimonies have discharged themselves and disappeared. Among the Romans, Fabius, for devouring his patrimony, was called Gurges [whirlpool]. Were this the practice now, he would have many great men surnamed from him, who, poor through gluttony, prey on the patrimonies of the poor, retain the property of the rich against their wills, and live on what is another's.—It were little to consume whole patrimonies in luxury, were it not that the virtues and nerves of the mind were also consumed and vices of all sorts crept in.—Shame to copy the luxury of Heathen, and despise their care for maintaining temperance.—We need not old examples. Such was the frugality of our Spaniards, 70 years ago, before they adopted foreign manners, that the rich had but mutton, roast and boiled, at their tables, nobles alone had poultry. Well were it then, if, in matter of food, we did only, what the Prophet in his time blamed." Spain has sunk under its luxury to a third-rate power. What can await England? What can await it, when the Prophet's blame were praise, and Dives is the pattern and ideal of the charity of most of us, and luxury, vanity, and self-indulgence are held to be the best way of ministering to the poor? Marvelous "imitation of Christ!" Once, to *forsake all* was to *follow* Christ. Now, to possess all, heap up all, to expend nothing save on self, and to *shew mercy on the poor* by allowing them to minister to our luxuries, is, according to the new philosophy of wealth, to be the counterfeit of Christian charity.

7. *Therefore now* [i. e. shortly] *shall they go captive with the first* [*at the head*] *of those who go captive.* They had sought eminence; they should have it. "[4] Ye who are first in riches, shall, the first, endure the yoke of captivity, as it is in Ezekiel[5], *begin from My sanctuary,* i. e. from the destruction of the Temple which is holy. For [6] *mighty men shall be mightily tormented;* and [7], *to whom men have committed much, of him they will ask the more.*"

And the banquet, probably, *the screech.* The root, *radsakh,* whose consonants contain most of those of our *screech,* signifies the loud sharp cry, which the mind cannot control, either in revelry or distress. Here it is probably, the drunken scream, or reckless cry of revelry, whose senseless shrillness is more piercing, in its way, than the scream of distress, of which Jeremiah[8] uses it. For it is the scream of the death of the soul. Amos seems to have purposely joined together similar harsh sibilants or guttural sounds, in order the more to express the harshness of that scream of luxurious self-indulgence. *Mirdsakh serukhim, the screech of the outstretched.* Of this he says, *it shall depart,* and for ever. *In that very day all his thoughts perish*[9]. It shall *depart;* but by what should it be replaced to those to whom it was their god and their all? On earth, by siege, pestilence, death or captivity: after death, by hell to the unrepentant.

8. *The Lord God,* He Who alone IS and Who Alone hath power, *hath sworn by Himself,* lit. *by His soul;* as our *self* comes from the same root as *soul.* "[4] So God saith in Isaiah[10], *Your new moons and your appointed feasts My soul hateth;* not that God hath a soul, but that He speaks after the way of

[1] S. Matt. xxii. 2, 4. [2] S. Luke xv. 23, 4. [3] 1 Kgs iv. 23. [4] S. Jer. [5] ix. 6.

[6] Wisd. vi. 6. [7] S. Luke xii. 48. [8] xvi. 5. [9] Ps. cxlvi. 4. [10] i. 14.

Before CHRIST cir. 787.

9 And it shall come to
pass, if there remain ten
men in one house, that
they shall die.
10 And a man's uncle
shall take him up, and he
that burneth him, to bring
out the bones out of the
house, and shall say unto
him that *is* by the sides of

human feelings. Nor is it any marvel that He condescends to speak of Himself, as having a soul, seeing He speaks of Himself as having the other members, feet, hands, bowels, which are less precious than the soul. In God the Father, the head, hands, and the rest are not members, but by these words a diversity of powers is expressed. So also by the soul is intended not a substance, but the inward affections, and the seat of thought whereby God indicates His Will." In truth, it is one and the same condescension in Almighty God, to use of Himself any words taken from our nature, our thoughts, acts, feelings, as those taken from the members of the body. It is a yet greater condescension that God should confirm the truth of His word by an oath. For *we* call God to witness, lest, by reason of the vast reign of falsehood among men, we should be thought not to speak true. But for God to act as though He needed the assurance of an oath in order to be believed, is more condescending, than for Him to speak as though He had a soul or limbs, such as He gave to man. Yet God, [1]*willing more abundantly to shew unto the heirs of His promise the immutability of His counsel, confirmed it by an oath. He sware by Himself saying, surely blessing I will bless thee. Now,* when Israel had, by apostasy, forfeited that blessing, and a portion of it was to be withdrawn from him, God, affirms by an oath that rejection of Israel. If the words, *by His soul*, are emphatic, they relate to those attributes in God of which man's holy affections are an image. God's love, justice, righteousness, holiness, were concerned, to vindicate the oppressed and punish the oppressor. To these He appeals. Our oaths mean, "As God is true, and as He avenges untruth, this which I say is true." So God says, "As I am God, this is true." God then must cease to be God, if He did not hate oppression.

I abhor the excellency of Jacob. The word *excellency* is used of the Majesty of God Himself; then, since man's relation to God is his only real greatness, God speaks of Himself as *the Excellency of Jacob*[2]; then of that *excellency* which God had given to *Jacob*[3]. That *excellency of their strength*, He had forwarned them in the law, that He would *break*[4]. Now that Israel took as his own what he held from God, his *excellency* became pride[5], and God says, *I abhor* it, as a thing loathsome and abominable, *and hate his palaces.* For they had been built, adorned, inhabited, filled with luxury, in the midst of, and out of, oppression and hard-hearted exaction. He calls them Jacob, perhaps as Hosea does[6], to remind them of the poverty and low estate of their forefather, out of which God had raised them, and the faithfulness of their forefather in it, in contrast with their luxury and unfaithfulness.

Therefore [*And*] *I will deliver up*; originally, *shut up*[7], then, *shut up in the hands of*[8], so that he should have no escape. Here, where the enemy is not spoken of, it may mean, that God *shut up the city*, so that there should be no going out or coming in, in the straitness of the siege, whereupon follows the fearful description of the ravages of the pestilence. *The city* is, what was to them, above others, *the* city, the place of their luxury pride and boast, where lay their strength, Samaria.

9. *If there shall remain ten men.* He probably still denounces the punishment of the rich inhabitants of the palaces, since in these only, of old, would there be found *ten men.* They died, it seems, at once, and so probably through the plague, the common companion. of the siege. The Prophet had before compared them to Sodom. It may be, that, in this mention of *ten men*, he tacitly refers to the history of that destruction. Then God promised, not to destroy the city, if there were ten righteous in it[9]. Here were *ten left*, not in one city, but in one house. Had God forgotten His loving-kindness? No! but, in Samaria, not even ten who *remained over*, and so had survived after the chastisement had begun, turned to God. All then were to be taken or destroyed. The miseries of its three years' siege by Shalmaneser may be filled up from those of its earlier siege by Benhadad[10], or from those of Jerusalem. The sufferings of a siege are in proportion to the obstinacy of the defence; and Samaria resisted for twice the time in which Jerusalem was reduced by famine at its first captivity.

10. *And a man's uncle—and he that burneth him*—lit. *and there shall take him up his uncle*

1 Heb. vi. 17, 13, 14. 2 Am. viii. 7. 3 Ps. xlvii. 4.
4 Lev. xxvi. 19.
5 Hence גאון is used of pride, Pr. xvi. 18. &c.
6 xii. 12. 7 Lev. xiv. 23, xiii. 4, 5, &c.
8 with ביד or (Am. i. 6, 9) ל. 9 Gen. xviii. 32.
10 2 Kgs vi. 24–29.

Before CHRIST cir. 787.

the house, *Is there* yet *any* with thee? and he shall say, No. Then shall he say, [r] Hold thy tongue: [s] for ‖ we may not make mention of the name of the LORD.

r ch. 5. 13.

s ch. 8. 3.

‖ Or, *they will not, or, have not.*

and his burner, i. e. his uncle who, as his next of kin, had the care of his interment, was himself the burner. Burial is the natural following out of the words, *dust thou art and unto dust thou shalt return.* The common burying-places (such as we find in the history of the Patriarchs) were the natural expression of the belief in the Resurrection. The bodies rested together, to be raised together. The heathen burned the bodies of Christian martyrs, and scattered their ashes in mockery of the Resurrection[1]. The heathen noticed that it was matter of piety with the Jews "[2] to bury rather than to burn bodies." The only exceptions are the history of Saul, and this place. Both were cases of emergency. The men of Jabesh-Gilead doubtless burnt the bodies of Saul and his sons[3], for fear the Philistines might disinter them, if buried, and renew their insults upon them. The Israelites still buried what would not be disturbed or could be concealed—the bones. David solemnly buried their remains in the sepulchre of Kish, Saul's father[4]. So probably here also, it is mentioned as an aggravation, that one who loved[5] them, had to burn their bodies. He does not say, why: but mentions it, as one feature of the common-suffering. Parents, brothers, all, gone, a man's uncle was his "burner." There was no other interment than this, the most alien from their affections and religion. It may have been on account of the extreme infection (the opening of a forgotten burying-place of those who died of the plague of London produced a virulent disease, though 1½ century had elapsed), or from the delay of burial, when, death reigning all round, there had been none to bury the dead.

He who is *by the sides*, i. e. the furthest part *of the house.* He was the one survivor of the ten, and he too, sick. The question, Is there *yet* any *with thee?* enquires whether there was any one, alive, to succor, or dead, to burn? There was none. All, even the bodies, had now been removed; one only remained, of all the hum, din, and throng, in that abode of luxury, one only *in the extremity* of its untenanted chambers. Probably the sick man was going to speak of God. The uncle breaks in upon his *No!* with *Hush! for we may not make mention of the Name of the Lord.* Times of plague are, with the most, times of religious despair. They who had not feared God in their prosperity, do nothing but fear Him then. Fear, without love, turns man more away from God. He feels *then* the presence and power of God Whom he had forgotten. He owns Him as the Author of his miseries; but, not having known Him before, he knows Him now in no other relation. The words then, *for not to be mentioned is the Name of the Lord*, are very probably the voice of despair. "It is useless to name Him now. We did not name His Name in life. It is not for *us* to name it now, in death." It might be the voice of impatient aversion, which would not bear to hear of God, the Author of its woe; or it might be the voice of superstition, which would not name God's Name, for fear of bringing fresh evil upon itself. All these grounds for not naming the Name of God and others yet worse, recur, again and again, under the pressure of a general sudden destruction. Such times bring out the soul to light, as it is. Souls, which have sinned away the grace of God and are beyond its reach, pass unobserved amid the thronging activity of ordinary life. They are arrested then. They must choose then or never. Their unchanged aversion from God, *then*, unveils what they had been before. They choose once more, deliberately, in the face of God's judgments, what they had habitually chosen before, and, by the dreadful nakedness of their choice of evil, become now unmitigatedly evil. The Prophet gives one instance of this utter misery of body and soul, because detail of misery sets the whole calamity more before men's eyes. In one picture, they see all. The words, or what the words imply, that, in extreme calamity, men mention not the Name of God, come true in different minds out of different characters of irreligion.

It has also been thought, that the brief answer, *hush!* closes the dialogue. The uncle asks, *is there yet with thee?* He answers, *None.* The other rejoins *Hush!* and the Prophet assigns the ground; *for the Name of the Lord is not to be named.* If men have not sought God earlier, they have, when his hand is heavy upon them, no heart, nor time, nor thought, nor faith to seek Him.

[1] See e. g. Ep. Eccl. Vienn. et Lugd. fin. Eus. H. E. v. 1.
[2] Tac. Hist. v. 5.
[3] 1 Sam. end.
[4] 2 Sam. xxi. 12–14.
[5] The name of the uncle is from "love" (דוד); probably, the one most loved out of the immediate household, "as חביבה, θεῖος from ἠθεῖος, amita from amata." Ges. It is not used of relationship or friendship generally, but only of the highest object of the soul's love, God. Cant. and Is. v. 1.

Before CHRIST cir. 787.

t Is. 55. 11.
u ch. 3. 15.
‖ Or, *droppings*.

11 For, behold, [t] the
LORD commandeth, [u] and
he will smite the great
house with ‖ breaches, and
the little house with clefts.
12 ¶ Shall horses run
upon the rock? will *one*
plow *there* with oxen? for
[x] ye have turned judgment
into gall, and the fruit of
righteousness into hemlock:
13 Ye which rejoice in
a thing of nought, which
say, Have we not taken

Before CHRIST cir. 787.

x Hos. 10. 4
ch. 5. 7.

11. *The Lord commandeth and He will smite.* "[1] If He commandeth, how doth He smite? If He smiteth, how doth He command? In that thing which He *commands* and enjoins His ministers, He Himself is seen to *smite.*—In Egypt the Lord declares that He slew the first-born, who, we read, were slain by *the destroyer* [2]." The *breaches* denote probably the larger, *the cleft* the smaller ruin. The greater pile was the more greatly destroyed.

12. The two images both represent a toil, which men would condemn as absurd, destructive, as well as fruitless. The horse's hoofs or his limbs would be broken; the plowing-gear would be destroyed. The Prophet gains the attention by the question. What then? they ask. The answer is implied by the *for*, which follows. Ye are they, who are so doing. As absurd is it to seek gain from injustice and oppression, to which God had annexed loss and woe, temporal and eternal. More easy to change the course of nature or the use of things of nature, than the course of God's Providence or the laws of His just retribution. They had changed the sweet laws of *justice* and equity *into* the *gall* of oppression, and the healthful *fruit of righteousness*, whereof they had received the seed from God, into the life-destroying poison of sin. Better to have *ploughed* the rock *with oxen* for food! For now, where they looked for prosperity, they found not barrenness, but death.

Others [3] understand the question as the taunt of unbelievers, trusting in the strength of Samaria, that when horses should run on their rocky eminence, or the oxen plough there, then might an enemy look for gain from investing the hill of Samaria. "Shall things which are against nature be done?" "Yes," the Prophet then would answer, "for ye have done against nature yourselves. Ye have *changed justice*, the solace of the oppressed, *into wormwood*, the bitterness of oppression. Well may what ye think above the laws of physical nature be done, when ye have violated the laws of moral nature. Well may the less thing be done, your destruction, secure as by nature ye seem, when ye have done the greater, violating the laws of the God of nature." Amos, however, when he refers to the sayings of the unbelievers, distinguishes them from his own.

13. *Who rejoice* (lit. *the rejoicers!* Amos, as is his wont, speaks of them with contempt and wonder at their folly, *the rejoicers!* much as we say, the cowards! the renegades!) *in a thing of nought*, lit. *a non-thing*, (*no-whit, nought*) not merely in a thing valueless, but in a *non-thing*, that has no existence at all, as nothing has any substantial existence out of God. This *non-thing* was their power, strength, empire, which they thought they had, but which was soon to shrivel away as a scroll.

Which say, (as before, *the sayers!* they who have this saying habitually in their mouth;) *have we not taken to ourselves horns?* The horn is the well-known symbol of strength which repels and tosses away what opposes it, as the bull doth its assailant. Moses, in his blessing, had used this symbol, of the strength of the tribe of Joseph, and as being a blessing, he spoke of it, as the gift of God [4]. *His glory is like the firstling of his bullock, and his horns are like the horns of buffalos; with them he shall push the people together to the ends of the earth; and they are the ten thousands of Ephraim, and they are the thousands of Manasseh.* To this blessing, doubtless, Zedekiah the false prophet referred [5], when he *made him horns of iron, and said* to Ahab, *Thus saith the Lord, with these shalt thou push the Syrians, until thou hast consumed them.* The Psalmist said, *through Thee will we push down our enemies*, as with a horn [6]; and adds, *For I will not trust in my bow, neither shall my sword save me. For Thou hast saved us from our enemies.* Israel ascribed God's gift to himself. He had been repeatedly and greatly victorious; he had conquered every enemy, with whom he had of old been at strife; he ascribed it to himself, and forfeited it. *By our own strength*, he said, instead of, *by the help of God*; as if we were to ascribe our Indian victories to our generals or our armies, and to substitute self-praise for Te Deums on days of thanksgiving.

"[7] The *sinner rejoiceth in a non-thing.* Sin *is a non-thing* 1) as being a thing of nought,

[1] S. Jer.
[2] Ex. xii. 23.
[3] Sanct.
[4] Deut. xxxiii. 17.
[5] 1 Kgs xxii. 11. Hengst. Auth. d. Pent. i. 101. 131,
[6] ננגח Ps. xliv. 5–7.
[7] from Lap.

Before CHRIST cir. 787.

to us horns by our own strength?

y Jer. 5. 15.

14 But, behold, [y] I will raise up against you a nation, O house of Israel, saith the LORD the God

Before CHRIST cir. 787.

i. e. vain and valueless. 2) Its pleasure is fleeting; whence the Psalmist says[1], *all the men, whose hands are mighty, have found nothing.* 3) Sin brings the sinner to nothing, i. e. destruction and death, temporal and eternal. 4) Sin is the privation of good; but privation is a mere negative; i. e. nothing. 5) Sin deprives of God Who is All and the Creator of all. 6) Sin is nothing, because it cleaves to and joys in creatures and opposes them and prefers them to the Creator. For creatures, compared to the Creator, are shadows of things, not the very things, and so are nothing. For the Being and Name of God is, I AM that I AM[2], i. e. I Am He Who Alone have true, full, solid, eternal, infinite, Being; but creatures participate from Me a shadow of their true being; for their being is so poor, brief, fleeting, unstable, perishing, that, compared to Mine, they may rather be said, not to be, than to be. So then as creatures have no true being, so neither have they true good, but only a shadow of good.—So also as to truth, wisdom, power, justice, holiness and other attributes. These have in God their real being; in creatures a shadow of being only. Whence God is called in Scripture Alone Wise[3], Alone Mighty[4], Alone Immortal[5], Alone Lord[6], Alone Holy[7], Alone Good[8]; because He Alone has true, full, uncreated and infinite Wisdom, Power, Goodness, &c. But the sinner, in that he delights in creatures not in the Creator, delights in a shadow, a nothing, not in the true Being. But, because these shadows of creatures amid the dimness of this life appear great to man in his blindness, (as the mountains, at sunset, cast broad and deep shadows,) he admires and pursues these shadows, like the dog in the fable, who, seeing the shadow of the meat in the water, magnified in the water, snatched at it, and so lost the meat and did not attain the shadow. O Lord, dispel our darkness, lighten our eyes, that we may love and seek, not the shadows of honors, riches, and pleasures, which, like meteors, dazzle here on earth our mind's eye, but may, with fixed gaze, behold, love, and compass the real honors, riches, pleasures themselves, which Thou hast from eternity laid up and prepared in heaven for those who love Thee."

[1] Ps. lxxvi. 5. [2] See ab. p. 119. [3] Rom. xvi. 27. [4] 1 Tim. vi. 15. [5] Ib. 16. [6] Is. xxxvii. 20. [7] Rev. xv. 4. [8] S. Luke xviii. 19. [9] Jud. ii. 16–18. [10] Ib. iii. 9–15. [11] Am. ii. 11, Jer. xxix. 15, and of the Prophet like Moses, Deut. xviii. 15. [12] Am. Ib. [13] 1 Sam. ii. 35. [14] 2 Sam. vii. 8.

14. *But* [*For*,]—it *was* a non-thing, a non-existent thing, a phantom, whereat they rejoiced;—*for behold I raise up a nation.* God is said to *raise up*, when, by His Providence or His grace, He calls forth those who had not been called before, for the office for which He designs them. Thus, He raised up judges[9], deliverers[10], prophets[11], Nazarites[12], priests[13], kings[14], calling each separately to perform what He gave them in charge. So He is said to *raise up* even the evil ministers of His good Will, whom, in the course of His Providence, He allows to raise themselves up aloft to that eminence, so often as, in fulfilling their own bad will, they bring about, or are examples of, His righteous judgment. Thus God *raised up Hadad* as *an adversary*[15] to Solomon, and again Rezon[16]; and the Chaldees[17]. So again God says to Pharaoh, *For this have I raised thee up*[18], *to shew in thee My power.* So here He says, *I will raise up against you a nation, and they shall afflict you from the entering in of Hamath.* Israel, under Jeroboam II., had recovered a wider extent of territory, than had, in her Northern portion, belonged to her since the better days of Solomon. Jeroboam[19] *recovered Damascus and Hamath,* which belonged *to Judah, unto Israel. He restored,* as God promised him by Jonah, *the coast of Israel from the entering of Hamath unto the sea of the plain. The entering of Hamath* expresses the utmost Northern boundary promised to Israel[20]. But this does not in itself express whether Hamath itself was included. Hamath however, and even Damascus itself, were incorporated in the bounds of Israel. The then great scourge of Israel had become part of its strength. Southward, Ammon and even Moab, had been taken into its borders. All the country on the other side of Jordan was theirs from Hamath and Damascus to the South of the Dead Sea, a space including four degrees of Latitude, as much as from Portsmouth to Durham. Amos describes the extension of the kingdom of Israel in the self-same terms as the Book of Kings; only he names as the southern extremity, *the river of the wilderness,* instead of *the sea of the wilderness*[21]. *The sea of the wilderness,* i. e. the Dead Sea, might in itself be either its Northern or its Southern extremity. The word used by Amos, defines

[15] 1 Kgs xi. 14. [16] Ib. 23. [17] Hab. i. 6. [18] העמדתיך Ex. ix. 16. [19] 2 Kgs xiv. 28, 25. [20] Num. xxxiv. 8. [21] 2 Kgs מלבוא חמת עד ים הערבה
Am. מלבוא חמת עד נחל הערבה

Before CHRIST cir. 787.

of hosts; and they shall afflict you from the [z] entering in of Hemath unto the || river of the wilderness.

Before CHRIST cir. 787.

[z] Num. 34. 8. 1 Kings 8. 65.

|| Or, *valley*.

it to be the Southern. For his use of the name, *river of the wilderness*, implies 1) that it was a well-known boundary, a boundary as well-known to Israel on the South[1], as *the entering in of Hamath* was on the North. 2) As a boundary-river, it must have been a river on the East of the Jordan, since Benjamin formed their boundary on the West of Jordan, and mountain passes, not rivers, separated them from it. 3) From its name, *river of the wilderness*, or *the Arabah*, it must, in some important part of its course, have flowed in the 'Arabah. The 'Arabah, (it is now well known,) is no other than that deep and remarkable depression, now called the Ghor, which extends from the lake of Gennesareth to the Red Sea[2]. The Dead Sea itself is called by Moses too *the sea of the Arabah*[3], lying, as it does, in the middle of that depression, and dividing it into two, the valley of the Jordan above the Dead Sea, and the Southern portion which extends uninterrupted from the Dead to the Red Sea; and which also (although Scripture has less occasion to speak of it) Moses calls the 'Arabah[4]. A river, which fell from Moab into the Dead Sea without passing through the Arabah, would not be called "a river of the Arabah," but, at the most "a river of the sea of the Arabah." Now, besides the improbability that the name, *the river of the Arabah*, should have been substituted for the familiar names, the Arnon or the Jabbok, the Arnon does not flow into the Arabah at all, the Jabbok is no way connected with the Dead Sea, the corresponding boundary in the Book of Kings. These were both boundary-rivers, the Jabbok having been the Northern limit of what Moab and Ammon lost to the Amorite; the Arnon being the Northern border of Moab. But there is a third boundary-river which answers all the conditions. Moab was bounded on the South by a river, which Isaiah calls *the brook of the willows*, Nahal Ha'arabim[5], across which he foretells that they should transport for safety all which they had of value. A river, now called in its upper part the Wadi-el-Ahsa, and then the Wadi-es-Safieh, which now too "[6] has more water than any South of the Yerka" [Jabbok], "divides the district of Kerek from that of Jebâl, the ancient Gebalene" (i.e. Moab from Idumæa). This river, after flowing from East to West and so forming a Southern boundary to Moab, turns to the North in the Ghor or Arabah, and flows into the S. extremity of the Dead Sea[7]. This river then, answering to all the conditions, is doubtless that of which Amos spoke, and the boundary, which Jeroboam restored, included Moab also, (as in the most prosperous times of Israel,) since Moab's Southern border was now his border.

Israel, then, had no enemy, West of the Euphrates. Their strength had also, of late, been increasing steadily. Jehoash had, at the promise of Elisha, thrice defeated the Syrians, and recovered cities which had been lost, probably on the West also of Jordan, in the heart of the kingdom of Israel. What Jehoash had begun, Jeroboam II., during a reign of forty-one years, continued. Prophets had foretold and defined the successes of both kings, and so had marked them out the more to be the gift of God. Israel ascribed it to himself; and now that the enemies, whom Israel had feared, were subdued, God says, *I will raise up an enemy, and they shall afflict thee from the entering in of Hamath unto the river of the wilderness.* The whole scene of their triumphs should be one scene of affliction and woe. This was fulfilled after some forty-five years, at the invasion of Tiglath-pileser.

VII. The visions of this chapter continue the direct prophecy of the last. That closed in the prophecy of the affliction of Israel through the Assyrian: this foretells three gradations, in which it took place. *That* spoke of a recovery of Israel after its extreme depression under Hazael; the first of these visions exhibit it as a field shorn to the ground, shooting out anew, but threatened with a fresh destruction. The chastisements are three-fold. Two, at the intercession of Amos, stop short of utter destruction; the 3d was final. Each also increased in severity. Such were the three invasions of the Assyrians. Pul, invited by Menahem, amid civil war, to establish him on his throne, exacted only a heavy fine. Tiglath-pileser, called in by Ahaz against Pekah, carried off the inhabitants of the East and North of Israel; the invasion of Shalmaneser ended the empire and its idolatry.

[1] This altogether excludes the Kidron (which Gesenius would make it). Indeed the Kidron is 1) no border-river at all, flowing *within* Judah. 2) It does not belong to the Arabah at all, flowing from Jerusalem, mostly through deep perpendicular defiles, to the Dead Sea (see ab. p. 141). 3) It falls into the W. side of the Dead Sea, not into its Northern extremity.

[2] Burckh. Syr. 441, 2. Rob. ii. 186, 7.
[3] Deut. iii. 17, iv. 49.
[4] Ib. ii. 8, 9 (translated *plain*). See more fully Stanley, Pal. 487.
[5] Is. xv. 7.
[6] Burckh. Ib. 401.
[7] See Van de Velde's map or Kiepert's in Porter's Hdbook, or Robinson's map.

Before CHRIST cir. 787.

CHAPTER VII.

1 *The judgments of the grasshoppers,* 4 *and of the fire, are diverted by the prayer of Amos.* 7 *By the wall of a plumbline is signified the rejection of Israel.* 10 *Amaziah complaineth of Amos.* 14 *Amos sheweth his calling,* 16 *and Amaziah's judgment.*

THUS hath the Lord
God shewed unto me;
and, behold, he formed
|| grasshoppers in the be-
ginning of the shooting up
of the latter growth; and,
lo, *it was* the latter growth
after the king's mowings.
2 And it came to pass,
that when they had made
an end of eating the grass
of the land, then I said, O
Lord God, forgive, I be-
seech thee: [a] || by whom
shall Jacob arise? for he
is small.
3 [b] The LORD repented
for this: It shall not be,
saith the LORD.

|| Or, *green worms.*

Before CHRIST cir. 787.

[a] Is. 51. 19. ver. 6.
|| Or, *who of* (or, for,) *Jacob shall stand?*
[b] Deut. 32. 36. ver. 56. Jonah 3. 10. James 5. 16.

1. *And behold He formed* (i. e. *He was forming*). The very least things then are as much in His infinite Mind, as what we count the greatest. He has not simply made "laws of nature," as men speak, to do His work, and continue the generations of the world. He Himself was still framing them, giving them being, as our Lord saith, *My Father worketh hitherto, and I work*[1]. The same power of God is seen in creating the locust, as the Universe. The creature could as little do the one as the other. But further. God was *framing* them for a special end, not of nature, but of His moral government, in the correction of man. He was *framing the locust*, that it might, at His appointed time, lay waste just those tracts which He had appointed to them. God, in this vision, opens our eyes, and lets us see Himself, framing the punishment for the deserts of the sinners, that so when hail, mildew, blight, caterpillars, or some other hitherto unknown disease, (which, because we know it not, we call by the name of the crop which it annihilates), waste our crops, we may think, not of secondary causes, but of our Judge. "[2] *Fire and hail, snow and vapors, stormy wind, fulfill His word*[3], in striking sinners as He wills. To be indignant with these, were like a dog who bit the stone wherewith it was hit, instead of the man who threw it." "[4] He who denies that he was stricken for his own fault, what does he but accuse the justice of Him Who smiteth?"

Grasshoppers, i. e. locusts. The name may very possibly be derived from their *creeping*[5] simultaneously, in vast multitudes, from the ground, which is the more observable in these creatures, which, when the warmth of spring hatches the eggs, creep forth at once in myriads. This first meaning of their name must, however, have been obliterated by use (as mostly happens), since the word is also used by Nahum of a flying locust[6].

The king's mowings must have been some regalia, to meet the state-expenses. The like custom still lingers on, here and there, among us, the "first mowth" or "first vesture," that with which the fields are first clad, belonging to one person; the pasturage afterward, or "after-grass," to others. The hay-harvest probably took place some time before the corn-harvest, and the *latter grass*, "after-grass,"(lekesh) probably began to spring up at the time of the *latter rain* (malkosh). Had the grass been mown after this rain, it would not, under the burning sun of their rainless summer, have sprung up at all. At this time, then, upon which the hope of the year depended, *in the beginning of the shooting up of the latter grass*, Amos saw, in vision, God form the locust, and *the green herb of the land* (the word includes all, that which is *for the service of man* as well as for beasts,) destroyed. Striking emblem of a state, recovering after it had been mown down, and anew overrun by a numerous enemy! Yet this need but be a passing desolation. Would they abide, or would they carry their ravages elsewhere? Amos intercedes with God, in words of that first intercession of Moses, *forgive now*[7]. *By whom*, he adds, *shall Jacob arise?* lit. *Who shall Jacob arise?* i. e. who is he that he should arise, so weakened, so half-destroyed? Plainly, the destruction is more than one invasion of locusts in one year. The locusts are a symbol, (as in Joel,) in like way as the following visions are symbols.

3. *The Lord repented for this.* God is said to *repent, to have strong compassion upon* or

[1] S. John v. 17. [2] Lap. [3] Ps. cxlviii. 8.
[4] S. Greg. on Job L. xxxii. c. 4. L.
[5] from the Arab. jabaa.
[6] See Pref. to Joel, p. 150. [7] Num. xiv. 19.

Before CHRIST cir. 787.

4 ¶ Thus hath the Lord
GOD shewed unto me: and,
behold, the Lord God called to contend by fire, and
it devoured the great deep,
and did eat up a part.
5 Then said I, O Lord
GOD, cease I beseech thee:
[c] by whom shall Jacob
arise? for he *is* small.
6 The LORD repented
for this: This also shall
not be, saith the Lord
GOD.

[c] ver. 2, 3.

over[1] evil, which He has either inflicted[2], or has said that He would inflict[3], and which, upon repentance or prayer, He suspends or checks. Here, Amos does not intercede until after the judgment had been, in part, inflicted. He prayed, when in vision the locust *had made an end of eating the grass of the land,* and when *the fire had eaten up a part.* Nor, until Israel had suffered what these visions foretold, was he *small,* either in his own or in human sight, or in relation to his general condition. The *this* then, *of which God repented* and said, *it shall not be,* is that further undefined evil, which His first infliction threatened. Evil and decay do not die out, but destroy. Oppression does not weary itself out, but increases. Visitations of God are tokens of His displeasure, and, in the order of His Justice, rest on the sinner. Pul and Tiglath-pileser, when they came with their armies on Israel, were instruments of God's chastening. According to the ways of God's Justice, or of man's ambition, the evil now begun, would have continued, but that God, at the prayer of the Prophet, said[4], *Hitherto shalt thou come, and no further.*

4. *God called to contend by fire;* i. e. He *called* His people to maintain their cause with Him *by fire,* as He says[5], *I will plead* in judgment *with him* [Gog] *with* [i. e. *by*] *pestilence and blood;* and, [6] *by fire and by His sword will the Lord plead with all flesh;* and, [7] *The Lord standeth up to plead and standeth to judge the people.* Man, by rebellion, challenges God's Omnipotence. He will have none of Him; he will find his own happiness for himself, apart from God and in defiance of Him and His laws; he plumes himself on his success, and accounts his strength or wealth or prosperity the test of the wisdom of his policy. God, sooner or later, accepts the challenge. He brings things to the issue, which man had chosen. He *enters into judgment*[8] with him. If man escapes with impunity, then he had chosen well, in rejecting God and choosing his own ways. If not, what folly and misery was his short-sighted choice; short-lived in its gain; its loss, eternal! *Fire* stands as the symbol and summary of God's most terrible judgments. It spares nothing, leaves nothing, not even the outward form of what it destroys. Here it is plainly a symbol, since it destroys *the sea* also, which shall be destroyed only by the fire of the Day of Judgment, when [9] *the elements shall melt with fervent heat, the earth also and the works that are therein shall be burned up.* The sea is called the *great deep,* only in the most solemn language, as the history of the creation or the flood, the Psalms and poetical books. Here it is used, in order to mark the extent of the desolation represented in the vision.

And did eat up a part, rather lit. *the portion*[10], i. e. probably, *the* definite *portion* fore-appointed by God to captivity and desolation. This probably our Version meant by *a part.* For although God calls Himself *the Portion* of Israel[11], and of those who are His[12], and reciprocally He calls the people *the Lord's portion*[13], and the land, *the portion*[14] of God's people; yet the land is nowhere called absolutely *the portion,* nor was the country of the ten tribes specially *the portion,* given by God. Rather God exhibits in vision to the Prophet, the ocean burned up, and *the portion* of Israel, upon which His judgments were first to fall. To this Amos points, as *the portion.* God knew *the portion,* which Tiglath-Pileser would destroy, and when he came and had carried captive the East and North of Israel, the pious in Israel would recognize the second, more desolating scourge, foretold by Amos; they would own that it was at the prayer of the Prophet that it was stayed and went no further, and would await what remained.

5. 6. As our Lord repeated the same words in the Garden, so Amos interceded with God with words, all but one[15], the same, and with the same plea, that, if God did not help, Israel was indeed helpless. Yet a second time God spared Israel. To human sight, what so strange and unexpected, as that the Assyrian and his army, having utterly destroyed the kingdom of Damascus, and carried away its people, and having devoured, like fire,

[1] נחם על. [2] Deut. xxxii. 36, 1 Chr. xxi. 15.
[3] Ex. xxxii. 12, Joel ii. 13, Jon. iii. 10, Jer. xviii. 8.
[4] Job xxxviii. 11. [5] Ezek. xxxviii. 22.
[6] Is. lxvi. 16. [7] Ib. iii. 13. [8] Ib. 14, &c.
[9] 2 S. Pet. iii. 10. [10] את החלק.
[11] Deut. xxxii. 9, Jer. x. 16, Zech. ii. 12. [12] Ps. xvi. 5, lxxiii. 26, &c. Jer. x. 16. [13] Jer. xii. 10.
[14] Mic. ii. 4. [15] חדל, *cease,* for סלח *forgive.*

Before CHRIST cir. 787.

7 ¶ Thus he shewed me:
and, behold, the Lord stood
upon a wall *made* by a
plumbline, with a plumb-
line in his hand.
8 And the LORD said
unto me, Amos, what seest
thou? And I said, A
plumbline. Then said the
Lord, Behold, [d] I will set
a plumbline in the midst
of my people Israel; [e] I
will not again pass by them
any more:

Before CHRIST cir. 787.

[d] See 2 Kings 21. 13. Is. 28. 17. & 34. 11. Lam. 2. 8.
[e] ch. 8. 2. Mic. 7. 18.

---

more than half of Israel, rolled back like an ebb-tide, swept away to ravage other countries, and spared the capital? And who, looking at the mere outside of things, would have thought that that tide of fire was rolled back, not by anything in that day, but by the Prophet's prayer some 47 years before? Man would look doubtless for motives of human policy, which led Tiglath-pileser to accept tribute from Pekah, while he killed Rezin; and while he carried off all the Syrians of Damascus, to leave half of Israel to be removed by his successor. Humanly speaking, it was a mistake. He "scotched" his enemy only, and left him to make alliance with Egypt, his rival, who disputed with him the possession of the countries which lay between them. If we knew the details of Assyrian policy, we might know what induced him to turn aside in his conquest. There were, and always are, human motives. They do not interfere with the ground in the mind of God, Who directs and controls them. Even in human contrivances, the wheels, interlacing one another, and acting one on the other, do but transmit, the one to the other, the motion and impulse which they have received from the central force. The revolution of the earth around its own centre does not interfere with, rather it is a condition of its revolving round the centre of our system, and, amidst the alternations of night and day, brings each several portion within the influence of the sun around which it revolves. The affairs of human kingdoms have their own subordinate centres of human policy, yet even thereby they the more revolve in the circuit of God's appointment. In the history of His former people God gives us a glimpse into a hidden order of things, the secret spring and power of His wisdom, which sets in motion that intricate and complex machinery which alone we see, and in the sight of which men lose the consciousness of the unseen agency. While man strives with man, prayer, suggested by God, moves God, the Ruler of all.

7. *Stood upon* [rather *over* [1]] *a wall* made by *a plumbline;* lit. *a wall of a plumbline,* i. e. (as our's has it) *made* straight, perpendicular, *by* it. The wall had been *made by a lead* or *plumbline;* by it, i. e. according to it, it should be destroyed. God had made it upright, He had given to it an undeviating rule of right, He had watched over it, to keep it, as He made it. Now *He stood over it,* fixed in His purpose, to destroy it. He marked its inequalities. Yet this too in judgment. He destroys it by that same rule of right wherewith He had built it. By that law, that right, those Providential leadings, that grace, which we have received, by the same we are judged.

8. *Amos?* "[2] He calls the Prophet by name, as a familiar friend, known and approved by Him, as He said to Moses [3], *I know thee by name.* For [4] *the Lord knoweth them that are His. What seest thou?* God had twice heard the Prophet. Two judgments upon His people He had mitigated, not upon *their* repentance, but on the single intercession of the Prophet. After that, He willed to be no more entreated. And so He exhibits to Amos a symbol, whose meaning He does not explain until He had pronounced their doom. *The plumbline* was used in pulling down, as well as in building up. Whence Jeremiah says [5], *The Lord hath purposed to destroy the wall of the daughter of Zion; He hath stretched out a line; He hath not withdrawn His hand from destroying; therefore He made the rampart and wall to lament:* and Isaiah [6]; *He shall stretch out upon it the line of wasteness* [7] *and the stone of emptiness* [7]: and God said of Judah [8], *I will stretch over Jerusalem the line of Samaria and the plummet of the house of Ahab.* Accordingly God explains the vision, *Behold I will set,* i. e. shortly, [lit. *am setting*] *a plumbline in the midst of My people Israel.* The wall, then, is not the emblem of Samaria or of any one city. It is the strength and defence of the whole people, whatever held it together, and held out the enemy. As in the vision to Belshazzar, the word *Tekel, He weighed,* was explained [9], *Thou art weighed in the balances and art found wanting,* so God here applies the plumbline, at once to convict and to destroy upon conviction. In this Judgment, as at the Last Day, God would not condemn, without having first made clear the

[1] This lies in the words נצב על. [2] Dion.
[3] Ex. xxxiii. 12, 17. [4] 2 Tim. ii. 19. [5] Lam. ii. 8.
[6] Is. xxxiv. 11. [7] תהו בהו as in Gen. i. 2.
[8] 2 Kgs xxi. 13. [9] Dan. v. 27.

Before CHRIST cir. 787.

9 [f] And the high places
of Isaac shall be desolate,
and the sanctuaries of
Israel shall be laid waste;
and [g] I will rise against
the house of Jeroboam with
the sword.

10 ¶ Then Amaziah
[h] the priest of Bethel sent
to [i] Jeroboam king of

f Beer-sheba. Gen. 26. 23. & 46. 1. ch. 5. 5. & 8. 14.
g Fulfilled, 2 Kings 15. 10.
h 1 Kings 12. 32.
i 2 Kings 14. 23.

justice of His condemnation. He sets it *in the midst of* His *people*, shewing that He would make trial of all, one by one, and condemn in proportion to the guilt of each. But the day of grace being past, the sentence was to be final. *I will not pass by them*, lit. *I will not pass over* [i. e. their transgressions] *to them*[1] *any more*, i. e. I will no more forgive them.

9. *The high places of Isaac.* He probably calls the ten tribes by the name of Isaac, as well as of Israel, in order to contrast their deeds with the blameless, gentle piety of Isaac, as well as the much-tried faithfulness of Israel. It has been thought too that he alludes to the first meaning of the name of Isaac. His name was given from the joyous laughter at the unheard-of promise of God, to give children to those past age; their high-places should be a laughter, but the laughter of mockery[2]. The *sanctuaries* were perhaps the two great idol-temples at Bethel and Dan, over against the one *sanctuary* of God at Jerusalem; the *high places* were the shrines of idolatry, especially where God had shewn mercy to the Patriarchs and Israel, but also all over the land. All were to be wasted, because all were idolatrous.

I will rise against the house of Jeroboam with the sword. God speaks after the manner of men, who, having been still, arise against the object of their enmity. He makes Himself so far one with the instruments of His sentence, that, what they do, He ascribes to Himself. Jeroboam II. must, from his military success, have been popular among his people. Successful valor is doubly prized, and he had both valor[3] and success. God had *saved Israel by* His *hand*[4]. A weak successor is often borne with for the merits of his father. There were no wars from without, which called for strong military energy or talent, and which might furnish an excuse for superseding a faineant king. Ephraim had no ambition of foreign glory, to gratify. Zechariah, Jeroboam's son, was a sensualist[5]; but many sensualists have, at all times, reigned undisturbed. Shallum who murdered Zechariah was simply a *conspirator*[6]; he represented no popular impulse, and was slain himself a month[7] after. Yet Amos foretells absolutely that the house of Jeroboam should perish by the sword, and in the next generation his name was clean put out.

10. *Amaziah, the priest of Bethel,* was probably the high-priest, in imitation of the High Priest of the order of Aaron and of God's appointment. For the many high places around Bethel required many idol-priests; and a splendid counterfeit of the ritual at Jerusalem, which should rival it in the eyes of Israel, was part of the policy of the first Jeroboam. Amaziah was at the head of this imposture, in a position probably of wealth and dignity among his people. Like *Demetrius the silversmith*[8], he thought that the craft whereby he had his wealth was endangered. To Jeroboam, however, he says nothing of these fears. To the king he makes it an affair of state. He takes the king by what he expected to be his weak side, fear for his own power or life. *Amos hath conspired against thee.* So to Jeremiah[9] *the captain of the ward* said, *Thou fallest away to the Chaldæans.* And the princes[10]; *Let this man be put to death, for thus he weakeneth the hands of the men of war that remain in this city, and the hands of all the people, in speaking such words unto them: for this man seeketh not the welfare of this people, but the hurt.* And of our Lord they said to Pilate, [11] *If thou let this Man go, thou art not Cæsar's friend. Whosoever maketh himself a king, is an enemy to Cæsar.* And of the Apostles[12]; *these men, being Jews, do exceedingly trouble our city, and teach customs which are not lawful for us to receive, neither to observe, being Romans;* and, [13] *these that have turned the world upside down are come hither also —and these all do contrary to the decrees of Cæsar, saying that there is another king, Jesus.* And so the heathen, who were ever conspiring against the Roman Emperors, went on accusing the early Christians as disloyal to the Emperors, factious, impious, because they did not offer sacrifices for them to false gods, but prayed for them to the True God[14]. Some doubtless, moved by the words of Amos, had forsaken the state-idolatry, reformed their lives, worshiped God with the Prophet; perhaps they were called in con-

1 as in viii. 2.
2 So the LXX, and, from them, S. Cyril and Theodoret.
3 2 Kgs xiv. 28. גבורתו personal bravery.
4 Ib. 27.
5 See on Hos. vii. 7. p. 45, and Introd. p. 5.
6 2 Kgs xv. 10.
7 Ib. 13, 14.
8 Acts xix.
9 Jer. xxxvii. 13.
10 Ib. xxxviii. 4.
11 S. John xix. 12.
12 Acts xvi. 20, 1.
13 Ib. xvii. 6, 7.
14 Tertul. Apol. § 28–38. pp. 68–80. Oxf. Tr. ad Scap. § 2. pp. 143, 4. Ib.

Before CHRIST cir. 787.

Israel, saying, Amos hath
conspired against thee in
the midst of the house of
Israel: the land is not able
to bear all his words.
11 For thus Amos saith,
Jeroboam shall die by the
sword, and Israel shall
surely be led away captive
out of their own land.
12 Also Amaziah said
unto Amos, O thou seer,
go, flee thee away into the
land of Judah, and there
eat bread, and prophesy
there:

Before CHRIST cir. 787.

tempt by his name, "Amosites" or "Judaizers," and were counted as *his* adherents, not as the worshipers of the one true God, *the God of their fathers.* Whence Amaziah gained the plea of a *conspiracy,* of which Amos was the head. For a *conspiracy* cannot be of one man. The word, by its force, signifies "banded[1];" the idiom, that he "banded" others "together against[2]" the king. To us Amaziah attests the power of God's word by His Prophet; *the land,* i. e. the whole people, *is not able to bear his words,* being shaken through and through.

11. *For thus Amos saith.* Amos had said, *Thus saith the Lord;* he never fails to impress on them, Whose words he is speaking. Amaziah, himself bound up in a system of falsehood and imposture, which, being a creature-worship, gave itself out as the worship of the true God, believed all besides to be fraud. Fraud always suspects fraud; the irreligious think devotion, holiness, saintliness to be hypocrisy: vice imagines virtue to be well-masked vice. The false priest, by a sort of law of corrupt nature, supposed that Amos also was false, and treats his words as the produce of his own mind.

Jeroboam shall die by the sword. Amos had not said this. The false prophet distorts the last words of Amos, which were yet in his ears, and reports to Jeroboam, as said of himself, what Amos had just said of his *house.* Amos *was* opposed to the popular religion or irreligion of which Jeroboam was the head, to the headship over which he had succeeded. Jeroboam, like the Roman Emperors, was High Priest, Pontifex Maximus, in order to get the popular worship under his control. The first Jeroboam had himself consecrated the calf-priests[2]. Amos bore also the message from God, that the reprieve, given to the house of Jehu, would not be extended, but would end. Amaziah would act on the personal fears of the king, as though there had been some present active conspiracy against him. A lie, mixed with truth, is the most deadly form of falsehood, the truth serving to gain admittance for the lie, and color it, and seeming to require explanation, and being something to fall back upon. Since thus much is certainly true, why should not the rest be so? In slander, and heresy which is slander against God, truth is used to commend the falsehood; and falsehood, to destroy the truth. The poison is received the more fearlessly because wrapt up in truth, but loses none of its deadliness.

And Israel shall surely be led away captive. This was a suppression of truth, as the other was a falsification of it. Amaziah omits both the ground of the threat, and the hope of escape urged and impressed upon them. On the one side he omits all mention of what even such a king as Jeroboam would respect, the denunciation of oppression of the poor, injustice, violence, robbery, and all their other sins against man. On the other hand, he omits the call to repentance and promises on it, *seek ye the Lord and live.* He omits too the Prophet's intercession for his people, and selects the one prophecy, which could give a mere political character to the whole. Suppression of truth is a yet subtler character of falsehood. Hence witnesses on oath are required to tell, not the truth only, but the whole truth. Yet in daily life, or in accusation of others, in detraction, or evil-speaking, men daily act, as though suppression were no lie.

12. Jeroboam apparently took no account of the false priest's message. Perhaps the memory of the true prophecies of Elisha as to the successes of his father, and of Jonah as to his own, fulfilled in his own person and still recent, inspired him with a reverence for God's prophets. To know his motive or motives, we must know his whole character, which we do not. Amaziah, failing of his purpose, uses his name as far as he dares. *Seer, go flee thee.* He probably uses the old title for a prophet, in reference to the visions which he had just related. Perhaps, he used it in irony also[3]. "Thou who seest, as thou

[1] קשר bound.

[2] קשר על "banded against, *con*spired." 1 Sam. xxii. 8, 13. 1 Kgs xv. 27, xvi. 9, 16, 2 Kgs x. 9, xiv. 19, xv. 10, 15, 25, xxi. 23. So also קֶשֶׁר, קשורים.

[3] "Either in irony, in that he lies throughout, or because seeing, &c." (as below) S. Jer.

Before CHRIST cir. 787.

13 [k] But prophesy not
again any more at Beth-el:
[l] for it *is* the king's ‖ chapel
and it *is* the † king's court.

[k] ch. 2. 12.
[l] 1 Kings 12. 32. & 13. 1.
‖ Or, *sanctuary.*
† Heb. *house of the kingdom.*

14 ¶ Then answered
Amos, and said to Amazi-
ah, I *was* no prophet,
neither *was* I [m] a prophet's

Before CHRIST cir. 787.

[m] 1 Kings 20. 35. 2 Kings 2. 5. & 4 38. & 6. 1.

deemest, what others see not, *visionary! visionist!" flee thee,* i. e. for thy good; (he acts the patron and the counsellor;) *to the land of Judah, and there eat bread, and there prophesy.* Worldly men always think that those whose profession is religious make *a gain of godliness.* "He is paid for it," they say. "Whose bread I eat, his song I sing." Interested people cannot conceive of one disinterested; nor the worldly, of one unworldly; nor the insincere, of one sincere. Amaziah thought then that Amos, coming out of Judah, must be speaking in the interests of Judah; perhaps, that he was in the pay of her king. Anyhow, prophecies, such as his against Israel, would be acceptable there and be well paid. The words are courteous, like so much patronizing language now, as to God or His revelation, His Prophets or His Apostles, or His Divine word. The words are measured: the meaning blasphemy. Perhaps, like the Scribes and Pharisees afterward, *he feared the people*[1]. "[2] Seeing that there were many among the people who heard him gladly, he dared not do him any open wrong, lest he should offend them."

13. *It is the king's chapel;* better, as in the E. M., *sanctuary*[3]. It is the name for *the sanctuary* of God[4]. *Let them make Me a sanctuary, that I may dwell among them. Ye shall reverence My sanctuary: I am the Lord*[5]. It is most often spoken of as, *The sanctuary*[6]; elsewhere, but always with emphasis, of reverence, sanctity, devotion, protection, it is called *His sanctuary; My sanctuary; Thy sanctuary; the sanctuary of the Lord of God, of his God*[7]; whence God Himself is called *a Sanctuary*[8], as a place of refuge. In three places only, is it called the sanctuary of Israel; *her sanctuary.* God, in His threat to cast them off, says[9], *I will bring your sanctuaries to desolation;* Jeremiah laments[10], *the heathen have entered into her sanctuary;* he says[11], *the place of our sanctuary is a glorious high throne from the beginning,* inasmuch as God was enthroned there. In this case too it is *the sanctuary for* Israel, not a mere property *of* Israel. *The sanctuary of God* could not be called the sanctuary of any man. One man could not so appropriate *the sanctuary.* God had ordained it for Himself. His presence had sanctified it. Heresy, in unconsciousness, lets out more truth than it means. A high priest at Jerusalem could not have said this. He knew that *the temple* was the *sanctuary* of God, and could not have called it *the king's sanctuary.* The sanctuary at Bethel had no other sanction, than what it had from the king. Jeroboam I. consecrated it and its priests[12]; and from him it and they had their authority. Amaziah wished to use a popular plea to rid himself of Amos. Bethel was *the king's sanctuary and the house,* not of God, but *of the kingdom,* i. e. *the house,* which had the whole royal sanction, which with its worship was the creature of royal authority, bound up in one with the kingdom, and belonging to it. Or it may be, *a royal house*[13], (not a palace, or court, for the king's palace was at Samaria, but) a *royal temple,* the state-Church. So the Arians betrayed their worldliness by dating one of their Creeds from the Roman Consuls of the year, its month and day, "[14] thereby to shew all thinking men, that their faith dates, not of old but now." Their faith was of yesterday. "They are wont to say," says St. Jerome, "the Emperor communicates with us, and, if any one resists them, forthwith they calumniate. 'Actest thou against the Emperor? Despisest thou the Emperor's mandate?' And yet we may think, that many Christian kings who have persecuted the Church of God, and essayed to establish the Arian impiety in the whole world, surpass in guilt Jeroboam king of Israel. He despised the message of a false priest, nor would he make any answer to his suggestions. But these, with their many Amaziah-priests, have slain Amos the prophet and the priest of the Lord by hunger and penury, dungeons and exile."

14. *I was no prophet.* The order of the words is emphatic. *No prophet I, and no prophet's son I; for a herdsman I, and dresser of sycamores.* It may be, Amos would meet, for the people's sake, Amaziah's taunt. He had a living, simple indeed, yet that of the prophets was as simple. But chiefly he tells them of the unusual character of his mission.

[1] S. Matt. xxi. 26, Acts v. 26. [2] S. Jer. [3] מקדש.
[4] Ex. xxv. 8. [5] Lev. xix. 30, xxvi. 2.
[6] המקדש 68 times. In reference to the time before it was built, it is called *a sanctuary,* Ex. xxv. 8, 2 Chr. xx. 8.
[7] In all, 23 times. [8] Is. viii. 14, Ezek. xi. 16.
[9] Lev. xxvi. 31. [10] Lam. i. 10. [11] Jer. xvii. 12.
[12] 1 Kings xii. 31–3.
[13] It has not the art. as בית המלכות has, Esth. i. 9.
[14] S. Ath. Counc. Arim. Sel. § 3. Treat. ag. Arian. p. 76. Oxf. Tr.

21

Before CHRIST cir. 787.

son; [n] but I *was* an herd-
man, and a gatherer of
|| sycamore fruit:
15 And the LORD took
me † as I followed the
flock and the LORD said
unto me, Go, prophesy unto
my people Israel.
16 ¶ Now therefore
hear thou the word of
the LORD: Thou sayest,
Prophesy not against
Israel, and [o] drop not *thy*
word against the house of
Isaac.
17 [p] Therefore thus saith
the LORD; [q] Thy wife shall
be an harlot in the city,
and thy sons and thy
daughters shall fall by
the sword, and thy land
shall be divided by line;
and thou shalt die in a
polluted land: and Israel
shall surely go into cap-
tivity forth of his land.

[n] ch. 1. 1. Zech. 13. 5.
|| Or, *wild figs.*
† Heb. *from behind.*
[o] Ezek. 21. 2. Mic. 2. 6.
[p] See Jer. 28. 12. & 29. 21, 25, 31, 32.
[q] Is. 13. 16. Lam. 5. 11. Hos. 4. 13. Zech. 14. 2.

He did not belong to the order of the prophets, nor had he been educated in the schools of the prophets, nor had he any human training. He was thinking of nothing less; he was doing the works of his calling, till *God took him from following the flock*, and gave him his commission. "[1] He premises humbly what he had been, what he had been made, not by merits, but by grace, that he had not assumed the prophetic office by hereditary right, nor had he begun to prophesy out of his own mind, but, being under the necessity of obeying, he had fulfilled the grace and the command of God Who inspired and sent Him." Twice he repeats, *The Lord took me; the Lord said unto me;* inculcating that, what Amaziah forbade, God bade. All was of God. *He* had but obeyed. "[2] As then the Apostles, when the Scribes and Pharisees forbade them to teach in the Name of Jesus, answered, [3] *We must obey God rather than man*, so Amos, when forbidden by the idol-priests to prophesy, not only prophesies, shewing that he feared God bidding, more than their forbidding, but he boldly and freely denounces the punishment of him who endeavored to forbid and hinder the word of God." "[1] Heaven thundered and commanded him to prophesy; the frog croaked in answer out of his marsh, *prophesy no more.*"

16. Amaziah then was in direct rebellion and contradiction against God. He was in an office forbidden by God. God's word came to him. He had his choice; and, as men do, when entangled in evil courses, he chose the more consciously amiss. He had to resign his lucrative office and to submit to God speaking to him through a shepherd, or to stand in direct opposition to God, and to confront God; and in silencing Amos, he would silence God. But, like one who would arrest the lightning, he draws it on his own head. Amos contrasts the word of Amaziah, and the word of God; "[1] *Hear thou the word of the Lord; Thou sayest; prophesy not against Israel. Therefore thus saith the Lord.* Not only will I not cease to prophesy against Israel, but I will also prophesy to thee. Hear now thine own part of the prophecy."

Drop not. The form of expression, (not the word) is probably taken from Moses[4]. *My doctrine shall drop as the rain, my speech shall distill as the dew; as the small rain upon the tender herb, and as the showers upon the grass.* Micah speaks of the word as used by those who forbade to prophesy, as though the prophecy were a continual wearisome *dropping.* God's word comes as a gentle dew or soft rain, not beating down but refreshing; not sweeping away, like a storm, but sinking in and softening even hard ground, all but the rock; gentle, so as they can bear it. God's word was to men, such as they were toward it; dropping like the dew on those who received it; wearing, to those who hardened themselves against it. It drops in measure upon the hearts which it fertilizes, being adapted to their capacity to receive it. And so contrariwise as to the judgments with which God's prophets are charged. "[2] The prophets do not discharge at once the whole wrath of God, but, in their threatenings, denounce little drops of it."

17. *Thy wife shall be a harlot.* These were, and still are, among the horrors of war. His own sentence comes last, when he had seen the rest, unable to hinder it. Against his and her own will, she should suffer this. "[2] Great is the grief, and incredible the disgrace, when the husband, in the midst of the city and in the presence of all, cannot hinder the wrong done to his wife[5]. For

[1] Rup.
[2] S. Jer.
[3] Acts v. 29.
[4] Deut. xxxii. 2.
[5] The recent horrors about Mount Lebanon have renewed this description, shewing how the wrong to the Christian woman was a devilish triumph over the helpless relation.

Before CHRIST cir. 787.

CHAPTER VIII.

1 *By a basket of summer fruit is shewed the propinquity of Israel's end.* 4 *Oppression is reproved.* 11 *A famine of the word threatened.*

THUS hath the Lord God
shewed unto me: and
behold a basket of summer
fruit.
2 And he said, Amos,
what seest thou? And I
said, A basket of summer
fruit. Then said the LORD
unto me, [a] The end is come
upon my people of Israel; a Ezek. 7. 2.
[b] I will not again pass by b ch. 7. 8.
them any more.
3 And [c] the songs of the c ch. 5. 23.
temple † shall be howlings † Heb. *shall howl.*
in that day, saith the Lord
God: *there shall be* many
dead bodies in every place;
[d] they shall cast them forth d ch. 6. 9. 10.
† with silence. † Heb. *be silent.*

the husband had rather hear that his wife had been slain, than defiled." What he adds, *thy daughters* (as well as his *sons*) *shall fall by the sword*, is an unwonted barbarity, and not part of the Assyrian customs, who carried off women in great numbers, as wives for their soldiery[1]. Perhaps Amos mentions the unwonted cruelty, that the event might bring home the more to the minds of the people the prophecies which relate to themselves. When this had been fulfilled before his eyes, "[2] Amaziah himself, who now gloried in the authority of the priesthood, was to be led into captivity, die in a land polluted by idols, yet not before he saw the people whom he had deceived, enslaved and captive." Amos closes by repeating emphatically the exact words, which Amaziah had alleged in his message to Jeroboam; *and Israel shall surely go into captivity forth of his land.* He had not said it before in these precise words. Now he says it, without reserve of their repentance, as though he would say, "Thou hast pronounced thine own sentence; thou hast hardened thyself against the word of God; thou hardenest thy people against the word of God; it remains then that it should fall on thee and thy people." "[3] How and when the prophecy against Amaziah was fulfilled, Scripture does not relate. He lies hid amid the mass of miseries[4]." Scripture hath no leisure to relate all which befalls those of the viler sort. "The majesty of Holy Scripture does not lower itself to linger on baser persons," whom God had rejected.

VIII. 1. *Thus hath the Lord God shewed me.* The sentence of Amaziah pronounced, Amos resumes just where he left off, before Amaziah broke in upon him. His vehement interruption is like a stone cast into the deep waters. They close over it, and it leaves no trace. Amos had authenticated the third vision; *Thus hath the Lord God shewed me.* He resumes in the self-same calm words. The last vision declared that the end was certain; this, that it was at hand.

A basket of summer fruit. The fruit was the latest harvest in Palestine. When *it* was gathered, the circle of husbandry was come to its close. The sight gives an idea of completeness. The symbol, and the word expressing it, coincide. The fruit-gathering (*kaits*), like our "crop," was called from "cutting." So was the word, *end*, "cutting-off," in *kets*. At harvest-time there is no more to be done for that crop. Good or bad, it has reached its end, and is cut down. So the harvest of Israel was come. The whole course of God's providences, mercies, chastenings, visitations, instructions, warnings, inspirations, were completed. *What could have been done more to My vineyard,* God asks[5], *that I have not done in it?* "To the works of sin, as of holiness, there is a beginning, progress, completion;" a "sowing of wild oats," as men speak, and a ripening in wickedness; a maturity of men's plans, as they deem; a maturity for destruction, in the sight of God. There was no more to be done. Heavenly influences can but injure the ripened sinner, as dew, rain, sun, but injure the ripened fruit. Israel was ripe, but for destruction.

3. *The songs of the temple shall be howlings,* lit. *shall howl*[6]. It shall be, as when mirthful music is suddenly broken in upon, and, through the sudden agony of the singer, ends in a shriek or yell of misery. When sounds of joy are turned into wailing, all must be complete sorrow. They are not hushed only, but are turned into their opposite. Since Amos is speaking to, and of, Israel, *the temple* is, doubtless, here the great idol-temple at Bethel, and *the songs* were the choral music, with which they counterfeited the temple-

[1] Fox Talbot, Ass. texts. [2] S. Jer.
[3] Rup. [4] See above, Introd. p. 153.
[5] Is. v. 4.
[6] הֵילִילוּ our "yell" or "howl," "ululo."

Before CHRIST cir. 787.

4 ¶ Hear this, O ye that [e]swallow up the needy, even to make the poor of the land to fail,

5 Saying, When will the ‖new moon be gone, that we may sell corn? and [f]the sabbath, that we may †set forth wheat, [g]making the ephah small, and the shekel great, and †falsifying the balances by deceit?

[e] Ps. 14. 4. Prov. 30. 14.

‖ Or, *month.*

[f] Neh. 13. 15, 16.

† Heb. *open.*

[g] Mic. 6. 10, 11.

† Heb. *perverting the balances of deceit,* Hos. 12. 7.

music, as arranged by David, praising (they could not make up their minds which,) Nature or "the God of nature," but, in truth, worshiping the creature. The temple was often strongly built and on a height, and, whether from a vague hope of help from God, (as in the siege of Jerusalem by the Romans,) or from some human trust, that the temple might be respected, or from confidence in its strength, or from all together, was the last refuge of the all-but-captive people. Their last retreat was often the scene of the last reeling strife, the battle-cry of the assailants, the shrieks of the defenceless, the groans of the wounded, the agonized cry of unyielding despair. Some such scene the Prophet probably had before his mind's eye; for he adds;

There shall be *many dead bodies,* lit. *Many the corpse in every place.* He sees it, not as future, but before him. The whole city, now so thronged with life, "the oppressor's wrong, the proud man's contumely," lies before him as one scene of death; every place thronged with corpses; none exempt; at home, abroad, or, which he had just spoken of, the temple; no time, no place for honorable burial. *They,* lit. *he casts forth, hush!* Each casts forth those dear to him, as [1] *dung on the face of the earth.* Grief is too strong for words. Living and dead are hushed as the grave. "Large cities are large solitudes," for want of mutual love; in God's retribution, all their din and hum becomes anew a solitude.

4. *Here ye this, ye that swallow* (or, better in the same sense, *that pant for*) *the needy;* as Job says [2], *the hireling panteth for the evening.* They *panted for the poor,* as the wild beast for its prey; and *that* to *make the poor* or (better, as the Hebrew text,) *the meek* [3], those not poor only, but who, through poverty and affliction, are *poor in spirit* also, *to fail.* The land being divided among all the inhabitants, they, in order *to lay field to field* [4], had to rid themselves of the poor. They did rid themselves of them by oppression of all sorts.

5. *When will the new moon be gone?* They kept their festivals, though weary and impatient for their close. They kept sabbath and festival with their bodies, not with their minds. The Psalmist said [5], *When shall I come to appear before the presence of God?* These said, perhaps in their hearts only which God reads to them, "when will this service be over, that we may be our own masters again?" They loathed the rest of the sabbath, because they had, thereon, to rest from their frauds. He instances *the new moons* and *sabbaths,* because these, recurring weekly or monthly, were a regular hindrance to their covetousness.

The *ephah* was a measure containing 72 Roman pints or nearly $1\frac{1}{10}$ English Bushel; the shekel was a fixed weight, by which, up to the time of the Captivity [6], money was still weighed; and that, for the price of bread also [7]. They increased the price both ways, dishonestly and in hypocrisy, paring down the quantity which they sold, and obtaining more silver by fictitious weights; and weighing in uneven balances. All such dealings had been expressly forbidden by God; and that, as the condition of their remaining in the land which God had given them [8]. *Thou shalt not have in thy bag divers weights, a great and a small. Thou shalt not have in thy house divers measures, a great and a small. But thou shalt have a perfect and just weight; a perfect and just measure shalt thou have, that thy days may be lengthened in the land which the Lord thy God giveth thee.* Sin in wrong measures, once begun is unbroken. All sin perpetuates itself. It is done again, because it has been done before. But sins of a man's daily occupation are continued of necessity, beyond the simple force of habit and the ever-increasing dropsy of covetousness. To interrupt sin is to risk detection. But then how countless the sins, which their poor slaves must needs commit hourly, whenever the occasion comes! And yet, although among us human law recognizes the Divine law and annexes punishment to its breach, covetousness sets both at nought. When human law was enforced in a city after a time of negligence, scarcely a weight was found to be honest. Prayer went up to God on *the sabbath,* and fraud on the poor went up to God in every transaction on the other six days. We admire the denunciations of Amos, and condemn the make-believe service of God. Amos denounces us, and we condemn ourselves. Righteous deal-

[1] Jer. viii. 2, &c. [2] vii. 2.
[3] The E. V. has followed the correction of the Kri. The textual reading is almost always the best.
[4] Is. v. 8. [5] Ps. xlii. 2.
[6] 2 Sam. xviii. 12, 1 Kings xx. 39, Jer. xxxii. 9.
[7] Is. lv. 2. [8] Deut. xxv. 13-15.

Before CHRIST cir. 787.

6 That we may buy the
poor for [h]silver, and the
needy for a pair of shoes;
yea, and sell the refuse of
the wheat?
7 The LORD hath sworn
by [i]the excellency of Jacob, Surely [k]I will never
forget any of their works.

[h] ch. 2. 6.
[i] ch. 6. 8.
[k] Hos. 8. 13. & 9. 9.

Before CHRIST cir. 787.

8 [l]Shall not the land
tremble for this, and every
one mourn that dwelleth
therein? and it shall rise
up wholly as a flood; and
it shall be cast out and
drowned, [m]as *by* the flood
of Egypt.
9 And it shall come to

[l] Hos. 4. 3.
[m] ch. 9. 5.

791.

ing in weights and measures was one of the conditions of the existence of God's former people. What must then be our national condition before God, when, from this one sin, so many thousand, thousand sins go up daily to plead against us to God?

6. *That we may buy*, or, indignantly, *To buy the poor!* lit. *the afflicted*, those in *low* estate. First, by dishonesty and oppression they gained their lands and goods. Then the poor were obliged to sell themselves. The slight price, for which a man was sold, shewed the more contempt for *the image of God*. Before[1], he said, *the needy* were *sold for a pair of sandals;* here, that they were bought for them. It seems then the more likely that such was a real price for man.

And sell the refuse [lit. the *falling*] *of wheat*, i.e. what fell through the sieve, either the bran, or the thin, unfilled, grains which had no meal in them. This they mixed up largely with the meal, making a gain of that which they had once sifted out as worthless; or else, in a time of dearth, they sold to men what was the food of animals, and made a profit on it. Infancy and inexperience of cupidity, which adulterated its bread only with bran, or sold to the poor only what, although unnourishing, was wholesome! But then, with the multiplied hard-dealing, what manifoldness of the *woe!*

7. *By the excellency of Jacob*, i.e. by Himself Who was its Glory, as Samuel calls Him [2]*the Strength* or the Glory of Israel. Amos had before said, *God sware by His Holiness*, and *by Himself* or *His soul*. Now, in like way, He pledges that Glory wherewith He was become the Glory of His people. He reminds them, *Who* was the sole Source of their glory; not their calves, but Himself, their Creator; and that He would not forget their deeds. *I will not forget any*, lit. *all;* as David and S. Paul say, *all flesh*, all living men, *shall not be justified*, i.e. none, no one, neither the whole nor any of its parts. Amos brings before the mind *all* their doings, and then says of all and each, the Lord will not forget them. God must cease to be God, if He did not do what He sware to do, punish the oppressors and defrauders of the poor.

8. *Shall not the land tremble for this?* "[3]For the greater impressiveness, he ascribes to the insensate earth sense, indignation, horror, trembling. For all creation feels the will of its Creator." *It shall rise up wholly as a flood*, lit. *like the river*. It is the Egyptian name for *river*[4], which Israel brought with it out of Egypt, and is used either for the Nile, or for one of the artificial *trenches*, derived from it. *And it shall be cast out and drowned*, lit. *shall toss to and fro* as the sea, *and sink*[5] *as the river of Egypt*. The Prophet represents the land as heaving like the troubled sea. As the Nile rose, and its currents met and drove one against the other, covered and drowned the whole land like one vast sea, and then sank again, so the earth should rise, lift up itself, and heave and quake, shaking off the burden of man's oppressions, and sink again. It may be, he would describe the heaving, the rising and falling, of an earthquake. Perhaps, he means that as a man forgat all the moral laws of nature, so inanimate nature should be freed from its wonted laws, and shake out its inhabitants or overwhelm them by an earthquake, as in one grave.

9. *I will cause the sun to go down.* Darkness is heaviest and blackest in contrast with the brightest light; sorrow is saddest, when it comes upon fearless joy. God commonly, in His mercy, sends heralds of coming sorrow; very few burst suddenly on man. Now, in the meridian brightness of the day of Israel, the blackness of night should fall at once upon him. Not only was light to be displaced by darkness, but *then*, when it was most opposite to the course of nature. Not by gradual decay, but by a sudden unlooked-for crash, was Israel to perish. Pekah was a military chief; he had reigned more than seventeen years over Israel in peace, when, together with Rezin king of Damascus, he attempted

[1] ii. 6. [2] 1 Sam. xv. 29. [3] Lap.

[4] יאר, the same as the Memph. *iaro*, כאור i. q. כיאר is the old reading, as appeared from Ecclus. xxiv. 27.

[5] The kethib נשקה is probably a 2d peculiarity as to a guttural in Amos (See ab. p. 152), as a different pronunciation of what stands in the kri, נשקעה

Before CHRIST cir. 787.

pass in that day, saith the
Lord God, [n] that I will
cause the sun to go down
at noon, and I will dark-
en the earth in the clear
day:

[n] Job. 5. 14. Is. 13. 10. & 59. 9, 10. Jer. 15. 9. Micah. 3. 6.

to extirpate the line of David, and to set a Syrian, one *son of Tabeal*[1], on his throne. Ahaz was weak, with no human power to resist; his *heart was moved, and the heart of his people, as the trees of the forest are moved with the wind*[2]. Tiglath-pileser came upon Pekah and carried off the tribes beyond Jordan[3]. Pekah's sun set, and all was night with no dawn. Shortly after, Pekah himself was murdered by Hoshea[4], as he had himself murdered Pekahiah. After an anarchy of nine years, Hoshea established himself on the throne; the nine remaining years were spent in the last convulsive efforts of an expiring monarchy, subdual to Shalmaneser, rebellious alliance with So, king of Egypt, a three years' siege, and the lamp went out[5].

And I will darken the earth at noon-day. To the mourner "all nature seems to mourn." "Not the ground only," says S. Chrysostom in the troubles at Antioch[6], "but the very substance of the air, and the orb of the solar rays itself seems to me now in a manner to mourn and to shew a duller light. Not that the elements change their nature, but that our eyes, confused by a cloud of sorrow, cannot receive the light from it's rays purely, nor are they alike impressible. This is what the Prophet of old said mourning, *Their sun shall set to them at noon, and the day shall be darkened.* Not that the sun was hidden, or the day disappeared, but that the mourners could see no light even in midday, for the darkness of their grief." No eclipse of the sun, in which the sun might seem to be shrouded in darkness at midday, has been calculated which should have suggested this image to the Prophet's mind. It had been thought, however, that there might be reference to an eclipse of the sun which took place a few years after this prophecy, viz. Feb. 9. 784, B. C. the year of the death of Jeroboam II[7]. This eclipse did reach its height at Jerusalem a little before mid-day, at 11 h 24 m A. M.[8]. An accurate calculation, however, shews that, although total in Southern latitudes, the line of totality was, at the longitude of Jerusalem or Samaria, about 11 degrees South Latitude, and so above 43 degrees South of Samaria, and that it did not reach the same latitude as Samaria until near the close of the eclipse, about 64 degrees West of Samaria in the Easternmost part of Thibet[9]. "[10]The central eclipse commenced in the Southern Atlantic Ocean, passed nearly exactly over St. Helena[11], reached the continent of Africa in Lower Guinea, traversed the interior of Africa, and left it near Zanzibar, went through the Indian Ocean and entered India in the Gulf of Gambay, passed between Agra and Allahabad into Thibet and reached its end on the frontiers of China." The Eclipse then would hardly have been noticeable at Samaria, certainly very far indeed from being an eclipse of such magnitude, as could in any degree correspond with the expression, *I will cause the sun to go down at noon.*

Archbishop Ussher suggests, if true, a different coincidence. "[12]There was an eclipse of the sun of about 10 digits in the

[1] Is. vii. 6. [2] Ib. 2. [3] 2 Kgs xv. 29. [4] Ib. 30.
[5] Ib. xvii. 1–9. [6] Hom. 2 on the Statues, § 2.
[7] Hitzig says, "Since the sun was to set at noon-day, and since, just before, mention was made of the death of Jeroboam" [rather of the destruction of the house of Jeroboam, vii. 9, the mention of his own death being merely a distortion of Amaziah], "we have to think of the total Eclipse which took place in the year of his death, Feb. 9. 784, which reached its centre at Jerusalem about 1."
[8] "9 A. M. Greenwich time, or at 11h.24m A. M. Jerusalem time." Letter of the Rev. Robert Main, Radcliffe Observer and President of the Royal Astron. Soc. Upon my enquiring as to the facts of this eclipse to which Hitzig had drawn attention, Mr. Main kindly directed Mr. Quirling his First Assistant to compute under his own superintendence the circumstances of the Eclipse of 784, B. C. Feb. 9. which had "originally been calculated by Pingré (Mém. de l'Acad. des. Inscr. vol. 52 in which the year is given 783 B. C. In l'Art de vérifier les Dates, T. i. the years are all altered by one unit, to make them agree with the mode of reckoning in ordinary chronology). Mr. Quirling, employing Hansen's lunar tables and Hansen's and Olufsen's solar tables, found, that on the given day, there was an eclipse, which would however be very small for Palestine, and that the apparent diameters of the sun and moon were so nearly equal that at no place could the totality be of more than 40s duration. The general conjunction was at 9h. A. M. (Greenwich time, i. e. 11h. 24m. Jerusalem time), of Feb. 9. and the Geo-centric Semi-diameters of the Sun and Moon were 16′ 17″. 25. and 16′ 0″. 88. at Greenwich noon." "Pingré's calculation must have been tolerably accurate; for he gives 11¼ A. M. Paris time."
[9] Mr. Main has kindly furnished me with a detailed account of the path of the central eclipse from which the following statements are taken. "It began—10° 13′ lat. 347° 49′ long. at 19h 1m (7h 1m A. M.) Greenwich Time, and ended at, + 32° 35′ lat. 100° 42′ long. at 22h 32m (10h 32m) Gr. Time." Samaria is 32° 15′ lat. 35° 14′ long. "The path of the central eclipse was—14 lat. 30° 6′ long.;—10 lat. 38° 14′ long."
[10] Mr. Main's letter.
[11] Every place here mentioned was "rigorously computed" by Mr. Quirling.
[12] Usserii Annales, A. M. 3213. p. 45. fol. [Prof. Donkin has verified Ussher's statement as to the eclipse Nov. 8. 771 B. C., and calculated that it was visible in Palestine at 12.55. P. M. Dr. Stanley, (J. Ch. ii. 363.) who reports this, supposes, in the way of his school, that Amos might be alluding to a past event, contrary to the date Am. i. 1, according to which he prophesied not later than 784 B. C. Ed. 2.]

Before CHRIST cir. 787.

10 And I will turn your feasts into mourning, and all your songs into lamentation; [o] and I will bring up sackcloth upon all loins, and baldness upon every head; [p] and I will make it as the mourning of an only *son*, and the end thereof as a bitter day.

[o] Is. 15. 2, 3. Jer. 48. 37. Ezek. 7. 18. & 27. 31.

[p] Jer. 6. 26. Zech. 12. 10.

Julian year 3923 (B. C. 791,) June 24, in the Feast of Pentecost; another, of about 12 digits, 20 years afterward, 3943, B. C. 771, Nov. 8, on the Day of the Feast of Tabernacles; and a third of more than 11 digits, on the following year 3944, May 5, on the Feast of the Passover. Consider whether that prophecy of Amos does not relate to it, *I will cause the sun to go down at noon, and I will darken the earth in the clear day, and I will turn your feasts into mourning.* Which, as the Christian Fathers have adapted in an allegorical sense to the darkness at the time of our Lord's Passion in the feast of the Passover, so it may have been fulfilled, in the letter, in these three great eclipses, which darkened the day of the three festivals in which all the males were bound to appear before the Lord. So that as, among the Greeks, Thales, first, by astronomical science, predicted eclipses of the sun[1], so, among the Hebrews, Amos first seems to have foretold them by inspiration of the Holy Spirit." The eclipses, pointed out by Ussher, must have been the one total, the others very considerable[2]. Beforehand, one should not have expected that an eclipse of the sun, being itself a regular natural phænomenon, and having no connection with the moral government of God, should have been the subject of the Prophet's prediction. Still it had a religious impressiveness then, above what it has now, on account of that wide-prevailing idolatry of the sun. It exhibited the object of their false worship, shorn of its light and passive. If Archbishop Ussher is right as to the magnitude of those eclipses in the latitude of Jerusalem, and as to the correspondence of the days of the solar year, June 24, Nov. 8, May 5, in those years, with the days of the lunar year upon which the respective feasts fell, it would be a remarkable correspondence. Still the years are somewhat arbitrarily chosen, the second only B. C. 771, (on which the house of Jehu came to an end through the murder of the weak and sottish Zechariah,) corresponding with any marked event in the kingdom of Israel. On the other hand, it is the more likely that the words, *I will cause the sun to go down at noon*, are an image of a sudden reverse, in that Micah also uses the words as an image[3], *the sun shall go down upon the prophets and the day shall be dark upon* [or, *over*] *them.*

10. *I will turn your feasts into mourning.* He recurs to the sentence which he had pronounced[4], before he described the avarice and oppression which brought it down. Hosea too had foretold[5], *I will cause all her mirth to cease, her feast-days, &c.* So Jeremiah describes[6], *the joy of our heart is ceased; our dance is turned into mourning.* The book of Tobit bears witness how these sayings of Amos lived in the hearts of the captive Israelites. The word of God seems oftentimes to fail, yet it finds those who are His. *I remembered,* he said[7], *that prophecy of Amos, your feasts shall be turned into mourning.*

The correspondence of these words with the miracle at our Blessed Lord's Passion, in that *the earth was darkened in the clear day, at noon-day,* was noticed by the earliest Fathers[8], and that the more, since it took place at the Feast of the Passover, and, in punishment for that sin, their *feasts were turned into mourning,* in the desolation of their country and the cessation of their worship.

I will bring up sackcloth (i. e. the rough coarse haircloth, which, being fastened with the girdle tight over the loins[9], was wearing to the frame) *and baldness upon every head.* The mourning of the Jews was no half-mourning, no painless change of one color of becoming dress for another. For the time, they were dead to the world or to enjoyment. As the clothing was coarse, uncomely, distressing, so they laid aside every ornament. the ornament of their hair also (as English widows used, on the same principle, to cover it). They shore it off; each sex, what was the pride of their sex; the men, their beards; the women, their long hair. The strong words, *baldness, is balded*[10], *shear*[11], *hew* off[12], *enlarge thy baldness*[13], are used to shew the completeness of this expression of sorrow.

[1] See Rawl. on Herod. i. 74. T. i. p. 212.

[2] Mr. Main tells me that, in the old mode of marking eclipses, the whole was divided into 12 digits, so that eclipses of 12 digits were total; those of 11 and 10, large.

[3] Mic. ii. 6. ובאה השמש על הנביאים Am. השמש והבאתי.

[4] ver. 3. [5] ii. 11. [6] Lam. v. 15. [7] Tob. ii. 6.

[8] S. Iren. iv. 33. 12. Tert. in Marc. iv. 42. S. Cypr. Test. ii. 23. p. 58. Oxf. Tr. S. Cyril, Cat. xiii. 25. Eus. Dem. Ev. x. 6.

[9] See ab. Joel i. 8, 13. pp. 107, 109. [10] Jer. xvi. 6.

[11] גזז Mic. i. 16, Jer. vii. 29.

[12] גרע (Is. xv. 2, Jer. xlviii. 37) although less strong than גרע, is harsher than the ordinary גלח.

[13] Mic. l. c.

Before CHRIST cir. 787.

11 ¶ Behold, the days come, saith the Lord GOD, that I will send a famine in the land, not a famine of bread, nor a thirst for water, but [q] of hearing the words of the LORD.

q 1 Sam. 3. 1. Ps. 74. 9. Ezek. 7. 26.

12 And they shall wander from sea to sea, and from the north even to the east, they shall run to and fro to seek the word of the LORD, and shall not find *it*.

13 In that day shall the

Before CHRIST cir. 787.

None exempted themselves in the universal sorrow; *on every head* came up *baldness*.

And I will make it (probably, the whole state and condition of things, everything, as we use our *it*) *as the mourning of an only son*. As, when God delivered Israel from Egypt, *there was not*, among the Egyptians, *a house where there was not one dead*[1], and one universal cry arose from end to end of the land, so now too in apostate Israel. The whole mourning should be the one most grievous mourning of parents, over the one child in whom they themselves seemed anew to live.

And the end thereof as a bitter day. Most griefs have a rest or pause, or wear themselves out. *The end* of this should be like the beginning, nay, one concentrated grief, a whole day of bitter grief summed up in its close. It was to be no passing trouble, but one which should end in bitterness, an unending sorrow and destruction; image of the undying death in hell.

11. *Not a famine for bread*. He does not deny that there should be bodily famine too; but this, grievous as it is, would be less grievous than the famine of which he speaks, *the famine of the word of the Lord*. In distress we all go to God. "[2] They who now cast out and despise the prophets, when they shall see themselves besieged by the enemy, shall be tormented with a great hunger of hearing the word of the Lord from the mouths of the prophets, and shall find no one to lighten their distresses. This was most sad to the people of God; [3] *we see not our tokens; there is not one prophet more; there is not one with us who understandeth, how long!*" Even the profane, when they see no help, will have recourse to God. Saul, in his extremity, [4] *enquired of the Lord* and *He answered him not, neither by dreams, nor by Urim, nor by prophets*. Jeroboam sent his wife to enquire of the prophet Ahijah about his son's health[5]. They sought for temporal relief only, and therefore found it not.

12 *They shall wander*, lit. *reel*. The word is used of the reeling of drunkards, of the swaying to and fro of trees in the wind, of the quivering of the lips of one agitated, and then of the unsteady seeking of persons bewildered, looking for what they know not where to find. *From sea to sea*, from the sea of Galilee to the Mediterranean, i. e. from East to West, *and from the North even to the sunrising*, round again to the East, whence their search had begun, where light should be, and was not. It may be, that Amos refers to the description of the land by Moses, adapting it to the then separate condition of Ephraim, [6] *your South border shall be from the extremity of the Salt sea* (Dead sea) *Eastward—and the goings out of it shall be at the sea, and for the Western border ye shall have the great sea for a border. And this shall be your North border—and the border shall descend and shall reach to the side of the sea of Chinnereth Eastward*. Amos does not mention *the South*, because *there* alone, where they might have found, where the true worship of God was, they did not seek. Had they sought God in Judah, instead of seeking to aggrandize themselves by its subdual, Tiglath-pileser would probably never have come against them. One expedition only in the seventeen years of his reign was directed Westward[7], and that was at the petition of Ahaz.

The principle of God's dealings, that, in certain conditions of a sinful people, He will withdraw His word, is instanced in Israel, not limited to it. God says to Ezekiel[8], *I will make thy tongue cleave to the roof of thy mouth, and thou shalt be dumb; and shalt not be to them a reprover; for it is a rebellious house;* and Ezekiel says[9], *Destruction shall come upon destruction, and rumor shall be upon rumor, and they shall seek a vision from the prophet, and the law shall perish from the priest and counsel from the ancients*. "[10] God turns away from them, and checks the grace of prophecy. For since they neglected His law, He on His side, stays the prophetic gift. *And the word was precious in those days, there was no open vision*, i. e. God did not speak to them through the prophets; He breathed not upon them the Spirit through which they spake. He did not appear to them, but is silent and hidden. There was silence, enmity between God and man."

13. In this hopelessness as to all relief,

[1] Ex. xii. 30.
[2] Rib.
[3] Ps. lxxiv. 9.
[4] 1 Sam. xxviii. 6.
[5] 1 Kings xiv. 2, 3.
[6] Num. xxxiv. 3-12.
[7] Rawl. Herod. i. 470.
[8] Ezek. iii. 26.
[9] vii. 26.
[10] from S. Chrys. in Is. vi. 1. Hom. 4. T. vi. p. 130.

Before CHRIST cir. 787.

fair virgins and young men
faint for thirst.
14 They that [r] swear by
[s] the sin of Samaria, and
say, Thy God, O Dan,
liveth; and, The † manner
[t] of Beer-sheba liveth; even
they shall fall, and never
rise up again.

[r] Hos. 4. 15.
[s] Deut. 9. 21.
† Heb. *way*: See Acts 9. 2. & 18. 25. & 19. 9, 23. & 24. 14.
[t] ch. 5. 5.

CHAPTER IX.

Before CHRIST cir. 787.

1 *The certainty of the desolation.*
11 *The restoring of the tabernacle of David.*

I SAW the Lord standing
upon the altar: and he
said, Smite the ‖ lintel of
the door, that the posts
may shake: and ‖ [a] cut

‖ Or, *chapiter*, or, *knop*.
‖ Or, *wound them*.
[a] Ps. 68. 21. Hab. 3. 13.

those too shall fail and sink under their sufferings, in whom life is freshest and strongest and hope most buoyant. Hope mitigates any sufferings. When hope is gone, the powers of life, which it sustains, give way. *They shall faint for thirst*, lit. "shall be mantled over, covered [1]," as, in fact, one fainting seems to feel as if a veil came over his brow and eyes. *Thirst*, as it is an intenser suffering than bodily hunger, includes sufferings of body and mind. If even over those, whose life was firmest, a veil came, and they fainted for thirst, what of the rest?

14. *Who swear*, lit. *the swearing*, they who habitually swear. He assigns, at the end, the ground of all this misery, the forsaking of God. God had commanded that all appeals by oath should be made to Himself, Who alone governs the world, to Whom alone His creatures owe obedience, Who alone revenges. [2] *Thou shalt fear the Lord thy God and serve Him and swear by His Name.* On the other hand Joshua warned them [3], *Neither make mention of the name of their gods nor cause to swear by them nor serve them.* But these *sware by the sin of Samaria*, probably *the calf at Bethel*, which was nigh to Samaria and the centre of their idolatry, whence Hosea calls it *thy calf* [4]. *Thy calf, O Samaria, hath cast thee off. The calf of Samaria shall be broken in pieces.* He calls it *the guilt of Samaria*, as the source of all their guilt, as it is said of the princes of Judah using this same word [5], *they left the house of the Lord God of their fathers, and served idols, and wrath came upon Judah and Jerusalem for this their trespass. And say, thy god, O Dan! liveth*, i. e. as surely as thy god liveth! by the life of thy god! as they who worshiped God said, *as the Lord liveth!* It was a direct substitution of the creature for the Creator, an ascribing to it the attribute of God; *as the Father hath life in Himself* [6]. It was an appeal to it, as the Avenger of false-swearing, as though it were the moral Governor of the world.

The manner of Beersheba liveth! lit. *the way.* This may be, either the religion and worship of the idol there, as S. Paul says, *I persecuted this way unto the death* [7], whence Mohammed learnt to speak of his imposture, as "the way of God." Or it might mean the actual *way to Beersheba*, and may signify all the idolatrous places of worship in the way thither. They seem to have made the way thither one long avenue of idols, culminating in it. For Josiah, in his great destruction of idolatry [8], *gathered all the priests from the cities of Judah, and defiled the high-places, where the priests sacrificed from Gebah to Beersheba:* only, this may perhaps simply describe the whole territory of Judah from North to South. Anyhow, Beersheba stands for the god worshiped there, as, *whoso sware by the Temple, sware*, our Lord tells us [9], *by it and by Him that dwelleth therein.*

IX. 1. *I saw the Lord.* He saw God in vision; yet God no more, as before, asked him what he saw. God no longer shews him emblems of the destruction, but the destruction itself. Since Amos had just been speaking of the idolatry of Samaria, as the ground of its utter destruction, doubtless this vision of such utter destruction of the place of worship, with and upon the worshipers, relates to those same idolaters and idolatries [10]. True, the condemnation of Israel would become the condemnation of Judah, when Judah's sins, like Israel's, should become complete. But directly, it can hardly relate to any other than those spoken of before and after, Israel. *The altar*, then, *over* [11] which Amos sees God *stand*, is doubtless the altar on which Jeroboam sacrificed, *the altar* which he set up over-against the altar at Jerusalem, the centre of the calf-worship, whose destruction the man of God foretold on the day of its dedication. There where, in counterfeit of the sacrifices which God had appointed, they offered would-be-atoning sacrifices and sinned in them, God appeared, standing, to behold, to judge, to condemn. *And He said, smite the lintel*, lit. *the chapter*, or *capital*, probably so

[1] The metaphor occurs both in Heb. and Arab.
[2] Deut. vi. 13, x. 20.
[3] Josh. xxiii. 7.
[4] Hos. viii. 5, 6.
[5] 2 Chr. xxiv. 18.
[6] S. John v. 26.
[7] Acts xxii. 4, add ix. 2, xix. 9, 23.
[8] 2 Kings xxiii. 8.
[9] S. Matt, xxiii. 21.
[10] S. Jer. Theod. understand it of "*the* altar" at Jerusalem.
[11] not, *upon*.

Before CHRIST cir. 787.

them in the head, all of
them; and I will slay the
last of them with the
b ch. 2. 14. sword: [b] he that fleeth of
them shall not flee away,
and he that escapeth of
them shall not be delivered.
c Ps. 139. 8. &c. 2 [c] Though they dig into
hell, thence shall mine
hand take them; [d] though
they climb up to heaven,
thence will I bring them d Job 20. 6. Jer. 51. 53. Obad. 4.
down;
3 And though they hide
themselves in the top of
Carmel, I will search and
take them out thence; and
though they be hid from
my sight in the bottom of

called from *crowning* the pillar with a globular form, like a pomegranate. This, the spurious outward imitation of the true sanctuary, God commands to be stricken, *that the posts*, or probably *the thresholds, may shake.* The building was struck from above, and reeled to its base. It does not matter, whether any blow on the capital of a pillar would make the whole fabric to shake. For the blow was no blow of man. God gives the command probably to the Angel of the Lord, as, in Ezekiel's vision of the destruction of Jerusalem, the charge to destroy was given to six men[1]. So the first-born of Egypt, the army of Sennacherib, were destroyed by an Angel[2]. An Angel stood with his sword over Jerusalem[3], when God punished David's presumption in numbering the people. At one blow of the heavenly Agent the whole building shook, staggered, fell.

And cut them in the head, all of them[4]. This may be either by the direct agency of the Angel, or the temple itself may be represented as falling on the heads of the worshipers. As God, through Jehu, destroyed all the worshipers of Baal in the house of Baal, so here He foretells, under a like image, the destruction of all the idolaters of Israel. He had said, *they that swear by the sin of Samaria—shall fall and never rise up again.* Here he represents the place of that worship, the idolaters, as it seems, crowded there, and the command given to destroy them all. All Israel was not to be destroyed. *Not the least grain* was to *fall upon the earth*[5]. Those then here represented as destroyed to the last man, must be a distinct class. Those destroyed in the temple must be the worshipers in the temple. In the Temple of God at Jerusalem, none entered except the priests. Even the space *between the porch and the altar* was set apart for the priests. But heresy is necessarily irreverent, because, not worshiping the One God, it had no Object of reverence. Hence the temple of Baal was full *from end to end*[6], and the worshipers of the sun at Jerusalem turned *their backs toward the Temple,* and *worshiped the sun toward the East, at the door of the Temple, between the porch and the altar*[7]. The worshipers of the calves were commanded to *kiss*[8] them, and so must have filled the temple, where they were.

And I will slay the last of them. The Angel is bidden to destroy those gathered in open idolatry in one place. God, by His Omniscience, reserved the rest for His own judgment. All creatures, animate or inanimate, rational or irrational, stand at His command to fulfill His will. The mass of idolaters having perished in their idolatry, the rest, not crushed in the fall of the temple, would fain flee away, but *he that fleeth shall not flee,* God says, to any good *to themselves*[9]; yea, although they should do what for man is impossible, they should not escape God.

2. Height or depth are alike open to the Omnipresent God. The grave is not so awful as God. The sinner would gladly *dig through* into hell, bury himself, the living among the dead, if so he could escape the sight of God. But *thence,* God says, *My hand shall take them,* to place them in His presence, to receive their sentence. Or if, like the rebel angels, they could *place* their *throne amid the stars*[10] *of* God, *thence will I bring them down,* humbling, judging, condemning.

3. He had contrasted heaven and hell, as places impossible for man to reach; as David says, [11] *If I ascend into heaven, Thou art there: If I make my bed in hell, behold Thee.* Now, of places in a manner accessible, he contrasts Mount Carmel, which rises abruptly out of the sea, with depths of that ocean which it overhangs. Carmel was in two ways a hiding place. 1) Through its caves (some say

[1] Ezek. ix. 2. [2] Ex. xii. 23, 2 Kgs xix. 34, 5.

[3] 2 Sam. xxiv. 1, 15, 16.

[4] Others render, *break them,* i. e. the capitals, *in pieces on the head of all of them;* but בצע signifies *cut, wound,* rather than *break;* and the plural ם, is more naturally referred to the same objects as כלם, than to the singular כפתור.

[5] ix. 9. [6] 2 Kings x. 21. [7] Ezek. viii. 16, xi. 1.

[8] Hos. xiii. 2. [9] the force of להם.

[10] Is. xiv. 12–14. [11] Ps. cxxxix. 8.

Before CHRIST cir. 787.

the sea, thence will I command the serpent, and he
shall bite them:
4 And though they go
into captivity before their
enemies, [e] thence will I
command the sword, and
it shall slay them: and [f] I

Before CHRIST cir. 787.

e Lev. 26, 33. Deut. 28. 65. Ezek. 5. 12.
f Lev. 17. 10. Jer. 44. 11.

1000[1], some 2000) with which it is perforated, whose entrance sometimes scarcely admits a single man; so close to each other, that a pursuer would not discern into which the fugitive had vanished; so serpentine within, that, "10 steps apart," says a traveler[2], "we could hear each others' voices, but could not see each other." "[3] Carmel is perforated by hundredfold greater or lesser clefts. Even in the garb of loveliness and richness, the majestic Mount, by its clefts, caves, and rocky battlements, excites in the wanderer who sees them for the first time, a feeling of mingled wonder and fear.—A whole army of enemies, as of nature's terrors, could hide themselves in these rock-clefts." 2) Its summit, about 1800 feet above the sea[4], "is covered with pines and oaks, and lower down with olive and laurel trees[5]." These forests furnished hiding places to robber-hordes[6] at the time of our Lord. In those caves, Elijah probably at times was hidden from the persecution of Ahab and Jezebel. It seems to be spoken of as his abode[7], as also one resort of Elisha[8]. Carmel, as the Western extremity of the land, projecting into the sea, was the last place which a fugitive would reach. If he found no safety there, there was none in his whole land. Nor was there by sea;

And though they be hid [rather, *hide themselves*] *from My sight in the bottom of the sea, thence will I command the serpent.* The sea too has its deadly serpents. Their classes are few; the individuals in those classes are much more numerous than those of the land-serpents[9]. Their shoals have furnished to sailors tokens of approaching land[9]. Their chief abode, as traced in modern times, is between the Tropics[10]. The ancients knew of them perhaps in the Persian gulf or perhaps the Red Sea[11]. All are "[12] highly venomous" and "[13] very ferocious." "[14] The virulence of their venom is equal to that of the *most* pernicious land-serpents." All things, with their will or without it through animal instinct, as the serpent, or their savage passions, as the Assyrian, fulfill the will of God. As, at His command, the fish whom He had prepared, swallowed Jonah, for his preservation, so, at His *command, the serpent* should come forth from the recesses of the sea to the sinner's greater suffering.

4. *Captivity*, at least, seemed safe. The horrors of war are over. Men enslave, but do not commonly destroy those whom they have once been at the pains to carry captive. Amos describes them in their misery, as *going* willingly, gladly, *into captivity before their enemies*, like a flock of sheep. Yet *thence* too, out of *the captivity*, God would command the sword, and it should slay them. So God had forewarned them by Moses, that captivity should be an occasion, not an end, of

1 "The caves in Carmel are exceeding many, especially on the W. It is said above 1000. In one part, there are 400 close together." v. Richter, 65. "more than 2000," Mislin, Les Saints Lieux, ii. 46. in Smith's Bibl. Dict.

2 Schulz, Leit. d. Hochstens, v. 186. Paulus, Reisen, vii. 43.

3 v. Schubert, iii. 205.

4 V. de Velde, Mem. 177.

5 Richter, 66.

6 Strab. 16. 2. 28.

7 1 Kings xviii. 19.

8 2 Kings ii. 25, iv. 25.

9 Cantor, in Zoolog. Trans. T. ii. n. xxi. p. 306.

10 "Intertropical, or near the tropics, between 90 and 230 degree long. meridian of Ferro." Schlegel, Essai sur la physion. d. serpens, p. 491. Cantor, ib. Orr; "The Hydrophidæ are found exclusively in the seas of the warmer parts of the Eastern Hemisphere, on the coasts of the Indian and Pacific Oceans. Some of them occur as far South as the coasts of N. Zealand and Australia. A few are found occasionally in salt-water tanks and canals, but they usually confine themselves to the Ocean, and rarely ascend beyond the mouths of rivers.—They are exceedingly venomous and are regarded with great dread by the fishermen in whose nets they are not unfrequently caught." Circle of the Sciences, T. iii. p. 111. Dr. Rolleston (Linacre Professor at Oxford) who kindly supplied me with these facts informs me that up to this time the hydrophidæ have only been found "in the Indian and the Pacific and the seas which are their dependencies;" but he drew my attention to the extreme warmth of the Red Sea and the causes of that warmth.

11 "It is in great measure from the statements of the Ancients, that the presence of the Hydrophidæ in the Red Sea and the Persian Gulf has been asserted; which may well be, although their observations need confirmation from further researches." Schlegel, p. 490. The accuracy of Pliny's statement as to their venom, which modern enquiry has confirmed, (Schlegel, p. 488. Duméril, Erpétologie vii. 1316–18. Cantor. p. 303, 6, 9, 10, 11. Orr, above) shews that he must have known the creature. "The most beautiful kind of snake in the world is that which lives in the waters too; they are called hydri; *inferior in venom to none of the serpents.*" N. H. xxix. 4. 22. More than half of the Red Sea is within the tropics, and it is, from its narrowness perhaps and the hot winds which blow over it from the deserts, one of the warmest seas; but it has been very little examined. Burckhardt says (Syria, 449) of the Gulf of Akaba, "the sands on the shore everywhere bore the impression of the passage of serpents, crossing each other in many directions. Ayd [an Arab fisher] told me that serpents were very common in these parts, that the fishermen were very much afraid of them." But these must have been land serpents. It is possible that both the Hebrews and Pliny knew of them through the commerce with India.

12 Cantor, p. 303.

13 Id. 307.

14 Id. 309.

Before CHRIST cir. 787.

will set mine eyes upon
them for evil, and not for
good.
5 And the Lord GOD of
hosts *is* he that toucheth
the land, and it shall [g] melt,
[h] and all that dwell therein
shall mourn: and it shall
rise up wholly like a flood;
and shall be drowned, as
by the flood of Egypt.
6 *It is* he that buildeth
his ‖ † [i] stories in the
heaven, and hath founded
his ‖ troop in the earth;
he that [k] calleth for the

g Mic. 1. 4.
h ch. 8. 8.
‖ Or, *spheres.*
† Heb. *ascensions.*
i Ps. 104. 3, 13.
‖ Or, *bundle.*
k ch. 5. 8.

slaughter. [1] *I will scatter you among the heathen, and will draw out a sword after you.* [2] *And among these nations shalt thou find no ease—and thy life shall hang in doubt before thee, and thou shalt fear day and night, and shalt have none assurance of thy life.* The book of Esther shews how cheaply the life of a whole nation was held by Eastern conquerors; and the book of Tobit records, how habitually Jews were slain and cast out unburied [3]. The account also that Sennacherib [4] avenged the loss of his army, and *in his wrath killed many,* is altogether in the character of Assyrian conquerors. Unwittingly he fulfilled the command of God, *I will command the sword and it shall slay them.*

I will set mine eyes upon them for evil. So David says, [5] *The eyes of the Lord are over the righteous, and His ears are open to their prayers. The Face of the Lord is against them that do evil, to root out the remembrance of them from off the earth.* The Eye of God rests on each creature which He hath made, as entirely as if He had created it alone. Every moment is passed in His unvarying sight. But, as man *sets his eye* on man, watching him and with purpose of evil, so God's Eye is felt to be on man in displeasure, when sorrow and calamity track him and overtake him, coming he knows not how, in unlooked-for ways and strange events. The Eye of God upon us is our whole hope and stay and life. It is on the Confessor in prison, the Martyr on the rack, the poor in their sufferings, the mourner in the chamber of death, for good. What when everywhere that Eye, the Source of all good, rests on His creature only for evil! *and not for good,* he adds; *not,* as is the wont and the Nature of God; *not,* as He had promised, if they were faithful; *not,* as perhaps they thought, *for good.* He utterly shuts out all hope of good. It shall be all evil, and no good, such as is hell.

5. And Who is He Who should do this? God, at Whose command are all creatures. This is the hope of His servants; whence Hezekiah begins his prayer, *Lord of hosts, God of Israel* [6]. This is the hopelessness of His enemies. *That toucheth the land* or *earth, and it shall melt,* rather, *hath melted.* His Will and its fulfillment are one. [7] *He spake, and it was; He commanded and it stood fast.* His Will is first, as the cause of what is done; in time they co-exist. He hath no need to put forth His strength; a touch, the slightest indication of His Will, sufficeth. If the solid earth, how much more its inhabitants! So the Psalmist says, [8] *The heathen raged, the kingdoms were moved; He uttered His voice, the earth melted.* The hearts of men melt when they are afraid of His Presence; human armies melt away, dispersed; the great globe itself shall dissolve into its ancient chaos at His Will.

6. *He that buildeth His stories.* The word commonly means *steps,* nor is there any reason to alter it. We read of *the third heaven* [9], *the heavens of heavens* [10]; i. e. heavens to which this heaven is as earth. They are different ways of expressing the vast unseen space which God has created, divided, as we know, through the distance of the fixed stars, into countless portions, of which the lower, or further removed, are but as *steps* to the Presence of the Great King, where, *above all heavens* [11], Christ sitteth at the Right Hand of God. It comes to the same, if we suppose the word to mean *upper chambers* [12]. The metaphor would still signify heavens above our heavens.

And hath founded His troop [lit. *band* [13]] *in the earth;* probably, *founded His arch upon the earth,* i. e. His visible heaven, which seems, like an arch, to span the earth. The whole then describes "all things visible and invisible;" all of this our solar system, and all beyond it, the many gradations to the Throne of God. "[14] He daily *buildeth His stories in the heavens,* when He raiseth up His saints from things below to heavenly places, presiding over them, ascending in them. In devout wayfarers too, whose *conversation is in Heaven* [15],

[1] Lev. xxvi. 33. [2] Deut. xxviii. 65, 6. [3] Tob. i. 17, ii. 3. [4] Ib. i. 18. [5] Ps. xxxiv. 15, 16. [6] Is. xxxvii. 16. [7] Ps. xxxiii. 9. [8] Ps. xlvi. 6. [9] 2 Cor. xii. 2. [10] Deut. x. 14, 1 Kings viii. 27, Ps. cxlviii. 4. [11] Eph. iv. 10

[12] as if מעלות were the same as עליות.

[13] It is used of "a bunch of hyssop" (Ex. xii. 22); "*bands* of a yoke" (Is. lviii. 6); "a band of men" (2 Sam. ii. 25); hence in Arab. Ijâd signifies an arch, as firmly held together, as our *apse* is from the Greek ἅπτω. [14] Dion. [15] Phil. iii. 20.

Before CHRIST cir. 787.

waters of the sea, and poureth them out upon the face of the earth: [l]The LORD is his name.

7 *Are* ye not as children of the Ethiopians unto me, O children of Israel? saith the LORD. Have not I brought up Israel out of the land of Egypt? and

l ch. 4. 13.

He ascendeth, sublimely and mercifully indwelling their hearts. In those who have the fruition of Himself in those Heavens, He ascendeth by the glory of beatitude and the loftiest contemplation, as He walketh in those who walk, and resteth in those who rest in Him."

To this description of His power, Amos, as before[1], adds that signal instance of its exercise on the ungodly, the flood, the pattern and type of judgments which no sinner escapes. God then hath the power to do this. Why should He not?

Are *ye not as children of the Ethiopians unto Me, O children of Israel!* Their boast and confidence was that they were children of the Patriarch, to whom God made the promises. But they, not following the faith nor doing the deeds of Israel, who was *a prince with God*, or of Abraham, the father of the faithful, had, for *Bene Israel*, children of Israel, become as *Bene Cushiim, children of the Ethiopians*, descendants of Ham, furthest off from the knowledge and grace of God, the unchangeableness of whose color was an emblem of unchangeableness in evil[2]. *Can the Ethiopian change his skin, or the leopard his spots? then may ye also do good, that are accustomed to do evil.*

Have I not brought up [*Did I not bring up*] *Israel out of the land of Egypt?* Amos blends in one their plea and God's answer. God, by bringing them up out of Egypt, had pledged His truth to them to be their God, to protect and preserve them. True! so long as they retained God as their God, and kept His laws. God chose them, that they might choose Him. By casting Him off, as their Lord and God, they cast themselves off and out of God's protection. By estranging themselves from God, they became as strangers in His sight. His act in bringing them up from Egypt had lost its meaning for them. It became no more than any other event in His Providence, by which He brought up *the Philistines from Caphtor*, who yet were aliens from Him, and *the Syrians from Kir*, who, He had foretold, should be carried back thither.

This immigration of the Philistines from Caphtor must have taken place before the return of Israel from Egypt. For Moses says[3], *The Caphtorim, who came forth from Caphtor*, had at this time *destroyed the Avvim who dwelt in villages unto Gazah, and dwelt in their stead.* An entire change in their affairs had also taken place in the four centuries and a half since the days of Isaac. In the time of Abraham and Isaac, Philistia was a kingdom; its capital, Gerar. Its king had a standing army, Phichol being *the captain of the host*[4]: he had also a privy councillor, Ahuzzath[5]. From the time after the Exodus, Philistia had ceased to be a kingdom, Gerar disappears from history; the power of Philistia is concentrated in five new towns, Gaza, Ashdod, Askelon, Gath, Ekron, with five heads, who consult and act as one[6]. The Caphtorim are in some sense also distinct from the old Philistines. They occupy a district not co-extensive with either the old or the new land of the Philistines. In the time of Saul, another Philistine clan is mentioned, the Cherethite. The Amalekites made a marauding inroad into the South country of the Cherethites[7]; which immediately afterward is called[8] *the land of the Philistines.* Probably then, there were different immigrations of the same tribe into Palestine, as there were different immigrations of Danes or Saxons into England, or as there have been and are from the old world into the new, America and Australia. They were then all merged in one common name, as English, Scotch, Irish, are in the United States. The first immigration may have been that from the Casluhim, *out of whom came Philistim*[9]; a second, from the Caphtorim, a kindred people, since they are named next to the Casluhim[10], as descendants of Mizraim. Yet a third were doubtless the Cherethim. But all were united under the one name of Philistines, as Britons, Danes, Saxons, Normans, are united under the one name of English. Of these immigrations, that from Caphtor, even if (as seems probable) second in time, was the chief; which agrees with the great accession of strength, which the Philistines had received at the time of the Exodus; whence the Mediterranean had come to be called by their name, *the sea of the Philistines*[11]; and, in Moses' song of thanksgiving, *the inhabitants of Philistia* are named on a level with *all the inhabitants of Canaan*[12]; and God led His people by the way of Mount Sinai, in order not to expose them at once to

1 v. 8.
2 Jer. xiii. 23.
3 Deut. ii. 23.
4 Gen. xxi. 22, xxvi. 26.
5 Ib. xxvi. 26.
6 See above, on i. 6–8.
7 1 Sam. xxx. 14.
8 Ib. 16.
9 Gen. x. 14.
10 Ib.
11 Ex. xxiii. 31.
12 Ib. xv. 14, 15.

Before CHRIST cir. 787.

the [m] Philistines from
[n] Caphtor, and the Syrians
from [o] Kir?
8 Behold, [p] the eyes of
the Lord God *are* upon
the sinful kingdom, and I
[q] will destroy it from off
the face of the earth; saving that I will not utterly
destroy the house of Jacob,
saith the LORD.
9 For, lo, I will com-
mand, and I will † sift the
house of Israel among all
nations, like as *corn* is
sifted in a sieve, yet shall
not the least † grain fall
upon the earth.

m Jer. 47. 4.
n Deut. 2. 23. Jer. 47. 4.
o ch. 1. 5.
p ver. 4.
q Jer. 30. 11. & 31. 35, 36. Obad. 16, 17.

† Heb. *cause to move.*
† Heb. *stone.*

---

so powerful an enemy [1]. A third immigration of Cherethim, in the latter part of the period of the Judges, would account for the sudden increase of strength, which they seem then to have received. For whereas heretofore those whom God employed to chasten Israel in their idolatries, were kings of Mesopotamia, Moab, Hazor, Midian, Amalek, and the children of the East [2], and Philistia had, at the beginning of the period, lost Gaza, Ashkelon, and Ekron [3], to Israel, and was repulsed by Shamgar, thenceforth, to the time of David, they became the great scourge of Israel on the West of Jordan, as Ammon was on the East.

The Jewish traditions in the LXX, the Vulgate, and three Targums, agree that Caphtor was Cappadocia, which, in that it extended to the Black Sea, might be called *I, sea-coast*, lit. "habitable land [4]," as contrasted with the sea which washed it, whether it surrounded it or no. The Cherethites may have come from Crete, as an intermediate resting-place in their migrations.

8. *Behold the eyes of the Lord* are *upon the sinful kingdom. The sinful kingdom* may mean each *sinful kingdom*, as St. Paul says [5], God *will render unto every man according to his deeds,—unto them who do not obey the truth but obey unrighteousness, tribulation and anguish upon every soul of man that doeth evil, of the Jew first, and also of the Gentile.* His *Eyes* are *on the sinful kingdom*, whatsoever or wheresoever it be, and so on Israel also: *and I will destroy it from off the face of the earth.* In this case, the emphasis would be on the, "I will not *utterly* destroy." God would destroy sinful kingdoms, yet Israel, although sinful, He would not *utterly* destroy, but would leave a remnant, as He had so often promised. Yet perhaps, and more probably, the contrast is between *the kingdom* and *the house of Israel. The kingdom*, being founded in sin, bound up inseparably with sin, God says, *I will destroy from off the face of the earth*, and it ceased for ever. Only, with the kingdom, He says, *I will not utterly destroy the house of Jacob*, to whom were the promises, and to whose seed, whosoever were the true Israel, those promises should be kept. So He explains;

9. *For lo! I will command!* lit. *lo! see, I am commanding.* He draws their attention to it, as something which shall shortly be; and inculcates that He is the secret disposer of all which shall befall them. *And I will sift the house of Israel among all nations.* Amos enlarges the prophecy of Hosea, *they shall be wanderers among the nations.* He adds two thoughts; the violence with which they shall be shaken, and that this their unsettled life, to and fro, shall be not *among the nations* only, but *in all* nations. In every quarter of the world, and in well-nigh every nation in every quarter, Jews have been found. The whole earth is, as it were, one vast sieve in the Hands of God, in which Israel is shaken from one end to the other. There has been one ceaseless tossing to and fro, as the corn in the sieve is tossed from side to side, and rests nowhere, till all is sifted. Each nation in whom they have been found has been an instrument of their being shaken, sifted, severed, the grain from the dirt and chaff. And yet in their whole compass, *not the least grain*, no solid corn, not one grain, should *fall to the earth.* The chaff and dust would be blown away by the air; the dirt which clave to it would fall through; but *no one grain.* God, in all these centuries, has had an eye on each soul of His people in their dispersion throughout all lands. The righteous too have been shaken up and down, through and through; yet not one soul has been lost, which, by the help of God's Holy Spirit, willed truly and earnestly to be saved. Before Christ came, they who were His, believed in Him Who should come; when He came, they who were His were converted to Him; as S. Paul saith [6], *Hath God cast away His people? God forbid! For I also am an Israelite, of the seed of Abraham, of the tribe of Benjamin—God hath not cast away His people which He foreknew—At this present time also there is a remnant, according to the election of grace.*

"[7] What is here said of all, God doth daily in each of the elect. For they are *the*

[1] Ex. xiii. 17.
[2] Judg. iii.—x. 5.
[3] Ib. i. 18.
[4] אי from אוי.
[5] Rom. ii. 6–9.
[6] Rom. xi. 1, 2, 5.
[7] Rib.

Before CHRIST cir. 787.

10 All the sinners of my
people shall die by the
sword, [r] which say, The
evil shall not overtake nor
prevent us.
11 ¶ [s] In that day will

r ch. 6. 3.

s Acts 15. 16, 17.

Before CHRIST cir. 787.

wheat of God, which, in order to be *laid up in* the heavenly *garner*, must be pure from chaff and dust. To this end He sifts them by afflictions and troubles, in youth, manhood, old age, wheresoever they are, in whatsoever occupied, and proves them again and again. At one time the elect enjoyeth tranquillity of mind, is bedewed by heavenly refreshments, prayeth as he wills, loveth, gloweth, hath no taste for ought except God. Then again he is dry, experienceth the heaven to be as brass, his prayer is hindered by distracting thoughts, his feet are as lead to deeds of virtue, his *hands hang down*, his *knees* are *feeble* [1], he dreads death; he sticks fast, languishes. He is shaken in a sieve, that he may mistrust self, place his hope in God, and the dust of vain-glory may be shaken off. He is proved, that it may appear whether he cleave to God for the reward of present enjoyment, or for the hope of future, for longing for the glory of God and for love of Himself. God suffereth him also to be sifted by the devil through various temptations to sin, as he said to the Apostle, *Simon, lo! Satan hath desired you, to sift you as wheat* [2]. But this is the power of God, this His grace to the elect, this the devil attaineth by his sifting, that the dust of immoderate self-love, of vain confidence, of love of the world, should fall off: *this* Satan effecteth not, that the least deed which appertaineth to the inward house and the dwelling which they prepare in their souls for God, should perish. Rather, as we see in holy Job, virtues will increase, grow, be strengthened."

10. *All the sinners of My people shall perish.* At the last, when the longsuffering of God has been despised to the uttermost, His Providence is exact in His justice, as in His love. As not *one grain should fall to the earth*, so not one sinner should escape. "[3] Not because they sinned aforetime, but because they persevered in sin until death. The Æthiopians are changed into sons of God, if they repent; and the sons of God pass away into Æthiopians, if they fall into the depth of sin."

Which say, The evil shall not overtake nor prevent us. Their security was the cause of their destruction. They perished the more miserably, being buoyed up by the false confidence that they should not perish. So it was in both destructions of Jerusalem. Of the first, Jeremiah says to the false prophet Hananiah [4], *Thus saith the Lord, Thou hast broken the yokes of wood; but thou shalt make for them yokes of iron;* and to Zedekiah [5], *Obey, I beseech thee, the voice of the Lord, which I speak unto thee; so shall it be well unto thee, and thy soul shall live. But if thou refuse to go forth—thou shalt not escape out of their hand, but shalt be taken by the hand of the king of Babylon, and thou shalt burn this city with fire.* At the second, while the Christians (mindful of our Lord's words) fled to Pella, the Jews were, to the last, encouraged by their false prophets to resist. "The cause of this destruction," at the burning of the temple, says their own historian [6], "was a false prophet, who on that day proclaimed to those in the city, 'God commands to go up to the temple, to receive the signs of deliverance.' There were too, at that time, among the people many prophets suborned by the tyrants, bidding them await the help from God, that they might not desert, and that hope might prevail with those, who were above fear and restraint. Man is soon persuaded in calamity. And when the deceiver promises release from the evils which are upon him, the sufferer gives himself wholly up to hope. These deceivers then and liars against God at this time mispersuaded the wretched people, so that they neither regarded, nor believed, the plain evident prodigies, which foretokened the coming desolation, but, like men stupefied, who had neither eyes nor mind, disobeyed the warnings of God."—Then, having related some of the prodigies which occurred, he adds [7];—"But of these signs, some they interpreted after their own will, some they despised, until they were convicted of folly by the capture of their country and their own destruction." So too now, none are so likely to perish forever, as they *who say, The evil shall not overtake us.* "I will repent hereafter." "I will make my peace with God before I die." "There is time enough yet." "Youth is for pleasure, age for repentance." "God will forgive the errors of youth, and the heat of our passions." "Any time will do for repentance; health and strength promise long life;" "I cannot do without this or that *now.*" "I will turn to God, only not yet." "God is merciful and full of compassion." Because Satan thus deludes thousands upon thousands to their destruction, God cuts away all such vain hopes with His word, *All the sinners of My people shall die which say, the evil shall not overtake nor come upon us.*

11. *In that day I will raise up.* Amos, as the prophets were taught to do, sums up his

1 Heb. xii. 12.
2 S. Luke xxii. 31.
3 S. Jer.
4 Jer. xxviii. 13.
5 Ib. xxxviii. 20, 23; add xxvii. 9, 10, 19.
6 Joseph. B. J. 6. 5. § 2. 3.
7 Ib. § 4.

Before CHRIST cir. 787.

† Heb. *hedge*, or, *wall*.

I raise up the tabernacle of David that is fallen, and † close up the breaches thereof; and I will raise up his ruins, and I will build it as in the days of old:

Before CHRIST cir. 787.

---

prophecy of woe with this one full promise of overflowing good. For the ten tribes, in their separate condition, there was no hope, no future. He had pronounced the entire destruction of *the kingdom* of Israel. The ten tribes were, thenceforth, only an aggregate of individuals, good or bad. They had no separate corporate existence. In their spiritual existence, they still belonged to the one family of Israel; and, belonging to it, were heirs of the promises made to it. When no longer separate, individuals out of its tribes were to become Apostles to their whole people and to the Gentiles. Of individuals in it, God had declared His judgment, anticipating the complete exactness of the Judgment of the Great Day. *All the sinners of* His *people* should *die* an untimely death *by the sword;* not one of those who were the true grain should perish with the chaff.

He now foretells, how that salvation, of those indeed His own, should be effected through the house of David, in whose line Christ was to come. He speaks of the house of David, not in any terms of royal greatness; he tells, not of its palaces, but of its ruins. Under the word *tabernacle*, he probably blends the ideas, that it should be in a poor condition, and yet that it should be the means whereby God should protect His people. The *succah, tabernacle*, (translated *booth* in Jonah[1]), was originally a rude hut, formed of *intertwined*[2] branches. It is used of the cattle-shed[3], and of the rough tents used by soldiers in war[4] or by the watchman in the vineyard[5], and of those wherein God *made the children of Israel to dwell, when* He *brought them out of the land of Egypt*[6]. The name of the feast of *Tabernacles, Succoth*, as well as the rude temporary huts[7] in which they were commanded to dwell, associated the name with a state of outward poverty under God's protection. Hence, perhaps, the word is employed also of the secret place of the Presence of God[8]. Isaiah, as well as Amos, seems, in the use of the same word[9], to hint that what is poor and mean in man's sight would be, in the Hands of God, an effectual protection. This *hut of David* was also at that time to be *fallen*. When Amos prophesied, it had been weakened by the schism of the ten tribes, but Azariah, its king, was mighty[10]. Amos had already foretold the destruction of the *palaces of Jerusalem by fire*[11]. Now he adds, that the abiding condition of the house of David should be a state of decay and weakness, and that from that state, not human strength, but God Himself should *raise* it. *I will raise up the hut of David, the fallen.* He does not say, of *that* time, "the hut that *is* fallen," as if it were already fallen, but *the hut, the fallen*[12], i. e. the hut of which the character should then be its falling, its caducity. So, under a different figure, Isaiah prophesied, *There shall come forth a rod out of the stump*[13] *of Jesse, and a Branch shall put forth from its roots.* When the trunk was hewn down even with the ground, and the rank grass had covered the *stump*, that *rod* and *Branch* should come forth which should rule the earth, and *to* which *the Gentiles should seek*[14]. From these words of Amos, "the Son of the fallen," became, among the Jews, one of the titles of the Christ. Both in the legal and mystical schools the words of Amos are alleged, in proof of the fallen condition of the house of David, when the Christ should come. "Who would expect," asks one[15], "that God would raise up the fallen tabernacle of David? and yet it is said, *I will raise up the tabernacle of David which is fallen down.* And who would hope that the whole world should become one band? as it is written[16], *Then I will turn to the people a pure language, that they may all call upon the name of the Lord, to serve him with one shoulder.* This is no other than the king Messiah." And in the Talmud[17]; "R. Nachman said to R. Isaac; Hast thou heard when 'the Son of the fallen' shall come? He answered, Who is he? R. Nachman; The Messiah. R. Isaac; Is the Messiah so called? R. Nachman; Yes; *In that day will I raise up the tabernacle of David which is fallen down.*"

And close up, lit. *wall up, the breaches thereof.* The house of David had at this time sustained breaches. It had yet more serious breaches to sustain thereafter. The first great breach was the rending off of the ten tribes. It sustained breaches, through the Assyrians; and yet more when itself was carried away captive to Babylon, and so many of its residue fled into Egypt. Breaches are repaired by new stones; the losses of the house of David were to be filled up by accessions from the Gentiles. God Himself should *close up the breaches;* so should they remain closed; and

---

1 Jon. iv. 5, Gen. xxxiii. 17. 2 from סכך i. q. שׂוך.
3 Gen. xxxiii. 17. 4 2 Sam. xi. 11.
5 Is. i. 8, Job xxvii. 18. 6 Lev. xxiii. 43.
7 Ib. 40, see on Hos. xii. 9. p. 79.
8 Ps. xviii. 11, Job xxxvi. 29. 9 Is. iv. 6.

10 2 Chr. xxvi. 6-15. 11 ii. 5. 12 הנפלת.
13 גזע Is. xi. 1. 14 Ib. 10.
15 Bereshith Rabba S. 88. fin. quoted by Schoettg. loc. gen. n. 18. p. 70. 16 Zeph. iii. 9.
17 Sanhedr. f. 96. 2. Schoettg. de Mess. p. 16.

Before CHRIST cir. 787.

[t] Obad. 19.
[u] Num. 24. 18.

12 [t] That they may possess the remnant of [u] Edom, and of all the heathen, † which are called by my name, saith the LORD that doeth this.

Before CHRIST cir. 787.

† Heb. *upon whom my name is called.*

---

the gates of hell should not prevail against the Church which He builded. Amos heaps on one another the words implying destruction. A *hut* and that *falling; breaches; ruins;* (lit. *his ruinated, his destructions*). But he also speaks of it in a way which excludes the idea of *the hut of David*, being "the royal Dynasty" or "the kingdom of Judah." For he speaks of it, not as an abstract thing, such as a kingdom is, but as a whole, consisting of individuals. He speaks not only of *the hut of David*, but of "*their* (*fem.*) breaches," "*his* ruins," that God would "build *her* up," "that *they* (masc.) may inherit;" using apparently this variety of numbers and genders[1], in order to shew that he is speaking of one living whole, the Jewish Church, now rent in two by the great schism of Jeroboam, but which should be reunited into one body, members of which should win the Heathen to the true faith in God. "I will raise up," he says, "the tabernacle of David, the fallen, and will wall up *their* breaches," [the breaches of the two portions into which it had been rent] and I will raise up *his* ruins [the "ruinated places" of David] and I will build *her* [as one whole] as in the days of old, [before the rent of the ten tribes, when all worshiped as one], that *they*, (masc.) i. e. individuals who should go forth out of her, "may inherit, &c."

12. *That they may possess*, rather, *inherit, the remnant of Edom.* The restoration was not to be for themselves alone. No gifts of God end in the immediate object of His bounty and love. They were restored, in order that they, the first objects of God's mercies, might win others to God; not Edom only, *but all nations, upon whom*, God says, *My Name is called.* Plainly then, it is no temporal subjugation, nor any earthly kingdom. The words, *upon whom the name is called*, involve, in any case, belonging to, and being owned by, him whose name is called upon them. It is said of the wife bearing the name of the husband and becoming his, *let thy name be called upon us*[2]. When Jacob specially adopts Ephraim and Manasseh as his own, he says, *let my name be named upon them, and the name of My fathers, Abraham and Isaac*[3]. In relation to God, the words are used of persons and of places especially appropriated to God; as the whole Jewish Church and people, His Temple[4], His Prophets[5], the city of Jerusalem[6] by virtue of the Temple built there. Contrariwise, Isaiah pleads to God, that the Heathen *were never called by Thy Name*[7]. This relation of being *called* by the *Name* of God, was not outward only, nor was it ineffective. Its characteristics were holiness imparted by God to man, and protection by God. Thus Moses, in his blessing on Israel if obedient, says[8], *The Lord shall establish thee an holy people unto Himself, as He hath sworn to thee, if thou shalt keep the commandments of the Lord thy God, and walk in His ways; and all the people of the earth shall see that the Name of the Lord thy God is called upon thee, and they shall fear thee.* And Jeremiah says to God[9], *Thy word was unto me the joy and rejoicing of my heart; for Thy name was called upon me, O Lord God of Hosts.*

Israel then, or the Jewish Church, was to inherit, or take into itself, not Edom only, but all nations, and that, by their belonging to God. Edom, as the brother of Israel and yet his implacable enemy, stands as a symbol of all who were alien from God, over against His people. He says, the *residue of Edom*, because he had foretold the destruction which was first to come upon Edom[10]; and Holy Scripture everywhere speaks of those who should be converted, as a *remnant* only. The Jews themselves are the keepers and witnesses of these words. Was it not foretold? It stands written. Is it not fulfilled? The whole world from this country to China, and from China round again to us, as far as it is Christian, and as, year by year, more are gathered into the fold of Christ, are the inheritance of those who were the seed of Abraham, Isaac and Jacob.

S. James quoted these words in the Council of Jerusalem, to show how the words of the Prophet were in harmony with what S. Peter had related, how[11] *God at the first did visit the Gentiles, to take out of them a people for His Name.* He quotes the words as they stood in the version which was understood by the Gentiles who came from Antioch. In it the words are paraphrased, but the meaning remains the same. The Greek translators took away the metaphor, in order, probably, to make the meaning more intelligible to Greeks, and paraphrased the Hebrew words, imagining other words, as like as might be

[1] Hengstenberg, Christologie, i. 447, 8 ed. 2.
[2] Is. iv. 1.
[3] Gen. xlviii. 16.
[4] 1 Kings viii. 43, Jer. vii. 10, 11, 14, 30, xxxiv. 15.
[5] Jer. xv. 16.
[6] Dan. ix. 18, 19.
[7] Is. lxiii. 19.
[8] Deut. xxviii. 9, 10.
[9] l. c.
[10] See ab. 106.
[11] Acts xv. 14.

Before CHRIST cir. 787.

x Lev. 26. 5.

13 Behold, [x]the days
come, saith the LORD, that
the plowman shall overtake the reaper, and the
treader of grapes him that
†soweth seed; [y]and the

Before CHRIST cir. 787.

† Heb. *draweth forth.*

y Joel 3. 18.

to the Hebrew[1]. They render, "that the residue of men may seek, and all the nations upon whom My name is called." The force of the prophecy lies in these last words, that "the Name of God should be called upon all nations." S. James, then, quoted the words as they were familiar to his hearers, not correcting those which did not impair the meaning. The so doing, he shews us incidentally, that even imperfection of translation does not empty the fullness of God's word. The words, "shall seek the Lord," although not representing anything expressed here in the original, occur in the corresponding prophecy of Isaiah as to the root of Jesse[2], *In that day there shall be a root* (i. e. a sucker from the root) *of Jesse, which shall stand for an ensign of the people, and to it shall the Gentiles seek.* It may be, that S. James purposely uses the plural, *the words of the prophets,* in order to include, together with the Prophet Amos, other prophets who had foretold the same thing. The statements, that the Jewish Church should inherit the Gentiles, that the Name of God should be called upon the Gentiles, and that the Gentiles should seek the Lord, are parts of one whole; that they should be called, that they should obey the call, and, obeying, be enrolled in the one family of God.

13. *Behold the days are coming.* The Day of the Lord is ever coming on: every act, good or bad, is drawing it on: everything which fills up the measure of iniquity or which "hastens the accomplishment of the number of the elect;" all time hastens it by. *The ploughman shall overtake the reaper and the treader of grapes him that soweth seed.* The image is taken from God's promise in the law[3]; *Your threshing shall reach unto the vintage, and the vintage shall reach unto the sowing time;* which is the order of agriculture. The harvest should be so copious that it should not be threshed out until the vintage: the vintage so large, that, instead of ending, as usual, in the middle of the 7th month, it should continue on to the seed-time in November. Amos appears purposely to have altered this. He describes what is wholly beyond nature, in order that it might the more appear that he was speaking of no mere gifts of nature, but, under natural emblems, of the abundance of gifts of grace. *The ploughman,* who breaks up the fallow ground, *shall overtake,* or *throng, the reaper.* The *ploughman* might *throng,* or *join on* to *the reaper,* either following upon him, or being followed by him; either preparing the soil for the harvest which the reaper gathers in, or breaking it up anew for a fresh harvest after the in-gathering. But the vintage falls between the harvest and the seed-time. If then by the *ploughmen thronging on the reaper,* we understand that the harvest should, for its abundance, not be over before the fresh seed-time, then, since the vintage is much nearer to the seed-time than the harvest had been, the words, *he that treadeth out the grapes, him that soweth the seed,* would only say the same less forcibly. In the other way, it is one continuous whole. So vast would be the soil to be cultivated, so beyond all the powers of the cultivator, and yet so rapid and unceasing the growth, that seed-time and harvest would be but one. So our Lord says[4], *Say not ye, There are yet four months, and* then *cometh harvest? Behold, I say unto you, Lift up your eyes, and look on the fields; for they are white already to harvest. Four months* ordinarily intervened between seed-time and harvest. Among these Samaritans, seed-time and harvest were one. They had not, like the Jews, had teachers from God; yet, as soon as our Lord taught them, they believed. But, as seed time and harvest should be one, so should the vintage be continuous with the following seed-time. *The treader of grapes,* the last crowning act of the year of cultivation, should join on to *him that soweth* (lit. *draweth* forth, soweth broadcast, scattereth far and wide the) *seed.* All this is beyond nature, and so, the more in harmony with what went before, the establishment of a kingdom of grace, in which *the Heathen* should have *the Name of God called upon* them. He had foretold[5] to them, how God would *send famine on the land, not a famine of bread, nor a thirst for water, but of hearing the words of the Lord.* Now, under the same image, he declares the repeal of that sentence. He foretells, not the fullness only of God's gifts, but their unbroken continuance. "[6] All shall succeed one another, so that no day should be void of corn, wine, and gladness." And they shall not follow only on one another, but shall all go on together in one perpetual round of toil and fruitfulness. There shall be one unceasing inpouring of riches; no break in the heavenly husbandry; labor shall at once yield fruit; the harvest shall

[1] As though there had stood אדם for אדום; and ידרשו for יירשו, the difference in each case lying in one letter.

[2] Is. xi. 10.
[3] Lev. xxvi. 5.
[4] S. John iv. 35.
[5] viii. 11.
[6] S. Jer.

Before CHRIST cir. 787.

mountains shall drop
‖ sweet wine, and all the
hills shall melt.
14 [z] And I will bring
again the captivity of my
people of Israel, and [a] they
shall build the waste cities,
and inhabit *them;* and they
shall plant vineyards, and
drink the wine thereof;
they shall also make gar-
dens, and eat the fruit of
them.
15 And I will plant

‖ Or, *new wine.*
z Jer. 30. 3.
a Is. 61. 4. & 65. 21. Ezek. 36. 33-36.

Before CHRIST cir. 787.

but encourage fresh labor. The end shall come swiftly on the beginning; the end shall not close the past only, but issue forth anew. Such is the character of the toils of the Gospel. All the works of grace go on in harmony together; each helps on the other; in one, the fallow-ground of the heart is broken up; in another, seed is sown, the beginning of a holy conversation; in another, is the full richness of the ripened fruit, in advanced holiness or the blood of Martyrs. And so, also, of the ministers of Christ, some are adapted especially to one office, some to another; yet all together carry on His one work. All, too, Patriarchs, Prophets, Apostles, shall meet together in one; they who, before Christ's Coming, "[1] sowed the seed, the promises of the Blessed Seed to come," and they who *entered into their labors,* not to displace, but to complete them; all shall rejoice together in that Seed which is Christ.

And the mountains shall drop sweet wine and all the hills shall melt. Amos takes the words of Joel, in order to identify their prophecies [2], yet strengthens the image. For instead of saying, *the hills shall flow with milk,* he says, *they shall melt, dissolve themselves* [3]. Such shall be the abundance and super-abundance of blessing, that it shall be as though the hills dissolved themselves in the rich streams which they poured down. The mountains and hills may be symbols, in regard either to their height, or their natural barrenness or their difficulty of cultivation. In past times they were scenes of idolatry [4]. In the time of the Gospel, all should be changed; all should be above nature. All should be obedient to God; all, full of the graces and gifts of God. What was exalted, like the Apostles, should be exalted not for itself, but in order to pour out the streams of life-giving doctrine and truth, which would refresh and gladden the faithful. And the lesser heights, *the hills,* should, in their degree, pour out the same streams. Everything, heretofore barren and unfruitful, should overflow with spiritual blessing. The mountains and hills of Judæa, with their terraced sides clad with the vine were a natural symbol fruitfulness to the Jews, but they themselves could not think that natural fruitfulness was meant under this imagery. It would have been a hyperbole as to things of nature; but what, in natural things, is a hyperbole, is but a faint shadow of the joys and rich delights and glad fruitfulness of grace.

14. *And I will bring again the captivity of My people.* Where all around is spiritual, there is no reason to take this alone as earthly. An earthly restoration to Canaan had no value, except as introductory to the spiritual. The two tribes were, in a great measure, restored to their own land, when Zachariah, being [5] *filled with the Holy Ghost, prophesied,* as then about to be accomplished, that *God hath visited and redeemed His people, and hath raised up a horn of salvation to us in the house of His servant David, as He spake by the mouth of His holy prophets—that we, being delivered from the hands of our enemies, might serve Him without fear, in holiness and righteousness before Him.* So our Lord said [6]; *ye shall know the truth, and the truth shall make you free.—Whosoever committeth sin, is the servant of sin.—If the Son shall make you free, ye shall be free indeed.* And Saint Paul [7], *The law of the Spirit of life in Christ Jesus has made me free from the law of sin and death.*

And they shall build the waste [rather *shall build waste* [8]] *cities.* "As they who are freed from captivity and are no longer in fear of the enemy, *build cities and plant vineyards* and gardens," so shall these unto God. "This," says one of old [1], "needs no exposition, since, throughout the world, amid the desert of Heathendom, which was before deserted by God, Churches of Christ have arisen, which, for the firmness of faith, may be called *cities,* and, for the gladness of *hope which maketh not ashamed, vineyards,* and for the sweetness of charity, gardens; wherein they dwell, who have builded them through the word; whence they drink the wine of gladness, who formed them by precepts; whence they eat fruits, who advanced them by counsels, because, as *he who reapeth,* so he too who *buildeth* such *cities,* and he who *planteth* such *vineyards,* and he who *maketh* such *gardens, receiveth wages and gathereth fruit unto life eternal* [9]."

15. *And I will plant them upon their own*

[1] Rup. [2] See ab. p. 94, 5, 149. [3] התמוגגנה.
[4] See above, p. 30. [5] S. Luke i. 68–70, 4, 5.

[6] S. John viii. 32, 4, 6. [7] Rom. viii. 2.
[8] There is no article. [9] S. John iv. 36.

Before CHRIST cir. 787.

them upon their land, and [b] they shall no more be

[b] Is. 60. 21. Jer. 32. 41. Ezek. 34. 28. Joel 3. 20.

Before CHRIST cir. 787.

land. The promises and threatenings of God are, to individuals, conditional upon their continuing to be of that character, to which God annexes those promises or threats. "[1] The God of all often promises, when those who receive the promises, by joying in iniquity hinder those promises from taking effect. At times also he threatens heavy things, and they who for their offences were the objects of those threats, being, through fear of them, converted, do not in act experience them." The two tribes received some little shadow of fulfillment of these promises on the return from Babylon. *They were planted in their own land.* The non-fulfillment of the rest, as well as the evident symbolic character of part of it, must have shewn them that such fulfillment was the beginning, not the end. Their land was *the Lord's land;* banishment from it was banishment from the special presence of God, from the palce where He manifested Himself, where alone the typical sacrifices, the appointed means of reconciliation, could be offered. Restoration to their own land was the outward symbol of restoration to God's favor, of which it was the fruit. It was a condition of the fulfillment of those other promises, the Coming of Him in Whom the promises were laid up, the Christ. He was not simply to be of David's seed, according to the flesh. Prophecy, as time went on, declared His birth at Bethlehem, His revelation in Galilee, His Coming to His Temple, His sending forth His law from Jerusalem. Without some restoration to their own land, these things could not be. Israel was restored in the flesh, that, after the flesh, the Christ might be born of them, where God foretold that He should be born. But the temporal fulfillment ended with that Event in time in which they were to issue, for whose sake they were; His Coming. They were but the vestibule to the spiritual. As shadows, they ceased when the Sun arose. As means, they ended, when the end, whereto they served, came. There was no need of a temporal Zion, when He Who was to send forth His law thence, had come and sent it forth. No need of a Temple when He Who was to be its Glory, had come, illumined it, and was gone. No need of one of royal birth in Bethlehem, when *the Virgin* had *conceived and borne a Son,* and *God* had been *with us.* And so as to other prophecies. All which were bound to the land of Judah, were accomplished. As the true Israel expanded and embraced all nations, the whole earth became *the land* of God's people. Palestine had had its prerogatives, because God manifested Himself there, was worshiped there. When God's people was enlarged, so as *to inherit the heathen,* and God was worshiped everywhere, His land too was everywhere. His promises accompanied His people, and these were in all lands. His words then, *I will plant them upon their own land, and they shall no more be pulled up out of their land which I have given them,* expanded with their expansion. It is a promise of perpetuity, like that of our Lord; *Lo! I am with you alway, even to the end of the world. The gates of hell shall not prevail against* the Church, the people of God. The world may gnash its teeth; kings may oppress; persecutors may harass; popular rage may trample on her; philosophy may scoff at her; unbelief may deny the promises made to her; the powers of darkness may rage around her; her own children may turn against her. In vain! "[2] She may be shaken by persecutions, she cannot be uprooted; she may be tempted, she cannot be overcome. For the Lord God Almighty, the Lord her God, hath promised that He will do it, Whose promise is the law to nature."

Saith the Lord thy God. "[3] O Israel of God, O Catholic Church, to be gathered out of Jews and Gentiles, doubt not, he would say, thy promised happiness. For thy God Who loveth thee and Who from eternity hath chosen thee, hath commanded me to say this to thee in His Name." "[4] He turneth too to the ear of each of us, giving us joy, in His word, *saith the Lord thy God.*" "[3] They too who are plants which God hath planted, and who have so profited, that through them many daily profit, *shall be planted upon their own ground,* i. e. each, in his order and in that kind of life which he has chosen, shall strike deep roots in true piety, and they shall be so preserved by God, that by no force of temptations shall they be uprooted, but each shall say with the holy prophet[5], *I am like a green olive tree in the house of God; I trust in the mercy of God forever and ever.* Not that every tree, planted in the ground of the Church militant, is so firm that it cannot be plucked up, but many there are, which are not plucked up, being protected by the Hand of Almighty God. O blessed that land, where no tree is plucked up, none is injured by any worm, or decays through any age. How many great, fruit-bearing, trees do we see plucked up in this land of calamity and misery! Blessed day, when we shall be there, where we need fear no storm!" Yet

[1] Theod.
[2] S. Jer.
[3] Rib. [4] Rup.
[5] Ps. lii. 9.

Before CHRIST cir. 787. pulled up out of their land which I have given them, saith the LORD thy God. Before CHRIST cir. 787.

this too abideth true; *none shall be plucked up*. Without our own will, neither passions within, nor temptations without, nor the malice or wiles of Satan, can *pluck* us *up*. None can *be plucked up*, who doth not himself loose his hold, whose root is twisted round the Rock, which is Thou, O Blessed Jesu. For Thou hast said[1], *they shall never perish, neither shall any pluck them out of My Hand.*

[1] S. John x. 28.

prophecy, but employed themselves about the Prophets. Unbelief, denying prophecy, had to find out two events in history, which should correspond with these events in the Prophet, a capture of Jerusalem, and a subsequent,—*it* could not say, consequent,—suffering on the part of Edom. And since Jerusalem was first taken under Shishak king of Egypt, in the 5th year of Rehoboam, B.C. 970, and Josephus relates[d], that B.C. 301, Ptolemy Lagus treacherously got possession of it under plea of offering sacrifice, treated it harshly, took many captive from the mountainous part of Judæa and the places round Jerusalem, from Samaritis, Gerizim, and settled them all in Egypt; unbelieving criticism had a wide range, in which to vacillate. And so it reeled to and fro between the first and last of these periods, agreeing that Obadiah did not prophesy, and disagreeing as to all besides. Eichhorn[e], avowedly on his principle of unbelief, that God's prophets, when they spoke of detailed events, as future, were really describing the past, assumed that the last five verses were written in the time of Alexander Janneus, two centuries later than the latest, about B.C. 82[f]. As though a Hebrew prophet would speak of one, detestable for his wanton cruelty[g], as a Saviour!

The real question as to the age of Obadiah turns upon two points, the one external, the other internal. The external is, whether in regard to those verses which he has in common with Jeremiah, Obadiah gathered into one, verses which lie scattered in Jeremiah, or whether Jeremiah, in renewing the prophecies against Edom, incorporated verses of Obadiah. The question, internal to Obadiah, is, whether he speaks of the capture of Jerusalem in the prophetic or the real past, and (as determining this), whether he reproves Edom for past malice at the capture of Jerusalem, or warns him against it in the future.

The English version in the text supposes that Obadiah reproves for past sin. For it renders; *Thou shouldest not have looked on the day of thy brother, in the day when he became a stranger; neither shouldest thou have rejoiced over the children of Judah in the day of their destruction; neither shouldest thou have spoken proudly in the day of their distress*[h]. The English margin gives the other, as a probable rendering, *do not behold, &c.* But it is absolutely certain that *al* with the future forbids or deprecates a thing future. In all the passages, in which *al* occurs in the Hebrew Bible[i], it signifies "do not." We might as well say that "do not steal" means "thou shouldest not have stolen," as say that *veal tēreh, and do not look,* means "thou shouldest not have looked." It is true that in a vivid form of question, belonging to strong feeling, the soul going back in thought to the time before a thing happened, can speak of the past as yet future. Thus David says[k], *The death of fools shall Abner die?* while mourning over his bier; or Job, having said to God, *why didst Thou bring me forth from the womb?* places himself as at that time and says[l] (literally), *I shall expire, and eye shall not see me; as if I had not been, I shall be; from the womb to the grave I shall be carried.* He contemplates the future, as it would have been, had he died in the birth. It was a relative future. We could almost, under strong emotion, use our "is to" in the same way. We could render, *Is Abner to die the death of fools?* But these cases have nothing to do with the uniform idiom; "do not." We must not, on any principle of interpretation, in a single instance, ascribe to a comon idiom, a meaning which it has not, because the meaning which it has, does not suit us. There *is* an idiom to express this. It is the future with *lo,* not with *al.*

It agrees with this, that just before[m], where our version renders, *thou wert as one of them,* the Hebrew (as, in our Bibles, is marked by the Italics) has only, *thou as one of them!* not expressing any time. The whole verse expresses no time as to Edom. *In the day of thy standing on the other side, in the day of strangers carrying captive his might, and strangers entered his gates and cast lots on Jerusalem, thou too as one of them.*

This too is a question not of rhetoric, but of morals. We cannot imagine that Almighty God, Who warns that he may not strike, would eight times repeat the exhortation,—a repetition which in itself has so much earnestness, "do not," "do not," "do not," in regard to sin which had been already ended. As to past sin, God exhorts to repent, to break it off, not to renew it. He does not exhort to that which would be a contradiction even to His own Omnipotence, not to do what had been already done.

According to the only meaning, then, which the words bear, Edom had not yet committed the sin against which Obadiah warns him, and so Jerusalem was not yet destroyed, when the Prophet wrote. For the sevenfold[n], *the day of thy brother,* (which is explained to be *the day of his calamity*), *the day of their destruction, the day of distress,* the mention whereof had just preceded, can be no other than *the day when strangers carried away his strength, and foreigners entered his gates, and cast lots on Jerusalem.* But no day was the day of utter destruction to Jerusa-

[d] Ant. xii. 1. 1. [e] Einl. ins. A. T. iv. § 570.
[f] i. e. three years before his death. Jos. Ant. xiii. 15. 4.
[g] See Jos. Ib. xiii. 14. and 15.

[h] ver. 12, and so in ver. 13, 14.
[i] Calasio's Concordance furnishes 207 instances.
[k] 2 Sam. iii. 33. [l] Job x. 18. 19.
[m] ver. 11. [n] ver. 12–14.

lem, except that of its capture by Nebuchadnezzar. Its capture by Shishak[o], or by the Chaldees under[p] Jehoiakim and Jehoiachin[q], left it uninjured; Jehoash, when he had defeated Amaziah, broke down a part of its walls only[r].

The relation of Obadiah to Jeremiah agrees with this. This argument in proof of that relation has been so carefully drawn out by Caspari[s], that little is needed except clearly to exhibit it. Few indeed, I should think, (unless under some strong contrary bias), could read the five first verses of Obadiah in the book of the Prophet himself, and, as they occur, scattered in the 49th chapter of Jeremiah, and not be convinced that Jeremiah reset the words of Obadiah in his own prophecy.

This is, in itself, probable, because Jeremiah certainly incorporated eight verses of Isaiah in his prophecy against Moab[t], and four of the same Prophet in his prophecy against Babylon[u], in addition to several allusions to his prophecies contained in a word or idiom, or mode of expression[v]. In like way, he closes his prophecy against Damascus, with a verse from the prophecy of Amos against it[x]; and he inserts a verse of Amos against Ammon in his own prophecy against that people[y]. This is the more remarkable, because the prophecy of Amos against each people consists of three verses only. This, of course, was done designedly. Probably in renewing the prophecies against those nations, Jeremiah wished to point out that those former prophecies were still in force; that they had not yet been exhausted; that the threatenings of God were not the less certain, because they were delayed; that His word would not the less come true, because He was long-suffering. The insertion of these former prophecies, longer or shorter, are a characteristic of Jeremiah's prophecies against the nations, occurring, as they do, in those against Babylon, Damascus, Moab, Ammon, and therefore probably in that also against Edom.

The eight verses, moreover, common to Obadiah and Jeremiah form one whole in Obadiah; in Jeremiah they are scattered amid other verses of his own, in precisely the same way as we know that he introduced verses of Isaiah against Moab. But beside this analogy of the relation of the prophecy of Jeremiah to that of Isaiah, it is plainly more natural to suppose that Jeremiah enlarged an existing prophecy, adding to it words which God gave him, than that Obadiah put together scattered sayings of Jeremiah, and yet that these sayings, thus severed from their context, should still have formed as they do, one compact, connected whole.

Yet this *is* the case as to these verses of Obadiah. Apart, for the time, from the poetic imagery, the connection of thought in Obadiah's prophecy is this; 1) God had commanded nations to come against Edom, 2) determining to lower it; 3) it had trusted proudly in its strong position; 4) yet God would bring it down; and that, 5) through no ordinary spoiler, but 6) by one who should search out its most hidden treasures; 7) its friends should be its destroyers; 8) its wisdom, and 9) might should fail it, and 10) it should perish, for its malice to its brother Jacob; the crowning act of which would be at the capture of Jerusalem; (11–14) but God's day was at hand, the heathen should be requited; (15, 16) the remnant of Zion, being delivered, would dispossess their dispossessors, would spread far and wide; (17–20) a Saviour should arise out of Zion, and the kingdom should be the Lord's. (21)

Thus, not the eight verses only of Obadiah, five of which recur in Jeremiah, and three others, to which he alludes, stand in close connection in Obadiah, but they form a part of one well-arranged whole. The connection is sometimes very close indeed; as when, to the proud question of Esau, *mi yorideni arets*[a], *who will bring me down to the ground?* God answers, *though thou place thy nest among the stars, mishsham* orideca[b], *thence will I bring thee down.*

Jeremiah, on the contrary, the mourner among the prophets, is plaintive, even in his prophecies against the enemies of God's people. Even in this prophecy he mingles words of tenderness[c]; *Leave thy fatherless children, I will preserve them alive; and let thy widows trust in Me.* Jeremiah, accordingly, has a succession of striking pictures; but the connection in him is rather one of oratory than of thought. His object is to impress; he *does* impress, by an accumulation of images of terror or desolation. Closeness of thought would not aid his object, and he neglects it, except when he retains the order of Obadiah. But plainly it is most probable,

[o] 1 Kings xiv. 25–27.
[p] 2 Kings xxiv. 2 Chr. xxxvi. 6, 7.
[q] 2 Chr. xxxvi. 10. [r] 2 Kings xiv. 13.
[s] Der Prophet Obadia, pp. 4. sqq.
[t] Jer. xlviii. 29, 30, from Is. xvi. 6; Jer. xlviii. 31, from Is. xv. 5, xvi. 7, 11; Jer. xlviii. 32, from Is. xvi. 8, 9. 10; Jer. xlviii. 34, from Is. xv. 4–6; Jer. xlviii. 36, from Is. xvi. 11, xv. 7; Jer. xlviii. 37, from Is. xv. 2, 3; also Jer. xlviii. 43, 44, from Is. xxiv. 17, 18.
[u] Jer. l. 16, from Is. xiii. 14; Jer. l. 39; from Is. xiii. 21. 20; and Jer. l. 40, from Is. xiii. 9.
[v] Jer. l. 2. refers to Is. xlvi. 1; Jer. l. 8, to Is. xlviii. 20; Jer. l. 23, to Is. xiv. 6, 4; Jer. l. 25, to Is. xiii. 5; Jer. l. 34, to Is. xlvii. 4; Jer. l. 38, to Is. xliv. 27; Jer. li. 11, to Is. xiii. 17.
[x] Jer. xlix. 27. from Am. i. 4.
[y] Am. i. 15, in Jer. xlix. 3, besides the allusion in ver. 2. תרועת מלחמה, and באש תצתנה.
[a] מי יורידני ארץ ver. 3. [b] משם אורידך ver. 4.
[c] xlix. 11.

that *that* is the original form of the prophecy, where the order is the sequence of thought. That sequence is a characteristic, not of these verses only of Obadiah, but of the whole. The whole twenty-one verses of the Prophet pursue one connected train of thought, from the beginning to the end. No one verse could be displaced, without injuring that order. Thoughts flow on, the one out of the other. But nothing is more improbable than to suppose that this connected train of thought was produced by putting together thoughts, which originally stood unconnected.

The slight variations also in these verses, as they stand in the two prophets, are characteristic. Wherever the two prophets in any degree vary, Obadiah is the more concise, or abrupt; Jeremiah, as belongs to his pathetic character, the more flowing. Thus Obadiah begins, *Thus saith the Lord God, of Edom. A report we have heard from the Lord, and a messenger among the heathen is sent; Arise and let us arise against her to battle.* The words, *Thus saith the Lord God, of Edom,* declare that the whole prophecy which follows came from God; then Obadiah bursts forth with what he had heard from God, *A report we have heard from the Lord.* The words are joined in meaning; the grammatical connection, if regarded, would be incorrect. Again, in the words, *we have heard,* the Prophet joins his people with himself. Jeremiah substitutes the more precise, *I have heard,* transposes the words to a later part of the prophecy, and so obviates the difficulty of the connection: then he substitutes the regular form, *shaluach,* for the irregular, *shullāch;* and for the one abrupt sentence, *Arise, and arise we against her to battle,* he substitutes the Hebrew parallelism, *Gather ye yourselves and come against her; and arise to battle.* Next, Obadiah has, *Behold! small have I made thee among the nations; despised art thou exceedingly.* Jeremiah connects the verse with the preceding by the addition of the particle *for,* and makes the whole flow on, depending on the word, *I have made. For behold! small have I made thee among the heathen, despised among men.* Obadiah, disregarding rules of parallelism, says; *The pride of thy heart hath deceived thee, dweller in rock-clefts, his lofty seat; who says in his heart, who will bring me down to the earth?* Jeremiah with a softer flow; *Thy alarmingness hath deceived thee, the pride of thy heart; dweller in the clefts of the rock, holding the height of a hill.* Obadiah has very boldly; *Though thou exalt as the eagle, and though amid stars set thy nest, thence will I bring thee down, saith the Lord.* Jeremiah contracts this, omits an idiom, for boldness, almost alone in Hebrew, *veim bein cocabim sim, and though amid stars set,* and has only, *when thou exaltest, as an eagle, thy nest, thence will I bring thee down, saith the Lord,* where also, through the omission of the words "amid stars," the word "thence" has, in Jeremiah, no exact antecedent. In like way Jeremiah smooths down the abrupt appeal, *If thieves had come to thee, if spoilers of the night (how art thou cut off!) will they not steal their enough? If grape-gatherers had come to thee, will they not leave gleanings?* Jeremiah changes it into two even half-verses; *If grape-gatherers had come to thee, will they not leave gleanings? If thieves by night, they had spoiled their enough.* Again, for the 5 bold words of Obadiah, *eik nechphesu Esau, nib'u matsmunaiv,* lit. *how are Esau outsearched, sought out his hidden places,* Jeremiah substitutes, *For I have laid bare Esau; I have discovered his hidden places, and he cannot be hid.*

Again, even an English reader of Jeremiah will have noticed that Jeremiah has many idioms or phrases or images, which he has pleasure in repeating. They are characteristic of his style. Now, in these verses which Obadiah and Jeremiah have in common, there is no one idiom which occurs elsewhere in Jeremiah; whereas, in the other verses of the prophecy of Jeremiah against Edom, in which they are, as it were, inlaid, there are several such, so to say, favorite turns of expressions. As such, there have been noticed, the short abrupt questions with which Jeremiah opens his prophecy against Edom[d]; *Is wisdom no more in Teman?* the hurried imperatives accumulated on one another[e], *Flee, turn, dwell deep;* the accumulation of words expressive of desolation[f]; *Bozrah shall become a desolation, a reproach, a waste and a curse; and all her cities, perpetual wastes;* the combination of the two strong words, *shall be stupefied, shall hiss,* in amazement at her overthrow; [g]*Every one who goeth by her shall be stupefied* [we say "struck dumb"] *and shall hiss at all her plagues.* Such again are the comparison to the overthrow of Sodom and Gomorrah[h]; the image of "the lion coming up from the pride of Jordan[i];" the burden of these prophecies, [k]*the day of the destruction of* Edom *and time of his visitation.* [l]*Wherefore hear ye the counsel of the Lord against Edom and His purposes which He has purposed toward Teman.* Then

[d] xlix. 7, comp. ii. 14, viii. 19, xiv. 19, xviii. 14, 20, xxii. 28, xxx. 6, xxxi. 20, xlix. 1.

[e] xlix. 8, comp. xlix. 30, xlviii. 6.

[f] xlix. 13, comp. xxiv. 9, xxv. 9, 18, xxix. 18, xlii. 18, xliv. 12, 22, besides other accumulations as in vii. 34, xxii. 5. or lesser degrees of accumulation, fullness of language being a characteristic of Jeremiah.

[g] xlix. 17, comp. xviii. 16, xix. 8, l. 13, Lam. ii. 15. from the vision, 1 Kings ix. 8, also Ezek. xxvii. 36, Zeph. ii. 15.

[h] xlix. 18, comp. l. 40. [i] xlix. 19, comp. i. 44.

[k] xlix. 8, comp. xlvi. 21, l. 27, 31, xlviii. 44, vi. 15, x. 15.

[l] xlix. 20 repeated l. 45. חשב מַחֲשָׁבוֹת occurs more in Jeremiah than in any other Book; xi. 19, xviii. 11, 18, xxix. 11, xlix. 30.

also, whole verses are repeated in these prophecies[m].

Out of 16 verses of which the prophecy of Jeremiah against Edom consists, four are identical with those of Obadiah; a fifth embodies a verse of Obadiah's; of the eleven which remain, ten have some turns of expression or idioms, more or fewer, which recur in Jeremiah, either in these prophecies against foreign nations, or in his prophecies generally. Now it would be wholly improbable that a prophet, selecting verses out of the prophecy of Jeremiah, should have selected precisely those which contain none of Jeremiah's characteristic expressions; whereas it perfectly fits in with the supposition that Jeremiah interwove verses of Obadiah with his own prophecy, that in verses so interwoven there is not one expression which occurs elsewhere in Jeremiah.

One expression, which has been cited as an exception, if it is more than an accidental coincidence, the rather confirms this. Obadiah, in one of the earlier verses which Jeremiah has not here employed, says, *To the border have sent thee forth the men of thy covenant; the men of thy peace have deceived thee, have prevailed against thee; thy bread* [i. e. the men of thy bread, they who ate bread with thee] *have laid a snare under thee.* In the middle of this threefold retribution for their misdealing to their brother Judah, there occur the words, *the men of thy peace*, which are probably taken from a Psalm of David[n]. But the word *hishshiucha*, "*have deceived thee*," corresponds to the word *hishshiecha*[o] in v. 3. "*deceived thee* hath the pride of thy heart." The deceit on the part of their allies was the fruit and consequence of their self-deceit through the pride of their own heart. The verse in Obadiah then stands in connection with the preceding, and it is characteristic of Obadiah to make one part of his prophecy bear upon another, to shew the connection of thoughts and events by the connection of words. The taunting words against Zedekiah, which Jeremiah puts into the mouth of the women left in the house, when they should be brought before the king of Babylon's princes, *Thy friends*, lit. *the men of thy peace, have set thee on, hissithuca*[p], *and have prevailed against thee*, may very probaby be a reminiscence of the words of Obadiah (although only the words, *men of thy peace*, are the same): but they stand in no connection with any other words in Jeremiah, as those of Obadiah do with the previous words.

The prophecy of Jeremiah in which he incorporated these words of Obadiah, itself also speaks of the destruction of Jerusalem as still future. For he says to Edom[q], *Lo! they whose judgment was not to drink the cup, shall indeed drink it; and shalt thou be unpunished? Thou shalt not be unpunished; for thou shalt indeed drink it.* It is plainly wrong (as even our own Version has done) to render the self-same expression *shatho yishtu* as past, in the first place, *have assuredly drunken*, and as future in the second, *ki shatho tishteh*[r], *for thou shalt surely drink of it.* Since they must be future in the second place, so must they also in the first. Jeremiah too elsewhere contrasts, as future, God's dealings with His own people and with the nations, in this self-same form of words. [s] *Thus saith the Lord of hosts, Ye shall certainly drink; for lo! I begin to bring evil on the city which is called by My Name, and shall ye be utterly unpunished? Ye shall not be unpunished; for I will call for a sword upon all the inhabitants of the earth, saith the Lord of hosts.* The form of words, [t] *hinneh bair anochi mechel leharea'*, in itself requires, at least a proximate future, (for *hinneh* with a participle always denotes a future, nearer or further) and the words themselves were spoken in the fourth year of Jehoiakim.

In that same fourth year of Jehoiakim, Jeremiah received from God the command to write in that roll which Jehoiakim burnt when a little of it had been read to him[u], *all the words that I have spoken unto thee against Israel and against Judah and against all the nations, from the day I spake unto thee, from the days of Josiah even unto this* day. After Jehoiakim had burnt the roll, that same collection was renewed, at God's command, *with many like words*[v]. Now immediately upon this, follows, in the book of Jeremiah, the collection of prophecies against the foreign nations, and in this collection three contain some notice that they were written in that 4th year of Jehoiakim, and only the two last, those against Elam and Babylon, which may have been added to the collection, bear any later date. The prophecy against Babylon is at its close marked as wholly by itself[w]. For Seraiah is bidden, when he had come to Babylon, and had *made an end of reading the book*, to *bind a stone* upon it, and *cast it into the Euphrates*, and say, *Thus shall Babylon sink, and shall not rise again from the evil which I bring upon her.* These chapters then as to Babylon, although connected with the preceding in that they are prophecies against enemies of God's people, are marked as in one way detached from them, *a book*[x] by themselves. And in conformity with this, they are stated, in the beginning, to have been written in the 4th year of Zedekiah. In like way, the prophecy against Elam,

[m] xlix. 18 repeated xlix. 33, l. 40, li. 43; and xlix. 22 in xlviii. 40, 1.
[n] Ps. xli. 10.
[o] השיאך, השיאוך.
[p] הסיתוך Jer. xxxviii. 22.
[q] xlix. 12.
[r] שתו ישתו, כי שתו תשתה.
[s] xxv. 28, 29.
[t] הנה בעיר ־אנכי מחל להרע.
[u] xxv. 1.
[v] xxxvi. 1, 2.
[w] Jer. li. 60–4.
[x] Ib. 60, 63.

which was uttered in the beginning of the reign of Zedekiah, was occasioned probably by misdeeds of that then savage people, serving, as they did, in the army of the Chaldees[y] against Jerusalem, when Nebuchadnezzar took Jehoiakim captive to Babylon. It is distinguished from the earlier prophecies, in that Elam was no inveterate enemy of God's people, and the instrument of his chastisement was not to be Babylon.

Those earlier prophecies (ch. xlvi–xlix. 33.) against Egypt, Philistia (including Tyre and Zidon), Moab, Ammon, Edom, Damascus, Kedar and the kingdoms of Hazor, all have this in common; 1) that they are directed against old and inveterate enemies of God's people; 2) they all threaten destruction from one source, the North[z], or Nebuchadnezzar himself, either naming[a] or describing him[b]. They are then probably one whole, a book of the visitations of God upon His enemies through Nebuchadnezzar. But the first of the two prophecies against Egypt relates to the expedition of Pharaoh Necho against Assyria, the utter overthrow of whose vast army at the Euphrates he foretells. That overthrow took place at Carchemish in the fourth year of Jehoiakim[c]. The next prophecy against Egypt relates to the expedition of Nebuchadnezzar against it, which followed immediately on the defeat of Pharaoh[d]. The third prophecy against Philistia was, *before Pharoah smote Gaza*[e]; but this was probably on his march against Assyria in that same fourth year of Jehoiakim, before his own power was broken for ever.

But since the prophecy of Obadiah was anterior to that of Jeremiah, it was probably long anterior to it. For Jeremiah probably incorporated it, in order to shew that there was yet a fulfillment in store for it. And with this it agrees, that Obadiah does employ in his prophecy language of Balaam, of a Psalm of David, of Joel and Amos, and of no later prophet. This could not have been otherwise, if he lived at the time, when he is placed in the series of the Minor Prophets. Had he lived later, it is inconceivable that, using of set purpose, as he does, language of Joel and Amos, his prophecy should exhibit no trace of any other later writing. The expressions taken from the book of Joel are remarkable, considering the small extent of both books. Such are undoubtedly the phrases; *it*, Jerusalem, *shall be holiness, kodesh*[f]; *In mount Zion there shall be a remnant*[g]; *For near is the Day of the Lord*[h]; *I will return thy recompense upon thy head*[i], the phrase *yaddu goral*[k] for "cast lots." These are not chance idioms. They are not language of imagery. They are distinguished in no poetical or rhetorical manner from idioms which are not used. They are not employed, because they strike the senses or the imagination. One prophet does not borrow the imagery of another. They are part of the religious language of prophecy, in which when religious truth had once been embodied, the prophets handed it on from one generation to another. These words were like some notes of a loved and familiar melody, which brought back to the soul the whole strain, of which they were a part. *The Day of the Lord* having been described in such awful majesty by Joel, thenceforth the saying, *near is the Day of the Lord*, repeated in his own simple words, conveyed to the mind all those circumstances of awe, with which it was invested. In like way the two words, *it shall be holiness*, suggested all that fullness of the outpouring of God's Spirit, the sole Source of holiness, with which the words were associated in Joel; they are full of the Gospel promise, that the Church should be not holy only, but the depository of holiness, the appointed instrument through which God would diffuse it. Equally characteristic is that other expression; *In Mount Sion shall be a remnant.* It gives prominence to that truth, so contrary to flesh and blood, which S. Paul had to develop, that *all* were *not Israel* who were *of Israel*[l]. It presented at once the positive and negative side of God's mercies, that there would be *salvation in Mount Zion*, but of a *remnant* only. So, on the other side, the use of the idiom *mechamas achica Yaakob*, repeated but intensified from that of Joel, *mĕchamas benĕ Yehudah*, continued on the witness against that abiding sin for which Joel had foretold the desolation of Edom, *his violence toward his brother Jacob.*

The promise in Amos of the expansion of Jacob, *that they may inherit the residue of Edom, and all nations upon whom My Name is called*, is, in like way, the basis of the detailed promise of its expansion in all directions, E. W. N. S. which Obadiah, like Amos, begins with the promise, that the people of God should inherit Edom: *And the South shall inherit Mount Esau, and the plain*

[y] Is. xxii. 6, Ezek. xxxii. 24.
[z] Jer. xlvi. 10, 20, 24, xlvii. 2.
[a] Jer. xlvi. 2, 13, 26, xlix. 28, 30.
[b] Jer. xlviii. 40, xlix. 22.
[c] Jer. xlvi. 2.
[d] Ib. 13.
[e] xlvii. 1.
[f] והיה קדש Ob. 17. והיתה ירושלם קדש Joel iv. 17.
[g] ובהר ציון תהיה פלטה Ob. 17. כי בהר ציון ובירושלם תהיה פלטה Joel iii. 5.
[h] כי קרוב יום יי על כל הגוים Ob. 15. כי קרוב יום יי בעמק החרוץ Joel i. 15.
[i] גמלך ישוב בראשך Ob. 15. אשיב גמלכם בראשכם. Joel iv. 4. והשבתי גמלכם בראשכם iv. 7.
[k] ידו גורל Ob. 11, Joel iv. 3; else only in Nah. iii. 10. Elsewhere with גורל there are united ידה, השליך, הפיל, נתן, הטיל not ידד.
[l] Rom. ix. 6.

the Philistines. Amos, taking Edom as a specimen and type of those who hated God and His people, promises that they and all nations should become the inheritance of the Church. Obadiah, on the same ground, having declared God's sentence on Edom, describes how each portion of the people of God should be enlarged and overspread beyond itself.

While thus alluding to the words of Amos, Obadiah further embodies an expression of Balaam, to which Amos also refers. Balaam says, *Edom shall be an heritage* (yereshah), *Seir also shall be an heritage to his enemies; and Jacob shall do valiantly; and one out of Jacob shall have dominion, and shall destroy the remnant* (sarid) *out of the city.* The union of these two declarations of Balaam (one only of which had been employed by Amos) cannot be accidental. They lie in the two adjacent verses in each. *The house of Jacob shall be a fire, and the house of Joseph a flame, and the house of Esau stubble, and they shall burn them, and devour them; and there shall be no remnant* (sarid) *to the house of Esau; for the Lord hath spoken it; and the south shall inherit* (yereshu) *the mount of Esau.* In the fourth verse, also, Obadiah has an idiom from the prophecy of Balaam, which occurs nowhere besides; *strong is thy dwelling, and place* (*vesim kinnecha*) *in the rock thy nest.*[m] This infinitive here is a very vivid but anomalous construction. It cannot be by accident, that this idiom occurs in these two places alone in the Hebrew Scriptures.

This employment of prophetic language of earlier prophets is the more remarkable, from the originality and freshness of Obadiah's own diction. In his 21 verses he has several words which occur nowhere else[n]. They are mostly simple words and inflections of words in use. Still they were probably framed by the Prophet himself. One, who himself adds to the store of words in a language, has no occasion to borrow them of another. Obadiah adopts that other prophetic language, not as needing it to express his own meaning, but in order to give to it a fresh force and bearing.

But on the same ground, on which Obadiah employs the language of prophets who lived before him, he would have used the words of later prophets, had he lived later.

The framing of single words or forms is the least part of the originality of Obadiah's style. Vividness, connectedness, power, are characteristics of it. As it begins, so it continues and ends. It has no breaks, nor interruptions. Thought follows on thought, as wave rolls upon wave, but all marshalled to one end, marching on, column after column, to the goal which God hath appointed for them. Each verse grows out of that which was before it, and carries on its thought. The cadence of the words in the original is a singular blending of pathos and strength. The pathos of the cadence consists in a somewhat long sustained measure, in which the Prophet dwells on the one thought which he wishes to impress; the force, in the few brief words in which he sums up some sentence. That lengthened flow will have struck even an English reader; the conciseness can only be seen in Hebrew. Those 5 words, *how are Esau outsearched! outsought his secret places!* have been already alluded to. Other such instances are, *Ein tebunah bo* with which v. 7. closes; *gam attah ceachad mehem,* "thou too as one of them," v. 11; *caasher 'asitha, ye'aseh lac* after the long exhortation in v. 12–14. or the 3 words *vehaiu celo haiu,* which close the description in v. 16, 17. or those three which so wonderfully sum up the whole prophecy, *vehayethah ladonai hammeluchah, and the kingdom shall be the Lord's.* Even the repetition which occurs in the Prophet, adds to the same effect, as in the two brief words, *beyom nochro, beyom obdam, beyom zarah, beyom eidam, beyom eido,* with which he closes each clause of the exhortation against malicious joy in the calamity of their brother. The characteristic, vivid detail in description, and, in the midst of it, great conciseness without sameness, occurs throughout Obadiah.

It would then be the more strange, that a prophecy so brief and so connected as that of Obadiah should have been severed into two (one part of which is to belong to some earlier prophet, the other is to have been written after the destruction of Jerusalem), but that the motive of this disruption of the prophecy is apparent. "The oracle on Edom preserved under the name of Obadiah *can,*" says one[o], "in its present form, be of no earlier date than the Babylonish Captivity. The destruction and entire desolation of Jerusalem is here described; the prophet himself wrote among the exiles." It *cannot* be of any earlier date, according to this writer, because, in his belief, there *cannot* be any certain prediction of details of the future, or any knowledge of that future, beyond those dim anticipations which man's own conscience and the survey of God's ordinary Providence may suggest; a *cannot,* which presupposes another *cannot,* that God *cannot* reveal Himself to His creatures.

But then this writer also could not altogether escape the impression, that great part of this prophecy must belong to a period long before the captivity. The only way

[m] Num. xxiv. 21, Ob. 4.

[n] פרק, our "fork," where two ways part, v. 14, נבעו, v. 16, לעו v. 7, מזור v. 9, קֶטֶל v. 6, מצפוניך *searched out,* v. 6, are words peculiar in this sense to Obadiah: חגוי סלע v. 3 occurs only in Cant. ii. 14.

[o] Ewald Proph. i. 398.

of reconciling these contradictions, this *must* of external evidence, and this *cannot* of anti-doctrinal prejudice, was to divide in twain this living whole, and to assign to the earlier period such portions relating to Edom, as contained no allusion to the destruction of Jerusalem. This then is done. "Further investigation," the writer proceeds, "shews, that the later prophet employed a fragment of an earlier prophet as to Edom. More than half of what is now extant, i. e. v. 1–10. half of v. 17. and v. 18. by their contents, language, and coloring, indicate very clearly such an earlier prophet; and moreover, about the same time Jeremiah employed the earlier fragment, in that very much out of verses 1-9. recurs in Jeremiah, but nothing of the words which belong most visibly to the later prophet, 11–16, 19–21."

i. Now, plainly, as Jeremiah is not here to tell us, why he did incorporate in his prophecy certain verses, and did not refer to certain other verses of Obabiah, it is, in the last degree, rash to make a positive inference from the mere fact of his not employing those verses, that he had them not to employ. He does embody in his prophecy the five first verses of Obadiah, and there the correspondence between the two Prophets almost ceases. The *thought* of ver. 6, but not one word of it recurs in Jeremiah [p]; to ver. 7. there is no allusion whatever; of ver. 8. again, the thought is retained, but only *one word*, and that, in a form altogether different [q]. This eighth verse is the last in Obadiah, to which Jeremiah refers. Ewald then has to manufacture his "earlier prophet" out of those five first verses, which Jeremiah does embody; of other two, of which the thought only recurs in Jeremiah; and five more [r], to which there is, in Jeremiah, no allusion whatever; and having culled these ad libitum out of the whole chapter, he argues against the non-existence of the rest on the ground that Jeremiah does not employ them, whereas Jeremiah equally does not employ five of those, the existence of which at that same time Ewald acknowledges, and to two others Jeremiah alludes but very distantly. Since Jeremiah's not alluding to five of these verses, does not prove, according to Ewald, that they did not then exist, neither does his not employing the remainder prove it as to them.

ii. Jeremiah assigns no ground for the punishment of Edom, except his pride; nor does he, in any of those prophecies as to those lesser nations, foretell anything as to the future of Judah. This was not assigned to him, as his subject here. He does in the prophecies against Egypt and Babylon; for those were the great dynasties, on whom, in human eyes, the existence of Judah depended. There he fortells, that God would *make a full end of* all *the nations whither* He had *driven* them, but not *of Jacob* His *servant* [s]. The future lot of Judah, as a whole, did not depend on those little nations. It may be on this ground, that Jeremiah foretells *their* destruction and the restoration of Moab and Ammon [t], and is silent as to Judah. Again, the immediate punishment of all these petty nations through Nebuchadnezzar was the subject of Jeremiah's prophecy, not ulterior suffering at the hands of Judah. Now these subjects, the *violence* of Esau against his *brother Jacob*, as the ground of Edom's punishment [u], the future enlargement of Jacob [v], and an ulterior retribution on Edom [w] through Judah, occupy most of those verses of Obadiah, to which there is no allusion in Jeremiah. This accounts (if there were any need to account for it) for the absence of allusion to almost all of Obadiah to which Jeremiah does not allude, both as to the part which Ewald accounts for in *his* way, and as to most of that part which he leaves unaccounted for.

But altogether, it must be said, that God's Prophets employ freely, as God taught them, what they do employ of the former Prophets. They do not copy them in a mechanical way, as if they were simply re-writing a work which lay before them, so that we should have to account for anything which they did not think good to repeat. In making the like use of Isaiah's prophecy as to Moab, Jeremiah makes no reference to the five first verses.

iii. So far from "writing among the exiles," Obadiah implies that the Captivity had not yet commenced. He speaks of Judah and Benjamin, as in their own land, and foretells that they shall enlarge themselves on all sides. Hosea and Amos had, at that time, prophesied the final destruction of the *kingdom* [x] of Israel and the dispersion [y] of the ten tribes. In conformity with this, Obadiah foretells to the two tribes, that they should occupy the vacated places of the land of promise. In contrast with this enlargement of Judah and Benjamin, he speaks of those already in captivity, and prophesies their restoration. He speaks of two bodies of present exiles, "the captivity of *this* host of the children of Israel," "the captivity of Jerusalem which is at Sepharad." Of these he probably says [z], *The captivity of this host of the children of Israel which* are among *the Canaanites as far as Zarephath, and the captivity of Jerusalem which* is *in Sepharad, shall possess*

[p] Jer. xlix. 10.
[q] *Shall I not destroy* (האבדתי) *the wise?* Ob. 8; *Is wisdom perished?* אבדה Jer. xlix. 7.
[r] 7–9, 10, 17, 18.
[s] Jer. xlvi. 27, 8; see also l. 4–8, 19, 20, 28, 33, 4, li. 5, 6, 10, 45.
[t] xlviii. 47, xlix. 6.
[u] 10–14. In 15, 16, Obadiah, having rehearsed the offence, repeats the sentence.
[v] 17–21.
[w] 18.
[x] Hos. i. 4, Am. v. 27. ab. p. 201, vi. 7, ix. 9.
[y] Hos. ix. 17. ab. pp. 61, 2; Am. ix. 9.
[z] ver. 20.

the cities of the South. Both these sets of captives must have been limited in number. Those *of Jerusalem at Sepharad* or Sardis[a], the capital of the Lydian empire, could only have been such as were exported by means of the slave trade. The only public settlement of Jews there, was in times long subsequent, about B. C. 200, when Antiochus the Great, in order to check the seditions in Lydia and Phrygia, "[b] removed thither at much cost 2000 Jewish families out of Mesopotamia and Babylonia, with their goods," on account of their tried faithfulness and zealous service to his forefathers. This removal, accompanied with grants of land, exemption from tribute for ten years, personal and religious protection, *was* a continuation of the commenced *dispersion;* it was not a *captivity.* They were the descendants of those who might have returned to their country, if they would. They were in the enjoyment of all the temporal benefits, for which their forefathers had bartered their portion in their own land. There was nothing peculiar why they should be singled out as the objects of God's promise. Jews were then dispersing everywhere, to be the future disciples or persecutors of the Gospel in all lands. Seleucus Nicator, a century before, had found Jews in Asia and Lower Syria, and had given them like privileges with the Macedonians and Greeks whom he settled there. Jews had shared his wars. Alexander had, at Alexandria, bestowed like privileges on the Egyptian Jews[c]. In such times, then, there was no *captivity at Sepharad;* no Lydian empire; nothing to distinguish the Jews there, from any others who remained willingly expatriated.

On the other side, the place which the Prophet assigns to those captives on their return is but a portion of Judah, *the cities of the South,* which he does not represent as unpeopled. In like way, whether the words as to Israel are rendered, "*which* are among *the Canaanites as far as Zarephath,*" or, "shall possess *the Canaanites as far as Zarephath,*" in either case the Prophet must be speaking of a very limited number. Had he been speaking in reference to the ten tribes or their restoration, he would not have assigned their territory, "Ephraim, Samaria, Gilead," to the two tribes, nor would he have assigned to them so small a tract. This limited number of captives exactly agrees with the state of things, supposing Obadiah to have lived, when, according to his place in the Canon, he did live, near the time of Joel. For Joel denounces God's judgments on Tyre, Zidon and Philistia for selling unto the Grecians the children of Judah and Jerusalem. These captives, of whom Obadiah speaks, were some probably yet unsold, at Sarepta, and some at Sepharad or Sardis among the Grecians. On the other hand, it is inconceivable that Obadiah would have contrasted the present captivity, "*this* captivity of the children of Israel," "the captivity of Jerusalem which is in Sepharad," with Judah and Benjamin in their ancient possessions, had Judah and Benjamin been, when he wrote, themselves in captivity in Babylon, or that he would have prophesied concerning some little fragment of Israel, that it should be restored, and would have passed over the whole body of the ten tribes, if, when he prophesied, it had been in captivity. Nor is there again any likelihood, that by "this captivity of Jerusalem in Sepharad," Obadiah means any captives, among whom he himself was, (which is the whole ground-work of this theory of Ewald) for, in that case, he would probably have addressed the consolation and the promise of return *to* them (as do the other prophets) and not have spoken *of* them only.

A few years hence, and this theory will be among the things which have been. The connection of thought in Obadiah is too close, the characteristics of his style occur too uniformly throughout his brief prophecy, to admit of its being thus dislocated. Nowhere, throughout his prophecy, can one word or form be alleged, of which it can even be said, that it was used more frequently in later Hebrew. All is one original, uniform, united whole.

"Obadiah," says Hugh of S. Victor, "is simple in language, manifold in meaning; few in words, abundant in thoughts, according to that, 'the wise man is known by the fewness of his words.' He directeth his prophecy, according to the letter, against Edom; allegorically, he inveighs against the world; morally, against the flesh. Bearing an image of the Saviour, he hinteth at His Coming Through Whom the world is destroyed, through Whom the flesh is subdued, through Whom freedom is restored." "Among all the prophets," says another[d], "he is the briefest in number of words; in the grace of mysteries he is their equal."

[a] "CPaRaD occurs three times in Cuneiform Inscriptions in a list of Asiatic nations after ARMIN between KaTaPaTUK (Cappadocia) and IaUNA (Ionia), Niebuhr Reiseb. T. ii. Tab. xxxi. l. 12. p. 152, in the Epitaph of Darius at Nakshi Rustam l. 28. before Ionia, in Col. 1 of the Inscription of Bisutun, l. 15." After it had been decyphered, De Sacy identified the CPRD of the Inscriptions with the "Sepharad" of Obadiah. (Burnouf, Mémoire sur deux Inscriptions Cunéiformes, 1836. p. 147.) Then Lassen (Hall. Encyclop. v. Persepolis, S. iii. Vol. 17. p. 36.) identified CRPD with SaRDis, the Greeks omitting the *v* or *ph*, and adding, according to their wont, their termination to the Asiatic name. S. Jerome's Hebrew instructor told him that it meant the "Bosphorus:" but this *may* have been his own conjecture, the letters "sphr" occurring in both; and if he took in the Prepos. ב, he had "bsphr" as the ground of his conjecture, taking in the ב which he ought not, and leaving out the ד which he ought to have accounted for.

[b] Jos. Ant. xii. 3. 4.

[c] Josephus (Ant. xii. 3. 1.) contrasts them with the ἐνοικισθεῖσιν.

[d] Isid. lib. alleg. S. Scr.

OBADIAH.

Before CHRIST cir. 587.

1 *The destruction of Edom,* 3 *for their pride,* 10 *and for their wrong unto Jacob.* 17 *The salvation and victory of Jacob.*

THE vision of Obadiah.
Thus saith the Lord
GOD [a]concerning Edom;
[b]We have heard a rumor
from the LORD, and an
ambassador is sent among
the heathen, Arise ye, and
let us rise up against her
in battle.

[a] Isai. 21. 11. & 34. 5. Ezek. 25. 12, 13, 14. Joel 3. 19. Mal. 1. 3.
[b] Jer. 49. 14, &c.

VER. 1. *The vision of Obadiah,* i. e. of *the worshiper of God.* The Prophet would be known only by that which his name imports, that he worshiped God. He tells us in this double title, through whom the prophecy came, and from Whom it came. His name authenticated the prophecy to the Jewish Church. Thenceforth he chose to remain wholly hidden. He entitles it *a vision,* as the prophets were called *seers*[1], although he relates, not the vision which he saw, but its substance and meaning. Probably the future was unfolded to him in the form of sights spread out before his mind, of which he spoke in words given to him by God. His language consists of a succession of pictures, which he may have seen, and, in his picture-language, described. "[2] As prophecy is called *the word,* because God spake to the prophets within, so it is called *vision,* because the prophet saw, with the eyes of the mind and by the light wherewith they are illumined, what God willeth to be known to them." The name expresses also the certainty of their knowledge. "[3] Among the organs of our senses, sight has the most evident knowledge of those things which are the object of our senses. Hence the contemplation of the things which are true is called *vision,* on account of the evidence and assured certainty. On that ground the prophet was called *seer.*"

Thus saith the Lord God concerning Edom. This second title states, that the whole which follows is from God. What immediately follows is said in Obadiah's own person; but all, whether so spoken or directly in the Person of God, was alike the word of God. God spake in or by the prophets, in both ways, since [4] *prophecy came not by the will of man, but holy men of God spake* as they were *moved by the Holy Ghost.* Obadiah, in that he uses, in regard to his whole prophecy, words which other prophets use in delivering a direct message from God, ascribes the whole of his prophecy to God, as immediately as other prophets did any words which God commanded them to speak. The words are a rule for all prophecy, that all comes directly from God.

We have heard a rumor, rather, *a report;* lit. *a hearing, a thing heard,* as Isaiah says[5], *Who hath believed our report?* *A report* is certain or uncertain, according to the authority from whom it comes. This *report* was certainly true, since it was *from the Lord.* By the plural, *we,* Obadiah may have associated with himself, either other prophets of his own day as Joel and Amos, who, with those yet earlier, as Balaam and David, had prophesied against Edom, or the people, for whose sakes God made it known to him. In either case, the Prophet does not stand alone for himself. He hears with "the goodly company of the Prophets;" and the people of God hear in him, as Isaiah says again[6], *that which I have heard from the Lord of hosts, the God of Israel, have I declared unto you.*

And an ambassador is sent among the heathen. The *ambassador* is any agent, visible or invisible, sent by God. Human powers, who wish to stir up war, send human messengers. All things stand at God's command, and whatever or whomsoever He employs, is *a messenger* from Him. He uses our language to us. He may have employed an angel, as He says[7], *He sent evil angels among them,* and as, through the permission given to *a lying spirit*[8], He executed His judgments on Ahab, of his own free will believing the evil spirit, and disbelieving Himself. So [9] *God sent an evil spirit between Abimelech and the men of Shechem,* allowing His rebellious spirit to bring about the punishment of evil men, by inflaming yet more the evil passions, of which they were slaves. Evil spirits, in their malice and rebellion, while stirring up the lust of conquest, are still God's *messengers,* in that He overrules them; as, to St. Paul[10], *the thorn in the flesh, the messenger of Satan to buffet him,* was still the gift of God. *It was given me,* he says.

Arise ye and let us rise. He who rouseth them, says, *Arise ye,* and they quickly echo the words, *and let us arise.* The will of God is fulfilled at once. While eager to accomplish their own ends, they fulfill, the more, the purpose of God. Whether the first agent be man's own passions, or the evil spirit who

[1] 1 Sam. ix. 9.
[2] Rib,
[3] Comm. in Is. § 8. ap. S. Basil. i. 383.
[4] 2 S. Pet. i. 21.
[5] liii. 1.
[6] xxi. 10.
[7] Ps. lxxviii. 49.
[8] 1 Kings xxii. 21–23.
[9] Jud. ix. 23.
[10] 2 Cor. xii. 7.

Before CHRIST cir. 587.

2 Behold, I have made thee small among the heathen: thou art greatly despised.

3 ¶ The pride of thine heart hath deceived thee, thou that dwellest in the clefts [c] of the rock, whose

Before CHRIST cir. 587.

c 2 Kings 14. 7.

stirs them, the impulse spreads from the one or the few to the many. But all catch the spark, cast in among them. The summons finds a ready response. *Arise*, is the command of God, however given; *let us arise*, is the eager response of man's avarice or pride or ambition, fulfilling impetuously the secret will of God; as a tiger, let loose upon man by man, fulfills the will of its owner, while sating its own thirst for blood. So Isaiah hears[1] *the noise of a multitude in the mountains, like as of a great people, a tumultuous noise of the kingdoms of nations gathered together*. The Medes and Persians thought at that time of nothing less, than that they were instruments of the One God, Whom they knew not. But Isaiah continues; *The Lord of hosts mustereth the host of the battle;* and, when it was fulfilled, Cyrus saw and owned it[2].

2. *Behold, I have made thee small.* God, having declared His future judgments on Edom, assigns the first ground of those judgments. Pride was the root of Edom's sin, then envy; then followed exultation at his brother's fall, hard-heartedness and bloodshed. All this was against the disposition of God's Providence for him. God had *made* him *small*, in numbers, in honor, in territory. Edom was a wild mountain people. It was strongly guarded in the rock-girt dwelling, which God had assigned it. Like the Swiss or the Tyrolese of old, or the inhabitants of Mount Caucasus now, it had strength for resistance through the advantages of its situation, not for aggression, unless it were that of a robber-horde. But lowness, as men use it, is the mother either of lowliness or pride. A low estate, acquiesced in by the grace of God, is the parent of lowliness; when rebelled against, it generates a greater intensity of pride than greatness, because that pride is against nature itself and God's appointment. The pride of human greatness, sinful as it is, is allied to a natural nobility of character. Copying pervertedly the greatness of God, the soul, when it receives the Spirit of God, casts off the slough, and retains its nobility transfigured by grace. The conceit of littleness has the hideousness of those monstrous combinations, the more hideous, because unnatural, not a corruption only but a distortion of nature. Edom never attempted anything of moment by itself. *Thou art greatly despised.* Weakness, in itself, is neither despicable nor *despised.* It is despised only, when it vaunts itself to be, what it is not. God tells Edom what, amid its pride, it was in itself, *despicable;* what it would thereafter be, *despised*[3].

3. *The pride of thy heart hath deceived thee.* Not the strength of its mountain-fastnesses, strong though they were, deceived Edom, but *the pride of his heart.* That strength was but the occasion which called forth the *pride.* Yet it was strong in its abode. God, as it were, admits it to them. *Dweller in the clefts of the rocks, the loftiness of his habitation.* "The whole Southern country of the Edomites," says S. Jerome, "from Eleutheropolis to Petra and Selah (which are the possessions of Esau), hath minute dwellings[4] in caves; and on account of the oppressive heat of the sun, as being a southern province, hath underground cottages." Its inhabitants, whom Edom expelled[5], were hence called Horites, i. e. dwellers in caves. Its chief city was called Selah or Petra, "rock." It was a city single of its kind amid the works of man. "[6] *The eagles* placed their nests in the rocky caves at a height of several hundred feet above the level of the valley." "[6] The power of the conception which would frame a range of mountain-rocks into a memorial of the human name, which, once of noble name and high bepraised, sought, through might of its own, to clothe itself with the imperishableness of the eternal Word, is here the same as in the contemporary monuments of the temple-rocks of Elephantine or at least those of the Egyptian Thebes." The ornamental buildings, so often admired by travelers, belong to a later date. Those nests in the rocks, piled over one another, meeting you in every recess, lining each fresh winding of the valleys, as each opened on the discoverer[7],

1 Is. xiii. 4.

2 Ezr. i. 1, 2.

3 בזוי is at once a passive participle and an adjective.

4 habitatiunculas.

5 Deut. ii. 12.

6 Schubert, Reise, ii. 428. ed. 2.

7 "The most striking feature of the place consists, not in the fact that there are occasional excavations and sculptures, like those above described, but in the innumerable multitude of such excavations along the whole coast of perpendicular rocks, adjacent to the main area, and in all the lateral vallies and chasms." Rob. ii. 139. "What remains are the mere débris of what the precipices once presented to view.—Many of the excavations are so difficult to reach and some are such mere wall or surface, that it appears as if the whole front of the rock, to a considerable depth, had fallen. The conduits, cisterns, flights of steps scattered over the rocks and among the precipices, indicate a larger number of rock-dwellings than remain now, very great as that number is.—As he pointed up two or three ravines, counting the holes in a single

Before CHRIST cir. 587.

habitation *is* high; [d] that saith in his heart, Who shall bring me down to the ground?

[d] Isai. 14. 13, 14, 15. Rev. 18. 7.

often at heights, where (now that the face of the rock and its approach, probably hewn in it, have crumbled away[1]) you can scarcely imagine how human foot ever climbed[2], must have been the work of the first hardy mountaineers, whose feet were like the chamois. Such habitations imply, not an uncivilized, only a hardy, active, people. In those narrow valleys, so scorched by a southern sun, they were at once the coolest summer dwellings, and, amid the dearth of fire-wood, the warmest in winter. The dwellings of the living and the sepulchres of the dead were, apparently, hewn out in the same soft red sandstone-rock, and perhaps some of the dwellings of the earlier rock-dwellers were converted into graves by the Nabatæans and their successors who lived in the valley. The central space has traces of other human habitations. "[3]The ground is covered with heaps of hewn stones, foundations of buildings and vestiges of paved streets, all clearly indicating that a large city once existed here." "[4]They occupy two miles in circumference, affording room in an oriental city for 30, or 40,000 inhabitants." Its theatre held "[5]above 3000." Probably this city belonged altogether to the later, Nabatæan, Roman, or Christian times. Its existence illustrates the extent of the ancient city of the rock. The whole space, rocks and valleys, imbedded in the mountains which girt it in, lay invisible even from the summit of Mount Hor[6]. So nestled was it in its rocks, that an enemy could only know of its existence, an army could only approach it, through treachery. Two known approaches[7] only, from E. and W., enter into it. The least remarkable is described as lying amid "[8]wild fantastic mountains," "rocks in towering masses," "over steep and slippery passes," or "winding in recesses below." Six[9] hours of such passes led to the Western side of Petra. The Greeks spoke of it as two days' journey from their "world[10]." Approach how you would, the road lay through defiles[11]. The Greeks knew but of "[12]one ascent to it, and that," (as they deemed) "made by hand;" [that from the E.] The Mohammedans now think the Sik or chasm, the two miles of ravine by which it is approached, supernatural, made by the rod of Moses when he struck the rock[13]. Demetrius, "the Besieger[14]," at the head of 8000 men, (the 4000 infantry selected

rock-face, and reminded me, how small a proportion these bore to the whole, I was indeed astonished." Miss Mart. Eastern Life, iii. 2, 3. "I do not doubt that by calculation of all in the outlying ravines, you might count up thousands, but in the most populous part that I could select, I could not number in one view more than fifty, and generally much fewer. It is these immense ramifications, rather than their concentrated effect, that is remarkable; and this, of course, can no more be seen in one view, than all the streets of London." Stanley, 88.

[1] Martin. ab. note 5. She speaks also of "short and odd staircases, twisting hither and thither among the rocks," iii. 19. "little flights of steps scattered over the slopes." ii. 319. "Wherever your eyes turn along the excavated sides of the rocks, you see steps often leading to nothing, or to something which has crumbled away; often with their first steps worn away, so that they are now inaccessible," Stanley, 91. "the thousand excavations" beyond, Ib. 90. "There [in the Sik] they are most numerous, the rock is honey-combed with cavities of all shapes and sizes." Ib. 91.

[2] "Had then the ancient builders of these rock-works wings like the eagle, with which they raised themselves to those perpendicular precipices?" "Who now, even with the feet of the chamois, could climb after them?" V. Schubert, ii. 429. Miss Martineau uses the same image of wings, Eastern Life, ii. 320, iii. 20.

[3] Burckhardt, Syr. p. 427. "On the left side of the river," he adds, "is a rising ground extending westward for nearly ¼ of an hour, entirely covered with similar remains. In the right bank, where the ground is more elevated, ruins of the same description are also seen."

[4] Robins. ii. 136.

[5] 3000. Burckhardt, Ib. "more than 3000." Rob. ii. 134.

[6] Stanley, 87. "Petra itself is entirely shut out by the intervening rocks.—The great feature of the mountains of Edom is the mass of red bald-headed sandstone rocks, intersected, not by valleys but by deep seams. In the heart of these rocks, itself invisible, lies Petra." See Woodcut.

[7] In regard to the brook of Wadi Musa, Robinson says, "no one could tell in what direction the waters, when swollen, find their way through the cliffs. This only is certain that the Wady does not, as Wady Musa, extend down to the Arabah." ii. 137. Dr. Wilson (1847) says, "the water found a subterraneous exit by the passage through the rocks on the W. side of the valley, through which they now flow." Lands, &c. i. 306. Any way, it was a passage impassable by man.

[8] Martineau, ii. 317, 8. She continues, "A little further on we stopped in a hollow of the hills.—Our path, our very narrow path, lay over these whitish hills, now up, now down, and then and then again we were slipping and jerking down slopes of gaudy rock. For nearly an hour longer we were descending the pass, down we went and still down, at length we came upon the platform above the bed of the torrent; near which stands the only edifice in Petra." Ib. 319, 20.

[9] Ib. ii. 316–19.

[10] τῆς οἰκουμένης. "The place was strong in the extreme, but unwalled, and two days journey, &c." Diod. Sic. xix. 95.

[11] See the accounts in Burckhardt, Syria, 421. Laborde, c. 8–10. Eng. Tr. Lindsay, pp. 220–30. Irby and M. c. 8. Rob. ii. 107. Stanley, 87, 98.

[12] Diod. Sic. xix. 97. "The corrosion of the surface of the rock by time and weather has so much the appearance of architectural intention, that it is at first difficult in Petra itself to distinguish the worn from the chiselled face of the precipices." Mart. ii. 317. "One striking feature of the whole scenery is, that not merely the excavations and buildings, but the rocks themselves are in a constant state of mouldering decay. You can scarcely tell where excavation begins or decay ends." Stanley, 88.

[13] Stanley, 89.

[14] Poliorcetes.

Before CHRIST cir. 587.

4 [e]Though thou exalt
thyself as the eagle, and
though thou [f]set thy nest
among the stars, thence
will I bring thee down,
saith the LORD.

e Job 20. 6. Jer. 49. 16. & 51. 53. Amos 9. 2.
f Hab. 2. 9.

for their swiftness of foot from the whole army[1]) made repeated assaults on the place, but "[2]those within had an easy victory from its commanding height." "[3]A few hundred men might defend the entrance against a large army." Its width is described as from 10 to 30 feet[4], "[5]a rent in a mountain-wall, a magnificent gorge, a mile and a half long, winding like the most flexible of rivers, between rocks almost precipitous, but that they overlap and crumble and crack, as if they would crash over you. The blue sky only just visible above. The valley opens, but contracts again. Then it is honey-combed with cavities of all shapes and sizes. Closing once more, it opens in the area of Petra itself, the torrent-bed passing now through absolute desolation and silence, though strewn with the fragments which shew that you once entered on a splendid and busy city, gathered along in the rocky banks, as along the quays of some great Northern river." Beyond this immediate rampart of rocks, there lay between it and the Eastern Empires that vast plateau, almost unapproachable by an enemy who knew not its hidden artificial reservoirs of waters. But even the entrance gained, what gain beside, unless the people and its wealth were betrayed to a surprise? Striking as the rock-girt Petra was, a gem in its mountain-setting, far more marvelous was it, when, as in the Prophet's time, the rock itself was Petra. Inside the defile, an invader would be outside the city yet. He might himself become the besieged, rather than the besieger. In which of these eyries along all those ravines were the eagles to be found? From which of those lairs might not Edom's lion-sons burst out upon them? Multitudes gave the invaders no advantage in scaling those mountain-sides, where, observed themselves by an unseen enemy, they would at last have to fight man to man. What a bivouac were it, in that narrow spot, themselves encircled by an enemy everywhere, anywhere, and visibly nowhere, among those thousand caves, each larger cave, may be, an ambuscade! In man's sight Edom's boast was well-founded; but what before God?

That saith in his heart. The heart has its own language, as distinct and as definite as that formed by the lips, mostly deeper, often truer. It needeth not the language of the lips, to offend God. As He answers the heart which seeks Him, so also He replies in displeasure to the heart which despises Him. *Who shall bring me down to the earth?* Such is the language of all self-sufficient security. "Can Alexander fly?" answered the Bactrian chief from another Petra. On the second night he was prisoner or slain[6]. Edom probably, under his Who? included God Himself, Who to him was the God of the Jews only. Yet men now too include God in their defiance, and scarcely veil it from themselves by speaking of "fortune" rather than God; or, if of a coarser sort, they do not even veil it, as in that common terrible saying, "He fears neither God nor devil." God answers his thought;

4. *Though thou exalt* thyself [or, thy nest] *like the eagle.* The eagle builds its nest in places well-nigh inaccessible to man. The Edomites were a race of eagles[7]. It is not the language of poetry or exaggeration; but is poetic, because so true. *And though thou set thy nest in the stars.* This is men's language, strange as it is. "[8]I shall touch the stars with my crown;" "I shall strike the stars with my lofty crown;" "since I have touched heaven with my lance." As Job says[9], *Though his excellency mount up to the heavens and his head reacheth unto the clouds*, yet *he shall perish forever, like his own dung.* And Isaiah to the king of Babylon, the type of Anti-Christ and of the Evil one[10], *Thou hast said in thy heart, I will exalt my throne above the stars of God; thy pomp is brought down to the grave, the worm is spread under thee, and the worms cover thee.* "[11]The heathen saw this. Æsop, when asked, what doeth God? said, 'He humbles the proud and exalts the humble.' And another[12], 'Whom morning's dawn beholdeth proud, The setting sun beholdeth bowed.'"

"[13]They who boast of being Christians, and are on that ground self-satisfied, promising themselves eternal life, and thinking that they need not fear Hell, because they are Christians and hold the faith of the Apostles, while their lives are altogether alien from

1 Diod. Ib. 96.
2 Schubert, Reise, ii. 428. ed. 2.
3 Burckhardt, 434. "The footing is extremely bad, and the passage so completely commanded from the sides, and so obstructed by huge masses of sandstone that had rolled down from above, that it was obvious a very small force would be capable of holding it against a great superiority of numbers." Captains Irby and M. c. 8.
4 Mart. iii. 11. "The width is not more than just sufficient for the passage of two horsemen abreast, the sides are in all parts perpendicular." I. & M. p. 127.
5 Stanley, 89–91.
6 Q. Curt. vii. 41. 2. L. Arr. iv. 18. 19.
7 See p. 235.
8 Ovid, Horace, Lysimachus in Plutarch de fort. Alex. L. ii. Lap.
9 xx. 6, 7.
10 xiv. 13, 11.
11 Lap.
12 Sen. Herc. fur. Ib.
13 Rib.

Before CHRIST cir. 587.

5 If [g]thieves came to thee, if robbers by night, (how art thou cut off!) would they not have stolen till they had enough? if the grape-gatherers came to thee, [h]would they not leave || *some* grapes?

6 How are *the things* of Esau searched out! *how* are his hidden things sought up!

g Jer. 49. 9.

h Deut. 24. 21. Is. 17. 6. & 24. 13.

|| Or, *gleanings?*

Christianity, are such Edomites, priding themselves because they dwell in clefts of the rocks. For it sufficeth not to believe what Christ and the Apostles taught, unless thou do what they commanded.—These spiritual Edomites, from a certain love or some fear of future torments, are moved by grief for sin, and give themselves to repentance, fastings, almsgiving, which is no other than to enter the clefts of the rocks; because they imitate the works of Christ and the holy Apostles who are called rocks, like those to whom John said[1], *O ye generation of vipers, who hath warned you to flee from the wrath to come?* But, since they have no humility, they become thereby the more inflated with pride, and the more of such works they do, the more pleasures they allow themselves, and become daily the prouder and the wickeder. *The pride* then *of* their *heart deceiveth* them, because they seem in many things to follow the deeds of the holy, and they fear no enemies, as though they *dwelt in clefts of the rocks.* They exalt their throne, in that, through the shadow of lofty deeds, they seem to have many below them, mount as high as they can, and place themselves, where they think they need fear no peril. But to them the Lord saith, *Though thou exalt thyself as the eagle,—thence will I bring thee down.* For, however exalted they be, and however they seem good and great, they are *brought down to the ground* and out from the caverns of the rocks, wherein they deemed that they dwelt securely, in that they lapse into overt shameful sin; whence all perceive, what they were then too, when they were thought to be righteous. And striking is it, that they are compared to *eagles.* For although the eagle fly aloft, yet thence it looks to the earth and the carcases and animals which it would devour, as Job writes of it[2], *She dwelleth and abideth upon the rock, upon the crag of the rock, and the strong place. From thence she seeketh the prey; her eyes behold afar off; her young ones also suck up blood, and where the slain are, there is she.* So these, while they pretend perfection, never turn their eyes away from earthly goods, always casting them on honors, or wealth, or pleasure, without which they count life to be no life. Well too is it called their *nest.* For, toil how they may, in seeking an assured, restful, security of life, yet what they build, is a nest made of hay and stubble, constructed with great toil, but lightly destroyed. This security of rest they lose, when they are permitted, by the just judgment of God, to fall into uncleanness, ambition or foulest sins, and are deprived of the glory which they unjustly gained, and *their folly becomes manifest to all.* Of such, among the Apostles, was the traitor Judas.—But the rich too and the mighty of this world, although they think that their possessions and what, with great toil, they have gained, when they have raised themselves above others, are most firm, it is but that nest which they have placed among the stars, soon to be dissipated by wind and rain."

5. *If thieves came to thee.* The Prophet describes their future punishment, by contrast with that which, as a marauding people, they well knew. Thieves and robbers spoil only for their petty end. They take what comes to hand; what they can, they carry off. Shortness of time, difficulty of transport, necessity of providing for a retreat, limit their plunder. When they have gorged themselves, they depart. *Their* plunder is limited. The *grape-gatherer* leaves gleanings. God promises to His own people, under the same image, that they should have a remnant left[3]. *Gleaning grapes shall be left in it.* It shall be, *as gleaning grapes, when the vintage is done.* The Prophet anticipates the contrast by a burst of sympathy. In the name of God, he mourns over the destruction which he fore-announces. He laments over the destruction, even of the deadly enemy of his people. *How art thou destroyed!* So the men of God are wont to express their amazement at the greatness of the destruction of the ungodly. [4]*How are they* brought *into desolation as in a moment!* [5]*How hath the oppressor ceased! How art thou fallen from heaven, O Lucifer son of the morning!* [6]*How is the hammer of the whole earth cut asunder and broken! how is Babylon become a desolation among the nations!* [7]*How is Sheshach taken! How is the praise of the whole earth surprised.*

6. *How are* the things *of Esau searched out!* lit. *How are Esau outsearched!* i. e. Esau, as a whole and in all its parts and in all its belongings, all its people and all its property,

[1] St. Matt. iii. 7. [2] Job xxxix. 28–30. [3] Is. xvii. 6, xxiv. 13.

[4] Ps. lxxiii. 19. [5] Is. xiv. 4, 12. [6] Jer. l. 23. [7] Ib. li. 41.

Before CHRIST cir. 587.

7 All the men of thy
confederacy have brought
thee *even* to the border:
†[1] the men that were at
peace with thee have deceived thee, *and* prevailed
against thee; † *they that*
eat thy bread have laid a

† Heb. *the men of thy peace.*
[1] Jer. 38. 22.
† Heb. the men *thy bread.*

one and all. The name *Esau* speaks of them as a whole; the plural verb, *are outsearched*, represents all its parts. The word signifies a diligent search and tracking out, as in Zephaniah[1], *I will search out Jerusalem with candles*, as a man holdeth a light in every dark corner, in seeking diligently some small thing which has been lost. *The hidden things*, i. e. his hidden treasures, *are sought up*. The enemy who should come upon him, should make no passing foray, but should abide there, seeking out of their holes in the rocks, themselves and their treasures. Petra, through its rocky ramparts, was well suited, as Nineveh in the huge circuit of its massive walls was well built, to be the receptacle of rapine. And now it was gathered, as all rapine is, first or last, for the spoiler. It was safe stored up there, to be had for the seeking. No exit, no way of escape. Edom, lately so full of malicious energy, so proud, should lie at the proud foot of its conqueror, as passive as the sheep in this large shamble, or as the inanimate hoards which they had laid up and which were now *tracked out*. Soon after Obadiah's prophecy, Judah, under Ahaz, lost again to Syria, Elath[2], which it had now under Uzziah recovered[3]. The Jews were replaced, it is uncertain whether by Edomites or by some tribe of Syrians[4]. If Syrians they were then friendly; if Edomites, Elath itself must, on the proximate captivity of Syria, have become the absolute possession of Edom. Either way, commerce again poured its wealth into Edom. To what end? to be possessed and to aggrandize Edom, thought her wealthy and her wise men; to be searched out and plundered, said the word of God. And it was so.

7. *All the men of thy confederacy have brought thee even to the border.* Destruction is more bitter, when friends aid in it. Edom had all along with unnatural hatred persecuted his *brother*, Jacob. So, in God's just judgment, its friends should be among its destroyers. Those *confederates* were probably Moab and Ammon, Tyre and Zidon, with whom they united to resist Nebuchadnezzar[5], and seduced Zedekiah to rebel, although Moab, Ammon, and Edom turned against him[6]. These then, he says, sent them *to the border*. "[7] So will they take the adversary's part, that, with him, they will drive thee forth from the borders, thrusting thee into captivity, to gain favor with the enemy." This they would do, he adds, through mingled treachery and violence. *The men of thy peace have deceived, have prevailed against thee.* As Edom turned peace with Judah into war, so those at peace with Edom should use deceit and violence against them, being admitted, perhaps, as allies within their borders, and then betraying the secret of their fastnesses to the enemy, as the Thessalians dealt toward the Greeks at Thermopylæ. It was to be no common deceit, no mere failure to help them. The men of *thy bread have laid a wound* (better, *a snare*[8]) *under thee.* Perhaps Obadiah thought of David's words[9], *mine own familiar friend, in whom I trusted, who did eat of my bread, hath lifted up his heel against me.* As they had done, so should it be done to them. *They that take the sword*, our Lord says[10], *shall perish by the sword;* so they who shew bad faith, are the objects of bad faith, as Isaiah says[11]. The proverb which says, "there is honor among thieves," attests how limited such mutual faith is. It lasts, while it seems useful. Obadiah's description relates to one and the same class, the allies of Edom; but it heightens as it goes on; not confederates only, but those confederates, friends; not friends only, but friends indebted to them, familiar friends; those joined to them through that tie, so respected in the East, in that they had eaten of their bread. Those banded with them should, with signs of friendship, conduct them to their border, in order to expel them; those at peace should prevail against them in war; those who ate their bread should requite them with a snare.

There is none understanding in him. The brief words comprise both cause and effect. Had Edom not been without understanding, he had not been thus betrayed; and when betrayed in his security, he was as one stupefied. Pride and self-confidence betray man to his fall; when he is fallen, self-confidence betrayed passes readily into despair. In the sudden shock, the mind collapses. Men do

[1] i. 12. [2] 2 Kings xiv. 6. [3] Ib. xiv. 22.

[4] The Hebrew text has ארומים, which the E. V. renders Syrians, but which is not the plural of ארם. The Kri corrects אדומים, which would indeed be the plural of אדום, but which is nowhere used for Edomites. It might have the meaning, however, that single "Edomites" (not, "the children of Edom" nationally) settled there. The Kri is, however, but a conjectural correction; the reading of the text has, in its favor, the general presumption everywhere in favor of the textual and harder reading. The LXX and Vulg. render "Edomites."

[5] Jer. xxvii. 3. [6] Zeph. ii. 8, Ezek. xxv.

[7] Theod.

[8] מזור from זור (a softer form probably of צור in a like meaning).

[9] Ps. xli. 9. [10] S. Matt. xxvi. 52.

[11] Is. xxxiii. 1. See ab. p. 182.

Before CHRIST cir. 587.

wound under thee : [k] *there*
is none understanding || in
him.
8 [l] Shall I not in that
day, saith the LORD, even
destroy the wise *men* out
of Edom, and understand-
ing out of the mount of
Esau ?
9 And thy mighty
[m] *men*, O [n] Teman, shall be
dismayed, to the end that

k Is. 19. 11, 12.
|| Or. *of it.*
l Job 5. 12, 13. Is. 29. 14. Jer. 49. 7.
m Ps. 76. 5. Amos 2. 16.
n Jer. 49. 7.

not use the resources which they yet have, because what they had overvalued, fails them. Undue confidence is the parent of undue fear. The Jewish historian relates, how, in the last dreadful siege, when the outer wall began to give way, "[1] fear fell on the tyrants, more vehement than the occasion called for. For, before the enemy had mounted, they were paralyzed, and ready to flee. You might see men, aforetime stouthearted and insolent in their impiety, crouching and trembling, so that, wicked as they were, the change was pitiable in the extreme.—Here especially one might learn the power of God upon the ungodly. For the tyrants bared themselves of all security, and, of their own accord, came down from the towers, where no force, but famine alone, could have taken them: For those three towers were stronger than any engines."

8. *Shall I not in that day even destroy the wise out of Edom?* It was then no common, no recoverable, loss of wisdom; for God, the Author of wisdom, had destroyed it. The heathen had a proverb, "whom God willeth to destroy, he first dements." So Isaiah foretells of Judah [2], *The wisdom of their wise shall perish, and the understanding of their prudent shall be hid.* Edom was celebrated of old for its wisdom. Eliphaz, the chief of Job's friends, the representative of human wisdom, was a Temanite [3]. A vestige of the name of the Shuhites, whence came another of his friends, probably still lingers among the mountains of Edom [4]. Edom is doubtless included among the *sons of the East* [5], whose wisdom is set as a counterpart to that of Egypt, the highest human wisdom of that period, by which that of Solomon would be measured. *Solomon's wisdom excelled the wisdom of all the children of the East country and all the wisdom of Egypt.* In Baruch, they are still mentioned among the chief types of human wisdom. [6] *It* (wisdom) *hath not been heard of in Chanaan, neither hath it been seen in Theman. The Agarenes that seek wisdom upon earth, the merchants of Meran and of Theman, the authors of fables and searchers-out of understanding, none of these have known the way of wisdom, or remember her paths.* Whence Jeremiah [7], in using these words of Obadiah, says, *Is wisdom no more in Teman? is counsel perished from the prudent? is their wisdom vanished?* He speaks, as though Edom were a known abode of human wisdom, so that it was strange that it was found there no more. He speaks of the Edomites *as prudent,* discriminating [8], full of judgment, and wonders that counsel should have *perished* from them. They had it eminently then, before it *perished.* They thought themselves wise; they were thought so; but God took it away at their utmost need. So He says of Egypt, [9] *I will destroy the counsel thereof. The counsel of the wise counsellors of Pharaoh is become brutish. How say ye unto Pharaoh, I am the son of the wise, the son of ancient kings? Where are they? who are thy wise? and let them tell thee now, and let them know, what the Lord of hosts hath purposed upon Egypt.* And of Judah, [10] *I will make void the counsel of Judah and Jerusalem in this place.* The men of the world think that they hold their wisdom and all God's natural gifts, independently of the Giver. God, by the events of His natural Providence, as here by His word, shews, through some sudden withdrawal of their wisdom, that it is His, not their's. Men wonder at the sudden failure, the flaw in the well-arranged plan, the one over-confident act which ruins the whole scheme, the over-shrewdness which betrays itself, or the unaccountable oversight. They are amazed that one so shrewd should overlook this or that, and think not that He, in Whose Hands are our powers of thought, supplied not just that insight, whereon the whole depended.

9. *And thy mighty, O Teman, shall be dismayed.* The heathen, more religiously than we, ascribed panic to the immediate action of one of their gods, or to Nature deified, Pan, i. e. the Universe: wrong as to the being whom they *ignorantly worshiped;* right, in ascribing it to what they thought a Divine agency. Holy Scripture at times discovers the hidden agency, that we may acknowledge God's Hand in those terrors which we cannot account for. So it relates, on occasion of Jonathan's slaughter of the Philistine garrison, [11] *there was a trembling in the host and in the field, and among all the people: the garrison and the spoilers, they also trembled, and the earth*

1 Jos. B. J. vi. 8. 4. 2 xxix. 14. 3 Job iv. 1.
4 "Ssihhan, a ruined place in the S. mountains of the Ghoeyr." Burckh. Syr. p. 414.
5 1 Kings iv. 30. 6 Bar. iii. 22, 3. 7 xlix. 7.
8 בנים.
9 Is. xix. 3, 11, 12.
10 Jer. xix. 7.
11 1 Sam. xiv. 15.

Before CHRIST cir. 587.

every one of the mount of
Esau may be cut off by
slaughter.
10 ¶ For *thy*[o] violence
against thy brother Jacob
shame shall cover thee,
and [p] thou shalt be cut off
for ever.
11 In the day that thou
stoodest on the other side,

o Gen. 27. 41. Ps. 137. 7. Ezek. 25. 12. & 35. 5. Amos 1. 11.

p Ezek. 25. 9. Mal. 1. 4.

quaked, so it became a trembling from God, or (in our common word,) a panic from God. All then failed Edom. Their allies and friends betrayed them; God took away their wisdom. Wisdom was turned into witlessness, and courage into cowardice; *to the end that every one from mount Esau may be cut off by slaughter*. The Prophet sums up briefly God's end in all this. The immediate means were man's treachery, man's violence, the failure of wisdom in the wise, and of courage in the brave. The end of all, in God's Will, was their destruction. [1] *All things work together to good to those who love God*, and to evil to those who hate Him.

By slaughter, lit. *from slaughter*, may mean either the immediate or the distant cause of their being *cut off*, either the means which God employed[2], that Edom was cut off by one great slaughter by the enemy; or that which moved God to give them over to destruction, their own *slaughter* of their brethren, the Jews, as it follows;

10. *For* thy *violence against thy brother Jacob*. To Israel God had commanded[3], *Thou shalt not abhor an Edomite; for he is thy brother.—The children that are begotten of them shall enter into the congregation of the Lord in their third generation*. Edom did the contrary to all this. *Violence* includes all sorts of ill-treatment, from one with whom "might is right," *because it is in the power of their hand*[4] to do it. This they had done to the descendants of their brother, and him, their twin-brother, Jacob. They helped the Chaldæans in his overthrow, rejoiced in his calamity, thought that, by this co-operation, they had secured themselves. What, when from those same Chaldees, those same calamities, which they had aided to inflict on their brother, came on themselves, when, as they had betrayed him, they were themselves betrayed; as they had exulted in his overthrow, so their allies exulted in their's! The *shame* of which the Prophet spake, is not the healthful distress at the evil of sin, but at its evils and disappointments. Shame at the evil which sin is, works repentance and turns aside the anger of God. Shame at the evils which sin brings, in itself leads to further sins, and endless, fruitless, shame. Edom had laid his plans, had succeeded; the wheel, in God's Providence, turned round and he was crushed.

So Hosea said[5], *they shall be ashamed through their own counsels;* and Jeremiah[6], *we lie down in our shame and our confusion covereth us;* and David[7], *let mine adversaries be clothed with shame, and let them cover themselves with their own confusion as with a mantle*. As one, covered and involved in a cloak, can find no way to emerge; as one, whom the waters cover[8], is buried under them inextricably, so, wherever they went, whatever they did, shame covered them. So the lost shall *rise to shame and everlasting contempt*[9].

Thou shalt be cut off for ever. One word expressed the sin, *violence;* four words, over against it, express the sentence; shame encompassing, everlasting excision. God's sentences are not completed at once in this life. The branches are lopped off; the tree decays; the axe is laid to the root; at last it is cut down. As the sentence on Adam, *in the day that thou eatest thereof thou shalt surely die*, was fulfilled, although Adam did not die, until he had completed 930 years[10], so was this on Edom, although fulfilled in stages and by degrees. Adam bore the sentence of death about him. The 930 years wore out at last that frame, which, but for sin, had been immortal. So Edom received this sentence of excision, which was, on his final impenitence, completed, although centuries witnessed the first earnest only of its execution. Judah and Edom stood over against each other, Edom ever bent on the extirpation of Judah. At that first destruction of Jerusalem, Edom triumphed, *Raze her, raze her, even to the ground*. Yet, though it tarried long, the sentence was fulfilled. Judah, the banished, survived; Edom, the triumphant, was, in God's time and after repeated trials, *cut off for ever*. Do we marvel at the slowness of God's sentence? Rather marvel we, with wondering thankfulness, that His sentences, on nations or individuals, are slow, yet stand we in awe, because, if unrepealed, they are sure. Centuries, to Edom, abated not their force or certainty; length of life changes not the sinner's doom.

11. *In the day that thou stoodest on the other side*. The time when they so stood, is not defined in itself, as a past or future. It is literally; *In the day of thy standing over against*, i. e. to gaze on the calamities of God's people; *in the day of strangers carrying away*

[1] Rom. viii. 28.
[2] as in Gen. ix. 11, *all flesh shall no more be cut off by* יכרת מ *the waters of the flood.*

[3] Deut. xxiii. 7, 8. [8, 9 Heb.] [4] Mic. ii. 2. [5] x. 6. [6] iii. 25. [7] Ps. cix. 29. [8] Ex. xv. 10. [9] Dan. xii. 2. [10] Gen. v. 5.

Before CHRIST cir. 587.

in the day that the strangers ‖ carried away captive
his forces, and foreigners
entered into his gates, and
q cast lots upon Jerusalem,
even thou *wast* as one of
them.
12 But ‖ thou shouldest
not have r looked on s the
day of thy brother in the
day that he became a
stranger; neither shouldest
thou have t rejoiced over
the children of Judah in
the day of their destruc-
tion; neither shouldest
thou have † spoken proud-
ly in the day of distress.
13 Thou shouldest not
have entered into the gate
of my people in the day of
their calamity; yea, thou
shouldest not have looked
on their affliction in the
day of their calamity, nor
have laid *hands* on their
‖ substance in the day of
their calamity.

‖ Or, *carried away his substance.*
q Joel. 3. 3. Nah. 3. 10.
‖ Or, *do not behold, &c.*
r Ps. 22. 17. & 54. 7. & 59. 10. Mic. 4. 11. & 7. 10.
s Ps. 37. 13. & 137. 7.
t Job 31. 29. Prov. 17. 5. & 24. 17, 18. Mic. 7. 8.
† Heb. *magnified thy mouth.*
‖ Or, *forces.*

his strength, i. e. *the strength of thy brother Jacob*, of whom he had just spoken, *and foreigners entered into his gates, and cast lots on Jerusalem, thou too as one of them. One of them* they were not. Edom was no stranger, no alien, no part of the invading army; he whose strength they carried away, was, he had just said, his *brother Jacob.* Edom burst the bonds of nature, to become what he was not, *as one of them.* He purposely does not say, *thou too wast* (hayitha) *as of them;* as he would have said, had he wished to express what was past. Obadiah seeing, in prophetic vision, the destruction of Jerusalem, and the share which the Edomites took thereat, describes it as it is before his eyes, as past. We see before us, the enemy carrying off all in which the human strength of Judah lay, his forces and his substance, and casting lots on Jerusalem, its people and its possessions. He describes it as past, yet not more so, than the visitation itself which was to follow, some centuries afterward. Of both, he speaks alike as past; of both, as future. He speaks of them as past, as being so beheld in *His* mind in Whose Name he speaks. God's certain knowledge does not interfere with our free agency. "[1] God compelleth no one to sin; yet foreseeth all who shall sin of their own will. How then should He not justly avenge what, foreknowing, He does not compel them to do? For as no one, by his memory, compelleth to be done things which pass, so God, by His foreknowledge, doth not compel to be done things which will be. And as man remembereth some things which he hath done, and yet hath not done all which he remembereth; so God foreknoweth all things whereof He is Himself the Author, and yet is not Himself the Author of all which He foreknoweth. Of those things then, of which He is no evil Author, He is the just Avenger.

12–14. *But thou shouldest not*, rather it means, and can only mean [2], (as in the E. M.) *And look not* (i. e. gaze not with pleasure [3]) *on the day of thy brother in the day of his becoming a stranger* [4]; *and rejoice not over the children of Judah in the day of their destruction; and enlarge not thy mouth in the day of distress. Enter not into the gate of My people in the day of their calamity; look not, thou too, on his affliction in the day of his calamity; and lay not* hands *on his substance in the day of his calamity; And stand not on the crossway, to cut off his fugitives; and shut not up his remnants in the day of distress.* Throughout these three verses, Obadiah uses the future only. It is the voice of earnest, emphatic, dehortation and entreaty, not to do what would displease God, and what, if done, would be punished. He dehorts them from malicious rejoicing at their brother's fall, first in look, then in word, then in act, in covetous participation of the spoil, and lastly in murder. Malicious gazing on human calamity, forgetful of man's common origin and common liability to ill, is the worst form of human hate. It was one of the contumelies of the Cross, *they gaze, they look* with joy *upon Me* [5]. The *rejoicing over* them was doubtless, as among savages, accompanied with grimaces [6]. Then follow words of insult. The *enlarging the mouth* is uttering a tide of large words, here against the people of God; in Ezekiel, against Himself [7]: *Thus with your mouth ye have en-*

[1] S. Aug. de lib. arb. iii. 4.
[2] See Introd. to Obad. p. 228. [3] as in Mic. vii. 10.
[4] Others, *of his strange unheard of calamity.* Others *of his* being rejected *as a stranger* by God, as 1 Sam. xxiii. 7; *estranged* as Jer. xix. 4. Either of these meanings suits the word נכר Job xxxi. 3, *rejection, reprobation*, or, as ours, *strange calamity.* Anyhow it is not *mere* calamity, as neither is it in Arabic.
[5] Ps. xxii. 17.
[6] as in Ps. xxxv. 19, xxxviii. 16.
[7] Ez. xxxv. 13.

Before CHRIST cir. 587.

14 Neither shouldest thou have stood in the crossway, to cut off those of his that did escape; neither shouldest thou have ‖ delivered up those of his that did remain in the day of distress.

‖ Or, *shut up*, Ps. 31. 8.

15 [u] For the day of the LORD *is* near upon all the heathen: [x] as thou hast done, it shall be done unto thee: thy reward shall return upon thine own head.

16 [y] For as ye have drunk upon my holy

Before CHRIST cir. 587.

[u] Ezek. 30. 3. Joel 3. 14.
[x] Ezek. 35. 15. Hab. 2. 8.
cir. 585.
[y] Jer. 25. 28, 29. & 49, 12. Joel 3. 17. 1 Pet. 4. 17.

larged against Me and have multiplied your words against Me. I have heard. Thereon follows Edom's coming yet closer, entering *the gate of* God's *people* to share the conqueror's triumphant gaze on his calamity. Then, the violent, busy, laying the hands on the spoil, while others of them stood in cold blood, taking the *fork* where the ways parted, in order to intercept the fugitives before they were dispersed, or to shut them up with the enemy, driving them back on their pursuers. The Prophet beholds the whole course of sin and persecution, and warns them against it, in the order, in which, if committed, they would commit it. Who would keep clear from the worst, must stop at the beginning. Still God's warnings accompany him step by step. At each step, some might stop. The warning, although thrown away on the most part, might arrest the few. At the worst, when the guilt had been contracted and the punishment had ensued, it was a warning for their posterity and for all thereafter. Some of these things Edom certainly did, as the Psalmist prays[1], *Remember, O Lord, to the children of Edom the day of Jerusalem, who said, Lay bare, lay bare, even to the foundation in her.* And Ezekiel[2] alluding to this language of Obadiah[3], *because thou hast had a perpetual hatred, and hast shed the blood of the children of Israel by the force of the sword in the time of their calamity, in the time that their iniquity had an end, therefore, as I live, saith the Lord God, I will prepare thee unto blood, and blood shall pursue thee; sith thou hast not hated blood, even blood shall pursue thee.* Violence, bloodshed, unrelenting, deadly hatred against the whole people, a longing for their extermination, had been inveterate characteristics of Esau. Joel and Amos had already denounced God's judgments against them for two forms of this hatred, the murder of settlers in their own land or of those who were sold to them[4]. Obadiah warns them against yet a third, intercepting their fugitives in their escape from the more powerful enemy. *Stand not in the crossway.* Whoso puts himself in the situation to commit an old sin, does, in fact, will to renew it, and will, unless hindered from without, certainly do it. Probably he will, through sin's inherent power of growth, do worse. Having anew tasted blood, Ezekiel says, that they sought to displace God's people and remove God Himself[5]. *Because thou hast said, these two nations and these two countries shall be mine, and we will possess it, whereas the Lord was there, therefore, as I live, saith the Lord God, I will even do according to thine anger, and according to thine envy, which thou hast used out of thy hatred against them.*

15. *For the day of the Lord is near upon all the heathen.* The Prophet once more enforces his warning by preaching judgment to come. *The day of the Lord* was already known[6], as a day of judgment upon *all nations*, in which God would *judge all the heathen*, especially for their outrages against His people. Edom might hope to escape, were it alone threatened. The Prophet announces one great law of God's retribution, one rule of His righteous judgment. *As thou hast done, it shall be done unto thee.* Heathen justice owned this to be just, and placed it in the mouth of their ideal of justice[7]. *Blessed he,* says the Psalmist[8], *that recompenses unto thee the deed which thou didst to us. Blessed,* because he was the instrument of God. Having laid down the rule of God's judgment, he resumes his sentence to Edom, and speaks to all in him. In the day of Judah's calamity Edom made itself as *one of them.* It, Jacob's brother, had ranked itself among the enemies of God's people. It then too should be swept away in one universal destruction. It takes its place with them, undistinguished in its doom as in its guilt, or it stands out as their representative, having the greater guilt, because it had the greater light. Obadiah, in adopting Joel's words[9], *thy reward shall return upon thine own head,* pronounces therewith on Edom all those terrible judgments contained in the sentence of retribution as they had been expanded by Joel.

16. *For as ye have drunk.* Revelry always followed heathen victory; often, desecration. The Romans bore in triumph the vessels of

[1] Ps. cxxxvii. 7. [2] xxxv. 5. 6.
[3] בעת אידם ver. 5. referring to the thrice repeated ביום אידו, ביום אידם. Ob. 13.

[4] Joel iii. 19. Am. i. 6, 9, 11. [5] Ez. xxxv. 10, 11.
[6] Joel i. 15, ii. 1, 31. [7] Rhadamanthus Aris. Eth. v. 5.
[8] Ps. cxxxvii. 8. [9] iii. 7.

Before CHRIST cir. 587.

mountain, *so* shall all the heathen drink continually,

Before CHRIST cir. 587.

the second temple, Nebuchadnezzar carried away the sacred vessels of the first. Edom, in its hatred of God's people, doubtless regarded the destruction of Jerusalem, as a victory of polytheism (the gods of the Babylonians, and their own god Coze), over God, as Hyrcanus, in his turn, required them, when conquered, to be circumcised. God's *holy mountain* is *the hill of Zion*, including mount Moriah on which the temple stood. This they desecrated by idolatrous revelry, as, in contrast, it is said that, when the heathen enemy had been destroyed, *mount Zion* should *be holiness*[1]. Brutal, unfeeling, excess had been one of the sins on which Joel had declared God's sentence, [2]*they cast lots on My people; they sold a girl for wine, that they might drink.* Heathen tempers remain the same; under like circumstances, they repeat the same circle of sins, ambition, jealousy, cruelty, bloodshed, and, when their work is done, excess, ribaldry, profaneness. The completion of sin is the commencement of punishment. *As ye*, he says, heathen yourselves and *as one of* the heathen, *have drunk* in profane revelry, on the day of your brother's calamity, *upon My holy mountain*, defiling it, *so shall all the heathen drink* continually. But what draught? a draught which shall never cease, *continually; yea, they shall drink* on, *and shall swallow down*, a full, large, maddening draught, whereby they shall reel and perish, *and they shall be as though they had never been.* "[3]For whoso cleaveth not to Him Who saith, I AM, is not." The two cups of excess and of God's wrath are not altogether distinct. They are joined, as cause and effect, as beginning and end. Whoso drinketh the draught of sinful pleasure, whether excess or other, drinketh therewith the cup of God's anger, consuming him. It is said of the Babylon of the world, in words very like to these[4]; *All nations have drank of the wine of her fornications—reward her as she has rewarded you; in the cup which she hath filled, fill to her double. All nations* are, in the first instance, all who had been leagued against God's people; but the wide term, *all nations*, comprehends all, who, in time, become like them. It is a rule of God's justice for all times. At each and at all times, God requites them to the uttermost. The continuous drinking is fulfilled in each. Each drinketh the cup of God's anger, till death and in death. God employs each nation in turn to give that cup to the other. So Edom drank it at the hand of Babylon, and Babylon from the Medes, and the Medes and Persians from the Macedonians, and the Macedonians from the Romans, and they from the Barbarians. But each in turn drank continuously, until it became as though it had never been. To swallow up, and be swallowed up in turn, is the world's history.

The details of the first stage of the excision of Edom are not given. Jeremiah distinctly says that Edom should be subjected to Nebuchadnezzar[5]. *Thus saith the Lord; make thee bonds and yokes, and put them upon thy neck, and send them to the king of Edom, and to the king of Moab, and to the king of the Ammonites, and to the king of Tyrus, and to the king of Zidon, by the hands of the messengers which come to Jerusalem unto Zedekiah king of Judah, and command them to say to their masters,—I have given all these lands into the hand of Nebuchadnezzar king of Babylon, My servant.* Holy Scripture gives us both prophecy and history; but God is at no pains to clear, either the likelihood of His history, or the fulfillment of His prophecies. The sending of messengers from these petty kings to Zedekiah looks as if there had been, at that time, a plan to free themselves jointly, probably by aid of Egypt, from the tribute to Nebuchadnezzar. It may be that Nebuchadnezzar knew of this league, and punished it afterward. Of these six kings, we know that he subdued Zedekiah, the kings of Tyre, Moab and Ammon. Zion doubtless submitted to him, as it had aforetime to Shalmaneser[6]. But since Nebuchadnezzar certainly punished four out of these six kings, it is probable that they were punished for some common cause, in which Edom also was implicated. In any case, we know that Edom was desolated at that time. Malachi, after the captivity, when upbraiding Israel for his unthankfulness to God, bears witness that Edom had been made utterly desolate[7]. *I have loved Jacob, and Esau I have hated, and laid his mountains and his heritage waste for the jackals of the wilderness.* The occasion of this desolation was doubtless the march of Nebuchadnezzar against Egypt, when, Josephus relates, he subdued Moab and Ammon[8]. Edom lay in his way from Moab to Egypt. It is probable, anyhow, that he then found occasion (if he had it not) against the petty state, whose submission was needed to give him free passage between the Dead Sea and the Gulf of Akaba, the important access which Edom had refused to Israel, as he came out of Egypt. There Edom was *sent forth to its borders*, i. e. misled to abandon its strong fastnesses, and so, falling into the hands of Nebuchadnezzar, it met with the usual lot of the conquered, plunder, death,

1 ver. 17.
2 iii. 3.
3 Gloss.
4 Rev. xviii. 3, 6.
5 xxvii. 2–4, 6.
6 Menander in Jos. Ant. ix. 14. 2.
7 Mal. i. 2, 3.
8 Ant. x. 9. 7.

Before CHRIST cir. 587. yea, they shall drink, and they shall ||swallow Before CHRIST cir. 587.

|| Or, *sup up*.

captivity. Malachi does not verbally allude to the prophecy of Obadiah; for his office related to the restored people of God, not to Edom. But whereas Obadiah had prophesied the slaughter of Edom and the searching out of his treasures, Malachi appeals to all the Jews, their immediate neighbors, that, whereas Jacob was in great degree restored through the love of God, Edom lay under His enduring displeasure; his mountains were, and were to continue to be[1], a waste; he was *impoverished;* his places were desolate. Malachi, prophesying toward[2] 415 B.C., foretold a further desolation. A century later, we find the Nabathæans in tranquil and established possession of Petra, having there deposited the wealth of their merchandise, attending fairs at a distance, avenging themselves on the General of Antigonus, who took advantage of their absence to surprise their retreat, holding their own against the conqueror of Ptolemy who had recovered Syria and Palestine; in possession of all the mountains around them, whence, when Antigonus, despairing of violence, tried by falsehood to lull them into security, they transmitted to Petra by fiery beacons the tidings of the approach of his army[3]. How they came to replace Edom, we know not. They were of a race, wholly distinct; active friends of the Maccabees[4], while the Idumæans were their deadly enemies. Strabo relates[5], that the Edomites "were expelled from the country of the Nabathæans in a sedition, and so joined themselves to the Jews and shared their customs." Since the alleged incorporation among the Jews is true, although at a later period, so may also the expulsion by the Nabathæans be, although not the cause of their incorporation. It would be another instance of requital by God, that "*the men of* their *confederacy brought* them *to* their *border, the men of* their *peace prevailed against* them." A mass of very varied evidence establishes as an historical certainty, that the Nabathæans were of Aramaic[6], not of Arabic, origin. They were inhabitants of Southern Mesopotamia, and, according to the oldest evidence short of Holy Scripture, were the earliest inhabitants, before the invasion of the Chaldæans[7]. Their country, Irak, "extended lengthways[8] from Mosul or Nineveh to Aba-

[1] Mal. i. 4. [2] See Introd. to Malachi. [3] Diod. Sic. xix. 94–8. [4] See 1 Macc. v. 24–27, ix. 35. Jos. Ant. xii. 8. 3. xiii. 1. 2. Aretas of Petra aided the Romans 3, B. C. against Jews and Idumæans. Ib. xvii. 10. 9.

[5] Strabo's words are, "The Idumæans are Nabatæans, but in a sedition having been expelled thence," [i. e. from the country of the Nabatæans,] "they, &c." The identifying of the Edomites and Nabathæans is a slight error in a Greek.

[6] The Arabian historians assert that the Nabathæans were Syrians; the Syrian writers equally claiming them as Syrians. This was first established out of the original unpublished writers by Quatremère (Nouveau Journal Asiatique, 1835. T. xv. reprinted, Mémoire sur les Nabatéens,) followed and illustrated by Larsow (de Dialect. ling. Syriac. reliquiis, Berlin, 1841.) and supplemented by Chwolson (die Ssabier, ii. 1. T. i. p. 697–711. and T. ii. 163. 844.) Their descendants who, according to the Arabic lexicographers, continued to live in "the marshes between the two Iraks," (Djauh. and Kam. in Quatr. p. 54, remained heathen (See Chwols. i. 821, 2. ii. 629, 664, 6). Whence the Syrians used the name Armoio, (as distinct from Oromoio) "Aramæon," to signify "Nabathæan," and "heathen." (Bar Ali, Lex, MS. sub v. See Larsow, p. 9–16.) Blau (in Zeitschr. d. Deutsch. Morg. Ges. 1855, pp. 235, 6.) contends that the Nabathæans of Petra were Arabs, on the following grounds; 1) the statements of Diodorus (xix. 94), Strabo (xvi. 2. 34. Ib. 4. 2 & 21), Josephus (Ant. i. 12, 4.), S. Jerome and some later writers. 2) The statement of Suidas (A. D. 980.) that Dusares, an Arab idol, was worshiped there. 3) The Arabic name of Aretas, king of Petra. 4) Arabic names of places, near Petra. Four such are alleged; *Arindela* (*if* the same as *this* Ghurundel) 18 hours from Petra (Porter, Handb. p. 58); *Negla*, (site unknown); *Auara*, a degree North, (Ptol. in Reland, 463); *Elji*, close to Petra. But as to 1) Diodorus, who calls the Nabathæans Arabs, says that they wrote *Syriac;* Strabo calls the *Edomites* Nabathæans, and the inhabitants of Galilee, Jericho, Philadelphia and Samaria, "a mixed race of Egyptians, Arabians, and Phœnicians" (§ 34), and speaks of "Nabathæan Arabia" as a distinct country (xvii. 1. 21) Josephus, and S. Jerome (Qu. in Gen. 25. 13) following him, include the whole country from the Euphrates to Egypt, and so some whose language was Aramaic. As to 2) Dusares, though at first an Arab idol, was worshiped far and wide, in Galatia, Bostra, even Italy (See coins in Eckhel, Tanini, in Zoega de Obelisc. pp. 205–7, and Zoega himself, p. 205). As to 3) the kings named by Josephus, (see the list in Vincent's Commerce, ii. 273-6) Arethas, Malchus, Obodas, may be equally Aramaic, and Obodas has a more Aramaic sound. Anyhow the Nabathæans, if placed in Petra by Nebuchadnezzar, were not conquerors, and may have received an Arab king in the four centuries between Nebuchadnezzar and the first Aretas known at Petra. What changes those settled in Samaria underwent! As to 4) the names of places are not altered by a garrison in a capital. Our English names were not changed even by the Norman conquest; nor those of Samaria by the Assyrian. How many live on till now! Then of the four names, none occurs until after the Christian era. There is nothing to connect them with the Nabathæans. They may have been given before or long after them.

[7] "The Nabathæans, who were inhabitants of the country of Babel before the Chaldæans." Babylonian Agric. quoted by Makrizi. Quatremère, p. 61. Chwolson, ii. 606.

[8] Yacut in Notices et Extraits, ii. 446. "Masudi says: The inhabitants of Nineveh formed a part of those whom we call Nabits or Syrians, who form one people and speak one language. That of the Nabits differs only in a few letters, but the basis of the language is the same" (Quatr. p. 59). "The Chaldees" [he means Nabathæans] "are an ancient people who dwelt in Irak and Mesopotamia; of them were the Nimrods, kings of the earth after the deluge; and of them was Bakhtnasr (Nebuchadnezzar) and their tongue was Syriac, and they did not disuse it, until the Persians came upon them and subdued their kingdom." (Hajji. Khal. pp. 70, 1.)

Before CHRIST cir. 587. down, and they shall be as though they had not been. Before CHRIST cir. 587.

dan, and in breadth from Cadesia to Hulvan." Syrian writers claimed that their's was the primæval language [1]; Mohammedan writers, who deny this, admit that their language was Syriac [2]. A learned Syriac writer [3] calls the three Chaldee names in Daniel, Shadrach, Meshach, Abednego, Nabathæan. The surviving words of their language are mostly Syriac [4]. Mohammedan writers suppose them to be descended from Aram son of Shem [5]. Once they were a powerful nation, with a highly cultivated language [6]. One of their books, written before the destruction of Nineveh and Babylon [7], itself mentions an ancient literature, specifically on agriculture, medicine, botany, and, that favorite study of the Chaldæans, astrology, "the mysteries," star-worship and a very extensive, elaborate, system of symbolical representation [8]. But the Chaldees conquered them; they were subjects of Nebuchadnezzar, and it is in harmony with the later policy of the Eastern Monarchies, to suppose that Nebuchadnezzar placed them in Petra, to hold in check the revolted Idumæans [9]. Diodorus [10] relates that the Nabathæans there "wrote in *Syriac*" a letter of remonstrance to Antigonus. "A tribe of Babylonians" were still, in the 6th century, "at Karak-Moab [11]," 60 geographical miles from Petra. Anyhow, B. C. 312,

[1] The Syrian Theodorus, quoted in the Alfehrest, says that "it was in this language that God spake to Adam." "Adam and his children spoke Syriac; some say, Nabathæan." (Ikhwan-alsafa, Quatr. 91.) "The primitive language which Adam spoke was that now used by the Chaldees; for Abraham was Chaldee by birth, and the language which he learnt of his fathers is that still used among us Syro-Chaldees." (Patriarch Michael, Chron. Ib. 91, 2.)

[2] "The Syriac writing is that of the Nabathæans and Chaldees. Ignorant men maintain that it is the primitive writing, on account of its great antiquity, and that it is used by the most ancient people; but it is an error." Ibn. Khaldun, Ib. 92.

[3] Abulfaraj, p. 74. "Nebuchadnezzar gave Hananiah, Mishael, and Azariah, Nabathæan names, Shadrach, &c.

[4] Words of the Nabathæan dialect are preserved both in Syriac and Arabic Lexica. On those in Syriac see Quatr. 104 sqq, Larsow, p. 15–26. The Arabic are given by Golius and Freytag.

[5] Masudi, (from Quatr. translation, p. 56.) "Among the sons of Mash, son of Aram, son of Shem, son of Noah, is Nabit, from whom are sprung all the Nabathæans and their kings." "Nabit, son of Mash, having fixed his residence at Babel, his descendants seized all Irak. These Nabathæans gave kings to Babel, who covered the land with cities, introduced civilization, and reigned with unequaled glory. Time has taken away their greatness and empire; and their descendants, in a state of dependence and humiliation, are now dispersed in Irak and other provinces." "After the deluge, men settled in different countries, as the Nabathæans who founded Babel, and the sons of Ham who settled in the same country under Nimrod." "The Chaldæans are the same as the Syrians, formerly called Nabathæans" (Ib. p. 59). "The Nimrods were the kings of the Syrians, whom the Arabs call Nabathæans." "The Nabathæans say that Iran was theirs, that the country belonged to them, and that they once possessed it, that their kings were the Nimrods, of whom was the Nimrod in the time of Abraham, and that Nimrod was the name of their kings" (Ib. 58); that Iran was named from them, Arian-shehr, land of lions, *ariam* (plur. of *aria*) "signifying in Nabathæan, *lion*." Ib. "The last king who fell before Ardeshir (Alexander) was a king of the Nabathæans, who lived in the towns of Irak." Ib. 60.

[6] In the 13th century, there were still three chief dialects of Syraic, 1) Aramæan, the dialect of Edessa, Haran, and Mesopotamia. 2) Palestine, that of Damascus, Lebanon, and the rest of inner (i. e. proper) Syria. 3) The Chaldee-Nabathæan, that of the mountaineers of Assyria, and the villages of Irak. (Abulfaraj, Hist. Arab. p. 70.) Of these the Nabathæan was once the purest; afterward, it appears to have been corrupted by contact with the proper Chaldæans, and (as is the wont in mountainous districts and among peasants) was debased among an uneducated people. Theodorus the Syrian says, "This language is the most elegant of the Syriac dialects—The inhabitants of Babel spoke it. When God confounded the languages, and men dispersed in different countries, the language of the inhabitants of Babel remained unchanged. As for the Nabathæan spoken in villages, it is a corrupt Syriac and full of vicious idioms." (in Arab. Hist. Quatr. 95.) Barhebræus says, "Syriac, more than any other language, being spread over countries far apart, underwent changes so great, that those who speak different dialects of it do not understand each other, but require an interpreter, as if they spoke foreign languages. The dialects are three, that of Syria, that of Palestine, and that of the Easterns. This, more than the rest, has adopted very anomalous forms, and assimilated itself to the Chaldee. The Syriac is spoken at Edessa, Melitene, Marde; of those who use the Eastern, the Nestorian Christians are conspicuous." (Gramm. Syr. Quatr. 97.)

"In the Fehrest (A. D. 987) it is said that Nabathæan was purer than Syriac, and that the people of Babylon spoke it, but that the Nabathæan spoken in villages was inelegant Syriac." H. Khal. p. 71. ed. Flüg. "The people of Suwad [Babylonia] spoke Syriac, and letters were written in a peculiar dialect, Syro-Persic." (Ibn Mocanna, Ib. 70.)

[7] Quatr. 45, 6. "The temples of Babylon were still standing." Id. Ibn Wahshiyyah the Chaldæan, who states that he translated the "Nabathæan Agriculture into Arabic from Chaldee," ascribed to it a fabulous antiquity. (ap. Makrizi in Chwols. i. 699.) Ibn Awwam, who used it largely, says that it was "built on the words of the greatest wise, and mentions their names and numbers." (p. 8, 9. Chw. i. 706.) "It was adapted to the climate of Babylon especially, and to countries with a similar climate." Ssagrit, its original author ap. Abn Awwam, i. p. 82. (Chw. i. 699.)

[8] Quatremère, p. 108 sqq. Chwols. i. 107. "The Chaldæans, before them the Syrians, and in their time the Nabathæans, gave themselves eagerly to the study of magic, astrology, and talismans." Ibn Khald. in Quatr. 61. "Chwolson states that he has found in the fragments of these different writings, very lofty speculations on philosophy and natural history, and a very remarkable political and social legislation. Libraries are mentioned; all the branches of religious and profane literature, history, biography, &c. appear there very developed." Renan, Hist. d. Langues Semit. iii. 2. T. i. p. 239.

[9] I find this same conjecture in Quatremère.

[10] xix. 96.

[11] Steph. Byz. v. 'Αδαρούπολις. quoted by Quatremère, p. 87.

Before CHRIST cir. 587.

17 ¶ [x] But upon mount Zion [a] shall be ‖ deliverance, ‖ and there shall be holiness; and the house of Jacob shall possess their possessions.

[x] Joel 2. 32.
[a] Amos 9. 8.
‖ Or, *they that escape.*
‖ Or, *it shall be holy.* Joel 3. 17.

18 And the house of Jacob [b] shall be a fire, and the house of Joseph a flame, and the house of Esau for stubble, and they shall kindle in them, and devour

Before CHRIST cir. 587.

[b] Is. 10. 17. Zech. 12. 6.

Edom had long been expelled from his native mountains. He was not there about B. C. 420, the age of Malachi. Probably then, after the expulsion foretold by Obadiah, he never recovered his former possessions, but continued his robber-life along the Southern borders of Judah, unchanged by God's punishment, the same deadly enemy of Judah.

17. *But* [*And*] *upon* [*in*] *Mount Zion shall be deliverance*, or, *an escaped remnant, and there* [*and it*] *shall be holiness.* The sifting times of the Church are the triumph of the world; the judgment of the world is the restoration of the Church. In the triumph of the world, the lot was cast on Jerusalem, her sons were carried captive and slain, her holy places were desecrated. On the destruction of the nations, Mount Zion rises in calm majesty, as before; *a remnant* is replaced there, after its sifting; it is again *holiness;* not holy only, but a channel of holiness; *and the house of Jacob shall possess their possessions;* (lit. *inherit their inheritances,*) either their own former possessions, receiving and *inheriting* from the enemy, what they had lost; or the *inheritances* of the nations. For the whole world is the inheritance of the Church, as Jesus said to the Apostles, sons of Zion, [1] *Go ye and teach all nations, baptizing them in the Name of the Father and of the Son and of the Holy Ghost.* [2] *Go ye into all the world and preach the Gospel to every creature.* Holiness is its title-deeds to the inheritance of the world, that holiness, which was in *the upper chamber* in *Mount Zion,* the presence of God the Holy Ghost, issuing in holy teaching, holy Scriptures, holy institutions, holy Sacraments, holy lives.

18. Having given, in summary, the restoration and expansion of Judah, Obadiah, in more detail, first mentions a further chastisement of Edom, quite distinct from the former. In the first, for which God summoned the heathen, there is no mention of Judah, the desolation of whose holy City, Jerusalem, for the time, and their own captivity is presupposed. In the second, which follows on the restoration of its remnant, there is no mention of heathen. Obadiah, whose mission was to Judah, gives to it the name of the whole, *the house of Jacob.* It alone had the true worship of God, and His promises. Apart from it, there was no oneness with the faith of the fathers, no foreshadowing sacrifice for sin. Does the *house of Joseph* express the same in other words? or does it mean, that, after that first destruction of Jerusalem, Ephraim should be again united with Judah? Asaph unites, as one, *the sons of Jacob and Joseph* [3], Israel and Joseph [4]; Israel, Jacob, Joseph [5]. Zechariah [6] after the captivity, speaks of *the house of Judah* and *the house of Joseph,* as together forming one whole. Amos, about this same time, twice speaks of Ephraim [7] under the name of Joseph. And although Asaph uses the name of Joseph, as Obadiah does, to designate Israel, including Ephraim, it does not seem likely that it should be used of Israel, excluding those whose special name it was. While then Hosea and Amos foretold the entire destruction of the *kingdom* of Israel, Obadiah foretells that some should be there, after the destruction of Jerusalem also, united with them. And after the destruction of Samaria, there did remain in Israel, of the poor people, many who returned to the worship of God. Hezekiah invited Ephraim and Manasseh to the passover [8], from Beersheba to Dan [9], addressing them as *the remnant, that are escaped out of the hands of the kings of Assyria* [10]. The more part *mocked* [11]; yet *divers of Asher, Manasseh and Zabulon* [12], came from the first, and afterward *many of Ephraim and Issachar* as well as *Manasseh and Zabulon* [13]. Josiah destroyed all the places of idolatry in Bethel [14] and *the cities of Samaria* [15], *of Manasseh and Ephraim and Simeon even unto Naphtali* [16]. *Manasseh, Ephraim, and all the remnant of Israel* gave money for the repair of the temple, and this was *gathered* by *the Levites who kept the doors* [17]. After the renewal of the covenant to keep the law, *Josiah removed all the abominations out of all the countries, that* pertained *to the children of Israel and made all found in Israel to serve the Lord their God* [18].

The heathen colonists were placed *by the king of Assyria in Samaria and the cities thereof* [19], probably to hold the people in the country in check. The remnant of *the house of Joseph* dwelt in the open country and the villages.

And the house of Esau for stubble. At some time after the first desolation by Nebuchad-

[1] S. Matt. xxviii. 19. [2] S. Mark xvi. 15. [3] Ps. lxxvii. 15. [4] Ps. lxxx. 1. [5] Ps. lxxxi. 4, 5. [6] x. 6. [7] v. 15, vi. 6. [8] 2 Chr. xxx. 1.

[9] Ib. 5. [10] Ib. 6. [11] Ib. 10. [12] Ib. 11. [13] Ib. 18. [14] 2 Kings xxiii. 15. [15] Ib. 19. [16] 2 Chr. xxxiv. 6. [17] Ib. 9. [18] Ib. 33. [19] 2 Kings xvii. 24.

Before CHRIST cir. 587.

them; and there shall not
be *any* remaining of the
house of Esau; for the
LORD hath spoken *it*.
19 And *they of* the south
[c] shall possess the mount of
Esau; [d] and *they of* the
plain the Philistines: and
they shall possess the fields
of Ephraim, and the fields
of Samaria: and Benjamin
shall possess Gilead.

c Amos 9. 12.

d Zeph. 2. 7.

nezzar, Esau fulfilled the boast which Malachi records, *we will return and build up the desolate places*[1]. Probably during the oppression of Judah by Antiochus Epiphanes, they possessed themselves of the South of Judah, bordering on their own country, and of Hebron[2], 22 miles from Jerusalem[3], where Judah had dwelt in the time of Nehemiah[4]. Judas Maccabæus was reduced to[5] *fortify Bethzur*, lit. *house of the rock*, (20 miles only from Jerusalem[6]) *that the people might have a defence against Idumæa.* Maresha and Adoraim, 25 miles S. W. of Jerusalem, near the road to Gaza, were cities of Idumæa[7]. The whole of Simeon was absorbed in it[8]. Edom was still on the aggressive, when Judas Maccabæus smote them at Arrabatene. It was "[9]because they beset Israel round about," that "Judas fought against the children of Esau in Idumea at Arrabatene and gave them a great overthow." His second battle against them was in Judæa itself. He "[10]fought against the children of Esau in the land toward the South, where he smote Hebron and her daughters, and pulled down its fortress and burned the towns thereof round about." About 20 years afterward, Simon had again to recover Bethzur[11], and again to fortify it, as still lying on the borders of Judah[12]. Twenty years later, John Hyrcanus, son of Simon[13], "[14]subdued all the Edomites, and permitted them to remain in the country, on condition that they would receive circumcision, and adopt the laws of the Jews." This they did, continues Josephus; "and henceforth became Jews." Outwardly they appear to have given up their idolatry. For although Josephus says, "[15]the Edomites *account* [not, accounted] Koze a god," he relates that, after this forced adoption of Jewish customs, Herod made Costobar, of the sacerdotal family, prefect of Idumæa and Gaza[15]. Their character remained unchanged. The Jewish historian, who knew them well, describes them as "[16]a tumultuous disorderly race, ever alive to commotions, delighting in change, who went to engagements as to a feast:" "[17]by nature most savage for slaughter." 3, B. C. they took part in the sedition against the Romans[18], using, as a pretext probably, the Feast of Pentecost, to which they went up with those of Galilee, Jericho, the country beyond Jordan, and "the Jews themselves." Just before the last siege of Jerusalem, the Zealots sent for them, on pretext that the city was betrayed to the Romans. "All took arms, as if in defence of their metropolis, and, 20,000 in number, went to Jerusalem[19]." After massacres, of which, when told that they had been deceived, they themselves repented, they returned; and were, in turn, wasted by Simon the Gerasene. "[20]He not only destroyed cities and villages, but wasted the whole country. For as you may see wood wholly bared by locusts, so the army of Simon left the country behind them, a desert. Some things they burnt, others they razed." After a short space, "he returned to the remnant of Edom, and, chasing the people on all sides, constrained the many to flee to Jerusalem[21]." There they took part against the Zealots[22], "were a great part of the war[23]" against the Romans, and perished, "[24]rivals in phrensy" with the worst Jews in the time of that extreme, superhuman, wickedness. Thenceforth their name disappears from history. The "greater part" of the remmant of the nation had perished in that dreadful exterminating siege; if any still survived, they retained no known national existence. Arabian tradition preserves the memory of three Jewish Arab tribes, none of the Edomites.

19. *And* they of *the South shall possess the mount of Esau.* The Church was now hemmed in within Judah and Benjamin. They too were to go into captivity. The Prophet looks beyond the captivity and the return, and tells how that original promise to Jacob[25] should be fulfilled; *Thy seed shall be as the dust of the earth, and thou shalt break forth to the West, and to the East, and to the North, and to the South; and in thee and in thy seed shall all the families of the earth be blessed.*

1 Mal. i. 4. 2 1 Macc. v. 65. 3 Eus. V. 'Αρκώ.
4 Neh. xi. 25. 5 1 Macc. iv. 61. 6 Eus.
7 Jos. Ant. xiii. 15. 4. 8 Ib. v. 1. 22.
9 1 Macc. v. 3. 10 Ib. 65. 11 Ib. xi. 65, 6.
12 Ib. xiv. 33. 13 Ib. xiii. 53. 14 Ant. xiii. 9, 1.
15 Ib. xv. 7, 9. 16 Id. B. J. iv. 4. 1. 17 Ib. iv. 5. 1.
18 Ant. xvii. 10. 2.
19 B. J. iv. 4. 2. It would seem from Josephus that their fighting men were already roduced to this number. "The princes of the Idumæans sped like madmen round the nation, and proclaimed the expedition throughout. *The* multitude was assembled, earlier than was commanded, and *all* took arms," &c.
20 Ib. iv. 9. 7. The Edomites were again in possession of Hebron. Simon took it.
21 Ib. 10. 22 Ib. 11. 23 Ib. vi. 8. 2. 24 Ib. vii. 8. 1.
25 Gen. xxviii. 14.

Before CHRIST cir. 587.

20 And the captivity of
this host of the children of
Israel *shall possess* that of
the Canaanites *even* [e] unto
Zarephath; and the cap-
tivity of Jerusalem,
‖ which *is* in Sepharad,
[f] shall possess the cities of
the south.
21 And [g] saviours shall

e 1 Kings 17. 9, 10.

Before CHRIST cir. 587.

‖ Or, shall possess *that which is in Sepharad.*

f Jer. 32. 44.

g 1 Tim. 4. 16. Jam. 5. 20.

Hosea and Amos had, at this time, prophesied the final destruction of the kingdom of Israel. Obadiah describes Judah, as expanded to its former bounds including Edom and Philistia, and occupying the territory of the ten tribes. *The South*[1], i. e. they of the *hot* and *dry* country to the South of Judah bordering on Edom, *shall possess the mountains of Esau,* i. e. his mountain country, on which they bordered. And *the plain,* they on the West, in the great maritime plain, the *shephēlah,* should spread over the country of the Philistines, so that the sea should be their boundary; and on the North, over the country of the ten tribes, *the fields of Ephraim and the fields of Samaria.* The territory of *Benjamin* being thus included in Judah, to it is assigned the country on the other side Jordan; *and Benjamin, Gilead.*

20. *And the captivity of this host of the children of Israel,* [it must, I believe, be rendered[2],] *which* are among *the Canaanites, as far as Zarephath, and the captivity of Jerusalem which* is *in Sepharad, shall possess the cities of the South.* Obadiah had described how the two tribes, whose were the promises to the house of David, should spread abroad on all sides. Here he represents how Judah should, in its turn, receive into its bosom those now carried away from them; so should all again be one fold.

Zarephath (probably "smelting-house," and so a place of slave-labor, pronounced Sarepta in S. Luke[3]) belonged to Sidon[4], lying on the sea[5] about half-way[6] between it and Tyre[7]. These were then, probably, captives, placed by Tyrians for the time in safe keeping in the narrow plain[8] between Lebanon and the sea, intercepted by Tyre itself[9] from their home, and awaiting to be transported to a more distant slavery. These, with those already sold to the Grecians and in slavery at Sardis, formed one whole. They stand as representatives of all who, whatever their lot, had been rent off from the Lord's land, and had been outwardly severed from His heritage.

21. *And saviours shall ascend on Mount Zion.* The body should not be without its head; saviours there should be, and those, successively. The title was familiar to them of old. [10] *The children of Israel cried unto the Lord, Who raised them up a saviour, and he saved them. And the Lord gave unto Israel a saviour*[11], in the time of Jehoahaz. Nehemiah says to God[12], *According to Thy manifold mercies, Thou gavest them saviours, who should save them from the hands of their enemies.* So there should be thereafter. Such were Judas Maccabæus and his brothers, and Hyrcanus, Alexander, Aristobulus. They are said to *ascend* as to a place of dignity, to *ascend on Mount Zion;* not to go up thither*ward,* but to dwell and abide *in*[13] it, which aforetime was defiled, which now was to be holy. He ends, as he began, with Mount Zion, the *holy hill,* where God was pleased to dwell[14], to reveal Himself. In both, is the judgment of Esau. Mount Zion stands over against Mount Esau, God's holy mount against the mountains of human pride, the Church against the world. And with this agrees the office assigned, which is almost more than that of man. He began his prophecy of the deliverance of God's people, *In Mount Zion shall be an escaped remnant;* he ends, *saviours shall ascend on Mount Zion:* he began, *it shall be*

---

1 נגב

2 The difficulty arises from the necessity of supplying something to fill up the construction of אשר כנענים lit. *which the Canaanites.* Our translation, following the Latin, has, *shall possess that of the Canaanites.* In this sense, we should have expected את אשר לכנענים, *that which belongs to the Canaanites,* the object having, in all the preceding instances, been marked by the את and אשר כנענים not being the Hebrew for "that which belongs to." On the other hand, the Hebrew accent, the parallelism, and the uniform use of the accusative here, point to the rendering, "*which* are among *the Canaanites,*" which is that of the Chaldee, while the construction is that of the LXX. and Syr וגלת החל הזה לבני ישראל corresponds with וגלת ירושלם; the אשר עד צרפת כנענים with אשר בספרד; and then the remainder, "shall inherit the cities of the South," ירשו את ערי הנגב, is the predicate of both, in exact correspondence with the previous clauses. Hence the Chaldee has supplied ב before כנענים, from the corresponding בספרד, and renders, "which are in the land of the Canaanites."

3 iv. 26.

4 1 Kings xvii. 9.

5 Phocas, Loc. Sanct. in Reland, 985.

6 Russegger, Reisen, iv 145. note. "Sarafend," in which the old name is nearly preserved, (Reland, ib.) is a little inland. It is 4½ hours both from Tyre and Sidon. (Russ. 145, 6.) The maps are wrong Id.

7 Jos. Ant. viii. 13. 2.

8 "Its breadth is nowhere more than ½ an hour, except around Tyre and Sidon, where the mountains retreat somewhat further. In some places they approach quite near to the shore." Rob. ii. 473.

9 In the term, "the Canaanites as far as Zarephath," the starting-point is naturally the confines of Canaan and Israel, and so Zarephath is the furthest point N. of Judah.

10 Judg. iii. 9, 15.

11 2 Kings xiii. 5.

12 Neh ix. 27.

13 not אל nor על but ב.

14 Ps ii. 6, lxviii 16.

Before CHRIST cir. 587.

come up on mount Zion to judge the mount of Esau; and the [h] kingdom shall be the LORD'S.

Before CHRIST cir. 587.

[h] Ps. 22. 28. Dan. 2. 44. & 7. 14, 27. Zech. 14. 9. Luke 1. 33. Rev. 11. 15. & 19. 6.

---

holiness; he closes, *and the kingdom shall be the Lord's. To judge the mount of Esau.* Judges, appointed by God, judge His people; saviours, raised up by God, deliver them. But once only does Ezekiel speak of man's judging another nation, as the instrument of God. [1] *I, the Lord, have spoken it—and I will do it; I will not go back, neither will I spare, neither will I repent; according to thy ways and according to thy doings shall they judge thee, saith the Lord God.* But it is the prerogative of God. And so, while the word *saviours* includes those who, before and afterward, were the instruments of God in saving His Church and people, yet all saviours shadowed forth or back the one Saviour, Who alone has the office of Judge, in Whose kingdom, and associated by Him with Him, [2] *the saints shall judge the world,* as He said to His Apostles[3], *ye which have followed Me, in the regeneration when the Son of man shall sit in the throne of His glory, ye also shall sit upon twelve thrones, judging the twelve tribes of Israel.* And the last words must at all times have recalled that great prophecy of the Passion, and of its fruits in the conversion of the Heathen, from which it is taken, the twenty-second Psalm. The outward incorporation of Edom in Judah through Hyrcanus was but a shadow of that inward union, when the kingdom of God was established upon earth, and Edom was enfolded in the one kingdom of Christ, and its cities, whence had issued the wasters and deadly foes of Judah, became the sees of Christian Bishops. And in this way too Edom was but the representative of others, aliens from and enemies to God, to whom His kingdom came, in whom He reigns and will reign, glorified for ever in His Saints, whom He has redeemed with His most precious Blood.

And the kingdom shall be the Lord's. Majestic, comprehensive simplicity of prophecy! All time and eternity, the struggles of time and the rest of eternity, are summed up in those three words[4]; Zion and Edom retire from sight; both are comprehended in that one kingdom, and God is *all in all.*[5] The strife is ended; not that ancient strife only between the evil and the good, the oppressor and the oppressed, the subduer and the subdued; but the whole strife and disobedience of the creature toward the Creator, man against his God. Outward prosperity had passed away, since David had said the great words[6], *the kingdom is the Lord's.* Dark days had come. Obadiah saw on and beyond to darker yet, but knits up all his prophecy in this; *the kingdom shall be the Lord's.* Daniel saw what Obadiah foresaw, the kingdom of Judah also broken; yet, as a captive, he repeated the same to the then monarch of the world, [7] *the hammer of the whole earth,* which had broken in pieces the petty kingdom of Judah, and carried captive its people[8]; *the God of heaven shall set up a kingdom, which shall never be destroyed.* Zechariah saw the poor fragments which returned from the captivity and their poor estate, yet said the same[9]; *The Lord shall be king over all the earth.* All at once that kingdom came; the fishermen, the tax-gatherer and the tentmaker were its captains; the scourge, the claw, thongs, rack, hooks, sword, fire, torture, the red-hot iron seat, the cross, the wild-beast, not employed, but endured, were its arms; the dungeon and the mine, its palaces; fiery words of truth, its [10] *sharp arrows in the hearts of the King's enemies;* for One spake by them, Whose *Word is with power.* The strong sense of the Roman, the acuteness of the Greek, and the simplicity of the Barbarian, cast away their unbelief or their misbelief, and joined in the one song[11], *The Lord God Omnipotent reigneth.* The imposture of Mohammed, however awfully it rent off countless numbers from the faith of Christ, still was forced to spread the worship of the One God, Who, when the Prophets spake, seemed to be the God of the Jews only. Who could foretell such a kingdom, but He Who Alone could found it, Who alone has for these eighteen centuries preserved, and now is anew enlarging it, God Omnipotent and Omniscient, Who waked the hearts which He had made, to believe in Him and to love Him? [12] Blessed peaceful kingdom even here, in this valley of tears and of strife, where God rules the soul, freeing it from the tyranny of the world and Satan and its own passions, inspiring it to know Himself, the Highest Truth, and to love Him Who is Love, and to adore Him Who is Infinite Majesty! Blessed kingdom, in which God reigns in us by grace, that He may bring us to His heavenly kingdom, where is the manifest vision of Himself, and perfect love of Him, blissful society, eternal fruition of Himself; "[13] where is supreme and certain security, secure tranquillity, tranquil security, joyous happiness, happy eternity, eternal blessedness, blessed vision of God for ever, where is perfect love, fear none, eternal day and One Spirit in all!"

[1] Ezek. xxiv. 14. [2] 1 Cor. vi. 2. [3] S. Matt. xix. 28. [4] והיתה ליהוה המלוכה. [5] 1 Cor. xv. 28. [6] Ps. xxii. 28. [7] Jer. l. 23.

[8] Dan. ii. 44, add vii. 14, 27. [9] Zech. xiv. 9. [10] Ps. xlv. 5. [11] Rev. xix. 6. [12] from Lap. [13] Medit. c. 37. ap. S. Aug. vi. p. 125. App.

INTRODUCTION

TO

THE PROPHET

JONAH.

THE Prophet Jonah, who was at once the author and in part the subject of the book which bears his name, is, beyond question, the same who is related in the book of Kings [a] to have been God's messenger of comfort to Israel, in the reign of Jeroboam II. For his own name, in English "Dove," as well as that of his father, Amittai, "The Truth of God," occurs nowhere else in the Old Testament; and it is wholly improbable that there should have been two prophets of the same name, sons of fathers of the same name, when the names of both son and father were so rare as not to occur elsewhere in the Old Testament. The place which the Prophet occupies among the twelve agrees therewith. For Hosea and Amos, prophets who are known to have prophesied in the time of Jeroboam, and Joel, who prophesied before Amos, are placed before him; Micah, who prophesied after the death of Jeroboam and Uzziah, is placed after him.

A remarkable and much-misunderstood expression of the Prophet shews that this mission fell in the later part of his life, at least after he had already exercised the prophetic office. Our translation has, *Jonah rose up to flee from the presence of the Lord.* It has been asked [b], "How could a *Prophet* imagine that he could flee from the presence of God?" Plainly he could not. Jonah, so conversant with the Psalms, doubtless knew well the Psalm of David [c], *Whither shall I go from Thy Spirit, and whither shall I flee from Thy presence?* He could not but know, what every instructed Israelite knew. And so critics should have known that such could *not* be the meaning. The words are used, as we say, "he went out of the king's presence," or the like. It is literally, *he rose to flee from being in the Presence of the Lord*, i. e. from standing in His Presence as His Servant and Minister [d]. Then he must have so stood before; he must have had the office, which he sought to abandon.

He was then a prophet of Israel, born at

[a] 2 Kings xiv. 25.
[b] Davidson, in Horne's Introd. ii. 958.
[c] Ps. cxxxix. 7.

[d] It is מלפני, not מפני. But לפני יהוה and מלפני יהוה, which correspond to one another, have very definite meanings. לפני יהוה is "before the Lord;" מלפני יהוה is "from being before the Lord." לפני יהוה is used in a variety of ways, of the place where God specially manifests Himself the tabernacle, or the temple. With verbs, it is used of passing actions, as sacrificing (with different verbs, Ex. xxix. 11, Lev. vii. 1–7, 2 Chr. vii. 4); of sprinkling the blood (Lev. iv. 16, &c. often); entering His Presence (Ex. xxxiv. 34, Lev. xv. 14); drawing near (Ex. xvi. 9); rejoicing in His Presence (2 Sam. vi. 5, 21, &c.); weeping before Him (Judg. xx. 23); or of abiding conditions, as walking habitually (Ps. lv. 14); dwelling (Is. xxiii. 18); or standing, as His habitual Minister, as the Levites (Deut. x. 8, 2 Chr. xxix. 11, Ezek. xliv. 15); or a prophet (1 Kings xvii. 1, Jer. xvi. 19); or the priest or the Nazarite (see ab. p. 176. col. 1). In correspondence with this, מלפני יהוה signifies "from before the Lord." It is used in special reference to the tabernacle, as of the fire which went forth from the Presence of God there (Lev. ix. 24, x. 2); the plague (Num. xvii. 11 Heb. [xvi. 46 Eng.]); the rods brought out (Num. xvii. 24 Heb. [10 Eng.]); or the shew bread removed thence (1 Sam. xxi. 6). And so it signifies, not that one fled *from* God, but that he removed from standing in His Presence. So *Cain went out from* the Presence of God (מלפני, Gen. iv. 16); and of an earthly ruler it is said, a man "went forth out of his presence" [Gen. xli. 46, xlvii. 10 &c.]; and to David God promises, "there shall not be cut off to thee a man from before Me," i. e., "from standing before Me," (מלפני 1 Kings viii. 25, 2 Chr.

Gath-hepher, "a small village" of Zabulon [e], which lies, S. Jerome says, "two miles from Sepphorim which is now called Diocæsarea, in the way to Tiberias, where his tomb also is pointed out." His tomb was still shewn in the hills near Sipphorim in the 12th century, as Benjamin of Tudela [f] relates; at the same place, "[g] on a rocky hill 2 miles East of Sepphuriah," is still pointed out the tomb of the Prophet, and "Moslems and the Christians of Nazareth alike regard the village (el-Meshhad) as his native village." The tomb is even now venerated by the Moslem inhabitants.

But although a prophet of Israel, he, like Daniel afterward or his great predecessor Elisha, had his mission also beyond the bounds of Israel. Whenever God brought His people into any relation with other people, He made Himself known to them. The mode of His manifestation varied; the fact remained uniform. So He made Himself known to Egypt through Joseph and Moses; to the Philistines at the capture of the ark; to the Syrians by Elisha; to Nebuchadnezzar and Belshazzar by Daniel, as again to Darius and Cyrus. The hindrances interposed to the edict of Darius perpetuated that knowledge among his successors. Yet further on, the High Priest Jaddua shewed to Alexander the prophecy of Daniel "[h] that a Greek should destroy the Persian Empire." For there is no ground to question the account of Josephus. The mission then of Jonah to Nineveh is in harmony with God's other dealings with heathen nations, although, in God's manifold wisdom, not identical with any.

To Israel the history of that mission revealed that same fact which was more fully declared by S. Peter [i]; *I perceive that God is no respecter of persons; but in every nation he that feareth Him and worketh righteousness, is accepted with Him.* This righteous judgment of God stands out the more, alike in the history of the mariners and of the Ninevites, in that the character of both is exhibited advantageously, in comparison with that of the Prophet. The Prophet brings out the awe, the humanity, the earnestness of the natural religion, and the final conversion of the sailors, and the zealous repentance of the Ninevites, while he neglects to explain his own character, or, in the least, to soften its hard angles. Rather, with a holy indifference, he has left his character to be hardly and unjustly judged by those who, themselves sharing his infirmities, share not his excellences. Disobedient once, he cares only to teach us what God taught him for us. The mariners were spared, the Hebrew Prophet was cast forth as guilty. The Ninevites were forgiven: the Prophet, rebuked.

That other moral, which our Lord inculcated, that the heathen believed and repented with less light, the Jews, amid so much greater light, repented not, also lay there, to be drawn out by men's own consciences. "To the condemnation of Israel," says S. Jerome [k], "Jonah is sent to the Gentiles, because, whereas Nineveh repented, Israel persevered in his iniquity." But this is only a secondary result of his prophecy, as all Divine history must be full of teaching, because the facts themselves are instructive. Its instructiveness in this respect depends wholly upon the truth of the facts. It is the real repentance of the Ninevites, which becomes the reproach of the impenitent Jew or Christian.

Even among the Jews, a large school, the Cabbalists, (although amid other error,) interpreted the history of Jonah as teaching the resurrection of the dead, and (with that remarkable correctness of combination of different passages of Holy Scripture which we often find) in union with the prophecy of Hosea. "[l] The fish's belly, where Jonah was enclosed, signifies the tomb, where the body is covered and laid up. But as Jonah was given back on the third day, so shall we

vi. 16; comp. Is. xlviii. 19, Jer. xxxiii. 18. of Israel) and David prays, "Cast me not away from Thy presence," lit. "from before Thee" (Ps. li. 11). Aben Ezra noticed the distinction in part, "And as I have searched in all Scripture, and I have not found the word ברח used otherwise than united with the word מפני, as in Ps. cxxxix. 7 and Judg. xi. 3, and in the prophecy of Jonah I have not found that he fled מפני, 'from the face of the Lord' but מלפני, 'from before the Presence of the Lord;' and it is written, 'As the Lord liveth, *before Whom* I stand' (לפניו). And so, on the other hand, it is always מלפני. And so it is, 'And Cain went out מלפני from before the presence of God'—And it is written 'to go into the clefts of the rocks and into the fissures of the cliff from the fear (לבוא־מפני פחד) of the Lord' (Is. ii. 21), and (in Jonah) it is written, to go with them from the Presence לבוא־מלפני of the Lord (Jon. i. 3), and the wise will understand." In one place (1 Chr. xix. 18) מלפני is used, not with ברח (of which alone Aben Ezra speaks) but with נוס. The idiom also is different, 1) since the two armies had been engaged face to face, (as Amaziah said, 'Let us look one another in the face,' 2 Kings xiv. 8, and the like idioms,) but 2) chiefly, in that מלפני יהוה is, by the force of the term, contrasted with the other idiom לפני יהוה, and therefore cannot be a mere substitute for מפני.

[e] Josh. xix. 13. [f] p. 44. 2. ed. Asher.

[g] Porter, in Smith, Bibl. Dict. p. 656. v. Gath-hepher. A Jewish traveller, A. D. 1637, places the tomb at Caphar Kena (קינא.) "There is buried Jonah son of Amittai, on the top of a hill in a beautiful Church of the Gentiles," in Hottinger Cippi Hebr. pp. 74, 5.

[h] Ant. xi. 8. 5. Justin alludes to the meeting, xi. 10.

[i] Acts x. 34, 5.

[k] in Jon. i. 1.

[l] Menasseh B. Israel de resurr. mort. c. 5. p. 36. from "the divine Cabbalists who, from the history of Jonah, prove, by way of allegory, the resurrection of the dead." Ib. p. 34.

also on the third day rise again and be restored to life. As Hosea says[m], *On the third day He will raise us up, and we shall live in His sight.*" Talmudic Jews[n] identified Jonah with their Messiah ben Joseph, whom they expected to die and rise again. The deeper meaning then of the history was not, at least in later times, unknown to them, a meaning which entirely depended on its truth.

The history of his mission, Jonah doubtless himself wrote. Such has been the uniform tradition of the Jews, and on this principle alone was his book placed among the prophets. For no books were admitted among the prophets but those which the arranger of the Canon *believed* (if this was the work of the great synagogue) or (if it was the work of Ezra) *knew*, to have been written by persons called to the prophetic office. Hence the Psalms of David, (although many are prophetic, and our Lord declares him to have been inspired by the Holy Ghost[o],) and the book of Daniel, were placed in a separate class, because their authors, although eminently endowed with prophetic gifts, did not exercise the pastoral office of the Prophet. Histories of the Prophets, as Elijah and Elisha, stand, not under their own names, but in the books of the prophets who wrote them. Nor is the book of Jonah a history of the Prophet, but of that one mission to Nineveh. Every notice of the Prophet is omitted, except what bears on that mission. The book also begins with just that same authentication, with which all other prophetic books begin. As Hosea and Joel and Micah and Zephaniah open, *The word of the Lord that came unto Hosea, Joel, Micah, Zephaniah*, and other prophets in other ways ascribe their books not to themselves, but to God, so Jonah opens, *And the word of the Lord came unto Jonah, the son of Amittai, saying.* This inscription is an integral part of the book; as is marked by the word, *saying*. As the historical books are joined on the sacred writings before them, so as to form one continuous stream of history, by the *and*, with which they begin, so the book of Jonah is tacitly joined on to other books of other prophets by the word, *and*, with which it commences[p]. The words, *The word of the Lord came to*, are the acknowledged form[q] in which the commission of God to prophesy is recorded. It is used of the commission to deliver a single prophecy, or it describes the whole collection of prophecies, with which any prophet was entrusted[r]; *The word of the Lord which came to Micah* or *Zephaniah*. But the whole history of the prophecy is bound up with, and a sequel of those words.

Nor is there anything in the style of the Prophet at variance with this.

It is strange that, at any time beyond the babyhood of criticism, any argument should be drawn from the fact that the Prophet writes of himself in the third person. Manly criticism has been ashamed to use the argument, as to the commentaries of Cæsar or the Anabasis of Xenophon[s]. However the genuineness of those works may have been at times questioned, here we were on the ground of genuine criticism, and no one ventured to use an argument so palpably idle. It has been pointed out that minds so different, as Barhebræus, the great Jacobite historian of the East[t], and Frederick the Great wrote of themselves in the third person; as did also Thucydides and Josephus[v], even after they had attested that the history, in which they so speak, was written by themselves.

But the real ground lies much deeper. It is the *exception*, when any sacred writer speaks of himself in the first person. Ezra and Nehemiah do so; for they are giving an account, not of God's dealings with His people, but of their own discharge of a definite office, allotted to them by man. Solomon does so in Ecclesiastes, because he is giving the history of his own experience; and the vanity of all human things, in themselves, could be attested so impressively by no one, as by one, who had all which man's mind could imagine.

On the contrary, the Prophets, unless they speak of God's revelations to them, speak of themselves in the third person. Thus Amos relates in the first person, what God shewed him in vision[w]; for God spoke to him, and he answered and pleaded with God. In relating his persecution by Amaziah, he passes at once to the third; [x] *Amaziah said to Amos; Then answered Amos and said to Amaziah.* In like way, Isaiah speaks of himself in the third person, when relating how God sent him to meet Ahaz[y]; commanded him to walk three years, naked and barefoot[z], Hezekiah's message to him, to pray for his people, and his own prophetic answer; his visit to Hezekiah in the king's sickness, his warning to him, his prophecy of his recovery, the sign which at God's command Isaiah gave him, and the means of healing he appointed[a]. Jeremiah, the mourner over his people more than any other prophet, speaks and complains to his God in the midst of his prophecy. In no other prophet do we see so much the workings of his inmost soul.

[m] vi. 2. (Eng.) see ab. p. 38.
[n] See in Eisenmenger, Entdecktes Judenthum, ii. 725.
[o] S. Matt. xxii. 43, S. Mark xii. 36.
[p] See more on Jon. i. 1.
[q] Gesenius, Thes. v. דבר. [r] Mic. i. 1, Zeph. i. 1.

[s] See Hengstenb. Auth. d. Pent. ii. 167–9.
[t] Hengst. ii. 170, from Ass. B. O. ii. 248 sqq.
[v] B. J, ii. 20. 4, 21, iii. 4, 6, 7, & 8.
[w] Am. vii. 1–8, viii. 1, 2, ix. 1.
[x] Ib. vii. 12, 14. [y] Is. vii. 3. [z] Ib. xx. 2, 3.
[a] Is. xxxvii, 2, 5, 6, 21, xxxviii. 1, 4, 21.

Such souls would most use the first person; for it is in the use of the first person that the soul pours itself forth. In relating of himself in the third person, the Prophet restrains himself, speaks of the event only. Yet it is thus that Jeremiah relates almost all which befell him; Pashur's smiting him and putting him in the stocks[b]; the gathering of the people against him to put him to death, his hearing before the princes of Judah and his deliverance[c]; the contest with Hananiah, when Hananiah broke off the symbolic yoke from his neck and prophesied lies in the name of God, and Jeremiah foretold his death[d], which followed; the letters of Shemaiah against him, and his own prophecy against Shemaiah[e]; his trial of the Rechabites and his prophecy to them[f]; the writing the roll, which he sent Baruch to read in God's house, and its renewal when Jehoiakim had burnt it, and God's concealing him and Baruch from the king's emissaries[g]; his purpose to leave Jerusalem when the interval of the last siege gave him liberty[h]; the false accusations against him, the designs of the princes to put him to death, their plunging him in the yet deeper pit, where was no water but mire, the milder treatment through the intercession of Ebed-melech; Zedekiah's intercourse with him[i]; his liberation by Nebuzaradan, his choice to abide in the land, his residence with Gedaliah[k]; Johanan's hypocritical enquiring of God by him and disobedience[l], his being carried into Egypt[m], the insolent answer of the Jews in Egypt to him and his denunciation upon them[n]. All this, the account of which occupies a space, many times larger than the book of Jonah, Jeremiah relates as if it were the history of some other man. So did God teach His prophets to forget themselves. Haggai, whose prophecy consists of exhortations which God directed him to address to the people, speaks of himself, solely in the third person. He even relates the questions which he puts to the priests and their answers still in the third person[o]; "then said Haggai;" "then answered Haggai." Daniel relates in the third person, the whole which he does give of his history; how when young he obtained exemption from the use of the royal luxuries and from food unlawful to him; the favor and wisdom which God gave him[p]; how God saved him from death, revealing to him, on his prayer, the dream of Nebuchadnezzar and its meaning; how Nebuchadnezzar made him ruler over the whole province of Babylon[q]; how he was brought into Belshazzar's great impious feast, and interpreted the writing on the wall; and was honored[r]; how, under Darius, he persevered in his wonted prayer against the king's command, was cast into the den of lions, was delivered, and *prospered in the reign of Darius and in the reign of Cyrus the Persian*[s]. When Daniel passes from history to relate visions vouchsafed to himself, he authenticated them with his own name, *I Daniel*[t]. It is no longer his own history. It is the revelation of God by him. In like way, S. John, when referring to himself in the history of his Lord, calls himself *the disciple whom Jesus loved*. In the Revelations, he authenticates his visions by his own name; [u]*I John*. Moses relates how God commanded him to write things which he wrote, in the third person. S. Paul, when he has to speak of his overpowering revelations, says[v], *I knew a man in Christ*. It seems as if he could not speak of them as vouchsafed to himself. He lets us see that it was himself, when he speaks of the humiliations[w], which God saw to be necessary for him. To ordinary men it would be conceit or hypocrisy to write of themselves in the third person. They would have the appearance of writing impartially of themselves, of abstracting themselves from themselves, when, in reality, they were ever present to themselves. The men of God were writing of the things of God. They had a God-given indifference how they themselves would be thought of by man. They related, with the same holy unconcern, their praise or their blame. Johah has exhibited himself in his infirmities, such as no other but himself would have drawn a Prophet of God. He has left his character, unexplained, unsoftened; he has left himself lying under God's reproof; and told us nothing of all that which God loved in him, and which made him too a chosen instrument of God. Men, while they measure Divine things, or characters formed by God, by what would be natural to themselves, measure by a crooked rule. [x]*It is a very small thing*, says S. Paul, *that I should be judged of you, or of man's judgment*. Nature does not measure grace; nor the human spirit, the Divine.

As for the few words, which persons who disbelieved in miracles selected out of the book of Jonah as a plea for removing it far down beyond the period when those miracles took place[y], they rather indicate the contrary. They are all genuine Hebrew words

[b] Jer. xx 1, 3. [c] Ib. xxvi. 7, 8, 12, 24.
[d] xxviii. 5, 6, 10, 12, 15 [e] xxix. 27, 29, 30.
[f] xxxv [g] xxxvi. 1, 4, 5, 26, 27, 32.
[h] xxxvii. 2–6, 12–21.
[i] xxxviii 1, 6, 12–28, xxxii. 2–5. [k] xl. 2–6
[l] xlii. [m] xliii. [n] xliv 15, 20, 24.
[o] Hagg i 1, 3, 12, 13, ii. 1, 10, 13, 14, 20.
[p] Dan. i 6–end [q] ii. 13-27, 46, 47, 49.
[r] v. 12, 13, 17, 29. [s] ch. vi.

[t] vii. 15, 28, viii. 1, 15, 27, ix. 2, x. 2, 7, xii. 5.
[u] Rev. i. 9, xxi. 2, xxii. 8. [v] 2 Cor. xii. 2-4.
[w] Ib. 7. [x] 1 Cor. iv. 3.
[y] "We heed not," says Rosenmuller, Præf. c. 7. "the opinion of those who think that Jonah himself committed to writing in this book what befel himself, *since we do not admit* that any real history is contained in it." "Formerly, when people saw in the book of Jonah pure history, no one doubted

or forms, except the one Aramaic name for the decree of the king of Nineveh, which Jonah naturally heard in Nineveh itself.

A writer [z], equally unbelieving, who got rid of the miracles by assuming that the book of Jonah was meant only for a moralizing fiction, found no counter-evidence in the language, but ascribed it unhesitatingly to the Jonah, son of Amittai, who prophesied in the reign of Jeroboam II. He saw the nothingness of the so-called proof, which he had no longer any interest in maintaining.

The examination of these words will require a little detail, yet it may serve as a specimen (it is no worse than its neighbors) of the way in which the disbelieving school picked out a few words of a Hebrew Prophet or section of a Prophet, in order to disparage the genuineness of what they did not believe.

The words are these:

1) The word *sephinah*, lit. "a decked vessel," is a genuine Hebrew word from *saphan*, "covered, ceiled [a]." The word was borrowed from the Hebrew, not by Syrians or Chaldees only but by the Arabians, in none of which dialects is it an original word. A word plainly is original in that language in which it stands connected with other meanings of the same root, and not in that in which it stands isolated. Naturally too, the term for a *decked* vessel would be borrowed by inland people, as the Syrians, from a notion living on the sea shore, not conversely. This is the first occasion for mentioning a *decked* vessel. It is related that Jonah went in fact "below deck," *was gone down into the sides of the decked vessel.* Three times in those verses [b], when Jonah did not wish to express that the vessel was decked, he uses the common Hebrew word, *oniyyah.* It was then of set purpose that he, in the same verse, used the two words, *oniyyah* and *sephinah.*

2) *Mallach* is also a genuine Heb. word from *melach*, *salt* sea, as ἁλιεύς from ἅλς "salt," then (masc.) in poetry "brine." It is formed strictly, as other Hebrew words denoting an occupation [c]. It does not occur in earlier books, because "seamen" are not mentioned earlier.

3) *Rab hachobel*, "chief of the sailors," "captain." *Rab* is Phœnician also, and this was a Phœnician vessel. It does not occur earlier, because "the captain of a vessel" is not mentioned earlier. One says "[d] it is the same as *sar*, *chiefly* in later Hebrew." It occurs, in *all*, only four times, and in all cases, as here, of persons not Hebrew; Nebuzaradan, *rab Tabbachim* [e], *captain* of the guard;" *rab Sarisim* [f], "chief of the eunuchs;" col *rab baitho* [g], "every officer of his house." *Sar*, on the other hand, is never used except of an *office* of authority, of one who had a place of authority given by one higher. It occurs as much in the later as in the earlier books, but is not used in the singular of an inferior office. It is used of military, but not of any inferior secular command. It would probably have been a solecism to have said *sar hachobel*, as much as if we were to say "prince of sailors." Chobel, which is joined with it, is a Hebrew not Aramaic word.

4) *Ribbo*, "ten thousand," they say, "is a word of later Hebrew." Certainly neither it, nor any inflection of it occurs in the Pentateuch, Judges, Samuel, Canticles, in all which we have the word *rebabah.* It is true also that the form *ribbo* or derivative forms occur in books of the date of the Captivity, as Daniel, Chronicles, Ezra, and Nehemiah [h]. But it also occurs in a Psalm of David [i], and in Hosea [k] who is acknowledged to have prophesied in the days of Jeroboam, and so was a contemporary of Jonah. It might have been, accordingly, a form used in Northern Palestine, but that its use by David does not justify such limitation.

5) *Yith' ashshath*, "thought, purposed," is also an old Hebrew word, as appears from its use in the number *eleven* [l], as the first number which is conceived in *thought*, the ten being numbered on the fingers. The root occurs also in Job, a Psalm [m], and the Canticles. In the Syriac, it does not occur; nor, in the extant Chaldee, in the sense in which it is used in Jonah. For in Jonah it is used of the merciful *thoughts* of God; in Chaldee, of the evil thoughts of man. Beside, it is used in Jonah not by the Prophet himself, but by the shipmaster, whose words he relates.

6) The use of the abridged forms of the relative *she* for *asher*, twice in composite words *beshellemi* [n], *beshelli* [o], (the fuller form, *baasher lemi* [p], also occurring) and once in union with a noun *shebbin* [q].

There is absolutely no plea whatever for making this an indication of a later style, and yet it occurs in every string of words, which have been assumed to be indications of such style. It is not Aramaic at all, but Phœnician [r]

that the Prophet Jonah himself wrote his wondrous lot." Bertholdt. Einl. § 564.

[z] Paulus, Memorabil. St. 6. p. 69.

[a] סְפַן "cover" occurs in Talmudic (as derived from the Hebrew) not in Chald. In Arabic it means "planed," smoothed, swept the earth, not "ceiled." So our deck is from the Dutch dekken, to cover.

[b] i. 3, 4, 5. [c] מַלָּח. [d] See Gesen. 1254.

[e] 2 Kings xxv. 8. [f] Dan. i. 3. [g] Esth. i. 8.

[h] In 1 Chron. xxix. 7. twice, Daniel once, Ezra twice; Nehemiah thrice.

[i] רבותים Ps. lxviii. 18. [k] viii. 12 Ch.

[l] עשתי עשר So A. E. Kim. [m] Ps. cxlvi. 4.

[n] i. 7. [o] i. 12. [p] i. 8. [q] iv. 10. (2).

[r] Ges. Thes. p. 1845. after Quatremère, Journ. Asiat. 1828. pp. 15. sqq. Journ. d. Savans, 1838. Oct. In Aramaic it is ד, די, דיל. "Every one skilled herein knows now, that in Punic אש is the relative pronoun." Roed. Ib. Add. Em. 113.

and old Hebrew. In Phœnician, *esh* is the relative, which corresponds the more with the Hebrew in that the following letter was doubled, as in the Punic words in Plautus, *syllohom, siddoberim*[s], it enters into two Proper names, both of which occur in the Pentateuch, and one, only there, *Methushael*[t], "a man of God," and *Mishael*[u], the same as Michael, "who is like God?" lit. "Who is what God is?" Probably, it occurs also in the Pentateuch in the ordinary language[v]. Perhaps it was used more in the dialect of North Palestine[w]. Probably it was also the spoken language[x], in which abridged forms are used in all languages. Hence perhaps its frequent use in the Song of Solomon[y], which is all dialogue, and in which it is employed to the entire exclusion of the fuller form; and that, so frequently, that the instances in the Canticles are nearly ¼ of those in the whole Old Testament[z]. In addition to this, half of the whole number of instances, in which it occurs in the Bible, are found in another short book, Ecclesiastes. In a book, containing only 222 verses, it occurs 66 times[a]. This, in itself, requires some ground for its use, beyond that of mere date. Of books which are really later, it does *not* occur in Jeremiah's prophecies, Ezekiel, Daniel, or any of the 6 later of the Minor Prophets, nor in Nehemiah or Esther. It occurs once only in Ezra[b], and twice in the first book of Chronicles[c], whereas it occurs four times in the Judges[d], and once in the Kings[e], and once probably in Job[f]. Its use belongs to that wide principle of condensation in Hebrew, blending in one, in different ways, what we express by separate words. The relative pronoun is confessedly, on this ground, very often omitted in Hebrew poetry, when it would be used in prose. In the Canticles Solomon does not once use the ordinary separate relative, *asher*. Of the 19 instances in the Psalms, almost half, 9, occur in those Psalms of peculiar rhythm, the gradual Psalms[g]; four more occur in two other Psalms[h], which belong to one another, the latter of which has that remarkable burden, *for His mercy endureth forever.* Three are condensed into a solemn denunciation of Babylon in another Psalm[i]. Of the ten Psalms, in which it occurs, four are ascribed to David, and one only, the 137th, has any token of belonging to a later date. In the two passages in the Chronicles, it occurs in words doubly compounded[c]. The principle of rhythm would account for its occurring four times in the five chapters of the Lamentations[k] of Jeremiah, while in the 52 chapters of his prophecies it does not occur once. In Job also, it is in a solemn pause[f]. Altogether, there is no proof whatever that the use of *she* for *asher* is any test of the date of any Hebrew book, since 1) it is not Aramaic, 2) it occurs in the earliest, and 3) not in the latest books: 4) its use is idiomatic, and nowhere except in the Canticles and Ecclesiastes does it pervade any book. Had it belonged to the ordinary idiom at the date of Ezra, it would not have been so entirely insulated as it is, in the three instances in the Chronicles and Ezra. It would not have occurred in the earlier books in which it does occur, and would have occurred in later books in which it does not. In Jonah, its use in two places is peculiar to himself, occurring nowhere else in the Hebrew Scriptures. In the first, its Phœnician form is used by the Phœnician mariners; in the 2d it is an instance of the spoken language in the mouth of the Prophet, a native of North Palestine, and in answer to Phœnicians. In the third instance, (where it is the simple relative) its use is evidently for condensation. Its use in any case would agree with the exact circumstances of Jonah, as a native of North Palestine, conversing with the Phœnician mariners. The only plea of argument has been gained by arguing in a circle, assuming without any even plausible ground that the Song of Solomon or Psalms of David were late, because they had this form, and then using it as a test of another book being late; ignoring alike the earlier books which have it and the later books which have it not, and its exceptional use (except in the Canticles and Ecclesiastes,) in the books which have it.

7) It is difficult to know to what end the use of *manah*, "appoint[l]" or "prepare," is

[s] Plaut. Pænul. v. 1. 4. 6. See Ges.

[t] Gen. iv. 18.

[u] Ex. vi. 22, Lev. x. 4; also in Daniel and Nehemiah.

[v] Gen. vi. 3.

[w] Hence perhaps in the song of Deborah, Judg. v. 7.

[x] Judg. vi. 17, 2 Kings vi. 11. Two of the instances in the Lamentations are words in the mouth of the heathen, Lam. ii. 15, 16.

[y] i. 6 (2), 7 (2), ii. 7, 17, iii. 1, 2, 3, 4 (4), 5, 7, iv. 1, 2 (2), 6, v. 2, 8, 9, vi. 5 (2), 6 (2), viii. 4. 8, 12.

[z] It occurs in all, I believe, 132 times, apart from its use as entering into the two proper names. Of these 29 are in the Canticles, 66 in Ecclesiastes, 19 in the Psalms, 1 in Genesis, 1 in Job, 4 in Judges, 1 in Kings, 4 in Lamentations, 1 in Ezra, 2 in Chronicles.

[a] Eccl. i. 3, 7, 9 (4), 10, 11 (2), 14, 17, ii. 9, 11 (2), 12, 13, 14, 15, 16, 17, 18 (3), 19 (2), 20, 21 (2), 22, 24, 26, iii. 13, 14, 15, 18, 22, iv. 2, 10, v. 4, 14 (2), 15 (2), 17, vi. 3, 10 (2), vii. 10, 14, 24, viii. 7, 14, 17 ix. 5, 12 (2), x. 3, 5, 14, 16, 17, xi. 3, 8, xii. 3, 7, 9.

[b] viii. 20.

[c] 1 Chr. v. 20. שעמהם, xxvii. 27. שבכרמים.

[d] v. 7, vi. 17, vii. 12, viii. 26.

[e] 2 Kings vi. 11. משלנו.

[f] xix. 29, ending with שדין.

[g] Ps. cxxii. 3, 4, cxxiii. 2, cxxiv 1, 6, cxxix. 6, 7, cxxxiii. 2, 3.

[h] cxxv. 2, 8, 10, cxxxvi. 23.

[i] cxxxvii. 8 (2), 9. The remaining are Ps. cxliv. 15. שככה and cxlvi. 3, 5.

[k] ii. 15, 16, iv. 19, v. 18.

[l] The word occurs in Arabic also in this sense, which is a primary meaning of the root, and allied to its use is the transposed Greek form, νέμω.

alleged, since it occurs in a Psalm of David[m]. Jonah uses it in a special way as to acts of God's Providence, "preparing" before, what He wills to employ. Jonah uses the word of the "preparing" of the fish, the palm-christ, the worm which should destroy it, the East wind. He evidently used it with a set purpose, to express what no other word expressed equally to his mind, how God prepared by His Providence the instruments which He willed to employ.

8) There remains only the word used for the decree of the king of Nineveh, *taam*. This is a Syriac word; and accordingly, since it has now been ascertained beyond all question, that the language of Nineveh was a dialect of Syriac, it was, with a Hebrew pronunciation[n], the very word used of this decree at Nineveh. The employment of the special word is a part of the same accuracy with which Jonah relates that the decree used was issued not from the king only, but from *the king and his nobles*, one of those minute touches, which occur in the writings of those who describe what they have seen, but supplying a fact as to the Assyrian polity, which we should not otherwise have known, that the nobles were in some way associated in the decrees of the king.

Out of these eight words or forms, three are naval terms, and, since Israel was no seafaring people, it is in harmony with the history, that these terms should first occur in the first prophet who left the land of his mission by sea. So it is also, that an Assyrian technical term should first occur in a prophet who had been sent to Nineveh. A fifth word occurs in Hosea, a contemporary of Jonah, and in a Psalm of David. The abridged grammatical form was Phœnician, not Aramaic, was used in conversation, occurs in the oldest proper names, and in the Northern tribes. The 7th and 8th do not occur in Aramaic in the meaning in which they are used by Jonah.

In truth, often as these false criticisms have been repeated from one to the other, they would not have been thought of at all, but for the miracles related by Jonah, which the devisers of these criticisms did not believe. A history of miracles, such as those in Jonah, would not be published at the time, unless they were true. Those then who did not believe that God worked any miracles, were forced to have some plea for saying that the book was not written in the time of Jonah. Prejudices against faith have, sometimes openly, sometimes tacitly, been the ruling principle on which earlier portions of Holy Scripture have been classed among the latter by critics who disbelieved what those books or passages related. Obviously no weight can be given to the opinions of critics, whose criticisms are founded, not on the study of the language, but on unbelief. It has recently been said, "[o] the joint decision of Gesenius, De Wette and Hitzig ought to be final." *A joint* decision certainly it is not. For De Wette places the book of Jonah before the captivity[p]; Gesenius[q] and Ewald[r], when prophecy had long ceased; Ewald, partly on account of its miracles, in the 5th century, B.C.; and Hitzig, with his wonted wilfulness and insulatedness of criticism, built a theory that the book is of Egyptian origin on his own mistake that the *kikaion* grew only in Egypt, and placed it in the 2d century, B.C., the times of the Maccabees[s]. The interval is also filled up. Every sort of date and contradictory grounds for those dates have been assigned. So then one places the book of Jonah in the time of Sennacherib[t], i.e. of Hezekiah; another under Josiah[u]; another before the Captivity[v]; another toward the end of the Captivity, after the destruction of Nineveh by Cyaxares[w]; a fifth lays chief stress on the argument that the destruction of Nineveh is not mentioned in it[x]; a sixth[y] prefers the time after the return from the Captivity to its close; a seventh doubted not, "from its argument and purpose, that it was written before the order of prophets ceased[z]," others of the same school are as positive from its arguments and contents, that it must have been written after that order was closed[a].

The style of the book of Jonah is, in fact pure and simple Hebrew, corresponding to the simplicity of the narrative and of the Prophet's character. Although written in prose, it has poetic language, not in the thanksgiving only, but whenever it suits the subject. These expressions are peculiar to Jonah. Such are, in the account of the storm, "the Lord *cast*[b] a strong wind," "the vessel *thought*[c] to be broken," "the sea shall be *silent*[d]" (hushed, as we say) i.e. calm; "the wind was advancing and storming[e],"

[m] Ps. lxi. 8. [n] טַעַם for טְעֵם.

[o] Mr. G. Vance Smith, Prophecies concerning Nineveh p. 257, who however (p. 294,) rightly rejects their grounds, the occurrence of the words discussed above, as inadequate. The only other ground is their unbelief.

[p] Einl. § 237. [q] Hall. A. L. Z. 1813. n. 23. p. 180.

[r] Propheten, p. 559. [s] Kl. Proph. Jonah, § 6.

[t] Goldhorn, Excurse zum B. Jonah, pp. 16 sqq.

[u] Rosenmuller, Prol. in Jon. § 7. [v] De Wette.

[w] Müller, in Memorabilien, P. vi. pp. 146 sqq.

[x] Bertholdt, § 564. [y] Jahn, Einl. § 129.

[z] Maurer, Præf. in Jon. p. 426.

[a] Ges. and Ew. above, Umbreit tacitly drops it out of "the twelve."

[b] הטיל i. 4; the word describing how the wind "swept *along*," as we say; Jonah also uses it of casting out, along, from the vessel, i. 5, 12, 15.

[c] חשבה i. 4, the only place where it is used of lifeless things.

[d] שׁתק i. 11, 12. used of the men in the vessel, Ps. cvii. 30; of ceasing of strife, Prov. xxvi. 20.

[e] הולך וסֹעֵר i. 11, 13.

as with a whirlwind; [the word is used as to the sea by Jonah only,] "the men ploughed" or "dug[f]" [in rowing] "the sea *stood*[g] from its raging." Also "let man and beast *clothe themselves*[h] with sackcloth," and that touching expression, "son of a night[i], it [the palma Christi] came to being, and son of a night [i.e. in a night] it perished." It is in harmony with his simplicity of character, that he is fond of the old idiom, by which the thought of the verb is carried on by a noun formed from it. "The men *feared* a great *fear*[k]," "It *displeased* Jonah a great *displeasure*[l]," "Jonah *joyed* a great *joy*[m]." Another idiom[n] has been observed, which occurs in no writer later than the judges.

But in the history every phrase is vivid and graphic. There is not a word which does not advance the history. There is no reflection. All hastens on to the completion, and when God has given the key to the whole, the book closes with His words of exceeding tenderness, lingering in our ears. The Prophet, with the same simplicity and beginning with the same words, says he did not, and he did, obey God. The book opens, after the first authenticating words, *Arise, go to Nineveh, that great city, and cry against it; for the wickedness is come up before Me.* God had bidden him arise[o]; the narrative simply repeats the word, *And Jonah arose*[p],—but for what? to flee in the very opposite direction *from being before the Lord*[q], i.e. from standing in His Presence, as His servant and minister. He lost no time, to do the contrary. After the miracles, by which he had been both punished and delivered, the history is resumed with the same simple dignity as before, in the same words; the disobedience being noticed only in the word, *a second time. And the word of the Lord came to Jonah a second time, saying, Arise, go to Nineveh, that great city, and cry unto it that cry which I say unto thee.* This time it follows, *And Jonah arose and went to Nineveh.*

Then in the history itself we follow the Prophet step by step. He arose to flee to Tarshish, went down to Joppa, a perilous, yet the only sea-port for Judæa[r]. He finds the ship, *pays its fare,* (one of those little touches of a true narrative); God sends the storm, man does all he can; and all in vain. The character of the heathen is brought out in contrast with the then sleeping conscience and despondency of the Prophet. But it is all in act. They are all activity; he, simply passive. They pray, (as they can) each man to his gods; he is asleep: they do all they can, lighten the ship, the ship-master rouses him, to pray to his God, since their own prayers avail not; they propose the lots, cast them; the lot falls on Jonah. Then follow their brief accumulated enquiries; Jonah's calm answer, increasing their fear; their enquiry of the Prophet himself, what they are to do to him; his knowledge that he must be cast over; the unwillingness of the Heathen; one more fruitless effort to save both themselves and the Prophet; the increasing violence of the storm; the prayer to the Prophet's God, not to lay innocent blood to them, who obeyed His Prophet; the casting him forth; the instant hush and silence of the sea; their conversion and sacrifice to the true God—the whole stands before us, as if we saw it with our own eyes.

And yet, amid, or perhaps as a part of, that vividness, there is that characteristic of Scripture-narratives, that some things even seem improbable, until, on thought, we discover the reason. It is not on a first reading, that most perceive the naturalness either of Jonah's deep sleep, or of the increase of the mariner's fear, on his account of himself. Yet that deep sleep harmonizes at least with his long hurried flight to Joppa, and that mood with which men who have taken a wrong step, try to forget themselves. He relates that he *was gone down*[s], i.e. before the storm began. The sailors' increased fear surprises us the more, since it is added, "they knew that he had fled from before the presence of God, *because he had told them.*" One word explained it. He had told them, from Whose service he had fled, but not that He, against Whom he had sinned, and Who, they would think, was pursuing His fugitive, was "the Maker of the sea," whose raging was threatening their lives.

Again, the history mentions only, that Jonah was cast over; that God prepared a fish to swallow him; that he was in the belly of the fish three days and three nights; that he, at the end of that time, prayed to God out of the fish's belly, and at the close of the prayer was delivered. The word "prayed" obviously includes "thanksgiving" as the act of adoring love from the creature to the Creator. It is said that *Hannah prayed*[t]; but her hymn, as well as Jonah's does not contain one petition. Both are the outpouring

[f] חתר "Æquor arare." Virg. Æn. ii. 780. Ov. Trist. i. 2, 76.

[g] יעמד־מזעפו i. 15. [h] יתכסו iii. 8.

[i] בִּן־לילה iv. 10. [k] i. 10, 16. ייראו יראה.

[l] iv. 1. ירע רעה. [m] Ib. 6. ישמח שמחה.

[n] עַד with the inf. (for בעוד) iv. 2. coll. Jud. iii. 26. (Delitzsch in Zeitschr. f. Luth. Theol. 1840. p. 118.) But two passages do not furnish an induction. הרבה for יותר iv. 11. (mentioned ib.) cannot prove anything, since it occurs, 2 Chr. xxv. 9.

[o] קום.

[p] ויקם, more expressive in the original, as being the first word in the clause; "The Lord said, *Arise; And arose* Jonah," to do the contrary.

[q] See ab. p. 371.

[r] 1 Kings v. 9, 2 Chron. ii. 16, and after the captivity, Ezr. iii. 7.

[s] i. 5.

[t] 1 Sam. ii. 1.

of thanksgiving from the soul, to which God had given what it *had* prayed for. As, before, it was not said, whether he prayed, on the ship-master's upbraiding, or no, so here nothing is said in the history, except as to the last moment, on which he was cast out on the dry ground. The prayer incidentally supplies the rest. *It* is a simple thanksgiving of one who *had* prayed, and *had* been delivered. [u] *I cried unto the Lord, and He heard me.* In the first mercy, he saw the earnest of the rest. He asks for nothing, he only thanks. But that for which he thanks is the deliverance from the perils of the *sea*. The thanksgiving corresponds with the plain words, that he *prayed out of the fish's belly*. They are suited to one so praying, who looked on in full faith to the future completion of his deliverance, although *our* minds might rather have been fixed on the actual peril. It is a thanksgiving of faith, but of stronger faith than many moderns have been able to conceive [v].

The hymn itself is a remarkable blending of old and new, as our Lord says [w]; *Therefore is the kingdom of heaven like a householder, who bringeth out of his treasure new and old.* The Prophet teaches us to use the Psalms, as well as how the holy men of old used them. In that great moment of religious life, the well-remembered Psalms, such as he had often used them, were brought to his mind. What had been figures to David or the sons of Korah, as [x], *the waters are come in even unto my soul;* [y] *all Thy billows and Thy waves passed over me,* were strict realities to him. Yet only in this last sentence and in one other sentence which doubtless had become a proverb of accepted prayer, [z] *I cried out of my trouble unto the Lord and He heard me,* does Jonah use exactly the words of earlier Psalms. Elsewhere he varies or amplifies them according to his own special circumstances. Thus, where David said, "the waters are *come in,* even unto my soul," Jonah substitutes the word which described best the condition from which God had delivered *him,* "The water *compassed me about,* even to the soul." Where David said [a], "*I am cut off* from before Thine eyes," expressing an abiding condition, Jonah, who had for disobedience been cast into the sea, uses the strong word, "[b] *I am cast out* from before Thine eyes." David says, "I said in my haste;" Jonah simply, "I said;" for he had deserved it. David said [c], "when my spirit was overwhelmed" or "fainted within me," "*Thou knewest my path;*" Jonah substitutes, "When my soul fainted within me, *I remembered the Lord* [d];" for when he rebelled, he forgat Him. David said, "[e] *I hate* them that observe lying vanities;" Jonah, who had himself disobeyed God, says mournfully, "[f] They that observe lying vanities, *forsake their own mercy,*" i. e. their God, Who is Mercy.

Altogether, Jonah's thanksgiving is that of one whose mind was stored with the Psalms which were part of the public worship, but it is the language of one who uses and re-casts them freely, as he was taught of God, not of one who copies. No one verse is taken entirely from any Psalm. There are original expressions everywhere [g]. The words, "I went down to the cuttings-off of the mountains," "the sea-weed bound around my head;" "the earth, its bars around me for ever;" perhaps the coral reefs which run along all that shore [h], vividly exhibit him, sinking, entangled, imprisoned, as it seems, inextricably; he goes on; we should expect some further description of his state; but he adds, in five simple words [i], *Thou broughtest up my life from corruption, O Lord My God.* Words, somewhat like these last, occur elsewhere [j] *thou hast brought up my soul from hell,* agreeing in the one word "brought up." But the majesty of the Prophet's conception is in the connection of the thought; the sea-weed was bound round his head as his grave-clothes; the solid bars of the deep-rooted earth, were around him, *and*—God brought him up. At the close of the thanksgiving, *Salvation is the Lord's,* deliverance is completed, as though God had only waited for this act of complete faith.

So could no one have written, who had not himself been delivered from such an extreme peril of drowning, as man could not, of himself, escape from. True, that no image so well expresses the overwhelmedness under affliction or temptation, as the pressure of storm by land, or being overflooded by the waves of the sea. Human poetry knows of "a sea of troubles," or "the triple wave of evils." It expresses how we are simply passive and powerless under a trouble, which leaves us neither breath nor power of motion; under which we can be but still, till, by

[u] ii. 3.

[v] "In the fish's belly, he prays as tranquilly as if on land," says even Jahn, as an objection. Einl. § 126.

[w] S. Matt. xiii. 52.

[x] Jon. ii. 5, Ps. lxix. 2.

[y] Jon. ii. 3, Ps. xlii. 8.

[z] Jon. ii. 2, Ps. cxx. 1.

[a] Ps. xxxi. 22. נגזרתי.

[b] Jon. ii. 4. [5] נגרשתי.

[c] Ps. cxlii. 8.

[d] ii. 7. (8).

[e] Ps. xxxi. 7.

[f] ii. 9.

[g] שאול מבטן ii. 3; נהר of the currents of the sea, 4; סוף חבוש לראשי, 6; קצבי הרים 7; הארץ בריחיה בעדי לעולם, Ib. חסדם יעזבו, 8.

[h] "Considerable quantities of coral are found in the adjacent sea." W. G. Browne, writing of Jaffa, Travels, p. 360. "Coral-reefs run along the coast as far as Gaza, which cut the cables in two, and leave the ships at the mercy of the storms. None lie here on the coast, which is fuller of strong surfs (brandings,) and unprotected against the frequent West winds." Ritter, ii. 399. ed. 1.

[i] ותעל משחת חיי יהוה אלהי.

[j] Ps. xxx. 3.

God's mercy it passes. "We are sunk, over-head, deep down in temptations, and the masterful current is sweeping in eddies over us." Of this sort are those images which Jonah took from the Psalms. But a description so minute as the whole of Jonah's would be allegory, not metaphor. What, in it, is most descriptive of Jonah's situation[k], as "binding of the sea-weed around the head, the sinking down to the roots of the mountains, the bars of the earth around him," are peculiar to this thanksgiving of Jonah; they do not occur elsewhere; for, except through miracle, they would be images not of peril but of death.

The same vividness, and the same steady directions to its end, characterizes the rest of the book. Critics have wondered[l], why Jonah does not say, on what shore he was cast forth, why he does not describe his long journey to Nineveh, or tell us the name of the Assyrian king, or what he himself did, when his mission was closed. Jonah speaks of himself, only as relates to his mission, and God's teaching through him; he tells us not the king's name, but his deeds. The description of the size of Nineveh remarkably corresponds alike with the ancient accounts and modern investigations. Jonah describes it as "a city of three days' journey." This obviously means its circumference; for, unless the city were a circle, (as no cities are,) it would have no one diameter. A person might describe the average length *and* breadth of a city, but no one who gave any one measure, by days or miles or any other measure, would mean anything else than its circumference. Diodorus (probably on the authority of Ctesias) states that "[m] it was well-walled, of unequal lengths. Each of the longer sides was 150 furlongs; each of the shorter, 90. The whole circuit then being 480 furlongs [60 miles] the hope of the founder was not disappointed. For no one afterward built a city of such compass, and with walls so magnificent." To Babylon "Clitarchus and the companions of Alexander in their writings, assigned a circuit of 365 furlongs, adding that the number of furlongs was conformed to the number of days in the year[n]." Ctesias, in round numbers, calls them 360[o]; Strabo, 385[p]. All these accounts agree with the statement of Strabo, "Nineveh was much larger than Babylon[q]." The 60 miles of Diodorus exactly correspond with the three days' journey of Jonah. A traveler of our own at the beginning of the 17th century, J. Cartwright, states that with his own eyes he traced out the ruinous foundations, and gives their dimensions. "[r] It seems by the ruinous foundation (*which I thoroughly viewed*) that it was built with four sides, but not equal or square. For the two longer sides had each of them (as we guess) 150 furlongs, the two shorter sides ninety furlongs, which amounteth to four hundred and eighty furlongs of ground, which makes the threescore miles, accounting eight furlongs to an Italian mile." No one of the four great mounds, which lie around the site of ancient Nineveh, Nimrud, Kouyunjik, Khorsabad, Karamless, is of sufficient moment or extent to be identified with the old Nineveh. But they are connected together by the sameness of their remains. Together they form a parallelogram, and this of exactly the dimensions assigned by Jonah. "[s] From the Northern extremity of Kouyunjik to Nimrud, is about 18 miles, the distance from Nimrud to Karamless, about 12; the opposite sides, the same." "A recent trigonometrical survey of the country by Captain Jones proves, I am informed," says Layard[t], "that the great ruins of Kouyunjik, Nimrud, Karamless, and Khorsabad form very nearly a perfect parallelogram."

This is perhaps also the explanation, how, seeing its circumference was three days' journey, Jonah entered a day's journey *in* the city and, at the close of the period, we find him at the East side of the city, the opposite to that at which he had entered.

His preaching seems to have lasted only this one day. He *went*, we are told, *one day's journey in the city*. The 150 stadia are nearly 19 miles, a day's journey, so that Jonah walked through it from end to end, repeating that one cry, which God had commanded him to cry. We seem to see the solitary figure of the Prophet, clothed (as was the prophet's dress) in that one rough garment of hair cloth, uttering the cry which we almost hear, echoing in street after street, "ōd arbaim yom venineveh nehpācheth," "yet forty days and Nineveh overthrown." The words which he says he cried and said, belong to that one day only. For on that one day only, was there still a respite of *forty days*. In one day, the grace of God prevailed. The conversion of a whole people upon one

[k] See below on ii. 5, 6.

[l] Hitzig. Jona, § 3. Jahn added, as the current objections, the omissions, "what vices prevailed in Nineveh," [it is incidentally said, "violence," iii. 8] how Jonah brought home to the inhabitants the sense of their guilt; by what calamity, earthquake, inundation or war, the city was to perish; whether, in the general repentance, idolatry was abolished." § 126. 4. All mere by-questions, not affecting the main issue, God's pardoning mercy to the penitent heathen!

[m] ii. 3. So too Q. Curtius v. 4. [n] Diod. ii. 7.

[o] in Diod. l. c. [p] xvi. 1. 5. [q] Ib. 3.

[r] Mr. John Cartwright, The Preacher's Travels, Nineveh, c. 4. Lord Oxford's Collection, i. 745. London, 1745, abridged in Purchas, T. ii. p. 1435.

[s] Layard, Nineveh, P. 2. c. 2. T. ii. 247 note.

[t] Ninev. and Bab. p. 640. Capt. Jones, although treating Ctesias' account as fabulous, states "the entire circuit is but 61½ English miles." Topography of Nineveh, Journ. As. Soc. T. xv. p. 303. See Plan, p. 254.

day's preaching of a single stranger, stands in contrast with the many years during which, God says [u], *since the day that your fathers came forth out of the land of Egypt unto this day, I have sent unto you all My servants the prophets, daily rising up early and sending them, yet they hearkened not unto Me.* Many of us have wondered what the Prophet did on the other thirty-nine days; people have imagined the Prophet preaching as moderns would, or telling them his own wondrous story of his desertion of God, his miraculous punishment, and, on his repentance, his miraculous deliverance. Jonah says nothing of this. The one point he brought out was the conversion of the Ninevites. This he dwells on in circumstantial details. His own part he suppresses; he would be, like S. John Baptist, but the voice of one crying in the wild waste of a city of violence.

This simple message of Jonah bears an analogy to what we find elsewhere in Holy Scripture. The great preacher of repentance, S. John Baptist, repeated doubtless oftentimes that one cry [x], *Repent ye, for the kingdom of heaven is at hand.* Our Lord vouchsafed to begin His own office with those self-same words [y]. And probably, among the civilized but savage inhabitants of Nineveh, that one cry was more impressive than any other would have been. Simplicity is always impressive. They were four words which God caused to be written on the wall amid Belshazzar's impious revelry [z]; *Mene, mene, tekel, upharsin.* We all remember the touching history of Jesus the son of Anan, an unlettered rustic, who, "[a] four years before the war, when Jerusalem was in complete peace and affluence," burst in on the people at the feast of tabernacles with one oft-repeated cry, "A voice from the East, a voice from the West, a voice from the four winds, a voice on Jerusalem and the temple, a voice on the bridegrooms and the brides, a voice on the whole people;" how he went about through all the lanes of the city, repeating, day and night, this one cry; and when scourged until his bones were laid bare, echoed every lash with "woe, woe, to Jerusalem," and continued as his daily dirge and his one response to daily good or ill-treatment, "woe, woe, to Jerusalem." The magistrates and even the cold Josephus thought that there was something in it above nature.

In Jerusalem, no effect was produced, because they had filled up the measure of their sins and God had abandoned them. All conversion is the work of the grace of God. That of Nineveh remains, in the history of mankind, an insulated instance of God's overpowering grace. All which can be pointed out as to the book of Jonah, is the latent suitableness of the instruments employed. We know from the Cuneiform Inscriptions that Assyria had been for successive generations at war [b] with Syria. Not until the time of Ivalush or Pul [c], the Assyrian monarch, probably, at the time of Jonah's mission, do we find them tributary to Assyria. They were hereditary enemies of Assyria, and probably their chief opponents on the North East. The breaking of their power then, under Jeroboam, which Jonah had foretold, had an interest for the Assyrians; and Jonah's prophecy and the fact of its fulfillment may have reached them. The history of his own deliverance, we know from our Lord's own words, did reach them. He *was a sign* [d] *unto the Ninevites.* The word, under which he threatened their destruction, pointed to a miraculous overthrow. It was a turning upside down [e], like the overthrow of the five cities of the plain which are known throughout the Old Testament [f], and still throughout the Mohammedan East, by the same name, "almoutaphikat [g], the overthrown."

The Assyrians also, amidst their cruelties, had a great reverence for their gods, and (as appears from the inscriptions, ascribed to them their national greatness [h]. The variety of ways in which this is expressed, implies a far more personal belief, than the statements which we find among the Romans, and would put to shame almost every English manifesto, or the speeches put into the mouth of the Queen. They may have been, then, the more prepared to fear the prophecy of their destruction from the true God. Layard relates that he has "known a Christian priest frighten a whole Mussulman town to repentance, by proclaiming that he had a Divine mission to announce a coming earthquake or plague [i]."

These may have been predisposing causes. But the completeness of the repentance, not outward only, but inward, "turning from their evil way," is, in its extent, unexampled.

[u] Jer. vii. 25, add 13, xi. 7, xxv. 3, 4, xxvi. 5, xxix. 19, xxxii. 33, xxxv. 14, 15, xliv. 4.
[x] S. Matt. iii. 2. [y] Ib. iv. 17, S. Mark i. 15.
[z] Dan. v. 25. [a] Jos. de B. J. vi. 5. 3.
[b] See above on Am. i. 3. p. 157.
[c] Rawl. Herod. i. 466, 7. [d] S. Luke xi. 30.
[e] as Judg. vii. 13, Job ix. 5, xxviii. 9.
[f] Gen. xix. 21, 25, Deut. xxix. 23, Am. iv. 11, Jer. xx. 16, Lam. iv. 6.
[g] from Cor. ix. 71, liii. 53, lxix. 9.
[h] Thus in one inscripton, "Ashur, the giver of sceptres and crowns, the appointer of sovereignty;" "the gods, the guardians of the kingdom of Tiglath-pileser, gave government and laws to my dominions, and ordered an enlarged frontier to my territory;" "they withheld the tribute due to Ashur my Lord;" "the exceeding fear of the power of Ashur, my Lord, overwhelmed them; my valiant servants (or powerful arms) to which Ashur the Lord gave strength." "In the service of my Lord Ashur;" "whom Ashur and Ninep have exalted to the utmost wishes of his heart;" "the great gods, guardians of my steps," &c. Journ. Asiat. Soc. 1860. xviii. pp. 164, 8, 170, 4, 6, (and others 172, 8, 180, 4) 192, 8, 206, 10, 14, and Rawl. Herod. i. 457, 587, and note 7.
[i] Ninev. and Babyl. p. 632 note.

The fact rests on the authority of *One greater than Jonah.* Our Lord relates it as a fact. He contrasts people with people, the penitent heathen with the impenitent Jews, the inferior messenger who prevailed, with Himself, Whom His own received not. [k] *The men of Nineveh shall raise up with this generation and shall condemn it, because they repented at the preaching of Jonas, and behold, a greater than Jonas is here.*

The chief subject of the repentance of the Ninevites agrees also remarkably with their character. It is mentioned in the proclamation of the king and his nobles, "let them turn every one from his evil way *and from the violence* that is in their hands." Out of the whole catalogue of their sins, conscience singled out *violence.* This incidental notice, contained in the one word, exactly corresponds in substance with the fuller description in the Prophet Nahum, "[l] Woe to the bloody city; it is all full of lies and *robbery; the prey* departeth not." "[m] The lion did tear in pieces enough for his whelps, and strangled for his lionesses, and filled his holes with *prey* and his dens with *ravin.*" "[n] Upon whom hath not thy wickedness [ill-doing] passed continually?" "The Assyrian records," says Layard[o], "are nothing but a dry register of military campaigns, spoilations and cruelties."

The direction, that the animals also should be included in the common mourning, was according to the analogy of Eastern custom. When the Persian general Masistius fell at the battle of Platæa[p], the "whole army and Mardonius above all, made a mourning, *shaving themselves, and the horses, and the beasts of burden,* amid surpassing wailing—Thus the Barbarians after their manner honored Masistius on his death." Alexander imitated apparently the Persian custom in his mourning for Hephæstion[q]. The characteristic of the mourning in each case is, that they include the animals in that same mourning which they made themselves. The Ninevites had a right feeling, (as God Himself says) that the mercies of God were over man and beast[r]; and so they joined the beasts with themselves, hoping that the Creator of all would the rather have mercy on their common distress. [s] *His tender mercies are over all His works:* [t] *Thou, Lord, shalt save both man and beast.*

The name of the king cannot yet be ascertained. But since this mission of Jonah fell in the latter part of his prophetic office, and so probably in the latter part of the reign of Jeroboam or even later, the Assyrian king was probably Ivalush III. or the Pul of Holy Scripture. Jonah's human fears would, in that case, have been soon fulfilled. For Pul was the first Assyrian Monarch through whom Israel was weakened; and God had foreshewn by Amos that through the third it would be destroyed. Characteristic, on account of the earnestness which it implies, is the account that the men of Nineveh proclaimed the fast, before tidings reached the king himself. This is the plain meaning of the words; yet on account of the obvious difficulty they have been rendered, *and word had come to the king*[u]. The account is in harmony with that vast extent of the city, as of Babylon, of which "[x] the residents related that, after the outer portions of the city were taken, the inhabitants of the central part did not know that they were taken." It could scarcely have occurred to one who did not know the fact.

The history of Jonah, after God had spared Nineveh, has the same characteristic touches. He leaves his own character unexplained, its severity rebuked by God, unexcused and unpalliated. He had some special repugnance to be the messenger of mercy to the Ninevites. *For this cause,* he says to God, *I fled before to Tarshish; for I knew that Thou art a merciful God, and repentest Thee of the evil.* The circumstances of his time explain that repugnance. He had already been employed to prophesy the partial restoration of the boundaries of Israel. He was the contemporary of Hosea who foretold of his people, the ten tribes[y], *they shall not dwell in the Lord's land, they shall eat unclean things in Assyria.* God, in giving him his commission to go to Nineveh, the capital of Assyria, and *cry against it,* assigned as the reason, *for its wickedness is come up before Me;* words which to Jonah would suggest the memory of the wickedness of Sodom and its destruction. Jonah was a Prophet, but he was also an Israelite. He was commanded by God to call to repentance the capital of the country by which his own people, nay the people of his God, were to be carried captive. And he rebelled. *We* know more of the love of God than Jonah, for we have known the love of the Incarnation and the Redemption. And yet, were it made known to us, that some European or Asiatic people were to carry our own people captive out of our land, more than would be willing to confess it of themselves, (whatever sense they might have of the awfulness of God's judgments, and what-

[k] S. Matt. xii. 41.
[l] iii. 1.
[m] ii. 12.
[n] iii. 19.
[o] Nineveh and Bab. p. 631.
[p] Herod. ix. 24. Plutarch Aristid. c. 14; see Rawlinson's note on Her. T. iv. p. 401.
[q] Plutarch Alex. c. 72. "he commanded to shave all the horses and mules, as mourning."
[r] See on Joel i. 20. p. 111.
[s] Ps. cxlv. 9.
[t] Ib. xxxvi. 7.
[u] The Vulg. has rightly, "et pervenit." Lapide explains this wrongly, "id est, quia pervenerat." The E. V. smooths the difficulty wrongly by rendering, "*For* word came."
[x] Herod. i. 191.
[y] ix. 3.

ever feelings belonging to our common humanity,) would still inwardly rejoice to hear, that such a calamity as the earthquake at Lisbon befell its capital. It is the instinct of self-preservation and the implanted love of country. Jonah's murmuring related solely to God's mercy shewn to them as to this world. For the Ninevites had repented, and so were in the grace of God. The older of us remember what awful joy was felt when that three days' mortal strife at Leipzig at length was won, in which 107,000 were killed or wounded [z]; or when out of 647,000 men who swept across Europe (a mass larger than the whole population of Nineveh) only "85,000 escaped; 125,000 were slain in battle, 132,000 perished by cold, fatigue and famine [a]." A few years ago, how were Sebastopol and the Krimea in men's mouths, although that war is reputed to have cost the five nations involved in it 700,000 lives, more, probably, than all the inhabitants of Nineveh. Men forget or abstract themselves from all the individual sufferings, and think only of the result of the whole. A humane historian says of the battle of Leipzig [b], "a prodigious sacrifice, but one which, great as it was, humanity has no cause to regret, for it delivered Europe from French bondage, and the world from revolutionary aggression." He says on the Russian campaign of Napoleon I. [c], "the faithful throughout Europe repeated the words of the Psalm, Efflavit Deus et dissipantur."

Look at Dr. Arnold's description of the issue of the Russian campaign. "[d] Still the flood of the tide rose higher and higher, and every successive wave of its advance swept away a kingdom. Earthly state has never reached a prouder pinnacle, than when Napoleon in June, 1812, gathered his army at Dresden, that mighty host, unequalled in all time, of 450,000, not men merely but, effective soldiers, and there received the homage of subject kings. And now, what was the principal adversary of this tremendous power? by whom was it checked, resisted, and put down? By none, and by nothing but the direct and manifest interposition of God. I know no language so well fitted to describe the victorious advance to Moscow, and the utter humiliation of the retreat, as the language of the prophet with respect to the advance and subsequent destruction of the host of Sennacherib. *When they arose early in the morning, behold they were all dead corpses*, applied almost literally to that memorable night of frost in which 20,000 horses perished, and the strength of the French army was utterly broken. Human instruments no doubt were employed in the remainder of the work, nor would I deny to Germany and to Russia the glories of that great year 1813, nor to England the honor of her victories in Spain or of the crowning victory of Waterloo. But at the distance of thirty years those who lived in the time of danger and remember its magnitude, and now calmly review what there was in human strength to avert it, must acknowledge, I think, beyond all controversy, that the deliverance of Europe from the dominion of Napoleon was effected neither by Russia nor by Germany nor by England, but by the hand of God alone." Jonah probably pictured to himself some sudden and almost painless destruction, which the word, *overthrown*, suggested, in which the whole city would be engulfed in an instant and the power which threatened his people, the people of God, broken at once. God reproved Jonah; but, before man condemns him, it were well to think, what is the prevailing feeling in Christian nations, at any signal calamity which befalls any people who threaten their own power or honor;—we cannot, in Christian times, say, their existence. "Jonah," runs an old traditional saying among the Jews [e], "sought the honor of the son [Israel], and sought not the honor of the Father."

An uninspired writer would doubtless at least have brought out the relieving points of Jonah's character, and not have left him under the unmitigated censure of God. Jonah tells the plain truth of himself, as S. Matthew relates his own desertion of his Lord among the Apostles, or S. Mark, under the guidance of S. Peter, relates the great fall of the great Apostle.

Amid this, Jonah remains the same throughout. It is one strong impetuous will, bent on having no share in that which was to bring destruction on his people, fearless of death and ready to give up his life. In the same mind he gives himself to death amid the storm, and, when his mission was accomplished, asks for death in the words of his great predecessor Elijah, when he fled from Jezebel. He probably justified his impatience to himself by the precedent of so great a prophet. But although he complains, he complains to God of Himself. Having complained, Jonah waits. It may be that he thought, although God did not execute His judgments on the 40th day, He might still fulfill them. He had been accustomed to the thought of the long-suffering of God, delaying even when He struck at last. "Considering with himself," says Theodorus, "the greatness of the threat, he imagined that something might perchance still happen even

[z] Alison, Hist. of Europe, c. 81. T. xii. p. 255.
[a] Ib. c. 73. T. xi. 199; c. 74. ib. 229.
[b] Alison, l. c.
[c] Alis. xi. 213.
[d] Lecture iii. pp. 177-9.
[e] "Words of the Rabbies of blessed memory." Kim. on Jon. i.

after this." The patience of God amid the Prophet's impatience, the still, gentle inquiry, (such as He often puts to the conscience now,) *Doest thou well to be angry?* and his final conviction of the Prophet out of his own feelings towards one of God's inanimate creatures, none would have ventured to picture, who had not known or experienced it.

In regard to the miracles in Jonah's history, over and above the fact, that they occur in Holy Scripture, we have our Lord's own word for their truth. He has set His seal on the whole of the Old Testament [f]; He has directly authenticated by His own Divine authority the physical miracle of Jonah's preservation for three days and nights in the belly of the fish [g], and the yet greater moral miracle of the conversion of the Ninevites [h]. He speaks of them both, as facts, and of the stay of Jonah in the fish's belly, as a type of His own stay in the heart of the earth. He speaks of it also as a miraculous sign [i].

The Scribes and Pharisees, unable to answer His refutation of their blasphemy, imputing His miracles to Beelzebub, asked of Him a miraculous sign [k] from Heaven. Probably, they meant to ask that one sign, for which they were always craving. Confounding His first Coming with His second, and interpreting, according to their wishes, of His first Coming all which the prophets foretold of the Second, they were ever looking out for that His Coming in glory *with the clouds of heaven* [l], to humble, as they thought, their own as well as His enemies. Our Lord answers, that this their craving for a sign was part of their faithlessness. *An evil and adulterous generation seeketh after a sign: and there shall no sign be given them, but the sign of the Prophet Jonas.* He uses three times their own word *sign*. He speaks of a miraculous sign, *the sign of Jonas*, a miracle which was the sign of something beyond itself. [h] *For as Jonas was three days and three nights in the whale's belly, so shall the Son of Man be three days and three nights in the heart of the earth.* He gave them the sign from earth, not from Heaven; a miracle of humility, not of glory; of deliverance from death, and, as it were, a resurrection. A *sign*, such as Holy Scripture speaks of, need not at all times be a miraculous, but it is always a real *sign*. Isaiah and his sons, by real names, given to them by God, or the prophet by his walking barefoot, or Ezekiel by symbolic acts, were signs; not by miraculous but still by real acts. In *this* case, the Jews asked for a miraculous sign; our Lord promises them a miraculous sign, although not one such as they wished for, or which would satisfy *them;* a miraculous sign, of which the miraculous preservation of Jonah was a type. Our Lord says, "[h] Jonah *was* three days and three nights in the whale's belly," and no one who really believes in Him, dare think that he was not.

It is perhaps a part of the simplicity of Jonah's narrative, that he relates these great miracles, as naturally as he does the most ordinary events. To God nothing is great or small; and the Prophet, deeply as he feels God's mercy, relates the means which God employed, as if it had been one of those every day miracles of His power and love, of which men think so little because God worketh them every day.

God prepared a great fish, he says, *God prepared a palmchrist; God prepared a worm; God prepared a vehement East wind.* Whether Jonah relates God's ordinary or His extraordinary workings, His workings in the way in which He upholdeth in being the creatures of His Will, or in a way which involves a miracle, i. e. God's acting in some unusual way, Jonah relates it in the same way, with the same simplicity of truth. His mind is fixed on God's Providence, and he relates God's acts, as they bore upon God's Providential dealings with him. He tells of God's preparing the East Wind which smote the palmchrist, in the same way in which he speaks of the supernatural growth of the palmchrist, or of God's Providence, in appointing that the fish should swallow him. He mentions this, which was in the order of God's Providence; he nowhere stops to tell us the "how." How God converted the Ninevites, how He sustained his life in the fish's belly, he tells not. He mentions only the great facts themselves, and leaves them in their mysterious greatness.

It is not strange, the heathen scoffers fixed upon the physical miracles in the history of Jonah for their scorn. They could have no appreciation of the great moral miracle of the conversion of a whole Heathen city at the voice of a single unknown Prophet. Such a conversion is unexampled in the whole revelation of God to man, greater in its immediate effects than the miracle of the Day of Pentecost. Before this stupendous power of God's grace over the unruly will of savage, yet educated, men, the physical miracles, great as they are, shrink into nothing. The wielding and swaying of half a million of human wills, and turning them from Satan to God, is a power of grace, as much above and beyond all changes of the unresisting physical creation, as the spirits and intelligences which God has created are higher than insentient matter. Physical miracles are a new exercise of the creative power of

[f] S. Luke xxiv. 24.
[g] S. Matt. xii. 40.
[h] Ib. 41, S. Luke xi. 32.
[i] S. Matt. xii. 38–40, S. Luke xi. 16, 29, 30.
[k] σημεῖον.
[l] Dan. vii. 13, 14, S. Matt. xvi. 27, xxiv. 30, xxvi. 64, S. Luke xxi. 27, 1 Thess. iv. 16, Rev. i. 7.

God: the moral miracles were a sort of first-fruit of the re-creation of the Gentile world. Physical miracles were the simple exercise of the Will of God; the moral miracles were, in these hundreds of thousands, His overpowering grace, pouring itself into the heart of rebellious man and re-creating it. As many souls as there were, so many miracles were there, greater even than the creation of man.

The miracles too are in harmony with the nature around. The Hebrews, who were, at this time, not a maritime people, scarcely knew probably of those vast monsters, which our manifold researches into God's animal kingdom have laid open to us. Jonah speaks only of *a great fish*. The Greek word[m], by which the LXX translated it, and which our Lord used, is, (like our "cetacea" which is taken from it,) the name of a genus, not of any individual fish. It is the equivalent of the *great fish* of Jonah. The Greeks use the adjective[n], as we do, but they also use the substantive which occurs in S. Matthew. This designates a class which *includes* the whale, but is never used to designate the whale. In Homer[o], it includes "dolphins and the dog." In the natural historians, (as Aristotle[p],) it designates the whole class of sea-creatures which are viviparous, "as the dolphin, the seal, the whale;" Galen[q] adds the Zygæna (a shark) and large tunnies; Photius says that "the Carcharias," or white shark, "is a species of it[r]." Oppian[s] recounts, as belonging to the Cete, several species of sharks[t] and whales[u], some with names of land animals[x], and also the black tunnies[y]. Ælian enumerates most of these under the same head[z]. Our Lord's words then would be rendered more literally, *in the fish's belly*[a], than *in the whale's belly*. Infidels seized eagerly on the fact of the narrowness of the whale's throat; their cavil applied only to an incorrect rendering of modern versions. Fish, of such size that they can swallow a man whole, and which are so formed as naturally to swallow their prey whole, have been found in the Mediterranean. The white shark, having teeth merely incisive, has no choice, except between swallowing its prey whole, or cutting off a portion of it. It cannot *hold* its prey, or swallow it piecemeal. Its voracity leads it to swallow at once all which it can[b]. Hence Otto Fabricius relates[c], "its wont is to swallow down dead and, sometimes also, living men, which it finds in the sea."

A natural historian of repute relates[d], "In 1758 in stormy weather a sailor fell overboard from a frigate in the Mediterranean. A shark was close by, which, as he was swimming and crying for help, took him in his wide throat, so that he forthwith disappeared. Other sailors had leapt into the sloop, to help their comrade, while yet swimming; the captain had a gun which stood on the deck discharged at the fish, which struck it so, that it cast out the sailor which it had in its throat, who was taken up, alive and little injured, by the sloop which had now come up. The fish was harpooned, taken up on the frigate, and dried. The captain made a present of the fish to the sailor who, by God's Providence, had been so wonderfully preserved. The sailor went round Europe exhibiting it. He came to Franconia, and it was publicly exhibited here in Erlangen, as also at Nurnberg and other places. The dried fish was delineated. It was 20 feet long, and, with expanded fins, nine feet wide, and weighed 3924 pounds. From all this, it is probable that this was the fish of Jonah."

This is by no means an insulated account of the size of this fish. Blumenbach[e] states, "the white shark, or Canis carcharias, is found of the size of 10,000 lbs, and horses have been found whole in its stomach." A writer of the 16th century on "the fish of Marseilles[f]" says, "they of Nice attested to me, that they had taken a fish of this sort, approaching to 4000 lbs weight, in whose body they had found a man whole. Those of Marseilles told something similar, that they had once taken a Lamia (so they still popularly call the Carcharias) and found in it a man in a coat of mail [loricatus.]" Rondelet says, "[g] sometimes it grows to such size, that, placed on a carriage, it can hardly be drawn by two horses. I have seen one of moderate size, which weighed 1000 lbs, and, when disembowelled and cut to pieces, it had to be put on two carriages." "I have seen on the shore of Saintonge a Lamia, whose mouth and throat were of such vast size, that it would easily swallow a large man."

Richardson[h], speaking of the white shark in N. America, says that they attain the length of 30 feet, i. e. a 3d larger than that

[m] κῆτος.

[n] κητώδη.

[o] δελφῖνάς τε κύνας τε καὶ εἴποτε μεῖζον ἕληται κῆτος. Od. xii. 37.

[p] Hist. Anim. iii. 20. T. ii. 258.

[q] de alim. fac. iii. 37. T. iv. 349. Sostratus in Athen. vii. 66. says that "the Pelamus (a tunny) when exceeding large is called κῆτος."

[r] Lex. V. καρχαρίας.

[s] Halieut. i. 360–382.

[t] The ζύγαινα, λάμνη or λάμια (our "lamia") κεντρίνης, γαλεός, ἀκανθίας, λεῖος, ῥίνη, and probably the πάρδαλις.

[u] The φύσαλοι, (i. q. physeter Linn.) and πρῆστις.

[x] λέων, πάρδαλις, κριὸς, ὕαινα, γαλεός, σκύμνος.

[y] μελανθύνων.

[z] de animal. ix. 49.

[a] S. Matt. xii. 40.

[b] "It swallows everything without chewing." P. du Tertre, Hist. des. Antilles, ii. 203.

[c] Fauna Gronlandica, p. 129.

[d] Müller, Vollstandige Natursystem des Ritters Karl von Linné. Th. iii. p. 268, quoted by Eichhorn, Einl. T. iv. § 574.

[e] Naturgesch. v. Squalus, Carcharias.

[f] P. Gyll. de Gall. et Lat. nom. pisc. Massil. c. 99. A. D. 1535.

[g] de piscib. xiii. 12, referred to by Bochart.

[h] Fauna Boreali-Americana, p. 289.

which swallowed the sailor whole. Lacepède speaks of fish of this kind as "more than 30 feet long[i]." "The contour," he adds[k], "of the upper jaw of a requin of 30 feet, is about 6 feet long; its swallow is of a diameter proportionate."

"[l] In all modern works on Zoology, we find 30 feet given as a common length for a shark's body. Now a shark's body is usually only about eleven times the length of the half of its lower jaw. Consequently a shark of 30 feet would have a lower jaw of nearly six feet in its semicircular extent. Even if such a jaw as this was of hard bony consistence instead of a yielding cartilaginous nature, it would qualify its possessor for engulfing one of our own species most easily. The power which it has, by virtue of its cartilaginous skeleton, of stretching, bending and yielding, enables us to understand how the shark can swallow entire animals as large or larger than ourselves. Such an incident is related to have occurred A. D. 1802, on the authority of a Captain Brown, who found the body of a woman entire with the exception of the head within the stomach of a shark killed by him at Surinam[m]."

In the Mediterranean there are traces of a yet larger race, now extinct[n]. "[o] However large or dangerous the existing race may be, yet from the magnitude of the fossil teeth found in Malta and elsewhere, some of which measure 4½ inches from the point to the base, and 6 inches from the point to the angle, the animal, to which they belonged, must have much exceeded the present species in size." "The mouth of a fish of this sort," says Bloch[p], "is armed with 400 teeth of this kind. In the Isle of Malta and in Sicily, their teeth are found in great numbers on the shore. Naturalists of old took them for tongues of serpents. They are so compact that, after having remained for many centuries in the earth, they are not yet decayed. The quantity and size of those which are found proves that these creatures existed formerly in great numbers, and that some were of extraordinary size. If one were to calculate from them what should, in proportion, be the size of the throat which should hold such a number of such teeth, it ought to be at least 8 or 10 feet wide. In truth, these fish are found to this day of a terrific size.— This fish, celebrated for its voracity and courage, is found in the Mediterranean and in almost every Ocean. It generally keeps at the bottom, and rises only to satisfy its hunger. It is not seen near shore, except when it pursues its prey, or is pursued by the mular[q], which it does not venture to approach, even when dead. It swallows all sorts of aquatic animals, alive or dead, and pursues especially the sea-calf and the tunny. In its pursuit of the tunny, it sometimes falls into nets, and some have been thus taken in Sardinia, which weighed 400 lbs and in which 8 or 10 tunnies were found still undigested. It attacks men wherever it can find them, whence the Germans call it 'menschenfresser' (men-eater.) Gunner[r] speaks of a sea-calf 'of the size of an ox, which has also been found in one of these animals; and in another a reindeer without horns, which had fallen from a rock.' This fish attains a length of 25–30 feet. Müller[s] says that one was taken near the Island of St. Marguerite which weighed 1500 lbs. On opening it, they found in it a horse, quite whole: which had apparently been thrown overboard. M. Brünniche says[t] that during his residence at Marseilles, one was taken near that city, 15 feet long, and that two years before, two, much larger, had been taken, in one of which had been found two tunnies and a man quite dressed. The fish were injured, the man not at all. In 1760 there was exhibited at Berlin a requin stuffed, 20 feet long, and 9 in circumference, where it was thickest. It had been taken in the Mediterranean. Its voracity is so great, that it does not spare its own species. Leem[u] relates, that a Laplander, who had taken a requin, fastened it to his canoe; soon after, he missed it. Some time after, having taken a larger, he found in its stomach the

[i] Lacep. Hist. des. Poissons, i. p. 189.

[k] Ib. 191. "We have ascertained, from several comparisons, that the contour of one side of the upper jaw, measured from the angle of the two jaws to the summit of the upper jaw nearly equals one-eleventh of the animal. One ought not then to be surprised, to read in Rondelet and other authors, that large requins can swallow a man whole."

[l] MS. statement furnished me by Dr. Rolleston, Linacre Prof. Oxford.

[m] Buffon, ed. C. Sonnini, Poissons, iii. p. 344. Ed. 1803.

[n] This appears from the following statement with which Prof. Phillips has kindly furnished me. "The earliest notice of them which has met my eye is in Scilla's very curious work, La vana Speculazione disingannata. Napoli, 1670. Tav. iii. fig. 1. gives a fair view of some of their teeth, which are stated to have been found in 'un Sasso di Malta'; he rightly enough calls them teeth of Lamia (i. e. Shark) petrified. Mr. Bowerbank, in Reports of the Brit. Association, 1851, gives measures of these teeth, and estimates of the size of the animal to which they belonged. His specimens are from Suffolk, from the Red Crag, where sharks' teeth, of several sorts, and a vast variety of shells, corals, &c. are mixed with some remains of mostly extinct mammalia. The marine races are also for the most part of extinct kinds. These deposits in Suffolk and Malta are of the later Tertiary period; specimens derived from them may be found on the shores no doubt, but there is also no doubt of their original situation being in the stratified earth-crust. The living sharks to which the fossil animal may have most nearly approached are included in the genus Carcharias, the teeth being beautifully serrated on the edges."

[o] Stark, Animal kingdom, p. 305.

[p] Hist. des Poissons, iv. 31. § xi.

[q] Physeter Macrocephalus, Linn. The Spermaceti whale.

[r] Dict. des Anim. iii. p. 683. Schrift. der Dront. Gesellch. T. ii. p. 299.

[s] L. S. T. iii. p. 267.

[t] Pisc. Mass. p. 6.

[u] Lappl. p. 150.

requin which he had lost." "[x] The large Australian shark (Carcharias glaucus), which has been measured after death 37 feet long, has teeth about 2⅝ inches long."

Such facts ought to shame those who speak of the miracle of Jonah's preservation through the fish, as a thing less credible than any other of God's miraculous doings. There is no greater or less to Omnipotence. The creation of the Universe, the whole stellar system, or of a fly, are alike to Him, simple acts of His Divine Will. *He spake, and it was*[y]. What to men seem the greatest miracles or the least, are alike to Him, the mere *Let it be* of His All-Holy Will, acting in a different way for one and the same end, the instruction of the intelligent creatures which He has made. Each and all subserve, in their several places and occasions, the same end of the manifold Wisdom of God. Each and all of these, which to us seem interruptions of His ordinary workings in nature, were from the beginning, before He had created anything, as much a part of His Divine purpose, as the creation of the Universe. They are not disturbances of His laws. Night does not disturb day which it closes, nor day night. No more does any work which God, before the creation of the world, willed to do, (for, [z] *known unto God are all His ways from the beginning of the world*,) interfere with any other of His workings. His workings in nature, and His workings above nature, form one harmonious whole. Each are a part of His ways; each is essential to the manifestation of God to us. That wonderful order and symmetry of God's creation exhibits to us some effluences of the Divine Wisdom and Beauty and Power and Goodness; that regularity itself sets forth those other foreknown operations of God, whereby He worketh in a way different from His ordinary mode of working in nature. "They who know not God, will ask," says S. Cyril [a], "how was Jonah preserved in the fish? how was he not consumed? how did he endure that natural heat, and live, surrounded by such moisture, and was not rather digested? For this poor body is very weak and perishable. Truly wonderful was it, surpassing reason and wontedness. But if God be declared its Author, who would any more disbelieve? For God is All-powerful, and transmouldeth easily the nature of things which are, to what He willeth, and nothing resisteth His ineffable Will. For that which is perishable can at His Will easily become superior to corruption; and what is firm and unshaken and undecaying is easily subjected thereto. For nature, I deem, to the things which be, is, what seemeth good to the Creator." S. Augustine well points out the inconsistency, so common now, of excepting to the one or the other miracle, upon grounds which would in truth apply to many or to all. "[b] The answer" to the mockery of the Pagans, "is that either all Divine miracles are to be disbelieved, or there is no reason why *this* should not be believed. For we should not believe in Christ Himself that He rose on the third day, if the faith of the Christians shrank from the mockery of Pagans. Since our friend does not put the question, Is it to be believed that Lazarus rose on the 4th day, or Christ Himself on the third day, I much marvel that he put this as to Jonah as a thing incredible, unless he think it easier for one dead to be raised from the tomb, than to be preserved alive in that vast belly of the fish. Not to mention how vast the size of marine creatures is said to be by those who have witnessed it, who could not conceive what numbers of men that stomach could contain which was fenced by those ribs, well known to the people at Carthage, where they were set up in public?—how vast must have been the opening of that mouth, the door, as it were, to that cave." "But, troth, they have found in a Divine miracle something which they need not believe; viz. that the gastric juice whereby food is digested could be so tempered as not to injure the life of man. How still less credible would they deem it, that those three men, cast into the furnace by the impious king, walked up and down in the midst of the fire! If then they refuse to believe *any* miracles of God, they must be answered in another way. But they ought not to question any *one*, as though *it* were incredible, but at once all which are as, or even more, marvelous. He who proposed these questions, let him be a Christian now, lest, while he waits first to finish the questions on the sacred books, he come to the end of his life, before he have passed from death to life.—Let him, if he will, first ask questions such as he asked concerning Christ, and those few great questions to which the rest are subordinate. But if he think to finish all such questions as this of Jonah, before he becomes a Christian, he little appreciates human mortality or his own. For they are countless; not to be finished before accepting the faith, lest life be finished without faith. But, retaining the faith, they are subjects for the diligent study of the faithful; and what in them becomes clear is to be communicated without arrogance, what still lies hid, to be borne without risk to salvation."

The other physical miracle of the rapid production of the Palma Christi, which God created to overshadow Jonah, was plainly

[x] Prof. Phillips, MS. letter. He adds, "but our fossil shark's teeth are 4½ to even 5 inches long. Its length has been inferred to have reached 65 feet."

[y] Ps. xxxiii. 9.
[z] Acts xv. 18.
[a] on Jon. c. 2. beg.
[b] Ep. 102. q. 6. § 31.

supernatural in that extreme rapidity of growth, else in conformity with the ordinary character of that plant. "The kikaion, as we read in the Hebrew, called kikeia [or, Elkeroa[c],] in Syriac and Punic," says S. Jerome[d], "is a shrub with broad leaves like vine-leaves. It gives a very dense shade, supports itself on its own stem. It grows most abundantly in Palestine, especially in sandy spots. If you cast the seed into the ground, it is soon quickened, rises marvelously into a tree, and a few days what you had beheld an herb, you look up to, a shrub.—The kikaion, a miracle in its instantaneous existence, and an instance of the power of God in the protection given by this living shade, followed the course of its own nature." It is a native of all North Africa, Arabia, Syria, India. In the valley of the Jordan it still grows to a "large size, and has the character," an eyewitness writes[e], "of a perennial tree, although usually described as a biennial plant." "[f]It is of the size of a small fig tree. It has leaves like a plane, only larger, smoother, and darker." The name of the plant is of Egyptian origin, kiki; which Dioscorides and Galen identify with the croton[g]; Herodotus with the Silicyprion[h], which, in the form seselicyprion, Dioscorides mentions as a name given to the kiki or kroton[f]; Pliny[i] with the Ricinus also (the Latin name for the croton), our Palma Christi; Hebrews[k] with the Arabic Elkeroa, which again is known to be the Ricinus. The growth and occasional perishing of the Palma Christi have both something analogous to the growth and decay related in Jonah. Its rapidity of growth is remarked by S. Jerome and Pliny, who says, "[i] in Spain it shoots up rapidly, of the height of an olive, with hollow stem," and branches[f].

"[l] All the species of the Ricinus shoot up quickly, and yield fruit within three months, and are so multipled from the seed shed, that, if left to themselves, they would occupy in short space the whole country." In Jamaica, "[m]it grows with surprising rapidity to the height of 15 or 16 feet." Niebuhr says[n], "it has the appearance of a tree. Each branch of the kheroa has only one leaf, with 6, 7, or 8 indentures. This plant was near a stream which watered it adequately. At the end of Oct. 1765, it had, in 5 months, grown about 8 feet, and bore, at once, flowers and fruit, green and ripe." This rapidity of growth has only a sort of likeness to the miracle, which quickened in a way far above nature the powers implanted in nature. The destruction may have been altogether in the way of nature, except that it happened at that precise moment, when it was to be a lesson to Jonah. "[o]On warm days, when a small rain falls, black caterpillars are generated in great numbers on this plant, which, in one night, so often and so suddenly cut off its leaves, that only their bare ribs remain, which I have often observed with much wonder, as though it were a copy of that destruction of old at Nineveh." The Ricinus of India and Assyria furnishes food to a different caterpillar from that of Amboyna[p], but the account illustrates the rapidity of the destruction. The word "worm" is elsewhere also used collectively, not of a single worm only[q], and of creatures which, in God's appointment, devour the vine[r]. There is nothing in the text, implying that the creature was one which gnawed the stem rather than the leaves. The peculiar word, *smote*[s], is probably used, to correspond with the mention of the sun *smiting*[t] on the head of Jonah.

These were miracles, like all the other miracles of Scripture, ways, in which God made Himself and His power known to us, shewing Himself the Lord of that nature which men worshiped and worship, for the

[c] *Elkeroa* is the reading of Erasmus and Victorius, who used MSS. and do not mention any conjecture. The Benedictines substituted *kikeion*, their MSS. having *Siccia*. In S. Jerome, Ep. ad. Aug. Ep. 112. n. 22. their MSS. had *ciceiam* or κηκηαμ. If this is right, S. Jerome must have meant Chaldee by Syriac, the word being retained in Jonathan. Only if S. Jerome had meant that the "Syriac" word was the same, one should have thought that he would have said so. The Peshito has probably been corrupted out of the LXX.

[d] on Jon. iv. 6. [e] Robinson, i. 553.

[f] Dioscor. iv. 164.

[g] Diosc. ib. Galen Lex. Hipp. p. 82; also Paul. Ægin. vii. 297.

[h] Herod. ii. 94. [i] xv. 7.

[k] Samuel B. Hophni, A. D. 1054, ap. Kim. Resh Lachish (2d cent. Wolf, Bibl. H. ii. 881, 2 coll. 844.) says that "the oil of Kik" (forbidden in the Mishnah Shabbath, c. 2. to be used for lights on the sabbath) is the kikaion of Jonah, (Kim.) "The oil of Kik" is the ἔλαιον κίκινον of Galen (Lex. Hipp. p. 58) the "oleum cicinum" of Pliny (xxiii. 4). Resh Lachish identified the kikaion with the Alekeroa' (Boch. Ep. ad Morin. Geogr. S. p. 918) which Ibn Baithar uses to translate the kiki, κροτών (Boch. Hieroz. ii. 24). R. Nathan, Maimonides on Tr. Shabbath, c. 2. n. 1, and "some" in Bartenora, (Ib.) also explain it of the keroa. R. Bar Bar Channach, (early 3d cent. Wolf, ib. 880. coll. 879) identifies it with the Zelulibah (Kim.) which again is explained to be the Elkeroa' (respons. Geonim in Boch. Hieroz. ii. 24. p. 42. ed. Leipz.) and whose oil is called "oil of keroa" i. e. the castor or croton oil (Buxt. Lex. Talm. v. צלוליבא.)

[l] Rumph. Herb. Amboin. vi. 46. T. iv. p. 92.

[m] Long's Jamaica, T. iii. p. 712.

[n] Descr. de l' Arab. p. 130.

[o] Rumph. Ib. p. 94.

[p] Sir W. Hooker kindly pointed this out to me, referring to a description and picture of the caterpillar, or silk-worm, the Phalæna Cynthia or the Arrindy silk-worm, in the Linn. Trans. T. iii. p. 42. He also kindly pointed out to me the drawing of the Ricinus in the Flora Græca, T. ix. Tab. 952, given on a reduced scale on the opposite page, as the best representation of the Palma Christi.

[q] התולעת, as we say, "the worm" which preys on the dead body, Is. xiv. 11 (and thence *the worm which dieth not.* Ib. lxvi. 24). תולעת שני, "the cochineal grub," kermez. [r] Deut. xxviii. 39.

[s] ותך Jon. iv. 7. [t] Ib. 8.

present conversion of a great people, for the conviction of Israel, a hidden prophecy of the future conversion of the heathen, and an example of repentance and its fruits to the end of time. They have no difficulty except to the rebelliousness of unbelief.

Other difficulties people have made for themselves. In a planked-roof booth such as ours, Jonah would not have needed the shadow of a plant. Obviously then, Jonah's booth, even if we knew not what it was, was not like our's. A German critic has chosen to treat this as an absurdity. "[u] Although Jonah makes himself a shady booth, he still further needs the overshadowing kikaion." Jonah however, being an Israelite, made booths, such as Israel made them. Now we happen to know that the Jewish succah, or booth, being formed of the interlaced branches of trees, did not exclude the sun. We know this from the rules in the Talmud as to the construction of the Succah or "tabernacle" for the feast of Tabernacles. It lays down,[v] "A Succah whose height is not ten palms, and which has not three sides, and which has more sun than shade [i. e. more of whose floor is penetrated by light through the top of the Succah, than is left in shade], is profane." And again [w], "Whoso spreadeth a linen cloth over the Succah, to protect him from the sun, it is profane." "[x] Whoso raiseth above it the vine or gourd or ivy, and so covers it, it is profane; but if the roof be larger than they, or if one cut them, they are lawful." "[y] With bundles of straw, and bundles of wood, and bundles of faggots, they do not cover it; and all these, if undone, are lawful." "[z] They cover it with planks according to R. Jonah; and R. Meir forbids; whoso putteth upon it one plank of four palms' breadth it is lawful, only he must not sleep under it." Yet all held [a] that a plank thus broad was to overlap the booth, in which case it would not cover it. The principle of all these rules is, that the rude hut, in which they dwelt during the feast of Tabernacles, was to be a shade, symbolizing God's overshadowing them in the wilderness; the Succah itself, not anything adscititious, was to be their shade; yet it was but an imperfect protection, and was indeed intended so to be, in order to symbolize their pilgrim-state. Hence the contrivances among those who wished to be at ease, to protect themselves; and hence the inconvenience which God turned into an instruction to Jonah. Even "the Arabs," Layard tells us [b] in a Nineveh summer, "struck their black tents and lived in sheds, constructed of reeds and grass along the banks of the river." "The heats of summer made it impossible to live in a white tent." Layard's resource of a "recess, cut into the bank of the river where it rose perpendicularly from the water's edge, screening the front with reeds and boughs of trees, and covering the whole with similar materials," corresponds with the hut of Jonah, covered by the Kikaion.

No heathen scoffer, as far as we know, when he became acquainted with the history of Jonah, likened it to any heathen fable. This was reserved for so-called Christians. Some heathen mocked at it, as the philosophers of Mars'-hill mocked at the resurrection of Christ [c]. "This sort of question" [about Jonah], said a heathen, who professed to be an enquirer, "I have observed to be met with broad mockery by the pagans [d]." They mocked, but they did not insult the history by likening it to any fable of their own. S. Jerome, who mentions incidentally that "[e] Joppa is the place in which, to this day, rocks are pointed out in the shore, where Andromeda, being bound, was once on a time freed by the help of Perseus," does not seem aware that the fable could be brought into any connection with the history of Jonah. He urges on the heathen the inconsistency of believing their own fables, which besides their marvelousness were often immoral, and refusing to believe the miracles of Scripture histories; but the fable of Andromeda or of Hesione do not even occur to him in this respect. "[f] I am not ignorant that to some it will seem incredible that a man could be preserved alive 3 days and nights in the fish's belly. These must be either believers or unbelievers. If believers, they must needs believe much greater things, how the three youths, cast into the burning fiery furnace, were in such sort unharmed, that not even the smell of fire touched their dress; how the sea retired, and stood on either side rigid like walls, to make a way for the people passing over; how the rage of lions, aggravated by hunger, looked, awestricken, on its prey, and touched it not, and many like things. Or if they be unbelievers, let them read the 15 books of Ovid's metamorphoses, and all Greek and Latin story, and there they will see—where the foulness of the fables precludes the holiness of a divine origin. *These things they believe*, and that to God all things are possible. Believing foul things, and defending them by alleging the unlimited power of God, they do not admit the same power as to things moral." In Alexandria and in the time of S. Cyril, the old heathen fables were tricked up again. He alludes then to Lycophron's version of

[u] Hitzig, Kl. Proph. p. 160.
[v] Massecheth Succa, i. 1. Dachs Succa, p. 1.
[w] Ib. § 3. p. 30. [x] § 4. p. 29. [y] § 5. p. 49.
[z] § 6. p. 51.

[a] Yom tob and Rashi on Gem. Succah, f. 14. 2.
[b] Ninev. i. 123. [c] Acts xvii. 32.
[d] in S. Aug. Ep. 102. See ab. p. 259.
[e] on Jon. i. 3. [f] on Jon. ii. 2.

the story of Hercules[g], in order, like S. Jerome, to point out the inconsistency of believing heathen fables and rejecting Divine truth. "We," he says, "do not use their fables to confirm things Divine, but we mention them to a good end, in answer to unbelievers, that *their* received histories too do not reject such relations." The philosophers wished at once to defend their own fables and to attack the Gospel. Yet it was an unhappy argumentum ad hominem. Modern infidelity would find a likeness, where there is no shadow of it. The two heathen fables had this in common; that, in order to avert the anger of the gods, a virgin was exposed to be devoured by a sea-monster, and delivered from death by a hero, who slew the monster and married the princess whom he delivered. This, as given by S. Cyril, was a form of the fable, long subsequent to Jonah. The original simple form of the story was this, "[h] Apollo and Poseidon, wishing to make trial of the insolence of Laomedon, appearing in the likeness of men, promised for a consideration to fortify Pergamus. When they had fortified it, he did not pay them their hire. Wherefore Apollo sent a pestilence, and Poseidon a sea-monster, cast on shore by the flood-tide, who made havoc of the men that were in the plain. The oracle said that they should be freed from these misfortunes, if Laomedon would set his daughter Hesione as food for the monster; he did so set her, binding her to the rocks near to the plain; Hercules, seeing her thus exposed, promised to save her, if he might have from Laomedon the horses, which Zeus had given in compensation for the rape of Ganymede. Laomedon saying that he would give them, he slew the monster and set Hesione free."

This simple story is repeated, with unimportant variations, by Diodorus Siculus[i], Hyginus[k], Ovid[l], Valerius Flaccus[m]. Even later, the younger Philostratus, depicting the story, has no other facts[n]. An old icon represents the conflict in a way inconsistent with the later form of the story[o].

The story of Andromeda is told by Apollodorus[p], in part in the very same words. The Nereids were angered by Cassiope the mother of Andromeda, for boasting herself more beautiful than they. Then follows the same history, Poseidon sending a flood-tide and a sea-monster; the same advice of the oracle; the setting Andromeda in chains, as food for the sea-monster; Perseus' arrival, bargain with the father, the killing of the sea-monster, the deliverance of Andromeda. Fable as all this is, it does not seem to have been meant to be fable. Pliny relates, "[q] M. Scaurus, when Ædile, exhibited at Rome, among other marvels, the bones of the monster to which Andromeda was said to have been exposed, which bones were brought from Joppa, a city of Judæa, being 40 feet long, in height greater than the ribs of the Indian elephant, and the vertebræ a foot and a half thick." He describes Joppa as "seated on a hill, with a projecting rock, in which they shew the traces of the chains of Andromeda[r]." Josephus says the same[s]. Pausanias relates, "[t] the country of the Hebrews near Joppa supplies water blood-red, very near the sea. The natives tell, that Perseus, when he had slain the monster to which the daughter of Cepheus was exposed, washed off the blood there." Mela, following perhaps his Greek authority[u], speaks in the present[v], "an illustrious trace of the preservation of Andromeda by Perseus, they *shew* vast bones of a sea-monster."

But, whether the authors of these fables meant them for matters of fact, or whether the fables had any symbolical meaning, they have not, in any form which they received until long after the time of Jonah, any connection with the book of Jonah.

The history of Andromeda has in common with the book of Jonah, this only, that, whereas Apollodorus and the ancients[w] placed the scene of her history in Æthiopia, writers who lived some centuries after the time of Jonah removed it to Joppa, the seaport whence Jonah took ship. "There are some," says Strabo[x], speaking of his own day, "who transfer Æthiopia to our Phœnicia, and say that the matters of Andromeda took place at Joppa; and this, not out of ignorance of places, but rather in the form of a myth." The transfer, doubtless, took place in the 800 years which elapsed between Jonah and Strabo, and was occasioned perhaps by the peculiar idolatry of the coast, the worship of Atargatis or Derceto. Pliny, at least, immediately after that statement about the chains of Andromeda at Joppa, subjoins, "[y] The fabulous Ceto is worshiped there." Ceto is doubtless the same as "Derceto," of which Pliny uses the same epithet a little after-

[g] on Jon. ii. beg. T. iii. p. 376.
[h] Apollodorus, iii. 4. 1. [i] iv. 42. [k] Fab. 89.
[l] Metam. iv. 202–15. [m] Argon. ii. 451–546.
[n] Imag. 12.
[o] in Chosil. and in Beyer, Spicil. Antiq. p. 154. It represents Hercules laurel-crowned and bene comatus. Fabric. ad Sext. Empiric. p. 270.
[p] ii. 43. [q] N. H. ix. 5.
[r] Ib. v. 13. [s] B. J. iii. 9. 3.
[t] iv. 35. [u] So Voss conjectures.
[v] i. 11.

[w] Euripides (in Plutarch de aud. poet.) speaks of the animal as "rushing from the Atlantic sea." (Fragm. Androm. T. ix. p. 45. ed. Matth.). Tacitus, in giving the heathen notions of the origin of the Jews, says, "*most* think that they are offspring of Æthiopians, whom, *when Cepheus was* king (of Æthiopia) fear and hatred compelled to change their abode." (Hist. v. 2.) Ovid still placed the scene in Æthiopia, (Met. iv. 668.) and ascribed the Oracle to Ammon. (670.)
[x] i. 2. 35. ed. Kr. [y] v. 13.

ward[z]. "There," at Hierapolis, "is worshiped the prodigious Atargatis, which the Greeks call Derceto." The Greeks appear (as their way was), on occasion of this worship of Ceto, to have transferred here their own story of Andromeda and the Cetos.

Ceto, i. e. Derceto, and Dagon were the corresponding male and female deities, under whose names the Philistines worshiped the power which God has implanted in nature to reproduce itself. Both were fish-forms, with human hands and face. Derceto or Atargatis was the Syriac Ter'to, whose worship at Hierapolis or Mabug had a far-known infamy, the same altogether as that of Rhea or Cybele[a]. The maritime situation of Philistia probably led them to adopt the fish as the symbol of prolific reproduction. In Holy Scripture we find chiefly the worship of the male god Dagon, lit. "great fish." He had temples at Gaza[b], and Ashdod[c], whither all the lords of the Philistines assembled. Five other places are named from his worship, four near the sea coast, and one close to Joppa itself[d]. But in later times the name of the goddess became more prominent, and, among the Greeks, exclusive. Atargatis or Derceto had, in the time of the Maccabees, a celebrated temple at Carnion[e], i. e. Ashteroth Carnaim in Gilead, and, according to Pliny, at Joppa itself. This furnished an easy occasion to the Greeks to transfer thither their story of the Cetos. The Greeks had peopled Joppa[f], before Simon retook it from Antiochus. In Jonah's time, it was Phœnician. It was not colonized by Greeks until 5 centuries later. Since then Andromeda is a Greek story which they transferred to Joppa with themselves, the existence of the Greek story, at a later date, can be no evidence for "a Phœnician legend," of which the rationalists have dreamed, nor can it have any connection with Jonah who lived half a millennium before the Greeks came, eight hundred years before the story is mentioned in connection with Joppa.

With regard to the fables of Hercules, Diodorus Siculus thought that there was a basis of truth in them. The story of Hercules and Hesione, as alluded to by Homer and told by Apollodorus, looks like an account of the sea breaking in upon the land and wasting it; a human sacrifice on the point of being offered, and prevented by the removal of the evil through the building of a sea-wall. Gigantic works were commonly attributed to superior agency, good or evil. In Homer, the mention of the sea-wall is prominent. "[g]He led the way to the lofty wall of mounded earth of the divine Hercules, which the Trojans and Minerva made for him, that, eluding the sea-monster, he might escape, when he rushed at him from the beach toward the plain." In any case a monster, which came up from the sea and wasted the land, is no fish; nor has the story of one who *destroyed* such a monster, any bearing on that of one whose life God *preserved* by a fish. Nor is the likeness really mended by the later version of the story, originating in an Alexandrian[h], after the book of Jonah had been translated into Greek at Alexandria. The writer of the Cassandra, who lived at least five centuries after Jonah, represents Hercules as "a lion, the offspring of three nights, which aforetime the jagged-toothed dog of Triton lapped up in his jaws; and he, a living carver of his entrails, scorched by the steam of a cauldron on the fireless hearths, shed the bristles of his head upon the ground, the infanticide waster of my country." In that form the story re-appears in a heathen philosopher[i] and an Alexandrian father[k], but, in both, as borrowed from the Alexandrian poet. Others, who were unacquainted with Lycophron, heathen[l]

[z] v. 19.

[a] Lucian, de dea Syra, attests the celebrity of this dreadful worship; among the Syrians S. James of Sarug attests its prevalence in Haran (Ass. B. O. i. 328.) and Bardesanes, in Syria generally with its special enormities. (in Cureton, Spicil. Syr. p. 32 Syr. p. 20 Gr.) Diodorus Sic. [ii. 4.] mentions the woman's face and fish-body of Derceto.

[b] Judg. xvi. 23.

[c] 1 Sam. v. 1. 1 Macc. x. 83, xi. 4.

[d] 1) *Bethdagon* ("temple of Dagon") in the S. W. of Judah (Josh. xv. 41.) and so, near Philistia; 2) Another, in Asher also near the sea; 3) *Caphar Dagon* ("village of D.") "a very large village between Jamnia and Diospolis." (Euseb. Onom. sub v.) 4) *Beit Dejan* [Beth Dagon] about 6 miles N. W. of Ramlah (Robinson, Bibl. R. ii. 232; see map) accordingly distinct from *Caphar Dagon*, and 4½ hours from Joppa; 5) Another *Beit Dejan*, E. of Nablus. (Ib. 282.)

[e] 2 Macc. xii. 26.

[f] 1 Macc. x. 75, xiv. 34.

[g] Il. xx. 144–8.

[h] "Lycophron the obscure," if it was his work, lived under Ptolemy Philadelphus, B. C. 283–247. Niebuhr, following and justifying an old Scholiast, (Kl. hist. Schrift. i. 438–50) places the writer of the Cassandra not earlier than 190, B. C. on the ground of allusions to Roman greatness (1226–82. 1446–51.) which he thinks inconsistent in a friend of Ptolemy's. Welcker (die Griech. Trag. p. 1259–62) thinks both passages interpolated.

[i] Sextus Empiricus, (about 3d century) adv. Gramm. i. 12. p. 255.

[k] S. Cyril Al. quoting Lycophron. Later Greek writers, as Isaac Comnenus (A. D. 1057,) add to Homer's fable, that Hercules leapt armed into the jaws of the monster, and so cut him up (de prætermissis ab Hom. in Allat. Excerpta Var. p. 274.). The Empress Eudocia (A. D. 1067, &c.) adds the new and false interpretation of τριέσπερος (Violet. in Villoison, Anecd. i. 344), but also the old explanation (Ib. p. 211). These, as also Theophylact (A. D. 1077,) and Sextus, show by their relation their acquaintance with Lycophron.

[l] See p. 262. 1. A scholiast on Homer (Il. xx. 245) having given the story, adds "The history is in Hellanicus." But 1) had this history been in Hellanicus, it would have been known to writers (as Apollodorus &c.) who used Hellanicus. 2) It is only a general statement, that the history in the main was in Hellanicus, not extending to details. 3) "Such statements as, 'thus relates Pherecydes,' 'The history is in Acusilaus,' do not always exhibit the account of the writers whom he quotes, but he

and Christian[m] alike, knew nothing of it. One Christian writer, at the end of the 5th century[n], a Platonic philosopher, gives an account, distinct from any other, heathen or Christian, probably confused from both. In speaking of marvelous deliverances, he says; "[o]As Hercules too is sung" [i.e. in Greek poetry], "when his ship was broken, to have been swallowed up by a ketos, and, having come within, was preserved." In the midst of the 11th century after our Lord, some writers on Greek fable, in order to get rid of the very offensive story of the conception of Hercules, interpreted the word of Lycophron which alludes to it, of his employing, in the destruction of the monster, three periods of 24 hours, called "nights" from the darkness in which he was enveloped. Truly, full often have those words of God been fulfilled, that [p]*men shall turn away their ears from the truth, and shall be turned unto fables.* Men, who refused to believe the history of Jonah, although attested by our Lord, considered Æneas Gazæus, who lived about 13 centuries after Jonah, to be an authentic witness of an imaginary Phœnician tradition[q], 13 centuries before his own time; and that, simply on the ground that he has his name from Gaza; whereas he expressly refers, not to Phœnician tradition but to Greek poetry.

Such are the stories, which became a traditional argument among unbelieving critics[r] to justify their disbelief in miracles accredited by our Lord. Flimsy spider-webs, which a critic of the same school brushes away[s], as soon as he has found some other expedient, as flimsy, to serve his purpose! The majestic simplicity of Holy Scripture and its moral greatness stand out the more, in contrast with the unmeaning fables, with which men have dared, amid much self-applause, to compare it. A more earnest, but misled, mind, even while unhappily disbelieving the miracle of Jonah, held the comparison, on ground of "reason, ludicrous; but not the less frivolous and irreverent, as applied to Holy Scripture[t]."

It was assumed by those who first wrote against the book of Jonah, that the thanksgiving in it was later than Jonah, "a cento from the Psalms." They objected that it did not allude to the history of Jonah. One critic repeated after the other[u], that the Psalm was a "mere cento" of Psalms. However untrue, nothing was less doubted. A later critic felt that the Psalm must have been the thanksgiving of one delivered from great peril of life in the sea. "The images," he says[v], "are too definite, they relate too exclusively to such a situation, to admit of being understood vaguely of any great peril to life, as may Psalms 18 and 42, (which the writer may have had in his mind) or Psalm 124." Another, to whom attention has been recently drawn, maintained the early date of the thanksgiving, and held that it contained so much of the first part of Jonah's history, that that history might be founded on the thanksgiving[w]. This was one step backward toward the truth. It is admitted that the thanksgiving is genuine, is Jonah's, and relates to a real deliverance of the real Prophet. But the thanksgiving would not suggest the history[x]. Jonah thanks God for his deliverance from the depths of the sea, from which no man could be delivered, except by miracle. He describes himself, not as struggling with the waves, but as sunk beneath them to the bottom of the sea, whence no other ever rose[y]. Jonah does not tell God, how He had

frequently interweaves a history out of many authors, and inserts what he had read elsewhere." See Sturz, Hellanici Fragm. n. xxvi. ed. Cant. Forbiger de Lycophr. 1827. p. 16. Porphyry speaks of the "Barbarian customs of Hellanicus," as, "a mere compound of the works of Herodotus and Damasus;" in Eus. Præp. Ev. x. 3.

[m] Not Theodorus or Theodoret, or S. Jerome (fond as he is of such allusions), nor the early author of the Orat. ad Græcos in S. Justin, although referring to the fables on Hercules.

[n] Æneas Gazæus. See Gall. T. x. Proleg. c. 12.

[o] Gall. x. 645. or p. 37. ed. Boiss. [p] 2 Tim. iv. 4.

[q] Friederichsen, Jonas, p. 311. 2, &c.

[r] Bauer, Rosenmüller, Gesenius, De Wette, Bertholdt, Gramberg (Religions-Id. ii. 510), Knobel, (Prophetismus, ii. 372.) Goldhorn. Friederichsen, Forbiger, &c.

[s] "What has the myth of Perseus, rightly understood, and with no foreign ingredients, in common with the history of Jonah, but the one circumstance, that a sea-creature is mentioned in each? And how different the meaning! Neither the myth of Perseus and Andromeda, nor the fully corresponding myth of Hercules and Hesione, can serve either to confirm the truth of the miracles in the book of Jonah" [as though the truth needed support from a fable], "nor to explain it as a popular heathen tradition, inasmuch as the analogy is too distant and indefinite to explain the whole. Unsatisfactory as such parallels are as soon as we look, not merely at incidental and secondary points, but at the central point to be compared," &c. Baur (in Illgen Zeitschr. 1837 p. 101.) followed by Hitzig. Winer also rejects it.

[t] "In classical philology we should simply add, 'to think this in earnest were ludicrous;' 'but not the less frivolous and irreverent,' we may well add in the criticism of Scripture." Bunsen, Gott. in d. Gesch. i. 354. Eichhorn would not decide which was taken from the other. Einl. 577. ed. 1.

[u] Eichhorn, De Wette, Rosenmuller, Bertholdt, Hitzig, Maurer, &c. (Eichhorn admits the beauty of the Psalms employed.)

[v] Ewald Poet. Büch. d. A. Test. i. 122.

[w] Bunsen, Ib. i. 359 sqq.

[x] The heathen ode in praise of the god of the waters which appears in Ælian (Hist. Anim. xii. 45) about 220, A. D. (Fabr. Bibl. Gr. iv. 21. 1.) contains the whole fable about Arion (B. C. 625, or 615,) being thrown overboard treacherously and borne to shore on the backs of dolphins. The ode then did not suggest the fable (as Bunsen makes it); for it contains it. The Dolphin, playing as it does about vessels, was a Greek symbol of the sea; and the human figure upon it a votive offering for a safe arrival. Welcker gives 6 fables of persons, dead or alive, brought ashore by Dolphins. (Welcker, Kl. Schrift, i. 90 1.) The symbol was turned by the fertile Greek into the myth.

[y] Bunsen, in his Epitome of the thanksgiving, omitted the characteristic part of it, p. 364.

delivered him. Who does? He rehearses to God the hopeless peril, out of which He had delivered him. On this the soul dwells; for this is the ground of its thankfulness. The delivered soul loves to describe to God the death out of which it had been delivered. Jonah thanks God for one miracle; he gives no hint of the other, which, when he uttered the thanksgiving, was not yet completed. The thanksgiving bears witness to a miracle; but does not suggest its nature. The history supplies it.

It is instructive that the writer who, disbelieving the miracles in the book of Jonah, "*restores* his history[z]" by effacing them, has also to "*restore* the history[a] of the Saviour of the world, by omitting His testimony to them. But this is to subject the revelation of God to the variations of the mind of His creatures, believing what they like, disbelieving what they dislike.

Our Lord Himself attested that this miracle on Jonah was an image of His own entombment and Resurrection. He has compared the preaching of Jonah with His own. He compares it as a real history, as He does the coming of the Queen of Sheba to hear the wisdom of Solomon. Modern writers have lost sight of the principle, that men, as individuals, amid their infirmities and sins, are but types of man; in their history alone, their office, their sufferings, can they be images of their Redeemer. God portrayed doctrines of the Gospel in the ritual of the law. Of the offices of Christ and, at times, His history, He gave some faint outline in offices which He instituted, or persons whose history He guided. But they are types only, in that which is of God. Even that which was good in any was no type of His goodness; nay, the more what is human is recorded of them, the less they are types of Him. Abraham who acted much, is a type, not of Christ, but of the faithful. Isaac, of whom little is recorded, except his sacrifice, becomes the type of Christ. Melchisedek, who comes forth once in that great loneliness, a King of Righteousness and of peace, a Priest of God, refreshing the father of the faithful with the sacrificial bread and wine, is a type, the more, of Christ's everlasting priesthood, in that he stands alone, without father, without known descent, without known beginning or end, majestic in his one office, and then disappearing from our sight. Joseph was a type of our Lord, not in his chastity or his personal virtues but in his history; in that he was rejected by his brethren, sold at the price of a slave, yet, with kingly authority, received, supported, pardoned, gladdened, feasted, his brethren who had sold him. Even so the history of Jonah had two aspects. It is, at once, the history of his mission and of his own personal conduct in it. These are quite distinct. The one is the history of God's doings in him and through him; the other is the account of his own soul, its rebellions, struggles, conviction. As a man, he is himself the penitent; as a Prophet, he is the preacher of repentance. In what was human infirmity in him, he was a picture of his people, whose cause he espoused with too narrow a zeal. Zealous too for the honor of God, although not with God's all-enfolding love, willing that that honor should be vindicated in his own way, unwilling to be God's instrument on God's terms, yet silenced and subdued at last, he was the image and lesson to those who murmured at S. Peter's mission to Cornelius, and who, only when they heard how God the Holy Ghost had come down upon Cornelius' household, *held their peace and glorified God, saying, then hath God to the Gentiles also granted repentance unto life*[b]. What coinciding visions to Cornelius and S. Peter, what evident miracles of power and of grace, were needed after the Resurrection to convince the Jewish converts of that same truth, which God made known to and through Jonah! The conversion of the Gentiles and the saving of a remnant only of the Jews are so bound together in the prophets, that it may be that the repugnance of the Jewish converts was founded on an instinctive dread of the same sort which so moved Jonah. It was a superhuman love, through which S. Paul contemplated *their fall* as *the riches of the Gentiles*[c].

On the other hand, that, in which Jonah was an image of our Lord, was very simple and distinct. It was where Jonah was passive, where nothing of his own was mingled. The storm, the casting over of Jonah, were the works of God's Providence; his preservation through the fish was a miracle of God's power; the conversion of the Ninevites was a manifold miracle of His grace. It might have pleased God to send to convert a heathen people one whom He had not so delivered; or to have subdued the will of the Prophet whom He sent on some other mission. But now sign answers to sign, and mission shadows out mission. Jonah was first delivered from his three days' burial in that living tomb by a sort of resurrection, and then, whereas he had previously been a Prophet to Israel, he thenceforth became a Prophet to the heathen, whom, and not Israel, he converted, and, in their conversion, his, as it were, resurrection was operative. The correspondence is there. We may lawfully dwell on subordinate details, how man was tempest-tost and buffeted by the angry waves of this perilous and bitter world; Christ, as one of us, gave His life for our lives, the storm at once was hushed, there is a deep calm of inward peace, and our haven was secured. But the great

[z] Bunsen, ib. 372. [a] Ib. 379.

[b] Acts xi. 18. [c] Rom. xi. 12.

JONAH.

Before CHRIST cir. 780.

CHAPTER I.

1 *Jonah, sent to Nineveh, fleeth to Tarshish.* 4 *He is bewrayed by a tempest,* 11 *thrown into the sea,* 17 *and swallowed by a fish.*

NOW the word of the LORD came unto [a]
|| Jonah the son of Amit-
tai saying,

Before CHRIST cir. 780.

[a] 2 Kings 14. 25.
|| Called, Matt. 12. 39. *Jonas.*

CHAP. I. ver. 1. *Now the word of the Lord,* lit. *And, &c.* This is the way in which the several inspired writers of the Old Testament mark that what it was given them to write, was united on to those sacred books which God had given to others to write, and formed with them one continuous whole. The word, *And,* implies this. It would do so in any language, and it does so in Hebrew as much as in any other. As neither we, nor any other people, would, without any meaning, use the word, *And,* so neither did the Hebrews. It joins the four first books of Moses together; it carries on the history through Joshua, Judges, the books of Samuel and of the Kings. After the captivity, Ezra and Nehemiah begin again where the histories before left off; the break of the captivity is bridged over; and Ezra, going back in mind to the history of God's people before the captivity, resumes the history, as if it had been of yesterday, *And in the first year of Cyrus.* It joins in the story of the book of Ruth before the captivity, and that of Esther afterward. At times, even prophets employ it, in using the narrative form of themselves, as Ezekiel, *And it was in the thirtieth year, in the fourth month, in the fifth day of the month, and I was in the captivity by the river of Chebar, the heavens opened and I saw.* If a prophet or historian wishes to detach his prophecy or his history, he does so; as Ezra probably began the book of Chronicles anew from Adam, or as Daniel makes his prophecy a whole by itself. But then it is the more obvious that a Hebrew prophet or historian, when he does begin with the word, *And,* has an object in so beginning; he uses an universal word of all languages in its uniform meaning in all language, to join things together.

And yet more precisely; this form, *And the word of the Lord came to—saying,* occurs over and over again, stringing together the pearls of great price of God's revelations, and uniting this new revelation to all those which had preceded it. The word, *And,* then joins on histories with histories, revelations with revelations, uniting in one the histories of God's works and words, and blending the books of Holy Scripture into one Divine book.

But the form of words must have suggested to the Jews another thought, which is part of our thankfulness and of our being, [1] *then to the Gentiles also hath God given repentance unto life.* The words are the self-same familiar words with which some fresh revelation of God's Will to His people had so often been announced. Now they are prefixed to God's message to the heathen, and so as to join on that message to all the other messages to Israel. Would then God deal thenceforth with the heathen as with the Jews? Would they have their prophets? Would they be included in the one family of God? The mission of Jonah in itself was an earnest that they would; for God, Who does nothing fitfully or capriciously, in that He had begun, gave an earnest that He would carry on what He had begun. And so thereafter, the great prophets, Isaiah, Jeremiah, Ezekiel, were prophets to the nations also; Daniel was a prophet among them, to them as well as to their captives. But the mission of Jonah might, so far, have been something exceptional. The enrolling his book, as an integral part of the scriptures, joining on that prophecy to the other prophecies to Israel, was an earnest that they were to be parts of one system. But then it would be significant also, that the records of God's prophecies to the Jews, all embodied the accounts of their impenitence. Here is inserted among them an account of God's revelation to the heathen, and their repentance. "[2] So many prophets had been sent, so many miracles wrought, so often had captivity been foreannounced to them for the multitude of their sins, and they never repented. Not for the reign of one king did they cease from the worship of the calves; not one of the kings of the ten tribes departed from the sins of Jeroboam? Elijah, sent in the Word and Spirit of the Lord, had done many miracles, yet obtained no abandonment of the calves. His miracles effected this only, that the people knew that Baal was no god, and cried out, *the Lord He is the God.* Elisha his disciple followed him, who asked for a double portion of the Spirit of Elijah, that he might work more miracles, to bring back the people.—He died, and, after his death as before it, the worship of the calves continued in Israel. The Lord marvelled and was weary of Israel, knowing that if He sent to the heathen they would hear, as he saith to Ezekiel. To make trial of this, Jonah was chosen, of whom it is recorded in the book of Kings that he prophesied the

[1] Acts xi. 18.

[2] Rup.

Before CHRIST cir. 780.

2 Arise, go to Nineveh,
that [b]great city and cry
against it; for [c]their wickedness is come up before me.

[b] Gen. 10. 11, 12. ch. 3. 2, 3. & 4. 11.

[c] Gen. 18. 20, 21. Ezra 9. 6. Jam. 5. 4. Rev. 18. 5.

restoration of the border of Israel. When then he begins by saying, *And the word of the Lord came to Jonah*, prefixing the word *And*, he refers us back to those former things, in this meaning. The children have not hearkened to what the Lord commanded, sending to them by His servants the prophets, but have hardened their necks and given themselves up to do evil before the Lord and provoke Him to anger; *and* therefore *the word of the Lord came to Jonah, saying, Arise and go to Nineveh that great city, and preach unto her*, that so Israel may be shewn, in comparison with the heathen, to be the more guilty, when the Ninevites should repent, the children of Israel persevered in unrepentance."

Jonah the son of Amittai. Both names occur here only in the Old Testament, Jonah signifies "Dove," Amittai, "the truth of God." Some of the names of the Hebrew prophets so suit in with their times, that they must either have been given them prophetically, or assumed by themselves, as a sort of watchword, analogous to the prophetic names, given to the sons of Hosea and Isaiah. Such were the names of Elijah and Elisha, "The Lord is my God," "my God is salvation." Such too seems to be that of Jonah. The "dove" is everywhere the symbol of "mourning love." The side of his character which Jonah records is that of his defect, his want of trust in God, and so his unloving zeal against those, who were to be the instruments of God against his people. His name perhaps preserves that character by which he willed to be known among his people, one who moaned or mourned over them.

2. *Arise, go to Nineveh, that great city.* The Assyrian history, as far as it has yet been discovered, is very bare of events in regard to this period. We have as yet the names of three kings only for 150 years. But Assyria, as far as we know its history, was in its meridian. Just before the time of Jonah, perhaps ending in it, were the victorious reigns of Shalmanubar and Shamasiva; after him was that of Ivalush or Pul, the first aggressor upon Israel. It is clear that this was a time of Assyrian greatness: since God calls it *that great city*, not in relation to its extent only, but its power. A large weak city would not have been called *a great city unto God*[1].

And cry against it. The substance of that *cry* is recorded afterward, but God told to Jonah now, what message he was to *cry* aloud to it. For Jonah relates afterward, how he expostulated now with God, and that his expostulation was founded on this, that God was so merciful that He would not fulfill the judgment which He threatened. Faith was strong in Jonah, while, like Apostles "the sons of thunder," before the Day of Pentecost, he knew not "what spirit *he* was of." Zeal for the people and, as he doubtless thought, for the glory of God, narrowed love in him. He did not, like Moses, pray[2], *or else blot me also out of Thy book*, or like St. Paul, desire even to be *an anathema from Christ*[3] for his people's sake, so that there might be more to love his Lord. His zeal was directed, like that of the rebuked Apostles, against others, and so it too was rebuked. But his faith was strong. He shrank back from the office, as believing, not as doubting, the might of God. He thought nothing of preaching, amid that multitude of wild warriors, the stern message of God. He was willing, alone, to confront the violence of a city of 600,000, whose characteristic was violence. He was ready, at God's bidding, to enter what Nahum speaks of as a den of lions; [4]*The dwelling of the lions and the feeding-place of the young lions, where the lion did tear in pieces enough for his whelps, and strangled for his lionesses.* He feared not the fierceness of their lion-nature, but God's tenderness, and lest that tenderness should be the destruction of his own people.

Their wickedness is come up before Me. So God said to Cain, [5]*The voice of thy brother's blood crieth unto Me from the ground:* and of Sodom[6], *The cry of Sodom and Gomorrah is great, because their sin is very grievous; the cry of it is come up unto Me.* The *wickedness* is not the mere mass of human sin, of which it is said [7], *the whole world lieth in wickedness*, but evil-doing[8] toward others. This was the cause of the final sentence on Nineveh, with which Nahum closes his prophecy, *upon whom hath not thy wickedness passed continually?* It had been assigned as the ground of the judgment on Israel through Nineveh. [9]*So shall Bethel do unto you, on account of the wickedness of your wickedness.* It was the ground of the destruction by the flood. [10]*God saw that the wickedness of man was great upon the earth.* God represents Himself, the Great Judge, as sitting on His Throne in heaven, Unseen but All-seeing, to Whom the wickedness and oppressiveness of man against man *goes up*, appealing for His sentence against the oppressor.

[1] Jon. iii. 3. [2] Ex. xxxii. 32. [3] Rom. ix. 3.
[4] Nah. ii. 11, 12. [5] Gen. iv. 10.
[6] xviii. 20, 21.

[7] I S. John v. 19.
[8] רעה is almost always evil, suffered or afflicted.
[9] Hos. x. 14, 15. [10] Gen. vi. 5.

Before CHRIST cir. 780.

3 But [d] Jonah rose up to flee unto Tarshish from the presence of the LORD, and went down to [e] Joppa;

[d] ch. 4. 2.

[e] Josh. 19. 46. 2 Chr. 2. 16. Acts 9. 36.

The cause seems ofttimes long in pleading. God is long-suffering with the oppressor too, that if so be, he may repent. So would a greater good come to the oppressed also, if the wolf became a lamb. But meanwhile, "[1] every iniquity has its own voice at the hidden judgment seat of God." Mercy itself calls for vengeance on the unmerciful.

3. *But* [*And*] *Jonah rose up to flee—from the presence of the Lord;* lit. *from being before the Lord*[2]. Jonah knew well, that man could not escape from the Presence of God, Whom he knew as the Self-existing, He Who alone IS, the Maker of heaven, earth and sea. He did not *flee* then *from His presence*, knowing well what David said, [3] *whither shall I go from Thy Spirit, or whither shall I flee from Thy presence? If I take the wings of the morning,* and *dwell in the uttermost parts of the sea, even there shall Thy hand lead me and Thy right hand shall hold me.* Jonah fled, not from God's Presence, but from standing before him, as His servant and minister. He refused God's service, because, as he himself tells God afterward[4], he knew what it would end in, and he misliked it. So he acted, as men often do, who mislike God's commands. He set about removing himself as far as possible from being under the influence of God, and from the place where he *could* fulfill them. God bid him go to Nineveh, which lay North-East from his home; and he instantly set himself to flee to the then furthermost West. Holy Scripture sets the rebellion before us in its full nakedness. *The word of the Lord came unto Jonah, go to Nineveh, and Jonah rose up;* he did something instantly, as the consequence of God's command. He *rose up*, not as other prophets, to obey, but to disobey; and that, not slowly nor irresolutely, but *to flee, from* standing *before the Lord.* He renounced his office. So when our Lord came in the Flesh, those who found what He said to be *hard sayings,* went away from Him, *and walked no more with Him*[5]. So the rich *young man went away sorrowful,* [6] *for he had great possessions.* They were perhaps afraid of trusting themselves in His Presence; or they were ashamed of staying there, and not doing what He said. So men, when God secretly calls them to prayer, go and immerse themselves in business; when, in solitude, He says to their souls something which they like not, they escape His Voice in a throng. If He calls them to make sacrifices for His poor, they order themselves a new dress or some fresh sumptuousness or self-indulgence; if to celibacy, they engage themselves to marry forthwith; or, contrariwise, if He calls them not to do a thing, they do it at once, to make an end of their struggle and their obedience; to put obedience out of their power; to enter themselves on a course of disobedience. Jonah, then, in this part of his history, is the image of those who, when God calls them, disobey His call, and how He deals with them, when he does not abandon them. He lets them have their way for a time, encompasses them with difficulties, so that they shall "[7] flee back from God displeased to God appeased."

"[8] The whole wisdom, the whole bliss, the whole of man lies in this, to learn what God wills him to do, in what state of life, calling, duties, profession, employment, He wills him to serve Him." God sent each one of us into the world, to fulfill his own definite duties, and, through His grace, to attain to our own perfection in and through fulfilling them. He did not create us at random, to pass through the world, doing whatever self-will or our own pleasure leads us to, but to fulfill His Will. This Will of His, if we obey His earlier calls, and seek Him by prayer, in obedience, self-subdual, humility, thoughtfulness, He makes known to each by His own secret drawings, and, in absence of these, at times by His Providence or human means. And then, "[9] to follow Him is a token of predestination." It is to place ourselves in that order of things, that pathway to our eternal mansion, for which God created us, and which God created for us. So Jesus says[10], *My sheep hear My voice and I know them, and they follow Me, and I give unto them eternal life, and they shall never perish, neither shall any* man *pluck them out of My Hand.* In these ways, God has fore-ordained for us all the graces which we need; in these, we shall be free from all temptations which might be too hard for us, in which our own special weakness would be most exposed. Those ways, which men choose out of mere natural taste or fancy, are mostly those which expose them to the greatest peril of sin and damnation. For they choose them, just because such pursuits flatter most their own inclinations, and give scope to their natural strength and their moral weakness. So Jonah, misliking a duty, which God gave him to fulfill, separated himself from His service, forfeited his past calling,

[1] S. Greg. Mor. v. 20.
[2] Not מִפְּנֵי יי but מִלִּפְנֵי; see Introd. p. 247.
[3] Ps. cxxxix. 7, 9, 10.
[4] iv. 2.
[5] S. John vi. 66.
[6] S. Matt. xix. 22.
[7] S. Aug. in Ps. lxx.
[8] from Lap.
[9] Bourdaloue.
[10] S. John x. 27, 28.

Before CHRIST cir. 780.

and he found a ship going to Tarshish: so he paid the fare thereof, and went down into it, to go with

Before CHRIST cir. 780.

lost, as far as in him lay, his place among "the goodly fellowship of the prophets," and, but for God's overtaking grace, would have ended his days among the disobedient. As in Holy Scripture, David stands alone of saints, who had been after their calling, bloodstained; as the penitent Robber stands alone converted in death; as S. Peter stands singly, recalled after denying his Lord; so Jonah stands, the one Prophet, who, having obeyed and then rebelled, was constrained by the overpowering Providence and love of God, to return and serve Him.

"[1] Being a Prophet, Jonah could not be ignorant of the mind of God, that, according to His great Wisdom and His unsearchable judgments and His untraceable and incomprehensible ways, He, through the threat, was providing for the Ninevites that they should not suffer the things threatened. To think that Jonah hoped to hide himself in the sea and elude by flight the great Eye of God, were altogether absurd and ignorant, which should not be believed, I say not of a prophet, but of no other sensible person who had any moderate knowledge of God and His supreme power. Jonah knew all this better than any one, that, planning his flight, he changed his place, but did not flee God. For this could no man do, either by hiding himself in the bosom of the earth or depths of the sea or ascending (if possible) with wings into the air, or entering the lowest hell, or encircled with thick clouds, or taking any other counsel to secure his flight. This, above all things and alone, can neither be escaped nor resisted, God. When He willeth to hold and grasp in His Hand, He overtaketh the swift, baffleth the intelligent, overthroweth the strong, boweth the lofty, tameth rashness, subdueth might. He who threatened to others the mighty Hand of God, was not himself ignorant of nor thought to flee, God. Let us not believe this. But since he saw the fall of Israel and perceived that the prophetic grace would pass over to the Gentiles, he withdrew himself from the office of preaching, and put off the command." "[2] The Prophet knoweth, the Holy Spirit teaching him, that the repentance of the Gentiles is the ruin of the Jews. A lover then of his country, he does not so much envy the deliverance of Nineveh, as will that his own country should not perish.—Seeing too that his fellow-prophets are sent to the lost sheep of the house of Israel, to excite the people to repentance, and that Balaam the soothsayer too prophesied of the salvation of Israel, he grieveth that he alone is chosen to be sent to the Assyrians, the enemies of Israel, and to that greatest city of the enemies where was idolatry and ignorance of God. Yet more he feared lest they, on occasion of his preaching, being converted to repentance, Israel should be wholly forsaken. For he knew by the same Spirit whereby the preaching to the Gentiles was entrusted to him, that the house of Israel would then perish; and he feared that what was at one time to be, should take place in his own time." "[3] The flight of the Prophet may also be referred to that of man in general who, despising the commands of God, departed from Him and gave himself to the world, where subsequently, through the storms of ill and the wreck of the whole world raging against him, he was compelled to feel the Presence of God, and to return to Him Whom he had fled. Whence we understand, that those things also which men think for their good, when against the Will of God, are turned to destruction; and help not only does not benefit those to whom it is given, but those too who give it, are alike crushed. As we read that Egypt was conquered by the Assyrians, because it helped Israel against the Will of God. The ship is emperilled which had received the emperilled; a tempest arises in a calm; nothing is secure, when God is against us."

Tarshish, named after one of the sons of Javan[4], was an ancient merchant-city of Spain, once proverbial for its wealth[5], which supplied Judæa with silver[6], Tyre with *all manner of riches*, with iron also, tin, lead[7]. It was known to the Greeks and Romans, as (with a harder pronunciation) Tartessus; but in our first century, it had either ceased to be, or was known under some other name[8]. Ships destined for a voyage, at that time, so long, and built for carrying merchandise, were naturally among the largest then constructed. *Ships of Tarshish* corresponded to the "East-Indiamen" which some of us remember. The breaking of *ships of Tarshish by the East Wind*[9] is, on account of their size and general safety, instanced as a special token of the interposition of God.

And went down to Joppa. Joppa, now Jaffa, was the one well-known port of Israel on the

[1] S. Greg. Naz. Apol. pro fuga, prope fin.
[2] S. Jer. on Jon. i. 3.
[3] Id. on i. 4.
[4] Gen. x. 4.
[5] Ps. lxxii. 10. Strabo iii. 2. 14.
[6] Jer. x. 9.
[7] Ezek. xxvii. 12, 25.
[8] Pliny (iii. 3) speaks of Carteia as so called by the Greeks; in iv. 36, he identifies Gades, the Carthaginian Gadir, with the Roman Tartesus. Strabo says, "some call the present Karteia, Tartessus." (l. c.)
[9] Ps. xlviii. 7.

Before CHRIST cir. 780.

them unto Tarshish [f] from the presence of the LORD.

[f] Gen. 4. 16. Job 1. 12. & 2. 7.

4 ¶ But [g] the LORD † sent out a great wind

[g] Ps 107. 25. † Heb. *cast forth.*

Before CHRIST cir. 780.

Mediterranean. Thither the cedars were brought from Lebanon for both the first and second temple[1]. Simon the Maccabee "[2] took it again for a haven, and made an entrance to the isles of the sea." It was subsequently destroyed by the Romans, as a pirate-haven[3]. At a later time, all describe it as an unsafe haven. Perhaps the shore changed, since the rings, to which Andromeda was fabled to have been fastened, and which probably were once used to moor vessels, were high above the sea. Perhaps, like the Channel Islands, the navigation was safe to those who knew the coast, unsafe to others. To this port Jonah *went down* from his native country, the mountain district of Zabulon. Perhaps it was not at this time in the hands of Israel. At least, the sailors were heathen. He *went down*, as the man who fell among the thieves, is said to have *gone down from Jerusalem to Jericho*[4]. He *went down* from the place which God honored by His Presence and protection.

And he paid the fare thereof. Jonah describes circumstantially, how he took every step to his end. He went down, found a strong-built ship going whither he wished, paid his fare, embarked. He seemed now to have done all. He had severed himself from the country where his office lay. He had no further step to take. Winds and waves would do the rest. He had but to be still. He went, only to be brought back again.

"[5] Sin brings our soul into much senselessness. For as those overtaken by heaviness of head and drunkenness, are borne on simply and at random, and, be there pit or precipice or whatever else below them, they fall into it unawares; so too, they who fall into sin, intoxicated by their desire of the object, know not what they do, see nothing before them, present or future. Tell me, Fleest thou the Lord? Wait then a little, and thou shalt learn from the event, that thou canst not escape the hands of His servant, the sea. For as soon as he embarked, it too roused its waves and raised them up on high; and as a faithful servant, finding her fellow-slave stealing some of his master's property, ceases not from giving endless trouble to those who take him in, until she recover him, so too the sea, finding and recognizing her fellow-servant, harasses the sailors unceasingly, raging, roaring, not dragging them to a tribunal but threatening to sink the vessel with all its men, unless they restore to her, her fellow-servant."

"[6] The sinner *arises*, because, will he, nill he, toil he must. If he shrinks from the way of God, because it is hard, he may not yet be idle. There is the way of ambition, of covetousness, of pleasure, to be trodden, which certainly are far harder. 'We wearied ourselves[7],' say the wicked, 'in the way of wickedness and destruction, yea, we have gone through deserts where there lay no way; but the way of the Lord we have not known.' Jonah would not arise, to go to Nineveh at God's command; yet he must needs arise, to flee to Tarshish from before the Presence of God. What good can he have who fleeth the Good? what light, who willingly forsaketh the Light? *He goes down to Joppa.* Wherever thou turnest, if thou depart from the Will of God, thou goest down.—Whatever glory, riches, power, honors, thou gainest, thou risest not a whit; the more thou advancest, while turned from God, the deeper and deeper thou goest down.—Yet all these things are not had, without paying the price. At a price and with toil, he obtains what he desires; he receives nothing gratis, but, at great price purchases to himself storms, griefs, peril. There arises a great tempest in the sea, when various contradictory passions arise in the heart of the sinner, which take from him all tranquillity and joy. There is a tempest in the sea, when God sends strong and dangerous disease, whereby the frame is in peril of being broken. There is a tempest in the sea, when, thro' rivals or competitors for the same pleasures, or the injured, or the civil magistrate, his guilt is discovered, he is laden with infamy and odium, punished, withheld from his wonted pleasures. [8] *They who go down to the sea* of this world, *and do business in mighty waters—their soul melteth away because of trouble; they reel to and fro and stagger like a drunken man, and all their wisdom is swallowed up.*"

4. *But* [*And*] *the Lord sent out* [lit. *cast along*]. Jonah had done his all. Now God's part began. This He expresses by the word, *And.* Jonah took *his* measures, *and* now God takes *His.* He had let him have his way, as He often deals with those who rebel against Him. He lets them have their way up to a certain point. He waits, in the tranquillity of His Almightiness, until they have completed their preparations; and then, when man has ended, He begins, that man may see the more that it is His doing. "[9] He

[1] 2 Chr. iii. 16, Ezr. ii. 7.
[2] 1 Macc. xiv. 5.
[3] Jos. B. J. iii. 9. 3, and Strabo xvi. 2. 28.

[4] S. Luke x. 30.
[5] S. Chrys. Hom. 5. de Pœnit. n. 3. T. ii. p. 312.
[6] Rib. [7] Wisd. v. 7. [8] Ps. cvii. 23–7. [9] Lap.

Before CHRIST cir. 780.

into the sea, and there was
a mighty tempest in the
sea, so that the ship was
† like to be broken.
5 Then the mariners
were afraid, and cried
every man unto his god,
[h] and cast forth the wares
that *were* in the ship into
the sea, to lighten *it* of
them. But Jonah was
gone down [i] into the sides
of the ship; and he lay,
and was fast asleep.

† Heb. *thought to be broken.*

h So Acts 27. 18, 19, 38.

i 1 Sam. 24. 3.

takes those who flee from Him in their flight, the wise in their counsels, sinners in their conceits and sins, and draws them back to Himself and compels them to return. Jonah thought to find rest in the sea, and lo! a tempest." Probably, God summoned back Jonah, as soon as he had completed all on his part, and sent the tempest, soon after he left the shore. At least, such tempests often swept along that shore, and were known by their own special name, like the Euroclydon off Crete. Jonah too alone had gone down below deck to sleep, and, when the storm came, the mariners thought it possible to put back. Josephus says of that shore, "[1] Joppa having by nature no haven, for it ends in a rough shore, mostly abrupt, but for a short space having projections, i. e. deep rocks and cliffs advancing into the sea, inclining on either side toward each other (where the traces of the chains of Andromeda yet shewn accredit the antiquity of the fable,) and the North wind beating right on the shore, and dashing the high waves against the rocks which receive them, makes the station there a harborless sea. As those from Joppa were tossing here, a strong wind (called by those who sail here, the black North wind) falls upon them at daybreak, dashing straightway some of the ships against each other, some against the rocks, and some, forcing their way against the waves to the open sea, (for they fear the rocky shore—) the breakers towering above them, sank."

The ship was like [lit. *thought*] *to be broken.* Perhaps Jonah means by this very vivid image to exhibit the more his own dullness. He ascribes, as it were, to the ship a sense of its own danger, as she heaved and rolled and creaked and quivered under the weight of the storm which lay on her, and her masts groaned, and her yard-arms shivered. To the awakened conscience everything seems to have been alive to God's displeasure, except itself.

5. *And cried, every man unto his God.* They did what they could. "[2] Not knowing the truth, they yet know of a Providence, and, amid religious error, know that there is an Object of reverence." In ignorance they had received one who offended God. And now God, *Whom they ignorantly worshiped*[3], while they cried to the gods, who, they thought, disposed of them, heard them. They escaped with the loss of their wares, but God saved their lives and revealed Himself to them. God hears ignorant prayer, when ignorance is not wilful and sin.

To lighten it of them, lit. *to lighten from against them, to lighten* what was so much *against them,* what so oppressed them. "[2] They thought that the ship was weighed down by its wonted lading, and they knew not that the whole weight was that of the fugitive Prophet." "[4] *The sailors cast forth their wares,* but the ship was not lightened. For the whole weight still remained, the body of the Prophet, that heavy burden, not from the nature of the body, but from the burden of sin. For nothing is so onerous and heavy as sin and disobedience. Whence also Zechariah[5] represented it under the image of lead. And David, describing its nature, said[6], *my wickednesses are gone over my head; as a heavy burden they are too heavy for me.* And Christ cried aloud to those who lived in many sins[7], *Come unto Me, all ye that labor and are heavy-laden, and I will refresh you.*"

Jonah was gone down, probably before the beginning of the storm, not simply before the lightening of the vessel. He could hardly have fallen asleep *then.* A heathen ship was a strange place for a prophet of God, not *as* a prophet, but as a fugitive; and so, probably, ashamed of what he had completed, he had withdrawn from sight and notice. He did not embolden himself in his sin, but shrank into himself. The conscience most commonly awakes, when the sin is done. It stands aghast as itself; but Satan, if he can, cuts off its retreat. Jonah had no retreat now, unless God had made one.

And was fast asleep. The journey to Joppa had been long and hurried; he had *fled.* Sorrow and remorse completed what fatigue

[1] B. J. iii. 9. 3. In the Ant. xv. 9. 6. he says that Herod made the port of Cæsarea, "between Dora [in Manasseh] and Joppa, small towns on the sea-shore, with bad harborage, on account of the strong blasts from the South-West, which, accumulating the sea-sand on the shore, admit of no quiet moorage, but merchants must mostly ride at anchor out at sea."

[2] S. Jer.

[3] Acts xvii. 23.

[4] S. Chrys. Ib.

[5] v. 7.

[6] Ps. xxxviii. 4.

[7] S. Matt. xi. 28.

Before CHRIST cir. 780.

6 So the shipmaster
came to him, and said unto
him, What meanest thou,
O sleeper? arise, [k]call
upon thy God, [l]if so be
that God will think upon
us, that we perish not.
7 And they said every
one to his fellow, Come,
and let us [m]cast lots, that

k Ps. 107. 28.
l Joel 2. 14.
m Josh. 7. 14, 16. 1 Sam. 10. 20, 21. & 14. 41, 42. Prov. 16. 33. Acts 1. 26.

began. Perhaps he had given himself up to sleep, to dull his conscience. For it is said, *he lay down and was fast asleep*. Grief produces sleep; whence it is said of the Apostles in the night before the Lord's Passion, when Jesus *rose up from prayer and was come to His disciples, He found them sleeping for sorrow*[1]. "[2]Jonah slept heavily. Deep was the sleep, but it was not of pleasure but of grief; not of heartlessness, but of heavy-heartedness. For well-disposed servants soon feel their sins, as did he. For when the sin has been done, then he knows its frightfulness. For such is sin. When born, it awakens pangs in the soul which bare it, contrary to the law of our nature. For so soon as *we* are born, we end the travail-pangs; but sin, so soon as born, rends with pangs the thoughts which conceived it." Jonah was in a deep sleep, a sleep by which he was fast held and bound[3]; a sleep as deep as that from which Sisera never woke[4]. Had God allowed the ship to sink, the memory of Jonah would have been that of the fugitive prophet. As it is, his deep sleep stands as an image of the lethargy of sin. "[5]This most deep sleep of Jonah signifies a man torpid and slumbering in error, to whom it sufficed not to flee from the face of God, but his mind, drowned in a stupor and not knowing the displeasure of God, lies asleep, steeped in security."

6. *What meanest thou?* or rather, *what aileth thee?* [lit. *what is to thee?*] The shipmaster speaks of it (as it was) as a sort of disease, that he should be thus asleep in the common peril. *The shipmaster*, charged, as he by office was, with the common weal of those on board, would, in the common peril, have one common prayer. It was the Prophet's office to call the heathen to prayers and to calling upon God. God reproved the Scribes and Pharisees by the mouth of the children who *cried Hosanna*[6]; Jonah by the shipmaster; David by Abigail[7]; Naaman by his servants. Now too he reproves worldly priests by the devotion of laymen, sceptic intellect by the simplicity of faith.

If so be that God will think upon us, [lit. *for us*] i. e. for good; as David says[8], *I am poor and needy, the Lord thinketh upon* [lit. *for*] *me*. Their calling upon their own gods had failed them. Perhaps the shipmaster had seen something special about Jonah, his manner, or his prophet's garb. He does not only call Jonah's God, *thy God*, as Darius says to Daniel *thy God*[9], but also *the God*, acknowledging the God Whom Jonah worshiped, to be *the God*. It is not any heathen prayer which he asks Jonah to offer. It is the prayer of the creature in its need to God Who can help; but knowing its own ill-desert, and the separation between itself and God, it knows not whether He will help it. So David says[10], *Remember not the sins of my youth nor my transgressions; according to Thy mercy remember Thou me for Thy goodness' sake, O Lord*.

"[2]The shipmaster knew from experience, that it was no common storm, that the surges were an infliction borne down from God, and above human skill, and that there was no good in the master's skill. For the state of things needed another Master Who ordereth the heavens, and craved the guidance from on high. So then they too left oars, sails, cables, gave their hands rest from rowing, and stretched them to heaven and called on God."

7. *Come, and let us cast lots*. Jonah too had probably prayed, and his prayers too were not heard. Probably, too, the storm had some unusual character about it, the suddenness with which it burst upon them, its violence, the quarter whence it came, its whirlwind force. "[5]They knew the nature of the sea, and, as experienced sailors, were acquainted with the character of wind and storm, and had these waves been such as they had known before, they would never have sought by lot for the author of the threatened wreck, or, by a thing uncertain, sought to escape certain peril." God, Who sent the storm to arrest Jonah and to cause him to be cast into the sea, provided that its character should set the mariners on divining, why it came. Even when working great miracles, God brings about, through man, all the fore-running events, all but the last act, in which He puts forth His might. As, in His people, he directed the lot to fall on Achan or on Jonathan, so here He overruled the lots of the heathen sailors to accomplish His end. "[5]We must not, on this precedent, forthwith trust in lots, or unite with this testimony that from the Acts of the Apostles, when Matthias

1 S. Luke xxii. 45.
2 S. Chrys. Ib.
3 The Hebrew form is passive, נרדם.
4 The same word is used Judg. iv. 21.
5 S. Jer.
6 S. Matt. xxi. 15.
7 1 Sam. xxv. 32–34.
8 Ps. xl. 17.
9 Dan. vi. 20.
10 Ps. xxv. 7.

Before CHRIST cir. 780.

we may know for whose
cause this evil *is* upon us.
So they cast lots, and the
lot fell upon Jonah.

n Josh. 7. 19. 1 Sam. 14. 43.

8 Then said they unto
him, [n]Tell us, we pray
thee, for whose cause this
evil *is* upon us; What *is*
thine occupation? and
whence comest thou? what
is thy country? and of
what people *art* thou?

Before CHRIST cir. 780.

was by lot elected to the Apostolate, since the privileges of individuals cannot form a common law." "Lots," according to the ends for which they were cast, were[1] for i) dividing; ii) consulting; iii) divining. i.) The lot for dividing is not wrong if not used, 1) "[2] without any necessity; for this would be to tempt God:" 2) "if[2] in case of necessity, not without reverence of God, as if Holy Scripture were used for an earthly end," as in determining any secular matter by opening the Bible[3]: 3) for objects which ought to be decided otherwise, (as, an office ought to be given to the fittest:) 4) in dependence upon any other than God. [4] *The lot is cast into the lap, but the whole disposing of it is the Lord's.* So then they are lawful "[5] in secular things which cannot otherwise be conveniently distributed," or "[6] when there is no apparent reason why, in any advantage or disadvantage, one should be preferred to another." S. Augustine even allows[7] that, in a time of plague or persecution, the lot might be cast to decide who should remain to administer the Sacraments to the people, lest, on the one side, all should be taken away, or, on the other, the Church be deserted. ii. The lot for consulting, i. e. to decide what one should do, is wrong, unless in a matter of mere indifference, or under inspiration of God, or in some extreme necessity where all human means fail. iii. The lot for divining, i. e. to learn truth, whether of things present or future, of which we can have no human knowledge, is wrong, except by direct inspiration of God. For it is either to tempt God Who has not promised so to reveal things, or, against God, to seek superhuman knowledge by ways unsanctioned by Him. Satan may readily mix himself unknown in such enquiries, as in mesmerism. Forbidden ground is his own province.

God overruled the lot in the case of Jonah, as He did the sign which the Philistines sought. "[8] He made the heifers take the way to Bethshemesh, that the Philistines might know that the plague came to them, not by chance, but from Himself." "[9] The fugitive (Jonah) was taken by lot, not by any virtue of the lots, especially the lots of heathen, but by the Will of Him Who guided the uncertain lots." "[10] The lot betrayed the culprit. Yet not even thus did they cast him over; but, even while such a tumult and storm lay on them, they held, as it were, a court in the vessel, as though in entire peace, and allowed him a hearing and defence, and sifted everything accurately, as men who were to give account of their judgment. Hear them sifting all as in a court.—The roaring sea accused him; the lot convicted and witnessed against him, yet not even thus did they pronounce against him—until the accused should be the accuser of his own sin. The sailors, uneducated, untaught, imitated the good order of courts. When the sea scarce allowed them to breathe, whence such forethought about the Prophet? By the disposal of God. For God by all this instructed the Prophet to be humane and mild, all but saying aloud to him; 'Imitate these uninstructed sailors. They think not lightly of one soul, nor are unsparing as to one body, thine own. But thou, for thy part, gavest up a whole city with so many myriads. They, discovering thee to be the cause of the evils which befell them, did not even thus hurry to condemn thee. Thou, having nothing whereof to accuse the Ninevites, didst sink and destroy them. Thou, when I bade thee go and by thy preaching call them to repentance, obeyedst not; these, untaught, do all, compass all, in order to recover thee, already condemned, from punishment.'"

8. *Tell us, for whose cause* [lit. *for what to whom.*] It may be that they thought that Jonah had been guilty toward some other. The lot had pointed him out. The mariners, still fearing to do wrong, ask him thronged questions, to know why the anger of God followed him; *what* hast thou done *to whom? what thine occupation?* i. e. either his ordinary occupation, whether it was displeasing to God? or this particular *business* in which he was engaged, and for which he was come on board. Questions so thronged have been ad-

[1] Aquin. 2. 2. q. 95. art. 8.
[2] Aquin. l. c.
[3] From S. Aug. Ep. 55. ad inquis. Januar.
[4] Prov. xvi. 33.
[5] Less. de justit. &c. ii. 43. Dub. 9. L.
[6] Id. quoting S. Aug. de doctr. Xt. i. 28. "If any have a superfluity which ought to be given to such as have not, and cannot be given to two, and two come to you, of whom neither is to be preferred to the other from want or any urgent necessity, you cannot do anything more just than choose by lot, to which that should be given which cannot be given to both." also in Aquin. l. c.
[7] Ep. 228. ad Honorat. n. 12.
[8] Lap.
[9] S. Jer.
[10] S. Chrys. Ib. p. 313.

Before CHRIST cir. 780.

9 And he said unto
them, I *am* an Hebrew;
and I fear ‖ the LORD, the
God of heaven, ° which
hath made the sea and the
dry *land*.
10 Then were the men
† exceedingly afraid, and
said unto him, Why hast
thou done this? For the
men knew that he fled
from the presence of the
LORD, because he had told
them.

‖ Or, JEHOVAH.
° Ps. 146. 6. Acts. 17. 24.
† Heb. *with great fear.*

mired in human poetry, S. Jerome says. For it is true to nature. They think that some one of them will draw forth the answer which they wish. It may be that they thought that his country, or people, or parents, were under the displeasure of God. But perhaps, more naturally, they wished to "know all about him," as men say. These questions must have gone home to Jonah's conscience. *What is thy business?* The office of Prophet which he had left. *Whence comest thou?* From standing before God, as His minister. *What thy country? of what people art thou?* The people of God, whom he had quitted for heathen; not to win them to God, as He commanded; but, not knowing what they did, to abet him in his flight.

What is thine occupation? They should ask themselves, who have Jonah's office to speak in the name of God, and preach repentance. "[1] What should be thy business, who hast consecrated thyself wholly to God, whom God has loaded with daily benefits? who approachest to Him as to a Friend? *What is thy business?* To live for God, to despise the things of earth, to behold the things of Heaven," to lead others heavenward.

Jonah answers simply the central point to which all these questions tended;

9. *I am an Hebrew.* This was the name by which Israel was known to foreigners. It is used in the Old Testament, only when they are spoken of by foreigners, or speak of themselves to foreigners, or when the sacred writers mention them in contrast with foreigners[2]. So Joseph spoke of his land[3], and the Hebrew midwives[4], and Moses' sister[5], and God in His commission to Moses[6] as to Pharaoh, and Moses in fulfilling it[7]. They had the name, as having passed the river Euphrates, "emigrants." The title might serve to remind themselves, that they were *strangers and pilgrims*[8], whose fathers had left their home at God's command and for God, "[9] *passers by*, through this world to death, and through death to immortality."

And I fear the Lord, i. e. I am a worshiper of Him, most commonly, one who habitually stands in awe of Him, and so one who stands in awe of sin too. For none really fear God, none fear Him as sons, who do not fear Him in act. To be afraid of God is not to fear Him. To be afraid of God keeps men away from God; to fear God draws them to Him. Here, however, Jonah probably meant to tell them, that the Object of his fear and worship was the One Self-existing God, He Who alone IS, Who made all things, in Whose hands are all things. He had told them before, that he had fled *from being before the* LORD. They had not thought anything of this, for they thought of the LORD, only as the God of the Jews. Now he adds, that He, Whose service he had thus forsaken, was *the God of heaven, Who made the sea and dry land*, that sea, whose raging terrified them and threatened their lives. The title, *the God of heaven*, asserts the doctrine of the creation of the heavens by God, and His supremacy. Hence Abraham uses it to his servant[10], and Jonah to the heathen mariners, and Daniel to Nebuchadnezzar[11]; and Cyrus in acknowledging God in his proclamation[12]. After his example, it is used in the decrees of Darius[13] and Artaxerxes[14], and the returned exiles use it in giving account of their building the temple to the Governor[15]. Perhaps, from the habit of intercourse with the heathen, it is used once by Daniel[16] and by Nehemiah[17]. Melchisedek, not perhaps being acquainted with the special name, the LORD, blessed Abraham in the Name of *God, the Possessor* or *Creator of heaven and earth*[18], i. e. of all that is. Jonah, by using it, at once taught the sailors that there is One Lord of all, and why this evil had fallen on them, because they had with them himself, the renegade servant of God. "[19] When Jonah said this, he indeed feared God and repented of his sin. If he lost filial fear by fleeing and disobeying, he recovered it by repentance."

10. *Then were the men exceedingly afraid.* Before, they had feared the tempest and the loss of their lives. Now they feared God. They feared, not the creature but the Creator. They knew that what they had feared

1 Sanch. 2 In all 32 times in the O. T. 3 Gen. xl. 15. 4 Ex. i. 19. 5 Ib. ii. 7. 6 Ib. iii. 18, vii. 16. ix. 1. 7 Ib. v. 3. 8 Heb. xi. 13. 9 Lap.

10 Gen. xxiv. 7. 11 Dan. ii. 37, 44. 12 2 Chr. xxxvi. 23, Ezr. i. 2. 13 Ezr. vi. 9. 10. 14 Ib. vii. 12, 21, 23. 15 Ib. v. 11, 12. 16 ii. 18. 17 i. 4, 5, ii. 4, 20. 18 Gen. xiv. 19. 19 Dion.

Before CHRIST cir. 780.

11 ¶ Then said they unto him, What shall we do unto thee that the sea † may be calm unto us? for the sea || † wrought, and was tempestuous.

12 And he said unto them, [p] Take me up, and cast me forth into the sea, so shall the sea be calm unto you: for I know that for my sake this great tempest *is* upon you.

† Heb. *may be silent from us.*
|| Or, *grew more and more tempestuous.*
† Heb. *went.*

Before CHRIST cir. 780.

p John 11. 50.

---

was the doing of His Almightiness. They felt how awful a thing it was to be in His Hands. Such fear is the beginning of conversion, when men turn from dwelling on the distresses which surround them, to God Who sent them.

Why hast thou done this? They are words of amazement and wonder. Why hast thou not obeyed so great a God, and how thoughtest thou to escape the hand of the Creator? "[1] What is the mystery of thy flight? Why did one, who feared God and had revelations from God, flee, sooner than go to fulfill them? Why did the worshiper of the One true God depart from his God?" "[2] A servant flee from his Lord, a son from his father, man from his God!" The inconsistency of believers is the marvel of the young Christian, the repulsion of those without, the hardening of the unbeliever. If men really believed in eternity, how could they be thus immersed in things of time? If they believed in hell, how could they so hurry thither? If they believed that God died for them, how could they so requite Him? Faith without love, knowledge without obedience, conscious dependence and rebellion, to be favored by God yet to despise His favor, are the strangest marvels of this mysterious world. All nature seems to cry out to and against the unfaithful Christian, *why hast thou done this?* And what a *why* it is! A scoffer has lately said truly, "[3] Avowed scepticism cannot do a tenth part of the injury to practical faith, that the constant spectacle of the huge mass of worldly unreal belief does." It is nothing strange, that the world or unsanctified intellect should reject the Gospel. It is a thing of course, unless it be converted. But, to know, to believe, and to disobey! To disobey God, in the name of God. To propose to halve the living Gospel, as the woman who had killed her child[4], and to think that the poor quivering remnants would be the living Gospel any more! As though the Will of God might, like those lower forms of His animal creation, be divided endlessly, and, keep what fragments we will, it would still be a living whole, a vessel of His Spirit! Such unrealities and inconsistencies would be a sore trial of faith, had not Jesus, Who [5] *knew what is in man*, forewarned us that it should be so. The scandals against the Gospel, so contrary to all human opinion, are but a testimony the more to the Divine knowledge of the Redeemer.

11. *What shall we do unto thee?* They knew him to be a prophet; they ask him the mind of his God. The lots had marked out Jonah as the cause of the storm; Jonah had himself admitted it, and that the storm was for *his* cause, and came from *his* God. "[2] Great was he who fled, greater He Who required him. They dare not give him up; they cannot conceal him. They blame the fault; they confess their fear; they ask *him* the remedy, who was the author of the sin. If it was faulty to receive thee, what can we do, that God should not be angered? It is thine to direct; ours, to obey."

The sea wrought and was tempestuous, lit. *was going and whirling*. It was not only increasingly tempestuous, but, like a thing alive and obeying its Master's Will, it was holding on its course, its wild waves tossing themselves, and marching on like battalions, marshalled, arrayed for the end for which they were sent, pursuing and demanding the runaway slave of God. "[2] *It was going*, as it was bidden; *it was going* to avenge its Lord; *it was going*, pursuing the fugitive Prophet. It was swelling every moment, and, as though the sailors were too tardy, was rising in yet greater surges, shewing that the vengeance of the Creator admitted not of delay."

12. *Take me up, and cast me into the sea.* Neither might Jonah have said this, nor might the sailors have obeyed it, without the command of God. Jonah might will alone to perish, who had alone offended; but, without the command of God, the Giver of life, neither Jonah nor the sailors might dispose of the life of Jonah. But God willed that Jonah should be cast into the sea, whither he had gone for refuge, that[6] *wherewithal* he had *sinned, by the same also he* might *be punished* as a man; and, as a Prophet, that he might, in his three days' burial, prefigure Him Who, after His Resurrection, should convert, not Nineveh, but the world, the cry of whose wickedness went up to God.

For I know that for my sake. "[7] In that he

[1] Dion. [2] S. Jer.
[3] In the Times. [4] 1 Kings iii. 26.
[5] S. John ii. 25
[6] Wisd. xi. 16. [7] Alb. M.

Before CHRIST cir. 780.

13 Nevertheless the men
† rowed hard to bring *it* to
the land; [q] but they could
not: for the sea wrought,
and was tempestuous
against them.

† Heb. *digged.*
q Prov. 21. 30.

14 Wherefore they cried
unto the LORD, and said,
We beseech thee, O LORD,
we beseech thee, let us not
perish for this man's life,
and [r] lay not upon us in-

Before CHRIST cir. 780.

r Deut. 21. 8.

---

says, *I know*, he marks that he had a revelation; in that he says, *this great storm*, he marks the need which lay on those who cast him into the sea."

13. *The men rowed hard*, lit. *dug*. The word, like our "ploughed the main," describes the great efforts which they made. Amid the violence of the storm, they had furled their sails. These were worse than useless. The wind was off shore, since by rowing alone they hoped to get back to it. They put their oars well and firmly in the sea, and turned up the water, as men turn up earth by digging. But in vain! God willed it not. The sea went on its way, as before. In the description of the deluge, it is repeated, [1] *the waters increased and bare up the ark, and it was lifted up above the earth; the waters increased greatly upon the earth; and the ark went upon the face of the waters.* The waters raged and swelled, drowned the whole world, yet only bore up the ark, as a steed bears its rider: man was still, the waters obeyed. In *this* tempest, on the contrary, man strove, but, instead of the peace of the ark, the burden is, the violence of the tempest; *the sea wrought and was tempestuous against them.* "[2] The Prophet had pronounced sentence against himself, but they would not lay hands upon him, striving hard to get back to land, and escape the risk of bloodshed, willing to lose life rather than cause its loss. O what a change was there. The people who had served God, said, Crucify Him, Crucify Him! These are bidden to put to death; the sea rageth; the tempest commandeth; and they are careless as to their own safety, while anxious about another's."

14. *Wherefore* [*And*] *they cried unto the Lord. They cried* no more *each man to his god*, but to the one God, Whom Jonah had made known to them; and to Him they cried with an earnest, submissive, cry, repeating the words of beseeching, as men, do in great earnestness; *we beseech Thee, O Lord, let us not, we beseech Thee, perish for the life of this man* (i. e. as a penalty for taking it, as it is said, [3] *we will slay him for the life of his brother*, and, [4] *life for life.*) They seem to have known what is said, [5] *your blood of your lives will I require; at the hand of every beast will I require it and at the hand of man; at the hand of every man's brother will I require the life of man. Whoso sheddeth man's blood, by man shall his blood be shed; for in the image of God made He man.* "[2] Do not these words of the sailors seem to us to be the confession of Pilate, who washed his hands, and said, *I am clean from the blood of this Man?* The Gentiles would not that Christ should perish; they protest that His Blood is innocent."

And lay not upon us innocent blood; innocent as to them, although, as to this thing, guilty before God, and yet, as to God also, more innocent, they would think, than they. For, strange as was this one disobedience, *their* whole life, they now knew, was disobedience to God; *his*, but one act in a life of obedience. If God so punishes one sin of the holy, [6] *where shall the ungodly and sinner appear?* Terrible to the awakened conscience are God's chastenings on some (as it seems) single offence of those whom He loves.

For Thou, Lord, [*Who knowest the hearts of all men,*] *hast done, as it pleased Thee.* Wonderful, concise, confession of faith in these new converts! Psalmists said it [7], *Whatsoever God willeth, that doeth He in heaven and in earth, in the sea and in all deep places.* But these had but just known God, and they resolve the whole mystery of man's agency and God's Providence into the three simple words [8], *as* [Thou] *willedst* [Thou] *didst.* "[2] That we took him aboard, that the storm ariseth, that the winds rage, that the billows lift themselves, that the fugitive is betrayed by the lot, that he points out what is to be done, it is of Thy Will, O Lord." "[2] The tempest itself speaketh, that *Thou, Lord, hast done as Thou willedst.* Thy Will is fulfilled by our hands." "[9] O! serve the counsel of God, that, of his own will, not by violence or by necessity, should he be cast into the sea. For the casting of Jonah into the sea signified the entrance of Christ into the bitterness of the Passion, which He took upon Himself of His own Will, not of necessity. [10] *He was offered up, and He willingly submitted Himself.* And as those who sailed with Jonah were delivered, so the faithful in the Passion of Christ. [11] *If ye seek Me, let these go their way, that the saying might be fulfilled which*

1 Gen. vii. 17, 18. 2 S. Jer. 3 2 Sam. xiv. 7. 4 Deut. xix. 21. 5 Gen. ix. 5, 6.

6 1 S. Pet. iv. 18. 7 Ps. cxxxv. 6, cxv. 3. 8 כאשר חפצת עשית. 9 Alb. M. 10 Is. liii. 7. 11 S. John xviii. 8, 9.

Before CHRIST cir. 780.

nocent blood: for thou, O
LORD, [s] hast done as it
pleased thee.

15 So they took up Jo-
nah, and cast him forth
into the sea: [t] and the sea
† ceased from her raging.

16 Then the men [u] feared
the LORD exceedingly, and
† offered a sacrifice unto
the LORD, and made
vows.

17 ¶ Now the LORD
had prepared a great fish
to swallow up Jonah. And
[x] Jonah was in the † belly
of the fish three days and
three nights.

s Ps. 115. 3.
t Ps. 89. 9. Luke 8. 24.
† Heb. *stood.*
u Mark 4. 41. Acts 5. 11.

Before CHRIST cir. 780.

† Heb. *sacrificed a sacrifice unto the LORD, and vowed vows.*
x Matt. 12. 40. & 16. 4. Luke 11. 30.
† Heb. *bowels.*

Jesus spake, Of them which Thou gavest Me, I have lost none."

15. *They took up Jonah.* "[1] He does not say, 'laid hold on him', nor 'came upon him' but *lifted* him; as it were, bearing him with respect and honor, they cast him into the sea, not resisting, but yielding himself to their will."

The sea ceased [lit. *stood*] *from his raging.* Ordinarily, the waves still swell, when the wind has ceased. The sea, when it had received Jonah, was hushed at once, to shew that God alone raised and quelled it. It *stood* still, like a servant, when it had accomplished its mission. God, Who at all times saith to it, [2] *Hitherto shalt thou come and no further, and here shall thy proud waves be stayed,* now unseen, as afterwards in the Flesh, [3] *rebuked the winds and the sea, and there was a great calm.* "[1] If we consider the errors of the world before the Passion of Christ, and the conflicting blasts of divers doctrines, and the vessel, and the whole race of man, i. e. the creature of the Lord, imperilled, and, after His Passion, the tranquillity of faith and the peace of the world and the security of all things and the conversion to God, we shall see how, after Jonah was cast in, the sea stood from its raging." "[1] Jonah, in the sea, a fugitive, shipwrecked, dead, saveth the tempest-tost vessel; he saveth the heathen, aforetime tossed to and fro by the error of the world into divers opinions. And Hosea, Amos, Isaiah, Joel, who prophesied at the same time, could not amend the people in Judæa; whence it appeared that the breakers could not be calmed, save by the death of [Him typified by] the fugitive."

16. *And the men feared the Lord with a great fear;* because, from the tranquillity of the sea and the ceasing of the tempest, they saw that the Prophet's words were true. This great miracle completed the conversion of the mariners. God had removed all human cause of fear; and yet, in the same words as before, he says, *they feared a great fear;* but he adds, *the Lord.* It was the great fear, with which even the disciples of Jesus feared, when they saw the miracles which He did, which made even Peter say, [4] *Depart from me, for I am a sinful man, O Lord.* Events full of wonder had thronged upon them; things beyond nature, and contrary to nature; things which betokened *His* Presence, Who had all things in His hands. They had seen *wind and storm fulfilling His word* [5], and, forerunners of the fishermen of Galilee, knowing full well from their own experience that this was above nature, they felt a great awe of God. So He commanded His people, *Thou shalt fear the Lord thy God* [6], *for thy good always* [7].

And offered a sacrifice. Doubtless, as it was a large decked vessel and bound on a long voyage, they had live creatures on board, which they could offer in sacrifice. But this was not enough for their thankfulness; *they vowed vows.* They promised that they would do thereafter what they could not do then; "[1] that they would never depart from Him Whom they had begun to worship." This was true love, not to be content with aught which they could do, but to stretch forward in thought to an abiding and enlarged obedience, as God should enable them. And so they were doubtless enrolled among the people of God, first-fruits from among the heathen, won to God Who overrules all things, through the disobedience and repentance of His Prophet. Perhaps, they were the first preachers among the heathen, and their account of their own wonderful deliverance prepared the way for Jonah's mission to Nineveh.

17. *Now the Lord had* [lit. *And the Lord*] *prepared.* Jonah (as appears from his thanksgiving) was not swallowed at once, but sank to the bottom of the sea, God preserving him in life there by miracle, as He did in the fish's belly. Then, when the sea-weed was twined around his head, and he seemed to be already buried till the sea should give up her dead, *God prepared the fish to swallow Jonah.* "[8] God could as easily have kept Jonah alive in the sea as in the fish's belly, but, in order to prefigure the burial of the Lord, He willed him to be within the fish whose

[1] S. Jer.
[2] Job xxxviii. 11.
[3] S. Matt. viii. 26.
[4] S. Luke v. 8.
[5] Ps. cxlviii. 8.
[6] Deut. vi. 13.
[7] Ib. 24.
[8] Dion.

Before CHRIST cir. 780.

CHAPTER II.

1 *The prayer of Jonah.* 10 *He is delivered from the fish.*

THEN Jonah prayed unto the LORD his God out of the fish's belly,

Before CHRIST cir. 780.

belly was as a grave." Jonah, does not say what fish it was; and our Lord too used a name, signifying only one of the very largest fish[1]. Yet it were no greater miracle to create a fish which should swallow Jonah, than to preserve him alive when swallowed. "[2]The infant is buried, as it were, in the womb of its mother; it cannot breathe, and yet, thus too, it liveth and is preserved, wonderfully nurtured by the will of God." He Who preserves the embryo in its living grave can maintain the life of man as easily without the outward air as with it. The same Divine Will preserves in being the whole creation, or creates it. The same Will of God keeps us in life by breathing this outward air, Which preserved Jonah without it. How long will men think of God, as if He were man, of the Creator as if He were a creature, as though creation were but one intricate piece of machinery, which is to go on, ringing its regular changes until it shall be worn out, and God were shut up, as a sort of mainspring within it, Who might be allowed to be a primal Force, to set it in motion, but must not be allowed to vary what He has once made? "We must admit of the agency of God," say these men[3] when they would not in name be Atheists, "once in the beginning of things, but must allow of His interference as sparingly as may be." Most wise arrangement of the creature, if it were indeed the god of its God! Most considerate provision for the non-interference of its Maker, if it could but secure that He would not interfere with it for ever! Acute physical philosophy, which, by its omnipotent word, would undo the Acts of God! Heartless, senseless, sightless, world, which exists in God, is upheld by God, whose every breath is an effluence of God's love, and which yet sees Him not, thanks Him not, thinks it a greater thing to hold its own frail existence from some imagined law, than to be the object of the tender personal care of the Infinite God, Who is Love! Poor hoodwinked souls, which would extinguish for themselves the Light of the world, in order that it may not eclipse the rushlight of their own theory!

And Jonah was in the belly of the fish. The time that Jonah was in the fish's belly was a hidden prophecy. Jonah does not explain nor point it. He tells the fact, as Scripture is wont. Then he singles out one, the turning point in it. Doubtless in those three days and nights of darkness, Jonah, (like him who after his conversion became S. Paul,) meditated much, repented much, sorrowed much, for the love of God, that he had ever offended God, purposed future obedience, adored God with wondering awe for His judgment and mercy. It was a narrow home, in which Jonah, by miracle, was not consumed; by miracle, breathed; by miracle, retained his senses in that fetid place. Jonah doubtless, repented, marvelled, adored, loved God. But, of all, God has singled out this one point, how, out of such a place, Jonah thanked God. As He delivered Paul and Silas from the prison, when they prayed with a loud voice to Him, so when Jonah, by inspiration of His Spirit, thanked Him, He delivered him. To thank God, only in order to obtain fresh gifts from Him, would be but a refined, hypocritical form of selfishness. Such a formal act would not be thanks at all. We thank God, because we love Him, because He is so infinitely Good, and so good to us, unworthy. Thanklessness shuts the door to His personal mercies to us, because it makes them the occasion of fresh sins of our's. Thankfulness sets God's essential Goodness free (so to speak) to be good to us. He can do what He delights in doing, be good to us, without our making His Goodness a source of harm to us. Thanking Him through His grace, we become fit vessels for larger graces. "[4] Blessed he who, at every gift of grace, returns to Him in Whom is all fullness of graces; to Whom when we shew ourselves not ungrateful for gifts received, we make room in ourselves for grace, and become meet for receiving yet more." But Jonah's was that special character of thankfulness, which thanks God in the midst of calamities from which there was no human exit; and God set His seal on this sort of thankfulness, by annexing this deliverance, which has consecrated Jonah as an image of our Lord, to his wonderful act of thanksgiving.

II. 1. *Then* [*And*] *Jonah prayed*, i. e. when the three days and nights were passed, he uttered this devotion. The word *prayed* includes thanksgiving, not petition only. It is said of Hannah that she *prayed*[5]; but her canticle is all one thanksgiving without a single petition. In this thanksgiving Jonah says how his prayers had been heard, but prays no more. God had delivered him from the sea, and he thanks God, in the fish's belly, as undisturbed as in a Church or an oratory, secure that God, Who had done so

[1] See ab. Introd. p. 257. [2] S. Cyr.
[3] Westminster Review.

[4] S. Bern. Serm. 27. c. pessim.vit. in gratitud. i. 1142. [5] 1 Sam. ii. 1.

Before CHRIST cir. 780.

2 And said, I [a]cried ||by
reason of mine affliction
unto the LORD, [b]and he
heard me; out of the belly
of ||hell cried I, *and* thou
heardest my voice.

3 [c]For thou hadst cast
me into the deep, in the
†midst of the seas; and
the floods compassed me
about: [d]all thy billows and
thy waves passed over me.

[a] Ps. 120. 1. & 130. 1. & 142. 1. Lam. 3. 55, 56.
|| Or, *out of mine affliction.*
[b] Ps. 65. 2.
|| Or, *the grave.* Is. 14. 9.
[c] Ps. 88. 6.
† Heb. *heart.*
[d] Ps. 42. 7.

much, would fulfill the rest. He called God, *his God*, Who had in so many ways shewn Himself his, by His revelations, by His inspirations, by His chastisements, and now by His mercy. "[1]From these words, *Jonah prayed unto the Lord his God out of the fish's belly*, we perceive that, after he felt himself safe in the fish's belly, he despaired not of God's mercy."

2. *I cried by reason of mine affliction*, or, *out of affliction* which came *to me*. So the Psalmist thanked God in the same words, though in a different order[2]; *To the Lord in trouble to me I called, and He heard me.* He *called*, and God heard and answered. "[1]He does not say, *I call*, but *I called;* he does not pray for the future, but gives thanks for the past." Strange cause of thankfulness this would seem to most faith, to be alive in such a grave; to abide there hour after hour, and day after day, in one unchanging darkness, carried to and fro helplessly, with no known escape from his fetid prison, except to death! Yet spiritual light shone on that depth of darkness. The voracious creature, which never opened his mouth save to destroy life, had swallowed him, to save it. "[1]What looked like death, became safe-keeping," and so the Prophet who had fled to avoid doing the Will of God and to do his own, now willed to be borne about, he knew not whither, at the will, as it seemed, of the huge animal in which he lay, but in truth, whither God directed it, and he gave thanks. God had heard him. The first token of God's mercy was the earnest of the whole. God was dealing with him, was looking on him. It was enough.

Out of the belly of hell cried I. The deep waters were as a grave, and he was counted *among the dead*[3]. Death seemed so certain that it was all one as if he were in the womb of hell, not to be re-born to life until the last Day. So David said[4], *The bands of death compassed me round about;* and, [5]*Thou hast drawn my life out of hell.* The waters choked his speech; but he cried with a loud cry to God Who knew the heart. *I cried; Thou heardest.* The words vary only by a kindred letter[6], *Shivva'ti, Shama'ta.* The real heart's-cry to God according to the mind of God and His hearing are one, whether, for man's good, He seem at the time to hear or no.

"[7]Not of the voice but of the heart is God the Hearer, as He is the Seer.—Do the ears of God wait for sound? How then could the prayer of Jonah from the inmost belly of the whale, through the bowels of so great a creature, out of the very bottomless depths, through so great a mass of waters, make its way to Heaven?" "[8]Loud crying to God is not with the voice but with the heart. Many, silent with their lips, have cried aloud with their heart; many, noisy with their lips, could, with heart turned away, obtain nothing. If then thou criest, cry within, where God heareth." "[9]Jonah cried aloud to God out of the fish's belly, out of the deep of the sea, out of the depths of disobedience; and his prayer reached to God, Who rescued him from the waves, brought him forth out of the vast creature, absolved him from the guilt. Let the sinner too cry aloud, whom, departing from God, the storm of desires overwhelmed, the malignant Enemy devoured, the waves of this present world sucked-under! Let him own that he is in the depth, that so his prayer may reach to God."

3. *For Thou hadst* [*didst*] *cast me into the deep.* Jonah continues to describe the extremity of peril, from which God had already delivered him. Sweet is the memory of perils past. For they speak of God's Fatherly care. Sweet is it to the Prophet to tell God of His mercies; but this is sweet only to the holy; for God's mercy convicts the careless of ingratitude. Jonah then tells God, how He had cast him vehemently forth into the *eddying*[10] *depth*, where, when Pharaoh's army *sank like a stone*[11], they never rose, and that, *in the heart* or centre *of the seas*, whence no strong swimmer could escape to shore. *The floods* or *flood*, [lit. *river*,] the sea with its currents, *surrounded* him, encompassing him on all sides; and, above, tossed its multitudinous waves, passing over him, like an army trampling one prostrate under foot. Jonah remembered well the temple-psalms, and, using their words, united himself with those other worshipers who sang them, and

[1] S. Jer. [2] See Introd. p. 252.
[3] Ps. lxxxviii. 4. [4] Ib. xviii. 5. [5] Ib. xxx. 3.
[6] שועתי שמעת.
[7] Tert. de Orat. § 17. p. 311. Oxf. Tr.
[8] S. Aug. in Ps. 30. Enarr. 4. § 10: see others referred to on Tert. l. c. p. 310. n. v.
[9] S. Greg. in Ps. 6. Pœnit. L.
[10] מצולה.
[11] Ex. xv. 5, add 10.

Before CHRIST cir. 780.

e Ps. 31. 22.
f 1 Kings 8. 38.
g Ps. 69. 1. Lam. 3. 54.

4 [e]Then I said, I am
cast out of thy sight, yet I
will look again [f]toward thy
holy temple.
5 The [g]waters compassed
me about, *even* to the soul:
the depth closed me round
about, the weeds were
wrapped about my head.
6 I went down to the
†bottoms of the moun-
tains; the earth with her
bars *was* about me for
ever: yet hast thou

† Heb. *cuttings off.*

taught us how to speak them to God. The sons of Korah[1] had poured out to God in these self-same words the sorrows which oppressed them. The rolling billows[2] and the breakers[3], which, as they burst upon the rocks, shiver the vessel and crush man, are, he says to God, *Thine*, fulfilling Thy Will on me.

4. *I am cast out of Thy sight*, lit. *from before Thine eyes.* Jonah had wilfully withdrawn from standing in God's presence. Now God had taken him at his word, and, as it seemed, cast him out of it. David had said in his haste, *I am cut off.* Jonah substitutes the stronger word, *I am cast forth*[4], driven forth, expelled, like the *mire and dirt*[5] which the waves drive along, or like the waves themselves in their restless motion[6], or the heathen (the word is the same) whom God had driven out before Israel[7], or as Adam from Paradise[8].

Yet [*Only*] *I will look again.* He was, as it were, a castaway, cast out of God's sight, unheeded by Him, his prayers unheard; the storm unabated, until he was cast forth. He could no longer look with the bodily eye even toward the land where God shewed the marvels of His mercy, and the temple where God was worshiped continually. Yet what he could not do in the body, he would do in his soul. This was his only resource. "If I be cast away, this one thing will I do, I will still look to God." Magnificent faith! Humanly speaking, all hope was gone, for, when that huge vessel could scarcely live in the sea, how should a man? when God had given it no rest, while it contained Jonah, how should He will that Jonah should escape? Nay, God had hidden His Face from him; yet he did this one, this only thing; only this, "once more, still *I will add to look to God.*" Thitherward would he look, so long as his mind yet remained in him. If his soul parted from him, it should go forth from him in that gaze. God gave him no hope, save that He preserved him alive. For he seemed to himself forsaken of God. Wonderful pattern of faith which gains strength even from God's seeming desertion! "I am cast vehemently forth from before Thine eyes; yet this one thing will I do; mine eyes shall be unto Thee, O Lord." The Israelites, as we see from Solomon's dedication-prayer, *prayed toward the temple*[9], where God had set His Name and shewn His glory, where were the sacrifices which foreshadowed the Great Atonement. Thitherward they looked in prayer, as Christians, of old, prayed toward the East, the seat of our ancient Paradise, where our Lord *shall appear unto them that look for Him, a second time unto salvation*[10]. Toward that Temple then he would yet look with fixed eye[11] for help, where God, Who fills heaven and earth, shewed Himself to sinners reconciled.

5. *The waters compassed me about even to the soul.* Words which to others were figures of distress, [12]*the waters have come even to the soul*, were to Jonah realities. Sunk in the deep seas, the water strove to penetrate at every opening. To draw breath, which sustains life, to him would have been death. There was but a breath between him and death. *The deep encompassed me*, encircling, meeting him whithersoever he turned, holding him imprisoned on every side, so that there was no escape, and, if there otherwise had been, he was bound motionless, *the weed was wrapped around my head*, like a grave-band. *The weed* was the well-known sea-weed, which, even near the surface of the sea where man can struggle, twines round him, a peril even to the strong swimmer, entangling him often the more, the more he struggles to extricate himself from it. But to one below, powerless to struggle, it was as his winding-sheet.

6. *I went down to the bottoms*, [lit. *the cuttings off*] *of the mountains*, the "roots" as the Chaldee[13] and we call them, the hidden rocks, which the mountains push out, as it were, into the sea, and in which they end. Such hidden rocks extend along the whole length of that coast[14]. These were his dun-

1 Ps. xlii. 7. 2 גליך.
3 משבריך. 4 See Introd. p. 252. 5 Is. lvii. 20.
6 Ib. 7 Ex. xxxiv. 11. and Piel often.
8 Gen. iii. 24.
9 1 Kings viii. 29, 30, 35, &c. 10 Heb. ix. 28.
11 הביט אל is, "look intently towards," as Moses at the bush, Ex. iii. 6.

12 Ps. lxix. 2. See ab. Introd. p. 252.
13 Jon. here.
14 "The road is very dangerous; for the bottom is a mere bank of rocks, which extend the whole length of the coast. It is thought that the sharp rocks which pierce to the surface of the sea are the remains of the Isle Paria, mentioned by Pliny v. 31." Mislin, Les Saints Lieux, ii. 137.

Before CHRIST cir. 780.

brought up my life [h] from
|| corruption, O LORD my
God.
7 When my soul fainted
within me I remem-
bered the LORD: [i] and
my prayer came in
unto thee, into thine holy
temple.
8 They that observe
[k] lying vanities forsake
their own mercy.

h Ps. 16. 10.
|| Or, *the pit.*
i Ps. 18. 6.

Before CHRIST cir. 780.

k 2 Kings 17. 15. Ps. 31. 6. Jer. 10. 8. & 16. 19.

geon-walls; *the earth, her bars,* those long submarine reefs of rock, his prison-bars, *were around* him *for ever:* the sea-weeds were his chains: and, even thus, when things were at their uttermost, *Thou hast brought up my life from corruption,* to which his body would have fallen a prey, had not God sent the fish to deliver him. The deliverance for which he thanks God is altogether past: *Thou broughtest me up.* He calls *the* LORD, *my* God, because, being the God of all, He was especially his God, for whom He had done things of such marvellous love. God loves each soul which He has made with the same infinite love with which He loves all. Whence S. Paul says of Jesus [1], *Who loved me and gave Himself for me.* He loves each, with the same undivided love, as if he had created none besides; and He allows each to say, *My God,* as if the Infinite God belonged wholly to each. So would He teach us the oneness of Union between the soul which God loves and which admits His love, and Himself.

7. *When my soul fainted,* lit. *was covered, within me,* was dizzied, overwhelmed. The word is used of actual faintness from heat [2], thirst [3], exhaustion [4], when a film comes over the eyes, and the brain is, as it were, mantled over. The soul of the pious never is so full of God, as when all things else fade from him. Jonah could not but have remembered God in the tempest; when the lots were cast; when he adjudged himself to be cast forth. But when it came to the utmost, then he says, *I remembered the Lord,* as though, in the intense thought of God then, all his former thought of God had been forgetfulness. So it is in every strong act of faith, of love, of prayer; its former state seems unworthy of the name of faith, love, prayer. It believes, loves, prays, as though all before had been forgetfulness.

And my prayer came in unto Thee. No sooner had he so prayed, than God heard. Jonah had thought himself cast out of His sight; but his prayer entered in thither. His *holy temple* is doubtless His actual Temple, whitherward he prayed. God, Who is wholly everywhere but the whole of Him nowhere, was as much in the Temple as in heaven; and had manifested Himself to Israel in their degree in the Temple, as to the blessed saints and angels in heaven.

8 *They that observe lying vanities,* i. e. (by the force of the Hebrew form [5],) that diligently watch, pay deference to, court, sue, *vanities of vanities,* vain things, which prove themselves vain at last, failing the hopes which trust in them. Such were actual idols, in which men openly professed that they trusted Such are all things in which men trust, out of God. One is not more vain than another. All have this common principle of vanity, that men look, out of God, to that which has its only existence or permanence from God. It is then one general maxim, including all men's idols, idols of the flesh, idols of intellect, idols of ambition, idols of pride, idols of self and self-will. Men *observe* them, as gods, watch them, hang upon them, never lose sight of them, guard them as though they could keep them. But what are they? *lying vanities,* breath and wind, which none can grasp or detain, vanishing like air into air. And what do they who so *observe* them? All alike *forsake their own mercy;* i. e. God, "Whose property is, always to have mercy," and Who would be Mercy to them, if they would. So David calls God, *my Mercy* [6]. Abraham's servant and Naomi praise God, that He *hath not forsaken His mercy* [7]. Jonah does not, in this, exclude himself. His own idol had been his false love for his country, that he would not have his people go into captivity, when God would; would not have Nineveh preserved, the enemy of his country; and by leaving his office, he left his God, *forsook* his *own Mercy.* See how God speaks of Himself, as wholly belonging to them, who are His. He calls Himself *their own Mercy.* "[8] He saith not, *they who* do *vanities,* (for [9] *vanity of vanities, and all things* are *vanity*) lest he should seem to condemn all, and to deny mercy to the whole human race; but *they who observe, guard vanities,* or lies; *they,* into the affections of whose hearts those *vanities* have entered; who not only *do vanities,* but who *guard* them, as loving them, deeming that they have found a treasure—These *forsake their own Mercy.* Although *mercy* be offended, (and under Mercy we may understand God Himself, for God is [10] *gracious and full of compassion;*

[1] Gal. ii. 20. [2] Jon. iv. 8. [3] Am. viii. 13. [4] Is. li. 20. [5] שמרים.

[6] Ps. cxliv 2. [7] Gen. xxiv. 27, Ruth ii. 20. [8] S. Jer. [9] Eccl. i. 2. [10] Ps. cxlv. 8.

Before CHRIST cir. 780.

9 But I will [l]sacrifice unto thee with the voice of thanksgiving; I will pay *that* that I have vowed. [m]Salvation *is* of the LORD.

[l] Ps. 50. 14, 23. & 116. 17. 18. Hos. 14. 2. Heb. 13. 15.
[m] Ps. 3. 8.

10 ¶ And the LORD spake unto the fish, and it vomited out Jonah upon the dry *land*.

slow to anger and of great mercy,) yet he doth not *forsake*, doth not abhor, *those who guard vanities*, but awaiteth that they should return: these contrariwise, of their own will, *forsake Mercy* standing and offering Itself."

9. *But* [*And*] *with the voice of thanksgiving will I* [*would I fain*] *sacrifice unto Thee; what I have vowed, I would pay.* He does not say, *I will;* for it did not depend upon him. Without a further miracle of God, he could do nothing. But he says, that he would nevermore forsake God. The law appointed sacrifices of thanksgiving[1]; these he would offer, not in act only, but with words of praise. He would *pay what he had vowed*, and chiefly himself, his life which God had given back to him, the obedience of his remaining life, in all things. For [2] *he that keepeth the law bringeth offerings enough; he that taketh heed to the commandments offereth a peace-offering.* Jonah neglects neither the outward nor the inward part, neither the body nor the soul of the commandment.

Salvation is of [lit. *to*] *the Lord.* It is wholly His; all belongs to Him, so that none can share in bestowing it; none can have any hope, save from Him. He uses an intensive form, as though he would say, strong *mighty salvation* [3]. God seems often to wait for the full resignation of the soul, all its powers and will to Him. Then He can shew mercy healthfully, when the soul is wholly surrendered to Him. So, on this full confession, Jonah is restored. The Prophet's prayer ends almost in promising the same as the mariners. They *made vows;* Jonah says, *I will pay that I have vowed.* Devoted service in the creature is one and the same, although diverse in degree; and so, that Israel might not despise the heathen, he tacitly likens the act of the new heathen converts and that of the Prophet.

10. *And the Lord spake unto the fish.* [4] *Wind and storm fulfill His word.* The irrational creatures have wills. God had commanded the Prophet, and he disobeyed. God, in some way, commanded the fish. He laid His will upon it, and the fish forthwith obeyed; a pattern to the Prophet when He released him. "[5] God's Will, that anything should be completed, is law and fulfillment and hath the power of law. Not that Almighty God commanded the fish, as He doth us or the Holy Angels, uttering in its mind what is to be done, or inserting into the heart the knowledge of what He chooseth. But if He be said to command irrational animals or elements or any part of the creation, this signifieth the law and command of His Will. For all things yield to His Will, and the mode of their obedience is to us altogether ineffable, but known to Him." "Jonah," says S. Chrysostom, "[6] fled the land, and fled not the displeasure of God. He fled the land, and brought a tempest on the sea: and not only himself gained no good from flight, but brought into extreme peril those also who took him on board. When he sailed, seated in the vessel, with sailors and pilot and all the tackling, he was in the extremest peril: when, sunk in the sea, the sin punished and laid aside, he entered that vast vessel, the fish's belly, he enjoyed great fearlessness; that thou mayest learn that, as no ship availeth to one living in sin, so when freed from sin, neither sea destroyeth, nor beasts consume. The waves received him, and choked him not; the vast fish received him and destroyed him not; but both the huge animal and the element gave back their deposit safe to God, and by all things the Prophet learnt to be mild and tender, not to be more cruel than the untaught mariners or wild waves or animals. For the sailors did not give him up at first, but after manifold constraint; and the sea and the wild animal guarded him with much benevolence, God disposing all these things. He returned then, preached, threatened, persuaded, saved, awed, amended, stablished, through that one first preaching. For he needed not many days, nor continuous exhortation; but, speaking those words he brought all to repentance. Wherefore God did not lead him straight from the vessel to the city; but the sailors gave him over to the sea, the sea to the vast fish, the fish to God, God to the Ninevites, and through this long circuit brought back the fugitive; that He might instruct all, that it is impossible to escape the Hands of God. For come where a man may, dragging sin after him, he will undergo countless troubles. Though man be not there, nature itself on all sides will oppose him with great vehemence."

"[7] Since the elect too at times strive to be sharp-witted, it is well to bring forward another wise man, and shew how the craft of mortal man is comprehended in the Inward

[1] Lev. vii. 12–15. [2] Ecclus. xxxv. 1. [3] ישועתה.
[4] Ps. cxlviii. 8. [5] S. Cyr. on Jon. ii. init.

[6] Hom. on the Statues, v. 6.
[7] S. Greg. Mor. vi. 31.

Before CHRIST cir. 780.

CHAPTER III.

1 *Jonah, sent again, preacheth to the Ninevites.* 5 *Upon their repentance,* 10 *God repenteth.*

AND the word of the LORD came unto Jonah the second time, saying,

Before CHRIST cir. 780.

Counsels. For Jonah wished to exercise a prudent sharpness of wit, when, being sent to preach repentance to the Ninevites, in that he feared that, if the Gentiles were chosen, Judæa would be forsaken, he refused to discharge the office of preaching. He sought a ship, chose to flee to Tarshish; but forthwith a tempest arises, the lot is cast, to know for whose fault the sea was troubled. Jonah is taken in his fault, plunged in the deep, swallowed by the fish, and carried by the vast beast thither whither he set at naught the command to go. See how the tempest found God's runaway, the lot binds him, the sea receives him, the beast encloses him, and, because he sets himself against obeying his Maker, he is carried a culprit by his prison-house to the place whither he had been sent. When God commanded, man would not minister the prophecy; when God enjoined, the beast cast forth the Prophet. The Lord then *taketh the wise in their own craftiness,* when He bringeth back to the service of His own Will, that whereby man's will contradicts Him." "[1]Jonah, fleeing from the perils of preaching and salvation of souls, fell into peril of his own life. When, in the ship, he took on himself the peril of all, he saved both himself and the ship. He fled as a man; he exposed himself to peril, as a prophet." "[2]Let them think so, who are sent by God or by a superior to preach to heretics or to heathen. When God calleth to an office or condition whose object it is to live for the salvation of others, He gives grace and means necessary or expedient to this end. For so the sweet and careful ordering of His Providence requireth.—Greater peril awaiteth us from God our Judge, if we flee His calling as did Jonah, if we use not the talents entrusted to us to do His Will and to His glory. We know the parable of the servant who buried the talent, and was condemned by the Lord."

And it vomited out Jonah. Unwilling, but constrained, it cast him forth, as a burden to it. "[3]From the lowest depths of death, Life came forth victorious." "[4]He is swallowed by the fish, but is not consumed; and then calls upon God, and (marvel!) on the third day is given back with Christ." "[5]What it prefigured, that that vast animal on the third day gave back alive the Prophet which it had swallowed, no need to ask of us, since Christ explained it. As then Jonah passed from the ship into the fish's belly, so Christ from the wood into the tomb or the depth of death. And as he for those imperilled in the tempest, so Christ for those tempest-tossed in this world. And as Jonah was first enjoined to preach to the Ninevites, but the preaching of Jonah did not reach them before the fish cast him forth, so prophecy was sent beforehand to the Gentiles, but did not reach them until after the resurrection of Christ." "[6]Jonah prophesied of Christ, not so much in words as by a suffering of his own; yet more openly than if he had proclaimed by speech His Death and Resurrection. For why was he received into the fish's belly, and given back the third day, except to signify that Christ would on the third day return from the deep of hell?"

S. Irenæus looks on the history of Jonah as the imaging of man's own history. "[7]As He allowed Jonah to be swallowed by the whale, not that he should perish altogether, but that, being vomited forth, he might the more be subdued to God, and the more glorify God Who had given him such unlooked-for deliverance, and bring those Ninevites to solid repentance, converting them to the Lord Who would free them from death, terrified by that sign which befell Jonah (as Scripture says of them, *They turned every man from his evil way, &c. . . . . .*) so from the beginning, God allowed man to be swallowed up by that vast Cetos who was the author of the transgression, not that he should altogether perish, but preparing a way of salvation, which, as foresignified by the word in Jonah, was formed for those who had the like faith as to the Lord as Jonah, and with him confessed, *I fear the Lord, &c.* that so man, receiving from God unlooked-for salvation, might rise from the dead and glorify God, &c. . . . . . This was the long-suffering of God, that man might pass through all, and acknowledge his ways; then, coming to the resurrection and knowing by trial from what he had been delivered, might be for ever thankful to God, and, having received from Him the gift of incorruption, might love Him more (for he to whom much is forgiven, loveth much) and know himself, that he is mortal and weak, and understand the Lord, that He is in such wise Mighty and Immortal, that to the mortal He can give immortality and to the things of time eternity."

III. 1. *And the word of the Lord came a*

[1] Lap. from S. Chrys. [2] from Lap. [3] S. Jer. [4] S. Greg. Naz l. c. [5] S. Aug. Ep. 102. q. 6 n. 34.

[6] de Civ. Dei, xviii. 30. 2. [7] iii. 20. p. 213. ed. Mass L.

Before CHRIST cir. 780.

2 Arise, go unto Nine-
veh, that great city, and
preach unto it the preaching that I bid thee.
3 So Jonah arose, and
went unto Nineveh, ac-
cording to the word of the
LORD. Now Nineveh was
an †exceeding great city
of three days' journey.

Before CHRIST cir. 780.

† Heb. *of God.* So Gen. 30. 8. Ps. 36. 6. & 80. 10.

---

second time to Jonah. "[1] Jonah, delivered from the whale, doubtless went up to Jerusalem to pay his vows and thank God there. Perhaps he hoped that God would be content with this his punishment and repentance, and that He would not again send him to Nineveh." Anyhow he was in some settled home, perhaps again at Gathhepher. For God bids him, *Arise, go.* "[2] But one who is on his way, is not bidden to *arise* and go." God may have allowed an interval to elapse, in order that the tidings of so great a miracle might spread far and wide. But Jonah does not supply any of these incidents[3]. He does not speak of himself[3], but of his mission only, as God taught him.

2. *Arise, go to Nineveh that great city, and preach* [or *cry*] *unto it.* God says to Jonah the self-same words which He had said before; only perhaps He gives him an intimation of His purpose of mercy, in that he says no more, *cry against her*, but *cry unto her.* He might *cry against* one doomed to destruction; to *cry unto her*, seems to imply that she had some interest in, and so some hope from, this cry. *The preaching that I bid thee.* This is the only notice which Jonah relates that God took of his disobedience, in that He charged him to obey exactly what He commanded. "[4] He does not say to him, why didst thou not what I commanded?" He had rebuked him in deed; He amended him and upbraided him not. "[4] The rebuke of that shipwreck and the swallowing by the fish sufficed, so that he who had not felt the Lord commanding, might understand Him, delivering." Jonah might have seemed unworthy to be again inspired by God. But *whom the Lord loveth, He chasteneth;* whom He chasteneth, He loveth. "[5] The hard discipline, the severity and length of the scourge, were the earnests of a great trust and a high destination." He knew him to be changed into another man, and, by one of His most special favors, gives him that same trust which he had before deserted. "[2] As Christ, when risen, commended His sheep to Peter, wiser now and more fervent, so to Jonah risen He commends the conversion of Nineveh. For so did Christ risen bring about the conversion of the heathen, by sending His Apostles, each into large provinces, as Jonah was sent alone to a large city." "[6] He bids him declare not only the sentence of God, but in the self-same words; not to consider his own estimation or the ears of his hearers, nor to mingle soothing with severe words, and convey the message ingeniously, but with all freedom and severity to declare openly what was commanded him. This plainness, though, may be, less acceptable to people or princes, is ofttimes more useful, always more approved by God. Nothing should be more sacred to the preacher of God's word, than truth and simplicity and inviolable sanctity in delivering it. Now alas, all this is changed into vain show at the will of the multitude and the breath of popular favor."

3. *And Jonah arose and went unto Nineveh,* as ready to obey, as before to disobey. Before, when God said those same words, *he arose and fled;* now, *he arose and went.* True conversion shews the same energy in serving God, as the unconverted had before shewn in serving self or error. Saul's spirit of fire, which persecuted Christ, gleamed in S. Paul like lightning through the world, to win souls to Him.

Nineveh was an exceeding great city; lit. *great to God*, i. e. what would not only appear great to man who admires things of no account, but what, being really great, is so in the judgment of God Who cannot be deceived. God *did* account it great, Who says to Jonah, *Should not I spare Nineveh that great city, which hath more than six score thousand that cannot discern between their right hand and their left?* It is a different idiom from that, when Scripture speaks of *the mountains of God, the cedars of God.* For of these it speaks, as having their firmness or their beauty from God as their Author.

Of three days' journey, i. e. sixty miles in circumference. It *was* a great city. Jonah speaks of its greatness, under a name which he would only have used of real greatness. Varied accounts agree in ascribing this size to Nineveh[7]. An Eastern city enclosing often, as did Babylon, ground under tillage, the only marvel is, that such a space was enclosed by walls. Yet this too is no marvel, when we know from inscriptions, what masses of human strength the great empires of old had at their command, or of the more than threescore pyramids of Egypt[8]. In population it was far inferior to our metropolis, of which, as of the suburbs of Rome of old, "[9] one would hesitate to say,

[1] Lap. [2] Castr. [3] See Introd. p. 253 [4] S. Jer. [5] from Sanch. [6] Mont.

[7] See ab. Introd. pp. 253, 4. [8] 67. Lepsius. [9] Dionys. Hal. T. i. p. 219. L.

Before CHRIST cir. 780.

[a] See Deut. 18. 22.

4 And Jonah began to
enter into the city a day's
journey, and [a]he cried, and
said, Yet forty days, and
Nineveh shall be over-
thrown.

Before CHRIST cir. 780.

5 ¶ So the people of
Nineveh [b]believed God,

[b] Matt. 12. 41. Luke 11. 32.

where the city ended, where it began. The suburban parts are so joined on to the city itself, and give the spectator the idea of boundless length." An Eastern would the more naturally think of the circumference of a city, because of the broad places, similar to the boulevards of Paris, which encircled it, so that men could walk around it, within it. "[1]The buildings," it is related of Babylon, "are not brought close to the walls, but are at about the distance of an acre from them. And not even the whole city did they occupy with houses; 80 furlongs are inhabited, and not even all these continuously, I suppose because it seemed safer to live scattered in several places. The rest they sow and till, that, if any foreign force threaten them, the besieged may be supplied with food from the soil of the city itself." Not Babylon alone was spoken of, of old, as "[2]having the circumference of a nation rather than of a city."

4. *And Jonah began to enter the city a day's journey.* Perhaps the day's journey enabled him to traverse the city from end to end, with his one brief, deep cry of woe; *Yet forty days and Nineveh overthrown*[3]. He prophesied an utter overthrow, a turning it upside down[4]. He does not speak of it as to happen at a time beyond those days. The close of the forty days and the destruction were to be one. He does not say strictly, *Yet forty days and Nineveh shall be overthrown*, but, *Yet forty days and Nineveh overthrown.* The last of those forty days was, ere its sun was set, to see Nineveh as *a thing overthrown.* Jonah knew from the first God's purpose of mercy to Nineveh; he had a further hint of it in the altered commission which he had received. It is perhaps hinted in the word *Yet.* "[5]If God had meant unconditionally to overthrow them, He would have overthrown them without notice. *Yet*, always denotes some long-suffering of God." But, taught by that severe discipline, he discharges his office strictly. He cries, what God had bidden him to cry, without reserve or exception. The sentence, as are all God's threatenings until the last, was conditional. But God does not say this. That sentence was now within forty days of its completion; yet even thus it was remitted. Wonderful encouragement, when one Lent sufficed to save some six hundred thousand souls from perishing! Yet the first visitation of the Cholera was checked in its progress in England, upon one day's national fast and humiliation; and we have seen how general prayer has often-times at once opened or closed the heavens as we needed. "A few years ago," relates S. Augustine[6], "when Arcadius was Emperor at Constantinople (what I say, some have heard, some of our people were present there,) did not God, willing to terrify the city, and, by terrifying, to amend, convert, cleanse, change it, reveal to a faithful servant of His (a soldier, it is said), that the city should perish by fire from heaven, and warned him to tell the Bishop! It was told. The Bishop despised it not, but addressed the people. The city turned to the mourning of penitence, as that Nineveh of old. Yet lest men should think that he who said this, deceived or was deceived, the day which God had threatened, came. When all were intently expecting the issue with great fears, at the beginning of night as the world was being darkened, a fiery cloud was seen from the East, small at first, then, as it approached the city, gradually enlarging, until it hung terribly over the whole city. All fled to the Church; the place did not hold the people. —But after that great tribulation, when God had accredited His word, the cloud began to diminish and at last disappeared. The people, freed from fear for a while, again heard that they must migrate, because the whole city should be destroyed on the next sabbath. The whole people left the city with the Emperor; no one remained in his house.—That multitude, having gone some miles, when gathered in one spot to pour forth prayer to God, suddenly saw a great smoke, and sent forth a loud cry to God." The city was saved. "What shall we say?" adds S. Augustine. "Was this the anger of God, or rather His mercy? Who doubts that the most merciful Father willed by terrifying to convert, not to punish by destroying? As the hand is lifted up to strike, and is recalled in pity, when he who was to be struck is terrified, so was it done to that city." Will any of God's warnings *now* move our great Babylon to repentance, that it be not ruined?

5. *And the people of Nineveh believed God;*

[1] Q. Curt. v. 4.
[2] Aristot. Polit. iii. 2. "You cannot judge whether a city is one or no by there being walls. For it would be possible to carry one wall round Peloponnesus; and perhaps Babylon is something of this sort, and *every city* which had the circumference of a nation rather than of a city, at the taking of which they say that some parts of the city did not hear of it for three days."
[3] Introd. p. 253.
[4] Ib. p. 255.
[5] Castr.
[6] de excid. urb. c. 6. (L.) add Paul. Diac. L. 13.

Before CHRIST cir. 780.

and proclaimed a fast, and
put on sackcloth, from the
greatest of them even to
the least of them.

6 For word came unto
the king of Nineveh, and
he arose from his throne,
and he laid his robe from

Before CHRIST cir. 780.

strictly, *believed in God.* To *believe in God* expresses more heart-belief, than to *believe God* in itself need convey. To *believe God* is to believe what God says, to be true; *to believe in* or *on God* expresses not belief only, but that belief resting in God, trusting itself and all its concerns with Him. It combines hope and trust with faith, and love too, since, without love, there cannot be trust. They believed then the preaching of Jonah, and that He, in Whose Name Jonah spake, had all power in heaven and earth. But they believed further in His unknown mercies; they cast themselves upon the goodness of the hitherto *unknown God.* Yet they believed in Him, as the Supreme God, *the* object of awe, *the* God (Elohim[1], Haelohim[2]), although they knew Him not, as He Is[3], the Self-Existent. Jonah does not say how they were thus persuaded. God the Holy Ghost relates the wonders of God's Omnipotence as common every-day things. They are no marvels to Him Who wrought them. *He commanded and they were done.* He spake with power to the hearts which He had made, and they were turned to Him. Any human means are secondary, utterly powerless, except in *His* hands Who Alone doth all things through whomsoever He doth them. Our Lord tells us that *Jonah* himself *was a sign unto the Ninevites*[4]. Whether then the mariners spread the history[5], or howsoever the Ninevites knew the personal history of Jonah, he, in his own person and in what befell him, was a sign to them. They believed that God, Who avenged *his* disobedience, would avenge their's. They believed perhaps, that God must have some great mercy in store for them, Who not only sent His Prophet so far from his own land to *them* who had never owned, never worshiped Him, but had done such mighty wonders to subdue His Prophet's resistance and to make him go to them.

And proclaimed a fast and put on sackcloth. It was not then a repentance in word only, but in deed. A fast was at that time entire abstinence from all food till evening; the haircloth was a harsh garment, irritating and afflictive to the body. They who did so, were (as we may still see from the Assyrian sculptures) men of pampered and luxurious habits, uniting sensuality and fierceness. Yet this they did at once, and as it seems, for the 40 days. They *proclaimed a fast.* They did not wait for the supreme authority. Time was urgent, and they would lose none of it. In this imminent peril of God's displeasure, they acted as men would in a conflagration. Men do not wait for orders to put out a fire, if they can, or to prevent it from spreading. Whoever they were who proclaimed it, whether those in inferior authority, each in his neighborhood, or whether it spread from man to man, as the tidings spread, it was done at once. It seems to have been done by acclamation, as it were, one common cry out of the one common terror. For it is said of them, as one succession of acts, *the men of Nineveh believed in God, and proclaimed a fast, and put on sackcloth from their great to their little*, every age, sex, condition. "[6] Worthy of admiration is that exceeding celerity and diligence in taking counsel, which, although in the same city with the king, perceived that they must provide for the common and imminent calamity, not waiting to ascertain laboriously the king's pleasure." In a city, 60 miles in circumference, some time must needs be lost, before the king could be approached; and we know, in some measure, the forms required in approaching Eastern monarchs of old.

6. *For word came*, rather, *And the matter*[7] *came*, i. e. the "whole *account*," as we say. *The word, word,* throughout Holy Scripture, as in so many languages, stands for that which is reported of[8]. *The* whole *account*, viz. how this stranger, in strange austere attire, had come, what had happened to him before he came, how he preached, how the people had believed him, what they had done, as had just been related, *came to the king.* The form of words implies that what Jonah relates in this verse took place after what had been mentioned before. People are slow to carry to sovereigns matters of distress, in which they cannot help. This was no matter of peril from man, in which the counsel or energy of the king could be of use. Anyhow it came to him last. But when it came to him, he disdained not to follow the example of those below him. He was not jealous of his prerogative, or that his advice had not been had; but, in the common peril, acted as his subjects had, and humbled him-

[1] iii. 5, 8. [2] Ib. 9.
[3] יהוה occurs once only in this chapter, of God speaking to Jonah, iii. 1.
[4] See ab. pp. 256, 7.
[5] Dion. suggests this as a conjecture. Aben Ezra quotes the same from R. Jesua. Kimchi says the same. [6] Mont. [7] It is, *the word*, הדבר.
[8] See Lex. of the Old or New Testament v. דבר, ἔπος, ῥῆμα. So in Arab. Aram. Æthiop. Ges. adds Pers. and Germ. "Sache" from "sagen," "Ding."

Before CHRIST cir. 780.

him, and covered *him* with
sackcloth, [e] and sat in
ashes.
7 [d] And he caused *it* to
be proclaimed and † pub-
lished through Nineveh by
the decree of the king and
his † nobles, saying, Let
neither man nor beast,
herd nor flock, taste any
thing: let them not feed,
nor drink water:

[e] Job 2. 8.
[d] 2 Chr. 20. 3. Joel 2. 15.
† Heb. *said.*
† Heb. *great men.*

self as they did. Yet this king was the king of Nineveh, the king, whose name was dreaded far and wide, whose will none who disputed, prospered. "[1] He who was accounted and was the greatest of the kings of the earth, was not held back by any thought of his own splendor, greatness or dignity, from fleeing as a suppliant to the mercy of God, and inciting others by his example to the same earnestness." The kings of Assyria were religious, according to their light. They ascribed all their victories to their god, Asshur[2]. When the king came to hear of One Who had a might, such as he had not seen, he believed in Him.

And he arose from his throne. He lost no time; he heard, *and he arose.* "[1] It denotes great earnestness, haste, diligence." *And he laid his robe from him.* This was the large costly upper garment, so called from its amplitude[3]. It is the name of the goodly Babylonian garment[4] which Achan coveted. As worn by kings, it was the most magnificent part of their dress, and a special part of their state. Kings were buried as they lived, in splendid apparel[5]; and rich adornments were buried with them[6]. The king of Nineveh dreads no charge of precipitancy nor man's judgment. "[1] He exchanges purple, gold, gems for the simple rough and sordid sackcloth, and his throne for the most abject ashes, the humblest thing he could do, fulfilling a deeper degree of humility than is related of the people." Strange credulity, had Jonah's message not been true; strange madness of unbelief which does not repent when a Greater than Jonah cries[7], *Repent ye, for the kingdom of heaven is at hand.* Strange garb for the king, in the eyes of a luxurious age; acceptable in His Who said[8], *if the mighty works which have been done in you had been done in Tyre and Sidon, they would have repented long ago in sackcloth and ashes.* "[9] Many wish to repent, yet so as not to part with their luxuries or the vanity of their dress, like the Greek who said he would 'like to be a philosopher, yet in a few things, not altogether.' To whom we may answer, 'delicate food and costly dress agree not with penitence; and that is no great grief which never comes to light.'" "[10] It was a marvelous thing, that purple was outvied by sackcloth. Sackcloth availed, what the purple robe availed not. What the diadem accomplished not, the ashes accomplished. Seest thou, I said not groundlessly that we should fear, not fasting but drunkenness and satiety? For drunkenness and satiety shook the city through and through, and were about to overthrow it; when it was reeling and about to fall, fasting stablished it." "[11] The king had conquered enemies by valor; he conquered God by humility. Wise king, who, for the saving of his people, owns himself a sinner rather than a king. He forgets that he is a king, fearing God, the King of all; he remembereth not his own power, coming to own the power of the Godhead. Marvelous! While he remembereth not that he is a king of men, he beginneth to be a king of righteousness. The prince, becoming religious, lost not his empire but changed it. Before, he held the princedom of military discipline; now, he obtained the princedom in heavenly disciplines."

7. *And he caused it to be proclaimed and published through Nineveh;* lit. *And he cried and said, &c.* The cry or proclamation of the king corresponded with the cry of Jonah. Where the Prophet's cry, calling to repentance, had reached, the proclamation of the king followed, obeying. *By the decree of the king and his nobles.* This is a hint of the political state of Nineveh, beyond what we have elsewhere. It was not then an absolute monarchy. At least, the king strengthened his command by that of his nobles, as Darius the Mede sealed the den of lions, into which Daniel was cast, with the signet of his lords as well as his own[12], *that the purpose might not be changed concerning him.*

Let neither man nor beast, &c. "[13] Are brutes too then to fast, horses and mules to be clothed with sackcloth? Yes, he says. For as, when a rich man dies, his relatives clothe not only the men and maidservants, but the horses too with sackcloth, and, giving them to the grooms, bid that they should follow to the tomb, in token of the greatness of the

[1] Mont.
[2] Cuneiform Inscriptions. See ab. p. 255. n. h.
[3] אדרת. It expresses size, not magnificence, since a wide garment of hair, such as the prophets afterwards wore, (Zech. xiii. 4, 2 Kings ii. 13, 14) was so called, Gen. xxv. 25.
[4] Josh. vii. 21.
[5] Jos. Ant. xvii. 8. 3.
[6] Id. xv. 3. 4. xvi. 7. 1.
[7] S. Matt. iv. 17.
[8] S. Matt. xi. 21.
[9] Rib.
[10] S. Chrys. Hom. v. de Pœnit. n. 4. ii. 314.
[11] S. Maximus in Jon. Bibl. Patr. T. vi. f. 28.
[12] Dan. vi. 17.
[13] S. Chrys. on the Statues, Hom. iii. 4.

Before CHRIST cir. 780.

8 But let man and beast
be covered with sackcloth,
and cry mightily unto God:
yea, [e] let them turn every

Before CHRIST cir. 780.

[e] Is. 58. 6.

calamity and inviting all to sympathy, so also when that city was about to perish, they clad the brute natures in sackcloth, and put them under the yoke of fasting. The irrational animals cannot, through words, learn the anger of God; let them learn through hunger, that the infliction is from God: for if, he says, the city should be overthrown, it would be one grave of us the inhabitants and of them also." It was no arbitrary nor wanton nor careless act of the king of Nineveh to make the dumb animals share in the common fast. It proceeded probably from an indistinct consciousness that God cared for them also, and, that *they* were not guilty. So the Psalmist looked on God's care of His creatures as a fresh ground for man's trust in Him[1], *O Lord, Thou preservest man and beast: How excellent is Thy loving-kindness, O Lord, therefore the children of men put their trust under the shadow of Thy wings.* As our Lord teaches that God's care of the sparrows is a pledge to man of God's minute unceasing care for him, so the Ninevites felt truly that the cry of the poor brutes would be heard by God. And God confirmed that judgment, when He told Jonah of the *much cattle*[2], as a ground for having pity on Nineveh. The moanings and lowings of the animals, their voices of distress, pierce man's heart too, and must have added to his sense of the common misery. Ignorance or pride of human nature alone could think that man's sorrow is not aided by these objects of sense. Nature was truer in the king of Nineveh.

8. *Let man and beast be covered with sackcloth.* The gorgeous caparisons of horses, mules and camels was part of Eastern magnificence. Who knows not how man's pride is fed by the sleekness of his stud, their "well-appointed" trappings? Man, in his luxury and pride, would have everything reflect his glory, and minister to pomp. Self-humiliation would have everything reflect its lowliness. Sorrow would have everything answer to its sorrow. Men think it strange that the horses at Nineveh were covered with sackcloth, and forget how, at the funerals of the rich, black horses are chosen and are clothed with black velvet.

And cry unto God mightily, "with might which conquereth judgment." A faint prayer does not express a strong desire, nor obtain what it does not strongly ask for, as having only half a heart.

And let them turn, every man from his evil way. "[a] See what removed that inevitable wrath. Did fasting and sackcloth alone? No, but the change of the whole life. How does this appear? From the Prophet's word itself. For he who spake of the wrath of God and of their fast, himself mentions the reconciliation and its cause. *And God saw their works.* What works? that they fasted? that they put on sackcloth? He passes by these, and says, *that every one turned from his evil ways, and God repented of the evil which He had said that He would do unto them.* Seest thou, that not the fast plucked them from the peril, but the change of life made God propitious to these heathen. I say this, not that we should dishonor, but that we may honor fasting. For the honor of a fast is not in abstinence from food, but in avoidance of sin. So that he who limiteth fasting to the abstinence from food only, he it is, who above all dishonoreth it. Fastest thou? Shew it me by its works. 'What works?' askest thou? If you see a poor man, have mercy; if an enemy, be reconciled; if a friend doing well, envy him not; if a beautiful woman, pass on. Let not the mouth alone fast; let eyes too, and hearing and feet, and hands, and all the members of our bodies. Let the hands fast, clean from rapine and avarice! let the feet fast, holding back from going to unlawful sights! let the eyes fast, learning never to thrust themselves on beautiful objects, nor to look curiously on others' beauty; for the food of the eye is gazing.—Let the ear too fast; for the fast of the ears is not to hear detractions and calumnies. Let the mouth too fast from foul words and reproaches. For what boots it, to abstain from birds and fish, while we bite and devour our brethren? The detractor preys on his brother's flesh."

He says, *each from his evil way,* because, in the general mass of corruption, each man has his own special heart's-sin. All were to return, but by forsaking, each, one by one, his own habitual, favorite sin.

And from the violence. Violence is singled out as the special sin of Nineveh, out *of all their evil way;* as the Angel saith[3], *tell His disciples and Peter.* This was the giant, Goliath-sin. When this should be effaced, the rest would give way, as the Philistines fled, when their champion was fallen to the earth dead. *That is in their hands,* lit. *in their palms*[4], the hollow of their hand. The hands being the instruments alike of using violence and of grasping its fruits, the violence cleaves to them in both ways, in its guilt and in its gains. So Job and David say[5], *while there was no violence in my hands;* and Isaiah[6], *the*

[1] Ps. xxxvi. 6, 7.
[2] iv. ult.
[3] S. Mark xvi. 7.
[4] בכפיהם.
[5] Job xvi. 17, 1 Chr. xii. 17.
[6] Is. lix. 6.

Before CHRIST cir. 780.

one from his evil way, and
from [f] the violence that *is*
in their hands.

[f] Is. 59. 6.

9 [g] Who can tell *if* God
will turn and repent, and
turn away from his fierce

[g] 2 Sam. 12. 22. Joel 2. 14.

work of wickedness is in their hands. Repentance and restitution clear the hands from the guilt of the violence: restitution, which gives back what was wronged; repentance, which, for love of God, hates and quits the sins, of which it repents. "Keep the winning, keep the sinning." The fruits of sin are temporal gain, eternal loss. We cannot keep the gain and escape the loss. Whoso keeps the gain of sin, loves it in its fruits, and will have them, all of them. The Hebrews had a saying, "[1] Whoso hath stolen a beam, and used it in building a great tower, must pull down the whole tower and restore the beam to its owner," i. e. restitution must be made at any cost. "He," they say[2], "who confesses a sin and does not restore the thing stolen, is like one who holds a reptile in his hands, who, if he were washed with all the water in the world, would never be purified, till he cast it out of his hands; when he has done this, the first sprinkling cleanses him."

9. *Who can tell* if *God will turn and repent?* The Ninevites use the same form of words, which God suggested by Joel to Judah. Perhaps He would thereby indicate that He had Himself put it into their mouths. "[3] In uncertainty they repented, and obtained certain mercy." "[4] It is therefore left uncertain, that men, being doubtful of their salvation, may repent the more vehemently and the more draw down on themselves the mercy of God." "[5] Most certain are the promises of God, whereby He has promised pardon to the penitent. And yet the sinner may well be uncertain whether he have obtained that penitence which makes him the object of those promises, not a servile repentance for fear of punishment, but true contrition out of the love of God." And so by this uncertainty, while, with the fear of hell, there is mingled the fear of the loss of God, the fear of that loss, which in itself involves some love, is, by His grace, turned into a contrite love, as the terrified soul thinks *Who* He is, Whom it had all but lost, Whom, it knows not whether it may not lose. In the case of the Ninevites, the remission of the temporal and eternal punishment was bound up in one, since the only punishment which God had threatened was temporal, and if this was forgiven, that forgiveness was a token that His displeasure had ceased.

"[6] They know not the issue, yet they neglect not repentance. They are unacquainted with the method of the loving-kindness of God, and they are changed amid uncertainty. They had no other Ninevites to look to, who had repented and been saved. They had not read the Prophets nor heard the Patriarchs, nor benefited by counsel, nor partaken of instruction, nor had they persuaded themselves that they should altogether propitiate God by repentance. For the threat did not contain this. But they doubted and hesitated about this, and yet repented with all carefulness. What account then shall we give, when these, who had no good hopes held out to them as to the issue, gave evidence of such a change, and thou, who mayest be of good cheer as to God's love for men, and hast many times received many pledges of His care, and hast heard the Prophets and Apostles, and hast been instructed by the events themselves, strivest not to attain the same measure of virtue as they? Great then was the virtue too of these men, but much greater the loving-kindness of God; and this you may see from the very greatness of the threat. For on this ground did He not add to the sentence, 'but if ye repent, I will spare,' that, casting among them the sentence unconditioned, He might increase the fear, and, increasing the fear, might impel them the more speedily to repentance." "[7] That fear was the parent of salvation; the threat removed the peril; the sentence of overthrow stayed the overthrow. New and marvelous issue! The sentence threatening death was the parent of life. Contrary to secular judgment, the sentence lost its force, when passed. In secular courts, the passing of the sentence gives it validity. Contrariwise with God, the pronouncing of the sentence made it invalid. For had it not been pronounced, the sinners had not heard it: had they not heard it, they would not have repented, would not have averted the chastisement, would not have enjoyed that marvelous deliverance. They fled not the city, as we do now [from the earthquake], but, remaining, established it. It was a snare, and they made it a wall; a quicksand and precipice, and they made it a tower of safety."

"[7] Was Nineveh destroyed? Quite the contrary. It arose and became more glorious, and all this intervening time has not effaced its glory, and we all yet celebrate it and marvel at it, that thenceforth it has become a most safe harbor to all who sin, not allowing them to sink into despair, but calling all to repentance, both by what it did and by what

[1] in Kimchi. [2] in Merc. [3] S. Aug. in Ps. 50. L. [4] S. Jer. [5] in Lap.

[6] S. Chrys. on Statues, Hom. v. n. 6. [7] Ib. n. 5.

Before CHRIST cir. 780.

anger, that we perish not?

10 ¶ [h] And God saw their works, that they

Before CHRIST cir. 780.

[h] Jer. 18. 8. Amos 7. 3, 6.

it gained from the Providence of God, persuading us never to despair of our salvation, but living the best we can, and setting before us a good hope, to be of good cheer that the end will anyhow be good." "[1] What *was* Nineveh? *They ate, they drank; they bought, they sold; they planted, they builded;* they gave themselves up to perjuries, lies, drunkenness, enormities, corruptions. This *was* Nineveh. Look at Nineveh now. They mourn, they grieve, are saddened, in sackcloth and ashes, in fastings and prayers. Where is that Nineveh? It is overthrown."

10. *And God saw their works.* "[2] He did not then first see them; He did not then first see their sackcloth when they covered themselves with it. He had seen them long before He sent the Prophet thither, while Israel was slaying the prophets who announced to them the captivity which hung over them. He knew certainly, that if He were to send the prophets far off to the Gentiles with such an announcement, they would hear and repent." God saw them, looked upon them, approved them, accepted the Ninevites not for time only, but, as many as persevered, for eternity. It was no common repentance. It was the penitence, which our Lord sets forth as *the* pattern of true repentance before His Coming. [3] *The men of Nineveh shall rise in judgment with this generation and shall condemn it, because they repented at the preaching of Jonah, and behold a greater than Jonah is here.* They believed in the One God, before unknown to them; they humbled themselves; they were not ashamed to repent publicly; they used great strictness with themselves; but, what Scripture chiefly dwells upon, their repentance was not only in profession, in belief, in outward act, but in the fruit of genuine works of repentance, a changed life out of a changed heart. *God saw their works, that they turned from their evil way.* Their whole way and course of life was evil; they broke off, not the one or other sin only, but all *their* whole *evil way.* "[4] The Ninevites, when about to perish, appoint them a fast; in their bodies they chasten their souls with the scourge of humility; they put on haircloth for raiment; for ointment they sprinkle themselves with ashes; and, prostrate on the ground, they lick the dust.—They publish their guilt with groans and lay open their secret misdeeds. Every age and sex alike applies itself to offices of mourning; all ornament was laid aside; food was refused to the suckling, and the age, as yet unstained by sins of its own, bare the weight of those of others; the dumb animals lacked their own food. One cry of unlike natures was heard along the city-walls; along all the houses echoed the piteous lament of the mourners; the earth bore the groans of the penitents; heaven itself echoed with their voice. That was fulfilled; [5] *The prayer of the humble pierceth the clouds.*" "[6] The Ninevites were converted to the fear of God, and laying aside the evil of their former life, betook themselves through repentance to virtue and righteousness, with a course of penitence so faithful, that they changed the sentence already pronounced on them by God." "[7] As soon as prayer took possession of them, it both made them righteous, and forthwith corrected the city which had been habituated to live with profligacy and wickedness and lawlessness. More powerful was prayer than the long usage of sin. It filled that city with heavenly laws, and brought along with it temperance, loving kindness, gentleness and care of the poor. For without these it cannot abide to dwell in the soul. Had any then entered Nineveh, who knew it well before, he would not have known the city; so suddenly had it sprung back from life most foul to godliness."

And God repented of the evil. This was no real change in God; rather, the object of His threatening was, that He might not do what He threatened. God's threatenings are conditional, "unless they repent," as are His promises, "if they *endure to the end* [8]." God said afterward by Jeremiah [9], At what *instant I shall speak concerning a nation and concerning a kingdom, to pluck up and to pull down and to destroy* it, *if that nation, against whom I had pronounced, turn from their evil, I will repent of the evil that I thought to do unto them.*

"[10] As God is unchangeable in nature, so is He unchangeable in Will. For no one can turn back His thoughts. For though some seem to have turned back His thoughts by their deprecations, yet this was His inward thought, that they should be able by their deprecations to turn back His sentence, and that they should receive from Him whereby to avail with Him.—When then outwardly His sentence seemeth to be changed, inwardly His counsel is unchanged, because He inwardly ordereth each thing unchangeably, whatsoever is done outwardly with change." "[11] It is said that He *repented,* because He

[1] S. Aug. Serm. 361. de res. n. 20. [2] Rup.
[3] S. Matt. xii. 41.
[4] S. Amb. de Pœnit. c. 6. L. [5] Ecclus. xxxv. 17.
[6] S. Chrys. Hom. quod nemo læditur nisi a seipso.
[7] de precat. i. inter dub. S. Chrys. T. ii. 781.
[8] S. Matt. x. 22. [9] xviii. 7, 8.
[10] S. Greg. Mor. xvi. n. 46.
[11] S. Aug. in Ps. cv. n. 35.

Before CHRIST cir. 780.

turned from their evil way; and God repented of the evil, that he had said that he would do unto them; and he did *it* not.

Before CHRIST cir. 780.

changed that which He seemed about to do, to destroy them. In God all things are disposed and fixed, nor doth He anything out of any sudden counsel, which He knew not in all eternity that He should do; but, amid the movements of His creature in time, which He governeth marvelously, He, not moved in time, as by a sudden will, is said to do what He disposed by well-ordered causes in the immutability of His most secret counsel whereby things which come to knowledge, each in its time, He both doth when they are present, and already did when they were future." "[1] God is subject to no dolor of repentance, nor is He deceived in anything, so as to wish to correct wherein He erred. But as man, when he repenteth willeth to change what he has done, so when thou hearest that God repenteth, look for the change. God, although He calleth it 'repenting,' doth it otherwise than thou. Thou doest it, because thou hast erred; He, because He avengeth or freeth. He changed the kingdom of Saul when He *repented.* And in the very place, where Scripture saith, *He repenteth,* it is said a little after, *He is not a man that He should repent.* When then He changes His works through His unchangeable counsels, He is said to repent, on account of the change, not of the counsel, but of the act." S. Augustine thinks that God, by using this language of Himself, which all would feel to be inadequate to His Majesty, meant to teach us that all language is inadequate to His Excellences. "[2] We say these things of God, because we do not find anything better to say. I say, 'God is just,' because in man's words I find nothing better; for He is beyond justice. It is said in Scripture, *God is just and loveth justice.* But in Scripture it is said, that *God repenteth,* 'God is ignorant.' Who would not start back at this? Yet to that end Scripture condescendeth healthfully to those words from which thou shrinkest, that thou shouldest not think that what thou deemest great is said worthily of Him. If thou ask, 'what then is said worthily of God?' one may perhaps answer, that 'He is just.' Another more gifted would say, that this word too is surpassed by His Excellence, and that this too is said, not worthily of Him, although suitably according to man's capacity: so that, when he would prove out of Scripture that it is written, *God is just,* he may be answered rightly, that the same Scriptures say that *God repenteth;* so, that, as he does not take that in its ordinary meaning, as men are wont to repent, so also when He is said to be just, this does not correspond to His supereminence, although Scripture said this also well, that, through these words such as they are, we may be brought to that which is unutterable." "Why predictest Thou," asks S. Chrysostom[3], "the terrible things which Thou art about to do? That I may not do what I predict. Wherefore also He threatened hell, that He may not bring to hell. Let words terrify you that ye may be freed from the auguish of deeds." "[4] Men threaten punishment and inflict it. Not so God; but contrariwise, He both predicts and delays, and terrifies with words, and leaves nothing undone, that He may not bring what He threatens. So He did with the Ninevites. He bends His bow, and brandishes His sword, and prepares His spear, and inflicts not the blow. Were not the Prophet's words bow and spear and sharp sword, when he said, *yet forty days and Nineveh shall be destroyed?* But He discharged not the shaft; for it was prepared, not to be shot, but to be laid up."

"[5] When we read in the Scriptures or hear in Churches the word of God, what do we hear but Christ? *And behold a greater than Jonas is here.* If they repented at the cry of one unknown servant, of what punishment shall not we be worthy, if, when the Lord preacheth, Whom we have known through so many benefits heaped upon us, we repent not? To them one day sufficed; to us shall so many months and years not suffice? To them the overthrow of the city was preached, and 40 days were granted for repentance: to us eternal torments are threatened, and we have not half an hour's life certain."

And He did it *not.* God willed rather that His prophecy should seem to fail, than that repentance should fail of its fruit. But it did not indeed fail, for the condition lay expressed in the threat. "Prophecy," says Aquinas[6] in reference to these cases, "cannot contain anything untrue." For "prophecy is a certain knowledge impressed on the understanding of the Prophets by revelation of God, by means of certain teaching. But truth of knowledge is the same in the Teacher and the taught, because the knowledge of the learner is a likeness of the knowledge of the Teacher. And in this way, Jerome saith that 'prophecy is a sort of sign of Divine foreknowledge.' The truth then of

[1] S. Aug. in Ps. cxxxi. n. 18.
[2] Id. Serm. 341. n. 9.
[3] De pœnit. Hom. v. n. 2. T. ii. p. 311 L.
[4] Id. in Ps. vii.
[5] Rib.
[6] 2. 2. q. 171. art. 6.

Before CHRIST cir. 780.

CHAPTER IV.

1 *Jonah, repining at God's mercy,* 4 *is reproved by the type of a gourd.*

BUT it displeased Jonah exceedingly, and he was very angry.

Before CHRIST cir. 780.

the prophetic knowledge and utterance must be the same as that of the Divine knowledge, in which there can be no error.—But although in the Divine Intellect, the two-fold knowledge [of things as they are in themselves, and as they are in their causes,] is always united, it is not always united in the prophetic revelation, because the impression made by the Agent is not always adequate to His power. Whence, sometimes, the prophetic revelation is a sort of impressed likeness of the Divine Foreknowledge, as it beholds the future contingent things in themselves, and these always take place as they are prophesied: as, *Behold, a virgin shall conceive.* But sometimes the prophetic revelation is an impressed likeness of Divine Foreknowledge, as it knows the order of causes to effects; and then at times the event is other than is foretold, and yet there is nothing untrue in the prophecy. For the meaning of the prophecy is, that the disposition of the inferior causes, whether in nature or in human acts, is such, that such an effect would follow" (as in regard to Hezekiah and Nineveh), "[1] which order of the cause to the effect is sometimes hindered by other things supervening." "The Will of God," he says again [2], "being the first, universal Cause, does not exclude intermediate causes, by virtue of which certain effects are produced. And since all intermediate causes are not adequate to the power of the First Cause, there are many things in the Power, Knowledge, and Will of God, which are not contained in the order of the inferior causes, as the resurrection of Lazarus. Whence one, looking to the inferior causes, might say, 'Lazarus will not rise again:' whereas, looking to the First Divine Cause, he could say, 'Lazarus will rise again.' And each of these God willeth, viz. that a thing should take place according to the inferior cause: which shall not take place, according to the superior cause, and conversely. So that God sometimes pronounces that a thing shall be, as far as it is contained in the order of inferior causes (as according to the disposition of nature or deserts), which yet doth not take place, because it is otherwise in the superior Divine cause. As when He foretold Hezekiah, [3] *Set thy house in order, for thou shalt die and not live;* which yet did not take place, because from eternity it was otherwise in the Knowledge and Will of God which is unchangeable. Whence Gregory saith [4], 'though God changeth the thing, His counsel He doth not change.' When then He saith, *I will repent* [5], it is understood as said metaphorically; for men, when they fulfill not what they threatened, seem to repent."

IV. 1. *And Jonah was displeased exceedingly.* It was an untempered zeal. The Prophet himself records it as such, and how he was reproved for it. He would, like many of us, govern God's world better than God Himself. Short-sighted and presumptuous! Yet not more short-sighted than those who, in fact, quarrel with God's Providence, the existence of evil, the baffling of good, "the prison-walls of obstacles and trials," in what we would do for God's glory. What is all discontent, but anger with God? The marvel is that the rebel was a prophet! "[6] What he desired was not unjust in itself, that the Ninevites should be punished for their past sins, and that the sentence of God pronounced against them should not be recalled, although they repented. For so the judge hangs the robber for theft, however he repent." He sinned, in that he disputed with God. Let *him* cast the first stone, who never rejoiced at any overthrow of the enemies of his country, nor was glad, in a common warfare, that they lost as many soldiers as we. As if God had not instruments enough at His Will! Or as if He needed the Assyrians to punish Israel, or the one nation, whose armies are the terror of Europe, to punish us, so that if they should perish, Israel should therefore have escaped, though it persevered in sin, or we!

And he was very angry, or, it may be, *very grieved.* The word expresses also the emotion of burning grief, as when Samuel was grieved at the rejection of Saul, or David at *the breach upon Uzzah* [7]. Either way, he was displeased with what God did. Yet so Samuel and David took God's doings to heart; but Samuel and David were grieved at God's judgments; Jonah, at what to the Ninevites was mercy, only in regard to his own people it seemed to involve judgment. Scripture says that he was displeased, because the Ninevites were spared; but not, why this displeased him. It has been thought, that it was jealousy for God's glory among the heathen, as though the Ninevites would think that God in Whose Name he spake had no certain knowledge of things to come; and so that his fault was mistrust in God's Wisdom or Power to vindicate His own honor.

[1] 2. 2. q. 174. art. 1.
[2] P. q. 19. art. 7. concl.
[3] Is. xxxviii. 1.
[4] Mor. xx. 32. n. 63.
[5] Jer. xviii. 8.
[6] Lap.
[7] 2 Sam. vi. 8, 1 Chr. xiii. 11.

Before CHRIST cir. 780.

2 And he prayed unto the
LORD, and said, I pray
thee, O LORD, *was* not this
my saying, when I was yet
in my country? Therefore
[a] ch. 1. 3. I [a] fled before unto Tarshish: for I knew that thou
[b] Ex. 34. 6. Ps. 86. 5. Joel 2. 13. *art* a [b] gracious God, and
merciful, slow to anger, and
of great kindness, and repentest thee of the evil.
3 [c] Therefore now, O [c] 1 Kings 19. 4.
LORD, take, I beseech thee,
my life from me; for [d] *it is* bet- [d] ver. 8.
ter for me to die than to live.
4 ¶ Then said the LORD,
‖ Doest thou well to be ‖ Or, *Art thou greatly angry?*
angry?

But it seems more likely, that it was a mistaken patriotism, which idolized the well-being of his own and God's people, and desired that its enemy, the appointed instrument of its chastisement, should be itself destroyed. Scripture being silent about it, we cannot know certainly. Jonah, under God's inspiration, relates that God pronounced him wrong. Having incurred God's reproof, he was careless about men's judgment, and left his own character open to the harsh judgments of men; teaching us a holy indifference to man's opinion, and, in our ignorance, carefulness not to judge unkindly.

2. *And he prayed unto the Lord.* Jonah, at least, did not murmur or complain of God. He complained to God of Himself. He expostulates with Him. Shortsighted indeed and too wedded to his own will! Yet his will was the well-being of the people whose Prophet God had made him. He tells God, that this it was, which he had all along dreaded. He softens it, as well as he can, by his word, *I pray Thee,* which expresses deprecation and submissiveness. Still he does not hesitate to tell God that this was the cause of his first rebellion! Perilous to the soul, to speak without penitence of former sin; yet it is to God that he speaks, and so God, in His wonderful condescension, makes him teach himself.

I knew that Thou art *a gracious God.* He repeats to God to the letter His own words by Joel[1]. God had so revealed Himself anew to Judah. He had, doubtless, on some repentance which Judah had shewn, turned away the evil from them. And now by sending him as a preacher of repentance, He implied that He would do the same to the enemies of his country. God confirms this by the whole sequel. Thenceforth then Israel knew, that to the heathen also God was intensely, infinitely full of gracious and yearning love[2], nay (as the form rather implies[3]) mastered (so to speak) by the might and intensity of His gracious love, *slow to anger* and delaying it, *great in loving-tenderness,* and abounding in it; and that toward them also, when the evil is about to be inflicted, or has been partially or wholly inflicted, He will repent of it and replace it with good, on the first turning of the soul or the nation to God.

3. *Therefore now, O Lord, take I beseech Thee my life from me.* He had rather die, than see the evil which was to come upon his country. Impatient though he was, he still cast himself upon God. By asking of God to end his life, he, at least, committed himself to the sovereign disposal of God. "[4] Seeing that the Gentiles are, in a manner, entering in, and that those words are being fulfilled, [5] *They have moved Me to jealousy with* that which is *not God, and I will move them to jealousy with* those which are *not a people, I will provoke them to anger with a foolish nation,* he despairs of the salvation of Israel, and is convulsed with great sorrow, which bursts out into words and sets forth the causes of grief, saying in a manner, 'Am I alone chosen out of so many prophets, to announce destruction to my people through the salvation of others?' He grieved not, as some think, that the multitude of nations is saved, but that Israel perishes. Whence our Lord also wept over Jerusalem. The Apostles first preached to Israel. Paul wishes to become an anathema for his [6] *brethren who are Israelites, whose is the adoption and the glory and the covenant, and the giving of the law and the service* of God, *and the promises, whose are the fathers, and of whom, as concerning the flesh, Christ* came." Jonah had discharged his office faithfully now. He had done what God commanded; God had done by him what He willed. Now, then, he prayed to be discharged. So S. Augustine in his last illness prayed that he might die, before the Vandals brought suffering and devastation on his country[7].

4. *And the Lord said, Doest thou well*[8] *to be angry?* God, being appealed to, answers the

[1] ii. 13.
[2] רחום חנון, both intensives. See on Joel ii. 13.
[3] In that both words, רחום, חנון, although adjectives, partake of the passive form.

[4] S. Jer. [5] Deut. xxxii. 21. [6] Rom. ix. 3–5.
[7] Posid. vit. S. Aug.
[8] הֵיטִיב, *do well,* is used almost adverbially of "*doing* a thing very perfectly," and by a deep irony in one place of doing evil very perfectly (see bel.

Before CHRIST cir. 780.

5 So Jonah went out
of the city, and sat on
the east side of the city,
and there made him a
booth, and sat under it in
the shadow, till he might
see what would become of
the city.

6 And the LORD God
prepared a ‖ † gourd, and
made *it* to come up over
Jonah, that it might be a
shadow over his head, to
deliver him from his grief.
So Jonah † was exceeding
glad of the gourd.

‖ Or, *palmchrist.*
† Heb. *Kikajon.*
† Heb. *rejoiced with great joy.*

appeal. So does He often in prayer, by some secret voice, answer the enquirer. There is right anger against the sin. Moses' anger was right, when he broke the tables[1]. God secretly suggests to Jonah that *his* anger was not right, as our Lord instructed[2] S. James and S. John that *theirs* was not. The question relates to the quality, not to the greatness of his anger. It was not the vehemence of his passionate desire for Israel, which God reproves, but that it was turned *against* the Ninevites. "[3] What the Lord says to Jonah, he says to all, who in their office of the cure of souls are angry. They must, as to this same anger, be recalled into themselves, to regard the cause or object of their anger, and weigh warily and attentively whether they *do well to be angry.* For if they are angry, not with men but with the sins of men, if they hate and persecute, not men, but the vices of men, they are rightly angry, their zeal is good. But if they are angry, not with sins but with men, if they hate, not vices but men, they are angered amiss, their zeal is bad. This then which was said to one, is to be watchfully looked to and decided by all, *Doest thou well to be angry?*"

5. *So Jonah went out of the city*[4]. The form of the words implies (as in the Eng. V.), that this took place after Jonah was convinced that God would spare Nineveh; and since there is no intimation that he knew it by revelation, then it was probably after the 40 days. "[5] The days being now past, after which it was time that the things foretold should be accomplished, and His anger as yet taking no effect, Jonah understood that God had pity on Nineveh. Still he does not give up all hope, and thinks that a respite of the evil has been granted them on their willingness to repent, but that some effect of His displeasure would come, since the pains of their repentance had not equalled their offences. So thinking in himself apparently, he departs from the city, and waits to see what will become of them." "He expected" apparently "that it would either fall by an earthquake, or be burned with fire, life Sodom." "[6] Jonah, in that he built him a tabernale and sat over against Nineveh, awaiting what should happen to it, wore a different, foresignifying character. For he prefigured the carnal people of Israel. For these too were sad at the salvation of the Ninevites, i. e. the redemption and deliverance of the Gentiles. Whence Christ came to call, not the righteous but sinners to repentance. But the overshadowing gourd over his head was the promises of the Old Testament or those offices in which, as the Apostle says, there was *a shadow of good things to come,* protecting them in the land of promise from temporal evils;—all which are now emptied and faded. And now that people, having lost the temple at Jerusalem and the priesthood and sacrifice (all which was a shadow of that which was to come) in its captive dispersion, is scorched by a vehement heat of tribulation, as Jonah by the heat of the sun, and grieves greatly; and yet the salvation of the heathen and the penitent is accounted of more moment than its grief, and the shadow which it loved."

6. *And the Lord God prepared a gourd,* [*a palmchrist,* E. M. rightly.] "[7] God again commanded the gourd, as he did the whale, willing only that this should be. Forthwith it springs up beautiful and full of flower, and straightway was a roof to the whole booth, and anoints him so to speak with joy, with its deep shade. The Prophet rejoices at it exceedingly, as being a great and thankworthy thing. See now herein too the simplicity of his mind. For he was grieved exceedingly, because what he had prophesied came not to pass; he rejoiced exceedingly for a plant. A blameless mind is lightly moved to gladness or sorrow. You will see this in children.—For as people who are not strong, easily fall, if some one gives them no very strong push, but touches them as it were with a lighter hand, so too the guileless mind is easily carried away by anything which delights or grieves it." Little as the

Mic. vii. 3), but it is nowhere used, of a passion or quality *existing* (passively) in a strong degree. The E. V. then is right. The E. M. *art thou greatly angry?* (the rendering of the LXX) is against the language.

[1] Ex. xxxii. 19. [2] S. Luke ix. 55. [3] Rup.
[4] Some render, contrary to grammar, "And Jonah had gone, &c."
[5] S. Cyr.
[6] S. Aug. Ep. 102. q. 6. n. 35. [7] S. Cyr.

Before CHRIST cir. 780.

7 But God prepared a
worm when the morning
rose the next day, and it
smote the gourd that it
withered.
8 And it came to pass,
when the sun did arise,
that God prepared a ‖ ve-
hement east wind; and the
sun beat upon the head of
Jonah, that he fainted, and
wished in himself to die,
and said, [e] *It is* better for
me to die than to live.

Before CHRIST cir. 780.

‖ Or, *silent.*

[e] ver. 3.

---

shelter of the palm-christ was in itself, Jonah must have looked upon its sudden growth, as a fruit of God's goodness toward him, (as it was) and then perhaps went on to think (as people do) that this favor of God shewed that He meant, in the end, to grant him what his heart was set upon. Those of impulsive temperaments are ever interpreting the acts of God's Providence, as bearing on what they strongly desire. Or again, they argue, 'God throws this or that in our way; therefore He means us not to relinquish it for His sake, but to have it.' By this sudden miraculous shelter against the burning Assyrian sun, which God provided for Jonah, He favored his waiting on there. So Jonah may have thought, interpreting rightly that God willed him to stay; wrongly, why He so willed. Jonah was to wait, not to see what he desired, but to receive, and be the channel of the instruction which God meant to convey to him and through him.

7. *When the morning rose*, i. e. in the earliest dawn, before the actual sunrise. For one day Jonah enjoyed the refreshment of the palm-christ. In early dawn, it still promised the shadow; just ere it was most needed, at God's command, it withered.

8. *God prepared a vehement*[1] [E. M. following the Chaldee, *silent*, i. e. sultry] *East wind.* The winds in the East, blowing over the sand-deserts, intensely increase the distress of the heat. A sojourner describes on two occasions an Assyrian summer. "[2] The change to summer had been as rapid as that which ushered in the spring. The verdure of the plain had perished almost in a day. Hot winds, coming from the desert, had burnt up and carried away the shrubs.—The heat was now almost intolerable. Violent whirlwinds occasionally swept over the face of the country." "[3] The spring was now fast passing away; the heat became daily greater; the corn was cut; and the plains and hills put on their summer-clothing of dull parched yellow. *The pasture is withered, the herbage faileth; the green grass is not.* It was the season too of the Sherghis, or burning winds from the South, which occasionally swept over the face of the country, driving in their short-lived fury everything before them.—We all went below [ground] soon after the sun had risen, and remained there [in the tunnels] without again seeking the open air until it was far down in the Western horizon." The "Sherghi" must be rather the East-wind, Sherki, whence Sirocco. At Sulimania in Koordistan (about 2½ degrees E. of Nineveh, and ¾ of a degree South) "[4] the so much dreaded Sherki seems to blow from any quarter, from E. to N. E.—It is greatly feared for its violence and relaxing qualities," "[5] hot, stormy and singularly relaxing and dispiriting." Suffocating heat is a characteristic of these vehement winds. Morier relates at Bushire; "[6] A gale of wind blew from the Southward

[1] The root חרש signifying to *cut*, then to *cut into*, "plough," then, passive, to be *cut off* from hearing or intercourse, "deaf," "dumb," (as in the Arab. and κωφὸς from κόπτω) and thence "silent," (as we speak of one voluntarily "dumb," i. e. silent), the meaning *silent* has been derived from this last sense; that of *vehement* comes either directly from the root, (as we speak of a "cutting" wind, although our cutting winds are cold), or from "deafening" (Kim.), as we speak of "a deafening noise," and as strong winds do hinder hearing; or, as matter of fact, from the strong dry winds in Autumn, in which way חרישית is derived directly from חריש *earing* (i. e. ploughing) *time*, Ex. xxxiv. 21. The English Version "vehement," lies more in the direct meaning of the root, than "silent," and agrees with the description, although not what one, unacquainted with Eastern nature, would expect. Next to this, the harvest or autumn wind seems perhaps the most probable.

[2] Layard, Nineveh, (1846) c. 5. i. 123.

[3] Nin. and Bab. [1850] pp. 364, 5.

[4] Rich's Koordistan, i. 125, add 133. "Just as the moon rose about 10, an intolerable puff of wind came from the N. E. All were immediately silent as if they had felt an earthquake, and then exclaimed in a dismal tone, 'the Sherki is come.' This was indeed the so much dreaded Sherki, and it has continued blowing ever since with great violence from the E. and N E. the wind being heated like our Bagdad Saum, but I think softer and more relaxing. This wind is the terror of these parts." Ib. 165. "The extraordinary prevalence of the Sherki or Easterly wind this year, renders this season intolerably hot and relaxing. They had not had 3 days together free from this wind since the beginning of the summer." Ib. 271. "In the summer the climate is pleasant, except when the Easterly wind blows, which it does with prodigious violence sometimes for 8 or 10 days successively. The wind is hot and relaxing in summer, and what is very curious, is it not felt at the distance of 2 or 3 hours." Ib. 113. "This is asserted by every one in the country." Ib. 125.

[5] Ib. ii. 35.

[6] 2d journey, p. 43. He continues, "Again from the 23d to the 25th, the wind blew violently from the S. E. accompanied by a most suffocating heat, and continued to blow with the same strength until the next day at noon, when it suddenly veered

Before CHRIST cir. 780.

9 And God said to Jonah, || Doest thou well to be angry for the gourd? And he said, || I do well to be angry, *even* unto death.

|| Or, *Art thou greatly angry?*

|| Or, *I am greatly angry.*

and Eastward with such violence, that three of our largest tents were leveled with the ground. The wind brought with it such hot currents of air, that we thought it might be the precursor of the *Samoun* described by Chardin, but upon enquiry, we found that the autumn was generally the season for that wind. The *Sam* wind commits great ravages in this district. It blows at night from about midnight to suurise, comes in a hot blast, and is afterward succeeded by a cold one. About 6 years ago, there was a *sam* during the summer months which so totally burnt up all the corn, then near its maturity, that no animal would eat a blade of it, nor touch any of its grain."

The sun beat upon the head of Jonah. "[1] Few European travelers can brave the perpendicular rays of an Assyrian sun. Even the well-seasoned Arab seeks the shade during the day, and journeys by night, unless driven forth at noontide by necessity, or the love of war."

He wished in himself to die. [lit. *he asked as to his soul, to die*]. He prayed for death. It was still the same dependence upon God, even in his self-will. He did not murmur, but prayed God to end his life here. When men are already vexed in soul by deep inward griefs, a little thing often oversets patience. Jonah's hopes had been revived by the mercy of the palmchrist; they perished with it. Perhaps he had before him the thought of his great predecessor, Elijah, how he too wished to die, when it seemed that his mission was fruitless. They differed in love. Elijah's preaching, miracles, toil, sufferings, seemed to him, not only to be in vain, but (as they must, if in vain), to add to the guilt of his people. God corrected him too, by showing him his own short-sightedness, that he knew not of *the seven thousand who had not bowed their knees unto Baal*, who were, in part, doubtless, *the travail of his soul.* Jonah's mission to his people seemed also to be fruitless; his hopes for their well-being were at an end; the temporal mercies of which he had been the Prophet, were exhausted; Nineveh was spared; his last hope was gone; the future scourge of his people was maintained in might. The soul shrinks into itself at the sight of the impending visitation of its country. But Elijah's zeal was *for* his people only and the glory of God in it, and so it was pure love. Jonah's was directed *against* the Ninevites, and so had to be purified.

9. *Doest thou well to be angry?* "[2] See again how Almighty God, out of His boundless loving-kindness, with the yearning tenderness of a father, almost disporteth with the guileless souls of the saints! The palmchrist shades him: the Prophet rejoices in it exceedingly. Then, in God's Providence, the caterpillar attacks it, the burning East-wind smites it, shewing at the same time how very necessary the relief of its shade, that the Prophet might be the more grieved, when deprived of such a good.—He asketh him skillfully, was he very grieved? and that for a shrub? He confesseth, and this becometh the defence for God, the Lover of mankind."

I do well to be angry, unto death. "[3] Vehement anger leadeth men to long and love to die, especially if thwarted and unable to remove the hindrance which angers them. For then vehement anger begetteth vehement sorrow, grief, despondency." We have each, his own palmchrist; and our palmchrist has its own worm. "[4] In Jonah, who mourned when he had discharged his office, we see those who, in what they seem to do for God, either do not seek the glory of God, but some end of their own, or at least, think that glory to lie where it does not. For he who seeketh the glory of God, and not *his own*[5] things, but those of Jesus Christ, ought to will what God hath willed and done. If he wills aught else, he declares plainly that he sought himself, not God, or himself more

round to the N. W. with a violence equal to what it had blown from the opposite point." And again (p. 97) "When there was a perfect calm, partial and strong currents of air would arise and form whirlwinds, which produced high columns of sand all over the plain. They are looked upon as the sign of great heat. Their strength was very various. Frequently they threw down our tents." Burckhardt, when professedly lessening the general impression as to these winds, says, "The worst effect [of the Semoum "a violent S. E. wind"] is that it dries up the water in the skins, and so far endangers the traveler's safety.—In one morning ⅓ of the contents of a full water-skin was evaporated. I always observed the whole atmosphere appear as if in a state of combustion; the dust and sand are carried high into the air, which assumes a reddish or blueish or yellowish tint, according to the nature and color of the ground, from which the dust arises. The Semoum is not always accompanied by whirlwinds: in its less violent degree it will blow for hours with little force, although with oppressive heat; when the whirlwind raises the dust, it then increases several degrees in heat. In the Semoum at Esne, the thermometer mounted to 121° in the shade, but the air seldom remains longer than a quarter of an hour in that state, or longer than the whirlwind lasts. The most disagreeable effect of the Semoum on man is, that it stops perspiration, dries up the palate, and produces great restlessness." Travels in Nubia, pp. 204, 5.

1 Layard, Nin. and Bab 366.
2 S. Cyr.
3 Lap.
4 Rib.
5 Phil. ii. 21.

Before CHRIST cir. 780.

‖ Or, *spared*.

10 Then said the LORD, Thou hast ‖had pity on the gourd, for the which thou hast not labored, neither madest it grow; which †came up in a night, and perished in a night:
11 And should not I spare Nineveh, ᶠthat great

Before CHRIST cir. 780.

† Heb. *was the son of the night.*

ᶠ ch. 1. 2. & 3. 2, 3.

than God.—Jonah sought the glory of God wherein it was not, in the fulfillment of a prophecy of woe. And choosing to be led by his own judgment, not by God's, whereas he ought to have joyed exceedingly, that so many thousands, being *dead, were alive again*, being *lost, were found*, he, when *there was joy in heaven among the angels of God over* so many repenting sinners, was *afflicted with a great affliction* and was angry. This ever befalls those who wish *that* to take place, not what is best and most pleasing to God, but what they think most useful to themselves. Whence we see our very great and common error, who think our peace and tranquillity to lie in the fulfillment of our own will, whereas this will and judgment of our own is the cause of all our trouble. So then Jonah prays and tacitly blames God, and would not so much excuse as approve that, his former flight, to *Him Whose eyes are too pure to behold iniquity.*—And since all inordinate affection is a punishment to itself, and he who departeth from the order of God hath no stability, he is in such anguish, because what he wills, will not be, that he longs to die. For it cannot but be that *his* life, who measures everything by his own will and mind, and who followeth not God as his Guide but rather willeth to be the guide of the Divine Will, should be from time to time troubled with great sorrow. But since *the merciful and gracious Lord* hath pity on our infirmity and gently admonisheth us within, when He sees us at variance with Him, He forsakes not Jonah in that hot grief, but lovingly blames him.—How restless such men are, we see from Jonah. The *palmchrist* grows over his head, and *he was exceeding glad of the palmchrist.* Any labor or discomfort they bear very ill, and being accustomed to endure nothing and follow their own will, they are tormented and cannot bear it, as Jonah did not the sun. If anything, however slight, happen to lighten their grief, they are immoderately glad. Soon gladdened, soon grieved, like children. They have not learned to bear anything moderately. What marvel then that their joy is soon turned into sorrow? They are joyed over a palmchrist, which soon greeneth, soon drieth, quickly falls to the ground and is trampled upon.—Such are the things of this world, which, while possessed, seem great and lasting; when suddenly lost, men see how vain and passing they are, and that hope is to be placed, not in them but in their Creator, Who is Unchangeable. It is then a great dispensation of God toward us, when those things in which we took especial pleasure are taken away. Nothing can man have so pleasing, green, and, in appearance, so lasting, which has not its own worm prepared by God, whereby, in the dawn, it may be smitten and die. The change of human will or envy disturbs court-favor; manifold accidents, wealth; the varying opinion of the people or of the great, honors; disease, danger, poverty, infamy, pleasure. Jonah's palmchrist had one worm; our's, many; if other were wanting, there is the restlessness of man's own thoughts, whose food is restlessness."

10. *Thou hadst pity on the palmchrist.* In the feeling of our common mortality, the soul cannot but yearn over decay. Even a drooping flower is sad to look on, so beautiful, so frail. It belongs to this passing world, where nothing lovely abides, all things beautiful hasten to cease to be. The natural God-implanted feeling is the germ of the spiritual.

11. *Should I not spare?* lit. *have pity* and so *spare.* God waives for the time the fact of the repentance of Nineveh, and speaks of those on whom man must have pity, those who never had any share in its guilt, the 120,000 children of Nineveh, "[1] who, in the weakness of infancy, knew not which hand, *the right* or *the left*, is the stronger and fitter for every use." He Who would have spared Sodom *for ten's sake*, might well be thought to spare Nineveh for the 120,000's sake, in whom the inborn corruption had not developed into the malice of wilful sin. If these 120,000 were the children under three years old, they were ⅕ (as is calculated) of the whole population of Nineveh. If of the 600,000 of Nineveh all were guilty, who by reason of age could be, above ⅕ were innocent of actual sin.

To Jonah, whose eye was evil to Nineveh for his people's sake, God says, as it were, "[1] Let the *spirit* which *is willing* say to the *flesh* which *is weak*, '*Thou grievest for the palmchrist*, that is, thine own kindred, the Jewish people; and *shall not I spare Nineveh that great city*, shall not I provide for the salvation of the Gentiles in the whole world, who are in ignorance and error? For there are many thousands among the Gentiles, who go after [2] *dumb idols even as they are led*, not out of

[1] Rup.

[2] 1 Cor. xii. 2.

Before CHRIST cir. 780.

g Deut. 1. 39.

city, wherein are more than sixscore thousand persons [g] that cannot discern between their right hand and their left hand; and *also* much [h] cattle?

Before CHRIST cir. 780.

h Ps. 36. 6. & 145. 9.

malice but out of ignorance, who would without doubt correct their ways, if they had the knowledge of the truth, if they were shewn the difference *between their right hand and their left*, i. e. between the truth of God and the lie of men.'" But, beyond the immediate teaching to Jonah, God lays down a principle of His dealings at all times, that, in His visitations of nations, He, [1] *the Father of the fatherless and judge of the widows*, takes especial account of those who are of no account in man's sight, and defers the impending judgment, not for the sake of the wisdom of the wise or the courage of the brave, but for the helpless, weak, and, as yet, innocent as to actual sin. How much more may we think that He regards those with pity who have on them not only the recent unefaced traces of their Maker's Hands, but have been reborn in the Image of Christ His Only-Begotten Son! The infants clothed with Christ[2] must be a special treasure of the Church in the Eyes of God.

"[3] How much greater the mercy of God than that even of a holy man; how far better to flee to the judgment-seat of God than to the tribunal of man. Had Jonah been judge in the cause of the Ninevites, he would have passed on them all, although penitent, the sentence of death for their past guilt, because God had passed it before their repentance. So David said to God; [4] *Let us fall now into the hand of the Lord; for His mercies are great; and let me not fall into the hand of man.* Whence the Church professes to God, that mercy is the characteristic of His power; '[5] O God, who shewest Thy Almighty power most chiefly in shewing mercy and pity, mercifully grant unto us such a measure of Thy grace, that we, running the way of Thy commandments, may obtain Thy gracious promises, and be made partakers of Thy heavenly treasure.'"

"Again, God here teaches Jonah and us all to conform ourselves in all things to the Divine Will, that, when He commandeth any work, we should forthwith begin and continue it with alacrity and courage; when He bids us cease from it, or deprives it of its fruit and effect, we should forthwith tranquilly cease, and patiently allow our work and toil to lack its end and fruit. For what is our aim, save to do the Will of God, and in all things to confirm ourselves to it? But now the Will of God is, that thou shouldest resign, yea destroy, the work thou hast begun. Acquiesce then in it. Else thou servest not the Will of God, but thine own fancy and cupidity. And herein consists the perfection of the holy soul, that, in all acts and events, adverse or prosperous, it should with full resignation resign itself most humbly and entirely to God, and acquiesce, happen what will, yea, and rejoice that the Will of God is fulfilled in this thing, and say with holy Job, *The Lord gave, The Lord hath taken away; blessed be the Name of the Lord*—S. Ignatius had so transferred his own will into the Will of God, that he said, 'If perchance the society, which I have begun and furthered with such toil, should be dissolved or perish, after passing half an hour in prayer, I should, by God's help, have no trouble from this thing, than which none sadder could befall me.' The saints let themselves be turned this way and that, round and round, by the Will of God, as a horse by its rider."

[1] Ps. lxviii. 5.
[2] Gal. iii. 27. [3] Lap.
[4] 2 Sam. xxiv. 14.
[5] Collect for the eleventh Sunday after Trinity.

END OF VOL. I.

The Minor Prophets
A Commentary

E. B. Pusey

Volume 2
MICAH TO MALACHI

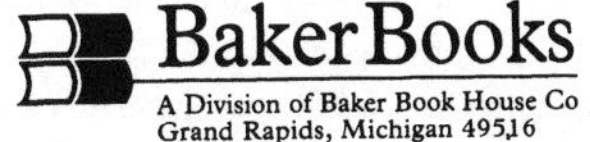

Heritage Edition

Fourteen Volumes 0834-4

1.	Genesis (Murphy)	0835-2	8.	Minor Prophets (Pusey)	0842-5
2.	Exodus to Esther (Cook)	0836-0	9.	The Gospels	0843-3
3.	Job	0837-9	10.	Acts and Romans	0844-1
4.	Psalms	0838-7	11.	I Corinthians to Galatians	0846-8
5.	Proverbs to Ezekiel (Cook)	0839-5	12.	Ephesians to Philemon	0847-6
6.	Isaiah	0840-9	13.	Hebrews to Jude	0848-4
7.	Daniel	0841-7	14.	Revelation	0849-2

When ordering by ISBN (International Standard Book Number), numbers listed above should be preceded by 0-8010-.

Reprinted from the 1847 edition published
by Blackie & Son, London

Reprinted 2005 by Baker Books
a division of Baker Book House Company
P.O. Box 6287, Grand Rapids, MI 49516-6287

Printed in the United States of America

For information about academic books, resources for Christian leaders, and all new releases available from Baker Book House, visit our web site:
http://www.bakerbooks.com/

CONTENTS.

I. MICAH.

II. NAHUM.

III. HABAKKUK.

IV. ZEPHANIAH.

V. HAGGAI.

VI. ZECHARIAH.

VII. MALACHI.

INTRODUCTION

TO

THE PROPHET

MICAH.

MICAH, or Micaiah, this Morasthite, was so called, probably, in order to distinguish him from his great predecessor, Micaiah, son of Imlah, in the reign of Ahab. His name was spoken in its fuller form, by the elders of the land whose words Jeremiah has preserved. And in that fuller form his name is known, where the Greek and Latin translations of the Scriptures are used [a]. By the Syrians, and by the Jews [b] he is still called, as by us, Micah. The fullest and original form is Micaiahu, "who is like the Lord?" In this fullest form, it is the name of one of the Levites sent by Jehoshaphat to teach the people [c], as also of the mother of king Asa [d], (the same name serving sometimes both for men and women). Then according to the habit of abridging names, in all countries, and especially those of which the proper name of the Lord is a part, it is diversely abridged into Micaihu, Micahu [e], whence Micah is readily formed, on the same rule as Micaiah itself from Micaiahu. The forms are all found indifferently. The idolatrous Levite in the time of the Judges [f], and the son of Imlah [g], are both called in the same chapter *Micaihu* and *Micah;* the father of one of Josiah's officers is called *Micaiah* in the book of Kings [h], *Micah* in the Chronicles [i].

The Prophet's name, like those of Joshua, Elijah, Elisha, Hosea, Joel, Obadiah, was significant. Joshua's, we know, was changed of set purpose [k]. The rest seem to have been given in God's Providence, or taken by the Prophets, in order to enunciate truths concerning God, opposed to the idolatries or self-dependence of the people. But the name of Micah or Micaiah, (as *the elders of the land* [l] called him on a solemn occasion, some 120 years afterward) contained more than teaching. It was cast into the form of a challenge. *Who is like the Lord?* The form of words had been impressed on Israel by the song of Moses after the deliverance at the Red sea [m]. In the days of Elijah and that first Micaiah, the strife between God and man, the true Prophet and the false, had been ended at the battle of Ramoth-Gilead; it ceased for a time, in the reigns of Jehu and his successors, because in consequence of his partial obedience, God, by Elisha and Jonah, promised them good: it was again resumed, as the promise to Jehu was expiring, and God's prophets had anew to proclaim a message of woe. *Hast thou found me, O mine enemy* [n]? and, [o] *I hate him, for he doth not prophesy good concerning me, but evil,* Ahab's words as to Elijah and Micaiah, were the types of the subsequent contradiction of the false prophets to Hosea and Amos, which closed only with the destruction of Samaria. Now, in the time of the later Micaiah, were the first dawnings of the same strife in Judah, which

[a] Μιχαίας is used by the LXX. in Jer. xxvi. 18 and Micah i. 1, as also in the other places where the name occurs, except Neh. xi. 17, 22, where for מִיכָא they have Μιχά. Josephus calls both prophets Μιχαίας, Micah son of Imlah, Ant. 8. 14. 5. and our prophet, Ant. 10. 6. 2. The Vulgate uses for both, Michæas.

[b] They substituted מִיכָה in the Kri in Jeremiah.

[c] 2 Chr. xvii. 7.
[d] Ib. xiii. 2.
[e] Ib. xviii. 8. Keth.
[f] מִיכָיְהוּ Jud. xvii. 1, 4; מִיכָה 5, 8, 9, 10.
[g] מִיכָיְהוּ 1 Kings xxii. 9, 2 Chr. xviii. 7; מִיכָה 2 Chr. xviii. 14.
[h] 2 Kings xxii. 12.
[i] 2 Chr. xxxiv. 20.
[k] Num. xiii. 16.
[l] Jer. xxvi. 17, 18.
[m] Ex. xv. 11.
[n] 1 Kings xxi. 20.
[o] Ib. xxii. 8, 18.

hastened and brought about the destruction of Jerusalem under Zedekiah, which re-appeared after the Captivity[p], and was the immediate cause of the second destruction under the Romans[q]. Micah, as he dwells on the meaning of names generally, so, doubtless, it is in allusion to his own, that, at the close of his prophecy, he ushers in his announcement of God's incomparable mercy with the words[r], *Who is a God like unto Thee?* Before him, whatever disobedience there was to God's law in Judah, there was no systematic, organized, opposition to His prophets. There is no token of it in Joel. From the times of Micah it is never missing. We find it in each prophet (however brief the remains of some are), who prophesied directly to Judah, not in Isaiah only, but in Habakkuk[s] and Zephaniah[t]. It deepened, as it hastened toward its decision. The nearer God's judgments were at hand, the more obstinately the false prophets denied that they would come. The system of false prophecy, which rose to its height in the time of Jeremiah, which met and thwarted him at every step[u], and deceived those who wished to be deceived, was dawning in the time of Micah. False prophecy arose in Judah from the self-same cause whence it had arisen in Israel, because Judah's deepening corruption drew down the prophecies of God's displeasure, which it was popular to disbelieve. False prophecy was a gainful occupation. The false prophets had men's wishes on their side. They had the people with them. *My people love to have it so*[x], said God. They forbade Micah to prophesy[y]; prophesied peace[z], when God foretold evil; prophesied for gain[a], and proclaimed war in the Name of God[b] against those who fed them not.

At such a time was Micah called. His name which he himself explains, was no chance name. To the Hebrews, to whom names were so much more significant, parts of the living language, it recalled the name of his great predecessor, his standing alone against all the prophets of Ahab, his prophecy, his suffering, his evidenced truth. The truth of prophecy was set upon the issue of the battle before Ramoth-Gilead. In the presence of Jehoshaphat, king of Judah, as well as of Ahab, the 400 prophets of Ashtaroth had promised to Ahab the prize he longed for. One solitary, discriminating voice was heard amid that clamorous multitude, forewarning Ahab that he would perish, his people would be scattered. On the one side, was that loud triumphant chorus of[c] *all the prophets, Go up to Ramoth-Gilead, and prosper; for the Lord shall deliver it into the king's hand.* On the other, one solemn voice, exhibiting before them that sad spectacle which the morrow's sun should witness[d], *I saw all Israel scattered upon the hills, as sheep that have not a shepherd, and the Lord said, these have no master, let them return every man to his house in peace.* Micaiah was smitten, imprisoned, and, apparently, ended his ministry, appealing from that small audience of the armies of Israel and Judah to the whole world, which has ever since looked back on that strife with interest and awe; [e] *Hear ye peoples, each one of them.* God, who guided the archer shooting *at a venture*[f], fulfilled the words which He had put into the Prophet's mouth. God's words had found Ahab, although *disguised;* Jehoshaphat, the imperilled[g], returned home, to relate the issue. The conflict between God's truth and idol falsehood was doubtless long remembered in Judah. And now when the strife had penetrated into Judah, to be ended some 170[h] years afterward in the destruction of Jerusalem, another Micaiah arose, his name the old watchword, *Who is like the Lord?* He prefixed to his prophecy that same summons[i] to the whole world to behold the issue of the conflict, which God had once accredited and, in that issue, had given an earnest of the victory of His truth, there thenceforth and for ever.

The prophet was born a villager, in Moresheth Gath, "a village[j]", S. Jerome says; ("a little village[k]", in S. Jerome's own days), "East of Eleutheropolis," where what was "[l]formerly his grave," was "now a church." Since it was his birthplace and his burial-place, it was probably his home also. In the beginning of the reign of Jehoiakim, *the elders of the land*[m] speak of him with this same title, *the Morasthite.* He lingers, in his prophecy, among the towns of the maritime plain (the Shephēlah) where his birthplace lay. Among the ten places in that neighborhood[n], which he selects for warning and for example of the universal captivity, is his native village, "the home he loved." But the chief scene of his ministry was Jerusalem. He names it in the beginning of his prophecy, as the place where the idolatries, and, with the idolatries, all the other sins of Judah were concentrated. The two capitals, Samaria and Jerusalem, were the chief objects of the word of God to him, because the corruption of each kingdom streamed forth from them. The sins which he rebukes are chiefly those of the capital. Extreme oppression[o], violence

[p] Neh. vi. 14. [q] See vol. i. pp. 334–336. [r] vii. 18. [s] i. 5, ii. 1. [t] i. 12. [u] See Jer. v. 13, 31, vi. 13–17, viii. 10–12, xiv. 13–16, xx. 1–6, xxiii. 9-end, xxvi. 7, 8, 11, xxvii. 14–18, xxviii., xxix. 8, 9, 21–32. [x] Jer. v. 31. [y] ii. 6. [z] iii. 5. [a] iii. 11.

[b] iii. 5. see note. [c] 1 Kings xxii. 12. [d] Ib. 17. [e] Ib. 28. [f] 34. [g] 30–3. [h] from the beginning of Jotham's reign. [i] Hengst. Christ. i. 475. [j] Onom. [k] Præf. to Mic. [l] Ep. 86. ad Eustoch. Epitaph. Paulæ § 14. i. 698. [m] Jer. xxvi. 17, 18. [n] i. 11–15. [o] iii. 2, 3, ii. 2.

among the rich[p], bribing among judges, priests, prophets[q]; building up the capital even by cost of life, or actual bloodshed[r]; spoilation[s]; expulsion of the powerless, women and children from their homes[t]; covetousness[u]; cheating in dealings[x]; pride[y]. These, of course, may be manifoldly repeated in lesser places of resort and of judgment. But it is *Zion and Jerusalem* which are so *built up with blood*[r]; *Zion and Jerusalem*, which are, on that ground, to be *plowed as a field*[z]; it is *the city* to which *the Lord's voice crieth*[a]; whose *rich men are full of violence*[p]; it is the *daughter of Zion*[b], which is to *go forth out of the city and go to Babylon*. Especially, they are the heads and princes of the people[c], whom he upbraids for perversion of justice and for oppression. Even the good kings of Judah seem to have been powerless to restrain the general corruption.

Micah, according to the title which he prefixed to his prophecy, was called to the prophetic office somewhat later than Isaiah. His ministry began later, and ended earlier. For Uzziah, in whose reign Isaiah began to prophesy, was dead before Micah was called to his office; and Micah probably was called away early in the reign of Hezekiah, whereas some of the chief public acts of Isaiah's ministry fell in the 17th and 18th years of the reign of Hezekiah. Joel, Amos, Obadiah, Jonah, had doubtless been withdrawn to their rest. Hosea alone, in "grey-haired might," was still protesting in vain against the deepening corruptions of Israel.

The contents of Micah's prophecy and his relation to Isaiah agree with the inscription. His prophecy has indications of the times of Jotham, perhaps also of those of Ahaz; one signal prophecy, we know historically, was uttered in the reign of Hezekiah.

It is now owned, well nigh on all hands, that the great prophecy, three verses of which Isaiah prefixed to his 2d chapter, was originally delivered by Micah. But it appears from the context in Isaiah, that he delivered the prophecy in that 2d chapter, in the reign of Jotham. Other language of Micah also belongs to that same reign. No one now thinks that Micah adopted that great prophecy from Isaiah. The prophecy, as it stands in Micah, is in close connection with what precedes it. He had said[d], *the mountain of the house shall be as the high places of the forest;* he subjoins instantly God's reversal of that sentence, *in the latter days.* [e]*And in the last days it shall be that the mountain of the house of the Lord shall be established on the top of the mountains, and peoples shall flow unto it.* He had said, *Zion shall be plowed as a field, and Jerusalem shall become heaps;* he adds forthwith, in reversal of this[f], *the law shall go forth from Zion, and the word of the Lord from Jerusalem.* The two sentences are joined as closely as they can be; *Zion shall be plowed as a field, and Jerusalem shall become heaps, and the mountain of the house shall become high places of a forest; and it shall be, in the last days, the mountain of the house of the Lord shall be* (abidingly)[g] *established on the top of the mountains.* Every reader would understand, that the elevation intended, was spiritual, not physical. They could not fail to understand the metaphor; or imagine that the Mount Zion, on part of which, (Mount Moriah,) the *house of the Lord* stood, should be physically placed on other hills. But the contrast is marked. The promise is the sequel of the woe; the abiding condition is the reversal of the sentence of its desolation. Even the words allude, the one to the other[h].

In Isaiah, there is no such connection. After the first chapter and its summary of rebuke, warning, threatening, and final weal or woe resting on each class, Isaiah, in his second chapter, begins his prophecy anew with a fresh title[i]; *The word that Isaiah the son of Amos saw concerning Judah and Jerusalem;* and to this he prefixes three verses from Micah's prophecy. He separates it in a marked way from the preceding summary, and yet connects it with some other prophecy by the word, *And*[j]. He himself marks that it is not in its original place here. So then, in the prophet Micah, the close connection with the foregoing marks that it *is* in its original place; Isaiah marked purposely that in his prophecy it is not.

But Isaiah's prophecy belongs to a time of prosperity; such as Judah had not, after the reign of Jotham. It was a time of great warlike strength, diffused through the whole land. The land was full[k], without end, of gold, silver, chariots, horses, of lofty looks and haughtiness. The images which follow[l] are shadows of the Day of Judgment, and extend beyond Judah; but the sins rebuked are the sins of strength and might, self-confidence, oppression, manifold female luxury and bravery[m]. Isaiah prophesies that God would take away their strength[n]. Then they still had it. Judah trusted not at that time in God nor in foreign alliances, but in self. Yet, from the time of Ahaz, trust in foreign help infected them to the end. Even Hezekiah, when he received the messengers of Merodach-baladan[o], fell into the snare; and Josiah probably lost his life, as a vassal

[p] vi. 12. [q] iii. 11; judges and priests, vii. 3. [r] iii. 10; bloodshed also, vii. 2. [s] ii. 8. [t] ii. 9. [u] ii. 2. [x] vi. 10, 11. [y] ii. 3. [z] iii. 12. [a] vi. 9. [b] iv. 10. [c] iii. 1, 9, 11, vi. 12, vii. 3. [d] iii. 12. [e] iv. 1. [f] iv. 2.

[g] It is not יִכּוֹנֵ׳ but יהיה־נכון.

[h] The הר בית יהוה iv. 1. to the הר הבית iii. 12; the תהיה יהיה. Hengst.

[i] ii. 1. [j] ii. 2. [k] Is. ii. 7, 11. [l] 12–21. [m] iii. 16, 23. [n] iii. 1–3. [o] Is. xxxix.

of Assyria [p]. This union of inherent strength and unconcernedness about foreign aid is an adequate test of days anterior to Ahaz.

But since Isaiah prefixed to a prophecy in the days of Jotham this great prophecy of Micah, then Micah's prophecy must have been already current. To those same days of strength it belongs, that Micah could prophesy as a gift, the cutting off [q] of *horses and chariots*, the destruction *of cities* and *strong towers*, all, in which Judah trusted instead of God. The prophecy is a counterpart of Isaiah's. Isaiah prophesied a day of Judgment, in which all these things should be removed; Micah foretold that their removal should be a mercy to those who trust in Christ.

On the other hand, the utter dislocation of society, the bursting of all the most sacred bands which bind man to man together, described in his last chapter [r], perhaps belong most to the miserable decay in the reign of Ahaz. The idolatry spoken of also belongs probably to the time of Ahaz. In Jotham's time [s], *the people sacrificed and burned incense still in the high places;* yet, under a king so highly praised [t], these are not likely to have been in Jerusalem. But Micah, in the very head of his prophecy, speaks of Jerusalem [u] as the centre of the idolatries of Judah. The allusion also to child-sacrifices belongs to the time of Ahaz, who sacrificed sons of his own [x], and whose sacrifice others probably imitated. The mention of the special idolatry of the time, [y] *the statutes of Omri are kept, and all the works of the house of Ahab*, belong to the same reign, it being recorded of Ahaz especially [z], *he walked in the ways of the kings of Israel and made also molten images for Baalim;* the special sin of the house of Ahab. That character too which he describes, that, amid all that idolatry, practical irreligion, and wickedness, they *leant upon the Lord, and said, Is not the Lord among us? none evil can come upon us* [a]; was just the character of Ahaz. Not until the end of his reign was he so embittered by God's chastisements, that he closed His temple [b]. Up to that time, even after he had copied the brazen altar at Damascus, he still kept up a divided allegiance to God. Urijah, the high Priest, at the king's command, offered the sacrifices for the king and the people, while Ahaz used *the brazen altar, to enquire by* [c]. This was just the half-service which God by Micah rejects. It is the old history of man's half-service, faith without love, which provides, that what it believes but loves not, should be done for it, and itself enacts what it prefers. Urijah was to offer the lawful sacrifices for the king and the people; Ahaz was to obtain knowledge of the future, such as he wished in his own way, a lying future, by lying acts.

Micah renewed under Hezekiah the prophecy of the utter destruction of Jerusalem, which he had pronounced under Jotham. The prophets did not heed repeating themselves. Eloquent as they were, they are the more eloquent because eloquence was not their object. Even our Lord, with Divine wisdom, and the more, probably, because He had Divine wisdom, repeated in His teaching the same words. Those words sank the deeper, because often repeated. So Micah repeated doubtless oftentimes those words, which he first uttered in the days of Jotham; *Zion shall be plowed like a field and Jerusalem shall become heaps, and the mountain of the house as the high places of the forest.* Often, during those perhaps thirty years, he repeated them in vain. At the last, they wrought a great repentance, and delayed, it may be for 136 years, the destruction which he was constrained to foretell. Early in the days of Jehoiakim, about 120 years afterward, in the public assembly when Jeremiah was on trial for his life, *the elders of the land* said explicitly, that the great conversion at the beginning of the reign of Hezekiah, nay, of that king himself, was wrought by the teaching of Micah. [d] *Then rose up*, says Jeremiah, *certain of the elders of the land, and spake to all the assembly of the people, saying, Micah the Morasthite prophesied in the days of Hezekiah king of Judah, saying, Thus saith the Lord of hosts, Zion shall be ploughed like a field, and Jerusalem shall become heaps, and the mountain of the house, as the high places of the forest. Did Hezekiah king of Judah, and all Judah, put him at all to death? Did he not fear the Lord, and besought the Lord, and the Lord repented Him of the evil which He had pronounced against them?*

It may have been that single prophecy which Micah so delivered; some have thought that it was his whole book. Jeremiah, at God's command, at one time uttered single prophecies; at another, the summary of all his prophecies. This only is certain, that the prophecy, whether these words alone or the book containing them, was delivered to all Judah, and that God moved the people through them to repentance.

The words, as they occur in Jeremiah, are the same, and in the same order, as they stand in Micah. Only in Jeremiah the common plural termination is substituted for the rarer and poetic form used by Micah [e]. The *elders*, then, who quoted them, probably knew them, not from tradition, but from the written book of the Prophet. But those elders speak of Micah, as exercising his prophetic office in the days of Hezekiah. They

[p] 2 Kings xxiii. 29, 2 Chr. xxxv. 20–22.
[q] Mic. v. 10, 11, 14.
[r] vii. 5, 6.
[s] 2 Kings xv. 35.
[t] 2 Kings xv. 34, 2 Chr. xxvii. 2, 6.
[u] i. 5.
[x] 2 Kings xvi. 3, 2 Chr. xxviii. 3.
[y] vi. 16.
[z] 2 Chr. xxviii. 2.
[a] iii. 11, vi. 6.
[b] 2 Chr. xxviii. 22–24.
[c] 2 Kings xvi. 15.
[d] Jer. xxvi. 17–19.
[e] עיים for עיין.

do not say, *he prophesied*, which might have been a single act; but *he was prophesying, hayah nibbah*, a form of speaking which is only used of an abiding, habitual, action. They say also, "he was habitually prophesying, and he said," i. e. as we should say, "in the course of his prophesying in the days of Hezekiah, he said." Still it was to *all the people of Judah* that he said it. The elders say so, and lay stress upon it by repeating it. *Did Hezekiah king of Judah and all Judah put him at all to death?* It must have been then on some of the great festivals, when *all Judah* was gathered together, that Micah so spake to them.

Probably, shortly afterward, in those first years of Hezekiah, Micah's office on earth closed. For, at the outset and in the summary of his prophecy, not incidentally, he speaks of the destruction of Samaria, which took place in the 4th year of Hezekiah, as still to come; and however practical or partial idolatry continued, such idolatry as he throughout describes, did not exist after the reformation by Hezekiah. This conversion, then, of the king and of some considerable part of Judah was probably the closing harvest of his life, after a long seed-time of tears. So God allowed His servant to *depart in peace.* The reformation itself, at least in its fullness, took place after the kingdom of Samaria had come to an end, since Hezekiah's messengers could, unhindered, invite all Israel to join in his great Passover. Probably, then, Micah lived to see the first dawnings only of the first reformation which God wrought by his words.

At the commencement, then, of Hezekiah's reign he collected the substance of what God had taught by him, re-casting it, so to speak, and retaining of his spoken prophecy so much as God willed to remain for us. As it stands, it belongs to that early time of Hezekiah's reign, in which the sins of Ahaz still lived on. Corruption of manners had been hereditary. In Jotham's reign too, it is said expressly, in contrast with himself[f], *the people were still doing corruptly.* Idolatry had, under Ahaz, received a fanatic impulse from the king, who, at last, set himself to close the worship of God[g]. The strength of Jotham's reign was gone; the longing for its restoration led to the wrong and destructive policy, against which Isaiah had to contend. Of this Micah says, such should not be the strength of the future kingdom of God. Idolatry and oppression lived on; against these, the inheritance of those former reigns, the sole residuum of Jotham's might or Ahaz' policy, the breach of the law of love of God and man, Micah concentrated his written prophecy.

This book also has remarkable symmetry. Each of its three divisions is a whole, beginning with upbraiding for sin, threatening God's judgments, and ending with promises of future mercy in Christ. The two later divisions begin again with that same characteristic, *Hear ye*[h], with which Micah had opened the whole. The three divisions are also connected, as well by lesser references of the later to the former, as also by the advance of the prophecy. Judah could not be trusted now with any simple declaration of God's future mercy. They supposed themselves, impenitent as they were and with no purpose of repentance, to be the objects of God's care, and secure from evil. Unmixed promise of good would but foment this irreligious apathy. Hence on the promises at the end of the first portion[i], *and their king shall pass before them and the Lord at the head of them*, he turns abruptly[k], *And I said, Hear, I pray you, Is it not for you to know judgment?* The promise had been to *Jacob* and *the remnant of Israel*[i]. He renews his summons to the[k] *heads of Jacob* and the *princes of the house of Israel.* In like way, the last section, opening with that wonderful pleading of God with His people, follows upon that unbroken declaration of God's mercies, which itself issues out of the promised Birth at Bethlehem.

There is also a sort of progress in the promises of the three parts[l]. In the first, it is of deliverance generally, in language taken from that first deliverance from Egypt. The 2d is objective, the Birth of the Redeemer, the conversion of the Gentiles, the restoration of the Jews, the establishment and nature of His kingdom. The third is mainly subjective, man's repentance, waiting upon God, and God's forgiveness of his sins.

Throughout, the metropolis is chiefly addressed, as the main seat of present evil[m] and as the centre of the future blessings; where the reign of the long-promised Ruler should be[n]; whence the revelation of God should go forth to the heathen[o]; whither the scattered and dispersed people should be gathered[p].

Throughout the prophecy also, Micah upbraids the same class of sins, wrong dealing of man to man, oppression of the poor by the rich[m]. Throughout, their future captivity and dispersion are either predicted[q], or assumed as the basis of the prediction of good[r]. Throughout, we see the contemporary of the prophet Isaiah. Beside that great prediction, which Isaiah inserted verbally from Micah, we see them, as it were, side by side, in that city of God's visitation and of His mercy, prophesying the same respite, the same place of captivity and deliverance from

[f] 2 Chr. xxvii. 2. [g] Ib. xxviii. 22–25, xxix. 7.
[h] ch. iii.–v. and vi. vii. [i] ii. 12. [k] iii. 1.
[l] Hengst. Christ. i. 477, 8. [m] See ab. p. 289.
[n] iv. 2, 7, 8. [o] iv. 1, 2.

[p] iv. 6, 7, vii. 11, 12.
[q] i. 11, 14–16, ii. 4, 5, 10, (utter abiding destruction of Jerusalem) iii. 12, iv. 10, v. 3.
[r] ii. 12, 13, iv. 6, 7, 10, vii. 11, 12, 15.

it, the same ulterior mercies in Christ. "[s]The more to establish the faith, God willed that Isaiah and Micah should speak together, as with one mouth, and use such agreement as might the more convict all rebels." Assyria was then the monarchy of the world; yet both prophets promise deliverance from it[t]; both foretell the captivity in the then subordinate Babylon[u]; both, the deliverance from it[x]. Both speak in the like way of the gathering together of God's people from lands[y], to some of which they were not yet dispersed. Isaiah prophesied the Virgin-Birth of Immanuel[z]; Micah, the Birth at Bethlehem of Him *Whose goings forth* have been *of old, from everlasting*[a]. Both speak in the like way of the reverence for the Gentiles thereafter for her[b], by reason of the presence of her God. Even, in outward manner, Micah, representing himself, as one who *went mourning* and *wailing, stripped and naked*[c], is a sort of forerunner of the symbolic acts of Isaiah[d]. Micah had this also common with Isaiah, that he has a predominance of comfort. He is brief in upbraiding[e], indignant in casting back the pleas of the false prophets[f], concise in his threatenings of woe[g], save where he lingers mournfully over the desolation[h], large and flowing in his descriptions of mercy to come[i]. He sees and pronounces the coming punishment, as absolutely certain; he does not call to repentance to avert it; he knows that ultimately it will not be averted; he sees it irrespectively of time, and says that it will be. Time is an accident to the link of cause and effect. Sin consummated would be the cause; punishment, the effect. He spoke to those who knew that God pardoned on repentance, who had lately had before them that marvelous instance in Nineveh. He dashes to the ground their false security, by reason of their descent from Jacob[k], of God's Presence among them in the Temple[l]; the multitude of their offerings amid the multitude of their sins[m]. He rejects in God's name, their false, outward, impenitent, penitence; and thereby the more implies that He would accept a true repentance. They knew this, and were, for a time, scared into penitence. But in his book, as God willed it to remain, he is rather the prophet of God's dealings, than the direct preacher of repentance to individuals. Yet he is the more an evangelic preacher, in that he speaks of repentance, only as the gift of God. He does not ignore that man must accept the grace of God; but, as Isaiah foretells of the days of the Gospel, *the idols He shall utterly abolish*[n], so Micah first foretells that God would abolish all wherein man relied out of God, all wherein he prided himself[o], every form of idolatry[p], and subsequently describes the future evangelic repentance, submission to, and waiting upon God and His righteousness[q]; and God's free plenary forgiveness[r].

Micah's rapid unprepared transitions from each of his main themes to another, from upbraiding to threatening, from threatening to mercy and then back again to upbraiding, is probably a part of that same vivid perception of the connection of sin, chastisement, forgiveness, in the will and mind of God. He sees them and speaks of them in the natural sequence in which they were exhibited to him. He connects most commonly the sin with the punishment by the one word, *therefore*[s], because it was an object with him to shew the connection. The mercies to come he subjoins either suddenly without any conjunction[t], or with the simple *and*. An English reader loses some of the force of this simplicity by the paraphrase, which, for the simple copula, substitutes the inference or contrast, *therefore, then, but, notwithstanding*[u], which lie in the subjects themselves. An English reader might have been puzzled, at first sight, by the monotonous simplicity of the, *and, and*, joining together the mention of events, which stand, either as the contrast or the consequence of those which precede them. The English version accordingly has consulted for the reader or hearer, by drawing out for him the contrast or consequence which lay beneath the surface. But this gain of clearness involved giving up so far the majestic simplicity of the Prophet, who at times speaks of things as they lay in the Divine Mind, and as, one by one, they would be unfolded to man, without explaining the relation in which they stood to one another. Micah knew that sufferings were, in God's purpose, travail-pains. And so, immediately after the denunciation of punishment, he adds so calmly, "[x]*And* in the last days it shall be;" "*And* thou, Bethlehem Ephratah." Or in the midst of his descriptions of mercies, he speaks of the intervening troubles, as the way to them. *Now*[y] *why dost thou cry aloud?—pangs have taken thee, as a woman in travail—be in pain—thou shalt go even unto Babylon; there shalt thou be delivered:* or, [z]*Therefore will He*

[s] Carpz. Introd. p. 365. in Häv. ii. 364.
[t] Is. x. 24–34, xiv. 25, xxx. 31, xxxi. 8, 9, xxxvii. 6, 7, 21–35, Mic. v 5, 6.
[u] Is. xxxix. 6, Mic. iv. 10.
[x] Is. xlviii. 20, Mic. ib.
[y] Is. xi. 11 sqq. Mic. vii. 12.
[z] vii. 14.
[a] v. 2 Eng. (1 Heb.)
[b] Is. xlix. 23, Mic. vii. 17. Häv. ib.
[c] i. 8. see note.
[d] Is. xx. 2, 3.
[e] i. 5, ii. 1, 2, 9–11.
[f] ii. 7, 11, iii. 5–7.
[g] ii. 3, 10, iii. 4, 12, vi. 13–16, vii. 4, 13.
[h] i. 10–16, ii. 4, 5.
[i] iv., v., vii. 7–20.
[k] ii. 7.
[l] iii. 11.
[m] vi. 6, 7.
[n] Is. ii. 18.
[o] v. 9, 10.
[p] v. 11–13.
[q] vii. 8, 9.
[r] Ib. 18, 19.
[s] Not i. 6, vi. 13. but i. 14, ii. 3, 5, iii. 6, 12.
[t] ii. 12, iv. 13.
[u] *Therefore*, i. 6, vi. 13, vii. 7; *then*, iii. 7, vii. 10; *but*, iii. 8, iv. 1, 4, 12, v. 2, vi. 16; *for*, iv. 5; *notwithstanding*, vii. 13.
[x] iv. 1, v. 2 (1 Heb.), add vii. 7.
[y] iv. 9.
[z] v. 3. [2 Heb.]

give thee up until the time, &c. i.e. because He has these good things in store for thee, *He will give thee up, until the time* comes.

With this great simplicity Micah unites great vividness and energy. Thus in predicting punishment, he uses the form of command, bidding them, as it were, execute it on themselves [a]; *Arise, depart:* as, in the Great Day, our Lord shall say, *Depart, ye cursed.* And since God does in us or by us what He commands to be done, he uses the imperative to Zion, alike as to her victories over God's enemies [b], or her state of anxious fear [c].

To that same vividness belong his rapid changes of person or gender; his sudden questions [d]; his unmarked dialogues. The changes of person and gender occur in all Hebrew poetry; all have their emphasis. He addresses the people or place as a whole (*fem.*), then all the individuals in her [e]; or turns away and speaks of it [f]; or contrariwise, having spoken of the whole in the third person, he turns round and drives the warning home to individuals [g]. The variations in the last verse of ch. vi. are unexampled for rapidity even in Hebrew.

And yet the flow of his words is smooth and measured. Without departing from the conciseness of Hebrew poetry, his cadence, for the most part, is of the more prolonged sort, as far as any can be called prolonged, when all is so concise. In some 8 verses, out of 104, he is markedly brief, where conciseness corresponds with his subject, as in an abrupt appeal as to their sins [h], or an energetic announcement of judgment [i] or of mercy [k], or in that remarkable prophecy of both [l], how God would, in mercy, cut off all grounds of human trust. Else, whereas in Nahum and Habakkuk, not quite $\frac{1}{3}$, and in the eleven last Chapters of Hosea much less than $\frac{1}{3}$, of the verses contain more than 13 words [m], in Micah above $\frac{3}{7}$ (as, in Joel, nearly $\frac{3}{7}$) exceed that number [n]. The verses are also distributed in that ever-varying cadence, whereby, in Hebrew poetry, portions of their short sentences being grouped together, the harmony of the whole is produced by the varied dispositions of these lesser groups of 2, 3, 4, and but rarely 5 words; scarcely any two verses exactly corresponding, but all being united by the blending of similar cadences. In Micah, as in all Hebrew poetry, the combination of 3 words is the most frequent, and this, sometimes by itself, sometimes in union with the number 4, making the sacred number 7; or, with 2, making a number which we find in the tabernacle, but which dwells more in the hearts of the disciples of the Crucified. The same exact rhythm seldom recurs, and that, naturally, chiefly in the shorter verses, the longer admitting or requiring more combinations. Wherever also there is more than one pause in the verse, a further and very considerable variety of rhythm may be produced, even when the several clauses of two verses contain the same number of words in the same order. The difference of cadence is far more influenced by the place, where the verse is divided, than by the exact number of words contained in it. The rhetorical force of the distribution of the words into the several clauses depends mainly upon the place of the Athnach or semicolon [o]. The same exact rhythm, (in which both the same number of words occur in the verse, and the verse is divided in the same place) recurs only seven times in Micah, in verses capable of a variation. The other four cases of repetition occur in short verses which have one division only [p] according to the place where the main division of the verse falls.

[a] ii. 10, add i. 11, 13, iv. 10. [b] iv. 13.
[c] v. 1. (iv. 14 Heb.)
[d] i. 5, ii. 7, iii. 1, iv. 9, vi. 3, 6, 10, 11, vii. 18.
[e] i. 11. twice.
[f] i. 2. twice; in i. 13. he returns to the 2d pers.
[g] ii. 3. [h] iii. 10 (5 words), vi. 11 (6 words).
[i] v. 8, and vii. 13, (7 words).
[k] vii. 11 (7 words), vii. 15 (5 words).
[l] v. 13 Heb. (5 words), v. 10 (6 words), v. 11 (7 words).

[m] Out of the 157 verses in Hosea's 11 last chapters, 111 contain fewer than 14 words each, 46 only 14 words or upwards; out of 46, of which the book of Nahum consists (excluding the title) 14 only have more than 13 words; out of 55 of Habakkuk, 17 only have more than 13.

[n] In Micah, 48 out of 104; in Joel, 30 out of 72; in Obadiah, 10 out of 21.

[o] There is less difference between a verse of 14 words, distributed 43, 43 and one of 11, distributed 32, 42, than in a verse whose 10 words were distributed 32,32 or 323,2.

[p] The following summary of these lesser divisions, which are mostly marked by the Hebrew accents, may perhaps give some little idea of the rhythm. Only the degree of subdivision must often be a matter of opinion or taste or ear. Thus, of 5 words which grammatically belong together, one might think that the cadence separated them into 3 and 2; another might take them altogether. But this is a matter of detail only; the principle is unmistakable. Again, words which have been artificially joined together in Hebrew by the Makkeph, I have considered as 2 words, if each had a distinct idea. Thus אֶת, when the mere sign of the object, I have not counted; when it is the preposition, "with," I have counted it. In the following list, the verses are ranged according to the number of the words contained in each verse, beginning with the highest. The numbers on the right hand indicate the lesser divisions into which each verse may be distributed. The comma in each set of numbers marks the place of the Athnach or semicolon. The Roman numerals indicate how often any cadence is repeated.

Number of Words in Each Lesser Division.

Words.	
24	333422,43 432,3264
22	46,534 14333,44
21	221,423232 4433,34
20	23333,33 333,3134 3333,44 4333,322
19	344,44 34,2253 32,4424
18	43,3233 342,423 3232,44
17	444,32 3433,22 3,4343 2223,332
16	222,433 3433,3 33,4222 44,44
15	32,325 3333,3 432,33 43,233 43,323 (ii) 134,133 43,332 3223,32
14	33,53 (ii) 34,34 23122,22 43,43 432,32 333,23 33,323 43,52 332,33 13,334 43,34 22,3313 2222,33 2222,51

His description of the destruction of the cities or villages of Judah corresponds in vividness to Isaiah's ideal march of Sennacherib [q]. The flame of war spreads from place to place; but Micah relieves the sameness of the description of misery by every variety which language allows. He speaks of them in his own person [r], or to them; he describes the calamity in past [s] or in future [t], or by use of the imperative [u]. The verbal allusions are crowded together in a way unexampled elsewhere. Moderns have spoken of them, as not after their taste, or have apologized for them. The mighty Prophet, who wrought a repentance greater than his great contemporary Isaiah, knew well what would impress the people to whom he spoke. The Hebrew names had definite meanings.

13	43,33 3,442 332,32 1322,5 222,322 432,4 43,33 322,42
12	32,322 422,22 143,22 224,4 23,34 53,22 24,24 43,23
11	32,33 42,32 (ii) 33,32 23,33 (ii) 24,32 33,23 (ii) 4322 22,43 32,42
10	5,5 33,4 32,32 (ii) 323,2 32,23 (ii) 22,33 2222,2 43,3
9	43,2 4,32 3,33 42,3 22,32 33,3
8	132,2 33,2
7	4,3 (ii) 3, 4 (ii) 3,22
6	3,3 (ii) 22,2
5	3,2 (ii)

To facilitate comparison, I subjoin a like analysis of the other prophets mentioned.

Hosea.

Eleven last chapters.

22	422253,4 3244,54
21	4433,34 5,242224
20	32,33324 3333,44
19	4343,32 3423,34
18	4,4334 332,2332 2232,423 44,3223
17	43,3322 3332,33 23,4323 3223,223 333,323 3223,43 3442,4
16	2323,24 32,3422 233,323 21214,24 3223,33 3232,33 33,253 42,433
15	344,4 2323,23 3332,4 (ii) 223,242 333,33
14	43,43 44,33 5,432 44,42 43,232 324,32 422,42 33,2222 33,44 3224,3 33,53 4,442 32,333 14,-333
13	33,43 (iii) 34,42 43,33 (ii) 4,333 4,54 34,33 323.32 223,33 22,234 33,34
12	4,44 432,21 33,33 (ii) 222,222 32,34 42,42 222,33 223,32 43,122 43,23 43,32 32,43
11	24,32 323,3 32,33 233,12 33,23 42,23 132,14 32,-42 32,33 33,32 4,43 23,222
10	43,3 (ii) 33,4 (ii) 3,34 3232 (ii) 44,2 24,4 222,22 4,33 33,22 322,3
9	5,13 25,2 3,33 (ii) 33,3 (iii) 232,2 2,322 32,22 (ii) 32,4 22,23 22,32 (ii) 4,32 13,32 2,34 5,4 24,3
8	32,3 (ii) 23,3 (iv) 2222 224 (ii)
7	13,3 (iii) 4,3 (iii) 3,4 (ii) 2,23 22,3 2,32 23,2 31,3 33,1 14,2
6	4,2 (ii) 3,3 (iii) 13,2 (ii)
5	3,2 (vii) 2111 113

Joel.

25	334,3534
24	322,144332
23	3544,223
22	423,4423
21	5422,422 3335,43
20	16,42313 34,3433
19	224,443
18	22,4433 33,435
17	3332,42 245,33 353,33 1422,35
16	334,42 2242,6 44,44
15	22233,3 2432,22 22222,32 344,4 23,2323 333, 33 34,35

We can well imagine how, as name after name passed from the Prophet's mouth, connected with some note of woe, all around awaited anxiously, to know upon what place the fire of the Prophet's word would next fall; and as at last it had fallen upon little and mighty round about Jerusalem, the names of the places would ring in their ears as heralds of the coming woe; they would be like so many monuments, inscribed beforehand with the titles of departed greatness, reminding Jerusalem itself of its portion of the prophecy, that [x] *evil* should *come from the Lord unto the gate of Jerusalem.*

Wonderful must have been his lightning-flash of indignation, as, when the false prophet or the people had forbidden God's word to be spoken, he burst upon them, [y] *Thou,*

14	53,33 334,4 36,23 1432,4 3332,3
13	34,33 3,55 33,34
12	44,4 34,23 2222,4 5,34 24,33 43,32 32,223
11	22,322 (ii) 223,22 2222,3 (ii) 32,33 3,224 32,42 222,5 4,331 44,3 223,22 2222,3
10	32,32 222,22 22,42 231,4
9	32,22 (iii) 2,43 5,22
8	3,23 22,22 4,22
7	133 3,4 (ii) 3,22 22,3
6	3,3 (iv)

Obadiah.

21	4333,323
19	4323,43
18	3332,133 34,344 4252,32
17	4242,32
16	5434 32422,3
15	334,23
14	43,43
13	332,23 42,34 4232,2
12	35,22
11	32,33 42,32
10	43,3
9	3,33
7	4,3 32,2
5	32

Nahum.

21	32232,72
19	2333,35 3233,44
18	32,337
16	34,2322 23,42131
15	323,43 33,522 22222,32 14123,4
14	44,33 (ii) 32221,13 3,2234 234,32
13	42,223 3332,2 323,32
12	33,33 32,34 322,32 (ii) 414,3 42,222 222,222
11	43,4 32,222 22,313 42,32 23,24 322,22
10	42,13 12,223 3,223 32,32
9	32,22 (ii) 23,22
8	23,3 (ii) 24,2 22,22
7	22,21
6	13,2 31,2
5	3,2

Habakkuk.

24	44,4444
20	4334.33
19	333,1423
18	43,254 3332,43
17	45,35 422,2232 54,44 333,53
15	34,44 332,322 33,234 34,233 43,44 13143,3 3333,3 333,42
14	43,322 332,33 33,44
13	32,422 33,43 23,44
12	323,22 (ii) 33,33 (ii)
11	222,32 32.42 32,33 322,4 42,14
10	322,3 3,34 4,33
9	33,3 (ii) 4,5 24,3 42,3 23,4
8	311,3 22,4 3,32
7	3,4 (ii) 4,3 (ii)
6	3,3 [iv]

q Is. x. 28–32. r i. 8, 10. see note. s 9, 10, 11, 12. t 8. u 11, 13, 16. x i. 12. y ii. 7.

called house of Jacob, shortened is God's Spirit? Or these His doings? And then follow the plaintive descriptions of the wrongs done to the poor, the peaceful[z], the mothers of his people and their little ones. And then again the instantaneous dismissal[a], *Arise and depart.* But, therewith, wonderful also is his tenderness. Burning as are his denunciations against the oppressions of the rich[b], (words less vehement will not pierce hearts of stone) there is an under-current of tenderness. His rebukes evince not indignation only against sin, but a tender sympathy with the sufferers. [c] He is afflicted in the afflictions which he has to denounce. He yearns for his people[d]; nay, until our Lord's Coming, there is scarcely an expression of such yearning longing: he hungers and thirsts for their good[e].

God's individual care of His people, and of each soul in it, had, since David's time[f] and even since Jacob[g], been likened to the care of the shepherd for each single sheep. The Psalm of Asaph[h] must have familiarized the people to the image, as relating to themselves as a whole, and David's deep Psalm had united it with God's tender care of His own in, and over, death. Yet the predominance of this image in Micah is a part of the tenderness of the Prophet. He adopts it, as expressing, more than any other natural image, the helplessness of the creature, the tender individual care of the Creator. He forestalls our Lord's words, *I am the good shepherd,* in his description of the Messiah, gathering *the remnant of Israel together, as the sheep of Bozrah*[i]; His people are as a flock, *lame and despised*[k], whom God would assemble; His royal seat, *the tower of the flock*[l]; the Ruler of Israel should *stand* unresting, *and feed them*[m]; those whom He should employ against the enemies of His people, are *shepherds*[n], under Him, the true shepherd. He sums up his prayer for his people to God as their Shepherd[o]; *Feed Thy people with Thy rod, the flock of Thine heritage.*

Directly, he was a Prophet for Judah only. At the beginning of his book, he condemns the idolatries of both capitals, as the central sin of the two kingdoms. The destruction of Samaria he pronounces at once, as future, absolutely certain, abiding[p]. There he leaves her, declares her *wound incurable,* and passes forthwith to Judah, to whom, he says, that wound should pass, whom that same enemy should reach[q]. Thereafter, he mentions incidentally the infection of Israel's sin spreading to Judah[r]. Else, after that first sentence on Samaria, the names of Jacob (which he had given to the ten tribes[s]) and Israel are appropriated to the kingdom of Judah[t]: Judah is mentioned no more, only her capital[u]; even her kings are called *the kings of Israel*[x]. The ten tribes are only included in the general restoration of the whole[y]. The future remnant of the two tribes, to be restored after the captivity of Babylon, are called by themselves *the remnant of Jacob*[z]: the Messiah to be born at Bethlehem is foretold as *the ruler in Israel*[a]: the ten tribes are called *the remnant of His brethren,* who were to *return to the children of Israel*[b], i. e. Judah.

This the more illustrates the genuineness of the inscription. A later hand would have been unlikely to have mentioned either Samaria or those earlier kings of Judah. Each part of the title corresponds to something in the prophecy; the name *Micah* is alluded to at its close; his birthplace, *the Morasthite,* at its beginning; the indications of those earlier reigns lie there, although not on its surface[c]. The mention of the two capitals, followed by the immediate sentence on Samaria, and then by the fuller expansion of the sins and punishment of Jerusalem, culminating in its sentence[d], in Micah, corresponds to the brief mention of the punishment of Judah in Amos the Prophet of Israel, and then the fuller expansion of the sins and punishments of Israel. Further, the capitals, as the fountains of idolatry, are the primary object of God's displeasure. They are both specially denounced in the course of the prophecy; their special overthrow is foretold[e]. The title corresponds with the contents of the prophecy, yet the objections of modern critics shew that the correspondence does not lie on the surface.

The taunt of the false priest Amaziah[f] to Amos may in itself suggest that prophets at Jerusalem did prophesy against Samaria. Amaziah, anyhow, thought it natural that they should. Both Isaiah and Micah, while exercising their office at Jerusalem, had regard also to Samaria. Divided as Israel and Judah were, Israel was not yet cut off. Israel and Judah were still, together, the one people of God. The prophets in each had a care for the other.

Micah joins himself on to the men of God before him, as Isaiah at the time, and Jeremiah, Habakkuk, Zephaniah, Ezekiel, subsequently, employed words or thoughts of

[z] 8, 9. [a] 10.
[b] ii. 1, 2, iii. 1–3, 9–11, vi. 10–12, vii. 2, 3.
[c] i. 8, 9, ii. 1, 2, vii. 5, 6. [d] i. 8–10, 16, iv. 9, 10.
[e] vii. 1. [f] Ps. xxiii. [g] Gen. xlix. 24.
[h] Ps. lxxiv. 1, lxxviii. 52, lxxix. 13, lxxx. 1.
[i] ii. 12. [k] iv. 6. [l] Ib. 8. [m] v. 4. [Eng. 3 Heb.]
[n] Ib. 5. [4 Heb.] [o] vii. 14.
[p] i. 6, 7. [q] i. 9. [r] i. 13. [s] i. 5.

[t] *Jacob*, ii. 7, iii. 1, 8, 9; *Israel*, i. 14, 15, iii. 1, 8, 9, v. 1, 3, vi. 2.
[u] See ab. p. 6. [x] i. 14.
[y] *Jacob, all of thee*, ii. 12; *the remnant of Israel*, ib.
[z] v. 7, 8, [8, 9 Heb.] [a] v. 2. (1 Heb.)
[b] Ib. 3. (2 Heb.) [c] See ab. p. 8.
[d] iii. 12.
[e] i. 6, 9, 12, iii. 10–12, iv. 10. [f] See vol. i. p. 321.

MICAH.

Before CHRIST cir. 758–726.

CHAPTER I.

1 *Micah sheweth the wrath of God against Jacob for idolatry.* 10 *He exhorteth to mourning.*

THE word of the LORD
that came to [a]Micah
the Morasthite in the days
of Jotham, Ahaz, *and*
Hezekiah, kings of Judah,
[b]which he saw concerning
Samaria and Jerusalem.
2 † Hear, all ye people;
[c]hearken, O earth, and
† all that therein is; and
let the Lord GOD [d]be witness against you, the Lord
from [e]his holy temple.

[a] Jer. 26. 18.
[b] Amos 1. 1.
† Heb. *Hear, ye people, all of them.*
[c] Deut. 32. 1. Is. 1. 2.
† Heb. *the fullness thereof.*
[d] Ps. 50. 7. Mal. 3. 5.
[e] Ps. 11. 4. Jonah 2. 7. Hab. 2. 20.

CHAP. I. VER. 1. *The word of the Lord that came to Micah—which he saw.* No two of the prophets authenticate their prophecy in exactly the same way. They, one and all, have the same simple statement to make, that this which they say is *from* God, and *through* them. A later hand, had it added the titles, would have formed all upon one model. The title was an essential part of the prophetic book, as indicating to the people afterward, that it was not written after the event. It was a witness, not to the prophet whose name it bears, but to God. The prophet bare witness to God, that what he delivered came from Him. The event bare witness to the prophet, that he said this truly, in that he knew what God alone could know,—futurity. Micah blends in one the facts, that he related in words given him by God, what he had seen spread before him in prophetic vision. His prophecy was, in one, *the word of the Lord which came to him*, and a sight *which* he *saw*.

Micah omits all mention of his father. His great predecessor was known as Micaiah *son of Imlah*. Micah, a villager, would be known only by the name of his native village. So Nahum names himself *the Elkoshite;* Jonah is related to be a native *of Gath-hepher;* Elijah, the Tishbite, a sojourner in the despised Gilead[1]; Elisha, of Abelmeholah; Jeremiah, of Anathoth; forerunners of *Him*, and taught by *His* Spirit Who willed to be born at Bethlehem, and, since this, although *too little to be* counted *among the thousands of Judah*, was yet a royal city and was to be the birthplace of the Christ, was known only as *Jesus of Nazareth, the Nazarene.* No prophet speaks of himself, or is spoken of, as born at Jerusalem, *the holy city.* They speak of themselves with titles of lowliness, not of greatness.

Micah dates his prophetic office from kings of Judah only, as the only kings of the line appointed by God. Kings of Israel are mentioned in addition, only by prophets of Israel. He names Samaria first, because, its iniquity being most nearly full, its punishment was the nearest.

2. *Hear, all ye people,* lit. *hear, ye peoples, all of them* Some 140, or 150 years had flowed by, since Micaiah, son of Imlah, had closed his prophecy in these words. And now they burst out anew. From age to age the word of God holds its course, ever receiving new fulfillments, never dying out, until the end shall come. The signal fulfillment of the prophecy, to which the former Micaiah had called attention in these words, was an earnest of the fulfillment of this present message of God.

Hearken, O earth, and all that therein is. The *peoples* or *nations* are never Judah and Israel only: *the earth and the fullness thereof* is the well-known title of the whole earth[2] and all its inhabitants. Moses[3], Asaph[4], Isaiah[5], call heaven and earth as witnesses against God's people. Jeremiah[6], as Micah here, summons *the nations* and the *earth.* The contest between good and evil, sin and holiness, the kingdom of God and the kingdom of Satan, everwhere, but most chiefly where God's Presence is nearest, is *a spectacle to the world, to angels and to men*[7]. The nations are witnesses of God against His own people, so that these should not say, that it was for want of faithfulness or justice or power[8], but in His righteous judgment, that He cast off whom He had chosen. So shall the Day of Judgment *reveal His righteousness*[9]. *Hearken, O earth.* The lifeless earth[10] *trembles at the Presence of God,* and so reproaches the dullness of man. By it he summons man to listen with great reverence to the Voice of God.

[1] 1 Kgs xvii. 1.

[2] In the two passages quoted for the contrary, Jer. viii. 16, Ezek. xii. 19, the context shews that ארץ is and can only be, *land*, not, *earth*, Jer. *The snorting of his horses is heard from Dan, and they came and devoured the land and the fullness thereof;* where *the land* to which they *came* could plainly be Judea only. In Ezekiel it is not even *the land*, but *her land. Say unto the people of the land; Thus saith the Lord God of the land of Israel,—that her land may be desolate from all the fullness thereof.*

[3] Deut. xxxii. 1. [4] Ps. l. 7. [5] i. 2. [6] vi. 19.

[7] 1 Cor. iv. 9.

[8] Ex. xxxii. 12, Num. xiv. 16, Josh. vii. 8, 9.

[9] Rom. ii. 5. [10] Ps. cxiv. 7, xcvii. 5.

Before CHRIST cir. 758-726.

3 For, behold, [f]the LORD cometh forth out of his [g]place, and will come down, and tread upon the [h]high places of the earth.

[f] Is. 26. 21.
[g] Ps. 115. 3.
[h] Deut 32. 13. & 33. 29. Amos 4. 13.

And let the Lord God be witness against you. Not in words, but in deeds ye shall know, that I speak not of myself but God in me, when, what I declare, He shall by His Presence fulfill. But the nations are appealed to, not merely because the judgments of God on Israel should be made known *to* them by the Prophets. He had not yet spoken of Israel or Judah, whereas he *had* spoken to the nations; *hear, ye peoples.* It seems then most likely that here too he is speaking to them. Every judgment is an earnest, a forerunner, a part, of the final judgment and an ensample of its principles. It is but "the last great link in the chain," which unites God's dealings in time with eternity. God's judgments on one imply a judgment on all. His judgments in time imply a Judgment beyond time. Each sinner feels in his own heart a response to God's visible judgments on another. Each sinful nation may read its own doom in the sentence on each other nation. God judges each according to his own measure of light and grace, accepted or refused. The Heathen shall be judged by *the law written in their heart*[1]; the Jew, by the law of Moses and the light of the prophets; Christians, by the law of Christ. *The word,* Christ saith[2], *that I have spoken, the same shall judge him at the last Day.* God Himself foretold, that the heathen should know the ground of His judgments against His people[3]. *All nations shall say, wherefore hath the Lord done thus unto this land? What meaneth the heat of this great anger? Then men shall say, Because they have forsaken the covenant of the Lord God of their fathers which He made with them, when He brought them forth out of the land of Egypt, &c.* But in that the heathen knew why God so punished His people, they came so far to know the mind of God; and God, Who at no time[4] *left Himself without witness,* bore fresh *witness* to them, and, so far as they neglected it, *against* them. A Jew, wherever he is seen throughout the world, is a witness to the world of God's judgments against sin.

"[5] Christ, *the faithful Witness,* shall *witness against* those who do ill, *for* those who do well."

The Lord from His holy temple. Either that at Jerusalem, where God shewed and revealed Himself, or Heaven of which it was the image. As David says[6], *The Lord* is *in His holy temple; the Lord's throne* is *in heaven;* and contrasts His dwelling in heaven and His coming down upon earth. [7] *He bowed the heavens also and came down;* and Isaiah, in like words[8], *Behold, the Lord cometh out of His place to punish the inhabitants of the earth for their iniquity.*

3. *For, behold, the Lord cometh forth,* i. e. (as we now say,) *is coming forth.* Each day of judgment, and the last also, are ever drawing nigh, noiselessly as the nightfall, but unceasingly. *Out of His Place.* "[9] God is hidden from us, except when He sheweth Himself by His Wisdom or Power of Justice or Grace, as Isaiah saith[10], *Verily, Thou art a God Who hidest Thyself.*" He seemeth to be absent, when He doth not visibly work either in the heart within, or in judgments without; to the ungodly and unbelieving He is absent[11], *far above out of their sight,* when He does not avenge their scoffs, their sins, their irreverence. Again He seemeth to go forth, when His Power is felt. "[9] Whence it is said[12], *Bow Thy heavens, O Lord, and come down;* and the Lord saith of Sodom[13], *I will go down now and see, whether they have done altogether according to the cry of it, which is come unto Me.* Or, *the Place* of the Infinite God is God Himself. For the Infinite sustaineth Itself, nor doth anything out of Itself contain It. God *dwelleth* also *in light unapproachable*[14]. When then Almighty God doth not manifest Himself, He abideth, as it were, in *His own Place.* When He manifests His Power or Wisdom or Justice by their effects, He is said to *go forth out of His Place,* i. e. out of His hiddenness. Again, since the Nature of God is Goodness, it is proper and co-natural to Him, to be propitious, have mercy and spare. In this way, *the Place* of God is His mercy. When then He passeth from the sweetness of pity to the rigor of equity, and, on account of our sins, sheweth Himself severe (which is, as it were, alien from Him) He *goeth forth out of His Place.*" "[15] For He Who is gentle and gracious, and Whose Nature it is to have mercy, is constrained, on your account, to take the seeming of hardness, which is not His."

He comes invisibly now, in that it is He Who punisheth, through whatever power or will of man He useth; He shews forth His Holiness through the punishment of unholiness. But the words, which are image-language now, shall be most exactly fulfilled in the end, when, in the Person of our Lord, He

[1] Rom. ii. 12-15. [2] S. John xii. 48. [3] Deut. xxix. 24, 5. [4] Acts xiv. 17. [5] Dion. [6] Ps. xi. 4. [7] Ps. xviii. 9.

[8] xxvi. 21. [9] Dion. [10] xlv. 15. [11] Ps. x. 5. [12] Ps. cxliv. 5, Is. lxiv. 1. [13] Gen. xviii. 21. [14] 1 Tim. vi. 16. [15] S. Jer.

Before CHRIST cir. 758-726.

4 And [l]the mountains shall be molten under him, and the valleys shall be cleft, as wax before the fire, *and* as the waters *that are* poured down †a steep place.

[l] Judg. 5. 5. Ps. 97. 5. Is. 64. 1, 2, 3. Amos 9. 5. Hab. 3. 6, 10.

† Heb. *a descent.*

shall *come* visibly to judge the world. "[1] In the Day of Judgment, Christ *shall come down,* according to that Nature which He took, *from His Place,* the highest heavens, and shall cast down the proud things of this world."

And will come down; not by change of place, or in Himself, but as felt in the punishment of sin; *and tread upon the high places of the earth;* to bring down the pride of those [2] who "[3] being lifted up in their own conceit and lofty, sinning through pride and proud through sin, were yet created out of earth. For [4] *why is earth and ashes proud?*" What seems mightiest and most firm, is unto God less than is to man the dust under his feet. The high places were also the special scenes of an unceasing idolatry. "God treadeth *in* the good and humble, in that He dwelleth, walketh, feasteth in their hearts [5]. But He *treadeth upon* the proud and the evil, in that He casteth them down, despiseth, condemneth them."

4. *And the mountains shall be molten under Him.* It has been thought that this is imagery, taken from volcanic eruptions [6]; but, although there is a very remarkable volcanic district just outside of Gilead [7], it is not thought to have been active at times so late as these; nor were the people to whom the words were said, familiar with it. Fire, the real agent at the end of the world, is, meanwhile, the symbol of God's anger, as being the most terrible of His instruments of destruction: whence God revealed Himself as *a consuming fire* [8], and, at this same time said by Isaiah [9]; *For behold, the Lord will come with fire—to render His anger with fury, and His rebuke with flames of fire.*

And the valleys shall be cleft as wax before the fire. It seems natural that the mountains should be cleft; but the valleys [10], so low already! This speaks of a yet deeper dissolution; of lower depths beyond our sight or knowledge, into the very heart of the earth. "[11] This should they fear, who will to be so low; who, so far from lifting themselves to heavenly things, pour out their affections on things of earth, meditate on and love earthly things, and forgetful of the heavenly, choose to fix their eyes on earth. These the wide gaping of the earth which they loved, shall swallow: to them the *cleft valleys* shall open an everlasting sepulchre, and, having received them, shall never part with them."

Highest and lowest, first and last, shall perish before Him. The pride of the highest, kings and princes, priests and judges, shall sink and melt away *beneath* the weight and Majesty of His glory; the hardness of the lowest, which would not open itself to Him, shall be cleft in twain before Him.

As wax before the fire [12], melting away before Him by Whom they were not softened, vanishing into nothingness. Metals melt, changing their form only; wax, so as to cease to be [13].

As the waters poured down (as a stream or cataract, so the word means [14]) *a steep place.* Down to the very edge, it is borne along, one strong, smooth, unbroken current; then, at once, it seems to gather its strength, for one great effort. But to what end? To fall, with the greater force, headlong, scattered in spray, foam and froth; dissipated, at times, into vapor, or reeling in giddy eddies, never to return. In Judæa, where the autumn rains set in with great vehemence [15], the waters must have been often seen pouring in their little tumultuous brooklets down the mountain side [16], hastening to disappear, and disappearing the faster, the more vehemently they rolled along [17]. Both images exhibit

[1] S. Jer. Theoph.
[2] See Am. iv. 13, Job ix. 8.
[3] Rup.
[4] Ecclus. x. 9.
[5] 2 Cor. vi. 16, Rev. iii. 20.
[6] Henderson here.
[7] See vol. i. p. 425.
[8] Deut. iv. 24.
[9] lxvi. 15.
[10] Hence some MSS. mentioned in De Rossi's cod. 319, have (as a conjecture) והגבעות "the hills."
[11] Sanch.
[12] See Ps. xcvii. 5.
[13] See S. Hil. in Ps. lvii. § 4. מסס is used, as to natural objects, only of such melting whereby the substance is wasted, as of manna (Ex. xvi. 21), wax (Ps. lxviii. 3, &c.), or the body through disease (1 Sam. xxv. 37); then, morally, chiefly of fear.
[14] See Ges. Thes. sub v. from the Punic, Monum. Phœn. p. 418. "There are many waterfalls in Lebanon, one very near and to the N. of the Damascus road. I have also seen one in Anti-libanus on the river Barada, a little above Abîl. The stream, named Sheba, which springs from the perpetual snows of Mount Hermon is extremely rapid and has a very steep fall to the Hasbeia which it joins in Merj-el-Huleh. The Jordan is a continual cataract between el-Huleh and the Lake of Gennesareth;" (Rev. G. Williams, MS. letter) "a fall of 600 feet in about 10 miles. On the Western bank, high above the rocky bed of the torrent, the water was running rapidly down the steep incline toward the river, which could hardly be less than 150 feet below us." (Id. Col. Church Chron. 1860. Jan. p. 30.). Porter describes the fall of the river Adonis (Five years, ii. 295.) From the height at which the streams rise in the Lebanon chain, there must be many greater or lesser falls.
[15] Hence the Hebrew name נשם, "heavy rain," for which we have no one word, is used of the autumn and winter rain, Cant. ii. 11.
[16] I have seen this effect for above half an hour (15 miles) on the mountain country near the lakes in a thunderstorm.
[17] "The decrease of the waters (swollen by the rains in the mountains) is usually as rapid as their rise." Burckhardt, Syria, p. 161.

Before CHRIST cir. 758–726.

5 For the transgression
of Jacob *is* all this, and
for the sins of the house of
Israel. What *is* the transgression of Jacob? *is it*
not Samaria? and what
are the high places of Judah? *are they* not Jerusalem?
6 Therefore I will make

the inward emptiness of sinners, man's utter helplessness before God. They need no outward impulse to their destruction. "[1] Wax endureth not the nearness of the fire, and the waters are carried headlong. So all of the ungodly, when the Lord cometh, shall be dissolved and disappear." At the end of the world, they shall be gathered into bundles, and cast away.

5. *For the transgression of Jacob is all this.* Not for any change of purpose in God; nor, again, as the effect of man's lust of conquest. None could have any power against God's people, unless it had been given him by God. Those mighty Monarchies of old existed but as God's instruments, especially toward His own people. God said at this time of Assyria, [2] *Asshur, rod of Mine anger, and the staff in his hand* is *Mine indignation;* and [3], *Now have I brought it to pass, that thou shouldest be to lay waste defenced cities* into *ruinous heaps.* Each scourge of God chastised just those nations, which God willed him to chasten; but the especial object for which each was raised up was his mission against that people, in whom God most shewed His mercies and His judgments. [4] *I will send him against an ungodly nation and against the people of My wrath will I give him a charge. Jacob* and *Israel,* in this place, comprise alike the ten tribes and the two. They still bare the name of their father, who, wrestling with the Angel, became *a prince with God,* Whom they forgat. The name of Jacob then, as of Christian now, stamped as deserters, those who did not the deeds of their father. *What,* [rather *Who* [5]] *is the transgression of Jacob? Who* is its cause? In whom does it lie? *Is* it *not Samaria?* The metropolis must, in its own nature, be the source of good or evil to the land. It is the heart whose pulses beat throughout the whole system. As the seat of power, the residence of justice or injustice, the place of counsel, the concentration of wealth, which all the most influential of the land visit for their several occasions, its manners penetrate in a degree the utmost corners of the land. Corrupted, it becomes a focus of corruption. The blood passes through it, not to be purified, but to be diseased. Samaria, being founded on apostasy, owing its being to rebellion against God, the home of that policy which set up a rival system of worship to *His,* forbidden by Him, became a fountain of evil, whence the stream of ungodliness overflowed the land. It became the impersonation of the people's sin, "the heart and the head of the body of sin."

And what [lit. *Who* [5]] are *the high places of Judah?* are they *not Jerusalem?* Jerusalem God had formed to be a centre of unity in holiness; *thither the tribes of the Lord* were to *go up to the testimony of Israel;* there was the unceasing worship of God, the morning and evening sacrifice; the Feasts, the memorials of past miraculous mercies, the foreshadowings of redemption. But there too Satan placed his throne. Ahaz brought thither that most hateful idolatry, the burning children to Moloch *in the valley of the son of Hinnom* [6]. There, [7] *he made him altars in every corner of Jerusalem.* Thence, he extended the idolatry to all Judah. [8] *And in every several city of Judah he made high places to burn incense unto other gods, and provoked to anger the Lord God of his fathers.* Hezekiah, in his reformation, with *all Israel,* [9] *went out to the cities of Judah, and brake the images in pieces and hewed down the statues of Asherah, and threw down the high places and the altars out of all Judah and Benjamin,* as much as out of *Ephraim and Manasseh.* Nay, by a perverse interchange, Ahaz took the *brazen altar,* consecrated to God, for his own divinations, and assigned to the worship of God the altar copied from the idol-altar at Damascus, whose fashion pleased his taste [10]. Since *God and mammon cannot* be *served* together, Jerusalem was become one great idol-temple, in which Judah brought its sin into the very face of God and of His Worship. The *Holy City* had itself become sin, and the fountain of unholiness. The one temple of God was the single protest against the idolatries which encompassed and besieged it; the incense went up to God, morning and evening, from it; from every head of every street of the city [11], and (since Ahaz had brought in the worship of Baalim [12], and the rites of idolatry continued the same,) from *the roofs* of all their *houses* [13], went up *the incense to Baal;* a worship which, denying the Unity, denied the Being of God.

6. *Therefore* [lit. *And*] *I will make Samaria*

[1] S. Jer. [2] Is. x. 5. [3] Ib. xxxvii. 26. [4] Ib. x. 6.
[5] מי always relates to a personal object, and apparent exceptions may be reduced to this. So AE. Kim. Tanch. Poc.
[6] 2 Chr. xxviii. 3. [7] Ib. 24. [8] Ib. 25.
[9] Ib. xxxi. 1. [10] 2 Kings xvi. 10–16.
[11] Ezek. xvi. 31, 2 Chr. xxviii. 24. [12] Ib. 2.
[13] Jer. xxxii. 29.

Before CHRIST cir. 758–726.

Samaria [k] as an heap of the
field, *and* as plantings of a
vineyard: and I will pour
down the stones thereof
into the valley, and I will
[l] discover the foundations
thereof.

[k] 2 Kings 19. 25. ch. 3. 12.

[l] Ezek. 13. 14.

7 And all the graven
images thereof shall be
beaten to pieces, and all
the [m] hires thereof shall
be burned with the fire,
and all the idols thereof
will I lay desolate: for she

[m] Hos. 2. 5, 12.

as an heap of the field, and as plantings of a vineyard. "[1] The order of the sin was the order of the punishment." Samaria's sins were the earliest, the most obstinate, the most unbroken, bound up with its being as a state. On it then God's judgments should first fall. It was *a crown of pride*[2], *resting on the head of the rich valleys*, out of which it rose. Its soil is still rich[3]. "The whole is now cultivated in terraces[4]," "to the summits[5]." Probably, since the sides of hills, open to the sun, were chosen for vineyards, it had been a vineyard, before Shemer sold it to Omri[6]. What it had been, that it was again to be. Its inhabitants cast forth, its houses and gorgeous palaces were to become heaps of stones, *gathered out*[7] to make way for cultivation, or to become the fences of the vegetation, which should succeed to man. There is scarce a sadder natural sight than the fragments of human habitation, tokens of man's labor or his luxury, amid the rich beauty of nature when man himself is gone. For they are tracks of sin and punishment, man's rebellion and God's judgment, man's unworthiness of the good natural gifts of God. A century or two ago, travelers "[8] speak of the ground [the site of Samaria] as strewed with masses of ruins." Now these too are gone. "[3] The stones of the temples and palaces of Samaria have been carefully removed from the rich soil, thrown together in heaps, built up in the rude walls of terraces, and rolled down into the valley below." "[9] About midway of the ascent, the hill is surrounded by a narrow terrace of woodland like a belt. Higher up too are the marks of slighter terraces, once occupied perhaps by the streets of the ancient city." Terrace-cultivation has succeeded to the terraced streets once thronged by the busy, luxurious, sinful, population.

And I will pour down the stones thereof into the valley, of which it was the crest, and which it now proudly surveyed. God Himself would cause it to be poured down (he uses the word which he had just used of the vehemence of the cataract[10]). "[11] The whole face of this part of the hill suggests the idea that the buildings of the ancient city had been thrown down from the brow of the hill. Ascending to the top, we went round the whole summit, and found marks of the same process everywhere."

And I will discover the foundations thereof. The desolation is entire; *not one stone left upon another.* Yet the very words of threatening contain hope. It was to be not a *heap* only, but *the plantings of a vineyard.* The *heaps* betoken ruin; the *vineyard*, fruitfulness cared for by God. Destroyed, as what it was, and turned upside down, as a vineyard by the share, it should become again what God made it and willed it to be. It should again become a *rich valley*, but in outward desolation. Its splendid palaces, its idol temples, its *houses of joy*, should be but heaps and ruins, which are cleared away out of a vineyard, as only choking it. It was built in rebellion and schism, loose and not held together, like a *heap* of stones, having no cement of love, rent and torn in itself, having been torn both from God and His worship. It could be remade only by being wholly unmade. Then should they who believed be branches grafted in Him Who said, [12] *I am the Vine, ye are the branches.*

7. *And all the graven images thereof shall be beaten to pieces.* Its idols in whom she trusts, so far from protecting her, shall themselves go into captivity, broken up for the gold and silver whereof they were made. The wars of the Assyrians being religious wars[13], the idolatry of Assyria destroyed the idolatry and idols of Israel.

And all the hires thereof shall be burned with fire. All forsaking of God being spiritual fornication from Him Who made His creatures for Himself, the *hires* are all which man would gain by that desertion of his God, employed in man's intercourse with his idols, whether as bribing his idols to give him what are the gifts of God, or as himself bribed by them. For there is no pure service, save that of the love of God. God alone can be loved purely, for Himself; offerings to Him Alone are the creature's pure

[1] S. Jer. [2] Is. xxviii. 1.
[3] Porter, Hdbook, p. 345. [4] Ib. 344.
[5] Rob. ii. 304. 307. [6] 1 Kings xvi. 24. [7] Is. v. 2.
[8] "Cotovicus in the 16th, and Von Troilo in the 17th century." Rob. ii. 307. note 1.
[9] Rob. ii. 304. [10] ver. 4.
[11] Narrative of Scottish Mission, pp. 293, 4. in Henderson.
[12] S. John xv. 5.
[13] See below Introd. to Nahum.

Before CHRIST cir. 758-726.

gathered *it* of the hire of
an harlot and they shall
return to the hire of an
harlot.

8 Therefore [n] I will wail
and howl, [o] I will go stripped and naked: [p] I will
make a wailing like the

Before CHRIST cir. 758-726.

n Is. 21. 3. & 22. 4. Jer. 4. 19.
o Is. 20. 2, 3, 4.
p Job 30. 29. Ps. 102. 6.

homage to the Creator, going out of itself, not looking back to itself, not seeking itself, but stretching forth to Him and seeking Him for Himself. Whatever man gives to or hopes from his idols, man himself is alike his object in both. The *hire* then is, alike what he gives to his idols, *the gold whereof he makes* his *Baal*[1], the offerings which the heathen used to lay up in their temples, and what, as he thought, he himself received back. For he gave only earthly things, in order to receive back things of earth. He hired their service to him, and his earthly gains were his hire. It is a strong mockery in the mouth of God, that they had these things from their idols. He speaks to them after their thoughts. Yet it is true that, although God overrules all, man does receive from Satan[2], *the god of this world*[3], all which he gains amiss. It is the price for which he sells his soul and profanes himself. Yet herein were the heathen more religious than the Christian worldling. The heathen did offer an ignorant service to they knew not what. Our idolatry of mammon, as being less abstract, is more evident self-worship, a more visible ignoring and so a more open dethroning of God, a worship of a material prosperity, of which we seem ourselves to be the authors, and to which we habitually immolate the souls of men, so habitually that we have ceased to be conscious of it.

And all the idols thereof will I lay desolate, lit. *make a desolation*. They, now thronged by their worshipers, should be deserted; their place and temple, a waste. He thrice repeats *all; all her graven images, all her hires, all her idols; all* should be destroyed. He subjoins a threefold destruction which should overtake them; so that, while the Assyrian broke and carried off the more precious, or burned what could be burned, and, what could not be burned, nor was worth transporting, should be left desolate, all should come to an end. He sets the whole the more vividly before the mind, exhibiting to us so many separate pictures of the mode of destruction.

For from the hire of a harlot she gathered them, *and to the hire of a harlot they shall return.* "[4]The wealth and manifold provision which (as she thought) were gained by fornication with her idols, shall go to another harlot, Nineveh; so that, as they went a whoring in their own land, they should go to another land of idols and fornication, the Assyrians." They [5]*turned their glory into shame, changing the glory of the incorruptible God into an image made like unto corruptible man;* and so it should turn to them into shame. It sprung out of their shame, and should turn to it again. "Ill got, ill spent." Evil gain, cursed in its origin, has the curse of God upon it, and makes its gainer a curse, and ends accursedly. "Make not ill gains," says even a Heathen[6], "ill gains are equal to losses;" and another[7], "Unlawful sweetness a most bitter end awaiteth."

Probably, the most literal sense is not to be excluded. The degrading idolatrous custom, related of Babylon and Cyprus[8], still continued among the Babylonians at the date of the book of Baruch[9], and to the Christian era[10]. S. Augustine speaks of it as having existed[11] among the Phœnicians, and Theodoret[12] says that it was still practiced by some in Syria. The existence of the idolatrous custom is presupposed by the prohibition by Moses[13]; and, in the time of Hosea self-desecration was an idolatrous rite in Israel[14]. In the day of Judgment, when the foundation of those who build their house upon the sand, shall be laid bare, the riches which they gained unlawfully shall be burned up; all the idols, which they set up instead of God, "[15]the vain thoughts, and useless fancies, and hurtful forms and images which they picture in their mind, defiling it, and hindering it from the steadfast contemplation of divine things, will be punished. They were the hire of the soul which went astray from God, and they who conceived them will, with them, become the prey again of that infernal host which is unceasingly turned from God."

8. *Therefore I will* [*would*[16]] *wail* [properly *beat*[17], i. e. on the breast], *and howl.* "Let me alone," he would say, "that I may vent my sorrow in all ways of expressing sorrow, beating on the breast and wailing, using all acts and sounds of grief." It is as we would say, "Let me mourn *on*," a mourning inexhaustible, because the woe too and the cause of

1 See Hos. ii. 8. vol. i. p. 32.
2 S. Matt. iv. 9.
3 2 Cor. iv. 4.
4 S. Jer.
5 Rom. i. 23.
6 Hesiod. 'E. κ. 'H. 354. L.
7 Pindar Isthm. vii. 67, 8. L.
8 Herod. i. 199.
9 vi. 43.
10 Strabo, xvi. 1. 20.
11 dabant. de Civ. Dei iii. 10.
12 on this place.
13 Deut. xxiii. 18.
14 See on Hos. iv. 14, p. 31.
15 Dion.
16 He thrice repeats the optative אספדה ואילילה אילכה.
17 ספד.

Before CHRIST cir. 758–726.

dragons, and mourning as
the † owls.
9 For ‖ her wound *is*
incurable; for [q] it is
come unto Judah; he is
come unto the gate of
my people, *even* to Jerusalem.

† Heb. *daughters of the owl.*

‖ Or, *she is grievously sick of her wounds.*

q 2 Kings 18. 13. Is. 1. 6, 7, 8.

Before CHRIST cir. 758–726.

grief was unceasing. The Prophet becomes in words, probably in acts too, an image of his people, doing as they should do hereafter. He mourns, because and as they would have to mourn, bearing chastisement, bereft of all outward comeliness, an example also of repentance, since what he did were the chief outward tokens of mourning.

I will [*would*] *go stripped* [*despoiled*[1]] *and naked.* He explains the acts, that they represented no mere voluntary mourning. Not only would he, representing them, go bared of all garments of beauty, as we say "half-naked[2]" but *despoiled* also, the proper term of those plundered and stripped by an enemy. He speaks of his doing, what we know that Isaiah did, by God's command, representing in act what his people should thereafter do. "[3] Wouldest thou that I should weep, thou must thyself grieve the first." Micah doubtless went about, not speaking only of grief, but grieving, in the habit of one mourning and bereft of all. He prolongs in these words the voice of wailing, choosing unwonted forms of words, to carry on the sound of grief[4].

I will make a wailing like the dragons [*jackals*[5]] *and mourning as the owls* [*ostriches*[6]]. The cry of both, as heard at night, is very piteous. Both are *doleful creatures*, dwelling in desert and lonely places. "The[7] jackals make a lamentable howling noise, so that travelers unacquainted with them would think that a company of people, women or children, were howling, one to another." "Its howl," says an Arabic natural historian[8], "is like the crying of an infant." "We heard them," says another[9], "through the night, wandering around the villages, with a continual, prolonged, mournful cry." The ostrich, forsaking its young[10], is an image of bereavement. "[11] As the ostrich forgets her eggs and *leaves them as though they* were *not her's*, to be trampled by the feet of wild beasts, so too shall I go childless, spoiled and naked." Its screech is spoken of by travelers as "[12] fearful, affrighting." "[13] During the lonesome part of the night they often make a doleful and piteous noise. I have often heard them groan, as if they were in the greatest agonies."

"[14] I will grieve from the heart over those who perish, mourning for the hardness of the ungodly, as the Apostle had[15] *great heaviness and continual sorrow in* his *heart* for his brethren, the impenitent and unbelieving Jews. Again he saith[16], *who is weak and I am not weak? Who is offended, and I burn not?* For by how much the soul is nobler than the body, and by how much eternal damnation is heavier than any temporal punishment, so much more vehemently should we grieve and weep for the peril and perpetual damnation of souls, than for bodily sickness or any temporal evil."

9. *For her* [Samaria's] *wound*[17], [lit. *her wounds, or strokes,* (the word is used especially of those inflicted by God[18],) each, one by one,] *is incurable.* The idiom is used of inflictions on the body politic[19] or the

1 *Barefoot* is expressed in Hebrew by יחף. Since then Micah does not use the received term for *barefoot*, and does use the word expressing "stripped," "despoiled," the E. V. is doubtless right, agreeing with the Latin against the LXX. and Syr.

2 See on Amos ii. 16. p. 178. n. 6. Seneca says: "Some things, though not [exactly] true, are comprised under the same word, for their likeness. So we call illiterate, one not altogether uninstructed, but who has not been advanced to higher knowledge. So he who has seen one illhabited and in rags, says that he had seen one 'naked.'" de benef. v. 13. Sanch.

3 Hor. A. P. 102, 3.

4 שילל and אילכה carry on the sound of אילילה. שילל, the textual reading, is doubtless right, although without example; אילכה has analogy with other words, but, common as the word is, stands alone in the word itself. Each bears out the other.

5 The תן, which occurs only in the plural תנים, is distinct from the תנין, plur. תנינים, although they touch on each other, in that תנין sing. is written תנים, Ezek. xxix. 3, and the poetic plur. of תן, תנין occurs in the text, Lam. iv. 3. The Syr. (and Chaldee, properly) and Tanchum oftentimes render it "jackal." Pococke first, of moderns, brought out this meaning. See his note here.

6 The בת יענה "female ostrich" (the תחמס probably being the male ostrich) may be so called from יען, (Syr. *glutton*, like its Arabic name na'am) or from its shrill cry, ענה.

7 Pococke, who had heard them in Syria, &c.

8 Demiri, in Bochart, iii. 12. T. iii. p. 181. ed. Leipz. "It howls by night only." Id.

9 Olearius, Itin. Mosc. et Pers. iv. 17. Boch. Ib. p. 183.

10 Job xxxix. 16.

11 S. Jer.

12 Sandys' Travels, L. ii. fin.

13 Shaw, Travels, T. ii. p. 349.

14 Dion.

15 Rom. ix. 1.

16 2 Cor. xi. 29.

17 The construction of the E. V. is beyond question preferable that of the E. M. It is the common emphatic idiom, in which the plural subject and singular predicate are joined to express, that the thing asserted is true not only of all generally but of each individually.

18 Lev. xxvi. 21, Nu. xi. 33, Deut. xxviii. 59, 61, &c.

19 Nah. iii. ult. Jer. xxx. 12, 15.

Before CHRIST cir. 758–726.

10 ¶ [r] Declare ye *it* not at Gath, weep ye not at all:
in the house of ‖ Aphrah [s] roll thyself in the dust.

[r] 2 Sam. 1. 20.
‖ That is, *dust*.
[s] Jer. 6. 26.

mind[1], for which there is no remedy. The *wounds* were very *sick*, or incurable, not in themselves or on God's part, but on Israel's. The day of grace passes away at last, when man has so steeled himself against grace, as to be morally dead, having deadened himself to all capacity of repentance.

For it is come unto [*quite up to*[2] *Judah; he*, [the enemy,] *is come* [lit. hath *reached*, touched,] *to* [*quite up to*[2]] *the gate of my people*, even *to* [*quite up to*[2]] *Jerusalem.* "[3] The same sin, yea, the same punishment for sin, which overthrew Samaria, shall even come unto, *quite up to Judah.* Then the Prophet suddenly changes the gender, and, as Scripture so often does, speaks of the one agent, the centre and impersonation of the coming evil, as sweeping on over Judah, *quite up to the gate of* his *people, quite up to Jerusalem.* He does not say here, whether Jerusalem would be taken[4]; and so, it seems likely that he speaks of a calamity short of excision. Of Israel's wounds only he here says, that they are *incurable;* he describes the wasting of even lesser places near or beyond Jerusalem, the flight of their inhabitants. Of the capital itself he is silent, except that the enemy *reached, touched, struck* against it, *quite up to it.* Probably, then, he is here describing the first visitation of God, when [5] *Sennacherib came up against all the fenced cities of Judah and took them*, but Jerusalem was spared. God's judgments come step by step, leaving time for repentance. The same enemy, although not the same king, came against Jerusalem who had wasted Samaria. Samaria was probably as strong as Jerusalem. Hezekiah prayed; God heard, the Assyrian army perished by miracle; Jerusalem was respited for 124 years.

10. *Tell it not in Gath.* Gath had probably now ceased to be; at least, to be of any account[6]. It shows how David's elegy lived in the hearts of Judah, that his words are used as a proverb, (just as we do now, in whose ears it is yearly read), when, as with us, its original application was probably lost. True, Gath, reduced itself, might rejoice the more maliciously over the sufferings of Judah. But David mentions it as a chief seat of Philistine strength[7]; now its strength was gone.

The blaspheming of the enemies of God is the sorest part of His chastisements. Whence David prays[8], *let not mine enemies exult over me;* and the sons of Korah, [9] *With a sword in my bones, mine enemies reproach me, while they say daily unto me, where* is *thy God?* and Ethan[10]; *Thou hast made all his enemies to rejoice. Remember, Lord, the reproach of Thy servant—wherewith Thine enemies have reproached, O Lord, wherewith they have reproached the footsteps of Thine anointed.* It is hard to part with home, with country, to see all desolate, which one ever loved. But far, far above all, is it, if, in the disgrace and desolation, God's honor seems to be injured. The Jewish people was then God's only home on earth. If *it* could be extinguished, who remained to honor Him? Victories over them seemed to their heathen neighbors to be victories over Him. He seemed to be dishonored without, because they had first dishonored Him within. Sore is it to the Christian, to see God's cause hindered, His kingdom narrowed, the Empire of Infidelity advanced. Sorer in one way, because he knows the price of souls, for whom Jesus died. But the world is now the Church's home. "The holy Church throughout all the world doth acknowledge Thee!" Then, it was girt in within a few miles of territory, and sad indeed it must have been to the Prophet, to see this too hemmed in. *Tell it not in Gath*, to the sons of those who, of old, defied God.

Weep not at all [lit. *weeping*[11], *weep not*].

[1] Jer. x. 19, xv. 18. נחלה in Nahum and Jer. xxx. 15. is exactly equivalent to the אנוש in Micah. In Jer. xxx. 12, אנוש לשברך stands parallel with it. Isaiah (xvii. 11) has כאב אנוש.

[2] עד in each of the three places.

[3] S. Jer.

[4] עד includes the whole country, *quite up to.* It does not necessarily include the place, *quite up to* which it reaches. It does not, probably, 2 Kings xviii. 8. See on Am. i. vol. i. p. 245.

[5] 2 Kings xviii. 13.

[6] See on Am. vi. 2. vol. i. p. 305.

[7] Parallel with Ashkelon.

[8] Ps. xxv. 2.

[9] Ps. xlii. 10.

[10] Ps. lxxxix. 42, 50.

[11] The conjecture of Reland (Pal. p. 534) "in Acco weep not," as if בכו were for בעכו, is against the Hebrew idiom, and one of the many abuses of Hebrew parallelism, as if Hebrew writers were tied down to exactness of parallelism, and because the Prophet mentions the name of a city in two clauses, he must in the third. The Prophet never would have used one of the commonest idioms in Hebrew, the emphatic use of the Inf. Abs. with the finite verb, unless he had meant it to be understood, as any one must understand the three Hebrew words, בכו אל תבכו. The sacred writers wrote to be understood. It is contrary to all principles of language, not to take a plain idiom in its plain sense. The Verss. Vulg. Aq. Symm. so render it. The LXX. (from a reading in which, οἱ Ἐνακείμ or οἱ ἐν Ἀχείμ, Reland made his οἱ ἐν Ἀχῷ) is full of blunders. They render also תבכו as if it were תבנו, ἀνοικοδομεῖτε; בבית, ἐξ οἴκου; לעפרה κατὰ γέλωτα. The ע is but seldom omitted in Hebrew. (Of the instances given by Gesenius, p. 976, בל for בעל is the Chaldee name of the idol; בי for בעי, uncertain, at most; למו for לעכו (Ps. xxvii. 8) wrong. There remains then in, Hebrew, only the single

Before CHRIST cir. 758–726.

11 Pass ye away, ‖thou †inhabitant of Saphir, having thy[t] shame naked: the inhabitant of ‖ Zaanan came not forth in the mourning of ‖ Beth-ezel; he shall receive of you his standing.

‖ Or, *thou that dwellest fairly.*
† Heb. *inhabitress.*
t Is. 20. 4. & 47. 2, 3. Jer. 13. 22. Nah. 3. 5.
‖ Or, *the country of flocks.*
‖ Or, *a place near.*

Weeping is the stillest expression of grief. We speak of "weeping in silence." Yet this also was too visible a token of grief. Their weeping would be the joy and laughter of God's enemies.

In the house of Aphrah, [probably, *In Beth-leaphrah*] *roll thyself in the dust* [better, as the text, *I roll myself in dust*[1]]. The Prophet chose unusual names, such as would associate themselves with the meanings which he wished to convey, so that thenceforth the name itself might recall the prophecy. As if we were to say, "In Ashe I roll myself in ashes."—There was an Aphrah near Jerusalem[2]. It is more likely that Micah should refer to this, than to the Ophrah in Benjamin[3]. He shewed them, in his own person, how they should mourn, retired out of sight and hidden, as it were, in the dust. "[4] Whatever grief your heart may have, let your face have no tears; go not forth, but, *in the house of dust,* sprinkle thyself with the ashes of its ruins."

All the places thenceforth spoken of were in Judah, whose sorrow and desolation are repeated in all. It is one varied history of sorrow. The names of her cities, whether in themselves called from some gifts of God, as Shaphir, (*beautiful;* we have *Fair*ford, *Fair*field, *Fair*burn, *Fair*light,) or contrariwise from some defect, Maroth, *Bitterness* (probably from brackish water) Achzib, *lying,* (doubtless from a winter-torrent which in summer failed) suggest, either in contrast or by themselves, some note of evil and woe. It is Judah's history in all, given in different traits; her "beauty" turned into shame; herself free neither to go forth nor to "abide;" looking for good and finding evil; the strong (Lachish) strong only to flee; like a brook that fails and deceives; her *inheritance* (Mareshah) inherited; herself, taking refuge in dens and caves of the earth, yet even there found, and bereft of her glory. Whence, in the end, without naming Judah, the Prophet sums up her sorrows with one call to mourning.

11. *Pass ye away* [lit. *Pass thou* (fem.) *away to* or *for yourselves*[5], disregarded by God and despised by man] *pass* the bounds of your land into captivity, *thou inhabitant of Shaphir, having thy shame naked,* [better, *in nakedness,* and *shame*[6]]. *Shaphir* [*fair*] was a village in Judah, between Eleutheropolis and Ashkelon[7]. There are still, in the Shephelah, two villages called Sawafir[8]. It, once *fair,* should now go forth in the disgrace and dishonor with which captives were led away.

The inhabitants of Zaanan came not forth. Zaanan (*abounding in flocks*) was probably the same as Zenan of Judah, which lay in the Shephēlah[9]. It, which formerly *went forth*[10] in pastoral gladness with the multitude of its flocks, shall now shrink into itself for fear.

The mourning of Beth-Ezel [lit. *house of root,* firmly rooted] *shall take from you its standing*[11]. It too cannot help itself, much less be a stay to others. They who have

pronunciation of Amos נשקה for נשקעה viii. 8. See ab. p. 216. Robinson observes, "The Semitic letter ע in particular, so unpronounceable by other nations, has a remarkable tenacity. Of the very many Hebrew names, containing this letter, which still survive in Arabic, our lists exhibit only two or three in which it has been dropped; and perhaps none in which it has been exchanged for another letter." (i. 255. n. 2.) His only instances are Jib for Gibeon (where the whole syllable has been dropped) i. 456; Jelbon for Gilboa (ii. 316); Yafa for Yaphia Josh. xix. 12, (doubtful) ii. 342; and Endor (which I doubt) ii. 360. Anyhow they are but three names, in which, in the transfer into another though cognate language, ע has been dropped at the end, and one at the beginning of a word, none in the middle. In fact also Acco (Acre) was probably never in the possession of Israel. It is only mentioned in the Old Testament, to say that *Asher did not drive out* its *inhabitants* (Judg. i. 31). This interpretation which has become popular, 1) violates the Hebrew idiom; 2) implies a very improbable omission of a "tenacious letter;" 3) is historically unnatural, in that the Prophet would thus forbid Judah to weep in a city where there were none even of Israel. Yet of late, it has been followed by Hitz. Maur. Umbreit, Ewald, thought probable by Gesenius and Winer, and adopted even by Dr. Henderson.

1 The Kethib התפלשתי is, as usual, to be preferred to the correction, the Kri, התפלשי.

2 R. Tanchum of Jerusalem, here.

3 Josh. xviii. 23, 1 Sam. xiii 17.

4 S. Jer. Rup.

5 עברי לכם.

6 The construction, עריה בשת, is like ענוה צדק *meekness, righteousness,* Ps. xlv. 5. בשת is the quality, *shame.*

7 Onom.

8 Scholz, Reisen, p. 255. Robinson, ii. 34, says, "There are three villages of this name near each other." "There is yet a village Suaphir, two hours S. E. of Ashdod." Schwartz (of Jerusalem) Das Heil. Land, p. 87. "a Sapheria one hour N. W. of Lod." [Lydda] (Ib. p. 105.)

9 Josh. xv. 27, coll. 33. "There is a village Zanabra, 1. hour S. E. of Moresha." Schwartz, 74.

10 צאן, whence צאנן, is itself probably connected with יצא.

11 I have preferred the division of the Syr. and Vulg. because, if joined as in the E. V. the last clause has no definite subject, and there is no allusion to the meaning of Beth haezel.

Before CHRIST cir. 750.

‖ Or, *was grieved.*
u Amos 3. 6.

12 For the inhabitant of
Maroth ‖ waited carefully
for good: but [u] evil came
down from the LORD unto
the gate of Jerusalem.
13 O thou inhabitant of
[x] Lachish, bind the chariot
to the swift beast: she *is*
the beginning of the sin to
the daughter of Zion: for
the transgressions of Israel
were found in thee.

Before CHRIST cir. 750.

x 2 Kings 18. 14, 17.

been wont to go forth in fullness, shall not go forth then, and they who abide, strong though they be, shall not furnish an abiding place. Neither in going out nor in remaining, shall anything be secure then.

12. *For the inhabitant of Maroth* [*bitterness*] *waited carefully for good.* She *waited carefully*[1] for the good which God gives, not for the Good which God *is*. She looked, longed for, good, as men do; but therewith her longing ended. She longed for it, amid her own evil, which brought God's judgments upon her. *Maroth* is mentioned here only in Holy Scripture, and has not been identified. It too was probably selected for its meaning. *The inhabitant of bitternesses, she,* to whom *bitternesses,* or, it may be, *rebellions*[2], were as the home in which she dwelt, which ever encircled her, in which she reposed, wherein she spent her life, *waited for good!* Strange contradiction! yet a contradiction, which the whole un-Christian world is continually enacting; nay, from which Christians have often to be awakened, to look for good to themselves, nay, to pray for temporal good, while living in bitternesses, bitter ways, displeasing to God. The words are calculated to be a religious proverb. "Living in sin," as we say, *dwelling in bitternesses, she looked for good! Bitternesses!* for it is[3] *an evil* thing *and bitter, that thou hast forsaken the Lord thy God, and that My fear is not in thee.*

But [*For*] *evil came down from the Lord unto the gate of Jerusalem.* It came, like the brimstone and fire which God rained upon Sodom and Gomorrah, but as yet *to the gate of Jerusalem,* not upon itself. "[4] Evil came down upon them from the Lord, i. e. *I* was grieved, *I* chastened, *I* brought the Assyrian upon them, and from *My* anger came this affliction upon them. But it was removed, *My* Hand prevailing and marvelously rescuing those who worshiped My Majesty. For the trouble shall *come to the gate.* But we know that Rabshakeh, with many horsemen, came to Jerusalem and all-but touched the gates. But he took it not. For in one night the Assyrian was consumed." The two *for's* are seemingly co-ordinate, and assign the reasons of the foreannounced evils[5], on man's part and on God's. On man's, in that he looked for what could not so come, good: on God's, in that evil, which alone could be looked for, which, amid man's evil, could alone be good for man, came from Him. Losing the true Good, man lost all other good, and dwelling in the bitterness of sin and provocation, he dwelt indeed in bitterness of trouble.

O thou inhabitant of Lachish, bind the chariot to the swift beast [*steed.*] Lachish was always a strong city, as its name probably denoted, (probably "compact[6].") It was one of the royal cities of the Amorites, and its king one of the five, who went out to battle with Joshua[7]. It lay in the low country, Shephēlah, of Judah[8], between Adoraim and Azekah[9], 7 Roman miles S. of Eleutheropolis[10], and so, probably, close to the hill-country, although on the plain; partaking perhaps of the advantages of both. Rehoboam fortified it. Amaziah fled to it from the conspiracy at Jerusalem[11], as a place of strength. It, with Azekah, alone remained, when Nebuchadnezzar had taken the rest, just before the capture of Jerusalem[12]. When Sennacherib took *all the defenced cities of Judah,* it seems to have been his last and proudest conquest, for from it he sent his contemptuous message to Hezekiah[13]. The whole power of the great king seems to have

1 חול is used in the sense of יחל, Gen. viii. 10, and in Hif. Jud. iii. 25, in Pil. Job xxvi. 15, and in Hithpal. Ps. xxxvii. 7. Here too it has the construction of יחל with ל, as it has in Job xxvi, and as it has not in the sense of the E. M. "was grieved." Such an idiom as חול לטוב, "to be in pain for (lost) good," does not occur in Hebrew, and would be equivocal, since the idiom *is* used for "longed for (expected) good." חול also, "grieved," occurs only Jer. v. 3. Used of the "writhing" of the birth-pangs, it is joined with no preposition; in the sense "feared," it is joined only with the מלפני, מן, מפני, of the object of fear.

2 מרתים from מרה occurs Jer. 1. 21.

3 Jer. ii. 19.

4 S. Cyr.

5 3–11.

6 from the Arab. The bilitteral root לך seems to have been an onomato-poet. In Arabic the sense of "striking" occurs in לכז, לכץ, לכע, לכם, לכך, לכא, לכת, לכח, לכד. Thence the idea of parts "impinging on one another," "cleaving close to," in לכא, לכת, לכד, [griping, לכז,] לכי; "cleaving close together," "compact," in לכד, לכע, לכך. These senses account for all the Arabic words, beginning with לך. The only Hebrew roots, so beginning, are לכד, took, and לכיש.

7 Josh. x. 3.

8 Ib. xv. 33. 39.

9 2 Chr. xi. 9.

10 Onom.

11 2 Kgs xiv. 19.

12 Jer. xxxiv. 7.

13 Is. xxxvi. 1, 2.

Before CHRIST cir. 750.

14 Therefore shalt thou
[y] give presents ‖ to More-
sheth-gath: the houses
of ‖ [z] Achzib *shall be*
a lie to the kings of
Israel.

[y] 2 Sam. 8. 2. 2 Kings 18. 14, 15, 16.

‖ Or, *for*.

Before CHRIST cir. 750.

‖ That is, *a lie*.

[z] Josh. 15. 44.

---

been called forth to take this stronghold. The Assyrian bas-reliefs, the record of the conquests of Sennacherib, if (as the accompanying inscription is deciphered), they represent the taking of Lachish, exhibit it as "[1] a city of great extent and importance, defended by double walls with battlements and towers, and by fortified out-works. In no other sculptures were so many armed warriors drawn up in array against a besieged city. Against the fortifications had been thrown up as many as ten banks or mounts compactly built,—and seven battering-rams had already been rolled up against the walls." Its situation, on the extremity probably of the plain, fitted it for a dépôt of cavalry. *The swift steeds* [2], to which it was bidden to bind the chariot, are mentioned as part of the magnificence of Solomon, as distinct from his ordinary horses [3]. They were used by the posts of the king of Persia [4]. They were doubtless part of the strength of the kings of Judah, the cavalry in which their statesmen trusted, instead of God. Now, its swift horses in which it prided itself should avail but to flee. Probably, it is an ideal picture. Lachish is bidden to bind its chariots to horses of the utmost speed, which should carry them far away, if their strength were equal to their swiftness. It had great need; for it was subjected under Sennacherib to the consequences of Assyrian conquest. If the Assyrian accounts relate to its capture, impalement and flaying alive [5] were among the tortures of the captive-people; and awfully did Sennacherib, in his pride, avenge the sins against God Whom he disbelieved.

She is *the beginning of the sin to the daughter of Zion.* "[6] She was at the gate through which the *transgressions of Israel* flooded Judah." How she came first to apostatise and to be the infectress of Judah, Scripture does not tell us [7]. She scarcely bordered on Philistia; Jerusalem lay between her and Israel. But the course of sin follows no geographical lines. It was the greater sin to Lachish that she, locally so far removed from Israel's sin, was the first to import into Judah the idolatries of Israel. Scripture does not say, what seduced Lachish herself, whether the pride of military strength, or her importance, or commercial intercourse, for her *swift steeds*, with Egypt, the common parent of Israel's and her sin. Scripture does not give the genealogy of her sin, but stamps her as the heresiarch of Judah. We know the fact from this place only, that she, apparently so removed from the occasion of sin, became, like the propagators of heresy, the authoress of evil, the cause of countless loss of souls. *Beginning of sin to*—, what a world of evil lies in the three [8] words!

14. *Therefore shalt thou give* [*bridal*] *presents to Moresheth Gath. Therefore!* since Judah had so become a partaker of Israel's sins, she had broken the covenant, whereby God had given her the land of the Heathen, and she should part with it to aliens. The *bridal presents*, lit. *the dismissals*, were the dowry [9] with which the father *sent away* [10] his daughter, to belong to another, her *lord* [11] or husband, never more to return. *Moresheth*, [lit. *inheritance*,] *the inheritance* which God gave her, was to be parted with; she was to be laden [12] with gifts to the enemy. Judah should part with her, and her own treasure also.

The houses of Achzib shall be a lie. Achzib, so called probably from *a winter brook* (achzab) was to become what its name imported, a resource which should fail just in the time of need, as the winter brooks in the drought of summer. [13] *Wilt Thou be unto me as a failing brook, waters which are not sure?* This Achzib, which is recounted between Keilah and Mareshah [14], was probably one of the oldest towns of Palestine, being mentioned in the history of the Patriarch Judah [15]. After having survived about 1000 years, it should, in time of need, fail. *The kings of Israel* are here the kings of Judah. When this prophecy was to be accomplished, the ten tribes would have ceased to have any political existence, the remnant in their own land would have no head to look to, except the line of David,

[1] Layard, Nin. and Bab. p. 149.

[2] The רכש was undoubtedly a swift horse, probably from its rapid striking of the earth. (Arab.) The word is used of riding horses in Syr. Chald. Talm. Nasor. see Ges. "horses of good breed and young," R. Jonah in Kim. Ib.

[3] 1 Kgs iv. 28. Eng. (v. 8. Heb.)

[4] Esther viii. 10, 14.

[5] Layard, Ib. and 150.

[6] S. Jer.

[7] Rosenm. and others from him, by mistake, attribute it to a supposed situation of Lachish, "lying on the frontier of" Israel; whereas it was part of the chain of fortified cities furthest removed from Israel on the S. W.

[8] ראשית חטאת ל.

[9] 1 Kgs ix. 16. [10] Jud. xii. 9. [11] בעל.

[12] שלוחים על מורשת גת lit. "bridal presents on Moresheth Gath." Hitzig thinks that in מורשת there is an allusion to כארשת, "espoused;" but this would be a contradictory image, since the bridal-presents were given in espousing, not to one already espoused, and they were to be given not to Gath but to the invader.

[13] Jer. xv. 18. [14] Josh. xv. 44.

[15] in the unlengthened form כזיב Gen. xxxviii. 5.

Before CHRIST cir. 750.

15 Yet will I bring
an heir unto thee, O
inhabitant of [a]Mare-
shah: ‖he shall come
unto [b]Adullam the glory
of Israel.
16 Make thee [c]bald,
and poll thee for thy [d]deli-

[a] Josh. 15. 44.
‖ Or, *the glory of Israel shall come, &c.*

Before CHRIST cir. 750.

[b] 2 Chr. 11. 7.
[c] Job 1. 20. Isai. 15. 2. & 22. 12. Jer. 7. 29. & 16. 6. & 47. 5. & 48. 37.
[d] Lam. 4. 5.

whose good kings had a care for them. Micah then, having prophesied the utter destruction of Samaria, speaks in accordance with the state of things which he foresaw and foretold[1].

15. *Yet will I bring an heir* [*the heir*[2], him whom God had appointed to be *the heir*, Sennacherib] *unto thee, O inhabitant of Mareshah. Mareshah*, (as the original form of its name denotes[3],) lay on the summit of a hill. "Its ruins only were still seen," in the time of Eusebius and S. Jerome, "in the second mile from Eleutheropolis[4]." "[5]Foundations still remain on the south-eastern part of the remarkable Tell, south of Beth-Jibrin." Rehoboam fortified it also[6]. Zerah the Æthiopian had *come to*[7] it, probably to besiege it, when Asa met him, and *God smote the Æthiopians before* him, *in the valley of Zephathah* thereat. In the wars of the Maccabees, it was in the hands of the Edomites[8]. Its capture and that of Adora are mentioned[9] as the last act of the war, before the Edomites submitted to John Hyrcanus, and were incorporated in Israel. It was a powerful city[10], when the Parthians took it. As Micah writes the name, it looked nearer to the word "inheritance[11]." *Mareshah* (*inheritance*) shall yet have *the heir* of God's appointment, the enemy. It shall not inherit the land, as promised to the faithful, but shall itself be inherited, its people dispossessed. While it, (and so also the soul now) held fast to God, they were the heritage of the Lord, by His gifts and grace; when, of their own free-will, those, once God's heritage, become slaves of sin, they passed and still pass, against their will, into the possession of another master, the Assyrian or Satan.

He [i. e. the heir, the enemy] *shall come unto Adullam, the glory of Israel*[12]; i. e. he who shall dispossess Mareshah, *shall come quite unto Adullam*, where, as in a place of safety, *the glory of Israel*, all in which she gloried, should be laid up. Adullam was a very ancient city, being mentioned in the history of the patriarch Judah[13], a royal city[14]. It too lay in the Shephelah[15]; it was said to be 10[16] or 12[17] miles East of Eleutheropolis; but for this, there seems to be scarcely place in the Shephelah. It was one of the 15 cities fortified by Rehoboam[18]; one of the 16 towns, in which (with their dependent villages) Judah settled after the captivity[19]. It contained the whole army of Judas Maccabæus[20]. Like Lachish, it had probably the double advantages of the neighborhood of the hills and of the plain, seated perhaps at the roots of the hills, since near it doubtless was the large *cave of Adullam* named from it. The line of caves, fit for human habitation, which extended from Eleutheropolis to Petra[21], began Westward of it. "[22]The valley which runs up from Eleutheropolis Eastward, is full of large caves; some would hold thousands of men. They are very extensive, and some of them had evidently been inhabited." "[22]The outer chamber of one cavern was 270 feet long by 126 wide; and behind this were recesses and galleries, probably leading to other chambers which we could not explore. The massive roof was supported by misshaped pieces of the native limestone left for that purpose, and at some places was domed quite through to the surface, admitting both light and air by the roof." The name of *Adullam* suggested the memory of that cave, the refuge of the Patriarch David, the first of their line of kings, in extreme isolation and peril of his life. Thither, the refuge now of the remaining *glory of Israel*, its wealth, its trust, its boast,—the foe should come. And so there only remained one common dirge for all.

16. *Make thee bald, poll* [lit. *shear*[23]] *thee for thy delicate children.* Some special ways of cutting the hair were forbidden to the Israelites, as being idolatrous customs, such as the rounding the hair in front, cutting it away from the temples[24], or between the eyes[25]. All shearing of the hair was not forbidden[26]; indeed to the Nazarite it was commanded, at the close of his vow. The removal of that chief ornament of the countenance was a natural expression of grief, which revolts at all personal appearance. It belonged, not to idolatry, but to nature[27]. *Thy*

[1] See ab. Introd. p. 5. [2] הירש.
[3] מראשה (from ראש) Jos. xv. 44. [4] Onom.
[5] Rob. ii. 67, 8. [6] 2 Chr. xi. 8. [7] Ib. xiv. 9. sqq.
[8] Jos. Ant. xii. 8. 6. [9] Ib. xiii. 9. 1. [10] Ib. xiv. 13. 9.
[11] מרשה like מורשה. In the Chron. it is spelled as in Micah.
[12] The Eng. Marg. has, in the same general sense, *unto Adullam shall come the glory of Israel.*
[13] Gen. xxxviii. 1. 12. 20. [14] Jos. xii. 15.
[15] Ib. xv. 35. [16] Eus. [17] S. Jer. [18] 2 Chr. xi. 7.
[19] Neh. xi. 30. [20] Macc. xii. 38.
[21] see S. Jer. ab. p. 235.
[22] Rev. G. Williams, MS. letter.
[23] see on Am. viii. 10. vol. i. p. 327.
[24] Lev. xix. 27. against Arab idolatry. See Herod. iii. 8. [25] Deut. xiv. 1. [26] as Hitzig says.
[27] See Job i. 20, early Greece, (Il. 23, 46, 135 sqq. Alcestis 429. non-Egyptian nations, (Herod. ii. 36.) Persians, (Ib. ix. 24.) Scythians, (Ib. iv. 71.) Thessalians, Macedonians (Plut. Pelop. 34.)

Before CHRIST cir. 750.

cate children; enlarge thy baldness as the eagle; for they are gone into captivity from thee.

delicate children. The change was the more bitter for those tended and brought up delicately. Moses from the first spake of special miseries which should fall on *the tender and very delicate. Enlarge thy baldness;* outdo in grief what others do; for the cause of thy grief is more than that of others. The point of comparison in *the Eagle* might either be the actual baldness of the head, or its moulting. If it were the baldness of the head, the word translated *eagle*[1], although mostly used of the Eagle itself, might here comprehend the Vulture[2]. For entire baldness is so marked a feature in the vulture, whereas the "bald-headed Eagle" was probably not a bird of Palestine[3]. On the other hand, David, who lived so long among the rocks of Palestine, and Isaiah seem to have known of effects of moulting upon the *Eagle* in producing, (although in a less degree than in other birds,) a temporary diminution of strength, which have not in modern times been commonly observed. For David says[4], *Thou shalt renew, like the eagle, thy youth,* which speaks of fresh strength after temporary weakness; and Isaiah[5], *They that trust in the Lord shall put forth*[6] *fresh strength; they shall put forth pinion-feathers*[7] *like eagles,* comparing the fresh strength which should succeed to that which was gone, to the eagle's recovering its strong pinion-feathers. Bochart however says unhesitatingly, "[8]At the beginning of spring, the rapacious birds are subject to shedding of their feathers which we call moulting." If this be so, the comparison is yet more vivid. For the baldness of the vulture belongs to

[1] The etymology, (Arab. nasara "tore with the beak,") belongs rather to the eagle with its sharp, than to the vulture with its long, piercing beak. (The Kamoos, Freytag's authority for rendering *nasr vulture,* only says "a bird," adding that it is the name of "the constellation," i. e. Aquila. In Ulug Begh Tab. Stell. 49, 50. the okab and the *nasr* both occur as names of the constellation. Kazwini in Ideler [Sternkunde p. 385] says that the 'okab is three stars of the form of the flying nasr.) Leo Afr. [Descr. Afr. ix. 56.] says that "the largest species of eagle is called Nesir." 2) Unless *nesher* be the golden Eagle, there is no Hebrew name for it, whereas it is still a bird of Palestine, and smaller eagles are mentioned in the same verse, Lev. xi. 13; viz. *the ossifrage,* פרס, and *the black eagle,* עזניה, so called from its strength, like the valeria, of which Pliny says, "the melanætos or valeria, least in size, remarkable for strength, blackish in color." x. 3. The same list of unclean birds contains also the *vulture,* דיה, Deut. xiv. 13, (as it must be, being a gregarious bird, Is. xxxiv. 15.) in its different species; (Deut. ib.) *the gier-eagle,* (i. e. Geyer) [vulture] eagle, gypaetos, or vultur percnopterus, (Hasselquist, Forskal, Shaw, Bruce in Savigny p. 77.) partaking of the character of both, (רחם Lev. xi. 18. Deut. xiv. 17.) together with the *falcon* (דאה Lev. xi. 14.) and *hawk,* with its subordinate species, (נץ למינהו) Lev. xi. 18. Deut. xiv. 15.

[2] In this case, *nesher,* being a name taken from a quality common to birds of prey, might at once be a generic term, corresponding to the modern term, (aves) *rapaces,* and might also designate what all account the king of birds. Its Greek name ἀετὸς is doubtless the Hebrew, עיט, (Bochart ii. 2. p. 170.) a generic name for birds of prey. The Gypaetos forms a link between the vulture and the eagle. Seeing the prey afar, lofty flight out of human sight, strength of pinion, building nests in the rocks, attributed in H. Scr. to the *nesher,* belong also to the vulture. The feeding on dead bodies belongs especially to the vulture, although affirmed of eagles also if the body be not decayed. The Arabic *nasr* seems to comprise the vulture also. See in Boch. ii. 27. T. iii. p. 79 sqq. Leipz. Savigny says, "Nisr is a generic name which has always been translated Aquila, but now the people and Arabic naturalists use it to designate the great vulture." (Descr. de l'Eg. i. 73.) and of 'Okab, "'Okab is a generic name, but it becomes specific for the small black eagle which, properly speaking, is the 'Okâb." (Ib. 85.)

[3] "The only 'bald-headed Eagle' is an American rather than an European species. Though it is not exclusively of the new world, it is yet rarely seen in the old, and then chiefly in the Northern latitudes." Dr. Rolleston, MS. letter, who kindly guided me to the modern authorities quoted above.

[4] Ps. ciii. 5.

[5] xl. 31.

[6] חלף, יחליפו כח to *succeed to* (as in Arab. whence Chaliph) is used of the fresh shoots of grass, (Ps. xc. 5, 6.) of the stump of a felled tree, putting forth fresh suckers, Job xiv. 7. then, causatively, of the *putting forth fresh strength,* in contrast with the exhaustion and utter stumbling of the young and strong. In Arab. conj. iv. one of its many special meanings is "put forth fresh feathers" after moulting.

[7] Bochart ii. 1. T. ii. p. 745. So the LXX *πτεροφυήσουσιν.* S. Jer. assument pennas. So also Syr. Saad. חעלה is used of bringing flesh on the bones, (Ez. xxxvii. 6.) putting on the figures of Cherubim on the veil, (2 Chr. iii. 14.) gold on a shield, (1 Kgs x. 17.) dress, 2 Sam. i. 24. Am. viii. 10. The E. V. (lit. "they shall ascend a pinion [i. e. with a pinion] like eagles,") would not be too bold, but for the correspondence of Ps. ciii. 5. The word אבר, rendered *wings* E. V., is, in Ezek. xvii. 3, distinguished from the *wing* itself and the *plumage;* as is אברה Job xxxix. 13. In Ps. lxviii. 14. אברות must be the pinion-feathers, not the pinions; and so אברה in Ps. xci. 4. In Job xxxix. 26, the denom. יאבר might mean the same, (Boch. Ib.) the first hemistich describing the acquiring the new feathers, the 2d the emigration of the hawks. The radical meaning of אבר is strength.

[8] Bochart, Hieroz. ii. 1. p. 744, 5. The Kamoos quotes, among the 10 characteristics of the *Anook,* (the Rachma, Heb. רחם), "It flies in the time of shedding its feathers and is not imperilled in its young plumage, &c." Boch. ii. 26. T. iii. p. 57. Demetrius Const. in his Ἱερακοσοφ. gives remedies for making fresh feathers put forth fast, (c. 17.) and grow quick, (c. 18.) and against diseases in moulting, (c. 32.) showing that birds of prey are liable to the same law as other birds. (See Buffon, Hist. Nat. i. 44, 5. 69, 70.) Cuvier says, "In certain states of moulting, you see in the plumage [of the royal eagle] the white at the base of the feathers. It is then called Falco Canadensis." (Règne Animal.) To this Grey adds, that the names Melanaetos and Mogilnik (in Gmelin) only describe it when moulting. (Cuvier Anim. Kingd. vi. 33.) So then the change at moulting is so great, that the royal eagle, when moulting, has been thought to be four different species.

Before CHRIST cir. 730.

CHAPTER II.

1 *Against oppression.* 4 *A lamentation.* 7 *A reproof of injustice and idolatry.* 12 *A promise of restoring Jacob.*

WOE to them [a] that de-
vise iniquity, and
[b] work evil upon their
beds! when the morning is
light, they practise it, be-

Before CHRIST cir. 730.

[a] Hos. 7. 6.
[b] Ps. 36. 4.

its matured strength, and could only be an external likeness. The moulting of the eagle involves some degree of weakness, with which he compares Judah's mournful and weak condition amid the loss of their children, gone into captivity[1].

Thus closes the first general portion of the prophecy. The people had cast aside its own Glory, God; now its sons, its pride and its trust, shall go away from it.

"[2] The eagle, laying aside its old feathers and taking new, is a symbol of penitence and of the penitents who lay aside their former evil habits, and become other and new men. True, but rare form of penitence!" S. Gregory the Great thus applies this to the siege of Rome by the Lombards. "[3] That happened to her which we know to have been foretold of Judea by the Prophet, *enlarge thy baldness like the eagle.* For baldness befalls man in the head only, but the eagle in its whole body; for, when it is very old, its feathers and pinions fall from all its body. She lost her feathers, who lost her people. Her pinions too fell out, with which she was wont to fly to the prey; for all her mighty men, through whom she plundered others, perished. But this which we speak of, the breaking to pieces of the city of Rome, we know has been done in all the cities of the world. Some were desolated by pestilence, others devoured by the sword, others racked by famine, others swallowed by earthquakes. Despise we them with our whole heart, at least, when brought to nought; at least with the end of the world, let us end our eagerness after the world. Follow we, wherein we can, the deeds of the good." One whose commentaries S. Jerome had read, thus applies this verse to the whole human race. "O soul of man! O city, once the mother of saints, which wast formerly in Paradise, and didst enjoy the delights of different trees, and wast adorned most beautifully, now being cast down from thy place aloft, and brought down unto Babylon, and come into a place of captivity, and having lost thy glory, make thee bald and take the habit of a penitent; and thou who didst fly aloft like an eagle, mourn thy sons, thy offspring, which from thee is led captive."

[1] In Greek also the loss of wealth by pillage is compared to moulting, not in Aristoph. Av. 284-6. only, but in Philostratus, "he moults as to the wealth," p. 273.
[2] Lap.
[3] in Ezek. Hom. 18, fin. L.
[4] Dion.
[5] Rup. Rib.

CHAP. II. The Prophet had declared that evil should come down on Samaria and Jerusalem for their sins. He had pronounced them sinners against God; he now speaks of their hard unlovingness toward man, as our Blessed Lord in the Gospel speaks of sins against Himself in His members, as the ground of the condemnation of the wicked. The time of warning is past. He speaks as in the person of the Judge, declaring the righteous judgments of God, pronouncing sentence on the hardened, but blessing on those who follow Christ. The sins thus visited were done with a high hand; first, with forethought:

1. *Woe*, all woe, woe from God; "[4] the woe of temporal captivity; and, unless ye repent, the woe of eternal damnation, hangeth *over* you." *Woe to them that devise iniquity.* They *devise* it, "[5] they are not led into it by others, but invent it out of their own hearts." They plot and forecast and fulfill it even in thought, before it comes to act. *And work evil upon their beds.* Thoughts and imaginations of evil are works of the soul[6]. *Upon their beds*[7], which ought to be the place of holy thought, and of communing with their own hearts and with God[8]. Stillness must be filled with thought, good or bad; if not with good, then with bad. The chamber, if not the sanctuary of holy thoughts, is filled with unholy purposes and imaginations. Man's last and first thoughts, if not of good, are especially of vanity and evil. The Psalmist says[9], *Lord, have I not remembered Thee in my bed, and thought upon Thee when I was waking?* These men thought of sin on their bed, and did it on waking. *When the morning is light*, lit. *in the light of the morning*, i. e. instantly, shamelessly, not shrinking from the light of day, not ignorantly, but knowingly, deliberately, in full light. Nor again through infirmity, but in the wantonness of might, *because it is in the power of their hand*[10], as, of old, God said[11], *This they begin to do, and now nothing will be restrained from them which they have imagined to do.* "[12] Impiously mighty, and mighty in impiety."

[13] See the need of the daily prayer, "Vouchsafe, O Lord, to keep us this day without sin;" and "Almighty God, Who hast brought

[6] Ps. lviii. 2.
[7] See Ps. xxxvi. 4.
[8] Ib. iv. 4.
[9] lxiii. 6.
[10] This phrase can have no other meaning, Gen. xxxi. 29. Prov. iii. 27; nor the corresponding phrase with the negative, Deut. xxviii. 32. Neh. v. 5.
[11] Gen. xi. 6.
[12] Rup.
[13] from lap.

Before CHRIST cir. 730.

cause [c] it is in the power of
their hand.
2 And they covet [d] fields,
and take *them* by violence;
and houses, and take *them*
away: so they || oppress a
man and his house, even a
man and his heritage.
3 Therefore thus saith
the Lord; Behold, against
[e] this family do I devise an
evil, from which ye shall

c Gen. 31. 29.
d Isai. 5. 8.
|| Or, *defraud.*
e Jer. 8. 3.

Before CHRIST cir. 730.

us to the beginning of this day, defend us in the same by Thy mighty power, that we may fall into no sin, &c." The illusions of the night, if such be permitted, have no power against the prayer of the morning.

2. *And they covet fields and take* them *by violence,* [*rend* them *away*] *and houses, and take* them *away.* Still, first they sin in heart, then in act. And yet, with them, to covet and to rob, to desire and to take, are the same. They were prompt, instantaneous, without a scruple, in violence. So soon as they coveted, they took [1]. Desired, acquired! Coveted, robbed! "They saw, they coveted, they took," had been their past history. They did violence, not to one only, but, touched with no mercy, to whole families, their little ones also; *they oppressed a man and his house.* They spoiled not goods only, but life, *a man and his inheritance;* destroying him by false accusations or violence and so seizing upon his inheritance [2]. Thus Ahab first coveted Naboth's vineyard, then, through Jezebel, slew him; and "[3] they *who devoured widow's houses,* did at the last plot by night against Him of Whom they said, *Come, let us kill Him, and the inheritance shall be our's; and in the morning, they practiced it,* leading Him away to Pilate." "[4] Who of us desires not the villas of this world, forgetful of the possessions of Paradise? You see men join field to field, and fence to fence. Whole places suffice not to the tiny frame of one man." "[5] Such is the fire of concupiscence, raging within, that, as those seized by burning fevers cannot rest, no bed suffices them, so no houses or fields content these. Yet no more than seven feet of earth will suffice them soon. [6] Death only owns, how small the frame of man."

3. Such had been their habitual doings. They had done all this, he says, as one continuous act, up to that time. They were habitually *devisers of iniquity, doers of evil* [7]. It was ever-renewed. By night they sinned in heart and thought; by day, in act. And so he speaks of it in the present. *They do it* [8]. But, although renewed in fresh acts, it was one unbroken course of acting. And so he also uses the form, in which the Hebrews spoke of uninterrupted habits, *They have coveted, they have robbed, they have taken* [9]. Now came God's part.

Therefore, thus saith the Lord, since they oppress whole families, *behold* I will set Myself *against this* whole *family* [10]; since they *devise iniquity, behold I* too, Myself, by Myself, in My own Person, *am devising.* Very awful is it, that Almighty God sets His own Infinite Wisdom against the devices of man and employs it fittingly to punish. "I am devising no common punishment, but one to bow them down without escape; *an evil from which* —He turns suddenly to them, *ye shall not remove your necks, neither shall ye go haughtily.*" "[5] Pride then was the source of that boundless covetousness," since it was pride which was to be bowed down in punishment. The punishment is proportioned to the sin. They had done all this in pride; they should have the liberty and self-will wherein they had wantoned, tamed or taken from them. Like animals with a heavy yoke upon them, they should live in disgraced slavery. The ten tribes were never able to *withdraw their necks* from the yoke. From the two tribes God removed it after the 70 years. But the same sins against the love of God and man brought on the same punishment. Our Lord again spake the woe against their covetousness [11]. It still shut them out from the service of God, or from receiving Him, their Redeemer. They still *spoiled the goods* [12] of their brethren. In the last dreadful siege, "[13] there were insatiable longings for plunder, searching-out of the houses of the rich; murder of men and insults of women were enacted as sports; they drank down what they had spoiled, with blood." And so the prophecy was for the third time fulfilled. They who withdraw from Christ's easy yoke of obedience shall not remove from the yoke of punishment; they who, through pride, will not bow down their necks, but *make* them *stiff,* shall be bent low, that they *go not* upright or *haughtily* any more. [14] *The Lord alone shall be exalted in that Day. For it is an evil time.* Perhaps he gives a more special meaning to

1 The force of חמדו ונזלו.

2 Comp. the woes, Is. v. 7. on oppression; 8 covetousness.

3 Theoph. 4 S. Jer. 5 Rib.

6 Juv. Sat. x. 172, 3. 7 חשבי און ,פעלי רע.

8 יעשוה. 9 חמדו גזלו נשאו.

10 as in Am. iii. 1. vol. i. p. 270.

11 S. Luke xvi. 13, 14. xi. 39. S. Matt. xxiii. 14, 23, 25. S. Mark xii. 40.

12 Heb. x. 34.

13 Jos. B. J. iv. 9. 10. add v. 1. 14 Is. ii. 11.

Before CHRIST cir. 730.

not remove your necks;
neither shall ye go haughtily: [f] for this time *is* evil.
4 ¶ In that day shall
one [g] take up a parable
against you, and [h] lament
† with a doleful lamenta-
tion, *and* say, We be utterly spoiled: [i] he hath
changed the portion of my
people: how hath he re-
moved *it* from me! || turn-
ing away he hath divided
our fields.

f Amos 5. 13. Eph. 5. 16.
g Hab. 2. 6.
h 2 Sam. 1. 17.
† Heb. *with a lamentation of lamentations.*
i ch. 1. 15.
|| Or, *instead of restoring.*

the words of Amos[1], that *a time of* moral *evil* will be, or will end in, *a time*, full of *evil*, i. e. of sorest calamity.

4. *In that day shall one take up a parable against you.* The *mashal* or *likeness* may, in itself, be any speech in which one thing is likened to another; 1) "figured speech," 2) "proverb," and, since such proverbs were often sharp sayings against others, 3) "taunting figurative speech." But of the person himself it is always said, he *is made*, *becomes a proverb*[2]. To *take up* or *utter* such a speech *against* one, is, elsewhere, followed by the speech itself; [3] *Thou shalt take up this parable against the king of Babylon, and say, &c.* [4] *Shall not all these take up a parable against him, and say, &c.* Although then the name of the Jews has passed into *a proverb of reproach*[5], this is not contained here. The parable here must be the same as the *doleful lamentation*, or dirge, which follows. No mockery is more cutting or fiendish, than to repeat in jest words by which one bemoans himself. The dirge which Israel should use of themselves in sorrow, the enemy shall take up in derision, as Satan does doubtless the self-condemnation of the damned. "[6] Men do any evil, undergo any peril, to avoid shame. God brings before us that deepest and eternal shame," *the shame and everlasting contempt*, in presence of Himself and angels and devils and the good[7], that we may avoid shame by avoiding evil.

And lament with a doleful lamentation. The words in Hebrew are varied inflections of a word imitating the sounds of woe. It is the voice of woe in all languages, because the voice of nature. *Shall wail a wail of woe*[8], It is the funeral dirge over the dead[9], or of the living doomed to die[10]; it is sometimes the measured mourning of those employed to call forth sorrow[11], or mourning generally[12]. Among such elegies, are still Zion-songs[13], (elegies over the ruin of Zion,) and mournings for the dead[14]. The word *woe* is thrice[15] repeated in Hebrew, in different forms, according to that solemn way, in which the extremest good or evil is spoken of; the threefold blessing, morning and evening, with the thrice-repeated name of God[16], impressing upon them the mystery which developed itself, as the Divinity of the Messiah and the personal agency of the Holy Spirit were unfolded to them. The dirge which follows is purposely in abrupt brief words, as those in trouble speak, with scarce breath for utterance. First, in two words, with perhaps a softened inflection[17], they express the utterness of their desolation. Then, in a threefold sentence, each clause consisting of three short words, they say what God had done, but name Him not, because they are angry with Him. God's chastisements irritate those whom they do not subdue[18].

The portion of my people He changeth;
How removeth He (it) as to *me!*
To a rebel[19] our fields He divideth.

They act the patriot. They, the rich, mourn over "the portion of *my* people" (they say) which they had themselves despoiled: they speak, (as men do,) as if things were what they ought to be: they hold to the theory and ignore the facts. As if, because God had divided it to His people, therefore it so remained! as if, because the poor were in theory and by God's law provided for, they were so in fact! Then they are enraged at God's dealings. *He removeth* the portion *as to me;* and to whom giveth He our fields?

[1] v. 13.
[2] Deut. xxviii. 37. 1 Kings ix. 7. 2 Chr. vii. 20. Ps. xliv. 15. lxix. 12. Jer. xxiv. 9. Ezek. xiv. 8.
[3] Is. xiv. 4. [4] Hab. ii. 6. [5] Jer. l. c.
[6] Rib. [7] Ps. lii. 6, 7, Is. lxvi. 24.
[8] נהה נהי נהיה from the sounds, הוי passim, הו הו Am. v. 16. הי Ezek. ii. 10. הה, i. q. אהה Ezek. xxx. 2.
[9] Jer. xxxi. 15. [10] Ez. xxxii. 18.
[11] Am. v. 16. Jer. ix. 17, 19.
[12] 1 Sam. vii. 2. Jer. ix. 18.
[8] ציונית Fürst s. v. [14] הזכרה Id.
[15] There is no plea for separating נהיה in the sense, "it has been," like "fuit Ilium." By itself נהיה would rather be, "it came to pass." אמר also, which follows, explains what the proverb and dirge is, as in Isaiah and Habakkuk. The single word נהיה, actum est, is no dirge. The feminine and masculine together make up a whole as in Is. iii. 1; or it might stand as a superlative, as in the Eng. Marg.
[16] Num. vi. 24–26.
[17] שדוד נשדנו The ׁ for the ּ repeating the sound oo.
[18] See ab. on Am. vi. 10. p. 207.
[19] שובבה, "backsliding," occurs Jer. xxxi. 22. and, of Ammon, xlix. 4. This rendering is favored by the contrast between the לי and the לשובב, and gives an adequate meaning to the ל in the לשובב; whereas, as part of the infinitive, it is superfluous, and unusual as superfluous.

Before CHRIST cir. 730.

[k] Deut. 32. 8, 9.

5 Therefore thou shalt have none that shall [k] cast a cord by lot in the congregation of the LORD.

Before CHRIST cir. 730.

To a rebel! the Assyrian, or the Chaldee. They had deprived the poor of their portion of *the Lord's land*[1]. And now they marvel that God resumes the possession of His own, and requires from them, not the fourfold[2] only of their spoil, but His whole heritage. Well might Assyrian or Chaldee, as they did, jeer at the word, *renegade. They* had not forsaken their gods;—but Israel, what was its whole history but a turning back? [3] *Hath a nation changed their gods, which yet* are *no gods? But My people have changed their glory for* that which *doth not profit.*

Such was the meaning in their lips. The word *divideth* had the more bitterness, because it was the reversal of that first *division* at the entrance into Canaan. Then, with the use of this same word[4], the division of the land of the heathen was appointed to them. Ezekiel, in his great symbolic vision, afterward prophesied the restoration of Israel, with the use of this same term[5]. Joel spoke of the parting of their land, under this same term, as a sin of the heathen[6]. Now, they say, God *divideth our fields,* not to us, but to the Heathen, whose lands He gave us. It *was* a change of act: in impenitence, they think it a change of purpose or will. But what lies in that, *we be utterly despoiled?* Despoiled of everything; of what they felt, temporal things; and of what they did not feel, spiritual things. Despoiled of the land of promise, the *good things* of this life, but also of the Presence of God in His Temple, the grace of the Lord, the image of God and everlasting glory. *Their portion* was *changed,* as to themselves and with others. As to themselves, riches, honor, pleasure, their own land, were changed into want, disgrace, suffering, captivity; and yet more bitter was it to see others gain what they by their own fault had forfeited. As time went on, and their transgression deepened, the exchange of the portion of that former people of God became more complete. The casting-off of the Jews was the grafting-in of the Gentiles. [7] *Seeing ye judge yourselves unworthy of everlasting life, lo! we turn to the Gentiles.* And so they who were[8] *no people,* became *the people of God,* and they who were His people, became, for the time, [9] *not My people:* and[10] *the adoption of sons, and the glory, and the covenants, and the lawgiving, and the service* of God, *and the promises,* came to us Gentiles, since to us Christ Himself our *God blessed for ever* came, and made us His.

How hath He removed. The words do not say what *He* removed. They thought of His gifts, the words include Himself[11]. They say How! in amazement. The change is so great and bitter, it cannot be said. Time, yea eternity cannot utter it. *He hath divided our fields.* The land was but the outward symbol of the inward heritage. Unjust gain, kept back, is restored with usury; [12] *it taketh away the life of the owners thereof.* The vineyard whereof the Jews said, *the inheritance shall be ours,* was taken from them and given to others, even to Christians. So now is that awful change begun, when Christians, leaving God, their only unchanging Good, turn to earthly vanities, and, for the grace of God which He withdraws, have these only for their fleeting portion, until it shall be finally exchanged in the Day of Judgment. [13] *Son, remember that thou in thy lifetime receivedst thy good things, and likewise Lazarus evil things; but now he is comforted and thou art tormented.*

Israel defended himself in impenitence and self-righteousness. He was already the Pharisee. The doom of such was hopeless. The prophet breaks in with a renewed, *Therefore.* He had already prophesied that they should lose the lands which they had unjustly gotten, the land which they had profaned. He had described it in their own impenitent words. Now on the impenitence he pronounces the judgment which impenitence entails, that *they* should not be restored

5. *Therefore thou shalt have none that shall cast a cord by lot in the congregation of the Lord. Thou,* in the first instance, is the impenitent Jew of that day. God had promised by Hosea[14] to restore Judah; shortly after, the Prophet himself foretells it[15]. Now he forewarns these and such as these, that they would have no portion in it. They had[16] *neither part nor lot in this matter.* They, the not-Israel then, were the images and ensamples of the not-Israel afterward, those who seem to be God's people and are not; members of the body, not of the soul of the Church; who have a sort of faith, but have not love. Such was afterward the *Israel after the flesh,* which was *broken off,* while the true Israel was restored, passing out of themselves into Christ. Such, at the end, shall be

[1] See on Hos. ix. 3. vol. i. p. 88.
[2] Ex. xxii. 1. 2 Sam. xii. 6. S. Luke xix. 8.
[3] Jer. ii. 11.
[4] Num. xxvi. 53, 55, 6. Josh. xiii. 7. xiv. 5. xviii. 2, 5, 10. xix. 51. [5] xlvii. 21. [6] iv. 2. [iii. 3. Eng.]
[7] Acts xiii. 46. [8] Rom. x. 19. [9] Hos. i. 9.

[10] Rom. ix. 4, 5.
[11] ימיש is mostly transitive; it was intransitive ii. 3, and is so (if not Kal) Prov. xvii. 13.
[12] Prov. i. 19. [13] S. Luke xvi. 25.
[14] See on Hos. v. 11. vol. i. p. 60.
[15] ii. 12. [16] Acts viii. 21.

Before CHRIST cir. 730.

‖ Or, *Prophesy not as they prophesy.*
† Heb. *Drop, &c.* Ezek. 21. 2.
[1] Isai. 30. 10. Amos 2. 12. & 7. 16.

6 ‖ † [1] Prophesy ye not,
say they to them that prophesy: they shall not prophesy to them, *that* they shall
not take shame.
7 ¶ O *thou that art*
named the house of Jacob,
is the spirit of the LORD
‖ straitened? *are* these his
doings? do not my words
do good to him that walk-
eth † uprightly?

‖ Or, *shortened?*
† Heb. *upright?*

those, who, being admitted by Christ into *their portion*, renounce the world in word not in deed. Such shall have "[1] no portion for ever *in the congregation of the Lord.* For [2] *nothing defiled shall enter there, nor whatsoever worketh abomination or a lie, but they which are written in the Lamb's book of life.*"

The ground of their condemnation is their resistance to light and known truth. These not only [3] *entered not in*, themselves, but, being hinderers of God's word, *them that were entering in*, they *hindered.*

6. *Prophesy ye not*, say they to them that *prophesy; they shall not prophesy to them, that they shall not take shame.* The words are very emphatic in Hebrew, from their briefness, *Prophesy not; they shall indeed prophesy; they shall not prophesy to these; shame shall not depart* [4]. The people, the false prophets, the politicians, forbade God and Micah to prophesy; *Prophesy not.* God, by Micah, recites their prohibition to themselves, and forewarns them of the consequences.

Prophesy ye not, lit. *drop not.* Amaziah and the God-opposing party had already given an ungodly meaning to the word [5]. "Drop not," "distill not," thus unceasingly, these same words, ever warning, ever telling of [6] *lamentation and mourning and woe; prophesying not good concerning* us, *but evil* [7]. So their descendants *commanded* the Apostles [8] *not to speak at all or to teach in the Name of Jesus.* [9] *Did we not straitly command you, that ye should not teach in this Name?* [10] *This man ceaseth not to speak blasphemous words against this holy place and the law.* God answers; *They shall certainly prophesy.* The Hebrew word is emphatic [11]. The Prophets had their commission from God, and Him they must obey, whether Israel [12] *would hear or whether they would forbear.* So must Micah and Isaiah [13] now, or Jeremiah [14], Ezekiel, and the rest afterward. *They shall not prophesy to these.* He does not say only, *They shall not prophesy to them*, but, *to these;* i. e. they shall prophesy to others who would receive their words: God's word would not be stayed; they who would hearken shall never be deprived of their portion; but *to these* who despise, *they shall not prophesy.* It shall be all one, as though they did not prophesy; the soft rain shall not bedew *them.* The barn-floor shall be dry, while the fleece is moist [15]. So God says by Isaiah [16]; *I will also command the clouds that they rain no rain upon it.* The dew of God's word shall be transferred to others. But so *shame* [lit. *shames* [17], manifold shame,] *shall not depart*, but shall rest upon them for ever. God would have turned away the shame from them; but they, despising His warnings, drew it to themselves. It was the natural fruit of their doings; it was in its natural home with them. God spake to them, that they might be freed from it. They silenced His Prophets; deafened themselves to His words; so it *departed not.* So our Lord says [18], *Now ye say, we see; therefore your sin remaineth;* and S. John Baptist [19], *The wrath of God abideth on him.* It hath not now first to come. It is not some new thing to be avoided, turned aside. The sinner has but to remain as he is; the shame encompasseth him already; and only *departeth* not. The *wrath of God* is already upon him, and *abideth on him.*

7. *O thou* that art *named the house of Jacob;* as Isaiah says [20], *Hear ye this, O house of Jacob, which are called by the name of Israel—which make mention of the God of Israel, not in truth, nor in righteousness. For they call themselves of the holy city, and stay themselves upon the God of Israel.* They boasted of what convicted them of faithlessness. They relied on being what in spirit they had ceased to be, what in deeds they denied, children of a believing forefather. It is the same temper which we see more at large in their descendants; [21] *We be Abraham's seed and were never in bondage to any man; how sayest Thou, ye shall be made free?* [22] *Abraham is our Father.* It is the same which S. John Baptist and our Lord and S. Paul reproved. [23] *Think not to say within yourselves, we have Abraham to our father.* [24] *If ye were Abraham's children, ye would do the works of Abraham. Now ye seek to kill Me, a Man that hath told you the truth—This did not*

[1] Rib. [2] Rev. xxi. 27. [3] S. Luke xi. 52.
[4] Poc. gives this distribution of the words from Abulwalid *v.* נטף.
[5] See on Am. vii. 16. vol. i. p. 322.
[6] Ezek. ii. 10. [7] 1 Kings xxii. 18.
[8] Acts iv. 18. v. 40. [9] Ib. v. 28. [10] Ib. vi. 13.
[11] יטיפון. [12] Ezek. ii. 5. 7. [13] xxviii. 9–14. 22.
[14] i. 7. 17. xxvi. 10–15. [15] Judg. vi. 37.
[16] Is. v. 6.
[17] כלמות as ישועות, omnigenæ salutes, manifold salvation.
[18] S. John ix. 41. [19] Ib. iii. 36. [20] xlviii. 1.
[21] S. John viii. 33. [22] Ib. 39.
[23] S. Matt. iii. 9. [24] S. John viii. 39, 40.

Before CHRIST cir. 730.

8 Even † of late my people is risen up as an enemy: ye pull off the robe † with the garment from them that pass by securely as men averse from war.

† Heb. *yesterday.*
† Heb. *over against a garment.*

Abraham. [1] *He is not a Jew which is one outwardly, neither is that circumcision which is outward in the flesh.*—*Behold thou art called a Jew, and restest in the law and makest thy boast of God, and knowest His Will and approvest the things that are more excellent*—&c. The Prophet answers the unexpressed objections of those who forbade to prophesy evil. "Such could not be of God," these said; "for God was pledged by His promises to *the house of Jacob.* It would imply change in God, if He were to cast off those whom He had chosen." Micah answers; "not God is changed, but you." God's promise was to Jacob, not to those who were but *named* Jacob, who called themselves after the name of their father, but did not his deeds. *The Spirit of the Lord was not straitened* [2], so that He was less long-suffering than heretofore. *These,* which He threatened and of which they complained, were *not His doings,* not what He of His own Nature did, not what He loved to do, not His, as the Author or Cause of them, but *theirs.* God is Good, but to those who can receive good, *the upright in heart* [3]. *God is only Loving unto Israel.* He is all Love; nothing but [4] Love: all His ways are Love; but it follows, unto *what* Israel, the true Israel, *the pure of heart.* [5] *All the paths of the Lord are mercy and truth;* but to whom? *unto such as keep His covenant and His testimonies.* [6] *The mercy of the Lord is from everlasting to everlasting;* but *unto them that fear Him.* But, they becoming evil, His good became to them evil. Light, wholesome and gladdening to the healthful, hurts weak eyes. That which is straight cannot suit or fit with the crooked. Amend your crookedness, and God's ways will be straight to you. *Do not My words do good?* He doth speak [7] *good words and comfortable words.* They are not only *good,* but *do good.* [8] *His word is with power.* Still it is with those who *walk uprightly;* whether those who forsake not, or those who return to, the way of righteousness. God flattereth not, deceiveth not, promiseth not what He will not do. He cannot [9] *speak peace where there is no peace.* As He saith, [10] *Behold the goodness and severity of God; on them which fell, severity, but toward thee, goodness, if thou continue in His goodness.* God Himself could not make a heaven for the proud or envious. Heaven would be to them a hell.

8. *Even of late* [lit. *yesterday* [11].] "[12] He imputeth not past sins, but those recent and, as it were, of yesterday." *My people is risen up vehemently* [13]. God upbraideth them tenderly by the title, *Mine own people,* as S. John complaineth [14], *He came unto His own, and His own received Him not.* God became not *their* enemy, but they arose as one man,—*is risen up,* the whole of it, as *His.* In Him they might have had peace and joy and assured gladness, but they arose in rebellion against Him, requiting Him evil for good, (as bad Christians do to Christ,) and brought war upon their own heads. This they did by their sins against their brethren. Casting off the love of man, they alienated themselves from the love of God.

Ye pull off [*strip off violently* [15]] *the robe with the garment,* lit. *over against the cloak.* The *salmah* [16] is the large enveloping cloak, which was worn loosely over the other dress, and served by night for a covering [17]. *Eder* [18], translated *robe,* is probably not any one garment, but the remaining dress, the comely, becoming [19], array of the person. These they stripped violently off from persons, peaceable, unoffending, off their guard, *passing by securely, men averse from war* [20] and strife. These they stripped of their raiment by day, leaving them half-naked, and of their covering for the night. So making war against God's

[1] Rom. ii. 17–28.
[2] קצר רוח, (as in part Zech. xi. 8,) as opposed to ארך אפום (Ex. xxxiv. 6. &c. longanimis, longsuffering,) and i. q. קצר אפים Prov. xx. 17, coll. 29.
[3] Ps. lxxiii. 1.
[4] The force of אך.
[5] Ps. xxv. 10.
[6] Ps. ciii. 17. S. Luke i. 50.
[7] Zech. i. 13.
[8] S. Luke iv. 32.
[9] Jer. vi. 14.
[10] Rom. xi. 22.
[11] אתמול is i. q. אתמול, in Is. xxx. 33.
[12] S. Jer.
[13] יקומם, in Isaiah (xliv. 26. lviii. 12. lxi. 4.) transitive, but only of the raising up, rebuilding of ruins. The use of קומם actively in that one sense is no ground for taking it so, where the idea is different. To *raise up* an adversary is expressed by הקים Mic. v. 4. Am. vi. 14. 1 Kings xi. 14. and so raising up evil also.
[14] i. 11.
[15] חפשטון. This is intensive, as in Arabic.
[16] שלמה here and Ex. xxii. 8. i. q. שמלה, elsewhere.
[17] Deut. xxii. 17.
[18] אדר occurs here only. There is no ground to identify it with the well-known אדרת. It is not likely that the common garment should have been called, this once, by a different name; nor that the אדרת, a wide enfolding garment, (see on Jonah iii. 6. vol. i. p. 416,) should have been worn together with the שלמה.
[19] This meaning seems to lie in the root; comp. στολή, array, apparel, dress.
[20] שובי is doubtless an adjective form, distinct from the participle שבי, (I.. lix. 20.) like סורי Jer. ii. 21.

Before CHRIST cir. 730.

‖ Or, *wives.*

9 The ‖ women of my
people have ye cast out
from their pleasant houses;
from their children have
ye taken away my glory
for ever.
10 Arise ye, and depart;
for this *is* not *your* [m] rest:

[m] Deut. 12. 9.

Before CHRIST cir. 730.

peaceful people, they, as it were, made war against God.

9. *The women of my people have ye cast out from their pleasant houses,* [lit. *from her pleasant house,*] each from her home. These were probably the widows of those whom they had stripped. Since the houses were their's, they were widows; and so their spoilers were at war with those whom God had committed to their special love, whom He had declared the objects of His own tender care, *the widows and the fatherless.* The widows they *drove vehemently forth*[1], as having no portion in the inheritance which God had given them, as God had driven out their enemies before them, each *from her pleasant house,* the home where she had lived with her husband and children in delight and joy.

From [*off*] *their* [*young*[2]] *children have ye taken away My glory.* Primarily, the glory, comeliness, was the fitting apparel which God had given them[3], and laid upon them[4], and which these oppressors stripped *off* from them. But it includes all the gifts of God, wherewith God would array them. Instead of the holy home of parental care, the children grew up in want and neglect, away from all the ordinances of God, it may be, in a strange land. *For ever.* They never repented, never made restitution; but so they incurred the special woe of those who ill-used the unprotected, the widow, and the fatherless. The words *for ever* anticipate the punishment. The punishment is according to the sin. They never ceased their oppression. They, with the generation who should come after them, should be deprived of God's *glory,* and cast out of His land forever.

10. *Arise ye and depart.* Go your way, as being cast out of God's care and land. It matters not whither they went. *For this is not your rest.* As ye have done, so shall it be done unto you. As ye cast out the widow and the fatherless, so shall ye be cast out; as ye gave no rest to those *averse from war,* so shall ye have none. [5] *He that leadeth into captivity shall go into captivity; he that killeth with the sword must be killed with the sword.* The land was given to them as a temporary rest, a symbol and earnest of the everlasting rest to the obedient. So Moses spake[6], *ye are not as yet come to the rest*[7] *and the inheritance which the Lord your God giveth you. But when ye go over Jordan, and dwell in the land which the Lord your God giveth you to inherit, and when He giveth you rest*[8] *from your enemies round about, so that ye dwell in safety,* &c. And Joshua[9], *Remember the word which Moses commanded you, saying, The Lord your God giveth you rest*[10]. But the Psalmist had warned them, that, if they hardened their hearts like their forefathers, they too would *not enter into* His *rest*[11].

Because it is polluted [lit. *because of* its *pollution*[12]] by idolatry, by violence, by uncleanness. So Moses (using the same word) says, *the land is defiled*[13] by the abominations of the heathen; and warns them, *that the land spue you not out, when you defile it, as it spued out the nations which were before you.* Ezekiel speaks of that *defilement*[14], as the ground why God expelled Israel[15]. *It shall destroy you, even with a sore* [lit. *sharp*] *destruction*[16]. It is a sore thing to abuse the creatures of God to sin, and it is unfit that we should use what we have abused. Hence Holy Scripture speaks, as though even the inanimate creation took part with God, *made subject to vanity, not willingly,* and could not endure those who employed it against His Will.

The words, *Arise, depart ye, for this is not your rest,* became a sort of sacred proverb, spoken anew to the soul, whenever it would find rest out of God. "[17] We are bidden to think of no rest for ourselves in any things of the world; but, as it were, *arising* from the dead, to stretch upwards, and walk after the Lord our God, and say, *My soul cleaveth hard*

[1] תנרשון is doubly intensive, as the intensive form with the emphatic ן. It is the word used of God's driving out the nations before Israel, (Ex. Jud. &c.) or of man being driven out of Paradise, (Gen. iii. 24,) Hagar being cast out. (Gen. xxi. 10.) The word itself, by its rough sound, expresses the more of harshness; and that as opposed to softness, תענוניה. This is the same word as that rendered *delicate,* i. 16.

[2] מעל עולליה.

[3] as Hos. ii. 11. דנני I. H. Mich.

[4] Ez. xvi. 14. Id.

[5] Rev. xiii. 10.

[6] Deut. xii. 9. 10. add 1 Kings viii. 56.

[7] אל המנוחה, the same word.

[8] הניח.

[9] i. 13.

[10] מניח.

[11] Ps. xcv. 11. comp. למנוחתך Ps. cxxxii. 8. מנוחתי 14.

[12] as pointed in most accurate copies, without Metheg.

[13] תטמא Lev. xviii. 27. בטמאכם 28.

[14] Ezek. xxxvi. 17.

[15] Ezek. xxxvi. 18. add Jer. ii. 7.

[16] This is the common rendering of חבל. Others, with Sal. B. Mel. have understood it of travail-pains, (Cant. viii. 5. Ps. vii. 15.) but this would have the opposite sense of bringing forth, re-birth, not of ejection. (See Is. lxvi. 8.) The sharp bitter pang would express the pains of travail, not its fruitlessness or that they were cast out any whither. Fruitlessness of travail-pangs is expressed, if intended, (as in Is. xxvi. 18.)

[17] S. Jer.

Before CHRIST cir. 730.

because it is [n] polluted, it
shall destroy *you*, even with
a sore destruction.
11 If a man ‖ [o] walking
in the spirit and falsehood
do lie, *saying*, I will prophesy unto thee of wine and
of strong drink; he shall
even be the prophet of this
people.
12 ¶ [p] I will surely assemble, O Jacob, all of

[n] Lev. 18. 25, 28. Jer. 3. 2.
‖ Or, *walk with the wind, and lie falsely.*
[o] Ezek. 13. 3.
[p] ch. 4. 6, 7.

after Thee. This if we neglect, and will not hear Him Who saith, *Awake thou that sleepest, and arise from the dead, and Christ shall give thee light*, we shall indeed slumber, but shall be deceived and shall not find rest; for where Christ enlighteneth not the risen soul, what seemeth to be rest, is trouble." All rest is wearisome which is not in Thee, O our God.

11. *If a man walking in the spirit and falsehood*, lit. *in spirit* [not *My* Spirit] *and falsehood*, i. e. in a lying spirit; such as they, whose woe Ezekiel pronounces [1], *Woe unto the foolish prophets who walk after their own spirit and what they have not seen* [2]; *prophets out of their own hearts*, who [3] *prophesied a vision of falsehood, and a destruction and nothingness* [4]; *prophesid falsehood; yea, prophets of the deceit of their hearts.* These, like the true prophets, *walked in spirit;* as Isaiah speaks of *walking in righteousness* [5], and Solomon of one *walking in the frowardness of the mouth* [6]. Their habitual converse was in a spirit, but of falsehood. If such an one *do lie*, saying, *I will prophesy unto thee of wine and strong drink.* Man's conscience must needs have some plea in speaking falsely of God. The false prophets had to please the rich men, to embolden them in their self-indulgence, to tell them that God would not punish. They doubtless spoke of God's temporal promises to His people, the land *flowing with milk and honey.* His promises of abundant harvest and vintage, and assured them, that God would not withdraw these, that He was not so precise about His law. Micah tells them in plain words, what it all came to; it was a prophesying of *wine and strong drink.*

He shall even be the prophet of this people, lit. *and shall be bedewing this people.* He uses the same words, which scorners of Israel and Judah employed in forbidding to prophesy. They said, *drop not;* forbidding God's word as a wearisome dropping. It wore away their patience, not their hearts of stone. He tells them, *who* might speak to them without wearying, of *whose* words they would never tire, *who* might do habitually [7] what they forbade to God,—one who, in the Name of God, set them at ease in their sensual indulgences. This is the secret of the success of everything opposed to God and Christ. Man wants a God. God has made it a necessity of our nature to crave after Him. Spiritual, like natural, hunger, debarred from or loathing wholesome food, must be stilled, stifled, with what will appease its gnawings. Our natural intellect longs for Him; for it cannot understand itself without Him. Our restlessness longs for Him; to rest upon. Our helplessness longs for Him, to escape from the unbearable pressure of our unknown futurity. Our imagination craves for Him; for, being made for the Infinite, it cannot be content with the finite. Aching affections long for Him; for no creature can soothe them. Our dissatisfied conscience longs for Him, to teach it and make it one with itself. But man does not want to be responsible, nor to owe duty; still less to be liable to penalties for disobeying. The Christian, not the natural man, longs that his whole being should tend to God. The natural man wishes to be well-rid of what sets him ill at ease, not to belong to God. And the horrible subtlety of false teaching, in each age or country, is to meet its own favorite requirements, without calling for self-sacrifice or self-oblation, to give it a god, such as it would have, such as might content it. "[8] The people willeth to be deceived, be it deceived," is a true proverb. *Men turn away their ears from the truth* [9] which they dislike; and so *are turned unto fables* which they like. They who *receive not the love of the truth,—believe a lie* [10]. If men *will not retain God in their knowledge*, God *giveth them over to an undistinguishing mind* [11]. They who would not receive our Lord, coming in His Father's Name, have ever since, as He said, *received* them *who came in their own* [12]. Men teach their teachers how they wish to be mistaught, and receive the echo of their wishes as the Voice of God.

12. *I will surely assemble, O Jacob, all of thee; I will surely gather the remnant of Israel.* God's

[1] Ezek. xiii. 3. [2] Ib. 2. 17.
[3] Jer. xiv. 14, הזון שקר, as here רוח ושקר.
[4] Ib. xxiii. 26. add נבאים שקר xxvii. 10, 14, 16. or בשקר Jer. xxix. 9. נבאי חלמות שקר Ib. xxiii. 32.
[5] xxxiii. 15. הל־ צדרות.
[6] הולך עקשות פה Pr. vi. 12. elsewhere with ב.
[7] The force of היה מטיף.
[8] Populus vult decipi, decipiatur.
[9] 2 Tim. iv. 4.
[10] 2 Thess. ii. 11. 12.
[11] Rom. i. 28. [12] S. John v. 43.

Before CHRIST cir. 730.

thee; I will surely gather the remnant of Israel; I will put them together [q] as the sheep of Bozrah, as the flock in the midst of their fold: [r] they shall make great noise by reason of *the multitude of* men.

q Jer. 31. 10.

r Ezek. 36. 37.

mercy on the penitent and believing being the end of all His threatenings, the mention of it often bursts in abruptly. Christ is ever the Hope as the End of prophecy, ever before the Prophets' mind. The earthquake and fire precede the still small voice of peace in Him. What seems then sudden to us, is connected in truth. The Prophet had said [1], where was not their rest and how they should be cast forth; he saith at once how they should be gathered to their everlasting rest. He had said, what promises of the false prophets would *not* be fulfilled [2]. But, despair being the most deadly enemy of the soul, he does not take away their false hopes, without shewing them the true mercies in store for them. "[3] Think not," he would say, "that I am only a prophet of ill. The captivity foretold will indeed now come, and God's mercies will also come, although not in the way, which these speak of." The false prophets spoke of worldly abundance ministering to sensuality, and of unbroken security. He tells of God's mercies, but after chastisement, to *the remnant of Israel*. But the restoration is complete, far beyond their then condition. He had foretold the desolation of Samaria [4], the captivity of Judah [5]; he foretells the restoration of *all Jacob*, as one. The images are partly taken (as is the Prophet's wont,) from that first deliverance from Egypt [6]. *Then*, as the image of the future growth under persecution, God multiplied His people exceedingly [7]; then [8] *the Lord went before them by day in a pillar of a cloud to lead them the way;* then God *brought them up* [9] *out of the house of bondage* [10]. But their future prison-house was to be no land of Goshen. It was to be a captivity and a dispersion at once, as Hosea had already foretold [11]. So he speaks of them emphatically [12], as a great throng, *assembling I will assemble, O Jacob, all of thee; gathering I will gather the remnant of Israel.* The word, which is used of the gathering of a flock or its lambs [13], became, from Moses' prophecy [14], a received word of the gathering of Israel from the dispersion of the captivity [15]. The return of the Jews from Babylon was but a faint shadow of the fulfillment. For, ample as were the terms of the decrees of Cyrus [16] and Artaxerxes [17], and widely as that of Cyrus was diffused [18], the restoration was essentially that of Judah, i. e. Judah, Benjamin and Levi [19]: the towns, whose inhabitants returned, were those of Judah and Benjamin [20]; the towns, to which they returned, were of the two tribes. It was not a gathering of *all Jacob;* and of the three tribes who returned, there were but few gathered, and they had not even an earthly king, nor any visible Presence of God. The words began to be fulfilled in the *many* [21] *tens of thousands* who believed at our Lord's first Coming; and *all Jacob*, that is, all who were Israelites indeed, *the remnant according to the election of grace* [22], were gathered within the one fold of the Church, under One Shepherd. It shall be fully fulfilled, when, in the end, *the fullness of the Gentiles shall come in, and all Israel shall be saved* [23]. *All Jacob* is the same as *the remnant of Israel*, the true Israel which remains when the false severed itself off; all the seed-corn, when the chaff was winnowed away. So then, whereas they were now scattered, *then*, God saith, *I will put them together* [in one fold] *as the sheep of Bozrah*, which abounded in sheep [24], and was also a strong city of Edom [25]; denoting how believers should be fenced within the Church, as by a strong wall, against which the powers of darkness should not prevail, and the wolf should howl around the fold, yet be unable to enter it, and Edom and the heathen should become part of the inheritance of Christ [26]. *As a flock in the midst of their fold*, at rest, "[27] like sheep, still and subject to their shepherd's voice. So shall these, having one faith and One Spirit, in meekness and simplicity, obey the one rule of truth. Nor shall it be a small number;" for the place where they

1 ver. 10. 2 ver. 11. 3 S. Jer.
4 i. 6. 5 i. 16. ii. 4. 6 Hengst. Christ. i. 499.
7 Ex. i. 12. 8 Ib. xiii. 21.
9 Ex. iii. 8, 17. Lev. xi. 45. The people *went up*. Ex. xiii. 18. add. xii. 38. i. 10.
10 See below, vi. 4.
11 See on Hos. vi. 11. vol. i. p. 70. ix. 17. p. 97.
12 קבץ אקבץ, אסף אאסף. 13 Is xl. 11. xiii. 14.
14 Deut. xxx. 3, 4. see Neh. i. 9.
15 See below, iv. 6. Ps. cvi. 47. cvii. 3. Is. xi. 12. xliii. 5. liv. 7. lvi. 8. Zeph. iii. 19, 20. Jer. xxiii. 3. xxix. 14. xxxi. 8, 10. xxxii. 37. Ezek xi. 17. xx. 34, 41. xxviii. 25. xxxiv. 13. xxxvii. 21. xxxviii. 8. xxxix. 27. Zech. x. 10.
16 Ezr. i. 2–4. 17 vii. 13. 18 Ib. i. 1.
19 Ib. i. 5. ii. 1. iv. 1. x. 7, 9. Josephus, who alone mentions that Ezra sent a copy of Artaxerxes' letter to him, "to all those of his nation who were in Media," and that "many of them, taking their property, came to Babylon, longing for the return to Jerusalem," adds, "but the whole people of Israelites [i. e. the great mass] remained where they were." Ant. xi 5. 2.
20 Ezr. ii. Neh. vii. 21 *μυριάδες* Acts xxi. 20.
22 Rom. xi. 5. 23 Ib. xi. 25, 6.
24 Is. xxxiv. 6.
25 See on Am. i. 12. vol. i. p. 252.
26 See on Am. ix. 12. vol. i. p. 337. 27 Rup.

Before CHRIST cir. 730.

13 The breaker is come up before them: they have broken up, and have passed through the gate, and are

Before CHRIST cir. 730.

shall be gathered shall be too narrow to contain them, as is said in Isaiah; *Give place to me, that I may dwell*[1].

They shall make great noise (it is the same word as our *hum*, "the hum of men,") *by reason of the multitude of men.* He explains his image, as does Ezekiel[2], *And ye are My flock, the flock of My pasture; men* are *ye; I, your God, saith the Lord God:* and, [3] *As a flock of holy things, as the flock of Jerusalem in her solemn feasts; so shall the waste cities be full of a flock of men, and they shall know that I am the Lord.* So many shall they be, that "throughout the whole world they shall make a great and public sound in praising God, filling Heaven and the green pastures of Paradise with a mighty hum of praise;" as St. John saw[4] *a great multitude which no man could number,* "[5] with one united voice praising the Good Shepherd, Who smoothed for them all rugged places, and evened them by His Own Steps, Himself the Guide of their way and the *Gate* of Paradise, as He saith, *I am the Door;* through Whom, *bursting through* and *going before,* being also the Door of the way, the flock of believers shall break through *It.* But this Shepherd is their *Lord* and *King.*" Not their King only, but the Lord God; so that this, too, bears witness that Christ is God.

13. *The Breaker is come up* (*gone up*) *before them; they have broken up,* (*broken through*[6]) and have passed *the gate, and have gone forth.* The image is not of conquest, but of deliverance. They *break through,* not to enter in but to *pass through the gate* and *go forth.* The wall of the city is ordinarily *broken through,* in order to make an entrance[7], or to secure to a conqueror the power of entering in[8] at any time, or by age and decay[9]. But here the object is expressed, to *go forth.* Plainly then they were confined before, as in a prison; and the gate of the prison was burst open, to set them free. It is then the same image as when God says by Isaiah[10]; *I will say to the North, give up; and to the South, Hold not back,* or[11], *Go ye forth of Babylon, Say ye, the Lord hath redeemed His servant Jacob;* or, with the same reminiscence of God's visible leading of His people out of Egypt, [12] *Depart ye, depart ye; for ye shall not go out with haste, nor yet by flight, for the Lord God shall go before you, and the God of Israel* will be *your reward;* or as Hosea describes their restoration[13]; *Then shall the children of Judah and the children of Israel be gathered together and appoint themselves one Head, and they shall go up out of the land*[14]. Elsewhere, in Isaiah, the spiritual meaning of the deliverance from the prison is more distinctly brought out, as the work of our Redeemer[15]. *I will give Thee for a covenant of the people, for a light of the Gentiles, to open the blind eyes, to bring out the prisoners from the prison, them that sit in darkness out of the prison-house;* and [16], *the Spirit of the Lord God is upon Me, because the Lord hath anointed Me to proclaim liberty to the captives, and the opening* of the prison *to* them that are *bound.*

From this passage, the "Breaker-through" was one of the titles of the Christ, known to the Jews[17], as One Who should be "[18] from below and from above" also; and from it they believed that "[19] captives should come up from Gehenna, and the Shechinah," or the Presence of God, "at their head." "[20] He then, Who shall break the way, the King and Lord Who shall *go up before them,* shall be the Good Shepherd, Who puts them together in the fold. And this He doth when, as He saith, [21] *He putteth forth His own sheep, and He goeth before them, and the sheep follow Him, for they know His Voice.* How doth He go before them but by suffering for them, leaving them an example of suffering, and opening the entrance of Paradise? The Good Shepherd *goeth up* to the Cross, [22] *and is lifted up from the earth, laying down* His *Life for* His *sheep,* to *draw all men unto* Him. He *goeth up,* trampling on death by His resurrection; He *goeth up* above the heaven of heavens, and sitteth on the Right Hand of the Father, opening the way before them, so that the flock, in their lowliness, may arrive where the Shepherd went before in His Majesty.

[1] xlix. 20. [2] xxxiv. 31. [3] Ib. xxxvi. 38.
[4] Rev. vii. 9. [5] Rup.
[6] פָּרַץ is to *break through,* as, enemies surrounding one, 2 Sam. v. 20. 1 Chr. xiv. 11. *break in pieces* so as to scatter, Ps. lx. 3. *break through or down* a wall, (see references in 30, 31, 33.) and with בְּ, "burst *upon,*" of God's inflictions, Ex. xix. 22, 24. 2 Sam. vi. 8. Ps. cvi. 29. 1 Chr. xiii. 11. xv. 13.
[7] Ps. lxxx. 13. lxxxix. 41. Is. v. 5. Neh. ii. 13.
[8] Prov. xxv. 28. 2 Kgs xiv. 13. 2 Chr. xxv. 23. xxvi. 6.
[9] 2 Chr. xxxii. 5. [10] xliii. 6. [11] Ib. xlviii. 20.
[12] lii. 11, 12. תֵצֵאוּ, as here יֵצְאוּ; and הֹלֵךְ לִפְנֵיכֶם corresponding to עָלָה לִפְנֵיהֶם.

[13] i. 11. (ii. 2. Heb.)
[14] עָלוּ מִן הָאָרֶץ in reference to Egypt, (see on Hos. i. 11. vol. i. p. 26) as here עָלָה.
[15] Is. xlii. 6, 7.
[16] Is. lxi. 1. [17] Huls. Theol. Jud. pp. 143, 144.
[18] R. Mos. Haddars. in Mart. Pug. Fid. p. 432. It is interpreted of the Messiah in the Bereshith Rabba, § 48. f. 47. 2. (Schöttg. de Mess. p. 61.) the Echa Rabbathi, f. 60. 2, (Ib. p. 69.) the Pesikta Rabbathi, f. 60. 1, (Ib. p. 135.) and the Midrash Mishle, ad c. vi. 1. (Ib. ad loc. p. 212.) So also Jonathan, Rashi, Tanchum, Abarbanel in Poc.
[19] Quoted by Pearson on the Creed, art. 6, note y.
[20] Rup. [21] S. John x. 4. [22] Ib. 15. xii. 32.

Before CHRIST cir. 730.

gone out by it: and [s] their king shall pass before them,

[t] and the LORD on the head of them.

Before CHRIST cir. 730.

[s] Hos. 3. 5.

[t] Is. 52. 12.

And when He thus breaketh through and openeth the road, they also *break through and pass through the gate and go out by it*, by that Gate, namely, whereof the Psalmist saith [1], *This is the Gate of the Lord; the righteous shall enter into It.* What other is this *Gate* than that same Passion of Christ, beside which there is no gate, no way whereby any can enter into life? Through that open portal, which the lance of the soldier made in His Side when crucified, and *there came thereout Blood and Water, they shall pass and go through*, even as the children of Israel passed through the Red Sea, which divided before them, when Pharaoh, his chariots and horsemen, were drowned." "[2] He will be in their hearts, and will teach and *lead* them; He will shew them the way of Salvation, [3] *guiding their feet into the way of peace*, and they shall pass through the strait and narrow gate which leadeth unto life; of which it is written [4], *Enter ye in at the strait gate; because strait is the gate and narrow is the way which leadeth unto life, and few there be that find it. And their King shall pass before them*, as He did, of old, in the figure of the cloud, of which Moses said [5], *If Thy Presence go not, carry us not up hence; and wherein shall it be known that I have found grace in Thy sight, I and Thy people, is it not in that Thou goest up with us?* and as He then did when He passed out of this world to the Father. *And the Lord on* (that is, *at*) *the head of them*, as of His army. "[6] For *the Lord is His Name*, and He is the Head, they the members; He the King, they the people; He the Shepherd, they the sheep of His pasture. And of this *passing through* He spake [7], *By Me if any man enter in, he shall be saved, and shall go in and out and find pasture.* For a man *entereth in*, when, receiving the faith, he becomes a sheep of this Shepherd, and *goeth out*, when he closeth this present life, and then findeth the pastures of unfading, everlasting life;" "[2] passing from this pilgrimage to his home, from faith to sight, from labor to reward." Again, as describing the Christian's life here, it speaks of progress. "[8] Whoso shall have entered in, must not remain in the state wherein he entered, but must *go forth* into the pasture; so that, in entering in should be the beginning, in *going forth and finding pasture*, the perfecting of graces. He who entereth in, is contained within the bounds of the world; he who goeth forth, goes, as it were, beyond all created things, and, counting as nothing all things seen, shall *find pasture* above the Heavens, and shall feed upon the Word of God, and say [9], *The Lord is my Shepherd*, (and feedeth me,) *I can lack nothing.* But this going forth can only be through Christ; as it followeth, *and the Lord at the head of them.*" Nor, again, is this in itself easy, or done for us without any effort of our own. All is of Christ. The words express the closeness of the relation between the Head and the members; and what He, our King and Lord, doth, they do, because He Who did it for them, doth it in them. The same words are used of both, shewing that what they do, they do by virtue of His Might, treading in His steps, walking where He has made the way plain, and by His Spirit. What they do, they do, as belonging to Him. He *breaketh through*, or, rather, in all is *the Breaker-through.* They, having broken through, *pass* on, because He *passeth before them.* He will [10] *break in pieces the gates of brass, and cut in sunder the bars of iron.* He *breaketh through* whatever would hold us back or oppose us, all might of sin and death and Satan, as Moses opened the Red Sea, for [11] *a way for the ransomed to pass over;* and so He saith, [12] *I will go before thee, I will break in pieces the gates of brass, and cut in sunder the bars of iron, and I will give thee the treasures of darkness, and hidden riches of secret places.* So then Christians, following Him, the *Captain of their salvation*, strengthened by His grace, must burst the bars of the flesh and of the world, the chains and bonds of evil passions and habits, force themselves through the narrow way and narrow gate, do violence to themselves, [13] *endure hardness, as good soldiers of Jesus Christ.* The title of our Lord, *the Breaker-through* [14], and the saying, *they break through*, together express the same as the New Testament doth in regard to our being partakers of the sufferings of Christ. [15] *Joint heirs with Christ, if so be that we suffer with Him, that we may be also glorified together.* [16] *If we be dead with Him, we shall also live with Him; if we suffer, we shall also reign with Him.* [17] *Forasmuch then as Christ hath suffered for us in the flesh—arm yourselves likewise with the same mind.*

The words may include also the removal of the souls of the just, who had believed in Christ before His Coming, into Heaven after His Resurrection, and will be fully completed when, in the end, He shall cause His faithful

[1] Ps. cxviii. 20. [2] Dion. [3] S. Luke i. 79. [4] S. Matt. vii. 13, 14. [5] Ex. xxxiii. 15, 16. [6] Rup. [7] S. John x. 9. [8] S. Jer. [9] Ps. xxiii. 1. [10] Is. xlv. 2. [11] Ib. li. 10. [12] Ib. xlv. 2, 3. [13] 2 Tim. ii. 3.

[14] פרץ. It is from the same word as Pharez, Judah's son, whose birth was typical. Gen. xxxviii. 29. [15] Rom. viii. 17. [16] 2 Tim. ii. 11, 12. [17] 1 Pet. iv. 1.

Before CHRIST cir. 710.

CHAPTER III.

1 *The cruelty of the princes.* 5 *The falsehood of the prophets.* 8 *The security of them both.*

AND I said, Hear, I pray
you, O heads of Jacob,
and ye princes of the house
of Israel; [a] *Is it* not for
you to know judgment?
2 Who hate the good,
and love the evil; who
pluck off their skin from
off them, and their flesh
from off their bones;
3 Who also [b] eat the
flesh of my people, and
flay their skin from off
them; and they break
their bones, and chop them
in pieces, as for the pot,
and [c] as flesh within the
caldron.

a Jer. 5. 4, 5.

b Ps. 14. 4.

c Ezek. 11. 3, 7.

---

servants, in body and soul, to *enter into the joy of their Lord.*

CHAP. III. ver. 1. *And I said.* God's love for us is the great incitement, constrainer, vivifier of His creature's love. Micah had just spoken of God's love of Israel; how He would gather them into one fold under One Shepherd, guard them, lead them, remove all difficulties before them, be Himself their Head and enable them to follow Him. He turns then to them. These are God's doings; this, God has in store for you hereafter. Even when mercy itself shall require chastisement, He doth not cast off forever. The desolation is but the forerunner of future mercy. What then do ye? The Prophet appeals to them, class by class. There was one general corruption of every order of men, through whom Judah could be preserved, princes[1], prophets[2], priests[3]. *The salt had lost its savor; wherewith could it be seasoned?* whereby could the decaying mass of the people be kept from entire corruption?

Hear, I pray you, O heads of Jacob, and ye princes of the house of Israel. He arraigns them by the same name, under which He had first promised mercy. He had first promised mercy to *all Jacob* and *the remnant of Israel.* So now he upraids the *heads of Jacob,* and *the princes of the house of Israel,* lest they should deceive themselves. At the same time he recalls them to the deeds of their father. Judah had succeeded to the birthright, forfeited by Reuben, Simeon and Levi; and in Judah all the promises of the Messiah were laid up. But he was not like the three great Patriarchs, *the father of the faithful,* or the meek Isaac, or the much-tried Jacob. The name then had not the reminiscences, or force of appeal, contained in the titles, *seed of Abraham,* or Isaac, or Israel.

Is it not for you to know judgment? It is a great increase of guilt, when persons neglect or pervert what it is their special duty and office to guard; as when teachers corrupt doctrine, or preachers give in to a low standard of morals, or judges pervert judgment. The *princes* here spoken of are so named from judging, "deciding[4]" causes. They are the same as the *rulers,* whom Isaiah at the same time upbraids, as being, from their sins, *rulers of Sodom*[5], whose [6] *hands* were *full of blood.* They who *do* not right, in time cease, in great measure, to know it. As God withdraws His grace, the mind is darkened and can no longer see it. So it is said of Eli's sons, they[7] *were sons of Belial, they knew not the Lord;* and, [8] *Into a malicious soul Wisdom shall not enter, nor dwell in a body that is subject unto sin.* Such "[9] attain not to know *the judgments of God* which are *a great deep:* and the depth of His justice the evil mind findeth not." But if men will not *know judgment* by doing it, they shall by suffering it.

2. *Who hate the good and love the evil;* i. e. *they* hate, for its own sake, *that* which is good, and love *that* which is evil. The Prophet is not here speaking of their *hating good* men, or *loving evil* men, but of their hating *goodness* and loving *wickedness*[10]. "[9] It is sin not to love good; what guilt to hate it! it is faulty, not to flee from evil, what ungodliness to love it!" Man, at first, loves and admires the good, even while he doth it not; he hates the evil, even while he does it, or as soon as he has done it. But man cannot bear to be at strife with his conscience, and so he ends it, by excusing himself and telling lies to himself. And then, he hates the truth or good with a bitter hatred, because it disturbs the darkness of the false peace with which he would envelop himself. At first, men love only the pleasure connected with the evil; then they make whom they can, evil, because goodness is a reproach to them: in

[1] 1–4. [2] 5–7 [3] 11.

[4] קָצִין from קצה, "cut, *decide,*" whence Cadhi.

[5] The word is the same, Is. i. 10.

[6] Ib. 15. [7] 1 Sam. ii. 12.

[8] Wisd. i. 4. [9] S. Jer.

[10] This appears from the Kethib רעה.

Before CHRIST cir. 710.

4 Then [d]shall they cry
unto the LORD, but he will
not hear them: he will
even hide his face from
them at that time, as they
have behaved themselves
ill in their doings.
5 ¶ Thus saith the
LORD [e]concerning the
prophets that make my

[d] Ps. 18. 41. Prov. 1. 28. Is. 1. 15. Ezek. 8. 18. Zech. 7. 13.

[e] Is. 56. 10, 11. Ezek. 13. 10. & 22. 25.

the end, they love evil for its own sake[1]. Heathen morality too distinguished between the incontinent and the unprincipled[2], the man who sinned under force of temptation, and the man who had lost the sense of right and wrong. "[3] *Every one that doeth evil, hateth the light.* Whoso longeth for things unlawful, hateth the righteousness which rebuketh and punisheth[4]."

Who pluck off their skin from off them, and their flesh from off their bones. He had described the Good Shepherd; now, in contrast, he describes those who ought to be "shepherds of the people," to feed, guard, direct them, but who were their butchers; who did not shear them, but flayed them; who fed on them, not fed them. He heaps up their guilt, act by act. First they flay, i. e. take away their outer goods; then they break their bones in pieces, the most solid parts, on which the whole frame of their body depends, to get at the very marrow of their life, and so feed themselves upon them. And not unlike, though still more fearfully, do they sin, who first remove the skin, as it were, or outward tender fences of God's graces; (such as is modesty, in regard to inward purity; outward demeanor, of inward virtue; outward forms, of inward devotion;) and so break the strong bones of the sterner virtues, which hold the whole soul together; and with them the whole flesh, or softer graces, becomes one shapeless mass, shred to pieces and consumed. So Ezekiel says[5]; *Woe to the shepherds of Israel that do feed themselves; should not the shepherds feed the flock? Ye eat the fat and ye clothe you with the wool, ye kill them that are fed, ye feed not the flock. The diseased have ye not strengthened, &c.*

4. *Then shall they cry unto the Lord. Then.* The Prophet looks on to the Day of the Lord, which is ever before his mind. So the Psalmist, speaking of a time or place not expressed, says, [6] *There were they in great fear.* He sees it, points to it, as seeing what those to whom he spoke, saw not, and the more awfully, because he saw, with super-human and so with certain vision, what was *hid from their eyes.* The *then* was not then, *in the time of grace,* but when the Day of grace should be over, and the Day of Judgment should be come. So of that day, when judgment should set in, God says in Jeremiah[7], *Behold I will bring evil upon them which they shall not be able to go forth of, and they will cry unto Me, and I will not hearken unto them.* And David[8], *They cried and* there was *none to save; unto the Lord, and He answered them not.* And Solomon[9]; *Whoso stoppeth his ears at the cry of the poor, he shall cry himself and shall not be heard.* And St. James[10], *He shall have judgment without mercy, that hath shewed no mercy.* The prayer is never too late, until judgment comes[11]; the day of grace is over, when the time of judgment has arrived. "They shall cry unto the Lord, and shall not be heard, because they too did not hear those who asked them, and the Lord shall turn His Face from them, because they too turned their face from those who prayed them."

He will even hide His Face. He will not look in mercy on those who would not receive His look of grace. *Your sins,* He says by Isaiah, *have hid His face from you, that He heareth not.* O what will that turning away of the Face be, on which hangs eternity!

As. There is a proportion between the sin and the punishment. [12] *As I have done, so God hath requited me. They have behaved themselves ill in their doings.* lit. *have made their deeds evil.* The word rendered *doings* is almost always used in a bad sense, *mighty deeds,* and so deeds with a high hand. Not ignorantly or negligently, nor through human frailty, but with set purpose they applied themselves, not to amend but to *corrupt their doings,* and make them worse. God called to them by *all* His *prophets, make good your doings*[13]; and they, reversing it, used diligence to *make their doings evil.* "[14] All this they shall suffer, because they were not rulers, but tyrants; not Prefects, but lions; not masters of disciples, but wolves of sheep; and they sated themselves with flesh and were fattened, and, as sacrifices for the slaughter, were made ready for the punishment of the Lord. Thus far against evil rulers; then he turns to the false prophets and evil teachers, who by flatteries subvert the people of God, promising them the knowledge of His word."

5. *The prophets that make My people err,* flattering them in their sins and rebellions,

[1] Rom. i. 32.
[2] The ἀκρατὴς and ἀκόλαστος of Aristotle.
[3] S. John iii. 20. [4] Dion. [5] xxxiv. 2–4. add 5–10.
[6] Ps. liii. 5. [7] xi. 11. [8] Ps. xviii. 41. [9] Prov. xxi. 13.
[10] ii. 13. [11] See on Hos. v. 6. vol. i. p. 58.

[12] Judg. i. 7. "As the Jews speak 'measure for measure'." Poc. from Abarb.
[13] Jer. xxxv. 15. היטיבו מעלליכם; here, הרעו מעלליהם.
[14] St. Jer.

Before CHRIST cir. 710

people err, that [f]bite with
their teeth, and cry, Peace;
and [g]he that putteth not
into their mouths, they
even prepare war against
him:
6 [h]Therefore night
shall be unto you, †that
ye shall not have a vision;
and it shall be dark
unto you, †that ye shall
not divine; [i]and the sun
shall go down over the
prophets, and the day
shall be dark over
them.

f ch. 2. 11. Matt. 7. 15.
g Ezek. 13. 18, 19.
h Is. 8. 20, 22. Ezek. 13. 23. Zech. 13. 4.
† Heb. *from a vision.*
† Heb. *from divining.*
i Amos 8. 9.

promising that they shall go unpunished, that God is not so strict, will not put in force the judgments He threatens. So Isaiah saith[1]; *O my people, they which lead thee, mislead thee;* and[2], *the leaders of this people are its misleaders, and* they that are *led of them are destroyed.* And Jeremiah[3], *The prophets have seen for thee vanity and folly; and they have not discovered thine iniquity to turn away thy captivity, and have seen for thee false burdens and causes of banishment.* No error is hopeless, save what is taught in the Name of God.

That bite with their mouths. The word[4] is used of no other biting than the biting of serpents. They were doing real, secret evil *while they cry,* i. e. *proclaim peace;* they bit, as serpents, treacherously, deadlily. They fed, not so much on the gifts, for which they hired themselves to [5]*speak peace when* there was *no peace,* as on the souls of the givers. So God says by Ezekiel[6], *Will ye pollute Me among My people for handfuls of barley and for pieces of bread, to slay the souls that should not die, and to save the souls alive that should not live, by your lying to My people that hear your lies? Because with lies ye have made the heart of the righteous sad, whom I have not made sad; and strengthened the hands of the wicked, that he should not return from his wicked way, by promising him life—therefore ye shall see no more vanity nor divine divinations.* It was with a show of peace that Joab slew Abner and Amasa, and with a kiss of peace Judas betrayed our Lord.

And he that putteth not into their mouths, they prepare war against him, lit. *and* (i. e. forthwith; it was all one; bribes refused, war proclaimed,) *they sanctify war against him.* Like those of whom Joel prophesied[7], they proclaim war against him in the Name of God, by the authority of God which they had taken to themselves, speaking in His Name Who had not sent them. So when our Lord fed the multitude, they would *take Him by force and make Him a king;* when their hopes were gone and they saw that His *Kingdom was not of this world,* they said, *Crucify him, crucify Him.* Much more the Pharisees, who, because He rebuked their covetousness, their devouring widows' houses, their extortion and excess, their making their proselytes more children of hell than themselves, said, *Thou blasphemest.* So, when the masters of the possessed damsel whom St. Paul freed, [8]*saw that the hope of their gains was gone,* they accused him, that he *exceedingly troubled their city, teaching customs not lawful to be received.* So Christians were persecuted by the Heathen as "[9]hating the human race," because they would not partake of their sins; as "[10]atheists," because they worshiped not their gods; as "[11]disloyal" and "public enemies," because they joined not in unholy festivals; as "unprofitable," because they neglected things not profitable but harmful. So men are now called "illiberal," who will not make free with the truth of God; "intolerant," who will not allow that all faith is matter of opinion, and that there is no certain truth; "precise," "censorious," who will not connive at sin, or allow the levity which plays, mothlike, around it and jests at it. The Church and the Gospel are against the world, and so the world which they condemn must be against them; and such is the force of truth and holiness, that it must carry on the war against them in their own name.

6. *Therefore night shall be unto you, that ye shall not have a vision.* In the presence of God's extreme judgments, even deceivers are at length still; silenced at last by the common misery, if not by awe. The false prophets had promised peace, light, brightness, prosperity; the night of trouble, anguish, darkness, fear, shall come upon them. So shall they no more dare to speak in the Name of God, while He was by His judgments speaking the contrary in a way which all must hear. They abused God's gifts and long-suffering

1 iii. 12. 2 ix. 16. (15, Heb.) 3 Lam. ii. 14.
4 נשך Gen. xlix. 17. Num. xxi. 8, 9. Prov. xiii. 32. Eccl. x. 8, 11. Am. v. 19. ix. 3. Hence, Kimchi, "While they proclaim peace, and flatter the people, it is as if they bit it with the teeth." So A. E. also and Tanch. in Poc.
5 Ezek. xiii. 10. 6 Ib. 19, 22, 23
7 See on Joel iii. vol. i. p. 207.
8 Acts xvi. 19–21.
9 Tertullian, Apol. c. 10. and note k. Oxf. Tr.
10 Ib. c. 35. ad Scap. c. 2.
11 Ib. 42, 43.

Before CHRIST cir. 710.

7 Then shall the seers
be ashamed, and the divi-
ners confounded: yea, they
shall all cover their † lips;
[k] for *there is* no answer of
God.
8 ¶ But truly I am full
of power by the spirit of

† Heb. *upper lip.*

Before CHRIST cir. 710.

k Ps. 74. 9. Amos 8. 11.

against Himself: they could misinterpret His long-suffering into favor, and they did it: their visions of the future were but the reflections of the present and its continuance; they thought that because God was enduring, He was indifferent, and they took His government out of His Hands, and said, that what He appeared to be now, He would ever be. They had no other light, no other foresight. When then the darkness of temporal calamity enveloped them, it shrouded in one common darkness of night all present brightness and all sight of the future.

"[1] After Caiaphas had in heart spoken falsehood and a prophecy of blood, although God overruled it to truth which he meant not, all grace of prophecy departed. [2] *The law and the prophets prophesied until John. The Sun of Righteousness went down over* them, inwardly and outwardly, withdrawing the brightness of His Providence and the inward light of grace." So Christ Himself forewarned; [3] *Walk while ye have the light, lest darkness come upon you.* And so it has remained ever since. [4] *The veil has been on their hearts.* The light is in all the world, but they see it not; it arose to lighten *the Gentiles*, but they *walk on still in darkness.* As opposed to holiness, truth, knowledge, Divine enlightening of the mind, bright gladness, contrariwise darkness is falsehood, sin, error, blindness of soul, ignorance of Divine things, and sorrow. In all these ways, did the Sun go down *over them*, so that the darkness weighed heavily *upon them.* So too the inventors of heresies pretend to see and to enter into the mysteries of Christ, yet find darkness instead of light, lose even what they think they see, fail even of what truth they seem most to hold; and they shall be in night and darkness, being *cast into outer darkness;* [5] *sinning against the brethren, and wounding the weak conscience of those for whom Christ died.*

7. *They shall cover their lips*, lit. *the hair of the upper lip* [6]. This was an action enjoined on lepers [7], and a token of mourning [8]; a token then of sorrow and uncleanness. With their lips they had lied, and now they should cover their lips, as men dumb and ashamed. *For there is no answer of God*, as these deceivers had pretended to have. When all things shall come contrary to what they had promised, it shall be clear that God did not send them. And having plainly no answer of God, they shall not dare to feign one *then.* "[9] Then not even the devils shall receive power to deceive them by their craft. The oracles shall be dumb; the unclean spirit shall not dare to delude." "[10] All this is spoken against those who, in the Church of Christ, flatter the rich, or speak as men-pleasers, out of avarice, ambition, or any like longing for temporal good, to whom that of Isaiah [11] fitteth; *the leaders of this people* [they who profess to *lead* them *aright*] *mislead them, and they that are led of them are destroyed.*"

8. *And truly I*, [lit. *contrariwise I*,] i.e. whereas they shall be void and *no word in them, I am full of* (or *filled with*) *power by the Spirit of the Lord and of judgment and might.* The false prophets [12] *walked after their own spirit.* Their only power or influence was from without, from favoring circumstances, from adapting themselves to the great or to the people, going along with the tide, and impelling persons whither they wished to go. The power of the true prophet was inherent, and that by gift of *the Spirit of the Lord* [13]. And so, while adverse circumstances silenced the false prophets, they called forth the more the energy of the true, whose power was from Him in Whose Hands the world is. The adverse circumstances to the false prophets were God's judgments; to the true, they were man's refractoriness, rebellion, oppressiveness. *Now* was the time of the false prophets; *now*, at a distance, they could foretell hardily, because they could not yet be convicted of untruth. When trouble came, they went *into the inner chamber to hide* [14] themselves. Micah, amid *the wild tumult of the people* [15], was fearless, upborne by Him who controls, *stills*, or looses it, to do His Sovereign Will.

I am filled with power. So our Lord bade His Apostles [16], *Tarry ye, until ye be endued with power from on high* [17]: *ye shall receive power, after that the Holy Ghost is come upon you;* and [18] *they were all filled with the Holy Ghost.* The three gifts, *power, judgment, might*, are the fruits of the One Spirit of God, through Whom the Prophet was filled with them. Of these, *power* is always strength residing in the person, whether it be the *power* [19] or *might of wisdom* [20] of Almighty God Himself,

[1] Rup. [2] S. Matt. xi. 13. [3] S. John xii. 35. [4] 2 Cor. iii. 15. [5] 1 Cor. viii. 12. [6] Kim. [7] Lev. xiii. 45. [8] Ezek. xxiv. 17, 22. [9] S. Jer. [10] Dion. [11] iii. 12. [12] Ezek. xiii. 3.

[13] The use of את before רוח יי only, shews plainly that the objects of the verb are כח, משפט, גבורה, and that the את is "with" "through," as in Gen. iv. 1. [14] 1 Kgs. xxii. 25. [15] Ps. lxv. 7. [16] S. Luke xxiv. 49. [17] Acts i. 8. [18] Ib. ii. 4. [19] Ex. xv. 6. xxxii. 11. Num. xiv. 17, &c. [20] Job xxxvi. 5.

Before CHRIST cir. 710.

the LORD, and of judg-
ment, and of might, [l] to
declare unto Jacob his
transgression, and to Israel
his sin.

[l] Is. 58. 1.

9 Hear this, I pray you,
ye heads of the house of Jacob, and princes of the house
of Israel, that abhor judgment, and pervert all equity.

Before CHRIST cir. 710.

---

or *power* which He imparts[1] or implants[2]. But it is always power lodged *in* the person, to be put forth by him. Here, as in St. John Baptist[3] or the Apostles[4], it is Divine power, given through God the Holy Ghost, to accomplish that for which he was sent, as St. Paul was endued with might[5], *casting down imaginations and every high thing that exalteth itself against the knowledge of God, and bringing into captivity every thought to the obedience of Christ.* It is just *that,* which is so wanting to human words, which is so characteristic of the word of God, *power. Judgment* is, from its form[6], not so much discernment in the human being, as "the thing judged," pronounced by God, the righteous judgment of God, and righteous judgment in man conformably therewith[7]. It was what, he goes on to say, the great men of his people *abhorred*[8], equity. With this he was filled. This was the substance of his message, right judgment to be enacted by them, to which he was to exhort them, or which, on their refusal, was to be pronounced upon them in the Name of God the Judge of all, and to be executed upon them. *Might* is courage or boldness to deliver the message of God, not awed or hindered by any adversaries. It is that holy courage, of which St. Paul speaks[9], *that utterance may be given unto me, that I may open my mouth boldly, to make known the mystery of the gospel, for which I am an ambassador in bonds, that therein I may speak boldly, as I ought to speak.* So too, after the Apostles had been [10]*straitly threatened that they should speak no more in the Name of Jesus, all,* having prayed, *were filled with the Holy Ghost,* and spake *the word of God with boldness.* "[11] Whoso is so strengthened and arrayed, uttereth fiery words, whereby hearers' hearts are moved and changed. But whoso speaketh of his own mind, doth good neither to himself nor others."

So then, of the three gifts, *power* expresses the Divine might lodged in him; *judgment,* the substance of what he had to deliver; *might* or *courage,* the strength to deliver it in face of human power, persecution, ridicule, death.

"[12] These gifts the Prophets know are not their own, but are from the Spirit of God, and are by Him inspired into them. Such was the spirit of Elijah, unconquered, energetic, fiery, of whom it is said, [13]*Then stood up Elias as fire, and his word burned like a lamp.* Such was Isaiah[14], *Cry aloud, spare not, lift up thy voice like a trumpet, and shew My people their transgression and the house of Jacob their sins.* Such was Jeremiah[15]; *Therefore I am full of the fury of the Lord; I am weary of holding in. I have set thee for a trier among My people, a strong fort; and thou shalt know and try their ways.* Such was John Baptist, who said[16], *O generation of vipers, who hath warned you to flee from the wrath to come?* Such was Paul, who, when he [17]*reasoned of temperance, righteousness and judgment to come,* made Felix tremble, though unbelieving and ungodly. Such were the Apostles, who, when they had received the Holy Spirit, [18]*brake,* with a mighty breath, *ships* and kings *of Tarshish.* Such will be Elias and Enoch at the end of the world, striving against Anti-Christ, of whom it is said[19], *If any man will hurt them, fire proceedeth out of their mouth and devoureth their enemies.*"

9. *Hear this, I pray you.* The Prophet discharges upon them that *judgment,* whereof, *by the Spirit of God,* he was *full,* and which they *abhorred; judgment* against their perversion of judgment. He rebukes the same classes as before[20], *the heads* and *judges,* yet still more sternly. They *abhorred judgment,* he says, as a thing loathsome and *abominable*[21], such as men cannot bear even to look upon; they not only dealt wrongly, but they *perverted,* distorted, *all equity:* "[22] that so there should not remain even some slight justice in the city." *All equity;* all of every sort, right, rectitude, uprightness, straight-forwardness[23], whatever was right by natural conscience or by God's law, they distorted, like the sophists making the worse appear the better cause. Naked violence crushes

---

[1] Deut. viii. 18. Judg. xvi. 5. 9, 19.
[2] Deut. viii. 17. and passim.
[3] S. Luke i. 17.
[4] S. Luke xxiv. 49.
[5] 2 Cor. x. 5.
[6] משפט.
[7] As in Prov. i. 3. Is. i. 21. v. 7.
[8] ver. 9.
[9] Eph. vi. 19, 20.
[10] Acts iv. 18, 31.
[11] Dion.
[12] Lap.
[13] Ecclus. xlviii. 1.
[14] lviii. 1.
[15] vi. 11, 27.
[16] S. Matt. iii. 7.
[17] Acts xxiv. 25.
[18] Ps. xlviii. 8.
[19] Rev. xi. 5.
[20] iii. 1.

[21] מתעבים, one of the two strongest Hebrew words to express abomination, comp. תועבה.
[22] S. Jer.
[23] Frequent as the adj. ישר, "right, upright," is, the abstract ישרה occurs here only in the O. T. The original force is "straight," "even," and hence "straight-forwardness, rectitude." The idea of "evenness" (which Ges. denies) belonged to the root in early times, the names of the two "plains," *Sharon,* and *Mishor* in Reuben (Deut. iii. 10. iv. 43.) being formed from it.

Before CHRIST cir. 710.

10 [m] They build up Zion with [n] † blood, and Jerusalem with iniquity.

m Jer. 22. 13. n Ezek. 22. 27. Hab. 2. 12. Zeph. 3. 3. † Heb. *bloods*.

11 [o] The heads thereof judge for reward, and [p] the priests thereof teach for

Before CHRIST cir. 710.

o Is. 1. 23. Ezek. 22. 12. Hos. 4. 18. ch. 7. 3. p Jer. 6. 13.

the individual; perversion of equity destroys the fountain-head of justice. The Prophet turns from them in these words, as one who could not bear to look upon their misdeeds, and who would not speak to them; *they pervert; building; her heads, her priests, her prophets;* as Elisha, but for the presence of Jehoshaphat, would not look on Jehoram, nor see him[1]. He first turns and speaks of them, as one man, as if they were all one in evil;

10. *They build up* [lit. *building, sing.*] *Zion with blood.* This may be taken literally on both sides, that, the rich built their palaces, "with wealth gotten by bloodshed[2], by rapine of the poor, by slaughter of the saints," as Ezekiel says[3], *her princes in the midst thereof* are *like wolves, to shed blood, to destroy souls, to get dishonest gain.* Or by *blood* he may mean that they indirectly took away life, in that, through wrong judgments, extortion, usury, fraud, oppression, reducing wages or detaining them, they took away what was necessary to support life. So it is said[4]; *The bread of the needy is their life, he that defraudeth him thereof is a man of blood. He that taketh away his neighbor's living slayeth him, and he that defraudeth the laborer of his hire is a bloodshedder.* Or it may be, that as David prayed to God, [5] *Build Thou the walls of Jerusalem,* asking Him thereby to maintain or increase its well-being, so these men thought to promote the temporal prosperity of Jerusalem by doings which were unjust, oppressive, crushing to their inferiors. So Solomon, in his degenerate days, made the *yoke* upon his people and his *service grievous*[6]. So ambitious monarchs by large standing-armies or filling their exchequers drain the life-blood of their people. The physical condition and stature of the poorer population in much of France was lowered permanently by the conscriptions under the first Emperor. In our wealthy nation, the term poverty describes a condition of other days. We have had to coin a new name to designate the misery, offspring of our material prosperity. From our wealthy towns, (as from those of Flanders,) ascends to heaven against us "[7] the cry of 'pauperism' i.e. the cry of distress, arrived at a condition of system and of power, and, by an unexpected curse, issuing from the very development of wealth. The political economy of unbelief has been crushed by facts on all the theatres of human activity and industry." Truly we *build up Zion with blood,* when we cheapen luxuries and comforts at the price of souls, use Christian toil like brute strength, tempt men to dishonesty and women to other sin, to eke out the scanty wages which alone our selfish thirst for cheapness allows, heedless of every thing save of our individual gratification, or the commercial prosperity, which we have made our god. Most awfully was *Zion built with blood,* when the Jews shed the innocent Blood, that [8] *the Romans* might not *take away* their *place and nation.* But since He has said[9], *Inasmuch as ye did it not unto one of the least of these My brethren, ye did it not unto Me,* and, [10] *Saul, Saul, why persecutest thou Me?* when Saul was persecuting Christ's members, then, in this waste of lives and of souls, we are not only wasting the Price of His Blood in ourselves and others, but are anew slaying Christ, and that, from the selfsame motives as those who crucified Him. [11] *When ye sin against the members, ye sin against Christ.* Our commercial greatness is *the price of* His *Blood*[12]. In the judgments on the Jews, we may read our own national future; in the woe on those through whom *the weak brother perishes for whom Christ died*[13], we, if we partake or connive at it, may read our own.

11. *The heads thereof judge for reward.* Every class was corrupted. One sin, *the root of all evil*[14], covetousness, entered into all they did. It, not God, was their one end, and so their God. *Her heads,* the secular authority, who[15] *sat to judge according to the law, judged,* contrary to the law, *for rewards.* They sat as the representatives of the Majesty of God, in Whose Name they judged, Whose righteous Judgment and correcting Providence law exhibits and executes, and they profaned it. To *judge for rewards* was in itself sin, forbidden by the law[16]. To refuse justice, unless paid for it, was unjust, degrading to justice. The second sin followed hard upon it, to judge unjustly, absolving the guilty, condemning the innocent, justifying the oppressor, legalizing wrong.

And her priests teach for hire. The Lord was *the portion and inheritance*[17] of the priest. He had his sustenance assigned him by God,

1 2 Kgs iii. 14. 2 S. Jer. 3 xxii. 27. 4 Ecclus. xxxiv. 21, 22. 5 Ps. li. 18. 6 1 Kgs. xii. 4. 7 Lacordaire, Conférences, T. ii. p. 300. 8 S. John xi. 48. 9 S. Matt. xxv. 45.

10 Acts ix. 4. 11 1 Cor. viii. 12. 12 S. Matt. xxvii. 6. 13 1 Cor. viii. 11. 14 1 Tim. vi. 10. 15 Acts xxiii. 3. 16 Ex. xxiii. 8. Deut. xvi. 19. 17 Num. xviii. 20. Deut. xviii. 2.

Before CHRIST cir. 710.

hire, and the prophets thereof divine for money: [q]yet will they lean upon the LORD, †and say, *Is* not the LORD among us? none evil can come upon us.

q Is. 48. 2. Jer. 7. 4. Rom. 2. 17.

† Heb. *saying.*

and, therewith, the duty to [1] *put difference between holy and unholy, and between clean and unclean, and to teach all the statutes,* which God had commanded. Their *lips* were to *keep knowledge* [2]. This men, which they were bound to *give*, they sold. But "[3] whereas it is said to the holy, [4] *Freely ye have received, freely give,* these, producing the answer of God upon the receipt of money, sold the grace of the Lord for a covetous price." Probably too, their sin co-operated with and strengthened the sin of the judges. Authorized interpreters of the law, they, to please the wealthy, probably misinterpreted the law. For wicked judges would not have given a price for a righteous interpretation of the law. The civil authorities were entrusted by God with power to execute the law; the priests were entrusted by Him with the knowledge to expound it. Both employed in its perversion that which God gave them for its maintenance. The princes obtained by bribery the misjudgment of the priests and enforced it; the priests justified the injustice of the Princes. So Arian Bishops, themselves hirelings [5], by false expositions of Scripture, countenanced Arian Emperors in the oppression of the faithful. "[6] They propped up the heresy by human patronage;" the Emperors "[7] bestowed on" them their "reign of irreligion." The Arian Emperors tried to efface the Council of Nice by councils of Arian Bishops [8]. Emperors perverted their power, the Bishops their knowledge. Not publicly only but privately doubtless also, these *priests taught* falsely *for hire,* lulling the consciences of those who wished to deceive themselves as to what God forbade, and to obtain from His priests answers in His Name, which might explain away His law in favor of laxity or sin. So people now try to get ill-advised to do against God's will what they are bent on doing; only they get ill-advised for nothing. One who receives money for giving an irresponsible opinion, places himself in proximate peril of giving the answer which will please those who pay him. "[9] It is Simony to teach and preach the doctrine of Christ and His Gospel, or to give answers to quiet the conscience, for money. For the immediate object of these two acts, is the calling forth of faith, hope, charity, penitence, and other supernatural acts, and the reception of the consolation of the Holy Spirit; and this is, among Christians, their only value. Whence they are accounted things sacred and supernatural; for their immediate end is to things supernatural; and they are done by man, as he is an instrument of the Holy Ghost."

"[10] Thou art permitted, O Priest, *to live* [11], not to luxuriate, from the altar. [12] *The mouth of the ox which treadeth out the corn* is *not muzzled.* Yet the Apostle [13] *abused not the liberty,* but [14] *having food and raiment,* was *therewith content;* [15] *laboring night and day, that he might not be chargeable to anybody.* And in his Epistles he calls God to witness that he [16] *lived holily and* without avarice in the Gospel of Christ. He asserts this too, not of himself alone but of his disciples, that he had sent no one who would either ask or receive anything from the Churches [17]. But if in some Epistles he expresses pleasure, and calls the gifts of those who sent, the *grace* [18] *of God,* he gathers not for himself but for the [19] *poor saints at Jerusalem.* But these *poor saints* were they who of the Jews first believed in Christ, and, being cast out by parents, kinsmen, connections, had lost their possessions and all their goods, the priests of the temple and the people destroying them. Let such poor receive. But if on plea of the poor, a few houses are enriched, and we eat in gold, glass and china, let us either with our wealth change our habit, or let not the habit of poverty seek the riches of Senators. What avails the habit of poverty, while a whole crowd of poor longs for the contents of our purse? Wherefore, *for our sake* who are such, *who build up Zion with blood and Jerusalem by iniquity, who judge for gifts, give answers for rewards, divine for money,* and thereon, claiming to ourselves a fictitious sanctity, say, *Evil will not come upon us,* hear we the sentence of the Lord which follows. *Sion and Jerusalem and the mountain of the temple,* i. e. the temple of Christ, *shall,* in the consummation and the end, when [20] *love shall wax cold* and the faith shall be rare [21], *be plowed as a field and become heaps as the high places of a forest;* so that, where once were ample houses and countless heaps of corn, there should only be a poor cottage, keeping up the show

1 Lev. x. 10, 11. add Deut. xvii. 10, 11. xxxiii. 10. Hag. ii. 11 sqq.
2 Mal. ii. 7. 3 S. Jer. 4 S. Matt. x. 8.
5 S. Ath. ag. Arians, i. 8. p. 191. and n. c. Oxf. Tr.
6 Id. ii. 43. p. 341.
7 Counc. Arim. § 3. p. 77.
8 Pusey's Councils of the Church, p. 118–180, &c.

9 Less de Justit. ii. 35. de Simonia Dub. 13. p. 389. L.
10 S. Jer. 11 1 Cor. ix. 13. 12 Ib. 9. 13 Ib. 18.
14 1 Tim. vi. 8. 15 1 Thess. ii. 6. 2 Thess. iii. 8.
16 1 Thess. ii. 10. 17 2 Cor. xii. 17, 18.
18 Ib. viii. 6. 7. 19 Rom. xv. 26.
20 S. Matt. xxiv. 12. 21 S. Luke xviii. 8.

Before CHRIST cir. 710.

12 Therefore shall Zion for your sake be [r] plowed *as* a field, [s] and Jerusalem shall become heaps, and [t] the

r Jer. 26. 18. ch. 1. 6. s Ps. 79. 1. t ch. 4. 2.

of fruit which has no refreshment for the soul."

The three places, Zion, Jerusalem, the Temple, describe the whole city in its political and religious aspects. Locally, Mount Zion, which occupies the South-West, "had upon it the Upper city," and "was by much the loftier, and length-ways the straighter." Jerusalem, as contrasted with Zion, represented the lower city, "[1] supported" on the East by Mount Acra, and including the valley of Tyropœon. South of Mount Acra and lower than it, at the South Eastern corner of the city, lay Mount Moriah or the Mount of the Lord's House, separated at this time from Mount Acra by a deep ravine, which was filled up by the Asmonæan princes, who lowered Mount Acra. It was joined to the N. E. corner of Mount Zion by the causeway of Solomon across the Tyropœon. The whole city then in all its parts was to be desolated.

And her prophets divine for money. The word rendered[2], *divine,* is always used in a bad sense. These prophets then were false prophets, *her prophets* and not God's, which *divined,* in reality or appearance, giving the answer which their employers, the rich men, wanted, as if it were an answer from God. [3] Yet they also *judge for rewards,* who look rather to the earthly than to the spiritual good; they *teach for hire,* who seek in the first place the things of this world, instead of teaching for the glory of God and the good of souls, and regarding earthly things in the second place only, as the support of life.

And say, Is not the Lord among us? And after all this, not understanding their sin, as though by their guilt they purchased the love of God, they said in their impenitence, that they were judges, prophets, priests, of God. *They do all this,* and yet *lean on the Lord;* they stay and trust, not in themselves, but in God; good in itself, had not they been evil! *And say, Is not the Lord among us? none evil can* [*shall*] *come upon us.* So Jeremiah says[4], *Trust ye not in lying words saying, The temple of the Lord, the temple of the Lord, The temple of the Lord are these.* "[5] He called them *lying words,* as being ofttimes repeated by the false prophets, to entice the credulous people to a false security" against the threatenings of God. As though God could not forsake His own people, nor cast away Zion which He had *chosen for an habitation for Himself,* nor profane His own holy place! Yet it was true that God *was among them,* in the midst of them, as our Lord was among the Jews, though they knew Him not. Yet if not in the midst of His people so as to hallow, God is in the midst of them to punish. But what else do we than these Jews did, if we lean on the Apostolic line, the possession of Holy Scripture, Sacraments, pure doctrine, without setting ourselves to gain to God the souls of our Heathen population? or what else is it for a soul to trust in having been made a member of Christ, or in any gifts of God, unless it be *bringing forth fruit with patience?* "[6] Learn we too hence, that all trust in the Merits of Christ is vain, so long as any wilfully persist in sin." "[6] Know we, that God will be in us also, if we have not faith alone, nor on this account rest, as it were, on Him, but if to faith there be added also the excelling in good works. For *faith without works is dead.* But when with the riches of faith works concur, then will God indeed be with us, and will strengthen us mightily, and account us friends, and gladden us as His true sons, and free us from all evil."

12. *Therefore shall Zion for your sake* [*for your sake shall Zion*] *be plowed as a field.* They thought to be its builders; they were its destroyers. They imagined to advance or secure its temporal prosperity *by bloods;* they (as men ever do first or last,) ruined it. Zion might have stood, but for these its acute, far-sighted politicians, who scorned the warnings of the prophets, as well-meant ignorance of the world or of the necessities of the state. They taught, perhaps they thought, that *for Zion's sake* they, (act as they might,) were secure. Practical Antinomians! God says, that, *for their sake,* Zion, defiled by their deeds, should be destroyed. The fulfillment of the prophecy was delayed by the repentance under Hezekiah. *Did he not,* the elders ask[7], *fear the Lord and besought the Lord, and the Lord repented Him of the evil which He had pronounced against them?* But the prophecy remained, like that of Jonah against Nineveh, and, when man undid and in act repented of his repentance, it found its fulfillment.

Jerusalem shall become heaps, [lit. *of ruins*[8],] and *the mountain of the house,* Mount Moriah, on which the *house of God* stood, *as the high*

[1] Jos. B. J. v. 4. 1.

[2] In Prov. xvi. 10. (quoted as an exception) it is used of that penetrating acuteness which is like a gift of divination; as we speak of "divining a person's thoughts, purposes," &c.

[3] From Dion.

[4] vii. 4.

[5] Sanch.

[6] J. H. Mich.

[7] Jer. xxvi. 19.

[8] עיין from עוה, "distort, pervert, subvert."

Before CHRIST cir. 710. mountain of the house as the high places of the forest. Before CHRIST cir. 710.

places of the forest, lit. *as high places of a forest.* It should return wholly to what it had been, before Abraham offered up the typical sacrifice of his son, a wild and desolate place covered with tangled *thickets*[1].

The prophecy had a first fulfillment at its first capture by Nebuchadnezzar. Jeremiah mourns over it; [2] *Because of the mountain of Zion which is desolate, foxes walk* [habitually [3]] upon it. Nehemiah said, [4] *Ye see the distress that we are in, how Jerusalem* lieth *waste;* and Sanballat mocked at the attempts to rebuild it, as a thing impossible; [5] *Will they revive the stones out of the heaps of dust, and these too, burned?* and the builders complained; [6] *The strength of the bearers of burdens is decayed* [lit. *sinketh* under them], *and there is much dust, and we are not able to build the wall.* In the desolation under Antiochus again it is related; [7] *they saw the sanctuary desolate, and the altar profaned, and the gates burned up, and shrubs growing in the courts, as in a forest or in one of the mountains.* When, by the shedding of the Blood of the Lord, they [8] *filled up the measure* of their *fathers*, and called the curse upon themselves, [9] *His Blood be upon us and upon our children*, destruction came upon them to the uttermost. With the exception of three towers, left to exhibit the greatness of Roman prowess in destroying such and so strong a city, they "[10] so levelled to the ground the whole circuit of the city, that to a stranger it presented no token of ever having been inhabited." He "*effaced* the rest of the city," says the Jewish historian, himself an eyewitness[11]. The elder Pliny soon after, A. D. 77, speaks of it, as a city which *had been* and was not. "[12] Where *was* Jerusalem, far the most renowned city, not of Judæa only, but of the East," "[13] a funeral pile." With this corresponds S. Jerome's statement, "[14] relics of the city remained for fifty years until the Emperor Hadrian." Still it was in utter ruins[15]. The toleration of the Jewish school at Jamnia[16] the more illustrates the desolation of Jerusalem where there was none. The Talmud[17] relates how R. Akiba smiled when others wept at seeing a fox coming out of the Holy of holies. This prophecy of Micah being fulfilled, he looked the more for the prophecy of good things to come, connected therewith. Not Jerusalem only, but well-nigh all Judæa was desolated by that war, in which a million and a half perished[18], beside all who were sold as slaves. "Their country to which you would expell them, is destroyed, and there is no place to receive them," was Titus' expostulation[19] to the Antiochenes, who desired to be rid of the Jews their fellow-citizens. A heathen historian relates how, before the destruction by Hadrian, "[20] many wolves and hyænas entered their cities howling." Titus however having left above 6000[21] Roman soldiers on the spot, a civil population was required to minister to their wants. The Christians who, following our Lord's warning, had fled to Pella[22], returned to Jerusalem[23], and continued there until the second destruction by Hadrian, under fifteen successive Bishops[24]. Some few Jews had been left there[25]; some very probably returned, since we hear of no prohibition from the Romans, until after the fanatic revolt under Barcocheba. But the fact that when toward

1 Gen. xxii. 13. סבך. 2 Lam. v. 18. 3 הִלְּכוּ.
4 Neh. ii. 17. 5 Ib. iv. 2. [iii. 34. Heb.]
6 Ib. 10. [iv. 4. Heb.] 7 1 Macc. iv. 38.
8 S. Matt. xxiii. 32. 9 Ib. xxvii. 25.
10 Joseph. B. J. vii. 1. 1. 11 Ib. vi. 9. 1.
12 Nat. Hist. v. 14.
13 Pliny says of Engedi, "Below these was the town Engadda, second only to Jerusalem in fertility and palm-groves, now a second funeral pile." [bustum] N. H. v. 18. See at length in Deyling de Æliæ Capit. Orig. in his Obss. sacr. v. 436–490. and on the whole subject Lightfoot, Chronicon de Excidio urb. Hieros. Opp. ii. 136 sqq. Tillemont, Hist. d. Emp. T. i. Ruine des Juifs; T. ii. Révoltes des Juifs; Munter, d. Jud. Krieg unt. Traj. u. Hadr. (translated in Dr. Robinson's Bibl. Sacr. T. iii. 1st series) who, however, gives too much weight to very late authorities. Jost, Gesch. d. Juden, B. xii.
14 Ep. 129. ad Dard. fin.
15 The Talmud speaks of R. Jose (who lived before Hadrian) "praying in one of the ruins of Jerusalem," but only when on a journey. Berachoth, f. 3. The context implies that they were utter ruins.
16 Gittin, f. 56. Jost, iii. 184. Anhang, p. 165.
17 Maccoth, fin. 18 Josephus' numbers.
19 Jos. B. J. vii. 5. 2. 20 Dio lxix. 14.
21 "The tenth legion and some troops of horse and companies of foot." (Jos. Ib. vii. 1. 2.) The legion was 6000 men; the troop, 64; the company, 100.
22 Eus. H. E. iii. 5.
23 S. Epiph. de Mens. c. 15. p. 171.
24 Eus. H. E. iv. 5. "from written documents."
25 Josephus makes Eleazar say in the siege of Masada, "Jerusalem has been plucked up by the roots, and the only memorial of it remaining is the camp of those who took it, still seated on its remains. Hapless elders sit by the dust of the temple, and a few women preserved by the enemy for the foulest insolence." B. J. vii. 8. The statement of S. Epiphanius (de Mens. 15. p. 170.) "in that part of Zion which survived after the desolation, there were both parts of dwellings around Zion itself and seven synagogues which alone stood in Zion as cabins, one of which survived till the time of Bishop Maximus and the Emperor Constantine, as a hut in a vineyard," is remarkably confirmed by the independent Latin statement of the Bourdeaux pilgrim. "Within the wall of Zion appears the place where David had his palace; and of seven synagogues, which were there, one only has remained, the rest are ploughed and sowed." Itin. Hieros. p. 592, ed. Wess. Optatus also mentions the 7 synagogues. (iii. 2. Edd. before Dupin, and all MSS. but one. See p. 53.) Before the destruction there are said to have been 480. Echa Rabbathi, f. 52. col. 2. f. 71. col. 4.

the close of Trajan's reign they burst out simultaneously, in one wild frenzy [1], upon the surrounding Heathen, all along the coast of Africa, Libya, Cyrene, Egypt, the Thebais, Mesopotamia, Cyprus [2], there was no insurrection in Judæa, implies that there were no great numbers of Jews there. Judæa, aforetime the centre of rebellion, contributed nothing [3] to that wide national insurrection, in which the carnage was so terrible, as though it had been one convulsive effort of the Jews to root out their enemies [4]. Even in the subsequent war under Hadrian, Orosius speaks of them, as "[5] laying waste the province of Palestine, *once their own*," as though they had gained possession of it from without, not by insurrection within it. The Jews assert that in the time of Joshua Ben Chananiah (under Trajan) "the kingdom of wickedness decreed that the temple should be rebuilt [6]." If this was so, the massacres toward the end of Trajan's reign altered the policy of the Empire. Apparently the Emperors attempted to extinguish the Jewish, as, at other times, the Christian faith. A heathen Author mentions the prohibition of circumcision [7]. The Jerusalem Talmud [8] speaks of many who for fear *became uncircumcised*, and renewed the symbol of their faith "[9] when Bar Cozibah got the better, so as to reign 2½ years among them." The Jews add, that the prohibition extended to the keeping of the sabbath and the reading of the law [10]. Hadrian's city, Ælia, was doubtless intended, not only for a strong position, but also to efface the memory of Jerusalem by the Roman and Heathen city which was to replace it. Christians, when persecuted, suffered; Jews rebelled. The recognition of Barcocheba, who gave himself out as the Messiah [11], by Akibah [12] and "all the wise [Jews] of his generation [13]," made the war national. Palestine was the chief seat of the war, but not its source. The Jews throughout the Roman world were in arms against their conquerors [14]; and the number of fortresses and villages which they got possession of, and which were destroyed by the Romans [15], shews that their successes were far beyond Judæa. Their measures in Judæa attest the desolate condition of the country. They fortified, not towns, but "[16] the advantageous positions of the country, strengthened them with mines and walls, that, if defeated, they might have places of refuge, and communication among themselves underground unperceived." For two years, (as appears from the coins struck by Barcocheba [17],) they

[1] sub uno tempore, quasi rabie efferati. Oros. L. vii. B. P. vi. 437. "as if rekindled by some dreadful seditious spirit." Eus. H. E. iv. 2.

[2] Oros. Dio mentions Cyrene, Egypt, Cyprus; to these Eusebius adds Mesopotamia; also in S. Jer. Chron. A. D. 117.

[3] Abulfaraj (A. D. 1270.) mentions an *invasion* of Judæa by one whom the Egyptian Jews made their king; and whom "the Roman armies sought and slew with some ten thousands of Jews everywhere." (Hist. Ar. p. 120. Chron. Syr. p. 56.) He is too late to be an authority; but his account equally implies that there was no rebellion *in* Judæa.

[4] Dio speaks of their destroying 220,000 Romans and Greeks in Cyrene; committing much the same horrors in Egypt; destroying 240,000 in Cyprus. lxviii. 32. The Jews, ascribing this to Barcocheba, say that they destroyed "in Africa a great multitude of Romans and Greeks like the sand on the sea-shore innumerable," and in Egypt more than 200,000 men; and in Cyprus, so as to leave none. Zemach David, f. 27. 1. in Eisenmenger, Entd. Jud. ii. 655. (The coincidence is remarkable, but the statement is too late to have any independent value.) Orosius says that "Libya was so desolated through the slaughter of its peasants, that, had not Hadrian re-colonized it, it would have remained empty." l. c.

[5] l. c. Sulpicius Severus in like way speaks of the Jews "wishing to rebel, essaying to plunder Syria and Palestine." ii. 4. [6] Bereshith Rabba, c. 64.

[7] Spartian Hadrian, c. 14. It was repealed by Antonine. See Munter, § 26.

[8] Yebammoth, f. 9. 1. and R. Nissim. (See in Lightfoot, Chron. Opp. ii. 143.) Berachoth f. 16. 2. in Jost B. xii. Anhang n. 21.

[9] R. Nissim in Lightfoot, l. c.

[10] Jost xii. 9. p. 228.

[11] Eus. H. E. iv. 6. Zemach David, f. 27. in Eisenmenger, Entd. Jud. ii. 654. "He was called Bar Cocheba, because he interpreted, as said of himself, *a star shall arise out of Jacob, &c.* (Num. xxiv. 17.) Shalshalet hakkabbala (in De Voisin on Martini, Pug. Fid. p. 265.) Sanhedrin, Chelek. (Mart. p. 320.)

[12] "And R. Akibah himself, when he saw him, said of him, This is the king Messiah, as it is in the Echa Rabbathi on the verse Lam. ii. 2." (Ib.) "He applied Hagg. ii. 6, 7. to him" (quoting v. 7. "*I will bring the desire of the nations to Jerusalem.*") Sanh. Chelek in Mart. See more of him Wolf, Bibl. Hebr. i. n. 1801. R. Bechai said, God revealed to him things unknown to Moses. (Ib.) See also Midrash Cant. in Mart. p. 320. Bartolocci, Bibl. Rabb. p. 274.

[13] Maimon. Yad Chazaka, Sanhedrin, c. 11. in Mart. p. 873. "R. Akiba and all the wise of his generation thought that he was the Messiah, until he was slain in his iniquities, and it was known that he was not." This was doubtless the ground of their death, mentioned in the Avoda Zara. See p. 128 sqq. F. C. Ewald, trans.

[14] "The Romans made no account of them at first, but when all Judæa was moved and all the Jews throughout the world were set in commotion and conspired and publicly and privately inflicted much evil on the Romans, and many foreigners helped them in hope of gain, and the whole world was shaken, Hadrian sent his best general against them." Dio Cass. lxix. 13.

[15] "50 fortresses of much account and 985 very well-known villages." Dio C. (almost a contemporary) Ib. 14. [16] Ib. 12.

[17] De Saulcy, Numismatique Judaique, p. 156–70. The coins bear the inscription "the 1st year of the redemption of Jerusalem," "the first" and "second year of the freedom of Jerusalem." Two of them are cast upon coins of Trajan and Vespasian. Ib. p. 162. The Abbé Barthélémi (App. to Bayer Num. Hebr. Sam. Vind. L. iii. p. ix.–xi.) mentions four of Trajan's, recast by Barcocheba. Bayer mentions coins of the 3d and 4th year, but anonymous. (Num. Hebr. Sam. p. 171.) De Saulcy supposes these to belong to the revolt against Vespasian. (p. 153, 4.) The title and the name "Simon" which probably Barcocheba took, were doubtless intended to recall the memory of the Maccabees. The Jerusalem Talmud speaks of money with the impress of Ben Coziba, ("son of a lie" as the Jews changed his name.) Lightfoot, Opp. ii. 143. Mr. Vaux, keeper of the coins, British Museum, tells me that these coins (of which some are in the British Museum) are certainly genuine. See also Madden, p. 161–182.

had possession of Jerusalem. It was essential to his claim to be a temporal Messiah. They proposed, at least, to "rebuild their temple[1]" and restore their polity." But they could not fortify Jerusalem. Its siege is just named[2]; but the one place which obstinately resisted the Romans was a strong city *near* Jerusalem[3], known before only as a deeply indented mountain tract, Bether[4]. Probably, it was one of the strong positions, fortified in haste, at the beginning of the war[5].

The Jews fulfilled our Lord's words[6], *I am come in My Father's Name and ye receive Me not; if another shall come in his own name, him ye will receive.* Their first destruction was the punishment of their Deicide, the crucifixion of Jesus, the Christ; their second they brought upon themselves by accepting a false Christ, a robber[7] and juggler[8]. "580,000 are said to have perished in battle[9]," besides "an incalculable number by famine and fire, so that all Judæa was made well-nigh a desert." The Jews say that "[10] no olives remained in Palestine." Hadrian "[11] destroyed it," making it "[12] an utter desolation" and "effacing all remains of it." "We read[13]," says St. Jerome[14], "the expedition of Ælius Hadrianus against the Jews, who so destroyed Jerusalem and its walls, as, from the fragments and ashes of the city to build a city, named from himself, Ælia." At this time[15] there appears to have been a formal act, whereby the Romans marked the legal annihilation of cities; an act esteemed, at this time, one of most extreme severity[16]. When a city was to be built, its compass was marked with a plough; the Romans, where they willed to unmake a city, did, on rare occasions, turn up its soil with the plough. Hence the saying, "[17] A city with a plough is built, with a plough overthrown." The city so ploughed forfeited all civil rights[18]; it was counted to have ceased to be. The symbolical act under Hadrian appears to have been directed against both the civil and religious existence of their city, since the revolts of the Jews were mixed up with their religious hopes. The Jews relate that both the city generally, and the Temple, were ploughed. The ploughing of the city was the last of those mournful memories, which made the month Ab a time of sorrow. But the ploughing of the temple is also especially recorded. S. Jerome says, "[19] In this [the 5th Month] was the Temple at Jerusalem burnt and destroyed, both by Nebuchadnezzar, and many years afterward by Titus and Vespasian; the city Bether, whither thousands of Jews had fled, was taken; the Temple was ploughed, as an insult to the conquered race, by Titus Annius Rufus." The Gemara says, "[20] When Turnus, [or it may be "when Tyrant] Rufus ploughed the porch," [of the temple.] Perhaps Hadrian meant thus to declare the desecration of the site of the Temple, and so to make way for the further desecration by his temple of Jupiter. He would declare the worship of God at an end. The horrible desecration of placing the temple of Ashtaroth over the Holy Sepulchre[21] was probably a part of the same policy, to make the Holy City utterly Heathen. The "Capitoline[22]" was part of its new name in honor of the Jupiter of the Roman Capitol. Hadrian intended, not to rebuild Jerusalem, but to build a new city under his own name. "[23] The city being thus bared of the Jewish nation, and its old inhabitants having been utterly destroyed, and

[1] S. Chrys. adv. Jud. v. 10. He does not apparently mean that they actually began it.

[2] Eus. Dem. Ev. ii. 38. vi. 18. The Samaritan Chronicle (c. 47. ed. Juynboll) gives an account of a siege by Adrian in which it mixes up fables and facts belonging to the siege of Titus, (which it omits,) but I do not see any traces of traditional fact.

[3] Eus. H. E. iv. 6.

[4] The Rev. G. Williams, (Holy City, i. 209–13,) has at once identified *Bether* with the name, *the mountains of Bether*, (Cant. ii. 17,) and ruins, "khirbet el yehûd," (ruins of the Jews) near the village still called Bittir near Jerusalem. (See Robinson's or Kiepert's map.) There are traces both of fortifications and excavations, such as Dio speaks of. *Bether* as well as *Bithron* beyond Jordan (2 Sam. ii. 29.) had their name from deep *incisions*. (See the use of בָּתַר, בַּתֵּר, בֶּתֶר, Gen. xv. 10.)

[5] Dio Cass. lxix. 12.

[6] S. John v. 43.

[7] "given to murder and robbery." Eus. H. E. iv. 6. See Maimonides above, n. 13.

[8] S. Jer. Apol. 2. c. Ruf. §31. He pretended to breathe fire, a trick ascribed by Florus iii. 19 to Eunus, author of the servile war in Sicily. Vallars.

[9] Dio l. c.

[10] Talm. Jesus. Pea 7 in Lightfoot, l. c.

[11] Appian de reb. Syr. 50. "Jerusalem, which Ptolemy king of Egypt first destroyed: then, when rebuilt, Vespasian razed to the ground, and again Hadrian, in my time."

[12] S. Chrys. l. c. §11.

[13] S. Jerome then took this statement from written history.

[14] in Joel i. 4.

[15] The Mishnah places it after the capture of Bether. "On the 9th of Ab, it was decreed against our fathers, that they should not enter the land; and the Temple was laid desolate the first and second time; and Bether was taken; and the city was ploughed." Taanith, c. 5. §6. Mishna ii. p. 382. ed. Surenhus. Rashi regards this as a fulfillment of Jer. xxvi. 18. and of this place. Ib. p. 383. col. 2. Buxtorf quotes also Yotseroth, (Jewish hymns,) c. Comm. f. 35. l. for the fact. Lex. Rabb. p. 916.

[16] Seneca de clem. i. 26. Deyl.

[17] Isidor. lxxv. 1. &c.

[18] "If the usufruct [annual produce] be left to a city, and the plough be passed over it, (as befell Carthage,) it ceases to be a city, and so by a sort of death it ceases to have the usufruct." Modestinus in l. Si usus fructus 21. ff quibus modis usus fructus amittatur. L.

[19] On Zech. viii. 16, 17. S. Jerome has the same order as the Talmud.

[20] Taanith, l. c. The Jerusalem Talmud has "the temple" for "the porch."

[21] Eus. Vit. Const. iii. 26. Socr. i. 17. Soz. ii. 1. S. Jer. Ep. 58, ad Paul. §3.

[22] Col. Æl. Capitol. i. 3. Colonia Ælia Capitolina.

[23] Eus. H. E. iv. 6.

an alien race settled there, the Roman city which afterward arose, having changed its name, is called Ælia in honor of the Emperor Ælius Hadrianus." It was a Roman colony[1], with Roman temples, Roman amphitheatres. Idolatry was stamped on its coins[2]. Hadrian excluded from it, on the North, almost the whole of Bezetha or the new city, which Agrippa had enclosed by his wall, and, on the South, more than half of Mount Zion[3], which was left, as Micah foretold, to be *ploughed as a field*. The Jews themselves were prohibited from entering the Holy Land[4], so that the heathen Celsus says, "[5]they have neither a clod nor a hearth left." Ælia, then, being a new city, Jerusalem was spoken of, as having ceased to be. The Roman magistrates, even in Palestine, did not know the name[6]. Christians too used the name Ælia[7], and that, in solemn documents, as the Canon of Nice[8]. In the 4th century the city was still called Ælia by the Christians[9], and, on the first Mohammedan coin [10] in the 7th century, it still bore that name. A series of writers speak of the desolation of Jerusalem. In the next century Origen addresses a Jew, "[11] If going to the earthly city, Jerusalem, thou shalt find it overthrown, reduced to dust and ashes, weep not, as ye now do." "[12] From that [Hadrian's] time until now, the extremest desolation having taken possession of the place, their once renowned hill of Zion—now no wise differing from the rest of the country, is cultivated by Romans, so that we ourselves have with our own eyes observed the place ploughed by oxen and sown all over. And Jerusalem, being inhabited by aliens, has to this day the stones gathered out of it, all the inhabitants, in our own times too, gathering up the stones out of its ruins for their private or public and common buildings. You may observe with your own eyes the mournful sight, how the stones from the Temple itself and from the Holy of holies have been taken for the idol-temples and to build amphitheatres." "[13]Their once holy place has now come to such a state, as in no way to fall short of the overthrow of Sodom." S. Hilary, who had been banished into the East, says, "[14]The Royal city of David, taken by the Babylonians and overthrown, held not its queenly dignity under the rule of its lords; but, taken afterward and burnt by the Romans, it now is not." S. Cyril of Jerusalem, Bishop of the new town, and delivering his catechetical lectures in the Church of the Holy Sepulchre, pointed out to his hearers the fulfillment of prophecy; "[15] The place [Zion] is now filled with gardens of cucumbers." "If they [the Jews] plead the captivity," says S. Athanasius[16], "and say that on that ground Jerusalem is not." "The whole world, over which they are scattered," says S. Gregory of Nazianzum[17], "is one monument of their calamity, their worship closed, and the soil of Jerusalem itself scarcely known."

It is apparently part of the gradual and increasing fulfillment of God's word, that the ploughing of the city and of the site of the Temple, and the continued cultivation of so large a portion of Zion, are recorded in the last visitation when its iniquity was full. It still remains *ploughed as a field*. "[18]At the time I visited this sacred ground, one part of it supported a crop of barley, another was undergoing the labor of the plough, and the soil, turned up, consisted of stone and lime filled with earth, such as is usually met with in the foundations of ruined cities. It is nearly a mile in circumference." "[19]On the S. E. Zion slopes down, in a series of cultivated terraces, sharply though not abruptly, to the sites of the Kings' gardens.—Here and round to the S. the whole declivities are sprinkled with olive trees, which grow luxuriantly among the narrow slips of corn."

[1] Col. Æl. Capitol. i. e. Colonia Ælia Capitolina.

[2] See Roman coins in De Saulcy, p. 171–187. from Hadrian, A. D. 136, to Hostilian, A. D. 250.

[3] See Pierotti's excellent map of Jerusalem, (also reduced in his "Jerusalem explored." n. 3.)

[4] Eusebius, l. c. affirms this on the authority of Aristo of Pella, a contemporary; Tertullian says, "they are not permitted, even in the right of strangers, to greet their native land so much as with the sole of their foot." (Apol. c. 21. p. 45 Oxf. Tr. and adv. Jud. c. 13.) S. Jerome affirms the same. (on Is. vi. 11–13. and on Dan. ix. end.) Celsus urges the fact of their total expulsion as a proof of God's breach of promise; (in Orig. c. Cels. viii. 69.) and Origen agrees as to the fact. S. Justin speaks of their expulsion (as a nation) after their defeat, (Dial. c. 110.) so that, when he speaks of Jerusalem only, (Apol. i. 47.) it may have been that he spoke of it alone, as sufficing for the prophecy which he was explaining. The prohibition was subsequently limited to Jerusalem, with the well-known concession to behold it without entering, one day in the year, to weep. Itin. Hieros. p. 591. S. Hil. on Ps. 58. § 7. S. Jer. on Zeph. i. 15, 16, &c. Both S. Chrysostom and S. Augustine speak of the Jews, as excluded from Jerusalem. "Dost thou for thy sins, O Jew, remain so long out of Jerusalem?" S. Chrys. adv. Jud. vi. 2. "They were excluded from the place where they crucified Christ; *now* that place is full of Christians who praise Him; it hath no Jew." S. Aug. in Ps. lxii. n. 18. "Now thou seekest a Jew in the city of Jerusalem, and findest not." in Ps. cxxiv. n. 3.

[5] L. c.

[6] Eus. de mart. Pal. c. 11.

[7] "In the suburbs of what is now Ælia." Eus. H. E. ii. 12. add. vi. 20. de mart. Pal. c. 11. (Deyl.)

[8] Can. vii.

[9] "From that [Hadrian's] time until now, it is called Ælia from the name of him who conquered and destroyed it." (S. Chrys. adv. Jud. v. 11 T. i. p. 645.) "Which is now Ælia." S. Jer. Ep. 129. ad. Dard. § 5.

[10] De Saulcy, p. 188.

[11] In Jos. Hom. xvii. 1. Opp. ii. 438.

[12] Eus. Dem. Ev. viii. 8. p. 406.

[13] Ib. v. 23. p. 250.

[14] S. Hil. in Ps. 131. § 18.

[15] Lect. xvi. 9. § 18. see Oxf. Tr.

[16] de Incarn. n. 39. T. i. p. 81. Ben.

[17] Orat. 6. § 18. Ben.

[18] Richardson's Travels, p. 359. quoted by Keith on Prophecy, p. 257.

[19] Porter, Hdbook, p. 92.

Before CHRIST cir. 710.

CHAPTER IV.

1 *The glory,* 3 *peace,* 8 *kingdom,*
11 *and victory of the church.*

BUT [a] in the last days it
shall come to pass, *that*
the mountain of the house

Before CHRIST cir. 710.

[a] Is. 2. 2, &c. Ezek. 17. 22, 23.

Not Christians only, but Jews also have seen herein the fulfillment upon themselves of Micah's words, spoken now "26 centuries ago."

IV. 1. *But* [*And*] *in the last days it shall come to pass.* God's promises, goodness, truth, fail not. He withdraweth His Presence from those who receive Him not, only to give Himself to those who will receive Him. Mercy is the sequel and end of chastisement. Micah then joins on this great prophecy of future mercy to the preceding woe, as its issue in the order of God's Will. *And it shall be.* He fixes the mind to some great thing which shall come to pass; *it shall be.* Then follows, in marked reference to the preceding privations, a superabundance of mercy. For *the mountain of the house,* which should be as a *forest* and which was *left unto* them *desolate,* there is *the mountain of the Lord's house established;* for *the heap of dust and the ploughed field,* there is the flowing-in of the Gentiles; for the *night* and *darkness,* that *there shall be no vision,* there is the fullness of revelation; for corrupt judgment, teaching, divining, a law from God Himself going forth through the world; for the building of Jerusalem with blood, one universal peace.

In the last days, lit. *the end*[1] *of the days,* i. e. of those days which are in the thoughts of the speaker. Politically, there are many beginnings and many endings; as many endings as there are beginnings, since all human polity begins, only to end, and to be displaced in its turn by some new beginning, which too runs its course, only to end. Religiously, there are but two consummations. All time, since man fell, is divided into two halves, the looking forward to Christ to come in humility; the looking forward to His Coming in glory. These are the two events on which man's history turns. To that former people the whole period of Christ's kingdom was one future, the fullness of all their own shadows, types, sacrifices, services, prophecies, longings, being. The *end of* their *days* was the beginning of the new Day of Christ: the coming of His Day was necessarily the close of the former days, the period of the dispensation which prepared for it. The Prophets then by the words, *the end of the days,* always mean the times of the Gospel[2]. *The end of the days* is the close of all which went before, the last dispensation, after which there shall be no other. Yet this too hast *last days* of its own, which shall close God's kingdom of grace and shall issue in the Second Coming of Christ; as the end of those former days, which closed the times of "the law," issued in His First Coming. We are then at once living in the *last times,* and looking on to a *last time* still to come. In the one way St. Peter speaks[3] of *the last times,* or *the end of the times*[4], *in* which *Christ was manifested for* us, in contrast *with the foundations of the world, before* which He *was foreordained.* And St. Paul contrasts God's [5] *speaking to the fathers in the Prophets,* and *at the end of these days*[6] *speaking to us in the Son;* and of our Lord coming [7] *at the end, consummation, of the times*[8], *to put away sins by the sacrifice of Himself;* and says that the things which befell the Jews [9] *were written for our admonition, unto whom the ends of the times*[10] [i. e. of those of the former people of whom he had been speaking] *are come;* and St. John speaks of this as [11] *the last time.* In the other way, they contrast *the last days,* not with the times before them but with their own, and then plainly they are a last and distant part of this their own *last time.* [12] *The Spirit speaketh expressly, that in the latter times some shall depart from the faith:* [13] *In the last days perilous times shall come:* [14] *There shall come at the end of the days scoffers:* [15] *They told you that there should be mockers in the last time.* The Jews distributed all time between "this world" and "the coming world[16]," including under "the coming world" the time of grace under the Messiah's reign, and the future glory. To us the

[1] Gesenius adduces, as the single instance in which אחרית is to mean "sequel," Is. xlvi. 10, where "the end" answers to "the beginning," ראשית אחרית. It is the *end* of the year, Deut. xi. 12; the *end* of a person, Pr. v. 4, Ps. xxxvii. 37; of a nation, Jer. xxxi. 17; of a thing, i. e. its issue, Pr. xxiii. 32; "the *end* of the sea," Ps. cxxxix. 9. The phrase is rendered rightly by the Ch. סוף יומיא.
The ἐπ' ἐσχάτου τῶν χρόνων of S. Paul, S. Peter and S. Jude is nearly the translation of באחרית הימים.

[2] Hos. iii. 5. Is. ii. 2. Jer. xxiii. 20. xxx. 24. xlviii. 47. xlix. 39. Ezek. xxxviii. 16. Dan. x. 14. Daniel uses it in Chaldee. (ii. 28.) Nebuchadnezzar's dream which he is interpreting ended in the kingdom of Christ. On the Jewish agreement, see on Hos. iii. 5. p. 25. n. 10.

[3] 1 Ep. i. 20.

[4] According to the reading ἐπ' ἐσχάτου τῶν χρόνων, preferred by Alter and Tischendorf.

[5] Heb. i. 1.

[6] ἐπ' ἐσχάτου τῶν ἡμερῶν τούτων, preferred by Griesbach, Matthiæ, Scholz, Tisch.

[7] Heb. ix. 26.

[8] ἐπὶ συντελείᾳ τῶν αἰώνων, comp. S. Matt. xiii. 40. xxiv. 3. [9] 1 Cor. x. 11. [10] τὰ τέλη τῶν αἰώνων.

[11] 1 Ep. ii. 18.

[12] 1 Tim. iv. 1. ἐν ὑστέροις χρόνοις.

[13] 2 Tim. iii. 1. ἐν ἐσχάταις ἡμέραις.

[14] 2 Pet. iii. 3. ἐπ' ἐσχάτου τῶν ἡμερῶν, preferred by Griesb., Alter, Matthæi, Scholz.

[15] Jude 18. ἐν ἐσχάτῳ χρόνῳ or ἐπ' ἐσχάτου τοῦ χρόνου, preferred by Scholz, Tisch.

[16] עולם הזה and עולם הבא. See Schöttg de Messia i. 2. 4. p. 23–27.

Before CHRIST cir. 710.

of the LORD shall be established in the top of the mountains, and it shall be exalted above the hills; and people shall flow unto it.

Before CHRIST cir. 710.

names have shifted, since this present world[1] is to us the kingdom of Christ, and there remains nothing further on this earth to look to, beyond what God has already given us. Our future then, placed as we are between the two Comings of our Lord, is, of necessity, beyond this world[2].

The mountain of the house of the Lord shall be [*abidingly*] *established.* He does not say merely, *it shall be established.* Kingdoms may be established at one time, and then come to an end. He says, *it shall be a thing established*[3]. His saying is expanded by Daniel; [4]*In the days of these kings shall the God of heaven set up a kingdom which shall not be destroyed for ever, and it shall abide for ever. The house of the Lord* was the centre of His worship, the token of His Presence, the pledge of His revelations and of His abiding acceptance, protection, favor. All these were to be increased and continuous. The image is one familiar to us in the Hebrew Scriptures. People were said to *go up*[5] to it, as to a place of dignity. In the Psalm on the carrying of the Ark thither, *the hill of God* is compared to the many-topped mountains of Basan[6], (the Hermon-peaks which bound Basan,) and so declared to be greater than they, as being the object of God's choice. The mountain where God was worshiped rose above the mountains of idolatry. Ezekiel, varying the image, speaks of the Gospel as an overshadowing cedar[7], *planted* by God *upon an high mountain and an eminent, in the mountain of the height of Israel, under* which *should dwell* all *fowl of every wing;* and, in his vision of the Temple, he sees this, the image of the Christian Church, [8]*upon a very high mountain.* Our Lord speaks of His Apostles and the Church in them, as [9]*a city set upon a hill which cannot be hid.* The seat of God's worship was to be seen far and wide; nothing was to obscure it. It, now lower than the surrounding hills, was then to be as on the summit of them. Human elevation, the more exalted it is, the more unstable is it. Divine greatness alone is at once solid and exalted. The new kingdom of God was at once to be *exalted above the hills,* and *established on the top of the mountains; exalted,* at once, above everything human, and yet *established,* strong as the mountains on which it rested, and unassailable, unconquerable, seated secure aloft, between heaven, whence it came and to which it tends, and earth, on which it just rests in the sublime serenity of its majesty.

The image sets forth the supereminence of the Lord's House above all things earthly. It does not define wherein that greatness consists. The flowing in of the nations is a fruit of it[10]. The immediate object of their coming is explained to be, to learn to know and to do the will of God[11]. But the new revelation does not form all its greatness. That greatness is from the Presence of God, revealing and evermore teaching His Will, ruling, judging, rebuking, peacemaking[12]. "[13]The *mountain of the Lord's House* was then *exalted above the hills* by the bodily Presence of Christ, when He, in the Temple built on that mountain, spake, preached, worked so many miracles; as, on the same ground, Haggai saith[14], *the glory of this latter house shall be greater than* the glory of *the former.*" "[15]This *mountain,* the Church of Christ, transcends all laws, schools, doctrines, religions, Synagogues of Jews and Philosophers, which seemed to rise aloft among men, like mountain-tops, yea, whatever under the sun is sublime and lofty, it will overpass, trample on, subdue to itself."

Even Jews have seen the meaning of this figure. Their oldest mystical book explains it[16]. "*And it shall be in the last days,* when namely the Lord shall visit the daughter of Jacob, then shall *the mountain of the house of the Lord be firmly established,* i. e. the Jerusalem which is above, which shall stand firmly in its place, that it may shine by the light which is above. (For no light can retain its existence, except through the light from above.) For in that time shall the light from above shine sevenfold more than before; according to that[17], *Moreover the light of the moon shall be as the light of the sun; and the light of the sun shall be sevenfold, as the light of seven days, in the day that the Lord bindeth up the breach of His people and healeth the stroke of their wound.*" Another, of the dry literal school, says[18], "It is well known that the house of the Temple is not high. The meaning then is, that its fame shall go forth far, and there shall return to it from all quarters

[1] S. Matt. xiii. 40. Eph. i. 21. Tit. ii. 12.

[2] S. Mark x. 30. S. Luke xviii. 30. xx. 35. Eph. l. c. Heb. vi. 5. Attention to this language of Holy Scripture and the distant future which it looks on to, should have saved misbelievers from imagining that Apostles erroneously expected a near end of the world.

[3] יהיה נכון, as in 1 Kgs ii. 45, of the throne of David. "It is an expression denoting continuance and perpetuity, that it shall continually remain on its settlement." Poc. from Abarb.

[4] ii. 44. [5] See on Hos. i. 11. vol. i. p. 26. [6] Ps. lxviii. 16, 17. [7] xvii. 22, 23. [8] xl. 2. [9] S. Matt. v. 14. [10] iv. 1, 2. [11] iv. 2. [12] iv. 3, 4. [13] Dion. [14] ii. 9. [15] Lap. [16] Zohar, f. 93. [17] Is. xxx. 26. [18] Aben Ezra.

Before CHRIST cir. 710.

2 And many nations shall come, and say, Come, and let us go up to the mountain of the LORD,

persons with offerings, so that it shall be, as if it were on the top of all hills, so that all the inhabitants of the earth should see it."

Some [1] interpret *the mountain* to be Christ, Who is called *the Rock* [2], on the confession of Whom, God-Man, *the house of the Lord*, i. e. the Church is built [3], *the precious Corner-stone* [4], which is laid, beside which *no foundation can* be laid [5]; *the great mountain*, of which Daniel [6] prophesied. It is *firmly established*, so that *the gates of Hell shall not prevail against the Church*, being built thereon; *exalted above hills and mountains*, i. e. above all beside, greater or smaller, which has any eminence; for He in truth is [7] *highly exalted and hath a Name above every name*, being [8] *at the Right Hand* of God *in the heavenly places, far above all principality and power and might and dominion, and every name that is named, not only in this world but also in that which is to come;* and *all things are under His Feet*. And this for us, in that He, the Same, is *the Head over all things to the Church which is His Body, the fullness of Him that filleth all in all*. "[9] He is God and Man, King and Priest, King of kings, and a Priest abiding for ever. Since then His Majesty reacheth to the Right Hand of God, neither mountains nor hills, Angels nor holy men, reach thereto; for [10] *to which of the Angels said God at any time, Sit thou on My Right Hand?*"

"[11] Aloft then is the Church of God raised, both in that its Head is in heaven and the Lord of all, and that, on earth, it is not like the Temple, in one small people, but [12] *set on a hill that it cannot be hid*, or remain unseen even to those far from it. Its doctrine too and life are far above the wisdom of this world, shewing in them nothing of earth, but are above; its wisdom is the knowledge and love of God and of His Son Jesus Christ, and its *life is hid with Christ in God*, in those who are justified in Him and hallowed by His Spirit." In Him, it is lifted above all things, and with the eyes of the mind beholdeth (as far as may be) the glory of God, soaring on high toward Him Who is the Author of all being, and, filled with Divine light, it owneth Him the Maker of all.

And people, [*peoples*, nations,] *shall flow unto* [lit. *upon*] *it*. A mighty tide should set in to the Gospel. The word [13] is appropriated to the *streaming in* of multitudes, such as of old poured into Babylon, the merchant-empress of the world [14]. It is used of the distant nations who should throng in one continuous stream into the Gospel, or of Israel streaming together from the four corners of the world [15]. So Isaiah foretells [16], *Thy gates shall be open continually; they shall not be shut day nor night; that they may bring unto thee the forces of the Gentiles, and that their kings* may be *brought*. These were to *flow upon it*, perhaps so as to cover it, expressing both the multitude and density of the throng of nations, how full the Church should be, as the swollen river spreads itself over the whole champaign country, and the surging flood-tide climbs up the face of the rock which bounds it. The flood once covered the highest mountains to destroy life; this flood should pour in for the saving of life. "[17] It is a miracle, if waters ascend from a valley and flow to a mountain. So is it a miracle that earthly nations should ascend to the Church, whose doctrine and life are lofty, arduous, sublime. This the grace of Christ effecteth, mighty and lofty, as being sent from heaven. As then waters, conducted from the fountains by pipes into a valley, in that valley bound up and rise nearly to their original height, so these waters of heavenly grace, brought down into valleys, i. e. the hearts of men, make them to bound up with them into heaven and enter upon and embrace a heavenly life."

2. *And many nations shall come.* Isaiah [18] added the world *all* to Micah's prophecy. So our Lord said, [19] *This Gospel of the kingdom shall be preached in all the world for a witness unto all nations;* and the elect are to be gathered out *of all nations and kindreds and people and tongues* [20]. *All nations shall flow into it.* The *all* might be many or few. Both prophets say that those *all* should be many. Judah probably knew already of many. The history of Genesis gave them a wide-expanding knowledge of the enlargement of mankind after the flood, in Europe, Asia, Africa, as they then existed in their nations. The sons of Japhet had already spread over the whole coast of our Western sea, and far

[1] Tert. c. Jud. i. 3. Orig. c. Cels. ii. 33. S. Cypr. Test. ii. 18. Euseb. Ecl. Proph. iv. 1. p. 171. ed. Ox. S. Jerome here, S. Aug. de Civ. D. xviii. 30. Ps. Basil on Is.
[2] 1 Cor. x. 4–6.
[3] S. Matt. xvi. 18. see Note Q. on Tertull. p. 492 sqq. Oxf. Tr.
[4] Is. xxviii. 16. 1 Pet. ii. 6. Eph. ii. 20.
[5] 1 Cor. iii. 11.
[6] Dan. ii. 35.
[7] Phil. ii. 9.
[8] Eph. i. 20–23.
[9] from Rup.
[10] Heb. i. 13.
[11] from S. Cyr.
[12] S. Matt. v. 14.
[13] נהרו (from נהר river, stream) is used only figuratively.
[14] Jer. li. 44.
[15] Ib. xxxi. 12. It is used in these places only, and Is. ii. 2.
[16] Is. lx. 11. add Rev. xxi. 25, 26.
[17] Lap.
[18] Is. ii. 2.
[19] S. Matt. xxiv. 14.
[20] Rev. vii. 9.

Before CHRIST cir. 710.

and to the house of the God of Jacob; and he will teach us of his ways, and we will walk in his

Before CHRIST cir. 710.

North; the Cimmerians[1], or Cwmry, Scandinavians[2], Carpathians[3], (probably Celts,) Armenians[4], (including the kindred Phrygians,) Scythians[5], Medes, Ionians[6], Æolians[7], Iberians[8], Cypriotes[9], Dardani[10], Tybarenes[11], Moschi[12], and the Turseni[13], or perhaps the Thracians. On the East, the sons of Shem had spread in Elam, Asshur, Arrapachitis[14]; they occupied the intervening tract of Aram; in the N. W. they reached to Lydia. Southward the sons of Joktan were in Arabia. Micah's hearers knew how, of the sons of Ham, Cush had spread far to the S. E. and S. from Babylonia to Æthiopia; Egypt they remembered too well, and, beyond it, they knew of the far-scattered tribes of the Libyans, who extended along the coast of Africa. Phœnician trade filled up this great outline. They themselves had, in Solomon's time, traded with India[15]; about this time, we know that they were acquainted with the furthest East, China[16]. Such was the sight before the human mind of the Prophet; such the extent of the nations whom his people knew of. Some were the deadly enemies of his people; some were to be its conquerors. He knew that the the ten tribes were to be abidingly *wanderers among the nations*[17], despised by them[18]; "a people, the strangers and sojourners of the whole world[19]." He knew many of those nations to be sunk in idolatry, viciousness; proud, contemptuous, lawless; he saw them fixed in their idolatries. *All people will walk every one in the name of his god.* But he saw what eye of man could not see, what the will of man could not accomplish, that He, whom now Judah alone partially worshiped, would turn the hearts of His creatures to Himself, to seek Him, not in their own ways, but as He should reveal Himself at Jerusalem. Micah tells them distinctly, that those who should believe would be a great multitude from *many nations*. In like way Isaiah expresses the great multitude of those for whom Christ should atone. [20] *He bare the sin of many.* [21] *By knowledge of Him shall My righteous Servant make many righteous.* And our Lord Himself says; [22] *The Son of man came to give His life a ransom for many.* [23] *This is my Blood—which is shed for many for the remission of sins.* In Micah's time not one people, scarcely some poor fragments of the Jewish people, went up to worship God at Zion, to call to remembrance His benefits, to learn of Him. Those who should thereafter worship Him, should be *many nations*.

And say, exhorting one another, in fervor and mutual love, as Andrew exhorted his brother Simon, and Philip Nathanael, and the woman of Samaria those of her city, to come to Christ: and so all since, who have been won by Him, by word or example, by preaching or by deed, in public or in private, bear along with them others to seek Him Whom they themselves have found.

Let us go up, leaving the lowness and earthliness of their former conversation, and mounting upward on high where Christ is, desiring righteousness, and athirst to know His ways.

To the house of the God of Jacob. They shall seek Him as Jacob sought Him, "[24] who left his father's house and removed into another land, was a man of heavy toils and served for hire, but obtained special help from God, and, undistinguished as he was, became most glorious. So too the Church, leaving all Heathen wisdom, and having its conversation in Heaven, and therefore persecuted and enduring many hardships, enjoys now glory with God."

And He, i. e. *the God of Jacob* of Whom he had just spoken, *shall teach us of His ways.* They do not go to God, because they know Him, but *that* they *may* know Him. They are drawn by a mighty impulse toward Him. Howsoever attracted, they come, not making bargains with God, (as some now would,) what they should be taught, that He should reveal to them nothing transcending reason, nothing exceeding or contradicting their

[1] Gomer.

[2] Ashkenaz, Scandinavia, Scanzia in Jornandes. Knobel, Völkertafel d. Genesis, p. 35.

[3] Riphath, from whom also the Montes Riphæi are named.

[4] Togarmah. [5] Magog. [6] Javan.

[7] Elishah, Αἰολεῖς or Αἰλεῖς, Knobel; *Elis*, Boch. iii. 4.

[8] Tarshish. "Tarseis, whence the Iberians." Eus. (Tuch ad loc.)

[9] Chittim. [10] Dodanim. [11] Tubal. [12] Meshech.

[13] Tiras, Tyrseni, (Tuch,) Thracians, Boch. iii. 2. Knob.

[14] Arphaxad, Gen. x. 22.

[15] As appears from the Tamul name for the peacock תֻּכִּי Tam. *tôgai* 1 Kgs x. 22; the Sanskrit or Malabar name for the ape, קוֹף *kapi*; (Ib. see Ges.) which came with the creatures themselves; a Sanskrit name for elephant, *ibha*, שֶׁנְהַבִּים ivory, lit. "elephant's tooth;" (Ib.) and a Malabar name for a wood, *al gum*, *val gu* (*ka*.) See Max Müller, Science of language, p. 205. ed. 3. Ophir itself, (which is mentioned in connection with these things,) Max Müller identifies, beyond question, with the Abiria of Ptolemy above Pattalene; the people, "called by Hindu Geographers *Abhira* and "the *Ahirs*" in "Macmurdo's account of the province of Cutch." Ib.

[16] Is. xlix. 12. see Gesenius Thes. p. 948–50.

[17] See on Hos. ix. 17. vol. i. p. 97.

[18] See on Hos. viii. 8. vol. i. p. 83.

[19] S. Greg. Naz. Or. 22. n. 2. [20] Is. liii. 12.

[21] Ib. 11. [22] S. Matt. xx. 28.

[23] Ib. xxvi. 28. add Rom. v. 15. [24] Theoph.

Before CHRIST cir. 710.

paths: for the law shall go forth of Zion, and the word of the LORD from Jerusalem.

notions of God; they do not come with reserves, that God should not take away *this* or *that* error, or should not disclose anything of His incomprehensibleness. They come in holy simplicity, to learn whatever He will condescend to tell them; in holy confidence, that He, the Infallible Truth, will teach them infallibly. They say, *of His ways*. For all learning is by degrees, and all which all creatures could learn in all eternity falls infinitely short of His truth and Holiness. Nay, in all eternity the highest creature which He has made and which He has admitted most deeply into the secrets of His Wisdom will be as infinitely removed as ever from the full knowledge of His Wisdom and His Love. For what is finite, enlarged, expanded, accumulated to the utmost degree possible, remains finite still. It has no proportion to the Infinite. But even here, all growth in grace implies growth in knowledge. The more we love God, the more we know of Him; and with increased knowledge of Him come higher perceptions of worship, praise, thanksgiving, of the character of faith, hope, charity, of our outward and inward acts and relations to God, the unboundedness of God's love to us and the manifoldness of the ways of pleasing Him, which, in His love, He has given us. Since then the whole Christian life is a growth in grace, and even St. Paul, [1]*forgetting those things which are behind and reaching forth to those which are before, pressed toward the mark for the high calling of God in Christ Jesus*, then St. Paul too was ever learning, in intensity, what he knew certainly by revelation, *of His ways*. Again, as each blade of grass is said to differ from another, so, and much more, each soul of man which God has created for Himself. No one ever saw or could imagine two human beings, in whom the grace of God had unfolded itself in exactly the same way. Each saint will have his distinct beauty around the Throne. But then each will have learnt *of His ways*, in a different proportion or degree. His greatest saints, yea His Apostles, have been pre-eminent, the one in one grace, another in another. St. John Baptist came as a pattern of repentance, and contempt of self; St John the Evangelist, stands out pre-eminent in deep tender burning personal love; St. Paul in zeal to spread the knowledge of Christ Crucified; St. Mary Magdelene in loving penitence. Even the Blessed Virgin herself, under inspiration, seems, in part, to speak of her *lowly lowness* [2], as that which God specially regarded in her, when He made her the Mother of God. Eternity only will set forth the fullness of the two words [3], *He will teach us of His ways*. For eternity will shew, how in all [4]*worketh that one and the self-same Spirit, dividing to every man severally as He will;* and how the countless multitude of the redeemed have corresponded to His gifts and drawings. "[5]The way of the life to God-ward is one, in that it looketh to one end, to please God; but there are many tracks along it, as there are many modes of life;" and each several grace is a part of the way to God.

And we will walk in His paths, "[6]by believing, hoping, loving, well-doing, and bearing patiently all trouble." "[7]For it sufficeth not to believe, unless we act as He commandeth, and strive to enter on His ways, *the strait and narrow path which leadeth unto life.* He Himself then, when He had said, [8]*Go, teach all nations, baptizing them in the Name of the Father, and of the Son, and of the Holy Ghost*, added, *teaching them to observe all things whatsoever I have commanded you*." They say too, *we will walk*, i.e. *go on from strength to strength*, not stand still after having labored for a while to do His Will, but hold on to all His ways and to Himself Who is *the Way, until they appear before the Lord in Zion.*

For the law, [lit. *law* [9],] *shall go forth from Zion*. These are the Prophet's words, declaring why the nations should so flock to Zion. For he says, *shall go forth*, but the nations were not gathered to Zion, until the Gospel was already gone forth. He speaks of it as *law* simply, not *the* Jewish *law* as such, but a rule of life [10] from God. Man's better nature is ill at ease, being out of harmony with God. It cannot be otherwise. Having been made in His likeness, it must be distressed by its unlikeness; having been made by Him for Himself, it must be restless without Him. What they indistinctly longed for, what drew them, was the hope to be conformed by Him to Him. The sight of superhuman holiness, life, love, endurance, ever won and

[1] Phil. iii. 13, 14.

[2] S. Luke i. 48. ταπείνωσις in Prov. xvi. 19. LXX. is, "lowliness." The whole phrase ἐπέβλεψεν ἐπὶ τὴν ταπείνωσιν τῆς δούλης αὐτοῦ, corresponds more to the use in 1 Kgs (Sam.) i. 11. 2 Kgs xvi. 12. 2 Kgs xiv. 26. Neh. ix. 9. Ps. ix. 13. LXX. where the prominent sense is *low estate*. Perhaps, as in עֳנִי, the two meanings are blended.

[3] יורנו מדרכיו. [4] 1 Cor. xii. 11. [5] Theoph.

[6] Dion. [7] Rup. [8] S. Matt. xxviii. end.

[9] תורה, not התורה.

[10] תורה is always *law*, not, as some have said, "religion," or "doctrine" generally. It is used without the article, in this sense, as rule of life, (Prov. vi. 23. xxviii. 4, 7, 9. xxix. 18.) such as the Heathen had not, (Lam. ii. 9.) but which should be revealed to them, (here, Is. ii. 3. li. 4.) The תורה corresponds with the יורנו.

Before CHRIST cir. 710.

3 ¶ And he shall judge among many people, and rebuke strong nations afar off; and they shall

wins those without to the Gospel or the Church. Our Lord Himself gives it, as the substance of Prophecy[1], *that repentance and remission of sins should be preached in His Name among all nations beginning at Jerusalem.* The image may be that of a stream, issuing forth from Jerusalem[2] and watering the whole world. "[3]The law of the Gospel and the word of the Apostles, beginning from Jerusalem, as from a fountain, ran through the whole world, watering those who approached with faith." But in that it *went forth,* it may be meant, that it left those from among whom it *went forth,* and "[4]Zion was indeed desolate of the law and Jerusalem bared of the Divine word." "[5]The word of God *passed* from Jerusalem to the Gentiles." "[6]For the shadow was done away, and the types ceased, and sacrifices were abolished, and everything of Moses was, in the letter, brought to a close."

He does not say here, through whom God would so teach, but he does speak of a direct teaching of God. He does not say only, "God will give us a law," or "will make a revelation of Himself." He speaks of a Personal, direct, continuous act of teaching by God, carried on upon earth, whether the teacher be our Lord's word spoken once on earth, which does *not pass away*[7], or God the Holy Ghost, as teaching in the Church and in the hearts which receive Him. The words which follow speak of a personal reign, as these speak of personal teaching.

3. *And He shall judge among many people and rebuke strong nations afar off.* Hitherto, they had walked each *in their own ways*[8]; now, they sought to be *taught in the ways of God.* Before, they had been lords of the world; now they should own a Judge higher than themselves. They were no common, but *mighty*[9] nations, such as had heretofore been the oppressors of Israel. They were to be many, and those mighty, nations. He should "[10]not only command, but *rebuke,* not weak or petty nations only, but mighty, and those not only near but afar." Mohammed had moral strength through what he stole from the law and the Gospel, and by his owning Christ as the Word of God. He was a heretic, rather than a heathen. Fearful scourge as he was, and as his successors have been, all is now decayed, and no *mighty nation* is left upon earth, which does not profess the Name of Christ.

He shall rebuke them; for it was an office of the Holy Ghost[11] *to reprove the world as to* its *sin, the righteousness* of Christ, *the judgment* of the *prince of this world.* The Gospel conquered the world, not by compromises or concordants, but by convicting it. It alone could *rebuke* with power; for it was, like its Author, all-holy. It could rebuke with efficacy; for it was the word of Him Who *knew what is in man.* It could rebuke with awe; for it knew the secrets of eternal Judgment. It could rebuke winningly; for it knew[12] *the love of Christ which passeth knowledge.* Its martyrs suffered and rebuked their judges; and the world was amazed at the impotence of power and the might of suffering. It rebuked the enthroned idolatry of centuries; it set in rebellion by its rebukes every sinful passion of man, and it subdued them. Tyrants, whom no human power could reach, trembled before its censures. Then only is it powerless, if its corrupted or timid or paralyzed ministers forfeit in themselves the power of rebuke.

And they shall beat their spears into ploughshares. "All things are made new in Christ." As the inward disquiet of evil men makes them restless, and vents itself toward others in envy, hatred, maliciousness, wrong, so the inward peace whereof He saith, *My peace I give unto you,* shall, wherever it reacheth, spread out abroad and, by the power of grace, bring to "[13]all nations unity, peace, and concord." All, being brought under the one empire of Christ, shall be in harmony, one with the other. As far as in it lies, the Gospel *is* a Gospel of peace, and makes peace. Christians, as far as they obey Christ, are at peace, both in themselves and with one another. And this is what is here prophesied. The peace follows from His rule. Where He judges and rebukes, there even the mighty *beat their swords into ploughshares.* The universal peace, amid which our Lord was born in the flesh, the first which there had been since the foundation of the Roman empire, was, in God's Providence, a fruit of His kingdom. It was no chance coincidence, since nothing is by chance. God willed that they should be contemporaneous. It was fitting that the world should be still, when its Lord, the Prince of peace, was born in it. That outward cessation of public strife, though but for a brief time, was an image how His peace spread backward as well as

[1] S. Luke xxiv. 47.
[2] See on Joel iii. 18. vol. i. p. 212.
[3] Theod.
[4] S. Cyr.
[5] S. Jer.
[6] Rup.
[7] S. Matt. xxiv. 35.
[8] Is. liii. 6.
[9] עצם, which originally signified bound together, (coll. Arab.) thence used of the closing of the eyes, (Is. xxix. 10. xxxiii. 15.) included the idea of number. The secondary idea of strength, (as we use "well-knit,") is so prominent, that the idea of number, in the verb, only occurs in Ps. xl. 13. Jer. xv. 8; in the adj. Num. xxxii. 1.
[10] Rib.
[11] S. John xvi. 8–11.
[12] Eph. iii. 19.
[13] Litany.

Before CHRIST cir. 710.

beat their swords into [b] plowshares, and their spears into ‖ pruning-hooks: nation shall not

b Is. 2. 4. Joel 3. 10.

Before CHRIST cir. 710.

‖ Or, *scythes.*

forward, and of the peace which through Him, our Peace, was dawning on the world. "[1] First, according to the letter, before That Child was born to us, [2] *on* Whose *shoulder the government is,* the whole world was full of blood; people fought against people, kings against kings, nations against nations. Lastly, the Roman state itself was torn by civil wars, in whose battles all kingdoms shed blood. But after that, at the time of the Empire of Christ, Rome gained an undivided empire, the world was laid open to the journeys of Apostles, and the gates of cities were open to them, and, for the preaching of the One God, one single empire was formed. It may too be understood as an image, that, on receiving the faith of Christ, anger and unrestrained revilings were laid aside, so that each *putteth his hand to the plough and looketh* not *back,* and, breaking in pieces the shafts of contumelies, seeketh to reap spiritual fruit, so that, *others laboring, we enter into their labors;* and of us it is said, *They shall come with joy, bringing their sheaves*[3]. Now no one fighteth; for we read, [4] *Blessed are the peacemakers;* no one learneth to [5] *strive, to the subverting of the hearers. And every one shall rest under his vine,* so as to press out that [6] *Wine which gladdeneth the heart of man,* under that [7] *Vine,* whereof the *Father is the Husbandman;* and *under his fig tree,* gathering the sweet [8] *fruits of the* Holy *Spirit, love, joy, peace,* and the rest."

The fathers had indeed a joy, which we have not, that wars were not between Christians; for although "just wars are lawful," war cannot be on both sides just; very few wars have not, on both sides, what is against the spirit of the Gospel. For, except where there is exceeding wickedness on one side, or peril of further evil, the words of our Lord would hold good, in public as in private, [9] *I say unto you, that ye resist not evil.*

This prophecy then is fulfilled 1) in the character of the Gospel. "[10] The law of the Gospel worketh and preserveth peace. For it plucketh up altogether the roots of all war, avarice, ambition, injustice, wrath. Then, it teacheth to bear injuries, and, so far from requiting them, willeth that we be prepared to receive fresh wrongs. He saith, [11] *If any one smite thee on the right cheek, turn to him the other also, &c.* [12] *I say unto you, Love your enemies, &c.* For neither did the old law give these counsels, nor did it explain so clearly the precept implied in them, nor had it that wonderful and most efficacious example of the patience and love of Christ, nor did it supply grace, whereby peace could be preserved; whereas now the first fruits of the Spirit are *love, joy, peace, long-suffering, gentleness, goodness.*" 2) The prophecy has been fulfilled within and without, among individuals or bodies of men, in body or mind, in temper or in deed, as far as the Gospel has prevailed. [13] *The multitude of them that believed were of one heart and of one mind;* one, through One indwelling Spirit; one, though a great multitude, through one bond of love. "[14] See how these Christians love one another;" "see how ready they are to die for one another," was, in the third century, a heathen proverb as to Christian love. "[15] They love one another, almost before they know one another." "[16] Their first lawgiver has persuaded them that they are all brethren." "We (which grieves you,)" the Christian answered [17], "so love one another, because we know not how to hate. We call ourselves 'brethren' which you take ill, as men who have one Father, God, and are sharers in one faith, in one hope, coheirs." For centuries too, there was, for the most part, public peace of Christians among themselves. Christian soldiers fought only, as constrained by the civil law, or against Barbarian invaders, to defend life, wife, children, not for ambition, anger, or pride. Christians could then appeal, in fulfillment of the prophecy, to this outward, the fruit of the inward, peace. "We," says an early martyr [18], "who formerly stained ourselves with mutual slaughter, not only do not wage war with foes, but even, in order not to lie and deceive those who consume us, willingly professing Christ, meet death." "From the coming of the Lord," says another martyr [19], "the New Testament, reconciling unto peace, and a life-giving law, went forth into all lands. If then another law and word, going forth from Jerusalem, produced such peace among the nations which received it, and thereby *reproved much people* of want of wisdom, then it would follow that the prophets spake of some other. But if *the law of liberty,* that is, the law of God preached by the Apostles, which went forth out of Jerusalem to all the world, worked

1 S. Jer. 2 Is. i
3 Ps. cxxvi. 6. 4 S. Matt. v. 9. 5 2 Tim. ii. 14.
6 Ps. civ. 15. 7 S. John xv. 1. 8 Gal. v. 22.
9 S. Matt. v. 39. 10 Rib. 11 S. Matt. v. 39–42.
12 Ib. 44–48. 13 Acts iv. 32.
14 Tertull. Apol. c. 39. "For they themselves hate one another." "For they themselves are more ready to slay one another," are Tertullian's statements as to the contemporary condition of the Heathen, which their amazement at Christian love rather confirms. 15 Minut. Felix, p. 81. ed. Ouz.
16 Lucian. de morte Peregrini, i. 507. ed. Græv.
17 Min. F. p. 312, 3.
18 S. Justin M. Apol. i. 39. 19 S. Iren. iv. 34. 4.

Before CHRIST cir. 710.

lift up a sword against nation, [e] neither shall they learn war any more.

Before CHRIST cir. 710.

[e] Ps. 72. 7.

such a transformation, that swords and spears of war He wrought into plough-shares and pruning-hooks, instruments of peace, and now men know not how to fight, but, when smitten, yield the other cheek, then the prophets spake of no other, but of Him who brought it to pass." "Even from this," says Tertullian[1], "you may know that Christ was promised, not as one mighty in war, but as a peace-bringer. Either deny that these things were prophesied, since they are plain to see; or, since they are written, deny that they are fulfilled. But if thou mayest deny neither, thou must own that they are fulfilled in Him, of Whom they are prophesied." "Of old[2]," says St. Athanasius, "Greeks and Barbarians, being idolaters, warred with one another, and were fierce toward those akin. For through their implacable warfare no one might pass land or sea, unarmed. Their whole life was passed in arms; the sword was to them for staff and stay. They worshiped idols, sacrificed to demons, and yet from their reverence for idols they could gain no help to correct their minds. But when they passed into the school of Christ, then, of a truth, pricked in mind, they wondrously laid aside their savage slaughters, and now think no more of things of war; for now all peace and friendship are alone their mind's delight. Who then did this, Who blended in peace those who hated one another, save the Beloved Son of the Father, the common Saviour of all, Christ Jesus, Who, through His love, endured all things for our salvation? For of old too, the peace which should hold sway from Him was prophesied, *they shall beat their swords into ploughshares.* Nor is this incredible, since now too, the Barbarians with innate savageness, while they yet sacrifice to their idols, are mad with one another, and cannot for one hour part with their swords. But when they have received the teaching of Christ, forthwith for ever they turn to husbandry; and, in lieu of arming their hands with swords, stretch them out to prayer. And altogether, instead of warring with one another, they arm themselves against the devil and demons, warring against them with modesty and virtue of soul. This is a token of the Godhead of the Saviour. For what men could not learn among idols, this they have learned from Him. Christ's disciples, having no war with one another, array themselves against demons by their life and deeds of virtue, chase them and mock their captain the devil, chaste in youth, enduring in temptation, strong in toils, tranquil when insulted, unconcerned when despoiled."

And yet later, S. Chrysostom says, "[3] Before the Coming of Christ, all men armed themselves and no one was exempt from this service, and cities fought with cities, and everywhere were men trained to war. But now most of the world is in peace; all engage in mechanical art or agriculture or commerce, and few are employed in military service for all. And of this too the occasion would cease, if we acted as we ought and did not need to be reminded by afflictions." "[4] After the Sun of righteousness dawned, so far are all cities and nations from living in such perils, that they know not even how to take in hand any affairs of war.—Or if there be still any war, it is far off at the extremity of the Roman Empire, not in each city and country, as heretofore. For then, in any one nation, there were countless seditions and multiform wars. But now the whole earth which the sun surveys from the Tigris to the British isles, and therewith Lybia too and Egypt and Palestine, yea, all beneath the Roman rule,—ye know how all enjoy complete security, and learn of war only by hearsay." S. Cyril[5] and Theodoret[5] carry on this account into the fifth century after our Lord's Coming. Christians then during those four centuries could point to a present fulfillment of prophecy, when we, for our sins, can only speak of the past. [6] *The Lord's hand is not shortened, that it cannot save: neither His ear heavy, that it cannot hear; but* our *iniquities have separated between* us, *and* our *God, and* our *sins have hid* His *Face from* us, *that He will not hear.* Those first Christians could urge against the Jews the fulfillment of their prophecies herein, where the Jews can now urge upon us their seeming non-fulfillment; "[7] In the time of King Messiah, after the wars of Gog and Magog, there shall be peace and tranquillity in all the world, and the sons of men shall have no need of weapons, but these promises were not fulfilled." The prophecy is fulfilled, in that the Gospel is a Gospel of peace and makes peace. Christians, as far as they obey Christ, are at peace both in themselves and with one another. The promises of God are perfect on His part: He is faithful to them. But He so wills to be freely loved by His intelligent creatures whom He formed for His love,

[1] adv. Marc. iii. 21.
[2] de Incarn. Verbi Dei, c. 51, 2.
[3] in Ps. xliv. § 3. T. v. p. 186.
[4] in Is. ii. n. 5. T. vi. p. 24, 5.
[5] on Is. ii. and here.
[6] Is. lix. 1, 2.
[7] R. Isaac, Munim. Fid. i. 5. 7. et all.

Before CHRIST cir. 710.

4 [d] But they shall sit
every man under his vine
and under his fig tree;
and none shall make *them*
afraid: for the mouth of
the Lord of hosts hath
spoken *it*.
5 For [e] all people will

[d] 1 Kings. 4. 25. Zech. 3. 10.

[e] Jer. 2. 11.

that He does not force our free-agency. We can fall short of His promises, if we will. To those only who will it, the Gospel brings peace, stilling the passions, quelling disputes, banishing contentions, removing errors, calming concupiscence, soothing and repressing anger, in individuals, nations, the Church; giving oneness of belief, harmony of soul, contentment with our own, love of others as ourselves; so that whatever is contrary to this has its origin in something which is not of Christ nor of His Gospel.

4. *But (And) they shall sit every man, under his vine and under his fig-tree.* Palestine was a home of the vine and the fig-tree. Vineyards were a common property, possessed by all but the very poor [1], or even by them [2]. The land was [3] *a land of bread and vineyards.* The vine was the emblem of the people, in Psalmists and Prophets [4]. The bunch of grapes or the vine-leaf appear as characteristic emblems on Jewish coins [5], chiefly in the times of their revolts under Vespasian and Hadrian [6]. The fig is also mentioned as part of the characteristic fruitfulness of Palestine [7]. It too was an universal property [8]. Both formed natural arbors; the fig had its name probably from its length [9], the vine from the arch made by its drooping boughs [10]. Both formed, in those hot countries, a grateful shade. The vine, rising with its single stem, was spread over trellis-work or by props, so as to enclose a considerable space [11]. Even in Italy, a single vine shaded a portico [12]. In Palestine it grew *by the walls of the house* [13]. Rabbins relate how their forefathers sat and studied under the fig-tree [14], as Nathanael was doubtless meditating or praying under one, when Jesus, being God, saw him [15].

It exhibits a picture of domestic peace, each family gathered in harmony and rest under the protection of God, each content with what they have, neither coveting another's, nor disturbed in their own. Wine is explained in Holy Scripture to be an emblem of gladness, and the fig of sweetness [16]. "[17] For exceeding sweet is the word of the Saviour, and it knoweth how to gladden man's heart; sweet also and full of joy is the hope of the future, wherewith we are enriched in Christ.

Such had been Israel's lot in the peaceful days of Solomon [18], the peace of whose times had already been made the image of the Gospel [19]; the coming of the Queen *of the South from the uttermost parts of the earth, to hear the wisdom of Solomon* [20], had made her kingdom to be selected as an emblem of those who should *fall down before* Christ and *serve Him* [21]. "[22] Such is that most quiet fearlessness which the law of Christ bringeth, as being the law of charity, peace, and concord."

And none shall make them afraid. "[23] Neither man, nor devil; for the Lord hath given us power to [24] *tread on serpents and scorpions, and over all the power of the enemy,* and said, *nothing shall by any means hurt you,* and bade us, [25] *fear not them which kill the body.*" Witness the might which He gave to His Apostles and Martyrs.

For the mouth of the Lord of Hosts hath spoken it. The Prophets often add this, when what they say, seems, for its greatness, past belief. Yet it will be, because He hath spoken it, *the Lord* Who changeth not, *the Lord of Hosts,* to Whose commands all creatures are subject, Whose word is truth with Whom to speak is to do.

5. *For all people will walk, every one in the*

[1] This is implied in the laws concerning them, as Ex. xxiii. 11. Lev. xix. 10. xxv. 3, 4. Deut. xx. 6, &c. comp. Num. xvi. 14. Deut. vi. 11. 1 Sam. viii. 14. xxii. 7. 2 Kgs. xviii. 32. Ps. cvii. 37. Prov. xxxi. 16.

[2] Neh. v. 4. Jer. xxxix. 10. [3] 2 Kgs. xviii. 32.

[4] Ps. lxxx. 8 sqq. Is. iii. 14. v. 1 sqq. xxvii. 2. Jer. ii. 21, xii. 10. Ezek. xv. xvii. 5–10. xix. 10. Hos. x. 1.

[5] The bunch of grapes appears on coins of Herod Archelaus, Madden, Jew, Coinage, p. 94, 5. also of Tiberius, Ib. p. 144. See De Saulcy, p. 134. 140, 1. The golden vine, given by Alexander to the Romans is mentioned by Strabo. (Jos. Ant. 14, 31.) The vine-tree stood at the porch of the Temple for receiving alms. Middoth 3. 8. in Levy Jüd. Münz. p. 134. Madden,.p 210.

[6] Madden, p. 162, 4, 7, 8. 170, 2, 3, 7. 180. 206, 7, 8, 9. See also De Saulcy, p. 160, 1, 2, 4, 5, 6, 7, &c.

[7] Deut. viii. 8. [8] 2 Kgs xviii. 32.

[9] תאנה (its name still in the East) from תאן i. q. תנן.

[10] גפן i. q. גבן.

[11] "We passed the evening, under a large vine, whose stem was about 1½ foot in diameter. Its height was 30 feet; its branches had to be propped up; and so it covered an arbor more than 50 feet wide and long. I remembered Micah. I have seen in this land the people living under both the fig and the vine; the fig between Jerusalem and Arimathea; the vine, here [Beitjin.]" Schulz. Leit. v. 285. in Paulus Reisen, vii. 103.

[12] Plin. N. H. xiv. 3. [13] Ps. cxxviii. 3.

[14] "R. Haia and his disciples—others say, R. Akiba, used to rise very early and sit and study under a fig-tree." Bereshith Rabba in Winer Reallex. [wrong reference.]

[15] S. John i. 48.

[16] Jud. ix. 11. 13. "The דבלה is the fig, distinguished for its more perfect sweetness, so that none such can be found, save in the land of Israel." Maimonid. in Demai c. ii. § 1. in Cels. Hierob. ii. 369. "It is appropriated to the food of man." Id. de jure anni 7 et jubil. c. v. § 8. Ib. Our Lord made it, as well as the grape, the figure of good fruit, which an evil nature could not bear. S. Matt. vii. 16. S. Luke vi. 44. [17] S. Cyr.

[18] 1 Kings iv. 25. [19] Ps. lxxii. [20] S. Matt. xii. 42.

[21] Ps. lxxii. 10, 11. [22] Lap. [23] Theoph.

[24] S. Luke x. 19. [25] S. Matt. x. 28.

Before CHRIST cir. 710.

walk every one in the name of his god, and [f] we will walk in the name of the Lord our God for ever and ever.

[f] Zech. 10. 12.

Before CHRIST cir. 710.

name of his god, and we will walk in the name of the Lord our God. Hitherto unsteadfastness had been the very characteristic sin of Israel. It was "[1] constant only in its inconstancy," ever [2] *falling away like their forefathers, starting aside like a broken bow.* The heathen persevered in their worship, because it was evil or had evil in it, not checking but feeding their passions. Israel did not persevere in his, because it required him to deny himself things unlawful. [3] *Hath a nation changed their gods which are yet no gods? But My people have changed their glory for that which doth not profit.* Henceforth, the Prophet professeth for his people, the true Israel, that he will be as steadfast in good, as the heathen in evil; so our Lord sets forth [4] *the children of this world in their generation,* as an example of wisdom to *the children of light.*

"[5] They who are eager to go up into the mountain of the Lord, and wish to learn thoroughly His ways, promise a ready obedience, and receive in themselves the glories of the life in Christ, and undertake with their whole strength to be earnest in all holiness. 'For let every one,' he saith, 'in every country and city go the way himself chooseth, and pass his life, as to him seemeth good; but our care is Christ, and His laws we will make our straight path; we will walk along with Him; and that not for this life only, present or past, but yet more for what is beyond.' [6] *It is a faithful saying. For they who* now *suffer with Him,* shall walk with Him forever, and *with Him be glorified, and with Him reign.* But *they* make Christ their care, who prefer nothing to His love, who cease from the vain distractions of the world, and seek rather righteousness and what is pleasing unto Him, and to excell in virtue. Such an one was the divine Paul; for he writeth, [7] *I am crucified with Christ;* and now no longer *I live, but Christ liveth in me;* and again [8], *I determined not to know anything among you, save Jesus Christ, and Him crucified.*"

To *walk* is so uniformly in Holy Scripture used of a person's moral or religious "ways [9]" (as we say), that the Prophet here too is doubtless speaking of the opposite religious ways of the Heathen and of the future people of God. The *name* was often, in Hebrew, expressive of the character; and, in regard to God Himself, that Name which He vouchsafed to give to Himself [10], expressed His Self-existence, and, as a result, His Unchangeableness and His Faithfulness. The names, by which it was foretold that Christ should be called, express both His Deity and attributes [11]; the human Name, which He bare and vouchsafes to bear yet, was significant of His office for us, Saviour [12]. *To praise the Name of the Lord* then, is to praise Him in that character or relation which He has revealed to us. "[13] He *walketh in the Name of the Lord,* who ordereth every act and motion worthily of the vocation wherewith he is called, and, [14] *whether he eateth or drinketh, doth all to the glory of God.*" This promise hath its own reward; for it is *for ever and ever.* They who *walk in the Name of the Lord,* shall *walk* [15] *before Him in the land of the living, for ever and ever.* Such walk on, with quickened steps, lingering not, *in the Name of the Lord our God,* i. e. doing all things in His Name, as His great Name requires, conformed to the holiness and all other qualities which His Name expresseth. *For ever and ever,* lit. *for ever and yet,* or, more strictly still, *for that which is hidden and yet,* which is the utmost thought of eternity we can come to. Time indeed has no relation to eternity; for time, being God's creature, is infinite. Still, practically to us, our nearest conception of eternity, is existence, on and on and on, an endless, unchanging, ever-prolonged future, lost in distance and *hidden* from us, and then, *and yet,* an ever-to-come *yet,* which shall never come to an end. Well then may we not faint, as tho' it were long to toil or to do without this or that, since the part of our way which lies amid toils and weariness is so short, and will soon be at an end; what lies beyond, in joy, is infinite in infinite joy, ever full and still ever a *yet* to come.

The Prophet says, *we will walk;* "[16] uniting himself in longing, hope, faith, to the sons of the New Testament, i. e. Christians, as his brethren, re-born by the grace of the same Christ;" "[17] ministers of the Old, heirs of the New Testament, because they loved through that same faith whereby we love; believing in the Incarnation, Passion, Resurrection of Christ yet to be, as we believe in it, having been."

[1] Rib. [2] Ps. lxxviii. 57. [3] Jer. ii. 11.
[4] S. Luke xvi. 8. [5] S. Cyr.
[6] 2 Tim. ii. 11, 12. Rom. viii. 17. Rev. iii. 4.
[7] Gal. ii. 20. [8] 1 Cor. ii. 2.
[9] As to *walk in God's statutes,* (Ezek. v. 6, 7, &c. and seven other places) *in His judgments,* (Ps. lxxxix. 31. Ez. xxxvi. 27.) *in His commandments,* (2 Chr. xvii. 4.) *in His law,* (Ps. lxxviii. 10 &c.) *in His fear,* (Neh. v. 9.) and, in the corresponding place in Isaiah, *in the light of the Lord.* (Is. ii. 5.) see Ges. Thes. v. הלך. p. 378. and above on Mic. ii. 11. p. 35. So again to *walk with God,* (Gen. v. 22.) or *before God,* (Ib. xvii. 1.) or *contrary to God.* (Lev. xxvi. 21.)
[10] יהוה See on Hos. xii. 5. vol. i. p. 119.
[11] Is. vii. 14. Immanuel, i. e. God with us; ix. 6. Wonderful, Counsellor, Mighty God, &c.
[12] S. Matt. i. 21. [13] Theoph. [14] 1 Cor. x. 31.
[15] Ps. cxvi. 9. [16] Tir. [17] S. Aug. c. 2 Epp. Pelag. iii. 4.

Before CHRIST cir. 710.

6 In that day, saith the
LORD, [g] will I assemble her
that halteth, [h] and I will
gather her that is driven
out, and her that I have
afflicted;
7 And I will make her
that halted [i] a remnant,
and her that was cast far
off a strong nation: and
the LORD [k] shall reign over
them in mount Zion from
henceforth, even for ever.
8 ¶ And thou, O tower

g Ezek. 34. 16. Zeph. 3. 19.
h Ps. 147. 2. Ezek. 34. 31. & 37. 21.
i ch. 2. 12. & 5. 3, 7, 8. & 7. 18.
k Is. 9. 6. & 24. 23. Dan. 7. 14, 27. Luke 1. 33. Rev. 11. 15.

6. *In that day*, i. e. in that day of Christ and of His Gospel, of grace and salvation, *the last days* of which he had been speaking. Hitherto he had prophesied the glory of Zion, chiefly through the coming-in of the Gentiles. Now he adds, how the Jews should, with them, be gathered by grace into the one fold, in that long last day of the Gospel, at the beginning, in the course of it, and completely at the end [1].

Her that halteth. The Prophet resumes the image of the scattered flock, under which he had before [2] foretold their restoration. This was no hope of his own, but *His* word Who cannot fail. The course of events, upon which he is entering, would be, at times, for their greatness and their difficulty, past human belief. So he adds straightway, at the outset, *saith the Lord.* To *halt* is used of bodily lameness [3], and that, of a flock, worn out by its wanderings [4]. It is used also of moral halting [5], such as had been a chief sin of Israel, serving partly God, partly Baal [6]; God, with a service of fear, Baal with a service of that counterfeit of love, sensuality. So it was *sick*, both in body and soul, and *driven out* [7] also, and *afflicted.*

7. *And her that was cast off a strong nation.* The prophecy, that there should be a remnant, was depressing. Yet what a remnant should it be! A remnant, which should multiply like the stars of heaven or the sand on the sea-shore. Israel had never been *a strong nation*, as a kingdom of this world. At its best estate, under David, it had subdued the petty nations around it, who were confederated to destroy it. It had never competed with the powers of this world, East or West, Egypt or Nineveh, although God had at times marvelously saved it from being swallowed up by them. *Now*, the remnant of Judah, which itself was but a remnant of the undivided people, was to become *a strong nation.* So Isaiah prophesied, [8] *A little one shall become a thousand, and a small one a strong nation.* Plainly not in temporal greatness, both because human strength was not, and could not be, its characteristic, and because the Prophet had been speaking of spiritual restoration.

"[9] *Strong* are they, whom neither torture nor allurements can separate from the love of Christ." "Strong are they, who are strong against themselves." Strong were they who said [10], *We ought to obey God rather than men*, and [11], *Who shall separate us from the love of Christ? shall tribulation, or distress, or persecution, or famine, or nakedness, or peril, or sword? Nay, in all these things we are more than conquerors through Him that loved us.* God does not only restore in the Gospel; He multiplies exceedingly. "[12] I will so clothe her with the spirit of might, that, as she shall be fruitful in number, so shall she be glorious in victories, so that of her it shall be said [13], *Who is she that looketh forth as the morning, fair as the moon, clear as the sun, terrible as* an army *with banners?*" For, not to name those, whose whole life is one warfare against invisible enemies and the evil desires of the flesh, who shall count the martyrs of Christ? We know that that *remnant* and *strong nation* owe wholly to grace all which they are, as they themselves in the Revelations give thanks; [14] *Thou wast slain and hast redeemed us to God by Thy Blood, out of every kindred and tongue and people and nation, and hast made us unto our God kings and priests, and we shall reign on the earth;* that same Lord, of Whom it is here said,

The Lord shall reign over them in Zion from henceforth even forever. The visible kingdom of God in Judah was often obscured, kings, princes, priests, and false prophets combining to encourage one another in rebellion against God. In the captivity it even underwent an almost total eclipse by the over-shadowing of earthly power, save when the Divine light flashed forth for an instant in the deeds or words of power and wisdom, related by Daniel. *Henceforth*, i. e. from the time, when *the law* should *go forth out of Zion*, God should *indeed* reign, and that kingdom should have no end.

8. *And thou, O tower of the flock.* "'Tower of Ader,' which is interpreted 'tower of the flock,' about 1000 paces (a mile) from Beth-

[1] Rom. xi. 26. [2] ii. 12, 13. [3] Gen xxxii. 32.
[4] Zeph. iii. 19.
[5] Ps. xxxv. 15. xxxviii. 18.
[6] 1 Kings xviii. 21. The word is different here.
[7] נִדָּחָה is used with the same image of the dispersed flock, Zeph. iii. 19. Ez. xxxiv. 4. 16. and הִדִּיחוּ Jer. l. 17.
[8] lx. 22. [9] Gloss. [10] Acts v. 29.
[11] Rom. viii. 35, 37. [12] Rup. [13] Cant. vi. 10.
[14] Rev. v. 9, 10.

Before CHRIST cir. 710.

of ‖ the flock, the strong hold of the daughter of Zion, unto thee shall it come, even the first domin-

‖ Or, *Edar:* Gen. 35, 21.

Before CHRIST cir. 710.

lehem," says St. Jerome[1] who lived there, "and foresignifying [in its very name] by a sort of prophecy the shepherds at the Birth of the Lord." There Jacob fed his sheep[2], and there (since it was hard by Bethlehem) the shepherds, keeping watch over their flocks by night, saw and heard the Angels singing, "Glory to God in the highest, and on earth peace, good will toward men." The Jews inferred from this place that the Messiah should be revealed there[3].

Stronghold [Ophel[4]] *of the daughter of Zion.* Ophel was a strong place in the South of Jerusalem, the last which the wall, enclosing Zion, reached, before, or as, it touched on the Eastern porch of the temple[5], with whose service it was connected. We know that, after the captivity, the Nethinim, who did the laborious service of the temple, dwelt there[6]. It lay very near to the priests' district[7]. It was probably, a lower acclivity, "swelling out," (as its name seems to mean[8],) from the mountain of the temple. In the last war, it was held together with "[9] the temple, and the adjoining parts to no slight extent, and the valley of Kedron." It was burnt[10] before the upper city was taken. It had been encircled by a wall of old; for Jotham "[11] built greatly *upon* its wall." Manasseh "[12] encircled it," (probably with an outer wall) "and raised it exceedingly," i. e. apparently raised artificially the whole level.

Yet, as a symbol of all Jerusalem, Ophel is as remarkable, as the "tower of the flock" is as to Bethlehem. For Ophel, although fortified, is no where spoken of, as of any account[13]. It is not even mentioned in the circuit of the walls, at their dedication under Nehemiah[14], probably as an outlying, spot. It was probably of moment chiefly, as giving an advantage to an enemy who might occupy it.

Both then are images of lowliness. The lonely Shepherd tower, for Bethlehem, the birthplace of David; Ophel for Jerusalem, of which it was yet but an outlying part, and deriving its value probably as an outwork of the temple. Both symbols anticipate the fuller prophecy of the littleness, which shall become great in God. Before the mention of the greatness of the *dominion to come,* is set forth the future poverty to which it should come. In lowliness Christ came, yet is indeed a Tower protecting and defending the sheep of His pasture, founded on earth in His Human Nature, reaching to Heaven in His Divine; [15] *a strong Tower; the righteous runneth into it, and is safe.*

Unto thee shall it come; (lit. *unto thee shall it come* [16], *and there shall arrive* &c.) He saith not at first what shall come, and so raises the soul to think of the greatness of that which should come. The soul is left to fill up what is more than thought can utter. *Unto thee,* (lit. *quite up to thee* [17].) No hindrances should withhold it from coming. Seemingly it was a great way off, and they in a very hopeless state. He suggests the difficulty even by his strength of assurance. One could not say, *it shall come quite up to thee,* of that which in the way of nature would readily come to any one. But amid all hindrances God's Might makes its way, and brings His gifts and promises to their end. *And there shall arrive.* He twice repeats the assurance, in equivalent words, for their fuller assurance, "[18] to make the good tidings the gladder by repeating and enforcing them."

The first or *former, dominion.* The word often stands, as our "former[19]," in contrast

[1] de loc. Hebr. Arculf A. D. 670 found "a Church of the Shepherds," a mile from Bethlehem. Early trav. in Pal. p. 6. The Migdal Edar is mentioned also in the Mass. Shekalim c. 7. 4. "Of the herds, in the space between Jerusalem and 'the tower of the flock' and on both sides, the males are for burnt-offerings, the female for peace-offerings. R. Jehuda says, whatever male animals are found (there) thirty days before the passover fit for it, are to be used thereto." in Sepp. Heil. Land. ii. 470.

[2] Gen. xxxv. 21.

[3] Ps. Jon. on Gen. xxxv. 21. "This is the place, where in the last days Messiah shall be revealed."

[4] Ophel, like many other Hebrew Proper names, did not lose its original appellative meaning, and so in the 6 places, where it occurs in the prose books, keeps the article; 2 Chron. xxvii. 3. xxxiii. 14. Neh. iii. 26, 7. xi. 21. and 2 Kings v. 24. in which last place it may very possibly be a place in Samaria, named after that in Jerusalem. It occurs without the art. here and Is. xxxii. 14. and in Josephus, Ὀφλᾶς. The E. V. retains the word as a Proper name in the historical books, 2 Chron. and Neh.

[5] "The oldest wall was hard to be taken on account of the ravines, and the ridge above them on which it was built.—On the West—turning to the S. over the pool of Siloam, and then again bending Eastward to Solomon's pool, and extending to a place which they call Ophlas, it was joined on to the Eastern porch of the temple." Jos. B. J. v. 4. 2.

[6] Neh. iii. 26. xi. 21. [7] Ib. iii. 28.

[8] Like *tum*ulus from *tumeo.* Fürst. It is used of a local tumor in Arab. and in Deut. xxviii. 27. 1 Sam. v. 6. 12. vi. 4. 5. and of the swelling of pride. Num. xiv. 44. Hab. ii. 4. [9] by John. Jos. B. J. v. 6. 1.

[10] Together with "the archive, Acra, the Council-hall." Ib. vi. 6. 3. after the destruction of the temple. Ib. vi. 4. 5–7. [11] 2 Chron. xxvii. 3. [12] Ib. xxxiii. 14.

[13] Josephus calls it, "that which was called Ophlas." B. J. v. 4. 2. vi. 6. 3.

[14] Neh. xii. 31–40. [15] Prov. xviii. 10.

[16] The Masorethes seem rightly to have marked this by the accents. [17] עָדֶיךָ. [18] Rup.

[19] So, the *former* time, (Is. viii. 23.) *deeds,* (2 Chron. ix. 29. xvi. 11, xx. 34,) *king,* (Num. xxvi. 26,) *tables,* (Ex. xxxiv. 1.) *benefits,* (Ps. lxxxix. 50.) *days,* (Deut. iv. 32, x. 10.) *kings,* (Jer. xxxiv. 5,) *prophets,* (Zech. i. 4, vii. 7. 12.) *temple,* (Ezr. iii. 12. Hagg. ii. 3. 9.) See Ges. Thes. p. 1251.

Before CHRIST cir. 710.

ion; the kingdom shall
come to the daughter of
Jerusalem.
9 Now why dost thou
cry out aloud? [l]*is there* no
king in thee? is thy counsellor perished? for [m]pangs
have taken thee as a woman
in travail.

[l] Jer. 8. 19.
[m] Is. 13. 8. & 21. 3. Jer. 30. 6. & 50. 43.

10 Be in pain, and la-
bor to bring forth, O
daughter of Zion, like a
woman in travail: for now
shalt thou go forth out of
the city, and thou shalt
dwell in the field, and thou
shalt go *even* to Babylon;
there shalt thou be de-

Before CHRIST cir. 710.

---

with the "later." It is not necessarily *the first*, strictly; and so here, not the *dominion* of David and Solomon exclusively. Rather the Prophet is placed in spirit in the later times when the kingdom should be suspended, and foretells that *the former dominion*, i. e. that of the line of David, should come to her, not in its temporal greatness, but the line itself. So the Angel said, [1] *He shall be great and shall be called the Son of the Highest, and the Lord God shall give unto Him the throne of His father David, and He shall reign over the house of Jacob for ever.*

The [*A*] *kingdom to the daughter of Jerusalem*, i. e. a kingdom, which should not be *of* her, but which should come *to* her; not her's by right, but by *His* right, Who should merit it for her, and, being King of kings, makes His own, [2] *kings and priests unto God and His Father.*

The Jews themselves seem to have taken these words into their own mouths, just before they rejected Him, when they hoped that He would be a king, such as they wished for. [3] *Blessed be the kingdom of our father David that cometh in the Name of the Lord.* And in a distorted form, they held it even afterward [4].

9. *Now.* The prophet places himself in the midst of their deepest sorrows, and out of them he promises comfort. *Why dost thou cry out aloud? is there no King in thee? is thy Counsellor perished* [5]? Is then all lost, because thou hast no visible king, none to counsel thee or consult for thee [5]? Very remarkably he speaks of their *King* and *Counsellor* as one, as if to say, "When all beside is gone, there is One Who abides. Though thou be a captive, God will not forsake thee. When thou hadst no earthly king, [6] *the Lord thy God* was *thy King.* He is the First, and He is the Last. When thou shalt have no other, He, thy King, ceaseth not to be." "[7] Thou shouldest not fear, so long as He, Who counselleth for thee, liveth; but He liveth for ever." Thy *Counsellor*, He, Who is called [8] *Counsellor*, Who counselleth for thee, Who counselleth thee, will, if thou obey His counsel, make birth-pangs to end in joy.

For pangs have taken thee, as a woman in travail, resistless, remediless, doubling the whole frame, redoubled until the end, for which God sends them, is accomplished, and then ceasing in joy. The truest comfort, amid all sorrow, is in owning that the travail-pains must be, but that the reward shall be afterward. "[7] It is meet to look for deliverance from God's mercy, as certainly as for punishment from our guilt; and that the more, since He who foretold both, willingly saves, punishes unwillingly." So the prophets adds.

10. *Be in pain, and labor to bring forth*, (lit. *Writhe and burst forth*,) as if to say, "thou *must* suffer, but thy suffering and thy joy shall be one. Thou canst not have the joy without the suffering. As surely as thou sufferest, thou shalt have joy. In all sorrow, lose not faith and hope, and [9] *thou shalt be sorrowful, but thy sorrow shall be turned into joy.*" "[10] Good daughter, be very patient in the pangs, bear up against your sorrows," so shall the birth be nigh. Yet for the time she must *go forth out of the city* into captivity. *And thou shalt dwell in the field*, houseless, under tents, as captives were wont to be kept, until all were gathered together to be led away; a sore exchange for her former luxury, and in requital of their oppression [11].

And thou shalt go even to Babylon. Not Babylon, but Assyria was the scourge of God in Micah's time. Babylon was scarcely known, *a far country* [12]. Yet Micah is taught of God to declare that thither shall the two tribes be carried captive, although the ten

---

[1] S. Luke i. 32, 3. [2] Rev. i. 6.
[3] S. Mark xi. 10.
[4] Targ. "And thou, O Messiah of Israel, who art hid on account of the sins of the congregation of Israel, to thee the kingdom will come," giving to עֹפֶל the sense of אפל. (as in the LXX. Vulg. Aq. Symm. Syr.) and thence obtaining the sense "hidden," in reference to their fable that He was born before the destruction of the temple and hidden by God.
[5] Comp. Hos. xiii. 10. [6] 1 Sam. xii. 12.
[7] Mont. [8] Is. ix. 6.
[9] S. John xvi. 20.
[10] S. Cyr. [11] Am. vi. Micah ii. 8, 9.
[12] 2 Kings xx. 14.

Before CHRIST cir. 710.

livered; there the LORD
shall redeem thee from the
hand of thine enemies.
11 ¶ [n] Now also many
nations are gathered
against thee, that say, Let
her be defiled, and let our
eye [o] look upon Zion.
12 But they know not
[p] the thoughts of the LORD,
neither understand they
his counsel: for he shall

n Lam. 2. 16.
o Obad. 12. ch. 7. 10.
p Is. 55. 8. Rom. 11. 33.

were carried captive by Assyria. *There*[1] *shalt thou be delivered, there the Lord shall redeem thee from the hand*[2] *of thine enemies.* God's judgments, or purifying trials, or visitation of His saints, hold their way, until their end be reached. They who suffer them cannot turn them aside; they who inflict them cannot add to them or detain them. The prisonhouse is the place of deliverance to Joseph and St. Peter; the Red-sea to Israel; the judges were raised up, when Israel was mightily oppressed; Jabesh-Gilead was delivered when the seventh day was come[3]; the walls of Jerusalem were the end of Sennacherib; Judah should have long been in the very hand and grasp of Babylon, yet must its clenched *hand* be opened.

11. *Now also.* [*And now.*] The prophet had already spoken of the future before them, with this word *Now.* Then, he distinctly prophesied the captivity to Babylon. Twice more he begins anew; as Holy Scripture, so often, in a mystery, whether speaking of evil or of good, of deliverance or of punishment, uses a threefold form. In these two, no mention is made of the enemy, and so there is some uncertainty. But the course must apparently be either backward or forward. They must either be two nearer futures before the Captivity, or two more distant after it. This second gathering might, in itself, either be that of the Assyrian hosts under Sennacherib out of all the nations subject to him; or that of the many petty nations in the time of the Maccabees, who took advantage of the Syrians' oppression, to combine to eradicate the Jews[4]. If understood of Sennacherib, the prophet, having foretold the entire captivity of the whole people to Babylon, would have prophesied the sudden destruction of a nearer enemy, whose miraculous and instantaneous overthrow should be the earnest of the destruction of Babylon and of their deliverance from it. This would suit well with the description, *He shall gather them as sheaves to the floor*, and would correspond well with the descriptions in Isaiah. On the other hand, whereas *this* description would suit any other event, in which man gathered his strength against God and was overthrown, the following words, *Arise and thresh, O daughter of Zion*, &c, fit better with the victories of the Maccabees, in which Israel was active, than with the overthrow of Sennacherib, in which they were wholly passive, and God did all for them, as Isaiah and Nahum foretell the same overthrow[5]. Then also, if the course of the description was backward, 1) the captivity in Babylon, 2) the destruction of Sennacherib, there is no earlier event to correspond with [6] *the smiting of the judge of Israel on the cheek.* The malice also of the nations gathered against Zion suits better with the abiding character of the petty nations, and of their hereditary envy against Israel and its high claims. To Nineveh and Babylon, Israel was but one little corner of ground, which rounded their territory and connected them with Egypt. They disdained them, even while they sought to subdue them. Micah describes the exultation of petty gratified rivalry.

That say, let her be defiled. The bad have a keen eye for the haltings and inconsistencies and falls of God's people, for which they are ever on the watch. Like Satan, they are first tempters, then the accusers; first desecrators, then sanctimonious justiciaries. God, in His judgment, leaves what has been inwardly defiled to be outwardly profaned. [7] *If any man defile the temple of God, him shall God destroy; for the temple of God is holy, which temple are ye.* [8] *The faithful city had become a harlot.* [9] *The land had become polluted by its inhabitants.* Now it was to be polluted by the enemy. Its seducers ask for the judgment of God. "It has become like us in its deeds; let it no more be distinguished from us by the name of the people of God."

And let our eye look upon Zion, with pleasure upon its desolation, and feed itself with its misery. "[10] Where the eye, there love; where the hand, there pain." [11] *They opened their mouth wide against me: they said, Aha, Aha, our eye hath seen.* The world hates the Church; Edom, Israel; it cannot be satisfied with beholding its chastisements[12]. The sufferings of the Martyrs were the choice spectacle of the Heathen.

1 See on Hos. ii. 15.
2 lit. "the hollow of the hand," and so "the grasp."
3 1 Sam. xi. 3. 10. 11.
4 1 Macc. v. 1, 2.
5 Is. x. 24–34. xiv. 24, 5. xvii. 12–14. xxix. 7, 8. Nah. i. 10–13.
6 v. 1–4. Heb.
7 1 Cor. iii. 17.
8 Is. i. 21.
9 Jer. iii. 9. Ps. cvi. 38. Is. xxiv. 5.
10 Proverb in Lap.
11 Ps. xxxv. 21.
12 Mic. vii. 10. Ob. 12.

Before CHRIST cir. 710.

gather them [q] as the
sheaves into the floor.
13 [r] Arise and thresh, O
daughter of Zion: for I
will make thine horn iron,
and I will make thy hoofs
brass: and thou shalt [s] beat
in pieces many people:
[t] and I will consecrate their
gain unto the LORD, and
their substance unto [u] the
Lord of the whole earth.

Before CHRIST cir. 710.

q Is. 21. 10.
r Is. 41. 15, 16. Jer. 51. 33.
s Dan. 2. 44.
t Isai. 18. 7. & 23. 18. & 60. 6, 9.
u Zeck. 4. 14. & 6. 5.

12. *But they know not the thoughts of the Lord, neither understand they His counsel.* The heathen did, for their own ends, what God willed for His. The first step was the same; God willed that His people should be punished; they willed to punish them. But all which lay beyond, they saw not; that God willed (on their repentance) to pardon His own people, but to punish themselves for their pride [1] and cruelty [2]. "[3] Almighty God corrects the elect through the reprobate, as with a rod; after which He condemns the reprobate eternally, as when the son has been disciplined, the rod is cast into the fire."

For He shall gather them as the sheaves into the floor. The multitude of the sheaves hinders not the threshing; the multitude of God's enemies hinders not their destruction. They think that they strengthen themselves, as they gather together; God sees them but as ripened and fitted for destruction, gathered into one bundle together, to perish together. God gathers them, not by constraint or force, but by giving free scope to their own wayward wills, and overruling these to His ends.

13. *Arise* (it may be,) from the dust in which they were lying, *I will make thine horn iron, and I will make thy hoofs brass.* Threshing in the East is partly with oxen, partly with wheels of iron, or with planks set with sharp flints on an open place made hard to this end. The Prophet joins another image, with this and represents Judah as being by God endued with strength, first as with a *horn* of *iron* [4] to cast the enemy to the ground, and then with *hoofs* of *brass*, wherewith to trample them to dust, as the stubble and chaff. *And I will consecrate their gain unto the Lord,* i. e. to Myself; the Lord gathered them into the floor by His Providence; the Lord gave His people strength to subdue them; and now, in His own Person, He says, I will complete My own work.

The very image of the "threshing" implies that this is no mere destruction. While the stubble is *beaten* or bruised to small pieces, and the chaff is far more than the wheat, and is carried out of the floor, there yet remains the seed-corn. So in the great judgments of God, while most is refuse, there yet remains over, what is severed from the lost heap and wholly *consecrated* to Him. Whatever things were the object of the "Cherem [5]" or "thing devoted to the Lord," could not be redeemed, but must remain wholly the Lord's. If it had life, it was to be put to death [6]. And so the use of the word here may the rather shew, how those converted to God, and who became *gain,* hallowed to Him, were to pass through death to life, to die to themselves that they might live to Him: what was evil was to be slain in them, that they themselves might live.

The Israelites and God's dealings with them are [7] *ensamples of us upon whom the ends of the world are come.* And so the whole section fits wonderfully with the condition of the single soul.

She who halteth is "[8] the soul, who would serve God, yet not so as wholly to give up the service of the world, which it had in Baptism renounced, who, after it had gone astray like a lost sheep, and been scattered amid the manifoldness of earthly things, was gathered again into the fold, to love One only, long for One only, give itself to One," its Good Shepherd, and over it the Lord reigneth for ever, if, taught by experience the deceitfulness of Satan's promises, and stung by the sense of its own thanklessness and vileness, and conscious of the peril of self confidence, it abideth more closely than others with God. *He shall gather her that is driven out,* i. e. "[9] He shall restore her, from whom He had, for the time, withdrawn His grace," *and her that was afflicted,* trouble being God's most effectual instrument, in recalling the soul to Himself. "[10] For *the Lord raiseth them that are bowed down. And will make her that halteth, a remnant,* placing her among the elect and holy, *and her that was cast off strong;* for Christ giveth oft to such souls great richness of Divine graces, so that [11] *where sin abounded, grace* should *much more abound.*" "[8] To it, when enlightened and purified by affliction and by repentance, it is promised, that its Lord, the Great King, shall come to it, and again reign in it, which is the great bliss of souls in grace. For then doth the soul really reign, when it submits wholly to Christ, Whom to serve is to reign, and so, under Him, receives power to command its

[1] Is. x. 7. 12. [2] Zech. i. 15. 19. [3] Dion. [4] 1 Kings xxii. 11.

[5] Lev. xxvii. 28. [6] Ib. 29. [7] 1 Cor. x. 11. [8] Rib. [9] Dion. [10] Ps. cxlvi. 8. [11] Rom. v. 20.

Before CHRIST cir. 710.

CHAPTER V.

1 *The birth of Christ.* 4 *His kingdom.* 8 *His conquest.*

NOW gather thyself in troops O daughter of troops: he hath laid siege against us: they shall [a]smite the judge of Israel with a rod upon the cheek.

[a] Lam. 3. 30. Matt. 5. 39. & 27. 30.

wrong desires, and rule itself;" that great and wonderful power which the Evangelist expresses in words so brief, [1] *To them gave He power to become the sons of God.* Thus He *maketh it strong,* so that [2] *neither death, nor life, nor angels, nor principalities, nor powers,* can *separate it from the love of God which is in Christ Jesus our Lord.* Then, "he describes the condition of the soul fluctuating between good and evil, called one way by God through inward inspirations, and another way by the enticements and habits of sin. And, wishing to follow God, yet not to be without its sinful pleasures, and knowing this to be impossible, it is in anguish and hesitates. Her the prophet justly rebukes, '*why thus cry aloud,* as though thou must be led captive by the Devil, not knowing or unable to extricate thyself? *Hast thou no King,* aided by Whose power, thou mayest fight against all enticements, habit, the flesh?' Paul felt this and cried aloud, [3] *I see another law in my members, warring against the law of my mind, and bringing me into captivity to the law of sin which is in my members. O wretched man that I am, who shall deliver me from the body of this death?*" You see his grief. But he despairs not. He knows that he has *a King. I thank God through Jesus Christ our Lord.* Or why grievest thou, as if thou hadst no *counsellor,* by whose counsels to free thee from these snares? *Thy Counsellor* indeed *perished* on the Cross, but for thy sake, that thou mayest live. He died, to destroy him who hath the power of death. But He rose the third day and is still with thee; at the Right Hand of the Father He still reigns Immortal forever. See how many counsels He has left thee in the Gospel, how many admonitions, whereby thou mayest lead a happy and tranquil life. Now *pain seizes thee like a woman in travail.* For such a soul *travails,* having conceived inspirations from God, which it wishes to obey, but that the flesh, overcome by concupiscence, resists, and so it never brings forth, nor experiences that joy, whereof the Lord speaketh, [4] *When she is delivered of the child, she remembereth no more the anguish, for joy that a man is born into the world.* Wherefore he adds; *be in pain,* for thou art indeed in travail; thou wilt not cease to be in pain, until thou bring forth. *Thou wilt go forth, &c.* "[5] God, by a provision of His great mercy, allows lukewarm souls, who will be at no pains to gain grace, to fall into foulest sins, in order that, owning at last their misery, they may cease to be lukewarm, and with great ardor of soul may embrace virtue. For, warned by the result, they understand that they themselves emboldened the tempter, (for he chiefly attacks the lukewarm and remiss,) and they become ardent in the conflict and in well-doing." Wherefore he says, *thou shalt go forth out of the city,* that City of God, whereof He *is the Builder and Maker* [6], which is gladdened by the river of His spirit; "and it dwells in the open field, unprotected, ready to be a prey, in the broad way of its own concupiscences, out of *the narrow road which leadeth to life, and goeth even to Babylon,* the city of 'confusion,' in tumult and din and unrest, and the distractions of this life." Yet even there shall it be delivered, like the poor Prodigal, who came to himself in a far country, when worn out by its hard service. Even there it must not despair, but remember, with him, its Father's house, its former home, the Heavenly Jerusalem. Its pains within or without, whereby it is brought back, are travail-pains. Though all is dark, it must not say, *I have no Counsellor.* For its Redeemer's Name is [7] *Counsellor,* "[8] one Counsellor of a thousand." "[9] Thine Intercessor never dies." Out of the very depth of misery will the Divine Mercy draw thee. Though thou seem held by the strong hand of the enemy, and he seems to triumph over thee and to jeer thee, [10] *There, there so would we have it, we have devoured him,* and hosts of devils seek thy utter destruction, and thou seem to be [11] *delivered over* to them *to the destruction of the flesh;* yet is it only *that the spirit may be saved in the Day of the Lord.* Even Satan, when he is tormenting souls, *knows not the thoughts of the Lord, nor understands His counsels,* how, by the very pain which he inflicts, God is bidding them, *Rise* and "[5] look up to heaven and long for heavenly things and trample on all which they had hitherto foully served, honor or vain glory or covetousness or lust;" how He will *exalt their horn in the Lord, make* it strong as *iron* that they should *do all things through Christ in strengthening them,* and conquer all through the might of Christ; how He should *bruise Satan under their feet shortly,* and they consecrate wholly to God their whole strength, every power of soul and body which hitherto had been the adversary's.

V. 1. *Now gather thyself in troops, O daughter*

[1] S. John i. 12. [2] Rom. viii. 38, 9. [3] Rom. vii. 23, 24. [4] S. John xvi. 21. [5] Rib. [6] Heb. xi. 10. [7] Is. ix. 6.

[8] Ecclus. vi. 6. [9] Christian Year. [10] Ps. xxxv. 25. [11] 1 Cor. v. 5.

Before CHRIST cir. 710.

2 But thou, [b]Beth-lehem Ephratah *though* thou

[b] Matt. 2. 6. John 7. 42.

Before CHRIST cir. 710.

of troops. The *daughter of troops* is still the same who was before addressed, Judah. The word is almost always[1] used of "bands of men employed in irregular, marauding, inroads." Judah is entitled *daughter of troops*, on account of her violence, the robbery and bloodshed within her[2], as Jeremiah says[3], *Is this house which is called by My Name become a den of robbers in your eyes?* She then who *had spoiled*[4] should now be *spoiled;* she who had formed herself in bands to lay waste, shall now be gathered thick together, in small bands[5], unable to resist in the open field; yet in vain should she so gather herself; for the enemy was upon her, in her last retreat.

This description has obviously no fulfillment, except in the infliction by the Romans. For there was no event, *before* the invasion by Sennacherib and accordingly in the prophet's own time, in which there is any seeming fulfillment of it. But then, the second deliverance must be that by the Maccabees; and this siege, which lies, in order of time, beyond it, must be a siege by the Romans. With this it agrees, that whereas, in the two former visitations, God promised, in the first, deliverance, in the second, victory, here the Prophet dwells on the Person of the Redeemer, and foretells that the strength of the Church should not lie in any human means[6]. Here too Israel had no *king*, but a *judge* only. Then the "gathering in robber-bands" strikingly describes their internal state in the siege of Jerusalem; and although this was subsequent to and consequent upon the rejection of our Lord, yet there is no reason why the end should be separated from the beginning since the capture by Titus was but the sequel of the capture by Pompey, the result of that same temper, in which they crucified Jesus, because He would not be their earthly king. It was the close of the organic existence of the former people; after which the *remnant* from among them with the Gentiles, not Israel after the flesh, were the true people of God.

He hath laid siege against us. The Prophet, being born of them, and for the great love he bore them, counts himself among them, as St. Paul mourns over his brethren after the flesh. *They shall smite the judge of Israel with a rod upon the cheek.* So St. Paul said to him who had made himself high priest,[7] *God shall smite thee, thou whited wall; for sittest thou to judge me after the law, and commandest me to be smitten contrary to the law.* It is no longer "the king" (for they had said,[8] *We have no King but Cæsar*) but *the judge of Israel*, they who against Christ and His Apostles gave wrong judgment. As they had smitten contrary to the law, so were the chief men smitten by Titus, when the city was taken. As they had done it, was done unto them. To be smitten on the face, betokens shame; to smite with the rod, betokens destruction. Now both shall meet in one; as, in the Great Day, the wicked[9] *shall awake to shame and everlasting contempt*, and shall *perish for ever.*

2. *But* [*And*] *thou, Bethlehem Ephratah.* With us, the chequered events of time stand in strong contrast, painful or gladdening. Good seems to efface evil, or evil blots out the memory of the good. God orders all in the continuous course of His Wisdom. All lies in perfect harmony in the Divine Mind. Each event is the sequel of what went before. So here the Prophet joins on, what to us stands in such contrast, with that simple, *And.* Yet he describes the two conditions as bearing on one another. He had just spoken of *the judge of Israel* smitten on the cheek, and, before[10], that Israel had neither *king* nor *counsellor;* he now speaks of *the Ruler in Israel*, the Everlasting. He had said, how Judah was to become mere *bands* of men; he now says, how the *little Bethlehem* was to be exalted. He had said before, that the *rule of old* was to come to *the tower of the flock*, *the daughter of Jerusalem;* now, retaining the word[11], he speaks of the Ruler, in Whom it was to be established. Before he had addressed *the tower of the flock;* now, *Bethlehem.* But he has greater things to say now, so he pauses[12], *And thou!* People have admired the brief appeal of the murdered Cæsar, "Thou too, Brutus." The like energetic conciseness lies in the words, *And thou! Bethlehem Ephratah.* The name Ephratah is not seemingly added, in order to distinguish Bethlehem from the Bethlehem of Zabulon, since *that* is but once named[13], and Bethlehem here is marked to be the *Bethlehem Judah*[14], by the addition, *too little to be among the thou-*

[1] i. e. except Job xxv. 3. (where it is used of the armies of God) and Job xxix. 25. In Job xix. 5. it is used metaphorically of the "host" of evils sent against Job. S. Jerome renders "filia latronis," and says that Aq. Symm. Theod. and Ed. V. agree with that rendering.

[2] ii. 8. iii. 2. &c. Hos. v. 10.

[3] Jer. vii. 11. comp. S. Matt. xxi. 13. [4] Is. xxxiii. 1.

[5] תתגודדי and בת גדוד are manifestly to be taken in corresponding senses. That of "gathering in troops" is the only known sense of התגודד, Jer. v. 7, except that of "making incisions in one's flesh," which is obviously irrelevant here.

[6] v. 8–15. [7] Acts xxiii. 3. [8] St. John xix. 15.

[9] Dan. xii. 2. [10] iv. 9.

[11] ממשלה iv. 8. מושל v. 1. Heb.

[12] As marked by the accent, "double Garesh." Casp. [13] Jos. xix. 15.

[14] Its name in Jud. xvii. 7–9. xix. 1, 2. 18. Ruth i. 1, 2. 1 Sam. xvii. 12.

Before CHRIST cir. 710.

be little [c] among the [d] thousands of Judah, *yet* out of

[c] 1 Sam. 23. 23. [d] Ex. 18. 25.

sands of Judah. He joins apparently the usual name, *Bethlehem,* with the old Patriarchal, and perhaps poetic[1] name *Ephratah,* either in reference and contrast to that former birth of sorrow near Ephratah[2], or, (as is Micah's wont,) regarding the meaning of both names. Both its names were derived from "fruitfulness;" "House of Bread" and "fruitfulness;" and, despite of centuries of Mohammedan oppression, it is fertile still[3].

It had been rich in the fruitfulness of this world; rich, thrice rich, should it be in spiritual fruitfulness. "[4] Truly is Bethlehem, 'house of bread,' where was born[5] *the Bread of life, which came down from heaven,*" "[6] Who with inward sweetness refreshes the minds of the elect," [7] *Angel's Bread,* and "[4] Ephratah, fruitfulness, whose fruitfulness is God," the Seed-corn, stored wherein, died and *brought forth much fruit,* all which ever was brought forth to God in the whole world.

Though *thou be little among the thousands of Judah,* lit. *small to be,* i. e. *too small to be among* &c. Each tribe was divided into its thousands, probably of fighting men, each thousand having its own separate head[8]. But the thousand continued to be a division of the tribe, after Israel was settled in Canaan[9]. The *thousand* of Gideon was *the meanest in Manasseh*[10]. Places too small to form a thousand by themselves were united with others, to make up the number[11]. So lowly was Bethlehem that it was not counted among the possessions of Judah. In the division under Joshua, it was wholly omitted[12]. From its situation, Bethlehem can never have been a considerable place. It lay and lies, East of the road from Jerusalem to Hebron, at six miles from the capital[13]. It was "[14] seated on the summit-level of the hill country of Judæa with deep gorges descending East to the Dead Sea and West to the plains of Philistia," "2704 feet above the sea[15]." It lay "[16] on a narrow ridge," whose whole length was not above a mile[16], swelling at each extremity into a somewhat higher eminence, with a slight depression between[17]. "[18] The ridge projects Eastward from the central mountain range, and breaks down in abrupt terraced slopes to deep valleys on the N. E. and S." The West end too "[19] shelves gradually down to the valley." It was then rather calculated to be an outlying fortress, guarding the approach to Jerusalem, than for a considerable city. As a garrison, it was fortified and held by the Philistines[20] in the time of Saul, recovered from them by David, and was one of the 15 cities [21] fortified by Rehoboam. Yet it remained an unimportant

[1] Ps. cxxxii. 6. [2] Gen. xxxv. 19. xlviii. 7.

[3] "The district country around Bethlehem abounds in fields, vineyards, hills, valleys, olive-yards, fig-trees, and is especially supported by wines and corn." Quaresm. Elucid. Terræ S. ii. 620. "Round the hill is fruitful garden and corn land." Russegger iii. 79. "The terraces, admirably kept, and covered with rows of luxuriant olives, intermixed with the fig and vine, sweep in graceful curves round the ridge, regular as stairs." Porter Hdbook, p. 206. "It is still one of the best-cultivated and most fertile parts of Palestine." Rev. G. Williams in Smith's Gr. and R. Geogr. Add. Volney ii. 298. [4] in vit. S. Jer. Ep. 108. de vit. Paulæ. n. 10.

[5] S. Joh. vi. 48, 51. [6] S. Greg. Hom. 8. in Ev.

[7] Ps. lxxviii. 25. [8] Num. i. 16. x. 4.

[9] Jos. xxii. 21. 30. 1 Sam. x. 19. xxiii. 23.

[10] Jud. vi. 15.

[11] As in 1 Chron. xxiii. 11. four brothers, not having many sons, were counted as one "house." Hengst.

[12] Jos. xv. The LXX interpolate it in Jos. xv. 59.

[13] Eus. S. Jer. de loc. Hebr. "6 miles [in the 6th mile, S. Jer.] from Ælia to the South, near the road which leadeth to Hebron." Itin. Hieros. p. 598. "From Jerusalem, as you go to Bethlehem, on the high road at 4 miles on the right is the monument where Rachel, Jacob's wife, was buried. Thence 2 miles on the left is Bethlehem where our Lord Jesus Christ was born." "Two parasangs," (6 miles) Benj. Tud (i. 40. ii. 90.) "6 miles," Arculf, (Early travels in Pal. p. 6.) Bernard (Ib. 29.) Sæ, wulf, (Ib. 44.) "2 hours." Maundrell, (Ib. 455.) Robinson. (i. 470.) [14] Thomson, The land ii. 509.

[15] van de Velde memoir p. 180. "convent at Bethlehem, 2704 Eng. feet." Russ.

[16] Arculf in Early Travels in Palestine p. 6.

[17] Ritter Erdk. xvi. 285. and Russ. in n. 15.

[18] Porter's Hdbook i. 207. "It stands upon an eminence surrounded by small valleys or depressions, devoted to the culture of the olive and vine." —"From this height there is a pretty steep slope on both the North and Southern sides, particularly the former, the two Wadis or gorges which form its boundaries. On the flanks of these Wadis are the principal gardens, vineyards, and plantations of olives and figs. They unite a little to the E. of the town, and form what is called the Wadi-et-Taamarah from the village of Beit-Taamr, in the neighborhood." Wilson, Lands i. 394. "A narrow ridge, surrounded on all sides by valleys." Arculf. Ib. "On the N. the other side of the deep, abruptly-sinking, valley, on the top of the hill, lay Bethlehem." V. Schubert ii. 493, coming from the south. "It stands on the slope of a hill, of difficult ascent, at least by night." Lord Lindsay p. 240. "The first sight of Bethlehem has something strangely picturesque. It lies quite on a bare summit in the Jura limestone of Palestine, 2338 Paris feet above the sea. The summit is divided by a shallow saddle-back. On the West side lies Bethlehem, on the East the great monastery and Church, like a fortress over the precipice, which falls into the deep valley." Russegger iii. 79. "The little city of David, seated on a lofty hill, shines, like a brilliant crown, among the mountains of Judah." Mislin. c. 32. iii. 6. From one spot, you can see the Church of Bethlehem, where our Saviour was born; the Church of the Holy Sepulchre where He was buried; the Mount of Olives whence He ascended to heaven." Id. Ib.

[19] Grove in Smith Dict. of Bib. "Toward the W. the hill is higher than the village, and then sinks down very gradually toward Wadi Ahmed." Rob. i. 470. [20] 2 Sam. xxiii. 14.

[21] 2 Chron. xi. 6. "A low wall without towers surrounds the brow of the hill, and overlooks the valley." Arculf. p. 6. "scarcely a ¼ of an hour." Ritter p. 286.

Before CHRIST cir. 710. thee shall he come forth unto me *that is* to be Before CHRIST cir. 710.

place. Its inhabitants are counted with those of the neighboring Netophah, both before[1] and after[2] the captivity, but both together amounted after the captivity to 179[3] or 188[2] only. It still does not appear among the possessions of Judah[4]. It was called a city[5], but the name included even places which had only 100 fighting men[6]. In our Lord's time it is called *a village*[7], a *city*[8], or a strong spot[9]. The royal city would become *a den of thieves.* Christ should be born in a lowly village. "[10] He Who had taken the form of a servant, chose Bethlehem for His Birth, Jerusalem for His Passion."

St. Matthew relates how the Chief Priest and Scribes in their answer to Herod's enquiries, *where Christ should be born*[11], alleged this prophecy. They gave the substance rather than the exact words, and with one remarkable variation, *art not the least among the princes of Judah.* St. Matthew did not correct their paraphrase, because it does not affect the object for which they alleged the prophecy, the birth of the Redeemer in Bethlehem. The sacred writers often do not correct the translations, existing in their time, when the variations do not affect the truth[12]. Both words are true here. Micah speaks of Bethlehem, as it was in the sight of men; the chief priests, whose words St. Matthew approves, speak of it as it was in the sight of God, and as, by the Birth of Christ, it should become. "[13] Nothing hindered that Bethlehem should be at once a small village and the Mother-city of the whole earth, as being the mother and nurse of Christ Who made the world and conquered it." "[14] That is *not the least*, which is the house of blessing, and the receptacle of Divine grace." "[15] He saith that the spot, although mean and small, shall be glorious. And in truth," adds S. Chrysostom, "the whole world came together to see Bethlehem, where, being born, He was laid, on no other ground than this only." "[16] O Bethlehem, little, but now made great by the Lord, He hath made thee great, Who, being great, was in thee made little. What city, if it heard thereof, would not envy thee that most precious Stable and the glory of that Crib? Thy name is great in all the earth, and *all generations call* thee *blessed.* [17] *Glorious things are* everywhere *spoken of thee, thou city of God.* Everywhere it is sung, that *this Man is born in her, and the Most High Himself shall stablish her.*

Out of thee shall He come forth to Me that is to be Ruler in Israel [lit. shall (one) come forth to Me *to be Ruler.*] Bethlehem was too small to be any part of the polity of Judah; out of her was to come forth One, Who, in God's Will, was to be its Ruler. The words *to Me* include both *of Me* and *to Me.* *Of Me,* i. e. "[18] by My Power and Spirit," as Gabriel said, [19] *The Holy Ghost shall come upon thee, and*

1 1 Chron. ii. 54.
2 Neh. vii. 26.
3 Ezr. ii. 21. 2.
4 Neh. xi. 25–30.
5 Ruth i. 19. Ezr. ii. 1. with 21. Neh. vii. 6. with 26.
6 Am. v. 3.
7 S. John vii. 42.
8 S. Luke ii. 4.
9 Jos. Ant. v. 2. 8. (χώριον)
10 S. Leo de Epiph. Serm. 1.
11 S. Matt. ii. 4–6.
12 See on Am. ix. 12. vol. i. p. 328. Pococke has employed much learning to make this passage verbally accord with the allegation of it by the chief priest recorded by S. Matthew (Notæ miscell. on the Porta Mosis, Works i. 134–9). He follows the eminent authority of Abulwalid (followed by R. Tanchum and a Hebr. Arab. Gloss.) in supposing צְעִיר, "little," to have had the opposite sense of "great," and that it actually had that meaning in Jer. xlviii. 4. Zech. xiii. 7. In neither of those passages, however, have צְעִיר, צָעַר, that meaning, nor do the cases alleged of words containing opposite meanings bear out such an one as this. For the two senses, although differing at last, can be traced up to one common source, which could not be done as to צְעִיר. Thus 1) קדשׁ, "holy," is used of idolatrous consecrations which were in fact horrible desecrations, (see on Hos. iv. 14. vol. i. p. 52.) 2) נפשׁ, "soul," is used of the "person," as we speak of "1000 souls." Thence the idiom נפשׁ מת, lit. "the soul of one dead," Lev. xxi. 11. Num. vi. 6; then in one idiom טמא לנפשׁ, "defiled as to the dead," but נפשׁ does not signify one alive or dead indifferently. 3) ברך, lit. "bent the knee," prayed, includes prayers for evil as well as for good, cursing as well as blessing. 4) חסד love, piety, hence perhaps, what is forbidden by natural piety, (Lev. xx. 17.) and a reproach; (Prov. xiv. 34. Ib. xxv. 10.) unless different roots have accidentally coalesced, (see Fürst Conc.) as in שׂכל, to use "insight," hence wisdom, and סכל vacillate, hence folly, meet in one Syriac word; or our *let,* "hinder," is from *lata,* "slow;" *latyan,* "retard;" Goth. our *let,* "allow," from "*letan*" i. q. lassen.) In Arabic this is the more common on account of the severance of the different tribes who spoke it, before Mohammed united them into one, as the same word receives modifications in different languages of Europe. The meaning, "great" also, if it could be obtained for צְעִיר, would still not yield the meaning desired. For להיות implies a comparison. It means *little to be in the thousands of Judah* i. e. too little. If צְעִיר were rendered *great,* it would still be "great to be among the thousands" &c. i. e. too great to be. Chald. Lxx. Syr. and the Latin in S. Aug. de Civ. D. xviii. 30. give another explanation, *it is little that thou shouldest be.* This does not agree better with the words in St. Matthew, and is against the idiom. In this idiom 1) צְעִיר is not used, but mostly מעט, or נקל Is. xlix. 6. or קטן 2 Sam. vii. 19. 2) The person spoken to is always expressed.

13 S. Greg. Naz. Orat. 18. in patr. § 17.
14 S. Chrys. Quod Christus sit Deus § 3. i. 561.
15 S. Ambr. Ep. 70. § 11.
16 S. Bern. Serm. 1 in Vig. Nativ. § 4. i. 763.
17 Ps. lxxxvii. 3.
18 Theoph.
19 S. Luke i. 35.

Before CHRIST cir. 710.

[e] ruler in Israel; [f] whose goings forth *have been* from of old, from † everlasting.

Before CHRIST cir. 710.

[e] Gen. 49. 10. Is. 9. 6. [f] Ps. 90. 2. Pro. 8. 22, 23. John 1. 1.

† Heb. *the days of eternity.*

the power of the Highest shall overshadow thee, therefore also that Holy Thing which shall be born of thee, shall be called the Son of God. To Me, as God said to Samuel[1], *I will send thee to Jesse the Bethlehemite; for I have provided Me a king among his sons.* So now, *one shall go forth* thence *to Me*, to do My Will, to My praise and glory, to reconcile the world unto Me, to rule and be Head over the true Israel, the Church. He was to *go forth out of* Bethlehem, as his native-place[2]; as Jeremiah[3] says, *His noble shall be from him, and his ruler shall go forth out of the midst of him*[4]; and Zechariah[5], *Out of him shall come forth the cornerstone; out of him the nail, out of him the battlebow, out of him every ruler together.* Before, Micah had said to *the tower of Edar, Ophel of the daughter of Zion, the first rule shall come to thee;* now, retaining the word, he says to Bethlehem, *out of thee shall come one to be a ruler*[6]. *The judge of Israel had been smitten;* now there should *go forth out of* the little Bethlehem, One, not to be a judge only, but a *Ruler.*

Whose goings forth have been *from of old, from everlasting*, lit. *from the days of eternity. Going forth* is opposed to *going forth;* a *going forth out of* Bethlehem, to *a going forth from eternity;* a *going forth*, which then was still to come, (the Prophet says, *shall go forth*,) to a *going forth* which had been long ago, "[7] not from the world but from the beginning, not in the days of time, but *from the days of eternity*. For[8] *in the beginning was the Word, and the Word was with God, and the Word was God. The Same was in the beginning with God. In the end of the days*, He was to go forth from Bethlehem; but, lest he should be thought then to have had His Being, the Prophet adds, His *goings forth are from everlasting.*" Here words, denoting eternity and used of the eternity of God, are united together to impress the belief of the Eternity of God the Son. We have neither thought nor words to conceive eternity; we can only conceive of time lengthened out without end. "[9] True eternity is boundless life, all existing at once," or "[10] duration without beginning and without end and without change." The Hebrew names, here used, express as much as our thoughts can conceive or our words utter. They mean literally, *from afore*, (i. e. look back as far as we can, that from which we begin is still "before,") "*from the days of that which is hidden.*" True, that in eternity there are no divisions, no succession, but one everlasting "now;" one, as God, in whom it is, is One. But man can only conceive of Infinity of space as space without bounds, although God contains space, and is not contained by it; nor can we conceive of Eternity, save as filled out by time. And so God speaks after the manner of men, and calls Himself [11] *the Ancient of Days*, "[12] being Himself the age and time of all things; before days and age and time," "the Beginning and measure of ages and of time." The word, translated *from of old*, is used elsewhere[13] of the eternity of God. [14] *The God of before* is a title chosen to express, that He is *before* all things which He made. [15] *Dweller of afore* is a title, formed to shadow out His ever-present existence. Conceive any existence *afore* all which else you can conceive, go back *afore* and *afore* that; stretch out backward yet *before* and *before* all which you have conceived, ages *afore* ages, and yet *afore*, without end,—then and there God was. That *afore* was the property of God. Eternity belongs to God, not God to eternity. Any words must be inadequate to convey the idea of the Infinite to our finite minds. Probably the sight of God, *as He is*, will give us the only possible conception of eternity. Still the idea of time prolonged infinitely, although we cannot follow it to infinity, shadows our eternal being. And as we look along that long vista, our sight is prolonged and stretched out by those millions upon millions of years, along which we can look, although even if each grain of sand or dust on this earth, which are countless, represented countless millions, we should be, at the end, as far from reaching to eternity as at the beginning. *The days of eternity* are only an inadequate expression, because every conception of the human mind must be so. Equally so is every other, [16] *From everlasting to everlasting;* [17] *from*

[1] 1 Sam. xvi. 1.

[2] When יצא is used of actual descent, it is in relation to the actual parent, to "go forth out of the womb," "out of the loins," "out of the bowels," "out of thee," Gen. xlvi. 26. Job i. 21. Jer. i. 5. Gen. xxxv. 11 xv. 4, xvii. 6. 2 Kings xx. 18. יצאי ירכו יצא, מבטן, מרחם, מחלצי, ממעי, ממך.

[3] xxx. 21. [4] משלו מקרבו יצא. [5] x. 4.

[6] משל (v. 1. Heb.) refers back to הממשלה iv. 8.

[7] Rup. [8] S. John i. 1. 2.

[9] S. Anselm Monol. c. 24. L.

[10] Rich. Vict. de Trin. ii. 4. L. [11] Dan. vii. 9.

[12] Dionys. de Div. Nom. c. 10. x. 5. [13] Hab. i. 12.

[14] אלהי קדם Deut. xxxiii. 27. So אל עולם Gen. xxi. 33. Is. xl. 28.

[15] ישב קדם Ps. lv. 20.

[16] מעולם עד עולם Ps. xc. 2. ciii. 17.

[17] מעולם Ps. xciii. 2. and of Divine Wisdom, or God the Son, Prov. viii. 23.

everlasting; [1] *to everlasting;* [2] *from the day,* i. e. since the day was. For the word, *from*, to our minds implies time, and time is no measure of eternity. Only it expresses præexistence, an eternal Existence backward as well as forward, the incommunicable attribute of God. But words of Holy Scripture have their full meaning, unless it appear from the passage itself that they have not. In the passages where the words, *for ever, from afore*, do not mean eternity, the subject itself restrains them. Thus *for ever*, looking onward, is used of time, equal in duration with the being of whom it is written, as[3], *he shall be thy servant for ever*, i. e. so long as he lives in the body. So when it is said to the Son[4], *Thy throne, O God, is for ever and ever*, it speaks of a kingdom which shall have no end. In like way, looking backward, [5] *I will remember Thy wonders from old*, must needs relate to time, because they are marvelous dealings of God in time. So again[6], *the heavens of old*, stand simply contrasted with the changes of man. But [7] *God of old* is the Eternal God. [8] *He that abideth of old* is God enthroned from everlasting In like manner the *goings forth* here, opposed to a *going forth* in time, (emphatic words being moreover united together,) are a going forth in eternity.

The word, *from of old*, as used of being, is only used as to the Being of God. Here too then there is no ground to stop short of that meaning; and so it declares the eternal *going-forth*, or Generation of the Son. The plural, *goings forth*, may here be used, either as words of great majesty[9], "God," "Lord," "Wisdom," (i.e. Divine[9]) are plural; or because the Generation of the Son from the Father is an Eternal Generation, before all time, and now, though not in time, yet in eternity still. As then the prophet saith, "*from* the *days* of eternity," although eternity has no parts, nor beginning, nor "*from*," so he may say *goings forth*, to convey, as we can receive it, a continual going-forth. We think of Eternity as unending, continual, time; and so he may have set forth to us the Eternal Act of the *Going Forth* of the Son, as continual acts.

The Jews understood, as we do now, that Micah foretold that the Christ was to be born at Bethlehem, until they rejected Him, and were pressed by the argument. Not only did the chief priests formally give the answer, but, supposing our Lord to be of Nazareth, some who rejected Him, employed the argument against Him. [10] *Some said, Shall Christ come out of Galilee? Hath not the Scripture said, that Christ cometh of the seed of David, and out of the town of Bethlehem, where David was?* They knew of two distinct things: that Christ was 1) to be *of the seed of David;* and 2) *out of the town of Bethlehem.* Christians urged them with the fact, that the prophecy could be fulfilled in no other than in Christ. "[11] If He is not yet born, who is to go forth as a Ruler out of the tribe of Judah, from Bethlehem, (for He must needs come forth out of the tribe of Judah, and from Bethlehem, but we see that now no one of the race of Israel has remained in the city of Bethlehem, and thenceforth it has been interdicted [12] that any Jew should remain in the confines of that country)—how then shall a Ruler be born from Judæa, and how shall he *come forth out of Bethlehem*, as the Divine volumes of the Prophets announce, when to this day there is no one whatever left there of Israel, from whose race Christ could be born?" The Jews at first met the argument, by affirming that the Messiah *was* born at Bethlehem on the day of the destruction of the temple[13]; but was hidden for the sins of the people. This being a transparent fable, the Jews had either to receive Christ, or to give up the belief that He was to be born at Bethlehem. So they explained it, "The Messiah shall go forth thence, because he shall be of the seed of David who was out of Bethlehem." But this would have been misleading language. Never did man so speak, that one *should be* born in a place, when only a remote ancestor had been born there. Micah does not say merely, that His family came out of Bethlehem, but that He Himself should thereafter come forth thence. No one could have said of Solomon or of any of the subsequent kings of Judah, that they *should* thereafter come forth from Bethlehem, any more than they could now say, 'one shall come forth from Corsica,' of any future sovereign of the line of Napoleon III., because the first Napoleon was a Corsican; or to us, 'one *shall come* out of Hanover,' of a successor to the present dynasty, born in England, because George I. came from Hanover in 1714.

[1] לעולם ישב Ps. ix. 8. xxix. 10.
[2] מיום Is. xliii. 13.
[3] Ex. xxi. 6.
[4] Ps. xlv. 6.
[5] Ib. lxxvii. 12.
[6] Ib. lxviii. 34.
[7] Deut. xxxiii. 27.
[8] ישב קדם Ps. lv. 20.
[9] הכמות, קדשים, אדני, אלהים Prov. i. 20. ix. 1.
[10] S. John vii. 41, 2.
[11] Tert. c. Jud. c. 13. R. Isaac, Chizzuk Emunah, in Wagenseil tela ignea Sat. p. 278. tries to evade it.

[12] By Hadrian. See ab. on iii. 12. p. 76. Reland p. 647, understands this of a prohibition to approach Bethlehem itself.

[13] See at length Martini Pugio fidei ii. 6. f. 279, from the Jerusalem Talmud Berachoth [f. 5.] and the old mystical books, Bereshith Rabba on Gen. xxx. 41, and the Echa R. on Lam. i. 16. (These last passages have been mutilated.) See also Schoettg. T. ii. p. 196. on Is. lxvi. 7. The fable of His concealment occurs in Jonath. on Micah iv. 8, (see ab. p. 62,) and in Trypho in S. Just. Dial. § 8.

Before CHRIST cir. 710.

3 Therefore will he give them up, until the time that [g] she which travaileth hath brought forth: then

[g] ch. 4. 10.

3. *Therefore*, since God has so appointed both to punish and to redeem, *He*, God, or the Ruler "Whose goings forth have been from of old from everlasting," Who is God with God, *shall give them up*, i. e. withdraw His protection and the nearness of His Presence, *giving them up* 1) into the hands of their enemies. And indeed the far greater part never returned from the captivity, but remained, although willingly, in the enemy's land, outwardly shut out from the land of the promise and the hope of their fathers[1]. But also, 2) all were, more than before, [2] *given up*, to follow their own ways. God was less visibly present among them. Prophecy ceased soon after the return from the captivity, and many tokens of the nearness of God and means of His communications with them, the Ark and the Urim and Thummim were gone. It was a time of pause and waiting, wherein the fullness of God's gifts was withdrawn, that they might look on to Him Who was to come. *Until the time that she which travaileth hath brought forth, i. e.* until [3] *the Virgin* who should *conceive and bear a Son and call His Name Emmanuel, God with us,* shall give birth to *Him* Who shall save them. And then shall be Redemption and joy and assured peace. God provides against the fainting of hearts in the long time before our Lord should come.

Then [*And.*] There is no precise mark of time such as our word *then* expresses. He speaks generally of what should be after the Birth of the Redeemer. *The remnant of His brethren shall return unto the children of Israel. The children of Israel* are the true Israel, *Israelites indeed*[4]; they who are such, not in name[5] only, but indeed and in truth. *His brethren* are plainly the brethren of the Christ; either because Jesus vouchsafed to be born [6] *of the seed of David according to the flesh,* and of them [7] *as concerning the flesh Christ came, Who is over all, God blessed for ever*; or as such as He makes and accounts and [8] *is not ashamed to call, brethren,* being sons of God by grace, as He is the Son of God by nature. As He says, [9] *Whosoever shall do the will of My Father which is in Heaven, the same is My brother and sister and mother*; and, [10] *My brethren are these who hear the word of God and do it. The residue* of these, the Prophet says, shall *return to,* so as to be joined with [11], *the children of Israel;* as Malachi prophesies, [12] *He shall bring back the heart of the fathers to* [13] *the children, and the heart of the children to* [13] *the fathers.* In the first sense, Micah foretells the continual inflow of the Jews to that true Israel who should first be called. All in each generation, who are the true Israel, shall be converted, made one in Christ, saved. So, whereas, since Solomon, all had been discord, and, at last, the Jews were scattered abroad everywhere, all, in the true Prince of Peace, shall be one[14]. This has been fulfilled in each generation since our Lord came, and shall be yet further in the end, when they shall haste and pour into the Church, and so *all Israel shall be saved*[15].

But "[16] the promise of God was not only to Israel after the flesh, but *to all*" also *that were afar off, even as many as the Lord our God should call*[17]. All these may be called *the remnant of His brethren,* even those that were, before, *aliens from the commonwealth of Israel* and *afar off,* [18] *but now, in Christ Jesus, made one* with them; all, brethren among themselves and to Christ their ruler. "[16] Having taken on Him their nature in the flesh, He is not ashamed to call them so, as the Apostle speaketh, confirming it out of the Psalm, where in the Person of Christ he saith[19], *I will*

[1] As in 2 Chron. xxxvi. 17.
[2] Acts vii. 42. Rom. i. 24. 26. 28.
[3] Is. vii. 14. The context requires, that the Mother here spoken of should be the Mother of the Messias. For the Birth is spoken of before (v. 2.) and *his brethren*, אחיו, in this v. can be no other than the brethren of *Him* Who is so born. The evasion, that it is only a figure for the end of the travail, gives an unmeaning sense, for it would signify, "He shall give them up, until He cease to give them up." It is also contrary to the idiom; since in the O. T. travail pangs are an emblem of suffering, not of the subsequent joy, and Israel is spoken of, both before and after, unfiguratively; "He shall give *them* up" and as "the children of Israel," so that a figurative mention of them in between would be unsuited to the context.
[4] S. John i. 47. [5] Rom. ix. 6. &c. [6] Ib. i. 3.
[7] Ib. ix. 5. [8] Heb. ii. 11. [9] S. Matt. xii. 50.
[10] S. Luke viii. 21.
[11] "על stands in its first meaning of 'place,' where one thing moves to another, and so abides on it;" Ewald, in Hengst. who quotes 2 Chr. xxx. 9, "when you return to (על) the Lord," and Mal. iii. 24. Heb. as to the religious meaning. So contrariwise, "they returned to (על) the iniquities of their forefathers." (Jer. xi. 10.) In all the cases mentioned by Fürst, (Conc. p. 1109–11,) the original idea "over" remains in some force; "the waters returned upon the Eg.," Ex. xiv. 26; "and they returned *unto* Pihahiroth (encamping there), Num. xxxiii. 7; "man would return *to* the dust," (so as to dwell there,) Job xxxiv. 15; "the dog returned *to* his vomit, (taking it up again,) Prov. xxvi. 11, "the wind returneth to its circuits," (so as to rest where it began,) Eccl. i. 6; "My prayer shall return *into* my bosom," (so as to rest there, or, from God in blessing upon himself,) Ps. xxxv. 13. In Neh. iv. 6. תשובו עלינו, "return so as to be with us," the idiom is the same as in this place.
[12] Mal. iii. 24. Heb. [13] על.
[14] See Hosea i. 11. Is. xi. 10. &c. [15] Rom. xi. 26.
[16] Poc. [17] Acts ii. 39.
[18] Eph. ii. 12–14. [19] Ps. xxii. 22.

Before CHRIST cir. 710.

[h] the remnant of his brethren shall return unto the children of Israel.

4 ¶ And he shall stand and ‖ [i] feed in the strength of the LORD, in the majesty of the name of the LORD his God; and they

Before CHRIST cir. 710.

h ch. 4. 7.

‖ Or, *rule*.
i Is. 40. 11. & 49. 10. Ezek. 34. 23. ch. 7. 14.

declare Thy name unto My brethren. There is no reason to take the name, *brethren*, here in a narrower sense than so to comprehend all [1] *the remnant whom the Lord shall call*, whether Jews or Gentiles. The word "brethren" in its literal sense includes both, and, as to both, the words were fulfilled.

4. *And He shall stand.* The Prophet continues to speak of personal acts of this Ruler Who was to be born. He was not to pass away, not to rule only by others, but by Himself. To *stand* is the attitude of a servant, as Jesus, although God and Lord of all, said of Himself, [2] *He shall come forth and serve them;* [3] *The Son of Man came not to be ministered unto, but to minister. He shall stand* as a Shepherd [4], to watch, feed, guard them, day and night; *He shall stand*, as St. Stephen saw Christ [5] *standing on the Right Hand of God*, "[6] to succor all those who suffer for Him." "[7] For to sit belongs to one judging; to stand, to one fighting or helping." *He shall stand*, as abiding, not to pass from them, as Himself saith, [8] *Lo, I am with you alway, even unto the end of the world:* and He shall *feed* His flock by His Spirit, His Word, His Wisdom and doctrine, His example and life; yea, by His own Body and Blood [9]. They whom He feedeth [13] *lack nothing.*

In the strength of the Lord. He, Who feedeth them with Divine tenderness, shall also have Divine might, His Father's and His own, to protect them; as He saith, [11] *My sheep hear My Voice, and I know them and they follow Me, neither shall any man pluck them out of My Hand. My Father Which gave them Me is greater than all, and no man is able to pluck them out of My Father's Hand. I and My Father are One. With authority*, it is said [12], *He commandeth even the unclean spirits and they come out.* His feeding or teaching also was [13] *with authority, and not as the scribes.*

In the Majesty of the Name of the Lord His God, as St. John says [14], *We beheld His Glory, the Glory as of the Only-Begotten of His Father;* and He saith, [15] *All power is given unto Me in heaven and in earth;* so that the Divine Glory should shine through the Majesty of His teaching, the power of His Grace, upholding His own, and the splendor of the miracles wrought by Him and in His Name. *Of the Name of the Lord;* as He saith again, [16] *Holy Father, keep through Thine own Name those whom Thou hast given Me, that they may be one as We are. While I was with them in the world, I kept them in Thy Name.* "[17] Whoever then is sent to feed His flock must *stand*, i. e. be firm and unshaken; feed, not sell, nor slay; and feed in might, i. e. in Christ." *His God*, as our Lord Himself, as Man, saith, [18] *Unto My Father, and your Father, and to My God and your God.* But that Majesty He Himself wields, as no mere man can; He Himself is invested with it. "[19] To ordinary kings God is strength [20], or gives strength [21]; men have strength in God; this Ruler is clad in the strength of the Lord, that same strength, which the Lord hath, Whose is strength. Of Him, as Israel's King, the same is said as of the Lord, as King of the whole earth [22]; only that the strength of the Messiah is not His own, but the Lord's. He is invested with the strength of the Lord, because He is Man; as Man, He *can* be invested with the *whole* strength of the Lord, only because He is also God."

And they shall abide (lit. *sit, dwell*) in rest and security and unbroken peace under Christ their Shepherd and their King; they shall not wander to and fro as heretofore. "[23] *He*, their Shepherd, shall *stand; they* shall *sit.*" "The word [24] is the more emphatic, because it stands so absolutely. This will be a sitting or dwelling, which will indeed deserve the name. The original promise, so often forfeited by their disobedience should be perfectly fulfilled; [25] *and ye shall dwell in your land safely, and I will give peace in the land, and ye shall lie down, and none shall make you afraid.* So Amos and Micah had before promised [26]. And this is the result of the greatness of the promised Ruler, as the

1 Joel ii. 32. 2 S. Luke xii. 37.
3 S. Matt. xx. 28. 4 See Is. lxi. 5.
5 Acts vii. 55. 6 Collect for S. Stephen's Day.
7 S. Greg. Hom. 29. in Evang. n. 7.
8 S. Matt. xxviii. 20. 9 S. John vi.
10 Ps. xxiii. 1. 11 S. John x. 27–30.
12 S. Luke iv. 36. 13 S. Matt. vii. 29.
14 S. John i. 14. 15 S. Matt. xxviii. 18.
16 S. John xvii. 11, 12. 17 Theoph.
18 S. John xx. 17. Lipmann, in Nizzachon, objects, that, "as God, He has no God; as Man, He is not from everlasting to everlasting," not knowing, as a Jew, the Divine Personality of our Lord, whence, He being "not two but one Christ," (Ath. Creed), both the attributes of His Divine and Human Nature can be said of Him. (in Poc.) R. Tanchum owns, that the Ruler here spoken of can, for His greatness, be no other than the Messiah. (Ib.)
19 Casp. 20 Ps. xxviii. 7. cxl. 7. 21 1 Sam. ii. 10.
22 Ps. xciii. 1. 23 from Casp. 24 יָשַׁב.
25 Lev. xxvi. 5, 6. "comp. Hos. ii. 20. [18 Eng.] Is. xiv. 30. xxxii. 18 Jer. xxiii. 8. Ezek. xxviii. 25, 6. xxxiv. 25, 28. xxxvii. 25. xxxviii. 8. Zech. xiv. 10, 11." Casp.
26 Am. ix. 14. Mic. iv. 4. Both use the same word as here.

Before CHRIST cir. 710.

shall abide: for now [k]shall
he be great unto the ends
of the earth.
5 And this *man* [l]shall
be the peace, when the Assyrian shall come into our
land: and when he shall
tread in our palaces, then

[k] Ps. 72. 8. Is. 52. 13. Zech. 9. 10. Luke 1. 32.
[l] Ps. 72. 7. Is. 9. 6. Zech. 9. 10. Luke 2. 14. Eph. 2. 14.

Before CHRIST cir. 710.

like promise of the Psalm is rested on the immutability of God[1]; *Thou art the Same, and Thy years shall have no end. The children of Thy servants shall dwell*[2], *and their seed shall be established before Thee.* For it follows,"

For now, (in the time which Micah saw as did Abraham with the eye of faith,) *now*, in contrast to that former time of lowliness. His life shall be divided between a life of obscurity, and a life of never-ending greatness.

Shall He be great unto the [*very*[3]] *ends of the earth*, embracing them in His rule, (as David and Solomon had foretold[4],) and so none shall harm those whom He, the King of all the earth, shall protect. The universality of protection is derived from an universality of power. To David God says, [5]*I have made thee a great name, like the name of the great that are in the earth.* Of Uzziah it is said[6], *His name went forth far; for he was marvelously helped, until he was strong;* but of the Messiah alone it is said, that His power should reach to the ends of the earth; as God prophesies of Himself, that His [7]*Name should be great among the Heathen.* So Gabriel said to His Mother, [8]*This*, Whom she should bear, *shall be great.*

5. *And this Man shall be the Peace. This*, emphatically, i. e. "This Same," as is said of Noah, [9]*This same shall comfort us*, or, in the song of Moses, of the Lord, [10]*This Same is my God.* Of Him he saith, not only that He brings peace, but that He Himself[11] is that Peace; as St. Paul saith, [12]*He is our Peace*, and Isaiah calls Him [13]*the Prince of peace*, and at His Birth the heavenly host proclaimed [14]*peace on earth;* and He [15]*preached peace to you which were afar off, and to them that were nigh;* and on leaving the world He saith, [16]*Peace I leave with you, My Peace I give unto you. He shall be our Peace*, within by His Grace, without by His Protection. "[17]Wouldest thou have peace with God, thine own soul, thy neighbor? Go to Christ Who is our Peace," and follow the footsteps of Christ. "Ask peace of Him Who is Peace. Place Christ in thy heart and thou hast placed Peace there."

When the Assyrian shall come into our land, and when he shall tread in our palaces. Assur stands for the most powerful and deadliest foe, "ghostly and bodily," as the Assyrian then was of the people of God. For since this plainly relates to the time after Christ's coming, and, (to say the least,) after the captivity in Babylon and deliverance[18] from it, which itself followed the dissolution of the Assyrian Empire, the Assyrians cannot be the literal people, who had long since ceased to be[19]. In Isaiah too the Assyrian is the type of Anti-Christ and of Satan[20]. As Christ is our Peace, so one enemy is chosen to represent all enemies who [21]*vex the Church*, whether the human agents or Satan who stirs them up and uses them. "By the Assyrian," says St. Cyril, "he here means no longer a man out of Babylon, but rather marks out the inventor of sin, Satan. Or rather, to speak fully, the implacable multitude of devils, which

[1] Ps. cii. 27, 28. [2] ישׁכונו. [3] עד.

[4] Ps. ii. 8. "the ends of the earth for His possession;" Ps. lxxii. 8. "from the river *unto* (עד) the ends of the earth." In both cases the אפסי ארץ as here. See "Daniel the Proph." p. 480.

[5] 2 Sam. vii. 9. [6] 2 Chron. xxvi. 15. add Ib. 8.

[7] Mal. i. 11. 14.

[8] S. Luke i. 32. οὗτος ἔσται μέγας,

[9] Gen. v. 29. [10] Ex. xv. 2.

[11] The word "this" *might* grammatically be taken as agreeing with "peace." "This [viz. this thing] shall be our peace," as Eccl. vi. 9, גם זה הבל, "this too is vanity;" Ex. iii. 15, זה זכרי, "this is My memorial," i. e. זה is not necessarily personal. But this would not alter the sense. For, "this thing is our peace," must necessarily refer to what had been said, viz. the greatness, majesty, tender care of the Messiah. It is most natural to take זה=οὗτος, as a person, since a person was the subject of the verse before.

[12] Eph. ii. 14. [13] Is. ix. 6. [14] S. Luke ii. 14.

[15] Eph. ii. 17. [16] S. John xiv. 27. [17] Lap.

[18] iv. 10.

[19] A disbeliever in prophecy writes, "If he would quote Micah as designating Bethlehem for the birthplace of the Messiah, he cannot shut his eyes to the fact that the Deliverer to come from thence was to be a *contemporary* shield against the Assyrian." Dr. Williams in Ess. and Rev. p. 68. Not "contemporary," unless it be certain that Psalmists and Prophets cannot identify themselves with the past and future of their people. The course of events interposed shews, that the deliverance was *not* to be contemporary. As the Psalmist speaking of the passage of the Red Sea, says, *there did we rejoice in Him*, (Ps. lxvi. 6.) making himself one with them; as Micah himself, speaking of times after the desolation of the land, (vii. 13.) says, "He will turn again, He will have compassion upon *us*;" (Ib. vii. 19.) nay, as our Lord Himself says to the Apostles, "I am with *you* alway, even to the end of the world," (S. Matt. xxviii. 20.) i. e. with them and their successors to the end of time; so Micah, who had sorrowed with his people in their sorrows, (i. 8. 10.) here rejoices with them in a deliverance far away, after God should for a long time have given them up, v. 3. and which he should not see. "Even L. Bauer translated, 'And if another Assur,' comparing the passage of Virgil which Castalio had already quoted, 'Alter erit tum Tiphys, et altera quæ vehat Argo Delectos heroas.'" Hengst.

[20] Is. x. and including Babylon Ch. xiv.

[21] Acts. xii. 1.

Before CHRIST cir. 710.

shall we raise against him seven shepherds, and eight † principal men.

6 And they shall † waste the land of Assyria with the sword and the land of [m]Nimrod ‖ in the entrances thereof: thus shall he [n]deliver *us* from the Assyrian, when he cometh into our land, and when he treadeth within our borders.

† Heb. *princes of men.*
† Heb. *eat up.*
[m] Gen. 10. 8, 10, 11.
‖ Or, *with her own naked swords.*
[n] Luke 1. 71.

spiritually ariseth against all which is holy, and fights against the holy city, the spiritual Zion, whereof the Divine Psalmist saith, *Glorious things are spoken of thee, thou city of God.* For Christ dwelleth in the Church, and maketh it, as it were, His own city, although by His Godhead filling all things. This city of God then is a sort of land and country of the sanctified and of those enriched in spirit, in unity with God. When then the Assyrian shall come against our city, i. e. when barbarous and hostile powers fight against the saints, they shall not find it unguarded." The enemy may tread on the land and on its palaces, i. e. lay low outward glory, vex the body which is of earth and the visible temple of the Holy Ghost, as he did St. Paul by *the thorn in the flesh, the minister of Satan to buffet him,* or Job in mind body or estate, but [1]*after that he has no more than he can do;* he cannot hurt the soul, because nothing can *separate us from the love of Christ,* and [2]Christ Who is our Peace is in us; and of the saint too it may be said, [3]*The enemy cannot hurt him.* [4]Much as the Church has been vexed at all times by persecutions of devils and of tyrants, Christ has ever consoled her and given her peace in the persecutions themselves: [5]*Who comforteth us in all our tribulation, that we may be able to comfort them which are in any trouble, by the comfort wherewith we are comforted of God. For as the sufferings of Christ abound in us,* so our *consolation also aboundeth by Christ.* The Apostles [6]*departed from the presence of the council, rejoicing that they were counted worthy to suffer shame for His Name.* And St. Paul writeth to the Hebrews, [7]*ye had compassion of me in my bonds, and took joyfully the spoiling of your goods, knowing that ye have in heaven a better and more enduring substance.*

Then shall we raise against him seven shepherds and eight principal men (lit. *anointed,* although elsewhere used of heathen princes.)

The *shepherds* are manifestly inferior, spiritual, shepherds, acting under the One Shepherd, by His authority, and He in them. The *princes of men* are most naturally a civil power, according to its usage elsewhere[8]. The *seven* is throughout the Old Testament a symbol of a sacred whole, probably of the union of God with the world[9], reconciled with it; *eight,* when united with it, is something beyond it[10]. Since then *seven* denotes a great, complete, and sacred multitude, by the *eight* he would designate "an incredible and almost countless multitude." "[4]So in defence of the Church, there shall be raised up very many shepherds and teachers (for at no time will it be forsaken by Christ;) yea by more and more, countlessly, so that, however persecutions may increase, there shall never be wanting more to teach, and exhort to, the faith."

6. *And they shall waste,* lit. *feed on,* and so *eat up.* They who were shepherds of their own people, should consume their enemies. Jeremiah uses the same image. [11]*The shepherds with their flocks shall come unto her; they shall pitch tents against her round about; they shall feed, each his space.* So Joshua and Caleb say, [12]*They,* (the inhabitants of Canaan,) are *bread for us.* So it was said to St. Peter, [13]*Arise, Peter, kill and eat;* and what once *was common,* defiled *and unclean,* shall turn to the nourishment and growth of the Church, and be incorporated into Christ, being made part of His Body.

And the land of Nimrod. Babylon, which should displace Assyria, but should carry on its work of chastising God's people, is joined by Micah, as by Isaiah[14], as an object of His judgment. In Isaiah, they are the actual Assyria[15] and Babylon[16] whose destruction is foretold, yet so as to shadow out rebellion against God in its intensest form, making itself independent of, or measuring itself against, God. Hence, probably, here alone in holy Scripture, Babylon is called *the land of Nimrod,* as indeed he founded it[17], but therewith was the author of the tower of Babel also, which was built in *rebellion* against God,

[1] S. Luke xii. 4. [2] Rup. [3] Ps. lxxxix. 22. [4] Rib. [5] 2 Cor. i. 4, 5. [6] Acts. v. 41. [7] x. 34.

[8] Jos. xiii. 21, Ps. lxxxiii. 12, Ezek. xxxii. 30. The word stands rather in contrast with משיח than as equivalent to it, since משיח is always used of one, anointed by God, נסיך, unless it be in this place, never.

[9] See Bähr Symbolik, ii. 107. sqq.

[10] See on Amos i. 3. vol. i. p. 234. This instance in Micah so far differs from the others, that the two numbers are not united with one substantive; and, unless *the shepherds* and *the princes of men* be the same class of persons, (which scarcely seems probable,) they have kindred, yet different, subjects.

[11] vi. 3. [12] Num. xiv. 9. [13] Acts x. 13. [14] Is. x. 5–34, xiii–xiv. 27. [15] Is. x. 12–15. [16] xiv. 13–15. [17] Gen. x. 10.

Before CHRIST cir. 710.

o ver. 3. Deut. 32. 2.
p Ps. 72. 6. & 110. 3.

7 And [o] the remnant of
Jacob shall be in the midst
of many people [p] as a dew
from the LORD, as the
showers upon the grass,
that tarrieth not for man,
nor waiteth for the sons of
men.

Before CHRIST cir. 710.

whence his own name was derived[1]. Assyria then, and the world-empire which should succeed it, stand as representing the God-opposed world.

In the entrances thereof, [lit. *in the gates thereof*[2].] The shepherds of Israel shall not act on the defensive only, but shall have victory over the world and Satan, carrying back the battle into his own dominions, and overthrowing him there. Satan's malice, so far from hurting the Church, shall turn to its good. Wherein he hoped to waste it, he shall be wasted; wherein he seemed to triumph, he shall be foiled. So it has been ever seen, how, under every persecution, the Church grew. "[3] The more it was pressed down, the more it rose up and flourished;" "[4] Shivering the assault of the Pagans, and strengthened more and more, not by resisting, but by enduring." Yet all, by whomsoever done, shall be the work of Christ Alone, enduring in martyrs, teaching in pastors, converting through the Apostles of Heathen nations. Wherefore he adds:

Thus, [*And*] *He shall deliver* us *from the Assyrian*. Not *they*, the subordinate shepherds, but He, the Chief Shepherd until *the last enemy shall be destroyed* and *death shall be swallowed up in victory, shall deliver*, whether by *them* or by Himself as He often so doth,—not *us* only (the saying is the larger because unlimited) but—*He shall deliver*, absolutely. Whosoever shall be delivered, He shall be their deliverer; all, whom He Alone knoweth, Who Alone [5] *knoweth them that are His*. [6] *Neither is there salvation in any other*. [7] *Whoso glorieth, let him glory in the Lord*. Every member of Christ has part in this, who, through the grace of God, "has power and strength to have victory and to triumph against the devil, the world, and the flesh"—not he, but the grace of God which is with him; and much more, all, whether Apostles or Apostolic men, or Pastors, or Bishops and Overseers, who, by preaching or teaching or prayer, bring those to the knowledge of the truth, who [8] *sat in darkness and the shadow of death*, and by whom [9] *God translates us into the kingdom of His dear Son*.

7. *And the remnant of Jacob*. Micah [10], as well as Isaiah [11], had prophesied, that *a remnant* only should *return unto the Mighty God*. These, though very many in themselves, are yet but a *remnant* only of the unconverted mass; yet this, [12] *the remnant, who shall be saved*, who believe in Christ, [13] *the little flock*, of whom were the Apostles and their disciples, *shall be, in the midst of many people*, whom they won to the faith, as John in Asia, Thomas in India, Peter in Babylon and Rome, Paul well-nigh in the whole world, what? something to be readily swallowed up by their multitude? No, but *as a dew from the Lord, as the showers from the grass, which tarrieth not for man, nor waiteth for the sons of men*, quickening to life that, which, like soon-withered [14] grass, no human cultivation, no human help, could reach.

In the Gospel and the grace of Christ there are both, gentleness and might; softness, as *the dew*, might as of *a lion*. For "[15] Wisdom reacheth from one end to another *mightily*; and *sweetly* doth she order all things." *The dew* is, in Holy Scripture, a symbol of Divine doctrine. [16] *My doctrine shall drop as the rain, my speech shall distill as the dew, as the small rain upon the tender herb, and as the showers upon the grass*. The dew comes down from heaven, is of heavenly not of earthly birth, transparent, glistening with light, reflecting the hues of heaven, gentle, slight, weak in itself, refreshing, cooling the strong heats of the day [17], consumed itself, yet thereby preserving life, falling on the dry and withered grass wherein all nature droops, and recalling it to freshness of life. And still more in those lands, where from the beginning of April to the end of October [18], the close of the latter and the beginning of the early rain, during all the hot months of summer, the life of all herb-

[1] Lit. "We will rebel." There is no other even plausible etymology.

[2] The E. V. has followed the analogy of the "Caspiæ pylæ," &c. and has paraphrased, "openings" or "gates" by "entrances," as if they were "the gates of the country;" which, however, belongs only to narrow entrances, such as Thermopylæ. The rendering in the E. M. "with their own drawn swords," (from Aq. and Ed. v. A. E. and Kim.) is owing to a slavish adherence to parallelism, פתיחות, &c. "drawn swords," (Ps. lv. 22.) is fem. after the analogy of חרב itself. The uniform meaning of פתח "opening," "door," "port," "gate," is plainly not to be deserted in a single case, on the ground of parallelism only. The fem. aff. also belongs naturally to the land, *her's*, not *their's*, i. e. the people's.

[3] S. Anton. in S. Athan. vit. ej. c. 79.

[4] S. Aug. de Ag. Christ. c. 12. and other fathers quoted Tertull. Apol. c. ult. n. a. Oxf. Tr.

[5] 2 Tim. ii. 19. [6] Acts iv. 12.

[7] 2 Cor. x. 17. [8] Ps. cvii. 10. [9] Col. i. 13.

[10] iv. 7. [11] x. 21. [12] Rom. ix. 27.

[13] S. Luke xii. 32.

[14] עשב. See Ps. cii. 5, 12, 2 Kings xix. 26, Is. xxxvii. 27. [15] Wisd. viii. 1. [16] Deut. xxxii. 2.

[17] Ecclus. xviii. 16, xliii. 22.

[18] Called איתן, because only "perennial" streams still flowed.

Before CHRIST cir. 710.

8 ¶ And the remnant
of Jacob shall be among
the Gentiles in the midst
of many people as a lion
among the beasts of the
forest, as a young lion
‖ Or, *goats*. among the flocks of ‖sheep:
who, if he go through,
both treadeth down, and
teareth in pieces, and none
can deliver.
9 Thine hand shall be
lifted up upon thine
adversaries, and all
thine enemies shall be
cut off.

Before CHRIST cir. 710.

---

age depends upon the dew alone[1]. *Showers*[2] are so called from the "multitude" of drops, slight and of no account in themselves, descending noiselessly yet penetrating the more deeply. So did the Apostles "[3] bedew the souls of believers with the word of godliness and enrich them abundantly with the words of the Gospel," themselves dying, and the Church living the more through their death[4], quenching the fiery heat of passions, and watering the dry and barren soil, that it might bring forth fruits unto Christ. Yet, they say[5], *the excellency of the power was of God and not of us*, and [6] *God gave the increase*. For neither was their doctrine [7] *of man nor by man;* but it came from heaven, the Holy Spirit teaching them invisibly and making *unlearned and ignorant* men *mighty in word and deed.* "[8] Whence these and these alone the Church of Christ looks up to, as furnishing the rule of truth." "[9] The herb, upon which this dew falleth, groweth to God without any aid of man, and flourisheth, and needeth neither doctrines of philosophers, nor the rewards or praises of men."

8. *And the remnant of Jacob shall be as a young lion.* "[10] What more unlike than the sweetness of the dew and the fierceness of the lion? What so different as the gentle shower distilling on the herb, and the savageness or vehemence of a *lion roaring among the flocks of sheeps?* Yet both are ascribed to *the remnant of Jacob.* Why? Because the Apostles of Christ are both tender and severe, tender in teaching and exhorting, severe in rebuking and avenging. How does Paul teach, [11] *God was in Christ reconciling the world unto Himself, and hath committed unto us the word of reconciliation; now then we are ambassadors for Christ, as though God did beseech you by us: we pray you in Christ's stead, be ye reconciled to God!* What sweeter than the dew of love, the shower of true affection? And so, on to that, "our heart is enlarged." They are such drops of dew as no one could doubt came from [12] *the Lord, the Father of our Lord Jesus Christ, the Father of mercies and the God of all comfort.* Yet the same Apostle after a little writes, [13] *This is the third time I am coming to you. I told you before and foretell you, and being absent now I write to them which heretofore have sinned and to all others, that if I come again, I will not spare, since ye seek a proof of Christ speaking in me.* See the severity of a master, like the roaring of *a lion among the beasts of the forest.* For such surely are they whom he rebukes for *the* [14] *uncleanness and fornication and lasciviousness which they had committed.* Was he not to such as a lion [15]? Was not Peter such, when he rebuked Ananias first and then Sapphira his wife, and they fell down and gave up the ghost? They *tread down* or [16] *cast down imaginations and every high thing that exalteth itself against the knowledge of God;* as Christ Himself, Who spake in them, is both a lamb and the [17] *Lion of the tribe of Judah*, and nothing is so terrible as [18] *the wrath of the Lamb.*

And none can deliver. "[19] For as the Apostles past from nation to nation, and trod down Heathenism, subduing it to Christ, and taking within their net the many converted nations, none could withdraw from the Apostles' doctrine those whom they had converted." The Heathen world "[20] cried out that the state is beset, that the Christians are in their fields, their forts, their islands." "[21] We are a people of yesterday, and yet we have filled every place belonging to you, cities, islands, castles, towns, assemblies, your very camp, your tribes, companies, palace, senate, forum! We leave you your temples only. We can count your armies, our numbers in a single province will be greater."

9. *Their hand shall be lifted up upon their adversaries.* The might of the Church is the Might of Christ in her, and the glory of the Church is His from Whom it comes and to Whom it returns. It is all one, whether this be said to Christ or to the *remnant of Jacob*, i. e. His Church. Her *enemies* are His, and her's only because they are His,

[1] On its importance to vegetable life, see Gen. xxvii. 28, Deut. xxxiii. 13, 28, Hag. i. 10, Zech. viii. 12.
[2] רְבִיבִים. It occurs Deut. xxxii. 2. Ps. lxv. 11. (Heb.) lxxii. 6, as especially refreshing.
[3] S. Cyr. [4] 2 Cor. iv. 12. [5] Ib. 7.
[6] 1 Cor. iii. 6, 7. [7] Gal. i. 12. [8] Rup. [9] Rib.
[10] Rup. [11] 2 Cor. v. 19—vi. 11. [12] Ib. i. 3.
[13] Ib. xiii. 1–3. [14] Ib. xii. 21.
[15] See again 1 Cor. v. 2–5. [16] 2 Cor. x. 5.
[17] Rev. v. 5. [18] Ib. vi. 16. [19] Dion.
[20] Apol. c. 1. p. 2. Oxf. Tr. [21] Ib. c. 37. p. 78.

Before CHRIST cir. 710.

q Zech. 9. 10.

r Is. 2. 6.

s Zech. 13. 2.

10 [q] And it shall come
to pass in that day, saith
the LORD, that I will cut
off thy horses out of the
midst of thee, and I will
destroy thy chariots:
11 And I will cut off
the cities of thy land, and
throw down all thy strong
holds:
12 And I will cut off
witchcrafts out of thine
hand and thou shalt have
no *more* [r] soothsayers:
13 [s] Thy graven images
also will I cut off, and thy
‖ standing images out of
the midst of thee; and
thou shalt [t] no more worship
the work of thine
hands.
14 And I will pluck up
thy groves out of the midst
of thee: so will I destroy
thy ‖ cities.
15 And I will [u] execute
vengeance in anger and
fury upon the heathen,
such as they have not
heard.

Before CHRIST cir. 710.

‖ Or, *statues.*

t Is. 2. 8.

‖ Or, *enemies.*

u Ps. 149. 7. ver. 8. 2 Thess. 1. 8.

and hate her as belonging to Him. They *shall be cut off*, either ceasing to be His enemies, or ceasing to be, as Julian or Arius or Anti-Christ, [1] *whom the Lord shall consume with the spirit of His Mouth and shall destroy with the brightness of His Coming.* And in the end, Satan also, over whom Christ gave the Apostles [2] *power to tread on all the power of the Enemy*, shall be *bruised under our feet* [3].

10. *And it shall come to pass in that day*, of grace in the kingdom of Christ and of His Presence in the Apostles and with the Church, *I will cut off thy horses out of the midst of thee.* The greater the glory and purity of the Church, the less it needs or hangs upon human aid. The more it is reft of human aid, the more it hangs upon God. So God promises, as a blessing, that He will remove from her all mere human resources, both what was in itself evil, and what, although good, had been abused. Most of these things, whose removal is here promised, are spoken of at the same time by Isaiah, as sin, or the occasion of sin, and of God's judgments to Judah. [4] *Soothsayers*, (the same word) *horses, chariots, idols the work of their hands; high towers, fenced walls.* "[5] I will take, from thee all arms wherewith, while unconverted, thou opposedst the faith," all which thou settest up as idols in place of God. (Such are witchcrafts, soothsayers, graven images, images of Ashtaroth.) "I will take from thee all outward means and instruments of defence which aforetime were turned into pride and sin;" as horses and chariots. Not such shall be the arms of the Church, not such her strongholds. *A horse is a vain thing to save a man.* Her arms shall be the despised Cross of shame; her warriors, they who bear it; their courage, to endure in holy patience and meekness; their might, the Holy Spirit within them; their victories, through death, not of others, but their Master's and, in His, their own. They shall overcome the world, as He overcame it, and through Him Alone and His Merits Who overcame it by suffering.

11–15. *I will cut off the cities of thy land.* So God promised by Zechariah [6], *Jerusalem shall be inhabited as towns without walls; for I will be unto her a wall of fire round about.* The Church shall not need the temptation of human defence; for God shall fence her in on every side. Great cities too, as the abode of luxury and sin, of power and pride, and, mostly, of cruelty, are chiefly denounced as the objects of God's anger. Babylon stands as the emblem of the whole city of the world or of the devil, as opposed to God. "[7] The first city was built by Cain; Abel and the other saints *had no continuing city* [8]" here. *Cities* then will include "[7] all the tumults and evil passions and ambition and strife and bloodshed, which Cain brought in among men. Cities are collectively called and are Babylon, *with whom*, (as in the Revelations we hear a voice from heaven saying),[9] *the kings of the earth committed fornication and the merchants of the earth are waxed rich through the abundance of her delicacies;* and of which it is written, [10] *And a mighty Angel took up a stone like a great millstone, and cast it into the sea, saying, Thus with violence shall that great city, Babylon, be thrown down, and shall be found no more at all.* "Great rest then is promised to holy Zion i. e. the Church, when the cities or strongholds of the land [strongholds, as they are, of earthliness] shall be destroyed.

[1] 2 Thess. ii. 8. [2] S. Luke x. 19. [3] Rom. xvi. 20. [4] Is. ii. 6–8. 15. [5] Rib. Lap.

[6] ii. 4, 5. [7] Rup. [8] Heb. xiii. 14. [9] Rev. xviii. 3. [10] Ib. 21.

Before CHRIST cir. 710.

CHAPTER VI.

1 *God's controversy for unkindness,* 6 *for ignorance,* 10 *for injustice,* 16 *and for idolatry.*

HEAR ye now what the
LORD saith; Arise;
contend thou ‖ before the
mountains, and let the hills
hear thy voice.
2 [a] Hear ye, O moun-
tains, [b] the LORD's controversy, and ye strong foun-

Before CHRIST cir. 710.

‖ Or, *with.*
[a] Deut. 32. 1. Ps. 50. 1, 4. Is. 1. 2.
[b] Hos. 12. 2.

For together with them are included all objects of desire in them, with the sight whereof the citizens of the kingdom of God, while pilgrims here, are tempted; whereof the wise man saith, *Vanity of vanities, all is vanity.*" The fulfillment reaches on to the Day of Judgment, when the Church shall finally receive glory from the Lord, and be [1] *without spot and wrinkle.* All looks on to that Day. The very largeness of the promise, which speaks, in its fullest sense, of the destruction of things, without which we can hardly do in this life, (as cities [2],) or things very useful to the needs of man, (as horses,) carries us on yet more to that Day when there will be no more need of any outward things; "[3] when the heavy body shall be changed, and shall have the swiftness of angels, and shall be transported whither it willeth, without *chariots* and *horses*; and all things which tempt the eye shall cease; and no evil shall enter; and there shall be no need of *divining,* amid the presence and full knowledge of God, and where the ever-present Face of God, Who is Truth, shall shine on all, and nothing be uncertain or unknown; nor shall they need to form in their souls images of Him Whom His own *shall see as He Is;* nor shall they esteem anything of self, or the work of their own hands; but God shall be All in all." In like way, the woe on those who obey not the truth, also looks on to the end. It too is final. There is nothing to soften it. Punishments in the course of life are medicinal. Here no mention is made of Mercy, but only of *executing vengeance;* and that, *with wrath and fury;* and that, *such as they have not heard.* For as *eye hath not seen, nor heart conceived the good things laid up in store for those who love* God, so neither the evil things prepared for those who, in act, shew that they hate Him.

Ch. VI. The foregoing prophecy closed with the final cleansing of the Church and the wrath of God resting on the wicked, when, as St. Paul saith, [4] *The Lord Jesus shall be revealed from heaven with His mighty angels, in flaming fire, taking vengeance on them that know not God, and that obey not the Gospel of our Lord Jesus Christ: who shall be punished with everlasting destruction from the presence of the Lord, and from the glory of His power; when He shall come to be glorified in His Saints, and to be admired in all them that believe.* The Prophet here begins his third and last summons to judgment, in the Name, as it were, of the All-Holy Trinity, against Whom they had sinned.

1. *Hear ye now what the Lord saith:* If ye will not hear the rebuke of man, hear now at last the word of God. "*Arise* thou, Micah." The prophet was not willing to be the herald of woe to his people; but had to *arise* at the bidding of God, that he might not [5] *be rebellious like that rebellious house. Stand up;* as one having all authority to rebuke, and daunted by none. He rouses the hearer, as shewing it to be a very grave urgent matter, to be done promptly, urgently, without delay. *Contend thou before* [better, as in E. M. *with* [6]] *the mountains.* Since man, who had reason, would not use his reason, God calls the mountains and hills, who [7] *unwillingly,* as it were, had been the scenes of their idolatry, as if He would say, "[8] Insensate though ye be, ye are more sensible than Israel, whom I endowed with sense; for ye feel the voice and command of God your Creator and obey Him; they do not. I cite you, to represent your guilty inhabitants, that, through you, they may hear My complaint to be just, and own themselves guilty, repent, and ask forgiveness." "The altars and idols, the blood of the sacrifices, the bones and ashes upon them, with unuttered yet clear voice, spoke of the idolatry and guilt of the Jews, and so pronounced God's charge and expostulation to be just. Ezekiel is bidden, in like way, to prophesy against *the mountains of Israel* [9], *I will bring a sword upon you, and I will destroy your high places, and your altars shall be desolate.* "[10] Lifeless nature without voice tells the glory of God; without ears it hears what the Lord speaks [11]."

2. *Hear, ye strong* [or, it may be, *ye enduring* [12],] *foundations of the earth.* Mountains

[1] Eph. v. 27.
[2] In ver. 14. Jon. has "I will cut off thy *enemies,*" whence E. M. But although עָר stands for צָר "enemy" 1 Sam. xxviii. 16, and plur. Ps. cxxxix. 20, (in both places with affix,) here every object mentioned is of things, *belonging* to Judah, its own.
[3] Rup.
[4] 2 Thess. i. 7–10.
[5] Ezek. ii. 8.
[6] This is the uniform sense of ריב with את as well as with עם. See Num. xx. 13, Jud. viii. 1, Prov. xxv. 9, Is. xlv. 9, l. 8, Jer. ii. 9, Neh. v. 7, xiii. 11, 17. (all, in Fürst Conc.)
[7] Rom. viii. 20.
[8] Lap.
[9] Ezek. vi. 2–5.
[10] Poc.
[11] Ps. xix. 3, S. Luke xix. 40.
[12] איתנים. See Ges. Lex. p. 644.

Before CHRIST cir. 710.

c Is. 1. 18. & 5. 3, 4. & 43. 26. Hos. 4. 1.

d Jer. 2. 5, 31.

dations of the earth: for
c the LORD hath a contro-
versy with his people,
and he will plead with
Israel.
3 O my people, d what
have I done unto thee?
and wherein have I wearied
thee? testify against me.
4 e For I brought thee
up out of the land of
Egypt, and redeemed thee
out of the house of ser-
vants; and I sent before

Before CHRIST cir. 710.

e Ex. 12. 51. & 14. 30. & 20. 2. Deut. 4. 20. Amos 2. 10.

and rocks carry the soul to times far away, before and after. They change not, like the habitable, cultivated, surface of the earth. There they were, before the existence of our short-lived generations; there they will be, until time shall cease to be. They have witnessed so many vicissitudes of human things, themselves unchanging. The prophet is directed to seize this feeling of simple nature. "They have seen so much before me," Yes! "then they have seen all which befell my forefathers; all God's benefits, all along, to them and to us, all their and our unthankfulness."

He will plead with Israel. God hath a strict severe judgment[1] with His people, and yet vouchsafes to clear Himself before His creatures, to come down from His throne of glory and place Himself on equal terms with them. He does not *plead* only, but mutually (such is the force of the word) *impleads with*[2] His people, hears if they would say aught against Himself, and then gives His own judgment[3]. But this willingness to hear, only makes us condemn ourselves, so that we should be without excuse before Him. We do owe ourselves wholly to Him Who made us and hath given us all things richly to enjoy. If we have withdrawn ourselves from His Service, unless He dealt hardly with us, we dealt rebelliously and ungratefully with Him. God brings all pleas into a narrow space. The fault is with Him or with us. He offers to clear Himself. He sets before us His good deeds, His Loving kindness, Providence, Grace, Long-suffering, Bounty, Truth, and contrasts with them our evil deeds, our unthankfulness, despitefulness, our breach of His laws, and disorderings of His creation. And then, in the face of His Goodness, He asks, "What evil have I done, what good have I left undone?" so that our evil and negligences should be but a requital of His. For if it is evil to return evil for evil, or not to return good for good, what evil is it to return evil for His exceeding good! As He says by Isaiah, [4] *What could have been done more to My vineyard and I have not done in it. Wherefore, when I looked that it should bring forth grapes, brought it forth wild grapes?* And our Blessed Lord asks; [5] *Many good works have I shewed you from My Father. For which of those works do ye stone Me?* [6] *Which of you convinceth Me of sin? And if I say the truth, why do ye not believe Me?* Away from the light of God, we may plead excuses, and cast the blame of our sins upon our temptations, or passions, or nature, i. e. on Almighty God Himself, Who made us. When His light streams in upon our conscience, we are silent. Blessed if we be silenced and confess to Him then, that we be not first silenced in the Day of Judgment. [7] *Righteous Job* said, [8] *I desire to reason with God;* but when his *eye saw Him,* he said, [9] *wherefore I abhor myself, and repent in dust and ashes.*

3. *O My people.* This one tender word[10], twice repeated[11], contains in one a whole volume of reproof. It sets before the eyes God's choice of them of His free grace, and the whole history of His loving-kindness, if so they could be ashamed of their thanklessness and turn to Him. "Mine," He says, "ye are by creation, by Providence, by great deliverances and by hourly love and guardianship, by gifts of nature, the world, and grace; such things have I done for thee; what against thee? *what* evil *have I done unto thee?*" [12] *Thy foot did not swell these forty years,* for He upbears in all ways where He leads. *Wherein have I wearied thee?* for [13] *His commandments are not grievous. Thou hast been weary of Me, O Israel,* God says by Isaiah[14], *I have not wearied thee with incense; thou hast wearied Me with thine iniquities.*

4. *For I brought thee up out of the land of Egypt, and redeemed thee out of the house of servants.* What wert thou? What art thou? Who made thee what thou art? God reminds them. They *were* slaves; they *are* His people in the heritage of the heathen, and that by

[1] רִיב.
[2] יִתְוַכָּח.
[3] Comp. Is. xliii. 26, Jer. ii. 5, 6, 9. So עֲנֵה בִי, "testify against Me," (ver. 3.) is a judicial term, lit. "answer against Me," i. e. "answer judicial interrogatories," then generally "depose," "testify," Num. xxxv. 30, Deut. xix. 18, Job xv. 6, Ruth i. 21, Is. iii. 9, lix. 12, Jer. xiv. 7.

[4] Is. v. 4.
[5] S. John x. 32.
[6] Ib. viii. 46.
[7] Job i. 8. ii. 3, Ezek. xiv. 20.
[8] Job xiii. 3.
[9] xlii. 5, 6.
[10] עַמִּי.
[11] Here and v. 5.
[12] Deut. viii. 4.
[13] 1 S. John v. 3.
[14] Is. xliii. 22–24.

Before CHRIST cir. 710.

thee Moses, Aaron, and
Miriam.
5 O my people, remem-
ber now what [f] Balak king
of Moab consulted, and
what Balaam the son of
Beor answered him from
[g] Shittim unto Gilgal; that
ye may know [h] the righteousness of the LORD.

f Num. 22. 5. & 23. 7. & 24. 10, 11. Deut. 23. 4, 5. Josh. 24. 9, 10. Rev. 2. 14.

Before CHRIST cir. 710.

g Num. 25. 1. & 33. 49. Josh. 4. 19. & 5. 10.
h Judg. 5. 11.

His *outstretched arm.* God mentions some heads of the mercies which He had shewn them, when He had made them His people, His redemption of them from Egypt, His guidance through the wilderness, His leading them over the last difficulty to the promised land. The use of the familiar language of the Pentateuch[1] is like the touching of so many key-notes, recalling the whole harmony of His love. *Moses, Aaron, and Miriam* together, are Lawgiver, to deliver and instruct; Priest, to atone; and Prophetess[2] to praise God; and the name of Miriam at once recalled the mighty works at the Red Sea and how they *then* thanked God.

5. *Remember now.* The word translated *now* is a very tender one, like our "*do* now remember" or "*do* remember," beseeching instead of commanding. "[3] I might command, but I speak tenderly, that I may lead thee to own the truth." *What Balak king of Moab consulted, and what Balaam the son of Beor answered him.* God did not only raise up Moses, Aaron, Miriam, out of their brethren, but He turned the curse of the alien Balaam into a blessing; and that, not for their righteousness, (for even then they were rebellious,) but against their deserts, out of His own truth and righteousness. Not that the curse of Balaam could in itself have hurt them; but, in proportion to his reputation, it would have infused great energy into their enemies, and its reversal must have struck a great panic into them and into others. Human might having failed in Sihon and Og, Balak sought superhuman. God shewed them by their own diviner, that it was against them. Even after they had seduced Israel, through Balaam's devilish counsel, Midian seems to have been stricken by God with panic, and not to have struck a blow[4].

From Shittim unto Gilgal. The words are separated by the Hebrew accent from what went before. It is then probably said in concise energy for, "Remember too from Shittim to Gilgal," i. e. all the great works of God *from Shittim*[5], the last encampment of Israel out of the promised land, where they so sinned in Baal-peor, *unto Gilgal*, the first in the promised land, which they entered by miracle, where the Ark rested amid the victories given them, where the Covenant was renewed, and [6] *the reproach of Egypt* was *rolled away.* Remember all, from your own deep sin and rebellion to the deep mercy of God.

That ye may know the righteousness [*righteousnesses*] *of the Lord;* His Faithfulness in performing His promises to Abraham, Isaac, and Jacob. God speaketh of His promises, not as what they were in themselves, mere mercy, but as what they became, through that gracious and free promise, *righteousness*, in that He had bound Himself to fulfill what He had, out of mere grace, promised. So in the New Testament He saith, [7] *God is not unrighteous that He should forget your works and labor which proceedeth of love;* and, [8] *He is faithful and just to forgive us our sins.* Micah speaks, by a rare idiom, of the *righteousnesses*[9] *of the Lord*, each act of mercy being a separate effluence of His Righteousness. The very names of the places suggest the righteous acts of God, the unrighteous of Israel. "[10] But we too, who desire with unveiled face to behold the glory of the Lord, and have Abraham really for our father, let us, when we have sinned, hear God pleading against us, and reproving us for the multitude of His benefits. For we too once served Pharaoh and the people of Egypt, laboring in works of mire and clay; and He redeemed us Who gave Himself a Redemption for all; that we, the redeemed of the Lord[11], *whom He redeemed out of the hand of the enemy and gathered from the lands*, might *say, His mercy endureth for ever.* He sent also before our face Moses, the spiritual Law, and Aaron the High Priest, not bearing the typical Ephod and Urim, but having in His Forehead the seal of holiness which God the Father sealed; and Miriam, the foreshewing of prophets. Recollect we too what *he* thought against us who willed to devour us, the true Balak, Satan, who laid snares for us through Balaam, *the destroyer of the people*, fearing lest we should cover his land and occupy it, withdrawing the earthly-minded from his empire."

[1] העלתיך מארץ מצדים see Gen. l. 24. בית עבדים Ex. xiii. 3. 14, xx. 2, Deut. viii. 14, xiii. 10; and united, as here, with פדה, Deut. vii. 8; xiii. 5.
[2] Ex. xv. 20. [3] Dion. [4] Num. xxxi. 49.
[5] See on Hos. ix. 10. vol. i. p. 93. and on Jo. iii. 18. vol. i. p. 212. [6] Jos. v. 9.
[7] Heb. vi. 10. [8] 1 S. John i. 9.
[9] צדקות יי, only occurs beside Jud. v. 11. (bis) 1 Sam. xii. 7 thence צִדְקֹתֶיךָ, Dan. ix. 16. Else only Ps. ciii. 6.
[10] From S. Jer. [11] Ps. cvii. 1-3.

Before CHRIST cir. 710.

6 ¶ Wherewith shall I
come before the LORD, *and*
bow myself before the high
God? shall I come before
him with burnt offerings,
with calves † of a year
old?
7 [i] Will the LORD be
pleased with thousands of
rams, *or* with ten thou-
sands of [k] rivers of oil?
[l] shall I give my firstborn
for my transgression, the
fruit of my † body *for* the
sin of my soul?
8 He hath [m] shewed

† Heb. *sons of a year?*
i Ps. 50. 9. & 51. 16. Isai. 1. 11.
k Job. 29. 6.
l 2 Kings 16. 3. & 21. 6. & 23. 10. Jer. 7. 31. & 19. 5. Ezek. 23. 37.
† Heb. *belly.*
m Deut. 10. 12. 1 Sam. 15. 22. Hos. 6. 6. & 12. 6.

6, 7. *Wherewith shall I come before the Lord?* The people, thus arraigned, bursts in, as men do, with professions that they would be no more ungrateful; that they will do anything, everything—but what they ought. With them it shall be but "Ask and have." They wish only to know, *with what* they shall come? They would *be beforehand*[1] with Him, anticipating His wishes; they would, with all the submission of a creature, *bow*[2], prostrate themselves before God; they acknowledge His High Majesty, who dwelleth on high[3], *the most High God*, and would *abase themselves*[4] before His lofty greatness, if they but knew, "how" or "wherewith." They would give of their best; sacrifices the choicest of their kind, which should be wholly His, whole-burnt-offerings, offered exactly according to the law[5], *bullocks of a year old;* then too, the next choice offering, the rams; and these, as they were offered for the whole people on very solemn occasions, in vast multitudes, *thousands* or ten thousands[6]; the *oil* which accompanied the burnt sacrifice, should flow in rivers[7]; nay, more still; they would not withhold their sons, their first born sons, from God, part, as they were, of themselves, *or* any *fruit of their own body*. They enhance the offering by naming the tender relation to themselves[8]. They would offer everything, (even what God forbade) excepting only what alone He asked for, their heart, its love and its obedience[9]. The form of their offer contains this; they ask zealously, "with *what* shall I come." It is an outward offering only, a *thing* which they would bring. Hypocritical eagerness! a sin against light. For to enquire further, when God has already revealed anything, is to deny that He has revealed it. It comes from the wish that He had *not* revealed what He *has* revealed. "[10] Whoso, after he hath found the truth, discusseth anything further, seeketh a lie." God had told them, long before, from the time that He made them His people, what he desired of them; So Micah answers,

8. *He hath shewed thee.* Micah does not tell them *now*, as for the first time; which would have excused them. He says, *He hath shewed thee; He*, about Whose mind and will and pleasure they were pretending to enquire, *the Lord* their God. He *had* shewn it to them. The law was full of it. He shewed it to them, when He said, [11] *And now, Israel, what doth the Lord thy God require of thee, but to fear the Lord thy God, to walk in all His ways, and to love Him and to serve the Lord thy God with all thy heart and with all thy soul, to keep the commandments of the Lord and His statutes which I command thee this day for thy good?* They had asked, "*with what* outward *thing*[12] shall I come before the Lord;" the prophet tells them, "what *thing* is *good*," the inward man of the heart, righteousness, love, humility.

And what doth the Lord require [*search, seek*] *of thee?* The very word[13] implies an earnest search within. He would say, "[14] Trouble not thyself as to any of these things, burnt-offerings, rams, calves, without thee. For God seeketh not thine, but thee; not thy substance, but thy spirit; not ram or goat, but thy heart." "[15] Thou askest, what thou shouldest offer for thee? Offer thyself. For what else doth the Lord seek of thee, but thee? Because, of all earthly creatures, He hath made nothing better than thee, He seeketh thyself from thyself, because thou hadst lost thyself."

To do judgment, are chiefly all acts of

[1] אֲקַדֵּם. [2] אִכַּף. [3] אֱלֹהֵי מָרוֹם.

[4] The word occurs only of one sinking, bowed down, amid persecutions, Ps. lvii. 7; of the "bowed down," whom God raiseth up, Ps. cxlv. 14, cxlvi. 8; and in Is. lviii. 5, of "ostentatious outward humiliation before God." So probably here, where alone the reflective occurs.

[5] Lev. ix. 2, 3.

[6] At Solomon's dedication, 22,000 oxen and 120,000 sheep, 1 Kings viii. 63; by Hezekiah, 2000 bullocks and 17,000 sheep, 2 Chron. xxx. 24; by Josiah, 30,000 lambs and kids for the paschal offerings and 3000 bullocks. Ib. xxxv. 7.

[7] Comp. Job xx. 17, "rivers" (נהרי as here) "of streams of honey and cream." Oil was used in all meal-offerings which accompanied the burnt-offering, Lev. ii. 1, 2. 4-7, vii. 10. 12, and so entered into the daily sacrifice, Ex. xxix. 40, and all sacrifices of consecration, Ex. xxix. 2, 23, Lev. vi. 15, 21, Num. viii. 8.

[8] See Deut. xxviii. 53. [9] Conc. Chalc. Act. 3.

[10] The enquiry, v. 7, was, *Will the Lord be pleased?* הירצה יי. The subject of, *He hath shewn thee*, is obviously that same Lord.

[11] Deut. x. 12, 13. [12] בַּמָּה, 6. מַה טוֹב, 8.

[13] דרש. [14] Rup. [15] S. Aug. Serm. 48. ad loc. § 2.

Before CHRIST cir. 710.

[n] Gen. 18. 19. Isai. 1. 17.

thee, O man, what *is* good; and what doth the LORD require of thee, but [n] to do justly, and to love mercy, and to † walk humbly with thy God?

Before CHRIST cir. 710.

† Heb. *humble thyself to walk.*

equity; *to love mercy,* all deeds of love. *Judgment,* is what right requires; *mercy,* what love. Yet, secondarily, "to do judgment" is to pass righteous judgments in all cases; and so, as to others, [1] *judge not according to the appearance, but judge righteous judgment;* and as to one's self also. Judge equitably and kindly of others, humbly of thyself. "[2] Judge of thyself in thyself without acceptance of thine own person, so as not to spare thy sins, nor take pleasure in them, because *thou* hast done them. Neither praise thyself in what is good in thee, nor accuse God in what is evil in thee. For this is wrong judgment, and so, not judgment at all. This thou didst, being evil; reverse it, and it will be right. Praise God in what is good in thee; accuse thyself in what is evil. So shalt thou anticipate the judgment of God, as He saith, [3] *If we would judge ourselves, we should not be judged of the Lord.*" He addeth, *love mercy;* being merciful, out of love, [4] *not of necessity, for God loveth a cheerful giver.* These acts together contain the whole duty to man, corresponding with and formed upon the mercy and justice of God [5]. All which is due, anyhow or in any way, is of *judgment;* all which is free toward man, although not free toward God, is of *mercy.* There remains, *walk humbly with thy God;* not, *bow* thyself only before Him, as they had offered [6], nor again *walk with Him* only, as did Enoch, Noah, Abraham, Job; but *walk humbly* (lit. *bow down* [7] *the going*) yet still *with thy God;* never lifting up thyself, never sleeping, never standing still, but ever walking on, yet ever *casting thyself down;* and the more thou goest on in grace, the more cast thyself down; as our Lord saith, [8] *When ye have done all these things which are commanded you, say, We are unprofitable servants; we have done that which was our duty to do.*

It is not a "crouching before God" displeased, (such as they had thought of,) but the humble love of the forgiven; *walk humbly,* as the creature with the Creator, but in love, *with thine* own *God. Humble* thyself with God, Who humbled Himself in the flesh; *walk on* with Him, Who is thy Way. Neither humility nor obedience alone would be true graces; but to cleave fast to God, because He is thine *All,* and to *bow thyself down,* because thou art nothing, and thine All is He and of Him. It is altogether a Gospel-precept; bidding us, [9] *Be ye perfect, as your Father which is in Heaven is perfect;* [10] *Be merciful, as your Father also is merciful;* and yet, in the end, have [11] *that same mind which was also in Christ Jesus, Who made Himself of no reputation.*

The offers of the people, stated in the bare nakedness in which Micah exhibits them, have a character of irony. But it is the irony of the truth and of the fact itself. The creature has nothing of its own to offer; [12] *the blood of bulls and goats cannot take away sin;* and the offerings, as they rise in value, become, not useless only but, sinful. Such offerings would bring down anger, not mercy. Micah's words then are, for their vividness, an almost proverbial expression of the nothingness of all which we sinners could offer to God. "[13] We, who are of the people of God, knowing that [14] *in His sight shall no man living be justified,* and saying, [15] *I am a beast with Thee,* trust in no pleas before His judgment-seat, but pray; yet we put no trust in our very prayers. For there is nothing worthy to be offered to God for sin, and no humility can wash away the stains of offences. In penitence for our sins, we hesitate and say, *Wherewith shall I come before the Lord?* how shall I come, so as to be admitted into familiar intercourse with my God? One and the same spirit revolveth these things in each of us or of those before us, who have been pricked to repentance, 'what worthy offering can I make to the Lord?' This and the like we revolve, as the Apostle saith; [16] *We know not what to pray for as we ought; but the Spirit itself maketh intercession for us with groanings which cannot be uttered.* 'Should I offer myself wholly as a burnt-offering to Him?' If, understanding spiritually all the Levitical sacrifices, I should present them in myself, and offer my first-born, i. e. what is chief in me, my soul, I should find nothing worthy of His greatness. Neither in ourselves, nor in ought earthly, can we find anything worthy to be offered to reconcile us with God. For the sin of the soul, blood alone is worthy to be offered; not the blood of calves, or rams, or goats, but our own; yet our own too is not offered, but given back, being due already [17]. The Blood of Christ Alone suf-

[1] S. John vii. 24. [2] S. Aug. l. c. [3] 1 Cor. xi. 31.
[4] 2 Cor. ix. 7. [5] Ps. ci. 1. lxi. 7. [6] v. 6.

[7] הַצְנֵעַ לֶכֶת The root only occurs beside in the form צְנוּעִים Prov. xi. 2, where it is opposed to *pride.* In the Targg. Afel is = Heb. הניח. The noun is also used of humility. The Arabic has no bearing upon it, all its meanings being derived from the original "formed."

[8] S. Luke xvii. 10. [9] S. Matt. v. 48.
[10] S. Luke vi. 36. [11] Phil. ii. 5, 7. [12] Heb. x. 4.
[13] from S. Jer. S. Cyr. Rup. Dion.
[14] Ps. cxliii. 2. [15] Ib. lxxiii. 22.
[16] Rom. viii. 26. [17] Ps. cxvi. 8.

Before CHRIST cir. 710.

‖ Or, *thy name shall see that which is.*

9 The LORD's voice crieth unto the city, and ‖ *the man of* wisdom shall see thy name: hear ye the rod, and who hath appointed it.

Before CHRIST cir. 710.

---

ficeth to do away all sin." "[1] The whole is said, in order to instruct us, that, without the shedding of the Blood of Christ and its Virtue and Merits, we cannot please God, though we offered ourselves and all that we have, within and without; and also, that so great are the benefits bestowed upon us by the love of Christ, that we can repay nothing of them."

But then it is clear that there is no teaching in this passage in Micah, which there is not in the law[2]. The developments in the Prophets relate to the Person and character of the Redeemer. The law too contained both elements; 1) the ritual of sacrifice, impressing on the Jew the need of an Atoner; 2) the moral law, and the graces inculcated in it, obedience, love of God and man, justice, mercy, humility, and the rest. There was no hint in the law, that half was acceptable to God instead of the whole; that sacrifice of animals would supersede self-sacrifice or obedience. There was nothing on which the Pharisee could base his heresy. What Micah said, Moses had said. The corrupt of the people offered a half-service, what cost them least, as faith without love always does. Micah, in this, reveals to them nothing new; but tells them that this half-service is contrary to the first principles of their law. *He hath shewed thee, O man, what is good.* Sacrifice, without love of God and man, was not even so much as the body without the soul. It was an abortion, a monster. For one end of sacrifice was to inculcate the insufficiency of all our good, apart from the Blood of Christ; that, do what we would, [3] *all* came *short of the glory of God.* But to substitute sacrifice, which was a confession that at best we were miserable sinners, unable, of ourselves, to please God, for any efforts to please Him or to avoid displeasing Him, would be a direct contradiction of the law, antinomianism under the dispensation of the law itself.

Micah changes the words of Moses, in order to adapt them to the crying sins of Israel at that time. He then upbraids them in detail, and that, with those sins which were patent, which, when brought home to them, they could not deny, the sins against their neighbor.

9. *The voice of the Lord crieth unto the city,* i. e. Jerusalem, as the metropolis of their wealth and their sin, the head and heart of their offending. *Crieth,* aloud, earnestly, intently, so that all might hear. So God says, [4] *Doth not wisdom cry? and understanding put forth her voice? She crieth at the gates,—unto you, O men, I cry, and my voice* is *to the sons of men;* and Isaiah prophesied of St. John Baptist, as [5] *the voice of one crying in the wilderness;* and our Lord saith, [6] *He that heareth you, heareth Me. And the man of wisdom shall see Thy Name.* The voice of God is in the hearing of all, but *the wise* only *seeth the Name of* God[7]. The word rendered *wisdom* means, *that which is*[8], and so, that which alone *is,* which alone has any real solid being, because it alone abides, *wisdom,* or counsel according to God. Such as are thus wise shall *see the Name of God,* (as Jeremiah says to his *generation*[9], *See ye the word of the Lord.*) They shall see His power and majesty and all which His Name expresses, as they are displayed severally in each work of His: He shall speak to them by all things wherein He is; and so seeing Him now *in a glass darkly,* they shall hereafter see all, His Glory, His Goodness, His Love, Himself, *face to face.*

Hear ye the rod, i. e. the scourge of the wrath of God. The name and the image recall the like propecies of Isaiah, so that Micah in one word epitomises the prophecies of Isaiah, or Isaiah expands the word of Micah. [10] *The rod in thine hand is My indignation;* [11] *As if the rod lifted up Him, Who is not wood;* [12] *He lifteth up his rod against thee;* [13] *Thou hast broken the rod* (which is) *on his*

---

1 Dion.
2 As is so often said, in order to depreciate the law, e. g. in Dr. Stanley's J. Church p. 448.
3 Rom. iii. 23.
4 Prov. viii. 1, 3, 4. 5 Is. xl. 3. S. Matt. iii. 3.
6 S. Luke x. 16.
7 This, the simplest, is the most energetic rendering. Other possible renderings of the simple words, וְתוּשִׁיָּה יִרְאֶה שְׁמֶךָ, come to the same. Such are, "And wisdom (i. e. wholly wise) is he who regards Thy Name;" or "Thy Name (i. e. Thou, such as Thy name expresses of Thee) beholdeth wisdom," i. e. the really wise, or religious; or, "And wisdom is it, that one regards Thy Name;" or, with the change of a vowel (יִרְאָה for יִרְאֶה), "and wisdom is it, to fear Thy Name." In regard to the use of the abstract, *wisdom,* for the concrete, *the wise,* Poc. compares Prov. xiii. 6, "wickedness overthrows sin," i. e. the sinner, and Ib. xx. 1. '*wine*' for *a man of wine.* He quotes also אמר קהלת, Eccl. i. 2. in illustration of the anomaly of gender, and vii. 8, מתנה יאבד.
8 There is no other even plausible etymology of תּוּשִׁיָּה, than יֵשׁ, whose 3d radical appears in אִיתַי in Daniel, and in Syriac, and in אִיתִיאֵל, Heb. See "Daniel the Proph." p. 49.
9 Jer. ii. 31. add "Ex. xx. 18, *and all the people saw* קולות *the voices,* or *thunderings,* and, *see the smell of my son,* Gen. xxvii. 27." Poc.
10 Is. x. 5. 11 Ib. 15. 12 Ib. 24. 13 Ib. ix. 3. Heb.

Before CHRIST cir. 710.

10 ¶ ‖ Are there yet the
treasures of wickedness in
the house of the wicked,
and the † scant measure
° *that is* abominable?
11 ‖ Shall I count *them*
pure with ᵖ the wicked
balances, and with the bag
of deceitful weights?
12 For the rich men
thereof are full of violence,
and the inhabitants thereof

‖ Or, *Is there yet unto every man an house of the wicked, &c.*
† Heb. *measure of leanness*, Amos 8. 5.
° Deut 25. 13–16. Prov. 11. 1. & 20. 10, 23.
‖ Or, *Shall I be pure with, &c.*

Before CHRIST cir. 710.

ᵖ Hos. 12. 7.

shoulder; [1] *The Lord hath broken the rod of the wicked;* [2] *whereon the grounded* [i. e. fixed by the decree of God] *staff shall pass.*

And Who hath appointed it, i. e. beforehand, fixing the time and place, when and where it should come. So Jeremiah says, [3] *How canst thou* (sword of the Lord) *be quiet, and the Lord hath given it a charge to Ashkelon and to the sea-shore? there hath He appointed it.* He Who has *appointed it,* changeth not His decree, unless man changeth; nor is He lacking in power to fulfill it. He will surely bring it to pass. All which can be thought of, of fear, terror, motives to repentance, awe, hope, trust, is in that word *Who.* It is God; hopes and fears may be infinite.

10. *Are there* [4] *yet,* still after all the warnings and long-suffering of God, *the treasures of wickedness in the house of the wicked? Treasures of wickedness* are treasures gotten by wickedness; yet it means too that the wicked shall have no treasure, no fruit, but his wickedness. He treasureth up treasures, but of wickedness; as St. James saith, [5] *Ye have heaped treasure together for the last days,* i. e. of the *miseries that shall come upon them* [6]. The words stand over against one another; *house of the wicked, treasures of wickedness;* as though the whole *house of the wicked* was but a "treasure-house of wickedness." Therein it began; therein and in its rewards it shall end. *Are there yet?* the Prophet asks. There shall soon cease to be. The treasure shall be spoiled; the iniquity alone shall remain.

And the scant ephah (lit. "*ephah of leanness*" E. M.) *which* is *abominable?* Scant itself, and, by the just judgment of God, producing scantness, emaciated and emaciating [7]; as He says, [8] *He gave them their desire, and sent leanness withal into their soul;* and St. James [9], *it shall eat your flesh as it were fire.* Even a heathen said, "[10] Gain gotten by wickedness is loss;" and that, as being "*abominable*" or "accursed" or, one might say, "bewrathed [11]," lying under the wrath and curse of God. "[12] What they minish from the measure, *that* they add to the wrath of God and the vengeance which shall come upon them; what is lacking to the measure shall be supplied out of the wrath of God." The Ephah was a corn-measure [13], containing about six bushels; the rich, in whose house it was, were the sellers; they were the necessaries of life then, which the rich retailers of corn were selling dishonestly, at the price of the lives of the poor [14]. Our subtler ways of sin cheat ourselves, not God. In what ways do not competitive employers use the *scant measure which is accursed?* What else is all our competitive trade, our cheapness, our wealth, but scant measure to the poor, making their wages *lean,* full and overflowing with the wrath of God?

11. *Shall I count them pure?* rather, (as E. M.) *Shall I be pure* [15]? The Prophet takes for the time their person and bids them judge themselves in him. If it would defile me, how are ye, with all your other sins, not defiled? All these things were expressly forbidden in the law. [16] *Ye shall do no unrighteousness in judgment, in mete-yard, in weight or in measure. Just balances, just weights, a just ephah and a just hin, shall ye have;* and, [17] *Thou shalt not have in thy bag divers weights, a great and a small. Thou shalt not have in thine house divers measures, a great and a small. For all that do such things, and all that do unrighteousness are an abomination unto the Lord thy God.* Yet are not these things common even now?

12. *For the rich men thereof,* i. e. *of the city* [18], *are full of violence.* It had been little, had thieves and robbers lived by violence, but now, (as Isaiah at the same time upbraids them,) [19] *her princes* were become *companions of thieves.* Not the poor out of distress, but the rich, out of wantonness and exceeding covetousness and love of luxury, not only did

[1] Ib. xiv. 5. [2] Ib. xxx. 32.
[3] Jer. xlvii. 7. יעד is used in regard to time, 2 Sam. xx. 5. It is used of both time and place in the Arab. Conj. iii. as in מוֹעֵד, and the Syr.
[4] אִשׁ i. q. יֵשׁ, as in 2 Sam. xiv. 19, the א occurring together with the י (here indicated by the vowel) in Arab. Chald. Syr. Sam. Pers. and Heb. אִיתַי See n. 5.
[5] S. Jam. v. 3. [6] Ib. 1. [7] See v. 14.
[8] Ps. cvi. 15. [9] v. 3.
[10] Chilon in Diog. Laert. i. 4. [11] זְעוּמָת.
[12] Rib. [13] Am. viii. 5.
[14] It seems necessary, I see, in so-called Christian London, to advertise in shops, that bread is of its alleged weight.
[15] זכה in Kal is only intransitive.
[16] Lev. xix. 35, 36.
[17] Deut. xxv. 13, 15, 16. add Prov. xi. 1. xvi. 11. xx. 10. [18] ver. 9. [19] Is. i. 23.

Before CHRIST cir. 710.

have spoken lies, and [q] their
tongue *is* deceitful in their
mouth.

[q] Jer. 9. 3, 5, 6, 8.

13 Therefore also will I
[r] make *thee* sick in smiting
thee, in making *thee* desolate because of thy sins.
14 [s] Thou shalt eat, but
not be satisfied; and thy
casting down *shall be* in
the midst of thee; and
thou shalt take hold, but
shalt not deliver; and
that which thou deliverest
will I give up to the
sword.

[r] Lev. 26. 16. Ps. 107. 17.

[s] Lev. 26. 26. Hos. 4. 10.

Before CHRIST cir. 710.

wrong but were *filled*, not so much with riches, as *with violence*. Violence is the very meat and drink wherewith they are filled, yea, and wherewith they shall be filled, when it is returned upon their heads.

And the inhabitants thereof have spoken lies. Fraud is itself lying, and lying is its inseparable companion. "[1] Lying followeth the gathering together of riches, and the hard wont to lay up riches hath a deceitful tongue." The sin, he saith, is spread throughout all *her inhabitants;* i. e. all of them, as their wont, have spoken lies, and, even when they speak not, the lie is ready; *their tongue is deceitful* (lit. *deceit*) *in their mouth.* It is *deceit*, nothing but deceit, and *that, deceit* which should "[2] overthrow" and ruin others. One intent on gain has the lie ever ready to be uttered, even when he speaks not. It lurks concealed, until it is needed.

13. *Therefore also will I,* [lit. *And I too,*] i. e. this dost thou, and thus will I too do. "[3] As thou madest sick the heart of the poor oppressed, so will I, by My grievous and severe punishments, *make thee sick,*" or *make thy wound incurable*, as in Nahum[4], *thy wound is grievous,* lit. *made sick. In making thee desolate because of thy sins.* The heaping up riches shall itself be the cause of thy being waste, deserted, desolate.

14. *Thou shalt eat, but not be satisfied.* The correspondence of the punishment with the sin shall shew that it is not by chance, but from the just judgment of God. The curse of God shall go with what they eat, and it shall not nourish them. The word, *thou*, is thrice repeated[5]. As God had just said, *I too*, so here, *Thou. Thou*, the same who hast plundered others, *shalt* thyself *eat, and not be satisfied;* "*thou* shalt sow, and not reap; *thou* shalt tread the olive, and thou shalt not anoint thee with oil." "Upon extreme but ill-gotten abundance, there followeth extreme want. And whoso," adds one[6], "seeth not this in our ways and our times is absolutely blind. For in no period have we ever read that there was so much gold and silver, or so much discomfort and indigence, so that those most true words of Christ Jesus seem to have been especially spoken of us, [7] *Take heed, for a man's life consisteth not in the abundance of the things which he possesseth.*" And is not this true of us now?

Thy casting down shall be in the midst of thee. Where thou hast laid up thy treasures, or rather thy wickedness, there thou shalt *sink down*, or give way, from inward decay, in the very centre of thy wealth and thy sin. They had said, [8] *Is not the Lord in the midst of us? None evil can come upon us.* Micah tells them of a different indweller. God had departed from them, and left them to their inherent nothingness. God had been their stay; without God, human strength collapses. Scarcely any destruction is altogether hopeless save that which cometh from within. Most storms pass over, tear off boughs and leaves, but the stem remains. Inward decay or excision alone are humanly irrecoverable. The political death of the people was, in God's hands, to be the instrument of their regeneration.

Morally too, and at all times, inward emptiness is the fruit of unrighteous fullness. It is disease, not strength; as even Heathen proverbs said; "the love of money is a dropsy; to drink increaseth the thirst," and "amid mighty wealth, poor;" and Holy Scripture, [9] *The rich He sendeth empty away.* And truly they must be empty. For what can fill the soul, save God? "[10] This is true too of such as, like the Bishop of Sardis, [11] *have a name that they live and are dead,*" "[12] such as do some things good, feed on the word of God, but attain to no fruit of righteousness;" "who corrupt natural and seeming good by inward decay; who appear righteous before men, are active and zealous for good ends, but spoil all by some secret sin or wrong end, as vain-glory or praise of men, whereby they lose the praise of God. *Their casting down shall be in the midst of* them. The

[1] S. Jer.
[2] רְמִיָּה from רמה. It is used of the tongue in Ps. lii. 4, ci. 7, cxx. 2, 3; of a bow, Ps. lxxviii. 57, Hos. vii. 16.
[3] Poc.
[4] iii. 19.
[5] אתה once in v. 14. twice in v. 15.
[6] Arias Montanus, a Spaniard. His Commentary on the Minor Prophets was published at Antwerp, 1571.
[7] S. Luke xii. 15.
[8] iii. 11.
[9] S. Luke i. 53, comp. 1 Sam. ii. 5.
[10] Rib.
[11] Rev. iii. 1.
[12] Dion.

Before CHRIST cir. 710.

15 Thou shalt [t] sow, but
thou shalt not reap; thou
shalt tread the olives, but
thou shalt not anoint thee
with oil; and sweet wine,
but shalt not drink wine.
16 ¶ For ‖ the statutes
of [u] Omri are [x] kept, and

[t] Deut. 28. 38, 39, 40. Amos 5. 11. Zeph. 1. 13. Hag. 1. 6.

‖ Or, *he doth much keep the &c.*

[u] 1 Kings 16. 25, 26.

[x] Hos. 5. 11.

meaning of the whole is the same, whether the word be rendered *casting down*, i. e. downfall, (lit. *sinking down*[1],) or *emptiness*, especially of the stomach, perhaps from the feeling of "sinking."

Thou shalt take hold to rescue or *remove* to a safe place from the enemy, those whom he would take from thee, *but shalt not* wholly *deliver; and that which thou deliverest* for a time, *will I give up to the sword*, i. e. the children for whose sake they pleaded that they got together this wealth; as, now too, the idols, for whose sake men toil wrongly all their life, are often suddenly taken away. Their goods too may be said to be *given to the sword*, i. e. to the enemy.

15. *Thou shalt sow, but thou shalt not reap.* Micah renews the threatenings of the law[2], which they had been habitually breaking. Those prophecies had been fulfilled before, throughout their history; they have been fulfilled lately in Israel for the like oppression of the poor[3]. Their frequent fulfillment spoke as much of a law of God's righteousness, punishing sin, as the yearly supply in the ordinary course of nature spoke of His loving Providence. It is the bitterest punishment to the covetous to have the things which they coveted, taken away before their eyes; it was a token of God's Hand, that He took them away, when just within their grasp. The prophet brings it before their eyes, that they might feel beforehand the bitterness of forgetting them. "[4] They should lose, not only what they gained unjustly, but the produce of their labor, care, industry, as, in agriculture, it is said that there is mostly much labor, little fraud, much benefit." Harvest is a proverb for joy; [5] *they joy before Thee according to the joy in harvest;* [6] *wine maketh glad the heart of man, and oil is to make him a cheerful countenance.* But the harvest shall be turned into sorrow, [7] the oil and wine shall be taken away, when all the labor had been employed. Yet, since all these operations in nature are adapted to be, and are used as, symbols of things spiritual, then the words which describe them are adapted to be spiritual proverbs. Spiritually, "[8] *he soweth and reapeth not, who* [9] *soweth to the flesh, and of the flesh reapeth corruption*, things corruptible, and inward decay and condemnation. He *treadeth the olive*, who, by shameful deeds contrary to the law, [10] *grieveth the Holy Spirit of God*, and therefore obtaineth not gladness of spirit; he maketh *wine, yet drinketh not wine*, who teacheth others, not himself." They too *take hold but do not deliver*, who *for awhile believe and in time of temptation fall away*, who repent for a while and then fall back into old sins, or in other ways *bring no fruit to perfection;* taking up the Cross for awhile and then wearying; using religious practices, as, more frequent prayer or fasting, and then tiring; cultivating some graces and then despairing because they see not the fruits. These tread the olive, but are not anointed with the oil of the Holy Spirit of grace, who "[11] end by doing for the sake of man, what they had thought to do out of the love for God, and abandon, for some fear of man, the good which they had begun."

16. *For the statutes of Omri are kept*, rather, (like E. M. *he doth much keep*,) *And he doth keep diligently for himself.* Both ways express much diligence in evil[12]. To "keep God's commandments" was the familiar phrase, in which Israel was exhorted, by every motive of hope and fear, to obedience to God. [13] *I know him*, God says of Abraham, *that he will command his children and his household after him, and they shall keep the way of the Lord, to do judgment and justice.* This was the fundamental commandment immediately after the deliverance from Egypt upon their first murmuring. [14] *The Lord made there* (at Marah) *for them a statute and ordinance, and said, If thou wilt diligently hearken to the voice of the Lord thy God, and wilt do that which is right in His sight, and wilt give ear to His commandments and keep all His statutes, I will put none of these diseases upon thee which I have brought upon the Egyptians.* In this character He revealed Himself on Mount Sinai, as [15] *shewing mercy unto thousands of them that love Me and keep My commandments.* This was their covenant, [16] *Thou hast avouched the Lord this day to be thy God and to walk in His ways, and to keep His statutes and His commandments and*

[1] It is possible, as Gesenius conjectures, that יֶשַׁח (a ἅπ. λεγ.) is a transposed form of the Arab. ושׁח; more probably it may be from the bi-literal שַׁח, which gave rise to the other forms, שׁוּח, שׁחח.
[2] Lev. xxvi. 16, Deut. xxviii. 30. 38–41.
[3] Am. v. 11. [4] Mont. [5] Is. ix. 3.
[6] Ps. civ. 15.
[7] Comp. Is. xvi. 9, 10, Jer. v. 17, xlviii. 37.
[8] Theoph. [9] Gal. vi. 8. [10] Eph. iv. 30. [11] Rib.
[12] In the construction of the E. V. (which is possible) the force of the union of the sing. verb with the plural noun would be that "the statutes of Omri, one and all, are kept diligently."
[13] Gen. xviii. 19. [14] Ex. xv. 25, 26. [15] Ib. xx. 6.
[16] Deut. xxvi. 17.

Before CHRIST cir. 710.

all the works of the house of [y] Ahab, and ye walk in their counsels; that I should make thee [z] a ‖ desolation, and the inhabitants thereof an hissing: therefore ye shall bear the [a] reproach of my people.

y 1 Kings 16. 30, &c. & 21. 25, 26. 2 Kin. 21. 3.
z 1 Kings 9. 8. Jer. 19. 8.
‖ Or, *astonishment.*
a Isai. 25. 8. Jer. 51. 51. Lam. 5. 1.

His judgments and to hearken unto His voice. This was so often enforced upon them in the law, as the condition upon which they should hold their land, if they kept *the covenant*[1], *the commandments*[2], *the judgments*[3], *the statutes*[4], *the testimonies*[5], *the charge*[6] of the Lord. Under this term all the curses of the law were threatened, if they [7] *hearkened not unto the voice of the Lord* their *God, to keep His commandments and His statutes which* He *commanded* them. Under this again the future of good and evil was, in Solomon, set before the house of David; of unbroken succession on his throne, if [8] *thou wilt keep My commandments;* but contrariwise, *if ye or your children will not keep My commandments and My statutes,* banishment, destruction of the temple, and themselves to be [9] *a proverb and a byword among all people.* This was the object of their existence, [10] *that they might keep His statutes and observe His laws.* This was the summary of their disobedience, [11] *they kept not the covenant of God.* And now was come the contrary to all this. They had *not* kept the commandments of *God;* and those commandments of man which were the most contrary to the commandments of God, they *had* kept and did keep diligently. Alas! that the Christian world should be so like them! What iron habit or custom of man, what fashion, is not kept, if it is against the law of God? How few are not more afraid of man than God? Had God's command run, *Speak evil one of another, brethren,* would it not have been the best kept of all His commandments? God says, *speak not evil;* custom, the conversation around, fear of man, say, *speak evil;* man's commandment is kept; God's is not kept. And no one repents or makes restitution; few even cease from the sin.

Scripture does not record, what was the special aggravation of the sin of Omri, since the accursed worship of Baal was brought in by Ahab[12], his son. But, as usual, "like father, like son." The son developed the sins of the father. Some special sinfulness of Omri is implied, in that Athaliah, the murderess of her children, is called after her grandfather, Omri, not after her father, Ahab[13]. Heresiarchs have a deeper guilt than their followers, although the heresy itself is commonly developed later. Omri settled for a while the kingdom of Israel, after the anarchy which followed on the murder of Elah, and slew Zimri, his murderer. Yet before God, *he did worse than all before him, and he walked in all the way of Jeroboam*[14]. Yet this too did not suffice Judah; for it follows, *And all the doings of the house of Ahab,* who again [15] *did evil in the sight of the Lord above all that were before him and served Baal;* Ahab, to whom none [16] *was like* in sin, *who did sell himself to work wickedness in the sight of the Lord.* These were they, whose statutes Judah now kept, as diligently and accurately as if it had been a religious act. They kept, not *the statutes of the Lord,* but *the statutes of Omri;* they kept, as their pattern before their eyes, *all the doings of the house of Ahab,* his luxury, oppression, the bloodshedding of Naboth; and they *walked* onward, not, as God bade them, *humbly with Him,* but *in their counsels.* And what must be the end of all this? *that I should make thee a desolation.* They acted, as though the very end and object of all their acts were *that,* wherein they ended, their own destruction and reproach[17].

Therefore ye shall bear the reproach of My people. The title of *the people of God* must be a glory or a reproach. Judah had gloried in being God's people, outwardly, by His covenant and protection; they were envied for the outward distinction. They refused to be so inwardly, and gave themselves to the hideous, desecrating, worship of Baal. Now then what had been their pride, should be the aggravation of their punishment. *Now* too we hear of people everywhere zealous for a system, which their deeds belie. Faith, without love, (such as their character had been,) feels any insult to the relation to God, which

[1] Ex. xix. 5. *the words of this covenant,* Deut. xxix. 9.

[2] המצוה or כל המצוה, or מצות י׳ Lev. xxii. 31, xxvi. 3, Deut. iv. 2, vi. 17, vii. 11, viii. 6, 11, x. 13, xi. 1, 8, 22, xiii. 5, Heb. 19, xv. 5. xix. 9, xxvii. 1. xxviii. 9, xxx. 10.

[3] משפטי Lev. xviii. 5, 26, xx. 22, Deut. vii. 11, viii. 11, xi. 1.

[4] חקות or חקים Lev. xviii. 5, 26, xx. 8, 22. Deut. iv. 40, vi. 17, vii. 11, x. 13, xi. 1, xxx. 10.

[5] עדות Deut. vi. 17.

[6] משמרת Lev. xviii. 30, Deut. xi. 1.

[7] Deut. xxviii. 15. [8] 1 Kings ix. 4–6.

[9] Ib. 7. [10] Ps. cv. 45. [11] Ib. lxxviii. 11.

[12] The worship of Baal was the result of Ahab's marriage with *Jezebel, the daughter* of one, whose name designates his devotedness to that idolatry, *Ethbaal,* (i. e. "with the help of Baal.") And this marriage is spoken of as Ahab's act, not his father's. 1 Kings xvi. 31.

[13] 2 Kings viii. 26. 2 Chron. xxii. 2.

[14] 1 Kings xvi. 25, 26. [15] Ib. 30–33. [16] Ib. xxi. 25.

[17] See on Hos. viii. 4. vol. i. p. 81.

Before CHRIST cir. 710.

CHAPTER VII.

1 *The church, complaining of her small number,* 3 *and the general corruption,* 5 *putteth her confidence not in man, but in God.* 8 *She triumpheth over her enemies.* 14 *God comforteth her by promises,* 16 *by confusion of the enemies,* 18 *and by his mercies.*

WOE is me! for I am as †when they have gathered the summer fruits, as [a]the grapegleanings of the vintage: *there is* no cluster to eat: [b]my soul desired the firstripe fruit.

Before CHRIST cir. 710.

† Heb. *the gatherings of summer.*
[a] Isai. 17. 6. & 24. 13.
[b] Is. 28. 4. Hos. 9. 10.

---

by its deeds it disgraces. Though they had themselves neglected God, yet it was a heavy burden to them to *bear* the triumph of the heathen over them, that God was unable to help them, or had cast them off. [1] *These are the people of the Lord and are gone forth, out of His land.* [2] *Wherefore should they say among the heathen, where is their God?* [3] *We are confounded, because we have heard reproach, shame hath covered our faces, for strangers are come into the sanctuaries of the Lord's house.* [4] *We are become a reproach to our neighbors, a scorn and derision to them that are round about us.* [5] *Thou makest us a reproach to our neighbors, a scorn and derision to them that are round about us. Thou makest us a byword among the heathen, a shaking of the head among the people. My confusion is daily before me, and the shame of my face hath covered me, for the voice of him that slandereth and blasphemeth, by reason of the enemy and the avenger.*

The words, *the reproach of My people*, may also include "[6]the reproach wherewith God in the law[7] threatened His people if they should forsake Him", which indeed comes to the same thing, the one being the prophecy, the other the fulfillment. The word *hissing* in itself recalled the threat to David's house in Solomon; [8]*At this house*, which is *high, every one that passeth by it shall be astonished and hiss.* Micah's phrase became a favorite expression of Jeremiah[9]. So only do God's prophets denounce. It is a marvelous glimpse into man's religious history, that faith, although it had been inoperative and was trampled upon without, should still survive; nay, that God, Whom in prosperity they had forsaken and forgotten, should be remembered, when He seemed to forget and to forsake them. Had the captive Jews abandoned their faith, the reproach would have ceased. The words, *ye shall bear the reproach of My people* are, at once, a prediction of their deserved suffering for the profanation of God's Name by their misdeeds, and of their perseverance in that faith which, up to that time, they had mostly neglected.

CHAP. VII. The Prophet's office of threatening woe is now over. Here, out of love, he himself crieth woe unto himself. He hath [10]*continual sorrow in heart* for his people. He bewails what he cannot amend, and, by bewailing, shews them how much more they should bewail it, over whose sins he sorrows; how certain the destruction is, since there is none to stand in the gap and turn away the wrath of God, no "ten righteous," for whose sake the city may be spared. "[11]These words flow out of the fount of pity, because the good zeal, wherewith the Holy seem to speak severely, is never without pity. They are wroth with the sins, they sympathize with the sinner." So Isaiah mourned for the judgment, which he prophesied against the world, [12]*Woe is me!* he sorrowed even for Moab[13]; and Joel, [14]*Alas for the day!* and Jeremiah in that exclamation of impassioned sorrow; [15]*Woe is me, my mother, that thou hast borne me a man of strife and a man of contention to the whole world!*

1. *Woe*[16] *is me! for I am, as when they have gathered the summer fruits*[17], *as the grape-gleanings of the vintage. The vineyard of the Lord of hosts*, Isaiah said at the same time[18], is *the house of Israel, and the men of Judah His pleasant plants.* Isaiah said, *it brought forth wild grapes;* Micah, that there are but gleanings, few and poor. It is as though Satan pressed the vineyard of the Lord, and made the most his prey, and few were left to those who glean for Christ; [19]*the foxes have eaten the grapes.* Some few remain too high out of their reach, or hidden behind the leaves, or, it may be, [20]falling in the time of gathering, fouled,

---

[1] Ezek. xxxvi. 20.
[2] Joel ii. 17. See vol. i. pp. 185, 186.
[3] Jer. li. 51. [4] Ps. lxxix. 4. [5] Ps. xliv. 13–16.
[6] Rib. and others in Poc. [7] Deut. xxviii. 36.
[8] 1 Kgs. ix. 8.
[9] שְׁרֵקָה Jer. li. 37. לִשְׁרֵקָה Jer. xix. 8. xxv. 9, 18. xxix. 18. Else it is only used by Hezekiah, 2 Chron. xxix. 8.
[10] Rom. ix. 2. [11] Rup. [12] Is. xxiv. 16.
[13] Ib. xv. 5. xvi. 11. [14] Joel i. 15. [15] Jer. xv. 10.
[16] אַלְלַי. The word occurs beside only in Job x. 15. but it is the cry of nature. Among the Greeks it is chiefly of joy or triumph, but of sorrow too; in Latin chiefly of sorrow, "ululo," our. "howl."
[17] lit. as *the gatherings of the fig-harvest.* It is one of those concise comparisons, which have to be filled up. In prose it would be, "I am as one who, at the gatherings of the fig-harvest, should still look for fruit on the trees." The meaning, "summer," E. M. is doubtless a secondary sense of the word, resulting from the fact, that the main fig harvest was about the summer solstice.
[18] Is. v. 7. [19] Cant. ii. 15. [20] Poc. from Tanch.

Before CHRIST cir. 710.

c Ps. 12. 1. & 14. 1, 3. Is. 57. 1.
|| Or, *godly*, or, *merciful*.
d Hab. 1. 15.

2 The c||good *man* is
perished out of the earth:
and *there is* none upright
among men: they all lie in
wait for blood; d they hunt
every man his brother with
a net.
3 ¶ That they may do
evil with both hands earnestly, e the prince asketh,

Before CHRIST cir. 710.

e Hos. 4. 18.

sullied, marred and stained, yet left." So in the gleaning there may be three sorts of souls; [1] *two or three in the top of the uppermost bough*, which were not touched; or those unripe, which are but imperfect and poor; or those who had fallen, yet were not wholly carried away. These too are all sought with difficulty; they had escaped the gatherer's eye, they are few and rare; it might seem at first sight, as though there were none. *There is no cluster to eat;* for the vintage is past, the best is but as a sour grape which sets the teeth on edge. *My soul desired the first-ripe fig* [2]. These are they which, having survived the sharpness of winter, ripen early, about the end of June; they are the sweetest [2]; but he longed for them in vain. He addressed a carnal people, who could understand only carnal things, on the side which they *could* understand. Our longings, though we pervert them, are God's gift. As they desired those things which refresh or recruit the thirsty body, as their whole self was gathered into the craving for that which was to restore them, so was it with him. Such is the longing of God for man's conversion and salvation; such is the thirst of His ministers; such, their pains in seeking, their sorrow in not finding. "[3] There were none, through whose goodness the soul of the prophet might spiritually be refreshed, in joy at his growth in grace, as St. Paul saith to Philemon, [4] *refresh my bowels in the Lord*. So our Lord saith in Isaiah, [5] *I said, I have labored in vain, I have spent my strength for nought and in vain.* [6] *Jesus was grieved at the hardness of their hearts.*

"[7] The first-ripe fig may be the image of the righteous of old, as the Patriarchs or the Fathers, such as in the later days we fain would see."

2. *The good* [or *godly*, or *merciful*, E. M.] *man*. The Hebrew word contains all. It is "he who loveth tenderly and piously" God, for His own sake, and man, for the sake of God. Mercy was probably chiefly intended, since it was to this that the prophet had exhorted [8], and the sins which he proceeds to speak of, are against this. But imaginary love of God without love of man, or love of man without the love of God, is mere self-deceit. *Is perished out of the earth*, i. e. by an untimely death [9]. *The good* had either been withdrawn by God *from the evil to come* [10], or had been cut off by those who *laid wait for blood;* in which case their death brought a double evil, through the guilt which such sin contracted, and then, through the loss of those who might be an example to others, and whose prayers God would hear. The loving and *upright*, all, who were men of mercy and truth, had ceased. They who were left, *all lie in wait for blood*, lit. *bloods* [11], i. e. bloodshedding; *all*, as far as man can see; as Elijah complains that he was left alone. Amid the vast number of the wicked, the righteous were as though they were not. Isaiah, at the same time, complains of the like sins, and that it was as though there were none righteous; [12] *Your hands are defiled with blood, and your fingers with iniquity; your lips have spoken lies, your tongue hath muttered perverseness. None calleth for justice, nor* any *pleadeth for truth.* Indirectly, or directly, they destroyed life [13]. To violence they add treachery. The good and *loving* had perished, and all is now violence; the upright had ceased, and all now is deceit. *They hunt every man his brother with a net.* Every man is the brother of every man, because he is man, born of the same first parent, children of the same Father: yet they lay wait for one another, as hunters for wild beasts [14].

3. *That they may do evil with both hands earnestly,* [lit. *upon evil both hands to do well,*] i. e. "both their hands are upon evil to do it well," or "earnestly [15]," as our translation gives the meaning; only the Hebrew expresses more, that evil is their good, and their good or excellence is in evil. Bad men gain a dreadful skill and wisdom in evil, as Satan has; and cleverness in evil is their delight. "[16] They call the evil of their hands good." *The prince asketh, and the judge* asketh (or, it may more readily be supplied, *judgeth*,

[1] Is. xvii. 6.
[2] The *bikkurah, boccore, Albacora.* (Span.) See Shaw's Travels p. 370. Its goodness was proverbial. See Hos. ix. 10, Is. xxviii. 4, Jer. xxiv. 2.
[3] Dion.
[4] Philem. 20.
[5] Is. xlix. 4.
[6] S. Mark iii. 5.
[7] From Rib.
[8] חסד vi. 8. חסיד vii. 2.
[9] אבד.
[10] Is. lvii. 1. where אבד is, in like way, used.
[11] See Hos. v. 2, and Mic. iii. 10, *They build up Zion with bloods:* Isaiah says in like way, *Your hands are full of bloods.* i. 15.
[12] Is. lix. 2, 3.
[13] See ab. p. 44, on iii. 10.
[14] Comp. Ps. xxxv. 7, lvii. 7, cxl. 6, Jer. v. 26.
[15] הֵיטֵב, like our, "do it well," can signify "do it thoroughly;" yet not so as to supersede the idea of its being "done well" in the mind of the actor. The two cases cited to the contrary, the thorough destruction of the calf, (Deut. ix. 21,) and of the house of Baal, (2 Kings xi. 18,) were, of course, good acts. So to "search well." Deut. xvii. 4, xix. 18.
[16] S. Jer.

Before CHRIST cir. 710.

f Is. 1. 23. ch. 3. 11
† Heb. *the mischief of his soul.*
g 2 Sam. 23. 6, 7. Ezek. 2. 6. See Is. 55. 13.

f and the judge *asketh* for a
reward; and the great *man*,
he uttereth † his mischievous desire: so they wrap it
up.
4 The best of them g *is*
as a brier: the most up-
right *is sharper* than a
thorn hedge: the day of
thy watchmen *and* thy
visitation cometh; now
shall be their perplexity.
5 ¶ h Trust ye not in a
friend, put ye not confi-
dence in a guide: keep the
doors of thy mouth from
her that lieth in thy bosom.
6 For i the son dishonor-
eth the father, the daughter
riseth up against her

Before CHRIST cir. 710.

h Jer. 9. 4.
i Ezek. 22. 7. Matt. 10. 21. 35, 36. Luke 12. 53. & 21. 16. 2 Tim. 3. 2, 3.

doth that which is his office,) against right *for a reward*, (which was strictly forbidden[1],) *and the great man he uttereth his mischievous desire*, (or *the desire of his soul.*) Even the shew of good is laid aside; whatever the heart conceives and covets, it utters;—mischief to others and in the end to itself. The mischief comes forth from the soul, and returns upon it. The *elders and nobles in the city*[2], as well as Ahab, took part, (as one instance,) in the murder of Naboth. The *great* man, however, here, is rather the source of the evil, which he induces others to effect; so that as many as there were great, so many sources were there of oppression. All, prince, judges, the great, unite in the ill, and this not once only, but they are ever doing it[3], and *so they wrap it up*, (lit. twist[4], intertwine it.) Things are twisted, either to strengthen, or to pervert or intricate them. It might mean, they *strengthen* it, that which their soul covets against the poor, or they *pervert* it, the cause of the poor.

4. *The best of them is as a brier;* the gentlest of them is a thorn, [5]strong, hard, piercing, which letteth nothing unresisting pass by but it taketh from it, "robbing the fleece, and wounding the sheep." *The most upright*, those who, in comparison of others still worse, seem so, *is sharper than a thorn hedge*. (lit. *the upright, than a thorn hedge.*) They are not like it only, but worse, and that in all ways; none is specified, and so none excepted; they were more crooked, more tangled, sharper. Both, as hedges, were set for protection; both, turned to injury. "[6]So that, where you would look for help, thence comes suffering." And if such be the best, what the rest?

The day of thy watchmen and thy visitation cometh. When all, even the good, are thus corrupted, the iniquity is full. Nothing now hinders the *visitation*, which *the watchmen*, or prophets, had so long foreseen and forewarned of. *Now shall be their perplexity*[7]; *now*, without delay; for the day of destruction ever breaketh suddenly upon the sinner. [8] *When they say, peace and safety, then sudden destruction cometh upon them.* [9] *Whose destruction cometh suddenly at an instant.* They had perplexed the cause of the oppressed; they themselves were tangled together, intertwined in mischief, as a thorn-hedge. They should be caught in their own snare; they had perplexed their paths and should find no outlet.

5. 6. *Trust ye not in a friend.* It is part of the perplexity of crooked ways, that all relationships are put out of joint. Selfishness rends each from the other, and disjoints the whole frame of society. Passions and sin break every band of friendship, kindred, gratitude, nature. "Every one *seeketh his own.*" Times of trial and of outward harass increase this; so that God's visitations are seasons of the most frightful recklessness as to everything but self. So had God foretold[10]; so it was in the siege of Samaria[11], and in that of Jerusalem both by the Chaldeans[12] and by the Romans[13]. When the soul has lost the love of God, all other is but seeming love, since *natural affection* is from Him, and it too dies out, as God gives the soul over to itself[14]. The words describe partly the inward corruption, partly the outward causes which shall call it forth. There is no real trust in any, where all are corrupt. The outward straitness and perplexity, in which they shall be, makes *that* to crumble and fall

1 Deut. xvi. 19. See ab. iii. 11.
2 1 Kings xxi. 8, 11.
3 The force of the partic. שׁוֹאֵל, דִּבֵּר.
4 עִבֵּת, the verb, is a ἅπ. λεγ. What remains of the root has the meaning of "twisted," (in עֲבֹת, "a rope") or "entangled," (in עָבֹת, עֲבֹת "thick boughs.")
5 The Heb. חֵדֶק seems to have been different from the Arab. which is a "solanum," (Cels. Hierob. ii. 35.) but Prov. xv. 19, (where it occurs beside), shews that it served as a hedge.
6 S. Jer.
7 In the Hebrew the two words "mesucah," "thorn hedge," and "mebucah," "perplexity," are alike in sound.
8 1 Thess. v. 3.
9 See Is. xxx. 13. comp. 2 Pet. ii. 1, "swift destruction;" Prov. i. 27, "cometh as a whirlwind," Ps. xxxv. 8, "unawares."
10 Deut. xxviii. 53.
11 2 Kings vi. 28.
12 Lam. iv. 3–16.
13 Jos. B. J. vi. 3. 8.
14 Rom. i. 28.

Before CHRIST cir. 710.

mother, the daughter in law against her mother in law; a man's enemies *are* the men of his own house.

7 Therefore [k] I will look unto the LORD; I will wait for the God of my salvation: my God will hear me.

[k] Isai. 8. 17.

to pieces, which was inwardly decayed and severed before. The words deepen, as they go on. First, *the friend*, or neighbor, the common band of man and man; then *the guide*, (or, as the word also means, one *familiar*, united by intimacy, to whom, by continual intercourse, the soul was *used*;) then the wife who lay in the bosom, nearest to the secrets of the heart; then those to whom all reverence is due, *father* and *mother*. Our Lord said that this should be fulfilled in the hatred of His Gospel. He begins His warning as to it, with a caution like that of the prophet; [1] *Be ye wise as serpents*, and *beware of men*. Then He says, how these words should still be true [2]. There never were wanting pleas of earthly interest against the truth. He Himself was *cut off*, lest [3] *the Romans should take away their place and nation*. The Apostles were accused, that they meant to *bring this Man's Blood upon* the chief priests [4]; or as [5] *ringleaders of the sect of the Nazarenes, pestilent fellows and movers of sedition, turning the world upside down, setters up of another king; troublers of the city; commanding things unlawful for Romans to practice; setters forth of strange gods; turning away much people;* endangering not men's craft only, but the honor of their gods; *evil doers*. Truth is against the world's ways, so the world is against it. Holy zeal hates sin, so sinners hate it. It troubles them, so they count it, *one which troubleth Israel* [6]. Tertullian, in a public defence of Christians in the second century, writes, "[7] Truth set out with being herself hated; as soon as she appeared, she is an enemy. As many as are strangers to it, so many are its foes; and the Jews indeed appropriately from their rivalry, the soldiers from their violence, even they of our own household from nature. Each day are we beset, each day betrayed; in our very meetings and assemblies are we mostly surprised." There was no lack of pleas. "[8] A Christian thou deemest a man guilty of every crime, an enemy of the gods, of the Emperors, of law, of morals, of all nature;" "factious," "authors of all public calamities through the anger of the heathen gods," "impious," "atheists," "disloyal," "public enemies." The Jews, in the largest sense of the word *they of their own household*, were ever the deadliest enemies of Christians, the inventors of calumnies, the authors of persecutions. "What other race," says [9] Tertullian, "is the seed-plot of our calumnies?" Then the Acts of the Martyrs tell, how Christians were betrayed by near kinsfolk for private interest, or for revenge, because they would not join in things unlawful. "[10] So many are the instances in daily life, [of the daughter rising against the mother] that we should rather mourn that they are so many, than seek them out."—"I seek no examples, [of those of a man's own househould being his foes] they are too many, that we should have any need of witness." "[11] Yet ought we not, on account of these and like words of Holy Scripture, to be mistrustful or suspicious, or always to presume the worst, but to be cautious and prudent. For Holy Scripture speaketh with reference to times, causes, persons, places." So St. John saith, [12] *Believe not every spirit, but try the spirits, whether they are of God.*

7. *Therefore*, (*And*,) when all these things come to pass and all human help fails, *I*, for my part, *will look unto*, (lit. *on*) *the Lord* God, the Unchangeable. The prophet sets himself, *I*, with emphasis, against the multitude of the ungodly. When all forsake, betray, fail, when [13] *love* is *waxed cold*, and men, in the last days, shall be [14] *lovers of their ownselves*, not *lovers of God*, I,—he does not say, "will trust," but—*will*, "[10] with the eye of the heart contemplating, loving, venerating God most High, and weighing His mercy and justice," *gaze intently* [15] with the devotion of faith toward Him, though I see Him not: yet so too I will rest *in* Him [16] and *on* Him, as the eyes are wont to rest in trust and love and dependence, and as, on the other hand, the Eyes of God [17] *espy into* man and dwell *on* him, never leaving him unbeheld. I will *espy* Him, although from afar, with the eyes

[1] S. Matt. x. 16. 17.
[2] Ib. 21, 35, 36.
[3] S. John xi. 48.
[4] Acts v. 28.
[5] Acts xxiv. 5. xvi. 20, 21. xvii. 6, 7, 18. 1 Pet. ii. 12.
[6] 1 Kings xviii. 17.
[7] Tert. Apol. c. 7. p. 17. Oxf. Tr.
[8] Ib. c. 2. p. 7. O. T. 38. 10. (and note k. Oxf. Tr.) 24, 28, 40, and notes e. f.; ad Scap. c, 2.
[9] Tert. ad Nat. i. 24. "The most atrocious calumnies against the Christians," S. Justin M. says, "were invented and circulated from country to country by the Jews." Apol. i. 49. See also Dial c. Tryph. § 16. 108. c. Cels. vi. 27.
[10] S. Jer.
[11] Dion.
[12] 1 John iv. 1.
[13] S. Matt. xxiv. 12.
[14] 2 Tim. iii. 2, 4.
[15] אֲצַפֶּה, intensive, (as in Ps. v. 4.) "will espy intently," as toward that which can be seen only by intent gazing; and with ב pers. "so as to dwell *upon*."
[16] Comp. Ps. xxv. 15. cxxiii. 1. cxli. 8.
[17] Ps. lxvi. 7.

Before CHRIST cir. 710.

8 ¶ [l] Rejoice not against me, O mine enemy: [m] when I fall, I shall arise; when I sit in darkness, [n] the LORD *shall be* a light unto me.

l Prov. 24. 17. Lam. 4. 21.
m Ps. 37. 24. Prov. 24. 16.
n Ps. 27. 1.

of the soul, as a watchman, (the word is the same,) looking for His Coming and announcing it to others; and until He comes, *I will wait* [*I would wait*] with trust unbroken by any troubles or delay, as Job saith, [1] *Though He slay me, yet will I put my trust in Him.* The word is almost appropriated to a longing waiting for God[2]. *For the God of my salvation.* This too became a wonted title of God[3], a title, speaking of past deliverances, as well as of confidence and of hope. Deliverance and salvation are bound up with God, and that, in man's personal experience. It is not only, "Saviour God," but "God, *my* Saviour," Thou who hast been, art, and wilt be, my God, my saving God. It is a prelude to the name of Jesus, our Redeeming God. *The Lord will hear me.* His purpose of waiting on God he had expressed wistfully. *I would wait*[4]; for man's longing trust must be upheld by God. Of God's mercy he speaks confidently, *the Lord will hear me*, He, Who is ever "more ready to hear than we to pray." He has no doubts, but, as Abraham said, [5] *the Lord will provide*, so he, *The Lord will hear me.* So, when Jehoshaphat prayed, [6] *We have no might against this great company that cometh against us, neither know we what to do, but our eyes* are *upon Thee;* God answered by the prophet, *Be not afraid nor dismayed by reason of this great multitude; for the battle is not yours, but God's.* Micah unites with himself all the faithful as one, "in the unity of the spirit," wherein all are one band, looking, waiting, praying for His Coming in His kingdom. "[7] God is our only refuge and asylum in things desperate, and rejoices to help in them, in order to shew His supreme Power and Goodness especially to those who believe, hope, and ask it. Therefore all mistrust and despondency is then to be supremely avoided, and a certain hope and confidence in God is to be elicited. This will call forth the help of God assuredly, yea though it were by miracle, as to Lot in Sodom, to Moses and the people from Pharaoh, to David from Saul, to Hezekiah from Sennacherib, to the Maccabees from Antiochus. This our proverbs express[8], how God aids, when there is least sign of it."

8. *Rejoice not against me, O mine enemy.* The Prophet still more makes himself one with the people, not only as looking for God, but in penitence, as Daniel bewails [9] *his own sins and the sins of his people.* The *enemy* is Babylon and *Edom*[10]; and then, in all times, (since this was written for all times, and the relations of the people of God and of its enemies are the same,) whosoever, whether devils or evil men, rejoice over the falls of God's people. *Rejoice not;* for thou hast no real cause; *the triumphing of the ungodly*, and the fall of the godly, [11] *is but for a moment. When I fall, I shall arise;* (lit. *when I have fallen, I have arisen;*) expressing both the certainty and speed of the recovery. To fall[12] and to arise is one. "[13] The fall of infirmity is not grave, if free from the desire of the will. Have the will to rise, He is at hand Who will cause thee to rise." "[14] Though I have sinned, Thou forgivest the sin; though I have fallen, thou raisest up; lest they, who rejoice in the sins of others, should have occasion to exult. For we who have sinned more, have gained more; for Thy grace maketh more blessed than our own innocence."

When I sit in darkness, the Lord shall be a light unto me. "[15] He does not say 'lie,' but *sit;* she was not as one dead, without hope of life, but she sat solitary as a widow, helpless, unable to restore herself, yet waiting for God's time. The darkness of the captivity was lightened by the light of the prophetic grace which shone through Daniel and Ezekiel, and by the faithfulness of the three

[1] Job xiii. 15.

[2] אוחילה לו, as in Ps. xxxviii. 16. xlii. 6, 12, xliii. 5, cxxx. 5, 2 Kings vi. 33, Lam. iii. 24. יחל is almost appropriated to one who so *waiteth* for God. Abs. Hifil, Lam. iii. 21. Pi. Job vi. 11, xiv. 14, Ps. lxxi. 14. יחיל, adj. Lam. iii. 26. and Prop. Name "Waiter" on God, as expressed in יחלאל. Pi. with ל, Ps. xxxi. 25, xxxiii. 22, lxix. 4; with אל, of God, Ps. cxxx. 7, cxxxi. 3; with ל, of the *word* of God, Ps. cxix. 74, 81, 114, 147; of His *mercy*, Ps. xxxiii. 18, cxlvii. 11; of His *judgments*, Ps. cxix. 43; of His *Arm*, Is. li. 5; of His *law*, Is. xlii. 4. Transitively, Ps. cxix. 49. So תוחלת, abs. Pr. x. 28. Lam. iii. 18; with ל, Ps. xxxix. 8.

[3] "God of *my* salvation," (ישעי,) Ps. xviii. 47, (2 Sam. xxii. 47.) xxv. 5, xxvii. 9, Hab. iii. 18. "God, my s." Ps. lxii. 8. "God of our s." Ps. lxv. 6, lxxix. 9, lxxxv. 5. "God of thy s." Is. xvii. 10. "God of his s." Ps. xxiv. 5. "Rock of our s." Ps. xcv. 1.

[4] אוחילה, optat.

[5] Gen. xxii. 8, 14.

[6] 2 Chron. xx. 12, 15.

[7] Lap.

[8] Deus ex machinâ.

[9] Dan. ix. 10.

[10] Obad. 10. 12. Ps. cxxxvii. 7.

[11] Ps. xxx 5.

[12] נפל is used of the fall of a people, Am. v. 2, viii. 14, Is. xxi. 9, Jer. li. 8; of a king and his people, 2 Kings xiv. 10; of many individuals, Is. viii. 15. In Prov. xxiv. 16. it is used of the fall of the righteous, from which he shall rise, in contrast with the stumbling (יכשלו) of the wicked, without recovery.

[13] S. Ambr. in Ps. 37. [38 Eng.] v. 15.

[14] Ib. v. 47.

[15] Mont.

Before CHRIST cir. 710.

9 [o] I will bear the indignation of the LORD, be-
[o] Lam. 3. 39. cause I have sinned against
him, until he plead my
cause, and execute judg-
[p] Ps. 37. 6. ment for me: [p] he will
bring me forth to the light,
and I shall behold his
righteousness.
10 || Then *she that is* mine
enemy shall see *it*, and
[q] shame shall cover her [q] Ps. 35. 26.

Before CHRIST cir. 710.

|| Or, *And thou wilt see her that is mine enemy, and cover her with shame.*

children, and the brightness of Divine glory shed abroad through them, when Nebuchadnezzar proclaimed to all people that their God was [1] *God of gods and Lord of kings*, and that none should [2] *speak anything amiss against Him.* Still more when, at the close of the captivity, they were delivered from sorrow, trouble, bondage, death, to joy, rest, freedom, life. Yet how much more in Christ, (for Whom this deliverance prepared,) when [3] *the people that walked in darkness have seen a great light: they that dwell in the land of the shadow of death, upon them hath the light shined. God is not only our light*, as "[4] restoring us" outwardly "to gladness, freedom, happiness, whereof light is a symbol, as darkness is of sorrow, captivity, adversity, death." Scripture speaks of God, in a directer way, as being Himself our light. [5] *The Lord is my light.* [6] *The Lord shall be unto thee an everlasting light.* He calls Himself, [7] *The light of Israel.* He is our light, by infusing knowledge, joy, heavenly brightness, in any outward lot. He does not say, "after darkness, comes light," but *when I shall sit in darkness*, then, *the Lord is light unto me.* The *sitting in darkness* is the occasion of the light, in that the soul or the people in sorrow turns to Him Who is their light. In their sin, which was so punished, they were turned away from the light.

9. *I will bear the indignation of the Lord, because I have sinned against Him.* This is the temper of all penitents, when stricken by God, or under chastisement from Him. [8] *It is the Lord, let Him do what seemeth Him good.* [9] *So let him curse, because the Lord hath said unto him, curse David. Who shall then say, Wherefore hast thou done so?* [10] *He putteth his mouth in the dust; if so be there may be hope.* The penitent owns the just sentence of God, and, knowing that he deserves far more than God inflicts, is thankful to endure it, until He remove it, *until He plead my cause and execute judgment for me,* i. e. until God Himself think the punishments inflicted, enough, and judge between me and those through whose hands they come. The judgments which God righteously sends, and which man suffers righteously from Him, are unrighteously inflicted by those whose malice He overrules, whether it be that of evil men (as the Assyrian or the Chaldæan or the Edomite) or of Satan. The close of the chastisements of His people is the beginning of the visible punishment of *their* misdeeds, who used amiss the power which God gave them over it. Whence it is said, [11] *Daughter of Babylon, the wasted! blessed he that rewardeth thee as thou hast served us.* But all is of the mercy of God. So He saith, *He shall bring me forth to the light* of His Countenance and His favor and His truth. Micah speaks in the name of those who were penitent, and so were forgiven, and yet, in that they were under punishment, seemed to lie under the wrath of God. For, although God remits at once the eternal penalty of sin, yet we see daily, how punishment pursues the forgiven sinner, even to the end of life. The light of God's love may not, on grounds which He knoweth, shine unchequered upon him. We should not know the blackness of the offence of sin, and should never know the depth of God's mercy, but for our punishment. The indignation of God toward the penitent is an austere form of His love. So then penitents may well say, in every grief or sickness or visitation or disappointment, *I will bear the indignation of the Lord, because I have sinned against Him.* He says, *I shall behold His righteousness,* because they had a righteous cause against man, although not toward God, and God in His just judgment on their enemies shewed Himself as the righteous Judge of the world.

10. *Then* [*And*] she that is *mine enemy shall see it, and shame shall cover her which said unto me, Where is He*[12], He of Whom thou boastest, *the Lord thy God?* The cause of her gladness then is, that the blasphemies of the enemy of God were to cease. This was the bitterest portion of her cup, that they said daily, "*Where is now thy God?* let Him come and save thee;" as though He could not, or as though He loved her not, and she vainly presumed on His help. Even when fallen, it was for *His* sake that she was hated, Who seemed to be overcome in her: as He was hated in His Martyrs, and they asked,

[1] Dan. ii. 47.
[2] Ib. iii. 29.
[3] Is. ix. 2.
[4] Lap.
[5] Ps. xxvii. 1.
[6] Is. lx. 19.
[7] Ib. x. 17.
[8] 1 Sam. iii. 18.
[9] 2 Sam. xvi. 10.
[10] Lam. iii. 29.
[11] Ps. cxxxvii. 8.
[12] אַיּוֹ. The pronoun is inserted emphatically.

Before CHRIST cir. 710.

which said unto me,
[r] Where is the LORD thy
God? [s] mine eyes shall behold her: now † shall she
be trodden down [t] as the
mire of the streets.

[r] Ps. 42. 3, 10. & 79. 10. & 115. 2. Joel 2. 17. [s] ch. 4. 11.

[t] 2 Sam. 22. 43. Zech. 10. 5.

† Heb. *she shall be for a treading down.*

"[1] Where is the God of the Christians?" Now the taunt was closed, and turned back on those who used it. The wheel, which they had turned against her, rolled round on themselves. They who had said, *Let our eye look on Zion*, now were ashamed that their hope had failed. *They* had longed to feed their sight *on* her miseries; Zion had her reverent gladness in *gazing* on [2] *the righteousness of God.* Babylon was trodden down by the Medes and Persians, and they whom she had let captive beheld it. Daniel was in the palace, when Belshazzar was slain.

The soul of one, who has known the chastening of God, cannot but read its own history here. The sinful soul is at once the object of the love of God and hath that about it which God hates. God hates the evil in us, even while He loves us, being, or having been, evil. He forgives, but chastens. His displeasure is the channel of His good-pleasure. Nathan said to David, [3] *The Lord hath put away thy sin*, but also, *the sword shall never depart from thy house.* It is part of His forgiveness to cleanse the soul with a [4] *spirit of burning.* "It seemeth to me," says St. Jerome, "that *Jerusalem* is every soul, which had been the temple of the Lord, and had had the vision of peace and the knowledge of Scripture, and which afterward, overcome by sins, hath fallen captive by its own consent, parting from that which is right in the sight of God, and allowing itself to sink among the pleasures of the world." So then "[5] captive, and tortured, she saith to Babylon, i. e. the confusion of this world and the power of the enemy which ruleth over the world, and sin who lordeth it over her, *Rejoice not against me, O mine enemy; when I fall, I shall arise;*" "[6] from sin by repentance, and from tribulation by the consolation of the Holy Spirit, Who, after weeping, poureth in joy. *For* [7] *the Lord helpeth them that are fallen*, and saith by the Prophet, [8] *Shall they fall and not arise?* and [9], *I have no pleasure in the death of the wicked; but that the wicked turn from his way and live. If I walk in darkness, the Lord is my light!* For although [10] *the rulers of the darkness of this world* have deceived me, and I [11] *sit in darkness and in the shadow of death*, and [12] *my feet stumble upon the dark mountains*, yet [13] *to them who sit in the region and shadow of death, light is sprung up,* and [14] *light shineth in darkness*, and [15] *the Lord is my light, and my salvation; whom then shall I fear?* and I will speak to Him and will say, [16] *Thy word is a lamp unto my feet, and a light unto my path.*" "He draweth me from the darkness of ignorance and from the black night of sin, and giveth a clear view of future bliss, and brighteneth the very inmost soul within." "[6] Even if a mist have come upon me and I have been in darkness, I too shall find the light, i. e. Christ; and the Sun of Righteousness arising on my mind shall make it white." *I will bear* patiently, yet gladly, *the indignation of the Lord*, "[6] all adversity, trial, tribulation, persecution, which can happen in this life;" *because I have sinned against Him*, "and such is the enormity of sin, offered to the Majesty and dishonoring the Holiness of God, and such punishment doth it deserve in the world to come, that if we weigh it well, we shall bear with joy whatever adversity can befall us." "[5] For although for a short time I be out of His Presence, and be [17] *given to an undistinguishing mind*, yet, seeing I suffer this rejection justly, I will bear the judgment, for I am not chastened in vain." [18] *All chastening for the present seemeth not to be joyous but grievous, nevertheless afterward it yieldeth the peaceable fruit of righteousness unto them who are exercised thereby.* "[19] The soul, feeling that it hath sinned, and hath the wounds of sins and is living in dead flesh and needs the cautery, says firmly to the Physician, 'Burn my flesh, cut open my wounds, all my imposthumes. It was my fault, that I was wounded; be it my pain, to endure such sufferings and to regain health.' And the true Physician shews to her, when whole, the cause of His treatment, and that He did rightly what He did. Then after these sufferings, the soul, being brought out of outer darkness, saith, *I shall behold His Righteousness*, and say, [20] *Thou, O Lord, art upright; Righteous are Thy judgments, O God.* But if Christ is [21] *made unto us wisdom and righteousness and sanctification and redemption*, he who, after the indignation of God, saith that he shall *see His Righteousness*, promiseth to himself the sight of Christ." "[5] Then, having considered in her mind the grace of the righteousness in Christ and the overthrow of sin, the soul, in full possession of herself,

[1] Ep. of Churches of Vienne and Lyons, in Eus. H. E. v. 1 fin.

[2] אראה בצדקתו ver. 9, corresponding to תראינה בה, v. 10.

[3] 2 Sam. xii. 10, 13. [4] Is. iv. 4. [5] S. Cyr.

[6] Dion. [7] Ps. cxlvi. 8. [8] Jer. viii. 4.
[9] Ezek. xxxiii. 11. [10] Eph. vi. 12.
[11] Ps. cvii. 10. [12] Jer. xiii. 16. [13] Is. ix. 2.
[14] S. John i. 5. [15] Ps. xxvii. 1. [16] Ps. cxix. 105.
[17] Rom. i. 28. [18] Heb. xii. 11. [19] S. Jer.
[20] Ps. cxix. 137. [21] 1 Cor. i. 30.

Before CHRIST cir. 710.

11 *In* the day that thy [u]walls are to be built, *in* that day shall the decree be far removed.

u Amos 9. 11, &c.

12 *In* that day *also* [x]he shall come even to thee from Assyria, ‖ and *from* the fortified cities, and from

Before CHRIST cir. 710.

x Is. 11. 16. & 19. 23. &c. & 27. 13. Hos. 11. 11.
‖ Or, *even to*.

---

crieth out, *Mine enemy shall see it, &c.* For, after that Christ came unto us, justifying sinners through faith, the mouth of the ungodly One is stopped, and the Author of sin is put to shame. He hath lost his rule over us, and sin is trodden down, *like mire in the streets*, being subjected to the feet of the saints. But the blotting-out of sin is the Day of Christ." "[1] And, because the end of all punishment is the beginning of good," God saith to the poor, penitent, tossed, soul, "*the walls* of virtues *shall be built up* in thee, and thou shalt be guarded on all sides, and the rule of thine oppressors shall be far removed, and thy King and God shall come unto thee, and *all the ends of the earth shall see the salvation of God.*" "[2] All this shall be most fully seen in the Day of Judgment."

11, 12. On this confession of unworthiness and trust the message of joy bursts in, with the abruptness [3] and conciseness of Hosea or Nahum:

A day to build thy fences; [i. e. cometh ;]
That day, far shall be the *decree;*
That day, and he shall come quite to thee[4];

and there follows, in a longer but still remarkably measured and interrupted cadence[5], the statement of the length and breadth from which the people shall come to her;

Up to and from Assyria and the cities of strong-land [Egypt ;]
Up to and from strong-land and even to river [Euphrates ;]
And sea from sea, and mountain to mountain.

It is not human might or strength which God promises to restore. He had before predicted, that the kingdom of the Messiah should stand, not through earthly strength[6]. He promises the restoration, not of city walls, but of the *fence* of the vineyard[7] of God, which God foretold by Isaiah that He would *break down*[8]. It is a peaceful renewal of her estate under God's protection, like that, with the promise whereof Amos closed his prophecy; [9] *In that day I will raise up the tabernacle of David that is fallen, and close up the breaches thereof.* This *decree*, which he says *shall be far* away, might in itself be the decree either of God or of the enemy[10]. The sense is the same, since the enemy was but the instrument of God. Yet it seems more in accordance with the language of the prophets, that it should be the decree of man. For the decree of God for the destruction of Jerusalem and the captivity of His people was accomplished, held its course, was fulfilled. The destruction, captivity, restoration, were parts of one and the same decree of God, of which the restoration was the last accomplished in time. The restoration was not the removal, but the complete fulfillment, of the decree. He means then probably,

---

[1] S. Jer. [2] Dion.

[3] Hence the omission of the preposition עַד before עָרֵי מָצוֹר and יָם, and of any preposition in the last clause, והר ההר.

[4] The three sentences, which begin with יוֹם, are manifestly each complete in itself.

[5] Ver. 12 is divided into four clauses, of which each consists of four words, and these in pairs;

"Yōm hoo, ve'adeica yabo
leminni asshur, ve'arē mātsōr,
ooleminni matsōr, ve' ad nahar
veyam miyyam, vehar hahar.

[6] v. 9–13.

[7] גָּדֵר is the wall of a vineyard, Num. xxii. 24, Is. v. 5, Ps. lxxx. 13; a wall pushed down, Ps. lxii. 4; one in which a serpent might lurk, Eccl. x. 8; a wall with gaps in it, Ezek. xiii. 5, xxii. 30; the wall of the court of the temple, Ib. xlii. 7; a fence, Ezr. ix. 9. It is no where used of "the wall of a city." גֶּדֶר too is the wall of the court of the temple, Ezek. xlii. 10; the wall of a vineyard, Prov. xxiv. 31. גְּדֵרָה is "a sheepfold," Num. xxxii. 16, 24, 36, 1 Sam. xxiv. 4, Zeph. ii. 6; fences under which locusts lodge, Nah. iii. 17; in the open field, Jer. xlix. 3, Hos. ii. 8. Heb.; fences, Ps. lxxxix. 41. Heb.

[8] Is. v. 5. [9] ix. 11.

[10] חֹק is used chiefly of a "statute" of God, either those positive laws given by Moses, (its common use) or such laws as God has impressed upon the physical world, Job xxvi. 10, xxviii. 26, xxxviii. 10, 33, Prov. viii. 29, Jer. v. 22. xxxi. 35, 6; of the time appointed by God for man's life, Job xiv. 5, 13; a decree of God, Job xxiii. 14, Ps. ii. 7, Zeph. ii. 2; of a portion of food appointed by God, Job xxiii. 12, Prov. xxx. 8, Ezek. xvi. 27; by man, Gen. xlvii. 22, Prov. xxxi. 15; of a statute made by man, Gen. xlvii. 26, 1 Sam. xxx. 25; a custom, Jud. xi. 39, (Plur. Jer. xxxii. 11, Ez. xx. 18.); a task appointed by man, Ex. v. 14. But in all cases the idea of "appointment," is prominent; so that although חֹק expresses the law of God determining the bounds of the sea or the term of man's life, it cannot therefore signify a mere point in space or time. רחק also, with which it is united by alliteration, (probably to fix the words in men's memories.) is not to "expand," but to "be far off." Then also יִרְחַק, corresponding to לִבְנוֹת which implies a future, must itself be a future, not a mere aorist or vivid present. These three observations together exclude such renderings as, "the decree for thy restoration shall be promulged far and wide;" "the decree of God shall not be confined to Babylon but shall extend to other countries." "In that day, the interval is distant:" (Ew.) "the bound set to her will be far off," i. e. Israel shall be enlarged.

Before CHRIST cir. 710.

the fortress even to the river, and from sea to sea, and *from* mountain to mountain.

Before CHRIST cir. 710.

that the *decree* of the enemy, whereby he held her captive, was to remove and *be far* off, not by any agency of her's[1]. The people were to stream to her of themselves. One by one, shall all thy banished, captive, scattered, children be brought *quite* home *unto thee* from all parts of the earth, whither they have been driven, *from Assyria, and from strong-land.* The name *Matsor,* which he gives to Egypt, modifying its ordinary dual name *Mitsraim,* is meant, at once to signify "Egypt[2]" and to mark the strength of the country; as, in fact, "[3] Egypt was on all sides by nature strongly guarded." A country, which was still strong relatively to Judah, would not, of itself, yield up its prey, but held it *straitly;* yet it should have to disgorge it. Isaiah and Hosea prophesied, in like way, the return of Israel and Judah from Assyria and from Egypt[4]. *And from strong-land even to the river* [Euphrates]; the ancient, widest, boundary of the promised land[5]; *and from sea to sea, and from mountain to mountain.* These last are too large to be the real boundaries of the land. If understood geographically, it would by narrowing those which had just been spoken of, from Egypt to the Euphrates. Joel likens the destruction of the Northern army to the perishing of locusts in the two opposite seas, the Dead sea and the Mediterranean[6]; but the Dead sea was not the entire Eastern boundary *of all Israel.* Nor are there any mountains on the South, answering to Mount Libanus on the North. Not the mountains of Edom which lay to the South-East, but *the desert*[7] was the Southern boundary of Judah. In the times too of their greatest prosperity, Edom, Moab, Ammon, Syria, had been subject to them. The rule of the Messiah *from sea to sea* had already been predicted by Solomon[8], enlarging the boundaries of the promised land to the whole compass of the world, *from the sea,* their bound westward, *to* the further encircling *sea* beyond all habitable land, in which, in fact, our continents are large islands[9]. To this, Micah adds a new description, *from mountain to mountain,* including, probably, all subdivisions in our habitable earth, as the words, *sea to sea,* had embraced it as a whole. For, physically and to sight, mountains are the great natural divisions of our earth. Rivers are but a means of transit. The Euphrates and the Nile were the centres of the kingdoms which lay upon them. Each range of mountains, as it rises on the horizon, seems to present an insuperable barrier. No barrier should avail to hinder the inflow to the Gospel. As Isaiah foretold that all obstacles should be removed[10], *every valley shall be exalted, and every mountain and hill shall be made low,* so Micah prophesies, *from mountain to mountain they shall come.*

The words are addressed as a promise and consolation to the Jews, and so, doubtless, the restoration of the Jews to their own land after the captivity is foretold here, as Micah had already foretold it[11]. But is the whole limited to this? He says, with remarkable indefiniteness, *there shall come*[12]. He does not say, *who* "shall come." But he twice sets two opposite boundaries, from which men should come; and, since these boundaries, not being coincident, cannot be predicted of one and the same subject, there must be two distinct incomings. The Jews were to come from those two countries, whither its people were then to be carried captive or would flee. From the boundaries of the world, the world was to come.

Thus Micah embraces in one the prophecies, which are distinct in Isaiah, that not only God's former people should *come from Egypt and Assyria,* but that Egypt and Assyria themselves should be counted as one with Israel[13]; and while, in the first place, the restoration of Israel itself is foretold, there follows that conversion of the world, which Micah had before promised[14], and which was the object of the restoration of Israel. This was fulfilled to Jews and heathen together, when the *dispersed* of the Jews were gathered into one in Christ, *the Son of David* according *to the flesh,* and the Gospel, *beginning at Jerusalem,* was spread abroad among all nations. The promise is thrice repeated, *It is the day,* assuring the truth thereof, as it were, in the Name of the All-Holy Trinity.

[1] This is conveyed by the simple neuter, ירחק, "shall be far off."

[2] As it certainly does in Isaiah at the same date, Is. xix. 6, xxxvii. 25, (2 Kings xix. 24.).

[3] Diod. Sic. i. 31.

[4] Is. xi. 11. xxvii. 13. Hos. xi. 11.

[5] Gen. xv. 18, Ex. xxiii. 31, Deut. i. 7, xi. 24, Jos. i. 4, 1 Kings iv. 21, 24.

[6] Joel ii. 20.

[7] Ex. xxiii. 31, Num. xxxiv. 3, Deut. xi. 24.

[8] Comp. Ps. lxxii. 8. See "Daniel the Prophet," p. 479 sqq.

[9] See Aristot. de mundo c. 3. in "Daniel the Prophet," p. 625. Strabo speaks as though Homer too knew the fact that the sea encircled the land, "hinting at those in East and West, in that they were washed by the Ocean."

[10] Is. xl. 4.

[11] Mic. iv. 10.

[12] יָבוֹא, not, "they shall come;" nor again is it, "he," Israel, "shall come," since they were to come *to* Israel, "there shall come *to thee;*" nor is it an individual, since one person could not come from all these places.

[13] Is. xix. 23–25.

[14] iv. 1–3.

Before CHRIST cir. 710.

13 ‖ Notwithstand-
ing the land shall be desolate because of them that
dwell therein, [y] for the fruit
of their doings.

‖ Or, *After that it hath been.*
y Jer. 21. 14. ch. 3. 12.

14 ¶ ‖ Feed thy people
with thy rod, the flock of
thine heritage, which
dwell solitarily *in* [z] the
wood, in the midst of Car-

Before CHRIST cir. 710.

‖ Or, *Rule.* Ps. 28. 9. ch. 5. 4.
z Is. 37. 24.

13. *Notwithstanding* [*And*] *the land* (i. e. that spoken of, the land of Judah) *shall be desolate*, not through any arbitrary law or the might of her enemies, but through the sins of the people, *because of them that dwell therein, for the fruit of their doings.* Truly "the fruit of *their* doings," what they did to please themselves, of their own minds against God. As they sow, so shall they reap. This sounds almost as a riddle and contradiction beforehand; "the walls built up," "the people gathered in," and "the land desolate." Yet it was all fulfilled in the letter as well as in spirit. Jerusalem was restored; the people was gathered, first from the captivity, then to Christ; and yet the land was again desolate *through the fruit of* their *doings* who rejected Christ, and is so until this day.

The prophet now closes with one earnest prayer [1]; to which he receives a brief answer, that God would shew forth His power anew, as when He first made them His people [2]. On this, he describes vividly the awed submission of the world to *their* God [3], and closes with a thanksgiving of marveling amazement at the greatness and completeness of the forgiving mercy of God [4], ascribing all to His free goodness [5].

14. *Feed Thy people with Thy rod.* The day of final deliverance was still a great way off. There was a weary interval before them of chastisement, suffering, captivity. So Micah lays down his pastoral office by committing his people to Him Who was their true and abiding Shepherd. Who that has had the pastoral office, has not thought, as *the night* drew nigh *in which no man can work*, "what will be after him?" Micah knew and foretold the outline. It was for his people a *passing through the valley of the shadow of death.* Micah then commits them to Him, Who had Himself committed them to him, Who alone could guide them through it. It is a touching parting with his people; a last guidance of those whom he had taught, reproved, rebuked, in vain, to Him the Good Shepherd Who led Israel like a flock. The *rod* is at times the shepherd's staff [6], although more frequently the symbol of chastisement. God's chastisement of His people is an austere form of His love. So He says, [7] *If his children forsake My law, I will visit their offences with a rod and their sin with scourges: nevertheless My loving-kindness will I not utterly take from them.*

The flock of Thine inheritance. So Moses had appealed to God, [8] *Destroy not Thy people and Thine inheritance which Thou hast redeemed through Thy greatness—They are Thy people and Thine inheritance;* and Solomon, in his dedication-prayer, that, on their repentance in their captivity, God would forgive His people, [9] *for they be Thy people and Thine inheritance which Thou broughtest forth out of Egypt;* and Asaph, [10] *O Lord, the heathen are come into Thine inheritance;* and again, [11] *Why doth Thine anger smoke against the sheep of Thy pasture? Remember the tribe of Thine inheritance which Thou hast redeemed;* and Joel, [12] *Spare Thy people and give not Thine heritage to reproach;* and a Psalmist, [13] *They break in pieces Thy people, O Lord, and afflict Thine heritage;* and Isaiah, [14] *Return for thy servants' sake, the tribes of Thine inheritance.* The appeal excludes all merits. Not for any deserts of their's, (for these were but evil,) did the Prophets teach them to pray; but because they were God's property. It was His Name, which would be dishonored in them; it was His work, which would seemingly come to nothing; it was He, Who would be thought powerless to save. Again, it is not God's way, to leave half-done what He has begun. [15] *Jesus, having loved His own which were in the world, loved them unto the end.* God's love in creating us and making us His, is the earnest, if we will, of His everlasting love. We have been the objects of His everlasting thought, of His everlasting love. Though we have forfeited all claim to His love, He has not forfeited the work of His Hands; Jesus has not forfeited the price of His Blood. So holy men have prayed; "[16] I believe that Thou hast redeemed me by Thy Blood: permit not the price of the Ransom to perish." "[17] O Jesus Christ, my only Saviour, let not Thy most bitter Passion and Death be lost or wasted in me, miserable sinner!"

Which dwell solitarily, or *alone.* Micah uses the words of Balaam, when he had been constrained by God to bless Israel. [18] *The people shall dwell alone and shall not be reckoned among the nations.* Moses had repeated them,

[1] v. 14. [2] v. 15. [3] v. 16, 17. [4] v. 18, 19. [5] v. 20.
[6] שבט Lev. xxvii. 32, Ps. xxiii. 4.
[7] Ps. lxxxix. 31, 33. [8] Deut. ix. 26, 29.
[9] 1 Kings viii. 51. [10] Ps. lxxix. 1.
[11] Ps. lxxiv. 1, 2. [12] Joel ii. 17. [13] Ps. xciv. 5.
[14] Is. lxiii. 17. [15] S. John xiii. 1.
[16] Bp. Andrewes Preces quotid. Græc. p. 150. Tracts for the Times, No. 88. p. 66.
[17] Paradise for the Christian Soul. On the Passion c. 5. [18] Num. xxiii. 9

Before CHRIST cir. 710.

mel: let them feed *in* Bashan and Gilead, as in the days of old.

15 [a] According to the days of thy coming out of the land of Egypt will I

[a] Ps. 68. 22. & 78. 12.

[1] *Israel shall dwell in safety alone.* This aloneness among other nations, then, was a blessing, springing from God's being in the midst of them[2], the deeds which He did for them[3], the law which He gave them[4]. So Moses prayed, [5] *Wherein shall it be known here, that I and Thy people have found grace in Thy sight? is it not in that Thou goest with us? So shall we be separated, I and Thy people, from all the people that are on the face of the earth.* It was, then, a separate appeal to God by all His former loving-kindness, whereby He had severed and elected His people for Himself.

In the wood, in the midst of Carmel. God [6] *turneth a fruitful land into barrenness for the wickedness of them that dwell therein. He turneth the wilderness into a standing water and dry ground into watersprings.* Isaiah at the same time used the like image, that [7] *Lebanon shall be turned into a fruitful field* [Carmel], *and the fruitful field* [Carmel] *shall be esteemed as a forest*[8]. The wild forest was to be like the rich domestic exuberance of Carmel[9]. He would say, "Feed Thy people in Babylon, which is to them a wild homeless tract, that it may be to them as their own peaceful Carmel." Without God, all the world is a wilderness; with God, the wilderness is Paradise.

Let them feed in Bashan and Gilead. The former words were a prayer for their restoration. Gilead and Bashan were the great pasture-countries of Palestine[10], "[11] a wide tableland, with undulating downs clothed with rich grass throughout," where the cattle ranged freely. They were the first possessions, which God had bestowed upon Israel; the first, which they forfeited. Micah prays that God, Who protected them in their desolation, would restore and protect them in the green pasture where He placed them. They are a prayer still to *the Good Shepherd* Who *laid* down His *life for His sheep*[12], our Lord Jesus Christ, that He would feed His flock whom He has redeemed, who have been *given* to Him as *an inheritance*[13], *the little flock*[14], to which *it is* the *Father's good pleasure to give the kingdom*, which cleaveth to Him and shall be heirs with Him[15]. "[16] Christ feedeth His own with a rod, guiding them gently, and repressing by gentle fears the tendency of believers to listlessness. He *bruiseth* as *with a rod of Iron*, not them, but the rebellious disobedient and proud, who receive not the faith; believers He instructs and forms tenderly, [17] *feeds them among the lilies*, and leads them into good pastures and rich places, namely the Divinely-inspired Scriptures, making the hidden things thereof clear through the Spirit to those of understanding, that they [18] *may grow up unto Him in all things which is the Head, even Christ*, with minds well-fed and nourished and gladdened with all spiritual delights. But the chosen and elect *dwell solitarily*, being apart from the rest who think only of the things of earth, and give themselves to the pleasures of sense. So then these, having the mind at rest, freed from the vain and abominable tumults, are placed apart as *in a wood* and in a *mountain*. By the *wood* you may understand, the rich and varied and solid instruction (as it were trees and flowers) both in doctrine and life; by the *mountain*, what is high and lofty. For none of the wisdom, accounted of in the Church, is low. They are *fed in Bashan and Gilead, as in the days of old*, rich pastures; for the mind of the holy is beautified, delighting itself in the contemplation of the inspired Scriptures, and filled, as it were, with a certain richness, and shares without stint all excellence in thought or in deed; and that, not for a brief and narrow season, but for ever. For what gladdeneth the flesh falleth therewith and fadeth and hasteth away like a shadow; but the participation of the good things from above and of the Spirit, stretcheth out along endless ages."

15. *According to the days of thy coming out*

[1] Deut. xxxiii. 28. In both cases, as in Micah, שכן is used; as also in Jer. xlix. 31, of Hazor dwelling in security alone. The idiom ישב בדד, "sit alone," is different. It occurs first of the separation of the leper, "he shall sit alone, without the camp shall his dwelling be (מושבו)," Lev. xiii. 46; then of an individual in sorrow, Jer. xv. 17, Lam. iii. 28; and, in one case, of the deserted city personified, Lam. i. 1. [2] Ex. xxxiii. 16, Deut. iv. 7. [3] Ex. xxxiv. 10, Deut. iv. 34. [4] Deut. iv. 8. 33. [5] Ex. xxxiii. 16. [6] Ps. cvii. 34, 5. [7] Is. xxix/17.

[8] והכרמל ליער יחשב. The phrase recurs Is. xxxii. 15, except that the Kethib omits the article, which makes the contrast of יער and כרמל exactly the same as in Micah.

[9] See on Am. i. 2. vol. i. p. 233.

[10] See on Am. i. 3. vol. i. p. 234; iv. 1. p. 280.

[11] Rev. G. H. Palmer in Dr. Stanley Pal. p. 320. See also Porter's Handbook, p. 307 sq. "One can scarcely get over the impression that he is roaming through some English park. The graceful hills, the rich vales, the luxuriant herbage, the bright wild-flowers, the plantations of evergreen oak, pine, and arbutus, now a tangled thicket, and now sparsely scattered over the gentle slope, as if intended to reveal its beauty, the little rivulets fringed with oleander, &c.—such are the features of the mountains of Gilead." p. 310. "The country from *Jerash* to *Wady Gâbes* [Jabesh Gilead] 8 hours, resembles in scenery that from es-Salt to Jerash. We have the thickly wooded hills, the deep and fertile valleys, and the luxuriant pasturage in every part of it." p. 316. See also Thomson, The Land and the Book, i. 304. [12] S. John x. 11, 15. [13] Ps. ii. 8. [14] S. Luke xii. 32. [15] Rom. viii. 17. [16] S. Cyr. [17] Cant. vi. 3. [18] Eph. iv. 15.

Before CHRIST cir. 710.

shew unto him marvelous *things*.
[b] Is. 26. 11.
16 ¶ The nations [b] shall
see and be confounded at
all their might: [c] they shall
lay *their* hand upon *their*
mouth, their ears shall be
deaf.

[c] Job 21. 5. & 29. 9.

Before CHRIST cir. 710.

of the land of Egypt. God answers the prayer, beginning with its closing words [1]. Micah had prayed, "Turn Thy people *like the days of old* [2];" God answers, "*like the days of thy coming* [2] *out of the land of Egypt.*" Micah had said, in the name of his people, [3] *I shall behold His Righteousness;* God answers, *I will make him to behold marvelous things.* The word *marvelous things* [4] was used of God's great marvels in the physical world [5], or the marvelous mercies of His Providence toward individuals or nations [6], and especially of those great miracles, which were accumulated at the deliverance from Egypt [7], and the entrance of the promised land [8] which was its completion. The reference to the Exodus must have led them to think of actual miracles; since, in regard to the Exodus, it is used of nothing else. But there were no miracles at the return from the captivity. [9] *When the Lord turned again the captivity of Zion,* said a Psalmist of the returned people, *we were like them that dream. The Lord hath done great things for us; we are glad.* Great things, but not miraculous. The promise then kept the people looking onward, until He came, [10] *a Prophet mighty in word and deed,* as to Whom St. Peter appealed to the people, that He was [11] *approved of God among you by miracles and wonders and signs, which God did by Him in the midst of you, as ye yourselves also know;* Who gave also to them who believed on Him power to do [12] *greater works than* He *did,* through His own power, *because* He went *to* His *Father;* and when they believed, He *shewed to him,* viz. to the whole people gathered into the One Church, Jew and Gentile, yet more *marvelous things*, things, every way more marvelous and beyond nature than those of old, [13] *the unsearchable riches of Christ, the mystery which from the beginning of the world hath been hid in God.*

16. *The nations shall see.* God had answered, what He would give to His own people, to *see.* Micah takes up the word [14], and says, what effect this sight should have upon the enemies of God and of His people. The world should still continue to be divided between the people of God and their adversaries. Those who are converted pass from the one to the other; but the contrast remains. Assyria, Babylon, Egypt, pass away or become subject to other powers; but the antagonism continues. *The nations* are they, who, at each time, waste, oppress, are arrayed against, the people of God. When the Gospel came into the world, the whole world was arrayed against it [15]. These then, he says, *shall see,* i. e. *the marvelous works* of God, which God should shew His people, *and be ashamed at,* i. e. *because of all their might,* their own might. They put forth their whole might, and it failed them against the *marvelous* might of God. They should array might against might, and *be ashamed* at the failure of *all their might* [16]. The word *all* is very emphatic; it implies that they had put forth *all,* and that *all* had failed them, and proved to be weakness. So the Heathen might was often put to shame and gnashed its teeth, when it could avail nothing against the strength to endure which God gave to His martyrs. Its strength to inflict and to crush was baffled before the hidden might of God's Spirit. *They shall lay their hand upon their mouth,* in token that they were reduced to silence, having no more to say [17]; for He promised, [18] *I will give you a mouth and wis-*

[1] Casp.

[2] כּימֵי עוֹלם ver. 14. כִּימֵי צֵאתְךָ ver. 16. The word עוֹלם is necessarily restrained to time, in that it relates to man's past, and *that,* according to the context, a limited past, the time of their coming out of Egypt. This does not interfere with its use as to eternity. See ab. on Mic. v. 2. p. 67.

[3] ver. 9. Casp.

[4] נִפְלָאוֹת.

[5] Job v. 9, xxxvii. 5, 14.

[6] Ps. ix. 2, xxvi. 7, lxxi. 17, lxxii. 18, &c.

[7] Ex. iii. 20, Jud. vi. 13, Neh. ix. 17, Ps. lxxviii. 4, 11, 32, cv. 2, 5, cvi. 7, 22.

[8] Ex. xxxiv. 10. Of the passage of the Jordan, Jos. iii. 5.

[9] Ps. cxxvi. 1, 3.

[10] S. Luke xxiv. 19.

[11] Acts ii. 22.

[12] S. John xiv. 12.

[13] Eph. iii. 8, 9.

[14] אַרְאֶנּוּ end of ver. 15; יִרְאוּ beg. of ver. 16. Casp.

[15] See ab. p. 92.

[16] This is the force of בּוֹשׁ with מִן. מִן designates, as usual, the cause and source of the shame; and mostly with this aggravation, that they had trusted in it, and it had failed them. See Hos. iv. 19, "*they shall be ashamed because of their sacrifices;* x. 6, *because of their own counsel*" (see on Hos. x. 6. vol. i. p. 10); "They shall be afraid and *ashamed because of Ethiopia, their expectation, and of Egypt, their glory,*" Is. xx. 5; "*because of the oaks, which ye have desired,*" Ib. i. 29; "*thou shalt be ashamed because of Egypt, as thou wast ashamed because of Assyria,*" Jer. ii. 36; "Moab shall be *ashamed because of Chemosh, as the house of Israel was ashamed because of Bethel their confidence,*" Ib. xlviii. 13; add xii. 13. The idiom itself, מִגְּבוּרָתָם בּוֹשִׁים, "*ashamed because of their might,*" occurs in Ezek. xxxii. 30, of the nations, which had perished in war. In a few cases, the idiom is used of the source of shame, where the idea of previous trust in them is less prominent, as in Ezek. xxxvi. 32, Zeph. iii. 11. But here, this is involved in the subject itself, and is illustrated by Ezek. xxxii. 30.

[17] See the use of the idiom in Jud. xviii. 19. Job. xxi. 5, xxix. 9, xl. 4, Prov. xxx. 32.

[18] S. Luke xxi. 15. comp. Acts v. 29.

Before CHRIST cir. 710.

17 They shall lick the [d] dust like a serpent, [e] they shall move out of their holes like || worms of the earth: [f] they shall be afraid of the LORD our God, and shall fear because of thee.

[d] Ps. 72. 9. Is. 49. 23.
[e] Ps. 18. 45.
|| Or, *creeping things.*
[f] Jer. 33. 9.

dom, which all your adversaries shall not be able to gainsay nor resist; and they had to own, [1] *indeed a notable miracle hath been done by them, and we cannot deny it. Their ears shall be deaf;* they shall be silent, as though they had heard nothing, as if they were both dumb and deaf [2]. Yet it seems too that they are wilfully deaf, *shutting their ears* out of envy and hatred, that they might not hear what great things God had done for His people, nor hear the voice of truth and be converted and healed. "[3] The nations and the Emperors of the nations saw, Jews and Gentiles saw, and were ashamed at all their might, because their might, great as it was accounted, upheld by laws and arms, could not overcome the mighty works, which the Good Shepherd did among His people or flock by His rod, i.e. by His power, through weak and despised persons, the aged, or oftentimes even by boys and girls. They were then ashamed at all their might which could only touch the [4] *earthen vessels,* but could not take away the *treasure* which was in them. What shall I say of the wisdom of those same nations? Of this too they were ashamed, as he adds, *They shall put their hands upon their mouths.* For, in comparison with the heavenly wisdom, which spake by them and made their tongues eloquent, dumb was all secular eloquence, owning by its silence that it was convicted and confounded."

17. *They shall lick the dust like a* [*the*] *serpent.* To *lick the dust,* by itself, pictures the extreme humility of persons who cast themselves down to the very earth [5]. To lick it "like *the* serpent" seems rather to represent the condition of those who share the serpent's doom [6], whose lot, viz. earth and things of earth, they had chosen [3]. *They shall move out of their holes,* or, better, *shall tremble,* (i.e. "come tremblingly,") *out of their close places* [7], whether these be *strong places* or *prisons,* as the word, varied in one vowel [8], means. If it be *strong places,* it means, that "[9] the enemies of God's people should, in confusion and tumultuously with fear, leave their strongholds, wherein they thought to be secure, not able to lift themselves up against God and those by Him sent against them." *Like worms of the earth,* lit. *creeping things,* or, as we say, *reptiles* [10], contemptuously. *They shall be afraid of,* or rather *come trembling to, the Lord our God;* it is not said *their,* but *our* God, Who hath *done so great things for us. And shall fear because of* [lit. *from*] *Thee, O* Lord, of Whom they had before said, *Where is the Lord thy God?*

It is doubtful, whether these last words express a "servile fear," whereby a man turns away and flees *from* [11] the person or thing which he fears, or whether they simply describe fear of God [12], the first step toward repentance. In Hosea's words [13], *they shall fear toward the Lord and His goodness,* the addition, *and His goodness,* determines the character of the fear. In Micah, it is not said that the fear brings them into any relation to God. He is not spoken of, as becoming, any how, *their* God, and Micah closes by a thanksgiving, for God's pardoning mercy, not to them but to His people.

And so the Prophet ends, as he began, with the judgments of God; to those who would repent, chastisement, to the impenitent, punishment: "sentencing Samaria, guilty and not repenting [3]," to perpetual captivity; "to Jerusalem, guilty but repenting, promising restoration. So from the beginning of the world did God; so doth He; so shall He unto the end. So did He shew Himself to Cain and Abel, who both, as we all, sinned in Adam. Cain, being impenitent, He wholly cast away; Abel, being penitent," *and through faith offering a better sacrifice than Cain,* and "*bringing forth fruits worthy of repentance,* He accepted." So He hath foreshewn as to the end [14]. "[3] And that we may know how uniformly our Judge so distinguisheth, at the very moment of His own Death while hanging between the two thieves, the one, impenitent and blaspheming, He left; to the other, penitent and confessing, He opened the gate of paradise; and, soon after, leaving the Jewish people unrepentant, He received the repentance of the

[1] Acts iv. 16.
[2] As in Ps. xxxviii. 14, "I was as a man that heareth not, and in whose mouth are no reproofs."
[3] Rup.
[4] 2 Cor. iv. 7.
[5] As in Ps. lxxii. 9. Is. xlix. 23.
[6] Gen. iii. 14, Is. lxv. 25.
[7] So our Version renders the word in Ps. xviii. 45, 2 Sam. xxii. 46.
[8] מַסְגֵּר masc. Is. xxiv. 22, xlii. 7, Ps. cxlii. 8; here and in Ps. xviii. 46, מִסְגֶּרֶת fem.
[9] Poc.
[10] The idiom occurs beside only in Deut. xxxii. 24, with the variation only of עָפָר for אֶרֶץ.
[11] ירא with מן Ps. iii. 7, xxvii. 1, Job v. 21. See Ges. Thes. p. 804.
[12] ירא with מן is used of a fear of God, whereby one is kept from evil. Lev. xix. 14. Yet also generally of fear of God, Ps. xxxiii. 8.
[13] Hos. iii. 5.
[14] S. Matt. xxv.

Before CHRIST cir. 710.

18 [g] Who *is* a God like
unto thee, that [h] pardoneth
iniquity, and passeth by
the transgression of [i] the
remnant of his heritage?
[k] he retaineth not his anger
for ever, because he delighteth *in* mercy.
19 He will turn again,
he will have compassion
upon us; he will subdue
our iniquities; and thou

g Ex. 15. 11.
h Ex. 34. 6, 7. Jer. 50. 20.
i ch. 4. 7. & 5. 3, 7, 8.
k Ps. 103. 9. Is. 57. 16. Jer. 3. 5.

Before CHRIST cir. 710.

Gentiles." Thus the Prophet parts with both out of sight; the people of God, feeding on the rich bounty and abundance of God, and His *marvelous* gifts of grace above and beyond nature, multiplied to them above all the wonders of old time; the enemies of God's people looking on, not to admire, but to be ashamed, not to be healthfully ashamed, but to be wilfully deaf to the voice of God. For, however to *lay the hand on the mouth* might be a token of reverent silence, the *deafness of the ears* can hardly be other than the emblem of hardened obstinacy. What follows, then, seems more like the unwilling creeping-forth into the Presence of God, when they cannot keep away, than conversion. It seems to picture the reprobate, who would not [1] *hear the Voice of the Son of God and live*, but who, in the end, shall be forced to hear it out of their *close places* or *prisons*, i. e. the grave, and come forth in fear, when they shall [2] *say to the mountains, Fall on us; and to the hills, Cover us.* Thus the Prophet brings us to the close of all things, the gladness and joy of God's people, the terror of His enemies, and adds only the song of thanksgiving of all the redeemed.

18. *Who is a God* (and, as the word means, *A Mighty God,*) *like unto Thee?* He saith not, [3] *Who hast made heaven and earth, the sea and all that therein is;* nor, [4] *Who telleth the number of the stars; and calleth them all by their names;* nor, [5] *Who by His strength setteth fast the mountains and is girded about with power;* but Who forgivest! For greater is the work of Redemption than the work of Creation. *That pardoneth,* and *beareth* and *taketh away* also, *and passeth by the transgression of the remnant of His heritage,* i. e. His heritage, which is a remnant still when [6] *the rest are blinded;* and this, not of its merits but of His mercy; since it is not His nature to *retain His anger for ever;* not for anything in them, but *because He delighteth in mercy,* as He saith, [7] *I am merciful, saith the Lord, and I will not keep anger for ever.* [8] *I am He that blotteth out thy transgressions for Mine own sake, and will not remember thy sins.* "[9] For although God for a time is angry with His elect, chastening them mercifully in this life, yet in the end He hath compassion on them, giving them everlasting consolations."

Moses, after the completion of his people's deliverance at the Red Sea, used the like appeal to God, in unmingled joy. Then the thanksgiving ran, [10] *glorious in holiness, awful in praises, doing wonders.* Now, it ran in a more subdued, yet even deeper, tone, taken from God's revelation of Himself after that great transgression on Mount Sinai, [11] *forgiving iniquity and transgression and sin.* With this, Micah identified his own name[12]. This was the one message which he loved above all to proclaim; of this, his own name was the herald to his people in his day. *Who is like the Lord,* the Pardoner of sin, the Redeemer from its guilt, the Subduer of its power? For no false god was ever such a claim made. The heathen gods were symbols of God's workings in nature; they were, at best, representatives of His Government and of His displeasure at sin. But, being the creatures of man's mind, they could not freely pardon, for man dared not ascribe to them the attribute of a freely-pardoning mercy, for which he dared not hope. *Who is a God like to Thee,* mighty, not only to destroy but to pardon? is the wondering thanksgiving of time, the yet greater amazement of eternity, as eternity shall unveil the deep blackness of sin over-against the light of God, and we, seeing God, as He Is, shall see what that Holiness is, against which we sinners sinned. The soul, which is truly penitent, never wearies of the wondering love, *Who is a God like unto Thee?*

19. *He will turn again,* Who seemed to be turned away from us when we were turned away from Him[13]. *He will subdue, or trample under foot,* our worst enemy, *our iniquities,* as He saith, [14] *He shall bruise Satan under your feet shortly.* Hitherto, sinful passions had not rebelled only, but had had the mastery over us. Sin subdued man; it was his lord, a fierce tyrant over him; *he* could not subdue *it.* Holy Scripture says emphatically of man under the law, that he was *sold under sin*[15], a slave under a hard master, oppressed, weighed down, and unable to throw off the bondage. [16] *We have before proved both Jews and Gen-*

1 S. John. v. 25.
2 S. Luke xxiii. 30, Rev. vi. 16.
3 2 Ex. xx. 11.
4 Ps. cxlvii. 4.
5 Ps. lxv. 6.
6 Rom. xi. 7.
7 Jer. iii. 12.
8 Is. xliii. 25.
9 Dion.
10 Ex. xv. 11.
11 נֹשֵׂא עָוֺן וָפֶשַׁע, Ex. xxxiv. 7; Micah, dividing the clauses, inserted עֹבֵר עַל before פשע. Casp.
12 See Introd. to Micah, ab. p. 5.
13 See Jo. ii. 14.
14 Rom. xvi. 20.
15 Ib. vii. 14.
16 Ib. iii. 9.

Before CHRIST cir. 710. will cast all their sins into the depths of the sea.

20 [1]Thou wilt perform the truth to Jacob, *and* the

Before CHRIST cir. 710.

[1] Luke 1. 72, 73.

tiles, that they are all under sin; [1] *the Scripture hath concluded all under sin.* Under the Gospel, God, he says, would subdue sin "under *us*," and make it, as it were, our "footstool[2]." It is a Gospel before the Gospel. God would pardon; and *He*, not *we*, would subdue sin to us. He would bestow, "[3]of sin the double cure, Save us from its guilt and power." [4] *Not I, but the grace of God, which was with me.*

And Thou wilt cast,—not, some ("[5]for it is impious to look for a half-pardon from God") but—*all their sins into the depths*[6] *of the sea,* so that as in the passage of the Red Sea there was not one Egyptian left of those who pursued His people, so neither shall there be one sin, which, through Baptism and on Repentance, shall not through His free mercy be pardoned. As they, which [7] *sank as lead in the mighty waters*, never again rose, so shall the sins, unless revived by us, not rise against us to condemnation, but shall in the Day of Judgment be sunk in the abyss of hell, as if they had never been.

20. *Thou wilt perform the truth to Jacob* and *the mercy to Abraham.* What was free *mercy to Abraham*, became, when God had once promised it, His *truth*. *Abraham* also stands for all those, who in him and his Seed should be blessed, those who were [8] *aliens from the commonwealth of Israel, and strangers from the covenants of promise, having no hope, and without God in the world*, in no covenant or relation with God, as well as those who were the children of the faith; heathen, as well as Jews. *Jacob* represents those who were immediately his children, such of the children of Israel, as were also the true Israel and *children of faithful Abraham.* In both ways the gift to Abraham was *mercy*, to Jacob, *truth*. So also St. Paul saith[9], "Jesus Christ was a Minister of the circumcision for the *truth* of God, to confirm the promises made to the fathers, and that the Gentiles might glorify God for *His mercy*." Yet *mercy and truth*[10], together, *are all the paths of the Lord;* they [11] *met together* in Christ; yea Christ Himself is full of Mercy as well as [12] *Truth:* and woe were it to that soul to whom He were Truth without mercy. "[13]For to be saved, we look not so much to the truth of the Judge as to the mercy of the Redeemer." And *mercy*, in the counsel of God, reacheth wider than *truth;* for *truth* is given to Jacob, the father of one nation, Israel; but mercy to Abraham, [14] *the father of many nations.* Isaac, it may be, is not here mentioned, because all to whom the blessing should come are already spoken of in Jacob and Abraham; in Jacob, all to whom the promise was first made; in Abraham, all nations of the world who should be blessed in his Seed, through the mercy of God overflowing the bounds of that covenant. Isaac is, in his sacrifice, chiefly a type of our Lord Himself.

Which Thou hast sworn unto our fathers. [15] *That by two immutable things, in which it was impossible for God to lie, we might have a strong consolation.*

From the days of old. [16] From eternity, in the counsel of God; in promise, from the foundation of the world, as is said in the hymn of Zacharias[17], *As He spake by the mouth of His holy Prophets, which have been since the world began.* [18]The inspired hymns of the Blessed Virgin Mary and of Zachariah take up the words of the prophet, and shew that they are already fulfilled in Christ, although they shall be more and more fulfilled unto the world's end, as Jew and Gentile are brought into His fold; [19] *He remembering His mercy, as He spake to our fathers, to Abraham and to his seed for ever.* [20] *To perform the mercy promised to our fathers, and to remember His holy covenant, the oath which He sware to our father Abraham that He would grant unto us.*

"I too," St. Jerome subjoins, "sealing the labor of my little work by calling upon the Lord, will say at the close of this tract, *O God, who is like unto Thee?* Take away the iniquity of Thy servant, pass by the sin of my decayed soul, and send not Thine anger upon me, nor rebuke me in Thy indignation; for Thou art full of pity and great are Thy mercies. Return and have mercy upon me; drown mine iniquities, and cast them into the depth of the sea, that the bitterness of sin may perish in the bitter waters. Grant the truth which Thou didst promise to Thy servant Jacob, and the mercy which Thou didst pledge to Abraham Thy friend, and free my

[1] Gal. iii. 22.

[2] כֶּבֶשׁ, "footstool," 2 Chr. ix. 18. (as in Syr. Ch.) from the same root.

[3] Hymn, "Rock of ages."

[4] 1 Cor. xv. 10.

[5] S. Amb. ap. Alb.

[6] מְצוֹלוֹת doubtless is meant to refer back to מְצוֹלוֹת, Ex. xv. 5, and so, to suggest the image of the destruction at the Red Sea, and its completeness.

[7] Ex. xv. 10.
[8] Eph. ii. 12.
[9] Rom. xv. 8, 9.
[10] Ps. xxv. 10.
[11] Ps. lxxxv. 10.
[12] S. John i. 14.
[13] Rup.
[14] Gen. xvii. 5, Rom. iv. 17.
[15] Heb. vi. 18.
[16] Alb.
[17] S. Luke i. 70.
[18] Poc.
[19] S. Luke i. 54, 55.
[20] Ib. 72–74.

INTRODUCTION

TO

THE PROPHET

NAHUM.

THE prophecy of Nahum is both the complement and the counterpart of the book of Jonah. When Moses had asked God to shew him His glory, and God had promised to let him see the outskirts of that glory, and to proclaim the Name of the Lord before him, *the Lord*, we are told, *passed by before him and proclaimed*, [a] *The Lord, the Lord God, merciful and gracious, longsuffering and abundant in goodness and truth, keeping mercy for thousands, forgiving iniquity and transgression and sin, and that will by no means clear* the guilty. God proclaimed at once His mercy and His justice. Those wondrous words echo along the whole of the Old Testament. Moses himself[b], David[c], other Psalmists[d], Jeremiah[e], Daniel[f], Nehemiah[g], plead them to God or rehearse some part of them in thanksgiving. Joel repeated them as a motive to repentance[h]. Upon the repentance of Nineveh, Jonah had recited to God the bright side of that His declaration of Himself, [i] *I knew that Thou art a gracious God and merciful, slow to anger and of great goodness*, repeating to God His words to Moses, and adding, *and repenting of the evil.* Nineveh, as appears from Nahum, had fallen back into the violence of which it had repented. Nahum then, in reference to that declaration of Jonah, begins by setting forth the awful side of the attributes of God. First, in a stately rhythm, which, in the original, reminds us of the gradual Psalms, he enunciates the solemn threefold declaration of the severity of God to those who will be His enemies.

[k] *A jealous God and Avenger is the Lord:*
An Avenger is the Lord, and lord of wrath;
An Avenger is the Lord to His adversaries:
And a Reserver of wrath *to His enemies.*

Then, he too recites that character of mercy recorded by Moses, [l] *The Lord is slow to anger, and great in power.* But anger, although slow, comes, he adds, not the less certainly on the guilty; [l] *and will not at all clear* the guilty. The iniquity is full. As a whole, there is no place more for repentance. Nineveh had had its prophet, and had been spared, and had sunk back into its old sins. The office of Nahum is to pronounce its sentence. That sentence is fixed. [m] *There is no healing of thy bruise.* Nothing is said of its ulterior conversion or restoration. On the contrary, Nahum says, [n] *He will make the place thereof an utter desolation.*

The sins of Nineveh spoken of by Nahum are the same as those from which they had turned at the preaching of Jonah. In Jonah, it is, [o] *the violence of their hands.* Nahum describes Nineveh as [p] *a dwelling of lions, filled with prey and with ravin,* the *feeding-place of young lions, where the lion tore enough for his whelps;* [q] *a city of bloods, full of lies and robbery,* from which *the prey departeth not.*

But, amid this mass of evil, one was eminent, in direct antagonism to God. The character is very peculiar. It is not simply of rebellion against God, or neglect of Him. It is a direct disputing of His Sovereignty. The prophet twice repeats the characteristic expression, *What will ye devise so vehemently* [r]

[a] Ex. xxxiv. 6, 7. [b] Num. xiv. 17, 18.
[c] Ps. lxxxvi. 15, ciii. 8, cxlv. 8.
[d] Ps. cxi. 4, cxii. 4, cxvi. 5. [e] xxxii. 18, 19.
[f] ix. 4. [g] ix. 17. [h] ii. 13. [i] Jon. iv. 2. [k] i. 2.

[l] Ib. 3. [m] iii. 19. [n] i. 8. [o] iii. 8.
[p] Nah. ii. 11, 12. [q] Ib. iii. 1.
[r] Ib. i. 9, מַה־תְּחַשְּׁבוּן. The verb is doubly intensive, both as Piel, and as having the intens. ן.

against the Lord? [s] *devising evil against the Lord;* and adds, *counsellor of evil.* This was exactly the character of Sennacherib, whose wars, like those of his forefathers, (as appears from the cuneiform inscriptions [t],) were religious wars, and who blasphemously compared God to the local deities of the countries, which his forefathers or himself had destroyed [u]. Of this enemy Nahum speaks, as *having* "gone forth;" *out of thee* (Nineveh) *hath gone forth* [x] *one, devising evil against the Lord, a counsellor of Belial.* This was past. Their purpose was inchoate, yet incomplete. God challenges them, [r] *What will ye devise so vehemently against the Lord?* The destruction too is proximate. The prophet answers for God, "[y] *He Himself*, by Himself, *is* already *making an utter end.*" To Jerusalem he turns, "[z] And *now* I will break his yoke from off thee, and will break his bonds asunder." Twice the prophet mentions the device against God; each time he answers it by the prediction of the sudden utter destruction of the enemy, while in the most perfect security. [a] *While they are intertwined as thorns, and swallowed up as their drink, they are devoured as stubble fully dry;* and, [b] *If they be perfect*, unimpaired in their strength, *and thus many, even thus shall they be mown down.* Their destruction was to be, as their numbers, complete. With no previous loss, secure and at ease, a mighty host, in consequence of their prosperity, all were, at one blow, mown down; "*and he* (their king, who *counselled against the Lord*) *shall pass away* and perish. "The abundance of the wool in the fleece is no hindrance to the shears," nor of the grass to the scythe, nor of the Assyrian host to the will of the Lord. After *he*, the chief, had thus *passed away*, Nahum foretells that remarkable death, in connection with the house of his gods; [c] *Out of the house of thy gods I will cut off the graven image and the molten image: I will make thy grave.* There is no natural construction of these words, except, *I will make* it *thy grave* [d]. Judah too was, by the presence of the Assyrian, hindered from going up to worship at Jerusalem. The prophet bids proclaim peace to Jerusalem; *keep thy feasts—for the wicked shall no more pass through thee.* It was then by the presence of the wicked, that they were now hindered from keeping their feasts, which could be kept only at Jerusalem.

The prophecy of Nahum coincides then with that of Isaiah, when Hezekiah prayed against Sennacherib. In the history [e], and in the prophecy of Isaiah, the reproach and blasphemy and rage against God are prominent, as an evil design against God is in Nahum. In Isaiah we have the messengers sent to blaspheme [f]; in Nahum, the promise, that *the voice of thy messengers shall no more be heard.* Isaiah prophesies the fruitlessness of his attempt against Jerusalem [g]; his disgraced return; his violent death in his own land [h]; Nahum prophesies the entire destruction of his army, his own passing away, his grave. Isaiah, in Jerusalem, foretells how the spontaneous fruits of the earth shall be restored to them [i], and so, that they shall have possession of the open corn-country; Nahum, living probably in the country, foretells the free access to Jerusalem, and bids them to [k] *keep* their *feasts*, and *perform* the *vows*, which, in their trouble, they had promised to God. He does not only foretell that they may, but he enjoins them to do it. The words, [l] *the emptiers have emptied them out and marred their vine branches*, may relate to the first expedition of Sennacherib, when, Holy Scripture says, he [m] *came up against all the fenced cities of Judah and took them*, and Hezekiah gave him *thirty talents of gold, and* 300 *talents of silver.* Sennacherib himself says [n], "Hezekiah, king of Judah, who had not submitted to my authority, forty-six of his principal cities, and fortresses and villages depending upon them of which I took no account, I captured, and carried away their spoil. And from these places I captured and carried off as spoil 200,150 people," &c. This must relate to the first expedition, on account of the exact correspondence of the tribute in gold, with a variation in the number of the talents of silver, easily accounted for [o]. In the first invasion Sennacherib relates that he besieged Jerusalem. "[p] Hezekiah himself I shut up in Jerusalem his capital city, like a bird in a cage, building towers round the city to fence him in, and raising banks of earth against the gates, so as to prevent escape." It is perhaps in reference to this, that, in the second invasion, God promises by Isaiah; [q] *He shall not come into this city, and shall not shoot an arrow there; and shall not present shield before it, and shall not cast up bank against it.* Still, in this second invasion also, Holy Scripture relates, that [r] *the king of Assyria sent Rabshakeh from Lachish to Jerusalem unto king Hezekiah with a great army.* Per-

[s] i. 11. [t] See on "Daniel the Prophet," pp. 444, 5.
[u] Is. xxxvi. 18–20, xxxvii. 10–13. [x] i. 11. יָצָא.
[y] i. 9. כָּלָה הוּא עֹשֶׂה. [z] i. 13. ועתה.
[a] i. 10. [b] i. 12. [c] i. 14.
[d] So Chald. Syr. S. Jer. and moderns, as soon as they have no bias, e.g. Ros. Ew. It is not *asah*, but *sim*; i.e. not ποιεῖν, but θεῖναι; not, in our sense, I will "make a grave," but "I will set" or "make" something else, viz. the house of his gods of which Nahum had just spoken, "to be his grave."

[e] 2 Kings xix. 4, 22–28. [f] Is. xxxvii. 4, 23–29.
[g] Ib. 33, 34. [h] Ib. 7.
[i] 2 Kings xix. 29, Is. xxxvii. 30.
[k] Nah. i. 15, ii. 1. [2 Heb.] [l] Ib. ii. 2. [3. Heb.]
[m] 2 Kings xviii. 13, 14, Is. xxxvi. 1.
[n] Dr. Hincks in Layard Nin. and Bab. pp. 143, 4. Sir H. Rawlinson, quoted ib. and Rawl. Bampt. L. p. 141.
[o] See Layard ib. pp. 144, 5. Rawl. B. L. p. 143.
[p] Sir H. Rawl. transl. in B. L. ib. [q] xxxvii. 33.
[r] Ib. xxxvi. 2. 2 Kings xviii. 17.

haps it is in regard to this second expedition, that God says, [s] *Though I have afflicted thee, I will afflict thee no more;* i. e. this second invasion should not desolate her, like that first. Not that God absolutely would not again afflict her, but not now. The yoke of the Assyrian was then broken, until the fresh sins of Manasseh drew down their own punishment.

Nahum then was a prophet for Judah, or for that remnant of Israel, which, after the ten tribes were carried captive, became one with Judah, not in temporal sovereignty, but in the one worship of God. His mention of Basan, Carmel and Lebanon alone, as places lying under the rebuke of God, perhaps implies a special interest in Northern Palestine. Judah may have already become the name for the whole people of God who were left in their own land, since those of the ten tribes who remained had now no separate religious or political existence. The idol-centre of *their* worship was gone into captivity.

With this agrees the old tradition as to the name of the birth-place of Nahum, *the Elkoshite.* "Some think," says St. Jerome [t], "that Elcesæus was the father of Nahum, and, according to the Hebrew tradition, was also a prophet; whereas Elcesi [u] is even to this day a little village in Galilee, small indeed, and scarcely indicating by its ruins the traces of ancient buildings, yet known to the Jews, and pointed out to me too by my guide." The name is a genuine Hebrew name, the *El*, with which it begins, being the name of God, which appears in the names of other towns also, as, El'ale, Eltolad, Elteke, Eltolem. The author of the shortlived Gnostic heresy of the Elcesaites, called Elkesai, ēlkasai, ēlxai, ēlxaios, Elkasaios [u], probably had his name from that same village. Eusebius mentions Elkese, as the place "whence was Nahum the Elkesæan." S. Cyril of Alexandria says, that Elkese was a village somewhere in Judæa.

On the other hand *Alcush*, a town in Mosul, is probably a name of Arabic origin, and is not connected with Nahum by any extant or known writer, earlier than Masius toward the end of the 16th century [x], and an Arabic scribe in 1713 [y]. Neither of these mention the tomb. "The tomb," says Layard [z], "is a simple plaster box, covered with green cloth, and standing at the upper end of a large chamber. The house containing the tomb is a modern building. There are no inscriptions, nor fragments of any antiquity near the place." The place is now reverenced by the Jews, but in the 12th century Benjamin of Tudela [a] supposed his tomb to be at Ain Japhata, South of Babylon. Were anything needed to invalidate statements above 2000 years after the time of Nahum, it might suffice that the Jews, who are the authors of this story, maintain that not Jonah only but Obadiah and Jephthah the Gileadite are also buried at Mosul [b]. Nor were the ten tribes placed there, but "[c] in the cities of the Medes." The name Capernaum, "the village of Nahum," is probably an indication of his residence in Galilee. There is nothing in his language peculiar to the Northern tribes. One very poetic word [d], common to him with the song of Deborah, is not therefore a "provincialism," because it only happens to occur in the rich, varied, language of two prophets of North Palestine. Nor does the occurrence of a foreign title [e] interfere with "purity of diction." It rather belongs to the vividness of his description.

The conquest of No-Ammon or Thebes and the captivity of its inhabitants, of which Nahum speaks, must have been by Assyria itself. Certainly it was not from domestic disturbances [f]; for Nahum says, that the people were carried away captive [g]. Nor was it from the Ethiopians [h]; for Nahum speaks of them, as her allies [i]. Nor from the Carthaginians [j]; for the account of Ammianus [k], that "when first Carthage was beginning to expand itself far and wide, the Punic generals, by an unexpected inroad, subdued the hundred-gated Thebes," is merely a mistaken gloss on a statement of Diodorus, that "[l] Hanno took Hekatompylos by siege;" a city, according to Diodorus himself [m], "in the desert of Libya." Nor was it from the Scythians [n]; for Herodotus, who alone speaks of their maraudings and who manifestly exaggerates them, expressly says, that Psammetichus induced the Scythians by presents not to enter Egypt [o]; and a wandering predatory horde does not besiege or take strongly-fortified towns. There remain then only the Assyrians. Four successive Assyrian Monarchs, Sargon, his son, grandson and great grandson, Sennacherib, Esarhaddon, Asshurbani-pal, from B.C. 718 to about B.C. 657,

[s] Nah. i. 12. [t] Præf. to Nah.
[u] 'Ελκεσαί, 'Ελκασαΐ, (Theod. Hær. Fab. i. 27.) 'Ηλκασαί, (Hippol. Philosoph. ix. 4. &c.) 'Ηλξαί, 'Ηλξαῖος, 'Ελκεσσαῖος, S. Epiph. Hær, xix. 5, xxx. 3, liii. 1. 'Ελκασαῖος or 'Ελκεσαιος, Method. Conviv. in Combef. Nov. Coll. p. 234. A.
[x] Assem. Bibl. Or. i. 525. [y] Ib. iii. 1. 352.
[z] Nin. i. 233. [a] Travels i. 310. ed. Asher.
[b] Niebuhr Voyage en Arabie ii. 289, 90.
[c] 2 Kings xvii. 6.
[d] דהר = דור of the "circling" of the forefeet of the horse in his speed, Nah. iii. 2, Jud. v. 22.

[e] טפסר, doubtless a Ninevite title, probably signifying "noble prince," from טבסר, as Prof. Lee conjectured. Lee denies that it bears in Persian the meaning ascribed to it by Bohlen. Richardson renders *tâbsâr*, "an elevated window;" Vüllers notes, "in others it occurs not." Gesenius was satisfied with no explanation of those before him.
[f] Ewald's theory. [g] iii. 10. [h] Vitringa, Grot
[i] iii. 9. [j] Heeren. [k] xvii.
[l] Excerpt. ex. L. xxiv. T. ii. p. 565.
[m] v. 18. T. i. p. 263.
[n] Gesenius Lit. Zeit. 1841. n. 1. [o] i. 105.

conquered in Egypt[p]. The hostility was first provoked by the encouragement given by Sabacho the Ethiopian (Sab'e[q], in the cuneiform inscriptions, S b k, in Egyptian), the So of Holy Scripture[r], to Hoshea to rebel against Shalmaneser[s]. Sargon, who, according to his own statement, was the king who actually took Samaria[t], led three expeditions of his own against Egypt. In the first, Sargon defeated the Egyptian king in the battle of Raphia[u]; in the second, in his seventh year, he boasts that Pharaoh became his tributary[x]; in a third, which is placed three years later, Ethiopia submitted to him[y]. A seal of Sabaco has been found at Koyunjik, which, as has been conjectured[z], was probably annexed to a treaty. The capture of Ashdod by the Tartan of Sargon, recorded by Isaiah[a], was probably in the second expedition, when Sargon deposed its king Azuri, substituting his brother Akhimit[b]: the rebellion of Ashdod probably occasioned the third expedition, in which as it seems, Isaiah's prophecy was fulfilled, that Egyptians and Ethiopians, young and old, should be carried captive by the king of Assyria. The king of Ashdod, Yaman, is related to have fled to Egypt, which was subject to Merukha or Meroe; and to have been delivered up by the king of Meroe who himself fled to some unnamed desert afar, a march of (it is conjectured) months[c]. The king of Meroe, first, from times the most distant, became tributary. "[d] His forefathers had not" in all that period "sent to the kings my ancestors to ask for peace and to acknowledge the power of Merodach." The fact, that his magnificent palace, "one of the few remains of external decoration," Layard says[e], "with which we are acquainted in Assyrian architecture," "seems" according to Mr. Fergusson[f], "at first sight almost purely Egyptian," implies some lengthened residence in Egypt or some capture of Egyptian artists.

Of Sennacherib, the son of Sargon, Josephus writes, "[g] Berosus, the historian of the Chaldee affairs, mentions the king Sennacherib, and that he reigned over the Assyrians, and that he warred against all Asia and Egypt, saying as follows." The passage of Berosus itself is wanting, whether Josephus neglected to fill it in, or whether it has been subsequently lost; but neither Chaldee nor Egyptian writers record expeditions which were reverses; and although Berosus was a Babylonian, not an Assyrian, yet the document, which he used, must have been Assyrian. In the second expedition of Sennacherib, Rabshakeh, in his message to Hezekiah, says, "[h] *Behold thou trustest upon the staff of this bruised reed, upon Egypt.* The expression is remarkable. He does not speak of Egypt, as a power, weak, frail, failing, but, passively, as *crushed*[i] by another. It is the same word and image which he uses in his prophecy of our Lord, *a bruised reed* (*kaneh ratsuts*) *shall He not break*, i. e. He shall not break that which is already bruised. The word implies, then, that the king of Egypt had already received some decided blow before the second expedition of Sennacherib. The annals of Sennacherib's reign, still preserved in his inscriptions, break off in the eighth of his twenty-two years[k], and do not extend to the time of this second expedition against Hezekiah[l]. Nor does Holy Scripture say, in what year this 2d expedition took place. In this he defeated "[m] the kings of Egypt and the king of Meroe at Altakou [Elteke] and Tamna [Timnatha]."

Sennacherib's son Esarhaddon appears for the time to have subdued Egypt and Ethiopia, and to have held them as kingdoms dependent on himself. "He *acquired* Egypt and the inner parts of Asia," is the brief statement of Abydenus[n]: (i. e. of Berosus.) "He established" (his son relates) "twenty kings, satraps, governors in Egypt[o]," among which can be recognized Necho, (the father of Psammetichus) king of Memphis and Sais; a king of Tanis, or Zoan (now Sân); Natho (or, according to another copy, Sept), Hanes, Sebennytus, Mendes, Bubastis, Siyout or Lycopolis, Chemmis, Tinis, and No. These were all subordinate kings; for so he entitles each separately in the list, although he sums up the whole, "[p] These are the names of the Kings, Pechahs, Satraps who in Egypt obeyed my father who begat me." Tearcho or Tarcho himself, "king of Egypt and Ethiopia[q]," was in like way subject to Esarhaddon. The account of the revolt, which his son Asshur-bani-pal quelled, implies also a fixed settlement in Egypt. The 20 kings were involved in the rebellion through fear of Tarcho, but there is notice of other servants of Esarhaddon who remained faithful and were

[p] See Rawlinson Five Empires ii. 409–486.
[q] Oppert, les rapports de l' Eg. et de l' Ass. p. 12.
[r] סוא. In the LXX, in different MSS. Σωά, Σοβά, Σωβά, Σουβά; in the Complut. Σουά Vulg. Sua. Sir G. Wilkinson in Rawl. Herod. [s] 2 Kings xvii. 4.
[t] Layard, Nin. and Bab. p. 618, Rawl. Herod. i. 472, Five Empires ii. 406.
[u] Rawl. Five Emp. ii. 414. [x] Rawl. Ib. pp. 415, 6.
[y] Rawl. Ib. pp. 416, 7.
[z] Rawl. Herod. i. 473, note 1. [a] xx. 1.
[b] Inscription in Oppert, les rapports de l' Eg. &c. p. 18.
[c] Ib. p. 19. [d] Ib. [e] Nin. and Bab. p. 130.
[f] Palaces of Nineveh and Persepolis restored, p. 223, quoted by Layard Ib. Rawl. Her. i. 474.
[g] Ant. x. 1. 4. [h] 2 Kings xviii. 21.
[i] רצוץ, "quassatum," Vulg. Gesenius says well, "It differs from שבר in this, that רצץ signifies, 'broke, crushed,' without severance of the parts; שבר signifies, 'broke asunder.'"
[k] Rawl. Her. i. 478. [l] See Rawl. i. 479, note 1.
[m] Inscr. in Oppert Rapports pp. 26, 27.
[n] In Eus. Chron. Arm. P. i. c. 9.
[o] Inscr. in Opp. Ib. pp. 51, 53. [p] Ib. p. 58.
[q] Ib. pp. 51, 62, 63.

maltreated by Taracho[r]. Asshur-bani-pal says also, that he strengthened his former garrisons[s]. One expedition of Esarhaddon (probably toward the close of his reign, since he does not mention it in his own annals which extend over eight years) is related by his son Asshur-bani-pal. "[t]He defeated Tirhakah in the lower country, after which, proceeding Southward, he took the city, where the Ethiopian held his court," and assumed the title, "[u]king of the kings of Egypt and conqueror of Ethiopia." On another inscription in a palace built for his son, at Tarbisi, now Sherif-khan, he entitles himself "[x]king of the kings of Egypt, Pathros, Ethiopia." We do not, however, find the addition, which appears to recur upon every conquest of a people not before conquered by Assyria, "which the kings, my fathers, had not subdued." This addition is so regular, that the absence of it, in itself, involves a strong probability of a previous conquest of the country.

The subdual apparently was complete. They revolted at the close of the reign of Esarhaddon (as his son Asshur-bani-pal relates) from fear of Taracho[y] rather than from any wish of their own to regain independence. Asshur-bani-pal accordingly, after the defeat of Taracho, forgave and restored them[z]. Even the second treacherous revolt was out of fear, lest Taracho shall return[a], upon the withdrawal of the Assyrian armies. This second revolt and perhaps a subsequent revolt of Urdamanie[b] a stepson of Taracho, who succeeded him, Asshur-bani-pal seems to have subdued by his lieutenants[c], without any necessity of marching in person against them. Thebes was taken and retaken; but does not appear to have offered any resistance. Taracho, upon his defeat at Memphis, fled to it, and again abandoned it as he had Memphis, and the army of Asshur-bani-pal made a massacre in it[d]. Once more it was taken, when it had been recovered by Urdamanie[e], and then, if the inscriptions are rightly deciphered, strange as it is, the carrying off of men and women from it is mentioned in the midst of that of "great horses and apes." "Silver, gold, metals, stones, treasures of his palace, dyed garments, *berom* and linen, great horses, men, male and female, immense apes —they drew from the midst of the city, and brought as spoils to Nineveh the city of my dominion, and kissed my feet."

All of those kings having been conquerors of Egypt, the captivity of No might equally have taken place under any of them. All of them employed the policy, which Sargon apparently began, of transporting to a distance those whom they had conquered[f]. Yet it is, in itself, more probable, that it was at the earlier than at the later date. It is most in harmony with the relation of Nahum to Isaiah that, in regard to the conquest of Thebes also, Nahum refers to the victory over Egypt and Ethiopia foretold by Isaiah, when Sargon's general, the Tartan, was besieging Ashdod. The object of Isaiah's prophecy was to undeceive Judah in regard to its reliance on Egypt and Ethiopia against Assyria, which was their continual bane, morally, religiously, nationally. But the prophecy goes beyond any mere defeat in battle, or capture of prisoners. It relates to conquest within Egypt itself. For Isaiah says, "[g]the king of Assyria shall lead into captivity Egyptians and Ethiopians, *young and old.*" They are not their choice young men[h], the flower of their army, but those of advanced age and those in their first youth[i], such as are taken captive, only when a population itself is taken captive, either in a marauding expedition, or in the capture of a city. The account of the captivity of No exactly corresponds with this. Nahum says nothing of its permanent subdual, only of the captivity of its inhabitants. But Esarhaddon apparently did not carry the Egyptians captive at all[k]. Every fact given in the Inscriptions looks like a permanent settlement. The establishment of the 20 subordinate kings, in the whole length and breadth of Egypt, implies the continuance of the previous state of things, with the exception of that subordination. No itself appears as one of the cities settled apparently under its native though tributary king[l].

In regard to the fulfillment of prophecy, they who assume as an axiom, or petitio principii, that there can be no prophecy of distant events, have overlooked, that while they think that, by assuming the later date, they bring Nahum's prophecy of the capture of Nineveh nearer to its accomplishment, they remove in the same degree Isaiah's prophecy of the captivity of Egyptians and Ethiopians, young and old, from *its* accomplishment. "Young and old" are not the prisoners of a field of battle; young and old of the Ethiopians would not be in a city of

[r] Inscr. in Opp. p. 64. [s] Ib. pp. 58, 68.
[t] Rawl. 5 Emp. ii. 474, 5.
[u] Ib. 475. He also entitles himself, "king of Assyria, Babylon, Egypt, Meroe and Ethiopia." Oppert Sargonides, p. 53. Rawl. Ib. 484.
[x] Inscript. Oppert Rapp. p. 41.
[y] Ib. p. 58. [z] Ib. [a] Ib. p. 59. [b] p. 77
[c] Ib. 70. where he speaks of *sapite-ya* (שֹׁפְטַי) "my judges" pp. 77, 78. In another inscription, however, Oppert observes that Asshurbanipal speaks, as if he had been there in person. pp. 73–76. It has been observed, long since, that the Assyrian monarchs speak at times of what was done by their generals as done by themselves. This, however, scarcely appears here, where he says "I returned in safety to Nineveh." p. 76.
[d] Ib. 66, 68.
[e] Ib. p. 79. In p. 75 it is said that Urdamanie abandoned No and fled to Kipkip.
[f] See on Am. i. 5, vol. i. p. 240.
[g] Is. xx. 4. [h] בחורים. [i] נערים וזקנים.
[k] Rawl. Ib. 474, 475. [l] Rawl. Ib. p. 485.

lower Egypt. If Isaiah's prophecy was not fulfilled under Sargon or Sennacherib, it must probably have waited for its fulfillment until this last subdual by Asshurbanipal. For the policy of Esarhaddon and also of Asshurbanipal, until repeated rebellions wore his patience, was of settlement, not of deportation. If too the prophecy of Nahum were brought down to the reign of Asshurbanipal, it would be the more stupendous. For the empire was more consolidated. Nahum tells the conqueror, flushed with his own successes and those of his father, that he had himself no more inherent power than the city whose people he had carried captive. Thebes too, like Nineveh, dwelt securely, conquering all, unreached by any ill, sea-girt, as it were, by the mighty river on which she rested. She too was strengthened with countless hosts of her own and of allied people. Yet she fell. Nineveh, the prophet tells her, was no mightier, in herself. Her river was no stronger defence than that sea of fresh water, the Nile; her tributaries would disperse or become her enemies. The Prophet holds up to her the vicissitudes of No-amon, as a mirror to herself. As each death is a renewed witness to man's mortality, so each marvelous reverse of temporal greatness is a witness to the precariousness of other human might. No then was an ensample to Nineveh, although its capture was by the armies of Nineveh. They had been, for centuries, two rivals for power. But the contrast had far more force, when the victory over Egypt was fresh, than after 61 years of alternate conquest and rebellion.

But, anyhow, the state of Nineveh and its empire, as pictured by Nahum, is inconsistent with any times of supposed weakness in the reign of its last king: the state of Judah, with reference to Assyria, corresponds with that under Sennacherib but with none below. They are these. Assyria was in its full unimpaired strength [m]. She still blended those two characters so rarely combined, but actually united in her and subsequently in Babylon, of a great merchant and military people. She had, at once, the prosperity of peace and of war. Lying on a great line of ancient traffic, which bound together East and West, India with Phœnicia, and with Europe through Phœnicia, both East and West poured their treasures into the great capital, which lay as a centre between them, and stretched out its arms, alike to the Indian sea and the Mediterranean. Nahum can compare its merchants only to that which is countless by man, the locusts or the stars of heaven [n]. But amid this prosperity of peace, war also was enriching her. Nineveh was still sending out its messengers (such as was Rabshakeh), the leviers of its tribute, the demanders of submission. It was still one vast lion-lair, its lions still gathering in prey from the whole earth [o], still desolating, continually, unceasingly, in all directions [p], and now, specially, devising evil against God and His people [q]. Upon that people its yoke already pressed, for God promises to break it off from them [r]; the people was *already* afflicted, for God says to it, *Though I have afflicted thee, I will afflict thee no more* [s], viz. by this invader. The solemn feasts of Judah were hindered through the presence of ungodly invaders; Belial, the counsellor of evil spoken of under that name, already passing through her [t]. War was around her, for he promises that one should publish peace upon her mountains [t]. This was the foreground of the picture. This was the exact condition of things at Hezekiah's second invasion, just before the miraculous destruction of his army. Sennacherib's yoke was heavy; for he had exacted from Hezekiah *three hundred talents of silver and thirty talents of gold* [u]; Hezekiah had not [x] *two thousand horsemen;* the *great host* [y] of the Assyrians encircled Jerusalem. They summoned it to surrender on the terms, that they should pay a new tribute, and that Sennacherib, whenever it pleased him, should remove them to Assyria [z].

At no subsequent period were there any events corresponding to this description. Manasseh was carried captive to Babylon by Esarhaddon; but probably this was no formidable or resisted invasion, since the book of Kings passes it over altogether, the Chronicles mention only that the Assyrian generals took Manasseh prisoner in a thicket [a], accordingly not in Jerusalem, and carried him to Babylon. Probably, this took place, in the expedition of Esarhaddon to the West, when he settled in the cities of Samaria people of different nations, his captives [b]. The capture of Manasseh was then, probably, a mere incident in the history. Since he was taken among the thickets, he had probably fled, as Zedekiah did afterward, and was taken in his place of concealment. This was simply personal. No taking of towns is mentioned, no siege, no terror, no exaction of tribute, no carrying away into captivity, except of the single Manasseh. The grounds of his restoration are not mentioned. The Chronicles mention only the religious aspect

[m] i. 12. ii. 12. [n] iii. 16. [o] ii. 12, 13. [p] iii. 19. [q] i. 9, 11. [r] i. 13. [s] i. 12. [t] i. 15. [u] 2 Kings xviii. 14. [x] Ib. 23. [y] Ib. 17. [z] Ib. 31, 32.

[a] 2 Chron. xxxiii. 11. The uniform meaning of לכר is "took, took prisoner;" of חוחים, "thorns;" the singular only, חוח, in one of the two places in Job, is "a hook," in the other it is a "thorn." לכר, which occurs 120 times in the O. T., never means "dragged captive." The meaning ascribed to the words, "bound him with chains," is wholly conjectural. לכר does not mean "bound," nor חוחים "chains."

[b] Ezr. iv. 2, 9, 10.

of his captivity and his restoration, his sin and his repentance. But it seems probable that he was restored by Esarhaddon, upon the same system of policy, on which he planted subjects of his own in Samaria and the country around Zidon, built a new town to take the place of Zidon, and joined in the throne of Edom one, brought up in his own palace. For, when restored, Manasseh was set at full liberty to fortify Jerusalem[c], as Hezekiah had done, and to put "[c] captains of war in all the cities of Judah." This looks as if he was sent back as a trusted tributary of Esarhaddon, and as a frontier-power against Egypt. At least, sixty years afterward, we find Josiah, in the like relation of trust to Nebuchadnezzar, resisting the passage of Pharaoh-Necho. However, the human cause of his restoration must remain uncertain. Yet clearly, in their whole history, there is nothing to correspond to the state of Judæa, as described by Nahum.

A recent critic writes, "[d] Nahum's prophecy *must* have been occasioned by an expedition of mighty enemies against Nineveh. The whole prophecy is grounded on the certain danger, to which Nineveh was given over; only the way in which this visible danger is conceived of, in connection with the eternal truths, is here the properly prophetic." Ewald does not explain how the danger, to which "Nineveh was given over" was *certain*, when it did not happen. The explanation must come to this. Nahum described a siege of Nineveh and its issue, as certain. The description in itself might be either of an actual siege, before the Prophet's eyes, or of one beheld in the Prophet's mind. But obviously no mere man, endowed with mere human knowledge, would have ventured to predict so certainly the fall of such a city as Nineveh, unless it was "given over to certain danger." But according to the axiom received in Ewald's school, Nahum, equally with all other men, could have had only human prescience. Therefore Nahum, prophesying the issue so confidently, must have prophesied when Nineveh was so "given over." The à priori axiom of the school rules its criticism. Meanwhile the admission is incidentally made, that a prophecy so certain, had it related to distant events, was what no man, with mere human knowledge, would venture upon. Ewald accordingly thinks that the prophecy was occasioned by a siege of Phraortes; which siege Nahum expected to be successful; which however failed, so that Nahum was mistaken, although the overthrow which he foretold came to pass afterward! The siege, however, of Nineveh by Phraortes is a mere romance. Herodotus, who alone attributes to Phraortes a war with Assyria, has no hint, that he even approached to Nineveh. He simply relates that Phraortes "subdued Asia, going from one nation to another, until, leading an army against the Assyrians, he perished himself, in the 22d year of his reign, and the greater part of his army." It is not necessary to consider the non-natural expositions, by which the simple descriptions of Nahum were distorted into conformity with this theory, which has no one fact to support it. Herodotus even dwells on the good condition of the Assyrian affairs, although isolated from their revolted allies, and seemingly represents the victory as an easy one. And, according to Herodotus, whose account is the only one we have, Phraortes (even if he ever fought with the Ninevites, and Herodotus' account is not merely the recasting of the history of another Median Frawartish who, according to the Behistun Inscription, claimed the throne of Media against Darius, and perished in battle with him[e]) had only an unorganized army. Herodotus says of Cyaxares, his son, "[f] He is said to have been more warlike far than his forefathers, and he first distributed Asiatics into distinct bands, and separated the spearmen and archers and horsemen from one another, whereas, before, everything had alike mixed into one confused mass." Such an undisciplined horde could have been no formidable enemy for a nation, whom the monuments and their history exhibit as so warlike and so skilled in war as the Assyrians.

Another critic[g], then, seeing the untenableness of this theory, ventures (as he never hesitated at any paradox) to place the prophet Nahum, as an eye-witness of the first siege of Cyaxares.

Herodotus states that Cyaxares, the son of Phraortes, twice besieged Nineveh. First, immediately after his father's death, to avenge it[f]; the second, after the end of the Scythian troubles, when he took it[h]. The capture of Nineveh was in the first year of Nabopolassor B. C. 625. The accession of Cyaxares, according to Herodotus, was B. C. 633. Eight years then only elapsed between his first siege and its capture, and, if it be true, that the siege lasted two years, there was an interval of six years only. But, at this time, the destruction of Nineveh was no longer a subject of joy to Judah. Since the captivity of Manasseh, Judah had had nothing to fear from Assyria; nor do we know of any oppression from it. Holy Scripture mentions none. The Assyrian monuments speak of expeditions against Egypt; but there was no temptation to harass Judah, which stood in the relation of a faithful tributary and an outwork against Egypt, and which, when Nineveh fell, remained in the same relation to its

[c] 2 Chron. xxxiii. 14. [d] Ewald, Proph. i. 349.
[e] In Rawl. i. 409. [f] i. 103.

[g] Hitzig, followed by Davidson, iii. 293.
[h] i. 106.

conquerors, into whose suzerainty it passed, together with the other dependencies of Assyria. The relation of Josiah to Babylon was the continuation of that of Manasseh to Esarhaddon.

The motive of this theory is explained by the words, " With a confidence, which leaves room for no doubt, Nahum expects a siege and an ultimate destruction of Nineveh. The security of his tone, nay that he ventures at all to hope so enormous a revolution of the existing state of things, must find its explanation in the circumstances of the time, out of the then condition of the world; but not till Cyaxares reigned in Media, did things assume an aspect, corresponding to this confidence." It is well that this writer doffs the courteous language, as to the " hopes," " expectations," " inferences from God's justice," and brings the question to the issue, " there is such absolute certainty of tone," that Nahum must have had either a Divine or a human knowledge. He acknowledges the untenableness of any theory which would account for the prophecy of Naḥum on any human knowledge, before Cyaxares was marching against the gates of Nineveh. Would human knowledge have sufficed then? Certainly, from such accounts as we have, Nineveh might still have stood against Cyaxares and its own rebel and traitorous general, but for an unforeseen event which man could not bring about, the swelling of its river.

But, as usual, unbelief fixes itself upon that which is minutest, ignores what is greatest. There are, in Nahum, three remarkable predictions. 1) The sudden destruction of Sennacherib's army and his own remarkable death in the house of his god. 2) The certain, inevitable, capture of Nineveh, and that, not by capitulation or famine, not even by the siege or assault, which is painted so vividly, but the river, which was its protection, becoming the cause of its destruction. 3) Its utter desolation, when captured. The first, men assume to have been the description of events past; the second, the siege, they assume to have been present; and that, when human wisdom could foresee its issue; the third, they generalize. The first is beyond the reach of proof now. It was a witness of the Providence and just judgment of God, to those days, not to our's. A brief survey of the history of the Assyrian Empire will shew, that the second and third predictions were beyond human knowledge.

The Assyrian Empire dated probably from the ninth century before Christ. Such, it has been pointed out, is the concurrent result of the statements of Berosus and Herodotus. Moses, according to the simplest meaning of his words, spake of the foundation of Nineveh as contemporary with that of Babylon. [i] *The beginning of* the *kingdom* of Nimrod, he relates, *was Babel and Erech, and Accad and Calneh, in the land of Shinar. Out of that land went forth Asshur, and builded Nineveh.* Oppressed probably and driven forth by Nimrod, Asshur and his Semitic descendants went forth from the plain of Shinar, the Babylonia of after-ages. Had Moses intended to express (what some have thought), that *Nimrod* " went forth out of that land to Assyria," he would doubtless have used the ordinary style of connected narrative; " [k] *And* he went forth thence." He would probably also have avoided ambiguity, by expressing that Nimrod " went forth *to* Asshur [l]," using a form, which he employs a little later. As it is, Moses has used a mode of speech, by which, in Hebrew, a parenthetic statement would be made, and he has not used the form, which occurs in every line of Hebrew narrative to express a continued history. No one indeed would have doubted that such was the meaning, but that they did not see, how the mention of Asshur, a son of Shem, came to be anticipated in this account of the children of Ham. This is no ground for abandoning the simple construction of the Hebrew. It is but the history, so often repeated in the changes of the world, that the kingdom of Nimrod was founded on the expulsion of the former inhabitants. Nimrod began his kingdom; "Asshur went forth."

It is most probable, from this same brief notice, that Nineveh was, from the first, that aggregate of cities, which it afterward was. Moses says, " [m] And he builded Nineveh and Rehoboth-Ir and Calach and Resen, between Nineveh and Calach; this is that great city [n]." This cannot be understood as said exclusively of Nineveh; since Nineveh was mentioned first in the list of cities, and the mention of the three others had intervened; and, in the second place where it is named, it is only spoken of indirectly and subordinately; it is hardly likely to be said of Resen, of whose unusual size nothing is elsewhere related. It seems more probable, that it is said of the aggregate of cities, that they formed together one great city, the very characteristic of Nineveh, as spoken of in Jonah.

Nineveh itself lay on the Eastern side of the Tigris, opposite to the present Mosul. In later times, among the Syrian writers, Asshur becomes the name for the country, distinct from Mesopotamia and Babylonia [o], from which it was separated by the Tigris,

[i] Gen. x. 10, 11.
[k] וַיֵּצֵא not מִן הָאָרֶץ הַהוּא יָצָא.
[l] אַשּׁוּרָה Gen. xxv. 18.

[m] Gen. x. 11, 12.
[n] הָעִיר הַגְּדֹלָה.
[o] Bar-Hebr. in Tuch de Nino urbe pp. 9, 10.

and bounded on the North by Mount Niphates.

This distinction, however, does not occur until after the extinction of the Assyrian empire. On the contrary, in Genesis, Asshur, in one place, is spoken of as West [p] of the Hiddekel or Tigris, so that it must at that time have comprised Mesopotamia, if not all on this side of the Tigris, i. e. Babylonia. In another place, it is the great border-state of Arabia on the one side, as was Egypt on the other. *The sons of Ishmael,* Moses relates [q], *dwelt from Havilah unto Shur that is before Egypt, as thou goest to Assyria;* i.e. they dwelt on the great caravan-route across the Arabian desert from Egypt to Babylonia. Yet Moses mentions, not Babylon, but Asshur. In Balaam's prophecy [r], Asshur stands for the great Empire, whose seat was at one time at Nineveh, at another at Babylon, which should, centuries afterwards, carry Israel captive.

Without entering into the intricacies of Assyrian or Babylonian history further than is necessary for the immediate object, it seems probable, that the one or other of the sovereigns of these nations had an ascendency over the others, according to his personal character and military energy. Thus, in the time of Abraham, Chedorlaomer king of Elam, in his expedition against the kings of Sodom and Gomorrah, took with him, as subordinate allies, the kings of Shinar, (or Babylon) and Ellasar, as well as *Tidal king of nations,* a king probably of Nomadic tribes. The expedition was to avenge the rebellion of the petty kings in the valley of Siddim against Chedorlaomer, after they had been for twelve years tributary. But, although the expedition closed with the attack on the five kings of Sodom and Gomorrah, Admah, Zeboim, and Zoar, its extent on the East side of the Jordan from Ashteroth Karnaim in Basan to Elparan (perhaps Elath on the Red Sea), and the defeat of the giant tribes, the Rephaim, Zuzim, Emim, Horites, the Amalekites and the Amorites in their several abodes, seems to imply one of those larger combinations against the aggressions of the East, which we meet with in later times [s]. It was no insulated conflict which spread over nearly three degrees of latitude. But it was the king of Elam, not the king of Babylon or of Asshur, who led this expedition; and those other kings, according to the analogy of the expeditions of Eastern monarchs, were probably dependent on him. It has been observed that the inscriptions of a monarch whose name partly coincides with that of Chedorlaomer, viz. Kudurmabuk, or Kudurmapula, shew traces of a Persian influence on the Chaldee characters; but cuneiform decipherers having desponded of identifying those monarchs [t], Chedorlaomer appears as yet only so far connected with Babylon, that its king was a tributary sovereign to him or a vice-king [u] like those of later times, of whom Sennacherib boasts, "Are not my princes altogether kings?"

Assyria, at this time, is not mentioned, and so, since we know of its existence at an earlier period, it probably was independent. Lying far to the North of any of the nations here mentioned, it, from whatever cause or however it may have been engaged, took no share in the war. Subsequently also, down to a date almost contemporary with the Exodus, it has been observed that the name of Asshur does not appear on the Babylonian inscriptions, nor does it swell the titles of the king of Babylon [x]. A little later than the Exodus, however, in the beginning of the 14th century B. C., Asshur and Egypt were already disputing the country which lay between them. The account is Egyptian, and so, of course, only relates the successes of Egypt. Thothmes III, in his fortieth year, according to Mr. Birch, received tribute from a king of Nineveh [y]. In another monument of the same monarch, where the line, following on the name Nineveh, is lost, Thothmes says that he "[z] erected his tablet in Naharaina (Mesopotamia) for the extension of the frontiers of Kami" [Egypt]. Amenophis III, in the same century, represented Asiatic captives [a], with the names of Patana [Padan-Aram], Asuria, Karukamishi [Carchemish"]. "On another column are Saenkar (Shinar), Naharaina, and the Khita (Hittites)." The mention of these contiguous nations strengthens the impression that the details of the interpretation are accurate. All

p Gen. ii. 14. There is no reason, with Keil, to disturb the rendering. קִדְמַת is most naturally rendered *Eastward,* in the other three places; Michmash was E. S. E. of Bethaven (1 Sam. xiii. 5), but was not *over-against* it, being some four miles from it, in a valley. The battle which began at Michmash, *passed over to Bethaven.* (1 Sam. xiv. 23.) The Philistines too were obviously facing Saul who was at Gilgal (1 Sam. xiii. 12). In Ezek. xxxix. 11, the words "*eastward of the sea,*" express that the carcases were outside the promised land. In Gen. iv. 16, Cain was not one to linger *over-against* the lost *Eden.* Probably he went *Eastward,* because then too the stream of population went Westward. In Isaiah vii. 20 the king of Assyria is spoken of as *beyond the river,* i. e. the Euphrates.

q Gen. xxv. 18.

r Num. xxiv. 22.

s Sir H. Rawl. in Rawl. Herod. i. 446.

t "On the one hand the general resemblance of Kudurmapula's legends to those of the ordinary Chaldæan monarchs is unquestionable; on the other hand, it is remarkable that there are peculiarities in the forms of the letters, and even in the elements composing the names upon his bricks which favor his connection with Elam." Sir H. Rawlinson in Rawl. Herod. i. 436.

u Rawl. Five Empires i. 206.

x Ib. p. 447.

y From statistical Tablet of Karnak, quoted by Layard Nin. and Bab. c. xxvi. p. 631, Birch in Archæologia Vol. xxxv. pp. 116–66.

z Ib. p. 630, note 1.

a Ib.

these inscriptions imply that Assyria was independent of Babylon. In one, it is a coordinate power; in the two others, it is a state which had measured its strength with Egypt, under one of its greatest conquerors, though, according to the Egyptian account, it had been worsted.

Another account, which has been thought to be the first instance of the extension of Babylonian authority so far northward, seems to me rather to imply the ancient self-government of Assyria. "[b] A record of Tiglath-pileser I. declares him to have rebuilt a temple in the city of Asshur, which had been taken down 60 years previously, after it had lasted for 641 years from the date of its first foundation by Shamas-Iva, son of Ismi-Dagon." Sir H. Rawlinson thinks that it is probable (although only probable)[c], that this Ismi-Dagon is a king, whose name occurs in the brick-legends of Lower Babylonia. Yet the Ismi-Dagon of the bricks does not bear the title of king of Babylon, but of king of Niffer only [d]: "his son," it is noticed, "does not take the title of king; but of governor of Hur [e]." The name Shamas-Iva nowhere occurs in connection with Babylonia, but it *does* recur, at a later period, as the name of an Assyrian Monarch [f]. Since the names of the Eastern kings so often continue on in the same kingdom, the recurrence of that name, at a later period, makes it even probable, that Shamas-Iva was a native king. There is absolutely nothing to connect his father Ismi-Dagon with the Ismi-Dagon king of Niffer, beyond the name itself, which, being Semitic, may just as well have belonged to a native king of Nineveh as to a king of Lower Babylonia. Nay, there is nothing to shew that Ismi-Dagon was not an Assyrian Monarch who reigned at Niffer; for the name of his father is still unknown; there is no evidence that his father was ever a king, or, if a king, where he reigned. It seems to me in the last degree precarious to assume, without further evidence, the identity of the two kings. It has, further, yet to be shewn that Lower Babylonia had, at that time, an *empire*, as distinct from its own local sovereignty. We know from Holy Scripture of Nimrod's kingdom in Shinar, a province distinct from Elymais, Mesopotamia, Assyria, and probably Chaldæa. In Abraham's time, 1900 B. C., we find again a king of Shinar. Shinar again, it is supposed, appears in Egyptian inscriptions, in the 14th century, B. C.[g]; and, if so, still distinct from Mesopotamia and Assyria. But all this implies a distinct kingdom, not an empire.

Again, were it ever so true, that Shamas-Iva was a son of a king in Lower Babylonia, that he built a temple in Kileh-Shergat, as being its king, and that he was king, as placed there by Ismi-Dagon, this would be no proof of the continual dependence of Assyria upon Babylonia. England did not continue a dependency of France, because conquered by William of Normandy. How was Alexander's empire broken at once! Spain under Charles the V. was under one sovereignty with Austria; Spain with France had, even of late, alike Bourbon kings. A name would, at most, shew an accidental, not a permanent, connection.

But there is, at present, no evidence implying a continued dependence of Assyria upon Babylon. Two facts only have been alleged; 1) that the cuneiform writing of inscriptions at Kileh-Shergat, 40 miles South of Nineveh, has a Babylonian character; 2) that, on those bricks, four names have been found of inferior Satraps.

But 1) the Babylonian character of the inscriptions would show a dependence of civilization, not of empire. Arts flourished early at Babylon, and so the graven character of the Inscriptions too may have been carried to the rougher and warlike North. The garment, worked at Babylon, was, in the 15th century B. C., exported as far as Palestine, and was, for its beauty, the object of Achan's covetousness[h].

2) In regard to the satraps whose names are found on the bricks of Kileh-Shergat, it does not *appear*, that they were tributary to *Babylon* at all; they may, as far as it appears, have been simply inferior officers of the Assyrian empire. Anyhow, the utmost which such a relation to Babylon would evince, if ever so well established, would be a temporary dependence of Kileh-Shergat itself, not of Nineveh or the Assyrian kingdom. Further, the evidence of the duration of the dependency would be as limited at its extent. Four satraps would be no evidence as to this period of 700 years, only a century less than has elapsed since the Norman conquest. The early existence of an Assyrian kingdom has been confirmed by recent cuneiform discoveries, which give the names of 8 Assyrian kings, the earliest of whom is supposed to have reigned about 3½ centuries before the commencement of the Assyrian Empire[i].

The "empire," Herodotus says[k], "Assyria held in Upper Asia for 520 years;" Berosus[l], "for 526 years." The Cuneiform Inscriptions give much the same result. Tiglath-pileser[m], who gives five years' annals of his own victories, mentions his grandfather's grandfather,

[b] Sir H. Rawlinson from the Shergat Cylinders in Rawl. Herod. Ess. vi. i. 433. note 1.
[c] Ib. p. 456. note 5. [d] Ib. p. 437. [e] Ib. § 7.
[f] Sir H. Rawlins., Journ. As. Soc. xvi. P. 1. Ann. Rep. p. xii. sq. Rawl. Herod. i. p. 466.

[g] Mr. Birch in Layard, Nin. and Bab. p. 631.
[h] Josh. vii. 21.
[i] Rawl. 5 Emp. ii. 291; comp. i. 212.
[k] i. 95. [l] Fragm. 11.
[m] Rawl. Her. i. 457.

the 4th king before him, as the king who "first organized the country of Assyria," who "established the troops of Assyria in authority." The expression, "established in authority," if it may be pressed, relates to foreign conquest. If this Tiglath-pileser be the same whom Sennacherib, in the 10th year of his own reign, mentions as having lost his gods to Merodach-ad-akhi, king of Mesopotamia, 418 years before [n], then, since Sennacherib ascended the throne about 703 B.C. [o], we should have B.C. 1112 for the latter part of the reign of Tiglath-pileser I., and counting this and the six preceding reigns at 20 years each [p], should have about 1252 B.C. for the beginning of the Assyrian empire. It has been calculated that if the 526 years, assigned by Berosus to his 45 Assyrian kings, are (as Polyhistor [q] states Berosus to have meant) to be dated back from the accession of Pul who took tribute from Menahem, and so from between B.C. 770 and B.C. 760, they carry back the beginning of the dynasty to about 1290 B.C. If they be counted, (as is perhaps more probable) from the end of the reign of Pul [r], i. e. probably B.C. 747, "the era of Nabonassar," the Empire would commence about 1273 B.C. Herodotus, it has been shewn [s], had much the same date in his mind, when he assigned 520 years to the Assyrian empire in upper Asia, dating back from the revolt of the Medes. For he supposed this revolt to be 179 years anterior to the death of Cyrus B.C. 529 (and so, B.C. 708)+a period of anarchy before the accession of Deioces. Allowing 30 years for this period of anarchy, we have 738 B.C.+520, i. e. 1258 B.C., for the date of the commencement of Assyrian empire according to Herodotus. Thus, the three testimonies would coincide in placing the beginning of that Empire anyhow between 1258 and 1273 B.C.

But this Empire started up full-grown. It was the concentration of energy and power, which had before existed. Herodotus' expression is "rulers of Upper Asia." Tiglath-pileser attributes to his forefather, that he "organized the country," and "established the armies of Assyria in authority." The 2d king of that list takes the title of "ruler over the people of Bel [t]," i. e. Babylonia. The 4th boasts to have reduced "all the lands of the Magian world." Tiglath-pileser I. claims to have conquered large parts of Cappadocia, Syria from Tsukha to Carchemish, Media and Muzr. According to the inscription at Bavian [u], he sustained a reverse, and lost his gods to a king of Mesopotamia, which gods were recovered by Sennacherib from Babylon. Yet this exception the more proves that conquest was the rule. For, had there been subsequent successful invasions of Assyria by Babylonia, the spoils of the 5th century backward would not have been alone recovered or recorded. If the deciphering of the Inscriptions is to be trusted, Nineveh was the capital, even in the days of Tiglath-pileser I. For Sennacherib brought the gods *back*, it is said, and put them in their places, i. e. probably where he himself reigned, at Nineveh. Thence then they were taken in the reign of Tiglath-pileser. Nineveh then was *his* capital also.

Of an earlier portion we have as yet but incidental notices; yet the might of Assyria is attested by the presence of Assyrian names in the Egyptian dynastic lists, whether the dynasties were themselves Assyrian, or whether the names came in through matrimonial alliances between two great nations [x].

With few exceptions, as far as appears from their own annals (and these are in the later times confirmed by Holy Scripture), the Assyrian Empire was, almost whenever we hear of it, one long series of victory and rapine. It is an exception, if any monarch is peaceful, and content to "repair the buildings [y]" in his residence, "leaving no evidence of conquest or greatness." Tiglathi-Nin, father of the warlike Asshur-i-danipal or Sardanapalus, is mentioned only in his son's monument, "[z] among his warlike ancestors, who had carried their arms into the Armenian mountains, and there set up stelæ to commemorate their conquests." Civil wars there were, and revolutions. Conquerors and dynasties came to an untimely end; there was parricide, fratricide; but the tide of war and conquest rolled on. The restless warriors gave no rest. Sardanapalus terms himself, "[a] the conqueror from the upper passage of the Tigris to Lebanon and the great sea, who all countries, from the rising of the sun to the going down thereof, has reduced under his authority." His son, Shalmanubar or Shalmaneser, in his thirty-five years of reign led, in person twenty-three military expeditions. 20,000,16,000, are the

n Dr. Hincks, from Bavian Inscription in Layard Nin. and Bab. pp. 212,3.

o His annals mention that, having expelled Merodach-baladan in the first year of his reign, he set up Belib in Babylon (Hincks in Layard Bab. and Nin. 140, 1); but, in the Canon of Ptolemy, the date of Belib is B. C. 703.

p Rawl. gives this as the average of Assyrian reigns (Five Empires ii. 93.). The whole calculation is his. An interregnum of 20 years, carries the whole back to the date of Berosus 1273 B. C.

q In Euseb. Chron. Arm. pp. 40, 1.

r 2 Kings xv. 19.

s Rawl. Herod. i. 407.

t Rawl. i. 458.

u Layard N. and B. 207-12. 614. Rawl. 459.

x Rawlinson's conjecture. Five Emp. ii. 335. The period is one of "obscurity," as Rawl. says, but that very obscurity forbids our deciding, as he does, that it was one of "extraordinary weakness and depression."

y Asshur-adan-akhi and three following kings. See Rawl. Her. i. 460. The accession of Asshur-adan-akhi was placed by some, referred to by Rawl. Ib., at B. C. 1050, by himself, at B. C. 950, Five Emp. ii. 291.

z Sir H. Rawl. Ib. in Rawl. Her. i. 460, n. 7.

a In Layard N. and B. pp. 361, 2 Rawl. p. 461.

numbers of his enemies left dead upon a field of battle with Benhadad and Hazael [b]. Cappadocia, Pontus, Armenia, Media, Babylonia, Syria, Phœnicia [c], 15 degrees of longitude and 10 of latitude, save where the desert or the sea gave him nothing to conquer, were the range of his repeated expeditions. He circled round Judæa. He thrice defeated Benhadad with his allies (on several occasions, twelve kings of the Hittites). His own army exceeded on occasions 100,000 fighting men. Twice he defeated Hazael. Israel under Jehu, Tyre, Sidon, 24 kings in Pontus, kings of the Hittites, of Chaldæa, 27 kings of Persia are among his tributaries [d]; "the shooting of his arrows struck terror," he says, "as far as the sea" [Indian Ocean]; "he put up his arrows in their quiver at the sea of the setting sun." His son Shamasiva apparently subdued Babylonia, and in the West conquered tribes near Mount Taurus, on the North the countries bordering on Armenia to the South and East, the Medes beyond Mount Zagros, and "[e] the Zimri [f] in upper Luristan." His son Ivalush III. or IV. received undisturbed tribute from the kingdoms which his fathers conquered, and ascribes to his god Asshur the grant of "[g] the kingdom of Babylon to his son." Thus "Assyria with one hand grasped Babylonia; with the other Philistia and Edom; she held Media Proper, S. Armenia, possessed all Upper Syria, including Commagene and Amanus, bore sway over all the whole Syrian coast from Issus to Gaza, and from the coast to the desert." Tiglath-pileser II. and Shalmaneser are known to us as conquerors from Holy Scripture [h]. Tiglath-pileser, we are told from the inscriptions, warred and conquered in Upper Mesopotamia, Armenia, Media, Babylonia, drove into exile a Babylonian prince, destroyed Damascus, took tribute from a Hiram king of Tyre, and from a Queen of the Arabs [h]. And so it continued, until nearly the close of the Monarchy.

The new dynasty which began with Sargon were even greater conquerors than their predecessors. Sargon, in a reign of seventeen or nineteen years, defeated the king of Elam, conquered in Iatbour beyond Elam, reigned from Ras, a dependency on Elam, over Poukoud (Pekod), Phœnicia, Syria, &c. to the river of Egypt, in the far Media to the rising sun, in Scythia, Albania, Parthia, Van, Armenia, Colchis, Tubal to the Moschi: he placed his lieutenants as governors over these countries, and imposed tribute upon them, as upon Assyrians; he, probably, placed Merodach-Baladan on the throne of Babylon, and after 12 years displaced him; he reduced all Chaldæa under his rule; he defeated "Sebech (i. e., probably, So), Sultan of Egypt, so that he was heard of no more;" he received tribute from the Pharaoh of Egypt, from a Queen of Arabia and from Himyar the Sabæan. To him first the king of Meroe paid tribute. He finally captured Samaria: he took Gaza, Kharkar, Arpad and Damascus, Ashdod (which it cost Psammetichus 29 years to reconquer), and Tyre, (which resisted Nebuchadnezzar for 13 years). He added to the Satrapy of Parthia, placed a Satrap or Lieutenant over Commagene and Samaria, Kharkar, Tel-Garimmi, Gamgoum, Ashdod, and a king of his own choice over Albania. He seized 55 walled cities in Armenia, 11, which were held to be "inaccessible fortresses;" and 62 great cities in Commagene; 34 in Media; he laid tribute on the "king of the country of rivers." He removed whole populations at his will; from Samaria, he carried captive its inhabitants, 27,800, and placed them in "cities of the Medes [i];" he removed those of Commagene to Elam; all the great men of the Tibareni, and the inhabitants of unknown cities, to Assyria; Cammanians, whom he had conquered, to Tel-Garimmi, a capital which he rebuilt; others whom he had vanquished in the East he placed in Ashdod: again he placed "Assyrians devoted to his empire" among the Tibareni; inhabitants of cities unknown to us, in Damascus; Chaldæans in Commagene [k]. "[l] The Comukha were removed from the extreme North to Susiana, and Chaldæans were brought from the extreme South to supply their place." "Seven kings of Iatnan, seven days' voyage off in the Western seas, whose names were unknown to the kings" his "fathers, hearing of" his "deeds, came before" him to Babylon with "presents:" as did the king of Asmoun, who dwelt in the midst of the Eastern sea (the Persian gulf). He placed his statue, "writing on it the glory of Asshur his master," in the capital of Van, in Kikisim (Circesium) as also in Cyprus, which he does not name, but where it has been discovered in this century [m]. The Moschian king, with his 3000 towns, who had never submitted to the

[b] Rawl. Ib. 464, 5.

[c] Nimrud Obelisk translated by Dr. Hincks, in Dubl. Univ. Mag. Oct. 1853. pp. 422, 5, 6. Rawl. Her. i. 462.

[d] Dr. Hincks, Athenæum N. 1476. p. 174. Rawl. Ib. Five Emp. ii. 360.

[e] Rawl. Herod. i. 466. Five Emp. ii. 374.

[f] Jer. xxv. 25.

[g] Rawl. Her. i. 467, Five Empires ii. 380.

[h] Rawl. Her. i. 470. [i] 2 Kings xvii. 6, xviii. 11.

[k] The above account of Sargon is taken from Oppert's Inscriptions Assyriennes des Sargonides, p. 19–40, extracted from the Annales de Philosophie Chrétienne T. vi. (5e sêrie). Oppert, p. 8, gives as the meaning of his name, "actual king," "roi de fait." Sargon himself, if Oppert has translated him rightly, gives as its meaning, "righteous prince," (שַׂר־כֵּן) p. 38.

[l] Rawl. 5 Emp. ii. 423. This statement is not in Oppert's Inscriptions.

[m] Now in the Royal Museum at Berlin. Layard, Bab. p. 618.

kings his predecessors, sent his submission and tribute to him.

Sennacherib, the son of Sargon, says of himself, "Assour, the great Lord, has conferred on me sovereignty over the peoples; he has extended my dominion over all those who dwell in the world. From the upper Ocean of the setting sun to the lower Ocean of the rising sun, I reduced under my power all who carried aloft their head." He defeated Merodach Baladan and the king of Elam together[n]; took in one expedition, "[n] 79 great strong cities of the Chaldæans and 820 small towns;" he took prisoners by hundreds of thousands; 200,150 in his first expedition against Hezekiah, from 44 great walled cities which he took and little villages innumerable[o]; 208,000 from the Nabathæans and Hagarenes[p]: he employed on his great buildings 360,000 men, gathered from Chaldæa and Aramæa, from Cilicia and Armenia[q]; he conquered populations in the North, which "had of old not submitted to the kings my brothers[r]," annexed them to the prefecture of Arrapachitis and set up his image[r]; he received tribute from the governor of Khararat[r], wasted the 2 residence-cities, 34 smaller cities of Ispahara king of Albania, joining a part of the territory to Assyria, and calling its city, Ilhinzas, the city of Sennacherib[s]; he reduced countries of "Media, whose names the kings his brothers had not heard[s]; he set a king, Toubaal, over the great and little Sidon, Sarepta, Achzib, Acco, Betzitti, Mahalliba; the kings of Moab, Edom, Bet-Amman, Avvad, Ashdod, submitted to him[t]; he defeated an "innumerable host" of Egyptians at Altakou[u] [Elteke]; sons of the king of Egypt fell into his hands; he captured Ascalon, Bene-Barak, Joppa, Hazor[u]; put back at Amgarron [Migron] the expelled king Padi, who had been surrendered to Hezekiah[x]; gave portions of the territory of Hezekiah to the kings of Ashdod, Migron, Gaza[y]; he drove Merodach-baladan again to Elam, captured his brothers, wasted his cities, and placed his own eldest son, Assurnadin, on the throne of Babylon[z]; took seven impregnable cities of the Toukharri, placed like birds' nests on the mountains of Nipour[z]; conquered the king of Oukkou in Dayi, among mountains which none of his ancestors had penetrated; took Oukkou and 33 other cities[a]; attached Elam, "crossing" the Persian gulf "in Syrian vessels[a];" capturing the men, and destroying the cities[b]; in another campaign, he garrisoned, with prisoner-warriors of his own, cities in Elam which his father had lost[c]; destroyed 34 large cities and others innumerable of Elam[c]. His account of his reign closes with a great defeat of Elam, whom the escaped Souzoub had hired with the treasures of the temples of Babylon, and of 17 rebel tribes or cities, at Khalouli, and their entire subdual[d]. He repelled some Greeks in Cilicia, set up his image there, with a record of his deeds, and built Tarsus, on the model of Babylon[e]. It has been noticed, what a "keen appreciation of the merits of a locality[f]" his selection of its site evinced. The destruction of his army of 185,000 men, at the word of God, might well deter him from again challenging the Almighty; but we have seen, in the wars of Napoleon I., that such losses do not break the power of an empire. It was no vain boast of Sennacherib, that he had *gathered all the earth, and carried captive the gods of the nations.* The boast was true; the application alone was impious. God owned in him the instrument which He had formed, *the rod of His anger.* He condemned him, only because *the axe boasted itself against Him Who hewed therewith.* Victorious, except when he fought against God, and employed by God to *tread down the people as the mire of the streets*[g], Sennacherib was cut off as God foretold, but left his kingdom to a victorious son.

His son, Esarhaddon, takes titles, yet more lofty than those of Sennacherib. He calls himself, "[h] King of Assyria, Vicar of Babylon, King of the Sumirs and Accads, King of Egypt, Meroe and Cush, who reigned from sunrising to sun-set, unequalled in the imposition of tributes." In Armenia, he killed Adrammelech[i], his half-brother, one of his father's murderers, who fled to Armenia, probably to dispute thence his father's crown. In every direction he carried his conquests further than his powerful father[k]. He speaks of conquests in the far Media, "[l] where none of the kings, our fathers," had conquered, whose kings bore well-known Persian names[m].

They and their subjects were carried off to Assyria. Others, who "[n] had not conspired against the kings my fathers and the land of Assyria, and whose territories my fathers had not conquered," submitted voluntarily in terror, paid tribute and received Assyrian governors. In the West, he pursued by sea a king of Sidon who rebelled, divided the Syrians in strange countries, and placed

[n] Oppert Sarg. p. 41.
[o] Ib. p. 45. [p] Layard Bab. p. 141.
[q] Rawl. Her. i. 476. [r] Opp. pp. 42, 3. [s] Ib. p. 43.
[t] pp. 43, 4. [u] p. 44. [x] pp. 44, 5. [y] p. 45.
[z] p. 46. [a] p. 47. [b] pp. 47, 8. [c] pp. 48.
[d] pp. 49–51.
[e] Polyhist. in Eus. Chr. i. c. 5. Abyden. ib. c. 9.
[f] Rawl. 5 Emp. ii. 456.
[g] Is. x. 5–15, xxxvi. 18–20. [h] Oppert p. 53.

[i] Abyden. in Eus. Chron. Arm. p. 53.
[k] The murder then of Sennacherib was no sign of the decadence of the empire, but one of the common fruits of the polygamy of Eastern monarchs.
[l] Oppert pp. 56, 7. [m] Sitirparna and Iparna.
[n] Ib. Two of the names again, Rawl. observes (5 Emp. ii. 473), are Aryan, Zanasana and Ramatiya; a 3d is Arpis.

mountaineers, whom his bow had subdued in the East, with a governor, in a castle of Esarhaddon which he built in Syria. He warred successfully in Cilicia, Khoubousna, and destroyed 10 large cities of the Tibareni and carried their people captive; trod down the country of Masnaki, transported rebels of Van; he established on the Southern shore that son of Merodach-baladan who submitted to him, removing the brother who trusted in Elam, himself reigned in Babylon[o], whither he carried Manasseh[p]. He reconquered "the city of Adoumou (Edom), (the city of the power of the Arabs,) which Sennacherib had conquered, and carried off its people to Assyria;" he named as Queen of the Arabs, Tabouya, born in his palace; put the son of Hazael on his father's throne. An expedition to "[q] a far country to the bounds of the earth beyond the desert," Bazi (Buz), reached by traversing 140 farsakhs (?) of sandy desert, then 20 farsakhs (?) of fertile land and a stony region, Khazi (Uz), looks like an expedition across Arabia, and, if so, was unparalleled except by Nushirvan. Some of the other names are Arabic. Anyhow, it was a country, whither none of his predecessors had gone; he killed 8 kings, carried off their subjects and spoils. He conquered the Gomboulou in their marshes. Twelve kings on the coast of Syria whom he recounts by name, (Ba'lou king of Tyre, Manasseh king of Judah, and those of Edom, Maan, Gaza, Ascalon, Amgarron, Byblos, Aradus, Ousimouroun, Bet-Ammon, Ashdod) and 10 kings of Yatnan in the sea (Cyprus),—Ægisthus (Ikistousi), King of Idalion (Idial), Pythagoras (Pitagóura) K. of Citium (Kitthim), Ki—,K. of Salamis (Silhimmi), Ittodagon ("Dagon is with him," Itoudagon), K. of Paphos (Pappa), Euryalus (Irieli), K. of Soli (Sillou), Damasou, K. of Curium (Kuri,) Ounagousou, K. of Limenion (Limini), Roumizu, K. of Tamassus (Tamizzi,) Damutsi of Amti-Khadasti, Puhali of Aphrodisium (Oupridissa)[r],—held their rule from him.

The names of the countries, from which he brought those whom he settled in Samaria, attest alike his strength and the then weakness of two of the nations, which afterward concurred to overthrow his empire. The colonists, according to their own letters to Artaxerxes[s], comprehended, among others, *Babylonians; Archevites* i. e. inhabitants of Erech, mentioned in Genesis[t], as, together with Babel, part of the beginning of the kingdom of Nimrod; *Susanchites*, i. e. inhabitants of Susiana or Chusistan; *Dehavites, Daans* in Herodotus[u], one of the wandering Persian tribes, whose name (Taia) still exists[x]; *Elamites*[y], or the dwellers on the Persian gulf, bordering on Susiana; *Apharsites* or the Persians in their original abode in Paraça, Paraiç, now Farsistan. It seems also probable that the *Apharsachites*[z] are those more known to us as Sacæ or Scythians, whom Esarhaddon says that he conquered[a]; and that the *Apharsachthites* (with the same word *Aphar* prefixed) are the Sittaceni on the Caspian. The *Dinaites* and the *Tarphelites* are as yet unidentified, unless the Tarpetes[b] of the Palus Mæotis near the Sittaceni, or the Tapiri [c] in Media be a corruption of the name. The Samaritan settlers add, *And the rest of the nations, whom the great and noble Asnapper carried captive, and settled in the cities of Samaria and the rest on this side the river.* Under this general term, they include the Mesopotamian settlers brought from Avvah and Sepharvaim, and those from Hamath[d], probably wishing to insist to the Persian Monarch on their Persian, Median, or Babylonian descent. They attest at the same time that their forefathers were not willingly removed but *transported, carried into exile*[e], and accordingly that Esarhaddon, in whose reign they were removed, had power in all these countries. The condensation also of settlers from twelve nations in so small a space as the cities of Samaria (analogous as it is to the dispersion of the Jews over so many provinces of their captors) illustrates the policy of these transportations, and the strength which they gave to the empire. Nations were blended together among those foreign to them, with no common bond except their relation to their conqueror. A check on those around them, and themselves held in check by them, they had no common home to which to return, no interest to serve by rebelling. Esarhaddon built 36 temples in Assyria by the labor of foreign slaves, his captives, who worshiped his gods[f].

This collection of people of twelve nations in the cities of Samaria represents moreover one portion only of the conquests of Esarhaddon, and, for the most part, that furthest from Judæa. For the principle of the policy was to remove them far from their own land. Ethiopian and Egyptian captives would be placed, not here whence they could easily return, but, like Israel in the cities of the Medes, whence they could find no escape.

The son of Esarhaddon, Asshurbanipal [g] II., yet further enlarged and consolidated

[o] Babyl. tablet in Rawl. Her. i. 482.
[p] 2 Chr. xxxiii. 11.
[q] Oppert p. 56. Rawl. 5 Emp. ii. 470, 1. Oppert does not identify the names of distances.
[r] Rawl. Herod. i. 483, 4. 5 Emp. ii. 483, Oppert p. 58.
[s] Ezr. iv. 9. [t] Gen. x. 10. [u] i. 125.
[x] Ritter Erdk. vii. 668. [y] Is. xxi. 2, xxii. 6.
[z] Ezr. v. 6. Rawl. Journ. of Asiat. Soc. xv. p. 164.
[a] Rawl. Her. i. 481. [b] Strabo xl. 2. 8. 11.
[c] Id. xl. 8. and 13. 2. [d] 2 Kgs xvii. 24.
[e] הִגְלִי Ezr. iv. 10.
[f] Assyr. texts p. 16, Oppert p. 57, Rawl. 5 Emp. ii. 482.
[g] Or Asordanes, Layard Nin. and B. p. 452.

the conquests of his conquering father. His expeditions into Egypt have been already dwelt upon; his victories were easy, complete. Tirhaka, himself a great conqueror, fled into unknown deserts beyond reach of pursuits. His step-son Urdaminie attempted to recover his kingdom, was defeated at once, fled and his capital was taken. In Asia, he took away the king of Tyre, who offended him; made conquests beyond Mt. Taurus, where his fathers had never been [h]; received an embassy from Gyges; attached to Assyria a tract of Minni or Persarmenia, took the capital of Minni; took Shushan [i] and Badaca, slew their kings, united Susiana to Babylonia; subdued anew Edom, Moab, Kedar, the Nabathæans; received the submission of the king of Urarda, Ararat [k]. While Assyria was extended wider than before, its old enemies were more incorporated with it, or, at least, more subdued; it was more at one within itself. Egypt, the great rival Empire, had tried to shake off the yoke, but was subdued; no people in Syria or the valley of the Euphrates stirred itself; the whole tract within the Taurus, once so rife with enemies, lay hushed under his rule: hushed were the Hittites, Hamathites, the Syrians of Damascus, the Tibareni who had once held their own against his father; war was only at the very extremities, in Minni or Edom, and that, rather chastisement than war; Babylon was a tranquil portion of his empire, except during the temporary rebellion of the brother, whom he had placed over it, and whom he pardoned. His death, amid the tranquil promotion of literature [l], when he had no more enemies to conquer or rebels to chasten, left his empire at the zenith of its power, some 22 years before its destruction. *Calno* had become, as Sennacherib boasted [m], *like Carchemish; Hamath like Arpad; Samaria as Damascus.* He [n] *had removed the bounds of the people* and *gathered all the earth, as one gathereth eggs, left* by the parent bird, undefended even by its impotent love. There was not a cloud on the horizon, not a token whence the whirlwind would come. The bas-reliefs attest, that neither the energy nor the cruelty of the Assyrians were diminished [o].

Of those twenty-two years, we have nothing reliable except their close. There was probably nothing to relate. There would not be anything, if Asshurbanipal had consolidated his empire, as he seems to have done, and if his son and successor inherited his father's later tastes, and was free from the thirst of boundless conquest, which had characterized the earlier rulers of Assyria. Anyhow, we know nothing authentic. The invasion of Assyria by Phraortes, which Herodotus relates, is held, on good grounds, to be a later history of a rebellion against Darius Hystaspes, adapted to times before the Medes became one nation [p]. There was no reason why it should not have been recorded, had it taken place, since it is admitted to have been a total defeat, in which Phraortes lost his life [q]. The invasion of the Scythians, which is to have stopped the siege of Nineveh under Cyaxares, was reported in a manifestly exaggerated form to Herodotus. The 28 years, during which Herodotus relates the Scythian rule to have lasted [r], is longer than the whole of the reign of the last king of Assyria; and yet, according to Herodotus, is to have been interposed between the two sieges of Cyaxares. And as its empire gave no sign of decay, so far as we can trace its history within 22 years before its destruction, so, with the like rapidity, did the empire rise, which was to destroy it. The account which Herodotus received, that the Medians had thrown off the yoke of Assyria before Deioces [s], is in direct contradiction to the Assyrian inscriptions. This was, they state, the time, not of the revolt, but of the conquest of Media. They are confirmed by Holy Scripture, which says that the Assyrian king [Sargon] placed *in the cities of the Medes* [t] his Israelitish captives. The utmost, which Herodotus ascribes to Deioces however, is, that he consolidated the six Median tribes and built a capital, Agbatana [u]. It is an union of wild hordes into one people, held together for the time by the will of one man and by their weariness of mutual oppressions. Even according to their accounts, Cyaxares (about B. C. 633, i. e. 8 years before the fall of Nineveh) first organized the Median army; the Greeks, in the time of Æschylus, believed Cyaxares to have been the first of the Median kings [x]; rebels in Media and Sagartia claimed the Median throne against Darius, as descended from Cyaxares, as the founder of the Monarchy [y].

Further, the subsequent history supports the account of Abydenus against Herodotus, that not the Medes, but the rebel general of the last Monarch of Nineveh was, with his Babylonian troops, the chief author of the destruction of Nineveh. The chief share of the spoil, where no motives of refined policy intervene, falls to the strongest, who had chief portion in the victory. "The Medes," says Herodotus, "took Nineveh, and conquered all Assyria, except the Babylonian

h Rawl. remarks that the names are new.
i The name is spelt as in Daniel.
k Rawl. 5 Emp. ii. 484–93.
l Ib. 495, 6.
m Is. x. 9.
n Ib. 13, 14.
o See plates in Layard Nin. and B. pp. 457, 8. Rawl. 5 Emp. iii. 504, and Layard Monuments Ser. 2. Pl. 47, 49. quoted Ib.
p Rawl. Herod. i. 408, 9.
q Herod. i. 402.
r Ib. 106.
s i. 95, 6.
t 2 Kgs xvii. 6.
u Her. i. 101.
x Persæ 761–4.
y Behistun Inscr., quoted by Rawl. Her. i. 409.

portion [z]." But Babylon was no spared province, escaping with its independence as a gain. Babylonia, not Media, succeeded to the Southern and Western dominions of the Assyrian empire, and the place, where Nineveh had stood, Cyaxares retaining the North. This was a friendly arrangement, since subsequently too we find a Babylonian prince in the expedition of Cyaxares against Asia Minor, and Medians assisting Nebuchadnezzar against the king of Egypt [a]. Abydenus represents the Babylonians and Medes, as equal [b], but exhibits the rebel general, as the author of the attack. "[c] After him [Sardanapal], Sarac held the empire of Assyria, who, being informed of a horde of mingled troops which were coming against him from the sea, sent Busalossor [Nebopalassar] general of his army, to Babylon. But he, having determined to revolt, betrothed to his son, Nebuchodrossor, Amuhea, daughter of Asdahag, prince of the Medes, and soon made a rapid attack on Nineveh. King Sarac, when he knew the whole, set the palace Evorita on fire. Then Nebuchodrossor, attaining to the empire, encircled Babylon with strong walls."

The "horde of mingled troops" "from the sea" were probably those same Susians and Elymæans, whom the Assyrians had, in successive reigns, defeated. If the account of Herodotus were true, the father of the Median Monarch had perished in conflict with Assyria. The grandfather of the Assyrian Monarch had himself reigned in Babylon. Assyria ruled Babylon by viceroys to the end. It has been noticed that Nahum mentions no *one* enemy who should destroy Nineveh. True, for no one enemy did destroy her.

Even now its fall is unexplained. The conquests of its Monarchs had not been the victories of talented individuals. They were a race of world-wide conquerors. In the whole history, of which we have the annals, they are always on the aggressive. They exacted tribute where they willed. The tide of time bore them on in their conquests. Their latest conquests were the most distant. Egypt, her early rival, had been subdued by her. The powers, which did destroy her, had no common bond of interest. They were united, for one reign, not by natural interests, but, as far as we see, by the ambition of two individuals. These crushed, at once and for ever, the empire which for so many centuries had been the ravager of the world. But who could have foreseen such a combination and such results, save God, in Whose hands are human wills and the fate of empires?

The fiery empire of conquerors sank like a tropic sun. Its wrath had burned, unassuaged, "from" (in their own words) "the rising to the setting sun." No gathering cloud had tempered its heat or allayed its violence. Just ere it set, in those last hours of its course, it seemed, as if in its meridian. Its bloodstained disk cast its last glowing rays on that field of carnage in Susiana; then, without a twilight, it sank beneath those stormy waves, so strangely raised, at once and for ever. All, at once, was night. It knew no morrow.

Its fall is inexplicable still. It may have accelerated its own destruction by concentrating the fierce Chaldees at Babylon. It was weakened by the revolt of its own general, and with him the defection of an army. Still, in those days, the city of 1200 towers, each 200 feet high, its ordinary wall 100 feet high and of such breadth, that three chariots could drive on it abreast [d], could not be taken by mounds, except by some most gigantic army with patience inexhaustible. Famine could not reduce a city, which, in its 60 miles in circumference, enclosed, like Babylon, space for [e] *much cattle*, and which could, within its walls, grow corn enough for its population of 600,000. With its perennial supply of provision, it might have laughed to scorn a more formidable foe than the Medes, Elamites and Babylonians, unaccustomed to sieges, except in as far as any had fought in its armies, while the Ninevites possessed the hereditary skill of centuries. Babylon, smaller than Nineveh [f], was at rest amidst the siege of the more powerful grandson of Cyaxares. Cyrus could only take it by stratagem; Darius Hystaspes, by treachery. Then, every Ninevite was a warrior. Their descendants, the Curds, are still among the fiercest and most warlike people of Asia. The bas-reliefs, which bear internal evidence of truth, exhibit a wonderful blending of indomitable strength of will, recklessness of suffering, inherent physical energy, unimpaired by self-indulgence. A German writer on art says [g], "You recognize a strong thickset race, of very powerful frame, yet inclined to corpulence, a very peculiar blending of energy and luxury.—The general impression of the figures, whether men, women or eunuchs, has uniformly something earnest and imposing." An English writer says still more vividly; "[h] All the figures indicate great physical development, animal propensities very strongly marked, a calm, settled ferocity, a perfect nonchalance amidst the most terrible scenes; no change of feature takes place, whether the individual is inflict-

[z] i. 106.
[a] Rawl. Herod. i. 415, 6.
[b] Conf. Tobit xiv. 15. "Before he died, he heard of the destruction of Nineveh, which was taken by Nabuchonosor and Ahasuerus."
[c] Euseb. Chron. P. 1. c. 9.
[d] Diod. Sic. ii. 3.
[e] Jon. iv. 11.
[f] Strabo xvi. p. 757.
[g] Kugler Kunst-Geschichte, (2) p. 75, 6. in Strauss Nahum p. li.
[h] Edwards in Kitto Scr. Lands. pp. 50, 1.

ing or experiencing horrid sufferings.—The pictures are very remarkable as indicating the entire absence of higher mental and moral qualities: and the exuberance of brutal parts of man's nature. At the same time there is not wanting a certain consciousness of dignity and of inherent power. There is a tranquil energy and fixed determination, which will not allow the beholder to feel any contempt of those stern warriors."

How then could it fall? The prophecy of Nahum describes, with terrible vividness, a siege; the rousing of its king from a torpor of indolence; [i] *he remembereth his nobles;* the orderly advance, the confused preparations for defence; and then, when expectation is strung, and we see besiegers and besieged prepared for the last decisive strife, there is a sudden pause. No human strength overthrows the city. [k] *The gates of the rivers shall be opened, and the palace shall be dissolved. And it is decreed, she shall be led away captive.* Her captivity follows on the opening of *the gates of the rivers.* The *rivers,* ordinarily her strength, were also her weakness. The annals of Sennacherib relate, how he repaired a palace which had been undermined by the Tigris. "[l] The small palace, which was become very ruinous in every part, because the river Tigris, during 16 years, had undermined and ravaged it, [I repaired.]" Dionysius, the Jacobite Patriarch, relates how in his own time, A. D. 763, "[m] the Tigris, overflowing, laid waste all the towns around it, and especially Mosul" (opposite to Nineveh). Barhebræus, in four different years, mentions the destruction of houses in Bagdad through the overflow of the Tigris [n]. He mentions also a city-wall, overthrown by an inundation, so that 3000 men were drowned in their houses [o]. Ives relates [p]; "The Bishop (of Babylon) remembers that" about 1733 "the Euphrates and Tigris were so overflown, that the whole country between them appeared as one large sea. Over all the plain between Bagdad and Hilla, people could pass only in boats. The water flowed quite up to the glacis, the ditch was full, the city also overflown, and the foundation of most of the buildings hurt; 300 houses were entirely destroyed. To prevent as much as possible" the recurrence of such a calamity, "the Turks now face the foundation-wall of their houses with a composition of charcoal, ashes, and Demar (bitumen)." "The river Khosar," also, which would be swollen by the same causes as the Tigris, "entered the city," says Ainsworth [q], "by an aperture in the walls on the East side, which appears to have formed part of the original plan and to have been protected by a gateway and walls, vestiges of which still remain." "The Khausser," says Mr. Rich [r], "is generally drawn off for irrigating the cotton-plantations in the alluvial ground of the river; when it is much overflowed, it discharges itself into the Tigris above the bridge." "[s] The Khausser now [Dec. 1. after "very heavy tropical rain,"] discharges itself direct into the Tigris, and brings an immense body of water." "[t] After rain, it becomes an impetuous torrent, overflowing its banks and carrying all before it." "[s] The stone-bridge was carried away one night by the violence of the Khausser, on a sudden inundation." On a lesser swelling of the river,—"[s] the water-wheels were removed" in precaution "and the bridge of boats opened." Cazwini, the Arabic geographer, speaks of "[u] the rivers of Nineveh."

Ctesias, being a writer of suspected authority, cannot safely be alleged in proof of the fulfillment of prophecy. Yet in this case his account, as it is in exact conformity with the obvious meaning of the prophecy of Nahum, so it solves a real difficulty, how Nineveh, so defended, could have fallen. It seems certain that the account of the siege taken from him by Diodorus, is that of the last siege. It has been remarked [x] that the only event of the siege, known from any other source, viz. that the last Assyrian king, when he had learned the combination of the Medes and Babylonians against him, set fire to his palace, is related also by Ctesias. Ctesias has also the same fact, that the Babylonian revolt was recent; the name of the revolted general in Ctesias, Belisis, is the latter half of that given to him by Abydenus [y], Nebopalassar, omitting only the name of the god, Nebo. The rest of the history is in itself probable. The success of the Assyrian monarch at first against the combined armies, and the consequent revelry, are that same blending of fierceness and sensuality which is stamped on all the Assyrian sculptures, continued to the end. The rest of his relation, which, on account of the facts of nature, which we know, but which, since they are gathered from sources so various, Ctesias probably did not know, is, in itself, probable, accounts for what is unaccounted for, and corresponds with the words of Nahum. It is, "[a] Sardanapalus, seeing the whole kingdom in the greatest danger, sent his three sons and two daughters with much wealth to Paphlagonia to Cotta the Governor, being the best-disposed of his subjects. He himself

[i] ii. 5, [6.] [k] ii. 6, 7. [7, 8.] [l] Assyr. Texts p. 7.
[m] Ass. B. O. ii. 112.
[n] A. D. 835, 941, 988, 1211. Barh. p. 153, 188, 204. 500.
[o] Ib. p. 153. [p] Voyage 1773. p. 281.
[q] Travels ii. 142, 3. [r] Koordistan, ii. 56.
[s] Ib. p. 64. [t] Layard N. and B. p. 77.

[u] Quoted by Tuch de Nino urbe p. 24.
[x] Rawl. Her. i. 413.
[y] Abydenus in Euseb. Chron. Can. P. i. c. 9.
[a] In Diod. Sic. ii. 27. Diodorus has "Euphrates" in conformity with his own error, that Nineveh was on that river.

sent by messengers to all his subjects for forces, and prepared what was needed for the siege. He had an oracle handed down from his forefathers, that no one should take Nineveh, unless the river first became an enemy to the city. Conceiving that this never would be, he held to his hopes, purposing to abide the siege and awaited the armies to be sent by his subjects." "The rebels, elated by their successes, set themselves to the siege, but on account of the strength of the walls, could in no wise injure those in the city." "But these had great abundance of all necessaries through the foresight of the king. The siege then being prolonged for two years, they pressed upon it; assaulting the walls and cutting off those therein from any exit into the country." "In the 3d year, the river, swollen by continuous and violent rains, inundated a part of the city and overthrew 20 stadia of the wall. Then the king, thinking that the oracle was fulfilled, and that the river was plainly an enemy to the city, despaired of safety. And, not to fall into the enemy's hands, he made an exceeding great pile in the palace, heaped up there all the gold and silver and the royal apparel, and having shut up his concubines and eunuchs in the house formed in the midst of the pile, consumed himself and all the royalties with them all. The rebels, hearing that Sardanapalus had perished, possessed themselves of the city, entering by the broken part of the wall."

Yet Nahum had also prophesied[b]; "the fire shall devour thy bars;" "fortify thy strong holds, there shall the fire devour thee;" "I will burn her chariots in the smoke," and all the ruins of Nineveh still speak from beneath the earth where they lie interred, that, overthrown as they have been by some gigantic power, fire consumed them within. "[c]The palaces of Khorsabad (Dur Sarjina) and Nimrud shew equal traces of fire with those of Koyunjik." "[d]The recent excavations have shown that fire was a great instrument in the destruction of the Nineveh palaces. Calcined alabaster, masses of charred wood and charcoal, colossal statues split through with the heat, are met with in parts of the Ninevite mounds, and attest the veracity of prophecy." "[e]It is evident from the ruins that Khorsabad and Nimroud were sacked, and set on fire."

Yet this does not exhaust the fullness of the prophecy. Nahum not only foretold the destruction of Nineveh, that it should *be empty, void, waste, there is no healing of thy bruise*, but in emphatic words, that its site also should be a desolation. *With an overrunning flood He shall make the place thereof* (*mekomah*) *a desolation*[f]. This was then new in the history of the world. Cities have remained, while empires passed away. Rome, Constantinople, Athens, Damascus, Alexandria, Venice, abide, although their political might is extinct. No or Thebes itself survived its capture by Sargon and a yet later loss of its inhabitants nearly two centuries, when the more fatal conquest of Cambyses, and perhaps the rise of Memphis perpetuated its destruction. Nahum foretells emphatically as to Nineveh, "He will make the *place* thereof an utter consumption." Not only would God destroy the then Nineveh; but the very *place* or site thereof should be an utter desolation. There was, *then*, no instance of so great a city passing away. Such had not been Babylonian, Assyrian, Egyptian policy. It had become an established policy in Sennacherib's time to remove populations, not to destroy cities. And these two policies were incompatible. For a conqueror who would remove populations must have, whither to remove them. Nineveh itself had conquered Babylon and Shushan, and the cities of the Medes; but had placed her own lieutenants in them. The mere destruction of such a city as Nineveh was "contrary to experience." Even later than this, Babylon, notwithstanding its rebellions, was spared by its first conqueror, and survived to be the grave of its second, Alexander. Xenophon describes Nineveh under the name of Mespila (of which Mosul has been supposed to be a corruption) "[g]a wall, void, large, lying against the city—the basement was of polished stone, full of shells, its width 50 feet, its height 50 feet. Thereon was built a wall of brick, its breadth 50 feet, the height 100; the circuit was six farsangs," i. e. 22½ miles. The shell remained; the tumult of life was gone. Its protecting bulwarks remained; all, which they protected, had disappeared. They had forgotten already on the spot what it had been or by whom it had perished. "[h]The Medes inhabited it formerly. It was said that Media, a king's wife, had fled thither, when the Medes were losing their power through the Persians. The Persian king, besieging this city, could not take it, either by time or force; but Zeus made the inhabitants senseless, and so it was taken." A little later, Alexander marched over its site to gain the world, not knowing that a world-empire, like that which he gave his life to found, was buried under

[b] iii. 13. 15. ii. 13.

[c] Rawl. Herod. i. 488. quoting "Layard Nin. and its Remains i. 12, 27, 40. &c. Nin. and B. [of Nimrud] p. 351, 357, 359. &c. Vaux Nineveh and Persepolis p. 196–8. Botta Letter ii. p. 26. iii. p. 41. &c." "They [the human-headed bulls] had suffered, *like all those previously discovered*, from the fire." Lay. N. and B. p. 71. "It [the wall] contained some fragments of calcined sculptured alabaster, evidently detached from the bas-reliefs on the walls." Ib. Add of Kouyunjik, Athenæum N. 900. Jan. 25. 1845. p. 99.

[d] Rawl. Ib. note 2.

[e] Bonomi p. 461.

[f] i. 8.

[g] Anab. iii. 4. 10.

[h] Ib. 12.

which the line by the Euphrates passed. If, for the downward course, the Euphrates itself was navigable, yet the desert presented a difficulty for caravans returning upward from the Persian gulf. Arrian, who mentions the two lines of travel, says that Alexander, having crossed the Euphrates at Thapsacus, chose the less direct line by the Tigris, as [x]having a better supply of all things, food for his cavalry, and a less scorching heat. The mention of Haran (afterward Carrhæ) Canneh, and Asshur in Ezekiel, (in one verse [y]) seems to indicate the continuation of the same line of commerce with Tyre, which must have existed from præhistoric times (i. e. from times of which we have no definite historic account), since there is no ground to question the statement of the Phœnicians themselves in Herodotus, that they had come from the Erythræan sea [z], i. e. the Persian gulf. The later hindrances to the navigation of the Tigris by the great dams (probably for irrigation), were of Persian date; but they could have had no great effect on the actual commerce; since for the greater part of the upward course on the Tigris line, this also must, on account of the rapidity of the river, have been by caravans. The route was still used in the middle ages [a]. "[b] The ancient road and the modern one on the upper Tigris follow, pretty nearly throughout, the same line, it being determined by the physical necessities of the soil." In the 16th century, "[c] from the head of the Persian gulf two commercial lines existed: by one of them goods were carried some way up the Euphrates, and then by land to Bir, Aleppo, Iskenderun. By the other they followed the Tigris to Baghdad and were carried by Diyar-Bekr and Sivas to Terabuzum." [But Mosul was necessarily on the way from Baghdad to Diyar Bekr]. Mosul still lies on the line of commerce, from the Persian gulf, Basrah, Baghdad, Mosul, Mardin, Diyar-Bekr to Iskenderun, the port of Aleppo [d], or Trebizond [Tarabuzum [e].] It still carries on some commerce with Kurdistan and other provinces [f] [beside Diyar-Bekr and Baghdad]. Col. Chesney, in 1850, advocated the advantages of extending the line of commerce by British stations at Diyar-Bekr and Mardin, in addition to and connection with those already existing at Baghdad and Mosul [g]. There is, in fact, a consent as to this. Layard writes; "[h] The only impediment between the Syrian coast and the Tigris and Euphrates in any part of their course, arises from the want of proper security. The navigation of the Persian gulf is, at all times, open and safe; and a glance at the map will shew that a line through the Mediterranean, the port of Suedia, Aleppo, *Mosul*, Baghdad, Busrah, and the Indian Ocean to Bombay is as direct as can well be desired. With those prospects, and with the incalculable advantages, which a flourishing commerce and a safe and speedy transit through, perhaps, the richest portions of its dominions would confer upon the Turkish empire, it would seem that more than Eastern apathy is shown in not taking some steps, tending to restore security to the country watered by the Tigris and Euphrates." Ainsworth suggests a still wider commerce, of which Mosul might be the centre. "[i] With a tranquil state of the surrounding country, Mosul presents mercantile advantages of no common order.—There are several roads open to Persia, across the mountains; a transit from five to seven days, and by which, considering the short distance and good roads from Mosul to Iskenderun, British manufactures might be distributed into the heart of Persia, in a time and at an expense, which the line of Trebizond Erzrum and Tabriz, that of Bushire and Baghdad, or the Russian line of Astrakhan Bakhu and Mazenderan can never rival."

But although marked out by these advantages for continuance, even when its power was gone, Nineveh was to perish and it perished. Nor ought it to be alleged, that in other cases too, "if the position of the old capital was deemed, from political or commercial reasons, more advantageous than any other, the population was settled in its neighborhood, as at Delhi, not amidst its ruins." For 1) there was, at the time of Nahum, no experience of the destruction of any such great city as Nineveh; 2) In the case of conquest, the capital of the conquering empire became, ipso facto, the capital of the whole; but this did not, in itself, involve

[x] Arr. iii. 7. The same route was recommended to Antiochus the great. Polyb. v. 51. Xenophon relates the scarcity in Cyrus' advancing army on the Euphrates route, Anab. i. 5. 4; Dio Cassius, the sufferings of the army of Severus L. lxxv. 1.

[y] Ezek. xxvii. 23. "Eden" (Ib.) is mentioned in 2 Kgs xix. 12, as having been subdued by Assyria; "Chalmad" remains unknown; "Sheba" spread too widely to the desert of Syria (Strabo xvi. 4. 21.) for the mention of it to be any indication that those thus grouped together did not live in the same direction.

[z] Herod. i. 1. vii. 89 and Rawlinson ib. and App. to B. vii. Essay 2. T. iv. pp. 241. sqq.

[a] Abulpharaj Hist. Dyn. p. 218 sqq. quoted by Tuch de Nino urbe p. 32. Col. Chesney counts Mosul among the flourishing commercial centres in the time of Abu'l Abbas A. D. 749. Expedition ii. 581.

[b] Ainsworth Travels ii. 337. Tuch quotes also Campbell's Land journey to India, p. 252, that "the merchants still, from the nature of the country, go from the Persian gulf to Armenia and Syria and thence again to Bagdad by the same route through Mosul and Arbela, by which large bodies of men went formerly." [c] Chesney's Expedition ii. 589.

[d] Ib ii. 595. [e] Ib. 596. [f] Ib. i. 21.

[g] "The Tigris being already provided with stations at Bagdad and Mosul—it only requires another at Diyar Bekr, and the neighboring town of Mardin, since the connection of the former places with the countries about it would speedily cause a revival of its ancient commerce." Chesney Expedition ii. 602.

[h] Nin. and Bab. p. 469. [i] Travels ii. 127.

the destruction of the former. Babylon, from having been the winter residence of Cyrus, became the chief residence of the Persian Emperor at the time of Alexander, and continued to exist for many centuries, after the foundation of Seleucia, although it ceased to be a great city[k]. And this, notwithstanding its two rebellions under Darius[l], and that under Xerxes[m]. There was no ground of human policy against Nineveh's continuing, such as Mosul became, any more than Mosul itself. It existed for some time, as a Christian See.

The grandeur, energy, power, vividness of Nahum, naturally can be fully felt only in his own language. The force of his brief prophecy is much increased by its unity. Nahum had one sentence to pronounce, the judgments of God upon the power of this world, which had sought to annihilate the kingdom of God. God, in His then kingdom in Judah, and the world, were come face to face. What was to be the issue? The entire final utter overthrow of whatever opposed God. Nahum opens then with the calm majestic declaration of the majesty of God; Who God is, against whom they rebelled; the madness of their rebellion, and the extinction of its chief: (c. 1); then in detail, what was to come long after that first overthrow, the siege and capture of Nineveh itself, (c. 2.); then, in wider compass, the overthrow of the whole power (c. 3.). It was to be the first instance, in the history of mankind, of a power so great, perishing and forever. Nahum's office was not, as Jonah's, to the people itself. There is then no call to repentance, no gleam of God's mercy toward them in this life. Nineveh was to perish wholly, as the habitable world had perished in the time of Noah. The only relief is in the cessation of so much violence. There is no human joy expressed at this destruction of the enemy of God and of His people; no sorrow, save that there can be no sorrow; "[n]who will bemoan her? whence shall I find comforters for her?"

In conformity with this concentration of Nahum's subject, there is little in outward style or language to connect him with the other Prophets. His opening (as already observed[o]) bears upon God's declarations of mercy and judgment; but, Nineveh having filled up the measure of its iniquites, he had to exhibit the dark side of those declarations; how much lay in those words, "that will by no means clear the guilty." "[p]Jonah and Nahum form connected parts of one moral history, the remission of God's judgment being illustrated in the one, the execution of it in the other: the clemency and the just severity of the Divine government being contained in the mixed delineation of the two books." His evangelic character just gleams through, in the eight tender words, in which he seems to take breath, as it were; "Tōb Yhvh lemaōz beyōmtsarah, veyōdēah chōsē bo," "Good is God (Yhvh), refuge in day of trouble, and knowing trusters in Him[q];" then again, in the few words, which I think Isaiah expanded, "Lo on the mountains the feet of a good-tidings-bearer, peace-proclaimer[r]." Else there is only the mingled tenderness and austereness of truth, which would sympathize with the human being, but that that object had, by putting off all humanity, alienated all which is man. "Who will bemoan her? Whence shall I seek comforters for thee?" Who? and Whence? None had escaped evil from her. "Upon whom hath not thy wickedness passed continually?"

It is difficult for us, who have to gather up our knowledge of the sacred language from the fragments which remain, in which also the number of words forms and idioms, which stand out singly here and there, seem but so many specimens of lost treasure, to judge with any certainty, whether any approximation of idiom, which we may observe, implies any connection between the writers in whom it occurs. Nahum has, especially in his picture of the capture of Nineveh, so many of those *ἅπαξ λεγόμενα*, consisting often of slight modifications[t], his language is so rich and so original, that one the more doubts whether

[k] See Dict. of Greek and Rom. Geogr. i. 358.
[l] Behistun Inscr. in Rawl. Herod. ii. 595–597. 608.
[m] Ctesias Exc. Pers. 22. [n] iii. 7. [o] p. 556.
[p] Davison on Prophecy, p. 369. [q] N. i. 7.

[r] Nah. ii. 1. הנה על ההרים רגלי מבשר משמיע שלום. Is. lii. 7. מה נאוו על ההרים רגלי מבשר משמיע שלום. It seems to me impossible that Nahum, had he been adapting the words of Isaiah, would have left out the tender מה נאוו at the beginning, or the triumphant softly-flowing continuation, מבשר טוב משמיע ישועה אמר לציון מלך אלהינו at the end.

[t] The following, at least in form or idiom, stand alone in Nahum; the condensed forms וַיַּבְּשֵׁהוּ (though with analogies) i. 4; סְבוּאִים i. 10; נָגוּזּוּ i. 12; מֹטֵ, else מוֹטָה as "yoke" i. 13; זמורים masc. ii. 3; מְתֻלָּעִים (denom. from תולעת) ii. 4; פְּלָדֹת Ib. בְּרוֹשִׁים like *μελία, ἐλάτη*, "abies," of the spear, (Ib. הָרְעָלוּ "are quivered;" verb too *ἅπ.*) Ib. יִשְׁתַּקְשְׁקוּן (form) ii. 5. יְרוֹצֵצוּ (form) Ib. סֹכֵךְ ("covered way") ii. 6. וְהֻצַּב "and it is decreed" ii. 8 (See Ib.) גֻּלְּתָה (form, the meaning is determined by גָּלָה See Ib.) Ib. מְנַהֲגוֹת ("moaning") Ib. מְתֹפְפוֹת (form and metaphor; Kal once Ps. lxviii. 26) Ib. לִבְבֵהֶן masc. plur. Ib. מימי היא ii. 9. תְּכוּנָה (like "apparatus") ii. 10. בּוּקָה and מְבוּקָה "void" and, as to the form, מְבֻלָּקָה (a fem. part. used as an abstract; elsewhere is only the act. part. kal. בּוֹלֵק Is. xxiv. 1) ii. 11. פִּיק "shaking" (of

in those idioms, in which he seems to approximate to other prophets, the expressions in common do not belong to the common stock of the language; and that the more, since mostly [u] part of the idiom only coincides, the rest is different [x]. As for the so-called Syriasms or other peculiarities of language which Hitzig would have to be evidences of a later date [y], and from some of which others would infer that Nahum lived at Nineveh itself,

knees) Ib מְחַנֵּק, form, ii. 13. (else Nif. 2 Sam. xvii. 23; noun, מַחֲנַק Job vii. 15) הבערתי בעשן (prægn. idiom) ii. 14. פֶּרֶק (in this sense) iii. 1. דהר (the verb) iii. 2. (noun, דהרה, Jud. v. 22.) מַעַר (i. q. עֶרְוָה iii. 5. שִׁקֻּצִים (only instance of etymol. meaning) iii. 6. רֹאִי (as, "spectacle") Ib. רֻתְּקָה (part. pass. fem. as noun Is. xl. 19) iii. 10. הִתְכַּבֵּד (of oppressive number) iii. 15. מִנְּזָרִים iii. 17. נָפֹשׁוּ iii. 18. כֵּהָה iii. 19.

[u] The correspondence is complete between Jo. ii. 6. כל פנים קבצו פארור. and Nah. ii. 11. פני כלם קבצו פארור.

[x] Dr Henderson (in addition to Nah. ii. 1, Is. lii. 7, see note r.) (connects a) שֶׁטֶף עֹבֵר כָּלָה יַעֲשֶׂה Nah. i. 8 and כלה הוא עשה i. 9 with שָׁטַף וְעָבַר Is. viii. 8 and כָּלָה וְנֶחֱרָצָה—עשה Is. x. 23; b) בוקה ומבוקה וּמְבֻלָּקָה N. ii. 11, with בוקק הארץ וּבוֹלְקָהּ Is. xxiv. 1. c) וחלחלה בכל מתנים ii. 11, מלאו מָתְנַי חלחלה Is. xxi. 3. But in) a כלה עשה is an idiom used not in Is. only but in Jeremiah (5 times) in Ezekiel (twice) Zephaniah and Nehemiah. It is then an ordinary Hebrew idiom. The peculiarity of Isaiah, that in both places (Is. x. 23, xxviii. 22) he adds ונחרצה, does not occur in Nahum. Nahum also has not the verb שָׁטַף, which Isaiah uses in 5 places; Isaiah does not use the noun שֶׁטֶף, which Nahum has, and which occurs in a Psalm of David (xxxii. 6). Nahum too speaks of a flood which shall pass over and overwhelm; Isaiah, of a man who should pass over and pass away. In b) there is only in common, that Isaiah joins the two like-sounding words בקק and בלק as active verbs (of which, the word common to the two prophets must be older than the Prophet Nahum (comp. "Balak" in the Pent.). Nahum unites two nouns, one from a different root בוק, the other a pass. intens. part. מְבֻלָּקָה, as an abstract noun. The gradual lengthening of the alliterate form occurs in Nahum only. Two of the three words in Nahum are ἅπ. λεγ. c) The mention of חלחלה, "great writhing anguish," in connection with the loins, is more remarkable, since חלחלה occurs in those places only and Ez. xxx. 4, 9 (with the same constr. with ב); yet מוּעָקָה (although not חלחלה) occurs with במתנים Ps. lxvi. 11. It may then only be an accidental coincidence of the same term.

O. Strauss thinks that d) Nah. i. 13 is from Is. x. 27; e) iii. 5 from Is. xlvii. 2. 3; f) Nah. iii. 7 from Is. li. 19. But in d and e there is no characteristic word the same; in Nah. i. 13 there is only the common imagery of breaking the yoke. מוֹט masc. occurs in Nahum only; נתק מוסרות in Ps. ii. 3 (of men rebelling) and Jerem. 3 times. It is then a common idiom. In f. there is the correspondence of the idiom מי יָנוּד לָךְ in Is. (which also occurs Jer. xv. 5) in N. מי ינוד לָהּ, but with the difference that in Is. God speaks of the heaviness of a sorrow which He will comfort; Nahum speaks of desolation which none can comfort. The construction of נוד with ל occurs Job ii. 11, xlii. 11, Jer. xvi. 5, xxii. 10, xlviii. 17; in Job and Ps. lxix. 21 נוד is united with נחם. The expression seems then to belong to the common stock of the language; the idiom מי אֲנַחֲמֵךְ "Who (in what character) shall I comfort thee?" is peculiar to Isaiah.

Hitzig further would have it, that, "נכבדים occurs in N. iii. 10 exactly as in Is. xxiii. 9 alone beside ;" whereas the only correspondence is, that Isaiah has the idiom, "honored of earth," "all honored of earth," נִכְבַּדֵּי אֶרֶץ; Nahum has, with the affix, "her honored," נִכְבַּדֶּיהָ as Ps. cxlix. 8. נִכְבְּדֵיהֶם.

[y] Of the forms or words, which Hitzig would make characteristic of a later time

1) שְׂעָרָה i. 3 is only orthographically different from the more common, סְעָרָה; yet not only does שְׂעָרָה occur Job ix. 17, and the masc. שַׂעַר, Is. xxviii. 2, but the verb is written with שׂ in the same meaning, Ps. l. 3, lviii. 10, Job xxvii. 21.

2) קַנּוֹא occurs in Jos. xxiv. 19, the oldest book next to the Pentateuch, and having much in common with it (see on Dan. p. 312 note 2), and in no later book. קַנָּא occurs 5 times in the Pentateuch; this form קַנָּא (not קַנּוֹא) survived in the Chaldee.

3) נָפֹשׁוּ iii. 18, is simply Nif. from פוּשׁ, a word as old as the Pentateuch, since the river, Pishon, פִּישׁוֹן, is derived from it. Hitzig obtains his "pronunciation" by making it kal, נפשׁ, a word not extant in Heb.

4) "The form of the suffix of the 2d person, ii. 14," מַלְאָכֵכֵה, which has been urged by all writers on his side, is the more singular ground of argument, because it turns entirely on the vowels, which only represent a tradition of the expiring language. Gesenius calls it "an especial form, which perhaps ought properly to be pronounced כָה, as masc., out of which the punctuator first made כֵה, in order in some sort of way to indicate the feminine" (Lehrg. p. 216). Written מַלְאָכְכָה, it is only the full and original form of the pronominal affix, כָה (from אַנְכָה for אַתָּה), as it is found in the Pentateuch, אַיֶּכָּה Gen. iii. 9, יָדְכָה Ex. xiii. 16, אֹתָכָה Ex. xxix. 35. Nahum chose it probably as a fuller form. It occurs in a Psalm of David, cxxxix. 5, at the close, כַּפֶּכָה, and in Jer. xxix. 25, בְּשִׁמְכָה: as also with the verb, יַעַצְרְכָה 1 Kgs xviii. 44, and, in the pause, תִּנְצְרֶכָּה Prov. ii. 11, יִמְצָאֶכָּה, 1 Kings xviii. 10. Mss. have, some מלאככֶה (19 De Rossi, 3 by correction, and 3 early Edd. De R.) "many have מלאככֶה;" 3 of De R. and 3 or 4 in the first instance, had the regular מלאככָה. The messengers were the king's messengers (Is. xxxvi. 2. 12. 13, xxxvii. 4. 6. 9. 17. 24.) and so the masculine form is in its place. Punctuators probably (as Ges. conjectured) wished to assimilate it to the preceding feminines; Ewald lays down that כֵה is a dialectic difference (p. 638 note) and uses it as an argument

"the wish has been father to the thought." One only solid ground there would be why Nahum should not have written his prophecy, when, according to all history, it could alone have any interest for Judah, long before the event itself, viz. if He to

for Nahum's living near Nineveh (Proph. i. 350). Davidson (iii. 301.) follows Hitzig.

5) "The form of the suffix of the 3d person, i. 13, ii. 4. comp. Hab. iii. 10." The form הוּ lies nearer to the original הוּא, than the contracted וֹ; it also occurs in the word לְמִינֵהוּ, 14 times in the Pentateuch (in Gen. 8 times, Levit. 5 times, Deut. once); it occurs most (Ges. observes, Lehrg. p. 213) in words ending in ֶה, as מַרְאֵהוּ 10 times (3 in Levit.) שָׂדֵהוּ 7 times (5 in Gen. Ex. Lev.) עָלֵהוּ in Ps. i. Ezek. twice, Jerem. once; מִקְנֵהוּ in Gen. 4 times, Exod. twice, Job twice: although רֵעֶה absolutely occurs 3 times only, רֵעֵהוּ is the rule: it occurs 114 times, of which 42 are in the Pentateuch. The form הוּ also occurs in פִּילַגְשֵׁהוּ Jud. xix. 24, אֹרֵהוּ Job xxv. 3. It is united with the plur. noun in אַשְׁרֵהוּ Prov. xix. 18, and רֵעֵהוּ for רעיהו 1 Sam. xxx. 26, Job xlii. 10; also יָדֵיהוּ Hab. iii. 10, עֵינֵיהוּ Job xxiv. 23. It is obviously used by Nahum for its more stately sound.

6) "The meaning of נִבֵּל iii. 6," is one attributed to it by Hitz. only.

7) "As Pilpel occurs more and more in later times, so חַלְחָלָה ii. 11, (comp. יִשְׁתַּקְשְׁקוּן ii. 5) only occurs in Is. xxi. 3, Ez. xxx. 4. 9." Pilpel is formed on exactly the same principle, as the other rarer intensive conjugations, the doubling of those letters of the root, most capable of being doubled. In כִּלְכֵּל, it occurs from Genesis downward. The use of the word חַלְחָלָה by two contemporaries, Isaiah and Nahum, was nothing remarkable.

8) "So, plainly שׁוּב ii. 3 could only in later times be used transitively, otherwise than as united with שְׁבוּת." Why? If שׁוּב is transitive in the phrase, שׁוּב שְׁבוּת, "restore the captivity" of Jacob, the corresponding phrase, שָׁב אֶת גְּאוֹן is but a variation of the phrase, such as would naturally occur in any original writer. שׁוּב is transitive, also in Ps. lxxxv. 5, and Ezek. xlvii. 7, (since if intrans., as Abulwalid pointed out, it would have been בשׁובי not בְּשׁוּבֵנִי) if not in Num. x. 36. Gesenius also pointed out that the corresponding Arab רָגַע is both transitive, and intransitive, so that the use of the causative conj. אַרְגַע is dialectic, according to Djauhari, or less pure (See Lane sub v. T. i. p. 1038). It is consistent in Hengst. to deny the transitive meaning of שׁוּב altogether, but not to make any idiomatic difference between שָׁב שְׁבוּת and שָׁב גְּאוֹן as belonging to different dates.

9) "מצורה (ii. 2) in the sense of munitio, first occurs in the Chronicles." In the Chronicles, the phrase is different. The idiom is a slight variation of the old masc., עִיר מָצוֹר Ps. xxxi., 22. lx., 11 (which the Chronicles too has, 2 C. viii. 5). The Chronicles, on whatever ground, mostly adopt the feminine form in speaking historically of the fortified cities built in Judah; once in the sing. עָרֵי מצולה 2 C. xiv. 5; else with two plurals ערי מצורות, 2 C. xi. 10. 23. xii. 4. xiv. 5. xxi. 3. In one place only, having ended a verse, xi. 10, "and in Benjamin עָרֵי מְצוּרוֹת," the writer begins the next, (omitting the ערי) "and he strengthened אֶת הַמְּצוּרוֹת." Nor is there anything characteristic of a later period in the use of the feminine; and, any how, since the Chronicles were compiled after the captivity, probably by Ezra, the use of the same form could have proved nothing, as to whether a book were written 85 years, sooner or later, before the captivity.

"Also the Hebrew of Nahum is in part impure; טפסר iii. 17, is probably not Semitic." It probably *is* Semitic (see above p. 108) and Assyrian. The occurrence of what probably is a title of an Assyrian commander, not only fits the times of Nahum, when Assyrian invasions had begun, but the occurrence of an official title, (like that of "Pechah" elsewhere, see Daniel the Prophet pp. 570, 571,) without any Syriasms, belongs to Nahum's time and life in Palestine. When three officers of Hezekiah understood Assyrian (Is. xxxvi. 11.), there is nothing surprising in the mention of an Assyrian title. Pechah is also an Assyrian title, occurring in the Inscriptions in the plural "pahati," Oppert Rapports p. 51. 52. 53. 57. 65. 74. "Tartan," in Isaiah and 2 Kings, is also probably an Assyrian title, since Rabsaris, "Chief of the Eunuchs," "Rab-shakeh, Chief-cupbearer," (with which Tartan is united in 2 Kings xviii. 17) are names of officers. Yet no satisfactory etymology has been found for "Tartan."

10) "מָכַר, iii. 4, stands in Arabic meaning." The coincidence with *Arabic* would have proved nothing; but Nahum uses מכר in its common meaning. In Arabic also it signifies "deceived," not (as Hitzig would have it) "meshed."

11) "נהג, ii. 8, in Syriac meaning." נהג, not in Syriac only, but in Arabic, signifies to be "violently out of breath;" but this, which is its only meaning which could be brought to bear on this passage, does not suit it, whereas that suggested by the Hebrew itself does. In Nahum it is evidently a modification of the biliteral הג, in the same sense as הָגָה which is used of the low moaning of the dove, Is. xxxviii. 14, lix. 11; and the subst. הֶגֶה "moaning" is united with קִינִים and הי (for נְהִי) Ezek. ii. 10. Another modification of the biliteral is הָגִיג Ps. v. 2, xxxix. 4.

12) "and דהר too, iii. 2 (only beside in the song of Deborah Jud. v. 22) is probably equally only a Syriasm;" i. e. supposing its meaning to be derived from דור "circle," the substitution of ה for ו occurs oftenest in Aramaic. In the root דור itself however, the nearest correspondence of Hebrew with any Semitic dialect is not with the Syriac but with the Arabic; דור "generation" and the Arab. דָהַר "prolonged time," but also the period of life (see Lane p. 923); whereas the Syr. דהרא only signifies "a mill." But Hitzig himself sets aside these last, with the observation, "these appearances however are sufficiently explained, if the home of Deborah was also Nahum's country, a border-country toward Syria, inhabited in part by non-Israelites."

13) Hitzig makes neither הֻצַּב the Queen's name and so Assyrian, nor פלדות, although he has his own fantastic meaning for each, derived from misapplication of the Arabic. The alleged Syriasm in פלדות rests on an odd ground-work. The Syriac word פלדא has not been found in any Syriac author; in one of three Syro-Arab Lexica (Bar-Bahlul's) it is explained by the Arabic word, "fûlâdso." This in its turn is interpreted by the Persian, which again has, in Vûllers, no Persian etymology. On the other hand the Arabic "faladsa" "cut," conj. ii. "cut to pieces," does give a good etymology for any sharp instrument, as the "scythe" of a scythed chariot.

Yet this is the evidence on which Davidson tells the unlearned (Introd. iii. 301), "The language is pure and classical with a few exceptions, as נהג to mourn, ii. 8, דהר iii. 2, פלדות ii. 4. which are Syri-

NAHUM.

Before CHRIST cir. 713.

CHAPTER I.

1 *The Majesty of God in goodness to his people, and severity against his enemies.*

THE burden [a] of Nineveh. The book of the vision of Nahum the Elkoshite.

Before CHRIST cir. 713.

[a] Zeph. 2. 13.

1. *The burden*[1]. "[2]The word 'massa' [burden] is never placed in the title, save when the vision is heavy and full of burden and toil." *Of Nineveh.* The prophecy of Nahum again is very stern and awful. Nineveh, after having "repented at the preaching of Jonah," again fell back into the sins whereof it had repented, and added this, that, being employed by God to chasten Israel, it set itself, not to inflict the measure of God's displeasure, but to uproot the chosen people, in whom was promised the birth of Christ[3]. It was then an Antichrist, and a type of him yet to come. Jonah's mission was a call to repentance, a type and forerunner of all God's messages to the world, while the day of grace and the world's probation lasts. Nahum, "the full of exceeding comfort," as his name means, or "the comforter" is sent to[4] *reprove the world of judgment.* He is sent, prominently, to pronounce on Nineveh its doom when its day of grace should be over, and in it, on the world, when it and [5]*all the works therein shall be burned up.* In few words he directly comforteth the people of God[6]; else the comfort even to her is indirect, in the destruction of her oppressor. Beside this, there is nothing of mercy or call to repentance, or sorrow for their desolation[7]; but rather the pouring out of the vials of the wrath of God on her and on the evil world, which to the end resists all God's calls and persecuteth His people. The book of Jonah proclaimeth God, *a gracious God and merciful, slow to anger and of great kindness, Who repenteth Him of the evil.* Nahum speaketh of the same attributes, yet closes with, *and will not at all acquit the wicked.* "[3]The Merciful Himself, Who is by Nature Merciful, the Holy Spirit, seemeth, speaking in the prophet, to *laugh at their calamity.*" All is desolation, and death. The aggression against God is retorted upon the aggressor; one reeling strife for life or death; then the silence of the graveyard. And so, in its further meaning, "[2]the prophecy belongs to the close of the world and the comfort of the saints therein, so that whatsoever they see in the world, they may hold cheap, as passing away and perishing and prepare themselves for the Day of Judgment, when the Lord shall be the Avenger of the true Assyrian."

So our Lord sets forth the end of the world as the comfort of the elect. *When these things begin to come to pass, then look up and lift up your heads, for your redemption draweth*

[1] So, beyond question, משׂא should be rendered. Since נשׂא is no where used of mere speaking, it is beforehand improbable that מַשָּׂא should mean "speech;" and this, apart from the consideration that "the speech of Babylon, Damascus, Egypt, Moab, Tyre, Dumah," "the valley of vision," "the desert of the sea," "Nineveh," would be an inexpressive expression for a speech concerning them. For, in one place only, (Is. xxi. 13.) is it expressed that the burden is *upon* (ב) Arabia. Else prepositions are only used to determine the relation of משא with the object (ב, Zech. ix. 1. על, Ib. xii. 1. אל, Mal i. 1.) when that object is already separated from משא; "the burden of the word of the Lord upon" Ib. נשׂא, "lift up" when used alone for נשׂא קול "lifted up" [the voice], is always used of "loud speaking," Is. xlii. 2, 11, Job xxi. 12, and so Is. iii. 7, "loudly protest." Eleven times in Isaiah (xiii. 1, xiv. 28, xv. 1, xvii. 1, xix. 1, xxi. 1, 11, 13, xxii. 1, xxiii. 1, xxx. 6.) in Ezek. xii. 10, Hab. i. 1, Mal. i. 1, משׂא is followed by a heavy prophecy, as it is here. Zech. ix. 1, also is a heavy prophecy, against those whom Alexander would conquer; Zech. xii. 2, begins with a heavy prophecy against Judah and Jerusalem. Prov. xxx. xxxi, are rebukes; in Prov. xxxi., it is expressly added, "wherewith his mother admonished him." The blasphemy also, rebuked by Jeremiah (xxiii. 33, 34, 36), presupposes that the meaning of מַשָּׂא, at which they mocked, was a heavy prophecy. "What fresh burden has God for us?" they asked mockingly, not believing that the evil which Jeremiah prophesied would come. In regard to the use of מַשָּׂא (1 C. xv. 22, 27,) where the E. V. has, "for song," if it related to the voice at all, it must (like the "on Alamoth," "on Sheminith" vv. 20, 21, which probably designate two notes of music, "treble" and the "octave," "bass") have signified some character of voice, as "alto," according to the meaning of נשׂא, "lift up." But, considering (as Hengstenberg has noticed, Christol. on Zech. ix. 1.) the use of מַשָּׂא in places where it can only mean "burden" as also throughout Num. iv. (19, 24, 27, 31, 32, 47, 49,) it seems probable, that in 1 C. xv. too, it signifies "bearing" (as in E. M. "carriage"). For the "bearing the ark" is spoken of immediately afterward as a matter of much skill. "When God helped the Levites, the bearers of the ark of the covenant of the Lord," נשׂאי ארון ברית יי (1 C. xv. 26); and the writer speaks of the dress of "all the Levites who bare the ark" "*and* the singers" v. 27, as two classes. Even Bertheau defends this meaning, and solidly. In Lam. ii. 14, מַשְׂאוֹת שָׁוְא is united with מַדּוּחִים "expulsions." The context seems to require more than is in the rendering, "sayings of vanity," which would be less strong than חָזוּ לָךְ שָׁוְא "have seen for thee vanity." "The burdens of vanity," which the false prophets professed to see, would be heavy prophecies against the enemy, that they should be driven from the land of Israel. Comp. Zedekiah's enquiry, Jer. xxi. 1, 2, and Hananiah's prophecy Jer. xxviii. 2. 11.

[2] S. Jer. [3] Rup. [4] S. John xvi. 6, 8. [5] 2 Pet. iii. 10. [6] i. 15.

[7] As in Jerem. iii. 12, viii. 18, 21.

Before CHRIST cir. 713.

2 ‖ God *is* [b] jealous, and [c] the Lord revengeth; the LORD revengeth, and † *is* furious; the LORD will

‖ Or, *The Lord is a jealous God, and a revenger, &c.*
b Ex. 20. 5. & 34. 14. Deut. 4. 24. Josh. 24. 19.
c Deut. 32. 35. Ps. 94. 1. Isa. 59. 18.
† Heb. *that hath fury.*

nigh[1]." This is the highest fulfillment of the prophecy; for "then will the wrath of God against the wicked be fully seen, Who now patiently waiteth for them for mercy."

The book of the vision of Nahum the Elkoshite. "[2] He first defines the object of the prophecy, whereto it looks; then states who spake it and whence it was;" the human instrument which God employed. The fuller title, "*The book of* the vision of Nahum," (which stands alone) probably expresses that it was not, like most prophecies, first delivered orally, and then collected by the prophet, but was always (as it is so remarkably) one whole. "The weight and pressure of this 'burden' may be felt from the very commencement of the book."

2. *God is jealous and the Lord revengeth.* Rather (as the E. M.) [3] *A God very jealous and avenging is the Lord.* The Name of God, YHVH, "He Who Is," the Unchangeable, is thrice repeated, and thrice it is said of Him that He is an Avenger. It sheweth both the certainty and greatness of the vengeance, and that He Who inflicteth it, is the All-Holy Trinity, Who have a care for the elect. God's jealousy is twofold. It is an intense love, not bearing imperfections or unfaithfulness in that which It loves, and so chastening it; or not bearing the ill-dealings of those who would injure what It loves, and so destroying them. To Israel He had revealed Himself, as *a*[4] *jealous God, visiting iniquity* but *shewing mercy;* here, as jealous for His people against those who were purely His enemies and the enemies of His people[5], and so His jealousy burneth to their destruction, in that there is in them no good to be refined, but only evil to be consumed.

The titles of God rise in awe; first, *intensely jealous*[6] and *an Avenger;* then, *an Avenger* and *a Lord of wrath;* One Who hath it laid up with Him, at His Command, and the more terrible, because it is so; the Master of it, (not, as man, mastered by it[7]); having it, to withhold or to discharge; yet so discharging it, at last, the more irrevocably on the finally impenitent. And this He says at the last, *an Avenger to* [8] *His adversaries,* (lit. "those who hem and narrow Him in"). The word *avenged*[9] is almost appropriated to God in the Old Testament, as to punishment which He inflicts, or at least causes to be inflicted[10], whether on individuals[11], or upon a people, (His own[12] or their enemies[13], for their misdeeds. In man it is a defect[14]. Personal vengeance is mentioned only in characters, directly or indirectly censured, as Samson[15] or Saul[16]. It is forbidden to man, punished in him, claimed by God as His own inalienable right. [17] *Vengeance is Mine and requital.* [18] *Thou shalt not avenge nor keep up against the children of My people.* Yet it is spoken of, not as a mere act of God, but as the expression of His Being. [19] *Shall not My soul be avenged of such a nation as this?*

And a Reserver of wrath for His enemies, the hardened and unbelieving who hate God, and at last, when they had finally rejected God and were rejected by Him, the object of His aversion. It is spoken after the manner of men, yet therefore is the more terrible. There is *that* in God, to which the passions of man correspond; they are a false imitation of something which in Him is good, a distortion of the true likeness of God, in which God created us and which man by sin defaced. "[20] Pride doth imitate exaltedness: whereas Thou Alone art God exalted over all. Ambition, what seeks it, but honors and glory? whereas Thou Alone art to be honored above

[1] S. Luke xxi. 28.

[2] S. Cyr. On the prophet, and his country which S. Cyril says, he had "learned by tradition to be expressed by the addition, the Elkoshite," see the Introduction p. 357.

[3] אֵל קַנָּא is used as an attribute of God Ex. xx. 5. xxxiv. 14. Dt. iv. 24. v. 9. vi. 15, as is אֵל קַנּוֹא, the form used here, Jos. xxiv. 19. It is observed that, in prose, אל is almost uniformly used with an adj. אל עליון, אל חי, אל גדול ונורא, אל רחום וחנון, אל דעות, אל עולם, אל ראי, or a noun אל שדי.

[4] Ex. xx. 5, 6.

[5] See Zech. i. 14.

[6] The form קַנּוֹא being intensive.

[7] בעל חמה occurs once only beside, and that, of man, Pr. xxix. 22; but בעל אף also Pr. xxii. 24.

[8] נקם with ל p., only beside Ez. xxv. 12.

[9] נקם.

[10] Nu. xxxi. 2, 3. Ps. cxlix. 9. Hence almost the same as, punished by law, Ex. xxi. 20. 21.

[11] Gen. iv. 15. 24. 1 Sam. xxiv. 12. 2 Sam. iv. 8. 2 Kings ix. 7. Jer. xi. 20. xv. 15. xx. 12.

[12] Lev. xxvi. 25. Ps. xcix. 8. Ez. xxiv. 8.

[13] Deut. xxxii. 41, 43. Ps. xviii. 48. Is. xxxiv. 8. xxxv. 4. xlvii. 3. lix. 17. lxi. 2. lxiii. 4. Mi. v. 14. Jer. xlvi. 10. l. 15. 28. li. 6. 11. 36. Ezek. xxv. 14. 17.

[14] מתנקם, a self-avenger, Ps. viii. 3. xliv. 17. It is punished by God Ezek. xxv. 12, 15, being moreover unjust; Jer. xx. 10. 12. Lam. iii. 60. coll. 64.

[15] Jud. xv. 7. xvi. 20.

[16] 1 Sam. xiv. 24. xviii. 25. Else only historically Pr. vi. 34. Esth. viii. 13. David thanks God for keeping him from it toward Nabal 1 Sam. xxv. 32, 33.

[17] Deut. xxxii. 35, comp. Ps. xciv. 1.

[18] Lev. xix. 18.

[19] Jer. v. 9. 29. ix. 9.

[20] S. Aug. Conf. B. ii. n. 13. 14.

Before CHRIST cir. 713.

take vengeance on his adversaries, and he reserveth *wrath* for his enemies.

3 The LORD *is* [d] slow to anger, and [e] great in power, and will not at all acquit

[d] Ex. 34. 6, 7. Neh. 9. 17. Ps. 103. 8. Jonah 4. 2.
[e] Job 9. 4.

all and glorious for evermore. The cruelty of the great would fain be feared; but who is to be feared but God Alone, out of Whose power what can be wrested or withdrawn, when, or where, or whither, or by whom? The tendernesses of the wanton would fain be counted love: yet is nothing more tender than Thy charity; nor is aught loved more healthfully than that Thy truth, bright and beautiful above all. Curiosity makes semblance of a desire of knowledge; whereas Thou supremely knowest all. Yea, ignorance and foolishness itself is cloaked under the name of simplicity and uninjuriousness: because nothing is found more single than Thee; and what less injurious, since they are his own works which injure the sinner? Yea, sloth would fain be at rest; but what stable rest beside the Lord? Luxury affects to be called plenty and abundance; but Thou art the fullness and never-failing plenteousness of incorruptible pleasures. Prodigality presents a shadow of liberality: but Thou art the most overflowing Giver of all good. Covetousness would possess many things; and Thou possessest all things. Envy disputes for excellency: what more excellent than Thou? Anger seeks revenge: who revenges more justly than Thou? Fear startles at things unwonted or sudden, which endanger things beloved, and takes fore-thought for their safety; but to Thee what unwonted or sudden, or who separateth from Thee what Thou lovest? Or where but with Thee is unshaken safety? Grief pines away for things lost, the delight of its desires; because it would have nothing taken from it, as nothing can from Thee. Thus doth the soul seek without Thee what she findeth not pure and untainted, till she returns to Thee. Thus all pervertedly imitate Thee, who remove far from Thee, and lift themselves up against Thee. But even by thus imitating Thee, they imply Thee to be the Creator of all nature; whence there is no place, whither altogether to retire from Thee." And so, in man, the same qualities are good or bad, as they have God or self for their end. "[1] The joy of the world is a passion. Joy in the Holy Spirit or to joy in the Lord is a virtue. The sorrow of the world is a passion. The sorrow according to God which worketh salvation is a virtue. The fear of the world which hath torment, from which a man is called fearful, is a passion. The holy fear of the Lord, which abideth for ever, from which a man is called reverential, is a virtue. The hope of the world, when one's hope is in the world or the princes of the world, is a passion. Hope in God is a virtue, as well as faith and charity. Though these four human passions are not in God, there are four virtues, having the same names, which no one can have, save from God, from the Spirit of God." In man they are "passions," because man is so far "passive" and suffers under them, and, through original sin, cannot hinder having them, though by God's grace he may hold them in. God, without passion and in perfect holiness, has qualities, which in man were jealousy, wrath, vengeance, unforgivingness, a "rigor of perfect justice toward the impenitent, which punisheth so severely, as though God had fury;" only, in Him it is righteous to punish man's unrighteousness. Elsewhere it is said, [2] *God keepeth not for ever*, or it is asked, [3] *will He keep for ever?* and He answers, [4] *Return, and I will not cause Mine anger to fall upon you; for I am merciful, saith the Lord, I will not keep for ever.* Man's misdeeds and God's displeasure remain with God, to be effaced on man's repentance, or [5] *by his hardness and impenitent heart man treasureth up unto himself wrath in the day of wrath and of the revelation of the righteous judgment of God, Who will reward each according to his works.*

3. *The Lord is slow to anger.* Nahum takes up the words of Jonah [6] as he spoke of God's attributes toward Nineveh, but only to shew the opposite side of them. Jonah declares how God is *slow to anger*, giving men time of repentance, and if they do repent, *repenting Him also of the evil;* Nahum, that the long-suffering of God is not *slackness*, that *He is long-suffering to usward, not willing that any should perish, but that all should come to repentance.*

And strong in power [7]. Divine long-suffering goes along with Divine power. God can be long-suffering, because He can, whenever He sees good, punish. His long-suffering is a token, not of weakness, but of power. He can allow persons the whole extent of trial, because, when they are past cure, He can end it at once. [8] *God is a righteous judge, strong*

[1] Rup.
[2] Ps. ciii. 9. The idiom נָטַר לְאֹיְבָיו stands alone.
[3] Jer. iii. 5.
[4] Ib. 12.
[5] Rom. ii. 5. 6.
[6] iv. 2.

[7] The full form וּגְדוֹל כֹּחַ, Cheth. belongs probably to the stately character of Nahum. The like occurs only in Ps. cxlv. 8. גְּדוֹל חסד.
[8] Ps. vii. 11.

Before CHRIST cir. 713.

the wicked: [f] the LORD
hath his way in the whirlwind and in the storm,

[f] Ps. 18. 7, &c. & 97. 2. Hab. 3. 5, 11, 12.

and the clouds *are* the dust
of his feet.
4 [g] He rebuketh the sea,

Before CHRIST cir. 713.

[g] Ps. 106. 9. Isa. 50. 2. Matt. 8. 26.

and patient, and God wratheth [1] *every day.* The wrath cometh only at the last, but it is ever present with God. He cannot but be displeased with the sin; and so the Psalmist describes in the manner of men the gradual approximation to its discharge. [2] *If he* (the sinner) *will not return* [from evil or to God], *He will whet His sword; He hath trodden His bow and directed it: He hath prepared for him instruments of death; He hath made his arrows burning.* We see the arrow with unextinguishable fire, ready to be discharged, waiting for the final decision of the wicked, whether he will repent or not, but that still *the Day of the Lord* will *come*[3]. He *will not at all acquit*[4]. The words occur originally in the great declaration of God's attributes of mercy by Moses, as a necessary limitation of them[5]; they are continued to God's people, yet with the side of mercy predominant[6]; they are pleaded to Himself[7]; they are the sanction of the third commandment[8]. He *will not acquit* of His own will, apart from His justice. So He saith[9], *I can of Mine own self do nothing,* i. e. (in part), not as unjust judges, who *call good evil and evil good,* following their own will, not the merits of the case; but, *as I hear, I judge, and My judgment is just.* He cannot even have mercy and spare unjustly, nor without the lowliness of penitence. Even if it be Jerusalem, over which He wept, or His *companion,* His *own familiar friend*[10], He, Who is no *accepter of persons,* cannot of mere favor forgive the impenitent.

The Lord hath His way in the whirlwind and in the storm. The vengeance of God comes at last swiftly, vehemently, fearfully, irresistibly. *When they say, Peace and safety, then sudden destruction cometh upon them*[11], and all creation stands at the command of the Creator against His enemies. *He shall take to Him His jealousy for complete armor, and make the creature His weapon, for the revenge of His enemies*[12].

And the clouds are the dust of His feet. Perhaps the imagery is from the light dust raised by an earthly army, of which Nahum's word is used[13]. The powers of heaven are arrayed against the might of earth. On earth a little dust, soon to subside; in heaven, the whirlwind and the storm, which sweep away what does not bow before them. The vapors, slight in outward seeming[14], but formed of countless multitudes of mist-drops, are yet dark and lowering, as they burst, and resistless. "The *Feet* of God are that power whereby He trampleth upon the ungodly." So it is said to the Son, *Sit Thou on My Right Hand until I make Thine enemies Thy footstool.* Tempests have also, without figure, been used to overthrow God's enemies[15].

4. *He rebuketh the sea and maketh it dry*[16], delivering His people, as He did from Pharaoh[17], the type of all later oppressors, and of Antichrist. *His word is with power; to destroy them at* once *with one rough word*[18]. The restlessness of the barren and troubled sea is an image of the wicked[19]. *And drieth up all the rivers,* as He did Jordan. His coming shall be far more terrible than when all *the hearts* of the inhabitants of the land *did melt*[20]. *Bashan languisheth and Carmel; and the flower of Lebanon languisheth.* Bashan was richest in pastures; Carmel, according to its name, in gardens and vineyards; Lebanon, in vines also and fragrant flowers[21], but chiefly in the cedar and cypress; it had its name from the whiteness of the snow, which rests on its summit. These mountains then together are emblems of richness, lasting beauty, fruitfulness, loftiness; yet all, even that which by nature is not, in the variety of seasons, wont to fade, dries up and withers before the rebuke of God. But if these thing are *done in a green tree, what shall be done in the dry?* All freshness, beauty, comeliness, shew of outward nature, shall fade as grass; all ornament of men's outward graces or gifts, all mere shew of goodness, shall fall off like a leaf and perish. If the glory of nature perishes before God, how much more the pride of man! Bashan also was the dwelling-place of the race of giants, and near Libanus was Damascus; yet their inhabitants *became as dead men*

[1] The word expresses continuously present action, וְזֹעֵם. The lxx added *strong and patient* to bring out the meaning.

[2] Ib. 12. 13. [3] 2 Pet. iii. 9, 10. [4] ונקה לא ינקה.

[5] Ex. xxxiv. 7. The Samaritan Pentateuch characteristically changes the words into ונקה לו ינקה "the innocent shall be held guiltless by him."

[6] Jer. xxx. 11. xlvi. 28. [7] Nu. xiv. 18.

[8] Ex. xx. 7. Deut. v. 11. [9] John v. 30.

[10] Ps. lv. 14. [11] 1 Thess. v. 3.

[12] Wisdom v. 17. [13] Ezek. xxvi. 10.

[14] אבק occurs six times in the O. T. It is by itself "light dust" Ex. ix. 9. De. xxviii. 24. Is. v. 24, but has דק added Is. xxix. 5.

[15] Ex. xiv. 27. Josh. x. 11. Judges v. 20. 1 Sam. ii. 10. and vii. 10. 2 Sam. xxii. 15.

[16] The contracted form, וַיַּבְּשֵׁהוּ is again for emphasis. The like contraction וַיַּדּוּ occurs in Lam. iii. 53. וַיַּגֶּה Ib. 33. וַיַּשְּׁרֵם 2 Chr. xxxii. 30. Kri.

[17] Ps. cvi. 9. [18] Wisd. xii. 9. [19] Is. lvii. 20.

[20] Josh. ii. 11. [21] Hos. xiv. 7, Cant. iv. 11.

Before CHRIST cir. 713.

and maketh it dry, and
drieth up all the rivers:
[h] Bashan languisheth, and
Carmel, and the flower of
Lebanon languisheth.
5 [i] The mountains quake
at him, and [k] the hills melt,
and [l] the earth is burned
at his presence, yea, the
world, and all that dwell
therein.
6 Who can stand before
his indignation? and [m] who
can † abide in the fierceness of his anger? [n] his
fury is poured out like
fire, and the rocks are
thrown down by him.

h Isa. 33. 9.
i Ps. 68. 8.
k Judg. 5. 5. Ps. 97. 5. Mic. i. 4.
l 2 Pet. 3. 10.
m Mal. 3. 2.
† Heb. *stand up.*
n Rev. 16. 1.

and their power shrank to nothing at the word of God.

5. *The mountains quaked at Him, and the hills melted*, as of their own accord. The words are a renewal of those of Amos[1]. Inanimate nature is pictured as endowed with the terror, which guilt feels at the presence of God. All power, whether greater or less, whatsoever lifteth itself up, shall give way in that Day, which shall be[2] *upon all the cedars of Lebanon that are high and lifted up, and upon all the oaks of Bashan, and upon all the high mountains, and upon all the hills that are lifted up. And the earth is burned* [rather *lifteth itself up*[3]]; as in an earthquake it seems, as it were, to rise and sink down, lifting itself as if to meet its God or to flee. What is strongest, shaketh; what is hardest, melteth; yea, the whole world trembleth and is removed. "[4] If," said even Jews of old, "when God made Himself known in mercy, to give the law to His people, the world was so moved at His Presence, how much more, when He shall reveal Himself in wrath!" The words are so great that they bear the soul on to the time, when the heaven and earth shall flee away from the Face of Him *Who sitteth on the throne, and the elements shall melt with fervent heat*[5]. And since all judgments are images of the Last, and the awe at tokens of God's Presence is a shadow of the terror of that coming, he adds,

6. *Who can stand before His indignation?* This question appeals to our own consciences, that we cannot[6]. It anticipates the self-conviction at every day of God's visitation, the forerunners of the last. The word rendered "indignation" is reserved almost exclusively to denote the wrath of God[7]. "[8] Who can trust in his own righteousness, and, for the abundance of his works or consciousness of his virtues, not be in need of mercy? *Enter not into judgment with Thy servant, O Lord, for in Thy sight shall no man living be justified;* and in Job it is said truly, *Behold He put no trust in His servants, and His Angels He charged with folly. How much less in them that dwell in houses of clay, whose foundation is in the dust, which are crushed before the moth*[9]? It were needless now to prove, that man's own deserts suffice to no one, and that we are not saved but by the grace of God, *for all have sinned and come short of the glory of God*[10]. Wherefore he saith, *before His indignation*, standing face to Face before Him in wrath."

lit. in the Face of: guilt cannot look in the face of man, how much less, of God. The bliss of the righteous is the punishment of the wicked, to behold God face to Face. For "[8] whoso trusteth in his own works deserveth His indignation, and thinking he standeth, righteously does he fall."

His fury is poured out[11] *like fire*, sweeping away, like a torrent of molten fire, him who presumeth that he can stand before His Face, as He did the cities of the plain[12], the image of the everlasting fire, which shall burn up His enemies on every side[13]. *And rocks are thrown down.* The rocks are like so many towers[14] of nature, broken down and crushed

[1] Am. ix. 13. התמוגג occurs beside only in Ps. cvii. 26, of the heart of man through terror. Delitzsch (on Hab. p. 156) supposed that the hithpael or hithpalel conveyed "the operation of an outward cause, completing itself within the subject, as it were in continued vibrations," alleging Ew. Lehrb. 124 a, coll. התבקע Mic. i. 4, התגעש Ps. xviii. 8, התרעע התפורר, Is. xxiv. 19, התקלקל Jer. iv. 24, but there is no ground for making the form at once passive and reflective; and it is less vivid.

[2] Is. ii. 13, 14.

[3] נשׂא intrans. as Ps. lxxxix. 10, בשׂוא גליו, of the sea. With this agrees the constr. מפניו "from His Presence," as the cause of its fear. The E. V. "is burned" is taken from Rashi.

[4] Jon. [5] Rev. xx. 11; 2 Pet. iii. 10.

[6] As in Jo. ii. 11, Mal. iii. 2; renewed Rev. vi. 17.

[7] The noun זַעַם (used here) occurs 21 times in the O. T.; of men only once; the verb זָעַם occurs 13 times, 5 times only of man's anger.

[8] Rup. [9] Job iv. 18, 19. [10] Rom. iii. 23.

[11] נתך is used of the pouring out of God's wrath, Jer. vii. 20, xlii. 18, 2 Chr. xii. 7 (as more commonly שׁפך); here its native meaning is brought out the more, by adding כאשׁ.

[12] Gen. xix. [13] Ps. xcvii. 3. l. 3, lxviii. 3, xviii. 8.

[14] נתץ (not in the dialects) is used 34 times of the "breaking down" of walls, buildings, a statue, altar, shrine; in Ps. lviii. 7. only, of the teeth of lions, and, by metaphor, of men in Ps. lii. 7, Job xix. 10. Three times it is used elliptically.

Before CHRIST cir. 713.

o 1 Chr. 16. 34. Ps. 100. 5. Jer 33. 11. Lam. 3. 25.
‖ Or, *strength*.
p Ps. 1. 6. 2 Tim. 2. 19.

7 o The LORD *is* good, a ‖ strong hold in the day of trouble; and p he knoweth them that trust in him.

8 q But with an overrunning flood he will make an utter end of the place thereof, and darkness shall pursue his enemies.

Before CHRIST cir. 713.

q Dan. 9. 26. & 11. 10, 22, 40.

by Him lit. *from Him.* It needeth not any act of God's. He wills and it is done. Those who harden themselves, are crushed and broken to pieces, the whole fabric they had built for themselves and their defences, crumbling and shivered. If then they, whose hearts are hard as rocks, and bold against all peril, and even Satan himself, whose [1] *heart is as firm as a stone, yea, as hard as a piece of the nether millstone,* shall be crushed then, who shall abide?

7. *The Lord is good: a stronghold in the day of trouble.* "Good and doing good," and full of sweetness; alike good and mighty; Good in giving Himself and imparting His goodness to His own; yea[2] *none is good, save God;* Himself the stronghold wherein His own may take refuge; both in the *troubles* of this life, in which [3] *He will not suffer us to be tempted above that we are able,* and in that Day, which shall *hem* them *in* on every side, and leave no place of escape except Himself.

And He knoweth them that trust in Him; so as to save them; as Rahab was saved when Jericho perished, and Lot out of the midst of the overthrow and Hezekiah from the host of Sennacherib. He *knoweth* them with an individual, ever-present, knowledge[4]. He says not only, "He shall own them," but He ever *knoweth them.* So it is said; [5] *The Lord knoweth the way of the righteous,*[6] *The Lord knoweth the days of the upright;* and our Lord says, [7] *I know My sheep;* and S. Paul, [8] *The Lord knoweth them that are His.* God speaks of this knowledge also in the past, of His knowledge, when things as yet were not, *I have known thee by name;* or of loving kindness in the past, [9] *I knew thee in the wilderness,* [10] *you alone have I known of all the families of the earth,* as contrariwise our Lord says, that He shall say to the wicked in the Great Day, [11] *I never knew you.* That God, being what He is, should take knowledge of us, being what we are, is such wondrous condescension, that it involves a purpose of love, yea, His love toward us, as the Psalmist says admiringly, *Lord, what is man that Thou takest knowledge of him*[12]?

Them that trust in Him. It is a *habit,* which has this reward; *the trusters in Him*[13], *the takers of refuge in Him.* It is a continued unvarying trust, to which is shewn this ever-present love and knowledge.

Yet this gleam of comfort only discloseth the darkness of the wicked. Since those who trust God are they whom God knoweth, it follows that the rest He knoweth not. On this opening, which sets forth the attributes of God toward those who defy Him and those who trust in Him, follows the special application to Nineveh.

8. *But with an overrunning flood He will make an utter end of the place thereof*[14], i. e. of Nineveh, although not as yet named, except in the title of the prophecy, yet present to the Prophet's mind and his hearers, and that the more solemnly, as being *the* object of the wrath of God, so that, although unnamed, it would be known so to be. Image and reality, the first destruction and the last which it pictures, meet in the same words. Nineveh itself was overthrown through the swelling of the rivers which flowed round it and seemed to be its defence[15]. Then also, the *flood* is the tide of the armies, gathered from all quarters, Babylonians[16], Medes, Persians, Arabians, Bactrians, which like a flood should sweep over Nineveh and leave nothing standing. It is also the flood of the wrath of God, in Whose Hands they were, and Who, by them, should *make a full end of it,* lit. *make the place thereof a thing consumed,* a thing which has ceased to be. For a while, some ruins existed, whose name and history ceased to be known; soon after, the ruins themselves were effaced and buried[17]. Such was the close of a city, almost coeval with the flood, which had now stood almost as many years

1 Job xli. 24. 2 S. Luke xviii. 19. 3 1 Cor. x. 13.
4 יוֹדֵעַ. 5 Ps. i. 6. 6 Ps. xxxvii. 18.
7 S. John x. 14. 27. 8 2 Tim. ii. 19. 9 Hos. xiii. 5.
10 Am. iii. 2. 11 S. Matt. vii. 23. 12 Ps. cxliv. 3.

13 It is the well known construction חוֹסֵי בוֹ, in which, the verb being united with its object by a preposition, (like our "trust in,") the "in Him" stands as gen. as marked by the stat. const. חוֹסֵי, as it were "all trusters of Him," as כל חסי בו Ps. ii. 12, כל חֹסֵי בך Ps. v. 12. Elsewhere the art. is used to express the class, החֹסים בו 2 Sam. xxii. 31 (Ps. xviii. 31.) Ps. xxxiv. 23, לַחוֹסִים בך, Ps. xxxi. 20. לַחוֹסִים בו Pr. xxx. 5. החוסה בי Is. lvii. 13.

14 So Ezek. xi. 13, xx. 17, כָּלָה being the second object of the verb, "He made them as a thing consumed," or כ'ע' is used abs. as in v. 9. or with אֶת Jer. v. 18.

15 See on ii. 6. 16 Diod. Sic. ii. 25.
17 See ab. Introd. pp. 122, 123.

Before CHRIST cir. 713.

r Ps. 2. 1.
s 1 Sam. 3. 12.

9 [r] What do ye imagine against the LORD? [s] he will make an utter end: affliction shall not rise up the second time.

Before CHRIST cir. 713.

as have passed since Christ came, but which now defied God. Marvelous image of the evil world itself, which shall flee away from the Face of Him Who sat on the throne[1], *and there was found no place for it.*

And darkness shall pursue His enemies; better, *He shall pursue His enemies* into *darkness*[2]. Darkness is, in the O. T., the condition, or state in which a person is, or lives; it is not an agent, which pursues. Isaiah speaks of the [3] *inhabitants of darkness*[4], *entering into darkness;* [5] *those who are in darkness. The grave is all* [6] *darkness,* [7] *darkness, and the shadow of death.* Hence even Jews rendered, "[8] He shall deliver them to hell." Into this darkness it is said, God shall pursue them, as other prophets speak of being *driven forth into darkness*[9]. The darkness, the motionless drear abode, to which they are driven, anticipates the being cast into *the outer darkness, where shall be weeping and gnashing of teeth.* "[10] The vengeance of God on" those who remain "His enemies" to the last, "ends not with the death of the body; but evil spirits, who are darkness and not light, pursue their souls, and seize them." They would not hear Christ calling to them, [11] *Walk, while ye have the light, lest darkness come upon you.* [12] *They are of those that rebel against the light; they know not the ways thereof, nor abide in the paths thereof.* [13] *They loved darkness rather than light.* And so they were driven into the darkness which they chose and loved.

9. The Prophet had in few words summed up the close of Nineveh; he now upbraids them with the sin, which should bring it upon them, and foretells the destruction of Sennacherib. Nineveh had, before this, been the instrument of chastising Israel and Judah. Now, the capture of Samaria, which had cast off God, deceived and emboldened it. Its king thought that this was the might of his own arm; and likened the Lord of heaven and earth to the idols of the heathen, and said, [14] *Who are they among all the gods of the countries, that have delivered their country out of mine hand, that the Lord should deliver Jerusalem out of mine hand?* He sent [15] *to reproach the living God* and [16] *defied the Holy One of Israel.* His blasphemy was his destruction. It was a war, not simply of ambition, or covetousness, but directly against the power and worship of God.

What will ye so mightily[17] *devise, imagine against the Lord? He* [18] Himself, by Himself, *is* already *making an utter end.* It is in store; the Angel is ready to smite. Idle are man's *devices,* when the Lord *doeth.* [19] *Take counsel together, and it shall come to nought; speak the word, and it shall not stand: for God is with us.* While the rich man was speaking comfort to his soul as to future years, God was making an utter end. *Thou fool, this night shall thy soul be required of thee.*

[20] *Affliction shall not rise up the second time:* as he says afterward, *Though I have afflicted thee, I will afflict thee no more*[21]. *God,* He had said, *is good for a refuge in the day of affliction;* now, personifying that affliction, he says, that it should be so utterly broken, that it should rise up no more to vex them, as when a serpent's head is, not wounded only but, crushed and trampled under foot, so that it cannot again lift itself up. The promises of God are conditioned by our not falling back into sin. He saith to Nineveh, "God will

[1] Rev. xx. 11.
[2] So S. Jer. The punctuators marked this by the Makkef, ירדף-חשך.
[3] Is. xlii. 7. [4] Ib. xlvii. 5. [5] Ib. xlix. 9.
[6] Ps. lxxxviii. 12. Job xvii. 13. [7] Job x. 21.
[8] Jon.
[9] Is. viii. 22. וַאֲפֵלָה מְנֻדָּח Jer. xxiii. 12. בָּאֲפֵלָה יִדַּחוּ וְנָפְלוּ בָהּ "in darkness, into which they shall be driven and fall therein."
[10] Rup. [11] S. John xii. 35. [12] Job xxiv. 13.
[13] S. John iii. 19. [14] 2 Kings xviii. 35.
[15] Ib. xix. 16. [16] See xix. 15–34.
[17] The Hebrew form is doubly emphatic, תְּחַשְּׁבוּן. The same construction occurs with אל, "towards," Hos. vii. 15, וְאֵלַי יְחַשְּׁבוּ רָע (in the same general sense as the stronger על Nah. i. 11, Dan. xi. 24), in אֶל שַׁדַּי יתגבר Job xv. 25, יָרוּץ אֵלָיו "runneth at" i. e. against Him (God) Ib. 26. חִשֵּׁב is not simply "think," but "excogitated," "calculated" (Lev. 5 times), "devised" Pr. xvi. 9; with ל and inf. "to do evil to" Pr. xxiv. 8. In kal, also, חָשַׁב מַחֲשָׁבָה is used for "devising against," alike with על Jer. xi. 19. xviii. 11. 18. xlix. 30, and with אֶל Jer. xlix. 20. l. 45; and with על in a good sense, Jer. xxix. 11. חִשֵּׁב is used also of "thinking over" the past, Ps. lxxvii. 6. cxix. 59; with לְ and inf. "thinking over," in order to know, Ps. lxxiii. 16; with acc. p. "take account of" Ps. cxliv. 3, 2 Kgs xii. 16; but in none of these cases with אל.
[18] The use of the pronoun in Heb. is again emphatic. [19] Is. viii. 10.
[20] Others have understood this, "affliction shall not rise up the second time," but shall destroy at once, utterly and finally (comp. 1 Sam. xxvi. 8. 2 Sam. xx. 10.): but 1) the idiom there, לא שנה לו, "he did not repeat to him," as we say, "he did not repeat the blow," is quite different: 2) it is said, "affliction shall not rise up," itself, as if it could not. The causative of the idiom occurs in 2 Sam. xii. 11. הִנְנִי מֵקִים עָלֶיךָ רָעָה "lo, I will cause evil to rise up against thee." [21] v. 12.

Before CHRIST cir. 713.

t 2 Sam. 23. 6, 7.
u ch. 3. 11.

10 For while *they be*
folden together [t] *as* thorns,
[u] and while they are
drunken *as* drunkards,
[x] they shall be devoured as
stubble fully dry.

11 There is *one* come
out of thee, [y] that imagin-

x Mal. 4. 1.
y 2 Kings 19. 22, 23.

Before CHRIST cir. 713.

not deliver Judah to thee, as He delivered the ten tribes and Samaria." Judah repented under Hezekiah, and He not only delivered it from Sennacherib, but never afflicted them again through Assyria. Renewal of sin brings renewal or deepening of punishment. The new and more grievous sins under Manasseh were punished, not through Assyria but through the Chaldeans.

The words have passed into a maxim, "God will not punish the same thing twice," not in this world and the world to come, i. e. not if repented of. For of the impenitent it is said, [1] *destroy them with a double destruction.* Chastisement here is a token of God's mercy; the absence of it, or prosperous sin, of perdition; but if any refuse to be corrected, the chastisement of this life is but the beginning of unending torments.

10. *For while they be folden together as thorns* [2], i. e. as confused, intertwined, sharp, piercing, hard to be touched, rending and tearing whosoever would interfere with its tangled ways, and seemingly compact together and strong; *and while they are drunken as their drink* [3], not "drinkers [4]" only but literally "drunken," swallowed up, as it were, by their drink which they had swallowed, mastered, overcome, powerless, *they shall be devoured as stubble fully dry* [5], rapidly, in an instant, with an empty crackling sound, unresisting, as having nothing in them which can resist. Historically, the great defeat of the Assyrians, before the capture of Nineveh, took place while its king, flushed with success, was giving himself to listlessness; and having distributed to his soldiers victims, and abundance of wine, and other necessaries for banqueting, the whole army [6] was negligent and drunken." In like way Babylon was taken amid the feasting of Belshazzar [7]; Benhadad was smitten, while [8] *drinking himself drunk in the pavilions, he and the kings, the thirty and two kings that helped him.* And so it may well be meant here too, that Sennacherib's army, secure of their prey, were sunk in revelry, already swallowed up by wine, before they were swallowed up by the pestilence, on the night when the Angel of the Lord went out to smite them, and, from the sleep of revelry, they slept the sleep from which they shall not awake until the Judgment Day. God chooseth the last moment of the triumph of the wicked, when he is flushed by his success, the last of the helplessness of the righteous, when his hope can be in the Lord Alone, to exchange their lots. [9] *The righteous is delivered out of trouble, and the wicked cometh in his stead.* Spiritually, " [10] the false fullness of the rich of this world, is real leanness; the greenness of such grass (for *all flesh is grass*) is real dryness. Marvelous words, *fully dry.* For what is dryness but emptiness?" They are perfected, but in dryness, and so perfectly prepared to be burned up. "The thorns had, as far as in them lay, choked the good seed, and hated the Seed-corn, and now are found, like stubble, void of all seed, fitted only to be burned with fire. *For those* who feast themselves *without fear is* [11] *reserved the blackness of darkness for ever.*"

11. *There is one come out of thee* i. e. Nineveh, *that imagineth* [12], deviseth [13], *evil* [14], *against the*

[1] Jer. xvii. 18.

[2] עַד סִירִים lit. "quite up to," so as altogether to equal; as עַד תַּכְלִית, Job. xi. 7, עַד בְּנֵי יְהוּדָה, 1 Chr. iv. 27.

[3] סֹבֶא, wine, Is. i. 22. Hos. iv. 18.

[4] As elsewhere סֹבְאִים, Deut. xxi. 20, Pr. xxiii. 20, 21, סוֹבָאִי Cheth. Ez. xxiii. 42.

[5] מָלֵא is best united with יבשׁ. מְלֵאָה is used of ripe corn, Ex. xxii. 28. Dt. xxii. 9; but this may be so called, from the ear being full. The idiom, in which מָלֵא is joined with the verb, קָרְאוּ אחריך מָלֵא Jer xii. 6, is different, being derived from a phrase, קִרְאוּ מַלְאוּ "cry aloud, fill," i. e with a full voice, Jer. iv. 5. Schultens compares Arab. נַעַל וַמַלַא "he did and filled"=did fully. For the imagery of the devouring of the stubble by fire, see Is. v. 24. xlvii. 14. Jo. ii. 5. Ob. 18.

[6] Diod. Sic. ii. 26.

[7] Dan. v. 1–30.

[8] 1 Kings xx. 16.

[9] Pr. xi. 8.

[10] Rup.

[11] Jude 12, 13.

[12] Those who explain this of the past, render, "Out of thee, Judah, is gone away, withdrawn, he who devised evil against the Lord." But a person is said to "go forth" out of that which is his abode, from the city, gate, &c. or, to war. In the exceptions, Is. xlix. 17, "thy destroyers and wasters shall go forth from thee," it is implied that thay had long sojourned there, and were to give place to the children, who should return. In Jer. xliii. 12, where it is said of Nebuchadnezzar, *he shall go forth thence in peace*, it is first said, *he shall set up his throne there and shall array himself with the land of Egypt, as a shepherd putteth on his garment;* i. e. he shall make it wholly his own.

[13] As Ps. xxxv. 4. חשׁבי רעתי.

[14] בליעל occurs 18 times, combined with עַד, בן, בת, בני, איש, אנשי, אדם, "a son, daughter, sons, man, men, witness." יועץ בי is a similar composition. Else it only occurs with דבר Ps. xli. 9, ci. 3, and as an adj. De. xv. 9; as personal 2 Sam. xxiii. 6. Nah. ii. 1. also הַאָמֹר בי Job xxxiv. 18. There is then no ground to take it here, or Ps. xviii. 5, and 2 Sam. xxii. 5, with נחלי, as signifying "destruction."

Before CHRIST cir. 713.

eth evil against the LORD,
† a wicked counsellor.
12 Thus saith the LORD;
‖ Though *they be* quiet,
and likewise many, yet
thus [z] shall they be † cut
down, when he shall [a] pass
through. Though I have

† Heb. *a counsellor of Belial.*
‖ Or, *If they would have been at peace, so should they have been many, and so should they have been shorn, and he should have passed away.*
[z] 2 Kings 19. 35, 37.
† Heb. *shorn.*
[a] Isa. 8. 8. Dan. 11. 10.

afflicted thee, I will afflict
thee no more.
13 For now will I
[b] break his yoke from off
thee, and will burst thy
bonds in sunder.
14 And the LORD hath
given a commandment

Before CHRIST cir. 713.

[b] Jer. 2. 20. & 30. 8.

Lord, Sennacherib, [1] *the rod of God's anger*, yet who "*meant* not so," as God meant. "And this was his counsel," as is every counsel of Satan, "that they could not resist him, and so should withdraw themselves from the land of God, [2] *into a land like their own*, but whose joy and sweetness, its vines and its fig-trees, should not be from God, but from the Assyrian, i. e. from Satan."

12. *Though they be quiet and likewise many, yet thus shall they be cut down.* lit. *If they be entire*[3], i. e. sound, unharmed, unimpaired in their numbers, unbroken in their strength, undiminished, perfect in all which belongeth to war; *and thus many, even thus shall they be mown down* (or *shorn*), *and he passeth away*[4]. With might outwardly unscathed, *without hand*[5], and *thus many* i. e. many, accordingly, as being unweakened; as many as they shall be, *so shall they be mown down*[6], *and he*, their head and king, *shall pass away* and perish[7]. Their numbers shall be, as their condition before, perfect; their destruction as their numbers, complete. It is wonderful how much God says in few words; and how it is here foretold that, with no previous loss, a mighty host secure and at ease, in consequence of their prosperity, all are at one blow *mown down*, like the dry grass before the scythe, are cut off and perish; and one, their king, *passeth away*, first by flight, and then by destruction. As they had shorn the glory of others[8], so should they be shorn and cut down themselves.

Though I have afflicted thee, I will afflict thee[9] *no more*, unless by new guilt thou compel Me. God always relieves us from trouble, as it were with the words[10], *sin no more, lest a worse thing come unto thee.* In the end, afflictions shall be turned into joy, and *God shall wipe away all tears from their eyes; and there shall be no more death, nor sorrow, nor crying, neither shall there be any more pain*[11].

13. *For now will I break his yoke from off thee.* God, lest His own should despair, does not put them off altogether to a distant day, but saith, *now.* Historically, the beginning of the fall is the earnest of the end. By the destruction of Sennacherib, God declared His displeasure against Assyria; the rest was matter of time only. Thus Haman's wise men say to him, [12] *If Mordecai be of the seed of the Jews, before whom thou hast begun to fall, thou shalt not prevail against him, but shalt surely fall before him;* as He saith in Isaiah, [13] *I will break the Assyrian in My land, and upon My mountains tread him under foot; then shall his yoke depart from off them, and his burden depart from off their shoulders.* "[14] In that He saith, not 'I will loose,' 'will undo,' but 'I will break,' 'will burst,' He sheweth that He will in such wise free Jerusalem, as to pour out displeasure on the enemy. The very mode of speaking shews the greatness of His displeasure against those who, when for the secret purpose of His judgments they have power given them against the servants of God, feed themselves on their punishments, and moreover dare to boast against God, as did the Assyrian, [15] *By the strength of my hand I have done it, and by my wisdom.*"

14. *And the Lord hath given a commandment*

[1] Is. x. 5–7.
[2] Is. xxxvi. 16, 17.
[3] שלם is used of physical entireness, completeness, or mental integrity. In one place only, Gen. xxxiv. 21, שְׁלֵמִים אִתָּנוּ is doubtless rendered rightly "peaceable with us," as שׁוֹלְמִי Ps. vii. 5, but not in the frequent idiom לֵבָב, לֵב שָׁלֵם, whether with or without "עִם, and never by itself.
[4] So it seems better to render it, than, as in the E. V., *and he shall pass through.* The word means alike "pass away" or "pass through," but the act spoken of is later than the *cutting down* of the army, and so probably the *passing away*, or flight of its king, to his destruction or final passing away.
[5] Dan ii. 34.
[6] גָּזַז is used of sheep-shearing, cutting off the hair in sorrow; גֵּז is "mown grass, fleece cut." Here alone, it is a metaphor, like that of יְגַלַּח, Is. vii. 20.
[7] Comp. Ps. xlviii. 4.
[8] Is. vii. 20.
[9] עִנִּה, "afflicted" relatively to God, is said of His chastisement of His people (Deut. viii. 2. 2 Kgs xvii. 20) or of individuals (Ps. lxxxviii. 8. xc. 15. cii. 24. cxix. 75. Job xxx. 11.) but no where of the enemies of God, whose *destruction* moreover is here spoken of. It cannot then refer to the Assyrian, as some have done. The double omission of the ' in עִנִּתִךְ was probably for the rhythm.
[10] S. John v. 14.
[11] Rev. xxi. 4.
[12] Esth. vi. 13.
[13] Is. xiv. 25.
[14] Rup.
[15] Is. x. 13.

Before CHRIST cir. 713.

concerning thee, *that* no
more of thy name be sown:
out of the house of thy
gods will I cut off the
graven image and the mol-
ten image: [c]I will make thy
grave; for thou art vile.
15 Behold [d]upon the

Before CHRIST cir. 713.

c 2 Kin. 19. 37.
d Isa. 52. 7. Rom. 10. 15.

concerning thee, O Assyrian. In the word "I have afflicted *thee*," the land of Israel is addressed, as usual in Hebrew, in the feminine; here, a change of gender in Hebrew shews the person addressed to be different. "[1] By His command alone, and the word of His power, He cut off the race of the Assyrian, as he says in Wisdom, of Egypt, [2] *Thine Almighty word leaped down from Heaven, out of Thy royal throne; as a fierce man of war into the midst of a land of destruction, and brought Thine unfeigned commandment as a sharp sword, and standing up filled all things with death*," or else it may be, He gave command to the Angels His Ministers. God commandeth beforehand, that, when it cometh to pass, it may be known "[3] that not by chance," nor by the will of man, "nor without His judgment but by the sentence of God" the blow came.

No more of thy name be sown, as Isaiah saith, [4] *the seed of evildoers shall never be renowned*. He prophesies, not the immediate but the absolute cessation of the Assyrian line. If the prophecy was uttered at the time of Sennacherib's invasion, seventeen years before his death, not Esarhaddon only, but his son Asshurbanipal also, whose career of personal conquest, the last glory of the house of the Sargonides and of the empire, began immediately upon his father's reign of thirteen years, was probably already born. Asshurbanipal in this case would only have been thirty-one, at the beginning of his energetic reign, and would have died in his fifty-second year. After him followed only an inglorious twenty-two years. The prophet says, *the Lord hath commanded*. The decree as to Ahab's house was fulfilled in the person of his second son, as to Jeroboam and Baasha in their sons. It waited its appointed time, but was fulfilled in the complete excision of the doomed race.

Out of the house of thy gods will I cut off graven image and molten image[5]; as thou hast done to others[6], it shall be done to thee. "[7] And when even the common objects of worship of the Assyrian and Chaldean were not spared, what would be the ruin of the whole city!" So little shall thy gods help thee, that "[8] there shalt thou be punished, where thou hopest for aid. *Graven and molten image* shall be thy grave; amid altar and oblations, as thou worshipest idols," thanking them for thy deliverance, "shall thy unholy blood be shed," as it was by his sons Adrammelech and Sharezer[9]. *I will make* it [10] *thy grave;* "[7] what God *maketh* remains immovable, cannot be changed. But He "maketh thy grave" in hell, where not only that rich man in the Gospel hath his grave; but all who are or have been like him, and especially thou, O Asshur, of whom it is written, [11]*Asshur is there and all her company; his graves are about him: all of them slain, fallen by the sword. Whose graves are set in the sides of the pit and her company is round about her grave: all of them slain, fallen by the sword, which caused terror in the land of the living. Graven and molten image*, the idols which men adore, the images of their vanity, the created things which they worship instead of the true God (as they *whose god is their belly*), in which they busy themselves in this life, shall be their destruction in the Day of Judgment.

For thou art vile. Thou honoredst thyself and dishonoredst God, so shalt thou be dishonored[12], as He saith, [13] *Them that honor Me I will honor, and they that despise Me shall be lightly esteemed*. So when he had said to Edom, [14] *thou art greatly despised*, he adds the ground of it, [15] *The pride of thine heart hath deceived thee. For thou art vile*. Great, honored, glorious as Assyria or its ruler were in the eyes of men, the prophet tells him, what he was in himself, being such in the eyes of God, light, empty, as Daniel said to Belshazzar, [16] *Thou art weighed in the balances, and found wanting*, of no account, vile[17].

15. *Behold upon the mountains, the feet of him that bringeth good tidings, that publisheth peace*. From mountain-top to mountain-top by beacon-fires they spread the glad tidings. Suddenly the deliverance comes, sudden its announcement. *Behold!* Judah, before hin-

[1] Alb. [2] Wisd. xviii. 15. 16. [3] S. Jer. [4] xiv. 20.

[5] פסל ומסכה are so joined De. xxvii. 15. Jud. xvii. 3, 4, xviii. 14.

[6] Is. xxxvii. 19. [7] Rup. [8] S. Jer.

[9] Is. xxxvii. 38.

[10] He does not use the word עשה "made," but שים "appointed" it, set it to be. "There I will make thy grave." Jon. Even Ew. has "making *them* thy grave."

[11] Ez. xxxii. 22, 23. [12] From Dion.

[13] I Sam. ii. 30. [14] Ob. 2. [15] Ib. 3. [16] Dan. v. 27.

[17] So in Job's confession of himself, xl. 4, which, as addressed to God, can only be said of his intrinsic worthlessness. It stands contrasted with those whom God honors (אִכַּבֵּד) 1 Sam. ii. 30; in Hif. "held cheap" (2 Sam. xix. 44, Ez. xxii. 7.) put to dishonor, Is. viii. 23. (contrasted with הכביד). In Gen. xvi. 4. 5, it is added "in the eyes of" another; it is used of a thing, 1 Sam. xviii. 23. 2 Kgs iii. 18. The physical sense "were lightened" (of the waters of the deluge, Gen. viii. 11.) does not authorize the interpretation of some, "art lessened in number;" nor would this be a ground why God should make its grave.

Before CHRIST cir. 713.

mountains the feet of him that bringeth good tidings, that publisheth peace! O Judah, † keep thy solemn feasts, perform thy vows: for †[e] the wicked shall no more pass through thee; [f] he is utterly cut off.

† Heb. *feast.*

† Heb. *Belial.*
[e] ver. 11, 12.
[f] ver. 14.

dered by armies from going up to Jerusalem, its cities taken[1], may now again *keep the feasts* there, and *pay the vows,* which "in trouble she promised;" *for the wicked* one, the ungodly Sennacherib, *is utterly cut off, he shall no more pass through thee;* "the army and king and empire of the Assyrians have perished." But the words of prophecy cannot be bound down to this. These large promises, which, as to this world, were forfeited in the next reign, when Manasseh was taken captive to Babylon, and still more in the seventy years' captivity, and more yet in that until now, look for a fulfillment, as they stand. They sound so absolute. "I will afflict thee *no more,*" "the wicked shall *no more* pass through thee," "he is utterly (lit. *the whole of him*) cut off." Nahum joins on this signal complete deliverance from a temporal enemy, to the final deliverance of the people of God. The invasion of Sennacherib was an avowed conflict with God Himself. It was a defiance of God. He would make God's people, his; he would *cut it off, that it be no more a people, and that the name of Israel may be no more in remembrance*[2]. There was a more "evil counsellor" behind, whose agent was Sennacherib. He, as he is the author of all murders and strife, so has he a special hatred for the Church, whether before or since Christ's Coming. Before, that he might cut off that Line from whom *the Seed of the woman* should be born, which should destroy his empire and crush himself, and that he might devour the Child who was to be born[3]. Since, because her members are his freed captives, and she makes inroads on his kingdom, and he hates them because he hates God and Christ Who dwells in them. As the time of the birth of our Lord neared, his hate became more concentrated. God overruled the hatred of Edom or Moab, or the pride of Assyria, to His own ends, to preserve Israel by chastising it. Their hatred was from the evil one, because it was God's people, the seed of Abraham, the tribe of Judah, the line of David. If they could be cut off, they of whom Christ was to be born according to the flesh, and so, in all seeming, the hope of the world, were gone. Sennacherib then was not a picture only, he was the agent of Satan, who used his hands, feet, tongue, to blaspheme God and war against His people. As then we have respect not to the mere agent, but to the principal, and should address him through those he employed (as Elisha said of the messenger who came to slay him, [4]*is not the sound of his master's feet behind him?*), so the Prophet's words chiefly and most fully go to the instigator of Sennacherib, whose very name he names, *Belial.* It is the deliverance of the Church and the people of God which he foretells, and thanks God for. To the Church he says in the Name of God, *Though I have afflicted thee, I will afflict thee* no more[5]. The *yoke* which He will burst is the yoke of *the* oppressor, of which Isaiah speaks, and which the Son, to be born of a Virgin, "the Mighty God, the Prince of Peace," was to *break*[6]; the yoke of sin and the bands of fleshly pleasure and evil habits, wherewith we were held captive, so that henceforth we should walk upright, unbowed, look up to heaven our home, and *run the way of Thy commandments when Thou hast set my heart at liberty.* Behold, then, *upon the mountains,* i. e. above all the height of this world, *the feet of him that bringeth good tidings,* i. e. of remission of sins and sanctification by the Spirit and the freedom and adoption as sons, and the casting out of the Prince of this world, *that publisheth peace. O Judah,* thou, the true people of God, *keep thy solemn feasts,* the substance of the figures of the law." "[7]He who is ever engaged on the words, deeds and thoughts of Him, Who is by nature Lord, the Word of God, ever liveth in His days, ever keepeth Lord's days. Yea he who ever prepareth himself for the true life and abstaineth from the sweets of this life which deceive the many, and who cherisheth not the mind of the flesh but chastens the body and enslaves it, is ever keeping the days of preparation. He too who thinketh that Christ our Passover was sacrificed for us, and that we must keep festival, eating the flesh of the Word, there is no time when he keepeth not the Passover, ever passing over in thought and every word and deed from the affairs of this life to God, and hasting to His city. Moreover whoso can say truthfully, *we have risen together with Christ,* yea and also, *He hath together raised us and together seated us in the heavenly places in Christ,* ever liveth in the days of Pentecost; and chiefly, when, going up into the upper room as the Apostles of Jesus, he giveth himself to supplication and prayer, that he may become meet for the rushing mighty wind

[1] 2 Kings xviii. 13. [2] Ps. lxxxiii. 4. [3] Rev. xii. 4.

[4] 2 Kings vi. 32. [5] v. 12. [6] ix. 4. and 6. [7] Orig. c. Cels. viii. n. 22.

Before CHRIST cir. 713.

CHAPTER II.

1 *The fearful and victorious armies of God against Nineveh.*

HE ||[a]that dasheth in pieces is come up before thy face: [b]keep the

[a] Jer. 50. 23. [b] Jer. 51. 11, 12. ch. 3. 14.

Before CHRIST cir. 713.

|| Or, *The disperser*, or, *hammer*.

from heaven, which mightily effaceth the evil in men and its fruits, meet too for some portion of the fiery tongue from God." "[1]Such an one will keep the feast excellently, having the faith in Christ fixed, hallowed by the Spirit, glorious with the grace of adoption. And he will offer to God spiritual sacrifice, consecrating himself for an odor of sweetness, cultivating also every kind of virtue, temperance, continence, fortitude, endurance, charity, hope, love of the poor, goodness, longsuffering: for *with such sacrifices God is well pleased.* Every power of the enemy, which before had dominion over him, *shall pass through no more,* since Christ commanded the unclean spirits to depart into the abyss and giveth to those who love Him power to resist the enemy, and subdue the passions, and destroy sin and *tread on serpents and scorpions and every power of the enemy.*"

And these feasts were to be kept "[2]in the spirit not in the letter. For what availeth it to keep any feast without, unless there be the feast of contemplation in the soul?" Wherefore he adds, *and pay thy vows,* i. e. thyself, whom in Baptism thou hast vowed: *for the Wicked One shall no more pass through thee.* "[2]For from what time, O Judah, Christ, by dying and rising again, hallowed *thy feasts,* he can *no longer pass through thee.* Thenceforth he perished wholly. Not that he has, in substance, ceased to be, but that the death of the human race, which through his envy came into this world, the two-fold death of body and soul, wholly perisheth. Where and when did this Belial perish? When died the death which he brought in, whence himself also is called Death? When Christ died, then died the death of our souls; and when Christ rose again, then perished the death of our bodies. When then, *O Judah* thou *keepest thy feasts,* remember that thy very feast is He, of Whom thou sayest that by dying He conquered death and by rising He restored life. Hence it is said, *Belial shall no more pass through thee.* For if thou look to that alone, that Sennacherib departed, to return no more, and perished, it would not be true to say, Belial hath wholly perished! For after him many a Belial, such as he was, passed through thee, and hurt thee far more. Perchance thou sayest, 'so long as Nineveh standest, how sayest thou, that Belial has wholly perished? So long as the world standeth, how shall I be comforted, that death hath perished? For lo! persecutors armed with death have stormed, and besides them, many sons of Belial, of whom Anti-Christ will be the worst. How then sayest thou, that Belial has wholly perished?' It follows, *the Scatterer hath gone up before thee.* To Judah in the flesh, Nebuchadnezzar who went up against Nineveh, was worse than Sennacherib. Who then is He Who went up before thee, and dispersed the world, that great Nineveh, that thou shouldest have full consolation? Christ who descended, Himself ascended; and as He ascended, so shall He come to *disperse* Nineveh, i. e. to judge the world. What any persecutor doth meanwhile, yea or the Devil himself or Anti-Christ, taketh nothing from the truth, that Belial hath *wholly perished. The prince of this world is cast out.* For nothing which they do, or can do, hinders, that both deaths of body and soul are swallowed up in *His* victory, Who hath ascended to heaven? Belial cannot in the members kill the soul, which hath been made alive by the death of the Head, i. e. Christ; and as to the death of the body, so certain is it that it will perish, that thou mayest say fearlessly that it hath perished, since Christ the Head hath risen."

Each fall of an enemy of the Church, each recovery of a sinful soul being a part of this victory, the words may be applied to each. The Church or the soul are bidden to *keep the feast* and *pay their* vows, whatever in their trouble they promised to God. "[3]It is said to souls, which confess the Lord, that the devil who, before, wasted thee and bowed thee with that most heavy yoke hath, in and with the idols which thou madest for thyself, perished; *keep thy feasts* and *pay* to God *thy vows,* singing with the Angels continually, for *no more shall Belial pass through thee,* of whom the Apostle too saith, *What concord hath Christ with Belial?* The words too, *Behold upon the mountains* the feet of him that bringeth good tidings, that publisheth peace" belong, in a degree, to all preachers of the Gospel. "[4]No one can preach peace, who is himself below and cleaveth to earthly things. For wars are for the good things of earth. If thou wouldest preach peace to thyself and thy neighbor, be raised above the earth and its goods, riches and glory. Ascend to the heavenly mountains, whence David also, lifting up his eyes, hoped that his help would come."

C. II. The Prophet, having foretold the destruction of Sennacherib, and in him how the enemy of Judah is wholly cut off, goes on to describe the destruction of Nineveh, and

[1] S. Cyr. [2] Rup. [3] S. Jer. [4] Theoph.

Before CHRIST cir. 713.

munition, watch the way,
make *thy* loins strong, fortify *thy* power mightily.
2 [c] For the LORD hath
turned away ‖ the excel-
lency of Jacob, as the excellency of Israel: for [d] the
emptiers have emptied
them out, and marred their
vine branches.

[c] Isa. 10. 12. Jer. 25. 29.
‖ Or, *the pride of Jacob as the pride of Israel.*
[d] Ps. 80. 12. Hos. 10. 1.

with it of his whole kingdom, and, under it, of Anti-Christ and Satan.

1. *He that dasheth in pieces*, rather, *the Disperser*[1], the instrument of God, whereby he should *break her in pieces like a potter's vessel*, or *should scatter* her in all lands, *is come up against thy face*, O Nineveh, i. e. either, *over against thee*[2], confronting her as it were, face to face, or directed *against thee*[3]. From the description of the peace of Judah, the Prophet turns suddenly to her oppressor, to whom, not to Judah, the rest of the prophecy is directed. Jacob and Israel are spoken *of*, not *to*[4]. The destroyer of Nineveh *went up against the face of Nineveh*, not in the presence of Judah and Jacob, who were far away and knew nothing of it. *Keep the munition.* While all in Judah is now peace, all in Nineveh is tumult. God Whom they had defied, saying that Hezekiah could not [5] *turn away the face of one captain of the least of* his *servants*, now bids them prepare to meet him whom He would send against them. *Gird up thy loins now, like a man*[6]. Thou who wouldest lay waste others, now, if thou canst, keep thyself. The strength of the words is the measure of the irony. They had challenged God; He in turn challenges them to put forth all their might.

Fence thy defences[7], we might say. Their strong walls, high though they were, unassailable by any then known skill of besiegers, would not be secure.

The prophet uses a kindred and allusive word, that their protection needed to be itself protected; and this, by one continued watchfulness. *Watch*, he adds, *the way:* espy out[8] (as far as thou canst), the coming of the enemy; *strengthen the loins*, the seat of strength[9]. Elsewhere they are said to be *girded up* for any exertion. *Fortify thy strength exceedingly.* The expression is rare[10]: commonly it is said of some part of the human frame, knees, arms, or mind, or of man by God.

The same words are strong mockery to those who resist God, good counsel to those who trust in God. *Keep the munition*, for *He Who keepeth thee will not sleep*[11]; *watch the way*, by which the enemy may approach from afar, for Satan approacheth, sometimes suddenly, sometimes very stealthily and subtly, *transforming himself into an angel of light.* "[12] *Watch* also *the way* by which thou art to go, as it is said, [13] *Stand ye in the ways, and see, and ask for the old paths, where is the good way, and walk therein;* so that, having stood in many ways, we may come to that Way which saith, *I am the Way.*" Then[14], *make thy loins strong*, as the Saviour commandeth His disciples, *Let your loins be girded about*[15], and the Apostle says, [16] *Stand therefore, having your loins girt about with truth;* for nothing so strengtheneth as the Truth. For Christ being the Truth, whoso with his whole heart hath belived in Christ, is strong against himself, and hath power over the loins, the seat of the passions. Then, since this warfare is hard, he adds, be strong, *fortify thy power mightily;* resist not listlessly, but vehemently; and that, in His strength Who hath strengthened our nature, taking it to Himself and uniting it with the Godhead. For without Him, strong though thou be, thou wilt avail nothing.

2. *For the Lord hath turned away* (rather *restoreth*) *the excellency of Jacob*, speaking of what should come, as already come. For Nineveh falls, because God restores His people, whom it had oppressed. The restoration of God's favor to His Church is the sea-

[1] מֵפִּ֫יץ is a partic. used as a proper name. מֵפִּיץ is indeed used as a noun=מַפֵּץ as united with the *sword* and arrow, and so an instrument of war, *battle axe* or the like (Prov. xxv. 18.), like מַפֵּץ (Jer. li. 20.), used of Nebuchadnezzar by God. Yet the like phrase עָלָה הַפֹּרֵץ (Mic. ii. 13.) and the use itself of עָלָה, "went up," make it probable that an agent is meant. הֵפִיץ is always "dispersed;" the sense, "broke in pieces," occurs only in פּוֹצֵץ Jer. xxiii. 29, פִּצְפֵּץ Job. xvi. 12, הִתְפֹּצֵץ Hab. iii. 6, תְּפוֹצוֹתֵיכֶם Jer. xxv. 34, and in נָפַץ, נִפֵּץ.

[2] As Gen. xxxii. 22, תעבר על פניו; Job iv. 15, רוח על פני יחלף.

[3] As Ps. xxi. 13, תכונן על פניהם which is supported by the use of עָלָה עַל, "went up against," as 2 Kgs xvii. 3, xviii. 25, Jo. i. 6.

[4] ver. 2. Jon., Rashi, Kim., Abarb. would have it, that Judah is addressed.

[5] Is. xxxvi. 9.

[6] Job. xl. 7.

[7] נָצוֹר מְצוּרָה The Imp. נְצוֹר would have expressed a simple command; the Infin. says, what has to be done.

[8] צַפֵּה.

[9] The use of the adj. אֵמְתָנִי "strong" Dan. vii. 7, shows that the meaning of the root was not lost, though occurring only in the adj. and מָתְנַיִם.

[10] It occurs Prov. xxiv. 5, of the man of understanding, and Am. ii. 14, of what man cannot do.

[11] Ps. cxxi. 3. [12] S. Jer. [13] Jer. vi. 16.

[14] From S. Jer. [15] Luke xii. 35. [16] Eph. vi. 14.

Before CHRIST cir. 713.

3 The shield of his
mighty men is made [e]red,
the valiant men *are* ||in
scarlet: the chariots *shall*
be with ||flaming torches
in the day of his preparation, and the fir trees shall
be terribly shaken.
4 The chariots shall
rage in the streets, they
shall justle one against
another in the broad ways:

e Isa. 63. 2, 3.
|| Or, *dyed scarlet.*
|| Or, *fiery torches.*

son of His punishment of their enemies; as, again, His displeasure against her enemies is a token of His favor to her. When Herod was smitten by God, [1] *the word of God grew and multiplied.* A long captivity was still before Judah, yet the destruction of the Assyrian was the earnest that every *oppressing city* should *cease* [2].

The excellency of Jacob. The word, *excellency,* is used in a good or bad sense; bad, if man takes the excellency to himself; good, as given by God. This is decisive against a modern popular rendering; "[3] *has returned to* the excellency of Jacob;" for Scripture knows of no *excellency of Jacob,* except God Himself or grace from God. Jacob, if separated from God or left by Him, has no excellency, to which God could return.

As the excellency of Israel. Both the ten and the two tribes had suffered by the Assyrian. The ten had been carried captive by Shalmanezer, the two had been harassed by Sennacherib. After the captivity of the ten tribes, the name Jacob is used of Judah only. It may be then, that the restoration of God's favor is promised to each separately. Or, [4] there may be an emphasis in the names themselves. Their forefather bore the name of *Jacob* in his troubled days of exile; that of *Israel* was given him on his return [5]. It would then mean, the afflicted people (Jacob) shall be restored to its utmost glory as Israel. The sense is the same.

For the emptiers have emptied them out. Their chastisement is the channel of their restoration. Unlike the world, their emptiness is their fullness, as the fullness of the world is its emptiness. The world is cast down, not to arise; for [6] *woe to him that is alone when he falleth: for he hath not another to help him up.* The Church *falleth,* but *to arise* [7]: the people is restored, because it had borne chastening [8]; *for the Lord hath restored the excellency of Jacob; for the emptiers have emptied them out and marred their vinebranches* [9], i. e. its fruit-bearing branches, that, as far as in them lay, it should not bear fruit unto God; but to cut the vine is, by God's grace, to make it shoot forth and bear fruit more abundantly.

3, 4. Army is arrayed against army; the armies, thus far, of God against the army of His enemy; all without is order; all within, confusion. The assailing army, from its compactness and unity, is spoken of, both as many and one. The might is of many; the order and singleness of purpose is as of one. *The shield,* collectively, not *shields. His mighty men;* He, who was last spoken of, was Almighty God, as He says in Isaiah; [10] *I have commanded My consecrated ones; I have also called My mighty ones, them that rejoice in My highness.*

Is reddened, either with blood of the Assyrians, shed in some previous battle, before the siege began, or (which is the meaning of the word elsewhere [11]), an artificial color, the color of blood being chosen, as expressive of fiery fierceness. *The valiant men are in scarlet;* for beauty and terror, as, again being the color of blood [12]. It was especially the color of the dress of their nobles [13], one chief color of the Median dress, from whom the Persians adopted their's [14]. *The chariots shall be with flaming torches,* literally *with the fire of steels* [15], or of sharp incisive instruments. Either way the words seem to indicate that the chariots were in some way armed with steel. For steel was not an ornament, nor do the chariots appear to have been ornamented with metal. Iron would have hindered the primary object of lightness and speed. Steel, as distinct from iron, is made only for incisiveness. In either way, it is probable, that scythed chariots were already in use. Against such generals, as the younger Cyrus [16] and Alexander [17], they were of no avail; but they

[1] Acts xii. 24. [2] Is. xxxiii. 1.
[3] See ab. Intr. p. 127. n. 8.
[4] Sanct. [5] Gen. xxxii. 28.
[6] Eccles. iv. 10. [7] Micah vii. 8.
[8] Ez. xxxvi. 3, 6, 7. [9] See Ps. lxxx. 12, 13.
[10] Is. xiii. 3.

[11] The form מְאָדָּם is used five times in Exodus of the artificial color of the dyed ramskins. But there is no proof of any such custom as to the shields. If reddened by actual blood, it must have been in a previous battle, since Nahum is thus far describing the preparations, בְּיוֹם הֲכִינוֹ. The gleaming of the brass of the shields in the sun (1 Macc. vi. 39) could hardly be called *their* being reddened.

[12] Ælian V. H. vi. 6. Val. Max. ii. 6. 2.

[13] Xenophon (Cyrop. viii. 3. 3) implies that they were costly treasures which Cyrus distributed.

[14] Strabo xi. 13. 9.

[15] On פלדות see Introd. pp. 127–129.

[16] At Cunaxa, Xen. Anab. i. 8.

[17] At Arbela, Arr. iii. 13, Q. Curt. iv. 51, and, upon experience, by Eumenes, "haud ignarus pugnæ," Liv. xxxvii. 41, Appian Syr. 33. Diodorus (xvii. 58.) describes their terrible vehemence, when not evaded. Uneven ground naturally disordered them. Tac. Agr. c. 36. Vegetius iii. 24.

Before CHRIST cir. 713.

† they shall seem like
torches, they shall run like
the lightnings.
5 He shall recount his
‖ worthies: they shall
stumble in their walk;
they shall make haste to
the wall thereof, and the
† defence shall be prepared.

† Heb. *their show.*

‖ Or, *gallants.*

† Heb. *covering,* or, *coverer.*

must have been terrific instruments against undisciplined armies. The rush and noise of the British chariots disturbed for a time even Cæsar's Roman troops[1]. They were probably in use long before.[2] Their use among the ancient Britons[3], Gauls[4] and Belgians[5], as also probably among the Canaanites[6], evinces that they existed among very rude people. The objection that the Assyrian chariots are not represented in the monuments as armed with scythes is an oversight, since those spoken of by Nahum may have been Median, certainly were not Assyrian. *In the day of His preparation*[7], when He mustereth the hosts for the battle; *and the fir-trees shall be terribly shaken;* i. e. fir-spears[8] (the weapon being often named from the wood of which it is made) shall be made to quiver through the force wherewith they shall be hurled.

The chariots shall rage (or *madden*[9], as the driving of Jehu is said to be *furiously*, lit. *in madness*) *in the streets.* The city is not yet taken; so, since this takes place *in the streets* and *broad ways*, they are the confused preparations of the besieged. *They shall justle one against another*, shall run rapidly to and fro, restlessly; *their show* (*E. M.*) is *like torches*, leaving streaks of fire, as they pass rapidly along. *They shall run* vehemently[10], *like the lightnings*, swift but vanishing.

5. *He shall recount his worthies.* The Assyrian king wakes as out of a sleep, lit. "he *remembers* his mighty men[11];" *they stumble in their walk*, lit. *paths*[12], not through haste only and eager fear, but from want of inward might and the aid of God. Those whom God leadeth stumble not[13]. "[14] Perplexed every way and not knowing what they ought to do, their mind wholly darkened and almost drunken with ills, they reel to and fro, turn from one thing to another, and in all" labor in vain.

They shall make haste to the walls thereof, and the defence (lit. *the covering*) *shall be prepared.* The Assyrian monuments leave no doubt that a Jewish writer[15] is right in the main, in describing this as a covered shelter, under which an enemy approached the city; "a covering of planks with skins upon them; under it those who fight against the city come to the wall and mine the wall underneath, and it is a shield over them from the stones, which are cast from off the wall."

The monuments, however, exhibit this shelter, as connected not with mining but with a battering ram, mostly with a sharp point, by which they loosened the walls[16]. Another covert was employed to protect single miners who picked out single stones with a pick-axe[17]. The Assyrians sculptures shew, in the means employed against or in defence of their engines, how central a part of the siege they formed[18]. Seven of them are represented in one siege[19]. The "ram[20]" is mentioned in Ezekiel as the well-known and ordinary instrument of a siege.

1 De bell. Gall. iv. 33, 34.

2 Ctesias, who speaks of them as long prior (quoted by Diod. Sic. ii. 5.) is, on Persian matters, much better authority than Xenophon who (Cyrop. vi. 1. as explained by Arrian, Tactic. c. 3.) attributes their invention to Cyrus. For Xenophon, who was a good witness as to what he saw, shews himself ignorant of the previous history (See ab. p. 123). He himself quotes Ctesias as an authority (Anab. i. 8.). The exaggerations of Ctesias are probably those of his Persian informants.

3 Sil. Ital. xvii. 417, 418. Tac. Agric. 35, 36. Mela iii. 6. Jornandes de reb. Goth. c. 2.

4 Mela iii. 6.

5 Lucan i. 426. S. Jerome in Is. ult.

6 The use of a little iron, more or less, in strengthening the wheels &c., could hardly entitle them to be called "chariots of iron." Jos. xvii. 16, 18. Jud. i. 19, iv. 3, 13.

7 הכין as in Jer. xlvi. 14, Ez. vii. 14, xxxviii. 7.

8 See on Hos. xiv. 8. vol. i. p. 140.

9 The words are adopted by Jeremiah xlvi. 9.

10 רִצִין Intensive from רוץ.

11 As iii. 18. Jud. v. 13. Neh. iii. 5.

12 So the Heb. text. Their many ways may be opposed to the oneness of the army of God (See v. 3).

13 Is. lxiii. 13.

14 S. Cyr.

15 Kimchi.

16 See in Rawlinson's 5 Empires ii. 78. "All of them [the battering-rams] were covered with a frame-work of ozier, wood, felt, or skins, for the better protection of those who worked the implement;—some appear to have been stationary, others in early times had six wheels, in the later times four only. Sometimes with the ram and its framework was a moveable tower, containing soldiers, who, at once, fought the enemy on a level and protected the engine."

17 See picture in Rawl. 5 Emp. ii. 82.

18 "Fire was the weapon usually turned against the ram, torches, burning tow or other inflammable substances being cast from the walls upon its framework." To prevent this [its being set on fire], the workers of the ram were sometimes provided with a supply of water; sometimes they suspended from a pole in front of their engine, a curtain of leather, or some other non-inflammable substance. In a bas-relief (Layard's *Monuments*, Series ii. Pl. 21.) where an enormous number of torches are seen in the air, every battering-ram is so protected. Or the besieged sought to catch the point of the ram by a chain, drawing it upwards; the besieger with metal hooks to keep it down." from Rawl. Ib. pp. 79, 80, referring further to Layard's *Monuments*, Series i. Pl. 17, 19.

19 Ib. p. 79.

20 Ezek. iv. 2.

Before CHRIST cir. 713.

6 The gates of the rivers shall be opened, and the palace shall be ‖ dissolved.

‖ Or, *molten*.

7 And ‖ Huzzab shall be ‖ led away captive, she shall be brought up, and

‖ Or, *discovered*.

Before CHRIST cir. 713.

‖ Or, *that which was established, or, there was a stand made.*

Thus v. 3. describes the attack; v. 4, the defence; the two first clauses of v. 5, the defence; the two last, the attack. This quick interchange only makes the whole more vivid.

"[1] But what availeth it to build the house, unless the Lord build it? What helpeth it to shut the gates, which the Lord unbarreth?" On both sides is put forth the full strength of man; there seems a stand-still to see, what will be, and God brings to pass His own work in His own way.

6. *The gates of the rivers shall be opened, and the palace shall be dissolved.* All gives way in an instant at the will of God; the strife is hushed; no more is said of war and death; there is no more resistance or bloodshed; no sound except the wailing of the captives, the flight of those who can escape, while the conquerors empty it of the spoil, and then she is left a waste. The swelling of the river and the opening made by it may have given rise to the traditional account of Ctesias, although obviously exaggerated as to the destruction of the wall. The exaggerated character of that tradition is not inconsistent with, it rather implies, a basis of truth. It is inconceivable that it should have been thought, that walls, of the thickness which Ctesias had described, were overthrown by the swelling of any river, unless some such event as Ctesias relates, that the siege was ended by an entrance afforded to the enemy through some bursting-in of the river, had been true. Nahum speaks nothing of the wall, but simply of the opening of *the gates of the rivers*, obviously the gates, by which the inhabitants could have access to the rivers [2], which otherwise would be useless to them except as a wall. These *rivers* correspond to the *rivers*, the artificial divisions of the Nile, by which No or Thebes was defended, or [3] *the rivers of Babylon* which yet was washed by the one stream, the Euphrates. But Nineveh was surrounded and guarded by actual rivers, the Tigris and the Khausser, and, (assuming those larger dimensions of Nineveh, which are supported by evidences so various [4]) the greater Zab, which was "called [5] the frantic Zab' on account of the violence of its current." "The Zab contained (says Ainsworth [6]), when we saw it, a larger body of water than the Tigris, whose tributaries are not supplied by so many snow-mountains as those of the Zab." Of these, if the Tigris be now on a level lower than the ruins of Nineveh, it may not have been so formerly. The Khausser, in its natural direction, ran through Nineveh where, now as of old, it turns a mill, and must, of necessity, have been fenced by *gates;* else any invader might enter at will; as, in modern times, Mosul has its "gate of the bridge." A break in these would obviously let in an enemy, and might the more paralyze the inhabitants, if they had any tradition, that the river alone could or would be their enemy, as Nahum himself prophesied. Subsequently inaccuracy or exaggeration might easily represent this to be an overthrow of the walls themselves. It was all one, in which way the breach was made.

The palace shall be dissolved. The prophet unites the beginning and the end. The river-gates were opened; what had been the fence against the enemy became an entrance for them: with the river, there poured in also the tide of the people of the enemy. *The palace*, then, the imperial abode, the centre of the empire, embellished with the history of its triumphs, sank, was *dissolved* [7], and ceased to be. It is not a physical loosening of the sun-dried bricks by the stream which would usually flow harmless by; but the dissolution of the empire itself. "[1] The temple i. e. his kingdom was destroyed." The palaces both of Khorsabad and Kouyunjik lay near the Khausser [8] and both bear the marks of fire [9].

7. The first word should be rendered, *And*

[1] S. Jer.

[2] Such explanations as "gates whereby the enemy poured in as rivers" (Ros.), or "gates of Nineveh which was guarded by rivers" (Ew.) or "of the streets, where the inhabitants surged like rivers" (Hitz.) are plainly not literal.

[3] Ps. cxxxvii. 1.

[4] See Introd. to Jonah, vol. i.

[5] Kaswini, quoted by Tuch p. 35.

[6] Ainsw. Tr. ii. 327.

[7] The word, which occurs 18 times, is used of the melting of the earth at the voice or presence or touch of God, Ps. xlvi. 7, Nah. i. 5, Am. ix. 5; of the "melting away" of a multitude, 1 Sam. xiv. 16; of all Philistia, Is. xiv. 31; (act.) of God working the dissolution of one being, Job xxx. 22, or of many, Is. lxiv. 6; of the hearts of people, melting for fear, Ex. xv. 15, Jos. ii. 9, 24, Ps. lxxv. 4, cvii. 26. Jer. xlix. 23, Ez. xxi. 20: once only it is used physically of water, of the clods softened by showers, Ps. lxv. 11; and in the ideal image "the hills shall melt," being dissolved, as it were, in the rich stream of the abundant vintage. Am. ix. 13.

[8] See Introduction to Jonah, vol. i. Asshurbanipal, the last great monarch of Assyria, built his palace on the mound of Kouyunjik. (Rawl. 5 Emp. ii. 496). "The Khosr-su, which runs on this side of the Khorsabad ruins, often overflows its banks, and pours its waters against the palace-mound. The gaps, N. and S. of the mound, may have been caused by its violence." Ib. i. 358.

[9] See ab. p. 122 n. c.

Before CHRIST cir. 713.

her maids shall lead *her* as
with the voice of [f] doves,
tabering upon their breasts.
8 But Nineveh *is* ‖ of
old like a pool of water:
yet they shall flee away.
Stand, stand, *shall they cry;*
but none shall ‖ look back.
9 Take ye the spoil of
silver, take the spoil of
gold: ‖ for *there is* none
end of the store *and* glory
out of all the † pleasant
furniture.
10 She is empty, and
void, and waste: and the
[g] heart melteth, and [h] the
knees smite together, [i] and

[f] Isa. 38. 14. & 59. 11.
‖ Or, *from the days* that *she* hath been.
‖ Or, *cause* them *to turn.*

Before CHRIST cir. 713.

‖ Or, *and* their *infinite store, &c.*
† Heb. *vessels of desire.*
[g] Isa. 13. 7.
[h] Dan. 5. 6.
[i] Jer. 30. 6.

it is decreed; She shall be laid bare. It is decreed[1]. All this took place, otherwise than man would have thought, because it was the will of God. *She* (the people of the city, under the figure of a captive woman) *shall be laid bare*[2], in shame, to her reproach; *she shall be brought up*[3], to judgment, or from Nineveh as being now sunk low and depressed; *and her maids*, the lesser cities, as female attendants on the royal city, and their inhabitants represented as women, both as put to shame and for weakness. The whole empire of Nineveh was overthrown by Nebopalassar. Yet neither was the special shame wanting, that the noble matrons and virgins were so led captives in shame and sorrow. They *shall lead her, as with the voice of doves*, moaning, yet, for fear, with a subdued voice.

8. *But Nineveh is of old like a pool of water* i. e. of many peoples[4], gathered from all quarters and settled there, her multitudes being like the countless drops, full, untroubled, with no ebb or flow, fenced in, *from the days that she hath been*, yet even therefore stagnant and corrupted[5], not "a fountain of living waters," during 600 years of unbroken empire; even lately it had been assailed in vain[6]; now its hour was come, the sluices were broken; the waters poured out. It was full not of citizens only, but of other nations poured into it. An old historian says[7], "The chief and most powerful of those whom Ninus settled there, were the Assyrians, but also, of other nations, whoever willed." Thus the pool was filled; but at the rebuke of the Lord they flee. *Stand, stand*, the Prophet speaks in the name of the widowed city; "shut the gates, go up on the walls, resist the enemy, gather yourselves together, form a band to withstand," *but none shall look back* to the mother-city which calls them; all is forgotten, except their fear; parents, wives, children, the wealth which is plundered, home, worldly repute. So will men leave all things, for the life of this world. [8] *All that a man hath, will he give for his life.* Why not for the life to come?

9. *Take ye the spoil of silver, take the spoil of gold.* Nineveh had not hearkened of old to the voice of the Prophet, but had turned back to sin; it cannot hearken now, for fear. He turns to the spoiler to whom God's judgments assigned her, and who is too ready to hear. The gold and silver, which the last Assyrian King had gathered into the palace which he fired, was mostly removed (the story says, treacherously) to Babylon. Arbaces is said to have borne this and to have removed the residue, to the amount of many talents, to Agbatana, the Median capital[9]. *For there is none end of the store.* Nineveh had stored up from her foundation until then, but at last for the spoiler. [10] *When thou shalt cease to spoil, thou shalt be spoiled.* Many [11] *perish and leave their wealth to others.* [12] *The wealth of the sinner is laid up for the just. And glory out of all the pleasant furniture,* [lit. as in the Margin, "glory out of all vessels of desire"] i. e. however large the spoil, it would be but a portion only; yet all their wealth, though more than enough for the enemy and for them, could not save them. Her "glory," was but a "weight" to weigh her down, that she should not rise again[13]. Their wealth brought on the day of calamity, availed not therein, although it could not be drawn dry even by the spoiler. "[14] They could not spoil so much as she supplied to be spoiled."

10. *She is empty and void and waste.* The

[1] This is the simple rendering of הֻצַּב, Hof. of נצב. In Ch. יַצִּיב, "firm," Dan. vi. 13; "reliable," Dan. ii. 45, vii. 16; יַצִּיבָא "certainly," Dan. iii. 24, מִן־יַצִּיב "of a certainty," Dan. ii. 8. Also in Phœn.; Ges. Thes. p. 66. The retention of Huzzab as a proper name for the queen, is derived from R. Samuel Hannagid in Ibn Ezra. The ground for this, alleged in Rashi, viz. the use of נִצְּבָה Ps. xlv. 10, betrays its origin. Kimchi, with the same etymology, explains it of the palace.

[2] The meaning of גֻּלְּתָה (ἅπ.) is determined by that of the active גִּלָּה, which is always "laid bare," not "carried captive."

[3] As in c. iii. 5. Is. xlvii. 2, 3.

[4] Rev. xvii. 1.

[5] See Jer. xlviii. 11.

[6] By Cyaxares Her. i. 106.

[7] Ctesias ap. Diod. ii. 3.

[8] Job ii. 4.

[9] Diod. Sic. ii. 28.

[10] Is. xxxiii. 1.

[11] Ps. xlix. 10.

[12] Pr. xiii. 22.

[13] Zech. v. 8. Ex. xv. 10.

[14] S. Jer.

Before CHRIST cir. 713.

much pain *is* in all loins,
and [k] the faces of them all
gather blackness.

[k] Joel 2. 6.

11 Where *is* the dwelling of [l] the lions, and the
feedingplace of the young
lions, where the lion *even*
the old lion, walked, *and*
the lion's whelp, and none
made *them* afraid?

[l] Job 4. 10, 11. Ezek. 19. 2–7.

12 The lion did tear in
pieces enough for his
whelps, and strangled for
his lionesses, and filled his
holes with prey, and his
dens with ravin.

13 [m] Behold, I *am*
against thee, saith the
LORD of hosts, and I will
burn her chariots in the

[m] Ezek. 29. 3. & 38. 3. & 39. 1 ch. 3. 5.

completeness of her judgment is declared first under that solemn number, Three, and the three words in Hebrew are nearly the same [1], with the same meaning, only each word fuller than the former, as picturing a growing desolation; and then under four heads (in all seven) also a growing fear. First *the heart,* the seat of courage and resolve and high purpose, *melteth;* then *the knees smite together,* tremble, shake, under the frame; then, *much pain is in all loins,* lit. "strong pains as of a woman in travail," writhing and doubling the whole body, and making it wholly powerless and unable to stand upright, shall bow the very loins, the seat of strength [2], *and,* lastly, *the faces of them all gather blackness* [3], the fruit of extreme pain, and the token of approaching dissolution.

11. *Where is the dwelling of the lions, and the feeding place of the young lions?* Great indeed must be the desolation, which should call forth the wonder of the prophet of God. He asks "where is it?" For so utterly was Nineveh to be effaced, that its place should scarcely be known, and now is known by the ruins which have been buried, and are dug up. The messengers of her king had asked, [4] *Where are the gods of Hamath and of Arpad? of Sepharvaim, Hena, and Ivah?* And now of her it is asked, "Where is Nineveh?" It had *destroyed utterly all lands,* and now itself is utterly destroyed. The lion dwelt, fed, walked there, up and down, at will; all was spacious and secure; he terrified all, and none terrified him; he tore, strangled, laid up, as he willed, booty in store; but when he had filled it to the full, he filled up also the measure of his iniquities, and his sentence came from God. Nineveh had set at nought all human power, and destroyed it; now, therefore, God appeareth in His own Person.

13. *Behold I,* Myself, *am against thee* [lit. *toward thee*]. God, in His long-suffering, had, as it were, looked away from him; now He looked toward [5] him, and in His sight what wicked one should stand? *Saith the Lord of hosts,* Whose power is infinite and He changeth not, and all the armies of heaven, the holy angels and evil spirits and men are in His Hand, whereto He directs or overrules them. *And I will burn her chariots in the smoke.* The Assyrian sculptures attest how greatly their pride and strength lay in their chariots. They exhibit the minute embellishment of the chariots and horses [6]. Almost inconceivably light for speed, they are pictured as whirled onward by the two [7] or, more often, three [8] powerful steeds with eye of fire [9], the bodies of the slain [10] (or, in peace, the lion [11]) under their feet, the mailed warriors, with bows stretched to the utmost, shooting at the more distant foe. Sennacherib gives a terrific picture of the fierceness of their onslaught. "The armor, the arms, taken in my attacks, swam in the blood of my enemies as in a river; the war-chariots, which destroy man and beast, had, in their course, crushed the bloody bodies and limbs [12]." All this their warlike pride should be but fuel for fire, and vanish in smoke, an emblem of pride, swelling, mounting like a column toward heaven, disappearing. Not a brand shall then be saved out of the burning; nothing half-consumed; but the fire shall burn, until there be nothing left to consume, as, in Sodom and Gomorrah [13], *the smoke of the country went up as the smoke of a furnace. And the sword* of the vengeance of God *shall devour the young lions,* his hope for the time to come, the flower of his youth; *and I will cut off thy prey,* what thou hast robbed, and so that thou shouldest rob no more, but that thy spoil should utterly cease *from the earth, and the voice of thy messengers shall be no more heard,*

[1] See ab. p. 125–6. *bookah, oomebookah, oomebullakah.*
[2] Prov. xxxi. 17.
[3] See on Joel ii. 6.
[4] 2 Kings xviii. 34.
[5] As in Ps. xxxvii. 20.
[6] See Rawl. 5 Empires ii. 4–21.
[7] Rawl. Ib. 10. 11. 13.
[8] Layard Monuments, Series i. Plate 18, 21, 23, 27, 28.
[9] See a striking illustration in Rawl. ii. 15. (from Boutcher.)
[10] Layard Ser. i. 27. 28. ii. 45. 46.
[11] Rawl. Ib. 13. Layard Ninev. ii. 77.
[12] In Oppert Sargonides p. 51. The general accuracy of the deciphering is alone presupposed.
[13] Gen. xix. 28.

Before CHRIST cir. 713.

smoke, and the sword shall devour thy young lions: and I will cut off thy prey from the earth, and the voice of [n]thy messengers shall no more be heard.

Before CHRIST cir. 713.

[n] 2 Kin. 18. 17, 19. & 19. 9, 23.

such as Rabshakeh, whereby they insulted and terrified the nations and blasphemed God.

In the spiritual sense, Nineveh being an image of the world, the prophecy speaks of the inroad made upon it through the Gospel, its resistance, capture, desolation, destruction. First, He that *ruleth with a rod of iron*, came and denounced *woe to it because of offenses;* then His *mighty* ones [1] in His Name. Their shield is red, *the shield of faith*, kindled and glowing with love. Their raiment too is red, because they wash it in the Blood of the Lamb, and conquer through the Blood of the Lamb, and many shed their own blood *for a witness to them. The day of His preparation* is the whole period, until the end of the world, in which the Gospel is preached, of which the prophets and apostles speak, as *the* day of salvation [2]; to the believing world a day of salvation; to the unbelieving, of preparation for judgment. All which is done, judgments, mercy, preaching, miracles, patience of the saints, martyrdom, all which is spoken, done, suffered, is part of the one preparation for the final judgment. The chariots, flashing with light as they pass, are [3] *the chariots of salvation*, bearing the brightness of the doctrine of Christ and the glory of His truth throughout the world, enlightening while they wound; the "spears" are the word of God, slaying to make alive.

On the other hand, in resisting, the world clashes with itself. It would oppose the Gospel, yet knows not how; is "maddened with rage, and gnashes its teeth, that it can prevail nothing [4]." On the *broad ways* which lead to death, where *Wisdom uttereth her voice* and is not heard, it is hemmed in, and cannot find a straight path; its chariots dash one against another, and yet they breathe their ancient fury, and run to and fro like lightning, as the Lord saith, *I beheld Satan, as lightning, fall from Heaven* [5]. Then shall they *remember their mighty* ones, all the might of this world which they ascribed to their gods, their manifold triumphs, whereby in Heathen times their empire was established; they shall gather strength against strength, but it shall be powerless and real weakness. While they prepare for a long siege, *without hand* their gates give way; the kingdom falls, the world is taken captive by a blessed captivity, suddenly, unawares, as one says in the second century; "[6] Men cry out that the state is beset, that the Christians are in their fields, in their forts, in their islands!" These mourn over their past sins, and beat their breasts, in token of their sorrow; yet sweeter shall be the plaint of their sorrow, than any past joy. So they shall mourn as doves, and their mourning is as melody and the voice of praise in the ear of the Most High. One part of the inhabitants of the world being thus blessedly taken, the rest are fled. So in all nearness of God's judgments, those who are not brought nearer, flee further. "*They flee, and look not back*, and none heareth the Lord speaking, *Return, ye backsliding children, and I will heal your backslidings* [7]. So then, hearing not His Voice, *stand, stand*, they flee away from His presence in Mercy, into darkness for ever. Such is the lot of the inhabitants of the world; and what is the world itself? The prophet answers what it has been. *A pool of water*, into which all things, the riches and glory, and wisdom, and pleasures of this world, have flowed in on all sides, and which gave back nothing. All ended in itself. The water came from above, and became stagnant in the lowest part of the earth. "[5] For all the wisdom of this world, apart from the sealed fountain of the Church, and of which it cannot be said, *the streams thereof make glad the city of God* nor are of those waters which, above the heavens, praise the Name of the Lord, however large they may seem, yet are little, and are enclosed in a narrow bound." These either are hallowed to God, like the spoils of Egypt, as when the eloquence of S. Cyprian was won through the fishermen [8], or the gold and silver are offered to Him, or they are left to be wasted and burned up. *All which is in the world, the lust of the flesh, and the lust of the eyes, and the pride of life, all under the sun*, remain here. "[9] If they are thine, take them with thee. *When he dieth, he shall carry nothing away, his glory shall not descend after him* [10]. True riches are, not wealth, but virtues, which the conscience carries with it, that it may be rich for ever." The seven-fold terrors [11], singly, may have a good sense [4], that the stony *heart* shall be melted, and the stiff *knees*, which before were not bent to God, be bowed in the Name of Jesus. Yet more fully are they the deepening horrors of the wicked in the Day of Judgment, when *men's hearts shall fail them for fear and for looking after those things which are coming on the earth* [12], closing with the everlasting confusion of face, *the shame and everlasting contempt*, to which the wicked

[1] From Dion. [2] Is. xlix. 8. 2 Cor. vi. 2.
[3] Habak. iii. 8. [4] S. Jer. [5] S. Luke x. 18.
[6] Tert. Apol. c. 1. and p. 3. not. 9. Oxf. Tr.

[7] Jer. iii. 22. [8] The Apostles. S. Aug.
[9] S. Bern. in Adv. Serm. 4. [10] Ps. xlix. 17.
[11] v. 10. [12] S. Luke xxi. 26.

Before CHRIST cir. 713.

CHAPTER III.

1 *The miserable ruin of Nineveh.*

† Heb. *city of bloods.*
a Ezek. 22. 2, 3. & 24. 6. 9. Hab. 2. 12.

WOE to the †[a] bloody city! it *is* all full of lies *and* robbery; the prey departeth not;

Before CHRIST cir. 713.

2 The noise of a whip, and [b]the noise of the

b Jer. 47. 3.

---

shall rise. As the vessel over the fire is not cleansed, but blackened, so through the judgments of God, whereby the righteous are cleansed, the wicked gather but fresh defilement and hate. Lastly, the Prophet asks, *Where is the dwelling of those who had made the world a den of ravin, where the lion,* even *the devil* who is *a roaring lion,* and all Anti-Christs[1], destroyed at will; where Satan made his dwelling in the hearts of the worldly, and *tore in pieces for his whelps,* i. e. slew souls of men and gave them over to inferior evil spirits to be tormented, and *filled his holes with prey,* the pit of hell with the souls which he deceived[2]? The question implies that they shall not be. [3] *They which have seen him shall say, Where is he?* God Himself answers, that He Himself will come against it to judgment, and destroy all might arrayed against God; and Christ [4] shall *smite the Wicked one with the rod of His Mouth,* and the [5] *sharp two-edged sword out of His mouth shall smite all nations,* and *the smoke of their torment ascendeth up for ever and ever*[6]; and it should no more oppress, nor "any messenger of Satan" go forth to harass the saints of God.

C. III. The prophecy of the destruction in Nineveh is resumed in a dirge over her; yet still as future. It pronounces a woe, yet to come[7].

1. *Woe to the bloody city,* lit. *city of bloods*[8], i.e. of manifold bloodshedding, built and founded in blood[9], as the prosperity of the world ever is. Murder, oppression, wresting of judgment, war out of covetousness, grinding or neglect of the poor, make it *a city of bloods.* Nineveh, or the world, is a city of the devil, as opposed to the "city of God." "[10] Two sorts of love have made two sorts of cities; the earthly, love of self even to contempt of God; the Heavenly, love of God even to contempt of self. The one glorieth in itself, the other in the Lord." "[11] Amid the manifold differences of the human race, in languages, habits, rites, arms, dress, there are but two kinds of human society, which, according to our Scriptures, we may call two cities. One is of such as wish to live according to the flesh; the other of such as will according to the Spirit." "Of these, one is predestined to live for ever with God; the other, to undergo everlasting torment with the devil." Of this city, or evil world, Nineveh, *the city of bloods,* is the type.

It is all full of lies and robbery, better, *it is all lie; it is full of robbery* [*rapine*]. *Lie* includes all falsehood, in word or act, denial of God, hypocrisy; toward man, it speaks of treachery, treacherous dealing, in contrast with open violence or rapine[12]. The whole being of the wicked is one lie, toward God and man; deceiving and deceived; leaving no place for God Who is the Truth; seeking through falsehood things which fail. Man [13] *loveth vanity and seeketh after leasing.* All were gone out of the way. "[14] There were none in so great a multitude, for whose sake the mercy of God might spare so great a city." *It is full,* not so much of booty as *of rapine* and violence. The sin remains, when the profit is gone. Yet it ceaseth not, but persevereth to the end; *the prey departeth*[15] *not;* they will neither leave the sin, nor the sin them; they neither repent, nor are weary of sinning. Avarice especially gains vigor in old age, and grows by being fed. *The prey departeth not,* but continues as a witness against it, as a lion's lair is defiled by the fragments of his prey.

2. *The noise* [lit. *voice*] *of the whip.* There is cry against cry; the voice of the enemy, brought upon them through the voice of the oppressed. Blood hath a voice which *crieth*[16] to heaven; its echo or counterpart, as it were, is the cry of the destroyer. All is urged on with terrific speed. The chariot-wheels quiver[17] in the rapid onset; the chariots bound, like living things[18]; the earth echoes

---

1 1 John ii. 18. 2 Dion. 3 Job xx. 7.
4 Is. xi. 4. 5 Rev. i. 16, xix. 15. 21. 6 Rev. xiv. 11.
7 הוֹי, when signifying "woe," is always of future woe, as lies in the word itself. It is used of classes of persons 25 times; against people, Samaria, Jerusalem or foreign nations, 13 times; of the past only as to the wailings at funerals. 1 Kgs xiii. 30, Jer. xxii. 18, xxxiv. 5.
8 As in E. M. The phrase occurs Ezek. xxii. 2, xxiv. 6. 9. So אִישׁ ד', אנשי', בית, "a man" (2 Sam. xvi. 7, 8. Ps. v. 7) "men" (Ps. xxvi. 9, lv. 24, lix. 3, cxxxix. 19, Pr. xxix. 10) "a house" (2 Sam. xxi. 1) "of bloods," guilty of manifold bloodshed.
9 Hab. ii. 12, Jer. xxii. 13.

10 S. Aug. de Civ. D. xiv. 28. 11 Ib. c. 1.
12 פֶּרֶק ἅπ. The verb is used of the merciless "tearing" of the lion, "rending and there is no deliverer." Ps. vii. 3. 13 Ps. iv. 2. 14 Alb.
15 ימישׁ is intrans. except in Mic. ii. 3, 4.
16 Gen. iv. 10.
17 רעשׁ of the chariots, Jer. xlvii. 3, of the war-horse, Job. xxxix. 24, of the loud tumult of battle, Is. ix. 4, Jer. x. 22.
18 רקד is used of the dancing of children, Job xxi. 11, of David before the ark, 1 Chr. xv. 29, of the satyrs, Is. xiii. 21. Even when used of the tremb-

Before CHRIST cir. 713.

rattling of the wheels, and of the pransing horses, and of the jumping chariots.

3 The horseman lifteth up both †the bright sword and the glittering spear: and *there is* a multitude of slain, and a great number of carcases; and *there is* none end of *their* corpses; they stumble upon their corpses:

† Heb. *the flame of the sword, and the lightning of the spear.*

4 Because of the multitude of the whoredoms of the wellfavored harlot, [c] the mistress of witchcrafts, that selleth nations through her whoredoms, and families through her witchcrafts.

c Isa. 47. 9. 12. Rev. 18. 2, 3.

with the whirling swiftness[1] of the speed of the cavalry. The Prophet within, with the inward ear and eye which heareth the *mysteries of the Kingdom of God*[2] and seeth things to come, as they shall come upon the wicked, sees and hears the scourge coming, with [3] a great noise, impetuously; and so describes it as present. Wars and rumors of wars are among the signs of the Day of Judgment. The *scourge*, though literally relating to the vehement onset of the enemy, suggests to the thoughts, the scourges of Almighty God, wherewith He chastens the penitent, punishes the impenitent; the *wheel*, the swift changes of man's condition in the rolling-on of time. [4] *O God, make them like a rolling thing.*

3. *The horseman lifteth up*, rather, *leading up*[5]: *the flash of the sword, and the lightning of the spear.* Thus there are, in all, seven inroads, seven signs, before the complete destruction of Nineveh or the world; as, in the Revelations, all the forerunners of the Judgment of the Great Day are summed up under the voice of seven trumpets[6] and seven vials. "[7] God shall not use horses and chariots and other instruments of war, such as are here spoken of, to judge the world, yet, as is just, His terrors are foretold under the name of those things, wherewith this proud and bloody world hath sinned. For so *all they that take the sword shall perish with the sword*[8]." They who, abusing their power, have used all these weapons of war, especially against the servants of God, shall themselves perish by them, and there shall be *none end of their corpses*, for they shall be corpses for ever: for, dying by an everlasting death, they shall, without end, be without the true life, which is God." *And there is a multitude of slain.* Death follows on death. The Prophet views the vast field of carnage, and everywhere there meets him only some new form of death, *slain, carcases, corpses*, and these in *multitudes*, an *oppressive heavy number*, without end, so that the yet living *stumble* and fall *upon the carcases* of the slain. So great the multitude of those who perish, and such their foulness; but what foulness is like sin?

4. *Because of the multitude of the whoredoms of the well-favored harlot.* There are *multitudes of slain*, because of the *multitude of whoredoms* and love of the creature instead of the Creator. So to Babylon Isaiah saith, "[9] they [loss of children and widowhood] shall come upon thee in their perfection *for* the multitude of thy sorceries, for the great abundance of thine enchantments." The actual use of *enchantments*[10], for which Babylon was so infamous, is not elsewhere attributed to the Assyrians. But neither is the word elsewhere used figuratively; nor is Assyria, in its intimate relation to Babylon, likely to have been free from the longing, universal in Heathendom, to obtain knowledge as to the issue of events which would affect her. She is, by a rare idiom, entitled "*mistress*[11] of

ling of the mountains before God, they are compared to living things, a calf, Ps. xxix. 6, rams, Ps. cxiv. 4. 6. It is used also of the locusts, Jo. ii. 5. [all]. Mostly, as here, it is intensive. In Syr. Pa. is "danced;" in Arabic the insulated רַקְדָאנ is used of "bounding as a kid." See Lane s. v.

1 The root only occurs beside Jud. v. 22. "Then smote [the earth] the horse-hoofs from the whirlings, the whirlings [probably "whirling speed" דהר i. q. דור] of his mighty ones" [i. e. steeds. Jer. viii. 16. xlvii. 3. l. 11.].

2 S. Matt. xiii. 11. 16.

3 2 Pet. iii. 10. The words in Hebrew are purposely chosen with rough sounds, (r) "*r*a'ash, dohe*r*, me*r*akkēdah."

4 Ps. lxxxiii. 14.

5 This division is the more likely, because the words stand very broken, mostly in pairs, describing, as it were, by the very order of the words, the successive onsets, wherewith the destruction from God should break in upon them.

6 Rev. vi. viii. The foreboding cry "woe! woe!" before the destruction of Jerusalem, an image also of the Day of Judgment, was also seven-fold. See above on c. ii. 10.

7 Rup.

8 S. Matt. xxvi. 52.

9 Is. xlvii. 9.

10 כְּשָׁפִים (always plural) are spoken of as to Jezebel, 2 Kgs ix. 22; Babylon, Is. l. c. and as to be abolished by God in Judah; Micah v. 11. Those who used them, מְכַשְּׁפִים, were employed by Pharaoh, Ex. vii. 11, and Nebuchadnezzar, Dan. ii. 2; were strictly forbidden to Israel (Ex. xxii. 17. De. xviii. 10.); their employment was one chief offence of Manasseh. (2 Chr. xxxiii. 6.)

11 בַּעֲלַת (fem.) only occurs beside in 1 Kgs xvii. 17, of the widow of Zarephath, who, as being a widow, was the mistress of the house, and of the witch of Endor, as בעלת אוב, 1 Sam. xxviii. 7.

Before CHRIST cir. 713.

5 [d] Behold, I *am* against thee, saith the LORD of hosts; and [e] I will discover thy skirts upon thy face, [f] and I will shew the nations thy nakedness, and the kingdoms thy shame.

[d] ch. 2. 13.
[e] Isa. 47. 2, 3. Jer. 13. 22, 26. Ezek. 16. 36. Mic. 1. 11.
[f] Hab. 2. 16.

enchantments," having them at her command, as instruments of power. Mostly, idolatries and estrangement from God are spoken of as *whoredoms*, only in respect of those who, having been taken by God as His own, forsook Him for false gods. But Jezebel too, of whose offences Jehu speaks under the same two titles [1], was a heathen. And such sins were but part of that larger all-comprehending sin, that man, being made by God for Himself, when he loveth the creature instead of the Creator, divorceth himself from God. Of this sin world-empires, such as Nineveh, were the concentration. Their being was one vast idolatry of self and of *the god of this world.* All, art, fraud, deceit, protection of the weak against the strong [2], promises of good [3], were employed, together with open violence, to absorb all nations into it. The one end of all was to form one great idol-temple, of which the centre and end was man, a rival worship to God, which should enslave all to itself and the things of this world. Nineveh and all conquering nations used fraud as well as force, enticed and entangled others, and so sold and deprived them of freedom [4]. Nor are people less sold and enslaved, because they have no visible master. False freedom is the deepest and most abject slavery. All sinful nations or persons extend to others the infection of their own sins. But, chiefly, the "wicked world," manifoldly arrayed with fair forms, and "beautiful in the eyes of those who will not think or weigh how much more beautiful the Lord and Creator of all," spreads her enticements on all sides, *the lust of the flesh, and the lust of the eye, and the pride of life,* "her pomps and vanities," worldly happiness and glory and majesty, and ease and abundance, deceives and sells mankind into the power of Satan. It is called *well-favored* [lit. *good of grace*], because the world has a real beauty, nor, "[5] unless there were a grace and beauty in the things we love, could they draw us to them." They have their beauty, because from God; then are they deformed, when "[6] things hold us back from God, which, unless they were in God, were not at all." We deform them, if we love them for our own sakes, not in Him; or for the intimations they give of Him. "[7] Praise as to things foul has an intensity of blame. As if one would speak of a skilled thief, or a courageous robber, or a clever cheat. So though he calls Nineveh *a well-favored harlot,* this will not be for her praise, (far from it!) but conveys the heavier condemnation. As *they,* when they would attract, use dainty babblings, so was Nineveh a skilled artificer of ill-doing, well provided with means to capture cities and lands and to persuade them what pleased herself." She selleth not *nations* only but *families,* drawing mankind both as a mass, and one by one after her, so that scarce any escape.

The adultery of the soul from God is the more grievous, the nearer God has brought any to Himself, in priests worse than in the people, in Christians than in Jews, in Jews than in Heathen; yet God espoused mankind to Him when He made him. His dowry were gifts of nature. If this be adultery, how much sorer, when betrothed by the Blood of Christ, and endowed with the gift of the Spirit!

5. *Behold I am against thee, saith the Lord of Hosts.* "[8] I will not send an Angel, nor give thy destruction to others; I Myself will come to destroy thee." "[7] She has not to do with man, or war with man: He Who is angered with her is *the Lord of hosts.* But who would meet God Almighty, Who hath power over all, if He would war against him?" In the Medes and Persians it was God who was against them. *Behold I am against thee,* lit. *toward thee.* It is a new thing which God was about to do. *Behold!* God in His long-suffering had seemed to overlook her. Now, He says, *I am toward thee,* looking at her with His all-searching eye, as her Judge. Violence is punished by suffering; deeds of shame by shame. All sin is a whited sepulchre, fair without, foul

[1] 2 Kgs ix. 22.
[2] 2 Kgs xvi. 7–9, 2 Chr. xxviii. 20, 21.
[3] Is. xxxvi. 16, 17.
[4] See Joel iii. 3. The word מָכַר, as the act of selling, implies elsewhere, "to part with into the hands of another." This is implied, even where (as in De. xxxii. 30, Ps. xliv. 13) it is not expressed to whom they were sold. But here the nations were not, as nations, sold by Assyria into the hands of others, but retained in its own power. Yet since מָכַר occurs 80 times throughout the O. T. in the one sense "sell," and its derivatives מִמְכֶּרֶת, מִמְכָּר, מֶכֶר, 14 times, it is against all idiom to assume that, in this one case, it meant "deceived" (as the Arab. מָכַר, with acc. p. and בְּ of thg.); nor were the enchantments an instrument of deceit; the word then must here too retain its sense of depriving of liberty, "selling" to slavery or death.
[5] S. Aug. Conf. iv. 13.
[6] Ib. x. 27 and iv. 12 and note m.
[7] S. Cyr.
[8] S. Jer.

Before CHRIST cir. 713.

6 And I will cast abom-
inable filth upon thee, and
g make thee vile, and will
set thee as h a gazingstock.
7 And it shall come to
pass *that* all they that look
upon thee i shall flee from
thee, and say, Nineveh is
laid waste: k who will bemoan her? whence shall I
seek comforters for thee?
8 l Art thou better than

g Mal. 2. 9.
h Heb. 10. 33.
i Rev. 18. 10.
k Jer. 15. 5.
l Amos 6. 2.

within. God will strip off the outward fairness, and lay bare the inward foulness. The deepest shame is to lay bare, what the sinner or the world veiled within. *I will discover thy skirts*[1], i. e. the long flowing robes which were part of her pomp and dignity, but which were only the veil of her misdeeds. *Through the greatness of thine iniquity have thy skirts been discovered*, says Jeremiah in answer to the heart's question, *why have these things come upon me?* *Upon thy face*, where shame is felt. The conscience of thy foulness shall be laid bare before thy face, thy eyes, thy memory continually, so that thou shalt be forced to read therein, whatsoever thou hast done, said, thought. *I will shew the nations thy nakedness*, that all may despise, avoid, take example by thee, and praise God for His righteous judgments upon thee. The Evangelist heard *much people in heaven saying Alleluia* to God that *He hath judged the whore which did corrupt the earth with her fornication*[2]. And Isaiah saith, *They shall go forth and look upon the carcases of the men that have transgressed against Me*[3].

6. *And I will cast abominable filth upon thee*, "[4]like a weight, that what thou wouldest not take heed to as sin, thou mayest feel in punishment." *Abominable things had God seen*[5] in her doings; with abominable things would he punish her. Man would fain sin, and forget it as a thing past. God *maketh* him to *possess the iniquities of his youth*[6], and bindeth them around him, so that they *make* him to appear what they are, *vile*[7]. [8]*These things hast thou done and I kept silence;—I will reprove thee and set them in order before thine eyes. And will set thee as a gazing-stock*, that all, while they gaze at thee, take warning from thee[9]. [10]*I will cast thee to the ground; before kings will I give thee, for them to gaze upon thee.* "[11]Whoso amendeth not on occasion of others, others shall be amended on occasion of him."

7. *All they that look upon thee shall flee from thee* through terror, lest they should share her plagues, as Israel did, when the earth swallowed up Corah, Dathan and Abiram; and they who [12]*had been made rich by Babylon, stand afar off, for the fear of her torment. All they who look on thee.* She was set as a thing to be *gazed at*[13]. He tells the effect on the gazers. *Each one who so gazed*[14] at her should *flee;* one by one, they should *gaze*, be scared, flee[15]. Not one should remain. *Who will bemoan her?* Not one should pay her the passing tribute of sympathy at human calamity, the shaking of the head at her woe[16]. Who had no compassion, shall find none.

8. *Art thou better*[17], more populous or more powerful, *than the populous No?* rather *than No-Ammon*, so called from the idol Ammon, worshiped there. No-Ammon, (or, as it is deciphered in the Cuneiform Inscriptions, *Nia*), meaning probably "the portion of Ammon[18]," was the sacred name of the capital of Upper Egypt, which, under its common name, Thebes, was far-famed, even in the time of Homer, for its continually accruing wealth, its military power, its 20,000 chariots, its vast dimensions attested by its 100 gates[19]. Existing earlier, as the capital of Upper Egypt, its grandeur began in the 18th dynasty, after the expulsion of the Hyksos, or Semitic conquerors of Egypt. Its Pharaohs were conquerors, during the 18th–20th dynasties, B. C. 1706–1110, about six centuries. It was then the centre of a world-empire. Under a disguised name[20], its rulers were celebrated in Geek story also, for their world-wide conquests. The Greek statements have in some main points been verified by the

1 שׁוּלַיִךְ always plural, for their profuseness, as we speak of "robes." It is the word used in the same image, Jer. xiii. 22. 26; Isaiah has the like, שֹׁבֶל. Is. xlvii. 2.

2 Rev. xix. 1. 2.
3 lxvi. 24.
4 Alb.
5 Jer. xiii. 27.
6 Job. xiii. 26.
7 Comp. Wisdom iv. 18.
8 Ps. l. 21.
9 Comp. 2 Chron. vii. 20.
10 Ezek. xxviii. 17.
11 Ptol. Prov. ap. Alb.
12 Rev. xviii. 15.
13 רֹאִי.
14 כָּל־רֹאַיִךְ.
15 Comp. Ps. xxxi. 11. lxiv. 8.
16 Comp. Job xvi. 4, 5.

17 תֵּיטְבִי, for תִּיטְבִי, as יֵיקַר Ps. lxxii. 14, אֵילְכָה Mic. i. 8.

18 As the LXX. (from their acquaintance with Egypt) render, μερὶς Ἀμμών. The Coptic MSS. Martyrologies mention "the place of Ammon," (Jablonski Opp. i. 163) and the Hieroglyphics. Lepsius, Chronol. d. Æg. i. 272. The common name Ap-t or T-ap was the original of the name Thebes, by which it became known to the West through the Greeks.

19 Il. ix. 381–4, [all the wealth] "as much as comes to the Egyptian Thebes, where most possessions are laid up in the houses, which hath a hundred gates, and from each, 200 men go forth with horses and chariots."

20 Sesostris. Herod. ii. 102–110, and notes in Rawl. Her.; Diod. i. 53–59, Strabo xv. 1. 6. xvi. 4. and 7. xvii. 1. 5.

Before CHRIST cir. 713.

‖ † populous [m] No, that was situate among the rivers, *that had* the waters round about it, whose ramparts *was* the sea, *and* her wall *was* from the sea?

Before CHRIST cir. 713.

‖ Or, *nourishing*. † Heb. *No Amon*.

m Jer. 46. 25, 26. Ezek. 30. 14–16.

decipherment of the hieroglyphics. The monuments relate their victories in far Asia, and mention Nineveh itself among the people who paid tribute to them. They warred and conquered from the Soudan to Mesopotamia. A monument of Tothmosis I. (1066 B.C.) still exists at Kerman, between the 20th and 19th degrees latitude, boasting, in language like that of the Assyrian conquerors; "All lands are subdued, and bring their tributes for the first time to the gracious god[1]." "The frontier of Egypt," they say[2], "extends Southward to the mountain of Aptâ (in Abyssinia) and Northward to the furthest dwellings of the Asiatics." The hyperbolic statements are too undefined for history[3], but widely-conquering monarchs could alone have used them. "[4]At all periods of history, the possession of the country which we call Soudan (the Black country) comprising Nubia, and which the ancients called by the collective name of Kous [Cush] or Æthiopia, has been an exhaustless source of wealth to Egypt. Whether by way of war or of commerce, barks laden with flocks, corn, hides, ivory, precious woods, stones and metals, and many other products of those regions, descended the Nile into Egypt, to fill the treasures of the temples and of the court of the Pharaohs: and of metals, especially gold, mines whereof were worked by captives and slaves, whose Egyptian name *noub* seems to have been the origin of the name Nubia, the first province S. of Egypt." "The conquered country of Soudan, called Kous in the hieroglyphic inscriptions, was governed by Egyptian princes of the royal family, who bore the name of 'prince royal of Kous.'"

But the prophet's appeal to Nineveh is the more striking, because No, in its situation, its commerce, the sources of its wealth, its relation to the country which lay between them, had been another and earlier Nineveh. Only, as No had formerly conquered and exacted tribute from all those nations, even to Nineveh itself, so now, under Sargon and Sennacherib, Nineveh had reversed all those successes, and displaced the Empire of Egypt by its own, and taken No itself. No had, under its Tothmoses, Amenophes, Sethos, the Ousertesens, sent its *messengers*[5], the leviers of its tribute, had brought off from Asia that countless mass of human strength, the captives, who (as Israel, before its deliverance, accomplished its hard labors) completed those gigantic works, which, even after 2000 years of decay, are still the marvel of the civilized world. Tothmosis I., after subduing the Sasou, brought back countless captives from Naharina[6] (Mesopotamia); Tothmosis III., in 19 years of conquests, (1603–1585 B.C.) "[7] raised the Egyptian empire to the height of its greatness. Tothmosis repeatedly attacked the most powerful people of Asia, as the Routen (Assyrians?) with a number of subordinate kingdoms, such as Asshur, Babel, Nineveh, Singar; such as the Remenen or Armenians, the Zahi or Phœnicians, the Cheta or Hittites, and many more. We learn, by the description of the objects of the booty, sent to Egypt by land and sea, counted by number and weight, many curious details as to the industry of the conquered peoples of central Asia, which do honor to the civilization of that time, and verify the tradition that the Egyptian kings set up stelæ in conquered countries, in memory of their victories. Tothmosis III. set up his stele in Mesopotamia, 'for having enlarged the frontiers of Egypt.'" Amenophis too is related to have "[8]taken the fortress of Nenii (Nineveh)." "[8]He returned from the country of the higher Routen, where he had beaten all his enemies to enlarge the frontiers of the land of Egypt:" "[8]he took possession of the people of the South, and chastised the people of the North:" "at Abd-el-Kournah" he was represented as "[9]having for his footstool the heads and backs of five peoples of the S. and four peoples of the N. or Asiatics." "[9]Among the names of the peoples, who submitted to Egypt, are the Nubians, the Asiatic shepherds, the inhabitants of Cyprus and Mesopotamia." "[10]The world in its length and its breadth" is promised by the sphinx to Tothmosis IV. He is represented as "[11] subduer of the negroes." Under Amenophis III., the Memnon of the Greeks, "[12]the Egyptian empire extended Northward to Mesopotamia, Southward to the land of Karou." He enlarged and beautified No,

1 Brugsch Hist. d'Eg. p. 88.
2 Ib. and (Tothmosis iii.) p. 109.
3 "Notwithstanding the length of the like texts, recording the victories gained by the Pharaohs, the historical subject is treated as accessory, as an occasion of repeating, for the thousandth time, the same formulas, the same hyperbolic words, the same ideas." Brugsch pp. 89.
4 Brugsch ib. p. 89–107.
5 Nah. ii. 13.
6 Brugsch p. 90.
7 Ib. p. 104, the summary of pp. 95–103.
8 Ib. p. 111.
9 Ib. 112.
10 On the sphinx of Gizeh Ib. p. 113.
11 In the Isle of Konosso near Philæ Ib. p. 114.
12 Ib. pp. 114, 115.

which had from him the temple of Louksor, and his vocal statue, "[1] all people bringing their tributes, their children, their horses, a mass of silver, of iron and ivory from countries, the roads whereto we know not." The king Horus is saluted as "[2] the sun of the nine people; great is thy name to the country of Ethiopia;" "[2] the gracious god returns, having subdued the great of all people." Setj I. (or Sethos) is exhibited[3], as reverenced by the Armenians, conquering the Sasou, the "Hittites, Naharina (Mesopotamia), the Routen (Assyrians?) the Pount, or Arabs in the S. of Arabia, the Amari or Amorites, and Kedes, perhaps Edessa." Rameses II., or the great[4] (identified with the Pharaoh of the Exodus[5]), conquered the Hittites in the N.; in the S. it is recorded, "[6] the gracious god, who defeated the nine people, who massacred myriads in a moment, annihilated the people overthrown in their blood, yet was there no other with him." The 20th Dynasty (B. C. 1288–1110) began again with conquests. "[7] Rameses III. triumphed over great confederations of Libyans and Syrians and the Isles of the Mediterranean. He is the only king who, as the monuments shew, carried on war at once by land and sea." Beside many names unknown to us, the Hittites, Amorites, Circesium, Aratus, Philistines, Phœnicia, Sasou, Pount, are again recognized. North, South East and West are declared to be tributary to him, and of the North it is said, "[8] The people, who knew not Egypt, come to thee, bringing gold and silver, lapis-lazuli, all precious stones." He adorned Thebes with the great temple of Medinet-Abou[9] and the Ramesseum[10]. The brief notices of following Rameses' speak of internal prosperity and wealth: a fuller account of Rameses XII. speaks of his "[11] being in Mesopotamia to exact the annual tribute," how "the kings of all countries prostrated themselves before him, and the king of the country of Bouchten [it has been conjectured, Bagistan, or Ecbatana] presented to him tribute and his daughter." "[12] He is the last Pharaoh who goes to Mesopotamia, to collect the annual tributes of the petty kingdoms of that country." On this side of the Euphrates, Egypt still retained some possessions to the time of Necho; for it is said, "[13] the king of Babylon had taken from the river of Egypt unto the river Euphrates all that pertained to the king of Egypt." Thebes continued to be embellished alike by "the high-priests of Ammon," who displaced the ancient line[14], and kings of the Bubastite Dynasty, Sesonchis I. or Sisak[15], Takelothis II.[16], and Sesonchis III[17]. The Ethiopian dynasty of Sabakos and Tearko or Tirhaka in another way illustrates the importance of No. The Ethiopian conquerors chose it as their royal city. Thither, in the time of Sabakos, Syria brought it tribute[18]; there Tirhaka set up the records of his victories[18]; and great must have been the conqueror, whom Strabo put on a line with Sesostris[19]. Its site marked it out for a great capital; and as such the Ethiopian conqueror seized it. The hills on either side retired, encircling the plain, through the centre of which the Nile brought down its wealth, connecting it with the untold riches of the south. "[20] They formed a vast circus, where the ancient metropolis expanded itself. On the West, the Lybian chain presents abrupt declivities which command this side of the plain, and which bend away above Bab-el-molouk, to end near Kournah at the very bank of the river. On the East, heights, softer and nearer, descend in long declivities toward Louksor and Karnak, and their crests do not approach the Nile until after Medamout, an hour or more below Karnak." The breadth of the valley, being about 10 miles[21], the city (of which, Strabo says, "[22] traces are now seen of its magnitude, 80 stadia in length") must have occupied the whole. "[23] The Ϛam city embraced the great space, which is now commonly called the plain of Thebes and which is divided by the Nile into two halves, an Eastern and a Western, the first bounded by the edge of the Arabian wilderness, the latter by the hills of the dead of the steep Libyan chain." The capital of Egypt, which was identified of old with Egypt itself[24], thus lay under the natural guardianship of the encircling hills which expanded to receive it, divided into two by the river which was a wall to both. The chains of hills, on either side were themselves fenced in on East and West by the great sand-deserts unapproachable by an army. The long valley of the Nile was the only access to an enemy. It occupied apparently the victorious army of Asshur-banipal[25] "a month and ten days" to march from Memphis to Thebes. "[26] At Thebes itself there are still remains of walls

[1] In Brugsch p. 116.
[2] Ib. pp. 124, 125. [3] Ib. pp. 128–132.
[4] Ib. pp. 137 sqq. [5] Ib. p. 156. [6] Ib. p. 158.
[7] Ib. p. 183. [8] Ib. p. 190. [9] Ib. p. 191.
[10] Ib. pp. 197, 198. [11] Ib. p. 207. [12] Ib. p. 210.
[13] 2 Kgs xxiv. 7. [14] Brugsch p. 212.
[15] Ib. pp. 224–227. [16] Ib. p. 223. [17] Ib. p. 235.
[18] Ib. p. 244.
[19] xv. 1. 6. He mentions him again for his extensive removals of people, which implies extensive conquests. i. 3. 21. [20] Joanne et Isambert, Itinéraire de l' Orient. p. 1039.

[21] Smith Bibl. Dict. v. Thebes. [22] xvii. 1. 46.
[23] Brugsch Geogr. d. Alt. Æg. p. 176.
[24] "In old times Thebes [the Thebais] was called Egypt." Herod. ii. 15. "Formerly Egypt was called Thebes." Aristot. Meteor. i. 14.
[25] Inscr. in Oppert, Rapports. pp. 74, 78, 85.
[26] Miss Harris, the learned daughter of a learned Egyptologist; "In several hieroglyphical inscriptions and notably in a papyrus in Miss Harris' possession, partly deciphered by her father and herself, there are minute accounts of fortresses existing at that date, about the time of the Exodus,

and fortifications, strong, skillfully constructed, and in good preservation, as there are also in other Egyptian towns above and below it. The crescent-shaped ridge of hills approaches so close to the river at each end as to admit of troops defiling past, but not spreading out or manœuvering. At each of these ends is a small old fort of the purely Egyptian, i. e. the Ante-Hellenic period. Both above and below there are several similar crescent sweeps in the same chain of hills, and at each angle a similar fort."

All successive monarchs, during more centuries than have passed since our Lord came, successively beautified it. Everything is gigantic, bearing witness to the enormous mass of human strength, which its victorious kings had gathered from all nations to toil for its and their glorification. Wonderful is it now in its decay, desolation, death; one great idol-temple of its gods and an apotheosis of its kings, as sons of its gods. "[1] What spires are to a modern city, what the towers of a cathedral are to the nave and choir, *that* the statues of the Pharaohs were to the streets and temples of Thebes. The ground is strewed with their fragments; the avenues of them towered high above plain and houses. Three of gigantic size still remain. One was the granite statue of Rameses himself, who sat on the right side of the entrance to his palace.—The only part of the temple or palace, at all in proportion to him, must have been the gateway, which rose in pyramidal towers, now broken down and rolling in a wild ruin down to the plain." It was that self-deifying, against which Ezekiel is commanded to prophesy; [2] *Speak and say; thus saith the Lord God; Behold, I am against thee, Pharaoh king of Egypt, the great dragon that lieth in the midst of his rivers, which hath said, My river is mine own, and I have made it for myself.* "[3] Everywhere the same colossal proportions are preserved. Everywhere the king is conquering, ruling, worshiping, worshiped. The palace is the temple. The king is priest. He and his horses are ten times the size of the rest of the army. Alike in battle and in worship, he is of the same stature as the gods themselves. Most striking is the familiar gentleness, with which, one on each side, they take him by each hand, as one of their own order, and then, in the next compartment, introduce him to Ammon, and the lion-headed goddess. Every distinction, except of degree, between divinity and royalty is entirely levelled." Gigantic dimensions picture to the eye the ideal greatness, which is the key to the architecture of No. "[3] Two other statues alone remain of an avenue of eighteen similar or nearly similar statues, some of whose remnants lie in the field behind them, which led to the palace of Amenophis III., every one of the statues being Amenophis himself, thus giving in multiplication what Rameses gained in solitary elevation." "[4] Their statues were all of one piece." Science still cannot explain, how a mass of nearly 890 tons[5] of granite was excavated at Syene, transported[6] and set up at Thebes, or how destroyed[7].

"[8] The temper of the tools, which cut adamantine stone as sharply and closely as an ordinary scoop cuts an ordinary cheese, is still a mystery." Everything is in proportion. The two sitting colossi, whose "breadth across the shoulders is eighteen feet, their height forty-seven feet, fifty-three above the plain, or, with the half-buried pedestal, sixty feet, were once connected by an avenue of sphinxes of eleven hundred feet with what is now 'Kom-el-Hettân,' or 'the mound of sand-stone,' which marks the site of another palace and temple of Amenophis III.; and, to judge from the little that remains, it must have held a conspicuous rank among the finest monuments of Thebes. All that now exists of the interior are the bases of its columns, some broken statues, and Syenite sphinxes of the king, with several lion-headed figures of black granite[9]." The four villages, where are the chief remaining temples, Karnak, Luksor, Medinet-Abou, Kournah, form a great quadrilateral[10], each of whose sides is about one and a half mile, and the whole compass accordingly six miles. The avenue of six hundred sphinxes, which joined the temple of Luksor with Karnak must have been one and a half mile long[11]: *one* of its obelisks is a remarkable ornament of Paris. Mostly massiveness is the characteristic, since strength and might were their

she supposes, and of their armaments and garrisons." Thebes then was fortified, as well as Nineveh, and Homer is confirmed by the Hieroglyphical inscriptions.

1 Stanley Sin. and Pal. Introd. p. xxxviii..

2 Ezek. xxix. 3. 3 Stanl. Ib. p. xxxix.

4 Wilkinson Anc. Eg. iii. 266.

5 "about 887 tons, 5½ hundred weight." Wilkinson Mod. Eg. ii. 145.

6 "The obelisks, transported from the quarries of Syene at the first cataract, in latitude 24° 5′ 23″ to Thebes and Heliopolis, vary in size from 70 to 93 feet in length. They are of one single stone, and the largest in Egypt (that of the great temple at Karnak) I calculate to weigh 297 tons. This was brought about 138 miles from the quarry to where it now stands; those taken to Heliopolis, more than 800 miles. The power, however, to move the mass was the same, whatever might be the distance, and the mechanical skill which transported it five or even one, would suffice for any number of miles. The two colossi of Amenophis iii., of a single block each, 47 feet in height, which contain about 11,500 cubic feet, are made of a stone not known within several days journey of the place; and at the Memnonium is another of Rameses which, when entire, weighed upwards of 887 tons, and was brought from E'Sooan to Thebes, 138 miles." Wilk. Anc. Eg. iii. 329, 330. 7 See Wilk. Mod. Eg. ii. 144.

8 Nozrani in Eg. and Syr. p. 278.

9 Wilkinson Mod. Eg. ii. 157, 158. 160. 162.

10 Joanne et Isambert, Itiner. de l' Orient pp. 1039, 1040.

11 Two kilometres, Joan. et Isamb. p. 1060.

ideal. Yet the massive columns still preserved, as in the temple of Rameses II.[1], are even of piercing beauty[1]. And for the temple of Karnak! Its enclosure, which was some two miles in circumference[2], bears the names of Monarchs removed from one another, according to the Chronology, by above two thousand years[3]. "[4] A stupendous colonnade, of which one pillar only remains erect, once extended across its great court, connecting the W. gate of entrance with that at its extremity. The towers of the Eastern gate are mere heaps of stones, poured down into the court on one side and the great hall on the other; giant columns have been swept away like reeds before the mighty avalanche, and one hardly misses them. And in that hall, of 170 feet by 329 feet, 134 columns of colossal proportions supported its roof; twelve of them, 62 feet high and about 35 in circumference, and on each side a forest of 66 columns, 42 feet 5 in. in height. Beyond the centre-avenue are seen obelisks, gateways and masses of masonry; every portion of these gigantic ruins is covered with sculpture most admirably executed, and every column has been richly painted."

"[5] Imagine a long vista of courts and doorways and colonnades and halls; here and there an obelisk shooting up out of the ruins, and interrupting the opening view of the forest of columns.—This mass of ruins, some rolled down in avalanches of stone, others perfect and painted, as when they were first built, is approached on every side by avenues of gateways. E. and W., N. and S., these vast approaches are found. Some are shattered, but in every approach some remain; and in some can be traced, beside, the further avenues, still in parts remaining by hundreds together, avenues of ram-headed sphinxes. Every Egyptian temple has, or ought to have, one of those grand gateways, formed of two sloping towers, with the high perpendicular front between." Then, over and above, is "their multiplied concentration.—Close before almost every gateway in this vast array were the colossal figures, usually in granite, of the great Rameses, sometimes in white and red marble, of Amenophis and of Thothmes. Close by them, were pairs of towering obelisks, which can generally be traced by pedestals on either side.—You have only to set up again the fallen obelisks which lie at your feet; to conceive the columns, as they are still seen in parts, overspreading the whole; to reproduce all the statues, like those which still remain in their august niches, to gaze on the painted walls and pillars of the immense hall, which even now can never be seen without a thrill of awe, and you have ancient Thebes before you." And most of those paintings were records of their past might. "[6] There remained on the massive buildings Egyptian letters, recording their former wealthiness; and one of the elder priests, bidden to interpret his native language, related that of old 700,000 of military age dwelt there; and with that army king Rhamses gained possession of Libya, Ethiopia, the Medes and Persians, the Bactrian and Scythian; and held in his empire the countries which the Syrians and Armenians and neighboring Cappadocians inhabit, the Bithynian also and Lycian to the sea. There were read too the tributes imposed on the natives, the weight of silver and gold; the number of arms and horses, and the gifts to the temples, ivory and frankincense, and what supplies of corn and utensils each nation should pay, not less magnificent than are now enjoined by Parthian violence or by Roman power."

That was situate lit. *the dweller, she that dwelleth.* Perhaps the Prophet wished to express the security and ease[7], in which she dwelt *among the rivers.* They encircled, folded round her, as it were, so that she was a little world in herself, secluded from all who would approach to hurt her. The Prophet's word, *rivers*[8], is especially used of the branches or canals of the Nile, which is also called *the sea*[9]. The Nile passed through No, and doubtless its canals encircled it.

[1] Memnonium. See Hoskins, Winter in upper and lower Eg. Frontispiece.

[2] 13 Stadia. (Diod. S. i. 46.) "It will be found to surpass the measurement of the historian by at least two or three stadia." Wilkins. ii. 249.

[3] Osirtasen i, placed at 2803. B.C. to Tirhaka, 693. B.C., Wilkinson Mod. Eg. ii. 250. 252.

[4] Lord Lindsay Letters on Egypt, &c., pp. 98, 99.

[5] Stanley, Sinai and Pal. p. xli. [6] Tac. Ann. ii. 60.

[7] In Zech. i. 11, this is brought out by the addition of the word וְשֹׁקָטֶת "and at rest;" in Zech. vii. 7, by וּשְׁלֵוָה, "and tranquil." In Rev. xviii. 7, "I sit a queen," the addition, "as a queen" points to the other meaning, of יֹשֵׁב, "*sat enthroned.*"

[8] Yeorim.

[9] Is. xviii. 2, xix. 5. In Arabic, the Nile is called "the sweet sea" in contrast with "the salt sea," or "the encircling sea;" a title given by Egyptian writers to the Mediterranean, as being connected with the Ocean. Egyptian writers mostly add an epithet to אַלְבַּחְר, to designate the sea, because אַלְבַּחְר, simply, is the Nile; as in India it is the Ganges; in Mesopotamia, the Euphrates. De Sacy Chrest. Arab. ii. 14, 15. ed. 2. The "white Nile" is called "Bahr-el-Abiad," the "blue Nile" Bahr-el-Azrek, and the great Ethiopian tributary to the Nile, the Albara, "Bahr-el-Aswad," "the black sea." Baker, Nile tributaries, p. 91. אַלְבַּחְר is also used of the Tigris. Lane sub v. At Thebes, the Nile is usually about half a mile in width, but, at the inundation, overflowing the plain, especially upon the western bank, for a breadth of two or more miles. Smith Bib. Dict. v. Thebes. "When the Nile overflows the country, the cities alone appear, surmounting it, like the islands in the Ægean; the rest of Egypt becomes a sea." Herod. ii. 97. "The water of the Nile is like a sea." Plin. H. N. xxxv. 11. "Homer gives to the river, the name 'Ocean,' because the Egyptians in their own language call the Nile, Ocean." Diod. S. i. 96.

Before CHRIST cir. 713.

9 Ethiopia and Egypt
were her strength, and
it was infinite; Put and
Lubim were † thy helpers.
10 Yet *was* she carried
away, she went into cap-
tivity: ⁿ her young chil-
dren also were dashed in
pieces ᵒ at the top of all
the streets: and they ᵖ cast

† Heb. *in thy help.*

ⁿ Ps. 137. 9. Isa. 13. 16. Hos. 13. 16.
ᵒ Lam. 2. 19.
ᵖ Joel 3. 3. Obad. 11.

Egypt is said by a Heathen to be "[1] walled by the Nile as an everlasting wall." *Whose rampart* was [*rampart* is] *the sea. Wall* and *rampart*[2] are, properly, the outer and inner wall of a city, the wall and forewall, so to speak. For all walls and all defences, her enfolding walls of sea would suffice. Strong she was in herself; strong also in her helpers.

9. *Ethiopia and Egypt were her strength;* lit. *Egypt* was *strength*[3], *and Ethiopia, and boundless.* He sets forth first the imperial might of No; then her strength from foreign, subdued power. The capital is a sort of impersonation of the might of the state; No, of Egypt, as Nineveh, of Assyria. When the head was cut off or the heart ceased to beat, all was lost. The might of Egypt and Ethiopia was the might of No, concentrated in her. They were *strength*, and that strength unmeasured by any human standard. *Boundless* was the *strength*, which Nineveh had subdued: *boundless*, the *store*[4] which she had accumulated for the spoiler; *boundless*[5] the carcases of her slain. *And it was infinite.* "The people that came up with the king out of Egypt, were without number[6]." The Egyptians connected with Thebes are counted by a heathen author[7] at seven millions. *Put* or *Phut*[8] is mentioned third among the sons of Ham, after Cush and Mizraim[9]. They are mentioned with the Ethiopians in Pharaoh's army at the Euphrates[10], as joined with them in the visitation of Egypt[11]; with Cush in the army of Gog[12]; with Lud in that of Tyre[13]; a country and river of that name were, Josephus tells us[14], "frequently mentioned by Greek historians." They dwelt in the Libya, conterminous to the Canopic mouth of the Nile[15].

And Lubim. These came up against Judah in the army of Shishak[6] against Rehoboam, and with the Ethiopians, "a huge host" under Zerah the Ethiopian against Asa[16]. The Ribou or Libou appear on the monuments as a people conquered by Menephthes[17] and Rameses III.[18] They were still to be united with Egypt and the Ethiopians in the times of Antiochus Epiphanes[19]; so their connection with Egypt was not broken by its fall. Those unwearied enemies had become incorporated with her; and were now her help. These were (E. M.) *in thy help;* set upon it, given up to it[20]. The prophet appeals to No herself, as it were, "Thou *hadst* strength." Then he turns away, to speak of her, unwilling to look on the miseries which he has to portray to Nineveh, as the preludes of her own. Without God, vain is the help of man.

10. *Yet* was *she* [*also*[21]] *carried away*, lit. *She also* became *an exile*[22] band, her people were carried away, with all the barbarities of Heathen war. All, through whom she might recover, were destroyed or scattered abroad; *the young*, the hope of another age, cruelly destroyed[23]; *her honorable men* enslaved[24], *all her great men* prisoners. God's judgments are executed step by step. Assyria herself was the author of this captivity, which Isaiah prophesied in the first years of Hezekiah when Judah was leaning upon Egypt[25]. It was repeated by all of the house of Sargon[26]. Jeremiah and Ezekiel foretold fresh desolation by Nebuchadnezzar[27]. God foretold to His people[28], *I gave Egypt for thy ransom, Ethiopia and Seba for thee;* and the Persian monarchs, who fulfilled prophecy in the restoration of Judah,

[1] Isocr. Busir. ap. Boch. Phal. i. 1. p. 7.

[2] חֵיל and חוֹמָה, joined Lam. ii. 8, חל וחומה. It included the space between the two walls (pomœrium) 2 Sam. xx. 15, 1 Kgs xxi. 23. It is the whole circuit of the wall as contrasted with the palaces of Zion, in Ps. xlviii. 14, cxxii. 7. As is common in Hebrew poetry, "wall and forewall," which together make one subject, are placed in the parallel columns. "Murus et antemurale" S. Jer. on Is. xxvii. "the lesser wall, which is before the greater," Rabb. ap. Kim. "the wall and the son of the wall." R. Chanina. Ib.

[3] Not lit. "*her* strength." It is עָצְמָה, not עָצְמָהּ; the abstract for the concrete, as אֵימָה Job xli. 6, גַּאֲוָה Ib. 7.

[4] ii. 10.

[5] iii. 3. וְאֵין קֵצֶה in each.

[6] 2 Chron. xii. 3.

[7] Cato in Steph. Byz. ap. Boch. iv. 27.

[8] Translated Lybians Jer. xlvi. 9, Ez. xxx. 5, xxxviii. 5.

[9] Gen. x. 6.

[10] Jer. l. c.

[11] Ez. xxx. 5.

[12] Ib. xxxviii, 15.

[13] Ib. xxix. 10.

[14] Jos. Ant. i. 6. 2.

[15] See Ges. Thes. s. v.

[16] 2 Chron. xvi. 8. coll. Ib. xiv. 9.

[17] B. C. 1341–1321 (Brugsch p. 172).

[18] 1288 B. C. Ib. 186, 190, 191.

[19] Dan. xi. 43.

[20] קומה בעזרתי Ps. xxxv. 2. בעזרי Ex. xviii. 4.

[21] The word is emphatic; "*She also*," *her* young children *also*. The same word *also* is repeated.

[22] הַגּוֹלָה might be either "captivity" or "the captives." But הלך בַגּולה occurs 5 times, בא בַגּולה, 3 times; but לַגּוֹלָה with neither.

[23] See Hos. xiv. Is. xiii. 16. 2 Kgs viii. 12.

[24] See Joel iii. 3.

[25] See Is. xx.

[26] See ab. pp. 117, 118.

[27] Jer. xlvi. 25, 26. and Ezekiel xxx. 14–16.

[28] Is. xliii. 3.

Before CHRIST cir. 713.

lots for her honorable men,
and all her great men were
bound in chains.

11 Thou also shalt be
[q] drunken: thou shalt be
hid, thou also shalt seek
strength because of the
enemy.

[q] Jer. 25. 17, 27. ch. 1. 10.

12 All thy strongholds
shall be like [r] fig trees with
the firstripe figs: if they
be shaken, they shall even
fall into the mouth of the
eater.

13 Behold, [s] thy people
in the midst of thee *are*

Before CHRIST cir. 713.

[r] Rev. 6. 13.

[s] Jer. 50. 37. & 51. 30.

---

fulfilled it also in the conquest of Egypt and Ethiopia. Both perhaps out of human policy in part. But Cambyses' wild hatred of Egyptian idolatry fulfilled God's word. Ptolemy Lathyrus carried on the work of Cambyses; the Romans, Ptolemy's. Cambyses burnt its *temples*[1]; Lathyrus its four-or five-storied private houses[2]; the Roman Gallus levelled it to the ground[3]. A little after it was said of her, "[4] she is inhabited as so many scattered villages." A little after our Lord's Coming, Germanicus went to visit, not it, but "[5] the vast traces of it." "[6] It lay overwhelmed with its hundred gates" and utterly impoverished. No was powerful as Nineveh, and less an enemy of the people of God. For though these often suffered from Egypt, yet in those times they even trusted too much to its help[7]. If then the judgments of God came upon No, how much more upon Nineveh! In type, Nineveh is the image of the world as oppressing God's Church; No, rather of those who live for this life, abounding in wealth, ease, power, and forgetful of God. If, then, *they* were punished, who took no active part against God, fought not against God's truth, yet still were sunk in *the cares and riches and pleasures of this life*, what shall be the end of those who openly resist God?

11. *Thou also.* As thou hast done, so shall it be done unto thee. The cruelties on No, in the cycle of God's judgments, draw on the like upon Nineveh who inflicted them. *Thou also*[8] *shalt be drunken* with the same cup of God's anger, entering within thee as wine doth, bereaving thee of reason and of counsel through the greatness of thy anguish, and bringing shame on thee[9], and a stupefaction like death. *Thou shalt be hid, a thing hidden*[10] from the eyes of men, *as though thou hadst never been.* Nahum had foretold her complete desolation: he had asked, where is she? Here he describes an abiding condition; strangely fulfilled, as perhaps never to that extent besides; her palaces, her monuments, her records of her glorious triumphs existed still in their place, but hidden out of sight, as in a tomb, under the hill-like mounds along the Tigris. *Thou also shalt seek strength*, or a *strong-hold from the enemy*[11], out of thyself, since thine own shall be weakness. Yet in vain, since God, is not such to thee[12]. "They *shall seek*, but not find." "For then shall it be too late to cry for mercy, when it is the time of justice." *He shall have judgment without mercy, that hath shewed no mercy*[13]

12. *All thy strong-holds shall be like figtrees, with the first ripe figs*, hanging from them[14]; eagerly sought after[15], to be consumed. Being ripe, they are ready to fall at once; *if they be shaken;* it needeth but the tremulous motion, as when trees wave in the wind[16], *they shall even fall into the mouth of the eater*, not costing even the slight pains of picking them from the ground[17]. So easy is their destruction on the part of God, though it cost more pains to the Babylonians. At the end of the world it shall be yet more fulfilled[18], for then God will use no human instrument, but put forth only His own Almightiness; and all strong-holds of man's pride, moral or spiritual, shall, of themselves, melt away.

13. *Behold, thy people in the midst of thee are women.* Fierce, fearless, hard, iron men, such as their warriors still are portrayed by themselves on their monuments, they whom no toil wearied, no peril daunted, shall be, one and all, their whole *people, women.* So

---

[1] Diod. Sic. i. 46. Strabo xvii. 1. 45.

[2] They had been destroyed shortly before Diodorus Sic. Ib. 45, 46.

[3] "She was destroyed to the ground." S. Jer. Chron. Eus. A. 1989.

[4] Strabo l. c.

[5] Tac. Ann. ii. 62.

[6] Juv. Sat. xv. 6.

[7] See Is. xxx. &c.

[8] גַם־אַתְּ takes up גַם־הִיא v. 10.

[9] The two images are united in Ob. 16.

[10] The force of the substantive verb with the pass. part. תְּהִי נַעֲלָמָה as in Zech. iii. 3; as, with the act. part., it expresses continued action; Gen. i. 6, xxxvii. 2, De. ix. 7, 22, 24, xxviii. 29, 2 Sam. iii. 6, Job i. 14, Ps. x. 14, cxxii. 2, Is. xxx. 20. See Ew. Lebrb. n. 168c.

[11] מָעוֹז מֵאוֹיֵב, as Is. xxv. 4, מַחֲסֶה מִזֶּרֶם, "a refuge from the storm."

[12] i. 7.

[13] S. Jas. ii. 13.

[14] תְּאֵנִים עִם בִּכּוּרִים, as Cant. iv. 13, רמונים עם פרי מגדים.

[15] See ab. p. 66 on Mic. v. 1. It is not here the specific word, בִּכּוּרָה, but בִּכּוּרִים, "the first-fruits," in the same sense, as in Nu. xiii. 20, בכורי ענבים "the first ripe grapes."

[16] נוּעַ is used of this, Is. vii. 2; here, as in Am. ix. 9. Nif.

[17] S. Jer.

[18] Rev. vi. 13.

Before CHRIST cir. 713.

women: the gates of thy land shall be set wide open unto thine enemies: the fire shall devour thy [t] bars.

Before CHRIST cir. 713.

[t] Ps. 147. 13. Jer. 51. 30.

Jeremiah to Babylon, "[1] they shall become, became, women." He sets it before the eyes. *Behold, thy people* are *women;* against nature they are such, not in tenderness but in weakness and fear. Among the signs of the Day of Judgment, it stands, *men's hearts failing them for fear*[2]. Where sin reigns, there is no strength left, no manliness or nobleness of soul, no power to resist. *In the midst of thee,* where thou seemest most secure, and, if any where, there were hope of safety. The very inmost self of the sinner gives way.

To thine enemies (this is, for emphasis, prefixed) not for any good to thee, but *to thine enemies shall be set wide open the gates of thy land,* not, *thy gates,* i. e. the gates of their cities, (which is a distinct idiom), but *the gates of the land* itself, every avenue, which might have been closed against the invader, but which was *laid open.* The Easterns[3], as well as the Greeks and Latins[4], used the word "gate" or "doors" of the mountain-passes, which gave an access to a land, but which might be held against an enemy. In the pass called "the Caucasian gates," there were, over and above, doors fastened with iron bars[5]. At Thermopylæ or, as the inhabitants called them, Pylæ[6], "gates," the narrow pass was further guarded by a wall[7]. Its name recalls the brilliant history, how such approaches might be held by a devoted handful of men against almost countless multitudes. Of Assyria, Pliny says, "[8] The Tigris and pathless mountains encircle Adiabene." When those *gates of the land* gave way, the whole land was laid open to its enemies.

The fire shall devour thy bars. Probably, as elsewhere, the *bars* of the gates, which were mostly of wood, since it is added expressly of some, that they were of the iron [9] or brass [10]. "[11] Occasionally the efforts of the besiegers were directed against the gate, which they endeavored to break open with axes, or to set on fire by application of a torch.—In the hot climate of S. Asia wood becomes so dry by exposure to the sun, that the most solid doors may readily be ignited and consumed." It is even remarked in one instance that the Assyrians "[12] have not set fire to the gates of this city, as appeared to be their usual practice in attacking a fortified place."

So were her palaces buried as they stood, that the traces of prolonged fire are still visible, calcining the one part and leaving others which were not exposed to it, uncalcined. "[13] It is incontestable that, during the excavations, a considerable quantity of charcoal, and even pieces of wood, either half-burnt or in a perfect state of preservation, were found in many places. The lining of the chambers also bears certain marks of the action of fire. All these things can be explained only by supposing the fall of a burning roof, which calcined the slabs of gypsum and converted them into dust. It would be absurd to imagine that the burning of a small quantity of furniture could have left on the walls marks like these which are to be seen through all the chambers, with the exception of one, which was only an open passage. It must have been a violent and prolonged fire, to be able to calcine not only a few places, but every part of these slabs, which were ten feet high and several inches thick. So complete a decomposition can be attributed but to intense heat, such as would be occasioned by the fall of a burning roof.

"Botta found on the engraved flag-stones scoria and half-melted nails, so that there is no

---

[1] Jer. l. 37, li. 30.

[2] S. Luke xxi. 26.

[3] Freytag (sub. v. באב) says that the Pyrenees are called in Arab. גבל אלאבואב "the mountain of gates," and' that the Portæ Caspiæ are called באב אלאבואב. "Bab Bmaria" is the name of a pass in Libanon to the Litany, Ritter Erdk. xvii. 93. 94. 138. 218; "Bab-el-Howa" "gate of the winds" is said to be a mountain gorge (Ritter xviii. 849. Buckingham gives the name to a gate of Bosra. Travels among Arabs ii. 200). Bab-el-Mardin is the name of a mountain-pass in the Masius chain (Ritter xi. 263. 393. 464), "a remaakable gap or notch in the chain of Mt. Masius, behind which is situated the city of Mardin." Forbes on the Sinjar Hills, Mem. R. Geogr. Soc. 1839 p. 421. The name "Bab-el-mandeb" shews that the name "door" is given to narrow straits also, as is that of πύλαι (See Lidd. and Scott Lex. v. πύλη). The Arab. תַּעְר only incidentally illustrates the idiom, being, not a "gate" (as Röd. in Ges. Thes.) but "a gap, interstice, hence a mountain-pass, an access to a country," and specifically "a border-country toward an enemy," and in the idiom שַׁדּ אלתעְר, "stopped the gap," like עמד בפרץ Ez. xxii. 30. The phrase, שׁערי הארץ, recurs Jer. xv. 7.

[4] The Κάσπιαι πύλαι (Strabo xi. 12. 13), the Αύδιαι Ib. xiii. 65). See further Lidd. and Sc. l. c.) the πύλαι τῆς Κιλικίας καὶ τῆς Συρίας, Xen. Anab. i. 4. 14, the "Amanicæ Pylæ" (Q. Curt. iii. 20). Pliny speaks of the "portæ Caucasiæ" (H. N. vi. 11) or "Iberiæ" (Albaniæ Ptol. v. 12.) Ib. 15.

[5] "After these are the Caucasian gates (by many very erroneously called the Caspian gates), a vast work of nature, the mountains being suddenly interrupted, where are doors, &c." Plin. H. N. vi. 11.

[6] Herod. vii. 201.

[7] Ib. 176. 208.

[8] Plin. N. H. vi. 9. quoted by Tuch ii. 1.

[9] Ps. cvii. 16, Is. xlv. 2.

[10] 1 Kgs iv. 13.

[11] Rawl. 5 Emp. ii. 83. who relates how "the city of Candahar was ignited from the outside by the Affghanees, and was entirely consumed in less than an hour." Note.

[12] Bonomi Nin. p. 205. ed. 2. on Botta plate 93. See also Ib. p. 221, 222. 225.

[13] Ib. Sect. iv. c. 1, pp. 245–247.

Before CHRIST cir. 713.

14 Draw thee waters for the siege, [u] fortify thy strong holds: go into clay, and tread the mortar, make strong the brickkiln.

[u] ch. 2. 1.

15 There shall the fire devour thee; the sword shall cut thee off, it shall eat thee up like [x] the cankerworm: make thyself

[x] Joel i. 4.

doubt that these appearances had been produced by the action of intense and long-sustained heat. He remembers, beside, at Khorsabad, that when he detached some bas-reliefs from the earthy substance which covered them, in order to copy the inscriptions that were behind, he found there coals and cinders, which could have entered only by the top, between the wall and the back of the bas-relief. This can be easily understood to have been caused by the burning of the roof, but is inexplicable in any other manner. What tends most positively to prove that the traces of fire must be attributed to the burning of a wooden roof is, that these traces are perceptible only in the interior of the building. The gypsum also that covers the wall inside is completely calcined, while the outside of the building is nearly everywhere untouched. But wherever the fronting appears to have at all suffered from fire, it is at the bottom; thus giving reason to suppose that the damage has been done by some burning matter falling outside. In fact, not a single bas-relief in a state to be removed was found in any of the chambers, they were all pulverized."

The soul which does not rightly close its senses against the enticements of the world, does, in fact, open them, and *death is come up into our windows*[1], and then "[2] whatever natural good there yet be, which, as *bars*, would hinder the enemy from bursting in, is consumed by the fire," once kindled, of its evil passions.

14. *Draw thee waters for the siege; fortify thy strongholds.* This is not mere mockery at man's weakness, when he would resist God. It foretells that they shall toil, and that, heavily. Toil is added upon toil. Nineveh did undergo a two years' siege. *Water* stands for all provisions within. He bids them, as before[3], strengthen what was already strong; *strongholds,* which seemed to "cut off" all approach. These he bids them strengthen, not repairing decays only but making them *exceeding strong*[4]. *Go into clay.* We seem to see all the inhabitants, like ants on their nest, all poured out, every one busy, every one making preparation for the defence. Why had there been no need of it? What needed she of towers and fortifications, whose armies were carrying war into distant lands, before whom all which was near was hushed? Now, all had to be renewed. As Isaiah in his mockery of the idol-makers begins with the forging of the axe, the planting and rearing of the trees, which were at length to become the idol[5], Nahum goes back to the beginning. The neglected *brick-kiln,* useless in their prosperity, was to be *repaired;* the clay[6], which abounded in the valley of the Tigris[7], was to be collected, mixed and kneaded by treading, as still represented in the Egyptian monuments. The conquering nation was to do the work of slaves, as Asiatic captives are represented, under their taskmasters[8], on the monuments of Egypt, a prelude of their future. Xenophon still saw the massive brick wall, on the stone foundation[9].

Yet, though stored within and fenced without, it shall not stand[10].

15. *There,* where thou didst fence thyself, and madest such manifold and toilsome preparation, *shall the fire devour thee.* All is toil within. The fire of God's wrath falls and consumes at once. Mankind still, with mire and clay, build themselves Babels. *They go into clay,* and become themselves earthly like the mire they steep themselves in. They make themselves strong, as though they thought *that their houses shall continue forever*[11], *and say,* [12] *Soul, take thine ease, eat, drink and be merry.* God's wrath descends. *Thou fool, this night thy soul shall be required of thee. It shall eat thee up like the canker-worm.* What in thee is strongest, shall be devoured with as much ease as the locust devours the tender grass. The judgments of God, not only overwhelm as a whole, but find out each tender part, as the locust devours each single blade.

Make thyself many as the cankerworm, as though thou wouldest equal thyself in oppressive number[13] to those instruments of the

[1] Jer. ix. 21. [2] S. Jer. [3] ii. 1.
[4] 2 Chr. xi. 12.
[5] Is. xliv. 12, sqq.
[6] חמר and טיט are united as synonymes Is. xli. 25, where the טיט is that which the potter treadeth, יוצר ירמס טיט.
[7] Rawl. 5 Emp. i. 476.
[8] Wilk. Anc. Eg. ii. 99. [9] Anab. iii. 4, 4.
[10] See Is. xxvii. 10, 11. [11] Ps. xlix. 11.
[12] S. Luke xii. 19, 20.
[13] התכבד expresses more than mere number. כָּבֵד retains always the idea of weight, gravity or oppressiveness. We say "heavy hail" Ex. ix. 18, 24. It is used of the plague of flies, Ib. viii. 20, and, as here, of the locusts, Ib. x. 14; of the host, with which Esau opposed Israel, Nu. xx. 20, (adding וּבְיָד חֲזָקָה); of that sent with Rabshakeh to Jerusalem, Is. xxxvi. 2. and of the great train of the Queen of Sheba, camels laden with very much gold and precious stones, 1 Kgs x. 2. כָּבֵד occurs above

Before CHRIST cir. 713.

many as the cankerworm,
make thyself many as the
locusts.
16 Thou hast multiplied
thy merchants above the
stars of heaven: the can-
kerworm ‖spoileth, and
fleeth away.

‖ Or, *spreadeth himself.*

vengeance of God, gathering from all quarters armies to help thee; yea, though thou make thy whole self[1] one oppressive multitude, yet it shall not avail thee. Nay, He saith, thou hast essayed to do it.

16. *Thou hast multiplied thy merchants above the stars of Heaven;* not numerous only but glorious in the eyes of the world, and, as thou deemest, safe and inaccessible; yet in an instant all is gone.

The commerce of Nineveh was carried back to præhistoric times, since its rivers bound together the mountains of Armenia with the Persian gulf, and marked out the line, by which the distant members of the human family should supply each others' needs. "Semiramis," they say[2], "built other cities on the Euphrates and the Tigris, where she placed emporia for those who convey their goods from Media and Parætacene. Being mighty rivers and passing through a populous country, they yield many advantages to those employed in commerce; so that the places by the river are full of wealthy emporia." The Phœnicians traced back their Assyrian commerce (and as it seems, truly) to those same præhistoric times, in which they alleged, that they themselves migrated from the Persian gulf. They commenced at once, they said[3], the long voyages, in which they transported the wares of Egypt and Assyria. The building of "Tadmor in the wilderness[4]" on the way to Tiphsach (Thapsacus) the utmost bound of Solomon's dominions[5], connected Palestine with that commerce. The great route for couriers and for traffic, extending for fifteen hundred or sixteen hundred miles in later times, must have lain through Nineveh, since, although no mention is made of the city which had perished, the route lay across the two rivers[6], the greater and lesser Zab, of which the greater formed the Southern limit of Nineveh. Those two rivers led up to two mountain-passes which opened a way to Media and Agbatana; and pillars at the summit of the N. pass attest the use of this route over the Zagros chain about 700 B.C.[7] Yet a third and easier pass was used by Nineveh, as is evidenced by another monument, of a date as yet undetermined[8]. Two other lines connected Nineveh with Syria and the West. Northern lines led doubtless to Lake Wan and the Black Sea[9]. The lists of plunder or of tribute, carried off during the world-empire of Egypt, before it was displaced by Assyria, attest the extensive imports or manufactures of Nineveh[10]; the titles of "Assyrian nard, Assyrian amomum, Assyrian odors, myrrh, frankincense[11], involve its trade with the spice countries: domestic manufactures of hers apparently were purple or dark-blue cloaks[12], embroidery, brocades[13], and these conveyed in chests of cedar; her metallurgy was on principles recognized now; in one practical point of combining beauty with strength, she has even been copied[14].

A line of commerce, so marked out by nature in the history of nations, is not changed, unless some preferable line be discovered. Empires passed away, but at the end of the 13th century trade and manufacture continued their wonted course and habitation. The faith in Jesus had converted the ancient heathenism; the heresy of Mohammedanism disputed with the faith for the souls of men; but the old material prosperity of the world held its way. Mankind still wanted the productions of each others' lands. The merchants of Nineveh were to be dispersed and were gone: itself and its remembrance were to be effaced from the earth, and it was so; in vain was a new Nineveh built by the Romans; that also disappeared; but so essential was its possession for the necessities of commerce, that Mosul, a large and populous town, arose over against its mounds, a city of the living over-against its buried glories; and, as *our* goods are known in China by the name of our great manufacturing capital, so a delicate manufacture imposed on the languages of Europe (Italian, Spanish, French, English, German) the name of Mosul[15].

iii. 3. of the heavy mass of corpses. In Ex. ix. 3, it is used of a grievous pestilence (Gesenius' instances Thes. s. v.).

1 The two genders, התכבר, התכבדי, are probably joined together, the more strongly to express universality, as מַשְׁעֵן וּמַשְׁעֵנָה, Is. iii. 1; and Nahum himself unites טֶרֶף and טְרֵפָה in two parallel clauses, ii. 13.

2 Diod. ii. 11.

3 Herod. i. 1.

4 1 Kgs ix. 18.

5 Ib v. 4. (iv. 24.)

6 Herod. ii. 52.

7 See Rawl. 5 Emp. ii. 180, 181.

8 Ib. 181, 182.

9 Ib. 182, 183.

10 "Dishes of silver with their covers; a harp of brass inlaid with gold; 823 pounds of perfumes" (Brugsch Hist. d' Eg. p. 100); "10 pounds of true lapis lazuli, 24 pounds of artificial lapis lazuli; vessels laden with ebony and ivory, precious stones, vases, (Ib. p. 203); beside many other articles, which cannot yet be made out.

11 See Rawl. 5 Emp. ii. 191, 192.

12 גלומי תְּכֵלֶת Ez. xxvii. 24.

13 ברומים

14 Layard Nin. and Bab. p. 191.

15 "All those cloths of gold and of silk which we call

Before CHRIST cir. 713.

y Rev. 9. 7.

17 [y] Thy crowned *are* as the locusts, and thy captains as the great grasshoppers, which camp in the hedges in the cold day, *but* when the sun ariseth

Before CHRIST cir. 713.

Even early in this century, under a mild governor, an important commerce passed through Mosul, from India, Persia, Kurdistan, Syria, Natolia, Europe[1]. And when European traffic took the line of the Isthmus of Suez, the communication with Kurdistan still secured to it an important and exclusive commerce. The merchants of Nineveh were dispersed and gone. The commerce continued over-against its grave.

The cankerworm spoileth and fleeth away; better, *the locust hath spread itself abroad (marauded) and is flown.* The prophet gives, in three words[2], the whole history of Nineveh, its beginning and its end. He had before foretold its destruction, though it should be oppressive as the locust; he had spoken of its commercial wealth; he adds to this, that other source of its wealth, its despoiling warfares and their issue. The heathen conqueror rehearsed his victory, "I came, saw, conquered." The prophet goes farther, as the issue of all human conquest, "I disappeared." *The locust* [Nineveh] *spread itself abroad* (the word is always used of an inroad for plunder[3]), destroying and wasting, everywhere: it left the world a desert, and was gone[4]. Ill-gotten wealth makes poor, not rich. Truly they who traffic in this world, are more in number than they who, seeking treasure in Heaven, shall *shine as the stars* for ever and ever. For *many are called, but few are chosen.* And when *all the stars of light* "shall abide and *praise God*[5], these men, though multiplied like the locust, shall, like the locust, pass away, destroying and destroyed. They abide for a while in the chillness of this world; when the Sun of righteousness ariseth, they vanish. This is the very order of God's Providence. As truly as locusts, which in the cold and dew are chilled and stiffened, and cannot spread their wings, *fly away* when the sun is hot and are found no longer, so shalt thou be dispersed and thy place not any more be known[6]. It was an earnest of this, when the Assyrians, like locusts, had spread themselves around Jerusalem in a dark *day of trouble and of rebuke and of blasphemy*[7], God was entreated and they were not. Midian *came up like the grasshopper for multitude*[8]. In the morning they had fled[9]. What is the height of the sons of men? or how do they spread themselves abroad?" At the longest, after a few years it is but as the locust *spreadeth himself and fleeth away*, no more to return.

17. *Thy crowned* are *as the locust, and thy captains as the great locusts.* What he had said summarily under metaphor, the prophet expands in a likeness. *The crowned*[10] are probably the subordinate princes, of whom Sennacherib said[11], *Are not my princes altogether kings?* It has been observed that the head-dress of the Assyrian Vizier has the orna-

'muslins' (Mossulini) are of manufacture of Mosul." Marco Polo, Travels c. 6. p. 37. ed. 1854. "The manufactures from fine transparent white cotton, like the stuffs now made in India under that name and like the bombazines manufactured at Arzingan, received in the following centuries the name 'muslins;' but not the silk brocades interwoven with gold, which had their name Baldachini from Baldak i. e. Bagdad, and perhaps were manufactured at that time at Mosul, unless indeed this name 'muslin' was then given to gold-brocades as wares of Mosul." Ritter Erdk. x. 274, 275. "There is a very large deposition of merchandise [at Mosul] because of the river, wherefore several goods and fruits are brought thither from the adjacent countries, both by land and water, to ship them for Bagdad." Rauwolf's Travels P. 2, c. 9. p. 205. A. 1573. Niebuhr still witnessed "the great traffic carried on there, as also linen manufactures, dyeing and printing [of stuffs]."

1 Olivier Voyage (1808) ii. 359. In 1766, one caravan, in which Niebuhr travelled, had 1300 camel-loads of gall-apples from Kurdistan. It supplied yearly 2000 centners of them. Nieb. ii. 274.

2 ילק פשט ויעף.

3 Jud. ix. 44 bis, 1 Sam. xxiii. 27, xxvii. 8, 10, xxx. 1, 1 Chr. xiv, 9, 13, 2 Chr. xxv. 13, xxviii. 18. The object, against which the attack is directed, is joined on with אל Jud. xx. 37, 1 Sam. xxvii. 8, 10, xxx. 1, or על, Jud. ix. 33, 44, 1 Sam. xxiii. 27, xxvii. 10; even as to the object of plunder, "camels" Job i. 17. The place (Hos. vi. 1) or country (1 Chr. xiv. 9, 13, 2 Chr. xxv. 13, xxviii. 18) is joined with ב, and once (1 Sam. xxx. 14) stands in the accus. The idiom פשט בגדיו, "put off his clothes," is distinct. The object of the verb is always added Lev. vi. 4, xvi. 23, 1 Sam. xix. 24, Cant. v. 3, Ez. xxvi. 16, xliv. 19, Neh. iv. 17; except that, in Is. xxxii. 11, it is implied by the context, "strip ye, make ye bare." Credner's theory then (followed by Ewald Proph. iii. 14. ed. 2.) that ילק signifies the locust in its last moulting, which strips off the involucra of its wings, is contrary to the use of פשט, as well as to that of ילק. See on Joel vol. i. p. 149. Gesenius, under פשט, contradicts the explanation which he had given under ילק from Credner.

4 עוף is used of shortness of human life; "like a dream he flieth away," (יעוף) Job xx. 8; "and we fly away" וַנָּעֻפָה, Ps. xc. 10. "Ephraim, like a bird, their glory flieth away," יתעופף, Hos. ix. 11, add Pr. xxiii. 5, of unjust wealth.

5 Ps. cxlviii. 3. 6 See c. i. 8. 7 Is. xxxvii. 3.

8 Judg. vi. 4, 5, vii. 12. 9 Judg. vii. 21.

10 The punctuation of מִנְּזָרַיִךְ is compared by Jewish grammarians too to מִקְּדָשׁ Ex. xv. 17; מַמְּגֻרוֹת Jo. i. 17.

11 Is. x. 8.

Before CHRIST cir. 713.

they flee away, and their
place is not known where
they *are*.
18 [z] Thy shepherds
slumber, O [a] king of As-
syria: thy || nobles shall
dwell *in the dust:* thy people is [b] scattered upon the
mountains, and no man
gathereth *them*.

z Ex. 15. 16. Ps. 76. 6. a Jer. 50. 18. Ezek. 31. 3, &c.

|| Or, *valiant ones.* b 1 Kin. 22. 17.

ment which "[1] throughout the whole series of sculptures is the distinctive mark of royal or quasi-royal authority." "[2] All high officers of state, *the crowned captains*, were adorned with diadems, closely resembling the lower band of the royal mitre, separated from the cap itself. Such was that of the vizier, which was broader in front than behind, was adorned with rosettes and compartments, and terminated in two ribbons with embroidered and fringed ends, which hung down his back." *Captain* is apparently the title of some military office of princely rank. One such Jeremiah[3], in a prophecy in which he probably alludes to this, bids place over the armies of Ararat, Minni, and Ashchenaz, to marshall them against Babylon, against which he summons the cavalry *like the rough locust.* The *captains* are likened to the *great caterpillars*[4], either as chief in devastation, or as including under them the armies under their command, who moved at their will. These and their armies now subsided into stillness for a time under the chill of calamity, like the locust "[5] whose nature it is, that, torpid in the cold, they fly in the heat." The stiffness of the locusts through the cold, when they lie motionless, heaps upon heaps, hidden out of sight, is a striking image of the helplessness of Nineveh's mightiest in the day of her calamity; then, by a different part of their history, he pictures their entire disappearance. "[6] The locusts, are commonly taken in the morning when they are agglomerated one on another, in the places where they passed the night. As soon as the sun warms them, they fly away." *When the sun ariseth, they flee away*[7], lit. *it is chased away*[8]. One and all; all as one. As at God's command the plague of locusts, which He had sent on Egypt, was removed[9]; *there remained not one locust in all the coasts of Egypt;* so the mighty of Nineveh were driven forth, with no trace where they had been, where they were. *The wind carried them away*[10]; *the wind passeth over him and he is not, and his place knoweth him no more*[11]. *The triumphing of the wicked is short, and the joy of the ungodly for a moment: though his excellency mount up to the heavens, and his head reach unto the clouds, yet he shall perish for ever; they which have seen him shall say, where is he? He shall fly away, as a dream, and shall not be found; neither shall his place any more behold him*[12].

Where they are. So Zechariah asks, *Your fathers, where are they*[13]? History, experience, human knowledge can answer nothing. They can only say, where they are *not*. God Alone can answer that much-containing word, *Where-they*[14]. They had disappeared from human sight, from their greatness, their visible being, their place on earth.

18. *Thy shepherds*, i.e. they who should counsel for the people's good and feed it, and *keep watch over their flocks by night*, but are now like their master, the *King of Assyria*, are his shepherds not the shepherds of the people whom they care not for; these *slumber*, at once through listlessness and excess, and now have fallen asleep in death, as the Psalmist says[15], *They have slept their sleep.* The prophet speaks of the future, as already past in effect, as it was in the will of God. All "the shepherds of the people[16]," all who could shepherd them, or hold them together, themselves sleep *the sleep of death; their mighty men dwelt*[17] in that abiding-place, where they shall not move or rise[18], the grave; and so as Micaiah, in the vision predictive of Ahab's death[19], *saw all Israel scattered on the*

[1] Rawl. 5. Empires i. 115.

[2] Gosse, Assyria p. 463, who remarks that "the Ten Thousand in Xerxes' army," crossed the Hellespont "crowned with garlands." Herod. vii. 55.

[3] Jer. li. 27. On the word, טפסר, see ab. p. 107. n. e.

[4] גוב גובי, doubtless the common superlative, like עבד עבדים Gen. ix. 25.

[5] S. Jer. copied by S. Cyr. and Theod.

[6] Casalis, on the proverb of the Bassouto, "locusts are taken in the heap." Etudes sur la langue Sechuana p. 87. Paris 1842, referred to by Ewald ad loc. who also refers to Ibn Babuta (in the Journ. As. 1843, March, p. 240.) "The chase of locusts is made before sunrise; for then they are benumbed by the cold and cannot fly."

[7] יוֹם קָרָה, "the cold day," (also Prov. xxv. 20), of course does not mean "night," (as Hitzig &c.) nor (as Ew. &c.) does זרח השמש mean anything but "sunrise," of which it is used 8 times beside, Gen. xxxii. 32, Ex. xxii. 2, Jud. ix. 33, 2 Sam. xxiii. 4, 2 Kgs iii. 22, Ps. civ. 22, Eccl. i. 5, Jon. iv. 8; but the locusts, having been benumbed by a cold day, plainly would not be warmed till the sunrise of the following day.

[8] נוֹדַד, passive. [9] Ex. x. 19. [10] Is. xli. 16.

[11] Ps. ciii. 16. [12] Job xx. 5–9. [13] Zech. i.

[14] אַיָּם, contracted for איה הם.

[15] Ps. lxxvi. 6, נמו שנתם.

[16] Homer, passim. [17] Comp. מִשְׁכָּן Is. xxii. 16.

[18] "They cannot rise" Rashi. "It means the rest of death, and so שכנה דומה נפשי Ps. xciv. 6, כבודי לעפר ישכן Ps. vii. 6." Sal. Ben Mel. "are still and move not." A. E. [19] 1 Kgs xxii. 17.

Before CHRIST cir. 713.

19 *There is* no †healing
of thy bruise; [c] thy wound
is grievous: [d] all that hear
the bruit of thee shall clap

† Heb. *wrinkling.* [c] Mic. 1. 9.

[d] Lam. 2. 15. Zeph. ii. 15. See Isa. 14. 8, &c.

Before CHRIST cir. 713.

hills, as sheep that have not a shepherd, so the people of the Assyrian monarch shall be *scattered on the mountains,* shepherdless, and that irretrievably; *no man gathereth* them.

19. *There is no healing* [lit. *dulling*] *of thy bruise;* it cannot be softened or mitigated; and so *thy wound is grievous* [lit. *sick*], incurable, for when the wound ever anew inflames, it cannot be healed. The word, *bruise,* is the more expressive, because it denotes alike the abiding wound in the body [1], and the shattering of a state, which God can heal [2], or which may be great, incurable [3]. When the passions are ever anew aroused, they are at last without remedy; when the soul is ever swollen with pride, it cannot be healed; since only by submitting itself to Christ, "broken and contrite" by humility, can it be healed. Nineveh sank, and never rose; nothing soothed its fall. In the end there shall be nothing to mitigate the destruction of the world, or to soften the sufferings of the damned. The *rich man, being in torments,* asked in vain that Lazarus might *dip the tip of his finger in water and cool my tongue.*

All that hear the bruit of thee shall clap the hands over thee, for none can grieve at thy fall.

Nineveh sinks out of sight amid one universal, exulting, exceeding joy [4] of all who heard the report of her. *For upon whom hath not thy wickedness passed continually?* "In that he asketh, *upon whom hath not thy wickedness passed continually?* he affirmeth most strongly that his evil did pass upon all continually." His *wickedness,* like one *continual* flood, which knew no ebb or bound, had *passed* upon the whole world and each one in it; now at length it had passed away, and *the whole earth is at rest, is quiet; they break forth into singing* [5].

It is not without meaning, that having throughout the prophecy addressed Nineveh (in the feminine), now, in the close [6], the prophet turns to him in whom all its wickedness is, as it were, gathered into one, the soul of all its evil, and the director of it, its king. As Nineveh is the image of the world, its pomps, wealth, luxury, vanity, wickedness, oppression, destruction, so its king is the image of a worse king, the Prince of this world. "[7] And this is the song of triumph of those, over whom *his wickedness has passed,* not rested, but they have escaped out of his hands. Nahum, 'the comforter,' had *rebuked the world of sin;* now he pronounces that *the prince of this world is judged. His shepherds* are they who serve him, who *feed the flock of the slaughter,* who guide them to evil, not to good. These, when they *sleep,* as all mankind, *dwell* there; it is *their* abiding-place; their sheep are *scattered on the mountains,* in the heights of their pride, because they are not of the sheep of Christ; and since they would not be gathered of Him, they are *scattered,* where *none gathereth.*" "The king of Assyria (Satan) knoweth that he cannot deceive the sheep, unless he have first laid the shepherds asleep. It is ever the aim of the devil to lay asleep souls that watch. In the Passion of the Lord, he weighed down the eyes of the Apostles with heavy sleep, whom Christ arouseth [8], *Watch and pray, lest ye enter into temptation;* and again, *What I say unto you, I say unto all, watch! And no man gathereth them,* for their shepherds themselves cannot protect themselves. In the Day of God's anger, *the kings of the earth and the great men, and the rich men and the chief captains, and the mighty men, and every bondman, and every free man, hid themselves in the dens and in the rocks of the mountains* [9]. Such are his shepherds, and his sheep; but what of himself? Truly his *bruise* or *breaking* can *not* be *healed; his wound* or smiting is *incurable;* that namely whereby, when *he came* to Him *in* Whom he *found nothing* [10], yet *bruised His heel,* and exacted of Him a sinner's death, *his* own *head was bruised.*" And hence *all who have ears to hear,* who hear not with the outward only, but with the inner ears of the heart, *clap the hands over thee,* i. e. give to God all their souls' thanks and praise, raise up their eyes and hands to God in heaven, praising Him Who had *bruised Satan under their feet.* Ever since, through the serpent, the evil and malicious One lied, saying, *ye shall not surely die,* eat and *ye shall be as gods,* hath *his evil, continually* and unceasingly, from one and through one, *passed upon all men.* As the Apostle saith, *As by one man, sin entered into the world, and death by sin, and so death passed upon all men, for that all have sinned* [11]. *Upon whom* then hath not *his sin passed?* Who hath not been *shapen in iniquity?* and whom did not *his mother conceive in sin?* Yet, it *passeth* only, for *the world itself also passeth away,* and we pass away from it, and all the evil it can do us, unless we share in its evil, is not abiding, but passing. This then is the cause, and a

[1] Lev. xxi. 19. [2] Ps. lx. 4, Is. xxx. 26.
[3] Jer. xxx. 12.
[4] תקעו כף, only here and Ps. xlvii. 2, expressing joy.

[5] Is. xiv. 7. [6] v. 18, 19.
[7] S. Jer. Rup.
[8] S. Mat. xxvi. 41. [9] Rev. vi. 15.
[10] S. John xiv. 30. [11] Rom. v. 12.

INTRODUCTION

TO

THE PROPHET

HABAKKUK.

HABAKKUK is eminently the prophet of reverential, awe-filled faith. This is the soul and centre of his prophecy. One word alone he addresses directly to his people. It is of marvel at their want of faith. [a] *Behold among the heathen and gaze attentively, and marvel, marvel; for I am working a work in your days; ye will not believe, when it is declared unto you.* He bids them *behold*, and *gaze*, for God is about to work in their own days; he bids them prepare themselves to *marvel*, and *marvel on;* for it was a matter, at which political wisdom would stagger; and they, since they had not faith, would not believe it. The counterpart to this, is that great blessing of faith, which is the key-stone of his whole book, [b] *the just shall live by his faith.*

Isaiah had foretold to Hezekiah that his treasures should be carried to Babylon, his sons be eunuchs in the palace of its king [c]. He had foretold the destruction of Babylon and the restoration of the Jews [d]. Prophecy in Habakkuk, full as it is, is almost subordinate. His main subject is, that which occupied Asaph in the 73d Psalm, the afflictions of the righteous amid the prosperity of the wicked. The answer is the same; the result of all will be one great reversal, the evil drawing upon themselves evil, God crowning the patient waiting of the righteous in still submission to His holy Will. *The just shall live by his faith,* occupies the same place in Habakkuk, as *I know that my Redeemer liveth,* does in Job [e], or *Thou shalt guide me with Thy counsel, and after that receive me into glory,* in Asaph [f].

His first subject [g] is, faith struggling under the oppressive sight of the sufferings of the good from the bad within God's people; the second [h], the sufferings at the hands of those who are God's instruments to avenge that wickedness. The third [i], that of his great hymn, is faith, not jubilant until the end, yet victorious, praying, believing, seeing in vision what it prays for, and triumphing in that, of which it sees no tokens, whose only earnest is God's old loving-kindnesses to His people, and His Name, under which He had revealed Himself, "He Who Is," the Unchangeable.

The whole prophecy is, so to speak, a colloquy between the prophet and God. He opens it with a reverential, earnest, appeal to God, like that of the saints under the heavenly Altar in the Revelations [k], *How long?* The prophet had prayed to God to end or mitigate the violence, oppressions, strife, contention, despoiling, powerlessness of the law, crookedness of justice, entrapping of the righteous by the wicked [l]. God answers [m], that a terrible day of retribution was coming, that He Himself would raise up the Chaldees, as the instruments of His chastisements, terrible, self-dependent, owning no law or authority but their own will, deifying their own power, sweeping the whole breadth of the land, possessing themselves of it, taking every fenced city, and gathering captives as the sand. This answers the one half of Habakkuk's question, as to the prosperity of the wicked among his people. It leaves the other half, as to the condition of the righteous, unanswered. For such scourges of God swept

[a] i. 5. [b] ii. 4. [c] Is. xxxix. 6, 7. [d] Is. xii. xiii. xlvii. [e] Job xix. 25.

[f] Ps. lxxiii. 24. [g] c. i. [h] c. ii. [i] c. iii. [k] Rev. vi. 10. [l] i. 2–4. [m] Ib. 6–11.

away the righteous with the wicked. Habakkuk then renews the question as to *them.* But, as Asaph began by declaring his faith, [n]*All-good is God to Israel*, the true Israel, *the pure of heart*, so Habakkuk, "Israel would not die, because He, their God, is Unchangeable." [o]*Art not Thou of old, O Lord, my God, my holy One? we shall not die; Thou, O Lord, hast set him* [the Chaldee] *for judgment, and Thou, O Rock, hast founded him to chasten.* Then he appeals to God, "Why then is this? *Thou art of purer eyes than to behold evil—wherefore keepest Thou silence, when the wicked devoureth him who is more righteous than he?*" This closes the first chapter and the first vision, in which he describes, with the vividness of one who saw it before him, the irresistible invasion of the Chaldæans. Israel was meshed as in a net; should that net be emptied [p]?

The second chapter exhibits the prophet waiting in silent expectation for the answer. This answer too dwells chiefly on those retributions in this life, which are the earnest of future judgments, the witness of the sovereignty of God. But although in few words, it does answer the question as to the righteous, that he has abiding life, that he lives and shall live. God impresses the importance of the answer in the words [q], *Write the vision* i. e. the prophecy, *and make it plain on the tables*, whereon the prophet was wont to write [r], *that he may run who reads it.* He says also, that it is for a time fixed in the mind of God, and that however, in man's sight, it might seem to *linger*, it would not be aught behind the time [s]. Then he gives the answer itself in the words, [t]*Behold his soul which is puffed up is not upright in him; and the just shall live by his faith.* The swelling pride and self-dependence of the Chaldee stands in contrast with the trustful submission of faith. Of the one God says, it has no ground of uprightness, and consequently will not stand before God; of faith, he says, *the righteous shall live by it.* But the life plainly is not the life of the body. For Habakkuk's ground of complaint was the world-wasting cruelty of the Chaldees. The woe on the Chaldee which follows is even chiefly for bloodshed, in which the righteous and the wicked are massacred alike. The simple word, *shall live*, is an entire denial of death, a denial even of any interruption of life. It stands in the same fullness as those words of our Lord, [u]*because I live, ye shall live also.* The other side of the picture, the fall of the Chaldees, is given in greater fullness, because the fulfillment of God's word in things seen was the pledge of the fulfillment of those beyond the veil of sense and time. In a measured dirge he pronounces a five-fold woe on the five great sins of the Chaldees, their ambition [v], covetousness [x], violence [y], insolence [z], idolatry [a]. It closes with the powerlessness of the Chaldee idols against God, and bids the whole world be hushed before the presence of the One God, its Maker, awaiting His sentence.

Then follows the prayer [b], that God would *revive* His *work* for Israel, which now seemed dead. He describes the revival as coming, under the images of God's miraculous deliverances of old. The division of the Red Sea and the Jordan, the standing-still of the sun and moon under Joshua, are images of future deliverances; all nature shakes and quivers at the presence of its Maker. Yet not it, but the wicked were the object of His displeasure. The prophet sees his people delivered as at the Red Sea, just when the enemy seemed ready to sweep them away, as with a whirlwind. And, in sight of the unseen, he closes with that wondrous declaration of faith, that all nature should be desolate, all subsistence gone, everything, contrary to God's promises of old to His people, should be around him, *and I will rejoice in the Lord, I will exult for joy in the God of my salvation.*

This prophecy is not less distinct, because figurative. Rather it is the declaration of God's deliverance of His people, not from the Chaldees only, but at all times. The evil is concentrated in one Evil one, who stands over against the One anointed. *Thou art gone forth for the salvation of Thy people; for salvation with Thine anointed One. Thou crushedst the head out of the house of the wicked One, laying bare the foundation unto the neck*, i. e. smiting the house, at once, above and below; with an utter destruction. It belongs then the more to all times, until the closing strife between evil and good, Christ and Antichrist, the ἄνομος and the Lord. It includes the Chaldee, and each great Empire which opposes itself to the kingdom of God, and declares that, as God delivered His people of old, so He would unto the end.

It may be that Habakkuk chose this name to express the strong faith, whereby he embraced the promises of God. At least, it means one who "strongly enfolds [c]."

Perhaps too it is on account of the form in

[n] Ps. lxxiii. 1.
[o] Hab. i. 12.
[p] Ib. 17.
[q] ii. 2.
[r] עַל הלחות.
[s] ii. 3.
[t] ii. 4.
[u] S. John xiv. 19.
[v] ii. 5. 8.
[x] ii. 9–11.
[y] ii. 12–14.
[z] ii. 15–17.
[a] ii. 18–20.
[b] c. iii.

[c] There is no other form exactly like חֲבַקּוּק. Yet it is manifestly intensive. It most resembles the form אהבהב "loved intensely." This form, in חֲצַרְצַר, הֲטַרְטַר, is changed into חֲצוֹצַר חֲטוֹטַר. Equally חֲבַקְבּוּק might be pronounced Habakkuk, the second ב being, as Delitzsch suggested, merged in the ק, for greater facility of pronunciation. The ו is a form like נַעֲצוּץ שַׁעֲרוּרָה, שְׁקַעֲרוּרוֹת,

which his prophecy is cast, as being spoken (with the exception of that one verse) to God or to the Chaldæan, not to his own people, that he added the title of Prophet to his name. *The burden which Habakkuk the prophet did see*[d]. For, however the name "prophet" includes all to whom revelations from God came, it is nowhere, in the Old Testament, added as the name of an office to any one, who did not exercise the practical office of the Prophet. Our Lord quotes David as *the Prophet*[e], and God says to Abimelech of Abraham[f], *He is a Prophet*, and, in reference to this, the Psalmist speaks of the Patriarchs, as Prophets[g]. *He reproved kings for their sakes, saying, Touch not Mine anointed and do My prophets no harm*, and Hosea speaks of Moses as a prophet[h], and St. Peter says of David[i], *He being a prophet.* But the title is nowhere in the Old Testament added to the name as it is here, *Habakkuk the prophet*, and as it is elsewhere Samuel the prophet[k], the prophet Gad[l], Nathan the prophet[m], Ahijah the prophet[n], the prophet Jehu[o], Elijah the prophet[p], Elisha the prophet[q], Shemaiah the prophet[r], the prophet Iddo[s], the prophet Obed[t], Isaiah the prophet[u], Jeremiah the prophet[v], Haggai the prophet[x], unless any have exercised the prophetic office. The title of *the Prophet* is not, in the Old Testament, added to the names of Jacob or even of Moses or David or Solomon or Daniel, although they all prophesied of Christ.

Since Holy Scripture often conveys so much incidentally, it may be that a large range of ministerial office is hinted in the words "write on *the* tables;" for "*the* tables" must have been well-known tables, tables upon which prophets (as Isaiah) and probably Habakkuk himself was accustomed to write. The writing of a few emphatic unexplained words in a public place, which should arouse curiosity, or startle passers-by, would be in harmony with the symbolical actions, enjoined on the prophets and used by them. The *Mene, Mene, Tekel, Upharsin*, had, from their mysteriousness, an impressiveness of their own, apart from the miracle of the writing.

The words appended to the prophecy, *to the chief singer*, (as we should say, "the leader of the band") *with* or *on my stringed instruments*, imply, not only that the hymn became part of the devotions of the temple, but that Habakkuk too had a part in the sacred music which accompanied it. The word so rendered, *neginothai*, could only mean *my stringed instruments*, or "my song accompanied with music," as Hezekiah says[y], *we will sing my songs on the stringed instruments, nenaggen neginothai.* But in Habakkuk's subscription, "To the chief musician *binginothai*," *neginoth* can have no other meaning than in the almost identical inscription of Psalms, "[z] To the chief musician *binginoth*," nor this any other than *with stringed instruments*, "instruments struck with the hand[a]." The addition, "with *my* stringed instruments," shews that Habakkuk himself was to accompany his hymn with instrumental music, and since the mention of *the chief musician* marks out that it was to form part of the temple-service, Habakkuk must have been entitled to take part in the temple-music, and so must have been a Levite. The Levitical order then had its prophet, as the sacerdotal in Jeremiah and Ezekiel. The tradition in the title to Bel and the Dragon, whatever its value, agrees with this; "[b] from the prophecy of Ambakum, son of Jesus, of the tribe of Levi."

This, however, does not give us any hint as to the time when Habakkuk prophesied. For, bad as were the times of Manasseh and Amon, their idolatry consisted in associating idols with God, setting them up in His courts, bringing one even into His temple[c], not in doing away His service. They set the two services, and the two *opinions*[d], side by side, adding the false, but not abolishing the true, "consenting to differ," leaving to the worshipers of God their religion, while forcing them to endure, side by side, what seemed an addition, but what was, in fact, a denial. Habakkuk then might have been allowed to present his hymn for the temple-service, while the king placed in the same temple the statue of Astarte, and required its devil's worship to be carried on there. The temple was allowed to go into some degree of decay, for Josiah had it repaired; but we read only of his removing idols[e], not of his having to restore the disused service of God. Of Ahaz it is recorded, that[f] *he shut up the doors of the house of the Lord*, which Hezekiah had to open[g]. Nothing of this sort is told of Manasseh and Amon.

Habakkuk, however, has two hints, which determine his age within a few years. He says that the invasion of the Chaldæans was to be in the days of those to whom he speaks;

אֲסַפְסֻף; yet it is impossible that the reduplication should be meaningless. (as Ew. 157. a. p. 405. ed. 7.)

[d] i. 1. add iii. 1. [e] S. Matt. xiii. 35.
[f] Gen. xx. 7. [g] Ps. cv. 14–15. [h] Hos. xii. 13.
[i] Acts ii. 30. [k] 2 Chr. xxxv. 18.
[l] 1 Sam. xxii. 5. [m] 1 Kgs i. 32. [n] 1 Kgs xi. 29.
[o] Ib. xvi. 7, 12. [p] Ib. xviii. 36. [q] 2 Kgs vi. 12.
[r] 2 Chr. xii. 5. [s] Ib. xiii. 22. [t] Ib. xv. 8.
[u] 2 Kgs xix. 2, xx. 1.

[v] Jer. xxviii. 6, xxxvi. 26, 2 Chr. xxxvi. 12.
[x] Ezr. v. 1, vi. 14. [y] Is. xxxviii. 20.
[z] Ps. iv. vi. liv. lv. lxi. lxvii. lxxvi.
[a] Coll. 1 Sam. xvii. 16, 23, xviii. 10, xix. 9, 2 Kgs iii. 15.
[b] Cod. Chis. of LXX from Origen's Tetraplar and the Syro-Hexaplar.
[c] 2 Kgs xxi. 7. [d] 1 Kgs xviii. 21.
[e] 2 Kgs xxiii. 6. [f] 2 Chr. xxxviii. 24.
[g] Ib. xxix. 3.

in your days[h]. Accordingly he must have spoken to adults, many of whom would survive that invasion of Nebuchadnezzar, in the 4th year of Jehoiakim B. C. 605. He can hardly have prophesied before B. C. 645, about the close of Manasseh's reign; for at this date, those who were 20 at the time of the prophecy, would have been 60, at the time of its commenced fulfillment at the battle of Carchemish. On the other hand, in that he speaks of that invasion as a thing incredible to those to whom he was speaking, he must have prophesied before Babylon became independent by the overthrow of Nineveh, B. C. 625. For when Babylon had displaced Nineveh, and divided the Empire of the East with Media and Egypt, it was not a thing incredible, that it would invade Judah in their own days, although it was beyond human knowledge to declare that it certainly would. The Babylonian Empire itself lasted only eighty-nine years; and, to human sight, Judah had as much or more to fear from Egypt as from Babylon. The Median Empire also might as well have swallowed up Judah for the time, as the Babylonian.

The relation of Zephaniah to Habakkuk coincides with this. Zephaniah certainly adopted the remarkable words[i], lit. [k] *Hush at the presence of the Lord God*, from Habakkuk's fuller form [l], *the Lord is in His holy temple; hush at His presence all the earth.*

But Zephaniah prophesied under Josiah, before the destruction of Nineveh B. C. 625, which he foretold [m]. Habakkuk was also, at latest, an earlier contemporary of Jeremiah who, in one place, at least, in his earlier prophecies, used his language [n], as he does so often, of set purpose, that of the prophets before him, in order to shew that the fullness of their prophecies was not yet exhausted. But Jeremiah began to prophesy in the thirteenth year of Josiah B. C. 629 [o]. Habakkuk, on the other hand, joins himself on with the old prophets and Psalms by the employment of language of Isaiah [p] and perhaps of Micah [q], by the use of language of Deuteronomy [r], and by the expansion of a Psalm of Asaph in his own Psalm [s], but does not systematically renew their prophecies like Jeremiah [t] or Zephaniah [u].

The ministry then of Habakkuk falls in the latter half of the reign of Manasseh or the earlier half of that of Josiah, (for the reign of Amon, being of two years only, is too short to come into account), and there is no decisive evidence for either against the other. In the reign of Manasseh, we are expressly told, that there were prophets, sent to foretell a destruction of Jerusalem as complete as that of Samaria, on account of the exceeding wickedness, into which Manasseh seduced his people. *The Lord spake by His servants, the prophets, saying, Because Manasseh king of Judah hath done these abominations, and hath made Judah also to sin with his idols, Therefore thus saith the Lord God of Israel, Behold, I am bringing such evil upon Jerusalem and Judah, that whosoever heareth of it, both his ears shall tingle. And I will stretch over Jerusalem the*

[h] i. 5.

[i] Dr. Davidson says, "Delitzsch [with many others] maintains from a comparison of Hab. ii. 20, with Zeph. i. 7, that the former preceded the latter.—The premises are by no means safe or valid" [and, following Umbreit,] "'Be silent before the Lord God' (Zeph. i. 7.) sounds like a proverb: part of it having been already used by Amos (vi. 10)," iii. 304. 305. Amos has only the single word הס "hush!" which is, of course no fragment of a proverb. Nor was there any lack of expressions to bid men be still before their Maker. Delitzsch (ad. loc. p. 102.) puts together the following; Ps. xcvi. 9. חילו מפניו כל-הארץ; xiv. 7. מלפני אדון הולי ארץ 1 Chr. xvi. 30, חילו מלפניו כל-הארץ; Ps. xxxiii. 8, ויראו מיי" כל הארץ, and the Psalm of Asaph," משמים השמעת דין ארץ יראה ושקטה; not to speak of other possible combinations, with חשה, החריש, דמם (which is thought to be only a stronger pronunciation of it. Kim. also explains הס by שתק.) When then a writer, who uses much the language of those before him, has an idiom which occurs once beside in Holy Scripture, there being many other expressions, which might equally have been used, any one unbiassed would think that he adopted the language of the other. Stähelin admits the connection, but inverts the argument, contrary to the character of both prophets.

[k] Zeph. i. 7. [l] Hab. ii. 20. [m] Zeph. ii. 13, sqq.

[n] Hab. i. 8, קַלּוּ מִנְּמֵרִים סוּסָיו וְחַדּוּ מִזְּאֵבֵי עֶרֶב seems to have suggested the like description of the Chaldee cavalry, Jer. iv. 13, קַלּוּ מִנְּשָׁרִים סוּסָיו, although, with the slight variation, which he commonly used, Jeremiah has כנשרים, after David probably on Saul and Jonathan, מִנְּשָׁרִים קַלּוּ 2 Sam. i. 23, the remaining instance of this likeness. זְאֵבֵי עֶרֶב recurs in Zeph. iii. 3, and זְאֵב עֲרָבוֹת in Jer. v. 6, only. Jer. xxii. 13, in the reign of Jehoiakim, is also a reminiscence of Habakkuk ii. 12; and Jer. li. 58, in the 4th year of Zedekiah, of Hab. ii. 13.

[o] Jer. i. 2, xxv. 3.

[p] Hab. ii. 14, is from Is. xi. 9; the form of Hab. i. 5, seems suggested by Is. xxix. 9; the standing on the watch-tower Hab. ii. 1, occurs in Is. xxi. 8; the writing on tables occurs in Is. viii. 1, xxx. 8, and Hab. ii. 2; the imagery, "he hath enlarged his desire as hell," (הרחוב כשאול נפשו) Hab. ii. 5, was probably suggested by Is. v. 14. הִרְחִיבָה שְׁאוֹל נַפְשָׁהּ; the introduction of a משל, Hab. ii. 6, as Is. xiv. 4, both over Babylon; the union of הלף and עבר Is. viii. 8, and Hab. i. 11; from Küper Jerem. p. 153. Havernick Symb. ad defend. authentiam vat. Ies. c. xiii.—xiv. 23. p. 37 sqq. in Delitzsch Hab. p. viii.

[q] Hab. ii. 12. and Mic. iii. 10.

[r] From Deut. xxxii. xxxiii. See below.

[s] Ps. lxxvii. 17–21, in Hab. iii. 10–15.

[t] On the relation of Jeremiah to Obadiah and Isaiah, see Introd. to Obad. vol. i. pp. 344–348.

[u] See Introd. to Zephaniah, below.

line of Samaria and the plummet of the house of Ahab; and I will wipe Jerusalem as a man wipeth a dish, wiping it and turning it upside down; and I will forsake the remnant of their inheritance, and deliver them into the hand of their enemies, and they shall become a prey and spoil to all their enemies [x].

The sinful great men of Manasseh's and Amon's court and judicature are but too likely to have maintained their power in the early years of the reign of Josiah. For a boy of eight years old (at which age Josiah succeeded his father [y]) could, amid whatsoever sense of right and piety, do little to stem the established wrong and ungodliness of the evil counsellors and judges of his father and grandfather. The sins, which Jeremiah denounces, as the cause of the future captivity of Jerusalem, are the very same, of which Habakkuk complains, "oppression, violence, spoil [z]." Jeremiah speaks, in the concrete, of total absence of right judgment [a], as Habakkuk, in the abstract, of the powerlessness of the law [b]. Zephaniah gives the like picture of those earlier years under Josiah [c]. But Habakkuk's description would not suit the later years of Josiah, when judgment and justice *were* done. *Did not thy father*, Jeremiah appeals to Jehoiakim [d], *eat and drink, and do judgment and justice, and then it was well with him; he judged the cause of the poor and needy, then it was well with him; was not this to know Me? saith the Lord* [e]. But while there is nothing to preclude his having prophesied in either reign, the earliest tradition places him in the close of the reign of Manasseh [f].

Modern critics have assigned an earlier or later date to Habakkuk, accordingly as they believed that God did, or did not, reveal the future to man, that there was or was not, superhuman prophecy. Those who denied that God did endow His prophets with knowledge above nature, fell into two classes; 1) Such as followed Eichhorn's unnatural hypothesis, that prophecies were only histories of the past, spoken of, as if it were still future, to which these critics gave the shameless title of "vaticinia post eventum [g]." These plainly involved the prophets in fraud. 2) Those who laid down that each prophet lived at a time, when he could, with human foresight, tell what would happen. Would that those who count certainty, as to even a near future, to be so easy a thing, would try their hands at predicting the events of the next few years or months, or even days [h], and, if they fail, acknowledge God's Truth! This prejudice, that there *could* be no real prophecy, ruled, for a time, all German criticism. It cannot be denied, that "the unbelief was the parent of the criticism, not the criticism of the unbelief." It is simple matter of history, that the unbelief came first; and, if men, à priori, disbelieved that there *could* be prophecy, it must needs be a postulate of their criticism, that what seemed to be prophecy *could* not have belonged to a date, when human foresight did not suffice for positive prediction. I will use the words of Delitzsch rather than my own;

"[i] The investigation into the age of Habakkuk could be easily and briefly settled, if we would start from the prejudice, which is the soul of modern criticism, that a prediction of the future, which rested, not on human in-

[x] 2 Kgs xxi. 11–14. [y] Ib. xxii. 1, 2 Chr. xxxiv. 1.

[z] חָמָס וָשֹׁד Jer. vi. 7, as Hab. i. 3, שֹׁד וחמס; Zeph. speaks of חמס ומרמה, i. 9.

[a] Jer. vi. 19. "My law they have despised it;" v. 28. "they have not judged the cause, the cause of the fatherless, and they prosper; and the judgment of the poor have they not judged."

[b] Hab. i. 4, "the law is chilled, and judgment will never go forth; for the wicked encompasseth the just; therefore judgment goeth forth perverted."

[c] Zeph. i. 9. where he too foretells the punishment of those, "which fill their masters' houses with violence and deceit, חָמָס וּמִרְמָה" and iii. 1–4.

[d] Jer. xxii. 15, 16.

[e] Dr. Davidson rightly says, "the spoiling and violence, there (i. 2, 3.) depicted, refer to the internal condition of the theocracy, not to external injuries" (p. 305); but then he contradicts himself and Jeremiah, when he says, (p. 305) following Ewald (Proph. ii. 30.), "The safest conclusion respecting the time of the prophet, is that he lived in the time of Jehoiakim (606–604. B. C.), *when the kingdom of Judah was in a good moral condition, justice and righteousness having entered into the life of the people after Josiah's reforms*, and idolatry having almost disappeared."

[f] "Seder Olam, from which Abarbanel, R. Dav. Ganz in Zemach David, p. 21, and Rabbins drew their opinion." Carpzoff Introd. P. iii. p. 410.

[g] Eichhorn (Einl.) Berthold (Einl.) Justi Habakkuk neu übersetzt 1841. Wolf, der Proph. Hab. &c. 1822.

[h] At every early stage of the great conflict (August 1870) it was remarkable how day after day journalists professed themselves to be at fault, as to the most immediate future. On one point only they were agreed that the war would be "long and severe." Then it was thought that one month would see its beginning and its end. "The course of the present war," says a journal not wanting in self-reliance, "has gone far to verify the paradox, that nothing is certain but the unexpected. At any rate, *nothing has happened but the unforeseen*. Neither king nor Emperor, neither French nor German government or people had formed any anticipation of the events of the month now ending. The French expected to invade Germany, and they have been invaded themselves. The Germans, though confident of ultimate success, expected a long and toilsome conflict, whereas a month has brought them almost to the gates of Paris. The calculation of all parties as to the political effects of the war have been equally mistaken." *The Times*, Aug. 31st. And yet men, who, with our full information, would not risk a prediction as to the issue of things immediately before their eyes, think it so easy for Jewish prophets, living in their own small insulated country, to foretell certainly that Babylon would prevail over Egypt, when they knew either country only as their own superior, and political sagacity and feeling was on the side of Egypt.

[i] Der Proph. Habakkuk Einleit. pp. iv–vi.

ferences or on a natural gift of divination, but on supernatural illumination, is *impossible.* For since Habakkuk foretold the invasion of the Chaldees, he must, in such case, have come forward at a time, at which natural acuteness could, with certainty, determine beforehand that sad event; accordingly in or after the time of the battle of Carchemish in the 4th year of Jehoiakim[j] 606 B. C. In this decisive battle Nebuchadnezzar defeated Pharaoh Necho, and it was more than probable that the king of Babylon would now turn against Judæa, since Jehoiakim, the son of Josiah, had been set on the throne by Pharaoh Necho[k], and so held with Egypt. And this is in reality the inference of modern critics. They bring the Chaldæans so close under the eyes of the prophet, that he could, by way of nature, foresee their invasion; and so much the closer under his eyes, the more deeply the prejudice, that there is no prophecy in the Biblical sense of the word, has taken root in them, and the more consistently they follow it out. 'Habakkuk prophesied under Jehoiakim, for,' so Jäger expresses himself, 'since Jehoiakim was on the side of the Egyptians, *it was easy to foresee, that*[l]; &c.' Just so Ewald; '[m]One might readily be tempted to think, that Habakkuk wrote, while the pious king Josiah was still living; but since the first certain invasion of the Chaldæans, of which our account speaks[n], falls within the reign of king Jehoiakim, somewhat between 608–604 B. C. we must abide by this date.' Hitzig defines the dates still more sharply, according to that principle of principles, to which history with its facts must adapt itself unconditionally. 'The prophet announces the arrival of the Chaldæans in Judæa, as something marvelous.' Well then, one would imagine, that it would follow from this, that at that time they had not yet come. But no! 'Habakkuk,' says Hitzig, 'introduces the Chaldæans as a new phænomenon, as yet entirely unknown; he *prophesied accordingly* at their *first* arrival into Palestine. But this beyond question falls in the reign of Jehoiakim[o]. In Jehoiakim's fourth year, i. e. 606, they had fought the battle at Carchemish; in 605 *the Chaldæan army seems to have been on its march;* the writing of Habakkuk is placed most correctly in the beginning of the year 604,' accordingly, at the time, when the Chaldæans were already marching with all speed straight on Jerusalem, and (as Hitzig infers from Hab. i. 9.) after they had come down from the North along the coast, were now advancing from the West, when they, as Ewald too remarks (resting, like Maurer on i. 2–4), '[p]already stood in the holy land, trampling everything under foot with irresistible might, and allowing their own right alone to count as right.' Holding fast to that naturalist *à priori,* we go yet further. In ii. 17, the judgment of God is threatened to the Chaldæan, on account of the violence practiced on Lebanon, and the destruction of its animals. Lebanon is, it is said, the holy land; the animals, its inhabitants: in iii. 14, 17, the prophet sees the hostile hordes storming in: the devastation wrought through the war stands clearly before his eyes. This is not *possible,* unless the Chaldæan were at that time already established in Judæa. However, then, c. i. was written *before* their invasion, yet c. ii., iii. must have been written after it. 'Wherefore,' says Maurer, 'since it is evident from Jer. xlvi. 2, and xxxvi. 9, that the Chaldæans came in the year B. C. 605, in the 9th month of the 5th year of the reign of Jehoiakim, it follows that c. i. was written at that very time, but c. ii. iii. at the beginning of B. C. 604, the 6th of Jehoiakim.'

"Turn we away from this cheap pseudo-criticism, with its ready-made results, which sacrifices all sense for historical truth to a prejudice, which it seems to have vowed not to allow to be shaken by anything. It seeks at any cost to disburden itself of any prophecy in Scripture, which can only be explained through supernatural agency; and yet it attains its end, neither elsewhere nor in our prophet. Chapter ii. contains a prediction of the overthrow of the Chaldæan empire and of the sins whereby that overthrow was effected, which has been so remarkably confirmed by history even in details, that that criticism, if it would be true to its principles, must assume that it was written while Cyrus, advancing against Babylon was employed in punishing the river Gyndes by dividing it off into 360 channels."

This major premiss, "there *can be* no superhuman prediction of the future," (in other words, "Almighty God, if He knows the future, cannot disclose it!") still lurks under the assumptions of that modern school of so-called criticism. It seems to be held no more necessary, formally to declare it, than to enounce at full length any axiom of Euclid. Yet it may, on that very ground, escape notice, while it is the unseen mainspring of the theories, put forth in the name of criticism. "That Habakkuk falls at a later time," says Stähelin, "is clear out of his prophecy itself; *for he speaks of the Chaldæans,* and the controversy is only, whether he announces their invasion, as Knobel, Umbreit, Delitzsch, Keil[q] hold, or presupposes it, as Ewald, Hit-

[j] Jer. xlvi. 2. [k] 2 Kgs xxiii. 34, 35.
[l] "Facile erat prævidere fore ut &c." Jäger de ord. proph. minor. chronol. ii. 18. sqq.
[m] Proph. iii. 30. ed. 2.
[n] 2 Kgs xxiv. 1. [o] Ib. 2.
[p] Proph. iii. 29. ed. 2.
[q] Stähelin mixed up Delitzsch and Keil, who believed in superhuman prediction, and Knobel &c.

zig, E. Meier maintain. To me the first opinion appears the right, since not only do i. 5. sqq. plainly relate to the future, but the detailed description of the Chaldæans points at something which has not yet taken place, at something hitherto unknown, and the terror of the prophet in announcing their coming, i. 12. sqq., recurs also iii. 1, 16, 17; and so, I think, that the time of Habakkuk's activity may be placed very soon after the battle of Carchemish, in the first half of the reign of Jehoiakim, and so his prophecy as contemporary with Jeremiah xxv." "Habakkuk," says De Wette, "lived and prophesied in the Chaldee period. It is, however, matter of dispute at what point of time in this period he lived. i. 5. sqq. clearly points to its beginning, the reign of Jehoiakim. Even ch. iii. seems to require no later point of time, since here the destruction of Judah is not yet anticipated. He was then Jeremiah's younger contemporary. Rightly do Perschke, Ranitz, Stickel, Knobel, Hitzig, Ewald, let the prophet prophesy a little before the invasion of the Chaldæans in Judah, which the analogy of prophecy favors;" for prophecy may still be human at this date, since so far it foretells only, what any one could foresee. A prophet of God foretells, these critics admit, an invasion which all could foresee, and does not foretell, what could not humanly be foreseen, the destruction of Jerusalem. The theory then is saved, and within these limits Almighty God is permitted to send His prophet. Condescending criticism!

Mostly criticism kept itself within these limits, and used nothing more than its axiom, "there was no prophecy." The freshness and power of prophetic diction in Habakkuk deterred most from that other expedient of picking out some two or three words as indicative of a later style. Stähelin however says; "His language too, although *on the whole* pure and without Aramaisms," (truly so! since there is not even an alleged or imagined Aramaism in his prophecy,) "still betrays, in single cases, the later period." And then he alleges that 1) one *verb* [r] "only occurs beside in the books of Kings and in Ezekiel;" 2) another word, "[s] *with the exception of Nahum*, only in Jeremiah and Malachi;" 3) "the image of the cup of destiny only occurs in prophecies subsequent to Jeremiah." Marvelous precision of criticism, which can infer the date of a book from the facts, 1) that a *verb*, formed from a *noun*, occurs four times only in Holy Scripture, in 2 Kings, Habakkuk, and Ezekiel, whereas the *noun* from which it is derived occurs in a Psalm, which fits no later time than David's [t]; 2) that a word, slightly varied in pronunciation from a common Hebrew word [u], occurs only in *Nahum*, Habakkuk, Jeremiah, and Malachi, once in each, when that word is the basis of the name of the river *Pishon*, mentioned in Genesis, and Stähelin himself places Nahum in the reign of Hezekiah; or that 3) no *prophet* before Jeremiah speaks of the image of the "cup of destiny [v]," whereas the portion given by God for good [w] or for ill [x], occurs under that same image in Psalms of David and Asaph; and if the question is to be begged as to the date of Isaiah li. 17, 22, the corresponding image of "drinking wine, of reeling," occurs in a Psalm of David [y], and being "drunk, but not with wine" is imagery of an earlier chapter in Isaiah [z]; the image occurs fully in Obadiah [a].

Such criticism is altogether childish. No

who denied it, joining himself on to the class in general and ignoring the radical difference. Dr. Davidson assumes the same principle. "As he mentions the Chaldæans by name, and his oracle refers to them, he lived in the Chaldæan period.—The safest conclusion respecting the time of the prophet is that he lived in the time of Jehoiakim 606–604. B. C." "To put the prophet in Manasseh's reign is incorrect *because* the Chaldæans were not a people formidable to the Jews at that time." (Introd. iii. pp. 304, 305.) And so Habakkuk, without superhuman knowledge, could not foretell it!

[r] "Thus the verb קָלַס occurs, only beside in the books of Kings and in Ezekiel." Stähelin. "The diction is pure and classical. Yet he has some late words, as קָלַס i. 10, which appears only in Kings and Ezekiel." Dr. Davidson. The primitive form קָלַס, which is alleged, does not occur at all; only קַלֵּס Ez. xvi. 31. and הִתְקַלֵּס with ב, "mock at," 2 Kgs ii. 23, Hab. i. 10, Ez. xxii. 5, as denominatives from קֶלֶס Ps. xliv. 14. lxxix. 4, and Jer. xx. 8. There is nothing to show that it is a late word, though occurring for the first time in the history of Elisha. In Aramaic, (not in Onk. or Jon. it has the opposite meaning, "praised." In the exceptions in Chaldee, Ges. seems rightly to conjecture, that it signifies ironical praise, as in Shem. rabba s. 27. In Ps. xliv. 14. קַלְסָא is retained for the Heb. קֶלֶס.

[s] "פּוּשׁ i. 8. with the exception of Nah. iii. 18. only besides in Jeremiah and Malachi." Stähelin, "פּוּשׁ i. 8. in Jeremiah and Malachi besides;" Dr. Davidson; who avoids the absurdity of arguing relative lateness of diction from a word, occurring in Nahum, by omitting this fourth instance, but therewith falsifying the facts before him.

[t] Ps. xliv. 14.

[u] פּוּשׁ (whence פִּישׁוֹן Gen. ii. 11.) an early variation of פּוּץ, ש for ץ, as Rashi observes on Nah. iii. 18.

[v] "The image of 'the cup of destiny' ii. 16, first occurs in the prophets after Jeremiah; and Hab. ii. 16. itself seems to refer to Jerem. xlix. 12." Stähelin pp. 288, 289. "The cup of judgment (ii. 16.) does not occur in the prophets before Jeremiah; whether Habakkuk refers in ii. 16. to Jer. xlix. 12. is doubtful, though Stähelin ventures to assert it;" Dr. Davidson (iii. 303) acknowledging, as usual, the source of his statements, where he dissents in one of them.

[w] David, Ps. xi. 6. Asaph, lxxv. 8.

[x] David. Ps. xvi. 5. xxiii. 5. [y] Ps. lx. 5. [3 Eng.]

[z] Is. xxix. 9. [a] ver. 16.

one would tolerate it, except that it is adduced to support a popular and foregone conclusion. It would be laughed to scorn, were it used by believers in revelation. In the small remains of the Hebrew Scriptures and language, an induction, if it is to be of any value, must be very distinct. The largeness of Greek literature enables critics to single out Homeric, Herodotean, Æschylean, Pindaric words. In Hebrew we meet with *ἅπαξ λεγόμενα* in perhaps every prophet, in many Psalms; but it requires far more than the occurrence of the word in one single place, to furnish any even probable inference, that it was framed by the Prophet or Psalmist himself. Still less can it be inferred safely that because, in the scanty remains of Hebrew, a word does not occur before e. g. a certain historical book, it did not exist before the date of that book. Rather the occurrence of any word in language so simple as that of the historical books, is an evidence that it did exist and was in common use at the time. Poets and orators coin words, in order to give full expression for their thoughts. The characteristic of the sacred historians, both of the Old and New Testament, is to relate the facts in most absolute simplicity. It would be a singular "history of the Hebrew language," which should lay down as a principle, that all those are later words, which do not happen to occur before the books of Kings, Habakkuk, or any other prophet, whom this criticism is pleased to rank among the later books. What are we to do with Habakkuk's own *ἅπαξ λεγόμενα?* Granted, that he framed some of them, yet it is impossible that he framed them all. As specimens of the results of such a critical principle, that words, occurring for the first time in any book, are characteristic of the date of that word, let us only take roots beginning with *s*. Had then the Hebrew no name for *nails* (as distinct from hooks, pegs[b],) before those whom these critics would make late writers[c], as Ecclesiastes and Isaiah xli? Or had they none for *ceiling* a building before the book of Kings[d]; although the ark had a third story[e], and Lot speaks of "the shadow of my roof[f]?" Or had they none for a "decked vessel" before Jonah[g], although the Indian names of Solomon's imports show that Ophir, whither his navy sailed, was in India, Ophir itself being Abhira in the province of Cutch[h]? Or had they no name for "divided opinions" before Elijah[i]? Seed *shed*, which sprang up in the second year, was known in the Pentateuch[k]; but that of the third year would, on that hypothesis, remain unknown till Hezekiah[l]; nor did the Hebrews express to "drag along the ground," till Hushai[m], and, after him, Jeremiah. They had no name for winter, as distinct from autumn, until the Canticles[n], and, but for the act of the Philistines in stopping up[o] Abraham's wells, it might have been said that Hebrew had no word for this act, till the time of Jehoshaphat[p].

Or as to the criticism itself, קלס is to be a later word, because, except in that Psalm of the sons of Corah, it occurs first in the history of Elisha[q]. Perhaps it is so rare (and this may illustrate the history of Elisha) because, as used, it seems to have been one of the strongest words in the language for "derision;" at least the verb is used in an intensive form only, and always of strong derision[r]. But then, did the old Hebrews never use derision? Happy exception for one nation, if they never used it wrongly or had no occasion to use it rightly! Yet even though (by a rare exception) Ewald allows the second Psalm to be David's, (Job however being placed about the 7th century B. C.) the evidence for לעג, as strong a word, would be of the time of David[s]. "Scorning" "scoffing,"

[b] יתד, וו.

[c] מַסְמְרִים Is. xli. 7, מִסְמְרִים 1 Chr. xxii. 3, מַסְמְרוֹת, Jer. x. 4, מסמרות, 2 Chr. iii. 9. מַשְׂמרוֹת Eccl. xii. 11.

[d] סָפַן, 1 Kgs vi. 9, סָפוּן 1 Kgs vii. 3, 7, Jer. xxii. 14, Hagg. i. 4, (ספון Dt. xxxiii. 21. שׂפוּן Ib. 19, is i. q. צפון). אחז, "hold together," occurs 1 Kgs vi. 6, 10, Ezek. xli. 6; טְלָל lit. "overshadowed" Neh. iii. 15; יָצוּעַ occurs also 1 Kgs vi. 5, 6, 10.

[e] שְׁלִשִׁים, Gen. vi. 16, as in 1 Kgs vi. 8. Ez. xlii. 3.

[f] קֹרָה Gen. xix 8. as being "beamed." Conf. קָרָה "laid beams," (met.) Ps. civ. 3. else 2 Chr. xxxiv. 11, Neh. ii. 8, iii. 3, 6; קורה beam 2 Kgs vi. 2, 5, 2 Chr. iii. 7. Cant. i. 17. מְקָרֶה Eccl. x. 18.

[g] סְפִינָה ἅπ. Jon. i. 5. See vol. i. p. 375.

[h] See ab. on Micah iv. p. 62.

[i] 1 Kgs xviii. 21. As "branches," סעִפִּים first occurs in Isaiah, (xvii. 6. xxvii. 10, and the denom. סֵעֵף, Ib. x. 33. and סַרְעַפּוֹת, סַעֲפּוֹת in Ezek. xxxi. 5. 6. 8.

[k] סָפִיחַ Lev. xxv. 5. 11. Else only with סחיש or שׁחים.

[l] סָחִישׁ 2 Kgs xix. 29, שָׁחִיס. Ib. xxxvii. 30.

[m] סחב 2 Sam. xvii. 13. Jer. xv. 3, xxii, 19, xlix. 20. So סחה "swept" occurs only Ezek. xxvi. 4. סְחִי Lam. iii. 45. but סחף is used by Solomon Prov. xxviii. 3.

[n] סְתָו Cant. ii. 11.

[o] סִתְּם Gen. xxvi. 15. 18.

[p] סָתַם 2 Kgs iii. 19. 25. 2 Chr. xxxii. 3. 4. Nif. of closing breaches in a wall. Neh. iv. 1.

[q] 2 Kgs ii. 23.

[r] Pih. Ez. xvi. 31. Hithp. 2 Kgs l. c., Hab. l. c., Ez. xxii. 5, who has also קַלָּסָה.

[s] לָעַג. The verb occurs Ps. ii. 4, xxii. 8, lix. 9, lxxx. 7, Prov. i. 26, xvii. 5, xxx. 17. Job ix. 23, xi. 3, xxi. 3, xxii. 19, Is. xxxiii. 19. xxxvii. 22, Jer. xx. 7,

(unless Psalm i. be allowed to be David's) did not begin till Solomon's time[t]. "Mocking" was yet later[u]. As belongs to a rude people, insult was only shewn in acts, of which התעלל is used[v]; and from those simple times of the Patriarchs, they had no stronger word than "to laugh at[w]." For this is the only word used in the Pentateuch[x].

But to what end all this? To prove that Habakkuk had no superhuman knowledge of what he foretold? Prophecy occupies, as I said, a subordinate place in Habakkuk. He renews the "burden" of former prophets, both upon his own people and upon the Chaldæans; but he does not speak even so definitely as they. His office is rather to enforce the connection of sin and punishment: he presupposes the details, which they had declared. Apart from those chapters, which pseudo-criticism denies to Isaiah[y], on account of the distinctness of the temporal prophecies, Isaiah had, in plainest words, declared to Hezekiah the carrying away of all the royal treasures to Babylon, and that his offspring should be eunuchs there[z]; Micah had declared not only the complete desolation of Jerusalem[a], but that the people should be "[b]carried to Babylon, and *there* delivered, *there* redeemed from the hands of the enemy." In the 13th year of Josiah, B. C. 628, and so, three years before the fall of Nineveh, while Babylon was still dependent on Nineveh and governed by a vice-roy, and while Nabopolassar was still in the service of the king of Nineveh, Jeremiah foretold, that [c]*evil should break forth from the North upon all the inhabitants of the land,* and *all the families of the kingdoms of the North shall come and set every one his throne at the entering of the gates of Jerusalem and against all the walls thereof round about and against all the cities of Judah,* to execute the *judgments* of God *against them for their wickedness.* This was his dirge over his country for twenty-three years[d], ere yet there was a token of its fulfillment. Babylon had succeeded to Nineveh in the West and South-West, and Judah had fallen to the share of Babylon; but the relation of Josiah to Nabopolassar was of a tributary sovereign, which rebellion only could disturb. The greater part of Nabopolassar's 21 year's reign are almost a blank[e]. Chastisement had come, but from the South, not from the North. Eighteen years had passed away, and Josiah had fallen, in resisting Pharaoh-Necho in discharge of his fealty to the king of Babylon. Pharaoh-Necho had taken away one king of Judah, Jehoahaz, the people's choice, whose continued fealty to Babylon represents their minds, and had set up another, Jehoiakim. For three years Judah's new allegiance was allowed to continue. Who, but God, could tell the issue of the conflict of those two great armies at Carchemish? Egypt with her allies, the Ethiopians, Phut and Lud, were come, *rising up like a flood*[f], *covering the earth* with her armies, as her rivers, when swollen, made her own land one sea. Necho had apparently in his alliance all the kings of the countries West of the Euphrates: for to them all, in connection with Egypt and subordinate to her, does Jeremiah at that moment give to drink the cup of the wrath of God; to [g]*Pharaoh king of Egypt, and his servants and his princes and all his people, and all the mingled people* [his auxiliaries] *and all the kings of the land of Uz,* and *all the kings of the land of the Philistines and Ashkelon and Azzah and Ekron and the remnant of Ashdod; Edom and Moab and the children of Ammon; and all the kings of Tyrus, and all the kings of Zidon and the kings of the isle beyond the sea* [probably Caphtor[h], or Crete, or Cyprus] *Dedan and Tema and Buz, and those whose hair is shorn* [Arabians[i]] *and all the kings of Arabia and all the kings of the mingled people that dwell in the desert, and all the kings of Zimri* [[k]descendants of Abraham and Keturah.] It was a mighty gathering. *All the kings of Elam, all the kings of the Medes, all the kings of the North far and near,* all was hostile to Babylon; for all were to drink of the cup beforehand, at the hands of the king of Babylon, *and* then *the king of Sheshach* [Babylon]

2 Chr. xxx. 10, Neh. ii. 19, iii. 33. לַעֵג Job. xxxiv. 7, Ps. cxxiii. 4, Hos. vii. 16, Ez. xxiii. 32, xxxvi. 4. with קֶלֶס Ps. xliv. 19. lxxix. 4.

[t] לֵץ part. occurs 14 times in Prov. Ps. i. 1. and Is. xxix. 20. ץ ׳ (the verb), Pr. ix. 12. לוצצים Hos. vi. 5. התלוצץ Is. xxviii. 22. הליץ Ps. cxix. 51 Pr. iii. 34, xiv. 9, xix. 28.

[u] התל Job xvii. 2, 1 Kgs xviii. 27.

[v] התעלל with ב of the pers. Num. xxii. 29, of Balaam's ass; 1 Sam. xxxi. 4, Jer. xxxviii. 19, 1 Chr. x. 4, of apprehended insult from an enemy.

[w] צִחֵק Gen. xix. 14, xxi. 9. insult in act, Ib. xxxix. 14, 17, revived from Genesis, Ez. xxiii. 32, elsewhere שחק.

[x] The exact meaning of שִׁמְצָה (Ex. xxxii. 25) is uncertain. The E. V. "shame" follows most of the Heb. Intt., yet with an improbable etymol. "Whisper" seems the most probable meaning of Job iv. 12. xxvi. 14, from which that of "ill-report" is possible. The Arabic gives nothing nearer than "hurried in speech."

[y] Is. xiii. xiv. 1–23, xl. sqq.

[z] Is. xxxix. 6, 7.

[a] Mic. iii. 12.

[b] Ib. iv. 10.

[c] Jer. i. 14–16.

[d] Ib. xxv. 3. see also v. 15–17, vi. 1. 22–25, x. 22. Also in the collection of all his prophecies from the time of Josiah, which God bade him make in the 4th year of Jehoiakim, Jer. xxxvi. 2. 29, he provides them also with a saying against idolatry (in Chaldee) for their use in their captivity in Chaldæa. x. 11.

[e] Rawl. 5 Emp. iii. 484.

[f] Jer. xlvi. 8. 9.

[g] Ib. xxv. 19–24.

[h] Jer. xlvii. 4.

[i] Herod. iii. 8.

[k] Gen. xxv. 2. 1 Chr. i. 32. (זִמְרִי for זִמְרָנִי.)

was *to drink after them.* Necho was one of the most enterprising monarchs[l]. Nabopolassar had shewn no signs of enterprise. Nebuchadnezzar, the first and last conqueror of the Babylonian empire, though the alliance with Media and his father's empire had been cemented by his marriage, had, as far as we know, remained inactive during 20 years of his father's life[m]. He was as yet untried. So little did he himself feel secure as to his inheritance of the throne, even after his success at the head of his father's army, that his rapid march across the desert, with light troops, to secure it, and its preservation for him by the chief priest, are recorded in a very concise history[n]. Neither Egypt nor Jehoiakim foresaw the issue. Defeat taught neither. Two voices only gave, in God's name, one unheeded warning. Pharaoh Hophra, the Apries of Herodotus, succeeded Pharaoh Necho in his self-confidence, his aggressions, his defeat. "I am against thee," God says[o], "Pharaoh, king of Egypt, the great dragon that lieth in the midst of his rivers, *which hath said, My river* is *mine own and I have made* it *for myself.*" "It is said," relates Herodotus[p], "that Apries believed that there was not a god which could cast him down from his eminence, so firmly did he think that he had established himself in his kingdom."

For a time, Nebuchadnezzar must have been hindered by Eastern wars, since, on Jehoiakim's rebellion and perjury, he sent only *bands of the Chaldees*, with *bands* of tributary nations, the Syrians, Moabites, Ammonites, against him[q]. But not in his time only, even after the captivity under his son Jehoiachin and his men of might[r], the conviction that Nebuchadnezzar could be resisted, still remained in the time of Zedekiah both in Egypt and Judah. Judah would have continued to hold under Babylonia that same position toward Egypt which it did under Persia, only with subordinate kings instead of governors. Apart from God's general promise of averting evil on repentance, Jeremiah, too, expressly tells Israel, "[s] If thou wilt put away thine abominations out of My sight, *thou shalt not remove;*" "[t] Then will I cause you to dwell in this place, in the land that I gave to your fathers, for ever and ever." And "in the beginning of the reign of Jehoiakim[u]," "[v] The Lord sent me to prophesy against this house and against this city all the words which ye have heard. Therefore now amend your ways and your doings and obey the voice of the Lord your God, *and the Lord will repent Him of the evil that He hath pronounced against you.*" Still later, to Zedekiah, "[w] The nations that bring their neck under the yoke of the king of Babylon and serve him, *them will I let remain still in their own land, saith the Lord; and they shall till it and dwell therein.*" "[x] I have sent unto you all My servants the prophets, rising up early and sending them, saying, Return ye now every man from his evil way and amend your doings, and go not after other gods to serve them, and *ye shall dwell in the land which I have given to you and to your fathers.*" Even on the very verge of the capture of Jerusalem, Jeremiah promised to Zedekiah[y]; "If thou wilt go forth to the king of Babylon's princes;—*this city shall not be burned with fire.*" Pharaoh Hophra was still strong enough to raise the siege of Jerusalem, when invested by the Chaldæan army[z]. Jeremiah had the king, his princes, his prophets, all the people of the land against him, because he prophesied that Jerusalem should be burned with fire, that those already taken captives should not return, until the whole had been carried away, and the seventy years of captivity were accomplished[a]. The warning and the promise of Jeremiah's inaugural vision had its accomplishment. "[b] I have made thee a defenced city, and an iron pillar, and brazen walls, *against the king of Judah, against the princes thereof and against the people of the land;* and they shall fight against thee, but they shall not prevail against thee; for I am with thee, saith the Lord, to deliver thee." Had it been matter of human foresight, how was it, that all nations, all their politicians, all their wise men, all their prophets, all Judah, kings, priests, princes, people, were blinded, (as in Him of Whom Jeremiah was a shadow,) and Jeremiah alone saw? "Vaticinia post eventum" are, in one sense, easy; viz. to imagine, after an event has taken place, that one could have foreseen it. And yet who, after the retreat to Corunna, could have foreseen the victories of the Peninsular war? Or, when that tide of 647,000 men[c] was rolling on toward Russia, who could imagine that only a small fraction of those hosts should return, that they should capture Moscow, but find it a tomb; and hunger and cold, reaching at last to 36 degrees below Zero, should destroy more than the sword? "[d] What was the principal adversary of this tremendous power? By whom was it checked

[l] As shewn in his attempt to make a canal across the isthmus of Suez (Herod. ii. 158.) and in the circumnavigation of Africa. Ib. iv. 42.

[m] The battle of Carchemish was in the 4th of Jehoiakim. Jer. xlvi. 1. 2.

[n] Berosus in Joseph. c. Ap. i. 19. Opp. ii. 450.

[o] Ezek. xxix. 3. [p] Herod. ii. 16.

[q] 2 Kgs xxiv. 2. [r] Ib. 14–16. [s] Jer. iv. 1.

[t] Ib. vii. 7, add xvii. 25, 26. xxii. 2–5.

[u] Ib. xxvi. 1. [v] xxvi. 12. add ib. 2, 3.

[w] xxvii. 11. [x] xxxv. 15. [y] xxxviii. 17.

[z] Jer. xxxvii. 5. [a] xxv. 11, 12. xxix. 10.

[b] Jer. i. 18, 19, renewed xv. 20.

[c] "Imperial muster rolls in Chambray Vol. i. App. No. 2." Alison Hist. of Europe x. 629.

[d] Dr. Arnold lect. on Hist. ii. 139.

and resisted and put down? By none and by nothing but the direct and manifest interposition of God."

The distinctness and perseverance of the prophecy are the more remarkable, because the whole of the greatness of the Chaldæan empire was that of one man. Assyria, in this one case, overreached itself in its policy of transporting conquered populations. It had, probably to check the rebellions of Babylon, settled there a wild horde, which it hoped would neither assimilate with its people, nor itself rebel. Isaiah relates the fact in simple words: [e] *Behold the land of the Chaldæans; this people was not; the Assyrian founded* [f] *it for them that dwelt in the wilderness.* This does not seem to me necessarily to imply, that the wild people, for whom Assyria founded it, were Chaldæans [g] or Curds, whom the king of Assyria had brought from their Northern dwellings in the *Card*uchæan mountains [h] near Armenia, where Sennacherib conquered. Isaiah simply uses the name, *the land of the Chaldæans,* as does Jeremiah [i] after him, as the name of Babylonia; the word *Babylonia,* had it existed, might have been substituted for it. Of this, he says, that *it was not,* i. e. was of no account [k], but that *Assur founded it for wild tribes,* whom he placed there. Whence he brought those tribes, Isaiah does not say. Æschylus (although indeed in later times) as well as Isaiah and Jeremiah, speak of the population of Babylon, as mingled of various nations; and the language is too large to be confined simply to its merchant-settlers. In Æschylus [l], "the all-mingled crowd," which "it sends out in long array," are its military contingents. It is its whole population, of which Isaiah and Jeremiah say, it will flee, each to his own land. [m] *It* [Babylon] *shall be as a chased roe, and as a sheep which no man gathereth; they shall, every man, turn to his own people, and flee every man to his own land. For fear of the oppressing sword they shall turn every one to his people:* [n] *And they shall flee, every one to his own land.*

Thus Babylonia received that solid accession of strength which ultimately made it a powerful people, sixty years before the beginning of the reign of Josiah; its ancient and new elements would take some time to blend: they did not assume importance until the capture of Nineveh; nor had Judah any reason to dread anything from them, until itself rebelled, early in the reign of Jehoiakim. But 18 years before the death of Josiah, while Judah was a trusted and faithful tributary kingdom, Jeremiah foretold that evil should come upon them from the North, i. e. as he himself explains it, from the Chaldees [o]. Even then if Habakkuk were brought down to be a contemporary of Jeremiah, still in the 13th year of Josiah, there was nothing to fear. Judah was not in the condition of an outlying country, which Babylonian ambition might desire to reduce into dependence on itself. It was already part of the Babylonian empire, having passed into it, in the partition with Assyria, and had no more to fear from it, than any of the conquered nations of Europe have now from those who have annexed them, unless they rebel. God alone knew the new ambition of the kings of the smitten and subdued Egypt, their momentary success, Josiah's death, Judah's relapse into the old temptation of trusting in Egypt—all, conditions of the fulfillment of Habakkuk's and Jeremiah's prophecies. Edom, Moab, Ammon, Tyre, Zidon, sent embassadors to Zedekiah, to concert measures of resistance against Nebuchadnezzar [p]; they were encouraged by their [q] *diviners, dreamers, enchanters, sorcerers, which spake* to them, *ye shall not serve the king of Babylon.* One alone told them that resistance would but bring upon them destruction, that submission was their only safety; there was prophecy against prophecy [r], among these nations, in Jerusalem, in Babylon [s]; the recent knowledge of the political aspect of Babylon deterred not the false prophets there; all, with one voice, declared the breaking the yoke of the king of Babylon: Jeremiah only saw, that they were framing for themselves [t] *yokes of iron.* Had Jehoiakim or Zedekiah, their nobles, and their people possessed that human fore-

[e] Is. xxiii. 13.

[f] Jon. unites Asshur with the preceding זה העם לא היה אשור and so Syr. and Oxf. Arab. S. Jer. divides as the E. V., though with an opposite sense. "Talis populus non fuit." The E. V. is from Kim. The rendering, "This people was not Asshur," i. e. no longer Asshur, or not like Asshur, is very obscure; and יסד is everywhere "grounded it, that it might be," (Comp. Ps. civ. 8, Hab. i. 12. and the common use of יסד "founded a city, building, temple,") not that it should cease to be.

[g] With this the only objection to the simple rendering falls away, that Jeremiah speaks of the Chaldees, as *an ancient nation.* Jer. v. 15.

[h] Xen. Cyrop. iii. 2. 7 and 12. Anab. iv. 3, 4. v. 5. 9. vii. 8. 14.

[i] Jer. xxiv. 5, l. 8. 25, li. 4; and, united with the name Babylon, xxv. 12, l. 1. 45, Ezek. xii. 13, as Isaiah does *Chasdim* alone, xlviii. 14, 20.

[k] Coll. לא עם Deut. xxxii. 21, לא איש Ps. xxii. 7. See the like in the Classics in Perizon. Orig. Bab. c. vi. p. 70. sqq. and from him in Vitr.

[l] Æsch. Pers. 52, 53, 54.

[m] Is. xiii. 14.

[n] Jer. l. 16.

[o] There ought to be no question as to the identity of the invasion from the north, Jer. i. 15, vi. 22, x. 22, and Jeremiah's own summary of his prophecies from the 13th of Josiah, xxv. 3–9 when he names Nebuchadnezzar; only then there would be definite prediction. Hence the mare's nest as to the dread of the Scythians, who marched down the sea coast and returned, being bought off by Psammetichus, doing no harm to Judah by this passing expedition.

[p] Jer. xxvii. 3.

[q] Ib. 9.

[r] Jer. v. 12–14. xiv. 14–16. xxiii. 16, 17, 21, 25–27, 30 sqq. xxvii. 14, 15–18, xxviii.

[s] Jer. xxix. 8, 9, 15, 21, 24, sqq.

[t] xxviii. 13, 14.

sight which that pseudo-critical school holds to be so easy, Judah had never gone into captivity to Babylon. But He Who *fashioneth the heart of man* knoweth alone the issue of the working of those hearts, which He over-rules.

From the necessity of its case, the pseudo-critical school lowers down the words, in which Habakkuk declares the marvelousness of the event which he foretells, and the unbelief of his people. "Look well," he bids them, "marvel ye, marvel on; for I will work a work in your days which ye will not believe, when it shall be told you." It is "something which had not hitherto been, something hitherto unknown," says Stahelin [u]. Yet things hitherto unknown, are not therefore incredible. "It is clear from the contents," says Bleek [v], "that the Chaldees had at that time already extended to the West their expeditions of conquest and destruction, and on the other side, that this had only lately begun and that they were not yet come to Judah and Jerusalem, so that here they were hitherto little known." "The appearance of the Chaldees as world-conquerors was, in Judah, then a quite new phenomenon," says Ewald [w]. "The description of the Chaldees altogether is of such sort, that they appear as a people still little known to the Jews," says Knobel [x]. "That which is incredible for the people consists therein, that God employs just the Chaldees, such as they are described in what follows, for the unexpected chastisement of Israel," says even Umbreit [y].

What was there incredible, that, when the king of Jerusalem had revolted from Babylon, and had sided with Egypt, its chief enemy, the Chaldæans, should come against it? As soon might it be said to be incredible that France should invade Prussia, when its hundred thousands were on their march toward the Rhine. During the reign of Manasseh it was incredible enough, that any peril should impend from Babylon; for Babylon was still subordinate to Assyria: in the early years of Josiah it was still incredible, for his thirty-one years were years of peace, until Pharaoh Necho disputed the cis-Euphratensian countries with Babylon. When the then East and West came to Carchemish, to decide whether the empire should be with the East or with the West, nothing was beyond human foresight but the result. Expectation lately hung suspended, perplexed between the forces of Europe. None, the most sagacious, could predict for a single day. Men might surmise; God only could predict. For three and twenty years Jeremiah foretold, that the evil would come from the North, not from the South. The powers were well-balanced. Take Habakkuk's prophecy as a whole—not that the Chaldæans should invade Judæa, (which in Jehoiakim's time was already certain) but that Egypt should be a vain help, and that the Chaldæans should mesh its people like *the fishes of the sea*, yet they should still have to disgorge them, because God's judgment would come upon them also. This too were incredible. Incredible it was to the kings, the wise, the politicians, the political prophets of Judæa, that Jerusalem itself should be taken. Incredible it was, and there was much human reason for the incredulity. Egypt and Assyria had been matched during centuries. Until the Sargonides, Egypt had, during centuries, the unbroken advantage. But the Sargonides had passed away. Yet Chaldæa had not, alone, prevailed against Assyria. Why should the yet untried Babylonian be so certain of success, when the whole West of the Euphrates was banded together against him, and fought within their own ground? *The kings of Elam and the kings of the Medes* [z] were now, as under Cyrus, enemies of Babylon. Babylon had enemies before and behind. But God had raised up Nebuchadnezzar to be *the hammer of the whole earth* [a], and had given those cis-Euphratensian lands which leagued against him *into the hands of Nebuchadnezzar the king of Babylon, My servant,* God says [b], *and all nations shall serve him and his son and his son's son, until the very time of his land come; and then many nations and great kings shall serve themselves of him.* Whence this combination of almost superhuman but short-lived might, this certainty of wide sway down to the third generation, this certainty of its cessation afterward? There was no time for decay. Alexander's empire was yet more short-lived, but it was divided among his successors. Alexander had, by his genius, founded his own empire, which the able generals, whom he had trained, divided among themselves. In the Chaldæan empire, we have an enterprising conspirator, who seizes an occasion, but does little beside which is recorded, nothing alone, nothing, beside that first grasp at power, for himself. He appears only as the ally of Media [c]: then a son, a world-wide conqueror, with a genius for consolidating the empire which he inherited, forming an impregnable city, which should also be a province, filling his empire with fortresses [d], but leaving none after him

[u] Einl. p. 218. [v] Einl. ins. A. T. pp. 545, 546.
[w] Die Proph. ii. 29. see also Delitzsch's quotation from him ab. p. 170.
[x] Die Proph. u. Hebr. ii. 292. Dr. Davidson's sentences are chiefly gleaned from him.
[y] Kl. Proph. p. 286.
[z] Jer. xxv. 25. [a] Ib. l. 23.
[b] Ib. xxvii. 6. 7. [c] Herod. i. 74.
[d] See Daniel the Prophet pp. 118. 122, Rawl. 5 Empires iii. 496 sqq.

to maintain what he had so consolidated. By whom could this be foreknown save by Him, with Whom alone it is, *to root out and to pull down and to destroy and to throw down, to build and to plant*[e]?

It has been common to praise the outside of Habakkuk's prophecy, the purity of his language, the sublimity of his imagery. Certainly it is, humanly speaking, magnificent: his measured cadence is impressive in its simplicity. He too has words and forms, which are peculiar to him among the remains of Hebrew[f]. But his eminence is rather the condensed thought, expressed often in the simplest words; as when, having carried on the tide of victory of the Chaldæan to its height, everything human subdued before him, all resistance derided, he gathers up his fall and its cause in those eight words, "[g]Then sweeps-he-by, wind, and-passes, and-is-guilty; this his-strength (is) his-god." Yet more striking is the religious greatness, in which he sums up the meaning of all this oppressiveness of man. "[h]*Thou*, Lord, has placed him for judgment, and, O Rock, has founded him to correct." Or, take the picture, prolonged relatively to his conciseness, of the utter helplessness of God's people, meshed, hooked, dragged in their net; their captors worshiping the instrument of their success, revelling in their triumph, and then the sudden question, "[i]*Shall they therefore empty their net?*" He waits to hear the answer from God. Or, again, the antiphonal dirge of the materials of the blood-built city over him[k]. Or the cutting off of every stay, sustenance, hope, promise of God, and, amid this universal crash, what does he? It is not as the heathen, "[l]fearless will the ruins strike him:" but, "[m]And I," as if it were the continuance and consequence of the failure of all human things; "I would exult in the Lord, I would bound for joy in the God of my salvation." His faith triumphs most, when all, in human sight, is lost.

> "Ill which Thou blessest is most good,
>   And unblest good is ill;
> And all is right which seems most wrong,
>   So it be Thy sweet Will."

[e] Jer. i. 10.

[f] The most remarkable, have, of course, been singled out of old; as, מִגַּמַּה, i. 9, עַבְטִיט, ii. 6, קִיקָלוֹן ii. 16. Others are partly emphatic forms, as מְזַעְזְעֶיךָ, ii. 7, or are in some way, even though slight, peculiar to him. מִיְעָקֶל, i. 4 (not in the verb), הִתַּמְּהוּ i. 5. יְהִיתַן ii. 17 (the form), מַסֵּכָה ii. 18. הֵעָרֵל ii. 16. מוֹדֵד, הִתְפּוֹצְצוּ, iii. 6. תְּעוֹר iii. 9. עֲלִיצֻתָם iii. 14. קְצוֹת ii. 10. עֻפְּלָה ii. 4. נָוֶה ii. 5. חֶבְיוֹן iii, 4. רֹגֶז iii, 2. תָּפוּשׂ ii. 19, מְעוֹרֵיהֶם ii. 15. חַדּוּ i. 8, כָּפִיס ii. 11. מְשִׁסּוֹת ii, 7. רַחֵם iii. 2, צָלַל quiver (of the lips) iii. 16, חֹמֶר (of sea) iii. 15. They will recur for notice in the Comm.

[g] Hab. i. 11. [h] Ib. 12. [i] Ib. 17. [k] ii. 11.

[l] Hor. Od. iii. 3. 8. [m] iii. 10.

HABAKKUK.

Before CHRIST cir. 626.

CHAPTER I.

1 *Unto Habakkuk, complaining of the iniquity of the land,* 5 *is shewed the fearful vengeance by the Chaldeans.* 12 *He complaineth that vengeance should be executed by them who are far worse.*

THE burden which Ha-
bakkuk the prophet did
see.
2 O LORD, how long
shall I cry, [a] and thou wilt
not hear! *even* cry out un-

a Lam. 3. 8.

CHAP. I., Ver. 1. *The burden*[1] *which Habakkuk the prophet did see.* The prophet's name signifies "strong embrace." The word in its intensive form is used both of God's enfolding the soul in His tender supporting love[2], and of man clinging and holding fast to Divine wisdom[3]. It fits in with the subject of his prophecy, faith, cleaving fast to God amid the perplexities of things seen. "[4] He who is spiritually Habakkuk, cleaving fast to God with the arms of love, or enfolding Him after the manner of one holily wrestling, until he be blessed, enlightened, and heard by Him, is the seer here." "Let him who would in such wise fervidly embrace God and plead with Him as a friend, praying earnestly for the deliverance and consolation of himself and others, but who sees not as yet, that his prayer is heard, make the same holy plaint, and appeal to the clemency of the Creator." "[5] He is called 'embrace' either because of his love to the Lord; or because he engages in a contest and strife and (so to speak) wrestling with God." For no one with words so bold ventured to challenge God to a discussion of His justice and to say to Him, "Why, in human affairs and the government of this world is there so great injustice?"

The prophet. The title, *the prophet,* is added only to the names of Habakkuk, Haggai, Zechariah. Habakkuk may the rather have added it to his name, because prominently he expostulates with God, like the Psalmists, and does not speak in the name of God to the people. The title asserts that he exercised the pastoral office of the prophets, although not directly in this prophecy[6].

Did see. "[7] God *multiplied visions,* as is written[8], and Himself spake to the prophets, disclosing to them beforehand what should be, and all but exhibiting them to sight, as if already present. But that they determined not to speak from their own, but rather transmit to us the words from God, he persuades us at the outset, naming himself a Prophet, and shewing himself full of the grace belonging thereto."

2. *O Lord, how long shall I cry,* lit. *how long have I cried so intensely* to Thee[9]? For it is ever the cry of the creature to Him Who alone can hear or help, its God[1]. Of this cry the Prophet expresses that it had already lasted long. In that long past had he cried to God and no change had come. There is an undefined past, and this still continues[10]. *How long,* as Asaph cries, *how long hast Thou been,* and, it is implied, wilt Thou be *wroth against the prayer of Thy people?* as we should say, *how long shall Thy wrath continue?* The words which the Prophet uses relate to domestic strife and wrong between man and man; violence[11], iniquity, strife, contention[12], nor are any of them used only of the oppression of a foreign enemy. He complains too of injustice too strong for the law, and the perversion of justice[13]. And on this the sentence is pronounced. The enemy is to be sent for *judgment* and *correction*[14]. They are then the sins of Judah which the Prophet rehearses before God, in fellow-suffering with the oppressed. God answers that they shall be removed, but by the punishment of the sinners.

Punishment does not come without sin, nor does sin endure without punishment. It is one object of the Old Testament to exhibit the connection between sin and punishment. Other prophets, as commissioned by God, first denounced the sins and then foretold the punishment of the impenitent. Habakkuk appeals to God's justice, as requiring

1 On the word *burden* see on Nah. i. 1. p. 129. n. 1.

2 חִבֵּק Cant. ii. 6. viii. 3. 3 Prov. iv. 8. 4 Dion.

5 S. Jer. Abarbanel has the like, "He strengthens himself in pleading his cause with God as to the prosperity of Nebuchadnezzar as if he was joined with God for the cause of his people." Pref. to Ezek. pp. 123, 4, 124. 1.

6 See ab. p. 20. 7 S. Cyr. 8 Hos. xii. 10.

9 שִׁוַּע only occurs in the intensive form, and always of the cry to God, expressed by אל. or implied, except perhaps Job xxxv. 9.

10 עַד־אָנָה שִׁוַּעְתִּי, as Ps. lxxx. 6. עַד־מָתַי עָשַׁנְתָּ and Exod. xvi. 28. עַד־אָנָה מֵאַנְתֶּם and Ex. x. 3, עַד־מָתַי מֵאַנְתָּ [all.]

11 חמס ושד are united of individual internal violence, Jer. vi. 7. xx. 8. Ez. xlv. 9. Am. iii. 10: even שד ושבר Is. lix. 7. and שד alone Ps. xii. 6. Job xxiv. 9. Pr. xxi. 7. xxiv. 2. Hab. ii. 17. כזב ושד Hos. xii. 2. און ועמל occur Ps. lv. 11, in Habakkuk's order; inverted in Ps. x. 7. און, עמל, שוא occur in three clauses in Is. lix. 4. עמל, און, with מרמה Job xv. 35.

12 i. 3. 13 i. 4. 14 i. 12.

Before CHRIST cir. 626.

to thee *of* violence, and
thou wilt not save!
3 Why dost thou shew
me iniquity, and cause *me*
to behold grievance? for
spoiling and violence *are*

Before CHRIST cir. 626.

its infliction. On this ground too this opening of the prophecy cannot be a complaint against the Chaldees, because *their* wrong would be no ground of the punishment which the prophet denounced, but the punishment itself, requiting wrong to man through human wrong.

"[1] The prophet considers the person of the oppressed, enduring the intolerable insolence and contumely of those wonted to do wrong, and very skillfully doth he attest the unutterable loving kindness of God. For he exhibits Him as very forbearing, though wont to hate wickedness. But that He doth not forthwith bring judgment on the offenders, he showed clearly, saying that so great is His silence and long-suffering, that there needeth a strong cry, in that some practise intolerable covetousness against others, and use an unbridled insolence against the weak. For his very complaints of God's endurance of evil attest the immeasurable loving kindness of God."

"[1] You may judge hence of the hatred of evil in the Saints. For they speak of the woes of others as their own. So saith the most wise Paul, [2] *who is weak and I am not weak? who is offended, and I burn not?* and bade us [3] *weep with those who weep*, shewing that sympathy and mutual love are especially becoming to the saints."

The Prophet, through sympathy or fellow-suffering with the sufferers, is as one of them. He *cries* for help, as himself needing it, and being in the misery, in behalf of which he prays. He says, *How long shall I cry?* standing, as it were, in the place of all, and gathering all their cries into one, and presenting them before God. It is the cry, in one, of all which is wronged to the God of Justice, of all suffering to the God of love. "When shall this scene of sin, and confusion, and wrong be at an end, and the harmony of God's creation be restored? How long shall evil not exist only, but prevail?" It is the cry of the souls under the altar[4], *How long, O Lord, Holy and True, dost Thou not judge and avenge our blood on them that dwell on the earth?* It is the voice of the oppressed against the oppressor; of the Church against the world; weary of hearing the Lord's Name blasphemed, of seeing wrong set up on high, holiness trampled under foot. It is in its highest sense His Voice, Who, to sanctify our longings for deliverance, said in the days of His Flesh, [5] *I cry in the daytime, but Thou hearest not.*

Even cry out aloud (it is the cry of anguish). "[6] We cry the louder, the more we cry from the heart, even without words; for not the moving of the lips, but the love of the heart sounds in the ears of God." *Even cry out unto Thee.* Whether as an exclamation or a continuance of the question, *How long?* the prophet gathered in one the prolonged cry of past and future. He *had* cried; he should cry on, *Violence*[7]. He speaks as if the one word, jerked out, as it were, wrung forth from his inmost soul, was, *Violence*, as if he said this one word to the God of Justice and love.

3. *Why dost Thou shew me iniquity, and cause me to behold*, or rather, *Why beholdest Thou*[8] *grievance?* God seemed to reverse what He had said by Balaam, [9] *He hath not beheld iniquity in Jacob, and hath not seen grievousness in Israel;* and in the Psalm, "[10] Thou hast seen, for *Thou* [emph.] beholdest grievousness *and wrong, to put it in Thy hand*," i.e. Thou layest it up in Thy hand, to cast it back on the head of the evildoer. Now He seemed to behold it and leave it unpunished, which yet Habakkuk says to God below, He could not do; [11] *Thou canst not look upon iniquity.* What then did this mean? What was the solution?

All forms and shapes of sin are multiplied; oppressive *violence*[12], such as *covered the earth* before the flood, and brought it down; which Nineveh had to put away[13], and it was spared; *iniquity*, i.e. what is unequal and contrary to truth, falsehood; *grievance* lit. burdensome wearisome *toil; spoiling*, or open robbery; *strife and contention*, both through perversion of the law and, without it, through endless jarrings of man with man. Sin recoils on the sinner. So what he beholds is not *iniquity* only, but (in the same word) *vanity; grievance;* which is a burden both to him who suffers, and yet more to him who inflicts it. For nothing is so burdensome as sin, nothing so empty as wickedness.

[1] S. Cyr. [2] 2 Cor. xi. 29. [3] Rom. xii. 15. [4] Rev. vi. 10. [5] Ps. xxii. 2. [6] Dion.

[7] אזעק חמס as חמס ושד אקרא Jer. xx. 8. הן אצעק חמס Job. xix. 7. [all of this construction.]

[8] Since הביט, occurring 67 times, is certainly no where else used causatively of its common meaning, *behold*, *look*, and Habakkuk himself uses it four times beside in that meaning הביטו, "look," i. 5. with אל, i. 13. with על ii. 13. with acc. pers. i. 13. it is wholly improbable that it should be used here of "causing to look;" the more, since he has not marked the supposed exceptional use by adding the affix, תביטני. There is no ground to assume a causative of a causative.

[9] Nu. xxiii. 21. [10] Ps. x. 14. [11] i. 13. [12] חמס Gen. vi. 11, 13. [13] Jonah iii. 8.

Before CHRIST cir. 626.

before me: and there are
that raise up strife and contention.
4 Therefore the law is
slacked, and judgment
doth never go forth: for
the [b] wicked doth compass
about the righteous; therefore
|| wrong judgment proceedeth.

Before CHRIST cir. 626.

b Job. 21. 7. Ps. 94. 3, &c. Jer. 12. 1.

|| Or, *wrested.*

And while to him who suffers, the suffering is temporal, to him who inflicts it, it is eternal. And yet the prophet and whoso prays against ungodliness, "[1] must commiserate him who doth wrong yet more, since they hurt what is most precious, their own soul, and that eternally." All then is full of evil. Whithersoever the Prophet looks, some fresh *violence is before* him; it confronts him on every side; *strife hath arisen*[2], come up, exists where it was not before; *contention lifteth itself*[3] on high, bowing down all beside.

4. *Therefore,* i.e. Because God seemed not to awake to avenge His own cause, men promised themselves that they might sin on with impunity. Sin produces sin, and wrong, wrong; it spreads like an infectious disease, propagating itself, and each, to whom it reaches, adds to its poison. At last, it reached those also, who should be in God's stead to restrain it. The Divine law itself is silenced, by the power of the wicked, by the sin of the judge, the hopelessness of all. When all around is evil, even those not yet lost are tempted to think; "Why should I be other than they? what evil befalls them? Why stand alone?" Even a Psalmist[4] speaks as if tempted to *speak even as they. These are the ungodly who prosper in the world; they increase in riches; verily I have cleansed my heart in vain, and washed my hands in innocency;* and Solomon[5], *Because sentence against an evil work is not executed speedily, therefore the heart of the sons of men is fully set in them to do evil.*

The law is slacked, lit. *is chilled*[6] (as we say, "is paralyzed,") through lack of the fire of love. This is what our Lord says, [7] *Because iniquity shall abound, the love of many shall wax cold.* The Divine law, the source of all right, being chilled in men's hearts, *judgment,* i. e. the sentence of human justice, as conformed to Divine, *doth never go forth*[8]. Human sense of right is powerless, when there is not the love of God's law. It seems ever ready to act, but ever falls short, like an arrow from an unstrung bow. The man seems ever *about* to do right; he judges, sees, aright; all but does it; yet at last always fails. It *goes not forth. The children are come to the birth, and there is not strength to bring forth*[9].

For the wicked doth compass about[10] the righteous, laying snares for him, as the Jews for our Lord; evil is too strong for a weak will to do right, and overbears it. Pilate sought in many ways, how he might deliver Jesus, yet at last did deliver Him into their hands.

Therefore wrong judgment proceedeth, lit. *judgment proceedeth wrested*[11]. He had said, "it *never* goes forth;" never, that is, in its true character; for, when it does *go forth,* it is distorted. "[12] For gifts or favor or fear or hate the guiltless are condemned and the guilty acquitted, as saith the Psalmist, [13] *How long will ye judge unjustly and accept the persons of the ungodly?*" "[14] *Judgment goes forth perverted* in the seat of man's judgment (the soul), when, bribed by the pleasures of sense, it leans to the side of things seen, and the Ungodly one, the rebel angel, besets and overpowers him who has the sense of right; for it is right that things seen should give way to things unseen; [15] *for the things which are seen are temporal, but the things which are not seen are eternal.*" Why then all this? and how long? Why does God bring it before him and He Who is *of purer eyes than to behold iniquity, behold grievance,* which His Holy Eyes could not endure? Neither the Unseen Presence of God nor the mission of the Prophet checks. If he rebuke, no one hearkened; if he intercedes for sinners, or against sin, God made as though He would

[1] Theoph.

[2] The Lxx. Syr. S. Jer. so divide; γέγονε κρίσις καὶ ὁ κριτὴς λαμβάνει, "et factum est judicium et contradictio potentior." So Tanchum. The E. V. has followed Jon. Kim. Aben Ezra.

[3] נשׂא intrans., as in Ps. lxxxix. 10; Nah. i. 5.

[4] Ps. lxxiii. 15, 12, 13.

[5] Eccl. viii. 11.

[6] It is used of Jacob's heart, who could not believe the good tidings, Gen. xlv. 26; the numbing of the comfortless heart of the penitent through grief (Nif.) Ps. xxxviii. 9. The Psalmist, holding on in prayer, denies it of himself. Ps. xxvii. 3. They quote "friget lex."

[7] S. Matt. xxiv. 12.

[8] According to the uniform use of לנצח, 31 times and נצח 6 times. This uniform usage cannot be overborne by the analogy of Is. xlii. 3. לאמת יוציא משפט, "He shall bring forth judgment to truth," as Syr. here, "with sincerity," Rashi, "according to truth."

[9] Is. xxxvii. 3.

[10] הכתיר, "encompass for hostile end," as כִּתֵּר Jud. xv. 43. Ps. xx. 13. "The wicked," רשע is collective, as implied by the word "encompass." "The righteous" is, in contrast, determined, את הצדיק.

[11] מעקל. The root occurs only in intensive forms; in the verb here only; crooked ways are עקלקלוֹת Jud. v. 6. Ps. cxxv. 5. the Serpent is called עקלתוֹן, Isa. xxvii. 1.

[12] Dion.

[13] Ps. lxxxii. 2.

[14] Theoph.

[15] 2 Cor. iv. 18.

Before CHRIST cir. 626.

5 ¶ [e] Behold ye among the heathen, and regard, and wonder marvellously; for *I* will work a work in your days, *which* ye will not believe, though it be told you.

6 For, lo, [d] ‖ I raise up

[e] Is. 29.14. Acts 13. 41.

[d] Deut. 28. 49. 50. Jer. 5. 15.

‖ fulfilled. 2 Chr. 36. 6.

not hear. God answers that, though to man's impatience the time seems long, judgment shall come, and that, suddenly and speedily. While the righteous is enquiring, *how long?* and the wicked is saying [1], *My Lord delayeth His coming*, He is come, and seen in the midst of them.

The whole tone of the words suddenly changes. The Jews flattered themselves that, being the people of God, He would not fulfill His threats upon them. They had become like the heathen in wickedness; God bids them look out among them for the instrument of His displeasure. It was an aggravation of their punishment, that God, Who had once chosen *them*, would now choose these whom He had not chosen, to chasten them. So Moses had foretold; [2] *They have moved Me to jealousy by that which is not God; they have provoked Me to anger with their vanities; and I will move them to jealousy with not-a-people, I will provoke them to anger with a foolish nation.* There were no tokens of the storm which should sweep them away, yet on the horizon. No forerunners yet. And so He bids them gaze on among the nations, to see whence it should come. They might have expected it from Egypt. It should come whence they did not expect, with a fierceness and terribleness which they imagined not. *Regard*, look narrowly, weigh well what it portends; *and wonder marvelously;* lit. *be amazed, amazed.* The word is doubled [3], to express how amazement should follow upon amazement; when the first was passing away, new source of amazement should come; for [4] *I will work a work in your days, which ye will not believe, though it be told you.* So incredible it will be, and so against their wills! He does not say, "ye would not believe if it were told you;" much less, "if it were told you *of others;*" in which case the chief thought would be left unexpressed. No condition is expressed. It is simply foretold, what was verified by the whole history of their resistance to the Chaldees until the capture of the city; "Ye will not believe, when it shall be told you." So it ever is. Man never believes, that God is in earnest, until His judgments come. So it was before the flood, and to Sodom, and Lot's sons-in-law; so it was to Ahab and Jezebel; so as to this destruction of Jerusalem by the Chaldæans, and that which is shadowed forth, by the Romans. So Jeremiah complained, [5] *They have belied the Lord, and said, it is not He; neither shall evil come upon us; neither shall we see sword nor famine*, and, [6] *I am in derision daily; every one mocketh me. For since I spake, I cried out, I cried violence and spoil; because the word of the Lord was made a reproach unto me, and a derision daily;* and Isaiah, [7] *Who hath believed our report?* and St. John Baptist speaks as though it were desperate; [8] *O generation of vipers, who hath warned you to flee from the wrath to come?* and our Lord tells them, [9] *Your house is left unto you desolate.* And yet they believed not, but delivered Him up to be put to death, *lest* that should be, which did come, *because* they put Him to death. [10] *If we let Him thus alone, all men will believe on Him; and the Romans shall come, and take away both our place and nation.* St. Paul [11], then, applies these words to the Jews in his day, because the destruction of the first temple by Nebuchadnezzar was an image of the destruction of the second (which by Divine appointment, contrary to man's intention, took place on the same day [12]), and the Chaldæans were images of the Romans, that second Babylon, heathen Rome; and both foreshowed the worse destruction by a fiercer enemy, the enemy of souls, the spiritual wasting and desolation which came on the Jew first, and which shall come on all who disobey the Gospel. So it shall be to the end. Even now the Jews believe not, Whose work their own dispersion is; His, Who by them was crucified, but Who hath [13] *all power in heaven and in earth.* The Day of Judgment will come like a thief in the night to those who believe not or obey not our Lord's words.

6. *For lo.* So God announces a future, in which His Hand shall be greatly visible,

[1] S. Matt. xxiv. 48. [2] Deut. xxxii. 21.

[3] As in Ps. cxviii. 11, סבוני גם סבבוני, Hos. iv. 18, אהבו הבו, Zeph. ii. 1. התקוששו וקושו. If suggested by Is. xxix. 9, התמהמהו ותמהו "be perplexed and marvel," Habakkuk changed the phrase, preserving the alliteration.

[4] The "I" is omitted in the Hebrew, probably for conciseness, as if it were the finite verb. Del. quotes as omissions of the 3d person, Ps. xxii. 29. lv. 20; of the second 1 Sam. ii. 24. vi. 3. Ps. vii. 10. Hab. ii. 10. Ewald adds "after הִנֵּה Gen. xli. 1. Ex. vii. 15. viii. 16, and without it, Ps. xxii. 29, xxxiii. 5. 7. lxvi. 7. xcvi. 13. Lehrb. p. 516. ed. 7.

[5] Jer. v. 12. [6] Ib. xx. 7, 8.

[7] Is. liii. 1. [8] S. Matt. iii. 7.

[9] Ib. xxiii. 38. S. Luke xiii. 35. [10] S. John xi. 48.

[11] Some of the words as there quoted (from the then received translation, the LXX.) differ; the sense is the same.

[12] Jos. de B. J. vii. 14. [13] S. Matt. xxviii. 18.

Before CHRIST cir. 626.

the Chaldeans, *that* bitter
and hasty nation, which
shall march through the
† breadth of the land, to
possess the dwellingplaces
that are not their's.
7 They *are* terrible and
dreadful: ‖ their judg-
ment and their dignity
shall proceed of them-
selves.
8 Their horses also are
swifter than the leopards,
and are more † fierce than
the [e] evening wolves: and
their horsemen shall spread
themselves, and their
horsemen shall come from

† Heb. *breadths.*

‖ Or, *from them shall proceed the judgment of these, and the captivity of these.*

Before CHRIST cir. 626.

† Heb. *sharp.*

[e] Jer. 5. 6. Zeph. 3. 3.

---

whether more or less distant. In His sight it is present. *I raise up.* God uses the free-will and evil passions of men or devils to His own ends; and so He is said to *raise up* [1] those whom He allows to be stirred up against His people, since the events which His Providence permits, favor their designs, and it rests with Him to withhold them. They lift themselves up for some end of covetousness or pride. But there is a higher order of things, in which God orders their actions to fulfill by their iniquities His righteousness. *The Chaldæans, that bitter* [2] *and hasty* [3] *nation.* "[4] To its might and warlike boldness almost all the Greeks who have written histories of the barbarians, witness." *Which shall march through the breadth of the land,* rather, *the earth,* lit. "to the breadths of the earth," reaching to its whole length and breadth, all its dimensions [5], as in the description of Gog and Magog, [6] *the number of whom is as the sand of the sea; and they went up on the breadth of the earth;* unhindered, not pent up, but spreading abroad, where they will, over the whole earth. All before it, is one wide even plain which it overspreads and covers, like a flood, and yet is not spent nor exhausted. *To possess the dwelling-places that are not theirs.* As God's people had done, so should it be done to them. Spoiling and violence within [7] attract oppression from without. The overcharged atmosphere casts down the lightning upon them. They had expelled the weak from their dwelling [8]; others shall possess theirs. Yet this scourge too shall pass by, since, although the Chaldæan did God's Will, he willed it not, but his own [9]. The words, *not theirs,* lit. *not to him* [*lo-lo* [10]] stand with a mysterious fullness of meaning. The dwelling places *not* being *his* by right, shall not remain *his,* although given to him, while God wills.

7. *They are terrible* [11] *and dreadful.* He describes them, first in themselves, then in act. They are terrible, and strike fear through their very being, their known character, before they put it forth in act. *Their judgment and their dignity shall proceed of themselves. Judgment* had *gone forth* in God's people *wrested* [12]; now shall it go forth against them at the mere will of their master, who shall own no other rule or Lord or source of his power. His own will shall be his only law for himself and others. His elevation [13] too is, in his own thought, from himself. He is self-sufficing; he holds from no other, neither from God nor man. His *dignity* is self-sustained; his *judgment* irresponsible, as if there were none [14] *higher than he.* He has, like all great world-powers, a real dignity and majesty. He infuses awe. The dignity is real but faulty, as being held independently of God. This is a character of Antichrist [15], a lawless insolence, a lifting up of himself.

8. *Their horses are swifter* [lit. *lighter,* as we say, "light of foot"] *than leopards.* The wild beast intended is the panther, the lightest, swiftest, fiercest, most blood-thirsty of beasts of prey. "[16] It runs most swiftly and rushes brave and straight. You would say, when you saw it, that it is borne through the air." "[17] It bounds exceedingly and is very exceed-

---

[1] הקים is so used, 1 Kings xi. 14, 23. Am. vi. 14, and of evil (in the abstract) 2 Sam. xii. 11. Zech. xi. 16, as also העיר Ezek. xxiii. 22. 2 Chr. xxi. 16. and against Babylon, Is. xiii. 17. xli. 2, 25. Jer. l. 9. li. 1. 11.

[2] מר. In Jud. xviii. 25. 2 Sam. xvii. 8, the less concise מר נפש is used.

[3] נמהר as Is. xxxii. 4.

[4] S. Jer.

[5] מרחבי (plur.) occurs here only. Isaiah has "the fullness of the breadth of Thy land, O Immanuel" viii. 8, and in the same sense v. 9. כל מרחקי ארץ "all the far places of the earth." (also ἅπ.)

[6] Rev. xx. 8. 9.

[7] i. 2–4.

[8] Mic. ii. 9.

[9] See Isa. x. 6, 7.

[10] לא לו.

[11] אָיֹם occurs here only and Cant. vi. 4. 10. compared with the "bannered host," but the root is common in אֵימָה.

[12] i. 4.

[13] שְׂאֵת is not in itself, "*self*-elevation" (as Kim. "that he will exalt himself above the nations") but simply "elevation;" from God, Gen. iv. 7, or His Providence, Ib. xlix. 3, Ps. lxii. 5. It is used of the majesty of God, Job xiii. 23.

[14] Eccl. v. 8.

[15] Dan. xi. 36. 2 Thess. ii. 4.

[16] Oppian Cyneg. iii. 75. sq.

[17] S. Cyr. See more fully in Daniel the Prophet p. 77. n. 3.

Before CHRIST cir. 626.

far; [r] they shall fly as the
eagle *that* hasteth to eat.
9 They shall come all
for violence: || † their faces
shall sup up *as* the east
wind, and they shall gather the captivity as the
sand.
10 And they shall scoff
at the kings, and the
princes shall be a scorn
unto them: they shall de-

r Jer. 4. 13.
|| Or, *the supping up of their faces, &c.* or, *their faces shall look toward the east.*
† Heb. *the opposition of their faces toward the east.*

Before CHRIST cir. 626.

ingly light to spring down on whatever it pursues." *More fierce* [1] *than the evening wolves* [2], i. e. than they are when fiercest, going forth to prey when urged to rabidness by hunger the whole day through. Such had their own judges been [3], and by such should they be punished. The horse partakes of the fierceness of his rider in trampling down the foe [4]. *Their horsemen shall spread themselves* [lit. *widespread are their horsemen*], *and their horsemen from far shall come.* Neither distance of march shall weary them, nor diffusion weaken them. So should Moses' prophecy be again fulfilled. [5] *The Lord shall raise against thee a nation from far, from the ends of the earth, as the eagle flieth; a nation whose tongue thou shalt not understand; a nation of fierce countenance, which shall not regard the person of the old, nor show favor to the young.*

They shall fly as the eagle that hasteth [lit. *hasting* [6]] *to eat,* " [7] not to fight, for none shall withstand; but with a course like the eagle's, to whom all fowl are subdued, *hasting* but to *eat.*" *Behold,* Jeremiah says of Nebuchadnezzar [8], *he shall fly as an eagle and spread his wings over Moab;* and, he repeats the words, [9] *over Bozrah. Our pursuers,* Jeremiah says [10], *are swifter than the eagles of the heavens.* Ezekiel likens him to [11] *a great eagle with great wings full of feathers;* in Daniel's vision he is [12] *a lion with eagle's wings.*

9. *They shall come all for violence. Violence* had been the sin of Judah [13], and now shall be her punishment. It had been *ever before* the prophet; all were full of it. Now should *violence* be the very end, one by one, of all the savage horde poured out upon them; *they all, each one of them* [14], *come for violence. Their faces shall sup up* [15] *as the east wind* [16]. "As at the breath of the burning wind all green things dry up, so at sight of these all shall be wasted." They shall sweep over everything impetuously, like the east wind, scorching, blackening, blasting, swallowing up all, as they pass over, as the East wind, especially in the Holy Land, sucks up all moisture and freshness. *And they shall gather the captivity* [i. e. *the captives*] *as the sand,* countless, as the particles which the East wind raises, sweeping over the sand-wastes, where it buries whole caravans in one death.

10. *And they* [lit. *he,* the word stands emphatically, *he,* alone against all *the kings* of the earth] *shall scoff at the kings* and all their might, taking them away or setting them up at his pleasure and caprice, subduing them as though in sport [17]; *and princes,* (lit. *grave* and *majestic*) *shall be a scorn unto them* [*him*] [18].

[1] lit. *sharp* "acer." חדד (except of the scales of the crocodile Job xii. 22) is used elsewhere only of the sharpening of iron against iron (Hif.) Pr. xxvii. 17; (Hof.), of the sword Ezek. xxi. 14, 15, 26. חדּה as an epithet of the sword (iv. times). In Arabic חַדַּ, conj. i. ii. iv. x. is to "sharpen;" חדּאד, חדאד "sharp," of a knife, sword; חדיד met., "sharp of intellect," &c. also of sword.

[2] Comp. Jer. v. 6. [3] Zeph. iii. 3.

[4] The horse and his rider are regarded as one. Nahum had spoken of the cavalry in the armies against Nineveh (Nah. iii. 2); in Judith they are numbered in the proportion of one-tenth to the footmen of Holofernes (Judith ii. 5, 15.). They were the more formidable to Judah which had footmen only. Under Persian rule Babylonia was a great breeding place for horses. Rawl. 5 Empires iii. 317.

[5] Deut. xxviii. 49, 50. מרחוק occurs in both.

[6] חָשׁ as partic. In the finite verb, it had been יחושׁ like יכסו ii. 14, יהלכו iii. 11, יטושׁ Job ix. 26. Del. [7] S. Jer. [8] Jer. xlviii. 40. [9] Ib. xlix. 22.

[10] Lam. iv. 19. [11] Ezek. xvii. 3. [12] Dan. vii. 4.

[13] v. 3. 4.

[14] As כלו Ps. xxix. 9, Is. i. 23, ix. 16, Jer. vi. 13, viii. 6. 10, xv. 10. כלה Jer. xx. 7.

[15] מגמּה, ἅπ. λεγ. The sense "swallowing" is given by Jos. Kimchi, A. E., Rashi, Ob. Sip., Menahem B. Saruk, taking גמם as i. q. גמא, quoting Job xxxix. 24 or Gen. xxiv. 17. Thence A. E. obtains the meaning "before, straight on," quoting Targ. Abulwalid, followed by Tanchum, compares the Arab. הַמַּ, "purposed," and thence derives the meaning "direction." The Arab. גַמַּ, (appetivit, Fr.) signifies "approached" not "desired." Gesenius "the *collection* of their faces," i. e. all of them, involves the use of a ἅπ. λεγ. to express, without emphasis, what is expressed everywhere by the common word, כל. Symm. has πρόσοψις, and so Syr.

[16] קדימה occurs else only in Ezek. xi. 1, and 16 times in c. xl.–xlviii. of the ideal city and temple as "Eastwards." But except in the far-fetched explanation of Abarb. (mentioned also by Tanchum) that they ravaged, not to settle, but to return home with their booty, "Eastwards" would have no meaning. Yet "forwards" is just as insulated a rendering as that adopted by J. and D. Kim., A. E., Rashi, Ob. Sip., Sal. B. Mel. Arab Tr. (following Jon.) "the East-wind;" קדימה standing as a met. instead of a simile the ה being regarded as paragogic, as in לילה. So also Symm. ἄνεμος καύσων. S. Jer., "ventus urens."

[17] Comp. Benhadad's drunken commands, 1 Kings xx. 18.

[18] Comp. Job xli. 29.

Before CHRIST cir. 626.

ride every strong hold; for they shall heap dust, and take it.

11 Then shall *his* mind change, and he shall pass over, and offend, [g] *imputing* this his power unto his god.

Before CHRIST cir. 626.

[g] Dan. 5. 4.

So Nebuchadnezzar *bound* Jehoiakim [1] *in fetters to carry him to Babylon;* then, on his submission made him for three years a tributary king [2], then on his rebellion sent bands of Chaldees and other tributaries against him [3]; and then, or when Nebuchadnezzar took Jehoiachin, Jeremiah's prophecy was fulfilled, that he should *be buried with the burial of an ass, dragged and cast forth beyond the gates of Jerusalem* [4], *his dead body cast out in the day to the heat and in the night to the frost* [5], then Nebuchadnezzar took away Jehoiachin; then Zedekiah. He had also many kings captive with him in Babylon. For on his decease Evil-Merodach brought Jehoiachin out of his prison after 27 years of imprisonment, *and set his throne above the throne of the kings that were with him in Babylon* [6]. Daniel says also to Nebuchadnezzar [7], *Thou, O king, art a king of kings: for the God of heaven hath given thee a kingdom, power and strength and glory. And wheresoever the children of men dwell, the beasts of the field and the fowls of heaven hath He given into thine hand and hath made thee ruler over all.*

They [*he*] *shall deride every strong hold*, as, aforetime, when God helped her, Jerusalem laughed the Assyrian to scorn [8]; *for they* [*he*] *shall heap dust, and take it*, as Nebuchadnezzar did Tyre, whose very name (*Rock*) betokened its strength. "[9] He shall come to Tyre, and, casting a mound in the sea, shall make an island a peninsula, and, amid the waves of the sea, land shall give an entrance to the city."

The *mount*, or heaped-up earth, by which the besiegers fought on a level with the besieged, or planted their engines at advantage, was an old and simple form of siege, especially adapted to the great masses of the Eastern armies. It was used in David's time [10]; and by the Assyrians [11], Egyptians [12], Babylonians [13], and afterward the Persians [14]. Here he describes the rapidity of the siege. To heap up dust and to capture were one.

It needed no great means; things slight as the dust sufficed in the hands of those employed by God. Portion by portion, [15] *the King of Babylon took all that pertained to the king of Egypt, from the river of Egypt unto the river Euphrates.*

11. *Then shall his mind change*, or, better, *Then he sweeps by* [16], *a wind* [17], *and passes* [18], *and is guilty; this his strength is his god.* The victory was completed, all resistance ended. He sweeps by, as his own Euphrates, when over-filled by the swelling [19] of all its tributary streams, riseth up over all its banks, and overwhelms all where it passes; as a wind which sweepeth [20] over the desert: *and passes over* all bounds and laws, human and Divine, *and is guilty* and stands guilty before God, making himself as God, *This his power is his god.* God had said to Israel, [21] *I will be to thee God.* The Chaldæan virtually said, *this my strength is to me my god.* This Nebuchadnezzar's own words speak; [22] *Is not this great Babylon, that I have built for the house of the kingdom by the might of my power, and for the honor of my majesty?* And the statue which was to be worshiped, was, very probably, of himself [23], as the intoxication of pride has made other heathen kings or conquerors, Alexander or Darius [24]. Belshazzar said, [25] *I will be like the Most High*, and the prince of Tyre said, [26] *I am a god*, and Anti-Christ shall [27] *exalt himself above all that is called god*, and, *as God, sit in the temple of God, shewing himself that he is god.* Such is all pride. It sets itself in the place of God,

[1] 2 Chr. xxxvi. 6. Dan. i. 2.
[2] 2 Kings xxiv. 1. [3] Ib. 2. [4] Jer. xxii. 19.
[5] Ib. xxxvi. 30. On the one hand, the expression "slept with his fathers" does not necessarily imply that Jehoiakim died a peaceful death, since it is used of Ahab (1 Kings xxii. 40) and Amaziah (2 Kings xiv. 20, 22.) On the other, Jeremiah's prophecy was equally fulfilled, if the insult to his corpse took place when Nebuchadnezzar took away Jehoiachin three months after his father's death. See Daniel the Prophet, pp. 399, 402, 403. Josephus attributes both the death and disgrace to Nebuchadnezzar. Ant. x. 6. 3.
[6] 2 Kgs xxv. 27, 28.
[7] Dan. ii. 37. 38. and iv. 22. [8] Is. xxxviii. 22.
[9] S. Jer. [10] 2 Sam. xx. 15. [11] 2 Kgs xix. 32.
[12] Ez. xvii. 17.
[13] Jer. vi. 6. xxxii. 24, xxxiii. 4, Ezek. iv. 2, xxi. 22 [27 Heb.], xxvi. 8.
[14] Herod. i. 162. [15] 2 Kings xxiv. 7.
[16] חלף is used of the overflowing of a river, Is. viii. 8. of a wind chasing, Ib. xxi. 1, of the invisible presence of God passing by, Job ix. 11. or a spirit, Ib. iv. 15. of the swift passing of our days, like ship or eagle, Ib. ix. 26. of idols utterly passing away, Is. ii. 18, of rain past and gone, Cant. ii. 11. It is, together with עבר, used of transgressing God's law, Is. xxiv. 5. It is always intrans., except as piercing the temples of man Jud. v. 26, or himself Job xx. 24.
[17] רוח, i. q. כרוח, metaphor for simile, as Ps. xi. 1. xxii. 14. (13 Eng.) xc. 4. Job xxiv. 5. Is. li. 12. &c. רוח can hardly be i. q. רוחו.
[18] עבר "pass over" (with חלף, as here.) Is. viii. 8. Nah. i. 8. Hab. iii. 10; "transgress," passim; "pass away," Ps. xxxvii. 6, Job xxxiv. 29, Nah. i. 12.
[19] Is. viii. 8. [20] Ib. xxi. 1.
[21] Ex. vi. 7. [22] Dan. iv. 30.
[23] See Daniel the Prophet, p. 443.
[24] See ib. p. 446. [25] Is. xiv. 14.
[26] Ezek. xxviii. 2. [27] 2 Thess. ii. 4.

Before CHRIST cir. 626.

h Ps. 90. 2. & 93. 2. Lam. 5. 19.

12 ¶ [h] *Art* thou not
from everlasting, O LORD
my God, mine Holy One?
we shall not die. O LORD,
[i] thou hast ordained them
for judgment; and, O

i 2 Kin. 19. 25. Ps. 17. 13. Is. 10. 5, 6, 7. Ezek. 30. 25.

it ceases to think itself His instrument, and so is a god to itself, as though its eminence and strength were its own, and its wisdom the source of its power[1], and its will the measure of its greatness. The words, with a Divine fullness, express severally, that the king shall *sweep* along, shall *pass* over all bounds and all hindrances, and shall *pass away*, shall *be guilty* and shall *bear his guilt*[2]: and so they comprise in one his sin and his punishment, his greatness and his fall. And so forty years afterward Nebuchadnezzar, [3] *whom he would, he slew; and whom he would, he kept alive; and whom he would, he set up; and whom he would, he put down; but when his heart was lifted up, and his mind hardened in pride, he was deposed from his kingly throne, and they took his glory from him;* [4] *there fell a voice from heaven, The kingdom is departed from thee;* and Belshazzar, [5] *in the same night that he lifted up himself against the Lord of heaven, was slain.*

12. The prophet, having summed up the deeds of the enemy of God in this his end, sets forth his questions anew. He had appealed against the evil of the wicked of his people; he had been told of the vengeance by the Chaldæans. [6] But the vengeance is executed by them who are far worse. How then? The answer is, "Wait to the end, and thou shalt see." What remains are the triumphs of faith; the second chapter closes with the entire prostration of the whole world before God, and the whole prophecy with joyous trust in God amid the entire failure of all outward signs of hope. Here, like the Psalmists[7] and Jeremiah[8], he sets down at the very beginning his entire trust in God, and so, in the name of all who at any time shall be perplexed about the order of God's judgments, asks how it shall be, teaching us that the only safe way of enquiring into God's ways is by setting out with a living conviction that they [9] *are mercy and truth.* And so the address to God is full of awe and confidence and inward love. For "[10] God placeth the oil of mercy in the vessel of trustfulness."

Art not Thou (the word has always an emphasis) *Thou*, and not whatsoever or whosoever it be that is opposed to Thee, (be it Nebuchadnezzar or Satan) *from everlasting* lit. *from before*[11]? Go back as far as man can in thought, God was still *before;* and so, much more *before* any of His creatures, such as those who rebel against Him. *O Lord,* it is the Proper Name of God, [12] *Which is and Which was and Which is to come,* I AM, the Unchangeable; *my God,* i. e., whereas his own might is (he had just said) the heathen's god, the Lord is his; *mine Holy One:*—one word, denoting that God is his God, sufficeth him not, but he adds (what does not elsewhere occur) *mine Holy One,* in every way, as hallowing him and hallowed by him: "[13] Who hallowest my soul, Holy in Thine Essence, and Whom as incomparably Holy I worship in holiness." All-Holy in Himself, He becometh the Holy One of him to whom He imparteth Himself, and so, by His own gift, belongeth, as it were, to him. The one word in Hebrew wonderfully fits in with the truth, that God becomes one with man by taking him to Himself. It is full of inward trust too, that he saith, "*my* God, *my* Holy One," as S. Paul saith, [14] *Who loved me, and gave Himself for me,* i. e., as S. Augustine explains it, "[15] O Thou God Omnipotent, Who so carest for every one of us, as if Thou caredst for him only; and so for all, as if they were but one." The title, *my Holy One,* includes his people with himself; for God was *his* God, primarily because he was one of the people of God; and his office was for and in behalf of his people. It involves then that other title which had been the great support of Isaiah[16], by which he at once comforted his people, and impressed upon them the holiness of their God, the holiness which their relation to their God required, *the Holy One of Israel.* Thence, since Habakkuk lived, for his people with himself, on this relation to God, as *my* God, *my Holy One,* and that God, the Unchangeable; it follows, "*We shall not die*[17]." There is no need of any mark of inference, "*therefore* we shall not die." It *is* an

[1] See Ezek. xxviii. 2–5.
[2] אשם includes both.
[3] Dan. v 19. 20.
[4] Ib. iv. 31.
[5] Ib. v. 23, 30.
[6] Heading of Chap. i.
[7] Asaph, Ps. lxxiii. Ethan Ps. lxxvi.
[8] Jer. xii. 1.
[9] Ps. xxv. 10.
[10] S. Bern. de Annunt. Serm. 3. n. 3.
[11] See on Micah v. 2.
[12] Rev. i. 8.
[13] Dion.
[14] Gal. ii. 9.
[15] Conf. iii. 11.
[16] Isaiah uses it in his prophetic answer to Hezekiah (2 Kgs xix. 22. Is. xxxvii. 23,) also in the earlier chapters 12 times and "his holy One" (of Israel) x. 17; in the chapters xl–lxvi, 14 times, and "his holy One" "your holy One" of or to Israel xlix. 7. xliii. 35. Else it occurs only in Ps. lxxviii. 41 (Asaph's), lxxxix. 19 (Ethan's), lxxi. 22 [Anon., but in Book ii.] and Jer. l. 29, li. 5.
[17] The "tikkune sopherim" or so-called "corrections of the scribes" I think, appear to almost any one who examines them, not to imply any correction of the text of Holy Scripture, but as meant to suggest what would have come naturally into the mind of the writer, unless for some reason he had chosen what stands written. Thus here, the obvi-

Before CHRIST cir. 626.

† mighty God, thou hast
† established them for correction.
13 [k] *Thou art* of purer
eyes than to behold evil,
and canst not look on ‖ iniquity: [l] wherefore lookest
thou upon them that deal
treacherously, *and* holdest
thy tongue when the wicked
devoureth *the man that is*
more righteous than he?

† Heb. *rock.* Deut. 32. 4.
† Heb. *founded.*
[k] Ps. 5. 5.
‖ Or, *grievance.*
[l] Jer. 12. 1.

Before CHRIST cir. 626.

---

inference, but it so lay in those titles of God, *He Is, My God, My Holy One*, that it was a more loving confidence to say directly, *we shall not die.* The one thought involved the other. God, the Unchangeable, had made Himself their God. It was impossible, then, that He should cast them off or that they should perish. *We shall not die*, is the lightning thought of faith, which flashes on the soul like all inspirations of God, founded on His truth and word, but borne in, as it were, instinctively without inference on the soul, with the same confidence as the Psalmist says[1], *The Lord hath chastened me sore; but He hath not given me over unto death;* and Malachi,[2] *I am the Lord, I change not; therefore ye sons of Jacob are not consumed.* "[3] Thou createdst us from the beginning; by Thy mercy we are in being hitherto." Thy *gifts and calling are without repentance*[4]. "Did we look to his might; none of us could withstand him. Look we to Thy mercy, Thine alone is it that we live, are not slain by him, nor led to deeds of death." *O Lord*, again he repeats the Name of God, whereby He had revealed Himself as their God, the Unchangeable; *Thou*, whose *mercies fail not, hast ordained them for judgment*, not for vengeance or to make a full end, or for his own ends and pleasure, but to *correct* Thine own[5] *in measure*, which he, exceeding, sinned.[6]

And O mighty God [lit. *Rock*]. It is a bold title. *My rock* is a title much used by David[7], perhaps suggested by the fastnesses amid which he passed his hunted life, to express, that not in them but in His God was his safety. Habakkuk purposely widens it. He appeals to God, not only as Israel's might and upholder, but as the sole Source of all strength, the Supporter of all which is upheld[8], and so, for the time, of the Chaldæan too. Hence he continues the simple image: *Thou hast founded him.* "[9] Thou hast made him to stand firm as the foundation of a building;" *to reprove* or *set before* those who have sinned against Thee, what they had done. Since then God was the Rock, Who had *founded them*, from Him Alone had they strength; when He should withdraw it, they must fall. How then did they yet abide, who abused the power given them and counted it their own? And this the more, since

13. *Thou art of purer eyes than to behold evil.* The prophet repeats his complaint, (as troubling thoughts are wont to come back, after they have been repelled,) in order to answer it more strongly. All sin is hateful in God's sight, and in His Holy Wisdom He cannot endure to *look toward iniquity.* As man turns away from sickening sights, so God's abhorrence of wrong is pictured by His not being able to *look toward* it. If He looked toward them, they must perish[10]. Light cannot coexist with darkness, fire with water, heat with cold, deformity with beauty, foulness with sweetness, nor is sin compatible with the Presence of God, except as its Judge and punisher. Thou *canst not look.* There is an entire contradiction between God and unholi-

---

ous contrast to "Thou art of old;" might be, (they would say) "Thou wilt continue to be;" "*Thou* wilt not die," ולא תמות; but since it were unbefitting to speak of death in regard to God, even in denying it, the prophet said לא נמות, "we shall not die." But no thoughtful Jewish critic could ever have believed that Habakkuk could have said to God, *Thou wilt not die.* It would also, while irreverent to God, have omitted the whole consolation to his people. Of Jewish Commentators, Kim., A. E., Abarb. Tanch., do not think it worth while to allude to the correction; Sal. B. Melech mentions it, to reject it; Rashi quotes it as the writing of the prophet. Several of the 18 Tikkune Sopherim are childish; no one of value. The Chaldee follows the suggestion, paraphrasing, "Thy word abideth for ever;" the LXX, not. Ewald corrects as the Chaldee. The Tikk. Soph. are given in Buxtorf Lex. Chald. pp. 2631, sqq. A glance will shew that they are no real corrections.

[1] Ps. cxviii. 18.
[2] Mal. iii. 6.
[3] S. Jer.
[4] Rom. xi. 29.
[5] Jer. x. 24. xxx. 11.
[6] See Isa. x. 5. xlvii. 6. Zech. i. 15.
[7] Ps. xviii. 2. 46. xix. 15. xxviii. 1. lxii. 6. 7. cxliv. 1. else only in Deut. xxxii. 1. Ps. xcii. 15. anon. Else Moses speaks in his Song of "the Rock," "our Rock," "their Rock," "Rock of his salvation." "the Rock who begat thee," [Deut. xxxii. 4, 31, 30. 15, 18.] and in reference to Deut. Ps. lxxviii. 35, and Hannah, "there is no rock like our God," 1 Sam. ii. 2, and David asks, "Who is a rock beside Thee?" 2 Sam. xxii. 31, and calls Him "the Rock of Israel," 2 Sam. xxiii. 3, "the Rock of my strength" Ps. lxii. 8, and Ethan says that God entitled David to call Him "Rock of my salvation," Ps. lxxxix. 26. and Asaph calls Him, "the Rock of my heart." Ps. lxxiii. 26. Isaiah in his song entitles God "the Rock of ages," Isa. xxvi. 4. also "the Rock of Israel," xxx. 29, "the rock of thy [Israel's] strength," xvii. 10. Else it occurs only in two anonymous Psalms, "the rock of my refuge," Ps. xciv. 22, "of our salvation," xcv. 1.
[8] "Thou Who art the Rock of all ages hast founded him to reprove by him all the nations of the earth." Kim.
[9] Kim.
[10] Ps. civ. 32.

Before CHRIST cir. 626.

14 And makest men as
the fishes of the sea, as the
|| creeping things, *that have*
no ruler over them?
15 They [m]take up all
of them with the angle,
they catch them in their
net, and gather them in
their || drag: therefore they
rejoice and are glad.
16 Therefore [n]they
sacrifice unto their net,

|| Or, *moving*.

[m] Jer. 16. 16. Amos 4. 2.

|| Or, *flue net*.

[n] Deut. 8. 17. Isai. 10. 13. & 37. 24, 25.

---

ness. And yet, *wherefore lookest thou upon*, viewest, as in Thy full sight [1], yea, as it would seem, with favor [2], bestowing on them the goods of this life, honor, glory, children, riches, as the Psalmist saith; [3] *Behold these are the ungodly, who prosper in the world, they increase in riches?* Why lookest thou upon *them that deal treacherously, holdest Thy tongue*, puttest restraint [4], as it were, upon Thyself and Thine own attribute of Justice, *when the wicked devoureth the man that is more righteous than he?* [5] *In God's sight no man living can be justified;* and in one sense Sodom and Gomorrah were less unrighteous than Jerusalem, and [6] *it shall be more tolerable for* them *in the day of Judgment*, because they sinned against less light; yet the actual sins of the Chaldee were greater than those of Jerusalem, and Satan's evil is greater than that of those who are his prey. To say that Judah was more righteous than the Chaldæan does not imply any righteousness of the Chaldæan, as the saying that [7] *God ransomed Jacob from the hand of* one *stronger than he*, does not imply any strength remaining to Israel. Then, also, in all the general judgments of God, the righteous too suffer in this world, whence Abraham intercedes for Sodom, if there were but ten righteous in it; lest [8] *the righteous* be *destroyed with the wicked*. Hence God also spared Nineveh in part as having [9] *more than sixscore thousand persons that cannot discern between their right hand and their left hand*, i. e. good from evil. No times were fuller of sin than those before the destruction of Jerusalem, yet the fury of the Assassins fell upon the innocent. And so the words, like the voice of the souls under the Altar [10], become the cry of the Church at all times against the oppressing world, and of the blood of the Martyrs from Abel to the end, *Lord, how long?* And in that the word Righteous [11] signifies both "one righteous man," and the whole class or generation of the righteous, it speaks both of Christ the Head and of all His members in whom (as by Saul) He was persecuted. The *wicked* also includes all persecutors, both those who slew the Lord Christ, and those who brought His servants before judgment-seats, and blasphemed His Name [12], and caused many to blaspheme, and slew whom they could not compel. And God, all the while, seemeth to look away and to regard not.

14. *And makest men as the fishes of the sea*, dumb, helpless, in a stormy, restless element, no cry heard, but themselves swept away in shoals, with no power to resist, *as the creeping things*, whether of the land (as it is mostly used), or the sea [13]. Either way it is a contemptuous name for the lowest of either. *That have no ruler over them;* none to guide, order, protect them, and so a picture of man deprived of the care and providence of God.

15. *They take up all of them* [lit. *he taketh up all of it*] the whole race as though it were one, *with an angle; they catch them*, [lit. *he sweepeth it away*] *in their* [*his*] *net*. One fisherman is singled out who partly by wiles [as by the bait of *an angle*], partly by violence, [the net or drag] sweeps away [14] and gathers as his own the whole kind. Nebuchadnezzar and the Chaldæans are herein a faint image of Satan, who casts out his baits and his nets in the stormy sea of this life, taking some by individual craft, sweeping others in whole masses, to do evil; and whoso hath no ruler, and will not have Christ to reign over him [15], he allures, hurries, drags away as his prey. "[16] Adam clave to his hook, and he drew him forth out of Paradise with his net; and covered him with his drags, his varied and manifold deceits and guiles. And *by one many became sinners*, and in Adam we *all died*, and all saints afterward were with him alike cast out of Paradise. And because he deceived the first man, he ceaseth not daily to slay the whole human race."

16. *Therefore they sacrifice unto their net, and burn incense unto their drag.* [lit. *he* sacrifices unto *his* &c.] Whatever a man trusts in, is

[1] The preposition אל is left out in this place, as if to make the contrast stronger. God cannot endure to *look toward* (אל) iniquity, and yet He does not only this, but beholdeth it, contemplateth it, and still is silent.

[2] So the word means mostly; "regard favorably;" except Ps. x. 14. where it is said that God beheld ungodliness to avenge it.

[3] Ps. lxxiii. 12.

[4] החריש translated "keep silent" Ps. xxxv. 22. l. 21. implies an acting on a person's self.

[5] Ps. cxliii. 2.

[6] S. Matt. x. 15. xi. 24. S. Mark vi. 11. S. Luke x. 12.

[7] Jer. xxxi. 11. Del.

[8] Gen. xviii. 23.

[9] Jon. iv. 11.

[10] Rev. vi. 10.

[11] Singular in Hebrew, yet so that it may be used of many.

[12] S. Jas. ii. 6, 7.

[13] Ps. civ. 25.

[14] The word גרר, *garar*, expresses by its sound the grating noise of the pebbles on the sea-shore. The word is singular, although it *might* be a collective.

[15] S. Luke xix. 4.

[16] S. Jer.

Before CHRIST cir. 626.

and burn incense unto their drag; because by them their portion *is* fat, and their meat || † plenteous.

|| Or, *dainty*.
† Heb. *fat*.

17 Shall they therefore empty their net, and not spare continually to slay the nations?

CHAPTER II.

Before CHRIST cir. 626.

1 *Unto Habakkuk, waiting for an answer, is shewed that he must wait by faith.* 5 *The judgment upon the Chaldean for unsatiableness,* 9 *for covetousness,* 12 *for cruelty,* 15 *for drunkenness,* 18 *and for idolatry.*

I WILL [a] stand upon my watch, and set me upon

a Is. 21. 8, 11.

his god. If a man relies to compass his end by his strength, or his wisdom, or his forethought, or his wealth, his armies or navies, these his forces are his God. So the Assyrian said,[1] *By the strength of my hand I did it; and by my wisdom, for I am prudent;* and God answered, *Shall the axe boast itself against him that heweth therewith?* The coarse forms of idolatry only embody outwardly the deep inward idolatry of the corrupt human mind. The idol is [2] *set up in the heart* first. There have not indeed been wanting savage nations, who in very deed worshiped their arms[3]; those of old worshiped spears as immortal gods[4]; Even now we are told of some North American Indians "[5] who designate their bow and arrow as the only beneficent deities whom they know." Among the civilized Romans, the worship of the eagles, their standards[6], to whom they did sacrifice[7], was no other nor better. The inward idolatry is only a more subtle form of the same sin, the evil spirit which shapes itself in the outward shew. Here the idolatry of self is meant, which did not join creatures with God as objects of worship; but, denying Him in practice or misbelief, became a God to itself[8]. So Habakkuk had said, *this his strength is his God.* His idol was himself.

Because by them their portion is fat, and their meat plenteous (lit. as in E. M., *well-fed*). All the choicest things of the world stood at his command, as Nebuchadnezzar boasted[9], and all the kingdoms of the world and their glory, all the knowledge and wisdom and learning of the world, and the whole world itself, were Satan's lawful prey[10]. "[11] Nebuchadnezzar, as by a hook and meshes and line, swept into his own land both Israel himself and other nations, encompassing them. Satan, as it were, by one line and net, that of sin, enclosed all, and Israel especially, on account of his impiety to Christ. *His food was choice.* For Israel was chosen above the rest, as from a holy root, that of *the fathers*, and having the *law* as a *schoolmaster*, and being called to the knowledge of the one true God. Yet he, having this glory and grace, was taken with the rest. *They* became his prey by error; but Israel, knowing Him Who is by nature God, slaying ungodlily Him Who was by nature His Begotten Son and Who came as Man, were taken in his nets."

17. *Shall they therefore empty their net, and not spare continually to slay the nations?* The prophet, like Isaiah[12], stands at the very last point, before the fury and desire of the enemy was fulfilled. Men, like fish, were gathered together for a prey; he who had taken them was rejoicing and exulting beforehand in his booty; his portion and meat were the choice of the earth; the prophet looks on, as it were, and beholds the net full; there is but one step more; "Shall he empty it? Shall he then devour those whom he has caught? and so cast his emptied net again unceasingly, pitilessly, to slay the nations?" This question he answers in the next chapter; A Deliverer will come.

II. 1. *I will stand* [*I would stand now*], as a servant awaiting his master, *upon my watch* [or *keep*[13]], *and set me* [plant myself firmly] *upon the tower* [lit. *fenced place*, but also one

[1] Is. x. 13. 15.

[2] Ezek. xiv. 4.

[3] The Scythians. Herod. iv. 62. Lucian Jov. Tragæd. 42. p. 275, Arnob. vi. § 11, Mela. ii. 1. Clem. Al. Protr. iv. p. 40, ed. Pott., Amm. Marc. xxvi. 2. The Quadi did the same. Id. xvii. 12. fin. The chance discovery of one of these sacred swords of the Scythian kings made Attila think himself "made prince of the whole world." Jordanes de Get. orig. c. 35, from Priscus, a contemporary.

[4] Justin L. 43. c. 3.

[5] Waitz die Indianer Nord-Americas 1867 p. 127. quoted by Ewald.

[6] See Tertull. Apol. c. 16 and note e. f. g. p. 38. Oxf. Tr.

[7] Joseph. de Bell. Jud. vi. 32.

[8] A heathen poet, wishing to express this irreverence, puts into a warrior's mouth this prayer: "Now may my right hand, to me god, and the weapon which I brandish, be my helper!" Virg. Æn. vii. 648. add Stat. x. 545. iii. 645, sq. So the *Times* said at the beginning of the late war, "The French almost worshiped the mitrailleuse as a goddess." They idolized, it would say, their invention, as if it could do what God alone could.

[9] Dan. iv. 30. comp. 22.

[10] S. Luke iv. 6. S. John xii. 31. Isa. xlix. 24.

[11] S. Cyr.

[12] Isa. xviii. 4, 5.

[13] Ib. xxi. 8. מִשְׁמָר in the same sense Jer. li. 12.

Before CHRIST cir. 626.

† Heb. *fenced place.*
[b] Ps. 85. 8.
|| Or, *in me.*
|| Or, *when I am argued with.*
† Heb. *upon my reproof*, or, *arguing.*

the †tower, [b]and will
watch to see what he will
say ||unto me, and what I
shall answer || †when I am
reproved.
2 And the LORD an-
swered me, and said,
[c]Write the vision, and
make *it* plain upon tables,
that he may run that readeth it.
3 For [d]the vision *is* yet

Before CHRIST cir. 626.

[c] Isai. 8. 1. & 30. 8.
[d] Dan. 10. 14. & 11. 27, 35.

---

straitened and narrowly hemmed in], *and will watch* (it is a title of the prophets [1], as espying, by God's enabling, things beyond human ken); I will *espy out*, to see a long way off, *to see* with the inward eye, *what He will say unto me* [lit. [2] *in me*]; first revealing Himself in the prophets "within to the inner man;" then, through them. *And what I shall answer when I am reproved* [3], or, *upon my complaint*, lit. *upon my reproof or arguing;* which might mean, either that others argued against him, or that he had argued, pleaded in the name of others, and now listened to hear what God would answer *in* him [4], and so he, as taught by God, should answer to his own plea. But he had so pleaded with God, repeatedly, *Why* is this? He has given no hint, that any complained of or reproved *him*.

"[5] By an image from those who, in war and siege, have the ward of the wall distributed to them, he says, *I will stand upon my watch.*" "[6] It was the wont of the Saints, when they wished to learn the things of God, and to receive the knowledge of things to come through His voice in their mind and heart, to raise it on high above distractions and anxieties and all worldly care, holding and keeping it unoccupied and peaceful, rising as to an eminence to look around and contemplate what the God of all knowledge should make clear to them. For He hateth the earth-bound and abject mind, and seeks hearts which can soar aloft, raised above earthly things and temporal desires." The prophet takes his stand, apart from men and the thoughts and cares of this world, on his lonely watch, as Moses on the rock, keeping himself and kept by God, and planted firm, so that nothing should move him, fenced around though straitened in [7], as in a besieged camp committed to his ward, looking out from his lofty place what answer God would give as to times long distant, and what answer he should give first to himself, and to those to whom his office lay, God's people.

2. The answer is, that it is indeed for a long time yet. *Write the vision*, that it may remain for those who come after and not be forgotten, *and make it plain* [8] *upon the tables*, whereon he was wont to write [9]; and that, in large lasting characters, *that he may run that readeth it*, that it may be plain to any, however occupied or in haste. So Isaiah too was bidden to write the four words, *haste-prey-speed-spoil.*

3. *For the vision is yet for an* [*the*] *appointed time.* [10] Not for the present, but to develop itself in the course of time, down to a season which God only knows; as it is subsequently repeated, [11] *for the end is yet for the appointed time;* [12] *for it is for the appointed time of the end;* and is explained, [13] *for the vision is yet for the days;* [14] *for it is for many days;* [15] *the house of Israel say, The vision that he seeth*, is *for many days* and he *prophesieth of the times far off;* yet it should haste toward the end, toward its fulfillment, so that, if it is not at once fulfilled, it should be surely waited for. "[16] It shall certainly be; not in vain hath it been shewn, but as certainly to be. For whatever hath been shewn to come and to be, will come and be."

But at the end it shall speak [17] [or *it breatheth,*

---

[1] Hence צוֹפֶה "watchman," the "prophet" Isa. lii. 8. Jer. vi. 17. Ezek. iii. 17. xxxiii. 7. Kal; of the prophets, Pih. Mic. vii. 4; of looking up to God, Ps. v. 4; with ב Mic. vii. 7.

[2] S. Jer.

[3] The Rabb. Kim. A. E. Rashi, Tanch. Sal. B. Mel., Abarb. take it as the E. V., probably thinking the other to be too bold an expression toward God.

[4] See Num. xii. 6. and on Zech. i. 19.

[5] Theod[s].

[6] S. Cyr.

[7] Symm. Theod. Aq. agree in this sense of narrowness.

[8] Etymologically, באר means "engrave," lit. *dig:* like so many other words, which come to mean "write," as כתב with חטב, חצב Ges.; ספר γράφειν, eingraben, graben, engrave, [Id.] but it only occurs as "make clear, explain," De. xxvii. 8. So Kim. &c.

[9] לוח is a table or tablet, on which Isaiah too was bidden to write what was to last, though in parallelism with a "book." Isa. xxx. 8. "the tablets which boys write on." A. E. comp. Ezek. xvii. 14. Jer. xxx. 2.

[10] Ewald ad loc.; but therewith the theory of a mere human foresight is abandoned.

[11] Dan. xi. 27. *for it is for the appointed time*, ib. 35.

[12] Ib viii. 19.

[13] Ib. x. 1, 14.

[14] Ib. viii. 26.

[15] Ezek. xii. 27.

[16] Theod[s].

[17] The E. V. follows the Rabbins [Kim. Comm., A. E., Tanch., Rashi, Abarb.] so far in rendering יָפֵחַ "speak." Yet in all the cases of both roots, יפח, פוח, except Prov. xii. 17, יָפִיחַ אֱמוּנָה, the root is used not of mere "speaking" but of "breathing out" like ἐμπνέων ἀπειλῆς (Acts xi. 1.) "breathing out threatening." In five cases it occurs in the one idiom, "breatheth out lies," יפיח כזבים, Pr. vi. 19, xiv. 5, 25, xix. 5, 9. In other idioms יפיח בהם יפיח לו, Ps. x. 5, xii. 6, it is still used of puffing at "contemptuously." Else the Kal is used of the cool air of the evening Cant. ii. 17. iv. 6, and Hifil

Before CHRIST cir. 626.

for an appointed time, but at the end it shall speak, and not lie: though it tarry, wait for it; because it will [e] surely come, it will not tarry.

Before CHRIST cir. 626.

e Heb. 10. 37.

hasteth to the end], not simply "to its own fulfillment," but to that *time of the end* which should close the period assigned to it, during which it should continually be putting itself forth, it should come true in part or in shadow, gleams of it should here and there part the clouds, which, until the end, should surround and envelop it. Being God's truth, he speaks of it as an animate living thing, not a dead letter, but running, hasting on its course, and accomplishing on its way that for which it was sent. The will and purpose of God hasteth on, though to man it seemeth to tarry; it can neither be hurried on, nor doth it linger; before *the appointed time* it cometh not; yet it hasteth toward it, and *will not be behindhand* when the time comes. It does *not lie*, either by failing to come, or failing, when come, of any jot or tittle. *Though it tarry* or *linger* [1], continually appearing, giving signs of itself, yet continually delaying its coming, *wait for it; because it will surely come, it will not be behindhand* [2], when the time comes. [3] *He cometh quickly* also, as He saith; because "[4] though the delay of His Coming and of the fulfillment of the vision seem long, yet, in comparison with eternity, it is very short. In His First Coming, He taught why God permitteth these things; in the Second, He shall teach by experience, how good it it is for the good to bear the persecution of the evil; whence S. Peter also has to say, [5] *The Lord is not slack concerning His promise, as some men count slackness.*" The words seem to belong, in the first instance, to the vision itself; but the vision had no other existence or fulfillment than in Him Who was the Object of it, and Who, in it, was foreshadowed to the mind. The coming of the vision was no other than His Coming. The *waiting*, to which he exhorts, expresses the religious act, so often spoken of, [6] of waiting for God, or His counsel, or His promised time. The sense then is wholly the same, when S. Paul uses the words of the Coming of our Lord Himself, [7] *Yet a little while, and He that shall come, will come and will not tarry.* S. Paul, as well as Habakkuk, is speaking of our Lord's Second Coming; S. Paul, of His Coming in Person, Habakkuk, of the effects of that Coming [8]; but both alike of the redressing of all the evil and wrong in the world's history, and the reward of the faithful oppressed. At His First Coming He said, [9] *Now is the judgment of this world; now shall the prince of this world be cast out.* He came to [10] *put down the mighty from their seat, and to exalt the humble and meek;* but much more in the Second, when [11] *He shall come to judge the world with righteousness and the people with His truth,* and to [12] *reward every man according to his works.* At all times He seemeth continually to linger, to give signs of His Coming, yet He cometh not; when the appointed season shall come, He shall be found not to be "later" than His word. Yea, all time shall shrink up into a little moment in the presence of a never-ending ever-present eternity.

"[13] Having named no one expressly, he says, *wait for him,* wait for him although delaying, and halt not in thy hope, but let it be rooted and firm, even if the interval be extended. For the God of all seemeth to suggest to the mind of the Prophet, that He who was foretold would surely come, yet to enjoin on him to wait for Him on account of the interval. He who believeth My word shall possess life, for this is the reward of those who honor God, and a good reward of His benevolence. He who admitteth faith and love to dwell in his heart hath as a requital, un-aging life and forgiveness of sins and sanctification by the Spirit." "[14] He shall live; for [15] *God is not the God of the dead but of the living,* "[16] *Whoso liveth and believeth in Me, shall never die.*"

It will not lie. God vouchsafes to speak of

of "causing to blow," Ib. iv. 16. Else it is only used (metaph.) of blowing up, kindling, (as we say) stirring up a city to strife Pr. xxix. 8, and blowing up the fire of the wrath of God, Ez. xxi. 36. הָתְיַפֵּחַ is used of the deep sigh of agony Jer. iv. 31. and יְפֵחַ חָמָס Ps. xxvii. 12. "breathing forth violence" stands united with "false witness" as in the Prov. If understood then of speaking, it would be "breathing of the end" (ל relating to the subject of the speech, as so often) which would be much the same as, breatheth panting toward the end, (like שׁאף ל, Eccl. i. 5.)

[1] התמהמה (no kal.) seems to be compound of מה, מה, *why, why?* the answer of one procrastinating. It occurs thrice in the Pent., twice in Judges, else only in 2 Sam. xv. 19, in the prophets Is. xxix. 9, and in Ps. cxix. 60. of religious procrastinating. In Arab. are the like forms מהמה and נהנה.

[2] לא תאחר.

[3] Rev. xxii. 7.

[4] from Dion.

[5] 2 S. Pet. iii. 9.

[6] Ps. xxxiii. 20. Isai. viii. 17. xxx. 18. lxiv. 3. Zeph. iii. 8. Dan. xii. 12. Ps. cvi. 13.

[7] Heb. x. 37.

[8] The vivid words, in themselves, rather express a personal agent; what would be figure as to the vision are simple words as to Him Who was foreshown. Whence the Lxx change the gender and interpret the clause of a person, "He who shall come."

[9] S. John xii. 31.

[10] S. Luke i. 52.

[11] Ps. xlvi. 13.

[12] S. Matt. xvi. 27.

[13] S. Cyr.

[14] Alb.

[15] S. Matt. xxii. 32.

[16] S. John xi. 26.

Before CHRIST cir. 626.

4 Behold, his soul *which* is lifted up is not upright in him: but the [f]just shall live by his faith.

Before CHRIST cir. 626.

[f] John 3. 36. Rom. 1. 17. Gal. 3. 11. Heb. 10. 38.

Himself, as we should be ashamed to speak of one whom we love, teaching us that all doubts question His truth. [1] *God is not a man, that He should lie: hath He said and shall He not do it?* [2] *The strength of Israel shall neither lie nor repent.* [3] *God that cannot lie, promised before the world began.* Therefore it follows, *wait for Him,* as Jacob says, [4] *I have waited for Thy salvation, O Lord.*

4. *Behold, his soul which is lifted up* [lit. *swollen* [5]] *is not upright in him.* The construction is probably that of a condition expressed absolutely. *Lo, swollen is it, not upright is his soul in him.* We should say, "His soul, if it be swollen [6], puffed up, is not upright in him." The source of all sin was and is pride. It is especially the sin of all oppressors, of the Chaldee, of Anti-Christs, and shall be of the Anti-Christ. It is the parent of all heresy, and of all corruption and rejection of the Gospel. It stands therefore as the type of all opposed to it. Of it he says, it is in its very inmost core [*in him*] lacking in uprightness. It can have no good in it, because it denies God, and God denies it His grace. And having nothing upright in it, being corrupt in its very inmost being, it cannot stand or abide. God gives it no power to stand. The words stand in contrast with the following, the one speaking of the cause of death, the other of life. The soul, being swollen with pride, shuts out faith, and with it the Presence of God. It is all crooked in its very inner self or being. S. Paul gives the result, [7] *if any man draw back, my soul hath no pleasure in him.* The prophet's words describe the proud man who stands aloof from God, in himself; S. Paul, as he is in the Eyes of God. As that which is swollen in nature cannot be straight, it is clean contrary that the soul should be swollen with pride and yet upright. Its moral life being destroyed in its very inmost heart, it must perish.

"[8] Plato saith, that properly is straight, which being applied to what is straight, touches and is touched everywhere. But God is upright, Whom the upright soul touches and is touched everywhere; but what is not upright is bent away from God. [9] *God is good unto Israel, the upright in heart.* [10] *The upright love thee.* [11] *The way of the just is uprightness, Thou, most Upright, doth weigh the path of the just.*"

But the just shall live by his faith. The accents emphasize the words [12], *The just, by his faith he shall live.* They do not point to an union of the words, *the just by his faith.* Isaiah says that Christ should *justify many by the knowledge of Himself* [13], but the expression, *just by his faith,* does not occur either in the O. or N. T. In fact, to speak of one really righteous [14] as being "righteous by his faith" would imply that men could be righteous in some other way. *Without faith,* S. Paul says at the commencement of his Old Testament pictures of giant faith, [15] *it is impossible to please God.* Faith, in the creature which does not yet see God, has one and the same principle, a trustful relying belief in its Creator. This was the characteristic of Abraham their father, unshaken, unswerving, belief in God Who called him, whether in leaving his own land and going whither he knew not, for an end which he was never to see; or in believing the promise of the son through whom that Seed was to be, in Whom all the nations of the world should be blessed; or in the crowning act of offering that son to God, knowing that he should receive him back, even from the dead. In all, it was one and the same principle. [16] *His belief was counted to him for righteousness,* though the immediate instance of that faith was not directly spiritual. In this was the good and bad of Israel. [17] *The people believed.* [18] *They believed the Lord and His servant Moses.* [19] *Then believed they His word, they sang His praise.* This contrariwise was their blame. [20] *In this ye did not believe the Lord.* [21] *Ye rebelled against the commandment of the Lord your God, and believed Him not, nor hearkened to His voice.* [22] *They forgat God their Saviour; they despised the pleasant land, they believed not His word.* And God asks, [23] *How long will it be, ere this people believe Me, for all the signs which I have shown among them?* [24] *Anger came upon Israel, because they believed not in God, and in His salvation trusted not.* [25] *For all this they sinned still, and believed not His wondrous works.* Even of Moses and Aaron God assigns this as the ground, why they should not bring His people into the land which He gave them, [26] *Because ye believed Me not, to sanctify Me in*

[1] Nu. xxiii. 19. [2] 1 Sam. xv. 29.
[3] Tit. i. 2. [4] Gen. xlix. 18.
[5] עֻפְּלָה See on Micah iv. 8. p. 62, note 8.
[6] In the Lxx ἐὰν ὑποστείληται. הנה is used thus absolutely, the condition being implied, Deut. xiii. 15, 16. In Ex. viii. 22. the future is used absolutely with הן.

[7] Heb. x. 39. [8] Alb. [9] Ps. lxxiii. 1.
[10] Cant. i. 4. [11] Is. xxvi. 7. [12] See Delitzsch.
[13] בדעתו יצדיק Is. liii. 11. [14] As צדיק always is.
[15] Heb. xi. 6. [16] Gen. xv. 6. [17] Ex. iv. 31.
[18] Ib. xiv. 31. [19] Ps. cvi. 12. [20] Deut. i. 32.
[21] Ib. ix. 23. [22] Ps. cvi. 21, 24. [23] Num. xiv. 11.
[24] Ps. lxxviii. 21, 22. [25] Ib. 32. [26] Num. xx. 20.

the eyes of the children of Israel (at Meribah). This was the watchword of Jehoshaphat's victory, [1] *Believe in the Lord your God and ye shall be established; believe His prophets, so shall ye prosper.* This continued to be one central saying of Isaiah. It was his own commission to his people; [2] *Go and say to this people; hear ye on, and understand not; see ye on and perceive not.* In sight of the rejection of faith, he spake prominently of the loss upon unbelief; [3] *If ye will not believe, surely ye shall not be established;* and, [4] *Who hath believed our report?* he premises as the attitude of his people toward Him, the Centre of all faith, Jesus. Yet still, as to the blessings of faith, having spoken of Him, [5] *Thus saith the Lord God, Behold, I lay in Zion for a foundation, a stone, a tried stone, a precious cornerstone,* he subjoins, *he that believeth in Him shall not make haste.*

So it had been the key-note of Habakkuk to his people, *Ye will not believe when it is declared unto you.* Here he is bid to declare contrariwise the blessing on belief. *The just shall live by his faith.* The faith, then, of which Habakkuk speaks, is faith, in itself, but a real, true confiding faith. It is the one relation of the creature to the Creator, unshaken trust. The faith may vary in character, according as God reveals more or less of Himself, but itself is one, a loving trust in Him, just as He reveals Himself. "[6] By this faith in God, each righteous person begins to live piously, righteously, holily, peacefully and divinely, and advanceth therein, since in every tribulation and misery, by this faith and hope in God he sustains, strengthens, and increases this life of the soul. He says then, *the just lives by faith,* i. e., the unbelieving and unrighteous displeases God, and consequently will not live by the true, right, peaceful and happy life of grace, present righteousness, and future glory, because God is displeased with him, and *he* places his hopes and fears, not in God, but in men and man's help and in created things. But the righteous who believeth in God shall live a right, sweet, quiet, happy, holy, untroubled life, because, fixed by faith and hope in God Who is the true Life, and in God's promises, he is dear to God, and the object of His care.

" This sentence, *the just shall live by faith,* is universal, belonging at once to Jews and Christians, to sinners who are *first* being justified, as also to those who are already justified. For the spiritual life of each of these begins, is maintained and grows through faith. When then it is said, *the just shall live by his faith,* this word, *his,* marks the cause, which both begins and preserves life. The just, believing and hoping in God, begins to live spiritually, to have a soul right within him, whereby he pleases God; and again, advancing and making progress in this his faith and hope in God, therewith advances and makes progress in the spiritual life, in rightness and righteousness of soul, in the grace and friendship of God, so as more and more to please God."

Most even of the Jewish interpreters have seen this to be the literal meaning of the words. It stands in contrast with, illustrates and is illustrated by the first words, *his soul is swollen, is not upright in him.* Pride and independence of God are the centre of the want of rightness; a steadfast cleaving to God, whereby *the heart,* as Abraham's, *was stayed on God,* is the centre and cause of the life of the righteous. But since this stayedness of faith is in everything the source of the life of the righteous, then the pride, which issues in want of rightness of the inmost soul, must be a state of death. Pride estranges the soul from God, makes it self-sufficing, that it should not need God, so that he who is proud cannot come to God, to be by Him made righteous. So contrariwise, since by his faith doth the righteous live, this must be equally true whether he be just made righteous from unrighteous, or whether that righteousness is growing, maturing, being perfected in him.

This life begins in grace, lives on in glory. It is begun, in that God freely justifies the ungodly, accounting and making him righteous for and through the Blood of Christ; it is continued in faith which worketh by love; it is perfected, when faith and hope are swallowed up in love, beholding God. In the Epistles to the Romans [7] and the Galatians [8] St. Paul applies these words to the first beginning of life, when they who had before been dead in sin, began to live by faith in Christ Jesus Who gave them life and made them righteous. And in this sense he is called "just," although before he comes to the Faith he is unjust and unrighteous, being unjustified. For St. Paul uses the word not of what he was before the faith, but what he is, when he lives by faith. Before, not having faith, he had neither righteousness nor life; having faith, he at once has both; he is at once *just* and *lives by his faith.* These are inseparable. The faith by which he lives, is a living faith, [9] *faith which worketh by love.* In the Epistle to the Hebrews [10], St. Paul is speaking of *their* endurance in the faith, once received, whose faith is not shaken by the trial of their patience. They who look on beyond things present, and fix their minds steadfastly on the Coming of Christ, will not suffer shipwreck of their faith, through any troubles of this time. Faith is the founda-

[1] 2 Chron. xx. 20. [2] Is. vi. 9. [3] Ib. vii. 9. [4] Ib. liii. 1. [5] Ib. xxviii. 16.

[6] Lap. in Rom. i. 17. [7] Rom. i. 17. [8] Gal. iii. 11. [9] Ib. v. 6. [10] Heb. x. 38.

Before CHRIST cir. 626.

‖ Or, *How much more.*

g Prov. 27. 20. & 30. 16.

5 ¶ ‖ Yea also, because he transgresseth by wine, *he is* a proud man, neither keepeth at home, who enlargeth his desire g as hell, and *is* as death, and cannot be satisfied, but gathereth unto him all nations, and heapeth unto him all people:

tion of all good, the beginning of the spiritual building, whereby it rests on The Foundation, Christ. *Without faith it is impossible to please God*, and so the *proud* cannot please Him. Through it, is union with Christ and thereby a divine life in the soul, even a life[1] *through faith in the Son of God*, holy, peaceful, self-possessed[2], enduring to the end, being [3] *kept by the power of God through faith unto salvation ready to be revealed in the last time.*

5. This general rule the Prophet goes on to apply in words which belong in part to all oppressors and in the first instance to the Chaldæan, in part yet more fully to the end and to Anti-Christ. *Yea also, because he transgresseth by wine* [or better, *Yea, how much more, since wine is a deceiver*[4]], as Solomon says[5], *Wine is a mocker, strong drink is raging, and whosoever erreth thereby shall not be wise*, and, [6] *In the end it biteth like a serpent and pierceth like an adder;* and Hosea, [7] *Whoredom and wine and new wine take away the heart.* As wine at first gladdens, then deprives of all reason, and lays a man open to any deceit, so also pride. And whereas all pride deceives, how much more[8], when men are either heated and excited by the abuse of God's natural gifts, or drunken with prosperity and hurried away, as conquerors are, to all excess of cruelty or lust to fulfill their own will, and neglect the laws of God and man. Literal drunkenness was a sin of the Babylonians under the Persian rule, so that even a heathen says of Babylon, "[9] Nothing can be more corrupt than the manners of that city, and more provided with all to rouse and entice immoderate pleasures;" and "the Babylonians give themselves wholly to wine, and the things which follow upon drunkenness." It was when flushed [10] with wine, that Belshazzar, *with his princes his wives and his concubines*, desecrated the sacred vessels, insulted God in honor of his idols, and in the night of his excess "was slain." Pride blinded, deceived, destroyed him. It was the general drunkenness of the inhabitants, at that same feast, which enabled Cyrus, with a handful of men, to penetrate, by means of its river, the city which, with its provisions for many years [11] and its impregnable walls, mocked at his siege. He calculated beforehand on its feast[12] and the consequent dissolution of its inhabitants; but for this, in the language of the heathen historian, he would have been caught "[13] as in a trap," his soldiery drowned.

He is a proud man[14], *neither keepeth at home.* It is difficult to limit the force of the rare Hebrew word rendered, [15] *keep at home;* for one may cease to dwell or abide at home either with his will or without it; and, as in the case of invaders, the one may be the result of the other. He who would take away the home of others becomes, by God's Providence, himself homeless. The context implies that the primary meaning is the restlessness of ambition; which abides not at home, for his whole pleasure is to go forth to destroy. Yet there sounds, as it were, an undertone, "he would not abide in his home, and he shall not." We could scarcely avoid the further thought, could we translate by a

[1] Gal. ii. 20. [2] S. Luke xxi. 19. [3] 1 S. Pet. i. 5.

[4] Jon. agrees "as one erring through wine." Kim. A. E. Rashi, Abarb. Tanch. (in one explanation) take it personally; Kim. supplying שתה "drinker of wine;" A. E. and Tanch. regarding יין as איש יין, quoting מרי Ez. ii. 8. and תפלה Ps. cix. 4. which they explain in the same way.

[5] Prov. xx. 1. [6] Ib. xxiii. 32. [7] Hosea iv. 11.

[8] אף כי as in 1 Sam. xxiii. 3. Ezek. xxiii. 40. It adds to the previous sentence; whether we should express it by *how much more*, if an affirmative had preceded; or *how much less*, if a negative. The *more* or *less* lies in the relation of the sentences, not in the אף כי.

[9] Q. Curt. v. 1. [10] See Daniel the Prophet, p. 450.

[11] Xen. Cyrop. vii. 4, 5, 6.

[12] "When then he [Cyrus] heard that there was a feast in Babylon, in which all the Babylonians drink and revel all the night, on this, &c." Ib. 11, on the drunkenness see Ib. 9. 10.

[13] Herod. i. 19.

[14] יהיר, in the only other-place, Pr. xxi. 24, stands in connection with זֵד and לֵץ; in Chald. it is "arrogant," (see instances in Levy Chald. Wört.) as in Nasor. (ap. Ges). The Arab. only supplies יְהַר "perseverance in litigation:" the meaning "prominence, swelling" is assumed only. The Arab. תַּיהוּר (in Ges. Hitz.) is from הָאַר (med. ו) and signifies "a sand-heap," not as heaped up, but as sinking asunder, "corruens," (the central meaning of הָאַר.)

[15] נוה, נאה, seems to be of the same root as *ναίω*, whence נְוַת בַּיִת "dweller in the house," Ps. lxviii. 13; נָוֶה, נָוָה, abode: נָוָית Pr. N. probably the same, and נְאוֹת also. The derived sense "becoming" (lit. "sit well on" "bene sedet alicui," Ges.) exists in נַאֲוָה Ps. xciii. 5; "beautiful," Cant. i. 10. Is. lii. 7; and in נָוָה Jer. vi. 2. It is the basis of Hif. אַנְוֵהוּ "will praise Him." Either gives a good sense. The Vulg. takes the derived sense "decorabitur."

Before CHRIST cir. 626.

6 Shall not all these [h]take up a parable against him, and a taunting proverb against him, and say, || Woe to him that increaseth *that which is* not his!

h Mic. 2. 4.

|| Or, *Ho, he.*

Before CHRIST cir. 626.

word which does not determine the sense, "he will not home," "he will not continue at home." The words have seemed to different minds to mean either; as they may[1]. Such fullness of meaning is the contrary of the ambiguity of Heathen oracles; they are not alternative meanings, which might be justified in either case, but cumulative, the one on the other. The ambitious part with present rest for future loss. Nebuchadnezzar lost his kingdom and his reason through pride, received them back when he humbled himself; Belshazzar, being proud and impenitent, lost both his kingdom and life.

Who enlargeth his desire, lit. *his soul.* The soul becomes like what it loves. The ambitious man is, as we say, "all ambition;" the greedy man, "all appetite;" the cruel man, "all savagery;" the vain-glorious, "all vainglory." The ruling passion absorbs the whole being. It is his end, the one object of his thoughts, hopes, fears. So, as we speak of "largeness of heart," which can embrace in its affections all varieties of human interests, whatever affects man, and "largeness of mind" uncramped by narrowing prejudices, the Prophet speaks of this "ambitious man widening his soul," or, as we should speak, "appetite," so that the whole world is not too large for him to long to grasp or to devour. So the Psalmist prays not to be delivered into the murderous *desire* of his enemies[2], (lit. *their soul,*) and Isaiah, with a metaphor almost too bold for our language, [3] *Hell hath enlarged her soul, and opened her mouth beyond measure.* It devours, as it were, first in its cravings, then in act.

As hell, which is insatiable[4]. He saith, *enlargeth;* for as hell and the grave are year by year fuller, yet there is no end, the desire *enlargeth* and becometh wider, the more is given to it to satisfy it. *And* [*he*[5]] *is* [*himself*] *as death,* sparing none. Our poetry would speak of a destroyer as being "like the angel of death;" his presence, as the presence of death itself. Where he is, there is death. He is as terrible and as destroying as the death which follows him. *And cannot be satisfied.* Even human proverbs say, "[6] The love of money groweth as much as the money itself groweth." "The avaricious is ever needy." [7] *He that loveth silver shall not be satisfied with silver.* For these fleeting things cannot satisfy the undying soul. It must hunger still; for it has not found what will allay its cravings[8].

But gathereth, lit. *And hath gathered*—He describes it, for the rapidity with which he completes what he longs for, as though it were already done, —*unto him all nations, and heapeth unto him all people.* One is still the subject of the prophecy, rising up at successive times, fulfilling it and passing away, Nebuchadnezzar, Alexander, Attila, Timur, Genghizchan, Hunneric, scourges of God, all deceived by pride, all sweeping the earth, all in their ambition and wickedness the unknowing agents and images of the evil One, who seeks to bring the whole world under his rule. But shall it prosper?

6. *Shall not all these*[9] *take up a parable against him, and a taunting proverb against him?* Nebuchadnezzar gathered [10] *all people, nations, and languages,* to *worship the golden image which he had set up.* The second Babylon, heathen Rome, sought to blot out the very Christian Name; but mightier were the three children than the King of Babylon; mightier, virgins, martyrs, and children than Nero or Decius. These shall rejoice over Babylon, that [11] *God hath avenged them on her.*

Woe to him that increaseth that which is not his! Truly wealth ill-gotten by fraud or oppression, *is not his,* who winneth it, before he had it, nor when he hath it, but a *woe.* It is *not his;* the *woe* is his. *Woe unto him.* He shall have no joy in what he gaineth, and what he hath he shall lose. *How long?* What is the measure of thine impiety and greediness and cruelty? Yet if these are like hell, without measure, there remains another *How long?* How long will the forbearance of God endure thee, which thou art daily exhausting?

This is then the end of all. The conqueror sweeps to him *all nations* and gathereth to him *all peoples.* To what end? As one vast choir in one terrible varied chant of all those thousand thousand voices, to sing a dirge over him of the judgments of God which his ill-doings to them should bring upon him, a

[1] A. E. Abarb. Tanch. Rashi, following Jon. take it of his privation of home. Kim. either of the shortness of Nebuchadnezzar's empire, or his own being driven forth with the wild animals, Dan. iv. 31–33. Del. illustrates the sense of forced "non-abiding" by בל ילין Ps. xlix. 13, "abideth not;" לא שכן ארץ Pr. x. 30, "shall not inhabit the earth;" שכן || נותר Pr. ii. 21.

[2] Ps. xxvii. 12. Comp. Ps. xli. 3 [2 Eng.] Ezek. xxvi. 27. [3] Is. v. 14. [4] Prov. xxx. 15.

[5] והוא. It is not an unmeaning change as though it belonged only to the simplicity of Hebrew construction; but emphatic, "and *he.*"

[6] Juv. Sat. xiv. 139. [7] Eccl. v. 10.

[8] S. Aug. Conf. and n. a. iv. 8.

[9] אלה כלם v. 6, referring to the כל העמים, כל הגוים v. 5. [10] Dan. iii. 4, 5. [11] Rev. xviii. 20.

Before CHRIST cir. 626.

how long? and to him that ladèth himself with thick clay!

7 Shall they not rise up suddenly that shall bite thee, and awake that shall vex thee, and thou shalt be for booties unto them?

fivefold Woe, woe, woe, woe, woe! Woe for its rapacity! Woe for its covetousness! Woe for its oppression! Woe for its insolence to the conquered! Woe to it in its rebellion against God! It is a more measured rhythm than any besides in Holy Scripture; each of the fivefold woes comprised in three verses, four of them closing with the ground, *because, for*. The opening words carry the mind back to the fuller picture of Isaiah. But Isaiah sees Babylon as already overthrown; Habakkuk pronounces the words upon it, not by name, but as certainly to come, upon it and every like enemy of God's kingdom. With each such fall, unto the end of all things, the glory of God is increased and made known. Having, for their own ends, been unconscious and even unwilling promoters of God's end, they, when they had accomplished it, are themselves flung away. The pride of human ambition, when successful, boasts "woe to the conquered." Since *whom the Lord loveth He chasteneth*, the ungodly saying of the heathen is reversed, and it stands, "Man sympathizes with the conquering side, God with the conquered." It is a terrible thought that men should have been the instruments of God, that they should, through ambition or other ends short of God, have promoted His ends which they thought not of, and then should be *weighed in the balance and found wanting*, and themselves be flung away.

"[1] Gentiles also departed from their worship under Satan, and having deserted him who aforetime called them, ran unto Christ. For Satan gathered what was *not his;* but Christ received what was His. For, as God, He is Lord of all."

And to him that ladeth himself with thick clay[2]. It is the character of these proverbs to say much in few words, sometimes in one, and more than appears. So the word translated *thick-clay*, as if it were two words, in another way means in an intensive sense, "a strong deep pledge." At best gold and silver are, as they have been called, red and white earth. "[3] What are gold and silver but red and white earth, which the error of man alone maketh, or accounteth precious? What are gems, but stones of the earth? What silk, but webs of worms?" These he "maketh heavy upon" or "against himself" [so the words strictly mean]. "For *he* weigheth himself down with thick clay, who, by avarice multiplying earthly things, hems himself in by the oppressiveness of his own sin, imprisons and, as it were, buries the soul, and heaps up sin as he heaps up wealth." With toil they gather what is not worthless only, but is a burden upon the soul, weighing it down that it should not rise Heavenwards, but should be bowed down to Hell. And so in that other sense while, as a hard usurer, he heaps up the *pledges* of those whom he oppresses and impoverishes, and seems to increase his wealth, he does in truth *increase against himself a strong pledge*, whereby not others are debtors to him, but he is a debtor to Almighty God Who careth for the oppressed. [4] *He that gathereth riches and not by right, shall leave them in the midst of his days and at his end shall be a fool.*

7. *Shall not they rise up suddenly that shall bite thee, and awake that shall vex thee?* The destruction of the wicked is ever sudden at last. Such was the flood[5], the destruction of Sodom, of Pharaoh, of the enemies of God's people through the Judges, of Sennacherib, Nineveh, Babylon by the Medes and Persians. Such shall the end be[6]. As he by his oppressions had *pierced* others (it is the word used of the oppression of usury[7]), so

[1] S. Cyr.

[2] The word עבטיט naturally suggests the division into עב and טיט which has been adopted by Syr. "cloud of mud," and S. Jer. doubtless from his Hebrew Instructor "densum lutum," as A. E., J. and D. Kimchi, Rashi, Abarb., R. Tanchum; Poc. Arab. Vers. which is not Saadiah's (Hunt. 206.) R. Samuel Hannagid, Joshua, Japhet, (quoted by A. E.) Sal. B. Mel., explaining it "abundance of clay." Kimchi (Shorashim) admits the possibility of its being derived from עבט sub v., but himself says it is a compound word. Saadiah Ben Denan Lex. Heb.-Arab. [Bodl. Or. 612.] alone positively derives it from עבט. The objection that there are no compound appellatives in Hebrew is contrary to the evidence of such words, as צַלְמָוֶת, בלימה, בליעל, and amid the predominance of compound words, as Proper Names, it would be monstrous to assume that a Prophet could not have compounded a word. On the other hand, the forms סגריר, כמריר, חכליל, שפריר, are remarkable analogies in favor of its being a single word. It was probably formed to suggest both thoughts, as it has.

[3] S. Bern. Serm. 4. in Adv. [4] Jer. xvii. 11.

[5] S. Luke xvii. 26. 27.

[6] S. Matt. xxiv. 43. 44. xxv. 13. S. Luke xvii. 26–30. xxi. 34. 35. 1 Thess. v. 3. 2 Pet. iii. 10. Rev. xvi. 15.

[7] כל דבר אשר יִשָּׁךְ lit. "everything which shall bite," De. xxiii. 20. הִשִּׁיךְ (De. xxiii. 20. 21 bis) is properly a denom. from נֶשֶׁךְ, explained to be "what bites the giver and takes something of his from him." Mezia 60. b. in Del. The הַמַּרְבָּה, v. 6. suggested תרבית, and this, favored by the conception

Before CHRIST cir. 626.

8 [l] Because thou hast spoiled many nations, all the remnant of the people shall spoil thee; [k] because of men's †blood, and *for* the violence of the land, of the city, and of all that dwell therein.

l Isai. 33. 1.
k ver. 17.
† Heb. *bloods.*

should it be done to him. "[1] The Medes and Persians who were before subject to the Babylonian empire, and whose kings were subject to Nebuchadnezzar and his successors, rose up and awaked, i. e., stirred themselves up in the days of Belshazzar to rebel against the successors of Nebuchadnezzar which sat on his throne, like a man who awaketh from sleep." The words *awake, arise,* are used also of the resurrection, when the worm of the wicked gnaweth and dieth not[2].

And thou shalt be for booties unto them? The common phrase is modified to explain the manifoldness of the plunder[3] which he should yield. So Jeremiah, [4] *Chaldœa shall be a spoil; all that spoil her shall be satisfied, saith the Lord.* "[5] We may hear Him Who saith, [6] *How can one enter into a strong man's house, and spoil his goods, except he first bind the strong man? and then he will spoil his house.* For, as soon as He was born of the holy Virgin, He began to *spoil his goods.* For the Magi came from the East—and worshiped Him and honored Him with gifts and became a first-fruits of the Church of the Gentiles. And being vessels of Satan, and the most honored of all his members, they hastened to Christ."

8. *Because,* [or *For*]. The Prophet assigns the reason of the *woes* he had just pronounced. *Thou*[7] [emph.], *thou hast spoiled many nations, all the remnant of the people shall spoil thee.* So Isaiah, [8] *When thou shalt cease to spoil, thou shalt be spoiled; when thou shalt make an end to deal treacherously, they shall deal treacherously with thee.* Boundless as his conquests were, each remaining people, tribe, or family shall be his foe. "[9] Having subdued very many, thou shalt be destroyed by few, and they who long endured thy tyranny, arising as from sleep, shall compass thy destruction; and thou shalt pay the penalty of thy countless slaughters and thy great ungodliness and thy lawless violence to cities which thou madest desolate of inhabitants." Nothing was too great or too little to escape this violence.

All the remnant. "[9] As thou, invading, didst take away the things of others, in like way shall what appertaineth to thee be taken away by those who are left for vengeance." Jeremiah foretold of Elam *in the beginning of the reign of Zedekiah*[10], (in expansion of the prophecy in the reign of Jehoiakim[11]); *Thus saith the Lord of hosts, Behold, I will break the bow of Elam, the chief of their might. And upon Elam I will bring the four winds from the four quarters of the heavens, and will scatter them toward all these winds, and there shall be no nation whither the outcasts of Elam shall not come. For I will cause Elam to be dismayed before her enemies; but it shall come to pass in the latter days, that I will bring again the captivity of Elam, saith the Lord.* Elam is also counted by Ezekiel[12] among those who, together with Pharaoh, should be brought down to the grave, with *Asshur, Meshech, Tubal, Edom and all the Zidonians,* by the king of Babylon. They were then all which remained[13] of the nations which he had conquered, who should be gathered against his house. *Because of men's blood and of the violence of* i. e. *to the land,* as *the violence of,* i. e. *to*[14], *Lebanon,* and *men's blood* is their blood which was shed. *To land, city, and all dwellers therein. Land* or *earth, city,* are left purposely undefined, so that while that in which the offence culminated should be, by the singular, specially suggested, *the violence to* Judah and Jerusalem, the cruelty condemned should not be limited to these. *The violence* was dealt out to the whole *land* or *earth,* and in it, to cities, and in each, one by one, to all its inhabitants. Babylon is called, [15] *the hammer of the whole earth;* [16] *a golden cup in the Lord's hand, that made all the earth drunken;* [17] *a destroying mountain, which destroyeth the whole earth; the whole earth is at*

of the Chaldæans as a pitiless creditor, concentrated in עבטיט, suggested נֹשֶׁךְ, (which is often united with תרבית); and this suggested the remarkable designation of those who were to execute the Divine retribution on the Chaldæans by the word, נשכים.

1 Abarb. quoted by Del.

2 See Isaiah xiv. 11. lxvi. 24.

3 היית למשסות. Elsewhere sing. למשסה.

4 Jer. l. 10. 5 See S. Cyr. 6 S. Matt. xii. 29.

7 כי אתה.

8 Isaiah xxxiii. 1.

9 Theod.

10 Jer. xlix. 34–39.

11 The prophecies against the heathen nations Jer. xlvi–li. were in the same order in the main as in Jer. xxv. 19–26, beginning with Egypt and ending in Babylon, and containing between these, the Philistines (with Tyre and Zidon incidentally), Moab, Ammon, Edom, Kedar, Hazor, Elam; Elam being in both cases the last before Babylon itself.

12 Ezek. xxxii. 17–32.

13 As יתר הגוים האלה Josh. xxiii. 12, יתר הפלטה Ex. x. 5; את יתר העם, את יתר ההמון 2 Kings xxv. 11; את יתר העם הנשארים Jer. xxxix. 9.

14 Hab. ii. 17, חמס is united with the gen. of the object, Gen. xvi. 5. Jud. ix. 24. Jo. iv. 19. Ob. 10. Jer. li. 35; with that of the subject, Ps. vii. 17, lviii. 3, Ezek. xii. 19. [all.]

15 Jer. l. 23. 16 Ib. li. 7. 17 Ib. 25.

Before CHRIST cir. 626.

9 ¶ Woe to him that
[l] || coveteth an evil covet-
ousness to his house, that
he may [m] set his nest on
high, that he may be de-
livered from the † power
of evil!
10 Thou hast consulted
shame to thy house by cutting off many people, and

[l] Jer. 22. 13.
|| Or, *gaineth an evil gain.*
[m] Jer. 49. 16. Obad. 4.
† Heb. *palm of the hand.*

Before CHRIST cir. 626.

rest and is quiet[1], after Babylon, *which made it to tremble*[2], is overthrown.

So Satan had by violence and deceit subdued the whole earth, yet Christ made him a spoil to those whom he had spoiled, and the strong man was bound and his goods spoiled and himself trampled underfoot. Yet here as throughout the prophets, it is a "remnant" only which is saved. "[3] Satan too was spoiled by the remnant of the people, i.e. by those justified by Christ and sanctified in the Spirit. For the remnant of Israel was saved."

9. *Woe to him that coveteth an evil covetousness to his house* [or, with accents, *that coveteth covetousness* or *unjust gain, an evil to his house.*] What man coveteth seems gain, but is *evil to his house* after him, destroying both himself and his whole family or race with him[4]. *That he may set his nest on high,* as an eagle, to which he had likened the Chaldee[5]. A heathen called "strongholds, the nests of tyrants." The nest was placed "on high" which means also "heaven," as it is said, [6] *though thou set thy nest among the stars;* and the tower of Babel was to [7] *reach unto heaven;* and the Anti-Christ, whose symbol the King of Babylon is, says, [8] *I will exalt my throne above the stars of God.* Babylon lying in a large plain, on the sides of the Euphrates, the image of its eagle's-nest on high must be taken,. not from any natural eminence, but wholly from the works of man. Its walls, and its hanging gardens were among "the seven wonders of the world." Eye witnesses speak of its walls, encompassing at the least 100 square miles[9], "[10] and as large as the land-graviat of Hesse Homberg;" those walls, 335, or 330 feet high, and 85 feet broad[11]; a fortified palace, near 7 miles in circumference; gardens, 400 Greek feet square, supporting at an artificial height arch upon arch, of "at least 75 feet," forest trees; a temple to its god, said to have been at least 600 feet high. Had we, creatures of a day, no one above us, Nebuchadnezzar's boast had been true[12], *Is not this great Babylon that I have builded for the house of the Kingdom by the might of my power and for the honor of my majesty?* He had built an *eagle's nest,* which no human arm could reach, encircled by walls which laughed its invaders to scorn, which no then skill could scale or shatter or mine. Even as one sees in a picture the vast mounds which yet remain[13], one can hardly imagine that they were, brick upon brick, wholly the work of man.

To be delivered from the hand [*grasp*] *of evil;* that it should not be able to reach him. *Evil* is spoken of as a living power[14], which would seize him, whose grasp he would defy. It was indeed a living power, since it was the Will of Almighty God, Whose servant and instrument Cyrus was, to chasten Babylon, when its sins were full. Such was the counsel, what the result? The *evil* covetousness which he wrought, brought on him the *evil,* from which, in that nest built by the hard toil of his captives, he thought to deliver himself.

10. *Thou hast consulted shame to thy house, the cutting off many people, and sinning against thy soul.* The wicked, whether out of passion or with his whole mind and deliberate choice and will, takes that *counsel,* which certainly brings *shame* to himself and his *house,* according to the law of God, whereby He [15] *visits the iniquities of the fathers upon the children unto the third and fourth generation of them that hate Him,* i.e. until by righteousness and restitution the curse is cut off. [16] *He that is greedy of gain troubleth his own house.* So Jeremiah says, [17] *Thus saith the Lord, Is it Me they are vexing? is it not themselves, for* [18] *the confusion of their faces?* i.e. with that end and object. Holy Scripture overlooks the means, and places us at the end of all. Whatever the wicked had in view, to satisfy ambition,

[1] Is. xiv. 7. [2] Ib. 16. [3] S. Cyr.

[4] בצע בצע elsewhere stand, without an epithet, it being itself evil, Prov. i. 19. xv. 27. Jer. vi. 13. viii. 10. and Ezek. xxii. 27. [all]

[5] i. 8. Comp. Jer. xx. 16. [6] Obad 4.

[7] Gen. xi. 4. [8] Is. xiv. 13.

[9] Herodotus, giving probably the extent of the outer wall, makes it a square 120 stades each way, and so 56 miles in circuit [i. 178]. Ctesias, giving probably the dimensions of the inner-wall, makes the circumference 360 stades, 41–42 miles, and so enclosing 100 square miles [Diod. Sic. ii. 7. sqq.].

[10] Rawl. 5 Empires iii. 340.

[11] It is remarkable that the larger dimensions are the oldest, given by eye-witnesses. Rawlinson has pointed out one case in which the later reduced the dimensions artificially, "softening down the cubits of Herodotus into feet." 5 Empires iii. 348 note. See the whole vivid description, Ib. pp. 338–361.

[12] Dan. iv. 30.

[13] See in Smith's Bible Dict. i. 152. Rawl. 5 Empires iii. 353.

[14] מִכַּף occurs in 19 other places with verbs signifying deliverance, [see Fürst Conc. p. 568.] and in all of living agents. [15] Ex. xx. 5.

[16] Prov. xv. 27. [17] Jer. vii. 19.

[18] למען בשֶׁת.

Before CHRIST cir. 626.

hast sinned *against* thy soul.

11 For the stone shall cry out of the wall, and the || beam out of the timber shall || answer it.

12 ¶ Woe to him that buildeth a town with

Before CHRIST cir. 626.

|| Or, *piece*, or, *fastening*.
|| Or, *witness against it*.

avarice, passion, love of pleasure, or the rest of man's immediate ends, all he was doing was leading on to a further end, shame and death. He was bringing about, not only these short-lived, but the lasting ends beyond, and these far more than the others, since that is the real end of a thing which abides, in which it at last ends. He consulted to cut off many people and was thereby (though he knew it not) by one and the same act, *guilty of* and *forfeiting his own soul*[1].

11. *For the stone shall cry out of the wall, and the beam out of the timber shall answer it.* All things have a voice, in that they are[2]. God's works speak that, for which He made them. [3] *The heavens declare the glory of God.* [4] *The valleys are clad with corn, they laugh, yea, they sing;* their very look speaks gladness. "[5] For the creation itself proclaims the glory of the Maker, in that it is admired as well made. Wherefore there are voices in things, although there are not words." Man's works speak of that in *him*, out of which and for which *he* made them. Works of mercy go up for a memorial before God, and plead there; great works, wrought amid wrong and cruelty and for man's ambition and pride, have a voice too, and *cry out* to God, calling down His vengeance on the oppressor. Here *the stones of the wall*, whereby the building is raised, and *the beam*, the tye-beam, *out of the timber*-work[6] wherewith it is finished, and which, as it were, crowns the work, join, as in a chorus, *answering* one another, and in a deep solemn wailing, before God and the whole world, together chant "Woe, Woe." Did not the blood and groans of men cry out to God, speechless things have a voice to appeal to Him[7]. Against Belshazzar the wall had, to the letter, words to speak.

Each three verses forming one stanza, as it were, of the dirge, the following words are probably not directly connected with the former, as if the woe, which follows, were, so to speak, the chant of these inanimate witnesses against the Chaldæans; yet they stand connected with it. The dirge began with woe on the wrongful accumulation of wealth from the conquered and oppressed people: it continues with the selfish use of the wealth so won.

12. *Woe to him that buildeth a town with blood, and establisheth a city by iniquity!* Nebuchadnezzar "[8] encircled the inner city with three walls and the outer city also with three, all of burnt brick. And having fortified the city with wondrous works, and adorned the gates like temples, he built another palace near the palace of his fathers, surpassing it in height and its great magnificence." He seemed to strengthen the city, and to stablish it by outward defences. But it was built through cruelty to conquered nations, and especially God's people, and by oppression, against His holy Will. So there was an inward rottenness and decay in what seemed strong and majestic, and which imposed on the outward eye; it would not stand, but fell. Babylon, which had stood since the flood, being enlarged contrary to the eternal laws of God, fell in the reign of his son. Such is all empire and greatness, raised on the neglect of God's laws, by unlawful conquests, and by the toil and sweat and hard service of the poor. Its aggrandizement and seeming strength is its fall. Daniel's exhortation to Nebuchadnezzar, [9] *Redeem thy sins by righteousness, and thine iniquities by shewing mercy on the poor*, implies that oppressiveness had been one of his chief sins.

[1] חטא נפשו Prov. xx. 2. comp. חמס נפשו Ib. viii. 36. The contemporaneousness of the act is expressed by the participle; the pronoun is omitted as in i. 5.

[2] The Arabs have an expression for it, לסאן אלחאל, lit. "The tongue of the situation."

[3] Ps. xix. 1. [4] Ib. lxv. 13. [5] S. Cyr.

[6] So the word is best understood, since the "beam" bears the same relation to the "woodwork" as the "stone" to the "wall," i. e. is a part of it, כפס in Ch. signifying "to bind," like כפת Dan. iii. 20, 21, 23, 24. So Kim. The other sense given, that it is a half-brick, such as is worked into the mode of building, called by us "bricknogging," which R. Tanchum of Jerusalem also knew in the East, seems unsuited here; 1) because it is speaking of magnificent building; the interlacing of brick with wood is for economy, since the wood, interlacing the bricks, holds them together, though the wall be thin; 2) the half-bricks naturally enter into this mode of building, but are neither the chief nor a prominent part of it. 3) Neither is the woodwork apparently in such way one, that it can stand as a whole. Tanchum and Parchon adopt this rendering, and Rashi on Taanit 11 *a* (ap. Del.) not in his Comm.; Symm. Theod. Syr. έ have σύνδεσμος, S. Jer. in the same sense, ἱμάντωσις, and LXX. κάνθαρος. The other sense given does not account for the wood "out of the timber," since it would rather be "out of the stone-work." S. Cyril says, "the other versions have ἔνδεσμος ξύλου, so that they named the crown of the house and the complexity of the wood, i. e., the band, κάνθαρος, because they as with many feet supported the roof which lay upon it.

[7] See S. Luke xix. 40.

[8] Berosus Hist. Chald. L. iii. ap. Joseph. Antiq. x. 11. and c. Ap. i. 20.

[9] Dan. iv. 27.

Before CHRIST cir. 626.

n † blood, and stablisheth a
city by iniquity!
13 Behold, *is it* not of
the LORD of hosts o that
the people shall labor in
the very fire, and the people shall weary themselves
|| for very vanity?
14 For the earth shall
be filled || with the p knowl-
edge of the glory of the
LORD, as the waters cover
the sea.
15 ¶ Woe unto him
that giveth his neighbor
drink, that puttest thy

n Jer. 22. 13. Ezek. 24. 9. Mic. 3. 10. Nah. 3 1.
† Heb. *bloods*.
o Jer. 51. 58.
|| Or, *in vain?*

Before CHRIST cir. 626.

|| Or, *by knowing the glory of the* LORD.
p Isai. 11. 9.

13. *Behold, is it not of the Lord of hosts that* [*the*] *people* [*nations*] *shall labor* [1] *in* [*for*] *the very fire* [lit. *to suffice the fire*]? By God's appointment, the end of all their labor is for the fire, what may *suffice* it to consume. This is the whole result of their labor; and so it is as if they had toiled for this; they built ceiled palaces and gorgeous buildings, only for the fire to consume them.

And peoples shall weary themselves for very vanity. They *wearied themselves*, and what was their reward? What had they to suffice and fill them? *Emptiness.* This is *from the Lord of hosts*, Whom all the armies of heaven obey and all creatures stand at His command against the ungodly, and in Whose Hand are all the hosts of earth, and so the oppressor's also, to turn as He wills.

Near upon the first stage of the fulfillment, Jeremiah reinforces the words with the name of Babylon; [2] *Thus saith the Lord of hosts! The broad walls of Babylon shall be utterly destroyed, and her high gates shall be burned with fire; and the people shall labor in vain* [*for vanity*], *and the folk in* [*for*] *the fire, and they shall be weary.*

14. *For the earth shall be filled with the knowledge of the glory of the Lord.* Habakkuk modifies in a degree the words of Isaiah which he embodies, marking that the destruction of Babylon was a stage only toward the coming of those good things which God taught His people to long for, not their very coming. All the world should be then full of the knowledge of the glory of the Lord, not, as yet, wholly of Himself. "[3] When Babylon shall be overthrown, then shall the power of the might of the Lord be known unto all. So shall the whole earth be filled with the glory of the Lord, as the waters cover the bottom of the sea. This as to the letter. But it is plain, that the Devil also and Anti-Christ, and the perverse teaching of heretics, built a city in blood; i. e., their own Church, with the destruction of those whom they deceive. . . . . . But when they fail in the fire, (either this fire which is felt, or consumed in the fire of the devil their prince, or burned up with the fire whereof the Lord says, *I came to send a fire upon the earth*, and so brought back from their former course, and doing penitence), the whole earth shall be filled with the glory of the Lord, when, at the preaching of the Apostles, their *sound shall go out into all the world*, as waters covering the sea, i. e., all the saltness and bitterness of the world which Satan had rained down and the earth had drunk, the waters of the Lord shall cover, and cause the place of their ancient bitterness not to appear." "[4] *For the Spirit of the Lord filled the earth*, and when He filled it, *the earth was filled with the knowledge of the glory of the Lord*, so that unlearned and ignorant men became wise and eloquent, and earthly became heavenly, yea, they who were earth became heaven, knowing the Glory of the Lord, declaring the Glory of God, not any how, but as waters cover the sea. Great as must be waters, which would cover the sea, or compared to which the sea were nothing, far greater is the miracle, when the abundance of heavenly wisdom, given to the simple, surpassed the sea, i. e., the wisdom of all mankind." This verse being already a received image of the spread of the Gospel [5], it would of itself be understood to include this also; but more generally, it declares how upon all the judgments of God, a larger knowledge of Him would follow. "[6] All things are full of Christ, Who is the Glory of the Father; wherefore also He said, [7] *I have glorified Thee on earth, I have finished the work which Thou gavest me to do.*"

15. From cruelty the Prophet goes on to denounce the woe on insolence. *Woe unto him that giveth his neighbor* (to whom he owes love) *drink* [lit. *that maketh him drink*]; *that puttest* [8] *thy bottle* [9] *to him, and makest him*

[1] יגע with ב "labor upon" Josh. xxiv. 13. Isa. lxii. 8. and boldly, of God, Ib. xliii. 22. and Hif. "cause to labor with" Isa. xliii. 23.

[2] Jer. li. 58. [3] S. Jer. [4] Rup. [5] Isaiah xi. 9. [6] S. Cyr. [7] S. John xvii. 4.

[8] סָפֵּחַ is rendered "approaching to" "joining" by Tanch., A. E., Rashi Kim. Sal. B. Mel. Abarb.; "pouring" Ch. Symm. Both senses exist in the verb; and the efforts of Ges. and Papenheim (ap. Del.) to reduce all the usages under either, force some.

[9] The E. V. has taken חמתך as irregular from חֵמֶת "flask," with Kim., A. E., Sal. ben Mel.; "poison," Ch. Abulw.; "wrath," Rashi, Abarb.; "flask" or "wrath," Tanch.

Before CHRIST cir. 626.

[q] bottle to *him*, and makest
him drunken also, that
thou mayest [r] look on their
nakedness!
16 Thou art filled || with
shame for glory: [s] drink
thou also, and let thy foreskin be uncovered: the
cup of the LORD's right
hand shall be turned unto
thee, and shameful spew-
ing *shall be* on thy glory.
17 For the violence of
Lebanon shall cover thee,
and the spoil of beasts,
which made them afraid,
[t] because of men's blood,
and for the violence of the
land, of the city, and of
all that dwell therein.

q Hos. 7. 5.
r Gen. 9. 22.
|| Or, *more with shame than with glory.*
s Jer. 25. 26, 27. & 51. 57.
t ver. 8.

drunken also, [1] *that thou mayest look* [*gaze with* devilish *pleasure*] *on their nakedness.* This may either be of actual insults (as in the history of Noah), in keeping certainly with the character of the later Babylonians, the last wantonness of unbridled power, making vile sport of those like himself (*his neighbor*), or it may be drunkenness through misery [2] wherein they are bared of all their glory and brought to the lowest shame. The *woe* falls too on all, who in any way intoxicate others with flattering words or feigned affection, mixing *poison* under things pleasant, to bring them to shame.

16. *Thou art filled with shame for glory.* Oppressors think to make themselves great by bringing others down, to *fill* themselves with riches, by spoiling others. They loved shame [3], because they loved that, which brought shame; they were filled with shame, in that they sated themselves with shamefulness, which was their shame within, before, in the just judgment of God, shame came on them from without. [4] *Their glory was in their shame.* They shall be filled, yea, he says, *they are* already filled [5]; they would satisfy, gorge themselves, with all their hearts' desires; they are *filled to the full*, but *with shame* instead of *glory* which they sought, or which they already had. *From* and *for* [6] a state of *glory*, they were filled with contempt.

Drink thou also, and let thy foreskin be uncovered: thy shame like those whom thou puttest to shame, only the greater in being uncircumcised. *The cup of the Lord's Right Hand shall be turned* [*round*] *unto thee* [or *against thee*]. It had gone round the circuit of the nations whom God had employed him to chasten, and now, the circle completed, it should be brought round to himself, [7] *With what measure ye mete, it shall be measured unto you again.* So Jeremiah says, [8] *And the king of Sheshach shall drink after them;* and of Edom, [9] *To thee also shall the cup be brought round.* Thou, a man, madest man to drink of the cup of *thine* anger: the cup shall be brought round to thee, but not by man; to thee it shall be given by *the Right Hand of the Lord*, which thou canst not escape; it shall be [10] *the cup of the wine of the fierceness of the wrath of Almighty God;* as Asaph had said, [11] *There is a cup in the Lord's hand; it is full of mixture, and He poureth out therefrom; but the dregs thereof all the ungodly of the earth shall suck them out, shall drink them.*

And shameful spewing [12] *shall be on thy glory.* "[13] With the shame of thy spewing shalt thou bring up all thou hast swallowed down, and from the height of glory shalt thou be brought to the utmost ills." The shame of the ungodly cometh forth from himself; the shame he put others to is doubled upon himself; and the very means which he had used to fill himself with glory and greatness, cover the glory which by nature he had, with the deeper disgrace, so that he should be a loathsome and revolting sight to all. Man veils foul deeds under fair words; God, in His word, unveils the foulness.

17. *For the violence of Lebanon* i. e., done to

[1] וְאַף שַׁכֵּר The inf. abs. continuing the previous action of the finite verb, as in Gen. xli. 43. Is. ix. 20. Jer. xiv. 5, or after the inf. constr. 1 Sam. xxii. 13. xxv. 26. 33. Jer. vii. 18. &c. See in Ewald Lehrb. p. 839. ed. 7.

[2] Isaiah xxix. 9.

[3] Hos. iv. 8.

[4] Phil. iii. 19.

[5] שָׂבַע has nowhere the reflective meaning, "satiated himself with" (as Del.); it simply expresses a state.

[6] מִן includes both.

[7] S. Matt. vii. 2.

[8] Jer. xxv. 26.

[9] Lam. iv. 21.

[10] Rev. xvi. 19.

[11] Ps. lxxvi. 8.

[12] קִיקָלוֹן *might* be simply an intensive, modified from קְלָקְלוֹן, as כּוֹכָב from כבכב, תְּצוֹצְרוֹת for חצרצרות, &c. Ew. Lehrb. p. 408. It was regarded as a compound word by S. Jerome's Hebrew instructor, "vomitus ignominiæ," the Midrash Ester Rabb. 121. c. (in Del.) Kim. Sal. B. Mel. as suggested by the mention of the drinking, (as in Jer. xxv. 27.). Ibn Ezra, Tanchum, Abarb. give both. In any case, as in עֲבַטִיט, the word was probably framed to suggest the two words, into which it is naturally resolved, קִיא קָלוֹן, like קִיא צֹאָה Is. xxviii. 8. and the image Is. xix. 14. The form is enlarged by Hab. from the previous קָלוֹן, but the doubling occurs in קְלֹקֵל Nu. xxi. 5.

[13] S. Jer.

Before CHRIST cir. 626.

18 ¶ [u] What profiteth the graven image that the maker thereof hath graven it; the molten image, and a [x] teacher of lies, that † the maker of his work trusteth therein, to make [y] dumb idols?

u Is. 44. 9, 10. & 46. 2.

x Jer. 10. 8, 14. Zech. 10. 2.

† Heb. *the fashioner of his fashion.*

y Ps. 115. 5. 1 Cor. 12. 2.

Lebanon, whether the land of Israel of which it was the entrance and the beauty [1], or the temple [2], both of which Nebuchadnezzar laid waste; or, more widely, it may be a symbol of all the majesty of the world and its empires, which he subdues, as Isaiah uses it, when speaking of the judgment on the world [3]. *It shall cover thee, and the spoil* [i. e., *spoiling, destruction*] *of beasts* [the inhabitants of Lebanon] *which made them afraid*, or more simply, *the wasting of wild beasts* [4] *shall crush* [5] *them*[selves]," i. e., as it is in irrational nature, that "the frequency of the incursions of very mischievous animals becomes the cause that men assemble against them and kill them, so their [the Chaldæans'] frequent injustice is the cause that they haste to be avenged on thee [6]." Having become beasts, they shared their history. They spoiled, scared, laid waste, were destroyed. "Whoso seeketh to hurt another, hurteth himself." The Chaldæans laid waste Judæa, scared and wasted its inhabitants; the end of its plunder should be, not to adorn, but to *cover* them, overwhelm them as in ruins, so that they should not lift up their heads again. Violence returns on the head of him who did it; they seem to raise a lofty fabric, but are buried under it. He sums up their past experience, what God had warned them beforehand, what they had found.

18. *What profiteth* [*hath profited* [7]] *the graven image, that the maker therefore hath graven it?* What did Baal and Ashtaroth profit you? What availed it ever but to draw down the wrath of God? Even so neither shall it profit the Chaldæan. As their idols availed them not, so neither need they fear them. Sennacherib and Nebuchadnezzar were propagandists of their own belief and would destroy, if they could, all other worship, false or true [8]: Nebuchadnezzar is thought to have set up his own image [9]. Anti-Christ will set himself up as God [10]. We may take warning at least by our own sins. If we had no profit at all from them, neither will the like profit others. This the Jews did, in the main, learn in their captivity.

The molten image and teacher of lies. It is all one whether by *teacher of lies* we understand the idol [11], or its priest [12]. For its priest gave it its voice, as its maker created its form. It could only seem to teach through the idol-priest. Isaiah used the title *teacher of lies*, of the false prophet [13]. It is all one. Zechariah combines them; [14] *The teraphim have spoken vanity, and the diviners have seen a lie, and have had false dreams.*

That the maker of his work trusteth therein. This was the special folly of idolatry. The thing made must needs be inferior to its maker. It was one of the corruptions of idolatry that the maker of his own work should trust in what was wholly *his* own *creation*, what, not God, but himself created, what had nothing but what it had from himself [15]. He uses the very words which express the relation of man to God, "the Framer" and "the thing framed." [16] *O your perverseness! Shall the framer be accounted as clay, that the thing made should say of its Maker, He made me not, and the thing framed say of its Framer, He*

1 See Is. xxxvii. 24. and, as a symbol, Jer. xxii. 6, 23. Ez. xvii. 3; but it is used as a symbol of Sennacherib's army, Is. x. 34, and the king of Asshur is not indeed spoken of under the name as a symbol (in Ezek. xxi. 3.) but is compared to it.

2 See on Zech. xii. 1.

3 Is. ii. 13.

4 בְּהֵמוֹת is used of beasts of prey, Deut. xxvii. 24.

5 As in Is. vii. 8. and מְחִתָּה Ps. lxxxix. 40, Pr. x. 14, xiii. 3, xiv. 14, xviii. 7.

6 R. Tanchum. He had after Abulwalid, which Kimchi quotes and approves, explained the first part of the verse; "This is a likeness framed as to him, that he was like a beast of prey which attacketh the animals in their lairs; and Lebanon is mentioned on account of the multitude of animals in it. He says then, thy wrong to the inhabitants of Lebanon shall overwhelm thee." He gives also the rendering, followed in the E. V., but prefers his own. He gives the two ways of deriving יחיתן from חתת and חית. Rashi follows the same construction. "The wasting of thy beasts and forces, because they have wasted My people Israel, it shall crush them [selves]."

7 מה הועיל. Samuel warned them, "Serve the Lord with all your heart, and turn ye not aside; for [it would be] after vanities, which will not profit, nor deliver, for they are vain:" and Jeremiah tells their past; "their prophets prophesied by Baal; and after things לא יועילו which profit not, have they gone." Elsewhere the idol is spoken of as a thing, "which *will* not profit" (fut.) "My people hath changed its glory בלא יועיל for that which profiteth not," Jer. ii. 8. 11. So Isaiah, "Who hath formed a god, לבלתי הועיל, not to profit." Is. xliv. 9. 10. "The makers of a graven image are all of them vanity, and their desirable things בל יועילו will not profit."

8 2 Kgs xviii. 33–35, xix. 12–18, xxv. 9, Is. x. 10, 11. See also Lectures on Daniel pp. 447–449 ed. 2.

9 Dan. iii. See Lectures on Dan. pp. 442.

10 2 Thess. ii. 4. Rev. xiii. 15–17.

11 Abarb. Kim.

12 AE. Tanch.

13 Is. ix. 14.

14 Zech. x. 2.

15 In Hebrew this is made stronger by the sameness of the words, יצר יצרו *yotser yitsro* E. M. "fashioner of his fashion." Again "dumb idols" are *elilim illemim*, the second word only slightly varying from the first.

16 Is. xxix. 16.

Before CHRIST cir. 626.

19 Woe unto him that
saith to the wood, Awake;
to the dumb stone, Arise,
it shall teach! Behold, it
is laid over with gold and
silver, [z] and *there is* no
breath at all in the midst
of it.

[z] Ps. 135. 17.

Before CHRIST cir. 626.

20 But [a] the LORD *is* in
his holy temple: † [b] let all
the earth keep silence before him.

[a] Ps. 11. 4.
† Heb. *be silent all the earth before him.*
[b] Zeph. 1. 7. Zech. 2. 13.

hath no hands? The idol-maker is "the creator of his creature," of his god whom he worships. Again the idol-maker makes *dumb idols* [lit. *dumb nothings*] in themselves nothings, and having no power out of themselves; and what is uttered in their name, are but *lies.* And what else are man's idols of wealth, honor, fame, which he makes to himself, the creatures of his own hands or mind, their greatness existing chiefly in his own imagination, before which *he* bows down himself, who is the image of God?

19. But then the greater is the *Woe* to him who deceiveth by them. The prophet passes away from the the idols as "nothings" and pronounces "woe" on those who deceive by them. He [1] first expostulates with them on their folly, and would awaken them. *What hath it profited* [2]? Then on the obstinate he denounces "woe." *Woe unto him that saith to the wood, Awake; to the dumb stone, Arise.* Self-made blindness alone could, in the light of truth, so speak; but yet more lies in the emphatic word, *It.* The personal pronoun stands emphatically in Hebrew; *He* shall teach, lo, *He* (this same of whom he speaks) this is *It* which *shall teach:* It, and not the living God. And yet this same *It* (the word is again emphatic) he points, as with the finger, to it, *behold, It is laid over with, held fast by* [3], *gold and silver,* so that no voice could escape, if it had any. *And there is no breath at all in the midst of it* [4], lit. *All breath, all which is breath, there is none within it;* he first suggests the thought, breath of every sort, and then energetically denies it all [5]; no life of any sort, of man, or bird, or beast, or creeping thing; [6] none, good or bad; from God or from Satan; none whereby it can do good or do evil; for which it should be loved or feared. Evil spirits may have made use of idols: they could not give them life, nor dwell in them.

The words addressed to it are the language of the soul in the seeming absence or silence of God [7], but mockery as spoken to the senseless stone, as Elijah had mocked the Baal-priests [8], *peradventure he sleepeth and must be awaked.*

20. And now having declared the nothingness of all which is not God, the power of man or his gods, he answers again his own question, by summoning all before the Presence of the Majesty of God.

And the Lord. He had, in condemning them, pictured the tumult of the world, the oppressions, the violence, bloodsheddings, covetousness, insolence, self-aggrandizement of the then world-empire, and had denounced woe upon it; we see man framing his idols, praying to the lifeless stones; and God, of Whom none thought, where was He? These were men's ways. "*And* the Lord," he joins it on, as the complement and corrective of all this confusion, *The Lord is in His holy temple,* awaiting, in His long-suffering, to judge. *The temple of God* is where God enshrines Himself, or allows Himself to be seen and adored. "God is wholly everywhere, the whole of Him no where." There is no contrast between His temple on earth, and His temple in heaven. He is not more locally present in heaven than in earth. It were as anthropomorphic but less pious to think of God, as confined, localized, in heaven as on earth; because it would be simply removing God away from man. Solomon knew, when he built the temple, that *the heaven and heaven of heavens could not contain* [9] God. The *holy temple,* which could be destroyed [10], toward which men were to pray [11], was the visible temple [12], where were the symbols of God's Presence, and of the atoning Sacrifice; but lest His presence should be localized, Solomon's repeated prayer is, [13] *hear Thou in heaven Thy dwelling place;* [14] *hear Thou in heaven.* There is then no difference, as though in earlier books the "holy temple" meant that at Jerusalem, in the later, "the heavens." In the confession at the offering of the *third year's tithes,* the prayer is, [15] *look down from Thy holy habitation, from heaven;* and David says, [16] *the Lord is in His holy temple, the Lord's throne is in heaven;*

[1] Rup.
[2] As in Ps. cxv. 5. 1 Cor. xii. 2.
[3] The meaning of תפש elsewhere. "Here it means 'surrounds,' for that which encircles a thing, is as if it held it on every side." Tanch.
[4] Comp. Jer. x. 14 repeated li. 17.
[5] As in the Hebraism of the N. T. οὐ δικαιωθήσεται πᾶσα σὰρξ Rom. iii. 20.
[6] Is. xli. 23. Jer. x. 5.
[7] Ps. vii. 7, xxxv. 23, xliv. 24. lix. 6, Is. li. 9. Del.
[8] 1 Kgs xviii. 26, 27.
[9] 1 Kgs viii. 27.
[10] Ps. lxxix. 1.
[11] Ps. v. 7. cxxxviii. 2. Jon. ii. 4.
[12] 1 Kgs viii. 29, 30, 35, 38, 42, 44, 48.
[13] Ib. 30, 39, 43, 49.
[14] Ib. 32, 34, 36, 45.
[15] De. xxvi. 15.
[16] Ps. xi. 4.

Before CHRIST cir. 626.

CHAPTER III.

1 *Habakkuk in his prayer trembleth at God's majesty.* 17 *The confidence of his faith.*

A PRAYER of Habakkuk the prophet [a] || upon Shigionoth.

Before CHRIST cir. 626.

a Ps. 7, title.
|| Or, *according to variable songs*, or, *tunes, called in Hebrew, Shigionoth.*

and, [1] *He heard my voice out of His temple—He bowed the heavens also and came down;* and, [2] *In His temple doth every one say, Glory.* The simple words are identical though not in the same order as those, in which David, in the same contrast with the oppression of man, ushers in the judgment and final retribution to good and bad, by declaring the unseen presence of God on His Throne in heaven, beholding and trying the sons of men.

In His Presence, all the mysteries of our being are solved. *The Lord is in His holy Temple,* not, as the idols in temples made with hands, but revealing Himself in the visible temple, "[3] dwelling in the Son, by Nature and Union, as He saith, [4] *The Father Who dwelleth in Me doeth the works;* in each one of the bodies and souls of the Saints by His Spirit[5], in the Blessed, in glory; in the Heavens, by the more evident appearance of His Majesty and the workings of His Power; "[6] everywhere by Essence, Presence, and Power, *for in Him we live, and move, and have our being;* nowhere as confined or inclosed." Since then God is in Heaven, beholding the deeds of men, Himself Unchangeable, Almighty, All-holy, *let all the earth keep silence before Him,* lit. *hush before Him all the earth,* waiting from Him in hushed stillness the issue of this tangled state of being. And to the hushed soul, hushed to itself and its own thoughts, hushed in awe of His Majesty and *His Presence, before His face,* God speaks[7].

III. 1. *A prayer*[8] *of Habakkuk.* The *prayer* of the prophet, in the strictest sense of the word, is contained in the words of verse 2. The rest is, in its form, praise and thanksgiving, chiefly for God's past mercies in the deliverance from Egypt and the entering into the promised land. But thanksgiving is an essential part of prayer, and Hannah is said to have *prayed,* whereas the hymn which followed is throughout one thanksgiving[9]. In that also these former deliverances were images of things to come, of every deliverance afterward, and, especially, of that complete Divine deliverance which our Lord Jesus Christ wrought for us from the power of Satan[10], the whole is one prayer. "Do, O Lord, as Thou hast done of old; forsake not Thine own works. Such were Thy deeds once; fulfill them now, all which they shadowed forth." It is then a prayer for the manifestation of God's power, and therewith the destruction of His enemies, thenceforth to the Day of Judgment. "[11] Having completed the discourse about Babylon, and having fore-announced most clearly, that those who destroyed the holy city and carried Israel captive shall be severely punished, he passes suitably to the mystery of Christ, and from the redemption which took place partially in one nation, he carries on the discourse to that universal redemption, whereby the remnant of Israel, and no less the whole world has been saved."

Upon Shigionoth. The title, *Shiggaion,* occurs but once besides [12]. *Upon,* in the titles of the Psalms, is used with the instrument[13], the melody[14], or the first words of the hymn, whose melody has been adopted[15]. The two first are mentioned by a Jewish Commentator[16] with others, "in his delight," or "his errors," in the sense, that God will forgive them. This, which the versions and Jewish commentators mostly adopt, would be a good sense, but is hardly consistent with the Hebrew usage. *Shiggaion of David,* as a title of a Psalm, must necessarily describe the Psalm itself, as *Midsmor of David, Michtam of David, Tephillah of David, Maschil of David.* But *Shiggaion,* as a "great error," is not a title: nor does it suit the character of the Psalm, which relates to calumny not to error. It probably, then, means a psalm with music expressive of strong emotion, "erratic" or "dithyrambic." Habakkuk's title, *on Shigionoth* [plur.] then would mean *upon,* or (as we should say,) "set to" music of psalms of this sort[17]. The number "three" remarkably predominates in this psalm[18], yet so that long measures are succeeded by very short.

[1] Ps. xviii. 6. 9. [2] Ib. xxix. 9.
[3] S. Jer. [4] S. John xiv. 10.
[5] 1 Cor. vi. 19. [6] Dion.
[7] See S. Augustine's words to his mother before her death, Conf. ix. 10.
[8] Tephilloth is a title of the collection of David's Psalms ending with Ps. lxxii. (Ib. ver. 20.) Three of David's Psalms are entitled Tephillah, Ps. xvii. lxxxvi. cxlii. Moses' Psalm xc., and anonymous cii.
[9] ותתפלל 1 Sam. ii. 1. [10] 1 Cor. x. 11.
[11] S. Cyr. [12] Ps. vii.
[13] on Neginoth, Ps. iv. vi. lv. Nehiloth, Ps. v. Gittith, Ps. viii. Shoshannim, Ps. xlv. Mahalath, Ps. liii.
[14] on Sheminith, Ps. vi. Alamoth Ps. xlvi.
[15] Perhaps "upon Muthlabben," Ps. ix. "on Aiieleth Shahar," Ps. xxii. "on Yonath-elem-rekokim," Ps. lvi. [16] R. Tanchum.
[17] Since שׁוה "erred" is common to Hebrew and Aramaic, it is improbable that שׁגיון should be i. q. Syr. סוגיתא a "hymn of praise," from סגי, beside that the Heb. שׁ does not interchange with Syr. ס.
[18] Ver. 6 has 15 words, in five combinations, of three words; vv. 3 and 10 have 12 words, in four 3s: vv. 4, 9, 19. have 9 words in three 3s: vv. 5, 12, 15 and 18 have 6 words in two 3s: ver. 17 is divided into 433433; ver. 8 is 33332; ver. 11 is 433; ver. 16 is

Before CHRIST cir. 626.

2 O LORD, I have heard †thy speech, *and* was afraid: O LORD, ||[b] revive thy work in the midst

† Heb. *thy report*, or, *thy hearing*.

|| Or, *preserve alive*.

[b] Ps. 85. 6.

Before CHRIST cir. 626.

2. *O Lord, I have heard* i. e. with the inward ear of the heart, *Thy speech*, (rather as E. M. *Thy report*, i. e. the report of Thee[1]) i. e. what may be heard and known of God, or, what he had himself heard[2]. The word contains in one both that which God had lately declared to the Prophet, the judgments of God upon the wicked of the people, and upon those who, with their own injustice, wrought on them the righteous judgments of God, and that the work of the Lord would be wrought in His time for those who in patience wait for it; and also still more largely, what might be heard of God, although, as it were, but a little whisper of His greatness and of the Majesty of His workings.

And was afraid, not "fearful" but *afraid* in awe, as a creature, and amazed at the surpassing wonderfulness of the work of God. Well may man stand in awe "[3] at the Incarnation of the Only Begotten Son, how earth should contain Him uncontained by space, how a Body was prepared for Him of the Virgin by the Holy Ghost, and all the works whereby He shall work the salvation of mankind, the Cross, the Death, Resurrection and Ascension, uniting things opposite, a Body with One incorporeal, Death with Life, Resurrection with Death, a Body in Heaven. All is full of wonder and awe." "[4] This is not a servile fear, but a holy fear which endureth forever, not one which *love casteth out*, but which it bringeth in, wherein angels praise, dominions adore, powers stand in awe at the Majesty of the Eternal God."

O Lord, revive Thy work. God's Word seems, often, as it were, dead and *come utterly to an end for evermore*[5], while it is holding on its own course, as all nature seems dead for a while, but all is laid up in store, and ready to shoot forth, as by a sort of resurrection. "[4] The Prophet prophesying prayeth, that it should come quickly, and praying prophesieth that it shall so come." All God's dealings with His people, His Church, each single soul, are part of one great work, perfect in itself[6]; glory and majesty[7]; all which the godly meditateth on[8]; which those busied with their own plans, do not look to[9]; it is manifested in great doings for them or with them, as in the Exodus the Psalmist says, [10] *We have heard with our ears, yea, our fathers have told us what work Thou didst in their days, in the times of old;* [11] *They proved Me and saw My work;* with it He makes His own glad[12]; after it has been withdrawn for a while, *He sheweth it to His servants*[13]; it issues in judgments on the ungodly, which men consider and declare[14].

The great work of God on earth, which includes all His works and is the end of all, is the salvation of man through Jesus Christ. This great work seemed, as it were, asleep, or dead, as trees in winter, all through those 4000 years, which gave no token of His Coming. Included in this great work is the special work of the Hand of God, of which alone it is said, *God said, Let Us make man in Our Image after Our Likeness*[15]; and, *we are the clay and Thou our Potter, and we are all the work of Thy Hands*[16]; and *Thy Hands have made me and fashioned me together round about*[17], —man; whom, being dead as to the life of the soul through the malice of Satan, Christ revived by dying and rising again. He was *dead in trespasses and sins*, and like a carcase putrefying in them, and this whole world one great charnel-house, through man's manifold corruptions, when Christ came to awaken the dead, and they who heard lived[18].

Again, the Centre of this work, the special Work of God, that wherein He made all things new, is the Human Body of our Lord, the Temple which was destroyed by Death, and within three days raised up.

The answer to Habakkuk's enquiry, *How long?* had two sides. It had given assurance as to the end. The trial-time would not be prolonged for one moment longer than the counsel of God had foredetermined. The relief would *come, come; it would not be behindhand.* But meantime? There was no comfort to be given. For God knew that deepening sin was drawing on deepening chastise-

3332223. This forces itself on every reader. Del. quotes the Meor. Enaim, i. 60, "The prayer of Habakkuk goeth on threes."

[1] Except in the one phrase שמע אזן "hearing of ear" (Job xlii. 5. Ps. xviii. 45.) the personal gen. after שֵׁמַע is that of the object, "the report of Jacob," Gen. xxix. 13. "of Solomon," 1 Kgs x. 1. 2 Chron. ix. 1. "of Tyre," Is. xxiii. 5 with the affix שִׁמְעֲךָ *the report of thee*, Nu. xiv. 15, De. ii. 25. Nah. iii. 19. שמעה *the report of her* [wisdom] Job xxviii. 22. שִׁמְעִי *the report of Me* [God], Is. lxvi. 19. שמעם *the report of them*, Jer. xxxvii. 5. l. 43.

[2] as שמועה Ob. 1, and thence Jer. xlix. 14. See on Hosea vii. 12.

[3] Theoph. from S. Cyr.

[4] Rup.

[5] Ps. lxxvii. 8.

[6] De xxxii. 4.

[7] Ps. cxl. 3.

[8] Ib. lxxvii. 3. cxliii. 35.

[9] Is. v. 12.

[10] Ps. xliv. 2. פֹּעַל פעלת.

[11] Ps. xcv. 9.

[12] Ib. xcii. 3.

[13] Ib. xc. 6.

[14] Ib. lxiv. 10. In all these cases sing. פֹּעַל.

[15] Gen. i. 26.

[16] Is. lxiv. 8.

[17] Job x. 8.

[18] S. John v. 25.

Before CHRIST cir. 626.

of the years, in the midst of the years make known; in wrath remember mercy.

Before CHRIST cir. 626.

ment. But in that He was silent as to the intervening time and pointed to patient expectation of a lingering future, as their only comfort, He implies that the immediate future was heavy. Habakkuk then renews his prayer for the years which had to intervene and to pass away. *In the midst of the years*, before that *time appointed*[1], when His promise should have its full fulfillment, before those years should come to their close, he prays; *revive Thy work*. The *years* include all the long period of waiting for our Lord's first Coming before He came in the Flesh; and now for His second Coming and the *restitution of all things*. In this long period, at times God seems to be absent, as when our Lord was asleep in the boat, while the tempest was raging; at times He bids *the storm to cease and there is a great calm*. This, in those long intervals, when God seems to be absent, and to leave all things to time and chance, and love waxes cold, and graces seem rare, is the prayer of Habakkuk, of Prophets and Psalmists, of the Church, [2]*Return, we beseech Thee, O God of hosts, look down from heaven, behold and visit this vine.* [3]*O God, why hast Thou cast us off for ever? Why withdrawest Thou Thy hand, Thy right hand? For God is my king of old, working salvation in the midst of the earth.* [4]*Awake, awake, put on strength, Thou Arm of the Lord; awake, as in the ancient days, in the generations of old. Art thou not It which did smite Rahab, didst wound the dragon? Art thou not It which didst dry the sea, the waters of the great deep, which didst make the depths of the sea a way for the ransomed to pass over?* [5]*Stir up Thy might and come, save us.* [6]*Renew our days, as of old.* So our Lord taught His Church to pray continually, whenever she prayed, *Thy kingdom come*, longing not for His final Coming only, but for the increase of His glory, and the greater dominion of His grace, and His enthronement in the hearts of men, even before its complete and final Coming. *In the midst of the years revive Thy work*, is the Church's continual cry.

In the midst of the years make known, lit. *Thou wilt make known: in wrath Thou wilt remember mercy;* and so (as we use the word *wilt*) the Prophet, at once, foretelleth, expresseth his faith, prayeth. God had made known His work and His power in the days of old. In times of trouble He seems *like a God who hideth Himself*. Now, he prays Him to *shine* forth and help; *make known* Thy work, before Thou fulfill it, to revive the drooping hopes of man, and that all may see that *Thy word is truth*. *Make* Thyself *known* in Thy work, that, when the time cometh to [7]*make an end of sin* by the Death of Thy Son, Thy Awful Holiness, and the love wherewith Thou hast [8]*so loved the world*, may be the more known and adored.

In wrath Thou wilt remember mercy. So David prayed, [9]*Remember Thy tender-mercies and Thy loving-kindnesses; for they are from old. Thou wilt remember* that counsel for man's redemption which has been from the foundation of the world: for we seem in our own minds to be forgotten of God, when He delayeth to help us. God remembereth mercy[10] in anger, in that in this life He never chastens without purposes of mercy, and His Mercy ever softeneth His judgments. His Promise of mercy, that the Seed of the woman shall bruise the serpent's head, went before the sentence of displeasure, [11]*Dust thou art, and unto dust shalt thou return.* "[12]He reveals His wrath that He may scare us from sin and so may not inflict it;" and when at last He inflicteth it, He hath mercy on the remnant who flee to His Mercy, that we be not like Sodom and Gomorrah. [13]*While we were yet sinners*, and God was wroth, *Christ died for us*, and [14]*He saved us, not for works which we had done, but out of His great Mercy*, and took away sin, and restored us to life and incorruption.

God had already promised by Micah, [15]*According to the days of thy coming out of the land of Egypt, I will show him marvelous things.* Isaiah had often used the great events of that deliverance as the symbols of the future. So now Habakkuk, in one vast panorama, as it were, without distinction of time or series of events, exhibits the future in pictures of the past. In the description itself which follows, he now speaks in the past, now in the future; of which times the future might be a vivid present; and the past a prophetic past. As a key to the whole, he says, *God shall come*, indicating that all which follows, however spoken, was a part of that future. In no other way was it an answer to that prayer, *Revive Thy work*. To foretell future deliverances in plain words, had been a comfort; it would have promised a continuance of that work. The unity and revival of the work is expressed, in that the past is made, as it was, the image of the future. That future was to be wondrous, superhuman; else the past miracles had been no image of it. It was

[1] מוֹעֵד.
[2] Ps. lxxx. 14.
[3] Ib. lxxiv. 1, 11, 12.
[4] Is. li. 9, 10.
[5] Ps. lxxx. 3.
[6] Lam. v. 21.
[7] Dan. ix. 24.
[8] S. John iii. 16.
[9] Ps. xxv. 6.
[10] S. Luke i. 54, 72.
[11] Gen. iii. 19.
[12] S. Jer.
[13] Rom. v. 8.
[14] Tit. iii. 5.
[15] Mic. vii. 15.

Before CHRIST cir. 626.

3 God came from ‖ Teman, [c] and the Holy One
from mount Paran. Selah.
His glory covered the

Before CHRIST cir. 626.

‖ Or, *the south.*

c Deut. 33. 2. Judg. 5. 4. Ps. 68. 7.

to be no mere repetition of the future; and to mark this, the images are exhibited out of their historical order.

3. *God came* (lit. *shall come*) *from Teman. God shall come,* as He came of old, clothed with majesty and power; but it was not mere power. The centre of the whole picture is, as Micah and Isaiah had prophesied that it was to be, a new revelation; [1] *The law shall go forth from Zion, and the word of the Lord from Jerusalem.* [2] *I will give Thee for a covenant to the people* [Israel], *for a light of the Gentiles.* So now, speaking of the new work in store, Habakkuk renews the imagery in the Song of Moses [3], in Deborah's Song [4], and in David [5]; but there the manifestation of His glory is spoken of wholly in time past, and Mount Sinai is named. Habakkuk speaks of that coming as yet to be, and omits the express mention of Mount Sinai, which was the emblem of the law [6]. And so he directs us to another Lawgiver, Whom God should *raise up like unto Moses,* yet with a law of life, and tells how He Who spake the law, God, shall come in likeness of our flesh.

And the Holy One from Mount Paran. In the earliest passage three places are mentioned, in which or from which the glory of God was manifested; with this difference however, that it is said, [7] *The Lord came from Sinai,* but His glory *arose,* as we should say *dawned* [8] unto *them from Seir,* and *flashed forth* [9] from Mount Paran [10]. Seir and Mount Paran are joined together by the symbol of the light which *dawned* or *shone forth* from them. In the second passage, the Song of Deborah, *Seir* and *the field of Edom* are the place whence God *came* forth; *Sinai melted* [11] at His presence. In the 68th Psalm the mention of Edom is dropped; and the march through the wilderness under the leading of God, is alone mentioned, together with the shaking of Sinai. In Habakkuk, the contrast is the same as in Moses; only *Teman* stands in place of *Seir* [12]. *Teman* and *Mount Paran* are named probably, as the two opposed

1 Is. ii. 3. Mic. iv. 2.
2 Is. xliv. 5.
3 Deut. xxxiii. 2.
4 Jud. v. 5.
5 Ps. lxviii. 7.
6 S. Cyr.
7 Deut. xxxiii. 2.

8 זרח is used in prose too, of the rising sun (with השמש) Gen. xxxii. 32, Ex. xxii. 3, Jud. ix. 33, 2 Sam. xxiii. 4, 2 Kgs iii. 22, Jon. iv. 8.

9 הופיע is used of the light of the sun Job iii. 4, x. 22; of the manifestation of God apart from any physical emblem Ps. l. 2, lxxx. 2, xciv. 1; and of God, favoring *the counsel of the wicked.* Job x. 3.

10 *Mount* Paran is only mentioned in Deuteronomy and Habakkuk, and was probably taken by Habakkuk from Moses, who himself knew it. *The wilderness of Paran* must have lain W. or S. of the *wilderness of Zin,* which formed the Southern border of Judah (Nu. xiii. 21. Josh. xv. 1.). The history of Ishmael implies that part of it lay toward Egypt (Gen. xii. 21.); that of *Hadad the Edomite,* shews that it lay between Midian and Egypt (1 Kgs xi. 18); but there being, (as far as it is ascertained), no natural boundary between it and the wilderness of Zin, the name Paran is apparently used in a wider sense as comprehending the desert of Zin, whence Kadesh is placed both in Paran (Nu. xiii. 26.) and more commonly in Zin (Nu. xx. 1, xxvii. 14, xxxiii. 36, 37, xxxiv. 4, Josh. xv. 3.), and the wilderness near it is also called *the wilderness of Kadesh* (Ps. xxix. 8.). The name of *the wilderness of Zin* does not occur after Joshua; and that of Paran may have extended over the whole desert cretaceous plateau up to the borders of Edom, now called Badiet-et-Tih, the "wilderness of the wanderings," whose Western extremity lies North of the crescent-shaped Jebel-et-Tih, which separates it from the lower part of the peninsula. (See Map in Sinaitic survey.) Hence Nabal is related to have fed his flocks in Paran (1 Sam. xxv. 5.) and Eilparan "the terebinth of Paran," (Gen. xiv. 6.) *by the wilderness,* the bound of the inroad of Chedorlaomer, may have had its name from the wilderness. *Mount* Paran might be anywhere connected with this wilderness on the West. "Mount Serbal is perhaps the most striking mountain in the peninsula; it rises abruptly to a height of more than 4000 feet above the valleys at its base, and its summit, a sharp ridge about three miles long, is broken into a series of peaks varying little in altitude, but rivaling each other in the beauty and grandeur of their outline. It is three miles from Wady Feiran;" "in one or two points from which its highest peak is visible." Ordnance Survey of Peninsula of Sinai pp. 143, 144. "When seen from a distance Serbal presents a boldness of outline and an appearance of massive isolation which entitled it to rank as one of the grandest and most distinctive features of the peninsula." (Palmer's desert of the Exodus p. 169.) What is now called Jebel Feiran is too low to be taken into account. It is but an eminence, rising on one side 810 feet above the Wady Feiran; on the other side, 795 feet, and above the sea 2800; so that in the same neighborhood Mount Serbal is above twice its height, 6443 feet above the sea at its highest peak. (Sinaitic Survey, Mount Serbal, sections.) This mountain has this advantage, that it is connected with Wady Feiran or Paran, through which Moses led Israel to Mount Sinai. The name is remarkable, as having been given by Israel, since it has a Hebrew etymology, "the beautiful" or "the leafy," and all travelers praise the richness of the valley, even amid the decay of fertility consequent on neglect. It has no Arabic etymology. (See Palmer, l. c. p. 20.) S. Jerome says, from his Hebrew teacher apparently, "Pharan is a place near to Mount Sinai." ad loc.

The striking mountain of Edom had its own name Hor, which in the eleven places in which it is named in the Pentateuch is always called הר ההר "Hor, the mountain." Nu. xx. 22, 23, 25, 27. xxi. 4. xxxii. 37, 38, 41. xxxiv. 7, 8. De. xxxii. 19. Prof. Palmer having shewn Ain Gadis to be Kadesh (l. c. c. iv. p. 373. sqq.) says, "To one encamped in the wilderness of Kadesh, i. e. in the open plain into which Wady Gadis debouches, Jebel Magrâh would be always the most conspicuous object in the scene." (Ib. p. 510.) This is a plateau, 70 miles long and 40–50 miles broad, "projecting into the Tih, much as the Tih projects into Sinai." Ib. p. 288, 9.

11 Jud. v. 4, 5.

12 As it stands connected with Edom, Ob. 9. Jer. lix. 7, 20, 21. with Dedan also, Jer. xlix. 8, Ezek. xxv. 13.

Before CHRIST cir. 626. heavens, and the earth was full of his praise. Before CHRIST cir. 626.

boundaries of the journeyings of Israel through the desert. They came to Mount Sinai through the valley, now called Wady Feiran[1] or Paran; Edom was the bound of their wanderings to their promised land[2]. God Who guided, fed, protected them from the beginning, led them to the end. Between *Paran* also and Edom or *Teman* was the gift of the Spirit to the seventy, which was the shadow of the day of Pentecost; there, was the brazen serpent lifted up, the picture of the healing of the Cross[3]. *If* Mount Paran *be* near Kadesh, then Moses in the opening of his song describes the glory of God as manifested from that first revelation of His law on Mount Sinai; then in that long period of Israel's waiting there to its final departure for the promised land, when Mount Hor was consecrated and God's awful Holiness declared in the death of Aaron.

He Who *shall come*, is God[4], the *Holy One* (a proper Name of God[5]). Perfect in Holiness, as God, the Son of God, and as Man also all-holy, with a human will, always exactly accompanying the Divine Will, which was

"the passion of His Heart
Those Three-and-thirty years."

On this there follows a pause denoted by Selah[6], (which occurs thrice according to the mystery of that number,) that the soul may dwell on the greatness of the majesty and mercy of God.

Selah. There is no doubt as to the general purport of the word, that it is a musical direction, that there should be a pause, the music probably continuing alone, while the mind rested on the thought, which had just been presented to it; our "interlude[7]." It is always placed at some pause of thought, even when not at the end of a strophe, or, as twice in this hymn[8], at the end of the verse. S. Gregory of Nyssa modifies this thought, supposing "Selah" to express a pause made by the writer, that "[9] while the psalmody, with which David's prophesying was accompanied, went on in its course, another illumining of the Holy Spirit, and an addition to the gift according to knowledge, came for the benefit of those who received the prophecy, he, holding in his verse, gave time for his mind to receive the knowledge of the thought, which took place in him from the Divine illumining. He defines it to be "a sudden silence in the midst of the Psalmody for the reception of the illumining."

His Glory covered the heavens, and the earth was full of His praise. This is plainly no created glory, but anticipates the Angelic Hymn, [10] *Glory to God in the highest, and on earth peace, good-will toward men*, or, as the Seraphim sing first, glory to God in Heaven, [11] *Holy Holy Holy is the Lord God of Sabaoth*, and then, *the whole earth is full of His glory;* and Uncreated Wisdom saith, [12] *I alone compassed the circuit of Heaven, and walked in the bottom of the deep.* Nor are they our material heavens, much less this lowest heaven over our earth, nor is *His glory* any lightning at Mount Sinai, but the boundless Majesty[13] of God, which rules, encompasses, fills, penetrates the orbs of heaven and all its inhabitants, and yet is not enclosed nor bounded thereby. Those who are made as the heavens by the indwelling of God He spiritually *covers*, filling[14] them with the light of glory and splendor of grace and brightness of

1 Sinaitic Survey c. 5. 149–155.
2 Nu. xx. 14–20. Deut. ii. 3 Rib.

4 The sing. אֱלוֹהַּ occurs 41 times in the book of Job; else only 16 times in all the O. T., and 8 times only of the true God, (twice in Moses' song Deut. xxxii. 15, 17; in a Psalm of David, Ps. cxxxix. 19, of Asaph, l. 22, Anon. Ps. cxiv. 7; in Proverbs xxx. 5, here, and in Nehemiah's prayer, (in which there are so many reminiscences from the Pentateuch. See in "Daniel the Prophet" pp. 356, 357.) Else it is used of the Godhead (*Who is God except*, &c. in David Ps. xviii. 32, *is there any God besides Me?* Is. xliv. 8); "any God" including the true God Dan. xi. 3. And five times it is used of a false god; in Hab. i. 11; three times in Dan. xi. 38, 39; and by Sennacherib 2 Chr. xxxii. 15. There is then no basis of induction as to its occurring in later Hebrew and poetic books; since its use is mostly a peculiarity of the book of Job, the other 16 cases are sporadic and in no one sense.

5 Whence in the Hebrew, though the subject, it has no article, as in Is. xl. 25, and Job vi. 11.

6 It occurs here only besides the Psalms. It occurs thrice in Ps. iii. xxxii. lxvi. lxviii.

7 διάψαλμα in Lxx. Theod. Symm. Syr.

8 Ps. lv. 20. lvii. 4. Hab. iii. 3, 9, alone, it is not at the end of the verse. Eight Psalms only, out of 39 Psalms which have it, have not the title "For the chief musician," Ps. 32, 48, 56, 82, 83, 87, 89, 143. 5 of these are מִזמוֹר; 2, מַשׂכּיל (32 and 89), one without any inscription (48). The most probable etymology seems to be סלה,=סלל and so our "alto;" whether the ה be added to סַל or it be an imperative with paragogic ה like אשׁיְעָה Ps. cxix. 117, נשׁתָּעָה Is. xli. 23, although there is no extant instance of this imperative. There is equally no instance of the form from סלל (as Ewald Ps. i. 179, Lehrb. § 216. c. p. 544) since נַתָּה 1 Kgs ii. 40, is only a Var. Read. for the received נַתָּה which is borne out by נִתָּה Jos. xix. 13.

9 Tract 2 in Ps. Inscr. &c. T. i. p. 329.
10 S. Luke ii. 14. 11 Is. vi. 3. 12 Ecclus. xxiv. 5.

13 הוד is used of the Divine Majesty Job xxxvii. 22. Ps. viii. 2. xx. 30. with הדר Ps. xcvi. 6, (1 Chr. xvi. 27,) civ. 1, cxi. 3, cxlv. 5, cxlviii. 11; ironically to man, as impossible for him, Job xl. 10. It is used as imparted to the Messiah Ps. xxi. 6, or being in Him, Ps. xlv. 4. 14 Dion.

Before CHRIST cir. 626.

4 And *his* brightness was as the light; he had

Before CHRIST cir. 626.

wisdom, as it saith, *Is there any number of His armies, and upon whom doth not His light arise*[1]? *and* so *the earth was full of His praise*, i. e. the Church militant spread throughout the world, as in the Psalm, [2] *The Lord's name is praised from the rising up of the sun unto the going down of the same*, and, [3] *O Lord, our Lord, how excellent is Thy name in all the earth. Who hast set Thy glory above the heavens.*

4. *And His Brightness*, that wherein God dwelleth, [4] *the brightness of the Lord's glory*, before which darkness fleeth[5], *was as the light*, or as the sun. Out of the midst of the darkness, wherewith God, as it were, [6] hid Himself, the Brightness of the *inapproachable Light* wherein He *dwelleth*, gleams forth[7], bright as *the* brightest *light* gathered into one, which man knows of and whereon he cannot gaze. So amid the darkness of the humiliation of His Presence in the flesh, [8] *we beheld His Glory, the Glory as of the Only-Begotten of the Father;* and [9] *the people that walked in darkness see a great light*, "not dim[10] nor weak, nor shadowed, like that of Moses, but pure unimaginable light of the knowledge of God." The Brightness too of His Flesh was like the light of the Godhead on Mount Tabor; for the Godhead flashed through. "[11] As often as He did His marvelous works, He put forth His *Brightness* (tempered for His creatures, since they could not approach the depth of His light, yet) *as light* to enlighten men to know Him. Yet the Brightness issues from the Light, co-existing with it, and in it, while issuing from it. And so the words aptly express, how He Who is the [12] *Brightness of the Father's Glory and the express Image of His Person*, the [13] *Brightness of the Eternal Light, the unspotted mirror of the Power of God, and the Image of His Goodness*, is as the Light from Whom He is, "[14] Light of Light," Equal to the Father by Whom He was Begotten; as S. John says, [15] *That was the true Light, which lighteneth every man that cometh into the world.* As He prayeth, [16] *Glorify Thou Me with Thine Own Self with the Glory Which I had with Thee before the world was.*

He had horns coming out of His Hand. "[17] Horns are everywhere in Holy Scripture the emblem of strength." It may be, that here "rays" are likened to horns, as the face of Moses is said, with the same image, to have "sent forth rays[18]" after he had long been in the presence of God. So it may be a mingled image of the Glory and might; Light, which was also might. But "horns," though they may be a symbol of "light," are not of "lightning;" and the Hand of God is used as an emblem of His Power, His protection, His bounty, His constraining force on His prophets. It is nowhere used of the side or sides[19]. We have two images combined here; "horns" which in every other place in which they are used as a metaphor, is an emblem of power; and "from the hand of" which, wherever it is used of a person, means that the thing spoken of had been in his hand or power really or virtually[20]. Both then combine in the meaning that the might came forth from the directing agency of God Who wielded it.

1 Job xxv. 3. 2 Ps. cxii. 3. 3 Ib. viii. 1.
4 Ezek. x. 4. 5 Ps. xviii. 12.
6 Ex. xix. 9, 16. xx. 21. 7 Ib. xxiv. 10.
8 S. John i. 14. 9 Is. ix. 2. 10 Theoph.
11 Rup. 12 Heb. i. 3. 13 Wisd. vii. 25.
14 Nicene Creed. 15 S. John i. 9.
16 Ib. xvii. 5. 17 S. Jer. Dion.

18 קֶרֶן Ex. xxxiv. 29. 30. 35. which is compared by Kim. Rashi, A. E. Abulw. Abarb. Tanch. Abendana. This is illustrated further by the use of "horns" as a hieroglyphic for the sun, Champollion Grammar p. 359. in Ges. and קרנתא "horns" of the sun, Buxt. (not in Levy). The title of Ps. xxii. עַל אַיֶּלֶת הַשַּׁחַר "according to the hind of the morning," may bear upon it, since אַיַּלְתָּא דשחרא in the Jerus. Talm. (originally quoted by Lightfoot, Horæ Hebr. on S. Mark xvi. 2) is used of the first rays of light, which usher in the dawn, the rays appearing solid like horns. In Arab. too עֻזַאלַת is a name of the sun, though Arab. authorities differ about its use, and עֻזאלת אלצֻחַא is the "sun at the time called צֻחַא," some part of the clear day. And Hariri uses "the horn of the gazelle" קַרְנ אלעֻזאלת (as explained by De Sacy) of those same first rays. But Kim. gives as the meanings of א. הש. hind (literally) or day-star, or sunrise.

19 As even Del. and Keil. יד is used of the side of the river Ex. ii. 5, and with the prepositions ל, אל, עד, בעד (See Ges.) but with מִן, once only *from the side of the country* Nu. xxiv. 4; on which, see note 20. end.

20 מיד occurs in the O. T. with the gen. of the noun or pronoun, 197 times; in the plural 5 times. Of these, the greatest number are with verbs of *delivering*, הציל, 71; הושיע, 18; *redeem*, פדה, 3, גאל, 3; *brought forth*, הוציא, 1; *rescued*, פרק, 1; *guard*, שמר, 2; *escape*, מלט, 9, פלט, 1; *flee*, ברח, 1; לקח, *took by force*, 11; *took, received*, 22; *took unawares from*, גזל, 2; *receive and offer*, הקריב, 1; *consecrate from*, הקדיש, 1; *sprinkled* (blood), זרה 2; *bought*, קנה, 7; *accept*, רצה, 2; *give*, נתן, 1; *collect*, אסף, 1; *eat from*, אכל 1; ברה, 2; *drank*, שתה 1; *seek*, בקש, 7; *require of*, דרש, 5; *judged and avenged*, שפט, 3; *avenged*, נקם, 1; *rend*, קרע, 3; *cause to fall from*, הפיל, 2; *strike from*, הכה, 2; *cut off from*,

Before CHRIST cir. 626.

‖horns *coming* out of his hand: and there *was* the hiding of his power.

‖ Or, *bright beams out of his side.*

When then did light or might, which lay, as it were, before in the Hand of God, go forth from it? For *the Hand of God* is always symbolic of His might, whether put forth, or for the time laid up in it. The form of the words remarkably corresponds to those of Moses, in the preface to the blessing on the tribes, which Habakkuk had in mind, [1] *From His right hand was a fiery law for them,* and S. Paul says that the glory of Moses' face which he received from the Presence of God, was a symbol of the glory of the law. [2] *The ministration of death written and engraven on stone was glorious, so that the children of Israel could not steadfastly behold the face of Moses for the glory of his countenance.* The law, being given by God, had a majesty of its own. The Psalms bear witness to its power in converting, enwisening, rejoicing, enlightening the soul [3]. They in whose heart it was, none of their steps slided [4]. The whole 119th Psalm is one varied testimony of its greatness and its power. It was a guide on the way; it was a schoolmaster unto Christ [5], by Whom it was fulfilled. But itself bare witness of the greater glory which should come forth from the Hand of God. [6] *If that which is done away were glorious, much more that which remaineth is glorious.* "[7] The horn signifieth power, when it is spoken of God the Father exhibiting to us God the Son: [8] *He hath raised up a horn of salvation for us,* and again, [9] *His horn shall be exalted in honor.* For all things which were marvelously done were glorious. The Only-Begotten came then in our form, and, in regard to the Flesh and the Manhood, enduring the appearance of our weakness, but, as God, invisible in might and easily subduing whom He willed."

And what has been the weapon of His warfare, whereby He has subdued the might of Satan and the hearts of men, but *the horns* of His Cross, whereto His Sacred Hands were once fastened by the sharp nails, where was the *hiding of His Power,* when His Almightiness lay hid in His Passion [10], and He was [11] *a worm and no man; a reproach of men and the despised of the people?* Now it is the Sceptre laid upon His Shoulder [12], the ensign and trophy of His rule, the Rod of His Strength [13], terrible to devils, salvation to man. In it lay His might, although concealed, as He said, [14] *I, if I be lifted up from the earth, will draw all men unto Me.* His Might was lodged there, although hidden. It was *the hiding-place of His power.* The Cross was [15] *to the Jews a stumbling-block, and unto the Greeks foolishness; but unto them which are called, both Jews and Greeks, Christ Crucified was the Power of God and the Wisdom of God.* Through the Cross was [16] *all power given to Him both in Heaven and earth.* [17] *There was given Him dominion and glory and a kingdom, that all people, nations, and languages should serve Him.* From Him shall go forth all power in earth; by His Hands shall be given the vacant thrones in Heaven, as He saith, [18] *To him that overcometh will I grant to sit with Me in My Throne, even as I also overcame and am set down with My Father in His Throne. There* too *was the hiding of His Power,* in that there, in His Cross, is our shelter [19], and in His pierced Side our hiding-place, where we may take refuge from Satan and our sins; for therein is Power. [20] *Neither shall any pluck them out of My Hand.* Light and darkness ever meet in God. His inapproachable light is darkness to eyes which would gaze on it. [21] *He covereth Himself with Light as with a garment.* His light is the very veil which hideth Him. His Light is darkness to those who pry into Him and His Nature; His darkness is light to those who by faith behold Him. He *emptied Himself* [22] and hid Himself; He hid the power of His Godhead in the weakness of the Manhood, and so [23] *He Who commanded the light to shine out of darkness, hath shined in our hearts, to give the light of the knowledge of the glory of God, in the Face of Jesus Christ.* "[24] In the Cross was for a while His might hidden, when He said to His Father, [25] *My soul is exceeding sorrowful even unto death,* and, *Father, if it be possible, let this cup pass from Me,* and on the Cross itself, [26] *Father, into Thy Hands I commend My Spirit.*"

הכרית, 1; נגזר, 1; *cast,* שלך; *reproach from,* חרפתי; *by writing from,* בכתב, 1; *letters from,* אגרת, 1; *officers appointed by* פקידים, 1. *strengthened from the hands of God,* 1. The verb *was,* היה, is expressed once; it lies in the sentence thrice; once only it means *from the side of a country,* Nu. xxiv. 4. in which there can be no ambiguity.

[1] Deut. xxxiii. 2. [2] 2 Cor. iii. 7. [3] Ps. xix. 8.
[4] Ib. xxxvii. 31. [5] Gal. iii. 24. [6] 2 Cor. iii. 11.
[7] S. Cyr. [8] S. Luke ii. 69. [9] Ps. cxi. 9.
[10] Is. liii. 3. [11] Ps. xxii. 6. [12] Is. ix. 6.
[13] S. John xii. 32.
[14] Ps. cx. 2. "The words, Horns are in His Hands, shew the insignia of His kingdom, by which horns, pushing and thrusting the invisible and opposing powers, He drove them away." Euseb. Dem. Evang. vi. 15. Add S. Cyprian Test. ad Quirin. ii. 21. p. 57. Oxf. Tr. "The horns in His Hands, what are they, but the trophy of the Cross?" S. Aug. de Civ. Dei xviii. 32. [15] 1 Cor. i. 23, 24. [16] S. Matt. xxviii. 18.
[17] Dan. vii. 14. [18] Rev. iii. 21.
[19] As in the proper names, Ezr. ii. 61. *Habaiah* "whom God hideth i. e., protecteth;" *Yehubbah* "hidden, protected." 1 Chron. vii. 34. Comp. Is. xxvi. 20. [20] S. John x. 28. [21] Ps. civ. 3.
[22] Phil. ii. 8. [23] 2 Cor. iv. 6. [24] S. Jer.
[25] S. Matt. xxvi. 38, 39. [26] S. Luke xxiii. 13.

Before CHRIST cir. 626.

d Nah. 1. 3.
|| Or, *burning diseases,* Deut. 32. 24.
e Ps. 18. 8.

5 [d] Before him went the
pestilence, and || [e] burning
coals went forth at his
feet.

6 He stood and measured the earth: he beheld,
and drove asunder the nations; [f] and the [g] everlast-

Before CHRIST cir. 626.

f Nah. 1. 5.
g Gen. 49. 26.

5. *Before Him went* [*goeth*] *the pestilence;* then to consume His enemies. [1] *I will send My fear before thee, and will destroy all the people, to whom thou shalt come,* and the lightnings are a token that [2] *they which hate Him, flee before Him, and the wicked perish at the Presence of God.* So, on His Ascension, Herod and Pilate were smitten by Him, and Elymas and Simon Magus before His Apostles, and whatsoever hath lifted itself up against Him hath perished, and Antichrist shall perish [3] *at the breath of His mouth,* and all the ungodly in the Day of Judgment.

And burning coals (rather, as E. M., *burning fever* [4]) *went forth at His Feet,* i. e., followed Him. Messengers of death went as it were before Him, as the front of His army, and the rear thereof was other forms of death [5]. Death and destruction of all sorts are a great army at His command, going before Him as heralds of His Coming, (such as are judgments in this world) or attendants upon Him, at the Judgment when He appeareth [6] in His Kingdom, when [7] *they shall gather out of His Kingdom all things that offend, and them which do iniquity, and shall cast them into a furnace of fire.*

6. *He stood* [8], *and measured* [9] *the earth.* Joshua, after he had conquered the land, meted it out and divided it among the people. He Who should come, should measure out the earth in its length and breadth, that *earth* which His glory *filleth. He stood,* as S. Stephen saw Him, [10] *standing at the Right Hand of God;* and Isaiah saith, [11] *The Lord standeth up to plead, and standeth to judge the people.* He had not need to go forth, but, in the abode of His glory, *He stood* and beheld and with His Eye *measured the earth,* as His own, whereas, before the Cross, it lay under [12] *the Prince of this world,* and he had said, [13] *it is delivered unto me, and unto whomsoever I will, I give it. He measureth* it, and gave it to His Apostles, [14] *All power is given unto Me in heaven and in earth. Go ye into all the world, and preach the Gospel to every creature,* and, [15] *their sound is gone out into all lands, and their words into the ends of the world.* He measureth it also, surveying and weighing all who dwell therein, their persons, qualities, deeds, good or bad, to requite them, as *Judge of quick and dead;* as David cast down Moab and measured them with a line, [16] *to put to death* and *to keep alive.*

He beheld, and drove asunder the nations, or, *made the nations to tremble* [17]. When Israel came out of Egypt and God divided the Red sea before them, they sang, [18] *The people shall hear and be afraid; terror shall take hold of the inhabitants of Palestina; the mighty men of Moab, trembling shall take hold of them; all the inhabitants of Canaan shall melt away; fear and dread shall fall on them; by the greatness of Thy power they shall be still as a stone.* Fear and awe were to be renewed. All nearness of God brings terror to sinful man. When the news came through the wise men, that they had [19] *seen in the East* the *star of* Him Who was *born, King of the Jews,* not *Herod the King* only *was troubled,* but *all Jerusalem with him.* Pilate [20] *was afraid* when he condemned Him: the High Priests wondered *whereunto this should grow,* and expostulated, [21] *ye have filled Jerusalem with your doctrine, and intend to bring this Man's blood upon us.* Heathendom was as a beleaguered city, mastered by an ubiquitous Presence, which they knew not how to meet. "[22] The state is beset: the Christians are in their fields, in their forts, in their islands. Every sex, age, condition, and now even rank is going over to this sect." The fierceness of the persecutions was the measure of their fear. They put forth all human might to stamp out the spark, lest their gods, and the greatness of the empire which they ascribed to their gods, should fall before this unknown power.

And the everlasting mountains were scattered;

[1] Ex. xxiii. 27. [2] Ps. lxviii. 1. 2. [3] Ib. xi. 4.

[4] De. xxxii. 2. (where also it is sing., as only beside in בְּנֵי רֶשֶׁף Job v. 7.) So A. E. "Burning coals" is from Kim. Tanch. gives as different opinions "sparks" or "arrows" or "pestilence;" but the meanings "sparks, arrows," are ascribed only to the plur. Ps. lxxvi. 4. lxxxviii. 48. Cant. viii. 6. The central meaning is probably "burning heat."

[5] "Before Him is sent the angel of death and His word goeth forth, a flame of fire." Jon.

[6] 2 Tim. vi. 1. [7] S. Matt. xiii. 51, 42.

[8] It is "a metaphor of his giving victory to Israel." Tanch.

[9] So Kim. A. E. Rashi. Tanch. Vulg. It is borne out by Hithpo. "extended himself," 1 Kgs xvii. 21. By an interchange of dentals מוד might be = מוט, and so Ch. LXX. but in no other case do the two forms coexist in Hebrew. [10] Acts vii. 56.

[11] Is. iii. 13. [12] 1 Cor. ii. 5. [13] S. Luke iv. 6.

[14] S. Matt. xxviii. 18. S. Mark xvi. 15.

[15] Ps. xix. 4. [16] 2 Sam. viii. 2.

[17] נִתֵּר being used of outward leaping of the locust, Lev. xi. 12, נָתַר, of the inward leaping of the heart, Job xxxvii. 1. either seems admissible. The inward terror was the forerunner and often the instrument of the outward dispersion.

[18] Ex. xv. 15, 16. [19] S. Matt. ii. 1–3.

[20] S. John xix. 8. [21] Acts v. 24, 28.

[22] Tertull. Apol. init. p. 2. Oxf. Tr.

Before CHRIST cir. 626.

ing mountains were scat-
tered, the perpetual hills
did bow: his ways *are*
everlasting.

7 I saw the tents of
‖ Cushan ‖ in affliction:
and the curtains of the
land of Midian did tremble.

‖ Or, *Ethiopia.*
‖ Or, *under affliction,* or, *vanity.*

the perpetual hills did bow; all power, great or small, gave way before Him. All which withstood was scattered asunder, all which in pride lifted itself up was brought low, although before the coming of the Saviour it had ever gone with neck erect, and none could humble its pride. There is something so marvelous about those ancient mountains. There they stood before man was on the earth; they are so solid, man so slight; they have survived so many generations of man; they will long survive us; they seem as if they would stand forever; the apter symbol how nothing should stand before the might of God. To the greater pride the heavier lot is assigned; the mountains lifted on high above the earth and, as it were, looking down upon it, are scattered or dispersed, as when a stone flieth in pieces under the stroke of the hammer. The "hills" are bowed down only; and this may be the pride of man humbled under the yoke of Christ.

His Ways are Everlasting. "Everlasting" is set over against "everlasting." The "everlasting" of the creature, that which had been as long as creation had been, co-existing with its whole duration, its most enduring parts, are as things past and gone; *the everlasting mountains, the hills of eternity,* have been scattered in pieces and bowed, and are no more. Over against these stands the ever-present eternity of God. *His ways are everlasting,* ordered everlastingly, existing everlastingly in the Divine Mind, and, when in act among us, without change in Him. The prophet blends in these great words, things seemingly contrary, *ways* which imply progress, *eternity* which is unchangeable. "[1] God ever worketh, and ever resteth; unchangeable, yet changing all; He changeth His works, His purpose unchanged." "[2] For Thou art Most High, and art not changed, neither in Thee doth to-day come to a close; yet in Thee it doth come to a close; because all such things also are in Thee. For they had no way to pass away, unless Thou heldest them together. And since *Thy years fail not,* Thy years are one To-day. How many of our's and our fathers' years have flowed away through Thy to-day; and from it received the measure and the mould of such being as they had; and still others shall flow away, and so receive the mould of their degree of being. But Thou art still the Same; and all things of to-morrow, and all beyond, and all of yesterday, and all behind it, Thou wilt do in this to-day, Thou hast done in this to-day."

To these His goings, a highway is made by the breaking down of all which exalted itself, as Isaiah had said,[3] *The loftiness of man shall be bowed down, and the haughtiness of men shall be made low, and the Lord Alone shall be exalted in that day;* and,[4] *The voice of him that crieth in the wilderness, Prepare ye the way of the Lord, make straight in the desert a highway for our God. Every valley shall be exalted, and every mountain and hill shall be made low.*

"[5] The Everlasting ways of the Everlasting God are Mercy and Truth,—by these Ways are the hills of the world and the proud demons, the princes of the darkness of this world, bowed down, who knew not the way of mercy and truth nor remembered Its paths. What hath he to do with truth, who is a liar and the father of it, and of whom it is written, *he abode not in the Truth?* But how far he is from Mercy, our misery witnesseth, inflicted on us by him. When was he ever merciful, who was *a murderer from the beginning?*—So then those swelling hills were bowed down from the Everlasting Ways, when through their own crookedness they sunk away from the straight ways of the Lord, and became not so much ways as precipices. How much more prudently and wisely are other hills bowed down and humbled by these ways to salvation! For they were not bowed from them, as parting from their straightness, but the Everlasting Ways themselves bowed down. May we not now see the hills of the world bowed down, when those who are high and mighty with devoted submission bow themselves before the Lord. and worship at His Feet? Are they not bowed down, when from their own destructive loftiness of vanity and cruelty, they are turned to the humble way of mercy and truth?"

7. *I saw* (in prophetic vision[6]), *the tents of Cushan in* (lit. *under*) *affliction.* On the Coming of the Lord there follows the visitation of those alien from Him[7]. Cushan-Rishathaim was the first, whose ambition God overruled to chasten His people[8]. It has been remarked[9], that as *king of Aram-Naha-*

[1] S. Aug. Conf. i. 4 p. 3. Oxf. Tr.
[2] Ib. 10. p. 6. [3] Is. ii. 17. [4] Ib. xl. 3.
[5] S. Bern. in Ps. Qui habitat. Serm. xi. 8.
[6] 1 Kgs xxii. 17.

[7] As in Joel ii. iii. Mic. iv. 1-10 and iv. 11. v. 1. v. 2. &c. v. 15. [8] Jud. iii. 8-10.
[9] R. S. Poole in Smith's Bible Dict., Art. Cushan. Often as Cush or Ethiopia is mentioned in the Old

Before CHRIST cir. 626.

8 Was the LORD displeased against the rivers? *was* thine anger against the rivers? *was* thy wrath against the sea, [h] that thou didst ride upon thine horses *and* ‖ thy chariots of salvation?

Before CHRIST cir. 626.

[h] Deut. 33. 26, 27. Ps. 68. 4. & 104. 3. ver. 15.

‖ Or, *thy chariots* were *salvation?*

raim or North Mesopotamia, he was probably sovereign of the Aram, from which Balak king of Moab, allied with Midian, sent for Balaam to curse Israel. *Midian* was the last enemy who, at the very entrance of the promised land, seduced God's people into idolatry and foul sin and lusts. Midian became then the object of the wrath of God [1]. They were also among the early oppressors of Israel, leaving [2] *no sustenance for Israel, neither sheep nor ox nor ass*, driving them for refuge to dwell in *the dens and the mountains, caves and fastnesses*, consuming the produce of their land *like locusts*, so that he whom God raised up as their subduer, was *threshing* even *in a wine-press to hide it from* them. Both the kingdom of Aram-Naharaim and Midian disappear from history after those great defeats. Midian, beside its princes, [3] lost, by mutual slaughter, *one hundred and twenty thousand men who drew sword.* It left its name as a proverb for the utter destruction of those who sought to exterminate the people of God. [4] *Do unto them as unto the Midianites; —make them and their princes like Oreb and Zeeb; all their princes as Zebah and as Zalmunnah, who said, let us take to ourselves the houses of God in possession.* It was an exterminating warfare, which rolled back on those who waged it. So Isaiah sums up an utter breaking-off of the yoke and the rod of the oppressor, as being [5] *as in the day of Midian.* The same word, *aven*, is nothingness, iniquity, and the fruit of iniquity, *trouble* [6], (since iniquity is emptiness and opposed to that which *is*, God and His Goodness, and ends in sorrow); so then Cushan is seen as lying as all sinners do, *weighed down* by and *under* what is very "emptiness." *Tents* and *curtains* are emblems of what shall pass away, under which the wicked shelter themselves from the troubles of this present life, as from heat and rain, "but which [7] in themselves decay, and are consumed by fire." *The curtains of Midian tremble.* The prophet uses the present to shew that he was not speaking of any mere past terror, but of that terror, which should still seize those opposed to God. The word "wrath" "*rogez*" echoes through the hymn [8]; here the wicked tremble, "*yirgezu*," under it, to perish; afterward the Prophet [9], to live.

8. *Was the Lord displeased against the rivers?* The Prophet asks the question thrice, as to the two miracles of the dividing of the Red Sea and the river Jordan, thereby the more earnestly declaring, that God meant somewhat by these acts and beyond them. He asks, as Daniel [10] and Zechariah [11] asked, what was the truth of the things which they saw. God's dealings with His former people were as much ensamples of what should be with us [12], as the visions shewn to the prophets. Hereafter too, there shall be [13] *signs in the sun, and in the moon, and in the stars; and upon the earth distress of nations, with perplexity, the sea and the waves roaring;* there shall be deepening plagues upon the sea and the rivers and fountains of waters; and *every living soul in the sea* shall *die* [14]. But God's purpose therein aforetime was not as to the sea or the rivers, but for the salvation of His elect; so shall it be to the end. Mighty as may be the *mighty waves of the sea* which lift themselves up against the Lord, *mightier on high is the Lord* [15]. "[16] As Thou didst dry up the Jordan and the Red sea, fighting for us; for Thou wert not wroth with the rivers or the sea, nor could things without sense offend Thee; so now mounting Thy chariots, and taking Thy bow, Thou wilt give salvation to Thy people; and the oaths which Thou swarest to our fathers and the tribes, Thou wilt fulfill for ever."

Thou didst ride upon Thy horses, as though God set His army, [17] *the Hosts which do His pleasure*, against the armies of earth, as the Prophet's servant had his eyes opened to see,

Testament, and in twelve of the sacred writers, Historians, Psalmists, Prophets; from Genesis to Esther (Moses, Job, Chronicles, Esther, David) (Ps. lxviii.), sons of Corah (Ps. lxxxvii.), Amos, Nahum, Zephaniah, Jeremiah, Ezekiel, and Ethiopians by Daniel, it is uniformly Cush not Cushan. Cush also is retained in Ch. and Syr. and was the name in use in the time of Josephus (Ant. i. 62.) One cannot then doubt, that Jon. and the Talmud (Sanh. 105 in Delitzsch) were right in regarding Cushan as designating him who is so called in the Holy Scriptures, not Ethiopia, which is never so called. Kim., Rashi, A. E., Abarb. follow the Targum. Only Tanchum, identifying the two clauses, says "Cushan is one of the names of Midian or one of its tribes, and it is also called Cush," Zipporah being identified with Moses' Cushite wife. Nu. xii. 1. Even Ewald says, "The people, כושן, which can neither according to language nor context stand for כוש:" though he guesses it to be a little people near Midian. ad loc.

[1] Nu. xxv. 17. [2] Jud. vi. 4. 11.
[3] Ib. viii. 10. [4] Ps. lxxxiii. 9, 11, 12.
[5] Is. ix. 4.
[6] Job v. 6. xxvi. 14; Jer. iv. 15. Hos. ix. 4. not in Ps. lv. 4. nor (as Ges.) in Job iv. 8. Ps. xxii. 8. Is. lix. 4.
[7] S. Greg. Mor. viii. 9. [8] ver. 2. [9] v. 16.
[10] vii. 16. [11] c. 1. [12] 1 Cor. x. 11.
[13] S. Luke xxi. 25. Rev. viii. 6. [14] Rev. xvi. 3.
[15] Ps. xciii. 4. [16] S. Jer. [17] Ps. ciii. 12.

Before CHRIST cir. 626.

9 Thy bow was made
quite naked, *according* to
the oaths of the tribes,
even thy word. Selah.
‖[1] Thou didst cleave the
earth with rivers.

[1] Ps. 78. 15, 16. & 105. 41.

‖ Or, *Thou didst cleave the rivers of the earth.*

---

[1] *the mountain was full of horses and chariots of fire round about Elisha.* "[2] Yet amidst so many thousands of horses and chariots, there was no rider; He was the Rider and Ruler of those horses, of Whom the Psalmist says, [3] *Thou that sittest above the Cherubim, shew Thyself.* With such horses and such chariots was Elijah also *taken up into Heaven.*"

And Thy chariots of salvation, lit, *Thy chariots are salvation.* Not, as in human armies, except as far as they are the armies of God, to destruction. The end of God's armies, His visitations and judgments, is the salvation of His elect, even while they who are inwardly dead, perish outwardly also. Nor, again, do they *prepare* for the deliverance for which He intends them. With God, to will is to do. His chariots *are* salvation. His help is *present help.* His *chariots* are the tokens and channels of His Presence to aid. And so, they who bore His *Name before the Gentiles, and kings, and the children of Israel, chosen vessels* to bear it, are, in a yet fuller sense, His *chariots,* which are *salvation.* They "[2] are holy souls, upon which the word of God cometh, to save them and others by them. [4] *I have compared thee,* saith the Spouse, *to a company of horses in Pharaoh's chariots.* However holy the soul, yet compared to God, it is like the chariot of Pharaoh; and a beast, yet still *a beast, before Thee*[5]." Yet such an one, as endowed with might and ready obedience, and swiftness and nobleness to bear the word of God, and through His might Whom they bore, not their own, nor making it their own, bearing down everything which opposed itself. "[6] The object of the Prophet, is to shew that the second dispensation is better and more glorious, and of incomparably better things than the old. For of old He led Israel forth, through the bodily service of Moses, changing into blood the rivers of Egypt, and doing signs and wonders; then dividing the Red Sea, and carrying over the redeemed, and choking in the waters the most warlike of the Egyptians. But when the Only-Begotten Word of God became Man, He withdrew the whole human race under heaven from the tyranny of Satan, not changing rivers into blood, nor pouring forth His anger upon waters, nor dividing waves of the sea, nor bringing destruction upon men, but rather destroying the murderous Serpent himself, and taking away the sin which had been invented by him and for him, and loosing the unconquered might of death, and calling all to the knowledge of God, through the holy Apostles, who, running forth their course under the whole Heaven and bearing about the Name of Christ, were very rightly had in admiration. He saith then, O Lord, most worthy to be heard are those things, of which Thou hast Thyself been the Doer, and what Thou hast anew wrought is far better than what Thou didst through Moses. For Thou wilt not inflict wrath on rivers, nor shew Thy might on the sea; not in these things will Thy Divine and marvelous power gleam forth, but *Thou wilt ride upon Thy horses,* and *Thy chariots are Salvation.* What may these horses be? The Blessed Disciples, Apostles and Evangelists, they who took on them wholly the yoke of all His Divine will, they, the noble, the obedient, ready for all things, whatsoever should please Him; who had Christ to sit upon them, whereof one is the Blessed Paul, of whom Himself saith, [7] *He is a chosen vessel unto Me, to bear My Name before the Gentiles.* Of fiery speed were these Horses, encompassing the whole earth; so then the chariots of God are said to be *ten thousand times ten thousand*[8]. For countless, each in their times, and after them, became leaders of the people, and subjected the neck of the understanding to the yoke of the Saviour, and bare about His Glory throughout the whole earth, and rightly divided the word of truth, and subdued the whole earth, as with the speed of horsemen."

His chariots are salvation; "[6] for they ran not in vain, but to save cities and countries and nations together, Christ overthrowing the empires of devils, who, so to speak, divided among themselves the whole earth, subduing its dwellers to their own will."

9. *Thy bow was made quite naked.* The word is repeated for emphasis. Lit. (In) *nakedness*[9] *it was laid naked;* the sheath being laid aside and cast away, as Isaiah says, [10] *Kir laid bare the shield.* The [11] *bow* represents the threat of the vengeance of Almighty God, from which it is at length discharged, if not turned aside; the longer the string is drawn, the sharper issueth the arrow. So then the more the coming of the day of judgment is delayed, the stricter is the severity of the judgment then issuing. So long as judg-

[1] 2 Kgs vi. 15.
[2] S. Jer.
[3] Ps. lxxx. 1.
[4] Cant. i. 9.
[5] Ps. lxxiii. 23.
[6] S. Cyr.
[7] Acts ix. 15.
[8] Ps. lxviii. 17.

[9] עֶרְיָה, acc. abs. as עֶרְיָה בֹשֶׁת Mic. i. 11., for the inf. abs.
[10] Is. xxii. 6.
[11] S. Greg. Mor. xix. 9. n. 54, Comp. S. Aug. in Ps. lix. n. 6.

Before CHRIST cir. 626.

[k] Ex. 19. 16, 18. Judg. 5. 4, 5. Ps. 68. 8. & 77. 18. & 114. 4.

10 [k] The mountains saw
thee, *and* they trembled:
the overflowing of the water passed by: the deep
uttered his voice, *and*
[l] lifted up his hands on high.

Before CHRIST cir. 626.

[l] Ex. 14. 22. Josh. 3. 16.

ment is delayed, the bow seems laid up in its sheath. God's judgments mostly strike suddenly [1] *as with a swift arrow,* because men regard them not, coming from a bow at a distance which they see not. His more signal judgments He makes bare in sight of all.

According to the oath of [*to*] *the tribes;* [2] *the oath which He sware unto our father Abraham,* which oath He often renewed to Abraham, Isaac and Jacob, and again to David[3]. This oath, the *word* and promise of God, was the pledge of the deliverance of His people, that they *should be saved from their enemies, and from the hand of all that hate them.* It lay, as it were, covered and hid, so long as God completed it not. *Selah.* A pause followeth, wherein to meditate on all which is contained in the *word* or promise of God, which is all time and eternity.

Thou didst cleave the earth with [i. e., *into*] *rivers.* Sea and river had become dry land for the passing through of God's people; again, the rock, struck by Moses' rod, was split, so that *rivers ran in the dry places.* Until that Rock, Which was Christ, was stricken, and [4] *out of His Side came Blood and water,* the whole world was desert and barren; then it was turned into streams of water, and "[5] now not four but twelve streams went forth from the Paradise of Scriptures." For from the One Fountain which is Christ, there issue many streams, even as many as convey the waters of His teaching, to *water the earth.*

10. *The mountains saw Thee, and they trembled,* lit. *they tremble.* While man is insensate, inanimate nature feels and attests the presence of its Maker. *It saw, it trembles.* To see, feel, tremble, were one. The Prophet does not follow a bare order of events, or bind himself to miracles which actually took place. The mountains tremble with earthquakes, or seem to be shaken by the thunders which they re-echo. And so they are signs, how what is firmest and closes up the way to man, trembles at the Presence of God. Whatever is lifted up shall be bowed down before Him[6]. But the word *trembled,* is that used especially of travail pangs[7], and so it may spiritually denote that "[8] they who conceive the fear of God shall bring forth unto salvation." *The overflowing* i. e., the impetuous, sweeping, flow, *of the water*[9] (or *of waters*), such as in themselves would bear all before them, *pass by* harmless. The more they swell, the more they expend themselves, and pass away. "The whole force of persecution, wherewith they vexed Thy people, at sight of Thee passed away," like a torrent which rages and disappears, and, by raging, the sooner wastes itself.

The deep uttered his voice, and lifted up his hands [10] *on high.* The noise of the waves, when God brought the strong East wind over it and [11] *rebuked* it, was as a cry to God; the waves, as they swelled, were like hands lifted up to Him, and stricken one against the other. There is no distinct ground against a slightly different rendering, [12] *the deep uttered his voice, the height lifted up his hands* i. e., to One yet higher, Whom height and depth owned as their Lord and worshiped.

[1] Ps. lxiv. 7.

[2] S. Luke i. 73. The E. V. takes the common words שבעות and מטות in their common senses, and אֹמֶר (which is a poetic word) agreeably to them. שְׁבוּעָה, "oath" occurs 27 times: the plur. שְׁבֻעוֹת here and Ezek. xxi. 28. The other meaning, *weeks,* which occurs 9 times (chiefly of the "feast of weeks," four times in De. xvi.), is plainly irrelevant here. מטות occurs 24 times beside of the tribes of Israel; twice only of the "rods" set against that of Aaron (Ex. vii. 12, Nu. xvii. 21.). אֹמֶר "speech" is used of the "promise of God," certainly Ps. lxxvii. 9. The construction is likewise easy, מטות is the gen. of the obj. after שבעות, and both in apposition with the preceding clause, and אֹמֶר with them. This construction and meaning of שבעות מטות, and meaning of אמר, and the construction with .ש.מ is that of Jon. followed by Kim. Rashi Abarb. Tanch. So also S. Jer. Only A. E. taking מַטּוֹת as spears, explains, that "His spears were sworn to establish the word of God."

[3] See Mic. end (ab. p. 104.) Ps. lxxxix. 3. cxxxii. 11.

[4] S. John xix. 24.

[5] S. Jer.

[6] See Zech. iv. 7.

[7] The LXX. so translate, "shall be in birth-pangs."

[8] Theoph.

[9] זרם is used apparently both of the "flow of waters and their strong current," as Tanch. explains it here; or of a violent storm breaking upon a thing. Its union with rain, Is. iv. 6, hail, Is. xxviii. 2. xxx. 30, the mountains, Job xxiv. 8, fits in with or requires the meaning "storm;" its union with mighty overflowing (שֹׁטְפִים) waters Is. xxviii. implies "a current;" "a storm against a wall" זרם קיר, Is. xxv. 4, might suit either; the verb זְרַמְתָּם, "hast swept them away," Ps. xc. 5, implies "a flood;" the mention of the clouds Ps. lxxvii. 18, "a storm." Kim. Rashi, Abarb. explain it here of water on the earth; A. E. of waters descending.

[10] רום = מרום which stands as the acc. of direction with *lifted up the eyes* Is. xxxvii. 23. xl. 26.

[11] Ps. cvi. 9.

[12] So S. Jer., Rashi, A. E.; רוֹם being a ἅπ. λεγ., one cannot say that it *might* not mean this. The metaphor would be dropped.

Before CHRIST cir. 626.

11 [m] The sun *and* moon
stood still in their habitation: ‖ at the light of
thine [n] arrows they went,
and at the shining of thy
glittering spear.

[m] Josh. 10. 12, 13.
‖ Or, *thine arrows walked in the light, &c.*
[n] Josh. 10. 11. Ps. 18. 14. & 77. 17, 18.

12 Thou didst march
through the land in indignation, [o] thou didst thresh
the heathen in anger.
13 Thou wentest forth
for the salvation of thy

Before CHRIST cir. 626.

[o] Jer. 51. 33. Amos. 1. 3. Mic. 4. 13.

11. *Sun* and *moon stood still in* [as one act[1], retiring *into*] *their habitation.* They withdrew, as it were, in the midst of the great tempest, wherein [2] *God cast down great stones from heaven upon* His enemies *and* they *died;* and *the sun stood still, and the moon stayed.* The sun too withdrew itself in the great darkness at the Crucifixion, as not bearing to look upon the Death of its Maker, when the majesty of the Sun of Righteousness was darkened o'er; and signs in the sun and in the moon there shall be to the end.

At the light of Thine arrows they went. "[3] There was no need of the sun by day, nor of the moon by night; for by the light of Thine arrows can the sons of men hold their way." "[4] This is a mystical interpretation, as you see; this is like the promise of the Most High; [5] *the sun shall be no more for thy light by day, neither for brightness shall the moon give light unto thee, and the Lord shall be to thee an everlasting light.*" The judgments of God are a light to His people, while they are the destruction of His enemies; in them they [6] *learn righteousness.* The arrows are God's judgments, as they threaten and wound from afar; *the shining of Thy glittering* [lit. *of the lightning of Thy*] *spear,* when close at hand. When all other light is withdrawn, and the *Sun,* our Lord, is hardly beheld in the darkness of the last days, and the *moon,* the Church, shall not give her light, Christ not shining upon her as before, because *iniquity shall abound, and the love of many shall wax cold,* and *stars,* many who seem to shine with the light of grace, *shall fall from heaven,* His own shall walk on and advance in holiness, "[7] from strength to strength[8], from good to better, from the way to their home," by the bright light of the lightning of God's Judgments, wherein His glory [9] shall be manifested. *Arrows and spears* are part of the spiritual armory of God, wherewith *the people are subdued unto Him;* "[10] armory, not wherewith He is girt but which He giveth to those who are meet; bright and as it were full of lightning. For most transparent is virtue." They went then at the light of Thine arrows; "[10] because to those who love sin virtue has no beauty, nor, as yet, any brightness. But to those who know her she is nothing less than lightning, bright and transparent, so that whoso hath her is easily known to all around. The disciples then, first having the lightning of Thine arms, shall lead others also to its Light. Admiring and conceiving in themselves those virtues which are the arms of Christ, they shine forth to others, a gleam, as it were, of the bright flash of light inherent in those graces." "[11] They were enlightened and began, by preaching, to send forth shining words of truth. But those words are Thine arrows, shining arrows, shewing by their light the way of life, and by their sharp point pricking the hearts of people unto repentance."

12. *Thou didst tread the earth in indignation.* The word *tread* [12] is used of very solemn manifestations of God[13], of His going to give to His own victory over their enemies[14]. Not *the land* only, as of old, but *the earth* is the scene of His judgments; the *earth* which was *full of His praise,* which He *meted out*[15], which contained the nations whom He chastened, the whole earth. *Thou dost thresh the heathen in anger.* Not then only, but at all times unto the end, *distress of nations and perplexity* are among the shoots of the fig-tree, which betoken that the everlasting [16] *summer is nigh at hand.* Jerusalem, when it had slain the Prince of Life, was given over to desolation and counted like the heathen. It became the synagogue, not the Church; and so in the destruction of Jerusalem (as it is an image of the destruction of the world) was that again fulfilled, *Thou dost march through the earth in indignation, Thou dost thresh the heathen in anger.*

13. *Thou wentest forth.* Even a Jew says of this place, "[17] The past is here used for the future; and this is frequent in the

[1] עָמַד sing. with the asyndeton שמש ירח; "Every word which needs ל (to) at the beginning has ה at the end, i. e. the ה replaces it." Rashi. Tanchum says the ה is for grandeur; Kim. Sal. b. Mel. say it is like ה in לילה. The "habitation" they explain to be heaven, like מעון.

[2] Jos. x. 11–13. [3] A. E. [4] Tanch. [5] Is. lx. 19. [6] Ib. xxvi. 9. [7] Dion. [8] Ps. lxxxiv. 7.

[9] The word "shining" is the same as "brightness," v. 4.

[10] S. Cyr. [11] Rup. [12] צעד.

[13] Jud. v. 4. Ps. lxviii. 8; of the procession of the ark 2 Sam. vi. 13. It is denied as to the idols, Jer. x. 5.

[14] "The voice of a treading" קול צעדה 2 Sam. v. 24. 1 Chr. xiv. 15.

[15] iii. 3, 6. [16] S. Luke xxi. 25–31. [17] Kimchi.

Before CHRIST cir. 626.

people, *even* for salvation with thine anointed; [p]thou woundest the head out of the house of the wicked, †by discovering the foundation unto the neck. Selah.

p Josh. 10. 24. & 11. 8, 12. Ps. 68. 21.

† Heb. *making naked.*

Before CHRIST cir. 626.

language of prophecy; for prophecy, although it be future, yet since it is, as it were, firmly fixed, they use the past concerning it." The Prophet speaks again in the past, perhaps to fix the mind on that signal going-forth, when God destroyed Pharaoh, the first enemy who essayed to destroy the chosen line. This stands at the head of all those dispensations, in which God put or shall put forth His might to save His people or destroy their enemies. All is with Him one everlasting purpose; the last were, as it were, embodied in the first: were it not for the last, the first would not have been. Prophecy, in speaking of the first, has in mind all the rest, and chiefly the chiefest and the end of all, the full salvation of His people through Jesus Christ our Lord. *Thou wentest forth*[1], i. e., "[2]Thou, the Unseen God, gavest signs which may be seen of Thy Presence or coming to men." *Thou wentest forth,* not by change of place, for Thou art not bounded; Thou art without change; but by shewing Thy power, and doing something anew openly *for the salvation of Thy people, even for salvation with*[3] *Thine Anointed,* God, from the first, helped His people through single persons, Moses, Joshua, each of the Judges, accustoming them to receive deliverance by one, and to gather together all their hopes in One. To Moses He said, [4]*I will be with thee,* and to Joshua, [5]*As I was with Moses, so I will be with thee,* and to Cyrus, [6]*I will go before thee,* preparing His people to receive that nearer Presence with His Christ, of which our Lord says: [7]*Believest thou not, that I am in the Father, and the Father in Me? The Father that Dwelleth in Me, He doeth the works.* "[8]The Son of God, God Invisible, became Man, visible; and with Him, so going forth, the Holy Spirit went forth *to the salvation of His people,* so as to give a visible sign of His Coming. For upon His Christ Himself, Him Who was anointed with the Holy Ghost[9], He *descended in a bodily Shape, as a Dove.* So He *went forth to the Salvation of His people,* i. e., to save His people with His Christ, our Saviour;" and again, on the Day of Pentecost, when that other Comforter came, *Whom,* He said, *I will send unto you from the Father,* and in Whose Presence His own promise was fulfilled, *Lo, I am with you always, even unto the end of the world.* His Presence was manifested both in the remission of sins, and the parting of graces among all, and in the [10]*signs and wonders, and divers miracles, and gifts of the Holy Ghost,* wherewith *God bare witness to the Apostles,* when [11]*they went forth, the Lord working with them, and confirming the word with signs following.* A going forth to judgment, at the end of the world, is foretold in the like image of warfare[12].

Thou woundedst [crushedst] the head out of the house of the wicked. One wicked stands over against One anointed, as in Isaiah, [13]*He shall smite the earth with the rod of His mouth, and with the breath of His lips shall He slay the wicked;* and David speaks of one, [14]*He shall smite the head over a great land;* and S. Paul speaks of [15]*that Wicked, whom the Lord shall consume with the spirit of His mouth, and shall destroy with the brightness of His Coming.* Him He shall destroy at once from above and below; overthrowing his kingdom from the foundation. From above, his head was crushed in pieces; from below, the house was razed from its very foundations. So Amos said, [16]*The Lord said, Smite the capital, and the lintel [threshold*[17]*] strike, and wound them in the head, all of them;* and with a different image, [18]*I destroyed his fruit from above, and his roots from beneath.* First, the head is struck off, crushed; then the house from the foundations to its neck; then as it were the headless walls. The image of *the neck* may

[1] Comp. בצעדך, בצאתך Jud. v. 4. Ps. lxviii. 8 of the great manifestation of God at Sinai; so of the judgment of the world, יֹצֵא מִמְּקוֹמוֹ Is. xxvi. 21.

[2] Rup.

[3] The E. V. is doubtless right. So Aquila, although a Jew, rendered, and the 5th Version. The 6th, a Christian, translated, "Thou wentest forth to save Thy people through Jesus, Thy Christ." So also the Vulgate and other old Jewish authorities. Rachmon (in Martini Pug. Fid. f. 534.) notes "that the word *eth* means *with*, as in Gen. xxxvii. 2. xxxix. 2." For although it might be used to mark the object only after a verbal noun, it is not likely that the construction would have been changed, unless the meaning were different. Had *eth* been only the sign of the object, there was no occasion for inserting it at all, and it would probably have been avoided, as only making the sentence ambiguous, in that it may more obviously be taken in the sense adopted by Aq. and the Vulgate and the E. V. The LXX and two early heretics who disbelieved the Divinity of our Lord (Theodot. and Symm.) render "to save Thy Christs." The LXX is wrong moreover, in that *the Anointed* is never used of the people, but of single persons only, who were shadows of the Christ. "Thine anointed" is understood of one individual, "the king of Judah," by A. E. "Saul and David," by Rashi; "Moses" by Abarb.; "Hezekiah" by Tanch.; but "Messiah Ben David" by Kim. Sal. b. Mel.

[4] Ex. iii. 12. [5] Josh. i. 5. [6] Is. xlv. 2.
[7] S. John xiv. 10. [8] Rup. [9] Acts x. 38.
[10] Heb. ii. 4. [11] S. Mark xvi. 20.
[12] Rev. xvii. 14. xix. 11. sqq. [13] Is. xi. 4.
[14] Ps. cx. 6. [15] 1 Thess. iv. 8. [16] Am. ix. 1.
[17] The same word is used Zeph. ii. 14. Ps. cxxxvii. 7. [18] Am. ii. 9.

Before CHRIST cir. 626.

14 Thou didst strike through with his staves the head of his villages: they †came out as a whirlwind to scatter me: their rejoicing *was* as to devour the poor secretly.

† Heb. *were tempestuous.*

be the rather used to recall, that as the house of God is built of living stones, so the kingdom of the evil one is made of living dead, who shall never cease to exist in an undying death. The bruising of Satan, the head or prince of this evil world, is the deliverance of the world. His head was bruised, when, by the Death of our Lord, *the Prince of this world* was *cast out;* he is *crushed out of the house of the wicked,* whenever he, the *strong man,* is bound and cast out, and "the soul of the sinner which had been his abode, becomes the house of God, and righteousness dwelleth there and walketh in her."

"[1] Thou didst not leave any error or vice in the world unshaken, either what was concealed, like the foundation of a house; or that which was open, as the neck of the body is open;" *to the neck,* where the destruction from above ceased, so that nothing remained unsmitten. "[1] For they being, by the fiery tongues which Thou shewedst without, made fervent and strong, wise and eloquent, ceased not, until they made known to all, what folly was this world's wisdom, what sacrilege its sacred worship." "[2] His secret counsels He laid bare, as the Apostle says, [3] *We are not ignorant of his devices;* and, *to another is given the discerning of spirits.*"

14. *Thou didst strike through with his staves the head of his villages*[4]. The destruction comes not upon himself only, but upon the whole multitude of his subjects; and this not by any mere act of Divine might, but *with his own staves,* turning upon him the destruction which he prepared for others. So it often was of old. When the Midianites and Amalekites and the children of the east[5] wasted Israel in the days of Gideon, [6] *the Lord set every man's sword against his fellow, even throughout all the host;* and when God delivered the Philistines into the hand of Jonathan[7]; so was it with *Ammon Moab and the inhabitants of Mount Seir,* at the prayer of Jehoshaphat and his army[8]. And so it shall be, God says, at the end, of the army of God; *every man's sword shall be against his brother*[9], and Isaiah says, [10] *every man shall eat the flesh of his own arm,* and Zechariah, [11] *a great tumult from the Lord shall be among them; and they shall lay every man hold on the hand of his neighbor, and his hand shall rise up against the hand of his neighbor.* So Pharaoh drove Israel to the shore of the sea, in which he himself perished; Daniel's accusers perished in the den of lions, from which Daniel was delivered unharmed[12]; and so Haman was hanged on the gallows which he prepared for Mordecai[13]. So it became a saying of Psalmists, [14] *He made a pit and digged it, and is fallen into the ditch which he made; his mischief shall return upon his own head, and his violent dealing shall come down upon his own pate:* and this from above, sent down by God. The heathen too observed that there was "no juster law than that artificers of death by their own art should perish." This too befell him, when he seemed to have all but gained his end. *They came* [*out*] *as a whirlwind to scatter me,* with whirlwind force, to drive them asunder to all the quarters of the heavens, as the wind scatters the particles of [15] cloud, or [16] *as the stubble which passeth away by the wind of the wilderness.* Pharaoh at the Red Sea or Sennacherib, sweep all before them. Pharaoh said, [17] *I will pursue, I will overtake, I will divide the spoil; my lust shall be satisfied upon them; I will draw my sword, my hand shall destroy them.*

Their rejoicing. It is no longer one enemy.

[1] Rup. [2] Dion. [3] 2 Cor. ii. 11. 1 Cor. xii. 10.

[4] The meaning "leaders, prefects of soldiers" has been obtained for פרן by Ges. &c. by a misapplication of the Arab. פַרַן "distinguished" which in conj. ii. signifies "defined for a person," but only in the idiom פרן עלי בראיה "defined for me by his own counsel," which gains its meaning only from the עלי. That of the E. V. is furnished, in most places, by the passages themselves. As in Ezek. xxxviii. 11, where "a land of פרזות" is expanded into "where they all dwell without wall; and bar and double gates they have not;" and Deut. iii. 5, "all these were fenced cities, with high wall, double gates and bar, beside cities of הפרזי," and 1 Sam. vi. 18, "from the fenced city to the village of הפרזי" and Zech. ii. 8. "Jerusalem shall dwell as פרזות for the multitude of men and cattle therein; and I, saith the Lord, will be a wall of fire around." In Esther ix. 19, cities הפרזות are contrasted with Shushan v. 18, and "the Perizzite," very possibly, was originally "paganus" "one who dwelt in villages." This rendering is adopted by chief Jewish interpreters; Kim. "cities of the plain, which have no fort nor wall." So Abulw. Tanch. "land;" Rashi, Abarb. "his cities and villages;" A. E. keeps the word, but implies the meaning, on Zech. ii. 8. Kim. Sal. b. Mel. obtained the sense of "forces" here, that they "shall come in great numbers, and so dwell in Jerusalem, as פרזים, who dwell in פרזות, who spread in the whole place, who have no wall to enclose them." This explains Jon. "the forces of Pharaoh," as hordes too large to be enclosed in walls, and perhaps the LXX. δυνάσται.

[5] Jud. vi. 3, 4. [6] Ib. vii. 22.
[7] 1 Sam. xiv. 12, 16, 20. [8] 2 Chron. xx. 22, 23.
[9] Ezek. xxxviii. 21. [10] Is. ix. 20.
[11] Zech. xiv. 13. [12] Dan. vi. 24. [13] Esth. vii. 10.
[14] Ps. vii. 5. add ix. 15, x. 2, xxxv. 8, lvii. 6, xciv. 23. cxli. 10. Prov. v. 22. xxvi. 27. Eccl. x. 8.
[15] Job xxxvii. 11. [16] Jer. xiii. 24. add xviii. 17. Is. xli. 16. Del. [17] Ex. xv. 9.

Before CHRIST cir. 626.

[q] Ps. 77. 19. ver. 8.
|| Or, *mud*.

15 [q] Thou didst walk through the sea with thine horses, *through* the || heap of great waters.

16 When I heard, [r] my belly trembled; my lips quivered at the voice: rottenness entered into my

Before CHRIST cir. 626.

[r] Ps. 119. 120. Jer. 23. 9.

The malice of the members was concentrated in the head; the hatred concentrated in him was diffused in them. The readiness of instruments of evil to fulfill evil is an incentive to those who conceive it; those who seem to ride the wave are but carried on upon the crest of the surge which they first roused. They cannot check themselves or it. So the ambitious conceiver of mischief has his own guilt; the willing instruments of evil have theirs. Neither could be fully evil without the other. Sennacherib had been nothing without those fierce warriors who are pictured on the monuments, with individual fierceness fulfilling his will, nor the Huns without Attila, or Attila without his hordes whose tempers he embodied. Satan would be powerless but for the willing instruments whom he uses. So then Holy Scripture sometimes passes from the mention of the evil multitude to that of the one head, on earth or in hell, who impels them; or from the one evil head who has his own special responsibility in originating it, to the evil multitude, whose responsibility and guilt lies in fomenting the evil which they execute.

Their rejoicing. He does not say simply "they rejoice to," but herein is their exceeding, exulting joy. The wise of this earth glories in his wisdom, the mighty man in his might, the rich in his riches: the truly wise, that he understandeth and knoweth God. But as for these, their exultation is concentrated in this,—savagery; in this is their jubilation; this is their passion. Psalmists and pious men use the word to express their exulting joy in God: men must have an object for their empassioned souls; and these, in cruelty.

As it were to devour the poor secretly. From the general he descends again to the individual, but so as now to set forth the guilt of each individual in that stormy multitude which is, as it were, one in its evil unity, when each merges his responsibility, as it were, in that of the body, the horde or the mob, in which he acts. *Their exultation,* he says, is that of the individual robber and murderer, who lies wait secretly in his ambush, to spring on the defenceless wanderer, to slay him and devour his substance. Premeditation, passion, lust of cruelty, cowardice, murderousness, habitual individual savagery and treachery, and that to the innocent and defenceless, are all concentrated in the words, *their exultation is, as it were, to devour the poor secretly,* i. e. *in their secret haunt.*

Pharaoh had triumphed over Israel. [1] *They are entangled in the land, the wilderness hath shut them in.* He rejoiceth in having them wholly in his power, as a lion has his prey in his lair, *in secret,* unknown to the Eyes of God Whom he regarded not, with none to behold, none to deliver. "[2] They gloried in oppressing the people of Israel, even as the cruel man glories in secretly rending and afflicting the needy, when without fear they do this cruelty, nor heed God beholding all as Judge." The invisible enemies too rejoice very greatly in the ruin of our souls. [3] *Lest mine enemy say, I have prevailed against him: for if I be cast down, they that trouble me will rejoice at it.* [4] *O Lord and governor of all my life, leave me not to their counsels and let me not fall by them.* Yet God left them not in his hands; but even *brake the head of Leviathan in pieces.*

15. *Thou didst walk through the sea with Thine horses.* God Himself is pictured as leading them on the way, Himself at the head of their multitude, having, as Asaph said of old, [5] *His path in the sea.* So Isaiah, [6] *Who leddest them in the depths;* and Zechariah, [7] *And he shall pass through the sea.* God was literally there; for [8] *in Him we live and move and have our being.* He Who "is wholly everywhere but the whole of Him nowhere" manifested His Presence there. Such anthropomorphisms have a truth, which men's favorite abstractions have not.

Through the heap [9] *of great waters,* as of old, [10] *the waters stood as a heap,* and *He made the waters to stand as a heap.* The very hindrances to deliverance are in God's Hands a way for His ends. The waves of the Red sea rose in heaps, yet this was but a readier way for the salvation of His people and the destruction of their enemies. "[2] God prepareth ever a way for His elect in this present evil world, and leadeth them along the narrow way which leadeth unto life."

16. *When I heard,* better, *I heard and* &c.

[1] Ib. xiv. 3. [2] Dion. [3] Ps. xiii. 4.
[4] Ecclus. xxiii. 1.
[5] דרכם בים as Ps. lxxvii. 20, בים דרכך.
[6] Is. lxiii. 13. [7] Zech. x. 11. [8] Acts xvii. 28.
[9] So Jon. Kim. (comparing Ex. xv. 8 and חמרים Ex. viii. 10.) Sal. b. Mel. Tanch. (mentioning the opinion of others that it is "mud" but choosing the other.) A. E. chooses the sense, "mud." Rashi paraphrases, "as the sand of the sea." For that of Ges., "the boiling of the waters," there is absolutely no authority.
[10] Ex. xv. 8. Ps. lxxviii. 13.

Before CHRIST cir. 626.

bones, and I trembled in myself, that I might rest in the day of trouble: when he cometh up unto the people, he will ‖invade them with his troops.

‖ Or, *cut them in pieces.*

The prophet sums up, resuming that same declaration with which he had begun, *I heard, I was afraid.* Only now he expresses far more strongly both his awe at God's judgments and his hopes. He had just beheld the image of the destruction of Pharaoh, the end of the brief triumphing of the wicked and of the trials of God's people. But awful as are all the judgments of God upon the enemies of His people, it was not this alone which was the object of his terror. *This* was deliverance. It was the whole course of God's dispensations, which he had heard; God's punishment of His people for their sins, and the excision of their oppressors, who, in His Providence, fulfilling their own evil end, executed His chastisements upon them. The deliverances, which shadowed out the future, had their dark side, in that they *were* deliverances. The whole course of this world is one series of man's unfaithfulnesses or sins, God's chastisements of them through their fellow-sinners, and His ultimate overthrow of the aggressors. Those first three centuries of glorious martyrdoms were, on the one side, the malice and hatred of Satan and the world against the truth; on the other side, the prophets of those days told their people that they were the chastisements of their sins. Future deliverance implies previous chastisement of those delivered. The prophet then, at the close, in view of all, for himself and all whose perplexities he represented and pleaded before God, chooses his and their portion. "Suffer here and rest forever!" "Endure here any terror, any failure of hopes, yet trust wholly in God, have rest in the day of trouble and sing the endless song!" Again he casts himself back amid all the troubles of this life.

I heard [i. e. that speech of God uttering judgments to come] *and my belly* [1], the whole inward self, bodily and mental, all his hidden powers, *trembled* [2], "vibrated" as it were, "[3] in every fibre of his frame," at the wrath of God; *my lips quivered* [4] *at the voice* of God, so that they almost refused their office and could hardly fulfill the prophetic duty and utter the terrors which he had heard; his very strongest parts, the *bones,* which keep the whole frame of man together, that he be not a shapeless mass, and which remain unconsumed long after the rest has wasted away in the grave, *rottenness entered into them,* corruption and mouldering eating into them [5]; *and I trembled in myself* [lit. *under me* [6]] so that he was a burden to himself and sank unable to support himself, *that I might rest in the day of trouble.* All up to this time was weariness and terror, and now at once all is repose; the prophet is carried, as it were, over the troubles of this life and the decay of the grave to the sweetness of everlasting rest [7]. I, the same, suffer these things, terror, quivering, rottenness in the very bones themselves. *I* [lit.] *who shall rest* [8] *in the day of trouble. I* who had not rest until then, shall enter into rest then in the very day of trouble to all who found their rest in the world not in God, the day of judgment. [9] *Blessed is the man whom Thou chastenest, O Lord, and teachest him in Thy law, that Thou mayest give him patience in time of adversity, until the pit be digged up for the ungodly.*

"[10] O my soul; had we daily to bear tortures, had we for a long time to endure hell

[1] בטן is used of the inward part of man, which "prepareth mischief," Job xv. 35; the spirit whereof constrains one, Ib. xxxii. 18; the chambers of which are searched out by the spirit of man, as the lamp of God, Prov. xx. 27; as cleansed by stripes Ib. 30; where the words of the wise are guarded, Ib. xxii. 18; which should not be filled with the East wind, Job xv. 2. In the like way in the N. T. "from his belly, κοιλία, shall flow living waters," S. John vii. 38. In Arab. בַּטְן is the "inner meaning;" בַּטַנַ "he knew the inner, the intrinsic, state of the case;" with ב p., "became intimate with;" conj. x. with acc., "penetrated a thing." So also אל בָּאטְן "that which is within," of facts, thoughts, mind. See Lane. All are derivative senses. בטן has nothing in common with Ar. בטל, as Ges.

[2] "ragaz," twice repeated in this verse, takes up, as it were, "rogez" wrath v. 2.

[3] Del.

[4] צלל occurs of the tingling of the ear, 1 Sam. iii. 11. 2 Kgs xxi. 12. Jer. xix. 3. "From the fear at the meaning of this sound which he has heard his lips trembled in speaking, and he uttered their words with a trembling sound." Tanch.

[5] רקב (the root) is used of the decay of wood and of the bones, and Pr. x. 7, of "the name of the wicked."

[6] As 2 Sam. ii. 23. "he died" as we say, "on the spot," sinking down dead.

[7] The very softness of the original word אָנוּחַ stands in contrast with the rigidness in the words ti*r*gaz, *r*akab, *r*egaz, tsa*r*ah.

[8] נוח is uniformly "rest." It is used of rest from labor, from calamities, [Is. xxiv. 7 Job iii. 26.] rest *in* a place, with ב, or *on* (עַל) it; of the Holy Spirit resting on a person (with עַל). But its meaning is uniformly of rest, not of silence as to a thing [as Ges.] nor does החריש furnish any analogy, since this in itself signifies "*kept* silence." Nor can it mean "wait patiently for," for נוח "rest" is the very opposite of "waiting for," חכה, which necessarily involves a degree, even if of subdued unrest. Then, too חִכָּה, קִוָּה, יִחַל, are used of waiting, looking for good, not for evil.

[9] Ps. xciv. 12, 13.

[10] Man. ap. App. S Aug. T. vi. c. 21.

Before CHRIST cir. 626.

17 ¶ Although the fig tree shall not blossom, neither *shall* fruit *be* in the vines; the labor of the olive shall † fail, and the fields shall yield no meat; the flock shall be cut off from the fold, and *there shall be* no herd in the stalls:

† Heb. *lie.*

Before CHRIST cir. 626.

itself, that we might see Christ in His glory and be the companion of His Saints, were it not worth enduring all sorrow, that we might be partakers of so exceeding a good, such exceeding glory?"

When he cometh up unto the people, he shall invade them with his troops, or, which is probably meant, *when he cometh up who shall invade them*[1]. It is a filling out of *the day of trouble*[2]. However near the trouble came, he, under the protection of God and in firm trust in Him, would be at rest in Him. The troubles of God's prophets are not the outward troubles, but the sins of their people which bring those troubles, the offence against the majesty of God, the loss of souls. Jeremiah was more at rest in the court of the prison, than when all the people did curse him[3] for telling them God's Truth. He who fears God and His judgments betimes, shall rest in perfect tranquillity when those judgments come. The immediate trouble was the fierce assault of the Chaldees whose terror he had described; and this, picturing, as through the prophecy, all other judgments of God even to the last, when devils shall contend about the souls of men, as Satan did about the body of Moses.

[1] This is the simplest construction, and is that adopted by Kim. Abarb. In the rendering "in the coming up of a people," the ל would, as Tanchum observes, be superfluous, and יְגוּדֵנוּ would be more natural than יְגוּדֶנּוּ. But the prophet would not needlessly make his language ambiguous. Had he meant, "in the coming up of *a* or *the* people," he would have used the common לעלות עם or לעלות העם. The construction of עלה with ל instead of על, "to" for "against," is exceptional. But עלה occurs with the equivalent אל of the person, and in one case with ל (as we say "go up to") Gen. xliv. 24, 34. xlv. 9. Ex. xix. 3, 24. xxiii. 1, 12. xxxii. 30. Deut. x. 1. Josh. x. 4, 6. Jud. iv. 5. xii. 3. xvi. 5. (לֹה) 18. 1 Sam. vi. 20. x. 3, xiv. 9, 12. xxiii. 19. 2 Kgs i. 11. xxii. 4, and this, in a hostile sense Jud. xx. 23, 2 Sam. v. 19, Jer. xlix. 28, 31. עם also, is used without the art. (as a sort of proper name) of the Jewish people, Is. xxvi. 11. xliv. 6. גוד occurs Gen. xlix. 19. there also with acc.; יתנודד, our, "troop" (verb) Jer. x. 7. See also Mic. v. 14, p. 79.

[2] יום צרה is a general term which occurs also Is. xxxvii. 3, more commonly with ב, ביוֹם צרה, Ps. xx. 2, l. 15, Pr. xxiv. 10, xxv. 19, Jer. xvi. 19, Ob. 12, 14, Nah. i. 7. Zeph. i. 15. as עת צרה occurs Jer. xxx. 7. Dan. xii. 1. בעת צרה, Is. xxxiii. 2. Jer. xiv. 8. xv. 11; ביום צרתי Gen. xxxv. 3, Ps. lxxvii. 3, lxxxvi. 7; בעת צרתכם Jud. x. 14. בעת צרתם Neh. ix. 27. There is no ground then to limit it to the Chaldæan or Assyrian period.

[3] Jer. xv. 10.

17. *Although* [lit. *For*[4]] *the figtree shall not blossom.* The Prophet repeats his confidence in God, premising his knowledge that all human hopes should fail. I know, he says, all stay and support shall fail; he numbers from the least to the greatest, the fruits of trees, the fig, vine and olive, for sweetness, gladness, cheerfulness[5], whereof the well-being of the vine and figtree furnishes the proverbial picture of peace and rest. These shall either not *shoot forth*, or shall at time of fruit-gathering have no *produce*[6], or having, as it were, labored to bring forth fruit shall *lie*[7], and fail: yet further "the staff of life" itself shall fail; *the fields shall yield no meat;* all the fields, as though they were but one[8], shall have one common lot, barrenness. Yet more; the flocks shall be cut off[9] from the fold; not those only, feeding abroad in fields and open plains, shall be driven away, but they shall be carried away by the enemy from the folds, where they seemed penned securely; and not these only, but *there shall be no herd in the stalls*[10], even the stronger animals shall utterly fail; every help for labor, or for clothing, or for food shall cease; he speaks not of privation, partial failure, but of the entire loss of all things,

[4] The adversative or exceptional force attributed to כי, always lies in the relation of the two sentences, not in the כי itself, which is always causative, "for" or "because."

[5] Ps. civ. 15.

[6] יבול occurs here only of the produce of trees; 10 times of the earth itself directly; in Ps. lxxvii. 1, its produce, as the result of human culture, is יגיעם, יבולם; and Job xx. 28 יבול ביתו. מעשׂה occurs here only of the fruit, being an application of the common idiom עשׂה פרי.

[7] כִּחֵשׁ as Hos. ix. 2.

[8] שְׁדֵמוֹת, (an old word Deut. xxxii. 32) with no known etymology, is used, in three out of the four places in which it certainly occurs, in relation to place: "fields of Gomorrah" Deut. l. c. "f. of Kidron 2 Kgs xxiii. 4." "f. of Heshbon" Is. xvi. 8. It occurs in a fifth, (if, as is probable, the Kri is right,) "all the fields unto the brook Kidron" i. e. reaching to it, Jer. xxxi. 40. As a collective, it is joined with a sing. verb here, and Is. xvi. 8.

[9] גזר occurs intrans. here only. In Arab. also it is commonly used, but intrans. of "water which sunk" or retired. See Lane.

[10] רפתים, here only, but clear from the context. In Buxtorf's instance, מצאה ברפת "found it in a stall," the word is very probably used in the sense ascribed to it here by tradition as "well known in the language of the ancient (doctors) who say in the sing. רפת בקר." Tanch. "House of oxen." Kim. "See Mishnah Bava Bathra ii. 3. vi. 4." Munk on Tanch. The Arab. רַפַּת "chopped straw" could hardly furnish a name for a stall.

Before CHRIST cir. 626.

s Job. 13. 15.
t Isai. 41. 16. & 61. 10.

18 [s]Yet I will [t]rejoice
in the LORD, I will joy
in the God of my salva-
tion.

19 The LORD God *is*
[u]my strength, and he will
make my feet like [x]hinds
feet, and he will make me

Before CHRIST cir. 626.

u Ps. 27. 1.
x 2 Sam. 22. 34. Ps. 18. 33.

---

no meat from the fields, *no* herd in the stalls; and what then? *And I will rejoice in the Lord, I will joy in the God of my salvation.* The words are very impressive, as they stand in the Hebrew. "For," he says, "the fig-tree shall not blossom, *and* there is no fruit in the vines, the labor of the olive *hath* failed;" (the Prophet does not look on, only to these things, but in his mind stands in the midst of them [1], they are done, and he amid them, feeling their effects) "and the field *hath* yielded no food; the flock hath been cut off from the fold, *and* there is no herd in the stall; *and I*"—He relates it as the result of all which had gone before; such and such was the state of fruit-trees, vintage, harvest, flocks and herds; such was the aspect of all nature, living or inanimate; all was barren, disappointing; all had failed and was gone; and then at last he comes to himself, *and I;* what is he doing, when all nature and every seeming hope is dead? thus and thus it is with them; *and I—will rejoice.* He almost uses the expression as to the exultation of the enemy, adopting the same word only in a softer form. "*Their exulting* joy was" concentrated in this, "as to devour the poor secretly;" *he* too had "exulting joy." There is a joy against joy: a joy of theirs in the possession of all which their rapacity covets, in the possession of all things: a joy of his amid the privation of all things. He contrasts the two joys, as David had of old; [2] *the men of the world, whose portion is in this life, whose belly Thou fillest with Thy hid treasure; they are sated of children and leave their substance to their babes: I,* he adds, *I shall behold Thy Presence in righteousness, I shall be sated, in the awakening, with Thine image.* So Habakkuk, *I will* not *rejoice* only, but *shout for joy* [3]; and not so only, but *I will bound for joy;* and this not for a time only; both words express a drawing, yearning [4] of the soul, and this yet more and more, *I will shout for joy and would shout on; I will bound for joy and would bound on.* But whence the source of this measureless unutterable joy? *In the Lord,* the Unchangeable God, *Who is and was and is to come,* I AM, (it is the incommunicable Name); in the God of my salvation: it is almost the Name of Jesus [5]; for JESUS is salvation, and the Name means "the Lord is Salvation;" whence the words are here rendered even by a Jew [6], "in God the Author of my redemption," and yet more sweetly by a father [7], "in God my Jesus." In Him his joy begins, to Him and in Him it flows back and on; before he ventures, amid all the desolation, to speak of joy, he names the Name of God, and, as it were, stays himself in God, is enveloped and wrapped round in God; *and I* (the words stand in this order) *and I in the Lord would shout for joy.* He comes, as it were, and places himself quite close to God, so that nothing, not even his joy should be between himself and God; "and *I* in *the Lord.*" All creation, as it had failed, ceases to be; all out of God: he speaks of nothing but himself and God, or rather himself *in God;* and as He, God, comes before his joy, as its source, so in Him does he lose himself, with joy which cannot be contained, nor expressed, nor rest, but utters itself in the glad motions of untiring love. *I would bound for joy in my Saving God.* Truly all our joy is, to be in Him in Whom is all Good, Who is all Goodness and all Love.

19. *The* LORD *God is my strength.* The prophet does not inwardly only exult and triumph in God, but he confesses also in words of praise, that in Him he hath all things, that He is All things in him. And as he had confessed the Father, under the Name whereby He revealed Himself to Moses, and the Son, "the Lord God of my salvation," so he confesses [8] God the Holy Ghost, Who, in us, is our strength. *He* is *our strength,* so that through Him, we *can do all things; He* is *our strength,* so that without Him, we can do nothing; *He* is *our strength,* so that when we put forth strength, we put forth nothing of our own, we add nothing of our own, we use not our own strength, of which we have none, but we *do* use His; and we have It ever ready to use, as if it were our own. For it is *not* our own and it *is* our

---

[1] The first future לא תפרח, "*shall* not *flourish*" determines that all which follows is future in act, though present to the prophet's mind.

[2] Ps. xvii. 13, 15.

[3] עלז, like ἀλαλάζω. It is used of exultation in the holiness of God, Ps. lx. 8. cviii. 8. before God, Ps. lxviii. 5, God being the implied Object, Zeph. iii. 14. Ps. xxviii. 7. xcvi. 12. cxlix. 5. of the evil in evil Jer. xi. 15. l. 11, li. 39. Ps. xciv. 3.

[4] This is the force of the optative אעלוזה. אָגִילָה, אֶעְלֹזָה, recurs in Ps. lx. 8. cviii. 8.

[5] Jesus in Heb. יֵשׁוּעַ, here יֶשַׁע.

[6] Chald. The Syr. "God my Redeemer." LXX. "God my Saviour."

[7] S. Aug. de Civ. D. xviii. 32. "To me what some MSS. have; 'I will rejoice in God my Jesus,' seems better than what they have, who have not set the Name itself, (but saving) which to us it is more loving and sweeter to name."

[8] Rup.

Before CHRIST cir. 626.

to [y] walk upon mine high places. To the chief singer on my † stringed instruments.

[y] Deut. 32. 13. & 33. 29.

† Heb. *Neginoth*, Ps. 4, title.

own; not our own, i. e., not from or of ourselves; but our own, since It is in us, yea He the Lord *our God* is *our strength*, not without us, for He is *our* strength, but in us. And so he says further, how we can use it as our own. *He will make my feet like hinds*, which bound upward through His imparted strength, and, when scared by alarms here below, flee fearless to their native rocks, spring from height to height, and at last shew themselves on some high peak, and standing on the Rock, look down on the whole world below their feet and upward on high. Even so, [1] when at the end of the world all shall fail, and *the love of many shall wax cold*, and the Church, which is likened to the fig tree the vine and the [2] olive, shall yield no fruits, and sweetness shall be corrupted by vanities, and the oil of mercy shall be dried up, and lamps go out, and its promises shall fail and it shall *lie*, having *a show of goodness, but denying the power of it; in words confessing God, and in works denying Him;* and through their own negligences, or the carelessness of pastors, the sheep of Christ shall perish from His very fold, and they who should be strong to labor [3] shall cease, God's elect shall joy in Him, "beholding His goodness, and loving Him in all things, and He will give them free affections, and fervid longings of holy love, whereby they shall not walk only, but *run the way of* His *commandments* and prevail over the enemies of their salvation."

[1] Chiefly from Dion. Comp. S. Jer.
[2] S. Luke xiii. 6. Is. v. 1. xxi. 33. &c. Rom. xi. 17.
[3] 1 Cor. ix. 9, 10.

Yet though this strength is inward, and used by man, still God Who gives it, Himself guides it. Not man shall *direct his own ways*, but *He will make me to walk* (as on a plain *way*) *upon my high places*. Steep and slippery places and crags of the rocks are but *ways* to the safe height above, to those whom God *makes to walk* on them; and since he has passed all things earthly, what are *his high places*, but the heavenly places, even his home, even while a pilgrim here, but now at the end, much more his home, when not *in hope* only, but in truth, he is *raised up together*, and *made to sit together in heavenly places in Christ Jesus* [4]?

And now what remains then, but that this song of praise should be for ever? And so it is not without meaning, nor was of old thought to be so [5], that there stand here, at the end, words which elsewhere in the Psalms always stand at the beginning. Nor is it anywhere else, "upon *my* stringed instruments." *To the chief singer on my stringed instruments.* To Him to Whom all praise is due, through Whom we praise Himself, His Spirit pleading in us, for us, *upon my stringed instruments.* He Himself, providing, as it were, and teaching the prelude of the endless song, and by His spirit, breathing upon the instrument which He has attuned, and it giving back faithfully, in union with the heavenly Choir with whom it is now blended, the Angelic Hymn, "Glory to God in the Highest."

[4] Eph. ii. 6.
[5] It is commented upon as part of the text by S. Cyril and S. Jerome.

felt any interest in denying it. Those who disbelieve definite prophecy invented for themselves a solution, whereby they thought that Zephaniah's prophecy need not be definite, even though uttered in the time of Josiah; so the fact remained unquestioned.

The unwonted fullness with which his descent is given implies so much of that personal knowledge which soon fades away, that those who speak of other titles, as having been prefixed to the books, or portions of books of the prophets, by later hands, have not questioned this. The only question is, whether he lived before or in the middle of the reformation by Josiah. Josiah, who came to the throne when eight years old B.C. 641, began the reformation in the twelfth year of his reign[l], when almost twenty; B.C. 630. The extirpation of idolatry could not, it appears, be accomplished at once. The finding of the ancient copy of the law, during the repairs of the temple in the eighteenth year of his reign[m], B. C. 624, gave a fresh impulse to the king's efforts. He then united the people with himself, bound all the people present to the covenant[n] to keep the law, and made a further destruction of idols[o] before the solemn passover in that year. Even after that passover some abominations had to be removed[p]. It has been thought that the words, [q] *I will cut off the remnant of Baal from this place*, imply that the worship of Baal had already in some degree been removed, and that God said, that He would complete what had been begun. But the emphasis seems to be rather on the completeness of the destruction, as we should say, that He would efface every remnant of Baal, than to refer to any effort which had been made by human authority to destroy it.

The prophet joins together, *I will cut off the remnant of Baal, the name of the Chemarim.* The cutting off *the name of the Chemarim*, or idolatrous priests, is like that of Hosea[r], *I will take away the names of Baalim out of her mouth, and they shall no more be remembered by their name.* As the cutting off of *the name of the Chemarim* means their being utterly obliterated, so, probably, does *the cutting off the remnant of Baal.* The worship of Baal was cut off, not through Josiah, but (as Zephaniah prophesied) through the captivity. Jeremiah asserts its continuance during his long prophetic office[s].

In the absence of any direct authority to the contrary, the description of idolatry by Zephaniah would seem to belong to the period, before the measures to abolish it were begun. He speaks as if everything were full of idolatry[t], the worship of Baal, the worship of the host of heaven upon the housetops, swearing by Malcham, and probably the clothing with strange apparel.

The state also was as corrupt[u] as the worship. Princes and judges, priests and prophets were all alike in sin; the judges distorted the law between man and man, as the priests profaned all which related to God. The princes were roaring lions; the judges, evening wolves, ever famished, hungering for new prey. This too would scarcely have been, when Josiah was old enough to govern in his own person. Both idolatry and perversion of justice were continued on from the reign of his father Amon. Both, when old enough, he removed. God Himself gives him the praise, that he [v] *did judgment and justice, then* it was *well with him; he judged the cause of the poor and needy, then* it was *well with him; was not this to know Me? saith the Lord.* His conversion was in the eighth year of his reign. Then, *while he was yet young*, he began to *seek after the God of David his father.*

The mention of the *king's children*[w], whom, God says, He would punish in the great day of His visitation, does not involve any later date. They might, anyhow have been brothers or uncles of the king Josiah. But, more probably, God declares that no rank should be exempt from the judgments of that day. He knew too that the sons of Josiah would, for their great sins, be then punished. The sun of the temporal rule of the house of David set in unmitigated wickedness and sorrow. Of all its kings after Josiah, it is said, they *did evil in the sight of the Lord;* some were distinguished by guilt; all had miserable ends; some of them aggravated misery.

Zephaniah then probably finished his course before that 12th year of Josiah, (for this prophecy is one whole) and so just before Jeremiah was, in Josiah's 13th year, called to his office, which he fulfilled for half a century, perhaps for the whole age of man.

The foreground of the prophecy of Zephaniah remarkably coincides with that of Habakkuk. Zephaniah presupposes that prophecy and fills it up. Habakkuk had prophesied the great wasting and destruction through the Chaldæans, and then their destruction. That invasion was to extend beyond Judah (for it was said *he shall scoff at kings*[x]), but was to include it. The instrument of God having been named by Habakkuk, Zephaniah does not even allude to him. Rather he brings before Judah the other side, the agency of God Himself. God

[l] 2 Chr. xxxiv. 3–7.
[m] 2 Kgs xxii. 2 Chr. xxxiv. 8–28.
[n] 2 Kgs xxiii. 3. 2 Chr. xxxv. 31.
[o] 2 Kgs xxiii. 4–20. 2 Chr. xxxiv. 33.
[p] 2 Kgs xxiii. 24.
[q] Zeph. i. 4.
[r] Hos. ii. 17.
[s] Jer. ii. 8. vii. 9. xi. 13. xix. 5. xxxii. 29.
[t] i. 4. 5.
[u] iii. 3, 4.
[v] Jer. xxii. 15, 16.
[w] See bel. on Zeph. i. 8.
[x] Hab. i. 10.

would not have them forget Himself in His instruments. Hence all is attributed to God. [y] *I will utterly consume all things from off the land, saith the Lord. I will consume man and beast; I will consume the fowls of the heaven, and the fishes of the sea, and the stumblingblocks with the wicked, and I will cut off man from the land, saith the Lord. I will also stretch out Mine hand upon Judah; and I will cut off the remnant of Baal. In the day of the Lord's sacrifice, I will punish the princes, &c. In the same day also I will punish all those &c. I will search Jerusalem with candles. The great day of the Lord is near, and I will bring distress upon, &c. O Canaan, land of the Philistines, I will even destroy thee. The Lord will be terrible upon them. Ye Ethiopians also, ye shall be slain by My sword. And He will destroy Nineveh.* The wicked of the people had [z] *said in their heart, The Lord will not do good, neither will He do evil.* Zephaniah inculcates, throughout his brief prophecy, that there is nothing, good or evil, of which He is not the Doer or Overruler.

But the extent of that visitation is co-extensive with that prophesied by Habakkuk. Zephaniah indeed speaks rather of the effects, the desolation. But the countries, whose desolation or defeat he foretells, are the lands of those, whom the Chaldæans invaded, worsted, in part desolated. Beside Judah, Zephaniah's subjects are Philistia, Moab, Ammon, Ethiopia (which included Egypt), Nineveh. And here he makes a remarkable distinction corresponding with the events. Of the Ethiopians or Egyptians, he says only, [a] *ye shall be slain by My sword.* Of Assyria he foretells [b] the entire and lasting desolation; the capitals of her palaces in the dust; her cedar-work bare; flocks, wild-beasts, pelican and hedgehog, taking up their abode in her. Moab and Ammon and Philistia have at first sight the two-fold, apparently contradictory, lot; *the remnant of My people,* God says, [c] *shall possess them; the coast shall be for the remnant of the house of Judah;* and, that they should be a perpetual desolation. This also was to take place, after God had brought back His people out of captivity. Now all these countries were conquered by the Chaldæans, of which at the time there was no human likelihood. But they were not swept away by one torrent of conquest. Moab and Ammon were, at first, allies of Nebuchadnezzar, and rejoiced at the miseries of the people, whose prophets had foretold their destruction. But, beyond this, Nineveh was at that time more powerful than Egypt. Human knowledge could not have discerned, that Egypt should suffer defeat only, Nineveh should be utterly destroyed. It was the wont of the great conquerors of the East, not to destroy capitals, but to re-people them with subjects obedient to themselves. Nineveh had held Babylon by viceroys; in part she had held it under her own immediate rule. Why should not Babylon, if she conquered Nineveh, use the same policy? Humanly speaking, it was a mistake that she did not. It would have been a strong place against the inroads of the Medo-Persian empire. The Persians saw its value so far for military purposes, as to build some fort there [d]; and the Emperor Claudius, when he made it a colony, felt the importance of the well-chosen situation [e]. It is replaced by Mosul, a city of some "[f] 20000 to 40000" inhabitants. Even after its destruction, it was easier to rebuild it than to build a city on the opposite bank of the Tigris. God declared that it should be desolate. The prediction implied destruction the most absolute. It and its palaces were to be the abode of animals which flee the presence of man; and it perished [g].

Again, what less likely than that Philistia, which had had the rule over Israel, strong in its almost impregnable towns, three of whose five cities were named for their strength, Gaza, *strong;* Ashdod, *mighty;* Ekron, *deep-rooting;* one of which, Ashdod, about this very time, resisted for 29 years the whole power of Egypt, and endured the longest siege of any city of ancient or modern times—what, to human foresight, less likely, than that Philistia should come under the power of the *remnant of the house of Judah,* when returned from their captivity? Yet it is absolutely foretold [h]. *The sea-coast shall be for the remnant of the house of Judah; they shall feed thereupon: in the houses of Ashkelon they shall lie down in the evening. For the Lord their God shall visit them, and restore their captivity.* As unlikely was it, that Moab and Ammon, who now had entered upon the territory of the two and a half tribes beyond Jordan, should themselves become the possession of the remnant of Judah. Yet so it was.

It is then lost labor, even for their own ends, when moderns, who believe not definite prophecy, would find out some enemy [i] whom

[y] Zeph. i. 2, 4, 8, 9, 13, 14, 17. ii. 5, 11, 12, 13.
[z] i. 12. [a] ii. 12. [b] ii. 13–15.
[c] ii. 9.
[d] Amm. Marcell. xxiii. 22. The Ninos taken by Meherdates A.D. 59. was on the site of the old Ninos, on the other side of the Tigris. Tac. Ann. xii. 13.
[e] The existence of the Nineve Claudiopolis is attested by coins. See Vaux in Smith's Dict. of Greek and Roman Geogr. v. Ninus.
[f] See Keith Johnstone, Dict. of Geography ed. 1864, and ed. 1867.
[g] See on Nahum, ab. pp. 122–125. [h] ii. 7.
[i] The Père Paul Pezron (Essai d'un Comm. lit. et. hist. sur les prophêtes 1697) assumed three irruptions of the Scythians: the first prophesied by Amos and Joel; the second, in the reign of Josiah about 631. B. C.; the third, prophesied (he thinks) by Ezek. xxxviii. xxxix. Baseless as all this is, the characteristic of the late writers is not the

Zephaniah may have had in mind in foretelling this wide destruction. It still remains that all that Zephaniah says beforehand was fulfilled. It is allowed that he could not foretell this through any human foresight. The avowed object in looking out for some power, formidable in Zephaniah's time, is, that he could not, by any human knowledge, be speaking of the Chaldæans. But the words stand there. They were written by Zephaniah, at a time when confessedly no human knowledge could have enabled man to predict this of the Chaldæans; nay, no human knowledge would have enabled anyone to predict so absolutely a desolation so wide and so circumstantially delineated.

That school however has not been willing to acquiesce in this, that Zephaniah does *not* speak of the instrument, through whom this desolation was effected. They will have it, that they know, that Zephaniah had in his mind one, who was *not* the enemy of the Jews or of Nineveh or of Moab and Ammon, and through whom no even transient desolation of these countries was effected. The whole argument is a simple begging of the question. "[k]The Egyptians cannot be meant; for the Cushites, who are threatened[l], themselves belong to the Egyptian army[m], and Psammetichus only besieged Ashdod which he also took, without emblazoning ought greater on his shield[n]. The Chaldæans come still less into account, because they did not found an independent kingdom until B. C. 625, nor threaten Judæa until after Josiah's death. On the other hand an unsuspicious and well-accredited account has been preserved to us, that somewhere about this time the Scythians overflowed Palestine too with their hosts. Herodotus relates[o], that the Scythians, after they had disturbed Cyaxares at the siege of Nineveh, turned toward Egypt; and when they had already arrived in Palestine, were persuaded by Psammetichus to return, and in their return plundered a temple in Ascalon."

It is true that Herodotus says that "a large Scythian army did, under their king Madyes, burst into Asia in pursuit of the Cimmerians and entered Media,—keeping Mount Caucasus on the right," and that "the Medes opposed and fought them and, being defeated, lost their rule[p]."

It is true also that Herodotus relates, that "[q]they went thence toward Egypt, and when they were in Palestine-Syria, Psammetichus king of Egypt, meeting them, turned them by gifts and entreaties from going further; that when in their return they were in Ascalon, a city of Syria, whereas most of the Scythians passed by without harming ought, some few of them, being left behind, plundered the temple of Venus Ourania." In this place also, it is true, Herodotus uses a vague expression, that "[r]for 28 years the Scythians ruled over Asia, and that all things were turned upside down by their violence and contempt. For beside the tributes, they exacted from each what they laid upon each, and beside the tribute, they drove together and took what each had. And most of them Cyaxares and the Medes entertaining as guests, intoxicated and slew. And then the Medes recovered their empire and *became masters of what they held before*."

But, apart from the inconsistency of the period here assigned to their power, with other history, it appears from the account itself, that by "all Asia" Herodotus means "all upper Asia," as he expresses himself more accurately, when relating the expedition of Darius against them. "[s]Darius wished to take revenge on the Scythians, because they first, making an inroad into Media and defeating in battle those who went against them, began the wrong. For the Scythians, as I have before said, *ruled upper Asia* for 28 years. For, pursuing the Cimmerians, they made an inroad into Asia, putting down the Medes from their rule; for these, before the Scythians came, ruled Asia." The Asia then, which Herodotus supposes the Scythians to have ruled, is co-extensive with the Asia which he supposes the Medes to have ruled previously. But this was all in the North; for having said that "[t]Phraortes subdued Asia, going from one nation to another," he adds that, having brought Persia under his yoke, "he led an army against those Assyrians who had Nineveh, and there lost most of his army and his own life." Apart then from the fabulousness of this supposed empire, established by Phraortes[u], (Cyaxares having been the real founder of the Median empire,) it is plain that, according to Herodotus himself, the Asia, in which the Scythians plundered and received tribute, were the lands North of Assyria. The expedition against Egypt stands as an insulated predatory excursion, the object of which having been mere plunder, they were bought off by Psammetichus and returned (he tells us) doing no mischief[v] in their way, except that a few lingerers plundered a temple at Ascalon. It was to Media that they first came; the Medes, whom they defeated; the Median

selection of the Scythians as the object of the prophecy (which were a thing indifferent) but the grounds alleged for that selection.

[k] Hitzig. [l] ii. 12.
[m] Jer. xlvi. 9.
[n] Herod. ii. 157. [o] Ib. i. 105.
[p] Ib. i. 103, 104. [q] Ib. 105.

[r] i. 106. He uses the same wide expression as to Cyrus, after the defeat of Crœsus. "Having subdued him, he thus ruled over all Asia," (i. 130); whereas he had not yet conquered Babylon.
[s] Ib. i. 106. [t] iv. 4.
[u] i. 102. See above p. 119. and Rawlinson Herod. quoted ib. [v] ἀσινέων. Her. l. c.

empire to which they succeeded; Cyaxares and the Medes, who treacherously destroyed most of them; the Medes, whose empire was restored by the destruction of some, and the return of the rest to their own land. With this agrees the more detailed account of the Scythians by Strabo, who impeaches the accuracy of the accounts of Herodotus [w]. Having spoken of the migrations of leaders, and by name, of "[x] Madyes the Scythian" (under whom Herodotus states the irruption to have taken place), he says, "[y] the Sacæ made the like inroad as the Cimmerians and the Trerians, some longer, some nigh at hand; for they took possession of Bactriana, and acquired the best land of Armenia, which they also left, named after them Sacasene, and advanced as far as to the Cappadocians and especially those on the Euxine, whom they now call of Pontus (Pontians). But the generals of the Persians who were at the time there, attacking them by night, while they were making a feast upon the spoils, utterly extirpated them." The direction which he says they took, is the same as that of the Cimmerians, whom Herodotus says that they followed. "[z] The Cimmerians, whom they also call Trerians, or some tribe of them, often overrun the right side of the Pontus, sometimes making inroads on the Paphlagonians, at others, on the Phrygians. Often also the Cimmerians and Trerians made the like attacks, and they say that the Trerians and Cobus [their king] were, at last expelled by Madyes king of the [Scythians]." Strabo also explains, what is meant by the tributes, of which Herodotus speaks. He is speaking of the Nomadic tribes of the Scythians generally: "[a] Tribute was, to allow them at certain stated times, to overrun the country [for pasturage] and carry off booty. But when they roamed beyond the agreement, there arose war, and again reconciliations and renewed war. Such was the life of the nomads, always setting on their neighbors and then being reconciled again."

The Scythians then were no object of fear to the Jews, whom they passed wholly unnoticed and probably unconscious of their existence in their mountain country, while they once and once only swept unharming along the fertile tracks on the sea-shore, then occupied by the old enemies and masters of the Jews, the Philistines. But Herodotus must also have been misinformed as to the length of time, during which they settled in Media, or at least as to the period during which their presence had any sensible effects. For Cyaxares, whom he represents as having raised the siege of Nineveh, in consequence of the inroad of the Scythians into Media, came to the throne, according to the numbers of Herodotus, B. C. 633. For the reign of Cyaxares having lasted according to him 40 years [b], that of Astyages 35 [c], and that of Cyrus 29 [d], these 104 years, counted back from the known date of the death of Cyrus, B. C. 529 or 530, bring us to B. C. 633 or 636 as the beginning of the reign of Cyaxares. But the invasion of the Scythians could not have taken place at the first accession of Cyaxares, since, according to Herodotus, he had already defeated the Assyrians, and was besieging Nineveh, when the Scythians burst into Media. According to Herodotus, moreover, Cyaxares "[e] first distributed Asiatics into troops, and first ordered that each should be apart, spearmen, and archers and cavalry; for before, all were mixed pele-mele together." Yet it would not be in a very short time, that those who had been wont to fight in a confused mass, could be formed into an orderly and disciplined army. We could not then, anyhow, date the Scythian inroad, earlier than the second or third year of Cyaxares. On the other hand the date of the capture of Nineveh is fixed by the commencement of the Babylonian Empire, Babylon falling to Nabopolassar. The duration of that empire is measured by the reigns of its kings [f], of whom, according to Ptolemy's Canon, Nabopolassar reigned 21 years; Nebuchadnezzar, (there called Nabocollasar) 43; Evil-Merodach (Iluaroadam) 2; Neriglissar (Niricassolassar) 4; Nabunahit (Nabonadius with whom his son Belshazzar was co-regent) 17; in all 87 years; and it ends in an event of known date, the capture of Babylon by Cyrus, B. C. 538. The addition of the 87 years of the duration of the empire to that date carries us back to the date assigned to the capture of Nineveh by Nabopolassar in conjunction with Cyaxares, B. C. 625. The capture then of Nineveh was removed by 8 or 9 years only from that, which Herodotus gives as the time of the accession of Cyaxares, and since the attack upon Nineveh can hardly have been in his first year, and the last siege probably occupied two, the 28 years of Scythian dominion would dwindle down into something too inconsiderable for history. Probably they represent some period from their first incursion into Media, to the final return of the survivors, during which they marauded in Media and Upper Asia. The mode, by which "the greater part" (Herodotus tells us) were destroyed, intoxication and subsequent murder at a banquet, implies that

[w] "More readily might we believe Homer and Hesiod in their tales of heroes, and the tragic poets, than Ctesias and Herodotus and Hellanicus and others of the same sort." xi. 6. 3.
[x] i. 3. 21. [y] xi. 8. 4.
[z] Prol. i. 3. 21. [a] xi. 8. 3.

[b] Herod. i. 106. [c] Ib. 130. [d] Ib. 214. [e] Ib. 103.
[f] Berosus, in his Chaldæan history, agrees as to these dates, only adding 9 months for the son of Neriglissar, Laborosoarchod, in Jos. Ant. x. 11. combined with cont. Apion. i. 20, and Eus. Præp. Evang. ix. 40.

judgment to come, or again to that his other great subject, God's love for the remnant of His people; yet mostly in fragments only and allusively. They were key-notes for those who knew the prophets. Thus, in calling on man to hushed submission before God, because a day of judgment was coming, he blends into one verse[r] Habakkuk's call, [s] *hush before the Lord*, and the warning words of Isaiah, Joel, Obadiah, [t] *nigh is the day of the Lord;* the image of the *sacrifice*, which God had commanded, and the remarkable word, *consecrated*, of God's instruments. The allusion is contained in single words, *sacrifice, consecrated;* the context in which they are embodied is different. The idea only is the same, that Almighty God maketh, as it were, a sacrifice to Himself of those who incorrigibly rebel against Him. Else Isaiah draws out the image at much length; [u] *A sword of the Lord is full of bloods; it is smeared with fat, with the blood of lambs and of goats; with the fat of kidneys of rams: for the Lord hath a sacrifice in Bozrah, and a great slaughter in the land of Edom.* Jeremiah uses the image in equal fullness of the overthrow of Pharaoh-Necho at the Euphrates; [v] *This is a day of the Lord God of hosts, a day of vengeance, that He may avenge Him of His adversaries: and the sword shall devour, and it shall be satiate and made drunk with blood; for the Lord God hath a sacrifice in the North country by the river Euphrates.* Ezekiel expands it yet more boldly [w]. Zephaniah drops everything local, and condenses the image into the words, *The Lord hath prepared a sacrifice; He hath consecrated His guests*, adding the new bold image, that they whom God employed were, as it were, His invited guests [x], whom He consecrated [y] thereto.

In like way, as to the day of the Lord itself, he accumulates all words of terror from different prophets; from Joel the words, [z] *a day of darkness and of gloominess; a day of clouds and of thick darkness:* to these he adds [a] *of shouting and the sound of the trumpet*, used by Amos in relation to the destruction of Moab; the two combinations, which precede, occur, the one in a different sense, the other with a slightly different grammatical inflection, in Job [b].

From Isaiah, Zephaniah adopts that characteristic picture of self-idolizing, which brings down God's judgments on its pride; (the city) [c] *that dwelleth securely, that said in her heart, I and no I beside.*

Even where Isaiah says, [d] *For a consumption and that decreed, the Lord God of hosts makes in the midst of all the earth* and, slightly varying it, [e] *For a consumption and that decreed, I have heard from the Lord God of hosts upon all the earth*, Zephaniah, retaining the two first words, which occur in both places, says more concisely, [f] *For a consumption, nought but terror, will He make all the inhabitants of the earth.* Yet simple as the words are, he pronounced, that God would not only *bring a desolation upon the earth*, or *in the midst of the earth*, but would make its inhabitants one consumption. Nahum had said of Nineveh, [g] *with an overflowing flood He will make the place thereof an utter consumption.* The most forceful words are the simplest.

He uses the exact words of Isaiah, [h] *From beyond the rivers of Cush*, than which none can be simpler, and employs the word of festive procession, though in a different form [i], and having thus connected his prophecy with Isaiah's, all the rest, upon which the prophecy turns, is varied.

In like way he adopts from Micah the three words [k], *her-that-halteth, and-will-gather her-that-is-driven-out.* The context in which he resets them is quite different.

It has been thought, that the words, [l] *I have heard the reproach of Moab*, may have been suggested by those of Isaiah, who begins his lament over Moab, *We have heard of the pride of Moab;* but the force and bearing of the words is altogether different, since it is God Who says, *I have heard*, and so He will punish.

The combination [m], *the exulters of pride*, is common to him with Isaiah: its meaning is

[r] i. 7. [s] Hab. ii. 20.

[t] Is. xiii. 6. Jo. i. 15. iv. 15. Ob. 15. The words יום יי are used of a day of God's judgments, Is. xiii. 9, Jo. ii. 1, 11, Am. v. 18, 20. Ezek. xiii. 5. Mal. iii. 23, not with קרוב. In Is. ii. 12, it is יוֹם לייי or in Jo. ii. 1. subordinately.

[u] Is. xxxiv. 6. [v] Jer. xlvi. 10.

[w] Ezek. xxxix. 17.

[x] Zephaniah's word, קְרֻאִים occurs beside only in 1 Sam. ix. 13.

[y] Isaiah's word (xiii. 3.) is מקדשי; Zephaniah's הקדיש.

[z] יום חשך ואפלה יום ענן וערפל Jo. ii. 2. Zeph. i. 15.

[a] שופר ותרועה Zeph. i. 16. Am. ii. 2.

[b] שואה ומשואה Job xxxviii. 27. צד ומצוקה xv. 24. Zeph. has צרה ומצ. צרות stands parallel with מצוקות Ps. xxv. 17.

[c] Is. xlvii. 8. Zeph. ii. 15. היושבת לבטח האמרה בלבבה אני ואפסי עוד.

[d] Is. x. 23. [e] Ib. xxviii. 22.

[f] כי כלה. He retains the simplest words, but substitutes אך נבהלה (a word formed by himself) for the ונחרצה of Isaiah.

[g] Nah. i. 8.

[h] מעבר לנהרי כוש Zeph. iii. 10. Is. xviii. 1.

[i] יובלון Zeph. יובל Is. xviii. 7.

[k] והצלעה והנדחה אקבצה Mic. iv. 6. Zeph. iii. 19.

[l] שמעתי חרפת מואב Zeph. ii. 8. שמענו גאון מואב Is. xvi. 6.

[m] עליזי גאותי Is. xiii. 3. עליזי גאותך Zeph. iii. 11.

uncertain; but it is manifestly different in the two places, since the one relates to God, the other to man.

The words, [n] *They shall build houses and shall not dwell therein; they shall plant vineyards and not drink the wine thereof*, are from the original threat in Deuteronomy, from which also the two words, [o] *They-shall-walk as-the-blind*, may be a reminiscence, but with a conciseness of its own and without the characteristic expressions of Deuteronomy, adopted by other sacred writers: [p] *They shall grope at noonday, as the blind gropeth in darkness.*

Altogether these passages are evidence that Zephaniah is of later date than the prophecies in which the like language occurs; and the fact that he does employ so much language of his predecessors furnishes a strong presumption in any single case, that he in that case also adopted from the other sacred writer the language which they have in common.

It is chiefly on this ground, that a train of modern critics[q] have spoken disparagingly of the outward form and style of Zephaniah. It has however a remarkable combination of fullness with conciseness and force. Thus, he begins the enumeration of those upon whom the destruction should fall, with the words, [r] *consuming I will consume all:* to an enumeration co-extensive with the creation, he adds unexpectedly, [s] *and the stumblingblocks with the wicked*, anticipating our Lord's words of the Day of Judgment, [t] *they shall gather the stumblingblocks and them that do iniquity:* to the different idolatries he adds those of a divided faith, [u] *swearers to the Lord and swearers by Malcham;* to those who turned away from God he adds those who were unearnest in seeking Him[v].

Again, after the full announcement of the destruction in the Day of the Lord, the burst, in those five words, [w] *sift-yourselves and-sift* (*on*) *nation unlonged for*, is, in suddenness and condensation, like Hosea; and so again, in five words, after the picture of the future desolation of Nineveh, the abrupt turn to Jerusalem, [x] *Woe rebellious and-defiled* (thou) *oppressive city*, and then follow the several counts of her indictment, in brief disjointed sentences, first negatively, as a whole; each in three or four words[y], *she-listened not to-voice; she-received not correction; in-the-Lord she-trusted not; to-her-God she-approached not;* then, in equally broken words, each class is characterized by its sins; [z] *her-princes in-her-midst* are *roaring lions; her-judges evening wolves; not gnawed-they-bones on-the-morrow; her-prophets empty-babblers, men of-deceits; her-priests profaned holiness, violated law.* Then in sudden contrast to all this contumacy, neglect, despite of God, He Himself is exhibited as *in the midst of her;* the witness and judge of all; there, where they sinned. [a] *The-Lord righteous in-her-midst; He-doth not iniquity; by-morning by-morning His-judgment He-giveth to-light; He-faileth not;* and then in contrast to the holiness and the judgments of God, follows in four words, the perseverance of man in his shamelessness, *and*—the fruit of all this presence and doings of the Holy and Righteous God and Judge is, *and-not knoweth* the *wrong-doer shame.* Zephaniah uses the same disjoining of the clauses in the description of God's future manifestation of His love toward them. Again it is the same thought[b], *The-Lord thy-God-*(is) *in-thy-midst;* but now in love; *mighty, shall-save; He-shall-rejoice over-thee with-joy; He-shall-keep-silence in-His-love; He-shall-rejoice over-thee with-jubilee.* The single expressions are alike condensed; [c] *she-hearkened not to-voice*, stands for what Jeremiah says at such much greater length, how God had sent all His servants [d] *the prophets, daily rising up early and sending them, but they hearkened not unto Me nor inclined their ear, but hardened their neck.* The words [e] *shall-be-silent in-His-love*, in their primary meaning, express the deepest human love, but without the wonted image of betrothal.

[f] *The whole people of Canaan* reminds one of Hosea; [g] *the-men-coagulated on-their-lees* is much expanded by Jeremiah[h], his word occurs before him in Job only and the song of Moses[i]. Single poetic expressions are, that Moab should become [k] *the possession of briars*, the word itself being framed by Zephaniah; in the description of the desolation of Nineveh, [l] *a voice singeth in the window; desolation* is *on the threshold*, the imagery is so bold, that modern criticism has thought that the word *voice* which occurs in the O. T. 328 times and with pronouns 157 times more, must signify "an owl," and *desolation* must stand for "a crow[m]." Very characteristic is the word, "*He* [n] *shall famish* all the gods of the earth," expressing with wonderful irony, the privation of their sacrifices, which was

[n] Zeph. i. 13. Deut. xxviii. 30, 39. The words are more exact than in Micah vi. 14. Am. v. 11.

[o] הלכו כעורים Zeph. i. 17. [p] Deut. xxviii. 29.

[q] Eichhorn, De Wette, Stähelin, and their followers. De Wette however does own, "In employing what is not his own, he is, at least, original in its expansion." Einl. 245. note b.

[r] i. 2. [s] i. 3. [t] S. Matt. xiii. 41. [u] Zeph. i. 5. [v] i. 6. [w] ii. 1. [x] ii. 1. [y] iii. 2. [z] Ib. 3, 4. [a] Ib. 5. [b] Ib. 17. [c] iii. 2. [d] Jer. vii. 24–28.

[e] iii. 17. Some modern commentators take umbrage at the beautiful expression. Ewald alters, with the LXX, into יחדיש which does not occur elsewhere. But the LXX renders "shall renew *thee;*" Ewald, "(God) *becomes young* (sich verjünget) in His love!"

[f] Zeph. i. 11. Comp. Hos. xii. 7. [g] i. 12. [h] Jer. xlviii. 11. [i] Job x. 10. Ex. xv. 8. [k] ii. 9. [l] ii. 14.

[m] "קול must answer to the Ethiopian קׂאֳע γλαὺξ and our *eule* (owl); and חרב seems equal ערב." Ewald Proph. ii. 25.

[n] See below on ii. 11.

the occasion of the first Heathen persecutions of the Christians.

When then a writer, at times so concise and poetic as Zephaniah is in these places, is, at others, so full in his descriptions, this is not prolixity, but rather vivid picturing; at one time going through all the orders of creation[o]; at another, different classes of the ungodly[p]; at yet another, the different parts of the scared woe-stricken city[q], to set before our eyes the universality of the desolation. Those who are familiar with our own great Northern poet of nature, will remember how the accumulation of names adds to the vividness of his descriptions. Yet here too there is great force in the individual descriptions, as when he pictures the petty plunderers for their master, and *fill their masters' houses*—not with wealth but—*with violence and fraud*[r], all which remains of wealth gained by fraud and extortion being the sins themselves, which dwell in the house of the fraudulent to his destruction.

In the strictly prophetic part of his office, Jerusalem having been marked out by Micah and Isaiah before him, as the place where God would make the new revelation of Himself, Zephaniah adds, what our Lord revealed to the Samaritan woman, [s]that Jerusalem should no longer be the abiding centre of worship. [t]*They shall worship Him, every man from his place, all the isles of the nations*, is a prophecy which, to this day, is receiving an increasing accomplishment. It is a prophecy, not of the spread of Monotheism, but of the worship of Him, to Whose worship at that time a handful of Jews could with difficulty be brought to adhere, the desertion or corruption or association of Whose worship with idolatry Zephaniah had to denounce and to foretell its punishment. The love which God should then shew to His own is expressed in words, unequaled for tenderness; and in conformity to that love is the increasing growth of holiness, and the stricter requirements of God's holy justice. Again, Zephaniah has a prelude to our Blessed Lord's words, [u]*to whom much is given, of him shall much be required*, or His Apostle's, of the great awe in working out our salvation[v]. Progress is a characteristic and condition of the Christian life; [w]*We beseech you, that as ye have received of us, how ye ought to walk and to please God, ye would abound more and more.* Even so Zephaniah bids[x] *all the meek of the earth, who have wrought His judgments* or *law* to *seek diligently* that *meekness*, which had already characterized them, and that, not in view of great things, but, if so be they might be saved; *it may be that ye may be hid in the day of the Lord's anger*, as S. Peter saith, [y]*If the righteous scarcely be saved, where shall the ungodly and the sinner appear?* It is again remarkable, how he selects meekness, as the characteristic of the new state of things, which he promises. He anticipates the contrast in the Magnificat, in which the lowest lowliness was rewarded by the highest exaltation. As it is said there, [z]*He hath put down the mighty from their seat and hath exalted the humble and meek,* so the removal of the proud *from within thee*, and the "leaving of an afflicted and poor people *within thee*[a]," is the special promise by Zephaniah.

Little is said of the captivity. It is a future variously assumed[b]. Judah in the furthest lands, *beyond the rivers of Ethiopia*, is *the daughter of My dispersed*[c]; the whole earth is the scene of their shame[d]; their praises should be commensurate with their shame, *when I turn back your captivity before your eyes*[e]. But this turning away of their captivity is the only notice, that their punishment should be the going into captivity. The captivity itself is pre-supposed, as certain and as known. So neither are there any images from temporal exaltation. All pride should be removed, as utterly unbefitting God's holy presence: *thou shalt no more be haughty in My holy mountain*[f]. The words expressive of the abasement of those within her are proportionably strong, [g]*My afflicted and poor.* Some are wont, in these days, to talk of God's prophets as patriots. They were such truly, since they loved the land of the Lord with a Divine love. But what mere "patriot" would limit his promises to the presence of "a poor people in a low estate," with an unseen presence of God? The description belongs to *His* kingdom, which was *not of this world*[h]: the only king whom Zephaniah speaks of, *the king of Israel*[i], is Almighty God. The blessing which he promises, is the corresponding blessing of peace, [k]*Fear thou not; thou shalt not see evil any more, none shall make them afraid.* But the words [k]*Let not thy hands be slack*, imply that they shall be aggressive on the world; that they were not to relax from the work which God assigned to them, the conversion of the world.

An allusion to the prophet Joel[l] makes it uncertain whether words of Zephaniah relate to the first Coming of our Lord, or the times which should usher in the Second, or to both in one; and so, whether, in accordance with his general character of gathering into one all God's judgments to His end, he

[o] i. 3. [p] Ib. 4–9. [q] Ib. 10, 11.
[r] Ib. 9. Amos has the like idea (iii. 10) but no word is the same except חמס.
[s] S. John iv. 21. [t] ii. 11.
[u] S. Luke xii. 48. [v] Phil. ii. 12.
[w] 1 Thess. iv. 1. [x] ii. 3.
[y] 1 S. Pet. iv. 18. [z] S Luke ii. 52.
[a] Zeph. iii. 12. [b] Ib. 13. [c] Ib. 10.
[d] Ib. 19. [e] Ib. 20. add. ii. 7. [f] Ib. 11.
[g] Ib. 12. [h] S. John xviii. 36.
[i] Zeph. iii. 15.
[k] iii. 16. [l] iii. 2. [iv. 2 Heb.]

ZEPHANIAH.

Before CHRIST cir. 630.

CHAPTER I.

God's severe judgment against Judah for divers sins.

THE word of the LORD
which came unto Zeph-
aniah the son of Cushi,
the son of Gedaliah, the
son of Amariah, the son
of Hizkiah, in the days of
Josiah the son of Amon,
king of Judah.
2 I †will utterly con-
sume all *things* from off
†the land, saith the LORD.

† Heb. *By taking away I will make an end.*
† Heb. *the face of the land.*

CHAP. I., Ver. 1. *The word of the Lord which came unto Zephaniah the son of Cushi, the son of Gedaliah, the son of Amariah, the son of Hezekiah.* It seems likely that more forefathers of the Prophet are named than is the wont of Holy Scripture, because the last so named was some one remarkable. Nor is it impossible that Zephaniah should have been the great grandson of the king Hezekiah; for although Holy Scripture commonly names the one son only who is in the sacred line, and although there is one generation more than to Josiah, yet if each had a son early, Zephaniah might have been contemporary with Josiah. The names seem also mentioned for the sake of their meaning; at least it is remarkable how the name of God appears in most. Zephaniah, "whom the Lord hid;" Gedaliah, "whom the Lord made great;" Amariah, "whom the Lord promised;" Hezekiah, "whom the Lord strengthened."

2. *I will utterly consume all things;* better *all*[1]. The word is not limited to "things" "animate" or "inanimate" or "men;" it is used severally of each, according to the context; here, without limitation, of "all." *God* and *all* stand over against one another; *God* and *all* which is not of God or in God. God, he says, will *utterly consume all from off the land* [*earth.*] The prophet sums up in few words the subject of the whole chapter, the judgments of God from his own times to the day of Judgment itself. And this Day Itself he brings the more strongly before the mind, in that, with wonderful briefness, in two words which he conforms, in sound also, the one to the other, [2] he expresses the utter final consumption of all things. He expresses at once the intensity of action and blends their separate meanings, *Taking away I will make an end of all;* and with this he unites the words used of the flood, *from off the face of the earth*[3]. Then he goes through the whole creation as it was made, pairing *man and beast,* which Moses speaks of as created on the sixth day, and the creation of the fifth day, *the fowls of the heaven and the fishes of the sea;* and before each he sets the solemn word of God, *I will end,* as the act of God Himself. The words can have no complete fulfillment, until [4] *the earth and the works that are therein shall be burned up,* as the Psalmist too, having gone through the creation, sums up, [5] *Thou takest away their breath, they die and return to their dust;* and then speaks of the re-creation, [6] *Thou sendest forth Thy Spirit, they are created; and Thou renewest the face of the earth,* and, [7] *Of old Thou hast laid the foundations of the earth, and the heavens are the work of Thy hands; they shall perish, but Thou shalt endure, yea, all of them shall wax old like a garment;* as

[1] כל is used absolutely in a title of God, "Who maketh all," עֹשֵׂה כֹּל, Is. xliv. 24; "Thou canst do all," i. e. art Almighty, Job xlii. 2; "Thou hast put all שַׁתָּה כל, under his feet," Ps. viii. 7; and of man, "mine eye hath seen all," Job xiii. 1; and personally, gathering in one all which he had said of God's doings, with לא חָסַר "want not any thing," De. viii. 9. חֹסֶר, חָסֵר "want of every thing," Jer. xliv. 18. De. xxviii. 48. 57; "all were [lit. *was*] ashamed" (with sing. verb) כל הֹבְאִישׁ Is. xxx. 5.

[2] So also Jeremiah viii. 13, in the same words, אסוף אֲסִיפֵם. Rashi makes them one word, supposing אָסֹף to be for אאסף. A. E. mentions those who thought that א in אסוף was prefixed, as in אָדוּשׁ Is. xxviii. 28; but it is unnatural to assume a rare and irregular form, when the word אסוף is the regular form from the common word אסף.

[3] האדמה signifies "earth," almost always in the phrase עַל פני האדמה, always in the phrase מֵעַל פני האדמה, unless they be limited by some addition, as "which the Lord sware that He would give thee." עַל פני האדמה is thus used Gen. vi. 1, vii. 23, Ex. xxxiii. 16, Nu. xii. 3, De. vii. 6, xiv. 2, 2 Sam. xiv. 7, Is. xxiii. 17, Jer. xxv. 26, Ezek. xxxviii. 20. מעל פני האדמה "from the face of the earth" occurs, unlimited by the context. Gen. iv. 14, vi. 7, vii. 4, viii. 8, Ex. xxxii. 12, De. vi. 15. 1 Sam. xx. 15. 1 Kgs xiii. 34. Jer. xxviii. 16. Am. ix. 8. ארמה is used of cultivable land, and so על פני האדמה is used in connection with rain falling on the ground, 1 Kgs xvii. 14; but מעל פ. הא. suffers no exception, unless it be restrained by an addition.

[4] 2 S. Pet. iii. 10

[5] Ps. civ. 29.

[6] Ps. civ. 30.

[7] Ib. cii. 25.

Before CHRIST cir. 630.

a Hos. 4. 3.

b Ezek. 7. 19. & 14. 3, 4, 7. Matt. 13. 41.

|| Or, *idols*.

3 [a]I will consume man
and beast; I will consume
the fowls of the heaven,
and the fishes of the sea,
and [b]the ||stumbling
blocks with the wicked;
and I will cut off man
from off the land, saith
the LORD.
4 I will also stretch out
mine hand upon Judah,
and upon all the inhabi-
tants of Jerusalem; and
[c]I will cut off the rem-

Before CHRIST cir. 630.

c Fulfilled, cir. 624. 2 Kin. 23. 4, 5.

---

a vesture shalt Thou change them, and they shall be changed. Local fulfillments there may, in their degree, be. S. Jerome speaks as if he knew this to have been. "[1] Even the brute animals feel the wrath of the Lord, and when cities have been wasted and men slain, there cometh a desolation and scarceness of beasts also and birds and fishes; witness Illyricum, witness Thrace, witness my native soil," [Stridon, a city on the confines of Dalmatia and Pannonia] "where, beside sky and earth and rampant brambles and deep thickets, all has perished." But although this fact, which he alleges, is borne out by natural history, it is distinct from the words of the prophet, who speaks of the fish, not of rivers (as S. Jerome) but of the sea, which can in no way be influenced by the absence of man, who is only their destroyer. The use of the language of the histories of the creation and of the deluge implies that the prophet has in mind a destruction commensurate with that creation. Then he foretells the final removal of offences, in the same words which our Lord uses of the general Judgment. [2] *The Son of Man shall send forth His Angels and they shall gather out of His kingdom all things that offend, and them that do iniquity.*

3. *The stumbling-blocks* [3] *with the wicked.* Not only shall the wicked be utterly brought to an end, or, in the other meaning of the word, *gathered into bundles to be taken away*, but all causes of stumbling too; everything, through which others can fall, which will not be until the end of all things. Then, he repeats, yet more emphatically, *I will cut off the whole race of man* [4] *from the face of the earth*, and then he closes the verse, like the foregoing, with the solemn words, *saith the Lord.* All this shall be fulfilled in the Day of Judgment, and all other fulfillments are earnests of the final Judgment. They are witnesses of the ever-living presence of the Judge of all, that God does take account of man's deeds. They speak to men's conscience, they attest the existence of a Divine law, and therewith of the future complete manifestation of that law, of which they are individual sentences. Not until the prophet has brought this circle of judgments to their close, does he pass on to the particular judgments on Judah and Jerusalem.

4. *I will also stretch out Mine Hand*, as before on Egypt [5]. Judah had gone in the ways of Egypt and learned her sins, and sinned worse than Egypt [6]. The *mighty Hand and stretched-out Arm*, with which she had been delivered, shall be again *stretched out*, yet not for her but *upon* her, *upon all the inhabitants of Jerusalem.* In this threatened destruction of all, Judah and Jerusalem are singled out, because *judgment* shall [7] *begin at the house of God.* They who have sinned against the greater grace shall be most signally punished. Yet the punishment of those whom God had so chosen and loved is an earnest of the general judgment. This too is not a partial but a general judgment "upon *all* the inhabitants of Jerusalem."

And I will cut off the remnant of Baal, i. e. to the very last vestige of it. Isaiah unites [8] *name and residue*, as equivalents, together with the proverbial, *posterity and descendant* [9]. Zephaniah distributes them in parallel clauses, "the *residue* [10] of Baal and the *name* of the Chemarim." Good and evil have each a root, which remains in the ground, when

---

1 S. Jer.

2 S. Matt. xiii. 41.

3 מִכְשֵׁלוֹת i. q. מִכְשֹׁלִים Jer. vi. 21, Ezek. xxi. 20. So Kim., Rashi, who limits it to idolatry (as Ges.) without reason. They are the wicked generally, not one class of them. In Is. iii. 6. (where alone the word occurs beside) it is used metaphorically of the state, "this ruin."

4 אֶת הָאָדָם, as in the history of the creation, Gen. i. 27, or the flood, Ib. vi. 7. vii. 21.

5 Ex. vi. 6, De. iv. 34, v. 15, vii. 19. xi. 2, xxvi. 8, and thence Jer. xxxii. 21, Ps. cxxxvi. 12. Isaiah had, in the same phrase, prophesied God's judgments against Israel in the burden v. 25, ix. 11, 16, x. 4.

6 Jer. ii. 10, 11.

7 1 S. Pet. iv. 17. Jer. xxv. 29.

8 Is. xiv. 22.

9 נִין וָנֶכֶד, which occur only together, Gen. xxi. 23, Job xviii. 19, Is. xiv. 22.

10 שְׁאָר is not limited, like שְׁאֵרִית, to that which remains over when a former or larger part has ceased or is gone. It is mostly "the rest," after others who had been named, yet still it may be the larger number; as, "the rest of those chosen," 1 Chr. xvi. 41; "the rest of their brethren, the priests and the Levites," Ezr. iii. 9 (8. Eng.); "the rest of the chief of the fathers," Ib. iv. 3; "the rest of their companions," Ib. 7; "the rest of the people," Neh. x. 29, xi. 1., "the rest of Israel," Ib. 20; "the rest of the Jews," Esth. ix. 16. So in Isaiah, "the rest of Syria" beside Damascus. Is. xviii. 3, and "the rest of the Spirit" Mal. ii. 15. (See Ib.)

Before CHRIST cir. 630.

nant of Baal from this place, *and* the name of [d]the Chemarims with the priests;

[d] Hos. 10. 5.

5 And them [e]that worship the host of heaven upon the housetops; [f]and them that worship *and*

Before CHRIST cir. 630.

[e] 2 Kin. 23. 12. Jer. 19. 13.

[f] 1 Kin. 18. 21. 2 Kin. 17. 33, 41.

the trunk has been hewn down. There is [1] *a remnant according to the election of grace*, when *the rest* have been *blinded;* and this is a [2] *holy seed* to carry on the line of God. Evil too has its remnant, which, unless diligently kept down, shoots up again, after the conversion of peoples or individuals. The [3] *mind of the flesh* remains in the regenerate also. The prophet foretells the complete excision of the whole *remnant of Baal*, which was fulfilled in it after the captivity, and shall be fulfilled as to all which it shadows forth, in the Day of Judgment. *From this place;* for in their phrensy, they dared to bring the worship of Baal into the very temple of the Lord [4]. "[5] Who would ever believe that in Jerusalem, the holy city, and in the very temple idols should be consecrated? Whoso seeth the ways of our times will readily believe it. For among Christians and in the very temple of God, the abominations of the heathen are worshiped. Riches, pleasures, honors, are they not idols which Christians prefer to God Himself?"

And the name of the Chemarim with the priests. Of the *idolatrous priests*[6] the very name shall be cut off, as God promises by Hosea, that He will [7] *take away the names of Baalim*, and by Zechariah, that He [8] *will cut off the names of the idols out of the land.* Yet this is more. Not the *name* only *of the Chemarim*, but themselves with their name, their posterity, shall be blotted out; still more, it is God Who cuts off all memory of them, blotting them out of the book of the living and out of His own. They had but *a name* before, [9] *that they were living, but were dead.* "[10] The Lord shall take away names of vain glory, wrongly admired, out of the Church; yea, the very names of the priests with the priests who vainly flatter themselves with the name of Bishops and the dignity of Presbyters without their deeds. Whence he markedly says, not, *and the deeds of priests with the priests*, but the *names;* who only bear the false name of dignities, and with evil works destroy their own names." The *priests* are *priests of the Lord*, who live not like priests, corrupt in life and doctrine and corrupters of God's people [11]. The judgment is pronounced alike on what was intrinsically evil, and on good which had corrupted itself into evil. The title of priest is no where given to the priest of a false God, without some mention in the context, implying that they were idolatrous priests; as the priests of Dagon [12], of the high-places as ordained by Jeroboam [13], of Baal [14], of Bethel [15], of Ahab [16], of those who were not gods [17], of On, where the sun was worshiped [18]. *The priests* then were God's priests, who in the evil days of Manasseh had manifoldly corrupted their life or their faith, and who were still evil. The *priests* of Judah, with its kings its princes and the people of the land, were in Jeremiah's inaugural vision enumerated as those, who *shall*, God says, [19] *fight against thee, but shall not prevail against thee.* [20] *The priests said not, Where is the Lord? and they that handle the law knew Me not.* In the general corruption, [21] *A wonderful and horrible thing is committed in the land, the prophets prophesy falsely, and the priests bear rule at their hands* [22]; [23] *the children of Israel and the children of Judah, their kings, their princes, their priests, and their prophets, and the men of Judah, and the inhabitants of Jerusalem, have turned unto Me the back, and not the face.* Jeremiah speaks specifically of heavy moral sins. [24] *From the prophet even unto the priest every one dealeth falsely;* [25] *both prophet and priest are profane;* [26] *for the sins of her prophets, the iniquities of her priests, that have shed the blood of the just in the midst of her.* And Isaiah says of their sensuality; [27] *the priests and the prophets have erred through strong drink; they are swallowed up of wine, they are out of the way through strong drink.*

5. *And them that worship the host of heaven upon the* [flat] *housetops.* This was fulfilled by Josiah who destroyed [28] *the altars that were on the top of the upper chamber of Ahaz.* Jeremiah speaks as if this worship was almost universal, as though well-nigh every roof had been profaned by this idolatry. [29] *The houses*

[1] Rom. xi. 5, 7. [2] Is. vi. 13. [3] φρόνημα σαρκός.
[4] 2 Kgs xxiii. 4. [5] Rib.
[6] The *chemarim* is the name of idolatrous priests generally, (it occurs also 2 Kgs xxiii. 5. Hos. x. 5). In 2 Kings, where is the account of the first fulfillment of this prophecy, they appear as priests of the idolatrous high-places, distinct from the priests of Baal and of the *host of heaven*. The name is probably the Syriac name of "priest," used in Holy Scripture of idolatrous priests, because the Syrians were idolaters. See Gesenius Gesch. d. Hebr. Sprache p. 58. In Chald. כומרא is limited to idolatrous priests. See Buxt. and Levy.

[7] Hos. ii. 17. [8] Zech. xiii. 2. [9] Rev. iii. 1.
[10] S. Jer. [11] See Jer. ii. 8. v. 31. [12] 1 Sam. v. 5.
[13] 1 Kgs xiii. 2, 33, 2 Kgs xxiii. 20. 2 Chr. xi. 15.
[14] 2 Kgs x. 19, xi. 18, 2 Chr. xxiii. 17.
[15] Am. vii. 10. [16] 2 Kgs x. 11. [17] 2 Chr. xiii. 9.
[18] Gen. xli. 45–50. &c. The name "Potipherah," probably belonging to "Phre," implies this.
[19] Jer. i. 18, 19. [20] Ib. ii. 7, 8. [21] Jer. v. 30, 31.
[22] על ידיהם. [23] Jer. xxxii. 32, 33.
[24] Ib. vi. 13. viii. 10. [25] Jer. xxiii. 11.
[26] Lam. iv. 13. [27] Is. xxviii. 7.
[28] 2 Kgs xxiii. 12. [29] Jer. xix. 13

of Jerusalem, and the houses of Judah, shall be defiled as the place of Tophet, because of all the houses upon whose roofs they have burned incense unto all the host of heaven, and have poured out drink-offerings unto other gods. [1] *The Chaldæans that fight against this city, shall come and set fire on this city, and burn it with the houses, upon whose roofs they have offered incense unto Baal, and poured out drink-offerings to other gods, to provoke Me to anger.* They worshiped *on the house-tops*, probably to have a clearer view of that magnificent expanse of sky, [2] *the moon and stars which* God had *ordained;* the *queen of heaven*, which they worshiped instead of Himself. There is something so mysterious in that calm face of the moon, as it [3] *walketh in beauty;* God seems to have invested it with such delegated influence over the seasons and the produce of the earth, that they stopped short in it, and worshiped the creature rather than the Creator. Much as men now talk of "*Nature*," admire "Nature," speak of its "laws," not as laws imposed upon it, but inherent in it, laws affecting us and our well-being; only not in their ever-varying vicissitudes, [4] *doing whatsoever God commandeth them upon the face of the world in the earth, whether for correction, or for His land or for mercy!* The idolaters [5] *worshiped and served the creature more than the Creator, Who is blessed for ever;* moderns equally make this world their object, only they idolize themselves and their discoveries, and worship their own intellect.

This worship *on the house-tops* individualized the public idolatry; it was a rebellion against God, family by family; a sort of family-prayer of idolatry. [6] *Did we*, say the mingled multitude to Jeremiah, *make our cakes to worship her, and pour out our drink-offerings unto her, without our men?* Its family character is described in Jeremiah. [7] *The children gather wood, and the fathers kindle the fire, and the women knead the dough to make cakes to the queen of heaven, and to pour out drink-offerings unto other gods.* The idolatry spread to other cities. [8] *We will certainly do*, they say, *as we have done, we and our fathers, our kings and our princes, in the cities of Judah, and in the streets of Jerusalem.* The incense went up continually *as a memorial to God* from the Altar of incense in the temple: the *roofs of the houses* were so many altars, from which, street by street and house by house the incense went up to her, for whom they dethroned God, *the queen of heaven.* It was an idolatry, with which Judah was especially besotted, believing that they received all goods of this world from them and not from God. When punished for their sin, they repented of their partial repentance and maintained to Jeremiah that they were punished for [9] *leaving off to burn incense to the queen of heaven.*

And them that worship the Lord, but with a divided heart and service; *that swear by* [rather [10] *to*] *the Lord*, swear fealty and loyal allegiance to Him, while they do acts which deny it, in that *they swear by Malcham*, better [it is no appellative although allied to one] *their king* [11], most probably, I think, "Moloch."

This idolatry had been their enduring idolatry in the wilderness, after the calves had been annihilated; it is *the* worship, against which Israel is warned by name in the law [12]; then, throughout the history of the Judges, we hear of the kindred idolatry of Baal [13], *the* Lord (who was called also "[14] eternal king" and from whom individuals named themselves "son of [the] king," "servant of [the] king [15]"), or the manifold Baals [16] and Ashtaroth or Astarte. But after these had been removed on the preaching of Samuel [17], this idolatry does not reappear in Judah until the intermarriage of Jehoram with the house of Ahab [18]. The kindred and equally horrible worship of [19] *Molech, the abomination of the children of Ammon*, was brought in by Solomon in his decay, and endured until his high-place was defiled by Josiah [20]. It is probable then that this was *their king* [21], of whom Zephaniah speaks, whom Amos [22] and after him Jeremiah, called *their king;* but speaking of Ammon. Him, the king of Ammon, Judah adopted as *their king.* They owned God as their king in words; Molech they owned by their deeds; *they worshiped and sware fealty to the Lord* and they *sware by their king;* his name was familiarly in their mouths; to him they appealed as the Judge and witness of the truth

[1] Jer. xxxii. 29. [2] Ps. viii. 3.
[3] Job xxxi. 26. [4] Ib. xxxvii. 12, 13.
[5] Rom. i. 25. [6] Jer. xliv. 19. [7] Ib. vii. 18.
[8] Ib. xliv. 17. [9] Ib. 2, 15, 18.
[10] As in the E. M., comp. 2 Chr. xv. 14. Is. xix. 18. xlv. 23. It can only mean this.
[11] מַלְכָּם as מַלְכְּכֶם Am. v. 26. and מַלְכָּם Jer. xlix. 1, 3. where the E. V. too renders, *their king.* On his worship see vol. i. pp. 301–303.
[12] Lev. xviii. 21, xx. 2–4.
[13] Always used with the article expressed or understood, הבעל, לַבַּעַל, בַּבַּעַל, unless the specific name (Bael-berith, Bael-zebub, Bael-peor) is mentioned.
[14] Numid. 1, 2, 3 in Ges. Thes. p. 795.
[15] עבדמלך, ברמלך ap. Ges. lc.
[16] הבעלים in Judges, 1 Sam., 2 Kgs, 2 Chron., Jeremiah, Hosea.
[17] 1 Sam. vii. 6. xii. 10.
[18] 2 Kgs viii. 16–18. 26, 27. 2 Chr. xxi. 6, 12, 13. xxii. 2–4.
[19] 1 Kgs xi. 7. [20] 2 Kgs xxiii. 13, 14.
[21] Molech is always an appellative, except 1 Kgs xi. 7. Else (by a pronunciation belonging probably to Ammon) it is הַמֹּלֶךְ Lev. xx. 5, or לַמֹּלֶךְ Lev. xviii. 21, xx. 2, 4, 2 Kgs xxiii. 10, Jer. xxxii. 35. As a proper name, it is *Milcom*, 1 Kgs xi. 5, 33, 2 Kgs xxiii. 13.
[22] See on Amos i. 15. vol. i. p. 255.

Before CHRIST cir. 630.

[g] that swear || by the LORD,
and that swear [h] by Malcham;

[g] Isai. 48. 1. Hos. 4. 15.
|| Or, *to the LORD.*
[h] Josh. 23. 7. 1 Kin. 11. 33.

of their words, his displeasure they invoked on themselves, if they sware falsely. "[1] Those in error were wont to swear by heaven, and, as matter of reverence to call out, 'By the king and lord Sun.' Those who do so must of set purpose and wilfully depart from the love of God, since the law expressly says, [2] *Thou shalt worship the Lord thy God, and serve Him* alone, *and swear by His Name.*"

The former class who *worshiped on the roofs* were mere idolaters. These *worshiped*, as they thought, *the Lord*, bound themselves solemnly by oath to Him, but with a reserve, joining a hateful idol to Him, in that they, by a religious act, owned it too as god. The act which they did was in direct words, or by implication, forbidden by God. The command to *swear by the Lord* implied that they were to swear by none else. It was followed by the prohibition to go after other gods[3]. Contrariwise to swear by other gods was forbidden as a part of their service. [4] *Be very courageous to keep and to do all that is written in the book of the Law of Moses, neither make mention of the name of their gods, nor cause to swear by them, neither serve them, but cleave unto the Lord your God.* [5] *How shall I pardon thee for this? Thy children have forsaken Me, and have sworn by those who are no gods.* [6] *They taught My people to swear by Baal.* They thought perhaps that in that they professed to serve God, did the greater homage to Him, professed and bound themselves to be His, (such is the meaning of *swear to the Lord*) they might, without renouncing His service, do certain things, *swear by their king*, although in effect they thereby owned him also as god. To such Elijah said, [7] *How long halt ye between two opinions? If the Lord be God, follow Him; but if Baal, then follow him;* and God by Jeremiah rejects with abhorrence such divided service. [8] *Ye trust in lying words, which will not profit. Will ye steal, murder, commit adultery, swear falsely, and burn incense unto Baal, and walk after other gods, and come and stand before Me in this house, which is called by My name, saying, We are delivered to do all these abominations.* And Hosea, [9] *Neither go ye to Beth-aven, and swear* there, *The Lord liveth.*

[1] S. Cyr.
[2] Deut. vi. 13.
[3] Ib. vi. 13, 14, x. 30. comp. Is. lxv. 16. Jer. iv. 2.
[4] Josh. xxiii. 6–8. comp. Amos viii. 14.
[5] Jer. v. 7.
[6] Ib. xii. 16.
[7] 1 Kgs xviii. 21.
[8] Jer. vii. 8–10.
[9] Hos. iv. 15. See vol. i., p. 53.
[10] S. Jer.
[11] 2 Tim. ii. 3, 4.
[12] Such is the uniform use of נָסוֹג. Its common construction is with אחוֹר; with מאחר, as here, Is. lix. 13; Kal, wlth מִן of pers., Ps. lxxx. 19; Nif. with מִן of thing, 2 Sam. i. 22.

Before CHRIST cir. 630.

6 And [i] them that are
turned back from the
LORD; and *those* that

[i] Isai. 1. 4. Jer. 2. 13, 17. & 15. 6.

Such are Christians, "[10] who think that they can serve together the world and the Lord, and please two masters, God and Mammom; who, *being soldiers of Jesus Christ* and having sworn fealty to Him, [11] *entangle themselves with the affairs of this life* and offer the same image to God and to Cæsar." To such, God, Whom with their lips they own, is not their God; their idol is, as the very name says, *their king*, whom alone they please, displeasing and dishonoring God. We must not only fear, love, honor God, but love, fear, honor all beside for Him Alone.

6. *And them that are turned back from* [lit. *have turned themselves back from following after*[12]] *the Lord.* From this half-service, the prophet goes on to the avowed neglect of God, by such as wholly fall away from Him, not setting His Will or law before them, but *turning away from* Him. It is their misery that they were set in the right way once, but themselves *turned themselves back*, now no longer *following* God, but [13] *their own lusts, drawn away and enticed* by them. How much more Christians, before whose eyes Christ Jesus is set forth, not as a Redeemer only but as an Example that they should [14] *follow His steps!*

And those that have not sought the Lord, nor enquired for Him. This is marked to be a distinct class. *And those who.* These did not openly break with God, or turn away overtly from Him; they kept (as men think) on good terms with Him, but, like *the slothful servant*, rendered Him a listless heartless service. Both words express diligent search[15]. God is not found then in a careless way. They who *seek* Him not *diligently*[16], do not find Him. *Strive*, our Lord says, [17] *to enter in at the strait gate; for many, I say unto you, shall seek to enter in, and shall not be able.* She who had lost the one piece of silver, *sought diligently*[18], till she had found it.

Thus he has gone through the whole cycle. First, that most horrible and cruel worship of Baal, the *idolatrous priests* and those who had the name of *priests* only, mingled with them, yet not openly apostatizing; then the milder form of idolatry, the star-worshipers; then those who would unite the wor-

[13] S. Jas. i. 14.
[14] 1 S. Pet. ii. 21.
[15] בִּקֵּשׁ, intensive; דָּרַשׁ of search below the surface.
[16] S. Matt. ii. 8.
[17] S. Luke xiii. 24.
[18] Ib. xv. 8.

Before CHRIST cir. 630.

[k]have not sought the
LORD, not enquired for
him.
7 [l]Hold thy peace at
the presence of the LORD
GOD: [m]for the day of the
LORD *is* at hand: for [n]the
LORD hath prepared a
sacrifice, he hath † bid his
guests.

Before CHRIST cir. 630.

k Hos. 7. 7.
l Hab. 2. 20. Zech. 2. 13.
m Isai. 13. 6.
n Isai. 34. 6. Jer. 46. 10. Ezek. 39. 17. Rev. 19. 17.
† Heb. *sanctified*, or *prepared*.

ship of God with idols, who held themselves to be worshipers of God, but whose real king was their idol; then those who openly abandoned God; and lastly those who held with Him, just to satisfy their conscience-qualms, but with no heart-service. And so, in words of Habakkuk and in reminiscence of his awful summons of the whole world before God, he sums up;

7. *Hold thy peace at the presence of the Lord God.* [lit. *Hush*, in awe *from the face of God.*] In the Presence of God, even the righteous say from their inmost heart, [1] *I am vile, what shall I answer Thee? I will lay mine hand upon my mouth.* [2] *Now mine eye seeth Thee, wherefore I abhor myself, and repent in dust and ashes.* [3] *Enter not into judgment with Thy servant, O Lord; for in Thy sight shall no man living be justified.* How much more must the [4] *man without the wedding garment* be *speechless*, and every false plea, with which he deceived himself, melt away before the Face of God! The voice of God's Judgment echoes in every heart, [5] *we indeed justly.*

For the Day of the Lord is at hand. Zephaniah, as is his wont, grounds this summons, which he had renewed from Habakkuk, to hushed silence before God, on Joel's prophetic warning[6], to shew that it was not yet exhausted. *A* day of the Lord, of which Joel warned, had come and was gone; but it was only the herald of many such days; judgments in time, heralds and earnests, and, in their degree, pictures of the last which shall end time.

"[7] All time is God's, since He Alone is the Lord of time; yet that is specially said to be His time when He doth anything special. Whence He saith, [8] *My time is not yet come;* whereas all time is His." The Day of the Lord is, in the first instance, "[9] the day of captivity and vengeance on the sinful people," as a forerunner of the Day of Judgment, or the day of death to each, for this too is near, since, compared to eternity, all the time of this world is brief.

For the Lord hath prepared a sacrifice. God had rejected sacrifices, offered amid unrepented sin; they were [10] *an abomination to Him.* When man will not repent and offer himself as [11] *a living sacrifice, holy and acceptable to God,* God, at last, rejects all other outward oblations, and the sinner himself is the sacrifice and victim of his own sins. The image was probably suggested by Isaiah's words, [12] *The Lord hath a sacrifice in Bozrah, and a great slaughter in the Land of Idumea;* and Jeremiah subsequently uses it of the overthrow of Pharaoh at the Euphrates, [13] *This is the day of the Lord of Hosts; that He may avenge Him of His adversaries; for the Lord God hath a sacrifice in the north country by the river Euphrates.* [14] *The Lord hath made all things for Himself, yea even the wicked for the day of evil.* All must honor God, either fulfilling the will of God and the end of their own being and of His love for them, by obeying that loving Will with their own free-will, or, if they repudiate it to the end, by suffering It.

He hath bid [lit. *sanctified* [15]] *His guests.* God had before, by Isaiah, called the heathen whom He employed to punish Babylon, [16] *My sanctified ones.* Zephaniah, by giving the title to God's instruments against Judah, declares that themselves, having become in deeds like the heathen, were as heathen to Him. The instruments of His displeasure, not they, were so far His chosen, His called [17]. Jeremiah repeats the saying, [18] *Thus saith the Lord against the house of the king of Judah;—I have sanctified against thee destroyers, a man and his weapons.* That is, so far, a holy war in the purpose of God, which fulfills His will; whence Nebuchadnezzar was [19] *His servant,* avenging His wrongs [20]. "[21] To be sanctified, here denotes not the laying aside of iniquity, nor the participation of the Holy Ghost, but, as it were, to be foreordained and chosen to the fulfillment of this end." That is in a manner hallowed, which is employed by God for a holy end, though the instrument, its purposes, its aims, its passions, be in themselves unholy. There is an awe about "the scourges of God." As with the lightning and the tornado, there is a certain presence of God with them, in that through them His Righteousness is seen; although they themselves have as little of God as the *wind and storm* which *fulfill His word.* Those who were

[1] Job xl. 4. [2] Ib. xlii. 5, 6. [3] Ps. cxliii. 2.
[4] S. Matt. xxii. 11, 12. [5] S. Luke xxiii. 41.
[6] See on Joel i. 14. vol. i. p. 164, and ii. 1. p. 168.
[7] Dion. [8] S. John vii. 6. [9] S. Jer
[10] Is. i. 11–15. [11] Rom. xii. 1.
[12] Is. xxxiv. 6. [13] Jer. xlvi. 10.
[14] Prov. xvi. 4. [15] See E. M.
[16] Is. xiii. 3. [17] קְרֻאָיו.
[18] Jer. xxii. 6, 7. [19] Ib. xxv. 9.
[20] See on Joel iii. 9. vol. i. p. 137 and Micah iii. 5. ab. p. 312. [21] S. Cyr.

Before CHRIST cir. 630.

8 And it shall come to pass in the day of the LORD's sacrifice, that I will † punish ° the princes,

Before CHRIST cir. 630.

° Jer. 39. 6. † Heb. *visit upon.*

once admitted to make offerings to God make themselves sacrifices to His wrath; these, still heathen and ungodly and in all besides reprobate, are His Priests, because in this, although without their will, they do His Will.

8. *I will punish* [lit. *visit upon*]. God seems oftentimes to be away from His own world. Men plot, design, say, in word or in deed, *who is Lord over us?* God is, as it were, a stranger in it, or as a man, who hath *taken a journey into a far country.* God uses our own language to us. *I will visit,* inspecting, (so to say), examining, sifting, reviewing, and when man's sins require it, allowing the weight of His displeasure to fall upon them.

The princes. The prophet again, in vivid detail (as his characteristic is), sets forth together sin and punishment. Amid the general chastisement of all, when all should become one *sacrifice,* they who sinned most should be punished most. The evil priests had received their doom. Here he begins anew with the mighty of the people and so goes down, first to special spots of the city, then to the whole, man by man. Josiah being a godly king, no mention is made of him. Thirteen years before his death [1], he received the promise of God, *because thine heart was tender, and thou hast humbled thyself before the Lord—I will gather thee unto thy fathers, and thou shalt be gathered unto thy grave in peace, and thou shalt not see all the evil which I will bring upon this place.* In remarkable contrast to Jeremiah, who had to be, in detail and continual pleading with his people, a prophet of judgment to come, until these judgments broke upon them, and so was the reprover of the evil sovereigns who succeeded Josiah, Zephaniah has to pronounce God's judgments only on the *princes* and *the king's children.* Jeremiah, in his inaugural vision, was forewarned, that [2] *the kings of Judah, its princes, priests, and the people of the land* should war against him, because he should speak unto them all which God should command him. And thenceforth Jeremiah impleads or threatens kings and the princes together [3]. Zephaniah contrariwise, his office lying wholly within the reign of Josiah, describes the princes again as [4] *roaring lions,* but says nothing of the king, as neither does Micah [5], in the reign, it may be, of Jotham or Hezekiah. Isaiah speaks of *princes,* as [6] *rebellious and companions of thieves.* Jeremiah speaks of them as idolaters [7]. They appear to have had considerable influence, which on one occasion they employed in defence of Jeremiah [8], but mostly for evil [9]. Zedekiah enquired of Jeremiah secretly for fear of them [10]. They brought destruction upon themselves by what men praise, their resistance to Nebuchadnezzar, but against the declared mind of God. Nebuchadnezzar unwittingly fulfilled the prophets's word, when he [11] *slew all the nobles of Judah, the eunuch who was over the war, and seven men of them that were near the king's person, and the principal scribe of the host.*

And the king's children. Holy Scripture mentions chief persons only by name. Isaiah had prophesied the isolated lonely loveless lot of descendants of Hezekiah who should be *eunuchs in the palace of the king of Babylon* [12], associated only with those intriguing pests of Eastern courts [13], a lot in itself worse than the sword (although to Daniel God overruled it to good) and Zedekiah's sons were slain before his eyes and his race extinct. Jehoiakim died a disgraced death, and Jehoiachin was imprisoned more than half the life of man.

And all such as are clothed with strange apparel. Israel was reminded by its dress, that it belonged to God. It was no great thing in itself; *a band of dark blue* [14] *upon the fringes at the four corners* of *their garments.* But *the band of dark blue* was upon the high-priest's mitre, with the plate engraved, [15] *Holiness to the Lord,* fastened upon it; *with a band of dark blue* also was the breastplate [16] bound to the ephod of the high-priest. So then, simple as it was, it seems to have designated the whole nation, as [17] *a kingdom of priests, an holy nation.* It was appointed to them, [18] *that ye may look upon it, and remember all the commandments of the Lord and do them, and that ye seek not after your own heart and your own eyes, after which ye use to go a whoring; that ye may remember and do all My commandments, and be holy unto your God.* They might say, "it is but *a band of blue;*" but the *band of blue* was the soldier's badge, which marked them as devoted to the service of their God; indifference to or shame of it involved indifference to or shame of the charge given them therewith, and to their calling as a peculiar people. The choice of the *strange apparel* involved the

1 2 Kgs xxii. 19. 20.
2 Jer. i. 18.
3 Ib. ii. 26, iv. 9, viii. 1, xxiv. 8, xxxii. 37, xxxiv. 21.
4 Zeph. iii. 3.
5 Mic. iii. 1, 9.
6 Is. i. 23.
7 Jer. xxxi. 32–34. xliv. 21.
8 Ib. xxvi. 16.
9 Ib. xxxvii. 15, xxxviii. 4, 16.
10 Ib. xxxvii. 17. xxxviii. 14–27.
11 Ib. xxxix. 6, lii. 25–27.
12 Is. xxxix. 7. See Daniel the prophet p. 16.
13 See Ib. p. 21, 22.
14 Nu. xv. 38. De. xxii. 12.
15 Ex. xxviii. 36.
16 Ib. xxxix. 21.
17 Ib. xix. 6.
18 Nu. xv. 39, 40.

Before CHRIST cir. 630.

and the king's children,
and all such as are clothed
with strange apparel.
9 In the same day also
will I punish all those that
leap on the threshold,
which fill their masters'
houses with violence and
deceit.
10 And it shall come to

Before CHRIST cir. 630.

choice to be as the nations of the world; [1] *we will be as the heathen, as the families of the countries.*

All luxurious times copy foreign dress, and with it, foreign manners and luxuries; whence even the heathen Romans were zealous against its use. It is very probable that with the foreign dress foreign idolatry was imported [2]. The Babylonian dress was very gorgeous, such as was the admiration of the simpler Jews. [3] *Her captains and rulers clothed in perfection, girded with girdles upon their loins, with flowing dyed attire upon their heads.* Ezekiel had to frame words to express the Hebrew idea of their beauty. Jehoiakim is reproved among other things for his luxury [4]. Outward dress always betokens the inward mind, and in its turn acts upon it. An estranged dress betokened an estranged heart, whence it is used as an image of the whole spiritual mind [5]. "[6] The garment of the sons of the king and the apparel of princes which we receive in Baptism, is Christ, according to that, *Put ye on the Lord Jesus Christ,* and *Put ye on bowels of mercy, goodness, humility, patience,* and the rest. Wherein we are commanded to be clothed with the new man from heaven according to our Creator, and to [7] *lay aside* the clothing of *the old man with his deeds.* Whereas then we ought to be clothed in such raiment, for mercy we put on cruelty, for patience, impatience, for righteousness, iniquity; in a word, for virtues, vices; for Christ, Antichrist. Whence it is said of such an one, [8] *He is clothed with cursing as with a garment.* These the Lord will visit most manifestly at His Coming." "[9] Thinkest thou that hypocrisy is *strange apparel?* Of a truth. For what stranger apparel than sheeps' clothing to ravening wolves? What stranger than for him who [10] *within is full of iniquity,* to appear outwardly *righteous before men?*"

9. *I will punish all those that leap on the threshold.* Neither language nor history nor context allow this to be understood of the idolatrous custom of Ashdod, not to tread on the threshold [11] of the temple of Dagon. It had indeed been a strange infatuation of idolatry, that God's people should adopt an act of superstitious reverence for an idol in the very instance in which its nothingness and the power of the true God had been shewn. Nothing is indeed too brutish for one who chooses an idol for the true God, preferring Satan to the good God. Yet the superstition belonged apparently to Ashdod alone; the worship of Dagon, although another form of untrue worship, does not appear, like that of Baal, to have fascinated the Jews; nor would Zephaniah, to express a rare superstition, have chosen an idiom, which might more readily express the contrary, that they "leapt *on* the threshold," not over it [12]. They are also the same persons, who *leap on the threshold,* and who *fill their masters' houses with violence and deceit.* Yet this relates, not to superstition, but to plunder and goods unjustly gotten. As then, before, he had declared God's judgments upon idolatry, so does he here upon sins against the second table, whether by open violence, or secret fraud, as do also Habakkuk [13], and Jeremiah [14]. All, whether open or hidden from man, every wrongful dealing, (for every sin as to a neighbor's goods falls under these two, violence or fraud) shall be avenged in that day. Here again all which remains is the sin. They enriched, as they thought, their masters, by art or by force; they schemed, plotted, robbed; they succeeded to their heart's wish; but, "ill-gotten, ill-spent!" They *filled their masters' houses* quite full; but wherewith? with violence and deceit, which witnessed against them, and brought down the judgments of God upon them.

10. *A cry from the fish-gate. The fish-gate* was probably in the North of the wall of *the second city.* For in Nehemiah's rebuilding, the restoration began at the sheep-gate [15], (so called doubtless, because the sheep for the

[1] Ezek. xx. 33.
[2] Jon. Rashi and S. Jer. connect it with idolatry.
[3] Ezek. xxiii. 12, 15. [4] Jer. xxii. 14, 15.
[5] Rom. xiii. 14, Col. iii. 12, Eph. iv. 24.
[6] S. Jer.
[7] Eph. iv. 22. [8] Ps. cix. 17. [9] Rup.
[10] S. Matt. xxiii. 28.
[11] מפתן is used 1 Sam. v. 4, 5, Ezek. ix. 3, x. 4, 18, xlvi. 2, xlvii. 1; elsewhere סף. There is a trace of this explanation in the Chald., "who walk in the laws of the Philistines," and in S. Jerome, doubtless from his Jewish teachers. Isaiah's reproof that they *have soothsayers like the Philistines*, ii. 6, is altogether different.
[12] דלג על is, in the only other place, Cant. ii. 8, "bounding *on* the mountains;" "bounding over" (like our "leapt a wall") happens to be expressed by an acc., 2 Sam. xviii. 30, Ps. xviii. 30; "passing over" had been expressed more clearly by פסח על, as in Ez. xii. 23, 27.
[13] Hab. i. 2, 3. [14] Jer. v. 27. [15] Neh. iii. 1.

Before CHRIST cir. 630.

pass in that day, saith the
LORD, *that there shall be*
p 2 Chr. 33. 14. the noise of a cry from [p] the
fish gate, and an howling
from the second, and a great
crashing from the hills.

sacrifices were brought in by it) which, as being near the temple, was repaired by the priests; then it ascended Northward, by two towers, *the towers of Meah* and *Hananeel;* then two companies repaired some undescribed part of the wall [1], and then another company *built the fish-gate* [2]. Four companies are then mentioned, who repaired, in order, to the *old gate*, which was repaired by another company [3]. Three more companies repaired beyond these; *and they left Jerusalem unto the broad wall* [4]. After three more sections repaired by individuals, two others repaired a *second measured portion, and the tower of the furnaces* [5]. This order is reversed in the account of the dedication of the walls. The people being divided [6] *into two great companies of them that give thanks*, some place near *the tower of the furnaces* was the central point, from which both parted to encompass the city in opposite directions. In this account, we have two additional gates mentioned, *the gate of Ephraim* [7], between *the broad wall* and the *old gate*, and *the prison-gate*, beyond *the sheep-gate*, from which the repairs had begun. *The gate of Ephraim* had obviously not been repaired, because, for some reason, it had not been destroyed. Else Nehemiah, who describes the rebuilding of the wall so minutely, must have mentioned its rebuilding. It was obviously to the North, as leading to Ephraim. But the tower of Hananeel must have been a very marked tower. In Zechariah Jerusalem is measured from North to South, [8] *from the tower of Hananeel unto the king's winepresses.* It was then itself at the North-East corner of Jerusalem, where towers were of most importance to strengthen the wall, and to command the approach to the wall either way. *The fish-gate* then, lying between it and *the gate of Ephraim*, must have been on the North side of the city, and so on the side where the Chaldæan invasions came; yet it must have been much inside the present city, because the city itself was enlarged by Herod Agrippa on the North, as it was unaccountably contracted on the South [9]. The then limits of Jerusalem are defined. For Josephus thus describes *the second wall.* " [10] It took its beginning from that gate which they called *Gennath*, which belonged to the first wall; it only encompassed the northern quarter of the city and reached as far as the tower of Antonia." The tower of Antonia was situated at the North-West angle of the corner of the temple. The other end of the wall, the Gennath or *garden* gate, must have opened on cultivated land; and Josephus speaks of the gardens on the N. and N. W. of the city which were destroyed by Titus in levelling the ground [11]. But near the tower of Hippicus, the North-Western extremity of the first wall, no ancient remains have been discovered by excavation [12]; but they *have* been traced North, from "an ancient Jewish semi-circular arch, resting on piers 18 feet high, now buried in rubbish." These old foundations have been traced at three places [13] in a line on the East of the Holy Sepulchre (which lay consequently outside the city) up to the judgment gate, but not North of it [14]. The line from West to East, i. e., to the tower of Antonia, is marked generally by "very large stones, evidently of Jewish work, in the walls of houses, especially in the lower parts [15]." They are chiefly in the line of the Via Dolorosa.

The fish-gate had its name probably from a

1 Neh. iii. 2. 2 Ib. 3. 3 Ib. 4–6. 4 Ib. 7, 8.
5 Ib. 9–11. 6 Ib. xii. 31–38. 7 Ib. 39.
8 Zech. xiv. 10. 9 See ab. p. 50. 10 B. J. v. 42.
11 Ib. v. 32.

12 Pierotti, "Jerusalem explored" p. 32, from whom this account is taken. Signor Pierotti's work is "the fruit of eight years of continual labor devoted to a study of the topography of Jerusalem upon the spot, in which I have been constantly occupied in excavating and removing the rubbish accumulated over the place during so many centuries, in retracing the walls, in examining the monuments and ancient remains, and in penetrating and traversing the conduits and vaults."—"I have," he says, "made excavations and watched those made by others, have formed intimacies with the inhabitants of the country, have sought for information on the spot, regardless of personal risk, have worked with my own hands underground, and so have obtained much knowledge of that which lies below the surface of the soil in Jerusalem." Jerusalem explored Pref. p. viii.

13 1) At the meat-bazaar near the convent of S. Mary the Great. "In digging down to the rock to lay the new foundations, 10 feet below the surface, I came upon large stones, boldly rusticated and arranged in a manner that reminded me of the Phœnician work of the time of Solomon." 2) on the East of the Church of the Resurrection. 3) "close to the West of the present *judgment gate.*" "In digging down for the rock, I found, 18 feet below the surface, a fragment of a wall, resembling, in all respects, that first described." Ib. p. 33.

14 This appeared from excavations made in repairing the then Russian consulate, and from "enquiries of all who in former years had built in this neighborhood." Ib.

15 "These were found when the Effendi Kadduti repaired and partly rebuilt the house in the Via Dolorosa at the *Station of Veronica.* A similar discovery was made by the Mufti in strengthening his house at the *Station of Simon of Cyrene*, and by the Effendi Soliman Giari, opposite to the Mufti's house on the North. The Armenian Catholic monks requested me to examine and level a piece of land, at the *Station of the first fall of Christ;* which, as representative of his nation, he had just bought. In the lower part of the wall enclosing it on the north, very large stones and an ancient gate were found. In the foundations of the Austrian hospice,

Before CHRIST cir. 630.

11 [q] Howl, ye inhabit-
ants of Maktesh, for all
the merchant people
are cut down; all they
that bear silver are cut
off.

q Jam. 5. 1.

Before CHRIST cir. 630.

fish-market (markets being in the open places near the gates [1]) the fish being brought either from the lake of Tiberias or from Joppa. Near it, the wall ended, which Manasseh, after his restoration from Babylon [2], *built without the city of David, on the West side of Gihon, in the valley.* This, being unprotected by its situation, was the weakest part of the city. "[3] The most ancient of the three walls could be considered as impregnable, as much on account of its extreme thickness, as of the height of the mountain on which it was built, and the depth of the valleys at its base, and David, Solomon and the other kings neglected nothing to place it in this state." Where they had made themselves strong, there God's judgment should find them.

And a howling from the second city, as it is supplied in Nehemiah, who mentions the prefect set over it [4]. It was here that Huldah the prophetess lived [5], who prophesied the evils to come upon Jerusalem, after Josiah should be *gathered to* his *grave in peace.* It was probably the lower city, which was enclosed by the second wall. It was a second or new city, as compared to the original city of David, on Mount Moriah. On this the enemy who had penetrated by the fish-gate would first enter; then take the strongest part of the city itself. Gareb [6] and Bezetha were outside of the then town; they would then be already occupied by the enemy before entering the city.

A great crashing from the hills. These are probably Zion, and Mount Moriah on which the temple stood, and so the capture is described as complete. Here should be not a cry or howling only, but an utter destruction [7]. Mount Moriah was the seat of the worship of God; on Mount Zion was the state, and the abode of the wealthy. In human sight they were impregnable. The Jebusites mocked at David's siege, as thinking their city impregnable [8]; but God was with David and he took it. He and his successors fortified it yet more, but its true defence was that *the Lord was round about His people* [9], and when He withdrew His protection, then this natural strength was but their destruction, tempting them to resist first the Chaldæans, then the Romans. Human strength is but a great *crash,* falling by its own weight and burying its owner. "This threefold cry [10], from three parts of the city, had a fulfillment before the destruction by the Romans. In the lower part of the city Simon tyrannized, and in the middle John raged, and *there was a great crashing from the hills,* i. e., from the temple and citadel where was Eleazar, who stained the very altar of the temple with blood, and in the courts of the Lord made a pool of blood of divers corpses." "[11] In the assaults of an enemy the inhabitants are ever wont to flee to the tops of the hills, thinking that the difficulty of access will be a hindrance to him, and will cut off the assaults of the pursuers. But when God smiteth, and requireth of the despisers the penalties of their sin, not the most towered city nor impregnable circuits of walls, not height of hills, or rough rocks, or pathless difficulty of ground, will avail to the sufferers. Repentance alone saves, softening the Judge and allaying His wrath, and readily inviting the Creator in His inherent goodness to His appropriate gentleness. Better is it, with all our might to implore that we may not offend Him. But since human nature is prone to evil, and [12] *in many things we all offend,* let us at least by repentance invite to His wonted clemency the Lord of all, Who is by nature kind."

11. *Howl, ye inhabitants of Maktesh,* lit. *Mortar* [13], "in which," S. Jerome says, "corn is pounded; a hollow vessel, and fit for the use of medical men, in which properly ptisans are wont to be beaten (or made). Striking is it, that Scripture saith not, 'who dwell in the valley or in the alley,' but who *dwell in the mortar,* because as corn, when the pestle striketh, is bruised, so the army of the enemy shall rush down upon you [14]." The place intended is probably so much of the valley of the Tyropœon, which intersected Jerusalem from North to South, as was en-

laid in 1857, to the north of the Armenian property, large stones were discovered, and also further to the East, in the new convent of the Daughters of Sion." Pierotti pp. 33, 34.

1 See 2 Kgs vii. 1. Neh. xiii. 16, 19.

2 2 Chr. xxxiii. 14.

3 Jos. de B. J. v. 4. 2.

4 Neh. xi. 9, E. V. "was second over the city" on account of the absence of the article, על העיר משנה. I prefer taking it, as in a sort of apposition, as Ewald does, Lehrb. n. 287, l. p. 734. ed. 8.

5 2 Kings xxii. 14. 2 Chr. xxxiv. 22. It is called by Josephus ἄλλη, "another" city, Ant. xv. 11, 5.

6 Jer. xxxi. 39.

7 Not, as some, "a cry of destruction" as in Is. xv. 5. Isaiah has indeed the words זעקת שבר "cry of destruction," but here שבר, יללה, צעקה are plainly parallel to one another.

8 2 Sam. v. 6.

9 Ps. cxxv. 2.

10 From Rup.

11 S. Cyr.

12 S. James iii. 2.

13 Prov. xxvii. 22. It is also a proper name in Jud. xv. 19, since Lehi in which it was situate (אשר בלחי), was a proper name, Ib. and 9, and 14.

14 S. Jer.

Before CHRIST cir. 630.

12 And it shall come to
pass at that time, *that* I
will search Jerusalem with
candles, and punish the
men that are † [r] settled on
their lees: [s] that say in

[r] Jer. 48. 11. Amos 6. 1. [s] Ps. 94. 7.

† Heb. *curded*, or, *thickened*.

closed by the second wall, on the North, and the first wall on the South. The valley "[1] extended as far as the fountain of Siloam," and united with the valley of Jehoshaphat a little below Ophel. It was "[2] full of houses," and, from its name as well as from its situation, it was probably the scene of petty merchandise, where the occasions in which men could and did break the law and offend God, were the more continual, because they entered into their daily life, and were a part of it. The sound of the pestle was continually heard there; another sound should thereafter be heard, when they should not bruise, but be themselves bruised. The name *Maktesh* was probably chosen to express how their false hopes, grounded on the presence of God's temple among them while by their sins they profaned it, should be turned into true fears. They had been and thought themselves *Mikdash*, "a holy place,. sanctuary;" they should be *Maktesh*[3], wherein all should be utterly bruised in pieces.

"[4] Whoso considereth the calamities of that siege, and how the city was pressed and hemmed in, will feel how aptly he calls them *the inhabitants of a mortar;* for, as grains of corn are brought together into a mortar, to the end that, when the pestle descendeth, being unable to fly off, they may be bruised, so the people flowing together, out of all the countries of Judæa, was narrowed in by a sudden siege, and through the savage cruelty of the above leaders of the sedition, was unutterably tortured from within, more than by the enemy without."

For all the merchant people [lit. *the people of Canaan*] *are cut down;* i.e., "[5] they who in deeds are like the people of Canaan," according to that, [6] *Thou art of Canaan and not of Judah*, and, [7] *Thy father is an Amorite and thy mother a Hittite.* So our Lord says to the reprobate Jews, [8] *Ye are of your father the devil.*

All they that bear [lit. [9] *all laden with*] *silver are cut off.* The silver, wherewith they *lade* themselves, being gotten amiss, is a load upon them, weighing them down until they are destroyed.

12. *I will search* [lit. *diligently*]. The word is always used of a minute diligent search, whereby places, persons, things, are searched and sifted one by one in every corner, until it be found whether a thing be there or no[10]. Hence also of the searching out of every thought of the heart, either by God[11], or in repentance by the light of God[12].

Jerusalem with candles: so that there should be no corner, no lurking-place so dark, but that the guilty should be brought to light. The same diligence, which Eternal Wisdom used, to *seek and to save that which was lost*, [13] *lighting a candle and searching diligently*, till It find each lost piece of silver, the same shall Almighty God use that no hardened sinner shall escape. "[14] What the enemy would do, using unmingled phrensy against the conquered, that God fitteth to His own Person, not as being Himself the Doer of things so foreign, but rather permitting that what comes from anger should proceed in judgment against the ungodly." It was an image of this, when, at the taking of Jerusalem by the Romans, they "[15] dragged out of common sewers and holes and caves and tombs, princes and great men and priests, who for fear of death had hid themselves." How much more in that Day when *the secrets of all hearts shall be revealed* by Him Who [16] *searcheth the hearts and reins, and to Whose Eyes*[17], *which are like flaming Fire, all things are naked and open!* The *candles* wherewith God searcheth the heart, are men's own consciences[18], His Own revealed word[19], the lives of true Christians[20]. These, through the Holy Ghost in each, may enlighten the heart of man, or, if he takes not heed, will rise in judgment against him, and shew the falsehood of all vain excuses. "[21] One way of escape only there is. If we judge ourselves, we shall not be judged. I will *search out my* own *ways* and my desires, that He Who *shall search out Jerusalem with candles*, may find nothing in me, unsought and unsifted.

[1] See Signor Pierotti's map.
[2] Jos. B. J. v. 4. 1.
[3] The two words do so occur in an epistle of the Samaritans (Cellar. Epist. Sichemit. p. 25) Ges.
[4] S. Jer. [5] Ch. [6] Hist. of Susannah 56.
[7] Ezek. xvi. 3. See also on Hosea xii. 7, ab. p. 121.
[8] S. John viii. 44.
[9] A passive adj. (קטיל from קטול). As an act. adj. (קטיל from קטֵל) it would rather imply that they cast it on others.
[10] Nif., of Esau by enemies Ob. 6, Pih., for Laban's idols, Gen. xxxi. 35; for Joseph's cup, Ib. xliv. 12; for David in hiding places, 1 Sam. xxiii. 23; Ahab's house, 1 Kgs xx. 6; for worshipers of God in Baal's temple, 2 Kgs x. 23; in Caves of Carmel, Am. ix. 3, (See vol. i. pp. 330–333); Divine wisdom Pr. ii. 4, God's ways, Ps. lxxvii. 7. The form is intensive here. [11] Pr. xx. 27. [12] Lam. iii. 40.
[13] S. Luke xv. 8. [14] S. Cyr.
[15] S. Jer. See Jos. de B. J. vi. 94. vii. 2 fin.
[16] Ps. vii. 9, xxvi. 2, Jer. xi. 20, xvii. 10, xx. 12, Rev. ii. 23. [17] Ib. i. 14. [18] Prov. xx. 27.
[19] Ps. cxix. 104. Pr. vi. 23. 2 Pet. i. 19.
[20] Phil. ii. 15. [21] S. Bern. Serm. 55 in Cant.

Before CHRIST cir. 626.

their heart, The LORD
will not do good, neither
will he do evil.
13 Therefore their
goods shall become a
booty, and their houses a
desolation: they shall also
build houses, but [t]not in-

Before CHRIST cir. 626.

[t] Deut. 28. 30, 39. Amos 5. 11.

For He will not twice judge the same thing. Would that I might so follow and track out all my offences, that in none I need fear His piercing Eyes, in none be ashamed at the light of His candles! Now I am seen, but I see not. At hand is that Eye, to Whom all things are open, although Itself is not open. Once [1] *I shall know, even as I am known.* Now *I know in part*, but I am not known in part, but wholly."

The men that are settled on their lees, stiffened and contracted [2]. The image is from wine which becomes harsh, if allowed to remain upon the lees, unremoved. It is drawn out by Jeremiah [3], *Moab hath been at ease* [4]*from his youth, and he hath settled on his lees, and hath not been emptied from vessel to vessel, neither hath he gone into captivity; therefore his taste remained in him, and his scent is not changed.* So they upon whom *no changes come, fear not God* [5]. The lees are the refuse of the wine, yet stored up (so the word [6] means) with it, and the wine rests, as it were, upon them. So do men of ease rest in things defiled and defiling, their riches or their pleasure, which they hoard up, on which they are bent, so that they "[7]lift not their mind to things above, but, darkened with foulest desires, are hardened and stiffened in sin."

That say in their heart, not openly scoffing, perhaps thinking that they believe; but people *do* believe as they love. Their most inward belief, the belief of their heart and affections, what they wish, and the hidden spring of their actions, is, *The Lord will not do good, neither will He do evil.* They act as believing so, and by acting inure themselves to believe it. They think of God as far away, [8] *Is not God in the height of heaven? And behold the height of the stars, how high they are! And thou sayest, How doth God know? Can He judge through the dark cloud? Thick clouds are a covering to Him, that He seeth not; and He walketh in the circuit of heaven.* [9] *The ungodly in the pride of his heart* (thinketh); *He will not enquire; all his devices* (speak), *There is no God. Strong are his ways at all times; on high are Thy judgments out of his sight.* [10] *They slay the widow and the stranger, and murder the fatherless, and they say, The Lord shall not see, neither shall the God of Jacob regard it.* [11] *Such things they did imagine and were deceived; for their own wickedness blinded them. As for the mysteries of God, they knew them not.* [12] *Faith without works is dead.* Faith which acts not dies out, and there comes in its stead this other persuasion, that God will not repay. There are more Atheists than believe themselves to be such. These act as if there were no Judge of their deeds, and at last come, themselves to believe that God will not punish [13]. What else is the thought of all worldlings, of all who make idols to themselves of any pleasure or gain or ambition, but "God will not punish?" "God cannot punish the [wrongful, selfish,] indulgence of the nature which He has made." "God will not be so precise." "God will not punish with everlasting severance from Him, the sins of this short life." And they see not that they ascribe to God, what He attributes to idols i. e., not-gods. [14] *Do good or do evil, that we may be dismayed and behold it together.* [15] *Be not afraid of them; for they cannot do evil, neither also is it in them to do good.* These think not that God does good; for they ascribe their success to their own diligence, wisdom, strength, and thank not God for it. They think not that He sends them evil. For they defy Him and His laws, and think that they shall go unpunished. What remains but that He should be as dumb an idol as those of the heathen?

13. *Therefore their goods*, lit. *And their strength.* It is the simple sequel in God's Providence. It is a continued narrative. God will visit those who say, that God does not interfere in man's affairs, *and*, it shall be seen [16] *whose words shall stand*, God's *or their's.* All which God had threatened in the law shall be fulfilled. God, in the fulfillment of the punishment, which He had foretold in the law [17], would vindicate not only His present Providence, but His continual gov-

[1] 1 Cor. xiii. 12.
[2] קפא is used in two cases of the (as it were) congealing of the waves when they *stood on an heap* Ex. xv. 8; of the curdling into cheese Job x. 10. Jon. paraphrases "who are tranquil in their possessions." The Arabic authorities, Abulw. Tanch. David B. Abr. agree in the sense "congealed," and do not call in the Arab. קַפַּ which is primarily "dried," then is used of the wrinkling of a cloth in drying, or of the face of the old, not "contracted" as Ges. On Zech. xiv. 6, see ibid.

[3] Jer. xlviii. 11. [4] שקט. [5] See Ps. lv. 19.
[6] שמרים. [7] Dion.
[8] Job xxii. 12–14.
[9] Ps. x. 4, 5. [10] Ib. xciv. 5, 6.
[11] Wisd. ii. 21–22. [12] S. Jas. ii. 20.
[13] Is. v. 19, Mal. ii. 17.
[14] Is. xli. 23. Perhaps Zeph. meant to suggest this by using words which God by Isaiah had used of idols.
[15] Jer. x. 5. [16] Ib. xliv. 28.
[17] Lev. xxvi. 32, 33. Deut. xxviii.

Before CHRIST cir. 626.

habit *them;* and they shall plant vineyards, but [u] not drink the wine thereof.

[u] Mic. 6. 15.

14 [x] The great day of the LORD *is* near, *it is* near, and hasteth greatly,

[x] Joel 2. 1, 11.

ernment of His own world. All which is strength to man, shall the rather fail, because it is strength, and they presume on it and it deceives them. Its one end is to *become a prey* of devils. Riches, learning, rule, influence, power, bodily strength, genius, eloquence, popular favor, shall all fail a man, and he, when stripped of them, shall be the more bared because he gathered them around him. "[1] Wealth is ever a runaway and has no stability, but rather intoxicates and inclines to revolt and has unsteady feet. Exceeding folly is it to think much of it. For it will not rescue those lying under the Divine displeasure, nor will it free any from guilt, when God decreeth punishment, and bringeth the judgment befitting on the transgressors. How utterly useless this eagerness after wealth is to the ungodly, he teacheth, saying, that *their strength shall be a prey* to the Chaldæan."

And their houses a desolation. "[1] For they are, of whom it may be said very truly, [2] *This is the man that took not God for his strength, but trusted unto the multitude of his riches, and strengthened himself in his wickedness.* But if indeed their houses are adorned costlily, they shall not be theirs, for they shall be burned, and themselves go into captivity, leaving all in their house, and deprived of all which would gladden. And this God said clearly to the king of Judah by Jeremiah, [3] *Thou hast builded thyself a large house and wide chambers, ceiled with cedar, and painted with vermilion. Shalt thou reign because thou closest thyself with cedar?*" "[4] As the house of the body is the bodily dwelling, so to each mind its house is that, wherein through desire it is wont to dwell," and *desolate* shall they be, being severed for ever from the things they desired, and for ever deserted by God. *They shall also build houses but not inhabit them,* as the rich man said to his soul, [5] *Soul, thou hast much goods laid up for many years.—Thou fool, this night thy soul shall be required of thee; then whose shall those things be, which thou hast provided?* Before the siege by the Romans, Jerusalem and the temple had been greatly beautified, only to be destroyed. *And they shall plant vineyards, but not drink the wine thereof.* This is the woe, first pronounced in the law [6], often repeated and ever found true. Wickedness makes joy its end, yet never finds it, seeking it where it is not, out of God.

14. *The great Day of the Lord is near.* The Prophet again expands the words of Joel, accumulating words expressive of the terrors of that Day, shewing that though [7] *the great and very terrible Day of the Lord, a day* (Joel had said [8]) *of darkness and gloominess, of clouds and of thick darkness,* which was then *coming* and *nigh at hand* [9], had come and was gone, it was only a forerunner of others; none of them final; but each, because it *was* a judgment and an instance of the justice of God, an earnest and forerunner of other judgments to the end. Again, *a great Day of the Lord* was *near.* This *Day* had itself, so to speak, many hours and divisions of the day. But each hour tolleth the same knell of approaching doom. Each calamity in the miserable reigns of the sons of Josiah was one stroke in the passing-bell, until the destruction of Jerusalem by the Chaldæans, for the time closed it. The judgment was complete. The completeness of that excision made it the more an image of every other like day until the final destruction of all which, although around or near to Christ, shall in the Great Day be found not to be His, but to have rejected Him. "[10] Truly was vengeance required, [11] *from the blood of righteous Abel to the blood of Zechariah, whom they slew between the temple and the Altar,* and at last when they said of the Son of God, [12] *His blood be upon us and upon our children,* they experienced a bitter day, because they had provoked the Lord to bitterness; a Day, appointed by the Lord, in which not the weak only but the mighty shall be bowed down, and wrath shall come upon them to the end. For often before they endured the wrath of the Lord, but that wrath was not to the uttermost. What need now to describe how great calamities they endured in both captivities, and how they who rejected the light of the Lord, walked in darkness and thick darkness, and they who would not hear the trumpet of the solemn feast-days, heard the shout of the enemy. But of the *fenced cities* and *lofty corner-towers* of Judæa, which are till now destroyed even to the ground, the eyes, I deem, can judge better than the ears. We especially, now living in that province, can see, can prove what is written. We scarcely discern slight traces of ruins of what once were great cities. At Shiloh, where was the tabernacle and ark of the testament of the Lord, scarcely the foundations of the altar are shewn. Rama and Bethoron and the other noble cities built by Solomon,

[1] S. Cyr. [2] Ps. lii. 7.
[3] Jer. xxii. 14, 15. [4] S. Greg. Mor. viii. 14.
[5] S. Luke xii. 19, 20. [6] Deut. xxviii. 39.

[7] Joel ii. 31. [8] Ib. 2. [9] Ib. 1.
[10] S. Jer. [11] S. Matt. xxiii. 35.
[12] Ib. xxvii. 25.

Before CHRIST cir. 626.

even the voice of the day
of the LORD: the mighty
man shall cry there bit-
terly.

15 [y] That day *is* a day
of wrath, a day of trouble
and distress, a day of
wasteness and desolation,

Before CHRIST cir. 626.

[y] Isai. 22. 5. Jer. 30. 7. Joel 2. 2, 11. Amos 5. 18. ver. 18.

are shewn to be little villages. Let us read Josephus and the prophecy of Zephaniah; we shall see his history before our eyes. And this must be said not only of the captivity, but even to the present day. The treacherous husbandmen, having slain the servants, and, at last, the Son of God, are prevented from entering Jerusalem, except to wail, and they purchase at a price leave to weep the ruin of their city, so that they who once bought the Blood of Christ, buy their tears; not even their tears are costless. You may see on the day that Jerusalem was taken and destroyed by the Romans, a people in mourning come, decrepit old women and old men, in aged and ragged wretchedness, shewing in their bodies and in their guise the wrath of the Lord. The hapless crowd is gathered, and amid the gleaming of the Cross of Christ, and the radiant glory of His Resurrection, the standard also of the Cross shining from Mount Olivet, you may see the people, piteous but unpitied, bewail the ruins of their temple, tears still on their cheeks, their arms livid and their hair dishevelled, and the soldier asketh a guerdon, that they may be allowed to weep longer. And doth any, when he seeth this, doubt of the *day of trouble and distress, the day of darkness and gloominess, the day of clouds and thick darkness, the day of the trumpet and alarm?* For they have also trumpets in their sorrow, and, according to the prophecy, the voice of *the solemn feast-day is turned into mourning.* They wail over the ashes of the Sanctuary and the altar destroyed, and over cities once fenced, and over the high towers of the temple, from which they once cast headlong James the brother of the Lord."

But referring the Day of the Lord to the end of the world or the close of the life of each, it too is *near; near,* the prophet adds to impress the more its nearness; for it is at hand to each; and when eternity shall come, all time shall seem like a moment, [1] *A thousand years, when past, are like a watch in the night;* one fourth part of one night.

And hasteth greatly. For time whirls on more rapidly to each, year by year, and when God's judgments draw near, the tokens of them thicken, and troubles sweep one over the other, events jostle against each other. *The voice of the day of the Lord.* That Day, when it cometh, shall leave no one in doubt what it meaneth; it shall give no *uncertain sound,* but shall, trumpet-tongued, proclaim the holiness and justice of Almighty God; its voice shall be the Voice of Christ, which [2] *all that are in the graves shall hear and come forth; they that have done good, unto the resurrection of life; and they that have done evil unto the resurrection of damnation.*

The mighty men shall cry there bitterly; for [3] *bitter is the remembrance of death to a man that liveth at rest in his possessions, unto the man that hath nothing to vex him, and that hath prosperity in all things;* and [4], *There is no mighty man that hath power over the spirit to retain the spirit; neither hath he power in the day of death; and there is no discharge in that war; neither shall wickedness deliver those that are given to it.* Rather, wrath shall come upon [5] *the kings* of the earth, *and the great men and the rich men and the mighty men, and* they shall will to *hide* themselves *from the Face of Him that sitteth on the Throne and from the wrath of the Lamb; for the great Day of His wrath is come: and who shall be able to stand?*

The mighty men shall cry there bitterly. The prophet has spoken of time, *the day of the Lord.* He points out the more vividly the unseen sight and place, *there;* so David says, [6] *There they feared a fear.* He sees the place; he hears the bitter cry. So nigh is it in fact; so close the connection of cause and effect, of sin and punishment. There shall be a great and *bitter cry,* when there shall be no place for repentance. It shall be a [7] mighty cry, but mighty in the bitterness of its distress. [8] *Mighty men shall be mightily tormented,* i. e., those who have been mighty against God, weak against Satan, and shall have used their might in his service.

15. *A day of wrath,* in which all the wrath of Almighty God, which evil angels and evil men have treasured to them for that day, shall be poured out: *the* day of wrath, because then they shall be brought face to face before the Presence of God, but thenceforth they shall be cast out of it for ever.

A day of trouble and distress. Both words express, how anguish shall narrow and hem them in; so that there shall be no escape; above them, God displeased; below, the flames of Hell; around, devils to drag them away, and Angels casting them forth *in bundles to burn them;* without, *the books* which

[1] Ps. xc. 4.
[2] S. John v. 28, 29.
[3] Ecclus. xli. 1.
[4] Eccl. viii. 8.
[5] Rev. vi. 15–17.
[6] Ps. xiv. 5.
[7] The Arab. word, צרח, is used of "a loud shrill cry." It occurs only here and (Hif.) in Is. xlii. 13.
[8] Wisd. vi. 6.

Before CHRIST cir. 626.

a day of darkness and
gloominess, a day of clouds
and thick darkness,
16 A day of [z] the trum-
pet and alarm against the
fenced cities, and against
the high towers.
17 And I will bring
distress upon men, that
they shall [a] walk like blind
men, because they have
sinned against the LORD:
and [b] their blood shall
be poured out as dust,
and their flesh [c] as the
dung.

z Jer. 4. 19.
a Deut. 28. 29. Isai. 59. 10.
b Ps. 79. 3.
c Ps. 83. 10. Jer. 9. 22. & 16. 4.

shall be opened; and within, conscience leaving them no escape.

A day of wasteness and desolation, in which all things shall return to their primeval void, before *the Spirit of God brooded upon the face of the waters,* His Presence being altogether withdrawn.

A day of darkness and gloominess; for sun and moon shall lose their brightness, and no brightness from the Lamb shall shine upon the wicked, but they shall be driven into *outer darkness.*

A day of clouds and thick darkness, hiding from them the Face of the Sun of Righteousness, and covering Him, so that their *prayers* should *not pass through*[1].

16. *A day of the trumpet and alarm*[2], i. e., of the loud blast of the trumpet, which sounds alarm and causes it. The word[3] is especially the shrill loud noise of the trumpet (for sacred purposes in Israel itself, as ruling all the movements of the tabernacle and accompanying their feasts); then also of the "battle cry." They had not listened to the voice of the trumpet, as it called them to holy service; now they shall hear [4] *the voice of the Archangel and the trump of God.*

Against the high towers, lit. *corners*[5], and so *corner-towers.* This peculiarity describes Jerusalem, whose walls "[6] were made artificially standing in a line curved inwards, so that the flanks of assailants might be exposed." By this same name[7] are called the mighty men and chiefs of the people, who, humanly speaking, hold it together and support it; on these chiefs in rebellion against God, whether devils or evil men, shall punishment greatly fall.

17. *I will bring distress upon men.* I will hem them in, in anguish on all sides. God Himself shall meet them with His terrors, wherever they turn. [8] *I will hem them in, that they may find it so.*

That they shall walk like blind men, utterly bereft of counsel, seeing no more than the blind which way to turn, grasping blindly and franticly at anything, and *going on* headlong to their own destruction. So God forewarned them in the law; [9] *Thou shalt grope at noon day, as the blind gropeth in darkness;* and Job, of the wicked generally, [10] *They meet with the darkness in the day-time, and grope in the noon-day as in the night;* and, [11] *They grope in the dark without light, and He maketh them to stagger like a drunken man;* and Isaiah foretelling of those times, [12] *We grope for the wall, as the blind; and we grope, as if we had no eyes; we stumble in the noon-day as in the night. Because they have sinned against the Lord,* and so He hath turned their wisdom into foolishness, and since they have despised Him, He hath made them objects of contempt[13]. *Their blood shall be poured out like dust,* as abundant and as valueless; utterly disregarded by Him, as Asaph complains, [14] *their blood have they shed like water;* contemptible and disgusting as what is vilest; *their flesh*[15] *as the dung,* refuse, decayed, putrefied, offensive, enriching by its decay the land, which had been the scene of their luxuries and oppressions. Yet the most offensive disgusting physical corruption is but a faint image of the defilement of sin. This punishment, in which the carrion-remains should be entombed only in the bowels of vultures and dogs, was especially threatened to Jehoiakim; [16] *He shall be buried with the burial of an ass, dragged and cast forth beyond the gates of Jerusalem.*

1 Lam. iii. 44.

2 "Alarm" seems to be used in the sense of "sounding alarm," alarum.

3 תרועה.

4 1 Thess. iv. 16.

5 See E. M. on iii. 6. It is the *corner* of a house, of a street, of a court, a city. Hence "the gate of the corner," 2 Kgs xiv. 13, 2 Chr. xxvi. 9, Jer. xxxi. 38. In 2 Chr. xxvi. 15, פנות cannot be "battlements" (as Ges. &c.) since the engines were erected upon them. Neither then here is there any ground to invent a new meaning for the word.

6 Tac. Hist. v. 11. Jos. de B. J. v. 5. 3.

7 Jud. xx. 2. 1 Sam. xiv. 38, Is. xix. 13. Zech. x. 4.

8 Jer. x. 18. Moses had said this of His instruments, *And He shall hem thee in, in all thy gates.* Deut. xxviii. 52.

9 Ib. 29. 10 Job v. 14. 11 Ib. xii. 25. 12 Is. lix. 10.

13 1 Sam. ii. 30.

14 Ps. lxxix. 3. שפך is used of the pouring out both liquids and solids.

15 Insulated as the use is, לחום must have had the meaning of the Arab. לַחְם "flesh." So LXX Ch. Vulg. Syr. David B. Abr. Abulw. Tanch., Anon-Arab. Tr., retain the word in Arabic; Abulw. notices that "the Heb. is akin to the Arabic word." Tanch. cites Job vi. 7.

16 Jer. xxii. 19.

Before CHRIST cir. 630.

[d] Prov. 11. 4. Ezek. 7. 19.

18 [d] Neither their silver
nor their gold shall be able
to deliver them in the day
of the LORD's wrath; but
the whole land shall be
[e] devoured by the fire of
his jealousy: for [f] he shall
make even a speedy rid-
dance of all them that
dwell in the land.

Before CHRIST cir. 630.

[e] ch. 3. 8.
[f] ver. 2, 3.

---

18. *Neither their silver nor their gold shall be able to deliver them in the day of the Lord's wrath.* Gain unjustly gotten was the cause of their destruction. For, as Ezekiel closes the like description; "[1] They shall cast their silver into the streets, and their gold shall be removed; their silver and their gold shall not be able to deliver them in the day of the wrath of the Lord; they shall not satisfy their souls nor fill their bowels: *because it is the stumbling block of their iniquity.*" Much less shall any possession, outward or inward, be of avail in the Great Day; since in death the rich man's [2] *pomp shall not follow him*, and every gift which he has misused, whether of mind or spirit, even the knowledge of God without doing His Will, shall but increase damnation. "Sinners will then have nothing but their sins."

Here the prophet uses images belonging more to the immediate destruction; at the close the words again widen, and belong, in their fullest literal sense, to the Day of Judgment. *The whole land*, rather, as at the beginning, *the whole earth shall be devoured by the fire of His jealousy; for He shall make even a speedy riddance of all them that dwell in the land:* rather, *He shall make an utter, yea altogether* [3] *a terrific destruction* [4] *of all the dwellers of the earth.* What Nahum had foretold of Nineveh [5], *He shall make the place thereof an utter consumption*, that Zephaniah foretells of all the inhabitants of the world. For what is this, *the whole earth shall be devoured by the fire of His jealousy*, but what S. Peter says, [6] *the earth also and the works that are therein shall be burned up?* And what is that he says, *He shall make all the dwellers of the earth an utter, yea altogether a hasty destruction*, but a general judgment of all, who belong to the world, whose home, citizenship, whose whole mind is in the world, not as true Christians, who are strangers and pilgrims here, and their [7] *citizenship is in Heaven?* These God shall make an utter, terrific, speedy destruction, a living death, so that they shall at once both be and not be; be, as continued in being; not be, as having no life of God, but only a continued death in misery. And this shall be through the jealousy of Almighty God, that Divine quality in Him, whereby He loves and wills to be loved, and endures not those who give to others the love for which He gave so much and which is so wholly due to Himself Alone. "[8] Thou demandest my love, and if I give it not, art wroth with me, and threatenest me with grievous woes. Is it then a slight woe to love Thee not?" What will be that anger, which is Infinite Love, but which becomes, through man's sin, Hate?

II. Having set forth the terrors of the Judgment Day, the prophet adds an earnest call to repentance; and then declares how judgments, forerunners of that Day, shall fall, one by one, on those nations around, who know not God, and shall rest upon Nineveh, the great beautiful ancient city of the world. "[9] See the mercy of God. It had been enough to have set before the wise the vehemence of the coming evil. But because He willeth not to punish, but to alarm only, Himself calleth to repentance, that He may not do what He threatened." "[10] Having set forth clearly the savageness of the war and the greatness of the suffering to come, he suitably turns his discourse to the duty of calling to repentance, when it was easy to persuade them, being terrified. For sometimes when the mind has been numbed, and exceedingly bent to evil, we do not readily admit even the will to repent, but fear often drives us to it, even against our will. He calls us then to friendship with Himself. For as they revolted, became aliens, serving idols and giving up their mind to their passions, so they would, as it were, retrace their steps, and lay hold of the friendship of God, choosing to serve Him, nay and Him Alone, and obey His commandments. Wherefore while we have time, while the Lord, in His forbearance as God, gives way, let us enact repentance, supplicate, say weeping, [11] *remember not the sins and offences of my youth;* let us unite ourselves with Him by sanctification and sobriety. So shall we be sheltered in the day of wrath, and wash away the stain of our falls, before the Day of the Lord come

---

[1] Ezek. vii. 19. [2] Ps. xlix. 17.

[3] אַךְ "nothing but."

[4] נִבְהָלָה unites here the senses of terror and destruction, as in Ps. civ. 29. *Thou hidest Thy face, they are troubled,* יִבָּהֵלוּן *and* perish; Is. lxv. 23, *they shall not bear* לַבֶּהָלָה for destruction, ‖ לֹא יִגְעוּ לָרִיק.

[5] See ab. on Nahum i. 8. p. 134.

[6] 2 Pet. iii. 13.

[7] Heb. xi. 13. Phil. iii. 20.

[8] S. Aug. Conf. i. 5. p. 3. Oxf. Tr.

[9] S. Jer. [10] S. Cyr. [11] Ps. xxv. 7.

Before CHRIST cir. 630.

CHAPTER II.

1 *An exhortation to repentance.* 4 *The judgment of the Philistines,* 8 *of Moab and Ammon,* 12 *of Ethiopia and Assyria.*

1 [a]GATHER yourselves together, yea, gather together, O nation ‖not desired;

Before CHRIST cir. 630.

a Joel 2. 16.
‖ Or, *not desirous.*

upon us. For the Judge will come, He will come from heaven at the due season, and will reward each according to his work."

1. *Gather yourselves together, yea gather together*[1], rather, *Sift yourselves, yea sift*[2]. The exact image is from gathering stubble or dry sticks, which are picked up one by one, with search and care. So must men deal with the dry and withered leaves of a past evil life. The English rendering however comes to the same meaning. We use, "collect one's self" for bringing one s self, all one's thoughts, together, and so, having full possession of one's self. Or *gathering ourselves* might stand in contrast with being "abroad," as it were, out of ourselves amid the manifoldness of things seen. "[3]Thou who, taken up with the business of the world, hurriest to and fro amid divers things, return to the Church of the saints, and join thyself to their life and assembly, whom thou seest to please God, and bring together the dislocated members of thy soul, which now are not knit together, into one frame of wisdom, and cleave to its embrace." *Gather yourselves* into one, wherein ye have been scattered; to the One God, from Whom they had wandered, seeking pleasure from His many creatures; to His one fold and Church, from which they had severed themselves outwardly by joining the worship of Baal, inwardly, by serving him and his abominable rites; joining and joined to the assembly of the faithful, by oneness of faith and life.

In order to repent, a man must know himself thoroughly; and this can only be done by taking act by act, word by word, thought by thought, as far as he can, not in a confused heap or mass, as they lie in any man's conscience, but one by one, each picked up apart, and examined, and added to the sear unfruitful heap, plucking them as it were, and gathering them out of himself, that so they may, by the Spirit of burning, the fire of God's Spirit kindling repentance, be burned up, and not the sinner himself be fuel for fire with them. The word too is intensive, "Gather together all which is in you, thoroughly, piece by piece" (for the sinner's whole self becomes chaff, dry and empty). To use another image, "Sift yourselves thoroughly, so that nothing escape, as far as your diligence can reach, and then—*And gather on,* i. e., "glean on;" examine yourselves, "not lightly and after the manner of dissemblers before God," but repeatedly, gleaning again and again, to see if by any means anything have escaped: continuing on the search and ceasing not. The first earnest search into the soul must be the beginning, not the end. Our search must be continued, until there be no more to be discovered, i. e. when sin is no more, and we see ourselves in the full light of the Presence of our Judge. For a first search, however diligent, never thoroughly reaches the whole deep disease of the whole man; the most grievous sins hide other grievous sins, though lighter. Some sins flash on the conscience, at one time, some at another; so that few, even upon a diligent search, come at once to the knowledge of all their heaviest sins. When the mist is less thick, we see more clearly what was before one dark dull mass of imperfection and misery. "[4]Spiritual sins are also with difficulty sifted, (as they are,) by one who is carnal. Whence it happens, that things in themselves heavier he perceives less or very little, and conscience is not grieved so much by the memory of pride or envy, as of impurities and crimes." So having said, "Sift yourselves through and through," he says, "sift on." A diligent sifting and search into himself must be the beginning of all true repentance and pardon. "[5]What remains, but that we give ourselves wholly to this work, so holy, and needful? [6]*Let us search and try our ways and our doings,* and let each think that he has made progress, not if he find not what to blame, but if he blame what he finds. Thou hast not sifted thyself in vain, if thou hast discovered that thou needest a fresh sifting; and so often has thy search not failed thee, as thou judgest that it must be renewed. But

[1] The Eng. Vers. follows the LXX Ch. Syr., S. Jer., which render "Gather yourselves together," as if, from the first meaning, "gather dry sticks or stubble" it came to signify "gather" generally, and thence, in the reflective form, "gather yourselves together."

[2] The word is first used of gathering dry stubble together (Ex. v. 7, 12.) then of "dry sticks" one by one (Nu. xv. 32, 33, 1 Kgs xvii. 10, 12.). A heathen speaks of "gathering out thorns" (ἐξακανθίζειν) i. e., minutely examining and bringing out to light every fault. (Cic. ad Att. vi. 6. 2.) And another writes to his steward, "Shalt thou with stronger hand pull out thorns from my field, or I from my mind?" Hor. Ep. i. 14. 4.

[3] S. Jer.

[4] S. Bern. de Cons. c. 5.

[5] Id. Serm. 58. in Cant. fin.

[6] Lam. iii. 40. The two words, *search* and *try,* חקר, חפר are both used of a deep search of a thing which lies deep and hidden. Both originally mean "dig." Both are used of a Divine knowledge of the inmost soul; the former of the mind as enlightened by God (Prov. xx. 27), the latter of God's searching it out Himself (Jer. xvii. 10. Ps. xliv. 22 (21) cxxxix. 1. Job xiii. 9, and of the Divine Wisdom, Job xxviii. 27.

Before CHRIST cir. 630.

2 Before the decree
bring forth, *before* the day
pass [b] as the chaff, before
[c] the fierce anger of the
LORD come upon you,
before the day of the
LORD's anger come upon
you.

[b] Job 21. 18. Ps. 1. 4. Isai. 17. 13. Hos. 13. 3.
[c] 2 Kin. 23. 26.

3 [d] Seek ye the LORD,
[e] all ye meek of the earth,
which have wrought his
judgment; seek righteous-
ness, seek meekness: [f] it
may be ye shall be hid in
the day of the LORD's
anger,

Before CHRIST cir. 630.

[d] Ps. 105. 4. Amos 5. 6.
[e] Ps. 76. 9.
[f] Joel 2. 14. Amos 5. 15. Jonah 3. 9.

---

if thou ever dost this, when there is need, thou dost it ever. But ever remember that thou needest help from above and the mercy of Jesus Christ our Lord Who is over all, God blessed for ever." The whole course of self-examination then lies in two words of Divine Scripture. And withal he warns them, instead of gathering together riches which shall *not be able to deliver them in the day of trouble*, to gather themselves into themselves, and so *judge* themselves *thoroughly*[1], *that they be not judged of the Lord*[2].

O nation not desired[3], i. e., having nothing in itself to be desired or loved, but rather, for its sin, hateful to God. God yearneth with pity and compassion over His creatures; He [4] *hath a desire to the work of His Hands.* Here Israel is spoken to, as what he had made himself, hateful to God by his sins, although still an object of His tender care, in what yet remained to him of nature or grace which was from Himself.

2. *Before the decree bring forth.* God's word is full (as it were) of the event which it foretelleth; it contains its own fulfillment in itself, and *travaileth* until it come to pass, giving signs of its coming, yet delaying until the full time. Time is said to bring forth what is wrought in it. *Thou knowest not, what a day shall bring forth.*

Before the day pass as the chaff, or, parenthetically, *like chaff the day passeth by.* God's counsels lie wrapt up, as it were, in the womb of time, wherein He hides them, until the moment which He has appointed, and they break forth suddenly to those who look not for them. The mean season is given for repentance, i. e., the day of grace, the span of repentance still allowed, which is continually whirling more swiftly by; and woe, if it be fruitless as chaff! Those who profit not by it shall also be as chaff, carried away pitilessly by the whirlwind to destruction. Time, on which eternity hangs, is a slight, uncertain thing, as little to be counted upon, as the light dry particles which are the sport of the wind, driven uncertainly hither and thither. But when it is *passed*, then *cometh*, not *to* them, but *upon* them, from Heaven, overwhelming them, [5] *abiding upon* them, not to pass away, *the heat of the anger of Almighty God.* This warning he twice repeats, to impress the certainty and speed of its coming [6]. It is the warning of our Lord, [7] *Take heed, lest that day come upon you unawares.*

3. *Seek ye the Lord.* He had exhorted sinners to penitence; he now calls the righteous to persevere and increase more and more. He bids them *seek diligently*[8], and that with a three-fold call, to seek Him from Whom they received daily the three-fold blessing [9], Father, Son, and Holy Ghost, as he had just before threatened God's impending judgment with the same use of the mysterious number, three. They, whom he calls, were already, by the grace of God, *meek*, and *had wrought His judgment.* "[10] Submitting themselves to the word of God, they had done and were doing the judgment of God, *judging themselves that they be not judged;* the beginning of which judgment is, as sinners and guilty of death, to give themselves to the Cross of the Lord, i. e., to be [11] *baptized* in *His Death and be buried with Him by Baptism into death;* but the perfection of that judgment or righteousness is, to *walk in newness of life, as He rose from the dead through the glory of the Father.*"

"[12] Since the meek already have God through grace as the Possessor and Dweller

---

[1] διακρινατε, which answers to the intensive form here, "judge yourselves through and through."

[2] 1 Cor. xi. 31, 32.

[3] The E. M. has "or not desirous," the word נכסף signifying to long, Gen. xxxi. 30. Ps. lxxxiv. 3. But in both places the object of desire is mentioned, "thy father's house," in Gen., "the courts of the Lord," in the Ps. Israel had strong but bad longings. "Not desirous" would not by itself convey, "having no desire to return to God," or as Ch., "who willeth not to return to the law." The same objection lies, over and above, to the rendering "unashamed," coll. Chald. כסף "turned pale" from shame, disgrace, horror. Buxt. For there is nothing to limit the "turning pale" to "shame." The root כסף in Heb. only means "longed," Ps. xvii. 12, Job xiv. 15, of which נכסף is here the passive. People turn pale from fear or horror, not from shame.

[4] Job xiv. 15. The word is the same.

[5] S. John iii. 36.

[6] Gen. xli. 32.

[7] S. Luke xvi. 34.

[8] The Hebrew form is intensive.

[9] Nu. vi. 23–26.

[10] Rup.

[11] Rom. vi. 3, 4.

[12] Dion.

Before CHRIST cir. 630.

4 ¶ For [g] Gaza shall be
forsaken, and Ashkelon a
desolation: they shall
drive out Ashdod [h] at the
noon day, and Ekron shall
be rooted up.

[g] Jer. 47. 4, 5. Ezek. 25. 15. Amos 1. 6, 7, 8. Zech. 9. 5, 6.

Before CHRIST cir. 630.

[h] Jer. 6. 4, & 15. 8.

---

in their heart, how shall they seek Him but that they may have Him more fully and more perfectly, knowing Him more clearly, loving Him more ardently, cleaving to Him more inseparably, that so they may be heard by Him, not for themselves only, but for others?" It is then the same Voice as at the close of the Revelation, [1] *the righteous, let him be still more righteous; the holy, let him be still more holy.* They are the *meek,* who are exhorted *diligently* to *seek meekness,* and they who had *wrought His judgment,* who are *diligently* to *seek Righteousness.* And since our Lord saith, [2] *Learn of Me, for I am meek and lowly of heart,* He bids "[3] those who imitated His meekness and did His judgment, to seek the Lord in their meekness." Meekness and Righteousness may be His Attributes, Who is All-gentleness and All-Righteousness, the Fountain of all, wheresoever it is, in gentleness receiving penitents, and, as *the Righteous Judge, giving the crown of righteousness* to those who *love Him and keep His commandments,* yea He joineth righteousness with meekness, since without His mercy no man living could be justified in His Sight. "[4] God is sought by us, when, of our choice, laying aside all listlessness, we thirst after doing what pleases Him; and we shall do judgment too, when we fulfill His Divine law, working out what is good unshrinkingly; and we shall gain the prize of righteousness, when crowned with glory for well-doing and running the well-reported and blameless way of true piety to God and of love to the brethren; for [5] *love is the fulfilling of the law.*"

It may be ye shall be hid in the day of the Lord's anger. "[6] Shall these too then scarcely be *hid in the day of the Lord's anger?* Doth not the Apostle Peter say the very same? [7] *If it first begin at us, what shall be the end of them that obey not the Gospel of God? And if the righteous scarcely be saved, where shall the ungodly and the sinner appear?* So then, although any be *meek,* although he *have wrought the judgment* of the Lord, let him ever suspect himself, nor think that he has *already attained,* since neither can any righteous be saved, if he be judged *without mercy.*" "[8] He saith, *it may be;* not that there is any doubt that the meek and they who perseveringly seek God, shall then be saved, but, to convey how difficult it is to be saved, and how fearful and rigorous is the judgment of God." To be hid is to be sheltered from wrath under the protection of God; as David says, [9] *In the time of trouble He shall hide me;* and, [10] *Thou shalt hide them [that trust in Thee] in the secret of Thy presence from the pride of man; Thou shalt keep them secretly in a pavilion from the strife of tongues.* And in Isaiah, [11] *A Man shall be as an hiding-place from the wind, and a covert from the tempest;* and, [12] *There shall be a tabernacle for a shadow in the daytime from the heat, and for a place of refuge, and for a covert from storm and from rain.*

4. *For.* As a ground for repentance and perseverance, he goes through Heathen nations, upon whom God's wrath should come. "[3] As Isaiah, Jeremiah, Ezekiel, after visions concerning Judah, turn to other nations round about, and according to the character of each, announce what shall come upon them, and dwell at length upon it, so doth this prophet, though more briefly." And thus under five nations, who lay West, East, South and North, he includes all mankind on all sides, and, again, according to their respective characters toward Israel, as they are alien from, or hostile to the Church; the Philistines[13], as a near, malicious, infesting enemy; Moab and Ammon[14], people akin to her (as heretics) yet ever rejoicing at her troubles and sufferings; Ethiopians[15], distant nations at peace with her, and which are, for the most part, spoken of as to be brought unto her; Assyria[16], as the great oppressive power of the world, and so upon it the full desolation rests. In the first fulfillment, because Moab and Ammon aiding Nebuchadnezzar, (and all, in divers ways, wronging God's people[17]), trampled on His sanctuary, overthrew His temple and blasphemed the Lord, the prophecy is turned against them. So then, before the captivity came, while Josiah was yet king, and Jerusalem and the temple were, as yet, not overthrown, the prophecy is directed against those who mocked at them. *Gaza shall be forsaken.* Out of the five cities of the Philistines, the Prophet pronounces woe upon the same four as Amos[18] before, Jeremiah[19] soon after, and Zechariah[20] later. Gath, then, the fifth, had probably remained with Judah since Uzziah[21] and Hezekiah[22]. In the sentence of the rest, regard is had (as is so frequent in the Old

[1] Rev. xxii. 11. [2] S. Matth. xi. 29. [3] S. Jer. [4] S. Cyr. [5] Rom. xiii. 10. [6] Rup. [7] 1 S. Pet. iv. 17, 18. [8] Dion. [9] Ps. xxvii. 5. [10] Ib. xxxi. 20. [11] Isai. xxxii. 2. [12] Ib. v. 6. [13] ii. 4–7. [14] Ib. 8–10.

[15] v. 12. [16] 13–15. [17] Is. xvi. 4, Am. i. 13–15. ii. 1–3. Jer. xlviii. 27–30, 42. xlix. 1. Ezek. xx. 3, 6, 8. [18] Am. i. 6–8. [19] Jer. xxv. 20. [20] Zech. ix. 5, 6. [21] 2 Chr. xxvi. 6. [22] 2 Kgs xviii. 8.

Testament) to the names of the places themselves, that, henceforth, the name of the place might suggest the thought of the doom pronounced upon it. The names expressed boastfulness, and so, in the Divine judgment, carried their own sentence with them, and this sentence is pronounced by a slight change in the word. Thus *'Azzah* (Gaza,) *strong* shall be *'Azoobah, desolated; Ekron, deep-rooting*[1], shall *Teaker, be uprooted;* the *Cherethites (cutters off)* shall become (*Cheroth*) *diggings; Chebel, the band* of the sea coast, shall be in another sense *Chebel,* an *inheritance*[2], divided by line to the remnant of Judah; and *Ashdod* (*the waster*[3]) shall be taken in their might, not by craft, nor in the way of robbers, but *driven forth* violently and openly in the *noon-day.*

For Gaza shall be forsaken. Some vicissitudes of these towns have been noted already[4]. The fulfillment of the prophecy is not tied down to time; the one marked contrast is, that the old heathen enemies of Judah should be destroyed, the house of Judah should be restored, and should re-enter upon the possession of the land, promised to them of old. The Philistine towns had, it seems, nothing to fear from Babylon or Persia, to whom they remained faithful subjects. The Ashdodites (who probably, as the most important, stand for the whole[5]) combined with Sanballat, *the Ammonites and the Arabians*[6], to hinder the rebuilding of the walls of Jerusalem. Even an army was gathered, headed by Samaria[7]. They gave themselves out as loyal, Jerusalem as rebellious[8]. The old sin remaining, Zechariah renewed the sentence by Zephaniah against the four cities[9]; a prophecy, which an unbeliever also has recognized as picturing the march of Alexander[10]. "[11] All the other cities of Palestine having submitted," Gaza alone resisted the conqueror for two or five months. It had come into the hands of the Persians in the expedition of Cambyses against Egypt[12]. The Gazæans having all perished fighting at their posts, Alexander sold the women and children, and re-peopled the city from the neighborhood[13]. Palestine lay between the two rival successors of Alexander, the Ptolemies and Seleucidæ, and felt their wars[14]. Gaza fell through mischance into the hands of Ptolemy[15], 11 years after the death of Alexander[16], and soon after, was destroyed by Antiochus[11] (B. C. 198), "preserving its faith to Ptolemy" as before to the Persians, in a way admired by a heathen historian. In the Maccabee wars, Judas Maccabæus chiefly destroyed the idols of Ashdod, but also [17] *spoiled their cities;* Jonathan set it on fire, with its idol-temple, which was a sort of citadel to it[18]; Ascalon submitted to him[19]; Ekron with its borders were given to him by Alexander Balas[20]; he burnt the suburbs of Gaza[21]; Simon took it, expelled its inhabitants, filled it with believing Jews and fortified it more strongly than before[22]; but, after a year's siege, it was betrayed to Alexander Jannæus, who slew its senate of 500 and razed the city to the ground[23]. Gabinius restored it and Ashdod[24]. After Herod's death, Ashdod was given to Salome[25]; Gaza, as being a Greek city[26], was detached from the realm of Archelaus and annexed to Syria. It was destroyed by the Jews in their revolt when Florus was "procurator," A. D. 55[27]. Ascalon and Gaza must still have been strong, and were probably a distinct population in the early times of Antipater, father of Herod, when Alexander and Alexandra set him over all Idumæa, since "he is said" then "[28] to have made friendship with the Arabs, Gazites and Ascalonites, likeminded with himself, and to have attached them by many and large presents."

Yet though the inhabitants were changed, the hereditary hatred remained. Philo in his Embassy to Caius, A. D. 40, used the strong language, "[29] The Ascalonites have an implacable and irreconcilable enmity to the Jews, their neighbors, who inhabit the holy land." This continued toward Christians. Some horrible atrocities, of almost inconceivable savagery, by those of Gaza and Ascalon A. D. 361, are related by Theodoret[30] and Sozomen[31]. "[32] Who is ignorant of the madness of the Gazæans?" asks S. Gregory

[1] It seems to me most probable that the origin of the meanings is preserved in the Ch. עִקַּר, "root," (which itself is the source of other metaphoric meanings, as, "the root of a thing;" "the root" i. e., the foundation "of faith," its fundamental doctrines; "the root," in Lexicography, see Buxtorf), and that the Chald. עֲקַר "pluck up, remove," and עָקַר, here and Eccl. iii. 2, is a denominative. The Proper Name is older probably than even Moses.

[2] ii. 5, 7.

[3] The root שדד has throughout, the meaning of "wasting," not of "strength." שַׁדַּי "the Almighty," is probably from a kindred root, שׁדה.

[4] See on Amos i. 6–8, vol. i. p. 244–247.

[5] Their language alone is mentioned Neh. ix. 24, אשדודית, in contrast with Jewish יהודית; but neither is it mentioned that the Jews married any other Philistine women. If Gath was destroyed, Ashdod lay nearest to them.

[6] Neh. iv. 7. [7] Ib. 2. [8] Ib. ii. 19. vi. 6.

[9] Zech. ix.

[10] Eichhorn Einl. iv. 605. See Daniel the Proph. p. 280. sqq.

[11] Polyb. Reliq. xvi. 40. [12] Mela i. 11.

[13] Arrian ii. 27. [14] Polyb. v. 68.

[15] Diod. Sic. xix. 84.

[16] Hecat. in Jos. c. Ap. i. 22 Opp. ii. 455.

[17] 1 Macc. v. 68. [18] Ib. x. 84. [19] Ib. 86. [20] Ib. 89.

[21] Ib. xi. 61. [22] Ib. xiii. 43–48.

[23] Jos. Ant. xiii. 13. 3. [24] Ib. xiv. 5. 3.

[25] Ib. xvii. 8. 1. [26] B. J. ii. 6. 3.

[27] κατέσκαπτον, Jos. B. J. ii. 18. 1.

[28] Ant. xiv. 1. 3.

[29] Philo Leg. ad Caium T. ii. p. 576 Mang. The words are ἀσυμβατός τις καὶ ἀκατάλλακτος δυσμένεια.

[30] Theod. H. E. iii. 7. [31] Soz. H. E. v. 10.

[32] Orat. 4. in Julian. c. 36.

of Nazianzus, of the times of Julian. This was previous to the conversion of the great Gazite temple of Marna into a Christian Church by Eudoxia[1]. On occasion of Constantine's exemption of the Maiumas Gazæ from their control, it is alleged, that they were "[2] extreme Heathen." In the time of the Crusades the Ascalonites are described by Christians as their "[3] most savage enemies."

It may be, that a likeness of sin may have continued on a likeness of punishment. But the primary prediction was against the people, not against the walls. The sentence, *Gaza shall be forsaken*, would have been fulfilled by the removal or captivity of its inhabitants, even if they had not been replaced by others. A prediction against any ancient British town would have been fulfilled, if the Britons in it had been replaced or exterminated by Danes, and these by Saxons, and these subdued by the Normans, though their displacers became wealthy and powerful in their place. Even on the same site it would not be the same Gaza, when the Philistine Gaza became Edomite, and the Edomite Greek, and the Greek Arabian[4]. Ashdod (as well as Gaza) is spoken of as a city of the Greeks[5]; New Gaza is spoken of as a mixture of Turks, Arabians, Fellahs, Bedouins out of Egypt, Syria, Petræa[6]. Felix Faber says, "there is a wonderful commixture of divers nations in it, Ethiopians, Arabs, Egyptians, Syrians, Indians and eastern Christians; no Latins[7]." Its Jewish inhabitants fled from it in the time of Napoleon: now, with few exceptions it is inhabited by Arabs[8].

But these, Ghŭzzeh, Eskalon, Akir, Sedud, are at most successors of the Philistine cities, of which there is no trace above the surface of the earth. It is common to speak of "remnants of antiquity," as being or not being to be found in any of them; but this means, that, where these exist, there are remains of a Greek or Roman, not of a Philistine city.

Of the four cities, *Akkaron*, Ekron, ("the firm-rooting") has not left a vestage. It is mentioned by name only, after the times of the Bible, by some who passed by it[9]. There was "a large village of Jews" so called in the time of Eusebius and S. Jerome[10], "between Azotus and Jamnia." Now a village of "[11] about 50 mud houses without a single remnant of antiquity except 2 large finely built wells" bears the name of Akir. S. Jerome adds, "Some think that Accaron is the tower of Strato, afterward called Cæsarea." This was perhaps derived from misunderstanding his Jewish instructor[12]. But it shows how entirely all knowledge of Ekron was then lost.

Ashdod or Azotus which, at the time when Zephaniah prophesied, held out a twenty-nine years' siege against Psammetichus, is replaced by "[13] a moderate sized village of mud houses, situated on the Eastern declivity of a little flattish hill," "entirely modern, not containing a vestige of antiquity." "A beautiful sculptured sarcophagus with some fragments of small marble shafts," "near the Khan on the S. W." belong of course to later times. "The whole south side of the hill appears also, as if it had been once covered with buildings, the stones of which are now thrown together in the rude fences." Its Bishops are mentioned from the Council of Nice to A. D. 536[14], and so probably continued till the Mohammedan devastation. It is not mentioned in the Talmud[15]. Benjamin of Tudela calls it Palmis, and says, "it is desolate, and there are no Jews in it[16]." "[17] Neither Ibn Haukal [Yacut], Edrisi, Abulfeda, nor William of Tyre mention it."

Ascalon and Gaza had each a port, Maiuma Gazæ, Maiuma Ascalon; lit. "a place on the sea" (an Egyptian name[18]) belonging to Ascalon or Gaza. The name involves that Ascalon and Gaza themselves, the old Philistine towns, were not on the sea. They were, like Athens, built inland, perhaps (as

[1] "This too we see to be fulfilled *in our times*. The temple of Serapis at Alexandria, and of Marna at Gaza, rose to be temples of the Lord." S. Jerome on Is. xvii.

[2] ἐς ἄγαν Ἑλληνίζουσιν. Soz. v. 3.

[3] William of Tyre (pp. 917, 840, 865) calls them "hydra immanissima," "hostes immanissimi"—"like restless gnats persevering in the purpose of injuring." comp. pp. 781, 787, 797. "Ascalona was ever an adversary of Jerusalem." Robertus Monachus p. 77. in v. Raumer Palæst. p. 173, ed. 4. It was called "the spouse of Syria," as an impregnable fortress.

[4] See on Amos i. 6. vol. i. p. 244.

[5] Ps. Epiphanius de vitis Proph. p. 246.

[6] Ritter xvi. 49.

[7] Fabri Evagatorium T. ii. p. 379.

[8] Schwartz, d. Heil. Land p. 91. 1853.

[9] "Passing through Azotus, between which and Jamnia, which is situate on the sea, [i. e. the maritime Jamnia] we left Accaron on one side." Fulcher. Carnot. A. D. 1100. Gesta Peregr. Franc. c. 23 p. 464 quoted Raumer's. verb.

[10] de locis Hebr. T. iii. p. 146. Vall.

[11] Porter Handb. p. 275.

[12] "The verse, *Ekron shall be uprooted*, the Talmud says, relates to Cæsarea, the daughter of Edom, which is situate among the sands. It does not mean that Ekron is Cæsarea, which would be absurd, but only shews its hatred against that city, and foretells its destruction, resting on a Biblical text, as is the habit of the talmudists." Neubauer Geogr. du Talmud p. 92. See also Ib. p. 12. Estori in his Kaftor uperach gives קסרי as another name of עקר, but Zunz quotes the Succah f. 276. as distinguishing קיסרי from קיסריון Cæsarea (on the geogr. of Pal. App. to Benj. Tud. ii. 441.)

[13] Porter Handb. pp. 272, 273.

[14] Reland p. 609.

[15] It does not appear in Neubauer, Geographie du Talmud.

[16] "Palmis, which is Ashdod of the Philistines." מג ed. Asher.

[17] Asher note Ib. T. ii. p. 99.

[18] "The name Maiuma seems to belong to the Egyptian language, and to offer the two words MA IOM "place by the sea." Quatremère, les sultans Mamlouks de Makrizi T. i. 2 App. p. 229.

has been conjectured) from fear of the raids of pirates, or of inroads from those who (like the Philistines themselves probably, or some tribe of them) might come from the sea. The port probably of both was built in much later times; the Egyptian name implies that they were built by Egyptians, after the time when its kings Necos and Apries, (Pharaoh-Necho and Pharaoh-Hophra, who took Gaza [1]) made Egypt a naval power [2]. This became a characteristic of these Philistine cities. They themselves lay more or less inland, and had a city connected with them of the same name, on the shore. Thus there was an "[3] Azotus by the sea," and an "Azotus Ispinus." There were "[4] two Iamniæ, one inland." But Ashdod lay further from the sea than Gaza; Yamnia, (the Yabneel of Joshua [5], in Uzziah's time, Yabneh [6]) further than Ashdod. The port of Yamnia was burnt by Judas [7].

The *name*, Maiumas, does not appear till Christian times, though "the port of Gaza" is mentioned by Strabo [8]: to it, Alexander brought from Tyre the machines, with which he took Gaza itself [9]. That port then must have been at some distance from Gaza. Each port became a town, large enough to have, in Christian times, a Bishop of its own. The Epistle of John of Jerusalem, inserted in the Acts of the Council of Constantinople, A. D. 536, written in the name of Palestine i., ii., and iii., is signed by a Bishop of Maiumen of Ascalon, as well as by a Bishop of Ascalon, as it is by a Bishop of Maiumas of Gaza as well as by a Bishop of Gaza [10]. Yabne, or Yamnia, was on a small eminence [11], 6½ hours from the sea [12]. The Maiumas Gazæ became the more known. To it, as being Christian, Constantine gave the right of citizenship, and called it Constantia from his son, making it a city independent of Gaza. Julian the Apostate gave to Gaza (which, though it had Bishops and Martyrs, had a heathen temple at the beginning of the 5th century) its former jurisdiction over it, and though about 20 furlongs off, it was called "the maritime portion of Gaza [13]." It had thenceforth the same municipal officers; but, "as regards the Church alone," Sozomen adds, "they still appear to be two cities; each has its own Bishop and clergy, and festivals and martyrs, and commemorations of those who had been their Bishops, and *boundaries of the fields around*, whereby the altars which belong to each Episcopate are parted." The provincial Synod decided against the desire of a Bishop of Gaza, in Sozomen's time, who wished to bring the Clergy of the Maiumites under himself, ruling that "although deprived of their civil privileges by a heathen king, they should not be deprived of those of the Church."

In A. D. 400, then, the two cities were distinct, not joined or running into one another.

S. Jerome mentions it as "[14] Maiumas, the emporium of Gaza, 7 miles from the desert on the way to Egypt by the sea;" Sozomen speaks of "[15] Gaza by the sea, which they also call Maiumas;" Evagrius, "[16] that which they also call Maiumas, which is over against the city Gaza," "[17] a little city." Mark the deacon A. D. 421, says, "[18] We sailed to the maritime portion of Gaza, which they call Maiumas," and Antoninus Martyr, about the close of the vi^th century, "[19] we came from Ascalon to Mazomates, and came thence, after a mile, to Gaza,—that magnificent and lovely city." This perhaps explains how an anonymous Geographer, enumerating the places from Egypt to Tyre, says so distinctly, "[20] after Rinocorura lies the new Gaza, being itself also a city; then the desert Gaza," (writing, we must suppose, after some of the destructions of Gaza); and S. Jerome could say equally positively; "[21] The site of the ancient city scarce yields the traces of foundations; but the city now seen was built in another place in lieu of that which fell."

Keith, who in 1844 explored the spot, found wide-spread traces of some extinct city.

"[22] At seven furlongs from the sea the manifold but minute remains of an ancient city are yet in many places to be found—Innumerable fragments of broken pottery, pieces of glass, (some beautifully stained) and of polished marble, lie thickly spread in every level and hollow, at a considerable elevation and various distances, on a space of several square miles. In fifty different places they profusely lie, in a level space far firmer than the surrounding sands," "from small patches to more open spaces of twelve or twenty thousand square yards." "The oblong sand-hill, greatly varied in its elevation and of an undulated surface, throughout

1 Jer. xlvii. 1.
2 See Herod. ii. 159, 161. and Rawlinson on ii. 182. Herod. T. ii. p. 277.
3 Ἄζωτος πάραλος. Excerpta in Græca notitia Patriarch. in Reland p. 215. Schwarz (d. heil. Land p. 91.) places Ashdod at an hour from the "Mediterranean."
4 Plin. N. H. v. 12.
5 Josh. xv. 11.
6 2 Chr. xxvi. 6.
7 2 Macc. xii. 9.
8 Strabo xvi. 2, 30. p. 759.
9 "The engines, with which he took Tyre, being sent for by him, arrive from the sea." Arr. ii. 27.
10 Conc. T. v. 1164. Col.
11 Irby and Mangles p. 57.
12 Michaud et Poujoulat Corresp. d'Orient v. p. 373, 374.
13 Soz. v. 3.
14 Vita S. Hilarion. n. 3. Opp. ii. 15. Vall.
15 Soz. vii. 21.
16 Ev. ii. 5.
17 Ib. 8.
18 Marcus Diac. A. D. 421, in vita S. Porphyrii, c. 8. ap. Bolland. Feb. 26.
19 Itin. B. Antonini, pp. 24, 25.
20 Hudson Geograph. Minores T. iv. p. 39.
21 T. iii. p. 218.
22 Keith on prophecy, from personal examination. pp. 378, 379.

which they recur, extends to the W. and W. S. W. from the sea nearly to the environs of the modern Gaza." "In attempts to cultivate the sand (in 1832) hewn stones were found, near the old port. Remains of an old wall reached to the sea.—Ten large fragments of wall were embedded in the sand. About 2 miles off are fragments of another wall. Four intermediate fountains still exist, nearly entire in a line along the coast, doubtless pertaining to the ancient port of Gaza. For a short distance inland, the débris is less frequent, as if marking the space between it and the ancient city, but it again becomes plentiful in every hollow. About half a mile from the sea we saw three pedestals of beautiful marble. Holes are still to be seen from which hewn stones had been taken."

On the other hand, since the old Ashkelon had, like Gaza, Jamnia, Ashdod, a sea-port town, belonging to it but distinct from itself, (the city itself lying distinct and inland), and since there is no space for two towns distinct from one another, within the circuit of the Ashkelon of the crusades, which is limited by the nature of the ground, there seems to be no choice but that the city of the crusades, and the present skeleton, should have been the Maiumas Ascalon, the sea-port. The change might the more readily take place, since the title "port" was often omitted. The new town obliterated the memory of the old, as Neapolis, Naples, on the shore, has taken place of the inland city (whatever its name was), or Utrecht, it is said, has displaced the [illegible] Roman town, the remains of which are three miles off at Vechten[1], or Sichem is called Neapolis, Nablous, which yet was 3 miles off[2]. Er-riha is, probably, at least the second representative of the ancient Jericho; the Jericho of the New Testament, built by Herod, not being the Jericho of the prophets. The Corcyra of Greek history gave its name to the island; it is replaced by a Corfu in a different but near locality, which equally gives its name to the island now. The name of Venetia migrated with the inhabitants of the province, who fled from Attila, some 23 miles, to a few of the islands on the coast, to become again the name of a great republic[3]. In our own country, "old Windsor" is said to have been the residence of the Saxon monarchs; the present Windsor, was originally "new Windsor:" old Sarum was the Cathedral city, until the reign of Henry iii: but, as the old towns decayed, the new towns came to be called Windsor, Sarum, though not the towns which first had the name. What is now called Shoreham, not many years ago, was called "new Shoreham," in distinction from the neighboring village[4].

William of Tyre describes Ashkelon as "[5]situated on the sea-shore, in the form of a semi-circle, whose chord or diameter lies on the sea-shore; but its circumference or arc on the land, looking East. The whole city lies as in a trench, all declining toward the sea, surrounded on all sides by raised mounds, on which are walls with numerous towers of solid masonry, the cement being harder than the stone, with walls of due thickness and of height proportionate; it is surmounted also with outer walls of the same solidity." He then describes its four gates, E. N. S. toward Jerusalem, Gaza, Joppa, and the W., called the sea-gate, because "by it the inhabitants have an egress to the sea."

A modern traveler, whose description of the ruins exactly agrees with this, says, "[6]the walls are built on a ridge of rocks that winds round the town in a semicircular direction and terminates at each end in the sea; the ground falls within the walls in the same manner, that it does without, so that no part of it could be seen from the outside of the walls. There is no bay nor shelter for shipping, but a small harbor advancing a little way into the town toward its eastern extremity seems to have been formed for the accommodation of such small craft as were used in the better days of the city." The harbor, moreover, was larger during the crusades, and enabled Ascalon to receive supplies of corn from Egypt and thereby to protract its siege. Sultan Bibars filled up the port and cast stones into the sea, A. D. 1270, and destroyed the remains of the fortifications, for fear that the Franks, after their treaty with the king of Tunis, should bring back their forces against Islamism and establish themselves there[7]. Yet Abulfeda, who wrote a few years later, calls it "one of the Syrian ports of Islam[8]."

This city, so placed on the sea, and in which too the sea enters, cannot be the Ash-

[1] Reland who lived at Utrecht, says that Roman antiquities were daily dug up at Vechten, where were the remains of a Roman fort. Pal. p. 105.

[2] S. Jerome.

[3] Gibbon c. 35.

[4] In like way Alresford, Basford, Brentford, Goole, Isleworth, must have been at one time, New Alr. New Basford &c. but, as the more considerable, have appropriated the name which belonged to both the old and new places.

[5] Willermus Tyr. Hist. xvii. 22. in Gesta Dei per Francos p. 924. The solidity of the walls and of the cement are described in the same way, in the latter part of the 17th. cent. by d'Arvieux and Padre Malone da Maleo Terra Santa p. 471.

[6] Dr. Richardson, Travels along the Mediterr. ii. p. 201.

[7] According to Ibn Férat in Reinaud Chroniques Arabes n. xcvi. Michaud, Biblioth. des. Croisades iv. 525.

[8] Ab. Tab. Syriæ p. 78. Köhler. תעֿר, a gap, opening, access, or an enemy's frontier, (Freytag) "is in ordinary Arabic, used for a port, as העֿר בירות 'the port of Beyrout,' and תעֿר דמיטה 'the port of Damietta.'" Prof. Chenery.

kelon, which had a port, which was a town distinct from it. The Ascalon of the Philistines, which existed down into Christian times, must have been inland.

Benjamin of Tudela in the 12th cent. who had been on the spot, and who is an accurate eyewitness[1], says, "From Ashdod are two parasangs to Ashkelonah[2]; this is new Ashkelon which Ezra the priest built on the seashore, and they at first called it Benibra[3], and it is distant from the old Ashkelon, which is desolate, four parasangs." When the old Ashkelon perished, is unknown. If, as seems probable from some of the antiquities dug up, the Ashkelon, at which Herod was born and which he beautified, was the seaport town, commerce probably attracted to it gradually the inhabitants of the neighboring town of Ascalon, as the population of the Piræus now exceeds that of Athens.

The present Ashkelon is a ghastly skeleton; all the frame-work of a city, but none there. "The soil is good," but the "peasants who cultivate it" prefer living outside in a small village of mud-huts, exposed to winds and sand-storms, because they think that God has abandoned it, and that evil spirits (the Jân and the Ghûl) dwell there[4].

Even the remains of antiquity, where they exist, belong to later times. A hundred men excavated in Ashkelon for 14 days in hopes of finding treasure there. They dug 18 feet below the surface, and fouud marble shafts, a Corinthian capital, a colossal statue with a Medusa's head on its chest, a marble pavement and white-marble pedestal[5]. The excavation reached no Philistine Ashkelon.

"Broken pottery," "pieces of glass," "fragments of polished marble," "of ancient columns, cornices &c.[6]" were the relics of a Greek Gaza.

Though then it is a superfluity of fulfillment, and what can be found belongs to a later city, still what can be seen has an impressive correspondence with the words *Gaza* is *forsaken;* for there are miles of fragments of some city connected with Gaza. The present Gaza occupies the southern half of a hill built with stone for the Moslem conquerors of Palestine. "[7] Even the traces of its former existence, its vestiges of antiquity, are very rare; occasional columns of marble or gray granite, scattered in the streets and gardens, or used as thresholds at the gates and doors of houses, or laid upon the front of watering-troughs. One fine Corinthian capital of white marble lies inverted in the middle of the street." These belong then to times later than Alexander, since whose days the very site of Gaza must have changed its aspect.

Ashkelon shall be a desolation. The site of the port of Ascalon was well chosen, strong, overhanging the sea, fenced from the land, stretching forth its arms toward the Mediterranean, as if to receive in its bosom the wealth of the sea, yet shunned by the poor hinds around it. It lies in such a living death, that it is "[8] one of the most mournful scenes of utter desolation" which a traveler "even in this land of ruins ever beheld." But this too cannot be the Philistine city. The sands which are pressing hard upon the solid walls of the city, held back by them for the time, yet threatening to overwhelm "the spouse of Syria," and which accumulated in the plain below, must have buried the old Ashkelon, since in this land, where the old names so cling to the spot, there is no trace of it.

Ekron shall be uprooted; and at Akîr and Esdûd "[9] celebrated at present, for its scorpions," the few stones, which remain, even of a later town, are but as gravestones to mark the burial place of departed greatness.

"[10] In like way, all who glory in bodily strength and worldly power and say, *By the strength of my hand I have done it,* shall be left desolate and brought to nothing in the day of the Lord's anger." And "the waster," they who by evil words and deeds injure or destroy others and are an offence unto them, these *shall be cast out* shamefully, *into outer darkness* "[11] when the saints shall receive the fullest brightness" in the *mid-day* of the Sun of Righteousness. The judgment shall not be in darkness, save to them, but in mid-day, so that the justice of God shall be clearly seen, and darkness itself shall be turned into

[1] p. נג. 2. ed. Asher. The enumeration of "about 200 Rabbanite Jews," with the names of the chief, "about 40 karaites, and about 300 Cuthæans" shews personal acquaintance. The former name of the "new Ascalon" and the supposed distance of the ruins of the old, he must have learned on the spot.

[2] Benj. Tud. pronounces the new city Ashkelon*a*, as the Latins did. When speaking himself, he says Ashkelon.

[3] "Benibra" looks like a corruption of בית נמרה, "a place of pure water," like "Bebaten, Bedora, Beestera, Begabar" &c. in Reland. 617. sqq. The Gadite town of that name becomes in Eus. βηθναβρίς. S. Jerome has another Benamerium, N. of Zoar, now N'mairah. Tristram Land of Moab p. 57. A well in Ascalon is mentioned by Eusebius. "There are many wells (named) in Scripture and are yet shewn in the country of Gerar, and at Ascalon." v. φρέαρ. William of Tyre says: "It has no fountains, either within the compass of the walls, or near it; but it abounds in wells, both within and without, which supply palatable water, fit for drinking. For greater caution the inhabitants had built some cisterns within, to receive rain-water. Benj. of T. also says, "There in the midst of the city is a well which they call Beer Ibrahim-al-khalil [the well of Abraham the friend (of God)] which he dug in the days of the Philistines." Keith mentions "20 fountains of excellent water opened up anew by Ibrahim Pasha." p. 274.

[4] Mr. Cyril Graham in Keith p. 376.

[5] Travels of Lady H. Stanhope, iii. 159–169.

[6] Keith p. 378.

[7] Robinson Travels ii. 38.

[8] Smith Ib. p. 66 note.

[9] Volney Voyage en Syrie c. 31. p. 311. Keith p. 370.

[10] S. Jer.

[11] Rup.

Before CHRIST cir. 630.

5 Woe unto the inhab-
itants of [i] the sea coast, the
nation of the Cherethites!
the word of the LORD *is*
against you; O [k] Canaan,
the land of the Philistines, I
will even destroy thee, that
there shall be no inhabitant.
6 And the sea coast
shall be dwellings *and* cottages for shepherds, [l] and
folds for flocks.
7 And the coast shall
be for [m] the remnant of

[i] Ezek. 25. 16.
[k] Jos. 13. 3.

Before CHRIST cir. 630.

[l] See Is. 17. 2. ver. 14.
[m] Isai. 11. 11. Mic. 4. 7. & 5. 7, 8. Hag. 1. 12. & 2. 2. ver. 9.

light, as was said to David, [1] *Thou didst this thing secretly, but I will do it before all Israel and before the sun;* and our Lord, [2] *Whatsoever ye have spoken in darkness shall be heard in the light; and that which ye have spoken in the ear in closets shall be proclaimed upon the housetops;* and St. Paul, [3] *the Lord shall come, Who both will bring to light the hidden things of darkness, and will make manifest the counsels of the heart.* And "they who by seducing words in life or in doctrine uprooted others, shall be themselves rooted up[4]."

5. The *woe* having been pronounced on the five cities apart, now falls upon the whole nation of the Cherethites or Philistines. The Cherethites are only named as equivalent to the Philistines, probably as originally a distinct immigration of the same people[5]. The name is used by the Egyptian slave of the Amalekite[6] for those whom the author of the first book of Samuel calls Philistines[7]. Ezekiel uses the name parallel with that of *Philistines,* with reference to the destruction which God would bring upon them[8].

The word of the Lord comes not to them, but *upon* them, overwhelming them. To them He speaketh not in good, but in evil; not in grace, but in anger; not in mercy, but in vengeance. Philistia was the first enemy of the Church. It shewed its enmity to Abraham and Isaac and would fain that they should not sojourn among them[9]. They were the hindrance that Israel should not go straight to the promised land[10]. When Israel passed the Red Sea, [11] *sorrow took hold of them.* They were close to salvation in body, but far in mind. They are called *Canaan,* as being a chief nation of it[12], and in that name lay the original source of their destruction. They inherited the sins of Canaan and with them his curse, preferring the restless beating of the barren, bitter sea on which they dwelt, "the waves of this troublesome world," to being a part of the true Canaan. They would absorb the Church into the world, and master it, subduing it to the heathen Canaan, not subdue themselves to it, and become part of the heavenly Canaan.

6. *The sea-coast*[13] *shall be dwellings and cottages,* lit. cuttings or diggings[14]. This is the central meaning of the word; the place of the Cherethites (the *cutters off*) shall be *cheroth* of shepherds, places which they dug up that their flocks might be enclosed therein. The tracts once full of fighting men, the scourge of Judah, should be so desolate of its former people, as to become a sheep-walk. Men of peace should take the place of its warriors.

So the shepherds of the Gospel with their flocks have entered into possession of warlike nations, turning them to the Gospel. They are shepherds, the chief of whom is that Good Shepherd, Who laid down His Life for the sheep. And these are the sheep of whom He speaks, [15] *Other sheep I have, which are not of this fold; them also I must bring, and they shall hear My Voice; and there shall be one fold and One Shepherd.*

7. *And the coast shall be.* Or probably[16], *It*

[1] 2 Sam. xii. 12. [2] S. Luke xii. 3. [3] 1 Cor. iv. 5.
[4] S. Matth. xv. 13. [5] See on Am. ix. 7. vol. i. p. 333.
[6] 1 Sam. xxx. 14. [7] Ib. 16.

[8] הכרתי את כרתים Ezek. xxv. 16. It may be that they were so called as coming from Crete as the LXX supposed, rendering "Cretans" in Ezek., and here (as also the Syr.) "sojourners of the Cretans." Hence perhaps also Tacitus' statement (Hist. v. 2.) that the Jews had been expelled from Crete. The other versions render the word as an appellative, "destroying" or "destroyed." Aq. and ε, ἔθνος ὀλέθριον, Theod. ἔθνος ὀλεθρίας Symm. ἔθνος ὀλὲθρευόμενον. S. Jer. gives perditorem.

[9] Gen. xxi. 34. xxvi. 14, 15, 28. [10] Ex. xiii. 17.
[11] Ib. xv. 14. [12] Gen. xv. 21.

[13] The words "band of the sea" are repeated with emphasis, vers. 5, 6, and the first words v. 7.

[14] So Kim. Ibn Denan has, "caves which shepherds inhabit;" Arab. transl. "domiciles which shepherds dig." Abulw., and Tanchum derive it from כָּרָה 2 Kgs. vi. 23. "a feast." Abulw. thinks this not improbable, as an irregular plural. Tanchum, "stations of shepherds where they turn their flocks to feed and sit down to eat, or places in which they dig for watering the flocks." The climate of Judæa, however, does not admit of underground habitations, like Nineveh, and in the country of the Philistines flocks would be supplied by wells with trenches. No Arabic authority suggests a derivation from וְכַר "nest" (as Ewald). The allusion to Cherethim would be lost by this invented root. Rashi has "a place where the shepherds eat." A. E. explains כְּרֹת, as if it were from כָּרַת, "which the shepherds כרתו for themselves." The Moabite stone has מכרתת l. 25. apparently, of "a ditch" "or moat."

[15] S. John x. 16.

[16] Grammatically, חבל may be either the subject or predicate. For even in prose (Josh xix. 29.) it is used without the article, of the sea-coast, the mention of the sea having preceded, "the goings forth

Before CHRIST cir. 630.

the house of Judah; they
shall feed thereupon; in
the houses of Ashkelon
shall they lie down in the
evening: ‖ for the LORD
their God shall [n] visit them,
and [o] turn away their captivity.
8 ¶ [p] I have heard the
reproach of Moab, and

‖ Or, *when, &c.*

[n] Ex. 4. 31. Luke 1. 68.
[o] Ps. 126. 1. Jer. 29. 14. ch. 3. 20.
[p] Jer. 48. 27. Ezek. 25. 8.

shall be a portion for the remnant of the house of Judah. He uses the word, employed in the first assignment of the land to Israel[1]; and of the whole people as belonging to God, "[2] Jacob is the *lot* of His inheritance." The *tract of the sea*, which, with the rest, was assigned to Israel, which, for its unfaithfulness, was seldom, even in part, possessed, and at this time, was wholly forfeited, should be a portion for the mere *remnant* which should be brought back. David used the word in his psalm of thanksgiving, when he had brought the ark to the city of David, how God had "[3] confirmed the covenant to Israel, saying, Unto thee will I give the land of Canaan, the *lot* of your inheritance;" and Asaph,[4] *He cast out the heathen before them and divided to them an inheritance by line.* It is the reversal of the doom threatened by Micah, [5] *Thou shalt have none, that shall cast a cord by lot in the congregation of the Lord.* The word is revived by Ezekiel in his ideal division of the land to the restored people[6]. [7] *The gifts and calling of God are without repentance.* The promise, which had slumbered during Israel's faithlessness, should be renewed to its old extent. "[8] There is no prescription against the Church." The boat threatens to sink; it is tossed, half-submerged, by the waves; but its Lord *rebukes the wind and the sea; wind and sea obey Him, and there is a great calm*[9].

For the remnant of the house of Juda Yet, who save He in Whose hand are human wills, could now foresee that Judah should, like the ten tribes, rebel, be carried captive, and yet, though like and worse than Israel in its sin[10], should, unlike Israel, be restored? The re-building of Jerusalem was, their enemies pleaded, contrary to sound policy[11]: the plea was for the time accepted; for the rebellions of Jerusalem were recorded in the chronicles of Babylon[12]. Yet the falling short of the complete restoration depended on their own wills. God turned again their captivity; but *they* only, *whose spirit God stirred*, willed to return. The temporal restoration was the picture of the spiritual. They who returned had to give up lands and possessions in Babylonia, and a remnant only chose the land of promise at such cost. Babylonia was as attractive as Egypt formerly.

In the houses of Ashkelon shall they lie down in the evening. One city is named for all. *They shall lie down*, he says, continuing the image from their flocks, as Isaiah, in a like passage[13], *The first-born of the poor shall feed, and the needy shall lie down in safety.*

The true Judah shall overspread the world; but it too shall only be a *remnant;* these shall, in safety, [14] *go in and out and find pasture. In the evening* of the world they shall find their rest; for then also in the time of Anti-Christ, the Church shall be but a remnant still. *For the Lord their God shall visit them*, for He is the Good Shepherd, Who came to seek the one sheep which was lost and Who says of Himself, [15] *I will seek that which was lost, and bring again that which was driven away, and will bind up that which was broken, and will strengthen that which was sick;* and Who in the end will more completely *turn away their captivity*, bring His banished to their everlasting home, the Paradise from which they have been exiled, and separate for ever the sheep from the goats who now oppress and scatter them abroad[16].

8. *I*, "[17] God, Who know all things, *I heard* i. e., have known within Me, in My mind, not anew but from eternity, and now I shew in effect that I know it; wherefore I say that I hear, because I act after the manner of one who perceiveth something anew." I, the just Judge, heard[18]. He was present and *heard*, even when, because He avenged not, He seemed not to hear, but laid it up in store with Him to avenge in the due time[19].

The reproach of Moab and the reviling of the children of Ammon, whereby they have reproached My people. Both words, *reproached, reviled*, mean, primarily, cutting speeches; both are

thereof were to the sea, מחבל to Mizpeh." Yet there is no emphasis in the repetition of the word from the preceding verse. The LXX renders חבל as the subject, the Ch. Vulg. as the predicate.

[1] "The ten *portions* of Manasseh;" Josh. xvii. 5. "Why hast thou given me one lot and one *portion?*" Ib. 14. "out of the *portion* of the children of Judah was the inheritance of the children of Simeon." Ib. xix. 9.

[2] Deut. xxxii. 9. [3] 1 Chr. xvi. 18. Ps. cv. 11.

[4] Ps. lxxviii. 55. [5] Mic. ii. 5. [6] Ezek. xlvii. 13.

[7] Rom. xi. 29.

[8] "Nullum tempus ecclesiæ," though said of its property.

[9] S. Matt. viii. 26, 27.

[10] Jer. iii. 8–11. Ezek. xvi. 46–52. xxiii. 11.

[11] Ezra ix. 12–16. [12] Ib. 19–22. [13] Is. iv. 30.

[14] S. John x. 9. [15] Ezek. xxxiv. 16. [16] Ib. 17–19.

[17] Dion.

[18] See Is. xvi. 6. Jer. xlviii. 39. Ezek. xxxv. 12, 13.

[19] Deut xxxii. 34, 35.

Before CHRIST cir. 630.

[q]the revilings of the children of Ammon, whereby they have reproached my people, and [r]magnified *themselves* against their border.

q Ezek. 25. 3, 6.

Before CHRIST cir. 630.

r Jer. 49. 1.

intensive, and are used of blaspheming God as unable to help His people, or reviling His people as forsaken by Him. If directed against man, they are directed against God through man. So David interpreted the taunt of Goliah, [1]*reviled the armies of the living God*, and the Philistine cursed David *by his gods*[2]. In a Psalm David complains, [3]*the reproaches of them that reproached Thee are fallen upon me;* and a Psalm which cannot be later than David, since it declares the national innocency from idolatry, connects with their defeats, the voice of him [4]*that reproacheth and blasphemeth* (joining the two words used here). The sons of Corah say, [5]*with a sword in my bones, mine enemies reproach me, while they say daily unto me, where is thy God?* So Asaph, [6]*The enemy hath reproached, the foolish people hath blasphemed Thy Name;* and, [7]*we are become a reproach to our neighbors. Wherefore should the heathen say, where is their God? render unto our neighbors—the reproach wherewith they have reproached Thee, O Lord.* And Ethan, [8]*Remember, Lord, the reproach of Thy servants—wherewith Thine enemies have reproached, O Lord, wherewith they have reproached the footsteps of Thine Anointed.*

In history the repeated blasphemies of Sennacherib and his messengers are expressed by the same words. In earlier times the remarkable concession of Jephthah, [9]*Wilt not thou possess what Chemosh thy god giveth thee to possess? so whomsoever the Lord our God shall drive out before us, them will we possess*, implies that the Ammonites claimed their land as the gift of their god Chemosh, and that that war was, as that later by Sennacherib, waged in the name of the false god against the True.

The relations of Israel to Moab and Ammon have been so habitually misrepresented, that a review of those relations throughout their whole history may correct some wrong impressions. The first relations of Israel toward them were even tender. God reminded His people of their common relationship and forbade him even to take the straight road to his own future possessions, across their land against their will. [10]*Distress them not, nor contend with them*, it is said of each, *for I will not give thee of their land for a possession; for I have given it unto the children of Lot for a possession.* Idolaters and hostile as they were, yet, for their father's sake, their title to their land had the same sacred sanction, as Israel's to his. *I*, God says, *have given it to them as a possession.* Israel, to their own manifest inconvenience, [11]*went along through the wilderness, and compassed the land of Edom, and the land of Moab, but came not within the border of Moab.* By destroying Sihon king of the Amorites and Og king of Bashan, Israel removed formidable enemies, who had driven Moab and Ammon out of a portion of the land which they had conquered from the Zamzummim and Anakim [12], and who threatened the remainder. [13]*Israel dwelt in all the cities of the Amorites.*

Heshbon, Dibon, Jahaz, Medeba, Nophah were *cities in the land of the Amorites, in* which *Israel dwelt.* The exclusion of Moab and Ammon from the congregation of the Lord to the tenth generation [14] was not, of course, from any national antipathy, but intended to prevent a debasing intercourse; a necessary precaution against the sensuousness of their idolatries. Moab was the first [15] in adopting the satanic policy of Balaam, to seduce Israel by sensuality to their idolatries; but the punishment was appointed to the partners of their guilt, the Midianites [16], not to Moab. Yet Moab was the second nation, whose ambition God overruled to chasten His people's idolatries. Eglon, king of Moab, united with himself Ammon and Amalek against Israel. The object of the invasion was, not the recovery of the country which Moab had lost to the Amorites but, Palestine proper. The strength of Moab was apparently not sufficient to occupy the territory of Reuben. They took possession only of *the city of palm trees*[17]; either the ruins of Jericho or a spot close by it; with the view apparently of receiving reinforcements or of securing their own retreat by the ford. This garrison enabled them to carry their forays over Israel, and to hold it enslaved for 18 years. The oppressiveness of this slavery is implied by the cry and conversion of Israel to the Lord, which was always in great distress. The memory of Eglon, as one of the oppressors of Israel, lived in the minds of the people in the days of Samuel [18]. In the end, this precaution of Moab turned to its own destruction; for, after Eglon was slain, Ephraim, under Ehud, took the fords, and

1 1 Sam. xvii. 26, 36, 45. coll. 10. 25.
2 1 Sam. xvii. 43.
3 Ps. lxix. 10 (9).
4 Ib. xliv. 16 (17).
5 Ib. xlii. 10.
6 Ib. lxxiv. 10, 18.
7 Ib. lxxix. 4, 10, 12.
8 Ib. lxxxix. 50, 51.
9 Jud. xi. 24.
10 Deut. ii. 9, 19.
11 Jud. xi. 18.
12 Deut. ii. 10, 20, 21.
13 Nu. xxi. 25, 31.
14 Deut. xxiii. 3.
15 Nu. xxv. 1, 3. The rank of the Midianitish lady who gave herself as a partner of the sin of the Simeonite chief (Ib. 6, 14, 15, 18.) shews how much store the Midianites set on that seduction.
16 Ib. 17. and xxxi.
17 Jud. iii. 13.
18 1 Sam. xii. 9.

the whole garrison, 10,000 of Moab's warriors, [1] *every strong man and every man of might*, were intercepted in their retreat and perished. For a long time after this, we hear of no fresh invasion by Moab. The trans-Jordanic tribes remained in unquestioned possession of their land for 300 years[2], when Ammon, not Moab, raised the claim, [3] *Israel took away my land*, although claiming the land down to the Arnon, and already being in possession of the Southernmost portion of that land, Aroer, since Israel smote him *from Aroer unto Minnith*[4]. The land then, according to a law recognized by nations, belonged by a twofold right to Israel; 1) that it had been won, not from Moab, but from the conquerors of Moab, the right of Moab having passed to its conquerors[5]; 2) that undisputed and unbroken possession "for time immemorial" as we say, 300 years, ought not to be disputed[6]. The defeat by Jephthah stilled them for near 50 years till the beginning of Saul's reign, when they refused the offer of the *men of Jabesh-Gilead* to serve them, and, with a mixture of insolence and savagery, annexed as a condition of accepting that entire submission, [7] *that I may thrust out all your right eyes, to lay it as a reproach to Israel.* The signal victory of Saul[8] still did not prevent Ammon, as well as Moab, from being among the enemies whom Saul *worsted*[9]. The term *enemies* implies that *they* were the assailants. The history of Naomi shews their prosperous condition, that the famine, which desolated Judah[10], did not reach them, and that they were a prosperous land, at peace, at that time, with Israel. If all the links of the genealogy are preserved[11], Jesse, David's father, was grandson of a Moabitess, Ruth, and perhaps on this ground David entrusted his parents to the care of the king of Moab[12]. Sacred history gives no hint, what was the cause of his terrible execution upon Moab. But a Psalm of David speaks to God of some blow, under which Israel had reeled. [13] *O God, Thou hast abhorred us, and broken us in pieces; Thou hast been wroth: Thou hast made the land to tremble and cloven it asunder; heal its breaches, for it shaketh; Thou hast shewed Thy people a hard thing, Thou hast made it drink wine of reeling;* and thereon David expresses his confidence that God would humble Moab, Edom, Philistia. While David then was engaged in the war with the Syrians of Mesopotamia and Zobah[14], Moab must have combined with Edom in an aggressive war against Israel. *The valley of salt*[15], where Joab returned and defeated them, was probably within Judah, since *the city of salt*[16] was one of the six cities of the wilderness. Since they had defeated Judah, they must have been overtaken there on their return[17].

Yet this too was a religious war. "*Thou,*" David says[18], "hast given a *banner to them that fear Thee,* to be raised aloft because of the truth."

There is no tradition, that the kindred Psalm of the sons of Corah, Psalm xliv. belongs to the same time. Yet the protestations to God of the entire absence of idolatry could not have been made at any time later than the early years of Solomon. Even were there Maccabee Psalms, the Maccabees were but a handful among apostates. They could not have pleaded the national freedom from unfaithfulness to God, nor, except in two subordinate and self-willed expeditions[19], were they defeated. Under the Persian rule, there were no armies nor wars; no immunity from idolatry in the later history of Judah. Judah did not in Hezekiah's time go out against Assyria; the one battle, in which Josiah was slain, ended the resistance to Egypt. Defeat was, at the date of this Psalm, new and surprising, in contrast with God's deliverances of old[20]; yet the inroad, by which they had suffered, was one of spoiling[21], not of subdual. Yet this too was a religious war, from their neighbors. They

[1] Jud. iii. 29. [2] Ib. xi. 26.
[3] Ib. 13. [4] Ib. 33.
[5] Grotius de jure belli et pacis, iii. c. vi. n. vii. and notes.
[6] Id. Ib. ii. c. iv. n. ii. and ix. and notes.
[7] 1 Sam. xi. 1, 2. [8] Ib. 11.
[9] הרשיע, not, "vexed." Ib. xiv. 47.
[10] Ruth i. 1. [11] Ib. iv. 21, 22.
[12] 1 Sam. xxii. 3, 4. [13] Ps. lx. 3–5. [14] Ib. tit.
[15] It was probably the narrow valley some three miles long between the Northern end of that remarkable salt mountain, the Jebel or Khasm Usdum and the dead sea. See the description in Tristram's Land of Isr., p. 326 sqq. At its N. extremity at the mouth of Wady Zuweirah there are considerable traces of (perhaps Roman) buildings. A tower placed here would command the entrance of the valley of salt, and this may well have been the site of the *city of salt.*
[16] Jos. xv. 62.
[17] Seetzen guessed (Reisen ii. 356) and Robinson considered it certain (ii. 109) that "the valley of salt" was the lower part of the 'Arabah, close to the Dead Sea, between Edom and Judæa. But i. This is spoken of as a "great plain" (Seetzen p. 355) and although the word גיא is twice used of as large valley; (1) the valley over against Baal Peor, where all Israel was encamped Deut. iii. 29, iv. 46; 2) that of Zephathah, where Asa, with an army of 580,000 men, defeated Zerah the Ethiopian with 1,000,000 (2 Chr. xiv. 10) this is the exception. In eleven other places it is used of a narrow valley. ii. The depression, South of the Dead Sea down to the Red Sea, had, in the time of Moses, the same title as now, the "Arabah," Deut. i. 1. ii. 8. iii. The space, near the Dead Sea, which is salt, "the Sebkha, or desolate sand-swamp" (Tristram Moab, p. 41.) is impracticable for men; much more for an army. "The Sebkha or salt-flat is a large flat, of at least 6 by 10 miles from N. to S. Taught by the experience of M. de Saulcy, we made no attempt to cross it to the northwards, as the mud would have been far too deep and treacherous for us to pass in safety" (Id. Land of Israel, p. 336.). "The land South of the Sebkha is not salt, but rich and fertile" (Id. p. 338). See de Saulcy Voyage en Syrie &c. p. 248–256.
[18] Ps. lx. 4. [19] 1 Macc. v. 56–60. 67.
[20] Ps. xliv. 1–3. [21] Ib. 10, 12.

were slain for the sake of God[1], they were covered with shame on account of the reproaches and blasphemies[2] of those who triumphed over God, as powerless to help; they were a scorn and derision to the petty nations around them. It is a Psalm of unshaken faith amid great prostration: it describes in detail what the lxth Psalm sums up in single heavy words of imagery; but both alike complain to God of what His people had to suffer for His sake.

The insolence of Ammon in answer to David's message of kindness to their new king, like that to the men of Jabesh Gilead, seems like a deliberate purpose to create hostilities. The relations of the previous king of Ammon to David, had been kind[3], perhaps, because David being a fugitive from Israel, they supposed him to be Saul's enemy. The enmity originated, not with the new king, but with *the princes of the children of Ammon*[4]. David's treatment of these nations[5] is so unlike his treatment of any others whom he defeated, that it implies an internecine warfare, in which the safety of Israel could only be secured by the destruction of its assailants.

Mesha king of Moab records one war, and alludes to others, not mentioned in Holy Scripture. He says, that before his own time, "Omri, king of Israel, afflicted Moab many days;" that "his son [Ahab] succeeded him, and he too said, 'I will afflict Moab.'" This affliction he explains to be that "[6] Omri possessed himself of the land of Medeba" [expelling[7], it is implied, its former occupiers] "and that" (apparently, Israel[8]) "dwelt therein," "[in his days and in] the days of his son forty years." He was also in possession of Nebo, and "the king of Israel" (apparently Omri,) "buil[t] Jahaz and dwelt in it, when he made war with me.[9]" Jahaz was near Dibon. In the time of Eusebius, it was still "pointed out between Dibon and Medeba[10]." Mesha says, "And I took it to annex it to Dibon." It could not, according to Mesha also, have been S. of the Arnon, since Aroer lay between Dibon and the Arnon, and Mesha would not have annexed to Dibon a town beyond the deep and difficult ravine of the Arnon, with Aroer lying between them. It was certainly N. of the Arnon, since Israel was not permitted to come within the border of Moab, but it was at Jahaz that Sihon met them and fought the battle in which Israel defeated him and gained possession of his land, *from the Arnon to the Jabbok*[11]. It is said also that [12] *Israel dwelt in the land of the Amorites from Aroer which is on the edge of the river Arnon*[13], *and the city which is in the river*[14] *unto Gilead.* [15] *Aroer on the edge of the river Arnon, and the city which is in the river* Arnon, again occur in describing the southern border of Reuben, among whose towns Jahaz is mentioned, with Beth-Baal-Meon and Kiriathaim, which have been identified.

The afflicting then of Moab by Omri, according to Mesha, consisted in this, that he recovered to Israel a portion of the allotment of Reuben, between 9 and 10 hours in length[16] from N. to S., of which, in the time of Israel's weakness through the civil wars which followed on Jeroboam's revolt, Moab must have dispossessed Reuben. Reuben had remained in undisturbed possession of it, from the first expulsion of the Amorites to the time at least of Rehoboam, about five hundred years[17]. "The men of Gad" still "dwelt in Ataroth," Mesha says, "from time immemorial."

The picture, which Mesha gives, is of a desolation of the southern portion of Reuben. For, "I rebuilt," he says, "Baal-Meon, Kiriathaim, Aroer, Beth-bamoth, Bezer, Beth-Diblathaim, Beth-baal-Meon." Of Beth-Bamoth, and probably of Bezer, Mesha says, that they had previously been destroyed[18]. But Reuben would not, of course, destroy his own cities. They must then have been destroyed either by Mesha's father, who reigned before him, when invad-

[1] Ps. xliv. 22. [2] Ib. 13, 14. [3] 2 Sam. x. 2. 3. [4] Ib. 3. [5] Ib. viii. 2. xii. 31.

[6] וירש עמרי את ארץ מה דבא.

[7] This lies in the word וירש.

[8] A gap in the broken stone probably contained the subject. I see that Schlottman also supplied, "Israel;" Dr. Ginsburg conjectured, less probably, "the enemy."

[9] In this place only Mesha speaks of the king of Israel's war with him in the past. Elsewhere he speaks of himself only as being on the offensive. "I fought against the city" [Ataroth]; "I fought against it" [Nebo]; "go down, fight against Horonaim." The king of Israel is apparently the same throughout, Omri.

[10] S. Jerome de situ loc. Hebr. Opp. iii. 230, v. Ἰεσσὰ, "Jassa, where Sihon king of the Amorites is defeated."

[11] Nu. xxi. 23–25. [12] Deut. ii. 36.

[13] "The ruins of Araayr (עַרָעִיר) the Aroer of the Scriptures, standing on the edge of the precipice." Burckhardt, travels in Syria p. 372.

[14] "Near the confluence of the Ledjoum and the Mojeb" [Arnon] "about 1 mile E. of the bridge across the Mojeb, there seems to be a fine verdant pasture ground, in the midst of which stands a hill with some ruins upon it." Burckhardt Ib. 373, 4.

[15] Josh. xiii. 16, 18.

[16] The distance is taken from Porter's Hand-book pp. 299–301.

[17] The beginning of Rehoboam's reign is, in the received Chronology, 477. B. C.

[18] I built Beth-Bamoth, for it was destroyed; I built Bezer, for" [the rest is conjecture. There are only two letters, which may be עצ or עז, perhaps עָזֻב "forsaken"] בנה probably, in such simple Hebrew, signifies, in regard to *all* the towns, built. It is the one word used of the king of Israel and of Mesha, "he built;" "I built," although it is rarely used of building on to existing towns and fortifying them. (1 Kgs xv. 17. 2 Chr. xi. 7.) It is probably here used of *re*-building; since the cause of the building was the previous destruction.

ing Reuben, or by Omri, when driving back Moab into his own land, and expelling him from these cities. *Possibly* they were dismantled only, since Mesha speaks only of Omri's occupying Medeba, Ataroth, and Jahaz. He held these three cities only, leaving the rest dismantled, or dismantling them, unable to place defenders in them, and unwilling to leave them as places of aggression for Moab. But whether they ever were fortified towns at all, or how they were desolated, is mere conjecture. Only they were desolated in these wars.

But it appears from Mesha's own statement, that neither Omri nor Ahab invaded Moab proper. For in speaking of his successful war and its results, he mentions no town S. of the Arnon. He must have been a tributary king, but not a foot of his land was taken. The subsequent war was not a mere revolt, nor was it a mere refusal to pay tribute, of which Mesha makes no complaint. Nor could the tribute have been oppressive to him, since the spoils, left in the encampment of Moab and his allies shortly after his revolt, is evidence of such great wealth. The refusal to pay tribute would have involved nothing further, unless Ahaziah had attempted to enforce it, as Hezekiah refused the tribute to Assyria, but remained in his own borders. But Ahaziah, unlike his brother Jehoram who succeeded him, seems to have undertaken nothing, except the building of some ships for trade[1]. Mesha's war was a renewal of the aggression on Reuben.

Heshbon is not mentioned, and therefore must, even after the war, have remained with Reuben.

Mesha's own war was an exterminating war, as far as he records it. "I fought against the city," [Ataroth], he says, "and took it, and killed all the mighty of the city for the well-pleasing of Chemosh and of Moab;" "I fought against it [Nebo] from break of day till noon and took it, and slew all of it, 7000 men; the ladies and maidens I devoted to Ashtar Chemosh;" to be desecrated to the degradations of that sensual idolatry. The words too "[2] Israel perished with an everlasting destruction" stand clear, whether they express Mesha's conviction of the past or his hope of the future.

The war also, on the part of Moab, was a war of his idol Chemosh against God. Chemosh, from first to last, is the agent. "Chemosh was angry with his land;" "Chemosh [was pleased] with it in my days;" "I killed the mighty for the well-pleasing of Chemosh;" "I took captive thence all [ ] and dragged it along before Chemosh at Kiriath;" "Chemosh said to me, Go and take Nebo against Israel;" "I devoted the ladies and maidens to Ashtar-Chemosh;" "I took thence the vessels of IHVH and dragged[3] them before Chemosh;" "Chemosh drove him [the king of Israel] out before [my face];" "Chemosh said to me, Go down against Horonaim." "Chemosh [ ] it in my days."

Contemporary with this aggressive war against Israel must have been the invasion by [4] *the children of Moab and the children of Ammon, the great multitude from beyond the sea, from Syria*, in the reign of Jehoshaphat, which brought such terror upon Judah. It preceded the invasion of Moab by Jehoshaphat in union with Jehoram and the king of Edom. For the invasion of Judah by Moab and Ammon took place, while Ahab's son, Ahaziah, was still living. For it was *after this*, that Jehoshaphat joined with Ahaziah in making ships to go to Tarshish[5]. But the expedition against Moab was in union with Jehoram who succeeded Ahaziah. The abundance of wealth which the invaders of Judah brought with them, and the precious jewels with which they had adorned themselves, shew that this was no mere marauding expedition, to spoil; but that its object was, to take possession of the land or at least of some portion of it. They came by entire surprise on Jehoshaphat, who heard of them first when they were at Hazazon-Tamar or Engedi, some 36½ miles from Jerusalem[6]. He felt himself entirely unequal to meet them, and cast himself upon God. There was a day of public humiliation of Judah at Jerusalem. [7] *Out of all the cities of Judah they came to seek the Lord.* Jehoshaphat, in his public prayer, owned, [8] *we have no might against this great company which cometh against us; neither know we what to do; but our eyes are upon Thee.* He appeals to God, that He had forbidden Israel to invade Ammon, Moab, and Mount Seir, so that they turned away from them and destroyed them not; and now these rewarded them by "[9] coming to cast us out of Thy possession which Thou hast given us to inherit." One of the sons of Asaph foretold to the congregation, that they might go out fearlessly; for they should not have occasion to fight. A Psalm, ascribed to Asaph, records a great invasion, the object of

[1] 2 Chr. xx. 35, 36.

[2] A break in the stone leaves the subject uncertain, "In my day said [ ], and I will look upon him and upon his house, and Israel perished with an everlasting destruction." Schlottman conjectures, probably, "Chemosh." Ganneau renders as if it were past, אָבַד, so Haug, Geiger, Neubauer, Wright; Schlottman, Nöldeke, and Ginsburg, as future, אֹבֵד, though Ginsburg alone renders, "And Israel said, I shall destroy it for ever," which is impossible.

[3] The word in Hebrew is used of contumelious dragging along the ground.

[4] 2 Chr. xx. 1, 2.

[5] Ib. 35, 36. "And *after this* did Jehoshaphat king of Judah join himself with Ahaziah."

[6] 300 stadia. Jos. Ant. ix. 1. 2.

[7] 2 Chr. xx. 4. [8] Ib. 13. [9] Ib. 10.

which was the extermination of Israel. [1] *They have said; Come and let us cut them off from* being *a nation,* that *the name of Israel may be no more in remembrance.* It had been a secret confederacy. [2] *They have taken crafty counsel against Thy people.* It was directed against God Himself, i. e. His worship and worshipers. [3] *For they have taken counsel in heart together; against Thee do they make a covenant.* It was a combination of the surrounding petty nations; Tyre on the N., the Philistines on the W.; on the South the Amalekites, Ishmaelites, Hagarenes; Eastward, Edom, Gebal, Moab, Ammon. But its most characteristic feature was, that Assur (this corresponds with no period after Jehoshaphat) occupies a subordinate place to Edom and Moab, putting them forward and helping *them. Assur also,* Asaph says[4], *is joined with them; they have become an arm to the children of Lot.* This agrees with the description, *there is come against thee a great multitude from beyond the sea, from Syria.*

Scripture does not record, on what ground the invasion of Moab by Jehoram and Jehoshaphat, with the tributary king of Edom, was directed against Moab proper; but it was the result doubtless of the double war of Moab against Reuben and against Judah. It was a war, in which the strength of Israel and Moab was put forth to the utmost. Jehoram had mustered all Israel[5]; Moab had gathered all who had reached the age of manhood and upward, [6] *every one who girded on a girdle and upward.* The three armies, which had made a seven days' circuit in the wilderness, were on the point of perishing by thirst and falling into the hands of Moab, when Elisha in God's name promised them the supply of their want, and complete victory over Moab. The eager cupidity of Moab, as of many other armies, became the occasion of his complete overthrow. The counsel with which Elisha accompanied his prediction, [7] *ye shall smite every fenced city and every choice city, and every good tree ye shall fell, and all springs of water ye shall stop up, and every good piece of land ye shall waste with stones,* was directed, apparently, to dislodge an enemy so inveterate. For water was essential to the fertility of their land and their dwelling there. We hear of no special infliction of death, like what Mesha records of himself. The war was ended by the king of Moab's sacrificing the heir-apparent of the king of Edom[8], which naturally created great displeasure against Israel, in whose cause Edom thus suffered, so that they departed to their own land and finally revolted.

Their departure apparently broke up the siege of Ar and the expedition. Israel apparently was not strong enough to carry on the war without Edom, or feared to remain with their armies away from their own land, as in the time of David, of which Edom might take the advantage. We know only the result.

Moab probably even extended her border to the South by the conquest of Horonaim[9].

After this, Moab is mentioned only on occasion of the miracle of the dead man, to whom God gave life, when cast into Elisha's sepulchre, as he came in contact with his bones. Like the Bedaween now, or the Amalekites of old, [10] *the bands of Moab came into the land, as the year came.* Plunder, year by year, was the lot of Israel at the hands of Moab.

On the East of Jordan, Israel must have remained in part (as Mesha says of the Gadites of Aroer) in their old border. For after this, Hazael, in Jehu's reign, smote Israel [11] *from Aroer which is by the river Arnon;* and at that time probably Ammon joined with him in the exterminating war in Gilead, destroying life before it had come into the world, *that they might enlarge their border*[12]. Jeroboam ii, B. C. 825, restored Israel *to the sea of the plain*[13], i. e., the dead sea, and, (as seems probable from the limitation of that term in Deuteronomy[14], *under Ashdoth-Pisgah Eastward*) to its Northern extremity, lower in latitude than Heshbon, yet above Nebo and Medeba, leaving accordingly to Moab all which it had gained by Mesha. Uzziah, a few years later, made the Ammonites tributaries[15] B. C. 810. But 40 years later B. C. 771, Pul, and, after yet another 30 years, 740, Tiglath-pileser having carried away the trans-jordanic tribes[16], Moab again possessed itself of the whole territory of Reuben. Probably before. For B. C. 726, when Isaiah foretold that [17] *the glory of Moab should be contemned with all that great multitude,* he hears the wailing of Moab throughout all his towns, and names all those which had once been Reuben's and of whose conquest or possession Moab had boasted[18], Nebo, Medeba, Dibon, Jahaz, Baiith; as also those not conquered then, [19] Heshbon, Elealeh; and those of Moab proper, Luhith, Horonaim, and its capitals, Ar-Moab and Kir-Moab. He hears their sorrow, sees their desolation and bewails with their weeping[20]. He had prophesied this before[21], and now, three

[1] Ps. lxxxiii. 4. [2] Ib. 3. [3] Ib. 5. [4] Ib. 8.
[5] 2 Kgs. iii. 6. [6] Ib. 21. [7] Ib. 19.
[8] See on Am. ii. 12. vol. i. p. 268.
[9] This is marked on the Moabite stone, as a subsequent and distinct expedition.
[10] 2 Kgs xiii. 20. [11] Ib. x. 33.
[12] See on Amos i. 13. vol. i. p. 252. [13] 2 Kgs xvi. 25.

[14] Deut. iii. 17. [15] 2 Chr. xxvi. 8.
[16] 1 Chr. v. 26. [17] Is. xvi. 14.
[18] Ib. xv. 1, 2, 4. [19] Ib. 4, 5. 1.
[20] Ib. xvi. 9.
[21] "That the prophecy must be from any other older prophet, is an inference from grounds of nought." Del.

years [1] before its fulfillment by Tiglath-Pileser, he renews it. This tender sorrow for Moab has more the character of an elegy than of a denunciation; so that he could scarcely lament more tenderly the ruin of his own people. He mentions also distinctly no sin there except pride. The pride of Moab seems something of common notoriety and speech. *We have heard* [2]. Isaiah accumulates words, to express the haughtiness of Moab; *the pride of Moab; exceeding proud; his pride and his haughtiness and his wrath* [3], pride overpassing bounds, upon others. His words seem to be formed so as to keep this one bared thought before us, as if we were to say "pride, prideful, proudness, pridefulness;" and withal the unsubstantialness of it all, *the unsubstantiality of his lies* [4]. Pride is the source of all ambition; so Moab is pictured as retiring within her old bounds, *the fords of Arnon*, and thence asking for aid; her petition is met by the counter-petition, that, if she would be protected in the day of trouble, the out-casts of Israel might lodge with her now: *be thou a covert to her from the face of the spoiler* [5]. The prophecy seems to mark itself out as belonging to a time, after the two and a half tribes had been desolated, as stragglers sought refuge in Moab, and when a severe infliction was to come on Moab: *the* [6] *remnant* shall be *small, small not great.*

Yet Moab recovered this too. It was a weakening of the nation, not its destruction. Some 126 years after the prophecy of Isaiah, 30 years after the prophecy of Zephaniah, Moab, in the time of Jeremiah, was in entire prosperity, as if no visitation had ever come upon her. What Zephaniah says of the luxuriousness of his people, Jeremiah says of Moab; [7] *Moab is one at ease from his youth; he is resting on his lees; and he hath not been emptied from vessel to vessel, neither hath he gone into captivity.* [8] They say, *We are mighty and strong men for the war.* Moab was [9] *a strong staff, a beautiful rod;* [10] *he magnified himself against the Lord;* [11] *Israel* was *a derision* to him; *he skipped for joy* at his distress. Jeremiah repeats and even strengthens Isaiah's description of his pride; [12] *his pride, proud,* he repeats, *exceedingly; his loftiness,* again *his pride, his arrogancy, and the haughtiness of his heart.* Its *strong holds* [13] were unharmed; all its cities, *far and near,* are counted one by one, in their prosperity [14]; its summer-fruits and vintage were plenteous; its vines, luxuriant; all was joy and shouting. Whence should this evil come? Yet so it was with Sodom and Gomorrah just before its overthrow. It was, for beauty, [15] *a paradise of God; well-watered everywhere; as the garden of the Lord, like the land of Egypt.* In the morning [16] *the smoke of the country went up as the smoke of the furnace.* The destruction foretold by Jeremiah is far other than the affliction spoken of by Isaiah. Isaiah prophesies only a visitation, which should reduce her people: Jeremiah foretells, as did Zephaniah, captivity and the utter destruction of her cities. The destruction foretold is complete. Not of individual cities only, but of the whole he saith, [17] *Moab is destroyed.* [18] *The spoiler shall come upon every city, and no city shall escape, and the valley shall perish and the high places shall be destroyed, as the Lord hath spoken.* Moab himself was to leave his land. [19] *Flee, save your lives, and ye shall be like the heath in the wilderness. Chemosh shall go forth into captivity; his priests and his princes together. Give pinions unto Moab, that it may flee and get away, and her cities shall be a desolation; for there is none to dwell therein.* It was not only to go into captivity, but its home was to be destroyed. [20] *I will send to her those who shall upheave her, and they shall upheave her, and her vessels they shall empty, all her flagons* (all that aforetime contained her) *they shall break in pieces.* [21] *Moab is destroyed and her cities;* [22] *the spoiler of Moab is come upon her; he hath destroyed the strongholds.* The subsequent history of the Moabites is in the words, [23] *Leave the cities and dwell in the rock, dwellers of Moab, and be like a dove which nesteth in the sides of the mouth of the pit.* The purpose of Moab and Ammon against Israel which Asaph complains of, and which Mesha probably speaks of, is retorted upon her. [24] *In Heshbon they have devised evil against it; come and let us cut it off from being a nation. Moab shall be destroyed from being a people, because he hath magnified himself against the Lord.*

Whence should this evil come? They had, with the Ammonites, been faithful servants of Nebuchadnezzar against Judah [25]. Their concerted conspiracy with Edom, Tyre, Zidon, to which they invited Zedekiah [26], was dissolved. Nebuchadnezzar's march against Judæa did not touch them; for they [27] *skipped with joy* at Israel's distresses. The connection of Baalis, king of the Ammonites, with Ishmael [28] the assassin of Gedaliah, whom the king of Babylon made governor over the land [29] out of their own people, probably brought down the vengeance of Nebuchadnezzar. For Chaldæans too were inciuded in

[1] Is. xvi. 13, 14. [2] Ib. 6.
[3] גאון מואב גֵא מאד גאותו וגאונו ועברתו.
[4] לא כן בדיו. [5] Is. xvi. 4, 5.
[6] Ib. 14. [7] Jer. xlviii. 11. [8] Ib. 14.
[9] Ib. 17. [10] Ib. 26. [11] Ib. 27.
[12] Ib. 29. [13] Ib. 18. [14] Ib. 1, 3, 5, 21–24.

[15] Gen. xiii. 10. [16] Ib. xix. 28.
[17] Jer. xlviii. 4. [18] Ib. 8. [19] Ib. xvii. 6.
[20] Ib. xlviii. 12. [21] Ib. 15. [22] Ib. 18.
[23] Ib. 28. [24] Ib. 2, 42.
[25] 2 Kgs xxiv. 2. [26] Jer. xxvii. 2 sqq.
[27] Ib. xlviii. 27. [28] Ib. xl. 14. xli. 10.
[29] 2 Kgs xxv. 22–26. Jer. xl. 6. xli. 1.

the slaughter[1]. The blow seems to have been aimed at the existence of the people; for the murder of Gedaliah followed upon the rallying of the Jews [2] *out of all the places whither they had been driven.* It returned on Ammon itself, and on Moab who probably on this, as on former occasions, was associated with it. The two nations, who had escaped at the destruction of Jerusalem, were warred upon and subdued by Nebuchadnezzar in the 23d year of his reign[3], the 5th after the destruction of Jerusalem.

And then probably followed that complete destruction and disgraced end, in which Isaiah, in a distinct prophecy, sees Moab trodden down by God as [4] *the heap of straw is trodden down in the waters*[5] *of the dunghill,* and he (Moab) *stretcheth forth his hands in the midst thereof, as the swimmer stretcheth forth his hands to swim, and He,* God, *shall bring down his pride with the treacheries of his hands.* It speaks much of the continued hostility of Moab, that, in prophesying the complete deliverance for which Israel waited, the one enemy whose destruction is foretold, is Moab and those pictured by Moab. [6] *We have waited for Him and He will save us—For in this mountain* (Zion) *shall the hand of the Lord rest, and Moab shall be trodden down under Him.*

After this, Moab, as a nation, disappears from history. Israel, on its return from the captivity, was again enticed into idolatry by Moabite and Ammonite wives, as well as by those of Ashdod and others[7], Canaanites, Hittites, Perizzites, Jebusites, Egyptians, Amorites[8]. Sanballat also, who headed the opposition to the rebuilding of Jerusalem, was a Moabite[9]; Tobiah, an Ammonite[10]. Yet it went no further than intrigue and the threat of war. They were but individuals, who cherished the old hostility. In the time of the Maccabees, the Ammonites, not Moab, *with a mighty power and much people* were in possession of the Reubenite cities to Jazar[11]. It was again an exterminating war, in which the Jews were to be destroyed[12]. After repeated defeats by Judas Maccabæus, the Ammonites *hired the Arabians*[13] (not the Moabites) *to help them,* and Judas, although victorious, was obliged to remove the whole *Israelite* population, [14] *all that were in the land of Gilead, from the least unto the greatest, even their wives, and their children, and their stuff, a very great host, to the end they might come into the land of Judæa.* The whole population was removed, obviously lest, on the withdrawal of Judas' army, they should be again imperilled. As it was a defensive war against Ammon, there is no mention of any city, south of the Arnon, in Moab's own territory. It was probably with the view to magnify descendants of Lot, that Josephus speaks of the Moabites as being "even yet a very great nation [15]." S. Justin's account, that there is "[16] even now a great multitude of Ammonites," does not seem to me to imply a national existence. A later writer says, "[17] Now not only the Edomites but the Ammonites and Moabites too are included in the one name of Arabians."

Some chief towns of Moab became Roman towns, connected by the Roman road from Damascus to Elath. Ar and Kir-Moab in Moab proper became Areopolis and Charac-Moab, and, as well as Medeba and Heshbon in the country which had been Reuben's, preserve traces of Roman occupancy. As such, they became Christian Sees. The towns, which were not thus revived as Roman, probably perished at once, since they bear no traces of any later building.

The present condition of Moab and Ammon is remarkable in two ways; 1) for the testimony which it gives of its former extensive population; 2) for the extent of its present desolation. "How fearfully," says an accurate and minute observer[18], "is this residence of old kings and their land wasted!" It gives a vivid idea of the desolation, that distances are marked, not by villages which he passes but by ruins[19]. "[20] From these ruined places, which lay on our way, one sees how thickly inhabited the district formerly was." Yet the ground remained fruitful. It was partly abandoned to wild plants, the wormwood and other shrubs[21];

[1] Jer. xli. 3. [2] Ib. xl. 12.
[3] Jos. Ant. x. 9, 7. [4] Is. xxv. 10–12.
[5] בְּמֵי Chethib. [6] Is. xxv. 9. 10.
[7] Neh. xiii. 23–26. [8] Ezr. ix. 1.
[9] Neh. ii. 10. iv. 1–8. [10] Ib. iv. 2, 9.
[11] 1 Macc. v. 6, 8. [12] Ib. 9, 10, 27.
[13] Ib. 39. [14] Ib. 45. [15] Ant. i. 11. 3.
[16] Dial. n. 119, p. 218. Oxf. Tr.
[17] Anon. in Job ap. Origen i. 852.
[18] Seetzen Reisen i. 412.
[19] e. g. "¾ of an hour further, we reached the ruins of el-Eale; 1½ hour further, we came to Hüsbân; beside some overthrown pillars, nothing important is found here. On the E., about 1½ hour, are the ruins of Shelûl: after an hour on this plain we came to 3 wasted places, close together; ½ an hour further, we reached the ruins of what formerly was Mádabá; ½ an hour further lay the ruined village of Tuéme: above an hour to the W. the important ruins of Maéin." Ib. 407, 8.

[20] Ib. 411.

[21] "A little N. of el-Eale we came on good soil, which however lay wholly uncultivated and was mostly overgrown with the prickly little Bullân, which gave the country the look of moor-ground." Seetzen Travels, i. 406. "The soil here (Heshbon) is in this district excellent, but it lies wholly uncultivated and serves only for pasture to the little herds of sheep, goats, kine and camels of the Arabs." Ib. p. 407. "The Arabs cultivate a little ground near Madaba." p. 409. "The land (the other side the Mujeb [Arnon] and so in Moab proper) had little grass, but there was an extraordinary quantity of wormwood on it. Yet the soil seems excellent for wheat, although no spot was cultivated. Large spots had the look of our moors from the quantity of wormwood and other little shrubs." p. 410. "Here and there, there were tokens of cultivation, wheatfields; the wheat was good." p. 412.

partly, the artificial irrigation, essential to cultivation in this land, was destroyed[1]; here and there a patch was cultivated; the rest remained barren, because the crops might become the prey of the spoiler[2], or the thin population had had no heart to cultivate it. A list of 33 destroyed places, which still retained their names, was given to Seetzen[3], "of which many were cities in times of old, and beside these, a great number of other wasted villages. One sees from this, that, in the days of old, this land was extremely peopled and flourishing, and that destructive wars alone could produce the present desolation." And thereon he adds the names of 40 more ruined places. Others say: "[4] The whole of the fine plains in this quarter" [the S. of Moab] "are covered with sites of towns, on every eminence or spot convenient for the construction of one; and as all the land is capable of rich cultivation, there can be no doubt that this country, now so deserted, once presented a continued picture of plenty and fertility." "[5] Every knoll" [in the highlands of Moab] "is covered with shapeless ruins.—The ruins consist merely of heaps of squared and well-fitting stones, which apparently were erected without mortar." "[6] One description might serve for all these Moabite ruins. The town seems to have been a system of concentric circles, built round a central fort, and outside the buildings the rings continue as terrace-walks, the gardens of the old city. The terraces are continuous between the twin hillocks and intersect each other at the foot." "[7] Ruined villages and towns, broken walls that once enclosed gardens and vineyards, remains of ancient roads; everything in Moab tells of the immense wealth and population, which that country must have once enjoyed."

The like is observed of Ammon[8]. His was direct hatred of the true religion. It was not mere exultation at the desolation of an envied people. It was hatred of the worship of God. "[9] Thus saith the Lord God; *Because thou saidst, Aha, against My sanctuary, because it was profaned;* and against the land of Israel, because it was desolated; and against the house of Judah, because they went into captivity." The like temper is shewn in the boast, "[10] *Because that Moab and Seir do say; Behold the house of Judah is like unto the heathen,*" i. e., on a level with them.

Forbearing and long-suffering as Almighty God is, in His infinite mercy, He does not, for that mercy's sake, bear the direct defiance of Himself. He allows His creatures to forget Him, not to despise or defy Him. And on this ground, perhaps, He gives to His prophecies a fulfillment beyond what the letter requires, that they may be a continued

[1] See Mr. Tristram's picture of "a ruin-covered ridge by an immense tank of solid masonry, 140 yards by 110 yards, at Ziza. From the surface of the water to the edge of the tank was 17 feet 6 inches. The masonry was simply magnificent. The whole system and artificial sluices were precisely similar to ancient works for irrigation in India and Ceylon.—Such works easily explain to us the enormous population, of which the ruined cities give evidence. Everywhere is some artificial means of retaining the occasional supplies of rain water. So long as these precious structures remained in order, cultivation was continuous and famines remained unknown.—The Islamite invasion left the miserable remnants of a dense and thriving nation entirely dependent on the neighboring countries for their supply of corn: a dependence which must continue till these border lands are secure from the inroad of the predatory bands of the East." Land of Moab pp. 183–186. At Kustul is "a massive wall in the plain, about 600 yards in length across the valley, and 18 feet thick, built to dam up the water in the gentle depression, the head of the wady." Ib. c. 12. p. 220. "Gôr el Mesráa, as far as the soil can be watered, evinces a luxuriant fertility. By far the greater part of it is a waste." Seetz. ii. 352. "Gôr el Záphia owes its fruitfulness entirely to the water of the Wady el Hössa, which is guided to the fields in many canals. But only a very small portion of this exceedingly rich soil is cultivated, the rest is overgrown with bushes and shrubs, wherein very many wild boars, hyenas and other wild animals live." Ib. 355. "This water too [of the Nimméry] is said formerly to have been used for watering some fields, of which there is now no trace." Ib. 354.

[2] "True, the land is not our's, but our people are many, and who shall dare to prevent them from going where they please? You will find them everywhere, if the land is good for them." Answer of Beni Sakkr Sheikh, Tristram Moab. c. 15. p. 28.

[3] Ib. 416.

[4] Irby and Mangles (May 14) p. 113.

[5] Tristram, Land of Moab, pp. 100, 101.

[6] Ib. 99.

[7] Palmer, desert of the Exodus ii. 473, 474.

[8] "East of Assalt, including Ammon, are thirty ruined or deserted places of which names are given in Dr. Smith's Arabic lists." Keith Prophecy p. 274. "All this country, formerly so populous and flourishing, is now changed into a vast desert." Seetzen Brief account &c. p. 34. Ib. p. 263. "The far greater part of this country is uninhabited, being abandoned to the wandering Arabs, and the towns and villages are in a state of total ruin." Id. p. 37. Ib. "Two hours from Szalt we came upon some peasants, who were ploughing some little fields near what was a little fountain." Seetzen i. 405. "The soil was excellent; but only here and there we saw a little spot cultivated, and this by the Aduân Arabs." p. 406. "The country that lay in our route [near Daboah] though now bare of wood, presented a great extent of fertile soil, lying entirely waste, though equal to any of the very best portions of Galilee and Samaria, and capable of producing sustenance for a large population. Around us, in every direction, were remains of more than 50 towns or villages, once maintained by the productive soil, over which they were so thickly studded." Buckingham Travels among the Arab tribes p. 66. "At Mahanafish we had arrived at a very elevated part of the plain, which had continued fertile throughout the whole distance from Ammon." p. 81. "S. S. E. of Yedoody we pushed our way over a continuous tract of fertile soil, capable of the highest cultivation. Throughout the whole extent of the plain were seen ruined towns in every direction, before, behind, on each side, generally seated on small eminences, all at a short distance from each other, and all, as far as we had yet seen, bearing evident marks of former opulence. There was not a tree in sight; but my guide assured me, that the whole of the plain was covered with the finest soil, and capable of being made the most productive corn-land in the world." Ib. p. 85.

[9] Ezek. xxv. 3.

[10] Ib. 8.

witness to Him. The Ammonites, some 1600 years ago, ceased to "be remembered among the nations." But as Nineveh and Babylon, and the cities of Sodom and Gomorrah, by being what they are, are witnesses to His dealings, so the way in which Moab and Ammon are still kept desolate is a continued picture of that first desolation. Both remain rich, fertile; but the very abundance of their fertility is the cause of their desolation. God said to Ammon, as the retribution on his contumely: "[1] therefore, behold, I give thee to the children of the East for a possession, and they shall set their encampments in thee, and place their dwellings in thee; *they* shall eat thy fruit and *they* shall drink thy milk; and I will make Rabbah a dwelling-place of camels, and the children of Ammon a couching-place for flocks." Of Moab He says also, "[2] I will open the side of Moab from the cities, which are on his frontiers, the glory of the country, unto the men of the East with the Ammonites." And this is an exact description of the condition of the land at this day. All travelers describe the richness of the soil. We have seen this as to Moab. But the history is one and the same. One of the most fertile regions of the world, full of ruined towns, destitute of villages or fixed habitations, or security of property, its inhabitants ground down by those, who have succeeded the Midianites and the Amalekites, *the children of the East.* "Thou canst not find a country like the Belka," says the Arabic proverb[3], but "the inhabitants cultivate patches only of the best soil in that territory when they have a prospect of being able to secure the harvest against the invasion of enemies." "We passed many ruined cities," said Lord Lindsay[4], "and the country has once been very populous, but, in 35 miles at least, we did not see a single village; the whole country is one vast pasturage, overspread by the flocks and herds of the Anezee and Beni Hassan Bedouins."

The site of Rabbath Amman was well chosen for strength. Lying "[5] in a long valley" through which a stream passed, "the city of waters" could not easily be taken, nor its inhabitants compelled to surrender from hunger or thirst. Its site, as the eastern bound of Peræa[6], "[7] the last place where water could be obtained and a frontier fortress against the wild tribes beyond," marked it for preservation. In Greek times, the disputes for its possession attest the sense of its importance. In Roman, it was one of the chief cities of the Decapolis, though its population was said to be a mixture of Egyptians, Arabians, Phœnicians[8]. The coins of Roman Emperors to the end of the second century contain symbols of plenty, where now reigns utter desolation[9]. In the 4th century, it and two other now ruined places, Bostra and Gerasa, are named as "most carefully and strongly walled." It was on a line of rich commerce filled with strong places, in sites well selected for repelling the invasions of the neighboring nations[10]. Centuries advanced. It was greatly beautified by its Roman masters. The extent and wealth of the Roman city are attested both by the remains of noble edifices on both sides of the stream, and [11] by pieces of pottery, which are the traces of ancient civilized dwelling, strewed on the earth two miles from the city. "[12] At this place, Ammân, as well as Gerasa and Gamala, three colonial settlements within the compass of a day's journey from one another, there were five magnificent theatres and one ampitheatre, besides temples, baths, aqueducts, naumachia, triumphal arches." "[13] Its theatre was the largest in Syria; its colonnade had at least 50 columns." The difference of the architecture shews that its aggrandizement must have been the work of different centuries: its "castle walls are thick, and denote a remote antiquity; large blocks of stone are piled up without cement and still hold together as well as if recently placed." It is very probably the same which Joab called David to take, after the city of waters had been taken; within it are traces of a temple with Corinthian columns, the largest seen there, yet "not of the best Roman times."

Yet Amman, the growth of centuries, at the end of our 6th century was destroyed. For "[14] it was desolate before Islam, a great ruin." "[15] No where else had we seen the vestiges of public magnificence and wealth in such marked contrast with the relapse into savage desolation." But the site of the old city, so well adapted either for a secure refuge for its inhabitants or for a secure depository for their plunder, was, on that very ground, when desolated of its inhabitants, suited for what God, by Ezekiel, said it would become, a place, where the men of the East should stable their flocks and herds, secure from straying. What a change, that its temples, the centre of the worship of its successive idols, or its theatres, its places of

[1] Ezek. xxv. 4, 5. [2] Ib. 8. 10.
[3] Burckhardt Syria p. 369. "On both sides of the road" (near Naour) "were the vestiges of ancient field-enclosures." Ib. 365.
[4] Travels p. 279.
[5] Irby and Mangles June 14. c. 8. p. 146.
[6] Jos. B. J. iii. 3. 3.
[7] Grote in Smith Bibl. Dict. v. Rabbah.
[8] Strabo xvi. 2. 33. p. 760. Cas.
[9] Ritter, West-Asien viii. 1157.
[10] Amm. Marc. xiv. 8. 13.
[11] Buckingham Arab Tribes p. 67, 73. [12] Ib. 77.
[13] See Burckhardt's description of its ruins. Travels in Syria pp. 357-360.
[14] Abulf. Tab. Syr. p. 91.
[15] Tristram Land of Israel p. 551.

Before CHRIST cir. 630.

9 Therefore *as* I live,
saith the LORD of hosts,
the God of Israel, Surely
[s] Moab shall be as Sodom,
and [t] the children of Ammon as Gomorrah, [u] *even*
the breeding of nettles,
and saltpits, and a perpetual desolation: [x] the residue of my people shall

s Isai. 15. Jer. 48. Ezek. 25. 9. Amos 2. 1.
t Amos 1. 13.
u Gen. 19. 25. Deut. 29. 23. Isai. 13. 19. & 34. 13. Jer. 49. 18. & 50. 40.
x ver. 7.

luxury or of pomp, should be stables for that drudge of man, the camel, and the stream which gave it the proud title of "city of waters" their drinking trough! And yet of the cities whose destruction is prophesied, this is foretold of Rabbah alone, as in it alone is it fulfilled! "Ammon," says Lord Lindsay [1], "was situated on both sides of the stream; the dreariness of its present aspect is quite indescribable. It looks like the abode of death; the valley stinks with dead camels; one of them was rotting in the stream; and though we saw none among the ruins, they were absolutely *covered* in every direction with their dung." "Bones and skulls of camels were mouldering there [in the area of the ruined theatre] and in the vaulted galleries of this immense structure." "It is now quite deserted, except by the Bedouins, who water their flocks at its little river, descending to it by a *wady*, nearly opposite to a theatre (in which Dr. Mac Lennan saw great herds and flocks) and by the *akiba*. Re-ascending it, we met sheep and goats by thousands, and camels by hundreds." Another says [2], "The space intervening between the river and the western hills is entirely covered with the remains of buildings, now only used for shelter for camels and sheep." Buckingham mentions incidentally, that he was prevented from sleeping at night "[3] by the bleating of flocks and the neighing of horses, barking of dogs &c." Another speaks of "[4] a small stone building in the Acropolis now used as a shelter for flocks." While he was "[5] traversing the ruins of the city, the number of goats and sheep, which were driven in among them, was exceedingly annoying, however remarkable, as fulfilling the prophecies." "[6] Before six tents fed sheep and camels." "[7] Ezekiel points just to these, (xx. 5.) which passage Seetzen cites [8]. And in fact the ruins are still used for such stalls."

The prophecy is the very opposite to that upon Babylon, though both alike are prophecies of desolation. Of Babylon Isaiah prophesies, "[9] It shall never be inhabited, neither shall it be dwelt in from generation to generation; neither shall the Arabian pitch tent there, neither shall the shepherds make fold there, but wild beasts of the desert shall lie there, and their houses shall be full of doleful creatures; and the ostriches shall dwell there, and the jackals shall cry in their desolate houses, and howling creatures in their pleasant palaces." And the ruins are full of wild beasts [10]. Of Rabbah Ezekiel prophesied that it should be "[11] a possession for the men of the East, and I," God says, "will make Rabbah a stable for camels, and the Ammonites a couching-place for flocks;" and man's lawlessness fulfills the will and word of God.

9. *Therefore as I live, saith the Lord of hosts.* Life specially belongs to God, since He Alone is Underived Life. [12] *He hath life in Himself.* He is entitled "the living God," as here, in tacit contrast with the dead idols of the Philistines [13], with idols generally [14]; or against the blasphemies of Sennacherib [15], the mockeries of scoffers [16], of the awe of His presence [17], His might for His people [18]; as the object of the soul's longings [19], the nearness in the Gospel, *children of the living God* [20]. *Since He can swear by no greater, He sware by Himself* [21]. Since mankind are ready mostly to believe that God means well with them, but are slow to think that He is in earnest in His threats, God employs this sanction of what He says, twice only in regard to His promises or His mercy [22]; everywhere else to give solemnity to His threats [23]. The appeal to the truth of His own being [24] in support of

1 The Holy Land pp. 279. 281, 283.
2 G. Robinson's travels in Palestine and Syria ii. 175.
3 Travels among the Arab tribes, Ruins of Ammon, p. 73.
4 Lord C. Hamilton in Keith p. 271.
5 Id. Ib. p. 269.
6 Seetzen Reisen i. 394.
7 Prof. Kruse Anmerkung. Ib. T. iv. p. 216.
8 l. 31.
9 Is. xiii. 20.
10 See Rich Mem. p. 27, 30. Buckingham ii. 307. Sir R. K. Porter Travels ii. 342. 387. Kenneir Memoirs p. 279. Keppel's Narr. i. 179, 180. Layard Nin. and Bab., quoted by Keith on Prophecy pp. 466, 467.
11 Ezek. xxv. 4, 5.
12 S. John v. 26.
13 1 Sam. xvii. 26, 36.
14 Jer. x. 10.
15 2 Kgs xix. 4. 16.
16 Jer. xxiii. 36.
17 Deut. v. 25 (26 Heb.)
18 Josh. iii. 10.
19 Ps. of sons of Korah. xlii. 2. lxxxiv. 2.
20 Hos. i. 10 [ii. 1. Heb.]
21 Heb. vi. 13.
22 Is. xlix. 18. Ezek. xxxiii. 10.
23 Num. xiv. 21, [of the glory which God should have in all the world from his chastisement of Israel] 28. Deut. xxxii. 40, [adding לְעוֹלָם] Jer. xxii. 24. Ez. v. 11. xiv. 16, 18, 20. xvi. 48. [as Judge] xvii. 16, 19. xviii. 3. [in rebuke] xx. 3, 31, 33. xxxiii. 27. xxxiv. 8. xxxv. 11. In the same sense, *I swear by Myself* Jer. xxii. 5. xlix. 13. *hath sworn by Himself* Am. vi. 8. by the excellency of Jacob, viii. 7.
24 Ges. Maurer, &c. [with a strange conception of God] render "ita *vivam*." Ewald rightly, "as true as I live."

Before CHRIST cir. 630.

spoil them, and the remnant of my people shall possess them.

10 This shall they have [y] for their pride, because they have reproached and

[y] Isai. 16. 6. Jer. 48. 29.

the truth of His words is part of the grandeur of the prophet Ezekiel in whom it chiefly occurs. God says in the same meaning, *by Myself have I sworn*, of promises which required strong faith [1].

Saith the Lord of Hosts. Their blasphemies had denied the very being of God, as God, to Whom they preferred or likened their idols; they had denied His power or that He could avenge, so He names His Name of power, *the Lord of the hosts* of heaven against their array against His border, I, *the Lord of hosts* Who can fulfill what I threaten, and *the God of Israel* Who Myself am wronged in My people, will make *Moab as Sodom, and the children of Ammon as Gomorrah.* Sodom and Gomorrah had once been flourishing cities, on the borders of that land, which Israel had won from the Amorite, and of which Moab and Ammon at different times possessed themselves, and to secure which Ammon carried on that exterminating war. For they were to the East of the plain *between Bethel and Ai*, where Lot made his choice, *in the plain or circle of Jordan* [2], the well known title of the tract, through which the Jordan flowed into the Dead Sea. Near this, lay Zoar, (Ziara [3]) beneath the caves whither Lot, at whose prayer it had been spared, escaped from its wickedness. Moab and Ammon had settled and in time spread from the spot, wherein their forefathers had received their birth. Sodom, at least, must have been in that part of the plain, which is to the East of the Jordan, since Lot was bidden to flee to the mountains, with his wife and daughters, and there is no mention of the river, which would have been a hindrance [4]. Then it lay probably in that "[5] broad belt of desolation" in the plain of Shittim, as Gomorrah and others of the Pentapolis may have lain in "the sulphur-sprinkled expanse" between El Riha [on the site of Jericho] and the dead sea, "covered with layers of salt and gypsum which overlie the loamy subsoil, literally fulfilling the descriptions of Holy Writ (says an eye witness), [6] *Brimstone and salt and burning, that it is not sown nor beareth, nor any grass groweth therein:* [7] *a fruitful land turned into saltness.* [8] *No man shall abide there, neither shall a son of man dwell in it.*" An elaborate system of artificial irrigation was carried through that cis-Jordanic tract, which decayed when it was desolated of man, and that desolation prevents its restoration.

The doom of Moab and Ammon is rather of entire destruction beyond all recovery, than of universal barrenness. For the imagery, that it should be the *breeding* [lit. *possession*] *of nettles* would not be literally compatible, except in different localities, with that of *saltpits*, which exclude all vegetation. Yet both are united in Moab. The soil continues, as of old, of exuberant fertility; yet in part, from the utter neglect and insecurity of agriculture it is abandoned to a rank and encumbering vegetation; elsewhere, from the neglect of the former artificial system of irrigation, it is wholly barren. The plant named is one of rank growth, since outcasts could lie concealed under it [9]. The preponderating authority seems to be for *mollâch* [10], the Bedawin name of the "mallow," Prof. E. H. Palmer says [11], "which," he adds, "I have seen growing in rank luxuriance in Moab, especially in the sides of deserted Arab camps."

The residue of My people shall spoil them, and the remnant of My people shall possess them. Again, a remnant only, but even these shall prevail against them, as was first fulfilled in Judas Maccabæus [12].

10. *This shall they have for their pride.* lit. *This to them instead of their pride.* Contempt and shame shall be the residue of the proud man; the exaltation shall be gone, and all which they shall gain to themselves shall be *shame.* Moab and Ammon are the types of heretics [13]. As they were akin to the people of God, but hating it; akin to Abraham through a lawless birth, but ever molesting the children of Abraham, so heretics profess to believe in Christ, to be children of Christ, and yet ever seek to overthrow the faith of Christians. As the Church says, [14] *My mother's children are*

[1] Gen. xxii. 16. (so often referred to) Is. xlv. 23, or by Thy Right Hand, i. e. the might which He would put forth.

[2] Gen. xiii. 1, 3, 11.

[3] See the description of Ziara "once a place of considerable importance" in Tristram, land of Moab pp. 328, 330.

[4] Gen. xix. 17–23.

[5] Tristram, Land of Israel, p. 367.

[6] Deut. xxix. 23. [7] Ps. cvii. 34. [8] Jer. xlix. 18.

[9] Job xxx. 7.

[10] Jon. has מַלּוּחִין: the Peschito, מָלוּחָא, and, remarkably, does not use a name coincident with the Heb. חרול sc. חונלא, a sort of vetch. Abulwalid prefers the מלוח, but mentions the חַרְשַׁף "artichoke" (Höst Nachrichten von Maroko u. Fez. p. 538) as an "opinion;" R. Tanchum adopts it, but gives חרמאן as an "opinion" and says that "altogether it belongs to the prickly plants;" Kimchi says, that "some count it a nettle; others, a thistle." On מלוח see Bochart Hieroz. ii. 223–228, ed. Leipz.

[11] Ms. letter.

[12] 1 Macc. v. 6–8.

[13] S. Jer. and Rup.

[14] Cant. i. 5.

Before CHRIST cir. 630.

magnified *themselves*
against the people of the
LORD of hosts.
11 The LORD *will be*
terrible unto them: for he
will † famish all the gods
of the earth; [z] and *men*
shall worship him, every

† Heb. *make lean.*
[z] Mal. 1. 11. John 4. 21.

angry with me. They seem to have escaped the overthrow of Sodom and Gomorrah (heathen sins), and to have found a place of refuge (Zoar); and yet they are in darkness and cannot see the light of faith; and in an unlawful manner they mingle, against all right, the falsehood of Satan with the truth of God; so that their doctrines become, in part, *doctrines of devils,* in part have some stamp of the original truth. To them, as to the Jews, our Lord says, *Ye are of your father the devil.* While they profess to be children of God, they claim by their names to have God for their Father (Moab) and to be of His people (Ammon), while in hatred to His true children they forfeit both. As Moab seduced Israel, so they the children of the Church. They too enlarge themselves against the borders of the Church, rending off its children and making themselves the Church. They too utter reproaches and revilings against it. "Take away their revilings," says an early father[1], "against the law of Moses, and the Prophets, and God the Creator, and they have not a word to utter." They too [2] *remove the old landmarks which the fathers* (the Prophets and Apostles) *have set.* And so, barrenness is their portion; as, after a time, heretics ever divide, and do not multiply; they are a desert, being out of the Church of God: and at last the remnant of Judah, the Church, possesses them, and absorbs them into herself.

11. *The Lord will be terrible unto* [*upon*] *them,* i. e. upon Moab and Ammon, and yet not in themselves only, but as instances of His just judgment. Whence it follows, *For He will famish all the gods of the earth.* "[3] Miserable indeed, to whom the Lord is terrible! Whence is this? Is not God by Nature sweet and pleasurable and serene, and an Object of longing? For the Angels ever desire to look into Him, and, in a wonderful and unspeakable way, ever look and ever long to look. For miserable they, whose conscience makes them shrink from the face of Love. Even in this life they feel this shrinking, and, as if it were some lessening of their grief, they deny it, as though this could destroy the truth, which they *hold down in unrighteousness*[4]."

For He will famish[5] *all the gods of the earth,* taking away [6] *the fat of their sacrifices,* and the *wine of their drink-offerings.* Within 80 years from the death of our Lord[7], the governor of Pontus and Bithynia wrote officially to the Roman Emperor, that "[8] the temples had been almost left desolate, the sacred rites had been for a long time intermitted, and that the victims had very seldom found a purchaser," before the persecution of the Christians, and consulted him as to the amount of its continuance. Toward the close of the century, it was one of the Heathen complaints, which the Christian Apologist had to answer, "[9] they are daily melting away the revenues of our temples." The Prophet began to speak of the subdual of Moab and Ammon; he is borne on to the triumphs of Christ over all the gods of the Heathen, when the worship of God should not be at Jerusalem only, but *they shall worship Him, every one from his place.*

Even all the isles of the heathen. For this is the very note of the Gospel, that "[10] each who through faith in Christ was brought to the knowledge of the truth, by Him, and with Him, *worshipeth from his place* God the Father; and God is no longer known in Judæa only, but the countries and cities of the Heathen, though they be separated by the intervening sea from Judæa, no less draw nigh to Christ, pray, glorify, thank Him unceasingly. For formerly [11] *His name* was *great in Israel,* but now He is well known to all everywhere; earth and sea are full of His glory, and so every one *worshipeth Him from his place;* and this is what is said, [12] *As I live, saith the Lord, all the earth shall be filled with the glory of the Lord.*" *The isles* are any distant lands on the seashore[13], especially the very distant[14]; but also Asia Minor[15] and the whole coast of Europe, and even the Indian Archipelago[16], since the ivory and ebony came from its *many isles.* Zephaniah revives the term, by which Moses had spoken

[1] Tert. de Præscr. Hær. c. 42, p. 493. Oxf. Tr.
[2] Ib. c. 37. p. 488.
[3] Rup.
[4] Rom. i. 18.
[5] There is no reason to abate the irony by rendering "destroy." נרזה is contrasted with משמן Is. xvii. 4, as is רזון Is. x. 16; רָזָה, of the land, with שְׁמֵנָה Nu. xiii. 20; of the sheep, with בְּרִיָּה Ez. xxxiv. 20. In Ps. cvi. 15. רזון is used met. for a wasting, emaciating sickness: in Mic. vi. 10, of "an ephah of emaciation" i. e. scant; in Is. xxiv. 6, רָזִי is sickness; (see Ew. Lehrb. 149. g.) [all.]
[6] Deut. xxxii. 38.
[7] Between A. D. 103–105.
[8] Pliny Epist. x. 32. p. 584. ed. Steph.
[9] Tert. Apol. c. 42. see p. 90. note o. Oxf. Tr.
[10] S. Cyr.
[11] Ps. lxxvi. 1.
[12] Nu. xiv. 21.
[13] Jer. xxv. 22. sqq. Ez. xxvi. 15. sqq. Ps. lxxii. 10.
[14] Is. lxvi. 19.
[15] Dan. xi. 1, 8.
[16] Ez. xxvii. 15. Ges. Thes. sub. v.

Before CHRIST cir. 630.

one from his place, *even* all [a]the isles of the heathen.

[a]Gen. 10. 5.

12 ¶ [b]Ye Ethiopians also, ye *shall be* slain by [c]my sword.

Before CHRIST cir. 630.

[b]Isai. 18. 1. & 20. 4. Jer. 46. 9. Ezek. 30. 9.

[c]Ps. 17. 13.

of the dispersion of the sons of Japhet; "[1]By these were the *isles of the Gentiles* divided in their lands, every one after his tongue." He adds the word, *all;* all, wherever they had been dispersed, every one from his place, shall worship God. One universal worship shall ascend to God from all everywhere. So Malachi prophesied afterward; "[2]From the rising up of the sun even to the going down of the same My Name shall be great among the Gentiles, and *in every place* incense shall be offered unto God and a pure offering; for My Name shall be great among the heathen, saith the Lord of hosts." Even a Jew [3]says here: "This, without doubt, refers to the time to come, when all the inhabitants of the world shall know that the Lord is God, and that His is the greatness and power and glory, and He shall be called the God of the whole earth." The *isles* or *coasts of the sea* are the more the emblem of the Church, in that, "[4]lying, as it were, in the sea of this world and encompassed by the evil events in it, as with bitter waters, and lashed by the most vehement waves of persecutions, the Churches are yet founded, so that they cannot fall, and rear themselves aloft, and are not overwhelmed by afflictions. For, for Christ's sake, the Churches cannot be shaken, and [5]*the gates of hell shall not prevail against them.*"

12. *Ye Ethiopians also, ye shall be slain by My sword.* lit. *Ye Ethiopians also, the slain of My sword are they.* Having summoned them to His throne, God speaks *of* them, not *to* them any more; perhaps in compassion, as elsewhere in indignation[6]. The Ethiopians were not in any direct antagonism to God and His people, but allied only to their old oppressor, Egypt. They may have been in Pharaoh Necho's army, in resisting which, as a subject of Assyria, Josiah was slain: they are mentioned[7] in that army which Nebuchadnezzar smote at Carchemish in the 4th year of Jehoiakim. The prophecy of Ezekiel implies rather, that Ethiopia should be involved in the calamities of Egypt, than that it should be itself invaded. "[8]Great terror shall be in Ethiopia, *when the slain shall fall in Egypt.*" "[9]Ethiopia and Lybia and Lydia &c. and all the men of the land that is in league, shall fall *with these,* by the sword." "[10]They also *that uphold Egypt* shall fall." Syene[10], the frontier-fortress over against Ethiopia, is especially mentioned as the boundary also of the destruction. "Messengers," God says[11], "shall go forth from Me to make the careless Ethiopians afraid," while the storm was bursting in its full desolating force upon Egypt. All the other cities, whose destruction is foretold, are cities of lower or upper Egypt[12].

But such a blow as that foretold by Jeremiah and Ezekiel must have fallen heavily upon the allies of Egypt. We have no details; for the Egyptians would not, and did not tell of the calamities and disgraces of their country. No one does. Josephus, however, briefly but distinctly says[13], that after Nebuchadnezzar had in the 23d year of his reign, the 5th after the destruction of Jerusalem, "reduced into subjection Moab and Ammon, he invaded Egypt, with a view to subdue it," "killed its then king, and having set up another, captured for the second time the Jews in it and carried them to Babylon." The memory of the devastation by Nebuchadnezzar lived on apparently in Egypt, and is a recognized fact among the Mohammedan historians, who had no interest in the fulfillment of Jewish prophecy, of which it does not appear that they even knew. Bokht-nasar [Nebuchadnezzar], they say, "[14]made war on the son of Nechas [Necho], slew him and ruined the city of Memphis and many other cities of Egypt: he carried the inhabitants captive, without leaving one, so that Egypt remained waste forty years without one inhabitant." Another says, "[15]The refuge which the king of Egypt granted to the Jews who fled from Nebuchadnezzar brought this war upon it: for he took them under his protection and would not give them up to their enemy. Nebuchadnezzar, in revenge, marched against the king of Egypt and destroyed the country." "One may be

[1]Gen. x. 5. The phrase, אִיֵּי הַגּוֹיִם, occurs only in these two places.
[2]Mal. i. 11. [3]Abarbanel. [4]S. Cyr.
[5]S. Matt. xvi. 18.
[6]Is. xxii. 16, "What hast thou here, and whom hast thou here, that thou hast hewed thee here a sepulchre? Hewing him out on high his sepulchre, graving in the rock a dwelling for him." Mic. i. 2, "Hear, ye people, all of them." Deut. xxxii. 15, "Thou art waxen fat, art grown thick, art covered with fatness; and he forsook God Who made him, and lightly esteemed the Rock of his salvation."

[7]Jer. xlvi. 9. [8]Ezek. xxx. 4.
[9]Ib. 5. [10]Ib. 6. [11]Ib. 9.
[12]Zoan, Aven, Pi-beseth, Tehaphnehes, Sin, on the Eastern boundary; Noph [Memphis] the capital of Lower Egypt; Pathros, probably a district of Upper Egypt; No [Thebes] its capital; Syene, its last town to the South.
[13]Ant. x. 9. 7. See further Sir G. Wilkinson, Manners and customs of the Ancient Egyptians, i. 173–179. Pusey's Daniel the Prophet pp. 275–277.
[14]Makrizi in De Sacy, Abdallatif Rélation de l'Egypte p. 247. [15]Abdallatif l. c. p. 184.

Before CHRIST cir. 630.

13 And he will stretch out his hand against the north, and [d] destroy Assyria; and will make Nineveh a desolation, *and* dry like a wilderness.

d Isai. 10. 12. Ezek. 31. 3. Nah. 1. 1. & 2. 10. & 3. 15, 18.

Before CHRIST cir. 630.

certain," says a good authority[1], "that the conquest of Egypt by Nebuchadnezzar was a tradition generally spread in Egypt and questioned by no one." Ethiopia was then involved, as an ally, and as far as its contingent was concerned, in the war, in which Nebuchadnezzar desolated Egypt for those 40 years. But, although this fulfilled the prophecy of Ezekiel, Isaiah, some sixty years before Zephaniah, prophesied a direct conquest of Ethiopia. *I have given*, God says[2], *Egypt as thy ransom, Ethiopia and Seba for thee.* It lay in God's purpose, that Cyrus should restore His own people, and that his ambition should find its vent and compensation in the lands beyond. It may be that, contrary to all known human policy, Cyrus restored the Jews to their own land, willing to bind them to himself, and to make them a frontier territory toward Egypt, not subject only but loyal to himself. This is quite consistent with the reason which he assigns; [3] *The Lord God of heaven hath given me all the kingdoms of the earth; and He hath charged me to build Him an house at Jerusalem which is in Judah;* and with the statement of Josephus, that he was moved thereto by "[4] reading the prophecy which Isaiah left, 210 years before." It is, alas! nothing new to Christians to have mixed motives for their actions: the exception is to have a single motive, "for the glory of God." The advantage to himself would doubtless flash at once on the founder of a great empire, though it did not suggest the restoration of the Jews. Egypt and Assyria had always, on either side, wished to possess themselves of Palestine, which lay between them. Anyhow, one Persian monarch did restore the Jews; his successor possessed himself of "Egypt, and part, at least, of Ethiopia." Cyrus wished, it is related[5], "to war in person against Babylon, the Bactrians, the Sacæ, and Egypt." He perished, as is known, before he had completed [6] the third of his purposed conquests. Cambyses, although after the conquest of Egypt he planned ill his two more distant expeditions, reduced "[7] the Ethiopians bordering upon Egypt" ["[8] lower Ethiopia and Nubia"], and these "brought gifts" permanently to the Persian Sovereign. Even in the time of Xerxes, the Ethiopians had to furnish their contingent of troops against the Greeks. Herodotus describes their dress and weapons, as they were reviewed at Doriscus[9]. Cambyses, then, did not lose his hold over Ethiopia and Egypt, when forced by the rebellion of Pseudo-Smerdis to quit Egypt.

13. Zephaniah began by singling out Judah amid the general destruction, [10] *I will also stretch out My Hand upon Judah;* he sums up the judgment of the world in the same way; *He will stretch out*, or, *Stretch He forth*[11], *His Hand against the North and destroy Asshur, and make Nineveh a desolation.* Judah had, in Zephaniah's time, nothing to fear from Assyria. Isaiah [12] and Micah [13] had already foretold, that the captivity would be to Babylon. Yet of Assyria alone the prophet, in his own person, expresses his own conformity with the mind of God. Of others he had said, *the word of the Lord is against you, O Canaan, and I will destroy thee; As I live, saith the Lord, Moab shall be as Sodom. Ye also, O Ethiopians, the slain of My sword are they.* Of Assyria alone, by a slight inflection of the word, he expresses that he goes along with this, which he announces.

[1] De Sacy l. c. who quotes Abulféda [see his hist. ante-Islam. p. 102. he could not find the names of Egyptian kings between Shishak and the Pharaoh who was the contemporary of Nebuch.] Masudi, Nosairi, also.

[2] Is. xliii. 3. [3] Ezr. i. 2, 3.

[4] Ant. xi. 1. 2. [5] Herod. i. 153.

[6] Ib. 214 and Rawl. notes p. 350. [7] Herod. iii. 97.

[8] Sir G. Wilkinson in Rawl. Herod. ii. 487. n. 10.

[9] Her. vii. 69. [10] i. 4.

[11] וְיָשֵׂם, וְיֵט. The ordinary force of the abridged form of the future with ו is consecutive, viz., that the action so joined on is the result of the preceding; "intercede with the Lord וְיָסֵר, that He may take away," lit. "and He may take away." Ex. x. 17. Gesenius' instances are all of this sort. In Hif. of the regular verb, Jud. xiv. 15, 1 Sam. vii. 3, Job xi. 6, xii. 7. Jer. xlii. 3. (Lehrg. p. 321.) verbs עו, Kal. Nu. xxv. 4, Jud. vi. 30, Is. l. 2, 1 Kgs xxi. 10, 2 Kgs. v. 10, 2 Chr. xxix. 10, xxx. 6, 8. (Ib. p. 403.) Hif. Ex. viii. 4, x. 17, Nu. xxi. 7. (Ib. p. 405) verb לה, Ez. x. 12, Is. ii. 20, Is. xxxviii. 21, 1 Kgs xx. 20, Jer. xxiii. 18. (Ib. p. 428). Such are also Hos. xiv. 6, 7, 9. Sometimes a prayer seems to be thus interwoven with prediction as, Nu. xxiv. 7, "her seed shall be in many waters, and exalted be (וְיָרֹם) his king above Amalek, and exalted shall be his kingdom" and Ib. 9, "And Israel doeth valiantly; and rule one (וְיֵרְדְּ) from Jacob." Is. xxxv. 1, 2, "Wilderness and dry-place shall be glad for them, and *let the desert rejoice* (וְתָגֵל) and it shall blossom as the Autumn-crocus. It shall blossom abundantly; *and joy it*, (וְתָגֵל) yea with joy and jubilee: the glory of Lebanon is given to it; they shall see the glory of the Lord, the excellency of our God." The peculiarity here is, that it stands so apart and independent of the preceding, with which ו connects it. The shade of meaning is so fine, that the Verss. and Rabbins pass over it, rendering simply future as do modern commentators, except Keil, and Ewald who corrects וְיֵאבַד וְיֵט arbitrarily and against history.

[12] Is. xxxix. 6. [13] Mic. iv. 10.

Before CHRIST cir. 630.

14 And [e] flocks shall lie down in the midst of her, all [f] the beasts of the nations: both the ‖ [g] cormorant and the bittern shall lodge in the ‖ upper lintels of it; *their* voice shall sing in the windows; desolation *shall be* in the thresholds: ‖ for he shall uncover the [h] cedar work.

[e] ver. 6
[f] Is. 13. 21, 22.
‖ Or, *pelican.*
[g] Is. 34. 11, 14.
‖ Or, *knops*, or, *chapiters.*
‖ Or, *when he hath uncovered.*
[h] Jer. 22. 14.

He does not say as an imprecation, "May He stretch forth His hand;" but gently, as continuing his prophecies, *and*, joining on Asshur with the rest; only instead of saying "He will stretch forth," by a form almost insulated in Hebrew, he says, *And stretch He forth His Hand.* In a way not unlike, David having declared God's judgments, *The Lord trieth the righteous; and the wicked and the lover of violence doth His soul abhor*, subjoineth, *On the wicked rain He snares*, signifying that he (as all must be in the Day of judgment), is at one with the judgment of God. This is the last sentence upon Nineveh, enforcing that of Jonah and Nahum, yet without place of repentance now. He accumulates words expressive of desolateness. It should not only be a *desolation* [1], as he had said of Ashkelon, Moab and Ammon, but a dry, parched [2], unfruitful [3] land. As Isaiah, under the same words, prophesies that the dry and desolate land [4] should, by the Gospel, be glad, so the gladness of the world should become dryness and desolation. *Asshur* is named, as though one individual [5], implying the entireness of the destruction; all shall perish, as one man; or as gathered into one and dependent upon one, its evil King. *The North* is not only Assyria, in that its armies came upon Judah from the North, but it stands for the whole power of evil [6], as Nineveh for the whole beautiful, evil, world. The world with "the princes of this world" shall perish together.

14. *And flocks shall lie down in the midst of her.* No desolation is like that of decayed luxury. It preaches the nothingness of man, the fruitlessness of his toils, the fleetingness of his hopes and enjoyments, and their baffling when at their height. Grass in a court or on a once beaten road, much more, in a town, speaks of the passing away of what has been, that man was wont to be there, and is not, or is there less than he was. It leaves the feeling of void and forsakenness. But in Nineveh not a few tufts of grass here and there shall betoken desolation, it shall be one wild rank pasture, where *flocks* shall not feed only, but *lie down* as in their fold and continual resting-place, not in the outskirts only or suburbs, but in the very centre of her life and throng and busy activity, *in the midst of her*, and none shall fray them away. So Isaiah had said of the cities of Aroer, [7] *they shall be for flocks, which shall lie down and none shall make them afraid*, and of Judah till its restoration by Christ, that it should be [8] *a joy of wild asses, a pasture of flocks.* And not only those which are wont to be found in some connection with man, but *all the beasts of a nation* [9], the troops of wild and savage and unclean beasts which shun the dwellings of man or are his enemies, these in troops have their lair there.

Both the pelican [10] *and the [hedgehog* [11]*] shall lodge in the upper lintels thereof.* The *chapiters* [E. M.] or capitals of the pillars of the temples and palaces shall lie broken and strewn upon the ground, and among those desolate fragments of her pride shall unclean animals haunt. The pelican has its Hebrew name from vomiting. It vomits up the shells which it had swallowed whole, after they had been opened by the heat of the stomach, and so picks out the animal contained in them [12], the very image of greediness and uncleanness. It dwells also not in deserts only but near marshes, so that Nineveh is doubly waste.

A voice shall sing in the windows. In the midst of the desolation, the muteness of the hedgehog and the pensive loneliness of the

[1] שְׁמָמָה Zeph. ii. 4. 9.
[2] צִיָּה of absence of water, Job xxx. 3. Ps. lxiii. 2. cv. 41. cvii. 35. Is. xli. 18. Jer. ii. 6. Ez. xix. 13. Hos. ii. 5.
[3] Is. liii. 2.
[4] מדבר וציה Is. xxxv. 1. Jer. joins מדבר ציה וערבה, l. 12.
[5] Asshur is used in this way of the people, considered in and with their king. Is. xxx. 31. xxxi. 8.
[6] See Is. xiv. 13. [7] Ib. xvii. 2.
[8] Ib. xxxii. 14. Comp. Jer. vi. 2.
[9] גּוֹי "nation," of gregarious creatures, locusts, Jo. i. 6, ii. 2; עַם, "ants," Pr. xxx. 25. "conies," Ib. 26. Comp. ἔθνεα χηνῶν &c. "apium populi," "equorum gentes," Virg. Georg. iv. 430. Arab. אֻמַּה Boch. Hieroz. ii. 468. Leipz.
[10] The most probable rendering, as explaining the etymology. The ὁ render "pelican" Ps. cii. 7. Lev. xi. 18; Aq. Symm. Th., Is. xxxiv. 11; Aq. here. The קוק of the Talmudists (קקא Jerus. Targ. ap. Levy Lex.) is probably the same. The pelican retires inland to consume its food. Tristram, Houghton, in Smith Bibl. Dict. v. Pelican. *note.*
[11] There seems a consent that the קִפֹּד is the hedgehog or porcupine (as in Aram. and Arab.) ο, S. Jer. R. Nathan, Rashi, although the Arab. etym. "rolled himself round" seems uncertain.
[12] Aristot. Anim. ix. 10.

Before CHRIST cir. 630.

l Isai. 47. 8.
k Rev. 18. 7.

15 This *is* the rejoicing
city [l] that dwelt carelessly,
[k] that said in her heart, I
am, and *there is* none beside me: how is she be-
come a desolation, a place
for beasts to lie down in!
every one that passeth by
her [l] shall hiss, *and* [m] wag
his hand.

Before CHRIST cir. 630.

l Job 27. 23. Lam. 2. 15. Ezek. 27. 36.
m Nah. 3. 19.

solitary pelican, the musing spectator is even startled by the gladness of a bird, joyous in the existence which God has given it. Instead of the harmony of music[1] and men-singers and women-singers in their palaces shall be the sweet music of some lonely bird, unconscious that it is sitting *in the windows* of those, at whose name the world grew pale, portions of the outer walls being all which remain of her palaces. *Desolation* shall be *in the thresholds*, sitting, as it were, in them; everywhere to be seen in them; the more, because unseen. Desolation is something oppressive; we *feel* its presence. There, as the warder watch and ward at the empty portals, where once was the fullest throng, shall *desolation sit*, that no one enter. *For He shall uncover* [*hath uncovered* E. M.] *the cedar-work:* in the roofless palaces, the carved *cedar-work* shall be laid open to wind and rain. Any one must have noticed, how piteous and dreary the decay of any house in a town looks, with the torn paper hanging uselessly on its walls. A poet of our own said of the beautiful ruins of a wasted monastery:

> "For the gay beams of lightsome day
> Gild, but to flout the ruins gray."

But at Nineveh it is one of the mightiest cities of the world which thus lies waste, and the bared *cedar-work* had, in the days of its greatness, been carried off from the despoiled Lebanon[2] or Hermon[3].

15. *This* utter desolation *is the rejoicing city* (so unlike is it, that there is need to point out that it is the same); this is she, who was full of joy, exulting exceedingly[4], but in herself, not in God; *that dwelt carelessly*, lit. *securely*, and so carelessly; saying *Peace and safety*[5], as though no evil would come upon her, and so perishing more certainly and miserably[6]. *That said in her heart*, this was her inmost feeling, the moving cause of all her deeds; *I am and there is none beside me;* literally, [7] *and there is no I beside*, claiming the very attribute of God (as the world does) of self-existence, as if it alone were *I*, and others, in respect of her, were as nothing. Pantheism, which denies the being of God, as Author of the world, and claims the life in the material world to be God, and each living being to be a part of God, is only this self-idolatry, reflected upon and carried out in words. All the pride of the world, all self-indulgence which says, *Let us eat and drink, for to-morrow we die*, all covetousness which ends in this world, speaks this by its acts, *I and no I beside.*

How is she become a desolation, has passed wholly into it, exists only as a desolation, *a place for beasts to lie down in*, a mere den for *the wild beasts. Every one that passeth by her shall hiss* in derision, *and wag* [or *wave*] *his hand*] in detestation, as though putting the hand between them and it, so as not to look at it, or, as it were, motioning it away. The action is different from that of [8] *clapping the hands* in exultation.

"It is not difficult," S. Jerome says, "to explain this of the world, that when the Lord hath stretched forth His Hand over the North and destroyed the Assyrian, the Prince of this world, the world also perishes together with its Princes, and is brought to utter desolation, and is pitied by none, but all hiss and shake their hands at its ruin. But of the Church it

[1] אֲרְזָה collective, like עֵצָה Jer. vi. 6.

[2] Is. xiv. 8. xxxvii. 24. Ezek. xxxi. 16. "In the fragment of another epigraph, we have mention of some objects also of wood, 'brought from Mt. Lebanon, (and taken up to the mound) from the Tigris.'" Layard, Nineveh and Babylon. p. 118. "At that time the countries that are upon Lebanon, I took possession of, to the great sea of the country of Akkari," (the Mediterranean,) from Inscription. Ib. p. 355, 356. "The conqueror from the upper passage of the Tigris to Lebanon and the Great Sea." Ib. p. 361. "Standing one day on a distant part of the mound, I smelt the sweet smell of burning cedar; the Arab workmen excavating in the small temple had dug out a beam, and the weather being cold, had at once made a fire to warm themselves. The wood was cedar, probably one of the very beams mentioned in the inscription, as brought from the forests of Lebanon, by the King who built the edifice. After a lapse of nearly 3000 years, it had retained its original fragrance." Ib. p. 357.

[3] Rawl. 5. Emp. i. 385.

[4] עָלֹז, (verb, perhaps i. q. ἀλαλάζω,) is exulting joy, the exultation being good or bad, according to its object, in God or in self and the world; in God, Ps. xxviii. 7, lxviii. 5, xcvi. 11, cxlix. 5, Hab. iii. 18; Zeph. iii. 14: in good, Pr. xxiii. 16; in God's gifts, Ps. lx. 8, cviii. 8; in evil, Ps. xciv. 3, Jer. xi. 15, xv. 17, l. 11, li. 39; over an enemy 2 Sam. i. 20. עַלִּיז (intens.) Is. xxii. 2, xxiii. 7, xxiv. 8, xxxii. 13, is used, as here, of a city, full of its tumultuous, self-confident excitement, as is the verb Is. xxiii. 12. and עָלֵז of an individual, Jer. v. 14. [all.]

[5] 1 Thess. v. 3.

[6] See Jud. xviii. 27.

[7] As we might say "no second I." This gives an adequate explanation of the י in אַפְסִי, as no other rendering does.

[8] Nah. iii. 19.

Before CHRIST cir. 630.

CHAPTER III.

1 *A sharp reproof of Jerusalem for divers sins.* 8 *An exhortation to wait for the restoration of Israel,* 14 *and to rejoice for their salvation by God.*

1 WOE to ‖ † her that is filthy and polluted, to the oppressing city!

‖ Or, *gluttonous.* † Heb. *craw.*

seems, at first sight, blasphemous to say that it shall be a pathless desert, and wild beasts shall dwell in her, and that afterward it shall be said insultingly over her; 'This is the city given up to ill, which *dwelt carelessly and said in her heart, I and none beside.*' But whoso should consider that of the Apostle, wherein he says, [1] *in the last days perilous times shall come,* and what is written in the Gospel, that [2] *because iniquity shall abound, the love of many shall wax cold,* so that then shall that be fulfilled, *When the Son of Man cometh, shall He find the faith on the earth?* he will not marvel at the extreme desolation of the Church, that, in the reign of Antichrist, it shall be reduced to a desolation and given over to beasts, and shall suffer whatever the Prophet now describes. For if for unbelief *God spared not the natural branches,* but *brake them off,* and *turned rivers into a wilderness and the water-springs into a dry ground,* and *a fruitful land into barrenness, for the iniquity of them that dwell therein,* why not as to those of whom He had said, [3] *He turneth the wilderness into a standing water, and dry ground into water-springs, and there He maketh the hungry to dwell;* and as to those whom *out of the wild olive He hath grafted into the good olive tree,* why, if forgetful of this benefit, they depart from their Maker and worship the Assyrian, should He not undo them and bring them to the same thirst wherein they were before? Which, whereas it may be understood generally of the coming of Anti-christ or of the end of the world, yet it may, day by day, be understood of those who feign to be of the Church of God, and *in works deny it, are hearers of the word not doers,* who in vain boast in an outward show, whereas herds i. e. troops of vices dwell in them, and brute animals serving the body, and all the beasts of the field which devour their hearts [and pelicans, i. e. gluttons [4], whose *god is their belly*] and hedgehogs, a prickly animal full of spikes which pricketh whatever it toucheth. After which it is subjoined, that the Church shall therefore suffer this, or hath suffered it, because it lifted itself up proudly and raised its head like a cedar, given up to evil works, and yet promising itself future blessedness, and despising others in its heart, nor thinking that there is any other beside itself, and saying, *I am, and there is no other beside me,* how is it become a solitude, a lair of beasts! For where before, dwelt the Father, and the Son, and the Holy Ghost, and Angels presided over its ministries, there shall beasts dwell. And if we understand that, every one that passeth by shall hiss, we shall explain it thus; when Angels shall pass through her, and not remain in her, as was their wont, they shall be amazed and marvel, and shall not support and bear her up with their hand, when falling, but shall lift up the hands and shall pass by. Or they shall make a sound as those who mourn. But if we understand this of the devil and his angels, who destroyed the vine also that was brought out of Egypt, we shall say, that through the soul, which before was the temple of God and hath ceased so to be, the serpent passeth, and hisseth and spitteth forth the venom of his malice in her, and not this only, but setteth in motion his works which figuratively are called *hands.*"

"[5] The earlier and partial fulfillment of prophecy does not destroy, it rather confirms, the entire fulfillment to come. For whoso heareth of the destruction of mighty cities, is constrained to believe the truth of the Gospel, that the fashion of this world passeth away, and that, after the likeness of Nineveh and Babylon, the Lord will in the end judge the whole world also."

C. III. I. The "woe," having gone round the heathen nations, again circles round where it began, the [6] *Jerusalem that killed the prophets and stoned those that were sent unto her.* Woe upon her, and joy to the holy Jerusalem, the *new Jerusalem* [7], *the Jerusalem which is from above, the mother of us all,* close this prophecy; both in figure; destruction of her and the whole earth, in time, the emblem of the eternal death; and the love of God, the foretaste of endless joy in Him.

Wo [8] *rebellious and polluted* [9]; *thou oppressive*

[1] 2 Tim. iii. 1–5. [2] S. Matt. xxiv. 12. [3] Ps. cvii. 33–36.
[4] Rib. [5] Rup. [6] S. Matt. xxiii. 37.
[7] Rev. iii. 12. xxi. 10.
[8] הוי with the partic., as a vocative, as in Am. v. 18. Is. xlv. 9, 10. Mic. i. 1. Hab. ii. 6, 9, 12, 15, 19, &c.
[9] מוֹרְאָה from מרא = מרה. This seems more probable than E. V. (from a meaning given to ראי Nah. iii. 6. and from מֻרְאָה crop of bird Lev. i. 16.) or LXX ἐπιφανὴς (as if מְרָאָה, as a few Mss. de R.) or S. Jer. "embittering," provocatrix (as if הַמֹּרָה = מֹרא), or Abarb. "terrible" (as from ירא which is expressed by Nif. נורא) or Drus. "made a spectacle;" παραδειγμα-τιζομένη, cf. מַרְאָה; but this is not used elsewhere, though the verb is so common.

Before CHRIST cir. 630.

2 She [a]obeyed not the
voice; she [b]received not
‖correction; she trusted
not in the LORD; she drew
not near to her God.
3 [c]Her princes within
her *are* roaring lions; her
judges *are* [d]evening wolves;
they gnaw not the bones
till the morrow.
4 Her [e]prophets *are*
light *and* treacherous per-

[a] Jer. 22. 21.
[b] Jer. 5. 3.
‖ Or, *instruction*.
[c] Ezek. 22. 27. Mic. 3. 9, 10, 11.
[d] Hab. 1. 8.
[e] Jer. 23. 11, 32. Lam. 2. 14. Hos. 9. 7.

city [1]! The address is the more abrupt, and bursts more upon her, since the prophet does not name her. He uses as her proper name, not her own name, "city of peace," but "rebellious," "polluted;" then he sums up in one, *thou oppressive city*.

Jerusalem's sin is threefold, actively rebelling against God; then, inwardly defiled by sin; then cruel to man. So then, toward God, in herself, toward man, she is wholly turned to evil, not in passing acts, but in her abiding state, 1) rebellious, 2) defiled, 3) oppressive. She is known only by what she has become, and what has been done for her in vain. She is rebellious, and so had had the law; defiled, and so had been cleansed; and therefore her state is the more hopeless.

2. *She obeyed not the Voice*, of God, by the law or the prophets, teaching her His ways; and when, disobeying, He chastened her, *she received not correction*, and when He increased His chastisements, she, in the declining age of the state and deepening evil, turned not unto Him, as in the time of the judges, nor ceased to do evil.

In the Lord she trusted not, but in Assyria or Egypt or her idols. Our practical relation to God is summed up in the four words, "Mistrust self; trust God." Man reverses this, and when "self-trust" has of course failed him, then he "mistrusts God." "[2]Such rarely ask of God, what they hope they may obtain from man. They strain every nerve of their soul to obtain what they want; canvass, flatter, fawn, bribe, court favor; and betake themselves to God when all human help fails. They would be indebted, not to God, but to their own diligence. For the more they receive of God, the less, they see, can they exalt their own diligence, the more they are bound to thank God, and obey Him the more strictly."

To her God she drew not nigh, even in trouble, when all draw nigh unto Him, who are not wholly alien from Him; she drew not near by repentance, by faith, hope or love, or by works meet for repentance, but in heart remained far from Him. And yet He was *her* own *God*, as He had shewn Himself in times past, Who changes not, while we change; is faithful to us, while we fail Him; is still our God, while we forget Him; *waits, to have mercy upon us;* shines on us while we interpose our earth-born clouds between us and Him. "[3]Not in body nor in place, but spiritually and inwardly do we approach to the uncircumscribed God," owning Him as our Father, to Whom we daily say "Our Father."

3. The prophet having declared the wickedness of the whole city, rehearses how each in Church and state, the ministers of God in either, who should have corrected the evil, themselves aggravated it. Not enemies, without, destroy her, but

Her princes within her, in the very midst of the flock, whom they should in God's stead *feed with a true heart*, destroy her as they will, having no protection against them. *Her judges are evening wolves* [4]; those who should in the Name of God redress all grievances and wrongs, are themselves like wild beasts, when most driven by famine. *They gnaw not the bones* [5] *till the morrow* or *on the morrow* [lit. *in the morning*]. They reserve nothing till the morning light, but do in darkness the works of darkness, shrinking from the light, and, in extreme rapacity, devouring at once the whole substance of the poor. As Isaiah says, [6]*Thy princes are rebellious and companions of thieves*, and [7]*The Lord will enter into judgment with the ancients of His people and the princes thereof: for ye have eaten up the vineyard: the spoil of the poor is in your houses.* And Ezekiel, [8]*Her princes in the midst thereof are like wolves, ravening the prey to shed blood, to destroy souls, to get dishonest gain.*

4. *Her prophets* are *light*, boiling and bubbling up, like water boiling over [9], empty

[1] העיר as a separate vocative, as Nu. xv. 15. Cant. vi. 1. Is. lii. 18. Mi. ii. 7. &c., and in the N. T. ὁ βασιλεὺς, S. Matt. xxvii. 29. ὁ υἱὸς, S. Mark x. 47. ὁ πατὴρ Ib. xiv. 36, &c.

[2] Rib. on Hos. vii. n. 39.

[3] Dion.

[4] See Hab. i. 8.

[5] The meaning of Piel, in Num. xxiv. 8, and met. Ez. xxiii. 34. as denom. from poetic גרם. "bone." The Verss. gave the meaning, dropping the metaphor, the Lxx. and Vulg. rendering "left;" Ch. "deferring to," Syr. "waiting for." In Arab. צרם signifies "cut off," spec. wool of sheep, fruit of palm-trees, and with ל p. "gaining for himself or his family." In Syr. it is 1) "cut off;" 2) "decreed;" not, "reserved." Abulw. Kim. Menach. render "break" as denom.

[6] Is. i. 23.

[7] Ib. iii. 14.

[8] Ez. xxii. 27.

[2] פחזות being used by Jeremiah (xxiii. 32.) of the false *prophets* who *prophesy false dreams and do tell them and cause My people to err by their lies and by their lightness*, it probably has the same meaning here; though פחז is used of the boiling over of

Before CHRIST cir. 630.

sons; her priests have polluted the sanctuary, they
have done [f] violence to the
law.

[f] Ezek. 22. 26.

5 [g] The just LORD [h] *is* in
the midst thereof; he will
not do iniquity: † every
morning doth he bring his

Before CHRIST cir. 630.

[g] Deut. 32. 4.
[h] ver. 15, 17. See Mic. 3. 11.
† Heb. *morning by morning.*

boasters claiming the gift of prophecy, which they have not; "boldly and rashly pouring out what they willed as they willed;" promising good things which shall not be. So they are *her* prophets, to whom they *prophesy smooth things*, "[1] the prophets of this people" not the prophets of God; *treacherous persons* [lit. men of treacheries] wholly given to manifold treacheries against God in Whose Name they spake and to the people whom they deceived. "[2] They spake as if from the mouth of the Lord and uttered everything against the Lord." *The leaders of the people*, those who profess to lead it aright, Isaiah says[3], *are its misleaders. Thy prophets*, Jeremiah says[4], *have seen vain and foolish things for thee; they have seen for thee false visions and causes of banishment.*

Her priests have polluted her sanctuary, lit. *holiness*, and so holy rites, persons[5], things, places (as the sanctuary), sacrifices. All these they polluted, being themselves polluted; they polluted first themselves, then the holy things which they handled, handling them as they ought not; carelessly and irreverently, not as ordained by God; turning them to their own use and self-indulgence, instead of the glory of God; then they polluted them in the eyes of the people, [6] *making them to abhor the offering of the Lord*, since, living scandalously, they themselves regarded the Ministry entrusted to them by God so lightly. Their office was to [7] *put difference between holy and unholy and between clean and unclean, and to teach the children all the statutes which the Lord hath spoken unto them by Moses;* that they [8] *should sanctify themselves and be holy, for I the Lord your God am holy.* But they on the contrary, God says by Ezekiel, [9] *have done violence to My law and have profaned My holy things; they have made no difference between holy and profane, and have taught none between clean and unclean. Holy* and *unholy* being the contradictory of each other, these changed what God had hallowed into its exact contrary. It was not a mere short-coming, but an annihilation (so to speak), of God's purposes.

"[10] The Priests of the Church then must keep strict watch, not to profane holy things. There is not one mode only of profaning them, but many and divers. For Priests ought to be purified both in soul and body, and to cast aside every form of abominable pleasure. Rather should they be resplendent with zeal in well-doing, remembering what S. Paul saith, [11] *walk in the Spirit and ye shall not fulfill the lust of the flesh.*"

They have oppressed, done violence, to the law, openly violating it[12]; or straining it, or secretly wresting and using its forms to wrong and violence, as in the case of Naboth and of Him, of Whom Naboth thus far bore the Image. "[13] *We have a law, and by our law He ought to die.* Law exists to restrain human violence; these reversed God's ordinances; violence and law changed places: first, they did violence to the majesty of the law, which was the very voice of God, and then, through profaning it, did violence to man. Forerunners herein of those, who, when Christ came, [14] *transgressed the commandment of God*, and *made it of none effect by their traditions;* [15] *omitting* also *the weightier matters of the law, judgment and mercy and faith; full of extortion and excess!*

5. But, beside these *evening wolves in the midst of her*, there standeth Another *in the midst of her*, Whom they knew not, and so, very near[16] to them although they would not draw near to Him. But He was near, to behold all the iniquities which they did in the very city and place called by His Name and in His very Presence; He was in her to protect, foster her with a father's love, but she, presuming on His mercy, had cast it off. And so He was near to punish, not to deliver; as a Judge, not as a Saviour. "[17] God is everywhere, Who says by Jeremiah, [18] *I fill heaven and earth.* But since, as Solomon attesteth, [19] *The Lord is far from the wicked*, how is He said here to be *in the midst* of these most wicked men? Because the Lord is far from the wicked, as regards the presence of love and grace; still in His Essence He is everywhere, and in this way He is equally present to all."

The Lord is in the midst thereof; He will not

sensuality (Gen. xlix. 4.) and of *empty wanton men*, Jud. ix. 4. In Arabic, פחז as well as פחר is used of vain-glory; in Syr. of "impurity."

[1] See Mic. ii. 11. [2] S. Jer.
[3] Is. ix. 15. [16. Eng.] [4] Lam. ii. 14.
[5] Ezra viii. 28. [6] 1 Sam. ii. 17.
[7] Lev. x. 10, 11. [8] Ib. xi. 44. xix. 2. &c.
[9] Ezek. xxii. 26. [10] S. Cyr.
[11] Gal. v. 16.

[12] The construction with the acc. of person occurs Ezek. xxii. 26, Prov. viii. 36, Jer. xxii. 3.
[13] S. John xix. 7. [14] S. Matt. xv. 6.
[15] Ib. xxiii. 23. 25.
[16] The words in Hebrew correspond with each other, being from the same root, קרבה "draw near;" בקרבה, "in the midst of her." ver. 2, 3, 5.
[17] Dion. [18] Jer. xxiii. 24.
[19] Pr. xv. 29.

Before CHRIST cir. 630.

judgment to light, he faileth not; but [l]the unjust
knoweth no shame.
6 I have cut off the na-
tions: their ||towers are
desolate; I made their
streets waste, that none
passeth by: their cities

l Jer. 3. 3. & 6. 15. & 8. 12.

|| Or, *corners*.

do iniquity. "[1] Since He is the primal rule and measure of all righteousness; therefore from the very fact that He doeth anything, it is just; for He cannot do amiss, being essentially holy. Therefore He will give to every man what he deserves. Therefore we chant, [2] *The Lord is upright, and there is no unrighteousness in Him.*" Justice and injustice, purity and impurity, cannot be together. God's Presence then must destroy the sinners, if not the sin. He was *in the midst of them,* to sanctify them, giving them His judgments as a pattern of theirs; *He will not do iniquity:* but if they heeded it not, the judgment would fall upon themselves. It were for God to become [3] *such an one as themselves,* and to connive at wickedness, were He to spare at last the impenitent.

Every morning [lit. *in the morning, in the morning*] one after the other, quickly, openly, daily, continually, bringing all secret things, all works of darkness, to light, as He said to David, [4] *Thou didst it secretly, but I will do this thing before all Israel, and before the sun. Doth He bring His judgments to light,* so that no sin should be hid in the brightness of His Light, as He said by Hosea, *Thy judgments are a light which goeth forth.* "[5] Morning by morning, He shall execute His judgments, i.e., in bright day and visibly, not restraining His anger, but bringing it forth in the midst, and making it conspicuous, and, as it were, setting in open vision what He had foreannounced." Day by day God gives some warning of His judgments. By chastisements which are felt to be His on this side or on that or all around, He gives ensamples which speak to the sinner's heart. *He faileth not.* As God said by Habakkuk, that His promises, although they seem to *linger,* were not *behind*[6] the real time, which lay in the Divine mind, so, contrariwise, neither are His judgments. His hand is never missing[7] at the appointed time. *But the unjust*[8], he, whose very being and character, *iniquity,* is the exact contrary to what he had said of the perfection of God, [9] *Who doth not iniquity,* or, as Moses had taught them in his song[10], *all His ways are judgment, a God of truth and without iniquity*[11], *just and right is He. Knoweth no shame,* as God saith by Jeremiah, [12] *Thou refusedst to be ashamed.* [13] *They were not at all ashamed, neither could they blush.* Even thus they would not be ashamed of their sins, [14] *that they might be converted and God might heal them.*

6. *I have cut off* [the] *nations.* God appeals to His judgments on heathen nations, not on any particular nation, as far as we know; but to past history, whether of those, of whose destruction Israel itself had been the instrument, or others. The judgments upon the nations before them were set forth to them, when they were about to enter on their inheritance, as a warning to themselves[15]. *Defile not ye yourselves in any of these things; for in all these have the nations defiled themselves, which I cast out before you: and the land is defiled; therefore I do visit the iniquity thereof upon it, and the land vomiteth out her inhabitants. And ye, ye shall keep My statutes and My judgments and shall not commit any of these abominations—And the land shall not spue you out when ye defile it, as it spued out the nations which were before you.* The very possession then of the land was a warning to them; the ruins, which crowned so many of its hill-tops[16], were silent preachers to them; they lived among the memories of God's visitations; if neglected, they were an earnest of future judgments on themselves. Yet God's judgments are not at one time only. Sennacherib appealed to their own knowledge, [17] *Behold, thou hast heard what the kings of Assyria have done to all lands by destroying them utterly. Have the gods of the nations delivered them which my fathers have destroyed?* Hezekiah owned it as a fact which he knew: [18] *Of a truth, Lord, the kings of Assyria have laid waste all the nations and their land.* And God owns him as His instrument: [19] *Now I have brought it to pass, that thou shouldest be to lay waste defenced cities into ruinous heaps:* and, [20] *I will send him against an ungodly nation, and against the people of My wrath will I give him a charge, to take the spoil and to take the prey, and to tread them down as the mire of the streets,* and says of him, *It is in his heart to destroy and to*

1 Dion. 2 Ps. xcii. 15. 3 Ib. l. 21.
4 2 Sam. xii. 12.
5 S. Cyr. 6 Hab. ii. 3.
7 נֶעְדָּר is used of one missing when a muster is made (1 Sam. xxx. 19, 2 Sam. xvii. 22, met. Is. xxxiv. 16, xl. 26, lix. 15.); here only of God, that He does not fail to visit at the time when He ought to be looked for.
8 עָוֶל. 9 לא יעשה עולה. 10 Deut. xxxii. 4.

11 ואין עָוֶל. 12 Jer. iii. 3. 13 Ib. vi. 15, viii. 12.
14 Is. vi. 10.
15 Lev. xviii. 24, 25, 26, 28, add Ib. xx. 23.
16 This will be brought out by the "Ordnance survey" of Palestine, when completed. Isaiah alludes to them, xvii. 9.
17 Is. xxxvii. 11, 13. 18 Ib. 18.
19 Ib. 26.
20 Ib. x. 6, 7, and the graphic picture ib. 13, 14.

Before CHRIST cir. 630.

are destroyed, so that
there is no man, that there
is none inhabitant.
7 [k] I said, Surely thou
wilt fear me, thou wilt receive instruction; so their
dwelling should not be cut
off, howsoever I punished

[k] So Jer. 8. 6.

cut off nations not a few. The king of Babylon too he describes as [1] *the man that made the earth to tremble, that did shake kingdoms, that made the world as a wilderness, and destroyed the cities thereof.* Habakkuk recently described the wide wasting by the Babylonians, and the helplessness of nations before him [2].

Their towers, corner towers [3], the most carefully fortified parts of their fortified cities, *are desolate; I made their streets waste.* The desolation is complete, within as well as without; ruin itself is hardly so desolate as the empty habitations and forsaken streets, once full of life, where

"The echoes and the empty tread
Would sound like voices from the dead."

7. *I said, surely thou wilt fear Me.* God speaks of things here, as they are in their own nature. *It could not but be*, that in the very presence of the Hand of God, destroying others but as yet sparing them, they must learn to fear Him; they must stand in awe of Him for His judgments on others; they must be in filial fear of Him for His loving longsuffering toward themselves. "Thou *wilt* receive instruction," corrected and taught through God's correction of others and the lighter judgments on themselves, as Solomon says, [4] *I looked, I set my heart: I saw, I received instruction.* He saith, *receive*, making it man's free act. God brings it near, commends it to him, exhorts, entreats, but leaves him the awful power to *receive* or to refuse. God speaks with a wonderful tenderness. "Surely thou *wilt* stand in awe of Me; thou *wilt* receive instruction; thou wilt now do what hitherto thou hast refused to do." There was (so to speak) nothing else left for them [5], in sight of those judgments. He pleads their own interests. The lightning was ready to fall. The prophet had, in vision, seen the enemy within the city. Yet even now God lingers, as it were, [6] *If thou hadst known in this thy day, the things which are for thy peace.*

So their [*her*] *dwelling should not be cut off.* His own holy land which He had given them. A Jew paraphrases [7], "And He will not cut off their dwellings from the land of the house of My Shechinah" (God's visible Presence in glory). Judah, who was before addressed *thou*, is now spoken of in the third person, *her;* and this also had wonderful tenderness. It is as though God were musing over her and the blessed fruits of her return to Him; "it shall not be needed to correct her further." *Howsoever I punished them:* lit. *all* (i.e., *all* the offences) *which I visited upon her*, as God saith of Himself, "[8] *visiting* the *sins* of the fathers *upon* the children," and this is mostly the meaning of the words [9] *visit upon.* Amid and notwithstanding all the offences which God had already chastised, He, in His love and compassion, still longeth, not utterly to remove them from His Presence, if they would but receive instruction *now;* but they would not. *How often*, our Lord says [10], *would I have gathered thy children together, even as a hen gathereth her chickens under her wings, and ye would not.* *But indeed*, probably, *Of a truth* [11] (it is a word strongly affirming what follows) *they rose early, they corrupted all their doings;* God gave them His warnings, awaited the result; they lost no time, they began with morning light; they hasted to rise, burthened [12] themselves, made sure of having the whole day before them, to—seek God as He had sent His Prophets, [13] *rising early and sending them?* No, nor even simply to do ill, but of set purpose to do, not this or that corruptly, but to *corrupt all their doings.* "[14] They with diligence and eagerness rose early, that, with the same haste wherewith they ought to have returned to Me, they might shew forth

[1] Is. xiv. 16, 17.
[2] Hab. i. 14–16.
[3] See on i. 16. Since also the subjects spoken of in this verse are places, the metaph. meaning of פנות "princes" i. e. corner-stones, is not probable here, although נשמו is, in four places, used of men.
[4] Prov. xxiv. 32.
[5] אַךְ, exclusively of all besides. All the meanings ascribed to אַךְ are but different ways of expressing in other languages the primary meaning, "nothing but."
[6] S. Luke xix. 42.
[7] Jon.
[8] Ex. xx. 5, xxxiv. 7. Nu. xiv. 18.
[9] Ex. xxxii. 34, Is. xiii. 11, Jer. xxiii. 2, Hos. i. 4, ii. 13, iv. 9, Amos iii. 2, 14; beside the separate cases of a) visiting upon, or b) visiting the sin. See Ges.
[10] S. Matt. xxiii. 37.
[11] אָכֵן probably (as Ges.)=הָכֵן Jos. iii. 17. iv. 5. The adversative force, which Gesenius (Thes. p. 670) and Ewald (Lehrb. n. 105. d. p. 274. ed. 8.) think to belong to a later style, lies (as so often in other Heb. particles) in the tacit contrast of the sentences. Gesenius' instances of this "later usage" are Ps. xxxi. 23. (David's) lxvi. 19. lxxxii. 7. Job xxxii. 8. Is. xlix. 4. liii. 4. Jer. iii. 20, and this place.
[12] The word means originally "placed on the back;" then is used of a traveler, who taking his baggage upon him, or setting it on his camels, sets out in very early dawn, or before it, as is the practice in hot countries.
[13] Jer. vii. 13, 25, xi. 7, xxvi. 5. xxix. 19.
[14] S. Jer.

Before CHRIST cir. 630.

them; but they rose early, *and* [l]corrupted all their doings.

8 ¶ Therefore [m]wait ye upon me, saith the LORD, until the day that I rise up to the prey: for my determination *is* to [n]gather the nations, that I may assemble the kingdoms, to pour upon them mine indignation, *even* all my fierce an-

[l] Gen. 6. 12.
[m] Ps. 27. 14. & 37. 34. Prov. 20. 22.
[n] Joel. 3. 2.

in deed what they had conceived amiss in their mind." There are as many aggravations of their sin as there are words. The four Hebrew words bespeak eagerness, wilfulness, completeness enormity, in sin. They *rose early*, themselves deliberately *corrupted*, of their own mind made offensive, *all* their *doings*, not slight acts, but *deeds*, great works done with a high hand [1].

8. *Therefore wait ye upon* [*for*] *Me*. God so willeth not to punish, but that all should lay hold of His mercy, that He doth not here even name punishment. Judah had slighted His mercies; He was ready to forgive *all* they had sinned, if they would *now* receive instruction; they in return set themselves to corrupt *all* their doings. They had wholly forsaken Him. *Therefore*—we should have expected, as elsewhere, "Therefore I will visit all your iniquities upon you." But not so. The chastisement is all veiled; the prophet points only to the mercy beyond. *Therefore wait ye for Me*. All the interval of chastisement is summed up in these words; i. e., since neither My mercies toward you, nor My chastisement of others, lead you to obey Me, *therefore* the time shall be, when My Providence shall not seem to be over you, nor My Presence among you [2]; but then, *wait ye for Me* [3] earnestly, intensely, perseveringly, *until the day, that I rise up to the prey*. *The day* is probably in the first instance, the deliverance from Babylon. But the words seem to be purposely enlarged, that they may embrace other judgments of God also. For the words to *gather the nations, assemble the kingdoms*, describe some array of nations against God and His people; gathering themselves for their own end at that time, but, in His purpose, gathering themselves for their own destruction, rather than the mere tranquil reunion of those of different nations in the city of Babylon, when the Medes and Persians came against *them*. Nor again are they altogether fulfilled in the destruction of Jerusalem, or any other event until now. For although then a vast number of the dispersed Jews were collected together, and were at that time "[4]broken off" and out of covenant with God, they could hardly be called *nations*, (which are here and before [5]spoken of in contrast with Judah), much less *kingdoms*. In its fullest sense the prophecy seems to belong to the same events in the last struggle of Anti-Christ, as at the close of Joel [6] and Zechariah [7]. With this agrees the largeness of the destruction; *to pour out upon them*, in full measure, emptying out so as to overwhelm them [8], *Mine indignation, even all My fierce anger; for all the earth shall be devoured with the fire of My jealousy*. The outpouring of *all* God's wrath, the devouring of the *whole* earth, in the fullest sense of the words, belongs to the end of the world, when He shall say to the wicked, "Depart from Me, ye cursed, into everlasting fire." In lesser degrees, and less fully, the substance of the prophecy has again and again been fulfilled to the Jewish Church before Christ, at Babylon and under the Maccabees; and to the Christian, as when the Mohammedans hemmed in Christendom on all sides, and the waves of their conquests on the East and West threatened to meet, overwhelming Christendom. The Church, having sinned, had to *wait* for a while *for God* Who by His Providence withdrew Himself, yet at last delivered it.

And since the whole history of the Church lies wrapt up in the Person of the Redeemer, *the day that I rise up to the prey*, is especially the Day in which the foundation of His Church was laid, or that in which it shall be completed; the Day whereon He rose again, as the first-fruits, or that Day in which He shall [9]*stand again on the earth*, to judge it; [10]*so coming even as He went up into Heaven*.

[1] עלילות are the "mighty works" of God, or deeds of man's might, and, as such, mostly great crimes in the sight of God. So even the heathen have formed from "facio," "facinus," of deeds which they too held to involve great guilt.

[2] See Hos. iii. 3–5.

[3] חִכָּה is mostly a longing persevering expectation for a thing or person which as yet comes not, when the delay requires patience; for God, with ל, Ps. xxxiii. 20, Is. viii. 7, lxiv 3; His promise, Hab. ii. 3, and (part. Kal in sense of Pi.) Is. xxx. 18; with negative Ps. cvi. 13; for death. Job iii. 20; of endurance, Dan. xii. 12. The only other cases are 'lying in wait,' Hos. vi. 9. waiting for the end of Job's words, Job xxxii. 4; for the issue of the message to Jehu, 2 Kgs ix. 3; till dawn, Ib vii. 9; and of God, waiting for us, till He can shew us mercy, Is. xxx. 18.

[4] Rom. xi. 20.

[5] v. 6.

[6] Joel iii. 2, 9–16.

[7] Zech. xiv.

[8] See Ps. lxix. 24, lxxix 6, Jer. vi. 11, x. 25, xiv. 16, Ezek. xxi. 31, Rev. xvi. 1.

[9] Job xix. 25. It is the same word.

[10] Acts i. 11.

Before CHRIST cir. 630.

ger; for all the earth [o]shall be devoured with the fire of my jealousy.

o ch. 1. 18.

9 For then will I turn to the people [p] a pure † language, that they may all

Before CHRIST cir. 630.

p Isai. 19. 18. † Heb. *lip*.

Then, *the prey*[1] must be, what God vouchsafes to account as His gain, *the prey* which is *taken from the mighty*[2], and *the lawful captivity, the prey of the terrible one*, which shall be delivered; even that spoil which the Father bestowed on Him *Who made His soul an offering for sin*[3], the goods of the strong man [4] whom He bound, and spoiled us, His lawful goods and captives, since we had *sold*[5] ourselves *under sin* to him. "[6] Christ lived again having spoiled hell, because [7] *it was not possible* [as it is written] *that He*, being by nature Life, *should be holden of death*.

Here, where spoken of with relation to the Church, *the jealousy* of Almighty God is that love for His people[8], which will not endure their ill-treatment by those who (as all Anti-Christian power doth) make themselves His rivals in the government of the world.

9. *For then*, in the order of God's mercies. The deliverance from Babylon was the forerunner of that of the Gospel, which was its object. The spread of the Gospel then is spoken of in the connection of God's Providence and plan, and time is overlooked. Its blessings are spoken of, as *then* given when the earnest was given, and the people, from whom according to the flesh Christ was to be born, were placed anew in the land where He was to be born. "[9] The prophet springs, as is his wont, to Christ and the time of the new law." And in Christ, the End of the law, the prophet ends.

I will turn, contrary to what they had before, *to the people*, lit. *peoples*, the nations of the earth, *a pure language*, lit. *a purified lip*. It is a real conversion, as was said of Saul at the beginning; [10] *God* [lit.] *turned to him another heart*. Before the dispersion of Babel the world was [11] *of one lip*, but that, impure, for it was in rebellion against God. Now it shall be again of *one lip;* and that, *purified*. The purity is of faith and of life, *that they may call upon the Name of the Lord*, not as heretofore on idols, but that every tongue should confess the one true God, Father Son and Holy Ghost, in Whose Name they are baptized. This is purity of faith. To [12] *call upon the Name of the Lord Jesus* is the very title of Christian worship; *all that called upon the Name* of Jesus, the very title of Christians[13]. *To serve Him with one consent*, lit. *with one shoulder*, evenly, steadfastly, *not unequally yoked*, but all with united strength, bearing Christ's *easy yoke* and *one another's burdens, fulfilling the law of Christ*. This is purity of life. The fruit of the lips is *the sacrifice of praise*[14]. God gave back one pure language, when, on the Day of Pentecost, the Holy Spirit, the Author of purity, came down in fiery tongues upon the Apostles, teaching them and guiding them *into the whole truth*[15], and to [16] *speak to every one in his own tongue, wherein he was born, the wonderful works of God*. Thenceforth there was to be a higher unity than that of outward language. For speech is not the outer sound, but the thoughts which it conveys and embodies. The inward thought is the soul of the words. The outward confusion of Babel was to hinder oneness in evil and a worse confusion. At Pentecost, the unity restored was oneness of soul and heart, wrought by One Spirit, Whose gift is the one Faith and the

[1] עַר commonly signifies "eternity," עַד or לָעַד; also Gen. xlix. 27, Is. xxxiii. 23. (as Ch עדא &c.) "prey;" nowhere, as Ew., "attack."

[2] Is. xlix. 24, 25.

[3] Ib. liii. 10, 12.

[4] S. Matt. xii. 29.

[5] Rom. vii. 14. coll. Is. l. 1, lii. 3.

[6] S. Cyr.

[7] Acts ii. 24.

[8] See on Nah. i. 2.

[9] Lap.

[10] 1 Sam. x. 9. ויהפן יי לו לב אחר, as here אהפך אל עמים שפה ברורה.

[11] Gen. xi. 1, 6, 7, 9. The Jews also saw that this was a reversal of the confusion of Babel. "God, blessed for ever, saith, 'in this world, on account of evil concupiscence (יצר הרע man's natural corruption) men were divided into 70 languages; but in the world to come, all shall agree with one mind to call upon My Name;'" alleging this place. Tanchuma f. 5. 1. ap. Schoettg. ad loc. "R. Chija said, 'thou hearest from holy Scripture, that all hangeth from the word of the mouth;' for after the tongues were confounded, it is added, 'and God dispersed them thence' But in the time to come, what is written? 'Then will I turn &c.'" Sohar, Gen f. 58. col. 217. (Schoettg. loc. gen n. 37). Again it is said, "when the days of the Messiah shall come, boys shall know the hidden things of wisdom; for then shall all things be revealed, as is said, Then v ill I turn &c." Ib. f. 74. col. 291. Ib. ad loc. And of its fulfillment in the conversion of the world, "Who would have expected that God would raise up the tabernacle of David, which was fallen? and yet it is read, In that day I will raise &c. (Am. ix. 11). And who would have hoped that the whole world would be one band? as in, Then will I turn &c." Bereshith rabba n. 88 fin. Schoettg. loci gen. n. 18, and on Gen. xli. 44; "Why is, 'they shall praise Thee' repeated four times in Ps. lxvii. 4? He means, 'They shall praise Thee with their heart; they shall praise Thee with their mouth; they shall praise Thee with their good deeds, and they shall praise Thee with all these, as it is said, For then will I turn &c.' and the Name of the Lord is no other than the King Messiah, according to, 'and the Name of the Lord cometh from far.'" in Mart. Pug. Fid f. 327. It is also quoted with other places, as to be fulfilled in the time of the Messiah, *Tikkune Sohar* p. 60 (Schoettg. Loc. gen. n. 80), R. Moseh in Ibn Ezra, and Ibn Ezra himself, of the second temple. Kimchi "after the wars of Gog."

[12] Acts xxii. 16. Rom. x. 13.

[13] Acts ix. 14, 21, 1 Cor. i. 2.

[14] Heb. xiii. 15.

[15] S. John xvi. 13.

[16] Acts ii. 8, 11.

Before CHRIST cir. 630.

call upon the name of the
LORD, to serve him with
one † consent.
10 q From beyond the
rivers of Ethiopia my suppliants, *even* the daughter
of my dispersed, shall bring
mine offering.

† Heb. *shoulder.*
q Ps. 68. 31. Isai. 18. 1, 7. & 60. 4, &c. Mal. 1. 11. Acts 8. 27.

one Hope of our calling, in the One Lord, in Whom we are one, grafted into the one body, by our Baptism[1]. The Church, then created, is the One Holy Catholic Church diffused throughout all the world, everywhere with one rule of Faith, *the Faith once for all delivered unto the saints,* confessing one God, the Trinity in Unity, and serving Him in the one law of the Gospel with one consent. Christians, as Christians, speak the same language of Faith, and from all quarters of the world, one language of praise goes up to the One God and Father of all. "[2] God divided the tongues at Babel, lest, understanding one another, they should form a destructive unity. Through proud men tongues were divided; through humble Apostles tongues were gathered in one. The spirit of pride dispersed tongues; the Holy Spirit gathered tongues in one. For when the Holy Spirit came upon the disciples, they spake with the tongues of all, were understood by all; the dispersed tongues were gathered into one. So then, if they are yet angry and Gentiles, it is better for them to have their tongues divided. If they wish for one tongue, let them come to the Church; for in diversity of the tongues of the flesh, there is one tongue in the Faith of the heart." In whatever degree the oneness is impaired within the Church, while there is yet one Faith of the Creeds, He Alone can restore it and *turn to her a purified language,* Who first gave it to those who waited for Him. Both praise and service are perfected above, where the Blessed, with one loud voice, [3] *shall cry, Salvation to our God which sitteth upon the Throne and unto the Lamb; blessing and glory and wisdom and thanksgiving and honor and power and might be unto our God for ever and ever.* And they who *have come out of great tribulation and have washed their robes and made them white in the Blood of the Lamb,* shall be *before the Throne of God and serve Him day and night in His Temple*[4]."

10. *From beyond the rivers*[5] *of Ethiopia.* The furthest Southern people, with whom the Jews had intercourse, stand as the type of the whole world beyond. The utmost bound of the known inhabited land should not be the bound of the Gospel. The conversion of Abyssinia is one, but the narrowest fulfillment of the prophecy. The whole new world, though not in the mind of the prophet, was in the mind of Him Who spake by the prophet.

My suppliants. He names them as what they shall be when they shall come to Him. They shall come, as needy, to the Fountain of all good, asking for mercy of the unfailing Source of all mercy. He describes the very character of all who come to God through Christ. *The daughter of My dispersed*[6]. God is, in the way of Providence, the Father of all, although, by sin, alienated from Him; whence S. Paul says, *we are the offspring of God*[7]. They were *dispersed,* severed from the oneness in Him and from His house and family; yet still, looking on them as already belonging to Him, He calls them, *My dispersed,* as by Caiaphas, being high-priest, He prophesied that *Jesus should die for that nation; and not for that nation only, but that also He should gather together in one the children of God that were scattered abroad*[8].

Shall bring Mine offering[9]. The offering is the same as that which Malachi prophesies shall continue under the New Testament, which offering was to be offered to the Name of God, not in Jerusalem, but [10] *in every place from the rising of the sun unto the going down of the same.* The dark skin of the Ethiopian is the image of ingrained sin, which man could not efface or change [11]: their conversion then declares how those steeped in sin shall be cleansed from all their darkness of mind, and washed white from their sins in Baptism and beautified by the grace of God. "[12] The word of prophecy endeth in truth. For not only through the Roman empire is

[1] Eph. iv 3–6.
[2] S. Aug. in Ps. liv. 6.
[3] Rev vii. 10, 12
[4] Ib. vii. 14, 15.
[5] See Isaiah xviii. 1.
[6] Ewald conjectures בת פוט because Nahum speaks of Cush, Phut and Lubin among the allies of No-Ammon or Thebes, and renders עתרי "my incenses;" first rendering עתר (Ez. viii. 11) "*the smoke of the cloud of incense.*" But this sense is not itself proved (in both Syr and Arab. incense is עטר not עתר) nor is incense plural; nor is there any parallelism of Cush and Phut in Nahum, but Phut and Lubim are historically named as allies of No.

[7] Acts xvii. 28.
[8] S. John xi. 51, 52.
[9] It is possible also to render, "from beyond the rivers of Ethiopia, My suppliants the daughter of My dispersed shall they bring as Mine offering;" and this some have preferred on account of the like place in Isaiah lxvi. 20. "And they shall bring all your brethren for an offering unto the Lord out of all nations &c." But the word מנחה alone is common to the two passages, and the words מעבר לנהרי כוש which occur in Is. xviii. 1, and יובל שי ליי Ib. 7, make me think that this place rather was in the prophet's mind
[10] Mal. i. 11
[11] Jer xiii. 23.
[12] S. Cyr.

Before CHRIST cir. 630.

11 In that day shalt thou not be ashamed for all thy doings, wherein thou hast transgressed against me: for then I will take away out of the midst of thee them that [r] rejoice in thy pride, and thou shalt no more be haughty † because of my holy mountain.

Before CHRIST cir. 630.

r Jer. 7. 4. Mic. 3. 11. Matt. 3. 9.
† Heb. *in my holy.*

---

the Gospel preached, but it circles round the barbarous nations. And there are Churches everywhere, shepherds and teachers, guides and instructors in mysteries, and sacred altars, and the Lamb is invisibly sacrificed by holy priests among Indians too and Ethiopians. And this was said plainly by another prophet also[1], *For I am a great King, saith the Lord, and My Name is great among the heathen, and in every place incense is offered to My Name and a pure sacrifice.*"

11. *In that day shalt thou not be ashamed for all thy doings*, because God, forgiving them, will blot them out and no more remember them. This was first fulfilled in the Gospel. "[2] No one can doubt that when Christ came in the flesh, there was an amnesty and remission to all who believed. *For we are justified not by works of righteousness which we have done, but according to His great mercy.* But we have been released from shame. For *He* hath restored us to freedom of access to God, Who for our sakes arose from the dead, and for us ascended to heaven in the presence of the Father. *For Christ, our Forerunner, hath ascended for us now to appear in the presence of God.* So then He took away the guilt of all and freed believers from failures and shame." St. Peter, even in heaven, must remember his denial of our Lord, yet not so as to be *ashamed* or pained any more, since the exceeding love of God will remove all shame or pain. "[3] Mighty promise, mighty consolation. Now, before that Day comes, the Day of My Resurrection, thou wilt be ashamed and not without reason, since thou ownest by a true confession, [4] *all our righteousnesses are as filthy rags.* But at that Day it will not be so, especially when that shall be which I promise thee in the Prophets and the Psalms, [5] *There shall be a Fountain opened for sin and for uncleanness;* whence David also, exulting in good hope of the Holy Spirit, saith, [6] *Thou shalt wash me and I shall be whiter than snow.* For though he elsewhere saith, [7] *they looked unto Him and were lightened, and their faces were not ashamed,* yet in this mortal life, when the Day of My Resurrection doth not fully shine upon thee, thou art after some sort ashamed; as it is written, [8] *What fruit had ye then in those things whereof ye are now ashamed?* but that shame will bring glory, and, when that glory cometh in its place, will wholly pass away. But when the fullness of that day shall come, the fullness of My Resurrection, when the members shall rise, as the Head hath risen, will the memory of past foulness bring any confusion? Yea the very memory of the miseries will be the richest subject of singing, according to that, [9] *My song shall be alway of the loving-kindness of the Lord.*" For how shall the redeemed forget the mercies of their redemption, or yet how feel a painful shame even of the very miseries, out of which they were redeemed by the fullness of the overstreaming Love of God?

For then will I take away out of the midst of thee them that rejoice in thy pride. [*those of thee who exult in pride* [10].] All confusion shall cease, because all pride shall cease, the parent of sin and confusion. The very gift of God becomes to the carnal a source of pride. Pride was to the Jew also the great hindrance to the reception of the Gospel. He made his *boast of the law*, yea, in God Himself, that he *knew His will*, and was *a guide of others* [11], and so was the more indignant, that the heathen was made equal to him, and that he too was called to repentance and faith in Christ. So, *going about to establish his own righteousness, he did not submit himself to the righteousness of God,* but shut himself out from the faith and grace and salvation of Christ, and rejected Himself. So, [3] *thy pride* may be the pride in being the people of God, and having Abraham for their father. *And thou shalt no more be haughty* [12] *in My holy mountain,* "but thou shalt stand in the great and everlasting abiding-place of humility, knowing perfectly, that thou now 'knowest in part' only, and confessest truly that no one ever could or can

---

[1] Mal. i. 11. [2] S. Cyr. [3] Rup.
[4] Is. lxiv. 6. [5] Zech. xiii. 1.
[6] Ps. li. 7. [7] Ib. xxxiv. 5.
[8] Rom. vi. 21. [9] Ps. lxxxix. 1.
[10] It cannot be "those that exult in thy highness;" for גאוה, as used of man, always has a bad sense, "self-exaltation."
[11] Rom. ii. 17, 18–20, 23.
[12] As in E. M., not, *because of.* גבה, as a mental quality, mostly occurs with לב and is used in a bad sense of high-mindedness=pride; Ps. cxxxi. 1, (David's), Pr. xviii. 12, Ez. xxviii. 2, 5, 17, 2 Chr. xxvi. 16, xxxii. 25; absol. in a bad sense, Is. iii. 16, Jer. xiii. 15, Ez. xvi. 50. It is used of eminence given by God, Job xxxvi. 7, and of the Messiah as exalted by Him, Is. lii. 13. Once only, 2 Chr. xvii. 6, גבה לבו is used in a good sense of Jehoshaphat, that, being exalted by God, "his heart was elevated in the ways of the law." The form לְגָבְהָה is like the inf. in Ex. xxix. 29, xxx. 18, xxxvi. 2, Lev. xv. 32, &c.

Before CHRIST cir. 630.

12 I will also leave in the midst of thee [s]an afflicted and poor people, and they shall trust in the name of the LORD.

13 [t]The remnant of Israel [u]shall not do iniquity, [x]nor speak lies; neither shall a deceitful tongue be found in their mouth: for

[s] Isai. 14. 32. Zech. 11. 11. Matt. 5. 3. 1 Cor. 1. 27, 28. Jam. 2. 5.

[t] Mic. 4. 7. ch. 2. 7.
[u] Isai. 60. 21.
[x] Isai. 63. 8. Rev. 14. 5.

by his own works be justified in the sight of God. [1] *For all have sinned and come short of the glory of God.*" Pride which is ever offensive to God, is yet more hideous in a holy place or a holy office, *in* Mount Sion where the temple was or in the Christian priesthood.

12. And *I will also leave* (*over*, as a remnant, it is still the same heavy prophecy, that *a remnant* only *shall be saved*[2]) *an afflicted and poor people.* Priests, (except that *great company* who *were obedient to the faith*[3]) scribes, lawyers, Pharisees, Sadducees were taken away; and there remained "[4] the people of the land," the [5] *unlearned and ignorant*, [6] *the weak things of the world and the things despised* who bore the very title of their Master[7], *the poor and needy; poor in Spirit*[8]; poor also in outward things, since *they who had lands, sold them* and they *had all things common*[9]. They were afflicted above measure outwardly in the [10]persecutions, *reproaches, spoiling of* their *goods*, stripes, deaths, which they endured for Christ's sake. They knew too their own poverty; "[11] knowing themselves to be sinners, and that they were justified only by faith in Jesus Christ." When the rest were cast out *of the midst of her*, these should be left *in the midst of her* (the words stand in contrast with one another) in the bosom of the Church. *And they shall trust in the name of the Lord.* "As they looked to be justified only in the Name of Christ," and "[12] trusted in the grace and power of God alone, not in any power or wisdom or eloquence or riches of this world, they converted the world to a faith above nature." "[13] Conformed in this too to Christ, Who for our sakes became poor and almost neglected both His divine glory and the supereminence of His nature, to subject Himself to the condition of a servant. So then those instructed in His laws after His example, think humbly of themselves. They became most exceedingly loved of God, and chiefly the divine disciples, who were set as lights of the world."

13. *The remnant of Israel*, the same poor people, the *true Israel* of whom God said, *I leave over* (the word is the same) *a poor people*, few, compared with the rest who were blinded; of whom the Lord said, *I know whom I have chosen*[14]. These *shall not do iniquity nor speak lies.* "[13]This is a spiritual adorning, a most beautiful coronet of glorious virtues. For where meekness and humility are and the desire of righteousness, and the tongue unlearns vain words and sinful speech, and is the instrument of strict truth, there dawns a bright and most perfect virtue. And this beseems those who are in Christ. For the beauty of piety is not seen in the Law, but gleams forth in the power of Evangelic teaching."

Our Lord said of Nathanael, [15] *Behold an Israelite indeed, in whom is no guile*, and to the Apostles, [16] *I send you forth as sheep among wolves; be ye therefore wise as serpents and harmless as doves;* and of the first Christians it is said, [17] *they, continuing daily with one accord in the temple, and breaking bread from house to house did eat their meat with gladness and singleness of heart, praising God and having favor with all the people.* This is the character of Christians, as such, and it was at first fulfilled; [18] *whosoever is born of God, doth not commit sin;* [19] *whosoever is born of God sinneth not; but he that is begotten of God keepeth himself, and that wicked one toucheth him not.* An Apologist, at the close of the second century, could appeal to the Roman Emperor[20], that no Christian was found among their criminals, "unless it be only as a Christian, or, if he be anything else, he is forthwith no longer a Christian. We alone then are innocent! What wonder if this be so, of necessity? And truly of necessity it is so. Taught "no humility without humiliation," is become a Christian proverb.

[1] Rom. iii. 23.
[2] Ib. ix. 27. See ab. on Mic. ii. 12. p. 36.
[3] Acts vi. 7.
[4] עם הארץ the uneducated, *this people that knoweth not the law* (S. John vii. 49), "one in whom there are moral not intellectual excellences." Rambam in Buxt. Lex. Talm. col. 1626.
[5] Acts iv. 13. [6] 1 Cor. i. 27, 28. [7] Ps. xli. 1.
[8] עני is not simply "poor," nor ענו simply "meek." עני is one "afflicted," in whom affliction has produced its fruits; ענו. one "meek" but in whom patience has been tried and perfected; as the same class are meant by the πτωχοὶ, S. Luke vi. 20, and the πτωχοὶ τῷ πνεύματι, S. Matt. v. 3; and,
[9] Acts ii. 44, 45, iv. 32, 35.
[10] Acts viii. 1, ix. 2, 13, 14. xii. 1, 2, xiii. 50, xiv. 5. 22. xxii. &c. Rom. viii. 17, 35, 36. xii. 14, 1 Cor. ix. 19, 2 Cor. i. 8, 9, xii. 10, 2 Thess. i. 4, 2 Tim. iii. 11, 12, Heb. x. 32–34, S James ii. 6, 7, 1 S. Pet. i. 6, 7. iv. 13, Rev. i. 9. vi. 9 &c.
[11] Rup. [12] Dion. [13] S. Cyr. [14] S. John xiii. 18.
[15] Ib. i. 47. [16] S. Mat. x. 16. [17] Acts ii. 46, 47.
[18] 1 S. John iii. 9. [19] Ib. v. 18.
[20] Tert. Apol. c. 44, 45. See also Justin M. i. n. 34. S. Athenagoras, n. 2, Minutius Felix p. 333. Theodoret de cur. Græc. aff. Disp. xii. circ. med. p. 1021 sqq. ed Schultz; Lactant. v. 9. quoted Ib.

Before CHRIST cir. 630.

y Ezek. 34. 28. Mic. 4. 4. & 7. 14.
z Isai. 12. 6. & 54. 1. Zech. 2. 10. & 9. 9.

[y] they shall feed and lie down, and none shall make *them* afraid.

14 ¶ [z] Sing, O daughter of Zion; shout, O Israel; be glad and rejoice with all the heart, O daughter of Jerusalem.

Before CHRIST cir. 630.

innocence by God, we both know it perfectly, as being revealed by a perfect Master; and we keep it faithfully, as being committed to us by an Observer, Who may not be despised." "[1] Being so vast a multitude of men, almost the greater portion of every state, we live silently and modestly, known perhaps more as individuals than as a body, and to be known by no other sign than the reformation of our former sins." Now in the Church, which "our earth dimm'd eyes behold," we can but say, as in regard to the cessation of war[2] under the Gospel, that God's promises are sure on His part, that still [3] *they that are Christ's have crucified the flesh with the affections and lusts*, that the Gospel is [4] *a power of God unto salvation*, that *the* [5] *preaching of the Cross is, unto us which are saved, the power of God;* [6] *unto them that are called, Christ is the power of God and the wisdom of God;* that those who will, [7] *are kept by God through faith unto salvation;* but that now too [8] *they are not all Israel, which are of Israel*, and that [9] *the faithlessness of man does not make the faith of God of none effect.* "[10] The Church of God is universally holy in respect of all, by institutions and administrations of sanctity; the same Church is really holy in this world, in relation to all godly persons contained in it, by a real infused sanctity; the same is farther yet at the same time perfectly holy in reference to the saints departed and admitted to the presence of God; and the same Church shall hereafter be most completely holy in the world to come, when all the members, actually belonging to it, shall be at once perfected in holiness and completed in happiness." Most fully shall this be fulfilled in the Resurrection. "[11] O blessed day of the Resurrection, in whose fullness no one will sin in word or deed! O great and blessed reward to every soul, which, although it hath now *done iniquity* and *spoken falsehood*, yet willeth not to do it further! Great and blessed reward, that he shall now receive such immovableness, as no longer to be able to do iniquity or speak falsehood, since the blessed soul, through the Spirit of everlasting love inseparably united with God its Creator, shall now no more be capable of an evil will!"

For they shall feed; on the hidden manna, "[12] nourished most delicately by the Holy Spirit with inward delights, and spiritual food, the bread of life." In the things of the body too was [13] *distribution made unto every man according as he had need. And they shall lie down* in the green pastures where He foldeth them; *and none shall make them afraid*, "[7] for they were ready to suffer and to die for the Name of the Lord Jesus [14]. [15] *They departed from the presence of the council rejoicing that they were counted worthy to suffer shame for His Name.* Before the Resurrection and the sending of the Holy Ghost, how great was the fearfulness, unsteadfastness, weakness of the disciples; how great, after the infusion of the Holy Spirit, was their constancy and imperturbableness, it is delightsome to estimate in their Acts," when they [16] *bare His Name before the Gentiles and kings, and the children of Israel*, and he who had been afraid of a little maid, said to the High Priest, [17] *We ought to obey God rather than men.* "[18] When Christ the Good Shepherd Who laid down His life for His sheep, shone upon us, we are fed in gardens and pastured among lilies, and lie down in folds; for we are folded in Churches and holy shrines, no one scaring or spoiling us, no wolf assailing nor lion trampling on us, no robber breaking through, no one invading us, to steal and kill and destroy; but we abide in safety and participation of every good, being in charge of Christ the Saviour of all."

14. *Sing, O daughter of Sion; shout, O Israel; be glad and rejoice with all the heart, O daughter of Jerusalem.* Very remarkable throughout all these verses is the use of the sacred number three, secretly conveying to the thoughtful soul the thought of Him, Father Son and Holy Ghost, the Holy and Undivided Trinity by Whose operation these things shall be. Threefold is the description of their being freed from sins; 1) they shall *not do iniquity*, 2) *nor speak lies*, 3) *neither shall a deceitful tongue be found in their mouth.* Threefold their blessedness; They shall 1) *feed*, 2) *lie down*, 3) *none make them afraid.* Threefold the exhortation to joy here; "[19] *Sing* to God the Father; *shout* to God the Son; *be glad and rejoice* in God the Holy Ghost, which Holy Trinity is One God, from Whom thou hast received it that

1 Id. ad Scap. n. 2, p. 145. Oxf. Tr.
2 See ab. on Mic. iv. 3 pp. 56, 57.
3 Gal. v. 24. See Dr. Pusey's Sermon, "The Gospel, the power of God." Lenten Sermons, pp. 300–321.
4 Rom. i. 16. 5 1 Cor. i. 18. 6 Ib. 24.

7 1 S. Pet. i. 5. 8 Rom. ix. 6. 9 Ib. iii. 3.
10 Bp. Pearson on the Creed, Art. ix.
11 Rup. 12 Dion.
13 Acts iv. 35. 14 Ib. xxi. 13. 15 Ib. v. 41.
16 Acts ix. 15. 17 Ib. v. 29. 18 S. Cyril. 19 Rup.

Before CHRIST cir. 630.

15 The LORD hath taken away thy judgments, he hath cast out thine enemy: [a]the king of Israel, *even* the LORD, [b]*is* in the midst of thee: thou shalt not see evil any more.

[a] John 1. 49.

[b] ver. 5, 17. Ezek. 48. 35. Rev. 7. 15. & 21. 3, 4.

thou art 1) *the daughter of Zion*, 2) *Israel*, 3) *the daughter of Jerusalem; the daughter of Zion* by faith, *Israel* by hope, *Jerusalem* by charity." And this hidden teaching of that holy mystery is continued; [1] *The Lord*, God the Father, *hath taken away thy judgments; He* God the Son, *hath cast out* (*cleared quite away*) *thine enemy; the king of Israel, the Lord*, the Holy Ghost, *is in the midst of thee!* The promise is threefold, 1) *thou shalt not see evil any more;* 2) *fear thou not;* 3) *let not thine hands be slack.* The love of God is threefold. 1) *He will rejoice over thee with joy;* 2) *He will rest in His love;* 3) *He will joy over thee with singing.* Again the words in these four verses are so framed as to be *ful*-filled in the end. All in this life are but shadows of that fullness. First, whether the Church or the faithful soul, she is summoned by all her names, *daughter of Zion* ("the thirsty" athirst for God) *Israel* ("Prince with God") *Jerusalem* ("City of Peace"). By all she is called to the fullest joy in God with every expression and every feeling. *Sing;* it is the inarticulate, thrilling, trembling burst of joy; *shout;* again the inarticulate yet louder swell of joy, a trumpet-blast; and then too, deep within, *be glad*, the calm even joy of the inward soul; *exult*, the triumph of the soul which cannot contain itself for joy; and this, *with the whole heart*, no corner of it not pervaded with joy. The ground of this is the complete removal of every evil, and the full Presence of God.

15. *The Lord hath taken away thy judgments;* her own, because brought upon her by her sins. But when God takes away the chastisements in mercy, He removes and forgives the sin too. Else, to remove *the judgments* only, would be to abandon the sinner. *He hath cast out*, lit. *cleared quite away* [2], as a man clears away all hindrances, all which stands in the way, so that there should be none whatever left—*thine enemy;* the one enemy, from whom every hindrance to our salvation comes, as He saith, [3] *Now shall the prince of this world be cast out. The King of Israel, even the Lord*, Christ the Lord, *is in the midst of thee*, of Whom it is said, [4] *He that sitteth on the throne shall dwell among them*, and Who Himself saith, [5] *Lo I am with you always unto the end of the world.* [6] *Where two or three are gathered together in My Name, there am I in the midst of you.* He Who had removed *from the midst of her* the proud, Who had left *in the midst of her* those with whom He dwelleth, shall Himself dwell *in the midst of her* in mercy, as He had before in judgment [7]. He cleanseth the soul for His indwelling, and so dwelleth in the mansion which He had prepared for Himself. *Thou shalt not see evil any more.* For even the remains of evil, while we are yet in the flesh, are overruled, and [8] *work together to good to those who love God.* They cannot separate between the soul and Christ. Rather, He is nearer to her in them. We are bidden to [9] *count it all joy when we fall into divers temptations*, for all sorrows are but medicine from a father's hand. "[10] And truly our way to eternal joy is to suffer here with Christ, and our door to enter into eternal life is gladly to die with Christ, that we may rise again from death and dwell with Him in everlasting life." So in the Revelation, it is first said that God should dwell with His people, and then that all pain shall cease. [11] *Behold the tabernacle of God is with men, and He will dwell with them and be their God. And God shall wipe all tears from their eyes; and there shall be no more death, neither sorrow nor crying, neither shall there be any more pain; for the former things are passed away.* "[12] In the inmost meaning of the words, he could not but bid her rejoice and be exceeding glad and rejoice with her whole heart, her sins being done away through Christ. For the holy and spiritual Zion, the Church, the multitude of believers, is justified in Christ Alone, and we are saved by Him and from Him, escaping the harms of our invisible enemies, and having in the midst of us the King and God of all, Who appeared in our likeness, the Word from God the Father, through Whom we see not evil, i. e. are freed from all who could do us evil. For He is the worker of our acceptableness, our peace, our wall, the bestower of incorruption, the dispenser of crowns, Who lighteneth the assaults of devils, Who giveth us to [13] *tread on serpents and scorpions and all the power of the enemy*—through Whom we are in good hope of immortality and life, adoption and glory, through Whom we shall not see evil any more."

[1] v. 15.
[2] Beside this place, the word is used of "the clearing of a house," Gen. xxiv. 31, Lev. xiv. 36; "a way," Is. xl. 3, lvii. 14, lxii. 10; Mal. iii. 1; "clearing ground," Ps. lxxx. 10.
[3] S. John xii. 31.
[4] Rev. vii. 15.
[5] S. Matt. xxviii. 20.
[6] Ib. xviii. 20.
[7] Verses 11, 12, 15, 5.
[8] Rom. viii. 28.
[9] S. James i. 2.
[10] Exhort. in Visit. of the sick.
[11] Rev. xxi. 3, 4.
[12] S. Cyril.
[13] S. Luke x. 19.

Before CHRIST cir. 630.

16 In that day [e] it shall
be said to Jerusalem, Fear
thou not: *and to* Zion,
[d] Let not thine hands be
|| slack.
17 The LORD thy God
[e] in the midst of thee *is*
mighty; he will save, [f] he
will rejoice over thee with
joy; † he will rest in his
love, he will joy over thee
with singing.

[c] Is. 35. 3, 4.
[d] Heb. 12. 12.
|| Or, *faint.*
[e] ver. 15.
[f] Deut. 30. 9. Isai. 62. 5. & 65. 19. Jer. 32. 41.
† Heb. *he will be silent.*

16. *In that day it shall be said to Jerusalem, Fear thou not;* for [1] *perfect love casteth out fear;* whence he saith, [2] *Fear not, little flock; it is your Father's good pleasure to give you the kingdom.* Who then and what should the Church or the faithful soul fear, since *mightier is He that is in her, than he that is in the world? And to Zion, Let not thine hands be slack,* through faint-heartedness[3], but work with all thy might; be ready to do or bear anything; since Christ worketh with, in, by thee, and [4] *in due time we shall reap, if we faint not.*

17. *The Lord thy God in the midst of thee is mighty; He will save.* What *can* He then not do for thee, since He is Almighty? What *will* He not do for thee, since *He will save?* Whom then should we fear? [5] *If God be for us, who can be against us?* But then was He especially *in the midst of* us, when God [6] *the Word became flesh and dwelt among us; and we beheld His Glory, the Glory as of the Only-Begotten of the Father, full of grace and Truth.* Thenceforth He ever is in the midst of His own. He with the Father and the Holy Spirit [7] *come unto them and make Their abode with them,* so that they are *the temple of God. He will save,* as He saith, [8] *My Father is greater than all, and no man is able to pluck them out of My Father's hand. I and My Father are One.* Of the same time of the Christ, Isaiah saith almost in the same words; [9] *Strengthen ye the weak hands and confirm the feeble knees, Say to them that are of a feeble heart, Be strong, fear not, behold your God will come, He will come and save you;* and of the Holy Trinity, [10] *He will save us.*

He will rejoice over thee with joy. Love, joy, peace in man are shadows of that which is in God, by Whom they are created in man. Only in God they exist undivided, uncreated. Hence God speaks after the manner of men, of that which truly is in God. God joyeth "with an uncreated joy" over the works of His Hands or the objects of His Love, as man joyeth over the object of *his* love. So Isaiah saith [11], *As the bridegroom rejoiceth over the bride, so shall thy God rejoice over thee.* As with uncreated love the Father resteth in good pleasure in His Well-beloved Son, so [12] *God is well-pleased with the sacrifices of loving deeds,* and, [13] *the Lord delighteth in thee;* and, [14] *I will rejoice in Jerusalem and joy in My people;* and, [15] *the Lord will again rejoice over thee for good.* And so in a two-fold way God meeteth the longing of the heart of man. The soul, until it hath found God, is evermore seeking some love to fill it, and can find none, since the love of God Alone can content it. Then too it longeth to be loved, even as it loveth. God tells it, that every feeling and expression of human love may be found in Him, Whom if any love, he only [16] *loveth Him, because He first loved us.* Every inward and outward expression or token of love are heaped together, to express the love of Him Who broodeth and as it were yearneth *over* (it is twice repeated) His own whom He loveth. Then too He loveth thee as He biddeth thee to love Him; and since the love of man cannot be like the love of the Infinite God, He here pictures His own love in the words of man's love, to convey to his soul the oneness wherewith love unites her unto God. He here echoes in a manner the joy of the Church, to which He had called her[17], in words the self-same or meaning the same. We have *joy* here for *joy* there; *singing* or the unuttered unutterable jubilee of the heart, which cannot utter in words its joy and love, and joys and loves the more in its inmost depths because it cannot utter it. A shadow of the unutterable, because Infinite Love of God, and this repeated thrice; as being the eternal love of the Ever-blessed Trinity. This love and joy the Prophet speaks of, as an exuberant joy, one which boundeth within the inmost self, and again is wholly *silent in His love,* as the deepest, tenderest, most yearning love broods over the object of its love, yet is held still in silence by the very depth of its love; and then, again, breaks forth in outward motion, and leaps for joy, and uttereth what it cannot form in words; for truly the love of God in its unspeakable love and joy is past belief, past utterance, past thought. "[18] Truly that joy wherewith *He will be silent in His love,* that exultation wherewith *He will joy over thee with singing,* [19] *Eye hath not seen nor*

[1] S. John iv. 18. [2] S. Luke xii. 32.
[3] See Heb. xii. 12. [4] Gal. vi. 9.
[5] Rom. viii. 31. [6] S. John i. 14.
[7] Ib. xiv. 23. [8] Ib. x. 29, 30.
[9] Is. xxxv. 3, 4. [10] Ib. xxxiii. 22.

[11] Ib. lxii. 5. [12] Heb. xiii. 16.
[13] Is. lxii. 4. [14] Ib. lxv. 19.
[15] Deut. xxx. 9. [16] 1 S. John iv. 19.
[17] Verse 14.
[18] Rup. [19] 1 Cor. ii. 9.

Before CHRIST cir. 630.

18 I will gather *them*
that [g] *are* sorrowful for the
solemn assembly, *who* are
of thee, *to whom* † the reproach of it *was* a burden.
19 Behold, at that time
I will undo all that afflict
thee: and I will save her
that [h] halteth, and gather
her that was driven out;
and † I will get them praise
and fame in every land
† where they have been
put to shame.

Before CHRIST cir. 630.

g Lam. 2. 6.
† Heb. *the burden upon it was reproach.*
h Ezek. 34. 16. Mic. 4. 6, 7.
† Heb. *I will set them for a praise.*
† Heb. *of their shame.*

ear heard, neither hath it entered into the heart of man." The Hebrew word[1] also contains the meaning, "He in His love shall make no mention of past sins[2], He shall not bring them up against thee, shall not upbraid thee, yea, shall not remember them." It also may express the still, unvarying love of the Unchangeable God. And again how the very silence of God, when He seemeth not to hear, as He did not seem to hear S. Paul, is a very fruit of His love. Yet that entire forgiveness of sins, and that seeming absence are but ways of shewing His love. Hence God speaks of His very love itself, *He will be silent in His love*, as, before and after, *He will rejoice, He will joy over thee.*

18–21. In these verses still continuing the number "three," the prophecy closes with the final reversal of all which, in this imperfect state of things, seems turned upside down, when those who now mourn shall be comforted, they who now bear reproach and shame shall have glory, and those who now afflict the people of God shall be undone.

18. *I will gather them that are sorrowful*[3] *for*[4] *the solemn assembly*, in which they were to *rejoice*[5] before God and which in their captivity God made to cease[6]. *They were of thee*, the true Israel who were [7] *grieved for the affliction of Joseph; to whom the reproach of it was a burden* [rather[8], *on whom reproach was laid*]: for this *reproach of Christ is greater riches than the treasures of Egypt*, and such shall inherit the blessing, [9] *Blessed are ye, when men shall hate you, and when they shall separate you from their company, and shall reproach you and cast out your name as evil, for the Son of Man's sake; rejoice ye in that day, and leap for joy; for, behold your reward is great in heaven.*

19. *Behold, at that time I will undo* [lit. *I deal with*[10]]. While God punisheth not, He seemeth to sit still[11], be silent[12], asleep[13]. Then He shall act, He shall *deal* according to their deserts with *all*, evil men or devils, *that afflict thee*, His Church. The prophecy looked for a larger fulfillment than the destruction of Jerusalem, since the Romans who, in God's Hands, avenged the blood of His Saints, themselves were among those who *afflicted her*. *And will save her*, the flock or sheep *that halteth*[14], "[15] imperfect in virtue and with trembling faith," *and gather*, like a good and tender shepherd[16], *her that was driven out;* scattered and dispersed through persecutions. All infirmities within shall be healed; all troubles without, removed.

And I will get them praise and fame [lit. *I will make them a praise and a name*] *in every land where they have been put to shame*[17]. Throughout the whole world have they been [18] *the offscourings of all things;* throughout the whole world should their praise be, as it is said, [19] *Thou shalt make them princes in all lands.* One of themselves saith[20], *Ye see your calling, brethren, how that not many wise men after the flesh, not many mighty, not many noble, are called. But God hath chosen the foolish things of the world to confound the wise; and God hath chosen the weak things of the world to confound the things which are*

[1] יחריש.

[2] Jer. xxxi. 34, xxxiii. 8, Mic. vii. 18.

[3] This is the common meaning of the root יגה, though not so frequent in the verb as in nouns, and 5 out of the 8 cases are in Lam. i. 4 (where the same form נוּגוֹת, Nif. occurs), 12. iii. 32, 33, the remaining being, this place, Job xix. 2, Is. li. 23. The other sense "removed" (even if הֻגָה 2 Sam. xx. 13, implies a פ׳ in this sense) comes to the same general meaning, though with less force. The Arab ונג׳, iv. is wrongly applied (e. g. Ges. Thes. p. 564) as "procul a se removit." It is simply "abstained from it," "refused one's self."

[4] מן is used of the ultimate cause. (See Ges. Thes. s. v. 2) b. p. 802.

[5] Lev. xxiii. 40. Deut. xii. 12, 18. xvi. 11, xxvii. 7.

[6] Lam. i. 4. ii. 6.

[7] Amos vi. 6.

[8] As in Ps. xv. 3, וחרפה לא נשא על קרבו, the construction being like מסתר פנים ממנו, Is. liii. 3.

[9] S. Luke vi. 22, 23.

[10] as Ru. ii. 19. in a good sense; Ez. vii. 27. xvii. 17, xxiii. 25, in a bad; אותו, אותם אותך, being probably for אִתָּם &c.

[11] Is. xviii. 4.

[12] Hab. i. 13.

[13] Ps. xliv. 23.

[14] See Micah iv. 6, 7.

[15] Dion.

[16] See Is. xl. 11.

[17] The article is inserted in a way very unusual and probably emphatic. Without it the words would mean, as in the E. V. "in every land of their shame." But it makes the meaning of the first words, בכל הארץ, complete in itself; and they mean, *in the whole earth.* בשתם then is probably in apposition, *in the whole earth, their shame*, i. e. the scene of *their shame;* comp. the construction הארון הברית Jos. iii. 14. 17 and those Deut. viii. 15. 1 Kgs iv. 13; and "Daniel the Prophet" p. 476. In the next verse, הארץ is undoubtedly "the earth."

[18] 1 Cor. iv. 13.

[19] Ps. xlv. 16.

[20] 1 Cor. i. 26–28.

Before CHRIST cir. 630.

20 At that time [1] will I bring you *again*, even in the time that I gather you: for I will make you a name and a praise among all people of the earth, when I turn back your captivity before your eyes, saith the LORD.

Isai. 11. 12. & 27. 12. & 56. 8. Ezek. 28. 25. & 34. 13. & 37. 21. Amos 9. 14.

mighty; and base things of this world, and things which are despised, hath God chosen, yea, and things which are not, to bring to nought things that are. "[1] These He maketh a praise and a name there, where they were without name and dispraised, confounding by them and bringing to nought those wise and strong and mighty, in whose sight they were contemptible."

20. *At that time will I bring you in* i. e. into the one fold, the one Church, the one *Household of God, even in the time that I gather you.* "That time" is the whole time of the Gospel; the one *day of salvation,* in which all who shall ever be gathered, shall be brought into the new Jerusalem. These words were fulfilled, when, at our Lord's first Coming, the remnant, the true Israel, those *ordained to eternal life* were brought in. It shall be fulfilled again, when "the fullness of the Gentiles shall be *come in,* and so all Israel shall be saved[2]." It shall most perfectly be fulfilled at the end, when there shall be no going out of those once *brought in,* and those who have gathered others into the Church, shall be *a name and a praise among all people of the earth,* those whom God hath [3] *redeemed out of every tribe and tongue and people and nation,* shining like stars for ever and ever.

When I turn back your captivity: "[1] that conversion, then begun, now perfected, when the dead shall rise and they shall be placed on the right hand, soon to receive the kingdom prepared for them from the foundation of the world. O mighty spectacle of the reversed captivity of those once captives; mighty wonder at their present blessedness, as they review the misery of their past captivity!" *Before your eyes,* so that we shall see what we now believe and hope for, the end of all our sufferings, chastisements, losses, achings of the heart, the fullness of our Redemption. That which our eyes have looked for, *our eyes shall behold and not another,* the everliving God as HE IS, face to Face; *saith the Lord,* Who is the Truth Itself, all Whose words will be fulfilled. [4] *Heaven and earth shall pass away, but My Words shall not pass away,* saith He Who is *God blessed for ever.* And so the Prophet closes in the thought of Him, Whose Name is I AM, the Unchangeable, the everlasting Rest and Centre of those who, having been once captives and halting and scattered among the vanities of the world, turn to Him, to Whom be glory and thanksgiving for ever and ever. Amen.

[1] Rup. [2] Rom. xi. 25, 26. [3] Rev. v. 9. [4] S. Mark xiii. 31.

THE MOABITE STONE. See pp. 263, 264.

I MESHA, son of Chemosh-gad, king of Moab the Dibonite. My father reigned over Moab thirty years, and I reigned after my father; and I made this shrine to Chemosh in Korchoh, a shr[ine of deli]verance, because he saved me from all [[1]] and because he let me look upon all who hate me, Om[r]i king of Israel; and he afflicted Moab many days, for Chemosh was wroth with his la[n]d; and his son succeeded him, and he too said, I will afflict Moab. In my days said [*Chemosh*[2]], and I will look upon him and upon his house, and Israel perisheth with an everlasting destruction. And Omri took possession of the land of Moh-deba and there dwelt in it [[2] Israel in *his days and in*] the days of his son, forty years; [*and looked*] on it Chemosh in my days, and I built Baal-Meon and I made in it the ditch [?] and I [built] Kiriathan. And the men of Gad dwelt in the land of [Atar]oth from time immemorial, and the kin[g of I]srael built for him A[ta]roth and I warred against the city; and I took it and I slew all the mi[ghty men] of the city, for the well-pleasing of Chemosh and Moab; and I took captive thence the [ ] and [dr]agged it [or them] before Chemosh in Kiriath and I made to dwell in it the men of Siran, and the men of Macharath. And Chemosh said to me, Go take Nebo against Israel [and I] went by night and I fought against it from the break of the morning to midday and I took it, and I slew the whole of it, seven thousand; [ ] the honorable women [and mai]dens, for to Ashtar Chemosh [I] dedicated [them] and I took thence [ves]sels of Yhvh and I dragged them before Chemosh. And the king of Israel buil[t] Yahats, and dwelt in it when he warred with me; and Chemosh drove him from [my] f[ace and] I took of Moab 200 men, all its chiefs and I took them against Yahats and took it to add to

[1] The stone has השלכן, whose meaning is conjectural. Nöldeke conjectures המלכן "the kings."

[2] Schlottman's conjecture. Likely conjectures I have put in [ ]; mere guess-work I have omitted.

Dibon. I built Korchoh the wall of the forest, and the wall of Ophel[1] and I built the gates thereof, and I built the towers thereof, and I built the king's house, and I made prisons for the gui[lt]y in the mi[dst] of the city; and there was no cistern within the city, in Korchoh, and I said to all the people, make yourselves every man a cistern in his house, and I cut the cutting for Korchoh by m[en] of Israel. I built [A]roer and I made the high road[2] at the Arnon. I built Beth-Bamoth, for it was destroyed. I built Bezer, for [it was] forsa[ken] me[n] of Dibon fifty; for all Dibon was obedience, and I reig[ned] from Bikran which I added to the land and I buil[t]——and Beth Diblathan and Beth-Baal-Meon and I took there the—of the land and Horonan dwelt in it————[and] Chemosh said to me, Go fight against Horonan and I it—Chemosh in my days and on [I] made

[1] חומת העפל occurs of Jerusalem, Neh. iii. 27.

[2] המסלת lit. "the way cast up" cannot possibly be a way over the river.

INTRODUCTION

TO

THE PROPHET

HAGGAI.

Haggai[a] is the eldest of the three-fold band, to whom, after the Captivity, the word of God came, and by whom He consecrated the beginnings of this new condition of the chosen people. He gave them these prophets, connecting their spiritual state after their return with that before the Captivity, not leaving them wholly desolate, nor Himself without witness. He withdrew them about 100 years after, but some 420 years before Christ came, leaving His people to long the more for Him, of Whom all the prophets spake. Haggai himself seems to have almost finished his earthly course, before he was called to be a prophet; and in four months his office was closed. He speaks as one who had seen the first house in its glory[b], and so was probably among the very aged men, who were the links between the first and the last, and who laid the foundation of the house in tears[c]. After the first two months[d] of his office, Zechariah, in early youth, was raised up to carry on his message; yet after one brief prophecy was again silent, until the aged prophet had ended the words which God gave him. Yet in this brief space he first stirred up the people in one month to rebuild the temple[e], prophesied of its glory through the presence of Christ[f], yet taught that the presence of what was holy sanctified not the unholy[g], and closes in Him Who, when Heaven and earth shall be shaken, shall abide, and they whom God hath chosen in Him[h].

It has been the wont of critics, in whose eyes the Prophets were but poets[i], to speak of the style of Haggai as "tame, destitute of life and power," shewing "[j] a marked decline in" what they call "prophetic inspiration." The style of the sacred writers is, of course, conformed to their mission. Prophetic descriptions of the future are but incidental to the mission of Haggai. Preachers do not speak in poetry, but set before the people their faults or their duties in vivid earnest language. Haggai sets before the people vividly their negligence and its consequences; he arrests their attention by his concise questions; at one time retorting their excuses[k]; at another asking them abruptly, in God's name, to say why their troubles came[l]. Or he puts a matter of the law to

[a] His name is explained by S. Jerome "festive." But although there are Prop. Names with *ai* which are Adjectives, as בַּרְזִלַּי, שֵׁשַׁי (Ezr. ix. 40. תַּלְמַי and שָׁשַׁי are foreign names) יְשִׁישַׁי, the termination *ai* is more frequently an abbreviation of the Name of God, which enters so largely into Hebrew names, as indeed we have חֲנַנְיָה 1 Chr. vi. 15. And this occurs not only, when the first part of the word is a verb, אֲחַסְבַּי, יֶהְדַּי, יַחְמַי, יַעְנַי, יַעֲשַׂי, אַחְזַי, יִשְׁמְרַי, יְרִיבַי, יְאַתְרַי, (as Köhler observes p. 2.) but when it is a noun, as מַתְּנַי, הִדַּי, אֲמִתַּי, שַׁלְמַי, צִלְּתַי, (coll. מַתַּנְיָה, and מַתַּנְיָהוּ) שִׁמְשַׁי Ezr. iv. פְּעֻלְּתַי (1 Chr. xxvi. 5.) perhaps שַׁבְּתַי, שִׁטְרַי or again אִתַּי.

[b] ii. 3.

[c] Ezr. iii. 12.

[d] The prophecies of Haggai and Zechariah are thus intertwined. Haggai prophesies in the 6th and 7th months of the 2d year of Darius Hystaspis, B. C. 520.) Hagg. i. 1. ii. 1) Zechariah first prophesies in the 8th month (Zech. i. 1.). Haggai resumes at the close of the 9th and there ends (ii. 10, 20). On the same day in the 11th month, the series of visions were given to Zechariah. (Zech. i. 7.)

[e] c. i.

[f] ii. 1–9.

[g] Ib. 12.

[h] Ib. 20–23.

[i] Eichhorn, De Wette, Bertholdt, Gesenius (Gesh. d. Hebr. Spr. p. 26.), Herzfeldt, (Gesch. d. Volkes Israel ii. 21) Stähelin.

[j] Dr. Davidson iii. 314.

[k] i. 4.

[l] i. 9.

the priests, that they may draw the inference, before he does it himself[m]. Or he asks them, what human hope had they[n], before he tells them of the Divine. Or he asks them (what was in their heart), "Is not this house poor[o]?" before he tells them of the glory in store for it. At one time he uses heaped and condensed antitheses[p], to set before them one thought; at another he enumerates, one by one, how the visitation of God fell upon all they had[q], so that there seemed to be no end to it. At another, he uses a conciseness, like S. John Baptist's cry, *Repent ye, for the kingdom of heaven is at hand*, in his repeated [r] *Set your heart to your ways*; and then, with the same idiom, *set your heart*[s] viz. to God's ways, what He had done on disobedience, what He would do on obedience. He bids them work for God, and then he expresses the acceptableness of that work to God, in the three words, [t] *And-I-will-take-pleasure in-it and-will-be-glorified.* When they set themselves to obey, he encouraged them in the four words, [u] *I with-you saith the-Lord.* This conciseness must have been still more impressive in his words, as delivered[v]. We use many words, because our words are weak. Many of us can remember how the House of Lords was hushed, so hear the few low, but sententious words of the aged general and statesman. But conceive the suggestive eloquence of those words, as a whole sermon, *Set your-heart on-your-ways.*

Of distant prophecies there are but two[w], so that the portion to be compared with the former prophets consists but of at most 7 verses. In these the language used is of the utmost simplicity. Haggai had but one message as to the future to convey, and he enforced it by the repeated use of the same word[x], that temporal things should be shaken, the eternal should remain, as S. Paul sums it up[y]. He, the long-longed for, the chosen of God, the signet on His Hand, should come; God would fill that house, so poor in their eyes, with glory, and there would He give peace. Haggai had an all-containing but very simple message to give from God. Any ornament of diction would but have impaired and obscured its meaning. The two or three slight idioms, noticed by one after another, are, though slight, forcible[z].

The office of Haggai was mainly to bring about one definite end, which God, Who raised him up and inspired him, accomplished by him. It is in the light of this great accomplishment of the work entrusted to him at the verge of man's earthly course, that his power and energy are to be estimated. The words which are preserved in his book are doubtless (as indeed was the case as to most of the prophets) the representatives and embodiment of many like words, by which, during his short office, he roused the people from their dejection indifference and irreligious apathy, to the restoration of the public worship of God in the essentials of the preparatory dispensation.

Great lukewarmness had been shewn in the return. The few looked mournfully to the religious centre of Israel, the ruined temple, the cessation of the daily sacrifice, and, like Daniel, [a] *confessed* their *sin and the sin of* their *people Israel, and presented* their *supplication before the Lord* their *God for the holy mountain of* their *God.* The most part appear, as now, to have been taken up with their material prosperity, and, at best, to have become inured to the cessation of their symbolical worship, connected, as it was, with the declaration of the forgiveness of their sins. Then too, God connected His declaration of pardon with certain outward acts: *they* became indifferent to the cessation of those acts. For few returned. The indifference was even remarkable among those, most connected with the altar. Of the 24 [b] orders of priests, $\frac{1}{6}$ only, 4 orders[c] returned; of the Levites only 74 individuals[d]; while of those assigned to help them, the Nethinim and the children of Solomon's servants, there were 392[e]. This coldness continued at the return of Ezra. The edict of Artaxerxes[f], as suggested by Ezra, was more pious than those appointed to the service of God. In the first instance no Levite answered to the invitation[g]; on the special urgency and message of Ezra, [h] *by the good hand of God upon us they brought us a man of understanding*, of the sons of Levi; some 3 or 4 chief Levites; their sons and brethren; in all, 38; but of the Nethinim, nearly six times as many, 220[i]. Those who thought more of temporal prosperity than of their high spiritual nobility and destination, had flourished doubtless in that exile as they have in their present homelessness, as [j] *wanderers among the nations.* Haman calculated apparently on being able to *pay* out of their spoils *ten thousand talents of silver*[k], some £300,000,000, two-thirds of

[m] ii. 12. 13. [n] ii. 19. [o] Ib. 3. [p] i. 6. [q] i. 11.
[r] i. 5–7. [s] ii. 15–18. [t] i. 8. [u] i. 13.
[v] See on ii. 5, 9. [w] ii. 6–9, 21–23.
[x] מרעיש, ii. 6, 22, והרעשתי ii. 7.
[y] Heb. xii. 26.
[z] See on ii. 3, 5, 17. The junction of אחת מעט ii. 6, is a mistake of the critics.
[a] Dan. ix. 20. [b] 1 Chr. xxiv. 3–19.
[c] Ezr. ii. 36–39. [d] Ib. 40. [e] Ib. 58.
[f] Ib. vii. 13–14. [g] Ib. viii. 15. [h] Ib. 18, 19.
[i] Ib. 20. [j] See on Hos. ix. 17. vol. i. p. 97, 98.

[k] Esther iii. 9. Ahasuerus apparently, in acceding to Haman's proposal, made over to him the lives and property of the Jews. *The silver* is *given unto thee, the people also, to do with them as it seemeth good to thee.* (Ib. 11.) The Jews' property, was confiscated with their lives. On the contrary, it was noticed, that the Jews, when permitted to defend their lives, did *not lay their hands on the prey*, which, by the king's decree, was granted to them, with authority to take the lives of those who *should assault them.* Esth. viii. 11. ix. 10, 15, 16.

the annual revenue of the Persian Empire[1] *into the king's treasuries.*

The numbers who had returned with Zerubbabel had been (as had been foretold of all restorations) *a remnant* only. There were 42,360 free men, with 7337 male or female slaves[m]. The whole population which returned was not above 212,000, freemen and women and children. The proportion of slaves is about $\frac{1}{12}$, since in their case adults of both sexes were counted. The enumeration is minute, giving the number of their horses, mules, camels, asses[n]. The chief of the fathers however were not poor, since (though unspeakably short of the wealth, won by David and consecrated to the future temple) *they*[o] *offered freely for the house of God, to set it up in its place*, a sum about £117,100[p] of our money. They had, beside, a grant from Cyrus, which he intended to cover the expenses of the building, the height and breadth whereof were determined by royal edict[q].

The monarch, however, of an Eastern empire had, in proportion to its size, little power over his subordinates or the governors of the provinces, except by their recall or execution, when their oppressions or peculations notably exceeded bounds. The returned colony, from the first, were in fear of the nations, *the peoples of those countries*[r], their old enemies probably; and the first service, *the altar to offer burnt-offerings thereon*, was probably a service of fear rather than of love, as it is said, [r] *they set up the altar upon its bases; for it was in fear upon them from the peoples of the lands, and they offered burnt-offerings thereon unto the Lord.* They hoped apparently to win the favor of God, that He might, as of old, protect them against their enemies. However, the work was carried on [s] *according to the grant that they had of Cyrus king of Persia;* and the foundations of the temple were laid amidst mixed joy at the carrying on of the work thus far, and sorrow at its poverty, compared to the first temple[t]. The hostility of the Samaritans discouraged them. Mixed as the religion of the Samaritans was, —its better element being the corrupt religion of the ten tribes, its worse the idolatries of the various nations, brought thither in the reign of Esarhaddon,—the returned Jews could not accept their offer to join in their worship, without the certainty of admitting, with them, the idolatries, for which they had been punished so severely. For the Samaritans pleaded the identity of the two religions. [u] *Let us build with you, for we serve your God, as ye do; and we do sacrifice unto Him since the days of Esarhaddon which brought us up hither.* But in fact this mixed worship, in which [v] *they feared the Lord and served their own gods*, came to this, that [w] *they feared not the Lord, neither did they after the law and commandment which the Lord commanded the children of Jacob.* For God claims the undivided allegiance of His creatures; *these* [x] *feared the Lord and served their graven images, both their children and their children's children: as did their fathers, so do they to this day.* But this worship included some of the most cruel abominations of heathendom, the sacrifice of their children to their gods[y].

The Samaritans, thus rejected, first themselves harassed the Jews in building, apparently by petty violence, as they did afterward in the rebuilding of the walls by Nehemiah. [z] *The people of the land weakened the hands of the people of Judah, and wore them out*[a] *in building.* This failing, they [b] *hired counsellors* (doubtless at the Persian court), *to frustrate their purpose, all the days of Cyrus king of Persia, until the reign of Darius king of Persia.* The object of the intrigues was probably to intercept the supplies, which Cyrus had engaged to bestow, which could readily be effected in an Eastern Court without any change of purpose or any cognizance of Cyrus.

In the next reign of Ahashverosh (i. e. Khshwershe, a title of honor of Cambyses) [c] they wrote accusations against the Jews, seemingly without any further effect, since none is mentioned. Perhaps Cambyses, in his expedition to Egypt, knew more of the Jews, than the Samaritans thought, or he may have shrunk from changing his father's decree, contrary to the fundamental principles of Persism, not to alter any decree, which the sovereign (acting, as he was assumed to do, under the influence of Ormuzd) had written[a]. Pseudo-Smerdis (who doubtless took the title of honor, Artachshatr) may, as an impostor, have well been ignorant of Cyrus' decree, to which no allusion is made[b]. From him the Samaritans, through Rehum the chancellor, obtained a decree prohibiting, until further notice, the rebuilding of *the city.* The accusers had overreached themselves; for the ground of their accusation was, the former rebellions of the city[c]; the prohibition accordingly extended only to the *city*[d], not to the temple. However, hav-

[1] 14,560 silver talents. Herod. iii. 95.

[m] Ezra ii. 64, 65, Neh. vii. 66, 67. In the time of Augustus, it was no uncommon thing for a person to have 200 slaves (Hor. Sat. i. 9. 11) it is said that very many Romans possessed 10000 or 20000 slaves. Athenæus vi. p. 272.

[n] 736 horses, 245 mules, 435 camels, 6720 asses. Ezra ii. 66, 67, Neh. vii. 68, 69.

[o] Ezr. ii. 68, 69.

[p] The golden daric being estimated at £1 2*s*., the 61,000 darics would be £67,100; the "maneh" being 100 shekels, and the shekel about 2*s*., the 5000 maneh of silver would be about £50,000.

[q] Ezr. iv. 3. [r] Ib. iii. 3. [s] Ezr. iii. 7. [t] Ib. 11–13.

[u] Ib. iv. 2. [v] 2 Kgs xvii. 33. [w] Ib. 34.

[x] Ib. 41. [y] Ib. 31. [z] בְּלָהּ Cheth.

[a] Ezr. iv. 4. [b] Ib. 5. [c] Ib. 6.

[a] See Daniel the prophet pp. 445–447.

[b] Ezr. iv. 7, sqq. [c] Ib. 12, 13, 15, 16. [d] Ib. 19. 21.

ing obtained the decree, they were not scrupulous about its application, and *made* the Jews *to cease* [e] *by arm and power*, the governor of the Jews being apparently unable, the governor of the cis-Euphratensian provinces being unwilling, to help. As this, however, was, in fact, a perversion of the decree, the Jews were left free to build, and in the second year of Darius Hystaspis, [f] *Haggai, and* then *Zechariah, prophesied in the name of the God of Israel* to Zerubbabel, the native Governor, and Joshua the high-priest, and *the Jews in Judah and Jerusalem; and they began to build the house of God in Jerusalem.* Force was no longer used. Those engaged in building appealed to the edict of Cyrus; the edict was found at Ecbatana [g], and the supplies which Cyrus had promised, were again ordered. The difficulty was at the commencement. The people had been cowed perhaps at first by the violence of Rehum and his companions; but they had acquiesced readily in the illegal prohibition, and had [h] *run each to his own house*, some of them to their [i] *ceiled houses.* All, employers or employed, were busy on their husbandry. But nothing flourished. The laborers' wages disappeared, as soon as gained [j]. East and West wind alike brought disease to their corn; both, as threatened upon disobedience in the law [k]. The East wind scorched and dried it up [l]; the warm West wind turned the ears yellow [m] and barren; the hail smote the vines, so that when the unfilled and mutilated clusters were pressed out, two-fifths only of the hoped-for produce was yielded; of the corn, only one half [n].

In the midst of this, God raised up an earnest preacher of repentance. Haggai was taught, not to promise anything at the first, but to set before them, what they had been doing, what was its result. [o] He sets it before them in detail; tells them that God had so ordered it for their neglect of His service, and bids them amend. He bids them quit their wonted ways; *go up into the mountain; bring wood; build the house.* Conceive in Christian England, after some potato-disease, or foot-and-mouth-disease (in Scripture language "*a murrain* among the cattle"), a preacher arising and bidding them, *consider your ways*, and as the remedy, not to look to any human means, but to do something, which should please Almighty God; and not preaching only but effecting what he preached. Yet such was Haggai. He stood among his people, his existence a witness of the truth of what he said; himself one, who had lived among the outward splendors of the former temple; a contemporary of those, who said [p] *the temple of the Lord, the temple of the Lord, the temple of the Lord* are *these;* who had held it to be impossible that Judah should be carried captive; who had prophesied the restoration of the vessels of God [q], which had been carried away, not, as God foretold, after the captivity, but as an earnest that the fuller captivity should not be [r]; yet who had himself, according to the prophecies of the prophets of those days, been carried into captivity, and was now a part of that restoration which God had promised. He stood among them "in gray-haired might," bade them do, what he bade them, in the name of God, to do; and they did it. When they had set about the work, he assured them of the presence of God with them [s]. A month later, when they were seemingly discouraged at its poorness, he promised them in God's name, that its glory should be greater than that of Solomon's [t]. Three days after, in contrast with the visitations up to that time, while there was as yet no token of any change, he promised them in the name of God, [u] *From this day will I bless you.*

He himself apparently saw only the commencement of the work; for his prophecies lay within the second year of Darius and the temple was not completed till the sixth [v]. Even the favorable rescript of Darius must have arrived after his last prophecy, since it was elicited by the enquiry of the governor, consequent upon the commenced rebuilding [w], three months only before his office closed [x].

While this restoration of the public worship of God in its intregrity was his main office, yet he also taught by parable [y] that the presence of what was outwardly holy did not, in itself, hallow those, among whom it was; but was itself unhallowed by inward unholiness.

Standing too amid the small handful of returned exiles, not, altogether, more than the inhabitants of Sheffield, he foretold, in simple all-comprehending words, that central gift of the Gospel, [z] *In this place will I give peace, saith the Lord.* So had David, the sons of Korah, Micah, Isaiah, Ezekiel prophe-

[e] Ezra iv. 23. [f] Ib. v. 1, 2. [g] Ib. vi. 2. [h] Hagg. i. 9. [i] Ib. 4. [j] Ib. 6. [k] Deut. xxviii. 22.

[l] שִׁדָּפוֹן comp. שְׁדוּפוֹת קָדִים Gen. xli. 6, 23, 27.

[m] יֵרָקוֹן Forskäl (in Niebuhr, Beschreibung v. Arabien, Pref. p. xlv.) took down from the mouth of "Muri, a Jew of Mecca, that, in the month Marchesvan, a warm wind sometimes blew, which turned the ears yellow and they yielded no grain; it was an unsteady wind, but spoils all it touches." "M. Forskäl remarks that the fields, near the canal of Alexandria are sown in October and reaped in Feb." Id. In Arabic the disease is called ירקאן. Ges. Thes.

[n] Hagg. ii. 16. [o] Ib. 5–11. [p] Jer. vii. 4. [q] Ib. xxvii. 16, xxviii. 3. [r] Ib. xxviii. 2. [s] Hagg. i. 13. [t] Ib. ii. 3–9. [u] ii. 19. [v] Ezr. vi. 15. [w] Ib. v. 3. sqq. [x] Hagg. i. 15. ii. 10, 20. [y] ii. 10–15. [z] ii. 9.

sied[a]; but the peace was to come, not then, but in the days of the Messiah. Other times had come, in which the false prophets had said[b], *Peace, peace, when there was no peace;* when God had taken away His peace from [c]*this people.* And now, when the chastisements were fulfilled, when the land lay desolate, when every house of Jerusalem lay burned with fire[d], and the "blackness of ashes" alone "marked where they stood;" when the walls were broken down so that, even when leave was given to rebuild them, it seemed to their enemies a vain labor to [e]*revive the stones out of the heaps of rubbish which were burned;* when [f]*the place of their fathers' sepulchres lay waste, and the gates thereof were consumed with fire;* when, for their sakes, Zion was [g]*ploughed as a field* and *Jerusalem* was *become heaps*—let any one picture to himself the silver-haired prophet standing, at first, alone, rebuking the people, first through their governor and the high-priest, then the collected multitude, in words, forceful from their simplicity, and obeyed! And then let them think whether anything of human or even Divine eloquence was lacking, when the words flew straight like arrows to the heart, and roused the people to do at once, amid every obstacle, amid every downheartedness or outward poverty, that for which God sent them. The outward ornament of words would have been misplaced, when the object was to bid a downhearted people, in the Name of God, to do a definite work. Haggai sets before his people cause and effect; that they denied to God what was His, and that God denied to them what was His to give or to withhold. His sermon was, in His words Whom he foretold; *Seek ye first the kingdom of God and His righteousness, and all these things shall be added unto you.* He spake in the name of God, and was obeyed.

"[h]The Holy Ghost, Who spake by the mouth of the prophets, willed that he by a foreboding name should be called Haggai, i. e. 'festive,' according to the subject whereof He should speak by his mouth. Yet was there not another festiveness in the prophet's heart, than the joy which he had or could have with the people, from the rebuilding of that temple made with hands, again to be defiled and burned with fire irrecoverably? Be it that the rebuilding of that temple, which he saw before him, was a matter of great festive joy; yet not in or for itself, but for Him, the festive joy of saints and angels and men, Christ; because when the temple should be rebuilt, the walls also of the city should be rebuilt and the city again inhabited and the people be united in one, of whom Christ should be born, fulfilling the truth of the promise made to Abraham and David and confirmed by an oath. So then we, by aid of the Holy Spirit, so enter upon what Haggai here speaketh, as not doubting that he altogether aimeth at Christ. And so may we in some sort be called or be Haggais, i. e. 'festive,' by contemplating that same, which because he should contemplate, he was, by a Divine foreboding, called Haggai.".

[a] Ps. lxxii. 3–7, lxxxv. 8, 10. Mic. v. 5. Is. ix. 6, 7. xxvi. 12. xxxii. 17. lii. 7. liii. 5. liv. 10, 13. lvii. 19. lx. 17. lxvi. 12. Ezek. xxxiv. 25. xxxvii. 26.

[b] Jer. vi. 14. viii. 11. xiv. 13.
[c] Ib. xvi. 5. [d] 2 Chr. xxxvi. 19.
[e] Neh. iv. 2. [f] Ib. ii. 3. [g] Mic. iii. 12. [h] Rup.

HAGGAI.

Before CHRIST cir. 520.

CHAPTER I.

1 *Haggai reproveth the people for neglecting the building of the house.* 7 *He inciteth them to the building.* 12 *He promiseth God's assistance to them being forward.*

IN [a] the second year of
Darius the king, in the
sixth month, in the first
day of the month, came
the word of the LORD † by
Haggai the prophet unto
[b] Zerubbabel the son of
Shealtiel, || governor of
Judah, and to [c] Joshua
the son of [d] Josedech, the
high priest, saying,

a Ezra 4. 24. & 5. 1. Zech. 1. 1.

† Heb. *by the hand of Haggai.*
b 1 Chron. 3. 17, 19. Ezra 3. 2. Matt. 1. 12. Luke 3. 27.
|| Or, *captain.*
c Ezra. 3. 2. & 5. 2.
d 1 Chr. 6. 15.

CHAP. I. 1. *In the second year of Darius,* i. e. Hystaspis. The very first word of prophecy after the Captivity betokens that they were restored, not yet as before, yet so, as to be hereafter, more than before. The earthly type, by God's appointment, was fading away, that the Heavenly truth might dawn. The earthly king was withdrawn, to make way for the Heavenly. God had said of Jeconiah, [1] *No man of his seed shall prosper, sitting upon the throne of David, and ruling any more in Israel:* and so now prophecy begins to be dated by the years of a foreign earthly ruler, as in the Baptism of the Lord Himself[2]. Yet God gives back in mercy more than He withdraws in chastisement. The earthly rule is suspended, that men might look out more longingly for the Heavenly.

In the sixth month. They counted by their own months, beginning with Nisan, the first of the ecclesiastical year, (which was still used for holy purposes and in sacred history) although, having no more any kings, they dated their years by those of the empire, to which they were subject[3]. In the sixth month, part of our July and August, their harvest was past, and the dearth, which they doubtless ascribed (as we do) to the seasons, and which Haggai pointed out to be a judgment from God, had set in for this year also. The months being lunar, *the first day of the month* was the festival of the new moon, a popular feast[4] which their forefathers had kept[5], while they neglected the weightier matters of the law, and which the religious in Israel had kept, even while separated from the worship at Jerusalem[6]. *In* its very *first day,* when the grief for the barren year was yet fresh, Haggai was stirred to exhort them to *consider their ways;* a pattern for Christian preachers, to bring home to people's souls the meaning of God's judgments. God directs the very day to be noted, in which He called the people anew to build His temple, both to shew the readiness of their obedience, and a precedent to us to keep in memory days and seasons, in which He stirs our souls to build more diligently His spiritual temple in our souls[7].

By the hand of Haggai. God doth well-nigh all things which He doeth for a man through the hands of men. He committeth His words and works for men into the hands of men as His stewards, to dispense faithfully to His household[8]. Hence He speaks so often of the law, which He commanded [9] *by the hand of Moses;* but also as to other prophets, Nathan[10], Ahijah[11], Jehu[12], Jonah[13], Isaiah[14], Jeremiah[15], and the prophets generally[16]. The very Prophets of God, although gifted with a Divine Spirit, still were willing and conscious instruments in speaking His words.

Unto Zerubbabel (so called from being born in Babylon) *the son of Shealtiel.* By this genealogy Zerubbabel is known in the history of the return from the captivity in Ezra and Nehemiah[17]. God does not say by Jeremiah, that Jeconiah should have no children, but that he should in his life-time be childless, as it is said of those married to the uncle's or brother's widow, [18] *they shall die childless.* Jeremiah rather implies that he should have children, but that they should die untimely before him. For he calls Jeconiah, [19] *a man who shall not prosper in his days; for there shall not prosper a man of his seed, sitting on the throne of David, and ruling any more in Israel.* He should die (as the word means) *bared*[20] of all, alone and desolate. The own father of Shealtiel appears to have been Neri[21], of the line of Nathan son

[1] Jer. xxii. 30.
[2] S. Luke iii. 1.
[3] See Zech. i. 7, vii. 1.
[4] Pr. vii. 20.
[5] Is. i. 13, 14.
[6] 2 Kgs iv. 23. add Am. viii. 5. Hos. ii. 11.
[7] Castro.
[8] S. Luke xii. 42.
[9] 12 times in the Pent.; 5 times in Joshua; in Judges once; in 1 Kgs viii.; 2 Chron. twice; Neh. ix. 14. Ps. lxxvii. 20.
[10] 2 Sam. xii. 25.
[11] 1 Kgs xii. 15, xiv. 18. 2 Chr. x. 15.
[12] Ib. xvi. 7.
[13] 2 Kgs xiv. 25.
[14] Is. xx. 2.
[15] Jer. xxxvii. 2.
[16] Hos. vii. 20. 2 Chr. xxix. 25.
[17] Ezr. iii. 2, 8. v. 2. Neh. xii. 1.
[18] Lev. xx. 20, 21.
[19] Jer. xxii. 30.
[20] ערירי from ערר, as the Samar. Vers. renders it in Lev. xx. 20, 21, "naked." Abraham uses it of his desolation in having no son. Gen. xv. 2. [all].
[21] S. Luke iii. 27.

Before CHRIST cir. 520.

2 Thus speaketh the
LORD of hosts, saying,
This people say, The time
is not come the time that
the LORD'S house should
be built.

of David; not, of the line of the kings of Judah. Neri married, one must suppose, a daughter of Assir, son of [1] Jeconiah whose grandson Shealtiel was; and Zerubbabel was the own son of Pedaiah, the brother of Shealtiel, as whose son he was in the legal genealogy inscribed, according to the law as to those who die childless [2]; or as having been adopted by Shealtiel being himself childless, as Moses was called the son of the daughter of Pharaoh [3]. So broken was the line of the unhappy Jehoiachin, two thirds of whose own life was passed in the prison [4], into which Nebuchadnezzar cast him.

Governor of Judah. The foreign name [5] betokens that the civil rule was now held from a foreign power, although Cyrus shewed the Jews the kindness of placing one of themselves, of royal extraction also, as his deputy over them. The lineage of David is still in authority, connecting the present with the past, but the earthly kingdom had faded away. Under the name *Sheshbazzar* Zerubbabel is spoken of both as *the prince* [6] and the *governor* [7] of Judah. With him is joined *Joshuah the son of Josedech, the high priest,* whose father went into captivity [8], when his grandfather Seraiah was slain by Nebuchadnezzar [9]. The priestly line also is preserved. Haggai addresses these two, the one of the royal, the other of the priestly, line, as jointly responsible for the negligence of the people; he addresses the people only through them. Together, they are types of Him, the true King and true Priest, Christ Jesus, Who by the Resurrection raised again the true temple, His Body, after it had been destroyed [10].

2. *Thus speaketh the Lord of hosts, saying, This people say.* Not Zerubbabel or Joshua, but *this people.* He says not, *My people,* but reproachfully *this people,* as, in acts, disowning Him, and so deserving to be disowned by Him. *The time is not come,* lit. *It is not time to come, time for the house of the Lord to be built* [11]. They might yet sit still; the time for them *to come* was not yet; for not yet was the *time for the house of the Lord to be built.* Why it was not time, they did not say. The government did not help them; the original grant by Cyrus [12] was exhausted; the Samaritans hindered them, because they would not own them, (amid their mishmash of worship, *worshiping,* our Lord tells them, they [13] *know not what,*) as worshipers of the same God. It was a bold excuse, if they said, that the 70 years during which the temple was to lie waste, were not yet ended. The time had long since come, when, 16 years before, Cyrus had given command that the house of God should be built. The prohibition to build, under Artaxerxes or Pseudo-Smerdis, applied directly to the city and its walls, not to the temple, except so far as the temple itself, from its position, might be capable of being used as a fort, as it was in the last siege of, Jerusalem. Yet in itself a building of the size of the temple, apart from outer buildings, could scarcely so be used. The prohibition did not hinder the building of stately private houses, as appears from Haggai's rebuke. The hindrances also, whatever they were, had not begun with that decree. Any how the death of Pseudo-Smerdis had now, for a year, set them free, had they had any zeal for the glory and service of God. Else Haggai had not blamed them. God, knowing that He should bend the heart of Darius, as He had that of Cyrus, requires the house to be built without the king's decree. It was built in faith, that God would bring through what He had enjoined, although outward things were as adverse now as before. And what He commanded He prospered [14].

There was indeed a second fulfillment of

[1] 1 Chr. iii. 17–19. [2] Deut. xxiii. 5–10.
[3] Ex. ii. 10. [4] Jer. lii. 31.

[5] See in Daniel the prophet pp. 570–572. Keil adduces a conjecture of Spiegel, "that *pechah* is from *pâvan*, 'protector' (from *pâ*) which in Sanskrit and old Persian occurs in compounds as *Khshatrapâvan*, Satrap, but in the Avesta occurs in the abridged form *pâvan*. Thence *might* be developed *pagvan*, as *dregvat* from *drevat*, *huôgva* from *huôva*." Max Müller kindly informs me; "Phonetically pavâo could hardly become pagvâo, and even this would still be considerably different from Pechah. The insertion of a *g* before a *v* in Zend is totally anomalous. It rests entirely on the uncertain identification of *dregvant*, "bad," with *drvant*, for in the second instance, *huova* is much more likely a corruption of *huogva*, than *vice versâ*. *Pavâo* in Zend would mean, protector, but like the Sanskrit *pâvân*, it occurs only at the end of compounds. The one passage, quoted in support of its occurring as a separate noun, seems to me to contain an etymological play, where *pavâo* is used as an independent noun in order to explain the two compounds, *pacca-pavâo* and *parâ-pavâo*, i. e., protecting behind and protecting in front, as if we were to say, 'he is a *tector*, both as a *pro-tector* and *sub-tector*.'"

[6] Ezr. i. 8. In relation to Cyrus, he is called by his Persian name Sheshbazzar, by which name he is mentioned in Tatnai's letter to Darius, as having been commissioned by Cyrus to rebuild the temple and as having done so (Ezr. vi. 14–16) while, in the history of the restoration, he is related to have done it under his domestic name Zerubbabel. On these changes of names by their masters, see Daniel the Prophet p. 16.

[7] Ezr. v. 14. [8] 1 Chr. vi. 15.
[9] 2 Kgs xxv. 18–21. [10] S. Jer.

[11] The first sentence being left incomplete, for, "It is not time to come to build the Lord's house."

[12] Ezr. iii. 7. [13] S. John iv. 22. [14] Ezr. v. vi.

Before CHRIST cir. 520.

3 Then came the word of the LORD [e] by Haggai the prophet saying,
4 [f] *Is it* time for you, O ye, to dwell in your ceiled houses, and this house *lie* waste?
5 Now therefore thus † saith the LORD of hosts; † [g] Consider your ways.

[e] Ezra 5. 1.
[f] 2 Sam. 7. 2. Ps. 132. 3, &c.
† Heb. *Set your heart on your ways.*
[g] Lam. 3. 40. ver. 7.

seventy years, from the destruction of the temple by Nebuchadnezzar B. C. 586, to its consecration in the 6th year of Darius B. C. 516. But this was through the wilfulness of man, prolonging the desolation decreed by God, and Jeremiah's prophecy relates to the people not to the temple.

"[1] The prophet addresses his discourse to the chiefs [in Church and state] and yet accuses directly, not their listlessness but that of the people, in order both to honor them before the people and to teach that their sins are to be blamed privately not publicly, lest their authority should be injured, and the people incited to rebel against them; and also to shew that this fault was directly that of the people, whom he reproves before their princes, that, being openly convicted before them, it might be ashamed, repent, and obey God; but that indirectly this fault touched the chiefs themselves, whose office it was to urge the people to this work of God." "[2] For seldom is the Prince free from the guilt of his subjects, as either assenting to, or winking at them, or not coercing them, though able."

Since also Christians are the temple of God, all this prophecy of Haggai is applicable to them. "[3] When thou seest one who has lapsed thinking and preparing to build through chastity the temple which he had before destroyed through passion, and yet delaying day by day, say to him, 'Truly thou also art of the people of the captivity, and sayest, *The time is not yet come for building the house of the Lord.*' Whoso has once settled to restore the temple of God, to him every time is suited for building, and the prince, Satan, cannot hinder, nor the enemies around. As soon as being thyself converted, thou callest upon the name of the Lord, He will say, *Behold Me.*" "[4] To him who willeth to do right, the time is always present; the good and right-minded have power to fulfill what is to the glory of God, in every time and place."

3. *And the word of the Lord came.* "[1] Before, he prophesied nothing, but only recited the saying of the people; now he refutes it in his prophecy, and repeats, again and again, that he says this not of himself, but from the mind and mouth of God." It is characteristic of Haggai to inculcate thus frequently, that his words are not his own, but the words of God. Yet "[1] the prophets, both in their threats and prophecies, repeat again and again, *Thus saith the Lord,* teaching us, how we should prize the word of God, hang upon it, have it ever in our mouth, reverence, ruminate on, utter, praise it, make it our continual delight."

4. *Is it time for you,* [*you*[5],] being what you are, the creatures of God, *to dwell in your ceiled houses*[6], more emphatically, *in your houses,* and those *ceiled,* probably with costly woods, such as cedar[7]. But where then was the excuse of want of means? They imitated, in their alleged poverty, what is spoken of as magnificent in their old kings, Solomon and Shallum, but not having, as Solomon first did, [8] *covered the house* of God *with beams and rows of cedar.* "[3] Will ye dwell in houses artificially adorned, not so much for use as for delight, and shall My dwelling-place, wherein was the Holy of holies, and the Cherubim, and the table of shew-bread, be bestreamed with rains, desolated in solitude, scorched by the sun?"

"[9] With these words carnal Christians are reproved, who have no glow of zeal for God, but are full of self-love, and so make no effort to repair, build, or strengthen the material temples of Christ, and houses assigned to His worship, when aged, ruinous, decaying or destroyed, but build for themselves curious, voluptuous, superfluous dwellings. In these the love of Christ gloweth not; these Isaiah threateneth, [10] *Woe to you who join house to house and field to field, and regard not the work of the Lord!*"

To David and Solomon the building of God's temple was their heart's desire; to early Christian Emperors, to the ages of faith, the building of Churches; now mostly, owners of lands build houses for this world's profit, and leave it to the few to build in view of eternity, and for the glory of God.

5. And now, thus saith the Lord of hosts; *Consider,* [lit. *set your heart upon*] *your ways,* what they had been doing, what they were doing, and what those doings had led to, and would lead to. This is ever present to the mind of the prophets, as speaking God's words, that our acts are not only *ways* in

[1] Lap. [2] à Castro from Alb.
[3] S. Jer. [4] S. Cyr.
[5] לכם אתם, the pers. pron. repeated emphatically.
[6] The force of ספונים in appos. to בתיכם.
[7] ספון בארז 1 Kgs vii. 6, 7. Jer. xxii. 14.
[8] 1 Kgs vi. 9. ויספן. [9] Dion.
[10] Is. v. 8, 12.

Before CHRIST cir. 520.

[h] Deut. 28. 38. Hos. 4. 10. Mic. 6. 14, 15. ch. 2. 16.

6 Ye have [h] sown much,
and bring in little; ye eat,
but ye have not enough;
ye drink, but ye are not
filled with drink; ye clothe
you, but there is none
warm; and [i] he that earneth wages earneth wages
to put it into a bag † with
holes.

Before CHRIST cir. 520.

[i] Zech. 8. 10.

† Heb. *pierced through.*

which we go, each day of life being a continuance of the day before; but that they are *ways* which lead somewhither in God's Providence and His justice; to some end of the *way*, good or bad. So God says by Jeremiah, [1] *I set before you the way of life and the way of death;* and David, [2] *Thou wilt shew me the path of life*, where it follows, *In Thy Presence is the fullness of joy and at Thy Right Hand there are pleasures for evermore;* and Solomon, [3] *Reproofs of instruction are the way of life;* and, he is in [4] *the way of life who keepeth instruction; and he who forsaketh rebuke, erreth;* and, [5] *The way of life is above to the wise, that he may depart from hell beneath;* and of the adulterous woman, [6] *Her house are the ways of hell, going down to the chambers of death;* and [7] *her feet go down unto death; her steps take hold on hell; lest thou shouldest ponder the path of life.* Again, [8] *There is a way that seemeth right unto a man, and the end thereof are the ways of death;* and contrariwise, [9] *The path of the righteous is a shining light, shining more and more until the midday.* [10] *The ways of darkness* are the ways which end in darkness; and when Isaiah says, [11] *The way of peace hast thou not known,* he adds, *whosoever goeth therein shall not know peace.* They who choose not peace for their way, shall not find peace in and for their end.

On these your ways, Haggai says, *set your hearts,* not thinking of them lightly, nor giving a passing thought to them, but fixing your minds upon them; as God says to Satan, [12] *Hast thou set thy heart on My servant Job?* and God is said to set His eye or His face upon man for good [13] or for evil [14]. He speaks also, not of setting the mind, applying the understanding, giving the thoughts, but of *setting the heart,* as the seat of the affections. It is not a dry weighing of the temporal results of their ways, but a loving dwelling upon them; for repentance without love is but the gnawing of remorse.

"[15] *Set your heart on your ways;* i. e., your affections, thoughts, works, so as to be circumspect in all things; as the Apostle says, [16] *Do nothing without forethought,* i. e., without previous judgment of reason; and Solomon, [17] *Let thine eyes look right on, and let thine eyelids look straight before thee;* and the son of Sirach, [18] *Son, do nothing without counsel and when thou hast done it thou wilt not repent.* For since, according to a probable proposition, nothing in human acts is indifferent, i. e., involving neither good nor ill deserts, they who do not thus *set* their *hearts upon* their *ways,* do they not daily incur well-nigh countless sins, in thought, word, desire, deed, yea and by omission of duties? Such are all fearless persons who heed not to fulfill what is written, [19] *Keep your heart with all watchfulness.*"

"[20] He *sows much* to his own heart, but *brings in little,* who by reading and hearing knows much of the heavenly commands, but by negligence in deeds bears little fruit. *He eats and is not satisfied,* who, hearing the words of God, coveteth the gains or glory of the world. Well is he said *not* to be *satisfied,* who *eateth* one thing, hungereth after another. *He* drinks and is not inebriated, who inclineth his ear to the voice of preaching, but changeth not his mind. For through inebriation the mind of those who drink is changed. He then who is devoted to the knowledge of God's word, yet still desireth to gain the things of the world, *drinks and is not inebriated.* For were he inebriated, no doubt he would have changed his mind and no longer seek earthly things, or love the vain and passing things which he *had* loved. For the Psalmist says of the elect, [21] *they shall be inebriated with the richness of Thy house,* because they shall be filled with such love of Almighty God, that, their mind being changed, they seem to be strangers to themselves, fulfilling what is written, [22] *If any will come after Me, let him deny himself.*"

6. *Ye have sown much.* The prophet expresses the habitualness of these visitations by a vivid present. He marks no time and so expresses the more vividly that it was at all times. It is one continually present evil. *Ye have sown much and there is a bringing in little; there is eating and not to satisfy; there is drinking and not to exhilarate; there is clothing and not to be warm* [23]. It is not for the one or the other years, as, since the first year of Darius Hystaspis; it is one continued

[1] Jer. xxi. 8. [2] Ps. xvi. 11. [3] Pr. vi. 23.
[4] Ib. x. 17. [5] Ib. xv. 24. [6] Ib. vii. 27.
[7] Ib. v. 5, 6. [8] Ib. xiv. 12. xvi. 25.
[9] Ib. iv. 18. [10] Ib. ii. 13. [11] Is. lix. 8.
[12] Job i. 8. [13] Jer. xxiv. 6. [14] Ib. xxi. 10.
[15] Dion. [16] 1 Tim. v. 21. [17] Pr. iv. 25.

[18] Ecclus. xxxii. 19. Vulg. [19] Pr. iv. 23.
[20] S. Greg. in Ezek. Hom. i. 10. n. 7. Opp. i. 1266.
[21] Ps. xxxvi. 8. [22] S. Matt. xvi. 24.
[23] לְחֹם לוֹ. The לוֹ is not pleonastic, but from the impersonal חַם לְ 1 Kgs i. 1, 2. Eccl. iv. 11. (bis).

Before CHRIST cir. 520.

7 ¶ Thus saith the LORD of hosts; Consider your ways.

8 Go up to the mountain, and bring wood, and build the house; and I will

Before CHRIST cir. 520.

visitation, coordinate with one continued negligence. As long as the sin lasted, so long the punishment. The visitation itself was twofold; impoverished harvests, so as to supply less sustenance; and various indisposition of the frame, so that what would, by God's appointment in nature, satisfy, gladden, warm, failed of its effect. *And he that laboreth for hire, gaineth himself hire into a bag full of holes* [lit. *perforated*]. The labor pictured is not only fruitless, but wearisome and vexing. There is a seeming result of all the labor, something to allure hopes; but forthwith it is gone. The heathen assigned a like baffling of hope as one of the punishments of hell. "[1] Better and wiser to seek to be blessed by God, Who bestoweth on us all things. And this will readily come to those who choose to be of the same mind with Him and prefer what is for His glory to their own. For so saith the Saviour Himself to us, [2] *Seek ye first the kingdom of God and His righteousness, and all these things shall be added unto you.*"

"[3] *He* loses good deeds by evil acts, who takes account of his good works, which he has before his eyes, and forgets the faults which creep in between; or who, after what is good, returns to what is vain and evil." "[4] Money is seen in the pierced bag, when it is cast in, but when it is lost, it is not seen. They then who look how much they give, but do not weigh how much they gain wrongly, cast their rewards into a pierced bag. Looking to the Hope of their confidence they bring them together; not looking, they lose them."

"[5] *They* lose the fruit of their labor, by not persevering to the end, or by seeking human praise, or by vain glory within, not keeping spiritual riches under the guardianship of humility. Such are vain and unprofitable men, of whom the Saviour saith, [6] *Verily I say unto you, they have their reward.*"

8. *Go up into the mountain.* Not Mount Lebanon, whence the cedars had been brought for the first temple; whence also Zerubbabel and Joshua had procured some out of Cyrus' grant [7], at the first return from the captivity. They were not required to buy, expend, but simply to give their own labor. They were themselves to *go up to the mountain,* i. e. the mountainous country where the trees grew, *and bring* them. So, in order to keep the feast of tabernacles, Ezra made a proclamation [8] *in all their cities and in Jerusalem, go ye up to the mountain and bring leafy branches of vines, olives, myrtles, palms.* The palms, anyhow, were timber. God required not goodly stones, such as had been already used, and such as hereafter, in the temple which was built, were the admiration even of disciples of Jesus [9], but which were, for the wickedness of those who rejected their Saviour, *not to be left, one stone upon another.* He required not costly gifts, but the heart. The neglect to build the temple was neglect of Himself, Who ought to be worshiped there. His worship sanctified the offering; offerings were acceptable, only if made with a free heart.

And I will have pleasure in it. God, Who has declared that He has no [10] *pleasure in thousands of rams, or ten thousands of rivers of oil,* had delight in [11] *them that feared Him,* that are *upright in their way* [12], that *deal truly* [13], in the *prayer* of the *upright* [14]; and so in the temple too, when it should be built to His glory.

And will be glorified [15]. God is glorified in man, when man serves Him; in Himself, when He manifests aught of His greatness; in His great doings to His people [16], as also in the chastisement of those who disobey Him [17]. God allows that glory, which shines ineffably throughout His creation, to be obscured here through man's disobedience, to shine forth anew on his renewed obedience. The glory of God, as it is the end of the creation, so is it His creature's supreme bliss. When God is really glorified, then can He shew forth His glory, by His grace and acceptance. "[18] The glory of God is our glory.

[1] S. Cyr. [2] S. Matt. vi. 33. [3] Lap.
[4] S. Greg. Reg. Past. iii. 21. fin. Opp. ii. 68.
[5] Dion. [6] S. Matt. vi. 2.
[7] Ezr. iii. 7. [8] Neh. viii. 15.
[9] S. Matt. xxiv. 1. [10] Mic. vi. 7. [11] Ps. cxlvii. 11.
[12] Pr. xi. 20. [13] Ib. xii. 22. [14] Ib. xv. 8.

[15] There is no ground for the Kri וְאִכָּבְדָה, *and so should I be glorified or honored.* It is a positive promise that God would shew forth His glory, as in וְאֶרְצֶה immediately before. God says, "do this, and I will do that." Comp. Zech. i. 3. Of 65 instances which Böttcher (Lehrb. n. 965. *c.*) gives of הָ after the imperative, 61 relate to some wish of the human agent; 4 only relate to God. Deut. v. 31, "stand here by Me, ואדברה, that I may speak unto thee;" Is. xli. 22, 23. irony, including men, "that we may consider and know; that we may know;" Ps. l. 7. "hear Me and *I would speak,* and *testify;*" Mal. iii. 7. "Return to Me and I would return unto you;" the return of the creature being a condition that God could return to it. On the other hand the Ch. Lam. v. 21, "Turn Thou us unto Thee, ונשוב, and we will return" expresses the absolute will to return; Ruth iv. 4, "tell me, ואדע, and I shall know," the certainty of the knowledge, upon which Boaz would act.

[16] Is. xxvi. 15, xliv. 23, lx. 21, lxi. 3.
[17] Ex. xiv. 4. Ezek. xxviii. 22.
[18] S. Aug. Serm. 380, n. 6.

Before CHRIST cir. 520.

take pleasure in it, and I
will be glorified, saith the
LORD.
9 [k] Ye looked for much,
and, lo, *it came* to little;
and when ye brought *it*
home, [l] I did ‖ blow upon
it. Why? saith the LORD
of hosts. Because of mine
house that *is* waste, and ye
run every man unto his
own house.

k ch. 2. 16.

l ch. 2. 17.
‖ Or, *blow it away.*

The more sweetly God is glorified, the more it profits us:" yet not our profit, but the glory of God is itself our end; so the prophet closes in that which is our end, *God will be glorified.*

"[1] Good then and well-pleasing to God is zeal in fulfilling whatever may appear necessary for the good condition of the Church and its building-up, collecting the most useful materials, the spiritual principles in inspired Scripture, whereby he may secure and ground the conception of God, and may shew that the way of the Incarnation was well-ordered, and may collect what appertains to accurate knowledge of spiritual erudition and moral goodness. Nay, each of us may be thought of, as the temple and house of God. For Christ *dwelleth in us* by the Spirit, and we are *temples of the living God,* according to the Scripture[2]. Let each then build up his own heart by right faith, having the Saviour as the *precious foundation.* And let him add thereto other materials, obedience, readiness for anything, courage, endurance, continence. So *being framed together by that which every joint supplieth,* shall we *become a holy temple, a habitation of God through the Spirit*[3]. But those who are slow to faith, or who believe but are sluggish in shaking off passions and sins and worldly pleasure, thereby cry out in a manner, *The time is not come to build the house of the Lord.*"

9. *Ye looked,* lit. *a looking;* as though he said, it has all been one looking, *for much,* for increase, the result of all sowing, in the way of nature: *and behold it came to little,* i. e. less than was sown; as Isaiah denounced to them of old by God's word, [4] *the seed of a homer shall yield an ephah,* i. e. one tenth of what was sown. *And ye brought it home, and I blew upon it,* so as to disperse it, as, not the wheat, but the chaff is blown before the wind. This, in whatever way it came to pass, was a further chastisement of God. The little seed which they brought in lessened through decay or waste. *Why? saith the Lord of hosts.* God asks by his prophet, what He asks in the awakened conscience. [5] *God with rebukes chastens man for sin.* Conscience, when alive, confesses for *what* sin; or it asks itself, if memory does not supply the special sin. Unawakened, it murmurs about the excess of rain, the drought, the blight, the mildew, and asks, not itself, why, in God's Providence, these inflictions came in these years? They felt doubtless the sterility in contrast with the exceeding prolificalness of Babylonia[6], as they contrasted the *light bread*[7], the manna, with [8] the plenteousness of Egypt. They ascribed probably their meagre crops (as we mostly do) to mere natural causes, perhaps to the long neglect of the land during the captivity. God forces the question upon their consciences, in that Haggai asks it in His Name, in Whose hands all powers stand, *saith the Lord of hosts.* They have not to talk it over among themselves, but to answer Almighty God, *why?* That *why?* strikes into the inmost depths of conscience!

Because of My house which is waste, and ye run lit. *are running,* all the while, *each to his own house*[9]. They were absorbed in their material interests, and had no time for those of God. When the question was of God's house, they stir not from the spot; when it is of their own concerns, they run. Our Lord says, [10] *Seek ye first the kingdom of God and His righteousness, and all these things shall be added unto you.* Man reverses this, seeks his own things first, and God withholds His blessing.

"[11] This comes true of those who prefer their own conveniences to God's honor, who do not thoroughly uproot self-love, whose penitence and devotion are shewn to be unstable; for on a slight temptation they are overcome. Such are they who are bold, self-pleasing, wise and great in their own eyes, who do not ground their conversation on true and solid humility."

"[12] To those who are slow to fulfill what is for the glory of God, and the things whereby His house, the Church, is firmly stayed, neither the heavenly dew cometh, which enricheth hearts and minds, nor the fruitfulness of the earth; i. e. right action; not food nor wine nor use of oil. But they will be

[1] S. Cyr. [2] 2 Cor. vi. 16. [3] Eph. iv. 16, ii. 21, 22.
[4] Is. v. 10. [5] Ps. xxxix. 11.
[6] Herod. i. 193. Theophr. Hist. Plant. viii. 7. Berosus Fr. 1. Strabo xvi. 1. 14. Pliny Nat. Hist. xviii. 17. Amm. Marc. xxiv. 9.
[7] Nu. xxi. 5. [8] Ib. xi. 5.
[9] רוץ with ל is used of the direction whither a man goes; if used of an action, hasting to do it; as *runneth to evil* (Is. lix. 7, Pr. i. 16.) Here לביתו cannot be "on account of his house," but to it, viz. for his business there.
[10] S. Matt. vi. 33. [11] Dion. [12] S. Cyr.

Before CHRIST cir. 520.

m Lev. 26. 19. Deut. 28. 23. 1 Kin. 8. 35.
n 1 Kin. 17. 1. 2 Kin. 8. 1.

10 Therefore [m]the heaven over you is stayed from dew, and the earth is stayed *from* her fruit.
11 And I [n]called for a drought upon the land, and upon the mountains, and upon the corn, and upon the new wine, and upon the oil, and upon *that* which the ground bringeth forth, and upon men, and upon cattle, and [o]upon all the labor of the hands.
12 ¶ [p]Then Zerubbabel the son of Shealtiel, and Joshua the son of Josedech, the high priest, with all the remnant of the people, obeyed the voice of the LORD their God, and the words of Haggai the prophet, as the LORD their God had sent him, and the

Before CHRIST cir. 520.

o ch. 2. 17.
p Ezra 5. 2.

ever strengthless and joyless, unenriched by spiritual oil, and remain without taste or participation of the blessing through Christ."

10. *Therefore, for you*, on your account [1]; for your sins [2], He points out the moral cause of the drought, whereas men think of this or that cause of the variations of the seasons, and we, e. g. take into our mouths Scripture-words, as *murrain of cattle*, and the like, and think of nothing less than why it was sent, or Who sent it. Haggai directs the mind to the higher Cause, that as they withheld their service from God, so, on their account and by His will, His creatures withheld [3] their service from them.

11. *And I called for a drought upon the land.* God called to the people and they would not hear. It is His ever-repeated complaint to them. *I called unto you, and ye would not hear.* He called to His inanimate creatures to punish them, and *they* obeyed. So Elisha tells the woman, whose son he had restored to life, [4] *The Lord hath called to the famine, and it shall also come to the land seven years.*

And upon men, in that the drought was oppressive to man. The Prophet may also allude to the other meaning of the word, "waste," "desolation." They had left the house of the Lord [5] waste, therefore God called for waste, desolation, upon them.

12. *Then Zerubbabel, and all the remnant of the people*, not, "the rest of people" but "the remnant [6]," those who remained over from the captivity, the fragment of the two tribes, which returned to their own land, *hearkened unto the voice of the Lord.* This was the beginning of a conversion. In this one thing they began to do, what, all along, in their history, and most in their decay before the captivity they refused to do—obey God's word. So God sums up their history, by Jeremiah, [7] *I spake unto thee in thy prosperity, thou saidst, I will not hear. This is thy way from thy youth, that thou hearkenedst not unto My voice.* Zephaniah still more briefly, [8] *she hearkened not unto* [any] *voice.* Now in reference, it seems, to that account of their disobedience, Haggai says, using the self-same formula, [9] *they hearkened unto the voice of the Lord,* [10] *according to the words of Haggai.* They obeyed, not vaguely, or partly, but exactly, *according to the words* which the messenger of God spake.

And they feared the Lord. "[11] Certainly the presence of the Divine Majesty is to be feared with great reverence." "[12] The fear of punishment at times transports the mind to what is better, and the infliction of sorrows harmonizes the mind to the fear of God; and that of the Proverbs comes true, [13] *He that feareth the Lord shall be recompensed*, and [14] *the fear of the Lord* tendeth *to life;* and Wisdom, [15] *The fear of the Lord is honor and glory*, and [16] *the fear of the Lord shall rejoice*

[1] As in Ps. xliv. 43. [2] Jon.

[3] כלא being everywhere transitive, and in this V. also, is probably transitive here.

[4] 2 Kgs viii. 1.

[5] חָרֵב, Hagg. i. 4, 9; חֹרֶב, i. 11.

[6] This is the almost uniform usage of שְׁארית, "remnant which remains over," mostly after the rest have been destroyed or carried captive. See vol. i. on Am. i. 8; add, *the remnant of Judah*, Jer. xl. 11, xlii. 19, xliii. 5, xliv. 12, 14, *of Israel*, Zeph. iii. 13. Ez. xi. 13; *whole remnant of the people*, Jer. xli. 10. 16; *of Ashdod*, Jer. xxv. 20; *of the coast of Caphtor*, Ib. xlvii. 4; *of their valley*, Ib. 5; *of the coast of the sea*, Ez. xxv. 16; *of the nations*, Ib. xxxvi. 3, 4, 5; *of the land*, אדמה, Is. xv. 9; *of My people*, Zeph. ii. 9; *of His heritage*, Mi. vii. 18; *thy remnant*, Is. xiv. 30, Ez. v. 10; *its remnant*, Is. xliv. 17; *their remnant*, Jer. xv. 9; and of those who had actually returned, Zech. viii. 6, 11, 12. In two places in which it signifies "the rest" (Jer. xxxix. 3, 1 Chr. xii. 38.) it is at least the rest of a whole, already mentioned. A third only, Neh. vii. 72. is uncertain. The word is used almost exclusively by the prophets.

[7] Jer. xxii. 21.

[8] לא שמעה בקול. See Introd. to Zeph. p. 225.

[9] וישמע בקול יי.

[10] This is the only place in which שמע על דברי is used.

[11] Dion. [12] S. Cyr. [13] Pr. xiii. 13.
[14] Ib. xix. 23. [15] Ecclus. i. 11. [16] Ib. 12.

Before CHRIST cir. 520.

people did fear before the
LORD,
13 Then spake Haggai
the Lord's messenger in the
LORD's message unto the
people, saying, [q] I *am* with
you, saith the Lord.
14 And [r] the Lord
stirred up the spirit of Zerubbabel the son of Shealtiel, [s] governor of Judah,
and the spirit of Joshua
the son of Josedech, the
high priest, and the spirit
of all the remnant of the
people; [t] and they came

q Matt. 28. 20. Rom. 8. 31.
r 2 Chr. 36. 22. Ezra 1. 1.
s ch. 2. 21.
t Ezra 5. 2, 8.

the heart, and giveth joy and gladness and a long life. See how gently and beseemingly God smites us."

"[1] See how the lovingkindness of God forthwith goes along with all changes for the better. For Almighty God changes along with those who will to repent, and promises that He will be with them; which what can equal? For when God is with us, all harm will depart from us, all good come in to us."

13. *And Haggai, the Lord's messenger.* Malachi, whose own name was framed to express that he was *the Lord's messenger*, and Haggai alone use the title, as the title of a prophet; perhaps as forerunners of the great prophet whom Malachi announced. Malachi also speaks of the priest, as [2] *the messenger of the Lord of hosts*, and prophesies of John Baptist as [3] *the messenger* of the Lord, who should *go before His face.* Haggai, as he throughout repeats that his words were God's words, frames a new word [4], to express, in the language of the New Testament [5]; that he had an embassy from God; *in the Lord's message.*

I am with you. All the needs and longings of the creature are summed up in those two words, *I with-you.* "Who art Thou and who am I? Thou, He Who Is; I, he who am not;" nothing, yea worse than nothing. Yet *if* [6] *God be for us*, S. Paul asks, *who can be against us?* Our Blessed Lord's parting promise to the Apostles, and in them to the Church, was, [7] *Lo I am with you alway*, even *to the end of the world.* The all-containing assurance goes beyond any particular promise of aid, as, "[8] I will help you, and will protect you, so that your building shall have its completion." This is one fruit of it; "[9] since I am in the midst of you, no one shall be able to hinder your building." But, more widely, the words bespeak *His* presence in love, Who knows all our needs, and is Almighty to support and save us in all. So David says, [10] *when I walk through the valley of the shadow of death, I will fear no evil; for Thou art with me:* and God says by another, [11] *I* will be *with him in trouble*, and by Isaiah, [12] *When thou passest through the waters, I* will be *with thee.*

14. *And the Lord stirred up the spirit.* The words are used of any strong impulse from God to fulfill His will, whether in those who execute His will unknowingly as Pul [13], to carry off the trans-Jordanic tribes, or the Philistines and Arabians against Jehoram [14], or the Medes against Babylon [15]; or knowingly, as of Cyrus to restore God's people and rebuild the temple [16], or of the people themselves to return [17]. "[9] The spirit of Zerubbabel and the spirit of Joshua were stirred, that the government and priesthood may build the temple of God: the spirit of the people too, which before was asleep in them; not the body, not the soul, but the spirit, which knoweth best how to build the temple of God." "[18] The Holy Spirit is stirred up in us, that we should enter the house of the Lord, and do the works of the Lord."

"[19] Again, observe that they did not set themselves to choose to do what should please God, before He was with them and stirred up their spirit. We shall know hence also, that although one choose zealously to do good and be in earnest therein, yet he will accomplish nothing, unless God be with him, raising him up to dare, and sharpening him to endure, and removing all torpor. For so the wondrous Paul says of those entrusted with the divine preaching, [20] *I labored more abundantly than they all*, yet added very wisely, *yet not I, but the grace of God which was with me*, and the Saviour Himself saith to the holy Apostles, [21] *Without Me ye can do nothing.* For He is our desire, He, our courage to any good work; He our strength, and, if He is with us, we shall do well, [22] *building ourselves to a holy temple, a habitation of God in the Spirit;* if He depart and withdraws, how should any doubt, that we should fail, overcome by sluggishness and want of courage?"

[1] S. Cyr. [2] Mal. ii. 7. [3] Ib. iii. 1.
[4] מלאכות. [5] 2 Cor. v. 20.
[6] Rom. viii. 31. [7] S. Matt. xxviii. 20.
[8] Dion. [9] S. Jer. [10] Ps. xxiii. 4.
[11] Ib. xci. 15. [12] Is. xliii. 2. [13] 1 Chr. v. 26.
[14] 2 Chr. xxi. 16. [15] Jer. li. 11.
[16] Ezr. i. 1. [17] Ib. 5. [18] ap. Lap.
[19] S. Cyr. [20] 1 Cor. xv. 11.
[21] S. John xv. 5. [22] Eph. ii. 21, 22.

Before CHRIST cir. 520.

and did work in the house
of the LORD of hosts, their
God.

15 In the four and
twentieth day of the sixth
month, in the second year
of Darius the king.

CHAPTER II.

1 *He encourageth the people to the work, by promise of greater glory to the second temple than was in the first.* 10 *In the type of holy things and unclean he sheweth their sins hindered the work.* 20 *God's promise to Zerubbabel.*

IN the seventh *month,* in
the one and twentieth
day of the month, came
the word of the LORD † by
the prophet Haggai, saying,
2 Speak now to Zerub-
babel the son of Shealtiel,
governor of Judah, and to
Joshua the son of Josedech,
the high priest, and to the
residue of the people, saying,
3 [a] Who *is* left among
you that saw this house in
her first glory? and how
do ye see it now? [b] *is it*
not in your eyes in comparison of it as nothing?

Before CHRIST cir. 520.

† Heb. *by the hand of.*

[a] Ezra 3. 12.

[b] Zech. 4. 10.

15. *In the four and twentieth day of the month.* The interval of twenty-three days must have been spent in preparation, since the message came on the first of the month, and the obedience was immediate.

II. 1. *In the seventh month, in the one and twentieth day of the month.* This was the seventh day of the feast of tabernacles[1], and its close. The eighth day was to be a sabbath, with its [2] *holy convocation,* but the commemorative feast, the dwelling in booths, in memory of God's bringing them out of Egypt, was to last seven days. The close then of this feast could not but revive their sadness at the glories of their first deliverance by God's *mighty hand and outstretched arm,* and their present fewness and poverty. This depression could not but bring with it heavy thoughts about the work, in which they were, in obedience to God, engaged; and that, all the more, since Isaiah and Ezekiel had prophesied of the glories of the Christian Church under the symbol of the temple. This despondency Haggai is sent to relieve, owning plainly the reality of its present grounds, but renewing, on God's part, the pledge of the glories of this second temple, which should be thereafter.

3. *Who is left among you?* The question implies that there were those among them, who had seen the first house in its glory, yet but few. When the foundations of the first temple were laid, there were many. [3] *Many of the priests and Levites and chief of the fathers, ancient men, that had seen the first house, when the foundations of this house were laid before their eyes, wept with a loud voice.* Fifty-nine years had elapsed from the destruction of the temple in the eleventh year of Zedekiah to the first of Cyrus; so that old men of seventy years had seen the first temple, when themselves eleven years old. In this second of Darius seventy years had passed, so that those of 78 or 80 years might still well remember it. Ezra's father, Seraiah, was slain in the eleventh year of Zedekiah; so he must have been born at latest a few months later; yet he lived to the second of Artaxerxes.

Is not such as it is[4], *as nothing?* Beside the richness of the sculptures in the former temple, everything, which admitted of it, was overlaid with gold; [5] *Solomon overlaid the whole house with gold, until he had finished all the house, the whole altar by the oracle, the two cherubim, the floor of the house, the doors of the holy of holies* and the ornaments of it, *the cherubims* thereon and *the palm trees he covered with gold fitted upon the carved work;* [6] *the altar of gold and the table of gold, whereupon the shewbread was, the ten candlesticks of pure gold, with the flowers and the lamps and the tongs of gold, the bowls, the snuffers and the basons and the spoons and the censers of pure gold, and hinges of pure gold for all the doors of the temple.* [7] *The porch that was in the front of the house, twenty cubits broad and* 120 *cubits high, was overlaid within with pure gold;* the house

[1] Lev. xxiii. 34, 36, 40–42.
[2] Ib. 36, 39.
[3] Ezr. iii. 12.
[4] Such is probably the force of כמוהו. Comp. כמוך כפרעה [Gen. xliv. 18] "one such as thou is like Pharaoh," and perhaps כמהו, Ex. ix. 18, and אשר כמוני, 2 Sam. ix. 8. הוא כאין (which Ewald says older writers would have used) would have been weaker.
[5] 1 Kgs vi. 22. 28, 30, 32, 35.
[6] Ib. vii. 48–50.
[7] 2 Chr. iii. 4–9.

Before CHRIST cir. 520.

[e] Zech. 8. 9.

4 Yet now [e] be strong,
O Zerubbabel, saith the
LORD; and be strong, O
Joshua, son of Josedech,
the high priest; and be
strong, all ye people of the
land, saith the LORD, and
work: for I *am* with you,
saith the LORD of hosts:
5 [d] *According to* the
word that I covenanted
with you when ye came

Before CHRIST cir. 520.

[d] Ex. 29. 45, 46.

glistened with precious stones; and the gold (it is added) was *gold of Parvaim*, a land distant of course and unknown to us. *Six hundred talents of gold* (about £4,320,000 [1],) were employed in overlaying the Holy of holies. *The upper chambers were also of gold; the weight of the nails was fifty shekels of gold.*

4. *Yet now be strong—and work.* They are the words with which David exhorted Solomon his son to be earnest and to persevere in the building of the first temple. [2] *Take heed now, for the Lord hath chosen thee to build an house for the sanctuary: be strong and do.* [3] *Be strong and of good courage, and do.* This combination of words occurs once only elsewhere [4], in Jehoshaphat's exhortation to *the* [5] *Levites and priests and chiefs of the fathers of Israel*, whom he had set as judges in Jerusalem. Haggai seems then to have adopted the words, with the purpose of suggesting to the down-hearted people, that there was need of the like exhortation, in view of the building of the former temple, whose relative glory so depressed them. The word *be strong* (elsewhere rendered, *be of good courage*) occurs commonly in exhortations to persevere and hold fast, amid whatever obstacles [6].

5. *The words which I covenanted.* The words stand more forcibly, because abruptly [7]. It is an exclamation which cannot be forced into any grammatical relation with the preceding. The more exact idiom would have been "Remember," "take to heart." But the Prophet points to it the more energetically, because he casts it, as it were, into the midst, not bound up with any one verb. This would be the rather done in speaking to the people, as David to his followers [8], *That which the Lord hath given us and hath preserved us and given the company against us into our hands!* i. e. "Would you deal thus with it?" The abrupt form rejects it as shocking. So here, *The word which I covenanted with you*, i. e. this, *I will be with you*, was the central all-containing promise, to which God pledged Himself when He brought them out of Egypt. He speaks to them as being one with those who came up out of Egypt, as if they were the very persons. The Church, ever varying in the individuals of whom it is composed, is, throughout all ages, in God's sight, one; His promises to the fathers are made to the children in them. So the Psalmist says, *There* (at the dividing of the Red Sea and the Jordan) *do we rejoice in Him*, as if present there; and our Lord promises to the Apostles, [9] *I am with you always even to the end of the world*, by an ever-present Presence with them and His Church founded by them in Him.

[1] Reckoning the silver shekel at 2*s*., the talent of silver,=3000 shekels, would be £300; reckoning the gold talent, as, in weight, double the silver talent, and the relation of gold to silver as 12 to 1, (H. W. Poole in Smith Bibl. Dict. p. 1734, 1735.) the gold talent would be £300 x 24,= £7,200; and 600 gold talents £4,320,000. This would not be so much as Solomon imported yearly, 666 talents = £4,795,200.

[2] 1 Chr. xxviii. 10.

[3] Ib. 20.

[4] 2 Chr. xix. 11.

[5] Ib. 8.

[6] Gesenius (v. חזק) refers to the following; 2 Sam. x. 12, (Joab to Abishai in the war with the Syrians); 2 Chr. xxv. 8. (the prophet to Amaziah); 2 Sam. xiii. 28 (Absalom to his servants about the murder of Amnon); Ps. xxvii. 14, xxxi. 25, (with the corresponding promise that God would *establish their hearts*); Is. xli. 6, (in mockery of the laborious process of making an idol). It occurs also, supported by וֶאֱמָץ Jos. i. 6, 7, 9, 18 (God's words to Joshua); Deut. xxxi. 7, (Moses to Joshua); Ib. 6, (to Israel); Josh. x. 25 (Joshua to the people); 2 Chr. xxxii. 7 (Hezekiah to the people); חזק itself is repeated Dan. x. 19. חזק וחזק.

[7] Less probable seems to me, 1) To make את הדבר depend on עשו in v. 4, as Kim. A. E. a) on account of the idiom in 1 Chr., in which, as here, עשה stands absolutely, "do work;" b) Haggai is exhorting them to this one work of rebuilding the temple, not to obedience to the law generally; c) he speaks of what God had promised them, not of their duties to God. 2) To supply זכרו "remember," or any like word, is arbitrary, unless it means that *we* should fill up the meaning by some such word. 3) To construe, "Remember the word which I covenanted with you, fear not" (Ew.); a) gives undue prominence to the absence of fear, which was one consequence of God's covenant that He would be their God, they His people, not the covenant itself; b) *Fear not*, is elsewhere the counterpart and supplement of the exhortation, "be strong," 2 Chr. xxv. 8, Is. xxxv. 41. c) In Ex. xx. 20, (referred to by Ew.) "fear not" is only Moses' exhortation on occasion of the terrors of the manifestation of God on Mt. Sinai. 4) It is doubly improbable, that it, as well as רוחי, should be the subject of the sing. עֹמֶדֶת. The את הדבר and the רוחי seem to be different constructions, in order to prevent this. Böttcher terms it, "an acc. abs. of the object," and cites Deut. xi. 2, Ezek. xliii. 7, xlvii. 17–19, ("unless one correct זאת for ואת") Zech. viii. 17. (Lehrb. n. 516. *e.*)

[8] 1 Sam. xxx. 23, which Ewald compares, Lehrb. n. 329. *a.* p. 811, ed. 8. and in his Die Proph. iii. 183. Only he, not very intelligibly, makes it a sort of oath, *By the word, By that which the Lord hath given us.* But he suggests the like broken sentence Zech. vii. 7.

[9] S. Matt. xxviii. 20.

Before CHRIST cir. 520.

out of Egypt, so [e] my spirit
remaineth among you:
fear ye not.

[e] Neh. 9. 20. Isai. 63. 11.

6 For thus saith the
LORD of hosts; [f] Yet once;
it *is* a little while, and [g] I

Before CHRIST cir. 520.

[f] ver. 21. Heb. 12. 26.
[g] Joel 3. 16.

My Spirit abideth among you, as the Psalmist says, [1] *they* [the heavens] *perish and Thou abidest;* [2] *The counsel of the Lord standeth forever;* [3] *His righteousness endureth forever.* The Spirit of God is God the Holy Ghost, with His manifold gifts. Where He is, is all good. As the soul is in the body, so God the Holy Ghost is in the Church, Himself its life, and bestowing on all and each every good gift, as each and all have need. As S. Paul says of the Church of Christ; [4] *There are diversities of gifts, but the same Spirit; and there are diversities of operations, but it is the same God, Who worketh all in all. All these worketh one and the self-same Spirit, dividing to every man severally as He will.* But above and beyond all gifts He is present as the Spirit of holiness and love, making the Church and those in whom He individually dwells, acceptable to God. Special applications, such as *the Spirit of wisdom and might;* a spirit such as He gave to Moses to judge His people [5]; the spirit of prophecy [6]; or the spirit given to Bezaleel and Aholiab for the work of the sanctuary [7]—these recognize in detail the one great truth, that all good, all wisdom, from least to greatest, comes from God the Holy Ghost; though one by one they would exclude more truth than they each contain.

6. *Yet once, it is a little while.* This, the rendering of S. Paul to the Hebrews, is alone grammatical [8]. *Yet once.* By the word *yet* he looks back to the first great shaking of the moral world, when God's revelation by Moses and to His people broke upon the darkness of the pagan world, to be a monument against heathen error till Christ should come; *once* looks on, and conveys that God would again shake the world, but *once* only, under the one dispensation of the Gospel, which should endure to the end.

It is a little while. "[9] The 517 years, which were to elapse to the birth of Christ, are called *a little time*, because to the prophets, ascending in heart to God and the eternity of God, all times, like all things of this world, seem, as they are, only a little thing, yea a mere point;" which has neither length nor breadth. So S. John calls the time of the new law, *the last hour;* [10] *Little children, it is the last hour.* It was *little* also in respect to the time, which had elapsed from the fall of Adam, upon which God promised the Saviour Christ [11]; little also in respect to the Christian law, which has now lasted above 1800 years, and the time of the end does not seem yet nigh.

I will shake the heavens and the earth, and the sea and the dry land. It is one universal shaking of all this our world and the heavens over it, of which the Prophet speaks. He does not speak only of [12] *signs in the sun and in the moon and in the stars*, which might be, and yet the frame of the world itself might remain. It is a shaking, such as would involve the dissolution of this our system, as St. Paul draws out its meaning; [13] *This word, once more, signifieth the removing of the things that are shaken, that those things which cannot be shaken may remain.* Prophecy, in its long perspective, uses a continual foreshortening, speaking of things in relation to their eternal meaning and significance, as to that which shall survive, when heaven and earth and even time shall have passed away. It blends together the beginning and the earthly end; the preparation and the result; the commencement of redemption and its completion; our Lord's coming in humility and in His Majesty. Scarce any prophet but exhibits things in their intrinsic relation, of which time is but an accident. It is the rule, not the exception. The Seed of the woman, Who should bruise the serpent's head, was promised on the fall; to Abraham, the blessing through his seed; by Moses, the prophet like unto him; to David, an everlasting covenant [14]. Joel unites the out-pouring of the Spirit of God on the Day of Pentecost, and the hatred of the world till the Day of Judgment [15]; Isaiah, God's judgments on the land and the Day of final judgment [16]; the deliverance from Babylon, and the first coming of Christ [17]; the glories of the Church, the new heavens and the new earth which shall remain forever, and the unquenched fire and undying worm of the lost [18]; Daniel, the persecutions of Antiochus Epiphanes, of Anti-

[1] Ps. cii. 27.
[2] Ib. xxxiii. 11.
[3] Ib. cxi. 3.
[4] 1 Cor. xii. 4, 6, 11.
[5] Alb. quoting Num. xi. 25.
[6] Jon. "My prophets shall teach you, fear not."
[7] Included by Lap.
[8] אחת 2 Kgs vi. 10, Ps. lxii. 12, Job. xl. 5: אחד, as an adj., follows the noun. In the only exception alleged by Ges., Dan. viii. 13, it is used of one certain angel, as contrasted with another. מעט is used of time, Job x. 20, xxiv. 24. עוד אחת ו is the like construction as עוד מעט ו Ex. xvii. 4, Ps. xxxvii. 10, Hos. i. 4.
[9] Lap.
[10] 1 S. John ii. 18.
[11] Gen. iii. 15.
[12] S. Luke xxi. 25.
[13] Heb. xii. 27.
[14] 2 Sam. xxiii. 5.
[15] Joel ii. 28–32, iii.
[16] Is. xxiv.
[17] Ib. xl.–lxvi.
[18] Ib. lxvi. 22–24.

Before CHRIST cir. 520.

will shake the heavens, and
the earth, and the sea, and
the dry *land;*

7 And I will shake all
nations, [h] and the desire of
all nations shall come: and

Before CHRIST cir. 520.

[h] Gen. 49. 10. Mal. 3. 1.

Christ, and the Resurrection[1]; Obadiah, the punishment of Edom and the everlasting kingdom of God[2]; Zephaniah, the punishment of Judah and the final judgment of the earth[3]; Malachi, our Lord's first and second Coming[4].

Nay, our Lord Himself so blends together the destruction of Jerusalem and the days of Anti-Christ and the end of the world, that it is difficult to separate them, so as to say what belongs exclusively to either[5]. The prophecy is an answer to two distinct questions of the Apostles, 1) *When shall these things* (viz. the destruction of the temple) *be?* 2) *and what shall be the sign of Thy coming and of the end of the world?* Our Lord answers the two questions in one. Some things seem to belong to the first Coming, as[6] *the abomination of desolation spoken of by Daniel*, and the flight from[7] *Judæa into the mountains.* But the exceeding deceivableness is authoritatively interpreted by St. Paul[8] of a distant time; and our Lord Himself, having said that *all these things*, of which the Apostles had enquired, should take place in that generation[9], speaks of His absence as of a man taking a far journey[10], and says that *not the angels in heaven knew that hour, neither the Son*[11]; which precludes the idea, that He had just before declared that the whole would take place in that generation. For this would be to make out, that He declared that the Son knew not the hour of His Coming, which He had just (on this supposition) declared to be in that generation.

So then, here. There was a general shaking upon earth before our Lord came. Empires rose and fell. The Persian fell before Alexander's; Alexander's world-empire was ended by his sudden death in youth; of his four successors, two only continued, and they too fell before the Romans; then were the Roman civil wars, until, under Augustus, the temple of Janus was shut. "[12]For it greatly beseemed a work ordered by God, that many kingdoms should be confederated in one empire, and that the universal preaching might find the peoples easily accessible who were held under the rule of one state." In the Heavens was the star, which led the wise men, the manifestation of Angels to the shepherds; the preternatural darkness at the Passion; the Ascension into the highest Heaven, and the descent of the Holy Ghost with[13] *a sound from heaven as* [*of*] *a rushing mighty wind.* "[14]God had moved them [heaven and earth] before, when He delivered the people from Egypt, when there was in heaven a column of fire, dry ground amid the waves, a wall in the sea, a path in the waters, in the wilderness there was multiplied a daily harvest of heavenly food [the manna], the rock gushed into fountains of waters. But He moved it afterward also in the Passion of the Lord Jesus, when the heaven was darkened, the sun shrank back, the rocks were rent, the graves opened, the dead were raised, the dragon, conquered in his waters, saw the fishers of men, not only sailing in the sea, but also walking without peril. The dry ground also was moved, when the unfruitful people of the nations began to ripen to a harvest of devotion and faith,—so that *more were the children of the forsaken, than* of *her which had a husband*, and[15] *the desert flourished like a lily.*" "[16]He moved earth in that great miracle of the birth from the Virgin: He moved the sea and dry land, when in the islands and in the whole world Christ is preached. So we see all nations moved to the faith."

And yet, whatever preludes of fulfillment there were at our Lord's first Coming, they were as nothing to the fulfillment which we look for in the Second, *when*[17] *the earth shall be utterly broken down; the earth, clean dissolved; the earth, moved exceedingly; the earth shall reel to and fro like a drunkard, and shall be removed like a hanging-cot in a vineyard*[18], *and the transgression thereof is heavy upon it; and it shall fall and not rise again;* whereon follows an announcement of the final judgment of men and angels, and the everlasting kingdom of the blessed in the presence of God.

Of that *day of the Lord*, St. Peter uses our Lord's image,[19] that it *shall*[20] *come as a thief in the night, in which the heavens shall melt with fervent heat, the earth also and the works therein shall be burned up.*

7. *And the desire of all nations shall come.*

[1] Dan. xi. xii.
[2] Ob. 18–21.
[3] See on Zeph. i. 2, 3. p. 235, 236.
[4] Mal. iii. 1–5. 17, 18. iv.
[5] The second question about the end of the world occurs only in S. Matthew (xxiv. 3); the first, *When shall these things be?* occurs in S. Mark also (xiii. 3) and S. Luke (xxi. 6). The words in S. Mark, *This generation shall not pass till all these things be done* (xiii. 30) seem to me to be cast in the form of their question, *When shall these things be?* viz. the things about which they had asked.
[6] S. Matt. xxiv. 15, 16.
[7] Ib. 24.
[8] 2 Thess. v. 2–10.
[9] S. Mark xiii. 30.
[10] Ib. 34.
[11] Ib. 32.
[12] S. Leo Hom. 82 in Nat. Ap. Petri et Pauli. c. 2. col. 322. Ball.
[13] Acts ii. 2.
[14] S. Ambr. Ep. 30 ad Iren. n. 11, 12. Opp. ii. 913 Ben.
[15] Is. xxxv. 1.
[16] S. Aug. de Civ. Dei. xviii. 25.
[17] Is. xxiv. 19, 20.
[18] מלונה. See a picture of one in Niebuhr.
[19] S. Matt. xxiv. 43.
[20] 2 S. Pet. iii. 10.

The words can only mean this, *the* central longing of all nations[1]; He whom they longed for, either through the knowledge of Him spread by the Jews in their dispersion, or mutely by the aching craving of the human heart, longing for the restoration from its decay. *The earnest expectation of the creature* did not begin with the Coming of Christ, nor was it limited to those, who actually came to Him. [2] *The whole creation,* Saint Paul saith, *groaneth and travaileth in pain together until now.* It was enslaved, and the better self longed to be free; every motion of grace in the multitudinous heart of man was a longing for its Deliverer; every weariness of what it was, every fleeting vision of what was better, every sigh from out of its manifold ills, were notes of the one varied cry, "Come and help us." Man's heart, formed in the image of God, could not but ache to be re-formed by and for Him, though *an unknown God,* Who should reform it.

This longing increased as the time drew nigh, when Christ should come. The Roman biographer attests the existence of this expectation, not among the Jews only, but in the East[3]; this was quickened doubtless among the heathen by the Jewish Sibylline book, in that, amid the expectations of one sent from heaven, who should found a kingdom of righteousness, which the writer drew from the Hebrew prophets, he inserted denunciations of temporal vengeance upon the Romans, which Easterns would share. Still, although written 170 years before our Lord came[4], it had not apparently much effect until the time, when, from the prophecies of Daniel it was clear, that He must shortly come[5]. Yet the attempt of the Jewish[6] and heathen [7] historian to wrest it to Vespasian, shews how great must have been the influence of the expectation, which they attempted to turn aside. The Jews, who rejected our Lord Whom Haggai predicted, still were convinced that the prediction must be fulfilled before the destruction of the second temple. The impulse did not cease even after its destruction. R. Akiba, whom they accounted "[8] the first oracle of his time, the first and greatest guardian of the tradition

[1] חמד is "coveted." It is the passion forbidden in the tenth commandment, Ex. xx. 14, (bis) Deut. v. 18, vii. 25, Ex. xxxiv. 24, Jos. vii. 21, Pr. vi. 25, Mi. ii. 2. In Pr. xii. 12, it is a passionate desire which ends in choice. It is united with "loved" and "hated," Ib. i. 22; of the passionate idolatry, Is. i. 29. It is used of God's passionless good-pleasure in that which He chooses, yet speaking after the manner of men, Ps. lxviii. 17, and of man's not longing for Jesus, Is. liii. 2. The Piel is used once of intense longing. Cant. ii. 3. Men covet things for some real or seeming good; and so the passive form of the verb, חָמוּד or נֶחְמָד, are things which are the object of coveting, and so things desirable; חמוד Job xx. 20, Ps. xxxix. 12, s. xliv. 9; נחמד Gen. ii. 9, iii. 6, Ps. xix. 11. Pr. xxi. 20. מַחְמָד with the gen. is "the desire of the eye," what it covets or desires, 1 Kgs xx. 6, Ex. xxiv. 16, 21, 25, Lam. ii. 4; or desirable things, belonging to one, Jo. iv. 5, Is. lxiv. 10, Lam. i. 10, 2 Chron. xxxvi. 19, or from it, מחמדי בטנם Hos. ix. 16. "the desires of the womb," "the desired children that their womb had borne," or with ל, "the desired things consisting in their silver," מחמד לכספם, Ib. ix. 6. or abs. Cant. v. 16. מחמד occurs in the same sense, Lam. i. 7, 11; חֲמֻדוֹת or א׳ש ח. of Daniel, as the object of the love of God, Dan. ix. 23, x. 11, 19; and of desirable things, Gen. xxvii. 15, 2 Chr. xx. 25, Dan. x. 3, xi. 38, 43, Ezr. viii. 27.

As to חֶמְדָּה itself, two idioms have been confused; 1) that in which it is accessory to another word, as כלי חמדה "vessels of desire," Hos. xiii. 15, Jer. xxv. 34, 2 Chr. xxxii. 27, Dan. xi. 8, Nah. ii. 10; ארץ חמדה, "land of desire," Ps. cvi. 24, Jer. iii. 19, Zech. vii. 14; בתי חמדתך "houses of thy desire," or "thy houses of desire," Ez. xxvi. 12; חלקת חמדתי "my portion of desire," Jer. xii. 10. These we might paraphrase "pleasant vessels," "pleasant land," as we might say "desirables." Not that the word חמדה means, in itself, "pleasant things," any more than the word "coveted" signifies *pleasant,* though those things only are "coveted," which are thought to be pleasant. The original sense of the root, to "desire," is obviously brought out the more, when the idea is not subsidiary, but the chief. There are four cases, in which *Chemdah* is so used. (1) "Jehoram died בלא חמדה, unregretted," we should say; "no one longing for him," 2 Chr. xxi. 20; (2) "To whom is כל חמדת ישראל, the whole longing of Israel?" 1 Sam. ix. 20; (3) The well-known words חמדת נשים *Chemdath Nashim,* "the desire of women," Dan. xi. 37. If (as this is now generally understood) this means "the object of the longing of women," so much the more must חמרת כל הגוים mean, "the object of the longing of all nations." They cannot mean, "the most desirable of all nations," "die liebsten aller Völker," Ew. formerly; "die edelsten aller Völker," Hitzig; "die auserlesensten derselben;" Umbreit. This must have been expressed by aid of the passive participle in any of the forms, by which a superlative is expressed. Nor can it mean "the costly things of all people;" ("die höhen Schätzen aller der völker," Ewald, "die Köstbarkeiten aller Nationen," Scholz). This, if expressed by the word at all, would have been, מַחֲמַדֵּי כל הגוים. Rashi, A. E., Kimchi, explain as if ב were omitted. R. Isaac (Chizzuk Emunah, in Wagens. Tela ignea p. 288) quotes 2 Kgs xii. 13, where " בית stands as the acc. of place; R. Tanchum omits the verse, Abulwalid the instance. It is not noticed by R. Parchon, Kimchi, Menahem ben Saruk, David b. Abraham, in their dictionaries. Abarbanel retains the meaning, "the desire of all nations," interpreting it of the holy land. He paraphrases ויבואו ח. כל הג. "that they shall come to the holy land and there shall He be avenged of them, and then at that time 'I will fill this house with glory.' v. p. רעת, 4. The Anon. Arab. (Hunt. 206) renders "the most precious things of all nations shall come."

[2] Rom. viii. 19–22.

[3] Suet. Vesp. c. 4.

[4] See Pusey's "Daniel the Prophet," pp. 364–368.

[5] Ib. pp. 230–235.

[6] Jos. B. J. vi. 5. 4.

[7] Tac. Hist. v. 13.

[8] "He was President of the academies of Lidda and Jafna, disciple and successor of Rabban Gamaliel, and a man of such learning and repute, that he was accounted among the Hebrews the first oracle &c." De Rossi Diz. stor. d. Autori Ebr. sub v.

and old law," of whom they said, that "[1] God revealed to him things unknown to Moses," was induced by this prophecy to acknowledge the impostor Bar-cochab, to the destruction of himself and of the most eminent of his time; fulfilling our Lord's words, [2] *I am come in My Father's name, and ye receive Me not; if another shall come in his own name, him ye will receive.* Akiba, following the traditional meaning of the great prophecy which rivetted his own eyes, paraphrased the words, "[3] Yet a little, a little of the kingdom, will I give to Israel upon the destruction of the first house, and after the kingdom, lo! I will shake heaven, and after that will come the Messiah."

Since the words can only mean "the Desire of all nations," he or that which all nations long for, the construction of the words does not affect the meaning. Herod doubtless thought to advance his own claims on the Jewish people by his material adorning of the temple; yet, although mankind do covet gold and silver, few could seriously think that, while a heathen immoral but observant poet could speak of "gold undiscovered and so better placed [4]," or our own of the "pale and common drudge 'Tween man and man," a Hebrew prophet could recognize gold and silver as *the desire of all nations.* R. Akiba and S. Jerome's Jewish teachers, after our Lord came, felt no difficulty in understanding it of a person. We cannot in English express the delicacy of the phrase, whereby manifoldness is combined in unity, the Object of desire containing in itself many objects of desire. To render "the desire of all nations" or "the desires of all nations" alike fail to do this. A great heathen master of language said to his wife, "fare you well, my longings [5]," i. e., I suppose, if he had analyzed his feelings, he meant that she manifoldly met the longings of his heart; she had in herself manifold gifts to content them. So St. Paul sums up all the truths and gifts of the Gospel, all which God shadowed out in the law and had given us in Christ, under the name of "[6] the good things to come." A pious modern writer [7] speaks of "the unseen *desirables* of the spiritual world." A psalmist expresses at once the collective, "God's Word" and the "words" contained in it, by an idiom like Haggai's, joining the feminine singular as a collective with the plural verb; [8] *How sweet are Thy word unto my taste* lit. *palate.* It is God's word, at once collectively and individually, which was to the Psalmist so *sweet.* What was true of the whole, was true, one by one, of each part; what was true of each part, was true of the whole. So here, the object of this longing was manifold, but met in one, was concentrated in One, [9] *in Christ Jesus, Who of God is made unto us wisdom and righteousness and sanctification and redemption.* That which the whole world sighed and mourned for, knowingly or unknowingly, light to disperse its darkness, liberty from its spiritual slavery, restoration from its degradation, could not come to us without some one, who should impart it to us.

But if Jesus was *the longed-for of the nations* before He came, by that mute longing of need for that which it wants (as the parched ground thirsteth for the rain [10]) how much more afterward! So Micah and Isaiah describe many peoples inviting one another [11] *Come ye, and let us go up to the mountain of the Lord, to the house of the God of Jacob; and He will teach us of His ways, and we will walk in His paths.* And in truth He became the *desire of the nations*, much more than of the Jews; as, St. Paul says [12], God foretold of old; *Moses saith, I will provoke you to jealousy by* them that are *not a people: by a foolish nation I will anger you. But Esaias is very bold and saith, I was found of them that sought Me not.*

So till now and in eternity, "[13] Christ is the longing of all holy souls, who long for nothing else, than to please Him, daily to love Him more, to worship Him better. So S. John longed for Him; *Come, Lord Jesus* [14]. So Isaiah; [15] *The desire of our soul is to Thy Name and to the remembrance of Thee: with my soul have I desired Thee in the night; yea, with my spirit within me, will I seek Thee early.* So S. Ignatius, "[16] Let fire, cross, troops of wild beasts, dissections, rendings, scattering of bones, mincing of limbs, grindings of the whole body, ill tortures of the devil come upon me, only may I gain Jesus Christ.—I seek Him Who for us died; I long for Him Who for us rose."

"[13] Hungerest thou and desirest food? Long for Jesus! He is the bread and refreshment of Angels. He is manna, *containing in Him*

[1] R. Bechai. See ab. p. 48. note 12.

[2] S. John v. 43.

[3] Sanhedrin. dist. *chelek* in Mart. Pug. fid. p. 305. R. Gedaliah B. Yechaiah quotes R. Akiba, rejecting his interpretation. "And not as Rabbi Akibah, who was interpreting this section; '*Yet once, it is a little and I shake the heaven and the earth.*' He interprets, that when Israel went to the captivity of Babylon, Haggai the prophet spake this section, and its meaning is, that in this house there will be little glory, and after this I will bring the desire of the heathen to Jerusalem." Shalsheleth Hakkabbala extracted in the Carm. R. Lipmanni confut. p. 619. in Wagenseil Tela ignea satanæ.

[4] "Aurum irrepertum et sic melius situm." Hor. Od. iii. 3. 49.

[5] "Valete, mea desideria, valete." Cic. Ep. ad Famil. xiv. 2. fin.

[6] Heb. x. 1. τῶν μελλόντων ἀγαθῶν.

[7] Dr. Watts Vol. i. Serm. 4.

[8] Ps. cxix. 103. מה נמלצו לחכי אמרתך.

[9] 1 Cor. i. 30.

[10] Euripides so uses ἐρᾶν, of the ground longing for the rain.

[11] Mi. iv. 2. Is. ii. 3.

[12] Rom. x. 19, 20; quoting Deut. xxxii. 21. Is. lxv. 2.

[13] Lap. [14] Rev. xxii. 20. [15] Is. xxvi. 8, 9.

[16] Ep. ad Rom. in Ruinart Acta Mart. p. 703.

Before CHRIST cir. 520.

I will fill this house with glory, saith the LORD of hosts.

8 The silver *is* mine and the gold *is* mine, saith the LORD of hosts.

Before CHRIST cir. 520.

all sweetness and pleasurable delight. Thirstest thou? Long for Jesus! He is the well of *living water*, refreshing, so that thou shouldest thirst no more. Art thou sick? Go to Jesus. He is the Saviour, the physician, nay, salvation itself. Art thou dying? Sigh for Jesus! He is *the resurrection and the life.* Art thou perplexed? Come to Jesus! He is *the Angel of great counsel.* Art thou ignorant and erring? Ask Jesus; He is *the way, the truth and the life.* Art thou a sinner? Call on Jesus! For *He shall save His people from their sins.* To this end He came into the world: *This is all His fruit, to take away sin.* Art thou tempted by pride, gluttony, lust, sloth? Call on Jesus! He is humility, soberness, chastity, love, fervor: *He bare our infirmities, and carried*, yea still beareth and carrieth, *our griefs.* Seekest thou beauty? He is *fairer than the children of men.* Seekest thou wealth? In Him are *all treasures*, yea in Him *the fullness of the Godhead dwelleth.* Art thou ambitious of honors? *Glory and riches are in His house. He is the King of glory.* Seekest thou a friend? He hath the greatest love for thee, Who for love of thee came down from heaven, toiled, endured the Sweat of Blood, the Cross and Death; He prayed for thee by name in the garden, and poured forth tears of Blood! Seekest thou wisdom? He is the Eternal and Uncreated Wisdom of the Father! Wishest thou for consolation and joy? He is the sweetness of souls, the joy and jubilee of Angels. Wishest thou for righteousness and holiness? He is *the Holy of holies;* He is *everlasting Righteousness*, justifying and sanctifying all who believe and hope in Him. Wishest thou for a blissful life? He is *life eternal*, the bliss of the saints. Long then for Him, love Him, sigh for Him! In Him thou wilt find all good; out of Him, all evil, all misery. Say then with S. Francis, 'My Jesus, my love and my all!' O Good Jesus, burst the cataract of Thy love, that its streams, yea seas, may flow down upon us, yea, inebriate and overwhelm us."

And I will fill this house with glory. The glory then was not to be anything, which came from man, but directly from God. It was the received expression of God's manifestation of Himself in the tabernacle[1], in Solomon's temple[2], and of the ideal temple[3] which Ezekiel saw, after the likeness of that of Solomon, that *the glory of the Lord filled the house.* When then of this second temple God uses the self-same words, that He will *fill it with glory*, with what other glory should He fill it than His own? In the history it is said, *the glory of the Lord filled the temple;* for there man relates what God did. Here it is God Himself Who speaks; so He says not, *the glory of the Lord*, but, *I will fill the house with glory*, glory which was His to give, which came from Himself. To interpret that *glory* of anything material, is to do violence to language, to force on words of Scripture an unworthy sense, which they refuse to bear.

The gold upon the walls, even had this second temple been adorned like the first did not fill the temple of Solomon. However richly any building might be overlaid with gold, no one could say that it is filled with it. A building is filled with what it contains; a mint or treasure-house may be filled with gold: the temple of God was *filled*, we are told, *with the glory of the Lord.* His creatures bring Him such things as they can offer; they bring [4] *gold and incense;* they [5] *bring presents* and *offer gifts;* they do it, moved by His Spirit, as acceptable to Him. God is nowhere said, Himself to give these offerings to Himself.

8. *The silver is Mine, and the gold is Mine.* These words, which have occasioned some to think, that God, in speaking of the glory with which He should fill the house, meant our material riches, suggest the contrary. For silver was no ornament of the temple of Solomon. Everything was overlaid with gold. In the tabernacle there were bowls of silver[6], in Solomon's temple they and all were of gold[7]. Silver, we are expressly told, *was nothing accounted of* [8] *in the days of Solomon: he* [9] *made silver to be in Jerusalem as stones—for abundance.* Rather, as God says by the Psalmist, [10] *Every beast of the forest is Mine, so are the cattle upon a thousand hills: I know all the fowls of the mountains, and the wild beasts of the field are Mine. If I were hungry, I would not tell thee: for the world is Mine, and the fullness thereof:* so here He tells them, that for the glory of His house He needed not gold or silver: for all the wealth of the world is His. They had no ground "[11] to grieve then, that they could not equal the magnificence of Solomon who had abundance of gold and silver." All was God's. He

[1] Ex. xl. 34, 35.
[2] 1 Kgs viii. 11. 2 Chr. v. 14. vii. 1–12.
[3] Ezek. xliii. 5. xliv. 4.
[4] Is. lx. 6.
[5] Ps. lxxii. 10.
[6] Nu. vii. 19, 25, 31. &c. The "charger" (קערה) which in the tabernacle was of silver (Nu. vii. 13. &c.) does not appear in the temple of Solomon.
[7] 1 Kgs vii. 50. 2 Chr. iv. 8.
[8] 1 Kgs x. 21.
[9] Ib. 27.
[10] Ps. l. 10–12.
[11] Lap.

Before CHRIST cir. 520.

l John 1. 14.

9 [l] The glory of this latter house shall be greater than of the former, saith the LORD of hosts: and in

Before CHRIST cir. 520.

---

would fill it with divine glory. The Desire of all nations, Christ, should come, and be a glory, to which all created glory is nothing.

"[1] God says really and truly, that the silver and gold is His, which in utmost bounty He created, and in His most just government administers, so that, without His will and dominion, neither can the bad have gold and silver for the punishment of avarice, nor the good for the use of mercy. Its abundance does not inflate the good, nor its want crush them: but the bad, when bestowed, it blinds: when taken away, it tortures."

"[2] It is as if He would say, Think not the temple inglorious, because, may be, it will have no portion of gold or silver, and their splendor. I need not such things. How should I? *For Mine is the silver and Mine the gold, saith the Lord Almighty.* I seek rather true worshipers: with their brightness will I guild this temple. Let him come who hath right faith, is adorned by graces, gleams with love for Me, is pure in heart, poor in spirit, compassionate and good." "These make the temple, i.e. the Church, glorious and renowned, being glorified by Christ. For they have learned to pray [3], *The glory of the Lord our God be upon us.*"

9. *The glory of this latter house shall be greater than of the former*, or, perhaps, more probably, *the later glory of this house shall be greater than the former;* for he had already spoken of the present temple, as identical with that before the captivity; "[4] Who is left among you that saw *this house* in her first glory, and how do you see *it* now?" He had spoken of its *first glory.* Now he says, in contrast, its later glory should be greater than that of its most glorious times [5]. In this case the question, whether the temple of Herod was a different material building from that of Zerubbabel, falls away. In either case, the contrast is between two things, either the temple in that its former estate, and this its latter estate after the captivity, or the two temples of Solomon and Zerubbabel. There is no room for a third temple. God holds out no vain hopes. To comfort those distressed by the poverty of the house of God which they were building, God promises a glory to this house greater than before. A temple, erected, after this had lain waste above 1800 years, even if Anti-Christ were to come now and to erect a temple at Jerusalem, could be no fulfillment of this prophecy.

In material magnificence the temple of Solomon, built and adorned with all the treasures accumulated by David and enlarged by Solomon, far surpassed all which Herod, amid his attempts to give a material meaning to the prophecy, could do. His attempt shews how the eyes of the Jews were fixed on this prophecy, then when it was about to be fulfilled. While taking pains, through the gradualness of his rebuilding, to preserve the identity of the fabric, he lavished his wealth, to draw off their thoughts from the king, whom the Jews looked for, to himself. The friendship of the Romans who were lords of all, was to replace the *all nations*, of whom Haggai spoke; he pointed also to the length of peace, the possession of wealth, the greatness of revenues, the surpassing expenditure beyond those before [6]. A small section of Erastians admitted these claims of the murderer of his sons. The Jews generally were not diverted from looking on to *Him Who should come.* Those five things, the absence whereof they felt, were connected with their atoning worship or God's Presence among them; "[7] the ark with the mercy-seat and the Cherubim, the Urim and Tummim, the fire from heaven, the Shechinah, the Holy Ghost." Material magnificence could not replace spiritual glory. The

---

[1] S. Aug. Serm. 50. (de Ag. 2.) n. 4, 5. [2] S. Cyr.

[3] Ps. xc. 17.

[4] ii. 3. So the LXX. "Wherefore great will be the last glory of this house above the first [glory]." In the other case, the order would have probably been, כבוד הבית האחרון הזה as in Ex. iii. 3, De. ii. 7, iv. 6, 1 Sam. xii. 16, 1 Kgs iii. 9, xx. 13, 28, Jon. i. 12; but, as Köhler observes, this is not quite uniform, as in 2 Chr. i. 10.

[5] This interpretation involves a change in the wording of the argument from this prophecy, as to the time of our Lord's first coming. For thus interpreted, it does not speak of a second house, and so does not, in terms, speak of the material building which was destroyed. R. Isaac made use of this: "a difficulty need not be raised, that he said, 'this house' of the house which is to be built, since of the first house, which in their time was of old waste, he said 'this house' in the words, 'who is left among you, who hath seen this house in its first glory?' and as 'this house' is spoken of the house of the sanctuary which was then desolate, which was passed away, so he saith, 'this house,' of the house which shall be." Chizzuch Emunah, c. 34. Wagens. p. 292.

[6] In his oration to the Jews, "Our forefathers built this temple to the supreme God after the return from Babylon, yet in size it lacks 60 cubits in height; for so much did the first, which Solomon built, exceed.—But since, by the counsel of God, I now rule, and we have a long peace, and ample funds and large revenues; and chief of all, the Romans, who, so to speak, are lords of all, are our friends and kindly disposed," (Joseph. Ant. xv. 11. 1.) and a little later (n. 3) "exceeding the expenditure of those aforetime, in a way in which no other appears to have adorned the temple." See Hengst. Christ. iii. 257, 258. ed. 2.

[7] Yoma 21. b.

Before CHRIST cir. 520.

this place will I give [k]peace, saith the LORD of hosts.

[k] Ps. 85. 8, 9. Luke 2. 14. Eph. 2. 14.

10 ¶ In the four and twentieth *day* of the ninth *month*, in the second year

Before CHRIST cir. 520.

explanations of the great Jewish authorities[1], that the second temple was superior to the first in structure (which was untrue) or in duration, were laid aside by Jews who had any other solution wherewith to satisfy themselves. "The Shechinah and the five precious things," says one[2], "which, according to our wise of blessed memory, were in it, and not in the second house, raised and exalted it beyond compare." Another[3] says, "When Haggai saith, 'greater shall be the glory of this later house than the first,' how is it, that the house which Zerubbabel built through the income which the king of Persia gave them was more glorious than the house which Solomon built? And though it is said that the building which Herod made, was exceeding beautiful and rich, we should not think that it was in its beauty like to the house which Solomon built. For what the wise of blessed memory have said of the beauty of the house of Herod is in relation to the house which Zerubbabel built. How much more, since Scripture saith not, 'Great shall be the *beauty* or the *wealth* of this latter house above the first,' but the *glory:* and the glory is not the wealth or the beauty, or the largeness of the dimensions of the building, as they said in their interpretations; for the 'glory' is in truth spoken of the glory of God, which filled the tabernacle, after it was set up, and of the glory of God which filled the house of God, which Solomon built, when he brought the ark into the holy of holies, which is the Divine cloud and the Light supreme, which came down thither in the eyes of all the people, and it is said, 'And it was when the priests came out of the holy place, the cloud filled the house of God, and the priests could not stand to minister because of the cloud, for the glory of God filled the house of God.' And this glory was not in the second house. And how shall it be said, if so, 'great shall be the glory of this later house above the first'?" The poor unconverted Jew did not know the answer to his question: "Through the Presence of God, in the substance of our flesh; through *the Son given to us*, Whose *name* should be *Mighty God*." The glory of this temple was in Him Who [4]*was made Flesh and dwelt among us, and we beheld His glory, the glory as of the Only Begotten of the Father, full of grace and truth.* "[5]There Christ, the Son of God, was, as a Child, offered to God: there He sat in the midst of the Doctors; there He taught and revealed things, hidden from the foundation of the world. The glory of the temple of Solomon was, that in it the majesty of God appeared, veiling itself in a cloud: in this, that same Majesty shewed itself, in very deed united with the Flesh, visible to sight: so that Jesus Himself said, [6]*He that hath seen Me hath seen the Father*. This it was which

[1] "Rab and Samuel disputed hereon, or, as others, R. Jochanan and R. Eliezer. The former said, 'it shall be more glorious in structure;' the latter, 'in years.'" Baba bathra c. 1. f. 30. R. Asariah quotes also from the Shir hashshirim Rabba on Cant. ii. 12 and viii. 1, and adds, "We have found that the best interpreters explained this prophecy literally as to the second house." This is followed by Kimchi, Rashi, A. E., Lipmann (Nizz. n. 260), Manasseh ben Israel (de term. vitæ) iii. 4. (Hilpert de gloria Templi post., Thes. Theol.-Phil. p. 1086 sqq.) Tanchum. Of the magnificence of the building they allege only that the building was in *size* equal to that of Solomon, while even in material magnificence it was beyond measure inferior. The relative duration they underrate; "the first, 410 years; the second 420;" for from the xi[th] of Solomon's reign, B.C. 1005, to the burning of the temple in the xi[th] of Zedekiah, were 417 years; but from the vi[th] of Darius when the 2d temple was finished, B.C. 515, to the burning of the temple under Titus A.D. 70, were 585 years. But mere duration is not glory. R. Isaac says as Abarbanel; "But it is a difficulty in what they say, that Scripture says not, 'great shall be the building of the house,' or, 'the time of the house,' only 'great shall be the glory of the house;' for what that the 2d house stood ten years more than the 1st, this was not such great glory, that for this the prophet should say what he said: and again though the days during which the 2d house stood were 100 years more than the duration of the first house, and though in its building it were twofold greater than the first house, how saith Scripture of it on this account, that its glory was greater than the first, since the glory which dwelt in the first house did not dwell in it?" Chizz. Em. l. c. pp. 287, 288. "Wherefore it is rather the true glory which is the abiding of the glory of the Shechinah in this house for ever; which did not abide continually in the first house; but in the second house the glory did not dwell at all; for they had not the ark and the mercy seat and the cherubim, or the Urim and Tummim, nor the Holy Spirit, nor the heavenly fire, nor the anointing oil, as it was in the 1st house." Ib. p. 293. Others made the glory to consist in the absence of idolatry, quoted Ib. p. 286. R. Lipmann Nizz. p. 42, makes in it to consist in the uninterruptedness of the worship of God there, whereas the temple was shut by Ahaz and Manasseh [as was the second at least desecrated by Antiochus Epiphanes for 3 years. 1 Macc. i. 54, iv. 59.]

[2] R. Asariah de Rossi *Imre Binah*, c. 51, in Hilpert l. c. n. 8. His own solution is that the glory was not in the temple itself, but in that kings brought presents to it. Ib. 10.

[3] Abarbanel Quæst. iv. in Hagg. f. רען. He says that "the interpreters, all of them explained it of the second house." p. רעח 2. Abarb subjoins a criticism, which R. Asaria, *Imre-Binah* c. 54, saw to be mistaken, that ראשון and אחרון could not be said of two things (of which אחד and שני are, he says, used) against which R. Asariah quotes Jer. l. 17. Gen. xxxiii. 2. Add Ex. iv. 8. Deut. xxiv. 3, 4. Ru. iii. 10, Is. viii. 23. [ix. 1. Eng.]

[4] S. John i. 14. [5] Lap. [6] S. John xiv. 9.

Before CHRIST cir. 520.

of Darius, came the word
of the LORD by Haggai
the prophet saying,
11 Thus saith the LORD
of hosts; [l]Ask now the

[l] Lev. 10. 10, 11. Deut. 33. 10. Mal. 2. 7.

priests *concerning* the law
saying,
12 If one bear holy
flesh in the skirt of his
garment, and with his

Before CHRIST cir. 520.

Malachi sang with joy: [1] *The Lord Whom ye seek shall suddenly come to His temple, even the Messenger of the covenant, whom ye delight in.*"

And in this place I will give peace. Temporal peace they had now, nor was there any prospect of its being disturbed. They were quiet subjects of the Persiam empire, which included also all their former enemies, greater or less. Alexander subdued all the bordering countries which did not yield, but spared themselves. Temporal peace then was nothing to be then given them; for they had it. In later times they had it not. The temple itself was profaned by Antiochus Epiphanes. "[2] Her sanctuary was laid waste like a wilderness. As had been her glory, so was her dishonor increased." Again by Pompey[3], by Crassus[4], the Parthians[5], before it was destroyed by Titus and the Romans. Jews saw this and, knowing nothing of the peace in Jesus, argued from the absence of outward peace, that the prophecy was not fulfilled under the second temple. "[6] What Scripture says, 'and in this place I will give peace,' is opposed to their interpretation. For all the days of the duration of the 2d house were *in strait of times* and not in peace, as was written in Daniel, *and threescore and two weeks: the street shall be built again and the fosse, and in strait of time*, and, as I said, in the time of Herod there was no peace whatever, for the sword did not depart from his house to the day of his death; and after his death the hatred among the Jews increased, and the Gentiles straitened them, until they were destroyed from the face of the earth."

But spiritual peace is, throughout prophecy, part of the promise of the Gospel. Christ Himself was to be [7] *the Prince of peace: of the increase of His government and of His peace* there was to be *no end;* in His days [8] *the mountains were to bring peace to the people; there should be abundance of peace, so long as the moon endureth; the work of righteousness* was to be *peace*[9]; *the chastisement of our peace* [that which obtained it] *was upon Him*[10]; *great* should be *the peace of her children*[11]; in the Gospel God would give *peace*, true *peace*, to the *far off and the near*[12]; He would extend [13] *peace to her like a river:* the good things of the Gospel was *the publishing of peace*[14]. The Gospel is described as [15] *a covenant of peace:* the promised king [16] *shall speak peace to the Heathen;* He Himself should be *our peace*[17]. And when He was born, the angels proclaimed [18] *on earth peace, goodwill toward men:* [19] *The Dayspring from on high visited us, to guide our feet into the way of peace.* He Himself says, [20] *My peace I leave with you.* He spake, that [21] *in Me ye might have peace.* S. Peter sums up *the word which God sent unto the children of Israel,* as [22] *preaching peace by Jesus Christ:* [23] *the kingdom of God is joy and peace;* [24] Christ *is our peace; made peace; preaches peace. God calleth us to peace*[25], in the Gospel: [26] *being justified by faith, we have peace with God through Jesus Christ our Lord;* [27] *the fruit of the Spirit is love joy peace.* Spiritual peace being thus prominent in the Gospel and in prophecy, as the gift of God, it were unnatural to explain *the peace* which God promised here to give, as other than He promised elsewhere; peace in Him Who is *our peace, Jesus Christ.*

"[28] Peace and tranquillity of mind is above all glory of the house; because peace passeth all understanding. This is peace above peace, which shall be given after the third shaking of heaven sea earth, dry land, when He shall destroy all powers and principalities [in the day of judgment].—And so shall there be peace throughout, that, no bodily passions or hindrances of unbelieving mind resisting, Christ shall be all in all, exhibiting the hearts of all subdued to the Father."

11–14. *Ask now the priests concerning the law.* The priests answer rightly, that, by the law, insulated unholiness spread further than insulated holiness. The flesh of the sacrifice hallowed whatever it should touch[29], but not further; but the human being, who was defiled by touching a dead body, defiled all he might touch[30]. Haggai does not

[1] Mal. iii. 1.
[2] 1 Macc. i. 39, 40.
[3] Jos. Ant. xiv. 4. 4. B. J. i. 7.
[4] Ant. xiv. 7. 1. B. J. i. 9. 8.
[5] Ant. xiv. 13. 3. 4.
[6] "Abraham B. Dior in his book of the Cabbala, p. 43" in R. Isaac Chizz. Em. l. c. p. 287. R. Isaac makes as if he had answered the explanation as to Jesus by quoting S. Matt. x. 34. l. c. p. 292, 293.
[7] Is. ix. 6, 7.
[8] Ps. lxxii. 3. 7.
[9] Is. xxxii. 17.
[10] Ib. liii. 5.
[11] Ib. liv. 13.
[12] Ib. lvii. 19.
[13] Ib. lxvi. 12.
[14] Ib. lii. 7.
[15] Ez. xxxiv. 25.
[16] Zech. ix. 10.
[17] Mi. v. 5.
[18] S. Luke ii. 14.
[19] Ib. i. 79.
[20] S. John xiv. 27.
[21] Ib. xvi. 33.
[22] Acts x. 36.
[23] Rom. xiv. 17.
[24] Eph. ii. 14, 15, 17.
[25] 1 Cor. vii. 15.
[26] Rom. v. 1.
[27] Gal. v. 22.
[28] S. Ambr. l. c. n. 14. Opp. ii. 913.
[29] Lev. vi. 19 (27 Eng.)
[30] Nu. xix. 22.

Before CHRIST cir. 520.

skirt do touch bread, or
pottage, or wine, or oil, or
any meat, shall it be holy?
And the priest answered
and said, No.
13 Then said Haggai,
If *one that is* [m] unclean by
a dead body touch any of
these, shall it be unclean?
And the priests answered
and said, It shall be un-
clean.
14 Then answered Hag-
gai, and said, [n] So *is* this
people, and so *is* this nation before me, saith the
LORD; and so *is* every
work of their hands; and
that which they offer there
is unclean.
15 And now, I pray
you, [o] consider from this
day and upward, from be-
fore a stone was laid upon
a stone in the temple of
the LORD:
16 Since those *days*
were, [p] when *one* came to
an heap of twenty *meas-
ures*, there were *but* ten:
when *one* came to the
pressfat for to draw out
fifty *vessels* out of the
press, there were *but*
twenty.
17 [q] I smite you with

[m] Num. 19. 11.
[n] Tit. 1. 15.
[o] ch. 1. 5.
[p] ch. 1. 6, 9. Zech. 8. 10.
[q] Deut. 28. 22. 1 Kin. 8. 37. ch. 1. 9. Amos 4. 9.

apply the first part; viz. that the worship on the altar which they reared, while they neglected the building of the temple, did not hallow. The possession of a holy thing does not counterbalance disobedience. Contrariwise, one defilement defiled the whole man and all which he touched, according to that, [1] *whosoever shall keep the whole law and yet offend in one point, he is guilty of all.*

In the application, the two melt into one; for the holy thing, viz. the altar which they raised out of fear on their return, so far from hallowing the land or people by the sacrifices offered thereon, was itself defiled. *This people* and *this nation* (not "My people") since they in act disowned Him. *Whatever they offer there*, i. e. on that altar, instead of the temple which God commanded, is unclean, offending Him Who gave all.

15. *And now, I pray you.* Observe his tenderness, in drawing their attention to it[2]. *Consider from this day and upward.* He bids them look backward, *from before a stone was laid upon a stone*, i. e. from the last moment of their neglect in building the house of God; *from since those* days *were*, or *from* the time backward *when those things were*, (resuming, in the word, *from-their-being*[3], the date which he had just given, viz. the beginning of their resuming the building backward, during all those years of neglect) *one came to a heap of twenty* measures. The precise measure is not mentioned[4]: the force of the appeal lay in the proportion: *the heap* of corn which, usually, would yield *twenty*, (whether bushels[5] or *seahs*[6] or any other measure, for the heap itself being of no defined size, neither could the quantity expected from it be defined) *there were ten* only; *one came to the press-vat to draw out fifty* vessels out of the *press*, or perhaps *fifty poorah*, i. e. the ordinary quantity drawn out at one time from the press[7], *there were*, or *it had become, twenty*, two-fifths only of what they looked for and ordinarily obtained. The dried grapes yielded so little.

17. *I smote you with blasting and mildew*, two diseases of corn, which Moses had foretold[8] as chastisements on disobedience and God's infliction, of which Amos had spoken in these self-same words[9]. Haggai adds *the hail*, as destructive of the vines[10]. *Yet* [*And*] *ye* turned *you not to Me* lit. *there were none—you*, (accusative[11]) i. e. who turned you unto Me. The words are elliptical, but express the entire absence of conversion, of any who turned to God.

[1] S. James ii. 10.
[2] As expressed by נא, here and 18.
[3] מִהְיוֹתָם.
[4] Ruth iii. 7. Neh. xiii. 15. 2 Chr. xxxi. 6–9.
[5] Vulg.
[6] LXX.
[7] פּוּרָה only occurs beside, Is. lxiii. 3; where it is the winefat itself. The LXX render it μετρηταὶ; Jon. גרבין (which they use for נבל 1 Sam. x. 3, xxv. 18, Jer. xiii. 12) Vulg. *lagenas.*
[8] Deut. xxviii. 27.
[9] Am. iv. 9.
[10] Ps. lxxviii. 47.
[11] אֶתְכֶם marking the acc., אין אתכם is not for אינכם, which itself, according to the common Hebrew construction, would require a participle, to express action on their part. See instances in Fürst Conc. p. 45. v. 'אינג, Ex. v. 19, De. i. 42, Is. i. 15, Jer. xiv. 12 (bis), xxxvii. 14; אינך Gen. xx. 7, xliii. 5, Ex. viii. 17, Jud. xii. 3, 1 Sam. xix. 11, 2 Sam. xix. 8, 1 Kgs xxi. 5, Neh. ii. 2, Eccl. xi. 5, 6. Jer. vii. 17; אינכם, De. i. 32, iv. 12, 2 Kgs xii. 8, Ez. xx. 39,

Before CHRIST cir. 520.

r ch. 1. 11.
s Jer. 5. 3. Amos 4. 6, 8, 9, 10, 11.
t Zech. 8. 9.

blasting and mildew and
with hail [r] in all the labors
of your hands; [s] yet ye
turned not to me, saith the
LORD.
18 Consider now from
this day and upward, from
the four and twentieth day
of the ninth *month*, *even*
from [t] the day that the
foundation of the LORD's
temple was laid, consider *it*.
19 [u] Is the seed yet in
the barn? yea, as yet the
vine, and the fig tree, and
the pomegranate, and the
olive tree, hath not brought
forth: from this day will I
bless *you*.
20 ¶ And again the
word of the LORD came

Before CHRIST cir. 520.

u Zech. 8. 12.

18. *From the day that the foundation of the Lord's house.* Zechariah, in a passage corresponding to this, uses the same words [1], *the day that the foundation of the house of the Lord of hosts was laid, that the temple might be built*, not of the first foundation, but of the work as resumed in obedience to the words by *the mouth of the prophets*, Haggai and himself, which, Ezra also says, was [2] *in the second year of Darius.* But that work was resumed, not now at the time of this prophecy, but three months before, on the 24th of the sixth month. Since then the word translated here, *from* [3], is in no case used of the present time, Haggai gives two dates, the resumption of the work, as marked in these words, and the actual present. He would then say, that even in these last months, since they had begun the work, there were as yet no signs for the better. There was yet no *seed in the barn*, the harvest having been blighted and the fruit-trees stripped by the hail before the close of the sixth month, when they resumed the work. Yet though there were as yet no signs of change, no earnest that the promise should be fulfilled, God pledges His word, *from this day I will bless you.*

Thenceforth, from their obedience, God would give them those fruits of the earth, which in His Providence had been, during their negligence, withheld. *God*, said St. Paul and Barnabas, [4] *left not Himself without witness, in that He did good, and gave us rain from heaven and fruitful seasons, filling our hearts with food and gladness.*

All the Old and New Testament, the Law, the Prophets and the Psalms, the Apostles and our Lord Himself, bear witness to the Providence of God Who makes His natural laws serve to the moral discipline of His creature, man. The physical theory, which presupposes that God so fixed the laws of His creation, as to leave no room for Himself to vary them, would, if ever so true, only come to this, that Almighty God knowing absolutely (as He must know) the actions of His creatures (in what way soever this is reconcilable with our free-agency, of which we are conscious), framed the laws of His physical creation, so that plenty or famine, healthiness of our cattle or of the fruits of the earth or their sickness, should coincide with the good or evil conduct of man, with his prayers or his neglect of prayer. The reward or chastisement alike come to man, whether they be the result of God's Will, acting apart from any system which He has created, or in it and through it. It is alike His Providential agency, whether He have established any such system with all its minute variations, or whether those variations are the immediate result of His sovereign

Mal. ii. 2, 9; אֵינֶנּוּ, De. xxi. 18, 20, Jud. iii. 25, 1 Sam. xi. 7, 2 Chr. xviii. 7, Esth. v. 13, Eccl. v. 11, viii. 7, 13, 16, ix. 2, Jer. xxxviii. 4, xliv. 16; אֵינָם, 2 Kgs xvii. 26, 34 bis, Eccl. iv. 17, ix. 5, Neh. xiii. 24, Jer. xxxii. 33, Ezek. iii. 7. וְאֵינְכֶם אֵלַי would have signified, "and ye were not [well disposed] toward Me," as in Hos. iii. 3, Jer. xv. 1, 2 Kgs vi. 11 (Ewald's instances Lehrb. n. 217 *c*), Gen. xxxi. 5; not (as required here) "ye turned you not unto Me," as in Am. iv. 6, 8, 9, 10, 11. Böttcher (Lehrbuch n. 516. d.) compares bene te (which implies a verb), en illum (where en is as a verb.) These however are exclamations, not parts of sentences. He thinks that אֵי is joined, 1) with a nom., and then an acc. after ו, 1 Sam. xxvi. 16; that יֵשׁ has an acc. Gen. xxiii. 8, 2 Kgs x. 15, and הֵן /אִ Zech. vii. 7.

[1] Zech. viii. 9.

[2] Ezr. iv. 24, v. 1.

[3] Such use of לְמִי would be inconsistent with any force of לְ. It is used of a *terminus à quo*, distant from the present, and is equivalent to "up to and from." So Jud. xix. 30, "No such deed was seen or done from the day that the children of Israel came up," i. e. looking back to that time and from it. So 2 Sam. vii. 6, "Since the time that I brought up the children of Israel out of Egypt," lit. "up to from the day." Add Ex. ix. 18, Deut. iv. 32, ix. 7, 2 Sam. vii. 11, xix. 25, Is. vii. 17, Jer. vii. 7, 25, xxv. 5, xxxii. 31, 1 Chr. xvii. 10, Mal. iii. 7. But there is no ground for thinking that Haggai used the word in any sense, in which it had not been used before him. The only construction consistent with the use of לְמִן elsewhere is, that the *terminus ad quem*, elsewhere expressed by וְעַד, having been expressed by the present מִיּוֹם, the distant *terminus à quo* is, as elsewhere, expressed by לְמִן.

[4] Acts xiv. 17.

Before CHRIST cir. 520.

unto Haggai in the four
and twentieth *day* of the
month, saying,
21 Speak to Zerubbabel,
[x] governor of Judah, saying, [y] I will shake the
heavens and the earth;
22 And [z] I will over-
throw the throne of king-
doms, and I will destroy
the strength of the king-
doms of the heathen; [a] I
will overthrow the chari-
ots, and those that ride in
them; and the horses and
their riders shall come
down, every one by the
sword of his brother.

x ch. 1. 14.
y ver. 6. 7. Heb. 12. 26.
z Dan. 2. 44. Matt. 24. 7.
a Mic. 5. 10. Zech. 4. 6. & 9. 10.

Before CHRIST cir. 520.

Will. If He has instituted any physical system, so that the rain, hail, and its proportions, size, destructiveness, should come in a regulated irregularity, as fixed in all eternity as the revolutions of the heavenly bodies or the courses of the comets, then we come only to a more intricate perfection of His creation, that in all eternity He framed those laws in an exact conformity to the perfectly foreseen actions of men good and evil, and to their prayers also: that He, knowing certainly whether the creature, which He has framed to have its bliss in depending on Him, would or would not cry unto Him, framed those physical laws in conformity therewith; so that the supply of what is necessary for our wants or its withholding shall be in all time inworked into the system of our probation. Only, not to keep God out of His own world, we must remember that other truth, that, whether God act in any such system or no, He [1] *upholdeth all things by the word of His power* by an ever-present working; so that it is He Who at each moment doth what is done, doth and maintains in existence all which He has created, in the exact order and variations of their being. [2] *Fire and hail, snow and vapor, stormy wind fulfilling His word,* are as immediate results of His Divine Agency, in whatever way it pleaseth Him to act, and are the expression of His Will.

21. *I will shake.* Haggai closes by resuming the words of a former prophecy to Zerubbabel and Joshua, which ended in the coming of Christ. Even thus it is plain, that the prophecy does not belong personally to Zerubbabel, but to him and his descendants, chiefly to Christ. There was in Zerubbabel's time no shaking of the heaven or of nations. Darius had indeed to put down an unusual number of rebellions in the first few years after his accession; but, although he magnified himself on occasion of their suppression, they were only so many distinct and unconcerted revolts, each under its own head. All were far away in the distant East, in Babylonia, Susiana, Media, Armenia, Assyria, Hyrcania, Parthia, Sagartia, Margiana, Arachosia [3]. The Persian *empire*, spread "[4] probably over 2,000,000 square miles, or more than half of modern Europe," was not threatened; no foreign enemy assailed it; one impostor only claimed the throne of Darius. This would, if successful, have been, like his own accession, a change of dynasty, affecting nothing externally. But neither were lasting, some were very trifling. Two decisive battles subdued Babylonia: of Media the brief summary is given; "[5] the Medes revolted from Darius, and having revolted were brought back into subjection, defeated in battle." The Susianians slew their own pretender, on the approach of the troops of Darius. We have indeed mostly the account only of the victor. But these are only self-glorying records of victories, accomplished in succession, within a few years. Sometimes the satrap of the province put the revolt down at once. At most two battles ended in the crucifixion of the rebel. The Jews, if they heard of them, knew them to be of no account. For the destroyer of the Persian empire was to come from the West [6]; the fourth sovereign was to stir up all against the realm of Grecia [7], and Darius was but the third. In the same second year of Darius, in which Haggai gave this prophecy, the whole earth was exhibited to Zechariah as [8] *sitting still and at rest.*

The overthrow prophesied is also universal. It is not one throne only, as of Persia, but *the throne,* i. e. the sovereigns, *of kingdoms;* not a change of dynasty, but a destruction of their *strength;* not of a few powers only, but *the kingdoms of the heathen;* and that, in detail; that, in which their chief strength lay, the chariots and horsemen and their riders, and this, man by man, *every one by the sword of his brother.* This mutual destruction is a feature of the judgments at the end of the world against Gog and Magog [9]; and of the yet unfulfilled prophecies of Zechariah [10]. Its stretching out so far does not hinder its par-

[1] Heb. i. 3.
[2] Ps. cxlviii. 8.
[3] Rawlinson v. Empires iv. pp. 407–415. chiefly from Behistun Inscription.
[4] Id. Ib. p. 2.
[5] Herod i. 130.
[6] Dan. viii. 5.
[7] Ib. xi. 2.
[8] Zech. i. 11.
[9] Ezek. xxxviii. 21.
[10] Zech. xiv. 17.

Before CHRIST cir. 520.

23 In that day, saith
the LORD of hosts, will I
take thee, O Zerubbabel,
my servant, the son of She-

tial fulfillment in earlier times. Zerubbabel stood, at the return from the captivity, as the representative of the house of David and heir of the promises to him, though in an inferior temporal condition; thereby the rather shewing that the main import of the prophecy was not temporal. As then Ezekiel prophesied, [1] *I will set up One Shepherd over them, and He shall feed them, My servant David;* [2] *And David My servant* shall be *king over them; and My servant David shall be their prince forever;* and Jeremiah, [3] *They shall serve the Lord their God and David their king, whom I will raise up unto them;* and Hosea, that [4] *after many days shall the children of Israel return and seek the Lord their God, and David their king,* meaning by David, the great descendant of David, in whom the promises centered, so in his degree, the promise to Zerubbabel reaches on through his descendants to Christ; that, amid all the overthrow of empires, God would protect his sons' sons until Christ should come, the King of kings and Lord of lords, Whose [5] *kingdom shall never be destroyed, but it shall break in pieces and consume all those kingdoms, and shall stand fast for ever.*

23. *I will make thee as a signet.* God reverses to Zerubbabel the sentence on Jeconiah for his impiety. To Jeconiah He had said, [6] *though he were the signet upon My right hand, yet would I pluck thee thence; and I will give thee into the hand of them that seek thy life.* The signet was very precious to its owner, never parted with, or only to those to whom authority was delegated (as by Pharaoh to Joseph [7], or by Ahasuerus to Haman [8] and then to Mordecai [9]); through it his will was expressed. Hence the spouse in the Canticles says, [10] *Set me, as a seal upon thy heart, as a seal upon thy arm.* The signet also was an ornament to him who wore it. *God is glorified in His saints* [11]; by Zerubbabel in the building of His house. He gave him estimation with Cyrus, who entrusted him with the return of his people, and made him (who would have been the successor to the throne of Judah, had the throne been re-established) his governor over the restored people. God promises to him and his descendants protection amid all shaking of empires. "[12] He was a type of Christ in bringing back the people from Babylon, as Christ delivered us from sin death and hell: he built the temple, as Christ built the Church; he protected his people against the Samaritans who would hinder the building, as Christ protects His Church: he was dear and joined to God, as Christ was united to Him, and hypostatically united and joined His Humanity to the Word. The true Zerubbabel then, i.e. Christ, the son and antitype of Zerubbabel, is the signet in the hand of the Father, both passively and actively, whereby God impresses His own Majesty thoughts and words and His own Image on men angels and all creatures." "[13] The Son is the Image of God the Father, having His entire and exact likeness, and in His own beauty beaming forth the nature of the Father. In Him too God seals us also to His own likeness, since, being conformed to Christ, we gain the image of God." "[12] Christ, as the Apostle says, is [14] *the Image of the invisible God, the brightness of His Glory and the express Image of His Person,* Who, as the Word and Seal and express Image, seals it on others. Christ is here called a *signet,* as Man not as God. For it was His Manhood which He took of the flesh and race of Zerubbabel. He is then, in His Manhood, the signet of God; 1) as being hypostatically united with the Son of God; 2) because the Word impressed on His Humanity the likeness of Himself, His knowledge, virtue, holiness, thoughts, words, acts and conversation; 3) because the Man Christ was the seal, i. e. the most evident sign and witness of the attributes of God, His power, justice, wisdom, and especially His exceeding love for man. For, that God might shew this, He willed that His Son should be Incarnate. Christ thus Incarnate is as a seal, in which we see expressed and depicted the love power justice wisdom &c. of God; 4) because Christ as a seal, attested and certified to us the will of God, His doctrine law commands, i.e. those which He promulgated and taught in the Gospel. *No one,* St. John saith, [15] *hath seen God at any time: the Only-Begotten Son Who is the Image of the Father, He hath declared Him.* Hence God gave to Christ the power of working miracles, that He might confirm His words as by a seal, and demonstrate that they were revealed and enjoined to Him by God, as it is in S. John, [16] *Him hath God the Father sealed.*" "[12] Christ is also the seal of God, because by His impress, i.e. the faith grace virtue and conversation from Him and by the impress in Baptism and the other Sacraments, He *willed to conform us to the Image of His Son* [17], that, [18] *as we have borne the image of*

[1] Ezek. xxxiv. 23. [2] Ib. xxxvii. 24, 25.
[3] Jer. xxx. 9. [4] Hos. iii. 5.
[5] Dan. ii. 44. [6] Jer. xxii. 24.
[7] Gen. xli. 42. [8] Esther iii. 10.
[9] Ib. viii. 2. [10] Cant. viii. 6.
[11] 2 Thess. i. 10. [12] Lap. [13] S. Cyr.
[14] Heb. i. 3. [15] S. John i. 18.
[16] S. John vi. 27. [17] Rom. viii. 29. [18] 1 Cor. xv. 49.

Before CHRIST cir. 520.

altiel, saith the LORD, [b]and will make thee as a signet: for [c]I have chosen thee, saith the LORD of hosts.

[b] Cant. 8. 6. Jer. 22. 24.
[c] Isai. 42. 1. & 43. 10

the earthly Adam, *we may also bear the image of the Heavenly.* Then, Christ, like a seal, seals and guards His faithful against all temptations and enemies. The seal of Christ is the Cross, according to that of Ezekiel, [1] *Seal a mark upon the foreheads of the men who sigh*, and in the Revelation, [2] *I saw another Angel having the seal of the living God.* For the Cross guardeth us against the temptations of the flesh, the world and the devil, and makes us followers, soldiers, and martyrs of Christ crucified. Whence the Apostle says, [3] *I bear in my body the marks of the Lord Jesus.*"

"This is said without doubt of the Messiah, the expected;" says even a Jewish controversialist[4], "who shall be of the seed of Zerubbabel; and therefore this promise was not fulfilled at all in himself: for at the time of this prophecy he had aforetime been governor of Judah, and afterward he did not rise to any higher dignity than what he was up to that day: and in like way we find that God said to Abraham our father in the covenant between the pieces, [5] *I am the Lord who brought thee out of Ur of the Chaldees to give thee this land to inherit it,* and beyond doubt this covenant was confirmed of God to the seed of Abraham, as He Himself explained it there afterward, when He said, *In that day God made a covenant with Abraham, saying, To thy seed have I given this land &c.*, and many like these.

Abarbanel had laid down the right principles, though of necessity misapplied. "[6]Zerubbabel did not reign in Jerusalem and did not rule in it, neither he nor any man of his seed; but forthwith after the building of the house, he returned to Babylon and died there in his captivity, and how saith he, 'In that day I will take thee?' For after the fall of the kingdom of Persia Zerubbabel is not known for any greatness, and his name is not mentioned in the world. Where then will be the meaning of 'And I will place thee as a signet, for thee have I chosen?' For the signet is as the seal-ring which a man putteth on his hand, it departeth not from it, night or day. And when was this fulfilled in Zerubbabel? But the true meaning, in my opinion, is, that God shewed Zerubbabel that this very second house would not abide; for after him should come another captivity, and of this he says, 'I shake the heaven &c.,' and afterward, after a long time, will God take His vengeance of these nations 'which have devoured Jacob and laid waste his dwelling place;' and so he says 'I will overthrow the thrones &c.,' and He sheweth him further that the king who shall rule over Israel at the time of the redemption is the Messiah of the seed of Zerubbabel and of the house of David; and God saw good to shew him all this to comfort him and to speak to his heart; and it is as if he said to him, 'It is true that thou shalt not reign in the time of the second temple, nor any of thy seed, but in that day when God shall overthrow the throne of the kingdoms of the nations, when He gathereth His people Israel and redeemeth them, then shalt thou reign over My people; for of thy seed shall he be who ruleth from Israel at that time forever, and therefore he saith, 'I will take thee, O Zerubabbel &c.,' for because the Messiah was to be of his seed he saith, that he will take him; and this is as he says, '[7]And David My servant shall be a prince to them for ever;' for the very Messiah, he shall be David, he shall be Zerubbabel, because he shall be a scion going forth out of their hewn trunk[8]."

For I have chosen thee. God's forecoming love is the ground of all the acceptableness of His creatures. [9] *We love Him, because He first loved us.* Zerubbabel was a devoted servant of God. God acknowledges his faithfulness. Only, the beginning of all was with God. God speaks of the nearness to Himself which He had given him. But in two words [10] He cuts off all possible boastfulness of His creature. Zerubbabel was all this, not of himself, but *because God had chosen* him. Even the Sacred Manhood of our Lord (it is acknowledged as a theological Truth) was not chosen for any foreseen merits, but for the great love, with which God the Father chose It, and God the Son willed to be in such wise incarnate, and God the Holy Ghost willed that that Holy Thing should be conceived of Him. So God says of Him, [11] *Behold My Servant whom I uphold, Mine elect in whom My soul delighteth;* and God bare witness to Him, [12] *This is My Beloved Son in Whom I am well pleased.*

[1] תו Ezek. ix. 4. [2] Rev. vii. 2. [3] Gal. vi. 17.
[4] R. Isaac Chiz. Em. l. c. pp. 289, 290.
[5] Gen. xv. 7, 18. [6] p. רעט.
[7] Ezek. xxxvii. 24. [8] Is. xi. 1.
[9] 1 S. John iv. 19. [10] כי בחרתיך.
[11] Is. xlii. 1. [12] S. Matt. iii. 17. xvii. 5.

INTRODUCTION

TO

THE PROPHET

ZECHARIAH.

Zechariah entered on his prophetic office, two months after Haggai's first prophecy. He was still a youth, when God called him[a], and so, since in the second year of Darius Hystaspis 18 years had elapsed from the first of Cyrus, he must have been brought in infancy from Babylon. His father Berechiah probably died young, since, in Ezra, the prophet is called after his grandfather, *Zechariah the son of Iddo*[b]. He succeeded his grandfather in the office of *the priests, the chief of the fathers*, (of which there were twelve) in the days of Joiakim the son of Joshua, the High priest[c]. Since then, while he prophesied together with Haggai, Joshua was still high-priest, and it is Joshua whom he sees in his vision in that same year[d], he must have entered on his prophetic office before he succeeded to that other dignity. Yet neither is there any reason to think that he ever laid it aside, since we hear not of any prophet, called by God, who did abandon it. Rather, like Jeremiah, he exercised both; called to the priesthood by the birth given to him by God, called to the prophetic office by Divine inspiration.

Like Jeremiah, Zechariah was called in early youth to the prophetic office. The same designation, by which Jeremiah at first excused himself as unfit for the office, is given to Zechariah, *youth*[e]. The term does not indeed mark any definite age; for Joseph, when he was so designated[f] by the chief butler, was 28[g]; Benjamin and Absalom had sons of their own[h]. They were probably so called as terms of affection, the one by his brother Judah[i], the other by David his father[k]. But his grandfather Iddo was still in the discharge of his office. The length of his ministry is equally unknown. Two years after his first entrance upon it[l], when Haggai's office was closed, he was bidden to answer from God those who enquired whether, now that they were freed from the captivity, they should keep the national fasts which they had instituted on occasion of some of the mournful events which had ushered it in. His remaining prophecies bear no date. The belief, that he lived and prophesied to old age, may have a true foundation, though to us unknown. We only know that he survived the high priest, Joshua, since his own accession to his office of head of the priests, in his division, was in the days of Joiakim, the son of Joshua.

His book opens with a very simple touching call to those returned from the captivity, linking himself on to the former prophets, but contrasting the transitoriness of all human things, those who prophesied and those to whom they prophesied, with the abidingness of the word of God. It consists of four parts, differing in outward character, yet with a remarkable unity of purpose and end. All begin with a foreground subsequent to the captivity; all reach on to a further end;

[a] Zech. ii. 4.
[b] Ezr. v. 1. vi. 14.
[c] Neh. xii. 10, 12, 16.
[d] Zech. iii. 1.
[e] נַעַר. Jer. i. 6, Zech. ii. 4.
[f] Gen. xli. 12.
[g] Joseph was 30, when he stood before Pharaoh (Ib. 46), but the interpretation of the dreams of Pharaoh's servants was given two years before. (Ib. 1.)
[h] Benjamin had 10 sons when Jacob went down into Egypt (Gen. xlvi. 21); Absalom's 3 sons (2 Sam. xiv. 27.) were dead (Ib. xviii. 18). Absalom was David's third son. (2 Sam. iii. 3.)
[i] Gen. xliii. 8. xliv. 22, 30, 33.
[k] 2 Sam. xviii. 5, 12, 29, 32.
[l] vii. 1.

the two first to the coming of our Lord; the third from the deliverance of the house then built, during the invasion of Alexander, and from the victories of the Maccabees, to the rejection of the true Shepherd and the curse upon the false; the last, which is connected with the third by its title, reaches from a future repentance for the death of Christ to the final conversion of the Jews and Gentiles.

The outward difference, that the first prophecy is in visions; the second, a response to an enquiry made of him; the two last in free delivery, obviously did not depend upon the prophet. The occasion also of the two first bodies of prophecy involved that they were written in prose. For the imagery was borne on the prophet's mind in visions. The office of the prophet was only to record them and the explanations given to him of parts of them, which could only be done in prose. He was so far like the Apostles, who enquired of our Lord, when in the flesh, the meaning of His parables. There is, as in the later chapters, abundance of imagery; and it may have pleased God to adapt the form of His revelation to the imaginative mind of the young prophet who was to receive it. But the visions are, as the name implies, pictures which the prophet *sees*, and which he describes. Even a rationalist writer saw this. "[m] Every vision must form a picture, and the description of a vision must have the appearance of being read from a picture. It follows from the nature of the description of a vision, that for the most part it cannot be composed in any elevated language. The simplest prose is the best vehicle for a relation (and such is the description of a vision), and elaborate ornament of language were foreign to it. The beauty, greatness, elevation of a vision, as described, must lie in the conception, or in the symmetry, or wondrous boldness in the grouping of the images. Is the whole group, piece by piece, in all its parts, to the most minute shading, faithful and described with the character of truth, the exhibition of the vision in words is perfect."

The four portions were probably of different dates, as they stand in order in the prophet's book, as indeed the second is dated two years later than the first [n]. For in the first part God's people are exhorted to come from Babylon [o], which command, many in the time of Ezra, obeyed, and doubtless individuals subsequently, when a prosperous polity was restored; in the latter part, Babylon is mentioned no more; only in one place, in the imagery of earlier prophets, the future gathering of God's people is symbolized under the previous deliverance from West and East, Egypt and Assyria [p].

But they agree in this, that the foreground is no longer, as in the former prophets, deliverance from Babylon. In the first part, the reference to the vision of the four empires in Daniel removes the promise of the Deliverer to the fourth Empire. For the series of visions having closed with the vision of the four chariots, there follows at once the symbolic act of placing the crown or crowns on the head of the high priest and the promise of the Messiah, Who should be king and priest [q]. In the later part the enemies spoken of are in one place the Greeks [r], subsequent to the protection of the temple under Alexander [s]; in another the final gathering of all nations against Jerusalem [t], which Joel also places at the end of all things [u], after the outpouring of the Spirit, as it was outpoured on the day of Pentecost.

In both parts alike, there is no mention of any king or of any earthly ruler; in both, the ruler to come is the Messias. In both, the division of the two kingdoms is gone. The house of Israel and house of Judah are united, not divided [v]; they had been distinct wholes, now they are in interests as one. Zechariah promises a future to both collectively, as did Jeremiah [w] long after the captivity of Israel, and Ezekiel promised that they should both again be one in the hand of God [x]. The *brotherhood between Judah and Israel* still existed, after they had weighed the thirty pieces of silver for the Good Shepherd. The captivity, in God's Providence, ended at once the kingdom of Israel and the religious schism, the object of which was to maintain the kingdom. Even before the captivity, [y] *divers of Asher and Manasseh and Zebulun humbled themselves, and came to Jerusalem*, to the passover of Hezekiah; nay, [z] *a great multitude of the people from Ephraim and Manasseh, Issachar and Zebulun*, who had neglected or despised the first invitation [a], came subsequently. In the great passover of Josiah, we hear [b] of *all Judah and Israel that were*

[m] Eichhorn Einl. n. 603. iv. pp. 435, 436. "The style in these visions borders closely on prose: for they relate what the Seer saw; and prose is the natural vehicle of relation." Ib. n. 605. p. 442. Eichhorn also draws attention to what he calls "the hymns, songs of victory or consolation, with which the visions are sometimes closed, and which are a more elevated finale." Ib.

[n] "In the 2d year of Darius." i. 1. "In the 4th year of Darius." vii. 1.

[o] ii. 7.

[p] Zech. x. 10. Comp. Is. xi. 11, 16, Hos. xi. 11.

[q] vi. 10–13.

[r] ix. 13.

[s] Ib. 8. See Pusey's "Daniel the Prophet." pp. 279–282.

[t] xii. 2, 3, 9. xiv. 2, 3, 14, 16.

[u] Joel iii. 2.

[v] "As ye were a curse among the heathen, O house of Judah and house of Israel" viii. 13; "these are the horns which scattered Judah, Israel, Jerusalem," i. 19. (ii. 2. Heb.) So in x. 6. "I will strengthen the house of Judah, and I will save the house of Joseph, and I will bring them again to place them."

[w] Jer. xxiii. 6. l. 20.

[x] Ez. xxxvii. 16–19.

[y] 2 Chr. xxx. 11.

[z] Ib. 18.

[a] Ib. 10.

[b] Ib. xxxv. 18.

present. The edict of Cyrus related to the [c] *people of the Lord God of heaven, and was published throughout all his kingdom,* which included [d] *the cities of the Medes,* whither Israel had been removed. The sacred history is confined to Jerusalem, whence the Gospel was to go forth; yet even [e] *the sons of Bethel,* the centre of the rival, idolatrous worship, which was *among the mountains of Ephraim,* were among those of the people of Israel who returned with Zerubbabel. It is inconceivable that, as the material prosperity of Palestine returned, even many of the ten tribes should not have returned to their country. But place was no condition of the unity of the Church. Those who returned recognized the religious oneness of all the twelve tribes, wherever dispersed. At the dedication of the house of God, they [f] *offered a sin-offering for all Israel, twelve he-goats, according to the number of the tribes of Israel.* At that passover were present, not only *the children of Israel which had come again out of the captivity,* but, [g] *all such as had separated themselves unto them from the defilements of the people of the land, to seek the Lord God of Israel,* i. e., Israelites, who had been defiled by the heathen idolatries. The *house of David* [h] is mentioned; for of his seed according to the flesh Messiah was to be born, but it is his *house,* not any earthly ruler in it.

In both parts alike, Zechariah connects his prophecies with the former prophets, the fulfillment of whose warnings he impressed upon his people in his opening exhortation to them [i], and in his answer to the question about keeping the fasts [k] which related to the destruction of the city and temple. In the first part, the title "[l] the Branch" is used as a proper name, recalling the title of the Messiah in Isaiah and Jeremiah, *the Branch of the Lord* [m], *a righteous Branch* [n], *a Branch of righteousness* [o], whom God would raise up to David. The prophecy of the mutual exhortation of peoples and cities to worship at Jerusalem [p] is an echo of those of Isaiah and Micah, prolonging them. The prophecy of the four chariots [q], the symbol of those world-empires, would be unintelligible without the visions in Daniel which it presupposes. The union of the offices of priest and king in the Messiah is a renewal of the promise through David [r]. In the last chapters, the continuousness of the prophet's diction admits still more of this interweaving of the former prophecies, and these alike from the earlier and later prophets. The censure of Tyre for its boast of its wisdom is a renewal of that of Ezekiel [s]; the prophecy against the Philistine cities, of that of Zephaniah [t]; the remarkable prediction that, when the king should come to Zion, chariots and horses, not of the enemy but of Judah should be cut off, is renewed from Micah [u]; the extent of his peaceful kingdom is from a psalm of Solomon [v]; the loosing of the exile from the pit, and God's rendering double unto them, are in Isaiah [w]. The description of the sifting, in which, two parts having been cut off, even the remaining third should be anew tried and cleansed, is condensed from Ezekiel, so that, *shall be cut off, shall expire,* correspond to the natural and violent deaths, by famine and by the sword, spoken of in Ezekiel [x]. The words, [y] *I have said, it is My people, and it will say, the Lord my God,* are almost verbally from Hosea, *I say to not-my-people, thou art My people, and it will say, my God;* only omitting the allusion to the significant name of the prophet's son. "[z] The first part of xiv. 10, *the whole land shall be turned as a plain from Gebah to Rimmon, and Jerusalem shall be exalted,* reminds of Isaiah and Ezekiel; the latter part, *it shall be inhabited in her place from the tower of Hananeel to the king's wine-presses, and men shall dwell in it and there shall be no more utter desolation, but Jerusalem shall dwell securely,* reminds of Jeremiah, [a] *The city shall be built to the Lord from the tower of Hananeel unto the gate of the corner; it shall not be plucked up nor thrown down any more.* The words, [b] *and every one that is left of all the nations shall go up to worship the king, the Lord of hosts, and to keep the feast of tabernacles,* reminds of Isaiah, [c] *From new-moon to his new-moon, and from sabbath to his sabbath shall all flesh come to worship before Me, saith the Lord.* v. 17–19 are an expansion of Isaiah lx. 12; v. 20 expresses the thought of Ez. xliii. 13: the prophecy, [d] *there shall be no more the Canaanite in the house of the Lord for ever,* refers back to Ezekiel [e]." The symbolizing of the Gospel by the life-giving waters which should flow forth from Jerusalem, originally in Joel iii. 18, is a miniature of the full picture in Ezekiel [f]. The promise, "[g] I will cut off *the names of the* idols *from* the land *and they shall be no more remembered,"* in part verbally

[c] Ezr. i. 1, 2. [d] 2 Kgs xvii. 6.
[e] Ezr. ii. 2, 28. [f] Ib. vi. 17. [g] Ib. 21.
[h] Zech. xii. 7. The *king's wine-presses* (Zech. xiv. 10.) is but the name of a locality in Jerusalem, which retained its former name. Wine-presses were often hewn out in the rock. Bleek, who alleged this, afterward (Einl. p. 563. note) laid no stress on it. [i] i. 4–6.
[k] vii. 7–14. [l] iii. 8. vi. 12.
[m] Is. iv. 2. [n] Jer. xxiii. 5.
[o] Ib. xxxiii. 15.
[p] Zech. viii. 20–22. comp. Mic. iv. 1, 2. Is. ii. 3.
[q] Zech. vi. coll. Dan. ii. vii. See below on c. vi. and "Daniel the Prophet" pp. 359–361.
[r] Zech. vi. 13. coll. Ps. cx.
[s] ix. 2. and Ezek. xxviii. 3.
[t] ix. 5. Zeph. ii. 4. [u] ix. 10. Mic. v. 10.
[v] Ib. Ps. lxxii. 8. [w] Ib. 12. Is. li. 14. lxi. 7.
[x] xiii. 8, 9. Ezek. v. 12. Hengst.
[y] Hengst. Zech. xiii. 9, Hos. ii. 25.
[z] Hengst. [a] Jer. xxxi. 38. 40. [b] Zech. xiv. 16.
[c] Is. lxvi. 23. [d] Zech. xiv. 21. [e] Ezek. xliv. 9.
[f] Zech. xiv. 8, Ezek. xlvii. 1–13.
[g] Zech. xiii. 2. Hos. ii. 17.

agrees with that of Hosea, "And I will remove *the names of the* Baalim *from* her mouth, *and they shall be no more remembered* by their names;" only, since the Baal-worship was destroyed by the captivity, the more general name of *idols* is substituted.

Equally, in descriptions not prophetic, the symbolizing of the wicked by the title of the goats, *I punished the goats*[h], is renewed from Ezekiel; *I judge between flock and flock, between the rams and the he-goats.* The description of the shepherds who destroyed their flocks retains from Jeremiah the characteristic expression, [i]*and hold themselves not guilty.* The minuteness of the enumeration of their neglects and cruelties is the same (amid differences of the words whereby it is expressed): "[k]the perishing shall he not visit, those astray shall he not seek, and the broken shall he not heal; the sound shall he not nurture, and the flesh of the fat shall he eat and their claws he shall split. In Ezekiel, "[l]Ye eat the fat and clothe you with the wool; the fat ye slay; the flock ye feed not; the diseased have ye not healed; and the broken have ye not bound, and the wandering have ye not sought." The imagery of Obadiah, that Israel should be a flame amidst corn to consume it, is retained; the name of Edom is dropped, for the prophecy relates to a larger gathering of enemies. Zechariah has, "[m]In that day I will make the governors of Judah like a hearth of fire among wood and like a lamp of fire in a sheaf of corn, and they shall eat on the right hand and on the left all nations round about:" Obadiah; "The house of Jacob shall be *fire* and the house of Jacob a *flame*, and the house of Esau stubble, and it shall kindle on them and shall eat them." Even so slight an expression as *the pride of Jordan*[n], as designating the cane-brake around it, is peculiar to Jeremiah[o].

Zechariah is eminently an Evangelic prophet, as much as Isaiah, and equally in both portions.

The use of different words in unlike subjects is a necessary consequence of that unlikeness. In contrast with that pseudo-criticism, which counts up the unlike words in different chapters of a prophet, the different words used by the same modern poet have been counted[p]. A finer perception will see the correspondence of a style, when the rhythm, subject, words, are different. No one familiar with English poetry could doubt that "the Bard," and "the Elegy in a country Churchyard," however different in subject and style and words, were by the same hand, judging alone from the labored selection of the epithets, however different. Yet there is not one characteristic word or idiom which occurs in both. But the recurrence of the same or like words or idioms, if unusual elsewhere, is a subordinate indication of sameness of authorship.

They are thus enumerated by the writers who have answered the attacks on the authorship of Zechariah.

"Common to both parts are the idioms, *from him who goeth and from him who returneth*, which do not occur elsewhere[q]; the whole Jewish people are throughout designated as "[r]the house of Israel and the house of Judah," or "[s]the house of Judah and the house of Joseph," or "[t]Judah Israel and Jerusalem," or "[u]Ephraim and Jerusalem," or "[v]Judah and Ephraim," or "[w]Judah and Israel." There is in both parts the appeal to future knowledge of God's doings to be obtained by experience[x]; in both, internal discord is directly attributed to God, Whose Providence permits it[y]; in both the prophet promises God's gifts of the produce of the earth[z]; in both he bids Jerusalem burst out for joy; in the first, "[a]*for lo,* God says, *I come and will dwell in the midst of thee;* in the second, [b]*behold thy King cometh unto thee.*

The purity of language is alike in both parts of the book. No one Syriasm occurs in

[h] Zech. x. 3. Ezek. xxxiv. 17.

[i] ולא יאשמו Zech. xi. 5. לא נאשם Jer. i. 7.

[k] Zech. xi. 16. [l] Ezek. xxxiv. 3, 4. [m] Zech. xii. 6. Obad. 18. [n] Zech. xi. 3. [o] Jer. xii. 5. xlix. 19. l. 44.

[p] Prof. Stanley Leathes, "The witness of the Old Testament to Christ. Note on the Authorship of Isaiah," (pp. 282, 283.) gives the following summary as to the occurrence of words in poems of Milton and Tennyson; "L'Allegro is a poem of 152 lines: it contains about 450 words; Il Penseroso is a poem of 176 lines, and contains about 578 words; Lycidas is a poem of 193 lines, which are longer than those of either of the other two, most of them being heroics: its words are about 725. It is plain, therefore, that Milton must have used for Il Penseroso 128 words not in L'Allegro, and for Lycidas 275 not in L'Allegro, and 147 not in Il Penseroso.

"But what is much more remarkable, is the fact that there are only about 125 words common to L'Allegro and Il Penseroso; only about 140 common to Lycidas and Il Penseroso; only about 61 common to all three. That is; Milton must have used for Il Penseroso 450 words not in L'Allegro, and for Lycidas 590 not in L'Allegro. He must have used for Lycidas some 585 words not in Il Penseroso, and more than 660 not occurring in both together. Also, there must be in L'Allegro some 325 words not in Il Penseroso, and 315 not in Lycidas: and there must be in Il Penseroso nearly 440 words not in Lycidas.

"Again, Tennyson's Lotos-Eaters contains about 590 words; Œnone has about 720. Thus the latter must contain 130 words not in the former: but a comparison shows that there are only about 230 words common to the two poems. That is, there must be 490 words in Œnone which are not in the Lotos-Eaters, and there must be in the Lotos-Eaters about 360 words not occurring in Œnone; that is,—the shorter poem has 360 words which the longer one does not contain."

[q] מעבר ומשב vii. 14, ix. 8. In Ez. xxxii. 27, the expression עִברו ושובו, "pass through and return," is not proverbial; in Ezek. xxxv. 7, it is "I will cut off from it" עֹבֵר וָשָׁב:

[r] viii. 13. [s] x. 6. [t] i. 19, [ii. 2. Heb.] [u] ix. 10. [v] ix. 13. [w] xi. 14. [x] ii. 13, 15. xi. 11. [y] viii. 10. xi. 6. [z] viii. 12. x. 1. [a] ii. 14. [10. Eng.] [b] ix. 9.

the earlier chapters[c]. The prophet, who returned as a child to Judæa, formed his language upon that of the older prophets.

In both there is a certain fullness of language, produced by dwelling on the same thought or word[d]: in both, the whole and its parts are, for emphasis, mentioned together[e]. In both parts, as a consequence of this fullness, there occurs the division of the verse into five sections, contrary to the usual rule of Hebrew parallelism.

This rhythm will appear more vividly in instances[f];

"[g] And *he* shall build the temple of the Lord;
And *he* shall bear majesty;
And he shall sit and rule on his throne;
And he shall be a priest on his throne;
And a counsel of peace shall be between them both.

[h] Ashkelon shall see, and shall fear;
Gaza, and shall tremble exceedingly;
And Ekron, and ashamed is her expectation;
And perished hath a king from Gaza,
And Ashkelon shall not be inhabited.

[i] And I will take away his blood from his mouth,
And his abominations from between his teeth:
And he too shall be left to our God,
And he shall be as a governor in Judah,
And Ekron as a Jebusite.

"[k] In that day, saith the Lord,
I will smite every horse with astonishment,
And his rider with madness;
And upon the house of Judah I will open my eyes,
And every horse of the nations I will smite with blindness."

With one considerable exception[l], those who would sever the six last chapters from Zechariah, are now at one in placing them before the captivity. Yet Zechariah here too speaks of the captivity as past. Adopting the imagery of Isaiah, who foretells the delivery from the captivity as an opening of a prison, he says, in the name of God, "[m] By the blood of thy covenant *I have sent forth thy* prisoners out of the pit wherein is no water." Again, "[n] The Lord of hosts hath visited His flock, the house of Judah. I will have mercy upon them [Judah and Joseph] and they shall be *as though I had not cast them off.*" The mention of the mourning of all the *families that remain*[o] implies a previous carrying away. Yet more; Zechariah took his imagery of the future restoration of Jerusalem, from its condition in his own time. "[p] It shall be lifted up and inhabited in its place from Benjamin's gate unto *the place* of the first gate, unto the corner-gate, and from the tower of Hananeel unto the king's winepresses." "The gate of Benjamin" is doubtless "the gate of Ephraim," since the road to Ephraim lay through Benjamin; but the gate of Ephraim existed in Nehemiah's time[q], yet was not then repaired, as neither was the tower of Hananeel[r], having been left, doubtless, at the destruction of Jerusalem, being useless for defence, when the wall was broken down. So [s] at the second invasion the Romans left the three impregnable towers, of Hippicus, Phasaelus, and Mariamne, as monuments of the greatness of the city which they had destroyed. Benjamin's gate, the corner gate, the tower of Hananeel, were still standing; "the king's winepresses" were naturally uninjured, since there was no use in injuring them; but *the first gate* was destroyed, since not itself, but *the place* of it is mentioned.

The prophecy of the victory over the Greeks fits in with times when Assyria or Chaldæa were no longer the instruments of God in the chastisement of His people. The notion that the prophet incited the few Hebrew slaves, sold into Greece, to rebel against

[c] וְאַסְעֲרֵם vii. 14 is no Syriasm (as so often alleged) but has Hebrew analogies as גֵּוָה Job xxii. 29. xxiii. 7, from נְאֵוָה for גַּאֲוָה (Ew. Lehrb. n. 62. b); but which of these critics would argue from the points except in favor of what he wished to maintain? Böttcher (Lehrbuch n. 437. g. 498. 3. p. 304.) regards the as emphatic. 2) "That מהלכים (iii. 7.) comes from a מַהְלֵךְ is self-evident." Ew. ad. loc. 3) עזר ל (i. 16.) is not "joined with acc. of object," but is simply our, "helped to evil."

[d] As in the repetition of שכנתי בתוכך ii. 14, 15; of ובאת, in vi. 10; ובנה את היכל יי והוא יבנה את היכל יי vi. 12, 13; ברחבתיה, ורחבות, ברחבות, 3 times in viii. 4. 5; יחזיקו-והחזיקו Ib. 23; וארעה את הצאן at the beginning and end of xi. 7; ישבה ירושלם לבטח and ישבה תחתיה at the end, xiv. 10, 11. ונלחם כיום הלחמו ביום קרב xiv. 3. In xiv. 4. the sentence ומש &c., explains the same event in different words: ונסתם-ונסתם כאשר נסתם xiv. 5.

[e] v. 4. "the house, and its stones, and its timbers," x. 4. "out of him the corner; out of him the nail; out of him the battle bow; out of him every oppressor together." x. 11. "the land shall mourn, every family apart," and then follows the enumeration of the families. 12, 13.

[f] This was observed by Köster, Meletemata crit. et exeg. in Zech. part. post. c. ix.–xiv. pp. 54–56.

[g] vi. 13. [h] ix. 5. [i] Ib. 7.

[k] xii. 4. Köster further refers to i. 4, 17. iii. 5, 9. and on the other hand to ix. 9, 10, 13, 15. x. 11. xi. 2, 7, 9, 17. xii. 10. xiv. 4, 8.

[l] Bottcher. [m] ix. 11. [n] x. 3–5. [o] xii. 14.

[p] xiv. 10. [q] Neh. viii. 16. xii. 39. [r] Ib. iii. 1.

[s] Jos. B. J. vii. 1.

their masters, is so absurd, that one wonders that any one could have ventured to forge it and put it upon a Hebrew prophet [t].

Since, moreover, all now, who sever the six last chapters from the preceding, also divide these six into two halves, the evidence that the six chapters are from one author is a separate ground against their theory. Yet not only are they connected by the imagery of the people as the flock of God [u], whom God committed to the hand of the Good Shepherd [v], and on their rejecting Him, gave them over to an evil shepherd [w]; but the Good Shepherd is One with God [x]. The poor of the flock, who would hold to the Shepherd, are designated by a corresponding word [y].

A writer has been at pains to shew that two different conditions of things are foretold in the two prophecies. Granted. The first, we believe, has its foreground in the deliverance during the conquests of Alexander, and under the Maccabees, and leads on to the rejection of the true Shepherd and God's visitation on the false. The later relates to a later repentance and later visitation of God, in part yet future. By what law is a prophet bound down to speak of one future only?

For those who criticize the prophets, resolve all prophecy into mere "anticipation" of what *might*, or might *not* be, denying to them all certain knowledge of any future, it is but speaking plainly, when they imagine the author of the three last chapters to have "anticipated" that God would interpose miraculously to deliver Jerusalem, then, when it was destroyed. It would have been in direct contradiction to Jeremiah, who for 39 years in one unbroken dirge predicted the evil which should come upon Jerusalem. The prophecy, had it preceded the destruction of Jerusalem, could not have been earlier than the reign of the wretched Jehoiakim, since the mourning for the death of Josiah is spoken of as a proverbial sorrow of the past. This invented prophet then would have been one of the false prophets, who contradicted Jeremiah, prophesying good, while Jeremiah prophesied evil; who encouraged Zedekiah in his perjury, the punishment whereof Ezekiel solemnly denounced [z], prophesying his captivity in Babylon as its penalty; he would have been one of those, of whom Jeremiah said, that they spake lies [a] in the name of the Lord. It was not "anticipation" on either side. It was the statement of those who spoke more certainly than we could say, "the sun will rise to-morrow." They were the direct contradictories of one another. The false prophets said, "[b] the Lord hath said, Ye shall have peace;" the true, "[c] they have said, Peace, peace, when there is no peace:" the false said, "[d] sword and famine shall not be in the land;" the true, "[d] By sword and famine shall their prophets be consumed;" the false said, "[e] ye shall not serve the king of Babylon; thus saith the Lord, even so will I break the yoke of Nebuchadnezzar, king of Babylon, from the neck of all nations within the space of two full years;" the true, "[f] Thus saith the Lord of hosts, Now have I given all these lands into the hand of Nebuchadnezzar the king of Babylon, My servant, and all nations shall serve him, and his son and his son's son." The false said, "[g] I will bring again to this place Jeconiah, with all the captives of Judah, that went into Babylon, for I will break the yoke of the king of Babylon;" the true, "[h] I will cast thee out and the mother that bare thee, into another country, where ye were not born, and there ye shall die. But to the land, whereunto they desire to return, thither they shall not return." The false said; "[i] The vessels of the Lord's house shall now shortly be brought again from Babylon;" the true, "[k] the residue of the vessels that remain in this city,—they shall be carried to Babylon."

If the writer of the three last chapters had lived just before the destruction of Jerusalem in those last reigns, he would have been a political fanatic, one of those who, by encouraging rebellion against Nebuchadnezzar, brought on the destruction of the city, and, in the name of God, told lies against God. "That which is most peculiar in this prophet," says one [l], "is the uncommon high and pious hope of the deliverance of Jerusalem and Judah, notwithstanding all visible greatest dangers and threatenings. At a time when Jeremiah, in the walls of the capital, already despairs of any possibility of a successful resistance to the Chaldees and exhorts to tranquillity, this prophet still looks all these dangers straight in the face with swelling spirit and divine confidence, holds, with unbowed spirit, firm to the like promises of older prophets, as Is. c. 29, and anticipates that, from that very moment when the blind fury of the destroyers would discharge itself on the sanctuary, a wondrous might would crush them in pieces, and that this must be the beginning of the Messianic weal within and without."

[t] Hitzig. Ewald avoids this; but would have it, that the prophet in Joel's time was stirring up the Jews to war with the Greeks. Other evasions see in Pusey's "Daniel the Prophet" pp. 281, 282. note.

[u] ix. 16. x. 3. [v] xi. 4–14. [w] Ib. 15–17.

[x] xi. 7-12. xiii. 7.

[y] עֲנִיֵּי הַצֹּאן, xi. 7, 11. הַצֹּעֲרִים, xiii. 7, the same as the צְעִירֵי הַצֹּאן Jer. xlix. 20, l. 45.

[z] Ezek. xiii. 10-19.

[a] Jer. xiv. 14, xxiii. 22, xxvii. 15, xxviii. 15, xxix. 8, 9.

[b] Jer. viii. 11. xxiii. 17. [c] Ezek. xiii. 2–10.

[d] Jer. xiv. 15. [e] Ib. xxvii. 9–14, xxviii. 11.

[f] Ib. xxvii. 4, 6, 7. [g] Ib. xxviii. 4.

[h] Ib. xxii. 26, 27. [i] Ib. xxvii. 16. [k] Ib. 19–22.

[l] Ewald Proph. ii. 52, 53. ed. 1868.

Chapter 14 is to this writer a modification of those anticipations. In other words there was a greater human probability, that Jeremiah's prophecies, not his, would be fulfilled: yet he cannot give up his sanguineness, though his hopes had now become fanatic. This writer says on chap. 14, "[m] This piece cannot have been written till somewhat later, when facts made it more and more improbable, that Jerusalem would not any how be conquered, and treated as a conquered city by coarse foes. Yet then too this prophet could not yet part with the anticipations of older prophets and those which he had himself at an earlier time expressed: so boldly, amid the most visible danger, he holds firm to the old anticipation, after that the great deliverance of Jerusalem in Sennacherib's time (Is. c. 37.) appeared to justify the most fanatic hopes for the future. (comp. Ps. 59). And so now the prospect moulds itself to him thus, as if Jerusalem must indeed actually endure the horrors of the conquest, but that then, when the work of the conquerors was half-completed, the great deliverance, already suggested in that former piece, would come, and so the Sanctuary would, notwithstanding, be wonderfully preserved, the better Messianic time would notwithstanding still so come."

It must be a marvelous fascination, which the old prophets exercise over the human mind, that one who can so write should trouble himself about them. It is such an intense paradox, that the writing of one convicted by the event of uttering falsehood in the name of God, incorrigible even by the thickening tokens of God's displeasure, should have been inserted among the Hebrew prophets, in times not far removed from those whose events convicted him, that one wonders that any one should have invented it, still more that any should have believed in it. Great indeed is "the credulity of the incredulous."

And yet this paradox is essential to the theories of the modern school which would place these chapters before the captivity. English writers, who thought themselves compelled to ascribe these chapters to Jeremiah, had an escape, because they did not bind down prophecy to immediate events. Newcome's criticism was the conjectural criticism of his day; i. e. bad, cutting knots instead of loosing them. But his faith, that God's word is true, was entire. Since the prophecy, placed at the time where he placed it, had no immediate fulfillment, he supposed it, in common with those who believe it to have been written by Zechariah, to relate to a later period. That German school, with whom it is an axiom, "that all definite prophecy relates to an immediate future," had no choice but to place it just before the destruction of the temple by the Chaldees, or its profanation by Antiochus Epiphanes; and those who placed it before the Captivity, had no choice, except to believe, that it related to events, by which it was falsified.

Nearly half a century has passed, since a leading writer of this school said, "[n] One must own, that the division of opinions as to the real author of this section and his time, as also the attempts to appropriate single oracles of this portion to different periods, leave the result of criticism simply *negative;* whereas on the other hand, the view itself, since it is not yet carried through exegetically, lacks the completion of its proof. It is not till criticism becomes *positive*, and evidences its truth in the explanation of details, that it attains its completion; which is not, in truth, always possible." Hitzig did what he could, "to help to promote the attainment of this end according to his ability." But although the more popular theory has of late been that these chapters are to be placed before the captivity, the one portion somewhere in the reigns of Uzziah, Jotham, Ahaz, or Hezekiah; the other, as marked in the chapters themselves, after the death of Josiah. there have not been wanting critics of equal repute, who place them in the time of Antiochus Epiphanes. Yet criticism which reels to and fro in a period of near 500 years, from the earliest of the prophets to a period, a century after Malachi, and this on historical and philological grounds, certainly has come to no definite basis, either as to history or philology. Rather, it has enslaved both to preconceived opinions; and at last, as late a result as any has been, after this weary round, to go back to where it started from, and to suppose these chapters to have been written by the prophet whose name they bear [o].

It is obvious that there must be some mistake either in the tests applied, or in their application, which admits of a variation of at least 450 years from somewhere in the reign of Uzziah (say B. C. 770) to "later than B. C. 330."

Philological and historical criticism, bearing on events (as it is assumed) of the day,

[m] Ewald Proph. p. 59.

[n] Hitzig. über d. abfassungszeit der Orakel Zach. ix-xiv, in the Theol. Studien u. Kritiken 1830. 1. p. 25.

[o] De Wette ed. 4 (after maintaining the contrary ed. 1-3) and Stähelin, Einl. 1862. "De Wette often assured me orally, that since he felt himself compelled to admit, that this portion evinces acquaintance with the latest prophets, he could not deny it to be Zechariah's." Stähelin p. 323. De Wette, Stähelin, Köster, Bürger, were of a different school from Hengstenberg, Havernick, Keil, or again from Jahn and Herbst. Stahelin says, "in the investigation I kept myself free from any influence from without, and first found the facts, which attest the post-exile origin of this section, given by Hengstenberg and de Wette, when I subsequently compared the labors of others, especially those two scholars." Messian. Weissag. p. 174. 1847.

which should, in its variations, oscillate between the reign of John or of Charles I, or (to bring it nearer to ourselves) the first half of the xiv[th] century or the latter part of the xviii[th], would not gain much attention. Indeed, it is instructive, that after the philological argument has figured so much in all questions about the date of books of Holy Scripture, it is virtually admitted to be absolutely worthless, except negatively. For, in regard to Zechariah, the argument is not used, except in proof that the same writer cannot have written prose and poetry, which would establish that Hosea did not write either his three first chapters or his nine last; or Ezekiel his inaugural vision, the visions of the ninth and tenth chapters, and the simple exhortations to repentance in his eighteenth and thirty-third. Only I know not on the same evidence, how, of modern writers, Scott and Southey could be supposed to have written their prose and their poetry. How easy it would be to prove that the author of Thalaba did not write the life of Wesley or the history of the peninsular war, nor Shakespeare Macbeth and any comedy which criticism may yet leave to him; still more that he cannot have written the deep tragic scenes of Hamlet and that of the grave-diggers.

Yet such negations have been practically considered as the domain of the philological neo-criticism. Style is to be evidence that the same prophet did not write certain prophecies; but, this being demonstrated, it is to yield no evidence, whether he wrote, when Hebrew was a dead language or in the time of its richest beauty. Individuals indeed have their opinions; but philological criticism, as a whole, or as relates to any acknowledged result, is altogether at fault. Having done its office of establishing, that, in the mind of the critic and his disciples, certain chapters are *not* Zechariah's, the witness is forthwith dismissed, as incompetent even to assist in proving anything beside. The rest is to be established by historical allusions, which are by some adapted to events in the reign of Uzziah, by others to those of the Maccabees: or rather, it being assumed that there is no prophecy, this latter class assumes that the book is to belong to the times of the Maccabees, because one part of it predicts their victories. Those who tell us [p] of the unity of the results of this modern criticism, must have been thinking of the agreement of its negations. As to the positive results, a table will best shew their harmony. Yet the fault is not in the want of an ill-exercised acumen of the critics; their principle, that nothing in the prophets can relate to any distant future, even though that future exactly realized the words, is the mainspring of their confusions. Since the words of Zechariah do relate to, and find their fulfillment in, events widely separated from each other, and the theory of the critics requires that they should belong to some proximate event, either in the present or some near future, they have to wrest those words from the events to which they relate, some in this way, some in that; and the most natural interpretations are those which are least admitted. Certainly since the descriptions in c. ix. suit with the wars of Alexander and the Maccabees, no one, but for some strong antecedent exigency, would assume that they related to some expected expedition of an Assyrian monarch, "[q] which may be conjectured as very probable, but which, for want of historical data, cannot be indicated more circumstantially," or to "[r] a plan of the Assyrians which was not then carried out," or [s] Uzziah's war with the Philistines [t], and some imagined "[u] attitude of Jeroboam II against Damascus and Hamath," or "[u] a concealed denunciation against Persia," against which Zechariah did not wish to prophesy openly, or to have had no special meaning at all [v].

It is marvelous, on what slight data this modern school has satisfied itself that these chapters were written before the captivity. To take the statement of an epitomator [w] of German pseudo-criticism: "*Damascus, Tyre, and Sidon, Philistia, Javan* (*ix.* 1, 6–12) *Assyria and Egypt* (*x.* 10.) *are the enemies of Judah.*" "*The historical stand-point is different from that of Zech. i-viii.*" Of all these, Javan, the Greeks, alone are spoken of as enemies of Judah, who before the captivity were known only as purchasers of Hebrew captives; the only known wars are those of the Maccabees.

"*The two kingdoms of Judah and Israel still exist. Surely the language,* 'that I might break the brotherhood between Judah and Israel,' *implies that both kingdoms existed as part of the covenant nation.*"

Zechariah speaks of Judah and Israel, but not as *kingdoms*. Before the captivity, except during the effects of the inter-marriage with Athaliah, there was not *brotherhood* but enmity. In the reigns of Amaziah and Ahaz there was war.

"*The house of David is spoken of xiii.* 1."

[p] Essays and Reviews, p. 340. "Among German commentators there is, for the first time in the history of the world, an approach to agreement and certainty. For example the diversity among German writers on prophecy is far less than among English ones."

[q] Bertholdt p. 1715. [r] Knobel ii. 170.

[s] Hitzig Vorbemerk. z. ii. and iii. Zech. Kl. Pr. p. 354.

[t] 2 Chr. xxvi. 6. [u] De Wette Einl. p. 337.

[v] "The uncertain hopes of the future, here expressed by the prophet, are not to be referred to certain events." Rosenmüller on Zech. ix. 13. ed. 1.

[w] Dr. S. Davidson iii. 321, 322.

The *house*, not the kingdom. The house existed after the captivity. Zerubbabel, whom the Persians made governor, was its representative.

"*Idols and false prophets* (*x.* 2. *xiii.* 2 *&c.*) *harmonize only with a time prior to the exile.*"

Idolatry certainly was not the prevailing national sin, after God had taught the people through the captivity. It is commonly taken for granted, that there was *none*. But where is the proof? Malachi would hardly have laid the stress on [x] *marrying the daughters of a strange god*, had there been no danger that the marriage would lead to idolatry. [y] Nehemiah speaks of the sin, into which Solomon was seduced by "outlandish women," as likely to recur through the heathen marriages; but idolatry was that sin. Half of the children could only speak the language of their mothers [z]. It were strange, if they had not imbibed their mothers' idolatry too. In a battle in the Maccabee war, it is related "[a] under the coats of every one that was slain they found things consecrated to the idols of the Jamnites, which is forbidden the Jews by their law."

The *Teraphim* were, moreover, an unlawful and forbidden means of attempting to know the future, not any coarse form of idolatry [b]; much as people now, who more or less earnestly have their fortunes told, would be surprised at being called idolaters. But Zechariah was probably speaking of sins which had brought on the captivity, not of his own day. The prediction repeated from an older prophet, that in the true Judah, the Church, God would *cut off* even *the names* and the memory *of idols*, does not imply that they existed [c].

False prophets continued after the captivity. Shemaiah, who *uttered a prophecy against* Nehemiah, *the prophetess Noadiah*, and *the rest of the prophets*, are known to us from Nehemiah's relation [d]. Such there were before our Lord came, of whom He said, that they [e] *were thieves and robbers:* He warned against them, [f] as *coming in sheep's clothing*, but *inwardly they are ravening wolves;* He foretold that [g] *many false prophets shall arise and deceive many;* the Acts tell us of the *false prophet* [h], *a Jew, Bar-jesus;* and *Theudas*, and *Judas* of Galilee [i]. S. John says, [k] *many false prophets have gone out into the world*. False prophets aggravated the resistance to the Romans and the final destruction of Jerusalem [l].

"*The mention of a king or kingdom, in xi.* 6, *xiii.* 7, *does not suit the age of Zechariah.*"

Zechariah had already implied that they had no king then, for he had bidden Zion to rejoice that her king *would come* to her; accordingly she had none. In xi. 6, God says, "I will no more pity the land; I will deliver man, every one into the hand of his king." It is an event, not of the prophet's time, but of the future; in xiii. 7, there is no mention of any king at all.

Such being the entire absence of proof that these chapters were written before the captivity [m], the proof that c. xi. relates to the time of Menahem is even absurd. The process with those who maintained this, has been, assuming as proved, that it was written before the captivity, and that it contained no prophecy of the future, to ask, to what period before the captivity does it relate? One verse [n] relates to civil confusion, such as is foretold also, with the same metaphor, by Isaiah and Jeremiah. The choice was large, since the kingdom of Israel had the curse of discord and irreligion entailed upon it, and no king ventured to cut off the entail by cutting off the central sin, the worship of the calves, which were to consolidate it by a worship, the rival of that at Jerusalem. Of the 18 kings between Jeroboam and Hosea, 9, including Tibni, died violent deaths. The choice was directed to Menahem, because of the words in Zechariah, *three shepherds also I cut off in one month*, and Shallum murdered Zachariah the son of Jeroboam; and he himself, after he had *reigned a full month in Samaria*, was murdered by Menahem. Here then were two kings cut off. But the third? Imagination is to supply it. One [o] conjectures Menahem; but *he* reigned 10 years, and so, he invents a meaning for the word, that the prophet does not mean *cut off*, but *denied* them, leaving it open whether he meant "removed" or merely "did not acknowledge them, as Menahem at first certainly found no recognition with the prophetic order (2 Kgs xv. 16, 19);" another [p] imagined "some third rival of Zachariah and Shallum, of whom there is no mention in the historical books;" but there is no room for a third king, since Shallum murdered Zachariah;

[x] Mal. ii. 11.
[y] Neh. xiii. 26.
[z] Ib. 23, 24.
[a] 2 Macc. xii. 40.
[b] See below on x. 2.
[c] See ab. p. 325, and bel. on xiii. 2.
[d] Neh. vi. 12. 14.
[e] S. John x. 8.
[f] S. Matt. vii. 15.
[g] Ib. xxiv. 11, 24. S. Mark xiii. 22.
[h] Acts xiii. 6.
[i] Acts v. 36, 37.
[k] 1 S. John iv. 1.
[l] "The cause of this destruction [of those who took refuge in the temple] was a false prophet, who at that day preached to those in the city, that God bade them go up to the temple, to receive the signs of salvation. But there were many at that time suborned by the tyrants to the people, bidding them wait the help from God, that they might not desert, and that hope might master to their ill, those who were beyond fear or watching.—The deceivers, telling lies against God, then misdeceived the wretched people." Jos. B. J. vi. 5. 2 and 3.
[m] The questions 1) whether the six last chapters were Zechariah's, and 2) whether they were written before the captivity, are entirely apart.
[n] xi. 6. Comp. Is. ix. 20. xlix. 26. Jer. xix. 9.'
[o] Hitzig ad loc. p. 373. ed. 3.
[p] Maurer, followed by Bunsen Bibelwerk on Zech., Dr. Davidson Intr. ii. 330.

and Menahem, Shallum; another [q] found in Hebrew words [r] which had crept into the LXX, an usurper Kobal-am, of whom he says truly, "we hear nothing;" another [s] conceived of some usurper after the murder of Zachariah or of Shallum (this is left free), who about this time *may* have set himself at the head of the kingdom, but scarcely maintained himself some weeks; another [t] says, "This refers probably to the Interregnum 784–773, in which many *may* have set themselves as kings, but none have maintained themselves." Another [u] "An anti-king *may* at this time have set himself up in other parts of the kingdom, whom Menahem overthrew as he did that murderer." Others [v] say of the whole, "The symbolical representation, verss. 3 sqq., admits of no detailed explanation, but can be understood only as a whole. It describes the evil condition of Judah under Ahaz." Another [w], equally certain that it relates to Ahaz, says, "the three shepherds, who perished in one and the same month, were probably men who, in the long anarchy before Hosea ascended the throne, contended for the sceptre."

Yet another is so confident in this interpretation as to the three kings, Shallum, Zechariah and Menahem, that, whereas the book of Kings says expressly that Shallum reigned "[x] a full month" lit. "a month of days," the commentator says, "The month cannot have been full [y]; Zechariah xi. 8 evidently refers to the three Kings, Sachariah, Sallum and Menahem," while others [z] will have it that Zechariah by *one month* means some indefinite space more than a month. This is indeed required (although not stated) by all these theories, since Shallum alone reigned "a full month," and, consequently, the other two kings (if intended at all by the term "shepherds") must have been cut off at some period, outside of that "one month."

Truly, theory is a very exacting taskmaster, though strangely fascinating. It is to be one of the triumphs of the neo-criticism to distinguish between the authorship of Zech. ix–xi and xii–xiv. *The* point alleged to prove that c. xi. belongs to the time of Menahem is one at variance with history. It is not that the whole is like, while in one point the likeness is imperfect. It is *the* point, alleged as the keystone of the whole, which fails. The words of God by the prophet are, "*Three shepherds* have I cut off in *one month.*" It lies on the surface of the history, that Zachariah, son of Jeroboam, was murdered by Shallum, after reigning 6 months; and that Shallum, after reigning one full month, was himself murdered by Menahem [a]. The succession of murders was not so rapid as when Zimri had murdered Elah, Baasha's son, and after reigning 7 days, committed suicide, lest he should fall into the hands of Omri [b]. Elah and Zimri were cut off in one month; Zachariah and Shallum, in two. But in neither case was there any visible result, except a partial retribution of God's justice. The last executioner of God's justice *slept with his fathers;* his retribution was after death. He was *not* cut off. And this is the proof, which is to supplant the testimony to Jesus. The Apostle's words come true, as so often beside: [c] *They shall turn away their ears from the truth and shall be turned unto fables.*

[d] *Thou art wearied in the greatness of thy way, yet saidst thou not, there is no hope.* One should have thought that some must have, at times, thought of the old days, when the prophecy was interpreted of the Good Shepherd and of the 30 pieces of silver which were the price of His Blood, and which *were* cast into the house of the Lord [e]. But this would have been fatal to "historical criticism," whose province was to find out events of the prophet's own day to fill up the words of prophecy.

The human authorship of any books of

[q] Ewald (Gesch. d. V. Israel iii. 644.), followed as elsewhere by Dr. Stanley, Jewish Church ii. 364.

[r] The original text of the LXX seems to have corresponded with the Hebrew. The meaning of the two Hebrew words, קבל עב, is very simple, "before people" i. e. publicly; קבל העם would (as Böttcher observed, Jen. Lit. Zeit. 1847. p. 1144) have signified "before the people publicly assembled together." The Syro-Hexaplar version by Paul of Tela translates the words, and introduces "Kebdaam" with Origen's asterism, and so, as not belonging to the LXX. The Alexandrian and two other MSS. (one of Constantinople cent. x.) also retain the rendering. The singular "conspired," which excludes "Keblaam" from the place which it commonly occupies, occurs in 3 MSS., the Syro-Hex. Georg. Slav-Ostrog. Verss. and the Complut.; "and smote him" is also sing. in 3 MSS. and Compl. The word "Keblaam" was doubtless only the Hebrew words, written by one, who did not know how to translate them, and is variously written and placed as if the scribes did not know what to do with it. Four MSS. make it the name of a place, "in Ieblaam." They are retained in the place of the Hebrew words in the Vat. MS., but more commonly are added to "Shallum son of Jabis:" in some MSS. and a note in the Syr. Hex., they are followed by "and Selem or Selēm his father." They are written, "Kebdaam, Kebdiam, Kebdam, Kaddaam, Kaibdaam, Keblaam, Keddaam, Kebdaan, Ieblaam Iebaan, Iebdaam, Bdaam, Beldaam." See LXX ed. Parsons.

[s] Bleek Einl. p. 559. [t] Knobel, Proph. ii. 171.

[u] Bunsen Gott in d. Gesch. i. 450.

[v] Bertholdt Einl. iv. 1716, and so seemingly Rosenmüller. "Single traits are not to be pressed here; that of v. 8, that Jehovah had slain 3 bad shepherds in one month, belongs merely to poetic individualising." Gramberg ii. 523.

[w] Herzfeld, Gesch. d. Volkes Isr. Excurs. ii. §3. p. 283. [x] 2 Kgs. xv. 13.

[y] Thenius on 2 Kgs l. c. p. 351.

[z] "Three kings were dethroned by sedition in nearly one month." G. L. Bauer, Addit. Schulzii. Scholia viii. "Three kings followed in a short time on each other." E. Meier Gesch. d. poet. nation. lit. d. Hebr. p. 307.

[a] 2 Kgs xv. 8–14. [b] 1 Kgs xvi. 15–18.

[c] 2 Tim. iv. 4. [d] Is. lvii. 10.

[e] S. Matt. xxvi. 14–16, xxvii. 3–10.

Holy Scripture, and so of these chapters of Zechariah is, in itself, a matter which does not concern the soul. It is an untrue imputation, that the date of books of the Bible is converted into matter of faith. In this case Jesus has not set His seal upon it; God the Holy Ghost has not declared it. But, as in other cases, what lay as the foundation of the theory was the unbelief that God, in a way above nature, when it seemed good to Him, revealed a certain future to His creature man. It is the postulate, (or axiom, as appears to these critics), that there is no superhuman prophecy, which gives rise to their eagerness, to place these and other prophetic books or portions of books where they can say to themselves that they do not involve such prophecy. To believers it has obviously no religious interest, at what time it pleased Almighty God to send any of His servants the prophets. Not the dates assigned by any of these self-devouring theories, but the grounds alleged in support of those dates, as implying unbelief in God's revelation of Himself, make the question one of religious interest, viz. to shew that these theories are as unsubstantial, as their assumed base is baseless.

It is an infelicity of the modern German mind, that it is acute in observing detailed differences, rather than comprehensive in grasping deeper resemblances. It has been more busied in discovering what is new, than in observing the grounds of what is true. It does not, somehow, acquire the power of balancing evidence, which is habitual to the practical minds of our own countrymen. To take an instance of criticism, apart from Theology, the genuineness of a work of Plato.

"The genuineness of the Laws," says their recent translator[f], "is sufficiently proved by more than 20 citations of them in the writings of Aristotle [whom Plato designated "[g] the intellect of the school," and who must have been intimate with him for some 17 years[h]] who was residing at Athens during the last years of the life of Plato, and who returned to Athens at the time when he was himself writing his Politics and Constitutions; 2) by the allusion of Isocrates, writing B. C. 346, a year after the death of Plato, and not more than 2 or 3 years after the composition of the Laws—3) by the reference of the comic poet Alexis, a younger contemporary of Plato (B. C. 356.); 4) by the unanimous voice of later antiquity, and the absence of any suspicion among ancient writers worth noticing."

Yet German acuteness has found out reasons, why the treatise should not be Plato's. Those reasons are plausible, as most untrue things are. As put together carefully by one who yet attaches no weight to them, they look like a parody of the arguments, produced by Germans to take to pieces books of Holy Scripture. Mutatis mutandis, they have such an absurdly ludicrous resemblance, that it provokes a smile. Some 50 years ago, there was a tradition at Göttingen, where Heyne had lived, that he attributed the non-reception of the theories as to Homer in England to the English Bishops, who "apprehended that the same principle would be applied to Holy Scripture." Now, for half a century more, both sets of critics have had full scope. The classical sceptics seem to me to have the advantage. Any one, who knew but a little of the uncritical criticism, applied to the sacred books, could imagine, what a jubilee of triumph it would have occasioned, could such differences as those pointed out between "the Laws" and other treatises of Plato, have been pointed out to detach any book of Holy Scripture from its traditional writer. Yet it is held inadequate by one, of whom an admirer said, that "[i] his peculiar mode of criticism cut the very sinews of belief." I insert the criticisms[k], (omitting the details of

[f] Prof. Jowett, Translation of Plato's Dialogues. T. iv. p. 1.

[g] Philopon. de Ætern. mundi vi. 27. in Smith Gr. & Rom. Biogr. i. 317.

[h] From B. C. 364. to Plato's death B. C. 347.

[i] Pall Mall Gaz. March 28, 1868.

[k] "The style of the Laws differs in several important respects from the other dialogues of Plato: 1) in the want of character, power and lively illustration; 2) in the frequency of mannerisms; 3) in the form and rhythm of the sentences; 4) in the use of words. On the other hand, there are many passages 5) which are characterized by a sort of ethical grandeur; and 6) in which perhaps, a greater insight into human nature, and a greater reach of practical wisdom is shewn than in any other of Plato's writings.

"The Laws fall very short of the other Platonic dialogues in the refinements of courtesy. Partly the subject did not properly take the form of dialogue and partly the dramatic vigor of Plato had passed away.—Plato has given the Laws that form which was most suited to his own powers of writing in the decline of life.

"The fictions of the Laws have no longer that verisimilitude, which we find in the Phædrus, and the Timæus or even in the Politicus—Nor is there any where in the Laws that lively ἐνάργεια, that vivid *mise en scène*, which is as characteristic of Plato, as of some modern novelists.

"We no longer breathe the atmosphere of humor which pervades the earlier writings of Plato, and which makes the broadest Aristophanic joke as well as the subtlest refinement of wit possible; and hence the impression made upon us is bald and feeble—The irony of the earlier dialogues, of which some traces occur in the 10th book, is replaced by a sort of severity which hardly condescends to regard human things.

"The figures of speech and illustrations are poor in themselves and are not assisted by the surrounding phraseology. In the Republic and in the earlier dialogues—notes are struck which are repeated from time to time, as in a strain of music. There is none of this subtle art in the Laws.—The citations from the poets have lost that fanciful character, which gave them their charm in the earlier dialogues.

2. "The clumsiness of the dialogue leads to frequent mannerisms—This finish of style [in the

illustration) because their failure may open the eyes of some to the utter valuelessness of this sort of criticism. The accuracy of the criticisms is not questioned; the statements are not said to be exaggerated; yet they are held invalid. The question then comes with great force to the conscience; "Why, rejecting arguments so forcible as to a treatise of Plato, do I accept arguments very inferior, as to such or such a book of the Old or New Testament,—certain chapters of Isaiah, or Ecclesiastes, or these chapters of Zechariah, or the Epistle to the Hebrews, or the Revelation of S. John the Divine,—except on grounds of theology, not of criticism, and how am I true to myself in rejecting such arguments as to human books, and accepting them as to Divine books?"

dialogue] is no longer discernible in the Laws. Again and again the speaker is charged or charges himself with obscurity; he repeats again and again that he will explain his views more clearly. —A tendency to a paradoxical form of statement is also observable.—More than in other writings of Plato the tone is hortatory; the Laws are sermons as well as laws; they are supposed to have a religious sanction, and to rest upon a religious sentiment in the mind of the citizens—Resumptions of subjects which have been half disposed of in a previous passage, constantly occur: the arrangement has neither the clearness of art, nor the freedom of nature. Irrelevant remarks are made here and there, or illustrations used which are not properly filled in. The dialogue is generally weak and labored; and is in the later books fairly given up; apparently, because unsuited to the subject of the work.

3. "From this [perfection of style in the Symposium and Phædrus] there are many fallings off in the Laws, first, in the structure of the sentences, which are rhythmical and monotonous:—second, they are often of enormous length, and the latter end frequently appears to forget the beginning of them: they seem never to have received the second thoughts of the author: either the emphasis is wrongly placed, or there is a want of point in the clause, or an absolute case occurs, which is not properly separated from the rest of the sentence; or words are aggregated in a manner, which fails to shew their relation to one another; or the connecting particles are omitted at the beginning of sentences; the use of the relative and the antecedent is more indistinct, the changes of number and person more frequent; examples of pleonasm, tautology and periphrasis, unmeaning antitheses of positive and negative, and other affectations, are more numerous than in the other writings of Plato; there is also a more common and sometimes unmeaning use of qualifying formulæ—and of double expressions—; again there is an over-curious adjustment of verb and participle, noun and epithet: many forms of affected variety: thirdly, the absence of metaphorical language is remarkable; the style is not devoid of ornament but the ornament is of a debased rhetorical kind, patched on it instead of growing out of the subject; there is a great command of words, and a labored use of them; forced attempts at metaphor occur in several passages—(compare also the unmeaning extravagance of language in other passages); poor and insipid illustrations are also common: fourthly, we may observe an unmeaning use of climax and hyperbole—

4. "The pecularities in the use of words, which occur in the Laws, have been collected by Zeller and Stallbaum; first, in the use of nouns, such as" [8 are given]; "secondly, in the use of adjectives, such as" [5 instances] "and of adverbs, such as" [3 instances] "thirdly in the use of verbs such as" [5 instances]——

"Zeller and Stallbaum have also collected forms of words in the Laws differing from the forms of the same words, which occur in other places [7 instances, "and the Ionic word——"]. Zeller has noticed a fondness for substantives ending in μα and σις, such as [9 instances "and others"]; also a use of substantives in the plural, which are commonly found only in the singular [five instances.] Also a peculiar use of prepositions in composition as in [five instances "and others"] also a frequent use of the Ionic datives plural in αισι and οισι.

"To these peculiarities he has added a list of peculiar expressions and constructions [9 are given]. He remarks also on the frequent use of the abstract for the concrete [11 instances]. He further notes some curious instances of the genitive case—and of the dative—and also some rather uncommon periphrases; also the pleonastic use of the enclitics τις and of γε, of ταvῦν, of ὡς, and the periphrastic use of the preposition περί. Lastly he observes the tendency to hyperbata or transposition of words; and to rhythmical uniformity as well as grammatical irregularity in the structure of the sentences.

"For nearly all the expressions, which are adduced by Zeller against the genuineness of the Laws, Stallbaum finds some sort of authority. There is no reason for suspecting their genuineness, because several words occur in them, which are not found in the other writings of Plato. An imitator will often preserve the usual phraseology of a writer, better than he would himself." From Prof. Jowett's Introduction to the Laws of Plato, T. iv. pp. 11-16.

TABLE OF DATES, WHICH IN THIS CENTURY HAVE BEEN ASSIGNED TO ZECHARIAH IX—XIV[a].

AFTER THE DATE OF ZECHARIAH.

c. ix–xiv.	"At the earliest, in the first half and middle of the fifth century."	Vatke[1].
	"The younger poet, whose visions were added to those of Zechariah."	Geiger[2].
	Last years of Darius Hystaspis, or first of Xerxes[3].	Gramberg[4].
	After the battle of Issus B. C. 333.	Eichhorn[5].
	After 330.	Böttcher[6].

[a] J. D. Michaelis, 1786, was uncertain. The opinions or doubts in the last century were altogether vague. "I have as yet no certainty, but am seeking: am also not opposed, if any deny these chapters to be Zechariah's." Neue Orient. u. Exeg. Biblioth. i. 128.

Augusti stated attack and defence, but gave no opinion, Einl. 1806. G. L. Bauer (1793) said generally, "c. ix.–xiv. seem not to be Zechariah's," but professed himself in utter uncertainty as to the dates. Scholia T. viii. On ix.–xiv. he says, "which seems not to be Zechariah's," but whether Flügge was right who thought c. ix. belonged to the time of Jeroboam ii., or Eichhorn, who doubted whether it was not later than Zechariah, he says, "I decide nothing, leaving the whole question uncertain." p. 74. On xi. he says, "we find no indication when the desolation was inflicted," though he would rather understand the Assyrians, than Ant. Epiph. or the Romans. pp. 96, 97. Of xii.–xiv. he leaves subject and time uncertain. pp. 109. 119. 121. Döderlein also seems uncertain, Auserl. theol. Biblioth. iv. 2. p. 81. (1787.)

[1] Biblische Theologie wissenschaftlich dargestellt. i. 553. "It seems to have been occasioned by the Persian-Egyptian wars, and by the feuds of the Jews with the neighboring people. Nehemiah found Jerusalem half destroyed [rather not rebuilt]. The want of historical accounts makes it impossible to explain to what details refer."

[2] (Rabbiner d. Synag. Gem. Breslau) Urschrift u. Uebersetz. d. Bibl. p. 55, 57. 1857.

[3] "When the fame of the Greeks, even in Palestine, must have been great enough to suggest to the poet the thought, that so mighty and warlike a people could only be conquered by Jehovah and his Israelites; then would mere peace and prosperity prevail.

[4] Religions-Ideen d. A. T. (with preface by Gesenius) ii. 520.

[5] Einl. ins. A. T. n. 605. iv. 445, 449. 450. 1824. "If it is true, that all prophecies start from the present, and prophets threaten with no people, and promise nothing of any, till the people itself is come on the scene and into relation with their people, the poet cannot have spoken of the relation of Alexander to the Jews, till after the battle of Issus." "Altogether, no explanation of the whole section (ix. 1.–x. 17.) is possible, if it be not gained from the history of Alexander the Great. History relates expressly, how after the battle of Issus he took possession of all Syria and Zidon without great difficulties; how, with an employment of military contrivance unheard of elsewhere, he conquered and destroyed island-Tyre; how, of the maritime cities of Philistia, with indomitable perseverance he is specified to have besieged and taken Gaza, punished with death the opposition of its commander and its inhabitants, can any require more to justify this explanation?" "The portions xi. xii.–xiii. 6. have no matter, from which their age could be determined; yet neither do they contain any thing to remove them to an early time; rather has the language much which is late; if then the contents of xiii. 7–end, set it late, they too may be accounted late. This last must either have been to comfort the people on the first tidings of the death of Judas Maccabi in the battle with Bacchides, or have no definite subject.—In that case it would belong to B. C. 161, yet one must own that there is not the same evidence for this, as that ix. 1.–x. 17, belongs to the time of Alexander.—These must be the proofs, that the 2d half of Zechariah cannot have the same author as the first, or one must allow what tradition gives out, and since there are great doubts against it, one must regret that one can come to no clear result as to Zechariah. *For the other proofs which could be brought are not decisive.*" pp. 450, 451.

Corrodi had on the same grounds assigned c. ix. to the time of Alexander; c. xiv. to that of Antiochus Epiphanes. Versuch e. Beleuchtung d. Gesch. d. Jud. u. Christl. Bibel-Canons i. 107.

[6] Ausf. Lehrbuch d. Hebr. Sprache. n. 45. p. 23. 1868. "The way in which Greece is named as a chief enemy of Zion (quite different from that of Joel iv. 6. Is. lxvi. 19.), chiefly shews that the sections Zech. ix. sqq. *which resist every assured collocation in the præ-exile* or ante-Macedonian *period*, could only have been written after Alexander's march through Palestine. With this agree the later coloring, the Levitical spirit, the style full of compilation and of imitation, as also the phantastic messianic hopes. These last must have been revived among the Jews after the overthrow through Alexander. In comparison with the lifeless language of these chapters, as to which we cannot at all understand how any can have removed them into so early præ-exile times, the Psalms attributed to the times of the Maccabees are amazingly fresh. On this, as well as other grounds, we can admit of no Psalms of the Maccabee times." Neue Aehrenlese ii. 215–127. One ground, which has by others of this school been alleged for not ascribing them to Zechariah, had been that they were so much *more* poetic &c. "In regard to language also, the style in the second Part is wholly different. c. 9. and 10, are energetic, vivid, &c." Hitzig, Vorbemerkk. z. d. ii. u. iii. Zech. n. 2. "Rosenmüller says truly:—How much the poetic, weighty, concise, fervid style of the six last chapters differs from the prosaic, languid, humble style of the eight first." Maurer on Zech. ix.–xiv. p. 667. "These prophecies [Zech. ix.–xiv.] cannot be from Zechariah, not on account of the un-symbolic style (comp. xi. 4–17.) but on account of the more forceful style" &c. De Wette Einl § 250 ed. 2.

TABLE OF DATES.

c. xiv.	Antiochus Epiphanes.	"many interpreters[1]."
c. ix.	On Hyrcanus i, as the Messiah.	Paulus[2].
	ZECHARIAH HIMSELF.	
	[Beckhaus[3] 1792] Jahn[4], Koster[5], Hengstenberg[6], Burger[7], De Wette (edd. 4–6). A. Theiner[8], Herbst[9], Umbreit[8], Hävernick[9], Keil[9], Stähelin[9], von Hoffmann[10], Ebrard, Schegg, Baumgarten[8], Neumann[8], Kliefoth[8], Köhler[8], Sandrock[11].	
	DATES BEFORE THE CAPTIVITY.	
ix–xiv.	Uzziah B.C. 772.	Hitzig[12], Rosenmüller[13].
ix–xi.	Under Ahaz, during war with Pekah.	Bertholdt[14].
ix–xi.	Beginning of Ahaz.	Credner[15], Herzfeld[16].
ix–xi.	Later time of Hezekiah.	Baur[17].
ix–xi.	Between B.C. 771–740, i. e. between the invasion of Pul, (2 Kgs xv. 19.) and the capture of Damascus by Tiglath-Pileser (2 Kgs xvi. 9.) i. e. between the 40th of Uzziah and the 3d of Ahaz.	Knobel[18].
ix–xi. and xiii. 7–9.	In the first 10 years of Pekah before the war with Ahaz [i. e. between B.C. 759–749].	Ewald[19].
ix–xi. xiii. 7–9.	"Very probably Uzziah's favorite prophet in his prosperous days."	Stanley[20].
ix–xi.	Contemporary with Isaiah under Ahaz toward B.C. 736.	Bunsen[21].
ix. x.	Perhaps contemporary with Zephaniah [in the time of Josiah].	De Wette[22].
xi.	Might be put in the time of Ahaz.	Id.
ix.	Perhaps out of the time of Zephaniah.	Gesenius[23].

[1] in Bertholdt Einl. iv. 1715.
[2] Comm. z. N. T. iii. 130–139. Else he follows Eichhorn 1832.
[3] ub. d. Integrität d. Proph. Schriften d. A. B. p. 337. sqq.
[4] Einl. ii. 675. sqq.
[5] Meletemata crit. et exeg. in Zach. proph. part. post. 1818.
[6] Beitrage zur Einl. ins. A. T. i. 361. sqq.
[7] Etudes exégét. et critiques sur le proph. Zacharie. Strasburg 1841.
[8] In their commentaries on Zechariah.
[9] In their Introductions to the O. T.
[10] Schriftbeweis ii. 2. p. 550.
[11] Prioris et posterioris Zach. partis vaticin. ab uno eodemque auct. profecta. 1857.
[12] Theol. Studien u. Kritiken 1830. 1. p. 25. sqq. followed by *v. Lengerke*, d. Buch Daniel, Einl. p. lxxvii.
[13] Scholia in V. T. vii. 4. p. 254. sqq. ed. 2. In ed. 1. he had followed Jahn.
[14] Einl. ins A. T. iv. n. 431. pp. 1712–1716. In p. 1722 he conjectures the prophet to have been Zechariah son of Jeberechiah (Is. viii. 2); a conjecture recommended by *Gesenius*, Jesaia i. 527 as "an acute combination." Ewald calls the theory of one or more Zechariahs, "an over-ingenious device (erklügelte) idle conjecture, a plea of those who will not look straight at the truth." Proph. i. 249.
[15] Joel. vol. i. p. 105.
[16] Gesch. d. Volkes Isr., Excurs. ii. n. 3. pp. 280–282.
[17] d. Proph. Amos, vol. i.
[18] Prophetismus d. Hebräer ii. 168–170.
[19] Kl. Proph. i. 248–251, followed mostly by *E. Meier* Gesch. d. poet. national. lit. d. Hebraer p. 308.
[20] Jewish Church ii. 444, add 364, 366.
[21] Gott. in d. Geschichte i. 453. In p. 247, he placed ch. ix. at "a generation after Ahaz."
[22] Einl. ins. A. T. n. 250. p. 338. edd. 1–3.
[23] On Is. xxiii. p. 713.

TABLE OF DATES.

ix.	Uzziah.	Bleek[1], Forberg[2].
x.	Ahaz, soon after war with Pekah and Rezin.	Bleek.
xi. 1–3.	Invasion of some Assyrian king.	
xii. 4–17.	Menahem, and end of Uzziah.	
ix.	Between the carrying away of 2½ tribes and the fall of Damascus.	Maurer[3].
x.	Between 739–731, the 7 years' anarchy between Hosea's murder of Pekah and his own accession.	
xi.	In reign of Hosea.	
ix.	Under Uzziah and Jeroboam.	
x.	The Anarchy after death of Jeroboam ii. [B.C. 784–772.]	v. Ortenberg[4].
xi. 1–3.	B.C. 716.	
xi. 4–17. xiii. 7–9.	Shortly after the war of Pekah and Rezin.	
ix–x.	Not before Jeroboam, nor before Uzziah's accession, but before the death of Zechariah son of Jeroboam.	Hitzig[5].
xi.	Beginning of reign of Menahem.	Hitzig[5].
xi.	Possibly contemporary with Hosea.	Bauer[6].
ix.	After capture of Damascus by Tiglath-Pileser.	Movers[7].
xii–xiv.	Manasseh, in view of a siege by Esarhaddon.	Hitzig[8].
	Between B.C. 607–604 (though falsified.)	Knobel[9].
	Soon after Josiah's death, by Uriah, Jeremiah's contemporary, B.C. 607 or 606.	Bunsen[10].
	Most probably, while the Chaldees were already before Jerusalem, shortly before Jerusalem was first conquered (599).	Schrader[11].
xii. 1–xiii. 6.	Under Joiakim or Jeconiah or Zedekiah in Nebuchadnezzar's last expedition (no objection that it was falsified).	Bertholdt[12].
xiii. 7.–end.	Soon after Josiah's death.	Bertholdt[13].
xii. 1–xiii. 6.	The last years of Jehoiakim, or under Jehoiachin or Zedekiah.	Bleek[14].
xiii.–7. end.	"Exceeding probably under Josiah or Jehoiakim."	Bleek[15].
xii. 1–xiii. 6.	Fourth year of Jehoiakim.	Maurer[16].
xiii. 7.–end.	Fifth.	
xii. 1–xiii. 6.	The latter half of 600 B.C.	v. Ortenberg[17].
xiv.	Later than xii. 1.–xiii. 6.	

1 Einl. ins. A. T. p. 555–560.
2 Comm. crit. et exeg. in part. post. Zach. P. i.
3 Maurer Comm. p. 669.
4 Die Bestandtheile d. Buchs Sacharia pp. 68. 72. 75, 79, followed by Kahnis Lutherische Dogm. i. 354–357.
5 D. Kl. Proph. ii. und iii. Zacharia, Vorbemerk. n. 4. p. 351. ed. 2., followed by *Schrader* in his re-writing of De Wette's Einl. n. 308, only placing c. ix. definitely in the time of Jeroboam ii.
6 "What I think, or rather, conjecture." Schulzii Scholia continuata viii. 100.
7 Phœnicien ii. 1. p. 383, 384.
8 Kl. Proph. ii. und iii. Sach. n. 5. 6. ed. 2, 3.
9 Prophetismus ii. 289.
10 Gott in d. Geschichte i. 451, 452.
11 De Wette's Einleitung, re-written from his Ed. vi. n. 308. a new § p. 382.
12 Einl. iv. 1717.
13 Ib. 1719.
14 Einl. p. 560.
15 Ib. 563.
16 Proph. Min. p. 670.
17 Bestandtheile &c. p. 87.

TABLE OF DATES.

xii–xiii. 6.	12 years after Habakkuk [about B.C. 607, Ewald] shortly before the destruction of Jerusalem.	Ewald [1].
xiii. 7–9.	Same date as ix. xi. (see above).	
xiv.	A little later than xii–xiii.	
	or, In the first rebellion against Nebuchadnezzar "[3] by Chananiah, or one of the many prophets who contradicted Jeremiah."	Ewald [2].
xii–xiii. 6. xiv.	Zedekiah, "Beginning of revolt."	Stanley [4]
xii. 1–xiii. 6. xiii. 7. end.	"Prophecies of fanatic contents, which deny all historical explanation, but xiii. 7. must rather be conceived as future than 'past,' as Bertholdt."	De Wette ed. 2 [5].
xii. 1–xiii. 6. xiv.	After death of Josiah, yet relating to the repentance for the putting the Messias to death, and so independent of the times in which it is placed.	Kahnis [6].

[1] Kl. Proph. ii. 52.

[2] Ib. ii. 59. "At a time when the earnest and more threatening condition of the world softened the proud certainty of victory, and occasioned the anticipation of the fulfillment of a judgment on the holy city." xiv. 1–2.

[3] Geschichte d. Volkes Isr. iii. 803. Ewald says that he often balanced between them, but always ended by coming back to the first, since xiv. 2. probably referred to the capture under Jehoiachin.

[4] Jewish Church. Sect. xi. "special authorities." p. 513. Passing him over in the history, he escapes the consequence which Ewald drew out, that he would have been a false prophet, although he says, that "in Hananiah," whose death Jeremiah prophesied for "telling lies in the name of the Lord," "passed away the last echo of the ancient invincible strain of the age of Isaiah." p. 545.

[5] Einl. n. 250. p. 338 ed. 1822.

[6] Lutherische Dogm. i. 359–361.

ZECHARIAH.

Before CHRIST cir. 520.

CHAPTER I.

1 Zechariah exhorteth to repentance. 7 The vision of the horses. 12 At the prayer of the angel comfortable promises are made to Jerusalem. 18 The vision of the horns, and the four carpenters.

IN the eighth month, [a] in
the second year of Da-
rius, came the word of the
LORD [b] unto Zechariah, the
son of Berechiah, the son
of Iddo the prophet, saying,
2 The LORD hath been
† sore displeased with your
fathers.
3 Therefore say thou
unto them, Thus saith the
LORD of hosts; Turn [c] ye
unto me, saith the LORD
of hosts, and I will turn
unto you, saith the LORD
of hosts.

[a] Ezra 4. 24. Hag. 1. 1.
[b] Ezra 5. 1. Matt. 23. 35.
† Heb. *with displeasure.*
[c] Jer. 25. 5. & 35. 15. Mic. 7. 19. Mal. 3. 7. Luke 15. 20. James 4. 8.

CHAP. I. 1. *In the eighth month*[1]. The date joins on Zechariah's prophecy to those of Haggai. Two months before, *in the sixth month*[2], had Haggai, conjointly with Zechariah[3], exhorted Zerubbabel and the people to resume the intermitted building of the temple. These had used such diligence, notwithstanding the partial discouragement of the Persian Government[4], that God gave them *in the seventh month,* the magnificent promise of the later glory of the temple through the Coming of Christ[5]. Still as Haggai too warned them, the conversion was not complete. So Zechariah in the eighth, as Haggai in the ninth[6] month, urges upon them the necessity of thorough and inward repentance, as the condition of partaking of those promises.

"[7] Thrice in the course of one saying, he mentions the most holy name of God; partly to instruct in the knowledge of Three Persons in one Nature, partly to confirm their minds more strongly in the hope of the salvation to come."

2. lit. *Wroth was the Lord against your fathers with wrath*[8], i. e., a wrath which was indeed such, whose greatness he does not further express, but leaves to their memories to supply. "[9] Seest thou how he scares them, and, setting before the young what befell those before them, drives them to amend, threatening them with the like or more grievous ills, unless they would wisely reject their fathers' ways, esteeming the pleasing of God worthy of all thought and care. He speaks of *great wrath.* For it indicates no slight displeasure that He allowed the Babylonians to waste all Judah and Samaria, burn the holy places and destroy Jerusalem, remove the elect Israel to a piteous slavery in a foreign land, severed from sacrifices, entering no more the holy court nor offering the thank-offering, or tithes, or first-fruits of the law, but precluded by necessity and fear even from the duty of celebrating his prescribed and dearest festivals. The like we might address to the Jewish people, if we would apply it to the mystery of Christ. For after they had *killed the prophets* and had *crucified the Lord of glory* Himself, they were captured and destroyed; their famed temple was levelled, and Hosea's words were fulfilled in them; [10] *The children of Israel shall abide many days without a king and without a prince, without a sacrifice and without an image, without an ephod and without teraphim.*"

3. *Therefore say thou.* lit. *And thou sayest,* i. e., this having been so, it follows that thou sayest or must say[11], *Turn ye unto Me.* In some degree they had turned to God, for Whose sake they had returned to their land; and again when, after some negligence[12], they renewed the building of the temple, and God had said, [13] *I am with you.* But there needed yet a more inward completer turning, whereon God promises a yet nearer presence, as Malachi repeats the words[14], and S. James exhorts[15], *Draw nigh to God and He will draw nigh to you.* Those who have turned to God need ever to turn more into the centre of the narrow way. As the soul opens itself more to God, God, Whose communication of Himself is ever hindered only by our closing the

[1] Not as Kim. in the 8th new-moon; for though חדש is used of the new-moon, Num. xxviii. 14, 1 Sam. xx. 5, 18, 24; Am. viii. 5. (not Ex. xix. 1. or Hos. v. 7.) it is not so used in dates, in which it would be ambiguous.
[2] Hagg. i. 1. [3] Ezr. v. 1, 2. [4] Ib. 3–5.
[5] Hagg. ii. 1–9. [6] Ib. 10–14. [7] Osor.
[8] As we might express by the indefinite article "a blow" for "such a blow." The LXX fill up ὀργὴν μεγάλην. Ewald (Lehrb. n. 281. p. 702.) quotes χαρᾷ χαίρει, S. John iii. 29.
[9] S. Cyr. [10] Hos. iii. 4. See vol. i. p. 44.
[11] The force of וְאָמַרְתָּ. The duty is implied in v. 2. [12] Hagg. i. 2–11. [13] Ib. 13.
[14] Mal. iii. 7. [15] S. James iv. 8.

Before CHRIST cir. 520.

d 2 Chron. 36. 15, 16.
e Isai. 31. 6. Jer. 3. 12. & 18. 11. Ezek. 18. 30. Hos. 14. 1.

4 Be ye not as your fa-
thers, [d] unto whom the
former prophets have cried,
saying, Thus saith the
LORD of hosts; [e] Turn ye
now from your evil ways,
and *from* your evil doings:
but they did not hear, nor
hearken unto me, saith the
LORD.

Before CHRIST cir. 520.

door of our hearts against Him, enters more into it. [1] *If a man love Me, he will keep My words, and My Father will love him, and We will come unto him, and make Our abode with him.*

"[2] Men are said to be converted, when leaving behind them deceitful goods, they give their whole mind to God, bestowing no less pains and zeal on Divine things than before on the nothings of life."

"[3] When it is said in Holy Scripture, *Turn unto Me and I will turn unto you*, we are admonished as to our own freedom; when we answer, *Turn us, Lord, unto Thee, and we shall be turned*, we confess that we are forecome by the grace of God."

4. *Be ye not like your fathers.* Strangely infectious is the precedent of ill. Tradition of good, of truth, of faith, is decried; only tradition of ill and error are adhered to. The sin of Jeroboam was held sacred by every king of Israel: [4] *The statutes of Omri were diligently kept, and all the works of the house of Ahab. They turned back and were treacherous like their forefathers; they turned themselves like a deceitful bow* [5], is God's summary of the history of Israel. "[6] Absurd are they who follow the ignorances of their fathers, and ever plead inherited custom as an irrefragable defence, though blamed for extremest ills. So idolaters especially, being called to the knowledge of the truth, ever bear in mind the error of their fathers and, embracing their ignorance as an hereditary lot, remain blind."

The former prophets. The prophets spake God's words, as well in their pastoral office as in predicting things to come, in enforcing God's law and in exhorting to repentance, as in announcing the judgments on disobedience. The predictive as well as the pastoral office were united in Nathan [7], Gad [8], Shemaiah [9], Azariah [10], Hanani [11], Elijah [12], Elisha [13], Micaiah the son of Imla, whose habitual predictions against Ahab induced Ahab to say [14], *I hate him, for he doth not prophesy good concerning me, but evil.* The specific calls to conversion here named and their fruitlessness, are summed up by Jeremiah as words of all the prophets. For ten years he says, [15] *The word of the Lord hath come unto me, and I have spoken unto you, rising early and speaking, and ye have not hearkened. And the Lord hath sent unto you all His servants the prophets, rising early and sending; but ye have not hearkened nor inclined your ear to hear. They said, Turn ye again now every one from his evil ways and from the evil of your doings, and dwell in the land that the Lord hath given unto you and to your fathers for ever and ever; and go not after other gods to serve and worship them, and provoke Me not to anger with the works of your hands, and I will do you no hurt. But ye have not hearkened unto Me, saith the Lord; that ye might provoke Me to anger with the works of your hands to your own hurt. Therefore, thus saith the Lord of hosts, Because ye have not heard My words &c.* The prophetic author of the book of Kings sums up in like way, of *all the prophets and all the seers.* [16] *The Lord testified against Israel and against Judah by the hand of all the prophets and all the seers*, saying, *Turn ye from your evil ways and keep My commandments, My statutes, according to all the law which I commanded your fathers, and which I sent to you by My servants the prophets, and they did not hear, and hardened their neck, like the neck of their fathers.*

The characteristic word [17], *turn from your evil ways and the evil of your doings* occurring in Jeremiah, it is probable, that this summary was chiefly in the mind of Zechariah, and that he refers not to Isaiah, Joel, Amos &c., (as all the prophets were preachers of repentance), but to the whole body of teachers, whom God raised up, analogous to the Christian ministry, to recall men to Himself.

The title, *the former prophets*, contrasts the office of Haggai and Zechariah, not with definite prophets before the captivity, but with the whole company of those, whom God sent as He says, so unremittingly.

And they hearkened not unto Me. "[18] They heard not the Lord warning through the pro-

[1] S. John xiv. 23. [2] Osor.
[3] Conc. Trid. Sess. vi. c. 5. [4] Mic. vi. 16.
[5] Ps. lxxviii. 57. [6] S. Cyr.
[7] 2 Sam. vii. 4–16, xii. 1–14. [8] 1 Sam. xxii. 5, xxiv. 11.
[9] 2 Chr. xi. 2–4, xii. 5–8. [10] Ib. xv. [11] Ib. xvi. 7–9.
[12] 1 Kgs xvii. 1, 14, xviii. 1, 41, xxi. 19, 21, 23, 29, 2 Kgs i. 4, 16.
[13] 2 Kgs iii. 17, 18. iv. 16, v. 27, vii. 1, 2, viii. 10–13, xiii. 14–19.
[14] 1 Kgs xxii. 8. [15] Jer. xxv. 3–8. [16] 2 Kgs xvii. 13.
[17] Zech. שובו נא מדרכיכם הרעים ומעליליכם Jer. xxv. 5. שבו נע איש מררכו הרעה ומרע מעלליכם. In Jer. xviii. 11. the second clause is, והיטיבודר כיכם ומעלליכם; in Jer. xxxv. 15, it is, והיטיבו מעלליכם. In Zech., the Kri מעלליכם substitutes Jeremiah's word for the ἀπ. λεγ. מעלילים.
[18] S. Jer.

Before CHRIST cir. 520.

5 Your fathers, where
are they? and the pro-
phets, do they live for
ever?

[f] Isai. 55. 1.

6 But [f]my words and
my statutes, which I com-
manded my servants the
prophets, did they not
‖take hold of your fa-
thers? and they returned
and said, [g]Like as the
LORD of hosts thought to
do unto us, according to
our ways, and according
to our doings, so hath he
dealt with us.

‖ Or, *overtake*.

[g] Lam. 1. 18. & 2. 17.

Before CHRIST cir. 520.

cir. 519.

7 ¶ Upon the four and
twentieth day of the
eleventh month, which *is*
the month Sebat, in the
second year of Darius,
came the word of the
LORD unto Zechariah, the
son of Berechiah, the son
of Iddo the prophet, say-
ing,
8 I saw by night, and
behold [h]a man riding upon

[h] Josh. 5. 13. Rev. 6. 4.

---

phets, attended not—not to the Prophets who spake to them but—not to Me, saith the Lord. For I was in them who spake and was despised. Whence also the Lord in the Gospel saith, [1] *He that receiveth you, receiveth Me.*"

5. *Your fathers, where are they*[2]? The abrupt solemnity of the question seems to imply an unexpected close of life which cut short their hopes, plans, promises to self. [3] *When they* said, *Peace and safety, then sudden destruction cometh upon them.* Yet not they only but the prophets too, who ministered God's word to them, these also being men, passed away, some of them before their time as men, by the martyr's death. Many of them saw not their own words fulfilled. But God's word which they spake, being from God, passed not away.

6. *Only My words and My decrees*[4], which God spake by them, *did not they overtake them?* Heathen reminiscence of God's justice acknowledged, "[5] Rarely hath punishment with limping tread parted with the forerunning miscreant." *All these curses,* Moses foretells[6], *shall come upon thee and overtake thee*[7], *until thou art destroyed.*

And they returned to God and said. The history of the Jews in Babylon is omitted in Holy Scripture, except as to His special dealings with Daniel and his three companions. Yet Jeremiah confesses in words, what Zechariah had apparently in his mind; [8] *The Lord hath done that which He purposed; He hath fulfilled His word, which He commanded in the days of old.* The Lamentations are one long confession of deserved punishment, such as Daniel too made in the name of his people with himself[9].

It was one long waiting for God and for the restoration of His visible worship. Yet repentance was a condition of their restoration.

7. *On the twenty-fourth day,* exactly five months after the building of the temple was resumed[10], and two months after Haggai's last prophecy[11]. The series of visions, leading onward, from the first deliverance from the enemies who oppressed them, to the Coming of Christ, is given as a reward to their first whole-hearted endeavor to restore their worship of Him. The visions are called *the word of the Lord,* because they were prophecy, made visible to the eye, conveying the revelation to the soul, and in part explained by Him.

8. *I saw in the night,* i. e. that following on *the twenty-fourth day.* The darkness of the night perhaps was chosen, as agreeing with the dimness of the restored condition. Night too is, "[12] through the silence of the senses and of the fancy, more suited for receiving Divine revelations."

A man riding upon a red horse. The man is an angel of God, appearing in form of man, as Daniel says, "[13] *The man* Gabriel, whom I had seen in the vision at the beginning, touched me." He is doubtless the same who appeared to Joshua in form of man, preparing thereby for the revelation of *God manifest in the flesh*—He, before whom Joshua fell on his face and in him worshiped God, through whom also

[1] S. Matt. x. 40.
[2] It is probably for emphasis, that (here alone) the full אַיֵּה הֵם stands for the contracted אַיָּם; our, "where are *they?*"
[3] 1 Thess. v. 3.
[4] As Ps. ii. 7. Zeph. ii. 2.
[5] Hor. Od. iii. 9. fin.
[6] Deut. xxviii. 45.
[7] The same word הִשִּׂיג (as here) occurs also Ib. 15; of the Divine wrath, Ps. lxix. 25; of iniquities, Ps. xl. 13.
[8] Lam. ii. 17. זמם is used of God, in connection with עשׂה in both places and in Jer. li. 12. זמם is used of God beside only in Jer. iv. 28. The verb is used only 13 times in all.
[9] Dan. ix. 4–16.
[10] Hagg. ii. 15.
[11] Ib. ii. 20.
[12] Dion.
[13] Dan. ix. 21.

Before CHRIST cir. 519.

a red horse, and he stood
among the myrtle trees
that *were* in the bottom;
and behind him *were there*
[i] red horses, || speckled, and
white.

i ch. 6. 2,-7.
|| Or, *bay.*

9 Then said I, O my
lord, what *are* these? And
the angel that talked with
me said unto me, I will
shew thee what these *be*.
10 And the man that
stood among the myrtle
trees answered and said,
[k] These *are they* whom the
LORD hath sent to walk
to and fro through the
earth.

k Heb. 1. 14.

Before CHRIST cir. 519.

God required the same tokens of reverence as He had from Moses [1]. *Joshua lifted up his eyes, and looked, and behold there stood a man over against him with a sword drawn in his hand, who said, as Captain of the Lord's host am I come.* He rides here, as Leader of the host who follow Him; to Him the others report, and He instructs the Angel who instructs the prophet. Red, being the color of blood, symbolizes doubtless "[2] the vengeance of God to be inflicted on the enemies of the Jews for their sins committed against the Jews," exceeding the measure of chastisement allowed by God. It probably was S. Michael [3], who is entitled in Daniel, *your prince* [4], *the great prince which standeth up for the children of thy people* [5].

And he was standing, almost as we say, stationary, abiding in that one place. The description is repeated [6], apparently as identifying this angel, and so he and *the angel of the* [7] *Lord* are probably one.

The myrtle trees [8], from their fragrance and lowness, probably symbolize the Church, as at once yielding a sweet odor, and in a low estate, or lowly. The natural habits of the myrtle make it the fitter symbol [9].

And behind him. The relation of the Angel as their chief is represented by their following him. This is consistent with their appearing subsequently as giving report to him. The red and white horses are well-known symbols of war and glory, whence He Who sits on *the white horse* [10] in the Revelations, *went forth conquering and to conquer.* The remaining color is somewhat uncertain. If it be *ashen gray*, it would correspond to *the pale horse* [11] of the Revelations, and the union of the two colors, black and white, is calculated to be a symbol of a chequered state of things, whereas a mingled color like "chestnut" is not suggestive of any symbol.

9. *What are these?* He asks, not *who*, but *what* [12] they import.

The angel that talked with me. lit. "spake *in* me." The very rare expression [13] seems meant to convey the thought of an inward speaking, whereby the words should be borne directly into the soul, without the intervention of the ordinary outward organs. God says to Moses, [14] *If there is a prophet among you, I, the Lord, will make Myself known unto him in a vision, I will speak* [lit.] *in him in a dream. My servant Moses is not so—In him will I speak mouth to mouth;* and Habakkuk says of the like inward teaching, [15] *I will watch to see,*

[1] Josh. v. 13–15. See on "the Angel of the Lord" in "Daniel the Prophet," pp. 519–525.
[2] Dion. [3] Dan. x. 13. [4] Ib. 21.
[5] Ib. xii. 1. S. Jerome observes, "The Jews suppose *the man on the red horse* to be the Angel Michael, who was to avenge the iniquities and sins against Israel." [6] ver. 10. [7] ver. 11.
[8] The name of the plant, הֲדַס, occurs in the Arabic of Yemen (Kam. p. 812 and Abulwalid) and is probably the basis of Esther's original name, הֲדַסָּה, perhaps i. q. Ἄτοσσα. Ges.
[9] מְצֻלָּה, ἅπ. in form is doubtless the same as צָלַל מְצוּלָה, being used of sinking in the water, Ex. xv. 10. "In profundo," S. Jer. (Virg. Georg. ii. 112, litora myrtetis gratissima, and Ib. iv. 124, amantes litora myrti.) The LXX κατασκιων would rather have been מְצִלָּה, and the myrtles make shade, but do not grow in a shady place. Hitz. Ew. Maur. correct מִצְלָּה, "the tent," (as Arab. מטלה) i. e. "of God," they say. But the tabernacle, while it existed, was not so called; nor did myrtles grow before it. Bottcher n. 641. γ.) מְצַלָּה, "schattendach."
[10] Rev. vi. 2.
[11] Rev. vi. 8, ψαροὶ, ὁ; varü, S. Jer., ξανθοὶ Aq. The קְוִחִין of the Targum is itself uncertain. It is a conjecture only of Levy, that it may be i. q. κυανοχαίτης, "dark-maned." Rashi and Kim. own that they do not know. The Peshito פְּיסְכֵּיא corresponds to the Heb. טלוא in Gen. xxx. 32. (bis) 33, 35 (bis) 39. but its meaning, in itself, is equally unknown. The Hebrew root occurs beside, only of a choice vine, pl. Is. xvi. 8, שֹׂרֵק Is. v. 2. Jer. ii. 21, שֹׂרֵקָה Gen. xlix. 11; in Arab. סריק, Abulw. But although this vine, growing only in Syria, has small blue-black grapes (Kim.), it is mere guess that it is so called from its color, or that שרק signifies red or dark. It is equally a guess that שרק is transposed from Arab. אַשְׁקַר "chestnut," (as distinct from "bay" כָּמִית). שַׁקְרָא is used of the color of fire.
[12] מָה, not מִי. [13] דִּבֵּר בִּי. [14] Nu. xii. 6–9.
[15] Hab. ii. 1. These are the only additional instances of the construction, unless Jer. xxxi. 20, be used of tender speaking, "in (elsewhere in the heart of) Ephraim."

Before CHRIST cir. 519.

11 [l]And they answered the angel of the LORD that stood among the myrtle trees, and said, We have walked to and fro through the earth, and, behold, all the earth sitteth still, and is at rest.

[l] Ps. 103. 20, 21.

12 ¶ Then the angel of the LORD answered and said, [m]O LORD of hosts, how long wilt thou not

[m] Ps. 102. 13. Rev. 6. 10.

what He will speak in me. It is the characteristic title of one attendant-angel, who was God's expositor of the visions to Zechariah[1]. "[2]By his ministry God shewed me things to come, in that that angel formed in the spirit and imaginative power of Zechariah phantasms or images of things which were foreshewn him, and gave him to understand what those images signified."

11. *And the man answered* to the question addressed to the attendant-angel. He himself took the word.

These are they whom the Lord sent to walk up and down. Satan says of himself that he came [3]*from going to and fro in the earth and from walking up and down in it.* As he for evil, so these for good. Their office was not a specific or passing duty, as when God sent His angels with some special commission, such as those recorded in Holy Scripture. It was a continuous conversation with the affairs of men, a minute course of visiting, inspecting our human deeds and ways, a part of the "[4]wonderful order," in which God has "ordained and constituted the services of Angels and men." Nor is it said that the Angels were limited, each to his own peculiar province, as we learn through Daniel, that certain great Angels, *Princes* among them, had the charge of empires or nations, even of the heathen[5]. These Angels had apparently only the office of inspecting and reporting to Angels of a higher order, themselves a subordinate order in the heavenly Hierarchy. Nor are they spoken of, as executing any judgments of God, or as pacifying the earth; they may have been so employed ; but they are only said to have reported the state in which they found it.

These *answered* the unexpressed inquiry of *the angel of the Lord,* as he had answered the unuttered question of the angel, attendant on Zechariah.

Sitteth still and is at rest, at rest, as the word seems to express[6], from its wonted state of tumult and war. Wars, although soon to break out again, were in the second year of Darius for the time suspended. The rest, in which the world was, suggests the contrast of the yet continuing unrest allotted to the people of God. Such rest had been promised to Israel, on its return from the captivity[7], but had not yet been fulfilled. Through the hostility of the Samaritans the building of the temple had been hindered and was just recommenced; the wall of Jerusalem was yet broken down[8]; its fire-burned gates not restored; itself was a waste[9]; its houses unbuilt[10]. This gives occasion to the intercession of *the Angel of the Lord.*

12. *And the Angel of the Lord answered* the implied longing, by intercession with God. As the angel-interpreter in Job had "[11]the office of no mere created angel, but one, anticipative of *His,* Who came at once to redeem and justify," so *the* Angel of the Lord, in whom God was, exercised at once a mediatorial office with God, typical of our Lord's High Priest's prayer[12], and acted as God.

These seventy years. The seventy years of the captivity, prophesied by Jeremiah[13], were on the eve of their conclusion at the time of Daniel's great prayer of intercession[14]; they ended with the capture of Babylon, and the edict of Cyrus, permitting the Jews to return[15]. Yet there seems to have been a secondary fulfillment, from the destruction of the temple and city, in Zedekiah's eleventh year[16], 588 B. C. to the second year of Darius, 519 B. C. Such double fulfillments of prophecy are not like alternative fulfillments. They are a more intricate and fuller, not an easier fulfillment of it. Yet *these* 70 *years* do not necessitate such a double fulfillment. It might express only a reverent wonder, that the 70 years being accomplished, the complete restoration was not yet brought to pass. "[17]God having fixed the time of the cap-

[1] i. 13, 14, 19 (ii. 2 Heb.) ii. 3. [7] iv. 1, 4, 5. v. 5. 10. vi. 4.
[2] Dion.
[3] Job ii. 2.
[4] Collect for S. Michael's day.
[5] See "Daniel the Prophet" pp. 525, 526.
[6] שקט is the word used in the book of Judges of the rest given to the land under judges until its fresh departure from God. Jud. iii. 11, 30, v. 31, viii. 28.; of the undisturbed life of the people of Laish, Jud. xviii. 7, 27; "from war," מִמִּלְחָמָה, is added, Jos. xi. 23, xiv. 15. of the rest after the war whereby Israel was put in possession of Canaan. It is used of the rest in Asa's days, 2 Chr. xiii. 23, Heb. given him by God, xiv. 4, 5. of the rest of the city after the death of Athaliah, 2 Kgs xi. 20, 2 Chr. xxiii. 21; of the earth, after the destruction of Babylon, Is. xiv. 7.
[7] with the same word שקט Jer. xxx. 10, xlvi. 27.
[8] Neh. i. 3.
[9] Ib. ii. 3.
[10] Ib. vii. 4.
[11] See "Daniel the Prophet" p. 523.
[12] S. John xvii.
[13] Jer. xxv. 11, 12. xxix. 10.
[14] Dan. ix. 2.
[15] 2 Chr. xxxvi. 22, 23. Ezr. i. 1.
[16] 2 Kgs xxv. 2, 8, 9.
[17] S. Cyr.

Before CHRIST cir. 519.

have mercy on Jerusalem
and on the cities of Judah,
against which thou hast
had indignation [n]these
three-score and ten
years?
13 And the LORD answered the angel that
talked with me *with* [o]good
words *and* comfortable
words.
14 So the angel that
communed with me said
unto me, Cry thou, saying,
Thus saith the LORD of
hosts; I am [p]jealous for
Jerusalem and for Zion
with a great jealousy.

n Jer. 25. 11, 12. Dan. 9. 2. ch. 7. 5.

o Jer. 29. 10.

p Joel 2. 18. ch. 8. 2.

tivity to the 70th year, it was necessary to be silent, so long as the time was not yet come to an end, that he might not seem to oppose the Lord's will. But, when the time was now come to a close and the fear of offending was removed, he, knowing that the Lord cannot lie, entreats and ventures to enquire whether His anger has come to an end, as had those who sinned; or whether, fresh sins having accrued, there shall be a further delay, and their forlorn estate shall be yet further extended. They then who worship God have a good and not uncertain hope, that, if they should offend from infirmity, yet have they those who should entreat for them, not men only, but the holy angels themselves, who render God gracious and propitious, soothing His anger by their purity, and in a manner winning the grieved judge. *Then* the Angel entreated for the synagogue to the Jews; but we, who believe and have been sanctified in the Spirit, [1] *have an Advocate with the Father Jesus Christ the righteous, and He is the propitiation for our sins*, and as the Divine Paul writes, [2] *God hath set Him forth as a propitiation through faith*, freeing from sin those who come to Him."

13. *And the Lord answered the angel that talked with me.* Either directly, at the intercession of *the angel of the Lord*, or mediately through an answer first given to him, and by him communicated to the subordinate angel. Neither is expressed.

Good words, as God had promised[3], *after seventy years shall be accomplished at Babylon, I will visit you and perform My good word unto you, causing you to return to this place;* and Joshua says, [4] *There failed not ought of any good word which the Lord spake unto the house of Israel.*

Comfortable words, lit. *consolations*[5]. Perhaps the Angel who received the message had, from their tender compassion for us, whereby they [6]*joy over one sinner that repenteth*, a part in these *consolations* which he conveyed.

14. *Cry thou.* The vision was not for the prophet alone. What he saw and heard, *that* he was to proclaim to others. The vision, which he now saw alone, was to be the basis and substance of his subsequent preaching[7], whereby he was to encourage his people to persevere.

I am jealous for Jerusalem, lit. *I have been*, not now only but in time past even when I did not shew it, *and am jealous*[8], with the tender love which allows not what it loves to be injured[9]. The love of God, until finally shut out, is unchangeable, He pursues the sinner with chastisements and scourges in His love, that he may yet be converted and live[10]. But for God's love to him and the solicitations of His grace, while yet impenitent and displeasing Him, he could not turn and please Him.

And for Zion, which especially He had chosen to put His Name there, and there to receive the worship of His people; [11] *the hill which God desired to dwell in*, [12] *which He loved.* "[13] With great and special love have I loved the people of the Jews and what pertained to them, and out of that love have I so diligently and severely corrected her excesses, that she may be more careful for the time to come, as a husband corrects most sharply a wife most dear to him, if she be unfaithful. Whence in the book of Maccabees it is written, "[14] It is a token of His great goodness, when wicked doers are not suffered any long time, but are forthwith punished. For not as with other nations, whom the Lord patiently forbeareth to punish, till they be come to the fullness of their sins, so dealeth He with us; lest, being come to the height of sin, afterward He should take vengeance of us. And therefore He never withdraweth His mercy from us, and though He punisheth

[1] 1 S. John ii. 1, 2. [2] Rom. iii. 25.
[3] Jer. xxix. 10.
[4] Josh. xxi. 43 (45 Eng.) add xxiii. 14, 15.
[5] as Is. lvii. 18. [6] S. Luke xv. 10.
[7] קרא, ab. 4. Jon. i. 2. Is. xl. 2, 6.
[8] Ewald compares ידעתי, οἶδα, novi; זכרתי, memini, Nu. xi. 5, חסיתי, הוחיל, Ps. xxxviii. 16. &c. Lehrb. n. 135. *b*. p. 129. ed. 8.
[9] See on Nah. i. 1, p. 129. [10] S. Aug. Conf. iii. 1.
[11] Ps. lxviii. 16.
[12] Ib. lxxviii. 68, add Ps. cxxxii. 13, 14.
[13] Dion. [14] 2 Macc. vi. 13–16.

Before CHRIST cir. 519.

15 And I am very sore
displeased with the heathen
that are at ease: for [q]I was
but a little displeased, and
they helped forward the
affliction.
16 Therefore thus saith
the LORD; [r]I am returned
to Jerusalem with mercies:
my house shall be built in
it, saith the LORD of hosts,
and [s]a line shall be
stretched forth upon Jerusalem.

q Isai. 47. 6.

r Isai. 12. 1. & 54. 8. ch. 2. 10. & 8. 3.

s ch. 2. 1, 2.

with adversity, yet doth He never forsake His people."

15. *I am sore displeased,* lit. *with great anger am I angered against the nations which are at ease.* The form of the words [1] shews that the greatness of the displeasure of God against those who oppress His people, is proportionate to the great and tender love toward themselves. God had been angered indeed [2] with His people; with their enemies He was *angered with a great anger;* and that the more, because they were *at ease*[3], in unfeeling self-enjoyment amid the miseries of others.

I was a little displeased[4]; little, in comparison with our deserts; little in comparison with the anger of the human instruments of His displeasure; little in comparison with their's who, in their anger, sought their own ends.

They helped forward the affliction[5]. "[6] He is wroth with the nations at ease, because He delivered His people to be corrected, but they used cruelty toward those delivered; He wills them to be amended as a son by a schoolmaster; they set themselves to slay and punish them, as an enemy. Like that in Isaiah, [7] *I gave them into thy hands; thou didst shew them no mercy; upon the ancients hast thou very heavily laid thy yoke.*"

Or it may be, *helped for evil,* in order to bring about evil, as in Jeremiah [8], *Behold I set My face against you for evil*[9], *and to destroy all Judah* i. e., as we should say, they were the instruments of God, "[10] coöperated in the execution of My justice toward you, but cruelly and with perverse intention. For although the Assyrians and Chaldæans wasted the Jewish people, God so ordaining in as far as He willed through them to punish in the present the sins of His people, yet they did it, not in view of God and out of zeal for righteousness, but out of pride covetousness and with the worst ends. Hence God says by Isaiah [11], *Wo to Asshur, the rod of Mine anger, and the staff in his hand is Mine indignation. Howbeit he thinketh not so, but his heart is to destroy and cut off nations not a few.*

16. *Therefore.* This being so, since God was so jealous for His people, so displeased with their persecutors, *thus saith the Lord,* "[10] *I* Who [12] *in wrath remember mercy, am returned*[13], not by change of place, Who am uncircumscribed, not existing in place, to the people of Judah and Jerusalem in mercies, manifoldly benefiting them by various effects of My love." The single benefits, the rebuilding of His House, and so the restoration of His public worship, and the rebuilding of Jerusalem, are but instances of that all-containing mercy, His restored presence in tender mercies [14]. *I am returned,* God says, although the effects of His return were yet to come.

A line shall be stretched forth over Jerusalem, before, when it stood, this had been done to destroy [15]; now, when destroyed, to rebuild [16].

"[17] The temple was built then, when the foundations of the walls were not yet laid. In man's sight it would have seemed more provident that the walls should be first builded, that then the temple might be builded more securely. To God, in Whom

[1] קצף גדול אני קֹצֵף על ver. 15, as contrasted with קנאתי ל. קנאה גדולה ver. 14.

[2] קצף קצפתי i. 2.

[3] שַׁאֲנָן, as applied to persons, is always used in a bad sense; the noun, 2 Kgs xix. 28, Is. xxxvii. 29; the adj. Is. xxxii. 9, 11, Job xii. 5, Am. vi. 1, Ps. cxxiii. 4, and here.

[4] קצפתי מעט is obviously contrasted with קצף גדול: others "for a little while." But beside this contrast, מעט is seldom, comparatively, used of time, and that, as indicated by the context. Gen. xlvii. 9, "my days have been few;" Lev. xxv. 52, "if a little remains of the years;" Ru. ii. 7, "she sat a little in the house;" Job x. 20, "are not my days few?" xxiv. 24, "they are exalted a little, and are not." Add Ps. xxxvii. 10, Jer. li. 33, Hos. i. 4, "yet a little, and." Hagg. ii. 6; "yet once, it is a little, and;" [all, except the doubtful Ps. viii. 6.]

[5] As 2 Chr. xx. 23, עָזְרוּ לְמַשְׁחִית "aided the destruction."

[6] S. Jer. [7] Is. xlvii. 6. [8] Jer. xliv. 11.

[9] לְרָעָה ולהכרית. [10] Dion. [11] Is. x. 5, 7.

[12] Hab. iii. 2. [13] שַׁבְתִּי, although ינטה, יבנה.

[14] רחמים occurs 27 times of the tender love of God; 12 times only, of the compassion of man, and in 6 of these, of compassion of man as given by God, נתן פ. לרחמים; 2ce with the word נכמרו.

[15] 2 Kgs xxi. 13, Is. xxxiv. 11.

[16] It is used of the creation of the earth, Job xxxviii. 5. The Chethib, probably קָוָה, occurs 1 Kgs vii. 23, Jer. xxxi. 19, and here. [17] Osor.

Before CHRIST cir. 519.

17 Cry yet, saying,
Thus saith the LORD of
hosts; My cities through
† prosperity shall yet be
spread abroad; [t] and the
LORD shall yet comfort
Zion, and [u] shall yet choose
Jerusalem.

† Heb. *good*.
[t] Isai. 51. 3.
[u] Isai. 14. 1. ch. 2. 12. & 3. 2.

18 ¶ Then lifted I up
mine eyes, and saw, and
behold four horns.
19 And I said unto the
angel that talked with me,
What *be* these? And he
answered me, [x] These *are*
the horns which have scat-

Before CHRIST cir. 519.

[x] Ezra 4. 1, 4, 7. & 5. 3.

Alone is the most firm stay of our life and salvation, it seemed otherwise. For it cannot be that he, to whom nothing is dearer than zeal for the most holy religion, should be forsaken of His help."

17. *Cry yet*, a further promise; not only should Jerusalem be rebuilt, but should as we say, *overflow with good*[1]; and God, Who had seemed to cast off His people, should yet comfort her, and should shew in act that He had chosen her[2]. Zechariah thrice[3] repeats the promise, given through Isaiah[4] to Jerusalem, before her wasting by the Chaldæans, reminding the people thereby, that the restoration, in the dawn whereof they lived, had been promised two centuries before. *Yet*, against all appearances. *My* cities shall overflow with good, as being God's; *yet* would the Lord comfort Zion; *yet* would He choose Jerusalem.

"[5] What is the highest of all goods? what the sweetest solace in life? what the subject of joys? what the oblivion of past sorrow? That which the Son of God brought upon earth, when He illumined Jerusalem with the brightness of His light and heavenly discipline. For to that end was the city restored, that in it, by the ordinance of Christ, for calamity should abound bliss; for desolation, fullness; for sorrow, joy; for want, affluence of heavenly goods."

This first vision having predicted the entire restoration, the details of that restoration are given in subsequent visions.

18. [6] *And I lifted up mine eyes*. "[7] Not those of the body (for such visions are invisible to the eyes of the flesh), but rather the inner eyes of the heart and mind." It seems as though, at the close of each vision, Zechariah sank in meditation on what had been shewn him; from which he was again roused by the exhibition of another vision.

I saw four horns. The mention of the horns naturally suggests the thought of the creatures which wielded them; as in the first vision that of the *horses* following the chiefs, implies the presence of the riders upon them. And this the more, since the word "fray them away" implies living creatures, liable to fear. "[8] The horn, in inspired Scripture, is always taken as an image of strength, and mostly of pride also, as David said to some, [9] *I said unto the fools, Deal not so foolishly, and to the ungodly, Lift not up the horns. Lift not up your horns on high and speak not with a stiff neck*. The prophet then sees *four horns*, i. e. four hard and warlike nations, who could easily uproot cities and countries."

These are the horns which have scattered. "[10] The four horns which scattered Judah, Israel and Jerusalem, are four nations, Babylonians, Medes and Persians, Macedonians and Romans; as the Lord, on the prophet's enquiry, explains here, and Daniel unfolds most fully[11]; who in the vision of the image with golden head, silver breast, belly and thighs of brass, feet of iron and clay, explained it of these four nations, and again in another vision of four beasts[12], lion, bear, leopard and another unnamed dreadful beast, he pointed out the same nations under another figure. But that the Medes and Persians, after the victory of Cyrus, were one kingdom, no one will doubt, who reads secular and sacred literature.—When this vision was beheld, the kingdom of the Babylonians had now passed away, that of the Medes and Persians was instant; that of Greeks and Macedonians and of the Romans was yet to come. What the Babylonians, what the Medes and Persians, what the Greeks i. e. the Macedonians, did to Judah, Israel and Jerusalem, a learned man acknowledgeth, especially under Antiochus, surnamed Epiphanes,

---

1 "affluent bonis," S. Jer.; "effluent bonis," Vulg. more exactly. The word פרץ is used of the "gushing forth of a fountain," Pr. v. 16; also of the dispersion of people; not of the spreading abroad of a people for good.

2 בחר is always "choose," not (as Ges. and others) "love." In all the cases, which Ges. cites as meaning "love," (Gen. vi. 2, 1 Sam. xx. 30, 2 Sam. xv. 15, Pr. i. 29, iii. 31, Is. i. 29) the sense would be injured by rendering, "loved."

3 here, ii. 12, iii. 2.

4 Is. xiv. 1. בחר עוד בישראל. Isaiah has the same cadence as Zechariah, though Zechariah only retains the characteristic words בחר עוד.

5 Osor.

6 The Eng. Vers. follows the LXX and S. Jer. in adding the 2d vision to the first chapter.

7 S. Cyril on ii. 1. 8 S. Cyr. 9 Ps. lxxv. 4.

10 S. Jer. Kimchi and Abarbanel agree with him in the general line. 11 Dan. ii. 12 Ib. vii.

Before CHRIST cir. 519.

tered Judah, Israel, and
Jerusalem.

20 And the LORD
shewed me four carpenters.

21 Then said I, What
come these to do? And he
spake, saying, These *are*
the horns which have scattered Judah, so that no
man did lift up his head:
but these are come to fray
them, to cast out the horns
of the Gentiles, which
[y] lifted up *their* horn over
the land of Judah to scatter it.

y Ps. 75. 4, 5.

CHAPTER II.

Before CHRIST cir. 519.

1 *God, in the care of Jerusalem, sendeth to measure it.* 6 *The redemption of Zion.* 10 *The promise of God's presence.*

I LIFTED up mine eyes
again, and looked, and
behold [a] a man with a
measuring line in his hand.

2 Then said I, Whither
goest thou? And he said
unto me, [b] To measure Jerusalem, to see what *is* the
breadth thereof, and what
is the length thereof.

a Ezek. 40. 3.

b Rev. 11. 1. & 21. 15, 16.

---

to which the history of the Maccabees belongs. After the Coming of our Lord and Saviour, when Jerusalem was encompassed, Josephus, a native writer, tells most fully, what the Israelites endured, and the Gospel fore-announced. These horns dispersed Judah almost individually, so that, bowed down by the heavy weight of evils, no one of them raised his head." Though these were successive in time, they are exhibited to Zechariah as one. One whole are the efforts against God's Church; one whole are the instruments of God, whether angelic or human, in doing or suffering, to repel them. Zechariah then exhibits these hostile powers as past and gone[1], as each would be at the end, having put forth his passing might, and perishing. They scattered, each in its day, and disappeared; for the next displaced it.

The long schism being ended, Judah and Israel are again one; and Jerusalem, the place of God's worship, belongs to Israel as well as to Judah[2].

The explanation of the number *four*, as symbolizing contemporaneous attacks from the four quarters of the heavens, fails in matter of fact, that, in these later times, the Jews suffered always from one power at a time. There was no such fourfold attack. In Zechariah's time all around was Persian.

"[3] Those horns, broken by the angels' ministry, portended that no guilt against the Church of Christ should be unpunished. Never will there be wanting fierce enemies from E. W. N. or S., whom God will strengthen, in order by them to teach His own. But when He shall see His work finished, i. e. when He shall have cleansed the stains of His own and brought back His Church to her former purity, He will punish those who so fiercely afflicted her."

Spiritually, "[4] those who destroy vices, build up virtues, and all the saints who, possessing these remedies, ever build up the Church, may be called 'builders.' Whence the Apostle says, [5] *I, as a wise builder, laid the foundation;* and the Lord, when wroth, said that He would [6] *take away* from Jerusalem *artificer and wise man.* And the Lord Himself, Son of the Almighty God and of the Creator of all, is called [7] *the son of the carpenter.*"

II. 1. *A man with a measuring line in his hand.* Probably the Angel of the Lord, of whom Ezekiel has a like vision. "[4] He who before, when he lift up his eyes, had seen in the *four horns* things mournful, now again lifts up his eyes to see a man, of whom it is written, [8] *Behold a man whose name is the Branch;* of whom we read above, [9] *Behold a man riding upon a red horse, and he stood among the myrtle trees, which were in the bottom.* Of whom too the Father saith; He builded My city,[10] *whose builder and maker is God.* He too is seen by Ezekiel in a description like this, [11] *a man whose appearance was like the appearance of brass,* i. e. burnished [12] and shining as fire, *with a line of flax in his hand and a measuring reed.*" The office also seems to be one of authority, not to measure the actual length and breadth of Jerusalem, but to lay down what it should be, "[13] to mark it out broad and very long."

[1] זֵרוּ.

[2] This is expressed by the use or omission of the את. Its use coordinates Judah and Israel; its omission subordinates Jerusalem.

[3] Osor. [4] S. Jer. [5] 1 Cor. iii. 10. [6] Is. iii. 3. [7] S. Matt. xiii. 55. [8] Zech. vi. 12. [9] Ib. i. 8. [10] Heb. xi. 10. [11] Ezek. xl. 3. [12] Ib. i. 7. [13] S. Cyr.

Before CHRIST cir. 519.

3 And, behold, the an-
gel that talked with me
went forth, and another
angel went out to meet
him,
4 And said unto him,
Run, speak to this young
man, saying, [e] Jerusalem
shall be inhabited *as* towns
without walls for the multitude of men and cattle
therein:

Before CHRIST cir. 519.

e Jer. 31. 27. Ezek. 36. 10, 11.

3. *The angel that talked with me went forth*, probably to receive the explanation which was given him for Zechariah; *and another angel*, a higher angel, since he gives him a commission, *went forth to meet him*, being (it seems probable) instructed by the Angel of the Lord, who laid down the future dimensions of the city. The indefiniteness of the description, *another angel*, implies that he was neither the Angel of the Lord, nor (were they different) Michael, or *the man with the measuring line*, but an angel of intermediate rank, instructed by one higher, instructing the lower, who immediately instructed Zechariah.

And said unto him, Run, speak unto this young man, the prophet himself, who was to report to his people what he heard. Jeremiah says, [1] *I am a youth;* and [2] *the young man, the young prophet*, carried the prophetic message from Elisha to Jehu. "Youth," common as our English term in regard to man, is inapplicable and unapplied to angels, who have not our human variations of age, but exist, as they were created.

Jerusalem shall be inhabited as towns without walls, or as villages [3], viz. an unconfined, uncramped population, spreading itself freely, without restraint of walls, and (it follows) without need of them. Clearly then it is no earthly city. To be inhabited as villages would be weakness, not strength; a peril, not a blessing. The earthly Jerusalem, so long as she remained unwalled, was in continual fear and weakness. God put it into the heart of His servant to desire to restore her; her wall was built, and then she prospered. He Himself had promised to Daniel, that [4] *Her street shall be rebuilt, and her wall, even in strait of times.* Nehemiah mourned 73 years after this, B.C. 443, when it was told him, [5] *The remnant that are left of the captivity there in the province* are *in great affliction and reproach: the wall of Jerusalem also is broken down, and the gates thereof are burned with fire.* He said to Artaxerxes, [6] *Why should not my countenance be sad, when the city, the place of my fathers' sepulchres, lieth waste, and the gates thereof are consumed with fire?* When permitted by Artaxerxes to return, he addressed the rulers of the Jews, [7] *Ye see the distress that we are in, how Jerusalem lieth waste, and the gates thereof are burned with fire; come, and let us build up the wall of Jerusalem, that we be no more a reproach; and they said, let us rise and build. So they strengthened their hands for this good work.* When [8] *the wall was finished and our enemies heard*, and *the heathen about us saw it, they were much cast down in their own eyes; for they perceived that this work was wrought of our God.*

This prophecy then looks on directly to the time of Christ. Wonderfully does it picture the gradual expansion of the kingdom of Christ, without bound or limit, whose protection and glory God is, and the character of its defences. It should *dwell as villages*, peacefully and gently expanding itself to the right and the left, through its own inherent power of multiplying itself, as a city, to which no bounds were assigned, but which was to fill the earth. "[9] For us God hath raised a Church, that truly holy and far-famed city, which Christ fortifieth, consuming opponents by invisible powers, and filling it with His own glory, and as it were, standing in the midst of those who dwell in it. For He promised; *Lo, I am with you always even unto the end of the world.* This holy city Isaiah mentioned: [10] *thine eyes shall see Jerusalem, a quiet habitation; a tabernacle that shall not be taken down; not one of the stakes thereof shall ever be removed, neither shall any of the cords thereof be broken;* and to her he saith, [11] *enlarge the place of thy tent, and let them stretch forth the curtains of thine habitation; spare not; lengthen thy cords and strengthen thy stakes. For thou shalt break forth on the right hand and on the left.* For the Church of Christ is widened and extended boundlessly, ever receiving countless souls who worship Him." "[12] What king or emperor could make walls so ample as to include the whole world? Yet, without this, it could not encircle that Jerusalem, the Church which is diffused through the whole world. This Jerusalem, the pilgrim part of the heavenly Jerusalem, is, in this present world, inhabited without walls, not being contained in one place or one nation. But in that world, whither it is daily being removed hence, much more can there not, nor ought to be,

1 נער Jer. i. 6.
2 הנער הנער הנביא 2 Kgs ix. 4.
3 See on Hab. iii. 14. p. 218.
4 Dan. ix. 25.
5 Neh. i. 3.
6 Ib. ii. 3.
7 Ib. 17, 18.
8 Ib. vi. 15, 16.
9 S. Cyr.
10 Is. xxxiii. 20.
11 Ib. liv. 2, 3.
12 Rup.

Before CHRIST cir. 519.

5 For I, saith the LORD,
will be unto her [d] a wall of
fire round about, [e] and will
be the glory in the midst
of her.
6 ¶ Ho, ho, *come forth*,
and flee [f] from the land of
the north, saith the LORD:
for I have [g] spread you
abroad as the four winds of
the heaven, saith the LORD.
7 [h] Deliver thyself, O
Zion, that dwellest *with* the
daughter of Babylon.

[d] Isai. 26. 1. ch. 9. 8.
[e] Isai. 60. 19. Rev. 21. 23.
[f] Isai. 48. 20. & 52. 11. Jer. 1. 14. & 50. 8. & 51. 6, 45.
[g] Deut. 28. 64. Ezek. 17. 21.
[h] Rev. 18. 4.

nor is, any wall around, save the Lord, Who is also the glory in the midst of it."

5. *And I*, Myself[1] in My own Being, *will be to her a wall of fire*, not protection only, an inner circle around her, however near an enemy might press in upon her, but destructive to her enemies. Isaiah says, [2] *No weapon that is formed against thee shall prosper, and every tongue that shall rise in judgment against thee thou shalt condemn.* Its defence, Isaiah says, shall be immaterial. [3] *We have a strong city; salvation shall God appoint for walls and bulwarks;* [4] *thou shalt call thy walls salvation and thy gates praise.* By a different figure it is said, [5] *I will encamp about mine house because of the army.*

And glory will I be in the midst of her, as Isaiah says, [6] *The Lord shall be unto thee an everlasting light, and thy God thy glory;* and of Christ, [7] *In that day shall the Branch of the Lord be Beauty and Glory—to the escaped of Israel.*

6. *Ho! ho! and flee.* Such being the safety and glory in store for God's people in Jerusalem, He Who had so provided it, the Angel of the Lord, bids His people everywhere to come to it, saving themselves also from the peril which was to come on Babylon. So Isaiah bade them, [8] *Go ye forth of Babylon; flee ye from the Chaldæans with a voice of singing; declare ye, tell this, utter it to the end of the earth; say ye, The Lord hath redeemed His servant Jacob.* [9] *Depart ye, depart ye, go ye out from thence; touch no unclean thing: go ye out of the midst of her; be ye clean, that bear the vessels of the Lord;* and Jeremiah, [10] *Flee ye out of the midst of Babylon, and deliver every man his soul; be not cut off in her iniquity, for this is the time of the Lord's vengeance; He will render unto her a recompense.* [11] *My people, go ye out of the midst of her, and deliver ye, every man his soul from the fierce anger of the Lord.*

The words, *flee, deliver thyself*, imply an imminent peril on Babylon, such as came upon her, two years after this prophecy, in the fourth year of Darius. But the earnestness of the command, its repetition by three prophets, the context in Isaiah and Jeremiah, imply something more than temporal peril, the peril of the infection of the manners of Babylon, which may have detained there many who did not return. Whence in the New Testament, the words are cited, as to the great evil city of the world; [12] *Wherefore come out from among them and be ye separate, and touch not the unclean thing, and I will receive you;* and under the name of Babylon; [13] *I heard another voice from heaven, saying, Come out of her, My people, that ye be not partakers of her sins, and that ye receive not of her plagues.*

For I have spread you abroad as the four winds of heaven. The north country, although its capital and centre was Babylon, was the whole Babylonian empire, called "the North [14]" because its invasions always came upon Israel from the North. But the book of Esther shews that, sixty years after this, the Jews were dispersed over the 127 provinces of the Persian empire, *from India* (the Punjaub) *to Ethiopia* [15], whether they were purposely placed by the policy of the conquerors in detatched groups, as the ten tribes were *in the cities of the Medes* [16], or whether, when more trusted, they migrated of their own accord. God, in calling them to return, reminds them of the greatness of their dispersion. He had dispersed them abroad as the four winds of heaven [17]: He, the Same, recalled them.

7. *Dwellest* with *the daughter of Babylon.* The unusual idiom [18] is perhaps chosen as expressive of God's tenderness, even to the people who were to be destroyed, from which Israel was to escape.

[1] אֲנִי emph. [2] Is. liv. 17.
[3] Ib. xxvi. 1. [4] Ib. lx. 18. [5] Zech. ix. 8.
[6] Is. lx. 19. [7] Ib. iv. 2.
[8] Is. xlviii. 20. [9] Ib. lii. 11. [10] Jer. li. 6. add. l. 8.
[11] Ib. li. 45. [12] 2 Cor. vi. 17. [13] Rev. xviii. 4.
[14] Jer. i. 13, 14, iii. 18, iv. 6, vi. 1. 22. xxiii. 8.
[15] Esther i. 1, iii. 8, 12–14. viii. 5, 9.
[16] 2 Kgs xvii. 6.
[17] "As the four winds of heaven are distant one from the other." Sal. b. Mel. Kim. AE. The LXX alone paraphrase, "For from the winds of heaven I will gather you." Others take the word of an intended diffusion of them, through the favor of God, the future being spoken of, as if past. But although פרשׂ is used of dispersion, beside, in Ps. lxviii. 15, Nif. Ez. xvii. 21, it is no where used of diffusion, only of the spreading out of what remained coherent, as hands, wings, a garment, tent, veil, cloud, letter, light. See instances Ges. Thes. p. 1132.

[18] יושבת בת בבל *dweller of the daughter of Babylon*, as Jer. xlvi. 19. יושבת בת מצרים, Ib. xlviii. 18, ישבת בת דיבון. In Jeremiah however, it is the same people, Egypt or Dibon; here, Israel as settled in Babylon.

Before CHRIST cir. 519.

8 For thus saith the LORD of hosts; After the glory hath he sent me unto the nations which spoiled you: for he that [l]toucheth you toucheth the apple of his eye.

[l] Deut. 32. 10. Ps. 17. 8. 2 Thess. 1. 6.

9 For, behold, I will [k]shake mine hand upon them, and they shall be a spoil to their servants: and [l]ye shall know that the LORD of hosts hath sent me.

Before CHRIST cir. 519.

[k] Isai. 11. 15. & 19. 16.

[l] ch. 4. 9.

---

8. *After the glory*[1], "[2]which it is promised to bring upon you." This being the usual construction, the words involve a great course of God's dealing, of first shewing favor to those who *will* receive favor, then abandoning or punishing the rest; as, when the eight souls had been received into the ark, the flood came; when Lot and his had escaped out of Sodom, the fire came down from heaven; when Israel had passed the Red Sea, Pharaoh's hosts were drowned; the election obtained what Israel sought for, the rest were blinded[3]. *The glory* then would be the glory, of which God says, *I will be the glory in the midst of you.*

But further He Who speaketh is Almighty God, *Thus saith the Lord of Hosts, He hath sent*[4] *me; For lo I wave My hand against them—and ye shall know that the Lord of hosts hath sent me; Lo I come and dwell in the midst of thee, saith the Lord, and many nations shall cleave unto the Lord in that day, and they shall be to Me a people and I will dwell in the midst of thee, and thou shalt know, that the Lord of hosts hath sent me unto you.* In all which series of promises, the *I*, of whom Israel were to know that the Lord of hosts had sent Him, is the *I*, Who affirms of Himself what belongs to Almighty God only, inflicting punishment on the enemies of Judah, indwelling the Church and people, receiving the Heathen as His own; and it is precisely by all these acts of power and love, that Israel shall know that the Lord of hosts had sent Him.

"[5] In what follows, *Thus saith the Lord of hosts, After glory, He hath sent Me &c.*, the Saviour is introduced speaking, Who, being Almighty God, saith that He was sent by the Father Almighty, not according to that whereby He was Almighty, but according to that, that, *after glory*, He was sent, [6] *Who being in the Form of God, thought it not robbery to be equal with God; but emptied Himself, taking the form of a servant, and was made obedient unto the Father even unto death; and that, the death of the Cross.* Nor is it marvel that Christ is called Almighty, in Whose Person we read in the Apocalypse of John, [7] *These things saith the faithful Witness—I am Alpha and Omega, the beginning and the ending, saith the Lord, which was and which is and which is to come, the Almighty,* [8] *to Whom all power is given in heaven and in earth;* and Who saith, [9] *All things of the Father's are Mine.* But if all things, i. e. God from God, Lord from Lord, Light from Light, therefore also Almighty from Almighty; for it cannot be, that diverse should be the glory of those whose Nature is One."

For he who toucheth, so as to injure[10], *you, toucheth the apple of His eye,* i. e. of Him Who sent Him, Almighty God[11], as in the song of Moses, [12] *He led him about, He instructed him, He kept him as the apple of His eye;* and David prays, [13] *Keep me as the apple of the eye.*

9. *For behold I will shake My hand against them,* as God promised of old against the enemies of His people[14], and they shall

[1] שלח is used with acc. pers., and אחרי also of persons, 2 Sam. iii. 26, 2 Kgs viii. 14, or with אחרי of pers. alone, 2 Kgs xiv. 9. שלח אחר is not elsewhere used like our "sent after a thing." So generally אחר is used with verbs of motion, הלך אחר, Gen. xxxvii. 17, 2 Kgs xxiii. 3; יבא אחר, Nu. xxv. 8; היה אחר, 1 Sam. xii. 14; רדף אחר, 2 Kgs xxv. 5; יצא אחר, 1 Sam. xi. 7: or, spiritually, ההלכים אחר מחשבותיהם Is. lxv. 2; אחר רוחם, Ez. xiii. 3; אחר עיני הלך לבי, Job xxxi. 7; but אחר is not used in our sense of **seeking,** "going after a thing," except in the one phrase ואחר כל ירוק ידרוש Job xxxix. 8, "searcheth after every green thing." It is the less probable here, because, apart from this, (beside the 5 duplicate passages in Isaiah and 2 Kings, 2 Sam. and 1 Chronicles) the construction of שלח with acc. of the person sent and אל of the person to whom he is sent, occurs in 71 passages, (Ges. cites 23 of them) and in no one case is the object for which they were sent, added by any preposition. Four are in Zechariah himself ii. 12, 15, iv. 9, vi. 15. To "send for" is expressed by שלח ל Jer. xiv. 3, 1 Kgs xx. 7.

[2] Jon. [3] Rom. xi. 7. [4] ver. 8–10. [5] S. Jer. [6] Phil. ii. 6. [7] Rev. i. 5, 8. [8] S. Matt. xxviii. 18. [9] S. John xvi. 15.

[10] נגע ב, as in Gen. xxvi. 11, Jos. ix. 19, 2 Sam. xiv. 10, Jer. xii. 14, Ezek. xvii. 10, Ps. cv. 15; with acc. Gen. xxvi. 29, Ru. ii. 9; of God, 1 Sam. vi. 9, Job i. 11. xix. 21.

[11] So S. Jer. Theod. Others, as S. Cyr., of his own eye, turning to evil to himself; but the analogy of the other passages is against it. בבת עין [ἅπ.] is doubtless the same as בת עין with the same reduplication as in Arab. Syr. Ch. The reduplication is plain in the Arab. בובוא from בַּאבַּא "papavit," not from a separate root, as Ges. Thes. p. 841.

[12] Deut. xxxii. 10. [13] Ps. xvii. 8.

[14] The same idiom, Is. xi. 15. xix. 16.

Before CHRIST cir. 519.

10 ¶ [m] Sing and rejoice,
O daughter of Zion: for,
lo, I come, and I [n] will
dwell in the midst of thee,
saith the LORD.

[m] Isai. 12. 6. & 54. 1. Zeph. 3. 14.
[n] Lev. 26. 12. Ezek. 37. 27. ch. 8. 3. John 1. 14. 2 Cor. 6. 16.

11 [o] And many nations
shall be joined to the LORD
[p] in that day, and shall be
[q] my people: and I will
dwell in the midst of thee,

Before CHRIST cir. 519.

[o] Isai. 2. 2, 3. & 49. 22. & 60. 3, &c. ch. 8. 22, 23.
[p] ch. 3. 10.
[q] Ex. 12. 49.

be a spoil to those who served them habitually[1].

And ye shall know that the Lord of hosts hath sent Me. "[2] He was sent, not as God, but as Man. For as God He is equal to the Father. For He saith, [3] *I am in the Father and the Father in Me*, and, *The Father Who dwelleth in Me He doeth the works*, and, [4] *I and My Father are one*, and [5] *He who hath seen Me hath seen the Father.* But He is sent, as Man, fulfilling the dispensation for us, not lessening the Divine Nature. The Prophet then intimated not the duality only, but the equality of the Persons."

10. *Sing and rejoice, O daughter of Zion.* It is a great jubilee of joy, to which Zion is invited. Thrice beside is she invited with this same word, and all for the restored or renewed Presence of God. [6] *Cry aloud for joy, thou barren which bare not*, as here, on the coming in of the Gentiles, [7] *Cry aloud for joy, O daughter of Zion; jubilate, O Israel; rejoice and exult with all the heart, O daughter of Jerusalem; the Lord, the King of Israel, is in the midst of thee.* [8] *Shout and cry aloud for joy, O inhabitant of Zion; for great in the midst of thee is the Holy One of Israel.* The source of joy is a fresh coming of God, *a coming*, whereby He should *dwell* abidingly among them: truly what is this, but the Incarnation? As S. John saith, [9] *The Word was made Flesh and dwelt among us;* and, [10] *Behold the tabernacle of God is with men, and He will dwell with them, and they shall be His people, and God Himself shall be with them and shall be their God.* "[11] Hence too you may learn how great a subject of contentment above is the Presence of the Saviour upon earth. He could not then but bid the spiritual Zion, [12] *which is the Church of the Living God*, the most sacred multitude of those saved by faith, to cry aloud for joy and rejoice. But it was announced that He should come and be in the midst of her. For S. John saith to us, *The Word* [13] *was in the world*, and, being God, was not severed from His creatures, but He was Himself the Source of life to all living, and holding all things together to well-being and life; but [13] *the world knew Him not:* for it worshiped the creature. But He came among us, when, taking our likeness, He was conceived by the holy Virgin, and [14] *was seen upon earth and conversed with men*, and the divine David witnesseth saying, [15] *Our God shall come manifestly, and shall not keep silence.* Then also was there a haven for the Gentiles. For now no longer was the race of Israel alone taught, but the whole earth was engoldened with the evangelical preachings, and in every nation and country *great is His Name.*"

"[16] This too is to be understood of the Person of the Lord, that He exhorts His people, being restored from the captivity to their former abode, to be *glad and rejoice*, because *the Lord* Himself *cometh* and *dwelleth in the midst of her*, and *many nations* shall believe in Him, of Whom it is said, [17] *Ask of Me and I will give Thee nations for Thine inheritance, and the ends of the earth for Thy possession*, and He shall *dwell in the midst of them*, as He saith to His disciples, [18] *Lo, I am with you always, even unto the end of the world.*"

11. *And many nations shall join themselves*, cleaving to Him by a close union. Isaiah had so spoken of single proselytes[19]; Jeremiah had used the word of Israel's self-exhortation after the return from Babylon; [20] *going and weeping, they shall go and seek the Lord their God*, saying, *Come and let us join ourselves unto the Lord, in a perpetual covenant* that *shall not be forgotten.* This Zechariah now predicts of *many nations.* The Jews were scarcely half-restored themselves, a mere handful. They had wrought no conversions among the heathen, yet prophecy continues its unbroken voice, *many nations shall join themselves unto the Lord.*

And shall be My people, lit. *be to Me a people.* This is exactly the history of the Christian Church, unity amid diversity; many nations still retaining their national

[1] The force of the part. עֹבְדֵיהֶם, instead of עֹבְדֵיהֶם. So עֹבֵד אדמה, Zech. xiii. 5. Is. xxx. 24; עֹבֵר אדמתו Pr. xii. 11; עֹבֵר אלהים Mal. iii. 18: העֹבד אתו Ib. 17. עֹבְדֵי הבעל 2 Kgs x. 19, 21, 22, 23, ע. פסל Ps. xcvii. 7. עֹבְדֵי העיר Ez. xlviii. 18, העֹבד העיר, Ib. 19. So כל העֹבד באהל מועד, Nu. iv. 37, 41. עֹבדתם אשר הם עֹבדים Ib. xviii. 21. הָעֹבֵד the laborer, Eccl. v. 11. In Gen. iv. 2, xlix. 15, Jos. xvi. 10, 1 Kgs v. 1, 2 Kgs xvii. 33, 41, it has this force from the preceding הָיָה.

[2] Theod. [3] S. John xiv. 10. [4] Ib. x. 30.
[5] Ib. xiv. 9. [6] Is. liv. 1. [7] Zeph. iii. 14, 15.
[8] Is. xii. 6. [9] S. John i. 14. [10] Rev. xxi. 3.
[11] S. Cyr. [12] 1 Tim. iii. 15. [13] S. John i. 10.
[14] Baruch iii. 37. [15] Ps. l. 3. [16] S. Jer.
[17] Ps. ii. 8. [18] S. Matt. xxviii. 20.
[19] Is. lvi. 3–6. [20] Jer l. 4, 5.

Before CHRIST cir. 519.

and [r] thou shalt know that
the LORD of hosts hath
sent me unto thee.
12 And the LORD shall
[s] inherit Judah his portion
in the holy land,
and [t] shall choose Jerusalem
again.

[r] Ezek. 33. 33. ver. 9.

[s] Deut. 32. 9.
[t] ch. 1. 17.

Before CHRIST cir. 519.

existence, yet owned by God as one people and His own. The words are those in which God adopted Israel in Egypt; [1] *I will take you to Me for a people, and I will be your God.* This was the covenant with them, [2] *that thou shouldest enter into covenant with the Lord thy God,—that He may establish thee to-day for a people unto Himself, and that He may be unto thee a God.* The contrary was the title of the heathen, [3] *not a people; with whom God said, I will move* Israel *to jealousy.* The closeness of union Jeremiah expresses; [4] *As the girdle cleaveth to the loins of a man, so have I caused to cleave to Me the whole house of Israel and the whole house of Judah, saith the Lord, that they might be unto Me for a people and for a name and for a praise and for a glory.* This was the object of the existence of Israel; to this it was to be restored [5] by conversion [6]; to this special privilege of Israel *many nations* were to be admitted; yet not so as to be separate from Israel, for He adds, *and I will dwell in the midst of thee,* Judah. God would dwell in His Church, formed of Israel and the Gentiles, yet so that the Gentiles should be grafted into Israel, becoming one with them.

12. *And the Lord shall inherit Judah His portion.* The *inheritance of the Lord* is the title which God commonly gave to Israel [7]. God is said to be the *portion* of Israel [8]; of the pious [9]; once only beside, is Israel said to be the portion of God [10]; once only is God said to inherit Israel, [11] *Pardon our iniquity and our sin, and take us for thine inheritance.* Zechariah unites the two rare idioms.

In the holy land. The land is again made holy by God, and sanctified by His Presence. So He calls the place where He revealed Himself to Moses, *holy ground* [12]. So it is said, [13] *the holy place,* [14] *the holy house,* [15] *the holy ark,* [16] *the holy city,* [17] *the holy mountain,* [18] *the holy people,* [19] *the holy chambers,* or, with reference to their relation to God Who consecrates them, [20] *My holy mountain,* [21] *Thy holy habitation,* [22] *Thy holy dwelling-place,* [23] *Thy holy temple,* [24] *Thy holy mountain,* [25] *Thy holy oracle,* [26] *Thy holy city,* [27] *cities,* [28] *His holy place,* [29] *His holy border.* It is not one technical expression, as people now by a sort of effort speak of "the holy land." Everything which has reference to God is holy. The land is holy, not for any merits of theirs, but because God was worshiped there, was specially present there. It was an anticipation and type of "Thy holy Church throughout all the world doth acknowledge Thee." This land their fathers had [30] *polluted with blood;* God says, [31] *they defiled My land;* Ezekiel called her eminently, [32] *the land that is not cleansed.* Now God said, [33] *I will remove the iniquity of the land,* and she was again *a holy land,* as hallowed by Him.

It is not a mere conversion of the heathen, but, as Isaiah [34] and Micah [35] foretold; a conversion, of which Jerusalem should be the centre, as our Lord explained to the Apostles after His Resurrection, [36] *that repentance and*

[1] Exod. vi. 7.
[2] Deut. xxix. 12, 13, add Lev. xxvi. 12, Deut. xxvii. 9. 1 Sam. xii. 22, 2 Sam. vii. 23, 24, 2 Kgs xi. 17, 1 Chr. xvii. 22, 2 Chr. xxiii. 16, Jer. vii. 23, xi. 4.
[3] Deut. xxxii. 21.
[4] Jer. xiii. 11.
[5] Ib. xxiv. 7, xxx. 22, xxxi. 1, xxxii. 38.
[6] Ez. xi. 20, xiv. 11, xxxvi. 28, xxxvii. 23, 27, Zech. viii. 8.
[7] Deut. iv. 20, ix. 26, 29, 1 Sam. xxvi. 19, 2 Sam. xiv. 16, xx. 19, xxi. 3, 1 Kgs viii. 51, Ps. xxviii. 9, xxxiii. 12, lxviii. 10, lxxviii. 62, 71, lxxix. 1, cvi. 40, Joel ii. 17, iii. 2, [Heb.] Is. xix. 25, xlvii. 6, Jer. xii. 7–9, l. 11.
[8] Jer. x. 16. li. 19.
[9] Ps. xvi. 5, lxxiii. 26, cxix. 57, cxlii. 6, Lam. iii. 24.
[10] Deut. xxxii. 9.
[11] Ex. xxxiv. 9.
[12] אדמת קדש, Ex. iii. 5.
[13] מקום הקדש, Lev. x. 17, xiv. 13.
[14] בית הק., 1 Chr. xxix. 3.
[15] ארון הק., 2 Chr. xxxv. 3.
[16] עיר הק., Neh. xi. 1, 18, Is. xlviii. 2, lii. 1.
[17] הר הק., Is. xxvii. 13, Jer. xxxi. 23, Zech. viii. 3.
[18] עם הק., Is. lxii. 12.
[19] לשכות הק. Ez. xlii. 13. [all.]
[20] הר קדשי Ps. ii. 6. Is. xi. 9. lvi. 7, lvii. 13, lxv. 11, 25, lxvi. 20, Ez. xx. 40. Jo. ii. 1, iv. 17, Ob. 16. Zeph. iii. 11.
[21] נוה קדשך Ex. xv. 13.
[22] מעון ק. Deut. xxvi. 15. *His holy hab.* Ps. lxviii. 6, Jer. xxv. 30, Zech. ii. 17.
[23] היכל ק. Ps. v. 8, lxxix. 1, cxxxviii. 2, Jon. ii. 5, 8, *His holy temple,* Mi. i. 2. Hab. ii. 20.
[24] הר ק. Ps. xv. 1, xliii. 3, Dan. ix. 16. *His holy hill,* Ps. iii. 5, xlviii. 2, xcix. 9.
[25] דביר ק. Ps. xxviii. 2.
[26] עיר ק. Dan. ix. 24.
[27] ערי ק. Is. lxiv. 9.
[28] מקום ק. Ps. xxiv. 3.
[29] גבול ק. Ps. lxxviii. 54.
[30] Ps. cvi. 38.
[31] Jer. ii. 7, iii. 9, xvi. 18.
[32] Ezek. xxii. 24.
[33] Zech. iii. 9.
[34] Is. ii. 3.
[35] Micah iv. 2.
[36] S. Luke xxiv. 47.

Before CHRIST cir. 519.

13 [a] Be silent, O all
flesh, before the LORD:
for he is raised up [x] out of
† his holy habitation.

[a] Hab. 2. 20. Zeph. 1. 7.
[x] Ps. 68. 5. Isai. 57. 15.
† Heb. *the habitation of his holiness.* Deut. 26. 15. Isai. 63. 15.

CHAPTER III.

1 *Under the type of Joshua, the restoration of the church,* 8 *Christ the Branch is promised.*

AND he shewed me
[a] Joshua the high
priest standing before the
angel of the LORD, and
[b] || Satan standing at his
right hand † to resist him.
2 And the LORD said
unto Satan, [c] The LORD rebuke thee, O Satan; even

Before CHRIST cir. 519.

[a] Hag. 1. 1.
[b] Ps. 109. 6. Rev. 12. 10.
|| That is, *an adversary.*
† Heb. *to be his adversary.*
[c] Jude 9.

remission of sins should be preached in His name among all nations, beginning at Jerusalem.

13. *Be silent,* lit. *hush*[1], *all flesh, before the Lord;* man in his weakness[2], *flesh and blood* in the language of the New Testament[3], before God his Maker. *All flesh,* the whole human race[4], is to be hushed before God, because His judgments, as His mercies, are over all.

For God ariseth. God seemeth to be quiescent, as it were, when He bears with us; to arise, when He puts forth His power, either for us, when we pray, [5] *Lord, awake to help me;* or in displeasure. His *holy habitation* is alike the tabernacle[6], temple[7], heaven[8], since His presence is in all.

III. 1. *And He,* God, (for the office of the attendant angel was to explain, not to shew the visions) *shewed me Joshua the High Priest, standing before the Angel of the Lord;* probably to be judged by him[9]; as in the New Testament, *to stand before the Son of Man;* for although *standing before,* whether in relation to man[10] or God[11], expresses attendance upon, yet here it appears only as a condition, contemporaneous[12] with that of Satan's, to accuse him. Although, moreover, the Angel speaks with authority, yet God's Presence in him is not spoken of so distinctly, that the High Priest would be exhibited as standing before him, as in his office before God.

And Satan, etymologically, *the enemy,* as, in the New Testament, [13] *your adversary the devil,* etymologically, *the accuser.* It is a proper name of the Evil one, yet its original meaning, *the enemy*[14], was not lost. Here, as in Job, his malice is shewn in accusation; [15] *the accuser of our brethren, who accused them before our God, day and night.* In Job[16], the accusations were calumnious; here, doubtless, true. For he accused Job of what would have been plain apostacy[17]; Joshua and Zerubbabel had shared, or given way to, the remissness of the people, as to the rebuilding of the temple and the full restoration of the worship of God[18]. For this, Haggai had reproved the people, through them[19]. Satan had then a real charge, on which to implead them. Since also the whole series of visions relates to the restoration from the captivity, the guilt, for which Satan impleads him with Jerusalem and Jerusalem in him, includes the whole guilt, which had rested upon them, so that for a time God had seemed to have *cast away His people*[20]. Satan *stands at his right hand,* the place of a protector[21], to shew that he had none to save him, and that himself was victorious.

2. *And the Lord said unto Satan, The Lord rebuke thee.* "[22] This they so explain, that the Father and the Son is Lord, as we read in the 110th Psalm, *The Lord said unto my*

[1] See on Hab. ii. 20. p. 207.

[2] Gen. vi. 3, 2 Chr. xxxii. 8, Job x. 4, Ps. lvi. 4, lxxviii. 39, Is. xxxi. 3, Jer. xvii. 5.

[3] S. Matt. xvi. 17, 1 Cor. xv. 50, Gal. i. 16.

[4] Gen. vi. 12, Ps. lxv. 3, cxlv. 21, Is. xl. 5, 6, xlix. 26, lxvi. 23, Jo. iii. 1, Ez. xxi. 4, 9, 10.

[5] Ps. lix. 4. add Ps. vii. 7, xliv. 24.

[6] 1 Sam. ii. 29, 32, Ps. xxvi. 9, lxviii. 6.

[7] 2 Chr. xxxvi. 15.

[8] Deut. xxvi. 15, Jer. xxv. 30, 2 Chr. xxx. 27.

[9] "Stand before" is used judicially, Nu. xxxv. 12, Deut. xix. 17. Jos. xx. 6, and of plaintiffs, Nu. xxvii. 2, 1 Kgs iii. 16; *stand before God,* Rev. xx. 12; *before the judgment-seat of Christ,* Rom. xiv. 10; and be acquitted, S. Luke xxi. 36.

[10] Joseph before Pharaoh, Gen. xli. 46; Joshua before Moses, Deut. i. 38; David before Saul, 1 Sam. xvi. 21; the young virgin before David. 1 Kgs i. 2; Solomon's servants, Ib. x. 8; his councillors, 2 Chr. x. 6; Gedaliah, of serving the Chaldæans, Jer. xl. 10; Nebuzaradan, Jer. lii. 12; Daniel and his companions, of office *before the king* of Babylon, Dan. i. 5. But it is also used of presence with a commission to the person; Moses before Pharaoh, Ex. viii. 20, ix. 13; of an office toward others, to minister unto them, as the Levites before the congregation, Nu. xvi. 9; degraded priests, "to serve them." Ezek. xliv. 11.

[11] The tribe of Levi, Deut. x. 8, 2 Chr. xix. 11; the High Priest, Jud. xx. 28, Ezek. xliv. 15; Elijah, 1 Kgs xvii. 1, xviii. 15; Elisha, 2 Kgs iii. 14, v. 16; Jonadab's descendants, Jer. xxxv. 19. It is used of standing to intercede with God, of Abraham, Gen. xviii. 22; Moses and Samuel, Jer. xv. 1; Jeremiah, Ib. 19. Also of worship, Jer. vii. 10.

[12] The two עֹמֵד express a correlative condition.

[13] 1 S. Pet. v. 8.

[14] As in other appellatives, הַיַּרְדֵּן (יַרְדֵּן twice only), הַבַּעַל, but in its contracted form, when the etymology was lost, בֵּל, &c. שָׂטָן as a Prop. Name, without the article, occurs 1 Chr. xxi. 1, Ps. cix. 6; with the article, eleven times here, and fourteen times in the first narrative chapters of Job.

[15] Rev. xii. 10.

[16] Job i. 8–11, ii. 3–5.

[17] Ib. i. 11. ii. 5.

[18] Ezr. iii. iv.

[19] Hagg. i. 1–11.

[20] Rom. xi. 1.

[21] Ps. xvi. 8. cix. 31, cxxi. 5, cxlii. 4.

[22] S. Jer.

Before CHRIST cir. 519.

the LORD that [d] hath chosen Jerusalem rebuke thee:
[e] *is* not this a brand plucked
out of the fire?
3 Now Joshua was
clothed with [f] filthy garments, and stood before the
angel.
4 And he answered and
spake unto those that stood

[d] ch. 1. 17. Rom. 8. 33.
[e] Amos 4. 11. Rom. 11. 5. Jude 23.
[f] Isai. 64. 6.

Lord, Sit Thou on My right hand. The Lord speaketh of another Lord; not that He, the Lord Who speaketh, cannot rebuke, but that, from the unity of nature, when the Other rebuketh, He Himself Who speaketh rebuketh. For [1] *he who seeth the Son, seeth the Father also.*" It may be that God, by such sayings [2], also accustomed men, before Christ came, to believe in the Plurality of Persons in the One Godhead.

The rebuke of God must be with power. [3] *Thou hast rebuked the nations, Thou hast destroyed the ungodly.* [4] *Thou hast rebuked the proud, accursed.* [5] *They perish at the rebuke of Thy Countenance.* [6] *At Thy rebuke, O God of Jacob, both the chariot and horse are cast into a deep sleep.* [7] *God shall rebuke him, and he fleeth far off, and shall be chased as the chaff of the mountains before the wind.* [8] *He rebuked the Red Sea and it dried up.* [9] *The foundations of the world were discovered at Thy rebuke, O Lord.* He [10] *rebuked the seed*, and it perished; *the devourer* [11], and it no longer devoured. The rebuke then of the blasted spirit involved a withering rejection of himself and his accusations, as when Jesus rebuked the unclean spirit and he departed out of his victim [12].

The Lord hath chosen Jerusalem. Joshua then is acquitted, not because the accusation of Satan was false, but out of the free love of God for His people and for Joshua in it and as its representative. [13] *Who shall lay anything to the charge of God's elect? It is God that justifieth. Who is he that condemneth?* The *high priest*, being [14] *himself also compassed with infirmity, needed daily to offer up sacrifices first for his own sins, and then for the people's.* As Isaiah said, on the sight of God, [15] *I am undone, because I am a man of unclean lips, and I dwell in the midst of a people of unclean lips*, and, until cleansed by the typical coal, dared not offer himself for the prophetic office, so here Satan, in Joshua, aimed at the whole priestly office, and in it, at Israel's relation to God.

Is not this a brand plucked out of the fire? "[16] As if he should say, Israel confessedly has sinned, and is liable to these charges. Yet it has suffered no slight punishment; it has endured sufferings, and has scarce been snatched out of them, as a half-burned *brand out of the fire.* For not yet had it shaken off the dust of the harms from the captivity; only just now and scarely had it escaped the flame of that most intolerable calamity. Cease then imputing sin to them, on whom God has had mercy."

3. *Now Joshua was clothed with filthy garments;* such, it is expressed, was his habitual condition [17]; he was one so clothed. The *filthy garment*, as defilement generally, is, in Scripture, the symbol of sin. [18] *We are all as the unclean, and all our righteousnesses are as filthy rags.* [19] *He that is left in Zion and he that remaineth in Jerusalem shall be called holy—when the Lord shall have washed away the filth of the daughters of Zion.* [20] *There is a generation, pure in its own eyes, and it is not washed from its filthiness.* The same is expressed by different words, signifying pollution, defilement by sin; [21] *Wo unto her that is filthy and polluted;* [22] *The land was defiled with blood;* [23] *they were defiled with their own works.* It is symbolized also by the [24] *divers washings* of the law, representing restored purity; and the use of the word by Psalmists and Prophets; [25] *Wash me thoroughly from mine iniquity;* [26] *wash you, make you clean; put away the evil of your doings from before Mine eyes;* [27] *O Jerusalem, wash thy heart from wickedness.* In later times at least, the accused were clothed in black [28], not in defiled [29] garments.

4. *And He spake to those who stood before Him*, the ministering Angels who had waited on the Angel of the Lord to do His bidding.

[1] S. John xiv. 9.
[2] As in those, "*the Lord rained upon Sodom and upon Gomorrah brimstone and fire from the Lord out of heaven,*" Gen. xix. 24, and others in which God speaks of Himself in the third person, *the Lord.* Gen. xviii. 14, 19.
[3] Ps. ix. 5. [4] Ib. cxix. 21. [5] Ib. lxxx. 16.
[6] Ib. lxxvi. 6. [7] Is. xvii. 13. [8] Ps. cvi. 9.
[9] Ib. xviii. 15. add. Nah. i. 4. [10] Mal. ii. 3.
[11] Ib. iii. 11. גער is used 11 times of God, only 3 times of man; Gen. xxxvii. 10, Ruth ii. 16, Jer. xxix. 27. גְּעָרָה 8 times of God; 3 times in Prov. and Eccl. vii. 5, of rebuke of man, and Is. xxx. 17.
[12] S. Mark i. 25, 26, ix. 25, S. Luke iv. 35, ix. 42.
[13] Rom. viii. 33, 34. [14] Heb. v. 2, 3. [15] Is. vi. 5.
[16] S. Cyr. [17] The force of the participle with היה.
[18] Is. lxiv. 6. [19] Ib. iv. 3, 4.
[20] Pr. xxx. 12. *Filth, filthiness*, in Is. iv. 4 also, is צוֹאָה, the abstract of the ἅπ. λεγ. in Zech., צוא.
[21] Zeph. iii. 1, מוֹרְאָה וְנִגְאָלָה. See ib.
[22] Ps. cvi. 38. חנף i. q. טנף Cant. v. 3.
[23] Ps. cvi. 39. טמא opp. to טָהוֹר. [24] Heb. ix. 10.
[25] Ps. li. 4, כַּבְּסֵנִי [2 Eng.] [26] Is. i. 16. רַחֲצוּ.
[27] Jer. iv. 14, כַּבְּסִי.
[28] Jos. Ant. xiv. 10. 4. "Whosoever is brought before the tribunal to be judged, is set, as lowly, before it, and is clothed with black raiment."
[29] As in Latin, "sordidati." Liv. ii. 54, vi. 20.

Before CHRIST cir. 519.

before him, saying, Take
away the filthy garments
from him. And unto him
he said, Behold, I have
caused thine iniquity to
pass from thee, [g]and I will
clothe thee with change of
raiment.
5 And I said, Let them
set a fair [h]mitre upon his
head. So they set a fair
mitre upon his head, and
clothed him with garments.
And the angel of the LORD
stood by.
6 And the angel of the
LORD protested unto
Joshua, saying,
7 Thus saith the LORD
of hosts; If thou wilt walk
in my ways, and if thou
wilt [i]keep my ‖charge,

g Isai. 61. 10. Luke 15. 22. Rev. 19. 8.

h Ex. 29. 6. ch. 6. 11.

i Lev. 8. 35. 1 Kin. 2. 3. Ezek. 44. 16.

‖ Or, *ordinance.*

See, I have caused thine iniquity to pass from thee; the pardoning words of the Lord to David by Nathan, [1] *The Lord too hath put away thy sin. And clothe thee*[2] *with change of raiment*[3], i. e. such as were taken off and reserved for great occasions. As the *filthy garments* were not necessarily other than the High Priest's vesture, symbolically defiled through the sins of the people, so neither need these be other than the priestly garments in their purity and freshness. The words imply the condition, not the nature of the vestment. "[4] The high-priest having been thus taken to represent the whole people, the filthy garments would be no unclear symbol of the wickedness of the people. For clad, as it were, with their sins, with the ill-effaceable spot of ungodliness, they abode in captivity, subject to retribution, paying the penalty of their unholy deeds. But when God had pity on them, He bade them be freed from their defilements, and in a manner re-clad with justifying grace. He indicates to them the end of their toils. For where remission of sin is, there follows of necessity freedom from the evils brought through sin."—He adds that *a clean mitre should be put upon his head,* "[5] that so we might understand that the glory of the priesthood ever, in a sort, concurs with the condition of the people. For the boast of the priesthood is the purity of those in their charge.—As then when the people was in sin, the raiment of the priest also was in a manner defiled, so if it were again well-approved, pure and bright is the fashion of the priesthood, and free its access to God. So the divine Paul having ministered to the Gentiles the Gospel of Christ, seeing them advancing in graces, writes, [6] *By your boast, brethren, which I have in Christ Jesus,* and, [7] *my joy and crown.*"

5. *And I said, let them set a fair mitre*[8] *on his head.* This seems to have been purposely omitted, in order to leave something, and that, the completion of all, to be done at the intercession of the prophet. The glory and complement of the High Priest's sacrificial attire was the *mitre* with the *holy crown upon it* and *the plate of pure gold, on which was graven, Holiness to the Lord*[9]; which was to *be upon* the High-priest's *forehead, that* he *may bear the iniquity of the holy things which the children of Israel shall hallow in all their holy gifts;* which was *always* to be *upon his forehead, that they may be accepted before the Lord.* The renewed gift of this was reserved for the intercession of man co-working with God.

And the angel of the Lord standing by, seeing that all was done aright, and, now that the acquittal was complete, *standing* to give the charge.

6. *And the angel of the Lord protested* solemnly (etymologically, *called* God *to witness*) as in, [10] *Did I not make thee swear by the Lord and protested unto thee,* laying it as an obligation upon him[11]. The charge is given to Joshua, and in him to all successive high-priests, while Israel should continue to be God's people, as the condition of their acceptance.

7. *If thou wilt walk in My ways and if thou wilt keep My charge.* Both of these are expressions, dating from the Pentateuch, for holding on in the way of life, well-pleasing to God and keeping the charge given by God[12]. It was the injunction of the dying David to Solomon, [13] *Keep the charge of the*

[1] 2 Sam. xii. 13, גם יי העביר חטאתך. The idiom occurs Ib. xxiv. 10. add. Job vii. 21.

[2] The inf. expresses the more, the contemporaneousness of the acts. See below vii. 5, xii. 10, and others in Ewald Lehrb. § 351. *c.* p. 853. ed. 8.

[3] מחלצות recurs Is. iii. 22. [4] S. Cyr.

[5] S. Cyr. [6] 1 Cor. xv. 31. [7] Phil. iv. 1.

[8] צניף is used of the turban of women, Is. iii. 23; or of nobles, Job xxix. 14: i. q. צנוף of royalty, Is. lxii. 3. Here it is put for מצנפת, the Pentateuch name for the high-priest's mitre, as distinct from the מִגְבָּעָה of ordinary priests.

[9] Ex. xxviii. 36–38, xxix. 6. [10] 1 Kgs ii. 42.

[11] העד with ב Gen. xliii. 3, Deut. viii. 19, xxxii. 46, Ps. l. 7, &c.

[12] שמר משמרת first used of Abraham, Gen. xxvi. 5, then Lev. xviii. 30, xxii. 9, Deut. xi. 1, Jos. xxii. 3.

[13] 1 Kgs ii. 3.

Before CHRIST cir. 519.

then thou shalt also [k]judge
my house, and shalt also
keep my courts, and I will
give thee †places to walk
among these that [l]stand by.
8 Hear now, O Joshua
the high priest, thou and
thy fellows that sit before
thee: for they *are* [m]†men
wondered at: for, behold,
I will bring forth [n]my servant the [o]BRANCH.

k Deut. 17. 9. Mal. 2. 7.
† Heb. *walks*.
l ch. 4. 14. & 6. 5.
m Ps. 71. 7. Isai. 8. 18. & 20. 3.
† Heb. *men of wonder*, or, *sign*, as Ezek. 12. 11. & 24. 24.
n Isai. 42. 1. & 49. 3, 5. & 52. 13. & 53. 11. Ezek. 34. 23, 24.
o Isai. 4. 2. & 11. 1. Jer. 23. 5. & 33. 15. ch. 6. 12. Luke 1. 78.

Lord thy God, to walk in His ways, to keep His statutes &c.

Then shalt thou also judge My house. Judgment, in the place of God, was part of the High-priest's office [1]. Yet these judgments also were given in the house of God. The cause was directed to be brought to God, and He through His priests judged it. Both then may be comprehended in the world, the oversight of the people itself and the judgment of all causes brought to it. "[2]Thou shalt judge those who minister in the house of My sanctuary."

And I will give thee place to walk among those who stand by[3], i.e. among the ministering spirits, who were [4]*standing before the Angel of the Lord.* This can be fully only after death, when the saints shall be received among the several choirs of angels. "[2]In the resurrection of the dead I will revive thee and give thee feet walking among these Seraphim." Even in this life, since [5]*our conversation is in heaven,* and the life of priests should be an angel-life, it may mean, that he should have free access to God, his soul in heaven, while his body was on this earth.

8. *Thou and thy companions which sit before thee; yea*[6] *men of marvelous signs are they*[7]. It seems probable that the words addressed to Joshua begin here; else *the men of signs* would be the companions of Joshua, to the exclusion of Himself. His companions are probably ordinary priests, who *sit* as sharing his dignity as priest, but *before him,* as inferiors. So Ezekiel says, [8]*I was sitting in my house, and the elders of Israel were sitting before me.* They are [9]*images of the things to come.* Isaiah's two sons, with their prophetic names, *Haste-spoil speed-prey,* and *a-remnant shall-return,* were with his own name, *salvation-of-the-Lord,* [10]*signs and portents* of the future Israel. Isaiah, walking naked and barefoot, was [11]*a sign and portent* against Egypt. God tells Ezekiel, that in the *removal of his stuff, as stuff for the captivity,* [12]*I have set thee for a portent unto the house of Israel. I,* he explains his act [13], *am your portent; like as I have done, so shall it be done unto you.* When forbidden to mourn on the death of his wife; [14]*Ezekiel is unto you for a portent; according to all that he hath done, shall ye do; and when this cometh, ye shall know that I am the Lord God.* Wherein then were Joshua and the other priests portents of what should be? One fact alone had stood out, the forgiveness of sins. Accusation and full forgiveness, out of God's free mercy, were the substance of the whole previous vision. It was the full reinstatement of the priesthood. The priesthood so restored was the portent of what was to come. To [15]*offer the offering of the people, and make an atonement for them;* [16]*to make an atonement for the children of Israel for all their sins once a year,* was the object of the existence of the priesthood. Typical only it could be, because they had but *the blood of bulls and goats to offer, which could,* in themselves, [17]*never take away sins.* But in this their act they were portents of what was to come. He adds here, *For, behold, I will bring My Servant the Branch.*

The Branch had now become, or Zechariah made it, a proper name. Isaiah had prophesied, [18]*In that day shall the Branch of the Lord be beautiful and glorious for the escaped of*

[1] Deut. xvii. 9–13, xix. 17, Mal. ii. 7. דין is used of judging a cause (with דין, Jer. v. 28, xxx. 13; with משפט, Ib. xxi. 12) or persons; with the personal pronoun, Gen. xxx. 6; or people, peoples, the ends of the earth, the poor and needy, 17 times: ביתי is used metaphorically of the people of God, only in Nu. xii. 7, *he is faithful in all My house,* or at most Jer. xii. 7, *I have left My house.* Here the parallel word *My courts,* shews that the house is the literal temple.

[2] Jon.

[3] Against the rendering, "those who shall make thee to go," i.e., guide thee, (מַהְלְכִים for מהליכים) there were valid objections; 1) that the Hif. is always הוליך, except היליך Ex. ii. 9. The Partic. מוליךְ occurs 9 times, once in Zech. v. 10. 2) It would have been probably "out of these" or at least "from among these." מהלכים is then probably from a sing. מַהְלֵךְ like מַהְפֵּךְ, מַעֲדֵר, מַחְצֵב) for מַהֲלָךְ Jon. iii. 3, 4, Ez. xlii. 4.

[4] verse 4.

[5] Phil. iii. 20.

[6] כי is inserted in the like way in Gen. xviii. 20, Ps. cxviii. 10–12, cxxviii. 2.

[7] The subject addressed in the nominative is resumed by the pronoun of the 3d person, as in Zeph. ii. 12.

[8] Ezek. viii. 1.
[9] Heb. x. 1.
[10] Is. viii. 18.
[11] Ib. xx. 3.
[12] Ezek. xii. 6.
[13] Ib. 11.
[14] Ib. xxiv. 24.
[15] Lev. ix. 7.
[16] Lev. xvi. 34.
[17] Heb. x. 4.
[18] Is. iv. 2.

Before CHRIST cir. 519.

9 For behold the stone
that I have laid before
Joshua; [p] upon one stone
shall be [q] seven eyes: be-

Before CHRIST cir. 519.

[p] Ps. 118. 22. Isai. 28. 16.

[q] ch. 4. 10. Rev. 5. 6.

Israel; and, in reference to the low estate of him who should come, [1] *There shall come forth a rod out of the stump of Jesse, and a Branch shall grow out of his roots;* and Jeremiah, [2] *Behold the days come, saith the Lord, that I will raise unto David a righteous Branch, and a king shall reign and prosper, and shall execute judgment and justice in the earth, and this is the name whereby He shall be called, The Lord our Righteousness;* and, [3] *In those days and at that time, will I cause the Branch of righteousness to grow up unto David, and he shall execute judgment and righteousness in the land.* Of him Zechariah afterward spoke as, [4] *a man whose name is the Branch.* Here Zechariah names him simply, as a proper name, *My servant* [the] *Branch*, as Ezekiel prophesied of [5] *My servant David.* The title *My servant*, which is Isaiah's chiefest title of the Messiah, occurs in connection with the same image of His youth's lowly estate, and of His atoning Death. [6] *He shall grow up before Him as a sucker, and as a root from a dry ground;* [7] *a scion shall grow out of his roots.* "[8] He alone was above all marked by this name, who never in anything withdrew from the Will of God." "[9] God had before promised to Joshua, i. e. to the priesthood of the law, that they should judge His house and fulfill the types of the legal worship. Yet not long after, the things of the law were to be translated into the true worship, and the unloveliness of the types to be recast into the lovely spiritual polity. [10] *A righteous king was to reign and princes to rule with judgment,* as the Prophet spake. Another priest was to arise, after the order, [11] *not of Aaron but of Melchisedec,* [12] *a minister of the sanctuary and of the true tabernacle which God pitched and not man.* For our Lord Jesus Christ entered the holy of holies, [13] *not by the blood of bulls and goats, but by His own Blood, having obtained eternal redemption,* and [14] *having by One Oblation perfected for ever them that are sanctified.* Lest then God should seem to have spoken untruly, in promising to the legal priesthood that it should ever have the oversight over His house, there was need to fore-announce the mystery of Christ, that the things of the law should cease and He Himself should judge His own house through the Scion from Himself, His Son."

"[8] Look ye to the Branch of the Lord; set Him as the example of life; in Him, as a most strong tower, place with most becoming faith all your hope of salvation and immortality. For He is not only a Branch, who shall fill you with the richness of Divine fruit, but a stone also, to break all the essays of the enemy."

9. *For behold the stone, that I have laid before Joshua.* This must be an expansion of what he had said, or the ground of it, being introduced by, *for.* It must be something future, to be done by God Himself, since God says, *I will grave the graving thereof;* something connected with the remission of sins, which follows upon that graving. The stone, then, cannot be the stone of foundation of the material temple [15]. For this had long before been laid. The head-corner-stone, the completion of the building [16], had nothing remarkable, why God should be said to grave it. The plumbline [17] was not a part even of the material temple. *The stone* is *one stone.* But to interpret it by other prophecy, one stone there is, of which God says, [18] *Behold I lay in Zion for a foundation, a stone, a tried stone, a precious corner-stone, a sure foundation, he that believeth shall not make haste;* that stone, of which our Lord reminded the Jews, [19] *the stone which the builders refused is become the head-stone of the corner;* [20] *Jesus Christ Himself, the chief corner-stone, in whom all the building, fitly framed together, groweth into an holy temple in the Lord, in whom ye also are builded together for an habitation of God through the Spirit.*

On this stone had Joshua, with all those typical priests, to look, in Whom Alone they and all have forgiveness, Whose Sacrifice their sacrifices pictured and pleaded. "It," says an old mystical Jewish book [21], "is the stone of foundation, on which the earth is founded, which God Himself laid, that the world might receive blessing from it." "[22] The Shechinah is called the stone, through which the world subsisteth; of which

[1] Is. xi. 1. [2] Jer. xxiii. 5, 6. [3] Ib. xxxiii. 15.
[4] Zech. vi. 12.
[5] עַבְדִּי דָוִד Ezek. xxxiv. 23, 24, xxxvii. 24, as here עַבְדִּי צמח.
[6] Is. liii. 2. [7] Ib. xi. 1. [8] Osor. [9] S. Cyr.
[10] Is. xxxii. 1. [11] Heb. vii. 11. [12] Ib. viii. 2.
[13] Ib. ix. 12. [14] Ib. x. 14. [15] Rashi.
[16] Kim. Nor, of course, were either foundation-stone or head-stone engraven.
[17] Also in Kim. [18] Is. xxviii. 16.
[19] Ps. cxviii. 22. S. Matt. xxi. 42. add Acts iv. 11. The passages of the Psalm and of Isaiah are united 1 S. Pet. ii. 4–7. [20] Eph. ii. 20, 21.
[21] Zohar Gen. fol. 124. col. 492.
[22] Ib. Num. f. 100. col. 397. quoted by Schoettg. de Mess. p. 218. "Both passages," he subjoins, "are again adduced as parallel, Zohar Deut. f. 118. col. 472." Jonathan seems to identify the Branch, the Messiah, and the Stone; "Lo I am bringing My Servant Messiah, and He shall be revealed. Lo, the stone which I have set before Joshua, upon one stone seven eyes, beholding it; lo, I revealed the vision thereof, saith the Lord of hosts, and will re-

Before CHRIST cir. 519.

hold, I will engrave the graving thereof, saith the Lord of hosts, and [r] I will remove the iniquity of that land in one day.

r Jer. 31. 34. & 50. 20. Mic. 7. 18, 19. ch. 13. 1.

it is said, *A stone of seven eyes*, and, *the stone which the builders refused*." This *stone*, God says, *I have laid* or *set before Joshua*, i. e. for him to consider; as He speaks to Solomon and his children, of *My commandments which I have set before you*[1]. "[2] That the stone is the Lord Jesus Christ, *the head corner-stone, elect, laid as a foundation;* and that the *seven eyes on the one stone* are the sevenfold Spirit of God which rested upon Him, is or ought to be unknown to no one. For to Him [3] *God giveth not the Spirit by measure*, and [4] *in Him dwelleth all the fullness of the Godhead bodily*. This stone was rejected by men, but chosen and honored by God." "[5] This stone then, on which the house of God and our whole salvation resteth, is placed by God before that high priest. That is, the most holy Name of Jesus, the virtue piety and largeness of Jesus is, by the Divine Spirit, shewed to the priest, that he might understand the End of the law and holiness, to Whom all the actions of life and the offices of the priesthood were to be referred. In which stone was foreshewn to the divine man, not the invisible strength only, but also the manifold light of the Divine intelligence. For it follows;"

Upon this *one stone* are *seven eyes*, whether they are *the eyes* of God, resting in loving care upon it, or whether, as the *wheels* in Ezekiel's vision were [6] *full of eyes round about*, the eyes are pictured as on the stone itself, marking that it symbolized a being with manifold intelligence. Zechariah speaks of the eyes of [7] *the Lord which run to and fro on the earth*, and S. John, of the [8] *Lamb, as it had been slain, having seven horns and seven eyes, which are the seven spirits of God, sent forth into all the earth*. Either symbol harmonizes with the context, and is admissible in language [9]. The care of God for this stone is expressed before and afterward, *I have laid it, I will engrave the graving thereof;* and so it corresponds to the [10] *It shall grow up before Him as a tender plant*. But the contrast, that on *one* stone there are *seven* eyes, perhaps rather suggests that the eyes are on the stone itself, and He, the *Living Stone*, is pictured with an universality of sight, whereby, with a Divine knowledge, He surveys and provides for the well-being of His whole Church. It has some analogy too to the sevenfold Spirit which was to rest upon Him. "[11] For this stone to have seven eyes is to retain in operation the whole virtue of the Spirit of sevenfold grace. For according to the distribution of the Holy Spirit, ones receives prophecy; another, knowledge; another, miracles; another, kinds of tongues; another, interpretation of words; but no one attaineth to have all the gifts of that same Spirit. But our Creator taking on Him our infirmities, because, through the power of His Divinity, He shewed that He had at once in Him all the virtues of the Holy Spirit, united beyond doubt the bright gleams of the sevenfold constellation." "None among men had together all the operations of the Holy Spirit, save the Mediator of God and man Alone, Whose is that same Spirit, Who proceeds from the Father before all worlds." "[12] The stone is one. For as we have in God One Spirit, one faith, one sacrament of that most pure laver, so we worship One Christ, the one only Deliverer of the human race, and Author of our righteousness and everlasting salvation; and strengthened by His guardianship, we hope for immortality and eternal glory. Who, though He be One, governs all things with ineffable wisdom. For His wisdom is aptly described by the seven eyes. For the number seven generally describes an universality of good."

Behold I will engrave the graving [13] *thereof*, as of a costly stone. What the graving is, is not explained; but manifestly it is every-

move the guilt of that land in one day." The Zohar chadash (f. 76. 1.) joins the mention of the stone in Dan. ii. 35, Ps. cxviii. 22, Gen. xlix. 24. and this place, in Schoettg. l. c. p. 140. n. cv.

[1] 1 Kgs ix. 6. The idiom is the same, נתתי לפניכם. See also Deut. iv. 8, xi. 32, Jer. ix. 12, xxvi. 4, xliv. 10; of two things, between which to choose, Deut. xi. 26, xxx. 15. In Ezek. xxiii. 24, נתתי לפניהם משפט, "I have placed before them judgment," which they are to consider and to execute.

[2] Rup. [3] S. John iii. 34. [4] Col. ii. 9. [5] Osor.

[6] Ezek. i. 18, x. 12. [7] iv. 10. [8] Rev. v. 6.

[9] In Ps. xxxii. 8. it is איעצה עליך עיני *I will counsel, My Eye upon thee;* in Ps. xxxiii. 18, "עין יי אל יראיו; in Ps. xxxiv. 16. עיני יי אל צדיקים; but "directed toward, or resting *upon*," are only shades of the same meaning. In Gen. xliv. 21. is ואשימה עיני עליו; Jer. xxiv. 6, ושמתי עיני עליהם and xl. 4, for good, אשים את עיני עליך.

[10] Is. liii. 2.

[11] S. Greg. on Job L. xxix. c. 31. n. 74. Opp. i. 951.

[12] Osor.

[13] פִּתּוּחַ only occurs besides of the carved wood of the house of God, 1 Kgs vi. 29, Ps. lxxiv. 6, or of the carving of a precious stone, Ex. xxviii. 11, 21, 36, xxxix. 6, 14, 30. פִּתֵּחַ is used of engraving things on wood, 1 Kgs vii. 36, 2 Chr. iii. 7; on precious stones, Ex. xxxviii. 9. The whole idiom, "skilled to *grave gravings*," to *grave all graving*, recurs 2 Chr. ii. 6, 13; *thou shalt grave on it* with the *engravings of a signet, holiness to the Lord;* Ex. xxviii. 36.

Before CHRIST cir. 519.

10 [s]In that day, saith
the LORD of hosts, shall
ye call every man his
neighbor [t]under the vine
and under the fig tree.

[s] ch. 2. 11.
[t] 1 Kin. 4. 25. Isai. 36. 16. Mic. 4. 4.

CHAPTER IV.

1 *By the golden candlestick is foreshewed the good success of Zerubbabel's foundation.* 11 *By the two olive trees the two anointed ones.*

AND [a]the angel that
talked with me came
again and waked me, [b]as a
man that is wakened out
of his sleep,

[a] ch. 2. 3.
[b] Dan. 8. 18.

thing which concurs to its beauty. "[1]This stone is of earth, and of the power and workmanship of God." "[2]It signifies Him Who had His birth in virgin-earth, but framed skillfully by the power of the Holy Spirit." That Precious stone was further graven, through the Providence and Will of God, when "[3]He caused it to be wounded by the nails of the Cross and the soldier's lance, and in His Passion took away the *iniquity of the earth in one day*, of which it is written, [4]*This is the day which the Lord hath made, we will rejoice and be glad in it*." Beautiful were the gifts and graces which Christ received, as Man; but beautiful beyond all beauty must be those glorious scars, with which He allowed His whole Body to be riven, that "[5]throughout the whole frame His love might be engraven." "[6]What even in the Body of the Lord can be lovelier or more lightful than those five Wounds, which He willed to retain in His immortal Being, lest the blessed should be deprived of that splendor, surpassing far the light of sun and stars?"

And I will remove the iniquity of the land in one day. On *one day* in the year was the typical atonement; in *one day* absolutely, God Himself would *make the iniquity of that land to depart. One day* is always emphatic[7], that things are crowded into it, which seemed too much for *one day*. Year by year came *the day of atonement*: its yearly repetition shewed that nothing lasting was effected. *On one day* that removal should be, which needed no renewal[8]. A Jewish writer confessed the mystery, while he said[9], "*One day;* I know not what that day is." Ask any Christian child, "On what day was iniquity removed, not from the land only, but from all lands?" he would say, "On the day when Jesus Died."

10. *Under the vine and under the fig tree.* Micah had already made the description of the peaceful days of Solomon[10], a symbol[11] of the universal fearless peace of the time of Christ. "[12]Christ by His Passion shall not only take away iniquity, but also bring peace, delight, free communication of all things, so that all things among Christians should be common. For the law of Christ enjoineth charity, forgiveness of injuries, patience, love of enemies &c., all which bring temporal peace."

IV. 1. *The angel came again.* The angel (as before[13]) had gone forth to receive some fresh instruction from a higher angel or from God.

And awakened me, as a man is awakened out of sleep. Zechariah, overwhelmed by the greatness of the visions, must have sunk down in a sort of stupor, as after the vision of the ram and he-goat, *as* Gabriel *was speaking with* him, Daniel says, [14]*I was in a deep sleep on my face toward the ground, and he touched me and set me upright;* and again at the voice of the angel, who, after his three weeks' fast[15], came to declare to him [16]*the scripture of truth;* and at the Transfiguration, [17]*Peter and they that were with him were heavy with sleep, and when they were awake, they saw His glory.* "[18]Wondrous and stupendous mysteries were they which were shewn to the divine man. He saw the Branch of the Lord; he saw His invincible might; he saw His brightness of Divine intelligence and Providence; he saw the amplitude of beauty and dignity. Nailed then and struck still with amazement, while he revolved these things in his mind, sunk in a sort of sleep, he is borne out of himself and, mantled around with darkness, understands that the secret things of Divine wisdom cannot be perfectly comprehended by the mind of any. This then he attained that, his senses being overpowered, he should see nothing, save that wherein is the sum of wisdom, that this

[1] S. Iren. Hær. iii. 21. 7. [2] Lap. as from S. Iren.
[3] S. Jer. [4] Ps. cxviii. 24.
[5] "Cernis, ut in toto corpore sculptus amor." in Lap. [6] Rib.
[7] Gen. xxvii. 45, "why should I be deprived of you both *in one day?*" 1 Sam. ii. 34, "*in one day* they shall die both of them;" 1 Kgs xx. 29, "Israel slew of the Syrians 100,000 footmen *in one day;*" 2 Chr. xxviii. 6, "Pekah slew in Judah 120,000 *in one day;*" Is. ix. 14, "shall cut off branch and rush *in one day;*" x. 17, "devour his thorns and briers *in one day:*" Is. xlvii. 9, "two things shall come to thee *in one day;*" Ib. lxvi. 8, "shall the earth be made to bring forth *in one day?*"
[8] It includes then the ἐφάπαξ of Heb. vii. 27, ix. 12, x. 10, though the idiom is different.
[9] Rashi. [10] 1 Kgs iv. 25.
[11] Mi. iv. 4. See ab. p. 59. [12] Lap.
[13] ii. 3. [14] Dan. viii. 18. [15] Ib. x. 9. [16] Ib. 21.
[17] S. Luke ix. 32. [18] Osor.

Before CHRIST cir. 519.

2 And said unto me,
What seest thou? And I
said, I have looked, and
behold [c] a candlestick all
of gold, † with a bowl upon
the top of it, [d] and his
seven lamps thereon, and
‖ seven pipes to the seven
lamps, which *are* upon the
top thereof:
3 [e] And two olive trees
by it, one upon the right
side of the bowl, and the
other upon the left *side*
thereof.
4 So I answered and
spake to the angel that
talked with me, saying,
What *are* these, my lord?
5 Then the angel that
talked with me answered
and said unto me, Knowest
thou not what these be?
And I said, No, my lord.
6 Then he answered and
spake unto me, saying,

c Ex. 25. 31. Rev. 1. 12.
† Heb. *with her bowl.*
d Ex. 25. 37. Rev. 4. 5.
‖ Or, *seven several pipes to the lamps, &c.*
e ver. 11. 12. Rev. 11. 4.

Before CHRIST cir. 519.

immensity of the Divine excellence cannot be searched out. By this sleep he was seized, when he was roused by the angel to see further mysteries." "[1] Such is the condition of our mind, so far inferior to that in the holy angels, that their state may be called wakefulness, our's a sleep."

2. *And I said*[2], *I have looked and behold a candlestick all of gold.* The candlestick is the seven-branched candlestick of the tabernacle[3], but with variations purposely introduced to symbolize the fuller and more constant supply of the oil, itself the symbol of God's Holy Spirit, Who

> "Enables with perpetual light
> The dullness of our blinded sight."

The first variation is *her bowl*[4] *on the top of the candlestick*, containing the oil; then (as dependent on this) the pipes to derive the oil into each lamp, *seven several*[5] *pipes to the seven lamps*, i. e., seven to each; and the *two olive trees* on either side of the bowl, whose extreme and fine branches poured through two golden pipes the golden oil into the bowl which supplied the lamps. The multiplied conduits imply the large and perfect supply of oil unceasingly supplied, the seven being symbolic of perfection or of the reconciling of God (symbolized by 3) unto the world (symbolized by 4, *its four quarters*); the spontaneous flow of the golden oil from the olive trees symbolizes the free gift of God.

4. "[6] Awakened from his state of sleep, even thus the prophet seemed slowly to understand what was shewn him. He asks then of the instructing angel. The angel, almost amazed, asks if he knowns it not, and when he plainly declares his ignorance, makes clear the enigma of the vision."

6. *This is the word of the Lord unto Zerubbabel.* "[6] As if he were to say, the meaning of the vision and scope of what has been exhibited is, 'God's doings have almost cried aloud to Zerubbabel that all these visions shall come to an end in their time, not effected by human might nor in fleshly strength, but in power of the Holy Ghost and through Divine Will.' For the Only Begotten became Man as we: but He warred not after the flesh, to set up the Church as a candlestick to the world, nor did He, through sensible weapons and armed phalanxes, make those two people His own, or place the spiritual lights on the candlestick; but in the might of His own Spirit He appointed in the Church [7] *first Apostles, then prophets and evangelists*, and all the rest of the saintly band, filling them with Divine gifts and enriching them abundantly by the influx of His Spirit."

[1] S Cyr.

[2] The Kri וְאָמַר must be right, "ויאמר, a manifest blunder, which the Kri corrects; countless Mss. correct in the text also, the Bibl. Brix., an old folio without date, and the Soncin. Prophets, 1486." De Rossi ad loc. All the Verss. agree with the Kri. The text would suppose that, in the silence of the prophet, the angel-interpreter related the vision which he also saw. But this is unlike all the other cases. Kim. supposes that the prophet speaks of himself in the third person. There is the same variation in 2 Sam. i. 8, Neh. v. 9, vii. 3.

[3] Ex. xxv. 31.

[4] גֻּלָּהּ ἁπ. λεγ. for גֻּלָּה, like other rare masculines, as תְּבוּנָם, Hos. xiii. 2; צִירָם, Ps. xlix. 15; בְּעָרְמָם Job v. 13; פִּנָּהּ Pr. vii. 8, as פִּנִּים Zech. xiv. 10; בִּמְגוּרָם Ps. lv. 16; סֻכּוֹ Ps. lxxvi. 3; שֵׂיבוֹ, 1 Kgs xiv. 4; מִטְּהָרוֹ, Ps. lxxxix. 45.

[5] lit. *seven and seven*, i. e., seven to each, as in Gen. vii. 2, without the ו, חמשת חמשת שקלים לַגֻּלְגֹּלֶת "five shekels apiece by the poll," Nu. iii. 47; "the fingers of his hands, and the fingers of his feet were שֵׁשׁ וָשֵׁשׁ, six and six, four and twenty in number," 2 Sam. xxi. 20; "his fingers (including as in 2 Sam. those of his feet) were six and six, twenty-four." 1 Chron. xx. 6.

[6] Osor.

[7] 1 Cor. xii. 28.

Before CHRIST cir. 519.

This *is* the word of the
LORD unto Zerubbabel,
saying, [f]Not by ‖might,
nor by power, but by my
spirit, saith the LORD of
hosts.
7 Who *art* thou, [g]O
great mountain? before
Zerubbabel *thou shalt be-*
come a plain: and he shall
bring forth [h]the headstone
thereof [i]*with* shoutings,
crying, Grace, grace unto
it.

f Hos. 1. 7.
‖ Or, *army*.
g Jer. 51. 25. Matt. 21. 21.
h Ps. 118. 22.
i Ezra 3. 11, 13.

"[1]*Not* then *in* great *power nor in* fleshly *might* were the things of Christ, but in power of the Spirit was Satan spoiled, and the ranks of the adverse powers fell with him; and Israel and those who aforetime served the creature rather than the Creator, were called to the knowledge of God through faith. But that He saved all under heaven, not by human arm, but by His own power as God Emmanuel, Hosea too protested [2], *I will have mercy upon the house of Judah and will save them by the Lord their God, and will not save them by bow nor by sword nor by battle nor by chariots nor by horses nor by horsemen.* But exceeding fittingly was this said to Zerubbabel, who was of the tribe of Judah and at that time administered the royal seat at Jerusalem. For that he might not think that, since such glorious successes were fore-announced to him, wars would in their season have to be organized, he lifts him up from these unsound and human thoughts, and bids him be thus minded, that the force was divine, the might of Christ, Who should bring such things to pass, and not human."

Having given this key of the whole vision, without explaining its details, God enlarges what He had said to Zerubbabel, as He had in the preceding chapter to Joshua [3].

7. *Who art thou, O great mountain* [4]? *Before Zerubbabel thou shalt be a plain.* The words have the character of a sacred proverb; [5]*Every one that exalteth himself shall be abased.* Isaiah prophesies the victories of the Gospel in the same imagery, [6]*Every valley shall be exalted and every mountain and hill shall be made low; and the crooked shall be made straight and the rough places plain.*' And in the New Testament S. Paul says, [7]*The weapons of our warfare are not carnal, but mighty through God to the pulling down of strongholds, casting down imaginations and every high thing that exalteth itself against God, and bringing into captivity every thought to the obedience of Christ.* As it is the character of Anti-Christ, that he [8]*opposeth and exalteth himself above everything that is called God*, so of Satan himself it had been said in the former vision, that he stood at the right hand of Joshua [9]*to resist him.* So then the mountain symbolizes every resisting power; Satan and all his instruments, who, each in his turn, shall oppose himself and be brought low. In the first instance, it was Sanballat and his companions, who opposed the rebuilding of the temple, on account of the "exclusiveness" of Zerubbabel and Joshua [10], because they would not make the temple the abode of a mixed worship of him whom they call *your God* and of their own idolatries. In all and each of his instruments, the persecuting Emperors or the heretics, it was the one adversary. "[11]The words seem all but to rebuke *the great mountain*, i. e. Satan, who riseth up and leadeth against Christ the power of his own stubbornness, who was figuratively spoken of before [9].—For that as far as it was allowed and in him lay, he warred fiercely against the Saviour, no one would doubt, who considered how he approached Him when fasting in the wilderness, and seeing Him saving all below, willed to make Him his own worshiper, shewing Him [12]*all the kingdoms of the world*, saying that all should be His, if He *would fall down and worship* him. Then out of the very choir of the holy Apostles he snatched the traitor disciple, persuading him to become the instrument of the Jewish perverseness. He asks him, *Who art thou?* disparaging him and making him of no account, *great* as the *mountain* was and hard to withstand, and in the way of every one who would bring about such things for Christ, of Whom, as we said, Zerubbabel was a type."

And he shall bring forth the headstone [13]. The foundation of the temple had long been laid. Humanly it still hung in the balance whether they would be permitted to complete it [14]: Zechariah foretells absolutely that they would. Two images appear to be

[1] S. Cyr. [2] Hos. i. 7. [3] Zech. iii. 8–10.

[4] הר הגדול; the construction as שער הראשון, xiv.10; לאיש העשיר 2 Sam. xii.4; עד בור הגדול, 1 Sam. xix. 22; איש אֶפְרָתִי הַזֶּה 1 Sam. xvii. 12; מָבוֹא השלישי Jer. xxxviii. 14; דָּבָר הַזֶּה Ib. xl. 3; סֵפֶר הַגָּלוּי הַזֶּה Ib. xxxii. 14. also 1 Kgs vii. 8, 12. Ges. Lehrg. n. 168. p. 659.

[5] S. Luke xiv. 11, xviii. 14.

[6] Is. xl. 4. The same word למישור, there with והיה.

[7] 2 Cor. x. 4, 5. [8] 2 Thess. ii. 4. [9] iii. 1.

[10] See ab. Introd. to Haggai. p. 293. [11] S. Cyr.

[12] S. Matt. iv. 8, 9.

[13] רֹאשָׁה is a form, perhaps framed by Zechariah, here in apposition to האבן.

[14] Ezr. v.

Before CHRIST cir. 519.

8 Moreover the word of
the LORD came unto me,
saying,
9 The hands of Zerub-
babel [k] have laid the foundation of this house; his
hands [l] shall also finish it;
and [m] thou shalt know that
the [n] LORD of hosts hath
sent me unto you.
10 For who hath de-
spised the day of [o] small
things? ‖ for they shall rejoice, and shall see the
† plummet in the hand of
Zerubbabel *with* those

[k] Ezra 3. 10.
[l] Ezra 6. 15.
[m] ch. 2. 9, 11. & 6. 15.
[n] Isai. 48. 16.
[o] ch. 2. 8. Hag. 2. 3.
‖ Or, *since the seven eyes of the Lord shall rejoice.*
† Heb. *stone of tin.*

used in Holy Scripture, both of which meet in Christ: the one, in which the stone spoken of is the foundation-stone; the other, in which it is the head corner-stone binding the two walls together, which it connects. Both were corner stones; the one at the base, the other at the summit. In Isaiah the whole emphasis is on the foundation; [1] *Behold Me Who have laid in Zion a stone, a tried stone, a precious corner-stone, well-founded.* In the Psalm, the building had been commenced; those who were building had disregarded and despised the stone, but *it became the head of the corner*, crowning and binding the work in one [2]. Both images together express, how Christ is the Beginning and the End, the First and the Last; the Foundation of the spiritual building, the Church, and its summit and completion; the unseen Foundation which was laid deep in Calvary, and the Summit to which it grows and which holds it firm together. Whence S. Peter unites the two prophecies, and blends with them that other of Isaiah, that Christ would [3] *be a stone of stumbling, and a rock of offence. To Whom coming, as unto a living stone, disallowed indeed of men but chosen of God and precious, ye also are built up a spiritual house—Whence also it is contained in the Scripture, Behold, I lay in Zion a chief corner-stone, elect, precious:—unto you which believe He is precious, but unto them which be disobedient, the same stone which the builders refused is made the head of the corner, and a stone of stumbling and a rock of offence, to them which stumble at the word being disobedient.*

A Jew paraphrases this of the Messiah; "[4] And He shall reveal His Messiah, whose name was spoken from the beginning, and he shall rule over all nations."

With shoutings[5], *grace, grace unto it*, i. e. all favor from God unto it, redoubled favors, grace upon grace. The completion of the building was but the commencement of the dispensation under it. It was the beginning not the end. They pray then for the continued and manifold grace of God, that He would carry on the work, which He had begun. Perseverance, by the grace of God, crowns the life of the Christian; our Lord's abiding presence in grace with His Church unto the end of the world, is the witness that He Who founded her upholds her in being.

8. *And the word of the Lord.* "[6] This word of the Lord is not addressed through 'the interpreting angel,' but direct from the Lord, and that through the 'Angel of the Lord.' [7] For though in the first instance the words, *the hands of Zerubbabel &c.*, relate to the building of the material temple, and announce its completion through Zerubbabel, yet the inference, *and thou shalt know that the Lord of hosts hath sent me unto you*, shews that the meaning is not exhausted thereby, but that here too this building is mentioned only as a type of the building of the spiritual temple [8]; and the completion of the typical temple is but a pledge of the completion of the true temple. For not through the completion of the material temple, but only through the building of the kingdom of God, shadowed forth by it, can Judah know, that the Angel of the Lord was sent to him."

10. The simplest rendering is marked by the accents. *For who hath despised*[9] *the day*

[1] Is. xxviii. 16.

[2] Ps. cxviii. 22. This is implied in the Midrash, quoted by De Lira. "They explain it of a certain stone of this building, which was frequently offered by the stone-masons for the building of the wall, but was always found too long or too short, and so was often rejected by them as unfit, but in the completion of the wall, in the coupling of the two walls, it is found most fit, which was then accounted a marvelous thing." in Ps. cxvii. (118) 22. ראש "head," is a natural metaphor for the summit; the tops of mountains, Gen. viii. 5 &c.; of a hill over valleys, Is. xxviii. 1, 4; of a tower, Gen. xi. 4; of columns, 1 Kgs vii. 19: the rounded top of a throne, Ib. x. 19; of a bed, Gen. xlvii. 31 [Heb.]; ear of corn, Job xxiv. 24; the starry heavens above us, Job xxii. 12; of the head of a people, tribes, nations, a family, in many places. Although used of the chief among things, it cannot, any more than κεφαλή, be used of "the base," as Gesenius would have it. Thes. p. 1251. v. ראשה.

[3] 1 S. Pet. ii. 4–7.

[4] Jon.

[5] תְּשֻׁאוֹת always plur.; of the cries of a city, Is. xxii. 2; of the exactor, Job xxxix. 7; crash of thunder, Ib. xxxvi. 29. [all]

[6] Keil.

[7] "comp. v. 9 b with ii. 13 b and 15 b."

[8] "as in vi. 12. sq."

[9] בַּז i. q. בָּז (and with its const. with ל) as טַח for טָח, Is. xliv. 18.

Before CHRIST cir. 519.

p 2 Chr. 16. 9. Prov. 15. 3. ch. 3. 9.

q ver. 3.

seven; [p] they *are* the eyes of
the LORD, which run to and
fro through the whole earth.
11 ¶ Then answered I,
and said unto him, What
are these [q] two olive trees
upon the right *side* of the
candlestick and upon the
left *side* thereof?

12 And I answered
again, and said unto him,
What *be these* two olive
branches which † through
the two golden pipes
|| empty † the golden *oil*
out of themselves?
13 And he answered me
and said, Knowest thou

Before CHRIST cir. 519.

† Heb. *by the hand.*

|| Or, *empty out of themselves* oil into *the gold.*

† Heb. *the gold.*

---

of small things [1]? *and* [i.e. *seeing that* [2],] *there have rejoiced and seen the plummet in the hand of Zerubbabel, these seven, the Eyes of the Lord, they are running to and fro in all the earth,* i.e. since God hath with joy and good-pleasure beheld the progress of the work of Zerubbabel, *who can despise the day of small things? The day of small things* was not only that of the foundation of the temple, but of its continued building also. The *old men* indeed, *that had seen the first house, wept with a loud voice, when the foundation of this house was laid before their eyes* [3]. But while in progress too, Haggai asks, [4] *Who is left among you that saw this house in its first glory? And how do ye see it now? is not in your eyes such as it, as nothing?* But that temple was to see the day of great things, when [5] *the later glory of this house shall be greater than the former, and in this place will I give peace, saith the Lord of hosts.*

They are the eyes of the Lord which run to and fro. He uses almost the words of the prophet Hanani to Asa [6], *the eyes of the Lord run to and fro throughout the whole earth, to shew Himself strong in behalf of those whose heart is perfect toward Him.* Yet this assurance that God's watchful Providence is over *the whole earth,* betokens more than the restoration of the material temple, whose only hindrance could be the will of one man, Darius.

The day of small things is especially God's day, Whose *strength is made perfect in weakness;* Who raised Joseph from the prison, David from the sheepfold, Daniel from slavery, and converted the world by the fishermen and the tentmaker, having Himself first become the Carpenter. "Wouldest thou be great? Become little." "Whenever," said S. Theresa [7], "I am to receive some singular grace, I first annihilate myself, sink into my own nothingness, so as to seem to myself to be nothing, be capable of nothing."

11. *And I answered and said.* The vision, as a whole, had been explained to him. The prophet asks as to subordinate parts, which seemed perhaps inconsistent with the whole. If the whole imports that everything should be done by the Spirit of God, not by human power, what means it that there are these *two* olive-trees? And when the Angel returned no answer, to invite perhaps closer attention and a more definite question, he asks again;

12. *What are the two spikes* [8] *of the olive?* comparing the extreme branches of the olive-tree, laden with their fruit, to the ears of corn, which *were by* or *in the hand of* [9] *the golden pipes* [10], *which empty forth the golden oil from themselves.* Zechariah's expression, *in the hand of* or, if so be, *by the hand* of the two pipes, shews that these two were symbols of living agents, for it is nowhere used except of a living agent, or of that which it personified as such [11].

[1] קטנות as נִעְמוֹת ,נִפְלָאוֹת ,רָעוֹת Ps. xvi. 11. sing. קְטַנָּה אוֹ גְדוֹלָה Num. xxii. 18.

[2] This is not a mere relation of a contemporaneous fact, in which the noun is placed first. (Ew. Lehrb. § 341 p. 835). It is a contrast; in which case the word, in which the contrast lies, is placed first, whether noun or verb. Here the contrast being between "despising" and "rejoicing," ושמחו is placed first. So in Ps. v. 12, וישמחו; Ib. xxv. 3, *all that trust in Thee shall not be ashamed; ashamed be they who &c.*; Ps. xxxviii. 17. *The arms of the ungodly shall be broken, and upholdeth the Lord the righteous.* " וסומך צדיקים.

[3] Ezr. iv. 12. [4] Hagg. ii. 3. [5] Ib. 9.

[6] 2 Chr. xvi. 9. עֵינַיִם is masc. in Zech. both here and iii. 9, which is rare, but also Ps. xxxviii. 11. עין m. Cant. iv. 9. Ch. Ps. lxxiii. 7.

[7] Rib. vita S. Ther. ap. Lap.

[8] שִׁבֲּלֵי, ἅπ. after the analogy of שִׁבֹּלֶת ,שִׁבֳּלִים of ears of corn.

[9] Kim., by his explanation "in the midst" and that the olive trees were pressed in the midst of the golden pipes, seems to mean that the branches with their olives fell into those pipes as hands, and yielded in them their oil; Rashi renders "near it" like אל ידי 2 Sam. xiv. 30, as בידו Job xv. 23.

[10] צנתרות is doubtless the same as Ch. צנתרין Esth. (ii.) i. 2, "tubes" צנורי תהוכא Eccl. i. 7, Targ. in Buxt., yet larger than the מוצק, both from its etymology, and since the oil was derived through *two* tubes to the bowl, but by 7 x 7 = 49 to the lamps.

[11] Of the 276 cases beside this, in which ביד occurs, in three only is it used of any other than a personal agent, and in these the agent is personified; Job viii. 4, *and he cast them away in the hand of their transgression;* Prov. xviii. 21, *death and life are*

Before CHRIST cir. 519.

not what these *be?* And I
said, No, my lord.

r Rev. 11. 4.

14 Then said he, [r] These
are the two † anointed
ones, [s] that stand by [t] the
Lord of the whole earth.

† Heb. *sons of oil.*

s ch. 3. 7. Luke 1. 19. t See Josh. 3. 11, 13. ch. 6. 5.

---

14. *These are the two sons of oil*, probably not as themselves anointed, (for another word is used for this [1], and the whole vision has turned on the use of oil as an instrument of light, not of anointing) but as themselves abundantly ministering the stream which is the source of light [2].

Which stand by the Lord of the whole earth, as His servants and ministers.

The candlestick is almost authoritatively interpreted for us, by the adoption of the symbol in the Revelation, where our Lord is exhibited [3] *as walking in the midst of the seven golden candlesticks*, and, it is said, [4] *the seven candlesticks are the seven Churches;* and our Lord says to the Apostles, on whom He founded the Church; [5] *Ye are the light of the world: men light a candle, and put it on a candlestick, and it giveth light to them that are in the house.*

"[6] The golden candlestick is the Church, as being honored in the world, most bright in virtues, raised on high exceedingly by the doctrines of the true knowledge of God. But there are seven lamps, having light, not of their own, but brought to them from without, and nourished by the supplies through the olive tree. These signify the holy Apostles, Evangelists, and those who, each in their season, were teachers of the Churches, receiving, like lamps, into their mind and heart the illumination from Christ, which is nourished by the supplies of the Spirit, casting forth light to those who are in the house." "[7] The pipes of the lamps, which pour in the oil, signify the unstinted prodigality of the loving-kindness of God to man."

The most difficult of explanation (as is plain from the variety of interpretations) is this last symbol of the spikes of the olive-tree, through whom flows the oil of the Holy Spirit to the candlesticks, and which yet represent created beings, ministers, and servants of God. Perhaps it represents that, in the Church, grace is ministered through men, as S. Paul says, [8] *Unto every one of us is given grace according to the measure of the gift of Christ. Wherefore he saith, when He ascended up on high, He led captivity captive and gave gifts unto men. And He gave some, apostles; and some, prophets; and some, evangelists; and some, pastors and teachers, for the perfecting of the saints, for the work of the ministry, for the edifying of the body of Christ—that we—may grow up into Him in all things which is the Head, even Christ, from Whom the whole body, fitly joined together and compacted by that which every joint supplieth, according to the effectual working in the measure of every part, maketh increase of the body unto the edifying of itself in love.* What S. Paul expresses by [9] *all the body, having nourishment ministered and being knit together by joints and bands, from the Head*, and so *increasing with the increase of God*, (as he elsewhere speaks of [10] *the ministration of the Spirit;* [11] *he that ministereth to you the Spirit*) *that* Zechariah may express by the oil being poured, through the living [12] tubes, the bowl, the sevenfold pipes, into the lamps, which shone with the God-given light. So S. Paul speaks again, of [13] *having this treasure in earthen vessels.* Joshua and Zerubbabel, as representatives of the priestly and royal offices, shadowed forth what was united in Christ, and so, in their several offices, they might be included in the symbol of the olive-tree, they could not exhaust it; for men who, having served God in their generation, were to pass away, could not be alone intended in a vision, which describes the abiding being of the Church.

"[14] Christ is both All-holy Priest and supreme Eternal King. In both ways He supplies to us the light which He brought. For from Him piety and righteousness flow unceasingly to the Church, that it never lack the heavenly light. The oil is expressed into tubes; thence passed through pipes into the vessel which contains the lamps; to designate the various suppliers of light, which, the nearer they are to the effluence of the oil, the more they resemble Him by Whom they are appointed to so Divine an office. The seven lamps are the manifold Churches, distinct in place but most closely bound together by the consent of one faith and by the

---

in the power, lit. *the hand, of the tongue;* Is. lxiv. 6, *thou hast made us to melt away by the hand of our iniquities.* With regard to בְּיַד, בְּיָדְךָ, this could not be otherwise; but also in the 92 cases in which בידו; 6, in which בידה: and 34, in which בידם, occurs, the pronoun relates to a personal agent.

[1] יִצְהָר, in the other 20 places where it occurs, is always united with other natural products: both תירוש (not יין), the fresh wine, and דגן "wheat." שמן is used of the oil as derived from the olive (שמן זית, Ex. xxvii. 20, Lev. xxiv. 2.) for the candlestick, Ex. xxvii. 20, as well as for the anointing oil, but not יצהר.

[2] So בן שמן Is. v. 1, and the other idioms of qualities, בן חיל, בן בליעל, בן עַוְלָה &c.

[3] Rev. i. 13. ii. 1. [4] Ib. i. 20. [5] S. Matt. v. 14, 15. cf. Phil. ii. 15. [6] S. Cyr. [7] Theod. [8] Eph. iv. 7, 8, 11, 12, 14–16. [9] Col. ii. 19. [10] 2 Cor. iii. 8. [11] Gal. iii. 5. [12] See ab. on ver. 12. [13] 2 Cor. iv. 7. [14] Osor.

Before CHRIST cir. 519.

CHAPTER V.

1 *By the flying roll is shewed the curse of thieves and swearers.* 5 *By a woman pressed in an ephah, the final damnation of Babylon.*

THEN I turned, and
lifted up mine eyes,
and looked, and behold a
flying [a] roll.

[a] Ezek. 2. 9.

2 And he said unto me,
What seest thou? And I
answered, I see a flying
roll; the length thereof *is*
twenty cubits, and the
breadth thereof ten cubits.
3 Then said he unto me,
This *is* the [b] curse that goeth forth over the face of

Before CHRIST cir. 519.

[b] Mal. 4. 6.

bond of charity. For although the Church is one, yet it is distinct according to the manifold variety of nations. They are said to be seven, both on account of the seven gifts of the Spirit, mentioned by Isaiah, and because in the numbers 3 and 4, is contained an emblem of piety and righteousness. There are 7 pipes to each lamp, to signify that each has need of many instruments, that the light may be maintained longer. For as there are diversities of gifts, so must there needs be the functions of many ministers, to complete one work. But the lamps are set in a circle, that the oil of one may flow more readily into others, and it, in turn, may receive from others their superabundance, to set forth the communion of love and the indissoluble community of faith."

V. 1. Hitherto all had been bright, full of the largeness of the gifts of God; of God's favor to His people[1]; the removal of their enemies[2]; the restoration and expansion and security of God's people and Church under His protection[3]; the acceptance of the present typical priesthood and the promise of Him, through Whom there should be entire forgiveness[4]: the abiding illumining of the Church by the Spirit of God[5]. Yet there is a reverse side to all this, God's judgments on those who reject all His mercies. "[6] Prophecies partly appertain to those in whose times the sacred writers prophesied, partly to the mysteries of Christ. And therefore it is the wont of the prophets, at one time to chastise vices and set forth punishments, at another to predict the mysteries of Christ and the Church."

And I turned and, or, *Again*[7] *I lifted up my eyes*, having again sunk down in meditation on what he had seen, *and behold a roll flying;* as, to Ezekiel was shewn *a hand with a roll of a book therein, and he spread it before me.* Ezekiel's roll also was [8] *written within and without, and there was written therein lamentation and mourning and woe.* It was a wide unfolded roll, as is involved in its *flying;* but its "[9] flight signified the very swift coming of punishment; its flying from heaven that the sentence came from the judgment-seat above."

2. *And he* (the interpreting angel) *said unto me.* It cannot be without meaning, that the dimensions of the roll should be those of the tabernacle[10], as the last vision was that of the candlestick, after the likeness of the candlestick therein. The explanations of this correspondence do not exclude each other. It may be that [11] *judgment shall begin at the house of God;* that the punishment on sin is proportioned to the nearness of God and the knowledge of Him; that the presence of God, which was for life, might also be to death, as S. Paul says; [12] *God maketh manifest the savor of this knowledge by us in every place; for we are unto God a sweet savor of Christ in them that are saved and in them that perish; to the one we are the savor of death unto death, and to the other the savor of life unto life;* and Simeon said, [13] *This child is set for the fall and rising again of many in Israel.*

Over the face of the whole earth, primarily *land*, since the perjured persons, upon whom the curse was to fall[14], were those who swore falsely by the name of God: and this was in Judah only. The reference to the two tables of the law also confines it primarily to those who were under the law. Yet, since the moral law abides under the Gospel, ultimately these visions related to the Christian Church, which was to be spread *over the whole earth.* The roll apparently was shewn, as

[1] Vision 1. i. 7-17. [2] Vision 2. Ib. 18–21.
[3] Vis. 3. c. ii. [4] Vis. 4. c. iii. [5] Vis. 5. c. iv.
[6] S. Aug. de Civ. Dei. xvii. 3. Rib.
[7] Gen. xxvi. 18, 2 Kgs i. 11, 13. Jer. xviii. 14.
[8] Ez. ii. 9, 10. [9] Rib.
[10] The length of the tabernacle is fixed by the 5 curtains which were to be on each side, *the breadth of each curtain four cubits.* Exod. xxvi. 1, 2. The whole, including the holy of holies, is determined by the *twenty boards* on each side, *a cubit and a half, the breadth of each board;* Ib. 16, 18. The breadth is fixed by the *six boards*, i. e. nine cubits, with the *two boards for the corners of the tabernacle in the two sides.* Ib. 22, 23. Josephus gives the whole thirty cubits long, (the holy of holies being ten cubits square) ten broad (Ant. 3. 6. 3.). Kimchi strangely neglects this, and refers to the porch of Solomon's temple, in which the dimensions of the tabernacle were repeated (1 Kgs vi. 3.), but which was itself only an ornament to the temple.
[11] 1 Pet. iv. 17. [12] 2 Cor. ii. 14–16.
[13] S. Luke ii. 34. [14] ver. 4.

Before CHRIST cir. 519.

the whole earth: for
||every one that stealeth
shall be cut off *as* on this
side according to it; and
every one that sweareth
shall be cut off *as* on that
side according to it.

|| Or, *every one of this* people *that stealeth holdeth* himself *guiltless as it* doth.

4 I will bring it forth,
saith the LORD of hosts,
and it shall enter into the
house of the thief, and into
the house of [c]him that
sweareth falsely by my
name: and it shall remain
in the midst of his house,
and [d]shall consume it with
the timber thereof and the
stones thereof.

Before CHRIST cir. 519.

c Lev. 19. 12. ch. 8. 17. Mal. 3. 5.

d See Lev. 14. 45.

---

written on both sides; the. commandments of the first table, in which perjury is forbidden, on the one side; those relating to the love of our neighbor, in which stealing is forbidden, on the other [1]. "[2] He calleth *curse* that vengeance, which goeth through the whole world, and is brought upon the workers of iniquity. But hereby both prophets and people were taught, that the God of all is the judge of all men, and will exact meet punishment of all, bringing utter destruction not on those only who live ungodly toward Himself, but on those also who are unjust to their neighbors. For let no one think that this threat was only against thieves and false-swearers; for He gave sentence against all iniquity. For since all the law and the prophets hang on this word, *Thou shalt love the Lord thy God with all thy heart and thy neighbor as thyself,* He comprised every sort of sin under false swearing and theft. The violation of oaths is the head of all ungodliness. One who so doeth is devoid of the love of God. But theft indicates injustice to one's neighbor; for no one who loves his neighbor will endure to be unjust to him. These heads then comprehend all the other laws."

Shall be cut off, lit. *cleansed away* [3], as something defiled and defiling, which has to be cleared away as offensive: as God says, [4] *I will take away the remnant of the house of Jeroboam, as a man taketh away dung, till it be all gone,* and so often in Deuteronomy, *thou shalt put the evil away from the midst of thee* [5], or *of Israel* [6], and in Ezekiel, [7] *I will disperse thee in the countries and will consume thy filthiness out of thee.* [8] *Set it empty upon the coals thereof, that the brass of it may be hot and may burn, and the filthiness of it may be molten, that the scum of it may be consumed.*

4. *I will bring it forth* out of the treasure-house, as it were; as he says, [9] *He bringeth forth the wind out of His treasures;* and, [10] *Is not this laid up in store with Me, sealed up among My treasures? To Me* belongeth *vengeance and recompense."*

And it shall remain, lit., "lodge for the night [11]," until it has accomplished that for which it was sent, its utter destruction. "[12] So we have seen and see at this day powerful families, which attained to splendor by rapine or ill-gotten goods, destroyed by the just judgment of God, that those who see it are amazed, how such wealth perceptibly yet insensibly disappeared." "[13] Why doth it overthrow the stones and the wood of the swearer's house? In order that the ruin may be a correction to all. For since the earth must hide the swearer, when dead, his house, overturned and become a heap, will by the very sight be an admonition to all who pass by and see it, not to venture on the like, lest they suffer the like, and it will be a lasting witness against the sin of the departed." Heathenism was impressed [14] with the doom of him who consulted the oracle, whether he should foreswear himself for gain [15]. "Swear," was the answer, "since death awaits too the man, who keeps

[1] מִזֶּה מִזֶּה, in two corresponding sentences, can only he partitive, as in Ex. xvii. 12, xxv. 19, xxvi. 13, xxxii. 15, of the two tables of the law, written on both sides; xxxvii. 8, xxxviii. 15, Nu. xxii. 24; Jos. viii. 22, and ten other places. So also מזה ומזה לארון Jos. viii. 33. מזה ומזה Ez. xlvii. 7, 12, as in other partitives מִפֹּה, מִפֹּה, or מִפּוֹ Ez. xl. 10, 12, 21, 26, xli. 2. מזה also, when used of place, always means "from here," i. e. a definite place where people are, Gen. xxxvii. 17, xlii. 15, Exod. xi. 1 (Maurer's instances).

[2] Theod.

[3] So is καθαριζω used Mark vii. 19, (See reff. notes 10–14.) For נקה is not simply "clear," but "cleanse out," as καθαίρω Soph. Tr. 1012, 1061, Plutarch Thes. n. 7, Mar. n. 6. "of monsters and robbers." (Gesenius in comparing Arab. אשתנקי, "emptied clean out" (Vita Tim. i. 576.), אשתחלץ, "appropriated it exclusively to himself" (Lane), אשתצפי "took away the whole" (Freyt.), "cleared it all off," misses the moral meaning of the Heb. word.

[4] 1 Kgs xiv. 10, add xxi. 21.

[5] Deut. xiii. 5 (6 Heb.), xvii. 7, xix. 19, xxi. 21, xxii. 21, 24, xxiv. 7.

[6] Ib. xvii. 12, xxiii. 22

[7] Ezek. xxii. 15.

[8] Ib. xxiv. 11.

[9] Jer. x. 13, li. 16.

[10] Deut. xxxii. 34, 35.

[11] לֵנֶה for לָנָה in verb ἅπ.; in part. pass. זוּרֶה Is. lix. 5.

[12] Lap.

[13] S. Chrys. on the statues 15. n. 13. p. 259. Oxf. Tr.

[14] "The story of Glaucus is alluded to by Plutarch (ii. p. 556 D) Pausanias (11. xviii. n. 2.) Juvenal (xiii. 199–208) Clemens (Strom. vi. p. 749) Dio Chrysostom (Or. lxiv. p. 640) and others." Rawl. Herod. iii. 477.

[15] Herod. vi. 85.

Before CHRIST cir. 519.

5 ¶ Then the angel that
talked with me went forth,
and said unto me, Lift up
now thine eyes, and see
what *is* this that goeth
forth.
6 And I said, What *is*
it? And he said, This *is*
an ephah that goeth forth.
He said moreover, This *is*
their resemblance through
all the earth.
7 And, behold there was
lifted up a ‖ talent of lead:

‖ Or, *weighty piece.*

the oath; yet Oath hath a son, nameless, handless, footless; but swift he pursueth, until he grasp together and destroy the the whole race and house." "[1] In the third generation, there was nought descended from him," who had consulted about this perjury, "nor hearthstone reputed to be his. It had been uprooted and effaced." A Heathen orator[2] relates, as well known, that "the perjurer escapes not the vengeance of the gods, and if not himself, yet the sons and whole race of the foresworn fall into great misfortunes." God left not Himself without witness.

"[3] The prophet speaks of the curse inflicted on the thieves and false swearers of his own day; but à fortiori he includes that which came upon them for slaying Christ. For this was the greatest of all, which utterly overthrew and consumed Jerusalem, the temple and polity, so that that ancient and glorious Jerusalem exists no longer, as Christ threatened. [4] *They shall lay thee even with the ground, and they shall not leave in thee one stone upon another.* This resteth upon them these" 1800 "years."

5. *Then the angel went forth* from the choirs of angels, among whom, in the interval, he had retired, as before[5] he had gone forth to meet another angel.

6. *This is the ephah that goeth forth.* "[6] We too are taught by this, that the Lord of all administers all things *in weight and measure.* So, foretelling to Abraham that his seed should be a sojourner and the cause thereof, He says, [7] *for the iniquity of the Amorites is not yet full*, i. e., they have not yet committed sins enough to merit entire destruction, wherefore I cannot yet endure to give them over to the slaughter, but will wait for the measure of their iniquity." The relation then of this vision to the seventh is, that the seventh tells of God's punishment on individual sinners; this, on the whole people, when the iniquity of the whole is full.

This is their *resemblance*, as we say, *their look*[8], i. e. the *look*, appearance, of the inhabitants [9] *in all the land.* This then being the condition of the people of the land, at the time to which the vision relates, the symbolical carrying away of the full measure of sin cannot be its forgiveness, since there was no repentance, but the taking away of the sin with the sinner. "[10] The Lord of all is good and loving to mankind; for He is patient toward sinners and endures transgressors, waiting for the repentance of each; but if one perseveres long in iniquity, and come to the term of the endurance allowed, it remains that he should be subjected to punishment, and there is no account of this long forebarance, nor can he be exempt from judgment proportioned to what he has done. So then Christ says to the Jewish people, rushing with unbridled phrensy to all strange excess, [11] *Fill ye up the measure of your fathers.* The measure then, which was seen, pointed to the filling up of the measure of the transgression of the people against Himself." "[12] The angel bids him behold the sins of the people Israel, heaped together in a perfect measure, and the transgression of all fulfilled—that the sins, which escaped notice, one by one, might, when collected together, be laid open to the eyes of all, and Israel might go forth from its place, and it might be shewn to all what she was in her own land." "[13] I think the Lord alluded to the words of the prophet, as though He would say, *Fill up the measure of sins* which your fathers began of old, as it is in Zechariah, i. e. ye will soon fill it; for ye so haste to do evil, that ye will soon fill it to the utmost."

7. *And behold there was lifted up a talent of*

[1] Herod. vi. 85, 86.
[2] Lycurgus Or. in Leocr. p. 157 fin. [3] Lap.
[4] S. Luke xix. 44. [5] ii. 3 (7 Heb.) [6] Theod.
[7] Gen. xv. 16.
[8] עֵין our *look*, as in Lev. xiii. 55. *and the leprosy hath not changed* עֵינוֹ *its look;* Nu. xi. 7, of the manna, *its look* (עֵינוֹ) *was like the look* (כְּעֵין) *of bdellium;* Ezek. x. 9. *the appearance of the wheels was like the look* (כְּעֵין) *of stone of Tarshish.* Add Ez. i. 4, 7, 16, 27, and Dan. x. 6. *like the look* (כְּעֵין) *of polished brass.*

[9] The ם relates to the persons, implied though not expressed in the כָּל הָאָרֶץ, as in Ps. lxv. 10, *thou preparest* דְּגָנָם *their corn;* xxxix. 7, *he heapeth up and knoweth not,* אֹסְפָם, *who gathereth them,* Eccl. v. 17, (18 Eng.) *to see good* (בְּכָל עֲמָלוֹ) *in all his labor;* Ib. vii. 1, *better is the day of death than the day* הִוָּלְדוֹ *of his birth;* Hagg. i. 6, lit. *to clothe, yet not for warmth* לוֹ, *to him.* Ew. Lehrb. n. 294. l. p. 754. ed. 8. [10] S. Cyr.
[11] S. Matt. xxiii. 32. [12] S. Jer. [13] Rib.

Before CHRIST cir. 519.

and this *is* a woman that
sitteth in the midst of the
ephah.
8 And he said, This *is*
wickedness. And he cast
it into the midst of the
ephah; and he cast the
weight of lead upon the
mouth thereof.
9 Then lifted I up mine
eyes, and looked, and, behold, there came out two
women, and the wind *was*
in their wings; for they
had wings like the wings
of a stork: and they lifted
up the ephah between the
earth and the heaven.
10 Then said I to the
angel that talked with me,
Whither do these bear the
ephah?
11 And he said unto me,
To [e] build it an house in [f] the land of Shinar: and
it shall be established, and
set there upon her own
base.

Before CHRIST cir. 519.

[e] Jer. 29. 5, 28.
[f] Gen. 10. 10.

lead, the heaviest Hebrew weight, elsewhere of gold or silver; the golden talent weighing, 1,300,000 grains; the silver, 660,000; here, being lead, it is obviously an undefined mass, though circular [1], corresponding to the Ephah. The Ephah too was the largest Hebrew measure, whose compass cannot now, with certainty, be ascertained [2]. Both probably were, in the vision, ideal. "[3] Holy Scripture calleth the punishment of sin, *lead*, as being by nature heavy. This the divine David teacheth us, [4] *mine iniquities are gone over my head: as an heavy burden, they are too heavy for me.* The divine Zechariah seeth sin under the image of a woman; for most evils are engendered by luxury. But he seeth the punishment, like most heavy lead, lying upon the mouth of iniquity, according to a Psalm, [5] *all iniquity shall stop her mouth.*" "[6] Iniquity, as with a talent of lead, weighs down the conscience."

This is a woman, lit. *one woman*, all sin being concentrated and personified in one, as he goes on to speak of her as *the*, personified, *wickedness* [7]. The *sitting* may represent her abiding tranquil condition in her sins, according to the climax in the first Psalm, [8] *and hath not sat in the seat of the scornful;* and, [9] *thou sittest and speakest against thy brother;* "[10] not standing as by the way, but sitting, as if of set purpose, of wont and habit." "[11] Whoso hath peace in sins is not far from lying down in them, so that, oppressed by a spirit of slumber, he neither sees light, nor feels any blow, but is kept down by the leaden talent of his obduracy."

8. *And cast her into the midst of the Ephah.* As yet then the measure was not full. "[12] She had the lower part within the Ephah, but the upper, especially the head, without. Though the Jews had slain the prophets and done many grievous things, the greatest sin of all remained to be done. But when they had crucified Christ and persecuted the Apostles and the Gospel, the measure was full; she was wholly within the Ephah, no part remained without, so that the measure was filled."

And he cast the weight of lead upon the mouth thereof, i.e. doubtless of the Ephah; as in Genesis [13], *a great stone was on the mouth of the well*, so that there should be no access to it.

9. *There came out two women.* It may be that there may be no symbol herein, but that he names women because it was a woman who was so carried; yet their wings were the wings of an unclean bird, strong, powerful, borne by a force not their own; with their will, since they flew; beyond their will, since the wind was in their wings; rapidly, inexorably, irresistibly, they flew and bore the Ephah between heaven and earth. No earthly power could reach or rescue it. God would not. It may be that evil spirits are symbolized, as being like to this personified human wickedness, such as snatch away the souls of the damned, who, by serving them, have become as they.

11. *To build it an house in the land of Shinar.* The name of Shinar, though strictly Babylonia, carries back to an older power than the world-empire of Babylon; which now too

[1] According to its etymology.

[2] It is thought that Josephus (Ant. 15. 9. 2.) put the μέδιμνος by mistake for the μετρητης, which is ¾ of the μεδιμνος; the μετρητής holding nine of our gallons, the μεδιμνος twelve. The Ephah was probably an Egyptian measure, since the LXX substitute οἰφί &c. corresponding to the Egyptian word for "measure," and Ephah has no Semitic etymology.

[3] Theod. [4] Ps. xxxviii. 4. [5] Ib. cvii. 42.

[6] S. Ambr. in Ps. 35. n. 9. Opp. i. 769.

[7] הרשעה, ἅπ. with art. as הצדקה absolutely, only in Dan. ix. 7. *Thine, O Lord*, is הצדקה, העולה does not occur at all.

[8] Ps. i. 1. [9] Ib. l. 20. [10] Lap.

[11] Sanct. [12] Rib. [13] Gen. xxix. 2.

Before CHRIST cir. 519.

CHAPTER VI.

1 *The vision of the four chariots.* 9 *By the crowns of Joshua is shewed the temple and kingdom of Christ the Branch.*

AND I turned, and lifted
up mine eyes, and
looked, and behold, there
came four chariots out
from between two moun-
tains; and the mountains
were mountains of brass.

2 In the first chariot
were [a]red horses; and in
the second chariot [b]black
horses;
3 And in the third char-
iot [c]white horses; and in
the fourth chariot grisled
and || bay horses.
4 Then I answered [d]and
said unto the angel that
talked with me, What *are*
these, my lord?

Before CHRIST cir. 519.

a ch. 1. 8. Rev. 6. 4.
b Rev. 6. 5.
c Rev. 6. 2.
|| Or, *strong.*
d ch. 5. 10.

was destroyed. *In the land of Shinar*[1] was that first attempt to array a world-empire against God, ere mankind was yet dispersed. And so it is the apter symbol of the antitheist or Anti-Christian world, which by violence, art, falsehood, sophistry, wars against the truth. To this great world-empire it was to be removed; yet to live there, no longer cramped and confined as within an Ephah, but in pomp and splendor. A house or temple was to be built for it, for its honor and glory; as Dagon[2] or Ashtaroth[3], or Baal[4] had their houses or temples, a great idol temple, in which the god of this world should be worshiped.

And it—"the house," *shall be established* firmly on its base, like the house of God, *and it*, (wickedness[5]) shall be tranquilly rested on its base, as an idol in its temple, until the end come. In the end, the belief of those of old was, that the Jews would have great share in the antagonism to Christ and His empire. At the first, they were the great enemies of the faith, and sent forth, S. Justin says[6], those everywhere who should circulate the calumnies against Christians, which were made a ground of early persecutions. In the end, it was believed, that Anti-Christ should be from them, that they would receive him as their Christ, the last fulfillment of our Lord's words, [7] *I am come in My Father's name and ye receive Me not; another shall come in his own name, him ye will receive.*

VI. 1. *Behold, four chariots going forth* "[8]by the secret disposal of God into the theatre of the world," *from between two mountains of brass.* Both Jews[9] and Christians have seen that the four chariots relate to the same four empires, as the visions in Daniel. "*The* two mountains." It may be that the imagery is from the two mountains on either side of the valley of Jehoshaphat, which Joel had spoken of as the place of God's judgment[10], and Zechariah afterward[11]. It may then picture that the judgments go forth from God. Anyhow the powers, symbolized by the four chariots, are pictured as closed in on either side by these mountains, strong as brass, unsurmountable, undecaying, "[12]that they should not go forth to other lands to conquer, until the time should come, fixed by the counsels of God, when the gates should be opened for their going forth." The mountains of brass may signify the height of the Divine wisdom ordering this, and the sublimity of the power which putteth them in operation; as the Psalmist says, [13] *Thy righteousnesses are like the mountains of God.*

2. 3. The symbol is different from that in the first vision. There[14], they were horses only, with their riders, to go to and fro to enquire; here they are war-chariots with their horses, to execute God's judgments, each in their turn. In the first vision also, there is not the characteristic fourfold division, which reminds of the four world-empires of Daniel[15]; after which, in both prophets, is the mention of the kingdom of Christ. Even if the *grisled* horses be the same as the *speckled* of the first vision, *the black horses* are wanting there, as well as the succession, in which they go forth. The only resemblance is, that there are horses of divers colors, two of which, red and white, are the same. The symbol of the fourth empire, *grizzled, strong*[16], remarkably corresponds with the strength and mingled character of the fourth empire in Daniel.

[1] Gen. xi. 2. [2] 1 Sam. v. 2–5.
[3] Ib. xxxi. 10. [4] 2 Kgs x. 23.
[5] The subjects are marked by the genders; ביה being masc., רשעה fem.
[6] S. Just. Dial. n. 17 (n. 91. Oxf. Tr.) and n. 108. p. 205. Eusebius quotes the first passage, H. E. iv. 18, and repeats the statement on Is. xviii.

[7] S. John v. 43. [8] Alb.
[9] Saadiah in Kim., Kim., Rashi, the Jews in the time of S. Jerome. Jon. paraphrases vi. 5, "four kingdoms." [10] Jo. iii. 2. [11] Zech. xiv. 4.
[12] Rib. [13] Ps. xxxvi. 6. [14] i. 8. [15] Dan. ii.
[16] The guess of Abulwalid and Kimchi that אמץ might be i. q., חָמוּץ *bright red*, Is. lxiii. 1, is at

Before CHRIST cir. 519.

e Ps. 104. 4. Heb. 1. 7, 14.
‖ Or, *winds.*
f 1 Kin. 22. 19. Dan. 7. 10. ch. 4. 14. Luke 1. 19.

5 And the angel answered and said unto me,
e These *are* the four ‖spirits
of the heavens, which go
forth from f standing before the Lord of all the
earth.

6 The black horses which
are therein go forth into
g the north country; and
the white go forth after
them; and the grisled go
forth toward the south
country.

Before CHRIST cir. 519.

g Jer. 1. 14.

5. *These are the four spirits of the heavens.* They cannot be literal winds: for spirits, not winds, *stand before God*, as His servants, as in Job, [1] *the sons of God came to present themselves before the Lord.* This they did, "[2] for these four kingdoms did nothing without the will of God." Zechariah sums up in one, what former prophets had said separately of the Assyrian, the Babylonian, Egyptian, Persian. [3] *O Assyria, the rod of Mine anger—I will send him against an ungodly nation, and against the people of My wrath I will give him a charge.* [4] *I will send and take all the families of the north, and Nebuchadrezzar, the king of Babylon, My servant, and will bring them against this land.* [5] *The Lord shall hiss for the fly, that is in the uttermost part of Egypt, and for the bee that is in the land of Assyria, and they shall come, and shall rest, all of them, in the desolate valleys.* [6] *I will call all the families of the kingdoms of the north, saith the Lord; and they shall come, and shall set every one his throne at the entering of the gates of Jerusalem.* Whatever the human impulse or the human means, all *stand before the Lord of the whole earth*, ministering to *His* will Whose are all things, the Judge of all, Who withholdeth the chastisement till the iniquity is full, and then, through man's injustice, executes His own just judgment. "[7] He says that they went forth from where they had stood before the Lord of the whole earth, to shew that their power had been obtained by the counsel of God, that they might serve His will. For no empire was ever set up on earth without the mind, counsel and power of God. He exalts the humble and obscure, He prostrates the lofty, who trust overmuch in themselves, arms one against the other, so that no fraud or pride shall be without punishment."

6. *The black horses which are therein go forth.* lit. *That chariot wherein the black horses are, these go forth.* "[2] Most suitably is the first chariot, wherein the red horses were, passed over, and what the second, third, fourth did is described. For when the prophet related this, the Babylonian empire had passed, and the power of the Medes possessed all Asia." Red, as the color of blood, represented Babylon as sanguinary; as it is said in the Revelation, [8] *There went out another horse, red, and power was given to him that sat thereon, to take peace from the earth, and that they should kill one another, and there was given him a sharp sword. The black* were to go forth to the North country, the ancient title of Babylon. For Babylon, though taken, was far from being broken. They had probably been betrayed through the weakness of their kings. Their resistance, in the first carefully prepared [9] revolt against Darius, was more courageous than that against Cyrus: and more desperate [10]. Since probably more Jews remained in it, than returned to their own country, what was to befall it had a special interest for them. They had already been warned in the third vision [11] to escape from it. The color *black* doubtless symbolizes the heavy lot, inflicted by the Medo-Persians; as in the Revelation it is said, [12] *the sun became black as sackcloth of hair;* and to the beast in Daniel's vision which corresponded with it, [13] it was *said, Arise, devour much flesh;* and in the Revelation [14], *he that sat on the black horse* was the angel charged

variance with the whole use of the Hebrew root, which occurs 40 times in the verb, אִמֵּץ; 7 times in the adj. אַמִּיץ; and once each in אַמְצָה, מַאֲמָץ, אֹמֶץ, beside the Proper Names אָמוֹץ, Isaiah's father; אַמְצִי, of two persons, אֲמַצְיָה, of four persons. The Arab. ומץ, which Eichhorn and Henderson compare, is no name of a color, but is used apparently of the "slight summer lightning." The ground with some was, that the word is united with names of colors; with Ewald, to replace the red horses, on which the prophet is silent. See "Daniel the prophet" p. 360. The single case too, in which ח and א are supposed to be interchanged in Heb., is that a Proper Name תַּחְרֵעַ 1 Chr. ix. 41, is written תַּאְרֵעַ Ib. viii. 35, but the pronunciation of Proper Names varies in all languages. See "Daniel the prophet" p. 405. Fürst's instances (Handwört. p. 368) are conjectures of his own. Within Arabic, אַתַּי, i. q., חַתַּי; ארמ i. q., חרמ; ארם i. q., חַרַתַּ; (Eichh. in Ges. Thes. p. 2.) are without authority; אבם is not owned by Lane; else, if it means "imprisoned," it would be a softer pronunciation of חַבַּס in this one sense; אצר and חצר are perhaps from the same biliteral root.

1 Job i. 6, ii. 1. The same idiom התיצב על.
2 S. Jer.
3 Is. x. 5.
4 Jer. xxv. 9.
5 Is. vii. 18, 19.
6 Jer. i. 15.
7 Osor.
8 Rev. vi. 4.
9 Herod. iii. 150.
10 See "Daniel the Prophet," pp. 129, 130. ed. 2.
11 ii. 7.
12 Rev. vi. 12.
13 Dan. vii. 5.
14 Rev. vi. 5, 6.

Before CHRIST cir. 519.

7 And the bay went forth, and sought to go that they might [h] walk to and fro through the earth: and he said, Get you hence, walk to and fro through the earth. So they walked to and fro through the earth.

[h] Gen. 13. 17. ch. 1. 10.

8 Then cried he upon me, and spake unto me, saying, Behold, these that

with the infliction of famine. Of the Medes, Isaiah had said[1], *I will stir up the Medes against them* [Babylon], *which shall not regard silver; and gold, they shall not delight in it. Their bows also shall dash the young men to pieces; and they shall have no pity on the fruit of the womb; their eye shall not spare children.*

The white went forth after them: for the Greek empire occupied the same portion of the earth as the Persian. White is a symbol of joy, gladness[2], victory[3], perhaps also, from its relation to light, of acute intelligence. It may relate too to the benevolence of Alexander to the Jewish nation. "[4] Alexander used such clemency to the conquered, that it seemed as though he might be called rather the founder than the destroyer of the nations whom he subdued."

And the grizzled, the Romans in their mingled character, so prominent in the fourth empire of Daniel[5], *go forth* to the south country, i. e. Egypt; as Daniel speaks of [6]*the ships of Chittim* and the intervention of the Romans first in regard to the expulsion of Antiochus Epiphanes from Egypt; in Egypt also, the last enduring kingdom of any successor of Alexander, that of the Ptolemies, expired. "30 years afterward, the Son of God was to bring light to the earth. The prophet so interweaves the prediction, that from the series of the four kingdoms it is brought to the Birth of the Eternal King[7]."

7. *And the strong went forth and sought to go, that they might walk to and fro through the earth.* The mention of their strength corresponds to the extent of the power and commission, for which they asked, to *go to and fro*, up and down, at their will, unhindered, through the whole earth. The Babylonian empire held Egypt only out of Asia; the Persian was conquered in its efforts against Europe, in Greece; Alexander's was like a meteor, gleaming but breaking into the four: the Roman combined East and West and within large limits tranquilly.

And he said go, walk to and fro in the earth. He commanded, and they, which were before withheld, went, *and they walked to and fro* [8] *on the earth*, ordering all things at their will, under the Providence of God, whereby He gave free access to the Gospel in all their wide empire. The Greek empire being extinguished, the Romans no longer went into any given country, but superintended and governed all human things in (it is the language of the New Testament) *all the world.* "[9] These same, the dappled and ashen grey horses were commanded to traverse the earth, and they did traverse it; for they mastered all under heaven, and ruled the whole earth, God consenting and arraying those who swayed the Roman might with this brilliant glory. For, as God, He knew beforehand the greatness of their future piety."

8. *Then* God, or *the Angel of the Lord*, who speaks of what belonged to God alone, *called me* (probably "loudly[10]"), so as to command his attention to this which most immediately concerned his people.

These have quieted My spirit in the North country, or rather, *have made My anger to rest*[11] *on*, i. e. have carried it thither and deposited it there, made it to rest upon them, as its abode, as S. John saith of the unbelieving, [12] *The wrath of God abideth on him.* Babylon had been the final antagonist and subduer of the people of God. It had at the outset destroyed the temple of God, and carried off its vessels to adorn idol-temples. Its empire closed on that night when it triumphed over God[13], using the vessels dedicated to Him, to the glorifying of their idols. *In that night was Belshazzar the king of the Chaldæans slain.* This final execution of God's anger upon that their destroyer was the earnest of the rest to *them;* and in this the visions pause.

[1] Is. xiii. 17, 18. [2] Eccl. ix. 8. [3] Rev. vi. 2.
[4] See note 16, p. 369. [5] Dan. ii. 41–43. [6] Ib. xi. 30.
[7] Osor. See "Daniel the Prophet," pp. 142–150.

[8] The fem. תתהלכנה may have been occasioned by the symbol מרכבות v. 1, or the explanation רוחות, v. 5; but since their going was consequent on the permission to go, which they asked and obtained, it must relate to the empire symbolized by the 4th chariot, not (as some) to all. [9] S. Cyr.

[10] הזעיק, with acc. p. is used elsewhere of calling together people. Jud. iv. 10, 13, 2 Sam. xx. 4, 5.

[11] הניח את רוחי, with ב, as Ez. v. 13. הניחותי חמתי בם, followed by בכלותי חמתי בם Ib. xxiv. 13: *thou shalt not be cleansed any more, until I have made my anger to rest upon thee.* The idiom, "to cause to rest upon" a person, involves that that person is the object, on whom it abides; not that anger or spirit was quieted in him whose it was, (as Kim.). רוח is "anger," Jud. viii. 3, Eccl. x. 4.

[12] S. John iii. 36.

[13] Dan. v. See in Daniel the Prophet pp. 450–453.

Before CHRIST cir. 519.

go toward the north coun-
try have quieted my [i]spirit
in the north country.
9 ¶ And the word of
the LORD came unto me,
saying,
10 Take of *them of* the
captivity, *even* of Heldai,
of Tobijah, and of Jeda-
iah, which are come from
Babylon, and come thou
the same day, and go into
the house of Josiah the
son of Zephaniah;

[i] Judg. 8. 3. Eccles. 10. 4.

9. *And the word of the Lord came to me.* The visions being closed, Zechariah marks the change by adopting the usual formula, with which the prophets authenticated, that they spake not of themselves, but by the Spirit of God. The act enjoined is a symbolic act, pointing and summing up and interpreting the visions, as some of the visions had been already expanded by fresh revelations following immediately upon them.

10. *Take of the captivity*, of that which they had brought with them [1]. *The captivity* was, in Jeremiah [2], and Ezekiel [3], the title of those who had been actually carried captive and were at that moment in captivity. Ezra continues it of those who had been in captivity, though now returned from exile. Yet not without a reference to the circumstances or causes of that captivity. It is *the captivity* [4] which Sheshbazzar brings from Babylon, or Ezra subsequently [5]; the *children of the captivity*, who set themselves to build the temple of God [6]; who dedicated it and kept the passover [7]. The title is used apparently as an aggravation of sin, like that which had been chastened by that captivity [8]. Here, the term seems to imply some blame, that they remained of their own accord in this state of severance from the altar, where alone special worship of God and sacrifice could be offered. They had been removed against their will; yet, as Christians often do, acquiesced in the loss, rather than forego their temporal advantages. Still they wished to take part in the work of restoring the public worship, and so sent these men, with their contribution of gold and silver, to their brethren, who had returned; as, in the first times of the Gospel, the Christians everywhere made collections for the poor saints, who dwelt in Jerusalem. And this their imperfect zeal was instantly accepted.

And go thyself, to make the act more impressive, *on that same day*, as matter of urgency, *and thou shalt come to the house of Josiah son of Zephaniah, whither they have come from Babylon* [9]. The exiles who had brought presents for the building of the temple, lodged, it seems, in the house of Josiah, whether they doubted or no that their presents would be accepted, since they chose Babylon, not Jerusalem for their abode. This acceptance of their gifts symbolized the incoming of those from afar. It is remarkable that all five names express a relation to God. *Tobiah*, "[10] The Lord is my good;" *Yedaiah*, "God knoweth" or "careth for;" *Josiah*, "The Lord supporteth [11];" *Zephaniah*, "The Lord hideth," and perhaps *Cheldai*, "The Lord's world [12]." They had taken religious instead of worldly names. Probably Zechariah was first to accept the offerings from the three exiles, and then to take the actual gold from the house of Josiah whither they had brought it. The pilgrims from Babylon and their host are included in one common blessing.

And make crowns; or *a crown* [13], as in Job, [14] *I would bind it as a crown unto me*, and our

[1] לקח מאת, as Ex. xxv. 2, xxx. 16, xxxv. 5, Lev. vii. 34.

[2] Jer. xxviii. 6, xxix. 1, 4, 20, 31. (גָּלוּת Ib. xxiv. 5, xxviii. 4, xxix. 22, xl. 1.)

[3] Ezek. i. 2, iii. 11, 15, xi. 24, 25.

[4] Ezr. i. 11.

[5] Ib. viii. 35.

[6] Ib. iv. 1.

[7] *the children of the captivity* Ib. vi. 16. Ch. 19, 20.

[8] הגולה Ib. ix. 4, x. 6, בני הגולה Ib. x. 7. 16, קהל הגולה Ib. 8.

[9] As in 1 Kgs xii. 2, אשר ברח *whither he had fled;* add Gen. xlv. 25, for the like accus. of place. Kim. renders, "who have come from Babylon" expressly including Josiah. Yet this too is an impossible construction.

[10] טוֹבִיָּהוּ. Tobias happens only to occur after the exile, in Ezr. ii. 60, Neh. vii. 62; 2) in Neh. ii. 10, vi. 1; 3) the Tobias here and 14; 4) Tobit and Tobias in his book.

[11] Josiah only occurs beside, as the name of the well-known king.

[12] חלדי. The name is preserved, though obelised, in the LXX. Ἐλδανὶ, Ελδαὶ; not from Aq. who has Ὀλδὰ. Jon. retains the name; the Syr. and S. Jer. Holdai, (the Syr. in v. 14. also.) The LXX only παρὰ τῶν ἀρχόντων.

[13] "great crown," Jon.; "a crown," Syr.

[14] עטרות Job xxxi. 36. The plural form is used only in these two places, and as, or in, the Proper Name of four towns; 1) עֲטָרוֹת a town of the Gadites, Nu. xxxii. 3, 34; 2) of Ephraim, Josh. xvi. 27, also עַטְרוֹת אַדָּר "crown of Addar," Ib. xvi. 5, xviii. 13; 3) of Judah עַטְרוֹת בֵּית יוֹאָב ("crown of the house of Joab") 1 Chr. ii. 54; and 4) and of Gad, עַטְרוֹת שׁוֹפָן, (mentioned with Ataroth) Nu. xxxii. 35. In all these it must needs be singular.

Before CHRIST cir. 519.

11 Then take silver and gold, and make [k] crowns, and set *them* upon the head of Joshua the son of Josedech the high priest;

[k] Ex. 28. 36. & 29. 6. Lev. 8. 9. ch. 3. 5.

Before CHRIST cir. 519.

Lord is seen in the Revelation, [1] *on His Head were many crowns.* The singular is used of [2] *a royal crown*, apparently of a festive crown [3]; and figuratively [4]; even of Almighty God Himself as a crown [5]; but no where of the mitre of the high-priest.

The characteristic of the act is, that *the crown* or crowns (it is not in the context said, which) were placed on the head of the one high priest, Joshua; *and thou shall place [it or them,* it is not said which] *upon the head of Joshua son of Josedech the high-priest, and shalt say unto him.* If crowns were made of each material, there were two crowns. But this is not said, and the silver might have formed a circlet in the crown of gold, as, in modern times, the iron crown of Lombardy, was called iron, because it had "[6] a plate of iron in its summit, being else of gold and most precious." In any case the symbolical act was completed by the placing of a royal crown upon the head of the high-priest. This, in itself, represented that He, Whom he and all other priests represented, would be also our King. It is all one then, whether the word designate one single crown, so entitled for its greatness, or one united royal crown, i. e., one crown uniting many crowns, symbolizing the many kingdoms of the earth, over which our High Priest and King should rule. Either symbol, of separate crowns [7], or an united crown [8], has been used in the same meaning, to symbolize as many empires, as there were crowns.

On Zerubbabel no crown was placed. It would have been confusing; a seeming restoration of the kingdom, when it was not to be restored; an encouragement of the temporal hopes, which were the bane of Israel. God had foretold, that none of the race of Jehoiakim should prosper, *sitting on the throne of David, or ruling any more in Israel.* Nehemiah rejects the imputation of Sanballat [9], *Thou hast also appointed prophets to preach of thee at Jerusalem,* There is *a king in Judah.* He answers, *There are no such things done as thou sayest; and thou feignest them out of thine own heart.* But Isaiah had foretold much of the king who should reign: Zechariah, by placing the royal crown on the head of Joshua, foreshewed that the kingdom was not to be of this world. The royal crown had been taken away in the time of Zedekiah, [10] *Thus saith the Lord God, Remove the diadem and take away the crown; this shall not be this; exalt the low and abase the high; an overthrow, overthrow, overthrow will I make* it; *this too is not; until he come whose the right is, and I will give it.*

But the Messiah, it was foretold, was to be both priest and king; [11] *a priest after the order of Melchizedec,* and *a king, set* by the Lord [12] *upon His holy hill of Zion.* The act of placing the crown on the head of Joshua the high-priest, pictured not only the union of the offices of priest and king in the person of Christ, but that He should be King, being first our High Priest. Joshua was already High Priest; being such, the kingly crown was added to him. It says in act, what S. Paul says, that [13] *Christ Jesus, being found in fashion as a man, humbled Himself and became*

[1] Rev. xix. 12. In Rev. xii. 3, the 7 crowns are for the 7 heads of the dragon. קִשֻּׁרִים is used of the one girdle, Jer. ii. 32.

[2] עטרת מלכם 2 Sam. xii. 30, 1 Chr. xx. 2; also of a king, Ps. xxi. 4, Cant. iii. 11, Jer. xiii. 18; perhaps Esther viii. 15, (coll. vi. 8.) possibly Ezek. xvi. 12, (coll. 13); fig., parallel with צנוף מלוכה Is. lxii. 3; comp. also צור מעטירה *Tyre the crowning* i. e., the kingmaker, in her colonies, Is. xxiii. 8.

[3] Is. xxviii. 1, 3, Lam. v. 16; of festive array, Ez. xxiii. 42

[4] Job xix. 9. [plur. Ib. xxxi. 36] Pr. iv. 9, xii. 4, xiv. 24, xvi. 31. xvii. 6.

[5] Is. xxviii. 5. is contrasted with "the crown of pride" Ib. 1, 3. [all]

[6] Ceremoniale Rom. L. 1. sect. 5. in Du Cange Glossar. v. Corona Ferrea.

[7] Ptolemy Philadelphus "set two crowns upon his head," the crown of Asia and of Egypt (1 Macc. xi. 13); Artabanus, "in whom the kingdom of Parthia ended," used two diadems (Herodian Hist. vi. 2. p. 119 Bekk.); "the Emperor of Germany received three crowns: first, silver (at Aix) for Germany; one of iron at Monza in the Milanese or Milan (for Lombardy); that of gold in divers places," (Alber. Index v. *Corona* in Du Cange v. Corona Imperialis) "the golden at Rome." Du Cang. Otto of Frisingen said that Frederic received 5 crowns; the first at Aix for the kingdom of the Franks; a second at Ratisbon for that of Germany; a third at Pavia for the kingdom of Lombardy; the fourth at Rome for the Roman empire from Adrian iv; the fifth of Monza for the kingdom of Italy." In our own memory, Napoleon I. having been crowned in France, was crowned with the iron crown at Monza.

[8] "The headdress of the king, on state occasions, was the crown of the upper or of the lower country, or the *pshent*, the union of the two. Every king, after the sovereignty of the Thebaid and lower Egypt had become once more vested in the same person, put on this double crown at his coronation, and we find in the grand representation given of this ceremony at Medeenet Haboo that the principal feature of the proclamation, on his ascension to the throne, was the announcement that Remeses had put on the crown of the upper and lower country.—When crowned, the king invariably put on the two crowns at the same time, though on other occasions he was permitted to wear each separately, whether in the temple, the city, or the field of battle." Wilkinson's Ancient Egypt, iii. 351-353.

[9] Neh. vi. 6-8. [10] Ezek. xxi. 31, 32 [26, 27, Eng.] [11] Ps. cx. 4. [12] Ib. ii. 6. [13] Phil. ii. 8, 9.

Before CHRIST cir. 519.

12 And speak unto him,
saying, Thus speaketh the
LORD of hosts, saying, Behold [l]the man whose name
is The [m]BRANCH; and
he shall ‖grow up out of
his place, [n]and he shall
build the temple of the
LORD:
13 Even he shall build

[l] See Luke 1. 73. John 1. 45.
[m] ch. 3. 8.

Before CHRIST cir. 519.

‖ Or, *branch up from under him.*
[n] ch. 4. 9. Matt. 16. 18. Eph. 2. 20, 21, 22. Heb. 3. 3.

---

obedient unto death, even the death of the Cross. Wherefore God also hath highly exalted Him.

12. The Prophet is taught to explain his own symbolic act. *Behold the Man whose name is the Branch*[1]. "Not for himself, but for Christ, Whose name Joshua bare, and Whose Priesthood and Princedom he represented," was the crown given him. The Prophet had already foretold the Messiah, under the name of the Branch. Here he adds,

And he shall grow up out of His place[2], lowly and of no seeming account, as God foretold by Jeremiah, [3]*I will cause the Branch of righteousness to grow up unto David;* and Jesus Himself said, [4]*Except a grain of wheat fall into the earth and die, it abideth alone; but if it die, it bringeth forth much fruit.* Alone He grew up before God, as a tender plant[5], unknown of man, known to God. It is that still, Divine life at Nazareth, of which we see only that one bright flash in the temple, the deep saying, ununderstood even by Joseph and Mary, and then, [6]*He went down with them and came to Nazareth and was subject unto them.*

And he shall build the temple of the Lord. The material temple was soon to be finished, and that by Zerubbabel, to whom this had been promised[7], not by Joshua. It was then a new temple, to be built from the foundation, of which He Himself was to be *the foundation*[8], as He said, [9]*On this rock I will build My Church;* and *in* Him [10]*all the building, fitly framed together, groweth unto an holy temple to the Lord.* "[11]He it is, Who built the house; for neither Solomon nor Zerubbabel nor Joshua son of Josedech could build a house worthy of the majesty of God. For [12]*the most High,* S. Stephen says, *dwelleth not in temples made with hands, as saith the prophet; Heaven is My throne and earth is My footstool; what house will ye build Me, saith the Lord?* For if they could have built a house for God, He would not have allowed His house to be burned and overthrown. What then is the house of God which Christ built? The Church, founded on faith in Him, dedicated by His Blood, stablished by the stayedness of Divine virtue, adorned with Divine and eternal riches, wherein the Lord ever dwelleth."

13. *Even He,* lit. *He Himself*[13]. The repetition shews that it is a great thing, which he affirms; *and He,* again emphatic, *He,* the same who shall build the temple of the Lord, *He shall bear the glory.* Great must be the

---

1 The consent of the ancient Jews in interpreting "the Branch" of the Messiah is very remarkable. "R. Berachiah (about A. D. 200, Wolf. Bibl. Hebr. ii. 870) said, that 'God, blessed for ever, saith to Israel, Ye say before Me, we are become orphans and have no father; the Redeemer too, Whom I am about to make to stand from you, He shall have no father, as is said, Behold the Man Whose name is the Branch, and he shall shoot [lit. from below him] from his place; and so saith Isaiah, And he grew up like a sucker before him.'" (Bereshith Rabba on Gen. xxxvi. 22. in Martini Pug. Fid. f. 594 quoted also by a Jewish convert, Joshua Hallorki, known among us as Hieron. de S. Fide, c. Jud. i. 5. Bibl. Max. Patr. xxvi. 536. His quotation is independent of Martini, since he adds the quotation from Ps. ii. "and elsewhere, 'The Lord said unto me, Thou art my Son,'") Jon. paraphrases, "Behold a Man, Whose name is Messiah, Who shall be revealed, and shall be multiplied," (ויתרבי, by which צמח is rendered Ps. lxxxv. 12.) "and *he* shall build the temple of the Lord, and *he* shall bear glory, and he shall sit and shall rule on his throne, and he shall be a great priest on his throne, and counsel of peace there shall be between them both." Rashi says, "He hints at the Messiah, and so paraphrases Jonathan, Behold a Man Whose name is Messiah, &c." (in Mart. p. 376. The printed edd. substitute "And some interpret it of king Messiah.") R. Nachman observes on the force of the word man, "Man (in Nu. i. 4.) is not said here but of the Messiah the Son of David, as is said, 'Behold the Man, Whose name is the Branch,' Jonathan paraphrases The Man Messiah, and so it is said, 'a man of sorrows and acquainted with grief.'" (Mart. p. 664). The Echa Rabati, f. 59, 2. and Jerus. Bereshith f. 5, 1. quote R. Joshua B. Levi (end of 2d cent., Wolf. B. H. ii. 842, coll. pp. 834, 841) as alleging this place in proof that "Branch is a name of the Messiah." Schöttgen [ad loc.]. Schöttgen quotes also the Pirke Elieser c. 38, "God will free Israel at the end of the 4th kingdom, saying, I have put forth a germ unto you, Behold my servant the Branch." Bammidbar R. sect. 18 f. 236, 1, Tanchuma f. 68, 3. "Behold the Man, whose name is the Branch. This is the Messiah, of Whom it is said (Jer. xxiii. 5.) And I will raise up unto David a righteous Branch." Midrash Mishle xix. 21 f. 57, 1. quotes, "R. Huna (3d cent.) said, The name of Messiah is Branch, as in, 'Behold a man.'" Ib. After all this Kimchi says, "*Some* interpret it of king Messiah."

2 מתחתיו as Ex. x. 23, "neither rose any from his place," מתחתיו.

3 Jer. xxxiii. 15. This is the natural construction, 1) צמח being the common word for the shooting of plants, (Gen. ii. 5, xli. 6, 23, Is. xliv. 4, Ez. xvii. 6,) the name of "the branch," having preceded, is the idiomatic subject to יצמח; 2) the impers. would have been plural, since the meaning would have been plural, *they* i. e. many, *shall grow up*, 3) it is unnatural to assume an impersonal, since a subject has been mentioned in the preceding clause to which it is united by ו; and 4) it is followed by a personal verb, with that same subject for its subject.

4 S. John xii. 24.

5 Is. liii. 2.

6 See S. Luke ii. 49–51.

7 iv. 10.

8 Is. xxviii. 16, 1 Cor. iii. 11, Eph. ii. 20, 21.

9 S. Matt. xvi. 18.

10 Eph. ii. 21.

11 Osor.

12 Acts vii. 48, 49.

13 הוא emph.

Before CHRIST cir. 519.

the temple of the LORD; and he [o]shall bear the glory, and shall sit and rule upon his throne; and [p]he shall be a priest upon his throne: and the counsel of peace shall be between them both.

o Isai. 22. 24.

p Ps. 110. 4. Heb. 3. 1.

Before CHRIST cir. 519.

---

glory, since it is affirmed of Him as of none beside, "*He* shall bear glory," "*He* should build the temple of the Lord," as none beside ever built it; *He* should *bear glory*, as none beside ever bare it, [1] *the glory as of the Only Begotten of the Father, full of grace and truth.* This word *glory* is almost always used of the special glory of God [2], and then, although seldom, of the Majesty of those, on whom God confers majesty as His representatives, as Moses, or Joshua [3], or *the glory of the kingdom* given to Solomon [4]. It is used also of Him, a likeness of Whom these vicegerents of God bare, in a Psalm whose language belongs (as Jews too have seen,) to One more than man [5], although also of glory given by God, either of grace or nature [6]. So in our Lord's great High Priest's prayer He says, [7] *Father, glorify Thou Me with Thine ownself with the glory which I had with Thee before the world was;* and prays, [8] *that they also whom Thou hast given Me, be with Me, where I am; that they may behold My glory which Thou hast given Me.* So S. Paul, applying the words of the eighth Psalm, says of our Lord, [9] *We see Jesus, Who was made a little lower than the angels, crowned with glory and honor;* and the angels and saints round the Throne say, [10] *Worthy is the Lamb which was slain to receive power and wisdom and strength and honor and glory and blessing,* and those on earth answer, *Blessing and honor and glory and power be unto Him that sitteth upon the Throne and unto the Lamb for ever and ever.* That glory Isaiah saw [11]; in His miracles He *manifested forth His glory* [12], which resided in Him; in His Transfiguration, the three Apostles *saw His glory* [13], shining out from within Him; *into* this *His glory* [14], He told the disciples at Emmaus, *the prophets* said, that He was *to enter*, having first suffered what He suffered; *in* this *His glory* He is to *sit*, when He judges [15]. *And He shall sit and rule on His Throne.* His rule shall be, not passing but abiding, not by human might, but in peaceful majesty, as God says, [16] *Yet have I set My king upon My holy hill of Zion,* and again, [17] *Sit Thou on My Right Hand, until I make Thine enemies Thy footstool;* and the angel said to Mary, [18] *The Lord God shall give unto Him the throne of His father David, and He shall reign over the house of Jacob for ever, and of His kingdom there shall be no end.*

And He shall be a priest upon His Throne. He shall be at once king and priest, as it is said, *Thou art a priest for ever after the order of Melchizedec.* When the Christ should reign, He should not cease to be our Priest. He, having *all power given to Him in heaven and earth,* reigneth over His Church and His elect by His grace, and over the world by His power, yet *ever liveth to make intercession for us.* "[19] Not dwelling now on what is chiefest, that [20] *by Him were all things created, that are in heaven and that are in earth, visible and invisible, whether they be thrones or dominions or principalities or powers; all things were created by Him and for Him, and He is before all things, and by Him all things consist,* how many crowns of glory belong to Him, One and the Same, God and man, Christ Jesus! *He* then *will bear glory and will sit upon His throne and shall be a priest on His throne.* How just this is, it is easier to think than to express, that *He should sit and rule all things, by Whom all things were made,* and He should be *a Priest for ever*, by Whose Blood all things are reconciled. *He shall rule* then *upon His throne*, and He *shall be a priest upon His throne*, which cannot be said of any of the saints, because it is the right of none of them, to call the throne of his rule or of his priesthood his own, but of this Only Lord and Priest, Whose majesty and throne are one and the same with the Majesty of God, as He saith, [21] *When the Son of Man shall come in His Majesty* [*Glory*], *then shall He sit upon the throne of His Majesty* [*Glory*]. And what meaneth that re-duplication, *and He shall rule on His Throne,* but that One and the Same, of Whom all this is said, should be and is King and Priest. He Who is King shall rule on His Throne, because kingdom and priesthood shall meet in One Person, and One shall occupy the double throne of kingdom and priesthood." He Alone should be our King; He Alone our Saviour: He

---

1 S. John i. 14.

2 הוד והדר Ps. xcvi. 6, (1 Chr. xvi. 27.) civ. 1, cxi. 3, Job xl. 10, of Christ, Ps. xlv. 4; הדר כבוד הדך Ps. cxlv. 5; הוד alone, Job xxxvii. 22, Is. xxx. 30, 1 Chr. xxix. 11, Ps. viii. 2, cxlviii. 13, Hab. iii. 3.

3 Nu. xxvii. 20.

4 1 Chr. xxix. 25.

5 Ps. xxi. 6. See in Schöttgen de Messia ad loc.

6 It is used of the inward glory given to regenerate Israel, Hos. xiv. 7. (6 Eng.); or as glorified by God, Zech. x. 3; of kingly glory, Jer. xxii. 18, Dan. xi. 21; of the inward glory of man, as such, Dan. x. 8, Pr. v. 9, or even of the horse, as the creation of God, Job xxxix. 20 [all].

7 S. John xvii. 5.

8 Ib. 24.

9 Heb. ii. 9.

10 Rev. v. 12, 13.

11 S. John xii. 41.

12 Ib. ii. 11.

13 S. Luke ix. 32.

14 Ib. xxiv. 26; add 1 S. Pet. i. 11, 12.

15 S. Matt. xix. 28, S. Luke ix. 26.

16 Ps. ii. 6.

17 Ib. cx. 1.

18 S. Luke i. 32, 33.

19 Rup.

20 Col. i. 16, 17.

21 S. Matt. xxv. 31.

Before CHRIST cir. 519.

14 And the crowns shall be to Helem, and to Tobijah, and to Jedaiah, and to Hen the son of Zephaniah, [q] for a memorial in the temple of the LORD.

q Ex. 12. 14. Mark 14. 9.

Alone the Object of our love, obedience and adoration.

And the counsel of peace shall be between them both. The counsel of peace is not merely *peace*, as S. Jerome seems to interpret: "He is both king and priest, and shall sit both on the royal and sacerdotal throne, and there shall be peaceful counsel between both, so that neither should the royal eminence depress the dignity of the priesthood, nor the dignity of the priesthood, the royal eminency, but both should be consistent in the glory of the One Lord Jesus." For had this been all, the simple idiom, *there shall be peace between them*, would have been used here, as elsewhere [1]. But *counsel of peace*, must, according to the like idioms [2], signify "a *counsel* devising or procuring *peace*" for some other than those who counsel thereon. We have the idiom itself, *counsellors of peace* [3].

They twain might be said of things [4]: but things are naturally not said to *counsel*, so that the meaning should be, that the thrones of the priests and of the Branch should counsel. For the throne is in each case merely subordinate. It is not as we might say, "the See of Rome," or "of Constantinople," or "of Canterbury," meaning the successive Bishops. It is simply the material throne, on which He sits. Nor is anything said of any throne of a priest, nor had a priest any throne. His office was *to stand before the Lord* [5], his intercessorial office to [6] *offer gifts and sacrifices for sin*. To [7] *offer up sacrifice, first for his own sins and then for the people's*, was his special office and honor. There are then not two thrones. One sits on His Throne, as King and Priest. It seems only to remain, that the *counsel of peace* should be between Jesus and the Father; as S. Jerome says, "I read in the book of some, that this, *there shall be a peaceful counsel between the two*, is referred to the Father and the Son, because He [8] *came to do not His own will, but the Will of the Father*, and [9] *the Father is in the Son, and the Son in the Father*." In Christ all is perfect harmony. There is a counsel of peace between Him and the Father Whose temple He builds. The Will of the Father and the Son is one. Both had one Will of love toward us, the salvation of the world, bringing forth peace through our redemption. God the Father [10] *so loved the world, that He gave His Only-Begotten Son, that whosoever believeth in Him should not perish but have everlasting life;* and God the Son [11] *is our peace, Who hath made both one, that He might reconcile both unto God in one body by the Cross, and came and preached peace to them which were afar off and to them that were nigh.* Others seem to me less naturally to interpret it of Christ in His two offices. "[12] There shall be the counsel of peace between them, the ruler and the priest, not that Christ is divided, but that those two princedoms, which were hitherto divided, (the priest and the king being different persons) should be united in the One Christ. *Between these two princedoms*, being inseparably joined in one, shall be the *counsel of peace*, because through that union we have peace; and through Him [13] *it pleased* the Father to *reconcile all things unto Himself, and that all things should be brought to peace through the Blood of His cross, whether things in earth or things in heaven*."

14. *And the crowns shall be to Helem.* There is no ground apparent to us, why the name *Helem* appears instead of *Holdai* [14], or *Hen* for *Josiah:* yet the same person must have been called both Hen *and* Josiah, since the father's name is the same in both places. They cannot both be intended as explanations of the former names, since *Helem* stands insulated in Hebrew, its meaning conjectural [15].

1 Jud. iv. 17, 1 Sam. vii. 14, 1 Kgs v. 16 (12 Eng.).

2 The verbal noun retaining the active force of the verb, as הַיּוֹעֲצִים עֲצַת רָע Ez. xi. 2. as in the verb יָעַצְתָּ בֹּשֶׁת לְבֵיתֶךָ Hab. ii. 10; הוּא זִמּוֹת יָעָץ, Is. xxxii. 7; נָדִיב נְדִיבוֹת יָעָץ, Ib. 8.

3 Pr. xii. 20.

4 שְׁנֵיהֶם is used of things, throughout Nu. vii. of the offerings of the princes of the 12 tribes; also Ex. xxvi. 24, xxxvi. 29, De. xxiii. 19, Pr. xx. 10, xxvii. 3, Eccl. xi. 6: but not with any verb implying action.

5 See ab p. 353, note 12.

6 Heb. v. 1, ix. 9.

7 Ib. vii. 27.

8 S. John v. 30, vi. 38.

9 Ib. xiv. 10.

10 Ib. iii. 16.

11 Eph. ii. 14, 16, 17.

12 Rup.

13 Col. i. 19, 20.

14 All MSS. and the Versions (except the Syr. which repeats here the names of v. 10) have or imply the names *Helem* and *Hen*. Aq. and Jon. have the names *Helem* here; Symm. translated it as *Holem*, τῷ ὁρῶντι ἐνύπνια. The LXX render the names common to both verses by the same words, (τῶν χρησίμων αὐτῆς, τῶν ἐπεγνωκότων αὐτὴν) but use different words for *Holdai* and *Helem*; for *Holdai* (v. 10) ἀρχόντων; for *Helem*, τοῖς ὑπομένουσι, as if יחילים. (The Prop. Name יחלאל is, in Gen. xlvi. 14, the third son of Zabulon, the patronymic יחלאלי, Nu. xxvi. 26, and the adj. יחיל Lam. iii. 26). The Jews in S. Jerome's time identified the three with Ananias Azarias and Misael, and *Hen*, "grace" with Daniel.

15 In Syr. the central meaning of חלד seems to be "crept," hence used of a "cancer" or a "mole." Neither חלדי nor חלם signify "strong." חלד is rather used of "the world" as "fleeting." חלד Arab. is perhaps originally "lingered," hence was "slow in becoming grey," "lingered," abode in a place ever, "everlastingly," *in heaven or hell.* It is

Before CHRIST cir. 519.

15 And [r] they *that are*
far off shall come and
build in the temple of the
LORD, and [s] ye shall know
that the LORD of hosts
hath sent me unto you.
And *this* shall come to
pass, if ye will diligently
obey the voice of the LORD
your God.

r Isai. 57. 19. & 60. 10. Eph. 2. 13, 19.
s ch. 2. 9. & 4. 9.

Perhaps then they were the own names of the individuals, and the names compounded with the name of *God,* honorable names which they had taken.

For a memorial in the temple of the Lord. They brought a passing gift, but it should be for a lasting memorial in their behalf. It is a renewal of the well-known term of the law[1]. The *two stones,* engraven with the names of the children of Israel, *upon the shoulders of the Ephod,* were to the end, that *Aaron* should *bear their names before the Lord upon his two shoulders for a memorial*[2]; *continually,* it is added of the *breastplate with its twelve precious stones*[3]; *the atonement money of the children of Israel* was to be *appointed for the service of the tabernacle of the congregation, that it may be a memorial for the children of Israel before the Lord, to make atonement for* their *souls*[4]; *to make an atonement for* their *souls before the Lord.* They were to *blow with the trumpets over* their *burnt-offerings, and over the sacrifice of* their *peace-offerings,* that *they may be to you for a memorial before your God*[5]. When Midian had been smitten before Israel, and not one of Israel had been slain, they brought all the gold which had accrued to them, and *Moses and Eleazar took the gold, and brought it into the tabernacle, a memorial for the children of Israel before the Lord*[6]. So the angel said to Cornelius, [7] *thy prayers and thy alms are come up for a memorial before God.* "[8] This is what we look for, that to all the saints and friends of God, whom these signify, those crowns which they made of their gold and silver for the Lord Jesus, shall be an everlasting memorial in that heavenly temple of the Lord." The tradition of the Jews, that this was literally observed[9], can hardly be without foundation. "[10] These their offerings shall be for grace to those who dedicated them and an occasion of doxology. For the piety of princes becomes to the rest a path to the love of God. But when Christ is crowned by us, then shall also the multitude of the Gentiles haste to the knowledge of Him."

And they who are far off shall come. They who came from Babylon with offerings to God, became types of the Gentiles, of whom the Apostle says, [11] *Now in Christ Jesus ye who sometimes were far off have become nigh through the blood of Christ;* and, [12] *He came and preached peace to you which were far off and to them that were nigh;* and [13] *the promise is to you and to your children, and to all that are far off, as many as the Lord our God shall call.*

And build in, or *upon, the temple of the Lord*[14], not "build it" for it was to be built by *the Branch,* but *build on,* labor on, it. It was a building, which should continually be enlarged; of which S. Paul says, [15] *I, as a wise master-builder, according to the grace given unto me, laid the foundation, and another buildeth thereon; let every man take heed how he buildeth thereupon.* "[16] What shall they build? Themselves, compacting themselves with the saints, and joining together in faith to oneness with those of Israel, Jesus Christ Himself being the head corner-stone and uniting together in harmony through Himself, what was of old divided. For He united [17] *the two peoples into one new man, making peace, and reconciling in His own Body all things unto the Father,* which being accomplished, we shall own the truth of the holy prophets, and know clearly that it was God Who spake in them and declared to us beforehand the mystery of Christ."

15. *And* this *shall be;* not as though the coming of Christ depended upon their faithfulness, but their share in it. *Ye shall know* (he had said) *that the Lord of hosts hath sent me unto you;* but whether this knowledge should reach to individuals, depends upon their obedience and their willingness to know; *it shall be,* [18] *if ye will diligently obey the voice of the Lord your God.* For *none of the wicked,* Daniel says[19], *shall understand;* and Hosea, [20] *Who is wise, and he shall understand these things? prudent, and he shall know them? For the ways of the Lord are right, and the just shall walk in them and the transgressors shall*

not used of strength. חלם is used of "good condition" of an animal, Job xxxix. 4; (as in Arab.); in Hif. is "restored one to health" (Is. xxxviii. 16), as Syr. in Ethp. In Syr. חלים is used of *recovered* health, S. Mark v. 34, S. John v. 11, Acts iv. 10; as opposed to sickness, S. Mark ii. 17; or sound *healthy* words, S. John vi. 3, 2 Tim. i. 11. In Arab. חלם conj. i. is "dreamt" ii. "was kind, forbearing," v. "became fat" (of animals). Other senses are derived from dreaming.

1 זִכָּרוֹן. 2 Ex. xxviii. 12, 22, xxxix. 7.

3 Ib. xxviii. 29. 4 Ib. xxx. 16. 5 Nu. x. 10.
6 Ib. xxxi. 50, 54. 7 Acts x. 4, 31. 8 Rup.
9 "The crowns were hung in windows in the height of the temple," as we learn from the tract Middot. a. f. 36. Rashi ad loc.
10 S. Cyr.
11 Eph. ii. 13. 12 Ib. 17. 13 Acts ii. 39.
14 בנה ב. Neh. iv. 4, 11 [10, 17 Eng.]
15 1 Cor. iii. 10. 16 S. Cyr.
17 Eph. ii. 15, 16.
18 So Marck. 19 Dan. xii. 10.
20 Hosea xiv. 9. [10 Heb.] see vol. i. p. 141.

Before CHRIST cir. 518.

CHAPTER VII.

1 *The captives enquire of fasting.* 4 *Zechariah reproveth their fasting.* 8 *Sin the cause of their captivity.*

518. AND it came to pass in
the fourth year of king
Darius, *that* the word of
the LORD came unto Zech-
ariah in the fourth *day* of
the ninth month, *even* in
Chisleu;
2 When they had sent
unto the house of God
Sherezer and Regem-me-
lech, and their men, † to
pray before the LORD,

† Heb. *to intreat the face of the* LORD; 1 Sam. 13. 12. ch. 8. 21.

stumble at them; and the wise man, [1] *he that keepeth the law of the Lord getteth the understanding thereof.* So our Lord said, [2] *If any man will do His will, he shall know of the doctrine, whether it be of God or whether I speak of Myself;* [3] *He that is of God heareth God's words: ye therefore hear them not because ye are not of God:* [4] *Every one that is of the truth heareth My voice.* "[5] Because he had said, *And ye shall know that the Lord hath sent me unto you,* he warns them, that the fruit of that coming will reach to those only, who should hear God and with ardent mind join themselves to His name. *For as many as believed in Him were made sons of God;* but the rest *were cast into outer darkness.* But *they* receive Christ, who hear His voice and do not refuse His rule. For He *was made the cause of eternal salvation to all who obey Him.*"

VII. 1. *In the fourth year of Darius.* Two years after the series of visions, shewn to him, and two years before the completion of the temple. Chisleu being December, it was the end of B. C. 518.

2. *When they had sent unto the house of God.* Rather, *And Bethel sent;* i. e. the inhabitants of Bethel sent. *The house of God* is nowhere in Holy Scripture called Bethel. Bethel is always the name of the place[6]. The *house of God* is designated by historians, Psalmists, prophets, by the name, *Beth-elohim,* more commonly *Beth-Ha-elohim, the God;* or *of the Lord,* YHVH[7]. Zechariah and Haggai use these names. It is not likely that the name, Beth-el, should have first been given to the house of God, when it had been desecrated by the idolatries of Jeroboam. Bethel also is, in the Hebrew order of the words, naturally the subject[8]. Nor is there any reason why they should have sent to Bethel, since they sought an answer from God. For it would be forced to say that they sent to Bethel, in order that those at Bethel should send to Jerusalem; which is not said. It were unnatural also that the name of the sender should not have been mentioned, when the names of persons inferior, because sent, are recorded[9]. Bethel, in Nehemiah's time[10], was one of the chief places of Benjamin. *Two hundred twenty and three* of *the men of Bethel and Ai*[11] had returned with Zerubbabel. The answer being to *the people of the land,* such were doubtless the enquirers, not those still in Babylon. The answer shews that the question was not religious, though put as matter of religion. It is remarkable that, whereas in the case of those who brought presents from Babylon, the names express some relation to God, these names are singularly, the one of a parricide son of

1 Ecclus. xxi. 11.
2 S. John vii. 17.
3 Ib. viii. 47.
4 Ib. xviii. 37.
5 Osor.
6 The LXX, Jon., Syr. render in the accusative, *to Bethel.* The Vulg. alone has "ad domum Dei."
7 Although בית is used alike of the "tent" and the "house," it is used but little of the "house of God" before Solomon's temple; בית יי Ex. xxiii. 19, xxxiv. 26, Deut. xxiii. 18, Jos. vi. 24, Jud. xix. 18, 1 Sam. i. 7, 24, iii. 15, 2 Sam. xii. 20; בית האלהים Jud. xviii. 31. Subsequently בית יי occurs in the books of Kings, 73 times; in the Chronicles, 92; in the Psalms, 7; in Isaiah, 6; in Jeremiah, 32; in Lam., 1; Ezek. 6; Hosea, 2; Joel, 3; Micah, 1; Haggai, 2; Zechariah, 5; Ezra, 7; in all 246; בית אלהים occurs Gen. xxviii. 17, 22; in two of David's Psalms (Ps. lii. 10, lv. 15,); once in the Chronicles, 2 Chron. xxxiv. 9; in all 5; and בית האלהים in Eccl. iv. 17; in Chronicles, 33 times (intermingled with בית יי); Daniel i. 2; Ezra, 7 times; Nehemiah, 8 times; in all 50.
8 So Ibn Ezra, although regarding Bethel as the name of a man, who sent the others. Rashi and S. Jerome's Hebrew instructors made Shareser and Regemmelech the senders. Rashi says that they sent to their kinsmen in Bethel, that these should come to *entreat the face of God* at Jerusalem. S. Jerome's teachers said more naturally, that "Shareser and Regemmelech sent to the house of God;" only "Bethel" is not so used, and the theory that they were "Persian officers of Darius fearing God," is inconsistent with the question as to a Jewish political fast of long standing. The interposition of the place whither they were sent, between the verb and the subject, without any mark that it is not the subject, would be unnatural. The E. V. follows Kimchi, taking וישלח as impersonal. But here it is a formal message from some definite person or persons. In Gen. xlviii. 1, ויאמר ליעקב is altogether like our "one told Jacob." In Esth. ix. 30, the subject is probably Mordecai, mentioned v. 29.
9 Abarbanel notices this difficulty.
10 Neh. xi. 31.
11 Ezr. ii. 28.

Before CHRIST cir. 518.

3 *And* to [a]speak unto
the priests which *were* in
the house of the LORD of
hosts, and to the prophets,
saying, Should I weep in
[b]the fifth month, separating myself, as I have done
these so many years?

[a] Deut. 17. 9, 10, 11. & 33. 10. Mal. 2. 7.
[b] Jer. 52. 12. ch. 8. 19.

4 ¶ Then came the word
of the LORD of hosts unto
me, saying,
5 Speak unto all the
people of the land, and to
the priests, saying, When
ye [c]fasted and mourned in
the fifth [d]and seventh

Before CHRIST cir. 518.

[c] Isai. 58. 5.
[d] Jer. 41. 1. ch. 8. 19.

Sennacherib[1], and of one, chief among the King of Babylon's princes[2]; the other probably a secular name, "the king's friend[3]."

"[4]I do not see why under the name of Bethel, the city so called is not understood. For since Jerusalem was not yet fortified, the Jews chose them sites in various places, where they should be less harassed. All hatred was concentrated on that city, which the neighbors wished not to be restored to its former greatness. Other cities they did not so molest. Bethel then, i. e. the assembly of the city, sent messengers to Jerusalem to offer sacrifices to God and consult the wise there."

To entreat the face of the Lord. They wished, it seems, (so to speak) to ingratiate themselves with God with an account of their past self-humiliation, on the day when the house of God was burned by Nebuchadnezzar. In regard to God, the word is always used of entreating Him by earnest prayer[5].

3. *Should I weep in the fifth month, separating myself? In the fifth month*, from the seventh to the tenth day, Jerusalem was in flames, fired by Nebuchadnezzar. [6] *He burnt the house of the Lord, and the king's house, and all the houses of Jerusalem and every great man's house he burnt with fire.*

"[7] Now since it is said that the temple is builded and we see that no cause of sorrow remaineth, answer, we pray, are we to do this or to change our sorrow into joy?"

Separating myself. This seems to be added, to intensify the fast which they had kept. The Nazarite was bound to [8] *separate himself from wine and strong drink*, and so, they severed themselves to the Lord, and consecrated themselves to Him[9]. These had severed themselves from food, from things pleasant, from pleasure, from sin, it may be, for the day, but not abidingly: they had not given themselves to God.

As I have done these so many years, lit. *how many*[10]. As if, although they knew that they were seventy years, they could not count them.

5. *Speak unto all the people of the land.* They of Bethel had spoken as one man, as Edom said to Israel, [11] *Thou shalt not pass by me;* and [12] *the men of Israel said to the Hivite; Perhaps thou dwellest in the midst of me, and how shall I make a league with thee?* God gives the answer not to them only, but to all like-minded with them, *all the people of the land*, the whole population (in our language); as Jeremiah says, [13] *ye and your fathers, your kings and your princes and all the people of the land*, and, [14] *the scribe who mustered the people of the land.*

When ye fasted and that, mourning. It was no mere abstinence from food (severe as the Jewish fasts were, one unbroken abstinence from evening to evening) but with real mourning, the word being used only of mourning for the dead[15], or, in a few instances[16], for a very great public calamity; probably with beating on the breast.

1 Is. xxxvii. 38, 2 Kgs xix. 37.

2 Nergal-Shar-ezer, "Nergal preserve the prince," Jer. xxxix. 3, 13. νεριγλισσάρ. The omission of the name of the idol left it less openly idolatrous, but retained the prayer originally idolatrous.

3 רֶגֶם occurs as a proper name, 1 Chr. ii. 47. The Kamoos and Fasee say that the Arab. רַגְמ is "friend," [see Lane] and, though this meaning is wholly insulated from the rest of the root, their authority is, of course, decisive.

4 Osor.

5 The explanation of the idiom, *stroked the face of*, in regard to which critics have so descanted about anthropomorphisms, is altogether imaginary. The phrase occurs, in all, 13 times in regard to God; three of these are in Zechariah, here, and viii. 21, 22; and beside Ex. xxxii. 11, 1 Sam. xiii. 12, 1 Kgs xiii. 6, (bis) 2 Kgs xiii. 4, Jer. xxvi. 19, Dan. ix. 13, Ps. cxix. 58, 2 Chr. xxxiii. 12, Mal. i. 9, and all the simplest prose. Of man it occurs only 3 times Ps. xlv. 13, Pr. xix. 6, Job xi. 19. In no dialect is there any trace of the meaning *lævis* or *palpo*. The Arab חַלַאַ is, any how, used of hard friction, as to bruising collyrium, rubbing off hair from skin [tanning], striking with sword, &c. חַלַא (ult. ו) is, "sweet;" חַלַי is "adorned with jewels."

6 2 Kgs xxv. 9, Jer. lii. 13. Jeremiah mentions *the tenth day;* the book of Kings, *the seventh.*

7 S. Jer.

8 Nu. vi. 3.

9 Ib. 5. See on Am. ii. 11. vol. i. p. 265.

10 כַמָה is used in exclamation, not interrogatively, here, Ps. lxxviii. 40, Job xxi. 17.

11 Nu. xx. 18.

12 Josh. ix. 7.

13 Jer. xliv. 21.

14 Ib. lii. 25.

15 Gen. xxiii. 2, l. 10, 1 Sam. xxv. 1, xxviii. 3, 2 Sam. i. 12, iii. 31, xi. 26, 1 Kgs. xiii. 29, 30, xiv. 13, 18, Eccl. xii. 5, Jer. xvi. 4, 5, 6, xxii. 18, [bis], xxv. 33, xxxiv. 5, Ezek. xxiv. 16, 23, Zech. xii. 10, 12.

16 Is. xxxii. 12, Jo. i. 13, Mic. i. 8, Jer. iv. 8, xlix. 3. In Eccl. iii. 4, it is "mourning" as opposed to רקד,

Before CHRIST cir. 518.

month [e] even those seventy
years, did ye at all fast
[f] unto me, *even* to me?
6 And when ye did eat,
and when ye did drink,
‖ did not ye eat *for yourselves*, and drink *for yourselves?*
7 ‖ *Should ye* not *hear*
the words which the LORD
hath cried † by the former
prophets, when Jerusalem
was inhabited and in prosperity, and the cities thereof round about her, when
men inhabited [g] the south
and the plain?
8 ¶ And the word of
the LORD came unto Zech-
ariah, saying,

e ch. 1. 12.
f See Rom. 14. 6.
‖ Or, be *not ye they that &c.*
‖ Or, Are *not* these *the words.*
† Heb. *by the hand of, &c.*
g Jer. 17. 26.

In the seventh month. The murder of Gedaliah, *whom the king of Babylon made governor of the land*, completed the calamities of Jerusalem, in the voluntary, but prohibited exile to Egypt, for fear lest the murder should be avenged on them[1].

Did ye at all fast unto Me, Me[2]? God emphatically rejects such fasting as their's had been, as something, unutterably alien from Him, *to Me, Me*[3]! Yet the fasting and mourning had been real, but irreligious, like remorse for ill-deeds, which has self only for its ground. He prepares the way for His answer by correcting the error of the question. "[4] Ye fasted to yourselves, not to Me. For ye mourned your sorrows, not your misdeeds; and your public fast was undertaken, not for My glory, but out of feeling for your own grief. But nothing can be pleasing to God, which is not referred to His glory. But those things alone can be referred to His glory, which are done with righteousness and devotion."

6. *And when ye eat and when ye drink, is it not ye who eat and ye who drink?* Conversely now that, after your return, ye feast for joy, this is no religious act; ye have all the good of it, there is no thanksgiving to God. Contrary to the Apostle's saying, [5] *Whether ye eat or drink, or whatever ye do, do all to the glory of God.* "[6] He eateth and drinketh to himself, who receiveth the nourishments of the body, which are the common gifts of the Creator, without the needy. And any one fasts to himself, if he doth not give to the poor what for the time he withdraweth from himself, but keepeth it to be thereafter offered to his appetite. Hence it is said by Joel, *sanctify a fast.* For to 'sanctify a fast' is to shew an abstinence worthy of God through other good deeds. Let anger cease, quarrels be hushed. For in vain is the flesh worn, if the mind is not refrained from evil pleasures, since the Lord says by the Prophet, [7] *Behold, in the day of your fast ye find pleasure. Behold, ye fast for strife and debate &c.*

7. Should ye *not* hear *the words*, or, Know ye *not the words?* The verb is presupposed in the emphatic question, as in, [8] *Shall I, the blood of these men?* David omits the word "drink" for abhorrence.

By the former prophets Isaiah and Jeremiah[9], *when Jerusalem was dwelling abidingly*[10], *at ease*, as the whole world then was, except herself, *and the south and the low-country*, both belonging to Judah, *were inhabited.* The restoration then was still very incomplete, since he contrasts their *then* condition with the present, as inhabited or no. *The mountain, the south, and the low country*, known still by its name of Sephēla to Greeks[11], made up the territory of Judah[12].

8. Instead of quoting the former prophets, Zechariah gives the substance of their exhortations, as renewed to himself.

"bounding" for joy [all]. The noun מספד is in like way used of "mourning" for the dead, Gen. l. 10, Jer. vi. 26, Nu. v. 16, Zech. xii. 10, 11, 12; for the destruction of a people or place, Jer. xlviii. 38, Ez. xxvii. 34, Mi. i. 8, 11; for imminent destruction, Am. v. 17, Esth. iv. 3: or great public calamity, Jo. ii. 12, Is. xvii. 12. In Ps. xxx. 12, it stands contrasted with a great outward expression of joy, dancing, מחול. [all.]

[1] Jer. xli.–xliii.

[2] צמתני. The affix is almost a dative, as in Is. xliv. 21, lxv. 5, Job xxxi. 18; and Ch. Dan. v. 6. שנוהי, for which, שנין עלוהו, occurs ver. 9.

[3] The pronoun repeated after the affix, as in בי אני 1 Sam. xxv. 24; פגריכם אתם Nu. xiv. 32, and with גם, ברכני גם אני Gen. xxvii. 38; 2 Sam. xvii. 5, 1 Kgs xxi. 19, Pr. xxiii. 15, Jer. xxv. 14, xxvii. 7.

[4] Osor. [5] 1 Cor. x. 31.

[6] S. Greg. in Evang. Hom. 16, n. 6. Opp. 1495.

[7] Is. lvii. 3, 4.

[8] 2 Sam. xxiii. 17.

[9] Is. lviii. 4, Jer. xiv. 12. Since Isaiah's is the chief passage and Jeremiah's scarcely more than allusive, Zechariah, just after the captivity, knew that the prophecy Is. lviii. was Isaiah's, not by a prophet after the captivity.

[10] בהיות–ישבת ושלוה as ab. i. 11, ישבת ושקטת; "the *state* of ease is conveyed by the היה with the act. partic.

[11] 1 Macc. xii. 38. "It is still called Sephēla." Eus. Onom.

[12] Josh. x. 40, Jud. i. 9, Jer. xvii. 26, xxxii. 44, xxxiii. 13.

Before CHRIST cir. 518.

9 Thus speaketh the
LORD of hosts, saying,
[h] † Execute true judgment,
and shew mercy and com-
passions every man to his
brother:
10 And [i] oppress not the
widow, nor the fatherless,
the stranger, nor the poor;
[k] and let none of you imagine evil against his
brother in your heart.

[h] Is. 58. 6, 7. Jer. 7. 23. Mic. 6. 8. ch. 8. 16. Matt. 23. 23.
† Heb. *Judge judgment of truth.*
[i] Ex. 22. 21, 22. Deut. 24. 17. Isai. 1. 17. Jer. 5. 28.
[k] Ps. 36. 4. Mic. 2. 1. ch. 8. 17.

11 But they refused to
hearken, and [l] † pulled
away the shoulder, and
† [m] stopped their ears, that
they should not hear.
12 Yea they made their
[n] hearts *as* an adamant
stone, [o] lest they should
hear the law, and the
words which the LORD of
hosts hath sent in his spirit
† by the former prophets:

Before CHRIST cir. 518.

[l] Neh. 9. 29. Jer. 7. 24. Hos. 4. 16.
† Heb. *they gave a backsliding shoulder.*
† Heb. *made heavy.*
[m] Acts 7. 57.
[n] Ezek. 11. 19. & 36. 26.
[o] Neh. 9. 29, 30.
† Heb. *by the hand of.*

9. *Thus spake the Lord,* i. e. through the former prophets, for he goes on to speak of their rejection in the past. *Execute true judgment.* He retains the words of Ezekiel[1]. The injunction itself runs throughout the prophets[2]. *Shew mercy,* i. e. tender love, to all; *compassion,* to the unhappy. Omit no act of love, God so loves the loving. "[3] Like S. Paul to the Romans[4], he names only the duties to the neighbor, but understands what relates to God. For the love of our neighbor presupposes the love of God, from which it springs." "[5] After strictness of justice, let mercy to all follow, and specially to brethren, of the same blood and of one faith. Brother and neighbor we ought to account the whole human race, since we are all born of one parent, or those who are of the household of faith, according to the parable of the Gospel[6], which willeth us to understand by neighbor, nor our kin, but all men."

10. *And oppress not.* He had commanded positive acts of love; he now forbids every sort of unlove. *He that oppresseth the poor,* Solomon had said[7], *reproacheth his Maker. The widow, the orphan, the stranger, the afflicted,* are, throughout the law, the special objects of God's care. This was the condition which God made by Jeremiah[8]; *If ye thoroughly amend your ways and your doings, if ye thoroughly execute judgment between a man and his neighbor; if ye oppress not the stranger the fatherless and the widow, and shed not innocent blood in this place, neither walk after other gods to your hurt, then will I cause you to dwell in this place.* It was on the breach of the covenant to set their brethren free in the year of release, that God said; [9] *I proclaim a liberty for you to the sword, to the pestilence and to the famine, and I will make you to be removed into all the kingdoms of the earth.*

And let none of you imagine, i. e. *devise*[10], as, by Micah, God retorted the evil upon them. They [11] *devised evil on their beds; therefore, behold, against this family do I devise an evil, from which ye shall not remove your necks.*

11. *But they gave a backsliding shoulder,* like a restive animal, which would not endure the yoke, dull and stupid as the beasts: as Hosea says, [12] *Israel slideth back like a backsliding heifer.* Nehemiah confesses the same; [13] *they gave a backsliding shoulder and hardened their neck and would not hear.*

And made heavy their ears, fulfilling in themselves what God foretold to Isaiah would be the result of his preaching, *make their ears heavy*[14]. The heart, which will not hearken, becomes duller by the outward hearing, as S. Paul says, [15] *The earth which drinketh in the rain that cometh oft upon it, and bringeth forth herbs meet for them by whom it is dressed, receiveth blessing from God; but that which beareth thorns and briars is rejected.*

12. *Harder than adamant.* The stone, whatever it be, was hard enough to cut ineffaceable characters[16]: it was harder than flint[17]. It would cut rocks; it could not be graven itself, or receive the characters of God.

This is the last sin, obduracy, persevering impenitence, which [18] *resisted the Holy Ghost,* and [19] *did despite to the Spirit of grace.* Not through infirmity, but of set purpose, they hardened themselves, lest [20] *they should convert and be healed.* They feared to trust them-

[1] מִשְׁפַּט אמת occurs beside in Ezek. xviii. 8, only. In Deut. xvi. 18, occurs משפט צדק.

[2] As Is. i. 17, 23, lviii. 6, 7, Jer. vii. 5, Ezek. xviii. 8. Hos. xii. 6 &c.

[3] Lap. [4] Rom. xiii. 9. [5] S. Jer.

[6] S. Luke x. 30 sqq. [7] Prov. xxiv. 31.

[8] Jer. vii. 5–7. [9] Ib. xxxiv. 17. [10] השב.

[11] Mic. ii. 1, 3. [12] Hos. iv. 16. [13] Neh. ix. 29.

[14] The same words; ואזניו הכבד Is. vi. 5, ואזניהם הכבידו Zech.

[15] Heb. vi. 7, 8.

[16] Jer. xvii. 1. "The sin of Judah is written with a pen of iron, with the point of a (שָׁמִיר) diamond." E. V.

[17] Ezek. iii. 9, "As an adamant harder than flint."

[18] Acts vii. 51. [19] Heb. x. 29. [20] Is. vi. 10.

Before CHRIST cir. 518.

[p] therefore came a great
wrath from the LORD of
hosts.

13 Therefore it is come
to pass, *that* as he cried,
and they would not hear;
so [q] they cried, and I would
not hear, saith the LORD
of hosts:

p 2 Chr. 36. 16. Dan. 9. 11.

q Prov. 1. 24—28. Isa. 1. 15. Jer. 11. 11. & 14. 12. Mic. 3. 4.

14 But [r] I scattered them
with a whirlwind among
all the nations [s] whom they
knew not. Thus [t] the land
was desolate after them,
that no man passed through
nor returned: for they laid
[u] the † pleasant land desolate.

Before CHRIST cir. 518.

r Deut. 4. 27. & 28. 64. Ezek. 36. 19. ch. 2. 6.
s Deut. 28. 33.
t Lev. 26. 22.
u Dan. 8. 9.
† Heb. *land of desire.*

selves to God's word, lest He should convert them by it.

Lest they should hear the law and the words which the Lord God sent by His Spirit by the hand of the former prophets. The Holy Ghost was the chief agent; *by His Spirit;* the inspired prophets were His instruments; *by the hand of.* Nehemiah confesses the same to God: [1] *Thou didst protest to them by Thy Spirit by the hand of Thy prophets.* Moses was one of the greatest prophets. The law then may be included, either as delivered by Moses, or as being continually enforced by all the prophets. Observe the gradations. 1) The words of God are not heard. 2) The restive shoulder is shewn; men turn away, when God, by the inner motions of His Spirit or by lesser chastisements, would bring them to the yoke of obedience. "[2] They would not bear the burden of the law, whereas they willingly bore that most heavy weight of their sins." 3) Obduracy. "[2] Their adamantine heart could be softened neither by promises nor threats." Therefore nothing remained but the *great wrath*, which they had *treasured to themselves against the day of wrath.* And so Zechariah returns to that, wherewith his message and visions of future mercy began, the *great wrath* which fell upon their fathers [3].

"[2] 'I sought not,' He says, 'for your tears; I enjoined not bitterness of sorrow; but what, had they been done, the calamity, for which those tears were meet, had never befallen you. What was it which I admonished you formerly by the former prophets to recall you from sin? What I bid you by Zechariah now. This I preach, admonish, testify, inculcate upon you.'"

13. *And it came to pass*, i. e. this which God had said, *As He cried and they heard not, so shall they cry and I will not hear, saith the Lord of hosts.* God had often said this. "It shall be too late to cry for mercy, when it is the time of justice." So Wisdom had said by Solomon; [4] *then*, i. e. *when distress and anguish cometh upon them, they shall call upon Me, but I will not answer; they shall seek Me early, and they shall not find Me.* So by Isaiah, [5] *When ye spread forth your hands, I will hide Mine eyes from you; yea, when ye make many prayers, I will not hear; your hands are full of bloods.* So by Hosea [6], by Micah [7], by Jeremiah [8]. It was one message which was verified in every day of chastisement, "there will be a 'too late;'" not a final "too late," until the end of ends comes, but a "too late" for them, a "too late" to avert that particular judgment of God, whereby the sinner's earthly trial and future were changed permanently [9].

14. *But I scattered them*, rather, *And I will scatter them* [10]. The saying continues what God had said that He had said, and which had come to pass. *Among all nations whom they knew not.* So God had repeatedly said by Jeremiah, [11] *I will cast you out of this land into a land that ye know not, ye nor your fathers; where I will not shew you favor.* This was the aggravation of the original woe in the law: [12] *The Lord shall bring a nation against thee from far, from the end of the earth, a nation whose tongue thou shalt not understand, a nation of fierce countenance.* There was no mitigation of suffering, when the common bond between man and man, mutual speech, was wanting.

That no man passed through nor returned, lit. *from passer through and from returner;* as in the prophecy of Alexander's march and return, [13] *because of him that passeth by and of him that returneth;* and of Seir God saith, [14] *I will cut off from him, passer-through and returner* [15]. As we say, there shall be no traffic more through her.

[1] Neh. ix. 30. [2] Osor.
[3] i. 7. קֶצֶף; here קֶצֶף גדול. [4] Prov. i. 27, 28.
[5] Is. i. 15. [6] Hos. v. 6. see vol. i. pp. 58, 59.
[7] iii. 4. see ab. pp. 40, 41. [8] Jer. xi. 14, xiv. 12.
[9] See Pusey's Parochial Sermons, Vol. I. Serm. 12. "Irreversible chastisements."
[10] The form וְאֵסָעֲרֵם for וָאֵ־, is remarkable chiefly, if the punctuation comes, (as is assumed) from Zechariah's time, for the care with which the vowel pronunciation has been preserved. It has no exact parallel. The conjugation recurs with the שׂ, Job xxvii. 21. See Introd. to Zech. p. 327. n. c.
[11] Jer. xvi. 13; add xv. 14, xvii. 4.
[12] Deut. xxviii. 49, 50. [13] ix. 8.
[14] Ezek. xxxv. 7.
[15] The form implies that the same did, or did not, pass and return, whence he came. Ezek. xxxii. 27.

Before CHRIST cir. 518.

CHAPTER VIII.

1 *The restoration of Jerusalem.* 9 *They are encouraged to the building by God's favor to them.* 16 *Good works are required of them.* 18 *Joy and enlargement are promised.*

AGAIN the word of the LORD of hosts came *to me*, saying,

2 Thus saith the LORD
of hosts; [a] I was jealous
for Zion with great jealousy, and I was jealous for
her with great fury.
3 Thus saith the LORD;
[b] I am returned unto Zion,
and [c] will dwell in the

Before CHRIST cir. 518.

[a] Nah. 1. 21. ch. 1. 14.

[b] ch. 1. 16.

[c] ch. 2. 10.

And they made the pleasant land[1] *desolate.* They were the doers of what they by their sins caused, by bringing down the judgments of God. Heretofore the land which God had given them, had been in our language "the envy" of all who knew it now they had made it into a desolation, one wide waste[2].

"[3] What is said in the beginning of the chapter against Jews who abstained indiscreetly, applies mystically to all, not inward, but rude Christians, who not being diligent enough but rather negligent about acts of piety and inward prayer and reformation of the powers of the soul, account highly of bodily exercises and outward observances, and use no slight scrupulosity as to things of less moment, and do not attend to the chief things, charity, humility, patience meekness. On these it must be inculcated, that if they wish their fasts and other outward exercises to please God, they must judge true judgment, and be compassionate, kind, liberal to their neighbors, keep their mind ever steadfast in God, cast away wholly all hardness of heart, and be soft and open to receive within them the word of God. Otherwise *their land will be desolate,* i. e. deprived of the indwelling of the Holy Spirit, and they scattered amid various vices." "[4] That which was formerly *a pleasant land,* and the hospice of the Trinity, is turned into a desert and dwelling-place of dragons."

VIII. "[3] After the Lord had, in the preceding chapter, manifoldly rebuked the Jewish people, He now comforts it with renewed promises, as a good physician, who after a bitter draught employs sweet and soothing remedies; as that most loving Samaritan poured in wine and oil." The chapter falls into two portions, each marked by the words, *The Word of the Lord of hosts came*[5], or *came unto me,* the first [6] declaring the reversal of the former judgments, and the complete, though conditional, restoration of God's favor; the 2d [7] containing the answer to the original question as to those fasts, in the declaration of the joy and the spread of the Gospel. The first portion has, again, a sevenfold, the second, a threefold subordinate division; marked by the beginning, *Thus saith the Lord of hosts.*

2. *Thus saith the Lord of hosts.* "[8] At each word and sentence, in which good things, for their greatness, almost incredible are promised, the prophet premises, *Thus saith the Lord of hosts,* as if he would say, Think not that what I pledge you are my own, and refuse me not credence as man. What I unfold are the promises of God."

I was jealous, lit. *I have been and am jealous for*[9]. He repeats in words slightly varied, but in the same rhythm, the declaration of His tender love wherewith He opened the series of visions, thereby assuring beforehand that this was, like that, an answer of peace. The form of words shews, that this was a jealousy *for,* not *with* her; yet it was one and the same strong, yea infinite love, whereby God, as He says, [10] *clave unto their fathers to love them and chose their seed after them out of all nations.* His jealousy of their sins was part of that love, whereby, "[3] without disturbance of passion or of tranquillity, He inflicted rigorous punishment, as a man fearfully reproves a wife who sins." They are two different forms of love according to two needs. "[11] The jealousy [12] of God is good, to love men and hate the sins of men. Contrariwise the jealousy of the devil is evil, to hate men and love the sins of men." "[13] Since God's anger had its origin in the vehemence of His love (for this sort of jealousy arises from the greatness of love), there was hope that the anger might readily be appeased toward her."

3. *I am returned.* "[3] Without change in

---

[1] ארץ חמדה occurs Ps. cvi. 24, Jer. iii. 19. On חמדה see ab. on Hagg. ii. 7. pp. 310, 311.

[2] This idiom שׂית לשׁמה or שׂום לשׁ. had been used by Jo. i. 7, Is. xiii. 9, Jer ii. 15, iv. 7, xviii. 16, xix. 8, xxv. 9, l. 3, li. 29.

[3] Dion.

[4] S. Jer.

[5] אלי, ver. 1, which is added in 22 Kenn. MSS., 13 De R.; 7 at first, 3 corrected; 2 early edd.; Jon. Syr., is only an explanatory addition. It is noted to be "wanting in correct MSS." De R.

[6] 1—17.

[7] 18—23.

[8] S. Jer.

[9] It is the inverted Hebrew parallelism 1, 2; 4, 3. *I am jealous for Zion with a great jealousy, and with great wrath am I jealous for her,* only substituting חמה גדולה for קצף גדול, in it.

[10] חָשַׁק בּ De. x. 15.

[11] Rup.

[12] Zelus.

[13] Osor.

Before CHRIST cir. 518.

midst of Jerusalem: and
Jerusalem [d] shall be called
a city of truth; and [e] the
mountain of the LORD of
hosts [f] the holy mountain.
4 Thus saith the LORD
of hosts; [g] There shall yet
old men and old women
dwell in the streets of Jerusalem,
and every man
with his staff in his hand
† for very age.

[d] Is. 1. 21, 26.
[e] Is. 2. 2, 3.
[f] Jer. 31. 23.
[g] See 1 Sam. 2. 31. Is. 65, 20, 22. Lam. 2. 20, &c. & 5. 11,—14.
† Heb. *for multitude of days.*

Myself, I am turned to that people from the effect of justice to the sweetness of mercy, *and I will dwell in the midst of Jerusalem,* in the temple and the people, indwelling the hearts of the good by charity and grace. Christ also, Very God and Very Man, visibly conversed and was seen in Zion." "[1] When He says, 'I am turned,' He shews that she was turned too. He had said, *Turn unto Me and I will turn unto you;* otherwise she would not have been received into favor by Him. As the fruit of this conversion, He promises her His presence, the ornaments of truth, the hope of security, and adorns her with glorious titles."

God had symbolized to Ezekiel the departure of His special presence, in that the *glory of the God of Israel* which was over the temple, at the very place where they placed *the image of jealousy* [2], [3] *went up from the Cherub, whereupon it was, to the threshold of the house;* then [4] *stood over the Cherubim;* and then [5] *went up from the midst of the city and stood upon the mountain, which is on the east side of the city,* so removing from them. He had prophesied its return in the vision of the symbolic temple, how [6] *the glory of the Lord came into the house by the way of the gate looking toward the East, and the Spirit took me up and brought me into the inner court, and behold, the glory of the Lord filled the house.* This renewed dwelling in the midst of them, Zechariah too prophesies, in the same terms as in his third vision [7], *I will dwell in the midst of Jerusalem.*

And Jerusalem shall be called the city of truth, being what she is called, since God would not call her untruly; so Isaiah says, [8] *afterward thou shalt be called the city of righteousness, the faithful city,* and [9] *they shall call thee the city of the Lord, the Zion of the Holy One of Israel.* So Zephaniah had prophesied, [10] *The remnant of Israel shall not do iniquity, nor speak lies.* Truth embraces everything opposite to untruth; faithfulness, as opposed to faithlessness; sincerity, as opposed to simulation; veracity, as opposed to falsehood; honesty, as opposed to untruth in act; truth of religion or faith, as opposed to untrue doctrine. "[11] *It shall be called the city of truth,* i. e. of the True God or of truth of life, doctrine, and justice. It is chiefly verified by the Coming of Christ, Who often preached in Jerusalem, in Whom the city afterward believed."

And the mountain of the Lord of hosts, Mount Zion, on which the temple shall be built, shall be called and be *the mountain of holiness.* This had been the favorite title of the Psalmists [12], and Isaiah [13]; and Obadiah had foretold, [14] *upon Mount Zion there shall be holiness;* and Jeremiah, [15] *As yet they shall use this speech in the land of Judah and in the cities thereof, when I shall bring again their captivity; The Lord shall bless thee, O habitation of justice, and mountain of holiness.* It should be called and be; it should fulfill the destination of its titles; as, in the Apostles' Creed we profess our belief of "the holy Catholic Church," and holiness is one of its characteristics.

4. *There shall yet dwell old men and old women.* "[11] Men and women shall not be slain now, as before in the time of the Babylonish destruction, but shall fulfill their natural course." It shall not be, as when [16] *He gave His people over unto the sword; the fire consumed their young men and their maidens were not given to marriage; the priests were slain by the sword and their widows made no lamentation;* apart from the horrible atrocities of heathen war, when the unborn children were destroyed in their mothers' womb [17], with their mothers. *Yet* [18], once more as in the days of old, and as conditionally promised in the law [19]. As death is the punishment of sin, so prolongation of life to the time which God has now made its natural term, seems the more a token of His goodness. This promise Isaiah had renewed [20], *There shall no more be an infant of days, nor an old man that hath not filled his days.* In those fierce wars neither young nor very old were spared. It implied then a long peace, that men should live to that utmost verge of human life.

[1] Osor. [2] Ezek. viii. 4, 5. [3] Ib. ix. 3.
[4] Ib. x. 4, 18. [5] Ib. xi. 23. [6] Ib. xliii. 4.
[7] ושכנתי בתוכך ii. 14. Heb. [10 Eng.]
[8] Is. i. 26.
[9] Ib. lx. 14. So Jer. iii. 17, *At that time they shall call Jerusalem the throne of the Lord.*
[10] Zeph. iii. 13. [11] Dion.
[12] David, Ps. ii. 6, iii. 4, xv. 1, sons of Korah, xliii. 3, xlviii. 1, lxxxvii. 1, and anon., Ps. xcix. 9.
[13] Is. xi. 9, lvi. 7, lvii. 13, lxv. 11, 25, lxvi. 20, also in Jo. ii. 1, iii. 17, Ob. 16, Zeph. iii. 11, Dan. ix. 16, 20.
[14] Ob. 17.
[15] Jer. xxxi. 23. [16] Ps. lxxviii. 63, 64.
[17] 2 Kgs xv. 16, Hos. xiii. 16, Am. i. 13.
[18] As in Zech. i. 17.
[19] De. iv. 10, v. 16, 33, vi. 2, xi. 9, xvii. 20, xxii. 7, xxxii. 47, Ezek. xx. 17.
[20] Is. lxv. 20.

Before CHRIST cir. 518.

5 And the streets of the
city shall be full of boys
and girls playing in the
streets thereof.

6 Thus saith the LORD
of hosts; If it be || marvel-
ous in the eyes of the remnant of this people in these

Before CHRIST cir. 518.

|| Or, *hard*, or, *difficult*.

The man, whose staff is in his hand for the multitude of days. The two opposite pictures, the old men, "[1] so aged that they support with a staff their failing and trembling limbs," and the young in the glad buoyancy of recent life, fresh from their Creator's hands, attest alike the goodness of the Creator, Who protecteth both, the children in their yet undeveloped strength, the very old whom He hath brought through "all the changes and chances of this mortal life," in their yet sustained weakness. The tottering limbs of the very old, and the elastic perpetual motion of childhood are like far distant chords of the diapason of the Creator's love. It must have been one of the most piteous sights in that first imminent destruction of Jerusalem[2], how [3] *the children and the sucklings swooned in the streets of the city;* how *the young children fainted for hunger in the top of every street.* We have but to picture to ourselves any city in which one lives, the ground strewed with these little all-but corpses, alive only to suffer. We know not, how great the relief of the yet innocent, almost indomitable joyousness of children is, until we miss them. In the dreadful Irish famine of 1847 the absence of the children from the streets of Galway was told me by Religious as one of its dreariest features[4]. In the dreary back-streets and alleys of London, the irrepressible joyousness of children is one of the bright sun-beams of that great Babylon, amid the oppressiveness of the anxious, hard, luxurious, thoughtless, care-worn, eager, sensual, worldly, frivolous, vain, stolid, sottish, cunning, faces, which traverse it. God sanctions by His word here our joy in the joyousness of children, that He too taketh pleasure in it, He the Father of all. It is precisely their laughing[5], the fullness of her streets of these merry creations of His hands, that He speaks of with complacency.

6. *If it should be marvelous in the eyes of the remnant of this people in those*[6] [not *these*] *days, shall it be marvelous in Mine eyes also? saith the Lord of hosts.* Man's anticipations, by reason of his imperfections and the chequered character of earthly things, are always disappointing. God's doings, by reason of His infinite greatness and goodness, are always beyond our anticipations, past all belief. It is their very greatness which staggers us. It is not then merely that the temporal promises seemed "too good to be true" (in our words) "[7] in the eyes of the people who had come from the captivity, seeing that the city almost desolate, the ruins of the city-walls, the charred houses shewed the doings of the Babylonians." It is in the day of the fulfillment, not of the anticipation, that they would seem marvelous in their eyes, as the Psalmist says, [8] *This is the Lord's doing: and it is marvelous in our eyes.* The temporal blessings which God would give were not so incredible. They were but the ordinary gifts of His Providence: they involved no change in their outward relations. His people were still to remain under their Persian masters, until their time too should come. It was matter of gladness and of God's Providence, that the walls of Jerusalem should be rebuilt: but not so marvelous, when it came to pass. The mysteries of the Gospel are a marvel even to the blessed Angels. That fulfillment being yet future, so the people, in whose eyes that fulfillment should be marvelous, were future also. And this was to be *a remnant* still. It does not say, *this people which is a remnant,* nor *this remnant of the people,* i. e., those who remained over out of the people who went into captivity, or *this remnant,* but "the remnant of *this* people," i. e. those who should remain over of it, i. e., of the people who were returned. It is the *remnant* of the larger whole, *this people*[9]. It is still *the remnant according to the election of grace; that election* which *obtained* what all Israel sought, but, seeking wrongly, were *blinded*[10].

Shall it be marvelous in Mine eyes also? It is an indirect question in the way of exclamation[11]. *It be marvelous in Mine eyes also,* rejecting the thought, as alien from the na-

[1] Dion. [2] Jer. vi. 11, ix. 21. [3] Lam. ii. 11. 19.

[4] See other pictures of that time in Pusey's "Chastisements neglected forerunners of greater," in "Occasional Sermons." [5] מְשַׂחֲקִים.

[6] בַּיָּמִים הָהֵם as in Gen. vi. 4, Ex. ii. 11, De. xvii. 9, בַּיָּמִים הָהֵמָּה are the times of the Gospel, Jo. iii. 2, iv. 1; bel. 25. [7] S. Jer.

[8] Ps. cxviii. 23. The phrase occurs beside only 2 Sam. xiii. 2.

[9] See on Am. i. 8, vol. i. p. 247, n. 28, and on Hagg. i. 12, p. 305. [10] Rom. xi. 5–7.

[11] As in 2 Sam. xvi. 17, *This thy kindness!* for, *Is this thy kindness?* Gen. xxvii. 24, *Thou, this my son Esau!* for, *Art thou my very son Esau?* 1 Sam. xxii. 7, *Yea, to you all the son of Jesse shall give!* for, *shall he give?* Job ii. 9, *Thou still holding fast thine integrity!* for, *art thou?* Jud. xiv. 16, *I have not told my father and my mother,* ולך אגיד *and to thee I shall tell!* i. e., shall I tell thee? Jer. xxv. 29, *For lo, on the city which is called by My Name, I begin to bring evil, and ye shall be utterly unpunished!* as we should say, "and ye be utterly unpunished." Ew. Lehrb. n. 324. p. 802. ed. 8.

Before CHRIST cir. 518.

days, [h] should it also be
marvelous in mine eyes?
saith the LORD of hosts.
7 Thus saith the LORD
of hosts; Behold, [i] I will
save my people from the
east country, and from
† the west country;
8 And I will bring them,
and they shall dwell in the
midst of Jerusalem: [k] and
they shall be my people,

[h] Gen. 18. 14. Luke 1. 37. & 18. 27. Rom. 4. 21.
[i] Is. 11. 11, 12. & 43. 5, 6. Ezek. 37. 21. Amos 9. 14, 15.

† Heb. *the country of the going down of the sun:* See Ps. 50. 1. & 113. 3. Mal. 1. 11.
[k] Jer. 30. 22. & 31. 1, 33. ch. 13. 9.

ture of God, to Whom [1] *all things are possible,* yea, what *with men is impossible.* As God says to Jeremiah, [2] *Behold, I am the Lord, the God of all flesh. Is there anything too hard for Me?* [3] *For with God nothing shall be impossible.* [4] *The things which are impossible with men are possible with God.* [5] *For with God all things are possible.* "[6] For He is the Lord of all powers, fulfilling by His will what exceedingly surpasseth nature, and effecting at once what seemeth Him good. The mystery of the Incarnation passeth all marvel and discourse, and no less the benefits redounding to us. For how is it not next to incredible, that the Word, Begotten of God, should be united with the flesh and be in the form of a servant, and endure the Cross and the insults and outrages of the Jews? Or how should one not admire above measure the issue of the dispensation, whereby sin was destroyed, death abolished, corruption expelled, and man, once a recreant slave, became resplendent with the grace of an adopted son?"

7. *I will save My people from the East country and from the West country,* "[7] i. e. the whole world; for Israel had been scattered in every part of the world." God had said to Israel, [8] *I will bring thy seed from the east and gather thee from the west; I will say to the north, Give up, and to the south, Keep not back.* The two tribes had been carried to Babylon and had been dispersed, or had been allowed to migrate to the various provinces of the Babylonian or Persian empire. But these were in the East, though commonly called the North, because they invaded Israel from the North. Those who had migrated to Egypt were in the South. As yet none were in the West. The dispersion, as well as the gathering, was still future. When our Lord came, they had migrated Westward. Greece, Italy, Asia minor, were full of them; and from all they were gathered. All S. Paul's Epistles written to named Churches, were written to Churches formed from converts in the West. In all these countries God would gather His one people, His Church, not of [9] *the Jews only, but also of the Gentiles,* grafted into them, as our Lord said, [10] *I say unto you, that many shall come from the East and from the West, and shall sit down with Abraham, and Isaac, and Jacob, in the kingdom of heaven; but the children of the kingdom* (the unbelieving Jews, who were not *the remnant*) *shall be cast out into outer darkness.*

8. *They shall dwell in the midst of Jerusalem,* not the literal Jerusalem; for this would not contain the Jews from all quarters of the world, whom, as they multiplied, the whole land could not contain; but the promised Jerusalem, the Jerusalem, which *should be inhabited* as *towns without walls,* to which the Lord should be *a wall of fire round about.*

And they shall be My people. He promises this as to those who were already His people; *I will save My people—and will bring them, and they shall dwell—and they shall be My people.* And this they were to be in a new way, by conversion of heart, as Jeremiah says, [11] *I will give them an heart to know Me, that I am the Lord, and they shall be My people, and I will be their God: for they shall return unto Me with their whole heart,* and, [12] *This* shall be *the covenant that I will make with the house of Israel; After those days, saith the Lord, I will put My law in their inward parts, and will write it in their hearts; and will be their God, and they shall be My people.*

"[13] The circuit of one city will not contain so great a multitude. But one confession of faith, one conspiration of sanctity, one communion of religion and righteousness, can easily enfold all born of the holy fathers, united to them in faith and piety. And God is specially called the God of all these. For He specially consults for these, loads them with benefits, fences them in with most strong protection, illumines them with His light, crowns them, when confirmed in the Image of His beauty, with glory immortal and Divine."

In truth and in righteousness. This too is on account of their former relation to God. Isaiah had upbraided them for a worship of God, [14] *not in truth and righteousness.* Jeremiah had said, [15] *Thou shalt swear, the Lord liveth, in truth, in judgment, and in righteousness.* God should be their God *in truth and righteousness;* "[16] truth in fulfilling His promises; righteousness in rewarding every man according to his works."

[1] S. Matt. xix. 26. [2] Jer. xxxii. 27. [3] S. Luke i. 37. [4] Ib. xviii. 27. [5] S. Mark x. 27. [6] S. Cyr. [7] Dion. [8] Is. xliii. 5, 6.

[9] Rom. ix. 24. [10] S. Matt. viii. 11, 12. [11] Jer. xxiv. 7, add xxx. 22. [12] Ib. xxxi. 33. [13] Osor. [14] Is. xlviii. 1. [15] Jer. iv. 2. [16] Rib.

Before CHRIST cir. 518.

and I will be their God, [l]in
truth and in righteousness.
9 ¶ Thus saith the
LORD of hosts; [m]Let your
hands be strong, ye that
hear in these days these
words by the mouth of [n]the
prophets, which *were* in
[o]the day *that* the foundation
of the house of the
LORD of hosts was laid,
that the temple might be
built.
10 For before these days
||there was no [p]hire for
man, nor any hire for
beast; [q]neither *was there*
any peace to him that went
out or came in because of
the affliction: for I set all
men every one against his
neighbor.

[l] Jer. 4. 2.
[m] Hag. 2. 4. ver. 18.
[n] Ezra 5. 1, 2.
[o] Hag. 2. 18.

Before CHRIST cir. 518.

|| Or, *the hire of man became nothing, &c.*
[p] Hag. 1. 6, 9, 10. & 2. 16.
[q] 2 Chr. 15. 5.

9 *Let your hands be strong.* The fulfillment of God's former promises are the earnest of the future; His former providences, of those to come. Having then those great promises for the time to come, they were to be earnest in whatever meantime God gave them to do. He speaks to them, as *hearing in these days*, i. e. that *fourth* year of Darius in which they apparently were, *these words from the mouth of the prophets, which* were *in the day* when *the foundation of the house of the Lord was laid, the temple, that it might be built.* Haggai was now gone to his rest. His voice had been silent for two years. But his words lived on. The fulfillment of what the prophets had then spoken in God's Name, was a ground, why their hands should be strong, now and thereafter, for every work which God gave or should give them to do. "[1]Some things are said to Jerusalem, i. e. to the Jews, which belong to them only; some relate to what is common to them and the other members of the Church, i. e. those who are called from the Gentiles. Now he speaks to the Jews, but not so as to seem to forget what he had said before. He would say, Ye who hear the words, which in those days when the temple was founded, Haggai and Zechariah spake, be strong and proceed to the work which ye began of fulfilling the will of the Lord in the building of the temple, and in keeping from the sins, in which ye were before entangled. For as, before ye began to build the temple, ye were afflicted with many calamities, but after ye had begun, all things went well with you, as Haggai said[2], so, if you cultivate piety and do not depart from God, ye shall enjoy great abundance of spiritual good." "[3]The memory of past calamity made the then tranquillity much sweeter, and stirred the mind to greater thanksgiving. He set forth then the grief of those times when he says;"

10. *There was no hire for man*, lit. *hire for man came not to pass*[4]. It was longed for, waited for, and came not. So little was the produce, that neither laborer nor beast of burden were employed to gather it in.

Neither was there peace to him who went out or came in because of the affliction, better, *of the adversary*. In such an empire as the Persian, there was large scope for actual hostility among the petty nations subject to it, so that they did not threaten revolt against itself, or interfere with the payment of tribute, as in the Turkish Empire now, or in the weak government of Greece. At the rebuilding of the walls, after this time, the Samaritans, *Arabians, Ammonites, Ashdodites conspired to fight against Jerusalem*, and to *slay them*[5]. They are summed up here in the general title used here, *our adversaries*[6].

For I set; lit. *and I set.* Domestic confusions and strife were added to hostility from without. Nehemiah's reformation was, in part, to stop the grinding usury in time of dearth or to pay the king's taxes, through which men sold lands, vineyards, even their children[7].

God (lit.) *let them loose, each against his neighbor*, in that He left them to their own ways and withheld them not.

[1] Rib. [2] Hagg. ii. 15–19. [3] Osor.

[4] נהיה .לא נהיה occurs only in 19 other places: "it came to pass," with כאת, "it was from," i. e. his doing, 1 Kings i. 27, xii. 24, 2 Chr. xi. 4; of a thing which had not its like, with כ or כמו Ex. xi. 6, Deut. iv. 32, Jo. ii. 2, Jud. xix. 30, Dan. xii. 1, or abs., Jud. xx. 3, 12, Jer. v. 30, xlviii. 19, Ezek. xxi. 12, xxxix. 8. There remain five insulated cases; "was made God's people," Deut. xxvii. 9; "a desire accomplished," Pr. xiii. 19; "hath not been done," (rejecting an imputation) Neh. vi. 8: "was departed," Dan. ii. 1; as if he had ceased to be, Ib. viii. 27.

[5] Neh. iv. 7–11.

[6] צרינו Neh. iv. 5 Heb. (11 Eng.), צר, as calamity, is very rare, except in the idiom בַּצַּר ל. It is used twice in the construct, as a sort of adj., לחם צר, *bread of affliction* Is. xxx. 20; עת צר *time of affliction*, Job xxxviii. 23; and as united with the synonyme ומצוקה, Job xv. 24, ומצוק, Ps. cxix. 143; absolutely, once only, Is. v. 30. The fem. צָרָה occurs, in all, 72 times.

[7] Neh. v. 1–12.

Before CHRIST cir. 518.

11 But now I *will* not
be unto the residue of this
people as in the former days,
saith the LORD of hosts.
r Hos. 2. 21, 22. Joel 2. 22. Hag. 2. 19. 12 [r] For the seed *shall*
† Heb. *of peace.* *be* † prosperous; the vine
shall give her fruit, and
s Ps. 67. 6. [s] the ground shall give her
t See Hag. 1. 10. increase, and [t] the heavens
shall give their dew; and
I will cause the remnant
of this people to possess all
these *things*.
13 And it shall come to
pass, *that* as ye were [u] a u Jer. 42. 18.
curse among the heathen,
O house of Judah, and
house of Israel; so will I

11. *And now.* The words imply a contrast of God's dealings, rather than a contrast of time. *I* am *not to the remnant of this people.* He had said, *I will be to them God;* so now He does not say that He will not *do* to them, *as in former days*, but *I am not to the remnant* of this people as heretofore. He would be, as He was in Jesus, in a new relation to them.

12. *For the seed* shall be *peace*[1]. "[2] Your seed shall be peace and a blessing, so that they will call it 'a seed of peace.'" The unusual construction is perhaps adopted, in order to suggest a further meaning. It is a reversal of the condition, just spoken of, when there was *no peace to him that went, or to him that returned.*

The vine shall give her fruit and the ground shall give her increase. The old promise in the law on obedience[3], as the exact contrary was threatened on disobedience[4]. It had been revived in the midst of promise of spiritual blessing and of the coming of Christ, in Ezekiel[5]. "[6] By the metaphor of sensible things he explains (as the prophets often do) the abundance of spiritual good in the time of the new law, as did Hosea[7], Joel[8], Amos[9], and many others." *And I will cause the remnant of the people to inherit.* "[6] As if he said, I promised these things not to you who live now, but to the future remnant of your people, i. e. those who shall believe in Christ and shall be saved, while the rest perish. These shall possess these spiritual goods, which I promise now, under the image of temporal." As our Lord said[10], *He that overcometh shall inherit all things, and I will be his God, and he shall be My son.*

13. *As ye were a curse among the nations, O house of Judah and house of Israel, so I will save you.* The ten tribes bore the name of Israel, in contrast with the two tribes with the name of Judah, not only in the history but in the prophets; as Hosea says[11], *I will no more have mercy upon the house of Israel*, and *on the house of Judah I will have mercy.* Here he unites both; both, in the time of their captivity, were *a curse*, were held to be a thing accursed, as it is said, [12] *He that is hanged is the curse of God*, i. e. a thing accursed by Him; and God foretold of Judah, that they should be [13] *a desolation and a curse*, and by Jeremiah, [14] *I will deliver them to be removed into all the kingdoms of the earth for hurt, a reproach and a proverb, a taunt and a curse in all places whither I shall drive them;* and in deed, when it was so, [15] *therefore is your land a desolation and an astonishment and a curse without an inhabitant, as at this day.* Now the sentence was to be reversed as to both. *As ye were a curse, among the nations*, naming each, *so I will save you.* There would have been no proportion between the curse and the blessing, unless both had been included under the blessing, as they were under the curse. But Israel had no share in the temporal blessing, not returning from captivity, as Zechariah knew they were not returned hitherto. Therefore the blessings promised must be spiritual. Even a Jewish commentator saw this. "[16] It is possible, that this may have been spoken of the second temple, on condition that they should keep the commandments of the Lord; or, it is still future, referring to the days of the Messiah: and this is proved by the following verse which

[1] It cannot be, *the seed shall. be safe*, (Jon.), for השלום is never used except of *peace;* nor is even שלום used as a predicate, except of human beings, either directly or as implied, as in Job v. 24, *thy tent*, שלום אהלך; Job xxi. 9, *their houses are peace from fear*, בתיהם שלום מפחד. The sense incolumitas, integritas, is wrongly assumed in Röd. Ges. Thes. Deut. xxix. 18, 1 Kgs ii. 33, Ps. xxxvii. 11, 37, lxxii. 3, 7, Is. lii. 7, lvii. 19, 21, Jer. iv. 10, vi. 14, except as far as this may be involved in "peace." Nor can זרע השלום be a noun. abs. before גפן, "a seed of peace, the vine shall yield her fruit;" for "seed" has no relation to the "vine."

[2] Kim. [3] Lev. xxvi. 4. [4] Ib. 20.
[5] Ezek. xxxiv. 27. [6] Rib. [7] Hos. ii. 21, 22.
[8] Jo. ii. 23–25, iii. 18. [9] Am. ix 13.
[10] Rev. xxi. 7. [11] Hos. i. 6, 7. [12] De. xxi. 23.
[13] 2 Kgs xxii. 19.

[14] Jer. xxiv. 9, add Ib. xxv. 18, *to make thee a desolation, an astonishment, a hissing and a curse;* and of those who went in rebellion to Egypt, *ye shall be an execration* [אלה] *and an astonishment and a curse and a reproach* (Ib. xlii. 18), and *that ye might be a curse and a reproach among all the nations of the earth* (Ib. xliv. 8.) [15] Ib. xliv. 22. [16] Kim. on ver. 12.

Before CHRIST cir. 518.

save you, and [x]ye shall be
a blessing: fear not, *but*
[y]let your hands be strong.
14 For thus saith the
LORD of hosts; [z]As I
thought to punish you,
when your fathers provoked me to wrath, saith
the LORD of hosts, [a]and I
repented not:
15 So again have I
thought in these days to do
well unto Jerusalem and
to the house of Judah: fear
ye not.
16 ¶ These *are* the

[x] Gen. 12. 2. Ruth 4. 11, 12. Is. 19. 24, 25. Zeph. 3. 20. Hag. 2. 19.
[y] ver. 9.
[z] Jer. 31. 28.
[a] 2 Chr. 36. 16. ch. 1. 6.

says, *O house of Judah and house of Israel.* During the second temple the house of Israel did not return."

And ye shall be a blessing. This is a revival and an application of the original promise to Abraham, [1]*thou shalt be a blessing;* which was continued to Jacob, [2]*God give thee the blessing of Abraham, to thee and to thy seed with thee.* And of the future king, of whom it is said, [3]*Thou gavest him length of days for ever and ever*, David says, *Thou hast made him blessings for ever*, and again, [4]*They shall be blessed in Him.* So Isaiah had said of the days of Christ, [5]*In that day shall Israel be the third with Egypt and with Assyria, a blessing in the midst of the land;* and symbolically of the cluster of grapes, [6]*Destroy it not: for a blessing is in it;* and Ezekiel, [7]*I will make them and the places round about My hill a blessing.* They were this; for of them, [8]*according to the flesh, Christ came, Who is over all, God blessed for ever;* of them were the Apostles and Evangelists, of them every writer of God's word, of them those who carried the Gospel throughout the world. "[9]Was this fulfilled, when the Jews were under the Persians? or when they paid tribute to the Greeks? or when they trembled, hour by hour, at the mention of the Roman name? Do not all count those who rule much happier than those oppressed by the rule of others? The prediction then was fulfilled, not then, but when Christ, the Sun of Righteousness, shone on the earth, and He chose from the Hebrews lights, through whom to dissipate darkness and illumine the minds of men who were in that darkness. The Jews, when restored from the captivity, seemed born to slavery." They were reputed to be of slaves the most despised. "But when they had through Christ been put in possession of that most sure liberty, they overthrew, through their empire, the power and tyranny of the evil spirits."

14. *As I thought to punish you* (lit. *to do evil to you*) *and repented not.* In like way God says in Jeremiah [10], *I have purposed and will not repent.*

15. *So have I turned and purposed* [11] *in these days to do well unto Jerusalem.* "[12]God, to be better understood, speaketh with the feelings and after the manner of men, although, in the passionless and unchangeable God, there is no provocation to anger, nor turning, implying change in Himself." So He says by Jeremiah, [13]*I know the thoughts that I think toward you, saith the Lord, thoughts of peace and not of evil.* And, with the same contrast as here, [14]*As I have watched over them to pluck up and to break down and to throw down, and to destroy and to afflict, so will I watch over them, to build and to plant, saith the Lord.* His having done what He purposed before was an earnest the more, that He would do what He purposed now. His chastisements were the earnests of His mercies; for they too were an austere form of His love. "[9]When the Lord stretches out His hand to strike those who are contumacious in guilt, none can hold His hand that He exact not the due punishment. Therefore He says, that He *repented not;* so, when He receives to grace those who repent of their sins, no one can any way delay the course of His benevolence. [15]*For the gifts and calling of God are without repentance.*"

And to the house of Judah. [16]He speaks to the two tribes, not to, or of, the ten, because Christ was to come to the two tribes, and Zechariah was prophesying to them, and they were to be admonished to prepare themselves in good works, lest the coming of Christ should not profit them, on account of their depraved ways. But the ten tribes were far off in the cities of the Medes, nor was Christ to come to them; but they were to hear the Gospel through the Apostles, and so he prophesies of the conversion of all to the glory of Christ, yet he could not admonish all, but those only to whom he was sent.

16. *These are the things that ye shall do.* He exhorts them to the same duties, to which the former prophets had exhorted their fathers [17], and, as before, first positively to *truth* and *peace;* then to avoid everything

[1] Gen xii. 2.
[2] Ib. xxviii. 4.
[3] Ps. xxi. 4, 6.
[4] Ib lxxii. 17.
[5] Is. xix. 24.
[6] Ib lxv. 8.
[7] Ezek. xxxiv. 26.
[8] Rom. ix. 5.

[9] Osor.
[10] Jer. iv. 28.
[11] On זמם see above on i. 6, p. 341, note 8.
[12] Dion.
[13] Jer. xxix. 11.
[14] Ib. xxxi. 28.
[15] Rom. xi. 29.
[16] Rib.
[17] vii. 9, 10.

Before CHRIST cir. 518.

things that ye shall do;
[b] Speak ye every man the
truth to his neighbor; † execute the judgment of
truth and peace in your
gates:
17 [c] And let none of you
imagine evil in your hearts
against his neighbor; and
[d] love no false oath: for
all these *are things* that I
hate, saith the LORD.
18 ¶ And the word of
the LORD of hosts came
unto me, saying,

[b] ch. 7. 9. ver. 19. Ephes. 4. 25.
† Heb. *judge truth, and the judgment of peace.*
[c] Prov. 3. 29. ch. 7. 10.
[d] ch. 5. 3, 4.

19 Thus saith the LORD
of hosts; [e] The fast of the
fourth *month,* [f] and the fast
of the fifth, [g] and the fast
of the seventh, [h] and the
fast of the tenth, shall be
to the house of Judah [i] joy
and gladness, and cheerful
|| feasts; [k] therefore love
the truth and peace.
20 Thus saith the LORD
of hosts; *It shall* yet *come
to pass,* that there shall
come people, and the in-
habitants of many cities:

Before CHRIST cir. 518.

[e] Jer. 52. 6, 7.
[f] Jer. 52. 12, 13. ch. 7. 3, 5.
[g] 2 Kin. 25. 25. Jer. 41. 1, 2.
[h] Jer. 52. 4.
[i] Esth. 8. 17. Isai. 35. 10.
|| Or, *solemn,* or, *set times.*
[k] ver. 16.

contrary to it. *Judgment of peace* must be judgment which issues in peace, as all righteous judgment righteously received, in which case each party acquiesces, must. "[1] If ye judge righteousness, there will be peace between the litigants, according to that proverb, '[2] He that hath his coat taken from him by the tribunal, let him sing and go his way' ["because," says a gloss[3], "they have judged the judgment of truth, and have taken away that which would have been stolen property, if he retained it," being in fact not his]. And they have quoted that, [4] *And all this people shall go to their place in peace.*" "[5] *All this people,* even he that is condemned in judgment. It is also interpreted of arbitration. What sort of judgment is that, in which there is peace? It is that of arbitration."

17. *For all these things do I hate.* lit. emphatic, [6] *For they are all these things which I hate.* This is the sum of what I hate; for they comprise in brief the breaches of the two tables, the love of God and of man.

19. *The fast of the fourth month.* On the ninth day *of the fourth month* [7] of Zedekiah's eleventh year, Jerusalem, in the extremity of famine, opened to Nebuchadnezzar, and his princes sat in her gate; in the *tenth month* [8] of his ninth year Nebuchadnezzar began the siege. Ezekiel was bidden [9] *on its tenth* day; *write thee the name of the day, of this same day,* as the beginning of God's uttermost judgments against *the bloody city* [10]. The days of national sorrow were to be turned into exuberant joy, *joy and gladness and cheerful feasts* [11], for the sorrows, which they commemorated, were but the harbingers of joy, when the chastisements were ended; only He adds, *love the truth and peace;* for such love whereby they would be Israelites indeed, in whose spirits is no guile, were the conditions of their participating the blessings of the Gospel, of which he goes on to speak;

20. It shall *yet* be *that.* The promises are those which God had already made by Isaiah [12] and Micah [13]. Yet where was the shew of their fulfillment? The Jews themselves, a handful: the temple unfinished; its completion depending, in human sight, upon the will of their heathen masters, the rival worship at Samaria standing and inviting to coalition. Appearances and experience were against it. God says virtually, that it was, in human sight, contrary to all expectations. But "weakness is aye Heaven's might." Despite of all, of the fewness of those who were returned, their downheartedness, broken condition, hopelessness, though all had hitherto failed, though, or rather because, all human energy and strength were gone, as

[1] Kim.
[2] Sanhedr. f. 7. a. quoted by Mc. Caul, p. 78.
[3] Rashi, quoted Ib.
[4] Exod. xviii. 23.
[5] Judah b. Korcha in Sanhr. f. 6 b. Ib.
[6] את כל אלה is a sort of noun abs., as Hagg. ii. 5.
[7] Jer. xxxix. 2, 3; lii. 6, 7.
[8] 2 Kgs xxv. 1, Jer. xxxix. 1, lii. 4.
[9] Ezek. xxiv. 1, 2.
[10] Ib. 6–14. The Jews in S. Jerome's time added, that in the fourth month Moses brake the tables of the law; in the fifth month was the rebellion on the return of the spies, and the sentence of the forty years' wandering. This is true. For since Moses went up into the mount in the third month (Ex. xix. 1, 16, xxiv. 12, 16.), the end of the forty days (Ib. 18), after which he came down and brake the tables (Ex. xxxii. 15, 19) would fall in the fourth month. Ribera calculates the fourth month thus: setting off from Sinai, 20th day of 2d month, Nu. x. 11; 3 days' journey, Ib. 33; halt of one month, Ib. xi. 20, 21; of 7 days, Ib. xii. 15; 40 days' search of spies, Ib. xiii. 25.
[11] טוב as יום טוב, Esth. viii. 17. ix. 19, 22, Eccl. vii. 14.
[12] Is. ii. 2, sqq.
[13] Mic. iv. 1. sqq.

Before CHRIST cir. 518.

21 And the inhabitants of one *city* shall go to another, saying, [l] Let us go || † speedily † to pray before the LORD, and to seek the LORD of hosts: I will go also.

22 Yea, [m] many people and strong nations shall come to seek the LORD of

[l] Isai. 2. 3. Mic. 4. 1, 2.
|| Or, *continually.*
† Heb. *going.*
† Heb. *to intreat the face of the* LORD, ch. 7. 2.
[m] Isai. 60. 3, &c. & 66. 23.

God had said before, *The Lord shall yet*[1] *choose Jerusalem*, so now, It shall *yet*[2] be *that.*

Nations and many cities shall come. He describes vividly the eagerness and mutual impulse, with which not only many but mighty nations should throng to the Gospel, and every fresh conversion should win others also, till the great tide should sweep through the world.

21. *The inhabitants of one* city *shall go to another.* It is one unresting extension of the faith, the restlessness of faith and love. "[3] They shall not be satisfied with their own salvation, careless about the salvation of others; they shall employ all labor and industry, with wondrous love, to provide for the salvation of others as if it were their own." It is a marvelous stirring of minds. Missionary efforts, so familiar with us as to be a household word, were unknown then. The time was not yet come. *Before the faith* in Christ *came*, the Jewish people were not to be the converters of mankind. They were to await for Him, the Redeemer of the world, through Whom and to Whom they were to be first converted, and then the world through those who were of them. This mutual conversion was absolutely unknown. The prophet[4] predicts certainly that it would be, and in God's time it was. *From you*, S. Paul writes to a small colony in Greece[5], *sounded out the word of the Lord, not only in Macedonia and Achaia, but also in every place your faith to God-ward is spread abroad.* [6] *Your faith*, he writes to the heathen capital of the world, *is spoken of throughout the whole world.* Within eighty years after our Lord's Ascension, the Roman governor of Bithynia reported, on occasion of the then persecution, that it spread as a contagion. "[7] The contagion of that superstition traversed not cities only but villages and scattered houses too." Before the persecution, the temples had been desolated, the solemn rites long intermitted, the sacrificed animals had very rarely found a purchaser. An impostor of the same date says, "[8] Pontus is full of atheists and Christians." "[9] There is no one race of men," it was said before the middle of the second century[10], "whether Barbarians or Greeks or by whatsoever name called, whether of those wandering houseless tribes who live in wagons or those pastoral people who dwell in tents, in which there are not prayers and Eucharists to the Father and Creator of all things, through the name of the crucified Jesus." "The word of our teacher," said another[11], "abode not in Judæa alone, as philosophy in Greece; but was poured out throughout the whole world, persuading Greeks and barbarians in their several nations and villages and every city, whole houses and each hearer individually, and having brought over to the truth no few even of the very philosophers. And if any ordinary magistrate forbid the Greek philosophy, forthwith it vanishes; but our teaching, forthwith at its first announcement, kings and emperors and subordinate rulers and governors with all their mercenaries and countless multitudes forbid, and war against us and try to extirpate; but it the rather flourishes." The second century had not closed, before another said, "[12] We are a people of yesterday, and yet we have filled every place belonging to you, cities, islands, castles, towns, assemblies, your very camp, your tribes, companies, palace, senate, forum! We leave you your temples only. We can count your armies; our numbers in a single province will be greater." "[13] Men cry out that the state is beset; that the Christians are in their fields, in their forts, in their islands. They mourn, as for a loss, that every sex, age, condition, and now even rank is going over to this sect." "[14] On whom besides have all nations believed, except on Christ Who hath already come?" Then having enumerated the nations mentioned in the Acts[15], he adds, "And now the varieties of the Getulians, and the many tracts of the Moors, all the bounds of the Spains, and the divers nations of the Gauls, and places of the Britons, unreached by the Romans but subdued to Christ; of Sarmatians, Dacians, Germans, and Scythians, and of many remote nations, and many provinces and islands, unknown to us, and which we can

[1] i. 17, ii. 16 [12 Eng.]
[2] עוד is premised emphatically.
[3] Osor.
[4] See below on ix. 12.
[5] 1 Thess. i. 8.
[6] Rom. i. 8.
[7] Plin. ad. Traj. Ep. x. 97.
[8] Alexander in Lucian. Alexander.
[9] S. Justin M. Dial. n. 117, on Mal. i. 10. p. 216. Oxf. Tr.
[10] Trypho says, "I escaped from the late war." (A. D. 132–135) Dial. init. p. 70.
[11] Clem. Alex. Strom. vi. fin.
[12] Tert. Apol. n. 37, p. 78. Oxf. Tr.
[13] Ib. n. 1. pp. 2. 3.
[14] Tert. adv. Jud. c. 7 p. 113 Rig.
[15] Acts ii. 9–11.

Before CHRIST cir. 518.

hosts in Jerusalem, and to
pray before the LORD.
23 Thus saith the LORD
of hosts; In those days *it
shall come to pass*, that ten
men shall [n] take hold out

[n] Isai. 3. 6. & 4. 1.

scarce enumerate. In all which places the name of Christ, Who hath already come, reigneth, seeing that before Him the gates of all cities are opened and none are shut against Him, before Whom [1] *the bars of iron are broken in pieces and the gates of brass are opened.* In all these places dwelleth a people called by the name of Christ. For who could reign over all, save Christ the Son of God, Who was foretold as about to reign over all nations forever?" Then having contrasted the limited rule of Solomon, Darius, the Pharaohs, Nebuchadnezzar, Alexander, "the Romans who protect their own empire by the strength of their legions and are unable to extend the might of their kingdom beyond these nations [Germans, Britons, Moors, Getulians], he sums up, "but the kingdom and the Name of Christ is extended everywhere, is believed in everywhere, is worshiped by all the nations above enumerated. Everywhere He reigns, everywhere is adored, is given everywhere equally to all. With Him no king hath greater favor; no Barbarian inferior joy; no dignities or birth enhance the merit of any; to all He is equal; to all, King; to all Judge; to all, God and Lord." A little later, a heathen owns, while calumniating, "[2] Those most foul rites of that impious coalition are growing throughout the whole world, as bad things come up most luxuriantly, evil ways creeping on daily." The Christian answers, "[3] That our number increases daily, this is no imputation of error, but a testimony to praise. For in a good mode of life, its own persevere, aliens accrue to it."

Let us go on and on, [4] perseveringly, until we attain *to entreat the face of the* Lord. It is not a Theism or Monotheism, but the God, Who had revealed Himself to Israel, Who, when our Lord came, was worshiped in Jerusalem, to which those invited say, *I too would go with thee.* Yet not so, but the words seem to speak of that which is a special gift of the Gospel, continued progress, "[5] *forgetting those things which are behind, and reaching forth unto those things which are before,* to *press toward the mark of the prize of the high calling of God in Christ Jesus. Let us go on and on;* whence it is a Christian proverb, "[6] not to go on is to go back." "[7] The whole life of a good Christian is a holy longing to make progress." "[8] The one perfection of man is, to have found that he is not perfect." "[9] If thou sayest, It sufficeth, thou art lost." "[10] To be unwilling to increase, is to decrease."

23. *Ten men of all languages of the nations. Ten* [11] is the symbol of a whole, all the numbers before it meeting in it and starting again from it. The day of Pentecost was to be the reversal of the confusion of Babel; all were to have one voice, as God had said, [12] *It* (the time) *shall come to gather all nations and tongues, and they shall come and see My glory.*

They shall lay hold of the skirt of one man who is a Jew, "[13] that is, of the Lord and Saviour, of Whom it is said, [14] *A prince shall not depart from Judah, nor a lawgiver from between his feet, until He shall come, for Whom it is laid up, and for Him shall the Gentiles wait;* for [15] *there shall be a rod of Jesse, and He who shall arise to rule over the Gentiles, to Him shall the Gentiles seek.* And when they shall lay hold of Him, they shall desire to tread in His steps, since God is with Him. Or else, whosoever shall believe out of all nations, *shall lay hold of a man who is a Jew,* the Apostles who are from the Jews, and shall say, *Let us go with you;* for we have known through the prophets and from the voice of all the Scriptures, that the Son of God, Christ, God and Lord, is with you. Where there is a most manifest prophecy, and the coming of Christ and His Apostles and the faith of all nations is preached, let us seek for nothing more."

"[16] Christ turning our sorrow into joy and a feast and good days and gladness, and transferring lamentation into cheerfulness, the accession to the faith and union to God by sanctification in those called to salvation shall not henceforth be individually; but the cities shall exhort each other thereto, and all nations shall come in multitudes, the later ever calling out to those before them, *I too will go.* For it is written, [17] *iron sharpeneth iron, so doth a man the countenance of another.*

[1] Is. xlv. 2.
[2] Cæcil. in Minut. Fel. p. 80. Ouz.
[3] Minut. Fel. Ib. p. 312. Other like sayings are in Origen, (de Princ. iv. 1. c. Cels. i. 7, 67, ii. 13, iii. 24,) Lactantius, (v. 13) Arnobius (i. p. 33, ii. 50, Lugd.), who argues thence to the divinity of the Gospel, Jul. Firmicus, (c. 21 B. P. iv. 172.)
[4] נלכה הלוך.
[5] Phil. iii. 13, 14.
[6] "non progredi est regredi."
[7] S. Aug. in 1 Ep. S. Joann. Hom. iv. n. 6. p. 1144. Oxf. Tr.
[8] Id. Serm. 120, [170. Ben.] c. 8. p. 877. Oxf. Tr.
[9] Id. Serm. 119, [169.] fin. ib. p. 871. Oxf. Tr.
[10] Nolle proficere deficere est. S. Bern. Ep. 254 ad Guarin. n. 4.
[11] As in Gen. xxxi. 7, *he hath changed my wages these ten times;* Lev. xxvi. 26, *when I have broken your staff of bread, ten women shall bake your bread in one oven;* Nu. xiv. 22, *those men which have seen My glory, have tempted Me now these ten times, and have not hearkened to My voice.*
[12] Is. lxvi. 18.
[13] S. Jer.
[14] Gen. xlix. 8–10.
[15] Is. xi. 10.
[16] S. Cyr.
[17] Pr. xxvii. 17.

Before CHRIST cir. 518.

of all languages of the nations, even shall take hold of the skirt of him that is a Jew, saying, We will go with you: for we have heard °*that* God *is* with you.

° 1 Cor. 14. 25.

CHAPTER IX.

Before CHRIST cir. 487.

1 *God defendeth his church.* 9 *Zion is exhorted to rejoice for the coming of Christ, and his peaceable kingdom.* 12 *God's promises of victory and defence.*

THE ᵃburden of the word of the LORD in

ᵃ Jer. 23. 33.

For the zeal of some is ever found to call forth others to fulfill what is good. But what is the aim proposed to the cities, that is, the Gentiles? *To entreat it and to seek the face of the Lord*, i. e. Christ, Who is the exact image of God the Father, and, as is written, [1] *the brightness of His glory, and the express image of His Person*, of Whom also the divine David saith, [2] *Shew Thy countenance to Thy servant.* For the Image and Countenance of God the Father hath shone upon us. Having Him propitious and kind, we lay aside the injury from sin, being justified through faith, [3] *not by works of righteousness, which we have done, but according to His great mercy.*—But how they shall come, he explains. By the *ten men* you are to understand the perfect number of those who come. For the number *ten* is the symbol of perfection. But that those of the Gentiles, who cleave to the holy Apostles, took in hand to go the same way with them, being justified by the faith in Christ, he sets evidently before us. For little children, if they would follow their fathers, lay hold of the hem of their dress, and, aided by the touch and hanging from their dress, walk steadily and safely. In like way, they too who [4] *worshiped the creature rather than the Creator*, choosing as their true fathers the bringers-in of the Gospel-doctrines, and joining themselves by like-mindedness to them, follow them, being still of childlike minds, and go the same way, ever shewing themselves zealous followers of their life, and by continued progress advancing [5] *to a perfect man, to the measure of the stature of the fullness of Christ.* But why do they follow them? Being persuaded that God is with them, i. e. Emmanuel, *God with us.* But that this calling belongs not only to those of the blood of Israel but to all nations throughout the world, he indicated by saying, that those who laid hold of that hem should be *of all languages.* But when were the nations called to the knowledge of the truth, and when did they desire to seek the face of the Lord and to entreat it, and to go the same way, as it were, as the holy Apostles, except when the Only-Begotten came to us, Who is [6] the *expectations of the nations;* to Whom also the divine David singeth, [7] *All the nations, whom Thou hast made, shall come and worship before Thee, O Lord?* For the multitude of the nations also is saved through Him."

The startling condescension of this passage is, that our Lord is spoken of as "a man, a Jew." Yet of His human Nature it is not only the simple truth, but essential to the truth. Pilate said to Him in scorn, *Am I a Jew*[8]*? Thine own nation and the Chief Priests have delivered Thee unto me.* But it was essential to the fulfillment of God's promises. The Christ was to be [9] *the Son of David.* [10] *Hath not the Scripture said, That Christ cometh of the seed of David, and out of the town of Bethlehem, where David was?* David, [11] *being a prophet and knowing that God had sworn with an oath to him, that of the fruit of his loins according to the flesh, He would raise up Christ to sit on his throne;* [12] *Of this man's seed hath God, according to promise, raised unto Israel a Saviour, Jesus.* Whence S. Paul begins his great doctrinal Epistle with this contrast, [13] *the Gospel of God concerning His Son Jesus Christ, which was made of the seed of David according to the flesh, and declared to be the Son of God with power.* He was that [14] *one Man among a thousand*, whom Solomon says, *I found;* but *a woman among all those have I not found;* the one in the whole human race. It was fulfilled in the very letter when [15] *they brought to Him all that were diseased, and besought Him that they might only touch the hem of His garment: and as many as touched were made perfectly whole.* [16] *The whole multitude sought to touch Him, for there went virtue out of Him and healed all.*

Even the Jews saw the reference to the Messiah. "[17] All nations shall come, falling on their faces before the Messiah and the Israelites, saying, Grant, that we may be Thy servants and of Israel. For as relates to the doctrine and the knowledge of the law, the Gentiles shall be their servants, according to that, *In those days ten men &c.*"

IX. 1. *The burden* [18] *of the word of the Lord*

[1] Heb. i. 3. [2] Ps. cxix. 135. [3] Tit. iii. 5. [4] Rom. i. 25. [5] Eph. iv. 13. [6] Gen. xlix. 10. [7] Ps. lxxxvi. 9. [8] S. John xviii. 35. [9] S. Matt. i. 1. xxii. 42. [10] S. John vii. 42. [11] Acts ii. 30. [12] Ib. xiii. 23. [13] Rom. i. 1-4. [14] Eccl. vii. 28.

[15] S. Matt. xiv. 35, 36.
[16] S. Luke vi. 19. add Ib. viii. 46, S. Mark v. 30.
[17] Pesikta Rabbathi, in Yalkut Shim 'oni ii. 56. 4. in Schöttgen ad loc.
[18] On the word "Burden" see above on Nah. i. 1. p. 129.

Before CHRIST cir. 487.

the land of Hadrach, and [b] Damascus *shall be* the rest thereof: when [c] the eyes of man, as of all the tribes of

Before CHRIST cir. 487.

[b] Amos 1. 3.

[c] 2 Chr. 20. 12. Ps. 145. 15.

in [or. *upon* [1]] *the land of Hadrach.* The foreground of this prophecy is the course of the victories of Alexander, which circled round the holy land without hurting it, and ended in the overthrow of the Persian empire. The surrender of Damascus followed first, immediately on his great victory at the Issus; then Sidon yielded itself and received its ruler from the conqueror, Tyre he utterly destroyed; Gaza, we know, perished; he passed harmless by Jerusalem. Samaria, on his return from Egypt, he chastised.

It is now certain that there was a city called Hadrach in the neighborhood of Damascus and Hamath, although its exact site is not known. "It was first found upon the geographical tablets [2] among the Assyrian inscriptions." "[3] In the catalogue of Syrian cities, tributary to Nineveh, (of which we have several copies in a more or less perfect state, and varying from each other, both in arrangement and extent) there are three names, which are uniformly grouped together and which we read Manatsuah, Magidá [Megiddo] and Du'ar [Dor]. As these names are associated with those of Samaria, Damascus, Arpad, Hamath, Carchemish, *Hadrach*, Zobah, there can be no doubt of the position of the cities [4]." In the Assyrian Canon, Hadrach is the object of three Assyrian expeditions, [5] 9183 (B.C. 818), 9190 (811) and 9200 (801). The first of these follows upon one against Damascus, 9182 (817). In the wars of Tiglath-pileser ii. (the Tiglath-pileser of Holy Scripture,) it has been twice deciphered; 1) in the war B. C. 738, 737, after the mention of "the cities to Saua the mountain which is in Lebanon were divided, the land of Bahalzephon to Ammana" (Ammon), there follows Hadrach [6]; and subsequently there are mentioned as joined to the league, "19 districts of Hamath, and the cities which were round them, which are beside the sea of the setting sun." 2) In his "war in Palestine and Arabia," "[7] the city of Hadrach to the land of Saua," and six other cities are enumerated, as "the cities beside the upper sea," which, he says, "I possessed, and six of my generals as governors over them I appointed." No other authority nearly approaches these times. The nearest authority is of the second century after our Lord, A.D. 116. "[8] R. Josè, born of a Damascene mother, said," answering R. Yehudah ben Elai [9], "I call heaven and earth to witness upon me, that I am of Damascus, and that there is a place called Hadrach." S. Cyril of Alexandria says [10] that "the land of Hadrach must be somewhere in the Eastern parts, and near to Emath (now Epiphania of Antioch) a little further than Damascus, the metropolis of the Phœnicians and Palestine." A writer of the 10th century [11] says that there was "a very beautiful mosque there, called the Mesjed-el-Khadra, and that the town was named from it." The conjecture that Hadrach might be the name of a king [12], or an idol [13], will now probably be abandoned, nor can the idea, (which before seemed the most probable and which was very old), that it was a symbolic name, hold any longer. For the Prophets *do* use symbolic names [14]; but then they are

[1] As Is. ix. 8, "The Lord sent a word *upon* Jacob (ביעקב) and it lighted on Israel" (בישראל).

[2] Published in the British Museum Series vol. ii. Pl. 53, Prof. Rawlinson.

[3] Sir H. Rawlinson, Athenæum, No. 1869, Aug. 22, 1863, p. 246, where he "published his reading, some time after he identified it." "It has since been identified by others."

[4] Sir H. Rawlinson adds in a note; "From the position on the lists, I should be inclined to identify it with Homs or Edessa which was certainly a very ancient capital, (being the Kedesh of the Egyptian records) and which would not otherwise be represented in the Assyrian inscriptions." Note 26. Ib.

[5] Oppert in the Révue Archéologique 1868. T. 2. p. 323. [6] G. Smith's Assyrian discoveries p. 276.

[7] Ib. p. 284.

[8] in Siphre sect. Debarim (ed. Friedm. p. 65.)

[9] In the time of Hadrian. Wolf Bibl. Hebr. i. 411.

[10] Here.

[11] David ben Abraham, MS. Opp. Add. f. 25, quoted by Neubauer, Geogr. du Talmud p. 298. The account of one Joseph Abassi that "it was once a large city, but now small; that the Arabs told much of its kings and princes; that it was said to have had giants and was about 10 miles from Damascus," no doubt relates to Edrei. See Hengstenberg Christol. ii. 92 sqq. A. v. Kremer, Beiträge zur Geographie des nördlichen Syriens (in d. Denkschriften d. Kais. Akad. d. Wissensch. [Wien] philos. hist. Classe, A. 1852. 2 Abth. p. 21 sqq.) and Topographie v. Damascus (Ib. 1854. 2 Abth. p. 1 sqq.; 1855 2 Abth. p. 1 sqq.) and Wetzstein d. Markt v. Damascus (ZDMG. 1857. p. 476 sqq.) Reisebericht üb. Hauran u. d. Trachonen (1860), carry out the evidence that no trace of such a place can now be found. Köhler ad loc. T. ii. p. 7.

[12] The idiom, *the land of*, is used of a people, Canaan, Benjamin, Israel, Judah, Zebulon, Naphtali, Sinim, Chittim, Egypt, Assyria, the Philistines; or of the actual king, speaking of his territory, (as Neh. ix. 22, *they possessed the land of Sihon, and the land of the king of Heshbon and the land of Og, king of Bashan*, (Sihon and Og and the king of Heshbon being, at the time spoken of, in actual possession of that land); but it is nowhere used of any past king or of an idol; much less would it be used in reference to an unknown king or idol. Scotland might, in oratory, be called "land of the Bruce," or England perhaps, "thou land of Mammon." But it would not be called, without emphasis, "land of Stephen" or "Edgar" or any obscure Saxon king.

[13] The people, not the land, is called "the people of Chemosh" (i.e. the people who worshiped it) Nu. xxi. 29. Jer. xlviii. 46. Nor is there any like name of an idol. "Derketo" (v. Alphen) would be תַּרְעֲתָא. Hitzig gave up the combination, by which he made the name of an idol. (Kl. Proph. Ed. 3.)

[14] As "Ariel," Is. xxix. 1, 2, 7; "The burden of the

names which they themselves frame. Micah again selects several names of towns, now almost unknown and probably unimportant, in order to impress upon his people some meaning connected with them[1], but then he does himself so connect it. He does not name it (so to say), leaving it to explain itself. The name Hadrach[2] would be a real name, used symbolically, without anything in the context to shew that it is a symbol.

The cities, upon which the burden or heavy prophecy fell, possessed no interest for Israel. Damascus was no longer a hostile power; Hamath had ever been peaceable, and was far away; Tyre and Sidon did not now carry on a trade in Jewish captives. But the Jews knew from Daniel, that the empire, to which they were in subjection, would be overthrown by Greece[3]. When that rapid attack should come, it would be a great consolation to them to know, how they themselves would fare. It was a turning point in *their* history and the history of the then known world. The prophet describes[4] the circuit, which the conqueror would take around the land which God defended; how the thunder-cloud circled round Judæa, broke irresistibly upon cities more powerful than Jerusalem, but was turned aside from the holy city *in going and returning*, because God encamped around it.

"[5]The selection of the places and of the whole line of country corresponds very exactly to the march of Alexander after the battle of Issus, when Damascus, which Darius had chosen as the strong depository of his wealth, of Persian women of rank, confidential officers and envoys[6]," was betrayed, but so opened its gates to his general, Parmenio. Zidon, a city renowned for its antiquity and its founders, surrendered freely; Tyre, here specially marked out, was taken after a 7 months' siege; Gaza too resisted for 5 months, was taken, and, as it was said, "plucked up[7]."

And Damascus shall be *the rest thereof.* God's judgment fell first upon Damascus. But the word "resting-place" is commonly used of quiet peaceful resting, especially as given by God to Israel; of the ark, the token of the Presence of God, after its manifold removals, and of the glorious dwelling-place of the Christ among men[8]. The prophet seems then purposely to have chosen a word of large meaning, which should at once express (as he had before[9]), that the word of God should fall heavily on Damascus and yet be its resting-place. Hence, about the time of our Lord, the Jews interpreted this of the coming of the Messiah, that "[10]Jerusalem should reach to the gates of Damascus. Since Damascus shall be the place of His rest, but the place of His rest is only the house of the sanctuary, as it is said, *This is My rest for ever; here will I dwell.*" Another added[11], "All the prophets and all prophesied but of the years of redemption and the days of the Messiah." Damascus, on the conversion of S. Paul, became the first resting-place of the word of God, the first-fruits of the Gentiles

desert of the sea," Ib. xxi. 1; "the sea," Jer. xlix. 23; "Sheshac," of Babylon, (whatever the explanation is, perhaps from sinking down, coll. שׁכך Gen. viii. 1) Jer. xxv. 26, li. 41; "the land Merathaim," ("double rebellion"), and "the inhabitants of Pekod" ("visitation") of Babylon (Jer. l. 21); not Dumah, which is probably a real proper name, Is. xxi. 11; nor לב קמי, (Jer. li. 1.) for כשׂדים; for כשׂדים could not be mentally substituted for it, since ישׁבי כשׂדים would be an impossible combination. For inhabitants are of a land, city &c; but כשׂדים are the people themselves.

[1] See ab. on Micah i. 10, p. 221.

[2] The word, divided into two halves, would signify, "sharp-soft." חד is used of sharpness (see on Hab. i. 8. comp. Ps. lvii. 5, Is. xlix. 2.); רך of delicacy, Deut. xxxiii. 54–56; of weakness, Ib. xx. 8, 2 Chr. xiii. 7. And so it would signify, what was in one respect or at one time "sharp," and in or at another, "soft." A Jewish tradition, extant in times soon after our Lord, so explained it: "Severe to the Gentiles, and tender to Israel." (R. Judah ben Elai, a disciple of R. Akibah. Wolf. Bibl. Hebr. ii. 690.) S. Jerome has the same from his Jewish teacher, "The burden of the word of the Lord is on the land of Hadrach; on which the Lord exercised both His austerity and clemency; austerity on those who would not believe, clemency on those who, with the Apostles, returned to Him." The name would have singularly suited Persia, whose empire Alexander was engaged in destroying, when this prophecy was fulfilled, and which was aimed at in them. It would describe them as they were, fierce and cruel, as conquerors, but infamous, even among the Heathen, for their incests. Sins of the flesh, destroying pure love, brutalizing the soul, disorganizing the frame, are parents of ferocity, from which voluptuousness seems at first sight most alien.

[3] Dan. viii. 20, 21. [4] See below on ver. 8.

[5] Pusey's "Daniel the Prophet," pp. 279, 280.

[6] Grote's Greece xii. 173, 4.

[7] *κατεσπασμένη*. Strabo xvi. 2. 30.

[8] מנוחה is used of rest or a place of rest, given by God, Deut. xii. 9, Ps. xxiii. 2, xcv. 11, Mi. ii. 10, Is. xxviii. 12, xxxii. 18; dwelling of God, Ps. cxxxii. 8, 14, Is. lxvi. 1; for the ark, 1 Chr. xxviii. 2; of the Messiah, Is. xi. 10. It is probably a proper name, Jud. xx. 43.

[9] הניח Zech. vi. 8.

[10] R. Johanan in Midrash Shir Hasshirim on Cant. vii. 4 in Raym. Pug. Fid. 643. This Midrash gives a second mystical interpretation of Hadrach. "Hadrach (חדרך) is the King Messiah, Who is to guide (להדרין) all who come into the world by repentance before God, Blessed for ever." Ib. "R. Johanan was a disciple of the elder Hillel and Shammai, according to the Pirkê Aboth c. 2; prince of Israel for 40 years, 5 of them after the destruction of the temple. Rashi on cod. Rosh Hasshana, end." Wolf Bibl. Hebr. ii. 844.

[11] Mar (quoted by Rashi) i. e. Rabbi ben Nachman "Rector of the Academy of Pombedita in 300." De Rossi Dict. St. v. Rabboth. Ibn Ezra has; "the rest of the prophecy shall be on Damascus; for this prophecy shall be fulfilled, connected with the second temple; For the eyes of man are to the Lord; for many from the men of Damascus shall return to worship the Lord and to turn to the obedience of Israel in Jerusalem." And so Kimchi, "Damascus shall be His resting-place, i. e. the Shechinah of His glory and prophecy."

Before CHRIST cir. 487.

Israel, *shall be* toward the
LORD.

2 And [d] Hamath also
shall border thereby; [e] Tyrus, and [f] Zidon, though it
be very [g] wise.

[d] Jer. 49. 23.

[e] Isai. 23. Ezek. 26, & 27, & 28. Amos 1. 9. [f] 1 Kin. 17. 9. Ezek. 28. 21. Obad. 20. [g] Ezek. 28. 3, &c.

whom the Apostle of the Gentiles gathered from East to West throughout the world.

When [or *For*] *the eyes of man, as* [lit. *and* i. e. especially beyond others] *of all the tribes of Israel,* shall be *toward the Lord.* This also implies a conversion of Gentiles, as well as Jews. For *man,* as contrasted with Israel, must be the heathen world, mankind[1]. "[2] The eyes of all must needs look in adoration to God, expecting all good from Him, because the Creator of all provided for the well-being of all, as the Apostle says, [3] *Is He the God of the Jews only? Is He not also of the Gentiles? Yea, of the Gentiles also.* God's time of delivering His people is, when they pray to Him. So Jehoshaphat prayed, [4] *O our God, wilt Thou not judge them? For we have no strength against this great company, which is come against us, and we know not what we shall do; but our eyes are on Thee*[5]; and the Psalmist says, [6] *The eyes of all wait toward Thee;* and, [7] *as the eyes of servants are unto the hand of their masters, and as the eyes of a maiden are unto the hand of her mistress, so our eyes are unto the Lord our God, until He have mercy upon us.* "For in those days," says a Jew, who represents the traditional interpretation[8], "man shall look to his Creator, and his eyes shall look to the Blessed One, as it was said above, *we will go with you,* and they shall join themselves, they and their cities, to the cities of Israel." And another[9]; "In those days the eyes of all mankind shall be to the Lord, not to idols or images; therefore the land of Hadrach and Damascus, and the other places near the land of Israel—shall be included among the cities of Judah, and shall be in the faith of Israel."

2. *And Hamath also shall border thereby*[10]. Near to it in place and character, it shall share its subdual. After the betrayal of Damascus, Parmenio was set over all Syria. "[11] The Syrians, not as yet tamed by the losses of war, despised the new empire, but, swiftly subdued, they did obediently what they were commanded."

And Zidon. Zidon, although probably older than Tyre[12], is here spoken of parenthetically, as subordinate. Perhaps, owing to its situation, it was a wealthy[13], rather than a strong place. Its name is "Fishing-town;" in Joshua, it is called "the great[14]," perhaps the metropolis; while Tyre is named from its strength[15]. It infected Israel with its idolatry[16], and is mentioned among the nations who oppressed them and from whom God delivered them on their prayers[17], probably under Jabin. In the time of the Judges, it, not Tyre, was looked to for protection[18]. In the times of Ezekiel it had become subordinate, furnishing "rowers[19]" to Tyre; but Esarhaddon, about 80 years before, boasts that he had taken it, destroyed its inhabitants, and repeopled it with men from the East, building a new city which he called by his own name[20]. Tyre too had been taken by Nebuchadnezzar[21]. At the restoration from the captivity, Sidon had the first place[22], which it retained in the time of Xerxes[23]. But Artaxerxes Ochus gained possession of it by treachery, when all Phœnicia revolted from Persia, and, besides those crucified, 40,000 of its inhabitants perished by their own hands[24], twenty years before the invasion of Alexander, to whom it submitted willingly[25].

The prophet having named Tyre and Zidon together, yet continues as to Tyre

[1] So Israel and *man* (האדם) are contrasted in Jer. xxxii. 20.

[2] Rib. [3] Rom. iii. 29. [4] 2 Chron. xx. 12.

[5] כי עליך עינינו.

[6] אליך ישברו Ps. cxlv. 15; without עיני Ps. civ. 27; and in the same sense, with ל, שִׂבַּרְתִּי לישועתך Ps. cxix. 166.

[7] Ps. cxxiii. 2. God's eye is said to be אֶל יְרֵאָיו, *toward them that fear Him.* Ps. xxxiii. 18, or in Ezra's Chaldee, *The eye of their God was upon the elders* (עַל שָׂבֵי) *of the Jews* (Ezr. v. 5.), or, *the eyes of the Lord thy God are upon it* (the land) בָּהּ, De xi. 12; but there is no construction like ליי עֵין אדם "the Lord hath an eye on (obj.) man" (as lxx. Jon. Syr.) The passages, *Whose eyes are opened* (פְּקֻחוֹת) *upon all the ways of the sons of men, to give* &c. (Jer. xxxii. 19), "His eyes behold the nations" (בגוים תצפינה Ps. lxvi. 7), are altogether different. "The eye of" must be construed as "his own eye."

[8] Rashi. [9] Kimchi.

[10] It might be also, *and Hamath too, which bordereth thereby,* viz. shall be *the place of its rest,* as well as Damascus, but it seems not so forcible.

[11] Q. Curtius iv. 1.

[12] "The Tyrians are often called Sidonians; the Sidonians are never called Tyrians."

[13] Its manufactures of silver bowls and of female robes of great beauty, are mentioned by Homer (Il. vi. 289, xxiii. 743, 744; Od. iv. 614–618.); Homer does not name Tyre.

[14] Jos. xi. 8, xix. 28. [15] Ib. xix. 29. [16] Jud. x. 6.

[17] Ib. 12. [18] Ib. xviii. 7, 28. [19] Ezek. xxvii. 8.

[20] Inscription of Esarhaddon (Annals of the past iii. 112). Such names, in the East, last only with the conquerors.

[21] See vol. i. pp. 249, 250, and, more fully, "Daniel the Prophet," pp. 289, 290.

[22] Ezr. iii. 7. [23] Herod. viii. 67, see also vii. 9. 6.

[24] Diod. xvi. 41 sqq. Mela i. 12. [25] Curt. iv. 3.

Before CHRIST cir. 487.

3 And Tyrus did build herself a strong hold, and [h] heaped up silver as the dust, and fine gold as the mire of the streets.

[h] Job 27. 16. Ezek. 28. 4, 5.

4 Behold, [i] the LORD will cast her out, and he will smite [k] her power in the sea; and she shall be devoured with fire.

[i] Isai. 23. 1.
[k] Ezek. 26. 17.

Before CHRIST cir. 487.

alone, as being alone of account in the days of which he is speaking, those of Alexander.

Although, rather, *because she is very wise.* Man's own wisdom is his foolishness and destruction, as *the foolishness of God* is his wisdom and salvation. God [1] *taketh the wise in their own craftiness.* [2] *For after that, in the wisdom of God, the world by wisdom knew not God, it pleased God by the foolishness of preaching to save them that believe.* Of the Hagarenes it is said, they [3] *seek wisdom upon earth; none of these know the way of wisdom, or remember her paths.* The wisdom of Tyre was the source of her pride, and so of her destruction also. [4] *Because thy heart is lifted up, and thou hast said, I am a god, I sit in the seat of God, in the midst of the seas; yet thou art a man and not God, though thou hast set thine heart as the heart of God; behold thou art wiser than Daniel, there is no secret that they can hide from thee. Therefore I will bring strangers upon thee—they shall bring thee down to the pit.* So of Edom Obadiah says, [5] *The pride of thy heart hath deceived thee, thou that dwellest in the clefts of the rock. Shall I not destroy the wise men out of Edom, and understanding out of the mount of Esau?*

3. *And Tyre did build herself a stronghold.* She built it for herself, not for God, and trusted to it, not to God, and so its strength brought her the greater fall. The words in Hebrew express yet more. "Tyre" (*Zor*) lit. "*the rock,*" *built herself mazor, tower*, a rock-like fort, as it were, a rock upon a rock for exceeding strength, binding her together. "[6] The walls, 150 feet high and of breadth proportionate, compacted of large stones, embedded in gypsum," seemed to defy an enemy who could only approach her by sea. "[7] In order to make the wall twice as strong they built a second wall ten cubits broad, leaving a space between of five cubits, which they filled with stones and earth." Yet high walls do not fence in only; they also hem in. *Mazor* is both "a stronghold" and "a siege." Wealth and strength, without God, do but invite and embitter the spoiler and the conqueror."

And she heaped up silver as the dust, and fine gold as the mire of the streets. Though he heap up silver as the dust, Job says. [8] *The King,* Solomon, *made silver in Jerusalem as stones* [9]. Through her manifold commerce she gathered to herself wealth, as abundant as the mire and the dust, and as valueless. "Gold and silver," said a heathen, "are but red and white earth." Its strength was its destruction. Tyre determined to resist Alexander, "[10] trusting in the strength of the island, and the stores which they had laid up," the strength within and without, of which the Prophet speaks.

4. *Behold.* Such were the preparations of Tyre. Over against them, as it were, the prophet sets before our eyes the counsels of God. "[11] Since they had severed themselves from the providence of God, they were now to experience His power." *The Lord will cast her out* [12], lit. deprive her of her possessions, give her an heir of what she had amassed, viz: the enemy; *and he will smite her power* or *wealth* [13], of which Ezekiel says, [14] *With thy wisdom and with thine understanding thou hast gotten thee riches, and hast gotten gold and silver into thy treasures: by the greatness of thy wisdom and by thy traffic thou hast increased thy riches, and thine heart is lifted up because of thy riches* [15]. All wherein she relied, and so too the stronghold itself, God would *smite in the sea.* The sea was her confidence and boast. She said [16] *I am a God; I sit in the seat of God, in the midst of the seas.*

The scene of her pride was to be that of her overthrow; the waves, which girt her round, should bury her ruins and wash over her site. Even *in the sea* the hand of God should find her, and *smite* her *in it*, and *into it*, and so that she should abide in it. "[17] They mocked at the king, as though he thought to prevail against Neptune [the sea]." "[18] Ye despise this land-army, through confidence in the place, that ye dwell in an island," was the message of Alexander, "but soon will I shew you that ye dwell on a continent."

Every device had been put in force in its defence: the versatility by which the inhabitants of an island, some 2½ miles in circumference, held at bay the conqueror of the

[1] Job v. 13. [2] 1 Cor. i. 21. [3] Baruch iii. 23. [4] Ezek. xxviii. 2, 8. [5] Ob. 3, 8. [6] Arrian ii. 21. [7] Diod. Sic. xvii. 43. [8] Job xxvii. 16. [9] 2 Chron. ix. 27. [10] Diod. Sic. xvii. 40. [11] Theod.

[12] יוריש, of God, is chiefly used of the driving out the Canaanitish nations before Israel, Ex. xxxiv. 24, Nu. xxxii. 21, Ps. xliv. 3, 1 Kgs xiv. 24, xxi. 26, 2 Kgs xvi. 3, xvii. 8. xxi. 2.

[13] חיל cannot be here the outer wall (on which see Nah. iii. 8, ab. p. 156, n. 2.) which was useless in island Tyre, whose walls rising from the sea needed no outer wall and admitted of no fosse or pomœrium.

[14] Ezek. xxviii. 4, 5. [15] חיל.
[16] Ezek. xxviii. 2.
[17] Diod. Sic. xvii. 41. [18] Q. Curt. iv. 7.

Before CHRIST cir. 487.

[1] Jer. 47. 1, 5. Zeph. 2. 4.

5 [1] Ashkelon shall see *it*,
and fear; Gaza also *shall*
see it, and be very sorrowful, and Ekron; for her
expectation shall be
ashamed; and the king

Before CHRIST cir. 487.

battle of Issus with unlimited resources, "[1] engineers from Cyprus and all Phœnicia," and "[2] a fleet of 180 ships from Cyprus," attests the wisdom in which the prophet says, she would trust. "[3] She had already a profusion of catapults and other machines useful in a siege, and easily prepared manifold others by the makers of war-engines and all sorts of artificers whom she had, and these invented new engines of all sorts; so that the whole circuit of the city was filled with engines." Divers who should loosen the mole; grappling hooks and nets to entangle near-assailants; melted metal or heated sand to penetrate between the joints of their armor; bags of sea-weed to deaden the blows of the battering machines; a fire-ship navigated so as to destroy the works of the enemy, while its sailors escaped; fiery arrows; wheels set in continual motion, to turn aside the missiles against them[4], bear witness to an unwearied inventiveness of defence. The temporary failures might have shaken any mind but Alexander's (who is even said to have hesitated[5]) but that he dared not, by abandoning the enterprise, lose the prestige of victory. Yet all ended in the massacre of 6, 7, or 8000 of her men, the crucifixion of 2000, the sale of the rest, whether 13,000 or 30,000, into slavery[6]. None escaped save those whom the Sidonians secreted in the vessels[7], with which they had been compelled to serve against her.

And she herself[8], when her strength is overthrown, *shall be devoured with fire.* "[7] Alexander, having slain all, save those who fled to the temples, ordered the houses to be set on fire."

5. *Ashkelon shall see and fear.* The words express that to *see* and *fear* shall be as one[9]. The mightiest and wealthiest, Tyre, having fallen, the neighbor cities of Philistia who had hoped that her might should be their stay, shall stand in fear and shame. Tyre, being a merchant-city, the mother-city of the cities of the African coast and in Spain, its desolation caused the more terror[10].

And the [*a*] *king shall perish from Gaza*, i. e. it shall have no more kings. It had been the policy of the world-empires to have tributary kings in the petty kingdoms which they conquered, thus providing for their continued tranquil submission to themselves[11]. The internal government remained as before: the people felt no difference, except as to the payment of the tribute. The policy is expressed by the title "king of kings," which they successively bore. Sennacherib speaks of the kings of Ascalon, Ekron and Gaza[12]. A contemporary of Alexander[13] mentions, that the king of Gaza was brought alive to Alexander on its capture. Alexander's policy was essentially different from that of the world-monarchs before him. *They* desired only to hold an empire as wide as possible, leaving the native kings, if they could; and only, if these were intractable, placing their own lieutenants. Alexander's policy was to blend East and West into one[14]. These petty sovereignties, so many insulated centres of mutual repulsion, were essentially at variance with this plan, and so this remnant of sovereignty of 1500 years was taken away by him, when, after a siege in which he himself was twice wounded, he took it. Alexander wholly depopulated it, and repeopled the city with strangers.

And Ashkelon shall not be inhabited. Ashkelon yielded at once to Jonathan, when he "camped against it[15]," after he had taken and "burned Ashdod and the cities round about it." In another expedition of Jonathan its inhabitants "[16] met him honorably," while "they of Gaza shut him out" at first. "[17] Simon—passed through the country unto Ascalon, and the holds there adjoining," without resistance, whereas "he turned aside to Joppe, and won it." He placed Jews in Gaza, but of Ascalon nothing is said. The ruins of a Christian city, built on its site, "khirbet-Ascalon," have been lately discovered in the hills near Tell Zakariyeh[18], and so, a little South of Timnath, a Philistine city in the days of Samson, whence

[1] Arr. ii. 21. [2] Q. Curt. iv. 13. [3] Diod. Sic. xvii. 41.
[4] Q. Curt. iv. 11–16. Arrian ii. 18–22.
[5] Diod. Sic. xvii. 42–46.
[6] Diod. xvii. 46. Q. Curt. iv. 19, Arr. ii. 24.
[7] Q. Curt. l. c. [8] והיא emph. [9] תֵּרֶא־וְתִירָא.
[10] Is. xxiii. 5–11.
[11] Herodotus states it to have been the wont of the Persian monarchs to put the sons even of revolted kings on their fathers' thrones (iii. 15), and in the review of the Persian troops under Xerxes mentions different tributary kings, among whom the king of Sidon had first rank; then the king of Tyre; then the rest (viii. 67). Josephus speaks of "the kings of Syria." (Ant. xi. 8. 5.)

[12] in Layard Nin. and Bab. p. 144.
[13] Hegesias in Dionys. Hal. de comp. verb. c. 18. T. V. p. 125, Reiske. There is much obscurity about the individual. Dion. Hal. has, "its king Baistis or Baistios;" Arrian (ii. 25) mentions Batis, an Eunuch and so a Persian officer, as "having supreme authority over Gaza;" κρατῶν τ. Γαζαίων πόλεως. Q. Curtius says, "Betis was over the city" (iv. 26). "Josephus (Ant. xi. 84.) says that "the name of the commandant of the garrison was Babēmēsēs."
[14] See "Daniel the Prophet," pp. 142–145.
[15] 1 Macc. x. 86. [16] Ib. xi. 60, 61. [17] Ib. xii. 33.
[18] "The name was given twice to Lieut. Conder and 3 times to Corporal Brophy by different wit-

Before CHRIST cir. 487.

shall perish from Gaza,
and Ashkelon shall not be
inhabited.
6 And a bastard shall
dwell in [m] Ashdod, and I
will cut off the pride of the
Philistines.

m Amos 1. 8.

7 And I will take away
his †blood out of his mouth,
and his abominations from
between his teeth: but he
that remaineth, even he,
shall be for our God, and
he shall be as a governor

Before CHRIST cir. 487.

† Heb. *bloods.*

Samson went to it, to gain the 30 changes of raiment[1]. Commentators have assigned reasons, why Samson might have gone so far as the maritime Ascalon, whereas, in fact, he went to a city close by.

That city, in 536 A.D., had its Bishop[2]. "[3] The site shews the remains of an early Christian Church or convent:" as a great lintel of stone[4], resembling somewhat the Maltese Cross, lies on the ground." It was probably destroyed by the inundation of Mohammedan conquest. In 1163 A. D. it was a ruin. The distance of the ruins from the Ascalon Maiumas corresponds to that assigned by Benjamin of Tudela, being twice the distance of that city from Ashdod[5]; but since he was at Beth Jibrin[6], he must have been not far from the spot where it has been lately discovered[7]. The Ashkelon, which was Herod's birth-place and which he beautified, must have been the well-known city by the sea; since the distance from Jerusalem assigned by Josephus[8] is too great for the old Ashkelon, and he speaks of it as on the sea[9].

6. *And a bastard shall dwell at Ashdod*[10].

nesses," "so that there is no doubt (Lieut. Conder subjoins) that it is a well-known site." Lieut. Conder's Report N. xxxiv. p. 153. [1] Jud. xiv. 19.

[2] See ab. p. 244. [3] Lieut. Conder, Ib. [4] "Such lintels are to be found in all that class of ruins, which date from about the 5th to the 7th century." Ib.

[5] He says that the new Ashkelon, that on the sea, is 2 parasangs from Ashdod, 4 from the old Ashkelon. [6] Travels, p. כב.

[7] Jeremiah, xlvii. 7, *How can it* (the sword of the Lord) *be quiet, seeing that the Lord has given it a charge against Ashkelon, and against the sea-shore?* has often been wrongly quoted in proof that Ashkelon was on the sea-shore." On the contrary, Jeremiah speaks of them as distinct; "against Ashkelon and against the sea-shore." The חוף הים, in the 3 other places, in which it occurs, is only a title for Philistia itself, as lying between the Shephelah and the sea. Thus in Deut. i. 7, Palestine is divided into the hill country, the 'Arabah, the Shephelah, the Nejeb, and the חוף הים. In Joshua, ix. 1, the division is, "the hill country, the Shephelah, and the whole coast of the great sea, כל חוף הים הגדול." Ezekiel (xxv. 16.) uses חוף הים, as equivalent to the Cherethim and Philistim, whom he had named in v. 5. Jeremiah names together the whole tract and a chief city of it, as the prophets so often speak of "Judah and Jerusalem."

[8] 520 stadia. B. J. iii. 2. 1. [9] Ib. iv. 11. 5.

[10] On the omission of Gath see on Am. i. 6.

[11] ἐκ πορνῆς, ὁ in Deut. xxiii. 3; "de scorto," Vulg. and so Saad.; "son of adultery," Syr. With this

The "mamzer" was one born unlawfully, whether out of marriage, or in forbidden marriage, or in adultery[11]. Here it is, probably, like our "spurious brood[12];" whether it was so itself or in the eyes of the Ashdodites; whence he adds,

I will cut off the pride of the Philistines. Pride would survive the ruin of their country, the capture of their cities, the loss of independence. It would not survive the loss of their nationality; for they themselves would not be the same people, who were proud of their long descent and their victories over Israel. The breaking down of nationalities, which was the policy of Alexander, was an instrument in God's hands in cutting off their pride.

7. *And I will take away his bloods out of his mouth.* The *abominations* being idol-sacrifices[13], the *bloods* will also be, the blood mingled with the wine of sacrifices, of which David says, [14] *Their drink-offerings of blood will I not offer;* and Ezekiel unites the offences, "[15] *Ye eat with the blood, and lift up your eyes toward your idols,* and shed blood."

But he that remaineth, better, *And he too*

agrees the opinion of R. Joshua A. D. 73, "every one, for whom they are guilty of death in the house of judgment." R. Joshua b. Azai says, 'I have found a roll of genealogies in Jerusalem, and there was written in it, 'M., a mamzer from a man's wife;' to confirm the words of R. Joshua." in Yebamoth c. 4, § 13. R. Akiba's opinion was, that "it was any near of kin, with whom marriage was forbidden;" Simon the Temanite said, "any liable to excision at the hands of God." Ib. in Ges. Thes. p. 781 sub. v. Of the etymologies, Kimchi's is perhaps the most probable, that it is from זור, the two מ's being added, as in מַמְּגֻרוֹת, Joel i. 17.

[12] The Lxx. Jon. Syr. agree in the rendering, "strangers," Jon. and the Syr. using the same word; נוכריא Pesh.; "and the children of Israel shall dwell in Ashdod, who were in it, as strangers" (כנוכראין). Jon. Aq. Symm. Theod. retain the Hebrew word, as do Onk. and Sam. in Deut.

[13] שִׁקּוּצִין always retains its appellative sense. It is not merely "idols," but idols, in that they were "abominations." It is generally in constr., "the abomination of" such a nation, 1 Kgs xi. 5, 7 [bis], 2 Kgs xxiii. 13 [bis], "the abomination of his, their, eyes," Ezek. xx. 7, 8; or with the personal pronoun as here, Deut. xxix. 16, Is. lxvi. 3, Jer. [5 times] Ezek. [6 times]. In a few places it stands absolutely, in its original appellative sense, Nah. iii. 6; allusively to the idol abominations, Hos. ix. 10; with art. the [idol] abominations (2 Kgs xxiii. 24, 2 Chr. xv. 8); and the abomination of desolation. Dan. ix. 27, xi. 31. xii. 11. [all].

[14] Ps. xvi. 4. [15] Ezek. xxxiii. 25.

Before CHRIST cir. 487.

in Judah, and Ekron as a Jebusite.

8 And [n]I will encamp about mine house because of the army, because of him that passeth by, and because of him that returneth: and [o]no oppressor

n Ps. 34. 3. ch. 2. 5.

o Isai. 60. 18. Ezek. 28. 24.

shall remain over to our God. Of the Philistines too, as of Israel, *a remnant shall be saved.* After this visitation their idolatry should cease; God speaks of the Philistine nation as one man; He would wring his idol-sacrifices and idol-enjoyments from him; he should exist as a nation, but as God's.

And he shall be as a governor in Judah, lit. "a captain of a thousand," merged in Judah as in a larger whole, as each tribe was divided into its "thousands," yet intimately blended, in no inferior position, with the people of God, as each converted nation became an integral yet unseparated whole in the people of God.

And Ekron as a Jebusite. Ekron was apparently the least important of the few remaining Philistine cities[1]; yet he shall be, as those of the Canaanite nations who were not destroyed, nor fled, but in the very capital and centre of Israel's worship, [2]*dwelt with the children of Benjamin and Judah,* and were, as a type of the future conversion and absorption of the heathen, incorporated into Judah.

8. *And I will encamp about my house (for*[3] *my house's sake) because of the army*[4]; *because,* it is added in explanation, *of him that passeth by and of him that returneth;* Alexander, who *passed by* with his army, on his way to Egypt, and *returned,* having founded Alexandria.

It was a most eventful march; one of the most eventful in the history of mankind. The destruction of the Persian empire, for which it prepared, was in itself of little moment; Alexander's own empire was very brief. As Daniel had foretold[5], he came, *cast down* Persia *to the ground, waxed very great,* and *when he was strong, the great horn was broken.* But with the marvelous perception which characterized him, he saw and impressed upon his successors the dependibleness of the Jewish people. When he came into Judæa, he sent to the high priest for aid against Tyre and for the like tribute as he used to pay to Darius, promising that he would not repent of choosing the friendship of the Macedonians[6]. The high priest refused on the ground of the oath, by which his people were bound in fealty to the earthly king of kings, whom Alexander came to subdue. Alexander threatened to teach all, through its fate, to *whom* fealty was due. This, after the conquest of Gaza, he prepared to fulfill. He came, he saw, he was conquered. [7]Jaddua and his people prayed to God. Taught by God in a dream not to fear, he went to meet the conqueror. The gates of the city were thrown open. There marched out, not an army such as encountered the Romans, but as he had been taught, a multitude in white garments, and the priests going before in their raiment of fine linen. The high priest, in his apparel of purple and gold, having on his head the mitre, and on it the golden plate[8], whereon was written the name of God, advanced alone, and the Conqueror, who was expected to give the city to be plundered, and the high priest to be insulted and slain, kissed the name of God, recognizing in the priest one whom he had seen in the like dress in a dream, who had bidden him, when hesitating, cross to Asia; for that he would go before his army and deliver the Persian empire to him.

The result is related to have been, that Alexander promised to allow the Jews in Judæa to live according to their own laws, remitted the tribute of every seventh year, acceded beforehand to the terms to be proposed by those in Babylonia and Media, and that many Jews joined his army, under condition that they might live under their own laws.

Rationalism, while it remains such, cannot admit of Daniel's prophecies which the high priest shewed him, declaring that a Greek should destroy the Persian empire, which Alexander rightly interpreted of himself. But the facts remain; that the conqueror, who, above most, gave way to his anger, bestowed privileges almost incredible

[1] See on Jo. i. 8, vol. i.

[2] Josh. xv. 63. Jud. i. 21.

[3] לְבֵיתִי.

[4] צָבָה, for צָבָא, according to the Masorites as in the verb also, Is. xxix. 7. So Symm. κωλύων στρατείας. The context also favors the reading; for unless the *passers by* and *returners* had been a powerful army, there had been no occasion for that defence of which God speaks. The correction מַצָּבָה would come to the same, "a military post;" only, in actual use, this is a "fort," "fortress," 1 Sam. xiv. 12, i. q. מַצָּב Ib. xiii. 23, xiv. 1, 4, 6, 11, 15, 2 Sam. xxiii. 14. מֻצָּב Is. xxix. 3, is a work on the offensive, not defensive. Ewald comes to the same sense, that God would protect her against any one coming against her.

[5] Dan. viii. 7, 8. [6] Jos. Ant. xi. 8, 3. [7] Ib. n. 5.

[8] Justin says, "then he, Alexander, goes to Syria, where many kings of the East with fillets met him. Of these, according to their deserts, he received some into alliance; others he deprived of their kingdom, putting other kings in their place." xi. 10.

Before CHRIST cir. 487.

shall pass through them any more: for now [p] have I seen with mine eyes.

[p] Ex. 3. 7.

9 ¶ [q] Rejoice greatly, O daughter of Zion; shout, O daughter of Jerusalem:

Before CHRIST cir. 487.

[q] Isai. 62. 11. ch. 2. 10. Matt. 21. 5. John 12. 15.

on a nation, which under the Medes and Persians had been "[1] the most despised part of the enslaved;" made them equal in privileges to his own Macedonians[2], who could hardly brook the absorption of the Persians, although in inferior condition, among themselves[3]. The most despised of the enslaved became the most trusted of the trusted. They became a large portion of the second and third then known cities of the world. They became Alexandrians, Antiochenes, Ephesians[4], without ceasing to be Jews. The law commanded faithfulness to oaths, and they who despised their religion respected its fruits.

The immediate successors of Alexander, Ptolemy Lagi[5] and Antiochus Nicator, followed his policy; Ptolemy especially on the ground of the fealty shewn to Darius; Nicator, as having observed their faithfulness as soldiers, who had served with him[6]; but they were so enrolled on this visit to Jerusalem. The Heathen kings multiplied, in their own purpose, faithful subjects to themselves; in God's design, they prepared in Asia and Egypt a seed-plot for the Gospel. The settlement of the Jews at Alexandria formed the language of the Gospel; that wonderful blending of the depth of the Hebrew with the clearness and precision of the Greek. Everywhere the seed of the preparatory dispensation was sown, to be fostered, grow and ripen with the harvest of the Gospel.

For now have I seen with Mine eyes. This is the counterpart of what the Psalmists and pious men so often pray, [7] *Awake to help me and behold;* [8] *Look down from heaven, behold and visit this vine;* [9] *Look upon my trouble from them that hate me;* [10] *Look upon my affliction and my trouble; look upon my enemies, for they are many;* [11] *Look upon my adversity and deliver me;* [12] *O Lord, behold my affliction;* [13] *Behold, O Lord, for I am in distress;* [14] *Look and behold my reproach;* [15] *Open Thine eyes, O Lord, and see;* [16] *Look down from heaven, and behold from the habitation of Thy holiness and glory.* With God, compassion is so intrinsic an attribute, that He is pictured as looking away, when He does not put it forth. With God, to behold is to help.

9. From the protection, which God promised to His people and to His House, the Prophet passes on to Him Who was ever in his thoughts, and for Whose sake that people and temple were preserved. He had described the great conqueror of this world,

[1] Tacitus limits the description to the time, "when the East belonged to the Assyrians, Medes and Persians." Hist. v. 8.

[2] "Alexander gave them (the Jews) a place to dwell in, and they obtained equal rank with the Macedonians. I know not what Apion would have said, had they been settled near the Necropolis and not near the palace, and were not their race now too called 'Macedonians.' If then he (Apion) has read the Epistles of Alexander the King, and has met with the rescripts of Ptolemy Lagi and the kings after him, and has lighted on the column which stands in Alexandria and contains the rights given by the great Cæsar to the Jews; if, I say, he knows these things, and, knowing them, has dared to write the contrary, he is unprincipled; if he knew nothing of them, he is ill-instructed." "Alexander collected some of our people there, not for want of such as should colonize the city which he founded with great earnestness. But carefully proving all as to good faith and probity, he gave this distinction to our people. For he honored our nation, as Hecatæus too says of us, that, for the probity and good faith which the Jews evinced toward him, he gave them in addition the territory of Samaria to hold, free from tribute. And Ptolemy Lagi too was like-minded with Alexander as to those who dwelt in Alexandria." Jos. Ib. This early equalizing of the Jews with Alexandrians is recognized in the edict of Claudius: "Having learnt that the Jews in Alexandria were from the first called Alexandrians, having been settled there together with the Alexandrians straightway at the earliest period, and having received from the kings equal citizenship, as appeared plain both from their letters and from the ordinances," &c. [in Jos. Ant. xix. 5, 2.] in Pusey's "Daniel the Prophet," p. 146, n. 3.

[3] Arr. vii. 6.

[4] "His (Apion's) marveling, how, being Jews, they were called Alexandrians, betrays the same ignorance. For all who are invited into a given colony, much as they differ in race, take their name from its founders. Those of us, who dwell at Antioch, are called Antiochenes. For Seleucus, the founder, gave them citizenship. And so too in Ephesus, and the rest of Ionia, they bear the same name with the natives, the Successors (of Alexander) having given it to them." Jos. c. Ap. ii. 4. See Pusey's "Daniel the Prophet," p. 146. n. 2.

[5] Ptolemy Lagi, "understanding that, those from Jerusalem were most reliable as to their oaths and fealty, (from the answer which they gave to the embassy of Alexander after he had conquered Darius,) having located many of them in the garrisons and given them equal rights of citizenship with the Macedonians in Alexandria, took an oath of them that they would keep fealty to the descendants of him who gave them this charge. And no few of the other Jews came of their own accord into Egypt, invited by the goodness of the soil and the liberality of Ptolemy." Jos. Ant. xii. 1. Ib. p. 145. n. 8.

[6] "They (the Jews) obtained the honor from the kings of Asia also, having served in the army with them. For Seleucus Nicator, in the cities which he founded in Asia and in lower Syria, and in the metropolis itself, Antioch, conferred on them citizenship, and made them rank with the Macedonians and Greeks who were settled therein, so that this citizenship remains even now also." Ant. xii. 3. Ib. p. 146. n. 1.

[7] Ps. lix. 4. [8] Ib. lxxx. 14. [9] Ib. ix. 13.
[10] Ib. xxv. 18, 19. [11] Ib. cxix. 153.
[12] Lam. i. 9. add 11, ii. 20. [13] Ib. i. 20.
[14] Ib. v. 1.
[15] Is. xxxvii. 17. Dan. ix. 18. [16] Is. lxiii. 15.

26

Before CHRIST cir. 487.

behold, [r] thy King cometh unto thee: he *is* just, and

[r] Jer. 23. 5. & 30. 9. Luke 19. 38. John 1. 49.

sweeping along in his course of victory. In contrast with such as he, he now exhibits to his people the character and procession of their king. *Rejoice greatly.* Not with this world's joy. God never exhorts man to *rejoice greatly* in this world's fleeting joys. He allows us to be glad, as children, before Him; He permits such buoyancy of heart, if innocent; but He does not command it. *Now* He commands His people to burst out into a jubilee of rejoicing: they were to dance and shout for gladness of spirit; "despising the poor exultation of this world and exulting with that exceeding" yet chaste joy, which befits the true bliss to be brought by their King and Saviour. "[1] This word, *greatly*, means that there should be no measure whatever in their exultation; for the exultation of the children of the bridegroom is far unlike to the exultation of the children of this world." "[2] He biddeth the spiritual Zion rejoice, inasmuch as dejection was removed. For what cause of sorrow is there, when sin has been removed, death trampled under foot, and human nature called to the dignity of freedom, and crowned with the grace of adoption and illumined with the heavenly gift?"

Behold, thy king cometh unto thee. He does not say "*a* king," but "*thy* king;" thy king, thine own, the long-promised, the long-expected; He Who, when they had kings of their own, given them by God, had been promised as *the* king[3]; [4] *the righteous Ruler among men*, of the seed of David; He Who, above all other kings, was *their* King and Saviour; Whose kingdom was to absorb in itself all kingdoms of the earth; *the King of kings, and Lord of lords.* Her king was to come *to her.* He was in a manner then "of her," and "not of her;" "of her," since He was to be *her king*, "not of her," since He was to "*come to* her." As Man, He was born of her: as God, the Word made flesh, He *came to* her. "[5] *To thee*, to be manifest unto thee[6]; to be thine by communion of nature[7]; as He is thine, by the earnest of the Eternal Spirit and the gift of the Father, to procure thy good. [8] *Unto us a Child is born, unto us a Son is given.*" Of this, His entry into Jerusalem was an image. But how should He come? "He shall come to thee," says an old Jewish writing[9], "to atone thee; He shall come to thee, to upraise thee; He shall come to thee, to raise thee up to His temple, and to espouse thee with an everlasting espousal."

He is just and having salvation. Just or righteous, and the Fountain of justice or righteousness. For what He is, *that* He diffuseth. Righteousness which God *Is*, and righteousness which God, made Man, imparts, are often blended in Holy Scripture[10]. This is also the source of the exceeding joy. For the coming of their king in righteousness would be, to sinful man, a cause, not of joy but of fear. This was the source of the Angel's message of joy; [11] *I bring you good tidings of great joy, which shall be to all people; for unto you is born this day, in the city of David, a Saviour.*

He is just, "[12] because in the Divine Nature, He is the Fountain of all holiness and justice." "[13] As Thou art righteous Thyself, Thou orderest all things righteously. For Thy power is the beginning of righteousness." According to the nature which He took, He was also most just; for He ever sought the glory of the Father, and [14] *He did no sin, neither was guile found in His Mouth.* In the way also of justice He satisfied for men, delivering Himself for their faults to the pain of the most bitter death, to satisfy the honor of the Divine Majesty, so that sin should not remain unpunished. Hence He saith of Himself; [15] *He that seeketh His glory that sent Him, the same is true, and no unrighteousness is in Him.* Of Whom also Stephen said to the Jews, [16] *Your fathers slew them which shewed before of the coming of the Just One, of Whom ye have been now the betrayers and murderers.* Righteousness is an awful attribute of God. It is a glory and perfection of His Being, for the perfect to gaze on and adore. Mercy, issuing in our salvation, is the attribute which draws us sinners. And this lies in the promise that He should *come to them*, however the one word *nosha'* be rendered[17]. The meaning of such a prophecy as this is secure, independent of single words. The whole context implies, that He should come as a ruler and deliverer, whether the word *nosha'* signify

[1] Rup. [2] S. Cyr.
[3] e.g. Ps. ii. lxxii. Is. xxxii. 1. Jer. xxiii. 5.
[4] 2 Sam. xxiii. 3. [5] Cocc. [6] 1 Tim. iii. 16.
[7] Heb. ii. 14. [8] Is. ix. 6.
[9] Zohar Levit. f. 3. col. 9 in Schöttg. on Hos. ii. 21.
[10] Is. xlv. 21. liii. 11, Jer. xxiii. 5, 6, xxxiii. 15, 16, Mal. iv. 2.
[11] S. Luke ii. 10, 11. [12] Dion. [13] Wisd. xii. 15, 16.
[14] 1 S. Pet. ii. 22. [15] S. John vii. 18. [16] Acts vii. 52.
[17] The Jewish Versions as well as the Christian render, actively, "Saviour," LXX, σώζων; Jon. פריק, as well as the Christian, the Syr. and S. Jerome. The participle נושע might, according to analogy, be a reflective, but it only occurs elsewhere as a passive; with ב p., Deut. xxxiii. 29, Is. xlv. 17; with ב r., Ps. xxxiii. 16. Imperat. "look unto Me and be ye saved," וְהִוָּשְׁעוּ Is. xlv. 22; being "saved by God" implied Nu. x. 9. Ps. xviii. 4. [2 Sam. xxii. 4.] lxxx. 4, 8, 20, cxix. 117, Pr. xxviii. 18, Is. xxx. 15, lxiv. 4, Jer. iv. 14, viii. 20, xvii. 14, xxiii. 6, xxx. 7, xxxiii. 16. [all]

Before CHRIST cir. 487.

|| having salvation; lowly, and riding upon an ass, and upon a colt the foal of an ass.

|| Or, *saving himself.*

Before CHRIST cir. 487.

"endued with salvation," (whereas the old versions rendered it, "Saviour") or whether it be, "saved." For as He came, not for Himself but for us, so, in as far as He could be said to be saved, He was "saved," not for Himself but for us. Of our Lord, as Man, it is, in like way, said, [1] *Thou shalt not leave His soul in Hell*, or, [2] *Whom God raised up, having loosed the pains of death, because it was not possible that He should be holden of it.* As Man, He was raised from the dead; as God, He raised Himself from the dead, for our sakes, for whom He died. For us, He was born a Saviour; for us, He was endued with salvation; for us, He was saved from being held of death; in like way as, of His Human Nature, the Apostle says, [3] *He was heard, in that He feared.* To us, as sinners, it is happiest to hear of the Saviour; but the most literal meaning "saved" has its own proper comfort: for it implies the Sufferings, by which that salvation was procured, and so it contains a hint of the teaching by Isaiah, *He was taken from oppression and from judgment;* upon which that same wide reign follows, of which David, in his picture of the Passion [4], and Isaiah [5] prophesy. "[6] This 'saved' does not imply, that He obtained salvation for His own otherwise than from Himself. *Mine own arm*, He saith in Isaiah, [7] *brought salvation unto Me.* But as Man, He obtained salvation from the indwelling Godhead. For when He destroyed the might of death, when, rising from the dead, He ascended into heaven, when He took on Him the everlasting kingdom of heaven and earth, He obtained salvation from the glory of the Father, i. e. from His own Divinity, to impart it to all His. The Hebrew word then in no way diminishes the amplitude of His dignity. For we confess, that the Human Nature of Christ had that everlasting glory added to It from His Divine Nature, so that He should not only be Himself adorned with those everlasting gifts, but should become the cause of everlasting salvation to all who obey Him."

Lowly. Outward lowliness of condition, is, through the grace of God, the best fosterer of the inward. The word *lowly* wonderfully expresses the union of both; lowness of outward state with lowliness of soul. The Hebrew word expresses the condition of one, who is bowed down, brought low through oppression, affliction, desolation, poverty, persecution, bereavement; but only if, at the same time, he had in him the fruit of all these, in lowliness of mind, submission to God, piety. Thus our Lord pronounces the blessedness of "the poor" and "the poor in spirit," i. e. poor in estate, who are poor in soul also. But in no case does it express lowliness of mind without lowness of condition. One lowly, who was not afflicted, would never be so called. The Prophet then declares that their king should come to them in a poor condition, *stricken, smitten, and afflicted* [8], and with the special grace of that condition, meekness, gentleness and lowliness of soul; and our Lord bids us, [9] *Learn of Me, for I am meek and lowly of heart.* "[10] He saith of Himself in the Gospel, [11] *The foxes have holes and the birds of the air have nests, but the Son of Man hath not where to lay His Head.* [12] *For though He was rich, He for our sakes became poor, that we through His poverty might be rich.*

Lowly and riding upon an ass. Kings of the earth ride in state. The days were long since by, when the sons of the judges rode on asses [13]. Even then the more distinguished rode on *white* (i. e. roan [14]) asses. The mule, as a taller animal, was used by David [15] and his sons [16], while asses were used for his household [17], and by Ziba, Shimei, Mephibosheth, Ahitophel [18], and, later, by the old prophet of Bethel [19]. David had reserved horses for 100 chariots [20], after the defeat of the Syrians, but he himself did not use them. Absalom employed *chariots and horses* [21] as part of his pomp, when preparing to displace his father; and Solomon multiplied them [22]. He speaks of it as an indignity or reverse; [23] *I have seen servants upon horses, and princes walking, as servants, upon the earth.* The burial of an ass became a proverb for a disgraced end [24]. There is no instance in which a king rode on an ass, save He Whose kingdom was not of this world. The prophecy, then, was framed to prepare the Jews to expect a prophet-king, not a king of this world. Their eyes were fixed on this passage. In the Talmud, in their traditional interpretations, and in their mystical books, they dwelt on these words. The mention of the ass, elsewhere, seemed to them typical of this ass, on which their Messiah should ride. "If a man in a dream seeth an ass," says

[1] Ps. xvi. 10. [2] Acts ii. 24. [3] Heb. v. 7.
[4] Ps. xxii. 27, 28. [5] Is. liii. 10–12. [6] Osor.
[7] Is. lxiii. 5. [8] Is. liii. 4. [9] S. Matt. xi. 29.
[10] Dion. [11] S. Matt. viii. 20. [12] 2 Cor. viii. 9.
[13] Jud. x. 4, xii. 14. [14] Ib. v. 10.
[15] 1 Kgs i. 33, 38, 44. [16] 2 Sam. xiii. 29, xviii. 9.
[17] Ib. xvi. 2.
[18] Ib. xvi. 1, xvii. 23, xix. 26, 1 Kgs ii. 40.
[19] 1 Kgs xiii. 13, 23, 27. [20] 2 Sam. viii. 4.
[21] Ib. xv. 1.
[22] 1 Kgs iv. 26, x. 26, 2 Chr. i. 14, ix. 25.
[23] Eccl. x. 7. [24] Jer. xxii. 19.

the Talmud[1], "he shall see salvation." It is an instance of a prophecy which, humanly speaking, a false Messiah could have fulfilled, but which, from its nature, none would fulfill, save the True. For *their* minds were set on earthly glory and worldly greatness: it would have been inconsistent with the claims of one, whose kingdom was of this

[1] Berachoth f. 56. 2 (in Schöttgen ad loc.). There was a general consent among the Jews, that this prophecy related to the Messiah. *R. Joseph* (probably "the pious," the disciple of Jochanan, the disciple of Hillel, Wolf, Bibl. Hebr. ii. 848, 844) used it as an argument against R. Hillel, who disbelieved in any Messiah. "R. Hillel, 'Israel has no Messiah, for they enjoyed him in the days of Hezekiah.' R. Joseph said, 'Lord, forgive R. Hillel!' When did Hezekiah live? In [the time of] the first temple. But Zechariah prophesied in [the time of] the second temple; 'Rejoice greatly, daughter of Zion, behold, thy king cometh unto thee, righteous and *nosha*'." He said also, "O that he may come, and that I may be worthy to sit in the shadow of the dung of his ass" Sanhedrin, f. 99. 1. "*R. Alexandri* said, that *R. Joshua ben Levi* set against each other the Scriptures, 'Lo, there came with the clouds of heaven one like unto the Son of Man,' and that, 'lowly and riding on an ass.' Deserve he [Israel], 'with the clouds of heaven;' deserve he not, 'lowly and riding on an ass.'" Ib. f. 98. "All these goods, which I will do to them through the merits of the Messiah, shall be extended in all those years." *R. Jannai* (about A. D. 130) said from *Raf*, "whoever looketh for salvation, God will give him rest in the garden of Eden, according to that, 'I will feed my flock and cause them to lie down' (Ezk. xxxiv. 15.) 'Just and nosha.' This is the Messiah, who justifieth his judgment against Israel because they mocked him, because he sat in prison, so he is called 'just.' But why נושע, but that he justifieth the judgment upon them. He says to them, 'ye are my sons; are ye not all to be saved only by the mercy of the Holy One, blessed be He?' 'Afflicted and riding on an ass.' This is the Messiah. But why is his name called עני, 'afflicted?' Because he was afflicted all those years in prison, and the transgressors of Israel mocked him, because he rideth upon an ass on account of the wicked who have no desert." (a dislocated passage, Schöttg. says, of the *Pesikta Rabbathi* f. 61. 1. 2. in Schottg. de Messia, loci gen. n. xcvii. p. 136. The Hebrew of the latter part is given by Wünsche d. Leiden des Messias p. 66.) And in a remarkable passage on Cant. i. 4, "Let us exult and rejoice in thee." "The Matrona is like a royal bride, whose husband the king, her sons and sons-in-law, were gone beyond sea. When they brought her word that her sons were returned, she said, 'What cause of joy have I? Let my daughters-in-law rejoice!' Another messenger came, that her sons-in-law were returned, she answered, 'What cause of joy have I? Let my daughters rejoice!' But when they told her that the king, her husband, was returned, she said, 'This is perfect joy, a joy above all joys!' So also in the time to come, the time of the Messiah, the prophets shall come to Jerusalem and say, (Is. lx. 4) 'thy sons shall come from far;' she will answer, 'What cause of joy have I?' The prophets will add, 'Thy daughters shall be nurtured by thy side; 'she will answer in like way. But when they shall say to her, 'Behold, thy king cometh unto thee, just and a Saviour,' then she shall say, 'This is perfect joy;' as in, 'Exult greatly, daughter of Zion,' and elsewhere, 'Sing and rejoice, O daughter of Zion.' Then she shall say, 'I will greatly rejoice in the Lord, my soul shall be joyful in my God (Is. lxi. 10.)'" *Shir hasshirim Rabba* fol. 7. 3 (in Schöttg. loc. gen. n. v., Martini f. 512). They quote the prophecy also as to the union of the royal and priestly offices of the Messiah. The *Bereshith Rabba* had on Gen. xiv. 18, "'And Melchizedec, king of Salem.' This is the name of Shem, the son of Noah. What would that teach, 'he brought forth bread and wine?' *R. Samuel Bar Nachman* said, He delivered to him the ways of the priesthood, and he offered bread and wine to God, as it is said, 'He was priest of the most High God, king of Salem.'—Otherwise; Melchizedec; this is what Scripture saith, 'The Lord sware and will not repent, Thou art a Priest for ever after the order of Melchizedec.' And who is he? This is the king, righteous and נושע, the king Messiah, according to, 'Behold thy king cometh unto thee, righteous and נושע.' And what would that teach, 'He brought forth bread and wine?' It is as is said, 'Be there a handful of corn upon the earth.' (Ps. lxxii. 16.) This is what is written, 'And he was a priest of the most High God.'" (in Mart. f. 654 end.) Or they argue from נושע, as to the free mercy of God, "God says to Israel, If your merit is not of such account, I do it for my own sake; for day by day, when you are in trouble, I am with you, as in, 'I am with him in trouble,' (Ps. xci. 15); and so I deliver myself, 'And he saw that there was no one, and wondered' (Is. lix. 16.); and elsewhere, 'Exult greatly, daughter of Zion—behold thy king cometh unto thee, just and נושע.' It is not written ומושיע ["and saving"] but ונושע ["and saved"]; whereby it is hinted that, though your merits are not of such account, God will act for His own sake, according to, 'For my salvation is near to come.'" (*Shemoth Rabba* sect. 30. fol. 129. 1. Schöttg. loc. gen. n. ix.) Martini quotes a like saying from the *Bereshith Rabba* on Gen. xlix. 8. "R. Berachiah the priest, son of Rabbi, said, See what is written, 'Rejoice greatly &c.' It is not written, 'Just and מושיע, a Saviour,' but 'Just and נושע saved,' and thus he says, (Is. lxii. 11.) 'Say ye to the daughter of Sion—it is not written, 'thy Saviour (מושיעך) cometh,' but, 'Behold thy salvation (ישעך) cometh.' As if one might so speak, 'Israel was redeemed, and it is as if God were redeemed,' and this is one of the hard Scriptures, that the salvation of Israel is the salvation of God." fol. 518. Martini quotes also from a comment on Isaiah lvii. 1. "The righteous perisheth." "This is Messiah, of Whom it is said, 'Just and saved.'" f. 334.

In other places, the riding upon the ass is dwelt upon. *Midrash Coheleth* on Eccl. i. 9. f. 73. 3. "*R. Berachiah* said from *R. Isaac*, As was the first redeemer, so also shall be the last redeemer. What did the first redeemer? (Ex. iv. 20.) 'And Moses took his wife and his sons and placed them on an ass;' the second, as is written, 'lowly and riding on an ass.'" (Martini f. 380, and 690, Schöttg. Hor. Hebr. on S. Matt. xxi. 5.) In the *Midrash Shemuel* f. 66. 1. the saying is ascribed to *R. Levi* (Schöttg. on this place). And the *Pirke R. Eliezer* c. 31, of Abraham's ass, "This is the ass, on which the son of David shall ride, according to, 'Rejoice greatly, daughter of Zion.'" (Ib.) The *Zohar* owns that the prophecy relates to the Messiah, but apologizes for it. "It is not the custom that the king and his Matrona should ride on an ass, but rather on horses, as in (Hab. iii. 7.) 'For thou shalt ride on thy horses, and thy chariots are salvation.' For they do not esteem a matrona so slightly, that she should ride on an ass, as the king wonteth not to ride on an ass, like one of the people. And therefore it is said of the Messiah, 'Poor and riding upon an ass.' And he is not there called king, until he ride upon his horses, which are the people of Israel." (on Levit. f. 38. col. 151. in Schöttg. de Mess. vi. 213. p. 543.) Or they say great things of the ass. "This ass is son of the she-ass, which was created within the six days in the twilight. This is the ass, which Abraham saddled, when he purposed to sacrifice Isaac. This is the ass, on which Moses was carried when he went to Egypt. This is the ass, on which the son of David shall ride hereafter." *Yalkut Reubeni* (f. 79, 3, 4 on Exod. iv.

Jews, of what nature His kingdom was. Hence the challenge; "[1] Let us look at the prophecy, that in words, and that in act. What is the prophecy? *Lo, thy king cometh unto thee, meek, and sitting upon an ass, and upon a colt;* not driving chariots as other kings, not in pomp nor attended by guards, but shewing herein also all gentleness. Ask the Jew then, What king, riding on an ass, came to Jerusalem? He could name none, save this One alone." An ancient writer says, "[2] The Greeks too" (not the Jews only) "will laugh at us, saying, that 'The God of the Christians, Who is called Christ, sat upon an ass.'" The same mockery was probably intended by Sapor[3] king of Persia, which the Jews met with equal pride. The taunt continues till now. "[4] It is not hid from you, O congregation of Christians, that 'rider upon an ass' indicates Christ." The Mohammedans appropriate the title "rider upon a camel" to Mohammad, as the grander animal[5]. The taunt of worshiping "Him Who sat upon an ass" was of the same class as those of the worship of the Crucified; "[6] one dead and crucified, who could not save himself;" "a crucified Man," "that great Man," or (if it suited them so to speak) "that great sophist who was crucified," but Who now, for above 1800 years, reigns, "to all, the King; to all, the Judge; to all, Lord and God." "[7] Christ did not only fulfill prophecies or plant the doctrines of truth, but did thereby also order our life for us, everywhere laying down for us rules of necessary use and, by all, correcting our life." Even Jews, having rejected our Lord, saw this. "Not from poverty," says one[8], "for behold the whole world shall be in his power—but from humility he will ride upon an ass; and further to shew that Israel [viz. the establishment of His kingdom or Church] shall not want horse nor chariot: therefore it is added, *And I will cut off the chariot from Ephraim and the horse from Jerusalem.*" And another[9]; "He, i. e. thy true king David, shall come to thee; and he mentions of his qualities that he shall be *righteous and nosha'* [10] in his wars; but his salvation

or, since as a Jew, he could not interpret it of Jesus, of interpreting it of any one in the time of the second temple. "Some of the interpreters make this consolation an announcement of the Expected (may he soon be revealed!) and this is found in most of the Midrashoth of the ancient wise (blessed be their memory!) and the obvious meaning of his words, 'and his dominion is from sea to sea and from the river unto the ends of ths earth' supports this; and some of them think, that from the context it relates to the circumstances of the second house, and this is supported by his words in the passage, 'And I will raise thy sons, O Zion, against thy sons, O Greece,' which was in the second house, through the Hasmonæans, and now the empire of Greece is dispersed and gone. How then should he promise help against it in the future? And altogether the word of the prophecies admits of the interpretation. And many vary therein from one meaning to the other. And therefore we will mention how the language can be explained according to each opinion. And God, most high, knows what is hidden! The meaning then of 'עני and riding upon an ass' is, in my opinion, in the first way, beautiful; that עני means one who humbles himself, like (Is. lxvi. 2) 'And to this man will I look, to the humble (עני) and contrite of spirit,' not weak in condition; on account then of his lowliness he will ride upon an ass." (He compares the reduplication to that in Gen. xlix. 11.) "Or," he says, "the whole of this may be a metaphor for self-abjection, not an actual history; and what is known, is that this is his condition at first for his weakness and lowness; afterward he will attain his later condition in strength and felicity. And so for the second way, this points to the return of the kingdom to Israel through the Hasmonæans, and his saying 'meek and riding upon an ass' indicates their first king, Judas the Hasmonæan, and he, at the outset, was weak, because he followed upon the oppression of Greece, according to what has been transmitted of that history; and that, 'his dominion shall be from sea to sea &c.' this is the kingdom to which he attained at last, and the extension of his house; and he means by this, 'from the red sea to the sea of the Philistines and from the river to the end of the habitable land;' and this is, 'And from the river &c.' and thus words, 'I will raise up thy sons, O Zion, against thy sons, O Greece,' will fit. And in the first way; 'from sea to sea' will be the encircling sea [the Ocean] and from the river which is the bound of the land of Israel to the furthest habitable earth." He answers the reference to Nehemiah, but ends by leaving the other two open. *Moses ben Nāchman* quotes it in illustration of the contempt of the Messiah spoken of in Isaiah lii. 13. liii. 3. 7. "Theirs [the kings'] astonishment was shewn by mocking him, when he first arrived, and by asking, how one 'despised, meek and riding upon an ass,' could conquer all the kings of the world who had laid hold on Israel?—He was 'despised,' for he had no army and no people, but was 'meek and riding on an ass,' like the first redeemer Moses our master, when he entered in Egypt with his wife and children riding upon an ass. (Ex. iv. 20.) 'He was oppressed and he was afflicted,' for when he first comes 'meek and riding upon an ass,' the oppressors and officers of every city will come to him, and afflict him with revilings and insult, reproaching both him and the God in whose name he appears, like Moses our master, who, when Pharaoh said, I know not the Lord, answered him not." In Jewish Commentaries on Is. liii. p. 80, 81.

The modern school, which rids itself of defini e prophecy, would have this relate to "the ideal Messiah." One does not see, how a literal prophecy, fulfilled to the letter, can relate to an ideal king; unless on the implied assumption, "There *can* be no prophecy of a definite event."

[1] S. Chrys. in S. Matt. Hom. 66. p. 656 marg. Ed. Oxon.

[2] Author of the Hom. in S. Matt. xxi. 2. in the Dubia of S. Athan. n. 6. Opp. ii. 77.

[3] "King Sapor said to R. Samuel, 'Ye say that the Messiah comes upon an ass, I will send him a horse [epithet uncertain] which I have, He answered, 'Hast thou one with 100 colors' (so Rashi) or, 'with 1000 qualities.' (Aruch and Reland Diss. ix. T. i. 288, 298.) Sanhedr. f. 98. 1. "In the deep humility of the Messiah," subjoins Lightfoot, "they dream of pride even in his ass." Hor. Hebr. on S. Matt. xxi. 5.

[4] Epist. Mohammedan. Anon. inserted by Hackspan Nizzach. pp. 397–401.

[5] The titles "rider on an ass," "rider on a camel," are derived from Is. xxi. 14.

[6] See Lucian de morte Peregrini c. 11, 13. Trypho in S. Justin Dial. n. 14. p. 83. Oxf. Tr. Celsus in Origen c. Cels. viii. 12. 14. 15. and others in Pusey's Lenten Sermons pp. 454, 455. Liddon's Bampton Lectures pp. 392–297. ed 2. Kortholt de calumniis Pagan. c. 4 pp. 31–36.

[7] S. Chrys. l. c. p. 655.

[8] Kimchi.

[9] Abarbanel in his Mashm'a Yeshu'ah p. 73.

[10] I leave the word *nosha'* untranslated, in order not to give any possible color to his words, though

Before CHRIST cir. 487.

10 And I [s]will cut off
the chariot from Ephraim,
and the horse from Jerusalem, and the battle bow
shall be cut off: and he
shall speak [t]peace unto the
heathen: and his dominion
shall be [u]from sea *even* to

[s] Hos. 1. 7. & 2. 18. Mic. 5. 10. Hag. 2. 22.

[t] Eph. 2. 14, 17.

[u] Ps. 72. 8.

shall not be from strength of his wars, for he shall come *lowly* and *riding upon an ass*[1]. And *riding on an ass*, this is not on account of his want, but to shew that peace and truth shall be in his days; and therefore he says forthwith, *And I will cut off the chariot from Ephraim and the horse from Jerusalem;* viz. that such shall be the peace and stillness in the world, that in Ephraim (i. e. the tribes) and in Jerusalem (i. e. the kingdom of Judah) they shall *trust* no more in horse and in rider, but *in the name of God.* And because it is the way of princes and chiefs to take example from the life of their kings, and to do as they, therefore he saith, that when the king Messiah rideth upon an ass, and *has no pleasure in the strength of a horse,* there will be no other in Jerusalem or the lands of the tribes, who will have pleasure in riding on a horse. And therefore he says, *And I will cut off the chariot from Ephraim and the horse from Jerusalem;* and he assigns the reason for this, when he says, *And the battle-bow shall be cut off, and he shall speak peace among the nations,* i. e. there shall be no more war in the world, because he shall *speak peace unto the nations, and by the word of his lips* [2] *he shall dispose peace unto them.*"

And upon a colt, the foal of an ass. The word rendered *colt,* as with us, signifies the young, as yet unbroken animal. In the fulfillment, our Lord directed His disciples to find [3]*an ass tied, and a colt with her, whereon never man sat.* The prophet foretold that He would ride on both animals; our Lord, by commanding both to be brought, shewed that the prophet had a special meaning in naming both. S. Matthew relates that both were employed. "They brought the ass and the colt, and put on *them* their clothes, and they set Him thereon." The untrained colt, an appendage to its mother, was a yet humbler animal. But as the whole action was a picture of our Lord's humility and of the unearthliness of His kingdom, so, doubtless, His riding upon the two animals was a part of that picture. There was no need of two animals to bear our Lord for that short distance. S. John notices especially, [4]*These things understood not His disciples at the first.* The ass, an unclean stupid debased ignoble drudge, was in itself a picture of unregenerate man, a slave to his passions and to devils, toiling under the load of ever-increasing sin. But, of man, the Jew had been under the yoke and was broken; the Gentiles were the wild unbroken colt. Both were to be brought under obedience to Christ.

10. *And I will cut off the chariot.* The horse is the symbol of worldly power, as the ass is of meekness. *Some,* says the Psalmist, [5]*put their trust in chariots, and some in horses; but we will remember the name of the Lord our God.* [6]*A horse is but a vain thing to save a man.* [7]*He delighteth not in the strength of a horse.* In scarcely any place in Holy Scripture is the horse spoken of in relation to man, except as the instrument of war. It represents human might, which is either to be consecrated to the Lord, or destroyed by Him [8]. As the [9]*stone, cut out without hands,* broke in pieces and absorbed into itself all the kingdoms of the world, so here He, Whose Kingdom should not be of this world, should supersede human might. His kingdom was to begin by doing away, among His followers, all, whereby human kingdoms are established. He first cuts off the chariot and the horse, not from His enemies, but from His own people; His people, not as a civil polity, but as the people of God. For the prophet speaks of them as Ephraim and Judah, but Ephraim had no longer a distinct existence.

And He shall speak peace unto the heathen, as the Apostle says, [10]*He came and preached peace to you which were afar off, and to them that were nigh.* He shall speak it to them, as He Who hath power to give it to them, peace with God, peace in themselves, the reconciliation of God and man, and the remission of their sins.

"[11]At His birth the heavenly host announced peace to men; all His doctrine has peace for its end; when His death was at hand, He especially commended peace to His disciples, that peace which the world knoweth not, which is contained in tranquillity of mind, burning zeal for charity. Divine grace. This same peace He brought to all who gathered themselves to His empire and guidance, that, emerging from intestine wars and foul darkness, they might behold the light of liberty, and, in all wisdom keep the grace of God."

And His dominion shall be from sea to sea.

he seems from the context to take it actively "Saviour."

[1] He says here that עני is like ענו.

[2] Is. xxvi. 12.

[3] S. Matt. xxi. 2, S. Mark xi. 2, S. Luke xix. 30.

[4] S. John xii. 16.

[5] Ps. xx. 7.

[6] Ib. xxxiii. 17.

[7] Ib. cxlvii. 10.

[8] See Mi. v. 10.

[9] Dan. ii. 34.

[10] Eph. ii. 17.

[11] Osor.

Before CHRIST cir. 487.

‖ Or, *whose covenant is by blood.* Ex. 24. 8. Heb. 10. 29. & 13. 20.

sea, and from the river
even to the ends of the
earth.
11 As for thee also, ‖ by
the blood of thy covenant
I have sent forth thy [x] prisoners out of the pit wherein *is* no water.
12 ¶ Turn you to the
strong hold, [y] ye prisoners

Before CHRIST cir. 487.

x Isai. 42. 7. & 51. 14. & 61. 1.

y Isai. 49. 9.

The bounds of the promised land, in its utmost range, on the West, were the Mediterranean sea; on the East, *the great river*, the Euphrates. The prophet pictures its extension, so as to embrace the whole world, taking away, first the one bound, then the other. *From sea to sea* is from the Mediterranean to the extremest East, where the Ocean encircles the continent of Asia; *from the river to the ends of the earth*, is from the Euphrates to the extremest West, embracing the whole of Europe; and whatever may lie beyond, to the ends of the earth, where earth ceaseth to be[1]. It is this same lowly and afflicted king, Whose entry into Jerusalem is on a despised animal, Who shall, by His mere will, make war to cease, Who shall, by His mere word, give peace to the heathen.

11. *As for thee also.* The Prophet turns from the deliverance of the whole world to the former people, the sorrows which they should have in the way, and the protection which God would bestow upon them for the sake of Him, Who, according to the flesh, was to be born of them. *Thou too;* he had spoken of the glories of the Church, such as her king, when He should come, should extend it, embracing earth's remotest bounds: he turns to her, Israel after the flesh, and assures her of the continued protection of God, even in her lowest estate. The deliverance under the Maccabees was, as those under the judges had been, an image of the salvation of Christ and a preparation for it. They were martyrs for the One God and for the faith in the Resurrection, and, whether by doing or by suffering, preserved the sacred line, until Christ should come.

By the blood of thy covenant. "[2] Not by the blood of those victims of old, but *by the blood of thy covenant*, wilt thou be united to the empire of Christ, and so obtain salvation. As the Lord Himself says, *This is the blood of covenant, which is shed for you.*" [3] *The gifts and calling of God are without repentance.* That symbolic blood, by which, fore-signifying the new Covenant, He made them His own people, [4] *Behold the blood of the covenant, which the Lord hath made with you concerning all these words*, endured still, amid all their unfaithfulness and breaches of it. By virtue of it God would send forth her imprisoned ones *out of the* deep, dry *pit, the dungeon* wherein they could be kept securely, because life was not threatened[5]. Out of any depth of hopeless misery, in which they seemed to be shut up, God would deliver them; as David says, [6] *He brought me up also out of a horrible pit, out of the miry clay, and set my feet upon a rock and established my goings;* and Jeremiah, [7] *They have cut off my life in the dungeon, and cast a stone upon me. I called upon Thy Name, O Lord; out of the low dungeon Thou hast heard my voice.* "[8] The dry and barren depth of human misery, where are no streams of righteousness, but the mire of iniquity."

12. *Turn ye to the stronghold*[9], i.e. Almighty God; as the Psalmists so often say [10], *The Lord is the defence of my life;* and Joel [11], *The Lord shall be a stronghold of the children of Israel;* and Nahum [12], *The Lord is a stronghold in the day of trouble;* And, David said, [13] *Thou hast been a shelter for me, a strong tower against the enemy* [14]; *the Name of the Lord is a strong tower, the righteous runneth into it and is safe;* and again, [15] *Be Thou to me a rock of strength, a house of defence to save me—Bring me forth out of the net that they have laid privily for me; for Thou art my stronghold.* The *stronghold*, "cut off" from all approach from an enemy, stands in contrast with the deep dungeon of calamity. The *return* must be a willing return, one in their own power; *return to the stronghold*, which is Almighty God, must be by conversion of heart and will. Even a Jewish commentator [16] paraphrases, "Turn ye to God; for He is a stronghold and tower of strength."

Ye prisoners of [*the*] *hope* [17] not, accordingly, any hope, or generally, *hope*, but *the* special

1 See "Daniel the Prophet." p. 483. 2 Osor.
3 Rom. xi. 29. Exod. xxiv. 8.
5 As in Gen. xxxvii. 24. 6 Ps. xl. 2.
7 Lam. iii. 53, 55, 56. 8 S. Aug. de Civ. Dei. xviii. 35. 3. 9 בצרון is ἅπ. λεγ.
10 Ps. xxvii. 1. add xxxi. 5, xxxvii. 39, xliii. 2, lii. 9.
11 Joel iv. 16. [iii. 16 Eng.] 12 Nah. i. 7.
13 מגדל עז Ps. lxi. 3. 14 Pr. xviii. 10.
15 Ps. xxxi. 3, 5. [2, 4, Eng.] 16 Kim.
17 התקוה. The only place, where it has the art. It is used 12 times with different pronouns; 6 times with the gen., of him whose expectation is spoken of; it is used absolutely 13 times, viz. 5 times of a hope which will not fail, in the idiom יש תקוה Ruth i. 12. Jer. xxxi. 17. כי יש ת. Job xi. 18, xiv. 7, Pr. xix. 18, modified by אולי Lam. iii. 29, with ל, a solid expectation which a person has, Job. v. 16, Pr. xxvi. 12, xxix. 20; given by God, Hos. ii. 17, Jer. xxix. 11; twice with the neg., the absence of *all* hope, Job vii. 6, Pr. xi. 7. [all.]

Before CHRIST cir. 487.

of hope: even to day do I
declare *that* [a] I will render
double unto thee;

[a] Isai. 61. 7.

13 When I have bent
Judah for me, filled the
bow with Ephraim, and
raised up thy sons, O Zion,
against thy sons, O Greece,
and made thee as the
sword of a mighty man.

Before CHRIST cir. 487.

hope of Israel, *the hope* which sustained them in all those years of patient expectations, as S. Paul speaks of [1] *the hope of Israel, for* which he says, *I am bound with this chain.* [2] *I stand to be judged for the hope of the promise made by God unto our fathers, unto which* promise *our twelve tribes, serving God instantly day and night, hope to come; for which hope's sake, King Agrippa, I am accused of the Jews.* And in his Epistles, [3] *the hope laid up for you in heaven;* [4] *the hope of the Gospel;* and, [5] *looking for the blessed hope and the glorious appearing of the great God and our Saviour Jesus Christ.* He writes also of "[6] keeping the rejoicing of *the* hope firm unto the end;" of "[7] the full assurance of *the* hope unto the end;" of "[8] fleeing to lay hold on *the* hope set before us; which hope we have as an anchor of the soul, both sure and steadfast." He does not speak of hope as a grace or theological virtue, but, objectively, as the thing hoped for. So Zechariah calls to them as bound, held fast by *the hope*, bound, as it were, to it and by it, so as not to let it go, amid the persecution of the world, or weariness of expectation; as S. Paul also says, [9] *before faith came, we were guarded,* kept in ward, *under the law, shut up unto the faith* [10] *which was about to be revealed.*

Even to-day, amid all contrary appearances, *do I declare, that I will render double unto thee;* as He had said by Isaiah [11], *For your shame ye shall have double.*

13. *When,* or *For I have bent* [12] *Judah for me,* as a mighty bow which is only drawn at full human strength, the foot being placed to steady it. It becomes a strong instrument, but only at God's Will. God Himself bends it. It cannot bend itself. *And filled the bow with Ephraim* [13]. The bow is filled, when the arrow is laid upon it. God would employ both in their different offices, as one. *And raised up* [14] *thy sons, O Zion, against thy sons, O Greece.* Let men place this prophecy where they will, nothing in the history of the world was more contradictory to what was in human sight possible. "[15] Greece was, until Alexander, a colonizing, not a conquering, nation. The Hebrews had no human knowledge of the site or circumstances of Greece. There was not a little cloud, like a man's hand, when Zechariah thus absolutely foretold the conflict and its issue. Yet here we have a definite prophecy later than Daniel, fitting in with his temporal prophecy, expanding part of it, reaching on beyond the time of Antiochus, and fore-announcing the help of God in two definite ways of protection; 1) *without war,* against the army of Alexander [16]; 2) *in the war* of the Maccabees; and these, two of the most critical periods in their history after the captivity [17]. Yet, being expansions of part of the prophecy of Daniel, the period, to which they belong, becomes clearer in the event by aid of the more comprehensive prophecies. They were two points in Daniel's larger prediction of the 3d empire."

And I will make thee as the sword of a mighty man. The strength is still not their own. In the whole history of Israel, they had only once met in battle an army of one of the

[1] Acts xxviii. 20. [2] Ib. xxvi. 6, 7. [3] Col. i. 5. [4] Ib. 23. [5] Tit. ii. 13. [6] Heb. iii. 6. [7] Ib. vi. 11. [8] Ib. 18, 19. [9] Gal. iii. 23.

[10] ἐφρουρούμεθα, συγκεκλεισμένοι εἰς.

[11] Is. lxi. 7. The same word, מִשְׁנֶה.

[12] דרך קשת, in different inflections is too common an idiom to leave any ambiguity, though the word קשת occurs in the following clause only. The idiom occurs Ps. vii. 13, xxxvii. 14, Is. v. 28, xxi. 15. Jer. xlvi. 9, l. 14, 29, li. 3, Lam. ii. 4, iii. 12, 1 Chr. v. 18, viii. 40, 2 Chr. xiv. 7. דרך is used twice in the same sense, when the arrow is made the object, Ps. lviii. 8, lxiv. 4.

[13] It is the common construction of מִלֵּא with a double acc., "fill a thing with;" which, in different idioms, occurs 38 times beside. [Gen. xxi. 19. xxvi. 15, xlii. 25, Ex. xxviii. 3, xxxi. 3, xxxv. 31, 35, 1 Sam. xvi. 1, 1 Kgs xviii. 35, 2 Kgs xxiii. 14, xxiv. 4, 2 Chr. xvi. 14, Job iii. 15, viii. 21, xv. 2, xxii. 18. xxiii. 4, Ps. xvii. 14, lxxxiii. 17, cvii. 9, cxxix. 7. Pr. i. 13, Is. xxxiii. 5, Jer. xiii. 13, xv. 17, xxxiii. 5, xli. 9, li. 14, 34, Ezek. iii. 3, ix. 7, x. 2, xi. 7, xxxii. 5, xxxv. 8. Nah. ii. 13, Zeph. i. 9, Hagg. ii. 7.] It is therefore entirely unidiomatic to render with Ges. &c., "pulled with full strength a bow, Ephraim." The Arab. אַמְלַאַ פי אלקַום does not bear this out, being for אמלא אלְנַזַע פִי אלקוס. The Syr. מְלָו קֶשְׁתָא Ps. xi. 2. קשתא דמליא Is. xxi. 15, probably mean, "filled the bow" "the bow filled" viz. with the arrow

[14] Since עורר occurs of rousing a person, Cant. ii. 7, iii. 5, viii. 4, 5, Is. xiv. 9, or living thing, Job iii. 8, or His might, (of God) Ps. lxxx. 3, it would be unidiomatic to interpret it here, "lift up as a spear," on the ground of the idioms עורר את חניתו, 2 Sam. xxiii. 18, 1 Chr. xi. 11, 20, עורר שוט, Is. x. 26, since here no instrument is mentioned, but a person, and עורר is not used of any one instrument, nor, by itself, signifies "wave."

[15] Pusey's "Daniel the Prophet" pp. 282, 283.

[16] Zech. ix. 1–8. [17] Ib. 9–16.

Before CHRIST cir. 487.

14 And the LORD shall
be seen over them, and
[a] his arrow shall go forth
as the lightning: and the
Lord GOD shall blow the
trumpet, and shall go [b] with
whirlwinds of the south.
15 The LORD of hosts
shall defend them; and
they shall devour, and
‖ subdue with sling stones;
and they shall drink, *and*
make a noise as through
wine; and they ‖ shall be
filled like bowls, *and* as
[c] the corners of the altar.

[a] Ps. 18. 14. & 77. 17. & 144. 6.

[b] Isai. 21. 1.

Before CHRIST cir. 487.

‖ Or, *subdue the stones of the sling.*

‖ Or, *shall fill both the bowls, &c.*

[c] Lev. 4. 18, 25. Deut. 12. 27.

world-Empires and defeated it, at a time, when Asa's whole population which could bear arms were 580,000 [1], and he met Zerah the Ethiopian with his million of combatants, besides his 500 chariots, and defeated him. And this, in reliance on the [2] *Lord his God*, to Whom he cried, *Lord, it is nothing to Thee to help, whether with many, or with them that have no power; help us, O Lord our God; for we rest on Thee, and in Thy Name we go against this multitude.* Asa's words found an echo in Judas Maccabæus[3], when the "small company with him asked him, How shall we be able, being so few, to fight against so great a multitude and so strong?" "It is no hard matter," Judas answered, "for many to be shut up in the hands of a few, and with Heaven it is all one to deliver with a great multitude or a small company. For the victory of battle standeth not in the multitude of an host; but strength cometh from Heaven." But his armies were but a handful; 3000, on three occasions [4], on one of which they are reduced by fear to 800 [5]; 10,000 on two occasions [6]; on another, two armies of 8000 and 3000, with a garrison, not trusted to fight in the open field [7]; on one, 20,000 [8]; once only 40,000, which Tryphon treacherously persuaded Jonathan to disperse [9]; these were the numbers with which, always against "great hosts," God gave the victory to the lion-hearted Judas and his brothers. But Who save He, in Whose hands are the hearts of men, could foresee that He, at that critical moment, would raise up that devoted family, or inspire that faith, through which they [10] *out of weakness were made strong, waxed valiant in fight, turned to flight the armies of the aliens?*

14. *And the Lord shall be seen over them* [11], "[12] He will reveal Himself," protecting them. "[13] He says plainly, that the Lord God will be with them and will fight in serried array with them and will with them subdue those who resist them." It is as if he would say, "When they go forth and preach everywhere, [14] *the Lord* shall *work with* them *and confirm the word with signs following.*" *And His arrow shall go forth as the lightning.* Habakkuk directly calls the lightnings the arrows of God [15]: *at the light of Thine arrows they went.* Here it is probably of an invisible agency, and so compared to that awful symbol of His presence, the lightning.

And the Lord God shall blow with the trumpet, as their Commander, ordering their goings. The blowing of the trumpet by the priests in war was commanded, as a reminiscence of themselves before God, [16] *If ye go to war in your land against the enemy that oppresseth you, then ye shall blow an alarm with the trumpets, and ye shall be remembered before the Lord your God, and ye shall be saved from your enemies.* Abijah said, [17] *God Himself is with us for our captain, and His priests with sounding trumpets to cry alarm against you.*

And shall go with whirlwinds of the south, as being the most vehement and destructive. So Isaiah, [18] *As whirlwinds in the south sweep by, He cometh from a desert, from a terrible land.* Such smote the four corners of the house where Job's children were [19], and they perished.

15. *The Lord of hosts shall defend them.* As God says [20], *I will defend this city to save it, for Mine own sake and for My servant David's sake.* The word is used by Isaiah only before Zechariah, and of the protection of Almighty God. The image of the complete protection on all sides stands first in God's words to Abraham [21], *I am thy shield;* David thence says to God, [22] *Thou, O Lord, art a shield around me.*

And they shall devour, and subdue, or more

[1] Chr. xiv. 8–10 sqq. [2] Ib. 11. [3] 1 Macc. iii. 16–19.
[4] 1 Macc. iv. 6, vii. 40. ix. 5. [5] Ib. ix. 6.
[6] Ib. iv. 29, x. 74. [7] Ib. v. 17–20. [8] Ib. xvi. 4.
[9] Ib. xii. 41–47. See more in detail in "Daniel the Prophet" p. 371. note 5. [10] Heb. xi. 34.
[11] עַל as with the word עטה, סכך, כסה, גנן.
[12] Jon. [13] S. Cyr. [14] S. Mark xvi. 20.
[15] Hab. iii. 11. The arrows of God, and the lightnings, stand in parallel or connected clauses, Ps. xviii. 14, lxxvii. 17, 18. cxliv. 6.
[16] Nu. x. 9. [17] 2 Chr. xiii. 12.
[18] Is. xxi. 1.
[19] Job i. 19. In Job xxxvii. 9, E. V. has followed Kim. who explains מן החדר by חַדְרֵי תימן Job ix. 9; but in this case the chief characteristic word would be omitted.
[20] Is. xxxvii. 35, 2 Kgs xix. 34. Is. xxxviii. 6, 2 Kgs xx. 6. It occurs again Zech. xii. 8.
[21] Gen. xv. 1, מָגֵן from the same root.
[22] Ps. iii. 4. (3 Eng.)

Before CHRIST cir. 487.

16 And the LORD their
God shall save them in
that day as the flock of his
^d Isai. 62. 3. Mal. 3. 17. people: for [d] *they shall be*
as the stones of a crown,
[e] lifted up as an ensign
upon his land. ^e Isai. 11. 12.
17 For [f] how great *is* his ^f Ps. 31. 19.

probably [1], *shall tread on, the stones of the sling,* as in the image of leviathan in Job, [2] *The son of the bow will not make him flee; sling-stones are to him turned into stubble; clubs are counted as stubble; he laugheth at the shaking of a spear.* Their enemies shall fall under them, as harmless and as of little account as the sling-stones which have missed their aim, and lie as the road to be passed over. It is not expressed what they shall devour, and so the image is not carried out, but left indefinite, as destruction or absorption only; as in that, [3] *thou shalt consume* [lit. *eat*] *all the people which the Lord thy God shall deliver thee;* and, [4] *they are our bread;* and in that, [5] *they shall devour* [lit. *eat*] *all the people round about,* where the image is of fire, not of eating. The one thought seems to be, that their enemies should cease to be, so as to molest them any more, whether by ceasing to be their enemies or by ceasing to be. There is no comparison here, (as in Balaam) with the lion; or of eating flesh or drinking blood, which, apart from the image of the wild beast, would be intolerable to Israel, to whom the use of blood, even of animals, was so strictly forbidden. They should disappear, as completely as fuel before the fire, or food before the hungry. The fire was invigorated, not extinguished, by the multitude of the fuel: the multitude of the enemies but nerved and braced those, whom they sought to destroy.

And they shall be filled like bowls, like the corners of the altar. They shall be consecrated instruments of God; they shall not prevail for themselves, but for Him; they shall be hallowed like the bowls of the temple, from which the sacrificial blood is sprinkled on His altar, or as *the corners of the altar* which receive it.

16. *And the Lord their God shall save them in that day.* Still all should be God's doing; they themselves were but as a flock, as sheep among wolves, ready for the slaughter; but they were *the flock, His people*[6], as He says, [7] *I will increase them like the flock, men, as the flock of holy things, as the flock of Jerusalem in her solemn feasts; so shall the waste cities be filled with flocks, men.* "[8] As a man saves his flock with all his strength, so He will save His people; for they are His flock." As in, [9] *Thou leddest Thy people like sheep by the hand of Moses and Aaron.*

They shall be as the stones of a crown. While God's enemies shall be trampled under foot, as a common thing which has failed its end, these shall be precious stones; a consecrated [10] diadem of king or priest, *raised aloft*[11], so that all can see. *On His land.* It was laid down, as the title-deed to its whole tenure, [12] *the land is Mine,* and much more our Christian land, bought and purified by the blood of Christ.

17. *For how great* is *His goodness.* For it is unutterable! As the Psalmist said, [13] *O Lord, our Lord, how excellent is Thy Name in all the earth!* and Jacob, [14] *How awful is this place!* and the Psalmist, *How awful are Thy doings!* The goodness and the beauty are the goodness and beauty of God, Whose great doings had been his theme throughout before. Of the goodness the sacred writers often speak [15], since of this we have extremest need. And this He shewed to Moses, [16] *I will cause all My goodness to pass before thy face.* Of this we know somewhat personally in this life; for beside the surpassing amazingness of it in the work of our redemption, we are surrounded by it, immersed in it, as in a fathomless, shoreless ocean of infinite love, which finds entrance into our souls, whenever we bar it not out.

Goodness is that attribute of God, whereby He loveth to communicate to all, who can or will receive it, all good; yea, Himself, "[17] Who is the fullness and universality of good, Creator of all good, not in one way, not in one kind of goodness only, but absolutely, without beginning, without limit, without measure, save that whereby without measurement He possesseth and embraceth all excellence, all perfection, all blessedness, all good." This Good His Goodness bestoweth on all and each, according to the capacity of each to receive it, nor is there

1 As in margin.
2 Job xli. 20, 21 (28, 29 Eng.) 3 Deut. vii. 16.
4 Nu. xiv. 9. 5 Zech. xii. 6.
6 כְּצֹאן עַמּוֹ in apposition, as in Ezek. כְּצֹאן אדם.
7 Ezek. xxxvi. 37, 38. 8 Kim. 9 Ps. lxxvii. 20.
10 The etymology implies this, properly "consecration," then the diadem of one consecrated, as the נֵזֶר הַקֹּדֶשׁ Ex. xxix. 6, xxxix. 30, Lev. viii. 9. or the נזר of the king.
11 Comp. Ar. נֵצִּ "lifted on high," נִצִּיץ "throne exalted."
12 Lev. xxv. 23. 13 Ps. viii. 1. 14 Gen. xxviii. 17.
15 טוּב "the goodness" of the Lord, Ps. xxv. 7, xxvii. 13, xxxi. 20, cxlv. 7, Is. lxiii. 7, Jer. xxxi. 12, 14. Hos. iii. 5.
16 אעביר כל טובי על פניך Ex. xxxiii. 19.
17 Blaise Palma in "Paradise of the Christian soul," P. 1. c. vi. n. 4. pp. 90, 91.

Before CHRIST cir. 487.

goodness, and how great *is*
his beauty! [g] corn shall make
the young men || cheerful,
and new wine the maids.

Before CHRIST cir. 487.

[g] Joel 3. 18. Amos 9. 14.

|| Or, *grow*, or, *speak*.

any limit to His giving, save His creature's capacity of receiving, which also is a good gift from Him. "From Him all things sweet derive their sweetness; all things fair, their beauty; all things bright, their splendor; all things that live, their life; all things sentient, their sense; all that move, their vigor; all intelligences, their knowledge; all things perfect, their perfection; all things in any wise good, their goodness."

The beauty of God belongs rather to the beatific vision. Yet David speaks of the Beauty of Christ[1], *Thou art exceeding fairer than the children of men;* and Isaiah says, [2] *Thine eyes shall behold the King in His beauty.* But the Beauty of God "eye hath not seen nor ear heard nor can heart of man conceive." Here, on earth, created beauty can, at least when suddenly seen, hold the frame motionless, pierce the soul, glue the heart to it, entrance the affections. Light from heaven kindles into beauty our dullest material substances; the soul in grace diffuses beauty over the dullest human countenance; the soul, ere it has passed from the body, has been known to catch, through the half-opened portals, such brilliancy of light, that the eye even for some time after death has retained a brightness, beyond anything of earth[3]. "[4] The earth's form of beauty is a sort of voice of the dumb earth. Doth not, on considering the beauty of this universe, its very form answer thee with one voice, 'Not I made myself, but God'?" Poets have said,

"[5] Old friends . . . . shall lovelier be,
As more of heaven in each we see,"

or,

"[6] When he saw,
"—God within him light his face."

and Holy Scripture tells us that when S. Stephen, *full of faith and of the Holy Ghost*, was about to speak of Jesus to the council which arraigned him, [7] *all that sat in the council, looking steadfastly at him, saw his face as it had been the face of an Angel.* It has been said, that if we could see a soul in grace, its beauty would so pierce us, that we should die. But the natural beauty of the soul transcends all corporeal beauty which so attracts us; the natural beauty of the last Angel surpasseth all natural beauty of soul. If we could ascend from the most beautiful form, which the soul could here imagine, to the least glorious body of the beatified, on and on through the countless thousands of glorious bodies, compared wherewith heaven would be dark and the sun lose its shining; and yet more from the most beautiful deified soul, as visible here, to the beauty of the disembodied soul, whose image would scarce be recognized, because "[8] the bodily eyes gleamed with angelic radiancy;" yea, let the God-enlightened soul go on and on, through all those choirs of the heavenly hierarchies, clad with the raiment of Divinity, from choir to choir, from hierarchy to hierarchy, admiring the order and beauty and harmony of the house of God; yea, let it, aided by divine grace and light, ascend even higher, and reach the bound and term of all created beauty, yet it must know that the Divine power and wisdom could create other creatures, far more perfect and beautiful than all which He hath hitherto created. Nay, let the highest of all the Seraphs sum in one all the beauty by nature and grace and glory of all creatures, yet could it not be satisfied with that beauty, but must, because it was not satisfied with it, conceive some higher beauty. Were God forthwith, at every moment to create that higher beauty at its wish, it could still conceive something beyond; for, not being God, its beauty could not satisfy its conception. So let him still, and in hundred thousand, hundred thousand, thousand years with swiftest flight of understanding multiply continually those degrees of beauty, so that each fresh degree should ever double that preceding, and the Divine power should, with like swiftness, concur in creating that beauty, as in the beginning He said, *let there be light and there was light;* after all those millions of years, he would be again at the beginning, and there would be no comparison between it and the Divine Beauty of Jesus Christ, God and Man. For it is the bliss of the finite not to reach the Infinite[9]. That city of the blest which is lightened by the glory of God, and the Lamb is the light thereof, sees It, enabled by God, as created eye can see It, and is held fast to God in one jubilant exstacy of everlasting love.

"[10] The Prophet, borne out of himself by consideration of the Divine goodness, stands amazed, while he contemplates the beauty and Deity of Christ: he bursts out with unwonted admiration! How great is His goodness, Who, to guard His flock, shall come

[1] Ps. xlv. 2. [2] Is. xxxiii. 17. [3] This I saw once.
[4] S. Aug. in Ps. cxliv. n. 13.
[5] Christian Year. Morning Hymn.
[6] Tennyson, In memoriam. T. has "*The* God."
[7] Acts vi. 5, 15.

[8] S. Flavian, of Successus a martyr, whom he saw after death. Passio SS. Montani, Lucii &c. cxxxi. in Ruinart, Acta martyr. sincera p. 241.
[9] abridged from Joannes a Jesu Maria, ars amandi Deum c. 3. Opp. ii. 301-304. [10] Osorius.

Before CHRIST cir. 487.

CHAPTER X.

1 *God is to be sought unto, and not idols.* 5 *As he visited his flock for sin, so he will save and restore them.*

ASK ye [a]of the LORD [b]rain [c]in the time of the latter rain; *so* the LORD shall make ‖ bright clouds, and give them

Before CHRIST cir. 487.

[a] Jer 14. 22.
[b] Deut. 11. 14.
[c] Job 29. 23. Joel 2. 23.
‖ Or, *lightnings.* Jer. 10. 13.

down on earth to lay down His life for the salvation of His sheep! How great His beauty, Who is the *brightness of the glory and the Image of the Father*, and comprises in His Godhead the measure of all order and beauty! With what firm might does He strengthen, with what joy does He overwhelm the souls which gaze most frequently on His beauty, and gives largely and bountifully that corn, by whose strength the youths are made strong. He supplieth abundantly the wine, whereby the virgins, on fire with His love, are exhilarated and beautified. But both are necessary, that the strength of the strong should be upheld by the *bread from heaven*, and that sound and uncorrupt minds, melted with the sweetness of love, should be re-created with wine, i. e. the sweetness of the Holy Spirit, and be borne aloft with great joy, in the midst of extreme toils. For all who keep holily the faith of Christ, may be called *youths*, for their unconquered strength, and virgins for their purity and integrity of soul. For all these that heavenly bread is prepared, that their strength be not weakened, and the wine is inpoured, that they be not only refreshed, but may live in utmost sweetness."

X. 1. *Ask ye of the Lord rain. Ask and ye shall receive*, our Lord says. Zechariah had promised in God's name blessings temporal and spiritual: all was ready on God's part; only, he adds, ask them of the Lord, the Unchangeable, the Self-same, not of Teraphim or of diviner, as Israel had done aforetime[1]. He had promised, [2]*If ye shall hearken diligently unto My commandments, to love the Lord your God, I will give you the rain of your land in his due season, the first rain and the latter rain, and I will send grass in thy field for thy cattle.* God bids them ask Him to fulfill His promise. The *latter rain*[3] alone is mentioned, as completing what God had begun by the former rain, filling the ears before the harvest. Both[4] had been used as symbols of God's spiritual gifts, and so the words fit in with the close of the last chapter, both as to things temporal and eternal. "[5]He exhorts all frequently to ask for the dew of the divine grace, that what had sprung up in the heart from the seed of the word of God, might attain to full ripeness."

The Lord maketh bright clouds, [rather] *lightnings*[6], *into rain*, as Jeremiah says, [7]*He causeth the vapors to ascend from the ends of the earth; He maketh lightnings into rain;* and the Psalmist, [8]*He maketh lightnings into rain*, disappearing as it were into the rain which follows on them. *And giveth them.* While man is asking, God is answering. *Showers of rain*[9], "rain in torrents," as we should say, or "in floods," or, inverted, "floods of rain." *To every one grass*, rather, *the green herb, in the field*, as the Psalmist says, [10]*He causeth the grass to grow for the cattle, and green herb for the service of men.* This He did with individual care, as each had need, or as should be best for each, as contrariwise He says in Amos, [11]*I caused it to rain upon one city, and caused it not to rain upon another city; one piece was rained upon, and the piece, whereon it rained not, withered.* The Rabbins observed these exceptions to God's general law, whereby He [12]*sendeth rain on the just and on the unjust*, though expressing it in their way hyperbolically; "[13]In the time when Israel doeth the will of God, He doeth their will; so that if one man alone, and not the others, wants rain, He will give rain to that one man; and if a man wants one herb alone in his field or garden, and not another, He will give rain to that one herb; as one of the saints used to say, This plot of ground wants rain, and that plot of ground wants not rain[14]." Spiritually the rain is divine doctrine bedewing the mind and making it fruitful, as the rain doth the earth. So Moses saith, [15]*My doctrine shall drop as the rain, my speech shall distill as the dew, as the*

[1] Hos. ii. 5–12, Jer. xliv. 15–28. [2] Deut. xi. 13–15.
[3] It is mentioned alone in Pr. xvi. 15.
[4] See vol. i. on Hos. vi. 3, p. 64; Jo. ii. 23. pp. 190, 191.
[5] Osorius.
[6] חזיזים, Its etymology is unknown, its meaning is determined by the idiom חזיז קולות Job xxviii. 26, xxxviii. 25. The Arab. חַז only signifies "made incisions, notches, cut the heart," (of misgivings of conscience.)
[7] Jer. x. 13, li. 16.
[8] Ps cxxxv. 7.
[9] As the words are transposed in Job xxxvii. 6, וגשם מטר וגשם מטרות עזו. גֶשֶׁם occurs, defined by גדול 1 Kgs xviii. 45; by שׁוטף Ezek. xiii. 11, 13, xxxviii. 22; by נְדָבוֹת Ps. lxviii. 10, המון הגשם 1 Kgs xviii. 41. "The clouds are full of גשם," Eccl. xi. 3. The waters of the flood are called הגשׁב Gen. vii. 12, viii. 2. Kim. compares the two synonymes, אדמת עָפר (Dan. xii. 2) טיט הַיָּוֵן Ps. xl. 3.
[10] Ps civ. 14. See also Gen. i. 30, iii. 18.
[11] Am. iv. 7. See note vol. i. p. 284.
[12] S. Matt. v. 49.
[13] Taanith f. ix. 2 in Kim. Mc. Caul pp. 111, 112.
[14] S. Cyril.
[15] Deut. xxxii. 2.

Before CHRIST cir. 487.

showers of rain, to every
one grass in the field.
2 For the [d] † idols have
spoken vanity, and the
diviners have seen a lie,
and have told false dreams;
they [e] comfort in vain:
therefore they went their
way as a flock, they || were
troubled, [f] because *there*
was no shepherd.
3 Mine anger was kin-
dled against the shepherds,
[g] and I † punished the
goats: for the LORD of
hosts [h] hath visited his
flock the house of Judah,
and [i] hath made them as

[d] Jer. 10. 8. Hab. 2. 18.
† Heb. *teraphims.* Judg. 17. 5.
[e] Job 13. 4.
|| Or, *answered that, &c.*

Before CHRIST cir. 487.

[f] Ezek. 34. 5.
[g] Ezek. 34. 17.
† Heb. *visited upon.*
[h] Luke 1. 68.
[i] Cant. 1. 9.

small rain upon the tender herb and as the showers upon the grass. "[1] The law of Moses and the prophets were the former rain."

2. *For the teraphim have spoken vanity,* rather, *spake vanity.* He appeals to their former experience. Their fathers had sought of idols, not of God; therefore they went into captivity. The *teraphim* were used as instruments of divination. They are united with the *ephod,* as forbidden, over against the allowed, means of enquiry as to the future, in Hosea, [2] *without an ephod and without teraphim;* they were united in the mingled worship of Micah [3]; Josiah *put* them *away* together with [4] *the workers with familiar spirits and the wizards,* to which are added, *the idols.* It was probably, a superstition of Eastern origin. Rachel brought them with her from her father's house, and Nebuchadnezzar used them for divination [5]. Samuel speaks of them, apparently, as things which Saul himself condemned. [6] *Rebellion is as the sin of divination, and stubbornness as iniquity* or *idolatry, and teraphim.* For it was probably in those his better days, that [7] *Saul had put away those that had familiar spirits and wizards out of the land.* Samuel then seems to tell him, that the sins to which he clave were as evil as those which he had, in an outward zeal, like Jehu, condemned. Anyhow, the *teraphim* stand united with the *divination* which was expressly condemned by the law [8]. The use of the teraphim by Rachel [9] and Michal [10] (for whatever purpose) implies that it was some less offensive form of false worship, though they were probably the *strange gods* [11] which Jacob bade his household to put away, or, anyhow, among them, since Laban calls them, [12] *my gods.*

Zechariah uses anew the words of Jeremiah and Ezekiel, [13] *Hearken ye not to your prophets, nor to your diviners, nor to your dreamers, nor to your enchanters, nor to your sorcerers;* and, [14] *let not your prophets and your diviners, that* be *in the midst of you, deceive you, neither hearken to your dreams, which ye cause to be dreamed;* and Ezekiel, [15] *While they see vanity unto thee, while they divine a lie unto thee.* The words not only joined on the Prophet's warning with the past, but reminded them of the sentence which followed on their neglect. The echo of the words of the former prophets came to them, floating, as it were, over the ruins of the former temple.

Therefore they went their way as a flock, which, having no shepherd, or only such as would mislead them, removed [16], but into captivity. *They were troubled* [17]. The trouble lasted on, though the captivity ended at the appointed time. Nehemiah speaks of the exactions of former governors, [18] *The former governors which were before me, laid heavy weights upon the people* [19], *and took from them in bread and wine, after forty shekels of silver; also their servants used dominion over* [20] *the people; and I did not so, because of the fear of God.*

Because there was no shepherd. As Ezekiel said of those times, [21] *They were scattered, because* there is *no shepherd; and they became meat to all the beasts of the field, when they were scattered: My flock was scattered upon all the face of the earth; and none did search or seek after them.*

3. *Mine anger was kindled against the shepherds.* As Ezekiel continued, [22] *Thus saith the Lord God; Behold I* am *against the shepherds, and I will require My flock at their hand.*

I punished the he-goats. The evil powerful

[1] S. Cyril.
[2] Hos. iii. 4. Every fresh attempt to find an etymology for תרפים attests the unsatisfactoriness of those before it, without finding anything better.
[3] Jud. xvii. 5, xviii. 14, 17, 18, 20.
[4] 2 Kgs xxiii. 24.
[5] Ezek. xxi. 21.
[6] 1 Sam. xv. 23.
[7] Ib. xxviii. 3.
[8] De. xviii. 13, 14.
[9] Gen. xxxi. 19, 34, 35.
[10] 1 Sam. xix. 13, 16.
[11] Gen. xxxv. 2, 4.
[12] Ib. xxxi. 30, 32.
[13] Jer. xxvii. 9.
[14] Ib. xxix. 8.
[15] Ezek. xxi. 29; add xxii. 28.
[16] The etym. meaning of נסע, "plucked up" pegs of tent, in order to removal, must have been lost in the idiom. The captivity is spoken of as past, and the idolatry as before the captivity, which was its punishment.
[17] עָנָה occurs in this sense Ps. cxvi. 10, cxix. 67, of man; with ב of wearisome labor Eccl. i. 13, iii. 10; of the lion, Is. xxxi. 4; of the song of the terrible, Ib. xxv. 5 [4 Eng.] all.
[18] Neh. v. 15.
[19] הכבידו with עַל p., like "made our, your, yoke heavy," 1 Kgs xii. 10, 14, 2 Chr. x. 10, 14. "thy yoke," Is. xlvii. 6. "my chain" Lam. iii. 7. or עבטיט Hab. ii. 6.
[20] שָׁלטו על
[21] Ezek. xxxiv. 5, 6.
[22] Ib. 10.

Before CHRIST cir. 487.

his goodly horse in the
battle.
4 Out of him came forth
[k]the corner, out of him [l]the
nail, out of him the battle
bow, out of him every op-
pressor together.
5 ¶ And they shall be as
mighty *men*, which [m]tread
down *their enemies* in the
mire of the streets in the
battle: and they shall fight,
because the LORD *is* with
them, and ‖the riders on
horses shall be confounded.
6 And I will strengthen

k Num. 24. 17. 1 Sam. 14. 38. Isai. 19. 13.
l Isai. 22. 23.
m Ps. 18. 42.
‖ Or, *they shall make the riders on horses ashamed.*

Before CHRIST cir. 487.

are called the *he-goats of the earth*[1]; and in Ezekiel God says, [2]*I will judge between cattle and cattle, between rams and he-goats;* and our Lord speaks of the reprobate as goats, the saved as sheep[3]. God *visited upon*[4] these in His displeasure, *because* He *visited His flock, the people of Judah,* to see to their needs and to relieve them.

And hath made them as the goodly horse, as, before, He said, [5]*I made thee as the sword of a mighty man.* Judah's might was not in himself; but, in God's hands, he had might like and above the might of this world; he was fearless, resistless; as S. Paul says, [6]*the weapons of our warfare are not carnal, but mighty through God to the pulling down of strongholds.*

4. *Out of him*[7] *came forth,* or rather, *From him is the corner,* as Jeremiah[8], *Their nobles shall be from themselves,* and *their governor shall go forth from the midst of them.* Her strength, though given by God, was to be inherent in her, though from her too was to come He Who was to be *the head-corner-stone,* the sure Foundation and Crowner of the whole building.

From thee the nail, an emblem of fixedness in itself, (as Isaiah says, [9]*I will fasten him a nail to a sure place*) and of security given to others dependent on Him, as Isaiah says further, [10]*And they shall hang upon him all the glory of his father's house, the offspring and the issue, from the vessels of cups to the vessels of flagons;* all, of much or little account, the least and the greatest. "[11]Christ is the corner-stone; Christ is the nail fixed in the wall, whereby all vessels are supported. The word of Christ is the bow, whence the arrows rend the king's enemies."

From it every exactor shall go forth together. God had promised[12] that no *oppressor,* or *exactor*[13], *shall pass through them any more.* He seems to repeat it here. *From thee shall go forth every oppressor together; go forth,* not to return: as Isaiah had said, [14]*Thy children shall make haste* to return; *thy destroyers and they that made thee waste shall go forth of thee.* "From it, its corner-stone; from it, the sure nail; from it, the battle bow; *from it,*"—he no longer unites closely with it, that which should be from it, or of it, but—*from it shall go forth every oppressor together;* one and all, as we say; a confused pêle-mêle body, as Isaiah, [15]*all that are found of thee are bound together;* [16]*together shall they all perish;* or, in separate clauses[17], *they are all of them put to shame; together they shall go into confusion.*

5. *And they* [the house of Judah[18], of whom he had said, *He hath made them as the goodly horse in the battle*] *shall be as mighty men, trampling on the mire of the streets.* Micah had said, [19]*she shall be a trampling, as the mire of the streets,* and David, [20]*I did stamp them as the mire of the street.* Zechariah, by a yet bolder image, pictures those trampled upon, as what they had become, *the mire of the streets,* as worthless, as foul; as he had said, [21]*they shall trample on the sling-stones. And they shall fight, because the Lord is with them,* not in their own strength, he still reminds them; they shall have power, because God empowers them; strength, because God instrengthens them[22]; in presence of which, the goodly war-horse of God, human strength, *the riders on horses, shall be ashamed.*

6. *I will bring them again to place them.* Zechariah seems to have condensed into one

[1] Is. xiv. 9. [2] Ezek. xxxiv. 17.
[3] S. Matt. xxv. 32.
[4] פקד על, as commonly, of chastisement; פקד, like ἐπεσκέψατο, of visiting to shew favor.
[5] ix. 13. [6] 2 Cor. x. 4.
[7] The word יצא does not suit פנה or יתד unless (which is not probable as to יתד) the metaphor was lost. [8] Jer. xxx. 21. [9] Is xxii. 23.
[10] Ib. 24. [11] Osor. [12] Zech. ix. 8.
[13] Is. xiv. 2. נֹגֵשׂ is no where used of a ruler or king, as in Æthiopic. The idea of "oppressors" remains in Is. iii. 12, (comp. נִגַּשׂ Ib. iii. 5) xiv. 2. add Is. lx. 17, where the contrast is of change of the inferior for the better; *for brass I will bring gold &c.* It is summed up and it ends in, *I will make their exactors righteousness.* [all alleged.]
[14] Is. xlix. 17. מִמֵּךְ יֵצֵאוּ. as here ממנו יצא
[15] With the same idiom, כָּל נִמְצָאַיִךְ אֻסְּרוּ יַחְדָּו כל יחדו; Is. xxii. 3.
[16] Is. xxxi. 3, יחדו כלם יכליון.
[17] Ib. xlv. 16, וגם נכלמו כלם יחדו הלכו בכלמה.
[18] They are the main subject in v. 3. The words in v. 4. could not be the subject: for neither corner-stone, nor nail, nor bow, can be said to be like mighty men &c.
[19] Mic. vii. 10. [20] 2 Sam. xxii. 43. [21] ix. 15.
[22] ἐν τῷ ἐνδυναμοῦντι με χριστῷ. Phil. iv. 13.

Before CHRIST cir. 487.

the house of Judah, and I
will save the house of Joseph, and [n]I will bring
them again to place them;
for I [o]have mercy upon
them: and they shall be
as though I had not cast
them off: for I *am* the
LORD their God, and [p]will
hear them.

n Jer. 3. 18. Ezek. 37. 21.
o Hos. 1. 7.
p ch. 13. 9.

7 And *they of* Ephraim
shall be like a mighty *man*,
and their [q]heart shall rejoice as through wine: yea,
their children shall see *it*,
and be glad; their heart
shall rejoice in the LORD.
8 I will [r]hiss for them,
and gather them; for I
have redeemed them: [s]and

Before CHRIST cir. 487.

q Ps. 104. 15. ch. 9. 15.
r Isai. 5. 26.
s Isai. 49. 19. Ezek. 36. 37.

word two[1] of Jeremiah, [2]*I will bring them again* unto this place, and *I will cause them to dwell* safely. "[3]The two ideas are here both implied, he will cause them to return to their land, and will cause them to dwell there in peace and security."

For I will have mercy upon them. "[4]For the goodness and lovingkindness of God, not any merits of our's, is the first and principal cause of our whole salvation and grace. Therefore the Psalmist says, [5]*neither did their own arm save them; but Thy right hand and Thine arm, and the light of Thy countenance, because Thou hadst a favor unto them.*

And they shall be, as though I had not cast them off. (etymologically, "loathed," "cast off as a thing abhorrent[6]".) God is ever "the God of the present." He does not half-forgive. [7]*Their sins and their iniquities I will remember no more.* God casts off the sinner, as being what he is, a thing abhorrent, as penitence confesses of itself that it is "[8]a dead dog, a loathsome worm, a putrid corpse." God will not clothe with a righteousness, which He does not impart. He restores to the penitent all his lost graces, as though he had never forfeited them, and cumulates them with the fresh grace whereby He converts him[9]. It is an entire re-creation. *They shall be, as though I had not cast them off.* [10]*I will settle you as in your old estates, and will do good, more than at your beginnings, and ye shall know that I am the Lord.*

For I am the Lord their God, and will hear them, as He says by Malachi[11], *I am the Lord; I change not.* His unchangeableness belongs to His Being; *I Am; therefore ye sons of Jacob are not consumed;* and by Hosea, [12]*The Lord of hosts, The Lord is His memorial, therefore turn thou to thy God.* Because God was *their God*, and as surely as He was *their God*, He would hear them. His Being was the pledge of His hearing. [13]*I, the Lord, will hear them; I, the God of Israel, will not forsake them.*

7. *And Ephraim, they shall be like a mighty man.* Prophecy, through the rest of the chapter, turns to Ephraim, which had not yet been restored. With regard to them, human victory retires out of sight, though doubtless, when their wide prison was broken at the destruction of the Persian empire, many were free to return to their native country, as others spread over the West in Asia Minor, Greece, Rome, and so some may have taken part in the victories of the Maccabees. Yet not victory, but strength, gladness beyond natural gladness, as through wine, whereby the mind is exhilarated above itself; and that, lasting, transmitted to their children, large increase, holy life in God, are the outlines of the promise.

Their heart shall rejoice in the Lord, "[5]as the principal object, the first, highest, most worthy Giver of all good, to Whom is to be referred all gladness, which is conceived from created goods, that [14]*whoso glorieth may glory in the Lord,* in Whom Alone the rational creature ought to take delight."

8. *I will hiss for them.* Formerly God had so spoken of His summoning the enemies of His people to chastise them. [15]*It shall be in that day, that the Lord shall hiss for the fly, that is in the uttermost part of the rivers of Egypt, and for the bee that is in the land of Assyria, and they shall come, and shall rest all of them in the desolate valleys, and in the holes of the rocks, and upon all thorns and upon all bushes.* [16]*He will hiss unto them from the ends of the earth, and behold they shall come with speed swiftly; none shall be weary or stumble among them.* He would gather them, like the countless num-

[1] הושבותִים from הֲשַׁבְתִּים, and הֲשִׁיבתִים.
[2] Jer. xxxii. 37.
[3] Kim. It is not a confusion of forms, but the blending of two words into one. So also Ibn E.
[4] Dion.
[5] Ps. xliv. 3.
[6] זנח. Arab used of "rancid" oil. Observe האזניתו Is. xix. 6.
[7] Heb. viii. 12.
[8] Bp. Andrewes' devotions. Morn. Pr.
[9] See vol. i. on Joel ii. 25 pp. 192, 193.
[10] Ezek. xxxvi. 11.
[11] Mal. iii. 6.
[12] Hos. xii. 5, 6. [6, 7 Heb.] See vol. i. pp. 119, 120.
[13] Is. xli. 17.
[14] 2 Cor. x. 17.
[15] Is. vii. 18, 19.
[16] Ib. v. 26, 27. The word is only used in this same sense in these three places.

Before CHRIST cir. 487.

they shall increase as they
have increased.
9 And [t]I will sow them
among the people: and
they shall [u]remember me
in far countries; and they
shall live with their children, and turn again.
10 [x]I will bring them
again also out of the land
of Egypt, and gather them
out of Assyria; and I will

[t] Hos. 2. 23.
[u] Deut. 30. 1.
[x] Is. 11. 11. 16. Hos. 11. 11.

bers of the insect creation, which, if united, would irresistibly desolate life. He would summon them, as the bee-owner, by his shrill call, summons and unites his own swarm. Now, contrariwise God would summon with the same His own people. The fulfillment of the chastisement was the earnest of the ease of the fulfillment of the mercy.

For I have redeemed them. Then they are His, being redeemed at so dear a price. "[1] For Christ, as far as in Him lay, redeemed all." God had done this in purpose, as S. John speaks of [2]*the Lamb slain from the foundation of the world.*

And they shall increase as they increased. "[3] As they increased in Egypt, so shall they increase at that time." The marvels of God's favor in Egypt shall be repeated. The increase there had been promised beforehand. [4]*Fear not to go down into Egypt; for I will there make of thee a great nation.* The fulfillment is recorded, [5]*the children of Israel were fruitful, and increased abundantly, and multiplied, and waxed exceeding mighty; and the land was filled with them.* God appointed that this should be part of their confession at their yearly prosperity, the offering of the basket of first-fruits; [6]*A Syrian ready to perish was my father, and he went into Egypt and sojourned there with a few, and became there a nation, great, mighty, and populous.* The Psalmist dwelt upon it. [7]*He increased His people greatly, and made them stronger than their enemies.* It became then one of the resemblances between the first deliverance and the last. "[1] For the Apostles and others converted from Judaism, had more spiritual children, all those whom they begat in Christ, than the synagogue ever had after the flesh."

9. *And I will sow them among the nations.* Such had been the prophecy of Hosea; [8]*I will sow her unto Me in the earth,* as the prelude of spiritual mercies, *and I will have mercy on her that had not obtained mercy, and I will say to not-my-people, Thou art My people, and they shall say, my God.* Hosea's saying, *I will sow her in the earth* i. e. the whole earth, and that *to Me*, corresponds to, and explains Zechariah's brief saying, *I will sow them among the nations.* The sowing, which was future to Hosea, had begun; but the purpose of the sowing, the harvest, was wholly to come; when it should be seen, that they were indeed sown by God, that *great* should *be the day of Jezreel*[9]. And Jeremiah said, [10]*Behold the days come, saith the Lord, that I will sow the house of Israel and the house of Judah, with the seed of man and with the seed of beast.* The word is used of sowing to multiply, never of mere scattering[11].

And they shall remember Me in far countries. So Ezekiel had said, [12]*And they that escape of you shall remember Me among the nations, whither they shall be carried captive—and they shall loath themselves for the evils which they have committed in all their abominations, and they shall know that I am the Lord.*

And shall live. As Ezekiel again says, [13]*Ye shall know that I am the Lord, when I open your graves, and bring you up out of your graves, O My people, and shall put My Spirit in you, and ye shall live. With their children.* A continuous gift, as Ezekiel, [14]*they and their children, and their children's children for ever: and My servant David* shall be *their prince for ever.*

And shall turn again to God, being converted, as Jeremiah had been bidden to exhort them; [15]*Go and proclaim these words toward the North,* the cities of the Medes whither they were carried captive, *and say, Return, thou backsliding Israel,* and *I will not cause Mine anger to fall upon you;* [16]*Turn, O backsliding children—and I will take you, one of a city, and two of a family, and will bring you to Zion, and I will give you pastors according to Mine heart.* [17]*Return, ye backsliding children; I will heal your backslidings.* And they answer, *Behold, we come unto Thee; for Thou art the Lord our God.* So Isaiah had said, [18]*A remnant shall return, the remnant of Jacob, unto the mighty God.* "[1] They shall return by recollection of mind and adunation and simplification of the affections toward God so as ultimately to intend that one thing, which alone is necessary."

10. *I will bring them again also out of the land of Egypt.* Individuals had fled to Egypt[19]; but here probably Egypt and Assyria stand,

[1] Dion. [2] Rev. xiii. 8. [3] Kim. [4] Gen. xlvi. 3.
[5] Ex. i. 7. [6] De. xxvi. 5. [7] Ps. cv. 24.
[8] Hos. ii. ult. See vol. i. pp. 27, 28, etc.
[9] Ib. i. 11. See vol. i. p. 25. [10] Jer. xxxi. 27.
[11] זרה (Kal and Pi.), "dispersed," is contrariwise never to "sow."

[12] Ezek. vi. 9. [13] Ib. xxxvii. 13, 14. [14] Ib. 25.
[15] Jer. iii. 12. [16] Ib. 14, 15. [17] Ib. 22.
[18] Is. x. 21. comp. שָׁבֶיהָ, "her converts," Is. i. 27, and וְשָׁבוּ in Solomon's prayer, 2 Chr. vi. 24.
[19] See Hos. viii. 13, vol. i., p. 86, ix. 3, p. 88.

Before CHRIST cir. 487.

bring them into the land of
Gilead and Lebanon; and
y *place* shall not be found — y Isai. 49. 20.
for them.
11 z And he shall pass — z Isai. 11. 15, 16.
through the sea with afflic-
tion, and shall smite the
waves in the sea, and all
the deeps of the river shall
dry up: and a the pride of — a Isai. 14. 25.
Assyria shall be brought
down, and b the sceptre — b Ezek. 30. 13.
of Egypt shall depart
away.

Before CHRIST cir. 487.

as of old, for the two great conflicting empires, between which Israel lay, at whose hands she had suffered, and who represent the countries which lay beyond them. Hosea unites, [1] *the West, Assyria, Egypt,* the three then known divisions of the world, Europe, Asia, Africa [2]. Asshur, after Nineveh perished, stands clearly for the world-empire of the East at Babylon [3], and then in Persia [4]. Balaam includes under Asshur, first Babylon, then the third world-empire [5]. Babylon, which was first subject to Nineveh, then subjected it, was at a later period known to Greek writers (who probably had their information from Persian sources) as part of Assyria [6].

And I will bring them into the land of Gilead and Lebanon, their old dwellings, East and West of Jordan. *And place shall not be found for them* [7], as Isaiah says, [8] *The children of thy bereaved estate shall yet say in thine ears, The place is too strait for me: give place, that I may dwell.*

11. *And He,* i. e. Almighty God, *shall pass through the sea, affliction* [9], as He says, [10] *When thou walkest through the waters, I* will be *with thee; and through the rivers, they shall not overflow thee. And shall smite the waves in the sea,* as in Isaiah, [11] *The Lord shall utterly destroy the tongue of the Egyptian sea.* The image is from the deliverance of Egypt: yet it is said, that it should not be any exact repetition of the miracles of Egypt; it would be as the Red Sea [12], which would as effectually shut them in, and in presence of which they might again think themselves lost, through which God would again bring them. But it would not be the Red sea itself; for *the sea* through which they should be brought, would be *affliction;* as our own poet speaks of "taking arms against a sea of troubles." "[13] The promise of succor to those who believe in Christ is under the likeness of the things given to those of old; for as Israel was conveyed across the Red sea, braving the waves in it; [14] *for the waters stood upright as an heap,* God bringing this to pass marvellously; and as [15] they passed the Jordan on foot, so he says, those who are called through Moses to the knowledge of Christ, and have been saved by the ministries of the holy Apostles, they shall pass the waves of this present life, like an angrily foaming sea, and, being removed from the tumult of this life, shall, undisturbed, worship the true God. And they shall pass through temptations, like sweeping rivers, saying with great joy, in like way, [16] *Unless the Lord had been for us, may Israel now say, the waters had drowned us, the stream had gone over our souls.*" *He shall smite the waves in the sea.* There, where the strength of the powers of this world is put forth against His people, there He will bring it down. *All the deeps of the river,* i. e. of the Nile [17], *shall be dried up.* The Nile as a mighty river is substituted for the

[1] Hos. xi. 10, 11, Is. xi. 15, 16; add Ib. xix. 23–25, xxvii. 13, lii. 4, Mic. vii. 12. See ab. p. 96.
[2] See on Hos. xi. 11. vol. i., p. 115.
[3] 2 Kgs xxiii. 29, Lam. v. 6; and, unless it refers to earlier history, Jer. ii. 18; also Judith i. 5, ii. 1, v. 1 &c.
[4] Ezra vi. 22. [5] Nu. xxiv. 22–24. coll. Dan. xi. 30.
[6] Thus Herodotus, in the familiar passages, speaks of "Assyria, all but the Babylonian portion." i. 106. "Those Assyrians, to whom Nineveh belongs." Ib. 102. "Assyria possesses a vast number of cities, whereof the strongest at this time was Babylon, whither after the fall of Nineveh the seat of government was removed." Ib. 178. "many sovereigns have ruled over this city of Babylon, and lent their aid to the building of its walls and the adornment of its temples: of whom I shall make mention in my Assyrian history." Ib. 184. "Babylon supplies food during four, the other regions of Asia during eight months [to the great king] by which it appears that Assyria in respect of resources is ⅓ of the whole of Asia." Ib. 192. "Little rain falls in Assyria. The whole of Babylonia is, like Egypt, intersected with canals. The largest is carried from the Euphrates into another stream called the Tigris, upon which the city Nineveh formerly stood." Ib. 193. so Strabo xiv. init., Arrian Exp. Al. vii. 2. 6. Ammian xxiii. 20.
[7] לא מצאו להם Jud. xxi. 14, is, "they found not (enough) for themselves;" thence here, Nif. "there was not found for them."
[8] Is. xlix. 20.
[9] צרה is in appos. to בַּיָּם. Against the rendering of the LXX ἐν θαλασσῇ στενῇ, 1) ים, as the sea, no where occurs as fem.; in 2 Kgs xvi. 17. it is "the brazen sea" which is spoken of; 2) the narrowness of the sea, if physical, would facilitate the crossing, not aggravate it; 3) omitting the art., בים צרה would be "in a sea of affliction," but would drop the reference to the sea, or "the red sea," "sea" becoming a mere metaphor.
[10] Is. xliii. 2. [11] Ib. xi. 15. [12] Ex. xiv. 10, 12.
[13] S. Cyr. [14] Ex. xv. 8. [15] Josh. iii. 17.
[16] Ps. cxxiv. 1–5.
[17] יאור, always the Nile, except Dan. xii. 5, where it is part of his revival of words of the Pentateuch. So Gesenius also. It has been conjectured that a canal now connecting the Tigris and Euphrates,

Before CHRIST cir. 487.

12 And I will strengthen them in the LORD; and [c] they shall walk up and down in his name, saith the LORD.

c Mic. 4. 5.

CHAPTER XI.

1 *The destruction of Jerusalem. The elect being cared for, the rest are rejected.* 10 *The staves of Beauty and Bands broken by the rejection of Christ.* 15 *The type and curse of a foolish shepherd.*

OPEN [a] thy doors, O Lebanon, that the fire may devour thy cedars.

a ch. 10. 10.

Jordan, symbolizing the greater putting forth of God's power in the times to come.

And the pride of Asshur shall be brought down. "[1] When the good receive their reward, then their enemies shall have no power over them, but shall be punished by Me, because they injured My elect.—By the Assyrians and Egyptians he understands all their enemies."

12. *I will strengthen them in the Lord*, as our Lord said to S. Paul, *My strength is made perfect in weakness*, and S. Paul said in turn, *When I am weak, then am I strong. And in His Name shall they walk up and down*, have their whole conversation "[2] in Him according to His will, and diligent in all things to speak and act in His grace and Divine hope." "[3] Christians walk in the Name of Christ, and there is written on the new white stone given to them *a new name*[4], and under the dignity of a name so great, they walk with God, as [5] Enoch walked and pleased God and was translated."

Saith the Lord: "[2] Again the Lord God speaks of the Lord God, as of Another, hinting the plurality of Persons in the Godhead."

XI. "[6] *All the ways of the Lord are mercy and truth*, saith the Psalmist[7], and, [8] *I will sing to Thee of mercy and judgment.* So is this prophecy divided. Above[9], almost all were promises of mercy, which are now fulfilled in deed; and from this, [10] *Open, O Lebanon, thy doors*, all are terrible edicts of truth and tokens of just judgment. How much sweetness and softness and pleasantness is therein, *Rejoice greatly, daughter of Zion: shout, O daughter of Jerusalem;* what bitterness and acerbity and calamity to those, to whom he says, *Open, O Lebanon, thy doors, that the fire may devour thy cedars; howl, O fir tree; howl, O ye oaks of Basan.* As then, before, we beheld His mercy in those who believed and believe; so now let us contemplate His just judgment on those who believed not." Gilead and Lebanon[11] had been named as the restored home of Ephraim; but there remained a dark side of the picture, which the prophet suddenly presents, with the names of those self-same lands, [12] *Open thy doors, O Lebanon; howl, O ye oaks of Basan.*"

1. *Open thy doors, O Lebanon.* Lebanon, whose cedars had stood, its glory, for centuries, yet could offer no resistance to him who felled them and were carried off to adorn the palaces of its conquerors[13], was in Isaiah[14] and Jeremiah[15] the emblem of the glory of the Jewish state; and in Ezekiel, of Jerusalem, as the prophet himself explains it[16]; glorious, beauteous, inaccessible, so long as it was defended by God; a ready prey, when abandoned by Him. The centre and source of her strength was the worship of God; and so Lebanon has of old been understood to be the temple, which was built with cedars of Lebanon, towering aloft upon a strong summit; the spiritual glory and the eminence of Jerusalem, as Lebanon was of the whole country, and "[17] to strangers who came to it, it appeared from afar like a mountain full of snow; for, where it was not gilded, it was exceeding white, being built of marble." But at the time of destruction, it was [18] *a den of thieves*, as Lebanon, amidst its beauty, was of wild beasts.

"[6] I suppose Lebanon itself, i. e. *the temple*, felt the command of the prophet's words, since, as its destruction approached, its doors opened without the hand of man. Josephus relates how "[19] at the passover, the Eastern gate of the inner temple, being of brass and very firm, and with difficulty shut at eventide by twenty men; moreover with bars strengthened with iron, and having very deep bolts, which went down into the threshold, itself of one stone, was seen at six o'clock at night to open of its own accord. The guards of the

called *Bahr-el-Nil*, may have had that name in the time of Daniel and been the river in his vision (Stanley Jewish Church iii. 12). 1) The *Bahr-el-Nil* is only the *modern* Arabic name for the Nile. 2) Had the canal been so called in Daniel's time and had he meant it (which is unlikely) he would naturally have called it by its name, not have translated it into the old Egyptian and Hebrew name.

[1] Rib. [2] Dion. [3] S. Jer. [4] Rev. ii. 17.

[5] Gen. v. 24. [6] Rup.
[7] Ps. xxv. 11. [8] Ib. ci. 1.
[9] " viii. 19–x. end." [10] "all c. xi."
[11] x. 10. [12] xi. 1, 2.
[13] See ab. on Zeph. ii. 14. and note 2. p. 276.
[14] Is. xiv. 8, xxxvii. 24. [15] Jer. xxii. 6, 7.
[16] Ezek. xvii. 3, 12. [17] Joseph. de Bello J. 5. 5, 6.
[18] S. Matt. xxi. 13.
[19] de Bell. J. 6. 5. 3 quoted by Rup.

Before CHRIST cir. 487.

2 Howl, fir tree; for
the cedar is fallen; be-
cause the ‖mighty are
spoiled: howl, O ye oaks
of Bashan; [b]for ‖the
forest of the vintage is
come down.
3 ¶ *There is* a voice of
the howling of the shep-
herds; for their glory is
spoiled: a voice of the roaring of young lions; for the
pride of Jordan is spoiled.
4 Thus saith the LORD
my God; [c]Feed the flock
of the slaughter;

‖ Or, *gallants.*

[b] Isai. 32. 19.
‖ Or, *the defenced forest.*

[c] ver. 7.

temple running told it to the officer, and he, going up, with difficulty closed it. This the uninstructed thought a very favorable sign, that God opened to them the gate of all goods. But those taught in the Divine words, understood that the safety of the temple was removed of itself, and that the gate opened." A saying of this sort is still exstant. "[1] Our fathers have handed down, forty years before the destruction of the house, the lot of the Lord did not come up on the right hand, and the tongue of splendor did not become white, nor did the light from the evening burn, and the doors of the temple opened of their own accord, until Rabban Johanan ben Zaccai rebuked them, and said, 'O temple, why dost thou affright thyself?, I know of thee that thy end is to be destroyed, and of this Zechariah prophesied, *Open thy doors, O Lebanon, and let the fire devour thy cedars.*'" The "forty years" mentioned in this tradition carry back the event exactly to the Death of Christ, the temple having been burned A. D. 73[2]. Josephus adds that they opened at the passover, the season of His Crucifixion. On the other hand, the shutting of the gates of the temple, when they had [3] *seized Paul and dragged him out of the temple*, seems miraculous and significant, that, having thus violently refused the preaching of the Gospel, and cast Paul out, they themselves were also shut out, denoting that an entrance was afterward to be refused them.

And let a fire devour thy cedars. Jerusalem, or the temple, were, after those times, burned by the Romans only. The destruction of pride, opposed to Christ, was prophesied by Isaiah in connection with His Coming[4].

2. *Howl, O cypress, for the cedar is fallen.* Jerusalem or the temple having been likened to Lebanon and its cedars, the prophet carries on the image, speaking of the priests princes and people, under the title of firs, cypresses and oaks, trees inferior, but magnificent. He shews that it is imagery, by ascribing to them the feelings of men. The more glorious and stately, *the cedars*, were destroyed. Woe then to the rest, *the cypress;* as our Lord says, [5] *If they do these things in the green tree, what shall be done, in the dry?* and S. Peter, [6] *If the righteous scarcely be saved, where shall the ungodly and the sinner appear?*

For the defenced[7] *forest is come down;* that which was closed and inaccessible to the enemy. All which was high and lifted up was brought low, *came down*, even to the ground[8].

3. *A voice of the howling of the shepherds, for their glory is spoiled.* It echoes on from Jeremiah before the captivity, [9] *Howl, ye shepherds—A voice of the cry of the shepherds, and an howling of the principal of the flock; for the Lord hath spoiled their pasture.* There is one chorus of desolation, the mighty and the lowly; the shepherds and the young lions; what is at other times opposed is joined in one wailing. *The pride of Jordan* are the stately oaks on its banks, which shroud it from sight, until you reach its edges, and which, after the captivity of the ten tribes, became the haunt of lions and their chief abode in Palestine, "on account of the burning heat, and the nearness of the desert, and the breadth of the vast solitude and jungles[10]."

4. *Thus saith the Lord my God, Feed the flock of the slaughter.* The fulfillment of the whole prophecy shews, that the person addressed is the prophet, not in, or for himself, but (as belongs to symbolic prophecy) as representing Another, our Lord. It is addressed, in the first instance, to Zechariah. For Zechariah is bidden, [11] *take unto thee yet the*

[1] Yoma f. 39 b. quoted by Mart. Pug. fid. f. 297. Eusebius (Dem. Evang. vii. 4) says, "He calls the temple Lebanon, as is his wont, since in other prophecies it has been shewn that the temple itself is called Lebanon. This the Jews themselves still confess."
[2] Euseb. Chron.
[3] Acts xxi. 30.
[4] Is. x. 34, xi. 1.
[5] S. Luke xxiii. 31.
[6] 1 S. Pet. iv. 18.
[7] As in E. M. The E. V. has followed the Kri, correcting יער הבציר for יער הבצור, probably in order to substitute the common nom. and gen. for the less usual construction of the subj. and adj. being defined by the art. of the adj. as in Zech. himself, iv. 7, xiv. 10.
[8] As in Is. xxxii. 19, ii. 12, sqq.
[9] Jer. xxv. 34, 36.
[10] S. Jer. See Jerem. xlix. 19, l. 44, 2 Kgs xvii. 25. The lion lingered there even to the close of the XIIth cent. Phocas in Reland Palæst. i. 274. S. Cyril says in the present, "there are very many lions there, roaring horribly and striking fear into the inhabitants."
[11] v. 15.

Before CHRIST cir. 487.

5 Whose possessors slay them, and [d] hold themselves not guilty: and they that sell them [e] say, Blessed be

[d] Jer. 2. 3. & 50. 7.

[e] Deut. 29. 19. Hos. 12. 8.

instruments of a foolish shepherd, in words addressed to himself, personally; *And the Lord said unto me.* But he who was to represent the foolish shepherd, had represented the True Shepherd, since it is said to him, "Take unto thee *yet.*" But He, the Shepherd addressed, who does the acts commanded, speaks with the authority of God. He says, [1] *I cut off three shepherds in one month;* [2] *I broke My covenant which I had made with all the peoples;* [3] *the poor of the flock waited upon Me;* [4] *I cut asunder Mine other staff, Bands, that I might break the brotherhood between Judah and Israel.* But in Zechariah's time, no three shepherds were cut off, the covenant made by God was not broken on His part, there was no such visible distinction between those who waited on God, and those who, outwardly too, rejected Him.

Feed the flock of the slaughter [5], those who were, even before the end, slain by their evil shepherds whom they followed, and who in the end would be given to the slaughter, as the Psalmist says, [6] *we are counted as sheep for the slaughter*, because they would not hear the voice of the True Shepherd, and were not His sheep. They were already, by God's judgment, a prey to evil shepherds; and would be so yet more hereafter. As a whole then, they were *sheep of the slaughter.* It is a last charge given to feed them. As our Lord says, [7] *Last of all, He sent unto them His Son, saying, They will reverence My Son.* This failing, nothing remained but that the flock would be given up, as they themselves say, [8] *He will miserably destroy those wicked men, and will let out His vineyard unto other husbandmen, which shall render Him the fruits in their seasons*, i.e. our Lord explains it, [9] *The kingdom of heaven shall be taken from them, and given to a nation bringing forth the fruits thereof.* Yet *a remnant should be saved*, for whose sake the larger flock was still to be fed: and, as our Lord, as Man, wept over Jerusalem, whose sentence He pronounced, so He still feeds those who would not turn to Him that they might be saved, and who would in the end be *a flock of slaughter*, [10] *Death their shepherd*, since they chose death rather than Life.

5. *Whose possessors* [*buyers* [11]] *slay them and hold themselves not guilty*, rather, *are not guilty*, either in their own eyes, or in the sight of God, since He gave them up and would no more avenge them. They contract no guilt. Aforetime God said; [12] *Israel* was *holiness to the Lord, the first-fruits of His increase; all that devour him shall be guilty* [13]: *evil shall come upon them, saith the Lord.* Now God reversed this, as He said by the same prophet, [14] *My people hath been lost sheep; their shepherds have caused them to go astray; they have turned them away* on *the mountains;—all that found them have devoured them; and their adversaries say, We are not guilty* [15]; *because they have sinned against the Lord, the habitation of justice, yea, the hope of their fathers, the Lord. The* offence of injuring Israel was that they were God's people: when He cast them forth, they who chastened them were His servants [16], His instruments, and offended only when through pride they knew not in Whose hands they themselves were [17], or through cruelty exceeded their office [18], and so they became guilty.

And they that sell them say, Blessed be the Lord, for I am rich. Even Sennacherib felt himself in part, or thought best to own himself, to be an instrument in God's hand [19]. But Titus when he "[20] entered Jerusalem, marveled at the strength of the city and its towers, which 'the tyrants' in phrensy abandoned. When then he had beheld their solid strength and the greatness of each rock, and how accurately they were fitted in, and how great their length and breadth, he said 'By the help of God we have warred: and God it was Who brought down the Jews from those bulwarks: for what avail the hands of man or his engines against such towers?' Much of this sort he said to his friends." The Jews also were *sold* in this war, as they had not been in former captures; and that, not by chance, but because the Roman policy was different from all, known by "experience" in the time of Zechariah. Into Babylon they had been carried captive, as a whole, because it was the will of God, after the *seventy years* to restore them. In this war, it was His will to destroy or disperse them; and so those above 17 were sent to Egypt to the works; those below 17 were sold. "[21] The whole number taken

[1] v. 8. [2] v. 10. [3] v. 11. [4] v. 14.
[5] צאן חֲהֲרֵגָה, as גֵיא הה. Jer. vii. 32, xix. 6. יום ה Ib. xii. 3.
[6] Ps. xliv. 22. צאן טבחה. [7] S. Matt. xxi. 37.
[8] Ib. 41. [9] Ib. 43. [10] Ps. xlix. 14.
[11] קֹנֵיהֶן stands opposed to מֹכְרֵיהֶן, as in Is. xxiv. 2, כַּקּוֹנֶה כַּמּוֹכֵר.

[12] Jer. ii. 3. [13] כל אכליו יאשמו. [14] Jer. l. 6, 7.
[15] לֹא נֶאְשָׁם. The same word.
[16] Jer. xxv. 9, xxvii. 6, xliii. 10.
[17] Is. x. 7. ואשם Hab. i. 11.
[18] Is. xlvii. 6, Zech. i. 18. [19] Is. xxxvi. 10.
[20] Jos. de B. J. 6. 9. 1.
[21] Jos. ib. § 2. 3.

Before CHRIST cir. 487.

the LORD; for I am rich:
and their own shepherds
pity them not.
6 For I will no more
pity the inhabitants of the
land, saith the LORD: but,
lo, I will † deliver the men
every one into his neighbor's hand, and into the
hand of his king: and
they shall smite the
land, and out of their
hand I will not deliver
them.

† Heb. *make to be found.*

prisoners during the wars were 1,100,000," beside those who perished elsewhere. "[1] Read we the ancient histories and the traditions of the mourning Jews, that at the Tabernaculum Abrahæ (where now is a very thronged mart every year) after the last destruction, which they endured from Adrian, many thousands were sold, and what could not be sold were removed into Egypt, and destroyed by shipwreck or famine and slaughter by the people. No displeasure came upon the Romans for the utter destruction, as there had upon the Assyrians and Chaldæans."

And their own shepherds (in contrast to those who *bought* and *sold* them, who accordingly were not their own, temporal or spiritual) they to whom God had assigned them, who should have fed them with the word of God, [2] strengthened the diseased, healed the sick, bound up the broken, and sought the lost, *pity them not.* He says what they should have done, in blaming them for what they did not do. They owed them a tender compassionate love[3]; they laid aside all mercy, and became wolves, as S. Paul says; [4] *After my departure shall grievous wolves enter in among you, not sparing the flock. Also of your own selves shall men arise, speaking perverse things, to draw away disciples after them.* They who owed them all love, shall have none. "[1] No marvel then, he says, if enemies shall use the right of conquest, when their very shepherds and teachers spared them not, and, through their fault, the flock was given over to the wolves." All were corrupted, High Priest, priests, scribes, lawyers, Pharisees, Sadducees. No one[5] had pity on them.

6. *For I will no more pity.* Therefore were they a *flock of the slaughter*, because God would *have no pity* on those who went after shepherds who *had no pity* upon them, but corrupted them; who [6] *entered not in themselves, and those who were entering in, they hindered.*

The inhabitants of the land, "that land, of which he had been speaking," Judæa. *And lo.* God, by this word, *lo*, always commands heed to His great doings with man; *I, I*, Myself[7], visibly interposing, *will deliver man*, the whole race of inhabitants, *every one into his neighbor's hand*, by confusion and strife and hatred within, *and into the hand of his king*, him whom they chose and took as their own king, when they rejected Christ as their King, repudiating the title which Pilate gave Him, to move their pity. Whereas He, their Lord and God, was their King, they formally [8] *denied Him in the presence of Pilate, when he was determined to let Him go; they denied the Holy One and the Just*, and said, [9] *We have no king but Cæsar.*

And they, the king without and the wild savages within, *shall smite*, bruise, crush in pieces, like a broken vessel[10], *the land, and out of their hand I will not deliver* them. Their captivity shall be without remedy or end. Holy Scripture often says, *there is no deliverer*[11], or [12] *none can deliver out of My hand*, or, since God delighteth in doing good, I[13], He[14], will deliver, or delivered[15] from the hands of the enemy, or their slavery, or their own fears, or afflictions, or the like. God nowhere else says absolutely as here, *I will not deliver*[16]. "Hear, O Jew," says S. Jerome, "who holdest out to thyself hopes most vain, and hearest not the Lord strongly asserting, *I will not deliver* them *out of their hands*, that thy captivity among the Romans shall have no end." In the threatened captivity before they were carried to

[1] S. Jer. [2] Ezek. xxxiv. 4.
[3] יחמלו. [4] Acts xx. 29, 30.
[5] This is expressed by the Hebrew idiom, "their shepherds [plur.] one by one, pity [sing.] them not." [6] S. Luke xi. 52. [7] אנכי emphatic.
[8] Acts iii. 13, 14. [9] S. John xix. 15.
[10] Of which כַּתַּת is used, Is. xxx. 14; of the golden calf, De. ix. 21. So כִּתֵּת, of the brazen serpent, 2 Kgs xviii. 4; the idols, 2 Chr. xxxiv. 7.
[11] אין מַצִּיל Jud. xviii. 28, 2 Sam. xiv. 6, Job v. 4, Ps. vii. 3, l. 22, lxxi. 11, Is. v. 29, xlii. 22, Hos. v. 14, Mic. v. 7, 8.
[12] De. xxxii. 39, Job x. 7, Ps. l. 22, lxxi. 11. Is. xliii. 13. Dan. viii. 4, 7.
[13] Ex. vi. 6, 2 Kgs xx. 6, Jer. xv. 21, xxxix. 17, Ezek. xxxiv. 27.
[14] 1 Sam. vii. 3, Ps. xviii. 15, lxxii. 12, 2 Kgs xvii. 39, Is. xix. 20, xxxi. 5, Job v. 19.
[15] Ex. xviii. 10, Josh. xxiv. 10, Jud. vi. 9, 1 Sam. x. 18, xiv. 10, 2 Sam. xxii. 1, Ps. xxxiv. 5, 18, liv. 9, Ezr. viii. 31, Jer. xx. 13.
[16] Once only on one of the brief repentances in the Judges, God answers their prayer, *I will not save you; go and cry to the gods which ye have chosen; let them save you:* but only to save them on their renewed repentance and prayer. Jud. x. 13–16.

Before CHRIST cir. 487.

7 And I will [f]feed the flock of slaughter, || *even* you, [g]O poor of the flock. And I took unto me two staves; the one I called Beauty, and the other I called || Bands; and I fed the flock.

[f] ver. 4.
|| Or, *verily the poor.*
[g] Zeph. 3. 12. Matt. 11. 5.
|| Or, *binders.*

Babylon, the prophet foretold the restoration: here only it is said of Judah, as Hosea had said of Israel, that there should be no deliverer out of the hand of the king whom they had chosen.

7. The prophetic narrative which follows, differs in its form, in some respects, from the symbolical actions of the prophets and from Zechariah's own visions. The symbolical actions of the prophets are actions of their own: *this* involves acts, which it would be impossible to represent, except as a sort of drama. Such are the very central points, the feeding of the flock, which yet are intelligent men who understand God's doings: the cutting off of the three shepherds; the asking for the price; the unworthy price offered; the casting it aside. It differs from Zechariah's own visions, in that *they* are for the most part exhibited to the eye, and Zechariah's own part is simply to enquire their meaning and to learn it, and to receive further revelation. In one case only, he himself interposes in the action of the vision[1]; but this too, as asking that it might be done, not, as himself doing it. Here, he is himself the actor, yet as representing Another, Who alone could cut off shepherds, abandon the people to mutual destruction, annulling the covenant which He had made. Maimonides, then, seems to say rightly; "[2]This, *I fed the flock of the slaughter*, to the end of the narrative, where he is said to have asked for his hire, to have received it, and to have cast it into the temple, to the treasurer, all this Zechariah saw in prophetic vision. For the command which he received, and the act which he is said to have done, took place in prophetic vision or dream." "This," he adds, "is beyond controversy, as all know, who are able to distinguish the possible from the impossible."

"[3]The actions, presented to the prophets are not always to be understood as actions but as predictions. As when God commands Isaiah, to make the heart of the people dull[4] i. e. to denounce to the people their future blindness, through which they would, with obstinate mind, reject the mercies of Christ. Or when He says, that He appointed Jeremiah [5]to destroy and to build; to root out and to plant. Or when He commanded the same prophet to cause the nations to drink the cup, whereby they should be bereft of their senses[6], Jeremiah did nothing of all this, but asserted that it would be. So here."

And I will feed the flock of the slaughter, rather *And* [our, so] *I fed*[7]. The prophet declares, in the name of our Lord, that He did what the Father commanded Him. He fed the flock, committed to His care by the Father, who, through their own obstinacy, became *the flock of slaughter.* What could be done, He did for them; so that all might see that they perished by their own fault. The symbol of our Lord, as the Good Shepherd, had been made prominent by Isaiah, Jeremiah and Ezekiel, [8]*Behold the Lord will come, as a Mighty One—He shall feed His flock like a shepherd: He shall gather the lambs with His arm and carry them in His bosom: He shall gently lead those that are with young.* And Jeremiah, having declared God's judgments on the then shepherds[9], [10]*I will gather the remnant of My flock out of all countries whither I have driven them, and will bring them again to their fold; and they shall be fruitful and increase. And I will set up shepherds over them which shall feed them. Behold the days come, saith the Lord, that I will raise unto David a righteous Branch, and a king shall reign and prosper—and this is the name whereby He shall be called, the Lord our Righteousness.* And Ezekiel with the like context[11]; [12]*Therefore will I save My flock and they shall be no more a prey; and I will judge between cattle and cattle. And I will set One Shepherd over them, and He shall feed them: My servant David, He shall feed them; and He shall be their Shepherd;* and, uniting both offices, [13]*David, My servant, shall be king over them, and they shall all have One Shepherd.* It was apparent then beforehand, Who this Shepherd was to be, to Whom God gave the feeding of the flock.

"Even *you*, or *for you, ye poor of the flock;* or, *therefore*, being thus commanded, [*fed I*]

[1] iii. 15.
[2] More Neboch. ii. 46, p. 123, 6. Buxt. Tr. p. 326. Abarbanel (ad loc.) regards the act as real, but symbolic. "God commanded him to do an act, in deed and awake, which was a declaration and a sign of what should be in God's guidance of Israel. See at length in McCaul's transl. of Kimchi on Zech. pp. 198–208.

[3] Osor. [4] Is. vi. 10. [5] Jer. i. 10. [6] Id. xxv. 15 sqq.
[7] ה retained in וָאֶרְעֶה as in verbs לה in 1 Sam. i. 7, 2 Sam. xxiii. 15, 1 Kgs xiv. 9, 2 Kgs ii. 8, 14 [bis] Jer. xx. 2.
[8] Is. xl. 10, 11. [9] Jer. xxiii. 2. [10] Ib. 3–6.
[11] Ezek. xxxiv. 1-21. [12] Ib. 22, 23.
[13] Ib. xxxvii. 24.

Before CHRIST cir. 487.

8 Three shepherds also I cut off[h] in one month; and my soul † loathed them, and their soul also abhorred me.

h Hos. 5. 7.

† Heb. *was straitened for them.*

the poor of the flock[1]. The whole flock was committed to Him to feed. He had to seek out all [2] *the lost sheep of the house of Israel.* "[3] *He fed*, for the time, the Jews destined to death, until their time should come;" the fruit of His labor was in the [4] *little flock*, "the faithful Jews who believed in Him, out of the people of the flock aforesaid, or the synagogue, Who in the primitive Church despised all earthly things, leading a most pure life." So He says, [5] *I will feed My flock and I will cause them to lie down, saith the Lord God: I will seek that which was lost, and bring again that which was driven away, and will bind* that which was *broken, and will strengthen that which was sick: but I will destroy the fat and the strong, I will feed them with judgment.*

The elect are the end of all God's dispensations. He fed all; yet the fruit of His feeding, His toils, His death, the travail of His soul, was in those only who are saved. So S. Paul says, [6] *Therefore I endure all things for the elect's sakes, that they may also obtain the salvation which is in Christ Jesus, with eternal glory.* He fed all; but the *poor of the flock* alone, those who were despised of men, because they would not follow the pride of the High Priests and Scribes and Pharisees, believed on Him, as they themselves say, [7] *Have any of the rulers or the Pharisees believed on Him?* and S. Paul says, [8] *Not many wise men after the flesh, not many mighty, not many noble are called; but God hath chosen the foolish things of the world to confound the wise; and God hath chosen the weak things of the world to confound the things that are mighty; and base things of the world, and things despised, hath God chosen, yea, and things which are not, to bring to nought things that are.*

And I took unto Me two [shepherd's] *staves*, as David says, [9] *Thy rod and Thy staff they comfort me. The one I called Beauty* or *Loveliness*[10], as the Psalmist longs to *behold the beauty* or *loveliness* of God in His temple[11], and says; let [12] *the beauty of the Lord our God be upon us.*

And the other I called Bands, lit. *Binders*[13]. The one staff represents the full favor and loving-kindness of God; when this was broken, there yet remained the other, by which they were held together as a people in covenant with God. *And I fed the flock.* This was the use of his staves; He tended them with both, ever putting in exercise toward them the loving beauty and grace of God, and binding them together and with Himself.

8. *And I cut off three shepherds in one month.* "[14] I have read in some one's commentary, that the shepherds, cut off in the indignation of the Lord, are to be understood of priests and false prophets and kings of the Jews, who, after the Passion of Christ, were all cut off in one time, of whom Jeremiah speaketh, [15] *The priests said not, Where is the Lord? and they that handle the law knew Me not; the pastors also transgressed against Me, and the prophets prophesied by Baal, and walked after* things which *do not profit*," and again, [16] *As the thief is ashamed when he is found, so is the house of Israel ashamed; they, their kings, their princes, and their priests and their prophets;* and [17] *they said, Come, let us devise devices against Jeremiah; for the law shall not perish from the priest, nor counsel from the wise, nor the word from the prophet.* "[18] He speaks of the kings of the Jews, and prophets and priests; for by the three orders they were shepherded." "[19] The true and good Shepherd having been already pointed out, it was right and necessary that the hirelings and false shepherds should be removed, the guides of the Jews in the law. The three shepherds were, I deem, those who exercised the legal priesthood, and those appointed judges of the people, and the interpreters of Scripture, i. e. the lawyers. For these too fed Israel. Those who had the glory of the priesthood were of the tribe of Levi only; and of them Malachi says, [20] *The priest's lips shall keep knowledge, and they shall seek the law at his mouth.* But those who received authority to judge were also selected, yet were appointed out of every tribe. In like way the lawyers, who were ever assessors to the judges, and adduced the words of the law in proof of every matter.— But we shall find that our Lord Jesus Christ

1 The masora parva says that "the לָכֵן is a feminine," i. e. so punctuated for לָכֶן, as in the 3d pers. כָּהֵם 2 Sam. xxiv. 3, Eccl. ix. 12; בָּהֵן Gen. xix. 29, xxx. 26. Yet לָכֵן being, so often, some 60 times, illative, *therefore*, it would be arbitrary to take it otherwise here, since even כֵּן itself nowhere occurs as a pronoun.

2 S. Matt. x. 6, xv. 24. 3 Dion. 4 S. Luke xii. 32. 5 Ezek. xxxiv. 15, 16. 6 2 Tim. ii. 10. 7 S. John xii. 48. 8 1 Cor. i. 26–28. 9 Ps. xxiii. 4.

10 κάλλος, ὁ; εὐπρέπεια, Aq. Sym. (Theodot. also, see Field Hexapl. on v. 10.) "decus." S. Jer.

11 "נֹעַם יי Ps. xxvii. 4. 12 Ps. xc. 17.

13 From the common חֶבֶל "rope;" in Arab. verb, "bound fast as with rope," "made covenant;" noun, "band of marriage, friendship, covenant of God or man, personal security," Lane. σχοίνισμα, ὁ Aq. Sym.; funiculos, S. Jer.

14 S. Jer. 15 Jer. ii. 8. 16 Ib. 26. 17 Ib. xviii. 18. 18 Theodoret. 19 S. Cyr. 20 Mal. ii. 7.

Before CHRIST cir. 487.

9 Then said I, I will not
feed you: [i] that that dieth,
let it die; and that that is
to be cut off, let it be cut off;
and let the rest eat every
one the flesh † of another.
10 ¶ And I took my
staff, *even* Beauty, and cut

i Jer. 15. 2. & 43. 11.

† Heb. *of his fellow*, or, *neighbor*.

Himself expressly pronounced woe on the Pharisees and scribes and lawyers. For He said, [1] *Woe unto you scribes and Pharisees.* And when one of the lawyers hereupon answered Him saying, [2] *Master, so saying Thou reproachest us also,* He said, *Woe unto you also, ye lawyers! for ye lade men with burdens grievous to be borne, and ye yourselves touch not the burdens with one of your fingers.* These *three Shepherds* then, priests and judges and lawyers [3], who remained in their own orders and places, until the coming of Christ, were very justly taken away *in one month.* For since [4] *they killed the Prince of life,* thereby also are they mown down, and that in the month of the first fruits, in which Emmanuel endured to be slain for us. They remained indeed administering Israel, even after the Saviour's Cross, through the long-suffering and compassion of Almighty God calling them to repentance; but, in the sentence passed by God, they were taken away, at that time, when they delivered to the Cross the Saviour and Redeemer of all. They were taken away then *in one month;*" Nisan. A. D. 33. The three offices, King, Divine Teacher, Priest, were to be united in Christ: they might have been held under Him: those who rejected them in Him, forfeited them themselves. These then He made to disappear, effaced them from the earth [5].

And My soul was straightened for them [6]. It is used of the Divine grief at the misery of His people [7]. *And their soul abhorred Me, nauseated Me* [8]. "[9] When it is said, *Their soul also abhorreth Me*, the meaning is, 'My soul did not loathe them first, but their soul first despised Me, therefore My Soul abhorred them.'" The soul which drives away God's good Spirit, comes at last to loathe Him and the thought and mention of Him.

9. *And I said, I will not feed you.* God, at last, leaves the rebellious soul or people to itself, as He says by Moses, [10] *Then My anger shall be kindled against them in that day, and I will forsake them, and will hide My Face from them, and they shall be devoured, and many evils and troubles shall find them:* and our Lord tells the captious Jews; [11] *I go My way, and ye shall seek Me and shall die in your sins.*

That which dieth, let it die. Zechariah seems to condense, but to repeat the abandonment in Jeremiah; [12] *Cast them out of My sight, and let them go forth. And it shall be, if they shall say unto thee, Whither shall we go forth? then thou shalt tell them, Thus saith the Lord, Such as* are *for death, to death; and such as* are *for the sword, to the sword; and such as* are *for the captivity, to the captivity.* First, God gives over to death without violence, by famine or pestilence, those whose lot it should be; another portion to violent death by the sword; *that which is cut off shall be cut off; and the rest,* the flock of slaughter, would be turned into wolves; and, as in the awful and horrible siege of Jerusalem, those who had escaped these deaths, *the left-over, shall eat every one of the flesh of his neighbor,* every law of humanity and of nature broken. "[13] So should they understand at last, how evil and bitter a thing it is for all who lived by My help to be despoiled of that help."

10. *And I took my staff Beauty, and cut it asunder.* Not, as aforetime, did He chasten His people, retaining His relation to them: for such chastening is an austere form of love.

[1] S. Luke xi. 44. [2] Ib. 45, 46.

[3] No other explanation of the 'three shepherds' seems to me at all to recommend itself. The Jews made them Moses Aaron and Miriam (Taanith f. 9a.) and from them, S. Jerome; J. Kim. and (as one solution) Ibn Ezra, suggested Haggai, Zechariah, Malachi; "'After whom,' the rabbis say, 'prophecy departed from Israel'" ("on account of the cutting off of prophecy at their death," opinion in Tanchum.) Abraham Lev. "the principality of the sons of David, and the monarchy of the Hasmonæans, and that of their servants." D. Kim., "the three sons of Josiah, Jehoahaz, Jehoiakim and Zedekiah:" Abarbanel, "the Maccabees, Judas Jonathan and Simon:" Rashi, "the house of Ahab and the house of Ahaziah, and his brethren and all the posterity of the kingdom of David (except Joash) slain by Ahab and Athaliah:" Tanchum, "Joshua the high-priest and the second priest and the anointed for war:" (Buxtorf refers for his office to Maimonides, Hilchos melachin umilchama c. 7. and massecheth Sota c. 8. Lex. Chald. col. 1267). "And it is said, Joshua, Zerubbabel and Nehemiah," Tanchum. Theodorus of Mops. interpreted it of "the priests" generally, not of any three classes of persons. Three classes, Priests, Pharisees and Sadducees, were adopted by some older; Pharisees Sadducees and Essenes by Lightfoot (Horæ Hebr. on S. John x.). On the abortive guesses of a German school, see ab. Introd. to Zechariah p. 509.

[4] Acts iii. 15.

[5] הכחוד lit. "hid," Job xx. 12, as כִּחֵד uniformly (15 times), thence ἀφανίζω. It is used of numbers; the 7 nations, Ex. xxiii. 23; of Israel, in the intention of their enemies, from being a nation, מגוי, Ps. lxxxiii. 5; of the house of Jeroboam from the face of the earth, 1 Kgs xiii. 34; of Sennacherib's army, 2 Chr. xxxii. 21.

[6] As in E. M.

[7] Jud. x. 16 also with ב p. Gesenius' comparison of Arab. נַזַע is wrong. Its primary meaning is "cut off from," See Lane p. 419.

[8] Such is the traditional meaning of בחל. "loathed My worship," Ch.; "loathed," Abulw. Tanch. coll. Syr. בַּחִילא. "one so nauseating as to vomit his food."

[9] Kim. [10] De. xxxi. 17. [11] S. John viii. 21.

[12] Jer. xv. 1, 2, and similarly xliii. 11. [13] Osor.

Before CHRIST cir. 487.

it asunder, that I might break my covenant which I had made with all the people.

11 And it was broken in that day: and ‖ so [k] the poor of the flock that waited upon me knew that

‖ Or, *the poor of the flock, &c. certainly knew.*
k Zeph. 3. 12. ver. 7.

it *was* the word of the LORD.

12 And I said unto them, † If ye think good, give *me* my price; and if not, forbear. So they [l] weighed for my price thirty *pieces* of silver.

Before CHRIST cir. 487.

† Heb. *If it be good in your eyes.*
l Matt. 26. 15. See Ex. 21. 32.

By breaking the staff of His tender love, He signified that this relation was at an end.

That I might dissolve My covenant which I had made with all the people, rather, *with all the peoples*, i. e. with all nations. Often as it is said of Israel, that they brake the covenant of God[1], it is spoken of God, only to deny that He would break it[2], or in prayer that He would not[3]. Here it is not absolutely the covenant with His whole people, which He brake; it is rather, so to speak, a covenant with the nations in favor of Israel, allowing thus much and forbidding more, with regard to His people. So God had said of the times of Christ[4]; *In that day I will make a covenant for them with the beasts of the field and with the fowls of the heaven, and with the creeping things of the ground;* and, [5] *I will make with them a covenant of peace, and will cause the evil beasts to cease out of the land;* and in Job [6] *thou shalt be in league with the stones of the field, and the beasts of the field shall be at peace with thee.* This covenant He willed to annihilate. He would no more interpose, as He had before said, [7] *I will not deliver from their hand.* Whoever would might do, what they would, as the Romans first, and well nigh all nations since, have inflicted on the Jews, what they willed; and Mohammedans too have requited to them their contumely to Jesus.

11. *And so the poor of the flock that waited upon Me*[8] *knew.* The rest were blinded; those who listened to God's word, observed His Prophet, waited on Him and observed His words, knew from the fulfillment of the beginning, that the whole was God's word. Every darkening cloud around the devoted city was an earnest, that the storm, which should destroy it, was gathering upon it. So our Lord warned, [9] *When ye shall see Jerusalem compassed with armies, then know that the desolation thereof is nigh. Then let them which are in Judæa flee to the mountains; and let them which are in the midst of it depart.* The *little flock which waited upon* the Good Shepherd, obeyed the warning, and, fleeing to Pella, escaped the horrible judgment which fell on those who remained. "[10] They remembered that it had been predicted many centuries before, and that the Lord, by Whose Spirit the prophet spake, foretold that in that city [11] *one stone should not be left upon another.*"

12. *And I said unto them, If ye think good, give Me My price.* God asks of us a return, not having any proportion to His gifts of nature or of grace, but such as we can render. He took the Jews out of the whole human race, made them His own, *a peculiar people*, freed them from *the bondage and the iron furnace of Egypt*, gave them *the land flowing with milk and honey*, fed and guarded them by His Providence, taught them by His Prophets. He, the Lord and Creator of all, was willing to have them alone for His inheritance, and, in return, asked them to love Him with their whole heart, and to do what He commanded them. [12] *He sent His servants to the husbandmen, that they might receive the fruits of the vineyard; and the husbandmen took His servants, and beat one, and killed another, and stoned another. Last of all, He sent unto them His Son,* to ask for those fruits, the return for all His bounteous care and His unwearied acts of power and love. "[13] Give Me," He would say, "some fruits of piety, and tokens of faith."

"[10] What? Does He speak of a price? Did the Lord of all let out His toil? Did He bargain with those, for whom he expended it for a certain price? He did. He condescended to serve day and night for our salvation and dignity; and as one hired, in view of the reward which He set before Him, to give all His care to adorn and sustain our condition. So He complains by Isaiah, that He had undergone great toil to do away our sins. But what

---

1 Lev. xxvi. 15, De. xxxi. 16, 20, Is. xxiv. 5, Jer. xi. 10, xxxi. 32, Ezek. xvi. 59, xliv. 7.
2 Lev. xxvi. 44, Jud. ii. 1. and, strongly, Jer. xxxiii. 20, 21.
3 Jer. xiv. 21.
4 Hos. ii. 18, [20, Heb.]
5 Ezek. xxxiv. 25.
6 Job v. 23.
7 v. 6.
8 השמרים אתי. שׁמר occurs more commonly w. acc. of thg., commandments &c. but w. acc. pers., in good sense, שׁמר אדניו "he that observeth his master," Pr. xxvii. 18; also of God, Hos. iv. 10; of idols, Ps. xxxi. 7; and of observing for evil, 1 Sam. xix. 11, Job x. 14.
9 S. Luke xxi. 20, 21.
10 Osor.
11 S. Matt. xxiv. 2.
12 S. Matt. xxi. 34–37.
13 Eus. Dem. Ev. x. 4. So Theod.

Before CHRIST cir. 487.

13 And the LORD said
unto me, Cast it unto the
[m] potter: a goodly price
that I was prized at of

Before CHRIST cir. 487.

[m] Matt. 27. 9, 10.

reward did He require? Faith and the will of a faithful heart, that thereby we might attain the gift of righteousness, and might in holy works pant after everlasting glory. For He needeth not our goods; but He so bestoweth on us all things, as to esteem His labor amply paid, if He see us enjoy His gifts. But He so asketh for this as a reward, as to leave us free, either by faith and the love due, to embrace His benefits, or faithlessly to reject it. This is His meaning, when He saith,"

And if not, forbear. God does not force our free-will, or constrain our service. He places life and death before us, and bids us choose life. By His grace alone we can choose Him; but we can refuse His grace and Himself. [1] *Thou shalt say unto them,* He says to Ezekiel, *Thus saith the Lord God, He that heareth, let him hear, and he that forbeareth, let him forbear.* This was said to them, as a people, the last offer of grace. It gathered into one all the past. As Elijah had said, [2] *If the Lord be God, follow Him; but if Baal, then follow him;* so He bids them, at last to choose openly, whose they would be, to whom they would give their service; and if they would refuse in heart, to refuse in act also. *Forbear,* cease, leave off, abandon; and that for ever.

So they weighed for My price thirty pieces of silver; the price of a slave, gored to death by an ox[3]. Whence one of themselves says, "[4] you will find that a freeman is valued, more or less, at 60 shekels, but a slave at thirty." He then, Whom the prophet represented, was to be valued at *thirty pieces of silver.* It was but an increase of the contumely, that this contemptuous price was given, not to Him, but for Him, the Price of His Blood. It was matter of bargain. [5] *Judas said, What will ye give me, and I will deliver Him unto you?* The High Priest, knowingly or unknowingly, fixed on the price, named by Zechariah. As they took into their mouths willingly the blasphemy mentioned in the Psalm; [6] *they shoot out the lip, they shake the head,* saying, *He trusted in the Lord,* that *He would deliver Him; let Him deliver Him, seeing that He delighted in Him;* so perhaps they fixed on the *thirty pieces of silver,* because Zechariah had named them as a sum offered in contumely to him, who offered to be a shepherd and asked for his reward.

13. *And the Lord said unto me, Cast it,* as a thing vile and rejected, as torn flesh was to be cast to dogs[7], or a corpse was cast unburied[8], or the dead body of Absalom was cast into the pit[9], or the dust of the idol-altars into the brook Kedron by Josiah[10], or the idols to the moles and the bats[11]; or Judah and Israel from the face of God[12] into a strange land[13]; Coniah and his seed, a vessel in which is no pleasure[14], into a land which they knew not; or the rebels against God, said, [15] *let us cast away their cords from us;* or wickedness was cast into the Ephah[16]; once it is added[17], *for loathing.*

Unto the potter. The words exactly correspond with the event, that the *thirty pieces of silver* were *cast* or flung away[18]; that their ultimate destination was the potter, whose field was bought with them; but that they were not cast directly to him, (which were a contemptuous act, such as would not be used whether for a gift or a purchase), but were cast to him *in the house of the Lord.* They were *flung away* by the remorse of Judas, and, in God's Providence, came to the potter. Whether any portion of this was a direct symbolic action of the prophet, or whether it was a prophetic vision, in which Zechariah himself was an actor, and saw himself in the character which he described, doing what he relates, cannot now be said certainly, since God has not told us. It seems to me more probable, that these actions belonged to the vision, because in other symbolic actions of the prophets, no other actors take part; and it is to the last degree unlikely, that Zechariah, at whose preaching Zerubbabel and Joshua and all the people set themselves earnestly to rebuild the temple, should have had so worthless a price offered to him; and the casting a price, which God condemned, into the house of God, at the command of God, and so implying His acceptance of it, were inconsistent. It was fulfilled, in act consistently, in Judas' remorse; in that he *flung*[19] *away the pieces of silver,* which had stained his soul with innocent blood, *in the*

[1] Ezek. iii. 27; add ii. 5, 7, iii. 11.
[2] 1 Kgs xviii. 21.
[3] Ex. xxi. 32.
[4] Maimonides More Neboch. c. 40. P. 3.
[5] S. Matt. xxvi. 15.
[6] Ps. xxii. 7, 8.
[7] Ex. xxii. 31.
[8] Is. xiv. 19, xxxiv. 3, Jer. xxiv. 16, xii. 19, xxvi. 23, xxxvi. 30.
[9] 2 Sam. xviii. 17.
[10] 2 Kgs xxiii. 12.
[11] Is. ii. 20, add Ezek. xx. 8.
[12] 2 Kgs xiii. 23, xvii. 20, xxiv. 21, Jer. lii. 3.
[13] De. xxix. 27 [28 Eng.]
[14] Jer. xxii. 28.
[15] Ps. ii. 3.
[16] Zech. v. 18.
[17] Ezek. xvi. 5.
[18] ῥίψας τὰ ἀργύρια ἐν τῷ ναῷ S. Matt. xxvii. 5.
[19] This is in itself (as Keil observed) decisive against the substitution of אוֹצָר for יוֹצֵר, as Jon. and the Syr. have, if it be interpreted of any act of Zechariah. If it were taken only of the result of the ordering of God's Providence, the man substance of the prophecy would equally remain, that the Good Shepherd was valued at this contemptuous price; and that the money itself was flung

Before CHRIST cir. 487.

them. And I took the thirty *pieces* of silver, and cast them to the potter in the house of the LORD.

Before CHRIST cir. 487.

temple, perhaps remembering the words of Zechariah; perhaps wishing to give to pious uses, too late, money which was the price of his soul; whereas God, even through the Chief Priests, rejected it, and so it came to the potter, its ultimate destination in the Providence of God. "[1] He saith, *cast it unto the potter*, that they might understand that they would be broken as a potter's vessel."

A goodly price, that I was prized at of them, lit. *the magnificence of the value*[2], *at which I was*

into the treasury; only in this case the second clause "to the treasury in the house of the Lord" would add nothing to the first, whereas, if יוצר be rendered in its natural sense "potter," this accounts for the use of the word "fling," and contains what was brought about by the joint agency of Judas and the Pharisees. But 2) no two words, in any language, are more distinct than אוצר and יוצר, both of them also being, in their several senses, common words. אוצר, "treasure," or at times, "treasury," occurs 79 times in the O. T.; יוצר, lit. "former," occurs 41 times beside these verses. There is not the slightest approximation of the meaning of the two roots; אצר is "treasured up;" יצר, "made." Since then, apart from inspiration, every writer wishes to be understood, it is, in the nature of things, absurd to suppose, that, had Zechariah meant to say, "cast into the treasury," he should not have used the word, which everywhere else, 79 times, is used to express it, but should have used a word, which is always, viz. 41 times, used of something else. The particular form moreover, with the art. occurs 11 times in the O. T. as "the potter;" once in Isaiah (xxix. 16), seven times in 2 chapters of Jeremiah, xviii. 2, 3, 4 (bis) 6 (bis) xix. 11, of "the potter," once only of Almighty God, (Ps. xxxiii. 15) and that, in a different idiom. Of God, it is never used as a substantive, "the Creator." It remains a part., "Maker of," it being added, of what He is the Maker. 'He that maketh the eye,' Ps. xciv. 9, the hearts, Ib. xxxiii. 15, light, Is. xlv. 7; the earth, Ib. 18; the universe, הַכֹּל Jer. x. 15, li. 19; mountains, Amos iv. 13; grasshoppers, Ib. vii. 1; the spirit of man, Zech. xii. 1; or with pronouns, my Maker Is. xlix. 5; thy Maker Is. xliii. 1; our Maker xliv. 2, 24, his Maker Is. xxvii. 11, xxix. 16, xlv. 9. 11. The rendering then of the Jews in S. Jerome's time, D. Kim., Abraham of Toledo apparently, Abarb., Alsheikh, "the Creator," is unidiomatic, as well as that of Rashi, J. Kim. Tanch., Isaac (xvii. cent.) Chizzuk Emunah (Wagnseil Tel. ign. Sat. p. 146.), "treasury," which the modern Anti-Messianic interpreters follow. Aquila has τὸν πλάστην; the LXX and Symm. χωνευτήριον, "foundry;" in that יצר is used with regard to metals, Is. xliv. 12, liv. 17, Hab. ii. 18, as well as, more commonly, of clay. יוצר is used of the "potter" 2 Sam. xvii. 28, 1 Chr. iv. 23, Ps. ii. 9, Is. xxx. 14, xli. 25, lxiv. 7, Jer. xix. 1, Lam. iv. 2 (beside the use of היוער above); also "the former thereof" contrasted with the clay, Is. xlv. 9. The Hebrew-Arabic translation, which Pococke so much valued (12th cent.) has twice אלצאי׳ג, (used chiefly of a gold-smith). Abulwalid does not notice it in either lexicon, nor Saadyah Ibn Danân nor Parchon. They must therefore have had nothing to remark on it, interpreting it as elsewhere, 'potter.'

It is not then necessary even to say, that the dicta as to the interchange of א and י in Hebrew are much too vague, the instances heterogeneous. All the words, in which א and י occur as the first letter, are allied words of the same meaning, not interchanged. Such are אחר and יחר, אשר and ישר, (whence the Proper Names אשראלה 1 Chr. xxv. 2. and ישראלה Ib. 14.). אחר and יחר ἀπ. λεγ. (2 Sam. xx. 5) are again allied, the Maltese also having a root *wacchar* (Vassali Lex. melit. pp. 82, 651, in Ges. v. יחר). אמן "was stable" was, probably, the basis of ימין. The use of the ἀπ. λεγ. האמינו for תימינו "turn to the right" Is. xxx. 21, would have been anyhow a substitution of the guttural for the י, not the י for the א, and any ambiguity is precluded by the contrast of תשמאילו "turn to the left." The Kri מיוזנים (Jer. v. 8) is only a bad correction for the Ch. מוזנים, and so not Biblical Hebrew. These are all the instances collected by Böttcher (Lehrb. n. 430.) In like way in the middle radical דָּאָה (Lev. x. 14) and דַּיָּה Deut. xiv. 13. Böttch, 1103, 4. adds תתימרו, which Saad. and Rashi, more probably, derive from ימר, Jer. ii. 11. In Ezek. vi. 6, ישם and אשם both occur, as variations, not of each other, but of שמם, vi. 4.

Other cases are simple omissions of the א, not an interchange at all; as קִיו from קיא (med. i. Arab. Æth.) Jer. xxv. 27, בריה for בריאה Ez. xxxiv. 20. ביר Jer. vi. 7 is a mere correction for בור. and so, again, not Biblical Hebrew. דויג (1 Sam. xxii. 18, 22 Ch.) is a mere corruption of דאג, as, in all languages proper names are the most easily corrupted. (See Daniel the prophet p. 405 ed. 2). אִשׁ (2 Sam. xx. 5. Mic. vi. 10) and the common יֵשׁ, each lose one letter of the original form, which has both. (See on Daniel the prophet p. 50 note. ed. 2) There is not then the slightest countenance for assuming that היוצר is *not*, what according to its form it *is*, "*the potter*."

[1] Osor.

[2] אדר occurs in this sense, here only. In Mi. ii. 8, it is used of a wide garment i. q. אַדֶּרֶת. יְקָר, "of value" only occurs else in כְּלִי יְקָר "a vessel of value" Pr. xx. 15; כל-יְקָר "every precious thing" Job. xxviii. 10; כָּל יְקָרָהּ "all its magnificence," Jer. xx. 5; "costliness," Ez. xxii. 25; not directly a "price."

"Jewish writers who could satisfy themselves that the 'thirty pieces of silver' were anything but what they are, some thirty precepts given to the sons of Noah (mystical interpretation in the גיד הנשה ap. Abarb. ad loc. p. 219. v.), or thirty dignities of royalty ("the wise of blessed memory," in Abarb. Ib. p. 292. v.) or the thirty righteous in each generation, promised (as they say) by God to Abraham (Midrash Aggadah in Rashi), or the thirty in that generation (Kim.), or who went up with Nehemiah, or were priests in his time [Tanchum has It is said, that perhaps it is an image of the thirty righteous or priests, who were the noblest of the followers of Zerubbabel or Nehemiah."] Ibn E., or thirty days of imperfect repentance (Kim.), or thirty years of the reigns of the kings of the pious Hasmonæans (Abrah. Toled. in McCaul on Zech. ad loc.), or who scrupled not to own that they could not explain them at all (Rashi);—Jewish writers, who could, in any of these ways, escape from thinking of those thirty pieces of silver, at which their forefathers priced the Blood of Jesus, doubt not that the Good Shepherd Who fed them, Whom

Before CHRIST cir. 487.

‖ Or, *Binders.*

14 Then I cut asunder mine other staff, *even* ‖ Bands, that I might break the brotherhood between Judah and Israel.

Before CHRIST cir. 487.

valued of them! The strong irony is carried on by the, *at which I was valued of them*, as in the idiom, *thou wert precious in my sight*[1]. Precious the thought of God to David[2]; precious the redemption of the soul of man[3]; and precious was the Shepherd Who came to them; precious was the value, whereat He was valued by them[4]. And yet He, Who was so valued, was Almighty God. For so it stands: *Thus saith the Lord God, Cast it unto the potter, the goodly price that I was prized at of them.* The name, *the potter*, connects the prophecy with that former prophecy of Jeremiah[5], denouncing the judgment of God for the shedding of innocent blood, whereby they had defiled *the valley of the son of Hinnom, which was at the entry of the gate of the pottery*[6], and which, through the vengeance of God there, should be called *the valley of slaughter*[7]. The price of this innocent Blood, by the shedding of which the iniquities of their fathers were filled up, should rest on that same place, for whose sake God said, [8] *I will break this people and this city, as one breaketh a potter's vessel, that cannot be made whole again.* So then S. Matthew may have quoted this prophecy as Jeremiah's, to signify how the woes, denounced on the sins committed in this same place, should be brought upon it through this last crowning sin, and *all the righteous blood which had been shed, should come upon that generation*[9].

14. *And I cut asunder mine other staff, Bands, to dissolve the brotherhood between Judah and Israel.* Hitherto prophecy had spoken of the healing of the great breach between Israel and Judah, in Christ. *The Lord*, Isaiah said, [10] *shall assemble the outcasts of Israel, and gather together the dispersed of Judah from the four corners of the earth. The envy of Ephraim shall depart, and the adversaries of Judah shall be cut off: Ephraim shall not envy Judah, and Judah shall not vex Ephraim;* and Hosea, [11] *Then shall the children of Judah and the children of Israel be gathered together and shall appoint themselves one Head;* and Jeremiah, [12] *In those days the house of Judah shall walk with the house of Israel.* And Ezekiel, in the midst of the captivity, in a symbolic action the counterpart of this, is bidden, [13] *Take thee one stick, and write upon it, For Judah, and for the children of Israel his companions; then take another stick, and write upon it, For Joseph, the stick of Ephraim and all the house of Israel his companions, and join them one to another into one stick, and they shall become one in thy hand;* and, when asked the meaning of this act, he was to say, *Thus saith the Lord God,* [14] *I will take the stick of Joseph, which is in the hand of Ephraim, and the tribes of Israel his fellows, and will put them with him,* even *with the stick of Judah, and will make them one stick, and they shall be one in Mine hand.* And dropping the symbol; [15] *Thus saith the Lord God, Behold, I will take the children of Israel from among the heathen, whither they be gone—and I will make*

they rejected, Who gave them up, Who speaks of Himself, "the goodly price that *I* was prized at of them' (however they may have distorted these words too) was Almighty God." Pusey's University Sermons pp. 151, 152.

[1] יקר בעיני פ 1 Sam. xxvi. 21, Ps. lxxii. 14, 2 Kgs i. 13, 14, Is. xliii. 4. [2] Ps. cxxxix. 17. [3] Ib. xlix. 9.

[4] יקר מֵעֲלֵיהֶם. See Ewald Lehrb. n. 219a. p. 573. ed. 8. [5] Jer. xix.

[6] שַׁעַר הַחַרְסוּת Ib. 2. See Ges. Thes. sub v. p. 522. [7] Jer. xix. 6. [8] Ib. 11.

[9] S. Augustine suggests that S. Matthew wished to lead the reader to connect the prophecy of Zechariah with Jerem. xxxii. 9. "All copies," he says, "have not 'Jeremiah' but only 'by the prophet;' but more Mss. have the name of Jeremiah; and those who have considered the Gospel carefully in the Greek copies, say that they have found it in the older Greek (copies); and there is no reason why the name should be added, so as to occasion a fault; but there was a reason *why* it should be removed from some copies, this being done by a bold unskillfulness [imperitia] being distracted by the question, that this testimony was not found in Jeremiah." "S. Matthew," he says further, "would have corrected it in his life-time at least, when admonished by others who could read this, while he was yet in the flesh, unless he thought that one name of a prophet instead of another did, not without reason, occur to his memory, which was ruled by the Holy Spirit, but that the Lord appointed that it should be so written," 1) to shew that all the prophets, speaking by the Spirit, agreed together by a marvelous consent, which is much more than if all the things of the prophets were spoken by the mouth of one man, and so that, whatever the Holy Spirit said by them, should be received undoubtingly, and each belonged to all and all to each &c. 2) to combine it with the selling the field of Hananeel, of which the evidence was put in an earthen vessel. de Cons. Evang. L. iii. n. 30, 31. T. iii. 2. p. 114–116.

None of the other cases of mixed quotation come up to this. S. Mark quotes two prophecies, of Malachi and of Isaiah as Isaiah's (S. Mark i. 2. 3). S. Matthew blends in one, words of Isaiah (lxii. 1) and Zechariah (ix. 9) as "the prophet" (S. Matt. xxi 4, 5). Our Lord unites Is. lvi. 7, and Jer. vii. 11, with the words, "It is written."

Of earlier fathers *Tertullian* simply quotes the prophecy as Jeremiah's (adv. Marc. iv. 40). *Origen* says, "Jeremiah is not said to have prophesied this anywhere in his books, either what are read in the Churches, or reported (referuntur) among the Jews. I suspect that it is an error of writing, or that it is some secret writing of Jeremiah wherein it is written." (in S. Matt. p. 916.) *Eusebius* says, "Consider since this, is not in the Prophet Jeremiah, whether we must think that it was removed from it by some wickedness, or whether it was a clerical error of those who made the copies of the Gospels carelessly." Dem. Ev. x. p. 481.

[10] Is. xi. 12, 13. [11] Hos. i. 11. [12] Jer. iii. 18.

[13] Ezek. xxxvii. 16, 17. [14] Ib. 19. [15] Ib. 21, 22, 23, 24.

Before CHRIST cir. 487.

15 ¶ And the Lord said
unto me, [n] Take unto thee
yet the instruments of a
foolish shepherd.
16 For, lo, I will raise
up a shepherd in the land,
which shall not visit those
that be ‖ cut off, neither
shall seek the young one,
nor heal that that is broken,
nor ‖ feed that that standeth still: but he shall eat
the flesh of the fat, and
tear their claws in pieces.

n Ezek. 34. 2, 3, 4.

‖ Or, *hidden.*

‖ Or, *bear.*

Before CHRIST cir. 487.

them one nation in the land upon the mountains of Israel: and one king shall be king to them all: and they shall be no more two nations, neither shall they be divided into two kingdoms any more at all—I will cleanse them, and they shall be My people and I will be their God, and David My servant shall be king over them, and they all shall have one Shepherd. Such should be the unity of those who would be gathered under the One Shepherd. And so it was. [1] *The multitude of them that believed were of one heart and of one soul;* and long afterward it was a proverb among the Heathen [2], "See how these Christians love one another." Zechariah is here speaking of those who had rejected the Good Shepherd, the Israel and Judah after the flesh, who shut themselves out from the promises of God. This had its first fulfillment in the terrible dissolution of every band of *brotherhood* [3] and of our common nature, which made the siege of Jerusalem a proverb for horror, and precipitated its destruction. "[4] Having thus separated the believing from the unbelieving, He bared the rest of His care. And what we now see bears witness to the prophecy. For the Jews, being deprived of prophets and priests and kings and temple and ark and altar and mercy-seat and candlestick and table and the rest, through which the legal worship was performed, have come to be deprived also of the guardianship from above; and, scattered, exiled, removed, serve against their will those who preach Christ: denying Him as Lord, they yield service to His servants. The prophet having foretold these things of Christ, our God and Saviour, and reproved the obstinacy of the Jews, naturally turns his prophecy straight to the God-opposed christ whom they expect, as they say. So said the Lord in the holy Gospels to them, [5] *I am come in My Father's name, and ye receive Me not; another will come in his own name, and him ye will receive.* This the blessed Paul also prophesied of them, [6] *Because they received not the love of the truth, that they might be saved, God shall send them strong delusion that they should believe a lie, that all might be damned, who believe not the truth, but have pleasure in unrighteousness.* The like does the blessed Zechariah prophesy, having received the power of the Holy Spirit."

15. *Take to thee yet the instrument* [7] *of a foolish* [8] *shepherd.* "[9] *Yet.* He had enacted one tragedy, in which he clearly set forth the future guilt of Judas; now another is set forth, the accumulated scoffing through Anti-Christ. For as Paul said, because they receive not the Spirit of truth, the All-righteous Judge shall send them a spirit of *delusion, that they should believe a lie* [10]. He calls him a foolish shepherd, for since the extremest folly consists in the extremest wickedness, he will be the most foolish, who reached the highest impiety, and this he will do by arrogating to himself divinity and claiming divine honors [11].

This is the only action, which the prophet had to enact or to relate. If it was a visible act, the instrument might be a staff which should bruise, an instrument which should bear a semblance to that of the good shepherd, but which should be pernicious. "[12] Good shepherds, who understood their business, had slight staves, that, if there should be occasion to strike, the stricken sheep might not be bruised; but one who understandeth not, beats them with thicker clubs." Or it may mean also, whatever he would use for the hurtful treatment of the sheep, such as he proceeds to speak of. He is spoken of as, in fact, foolishly sinful [8]: for sin is the only real folly, and all real folly has sin mingled in it. The short-lived wisdom of the foolish shepherd for his own ends should also be his destruction.

16. *I will raise up.* God supplies the strength or wisdom which men abuse to sin. He, in His Providence, disposeth the circumstances, of which the ambitious avail them-

[1] Acts iv. 32.

[2] Tert. Apol. n. 39. p. 82. and notes, Oxf. Tr.

[3] אַחֲוָה The word occurs only here, but is in Arab. Syr. Ch. Zab.

[4] Theod.

[5] S. John v. 43.

[6] 2 Thess. ii. 10–12.

[7] Ezekiel has the idiom, "his instrument of destruction," כְּלִי מַשְׁחֵתוֹ ix. 1; "his instrument of slaughter," כ. מַפָּתוֹ Ib. 2; Isaiah, "for his work," כלי למעשהו liv. 16.

[8] אֱוִלִי ἅπ., אויל being often a subst., אויל is a sinful fool, Job. v. 2, 3, and throughout the Proverbs, though more marked in some places, Pr. vii. 22, xiv. 3, xv. 5, xx. 3, xxiv. 7, xxvii. 22; and in the plural, Ps. cvii. 17, Pr. i. 7. x. 21, xiv. 9.

[9] Osor. [10] 2 Thess. ii. 10, 11. [11] Ib. 4. [12] S. Cyr.

Before CHRIST cir. 487.

17 °Woe to the idol shepherd that leaveth the flock! the sword *shall be* upon his arm, and upon his right eye: his arm shall be clean dried up, and his right eye shall be utterly darkened.

° Jer. 23. 1. Ezek. 34. 2. John 10. 12, 13.

Before CHRIST cir. 487.

---

selves. Anti-Christ, whom the Jews look for, will be as much an instrument of God for the perfecting the elect, as the Chaldees [1] or the Assyrians [2] whom God raised up, for the chastisement of His former people, or the Medes against Babylon [3].

Which shall not visit them that be cut off. Zechariah uses the imagery, yet not the exact words of Jeremiah [4] and Ezekiel [5]. Neglect of every duty of a shepherd to his flock, to the sick, the broken, the sound; direct injury of them, preying upon them, make up the picture.

Which shall not visit, or tend, *that which is cut off:* fulfilling God's judgment [6], *that which is to be cut off, let it be cut off.*

Neither shall seek the young one, better, *the scattered* [7], *dispersed,* as the Good Shepherd [8] *came to seek and to save that which was lost. Nor heal that which is broken; bound not,* Ezekiel says [9]. "[10] The broken legs of sheep are healed no otherwise than those of men; rolled in wool impregnated with oil and wine, and then bound up with splinters placed round about it."

Nor feed that which standeth still, better, *the whole* [11], as the word always means, "in its good estate," like our prayer, "that Thou wouldest strengthen those who do stand."

17. *Wo to the idol shepherd,* (a *shepherd of nothingness,* one who hath no quality of a shepherd [12];) *who leaveth the flock.* The condemnation of the evil shepherd is complete in the abandonment of the sheep; as our Lord says, [13] *He that is an hireling and not the Shepherd, whose own the sheep are not, seeth the wolf coming and leaveth the sheep and fleeth: and the wolf catcheth them and scattereth the sheep. The hireling fleeth, because he is an hireling and careth not for the sheep.*

Or it may equally be, *Shepherd,* [14] *thou idol,* including the original meaning of nothingness, such as Anti-Christ will be, "[15] while he calleth himself God, and willeth to be worshiped." "[15] This shepherd shall therefore arise in Israel, because the true Shepherd had said, *I will not feed you.* He is prophesied of by another name in Daniel the Prophet [16], and in the Gospel [17], and in the Epistle of Paul to the Thessalonians [18], as *the abomination of desolation,* who shall sit in the temple of the Lord, and make himself as God. He cometh, not to heal but to destroy the flock of Israel. This shepherd the Jews shall receive, whom the *Lord Jesus shall slay with the breath of His mouth, and destroy with the brightness of His coming.*"

The sword shall be upon [*against*] *his arm and right eye.* His boast shall be of intelligence, and might. The punishment and destruction shall be directed against the instrument of each, the eye and the arm. "[15] The eye, whereby he shall boast to behold acutely the mysteries of God, and to see more than all prophets heretofore, so that he shall call himself son of God. But the word of the Lord shall be upon his arm and upon his right eye, so that his strength and all his boast of might shall be dried up, and the knowledge which he promised himself falsely, shall be obscured in everlasting darkness." "[19] Above and against the power of Anti-Christ, shall be the virtue and vengeance and sentence of Christ, Who shall *slay* him *with the breath of His mouth.*" The right arm, the symbol of might, and the right eye which was to direct its aim, should fail together, through the judgment of God against him. He, lately boastful and persecuting, shall become blind and powerless, bereft alike of wisdom and strength.

The "right" in Holy Scripture being so often a symbol of what is good, the left of what is evil, it may be also imagined, that "[20] the left eye, i. e. the acumen and cunning to devise deadly frauds, will remain uninjured: while the *right eye,* i. e. counsel to guard against evil, will be sunk in thick

---

1 הִנְנִי מֵקִים Hab. i. 6. 2 Am. vi. 14.

3 הִנְנִי מֵעִיר. Is. xiii. 17. 4 Jer. xxiii. 1, 2.

5 Ezek. xxxiv. 3, 4. 6 ab. v. 9.

7 *τὸ ἐσκορπισμένον, ὁ;* dispersum, S. Jer. "who have wandered or gone astray," Syr. "He who hireth a flock is forbidden לנערה. What is this! To lead it from place to place." Talm. Hieros. Tr. Sheviith c. 3, in Burt. Lex. p. 1363. Arab. מן אין נערת אלינא "Whence camest thou to us?" c. פי, "traversed country" (Kam.). נער is not used of young of animals.

8 S. Luke xix. 10, S. Matt. xviii. 11.

9 Ezek. xxxiv. 4. 10 Colum. de re rust. viii. 5.

11 "Which was set firm, or set himself firm." Nif. as in Ps. xxxix. 6, "Every man in his firm estate (נִצָּב) is all vanity." *τὸ ὁλόκληρον, ὁ.* "id quod stat," S. Jer. So Syr. The Arab. "נַצַּב was weary" (quoted C. B. Mich. Ges.) has only this force as intrans.; נַצַּב c. acc. r., and אנתצב agree with Heb. Yet Jon. renders as Eng.

12 רֹעִי האליל, as רֹפְאֵי אֱלִל, "physicians of no value," Job xiii. 4. 13 S. John x. 12, 13.

14 רֹעִי, as a form for רֹעֶה, occurs in Is. xxxviii. 12. אֹהֶל רֹעִי.

15 S. Jer. 16 Dan. ix. 17 S. Mark xiii.

18 2 Thess. ii. 19 Dion. 20 Osor.

Before CHRIST cir. 487.

CHAPTER XII.

1 *Jerusalem a cup of trembling to herself,* 3 *and a burdensome stone to her adversaries.* 6 *The victorious restoring of Judah.* 9 *The repentance of Jerusalem.*

THE burden of the word of the LORD for Israel, saith the LORD, [a] which stretcheth forth the heavens, and layeth the foundation of the earth, and

Before CHRIST cir. 487.

[a] Isai. 42. 5. & 44. 24. & 45. 12, 18. & 48. 13.

darkness. And so, the more he employs his ability to evil, the more frantically will he bring to bear destruction upon himself."

XII. "[1] From 'I will make Jerusalem' to 'Awake, O sword,' there is a threefold exposition. For some of the Jews say that these things have already been fulfilled in part from Zorobabel to Cn. Pompey who, first of the Romans, took Judæa and the temple, as Josephus relates. Others think that it is to be fulfilled at the end of the world, when Jerusalem shall be restored, which the miserable Jewish race promiseth itself with its anointed, of whom we read above as the foolish shepherd. But others, i. e. we who are called by the name of Christ, say that these things are daily fulfilled, and will be fulfilled in the Church to the end of the world."

1. *The burden of the word of the Lord for,* rather, *upon*[2] *Israel.* If this prophecy is a continuation of the last, notwithstanding its fresh title, then *Israel* must be the Christian Church, formed of the true Israel which believed, and the Gentiles who were grafted into them. So S. Cyril; "Having spoken sufficiently of the Good Shepherd Christ, and of the foolish, most cruel shepherd who butchered the sheep, i. e. Anti-Christ, he seasonably makes mention of the persecutions which would from time to time arise against Israel; not the Israel according to the flesh, but the spiritual, that Jerusalem which is indeed holy, [3] *the Church of the Living God.* For as we say, that *he* is spiritually a Jew, who hath the [4] *circumcision in the heart,* that through the Spirit, *and not* in the flesh *through the letter;* so also may *Israel* be conceived, not that of the blood of Israel, but rather that, which has a mind beholding God. But such are all who are called to sanctification through the faith in Christ, and who, in Him and by Him, know of God the Father. For this is the one true elected way of beholding God."

Since the Good Shepherd was rejected by all, except the *poor of the flock,* the *little flock* which believed in Him, and thereupon the *band* of *brotherhood* was dissolved between Israel and Judah, *Israel* in those times could not be Israel after the flesh, which then too was the deadly antagonist of the true Israel, and thus early also chose Anti-Christ, such as was Bar-Cochba, with whom so many hundreds of thousands perished. There was no war then against Jerusalem, since it had ceased to be [5].

But Zechariah does not say that this prophecy, to which he has annexed a separate title, follows, in time, upon the last; rather, since he has so separated it by its title, he has marked it as a distinct prophecy from the preceding. It may be, that he began again from the time of the Maccabees and took God's deliverances of the people Israel then, as the foreground of the deliverances to the end [6]. Yet in the times of Antiochus, it was one people only which was against the Jews, and Zechariah himself speaks only of the Greeks [7]; here he repeatedly emphasizes that they were *all nations* [8]. It may then rather be, that the future, the successive efforts of the world to crush the people of God, and its victory amid suffering, and its conversions of the world through the penitent looking to Jesus, are exhibited in one great perspective, according to the manner of prophecy, which mostly exhibits the prominent events, not their order or sequence. "[9] The penitential act of contrite sinners, especially of Jews, looking at Him *Whom they pierced,* dates from the Day of Pentecost, and continues to the latter days, when it will be greatly intensified and will produce blessed results, and is here concentrated into one focus. The rising up of God's enemies against Christ's Church, which commenced at the same time, and has been continued in successive persecutions from Jews, Gentiles, and other unbelievers

[1] S. Jer.
[2] See on Nah. i. 1, p. 129. The עַל of the title is repeated in the עַל־יְהוּדָה עַל־יְרוּשָׁלַם ver. 2.
[3] 1 Tim. iii. 15. [4] Rom. ii. 29.
[5] See at length, ab. on Mic. iii. 12, pp. 46–50.
[6] So Lap. "That Zechariah speaks literally of the times of the Maccabees which were shortly to follow, appears both from the sequence of the times, and the connection and congruency of these oracles with the deeds of the Maccabees, as also because v. 10. ends in the Passion of Christ. For this followed the times of the Maccabees. As then Isaiah, Jeremiah, Hosea, Daniel, Ezekiel &c. foretold what was shortly to befall the Jews from Salmanassar, Nebuchadnezzar, Cyrus, Darius, so Zechariah foretells what should presently befall them from Antiochus under the Maccabees." Synops. c. xii. [7] Zech. ix. 13. [8] כָּל הָעַמִּים xii. 2, 3, 6, 9.
[9] Bp. C. Wordsworth here, and the like in Keil on xiv. 20. p. 661.

Before CHRIST cir. 487.

[b] formeth the spirit of man within him.

2 Behold, I will make
Jerusalem [c] a cup of || trembling unto all the people round about, || when

[b] Num. 16. 22. Eccles. 12. 7. Isai. 57. 16. Heb. 12. 9.

[c] Isai. 51. 17, 22, 23.

|| Or, *slumber*, or, *poison*. || Or, *and also against Judah* shall he be *which shall be in siege against Jerusalem.*

in every age, and which will reach its climax in the great Anti-Christian outbreak of the last times, and be confounded by the Coming of Christ to judgment, is here summed up in one panoramic picture, exhibited at once to the eye."

Which stretcheth forth the heavens. God's creative power is an ever-present working, as our Lord says, [1] *My Father worketh hitherto and I work.* His preservation of the things which He has created is a continual re-creation. All "forces" are supported by Him, Who Alone hath life in Himself. He doth not the less *uphold all things by the word of His power*, because, until the successive generations, with or without their will, with or against His Will for them, shall have completed His Sovereign Will, He upholds them uniformly in being by His Unchanging Will. Man is ever forgetting this, and because, [2] *since the fathers fell asleep, all things continue as from the beginning of the creation*, they relegate the Creator and His creating as far as they can to some time, as far back as they can imagine, enough to fill their imaginations, and forget Him Who made them, in Whose hands is their eternity, Who will be their Judge. So the prophets remind them and us of His continual working, which men forget in the sight of His works; [3] *Thus saith the Lord; He that createth the heavens, and stretcheth them out; He that spreadeth forth the earth and its produce, Who giveth breath to the people upon it, and spirit to them that walk therein*; and, [4] *I am the Lord Who maketh all things, Who stretcheth out the heavens alone, Who spreadeth abroad the earth by Myself*; speaking at once of that, past in its beginning yet present to us in its continuance, but to Him ever-present present; and of things actually present to us, [5] *that frustrateth the tokens of the liars*; and of things to those of that day still future, [6] *that confirmeth the word of His servant, and performeth the counsel of His messengers*: the beginning of which was not to be till the taking of Babylon. And the Psalmist unites past and present in one, [7] *Donning light as a garment, stretching out the heavens as a curtain; Who layeth the beams of His chambers on the waters, Who maketh the clouds His chariot; Who walketh on the wings of the wind; Who maketh His angels spirits, His ministers a flame of fire; He founded the earth upon its base.* And Amos, [8] *He that formeth the mountains and createth the winds, and declareth unto man his thoughts*;—adding whatever lieth nearest to each of us.

And formeth the spirit of man within him, both by the unceasing creation of souls, at every moment in some spot in our globe, or by the re-creation, for which David prays, [9] *Create in me a clean heart, O God, and renew a right spirit within me.* He Who formed the hearts of men can overrule them as He wills. "[10] But the spirit of man is formed by God in him, not by being called to the beginnings of being, although it was made by Him, but, as it were, transformed from weakness to strength, from unmanliness to endurance, altogether being transelemented from things shameful to better things."

"[10] It is the wont of the holy Prophets, when about to declare beforehand things of no slight moment, to endeavor to shew beforehand the Almightiness of God, that their word may obtain credence, though they should declare what was beyond all hope, and (to speak of our conceptions) above all reason and credibility."

2. *I will make Jerusalem a cup of trembling* [11]. For encouragement, He promises the victory, and at first mentions the attack incidentally. Jerusalem is as a cup or basin, which its enemies take into their hands; a stone, which they put forth their strength to lift; but they themselves reel with the draught of God's judgments which they would give to others, they are torn by the stone which they would lift to fling. The image of the *cup* is mostly of God's displeasure, which is given to His own people, and then, His judgment of chastisement being exceeded, given in turn to those who had been the instruments of giving it [12]. Thus Isaiah speaks of *the cup of trembling.* [13] Thou, *Jerusalem, hast drunk the dregs of the cup of trembling, hast wrung them out. Therefore hear thou this, thou afflicted and drunken but not with wine. Thus saith thy Lord, the Lord, and thy God that pleadeth the cause of His people, Behold, I have taken out of thine hand the cup of trembling, the dregs of the cup of My fury; thou shalt no more drink it again: but I will put it into the hand of them that afflict thee.* Jere-

[1] S. John v. 17. [2] 2 S. Pet. iii. 4. [3] Is. xlii. 5.
[4] Ib. xliv. 24. [5] Ib. 25. [6] Ib. 26.
[7] Ps. civ. 2–5. [8] Am. iv. 13. add v. 8.
[9] Ps. li. 10. [10] S. Cyr.
[11] רעל ἅπ. in the sense. The form תרעלה occurs in the like idioms, כוס תרעלה, Is. li. 17, 22; יין תרעלה Ps. lx. 5.
[12] See on Obad. 16, vol. i. pp. 362–365.
[13] Is. li. 17, 21–23.

Before CHRIST cir. 487.

d ver. 4, 6, 8, 9. 11. & ch. 13. 1. & 14. 4, 6, 8, 9. 13.

they shall be in the siege
both against Judah *and*
against Jerusalem.
3 ¶ [d] And in that day will
I make Jerusalem [e] a burdensome stone for all people; all that burden themselves with it shall be cut in

Before CHRIST cir. 487.

e Matt. 21. 44.

miah speaks of *the cup of God's anger*, as given by God first to Jerusalem, then to all whom Nebuchadnezzar should subdue, then to Babylon itself [1]; and as *passing through* to Edom also [2]; Ezekiel, of *Aholibah* [3] (Jerusalem) *drinking the cup of Samaria*. In Jeremiah alone, Babylon is herself the cup. [4] *Babylon is a golden cup in the Lord's hand, that made all the nations drunken; the nations have drunken of the wine; therefore the nations are mad.* Now Jerusalem is to be, not an ordinary cup, but a large *basin* [5] or vessel, from which all nations may drink what will make them reel.

And also upon Judah will it be in the siege against Jerusalem, i. e. *the burden of the word* [6] *of the Lord which was on Israel* should be *upon Judah*, i. e. upon all, great and small.

3. *I will make Jerusalem a burdensome stone to all nations.* What is *a stone to all nations?* It is not a rock or anything in its own nature immovable, but *a stone*, a thing rolled up and down, moved, lifted, displaced, piled on others, in every way at the service and command of men, to do with it what they willed. So they thought of that [7] *stone cut out without hands;* that [8] *tried stone and sure foundation, laid in Zion;* that *stone* which, God said in Zechariah [9], *I have laid;* of which our Lord says, [10] *the stone, which the builders rejected, is become the head of the corner;* [11] *whosoever shall fall on this stone shall be broken, but on whomsoever it shall fall, it will grind him to powder.* The Church, built on the stone, seems a thing easily annihilated; ten persecutions in succession strove to efface it; Diocletian erected a monument, commemorating that the Christian name was blotted out [12]. It survived; he perished. The image may have been suggested by the custom, so widely prevailing in Judæa, of trying the relative strength of young men, by lifting round stones selected for that end [13]. "[14] The meaning then is, I will place Jerusalem to all nations like a very heavy stone [15] to be lifted up. They will lift it up, and according to their varied strength, will waste it; but it must needs be, that, while it is lifted, in the very strain of lifting the weight, that most heavy stone should leave some scission or rasure on the bodies of those who lift it. Of the Church it may be interpreted thus; that all persecutors, who fought against the house of the Lord, are inebriated with that cup, which Jeremiah gives to all nations, to drink and be inebriated and fall and vomit and be mad. Whosoever would uplift the stone shall lift it, and in the anger of the Lord, whereby He chastens sinners, will hold it in his hands; but he himself will not go unpunished, the sword of the Lord fighting against him."

All that burden themselves with it will be cut to pieces [16], more exactly, *scarified, lacerated;* shall bear the scars. *Though* (rather, *and*) *all the people* [*peoples, nations*] *of the earth shall be gathered together against it.* The prophet marshals them all against Jerusalem, only to

[1] Jer. xxv. 15–26. [2] Lam. iv. 21. Jer. xlix. 12.
[3] Ezek. xxiii. 31–33. [4] Jer. li. 7.
[5] סף is the basin, which received the blood of the Paschal lamb, Ex. xii 22; סִפִּים, with beds and earthen vessels, were brought to David by Barzillai and the others, 2 Sam. xvii. 28. Else they are only mentioned as instruments of the temple-services. 1 Kgs vii. 50, 2 Kgs xii. 14, Jer. lii. 19.
[6] מַשָּׂא is the only natural subject, as in ix. 1, *the burden of the Lord is on the land of Hadrach*, but it is subjoined, *Damascus is the resting place thereof, &c.* The E. V. does not seem grammatical. The E. M. is too elliptical, as also that other, "it will be laid upon Jerusalem *to be* in the siege against Jerusalem." Had "the cup of trembling" been the subject, it had probably been ליהודה, as לכל העמים. Nor can מצור be the subject; for countries, as Judah, are not the objects of siege.
[7] Dan. ii. 45. [8] Is. xxviii. 16. [9] Zech. iii. 9.
[10] S. Luke xx. 17.
[11] S. Matt. xxi. 44. S. Luke xx. 18.
[12] Baronius speaks of two inscriptions as still existing at Clunia (Corunna dal Conde) in Spain. The one has, "amplificato per Orientem et Occid. Impe. Rom. et nomine Christianor. deleto qui remp. evertebant;" the other, "superstitione Christi ubiq. deleta. Cultu Deorum propagato." A. 304. n. I.
[13] "It is the custom in the cities of Palestine, and that old usage is kept up to this day throughout Judæa, that in villages towns and forts, round stones are placed, of very great weight, on which young men are wont to practise themselves, and according to their varying strength, lift them, some to the knees, others to the navel, others to the shoulders and head; others lift the weight above the head, with their two hands raised straight up, shewing the greatness of their strength. In the Acropolis at Athens, I saw a brass globe, of very great weight, which I, with my little weak body, could scarcely move. When I asked its object, I was told by the inhabitants, that the strength of wrestlers was proved by that mass, and that no one went to a match, until it was ascertained by the lifting of that weight, who ought to be set against whom." S. Jer.
[14] S. Jer.
[15] lit. "a stone of lading," which whoso lifteth would be laden or burthened. It is the only noun formed from עמס; and the root itself existed only in Hebrew.
[16] שׂרט is a root, revived by Zechariah from the Pentateuch. It occurs only Lev. xix. 28, xxi. 5, of the forbidden incisions for the dead. Arab. שַׁרַט and Syr. סְרַט, "scarified" Syr. אתסְרט "was branded."

Before CHRIST cir. 487.

pieces, though all the people of the earth be gathered together against it.

4 In that day, saith the
LORD, [f] I will smite every
horse with astonishment,
and his rider with madness: and I will open mine eyes upon the house of Judah, and will smite every horse of the people with blindness.

f Ps. 76. 6. Ezek. 38. 4.

5 And the governors of Judah shall say in their
heart, || The inhabitants of
Jerusalem *shall be* my strength in the LORD of hosts their God.

|| Or, *There is strength to me and to the inhabitants, &c.* Joel 3. 16.

6 ¶ In that day will I make the governors of Ju-

say how they should perish before it. So in Joel God says, [1] *I will also gather all nations, and will bring them down to the valley of Jehoshaphat*, speaking of that last closing strife of Anti-Christ against God. Wars against Israel had either been petty, though Antitheistic, wars of neighboring petty nations, pitting their false gods against the True, or one, though world-empire wielded by a single will. The more God made Himself known, the fiercer the opposition. The Gospel claiming [2] *obedience to the faith among all nations*, provoked universal rebellion. Herod and Pontius Pilate became friends through rejection of Christ; the Roman Cæsar and the Persian Sapor, Goths and Vandals, at war with one another, were one in persecuting Christ and the Church. Yet in vain;

4. *In that day, saith the Lord, I will smite every horse with astonishment, stupefying.* Zechariah revives the words concentrated by Moses, to express the stupefaction at their ills, which God would accumulate upon His people, if they perseveringly rebelled against Him. Each expresses the intensity of the visitation [3]. *The horse and his rider* had, through Moses' song at the Red Sea, become the emblem of worldly power, overthrown. That song opens; [4] *I will sing unto the Lord; for He hath triumphed gloriously: the horse and his rider hath He cast into the sea.* The scared cavalry throws into confusion the ranks, of which it was the boast and strength.

And on the house of Judah I will open My eyes, in pity and love and guidance, as the Psalmist says, [5] *I will counsel, with Mine eye upon thee*, in contrast with *the blindness* with which God would smite the powers arrayed against them.

5. *And the princes of Judah.* He pictures the onemindedness of the Church. No one shall assume anything to himself; each shall exalt the strength which the other was to him; but all, *in the Lord. The princes of Judah* shall say *in their heart*, not outwardly or politically, but in inward conviction, *strength to me* [6] (all speak as one) *are the inhabitants of Jerusalem in the Lord of hosts their God.* The highest in human estimation acknowledge that their strength is in those who are of no account in this world; as, in fact, the hearts of the poor are evermore the strength of the Church; but that, *in the Lord of hosts;* in Him, in Whose hands are the powers of heaven and earth, over against the petty turmoil on earth. God had chosen Jerusalem [7]; therefore she was invincible. "That most glorious prince of Judah, Paul, said, '*I can do all things in Christ Who instrengtheneth me.*'"

6. *I will make the governors of Judah like a hearth* or *cauldron* [8] of fire, large, broad, deep, and full of fire, *among the wood* which is prepared for burning [9], *and like a torch of fire in a sheaf.* The fire could not kindle the wood or the sheaf, of itself, unless applied to it. All is of the agency of God: *I will make.*

"[10] He foretells the increase of the Church, which by such persecutions shall not be diminished, but shall be marvelously increased. The preachers of the Church shall raise up all the peoples round about, shall destroy all unbelief, and shall kindle the

[1] Jo. iii. 2. See vol. i. pp. 200, 201, and p. 207 on Jo. iii. 9. [2] Rom. i. 5.

[3] Deut. xxvii. 28, תִּמְּהוֹן (the only noun derived from תָּמַהּ) (and with the same word, יַכֶּה) עִוָּרוֹן occurs only there beside; שִׁגָּעוֹן, beside, only in 2 Kgs ix. 20. Only לֵבָב is omitted after תמהון since it stands in connection with the horse in the parallelism. [4] Ex. xv. 1. [5] Ps. xxxii. 8.

[6] אַמְּצָה ἅπ.; as is the form אֹמֶץ, Job xvii. 19, כַּאֹמֶץ Ib. xxxvi. 19. [7] Zech. i. 17, ii. 12. iii. 2.

[8] כִּיּוֹר, in 1 Sam. ii. 14, is 'a vessel, in which the food is cooked;' in 2 Chr. vi. 13 'a pulpit;' so that the vessel, to which it is likened, must have been large; as must have been the brazen laver of the tabernacle (Ex. Lev.) or temple (2 Kgs), of which the word is elsewhere used. Each laver of Solomon's temple *contained forty baths*, or about 300 gallons, and was four cubits (1 Kgs vii. 38) square apparently (coll. 27.).

[9] עֵצִים (pl.) is used of wood cut up, 1) for burning, especially on an altar, or 2) for building, unless it is plain from the context, that they are living trees, as in Jos. x. 26, Jud. ix. 48, in Jotham's fable Ib. 9–15, or Ps. xcvi. 12, civ. 16, Cant. iv. 14, Is. vii. 2. &c. [10] Rib.

Before CHRIST cir. 487.

g Obad. 18.

dah [g] like an hearth of fire among the wood, and like a torch of fire in a sheaf; and they shall devour all the people round about, on the right hand and on the left: and Jerusalem shall be inhabited again in her own place, *even* in Jerusalem.

7 The LORD also shall save the tents of Judah first, that the glory of the house of David and the glory of the inhabitants of Jerusalem do not magnify *themselves* against Judah.

8 In that day shall the LORD defend the inhabitants of Jerusalem; and [h] he that is || † feeble among them at that day shall be

Before CHRIST cir. 487.

h Joel 3. 10.
|| Or, *abject.*
† Heb. *fallen.*

hearts of hearers with the fire of the Divine word." *On the right hand and on the left.* "[1] He indicates the strength and success of the preachers, whom no one can resist nor hinder," as our Lord says, [2] *I will give you a mouth and wisdom, which all your adversaries shall not be able to gainsay nor resist.*

And Jerusalem shall again, rather, *yet, be inhabited.* "Yet" is a sort of burden in Zechariah's prophecies[3]. "[4] They at once burned up by the flame all the defilement of vices, and kindled the minds of men with the torch of Divine love; at once consumed the enemy and cast a heavenly fire into the human heart: *yet;* in despite of all appearances, of all which is against her. *She shall yet dwell in her own place in Jerusalem;* for, however the waves of this world chafe and lash themselves into foam against her, they break themselves, not her; as soon as they have reached their utmost height, they fall back; if they toss themselves, and, for a moment, hide her light, they fall down at all sides, and the ray shines out, steady as before; for she is *founded on a rock*, against which [5] *the gates of hell* should not *prevail.*

7. *The Lord also shall save the tents of Judah first.* Still it is, *the Lord shall save.* We have, on the one side, *the siege*, the gathering of all the peoples of the earth *against Jerusalem, the horse and his rider.* On the other, no human strength; not, as before, in the prophecy of the Maccabees, the bow, the arrow, and the sword, though in the hand of God[6]. It is thrice, *I will make*[7]; *I will smite*[8]; and now, *The Lord shall save.* By *the tents*, he probably indicates their defencelessness. God would *save* them first; that *the glory*[9] *of the house* of David—*be not great against* or *over Judah*, may not overshadow it; but all may be as one; for all is the free gift of God, the mere grace of God, that [10] *he that glorieth may glory in the Lord*, and both "[11] may own that, in both, the victory is the Lord's."

"[12] *In Christ Jesus is neither Jew nor Greek; neither bond nor free*[13], neither rich nor poor; *but all are one*, viz. a new creation; yea in Christendom the poor are the highest, both because Christ [14] *preached to the poor*, and pronounced the [15] *poor blessed*, and He made the Apostles, being poor, nobles in His kingdom, through whom He converted kings and princes, as is written, [16] *ye see your calling, brethren, that not many wise men after the flesh, not many mighty, not many noble* are called, *but God hath chosen the foolish things of the world to confound the wise, and the weak things of the world to confound the things which are mighty &c.;* and, [17] *Hath not God called the poor in this world, rich in faith, and heirs of the kingdom, which God has promised to them that love Him?* The rich and noble have greater hindrances to humility and Christian virtues, than the poor. For honors puff up, wealth and delights weaken the mind; wherefore they need greater grace of Christ to burst their bonds than the poor. Wherefore, for the greater grace shewn them, they are bound to give greater thanks unto Christ."

8. *In that day the Lord shall defend the inhabitants of Jerusalem; and he that is feeble*, rather, *he that stumbleth among them, shall be as David.* The result of the care and the defence of God is here wholly spiritual, "the strengthening of such as do stand, and the raising up of such as fall." It is not simply one feeble, but one *stumbling*[18] and ready to

[1] Rib.
[2] S. Luke xxi. 15.
[3] See reff. note 2.
[4] Osor.
[5] S. Matt. xvi. 18.
[6] Zech. ix. 13.
[7] ver. 2, 3, 6.
[8] ver. 4 bis.
[9] תפארת is nowhere "gloriatio," as Ges., but simply "glory," "beauty," though, rarely, it is implied in the context, that he who has it, is proud of it, as Is. iii. 18. x. 12, xiii. 9.
[10] Jer. ix. 24, 1 Cor. i. 31, 2 Cor. x 17.
[11] S. Jer.
[12] Lap.
[13] Gal. iii. 28.
[14] S. Luke iv. 18.
[15] Ib. vi. 20.
[16] 1 Cor. i. 26.
[17] S. James ii. 5.
[18] 1 Sam. ii. 4, is the only case alleged by Ges., in which נִכְשָׁל is to signify "weak." Yet here too "stumble," as in the E. V., is the natural rendering. In the other 19 cases it is confessedly stumbling, though in some it is stumbling, so as to fall.

Before CHRIST cir. 487.

as David; and the house
of David *shall be* as God,
as the angel of the LORD
before them.
9 ¶ And it shall come
to pass in that day, *that* I
will seek to [l] destroy all the
nations that come against
Jerusalem.
10 [k] And I will pour
upon the house of David,
and upon the inhabitants

Before CHRIST cir. 487.

l Hag. 2. 22. ver. 3.
k Jer. 31. 9. & 50. 4. Ezek. 39. 29. Joel 2. 28.

fall, who becomes as David, the great instance of one who fell, yet was raised. Daniel says of a like trial-time, [1] *And some of those of understanding shall stumble, to try them and to purge and to make them white, to the time of the end.* "[2] Such care will God have of protecting the sons of the Church, when it shall be infested with persecutions, that he who shall have fallen through human infirmity, either deceived by heretics or overcome by fear of tortures, shall arise the more fervent and cautious, and with many tears shall make amends for his sins to God, as did David. *He who stumbled shall be as David,* because the sinner returneth to repentance. This is not said of all times, nor of all (for many have stumbled, who never rose) but chiefly of the first times of the Church and of men of great sanctity, such as were many then."

And the house of David shall be as God. They who stumbled became really like David; but he, though mighty and a great saint of God, though he once fell, was man. How then could the house of David be really like God? Only fully in Him, Who, [3] *being in the form of God, thought it not robbery to be equal with God;* Who said, [4] *He who hath seen Me, hath seen My Father also;* [5] *I and the Father are one.* And this the prophet brings out by adding, *as the Angel of the Lord before them,* i.e. that one Angel of the Lord, in whom His very Presence and His Name was; Who went before them, to guide them[6]. Else, having said, *like God,* it had been to lessen what he had just said, to add, *like the Angel of the Lord.* Our Lord prayed for those who are truly His, [7] *As Thou, Father, art in Me and I in Thee, that they may be one in Us; that they may be one as We are one, I in them, and Thou in Me, that they may be perfect in one;* and S. Paul saith, [8] *Christ is formed in us;* [9] *Christ dwelleth in our hearts by faith;* [10] *Christ liveth in me;* [11] *Christ is in you;* [12] *Christ is our life;* [13] *Christ is all and in all;* [14] *we grow into Him which is the Head, even Christ;* [15] *we are in Christ;* and S. Peter, we are [16] *partakers of the Divine nature;* and S. John, [17] *As He is, so are we in this world.* Then in a degree the glory of Christ passeth over to those who dwell in Him, and in whom He dwells by the Spirit, as S. Paul says; [18] *Ye received me, as an angel of God, as Christ Jesus.*

9. *In that day, I will seek to destroy.* Woe indeed to those, whom Almighty God shall "*seek* to destroy!" Man may seek earnestly to do, what at last he cannot do. Still it is an earnest seeking. And whether it is used of human seeking which fails[19], or which succeeds[20], inchoate[21] or permitted[22], it is always used of seeking to do, what it is a person's set purpose to do if he can[19]. Here it is spoken of Almighty God[23]. "[2] He saith not, 'I will destroy' but *I will seek to destroy,* i.e. it shall ever be My care to destroy all the enemies of the Church, that they may in no way prevail against it: this I will do alway to the end of the world."

10. *And I will pour,* as He promised by Joel[24], *I will pour out My Spirit upon all flesh,* largely, abundantly, *upon the house of David and the inhabitants of Jerusalem,* all, highest and lowest, from first to last, the *Spirit of grace and supplication,* i.e. the *Holy Spirit* which conveyeth *grace,* as [25] *the Spirit of wisdom and understanding* is *the Spirit* infusing *wisdom and understanding,* and *the Spirit of counsel and might* is that same Spirit, imparting the gift *of counsel* to see what is to be done and *of might* to do it, and the Spirit *of the knowledge and of the fear of the Lord* is that same *Spirit,* infusing loving acquaintance with God, with awe at His infinite Majesty. So *the Spirit of grace and supplication,* is that same Spirit,

[1] Dan. xi. 35. [2] Rib. [3] Phil. ii. 6.
[4] S. John xiv. 9. [5] Ib. x. 30.
[6] See "Daniel the prophet" pp. 519–523.
[7] S. John xvii. 21, 22, 23. [8] Gal. iv. 19.
[9] Eph. iii. 17. [10] Gal. ii. 20.
[11] Rom. viii. 10.
[12] Col. iii. 4. [13] Ib. 11. [14] Eph. iv. 15.
[15] Rom. xvi. 7, 2 Cor. v. 17, Gal. i. 22.
[16] 2 Pet. i. 4. [17] 1 S. John iv. 17. [18] Gal. iv. 14.

[19] בִּקֵּשׁ with ל and inf. "Pharaoh sought to slay Moses," Ex. ii. 15; "Saul, my father, seeketh to slay thee," 1 Sam. xi. 2; "Saul sought to smite David," Ib. 20; Solomon, to kill Jeroboam, 1 Kgs xi. 40; "Sought to lay hand on the king," Esth. vi. 2; Haman sought to destroy the Jews. Ib. iii. 6. The inf. without ל, occurs Jer. xxvi. 21.

[20] 1 Sam. xiv. 4, xxiii. 10, Eccl. xii. 10.

[21] "sought to turn away," De. xiii. 11. "seekest to destroy a city," 2 Sam. xx. 19.

[22] 1 Kgs xi. 22, Zech. vi. 7.

[23] In Ex. iv. 24 only, it is said, "God sought to slay Moses," i.e. shewed that He would, unless his son had been circumcised.

[24] Jo. ii. 28. See vol. i. pp. 193, 194. [25] Is. xi. 2.

Before CHRIST cir. 487.

[l]John 19. 34, 37. Rev. 1. 7.

of Jerusalem, the spirit of grace and of supplications: and they shall [l]look upon me whom they have pierced, and they shall mourn for him, [m]as one

[m]Jer. 6. 26. Amos 8. 10.

infusing grace and bringing into a state of favor with God, and a *Spirit of supplication*[1] is that Spirit, calling out of the inmost soul the cry for a yet larger measure of the grace already given. S. Paul speaks of [2]*the love of God poured out in our hearts by the Holy Spirit which is given unto us*; and of [3]*insulting the Spirit of grace*, rudely repulsing the Spirit, Who giveth grace. "[4]When God Himself says, '*I* will pour out,' He sets forth the greatness of His bountifulness whereby He bestoweth all things."

And they shall look, with trustful hope and longing, *on Me*[5], Almighty God, *Whom they*

[1] תחנונים is chosen in allusion to חן "grace." תחנונים is, almost everywhere, the cry to God for His grace and favor. It occurs mostly in the Psalms united with קול. "the voice of my supplications," Ps. xxviii. 2, 6, xxxi. 23, xxxvi. 6, cxvi. 1, cxxx. 2, cxi. 7; also of the cry to God, without קול, Ps. cxliii. 1, Dan. ix. 3, 17, 18, 33, Jer. iii. 21. xxxi. 9. It is used of man to man, only Prov. xviii. 23, and else, in irony, of what leviathan would not do to man, Job xl. 27, 6. [xli. 3. Eng.]

[2] Rom. v. 5.

[3] Heb. x. 29, τὸ πνεῦμα τῆς χάριτος ἐνυβρίσας.

[4] Osor.

[5] There is no critical doubt about the reading, אלי, *to Me*. It is the reading of all the old Verss., Jewish or Christian; LXX. Aq. Sym. Theod. Chald. Syr. Vulg. In the ixth cent., the Jews had begun to make a marginal correction into אליו, but did not venture to change the text. "Where we, according to the faith of Holy Scripture, read, in the Person of God, 'and they shall look to Me Whom they pierced,' though, in the text itself of the book, they were deterred by God's Providence from making a change, yet without, in the margin, they have it noted, 'they shall look to *him* whom they pierced.' And so they hand down to their disciples, that they should transcribe, as it is contained in the text, and read, as they have noted, outside; so that they may hold, according to their phrensy, that the Jews look to him, whom Gog and Magog pierced." Rabanus Maurus c. Jud. n. 12. In the 13th. cent. Martini says, that "*all* the old MSS. of the Jews have אלי;" and that the "perfidy of *some modern* Jews, unable to deprave so evident a testimony to the divinity of the Messiah, say, that it is not אלי but אליו." f. 666. In f. 328, he again says, "*some* Jews falsify the text;" and (f. 329) that "*now* (jam) in many MSS. they have corrupted their text, but that they are refuted by the Targum, the Talmud, *and by many ancient* MSS., in which this text is *not yet* corrupted, and by the exposition of Rashi." R. Isaac, at the end of the 16th. cent. A. D. 1593, quoted the reading אלי without doubt, though he was expressly controverting the Christian argument. "They say, that hereafter the sons of Israel shall mourn, because they pierced and slew the Messiah sent to them, Jesus who is compounded of Godhead and Manhood, and they say, that this is (the meaning of) 'they shall look *to me* whom they pierced.'" (Chizzuk Emunah in Wagenseil Tela ign. Sat. pp. 303, 304.) He explains it of the wars of Gog and Magog. 'If they shall see that they [their enemies] shall pierce through even one of them, they shall be amazed and shall look *to me*, *eth asher dakaroo*, i. e. on account of him, whom they pierced—So that the Nazarenes have no help from the words והביטו אלי את אשר דקרו;' (Ib. pp. 307, 308;) and he subjoins, that if he who was wounded had been the same as he to whom they should look, it ought to have gone on in the first person, ספדו עלי, and והמר עלי, like והביטו אלי. Ib. 309. R. Lipmann (A. D. 1399) uses the same argument, "He should have said, *and they shall mourn for me*, as he began, *they shall look to me*." p. 144 ed. Hacksp. *Ibn Ezra* agrees with this, for he explains it in the first person, "Then shall all nations look to me (אלי) to see what I shall do to those who have slain Messiah b. Joseph." *Alsheikh's* commentary requires the same, "And I will yet do a third thing. And this that they shall look אלי, is that they shall hang their eyes on Me in perfect repentance when they see &c." and *R. Obadiah Siporno*, (Bibl. Rabb.) "and they shall look to Me in their prayer." Rashi also gives the Targ. "and they shall seek *of Me*" מן קדמי as the interpretation of והביטו אלי "they shall look to me." *R. Tanchum* of Jerusalem, "a learned son of a learned father," in the latter part of the 13th cent. (Grätz vii. 144, 145) knew in the East of no other reading. He explains it; "They shall flee to Me, when they see the slaying of those whom the enemy had slain of them" (Poc. 344). His contemporary, *Parchon*, in his lexicon *Mechabberoth*, cites the passage with אלי, and explains the word "piercing of a sword in the body," v. דקר. The Heb. Arab. version, so often quoted by Pococke (Hunt. 206) renders, "And they turned to me, whom they rent (בענו the word, used by Abulwalid, only Abulwalid further explains this by שק.) Abulwalid does not notice the *reading* in either of his lexica, nor Menahem b. Sarug, nor David b. Abraham.

With regard to MSS., even in later times Peter Niger [Schwarz] (a learned Benedictine of the 17th cent.) wrote, "some false and lying Jews say that it is not written, 'And they shall look on me whom they have pierced,' but 'they shall seek to him whom they have pierced'—I answer, that on my conscience and on the Christian truth I say, I have seen many Jewish Bibles [Spanish, doubtless, since he studied Hebrew in Spain] and I never, in any Bible, found it written other than *vehibbitu elai* 'and they shall look to me,' and not *vehibbitu elav*, 'and they shall look to him,' as I will shew any one who desires to see." Stella Messiæ Tract. ii. c. 2. A. D. 1477 in Wolf Bibl. Hebr. iv. p. 543. Norzi, a Jewish critic, says that אליו is not found in the Scriptures, only in *Rashi and the Gemara*. The codex Babyl. Petropol. (I am told, of the ixth cent.) has אלי. In the collated MSS. there is the variation, common where there is a real or virtual kri, 33 Kenn. MSS. and 6 de R. have אליו; 3 have אליו marked on the marg., one as a kri; 7 K. and 5 de R. had אלי corrected into אליו; 4 K., 5 de R. had אליו corrected into אלי: 11 K., 5 de R. had a kri in marg. אליו. "The most and best MSS have אלי." De R. Ewald's ground for rejecting the reading אלי illustrates the Jewish. "דקר is, from the context which speaks of mourning for the dead, and the

Before CHRIST cir. 487.

mourneth for *his* only *son*, and shall be in bitterness for him, as one that is in bitterness for *his* firstborn.

Before CHRIST cir. 487.

have pierced[1]; the Head with the thorns, the Hands and Feet with the nails, the Side with the soldier's lance. The prophecy began to be fulfilled as soon as the deed was completed, and Jesus had yielded up His Spirit: when [2] *all the people that came together to that sight, beholding the things which were done, smote their breasts and returned.* "[3] When they had nailed the Divine Shrine to the Wood, they who had crucified Him, stood around, impiously mocking.—But when He had laid down His life for us, [4] *the centurion and they that were with him, watching Jesus, seeing the earthquake and those things which were done, feared greatly, saying, Truly this was the Son of God.*" As it ever is with sin, compunction did not come till the sin was over: till then, it was overlaid; else the sin could not be done. At the first conversion, the three thousand *were pricked*[5] *in the heart,* when told that He [6] *Whom they had taken and with wicked hands had crucified and slain,* is *Lord and Christ.* This awoke the first penitence of him who became S. Paul. *Saul, Saul, why persecutest thou Me?* This has been the centre of Christian devotion ever since, the security against passion, the impulse to self-denial, the parent of zeal for souls, the incentive to love; this has struck the rock, that it gushed forth in tears of penitence: this is the strength and vigor of hatred of sin, to look to Him Whom our sins pierced, *Who* S. Paul says, *loved me and gave Himself for me.* "[7] We all lifted Him up upon the Cross; we transfixed with the nails His Hands and Feet; we pierced His Side with the spear. For if man had not sinned, the Son of God would have endured no torment."

And they shall mourn for Him, as one mourneth for an only son, and shall be in bitterness for Him, as one that is in bitterness for a first-born. We feel most sensibly the sorrows of this life, passing as they are; and of these, the loss of an only son is a proverbial sorrow. [8] *O daughter of My people, gird thee with sackcloth and wallow thyself in ashes,* God says; *make thee the mourning of an only son, most bitter lamentation.* [9] *I will make it as the mourning of an only son.* The dead man carried out, *the only son of his mother and she was a widow,* is recorded as having touched the heart of Jesus. "[10] And our Lord, to the letter, was the Only-Begotten of His Father and His mother." He was [11] *the first-begotten of every creature,* and [12] *we saw His glory, the glory as of the Only-Begotten of the Father, full of grace and truth.* This mourning for Him Whom our sins pierced and nailed to the tree, is continued, week by week, by the pious, on the day of the week, when He suffered for us, or in the perpetual memorial of His Precious Death in the Holy Eucharist, and especially in Passion-Tide. God sends forth anew *the Spirit of grace and supplication,* and the faithful mourn, because of their share in His Death. The prophecy had a rich and copious fulfillment in that first conversion in the first Pentecost; a larger fulfillment awaits it in the end, when, after the destruction of Anti-Christ, [13] *all Israel shall* be converted and *be saved.* There is yet a more awful fulfillment; when [14] *He cometh with clouds, and every eye shall see Him, and they which pierced Him, and all kindreds of the earth shall wail because of Him.* But meanwhile it is fulfilled in every solid conversion of Jew Heathen or careless Christian, as well as in the devotion of the pious. Zechariah has concentrated in few words the tenderest devotion of the Gospel, *They shall look on Me Whom they pierced.* "[15] Zechariah teaches that among the various feelings which we can elicit from the meditation on the Passion of Christ, as admiration, love, gratitude,

language of the prophet (xiii. 3) clear; but for אלי, we must, with many MSS., read אליו. The first person were wholly unsuited here. It is at variance with the following וספדו עליו, and introduces into the Old Testament the senselessness, that one is to weep over Jahve, (for Jahve [Almighty God] must be the subject,) as over one dead, (who should never come back again!)." De Rossi suggests that the אליו came in accidentally, the scribe having in his mind Ps. xxxiv. 6, הביטו אליו.

[1] There can equally be no question about the meaning of דקרו (as even Ew. and Hitz. admit) or about the construction. דקר (which occurs 11 times, is everywhere "thrust through." In one place only, Lam. iv. 9. מְדֻקָּרִים. "thrust through," occurs as a synonyme of חַלְלֵי רעב "those wounded by hunger" and that, in contrast with חַלְלֵי חֶרֶב "wounded by the sword." So also the noun, מַדְקְרוֹת חרב, "the piercings of the sword," Ps. xii. 18. In regard to the construction, את אשר occurs in 97 places in the Bible, and in every place in the meaning "he who," "that which," "this that." In one place only Deut. xxix. 13, 14, את having been previously used as a preposition, "and not with you only, (אִתְּכם) do I make this covenant," the את is again used as a preposition, carrying on the construction, "but with him who, את אשר. Frischmuth (de Messia confixo) mentions 14 ways, by which "because" might without ambiguity have been expressed (see Pusey's Univ. Sermons p. 142). There is then no excuse for the renderings ἀνθ' ὧν, LXX. or Aq. σὺν ᾧ. Theod. has πρὸς μὲ εἰς ὃν ἐξεκέντησαν.

[2] S. Luke xxiii. 48. [3] S. Cyr. [4] S. Matt. xxvii. 54. [5] κατενύγησαν Acts ii. 37. [6] Ib. 23, 36. [7] Osor. [8] Jer. vi. 26. [9] Amos viii. 10. [10] Alb. [11] Col. i. 15. [12] S. John i. 14. [13] Rom. xi. 26. [14] Rev. i. 7. [15] Lap.

Before CHRIST cir. 487.

11 In that day shall
there be a great [n] mourning in Jerusalem, [o] as the
mourning of Hadadrim-
mon in the valley of Me-
giddon.
12 [p] And the land shall
mourn, † every family
apart; the family of the
house of David apart, and
their wives apart; the family of the house of [q] Nathan apart, and their wives
apart;
13 The family of the
house of Levi apart, and
their wives apart; the
family || of Shimei apart,
and their wives apart;
14 All the families that
remain, every family apart,
and their wives apart.

[n] Acts 2. 37.
[o] 2 Kin. 23. 29. 2 Chr. 35. 24.
[p] Matt. 24. 30. Rev. 1. 7.
† Heb. *families, families.*
[q] 2 Sam. 5. 14. Luke 3. 31.
|| Or, *of Simeon* as LXX.

compunction, fear, penitence, imitation, patience, joy, hope, the feeling of compassion stands eminent, and that it is this, which we peculiarly owe to Christ suffering for us. For who would not in his inmost self grieve with Christ, innocent and holy, yea the Only-Begotten Son of God, when he sees Him nailed to the Cross and enduring so lovingly for him sufferings so manifold and so great? Who would not groan out commiseration, and melt into tears? Truly says S. Bonaventure in his 'goad of Divine love:' 'What can be more fruitful, what sweeter than, with the whole heart, to suffer with that most bitter suffering of our Lord Jesus Christ?' "

11. *As the mourning of Hadadrimmon in the valley of Megiddon.* This was the greatest sorrow, which had fallen on Judah. Josiah was the last hope of its declining kingdom. His sons probably shewed already their unlikeness to their father, whereby they precipitated their country's fall. In Josiah's death the last gleam of the sunset of Judah faded into night. Of him it is recorded, that *his pious acts, according to what was written in the law of the Lord,* were written in his country's history [1]; for him the prophet *Jeremiah wrote a dirge* [2]; *all* the minstrels of his country *spake of him in their dirges* [2]. The dirges were *made an ordinance* which survived the captivity; *to this day* [2], it is said at the close of the Chronicles. Among the gathering sorrows of Israel, this lament over Josiah was written in the national collection of *dirges* [2]. *Hadadrimmon,* as being compounded of the name of two Syrian idols, is, in its name, a witness how Syrian idolatry penetrated into the kingdom, when it was detached from the worship of God. It was "[3] a city near Jezreel, now called Maximinianopolis in the plain of Megiddon, in which the righteous king Josiah was wounded by Pharaoh Necho." This "[4] was 17 miles from Cæsarea, 10 from Esdraelon." Its name still survives in a small village, south of Megiddon [5], and so, on the way back to Jerusalem.

12–14. This sorrow should be universal but also individual, the whole land, and that, family by family; the royal family in the direct line of its kings, and in a branch from Nathan, a son of David and whole brother of Solomon [6], which was continued on in private life, yet was still to be an ancestral line of Jesus [7]: in like way the main priestly family from Levi, and a subordinate line from a grandson of Levi, *the family of Shimei* [8]; and all the remaining families, each with their separate sorrow, each according to Joel's call, [9] *let the bridegroom go forth of his chamber and the bride out of her closet,* each denying himself the tenderest solaces of life.

"[10] The ungrateful and ungodly, daily, as far as in them lies, crucify Christ, as S. Paul says, [11] *crucifying to themselves the Son of God afresh and putting Him to an open shame.* And on these Christ, out of His boundless pity, poureth forth a spirit of grace and supplication, so that, touched with compunction, with grieving and tearful feeling, they look on Christ, suffering with His suffering, and bewailing their own impurities."

"[12] The likeness is in the sorrow, not in its degree. Josiah had restored religion, removed a dire superstition, bound up relaxed morals by healthful discipline, recalled to its former condition the sinking state. In their extremest needs light shone on them, when there came his unlooked-for death, Therewith the whole state seemed lost. So in the Death of Christ, they who loved Him, saw His Divine works, placed their whole hope

[1] 2 Chr. xxxv. 26, 7. [2] Ib. 25. [3] S. Jer.
[4] Itin. Hieros. in Reland p. 891.
[5] "About ¾ of an hour to the S. of Megiddo lies a small village called Rumûni." Van de Velde Travels i. 355.
[6] 1 Chr. iii. 5. [7] S. Luke iii. 31.
[8] Nu. iii. 21. Had the allusion been to the tribe of Simeon, as supplying the teachers of Israel, as S. Jerome thought, it had been, not שִׁמְעִי, but שמעני as in Nu. xxv. 14, Jos. xxi. 4. 1 Chr. xxvii. 15.
[9] Jo. ii. 16. [10] Dion. [11] Heb. vi. 6 [12] Osor.

Before CHRIST cir. 487.

CHAPTER XIII.

1 *The fountain of purgation for Jerusalem,* 2 *from idolatry, and false prophecy.* 7 *The death of Christ, and the trial of a third part.*

[a] ch. 12. 3.
[b] Heb. 9. 14. 1 Pet. 1. 19. Rev. i. 5.

IN [a] that day there shall
be [b] a fountain opened
to the house of David and
to the inhabitants of Jerusalem for sin and for † uncleanness.
2 ¶ And it shall come
to pass in that day, saith
the LORD of hosts, *that* I
will [c] cut off the names of
the idols out of the land,
and they shall no more be

Before CHRIST cir. 487.

† Heb. *separation for uncleanness.*

[c] Ex. 23. 13. Josh. 23. 7. Ps. 16. 4. Ezek. 30. 13. Hos. 2. 17. Mic. 5. 12, 13.

of salvation in His goodness, suddenly saw the stay of their life extinct, themselves deprived of that most sweet intercourse, all hope for the future cut off. But the grief in the death of Christ was the more bitter, as He awoke a greater longing for Himself, and had brought a firmer hope of salvation."

XIII. 1. *In that day there shall be a fountain opened.* Zechariah often repeats, *in that day* [1], resuming his subject again and again, as a time not proximate, but fixed and known of God, of which he declared somewhat. It is *that day* which [2] *Abraham desired to see, and saw it,* whether by direct revelation, or in the typical sacrifice of Isaac, *and was glad:* it was [3] *that day* which *many prophets and kings and righteous men desired to see,* and in patience waited for it: *the* one *day of salvation* of the Gospel. He had spoken of repentance, in contemplation of Christ crucified; he now speaks of forgiveness and cleansing, of sanctification and consequent obedience. The *fountain shall be* not simply *opened,* but shall remain open [4]. Isaiah had already prophesied of the refreshment of the Gospel. [5] *When the poor and needy seek water and* there is *none,* and *their tongue faileth for thirst, I, the Lord, will hear them, I, the God of Israel, will not forsake them. I will open rivers in high places and fountains in the midst of the valleys;* here it is added, *for sin and for uncleanness.* There were *divers* [6] symbolical *washings* under the law; the Levites were [7] *sprinkled with the water of purifying,* lit. *the water of taking away of sin: living waters* [8], put to the ashes of an heifer, were appointed as a [9] *water for* (removing) *defilements; a cleansing of sin* [10]. Now, there should be one ever-open fountain for all *the house of David.* "[11] Who that fountain is, the Lord Himself teacheth through Jeremiah, [12] *they have forsaken Me, the fountain of living waters;* and in the Gospel He says, [13] *If any man thirst, let him come unto Me and drink;* and [14] *The water which I shall give him, is a fountain of living water, gushing up to everlasting life.* This was *open to the house of David;* for of that kindred He took human nature. It was opened also *for the dwellers of Jerusalem,* for the sprinkling of holy Baptism, through which we have received remission of sins." "[15] That, receiving Divine and holy Baptism, we are sprinkled with the Blood of Christ to the remission of sins, who can doubt?" "[16] Of this fountain much was foretold by Ezekiel [17], that a fountain should issue forth from the temple of the Lord, and *go down into the desert,* and *every soul, to whom it shall come, shall live;* and Joel, [18] *A fountain shall come forth of the house of the Lord, and water the valley of Shittim.* Of this fountain Peter said to the Jews, when *pricked in the heart* and seeking forgiveness, [19] *Let every one of you be baptized in the Name of Jesus Christ for the remission of sins.*"

2. *I will cut off the names of the idols.* This had been a fence against idolatry. To name evil is a temptation to evil. Wrong words are the parents of wrong acts. To speak of evil awakens curiosity or passion; curiosity is one of the strongest incentives to act. All

[1] xii. 3, 4, 6, 8, 9, 11, xiii. 1, 2, 4, xiv. 6, 8, 13, 20.
[2] S. John viii. 56.
[3] S. Matt. xiii. 17, S. Luke x. 24.
[4] The force of יִהְיֶה נִפְתָּח.
[5] Is. xli. 17, 18.
[6] Heb. ix. 10.
[7] מֵי הַטָּאת Num. viii. 7.
[8] Ib. xix. 17.
[9] מֵי נִדָּה Ib. xix. 9, 13, 20, 21 bis xxxi. 23.
[10] חַטָּאת Ib. xix. 9.
[11] Theod.
[12] Jer. ii. 13. The word is the same, מְקוֹר, and Ib. xvii. 13. מקור is, etymologically, a place "dug;" but a "mere well" could not be "a fountain of living water." They dug to obtain anyhow a larger supply of water. Is. xxxvii. 25; Isaac's servants by digging obtained "a well of living" i.e. flowing "water" Gen. xxvi. 19. It is parallel with מעין Hos. xiii. 15., where cistern or reservoir would be unmeaning. Metaphorically, *fountain of living waters* Jer. xxii. 13. *fountain of life* Ps. xxxvi. 10. Pr. x. 11. xiii. 14. xiv. 27. xvi. 22. *of wisdom* Ib. xviii. 4. *of tears* Jer. viii. 23. *of blood* Lev. xii. 7. xx. 18. *of Israel* Ps. lxviii. 17, are like one fountain which supplies a stream, rather than a reservoir, and מים חיים is of running water, Gen. l. c. Lev. xiv. 5, 6, 50–52. xv. 13. Num. xix. 17. Cant. ix. 15. Zech. xiv. 8. מקור מְשֻׁחָת Pr. xxv. 28. is rather "a fountain corrupted," spoiled from without, than stagnant water in a reservoir, where the spoiling is from itself. In Jer. li. 36. מקור (sing.) stands collectively for the whole supply of water. Tanchum has מנבע מא.
[13] S. John vii. 37.
[14] Ib. iv. 14.
[15] S. Cyr.
[16] Dion.
[17] Ezek. xlvii. 1, 8, 9.
[18] Jo. iii. 18. See vol. 1. pp. 212, 213.
[19] Acts ii. 37, 38.

Before CHRIST cir. 487.

d 2 Pet. 2. 1.

remembered: and also I
will cause [d] the prophets
and the unclean spirit to
pass out of the land.
3 And it shall come to
pass, *that* when any shall
yet prophesy, then his father and his mother that
begat him shall say unto
him, Thou shalt not live;
for thou speakest lies in the
name of the LORD: and
his father and his mother
that begat him [e] shall thrust
him through when he pro-
phesieth.

Before CHRIST cir. 487.

e Deut. 13. 6. 8. & 18. 20.

public mention of terrible crimes (it has been observed) produces imitation of the specific form of crime. Hence it was commanded, [1] *make no mention of the name of other gods, neither let it be heard out of thy mouth.* And Joshua names it in his dying charge to Israel, [2] *Be ye therefore very strong to keep and to do all that is written in the book of the law of Moses—neither make mention of the name of their gods, nor cause to swear* by them. Hence they *changed* the *names* of cities [3], which bare idol names. David speaks of it, as part of fealty to God. [4] *I will not take their names upon my lips.* Hosea prophesies of the times of the new covenant; [5] *I will take away the names of Baalim out of her mouth, and they shall be no more remembered by their name.* Isaiah, [6] *The idols he shall utterly abolish.* Zechariah foretells their abolition with a turn of words, formed apparently on those of Hosea [7]; but slightly varied, because the worship of Baal, such a plague-spot in the time of Hosea, one, which continued until the year before the captivity [8], was gone. He implies nothing as to his own times, whether idolatry still existed. He predicts its entire abolition in the whole compass of the enlarged Judah, i. e. of Christendom.

And also I will cause the prophets and the unclean spirit to pass out of the land. False prophecy sets itself to meet a craving of human nature to know something of its future. False prophets there were, even in the time of Nehemiah [9], and those in some number, hired to prophesy against the word of God. Our Lord warns against them. [10] *Beware of false prophets, which come to you in sheep's clothing, but inwardly they are ravening wolves.* [11] *Many false prophets shall arise and shall deceive many. Many false prophets,* S. John says, [12] *are gone out into the world.* False prophets attended the decline of Judaism. Such was the author of the Jewish Sibylline book, prophesying the destruction of the Romans [13], and fixing the mind of his people on temporal aggrandizement [14]: false prophets were suborned by the Jewish "tyrants" and encouraged the Jews in the resistance which ruined the devoted city [15]: false prophets have arisen in Christianity; but, like the Phrygian women who led Tertullian astray, they "went out," were cast out "from it, as not being of it." "[16] After that the Only-Begotten Word of God appeared to us, the dull and childish toys of idolatry perished and were utterly destroyed, and with it were taken away the strange and impious devices of the false prophets, who were full of the evil, unclean spirit, and could be readily detected as laboring under a kindred disease to the idolaters. For both had one president of impiety, Satan." Not 50 years after the Crucifixion, a heathen [17] wrote his work, "on the failure of oracles." The outpouring of the Holy [18] *Spirit of grace and supplication,* should sweep away [19] *the unclean spirit,* (Zechariah alone anticipates the language of the New Testament [19]) which became [20] *a lying spirit in the mouth of the prophets* of those who sought to them.

3. *His father and mother that begat him* [21] *shall say unto him, Thou shalt not live.* The prophet describes the zeal against false prophecy, with reference to the law against those who seduced to apostasy from God. [22] The nearest relations were themselves to denounce any who had secretly tried to seduce them, and themselves, as the accusers, to cast the first stone at them. "[16] Such shall in those times be the reverence to God-wards, so careful shall they be of perfect probity and laudable life, that parents themselves shall be stimu-

1 Ex. xxiii. 13. 2 Jos. xxiii. 6, 7.
3 Nebo and Baalmeon, Num. xxxii. 38.
4 Ps. xvi. 4. 5 Hos. ii. 17. 6 Is. ii. 18.
7 Hos. ii. 19. Heb. "*I will* remove the *names* of Baalim *out of* his mouth; *and they shall be no more remembered,* ולא יִזָּכרו עוד, by their names" Zech. *I will* cut off *the names* of the idols *from* the land, *and they shall be no more remembered,* ולא יִזָּכרו עוד.
8 Jer. xxxii. 19. The prophecy was in the tenth year of Zedekiah, ver. 1. So far then from its implying a date before the captivity (Speaker's Comm. p. 735.), there could have been no ground for the change *then.*
9 See Introd. p. 330. 10 S. Matt. vii. 15.
11 Ib. xxiv. 11. 12 1 S. John iv. 1.
13 See Pusey's "Daniel the Prophet" p. 162.
14 Ib. pp. 364–368 15 Jos. B. J. vi. 5. 2.
16 S. Cyr. 17 Plutarch A. D. 80. 18 Zech. xii. 10.
19 רוּחַ הַטֻּמְאָה here only in the O. T.; πνεῦμα ἀκάθαρτον, in our Lord's words, S. Matt. xii. 43. S. Mark v. 8. S. Luke viii. 29, xi. 24. add Rev. xviii. 2, xvi. 13.
20 1 Kgs xxii. 21–23. 21 ילדיו. 22 De xiii. 6–10.

Before CHRIST cir. 487.

4 And it shall come to
pass in that day, *that* [f] the
prophets shall be ashamed
every one of his vision,
when he hath prophesied;
neither shall they wear
[g] † a rough garment † to
deceive:

[f] Mic. 3. 6, 7.
[g] 2 Kin. 1. 8. Isai. 20. 2. Matt. 3. 4.
† Heb. *a garment of hair.*
† Heb. *to lie.*

5 [h] But he shall say, I
am no prophet, I *am* an
husbandman; for man
taught me to keep cattle
from my youth.
6 And *one* shall say unto
him, What *are* these
wounds in thine hands?

Before CHRIST cir. 487.

[h] Amos 7. 14.

lated against their children, if they should speak falsely anything from their own heart, as though God spake by them—How true that word is, and how accredited the prophecy! This indicates clearly a great advance toward godliness, God transforming things for the better. What aforetime was held in great esteem, is now hated and accursed and held intolerable."

4. *The prophets shall be ashamed, every one of them.* They who before their conversion, gave themselves to such deceits, shall be ashamed of their deeds; as, after the defeat of the seven sons of the chief priest Sceva, [1] *fear fell on them all, and the name of the Lord Jesus was magnified, and many that believed came and confessed and shewed their deeds: many of them also which used curious arts brought their books together and burned them before all, and they counted the price of them, and found* it *fifty thousand* pieces *of silver. So mightily,* S. Luke subjoins, *grew the word of God and prevailed.*

Neither shall wear a rough garment to deceive, feigning themselves ascetics and mourners for their people, as the true prophets were in truth. The sackcloth, which the prophets wore [2], was a rough garment of hair [3], worn next to the skin [4], whence Elijah was known to Ahaziah, when described as [5] *a hairy man, and girt with a girdle of leather about his loins.* It was a wide garment, enveloping the whole frame [6], and so, afflictive to the whole body. " [7] This was the habit of the prophets, that when they called the people to penitence, they were clothed with sackcloth."

5. *And he shall say,* repudiating his former claims, *I am a husbandman* [8]: for *a man hath taught* [9] *me from my youth.* There was no room then for his having been a false prophet, since he had had from his youth one simple unlettered occupation, as Amos said truly of himself; [10] *I was no prophet, neither was I a prophet's son: but I was an herdsman and a gatherer of sycamore fruit.* The prophet does not approve the lie, any more than our Lord did the injustice of *the unjust steward.* Our Lord contrasted the wisdom *in their generation* of a bad man for his ends, with the unwisdom of *the children of light,* who took no pains to secure their God. Zechariah pictures vividly, how men would anyhow rid themselves of all suspicion of false-prophesying.

6. *And* one *shall say unto him, What* are *those wounds in thy hands?* The words are simple; the meaning different [11], according as they are united with what immediately precedes, or the main subject, Him Whom

[1] Acts xix. 13–20. [2] Is. xx. 2.
[3] Ib. xxii. 12, Jer. iv. 8, vi. 26.
[4] 1 Kgs xxi. 27, 2 Kgs vi. 30, Job xvi. 15.
[5] 2 Kgs i. 8.
[6] אדרת שער occurs Gen. xxv. 25, as describing the whole appearance of the new-born Esau; אדרת alone, of Elijah's mantle, 1 Kgs xix. 13, 19, 2 Kgs ii. 8, 13, 14; of the robes of the king of Nineveh Jon. iii. 6. אדרת שׁנער is the large Babylonian garment which incited Achan's covetousness. Jos. vii. 21–24. [all] [7] S. Jer.
[8] The phrase עֹבֵד אֲדָמָה is from Gen. iv. 2.
[9] הקנה, occurring in this place only, is uncertain. Against the modern rendering "sold" (which would be the obvious causative of קנה), or "bought" (taking *Hifil* as *Kal*) it seems decisive, that this would be contrary to the Levitical law. For since, if bought or sold as a slave, he would have been set free in the 7th year, he would not have been sold or bought from his youth. הקנה might equally be, "made me to possess," as "made another to possess me." In either case it governs a double accusative, of which one only is expressed. Kim. "made me a shepherd and husbandman: Rashi, quoting Menahem, "set me to keep his flocks," Ibn Ezra. "made me to possess ground i.e. made me a husbandman." Tanchum "tilled his land, which his father put him in possession of by inheritance." Hunt. 206. translates הקנני by אשתראנו "bought me."
[10] Am. vii. 14.
[11] A prevalent modern explanation has been of the self-inflicted wounds of the prophets of Baal. But 1) the idolatrous incisions have a technical name, יתגודד "cut himself;" De. xiv. 1, 1 Kgs xviii. 28, Jer. xvi. 16, xli. 5, xlvii. 5. גדודים Jer. xlviii. 37. 2) מַכָּה, מַכּוֹת, מַכִּים, are used of fresh unhealed wounds themselves, not of the scars. Pr. xx. 30, 1 Kgs xxii. 35, 2 Kgs viii. 29, ix. 15, Is. i. 6, xxx. 26, Mi. i. 9, Nah iii. 19, Jer. vi. 7, x. 19, xv. 18, xxx. 12, 17. 3) Self-infliction was characteristic of the idolatrous cuttings. They were probably to appease the displeased god or goddess. The only support of it, that מאהבים is used of idolatrous, and so adulterous, objects of love, is neutralized by the fact that the metaphor of male and female is never dropped. Of 14 times in which it occurs, 11 times, in Hosea, Jeremiah, Ezekiel, it is united with the fem. pronoun, מְאַהֲבֶיהָ, מְאַהֲבַיִךְ; 3 times in the first pers. of the city personified.

Before CHRIST cir. 487.

Then he shall answer, *Those* with which I was wounded *in* the house of my friends.

7 ¶ Awake, O sword, against [i] my shepherd, and against the man [k] *that is* my fellow, saith the LORD of hosts: [l] smite the shepherd,

Before CHRIST cir. 487.

[i] Isai. 40. 11. Ezek. 34. 23.
[k] John 10. 30. & 14. 10, 11. Phil. 2. 6.
[l] Matt. 26. 31. Mark 14. 27.

---

they pierced, for Whom they were to mourn, and, on their mourning, to be cleansed, and of Whom it is said in the next verse, *Awake, O sword, against My Shepherd.* S. Jerome and others[1] explain it of the punishment inflicted by parents. "These wounds and bruises I received, condemned by the judgment of my parents, and of those who did not hate but loved me. And so will truth prevail dissipating falsehood, that he too, who was punished for his own fault, will own that he suffered rightly." But wounds of chastisement are not inflicted on the hands, and the punishment of false prophecy was not such wounds[2], but death. Wounds in the hands were no punishment, which parents would inflict. They were the special punishment of the cross[3], after sustaining which, One only lived. The most literal interpretation, then, of the wounds in the hands harmonizes with the piercing before, and the smiting of the Good Shepherd which follows, of Whom David too prophesied, [4] *They pierced My Hands and My Feet.* "[5] What are those wounds o. Thy hands? How long, think you, and how and by whom will this be said to Him? For ever and ever, unceasingly, and with unspeakable admiration it will be said, both by God the Father, [6] *to Whom He was obedient unto death, the death of the Cross:* it will be said also both by the holy [7] *angels* who *desire to look into* Him, and by men whom He has redeemed. O great miracle, wonderful spectacle, especially in the Lord of all, to bear wounds in the midst of His Hands! And He shall say; *With these I was wounded in the house of those who loved Me.* O great sacrilege, sacrilegious homicide, that such wounds were inflicted in the house of those who loved. He will not say, 'with these I was wounded by those who loved Me,' but 'in the house of those who loved Me.' For they who inflicted them, loved Him not. But they were the house of Abraham and Isaac and Jacob and David, and the rest like them, who loved Me, and expected Me, Who was promised to them. Yet so to speak is not to answer the question, *what are these wounds?* For it is one thing to ask, what are these wounds, another to say, where they were inflicted. Having said, that they were inflicted in the house of those who loved Me, He says, what they are, *the Cup which My Father hath given Me to drink.* For what He subjoins, is the Voice of the Father giving the Cup. *Sword, awake &c.* is as though he said, Ask ye, What are these wounds? I say, 'the tokens of obedience, the signs of the Father's will and command. The Lord of hosts, God the Father *hath not spared* Me, *His own Son, but hath given* Me *for* you *all.* And He said, *Awake, o sword, against My Shepherd, and against the Man cohering to Me,* which is as much as, 'O Death, have thou power over My Son, My good Shepherd, the Man Who cohereth to Me, i. e. Who is joined in unity of Person with the Word Who is consubstantial with Me!' And then, as though the sword asked, how or how far shall I arise against this Thy Shepherd, he subjoins, *Smite the shepherd, and the sheep shall be scattered.* Hence the Shepherd Himself, when about to be smitten, spake, [8] *All ye shall be offended because of Me this night. For it is written, I will smite the Shepherd and the sheep shall be scattered.* So then to those who say, *what are those wounds in the midst of Thy hands?* is appositely subjoined the Voice of the Father, saying, *Awake, O sword, against My Shepherd &c.* in the meaning, 'They are monuments of the Father's love, the tokens of My Obedience, because He *spared not His own Son,* and I *became obedient* to Him for you all, *even unto death, and that, the death of the Cross.*'"

7. *Awake, O sword.* So Jeremiah apostrophises the sword, [9] *O thou sword of the Lord, when wilt thou be quiet?* The prophets express what *will be,* by a command that it should be; [10] *Make the heart of this people heavy.* But by this command he signifies that human malice, acting freely, could do

---

[1] So S. Cyr. also; but S. Cyril was misled by the rendering of the LXX, συμποδιοῦσιν, whereas Aq. Symm. Theod. have ἐκκεντήσουσιν.

[2] Hence Kim. explains it of the binding him hand and foot to keep him at home; Rashi of scourging the back, which would be the very opposite of בין ידים, and would not be visible. Ibn Ezra makes it refer to the ודקרוהו ver. 3. Tanchum explains "when one asks as to the marks of beating which are on his body," and, paraphrasing בין ידיך, explains "in front of thee." The Arab. version [Hunt. 206] has simply בין ידאך.

[3] S. Jerome makes the question answered in the words, "They are the wounds &c." inconsistently, "Why hangest thou on the Cross? why are thy hands transfixed by nails? What hast thou done, to be subjected to this punishment and torture?"

[4] Ps. xxii. 16. [5] Rup. [6] Phil. ii. 8.

[7] 1 S. Pet. i. 12.

[8] S. Matt. xxvi. 31. [9] Jer. xlvii. 6. [10] Is. vi. 10.

Before CHRIST cir. 487.

and the sheep shall be scattered: and I will turn mine hand upon [m] the little ones.

Before CHRIST cir. 487.

[m] Matt. 18. 10, 14. Luke 12. 32.

no more than [1] His *Hand and* His *counsel determined before to be done.* The envy and hatred of Satan, the blind fury of the Chief priests, the contempt of Herod, the guilty cowardice of Pilate, freely accomplished that Death, which God had before decreed for the salvation of the world. The meaning then is, "[2] the sword shall be aroused against My Shepherd, i. e. I will allow Him to be smitten by the Jews. But by *the sword* he designates death, persecution, wounding &c. as above, the [3] *sword upon his right arm,* and, where the Passion of Christ is spoken of, [4] *Deliver my soul from the sword.* So also, [5] *All the sinners of the people shall die by the sword,*" "[6] which cannot be taken literally; for many sinners perish by shipwreck, poison, drowning, fire." Amos then "[5] so spake, because many died by war, yet not all by the sword, but others by pestilence and famine, all which he includes under *the sword.* This smiting began, when the Lord was taken, and His sheep began to be scattered; but the prophecy which, before, was being gradually fulfilled, was fully fulfilled in His Death, and the Apostles were dispersed till the day of the Resurrection at eventide."

Against the Man, My Fellow[7], i. e. One united by community of nature. A little before, God had spoken of Himself as priced at *the thirty pieces of silver*, yet as breaking the covenant which He had made with all nations for His people; as *pierced through*, yet as *pouring the spirit of grace and supplication* on those who pierced Him, that they should mourn their deed, and as, thereon, ever cleansing them from sin. As Man, God was sold, was pierced. "[8] God, in flesh, not working with aught intervening as in the prophets, but having taken to Him a Manhood connatural[9] with Himself and made one, and through His flesh akin to us, drawing up to Him all humanity. What was the manner of the Godhead in flesh? As fire in iron, not transitively but by communication. For the fire does not dart into the iron, but remains there and communicates to it of its own virtue, not impaired by the communication, yet filling wholly its recipient." The bold language of the Fathers only expressed the actuality of the Incarnation. Since the Manhood was taken into God, and in Him dwelt all the fullness of the Godhead bodily, and God and Man were one Christ, then was it all true language. His Body was "[10] the Body of God;" His flesh "[11] the flesh of the Word;" and it was lawful to speak of "[12] the flesh of the Deity," of "[13] the Passion of the Word," "[14] the Passion of Christ, my God," "[15] the Passion of God," "[16] God dead and buried," "[17] God suffered," "[18] murderers of God," "[19] the Godhead dwelt in the flesh bodily, which is all one with saying that, being God, He had a proper body, and using this as an instrument, He became Man for our sakes, and, because of this, things proper to the flesh are said to be His, since He was in it, as hunger, thirst, suffering, fatigue and the like, of which the flesh is capable, while the works proper to the Word Himself, as raising the dead and restoring the blind, He did through His own Body," is but a continuance of the language of Zechariah, since He Who was sold, was priced, was Almighty God. Jesus being God and Man, the sufferings of His Humanity were the sufferings of God, although, as God, He could not suffer. Now, conversely, God speaks of the Shepherd Who was slain, as *My Fellow*, united in Nature with Himself, although not the Manhood of Jesus which suffered, but the Godhead, united with It in one Person, was Consubstantial with Himself. The name might perhaps be most nearly represented by "connatural." "[20] When then the title is employed of the relation of an individual to God, it is clear that that individual can be no mere man, but must be one, united with God by unity of Being. The Akin of the Lord is no other than He Who said in the Gospel [21] *I and My Father are One*, and Who is designated as [22] *the Only-Begotten Son, Who is in the Bosom of the Father.* The word, the Pentateuch by Zechariah, received no modification in the Hebrew of the intermediate period.

[1] Acts iv. 28. [2] Rib. [3] ch. xi. 17.
[4] Ps. xxii. 20. [5] Am. ix. 10. [6] S. Jer.

[7] The word עמית, in form, abstract, is always personal. It stands alone in the dialects, having probably been framed by Moses, to express more than "neighbor," "our common nature," as we speak. It occurs 11 times in Leviticus (v. 21 bis, [vi. 2 Eng.] xviii. 20, xix. 11, 15, 17, xxiv. 19, xxv. 14 (bis) 15, 17.) always with the pronominal affix, "thy" or "his;" and always in enjoining things or forbidding things by virtue of our common humanity. Though feminine in form, it is always masc. in fact, as in, "the wife of" עמיתך Lev. xviii. 20, and עליו, Ib. xix. 17. The word, being revived out of

[8] Hom. in Sanct. Christi gener. App. S. Basil. Opp. ii. 596 quoted in Newman on S. Ath. ag. Arian. p. 444. note k. Oxf. Tr.

[9] "συμφυῆ i. e. joined on to His Nature." Ib.

[10] S. Ath. ag. Arians iii. 9. p. 444. Oxf. Tr.

[11] Ib. n. 34 p. 449. [12] S. Leo, Serm. 65. fin.

[13] Tert. de carn. Christi, 5. [14] S. Ignat. Rom. 6.

[15] Tert. l. c. Ib. [16] Vigil. c. Eut. ii. p. 502.

[17] S. Melito in Anast. Hodeg. 12.

[18] Tert. l. c. all quoted on S. Ath. l. c. note i.

[19] S. Ath. ag. Ar. iii. n. 31 p. 443 O. T. See more ibid. [20] Hengst. Christ. iii. 530 ed. 2.

[21] S. John x. 30. [22] Ib. i. 18.

Before CHRIST cir. 487.

8 And it shall come to pass *that* in all the land, saith the LORD, two parts therein shall be cut off *and* die; [n] but the third shall be left therein.

Before CHRIST cir. 487.

[n] Rom. 11. 5.

it seems, was especially chosen, as being used in the Pentateuch, only in the laws against injuring a fellow-man. The prophet thereby gives prominence to the seeming contradiction between the command of the Lord, *Awake, O sword, against My Shepherd,* and those of His own law, whereby no one is to injure his fellow. He thus points out the greatness of that end, for the sake of which the Lord regards not that relation, Whose image among men He commanded to be kept holy. He speaks after the manner of men. He calls attention to the greatness of that sacrifice, whereby He [1] *spared not His own Son, but freely gave Him up for us all.* The word '*Man*' forms a sort of contrast with *My Fellow.* He Whom the sword is to reach must unite the Human Nature with the Divine." Jews too have seen that the words, *My Fellow,* imply an equality with God; only since they own not Him, Who was God and Man, they must interpret it of a false claim on the part of man[2], overlooking that it is given Him by God.

And I will turn My hand [3] *upon the little ones,* doing to them as He had done to the Shepherd. So our Lord forewarned them: [4] *If they have persecuted Me they will also persecute you:* [5] *If the world hate you, ye know that it hated Me, before it hated you:* [6] *Ye shall be hated of all men for My name's sake:* [7] *they will deliver you up to the councils and scourge you in the synagogues; and ye shall be brought before governors and kings for My name's sake:* [8] *they shall deliver you up to be afflicted, and shall kill you: and ye shall be hated of all men for My name's sake;* and to the Scribes and Pharisees, [9] *I send unto you prophets and wise men and scribes, and some of them ye shall kill and crucify, and some* of them *shall ye scourge in your synagogues and persecute them from city to city, that upon you may come all the righteous blood shed upon the earth.*

The little ones [10], as Jeremiah speaks of [11] *the least of the flock,* and the Lord said, [12] *fear not, little flock,* little and weak in itself, but mighty in Him and in His grace. Three centuries of persecution, alike in the Roman empire and beyond it in Persia, fulfilled the prophet's words and deepened the foundation of the Church and cemented its fabric.

8. *In all the land, two parts therein shall be cut off and die.* "In all the land of Israel," says a Jewish interpreter [13];—the land, in which the Good Shepherd had been slain and the sheep scattered, *that upon you,* our Lord had said, *may come all the righteous blood.* As David punished Moab, [14] *with two lines measured he to put to death, and with one full line to keep alive;* and Ezekiel prophesied, [15] *A third part of thee shall die with the pestilence, and with famine shall they be consumed in the midst of thee: and a third part shall fall by the sword round about thee;* so now, the greater part should be destroyed, but a remnant should be saved. *But the third part shall be left therein. Even so then at this present time also,* S. Paul says [16], *there is a remnant according to the election of grace.* "[17] The third part only shall be saved from the common de-

[1] Rom. viii. 32.

[2] Ibn Ezra interprets it in this sense, "He prophesieth again many wars, which shall be in all the earth, at the death of Messiah ben Joseph, and the meaning of My Shepherd, is every king of the nations, whom God made to rule over the earth; and he estimates of himself that he is as God; therefore (he saith) and against the man my fellow." Kimchi adopting the interpretation, adds "i. e. who thinks himself my fellow." R. Isaac (Chizzuk Emunah, Wagenseil Tela Ignea Satanæ p. 310) interprets the whole of the king of Ishmael, called also the king of Turkey, and ruling over Asia and Africa, under whose hand the majority of the people of Israel are in captivity. God calls him my shepherd, because He has given His people into his hand to feed them in their captivity. He calls him 'the man my fellow and companion,' because in the pride and greatness of his heart he accounteth himself like God, like that, Behold man is become like one of us (Gen. iii.)." Abarbanel gives, as the one of three interpretations which he prefers, a modification of R. Isaac's, explaining the words "my shepherd" of Mohammed, and directing his interpretation of "the man, my fellow" against our Lord. "The words, 'the man my fellow' are spoken of Jesus the Nazarene, for according to the sentiment of the children of Edom and their faith, he was the Son of God, and of the same substance, and therefore he is called according to their words, 'The man, my fellow." Rashi alone has "My shepherd, whom I set over the sheep of my captivity, and the man my fellow whom I associated with myself, to keep my sheep, even as I did;" but "I smite the shepherd," he explains "the wicked king of Moab," or "king of the border of wickedness" [i. e. Edom] or in one MS. "the wicked Roman king, who shepherdeth my flock." *R. Tanchum* has, "that they think in themselves on account of my setting them over the creation that they are my administrators in the kingdom and government." The Heb. Ar. [Hunt. 206] "against the man, my companion" (עלי אלרגל כאחבי).

[3] Such is the force of השיב על Am. i. 9, turning the hand against Ekron or against the other cities of Philistia; in Is. i. 25, upon Judah, and thoroughly cleansing her by affliction; Ezek. xxxviii. 12, of Gog against the restored Israel; Ps. lxxxi. 15 of God's turning upon its adversaries, His Hand which was now upon her [all]. It were in itself improbable that here alone should be in a good sense, as Ges.

[4] S. John xv. 20.

[5] Ib. 18.

[6] S. Matt. x. 22, S. Luke xxi. 17.

[7] S. Matt. x. 17, 18; add S. Luke xxi. 12.

[8] S. Matt. xxiv. 9.

[9] Ib. xxiii. 34, 35.

[10] הַצְּעִרִים ἅπ.

[11] Jer. xlix. 20 צְעִירֵי הַצֹּאן

[12] S. Luke xii. 32.

[13] Kim.

[14] 2 Sam. viii. 2.

[15] Ezek. v. 12.

[16] Rom. xi. 5.

[17] Osor.

Before CHRIST cir. 487.

9 And I will bring the third part [o]through the fire, and will [p]refine them as silver is refined, and will try them as gold is tried: [q]they shall call on my name, and I will hear them: [r]I will say, It *is* my people: and they shall say, The LORD *is* my God.

o Isai. 48. 10. p 1 Pet. 1. 6, 7. q Ps. 50. 15. & 91. 15. ch. 10. 6. r Ps. 144. 15. Jer. 30. 22. Ezek. 11. 20. Hos. 2. 23. ch. 8. 8.

CHAPTER XIV.

1 *The destroyers of Jerusalem destroyed.* 4 *The coming of Christ, and the graces of his kingdom.* 12 *The plague of Jerusalem's enemies.* 16 *The remnant shall turn to the Lord,* 20 *and their spoils shall be holy.*

Before CHRIST cir. 487.

BEHOLD, [a]the day of
1 the LORD cometh, and
thy spoil shall be divided
in the midst of thee.

a Isai. 13. 9. Joel 2. 31. Acts 2. 20.

struction; yet not so, that they should suppose that glory was to be obtained amid ease."

9. *I will bring the third part through the fire.* Such is always God's ways. [1] *Thou hast proved us, O God; Thou hast tried us, like as silver is tried. Thou broughtest us into the snare, Thou laidest trouble upon our loins: we went through fire and water, and Thou broughtest us out into a wealthy place.* [2] *I have refined thee, but not with silver, I have chosen thee in the furnace of affliction;* and, [3] *Through much tribulation we must enter into the kingdom of God.*

"[4] In adversity virtue is most tried, and it is shewn what advance a person has made; for *patience* hath *a perfect work* [5]; and it is called the touchstone of all other virtues, as is written; '[6] God tried His elect as gold in the furnace and received them as a burnt offering;' and, '[7] All the faithful who have pleased the Lord have passed through many tribulations.' And the angel Raphael saith to Tobias, '[8] Because thou wert accepted of God, need was that temptation should prove thee.'" "Adversities are granted to the elect of God, and therefore to be rejoiced in with the whole heart." "[9] Fire, crosses, racks were prepared; swords executioners torturers were put in action; new forms of suffering were invented, and yet Christian virtue remained moveless, unconquered: the fiercer the onslaught, the more glorious was the triumph." "[10] The more suffered, the more believed in Christ." "[9] Whose virtue they admired, these they imitated, and shared the suffering, that they might be partakers of the glory. This was that fire, whereby God willed that His own should be tried and purified, that, with Christ Whom they gave themselves to imitate, they might enjoy everlasting glory."

I will bless him and will say, It is My people, "[4] not only by creation as the rest, but by devotion and worship, by predestination and infusion of grace, by singular Providence, by mutual love; *and it shall say, The Lord is my God,* Whom Alone above all things, I long for, love, worship."

This promise is oftentimes renewed through the prophets, oftentimes fulfilled in Christ, whenever the Church is recalled from listlessness by fiery trials, and through them her children are restored to deeper devotedness and closer union with God.

XIV. "The Jews," S. Jerome says, "say that these things are to be fulfilled under Gog; others that they were accomplished in part, in the times of the Macedonians, Egyptians, and other nations. We, leaving the truth of the time to the judgment of the Lord, would explain what is written." Eusebius [11] points out that it cannot be said to have been fulfilled under Antiochus Epiphanes; "If any think that these things are, then let him consider again and again, whether he can refer the rest of the prophecy also to the times of Antiochus; as, that [12] *the feet of the Lord* stood *on the mount of Olives,* that [13] *the Lord in that day,* became *king over the whole earth;* and so, as to the rest of the prophecy." And although more was fulfilled in the last siege by the Romans, still those who would explain it solely of this, are obliged to mingle explanations partly literal, as that Jerusalem should be the earthly Jerusalem, which was destroyed, partly metaphorical, as to the mount of Olives, its division into two parts &c. It seems then probable that, like the kindred prophecy of Joel [14], it relates chiefly to the time of the end, and that as our Lord unites the destruction of Jerusalem with His Coming in the Day of Judgment, so here are united that first destruction with the last rebellion of man, in the times of Anti-Christ. Since then much or most may be yet future, it seems safer, as S. Jerome suggests, to explain the Prophet's symbolic language, leaving the times of the fulfillment to Him, in Whose hands they are.

1. *Behold the Day of the Lord cometh,* lit. *a day cometh, the Lord's,* in which He Himself

1 Ps. lxvi. 9–11. 2 Is. xlviii. 10. 3 Acts xiv. 22. 4 Dion. 5 S. James i. 4. 6 Wisd. iii. 6. 7 Judith viii. 23. Vulg. 8 Tobit. xii. 13 Vulg. 9 Osor.

10 S. Aug. in Ps. xc. Serm. i. n. 8. See more in Tert. Apol. c. ult. p. 105. note a. Oxf. Tr. 11 Dem. Evang. vi. 18. 12 ver. 4. 13 ver. 9. 14 Jo. ii. 30, iii. 18. See vol. 1. pp. 196–212.

Before CHRIST cir. 487.

2 For [b] I will gather all
nations against Jerusalem
to battle; and the city shall
be taken, and [c] the houses
rifled, and the women rav-
ished; and half of the city
shall go forth into captivity, and the residue of the
people shall not be cut off
from the city.
3 Then shall the LORD
go forth, and fight against
those nations, as when he
fought in the day of battle.

[b] Joel 3. 2.
[c] Isai. 13. 16.

Before CHRIST cir. 487.

shall be Judge, and no longer leave man to fulfill his own will, and despise God's; in which His glory and holiness and the righteousness of all His ways shall be revealed.

And thy spoil shall be in the midst of thee. "[1] How great will the strait be, that the spoils should be divided in the midst of her. It often happens that what, by a sudden assault, is plundered in the city, is divided in the field or in solitude, lest the enemy should come upon them. But now there will be such a heavy weight of ills, such will be the security of conquest, that the spoils shall be divided in the midst of the city."

2. *I will gather all nations against Jerusalem to battle.* This is a feature which belongs to the end. It had been dwelt upon by Joel[2]; Ezekiel spoke of the [3] *many nations* which should come under Gog. S. John foretells of an universal strife at the end, when [4] *The spirits of devils, working miracles, go forth unto the kings of the earth and of the whole world, to gather them to the battle of that great day of God Almighty;* and [5] *Satan shall be loosed out of his prison and shall go out to deceive the nations which are in the four quarters of the earth, Gog and Magog, to gather them together to battle, the number of whom is as the sand of the sea. And they went up on the breadth of the earth, and compassed the camp of the saints round about, and the beloved city.* Since no creature can do aught but what God wills, and, in his phrensy against God's people, is but His instrument, [6] *to try them and to purge and to make white to the time of the end;* and the strength of body or intellect, which is abused against His law, He continuously in the order of nature supplies, God may be said to do what Satan does against Him. Satan, in his blind fury, crowns martyrs, fills the thrones of heaven, works, against his will, the All-wise Will of God.

And the houses rifled, and the women &c. The horrors of heathen war repeat themselves through men's ever-recurring passions. What was foretold as to Babylon is repeated in the same words as to the Church of God. Seemingly *all things* come *alike to all:* [7] *there is one event to the righteous and to the wicked; to the good and to the clean and to the unclean: to him that sacrificeth and to him that sacrificeth not: as is the good, so is the sinner.* The outward event is the same, the hidden part is known to God Alone. *And the residue of the people shall not be cut off from the city,* unlike the lot of the earthly Jerusalem, in the destruction both by Nebuchadnezzar (which was past) and the Romans[8]. At the first, [9] *Nebuzaradan, the captain of the guard, carried away the rest of the people left in the city, and the fugitives that fell away to the king of Babylon, with the remnant of the multitude,* so that Jeremiah mourned over it, [10] *Because of the mountain of Zion which is desolate, foxes walk* [habitually] *upon it.* The Romans "[11] effaced the city." Now *a remnant* is *not cut off,* because [12] *for the elect's sake those days shall be shortened;* for our Lord had said[13], that *the gates of hell should not prevail against* His Church.

3. *The Lord shall go forth and shall fight,* "[14] is to be taken like that in Habakkuk, [15] *Thou wentest forth for the salvation of Thy people, for salvation with Thine Anointed,* and in Micah, [16] *For behold, the Lord cometh forth out of His place, and will come down and will tread upon the high places of the earth, and the mountains shall be molten under Him, and the valleys shall be cleft;* and Isaiah also, [17] *The Lord shall go forth as a mighty man; He shall stir up jealousy like a man of war; He shall cry; He shall prevail over His enemies.* "God is said to *go forth,* when by some wondrous deed He declares His Presence—His Deity is, as it were, laid up, so long as He holds Himself in, and does not by any token shew His power. But He *goes forth,* and bursts forth, when He exercises some judgment, and worketh some new work, which striketh terror." God then will *go forth out of His place,* when He is constrained to break through His quietness and gentleness and clemency, for the amendment of sinners. He Who elsewhere speaketh through the prophet, [18] *I, the Lord, change not,* and to Whom it is said, [19] *Thou art the same,* and in the Epistle of James, [20] *With Whom is no change,* now *goeth forth* and fighteth *as in the day of*

[1] S. Jer. [2] iii. 2–9, 11. [3] Ezek. xxxviii. 6, 15, 22.
[4] Rev. xvi. 14. [5] Ib. xx. 7, 8, 9.
[6] Dan. xi. 35. xii. 10. [7] Eccl. ix. 2.
[8] See on Mic. iii. 12. pp. 46–50. [9] 2 Kgs xxv. 11.

[10] Lam. v. 18. [11] See on pp. 46, 47.
[12] S. Matt. xxiv. 32. [13] Ib. xvi. 18. [14] S. Jer.
[15] Hab. iii. 13. [16] Mic. i. 3, 4. [17] Is. xlii. 13.
[18] Mal. iii. 6. [19] Ps. cii. 28. [20] S. James i. 17.

Before CHRIST cir. 487.

d See Ezek. 11. 23.

4 ¶ And his feet shall stand in that day [d] upon the mount of Olives, which *is* before Jerusalem on the east, and the mount of Olives shall cleave in the midst thereof toward the east and toward the west, [e] *and there shall be* a very great valley; and half of the mountain shall remove toward the north, and half of it toward the south.

e Joel 3. 12, 14.

battle, when He overwhelmed Pharaoh in the Red sea; and *fought for Israel*." *The Lord shall fight for you*, became the watchword of Moses [1] and the warrior Joshua in his old age [2], after his life's experience [3], and Nehemiah [4]. *Be not afraid by reason of this great multitude*, said Jahaziel, son of Zachariah [5], when *the Spirit of the Lord came upon* him; *for the battle is not your's, but God's.*

As He fought in the day of battle. "[6] All wars are so disposed by the power of God, that every victory is to be referred to His counsel and will. But this is not seen so clearly, when men, elate and confident, try to transfer to themselves all or the greater part of the glory of war. Then may the war be eminently said to be the Lord's, when no one drew sword, as it is written, [7] *The Lord shall fight for you, and ye shall hold your peace.* Of all God's wars, in which human insolence could claim no part of the glory, none was more wondrous than that, in which Pharaoh and his army were sunk in the deep. *The Lord*, said Moses [8], *is a man of war: the Lord is His Name. That day of battle* was the image of one much greater. In that, Pharaoh's army was sunk in the deep; in this, the power of evil, in Hell: in that, what could in some measure be conquered by human strength, was subdued; in this, a tyranny unconquerable; in that, a short-lived liberty was set up; the liberty brought by Christ through subdual of the enemy, is eternal. As then the image yields to the truth, earthly goods to heavenly, things perishable to eternal, so the glory of that ancient victory sinks to nothing under the greatness of the latter."

4 *And His feet shall stand in that day upon the mount of Olives*, "over against Jerusalem to the East, wherein riseth the Sun of Righteousness." The Mount of Olives is the central eminence of a line of hills, of rather more than a mile in length, overhanging the city, from which it is separated only by the narrow bed of the valley of the brook Cedron. It rises 187 feet above Mount Zion, 295 feet above Mount Moriah, 443 feet above Gethsemane, and lies between the city and the wilderness toward the dead sea: around its Northern side, wound the road to Bethany and the Jordan [9]. There, probably, David worshiped [10]; his son, in his decay, profaned it [11]; Josiah desecrated his desecrations [12]; there [13] *upon the mountain, which* is *on the East side of the city, the glory of the Lord stood*, when it had *gone up from the midst of the city*; it united the greatest glory of the Lord on earth, His Ascension, with its deepest sorrow, in Gethsemane. Since the Angel said, [14] *This same Jesus, which is taken up from you into heaven, shall so come in like manner as ye have seen Him go into heaven*, the old traditional opinion is not improbable, that our Lord shall come again to judge the earth, where He left the earth, near the place of His Agony and Crucifixion for us. So shall *the Feet* of God literally *stand upon the Mount of Olives.* Else it may be that "[15] the *Feet* of the uncircumscribed and simple God are to be understood not materially, but that the loving and fixed assistance of His power is expressed by that name."

Which is true, or whether, according to an old opinion, the last act of Anti-Christ shall be an attempt to imitate the Ascension of Christ (as the first Anti-Christ Simon Magus was said to have met his death in some attempt to fly [16]) and be destroyed by His Coming there, the event must shew.

And the Mount of Olives shall cleave [*be cleft*] *in* [*from*] *the midst thereof toward the East and toward the West*, i. e. the cleft shall be East and West, so as to form *a very great valley* through it—from Jerusalem toward the Jordan Eastward; and this shall be, in that *half of the mountain shall remove Northward, and half thereof Southward.* If this be literal, it is to form an actual way of escape from Jerusalem; if figurative, it symbolizes how that which would be the greatest hindrance to escape, the mountain which was higher than the city, blocking, as it were, the way, should itself afford the way of escape; as Zechariah speaks, [17] *O great mountain, before Zerubbabel* thou shalt become *a plain;* and Isaiah,[18] *Every valley shall be ex-*

1 Exod. xiv. 14. Deut. i. 30, xiii. 22, xx. 4.
2 Josh. xxiii. 10; comp. x. 14, 42, xxiii. 3.
3 Ib. x. 14, 42, xxiii. 3.
4 Neh. iv. 20.
5 2 Chr. xx. 15.
6 Osor.
7 Ex. xiv. 14.
8 Ib. xv. 3.
9 Van de Velde, Memoir 179.
10 2 Sam. xv. 32.
11 1 Kgs xi. 7.
12 2 Kgs xxiii. 13.
13 Ezek. xi. 23.
14 Acts i. 11.
15 Dion.
16 The evidence would be late, except as seemingly confirmed by a like history in Suetonius vi. 12.
17 Zech. iv. 7.
18 Is. xl. 4.

Before CHRIST cir. 487.

‖ Or, *my mountains.*

‖ Or, *when he shall touch the valley of the mountains to the place he separated.*

cir. 787.

5 And ye shall flee *to*
the valley of ‖ the moun-
tains; ‖ for the valley of
the mountains shall reach
unto Azal: yea, ye shall
flee, like as ye fled from
before the [f] earthquake in
the days of Uzziah king of
Judah: [g] and the LORD
my God shall come, *and*
[h] all the saints with thee.
6 And it shall come to

Before CHRIST cir. 487.

f Amos 1. 1.
g Matt. 16. 27. & 24. 30, 31. & 25. 31. Jude 14.
h Joel 3. 11.

---

alted and every mountain and hill shall be brought low, and the crooked shall be made straight, and the rough places plain; i. e. every obstacle should be removed.

5. *And ye shall flee to the valley of the mountains,* rather, *along* [1] *the valley of My mountains* [2] viz. of those mountains, which God had just formed by dividing the mount of Olives. *For the valley of the mountains shall reach unto Azal,* i. e. *Azel,* the same word which enters into Beth-Azel of Micah, where the allusion probably is to its firm-rootedness. It is more probable that the name of a place should have been chosen with an allusive meaning, as in Micah, than that an unusual appellative should have been chosen to express a very common meaning. S. Cyril had heard of it as the name of a village at the extremity of the mountain [3]. Else it might very probably have been destroyed in the destructive Roman wars. The Roman camp in the last siege must have been very near it [4]. The destruction of villages, after the frantic revolt under Bar-Chocab, was enormous [5].

Yea, ye shall flee like as ye fled from before the earthquake. An earthquake in the time of Uzziah, whose memory survived the captivity to the time of Zechariah, nearly two centuries, must have been very terrible, but no historical account remains of it, Josephus having apparently described the past earthquake in the language which Zechariah uses of the future [6]. Such an earthquake is the more remarkable a visitation in Jerusalem, because it was out of the line of earthquakes. These were to the North and East of Palestine: within it, they were almost unknown [7]. Interpositions of God even in man's favor, are full of awe and terror. They are tokens of the presence of the All-Holy among the unholy. Fear was an accompaniment of special miracles in the Gospel, not only among the poor Gadarenes [8], or the people [9], but even the Apostles [10]; apart from the effect of the sight of Angels on us who are in the flesh [11]. It is then quite compatible, that the valley so formed should be the means of deliverance, and yet an occasion of terror to those delivered through it. The escape of the Christians in Jerusalem to Pella, during the break of the siege, after the withdrawal of Cestius Gallus was a slight image of this deliverance.

And the Lord thy God shall come, and all the saints with Thee, O God. The prophet, having spoken of God as *my God,* turns suddenly to speak to Him, as present. "[12] This is manifestly said of the second Coming of the Saviour, of which John too in his Apocalypse says, [13] *Behold He shall come with the clouds, and every eye shall see Him, and they also which pierced Him.* And the Lord Himself in the Gospel declareth, that [14] *the Son of Man shall come in the clouds of heaven with power and great glory.* He shall *come with the clouds,* i. e. with the Angels, who are *ministering spirits* and are sent for different offices, and with the Prophets and Apostles." "[15] Whenever Scripture says that the saints and angels come with Christ, it is always speaking of His second Coming, as in that, [16] *When the Son of Man shall come in His glory and all His holy Angels with Him,* and in the Epistle of Jude [17], *Behold the Lord cometh with ten thousand of His saints, to execute judgment.*"

6. *The light shall not be clear nor dark,* or, more probably, according to the original

---

[1] According to the principle of words of motion, בוא עבר יצא הלך. See Ew. Lehrb. n. 282a, 1. pp. 706, 707, ed. 8.

[2] E. vers has followed Kim.; yet there is no need to assume that הָרַי is an old plur. form.

[3] אָצַל for אָצֵל, in pause, as in the man's name both forms occur 1 Chr. viii. 38, ix. 44. The LXX had 'Ασαήλ in S. Jerome's time; Aq. 'Ασέλ; Theod. 'Ασήλ; Symm. alone translates it, πρὸς τὸ παρακείμενον. Jon. retains אָצַל. So Kim., I. E., Abarb. The Syr. and Sym. (whom S. Jerome follows,) paraphrases. So Menahem and Rashi, giving an impossible explanation, "height." S. Cyril says, "it is a village, it is said, at the extremity of the mountain."

[4] Jos. B. J. v. 1. 8.

[5] "985 very well known villages." Dio Cass. lxix. 14. See ab. p. 48.

[6] See Introd. to Amos vol. i. pp. 224, 225.

[7] See Am. iv. 11, vol. i. p. 286.

[8] S. Mark v. 15, S. Luke viii. 25.

[9] On the restoration of Zacharias' speech, S. Luke i. 65; of the son of the widow of Nain Ib. vii. 16.

[10] At the walking on the sea, S. Matt. xiv. 26, S. John vi. 19; the rebuking of the wind, S. Mark vi. 48, S. Luke viii. 25; the Transfiguration, S. Matt. xvii. 6, S. Mark ix. 6; the draught of fishes, S. Luke v. 3–10.

[11] To Zacharias, S. Luke i. 12; the B. Virgin, Ib. 29, 30; the shepherds, Ib. ii. 9; to the women after the Resurrection, S. Mark xvi. 8; the Apostles "supposing they had seen a spirit." S. Luke xxiv. 37.

[12] S. Jer. on vv. 6, 7.

[13] Rev. i. 7.

[14] S. Matt. xxiv. 30.

[15] Rib.

[16] S. Matt. xxv. 31.

[17] S. Jude 14, 15.

Before CHRIST cir. 487.

pass in that day, || *that* the
light shall not be † clear,
nor † dark:
7 But || it shall be [l] one
day [k] which shall be known
to the LORD, not day, nor
night: but it shall come to
pass, *that* at [l] evening time
it shall be light.
8 And it shall be in that
day, *that* living [m] waters
shall go out from Jerusa-
lem; half of them toward
the || former sea, and half

|| *i. e.* it shall not be clear in some places, and dark in other places of the world.
† Heb. *precious.*
† Heb. *thickness.*
|| Or, *the day shall be one.*
[i] Rev. 22. 5.
[k] Matt. 24. 36.

Before CHRIST cir. 487.

[l] Isai. 30. 26. & 60. 19, 20. Rev. 21. 23.
[m] Ezek. 47. 1. Joel 3. 18. Rev. 22. 1.
|| Or, *eastern.* Joel 2. 20.

reading[1], *In that day there will be no light; the bright ones*[2] *will contract themselves*, as it is said, [3] *The stars shall withdraw their shining.*

This is evermore the description of the Day of Judgment, that, in the presence of God Who is Light, all earthly light shall grow pale. So Joel had said, [4] *The sun and moon shall be darkened, and the stars shall withdraw their shining.* And Isaiah,[5] *The moon shall be confounded and the sun ashamed, when the Lord of hosts shall reign in Mount Zion and in Jerusalem and before His ancients gloriously;* and, [6] *Behold the day of the Lord cometh,—The stars of heaven and the constellations thereof shall not give their light: the sun shall be darkened in his going forth, and the moon shall not cause her light to shine.* All know well our Lord's words[7]. S. John, like Zechariah, unites the failure of the heavenly light [8] *with a great earthquake, and the sun became as sackcloth of hair: and the moon became as blood; and the stars of heaven fell upon the earth.*

7. *And it shall be one day: it shall be known unto the Lord: not day, and not night; and at the eventide it shall be light.* One special *day; one*, unlike all beside; known unto God, and to Him Alone. For God Alone knows the day of the consummation of all things, as He saith, [9] *Of that day and that hour knoweth no one, neither the angels in Heaven, nor the Son,* (so as to reveal it) *but the Father only.* Neither wholly *day*, because overclouded with darkness; nor wholly *night*, for the streaks of light burst through the darkness chequered of both; but in *eventide*, when all seems ready to sink into the thickest night, *there shall be light.* Divine light always breaks in, when all seems darkness; but then the chequered condition of our mortality comes to an end, then comes the morning, which has no evening; the light which has no setting; "perpetual light, brightness infinite;" when[10] *the light of the moon shall be as the light of the sun, and the light of the sun shall be sevenfold;* and[11] *the glory of God doth lighten* the eternal city, *and the Lamb is the light* thereof; and [12] *in Thy light we shall see light.* "[13] Christ shall be to us eternal light, a long perpetual day."

And it shall be, that living waters. "[14] This is what is said in the prophecy of Joel, [15] *A fountain shall come forth from the house of the Lord;* and in that of Ezekiel, [16] *And behold there ran out waters.*" Zechariah leaves to the mind to supply what the former prophets had said of the fertilizing life-giving character of those waters. He adds that they should pervade the whole land, West as well as East; *to the former*, rather *the Eastern sea*[17], into which they would by nature flow, and toward *the hinder*, i. e. the Western sea, the Mediterranean, which natural waters could not *reach*. This their flow, he adds, should be perpetual. "[18] These streams shall not

[1] The E. V. follows Kim. "The light shall be neither יקרות 'preciousnesses' nor קפאון 'thickness.'"

[2] יְקָרוֹת יְקָפְאוּן.

[3] יְקָרוֹת as Job xxxi. 26. "the moon, יָקָר הֹלֵךְ, walking in beauty." יְקָפְאוּן "shall contract themselves," as it is said in Ex. xv. 8, קָפְאוּ תְהֹמֹת "the depths (lit.) coagulated in the heart of the sea." According to the Kri, יְהַרְאוּן, the meaning of יקרות is mere conjecture. Kimchi (Lex.) Ibn Ezra Rashi suppose it to be used of "clear light," as contrasted with cloudy, expressed by קִפָּאוֹן, so that the meaning of the whole should be the same as that of v. 7. Our version follows this. Abulwalid and Parchon explain it of heavy thick clouds, and make the words synonymous. Tanchum mentions both. The LXX seem further to have read וקרות, καὶ ψύχη; but it is not supported by any MS. or any other version: for the "but" in Symm. Chald. Syr. may only express the contrast of the sentences; "there shall not be light;—and—," as Asyndeton. The LXX. however, "There shall not be light and cold and ice," could only mean to deny the presence of any of them, not (as Ewald) "there shall be no alternation of light with cold and ice." Proph. ii. 62. Light too and cold are not alternatives. The Kri וקפאון, as always, occurs in some MSS., 8 Spanish of De Rossi, 2 at first, 15 old editions. The Jewish authorities (as far as I know) including Abulwalid Tanchum Parchon &c., take no notice of the Kethibh.

[4] Joel iii. 15. [5] Is. xxiv. 23. [6] Ib. xiii. 9, 10. [7] S. Matt. xxiv. 29. [8] Rev. vi. 12, 13. [9] S. Mark xiii. 32. [10] Is. xxx. 26. [11] Rev. xxi. 23. [12] Ps. xxxvi. 9. [13] S. Cyr. [14] Kim. [15] Joel iii. 18. [16] Ezek. xlvii. 2.

[17] Joel ii. 20, where the preternaturalness of the deliverance is pictured by the driving the *locust*, the symbol of the enemy, into two opposite seas. The Eastern sea, i. e. the dead sea, is spoken of there and Ezek. xlvii 18; the hinder sea, i. e. the Mediterranean, Joel ii. 20, Deut. xi. 24, xxxiv. 2.

[18] See Joel vol. i. pp. 212–215.

Before CHRIST cir. 487

of them toward the hinder
sea: in summer and in winter shall it be.
9 And the LORD shall
be [n] king over all the earth:
in that day shall there be
[o] one LORD, and his name
one.

n Dan. 2. 44. Rev. 11. 15.
o Eph. 4. 5, 6.

10 All the land shall be
|| turned [p] as a plain from
Geba to Rimmon south of
Jerusalem: and it shall be
lifted up, and [q] || inhabited
in her place, from Benja-
min's gate unto the place
of the first gate, unto the

Before CHRIST cir. 487.

|| Or, *compassed.*
p Isai. 40. 4.
q ch. 12. 6.
|| Or, *shall abide.*

dry up and their waters shall not fail[1];" therefore drought shall not lessen them, nor winter-cold bind them. "[1] From Jerusalem as from a fountain shall stream forth living waters of wisdom and grace to all nations."

"[2] Again he tells us, under a figure, that exceeding great and large shall be that outpouring of the Holy Spirit upon the saints, especially when they shall be removed to that holy eternal life in the world to come. For now through faith in Christ we are enriched, as with an earnest, with the first-fruits of the Holy Spirit. But after the Resurrection, sin being wholly taken away, the Holy Spirit will be in us, not as an earnest or in a measure; but richly bounteously and perfectly shall we enjoy the grace through Christ. He calleth, then, *living water*, the Spirit which, he says, will come forth from the Jerusalem which is from above.—But that the holy Scripture is wont to liken the Divine Spirit to *water*, the Giver thereof, the Son, accredits, saying[3], *he that believeth on Me, as the Scripture hath said, Out of his belly shall flow rivers of living water.* This the Evangelist explains, [4] *This spake He of the Spirit, which they who believe in Him should receive.* Since then the Spirit is life-giving, rightly does he liken it to that, which is life-giving to the frame."

9. *And the Lord shall be king over all the earth.* Such should be the influence of the living water, i. e. of the Spirit of God. God Who has ever reigned and will reign, [5] *a great King over all the earth*, shall be owned by His creatures, as what He is.

There shall be one Lord, more exactly, *The Lord shall be One, and His Name One.* He had before prophesied, [6] *I will cut off the names of the idols out of the land.* The Church being thus cleansed, no other lord or object of worship should be named but *Himself.* This is one of those prophecies, of continued expansion and development, ever bursting out and enlarging, yet never, until the end, reaching its full fulfillment. "[7] Since in this life we contemplate God in His effects, in which His whole perfection shineth not forth, now we know Him obscurely and imperfectly, His perfections being in divers diversely represented. In our home we shall see Him as He is, face to Face, through His Essence. Therefore then He will be represented by one name, as He shall be beheld by one gaze."

10. *All the land shall be turned as a plain from Rimmon to Gebah.* "[8] All the land, which is round about Jerusalem, which is now mountains, as is said, [9] *The mountains are round about Jerusalem*, shall be level as a plain, but Jerusalem itself shall be exalted[10], and high above all the earth." The dignity of the Church, as [11] *a city set upon a hill, which cannot be hid*, is symbolized here by the sinking of all around and its own uprising; as in Micah and Isaiah, [12] *The mountain of the Lord's house shall be established on the top of the mountains, and shall be exalted above the hills.* *Gebah*, lit. *hill*, now, *Jeva*, was a frontier-garrison, held once by the Philistines[13], and fortified by Asa[14], in the northern boundary of Benjamin[15], together with Michmash[16] (now Mûkhmas), commanding an important pass, by which Jerusalem was approached[17]. *Rimmon, south of Jerusalem* is mentioned in Joshua among the southern towns of Judah[18], given to Simeon[19]. Both survived the Captivity[20]. They mark then the N. and S. of the kingdom of Judah, a long mountain chain, which is pictured as sinking down into a plain, that Jerusalem alone might be exalted.

[1] Kim. קוץ וחרף make up the whole year. Gen. viii. 22, Ps. lxxiv. 17. חרף is winter Pr. xx. 4, Am. iii. 15, Jer. xxxvi. 22.

[2] S. Cyr. [3] S. John vii. 38. [4] Ib. 39.
[5] Ps. xlvii. 3, 8. [6] Zech. xiii. 2. [7] Dion. [8] Kim.
[9] Ps. cxxv. 2.

[10] ראמה, as וקאם, Hos. x. 14. א is substituted in the name of the animal ראם, רְאֵמִים; the appell., רָאמות Pr. xxiv. 7; the precious substance, Ezek. xxvii. 16, Job xxviii. 18; the town, Deut. iv. 43, Jos. xx. 8, 1 Chr. vi. 65.

[11] S. Matt. v. 14. [12] Is. ii. 2. Mic. iv. 1.
[13] 1 Sam. xiv. 5. [14] 1 Kgs xv. 22.

[15] From Gebah to Beer-sheba," 2 Kgs xxiii. 8, as here, "from Gebah to Rimmon." It is named among the northern towns of Benjamin, Jos. xviii. 24.

[16] 1 Sam. l. c. [17] Is. x. 28, 29.
[18] Jos. xv. 32. [19] Ib. xix. 7, 1 Chron. iv. 32.
[20] Gebah, mentioned with Michmash, Neh. xi. 31, Rimmon, Ib. 29.

Before CHRIST cir. 487.

corner gate, [r] and *from* the
tower of Hananeel unto
the king's winepresses.
11 And *men* shall dwell
in it, and there shall be
[s] no more utter destruction;
[t] but Jerusalem ‖ shall be
safely inhabited.
12 ¶ And this shall be
the plague wherewith the
LORD will smite all the
people that have fought
against Jerusalem; Their
flesh shall consume away
while they stand upon their
feet, and their eyes shall
consume away in their
holes, and their tongue
shall consume away in their
mouth.
13 And it shall come to
pass in that day, *that* [u] a
great tumult from the
LORD shall be among

r Neh. 3. 1. & 12. 39. Jer. 31. 38.
s Jer. 31. 40.
t Jer. 23. 6.
‖ Or, *shall abide.*
u 1 Sam. 14. 15, 20.

From Benjamin's gate unto the place of the first gate. Benjamin's gate[1] must obviously be a gate to the North, and doubtless the same as *the gate of Ephraim*[2], the way to Ephraim lying through Benjamin. This too has probably reference to the prophecy of Jeremiah, that [3] *the city shall be built to the Lord from the tower of Hananeel unto the gate of the corner.* [4] *Jehoash, king of Israel, brake down the wall of Jerusalem from the gate of Ephraim to the corner-gate, four hundred cubits,* after the war with Amaziah. Zechariah seems to speak of Jerusalem, as it existed in his time. For the tower of Hananeel[5] still existed; the *first gate* was probably destroyed, since he speaks not of it, but of its *place;* the gate of Benjamin and the corner-gate probably still existed, since Nehemiah[6] mentions the building of the sheep-gate, the fish-gate, the old gate, or gate of the old city, the valley-gate, the dung-gate, the gate of the fountain; but not these.

11. *And they shall dwell in it,* in peace, going forth from it, neither into *captivity,* nor in flight[7]; for God should exempt from curse the city which He had chosen, against which the gates of hell shall not prevail, and He says of the heavenly Jerusalem, [8] *there shall be no more curse.*

12. Again, upon the restoration of His people follows the destruction of His enemies. It shall, first and chiefly, be God's doing, not man's. *This shall be the plague.* The word is used of direct infliction by pestilence, *wherewith the Lord shall smite*[9] *all the people* [*peoples*] *that fought against Jerusalem.* The awful description is of living corpses. "[10] The enemies of Jerusalem shall waste, not with fever or disease, but by a plague from God, so that, being sound, standing, living, in well-being, they should waste and consume away," as Isaiah speaks of the [11] *carcases of the men, that have transgressed against Me; for their worm shall not die—and they shall be an abhorring unto all flesh.*

Their flesh shall consume away, rather, *wasting away the flesh of each one.* It is the act of God, in His individual justice to each one of all those multitudes gathered against Him. One by one, *their eyes,* of which they said, [12] *let our eye look on Zion,* i. e. with joy at its desolation, *shall consume away in their holes, and their tongue,* wherewith they blasphemed God[13], *shall consume away in their mouths.* Appalling, horrible, picture! *standing on their feet,* yet their flesh mouldering away as in a grave-yard, their sightless balls decaying in their holes, the tongue putrefying in their mouth, a disgust to themselves and to others! Yet what, compared to the horrible inward decay of sin, whereby men [14] *have a name that they live and are dead?* "[15] Let us read Ecclesiastical histories, what Valerian, Decius, Diocletian, Maximian, what the savagest of all, Maximin, and lately Julian suffered, and then we shall prove by deeds, that the truth of prophecy was fulfilled in the letter also."

13. *A great tumult,* and panic fear, such as

[1] Mentioned beside, Jer. xx. 2. xxxvii. 12, 17. Jeremiah goes through it, "to go into the land of Benjamin." Jer. xxxvii. 12, 13.
[2] Mentioned 2 Chr. xxv. 23, Neh. viii. 16, xii. 39.
[3] Jer. xxxi 38. [4] 2 Kgs xiv. 13. 2 Chr. xxv. 23.
[5] Neh. iii. 1. [6] Neh. iii. 1, 3, 6, 13, 14, 15.
[7] v. 2, 5. [8] Rev. xxii. 3.
[9] נָגַף occurs 20 times of God's striking; 2ce of a foot stumbling; once (like נגח) of an ox goring another, once of a man's accidental blow, both in Ex. . מַגֵּפָה, in like way, occurs 17 times of death inflicted by God (once only of an individual, Ezekiel's wife, Ez. xxiv. 16), and 3 times only, of slaughter in battle by men, 1 Sam. iv. 17, 2 Sam. xvii. 9, xviii. 7. The form Hif., המק; is ἅπ. Nif. is used of a putrefying wound, Ps. xxxviii. 6, and מק subst. Is. iii. 24. Nif. is also used of man's wasting away through (ב) his sins Lev. xxvi. 39 (bis) Ez. xxiv. 33, xxxiii. 10 [not 'under the weight of' as Ges.] and of the dissolution of the host of heaven, Is. xxxiv. 4.
[10] Lap. [11] Is. lxvi. 24. [12] Mi. iv. 11.
[13] comp. Ps. xii. 3. Is. xxxvi. 15, 18. xxxvii. 3, 4. 17, 23, 29. [14] Rev. iii. 1. [15] S. Jer.

Before CHRIST cir. 487.

them; and they shall
lay hold every one on
the hand of his neigh-
bor and [x] his hand shall
rise up against the
hand of his neighbor.
14 And ‖ Judah also
shall fight ‖ at Jerusalem;
[y] and the wealth of all the
heathen round about shall

x Judg. 7. 22. 2 Chr. 20. 23. Ezek. 38. 21.

‖ Or, *thou also, O Judah, shalt.*
‖ Or, *against.*
y Ezek. 39. 10, 17, &c.

Before CHRIST cir. 487.

God said He would send upon the Canaanites before Israel[1], or on Israel itself, if disobedient[2]; or which fell on the Philistines after Jonathan's capture of the garrison at Michmash, when every man's [3]*sword was against his fellow.* There is no real unity, except in God; elsewhere, since each seeks his own, all must be impregnated with mutual suspicion, ready at any moment to be fanned into a flame; as when, at the blowing of Gideon's trumpets, [4]*the Lord set every man's sword against his fellow;* or when, at Jehoshaphat's prayer[5], *the children of Ammon and Moab stood up against the inhabitants of Mount Seir, utterly to slay and destroy; and when they had made an end of the inhabitants of Seir, every one helped to destroy another.*

And they shall lay hold, every one on the hand of his neighbor. Every one shall be every one's foe. Each shall, in this tumultuous throng, grasp the other's hand, mastering him powerfully[6]. *And his hand shall rise up* [7]*against the hand of his neighbor,* as was prophesied of Ishmael, [8]*his hand will be against every man, and every man's hand against him.*

14. *And Judah also shall fight at Jerusalem.* This seems more probable than the alternative rendering of the E. M., "against." For Judah is united with Jerusalem as one, in the same context[9]; and, if it had shared with the heathen, it must also have shared their lot. It is Judah itself, not "a remnant of Judah," as it is [10]*every one that is left of all the nations,* which is thus united to Jerusalem: it is that same Judah, as a whole, of which it is said, *it shall fight.* Nor is anything spoken of "conversion," which is said of those left from the heathen nations, who had fought against her. Yet for Judah to have joined an exterminating Heathen war against Jerusalem, even though constrained, had, like the constrained sacrifices to Heathen gods, been apostasy. But there is not even a hint that, as Jonathan apologetically paraphrases[11], they were "constrained." The war is to be Judah's free act: *Judah also shall fight.* Again, those gathered against Jerusalem, and their warfare against it, had been described at the outset, as [12]*all nations:* here the subject is not the gathering or fighting, but the overthrow. Nor is there any decisive contrary idiom; for, although when used of people, it always means "fight against," yet, of place, it as often, means "fight in[13]." Probably then the Prophet means, that not only should God fight for His people, but that *Judah also* should do its part, as S. Paul says, [14]*We, then, as workers together with Him;* and, [15]*we are laborers together with God;* and, [16]*I labored more abundantly than they all; yet not I, but the grace of God which was with me;* or, [17]*work out your own salvation with fear and trembling; for it is God which worketh in you both to will and to do of His good pleasure.* God so doth all things in the Church, for the conversion of the heathen, and for single souls, as to wait for the cöoperation of His creature. "[18]God made thee without thee; He doth not justify thee without thee."

1 De vii. 23. 2 Ib. xxviii. 20. 3 1 Sam. xiv. 20. The same word is used. 4 Jud. vii. 22. 5 2 Chr. xx. 32.

6 החזיק, with acc., is used adversely though figuratively. Anguish (Jer. vi. 24, l. 43) amazement (Ib. viii. 21) pangs (Mic. iv. 9) are said to seize on—; and David "I seized (החזקתי) by the beard the lion and the bear," 1 Sam. xvii. 35. It is used of a man grasping with violence (with ב) De. xxii. 25, 2 Sam. xiii. 11; forcibly detaining prisoners, Ex. ix. 2, Jer. l. 33; the head of an opponent, "they seized each his fellow by the head, and his sword in his fellow's side," 2 Sam. ii. 16; "the ears of a dog," Pr. xxvi. 17. Here the context precludes ambiguity; the use of the acc. is poetic.

7 עלה "rise" = "be raised up," as even of inanimate things, Am. iii. 5, Pr. xxvi. 9, Job. v. 26; of a people carried away, Ib. xxxvi. 20. Gesenius' instances, Thes. p. 1023 n. 2.

8 Gen. xvi. 12. 9 v. 21. 10 v. 16.

11 "Yea, and those of the house of Judah the nations will bring, constrained, to carry war against Jerusalem." Jon. 12 v. 2, 3.

13 On the one hand, נלחם בעיר "fought against the city," Jud. ix. 45; בְּרַבָּה "against Rabbah" 2 Sam. xii. 27; בִּקְעִילָה "against Keilah," 1 Sam. xxiii. 1: on the other, בְּתַעְנַךְ "fought at Taanach," Jud. v. 19; בִּרְפִידִם, "at Rephidim," Ex. xvii. 8; בְּבִקְעַת מְגִדּוֹ "in the valley of Megiddo," 2 Chr. xxxv. 22, and so probably in the immediate context, (Ib. 20) בְּכַרְכְּמִישׁ, "at Carchemish," since it is hardly probable, that Carchemish should be mentioned as *the* object of such an expedition, and the decisive battle between Egypt and Chaldæa was "*at*," not "*in* Carchemish," בְּכַרְכְּמִשׁ, where Nebuchadnezzar smote his army. Jer. xlvi. 2. For such a large army as Pharaoh's would not have been shut up in a town, which was of importance only as a key to the passage of the Euphrates. Also in Isaiah xxx. 32, the Chethib בָּה must be "in her," Zion, which the Kri has corrected into the more common idiom, בָּם, "against them." The LXX. renders thus, παρατάξεται ἐν Ἱερουσαλήμ.

14 2 Cor. vi. 1. 15 1 Cor. iii. 9. 16 Ib. xv. 10.

17 Phil. ii. 12. 18 S. Aug. Serm. 169. n. 13. Opp. v. 815. (on N. T. p. 866 O. T.)

Before CHRIST cir. 487.

be gathered together, gold, and silver, and apparel, in great abundance.

z ver. 12.

15 And [z] so shall be the plague of the horse, of the mule, of the camel, and of the ass, and of all the beasts that shall be in these tents, as this plague.

16 ¶ And it shall come to pass, *that* every one that is left of all the nations which came against Jerusalem shall even [a] go up from year to year to worship the King, the LORD of hosts, and to keep [b] the feast of tabernacles.

a Is. 60. 6, 7, 9. & 66. 23.
b Lev. 23. 34, 43. Neh. 8. 14. Hos. 12. 9. John 7. 2.

And the wealth of all the heathen round about shall be gathered. Whatever the world had taken in their war against the Church shall be abundantly repaid. *All the heathen* had combined to plunder Jerusalem [1]; *the wealth of all the heathen* shall be gathered to requite them. "[2] As Isaiah says, The nations, converted to Christ, brought all their wealth to the Church, whence he congratulates the Church, saying, "[3] *Thou shalt also suck the milk of the Gentiles, and shalt suck the breasts of kings—For brass I will bring gold, and for iron I will bring silver;* under which he typically understands, "[4] wisdom, philosophy, eloquence, learning, and all the other arts and sciences, liberal and mechanical, wherewith the heathen shall be adorned, who are converted to the faith. So shall the gifts of nature be perfected by the gifts of grace, and *they* shall defend the Church who erstwhile attacked it."

15. *And so shall be the plague of the Lord &c.* "[4] So, when God sendeth the plague, all the irrational animals of Anti-Christ and his satellites shall perish, as the aforesaid men, who used them, perished. For, for the sins of men, God, to their greater confusion, sometimes slays their beasts, sometimes also for their loving correction." "[5] The imagery is from the Mosaic law of the ban. If a whole city became guilty of idolatry, not the inhabitants only, but the beasts were to be destroyed [6], so that here, in miniature, should be repeated the relation of the irrational to the rational part of the creation, according to which, for the sins of men, *the creature is*, against its will, *made subject to vanity.* Analogous is it also, that on the offence of Achan [7], beside him and his children, his oxen, asses and sheep were [stoned and] burned with him."

16. *Every one that is left of the nations.* God so gives the repentance, even through His visitations, that, in proportion to the largeness of the rebellion and the visitation upon it, shall be the largeness of the conversion. [8] *Jerusalem shall be trodden down of the Gentiles, until the times of the Gentiles shall be fulfilled.* And S. Paul, [9] *Blindness in part is happened to Israel, until the fullness of the Gentiles shall be come in; and so all Israel shall be saved.* Hitherto prophets had spoken of a [10] *remnant* of Jacob, who should *return to the mighty God*, and should be saved; now, upon this universal rebellion of the heathen. He foretells the conversion of a remnant of the heathen also.

Shall even go up from year to year to worship the King, the Lord of hosts. There is a harmony between the rebellion and the repentance. The converted shall go to worship God there, where they had striven to exterminate His worshipers. The prophet could only speak of the Gospel under the image of the law. *The Feast of Tabernacles* has its counterpart, not, like the Pascha or the Pentecost, in any single feast, but in the whole life of the Gospel. It was a thanksgiving for past deliverance; it was a picture of their pilgrim-life from the passage of the Red sea, until the parting of the Jordan opened to them the entrance to their temporary rest in Canaan [11]. "[12] In that vast, wide, terrible wilderness, where was no village, house, town, cave, it made itself tents, wherein to sojourn with wives and children, avoiding by day the burning sun, by night damp and cold and hurt from dew; and it was [13] *a statute forever in their generations; ye shall dwell in booths seven days; all, that are Israelites born, shall dwell in booths, that your generations may know, that I made the children of Israel to dwell in booths, when I brought them out of the land of Egypt.*" "[2] Much more truly do Christians keep the feast of tabernacles, not once in the year only, but continually, unceasingly. This is, what S. Peter admonisheth, [14] *Dearly beloved, I beseech you, as strangers and pilgrims, abstain from fleshly lusts.* And S. Paul often teacheth that we, like Abraham, are strangers on earth, but [15] *citizens* of heaven *with the saints, and of the household of God. Faith*, he says, [16] *is the substance of things hoped for, the evidence of things not seen. By*

[1] ver. 2. [2] Lap. [3] Is. lx. 16, 17. [4] Dion. [5] Hengst. [6] Deut. xiii. 15. [7] Josh. vii. 24, 25. [8] S. Luke xxi. 24. [9] Rom. xi. 25, 26. [10] Is. x. 21.

[11] See at greater length Hos. xii. 9. vol. i. p. 122. [12] S. Jer. [13] Lev. xxiii. 41–43. [14] 1 S. Pet. ii. 11. [15] Eph. ii. 19. [16] Heb. xi. 1, 9, 10.

Before CHRIST cir. 487.

a Is. 60. 12.

17 [a] And it shall be, *that*
whoso will not come up of
all the families of the earth
unto Jerusalem to worship
the King, the LORD of
hosts, even upon them shall
be no rain.
18 And if the family of

faith Abraham sojourned in the land of promise as in a strange country, dwelling in tabernacles with Isaac and Jacob, the heirs with him of the same promise; for he looked for a city which hath foundations, whose builder and maker is God." "[1] As long as we are in progress, in the course and militant, we dwell in tabernacles, striving with all our mind to pass from the tabernacles to the firm and lasting dwelling-place of the house of God. Whence also holy David said, [2] *I am a stranger with Thee and a sojourner, as all my fathers were.* So speaketh he, who is still in Egypt and yet placed in the world. But he who goeth forth out of Egypt, and entereth a desert from vices, holdeth his way and says in the Psalm, [3] *I will pass through to the place of the tabernacle of the Wonderful unto the house of God.* Whence also he says elsewhere, [4] *How amiable are Thy dwellings. Thou Lord of hosts; my soul longeth, yea, even fainteth for the courts of the Lord;* and a little after, [5] *Blessed are they who dwell in thy house, they shall be alway praising Thee.* [6] *The voice of rejoicing and salvation* is *in the tabernacles of the righteous.* [7] *One thing have I desired of the Lord, that will I seek after; that I may dwell in the house of the Lord all the days of my life, to behold the beauty of the Lord and to enquire in His temple.* Whoso dwelleth in such tabernacles, and hastes to go from the tabernacles to the court, and from the court to the house, and from the house to the temple of the Lord, ought to celebrate the feast of Tabernacles &c." It symbolizes how, "[8] in the New Testament, Christians, being delivered through Christ from the slavery to sin and satan, and sojourning in this vale of misery, by making progress in virtues go up to the home of the heavenly paradise, the door of glory being open by the merit of the Lord's Passion, and so the faithful of Christ celebrate the feast of tabernacles; and, after the destruction of Anti-Christ, they will celebrate it the more devoutly, as there will then be among them a fuller fervor of faith."

17. *Whoso will not go up.* "[9] To those who *go not up*, he threatens the same punishment as persecutors would endure. For enemies, and they who will not love, shall have the same lot. This is, I think, what Christ Himself said, [10] *Whoso is not with Me is against Me, and whoso gathereth not with Me scattereth.*"

Upon them there shall be no rain. Rain was the most essential of God's temporal gifts for the temporal well-being of His people. Moses marked out this, as his people were entering on the promised land, with recent memory of Egypt's independence of rain in Egypt itself, and that this gift depended on obedience. [11] *The land, whither thou goest in to possess it,* is *not as the land of Egypt, whence ye came out, where thou sowedst thy seed and wateredst* it *with thy foot, as a garden of herbs:* but *a land of hills and valleys,—it drinketh water of the rain of heaven; a land which the Lord thy God careth for; the eyes of the Lord* are *always upon it, from the beginning of the year even unto the end of the year. And it shall be, if ye shall hearken diligently unto My commandments—I will give* you *the rain of your land in its season, the first rain and the latter rain, that thou mayest gather in thy corn and thy wine and thine oil. And I will send grass in thy fields for thy cattle, that thou mayest eat and be full.* But the threat on disobedience corresponded therewith. [12] *Take heed to yourselves,* Moses continues, *that your heart be not deceived, and ye turn aside and serve other gods—and the Lord's wrath be kindled against you, and He shut up the heaven, that there be no rain, and that the land yield not her fruit, and ye perish quickly from off the good land, which the Lord giveth you;* and, [13] *Thy heaven, that* is *over thee, shall be brass, and the earth, that* is *under thee,* shall be *iron; the Lord shall make the rain of thy land powder and dust.* Amos speaks of the withdrawal of rain as one of God's chastisements [14]: the distress in the time of Ahab is pictured in the history of the woman of Sarepta [15], and Ahab's directions to Obadiah [16]. But it is also the symbol of spiritual blessings; both are united by Hosea [17] and Joel [18], as Joel and Amos also speak of spiritual blessings exclusively under the figure of temporal abundance [19]. In Isaiah it is simply a symbol, [20] *Drop down, ye heavens, from above, and let the skies pour down righteousness; let the earth open, and let them bring forth salvation, and let righteousness spring up together.*

18. *And if the family of Egypt go not up,*

[1] S. Jer. [2] Ps. xxxix. 12. [3] Ib. xli. 5. Vulg.
[4] Ib. lxxxiv. 1. [5] Ib. 4. [6] Ib. cxviii. 15.
[7] Ib. xxvii. 4. [8] Dion. [9] S. Cyr.
[10] S. Luke xi. 23. [11] De. xi. 10–15 [12] Ib. 16, 17.
[13] Ib. xxviii. 23, 24. [14] Am. iv. 7. See vol. i. p. 281.
[15] 1 Kgs xvii. 9–16. [16] Ib. xviii. 5.
[17] Hosea vi. 3 See vol. i. p. 64.
[18] Jo. ii. 23. See vol. i. pp. 190, 191.
[19] Jo. iii. 18. See vol. i. pp. 212–215. Am. ix. 13. See vol. i. p. 338.
[20] Is. xlv. 8. See also Ib. v. 6, both together Ib. xxx. 23.

Before CHRIST cir. 487.

Egypt go not up, and
come not, †[d]that *have* no
rain; there shall be the
plague, wherewith the
LORD will smite the heath-
en that come not up to keep
the feast of tabernacles.
19 This shall be the
||punishment of Egypt,
and the punishment of all

† Heb. *upon whom* there is *not.*

d Deut. 11. 10.

|| Or, *sin.*

Before CHRIST cir. 487.

and come not, that have *no* rain; rather, *and there shall not be*[1]. It may be that the prophet chose this elliptical form, as well knowing that the symbol did not hold as to Egypt, which, however it ultimately depended on the equatorial rains which overfilled the lakes which supply the Nile, did not need that fine arrangement of the rains of Autumn and Spring which were essential to the fruitfulness of Palestine. The omission leaves room for the somewhat prosaic supply of Jonathan, "The Nile shall not ascend to them." More probably the words are left undefined with a purposed abruptness, *there shall not be upon them,* viz. whatever they need: the omission of the symbol in these two verses might the more suggest, that it is a symbol only. Egypt, the ancient oppressor of Israel, is united with Judah as one, in the same worship of God, as Isaiah had said, [2]*In that day shall Israel be the third with Egypt and with Assyria;* and since it is united in the duty, so also in the punishment for despising it.

"[3]Let not Egypt be proud, that it is watered by the Nile, as if it needed no rain: i. e. let no one be secure in this life. For though we stand by faith, yet may we fall. For although bedewed by the efflux of Divine grace, and filled with its richness, yet if we give not thanks continually for such great gifts, God will count us as the rest, to whom such copious goodness never came. The safety of all then lies in this, that while we are in these tabernacles, we cherish the Divine benefits, and unceasingly praise the Lord, Who hath heaped such benefits upon us."

"[4]Under the one nation of the Egyptians, he understands those who are greatly deceived, and chose idolatry most unreasonably, to whom it will be a grave inevitable judgment, the pledge of destruction, that they despise the acceptable grace of salvation through Christ. For they are murderers of their own souls, if, when they could lay hold of eternal life and the Divine gentleness, open to all who will choose it and put off the burden of sin, they die in their errors; the stain and pollution from transgression and error uncleansed, although the Divine light illumined all around and called those in darkness to receive sight. Of each of these I would say, [5]*Better* is *an untimely birth than he; for he cometh in with vanity, and departeth in darkness, and his name shall be covered with darkness.* [6]*Good had it been for* them, *if* they *had never been born,* is the Saviour's word. That this is not said of the Egyptians only, but shall come true of all nations, who shall altogether be punished, if they are reckless of the salvation through Christ and honor not His festival, he will establish in these words;

19. *This shall be the sin of Egypt and the sin of all nations that come not up to keep the feast of tabernacles.* For before the coming of the Saviour, good perhaps had been in part the excuse of the heathen, that they had been called by none. For no one had preached unto them. Wherefore the Saviour also, pointing out this in the Gospel parables, said, [7]*the laborers,* called *at the eleventh hour, said, No man hath hired us.* But when Christ cast His light upon us, [8]*bound the strong man,* removed from his perverseness those subject to him, justified by faith those who came to Him, laid down His life for the life of all, they will find no sufficient excuse who admit not so reverend a grace. It will be true of the heathen too, if Christ said of them, [9]*If I had not come and spoken unto them, they had not had sin: but now they have no cloke for their sin.*"

The prophet says *sin,* not punishment[10], for sin includes *the punishment,* which is its

[1] The E. V., following Kim., takes ולא עליהם as a subordinate clause, "and there is not upon them," viz. rain at any time; but it is unnatural that, in two consecutive verses, the words should be taken in such divergent senses. The omission of ולא by the LXX., followed so far (as so often) by the Pesh., is supported only by 4 Kenn. MSS., against those in S. Jerome's time, and Symm. Theod. Jon., and is evidently a makeshift, followed by Ewald.

[2] Is. xix. 24. [3] Osor. [4] S. Cyr.

[5] Eccl. vi. 3, 4. [6] S. Matt. xxvi. 24. [7] Ib. xx. 7.

[8] Ib. xii. 29. [9] S. John xv. 22.

[10] The E. V. follows Kim. in rendering "punishment." Ges. combines the two in his rendering of אָשַׁם, n. 2 "culpam sustinuit," not in his "culpæ pœnas dedit." The rendering "shall be guilty" unites sin and punishment in his instances, Ps. xxxiv. 22, 23, Is. xxiv. 6, Jer. ii. 3, Hos. x. 2, [E. V., in the same sense, "shall be found faulty"] xiv. 1 [xiii. 16 Eng.] Pr. xxx. 10, ["be found guilty," E. V.] So also in חטא Lam. iii. 39, חַטָּאת Ib. iv. 6. When the Lord said, *It shall be more tolerable in the day of judgment for Sodom and Gomorrah than for that city,* He meant, that both guilt and punishment would be greater. In Is. v. 18, חַטָּאָה, and, Ib. xl. 2, חַטָּאת is "sin." So also עָוֹן Is. v. 18, Ps. xxxi. 11.

Before CHRIST cir. 487.

nations that come not up to
keep the feast of tabernacles.
20 ¶ In that day shall
there be upon the || bells of
the horses, [e] HOLINESS
UNTO THE LORD; and
the pots in the LORD'S
house shall be like the
bowls before the altar.
21 Yea, every pot in
Jerusalem and in Judah
shall be holiness unto the

|| Or, bridles.

e Isai. 23. 18.

Before CHRIST cir. 487.

due, and which it entails: it does not express the punishment, apart from the sin. It was *the sin* which comprised and involved all other sin, the refusal to worship God as He had revealed Himself, and to turn to Him. It was to say, [1] *We will not have* Him *to reign over us.*

20. *In that day there shall be upon the bells* [2] *of the horses, Holiness unto the Lord.* He does not say only, that they should be consecrated to God, as Isaiah says of Tyre, [3] *Her merchandise and her hire shall be holiness to the Lord;* he says that, *the bells of the horses,* things simply secular, should bear the same inscription as the plate on the high priest's forehead. Perhaps the comparison was suggested by the bells on the high priest's dress [4]; not the lamina only on his forehead, but bells (not as his, which were part of his sacred dress), bells, altogether secular, should be inscribed with the self-same title, whereby he himself was dedicated to God.

Holiness to the Lord. He does not bring down what is sacred to a level with common things, but he uplifts ordinary things, that they too should be sacred, as S. Paul says, [5] *whether ye eat or drink or whatsoever ye do, do all to the glory of God.*

And the pots of the Lord's house shall be like bowls before the altar. The pots are mentioned, together with other vessels of the Lord's house [6], but not in regard to any sacred use. They were used, with other vessels, for dressing the victims [7] for the partakers of the sacrifices. These were to be sacred, like those made for the most sacred use of all, *the bowls for sprinkling* [8], whence that sacrificial blood was taken, which was to make the typical atonement.

21. *And every pot in Jerusalem and in Judah shall be holiness to the Lord.* Everything is to be advanced in holiness. All the common utensils everywhere in the people of God shall not only be holy, but *holiness,* and capable of the same use as the vessels of the temple.

And there shall be no more the Canaanite in the house of the Lord of hosts. The actual Canaanite had long since ceased to be; the Gibeonites, the last remnant of them, had been absorbed among the people of God. But *all Israel* were not *of Israel.* Isaiah had called its princes and people, [9] *rulers of Sodom, people of Gomorrah.* Ezekiel had said, [10] *Thus saith the Lord God unto Jerusalem; Thy birth and thy nativity is of the land of Canaan; thy father was an Amorite, and thy mother a Hittite.* Hosea used at least the term of two-fold meaning, [11] *Canaan, in whose hands are the balances of deceit;* and Zephaniah, [12] *All the people of Canaan are destroyed.* After the time of the Canon, Daniel is introduced saying, "[13] O thou seed of Canaan and not of Judah." Ezekiel had spoken of ungodly priests, not only as uncircumcised in heart (according to the language of Deuteronomy [14]), but uncircumcised in flesh also, altogether alien from the people of God [15]. The prophet then speaks, as Isaiah, [16] *It shall be called the way of holiness; the unclean shall not pass over it,* and Joel, [17] *then shall Jerusalem be holy, and there shall no strangers pass through her any more.* This shall have its full fulfillment in the time of the end. [18] *There shall in no wise enter into it anything that defileth, neither* whatsoever *worketh abomination or a lie;* and, *without* are *dogs and sorcerers and whoremongers and murderers and idolaters, and whatsoever loveth and maketh a lie.*

"[19] Although born of the blood of Israel, those of old eagerly imitated the alien Canaanites. But after that the Only-Begotten Word of God came among us, and, having justified by faith, sealed with the Holy Spirit, those who came to His grace, our mind hath been steadfast, unshaken, fixed in piety. Nor will any one persuade those who are sanctified, to honor any other god

[1] S. Luke xix. 14.

[2] מְצִלָּה, ἁπ. Yet the rendering "bells" has the analogy of מְצִלְתַּיִם 1 Chr. xiii. xv. xvi. xxv. 2 Chr. v. xxix. Ezr. iii. 10, Neh. xii. 27. The other guesses, "bridles" (lxx. Syr.), "trappings of horses" [Jon.] or "warlike ornaments" (S. Jerome's Jewish teacher) have none; the βυθὸν of Aq. and περίπατον συσκιον of Symm. (as from מְצֻלוֹת) give no meaning.

[3] Is. xxiii. 18.

[4] פעמון Ex. xxviii. 34, xxxix. 25, 26, used of it only, and there only.

[5] 1 Cor. x. 31.

[6] Ez. xxxviii. 3, 1 Kgs vii. 45, 2 Kgs xxv. 14, 2 Chr. iv. 11, 16, Jer. lii. 18, 19.

[7] 2 Chr. xxxv. 13.

[8] מזרקים.

[9] Is. i. 10.

[10] Ezek. xvi. 3.

[11] Hosea xii. 7. See vol. i. p. 121.

[12] Zeph. i. 11. See ab. p. 244.

[13] Hist. of Sus. ver. 56.

[14] Deut. x. 16, xxx. 6.

[15] Ezek. xliv. 7.

[16] Is. xxxv. 8.

[17] Joel iii. 17. See vol. i. p. 211.

[18] Rev. xxi. 27, xxii. 15.

[19] S. Cyr.

Before CHRIST cir. 487.

LORD of hosts: and all they that sacrifice shall come and take of them, and seethe therein: and in that day there shall be no more the [f] Canaanite in [g] the house of the LORD of hosts.

Before CHRIST cir. 487.

f Isai. 35. 8. Joel 3. 17. Rev. 21. 27. & 22. 15.

g Eph. 2. 19, 20, 21, 22.

save Him Who is, by nature and in truth, God, Whom we have known in Christ. For in Himself He hath shewn us the Father, saying, [1] *He that hath seen Me hath seen the Father*. Wherefore *in that day*, i. e. at that time, he says, *there shall be no Canaanite*, i. e. alien and idolater, *in the house of the Lord Almighty*." "[2] But may the Almighty God bring the saying true at this time also, that no Canaanite should be seen among us, but that all should live according to the Gospel-laws, and await that blessed hope and the appearance of our great God and Saviour Jesus Christ, with Whom be glory to the Father with the Holy Ghost, now and ever and to endless ages. Amen."

[1] S. John xiv. 9.

[2] Theod.

Yet he probably bore a great part in the reformation, in which Nehemiah cöoperated outwardly, and to effect which, after he had, on the expiring of his 12 years of office [m], returned to Persia, he obtained leave to visit his own land again [n], apparently for a short time. For he mentions his obtaining that leave, in connection with abuses at Jerusalem, which had taken place in his absence, and which he began reforming, forthwith on his arrival. But three chief abuses, the neglect of God's service, the defilement of the priesthood and of their covenant, and the cruelty to their own Jewish wives, divorcing them to make way for idolatresses, are subjects of Malachi's reproofs. Nehemiah found these practices apparently rampant. It is not then probable that they had been, before, the subjects of Malachi's denunciation, nor were his own energetic measures probably fruitless, so that there should be occasion for these denunciations afterward. It remains, then, as the most probable, that Malachi, as the prophet, cöoperated with Nehemiah, as the civil authority, as Haggai and Zechariah had with Zerubbabel. "[o] So Isaiah cöoperated with Hezekiah; Jeremiah with Josiah. Of a mere external reformation there is no instance" in Jewish history.

It does not appear, whether Nehemiah, on his return, was invested by the king of Persia with extraordinary authority for these reforms, or whether he was appointed as their governor. The brief account affords no scope for the mention of it. It is not then any objection to the contemporaneousness of Malachi and Nehemiah, that, whereas Nehemiah, while governor, *required not the bread of the governor*, i. e. the allowance granted him by the Persian government, as an impost upon the people, Malachi upbraids the people that they would not offer to their governor the poor things which they offered to Almighty God, or that the governor would not accept it, in that it would be an insult rather than an act of respect. For 1) the question in Malachi is of a free-offering, not of an impost; 2) Nehemiah says that he did not *require it*, not that he would not accept it; 3) there is no evidence that he was now governor, nor 4) any reason why he should not accept in their improved condition, what he did not *require*, [p] *because the bondage was heavy upon this people.* Presents were, as they are still, a common act of courtesy in the East.

Like S. John Baptist, though afar off, he prepared the way of the Lord by the preaching of repentance. More than other prophets, he unveils priests and people to themselves, interprets their thoughts to them, and puts those thoughts in abrupt naked language, picturing them as demurring to every charge which he brought against them. They were not, doubtless, conscious hypocrites. For conscious hypocrisy is the sin of individuals, aping the graces which others possess and which they have not, yet wish to be held in estimation for having. Here, it is the mass which is corrupt. The true Israel are the exception; [q] *those who feared the Lord, the jewels of* Almighty God. It is the hypocrisy of self-deceit, contented with poor, limited, outward service, and pluming itself upon it. Malachi unfolds to them the meaning of their acts. His thesis is themselves, whom he unfolds to them. He interprets himself, putting into their mouths words, betokening a simple unconsciousness either of God's goodness or their own evil. [r] *Yet ye say, Wherein hast Thou loved us?* This was their inward thought, as it is the thought of all, ungrateful to God. But his characteristic is, that he puts these thoughts into abrupt, bold bad words, which might startle them for their hideousness, as if he would say, "This is what your acts mean." He exhibits the worm and the decay, which lay under the whited exterior. [s] *Ye say, Wherein have we despised Thy Name?* Perhaps, they were already learning, not to pronounce the proper Name of God, while they caused it to be despised. Or they pronounced it with reverent pause, while they shewed that they held cheap God and His service. [t] *Ye say, The table of the Lord* is *contemptible.* [u] *Ye say, the table of the Lord* is *polluted; and the fruit thereof, his meat,* is *contemptible.* Their acts said it. What a reading of thoughts! [v] *Ye said also, Behold, what a weariness!* It is the language of the heart in all indevotion. [w] *Ye say, Wherefore?* as if innocently unconscious of the ground of God's judgment. [x] *Wherein have we robbed Thee?* The language of those who count the earth as their own. [y] *Ye say, Wherein have we wearied* Him? *When ye say, Every one that doeth evil* is *good in the sight of the Lord, and in them doth He delight, or, Where is the God of judgment?* The heart's speech in all envy at the prosperity of the wicked!

Yet the object of all this unfolding them to themselves, is their repentance. We have already the self-righteousness of the Pharisees, and the Sadducees' denial of God's Providence. And we have already the voice of S. John Baptist, *of the wrath to come.* They professed to [z] *delight* in the coming of *the messenger of the covenant;* yet their deeds were such as would be burned up with the fire of His Coming, not, rewarded.

Pharisees and Sadduces are but two offshoots of the same ungodliness; Pharisees,

[m] Neh. v. 14. [n] Ib. xiii. 6. [o] Hengst. Christ. iii. 583. [p] Neh. v. 18. [q] Mal. iii. 16. [r] i. 2. [s] i. 6.

[t] Ib. 7. [u] Ib. and 12. [v] Ib. 13. [w] ii. 14. [x] iii. 8. [y] ii. 17. [z] iii. 1. iv. 1.

while they hoped by outward acts to be in favor with God, they become, at least, secret Sadducees, when the hope fails. First, they justify themselves. God had said to them, [a] *Ye are departed out of the way: I have made you base, as ye have not kept My ways.* They say [b], *It is vain to serve God; and what profit, that we have kept His ordinance?* (affirming that they had done, what God called them to repentance for not doing). God said [c], *Ye have covered the altar of the Lord with tears,* the tears of their wronged wives; they insist on their own austerities, [b] *we have walked mournfully before the Lord our God.* Then comes the Sadducee portion. God had called them to obedience and said, [d] *Prove Me now herewith: they say,* [e] *the workers of wickedness have proved God, and are saved.* God promised, [f] *All nations shall call you blessed;* they answer, [g] *and now we call the proud blessed. What have we spoken against Thee?* is the last self-justifying question, which Malachi records of them; and this, while reproaching God for the uselessness of serving Him, and choosing the lot of those who rejected Him.

Thereon Malachi abandons this class to their own blindness. There was hope amid any sin, however it rebelled against God. This was a final denial of God's Providence and rejection of Himself. So Malachi closes with the same prophecy, with which S. John Baptist prepared our Lord's coming, *His* [h] *fan is in His hand, and He will thoroughly purge His floor, and will gather the wheat into His garner, but the chaff He shall burn with fire unquenchable.* The unspeakable tenderness of God toward *those who fear His name,* and the severity to those who finally rebel, are perhaps nowhere more vividly declared, than in these closing words of the Old Testament. Yet the love of God, as ever, predominates; and the last prophet closes with the word "Remember," and with one more effort to avert the curse which they were bringing upon themselves. Yet no prophet declares more expressly the rejection of the people, to whom he came to minister, the calling of the Gentiles, the universal worship, in all the earth, of Him Who was hitherto worshiped by the Jews only; and that, not at Jerusalem, but each offering, in his own place, the sacrifice which hitherto (as they had recently experienced, in their captivity at Babylon) could be offered up in Jerusalem only. To him alone it was reserved to prophesy of the unbloody Sacrifice, which should be offered unto God *in every place* throughout the world *from the rising of the sun unto the going down thereof.* It has been said, "[i] Malachi is like a late evening, which closes a long day, but he is at the same time the morning twilight which bears in its bosom a glorious day."

"[k] When Prophecy was to be withdrawn from the ancient Church of God, its last light was mingled with the rising beams of *the Sun of Righteousness.* In one view it combined a retrospect of the Law with the clearest specific signs of the Gospel advent. [l] *Remember ye the law of Moses My servant, which I commanded him in Horeb, for all Israel,* with *the statutes and the judgments. Behold I will send you Elijah the prophet, before the great and dreadful day of the Lord.* Prophecy had been the oracle of Judaism and of Christianity, to uphold the authority of the one, and reveal the promise of the other. And now its latest admonitions were like those of a faithful departing minister, embracing and summing up his duties. Resigning its charge to the *personal* Precursor of Christ, it expired with the Gospel upon its lips."

A school, which regards the "prophets" chiefly as "poets," says that "the language is prosaic, and manifests the decaying spirit of prophecy." The office of the prophets was, to convey in forceful words, which God gave them, His message to His people. The poetic form was but an accident. God, Who knows the hearts of His creatures whom He has made, knows better than we, why He chose such an instrument. Zechariah, full of imagination, He chose some years before. But He preserved in history the account of the words which Zechariah spoke, not the words wherewith he urged the rebuilding of the temple, in his own book. Had Malachi spoken in imaginative language, like that of Ezekiel, to whom God says, [m] *thou art unto them like a very lovely song of one that hath a pleasant voice and can play well on an instrument, and they hear thy words and they do them not,* it may be that they would have acted then, as they did in the time of Ezekiel. It may be, that times like those of Malachi, apathetic, self-justifying, murmuring, self-complacent, needed a sterner, abrupter, more startling voice to awaken them. *Wisdom was justified of her children.* God wrought by him a reformation for the time being: He gave through him a warning to the generation, when our Lord should come, that He should come, as their Judge as well as their Saviour, and, how they should stand in the day of His

[a] ii. 8, 9. [b] iii. 14.
[c] ii. 13. [d] iii. 10 וּבְחָנוּנִי [e] iii. 15. בָּחֲנוּ
[f] ואשרו אתכם iii. 12.
[g] אנחנו מאשרים iii. 15. These last contrasts are Hengstenberg's Christ. iii. 597. ed. 2.
[h] S. Luke iii. 17.
[i] Nägelsbach in Herzog Real-Encycl.

[k] Davison on prophecy pp. 456, 457. "Malachi, the last of the prophets, as in order, so in time; and even for that reason, by me chosen to fix my thoughts on, before others, because nearest, therefore, in conjunction with the Gospel; to which it leads us by the hand, and delivers us over; for that begins, where he ends." Pococke, Dedication.
[l] iv. 4. [m] Ezek. xxxiii. 32.

MALACHI.

Before CHRIST cir. 397.

CHAPTER I.

1 *Malachi complaineth of Israel's unkindness,* 6 *Of their irreligiousness,* 12 *and profaneness.*

THE burden of the word
of the LORD to Israel
†by Malachi.
2 [a]I have loved you,
saith the LORD. Yet ye
say, Wherein hast thou
loved us? *Was* not Esau
Jacob's brother? saith the
LORD: yet [b]I loved
Jacob.
3 And I hated Esau,
and [c]laid his mountains

† Heb. *by the hand of Malachi.*
[a] Deut. 7. 8. & 10. 15.

Before CHRIST cir. 397.

[b] Rom. 9. 13.
[c] Jer. 49. 18. Ezek. 35. 3, 4, 7, 9, 14, 15. Obad. 10, &c.

CHAP. I. 1. *The burden of the word of the Lord to Israel.* "[1]The word of the Lord is heavy, because it is called a *burden,* yet it hath something of consolation, because it is not 'against,' but *to Israel.* For it is one thing when we write *to* this or that person; another, when we write 'against' this or that person; the one being the part of friendship, the other, the open admission of enmity."

By the hand of Malachi; through him, as the instrument of God, deposited with him; as S. Paul speaks of [2]*the dispensation of the Gospel,* [3]*the word of reconciliation,* [4]*the Gospel of the uncircumcision,* being *committed* to him.

2. *I have loved you, saith the Lord.* What a volume of God's relations to us in two simple words, *I-have-loved you*[5]. So would not God speak, unless He still loved. "I have loved and do love you," is the force of the words. When? and since when? In all eternity God loved; in all our past, God loved. Tokens of His love, past or present, in good or seeming ill, are but an effluence of that everlasting love. He, the Unchangeable, ever loved, as the Apostle of love says; [6]*we love Him, because He first loved us.* The deliverance from the bondage of Egypt, the making them His [7]*peculiar people, the adoption, the covenant, the giving of the law, the service of God and His promises,* all the several mercies involved in these, the feeding with manna, the deliverance from their enemies whenever they returned to Him, their recent restoration, the gift of the prophets, were so many single pulses of God's everlasting love, uniform in itself, manifold in its manifestations. But it is more than a declaration of His everlasting love. "I have loved *you;*" God would say; with "[8]a special love, a more than ordinary love, with greater tokens of love, than to others." So God brings to the penitent soul the thought of its ingratitude: I have loved *you:* I, you. *And ye have said, Wherein hast Thou loved us?* It is a characteristic of Malachi to exhibit in all its nakedness man's ingratitude. This is the one voice of all men's murmurings, ignoring all God's past and present mercies, in view of the one thing which He withholds, though they dare not put it into words: *Wherein hast Thou loved us?* [9]*Within a while they forgat His works, and the wonders that He had shewed them:* [10]*they made haste, they forgat His works.*

Was not Esau Jacob's brother! saith the Lord: and I loved Jacob, and Esau have I hated. "[11]While they were yet in their mother's womb, before any good or evil deserts of either, God said to their mother, [12]*The elder shall serve the younger.* The hatred was not a proper and formed hatred, (for God could not hate Esau before he sinned) but only a lesser love," which, in comparison to the great love for Jacob, seemed as if it were not love. "[11]So he says, [13]*The Lord saw that Leah* was *hated;* where Jacob's neglect of Leah, and lesser love than for Rachel, is called 'hatred;' yet Jacob did not literally hate Leah, whom he loved and cared for as his wife." This greater love was shewn in preferring the Jews to the Edomites, giving to the Jews His law, Church, temple, prophets, and subjecting Edom to them; and especially in the recent deliverance, "[11]He does not speak directly of predestination, but of prælection, to temporal goods." God gave both nations alike over to the Chaldees for the punishment of their sins; but the Jews He brought back, Edom He left unrestored.

3. *And I made his mountains a waste, and his heritage for the jackals*[14] *of the wilderness.*

[1] S. Jer. [2] 1 Cor. ix. 17, Tit. i. 3. [3] 2 Cor. v. 19.
[4] Gal. ii. 7. · 1 Tim. 18. [5] אהבתי אתכם.
[6] 1 S. John iv. 19. [7] Rom. ix. 4. [8] Poc.
[9] Ps. lxxviii. 11. [10] Ib. cvi. 13. [11] Lap.
[12] Gen. xxv. 23. [13] Ib. xxix. 31.
[14] תנות, in this fem. form, is but a variation from the form elsewhere, תנים, as we have אַיָּל and אַיֶּלֶת, Ewald. Lehrb. n. 147b. p. 458. ed. 8. Ges.'s rendering "dwellings" (after the LXX. δώματα ἐρήμου, and Syr.) fails in many ways. The Arab תַּנָאָה which he, after Pococke, compares, is a nomen actionis, "a remaining, staying, dwelling, abiding [in a country, town, place], not "the dwelling" itself. 2) he supposes תַּנּוֹת to be = תַּנְאוֹת (with dag. forte euphon.) as מִקְשָׁה for מִקְשָׁאָה, כִּכְלָה for מִכְלָאָה," (see Rod. in Ges. Thes.) But this would be to derive it from תנא, with the characteristics of תנן and none of תנא. 3) "dwellings of the

Before CHRIST cir. 397.

and his heritage waste for
the dragons of the wilderness.
4 Whereas Edom saith,
We are impoverished, but
we will return and build
the desolate places; thus
saith the LORD of hosts,
They shall build, but I
will throw down; and they
shall call them, The border
of wickedness, and, The
people against whom the
LORD hath indignation for
ever.
5 And your eyes shall
see, and ye shall say,
[d] The LORD will be magnified || † from the border of
Israel.

Before CHRIST cir. 397.

d Ps. 35. 27.
|| Or, *upon*.
† Heb. *from upon*.

Malachi attests the first stage of fulfillment of Joel's prophecy, [1] *Edom shall be a desolate wilderness.* In temporal things, Esau's blessing was identical with Jacob's; *the fatness of the earth and of the dew of heaven from above;* and the rich soil on the terraces of its mountain-sides, though yielding nothing now except a wild beautiful vegetation, and its deep glens, attest what they once must have been, when artificially watered and cultivated. The first desolation must have been through Nebuchadnezzar [2] in his expedition against Egypt, when he subdued Moab and Ammon; and Edom lay in his way, as Jeremiah had foretold [3].

4. *Whereas Edom saith* [4], *We are impoverished* [5], or, more probably, *we were crushed.* Either gives an adequate sense. Human self-confidence will admit anything, as to the past; nay, will even exaggerate past evil to itself, "Crush us how they may, we will arise and repair our losses." So Ephraim said of old, "[6] *in the pride and stoutness of heart, The bricks are fallen down, but we will build with hewn-stones: the sycamores are cut down, but we will change* them into *cedars.* It is the one language of what calls itself, "indomitable;" in other words, "untameable," conquerors or every other gambler; "we will repair our losses." All is again staked and lost.

They shall call them the border of wickedness. Formerly it had its own proper name, *the border of Edom*, as other countries, [7] *all the border of Egypt*, [8] *the border of Moab*, [9] *the whole border of Israel*, [10] *the border of Israel*, [11] *the whole border of the Amorite.* Henceforth it should be known no more by its own name; but as *the border of wickedness*, where wickedness formerly dwelt, and hence the judgment of God and desolation from Him came upon it, "an accursed land." Somewhat in like way Jeremiah says of Jerusalem, [12] *Many nations shall pass by this city, and they shall say, every man to his neighbor, Wherefore hath the Lord done this unto this great city? Then they shall answer, Because they have forsaken the covenant of the Lord their God, and worshiped other gods and served them.* Only Israel would retain its name, as it has; Edom should be blotted out wholly and for ever.

5. *And your eyes shall see.* Malicious pleasure in looking on at the misery of Judæa and Jerusalem, had been a special sin of Edom: now God would shew Judah the fruit of its reversal, and His goodness toward themselves. "[13] Ye have assurance of His love toward you and providence over you, when ye see that ye are returned to your own land, and can inhabit it, but they cannot do this: but *they build and I throw down*, and ye therefore praise and magnify My name for this, and ye shall say, *The Lord shall be magnified on the border of Israel*, i. e. His greatness shall be always manifest upon you;" high above and exalted over the border of Israel [14], which shall retain its name, while Edom shall have ceased to be. Wickedness gives its name to Edom's border, as in Zechariah's vision it was removed and settled in Babylon [15].

wilderness," is the contradictory of what is meant, complete desolation. [1] Joel iii. 19. vol. i. pp. 214, 215.

[2] Jos. Ant. x. 11. See vol. i. on Obad. 16. p. 362.

[3] Jer. xxv. 9, 21.

[4] תאמר, Edom, for Idumæa, and so fem.

[5] So Jon. and Syr. here κατέστραπται, LXX: destructi sumus, Vulg. R. Tanchum gives both, here and on Jer. v. 17, and Sal. b. Mel. here out of Kim. on Jer. v. 17," Poc. On Jerem., Tanchum says the meaning "cut off" suits best the mention of the sword. Perhaps רשש may be = רצץ, and תרשׁישׁ, "Tarshish," may be so called, as a boast, "she crushes." Syr., in Jerem. also has "impoverished;" Jon. "destroy;" S. Jer. "conteret." The αλοήσουσι of the LXX. probably implies a misreading, ידשׁשׁ.

[6] Is. ix. 9, 10. [7] Ex. x. 14, 19. [8] De. ii. 18.

[9] 1 Sam. xi. 3, 7, xxvii. 1, 1 Chr. xxi. 12.

[10] 2 Chr. xi. 13. [11] Jud. xi. 22.

[12] Jer. xxii. 8, 9. Comp. Deut. xxix. 23–28.

[13] Tanchum in Poc. here. Tanchum gives, as constructions of others, "the Lord, Who protecteth the border of Israel," or "ye from the border of Israel," or, "it had been fitting that ye should do this and abide in it; but ye have done the contrary," as he explains afterward.

[14] מעל, as in Eccl. v. 7, גָּבֹהַּ מֵעַל גָּבֹהַּ "One high from above the high;" Ezek. i. 25. "a voice from the firmament (מעל) from above their heads," Gen. i. 7, "the waters above the firmament."

[15] Zech. v. 8, 11.

Before CHRIST cir. 397.

e Ex. 20. 12.
f Luke 6. 46.

6 ¶ A son [e] honoreth *his* father, and a servant his master: [f] if then I *be* a father, where *is* mine honor? and if I *be* a master, where *is* my fear? saith the LORD of hosts unto you, O priests, that despise my

6. *A son honoreth his father, and a slave his lord.* Having spoken of the love of God, he turns to the thanklessness of man. God appeals to the first feelings of the human heart, the relation of parent and child, or, failing this, to the natural self-interest of those dependent on their fellow-men. *A son* by the instinct of nature, by the unwritten law written in the heart, *honoreth his father.* If he fail to do so, he is counted to have broken the law of nature, to be an unnatural son. If he is, what by nature he ought to be, he does really honor him. He does not even speak of love, as to which they might deceive themselves. He speaks of *honor*, outward reverence only; which whoso sheweth not, would openly condemn himself as an unnatural son, a bad slave. "Of course," the Jews would say, "children honor parents, and slaves their masters, but what is that to us?" God turns to them their own mental admission.

If I am a Father. "[1] Although, before ye were born, I began to love you in Jacob as sons, yet choose by what title ye will name Me: I am either your Father or your Lord. If a Father, render me the honor due to a father, and offer the piety worthy of a parent. If a Lord, why despise ye Me? why fear ye not your Lord?" God was their Father by creation, as He is Father of all, as Creator of all. He had come to be their Father in a nearer way, by temporal redemption and adoption as His peculiar people, creating them to be a nation to His glory. This they were taught to confess in their psalmody, [2] *He hath made us, and not we ourselves; we are His people and the sheep of His pasture.* This title God had given them in sight of the Egyptians, [3] *Israel is My son, My firstborn:* of this Hosea reminded them; [4] *When Israel was a child, then I loved him, and called My son out of Egypt;* and Jeremiah reassured them, [5] *I am a Father to Israel and Ephraim is My first-born:* this, Isaiah had pleaded to God; [6] *Doubtless Thou art our Father, though Abraham be ignorant of us, and Israel acknowledge us not. Thou, O Lord, art our Father, our Redeemer, Thy name is from everlasting.* [7] *And now, O Lord, Thou* art *our Father; we the clay, and Thou our potter; and we all, the work of Thy hands.* God had impressed this His relation of Father, in Moses' prophetic warning; [8] *Do ye thus requite the Lord, O foolish people and unwise? Is not He thy Father that hath bought thee? hath He not made thee and established thee?* "[9] God is the *Father* of the faithful; 1) by creation; 2) by preservation and governance; 3) by alimony; 4) by fatherly care and providence; 5) by faith and grace, whereby He justifies and adopts us as sons and heirs of His kingdom."

If I am a Father. He does not throw doubt, that He is our Father; but, by disobedience, we in deeds deny it. Our life denies what we in words profess. *Where is My honor?* "[10] Why obey ye not My precepts, nor honor Me with acts of adoration; praying, praising, giving thanks, sacrificing, and reverently fulfilling every work of God? For [11] *cursed is he that doeth the work of the Lord deceitfully.*"

And if I am your Lord, "as I certainly am, and specially by singular providence." "[12] He is our Lord by the same titles, that He is our Father, and by others, as that He has redeemed us, and purchased us to Himself by the Blood of His Son; that He is the Supreme Majesty, Whom all creation is bound to serve; that, setting before us the reward of eternal glory, He has hired us as servants and laborers into His vineyard." God Alone is Lord through universal sovereignty, underived authority, and original source of laws, precepts, rights; and all other lords are but as ministers and instruments, compared to Him, the Lord and original Doer of all. Hence He says, [13] *I am the Lord; that is My Name, and My glory will I not give to another.*

Where is My fear? which ought to be shewn Me. "[14] If thou art a servant, render to the Lord the service of fear; if a son, shew to thy Father the feeling of piety. But thou renderest not thanks, neither lovest nor fearest God. Thou art then either a contumacious servant or a proud son." "[12] Fear includes reverence, adoration, sacrifice, the whole worship of God." "[15] Whoso feareth is not over-curious, but adores; is not inquisitive, but praises, and glorifies."

"[10] Fear is twofold; servile, whereby punishment, not fault, is dreaded; filial, by which fault is feared. In like way service is twofold. A servant with a service of fear, purely servile, does not deserve to be called

1 S. Jer, 2 Ps. c. 3
3 Ex. iv. 22. 4 Hos. xi. 1. See vol. i. p. 109.
5 Jer. xxxi. 9. 6 Is. lxiii. 16. 7 Ib. lxiv. 8.
8 Deut. xxxii. 6. 9 Lap.

10 Dion. 11 Jer. xlviii. 10. 12 Lap. 13 Is. xlii. 8.
14 Lap. as from S. Ambr.
15 S. Chyrs. de Incompr. Dei. Hom. ii. T. 1. p. 459. Ben.

Before CHRIST cir. 397.

name. [g]And ye say, Wherein have we despised thy name?

g ch. 2. 14, 17. & 3. 7, 8, 13.

7 ‖Ye offer [h] polluted bread upon mine altar; and ye say, Wherein have

‖ Or, Bring unto, &c.

h Deut. 15. 21.

a son of God, nor is in a state of salvation, not having love. Whence Christ, distinguishing such a servant from a son of God by adoption, saith, [1] *The servant abideth not in the house forever, but the son abideth ever:* and again, [2] *The servant knoweth not what his Lord doeth.* But a servant, whose service is of pure and filial love, is also a son, of whom the Saviour saith, [3] *Well done, good and faithful servant, enter thou into the joy of thy Lord.* But since a distinction is made here between the son and the servant, he seems to be speaking of servile fear, which, although it doth not good well and meritoriously, i. e. with a right intention and from love, yet withdraws from ill, and is the beginning of wisdom, because it disposeth to grace. Whence it is written, '[4] The fear of the Lord driveth away sins,' and again Scripture saith, [5] *By the fear of the Lord men depart from evil.*"

"[6] God requireth to be feared as a Lord, honored as a Father, loved as a Husband. Which is chiefest of these? Love. Without this, fear has torment, honor has no grace. Fear, when not enfreed by love, is servile. Honor, which cometh not from love, is not honor, but adulation. Honor and glory belong to God Alone; but neither of them will God accept, unless seasoned with the honey of love."

Saith the Lord unto you, O priests, who despise My Name, lit. *despisers of My Name,* habitually beyond others. The contempt of God came specially from those bound most to honor him. Priests, as consecrated to God, belonged especially to God. "[7] Malachi begins his prophecy and correction by the correction of the priests; because the reformation of the state and of the laity hangs upon the reformation of the clergy and the priest; for [8] *as is the priest, such also is the people.*" He turns, with a suddenness which must have been startling to them, to them as the centre of the offending.

And ye say, Wherein have we despised Thy Name? Before, it was ignorance of God's love: now it is ignorance of self and of sin. They affect to themselves innocence and are unconscious of any sin. They said to themselves doubtless, (as many do now) "we cannot help it; we do the best we can, under the circumstances." Without some knowledge of God's love, there can be no sense of sin; without some sense of sin, no knowledge of His love. They take the defensive, they are simply surprised, like Cain, [9] *Am I my brother's keeper?* or many of the lost in the Day of judgment, [10] *Many will say to Me in that day, Lord, Lord, have we not prophesied in Thy Name? and in Thy Name have cast out devils? and in Thy Name done many wonderful works?* and yet were all the while *workers of iniquity,* to whom He will say, *I never knew you:* and, [11] *Lord, when saw we Thee an hungered, or athirst, or a stranger, or naked, or sick, or in prison, and did not minister unto Thee?* And yet they *shall go away into everlasting punishment.*

7. *Offering polluted bread upon Mine altar.* This, continuing on the words, *despisers of My Name*[12], is the answer to their question, *Wherein have we despised Thy Name? Bread* might stand, in itself, either for the shewbread, or for the "minchah," meal-offering, which was the necessary accompaniment of sacrifices and sometimes the whole. But here the *polluted bread* cannot be the shewbread, since this was not put upon the altar, but upon its own table; and although the altar is, as here, also called "a table[13]" in regard to the sacrifice hereon consumed, "the table" of the shewbread is nowhere called "altar." The prophet then means by *bread,* either the meal-offering, as representing the sacrifice, or the offerings by fire altogether, as in Ezekiel, [14] *When ye offer My bread, the fat and the blood;* and in Leviticus, [15] *the offerings of the Lord, made by fire, the bread of their God, do they offer;* and of the *peace-offering*[16], *the priest shall burn it upon the altar; the bread of the offering made by fire unto the Lord:* and specifically, of animals with blemish, as these, it is forbidden, [17] *Neither from a*

[1] S. John viii. 35. [2] Ib. xv. 15.
[3] S. Matt. xxv. 21, 23. [4] Ecclus. i. 21. [5] Pr. xvi. 6.
[6] S. Bern. Serm. 83 in Cant. n. 4. Opp. i. 1560 Ben. Lap. [7] Lap. [8] Hos. iv. 9. [9] Gen. iv. 9.
[10] S. Matt. vii. 22, 23. [11] Ib. xxv. 44, 46.

[12] The collocation of מגישים is probably subordinate to the verb, expressed in the question, *ye despise, offering;* as the participle often is to the expressed finite verb. Nu. xxvi. 27. Jud. viii. 4. Ps. vii. 3. lxxviii. 4, Job xiv. 20, xxiv. 5, Ezr. x. 1, Jer. xliii. 2 (instances out of those in Ewald Lehrb. § 341. *b* 3. p. 836. ed. 3.) This case is however more developed than the rest, as not being contemporaneous only, but in explanation of that expressed by the finite verb. הגיש is used with ל, of offerings to God, Am. v 25, Mal. ii. 12; with על, here only.

[13] In Ezek. xli. 22, the "altar" is called *the table that is before the Lord,* and in regard to the offering of the sacrifice, it is said, *they shall come near to my table,* Ezek. xli. 15, 16. [14] Ezek. xliv. 7.

[15] Lev. xxi. 6: more briefly, *the bread of thy God,* ib. 8, *of his God,* ib. 17 and (parallel with *to offer the offerings of the Lord made by fire,*) 21; *to eat the bread of his God* (in contrast with offering it) ib. 22, and in Nu. xxxiii. 2, "*thy offering, thy bread for thy sacrifices made by fire, shall ye observe to offer to Me.*"
[16] Lev. iii. 11. [17] Ib. xxii. 25.

Before CHRIST cir. 397.

we polluted thee? In that
ye say, [i] The table of the
LORD *is* contemptible.
8 And [k] if ye offer the
blind † for sacrifice, *is it*
not evil? and if ye offer
the lame and sick, *is it* not
evil? offer it now unto thy
governor; will he be
pleased with thee, or [l] accept thy person? saith the
LORD of hosts.

[i] Ezek. 41. 22. ver. 12.
[k] Lev. 22. 22. Deut. 15. 21. ver. 14.
† Heb. *to sacrifice.*
[l] Job 42. 8.

stranger's hand shall ye offer the bread of your God of any of these, because their corruption is in them, blemishes in them: they shall not be accepted for you. It was, as it were, a feast of God with man, and what was withdrawn from the use of man by fire, was, as it were, consumed by God, to Whom it was offered.

It was *polluted*, in that it was contrary to the law of God which forbade to sacrifice any animal, *lame or blind* or with *any ill blemish*, as being inconsistent with the typical perfection of the sacrifice. Even the Gentiles were careful about the perfection of their sacrifices.

"[1] Blind is the sacrifice of the soul, which is not illumined by the light of Christ. Lame is *his* sacrifice of prayer, who comes with a double mind to entreat the Lord." "[2] He offereth one weak, whose heart is not established in the grace of God, nor by the anchor of hope fixed in Christ. These words are also uttered against those who, being rich, offer to the Creator the cheaper and least things, and give small alms."

And ye say, Wherewith have we polluted Thee[3]? It is a bold expression. Yet a word, to which we are but too ill-accustomed, which expresses what most have done, "dishonor God," comes to the same. Though less bold in expression, they are yet like in meaning. [4] *Will ye pollute Me any more among My people?* or, [5] *that My Name should not be polluted before the heathen.* [6] *My holy Name shall Israel no more defile;* [7] *I will not let them pollute My Name any more.* "[8] Much more in the new law, in which the Sacrifice is Christ Himself our God, whence the Apostle says expressly, [9] *Whoso eateth this bread and drinketh* this *Cup of the Lord unworthily, shall be guilty of the Body and Blood of the Lord.* "[1] For when the Sacraments are violated, Himself, Whose Sacraments they are, is violated." God speaks of our acts with an unveiled plainness, which we should not dare to use. "[2] As we are said to *sanctify God*, when we minister to Him in holiness and righteousness, and so, as far as in us lies, shew that He is holy; so we are said to *pollute* Him, when we conduct ourselves irreverently and viciously before Him, especially in His worship, and thereby, as far as in us lies, shew that He is not holy and is to be dishonored."

In that ye say, the table of the Lord is contemptible, lit. *contemptible is it*[10], and so any contemptible thing might be offered on it. They said this probably, not in words, but in deeds. Or, if in words, in plausible words. "[11] God doth not require the ornamenting of the altar, but the devotion of the offerers." "[1] What good is it, if we offer the best? Be what we offer, what it may, it is all to be consumed by fire." "[8] The pretext at once of avarice and gluttony!" And so they kept the best for themselves. They were poor, on their return from the captivity. Anyhow, the sacrifices *were* offered. What could it matter to God? And so they dispensed with God's law.

"[12] So at this day we see some priests and prelates, splendid in their tables and feasts, sordid in the altar and temple; on the table are costly napkins and wine; on the Altar torn linen and wine-mace[13] rather than wine." "[1] We pollute the bread, that is, the Body of Christ, when we approach the Altar unworthily, and, being defiled, drink that pure Blood, and say, *The table of the Lord is contemptible;* not that any one dareth to say this, but the deeds of sinners pour contempt on the Table of God."

8. *And if ye offer the blind for sacrifice, is it not evil?* Others, *it is not evil*, as we should say, "there is no harm in it." Both imply, alike, an utter unconsciousness on the part of the offerer, that it was evil: the one, in irony, that this was always their answer, "there is nothing amiss;" the other is an indignant question, "is there indeed nought amiss?" And this seems the most natural.

The sacrifice of the *blind* and *lame* was expressly forbidden in the law[14], and the sick in manifold varieties of animal disease. *Whatever hath a blemish ye shall not offer,*

[1] S. Jer. [2] Dion.

[3] The conj. גאל occurs only here: the pass. נגאל, here and 12, Ezr. ii. 62, Neh. vii. 64, in one idiom.

[4] Ezek. xiii. 19. [5] Ib. xx. 9, 14, 22. [6] Ib. xliii. 7. [7] Ib. xxxix. 7. [8] Lap.

[9] 1 Cor. xi. 27.

[10] נבזה הוא; the noun being prefixed absolutely, as in Gen. xxxiv. 21, "*these men, peaceful* are *they*," Ib. xlii. 11; "*all of us, sons of one man* are *we*." Ewald n. 297. *b.* pp. 761, 762.

[11] Remig.

[12] Lap. referring to Card. Bellarmine de gemitu columbæ.

[13] "villum ("the refuse of kernels and skins,"), potius quam vinum."

[14] Deut. xv. 21.

Before CHRIST cir. 397.

9 And now, I pray you,
beseech † God that he will
be gracious unto us: [m] this
hath been † by your means:
will he regard your per-
sons? saith the LORD of
hosts.
10 Who *is there* even
among you that would shut
the doors *for nought?*
[n] neither do ye kindle *fire*
on mine altar for nought.
I have no pleasure in you,
saith the LORD of hosts,
[o] neither will I accept an
offering at your hand.

† Heb. *the face of God.*
m Hos. 13. 9.
† Heb. *from your hand.*
n 1 Cor. 9. 13
o Isai. 1. 11. Jer. 6. 20. Amos 5. 21.

[1] *blind or* with limb *broken, or wounded or mangy or scabby or scurfy.* Perfectness was an essential principle of sacrifice; whether, as in the daily sacrifice, or the sin or trespass-offering, typical of the all-perfect Sacrifice, or in the whole-burnt-offering, of the entire self-oblation. But these knew better than God, what was fit for Him and them. His law was to be modified by circumstances. He would not be so particular, (as men now say so often.)

Is it then fit to offer to God what under the very same circumstances man would not offer to man? Against these idle, ungrateful, covetous thoughts God saith,

Offer it now unto thy governor. He appeals to our own instinctive thought of propriety to our fellow creature, which may so often be a test to us. No one would think of acting to a fellow-creature, as they do to Almighty God. Who would make diligent preparation to receive any great one of the earth, and turn his back upon him, when come? Yet what else is the behavior of most Christians after Holy Communion? If thou wouldest not do this to a mortal man, who is but dust and ashes, how much less to God Almighty, the King of kings and Lord of lords! "[2] The words are a reproof to those most negligent persons, who go through their prayers to God without fear, attention, reverence or feeling; but if they have to speak to some great man, prelate or prince, approach him with great reverence, speak carefully and distinctly and are in awe of him. Do not thou prefer the creature to the Creator, man to God, the servant to the Lord, and that Lord, so exalted and so Infinite."

9. *And now entreat, I pray you, God* [3], *that He will be gracious unto you.* This is not a call to repentance, for he assumes that God would not accept them. It is rather irony; "go now, seek the favor of God, as ye would not that of your governor." *From your hand,* not from your fathers, not from aliens, *hath this been: will He accept persons from you?* The unusual construction seems to imply a difference of meaning; as if he would say, that it consisted not with the justice of God, that He should be an *accepter of persons,* (which He declares that He is not) which yet He would be, were He to accept them, while acting thus.

10. *Who* is there *even among you?* This stinginess in God's service was not confined to those offices which cost something, as the sacrifices. Not even services absolutely costless, which required only a little trouble, as that of closing the folding-doors of the temple or the outer court, or bringing the fire to consume the sacrifices, would they do without some special hire. All was mercenary and hireling service. Others have rendered it as a wish, *who is there among you!* i. e. would that there were one among you, who would close the doors altogether; so shall ye not kindle fire on Mine altar for nought, i. e. fruitlessly! But apart from the difficulty of the construction, it is not God's way to *quench the smouldering flax.* He Who bids, *Gather up the fragments that remain, that nothing be lost,* accepts any imperfect service rather than none. He does not break off the last link, which binds man to Himself. Then, if or when God willed His service to surcease, He would do it Himself, as He did by the destruction of the temple before the Captivity, or finally by the Romans. It would have been an ungodly act, (such as was only done by Ahaz, perhaps the most ungodly king of Israel [4]), and one which especially called down His wrath [5], to close the doors, and therewith to break off all sacrifice. Manasseh carried the worship of false gods into the temple itself; Ahaz, as far as in him lay, abolished the service of God. A prophet of God could not express a wish, that pious Israelites (for it is presupposed that they would do this out of zeal for God's honor) should bring the service of God to an end.

He sums up with an entire rejection of them, present and future. *I have no pleasure in you;* it is a term of repudiation [6], sometimes of disgust [7], *neither will I accept an offer-*

[1] Lev. xxii. 22.

[2] Dion.

[3] אל seems to be used purposely in contrast with man, as in Is. xxxi. 3, *The Egyptians are men and not God.*

[4] 2 Chron. xxviii. 24.

[5] Ib. xxix. 8.

[6] אין חפץ ב 1 Sam. xviii. 25. Eccl. v. 3. [4 Eng.]

[7] כלי אין חפץ בו Jer. xxii. 28, xlviii. 38, Hos. viii. 8.

Before CHRIST cir. 397.

11 For [p] from the rising
of the sun even unto the
going down of the same
my name *shall be* great
[q] among the Gentiles; [r] and
in every place [s] incense
shall be offered unto my
name, and a pure offering:

p Ps. 113. 3. Isai. 59. 19.

q Isai. 60. 3, 5.
r John 4. 21, 23. 1 Tim. 2. 8.
s Rev. 8. 3.

ing at your hands. He says not simply, [1] *your burnt-offerings are not acceptable, nor your sacrifices sweet unto Me*, but, *I will not accept* it. Such as they were, such they would be hereafter. God would not accept their sacrifices, but would replace them.

11. *For.* The form of words does not express whether this declaration relates to the present or the future. It is a vivid present, such as is often used to describe the future. But the things spoken of shew it to be future. The Jewish sacrifices had defects, partly incidental, partly inherent. Incidental were those, with which the Prophet had upbraided them; inherent, (apart from their mere typical character) that they never could be the religion of the world, since they were locally fixed at Jerusalem. Malachi tells them of a new sacrifice, which should be offered throughout the then heathen world, grounded on His new revelation of Himself to them. *For great* shall be *My Name among the heathen.* The prophet anticipates an objection [2], which the Jews might make to him. [3] *What then will God do unto His great Name?* Those by which He would replace them, would be more worthy of God in two ways, 1) in themselves, 2) in their universality. *Then*, whatsoever the heathen worshiped, even if some worshiped an *unknown God*, His *Name* was not known to them, nor *great among* them. Those who knew of Him, knew of Him, not as the Lord of heaven and earth, but as the God of the Jews only; their *offerings* were not *pure*, but manifoldly defiled. A Hebrew prophet could not be an apologist for heathen idolatry amidst its abominations, or set it on a level with the worship which God had, for the time, appointed; much less could he set it forth as *the* true acceptable service of God [4]. Malachi himself speaks of it, as an aggravation of cruelty in their divorcing of their wives, that they [5] *married the daughter of a strange god.* The worship of those Jews, who remained, out of secular interests, in foreign countries, could not be represented as *the* "pure offering;" for they made no offerings: then as now, these being forbidden out of Jerusalem; nor would the worship of such Jews, as were scattered in the large empire of Persia, be contrasted with that at Jerusalem, as *the* pure worship; else why should the Jews have returned? It would have been an abolition of the law before its time. Malachi prophesies then, as had Micah, Isaiah, Zephaniah [6], of a new revelation of God, when, and in which, men should *worship Him, every one from his place, even all the isles of the heathen.*

Our Lord Himself explains and expands it in His words to the Samaritan woman; [7] *Woman, believe Me, the hour cometh, when ye shall neither in this mountain, nor yet at Jerusalem, worship the Father.—The hour cometh, and now is, when the true worshipers shall worship the Father in spirit and in truth; for the Father seeketh such to worship Him. God is a Spirit: and they that worship Him must worship Him in spirit and in truth*, and declared the rejection of the Jews, sealing their own sentence against themselves, [8] *I say unto you, The kingdom of God shall be taken from you, and given to a nation bringing forth the fruits thereof;* and before, [9] *Many shall come from the East and West, and shall sit down with Abraham and Isaac and Jacob in the kingdom of heaven, and the children of the kingdom shall be cast out into outer darkness.*

Incense shall be *offered unto My name*, lit. I think, *there* shall be *incense, oblation made unto My name* [this is a mere question of construction [10]], *and a pure oblation.*

[1] Jer. vi. 20. [2] Poc. [3] Jos. vii. 9.

[4] So in Rashi; Our rabbis say, that "they [the heathen] called Him [the Lord] God of gods; he too who hath an idol, knoweth, that He [the Lord] is God, that He is above all those things, and that in every place the Gentiles also, of their own accord, offer unto my name. But our rabbis have expounded, that they [those spoken of] are the disciples of the wise, who in every place are occupied in the rules of the Divine worship; so also all the prayers of Israel, which they make in every place, these are like a pure oblation (Minchah), and so Jonathan interprets, 'at whatever time ye shall do My will, I receive your prayers, and My great name is sanctified by you, and your prayer is like a pure oblation before Me.'" See Ibn Ezra, D. Kim., Tanchum, Abarb., in Poc.

[5] Mal. ii. 11. [6] Zeph. ii. 11.

[7] S. John iv. 21, 23, 24. [8] S. Matt. xxi. 41, 43.

[9] Id. viii. 11, 12.

[10] מֻקְטָר מֻגָּשׁ are, I think most probably, two independent impersonal passive participles, taken as future, "will be incensed, offered [wird geräuchert, dargebracht as Ewald] (Lehrb. 295 a) הוּחַל, "there is begun," שֻׁדַּד, "there is wasted," מְדֻבָּר "there is spoken" (Ps. lxxxvii. 3), and this place. Tanchum praises Abulwalid for taking מקטר as a noun = קטורה (Lib. Rad. col. 634). He adds, "The rest (עָ׳ירה) take them as adjectives with an unexpressed substantive." This, I think right: for, although מקטר might be 'what is incensed,' and so a subst., הגיש is used elsewhere of offering a sacrifice, not of offering incense, and so מקטר could not be the subject to it.

This sacrifice, which should be offered, is designated by the special name of *meal-offering*[1]. God would not accept it from the Jews; He would, from the Heathen. It was a special sacrifice, offered by itself as an unbloody sacrifice, or together with the bloody sacrifice. [2] *It is most holy, as the sin-offering and as the trespass-offering.* In the daily sacrifice it was offered morning and evening, with the lamb. As this was typical of the precious blood-shedding of the *Lamb without spot* upon the Cross, so was the meal-offering which accompanied it, of the Holy Eucharist.

The early Christians saw the force of the prediction, that sacrifice was contrasted with sacrifice, the bloody sacrifices which were ended by the "One full perfect and sufficient Sacrifice Oblation and Satisfaction" made by our Lord "on the Altar of the Cross for the sins of the whole world," and those sacrifices which He commanded to be made on our Altars, as a memorial of Him. So S. Justin, who was converted probably A.D. 133, within 30 years from the death of S. John, says, "[3] God has therefore beforehand declared, that all who through this name offer those sacrifices, which Jesus, Who is the Christ, commanded to be offered, that is to say, in the Eucharist of the Bread and of the Cup, which are offered in every part of the world by us Christians, are well-pleasing to Him. But those sacrifices, which are offered by you and through those priests of yours, He wholly rejects, saying, *And I will not accept your offerings at your hands. For from the rising of the sun even to the going down of the same, My Name is glorified among the Gentiles; but ye profane it.*"

He points out further the failure of the Jewish explanation as to *their* sacrifices, in that the Church was everywhere, not so the Jews. "[3] You and your teachers deceive yourselves, when you interpret this passage of Scripture of those of your nation who were in the dispersion[4], and say that it speaks of their prayers and sacrifices made in every place, as pure and well-pleasing, and know that you speak falsely, and endeavor in every way to impose upon yourselves; first, because your people are not found, even now, from the rising to the setting of the sun, but there are nations, in which none of your race have ever dwelt: whilst there is not one nation of men, whether Barbarians, or Greeks, or by whatsoever name distinguished, whether of those (nomads) who live in wagons, or of those who have no houses, or those pastoral people that dwell in tents, among whom prayers and thanksgivings are not offered to the Father and Creator of all things, through the name of the crucified Jesus. And you know that at the time when the prophet Malachi said this, the dispersion of you through the whole world, in which you now are, had not yet taken place; as is also shewn by Scripture."

S. Irenæus in the same century, "[5] He took that which is part of the creation, viz. bread, and gave thanks, saying, *This is My Body.* And the Cup likewise, which is of the creation which appertains unto us, He professed to be His own Blood, and taught men the new oblation of the New Testament; which the Church receiving from the Apostles offers unto God in the world:—unto Him Who giveth us nourishment, the first-fruits of His own gifts, in the New Testament; of which in the twelve prophets Malachi gave beforehand this intimation [quoting Mal. i. 10, 11]; most evidently intimating hereby, that while the former people should cease to make offerings to God, in every place sacrifice should be offered unto Him, and that in pureness; His Name also is glorified among the Gentiles. Now what other name is there, which is glorified among the Gentiles, than that which belongs to our Lord, by Whom the Father is glorified, and man is glorified? And because man belongs to His Own Son, and is made by Him, He calls him His Own. And as if some King were himself to paint an image of his own son, he justly calls it his own image, on both accounts, first that it is his son's, next, that he himself made it: so also the Name of Jesus Christ, which is glorified in the Church throughout the whole world, the Father professes to be His own, both because it is His Son's, and because He Himself wrote and gave it for the salvation of men. Because therefore the Name of the Son properly belongs to the Father, and in God Almighty through Jesus Christ the Church makes her offering, well saith He on both accounts, *And in every place incense is offered unto My Name, and a pure sacrifice.* And *incense*, John in the Apocalypse declares to be *the prayers of the Saints.* Therefore the offering of the Church, which the Lord hath taught to be offered in the whole world, is accounted with God as a pure sacrifice, and accepted of Him."

Tertullian contrasts the "[6] sacerdotal law through Moses, in Leviticus, prescribing to the people of Israel, that sacrifices should in no other place be offered to God than in the land of promise, which the Lord God was about to give to the people Israel and to their brethren, in order that on Israel's introduction thither, there should be there

[1] Lev. ii. 7 (14 Eng.) sqq.
[2] Ib. vi. 17. [10. Heb.]
[3] Dial. c. Tryph. § 117 pp. 215, 216 Oxf. Tr. also § 28, 29 pp. 104, 105. Ib.
[4] The Jews then must have interpreted it of themselves in the present, and so of the times of Malachi after the return of others from Babylon.
[5] iv. 17. 5. pp. 356, 357. Oxf. Tr. See also his Fragment xxxvi. p. 554, 555. Oxf. Tr.
[6] c. Jud. i. 5. p. 214 Edinb. Tr. Add c. Marcion. iii. 22.

celebrated sacrifices and holocausts, as well for sins as for souls, and nowhere else but in the holy land [1]," and this subsequent prediction of "the Spirit through the prophets, that in every place and in every land there should be offered sacrifices to God. As He says through the angel Malachi, one of the twelve prophets, (citing the place)."

S. Hippolytus, a disciple of S. Irenæus, A.D. 220. martyr, in a commentary on Daniel, says that "[2] when Anti-Christ cometh, the sacrifice and libation will be taken away, which is now in every place offered by the Gentiles to God." The terms "Sacrifice offered in every place" are terms of Malachi.

So S. Cyprian, in his Testimonies against the Jews, sums up the teaching of the passage under this head, "[3] That the old sacrifice was to be made void, and a new sacrifice instituted."

In the "[4] Apostolic Constitutions," the prophecy is quoted as "said by God of His œcumenical Church."

Eusebius says, "[5] The truth bears witness to the prophetic word, whereby God, rejecting the Mosaic sacrifices, foretells that which shall be among us. *For from the rising of the sun &c.* We sacrifice then to the supreme God the sacrifice of praise; we sacrifice the Divine, reverend and holy oblation: we sacrifice, in a new way according to the New Testament, the pure sacrifice. The broken heart is also called a sacrifice to God—We sacrifice also the Memory of that great Sacrifice, performing it according to the mysteries which have been transmitted by Him."

S. Cyril of Jerusalem [6] speaks of it only as prophesying the rejection of the Jews and the adoption of the Gentiles.

In the liturgy of S. Mark [7], it is naturally quoted, only, as fulfilled "in the reasonable and unbloody sacrifice, which all nations offer to Thee, O Lord, from the rising of the sun to the setting thereof," not in reference to the cessation of Jewish sacrifices.

S. Chrysostom dwells on its peculiar force, coming from so late a prophet [8]. "Hear Malachi, who came after the other prophets. For I adduce, for the time, no testimony either of Isaiah or Jeremiah or any other before the Captivity, lest thou shouldest say that the terrible things which he foretold were exhausted in the Captivity. But I adduce a prophet, after the return from Babylon and the restoration of your city, prophesying clearly about you. For when they had returned, and recovered their city, and rebuilt the temple and performed the sacrifices, foretelling this present desolation then future, and the taking away of the sacrifice, Malachi thus speaks in the Person of God [ver. 10 fin.—12 beg.]. When, oh Jew, happened all this? When was incense offered to God in every place? when a pure sacrifice? Thou couldest not name any other time, than this, after the Coming of Christ. If the prophet foretelleth not this time and our sacrifice, but the Jewish, the prophecy will be against the law. For if, when Moses commandeth that sacrifice should be offered in no other place than the Lord God should choose, and shutteth up those sacrifices in one place, the prophet says that incense should be offered in every place and a pure sacrifice, he opposeth and contradicteth Moses. But there is no strife nor contention. For Moses speaketh of one sacrifice, and Malachi of another. Where doth this appear? [From the place, not Judæa only; from the mode, that it should be pure; from the offerers, not Israel, but the nations,] from East to West, shewing that whatever of earth the sun surveys, the preaching will embrace.—He calls the former sacrifice impure, not in its own nature but in the mind of the offerers; if one compares the sacrifice itself, there is such a boundless distance, that this [that offered by Christians] might in comparison be called 'pure.'"

Even the cold, but clear, Theodoret has, "[9] Foretelling to the Jews the cessation of the legal priesthood, he announces the pure and unbloody sacrifice of the Gentiles. And first he says to the Jews, *I have no pleasure in you, saith the Lord of hosts, and I will not accept a sacrifice at your hands.* Then he foreshews the piety of the Gentiles, *For from the rising of the sun &c,* (Mal. i. 11.) You then I will wholly reject; for I detest altogether what you do. Wherefore also I reject the sacrifice offered by you; but instead of you, I have the whole world to worship Me. For the dwellers in the whole earth, which the rising and setting sun illumines, will everywhere both offer to Me incense, and will sacrifice to Me the pure sacrifice, which I love. For they shall know My name and My will, and shall offer to Me reverence due. So the Lord said

[1] Lev. xvii. 1–6, Deut. xii. 5–14, 26, 27.

[2] Interpret. in Dan. n. xxii. p. 110, published from the Chisian codex of cent. x. in Daniel sec. LXX. Romæ 1772. The passage is quoted loosely by S. Jerome in Dan. c. 9. Opp. v. 689. Vall.

[3] Testim. ad Quirin. i. 16. pp. 23 and 31. Oxf. Tr.

[4] vii. 30 [on their age, especially of that of their substance, see Pusey, The Real Presence the doctrine of the early Church pp. 605–609.]

[5] Dem. Ev. i. 10. fin. He also quotes the passage in proof of the abolition of the Jewish sacrifices, although without allusion to the Eucharistic sacrifice, Ib. i. 6. p. 19; and in ii. 29. pp. 55, 56, of the rejection of the Jewish nation and their bodily worship according to the law of Moses, and the spiritual worship given to all nations through Christ."

[6] Cat. xviii. 25. [7] Assem. Cod. Lit. vii. 19, 20.

[8] Ad. Jud. v. 12. Opp. i. 647, 648 Montf. See also his Expos. in Ps. 112. n. 2. Opp. v. 288, 289, and Quod Christus sit Deus Opp. i. 582, "Seest thou, how plainly he both cast out Judaism and exhibited Christianity effulgent and extended over the whole world?"

[9] ad. loc.

Before CHRIST cir. 397.

t Isai. 66. 19, 20.

u ver. 7.

[t] for my name *shall be* great
among the heathen, saith
the LORD of hosts.
12 ¶ But ye have profaned it, in that ye say,
[u] The table of the LORD
is polluted: and the fruit
thereof, *even* his meat *is*
contemptible.
13 Ye said also, Behold,
what a weariness *is it!*
‖ and ye have snuffed at
it, saith the LORD of
hosts: and ye brought

‖ Or, *whereas ye might have blown it away.*

to the Samaritan woman, *Woman, believe Me, that the hour cometh and now is, when neither in this mountain, nor in Jerusalem shall ye worship the Father.*—The blessed Paul, being instructed in this, says, [1] *I will that men pray everywhere* &c, and the Divine Malachi clearly taught us in this place the worship now used; for the circumscribed worship of the priests is brought to an end, and every place is accounted fit for the worship of God, and the sacrifice of irrational victims is ended, and He, our spotless Lamb, Who taketh away the sin of the world, is sacrificed."

Lastly, S. Augustine, "[2] Malachi, prophesying of the Church which we see propagated through Christ, says most plainly to the Jews in the person of God, *I have no pleasure in you, and will not receive an offering at your hands. For from the rising of the sun* &c. Since we see this sacrifice through the priesthood of Christ after the order of Melchisedek, now offered to God in every place from the rising of the sun to its setting; but the sacrifice of the Jews, of which it is said, *I have no pleasure in you, neither will I accept an offering from your hands*, they cannot deny to have ceased; why do they yet expect another Christ, since what they read as prophesied and see fulfilled, could not be fulfilled, except through Him?"

12. *And ye have profaned* [[3] *are habitually profaning it*], *in that ye say.* It was the daily result of their daily lives and acts. "[4] It is probable that the priests did not use such words, but that by their very deeds, they proclaimed this aloud: as in the, *The fool hath said in his heart, There is no God.* For in that he is seen to be a despiser, though he say it not in words, yet, by their very deeds and by the crookedness of their lives, they all-but cry out, There is no God. For they who live as though God beheld not, and do all things recklessly and unholily, by their own deeds and works deny God. So they who are not earnest to preserve to the holy Altar the reverence becoming to it, by the very things which they do, say,

The table of the Lord is despised. Not *the table of shewbread,* since it is so called in reference to the sacrifice offered thereon. Ezekiel had probably so called the altar, which he saw in his vision of the new temple[5]. It is what was before called *the altar;* an *altar*, in regard to the sacrifices offered to God; a *table*, in regard to the food of the sacrifice therefrom received. Both names, "altar[6]" and "table[7]" being received in the New Testament, both were received in the early Church. For each represented one side of the great Eucharistic action, as it is a Sacrifice and a Sacrament. But the title "altar" was the earliest[8].

It may be here a different profaneness of the priests. They connived at the sin of the people in sacrificing the maimed animals which they brought, and yet, since they had their food from the sacrifices, and such animals are likely to have been neglected and ill-conditioned, they may very probably have complained of the poverty of their lot, and despised the whole service. For the words used, *its produce, the eating thereof is contemptible* belong to their portion, not to what was consumed by fire. With this agrees their cry,

13. *What a weariness!* What an onerous service it is! The service of God is its own reward. If not, it becomes a greater toil, with less reward from this earth, than the things of this earth. Our only choice is between love and weariness.

And ye have snuffed [*puffed*] *at it*[9], i. e. at the altar; as a thing contemptible. *Ye have brought* that which was *taken by violence*[10]. In despising any positive law of God, they despised the lawgiver; and so, from contempt of the ceremonial law, they went on to break the moral law. It were in-

[1] 1 Tim. ii. 8. [2] de Civ. Dei. xviii. 35. 3.
[3] אתם מחללים אתו
[4] S. Cyr. [5] Ezek. xliv. 16.
[6] S. Matt. v. 23, Heb. xiii. 10. [7] 1 Cor x. 21.
[8] S Ignat. ad Philad. n. 4. p. 32. Cotel.
[9] This too is one of the Tikkunē Sopherim, as if, had it not been profane, the prophet would have said, *at Me.* On the character of these hypothetic corrections, see on Hab. i. 12. p. 186. n. 17.
[10] This is the one sense of גזל, which occurs in 34 separate passages (beside two met. Job. xxiv. 19, Pr. iv. 16.) It is used specially of the robbery of the poor, whether by wrong judgment (Eccl. v. 7, [Heb.] Is. x. 2) or open violence. The meaning "torn" was gained, as if the animal had been carried off by beasts (θηριάλωτον), the *eating* of which was forbidden, Ex. xxii. 30, Lev. vii. 24, xxii. 8. Ezek. iv. 14, xliv. 31. But this had its own name, טְרֵפָה, and could not be used in sacrifices, since it was dead already.

Before CHRIST cir. 397.

that which was torn, and the lame, and the sick: thus ye brought an offering: [x]should I accept this of your hand? saith the LORD.
14 But cursed *be* [y]the deceiver, || which hath in his flock a male, and voweth, and sacrificeth unto the Lord a corrupt thing: for [z]I *am* a great King, saith the LORD of hosts, and my name *is* dreadful among the heathen.

x Lev. 22. 20, &c.
y ver. 8.
|| Or, *in whose flock is.*
z Ps. 47. 2. 1 Tim. 6. 15.

---

deed a mockery of God, to break a law whereby He bound man to man, and therefrom to seek to appease Himself. Yet in rough times, people, even in Christianity, have made their account with their souls, by giving to the poor a portion of what they had taken from the rich. "God," it was said to such an one, "rejects the gifts obtained by violence and robbery. He loves mercy, justice and humanity, and by the lovers of these only will He be worshiped." "[1]He that sacrificeth of a thing wrongfully gotten, his offering is ridiculous, and the gifts of unjust men are not accepted. The Most High is not pleased with the offerings of the wicked, neither is He pacified for sin by the multitude of sacrifices. Whoso bringeth an offering of the goods of the poor doeth as one that killeth the son before the father's eyes."

14. *Cursed is the deceiver.* "[2]The fraudulent, hypocritical, false or deceitful dealer, who makes a show of one thing, and doth or intends another, nor doth to his power what he would make a show of doing; as if he could deceive God in doing in His service otherwise than He required, and yet be accepted by Him." The whole habit of these men was not to break with God, but to keep well with Him on as easy terms as they could. They even went beyond what the law required in making vows, probably for some temporal end, and then substituted for that which had typical perfection, the less valuable animal, the ewe[3], and that, diseased. It was probably, to prevent self-deceit, that the law commanded that the oblation for a vow should be [4]*a male without blemish, perfect;* lest (which may be a temptation in impulsive vows) repenting of their vow, they should persuade themselves, that they had vowed less than they had. Ordinarily, then, it would not have been allowed to one, who had not the best to offer, to vow at all. But, in their alleged poverty, the prophet supposes that God would so far dispense with His own law, and accept the best which any one had, although it did not come up to that law. Hence the clause, *which hath in his flock a male.* "[5]If thou hast not a male, that curse in no wise injureth thee. But saying this, he sheweth, that they have what is best, and offer what is bad."

They sinned, not against religion only, but against justice also. "[6]For as a merchant, who offers his goods at a certain price, if he supply them afterward adulterated and corrupted, is guilty of fraud and is unjust, so he who promised to God a sacrifice worthy of God, and, according to the law, perfect and sound, is fraudulent and sins against justice, if he afterward gives one, defective, mutilated, vitiated, and is guilty of theft in a sacred thing, and so of sacrilege."

Clergy or "all who have vowed, should learn hence, that what they have vowed should be given to God, entire, manly, perfect, the best.—For, reverence for the supreme and Divine Majesty to Whom they consecrate themselves demandeth this, that they should offer Him the highest, best and most perfect, making themselves a whole-burnt-offering to God."

"[7]They who abandon all things of the world, and kindle their whole mind with the fire of Divine love, these become a sacrifice and a whole-burnt-offering to Almighty God." "[8]Man himself, consecrated and devoted in the name of God, is a sacrifice." He then offers a corrupt thing who, like Ananias, keeps back *part of the price,* and is the more guilty, because, while it was his own, it was in his own power.

I am a great King. "[9]As God is Alone Lord through His universal Providence and His intrinsic authority, so He Alone is King, and a King so great, that of His greatness or dignity and perfection there is no end."

My Name is dreadful among the heathen. Absence of any awe of God was a central defect of these Jews. They treated Him, as they would not a fellow-creature, for whom they had any respect or awe or fear. Some remaining instinct kept them from parting

[1] Ecclus. xxxiv. 18–20. [2] Poc.

[3] מָשְׁחָת fem. for מָשְׁחַתֶת, as מְשָׁרַת for מְשָׁרֶתֶת, Kgs i. 15. and מַחֲבַת Lev. ii. 5, Ewald Lehrb. n. 188. p. 495 ed. 8. Keil would read מָשְׁחָת (masc.) and make it a separate case, "the deceiver, whereas in his flock is a male; and he who voweth &c.:" but then nothing would be said, wherein the deceit consisted.

[4] Levit. xxii. 19, 21. [5] S. Jer. [6] Lap.

[7] S. Greg. in Ezek. L. i. Hom. xii. 30. Opp. i. 305 Ben. L.

[8] S. Aug. de Civ. Dei. x. 6. L. [9] Dion.

Before CHRIST cir. 397.

CHAPTER II.

1 *He sharply reproveth the priests for neglecting their covenant,* 11 *and the people for idolatry,* 14 *for adultery,* 17 *and for infidelity.*

AND now, O ye priests,
this commandment *is*
for you.
2 [a] If ye will not hear,
and if ye will not lay *it* to
heart, to give glory unto
my name, saith the LORD
of hosts, I will even send
a curse upon you, and I
will curse your blessings:
yea, I have cursed them
already, because ye do not
lay *it* to heart.

[a] Lev. 26. 14, &c. Deut. 28, 15, &c.

with Him; but they yielded a cold, wearisome, heartless service. Malachi points to the root of the evil, the ignorance, how awful God is. This is the root of so much irreverence in people's theories, thoughts, conversations, systems, acts, of the present day also. They know neither God or themselves. The relation is summed up in those words to a saint[1], "Knowest thou well, Who I am, and who thou art? I am He Who Is, and thou art she who is not." So Job says in the presence of God, [2]*I have heard of Thee by the hearing of the ear, but now mine eye seeth Thee: wherefore I abhor myself and repent in dust and ashes.* To correct this, God, from the beginning, insists on the title which He gives Himself. [3]*Circumcise the foreskin of your hearts and be no more stiff-necked: for the Lord your God is God of gods and Lord of lords, the great God, the mighty and the terrible;* and in warning, [4]*If thou wilt not observe* to do all *the words of this law that are written in this book, that thou mayest fear this glorious and fearful name, The Lord thy God,* then *the Lord thy God will make thy plagues wonderful* &c.

II. 1. *And now this is My commandment unto you,* not a commandment, which He gave them, but a commandment in regard to them. As God said of old, upon obedience, [5]*I will command My blessing unto you,* so now He would command what should reach them, but a curse. "[6]He returns from the people to the priests, as the fountain of the evil, whose carelessness about things sacred he had rebuked before. Let the priests of the new law hear this rebuke of God, and conceive it dictated to them by the Holy Spirit to hear, from whom God rightly requires greater holiness, and so will punish them more grievously, if careless or scandalous in their office." All Christians are, in some sense, [7]*a royal, holy priesthood,* over and above the special "Christian priesthood;" as the Jews, over and above the special priesthood of Aaron, were *a* [8]*kingdom of priests.* What follows then belongs, in their degree, to them and their duties.

2. *If ye will not lay to heart,* viz. the rebukes addressed to them, *to give glory to God.* For the glory of God is the end and aim of the priesthood. This should be the principle and rule of their whole life, "[9]to the greater glory of God." *I will send the curse upon you,* viz. that which He had threatened in the law upon disobedience; and will *curse your blessings,* will turn your blessings into a curse. He does not say, I will send you curses instead of blessings, but, I will make the blessings themselves a curse. [10]*The things which should have been to their wealth became to them an occasion of falling;* to the proud, the things which lift them up; to the gluttonous, their abundance; to the avaricious, their wealth; which, if used to the glory of God, become blessings, do, when self not God is their end, by God's dispensation and Providence, become a curse to them. "[11]The goods of nature, the goods of fortune, the goods of the Church allowed to you, I will turn to your greater damnation, permitting you to abuse them to pride; and your damnation shall be the more penal, the more good things ye have received from Me. Whence Christ declares in the Gospel, [12]*Unto whomsoever much is given, of him shall be much required.*"

Yea, I have cursed them [lit. *it*], i.e. each one of the blessings, *already.* God's judgments as well as His mercies are individual with a minute care, shewing that it is His doing. The curse had already gone forth, and had begun to seize upon them from the time that they began to despise His Name. His judgments do not break in at once, but little by little, with warnings of their approach, that so we may turn to Him, and *escape the wrath to come.*

[1] S. Catherine of Sienna. [2] Job xlii. 5, 6.
[3] Deut. x. 16, 17, vii. 21. Nehemiah uses it in his prayers (i. 5, ix. 32) and Daniel (ix 4.) It occurs also Neh. iv. 8 (14 Eng.) Ps. xlvii. 3, lxviii. 36, lxxxix. 8, xcvi. 4, xcix. 3, cxi. 9, Zeph. ii. 11.
[4] Deut. xxviii. 58, 59.
[5] Lev. xxv. 21, וצויתי את ברכתי לכם.
[6] Lap. [7] 1 S. Pet. ii. 9. [8] Ex. xix. 6.
[9] "Ad majorem Dei. gloriam," the motto of S. Ignatius Loyola.
[10] Ps. lxix. 23.
[11] Dion. [12] S. Luke xii. 48.

Before CHRIST cir. 397.

3 Behold, I will ‖ cor-
rupt your seed, and
† spread dung upon your
faces, *even* the dung of
your solemn feasts; and
‖ *one* shall [b] take you away
with it.
4 And ye shall know
that I have sent this commandment unto you, that
my covenant might be
with Levi, saith the LORD
of hosts.
5 [c] My covenant was
with him of life and
peace; and I gave them

‖ Or, *reprove.*
† Heb. *scatter.*
‖ Or, *it shall take you away to it.*
[b] 1 Kin. 14. 10.

Before CHRIST cir. 397.

[c] Num. 25. 12. Ezek. 34. 25. & 37. 26.

3. *Lo, I will rebuke the seed*[1] *for your sake,* i. e. that it should not grow. He Who worketh by His sustaining will all the operations of nature, would at His will withhold them. Neither priests nor Levites cultivated the soil; yet, since the tithes were assigned to them, the diminution of the harvest affected them. The meal-offering too was a requisite part of the sacrifice[2].

And spread dung upon your faces, the dung[3] *of your solemn feasts,* or, *of your sacrifices*[4]. It was by the law carried without the camp and burned with the animal itself. They had brought before the face of God maimed, unfitting sacrifices; they should have them cast back, with their refuse, upon them; "[5] as a lord that rejecteth a gift, brought to him by his servant, casts it back in his face." "[6] *Of your sacrifices,* not of Mine; for I am not worshiped in them: ye seek to please, not Me, but yourselves." So God said of Eli, [7] *them that honor Me I will honor, and they that despise Me shall be lightly esteemed.*

And one shall take you away with it, lit. *to it.* They should be swept away, as if they were an appendage to it, as God said, [8] *I will take away the remnant of the house of Jeroboam, as a man taketh away dung, till all be gone.* As are the offerings, so shall it be with the offerers.

4. *And ye shall know that I have sent this commandment unto you:* this, which He had just uttered. They who believe not God when threatening, know that He is in earnest and not to be trifled with, through His punishing. *That My covenant might be with Levi*[9]. God willed to punish those who at that time rebelled against Him, that He might spare those who should come after them. He chastened the fathers, who shewed their contempt toward Him, that their sons, taking warning thereby, might not be cut off. He continues to say, what the covenant was, which He willed still to be, if they would repent.

5. *My covenant was with him life and peace;* lit. *the life and the peace;* that, which alone is true *life and peace.* The covenant was not with Levi himself, but with Aaron, his representative, with whom the covenant was made in the desert, as is indeed here expressed; and, in him, with all his race[10] after him, who succeeded him in his office; as, when it is said, that [11] *Aaron and his sons offered upon the altar of burnt offering,* it must needs be understood, not of Aaron in person alone and his sons then living, but of any of his race that succeeded in his and their room. So our Lord promised to be with His Apostles, [12] *always to the end of the world,* i. e. with them and those whom they should appoint in their stead, and these others, until He should Himself come. God promised, if they would keep the law, that they should live in peace on the earth; yea, that they should have peace of mind and a life of grace. *Life* is an indefectible being, which man does not forfeit by sin, to which death is no interruption, changing only the place of the soul's life.

And I gave them to him, in, or as, *fear,* "[13] *Fear,* not servile but filial and pure, as S. Paul bids Christians, [14] *work out your own salvation with fear and trembling.*" God gave them an awful gift, to be held with fear

[1] Keil objects to this rendering of the text and adopts the punctuation הַזְּרֹעַ from lxx. Aq. Vulg. "the arm," i. e. render it useless and incapable of discharging its office. But when גער is used of other than men themselves, it is a whole, as to which the metaphor is used," either being animate, as "the devourer," Mal. iii. 11, or pictured as animate, as "the sea," Ps. cvi. 9. Nah. i. 4.

[2] See also Joel i. 13. ii. 14.

[3] פֶּרֶשׁ is only used of the dung, as it lies in the animal killed for sacrifice, Ex. xxix. 4, Lev. iv. 11, viii. 7, xxi. 27, Nu. xix. 5, and here.

[4] חַג is certainly the animal sacrificed at the feast, Ex. xxiii. 18, Ps. cxviii. 27, and so probably here. So Kim.

[5] Abarb. Poc. [6] Rib. [7] 1 Sam. ii. 30.

[8] 1 Kgs xiv. 10.

[9] Keil says that היה means indeed to "exist," but not to "continue existence." But the continuance is involved in the existence in the future, for the being in the future involves the continued being. His own rendering, "that this should be My covenant with Levi;" requires a more definite subject; and it should rather be, "that My covenant with Levi should come to this." In ver. 5, 6, he speaks of the past emphatically, "My covenant *was* with him," "the law of truth *was* in his mouth." So it shall be with you, if you become like him.

[10] By the art. in הלוי v. 8. See Num. xxv. 12, 13.

[11] 1 Chr. vi. 49. [12] S. Matt. xxviii. 20. [13] Dion.

[14] Phil. ii. 12.

Before CHRIST cir. 397. to him [d] *for* the fear wherewith he feared me, and
[d] Deut. 33. 8, 9. was afraid before my name.

6 [e] The law of truth Before CHRIST cir. 397.
was in his mouth, and in-
iquity was not found in [e] Deut. 33. 10.

and awe, for its very preciousness, as one would hold anxiously what is very precious, yet very fragile and easily marred.

And he feared Me, and was afraid before My Name. Malachi unites two words, the second expressive of strong fear, by which a man is, as it were, crushed or broken. They are often united in Hebrew, but as expressing terror, which men are bidden not to feel before men. Toward man it is ever said, [1] *fear not, neither be ye dismayed;* toward God Alone, it is a matter of praise. Man's highest fear is too little; for he knows not, Who God is. So Isaiah says, [2] *Fear ye not their fear* [*the fear of this people*], *nor be afraid. Sanctify the Lord of hosts Himself, and let Him be your fear and let Him be your dread.* "[3] What can be more precious (than this fear)? For it is written, [4] *He who feareth the Lord will be rewarded.* '[5] The fear of the Lord is honor and glory and gladness and a crown of rejoicing.' He saith, *the fear, wherewith he feareth Me and was afraid*, i. e. he received the fear of God in his whole heart and soul. For these reduplications and emphases suggest to the hearer how rooted in virtue are those thus praised."

6. *The law of truth was in his mouth.* Apart from those cases, which were brought to the priests at the tabernacle[6], in which their voice was the voice of God through them, to teach the law was part of the office both of the priest and Levite. Of the priest God says; [7] *that ye may teach the children of Israel all the statutes, which the Lord hath spoken unto them by the hand of Moses:* of the tribe of Levi generally Moses says, [8] *They shall teach Jacob Thy judgments and Israel Thy law.* After the schism of the ten tribes, a prophet says to Asa, that *Israel* had [9] *for a long time* been *without the true God and without a teaching priest and without law.* They are evil times, of which Ezekiel says, [10] *the law shall perish from the priest;* and God says of corrupt priests, [11] *The priest said not, where is the Lord? and they that handle the law knew Me not.* [12] *They did violence to My law.* On their return from the captivity Ezra was known to Artaxerxes as [13] *a scribe of the law of the God of heaven*, and he looked upon him apparently, as one who should keep the people in good order by teaching it. [14] *Thou, Ezra, after the wisdom of thy God which is in thy hand, set magistrates and judges, which may judge all the people which are beyond the river, all such as know the laws of thy God, and teach ye them that know them not: and whosoever will not do the law of thy God or the law of the king, let judgment be executed speedily upon him.* Ezra says of himself, that he [15] *had prepared his heart to seek the law of the Lord and to do it and to teach in Israel statutes and judgments.*

"[16] God's [17] *law is the truth:* the true doctrine of this law did he teach the people, and instruct them in the true meaning and intent thereof, that, according to the right rule, they might frame all their actions; nothing of it did he conceal from them, nor teach any thing contrary to it or false. This was in his mouth; nothing contrary to it was found in his lips."

And iniquity was not found in his lips. He expresses the perfectness of that teaching, first positively, then negatively. The true priest taught truth without any admixture of wrong. "[18] Not he only is a betrayer of the truth, who, transgressing the truth, openly teaches a lie for the truth; but he too, who does not freely utter the truth, which he ought to utter freely, or who does not freely defend the truth which he ought to defend freely, is a betrayer of the truth. [19] *For with the heart man believeth unto righteousness, and with the mouth confession is made unto salvation.*" "Nothing," says S. Ambrose [20] to the Emperor Theodosius, "is so perilous to the priest with God, so disgraceful with men, as not to utter freely what he thinks. For it is written, [21] *I spake of Thy testimonies before kings, and was not ashamed.* And therefore a priest's silence ought to displease your Clemency; his freedom, to please you. For you are involved in the peril of my silence, art aided by the good of my free speech."

He walked with Me. To awe of God, truthfulness of teaching, he adds a devout continual intercourse with God. Like the patriarchs of old, Enoch and Noah, he [22] *walked with God.* He not only lived in the Presence, but walked up and down with Him, through his whole life, as a Friend;

[1] Deut. i. 21, xxxi. 8, Josh. i. 9, x. 25, 1 Chr. xxii. 13, xxviii. 20, 2 Chr. xx. 15, 17, xxxii. 7, Is. li. 7, Jer. xxiii. 4, xxx. 10, xlvi. 27, Ez. ii. 6, iii. 9.
[2] Is. viii. 12, 13. [3] S. Cyr. [4] Pr. xiii. 13.
[5] Ecclus. i. 11.
[6] Deut. xvii. 9, 10, 11, xix. 17; (add Deut. xxi. 5, Ezek. xliv. 23, 24.) hence the use of אלהים Ex. xxi. 6, xxii. 7, 8.
[7] Lev. x. 11. [8] Deut. xxxiii. 10. [9] 2 Chr. xv. 3.
[10] Ezek. vii. 26. [11] Jer. ii. 8.
[12] Ezek. xxii. 26, Zeph. iii. 4. [13] Ezr. vii. 12, 21.
[14] Ib. 25, 26. [15] Ib. 10. [16] Poc. [17] Ps. cxix. 142.
[18] Opus imp. in S. Matt. ap. S. Chrys. Hom. 25. T. vi. App. p. cix. Ben.
[19] Rom. x. 10.
[20] S. Ambr. Ep. xi. ad Theod. n. 2. 3. Ben. L.
[21] Ps. cxix. 46. [22] Gen. v. 24, vi. 9.

Before CHRIST cir. 397.

his lips: he walked with
me in peace and equity,
and did [f]turn many away
from iniquity.
7 [g]For the priest's lips
should keep knowledge,
and they should seek the
law at his mouth: [h]for
he *is* the messenger of the
LORD of hosts.

[f] Jer. 23. 22. Jam. 5. 20.
[g] Lev. 10. 11. Deut. 17. 9, 10. & 24. 8. Ezra 7. 10. Jer. 18. 18. Hag. 2. 11, 12.
[h] Gal. 4. 14.

"having respect in all things to Him and His glory."

In peace and equity. The inward peace with God overflowing in peace to men. The brief words comprise the duties of both tables; as that, [1] *Follow peace with all men, and holiness, without which no man shall see God;* [2] *Live in peace, and the God of love and peace shall be with you;* [3] *blessed are the peacemakers, for they shall be called the children of God.* "[4] God's covenant with him was of *peace*[5]; so he observed it on his part." Even *equity,* or real considerate justice, would alienate those, whom it found wrong, so he joins with it *peace,* that even equity was not administered but with love. "[6] To have peace with God, what is it but to will to be mended and to do what He willeth, and in nothing to offend Him?"

And turned away many from iniquity. They, the true priests of the Old Testament then, were not satisfied with their own sanctification, but were zealous for the salvation of souls. What a history of zeal for the glory of God and the conversion of sinners in those, of whom the world knows nothing; of whose working, but for the three words [7] in the closing book of the Old Testament, we should have known nothing! The Prophets upbraid the sins of the many; the Psalms are the prayers given to and used by the pious; such incidental sayings as these, record some of the fruits. "Be of the disciples of Aaron," said Hillel[8], "who loved peace and followed peace, and who loved men and brought them near to the law." Yet even under the Gospel S. Gregory complains, "[9] The world is full of priests; yet in the harvest of God the laborers are few. For we undertake the priestly office, but do not fulfill its work. We receive the fruit of holy Church in daily stipend, but labor not for the everlasting Church in preaching." "[10] There are many priests," says a writer in the IVth cent., "and few priests; many in name, few in deed. See then, how ye sit on your thrones; for the throne maketh not the priest, but the priest the throne; the place sanctifieth not the man, but the man the place. Whoso sitteth well on the throne, receiveth honor from the throne; whoso ill, doth injustice to the throne. Thou sittest in judgment. If thou livest well and teachest well, thou wilt be a judge of all; if thou teachest well and livest ill, thine own only. For by teaching well and living well thou instructest the people, how it ought to live; by teaching well and living ill, thou teachest God, how He should condemn thee." "[11] We who are called priests, above the ills which we have of our own, add also the deaths of others. For we slay as many as we, in tepidity and silence, see daily go to death.—He who is placed under thee dies without thee, when in that which causes his death, thou hast withstood him. For to that death, which thou hast not withstood, thou wilt be added."

7. *For the priest's lips should keep knowledge.* "[12] He assigns the reason for what he had just said, *the law of truth was in his mouth;* they had done what it was their duty to do; as in Ecclesiasticus it is said of Aaron; '[13] God gave unto him His commandments, and authority in the statutes of judgments, that he should teach Jacob the testimonies, and inform Israel in His laws.' So S. Paul requires of Titus to ordain such Bishops, as shall be able to [14] *exhort by sound doctrine and to convince gainsayers.* Wherefore S. Ambrose [15] calls the Bible, which contains the law of God, 'the book of priests,' as specially belonging to them, to be specially studied by them. S. Jerome notes that he says *keep,* not 'give forth,' that they should speak seasonably, and give their fellow-servants meat in due season."

For he is the messenger [or *angel*] *of the Lord of hosts.* Malachi gives to the priest the title which belongs to the lowest order of the heavenly spirits, as having an office akin to theirs; as Haggai does to the prophet [16], as an extraordinary *messenger* of God; and S. Paul tells the Galatians, [17] *ye received me as an angel of God, as Christ Jesus;* and Christ, by S. John, speaks to the Bishops of the seven Churches, good or bad, or of mixed good and bad, as *the angels* [18] *of* those *Churches.*

[1] Heb. xii. 14. Rom. xii. 18. [2] 2 Cor. xiii. 11. [3] S. Matt. v. 9. [4] Poc. [5] ver. 5. [6] S. Cyr.

[7] ורבים השיב מעון.

[8] Pirke Aboth c. i. § 13 Poc.

[9] S. Greg. Hom. xvii. in Evang. n. 3 and 8. Opp. i. 1496, 1499. Ben. L.

[10] Op. Imperf. in S. Matt. cxxiii. Hom. xliii. App. p. clxxxiii. Ben. L.

[11] S. Greg. Hom. in Ezek. L. i. Hom. xi. nn. 9. and 11. Opp. i. 1285. L.

[12] Lap. [13] Ecclus. xlv. 17. [14] Tit. i. 9.

[15] de fide iii. c. 15. n. 128. Opp. i. 519. Ben.

[16] Hagg. ii. 11. [17] Gal. iv. 14. [18] Rev. i. 20.

Before CHRIST cir. 397.

[i] 1 Sam. 2. 17. Jer. 18. 15.
‖ Or, *fall in the law.*
[k] Neh. 13. 29.

8 But ye are departed out of the way; ye [i] have caused many to ‖ stumble at the law; [k] ye have corrupted the covenant of Levi, saith the LORD of hosts.

9 Therefore [l] have I also made you contemptible and base before all the people, according as ye have not kept my ways, but ‖ † have been partial in the law.

Before CHRIST cir. 397.

[l] 1 Sam. 2. 30.
‖ Or, *lifted up the face against.*
† Heb. *accepted faces.*

"[1] Since in the heavenly hierarchy the order of Angels is the lowest, and in the Eucharistical hierarchy the order of the priesthood is the highest," "[2] most truly is the priest of God called angel, i. e. messenger, because he intervenes between God and man, and announces the things of God to the people; and therefore were the Urim and Thummim placed on the priest's *breastplate of* judgment, that we might learn, that the priest ought to be learned, a herald of Divine truth." Much more in the New Testament. "[3] Who, as it were in a day, can form one of earth, to be the defender of truth, to stand with angels, to give glory with Archangels, to transmit the sacrifices to the altar above, to be partaker of the priesthood [4] of Christ, to reform the thing formed, and present the image, to re-create for the world above, to be a god [5] and make men *partakers of the Divine Nature* [6]?" "[7] The priesthood is enacted on earth, but is ranked with the heavenly ranks. Very rightly. For not man, not angel, not archangel, not any other created power, but the Paraclete Himself hath ordained this office, and persuaded them, while yet abiding in the flesh, to conceive the ministry of the Angels. Wherefore, he who is consecrated as priest, ought to be pure, as if he stood among the heavenly powers." "[8] The throne of the priesthood is placed in the heavens, and he is entrusted with ministering things of heaven. Who saith this? The King of heaven Himself. For He saith, *Whatsoever ye shall bind on earth, shall be bound in heaven, and whatsoever ye shall loose on earth, shall be loosed in heaven.*—So the priest standeth in the middle between God and human nature, bringing down to us Divine benefits, and transmitting thither our supplications."

8. *But ye* [9] *are departed out of the way* "[10] of knowledge, truth, equity, fear of God, which I appointed to Aaron and the Levites." *Ye have caused many to stumble at the law.* He does not simply say, *in the law*, but *at* it. The law was what they stumbled at. They did not only misunderstand the law, through the false teaching of the priests, as though it allowed things which in truth were sins (although this too); itself was their source of stumbling. As Jesus Himself was *a rock of offence* whereon they stumbled, because through His Divine holiness He was not what they expected Him to be, so contrariwise the law became an offence to them through the unholiness and inconsistency of the lives and ways of those who taught it; much as we now hear Christianity spoken against, because of the inconsistency of Christians. So S. Paul saith to the Jews, [11] *The name of God is blasphemed among the Gentiles through you, as it is written;* and, for the sins of Eli's sons [12], *men abhorred the offering of the Lord.*

And have corrupted the covenant of Levi; as it is said in Nehemiah, [13] *They have defiled the priesthood, and the covenant of the priesthood and of Levi,* that *covenant* which was *life and peace* [14], and therefore forfeited them.

9. *Therefore have I made you contemptible.* They had said in their hearts, [15] *The table of the Lord is contemptible.* So God would requite them "[16] measure for measure." Yet not only so, but in their office as judges, against the repeated protestations in the law, [17] *Thou shalt not respect the person of the poor, nor honor the person of the mighty, in righteousness shalt thou judge thy neighbor;* [18] *ye shall not respect persons in judgment;* [19] *thou shall not wrest judgment,* he says,

Ye have accepted persons in the law. You have interpreted the law differently for rich and poor, or have put it in force against the poor, not against the rich. It would include actual bribery; but there are many more direct offences against equal justice. How differently is the like offence against the eighth commandment visited upon the poor who have real temptation to it, and the rich who have none, but the lust of the eyes!

"Crows he condones, vexes the simple dove."

That contempt which they cast upon God and His law, by wresting it out of respect to

[1] Dion. [2] S. Jer.
[3] S. Greg. Naz. Orat. ii. n. 73. p. 48 Ben.
[4] συνιερευσοντα.
[5] Θεον ἐσόμενον και θεοποιήσοντα. [6] 2 S. Pet. i. 4.
[7] S. Chrys. de Sacerdotio iii. 4. Opp. i. 382 Ben.
[8] Id. in Is. vi. 1. Hom. v. 1. Opp. vi. 132.
[9] ואתם, emphatic. [10] Lap.
[11] Rom. ii. 24. [12] 1 Sam. ii. 17. Poc. [13] Neh. xiii. 29.
[14] ii. 5. [15] i. 7. [16] Kim. [17] Lev. xix. 15.
[18] Deut. i. 17. [19] Ib. xvi. 19.

Before CHRIST cir. 397.

[m] 1 Cor. 8. 6. Eph. 4. 6.
[n] Job 31. 15.

10 [m] Have we not all
one father? [n] hath not one
God created us? why do
we deal treacherously
every man against his
brother, by profaning the
covenant of our fathers?
11 ¶ Judah hath dealt
treacherously, and an
abomination is committed
in Israel and in Jerusa-
lem; for Judah hath pro-
faned the holiness of the
LORD which he || loved,
[o] and hath married the
daughter of a strange god.

|| Or, *ought to love.*
[o] Ezra 9. 1. & 10. 2. Neh. 13. 23.

persons, that so they might gain favor and respect from them, so honoring them more than Him, and seeking to please them more than Him, will He cast back on them making them contemptible even in the eyes of those, from whom they thought by that means to find respect.

10. *Have we not all one Father*[1]? *Hath not one God created us?* Malachi turns abruptly to another offence, in which also the priests set an evil example, the capricious dismissal of their Hebrew wives and taking other women in their stead. Here, as before, he lays down, at the outset, a general moral principle, which he applies. The *one Father*, (it appears from the parallel), is manifestly Almighty God, as the Jews said to our Lord, [2] *We have one Father, even God.* He created them, not only as He did all mankind, but by the spiritual relationship with Himself, into which He brought them. So Isaiah speaks, [3] *Thus saith the Lord that created thee, O Jacob, and He that formed thee, O Israel. Every one that is called by My Name; I have created Him for My glory; I have formed him; yea I have made him. This people have I formed for Myself; they shall shew forth My praise.* And from the first in Moses' song, [4] *Is not He thy Father that created*[5] *thee? Hath He not made thee and established thee?* This creation of them by God, as His people, gave them a new existence, a new relation to each other; so that every offence against each other was a violation of their relation to God, Who had given them this unity, and was, in a nearer sense than of any other, the common Father of all. *Why then,* the prophet adds, *do we deal treacherously, a man against his brother, to profane the covenant of our fathers?* He does not yet say, wherein this treacherous dealing consisted; but awakens them to the thought, that sin against a brother is sin against God, Who made him a brother; as, and much more under the Gospel, in which we are all members of one mystical body; [6] *when ye sin so against the brethren, and wound their weak conscience, ye sin against Christ.* He speaks of the sin, as affecting those who did not commit it. Why do *we* deal treacherously? So Isaiah, before his lips were cleansed by the mystical coal, said, [7] *I am a man of unclean lips, and I dwell in the midst of a people of unclean lips,* and the high-priest Joshua was shewn in the vision, clothed with defiled garments[8]; and the sin of Achan became the *sin* of *the children of Israel*[9], and David's sinful pride in numbering the people was visited upon all[10]. He teaches beforehand, that, [11] *whether one member suffer, all the members suffer with it, or one member be honored, all the members rejoice with it.* They *profaned* also *the covenant of their fathers,* by marrying those whom God forbade, and who would seduce, as heathen wives had Solomon, from His worship. S. Paul in sanctioning the remarriage of widows, adds, *only*[12] *in the Lord,* i. e. Christian husbands. "[13] He who treated as null the difference between the Israelites and a heathen woman, shewed that the difference between the God of Israel and the God of the heathen had before become null to him, whence it follows;

11. *Treacherously has Judah dealt; an abomination is committed in Israel.* The prophet, by the order of the words, emphasizes the *treachery* and the *abomination.* This have they done; the very contrary to what was required of them as the people of God. He calls the remnant of Judah by the sacred name of the whole people, of whom they were the surviving representatives. The word "abomination[14]" is a word belonging to the Hebrew, and is used especially of

[1] Jews (Ibn E., Tanchum, Kim. Abarb. ap. Poc.) have understood the *one father* to be Jacob; S. Cyril, to be Abraham. The parallelism is, I think, decisive against both. Although Abraham is specially spoken of as their father, yet the appeal to that relation would not hold against the marriage, condemned here, since he was the father of the descendants of Ishmael as of Isaac, of the bitterest foes of Israel, the heathenish Edomites. Ammon and Moab, inveterate persecutors of Israel, were his near kindred. Ammonitesses and Moabitesses were as much forbidden by Ezra (ix. 2) as women of the different nations of Canaan, Ashdod or Egypt.

[2] S. John viii. 41.

[3] Is. xliii. 1. 7. 21. add xliv. 2, 21, 24.

[4] Deut. xxxii. 6.

[5] אבִיךָ קנֶךָ.

[6] 1 Cor. viii. 12.

[7] Is. vi. 5.

[8] Zech. iii. 3, 4. See ab. pp. 354, 355.

[9] Josh. vii. 1, 11.

[10] 2 Sam. xxiv.

[11] 1 Cor. xii. 26.

[12] Ib. vii. 39.

[13] Hengst. Christ. iii. 595.

[14] תּוֹעֵבָה.

Before CHRIST cir. 397.

12 The LORD will cut
off the man that doeth
this, || the master and the
scholar, out of the tabernacles of Jacob, [p] and him
that offereth an offering
unto the LORD of hosts.
13 And this have ye
done again, covering the
altar of the LORD with
tears, with weeping, and
with crying out, insomuch
that he regardeth not the
offering any more, or re-
ceiveth *it* with good will
at your hand.

|| Or, *him that waketh, and him that answereth.*

p Neh. 13. 28, 29.

Before CHRIST cir. 397.

---

things offensive to, or separating from, Almighty God; idolatry, as the central dereliction of God, and involving offences against the laws of nature, but also all other sins, as adultery, which violate His most sacred laws and alienate from Him.

Hath profaned the holiness of the Lord which He loved, in themselves, who had been separated and set apart by God to Himself as a [1] *holy nation.* [2] *Israel* was *holiness to the Lord.* "[3] The Lord is holy, perfect holiness; His name, holy; all things relating to Him, holy; His law, covenant and all His ordinances and institutions holy; Israel, His peculiar people, an holy people; the temple and all things therein consecrated to Him, holy; Jerusalem, the city of the great God, holy; yea, the whole land of His inheritance, holy; so that whosoever doth not observe those due respects which to any of these belong, may be said to have *profaned the holiness which He loved.*"

Unlawful marriages and unlawful lusts were in themselves a special profanation of that holiness. The high priest was to [4] *take a virgin of his own people to wife*, and *not* to *profane his seed among the people.* The priests who *married strange wives, defiled the priesthood and the covenant of the priesthood* [5]. The marriage with idolatresses brought, as one consequence, the profanation by their idolatries. The prohibition is an anticipation of the fuller revelation in the Gospel, that [6] the body is the temple of the Holy Ghost, and so, that *sins against the body* are profanations of the temple of God. "[3] As those who acknowledge, worship and serve the true God are called His [7] *sons and daughters*, so they that worshiped any strange god are, by like reason, here called the daughters of that god. Hence the Jews say, '[8] He that marrieth a heathen woman is, as if he made himself son-in-law to an idol.'"

Hath married the daughter of a strange god. And so he came into closest relation with idols and with devils.

12. *The Lord will cut off the man that doeth this, the master and the scholar*, lit. *The Lord cut off from the man that doeth this, watcher* [9] *and answerer.* A proverbial saying apparently, in which the two corresponding classes comprise the whole [10]. Yet so, probably, that the one is the active agent; the other, the passive. The one as a *watcher* goes his rounds, to see that nothing stirreth against that which he is to guard; the other *answereth*, when roused. Together, they express the two opposite classes, active and passive sin; those who originate the sin, and those who adopt or retain it at the instigation of the inventor or active propagator of it. It will not exempt from punishment, that he was led into the sin.

From the tabernacles of Jacob. Perhaps "he chose the word, to remind them of their unsettled condition," out of which God had brought them.

And him that offereth an offering unto the Lord of hosts; i. e. him, who, doing these things, offereth an offering to God, to bribe Him, as it were, to connivance at his sin. In the same meaning, Isaiah says, that God hateth [11] *iniquity and the solemn meeting*, and, [12] *I hate robbery with burnt-offering;* or Solomon, [13] *The sacrifice of the wicked is an abomination to the Lord;* [14] *he that turneth away his ear from hearing the law, his prayer shall be an abomination.* And God by Amos says, [15] *I hate, I despise, your feast-days, and will not accept your solemn assemblies.* In one sense the sacrifice was an aggravation, in that the worship of God made the offence either a sin against light, or implied that God might be bribed into connivance in the breaking of His laws. The ancient discipline of removing from Communion those guilty of grievous sin was founded on this principle.

13. *And this ye have done again*, adding the second sin of cruelty to their wives to the

---

[1] Ex. xix. 6. [2] Jer. ii. 3. [3] Poc.
[4] Lev. xxi. 14, 15. [5] Neh. xiii. 29.
[6] 1 Cor. vi. 15–20.
[7] Deut. xxxii. 19, 2 Cor. vi. 18.
[8] Maim. in Issure biah, c. 12. § 1. Poc.
[9] Not "the awakener," as if עֵר were active: for עור is always intransitive, except in the correction of the text, Job xli. 2. In Chald. עִיר is "a watcher." Dan. iv. 10, 14.
[10] Dietrich, Abhandll. zur Hebr. Gram. p. 201 sqq., has instances from the Arabic, but not so energetic as those in the O. T., except when they are the same.
[11] Is. i. 13. [12] Ib. lxi. 8. [13] Prov. xv. 8.
[14] Ib. xxviii. 9. [15] See vol. i. p. 299 on Am. v. 21.

Before CHRIST cir. 397.

14 ¶ Yet ye say,
Wherefore? Because the
LORD hath been witness
between thee and [q] the wife of thy youth, against — q Prov. 5. 18.
whom thou hast dealt
treacherously: [r] yet *is* she — r Prov. 2. 17.
thy companion, and the
wife of thy covenant.
15 And [s] did not he — s Matt. 19. 4, 5.
make one? Yet had he
the || residue of the spirit. — || Or, *excellency.* † Heb. *a seed of God.*
And wherefore one? That
he might seed † [t] a godly — t Ezra 9. 2. 1 Cor. 7. 14.

Before CHRIST cir. 397.

---

taking foreign women; *they covered the altar of God with tears*, in that they by ill-treatment occasioned their wives to weep there to God; and God regarded this, as though they had stained the altar with their tears.

Insomuch that He regardeth not the offering any more. God regarded the tears of the oppressed, not the sacrifices of the oppressors. He would not accept what was thus offered Him as a thing well-pleasing [1] to Him, acceptable to win His good pleasure.

14. *And ye say, Wherefore?* They again act the innocent, or half-ignorant. What had they to do with their wives' womanly tears? He Who knows the hearts of all was Himself the witness between them and the wife of youth of each; her to whom, in the first freshness of life and their young hearts, each had plighted his troth, having been entrusted by her with her earthly all. [2] *The Lord*, said even Laban, when parting from his daughters, *watch between me and thee, when we are absent, the one from the other; if thou shalt afflict my daughters, or if thou shalt take wives beside my daughters, no man* is *with us; see, God* is *witness between me and thee.*

And he dealt treacherously against her, violating his own faith and her trusting love, which she had given once for all, and could not now retract. *And she is thy companion;* she has been another self, the companion of thy life, sharing thy sorrows, joys, hopes, fears, interests; different in strength, yet in all, good and ill, sickness and health, thy associate and companion; the help meet for the husband and provided for him by God in Paradise; and above all, *the wife of thy covenant*, to whom thou didst pledge thyself before God. These are so many aggravations of their sin. She was the wife of their youth, of their covenant, their companion; and God was the witness and Sanctifier of their union. Marriage was instituted and consecrated by God in Paradise. Man was to leave father and mother (if so be), but to cleave to his wife indissolubly. For they were to be [3] *no more twain, but one flesh.* Hence, as a remnant of Paradise, even the heathen knew of marriage, as a religious act, guarded by religious sanctions. Among God's people, marriage was a [4] *covenant of their God.* To that original institution of marriage he seems to refer in the following;

15. *And did not He*, God, of Whom he had spoken as the witness between man and his wife, *make one*, viz. Adam first, to mark the oneness of marriage and make it a law of nature, appointing "that out of man (created in His own image and similitude,) woman should take her beginning, and, knitting them together, did teach that it should never be lawful to put asunder those, whom He by matrimony had made one [5]?" "[6] Between those two, and consequently between all other married, to be born from them, He willed that there should be one indivisible union; for Adam could be married to no other save Eve, since no other had been created by God, nor could Eve turn to any other man than Adam, since there was no other in the world. 'Infringe not then this sanction of God, and unity of marriage, and degenerate not from your first parents, Adam and Eve.'" "[7] If divorce had been good, Jesus says, God would not have made one man and one woman, but, having made one Adam, would have made two women, had He meant that he should cast out the one, bring in the other; but now by the mode of creation, He brought in this law, that each should have, throughout, the wife which he had from the beginning. This law is older than that about divorce, as much as Adam is older than Moses."

Yet had he the residue of the spirit; [8] *the breath of life, which He breathed into* Adam, *and man became a living soul.* All the souls, which God would ever create, are His, and He could have called them into being at once. Yet in order to designate the unity of marriage, He willed to create but one. So our Lord argues against divorce, [9] *Have ye not read, that He which made them at the beginning, made them male and female?* They both together are called *one man* [10], and therefore should be of one mind and spirit also, the unity of which they ought faithfully to preserve.

---

1 רצון. 2 Gen. xxxi. 49, 50.
3 S. Matt. xix. 6. 4 Prov. ii. 17.
5 Marriage Service. 6 Lap.

7 S. Chrys. de libello repud. n 2. Opp. iii. 28. Ben. Rib.
8 Gen. ii. 7. 9 S. Matt. xix. 4–6. 10 Gen. i. 27.

Before CHRIST cir. 397.

seed. Therefore take heed
to your spirit, and let none
deal ‖treacherously
against the wife of his
youth.
16 For [u] the LORD, the
God of Israel, saith ‖that
he hateth † putting away:
for *one* covereth violence
with his garment, saith
the LORD of hosts: there-
fore take heed to your
spirit, that ye deal not
treacherously.
17 ¶ [x] Ye have wearied
the LORD with your words.
Yet ye say, Wherein have
we wearied *him?* When
ye say, Every one that doeth evil *is* good in the
sight of the LORD, and he
delighteth in them; or,
Where *is* the God of judgment?

‖ Or, *unfaithfully.*

[u] Deut. 24. 1. Matt. 5. 32. & 19. 8.

‖ Or, *if he hate her, put her away.*

† Heb. *to put away.*

[x] Isai 43. 24. Amos 2. 13. ch 3. 13, 14, 15.

And wherefore one? Seeking a seed of God, i. e. worthy of God; for from religious marriage, religious offspring may most be hoped from God; and by violating that law, those before the flood brought in a spurious, unsanctified generation, so that God in His displeasure destroyed them all. *And take heed to your spirit*[1], which ye too had from God, which was His, and which He willed in time to create. He closes, as he began, with an appeal to man's natural feeling, *let none deal treacherously against the wife of his youth.*

16. *He hateth putting away*[2]. He had allowed it *for the hardness of their hearts,* yet only in the one case of some extreme bodily foulness[3], discovered upon marriage, and which the woman, knowing the law, concealed at her own peril. Not subsequent illness or any consequences of it, however loathsome (as leprosy), were a ground of divorce, but only this concealed foulness, which the husband *found* upon marriage. The capricious tyrannical divorce, God saith, *He hateth:* a word[4] naturally used only as to sin, and so stamping such divorce as sin.

One *covereth violence with his garment*[5] or, *and violence covereth his garment*[6], or, it might be, in the same sense, *he covereth his garment with violence*[7], so that it cannot be hid, nor washed away, nor removed, but envelopes him and his garment; and that, to his shame and punishment. It was, as it were, an outer garment of violence, as Asaph says, [8] *violence covereth them as a garment;* or David, [9] *he clothed himself with cursing as with a garment.* It was like a garment with *fretting leprosy,* unclean and making unclean, to be burned with fire[10]. Contrariwise, the redeemed saints had [11] *washed their robes and made them white in the Blood of the Lamb.* Having declared God's hatred of this their doing, he sums up in the same words, but more briefly; *and* this being so, *ye shall take heed to your spirit, and not deal treacherously.*

17. *Ye have wearied the Lord with your words.* "[12] By your blasphemous words, full of unbelief and mistrust, you have in a man-

[1] The רוחכם, "your spirit," manifestly refers back to "the residue of the spirit," שאר רוח which, he says, was God's.

[2] The E. M. "*If he hate* her, *put* her *away,*" (which follows Jon.) seems to enjoin what Malachi reproves these for, their cruelty to their wives, as also it gives an unbounded license of divorce.

[3] ערות דבר Deut. xxiv. 1, used of disgusting foulness in the chapter before, xxiii. 15.

[4] Things spoken of as objects of God's hatred, are, "a proud look, a lying tongue, hands that shed innocent blood, a heart that deviseth wicked imaginations, feet that be swift in running to mischief, a false witness that speaketh lies, and he that soweth discord among brethren," Prov. vi. 16–19; "pride, arrogancy, the evil way, and the froward mouth," Ib. viii. 13; idolatry, De. xvi. 22, Jer. xliv. 4, "robbery with burnt-offering," Is. lxi. 8; heathen abominations, Deut. xii. 31; worship with sin, Am. v. 21, Is. i. 14.

[5] No Jewish-Arabic writer notices the meaning, which Pococke suggested, and Gesenius, Fürst, Ewald follow; as if לבוש signified "wife," because in the Koran לבאס is used, not directly for 'husband' or "wife," but in its original sense, "covering," of each reciprocally, הנ לבאס לכם ואנתם לבאס להן "they (your wives) are a garment to you, and you are a garment to them." So Abimelech said to Sarah, "*he* [Abraham] is *to thee a covering* (כסות) *of the eyes, unto all which are with thee,* (Gen. xx. 16). But לבאס does not signify, either husband or wife. In Arabic, חלה and אזאר loose dresses, (See Lane Arab. Lex. p. 53, 621) are used metaph. of a wife; (אזאר also of a person's self or family as well). But there is no trace of this in Heb.

[6] According to the constr., Nu. xvi. 33, Lev. iv. 8, Job xxi. 26, where the thing covering is the nominative and על is put before the thing covered. So Vulg. and LXX. originally, as shewn by the Arabic transl., though now the LXX. has ἐνθυμήματα for ἐνδύματα. (De Dieu.)

[7] In Ez. xxiv. 7, Job xxxvi. 32, the thing covering is in the acc., with על of thing covered.

[8] Ps. lxxiii. 6. [9] Ib. cix. 18. [10] Lev. xiii. 47–58. [11] Rev. vii. 14. [12] Dion.

Before CHRIST cir. 397.

CHAPTER III.

1 *Of the messenger, majesty and grace of Christ.* 7 *Of the rebellion,* 8 *sacrilege,* 13 *and infidelity of the people.* 16 *The promise of blessing to them that fear God.*

BEHOLD, [a] I will send
my messenger, and he
shall [b] prepare the way before me: and the Lord,
whom ye seek, shall sud-
denly come to his temple,

Before CHRIST cir. 397.

a Matt. 11. 10. Mark 1. 2. Luke 1. 76. & 7. 27.
b Isai. 40. 3.

ner wearied God. He speaks of God, after the manner of men, as a man afflicted by the ills of others. Whence also the Lord says in Isaiah, [1] *I am weary to bear them,* and [2] *thou hast made Me to serve with thy sins; thou hast wearied Me with thine iniquities.* In like way the Apostle says, [3] *Grieve not the Holy Spirit of God.*"

With the same contumacy as before, and unconsciousness of sin, they ask, *Wherein?* It is the old temptation at the prosperity of the wicked. "Does God love the wicked? if not, why does He not punish them?" "[4] The people, when returned from Babylon, seeing all the nations around, and the Babylonians themselves, serving idols but abounding in wealth, strong in body, possessing all which is accounted good in this world, and themselves, who had the knowledge of God, overwhelmed with want, hunger, servitude, is scandalized and says, 'There is no providence in human things; all things are borne along by blind chance, and not governed by the judgment of God; nay rather, things evil please Him, things good displease Him; or if God does discriminate all things, where is His equitable and just judgment?' Questions of this sort minds, which believe not in the world to come, daily raise to God, when they see the wicked in power, the saints in low estate; such as Lazarus, whom we read of in the Gospel, who, before the gate of the rich man in his purple, desires to support his hungry soul with the crumbs which are thrown away from the remnants of the table, while the rich man is of such savagery and cruelty, that he had no pity on his fellow-man, to whom the tongues of the dogs shewed pity; not understanding the time of judgment, nor that those are the true goods, which are for ever, say, He is pleased with the evil, and, Where is the God of judgment?"

Where is the God of the judgment? "[5] i. e. of that judgment, the great, most certain, most exact, clearsighted, omniscient, most just, most free, wherein He regards neither powerful nor rich nor gifts, nor aught but justice? For He is *the God of the judgment,* to Whom it belongs by nature to judge all men and things by an exact judgment: for His nature is equity itself, justice itself, providence itself, and that, most just, most wise.—To Him it belongs to be the Judge of all, and to exercise strict judgment upon all; and He will exercise it fully on that decisive and last day of the world, which shall be the horizon between this life and the next, parting off time from eternity, heaven from hell, the blessed from the damned forever, through Christ, Whom He constituted Judge of all, quick and dead."

III. 1. God answers their complaints of the absence of His judgments, that they would come, but would include those also who clamored for them. For no one who knew his own sinfulness would call for the judgment of God, as being himself, *chief of sinners.* S. Augustine pictures one saying to God, "Take away the ungodly man," and that God answers, "Which?"

Behold, I send My messenger before My face, and he shall prepare My way before Me. They, then, were not prepared for *His* Coming, for Whom they clamored. The messenger is the same whom Isaiah had foretold, whose words Malachi uses [6]; [7] *The voice of one crying in the wilderness, Prepare ye the way of the Lord, make straight in the desert a high-way for our God.* [8] *Thou, child,* was the prophecy on S. John Baptist's birth, *shalt be called the prophet of the Highest; for thou shalt go before the face of the Lord to prepare His way, to give knowledge of salvation unto His people, for the remission of their sins.* Repentance was to be the preparation for the kingdom of Christ, the Messiah, for Whom they looked so impatiently.

He Who speaks, is He Who should come, God the Son. For it was before Him Who came and dwelt among us, that the way was to be prepared. He speaks here in His Divine Nature, as the Lord Who should send, and Who should Himself come in our flesh. In the Gospel, when He *was* come in the flesh, He speaks not of His own Person but of the Father, since "[9] indivisible are the operations of the Trinity, and what the One doth, the other Two do, since the Three are of one nature, power and operation." Whence Christ, in order to give no excuse to the Jews to speak against Him before the time, refers

[1] Is. i. 14. [2] Ib. xliii. 24. [3] Eph. iv. 30.
[4] S. Jer. [5] Lap.
[6] פַּנָּה דרך had been used only by Isaiah, xl. 3, lvii. 14, lxii. 10, although פַּנָּה לְפָנֶיהָ, abs., had been used Ps. lxxx. 10.
[7] Is. xl. 3. [8] S. Luke i. 76. [9] Lap.

Before CHRIST cir. 397.

[e] even the messenger of the
covenant, whom ye delight

[e] Isai. 63. 9.

in: behold, [d] he shall come,
saith the LORD of hosts.

Before CHRIST cir. 397.

[d] Hag. 2. 7.

it, as He does His life[1], His doctrine[2], words[3] and works[4] to the Father.

"[5] Those works, which do not relate to that which belongs peculiarly to each Person, being common, are ascribed now to One Person, now to Another, in order to set forth the One Substance in the Trinity of Persons." Thus, S. John says[6], Isaiah spoke of the unbelief of the Jews, when he *saw* the *glory* of God the Son *and spake of Him*, and S. Paul says[7] that the *Holy Ghost spake* then *by* him.

And he shall prepare the way before Me. "[8] The same is God's way here, and Christ's there, an evident proof that Christ is one God with the Father, and that, in Christ, God came and was manifest in the flesh." The prophets and all who turned men to righteousness, or who retained the knowledge of the truth or of righteousness or of God in the world, did, in their degree, prepare the way for Christ. But John was His immediate forerunner *before His Face*, the herald of His immediate approach; whence he is called "[9] the end of the law, and the beginning of the Gospel," "[10] the lamp before the Light, the voice before the Word, the mediator between the Old and the New Testament;" "[11] the link of the law and of grace; a new morning star; a ray, before the true Sun should burst forth," the end of night, the beginning of day.

And the Lord, Whom ye seek, shall suddenly come to His temple. He, Whose Coming they sought for, was Almighty God, *the God of Judgment*[12]. He Who should come, was *the Lord*, again Almighty God, since, in usage too, none else is called "*the* Lord[13]," as none else can be. The temple also, to which He was to come, the temple of God, is His own. *The messenger*, or *the Angel of the covenant*, plainly, even from the parallelism, is the same as *the Lord.* It was *one*, for whom they looked; one, of whose absence they complained; [14] *where is the God of judgment?* one, who should come to His temple[15]; one, whose coming they sought and prepared to *have pleasure in*[16]; one, of whom it is repeated, *lo, He cometh*[17]; one, in the day of whose coming, at whose appearing, it was asked, *who shall stand?* "[18] All Christian interpreters are agreed that this Lord is Christ, [19] *Whom God hath made both Lord and Christ*, and [20] *Who is Lord over all;* by Whom all things were made, are sustained and governed; Who is (as the root of the word[21] imports) the basis and foundation, not of any private family, tribe or kingdom, but of all; [22] *by Whom are all things and we by Him:* and Whose we are also by right of redemption; and so He is [23] *Lord of lords and King of kings*, deservedly called *the* Lord." As then the special presence of God was often indicated in connection with *the Angel of the Lord*, so, here, He Who was to come was entitled the Angel or messenger of the covenant, as God also calls Him the covenant itself, [24] *I will give Thee for a covenant of the people, a light of the Gentiles.* He it was, [25] *the Angel of His Presence*, Who saved His former people, *in* Whom His *Name was*, and Who,

[1] S. John vi. 57. [2] Ib. vii. 16.

[3] Ib. iii. 11, v. 43, viii. 38, 40, 47, 55, xii. 49, xiv. 10, 24.

[4] Ib. iv. 34, v. 19, 20, 26, 30, 36, vi. 38, viii. 28, ix. 4, x. 25, 32, 37, 38, xiv. 10, 11.

[5] Rib. [6] S. John xii. 41. [7] Acts xxviii. 25.

[8] Poc.

[9] S. Thom. 3 p. q. 38. art. 1. ad 2. See Tert. in Marc. iv. 33. pp. 317, 318. Edinb. Tr.

[10] S. Greg. Naz. Orat. 21. n. 3 p. 387 Ben.

[11] S. Chrysol. Serm. 21. Bibl. Patr. vii. 917.

[12] Rashi, "The God of judgment." Ibn Ezra says, "This is the glory; this is *the messenger of the covenant;* for the sense is doubled." Abarbanel, "Haadon is the Name which is glorified, who will then come to His temple, the house of His sanctuary, and His glorious name and His Shechinah shall dwell there; and this is what they sought in their murmurings." In the "Mashmia' yeshu'ah," "he says, "Haadon may be explained of the king Messiah." Kimchi also gives it as his first explanation; "Haadon, he is the king Messiah, and he is the angel of the covenant;" but he gives an alternative explanation, "or he calls Elijah the messenger of the covenant." Saadiah Gaon admits the '*Me*,' before whom the messenger is sent, to be the Messiah b. David. "The forerunner of the Messiah b. David will be like his embassador, and as one who prepareth the people, and cleareth the way, as in what is said, Behold I send &c." Sepher Haemunoth Tr. 8 de redemptione, (quoted by Voisin on the P. F. f. 127.) The author of the older Nizzachon (whether seriously or to have something to say) said, "He is sent and is not God." Wagenseil p. 126. Tanchum says, "they are promised a time, in which transgressors will be requited with a swift retribution by the just king whom God will raise up to the rule, and he is the king Messiah."

The Jews are agreed also that the messenger is no ordinary person. Ibn Ezra supposes him to be the Messiah b. Joseph, holding accordingly that he, before whose face he should come, was the Messiah ben David: Kimchi, that it was an angel from heaven (as in Ex. xxiii. 20.) to guard them in the way. But to guard *in* the way is not to prepare the way *before* him; Rashi and the author of the Abkath rochel, "the angel of death who should clear away the wicked;" Abarbanel, that it was Malachi himself; but he who is promised through Malachi, was yet to come.

[13] האדון Ex. xxiii. 17, xxxiv. 23, Is. i. 24, iii. 1, x. 16, 33, xxix. 4. [all, beside this place.]

[14] ii. 17. [15] יבוא אל היכלו, iii. 1.

[16] מבקשים, רפצים Ib. [17] חנה בא. [18] Poc.

[19] Acts ii. 36. [20] Ib. x. 36.

[21] Poc., (as Abulwalid, Menahem, Parchon, Kimchi) derives אדון from אדן.

[22] 1 Cor. viii. 6. [23] Rev. xvii. 14, xix. 16.

[24] Is. xlii. 6. [25] Ib. lxiii. 9.

Before CHRIST cir. 397.

e ch. 4. 1.
f Rev. 6. 17.

2 But who may abide
e the day of his coming?
and f who shall stand when
he appeareth? for g he *is*
like a refiner's fire, and
like fullers' soap:

Before CHRIST cir. 397.

g See Is. 4. 4. Matt. 3. 10, 11, 12.

by the prerogative of God, would [1] *not pardon* their *transgressions*. He should be [2] *the Mediator of the new* and *better covenant* which is promised; [3] *not according to the covenant, that I made with their fathers, in the day when I took them by the hand to lead them out of the land of Egypt*, which *My covenant they brake, although I was a husband unto them, saith the Lord; but this shall be the covenant, that I will make with the house of Israel after those days, saith the Lord, I will put My law in their inward parts, and write it in their hearts, and will be their God and they shall be My people.*

Whom ye seek, are seeking, Whom ye delight in, i. e. profess so to do; *He will come*, but will be very different from Him whom ye look for, an Avenger on your enemies. Judgment will come, but it will begin with yourselves.

Shall suddenly come, "[4] unawares, when men should not think of them; whence perhaps it is that the Jews reckon the Messiah among what shall come *unawares*[5]. As, it is here said of His first Coming, so it is said of His second Coming (which may be comprehended under this here spoken of) that except they diligently watch for it, [6] *it shall come upon them unawares*, [7] *suddenly*, [8] *in such an hour as they think not.* "[9] The Lord of glory always comes, like a thief in the night, to those who sleep in their sins."

Lo, He will come: he insists again and calls their minds to that Coming, certain, swift, new, wonderful, on which all eyes should be set, but His Coming would be a sifting-time.

2. *And who may abide the day of His coming? And who shall stand when He appeareth?* The implied answer is, "No one;" as in the Psalm, [10] *If Thou, Lord, wilt mark iniquities, O Lord, who shall stand?* Joel had asked the same, [11] *The day of the Lord is great and very terrible; and who can abide it?* "[12] How can the weakness of man endure such might; his blindness, such light; his frailty, such power; his uncleanness, such holiness; the chaff, such a fire? *For He is like a refiner's fire.* Who would not fail through stupefaction, fear, horror, shrinking reverence, from such majesty?"

Malachi seems to blend, as Joel, the first and second coming of our Lord. The first Coming too was a time of sifting and severance, according as those, to whom He came, did or did not receive Him. The severance was not final, because there was yet space for repentance; but it was real, an earnest of the final judgment. [13] *For judgment*, our Lord says, *I am come into this world, that they which see not may see, and they which see might be made blind;* and again, [14] *Now is the judgment of this world;* and, [15] *He that believeth not is condemned already, because he hath not believed on the name of the Only-Begotten Son of God;* [16] *He that believeth not the Son, shall not see life, but the wrath of God abideth on him.* As, on the other hand, He saith, [17] *whoso eateth My Flesh and drinketh My Blood hath eternal life;* and [18] *he that believeth on the Son hath everlasting life;* "*hath,*" He saith; not, "shall have;" *hath* it, in present reality and earnest, though he may forfeit it: so the other class *is condemned already*, although the one may repent and be saved, the other may [19] *turn from his righteousness and commit iniquity;* and if he persevere in it, *shall die therein.* It is then one ever-present judgment. Every soul of man is in a state of grace or out of it; in God's favor or under His wrath; and the judgment of the Great Day, in which the secrets of men's hearts shall be revealed, will be but an outward manifestation of that now hidden judgment. But the words, in their fullest sense, imply a passing of that judgment, in which men do or do not stand, as in those of our Lord, [20] *As a snare shall that day come on all those that dwell on the face of the whole earth. Watch ye, therefore, and pray always, that ye may be accounted worthy to escape all these things which shall come to pass, and to stand before the Son of Man;* and S. Paul, [21] *Take unto you the whole armor of God, that ye may be able to withstand in the evil day, and, having done all, to stand;* and in the Revelation, [22] *They said to the mountains and rocks; Fall on us, and hide us from the wrath of Him that sitteth upon the throne, and from the wrath of the Lamb. For the great day of His wrath is come, and who shall*

1 Ex. xxiii. 21. 2 Heb. xii. 24, viii. 6.
3 Jer. xxxi. 32, 33, Heb. viii. 9. 4 Poc.
5 "Buxt. Lex. Ch. et Talm. v. נסח" Poc.
6 S. Luke xxi. 35.
7 S. Mark xiii. 36.
8 S. Matt. xxiv. 44. 9 Schmieder.
10 Ps. cxxx. 3.
11 Jo. ii. 11, ומי יכילנו; Jer. x. 10, "*The nations shall not abide* (יָכִלוּ) *His indignation.*" Vulg. has, cogitare, i. e. who shall comprehend? But כלכל, in this sense, is used of actual containing, *the heaven of heavens cannot contain* the Infinite God, (1 Kgs viii. 27, 2 Chr. ii. 5, [6 Eng.] vi. 18.) not of intellectually comprehending.
12 Lap. 13 S. John ix. 39. 14 Ib. xii. 31.
15 Ib. iii. 18. 16 Ib. 36.
17 Ib. vi. 54. 18 Ib. 47.
19 Ezek. xxxiii. 18. 20 S. Luke xxi. 35, 36.
21 Eph. vi. 13. 22 Rev. vi. 16, 17.

Before CHRIST cir. 397.

h Isai. 1. 25. Zech. 13. 9.

3 And [h] he shall sit *as*
a refiner and purifier of
silver: and he shall purify
the sons of Levi, and
purge them as gold and
silver, that they may [i] offer unto the LORD an of-
fering in righteousness.

Before CHRIST cir. 397.

i 1 Pet. 2. 5.

be able to stand? Asaph says of a temporal, yet, for this life, final destruction; [1] *At Thy rebuke, O God of Jacob, both the chariot and horse are cast into a deep sleep. Thou art to be feared, and who may stand in Thy sight, when Thou art angry?*

For He is like a refiner's fire, and like fuller's soap. Two sorts of materials for cleansing are mentioned, the one severe, where the baser materials are inworked with the rich ore; the other mild, where the defilement is easily separable. "[2] He shall come like a refining fire; [3] *a fire shall burn before Him, and it shall be very tempestuous round about Him. Then He shall call the heaven from above, and the earth, that He may judge His people;* streams of fire shall sweep before, bearing away all sinners. For the Lord is called a fire, and a [4] *consuming fire*, so as to burn our [5] *wood, hay, stubble.* And not fire only, but *fuller's soap* [6]. To those who sin heavily, He is a refining and *consuming fire*, but to those who commit light sins, *fuller's soap*, to restore cleanness to it, when washed." Yet, though light in comparison, this too had its severity; for clothes which were washed (of which the word is used) were trampled [7] on by the feet. "[8] The nitrum and the fuller's soap is penitence." Yet the whiteness and purity so restored, is, at the last, perfected. Inspiration could find no more adequate comparison for us, for the brightness of our Lord's raiment from the glory of the Transfiguration, than, [9] *exceeding white as snow; so as no fuller on earth can white them.*

Our Lord is, in many ways, as a fire. He says of Himself; [10] *I am come to send a fire upon earth, and what will I, if it be already kindled?* S. John Baptist said of Him, [11] *He shall baptize you with the Holy Ghost and with fire.* He kindles in the heart "a fire of love," which softens what is hard, will

"[12] Wash whate'er of stain is here,
Sprinkle what is dry or sere,
Heal and bind the wounded sprite;
Bend whate'er is stubborn still,
Kindle what is cold and chill,
What hath wandered guide aright."

But as God is *a consuming fire*, Who must burn out the dross, unless we be [13] *reprobate silver* which *the founder melteth in vain*, either He must, by His grace, consume the sin within us, or must consume us with it, in hell.

3. *And He shall sit* [14], as a King and Judge on His throne, with authority, yet also to try accurately the cause of each, separating seeming virtues from real graces; hypocrites, more or less consciously, from His true servants.

He shall purify [15] *the sons of Levi.* These had been first the leaders in degeneracy, the corrupters of the people by their example and connivance. Actually [16] *a great company of the priests were obedient to the faith.* Barnabas also was a Levite [17]. But more largely, as Zion and Jerusalem are the titles for the Christian Church, and Israel who believed was the true Israel, so *the sons of Levi* are the true Levites, the Apostles and their successors in the Christian priesthood.

It was through three centuries of persecutions that the Church was purified by fire.

That they may offer, lit. *and they shall be unto the Lord offerers of a meal-offering in righteousness*, i. e. they shall be such, and that, habitually, abidingly. Again, here and in the next words, *and the meal-offering of Judah shall be pleasant unto the Lord*, it is remarkable, that the *meal-offering*, to which the Holy Eucharist corresponds, is alone mentioned. Of bloody offerings Malachi is silent; for they were to cease.

1 Ps. lxxvi. 6, 7. 2 S. Jer. 3 Ps. l. 3, 4.
4 Deut. iv. 24. 5 1 Cor. iii. 12.

6 בֹּרית is a generic name for materials for cleansing; but various plants, possessing alkaline qualities, grew and grow in Palestine, and "kali" is still an article of trade. Being united with נתר Jer. ii. 22, it has been supposed the "borith" is a vegetable, as contrasted with נתר, a mineral. "For the herb *Borith*, the LXX. have translated ποαν, to signify the herb of fullers, which according to the wont of Palestine grows in luxuriant moist places, and has the same virtue for cleansing defilements as nitrum." S. Jer. on Jerem. ii. 21.

7 כבס, (only used in Piel, except in the part. of the obsolete Kal. Comp., with Ges., כבש and בוס.

8 S. Jer. ib. 9 S. Mark ix. 3. 10 S. Luke xii. 49.

11 Ib. iii. 16.

12 Transl. of Whitsun-hymn, Veni Sancte Spiritus, in Hymns for the Week and the Seasons p. 105. 1848.

13 Jer. vi. 29, 30.

14 The usual word for sitting on a throne, Ex. xii. 29, Deut. xvii. 18, 1 Kgs i. 13, 17, 46, 48, ii. 12, 24, iii. 6, viii. 20, 25, xvi. 11, xxii. 10, 2 Kgs x. 30, xi. 19, xiii. 13, xv. 12, Ps. cxxxii. 12, Pr. xx. 8, Is. xvi. 5, Jer. xiii. 13, xvii. 25, xxii. 4, 30, xxxiii. 17, xxxvi. 30, Zech. vi. 13; or for judgment, Ex. xviii. 13. Jud. v. 10, Ps. cxxii. 5, Is. xxviii. 6, Jer. xxix. 16, Dan. vii. 9, 26, Jo. iii. 12. Of God, Ps. ii. 4, ix. 5, 8, xxix. 10, xlvii. 8, lv. 20, 1 Kgs xxii. 19, Is. vi. 1. and others.

15 זקק, probably originally "strained," used of wine, Is. xxvi. 6, but thence perhaps, the first meaning being lost, of precious metals; gold, Job xxviii. 1, 1 Chr. xxviii. 18, silver, Ps. xii. 7, 1 Chr. xxix. 4.

16 Acts vi. 7. 17 Ib. iv. 36.

Before CHRIST cir. 397.

4 Then [k]shall the offering of Judah and Jerusalem be pleasant unto the LORD, as in the days of old, and as ||in former years.

[k] ch. 1. 11.

|| Or, *ancient*.

5 And I will come near to you to judgment; and I will be a swift witness against the sorcerers, and against the adulterers, [l]and against false swearers, and

Before CHRIST cir. 397.

[l] Zech. 5. 4. Jam. 5. 4, 12.

In righteousness, as Zacharias prophesied, *that we might serve Him in holiness and righteousness before Him all the days of our life.*

4. *Then* [*And*] *shall the offering of Judah and Jerusalem.* The *law*, the new revelation of God, was to [1]*go forth from Zion and the word of the Lord from Jerusalem.* Judah and Jerusalem then are here the Christian Church. They *shall be pleasant* [lit. *sweet*] *unto the Lord.* It is a reversal [using the self-same word] of what God had said of them in the time of their religious decay, [2]*they shall not offer wine-offerings to the Lord, neither shall they be sweet unto Him;* [3]*your burnt-offerings are not acceptable, nor your sacrifices sweet unto Me.*

As in the days of old, before the days of degeneracy; as it stands in the ancient Liturgies, "[4]Vouchsafe to look upon them [the consecrated oblations] with a propitious and serene Countenance, and to accept them, as Thou vouchsafedst to accept the gifts of Thy righteous Abel and the sacrifice of our Patriarch Abraham, and the holy sacrifice, the immaculate offering, which Thy high priest Melchisedec offered unto Thee." "[5]The oblation of the sacrament of the Eucharist, made by the Jews who should believe in Christ, which is known to have been first instituted by Christ in the city of Jerusalem, and afterward to have been continued by His disciples[6], shall be pleasing unto the Lord, as the sacrifices of the Patriarchs, Melchisedec, Abraham, and the holy priests in the law, as Aaron; yea, the truth takes precedence of the figure and shadow; the sacrifice of the new law is more excellent and acceptable to God, than all the sacrifices of the law or before the law. With this agrees what the Lord saith to the synagogue, [7]*I will turn My hand upon thee, and purely purge away thy dross, and take away all thy tin; and I will restore thy judges as at the first, and thy counsellors, as at the beginning: and the destruction of the transgressors, and of the sinners, shall be together, and they that forsake the Lord shall be consumed.*" So now it follows;

5. *And I will come near to you to judgment.* They had clamored for the coming of *the God of judgment;* God assures them that He will come to judgment, which they had desired, but far other than they look for. The few would be purified; the great mass of them (so that He calls them *you*), the main body of those who had so clamored, would find that He came as a Judge, not for them but against them.

And I will be a swift witness. "[5]In judging I will bear witness, and witnessing, I, the Same, will bring forth judgment, saith the Lord; therefore the judgment shall be terrible, since the judge is an infallible witness, whom the conscience of no one will be able to contradict."

God would be a *swift witness*, as He had said before, *He shall come suddenly.* Our Lord calls Himself [8]*the Faithful and True witness*, when He stands in the midst of the Church, as their Judge. God's judgments are always unexpected by those, on whom they fall. The sins are those specially condemned by the law; the use of magical arts as drawing men away from God, the rest as sins of special malignity. Magical arts were rife at the time of the Coming of our Lord[9]; and

[1] Is. ii. 3. [2] Hos. ix. 4. [3] Jer. vi. 20.

[4] Canon Missæ. So in S. James' Liturgy, in the prayer of the incense, "O God, Who didst receive the gift of Abel, and the sacrifice of Noah and Abraham, the incense of Aaron and Zachariah." Ass. Cod. Lit. T. v. p. 5. "Receive from the hand of us sinners this incense, as Thou didst receive the oblation of Abel and Noah and Aaron and all Thy saints." Ib. p. 6. "Grant us, Lord, with fear and a pure conscience to present to Thee this spiritual and unbloody Sacrifice, which, when Thou hast received on Thy holy supercelestial and spiritual altar, as a sweet savor, do Thou send back to us the grace of Thine All-holy Spirit, and look upon us, O God, and regard this our reasonable service, and accept it, as Thou didst accept the gifts of Abel, the sacrifice of Noah, the priesthoods of Moses and Aaron, the peace-offerings of Samuel, the repentance of David, the incense of Zachary. As Thou didst receive this true worship from the hand of Thine Apostle, so, in Thy goodness, receive also from us sinners the gifts which lie before Thee, and grant that our oblation may be acceptable, hallowed in the Holy Spirit, &c." Ib. p. 29, 30.

[5] Dion. [6] S. Matt. xxvi. [29] Acts ii. 42, 46.

[7] Is. i. 25, 26, 28.

[8] Rev. iii. 14, i. 5, "I, and not other witnesses, having seen with My own eyes." Theod. S. Jer.

[9] See Introduction to Zechariah pp. 330, 331, and on Zech. xiii. 2. p. 442. Lightfoot, on S. Matt. xxiv. 24., quotes Maimonides, alleging that one "elected in the Sanhedrin ought to be learned in the arts of astrologers, diviners, soothsayers &c. that he might be able to judge those guilty thereof." Sanhedrin c. 2. He mentions the belief that many had perished thereby (Hieros. Sanhedr. f. 18, 3). 80 women hung in one day for it at Ascalon, (Ib. f. 23, 3. Babyl. Sanh. f. 44, 2;) for that "the Jewish women had greatly broken out into such practices." Gloss Ib.

Before CHRIST cir. 397.

against those that ‖ oppress
the hireling in *his* wages,
the widow, and the fatherless, and that turn aside
the stranger *from his right*,
and fear not me, saith the
LORD of hosts.

‖ Or, *defraud*.

6 For I *am* the LORD,

adultery, as shewn in the history of the woman taken in adultery, when her accusers were convicted in their own consciences[1].

Oppress the hireling, lit. *oppress the hire*,[2] i. e. deal oppressively in it. *Behold*, says S. James[3], *the hire of the laborers who have reaped down your fields, which is by you kept back by fraud, crieth; and the cries of them which have reaped are entered into the ears of the Lord of Sabaoth*. The mere delay in the payment of the wages of the laborer brought sin unto him, against whom he cried to God[4]. It is no light sin, since it is united with the heaviest, and is spoken of as reaching the ears of God. The widow and the fatherless stand in a relation of special nearness to God.

And fear not Me. He closes with the central defect, which was the mainspring of all their sins, the absence of the fear of God. The commission of any of these sins, rife as they unhappily are, proves that those who did them had no fear of God. "[5] Nothing hinders that this should be referred to the first Coming of Christ. For Christ, in preaching to the Jews, exercised upon them a judgment of just rebuke, especially of the priests, Scribes and Pharisees, as the Gospels shew."

6. *I* am *the Lord, I change not*, better, more concisely, *I, the Lord*[6], *change not*. The proper name of God, *He Who Is*, involves His Unchangeableness. For change implies imperfection; it changes to that which is either more perfect or less perfect: to somewhat which that being, who changes, is not or has not. But God has everything in Himself perfectly. "[7] Thou Alone, O Lord, Art what Thou Art, and Thou Art Who Art. For what is one thing in the whole and another in parts, and wherein is anything subject to change, is not altogether what Is. And what beginneth from not being, and can be conceived, as not being, and only subsisteth through another thing, returns to not-being; and what hath a 'has been,' which now is not, and a 'to be,' which as yet is not, that *is* not, properly and absolutely. But Thou Art what Thou Art. For whatever Thou Art in any time or way, *that* Thou Art wholly and always; and Thou Art, Who Art properly and simply, because Thou hast neither 'to have been' or 'to be about to be;' but only to be present; and canst not be conceived, ever not to have been." "[8] There is only one simple Good, and therefore One Alone Unchangeable, which is God."

Our life is a "becoming" rather than a simple "being;" it is a continual losing of what we had, and gaining what we had not; for "[9] in as far as any one is not what he was, and is what he was not, so far forth he dieth and ariseth;" dieth to what he was, ariseth to be something otherwise.

"[10] Increase evidences a beginning; decrease, death and destruction. And therefore Malachi says, *I am God, and I change not*, ever retaining His own state of being; because what has no origin cannot be changed."

So the Psalmist says, [11] *As a vesture, Thou shalt change them and they shall be changed, but Thou art the Same, and Thy years shall not fail;* and Balaam, controlled by God, [12] *God is not a man, that He should lie, or the son of man, that He should repent;* and, [13] *with Whom is no variableness, neither shadow of turning*.

Of this unchangeableness of God, His holy ones partake, as far as they fix themselves on God. "[14] The soul of man hangs upon Him, by Whom it was made. And because it was made, to desire God Alone, but everything which it desires below is less than He, rightly doth not *that* suffice it, which is not God. Hence is it, that the soul is scattered hither and thither, and is repelled from everything, toward which it is borne, through satiety of them. But holy men guard themselves by

[1] S. John viii. 9, *adulterous generation*. S. Matt. xii. 39. Lightfoot on S. John viii. 3 quotes Sotah f. 47. 1. "From the time that homicides were multiplied, the beheading of the heifer ceased: from the time that adulterers were multiplied, the bitter waters ceased:" and Maimonides on Sotah, c. 3, "When the adulterers multiplied under the 2d Temple, the Sanhedrin abolished the ordeal of the adulteresses by the bitter water; relying on its being written, 'I will not visit your daughters when they commit whoredom, nor your spouses when they commit adultery.'" Lightfoot subjoins, "The Gemarists teach that Johanan b. Zacchai was the author of that advice, who was still alive, in the Sanhedrin, and perhaps among those who brought the adulteress before Christ. For some things make it probable, that the *Scribes and Pharisees*, mentioned here, were elders of the Synagogue." S. Justin reproaches them with having fresh wives, wherever they went throughout the world. Dial. fin. p. 243. Oxf. Tr.

[2] עשקי שכר שכיר, as in Mi. ii. 2, עשקו גבר וביתו *oppress a man and his house*.

[3] S. Jas. v. 4. [4] Deut. xxiv. 14, 15. [5] Dion.

[6] *The Lord* is in apposition to *I*, as, in the following clause, *the sons of Jacob* to *ye*. The two clauses correspond in form,

I, (אני) the Lord, change not;
Ye, (ואתם) sons of Jacob, are not consumed.

[7] S. Anselm Prosl. c. 22. p. 34 Ben.

[8] S. Aug. de Civ. Dei xi. 10.

[9] S. Aug. Conf. xi. 7. p. 291. Oxf. Tr.

[10] Novatian de Trin. c. 4. [11] Ps. cii. 27.

[12] Nu. xxiii. 19. [13] S. Jas. i. 17.

[14] S. Greg. Mor. xxvi. 44. n. 79. Ben.

Before CHRIST cir. 397.

[m] I change not; [n] therefore
ye sons of Jacob are not
consumed.
7 ¶ Even from the days
of [o] your fathers ye are
gone away from mine or-
dinances, and have not
kept *them*. [p] Return unto
me, and I will return unto
you, saith the LORD of
hosts. [q] But ye said,
Wherein shall we return?
8 ¶ Will a man rob
God? Yet ye have robbed
me. But ye say, Wherein
have we robbed thee? [r] In
tithes and offerings.
9 Ye *are* cursed with a
curse: for ye have robbed
me, *even* this whole nation.

m Num. 23. 19. Rom. 11. 29. Jam. 1. 17.
n Lam. 3. 22.
o Acts 7. 51.
p Zech. 1. 3.
q ch. 1. 6.
r Neh. 13. 10, 12.

cautious observation, lest they should be relaxed from their intentness by change, and because they desire to be the same, wisely bind themselves to the thought, whereby they love God. For in the contemplation of the Creator, they will receive this, that they should ever enjoy one stability of mind. No changeableness then dissipates them, because their thought ever perseveres, free from unlikeness to itself. This therefore they now imitate, striving with effort, which hereafter they shall with joy receive as a gift. To which unchangeableness the prophet had bound himself by the power of love, when he said, [1] *One thing I required of the Lord, which I will require, that I may dwell in the house of the Lord.* To this unity Paul clave intently, when he said, [2] *One thing I do, forgetting those things which are behind and stretching forth to those things which are before, I press forward toward the mark for the prize of the high calling of God in Christ Jesus.*"

And ye sons of Jacob are not consumed. Man would often have become weary of man's wickedness and waywardness. We are impatient at one another, readily despair of one another. God might justly have cast off them and us; but *He* changes not. He abides by the covenant which He made with their fathers; He consumed them not; but with His own unchangeable love awaited their repentance. Our hope is not in ourselves, but in God.

7. *Even from the days of your fathers. Back to those days and from them* [3], *ye are gone away from My ordinances.* "[4] I am not changed from good; ye are not changed from evil. I am unchangeable in holiness; ye are unchangeable in perversity."

Return unto Me. The beginning of our return is from the preventing grace of God. [5] *Turn Thou me, and I shall be turned; for Thou art the Lord my God,* is the voice of the soul to God, preparing for His grace; [6] *turn us, O God of our salvation.* For, not in its own strength, but by His grace can the soul turn to God. *Turn thou to Me and I will return unto you,* is the Voice of God, acknowledging our free-will, and promising His favor, if we accept His grace in return.

And ye say, Wherein shall we return? Strange ignorance of the blinded soul, unconscious that God has aught against it! It is the Pharisaic spirit in the Gospel. It would own itself doubtless in general terms a sinner, but when called on, wholly to turn to God, as being wholly turned from Him, it asks, "In what? What would God have of me?" as if ready to do it.

8. *Shall a man rob* or *cheat,* defraud God? God answers question by question, but thereby drives it home to the sinner's soul, and appeals to his conscience. The conscience is steeled, and answers again, *In what?* God specifies two things only, obvious, patent, which, as being material things, they could not deny. *In tithes and offerings.* The *offerings* included several classes of dues to God, a) the first fruits [7]; b) the annual half-shekel [8]; c) the offerings made for the tabernacle [9], and the second temple [10] at its first erection; it is used of ordinary offerings [11]; d) of the tithes of their own tithes, which the Levites paid to the priests [12]; e) of the portions of the sacrifice which accrued to the priests [13].

9. *Ye have been cursed with the curse* (not "with *a* curse"). The curse threatened had come upon them: but, as fore-supposed in Leviticus by the repeated burthen, *If ye still walk contrary to Me,* they had persevered in evil. God had already shewn His displeasure. But they, so far from being amended by it, were the more hardened in their sin. Perhaps as men do, they pleaded their punishment, as a reason why they should not amend. They *defrauded* God, under false pretences. They were impoverished by His curse, and

1 Ps. xxvii. 4. 2 Phil. iii. 13, 14. 3 למימי.
4 Rup.
5 Jer. xxxi. 18. Lam. v. 21.
6 Ps. lxxxv. 4. 7 תרומה Num. xv. 19, 20.
8 Ex. xxx. 13–15.
9 Ib. xxv. 2, 3, xxxv. 5, 21, 24, xxxvi. 3, 6.
10 Ezr. viii. 25.
11 2 Chr. xxxi. 10. 12 (where המעשר and התרומה are joined, as here, but in inverse order.)
12 Nu. xviii. 26, 28, 29. 13 Lev. vii. 14.

Before CHRIST cir. 397.

[s] Prov. 3. 9, 10.
[t] 1 Chr. 26. 20. 2 Chr. 31. 11. Neh. 10. 38. & 13. 12.

10 [s] Bring ye all the
tithes into [t] the storehouse,
that there may be meat in
mine house, and prove me
now herewith, saith the
LORD of hosts, if I will
not open you the [u] windows
of heaven, and † [x] pour

Before CHRIST cir. 397.

[u] Gen. 7. 11. 2 Kin. 7. 2.
† Heb. *empty out.*
[x] 2 Chr. 31. 10.

---

so they could not afford to pay the tithes; as men say, "the times are bad; so we cannot help the poor" of Christ. *And Me ye still are defrauding*[1]; *Me*, ye; man, God. And that not one or other, but *this whole people*. It was a requital as to that, in which they had offended. "[2] Because ye have not rendered tithes and first-fruits, therefore ye are cursed in famine and penury." "[2] Because the people did not render tithes and first-fruits to the Levites, the Lord saith, that He Himself suffered fraud, Whose ministers, constrained by hunger and penury, deserted the temple. For, if He is visited by others in prison, and sick, is received and cared for, and, hungry and athirst, receives food and drink, why should He not receive tithes in His ministers, and, if they are not given, be Himself deprived of His portion?"

10. *Bring the whole tithes*, not a part only, keeping back more or less, and, as he had said, *defrauding* God, offering, like Ananias, a part, as if it had been the whole; *into the treasury*, where they were collected in the time of Hezekiah[3], and again, at this time, by the direction of Nehemiah, *so that there shall be food*[4], not superfluity, *in My house*, "[5] for those who minister in the house of My sanctuary." [6] *The Levites and singers had*, before the reformation, *fled every one to his field*, because *the portion of the Levites had not been given them*. On Nehemiah's remonstrance, aided by Malachi, *the tithe of corn and the wine and the new oil were brought into the treasuries*.

Bring the whole tithes. "[7] Thou knowest that all things which come to thee are God's, and dost not thou give of His own to the Creator of all? The Lord God needeth not: He asketh not a reward, but reverence: He asketh not anything of thine, to restore to Him. He asketh of thee *first-fruits and tithes*. Niggard, what wouldest thou do, if He took nine parts to Himself, and left thee the tenth?—What if He said to thee; 'Man, thou art Mine, Who made thee; Mine is the land which thou tillest; Mine are the seeds, which thou sowest; Mine are the animals, which thou weariest; Mine are the showers, Mine the winds, Mine the sun's heat; and since Mine are all the elements, whereby thou livest, thou who givest only the labor of thine hands, deservest only the tithes.' But since Almighty God lovingly feeds us, He gives most ample reward to us who labor little: claiming to Himself the tithes only, He has condoned us all the rest."

And prove Me now herewith, in or *by this thing.* God pledges Himself to His creatures, in a way in which they themselves can verify. "If you will obey, I will supply all your needs; if not, I will continue your dearth." By whatever laws God orders the material creation, He gave them a test, of the completion of which they themselves could judge, of which they themselves must have judged. They had been afflicted with years of want. God promises them years of plenty, on a condition which He names. What would men think now, if any one had, in God's name, promised that such or such a disease, which injured our crops or our cattle, should come at once to an end, if any one of God's laws should be kept? We should have been held as fanatics, and rightly; for we had no commission of God. God authenticates those by whom He speaks; *He* promises, Who alone can perform.

"[8] There be three keys which God hath reserved in His own hands, and hath not delivered to any to minister or substitute, the keys of life, of rain, and of the resurrection. In the ordering of the rain they look on His great power, no less than in giving life at first, or afterward raising the dead to it; as S. Paul saith, [9] *God left not Himself without witness, in that He did good and gave rain from heaven and fruitful seasons.*"

If I will not open the windows of heaven[10]. In the time of the flood, they were, as it were,

---

[1] קְבְעִים. According to its probable etym. ("withdrew and so hid," Arab.), it might be defrauding rather than open robbery. But it has not this metaph. meaning in Arabic. Abulw. Tanchum, Hunt. 206., render it of open violence עצב. קבע occurs, beside, in Hebrew only in Pr. xxii. 23, *The Lord will plead their cause and will spoil those who spoil them*, i. e. He will requite them as they have done; in the same bold language, as in Ps. xviii. 17.

[2] S. Jer.

[3] 2 Chr. xxxi. 11. sqq. Neh. x. 38, 32, xii. 44. xiii. 12.

[4] טרף, food, as Pr. xxxi. 15, Ps. cxi. 5.

[5] Jon.

[6] Neh. xiii. 10–23.

[7] App. Serm. S. Aug. 277. Opp. v. App. p. 461. "Not S. Augustine's; more like Cæsarius than S. Aug." Ben.

[8] Poc. quoting Sanhedr. c. Chelek, and Taanith c. 1.

[9] Acts xiv. 17.

[10] The exact expression occurs only in the history of the flood, Gen. vii. 11, viii. 2; in the scoffing courtier's speech, ironically, of God "making windows in heaven" (בַשָּׁמַיִם), 2 Kgs vii. 2. and, perhaps in reference to the flood, Isaiah says, "*windows* from on high *are opened*, and the foundations of the earth do shake." Is. xxiv. 18.

Before CHRIST cir. 397.

you out a blessing, that
there shall not *be room*
enough *to receive it.*
11 And I will rebuke
[y] the devourer for your
sakes, and he shall not
† destroy the fruits of your
ground; neither shall your
vine cast her fruit before
the time in the field, saith
the LORD of hosts.
12 And all nations shall
call you blessed: for ye
shall be [z] a delightsome
land, saith the LORD of
hosts.
13 ¶ [a] Your words have
been stout against me,

y Amos 4. 9.

† Heb. *corrupt.*

z Dan. 8. 9.

a ch. 2. 17.

opened, to man's destruction: now, God would rain abundantly *for you*, for their sakes. *And pour you out*, lit. *empty out to you*, give to them fully, holding back nothing. So in the Gospel it is said, that the love of God is *shed abroad*[1], poured out and forth *in our hearts by the Holy Ghost which is given to us.*

That *there be not* room *enough* to receive it; lit. *until there be no sufficiency*[2]. The text does not express what should not suffice, whether it be on God's part or on man's. Yet it were too great irony, if understood of God. His superabundance, *above all which we can ask or think*, is a first principle in the conception of God, as the Infinite Source of all being. But to say of God, that He would pour out His blessing, until man could not contain it, is one bliss of eternity, that God's gifts will overflow the capacity of His creatures to receive them. The *pot of oil* poured forth the oil, until, on the prophet's saying, [3] *Bring me yet a vessel*, the widow's son said, There is *not a vessel more. And the oil stayed.* God's gifts are limited only by our capacity to receive them.

11. *And I will rebuke the devourer*, the locust, caterpillar, or any like scourge of God. It might be, that when the rain watered the fields, the locust or caterpillar &c. might destroy the corn, so that the labors of man should perish; wherefore he adds, *I will rebuke the devourer.* Neither shall *your vine cast her fruit*[4] *before the time*, holding out a fair promise, but cut off by the frost-wind or the hail; the blossoms or the unripe fruit strewing the earth, as a token of God's displeasure.

12. *All nations shall call you blessed.* The promise goes beyond the temporal prosperity of their immediate obedience. Few could know or think much of the restored prolificalness of Judæa; none could know of its antecedents. A people, as well as individuals, may starve, and none know of it. Had the whole population of Judah died out, their Persian masters would not have cared for it, but would have sent fresh colonists to replace them and pay the tribute to the great king. The only interest, which *all nations* could have in them, was as being the people of God, from whom He should come, *the Desire of all nations, in* Whom *all the families of the earth* would *be blessed.* Of this, God's outward favor was the earnest; they should have again the blessings which He had promised to His people.

And ye shall be called a delightsome land, lit. *a land of good pleasure.* It was not so much the land as the people; *ye shall be called.* The land stands for the people upon it, in whom its characteristics lay. The river Jordan was not so bright as Abana and Pharpar: "the aspect of the shore" is the same, when the inhabitants are spiritually or morally dead; only the more beautiful, in contrast with the lifeless "spirit of man." So Isaiah says, [5] *The nations shall see thy righteousness, and all kings thy glory; and thou shalt be called by a name, which the mouth of the Lord shall name—Thou shalt no more be called Forsaken, nor shall thy land be called Desolate, but thou shalt be called My-delight-is-in-her, and thy land Married: for the Lord delighteth in thee and thy land shall be married.* God and man should delight in her.

13. *Your words have been stout against Me*, probably *oppressive to* [6] *Me*, as it is said, *the famine was strong upon the land. And ye have said, What have we spoken among ourselves*[7] *against Thee?* Again, the entire unconscious-

[1] ἐκκέχυται Rom. v. 5.

[2] In Ps. lxxii. 3 (quoted by Ges. Ros. &c.) "*there shall be abundance of peace* עַד בְּלִי יָרֵחַ, lit "*until there be no moon*," has a literal meaning, that the peace should last until the end of our creation, without saying anything of what lies beyond.

[3] 2 Kgs iv. 6.

[4] שִׁכֵּל, used elsewhere as to the animal world, is used of a land, 2 Kgs ii. 19, whence מְשַׁכֶּלֶת Ib. 21. of "immaturity." Pliny speaks of "arborum abortus." H. N. xii. 2, 6. Ges.

[5] Is. lxii. 2–4.

[6] חזק, with ב on the land, Gen. xli. 56, 57; the city, 2 Kgs xxv. 3, Jer. lii. 6; with על, of persons, Gen. xlvii. 20; hand of God was strong upon the prophet, Ez. iii. 14; they were urgent, pressed upon. Ez. xii. 33

[7] The force of Nif. as in iii. 16. Ps. cix. 23, Ezek. xxxiii. 30. The constr. with על as Pih. in Ps. cix. 20, Hos. vii. 13, Jer. xxix. 32.

Before CHRIST cir. 397.

saith the LORD. Yet ye
say, What have we spoken
so much against thee?
14 [b] Ye have said, It *is*
vain to serve God: and
what profit *is it* that we
have kept † his ordinance,
and that we have walked
† mournfully before the
LORD of hosts?
15 And now [c] we call
the proud happy; yea,
they that work wickedness
† are set up; yea, *they that*
[d] tempt God are even delivered.

b Job 21. 14, 15, & 22. 17. Ps. 73. 13. Zeph. 1. 12.

† Heb. *his observation.*

† Heb. *in black.*

c Ps. 73. 12. ch. 2. 17.

† Heb. *are built.*

d Ps. 95. 9.

ness of self-ignorance and self-conceit! They had criticised God, and knew it not. "[1] Before, he had said, [2] *Ye have wearied the Lord with your words, and ye said, Wherein have we wearied Him? When ye said, Every one that doeth evil* is *good in the sight of the Lord &c.* Now he repeats this more fully. For the people who returned from Babylon seemed to have a knowledge of God, and to observe the law, and to understand their sin, and to offer sacrifices for sin; to pay tithes, to observe the sabbath, and the rest, commanded in the law of God, and seeing all the nations around them abounding in all things, and that they themselves were in penury, hunger and misery, was scandalized and said, 'What does it benefit me, that I worship the One True God, abominate idols, and, pricked with the consciousness of sin, walk mournfully before God?' A topic, which is pursued more largely in the 73d Psalm." Only the Psalmist relates his temptations to God, and God's deliverance of him from them; these adopted them and spake them against God. They claim, for their partial and meagre service, to have fulfilled God's law, taking to themselves God's words of Abraham, *he kept My charge*[3].

14. *Ye have said, It is vain to serve the Lord:* "[4] as receiving no gain or reward for their service. This is the judgment of the world, whereby worldlings think pious, just, sincere, strict men, vain, i. e. especially when they see them impoverished, despised, oppressed, afflicted, because they know not the true goods of virtue and eternal glory, but measure all things by sight, sense and taste.—Truly, if the righteous had not hope of another and better life, in vain would they afflict themselves, and bear the afflictions of others. For, as the Apostle says, [5] *If in this life only we have hope in Christ, we are of all men most miserable.* But now, hoping for another blessed and eternal life for the slight tribulations of this, we are the happiest of all men."

And we have walked mournfully[6]. Again they take in their mouths the words of Psalmists, that they took the garb of mourners, going about mourning before God for their country's afflictions.

15. *And now we call the proud happy* [*blessed*]. This being so, they sum up the case against God. God had declared that all nations should *call* them *blessed*[7], if they would obey. They answer, using His words; *And now we,* (they lay stress on the word, [8] *we,*) *pronounce blessed,* in fact, those whom God had pronounced cursed: [9] *Thou hast rebuked the proud, who are cursed.* Their characteristic, among other bad men, is of insolence [10], arrogance, *boiling* over with self-conceit, and presumptuous toward God. The ground of Babylon's sentence was, [11] *she hath been proud toward the Lord, the Holy One of Israel;* Jethro says of the Egyptians, as a ground of his belief in God, [12] *for, in the thing that they dealt proudly,* He was *above them.* It describes the character of the act of Israel, when God bade them *not go up, neither fight,* and they *would not hear, and went up presumptuously into the battle*[13]; the contumacious act of those, who, appealing to the judgment of God, afterward refused it [14]; of Johanan's associates, who accuse Jeremiah of speaking falsely in the name of God [15]; they are persons who rise up [16], forge lies against [17], dig pits for [18], deal perversely with [19], hold in derision [20], oppress [21], the pious. Whether or no, they mean specifically the heathen, those, whom these pronounced *blessed,* were those who were contemptuous toward God.

Yea, the workers of wickedness, those who habitually work it, whose employment it is, *are built up;* yea, *they have tried God and have escaped.* God had promised that, if [22] *they*

[1] S. Jer. [2] ii. 17.

[3] וישמר משמרתי Gen. xxvi. 5; add Lev. xviii. 30, xxii. 9, Deut. xi. 1, Jos. xxii. 3. 2 Kgs ii. 3, 2 Chr. xiii. 11, xxiii. 6, Zech. iii. 7.

[4] Lap. [5] 1 Cor. xv. 19.

[6] הלכנו קדרנית. The form ק is one found only here; the phrase in the Ps. is קֹדֵר הלך Ps. xxxv. 14, xxxviii. 7, xlii. 10, xliii. 2.

[7] verse 12. [8] אנחנו emph.

[9] Ps. cxix. 21. [10] Pr. xxi. 24.

[11] זדה אל Jer. l. 29. It is used in regard to Babylon together with עריצים (as in Ps. lxxxvi. 14.) Is. xiii. 11.

[12] Ex. xviii. 11. It is used of Egypt toward Israel. Neh. ix. 16.

[13] Deut. i. 41, 43. [14] Ib. xvii. 12, 13.

[15] Jer. xliii. 2. [16] Ps. lxxxvi. 14. [17] Ib. cxix. 69.

[18] Ib. 85. [19] Ib. 78. [20] Ib. 51.

[21] Ib. 122. [22] Jer. xii. 16.

Before CHRIST cir. 397.

e Ps. 66. 16. ch. 4. 2. f Heb. 3. 13. g Ps. 56. 8. Isai. 65. 6. Rev. 20. 12.

16 ¶ Then they [e]that
feared the LORD [f]spake
often one to another: and
the LORD hearkened, and
heard *it*, and [g]a book of
remembrance was written
before him for them that
feared the LORD, and that
thought upon his name.
17 And [h]they shall be
mine, saith the LORD of
hosts, in that day when I

h Ex. 19. 5. Deut. 7. 6. Ps. 135. 4. Tit. 2. 14. 1 Pet. 2. 9.

---

will diligently learn the ways of My people, they shall be built up in the midst of My people; these say, the workers of wickedness *had* been *built up:* God had bidden themselves, [1] *make trial of Me in this;* these answer, the wicked *had* made trial of Him, and had been unpunished.

16. *Then they that feared the Lord spake often among themselves.* The proud-speaking of the ungodly called out the piety of the God-fearing. "[2]The more the ungodly spake against God, the more these *spake among themselves* for God." Both went on till the great Day of severance. True, as those said, the distinction between righteous and wicked was not made yet, but it was stored up out of sight. They *spake among themselves,* strengthening each other against the ungodly sayings of the ungodly.

And the Lord hearkened and heard it. God, Whom these thought an idle looker-on, or regardless, all the while (to speak after the manner of men) was *bending the ear*[3] from heaven *and heard.* Not one pious loyal word for Him and His glory, escaped Him.

And a book of remembrance was written before Him. Kings had their chronicles written[4], wherein men's good or ill deeds toward them were recorded. But the image is one of the oldest in Scripture, and in the self-same words, [5]*the Lord said to Moses, Write this, a memorial in a book.* God can only speak to us in our own language. One expression is not more human than another, since all are so. Since with God all things are present, and memory relates to the past, to speak of God as "remembering" is as imperfect an expression in regard to God, as to speak of "a book." "[6]Forgetfulness hath no place with God, because He is in no way changed; nor remembrance, because He forgetteth not." Both expressions are used, only to picture vividly to our minds, that our deeds are present with God, for good or for evil; and in the Day of Judgment He will make them manifest to men and angels, as though read out of a book, and will requite them. So Daniel had said, [7]*the judgment was set, and the books were opened.* And S. John says, [8]*The books were opened, and another book was opened, which is the book of life; and the dead were judged out of those things which were written in the books, according to their works.* So Moses says to God, [9]*If not, blot me out of Thy book which Thou hast written;* and David, prophesying, prays, [10]*Let them be blotted out of the book of the living, and not be written among the righteous;* and our Lord bids His disciples, [11]*Rejoice in this, that your names are written in heaven.*

And that thought upon His name, rather, *esteemed, prized,* it, in contrast with those who [12]*despised;* as, of Christ, when He should come, it is said, [13]*He was despised, and we esteemed Him not.* "[14]The thinking on His Name imports, not a bare thinking of, but a due esteem and awful regard of, so as with all care to avoid all things which may tend to the dishonor of it, as always in His presence and with respect to Him and fear of Him." "[15]Those are meant who always meditate on the ways of the Lord and the knowledge of His Godhead; for His name is Himself, and He is His Name;" "[16]the wise in heart who know the mystery of the awful glorious Name."

17. *And they shall be Mine, saith the Lord of hosts, in that day when I make up My jewels*[17], or perhaps better, *And they shall be to Me, saith the Lord of hosts, in that day which I make* (or, *in which I do* this) *a peculiar treasure*[18]. "[19]In the day of judgment, those who fear Me and believe and maintain My providence shall be to Me a peculiar treasure, i. e. a people peculiarly belonging and precious to Me, blessed in the vision and fruition of Me. For as in the old law, Israel was a peculiar treasure[20], a special people[21] and inher-

---

[1] ch. iii. 10. [2] à Castro.
[3] ויקשב. [4] ספר הזכרנות Esth. vi. 1.
[5] כתב זאת זִכָּרוֹן בספר Ex. xvii. 14.
[6] S. Aug. in Ps. xxxvii. n. 5. [7] Dan. vii. 10.
[8] Rev. xx. 12. [9] Ex. xxxii. 32.
[10] Ps. lxix. 28.
[11] S. Luke x. 20. [12] Mal. i. 6. [13] Is. liii. 3.
[14] Poc. [15] Kim. ib. [16] Ibn Ezr. ib.
[17] The grounds for this rendering are 1) the recurrence of the words, יום אשר אני עשה, ver. 21. Heb. [iv. 3. Eng.], and the והייתם לי סגלה Ex. xix. 5; so that we have both phrases elsewhere. In Deut. vii. 6, there is the equivalent להיות לו לעם סגלה, and the like, Deut. xiv. 2, Ps. cxxxv. 4.
[18] Beside the places in which Israel is spoken of such, it occurs only of David's treasures, laid up for building the temple 1 Chr. xxix. 3. and of the public treasures of kings and provinces. Eccl. ii. 8.
[19] Lap. [20] סגלה Ex. xxix. 5, Ps. cxxxv. 4.
[21] עם סגלה Deut. vii. 6.

Before CHRIST cir. 397.

make up my ‖ [l] jewels;
and [k] I will spare them, as
a man spareth his own son
that serveth him.

18 [l] Then shall ye re-
turn, and discern between
the righteous and the
wicked, between him that
serveth God and him that
serveth him not.

‖ Or, *special treasure.*
[i] Isai. 62. 3.
[k] Ps. 103. 13.
[l] Ps. 58. 11.

CHAPTER IV.

Before CHRIST cir. 397.

1 *God's judgment on the wicked,* 2 *and his blessing on the good. He exhorteth to the study of the law,* 5 *and telleth of Elijah's coming and office.*

FOR, behold, [a] the day
cometh, that shall burn
as an oven; and all [b] the
proud, yea, and all that do

[a] Joel 2. 31. ch. 3. 2. 2 Pet. 3. 7.
[b] ch. 3. 18.

itance of God, chosen out of all nations, so in the new law Christians, and those who are righteous through grace, are the special treasure of God, and in heaven shall be His special treasure in glory, possessed by God and possessing God.' The *peculiar treasure*, is something, much prized, made great store of, and guarded. Such are Christians, bought at a great price, even by the precious Blood of Christ; but much more evidently such shall they be, Malachi says, in all eternity, which that Day of final retribution shall decide, "[1] joying in the participation of their Creator, by Whose eternity they are fixed, by Whose truth they are assured, by Whose gift they are holy."

And I will spare them. It is a remarkable word, as used of those who should be to Him a *peculiar treasure*, teaching that, not of their own merits, they shall be such, but by His great mercy. It stands in contrast with the doom of the wicked, whom that day shall sentence to everlasting loss of God. Still, the saved also shall have needed the *tender mercy*[2] of God, whereby He pardoned their misdeeds and had compassion upon them. [3] *If Thou, Lord, shalt lay up iniquities, O Lord, who shall stand?* Among those whom God will spare on that day, will be countless, whom the self-righteous despised as sinners. "[4] I will spare them, although formerly sinners; I will spare them, repenting, and serving Me with the service of a pious confession, as a man spareth his own son which served him." For our Lord saith of the son, who refused to go work in his Father's vineyard, and afterward repented and went, that he [5] *did the will of his Father.*

18. *Then shall ye return*, or *turn*, not, "return" in the sense of *returning* to God, for in that day will be the time of judgment, not of repentance; nor yet, "then shall ye again see;" for this is what they denied; and, if they had ceased to deny it, they would have been converted, not in that day, but before, when God gave them grace to see it. They shall turn, so as to have other convictions than before; but, as Judas. The Day of judgment will make a great change in earthly judgment. Last shall be first, and first last; this world's sorrow shall end in joy, and worldly joy in sorrow; afflictions shall be seen to be God's love: [6] *Thou in very faithfulness hast afflicted me;* and the unclouded prosperity of the ungodly to be God's abandonment of them. The picture of the surprise of the wicked in the Day of judgment, in the Wisdom of Solomon, is a comment on the Prophet. "[7] Then shall the righteous man stand in great boldness before the face of such as have afflicted him, and made no account of his labors; when they see it, they shall be troubled with terrible fear, and shall be amazed with the strangeness of his salvation, so far beyond all they looked for: and they, repenting and groaning for anguish of spirit, shall say within themselves, This was he whom we had sometimes in derision and a proverb of reproach: we fools counted his life madness and his end to be without honor: how is he numbered among the children of God, and his lot is among the saints!"

IV. 1. *For, behold, the day cometh, which shall burn as an oven.* He had declared the great severance of the God-fearing and the God-blaspheming, those who served and those who did not serve God; the righteous and the wicked; now he declares the way and time of the severance, the Day of Judgment. Daniel had described the fire of that day, [8] *The throne* [*of the Ancient of days*] *was a fiery flame; his wheels a burning fire: a fiery stream issued and came forth from Him: the judgment was set and the books were opened.* Fire is ever spoken of, as accompanying the judgment. [9] *Our God shall come, and shall not keep silence, a fire shall devour before Him;* [10] *Behold the Lord will come with fire: for by fire and by the sword will the Lord plead with all*

[1] S. Aug. in Civ. Dei x. 7.

[2] חמל has originally the meaning of tender compassion.

[3] Ps. cxxx. 3. [4] Rup. [5] S. Matt. xxi. 31.
[6] Ps. cxix. 75. [7] Wisd. v. 1–5.
[8] Dan. vii. 9, 10. [9] Ps. l. 3. [10] Is. lxvi. 15, 16.

Before CHRIST cir. 397.

wickedly, shall be [c]stubble:
and the day that cometh
shall burn them up, saith
the LORD of hosts, that it
shall [d]leave them neither
root nor branch.
2 ¶ But unto you that
[e]fear my name shall the

[c] Obad. 18.
[d] Amos 2. 9.
[e] ch. 3. 16.

flesh: [1] *every man's work shall be made manifest, for the Day shall declare it, because it shall be revealed by fire: and the fire shall try every man's work, of what sort it is.* S. Peter tells us that fire will be of this burning world; [2] *the heavens and the earth which are now, by the same word are kept in store, reserved unto fire against the day of judgment and perdition of ungodly men; —in the which the heavens shall pass away with a great noise, and the elements shall melt with fervent heat, the earth also and the works that are therein shall be burned up.*

The *oven*, or furnace, pictures the intensity of the heat, which is white from its intensity, and darts forth, fiercely, shooting up like a living creature, and destroying life, as the flame of the fire of Nebuchadnezzar's [3] *burning fiery furnace slew those men that took up Shadrach Meshach and Abednego.* The whole world shall be one burning furnace.

And all the proud and all that do wickedly. All those, whom those murmurers pronounced *blessed* [4], yea and *all* who should thereafter be like them (he insists on the universality of the judgment), *every doer of wickedness*, up to that day and those who should then be, *shall be stubble.* "[5] The proud and mighty, who in this life were strong as iron and brass, so that no one dared resist them, but they dared to fight with God, these, in the Day of Judgment, shall be most powerless, as stubble cannot resist the fire, in an everliving death."

That shall leave them neither root nor branch "i. e. [6] they shall have no hope of shooting up again to life; that life, I mean, which is worthy of love, and in glory with God, in holiness and bliss. For when the root has not been wholly cut away, nor the shoot torn up as from the depth, some hope is retained, that it may again shoot up. For, as it is written, [7] *There is hope of a tree, if it be cut down, that it will sprout again, and that the tender branch thereof will not cease.* But if it be wholly torn up from below and from its very roots, and its shoots be fiercely cut away, all hope, that it can again shoot up to life, will perish also. So, he saith, will all hope of the lovers of sin perish. For so the Divine Isaiah clearly announces, [8] *their worm shall not die and their fire shall not be quenched, and they shall be an abhorring to all flesh.*"

2. *But* (And) *unto you, who fear My Name, shall the Sun of Righteousness arise.* It is said of God, [9] *The Lord God is a sun and a shield,* and, [10] *The Lord shall be to thee an everlasting light, and thy God thy glory; thy sun shall no more go down; for the Lord shall be thine everlasting light;* and Zacharias, speaking of the office of S. John Baptist in the words of Malachi, *thou shalt go before the face of the Lord to prepare His way,* speaks of [11] *the tender mercy of our God, whereby the Dayspring from on high hath visited us, to give light to them that sit in darkness.* "[12] He Who is often called Lord and God, and Angel and Captain of the Lord's host, and Christ and Priest and Word and Wisdom of God and Image, is now called *the Sun of Righteousness.* He, the Father promises, will arise, not to all, but to those only who fear His Name, giving them the light of the Sun of Righteousness, as the reward of their fear toward Him. This is God the Word Who saith, *I am the Light of the world,* Who was *the Light of every one who cometh into the world.*" Primarily, Malachi speaks of our Lord's second Coming, when [13] *to them that look for Him shall He appear, a second time unto salvation.* For as, in so many places [14], the Old Testament exhibits the opposite lots of the righteous and the wicked, so here the prophet speaks of the Day of Judgment, in reference to the two opposite classes, of which he had before spoken, the proud and evil doers, and the fearers of God. The title, *the Sun of Righteousness,* belongs to both Comings; "[5] in the first, He diffused rays of righteousness, whereby He justified and daily justifies any sinners whatever, who will look to Him, i. e. believe in Him and obey Him, as the sun imparts light, joy and life to all who turn toward it." In the second, the righteousness which He gave, He will own and exhibit, cleared from all the misjudgment of the world, before men and Angels. Yet more, healing is, throughout Holy Scripture, used of the removal of sickness or curing of wounds, in the individual or state or Church, and, as to the individual, bodily or spiritual. So David thanks God, first for the forgiveness, [15] *Who forgiveth all thine iniquities;* then for healing of his soul, *Who healeth all thy diseases;* then for salvation, *Who redeemeth thy life from destruction;* then for the crown laid up for him, *Who crowneth thee with*

[1] 1 Cor. iii. 13. [2] 2 S. Pet. iii. 7–10. [3] Dan. iii. 22.
[4] ch. iii. 15. [5] Lap. [6] S. Cyr. [7] Job xiv. 7.
[8] Is. lxvi. ult. [9] Ps. lxxxiv. 11. [10] Is. lx. 19, 20.
[11] S. Luke i. 76, 78, 79.
[12] Eus. Dem. Ev. iv. 29. [13] Heb. ix. 28.
[14] As. Ps. i. 6, ii. 12, iii. 7, 8, v. 10–12, vi. 8–10, vii. 16, 17, ix. 17–20, x. 16–18, xi. 6, 7, xvii. 13–15, xx. 8, xxvi. 9–12, xxxi. 23, xxxii. 10, 11, xxxiv. 21, 22, xxxv. 26–28, xxxvi. 10–12, xxxvii. 38–40, xl. 15–17, l. 22, 23, lii. 5–9, lv. 22, 23, lviii. 10, 11, lxiii. 10, 11, lxiv. 9, 10, lxxiii. 27, 28, civ. 33–35, cxii. 9, 10, cxxvi. 5, cxlix. 9.
[15] Ps. ciii. 3–5.

Before CHRIST cir. 397.

[f] Sun of righteousness
arise with healing in his
wings; and ye shall go
forth, and grow up as
calves of the stall.
3 [g] And ye shall tread
down the wicked; for they
shall be ashes under the
soles of your feet in the
day that I shall do *this*,
saith the LORD of hosts.
4 ¶ Remember ye the

Before CHRIST cir. 397.

[f] Luke 1. 78. Eph. 5. 14. 2 Pet. 1. 19. Rev. 2. 28.
[g] 2 Sam. 22. 43. Mic. 7. 10. Zech. 10. 5.

---

loving-kindness and tender mercies; then, with the abiding sustenance and satisfying joy, *Who satisfieth thy mouth with good things.* Healing then primarily belongs to this life, in which we are still encompassed with infirmities, and even His elect and His Saints have still, whereof to be healed. The full then and complete healing of the soul, the integrity of all its powers will be in the life to come. There, will be "[1] understanding without error, memory without forgetfulness, thought without distraction, love without simulation, sensation without offence, satisfying without satiety, universal health without sickness." "[2] For through Adam's sin the soul was wounded in understanding, through obscurity and ignorance; in will, through the leaning to perishing goods; as concupiscent, through infirmity and manifold concupiscence. In heaven Christ will heal all these, giving to the understanding light and knowledge; to the will, constancy in good; to the desire, that it should desire nothing but what is right and good. Then too the healing of the soul will be the light of glory, the vision and fruition of God, and the glorious endowments consequent thereon, overstreaming all the powers of the soul and therefrom to the body." "[3] God has made the soul of a nature so mighty, that from its most full beatitude, which at the end of time is promised to the saints, there shall overflow to the inferior nature, the body, not bliss, which belongs to the soul as intelligent and capable of fruition, but the fullness of health that is, the vigorousness of incorruption."

And ye shall go forth, as from a prison-house, from the miseries of this lifeless life, *and grow up,* or perhaps more probably, *bound*[4], as the animal, which has been confined, exults in its regained freedom, itself full of life and exuberance of delight. So the Psalmist, [5] *The saints shall exult in glory.* And our Lord uses the like word[6], as to the way, with which they should greet persecution to the utmost, for His Name's sake. Swiftness of motion is one of the endowments of the spiritual body, after the resurrection; as the angels, to whom the righteous shall be like[7], [8] *ran and returned as the appearance of a flash of lightning.*

3. *And ye shall tread down the wicked; for they shall be ashes under the soles of your feet.* It shall be a great reversal. *He that exalteth himself shall be abased, and he that humbleth himself shall be exalted.* Here the wicked often have the pre-eminence. This was the complaint of the murmurers among the Jews; *in the morning* of the Resurrection [9] *the upright shall have dominion over them.* The wicked, he had said, shall be *as stubble,* and that day [10] *shall burn them up;* here, then, they are as the ashes, the only remnant of the stubble, as the dust under the feet. "[11] The elect shall rejoice, that they have, in mercy, escaped such misery. Therefore they shall be kindled inconceivably with the Divine love, and shall from their inmost heart give thanks unto God." And being thus of one mind with God, and seeing all things as He seeth, they will rejoice in His judgments, because they are His. For they cannot have one slightest velleity, other than the all-perfect Will of God. So Isaiah closes his prophecy, [12] *And they shall go forth, and look upon the carcases of the men, that have transgressed against Me; for their worm shall not die, neither shall their fire be quenched, and they shall be an abhorring to all flesh.* So [13] *The righteous shall rejoice, when he seeth the vengeance;* and another Psalmist, [14] *The righteous shall see and rejoice; and all wickedness shall stop her mouth;* and Job, [15] *The righteous see and are glad, and the innocent laugh them to scorn.*

4. *Remember ye the law of Moses, My servant.* [16] *The law was our schoolmaster to bring us unto Christ.* They then who were most faithful to the law, would be most prepared for Christ. But for those of his own day, too, who were negligent both of the ceremonial and moral law, he says, "[11] Since the judgment of God will be so fearful, remem-

---

[1] Pomerius de vit. contempl. i. 4. [2] Lap.
[3] S. Aug. Ep. 118 ad Diosc. n. 14 Opp. ii. 334. L.
[4] So LXX. Vulg. Syr. (and on Jer. l. 11) Jon. (here "go" only); of modern Jews, Tanchum here and on Jer. l. 11. Pococke says more cautiously than moderns generally, "*not far from* this signification is the Arab. פָּאשׁ, which signifies to 'vaunt' or 'boast' or 'go strutting' or 'proudly.'" For "arrogance," not "exuberance of joy," seems the meaning of the Arabic word. The E. V., "grow," "enlarge," follows the interpretation given by most Heb. Comm. or lexicographers.
[5] Ps. cxlix. 5. [6] σκιρτήσατε S. Luke vi. 23.
[7] S. Luke xx. 36. [8] Ezek. i. 14. [9] Ps. xlix. 14.
[10] iv. 1. [11] Dion. [12] Is. lxvi. 24.
[13] Ps. lviii. 10. [14] Ib. cvii. 42.
[15] Job xxii. 19. [16] Gal. iii. 24.

Before CHRIST cir. 397.

[h] law of Moses my servant, which I commanded unto him [i] in Horeb for all Israel, *with* [k] the statutes and judgments.

h Ex. 20. 3. &c.
i Deut. 4. 10.
k Ps. 147. 19.

5 ¶ Behold, I will send you [l] Elijah the prophet [m] before the coming of the great and dreadful day of the LORD:

Before CHRIST cir. 397.

l Matt. 11. 14. & 17. 11. Mark 9. 11. Luke 1. 17.
m Joel 2. 31.

---

ber now unceasingly and observe the law of God given by Moses."

Which I commanded[1] *unto him for* [lit. *upon*, incumbent *upon*] *all Israel.* Not Moses commanded them, but God by His servant Moses; therefore He "[2] would in the day of judgment take strict account of each, whether they had or had not kept them. He would glorify those who obeyed, He would condemn those who disobeyed them." They had asked, *Where is the God of judgment? What profit, that we have kept the ordinance?* He tells them of the judgment to come, and bids them take heed, that they did indeed keep them; for there was a day of account to be held for all.

With *the statutes and judgments,* better, *statutes and judgments,* i. e. consisting in them; it seems added as an explanation of the word, *law,* individualizing them. Duty is fulfilled, not in a general acknowledgment of law, or an arbitrary selection of some favorite commandments, which cost the human will less; as, in our Lord's time, they minutely observed the law of tithes, but [3] *omitted weightier matters of the law, judgment, mercy, and faith.* It is in obedience to the commandments, one by one, one and all. Moses exhorted to the keeping of the law, under these same words: [4] *Now, therefore hearken, O Israel, unto the statutes and judgments which I teach you, to do them, that ye may live.—Ye shall not add unto the word that I command you, neither shall ye diminish it.—Behold, I have taught you statutes and judgments, even as the Lord my God commanded me.— What nation* so *great, that hath statutes and judgments, righteous as all this law, which I set before you this day? The Lord commanded me at that time, to teach you statutes and judgments, that ye might do them in the land, whither ye go to possess it.*

5. *Behold I will send* [*I send,* as a future, proximate in the prophet's mind] *you Elijah the prophet.* The Archangel Gabriel interprets this for us, to include the sending of S. John Baptist. For he not only says [5] that he shall *go before* the Lord *in the spirit and power of Elias,* but describes his mission in the characteristic words of Malachi, *to turn the hearts of the fathers to the children:* and those other words also, *and the disobedient to the wisdom of the just,* perhaps represent the sequel in Malachi, *and the hearts of the children to the fathers;* for their hearts could only be so turned by conversion to God, Whom the fathers, patriarchs and prophets, knew, loved and served; and Whom *they* served in name only. S. John Baptist, in denying that he was Elias[6], denied only, that he was that great prophet himself. Our Lord, in saying, [7] *This is Elias, which was for to come,* [8] *that Elias is come already and they knew him not, but have done unto him whatsoever they listed,* met the error of the Scribes, that He could not be the Christ, because Elias was not yet come [9]. When He says, [10] *Elias truly shall first come and restore all things,* He implies a coming of Elias, other than that of S. John Baptist, since *he* was already martyred, and *all things* were not yet *restored.* This must also be the fullest fulfillment. For *the great and terrible Day of the Lord* is the Day of judgment, of which all earthly judgments, however desolating, (as the destruction of Jerusalem) are but shadows and earnests. Before our Lord's coming all things looked on to His first Coming, and, since that Coming, all looks on to the Second, which is the completion of the first and of all things in time.

Our Lord's words, *Elias truly shall first come and restore all things,* seem to me to leave no question, that, as S. John Baptist came, in the spirit and power of Elias, before His First Coming, so, before the Second Coming, Elias should come in person, as Jews and Christians have alike expected. This has been the Christian expectation from the first. *S. Justin Martyr* asked his opponent [11], "Shall we not conceive that the Word of God has proclaimed Elias to be the forerunner of the great and terrible day of His second Coming?" "Certainly," was Trypho's reply. S. Justin continues, "Our Lord Himself taught us in His own teaching that this very thing shall be, when He said that *Elias also shall come;* and we know that this shall be fulfilled, when He is about to come from Heaven in glory." *Tertullian* says [12], "Elias is to come again, not after a departure from life, but after a translation; not to be re-

---

1 צִוָּה with double accus. 2 Lap.
3 S. Matt. xxiii. 23. 4 Deut. iv. 1, 2, 5, 8, 14.
5 S. Luke i. 17. 6 S. John i. 21.
7 S. Matt. xi. 14. 8 Ib. xvii. 12.
9 The error of the Jews consisted, not in their rooted belief, as founded on these words, that Elijah should come before the great and terrible Day of the Lord, but in their denial that He should have any forerunner of His Coming in His great humility. They erred, not in what they believed, but in what they disbelieved.
10 S. Matt. xvii. 11. 11 Dial. c. 49. p. 131. Oxf. Tr.
12 De anima c. 35. p. 539. Rig.

stored to the body, from which he was never taken; but to be restored to the world, from which he was translated; not by way of restoration to life, but for the completion of prophecy; one and the same in name and in person." "[1] Enoch and Elias were translated, and their death is not recorded, as being deferred; but they are reserved as to die, that they may vanquish Antichrist by their blood." And, in proof that the end was not yet, "[2] No one has yet received Elias; no one has yet fled from Antichrist." And the ancient *author of the verses against Marcion;* "[3] Elias who has not yet tasted the debt of death, because he is again to come into the world." *Origen* says simply in one place[4], that the Saviour answered the question as to the objection of the Scribes, "not annulling what had been handed down concerning Elias, but affirming that there was another coming of Elias before Christ, unknown to the scribes, according to which, not knowing him, and, being in a manner, accomplices in his being cast into prison by Herod and slain by him, they had done to him what they listed." *S. Hippolytus* has; "[5] As two Comings of our Lord and Saviour were indicated by the Scriptures, the first in the flesh, in dishonor, that He might be set at naught—the second in glory, when He shall come from Heaven with the heavenly host and the glory of the Father—so two forerunners were pointed out, the first, John, the son of Zacharias, and again—since He is manifested as Judge at the end of the world, His forerunners must first appear, as He says through Malachi, *I will send to you Elias the Tishbite before the great and terrible day of the Lord shall come.*"

S. Hilary; "[6] The Apostles enquire in anxiety about the times of Elias. To whom He answereth, that *Elias will come and restore all things,* that is, will recall to the knowledge of God, what he shall find of Israel; but he signifies that John came *in the spirit and power of Elias,* to whom they had shewn all severe and harsh dealings, that, foreannouncing the Coming of the Lord, he might be a forerunner of the Passion also by an example of wrong and harass." "[7] We understand that those same prophets [Moses and Elias] will come before His Coming, who, the Apocalypse of John says, will be slain by Antichrist, although there are various opinions of very many, as to Enoch or Jeremiah, that one of them is to die, as Elias."

Hilary the Deacon, A.D. 355, has on the words, *I suppose God hath set forth us the Apostles last;* "[8] He therefore applies these to his own person, because he was always in distress, suffering, beyond the rest, persecutions and distresses, as Enoch and Elias will suffer, who will be Apostles at the last time. For they have to be sent before Christ, to make ready the people of God, and fortify all the Churches to resist Antichrist, of whom the Apocalypse attests, that they will suffer persecutions and be slain." "[9] When the faithless shall be secure of the kingdom of the devil, the saints, i. e. Enoch and Elias being slain, rejoicing in the victory, and *sending gifts, one to another,* as the Apocalypse says[10], sudden destruction shall come upon them. For Christ at His Coming, shall destroy them all." *S. Gregory of Nyssa* quotes the prophecy under the heading, that "[11] before the second Coming of our Lord, Elias should come."

S. Ambrose; "[12] Because the Lord was to come down from heaven, and to ascend to heaven, He raised Elias to heaven, to bring him back to the earth at the time He should please." "[13] The beast, Antichrist, ascends from the abyss to fight against Elias and Enoch and John, who are restored to the earth for the testimony to the Lord Jesus, as we read in the Apocalypse of John."

S. Jerome gives here the mystical meaning; "God will send, in Elias, (which is interpreted 'My God' and who is of the town Thisbe, which signifies 'conversion' or 'penitence')the whole choir of the Prophets, to *convert the heart of the fathers to the sons,* viz. Abraham and Isaac and Jacob and all the patriarchs, that their posterity may believe in the Lord the Saviour, in whom themselves believed: for *Abraham saw the day of the Lord and was glad.*" Here, he speaks of the "coming of Elias before *their* anointed," as a supposition of Jews and Judaizing heretics. But in commenting on our Lord's words in S. Matthew, he adheres twice to the literal meaning. "[14] Some think that John is therefore called Elias, because, as, according to Malachi, at the second Coming of the Saviour[15], Elias will precede and announce the Judge to come, so did John at His first Coming, and each is a messenger, of the first or second Coming of the Lord:" and again concisely, "[15] He who is to come in the second Coming of the Saviour in the actual body, now comes through John in spirit and power;" and he speaks of Enoch and Elias as "[16] the *two witnesses* in the Revelation,

[1] Id. ib. c. 50, p. 549.
[2] de res. carnis c. 22. p. 385. Rig.
[3] Carm. incert. Auct. adv. Marcion. L. iii. p. 302. col. 1 Rig.
[4] in S. Matt. xvii. 10. Opp. iii. 567.
[5] de Antichristo c. 44–46 pp. 21, 22.
[6] in Matt. c. xvii. n. 4. Opp. p. 694, 695.
[7] Id. Ib. c. xx. n. 10. p. 710. Ben.
[8] App. S. Ambros. ii. 125. in 1 Cor. iv. 9.
[9] Ib. p. 282. in 1 Thess. v. 1.
[10] Rev. xi. 10.
[11] adv. Jud. Opp. ii. p. 266.
[12] de pœnit. i. 8.
[13] in Psalm 45, n. 10. Opp. i. 930. "Only one MS. has, 'and John.'" Ben. note.
[14] On S. Matt. xi. 14, 15.
[15] On S. Matt. xvii. 11, 12.
[16] Ep 59 [al. 148] ad Marcell. Opp. i. 326. Vall.

since, according to the Apocalypse of John, Enoch and Elias are spoken of, as having to die."

S. Chrysostom, "[1] When He saith that Elias *cometh and shall restore all things*, He means Elias himself, and the conversion of the Jews, which shall then be; but when He saith, *which was to come*, He calls John, Elias, according to the manner of his ministry."

In *S. Augustine's* time it was the universal belief. "[2] When he [Malachi] had admonished them to remember the law of Moses, because he foresaw, that they would for a long time not receive it spiritually, as it ought, he added forthwith; *And I will send you Elias the Thisbite &c.* That when, through this Elias, the great and wonderful prophet, at the last time before the judgment, the law shall have been expounded to them, the Jews shall believe in the true Christ, i. e. in our Christ, is everywhere in the mouths and hearts of the faithful. For not without reason is it hoped, that he shall come before the Coming of the Saviour, as Judge, because not without reason is it believed that he still lives. For he was carried in a chariot of fire from things below; which Scripture most evidently attests. When he shall come then, by expounding the law spiritually, which the Jews now understand carnally, he shall turn the heart of the fathers to the children."

S. Cyril of Alexandria, his antagonist *Theodoret*, and *Theodore* of Mopsuestia, who was loose from all tradition, had the same clear belief. *S. Cyril;* "It is demonstrative of the gentleness and long-suffering of God, that Elias also the Tishbite shall shine upon us, to foreannounce when the Judge shall come to those in the whole world. For the Son shall come down, as Judge, in the glory of the Father, attended by the angels, and shall *sit on the throne of His glory*, judging *the world in righteousness*, and *shall reward every man according to his works*. But since we are in many sins, well is it for us, that the Divine Prophet goes before Him, bringing all those on earth to one mind; that all, being brought to the unity through the faith, and ceasing from evil intents, may fulfill that which is good, and so be saved when the Judge cometh down. The blessed Baptist John came before Him *in the spirit and power of Elias*. But, as he preached saying, *Prepare ye the way of the Lord, make His paths straight*, so also the divine Elias proclaims His then being near and all-but-present, that He may *judge the world in righteousness*." *Theodoret;* "[3] Malachi teaches us how, when Antichrist shall presume on these things, the great Elias shall appear, preaching to the Jews the Coming of Christ: and he shall convert many, for this is the meaning of, *he shall turn the heart of the fathers to the children*, i. e. the Jews (for these he calls fathers, as being older in knowledge) to those who believed from the Gentiles. They who shall believe through the preaching of the great Elias, and shall join themselves to the Gentiles who seized the salvation sent to them, shall become one Church. He hints, how when these things are done by Antichrist, S. Michael the Archangel will set all in motion, that Elias should come and foreannounce the Coming of the Lord, that the then Jews may obtain salvation." And on this place, "Knowing well, that they would neither obey the law, nor receive Him when He came, but would deliver Him to be crucified, He promises them, in His unspeakable love for man, that He will again send Elias as a herald of salvation, *Lo, I will send you Elias the Tishbite*. And signifying the time, He added, *Before the great and terrible Day of the Lord shall come:* He named the Day of His Second Coming. But He teaches us, what the great Elias shall do, when he comes, *Who shall bring back the heart of the father to the son &c.* And pointing out the end, for which Elias should first come, *Lest I come and smite the earth utterly*. For lest, finding you all in unbelief, I send you all to that endless punishment, Elias will first come, and will persuade you, O Jews, to unite you indissolubly with those, who from the Gentiles believe in Me, and to be united to My one Church."

Theodore of Mopsuestia paraphrases: "In addition to all which I have said, I give you this last commandment, to remember My law, which I gave to all Israel through Moses, plainly declaring what they ought to do in each thing, and as the first token of obedience, to receive the Lord Christ when He cometh, appearing for the salvation of all men: Who will end the law, but shew His own perfection. It had been well, had you immediately believed Him when He came, and known Him, as He Whom Moses and all the prophets signified, Who should put an end to the law, and reveal the common salvation of all men, so that it should be manifest to all, that this is the sum and chief good of the whole dispensation of the law, to bring all men to the Lord Christ, Who, for those great goods, should be manifested in His own time. But since, when He manifested Himself, ye manifested your own ungainliness, the blessed Elias shall be sent to you before the second Coming of Christ, when He will come from Heaven, to unite those who, for religion, are separated from each other, and, through the knowledge of religion, to bring the fathers to one-mindedness with the children, and in a word, to bring all men to one and the same harmony, when those, then

[1] In S. Matt. Hom. 57. Opp. vii. 577. [2] de Civ. Dei, xx. 29. Opp. vii. 613. [3] On Daniel, c. xii. init.

though that selfishness is the parent of general discord, of fraud, violence, and other misdeeds. Nay, conversion of children or parents becomes rather a source of discord, embittering the unconverted. Whence our Lord says, *Think not, that I* [1] *am come to send peace on the earth. I came not to send peace on earth, but a sword. For I am come to set a man at variance against his father, and the daughter against her mother, and the daughter-in-law against her mother-in-law: and a man's foes shall be they of his own household;* a prophecy fulfilled continually in the early persecutions, even to the extent of those other words of our Lord, [2] *the brother shall deliver up the brother to death, and the father the child; and the children shall rise up against their parents, and cause them to be put to death.* It is fulfilled also in the intense hatred of the Jews at this day, to any who are converted to Christ; a hatred which seems to have no parallel in the world. Nor do the words seem to mean that fathers and children should be united in one common conversion to God, as one says, "[3] All shall be one heart to return to the Lord, both fathers and children;" for he speaks primarily of their mutual conversion to one another, not to God.

The form of the expression seems to imply that the effect of the preaching of Elias shall be, to bring back the children, the Jews then in being, to the faith and love which their fathers, the Patriarchs, had; that "[4] as these believed, hoped for, longed exceedingly for, and loved Christ to come, so their sons should believe, hope in, long exceedingly for and love Christ, Who was come, yea is present; and so the heart of fathers, which before was turned from their unbelieving children, he should turn to them, now believing, and cause the Patriarchs to own and love the Jews believing in Christ, as indeed their children; for [5] *your father Abraham rejoiced to see My day; he saw it and was glad,* Christ saith."

Lest I come and smite the earth with a curse, i. e. with an utter destruction, from which there should be no redemption. In the end, God will so smite the earth, and all, not converted to Him. The prayer and zeal of Elijah will gain a reprieve, in which God will spare the world for the gathering of His own elect, the full conversion of the Jews, which shall fulfill the Apostle's words, [6] *So shall all Israel be saved.*

After the glad tidings, Malachi, and the Old Testament in him, ends with words of awe, telling us of the consequence of the final hardening of the heart; the eternal severance, when the unending end of the everlasting Gospel itself shall be accomplished, and its last grain shall be gathered into the garner of the Lord. The Jews, who would be wiser than the prophet, repeat the previous verse [7], because Malachi closes so aw-

[1] S. Matt. x. 34–36. [2] Ib. 21.

[3] Ibn Ezra. The Jews, although mostly agreed, that Elijah will come, are disagreed as to the end of his coming. By some he is spoken of as a Redeemer. *Tanchuma*, (f. 31. 1.) "God said to Israel, In this world I sent an angel to cast out the nations before you, but in the future [or, in the world to come, Yalkut Shim'oni f. 98–29] myself will lead you and will 'send you Elijah the prophet.'" Pesikta rabbathi (in Yalkut Shim'oni ii. f. 32. 4) "Both redeemed Israel: Moses in Egypt, and Elias in that which is to come." (Id. ib. f. 53. 2.) "I send you a redeemer." Midrash Shocher tof Ib. f. 884, "Israel said, 'It is written of the first redemption, '*He sent Moses His servant, Aaron whom He had chosen;* send me two like them.' God answered; 'I will send you Elijah the prophet: this is one, the other is he, of whom Isaiah spoke (xlii. 1.) *Behold, my servant whom I have chosen.*'" "Shemoth Rabba [Sect. 3. col. 108. 2. ad loc.] 'In the second redemption, ye shall be healed and redeemed by the word *I*, i. e. *I will send.*" Or, as a comforter, "I will send you Elias, he shall come and comfort you." Debarim rabba sect. 3. fin. Or to pronounce some things clean, others unclean. Shir hashirim rabba f. 27. 3. [all the above in Schöttgen ad loc.] Others, in different ways, to settle, to which tribe each belongs. Kimchi on Ezek. xlvii. and this with different explanations as to strictness. (See Edaioth fin. Mishnah T. iv. p. 362. Surenhus.) "Rabbi Simeon says, 'To remove controversies.' And the wise, and doctors say, To make peace in the world, as is said, "Behold I send." R. Abraham B. David explains the peace to be "from the nations," and adds, "to announce to them the coming of the redeemer, and this in one day before the coming of the Messiah;" and to "turn the hearts &c." he explains "the hearts of the fathers and children (on whom softness had fallen from fear, and they fled, some here, some there, from their distresses) on that day they shall return to their might and to one another and shall comfort each other." Abarbanel says, that Elijah shall be the instrument of the resurrection, and that, through those who rise, the race of man shall be directed in the recognition of God and the true faith." Ibn. Ezra, "that he shall come at the collection of the captives, as Moses at the redemption of Egypt, not for the resurrection." [These are collected by Frischmuth de Eliæ adventu. Thes. Theol. Phil. V. T. T. i. p. 1070. sqq.] R. Tanchum, from Maimonides, says, "This is without doubt a promise of the appearance of a prophet in Israel, a little before the coming of the Messiah; and some of the wise think that it is Elias the Tishbite himself, and this is found in most of the *Midrashoth*, and some think that it is a prophet like him in rank, occupying his place in the knowledge of God and the manifesting His Name and that so he is called Elijah. And so explained the great Gaon, Rab Mosheh ben Maimon, at the end of his great book on jurisprudence, called 'Mishneh Torah.' And, perhaps he [the person sent] may be Messiah ben Joseph, as he says again—And the exactness of the matter in these promises will only be known, when they appear: and no one has therein any accredited account, but each of them says what he says, according to what appears to him, and what preponderates in his mind of the explanation of the truth." "The turning of the heart of the father to the children," he explains to be, "the restoration of religion, until all should be of one heart in the obedience to God." [5] Lap.

[4] S. John viii. 56.

[6] Rom. xi. 26.

[7] The Masora at the end of Malachi notices, that in the reading of יתקק, i. e. Isaiah, the Twelve [as one book, ending with Malachi], the Lamentations Ecclesiastes, the last verse but one is repeated.